The University Atlas

Twentieth Edition

Edited by

Harold Fullard, M.Sc.,
DIRECTOR OF CARTOGRAPHY

& H. C. Darby, C.B.E., Litt. D., F.B.A.
EMERITUS PROFESSOR OF GEOGRAPHY
UNIVERSITY OF CAMBRIDGE

George Philip & Son Limited, London

First Edition   February 1937
Second Edition   August 1940
Third Edition   February 1944
Fourth Edition   July 1945
Fifth Edition   November 1946
Sixth Edition   November 1948
Seventh Edition   January 1953
Eighth Edition
Completely redesigned. © May 1958
Ninth Edition   © August 1960
Tenth Edition   © April 1962
Eleventh Edition   © June 1964
Twelfth Edition
Redesigned.   © March 1967
Thirteenth Edition   © June 1969
Fourteenth Edition © January 1972
Fifteenth Edition   © February 1973
Sixteenth Edition   © August 1974
Seventeenth Edition   © March 1975
Eighteenth Edition   © August 1977
Nineteenth Edition   © August 1978
Twentieth Edition © January 1980

ISBN 0 540 05366 X

Printed in Great Britain
by George Philip Printers, Ltd., London.

AN 1216

To be kept in Library Office
Under no circumstances to leave
the Library.

Preface

During the course of over forty years since its original publication the University Atlas has been through nineteen editions, each of which has in its turn been revised and improved.

For the eighth edition in 1958, the atlas was completely redesigned because it was considered that only an entirely new version would meet the needs of the post-war years. In that edition we made two significant changes: a substantial increase in the scale of the sectional maps, and a re-arrangement of the atlas into an easily portable size, convenient for frequent use and able to stand on a bookshelf.

For the twelfth edition in 1967, the style of colouring of the maps was completely changed to provide lighter and clearer layer colours. This in turn made possible the inclusion of hill-shading to complement the layer colouring and bring out clearly relief features without impairing the detail of names, settlements and communications.

For the nineteenth edition in 1978 the content of the atlas was completely re-examined, and the lay-out of a large number of maps was redesigned – in particular those covering Asia, Australasia and Latin America. This enabled larger scales to be provided for (a) China, south-east Asia, Japan, the Tashkent area and the southern Urals; (b) south-east Australia and New Guinea; and (c) Mexico, the West Indies and eastern Brazil. Other new maps covered the Indian Ocean, the North Sea, the French departments, the Benelux countries, Switzerland, Alaska and California. The design of yet other maps was altered to secure a more effective presentation, e.g., the world maps of climate.

As in previous editions, international boundaries have been drawn to show the de facto situation where there are rival claims to territory. The preliminary matter includes a summary of the projections used, and also climatic graphs for over 200 stations.

Spellings of names are in the forms given in the latest official lists, and generally agree with the rules of the Permanent Committee on Geographical Names and the United States Board on Geographic Names. A list of changed place names and names for which alternatives are often used appears with the index which contains over 50,000 entries.

We gratefully acknowledge the help of many official organisations and individuals, and especially thank the Meteorological Office for extracting data for the climate graphs.

H. FULLARD
H.C. DARBY

Contents

World

Europe & The British Isles

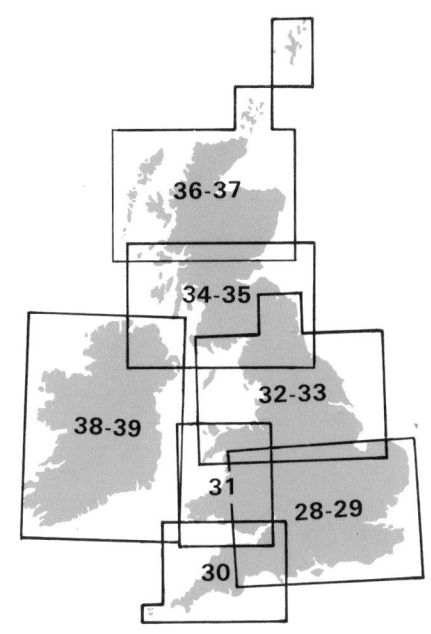

Europe

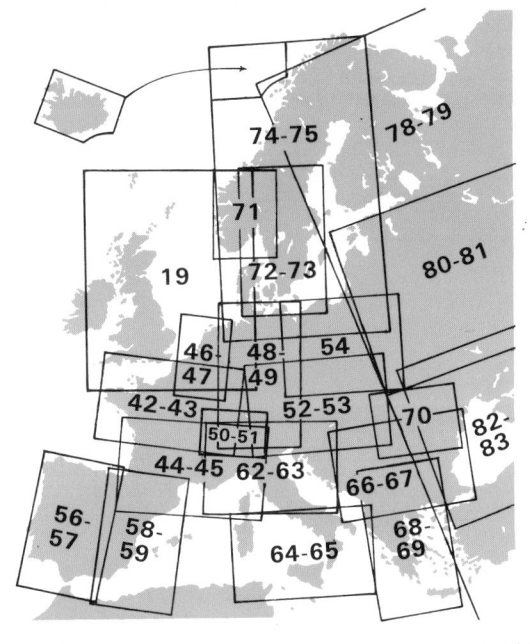

Asia

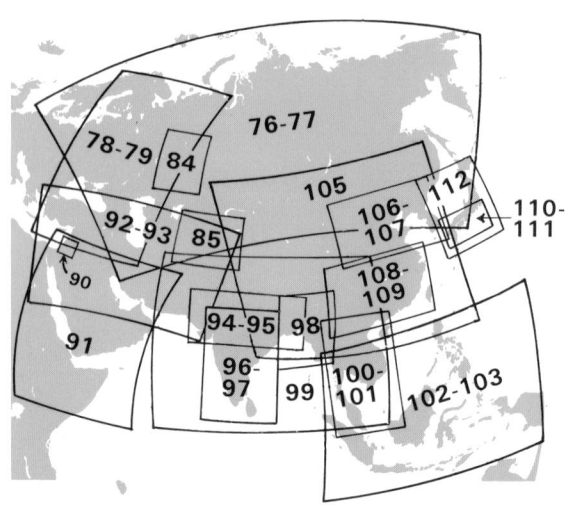

Africa

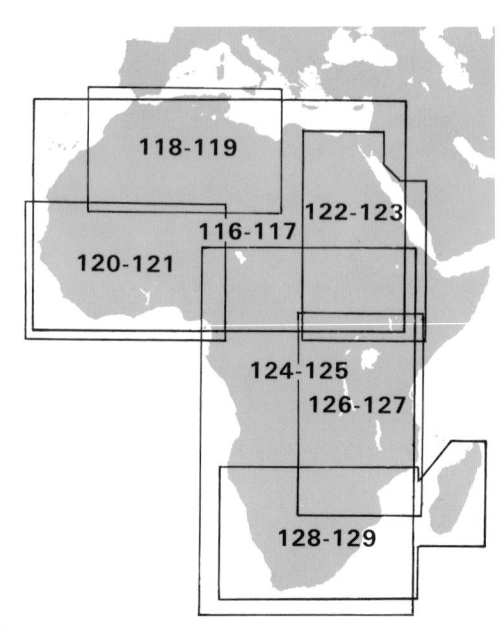

Australasia

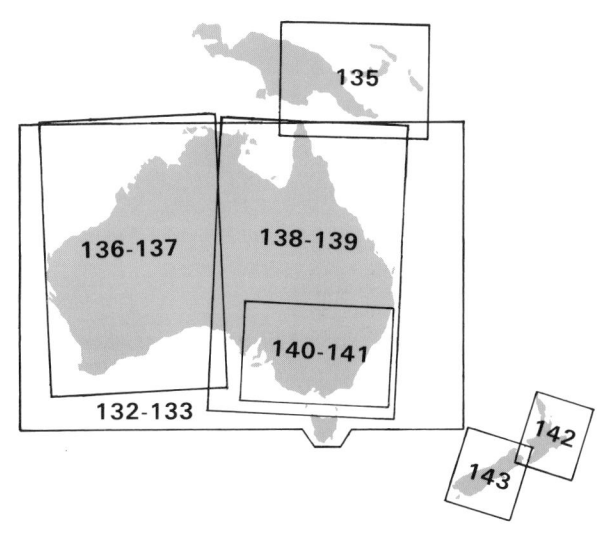

The Americas

Index

Principal Countries of the World

Country	Area in thousands of square km	Population in thousands	Density of population per sq. km	Capital Population in thousands
Afghanistan	647	19 803	31	Kabul (588)
Albania	29	2 548	88	Tiranë (175)
Algeria	2 382	17 304	7	Algiers (1 504)
Angola	1 247	6 761	5	Luanda (475)
Argentina	2 777	25 719	9	Buenos Aires (8 925)
Australia	7 687	14 078	2	Canberra (211)
Austria	84	7 514	89	Vienna (1 859)
Bangladesh	144	76 815	533	Dacca (1 730)
Belgium	31	9 889	319	Brussels (1 075)
Belize	23	144	6	Belmopan (5)
Benin	113	3 197	28	Porto-Novo (104)
Bhutan	47	1 202	26	Thimphu (10)
Bolivia	1 099	5 789	5	Sucre (263) La Paz (697)
Botswana	600	693	1	Gaborone (18)
Brazil	8 512	109 181	13	Brasilia (517)
Brunei	6	177	31	Bandar Seri Begawan (41)
Bulgaria	111	8 761	79	Sofia (962)
Burma	677	30 834	46	Rangoon (3 189)
Burundi	78	3 864	138	Bujumbura (107)
Cambodia	181	8 354	46	Phnom Penh (2 000)
Cameroon	475	6 591	14	Yaoundé (274)
Canada	9 976	23 143	2	Ottawa (693)
Central African Emp.	623	1 716	3	Bangui (187)
Chad	1 284	4 116	3	Ndjamena (193)
Chile	757	10 454	14	Santiago (3 263)
China	9 597	852 133	89	Peking (7 570)
Colombia	1 139	24 372	21	Bogota (2 855)
Congo	342	1 390	4	Brazzaville (290)
Costa Rica	51	2 012	39	San José (395)
Cuba	115	9 405	82	Havana (1 755)
Cyprus	9	639	69	Nicosia (116)
Czechoslovakia	128	14 918	117	Prague (1 096)
Denmark	43	5 073	118	Copenhagen (1 378)
Djibouti	22	108	5	Djibouti (62)
Dominican Republic	49	4 895	99	Santo Domingo (818)
Ecuador	284	7 305	26	Quito (597)
Egypt	1 001	38 067	38	Cairo (5 715)
El Salvador	21	4 123	196	San Salvador (337)
Equatorial Guinea	28	316	11	Rey Malabo (37)
Ethiopia	1 222	28 688	23	Addis Ababa (1 161)
Fiji	18	580	32	Suva (96)
Finland	337	4 727	14	Helsinki (868)
France	547	52 915	97	Paris (9 863)
French Guiana	91	62	1	Cayenne (25)
Gabon	268	530	2	Libréville (251)
Gambia	11	538	49	Banjul (48)
Germany, East	108	16 786	155	East Berlin (1 094)
Germany, West	249	61 498	247	Bonn (283)
Ghana	239	10 309	43	Accra (738)
Greece	132	9 165	69	Athens (2 540)
Greenland	2 176	50	0.02	Godthaab (4)
Guatemala	109	6 256	57	Guatemala (707)
Guinea	246	4 529	18	Conakry (526)
Guinea-Bissau	36	534	15	Bissau (65)
Guyana	215	783	4	Georgetown (164)
Haiti	28	4 668	167	Port-au-Prince (494)
Honduras	112	2 831	25	Tegucigalpa (302)
Hong Kong	1	4 383	4 174	Victoria (849)
Hungary	93	10 596	114	Budapest (2 055)
Iceland	103	220	2	Reykjavik (98)
India	3 288	610 077	186	Delhi (3 630)
Indonesia	1 904	139 616	73	Jakarta (4 576)
Iran	1 648	33 400	20	Tehran (4 002)
Iraq	435	11 505	26	Baghdad (2 969)
Irish Republic	70	3 162	45	Dublin (815)
Israel	21	3 584	171	Jerusalem (344)
Italy	301	56 323	187	Rome (2 868)
Ivory Coast	322	6 677	21	Abidjan (850)
Jamaica	11	2 060	187	Kingston (573)
Japan	372	112 768	303	Tokyo (11 623)
Jordan	98	2 779	28	Amman (598)
Kenya	583	13 847	24	Nairobi (630)
Korea, North	121	16 246	134	Pyongyang (1 500)
Korea, South	98	35 860	345	Seoul (6 889)
Kuwait	16	1 031	57	Kuwait (295)
Laos	237	3 383	14	Vientiane (174)
Lebanon	10	2 961	296	Beirut (939)
Lesotho	30	1 214	40	Maseru (29)
Liberia	111	1 751	16	Monrovia (172)
Libya	1 760	2 444	1	Tripoli (551)
Luxembourg	3	358	138	Luxembourg (78)
Madagascar	587	8 266	14	Tananarive (378)
Malawi	118	5 175	44	Lilongwe (102)
Malaysia	330	12 300	37	Kuala Lumpur (452)
Mali	1 240	6 035	5	Bamako (197)
Malta	0.3	304	950	Valletta (14)
Mauritania	1 031	1 481	1	Nouakchott (135)
Mauritius	2	895	448	Port Louis (141)
Mexico	1 973	62 329	32	Mexico (11 340)
Mongolia	1 565	1 488	1	Ulan Bator (282)
Morocco	447	17 828	40	Rabat (596)
Mozambique	783	9 444	12	Maputo (384)
Namibia	824	852	1	Windhoek (36)
Nepal	141	12 904	92	Katmandu (333)
Netherlands	41	13 825	339	Amsterdam (1 002)
New Zealand	269	3 140	12	Wellington (327)
Nicaragua	130	2 233	17	Managua (500)
Niger	1 267	4 727	4	Niamey (130)
Nigeria	924	64 750	70	Lagos (1 477)
Norway	324	4 035	12	Oslo (469)
Oman	212	791	4	Muscat (25)
Pakistan	804	72 368	90	Islamabad (77)
Panama	76	1 719	23	Panama (404)
Papua New Guinea	462	2 829	6	Port Moresby (76)
Paraguay	407	2 724	7	Asunción (473)
Peru	1 285	16 090	13	Lima (3 302)
Philippines	300	43 751	146	Manila (1 438)
Poland	313	34 636	111	Warsaw (1 400)
Portugal	92	9 449	103	Lisbon (1 612)
Puerto Rico	9	3 213	361	San Juan (695)
Zimbabwe-Rhodesia	391	6 530	17	Salisbury (502)
Rumania	238	21 446	90	Bucharest (1 934)
Rwanda	26	4 289	165	Kigali (54)
Saudi Arabia	2 150	9 240	4	Riyadh (667)
Senegal	196	5 115	26	Dakar (726)
Sierra Leone	72	3 111	43	Freetown (214)
Singapore	0.6	2 295	3 825	Singapore (2 250)
Somali Republic	638	3 261	5	Mogadishu (230)
South Africa	1 221	26 129	21	Pretoria (562) Cape Town (1 096)
Spain	505	35 971	71	Madrid (3 520)
Sri Lanka	66	14 270	216	Colombo (618)
Sudan	2 506	16 126	6	Khartoum (784)
Surinam	163	435	3	Paramaribo (182)
Swaziland	17	497	29	Mbabane (21)
Sweden	450	8 222	18	Stockholm (1 353)
Switzerland	41	6 346	155	Berne (288)
Syria	185	7 596	41	Damascus (923)
Taiwan	36	15 500	431	Taipei (1 922)
Tanzania	945	15 607	17	Dar-es-Salaam (517)
Thailand	514	42 960	84	Bangkok (3 967)
Togo	56	2 283	41	Lomé (214)
Trinidad and Tobago	5	1 067	209	Port of Spain (68)
Tunisia	164	5 737	35	Tunis (648)
Turkey	781	40 163	51	Ankara (1 554)
Uganda	236	11 943	51	Kampala (331)
United Arab Emirates	84	229	3	Abu Dubai (236)
U.S.S.R.	22 402	256 900	11	Moscow (7 632)
United Kingdom	244	55 852	228	London (7 168)
United States	9 363	215 800	23	Washington (2 861)
Upper Volta	274	6 174	23	Ouagadougou (125)
Uruguay	178	3 101	17	Montevideo (1 230)
Venezuela	912	12 361	14	Caracas (2 175)
Vietnam	330	46 523	140	Hanoi (920)
Western Samoa	2.8	159	56	Apia (33)
Yemen (Sana)	195	6 870	35	Sana (150)
Yemen (South)	333	1 749	6	Aden (285)
Yugoslavia	256	21 560	84	Belgrade (1 204)
Zaïre	2 345	25 629	11	Kinshasa (2 008)
Zambia	753	5 138	7	Lusaka (448)

Climate Graphs

The climate graphs should be used in conjunction with the maps illustrating the climate of the World, and also the more detailed maps of the climates of the Continents and the British Isles. For each of the Continents and the British Isles about thirty different stations have been selected so that practically every type of climate throughout the world is covered by the graphs. Complete temperature, pressure and rainfall statistics have been obtained for all except a few stations where pressure statistics were not available. Wherever possible the graphs show average observations based upon long period means, and in all other cases over as long a period as possible. The latest available statistics have been consulted throughout.

Small maps are given on each sheet of graphs showing the location of every station. The figure after the name of the station gives the height in metres of the station above sea-level, so that comparisons between stations can be made after allowing for elevation. For temperature, measurements are given in degrees Centigrade; for pressure, millibars; and for rainfall, in millimetres. The temperature graphs show the monthly means of daily maximum and minimum actual temperatures: from these the mean monthly actual temperatures can easily be determined. The mean annual range of temperature is given above the temperature graphs.
The pressure graphs show the mean monthly pressure at sea-level, except in cases of high-level stations, where the height to which the pressure has been reduced is noted.

The rainfall graphs show the average monthly rainfall, and above them is given the average total annual rainfall. These graphs have been drawn to show the rainfall on the same scale for all stations to facilitate true comparisons between them. Where the rainfall graph extends over to the temperature graph the rainfall scale has been continued at the side of the graph.

On the temperature maps the actual temperatures and sea-level isotherms for the two extreme months of the year, January and July, are given. This information is supplemented by the graphs so that a far more complete picture of temperature changes can now be visualized. A comparison of stations in high latitudes with those in low latitudes renders apparent the importance of the seasonal changes due to insolation. In high latitudes the annual range of temperature is considerable. It decreases gradually as the equator is approached where there is scarcely any variation throughout the year. Another important factor in determining the range is the position of a station in relation to the sea, which exercises a strong moderating influence. The graphs for Africa illustrate the differences in seasons in the northern and southern hemispheres. The influence of the sea also shows itself in the small differences between the mean daily maxima and minima of seaside stations as compared with inland stations. Those most remote from the sea experience a large diurnal range.

The graphs reveal very clearly the intimate connection existing between temperature and pressure. This is perhaps nowhere more clearly indicated than in Asia, where the intense winter cold of the interior coincides with a high pressure system, and the warmth of summer with a low pressure system. As the graphs deal only with land stations all the great pressure systems of the world cannot be demonstrated. Their influence is discernible however in the pressure graphs for many of the stations, e.g., the permanent low pressure system centred on Iceland and the permanent high pressure system based on the Azores, seen in the graphs for Reykjavík and Lisboa respectively, and the permanent equatorial low pressures. One further factor having an important bearing on local climate in high mountain regions deserves mention, namely, the influence of height in reducing pressure. Reduced to sea-level, the pressures for Quito and Guayaquil would appear to be the same, but the graphs reveal the differences which actually exist.

The rainfall maps in the atlas show broadly seasonal rainfall for summer and winter. These are now supplemented by the rainfall graphs, a study of which enables greater distinctions to be drawn between the various rainfall regions, by showing both the amount of precipitation and the months in which it occurs—factors of prime significance for vegetation. In classifying the different rainfall regimes attention should be paid to the factor of relief and the connection noted between the low pressures and convectional rains of equatorial regions.

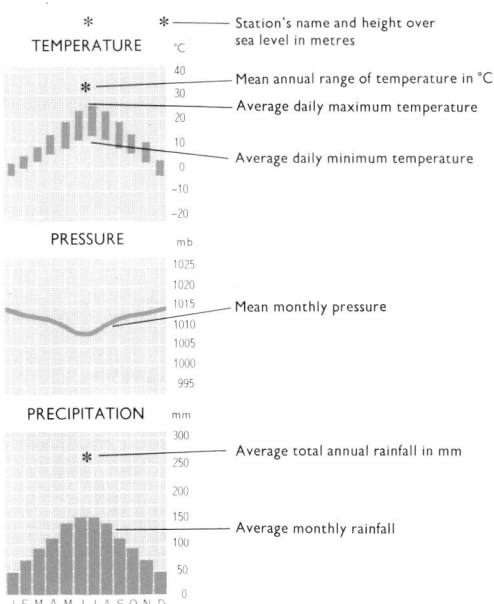

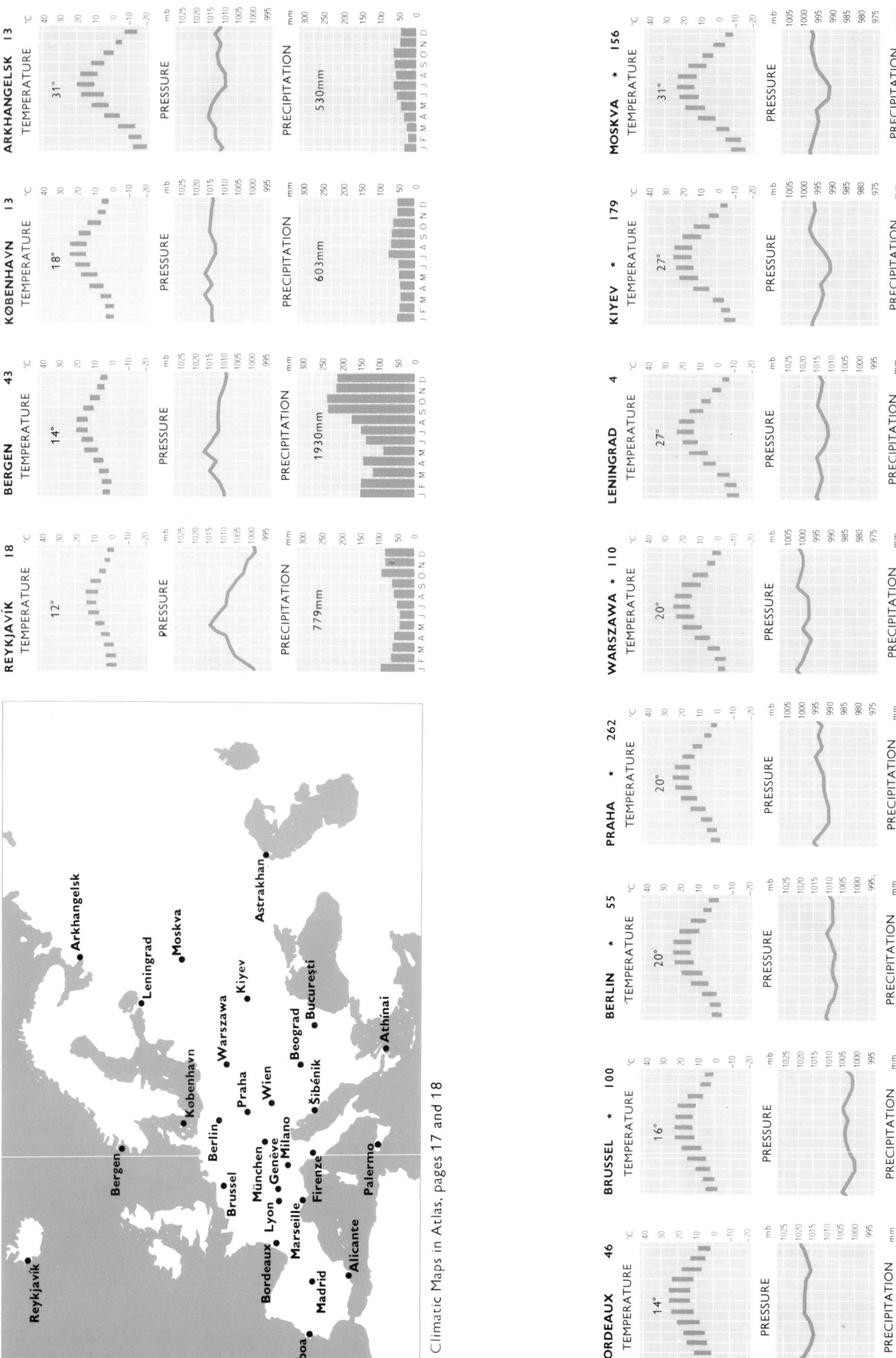

See Climatic Maps in Atlas, pages 17 and 18

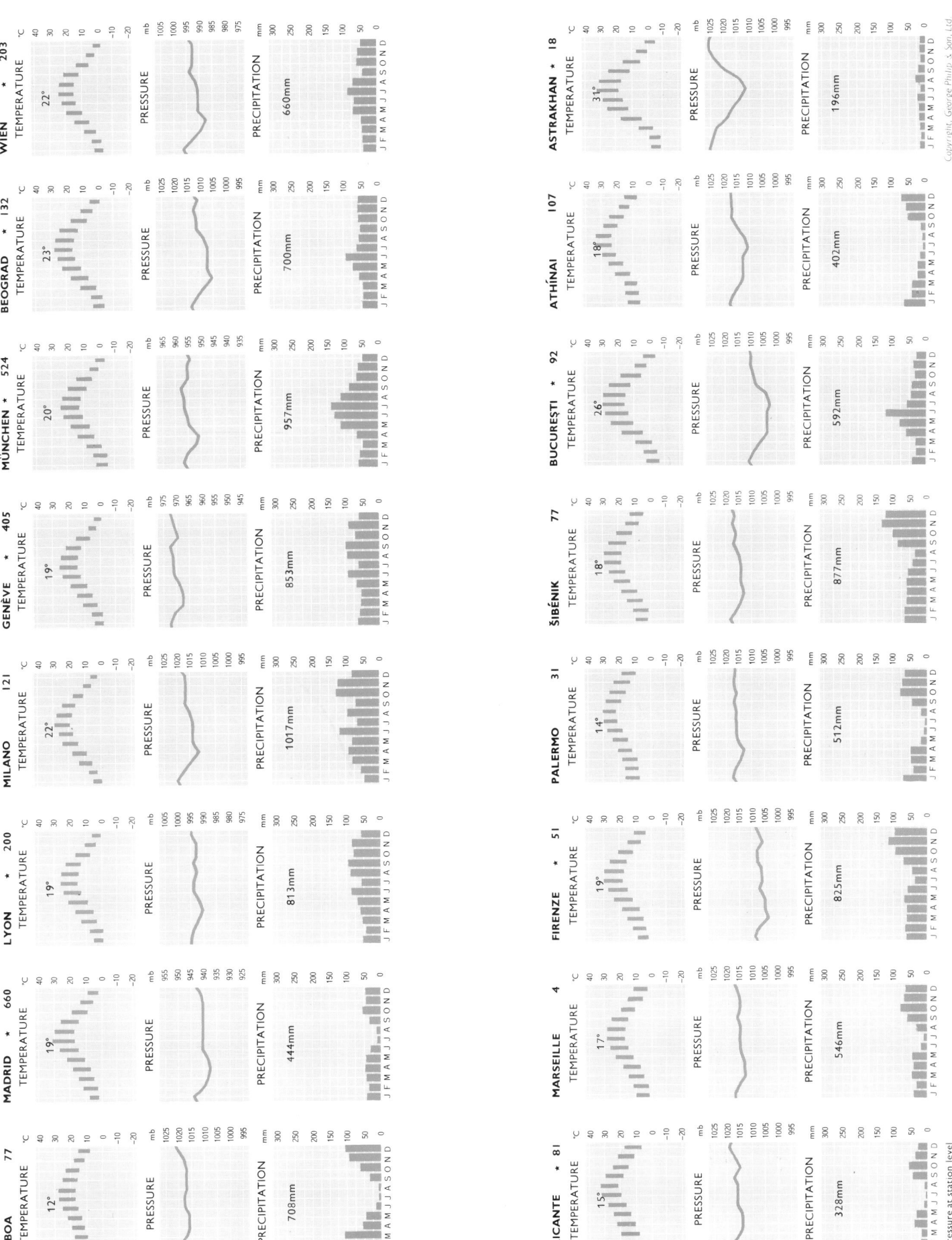

★ Pressure at station level

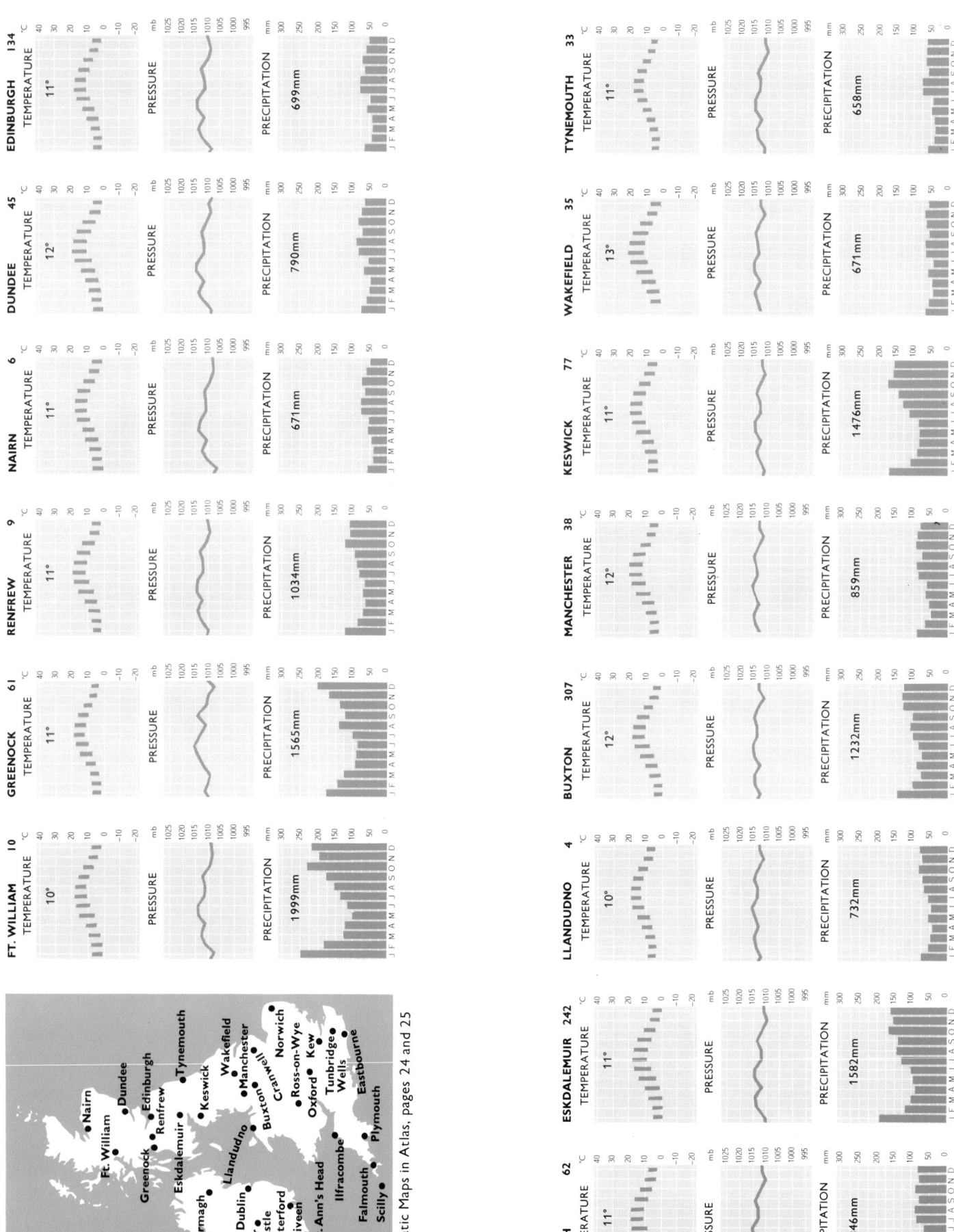

See Climatic Maps in Atlas, pages 24 and 25

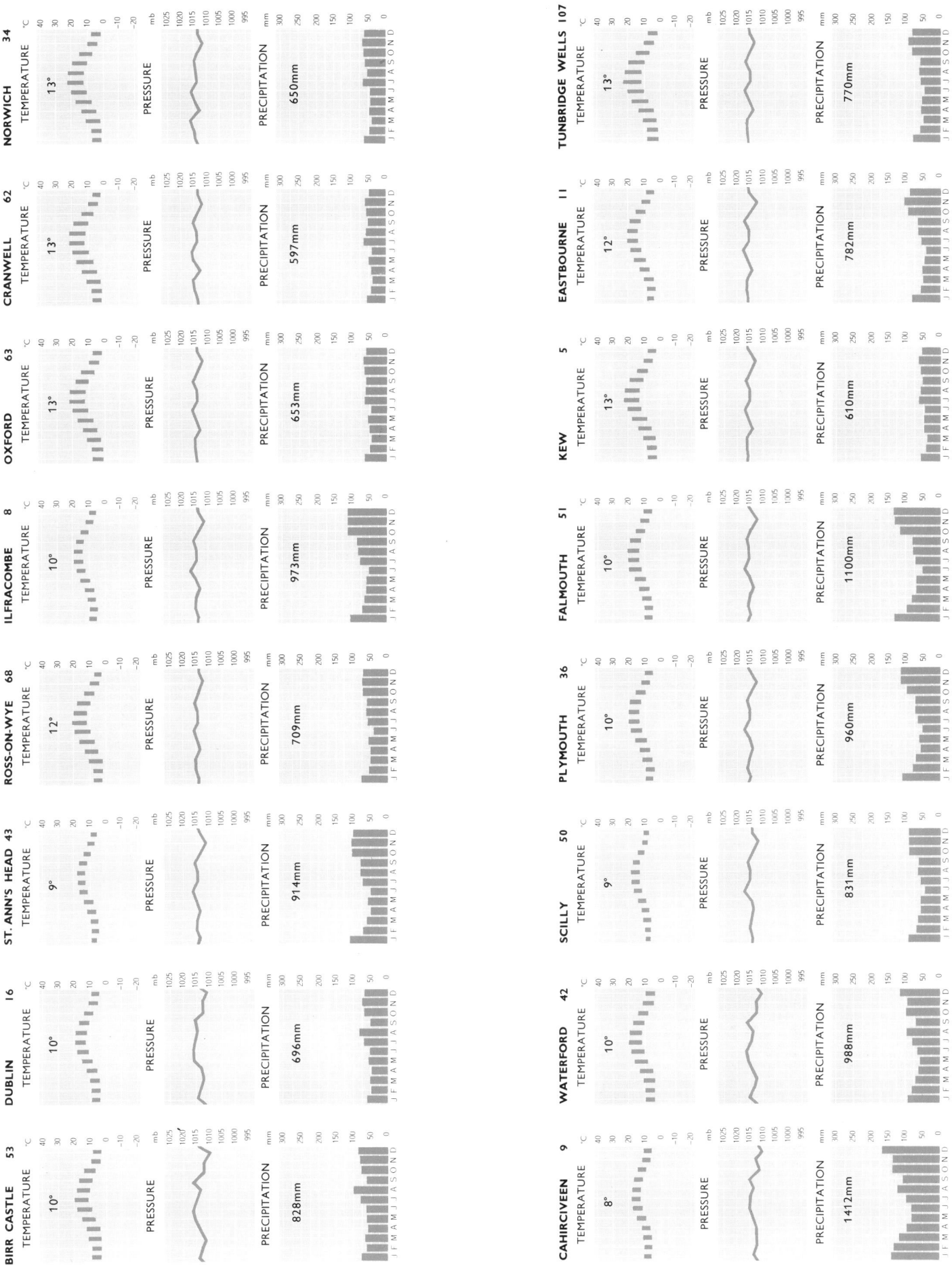

NORWICH 34

TEMPERATURE

13°

PRESSURE

PRECIPITATION

650mm

CRANWELL 62

TEMPERATURE

13°

PRESSURE

PRECIPITATION

597mm

OXFORD 63

TEMPERATURE

13°

PRESSURE

PRECIPITATION

653mm

ILFRACOMBE 8

TEMPERATURE

10°

PRESSURE

PRECIPITATION

973mm

ROSS-ON-WYE 68

TEMPERATURE

12°

PRESSURE

PRECIPITATION

709mm

ST. ANN'S HEAD 43

TEMPERATURE

9°

PRESSURE

PRECIPITATION

914mm

DUBLIN 16

TEMPERATURE

10°

PRESSURE

PRECIPITATION

696mm

BIRR CASTLE 53

TEMPERATURE

10°

PRESSURE

PRECIPITATION

828mm

TUNBRIDGE WELLS 107

TEMPERATURE

13°

PRESSURE

PRECIPITATION

770mm

EASTBOURNE 11

TEMPERATURE

12°

PRESSURE

PRECIPITATION

782mm

KEW 5

TEMPERATURE

13°

PRESSURE

PRECIPITATION

610mm

FALMOUTH 51

TEMPERATURE

10°

PRESSURE

PRECIPITATION

1100mm

PLYMOUTH 36

TEMPERATURE

10°

PRESSURE

PRECIPITATION

960mm

SCILLY 50

TEMPERATURE

9°

PRESSURE

PRECIPITATION

831mm

WATERFORD 42

TEMPERATURE

10°

PRESSURE

PRECIPITATION

988mm

CAHIRCIVEEN 9

TEMPERATURE

8°

PRESSURE

PRECIPITATION

1412mm

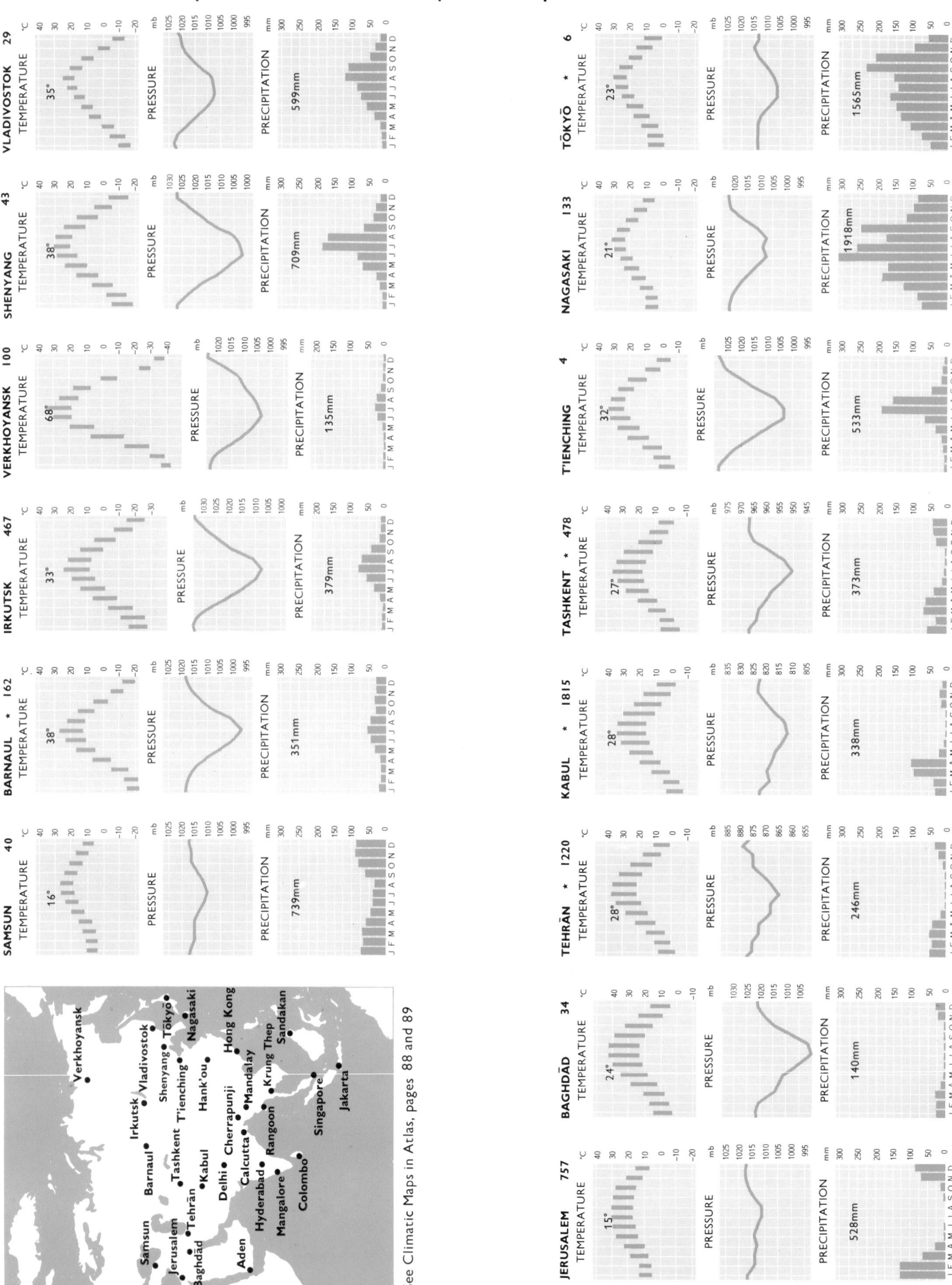

See Climatic Maps in Atlas, pages 88 and 89

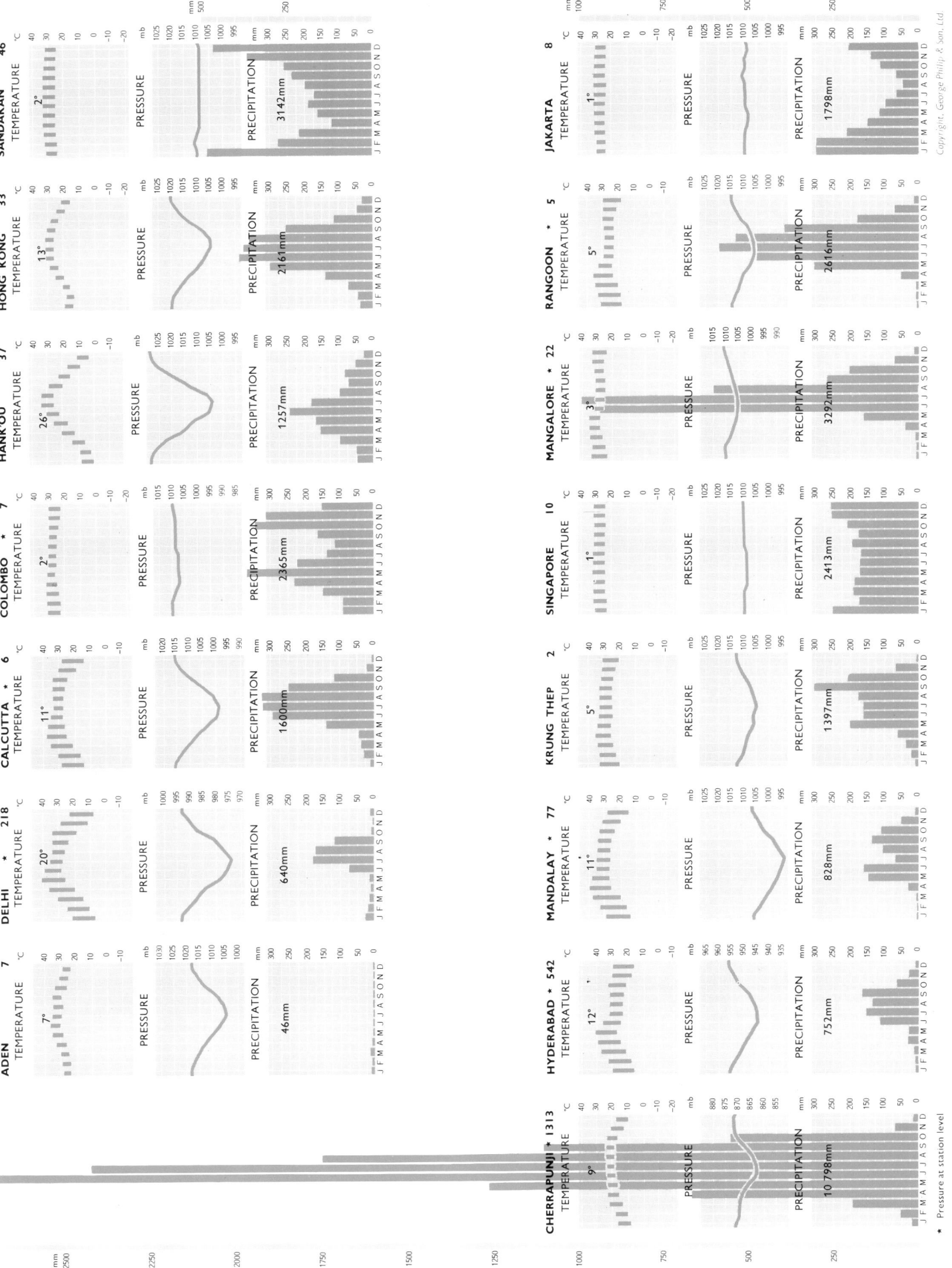

XV

SANDAKAN 46
TEMPERATURE
2°
PRESSURE
PRECIPITATION
3142mm

HONG KONG 33
TEMPERATURE
13°
PRESSURE
PRECIPITATION
2161mm

HANK'OU 37
TEMPERATURE
26°
PRESSURE
PRECIPITATION
1257mm

COLOMBO ★ 7
TEMPERATURE
2°
PRESSURE
PRECIPITATION
2365mm

CALCUTTA ★ 6
TEMPERATURE
11°
PRESSURE
PRECIPITATION
1600mm

DELHI ★ 218
TEMPERATURE
20°
PRESSURE
PRECIPITATION
640mm

ADEN 7
TEMPERATURE
7°
PRESSURE
PRECIPITATION
46mm

JAKARTA 8
TEMPERATURE
1°
PRESSURE
PRECIPITATION
1798mm

RANGOON ★ 5
TEMPERATURE
5°
PRESSURE
PRECIPITATION
2616mm

MANGALORE ★ 22
TEMPERATURE
3°
PRESSURE
PRECIPITATION
3292mm

SINGAPORE 10
TEMPERATURE
1°
PRESSURE
PRECIPITATION
2413mm

KRUNG THEP 2
TEMPERATURE
5°
PRESSURE
PRECIPITATION
1397mm

MANDALAY ★ 77
TEMPERATURE
11°
PRESSURE
PRECIPITATION
828mm

HYDERABAD ★ 542
TEMPERATURE
12°
PRESSURE
PRECIPITATION
752mm

CHERRAPUNJI ★ 1313
TEMPERATURE
9°
PRESSURE
PRECIPITATION
10 798mm

★ Pressure at station level

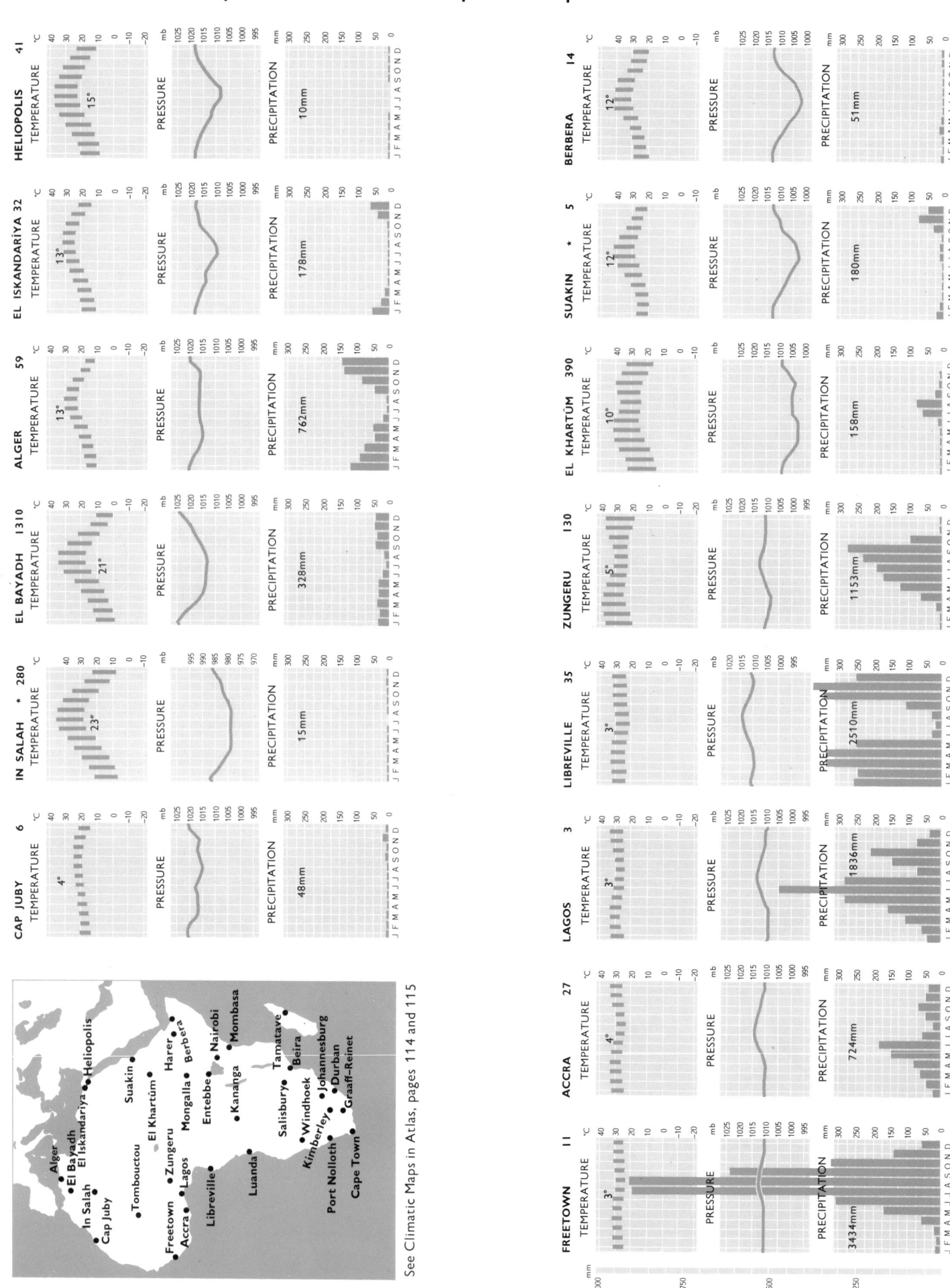

See Climatic Maps in Atlas, pages 114 and 115

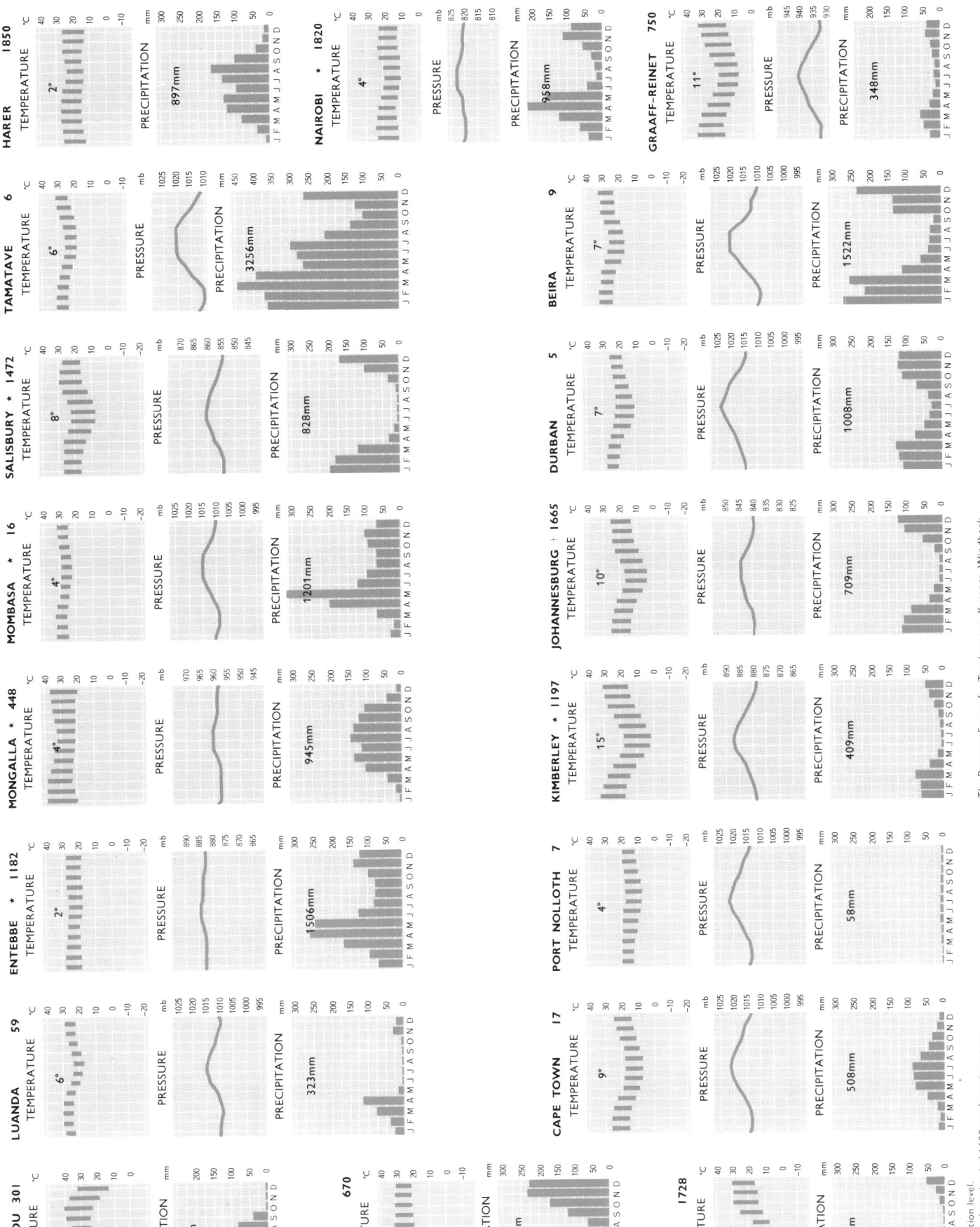

The Pressure figures for Tombouctou, Kananga, Windhoek and Harer, are unavailable owing to lack of reliable data.

* Pressure at station level.
† Pressure reduced to a level of 1600 geodynamic metres.
‡ Pressure reduced to a level of 700 geodynamic metres.

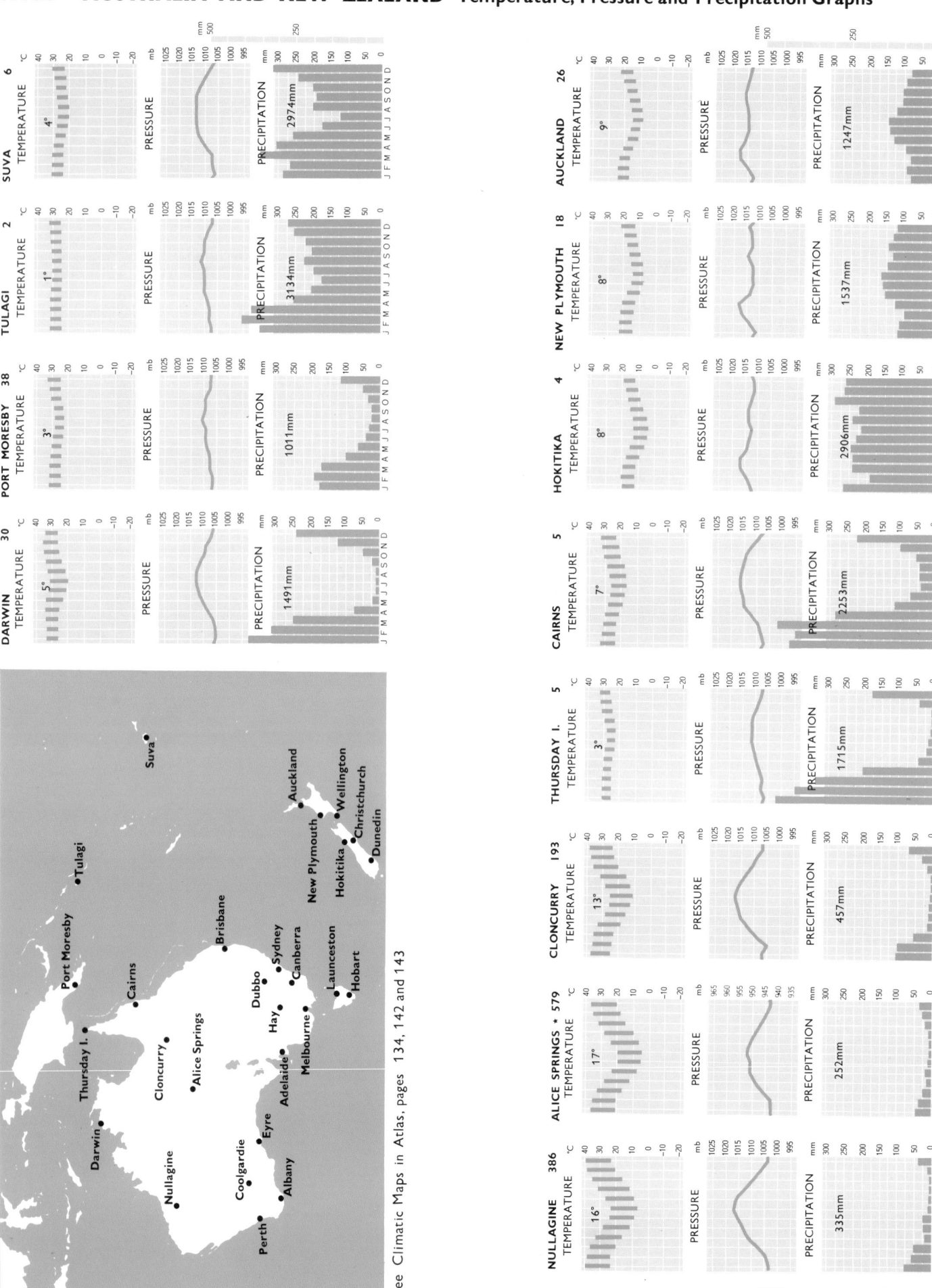

See Climatic Maps in Atlas, pages 134, 142 and 143

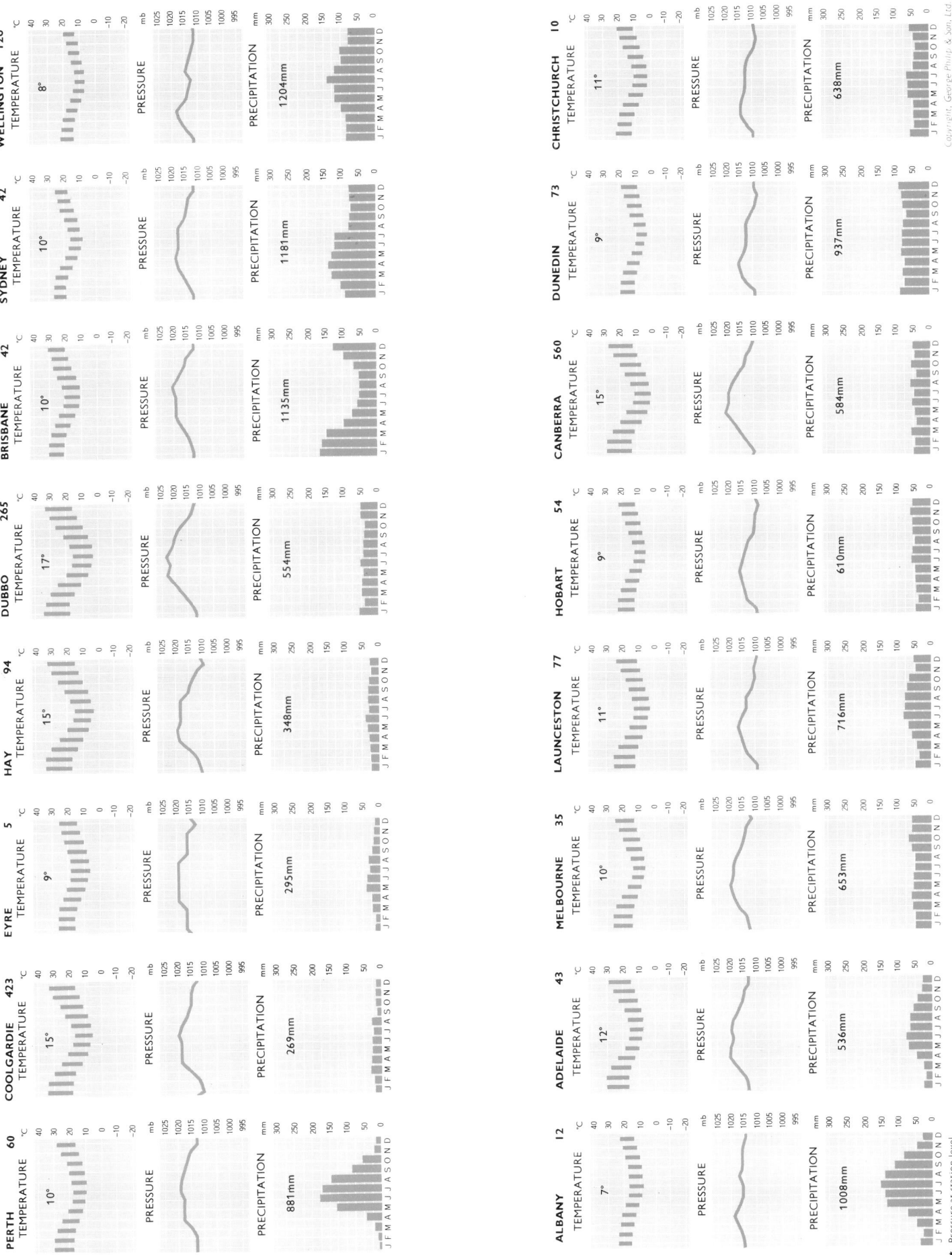

★ Pressure at station level

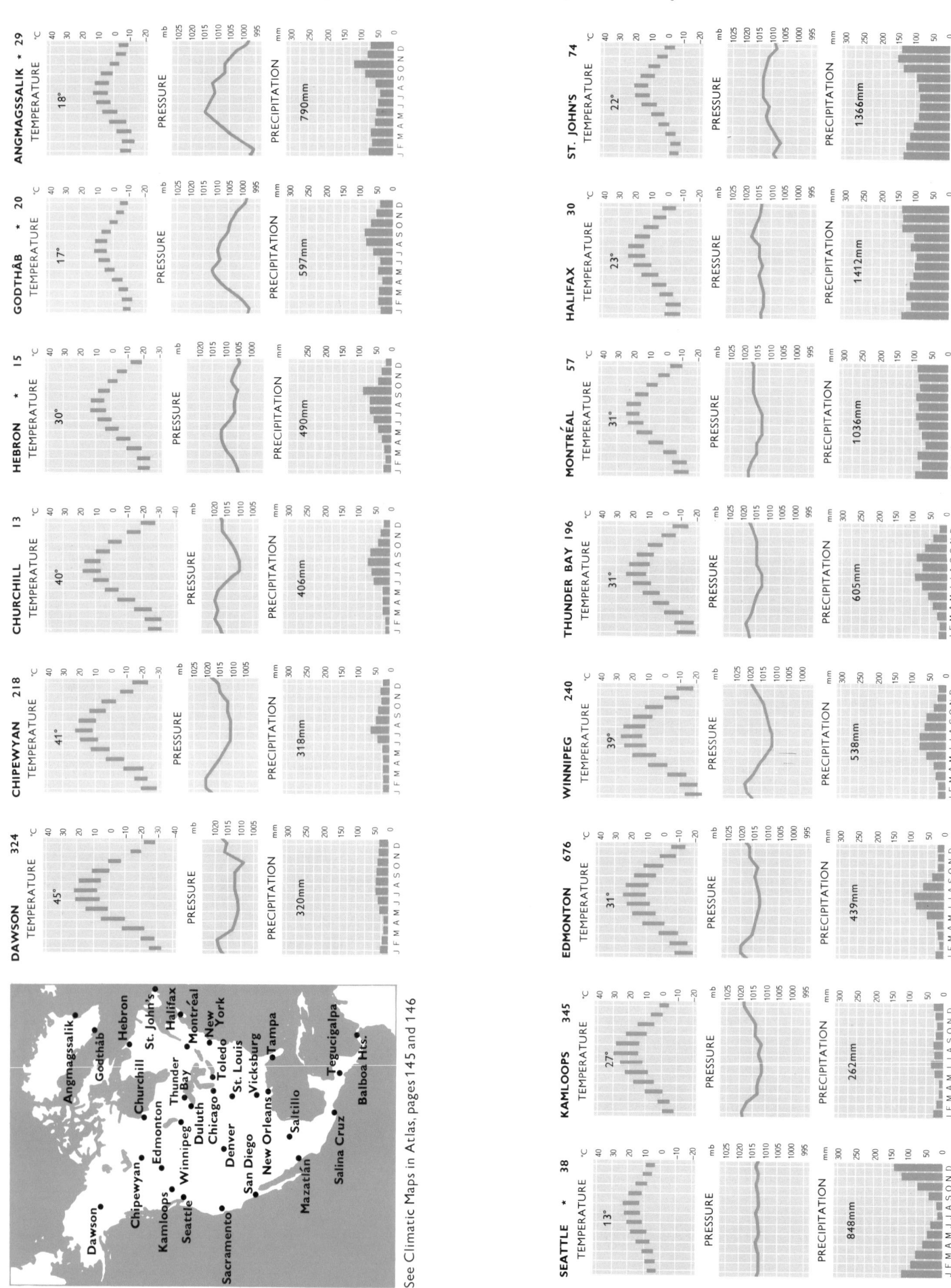

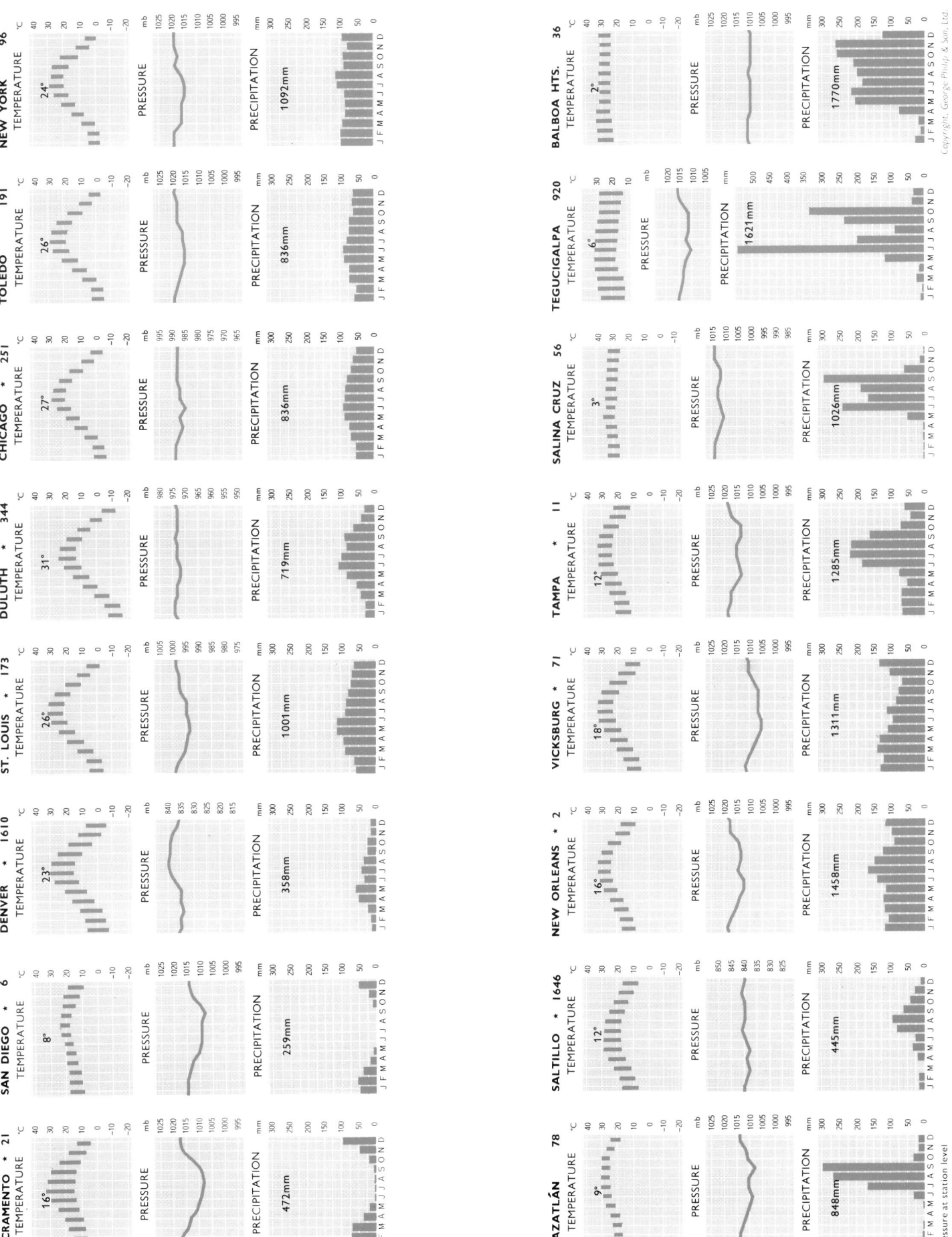

SACRAMENTO ★ 21
TEMPERATURE — 16°
PRESSURE
PRECIPITATION — 472mm

SAN DIEGO ★ 6
TEMPERATURE — 8°
PRESSURE
PRECIPITATION — 259mm

DENVER ★ 1610
TEMPERATURE — 23°
PRESSURE
PRECIPITATION — 358mm

ST. LOUIS ★ 173
TEMPERATURE — 26°
PRESSURE
PRECIPITATION — 1001mm

DULUTH ★ 344
TEMPERATURE — 31°
PRESSURE
PRECIPITATION — 719mm

CHICAGO ★ 251
TEMPERATURE — 27°
PRESSURE
PRECIPITATION — 836mm

TOLEDO 191
TEMPERATURE — 26°
PRESSURE
PRECIPITATION — 836mm

NEW YORK 96
TEMPERATURE — 24°
PRESSURE
PRECIPITATION — 1092mm

MAZATLÁN 78
TEMPERATURE — 9°
PRESSURE
PRECIPITATION — 848mm

SALTILLO ★ 1646
TEMPERATURE — 12°
PRESSURE
PRECIPITATION — 445mm

NEW ORLEANS ★ 2
TEMPERATURE — 16°
PRESSURE
PRECIPITATION — 1458mm

VICKSBURG ★ 71
TEMPERATURE — 18°
PRESSURE
PRECIPITATION — 1311mm

TAMPA ★ 11
TEMPERATURE — 12°
PRESSURE
PRECIPITATION — 1285mm

SALINA CRUZ 56
TEMPERATURE — 3°
PRESSURE
PRECIPITATION — 1026mm

TEGUCIGALPA 920
TEMPERATURE — 6°
PRESSURE
PRECIPITATION — 1621mm

BALBOA HTS. 36
TEMPERATURE — 2°
PRESSURE
PRECIPITATION — 1770mm

★ Pressure at station level

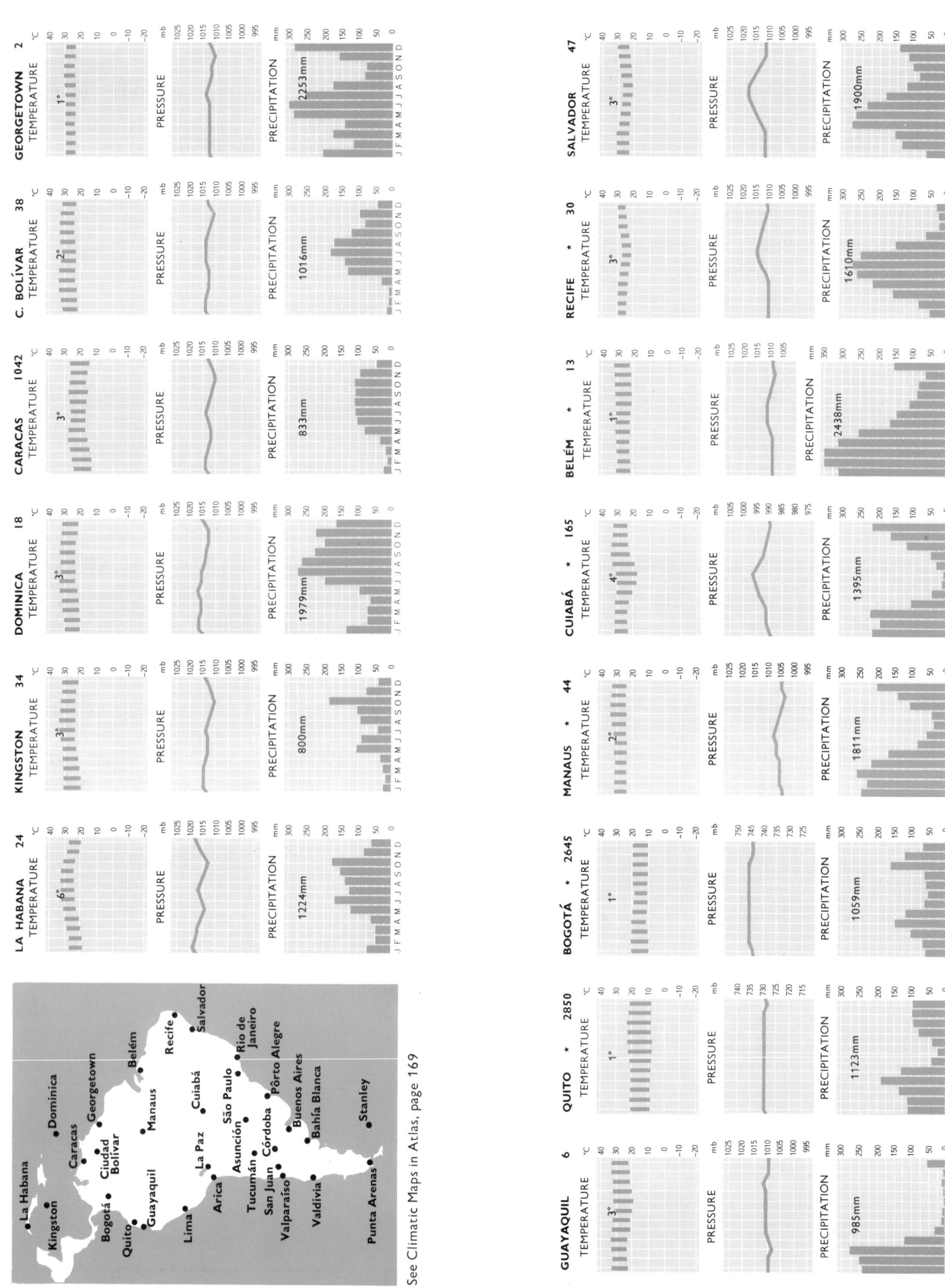

See Climatic Maps in Atlas, page 169

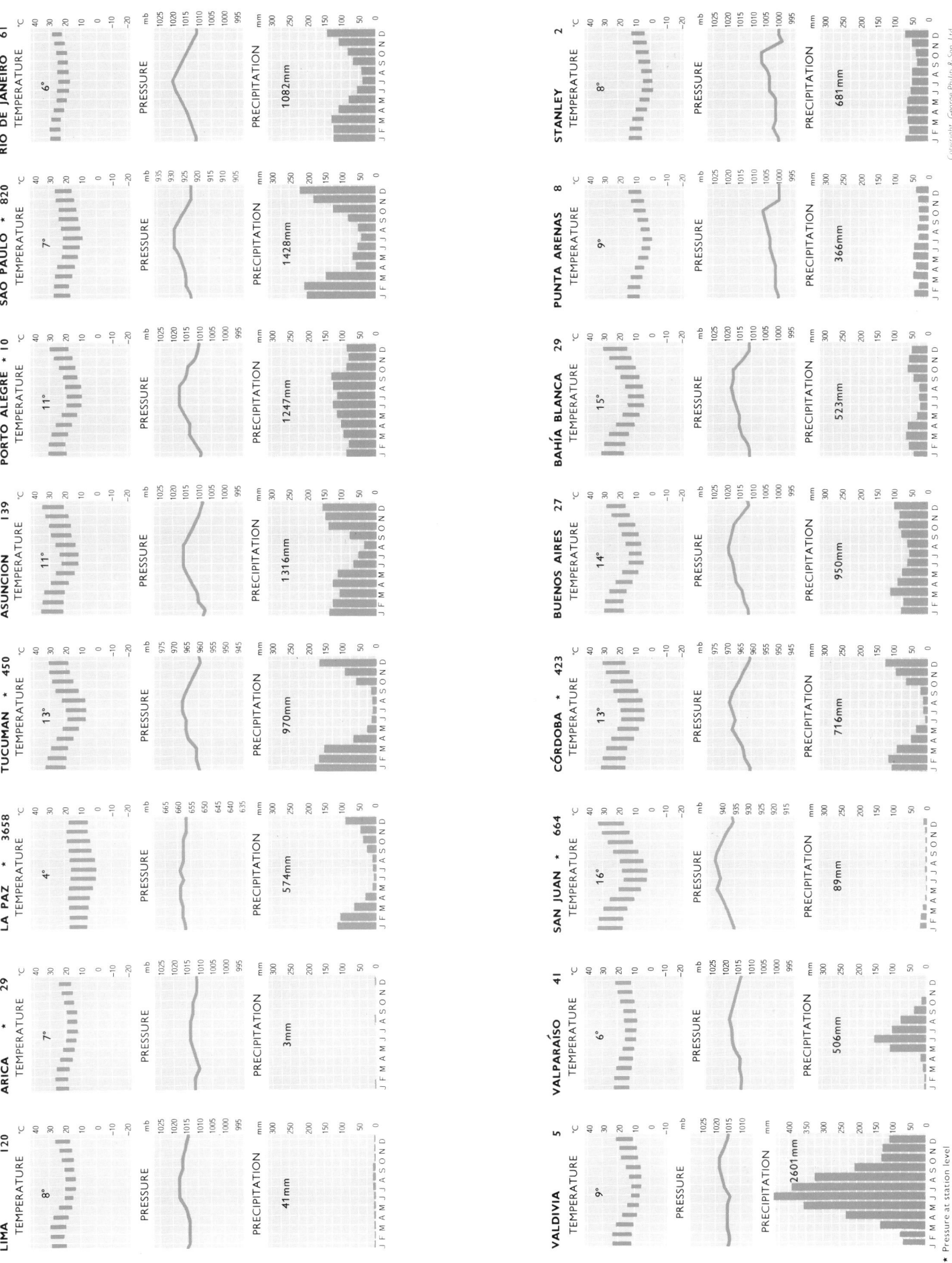

RIO DE JANEIRO 61 — TEMPERATURE 6° — PRESSURE — PRECIPITATION 1082mm

STANLEY 2 — TEMPERATURE 8° — PRESSURE — PRECIPITATION 681mm

SÃO PAULO * 820 — TEMPERATURE 7° — PRESSURE — PRECIPITATION 1428mm

PUNTA ARENAS 8 — TEMPERATURE 9° — PRESSURE — PRECIPITATION 366mm

PÔRTO ALEGRE * 10 — TEMPERATURE 11° — PRESSURE — PRECIPITATION 1247mm

BAHÍA BLANCA 29 — TEMPERATURE 15° — PRESSURE — PRECIPITATION 523mm

ASUNCIÓN 139 — TEMPERATURE 11° — PRESSURE — PRECIPITATION 1316mm

BUENOS AIRES 27 — TEMPERATURE 14° — PRESSURE — PRECIPITATION 950mm

TUCUMÁN * 450 — TEMPERATURE 13° — PRESSURE — PRECIPITATION 970mm

CÓRDOBA * 423 — TEMPERATURE 13° — PRESSURE — PRECIPITATION 716mm

LA PAZ * 3658 — TEMPERATURE 4° — PRESSURE — PRECIPITATION 574mm

SAN JUAN * 664 — TEMPERATURE 16° — PRESSURE — PRECIPITATION 89mm

ARICA * 29 — TEMPERATURE 7° — PRESSURE — PRECIPITATION 3mm

VALPARAÍSO 41 — TEMPERATURE 6° — PRESSURE — PRECIPITATION 506mm

LIMA 120 — TEMPERATURE 8° — PRESSURE — PRECIPITATION 41mm

VALDIVIA 5 — TEMPERATURE 9° — PRESSURE — PRECIPITATION 2601mm

* Pressure at station level

Projections Used

GENERAL REFERENCE

Abbreviations of measures used — ft Feet; mm {Millimetres / Millimeters} cm {Centimetres / Centimeters} m {Metres / Meters} km {Kilometres / Kilometers} mb Millibars

City and Town symbols in order of size

∴ Sites of Archæological or Historical Importance

International Boundaries

International Boundaries (Undemarcated or Undefined)

Internal Boundaries

Principal Roads

Tracks, Seasonal and other Roads

Road Tunnels

Principal Railways

Other Railways

Railways under construction

Railway Tunnels

Principal Canals

Principal Oil Pipelines

Principal Air Routes

☼ Principal Airports

_ _ 3386 _ _ Principal Shipping Routes (Distances in Nautical Miles)

Perennial Streams

Seasonal Streams

Seasonal Lakes, Salt Flats

Swamps, Marshes

Wells in Desert

Permanent Ice

Passes

▲ 8848 Height above sea-level
▼ 8050 Depth below sea-level } in metres
1134 Height of lake-level

CONVERSION SCALE
ft   m
30 000 — 9000
      — 8000
24 000 — 7000
      — 6000
18 000 — 5000
      — 4000
12 000 — 3000
9000 — 2000
6000 — 1000
3000 — 500
Sea-Level 0 — 0 Sea-Level
      — 500
      — 1000
1000 — 2000
      — 3000
2000 — 4000
      — 5000
3000 — 6000
      — 7000
4000 — 8000
      — 9000
5000 — 10 000
      — 11 000
6000 — 12 000
7000
fathoms   m

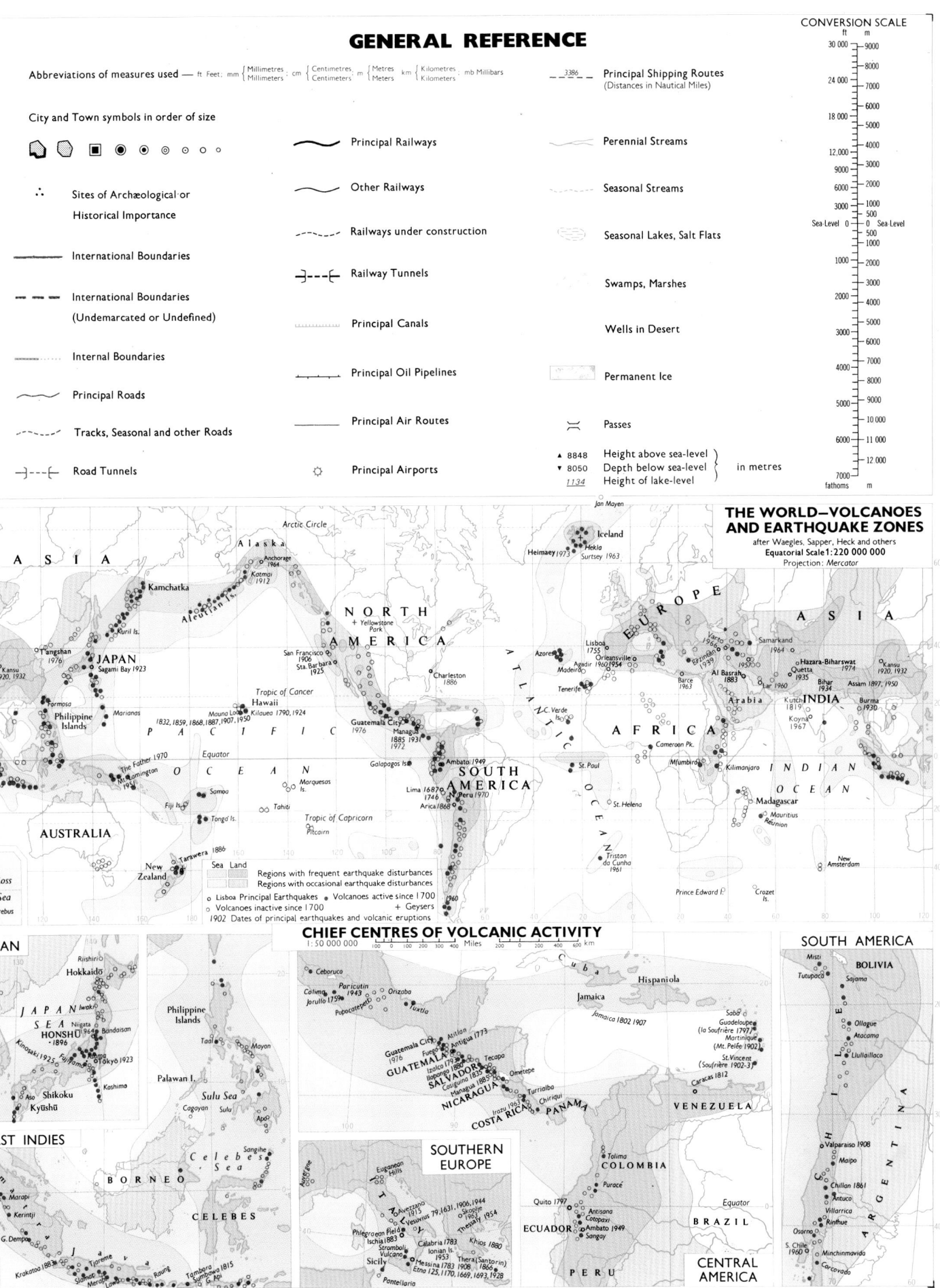

THE WORLD—VOLCANOES AND EARTHQUAKE ZONES
after Waegles, Sapper, Heck and others
Equatorial Scale 1:220 000 000
Projection: Mercator

Regions with frequent earthquake disturbances
Regions with occasional earthquake disturbances
○ Lisboa Principal Earthquakes   • Volcanoes active since 1700
○ Volcanoes inactive since 1700   + Geysers
1902 Dates of principal earthquakes and volcanic eruptions

CHIEF CENTRES OF VOLCANIC ACTIVITY
1:50 000 000

JAPAN

EAST INDIES

PHILIPPINE ISLANDS

SOUTHERN EUROPE

CENTRAL AMERICA

SOUTH AMERICA

COPYRIGHT. GEORGE PHILIP & SON. LTD.
HHK

GEOLOGY
after
Beyschlag, Nalivkin and others

1:90 000 000

Ⓐ

Arctic Circle

Tropic of Cancer

Equator

Tropic of Capricorn

Antarctic Circle

Ⓒ GEOLOGICAL CYCLES

Quaternary	Recent	
Tertiary (Cainozoic)	Pliocene	Alpine Folding
	Miocene	
	Oligocene	
	Eocene	
Secondary (Mesozoic)	Cretaceous	Laramide Folding
	Jurassic	
	Triassic	
Primary Upper (Palæozoic)	Permian	Hercynian Folding
	Carboniferous	
	Devonian	
Lower	Silurian	Caledonian Folding
	Ordovician	
	Cambrian	
Archæan	Pre-Cambrian	

Ⓑ An Interpretation of
STRUCTURE
showing
the distribution of rigid masses and folded regions
after L. Kober and others

Pre-Cambrian tables composite in structure, rigid since the Cambrian period and forming stable elements separating the geo-synclines of later times.

Regions of Caledonian folding; Siluro-Devonian earth movements.

Regions of Hercynian folding; Carbo-Permian earth movements.

Regions of Tertiary folding; Cretaceo-Tertiary earth movements.

The Great Rift Valley

Main Trend lines

L A U R E N T I A

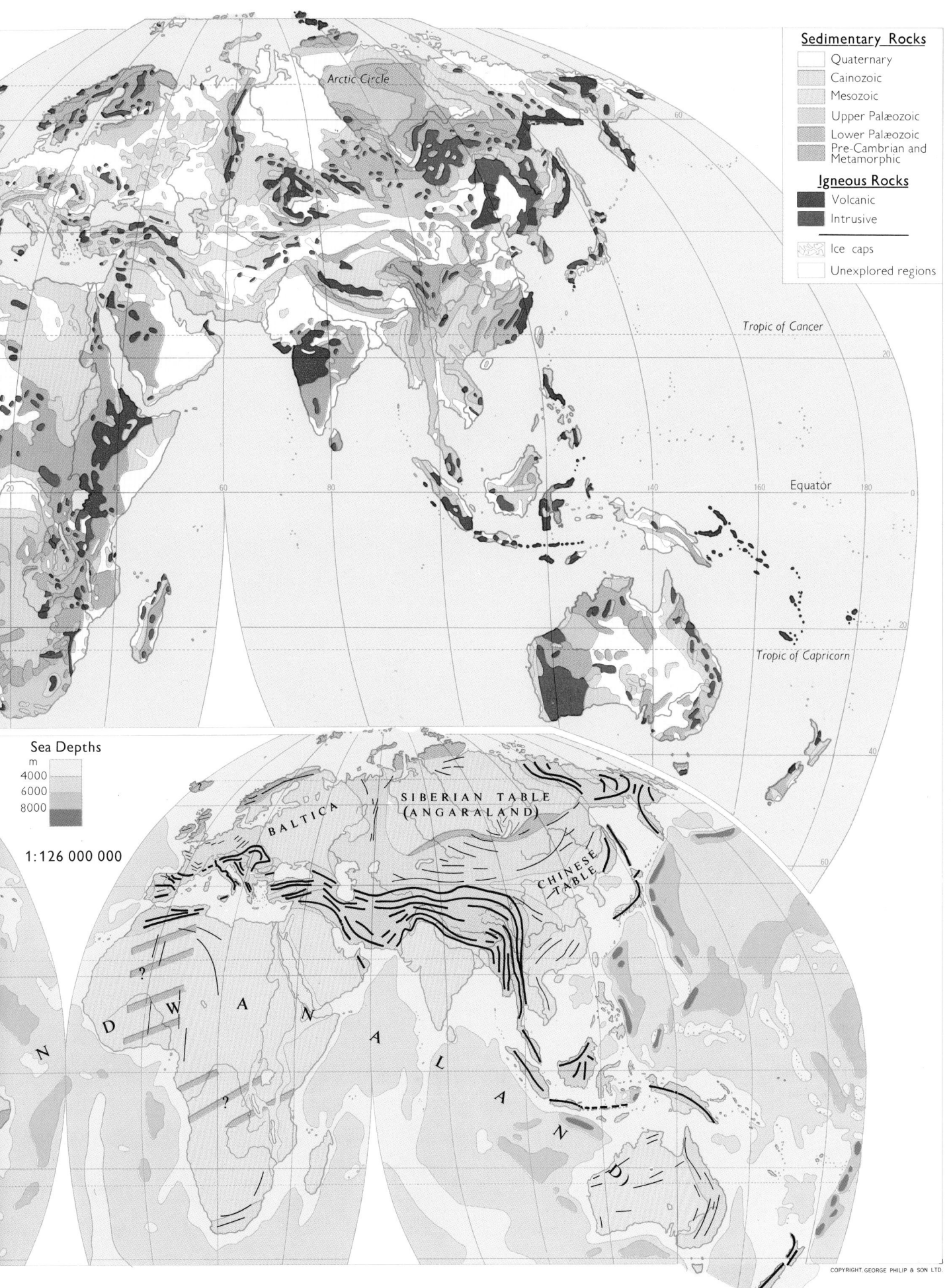

3

Sedimentary Rocks
- Quaternary
- Cainozoic
- Mesozoic
- Upper Palæozoic
- Lower Palæozoic
- Pre-Cambrian and Metamorphic

Igneous Rocks
- Volcanic
- Intrusive

- Ice caps
- Unexplored regions

Arctic Circle

Tropic of Cancer

Equator

Tropic of Capricorn

60

20

140   160   180   0

20

40

60

Sea Depths
m
4000
6000
8000

1:126 000 000

BALTICA

SIBERIAN TABLE
(ANGARALAND)

CHINESE
TABLE

G O N D W A N A L A N D

?

?

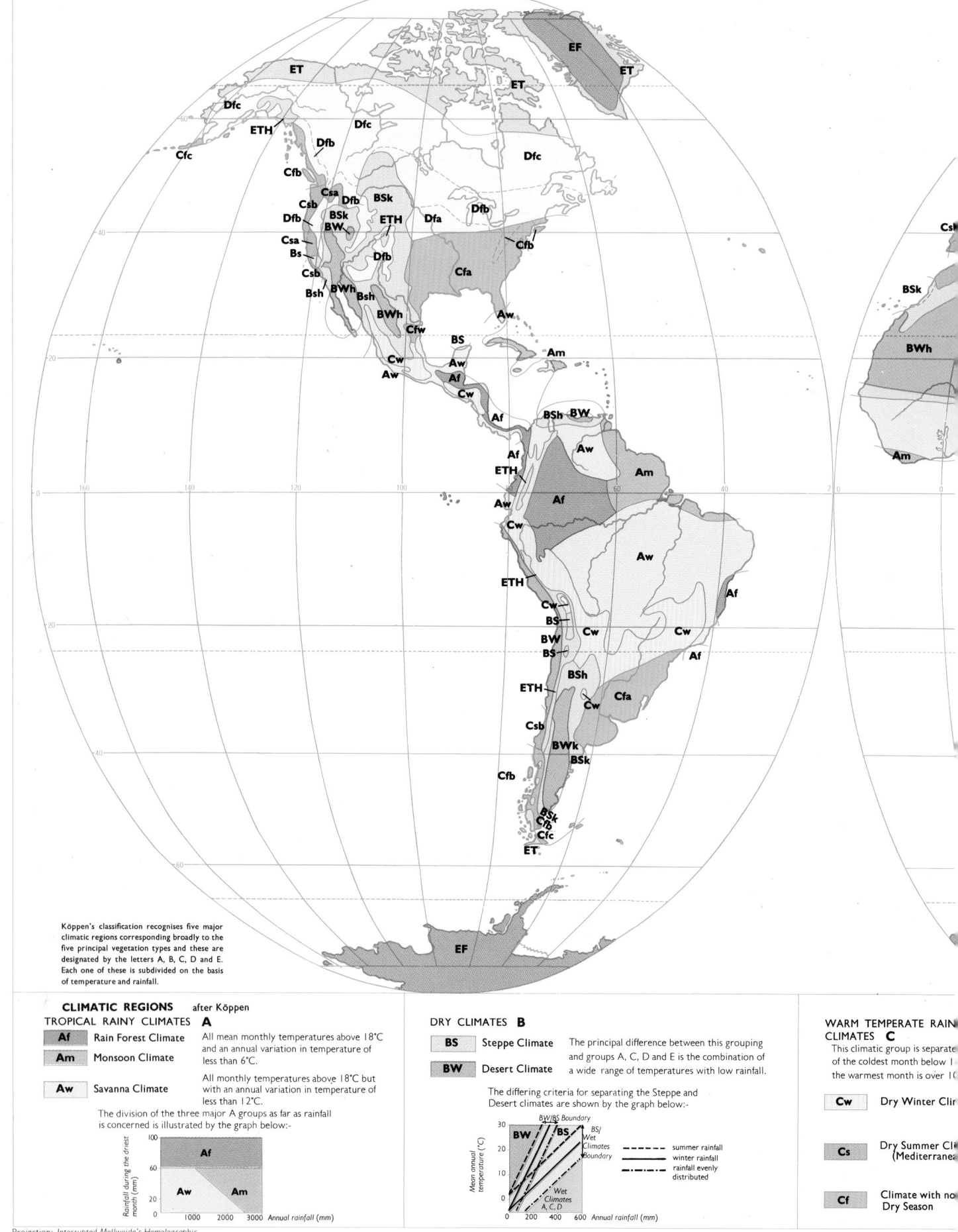

Köppen's classification recognises five major
climatic regions corresponding broadly to the
five principal vegetation types and these are
designated by the letters A, B, C, D and E.
Each one of these is subdivided on the basis
of temperature and rainfall.

CLIMATIC REGIONS after Köppen

TROPICAL RAINY CLIMATES **A**

Af	Rain Forest Climate
Am	Monsoon Climate
Aw	Savanna Climate

All mean monthly temperatures above 18°C
and an annual variation in temperature of
less than 6°C.

All monthly temperatures above 18°C but
with an annual variation in temperature of
less than 12°C.

The division of the three major A groups as far as rainfall
is concerned is illustrated by the graph below:-

DRY CLIMATES **B**

BS	Steppe Climate
BW	Desert Climate

The principal difference between this grouping
and groups A, C, D and E is the combination of
a wide range of temperatures with low rainfall.

The differing criteria for separating the Steppe and
Desert climates are shown by the graph below:-

- - - - summer rainfall
———— winter rainfall
—·—·— rainfall evenly
distributed

WARM TEMPERATE RAIN
CLIMATES **C**

This climatic group is separate
of the coldest month below 1
the warmest month is over 10

Cw	Dry Winter Clin
Cs	Dry Summer Cl
(Mediterranea
Cf	Climate with no
Dry Season

Projection: *Interrupted Mollweide's Homolographic*

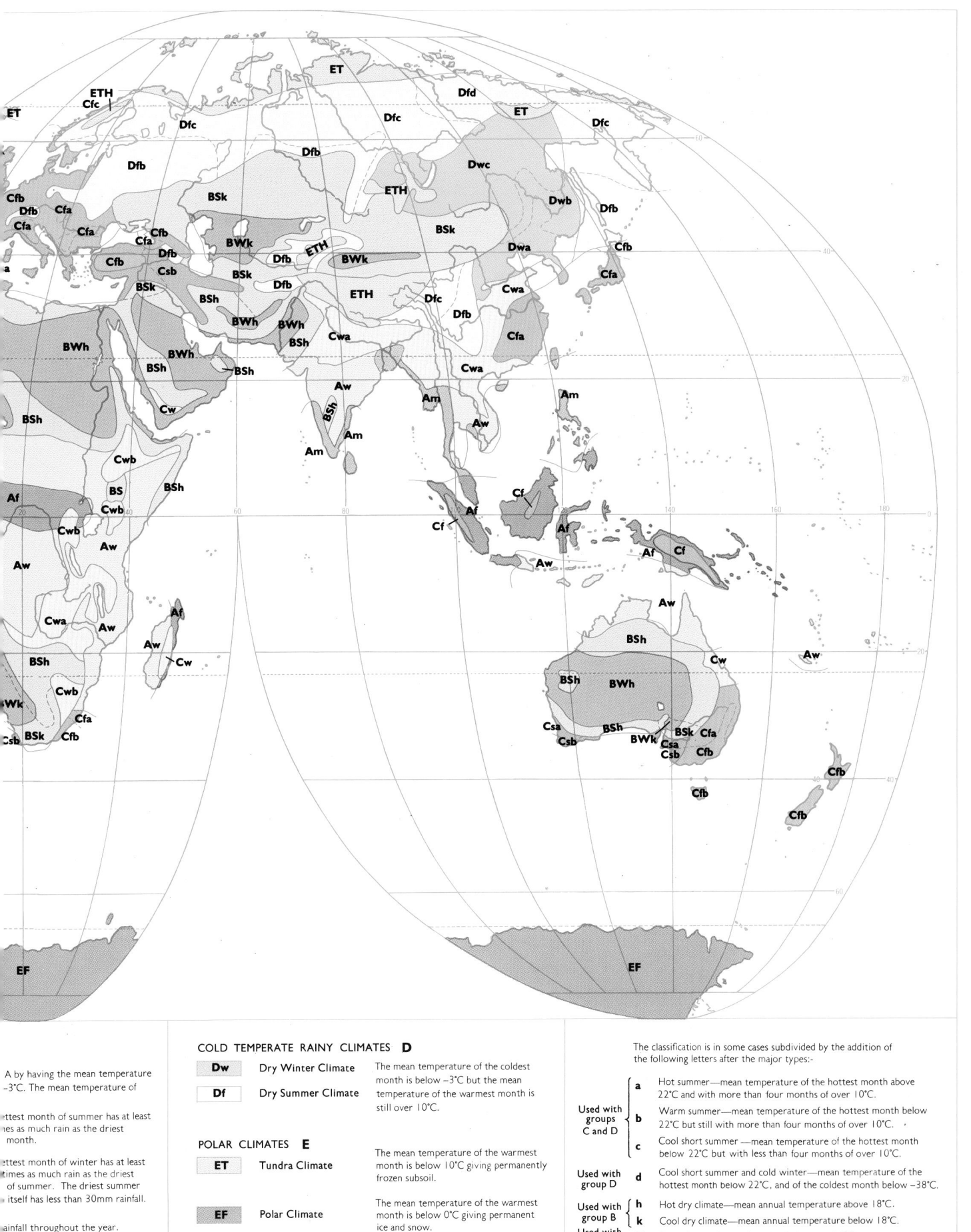

ETH
Cfc
ET
Dfd
ET
Dfc
Dfc
Dfb
Dfb
Dwc
Cfb
Dfb
Dwb
Cfb
BSk
Dfb
Dfb
ETH
Dwa
Cfb
Cfb
Cfa
Cfa
Cfa
Cfb
BWk
Dfb
Cfa
Cfb
ETH
BWk
Dwa
Cfa
Csb
BSk
Dfb
Cwa
BSh
Dfb
Cwa
Dfc
Cfa
BWh
BWh
BSh
ETH
Dfb
Cwa
BWh
BSh
BSh
Cwa
BSh
BWh
BSh
Cw
Am
Am
Aw
Am
Af
Cwb
BSh
Aw
BS
Cwb
Af
Am
Cwb
Af
Aw
Cf
Cf
Aw
Af
Af
Cf
Aw
Af
Cwa
Af
Aw
Aw
Aw
Aw
BSh
Cw
BSh
Cw
Cwb
BWh
Wk
Csa
BSh
BSk Cfa
BSk Cfa
Csb
BWk
Csa
Cfb
Csb
Csb
Cfb
Cfb
Cfb
EF
EF

A by having the mean temperature
–3°C. The mean temperature of

ttest month of summer has at least
es as much rain as the driest
month.

ttest month of winter has at least
imes as much rain as the driest
of summer. The driest summer
itself has less than 30mm rainfall.

ainfall throughout the year.

COLD TEMPERATE RAINY CLIMATES D

| Dw | Dry Winter Climate | The mean temperature of the coldest |
| Df | Dry Summer Climate | month is below –3°C but the mean temperature of the warmest month is still over 10°C. |

POLAR CLIMATES E

| ET | Tundra Climate | The mean temperature of the warmest month is below 10°C giving permanently frozen subsoil. |
| EF | Polar Climate | The mean temperature of the warmest month is below 0°C giving permanent ice and snow. |

The classification is in some cases subdivided by the addition of the following letters after the major types:-

Used with groups C and D	a	Hot summer—mean temperature of the hottest month above 22°C and with more than four months of over 10°C.
	b	Warm summer—mean temperature of the hottest month below 22°C but still with more than four months of over 10°C.
	c	Cool short summer —mean temperature of the hottest month below 22°C but with less than four months of over 10°C.
Used with group D	d	Cool short summer and cold winter—mean temperature of the hottest month below 22°C, and of the coldest month below –38°C.
Used with group B	h	Hot dry climate—mean annual temperature above 18°C.
	k	Cool dry climate—mean annual temperature below 18°C.
Used with group E	H	Polar climate due to elevation being over 1500m

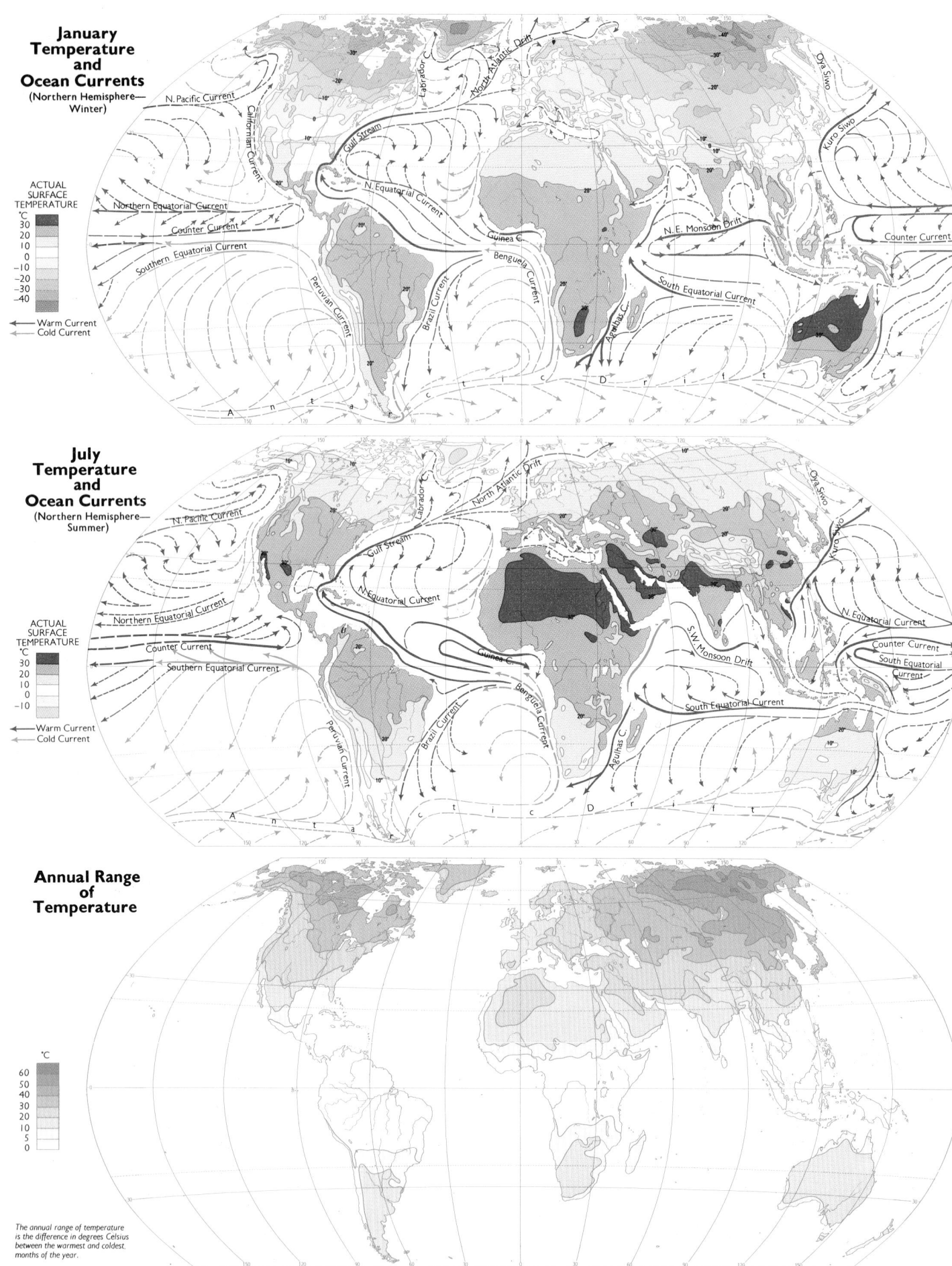

January Temperature and Ocean Currents
(Northern Hemisphere—Winter)

ACTUAL
SURFACE
TEMPERATURE

°C
30
20
10
0
-10
-20
-30
-40

→ Warm Current
→ Cold Current

N. Pacific Current
Californian Current
Labrador C.
North Atlantic Drift
Oya Siwo
Gulf Stream
N. Equatorial Current
Kuro Siwo
Northern Equatorial Current
Counter Current
Guinea C.
N. E. Monsoon Drift
Counter Current
Southern Equatorial Current
Benguela Current
South Equatorial Current
Peruvian Current
Brazil Current
Agulhas C.
A n t a r c t i c   D r i f t

July Temperature and Ocean Currents
(Northern Hemisphere—Summer)

ACTUAL
SURFACE
TEMPERATURE

°C
30
20
10
0
-10

→ Warm Current
→ Cold Current

N. Pacific Current
Labrador C.
North Atlantic Drift
Oya Siwo
Gulf Stream
N. Equatorial Current
Kuro Siwo
Northern Equatorial Current
N. Equatorial Current
Counter Current
Counter Current
Southern Equatorial Current
Guinea C.
S.W. Monsoon Drift
South Equatorial Current
South Equatorial Current
Benguela Current
Peruvian Current
Brazil Current
Agulhas C.
A n t a r c t i c   D r i f t

Annual Range of Temperature

°C
60
50
40
30
20
10
5
0

The annual range of temperature is the difference in degrees Celsius between the warmest and coldest months of the year.

Projection: *Hammer Equal Area*

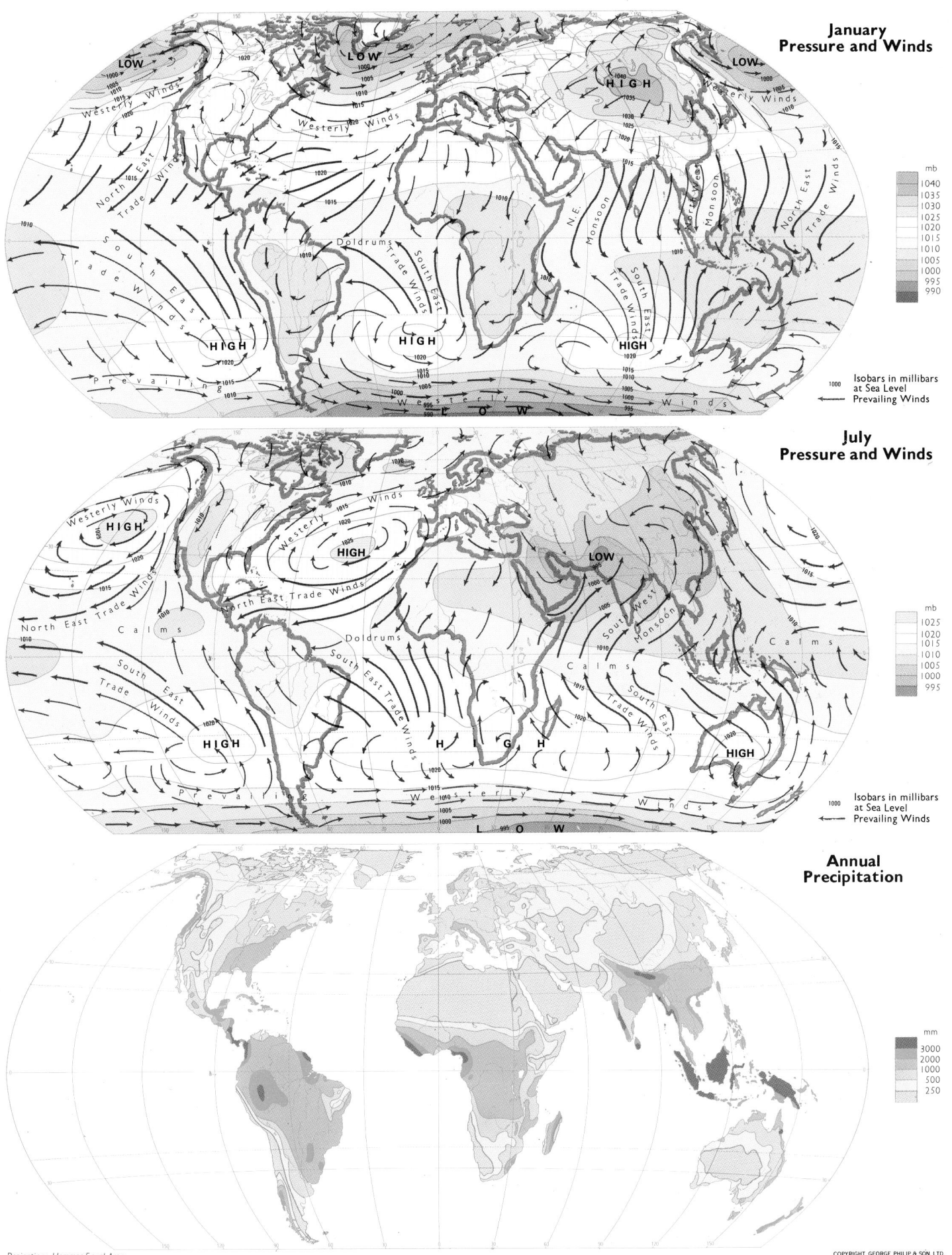

January
Pressure and Winds

mb
1040
1035
1030
1025
1020
1015
1010
1005
1000
995
990

1000 Isobars in millibars
at Sea Level
Prevailing Winds

July
Pressure and Winds

mb
1025
1020
1015
1010
1005
1000
995

1000 Isobars in millibars
at Sea Level
Prevailing Winds

Annual
Precipitation

mm
3000
2000
1000
500
250

Projection: *Hammer Equal Area*

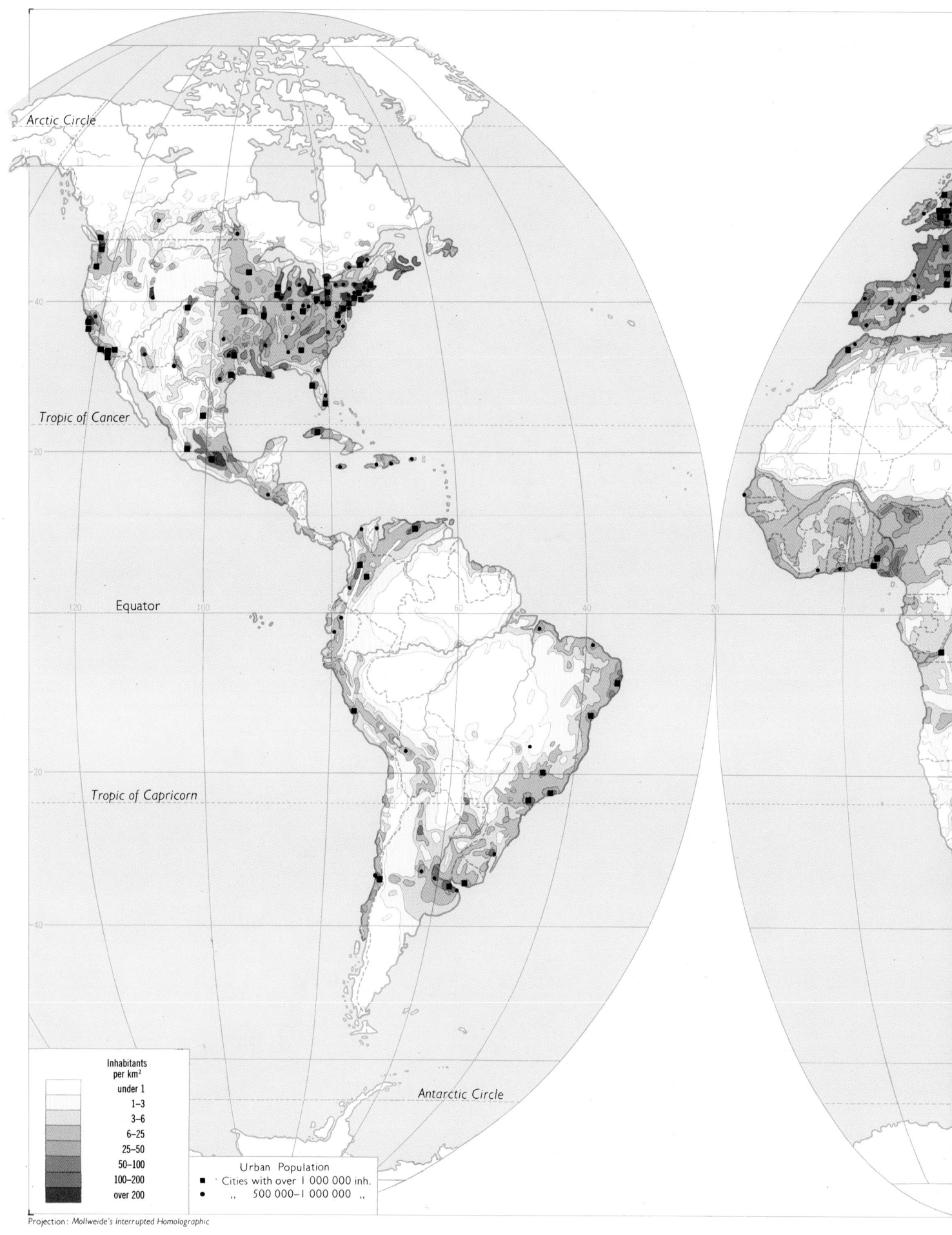

Arctic Circle

Tropic of Cancer

Equator

Tropic of Capricorn

Antarctic Circle

120   100   60   40   20   0

Inhabitants
per km²

	under 1
	1–3
	3–6
	6–25
	25–50
	50–100
	100–200
	over 200

Urban Population
■ Cities with over 1 000 000 inh.
● ,,   500 000– 1 000 000 ,,

Projection: Mollweide's Interrupted Homolographic

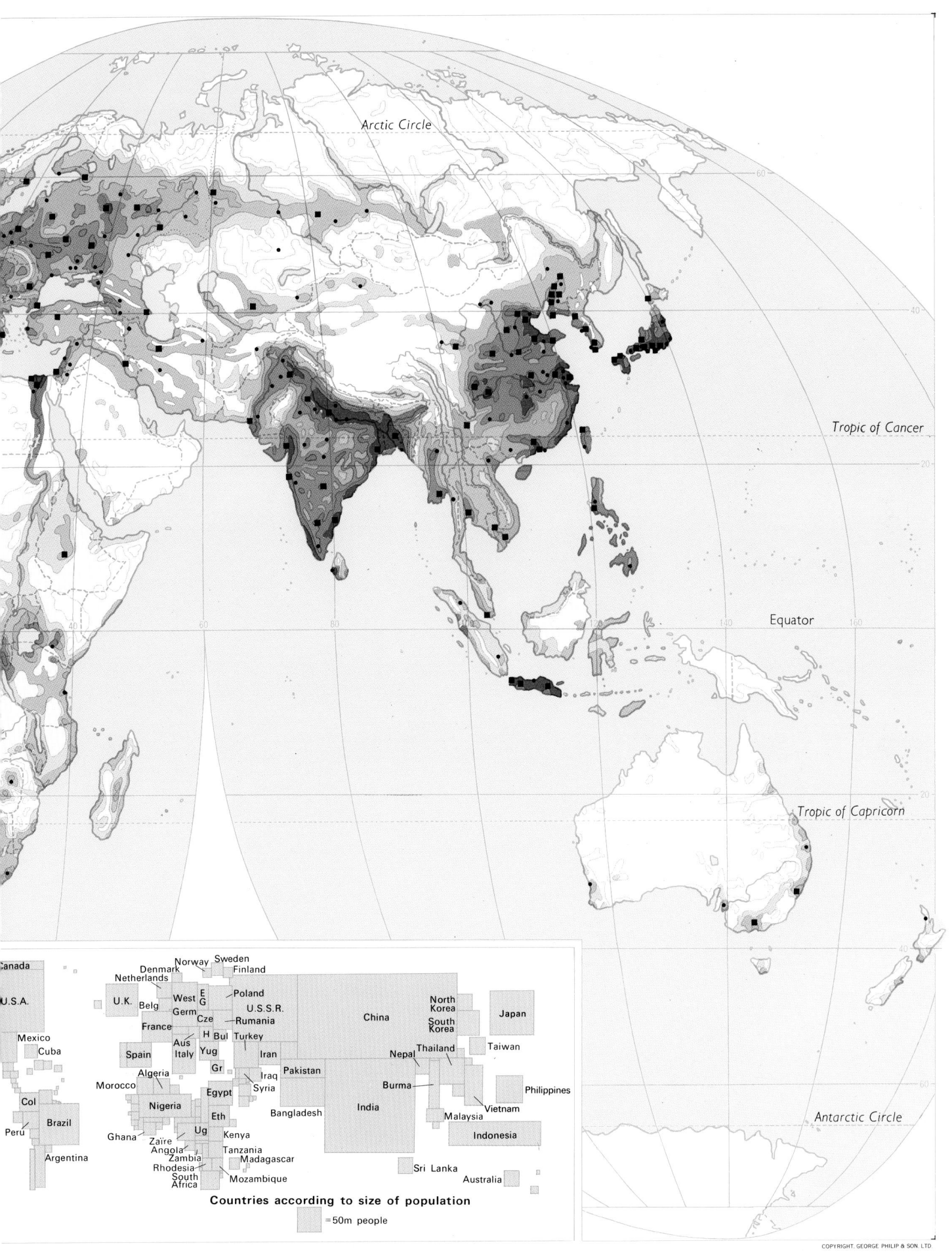

Arctic Circle

60

40

Tropic of Cancer

20

Equator

140   160

Tropic of Capricorn

20

Antarctic Circle

Canada

U.S.A.

Mexico
Cuba

Col
Peru
Brazil
Argentina

Norway Sweden
Denmark   Finland
Netherlands

U.K. Belg West E Poland
Germ G Cze Rumania
France   H Bul Turkey
Aus Yug
Spain Italy   Iran
Algeria Gr   Iraq
Morocco   Egypt Syria
Nigeria   Eth
Ghana   Bangladesh
Zaïre Ug Kenya
Angola Tanzania
Zambia Madagascar
Rhodesia Mozambique
South
Africa

U.S.S.R.

China

Pakistan

India

Sri Lanka

North
Korea
South
Korea

Nepal Thailand

Burma   Vietnam
Malaysia

Indonesia

Australia

Japan

Taiwan

Philippines

Countries according to size of population

=50m people

ARCTIC REGIONS

EUREKA
TEMPERATURE
Range 51.7°C   ℃
10
0
-10
-20
-30
Eureka   -40
80°00N
85°56W

PRESSURE
M.S.L.   mb
1025
1020
1015
1010

ANNUAL
PRECIPITATION   mm
Total 58.2mm.   50
0
J F M A M J J A S O N D

Arctic Explorers
Cook 1778
Franklin 1826–47
McClure 1850–53
Nordenskiöld ("Vega")1878–79
De Long 1881
Nansen ("Fram") 1893–96
Abruzzi & Cagni 1899–1900
Sverdrup 1902
Peary 1892–1906
Amundsen 1903–6 & 1926
Peary 1908–9
Knud Rasmussen 1912
Koch 1913
Stefánsson 1914–15
Byrd 1926 (by air)
Wilkins 1928 (by air)
Lindsay 1934
Papanin (Drift of Soviet
Expedition) 1937–38
"Sedov" 1937–40
Knuth (Danish Pearyland
Expedition) 1948–49

Projection: *Zenithal Equidistant*

Seas open all yea
Extreme limits c
drift-ice
Seas covered by
pack-ice in Sprin
Seas permanently
covered by pack-
Ice-caps and
permanent ice sh

Progress of Exploration
Coasts explored before   1800
  ,,   ,,   between 1800 & 18
  ,,   ,,   between 1850 & 19
  ,,   ,,   since   1900
+ Byrd   Highest latitudes reached by explorer
1926   with da

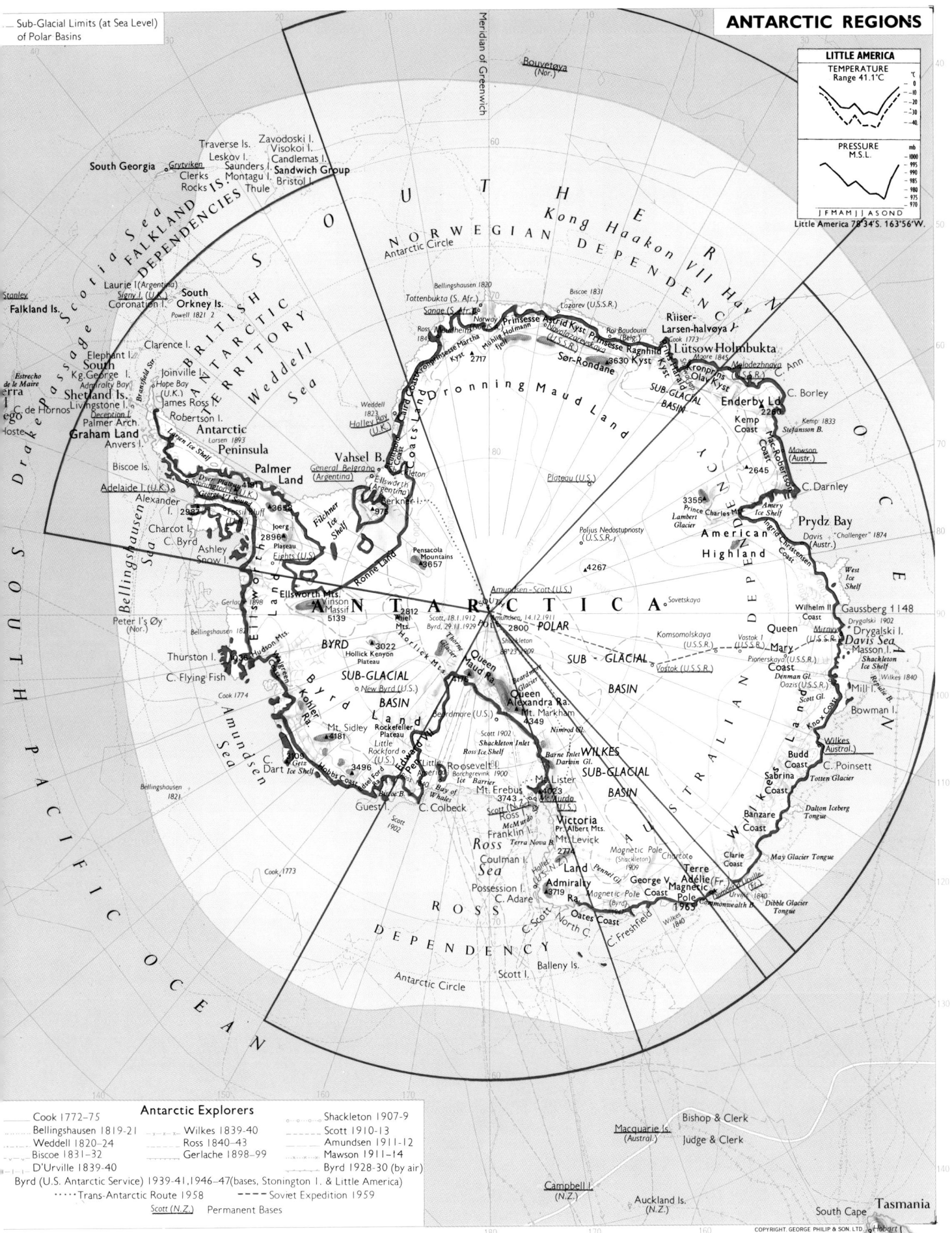

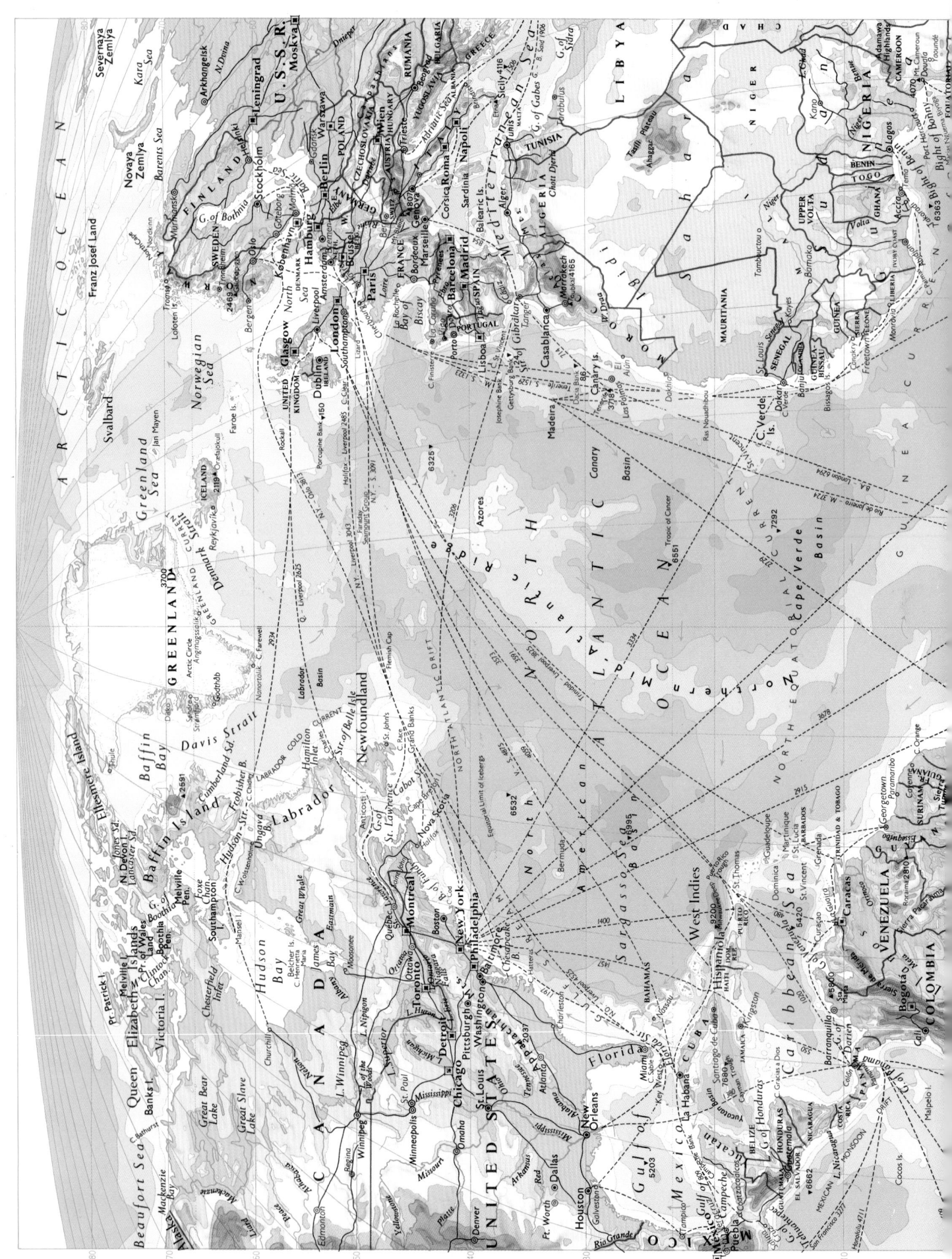

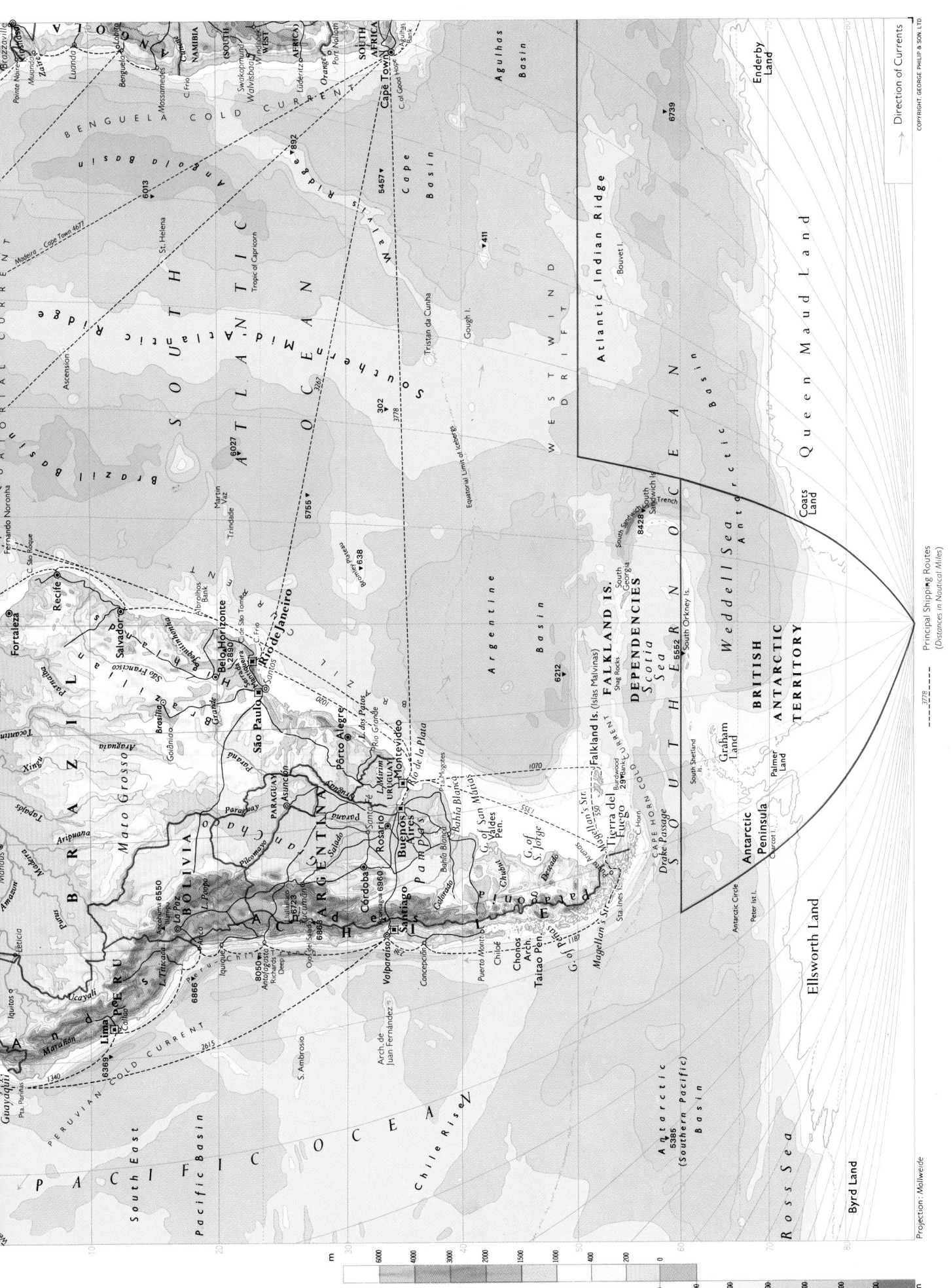

PACIFIC OCEAN

SOUTH ATLANTIC OCEAN

Southern

South East Pacific Basin

Pacific Basin

Chile Risen

Antarctic (Southern Pacific) Basin 5385

Mid Atlantic Ridge

Brazil Basin

Argentine Basin 6212

Brazil Basin

Angola Basin 6013

Cape Basin

Agulhas Basin

BENGUELA COLD CURRENT

EQUATORIAL CURRENT

Atlantic Indian Ridge

WEST WIND DRIFT

Queen Maud Land

Enderby Land

Coats Land

Weddell Sea

Antarctic Basin

SOUTHERN OCEAN

BRITISH ANTARCTIC TERRITORY

Ross Sea

Byrd Land

Ellsworth Land

Antarctic Peninsula

Graham Land

Palmer Land

FALKLAND IS. DEPENDENCIES

Scotia Sea

South Georgia

South Sandwich Is. 8428 Trench

South Orkney Is.

South Shetland

Antarctic Circle

Peter I st. I.

CAPE HORN COLD CURRENT

Drake Passage

Tierra del Fuego

C. Horn

Magellan's Str.

G. of Penas

Taitao Pen.

Chonos Arch.

Chiloé

Puerto Montt

Concepción

Valparaiso

Santiago

PERUVIAN COLD CURRENT

Lima El Callao 6369

Guayaquil

Pta. Parinas

Ucayali

Marañón

Iquitos

Leticia

BRAZIL

PERU

BOLIVIA

La Paz

Titicaca

CHILE

Antofagasta

Iquique

Arica

ARGENTINA

Córdoba 6960

Santiago

Tucumán 6723

Mendoza

Aconcagua 6550

Llullaillaco 6723

Rosario

Buenos Aires

Montevideo

URUGUAY

Río de la Plata

Bahia Blanca

Colorado

Pampas

Chubut

G. of S. Jorge

G. of San Matías

Valdés Pen.

PARAGUAY

Asunción

Paraguay

Paraná

São Paulo

Pôrto Alegre

Rio Grande

Rio de Janeiro 2890

Belo Horizonte

Salvador

Recife

Fortaleza

Fernando Noronha

Abrolhos Bank

Trindade

Martin Vaz

6027

5755

302 3778

638

5457 892

Tropic of Capricorn

Ascension

St. Helena

Tristan da Cunha

Gough I. 411

Bouvet I.

6739

Equatorial Limit of Icebergs

Cape Town 1070

C. of Good Hope

Agulhas Bank

SOUTH AFRICA

NAMIBIA (SOUTH WEST AFRICA)

Windhoek

Walvisbaai

Swakopmund

Lüderitz

Orange

C. Frio

Mossâmedes

Benguela

Lobito

Luanda

ANGOLA

Zaïre

Pointe Noire

Brazzaville

Madeira — Cape Town 4677

8050 Richards Deep

6866

1340

2615

1187

5552

5385

1335

590 Burdwood Bank 29

Falkland Is. (Islas Malvinas)

Shag Rocks

COPYRIGHT. GEORGE PHILIP & SON LTD.

Projection: Mollweide

Direction of Currents

Principal Shipping Routes
(Distances in Nautical Miles)

---- 3778

1 : 20 000 000

1:40 000 000

400   0   400   800   1200   1600 km

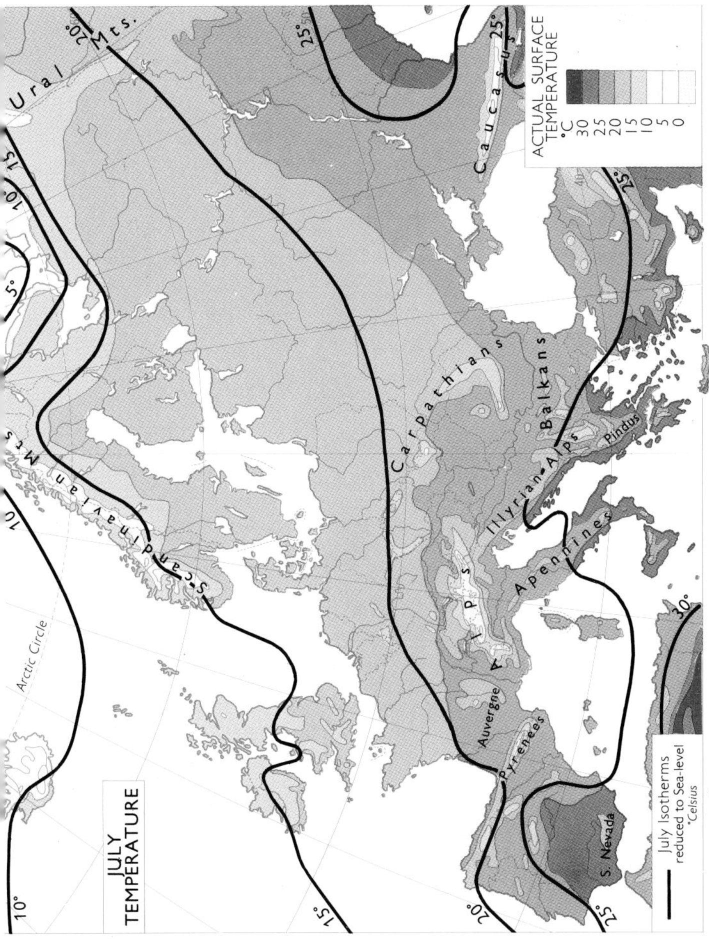

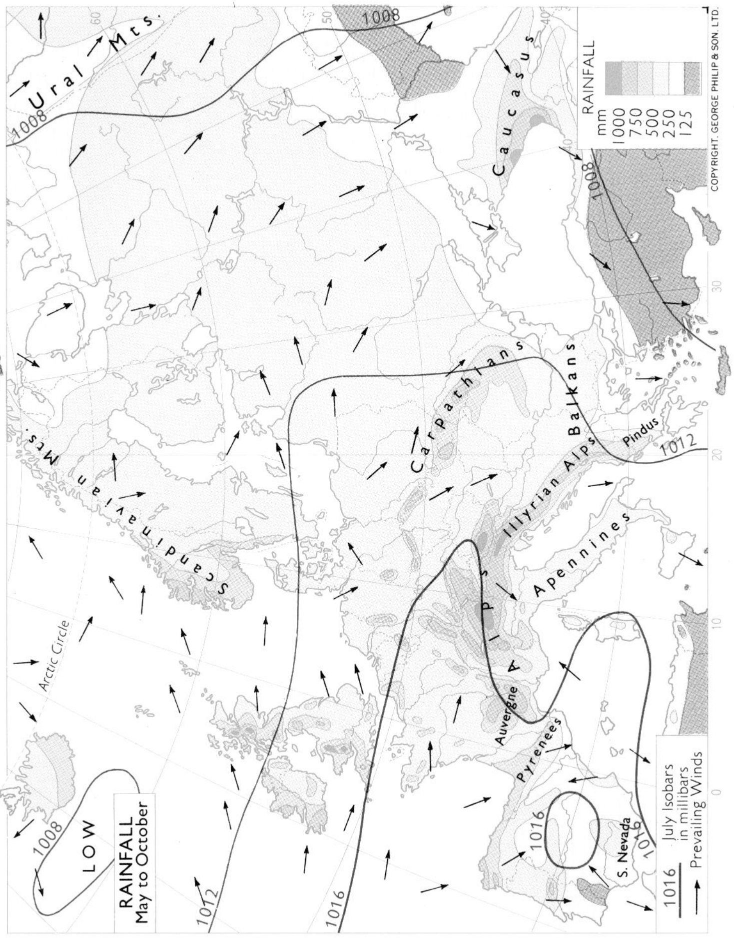

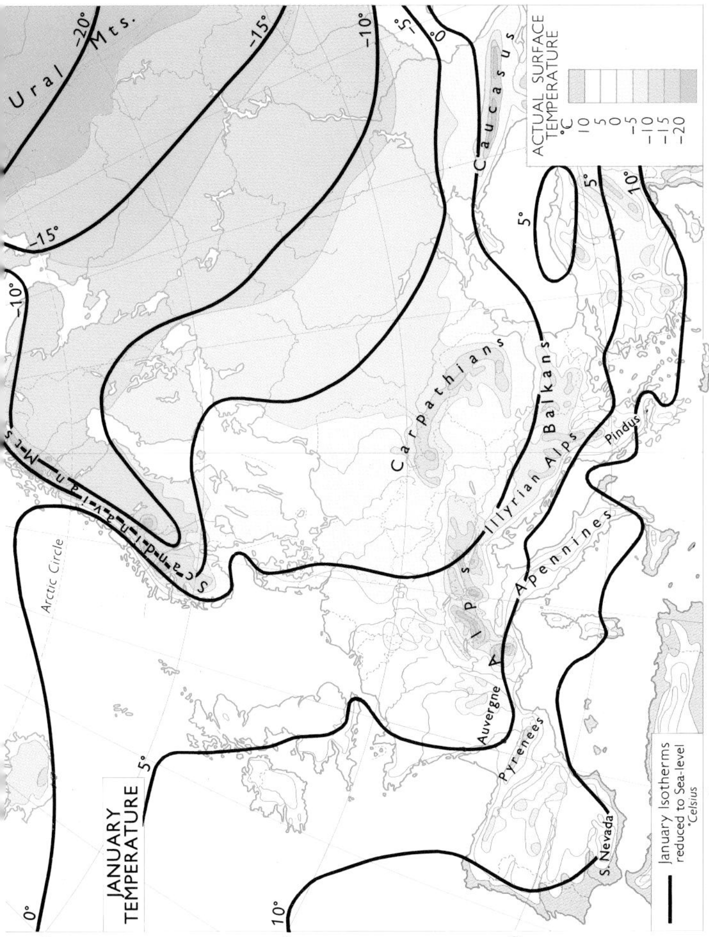

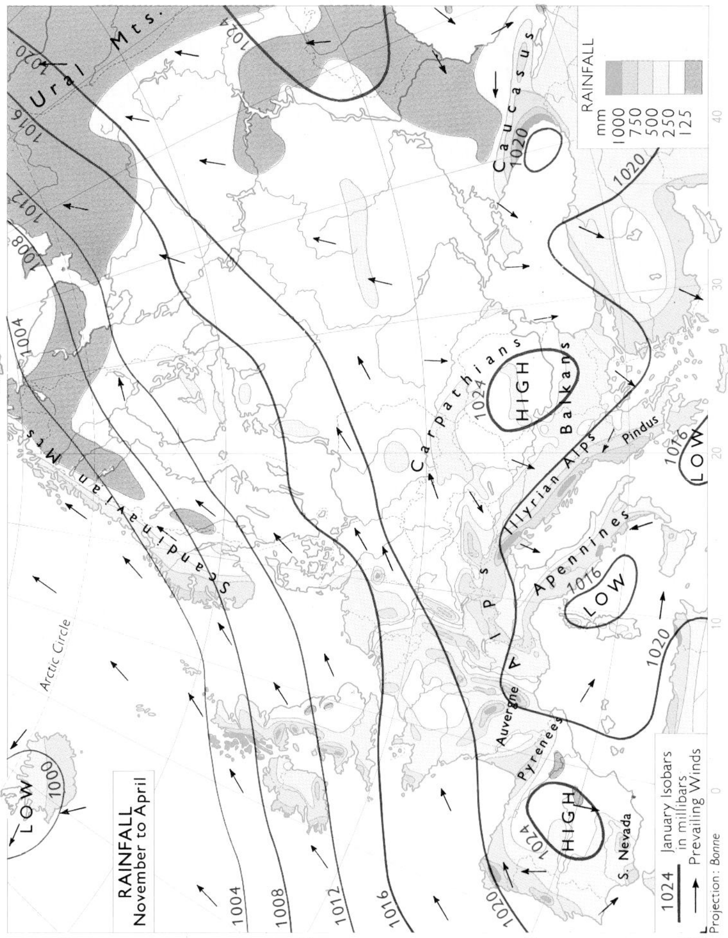

Top-left map — JULY TEMPERATURE

Ural Mts.
Caucasus
Scandinavian Mts.
Carpathians
Illyrian Alps
Balkans
Pindus
Alps
Apennines
Auvergne
Pyrenees
S. Nevada
Arctic Circle

ACTUAL SURFACE
TEMPERATURE
°C
30
25
20
15
10
5
0

JULY
TEMPERATURE

—— July Isotherms
reduced to Sea-level
°Celsius

20° 25° 15° 10° 5° 30° 15° 20° 25°

Top-right map — RAINFALL May to October

Ural Mts.
Caucasus
Scandinavian Mts.
Carpathians
Illyrian Alps
Balkans
Pindus
Alps
Apennines
Auvergne
Pyrenees
S. Nevada
Arctic Circle

RAINFALL
mm
1000
750
500
250
125

COPYRIGHT: GEORGE PHILIP & SON LTD.

1008 1008 1008 1012 1016 1008 1012 1016

LOW

RAINFALL
May to October

—— July Isobars
in millibars
→ Prevailing Winds
1016

Bottom-left map — JANUARY TEMPERATURE

Ural Mts.
Caucasus
Scandinavian Mts.
Carpathians
Illyrian Alps
Balkans
Pindus
Alps
Apennines
Auvergne
Pyrenees
S. Nevada
Arctic Circle

ACTUAL SURFACE
TEMPERATURE
°C
10
5
0
-5
-10
-20

-20° -15° -10° -5° 0° 5° 10°
-10° -15° 5° 10° 5° 10° 0°

JANUARY
TEMPERATURE

—— January Isotherms
reduced to Sea-level
°Celsius

60 50 40

Bottom-right map — RAINFALL November to April

Ural Mts.
Caucasus
Scandinavian Mts.
Carpathians
Illyrian Alps
Balkans
Pindus
Alps
Apennines
Auvergne
Pyrenees
S. Nevada
Arctic Circle

RAINFALL
mm
1000
750
500
250
125

1020 1016 1012 1020 1020 1020
HIGH
LOW
LOW
LOW
1016
HIGH
1004 1008 1012 1016 1020 1024 1024

RAINFALL
November to April

—— January Isobars
in millibars
→ Prevailing Winds
1024

HHK   Projection: Bonne

1:35 000 000

400   0   400   800   1200 km

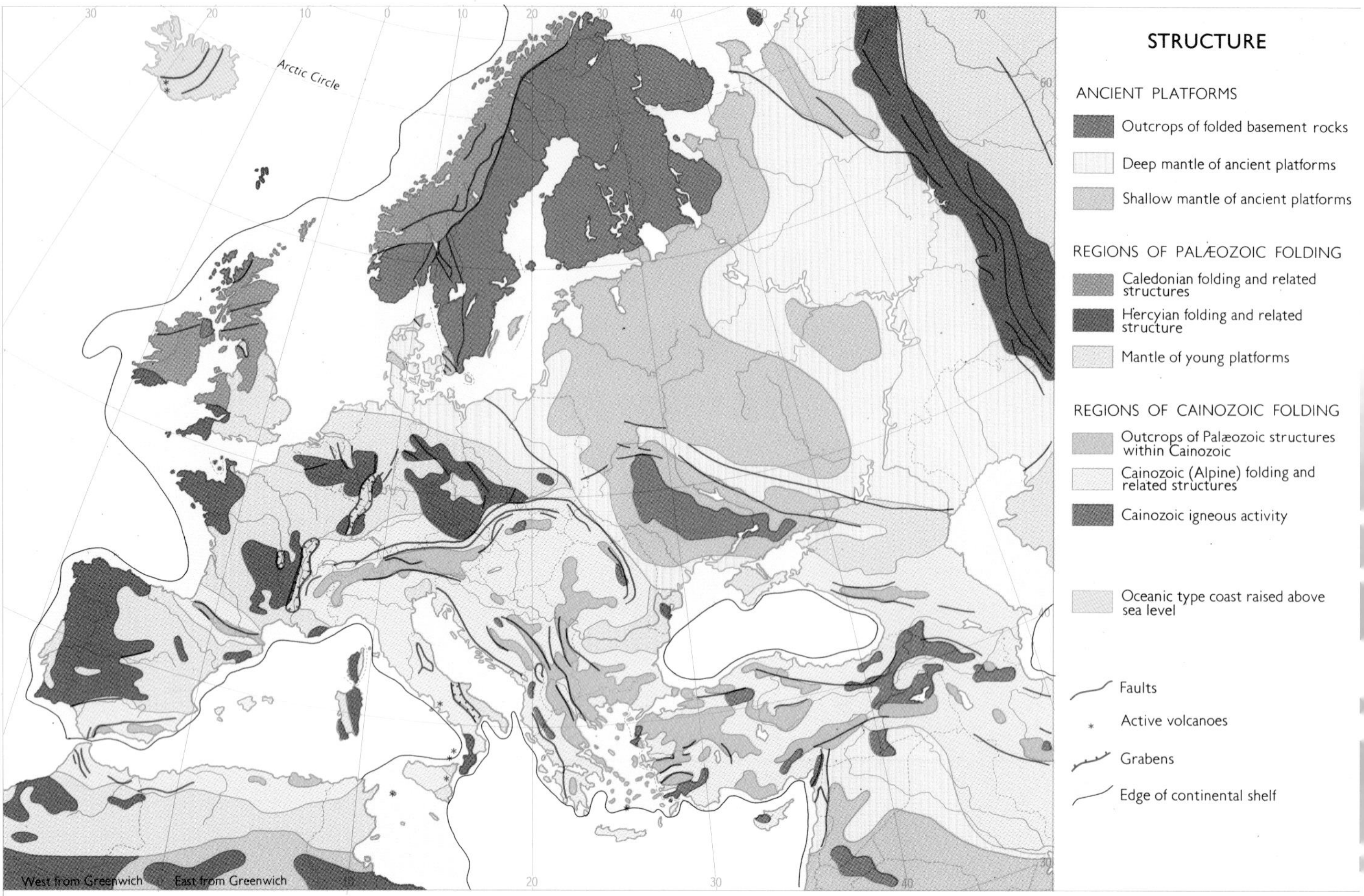

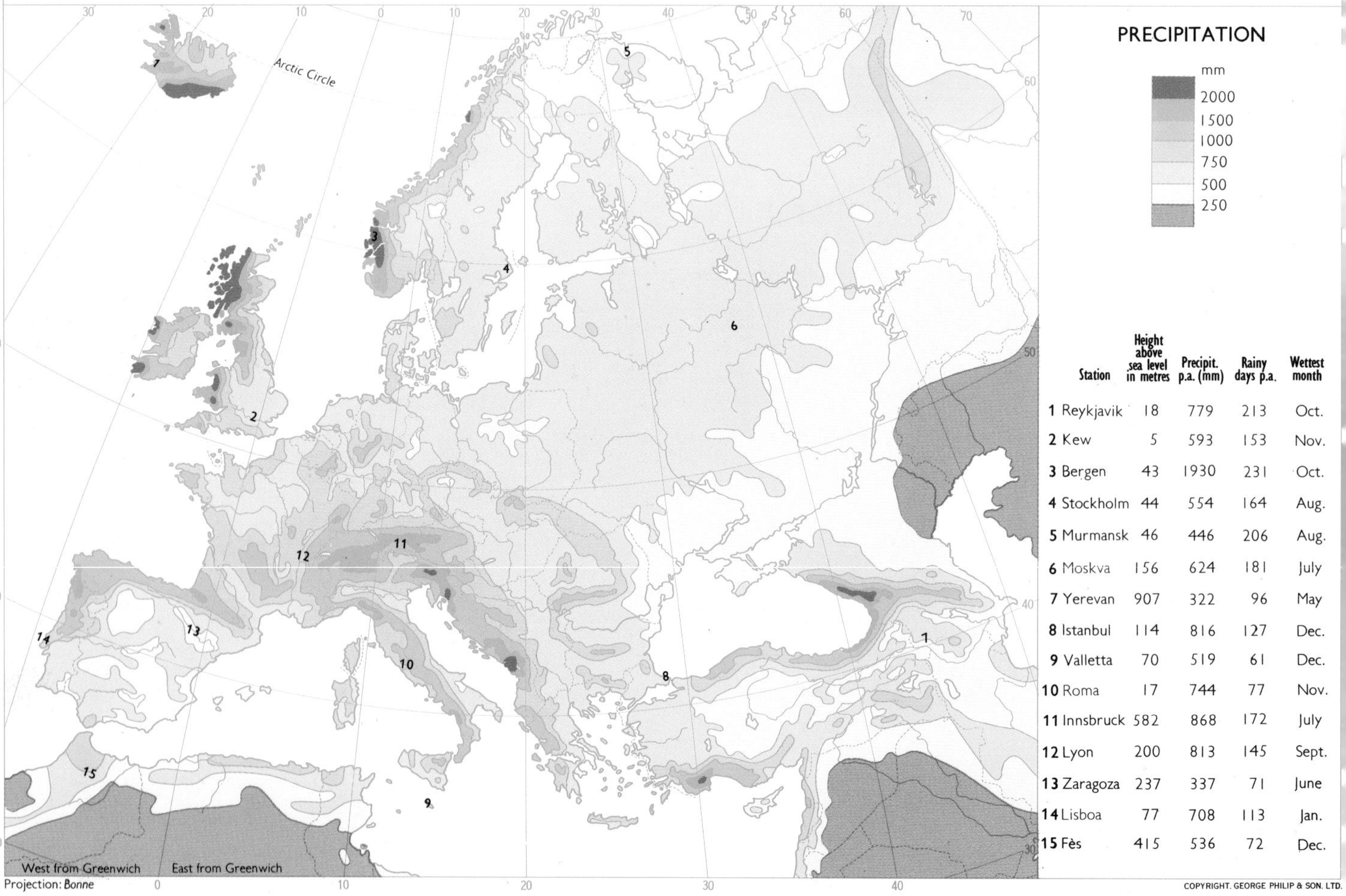

STRUCTURE

ANCIENT PLATFORMS

- Outcrops of folded basement rocks
- Deep mantle of ancient platforms
- Shallow mantle of ancient platforms

REGIONS OF PALÆOZOIC FOLDING

- Caledonian folding and related structures
- Hercyian folding and related structure
- Mantle of young platforms

REGIONS OF CAINOZOIC FOLDING

- Outcrops of Palæozoic structures within Cainozoic
- Cainozoic (Alpine) folding and related structures
- Cainozoic igneous activity

- Oceanic type coast raised above sea level

- Faults
- Active volcanoes
- Grabens
- Edge of continental shelf

Arctic Circle

West from Greenwich   East from Greenwich

PRECIPITATION

mm
2000
1500
1000
750
500
250

Arctic Circle

Station	Height above sea level in metres	Precipit. p.a. (mm)	Rainy days p.a.	Wettest month
1 Reykjavik	18	779	213	Oct.
2 Kew	5	593	153	Nov.
3 Bergen	43	1930	231	Oct.
4 Stockholm	44	554	164	Aug.
5 Murmansk	46	446	206	Aug.
6 Moskva	156	624	181	July
7 Yerevan	907	322	96	May
8 Istanbul	114	816	127	Dec.
9 Valletta	70	519	61	Dec.
10 Roma	17	744	77	Nov.
11 Innsbruck	582	868	172	July
12 Lyon	200	813	145	Sept.
13 Zaragoza	237	337	71	June
14 Lisboa	77	708	113	Jan.
15 Fès	415	536	72	Dec.

West from Greenwich   East from Greenwich

Projection: Bonne

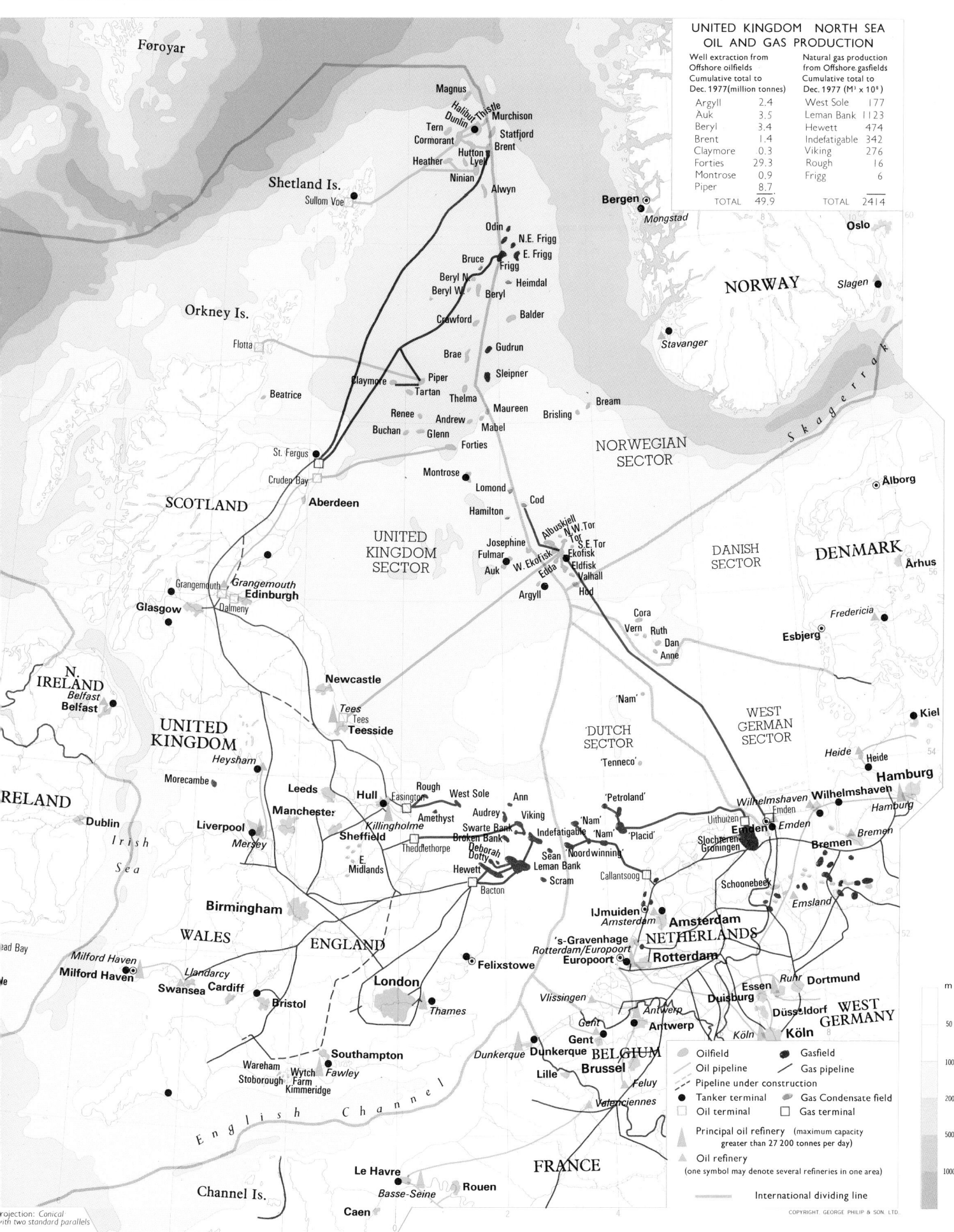

1:6 000 000

50   0   50   100   150   200   250 km

UNITED KINGDOM NORTH SEA OIL AND GAS PRODUCTION			
Well extraction from Offshore oilfields Cumulative total to Dec. 1977(million tonnes)		Natural gas production from Offshore gasfields Cumulative total to Dec. 1977 (M³ x 10⁸)	
Argyll	2.4	West Sole	177
Auk	3.5	Leman Bank	1123
Beryl	3.4	Hewett	474
Brent	1.4	Indefatigable	342
Claymore	0.3	Viking	276
Forties	29.3	Rough	16
Montrose	0.9	Frigg	6
Piper	8.7		
TOTAL	49.9	TOTAL	2414

Føroyar

Magnus
Halibut Thistle
Dunlin Murchison
Tern
Cormorant   Statfjord
Hutton   Brent
Heather   Lyell
Ninian
Shetland Is.
Sullom Voe   Alwyn

Odin
N.E. Frigg
Bruce   E. Frigg
Frigg
Beryl N   Heimdal
Beryl W   Beryl
Crawford   Balder
Brae   Gudrun
Orkney Is.
Flotta
Piper   Sleipner
Claymore   Tartan
Beatrice   Thelma
Renee   Maureen   Brisling
Buchan   Andrew   Mabel
Glenn   Bream
St. Fergus   Forties
Cruden Bay   Montrose
SCOTLAND   Lomond
Aberdeen   Cod
Hamilton
UNITED   Albuskjell
KINGDOM   Josephine   N.W. Tor
SECTOR   Fulmar   Tor   S.E. Tor
Auk   W. Ekofisk   Ekofisk
Edda   Eldfisk
Argyll   Valhall
Hod

Bergen
Mongstad
Oslo
NORWAY   Slagen
Stavanger

NORWEGIAN
SECTOR

Skagerrak

DANISH
SECTOR   DENMARK
Ålborg
Århus

Cora
Vern   Ruth
Dan
Anne

Esbjerg
Fredericia

Grangemouth
Edinburgh
Glasgow   Dalmeny

N.
IRELAND
Belfast
Belfast

UNITED
KINGDOM

IRELAND
Dublin

Irish
Sea

Newcastle
Tees
Tees
Teesside

Heysham
Morecambe
Leeds
Liverpool   Hull   Easington
Manchester   Rough   West Sole   Ann
Mersey   Amethyst   Audrey   Viking
Killingholme   Swarte Bank
Sheffield   Broken Bank   Indefatigable
Theddlethorpe   Deborah   Sean
E.   Dotty   Leman Bank
Midlands   Hewett   Scram
Bacton

Birmingham

WALES
ENGLAND

Milford Haven
Milford Haven   Llandarcy
Swansea   Cardiff
Bristol

London
Felixstowe
Thames

'Nam'

WEST
GERMAN
SECTOR
Kiel

'DUTCH
SECTOR
'Tenneco'

Heide
Heide
Hamburg
Hamburg

'Petroland'
'Nam'
'Nam'   'Placid'
'Noordwinning'
Callantsoog

Uithuizen   Wilhelmshaven   Wilhelmshaven
Emden
Emden   Emden   Bremen
Slochteren   Bremen
Groningen

Schoonebeek

IJmuiden
Amsterdam   Amsterdam
's-Gravenhage
Rotterdam/Europoort
Europoort   Rotterdam

Emsland

NETHERLANDS

Ruhr   Dortmund
Essen
Duisburg
Düsseldorf   WEST
GERMANY
Köln
Köln

Vlissingen
Antwerp
Gent
Dunkerque   Gent   Antwerp
Dunkerque   BELGIUM
Lille   Brussel
Brussel

Southampton
Wareham   Wytch
Stoborough   Farm   Fawley
Kimmeridge

Feluy
Valenciennes

English   Channel

Le Havre   Rouen
Channel Is.   Basse-Seine
Caen

FRANCE

◖ Oilfield	◗ Gasfield
◜ Oil pipeline	◝ Gas pipeline
--- Pipeline under construction	
● Tanker terminal	◗ Gas Condensate field
☐ Oil terminal	☐ Gas terminal
▲ Principal oil refinery (maximum capacity greater than 27 200 tonnes per day)	
▲ Oil refinery (one symbol may denote several refineries in one area)	
International dividing line	

m
50
100
200
500
1000

Projection: Conical
with two standard parallels

COPYRIGHT. GEORGE PHILIP & SON. LTD.

1:20 000 000

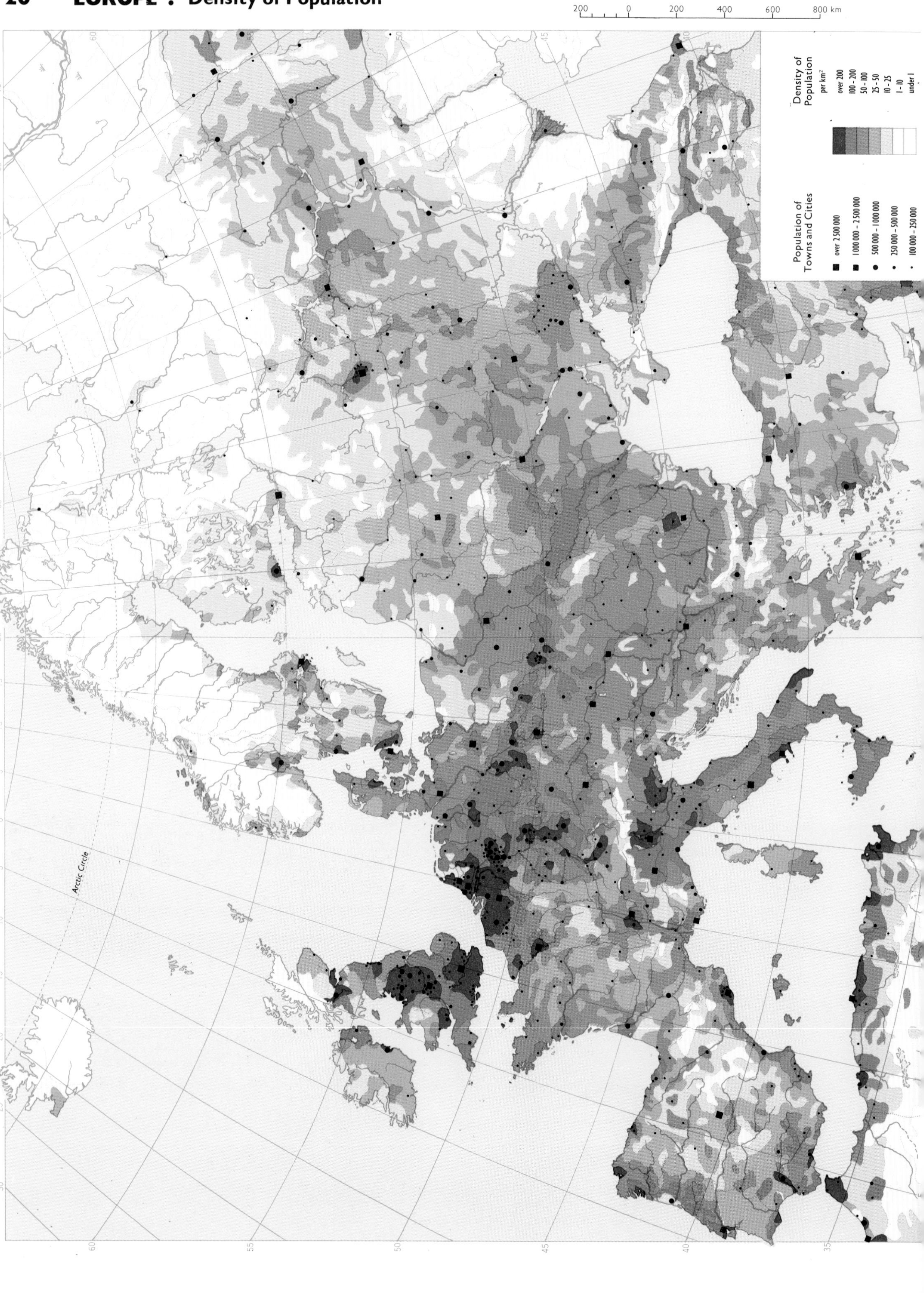

200   0   200   400   600   800 km

Density of
Population
per km²

over 200
100 - 200
50 - 100
25 - 50
10 - 25
1 - 10
under 1

Population of
Towns and Cities

over 2 500 000
1 000 000 - 2 500 000
500 000 - 1 000 000
250 000 - 500 000
100 000 - 250 000

Arctic Circle

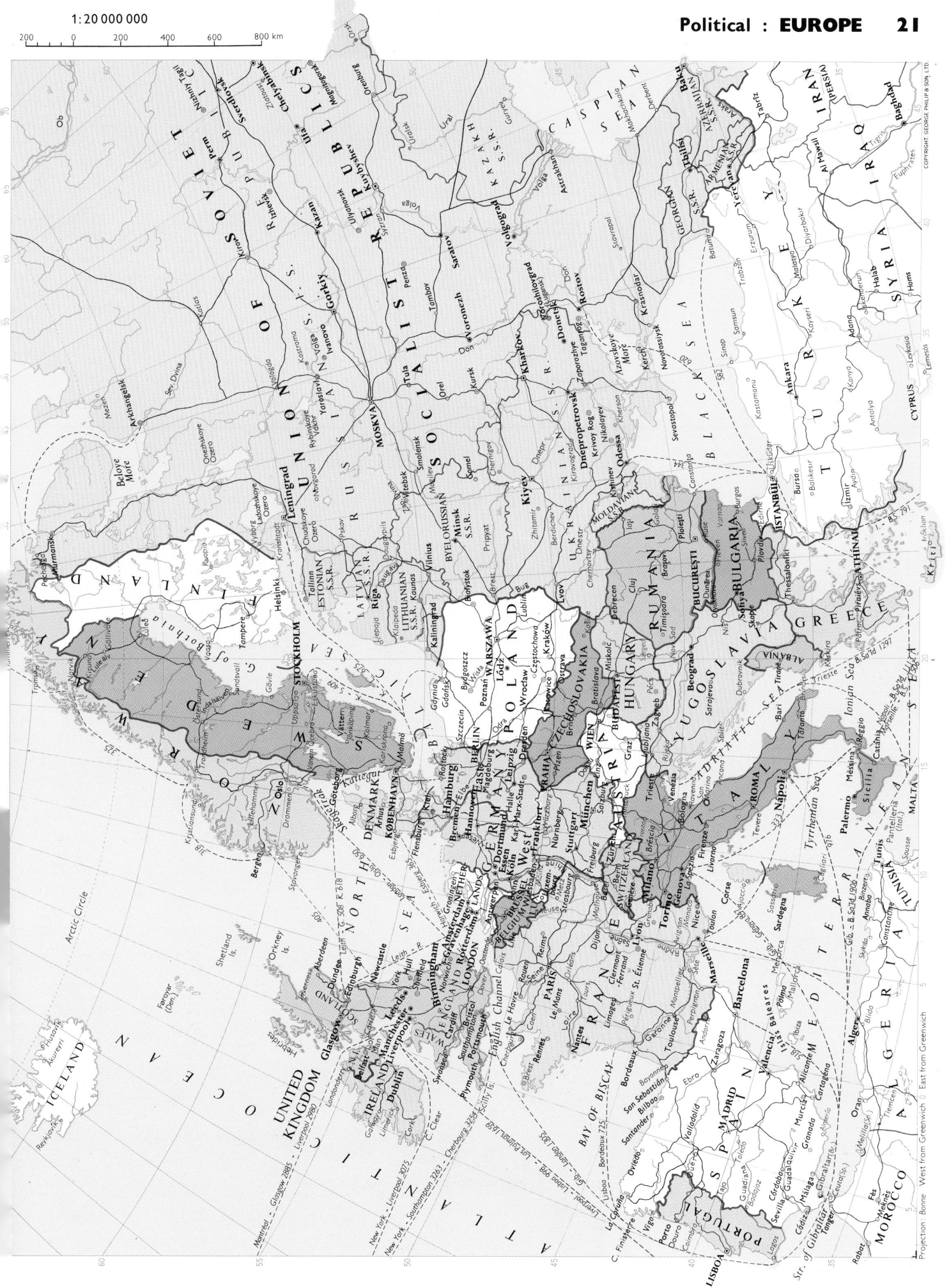

1 : 20 000 000

200   0   200   400   600   800 km

COPYRIGHT GEORGE PHILIP & SON, LTD

U N I O N   O F   S O V I E T   S O C I A L I S T   R E P U B L I C S

R U S S I A N   S.F.S.R.

Ob

Perm

Sverdlovsk

Chelyabinsk

Orenburg

Ufa

Kirov

Kazan

Gorkiy

Kuybyshev

Penza

Saratov

Tambov

Volgograd

Astrakhan

A Z A K H   S.S.R.

Ural

Volga

Don

C A S P I A N   S E A

Baku

I R A N (PERSIA)

Tabrïz

AZERBAIJAN S.S.R.

ARMENIAN S.S.R.

Yerevan

GEORGIAN S.S.R.

Tbilisi

Batumi

Erzurum

Diyarbakir

Al Mawsil

Baghdad

S Y R I A   I R A Q

Halab

Homs

Euphrates

Tigris

Arkhangelsk

Mezen

Sev. Dvina

Vologda

Kostroma

Ivanovo

Yaroslavl

Ryazan

Tula

MOSKVA

Orel

Kursk

Voronezh

Rostov

Donetsk

Kharkov

U K R A I N I A N   S.S.R.

Kiyev

Dnepropetrovsk

Odessa

Krivoy Rog

Nikolayev

Kherson

B L A C K   S E A

T U R K E Y

Ankara

Izmir

Konya

Adana

CYPRUS

Kríti

Iráklion

ATHÍNAI

G R E E C E

Thessaloníki

ALBÁNIA

Tiranë

BULGARIA

Sofiya

Plovdiv

Burgas

Varna

R U M A N I A

BUCUREŞTI

Ploieşti

Braşov

Cluj

Timişoara

MOLDAVIAN S.S.R.

BYELORUSSIAN S.S.R.

Minsk

Pripyat

Leningrad

Helsinki

Tampere

F I N L A N D

Tallinn

ESTONIAN S.S.R.

Riga

LATVIAN S.S.R.

LITHUANIAN S.S.R.

Kaunas

Vilnius

Kaliningrad

WARSZAWA

P O L A N D

Łódź

Kraków

Lwów

Gdańsk

Poznań

Wrocław

N O R W A Y

Narvik

S W E D E N

STOCKHOLM

Göteborg

Oslo

Bergen

DENMARK

KØBENHAVN

N O R T H   S E A

B A L T I C   S E A

G E R M A N Y

East

West

BERLIN

Hamburg

Bremen

Hannover

München

Frankfurt

Köln

Dortmund

Essen

Stuttgart

Leipzig

Dresden

CZECHOSLOVAKIA

PRAHA

A U S T R I A

WIEN

HUNGARY

BUDAPEST

Y U G O S L A V I A

Beograd

Zagreb

Sarajevo

Dubrovnik

I T A L Y

ROMA

Napoli

Milano

Torino

Genova

Venezia

Bologna

Firenze

Palermo

Sicilia

Sardegna

Tyrrhenian Sea

MALTA

Ionian Sea

A D R I A T I C   S E A

SWITZERLAND

NETHER-LANDS

Amsterdam

Rotterdam

BELGIUM

BRUSSEL

Antwerpen

F R A N C E

PARIS

Lyon

Marseille

Bordeaux

Nantes

Toulouse

BAY OF BISCAY

ENGLISH CHANNEL

UNITED KINGDOM

LONDON

Birmingham

Manchester

Liverpool

Leeds

Glasgow

Edinburgh

SCOTLAND

ENGLAND

WALES

Cardiff

IRELAND

Dublin

Belfast

ICELAND

Reykjavik

A T L A N T I C   O C E A N

Arctic Circle

S P A I N

MADRID

Barcelona

Valencia

Sevilla

Zaragoza

Málaga

Baleares

Mallorca

P O R T U G A L

LISBOA

Porto

M O R O C C O

Rabat

A L G E R I A

Oran

TUNISIA

Tunis

M E D I T E R R A N E A N   S E A

West from Greenwich   0   East from Greenwich

Projection : Bonne

11 · 8 · 5 · 791

1 : 4 000 000

50   0   50   100   150 km

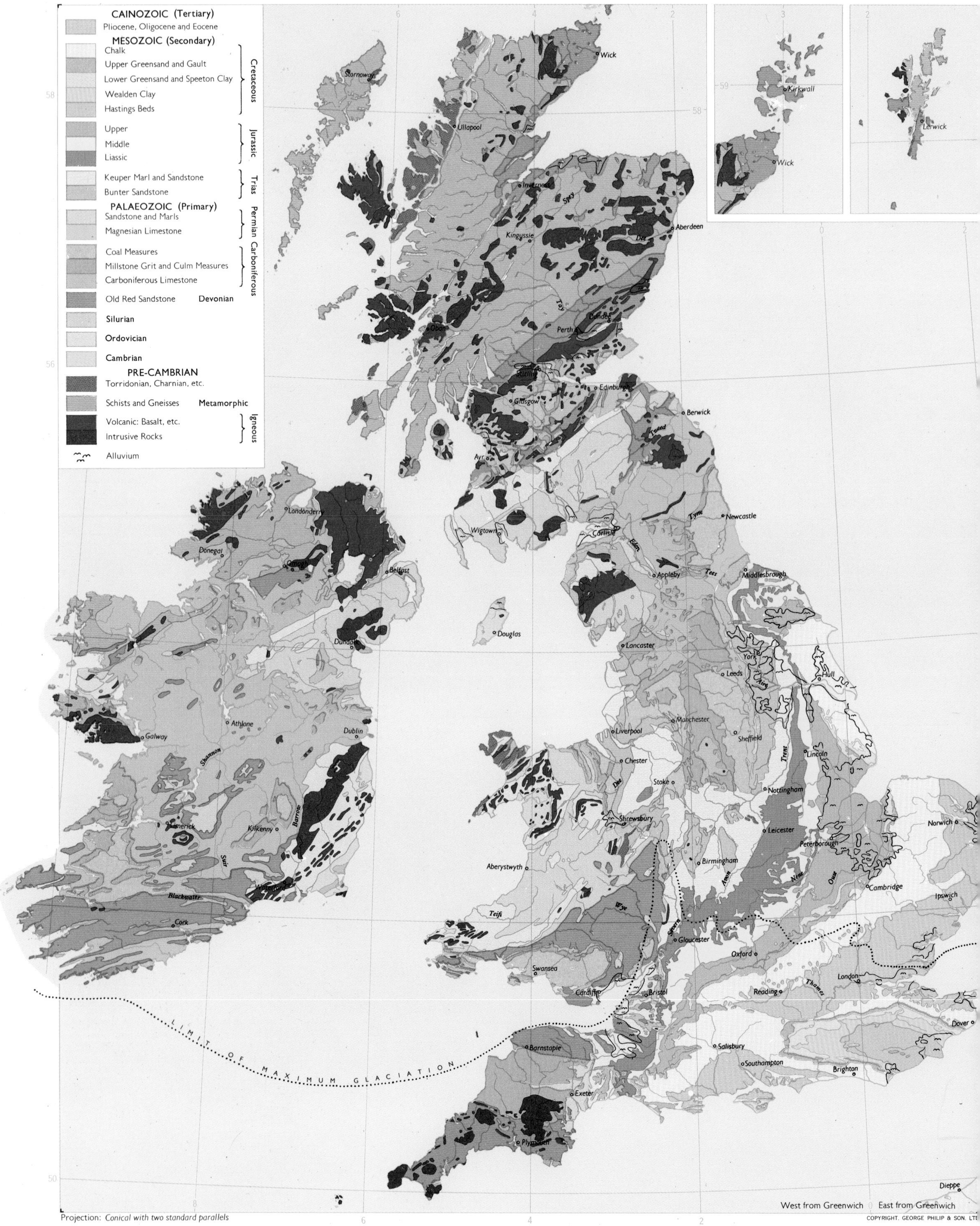

CAINOZOIC (Tertiary)
Pliocene, Oligocene and Eocene

MESOZOIC (Secondary)
Chalk — *Cretaceous*
Upper Greensand and Gault
Lower Greensand and Speeton Clay
Wealden Clay
Hastings Beds

Upper — *Jurassic*
Middle
Liassic

Keuper Marl and Sandstone — *Trias*
Bunter Sandstone

PALAEOZOIC (Primary)
Sandstone and Marls — *Permian*
Magnesian Limestone

Coal Measures — *Carboniferous*
Millstone Grit and Culm Measures
Carboniferous Limestone

Old Red Sandstone   **Devonian**

Silurian

Ordovician

Cambrian

PRE-CAMBRIAN
Torridonian, Charnian, etc.

Schists and Gneisses   **Metamorphic**

Volcanic: Basalt, etc. — *Igneous*
Intrusive Rocks

Alluvium

Stornoway
Wick
Kirkwall
Lerwick
Ullapool
Inverness
Skye
Kingussie
Aberdeen
Oban
Dee
Perth
Tay
Dundee
Stirling
Glasgow
Edinburgh
Ayr
Berwick
Tweed
Londonderry
Newcastle
Donegal
Tyne
Omagh
Belfast
Wigtown
Carlisle
Eden
Appleby
Tees
Middlesbrough
Douglas
Lancaster
York
Ouse
Hull
Leeds
Athlone
Manchester
Liverpool
Leeds
Sheffield
Galway
Shannon
Chester
Lincoln
Dublin
Dee
Trent
Nottingham
Stoke
Limerick
Barrow
Kilkenny
Swir
Shrewsbury
Leicester
Peterborough
Norwich
Aberystwyth
Birmingham
Avon
Nene
Cambridge
Ipswich
Teifi
Wye
Blackwater
Gloucester
Cork
Oxford
London
Thames
Swansea
Reading
Cardiff
Bristol
Dover
Barnstaple
Salisbury
Southampton
Brighton
Exeter
Plymouth
Dieppe

LIMIT OF MAXIMUM GLACIATION

West from Greenwich   East from Greenwich

Projection: *Conical with two standard parallels*

1 : 4 000 000

50   0   50   100   150 km

ATLANTIC

OCEAN

NORTH

SEA

IRISH SEA

St. George's Channel

Bristol Channel

ENGLISH CHANNEL

Strait of Dover

Dogger Bank

Devil's Hole ▼238

Mull Head N. Ronaldsay
Westr.
Rousay Start Point
Mainland Sanday Stronsay
Hoy Sound Orkney
Hoy Is.
Dunnet Hd. S. Ronaldsay
John o' Groats Duncansby Hd.
Pentland Firth

Shetland Is.
St. Magnus B.
Unst
Fetlar
Yell
Out Skerries
Whalsay
Mainland
Bressay
Sumburgh Hd.

Foula

Fair Isle

m
1000
400
200
100
0   0
50
100
200
m

West from Greenwich   East from Greenwich

1 : 4 000 000

50   0   50   100   150 km

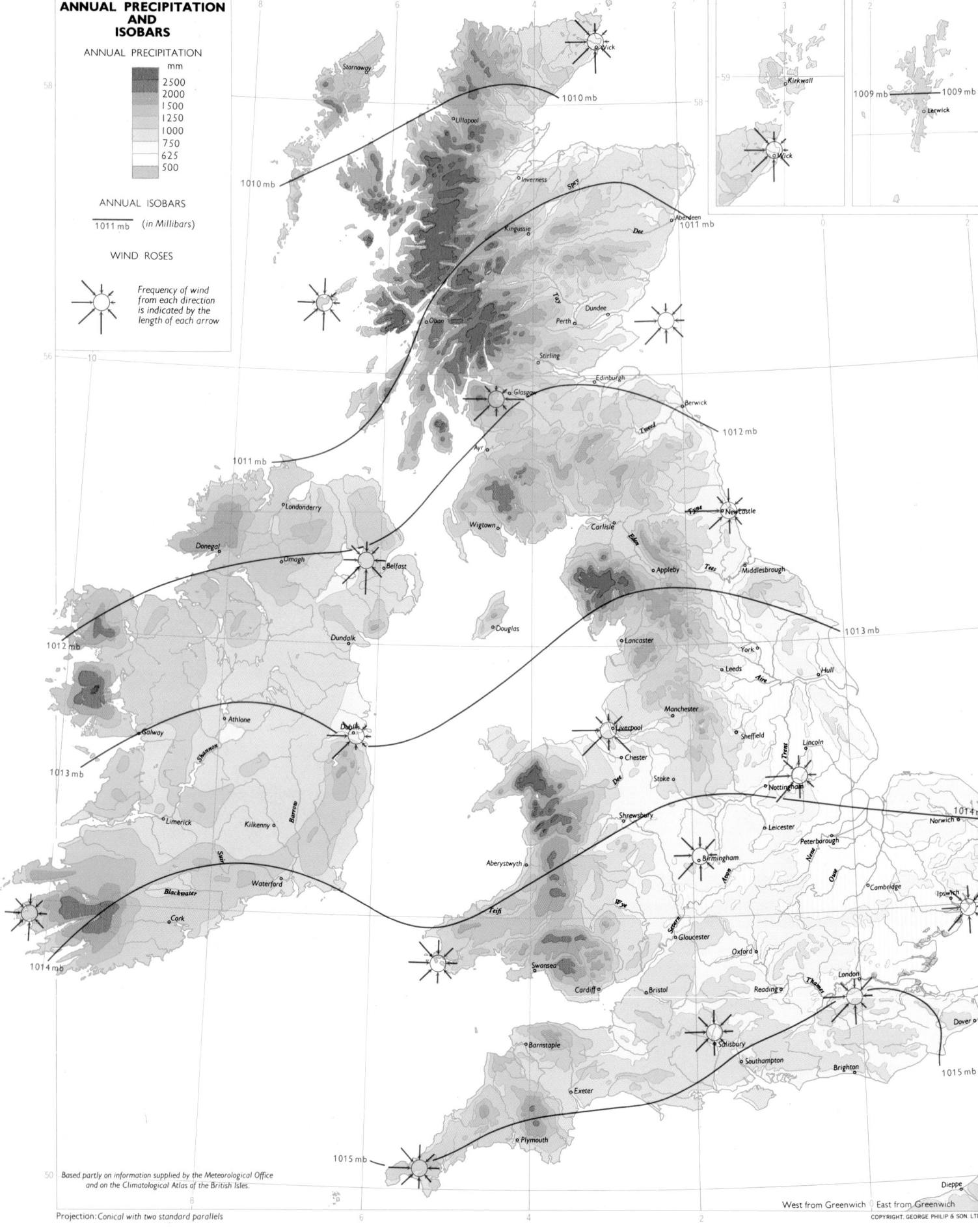

ANNUAL PRECIPITATION AND ISOBARS

ANNUAL PRECIPITATION

mm
2500
2000
1500
1250
1000
750
625
500

ANNUAL ISOBARS

1011 mb   (in Millibars)

WIND ROSES

Frequency of wind
from each direction
is indicated by the
length of each arrow

Based partly on information supplied by the Meteorological Office
and on the Climatological Atlas of the British Isles.

Projection: Conical with two standard parallels

West from Greenwich   East from Greenwich

COPYRIGHT. GEORGE PHILIP & SON. LTD.

1 : 8 500 000

50   0   50   100   150   200   250   300 km

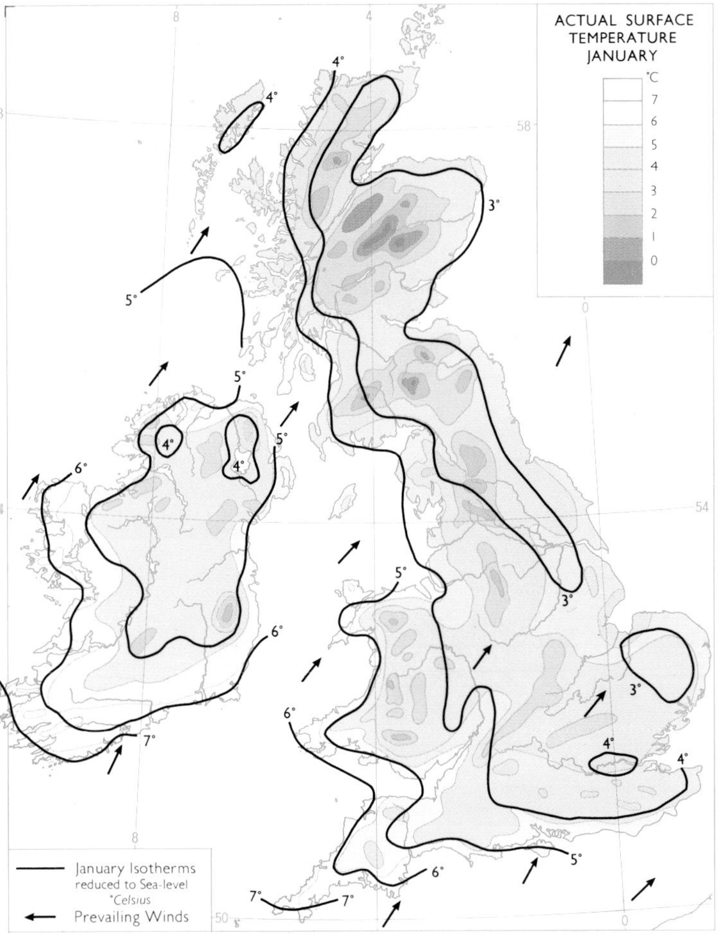

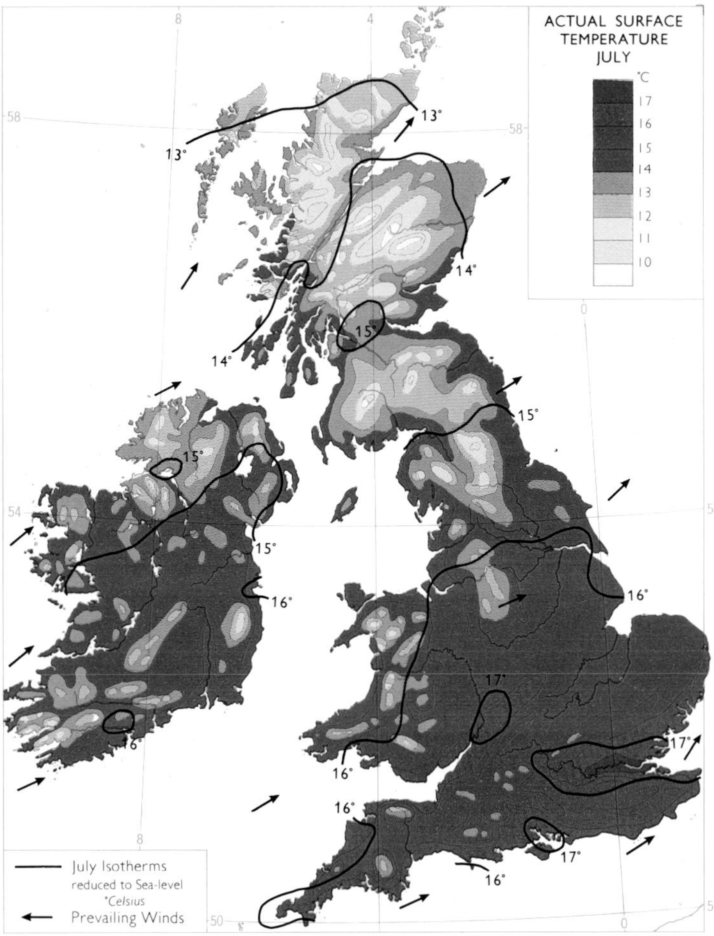

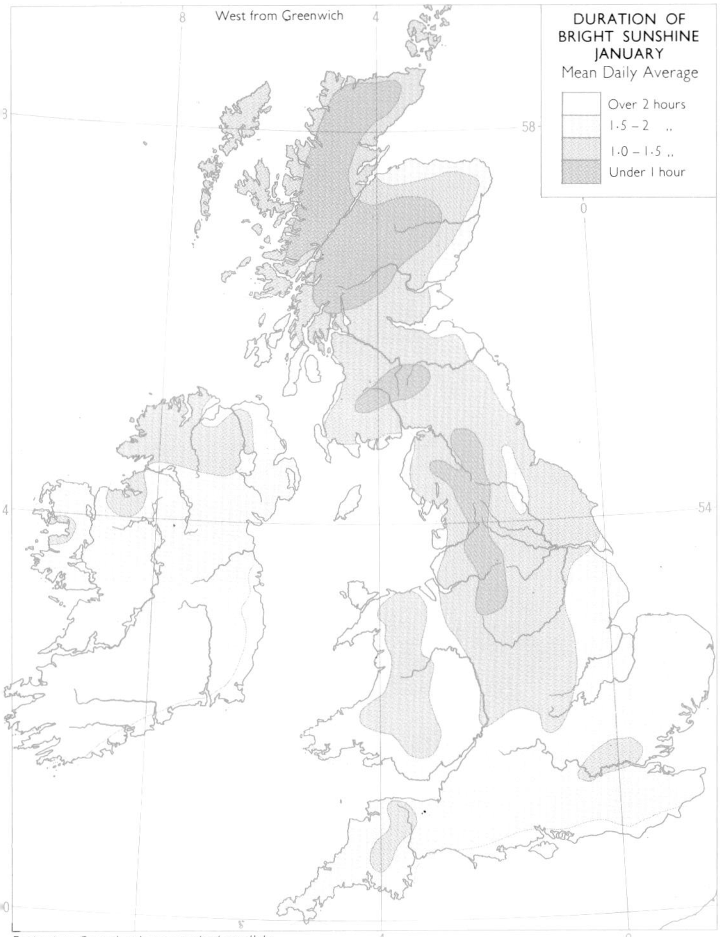

ACTUAL SURFACE TEMPERATURE JANUARY

°C
7
6
5
4
3
2
1
0

4°
4°
3°
5°
5°
5°
5°
4°
4°
6°
6°
6°
5°
3°
7°
6°
3°
4°
4°
6°
5°
7°
7°

— January Isotherms
reduced to Sea-level
°Celsius
← Prevailing Winds

ACTUAL SURFACE TEMPERATURE JULY

°C
17
16
15
14
13
12
11
10

13°
13°
13°
14°
14°
15°
14°
15°
15°
15°
15°
16°
16°
16°
17°
17°
17°
16°
16°
17°
16°

— July Isotherms
reduced to Sea-level
°Celsius
← Prevailing Winds

West from Greenwich

DURATION OF BRIGHT SUNSHINE JANUARY
Mean Daily Average

Over 2 hours
1·5 – 2   „
1·0 – 1·5   „
Under 1 hour

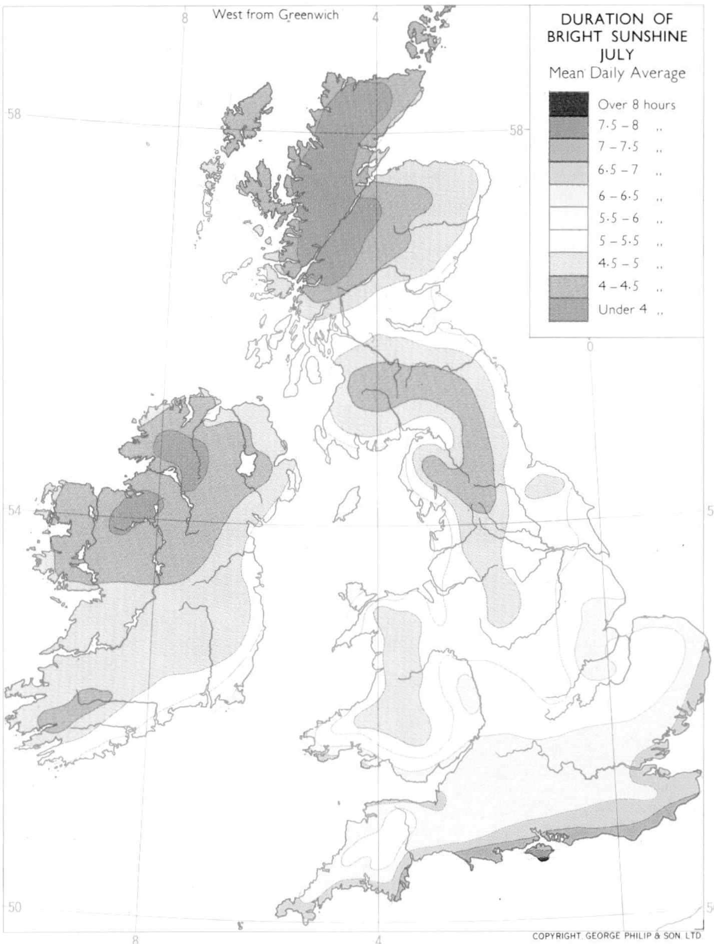

West from Greenwich

DURATION OF BRIGHT SUNSHINE JULY
Mean Daily Average

Over 8 hours
7·5 – 8   „
7 – 7·5   „
6·5 – 7   „
6 – 6·5   „
5·5 – 6   „
5 – 5·5   „
4·5 – 5   „
4 – 4·5   „
Under 4   „

Projection: Conical with two standard parallels

1:4 000 000

50   0   50   100   150 km

ATLANTIC

OCEAN

NORTH

SEA

IRISH SEA

St. George's Channel

Cardigan Bay

Bristol Channel

ENGLISH CHANNEL

Projection: Conical with two standard parallels

West from Greenwich   East from Greenwich
COPYRIGHT. GEORGE PHILIP & SON. LTD.

1:4 000 000

50   0   50   100   150 km

The DISTRICTS of Northern Ireland have been numbered and can be identified by reference to this table.

1	Londonderry	14	Craigavon
2	Limavady	15	Armagh
3	Coleraine	16	Newry & Mourne
4	Ballymoney	17	Banbridge
5	Moyle	18	Down
6	Larne	19	Lisburn
7	Ballymena	20	Antrim
8	Magherafelt	21	Newtownabbey
9	Cookstown	22	Carrickfergus
10	Strabane	23	North Down
11	Omagh	24	Ards
12	Fermanagh	25	Castlereagh
13	Dungannon	26	Belfast

1	Merseyside
2	Greater Manchester
3	West Yorkshire
4	South Yorkshire
5	West Glamorgan
6	Mid Glamorgan
7	South Glamorgan

Orkney Is.

Shetland Is.

ORKNEY

SHETLAND

HIGHLAND

ATLANTIC OCEAN

WESTERN ISLES

SCOTLAND

HIGHLAND

GRAMPIAN

TAYSIDE

CENTRAL

FIFE

STRATHCLYDE

LOTHIAN

BORDERS

NORTH SEA

DUMFRIES AND GALLOWAY

NORTHUMBERLAND

TYNE & WEAR

DURHAM

CLEVELAND

CUMBRIA

NORTH YORKSHIRE

HUMBERSIDE

IRISH SEA

LANCASHIRE

LINCOLN

NOTTS

DERBY

CHESHIRE

CLWYD

GWYNEDD

POWYS

DYFED

WALES

SALOP

STAFFORD

WARWICK

LEICESTER

NORTHAMPTON

NORFOLK

SUFFOLK

CAMBRIDGE

BEDFORD

HEREFORD

WORCESTER

GLOUCESTER

OXFORD

BUCKS

HERTFORD

ESSEX

LONDON

SURREY

KENT

BERKS

WILTS

AVON

SOMERSET

HANTS

WEST SUSSEX

EAST SUSSEX

DORSET

DEVON

CORNWALL

ISLE OF WIGHT

GWENT

NORTHERN IRELAND

ULSTER

DONEGAL

IRELAND

CONNACHT

MAYO

SLIGO

LEITRIM

ROSCOMMON

GALWAY

CLARE

LIMERICK

KERRY

CORK

MUNSTER

TIPPERARY

WATERFORD

LEINSTER

WEXFORD

WICKLOW

KILKENNY

CARLOW

LAOIS

OFFALY

KILDARE

DUBLIN

MEATH

WESTMEATH

LONGFORD

CAVAN

MONAGHAN

ENGLISH CHANNEL

Bristol Channel

St. George's Channel

Cardigan Bay

Projection : Conical with two standard parallels

West from Greenwich   East from Greenwich

COPYRIGHT. GEORGE PHILIP & SON. LTD.

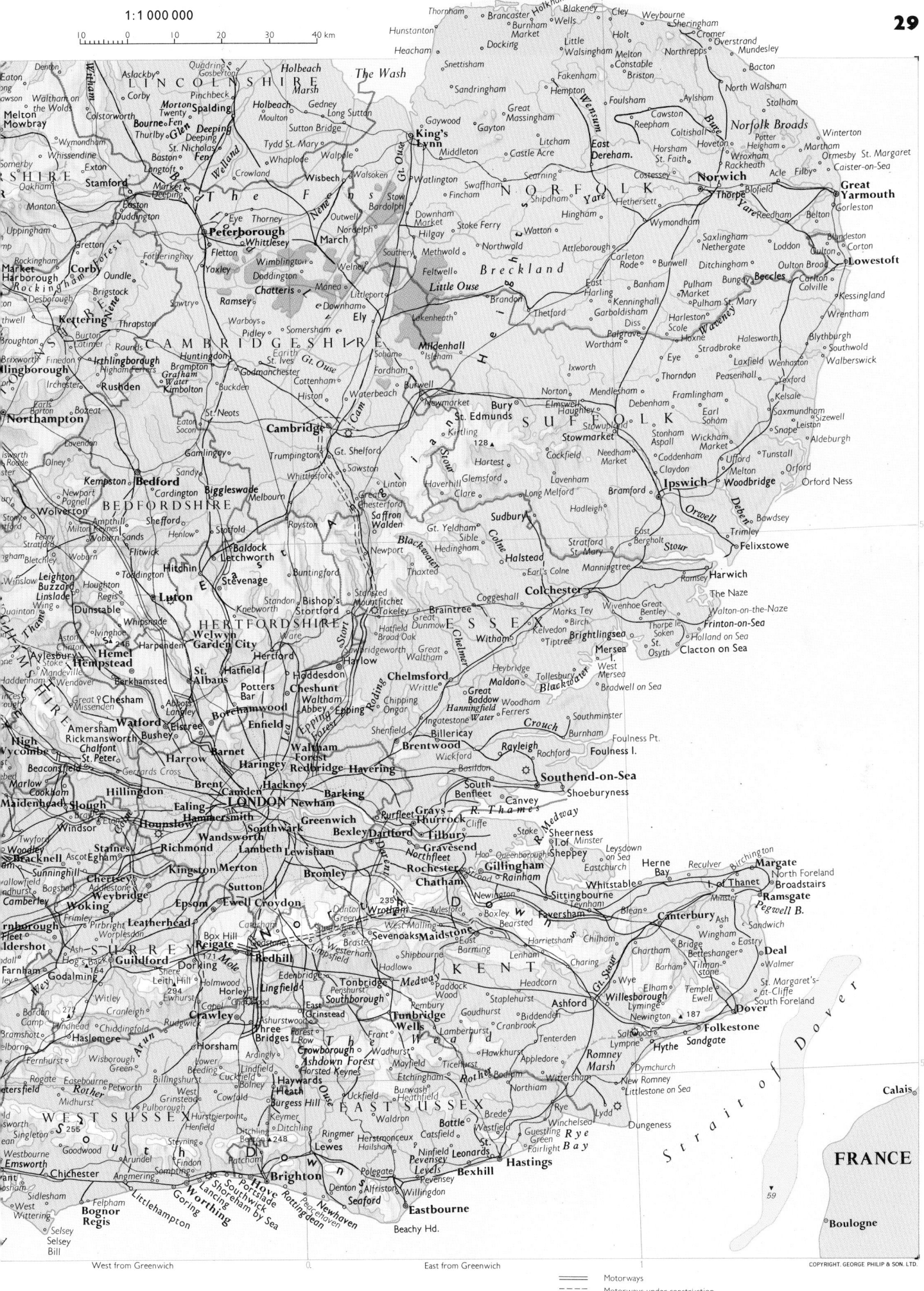

1:1 000 000

10   0   10   20   30   40 km

LINCOLNSHIRE

The Wash

Thornham · Brancaster Holkham Blakeney Cley Weybourne Sheringham
Hunstanton · Burnham Wells Little Overstrand Mundesley
Heacham · Docking Walsingham Melton Constable Briston Northrepps Cromer
Snettisham · Sandringham Fakenham Bacton
Hempton Aylsham North Walsham Stalham
Holbeach Gedney Long Sutton Gaywood Gayton Litcham Castle Acre Reepham Coltishall Hoveton Potter Heigham Martham Winterton
Spalding Moulton Sutton Bridge King's Lynn Middleton East Dereham St. Faith Wroxham Rackheath Acle Filby Ormesby St. Margaret Caister-on-Sea
Wisbech Walsoken Walpole Watlington Swaffham Searning Costessey Norwich Thorpe Blofield Yare Great Yarmouth Gorleston
Peterborough Whittlesey March Welney Downham Market Stoke Ferry Hilgay Watton Hingham Hethersett Saxlingham Nethergate Wymondham Reedham Belton Blundeston Corton
Chatteris Manea Littleport Brandon Breckland Thetford East Harling Banham Bunwell Ditchingham Loddon Oulton Broad Lowestoft
Ely Mildenhall Islesham Little Ouse Kenninghall Garboldisham Diss Pulham Market Bungay Beccles Carlton Colville Kessingland
Cambridge Newmarket Bury St. Edmunds Kirtling Norton Mendlesham Debenham Framlingham Saxmundham Sizewell Leiston Aldeburgh Snape Orford Orford Ness

SUFFOLK

IPSWICH Woodbridge

ESSEX

Colchester Harwich The Naze Frinton-on-Sea Walton-on-the-Naze Clacton on Sea

Chelmsford Maldon Blackwater Bradwell on Sea

Southend-on-Sea Shoeburyness Foulness Pt. Foulness I.

LONDON

R. Thames

KENT

Canterbury Ramsgate Broadstairs Margate North Foreland Deal Dover South Foreland Folkestone Hythe Sandgate

Strait of Dover

Calais

FRANCE

Boulogne

SURREY

WEST SUSSEX

EAST SUSSEX

Brighton Hove Worthing Eastbourne Beachy Hd. Hastings Bexhill

COPYRIGHT. GEORGE PHILIP & SON. LTD.

Motorways
Motorways under construction

1 : 1 000 000

10   0   10   20   30   40 km

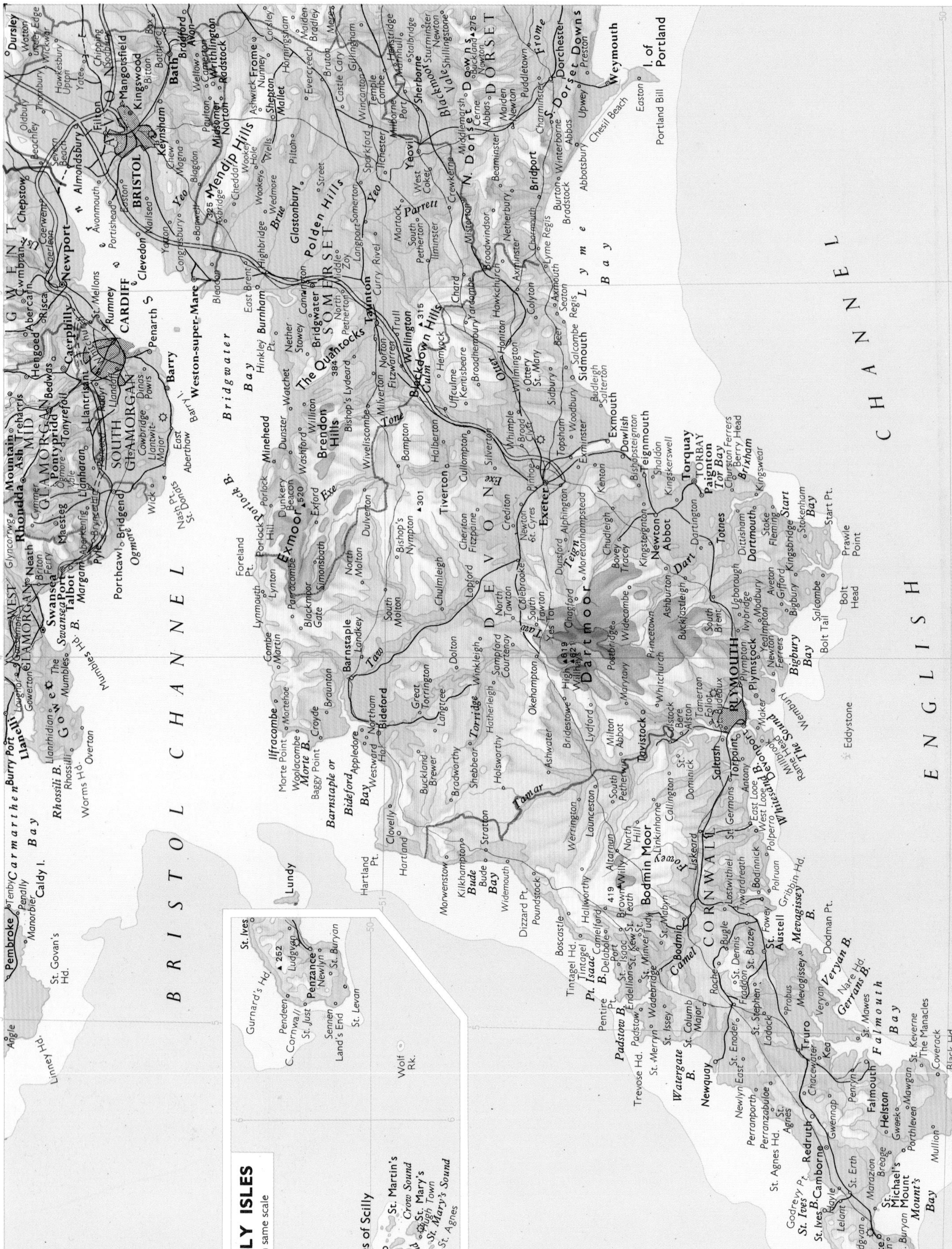

SCILLY ISLES
on same scale

Isles of Scilly

BRISTOL CHANNEL

ENGLISH CHANNEL

GWENT

GLAMORGAN

SOMERSET

DEVON

CORNWALL

DORSET

Dartmoor

Exmoor

Bodmin Moor

Bristol · Cardiff · Newport · Swansea · Weston-super-Mare · Bridgwater · Taunton · Exeter · Plymouth · Torquay · Paignton · Weymouth · Dorchester

m   600   400   200   100   0

0   50   m

1:1 000 000

10 0 10 20 30 40 km

Cardigan

Bay

BRISTOL CHANNEL

Bridgwater Bay

Projection : Conical with two standard parallels

West from Greenwich

═══ Motorways
═ ═ ═ Motorways under construction

Based upon the Ordnance Survey Map with the permission
of the Controller of Her Majesty's Stationery Office.
Crown Copyright Reserved.

COPYRIGHT.GEORGE PHILIP & SON. LTD.

Projection: Conical with two standard parallels

Motorways
Motorways under construction

1:1 000 000

10 0 10 20 30 40 km

Continuation
Northwards
on same scale

NORTH

SEA

Berwick on
Tweed
Tweedmouth
Scremerston

M e r s e
Westruther
Greenlaw
Swinton
Norham
Holy I.
Gordon
Leitholm
Coldstream
Beal
Earlston
Budle Bay
Farne Is.
Kelso
Maxwellheugh
Flodden
Barmoor
Castle
Lowick
Bamburgh
Newtown
St.
Boswells
Roxburgh
Mindrum
Doddington
Seahouses
N. Sunderland
Beadnell
Ancrum
Jedburgh
Morebattle
Town
Yetholm
Wooler
Chatton
Embleton

B O R D E R S
Bonchester
Bridge
The Cheviot
816
Breamish
Aln
Glanton
Alnwick
Lesbury
Alnmouth
Longhoughton

Alwinton
Rothbury
Longframlington
Shilbottle
Warkworth
Amble
Coquet I.
Catcleugh
Coquet
Rothbury
Felton
Hauxley
Broomhill

Peel Fell
602
Rochester
Elishaw
Ridsdale
Simonside
441
Weldon
Thirston
Druridge B.
Widdrington
Ellington

Kielder
Otterburn
Longhorsley
Pegswood
Ashington
Newbiggin

N. Tyne
Falstone
N O R T H U M B E R L A N D
Camba
Morpeth
Bedlington
Blyth
Sighty
Crag
519
Bellingham
Redesmouth
Kirkwhelpington
Whalton
Wansbeck
Cowpen
Cramlington
Seaton Delaval

Wark
Birtley
Colwell
Belsay
Stannington
Ponteland
Hartley
Whitley B.

Humshaugh
Chollerton
Stamfordham
Tynemouth
NEWCASTLE
UPON TYNE
Earsdon
South
Shields
Gilsland
Greenhead
HADRIAN'S WALL
Haydon
Bridge
Chollerford
Brunton
Heddon
Prudhoe
Ryton
Blaydon
Wallsend
Jarrow
TYNE AND
Gateshead
Newburn
WEAR
Haltwhistle
Hexham
Corbridge
Tyne
Sunderland

Cold Fell
622
Lambley
Catton
Slaley
Stanley
Birtley
Washington
Houghton
le Spring
Allen
Allendale
Town
Derwent
Leadgate
Consett
Chester le
Street
Alston
Edmondbyers
Castleside
Annfield Plain
Hetton le Hole
Easington
Allenheads
Collier Law
516
Lanchester
Sacriston
Durham

TYNE AND WEAR
Gateshead
Sunderland
Hartley
Seaton Delaval
Whitley Bay
Tynemouth
South Shields
Jarrow
Washington
Hebburn
Wallsend
Ryhope
Houghton le Spring
Seaham
Murton
Easington Colliery
Horden
Peterlee
Castle Eden
Hetton le Hole
Wheatley
Hill
Trimdan
Willington
Cornforth
Ferryhill
Hartlepool
Sedgefield
Shildon
Wolviston
Greatham
Grangetown
Redcar
Marske by the Sea
Saltburn by the Sea
Dalton
Newton
Aycliffe
Barton
Billingham
Stockton
on Tees
Tees
B.
Eston
Skelton
Brotton
Staithes
Catterick
Wiske
Thornaby
on Tees
Middlesbrough
Loftus
Kettle Ness
Guisborough
Hinderwell
Lythe
Northallerton
Stokesley
Great
Ayton
C L E V E L A N D
Castleton
Egton
Whitby
Hawsker
Robin Hood's Bay
Bedale
Osmotherley
Cleveland Hills
454
Esk
Sleights
Fylingdales
Moor
Broughton
Leven
North York
Moors
Eller Beck
Bridge
Hayburn Wyke
Carlton
Miniott
Hambleton
Hills
Laskill
Hodge
Dove
Seven
Rosedale
Abbey
Cloughton
Scalby Ness
Thirsk
Sowerby
Rievaulx
Helmsley
Kirkby
Moorside
Saltergate
Scalby
Scarborough
Y O R K S H I R E
Ampleforth
Vale of Pickering
Pickering
Ebberston
Thornton
Dale
Seamer
Ripon
Boroughbridge
Easingwold
Stillington
Hovingham
Rye
Snainton
Ayton
Filey
Aldborough
Whixley
Green
Hammerton
Sheriff Hutton
Malton
Norton
Rillington
Sherburn
Hunmanby
Filey Bay
Knaresborough
Ouse
Strensall
Haxby
Fridaythorpe
246
Kilham
Burton
Fleming
Flamborough
Harrogate
Spofforth
Marston
Moor
Huntington
Sledmere
Wetwang
Burton
Agnes
Rudston
Flamborough
Head
Wetherby
York
Stamford Bridge
Nafferton
Wharfe
Nidd
Tadcaster
Pocklington
Driffield
Skipsea
LEEDS
Harewood
Escrick
Barmby
Moor
Bridlington
Otley
Scarcroft
Riccall
Market Weighton
Beeford
Bridlington
Bay
Morley
Rothwell
Cawood
Holme
Hornsea
Castleford
Sherburn
Selby
H U M B E R S I D E
Leven
WEST
Knottingley
Aire
Beverley
Aldbrough
YORKSHIRE
Normanton
Pontefract
Snaith
Cottingham
Sproatley
Holderness
Batley
Goole
South
Cave
Hedon
Marfleet
Withernsea
Wakefield
Ossett
Thorne
Brough
HULL
Paull
Keyingham
Kirkburton
Hemsworth
Whitton
Hessle
New
Holland
Burstwick
Patrington
South
Kirkby
Cudworth
Crowle
Winterton
Barton upon
Humber
Barrow upon
Humber
Sunk
Island
Easington
Darton
Barnsley
Adwick le
Street
Stainforth
Bentley
Roxby
Immingham
Stallingborough
Wombwell
Bolton-on-
Dearne
Isle
of
Scunthorpe
Broughton
Keelby
Laceby
Grimsby
Spurn Hd.
Swinton
Mexborough
New
Rossington
Axholme
Brigg
Barnetby
Cleethorpes
Conisbrough
Doncaster
Epworth
Waltham
Mouth of the Humber
SOUTH YORKSHIRE
Idle
Belton
Owston
Ferry
Kirton in
Lindsey
Waddingham
Caistor
Halton le Clay
Rotherham
Wath
Tetney
Donna Nook
Rawmarsh
Blyton
Misterton
North
Thoresby
Maltby
Tickhill
Bawtry
Corringham
Usselby
Caenby
Corner
North Somercoates
SHEFFIELD
Blyth
Barnby Moor
Gainsborough
West
Rasen
Binbrook
Saltfleet
Beighton
Beckingham
Market Rasen
Louth
Saltfleetby
Eckington
Led
Kexby
South
Elkington
Worksop
East
Retford
Faldingworth
Sturton
Manby
Staintan
Withern
Mablethorpe
Whitwell
Wragby
Scamblesby
Sutton-on-Sea
Staveley
Saxilby
L I N C O L N S H I R E
Chesterfield
East
Markham
Nettleham
Alford
Withern
Bolsover
Ollerton
Skellingthorpe
Lincoln
Bardney
Willoughby
Warsop
Tuxford
Hogsthorpe
Shirebrook
North
Hykeham
Branston
Horncastle
Ulceby
Cross
Partney
Burgh le
Marsh
Ingoldmells Pt.
Clay Cross
Mansfield
Woodhouse
Bracebridge
Heath
Metheringham
Spilsby
Skegness
Matlock
Mansfield
Waddington
Woodhall
Spa
Sutton
in Ashfield
Kirkby-in-
Ashfield
Navenby
Scopwick
Mareham
le Fen
Wainfleet
All Saints
Alfreton
Rainworth
Eakring
Collingham
Billinghay
Coningsby
West
Fen
Gibraltar
Pt.
E. Kirkby
Leadenham
Ruskington
Sibsey
East Fen
Belper
Heanor
Eastwood
Bulwell
Arnold
Southwell
Newark
on-Trent
Bolderton
Cranwell
Wrangle
Old Leake
Ilkeston
Ripley
Hucknall
NOTTINGHAM
Carlton
Ancaster
Sleaford
Brothertoft
Holland Fen
Boston
Derby
Stapleford
Beeston
Radcliffe
Bennington
Gt.
Gonerby
Honington
Swineshead
Heckington
The Wash
Long
Eaton
West
Bridgford
Bingham
Bottesford
Grantham
Redmile
Denton
Ropsley
Donington
Sutterton
Kirton
Fishtoft
Holbeach
Aslackby
Gosberton
Quadring

Thornham
Brancaster
Holkham
Blakeney
Cley
Weybourne
Hunstanton
Burnham
Market
Wells
Holt
Heacham
Docking
Little
Walsingham
Melton
Snettisham
Walsingham
N O R F O L K
Fakenham
Briston

West from Greenwich
East from Greenwich

1:1 000 000

35

10 0 10 20 30 40 km

Motorways

Motorways under construction

SHETLAND ISLANDS
on same scale

Herma Ness
Baltasound
Haroldswick
Bluemull Sd.
Unst
Balta
Cullivoe
Uyeasound
Mu Ness
Ramna
Stacks
Whale
Firth
Fetlar
Point of Fethaland
Colgrave Sd.
North
Roe
Mid Yell
Yell
The Snap
The
Faither
Ronas Hill
450
Burravoe
Esha
Ness
Hillswick
Lunna Ness
St. Magnus
Bay
SHETLAND
Skaw
Taing
Out
Skerries
Muckle Roe
Brae
Voe
Whalsay
Papa
Stour
The Håa
Sd. of Papa
Sandness
S Nesting
Bay
Walls
Score Hd.
Easter
Skeld
Vaila
Lerwick
I. of Noss
Gruting Voe
Scalloway
Bressay
Bressay
Hamnavoe
West
Burra
Bard Hd.
Kettla Ness
Hellia
Ness
Hoswick
Mousa
St. Ninian's I.
Scousburgh
Fitful Hd.
Boddam
B. of Quendale
Sumburgh Hd.

Butt of Lewis
Port of Ness
C. Wra
South Dell
L. Inchard
Ness
Cellar Hd.
L. Laxford
Borve
Handa I.
Barvas
Tolsta Hd.
Gallan Hd.
Great
Bernera
Carloway
Shawbost
North Tolsta
Broad Bay
Eddrachillis
Bay
Pt. of Stoer
Scou
Drumbeg
Uig
291
Newmarket
Tiumpan Hd.
Quina
Callanish
Stornoway
Melbost
Eye
Peninsula
Assynt
L. Roag
Lewis
Portaguiran
Bayble
Lochinver
Aird Brenish
575
Gisla
Lochs
Chicken Hd.
Stoer
Loch
Langavat
Balallan
L. Erisort
Crossbost
Park
Cromore
Rhu Coigach
Enard
Bay
Kintaravay
Gravir
Kebock Hd.
Summer
Isles
L. Lurgainn
Scarp
Husinish
N. Harris
Ardvourlie
571
L. Shell
Stra
Husinish
Pt.
Castle
799
Beinn Mhor
Coi
Ullapool
Taransay
W. L. Tarbert
Ardhasig
Tarbert
Sd. of Shiant
Greenstone
Pt.
Gruinard B.
L. Broom
Toe Hd.
L. Seaforth
Shiant Is.
Mellon
Charles
Sd. of Taransay
WESTERN
Scalpay
An Teallach
1062
Aultbea
L. na Sealga
Scarastavore
E. L. Tarbert
North Minch
L.
Ewe
S. Harris
Melvaig
Fionn
Loch
Pabbay
Sound of Harris
Leverburgh
Poolewe
Brgemo
Sd. of Pabbay
Rodel
Berneray
Renish Pt.
ISLES
Longa I.
L. Gairloch
Gairloch
L.
Maree
981
Haskeir Is.
Rubha Hunish
Henderson
Kerrysdale
Talladale
Slooch
W
Griminish Pt.
Kilmaluag
Kinlochewe
Sollas
Vaternish Pt.
Uig
Little
1053
Torridon
Fasag
Paible
North Uist
L. Maddy
Waternish
Loch
Snizort
Rona
L. Torridon
Shieldaig
Achnashellach
Lochmaddy
Minch
Dunvegan
Head
Trotternish
Sound of Raasay
Applecross
Forest
Clachan
Stein
The Storr
718
Coulags
Carron
Monar For
1052 L. Mona
Monach Is.
Baleshare
Carinish
347
Eaval
Milovaig
Lephin
Applecross
Lochcarron
Sgurr
Gramisdale
Grimsay
Ronay
Dunvegan
Raasay
Toscaig
Kishorn
Stromemore
Carn Eige
1182
Benbecula
Wiay
488
Roskhill
Portree
Raasay
Is.
Crowlin
Is.
Plockton
Stromeferry
Mulla
Ardivachar Pt.
Bagh nam
Faoileann
Bracadale
Coillore
L. Bracadale
L. Harport
Carron
Auchtertyre
L. Bee
Fermlea
Scalpay
Kyle of
Dornie
Carbost
Lochalsh
South
Uist
605 Hecla
Minginish
Drynoch
Sligachan
Kyleakin
L. Alsh
Glenelg
Howmore
620 B. Mhor
Cuillin
Hills
1009
Bla Bheinn
928
Broadford
Invershiel
A Chrail
1120
Rubha
Ardvule
L. Eynort
Glenbrittle
Rubh' an
Dunain
Soay Sd.
L. Scavaig
Elgol
The Saddle
1010
Glen Shiel
Daliburgh
Lochboisdale
L. Boisdale
Soay
L. Eishort
Isle
Ornsay
L. Hourn
Quoich
Teangue
Armadale
Tomdou
Sound of Eriskay
Sd. of Eriskay
Eriskay
Canna
Ardvasar
Sound of Sleat
Knoydart
Glen Ga
1040
Greian
Hd.
Sanday Canna
Kinloch
Pt. of
Sleat
Inverie
Sgurr na
Ciche
Barra
384
Bruernish Pt.
Sd. of Canna
Rhum
810
Mallaig
L. Nevis
983
L. Arkaig
Gail
Caledonia
Castlebay
Morar
Culvain
Canal
Vatersay
Eigg
Arisaig
Loch Morar
882
L. Eil
Sandray
Sd. of Eigg
394
Lochailort
Glenfinnan
Kinlocheil
Corpac
Pabbay
Sound of Rhum
Moidart
Corpach
Mingulay
Muck
Shona
I.
Kinlochmoidart
L. Moidart
Moidart
Loch Shiel
S
Berneray
Barra Head
888
Ardnamurchan
Ardgour
Corran
North
Pt. of Ardnamurchan
Kilchoan
527
Ardour
Ballachulish
241
Sorisdale
Mingary
Strontian
L.
Kilbig
Sunart
South
Ballachulish
Coll
Sunart
Morvern
Clabhach
Caliach
Pt.
Tobermory
Drimnin
Arinagour
Calgary
Dervaig
Sd. of Mull
L. Frisa
Portnacroish
St. Ba
Tiree
Scarinish
Treshnish
Isles
L. Tuath
Lochaline
Loch Linnhe
Loch
Etive
Hynish B. Passage of Tiree
Lismore I.
Hynish

m
1000
800
600
400
200
100
0
50
100
m

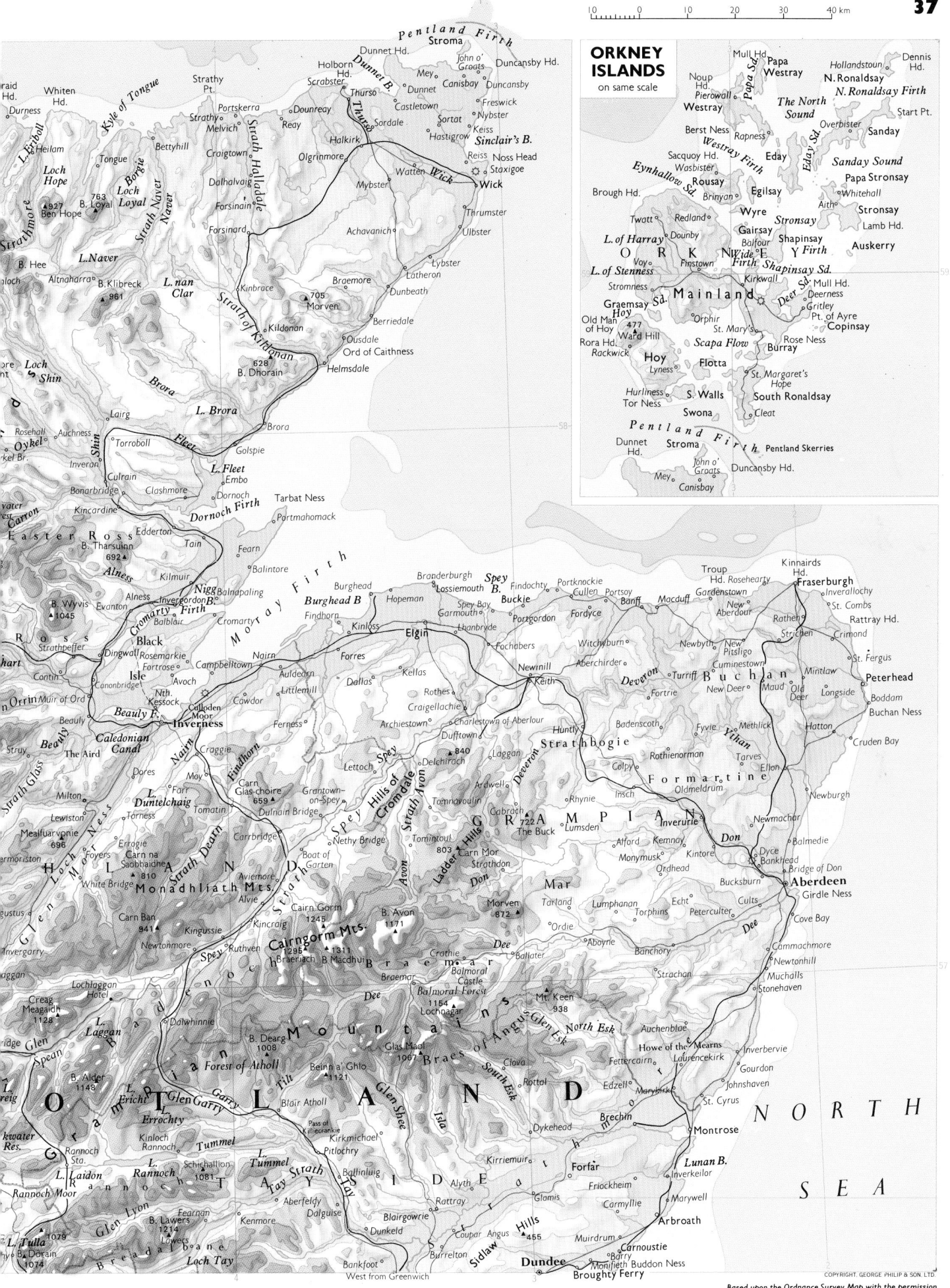

1:1 000 000

10   0   10   20   30   40 km

ORKNEY ISLANDS
on same scale

Mull Hd.   Papa   Hollandstoun   Dennis Hd.
Noup   Westray
Hd.   Pierowall   Papa Sd.   N. Ronaldsay
Westray   N. Ronaldsay Firth
Berst Ness   The North
Rapness   Sound   Overbister   Start Pt.
Eynhallow Sd.   Wasbister   Sanday
Brough Hd.   Sacquoy Hd.   Rousay   Eday   Sanday Sound
Wasbister   Egilsay   Papa Stronsay
Twatt   Redland   Brinyan   Whitehall
L. of Harray   Douby   Gairsay   Wyre   Stronsay
Voy   Finstown   Balfour   Shapinsay   Aithe   Lamb Hd.
O R K   Wide   Firth   Auskerry
L. OF STENNESS   Firth   Shapinsay Sd.
Stromness   Kirkwall   Mull Hd.
Graemsay Sd.   M a i n l a n d   Deer Sd.   Deerness
Old Man   Hoy   Orphir   Gritley
of Hoy   Ward Hill   St. Mary's   Pt. of Ayre   Copinsay
Rora Hd.   477   Scapa Flow   Rose Ness
Rackwick   Burray
Hoy   Lyness   Flotta   St. Margaret's
Hope
Hurlliness   S. Walls   South Ronaldsay
Tor Ness   Swona   Cleat
P e n t l a n d   F i r t h
Dunnet   Stroma   Pentland Skerries
Hd.
Mey   John o'
Groats   Duncansby Hd.
Canisby

DISTRICTS IN
NORTHERN IRELAND
1 Londonderry
2 Limavady
3 Coleraine
4 Ballymoney
5 Moyle
6 Larne
7 Ballymena
8 Magherafelt
9 Cookstown
10 Strabane
11 Omagh
12 Fermanagh
13 Dungannon
14 Craigavon
15 Armagh
16 Newry and Mourne
17 Banbridge
18 Down
19 Lisburn
20 Antrim
21 Newtownabbey
22 Carrickfergus
23 Ards
24 North Down
25 Castlereagh
26 Belfast

NORTHERN IRELAND

ULSTER

CONNACHT

LEITRIM

DONEGAL

LONDONDERRY

ANTRIM

DOWN

ARMAGH

TYRONE

FERMANAGH

MONAGHAN

CAVAN

LOUTH

MEATH

WESTMEATH

LONGFORD

ROSCOMMON

SLIGO

MAYO

GALWAY

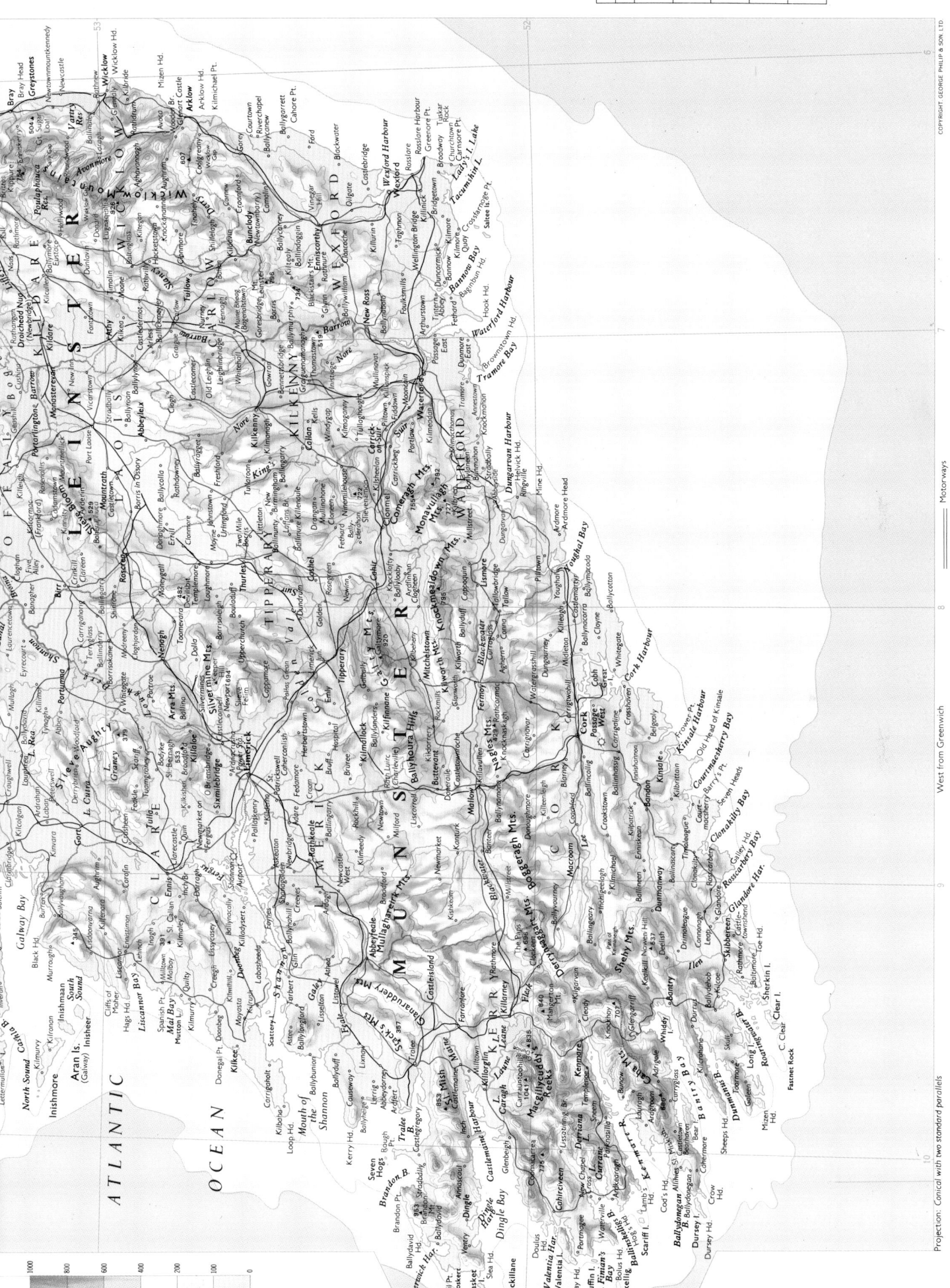

1 : 4 000 000

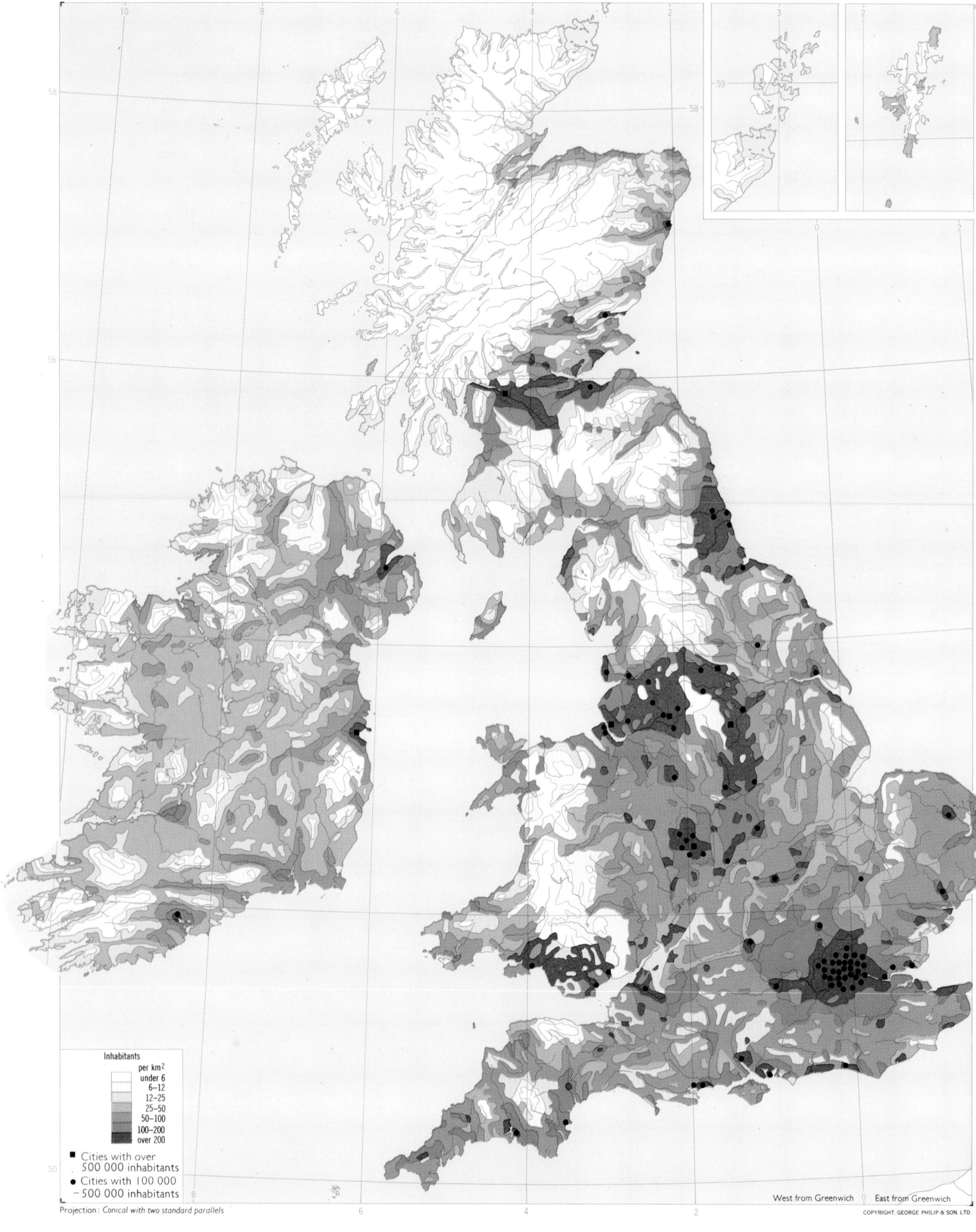

Inhabitants
per km²
under 6
6–12
12–25
25–50
50–100
100–200
over 200

■ Cities with over
500 000 inhabitants

● Cities with 100 000
–500 000 inhabitants

Projection: Conical with two standard parallels

West from Greenwich   East from Greenwich

COPYRIGHT. GEORGE PHILIP & SON. LTD.

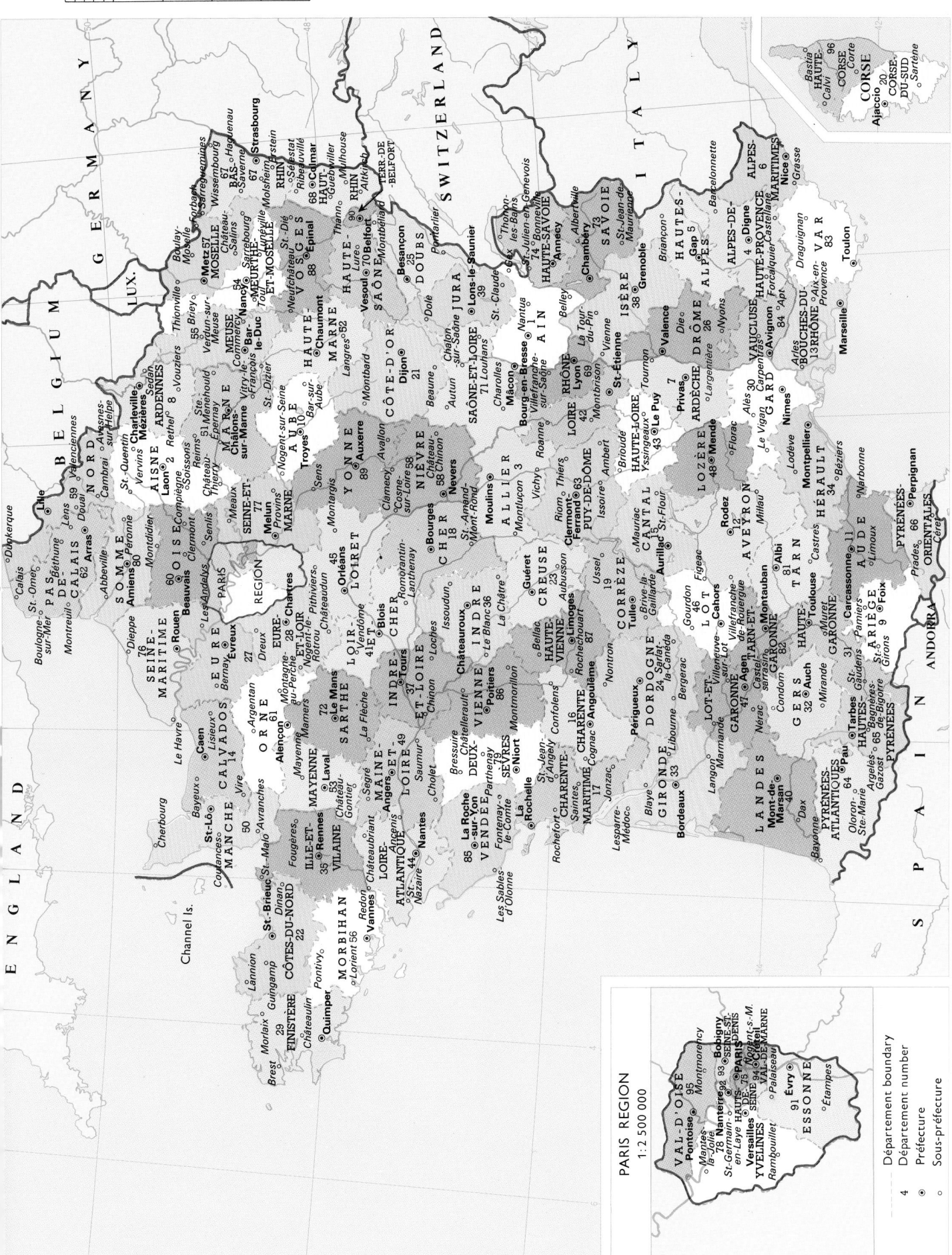

ENGLAND

ENGLISH CHANNEL

E n g l i s h   C h a n n e l

CHANNEL

Guernsey

St. Peter Port

ISLANDS

Jersey

St. Helier

Baie de la Seine

Golfe de St - Malo

Mer d'Iroise

BRETAGNE

Montagne Noire

MORBIHAN

Belle-Ile

Baie de Bourgneuf

Ile de Noirmoutier

Ile d'Yeu

Pertuis Breton

Ile de Ré

Pertuis d'Antioche

Ile d'Oléron

ANGOUMOIS

CHARENTE

NORMANDIE

CALVADOS

Collines de Normandie

Collines du Perche

MAINE

ANJOU

LOIRE

TOURAINE

VIENNE

POITOU

DEUX-SÈVRES

AUNIS

Projection: Conical with two standard parallels

West from Greenwich   0   East from Greenwich

1 : 2 500 000

10 0 10 20 30 40 50 60 70 80 90 100 km

SWITZERLAND

FRANCE

ITALY

LIGURIAN SEA

Golfo di Génova

MEDITERRANEAN SEA

Lion

CORSICA

COPYRIGHT. GEORGE PHILIP & SON. LTD.

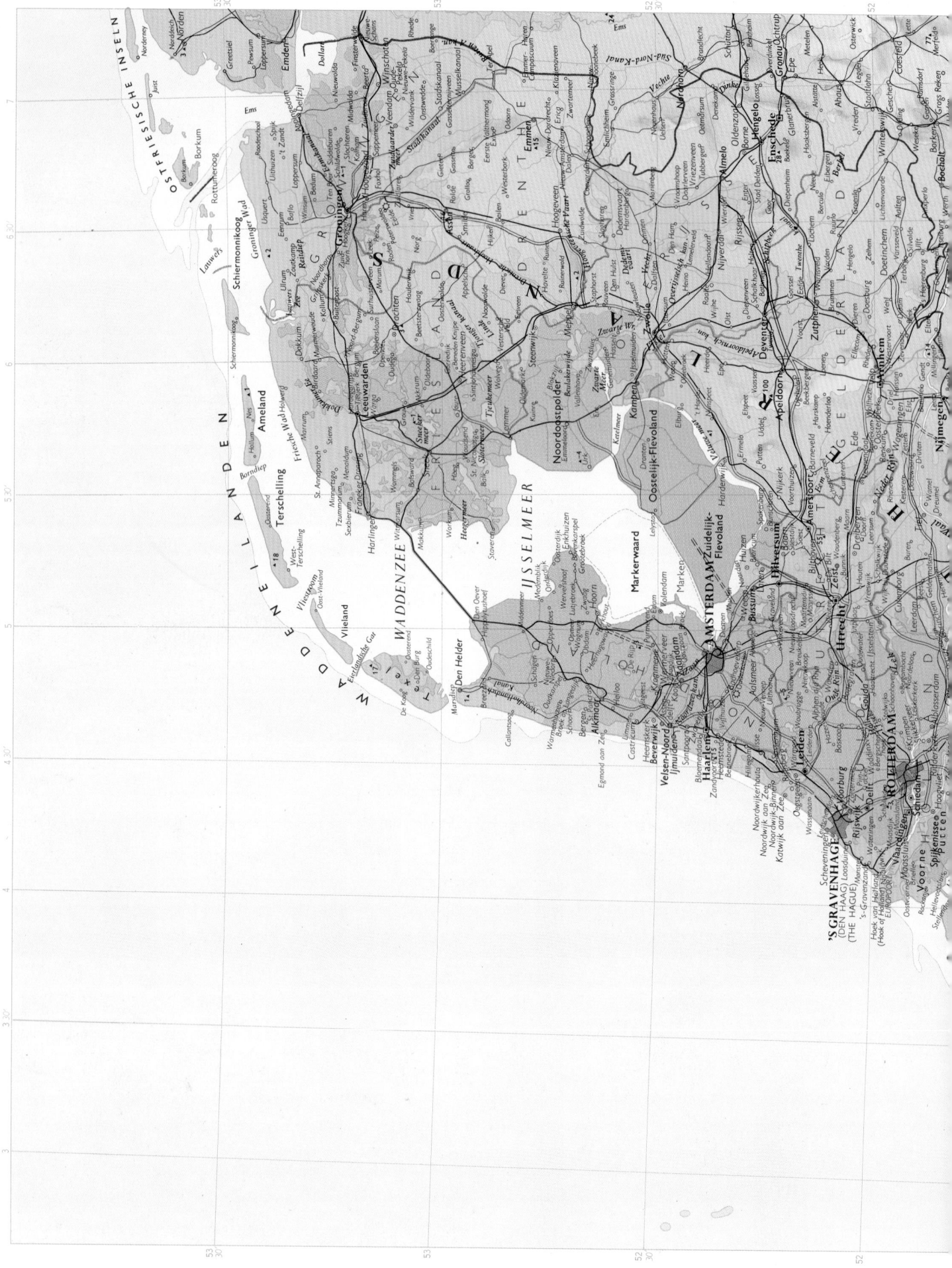

1:1 250 000

10 5 0 10 20 30 40 50 km

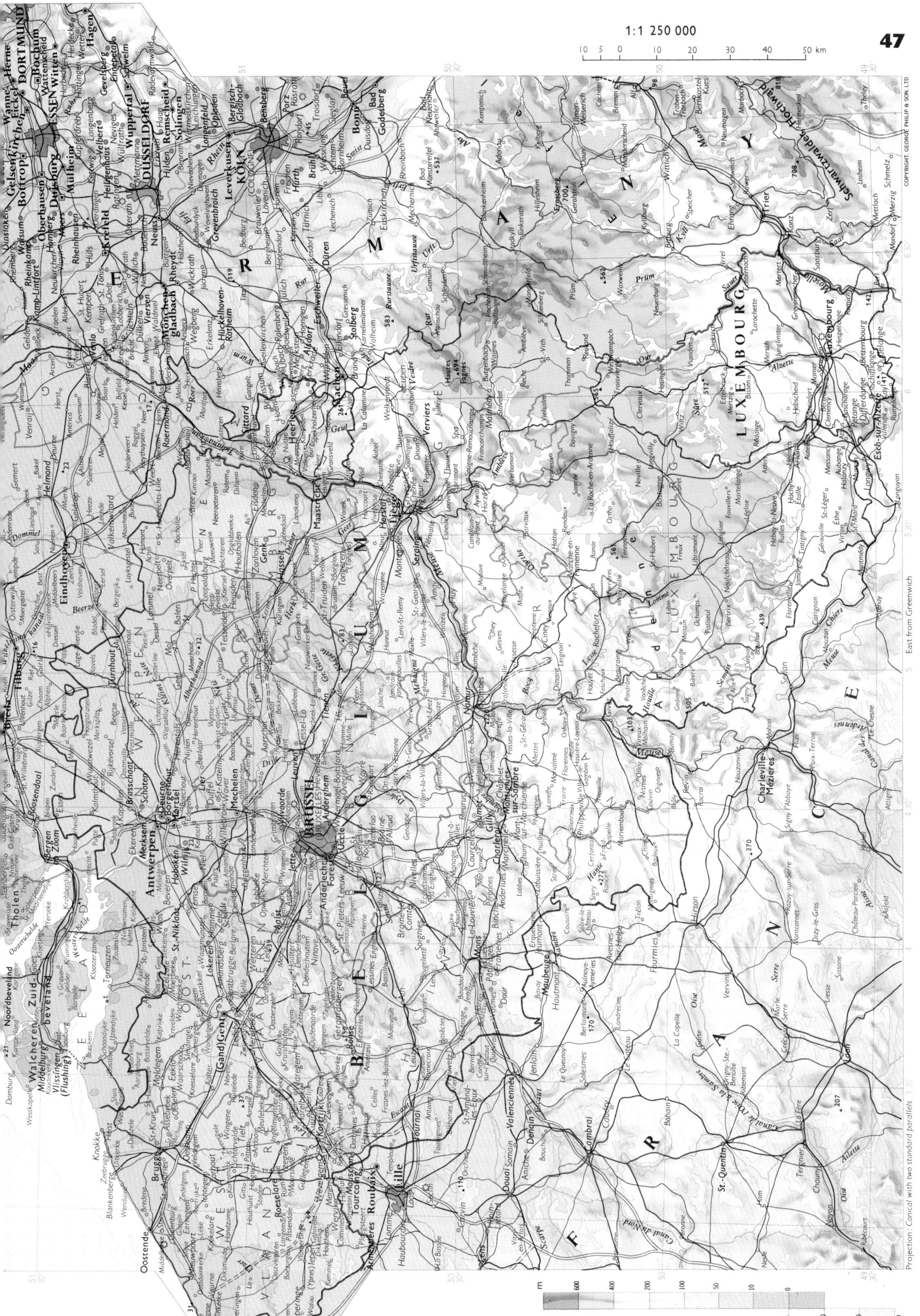

Projection: Conical with two standard parallels

East from Greenwich

LUXEMBOURG

GERMANY

FRANCE

BELGIË · BELGIE

NEDERLAND

DORTMUND · ESSEN · DÜSSELDORF · KÖLN · Bonn

BRUSSEL · Antwerpen · (Gand) Gent · Lille · Tourcoing · Roubaix · Eindhoven · Luxembourg · Charleville-Mézières · Cambrai · St-Quentin

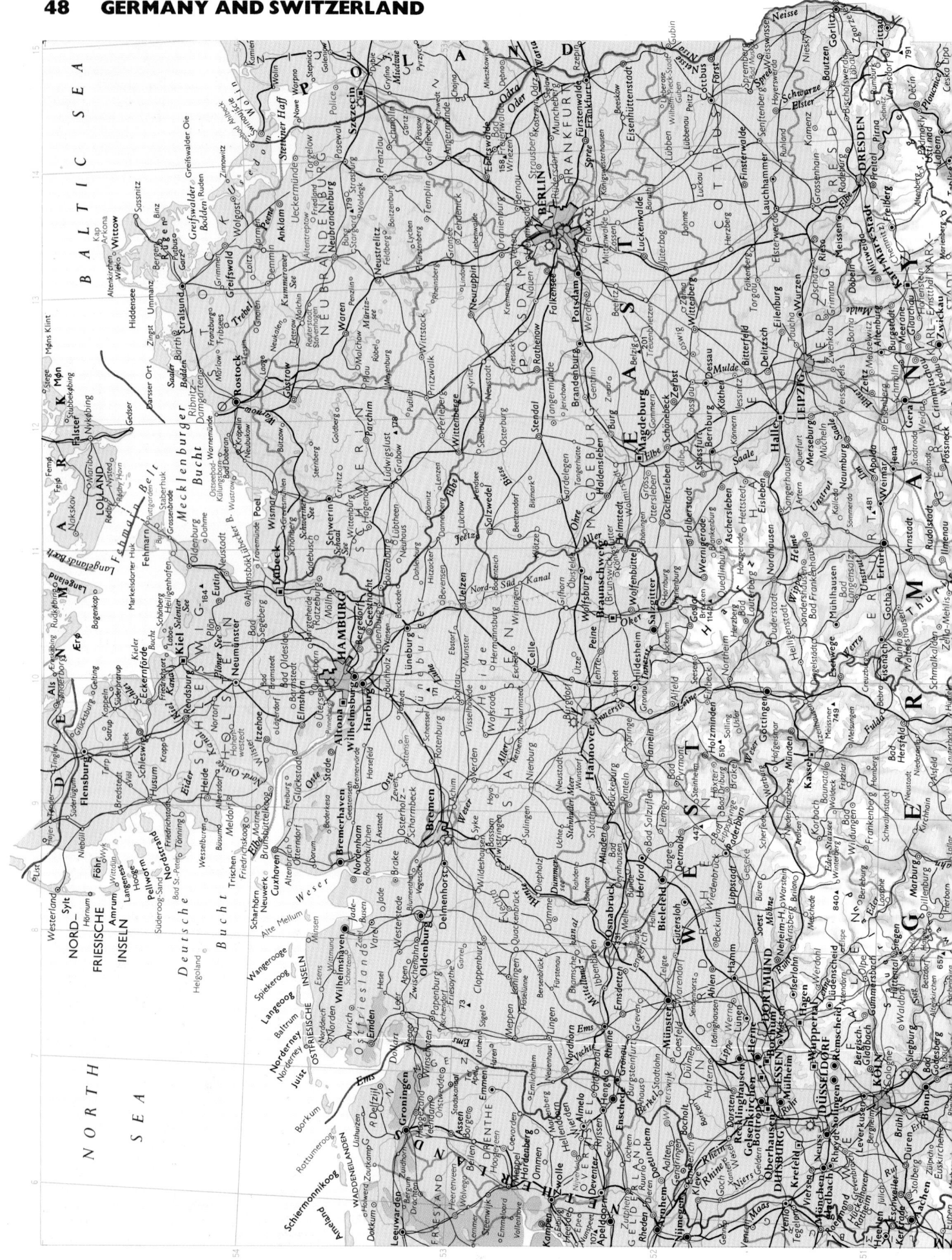

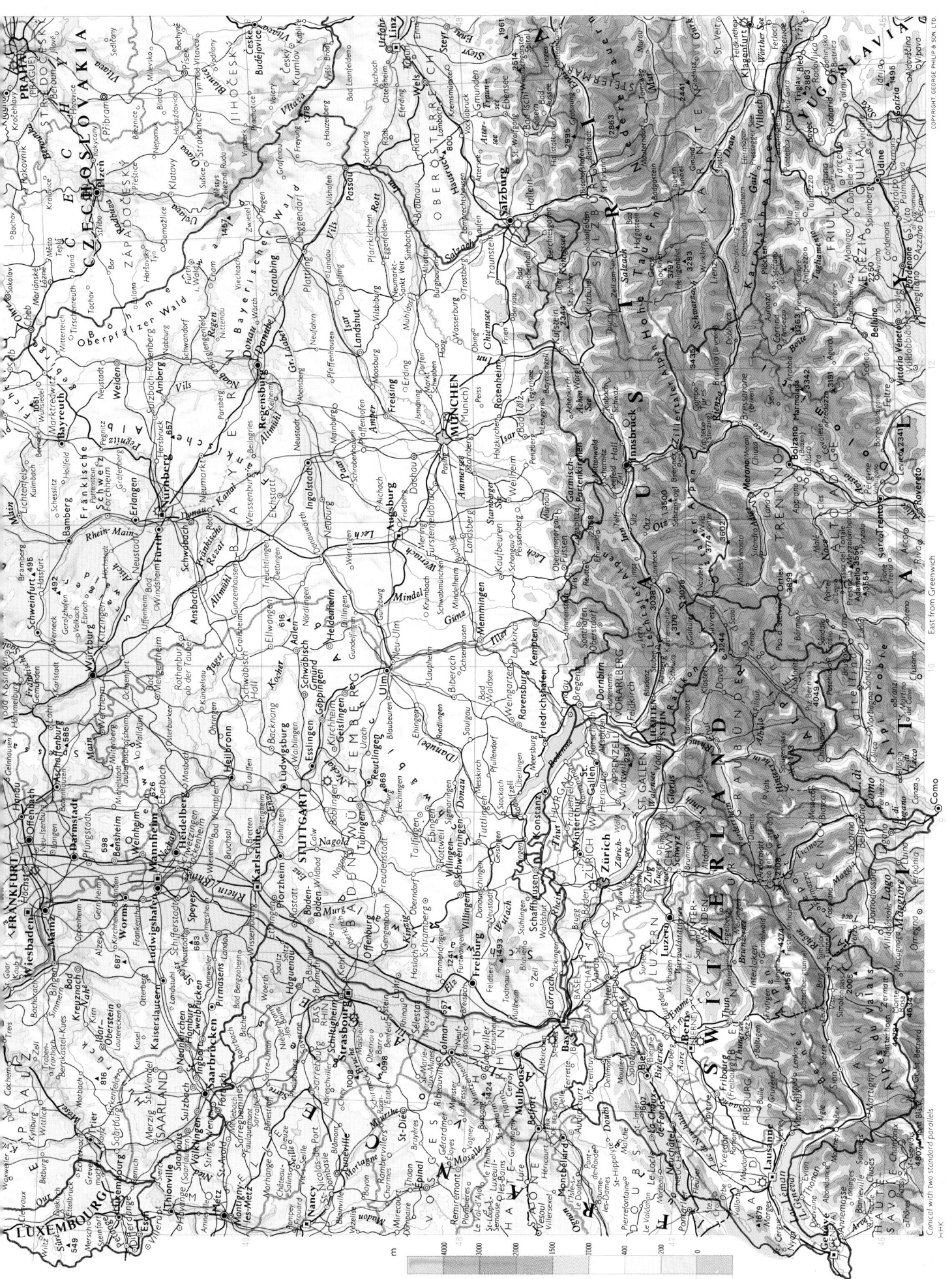

1 : 2 500 000

10 0 10 20 30 40 50 60 70 80 90 100 km

COPYRIGHT GEORGE PHILIP & SON LTD.

East from Greenwich

Conical with two standard parallels
H-HK

Projection: Conical with two standard parallels

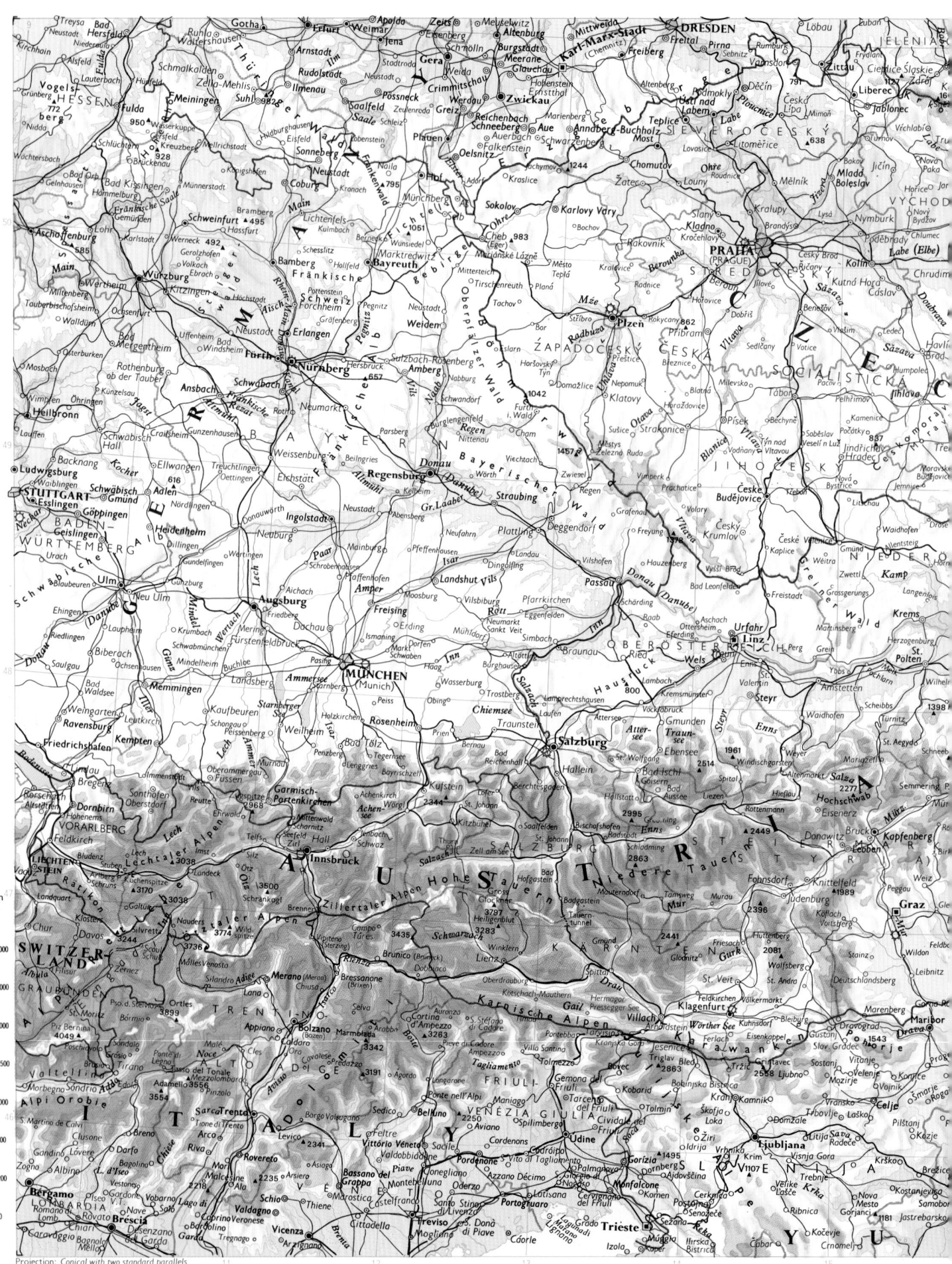

Projection: Conical with two standard parallels

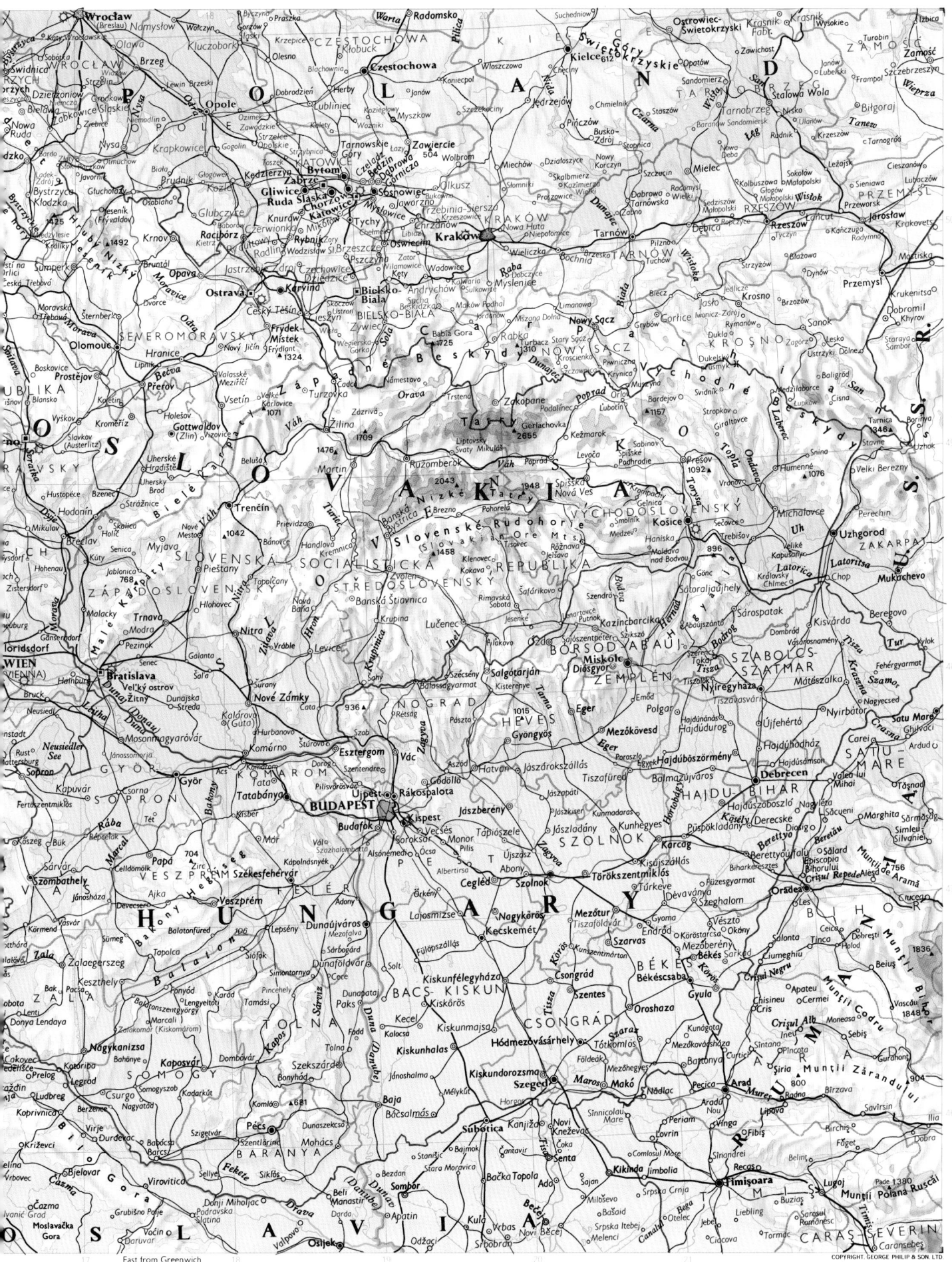

1:2 500 000

10 0 10 20 30 40 50 60 70 80 90 100 km

53

East from Greenwich

COPYRIGHT. GEORGE PHILIP & SON. LTD

1:3 000 000

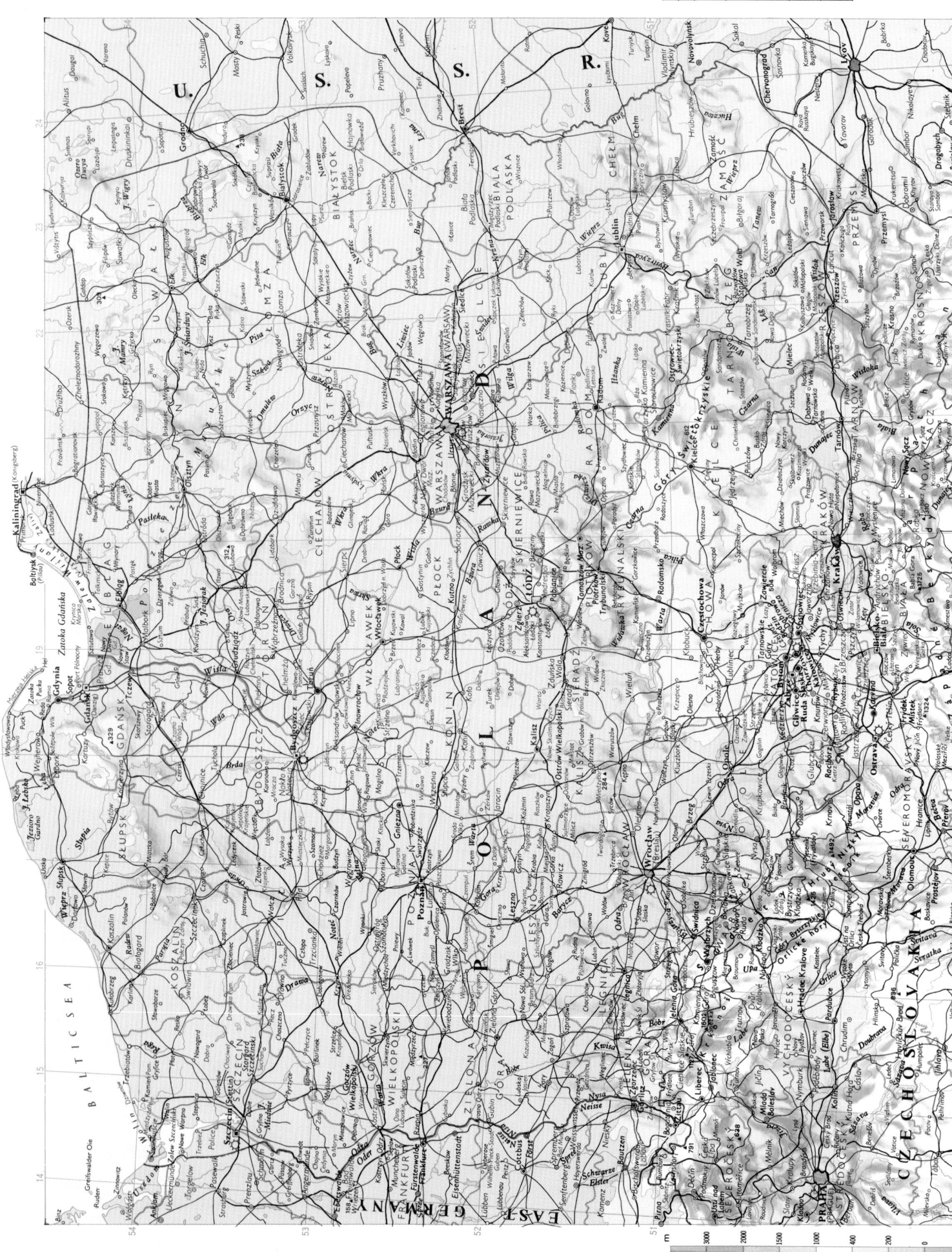

1:5 000 000

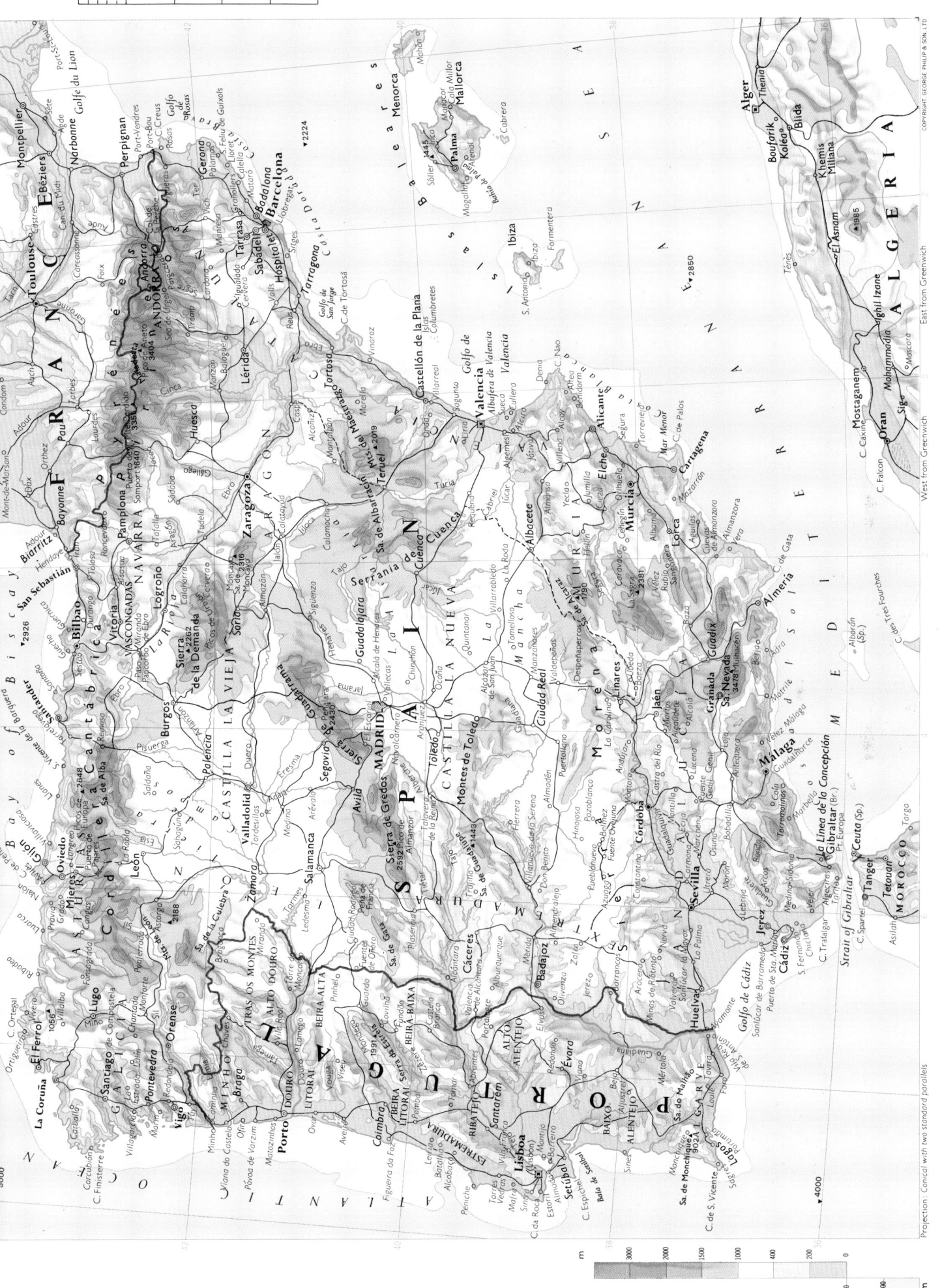

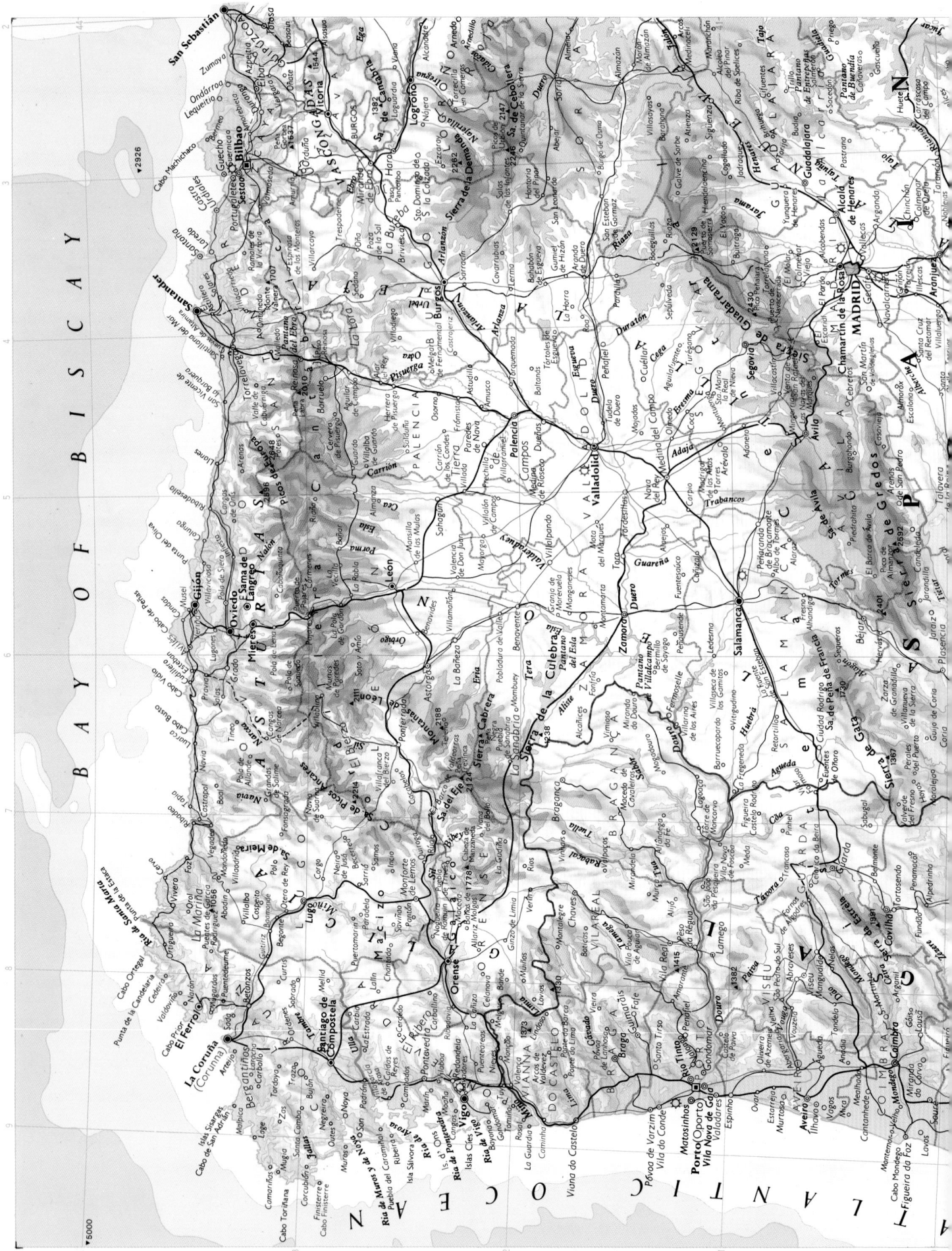

1 : 2 500 000

10 0 10 20 30 40 50 60 70 80 90 100 km

MEDITERRANEAN

SEA

MOROCCO

Projection: Conical with two standard parallels

COPYRIGHT GEORGE PHILIP & SON, LTD.

1:2 500 000

10 0 10 20 30 40 50 60 70 80 90 100 km

MEDITERRANEAN SEA

BALEARIC IS.

Valencia

Cabo de Salinas
Cabrera
Isla Conejera

Isla de Tagomago
Ibiza (Iviza)
Punta Grosa
San Juan Bautista
San Miguel de Abad
San Antonio Abad
Isla Cunillera
San José
Ibizo
Isla del Vedrá
▲475
Cabo Berbería
San Francisco Javier
San Pedro
Isla del Espardell
Formentera
192
Punta de Cala Codolar

2850

ALGERIA

ALGER
(Algiers)
Bou Ismail
Koléa
Cherchel
Blida
El Arba
Boufarik
Médéa
Berrouaghia
Kasr el Boukhari
Gourayo
Miliana
Khemis Miliana
1985
Chabounia
Guelt es Stel
Ksar-Chellala
Bl. Toguine
Ténès
El Asnam
Tissemsilt
Zemmora
Tiaret
Hamadia

C. Kramis
Aïn Tédélès
Ighil Izane
Mascara
Mostaganem
Arzew
Mohammadia
Sig
C. Caxine
C. Falcon
ORAN
Misserghin
Sidi-Bel-Abbès
Aïn Témouchent
Beni Saf
Ghazaouet
Nedroma
Berkane
MOROCCO
C. Tres Forcas
Melilla (Sp.)
Nador
C. del Agua

East from Greenwich

West from Greenwich

Denia
Cabo de San Antonio
Jávea
Cabo de la Nao
Benidorm
Villajoyosa
Alicante
Santa Pola
Isla de Tabarca
Elche
Cabo de las Huertas
Torrevieja
Guardamar del Segura
San Pedro del Pinatar
Mar Menor
Cabo de Palos
Cartagena
Puerto Mazarrón
Golfo de Mazarrón
Cabo Cope
Águilas
Cabo del Almanzora
Cuevas del Almanzora
Garrucha
Mojácar
Carboneras
Punta de los Muertos
Cabo de Gata
Punta del Río
Golfo de Almería
Punta del Sabinal
Almería
Adra
Cabo Sacratif
Motril

Alborán (Sp.)

Projection: Conical with two standard parallels

m
3000 2000 1500 1000 400 200 0

m
200 2000

LONDON
Bristol
Exmoor
Southampton
Brighton
Plymouth
Portsmouth
Land's End
Dartmoor
Scilly Is.
Lizard Pt.
English Channel
Channel Is.
I. d'Ouessant
Pte. de St-Mathieu
Brest
Pte. de Penmarch
's-Gravenhage
Hoek van Holland
Harwich
Oostende
Calais
Dunkerque
Str. of Dover
Dover
Folkestone
Boulogne
Arras
Douai
Lille
Somme
Amiens
Rotterdam
NETH.
Antwerpen
Gent
Brussel
BELGIUM
Namur
Liège
Mechelen
Aachen
Bonn
Maas
Ardennes
LUX.
Trier
Verdun
Metz
Nancy
Toul
Épinal
Belfort
W.
Osnabrück
Münster
Dortmund
Essen
Düsseldorf
Köln
Koblenz
Rhein
Wiesbaden
Mainz
Frankfurt
Darmstadt
Mannheim
Heidelberg
Karlsruhe
Strasbourg
Freiburg
Basel
Bern
Hannover
Braunschweig
Kassel
Harz
Halle
Fulda
Erfurt
Würzburg
Nürnberg
Stuttgart
Augsburg
München
Ulm
Bodensee
Zürich
LIECHT.
Inn
Innsbruck
Donau
Regensburg
Salzburg
Potsdam
Magdeburg
Elbe
Leipzig
Plauen
Erzgeb.
Karl-Marx-(Chemnitz)
Dres.
Praha
Plzeň
Böhmerwald
GERMANY
Thüringer Wald
Spree
Mulde
BERLIN
E.
Weser

Cherbourg
Le Havre
Dieppe
Rouen
Caen
St-Malo
Jersey
Rennes
Alençon
Versailles
PARIS
Reims
Châlons
Marne
Le Mans
Sarthe
Angers
Orléans
Loire
Troyes
Yonne
Seine
Nantes
St-Nazaire
Belle-Ile
Loire
Vannes
Lorient
Tours
Cher
Bourges
Dijon
Chalon
Mâcon
Creusot
Vichy
Clermont-Ferrand
Mt. Dore
1886
St-Étienne
Lyon
Isère
Grenoble
Mt. Blanc
4807
Genève
Lausanne
Lac Leman
SWITZERLAND
Simplon
Passo di
Ortles
3899
Brenner
1371
Bergamo
Brescia
L. di Garda
Como
Milano
Torino
Po
Verona
Pádova
Vicenza
Venézia
G. di Venézia
Trieste

FRANCE
Poitiers
La Rochelle
Rochefort
Angoulême
Limoges
Charente
Périgueux
Bordeaux
Dordogne
Bayonne
Biarritz
Pau
Adour
Garonne
Toulouse
Tarn
Lot
Auvergne
Cévennes
Rhône
Nîmes
Montpellier
Béziers
Sète
Narbonne
Golfe du Lion
Perpignan
C. Creus
Avignon
Marseille
Toulon
Nice
Cannes
Menton
MONACO
Golfo di Génova
Ligurian Sea
C. Corse
Mt Cinto 2710
Bastia
Elba
Ajaccio
Corse
(Corsica)
Civitavecchia
Durance

Bay of Biscay
5365
5098

C. Ortegal
La Coruña
El Ferrol
C. Finisterre
Pontevedra
Santiago
Vigo
Orense
Miño
Braga
Bragança
Porto
Douro
Coimbra
PORTUGAL
Sa. da Estrela
Torres Vedras
Lisboa
Tejo
Évora
Setúbal
Faro
C. Trafalgar
Cádiz
Jerez
Str. of Gibraltar
Tanger
Ceuta(Sp.)
Tétouan
Larache
Ouezzane
Rabat
Meknès
Fès
MOROCCO
Haut Atlas
3737
Atlas
Gijón
Oviedo
Santander
Picos de Europa
León
Palencia
Cordillera Cantábrica
Valladolid
Compos
Duero
SPAIN
Salamanca
Ciudad Rodrigo
Alcántara
Cáceres
Badajoz
Guadiana
Sierra Morena
Córdoba
Linares
Guadalquivir
Sevilla
Jaén
Granada
Genil
Sa. Nevada 3478
Mulhacén
Málaga
Almería
C. de Gata
Huelva
Tinto
Bilbao
San Sebastián
Vitoria
Pamplona
Burgos
Ebro
Sa. de Guadarrama
MADRID
Tajo
Guadalajara
Toledo
La Mancha
Ciudad Real
Albacete
Segura
Murcia
Lorca
Cartagena
Zaragoza
Lérida
Pica de Aneto 3404
Andorra
Pyrenees
Barcelona
Tarragona
Ebro
Tortosa
Teruel
Cuenca
Júcar
Castellón
Valencia
Alicante
C. Nao
Islas Baleares
Ibiza
Ibiza
Formentera
Cabrera
Palma
Mallorca (Majorca)
Menorca (Minorca)
Mahón
ROMA
SAN MARINO
Arezzo
Perúgia
Siena
Livorno
Arno
Firenze
Bologna
Modena
Parma
Réggio
Ferrara
Ravenna
Forlì
Rimini
Ancona
Mti. Sábini
Gran Sasso 2914
Pisa
La Spézia
Génova
Alessándria
Mediterranean
Gaeta
Volturno
Nápoli
Capri
Saler
Sardegna
(Sardinia)
Sássari
Olbia
Caprera
Mt. del Gennargentu 1834
Cagliari
Tyrrhenian Sea
3719
Isole Eólie
(Æolian Is.)
Palermo
Trápani
Ísole Egadi
Marsala
Sicily
Agrigento
Caltanissetta
C. Bon
Binzert
Tunis
Carthage
G. de Hammamet
Sousse
Kairouan
Pantelleria (It.)
Gozo
Valletta
MALTA
Lampedusa (It.)
Sfax
Îles Kerkenna
Gabès
Djerba
Tarābulus
Jabal Nafūsah
Mizdah

Orán
Mostaganem
Ghdzaouet
Tlemcen
Oujda
Moulouya
Figuig
Béchar
Beni Abbès
Ain Sefra
El Golea
Ghardaia
Sidi Bel Abbès
Chelif
El Asnam
Hauts Plateaux
Chott ech Chergui
Djelfa
Sahara
ALGERIA
Alborán (Sp.)
Melilla (Sp.)
Alger
Béjaïa
Skikda
Constantine
Chott el Hodna
Biskra
Chott Melrhir
Tébessa
Touggourt
Chott el Djerid
Ouargla
Hassi Messaoud
Ft. Lallemand
TUNISIA
Tozeur
O. Djedi
Annaba
Sahara
Atlas Saharien
2887
2850
L

Projection: Conical with two standard parallels.
West from Greenwich
East from Greenwich

m
4000
2000
1000
400
200
0
0
200
1000
2000
3000
m

10
45
40
35
30
5
0
5
10

1:10 000 000

100   0   100   200   300   400 km

POLAND
Poznań
Łódź
Wrocław
Chorzów
Kraków
Płock
Wisła (Vistula)
Warszawa
Radom
Kielce
Lublin
Brest
Pinsk
Polesye
Pripyat
Chernigov
Desna
Sumy
Konotop
Nezhin
Belgorod
Kozanskaya
Kharkov
Volgograd

OSTRAVA
Jablunkovsky Pr.
550
SLOVAKIA
Bratislava
Banská Stiavnica
Miskolc
Košice
Tatry
2655
Carpathians
Tarnów
Przemyśl
Lvov
Rovno
Lutsko
Styr
Bug
Goryn
Berdichev
Zhitomir
Vinnitsa
Kiyev
Pereyaslav-Khmelnitskiy
Belaya Tserkov
Cherkassy
Poltava
Kremenchug
(Dnieper)
Slavyansk
Artemovsk
Voroshilovgrad
(Lugansk)
Kamensk-Shakhtinskiy
Tsimlyanskoye Vdkhr.

HUNGARY
Budapest
Kecskemét
Szeged
Hódmezővásárhely
Pécs
Balaton
Debrecen
Oradea
Cluj
Kolomyya
Prut
Chernovtsy
Botoşani
Iaşi
Beltsy
MOLD. S.S.R.
MOLDAVIAN
S.S.R.
Kishinev
Bendery
Tiraspol
Balta
Uman
Pervomaysk
Voznesensk
Kirovograd
Krivoy Rog
Dnepropetrovsk
Zaporozhye
Makeyevka
Donetsk
Gorlovka
Shakhty
Novocherkassk
Rostov

HOSLOVAKIA
Vah
Hron
Tisza
Tokaj
Körös
Maros
Mureş
Arad
Timişoara
Sombor
Subotica
Novi Sad
Petrovaradin
Pietrosul
2305
Pietrosul
2102
RUMANIA
Sibiu
Braşov
(Oraşul Stalin)
2635
Carpaţii Meridionali
Negoiu
2543
Ploieşti
Galaţi
Brăila
Ismail
Sulina
Dnes
Belgorod
Dnestrovskiy
Odessa
Nikolayev
Kherson
Berdyansk
Melitopol
Perekop
Dneprodzerzhinsk
Zhdanov
(Mariupol)
Taganrog
Yeisk
Azov
Don
Manych
Oz. Manych
Gudilo

Raab
Bulaton
GOSA
BOSNAS
Brod
Novi Sad
Sava
Beograd
Smederevo
Sarajevo
Mostar
Durmitor
2522
CRNA GORA
Dubrovnik
(Ragusa)
Kotor
Cetinje
Shkodra
2764
Tirana
Durrësi
Elbasan
ALBANIA
Vlora
Str. of Otranto
C. Sta. Maria di Leuca
1929
Banja Luka
Bosna
Sava
Morava
Kragujevac
Niš
Sofiya
2925
Musala
Skopje
Vardar
Bitola
Strumica
Sérrai
Kaválla
Thessaloníki
Gökçeada
Límnos
Athos
2033
Óros Ólimbos
2917

Pietrosul
Pleven
Turnovo
Shipchenski prokhod
Stara Planina
Tolbukhin
Bucureşti
Craiova
Orşova
Porţile de Fier
Turnu-Severin
Vidin
Iskŭr
Dunărea (Danube)
Ruse
Silistra
Constanţa
Varna
Burgas
BULGARIA
Plovdiv
Rhodopi Planina
Maritsa
Edirne
Sliven
Tŭrnovo

BLACK SEA
2211
Ince Burnu
Sinop
Karkinitskiy Zaliv
M. Tarkhankut
Yevpatoriya
Simferopol
1545
Krymskaya
(Crimea)
Sevastopol
Balaklava
Yalta
Feodosiya
Kerch
Sea of Azov
Novorossiysk
Tuapse
Sukhumi
Poti
Batumi
Krasnodar
Kuban
Maykop
Armavir
Stavropol
Tikhoretsk

Istanbul
Karadeniz Boğazı
(Bosporus)
Üsküdar
Zonguldak
Ereğli
Kastamonu
2565
Inebolu
Samsun
Giresun
Tirebolu
Şebin Karahisar
Trabzon
Rize
Kuzey Anadolu Dağları
Amasya
Çorum
Tokat
Sivas
Erzincan
Fırat
Keban

Izmit
İznik Gölü
Bursa
Bilecik
Sakarya
Beypazarı
Ankara
Kızıl Irmak
Yozgat
Kırşehir
Tuz Gölü
Aksaray
Niğde
Kayseri
3770
Erciyes Dağı
Gürün
Malatya
Maraş
Gaziantep

Marmara Denizi
Tekirdağ
Gelibolu (Gallipoli)
Çanakkale
Troy
Boğazı
Balıkesir
Eskişehir
Kütahya
Sivrihisar
Afyon Karahisar
Bolvadin
TURKEY
Konya
Beyşehir Gölü
Eğridir Gölü
Eğridir
Isparta
Burdur
Toros Dağ
Karaman
Tarsus
Mersin
Adana
Seyhan
Osmaniye
İskenderun Körfezi
İskenderun
Halab
Antakya
SYRIA

GREECE
Notía Píndhos
Préveza
Voríai Sporádhes
Lárisa
Vólos
Évvoia
Lésvos
Khíos
Aegean Sea
İzmir
Manisa
Turgutlu
Büyük Menderes
Aydın
Denizli
Muğla
Alaşehir
Mýkonos
Sámos
Ikaría
Náxos
Kikládhes
Íos
Thíra
Dhodhekánisos
Ródhos
4486
Megísti
(Kastellórizon)
Antalya
Antalya Körfezi
Elmalı
3086
Fethiye
Silifke

Kefallinía
Pátrai
Olympia
Zákinthos
Korinthiakós Kólpos
Návpaktos
Korinthos
Athínai
Piraiévs
Sýros
Andros
Peloponnisos
Kalamáta
Spárti
Pílos
5121
Ákra Taínaron
Kíthira
Andikíthira
Khaniá
Ídhi Óros
2456
Kríti
Iráklion
Kárpathos

Ionian Sea
Spartivento
gio

Thíval
Návplion

AEGEAN SEA
4135
3174

Kérkira
Kérkira
Levkás
Ithákon

CYPRUS
Tróodhos
1951
Morfou
Levkosía (Nicosia)
Ammókhostos
(Famagusta)
Lárnax
Lemesós
Al Ladhiqiyah
Baniyas
Tarabulus
Ḥamā
Homs
Hamā
3083
Bayrût
(Beirut)
LEBANON
Zahle
Dimashq
(Damascus)
ash Sheikh
2814
Jabal ad Durûz
Sayda
'Akko
Haifa
Tel Aviv-Yafo
ISRAEL
Jerusalem
Amman
JORDAN
Bahr el Miyet
395
Gaza
Petra
Ma'ân
Al 'Aqabah
Khalij al 'Aqaba
Busra

Cyrene
Derna
Al Marj
(Barce)
Khalîj Bômba
Tobruq
Banghāzī
Khalîj Surt
Barqa
Khalîg el Salûm
Salûm
Matrûh
El 'Alamein
El Iskandarîya
Rashîd
Dumyât
Bûr Saîd
El Qantara
Ismaʻilîya
El 'Arish
LIBYA
B   Y   A
Bahra el Burullus
Bahra el Burullus
El Mahalla el Kubra
Tanta
Suez
Buheirat Murrat-el-Kubra
Canal
Is
Suweis
Gebel el Tîh
EGYPT
EL QÂHIRA
El Faiyûm
Beni Suêf
Nile
Khalîg es Suweis
2637
Es Sinâ'
Gebel

COPYRIGHT. GEORGE PHILIP & SON. LTD.

- - - - - - Division between Greeks
and Turks in Cyprus;
Turks to the north.

1 : 2 500 000

10 0 10 20 30 40 50 60 70 80 90 100 km

HUNGARY

SOMOGY

ZALA

Graz

Klagenfurt

Villach

Maribor

Ljubljana

Zagreb

YUGOSLAVIA

FRIULI-VENEZIA GIULIA

VENETO

Udine

Trieste

Golfo di
Venézia
(Venice)

Venézia
Laguna
Veneta

Pádova (Padua)

Méstre

Treviso

Ferrara

Ravenna

Rímini

San Marino

Ancona

MARCHE

Perúgia

UMBRIA

L. Trasimeno

Arezzo

ABRUZZI

L'Aquila

Pescara

Chieti

LAZIO

ROMA
(ROME)

Vatican City

Tívoli

A D R I A T I C   S E A

Golfo di Venézia

DALMACIJA

BOSNA

HERCEGOVINA

Banja Luka

Split

Brač

Hvar

Korčula

Lastovo

Mljet

Vis

Pag

Zadar

Rijeka (Fiume)

Pula

Cres

Krk

Dugi Otok

Palagruža

Pianosa

Tremiti

Vasto

Térmoli

Monte Sant'Ángelo

Vieste

MOLISE

FOR CONTINUATION SEE PAGE 66

Iles Sanguinaires
G. d'Ajaccio
Tarravo
Pietrosa
C. di Muro Propriano
CORSE
Zonza Solenzara
2136
Levie Favone
G. de Valinco Sartène
CORSICA
Porto-Vecchio
Bonifacio
CORSE-DU-SUD
Iles Cerbicales
I. de
Cavallo
Bouches de Bonifacio
Santa Teresa Maddalena
Gallura
La Maddalena Caprera
Punta dello Scorno
Golfo dell' Pto. Cervo
Arzachena
Costa
Smeralda
Asinara
Asinara Coghinas Àggius
Calangiànus G. di Òlbia
Porto Tórres Témpio Pausania
Tavolara
Sorso 1362 Òlbia
Sássari M. Limbara
Sénnori
C. dell'Argentiera Osilo Oschiri
L. di Coghinas
Fertília Ozieri *Posada* Tanaunella
Ìttiri Pattada Budduso
Alghero 1259 Siniscola
Villanova Bonórva 1150 Bitti C. Comino
Monteleone
Orune
Tèma Bosa Màcomer Nùoro Dorgali
Orosei
Oliena
SARDEGNA *Golfo di*
Orosei
L. del Tirso Fonni Báunei
Ghilarza Sòrgono **Monti del**
Tirso **Gennargentu** C. di Monte Santu
Córbas 1834 **SARDEGNA** Arbatax
Oristano Làconi Lanusei
M. Arci Iérzu
Golfo di 812
Oristano Àrborea Nurri
Terralba Mándas **SARDINIA**
Ìsili
S. Gavino Senorbì
Gúspini Monreale Flumendosa
C. Pécora Arbus Villacidro Serramanna S. Vito
1236 Dolianova Muravera
Fluminimaggiore M. Línas Sestu Sinnai 1069
Serpèdat C. Ferrato
Iglesias Cìxerri Àssemini Selárgius
Portoscuso Gonnesa Síliqua Quartu Sant'Elena
Carloforte **Carbónia** **Cágliari**
San Pietro 1116 *Golfo di* Serpentara
Sant'Antíoco Santadi *Cágliari*
Sant' Porto Botte C. Carbonara
Antíoco Pula Teulada
G. di Pálmas
C. Spartivento

ROMA
(Rome) Tívoli
Vatican City Subiaco Trevaco del
Fregene Palestrina
Frascati Valmontone Anagni Alatri Véroli
Lido di Óstia Albano Cori Ferentino Frosinone
(Lido di Roma) Prática Laziale Velletri Ceccano
di Mare Aprília Cisterna di Latina Ceprano 153
Ánzio Latina Sezze Priverno Sonnino Fondi
Nettuno Pontínia Sabáudia Terracina
Monte Circeo 541 Gaeta Minty
Golfo di
Palmarola Zannone *Gaeta* Gang
Ísole Ponza 283
Ponziane
Ventotene

T Y R R H E N I A N

3719

S E A

3589

Iles de la
Galite Ústica

Levanzo **Trápani** C. San Vito del Golfo **PALERMO**
Érice 1110 G. di Castellammare Terrasini Bogheria
Ísole Égadi Alcamo S. Giuseppe Monreale
Maréttimo Pàceco Calatafimi Partinico Iato Mariheo
Favignana Salemi Camporeale 1613
Favignana Corleone Prizzi
Marsala Gibellina Bisacquino
Partanna Sambuca Lercara Frido S I C
Castelvetrano di Sicilia Prizzi
Mazara Menfi Búrgio Mussom
del Vallo Campobello di Mazara Sciacca Platani Racalm
Belice Caltabel Ribera Raffadali
Sicilian Channel Cattólica Eráclea Siculiana Agrigento Favate
Porto Empédocle Agrigento
Palma di Montech
Campot

C. Blanc Cani
Bizerte Plane
(Binzert)
C. Serrat **Menzel-Bourguiba** Zembra
Mateur C. Bon
Golfe de Tunis
El Kala Tébourba **TUNIS** Halq el Oued
ALGERIA Tabarka (La Goulette) Kelibia
Bou Salem Béja Mejerda Menzel
Téboursouk Temime
T U N I S I A Soliman Pantelleria Pantelleria
Medjerda Nabeul 836 (It.)
Mellégue **M E D I T E**
Zaghouan Hammamet
1319

Projection: Conical with two standard parallels   East from Greenwich

m
3000
2000
1500
1000
400
200
0   0
200
2000
4000
m

1:2 500 000

10 0 10 20 30 40 50 60 70 80 90 100 km

ADRIATIC

SEA

G. di Manfredónia

Monte Gargano

Testa del Gargano

L. di Lésina

S. Severo

Manfredónia

Fóggia

Lucera

Campobasso

Benevento

Avellino

Salerno

G. di Salerno

Agrópoli

Castellabate

Punta Licosa

Pollica

Pisciotta

C. Palinuro

G. di Policastro

Camerota

Scalea

Belvedere Marittimo

Páola

Barletta

Trani

Biscéglie

Molfetta

Bari

Andria

Corato

Ruvo

Bitonto

Cerignola

Canosa

Minervino Murge

Gravina

Altamura

Matera

Potenza

BASILICATA

PUGLIA

CALABRIA

Táranto

Golfo di Táranto

Brindisi

Lecce

Gallípoli

Otranto

C. Santa Maria di Leuca

ALBANIA

Durrës (Durazzo)

Tirana (Tiranë)

Vlora (Valona)

Strait of Otranto

Kérkira (Corfu)

Cosenza

Rossano

Crotone

Catanzaro

Golfo di Squillace

Golfo di Sant'Eufémia

Vibo Valéntia

IONIAN

SEA

Isole Eólie o Lípari (Æolian Is.)

Strómboli

Lípari

Vulcano

Milazzo

Barcellona

Messina

Réggio

Catánia

Golfo di Catánia

SICILIA

Siracusa

Augusta

Ragusa

Módica

Noto

G. di Noto

C. Passero

RANEAN SEA

COPYRIGHT. GEORGE PHILIP & SON. LTD.
HHK

FOR CONTINUATION SEE PAGE 63

1 : 2 500 000

10 0 10 20 30 40 50 60 70 80 90 100 km

East from Greenwich

COPYRIGHT GEORGE PHILIP & SON LTD.

Projection: Conical with two standard parallels

Continuation Eastwards
on same scale

S E A   O F   C R E T E
(Sea of Candia)

A R K H I P É L A G O S
K I K L Á D H E S
(C Y C L A D E S)

D H O D H E K Á N I S O S
(D O D E C A N E S E)

Stenón Karpáthos

Stenón Kasos

m
3000
2000
1500
1000
400
200
0

0
200
2000
m

1:2 500 000

1:2 500 000

10 0 0 10 20 30 40 50 60 70 80 90 100 km

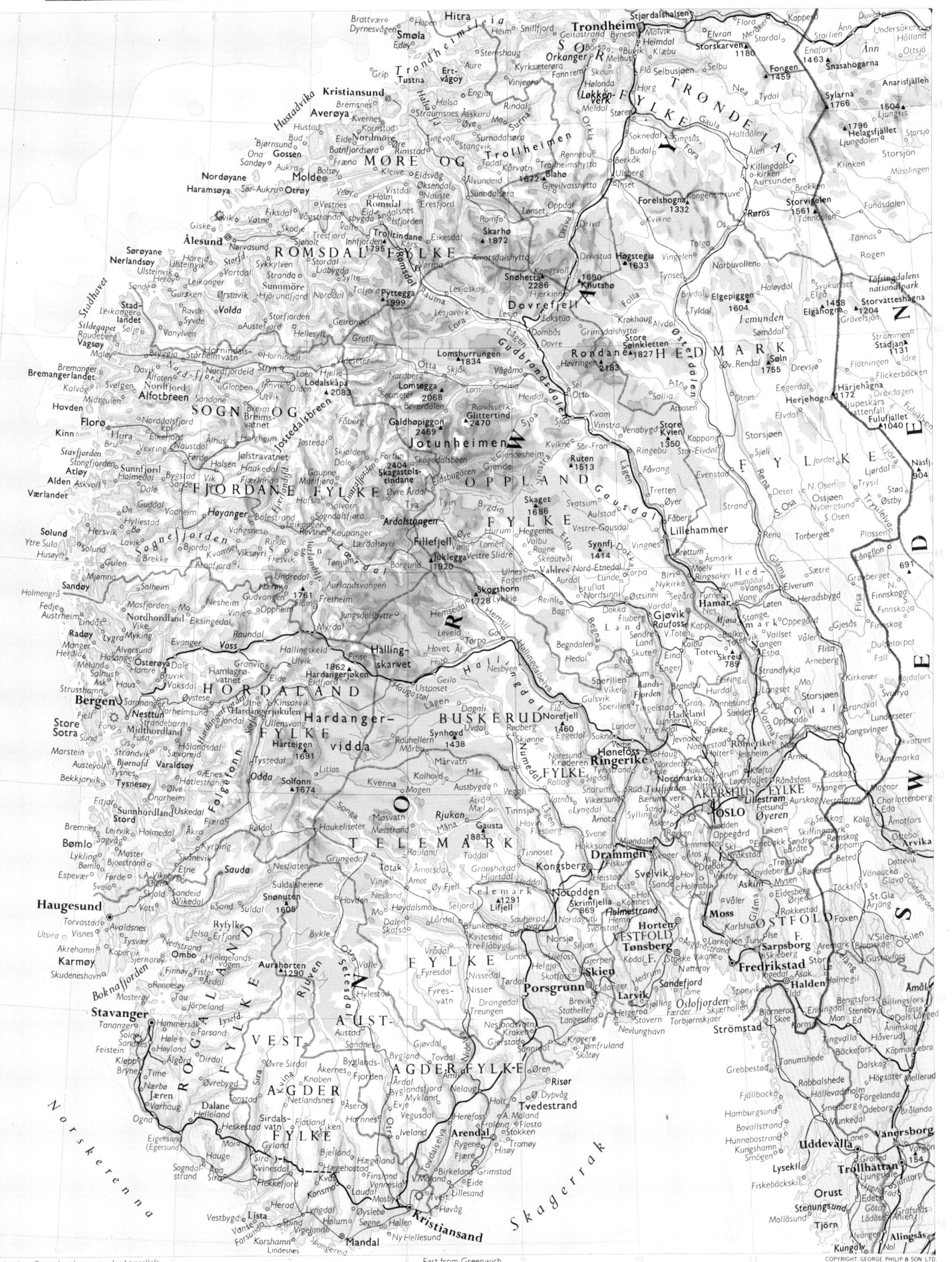

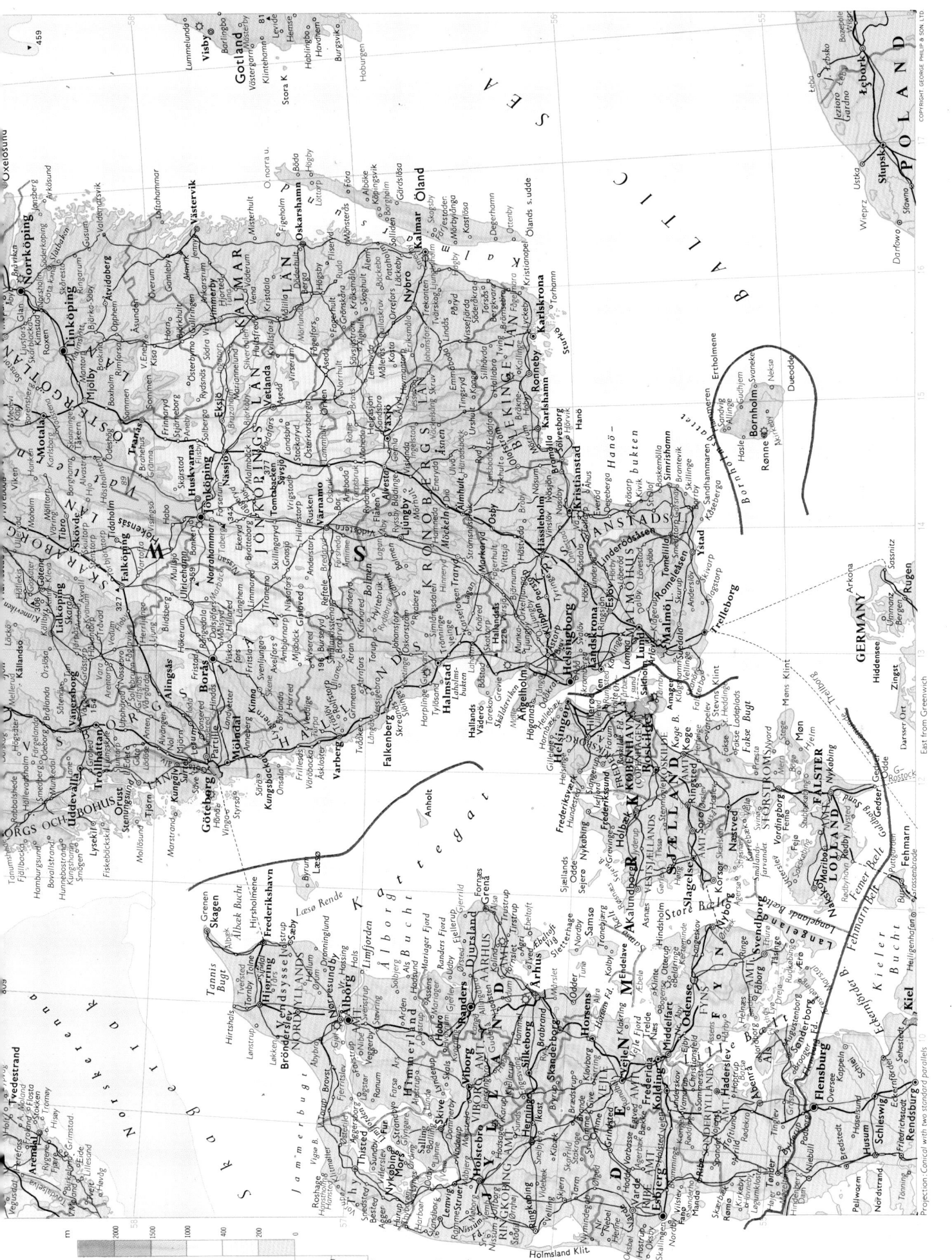

1 : 2 500 000

10 0 10 20 30 40 50 60 70 80 90 100 km

POLAND

BALTIC SEA

Gotland
Visby

Öland

Bornholm
Rønne

GERMANY

Oxelösund

Norrköping

Linköping

KALMAR LÄN

Kalmar

Nybro

Karlskrona

BLEKINGE LÄN

Ronneby

Karlshamn

Kristianstad

KRISTIANSTADS

Simrishamn

Ystad

MALMÖHUS

Malmö

Lund

Landskrona

Helsingborg

Trelleborg

Motala

ÖSTERGÖTLANDS LÄN

VÄSTERGÖTLANDS LÄN

SKARABORG

Jönköping

Nässjö

Huskvarna

JÖNKÖPINGS LÄN

Norrahammar

Värnamo

KRONOBERGS LÄN

Växjö

Ljungby

Älmhult

Falköping

Skövde

Lidköping

Vänersborg

Trollhättan

Alingsås

Borås

ÄLVSBORGS LÄN

HALLANDS

Halmstad

Falkenberg

Varberg

Uddevalla

GÖTEBORGS OCH BOHUS

Göteborg

Mölndal

Kungälv

Kungsbacka

Helsingør

KØBENHAVN

(COPENHAGEN)

Roskilde

SJÆLLAND

Næstved

Slagelse

Ringsted

Korsør

Frederikshavn

Skagen

Hjørring

Ålborg

NORDJYLLANDS

NØRREJYLLAND

VIBORG AMT

Randers

ÅRHUS

Djursland

Skive

Holstebro

Thisted

Silkeborg

Herning

RINGKØBING

Horsens

Vejle

VEJLE AMT

Kolding

Fredericia

Esbjerg

RIBE

SØNDERJYLLANDS AMT

Haderslev

Åbenrå

Sønderborg

Flensburg

Schleswig

Rendsburg

Kiel

FYN

Odense

Middelfart

Svendborg

Nyborg

Rudkøbing

LOLLAND

Maribo

Nykøbing

FALSTER

Gedser

Rostock

Rügen

Kattegat

Danmark

Norge

Arendal

Tvedestrand

m
2000 1500 1000 400 200

459

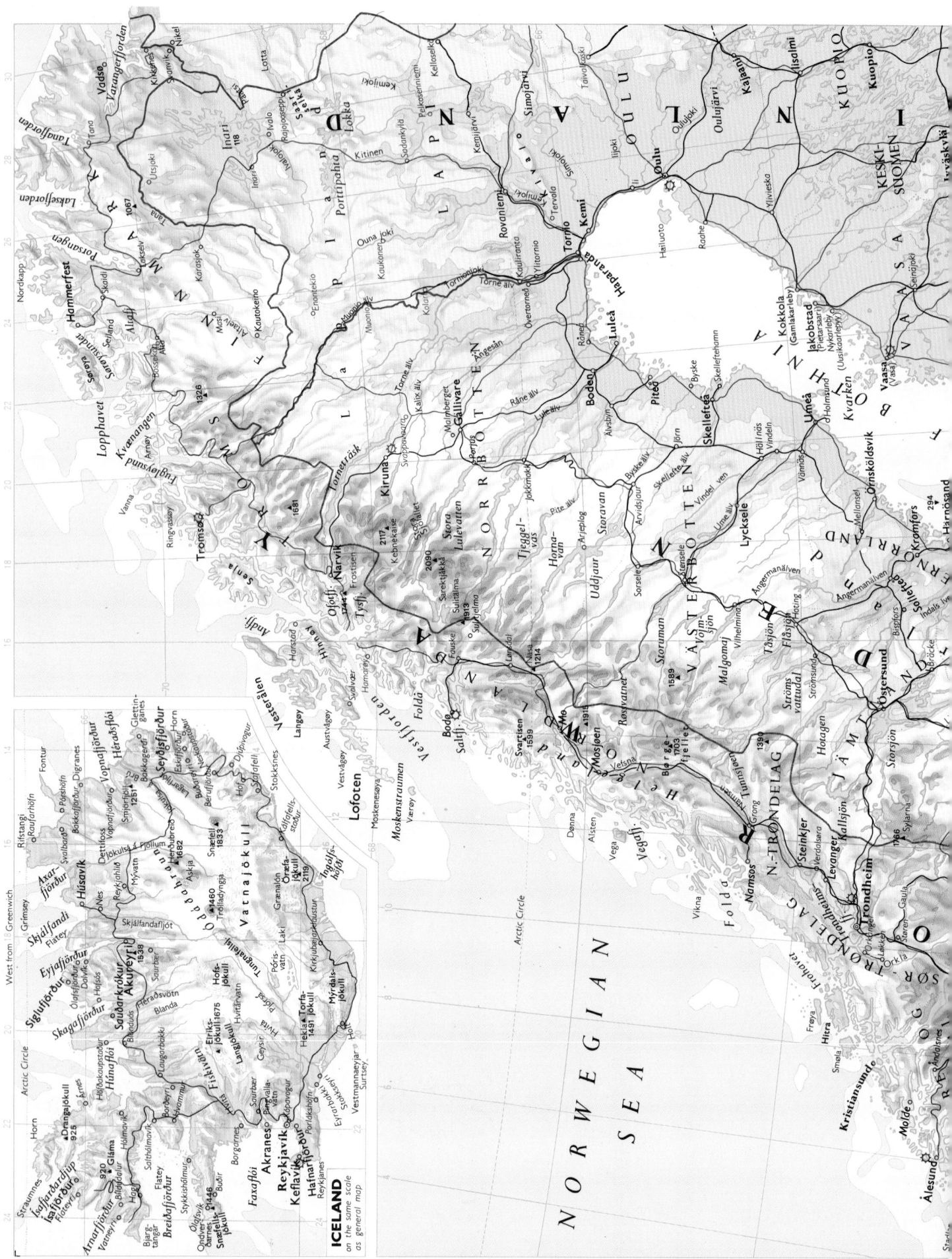

ICELAND
on the same scale
as general map

1 : 5 000 000

50 · 0 · 50 · 100 · 150 · 200 km

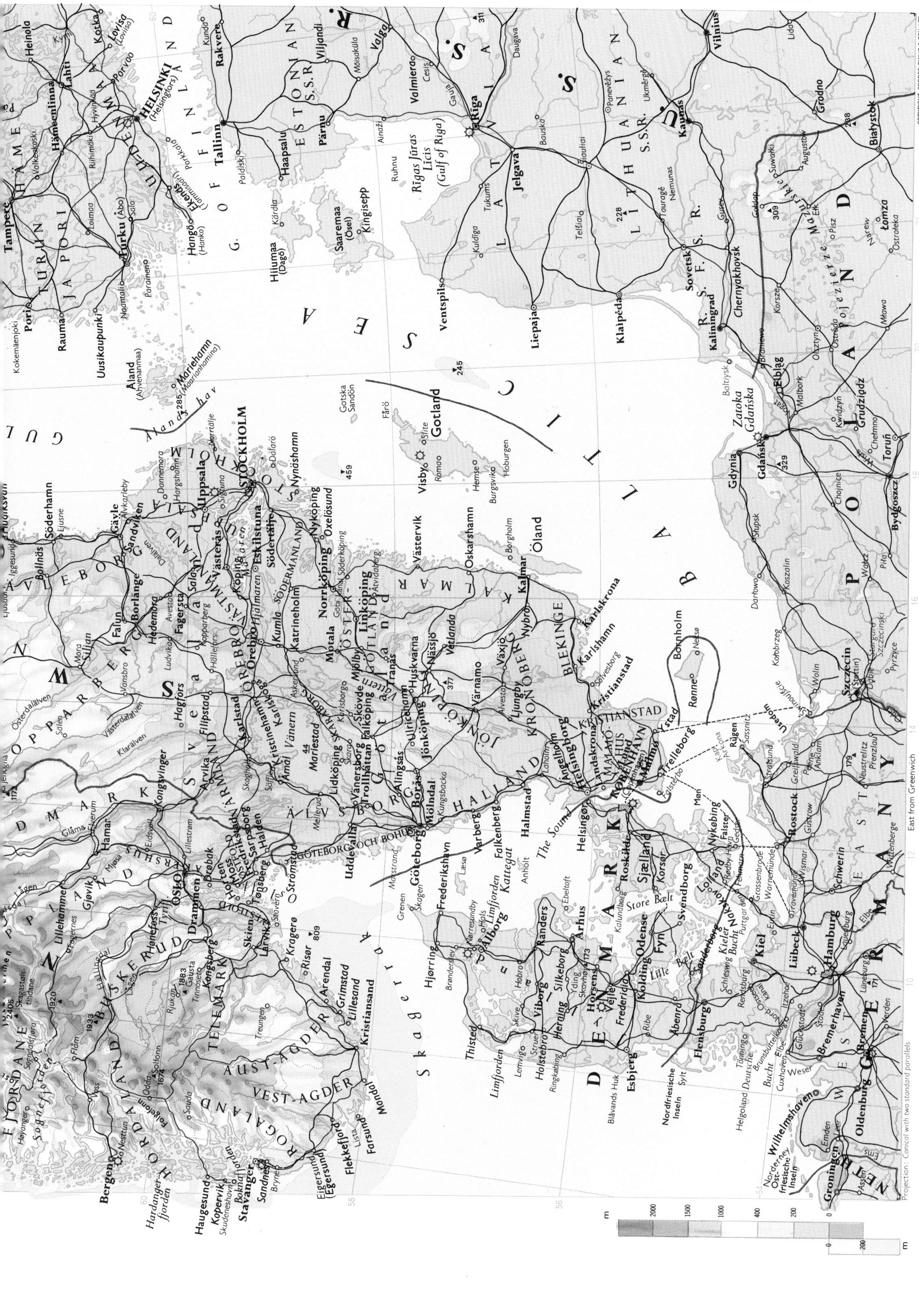

B A L T I C   S E A

Countries / Regions
- F I N L A N D
- E S T O N I A N   S.S.R.
- R. S. F. S. R.
- L A T V I A N   S.S.R.
- L I T H U A N I A N   S.S.R.
- P O L A N D
- G E R M A N Y (EAST / WEST)
- D E N M A R K
- N O R W A Y

Major places
HELSINKI (Helsingfors), Tampere, Turku (Åbo), Tallinn, Riga, Vilnius, Kaunas, Grodno, Białystok, Łomża, Kaliningrad, Chernyakhovsk, Elbląg, Gdańsk, Gdynia, Szczecin (Stettin), Bydgoszcz, Grudziądz, Toruń, STOCKHOLM, Uppsala, Gävle, Västerås, Örebro, Norrköping, Linköping, Jönköping, Göteborg, Malmö, Kristianstad, Karlskrona, Gotland, Visby, Öland, Kalmar, Bornholm, Rønne, Rostock, Lübeck, Hamburg, Bremen, Bremerhaven, Wilhelmshaven, Oldenburg, Groningen, KØBENHAVN (Copenhagen), Odense, Århus, Ålborg, Esbjerg, Kiel, Flensburg, Schwerin, OSLO, Drammen, Bergen, Stavanger, Kristiansand

East from Greenwich

Projection - Conical with two standard parallels

m 2000 1500 1000 400 200 0

m 200 0

R.S.F.S.R.
1. Daghestan A.S.S.R.
2. Kabardino–Balkar A.S.S.R.
3. Mari A.S.S.R.
4. Mordovian A.S.S.R.
5. North Ossetian A.S.S.R.
6. Tatar A.S.S.R.
7. Udmurt A.S.S.R.
8. Chuvash A.S.S.R.
9. Checheno–Ingush A.S.S.R.
AZERBAIJAN
10. Nakhichevan A.S.S.R.
GEORGIA
11. Abkhaz A.S.S.R.
12. Adzhar A.S.S.R.

Projection: Conical Orthomorphic with two standard parallels

East from Greenwich

1 : 20 000 000

200   0   200   400   600   800 km

OCEAN

Mys Dezhneva
(East C.)

St. Lawrence I.
(U.S.A.)

Mys Arkticheskiy

Ostrov
Komsomolets

Ostrov Oktyabrskoy
Revolyutsii

Severnaya
Zemlya

Ostrov Bolshevik

Proliv Vilkitskogo

Ostrova Delong

Novosibirskiye Ostrova

Ostrov
Faddeyevskiy

Ostrov
Novaya Sibir

East Siberian Sea

Ostrov Vrangelya

Chukotskiy Khrebet

Chukotskoye
More

Koryakskiy Khrebet

2562

Bering
Sea

Kamandorskiye
Ostrova

Poluostrov
Kamchatka

4750

Petropavlovsk-
Kamchatskiy

Sea of
Okhotsk

Sakhalin

Hokkaido

Sapporo

Hakodate

Sea of JAPAN

Honshū

Niigata

Kanazawa

A L   S O C I A L I S T   R E P U B L I C

Yakutsk

Okhotsk

Khabarovsk

Vladivostok

Nakhodka

M O N G O L I A

Ulaanbaatar
(Ulan Bator)

Irkutsk

Ulan Ude

Chita

Blagoveshchensk

Harbin

Shenyang
(Mukden)

Anshan

Fushun

Peip'ing
(Kalgan)

Paot'ou

Seoul

Pusan

North
KOREA

P'yongyang

South
KOREA

Taejon

COPYRIGHT. GEORGE PHILIP & SON. LTD.

	Boundaries of U.S.S.R.
	Boundaries of S.S.R.
	Boundaries of A.S.S.R.

1 : 10 000 000

100   0   100   200   300   400 km

Kabardino-Balkar A.S.S.R.
North Ossetian A.S.S.R. (Azer.)
Nakhichevan A.S.S.R. (Azer.)
Checheno-Ingush A.S.S.R.
Karagiye Depression

Projection: Conical with two standard parallels

East from Greenwich

Division between Greeks and Turks
in Cyprus; Turks to the North.

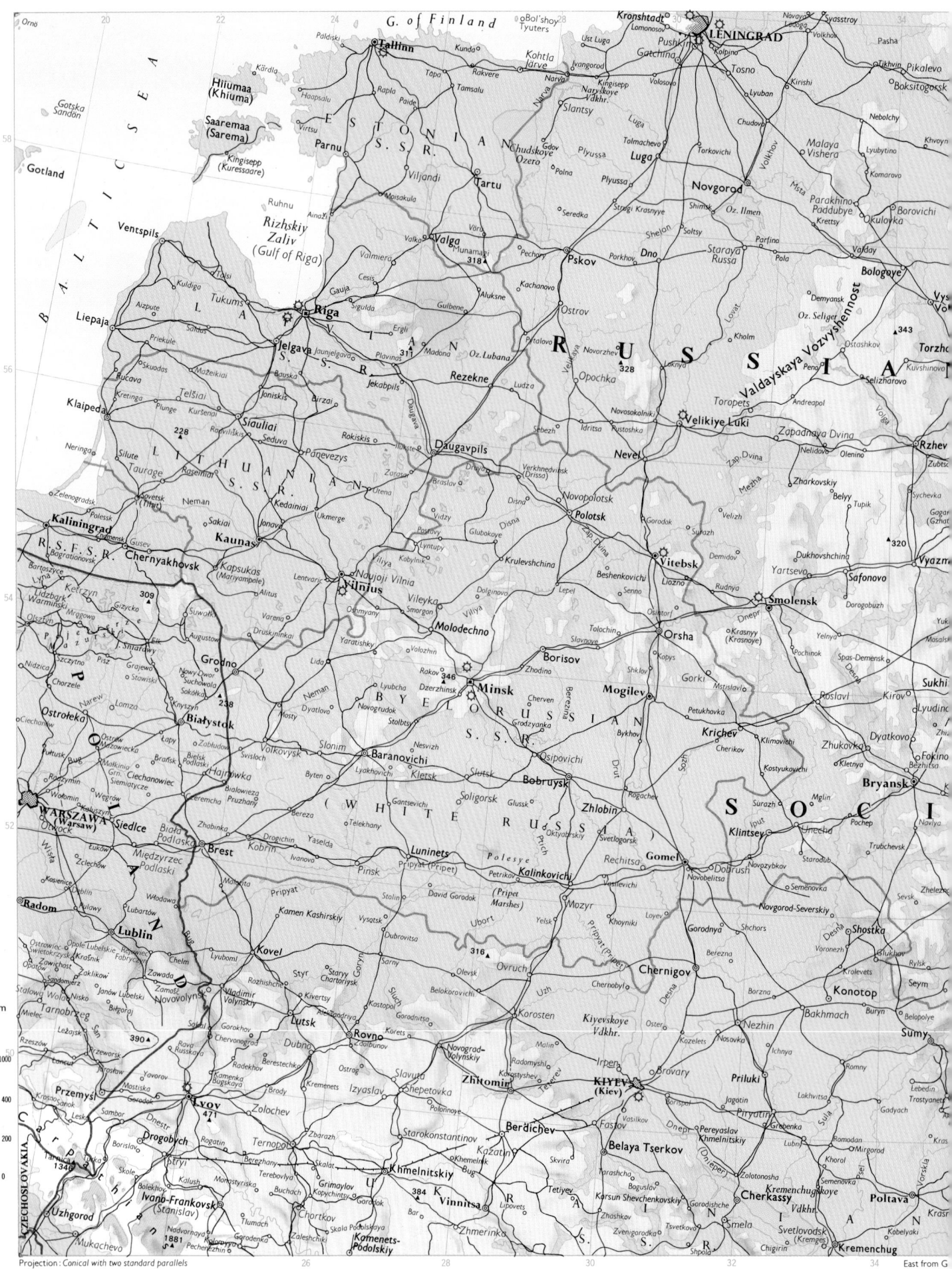

Projection: Conical with two standard parallels

East from G

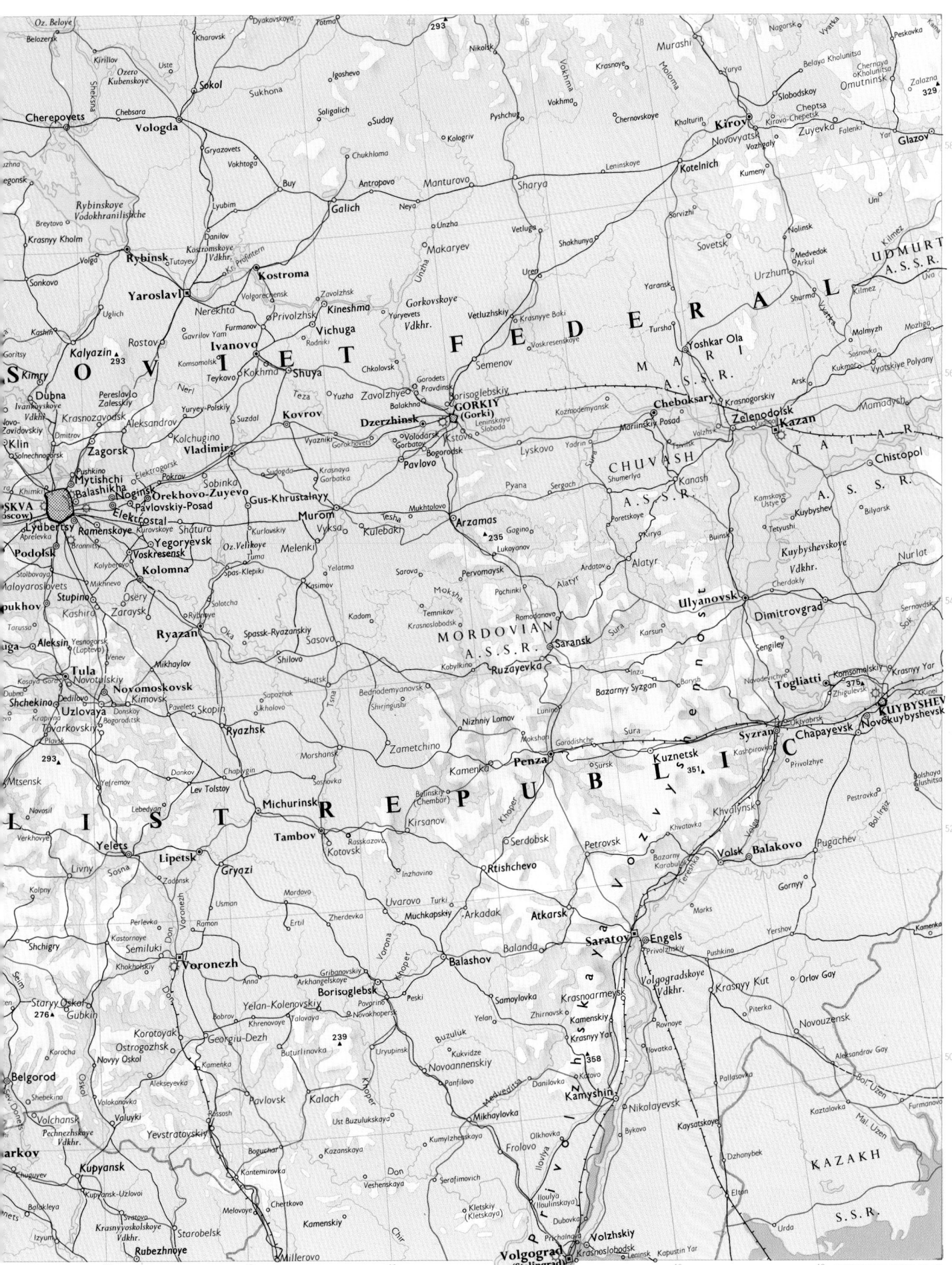

1 : 5 000 000

50   0   50   100   150   200 km

O_{z. Beloye}

Belozersk
Kirillov
Ozero
Uste
Kubenskoye

Cherepovets
Vologda
Chebsara
Sokol

Sukhona

Gryazovets
Vokhtoga

Rybinskoye
Vodokhranilishche

Breytovo
Krasnyy Kholm

Volga
Rybinsk
Tutayev
Danilov
Kostromskoye Vdkhr.
Kr. Profintern

Sonkovo

Kashin

Yaroslavl
Nerekhta
Volgorechensk
Zavolzhsk

Goritsy
Kalyazin
293
Rostov
Gavrilov Yam
Furmanov
Privolzhsk
Vichuga

Skimry
Uglich
Nerl
Ivanovo
Teykovo
Kokhma
Shuya

Dubna
Pereslavlo
Zalesskiy
Yuryev-Polskiy
Suzdal

Ivankovskoye
Vdkhr.
Krasnozavodsk
Aleksandrov
Kolchugino

Klin
Zagorsk
Vladimir

MORDOVIAN
A.S.S.R.

MOSKVA
(Moscow)

COPYRIGHT. GEORGE PHILIP & SON. LTD.
HHK

Projection: Conical with two standard parallels

1 : 5 000 000

50   0   50   100   150   200 km

83

Yelan-Kolenovskiy
Povorino
Peski
Krasnoarmeysk
Krasnyy Kut
Orlov Gay   Oz.Chalkar   Chalkar
Dzhambeyty
Georgiu-Dezh
Khrenovoye   Talovaya   Novokhopersk   Samoylovka   Zhirnovsk
Krasnyy   Yar   Ravnoye   Piterka   Novouzensk
Kazakh
Buturlinovka   239   Uryupinsk   Yelan   Krasnyy   Novatka
Volgogradskoye   S.   S.   R.
Kamenka   Novoannenskiy   Buzuluk   Kukvidze   Yar   358   Vdkhr.   Pallasovka   Aleksandrov Gay   Mergenevskiy   Karsha
Pavlovsk   Kalach   Panfilovo   Danilovka   Nikolayevsk   Kaztalovka   Mal.Uzen   Furmanovo   Ural   Bazartobe
Rossosh   Ust Buzulukskaya   Medveditsa   Mikhaylovka   Kotovo   Kamyshin   Pribalnaya   Urda   Bol.Uzen   Antonovo
Boguchar   Kazanskaya   Kumylzhenskaya   Frolovo   Olkhovka   Kamyshin   Dubovka   Elton   Bykovo   Dzhanybek   Inderborskiy
Kantemirovka   Don   Veshenskaya   Serafimovich   Iloviya   Privolzhskaya   Volzhskiy   Leninsk   Kapustin Yar   Shungay   Zelënyy
obelsk   Millerovo   Chir   Sovetskaya   Kletskiy   (Iloulinskaya)   Volgograd   (Stalingrad)   Krasnoslobodsk   Kapustin Yar   Verkhniy Baskunchak   Makhambet   (Yamankhalinka)   Topol
Voroshilovgrad   (Lugansk)   Kamensk-Shakhtinskiy   Morozovsk   Surovikino   Kalach na Donu   Krasnoarmeysk   Akhtubinsk   (Petropavlovsky)   Vladimirovka   Novobogatinskoye
Krasnodon   Sverdlovsk   Belaya Kalitva   Krasnodonetskaya   Chernyshkovskiy   Volga   Guryev
Gukovo   Shakhty   Ust-Donetsk   Tsimlyanskoye   Vdkhr.   Kotelnikovo   Kapanovka   Yenotayevka   -28
Shakhtinsk   Krasnyy Sulin   Sinegorski   Tsimlyansk   Volgodonsk   Dubovskoye   Zavetnoye   Krasnyy Yar
Kamenolomni   Konstantinovskiy   Bolshaya Martynovka   Zhivnovka   A.   S.   S.   R.   Astrakhan
Tuzlov   Novocherkassk   Manych   Proletarskaya   Yegorlykskaya   Kuberle   K A L M Y K   Krasnye   Kamyzyak
Rostov   Bataysk   Veselovskoye   Vdkhr.   Remontnoye   A.S.S.R.   Kirovskiy
Zernograd   Mechetinskaya   Gigant   Elista   (Stepnoi)   Mumra
Kushchevskaya   Yegorlyksk   Salsk   Oz. Manych-   Gudilo   Leninsk   Privutnoye   Liman
Belaya   Glina   Peschanokopskoye   Krasnoye   Kaspiyskiy   Kultay
Pavlovskaya   Divnoye   Kalaus   Beloye Ozero
Tikhoretsk   Krasnogvardeyskoye   Ipatovo   Kuma   O.Kulaly   Mangyshlakskiy   Zaliv
Korenovsk   Kropotkin   Novoaleksandrovskaya   Izobil'nyy   Svetlograd   (Petrovskoye)   Arzgir   Staryy Biryuzyak   M. Tyub Karagan   Fort Shevchenko   P-ov.   Mangyshlak
Ust-Labinsk   Armavir   Kurgannyi   (Kurganinaya)   Stavropol   Blagodarnoye   Bryanskoye   O.Chechen   Shevchenko
Krasnodar   Kuban   831   Nevinnomyssk   Prikumsk   Vladimirovka   Tyuleniy
Maykop   Labinsk   Kursavka   Zelenokumsk   (Vorontsovo-Aleksandrovskoye)   Aleksandriyskaya   Lopatin
Apsheronsk   Urup   Cherkessk   Mineralnyye Vody   Georgievsk   Kizlyar   800
Neftegorsk   Laba   Dakhovskaya   Yessentuki   Pyatigorsk   Prokhladnyy   Mozdok   CHECHENO-   Terek
Sochi   Bolshoy   Krasnaya Polyana   Kislovodsk   Karachayevsk   Nalchik   Mayskiy   Malgobek   INGUSH   Gudermes   Sulak
Matsesta   Teberda   Nartkala   Beslan   Groznyy   A.S.S.R.   Kumtorkala   Makhachkala
Adler   Gagra   Caucasus   KABARDINO   BALKAR   Elbrus   5633   Ordzhonikidze   5203   Kizil Yurt   Buynaksk   Kaspiysk
Gudauta   Novyy Afon   Klukhori   A.S.S.R.   Sadon   Balta   Khunzakh   Izberbash   Novokayakent
ABKHAZ   A.S.S.R.   Inguri   Kazbek   6047   Tebulos   4492   Agvali   Kakhib   Dagestanskiye Ogni
Sukhumi   Tkvarcheli   Dzhvari   Rioni   Oni   Tlyarata   Akusha   D A G E S T A N   A.S.S.R.
Ochamchire   Gali   GEORGIA   Mountains   Madzhalis   Derbent
Anaklia-Tskhaka   Sachkhere   Tskhinvali   (Staliniri)   Dusheti   Telavi   Kvareli   Samur   Akhty
Kutaisi   Tkibuli   Chiatura   Khashuri   Gori   Kvareli   Kasumkent   Mikhaylovka
Poti   Samtredia   Zestafoni   Kaspi   Mtskheta   Lagodekhi   Sheki   Khachmas
Kobuleti   S.   S.   R.   Borzhomi   Tbilisi   Signakhi   (Nukha)   Bazar Dyuzi   4466   Divichi
Makharadze   Khulo   Akhaltsikhe   Khrami   Rustavi   Citeli   Alazan   Mingechaurskoye   Baba dag   3629   Siazan
Batumi   ADZHAR   A.S.S.R.   Akhalkalaki   Shaumyani   Mirzaani   Iori   Vdkhr.   Kutkashen
Hopa   Barçka   Citli Çkaro   Shaumyani   Akstafa   Kura   Agdash
Pazar   Akhalkalaki   Alaverdi   Mingechaur   Geokchay   Shemakha   Sumgait
Rize   Çildir   Tauz   Shamkhor   ZERBAIJAN   BAKU
Trabzon   Artvin   Ardahan   3182   Kirovakan   Dilizhan   Kirovabad   Chanlar   S.   S.   R.   Kazi Magomed
Surmene   Kars   Leninakan   Artik   Aragats   4090   Mir-Bashir   Berda   Sabirabad   M. Byandovan
Çakirgol   3937   Oltu   Narman   Sarikamis   Diior   Charentsavan   Ozero   Sevan   Terter   Agdzhabedi   Al-Bayramly
Of   Ispir   ARMENIAN   Kagizman   Kamo   Agdam   Imishly   Zyrya
Bayburt   Çoruh   Echmiadzin   S.S.R.   Martuni   Surakhany
3063   Tortum   Aras   Yerevan   M. Byandovan

C A S P I A N   S E A

Prikaspiyskaya Nizmennost

Ergeni Vozvyshennost

COPYRIGHT. GEORGE PHILIP & SON. LTD.

1:5 000 000

50   0   50   100   150   200 km

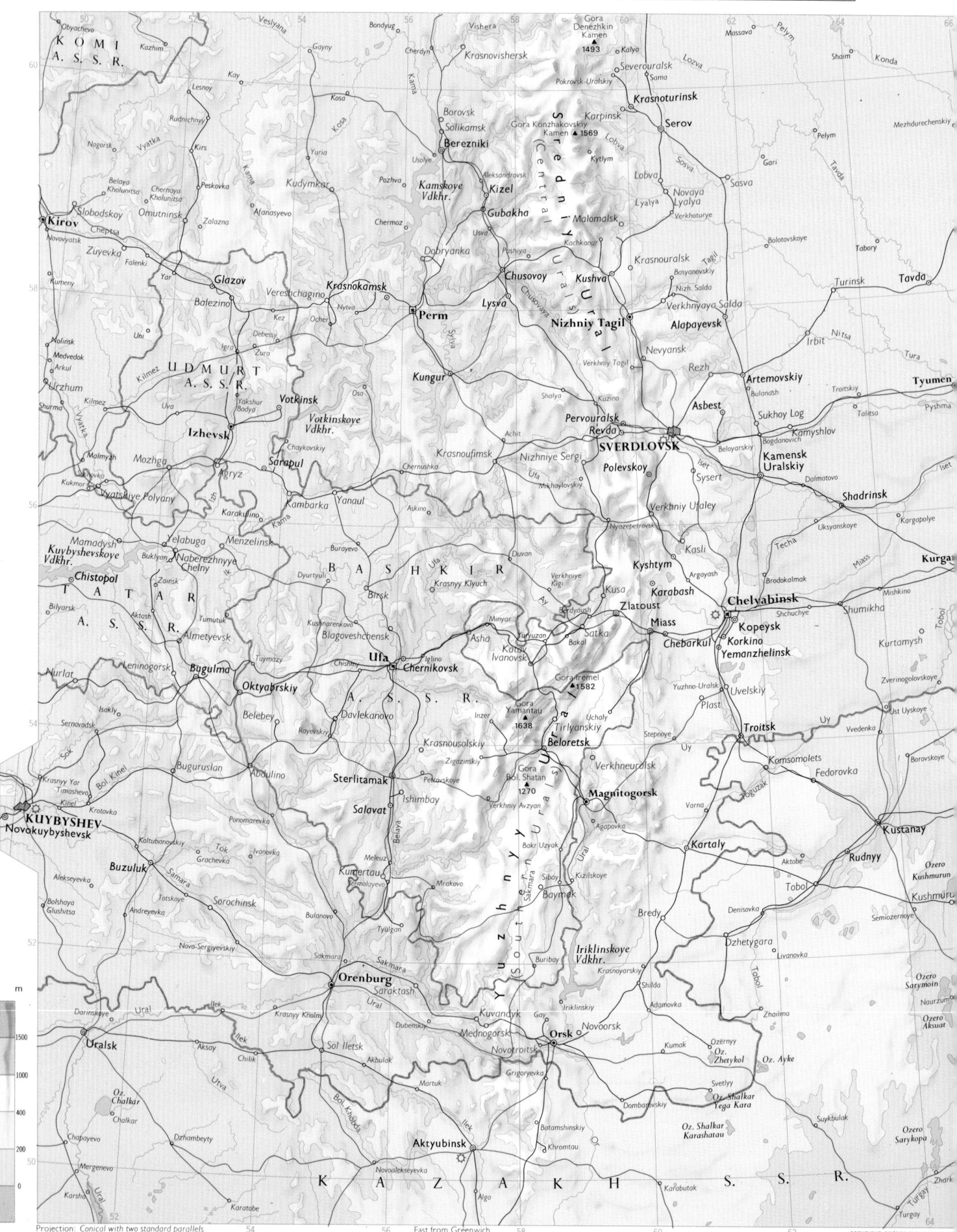

Projection: Conical with two standard parallels   East from Greenwich   COPYRIGHT. GEORGE PHILIP & SON. LT

m

1500
1000
400
200
50
0

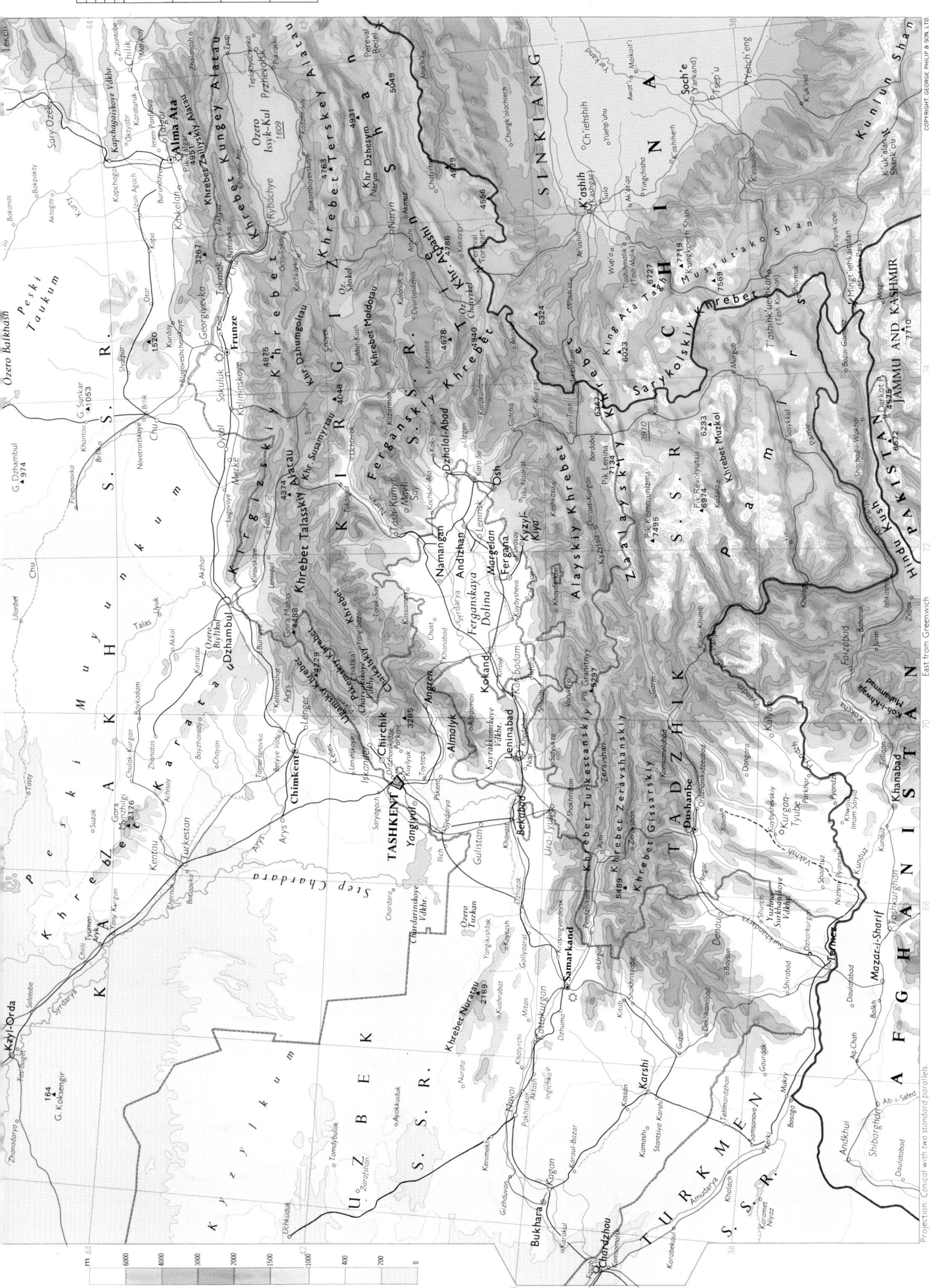

1 : 5 000 000

50   0   50   100   150   200 km

COPYRIGHT GEORGE PHILIP & SON, LTD.

East from Greenwich

Projection Conical with two standard parallels.

S   I   N   K   I   A   N   G

C   H   I   N   A

J A M M U   A N D   K A S H M I R

P A K I S T A N

A F G H A N I S T A N

K   A   Z   A   K   H   S   S   R

U   Z   B   E   K   S   S   R

K   I   R   G   I   Z   S   S   R

TADZHIK S.S.R.

TURKMEN S.S.R.

Ozero Balkhash

Peski Taukum

Peski Muyunkum

Kyzylkum

Step Chardara

Alma Ata

Frunze

TASHKENT

Chirchik

Chimkent

Samarkand

Bukhara

Dushanbe

Termez

Mazar-i-Sharif

Kashih (Kashgar)

Kokand

Fergana

Margelan

Andizhan

Namangan

Osh

Dzhalal-Abad

Angren

Almalyk

Leninabad

Bekabad

Gulistan

Karshi

Kagan

Kzyl-Orda

Turkestan

Khrebet Zailiyskiy Alatau

Khrebet Kungey Alatau

Ozero Issyk-Kul 1609

Khrebet Terskey Alatau

Kirgizskiy Khrebet

Khrebet Talasskiy Alatau

Khrebet Susamyrtau

Khr. Dzhungoltau

Khrebet Moldotau

Ferganskiy Khrebet

Ferganskaya Dolina

Alayskiy Khrebet

Zaalayskiy Khrebet

Khrebet Turkestanskiy

Khrebet Zeravshanskiy

Khrebet Gissarskiy

Khrebet Nuratau

Karatau

Khrebet

P a m i r

Pik Lenina 7134

Pik Kommunizma 7495

Kungkoch Shan

Mussurtako Shan

Sarykolskiy Khrebet

King Ata Tag 6727

Kunlun Shan

5049

4931

4763

4875

4374

4448

4678

5324

4556

6023

6247

6233

6974

5287

5489

3267

1520

1053

974

164

2176

2169

1:50 000 000

500   0   500   1000   1500   2000 km

P A C I F I C   O C E A N

A R C T I C   O C E A N

I N D I A N   O C E A N

Aleutian Is.
7822
Kamchatka Peninsula
Bering Sea
Bering Str.
C. Dezhneva
Sredinny Ra.
Klyuchevskaya Vol.
4750
Kurili Is.
Hokkaido
Honshu
Shikoku
Kyushu
Sakhalin
Japan Alps
Sea of Okhotsk
Sea of Japan
Korea Str.
Gydan Ra. (Kolyma)
Kolyma
Indigirka
Verkhoyansk Range
Stanovoy Range
Aldan
Amur
Sikhote Alin Ra.
Yablonovy Ra.
Sungari
Manchurian Plain
Great Khingan Mts.
Korea
Yellow Sea
East China Sea
Ryukyu Is.
Formosa
Bonin Is.
4454
Tropic of Cancer
Guam
Caroline Is.
10 022
Pelew Is.
Mindanao
10 497
Philippine Is.
Luzon
Halmahera
Moluccas
Ceram
Banda Sea
Arafura Sea
New Guinea
Celebes Sea
Celebes
Sulu Sea
Borneo
Palawan
Hainan
Kinabalu
4101
Makassar Strait
Java Sea
East Indies
Sunda Is.
Timor
Flores
Bali
Sumatra
Malay Peninsula
Str. of Malacca
Lena
Olenek
Severnaya Zemlya
Chelyuskin
Taimyr Peninsula
Laptev Sea
New Siberian Is.
Wrangel I.
Kara Sea
Novaya Zemlya
Yenisei
Lower Tunguska
Kotuy
Angara
Central Siberian Plateau
West Siberian Plain
Ob
Irtysh
Tobol
Irtysh
Narodnaya
1894
Ural Mountains
L. Baikal
Selenga
Sayan Mts.
Altai
Plateau of Mongolia
Belukha
4506
Tien Shan
Tarim Basin
Turfan Basin
Lop Nor
Takla Makan
Koko Nor
Kunlun Shan
Plateau of Tibet
Great Plain of China
Hwang
Po Hai
Si-kiang
G. of Tonkin
Mekong (Red)
Yangtze
Salween
Irrawaddy
Tsangpo
Everest
8848
Himalaya
Karakoram Ra.
8611
Pamirs
Communism Pk.
7495
Hindu Kush
Sulaiman Range
Indus
Sutlej
Ganga
Brahmaputra
Yamuna
Bay of Bengal
Andaman Is.
Nicobar Is.
Polk Strait
Ceylon
Equator
Maldive Is.
Laccadive Is.
C. Comorin
Western Ghats
Eastern Ghats
Deccan
India
Krishna
Godavari
Gulf of W.
Narmada
Thar Desert
Svalbard
Koluyev
Kola Pen.
North Cape
White Sea
N. Dvina
Finland
Baltic Sea
Scandinavia
Greenland
Iceland
British Isles
North Sea
Central Russian Uplands
Vistula
Oder
Elbe
Rhine
Danube
Carpathians
Dnepr
Don
Volga
Ural
Aral Sea
Syr Darya
Amu Darya
Turan Plain
1640
Chu
Ili
Caspian Sea
Elburz Mts.
Demavend
5604
Great Salt Desert
Plateau of Iran
Zagros
Helmand
Harirud
G. of Oman
Persian Gulf
Arabian Sea
Tigris
Euphrates
Mesopotamia
Caucasus
Elbrus
5633
Ararat
5165
Taurus Mts.
Anatolia
Cyprus
Black Sea
Bosporus
Adriatic Sea
Mediterranean Sea
Suez Canal
Sinai Pen.
Dead Sea
Syrian Desert
Red Sea
Nile
Libyan Desert
Arabia
Rub'al Khali
Socotra
Râs Asir (C. Guardafui)
G. of Aden
Somali Peninsula
Seychelles
Amirantes
Lake Victoria
N o r t h   E u r o p e a n   P l a i n
S   t   e   p   p   e
G. of Siam
Menam
Palk Strait

m   6000   4000   2000   1000   400   200   0

Arctic Circle

Tropic of Cancer

1:50 000 000

500   0   500   1000   1500   2000 km

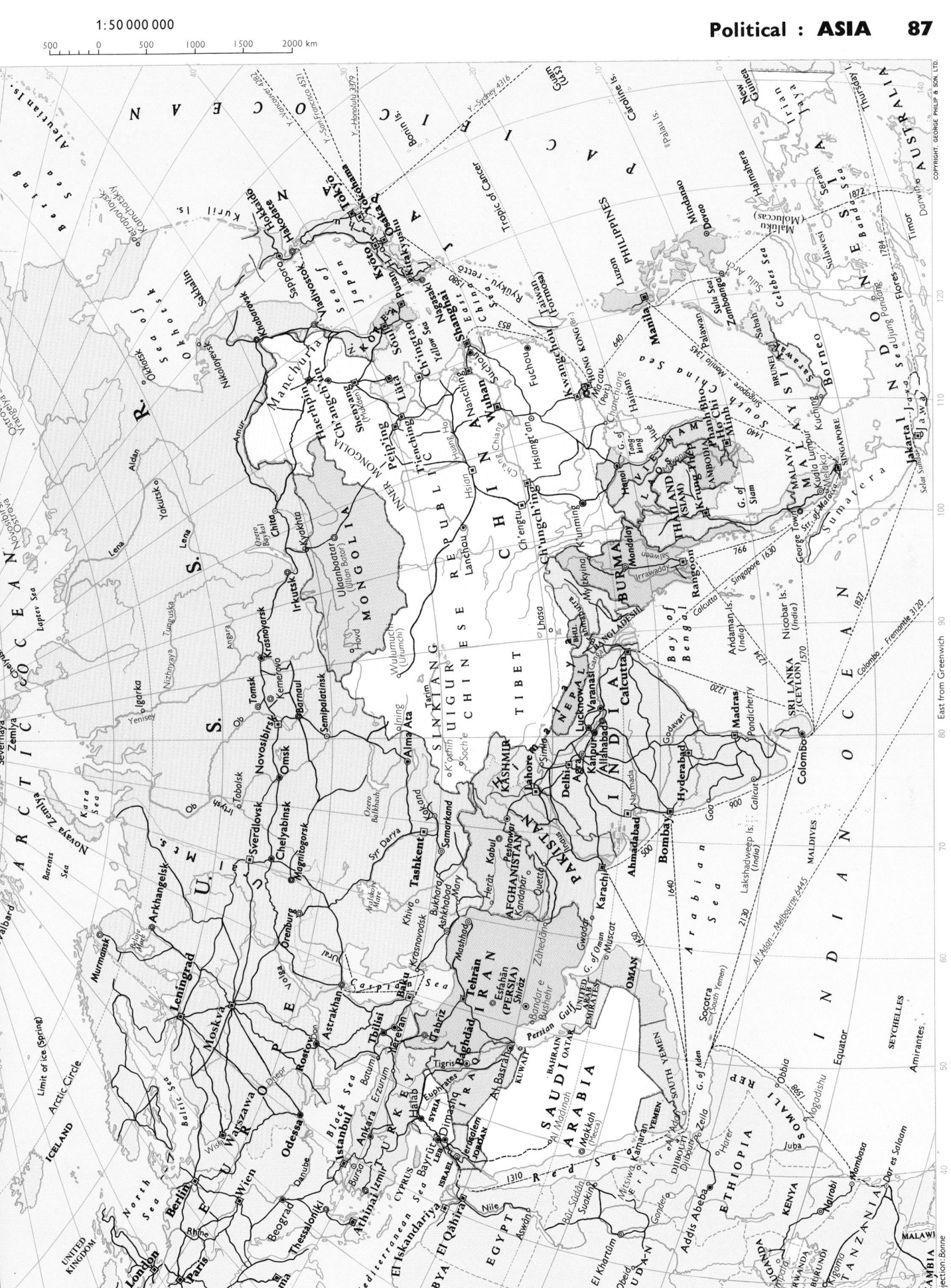

COPYRIGHT. GEORGE PHILIP & SON, LTD.

East from Greenwich

Projection: Bonne

1:100 000 000

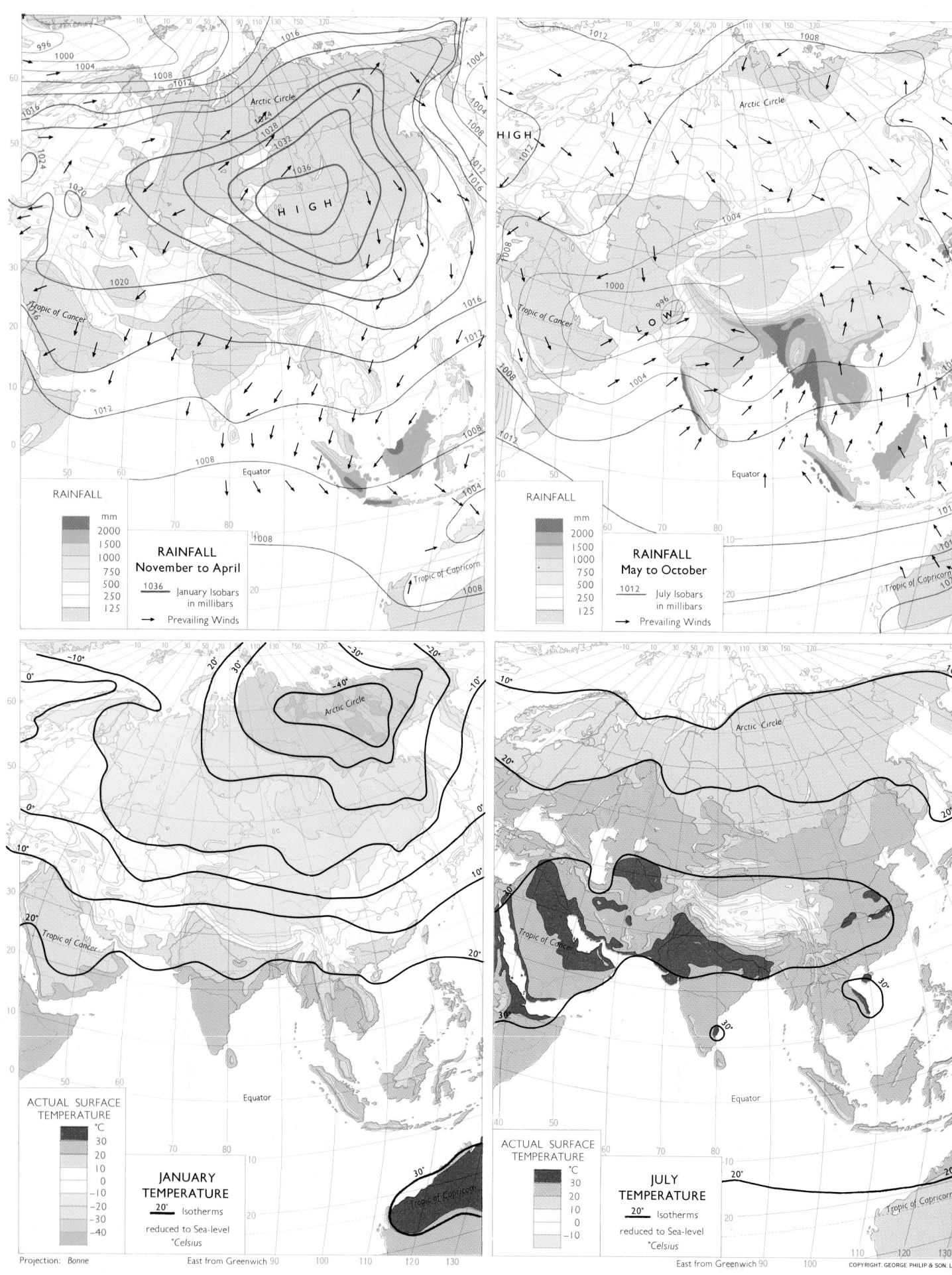

RAINFALL

mm	
	2000
	1500
	1000
	750
	500
	250
	125

RAINFALL
November to April

—— 1036 —— January Isobars
in millibars

→ Prevailing Winds

RAINFALL

mm	
	2000
	1500
	1000
	750
	500
	250
	125

RAINFALL
May to October

—— 1012 —— July Isobars
in millibars

→ Prevailing Winds

ACTUAL SURFACE
TEMPERATURE

°C	
	30
	20
	10
	0
	−10
	−20
	−30
	−40

**JANUARY
TEMPERATURE**

—— 20° —— Isotherms

reduced to Sea-level
°Celsius

ACTUAL SURFACE
TEMPERATURE

°C	
	30
	20
	10
	0
	−10

**JULY
TEMPERATURE**

—— 20° —— Isotherms

reduced to Sea-level
°Celsius

Projection: *Bonne*

East from Greenwich 90

East from Greenwich 90

COPYRIGHT. GEORGE PHILIP & SON L'°

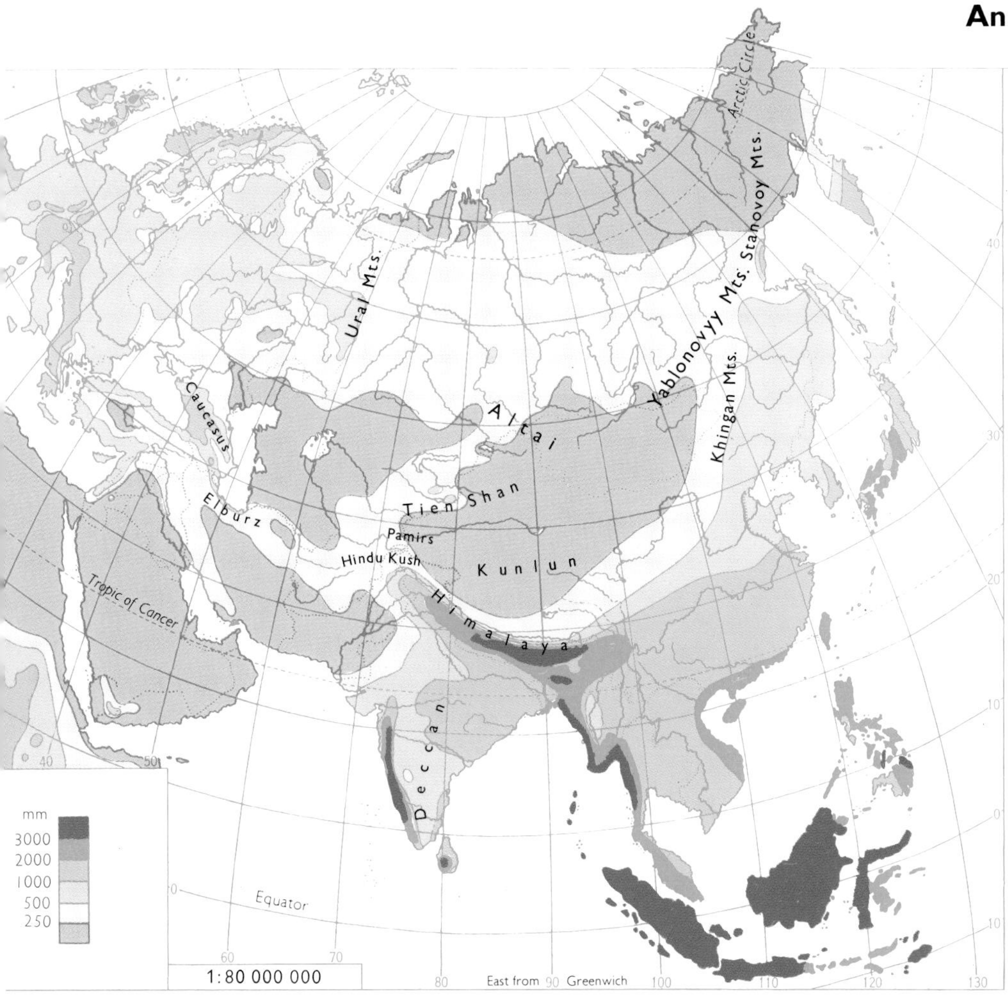

Arctic Circle

Ural Mts.

Stanovoy Mts.

Yablonovyy Mts.

Khingan Mts.

Caucasus

Altai

Elburz

Tien Shan

Pamirs

Hindu Kush

Kunlun

Tropic of Cancer

Himalaya

Deccan

Equator

**INDIA:
MONSOONS**

THEIR EVOLUTION

IS SHOWN BY

MONTHLY

CLIMATE

MAPS

RAINFALL

mm per month

mm
25
50
100
200
400

—— ISOTHERMS
*Temperature in
degrees Celsius*

—— ISOBARS
(Pressure in millibars)

← WINDS

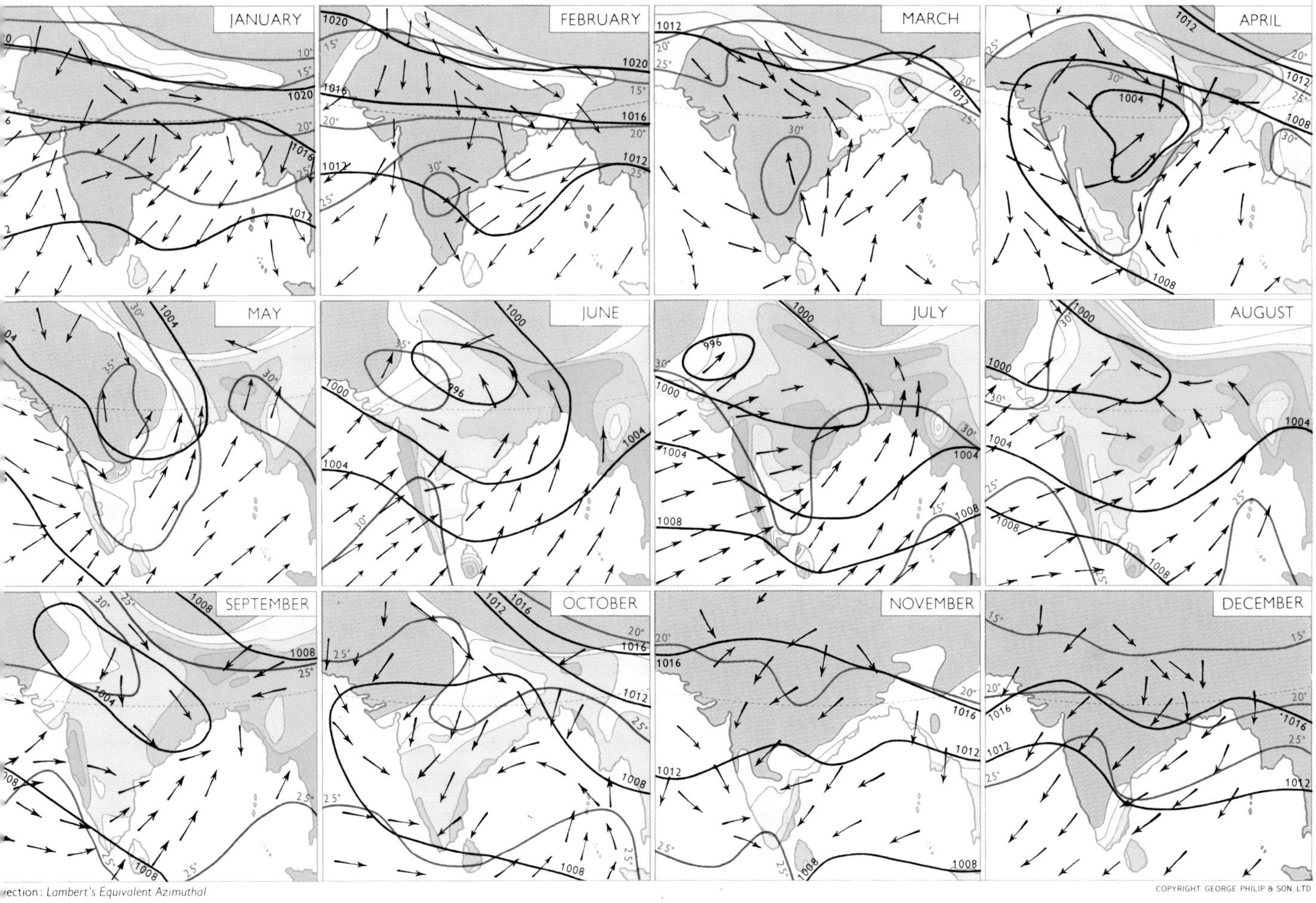

mm
3000
2000
1000
500
250

1:80 000 000

East from Greenwich

JANUARY

FEBRUARY

MARCH

APRIL

MAY

JUNE

JULY

AUGUST

SEPTEMBER

OCTOBER

NOVEMBER

DECEMBER

Projection: Lambert's Equivalent Azimuthal

1:15 000 000

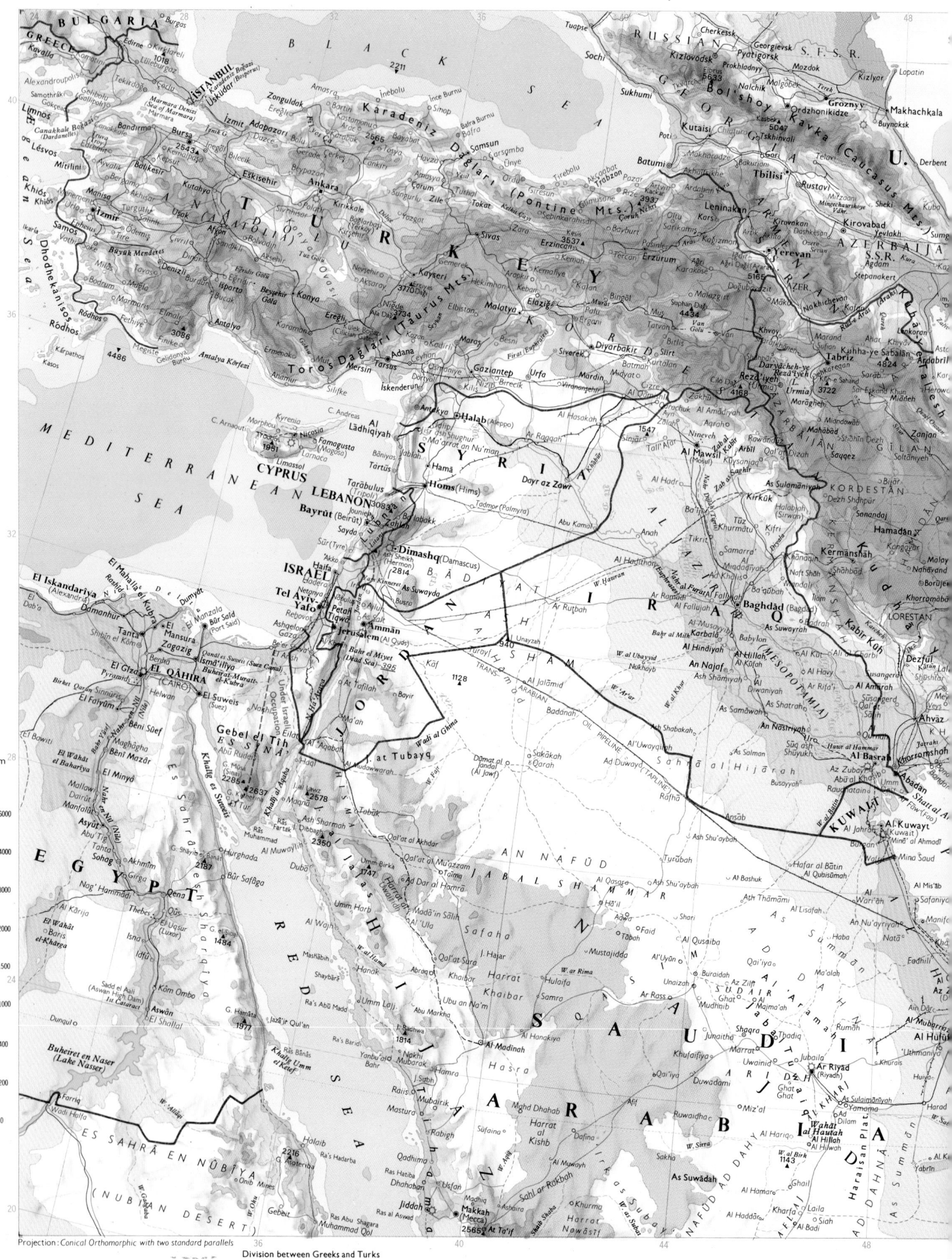

m
6000
4000
3000
2000
1500
1000
400
200
0
0
200
2000
m

Projection: Conical Orthomorphic with two standard parallels

Division between Greeks and Turks
in Cyprus; Turks to the North.

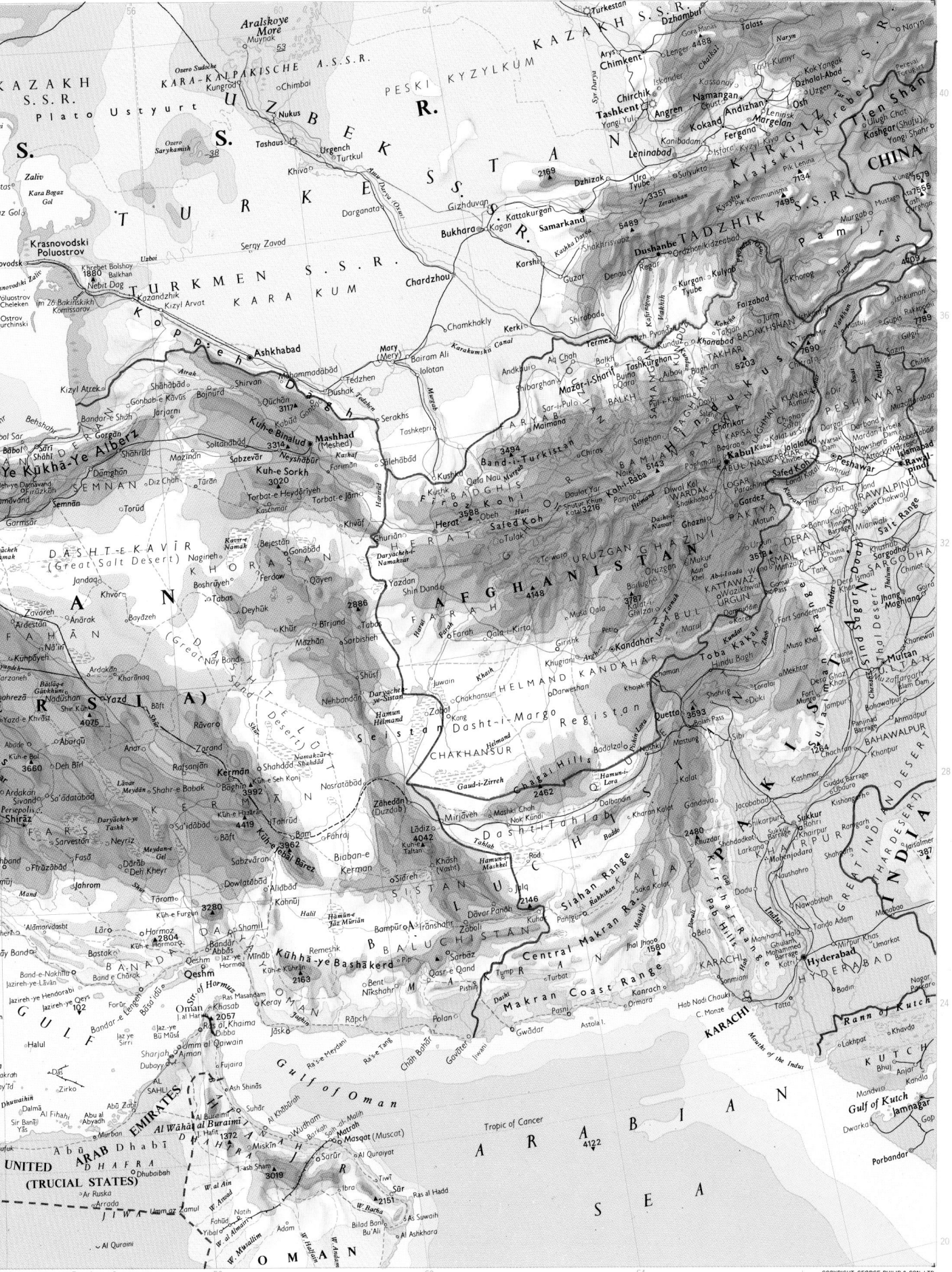

1:10 000 000

100   0   100   200   300   400 km

East from Greenwich

COPYRIGHT. GEORGE PHILIP & SON. LTD.

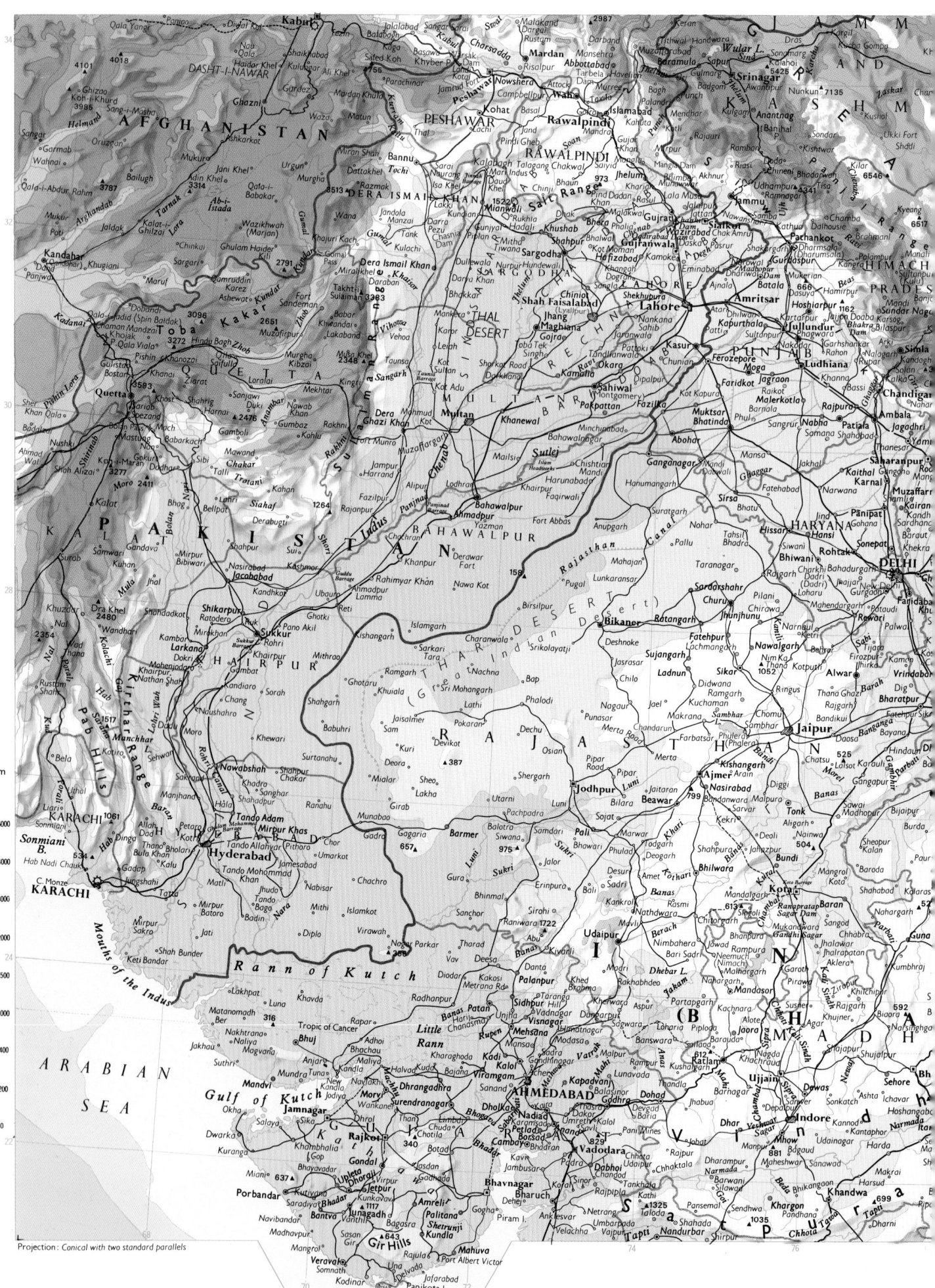

Projection: Conical with two standard parallels

JAMMU AND KASHMIR
On same scale as Main Map

U.S.S.R.

CHINESE REPUBLIC

TIBET

PESHAWAR
Srinagar
Anantnag
Jammu
Sialkot
Rawalpindi
Islamabad

HIMACHAL PRADESH

KASHMIR

KARAKORAM

Kunlun Shan

SODA PLAINS

Aksai Chin

Nanga Parbat
Mt. Everest 8848
Kanchenjunga

SIKKIM
Gangtok

BHUTAN

ASSAM

Bareilly
Lucknow
KANPUR
Allahabad
Varanasi
Gorakhpur
Faizabad
Patna
Gaya
Darbhanga
Muzaffarpur

Jabalpur
Ranchi
Jamshedpur
Durgapur
CALCUTTA
Kharagpur

BANGLADESH
DACCA
Khulna
Barisal

Mouths of the Ganga
The Sandheads

COPYRIGHT. GEORGE PHILIP & SON. LTD.

East from Greenwich

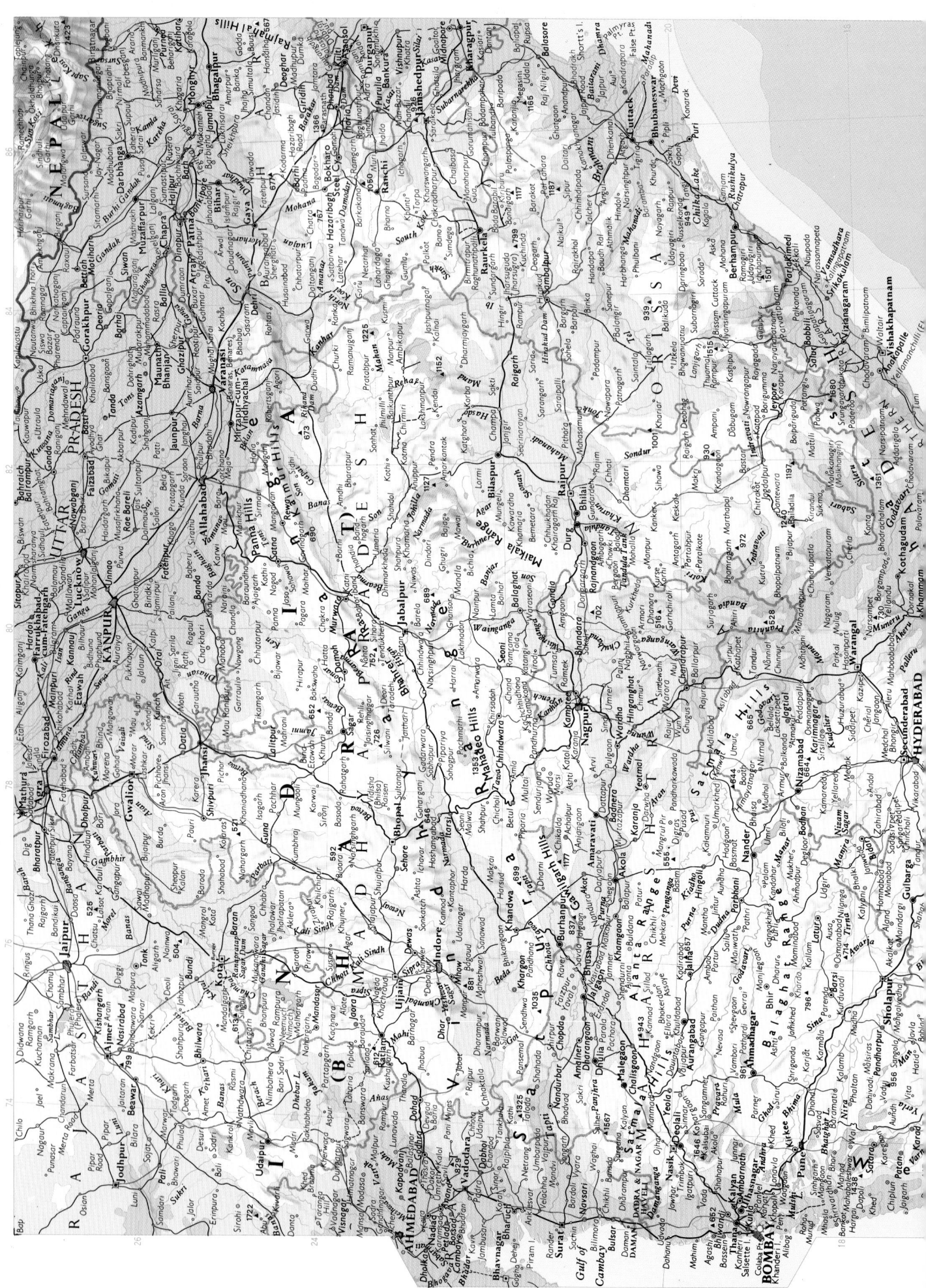

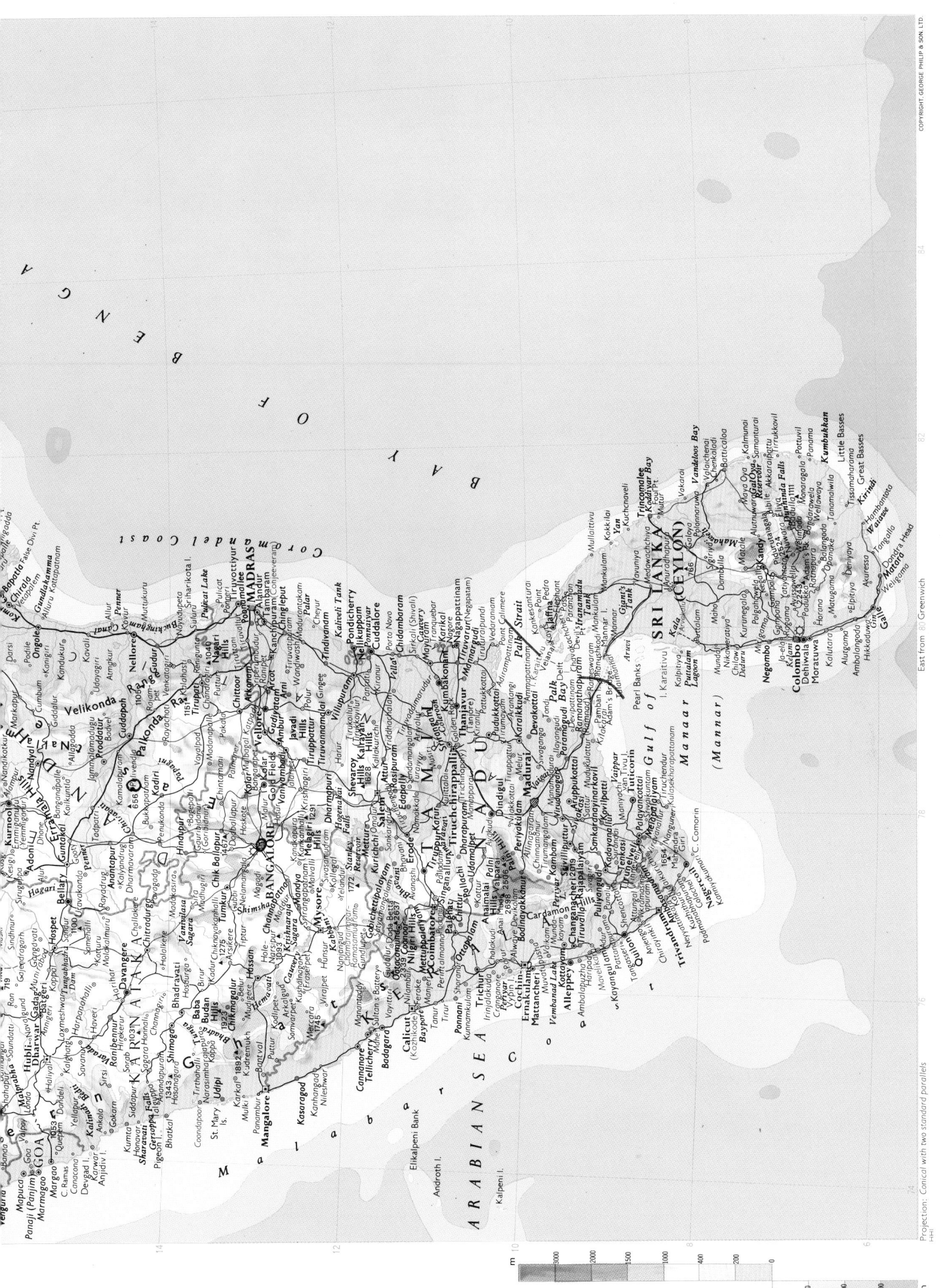

1:6 000 000

50   0   50   100   150   200   250 km

BAY OF BENGAL

Coromandel Coast

MADRAS

BANGALORE

KARNATAKA

TAMIL NADU

Mysore

SRI LANKA (CEYLON)

Anuradhapura

Colombo

Gulf of
Mannar
(Mannar)

Palk Strait

Pondicherry
Cuddalore

Madurai

GOA

ARABIAN SEA

Mangalore

Calicut
(Kozhikode)

Cochin

Trivandrum

C. Comorin

Laccadive Sea

Elikalpeni Bank

Androth I.

Kalpeni I.

Little Basses

Great Basses

Kumbukkan

Trincomalee

Vandaloos Bay

Negombo

Galle

Nellore

Kurnool

Cuddapah

Bellary

Hubli-Dharwar

Hospet

Davangere

Shimoga

Coimbatore

Salem

Tiruchchirappalli
(Trichinopoly)

Thanjavur
(Tanjore)

Nagappattinam
(Negapatam)

East from 80 Greenwich

Projection: Conical with two standard parallels
HH-I

m   3000   2000   1500   1000   400   200   0

0   200   2000   4000   m

1:6 000 000

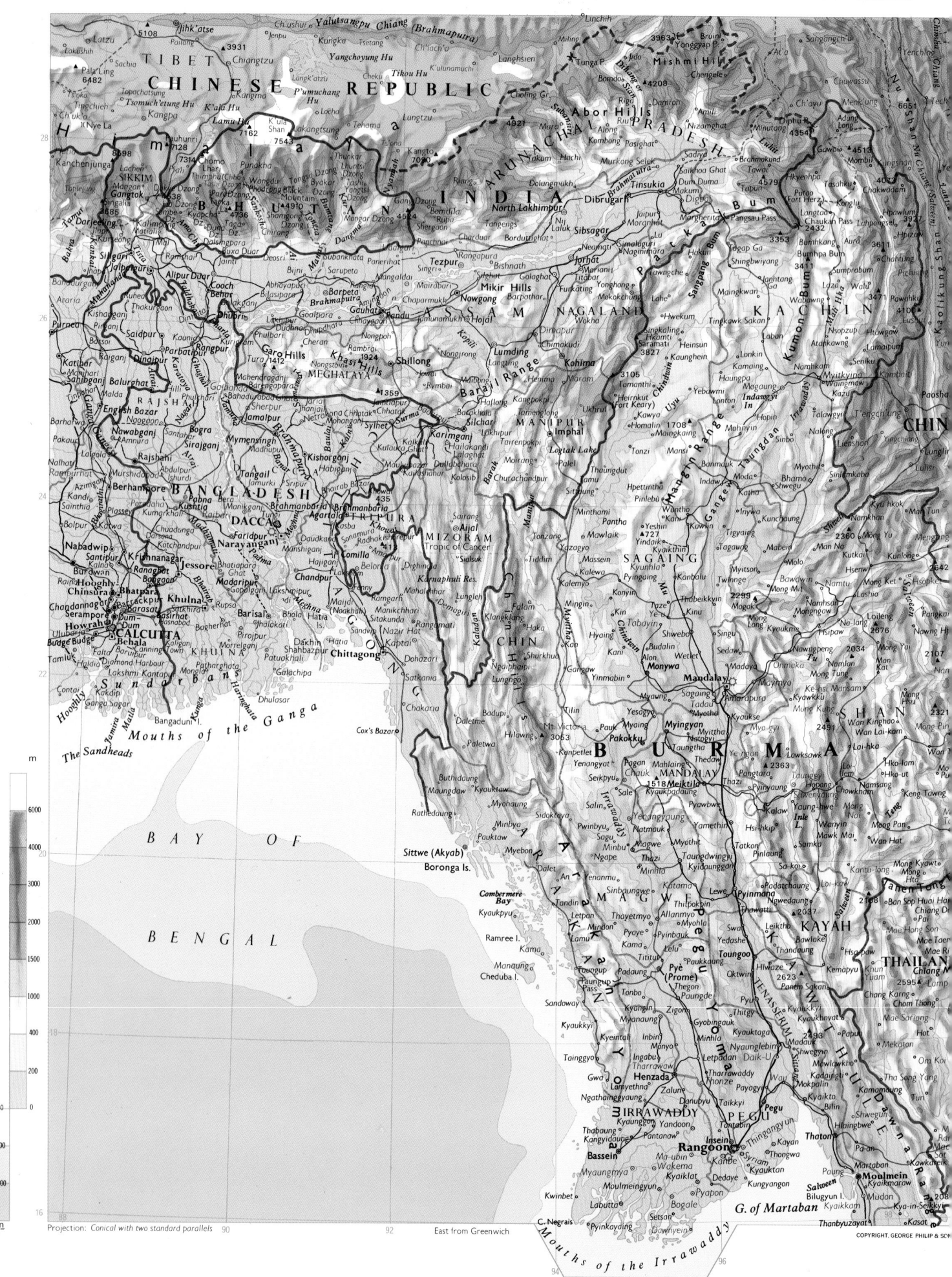

Projection: Conical with two standard parallels

1:20 000 000

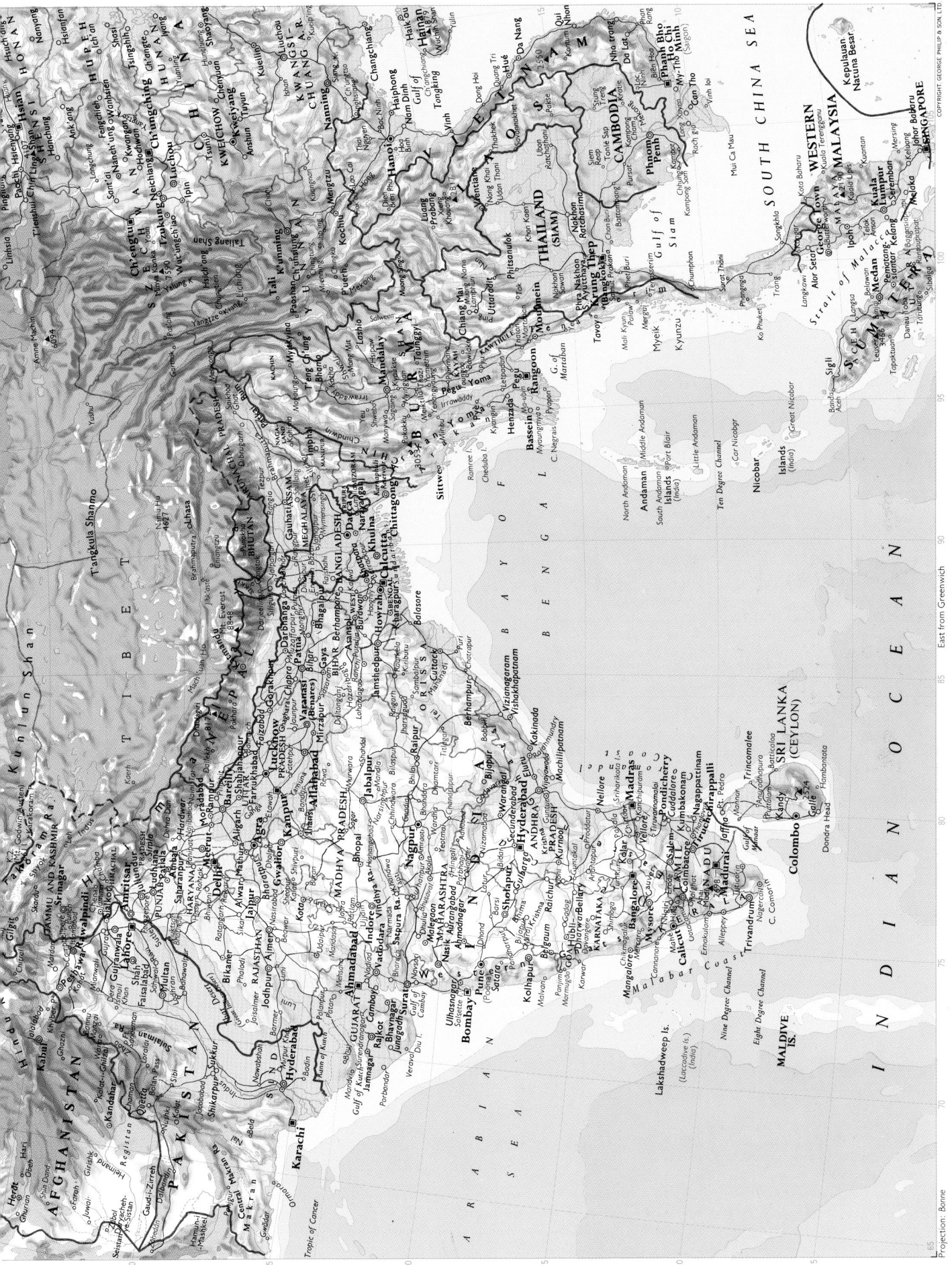

200   0   200   400   600   800 km

East from Greenwich

Projection: Bonne

m   6000   4000   2000   1000   400   200   0

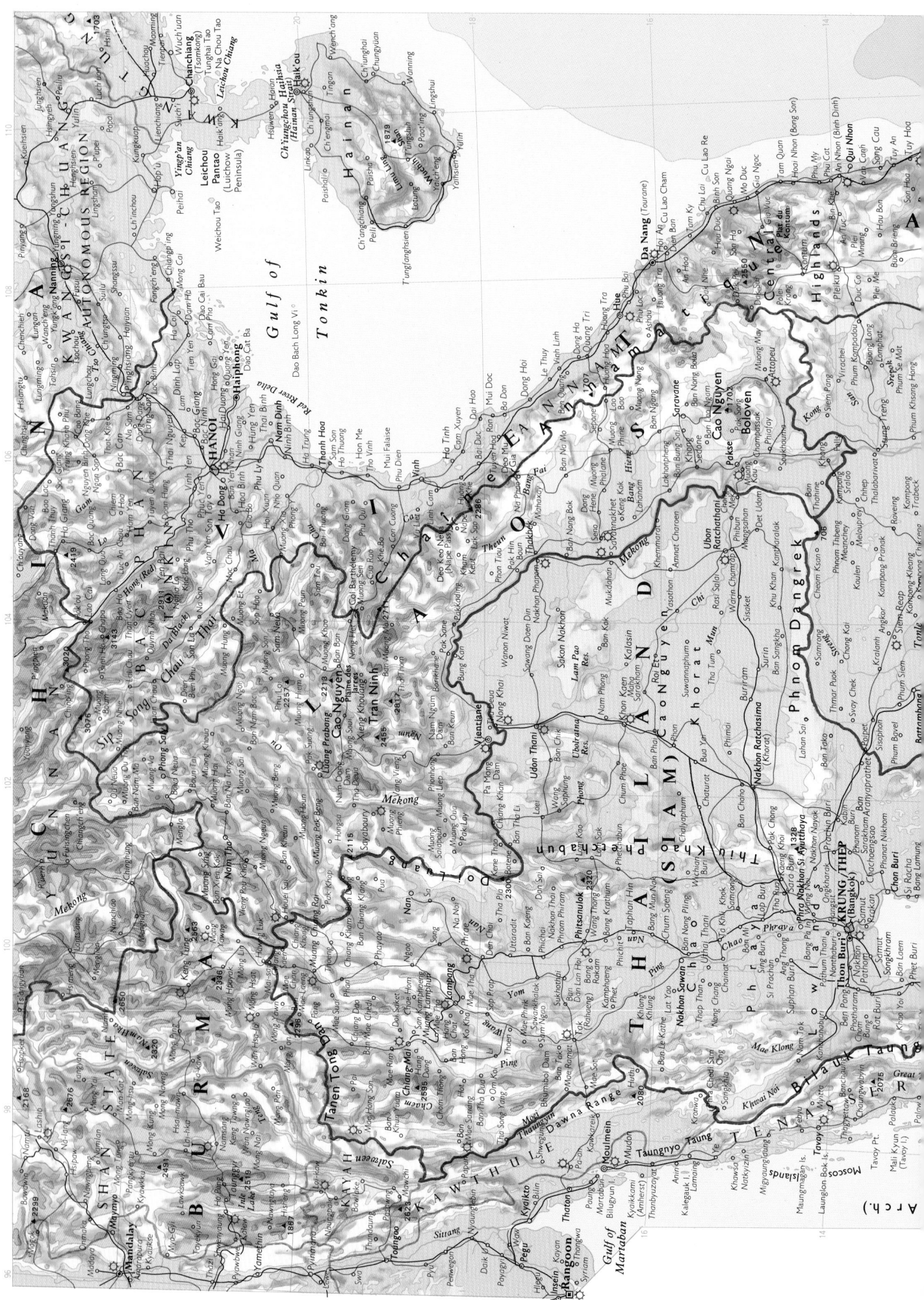

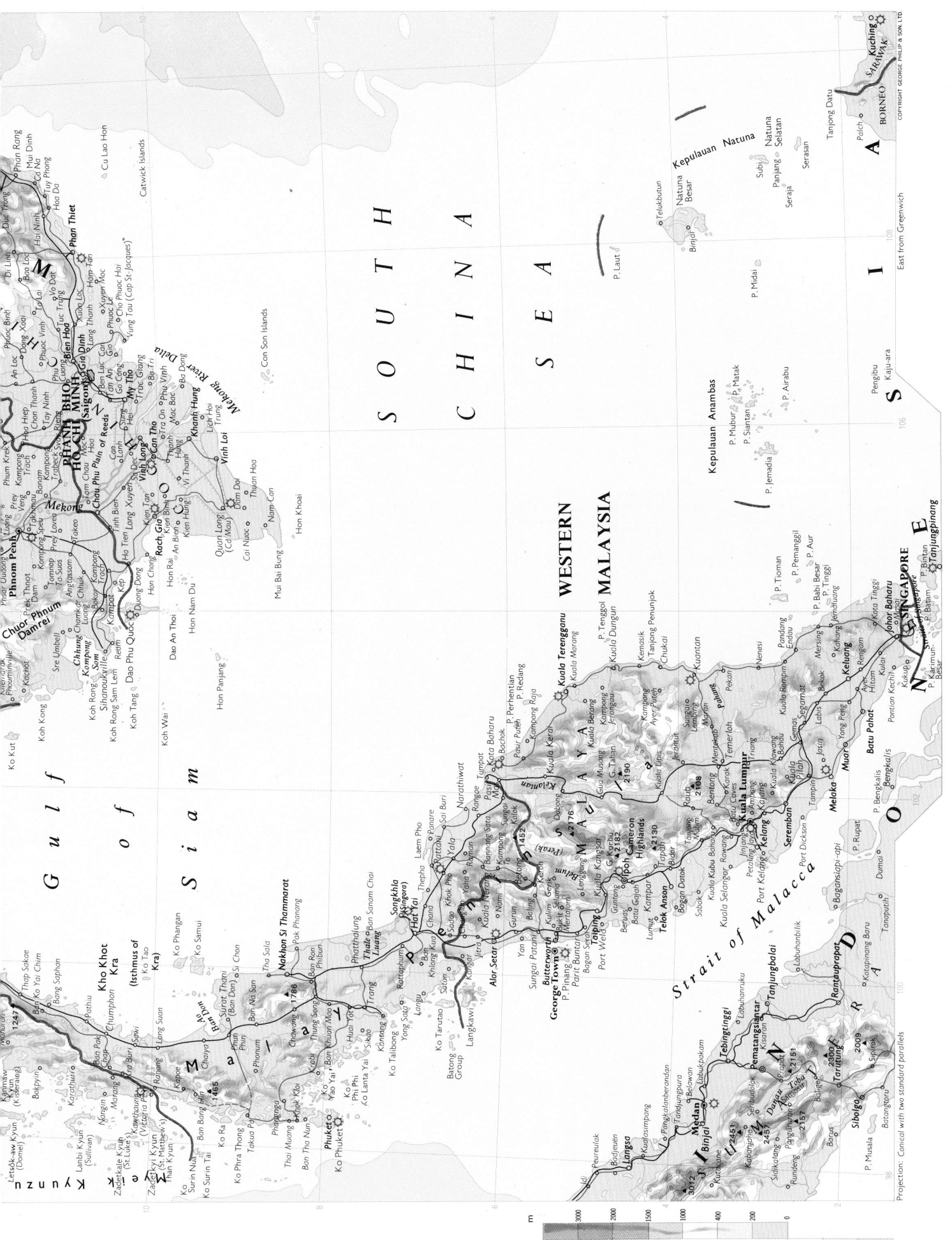

Projection: Mercator

East from Greenwich

1:12 500 000

100   0   100   200   300   400   500 km

114

JAVA AND MADURA

1:7 500 000

50   0   50   100   150   200   250   300 km

LUZON

Polillo Islands

Lamon Bay

Manila

Manila Bay

Catanduanes

Marinduque

Mindoro

Burias

Sibuyan

Tablas

Masbate

Sea

Panay

Samar

Visayan

Sea

Leyte

Tacloban

Iloilo

Bacolod

Cebu

Guimaras

Bohol

Negros

Dinagat

Siargao

Mindanao Sea

Camiguin

Cagayan
de Oro

Mindanao

Butuan

Zamboanga

Davao

Basilan

Jolo

Sulu   Arch

Sarangani Bay

Sarangani
Is.

PACIFIC

OCEAN

Yap Islands

Ulithi Atoll

Palau
Islands

Babelthuap

Koror

Angaur

Caroline Islands
(U.S. Trust Territory of the Pacific Islands)

Sorol Atoll

Ngulu Atoll

Sonsorol
Islands

Pulo-Anna

Merir

Tobi   Helen Atoll

CELEBES

SEA

Kepulauan
Nenusa

Kepulauan
Talaud

Pulau
Sangihe

Kepulauan
Sangihe

Siau

Manado

Halmahera

Morotai

Tobelo

Ternate

Tidore

Gorontala

UTARA

Teluk Tomini

SULAWESI
(CELEBES)

TENGAH

Teluk
Tolo

Waigeo

Dampier

Sorong

Jazirah Doberai
(Vogelkop)

Manokwari

Kepulauan
Schouten

Biak

Yapen

Selat Yapen

Equator

Misool

Salawati

Kepulauan
Obi

Kepulauan
Sula

Sanana

Buru

Namlea

SERAM (Ceram)

Ambon

Banda Sea

IRIAN JAYA

Pegunungan Maoke

Pegunungan
Sudirman

Jayawijaya

PAPUA NEW GUINEA

Jayapura

Teluk
Cendrawasih

Pegunungan Van Rees

Fakfak

Teluk Berau

Teluk
Flamingo

Merauke

Kepulauan
Kai

Kepulauan
Aru

Wokam

Kobroor

Kepulauan
Tanimbar

Yamdena

Saumlaki

MALUKU

BANDA SEA

Flores

TIMOR

NUSA TENGGARA TIMUR

Kupang

Roti

Sawu Sea

ARAFURA
SEA

COPYRIGHT GEORGE PHILIP & SON LTD

130   135   140

1 : 30 000 000

200   0   200   400   600   800   1000 km

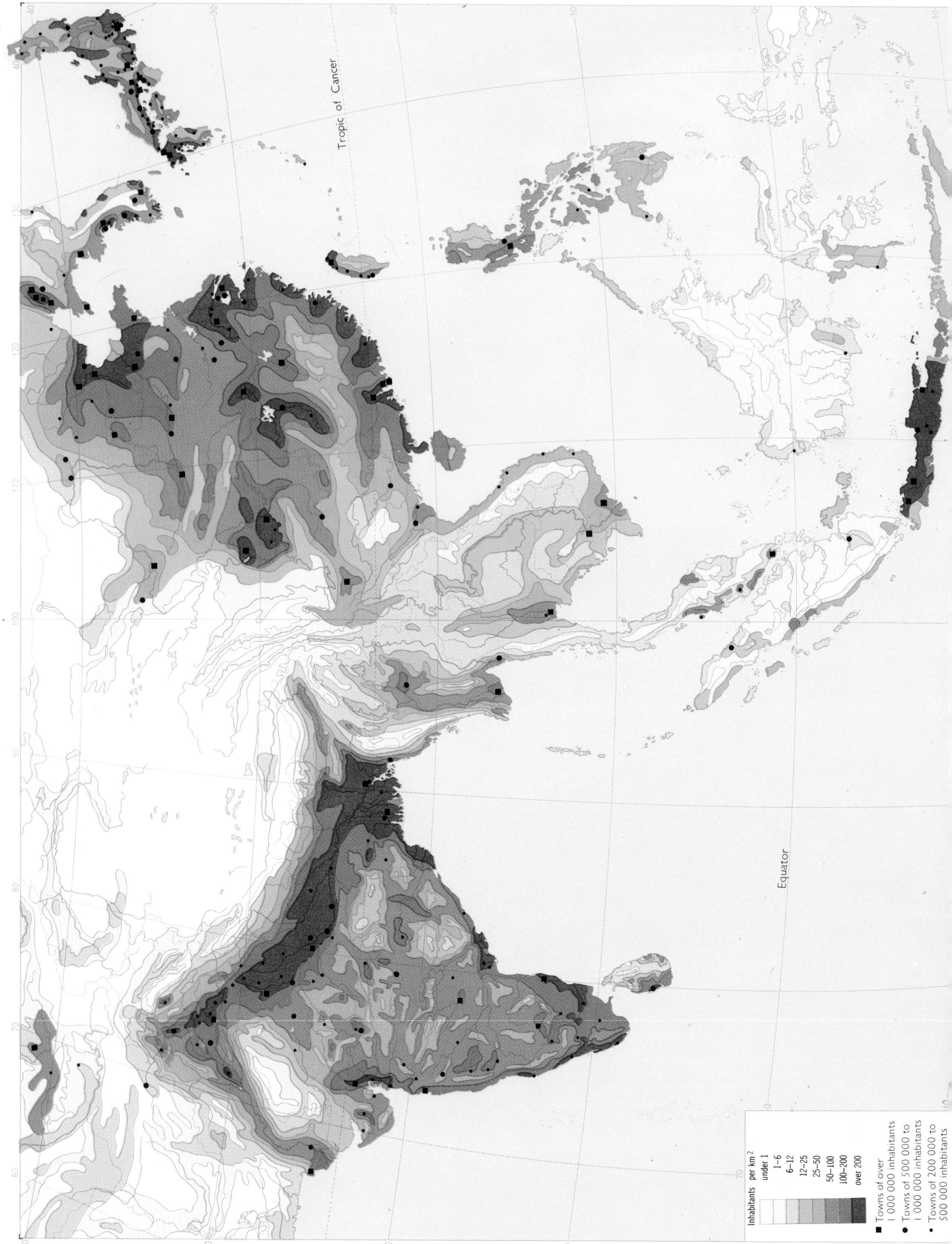

Tropic of Cancer

Equator

Inhabitants	per km²
	under 1
	1–6
	6–12
	12–25
	25–50
	50–100
	100–200
	over 200

■ Towns of over 1 000 000 inhabitants

● Towns of 500 000 to 1 000 000 inhabitants

• Towns of 200 000 to 500 000 inhabitants

1:20 000 000

200   0   200   400   600   800 km

COPYRIGHT GEORGE PHILIP & SON LTD.

East from Greenwich

Projection: Bonne

UNION OF SOVIET SOCIALIST REPUBLICS

MONGOLIA

KAZAKH S.S.R.

KIRGIZ S.S.R.

SINKIANG-UIGHUR

Takla Makan

Kunlun Shan

TIBET

C H I N A

NEPAL

BHUTAN

BANGLADESH

INDIA

BURMA

THAILAND (SIAM)

LAOS

VIETNAM

NORTH KOREA

SOUTH KOREA

JAPAN

YELLOW SEA

EAST CHINA SEA

SOUTH CHINA SEA

BAY OF BENGAL

PHILIPPINES

TAIWAN (Formosa)

SHANGHAI

Hong Kong

PEIPING

Tientsin

CALCUTTA

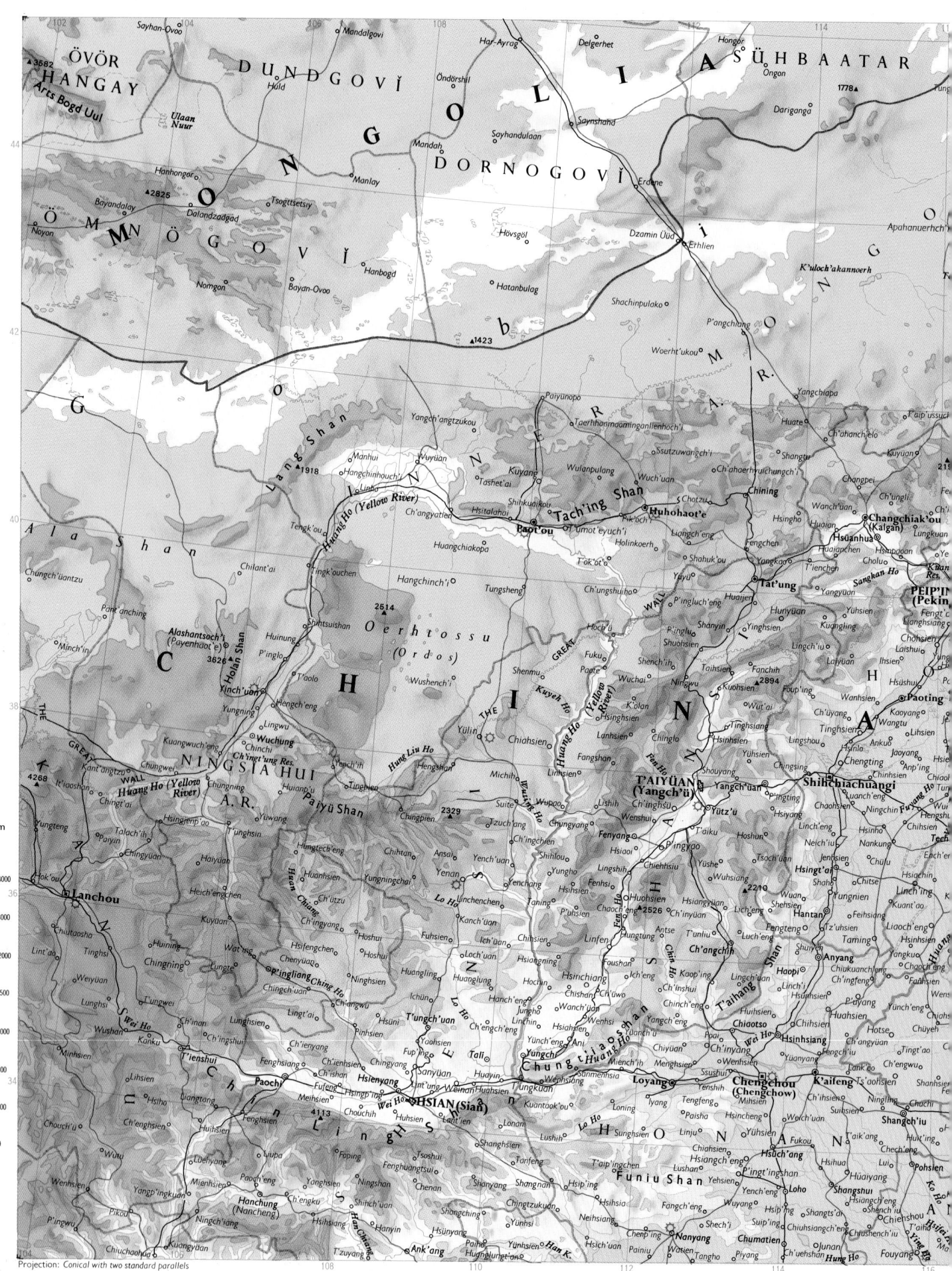

ÖVÖR
▲3582
HANGAY
Arts Bogd Uul

DUNDGOVĬ

Sayhan-Ovoo
Ulaan
Nuur
Hanhongor
Bayandalay
▲2825
Noyon
Dalandzadgad
Nomgon
Bayan-Ovoo
Hanbogd

MONGOLIA

Mandalgovi
Hüld
Manlay
Tsogttsetsiy

Öndörshil

Har-Ayrag

SÜHBAATAR
Hongor
Ongon

Delgerhet

Mandah
Sayhandulaan

Saynshand

DORNOGOVĬ

Hatanbulag
Shachinpulako

1778▲
Dariganga

Apahanuerhch'i

Dzamin Üüd
Erhlien

P'angchiang

K'uloch'akannoerh

▲1423

Woerht'ukou

Paiyünopo
Taerhhanmaominganlienhoch'i

Yangch'angtzukou

Lang Shan
1918

Manhui
Hangchinhouch'i
Linho

Wuyüan

Kuyang
Wulanpulang
Wuch'uan

Shihkuaikou
Hsitalahai
Ch'angyatien

Tengk'ou

Huang Ho (Yellow River)

Ala Shan

Chüngch'üantzu

Alashansoch'i
(Payenhaot'e)

Hoton Shan
3626

Yinch'uan

Hengch'eng

Yungning

Wuchung

Chinchi

Chungwei

NINGSIA HUI

A.R.

Paiyü Shan

Huang Ho (Yellow River)

m
4000
3000
2000
1500
1000
400
200
0 0
200
2000
m

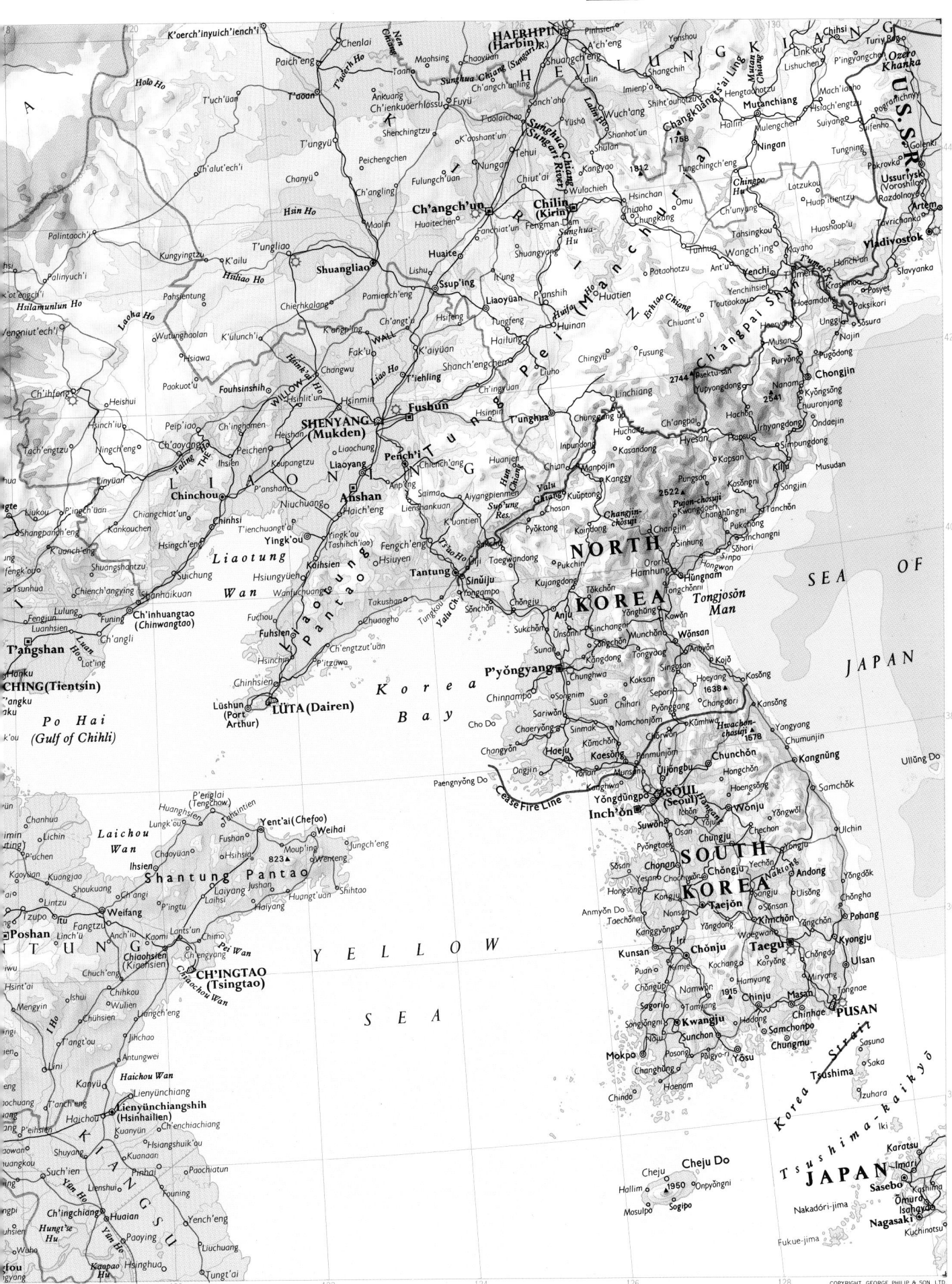

COPYRIGHT. GEORGE PHILIP & SON, LTD.

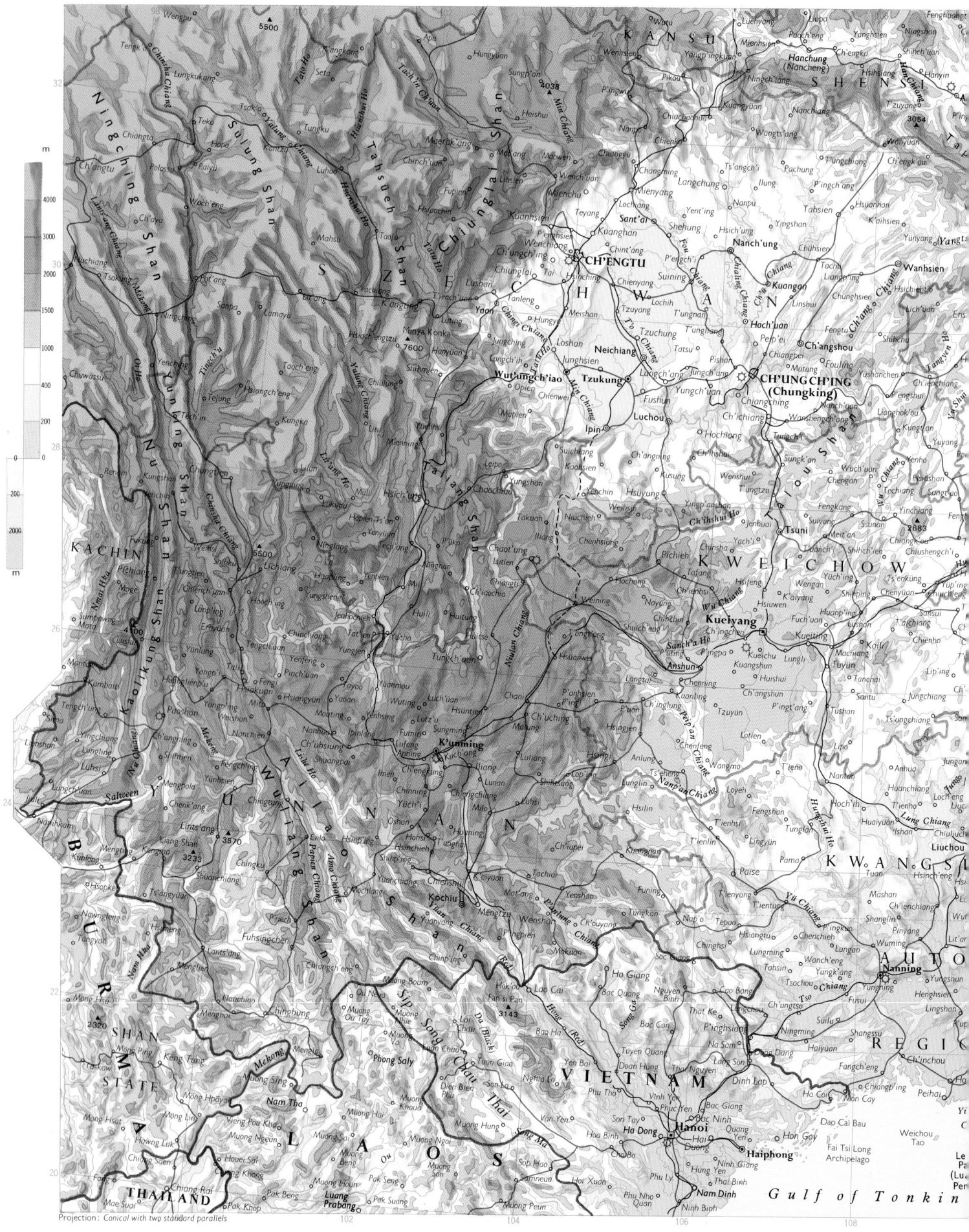

SOUTH CHINA SEA

SEA OF JAPAN

SOUTH KOREA

Oki-Shotō
Daimanji-San
Dōgo ▲608
Saigō

CHŪGOKU - DISTRICT

Shimane-Hantō
Jizō-Zaki
Iwami
Kasumi
Hi-no-Misaki Hirata Shinji Sakaiminato
Matsue
Taisha Izumo Ko Yasugi Yonago Kurayoshi Tottori Hid
Shinji Dai-Sen TOTTORI Wakasa
Gōtsu Ōda Daito Katsuyama Tsuyama Yamazaki
Yunotsu Sanbe-San Niimi Yonahara Sayō
Hamada SHIMANE Dōgo-San Tōjō Ochiai Tatsuno
Miyoshi OKAYAMA Aioi
Chūgoku Shōbara Takahashi Bizen Akō Kak
Masuda HIROSHIMA Fuchū Ibara Okayama Saidaiji
Kake Ōta-Gawa Kabe Saijō Mihara Kurashiki Tamano Shōdo-Shima
Ōmi-Shima Hagi Aono-Yama ▲908 Kanmuri Yama Fukuyama Kasaoka Kojima Tonoshō Harim
Tsuno-Shima Ato ▲1339 Onomichi In'no-shima Marugame Takamatsu Nad
Nagato Itsukaichi Takehara Tadotsu Saidate Awaji
Mi-Shima YAMAGUCHI Kure Zentsūji Kotohira AGAWA Hiketa
Hibiki- Mine Yamaguchi Ōtake Ondo Niigata Ōmi Tsurishima Miki Naruto
Nada Toyoura San'yō Ōgōri Hōfu Nan'yō Iwakuni Kurahashi- Takuma Kan'onji Hiuchi- Komatsujima
Genkai- Tokuyama Hiroshima-Wan Jima Aki-Nada Nada
Nada Shimonoseki Kudamatsu Yanai Yashiro- Hōjō Niihama Sanyuki-Sammyaku Tok
Onoda Ube Hikari Jima Matsuyama Nyūgawa Kawanoe Anbu
Higasi-Suidō Nakama Suō-Nada Iwai-Jima Heigun-To Matsusaka Saijō Iyo-mishima TOKUSHIMA Komatsujima
Iki Katsumoto KITAKYŪSHŪ Hime-Jima Naga-Shima S Iya SHIKOKU Tsurugi-San Mugi
Gō-no-ura Fukuma Nagahama Ishizuchi-Yama Sanchi ▲1955
Iki-Kaikyō Nogata Yukuhashi Ōzu EHIME ▲1981 Aki Tōyō
Ō-Shima Yobuko Iizuka Takawa Nakatsu Utago-Yama Kunisaki Iyo-Nada Kuma KŌCHI Muroto
Ikitsuki- FUKUOKA Maebaru Yamada Buzen ▲721 Sada-Misaki-Hantō Yawatahama Uchiko Otoyo Tosa-yamada
Shima Umi Usa Bungotakada Nagahama Nankoku
Hirado Karatsu FU Asō Hita Hiji Kitsuki Uwa Sagawa Kōchi
Hirado- Matsuura Tsukushi Sanchi Amagi Tosu Beppu-Wan Ōzu Susaki Muroto-Misaki
Shima Imari SAGA Setui-San Kurume Yufu-Dake Beppu Ekawasaki Uwajima Hiromi Tosa-Wan
Ō-Shima Arita Taku Yame Kurogi ▲584 ŌITA Ōita Uchiko Kubokawa Ashizuri-Zaki
Takeo Saga Chikugo Kuju-San Usuki Saga SHIKOKU
Sasebo Kashima Okawa Yanagawa Setaka ▲1787 Tsukumi Jahen Nakamura SHIKOKU - DISTRICT
Ureshino Tara Yamaga Oguni Asō Saiki Sukumo Tosa-shimizu
Ōmura- ▲983 Tamana Aso-zan Taketa Kamae
NAGA Wan Tara-Dake Ōmuta ▲1592 Sōbo-Yama Oki-no-Shima
Isahaya Arao Kikuchi ▲1758 Tsurumi-Saki
Omura Ōzu Kumamoto Takachiho Bungo-Suidō
Unzen-Dake Mashiki Hinokage Nobeoka
Nagasaki ▲1360 Shimabara KUMAMOTO Asō Tsurumi-Suidō
Obama Uto Shiba Hyūga
Nomo-Zaki Oyana Misumi Takachiho Hososhima
Amakusa- Hondo Kami- Kunimi-Dake MIYAZAKI
Amakusa- Jima ▲739
Shotō Shimo- Yatsushiro Itsuki Hitoyoshi Yunomae
Nada Jima Yatsushiro-Kai Saito Takanabe
Ushibuka Minamata KYŪSHŪ Saito
Naga-Shima Kyūshū Sanchi KYŪSHŪ - DISTRICT
Kami-koshiki Izumi Ebino Kobayashi
Jima Akune Okuchi Yoshimatsu Saito Kaji
Koshiki- Miyanojō Kurino ▲700 Miyazaki
Rettō Sendai Kirishima Yama
Shimo-koshiki- Kushikino Kokubu Miyakonojō
Jima Kajiki Hayato
Kagoshima On-Take Nichinan
Taniyama ▲118 Tarumizu Shibushi
Fukiage Satsuma-Hantō Kanoya Aburatsu Kushima
Noma-Saki Kaseda Chiran OSHIMA Kagoshima-Wan
Makurazaki Koyama Shibushi-Wan
Bō-no-Misaki Kaimon-Dake Ibusuki Ōsumi-Hantō
▲924 Yamagawa

Projection:
Lambert's Conformal
Conic

Sata-Misaki

130 131 132 133 134
36 35 34 33 32 31

1:2 500 000

10 0 10 20 30 40 50 60 70 80 90 100 km

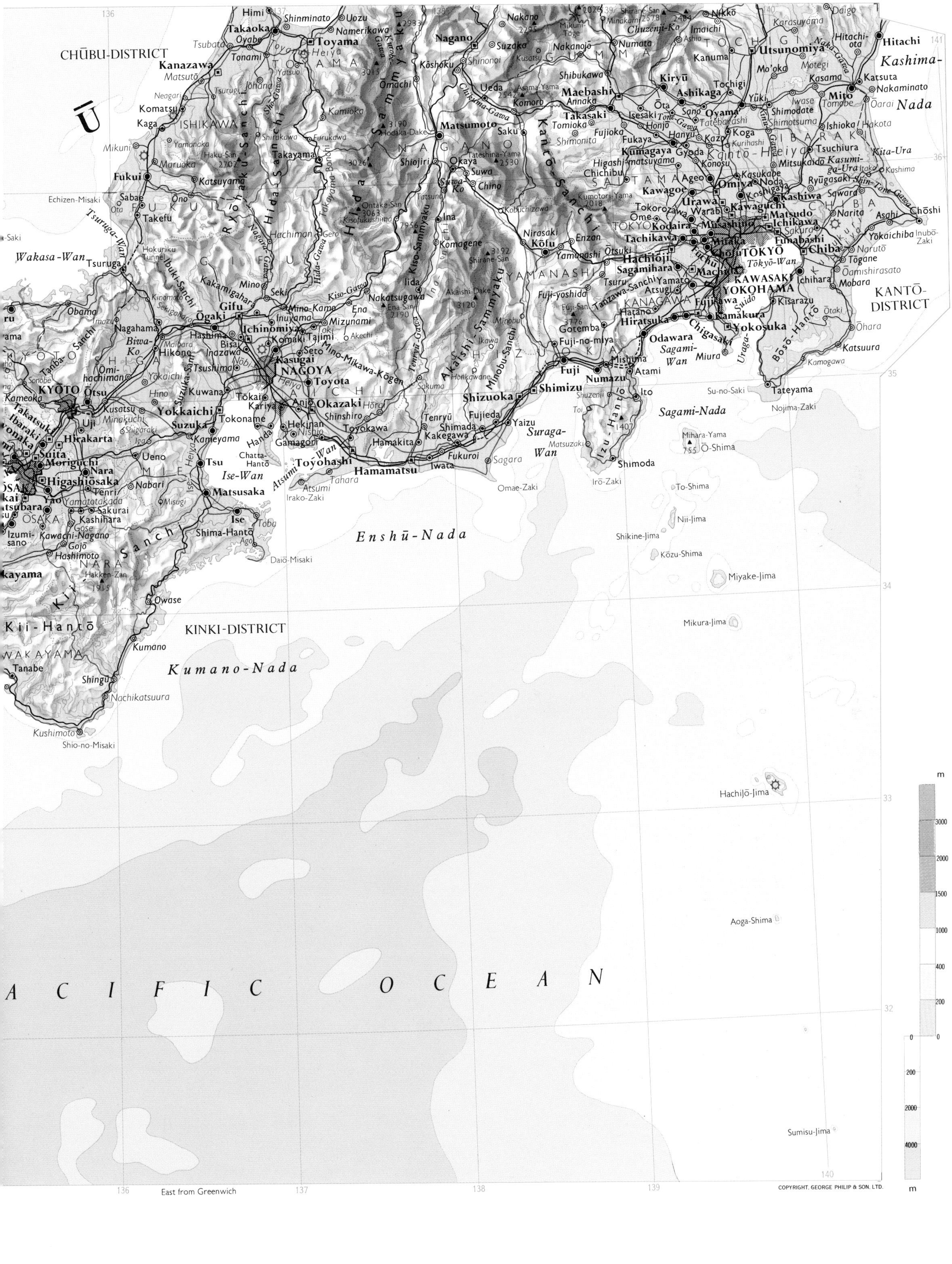

III

CHŪBU-DISTRICT

Ū

Himi 137 Shinminato Uozu Namerikawa Nakano 2026 39 Shirane-San 2578 Nikko Daigo
Takaoka Namerikawa Heiyo Nakanojo Chūzenji-Ko Imaichi Karasuyama Hitachi-ota **Hitachi**
Tsubata Oyabe TOYAMA Nagano Suzaka Numata Ashio TOCHIGI **Utsunomiya** *Kashima-*
Kanazawa Tonami Toyama **Nagano** Koshoku Shinonoi Kusatsu Kanuma Mo'oka Motegi Kasama Katsuta Nakaminato *Nada*
Matsuto ISHIKAWA Ueda Asama-Yama Maebashi GUMMA Kiryū Tochigi Mito Tombe Ōarai
Komatsu Neagari Kamioka 3190 Komoro **Maebashi** Ashikaga Yūki Shimodate IBARAKI Ishioka Hakota
Kaga Yamanaka Takayama 2702 Haku-San **Matsumoto** Saku Annaka Takasaki Isesaki Toni Honjo Fukaya Konosu Kasukabe Kasumi-ga-Ura Kashima Kita-Ura
Fukui Maruoka 3026 Shiojiri Okaya NAGANO Tomioka Shimonita Kumagaya Gyoda SAITAMA Ageo Kita-Ura
Echizen-Misaki FUKUI Katsuyama Furukawa Hodaka-Dake Chino Suwa-Ko Chichibu Higashi-matsuyama Kawagoe Kasukabe Koshigaya Ryūgasaki Narita
Sabae Ono 3063 Ina Tateshina-Yama 2530 Ageo Tokorozawa Urawa Warabi Kawaguchi Matsudo CHIBA Asahi Chōshi
Wakasa-Wan Takefu Hachiman Kisofukushima 2956 Komagane Nirasaki Kōfu Ōme Kodaira Musashino Ichikawa Sakura Inubo-Zaki
Tsuruga Iida Akaishi-Dake Shirane-San Enzan YAMANASHI **TOKYO** Tachikawa Ōtsuki Yamanashi Hachioji Fuchu TOKYO Funabashi Naruto Tōgane
Obama Nagahama GIFU Seki Kiso-Gawa Nakatsugawa 3120 Tsuru Fuji-yoshida Machida KAWASAKI Chiba
Tsuruga-Wan Mino Toki Mizunami Ena Minobu Fuji-San 3776 Hadano Atsugi YOKOHAMA Mobara
Hikone Ōgaki Ichinomiya Komaki Tajimi Seto Tino-Mikawa-Kogen Gotemba Hiratsuka Sagamihara Kamakura Yokosuka
KYŌTO Ōtsu SHIGA Hashima Inazawa Nōbi Fuji-no-miya SHIZUOKA Sagami-Wan Chigasaki Ōhara
Biwa-Ko Maibara Kusatsu Kuwana NAGOYA Toyota Tenryū-Gawa Fuji KANAGAWA Uraga Katsuura
Kameoka Minakuchi Yokkaichi Kariya Okazaki Shinshiro Numazu Mishima Atami Miura Bōsō-Hantō
Ibaraki Uji Hino Tōkai Anjo Shimada Shizuoka Shimizu Ito Su-no-Saki Tateyama
Hirakarta Shigaraki Igas Suzuka Tokoname Hekinan Nishio Toyokawa Fujieda Yaizu Suruga-Wan Shuzenji Nojima-Zaki
SUITA Iga Kameyama Handa Gamagori Kakegawa Sagara Toi IZU-Hantō Mihara-Yama
Moriguchi Ueno MIE Tsu Chatta-Hantō Hamakita Fukuroi Iwata Omae-Zaki Shimoda 755 Ō-Shima
Nara Nabari Matsusaka Atsumi Tahara Hamamatsu **Hamamatsu** Irō-Zaki
OSAKA Higashiōsaka Yao Tenri Ise-Wan Atsumi Irako-Zaki *Sagami-Nada*
sakai Yamatotakada Sakurai Misugi Ise Tōba To-Shima
Matsubara Kashihara Shima-Hantō Ago Daiō-Misaki *Enshū-Nada* Nii-Jima
Izumi-sano Kawachi-Nagano Gose Gojo Shikine-Jima
kayama NARA Hashimoto *Kii-Hantō* Owase Kōzu-Shima
Hakken-Zan 1915 **KINKI-DISTRICT** Miyake-Jima
WAKAYAMA Kumano *Kumano-Nada*
Tanabe Shingū Mikura-Jima
Nachikatsuura
Kushimoto Shio-no-Misaki To-Shima

KANTŌ-DISTRICT

m

3000
2000
1500
1000
400
200
0

200
2000
4000

m

P A C I F I C   O C E A N

Hachijō-Jima
Aoga-Shima
Sumisu-Jima

East from Greenwich

136 137 138 139 140 141

36

35

34

33

32

COPYRIGHT. GEORGE PHILIP & SON. LTD.

1 : 7 500 000

50   0   50   100   150   200   250   300 km

CHINA

U. S. S. R.

Mutankiang
Ningan
Motoshih
Turii Rog
Ozero
Khanka
Spassk-Dalni
Varfolomeyevka
Verkhove
Tetyukhe
Ussurysk
(Voroshilov)
Ugloyaya
Yenki
Hunchun
Nakhodka
Suchan
Vladivostok
Zaliv Petra
Velikogo
Najin

KOREA
Chongjin
Songjin
Tanchon

Rebun-Tō
Rishiri-Tō
Wakkanai
Teshio
Sea of Okhotsk
Enbetsu
Otoineppu
Monbetsu
Yūbetsu
HOKKAIDŌ
Teshio
Abashiri-Wan
Abashiri
Rumoi
Shibatsu
Kitami
Asahigawa
Daisetsu-Zan
2290
Ishikari-Wan
(Otaru-Wan)
Bibai
Iwamisawa
Obihiro
Kushiro
Kamui-
Misaki
Otaru
Yūbari
2052
Poroshiri Dake
Sapporo
Tomakomai
Shiraoi
Muroran
Uchiura-
Wan
Setana
Mombetsu
Samani
Urakawa
Okushiri-Tō
Esashi
Hakodate
Esan-Misaki
Erimo-Misaki
Matsumae
Tsugaru-Kaikyō
Shiriya-Zaki

KOREA
Kosŏng
Samchok
Ullung Do
Pusan
Antong
Kokai

SEA OF

JAPAN

Mutsu-Wan
Mutsu
Aomori
Hirosaki
Towada-Ko
Hachinohe
Kuji
Yoneshiro
Iwate-san
2041
Miyako
Akita
Morioka
Omono
Honjō
Hanamaki
Kitakami
Kamaishi
Yokote
Ichinoseki
Sakata
Mogami
Shinjō
Tsuruoka
Yamagata
Kogota
Ishinomaki
TŌHOKU
Sado
Yamagata
Yonezawa
Shiogama
Sendai
Iwanuma
Niigata
Shibata
Agano
Fukushima
Bandai-San
1819
Suzu-
Misaki
Wajima
Nagaoka
Aizuwakamatsu
Kōriyama
Iwaki
Nanao
Tajimi
Noetsu
Takada
Nikkō
Hitachi
Naoetsu
Kashiwazaki
Himi
Toyama-Wan
Nagano
Maebashi
Kiryū
Utsunomiya
Nakaminato
Kanazawa
Takaoka
Toyama
Ueda
Tochigi
Mito
CHŪBU
Matsumoto
Takasaki
Chichibu
Gyoda
Tsuchiura
Fukui
Takayama
Suwa
Kawagoe
Ōmiya
Shin-Tone
Sawara
Chōshi
Ontake-San
3063
Ida
Kōfu
Urawa
Ichikawa
KANTŌ
Oki-Shotō
Takefu
Tsuruga
Kiso
Fuji-San
3776
TOKYO
Chiba
Gifu
Ichinomiya
Fuji-no-miya
Kawasaki
Yokohama
Yokosuka
Hi-no-
Misaki
Matsue
Tottori
Toyooka
Biwa-Ko
Maizuru
Hikone
Kuwana
Yokkaichi
Okazaki
Nagoya
Shimizu
Numazu
Fujisawa
Izumo
Yonago
Kyōto
Hikone
Shizuoka
Atami
CHŪGOKU
Hamada
Tsuyama
Fukuyama
Akashi
Kōbe
Amagasaki
Osaka
Nara
Tsu
Ise-Wan
Hamamatsu
Ō-Shima
Masuda
Hōfu
Onomichi
Kurashiki
Himeji
Sakai
Matsusaka
Toyohashi
Katsuura
Hiroshima
Miharo
Kishiwada
Toba
Tateyama
Yamaguchi
Kure
Wakayama
Owase
Daiō-Misaki
Shimonoseki
Tokuyama
Marugame
Nii-Jima
Ube
Suō-Nada
Setonaikai
Takamatsu
Tokushima
Miyake-Jima
Fukuoka
Kitakyūshū
Nakatsu
Niihama
Kōchi
Shingū
Mikura-Jima
Karatsu
Saga
Kurume
Beppu
Matsuyama
Muroto-Misaki
Sasebo
Kashima
Ōita
SHIKOKU
Kawatahama
Shio-no-Misaki
Imari
Omuta
Aso-zan
1592
Usuki
Uwajima
Nakamura
SHIKOKU
Isahaya
Kumamoto
Saiki
Bango-Suidō
Ashizuri-zaki
Nagasaki
Shimabara
Yatsushiro
Nobeoka
Shimō-
Shima
Minamata
KYŪSHŪ
Sendai
Miyazaki
Kobayashi
Kagoshima
Kanoya
Miyakonojō
Makurazaki
KYŪSHŪ
Kagoshima-Wan
Ōsumi-Kaikyō
Shibushi-Wan
Ōsumi-Shotō
Nishinoomote
Tane-ga-Shima
Kuchinoerabu-Jima
Tokara-Kaikyō
Yaku-Jima
Naka-no-Shima
Suwanose-Jima

PACIFIC

OCEAN

Hachijo-Jima

Aoga-Shima

Nakadori-
Jima
Iki
Tsushima
Tsushima-Kaikyō
KOREA STRAIT
Fukue-
Jima

Ōsumi-Sh
Kuchinoerabu-Jima
Tokara-Kaikyō
Satsuna-Sh
Naka-no-
Shima
Suwanose-Ji
Nansei-Shotō
(Ryūkyū Islands)
Naze
Kikai-Ji
Amami Ō-Sh
Setouchi
Tokunoshima
Okinoerabu-
Jima
Okinawa-Shotō
Okinawa-
Jima
Ishikawa
Koza
Kerama-
Shotō
Ginowan
Naha
Nansei-Shotō Trench
7507
Miyako-Jima
Hirara

RYŪKYŪ ISLAND
Continuation southwards
in same scale

Yaeyama-
Shotō
Yonaguni
Iriomote-
Jima
Ishigaki-
Jima
Ishigaki

PACIFIC   OCEAN

m
1500
1000
400
200 30
0
0
200
m

Projection: Bonne   East from Greenwich   COPYRIGHT. GEORGE PHILIP & SO

1 : 40 000 000

400   0   400   800   1200   1600 km

DENSITY OF POPULATION
1 : 80 000 000
Inhabitants

per km²	per km²
under 1	12- 25
1- 3	25- 50
3- 6	50-100
6-12	over 100

Towns of over 200 000 inhabitants

Projection: Zenithal Equidistant

LES.   Lesotho
O.F.S. Orange Free State
SWAZ. Swaziland

COPYRIGHT. GEORGE PHILIP & SON. LTD.

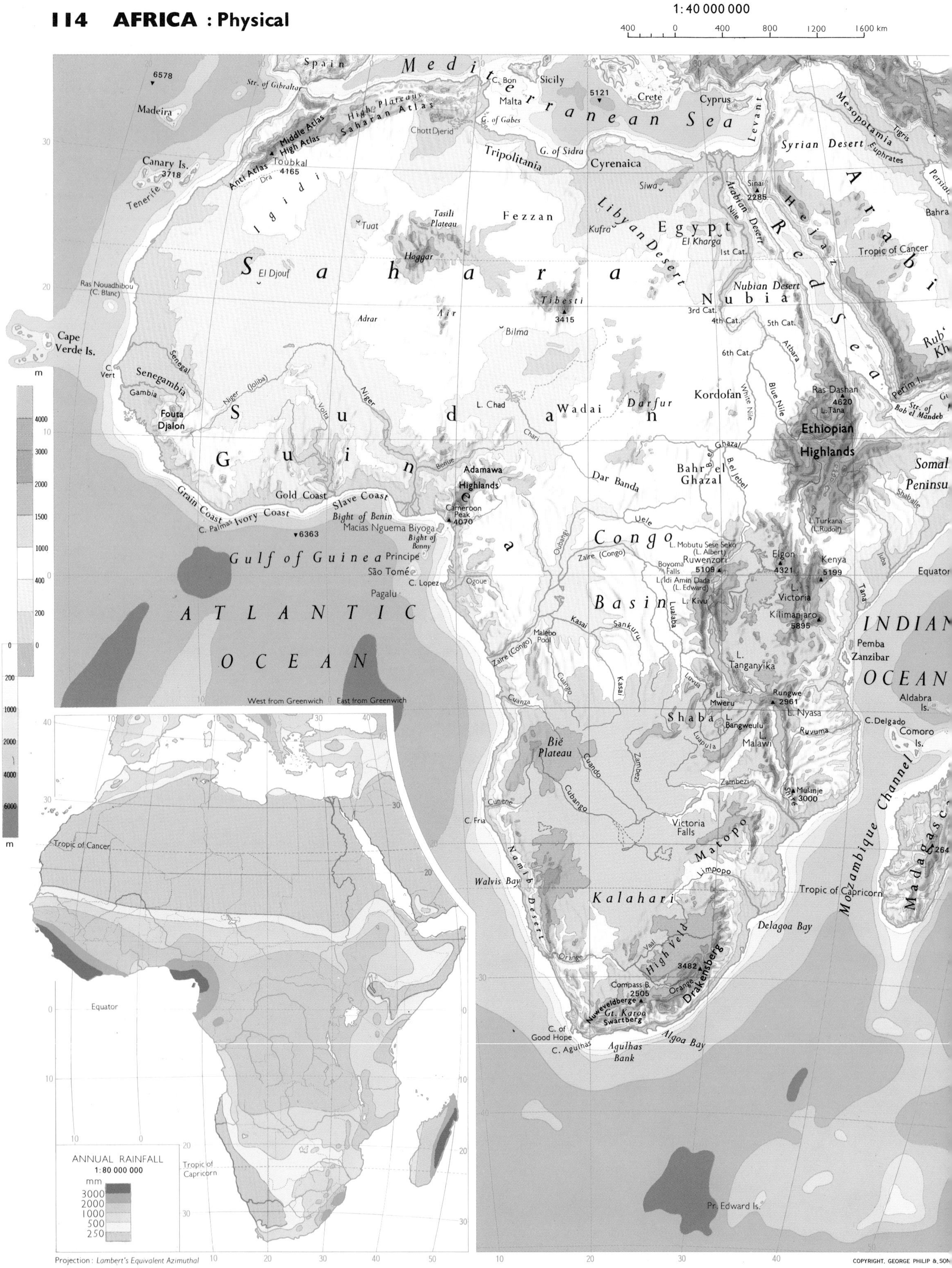

1:40 000 000

400   0   400   800   1200   1600 km

Spain
Mediterranean Sea
Madeira
6578
Str. of Gibraltar
C. Bon Sicily
Malta Crete Cyprus
5121
High Plateaus
Middle Atlas High Atlas Saharan Atlas
G. of Gabes
Canary Is. Toùbkal
3718 4165
Chott Djerid
Tripolitania G. of Sidra Cyrenaica
Tenerife
Dra
Siwa
Sinai 2285
Ras Nouadhibou (C. Blanc)
S a h a r a
El Djouf
Tuat Tasili Plateau Fezzan
Kufra *Libyan Desert* Egypt El Kharga 1st Cat.
Adrar Hoggar Air
Tibesti 3415
Bilma
Nubian Desert
Nubia 3rd Cat. 4th Cat. 5th Cat.
6th Cat.
Cape Verde Is.
C. Vert
Senegal Senegambia
Gambia
Foura Djalon
Niger (Joliba)
Volta
Niger
S u d a n
L. Chad Wadai Darfur Kordofan
White Nile Blue Nile
Ras Dashan 4620 L. Tana
Ethiopian Highlands
Chari Benue
Bahr el Ghazal Bahr el Jebel
Somali Peninsula
G u i n e a
Gold Coast Slave Coast
Grain Coast Ivory Coast
C. Palmas
Adamawa Highlands
Cameroon Peak 4070
Dar Banda
Uele *Congo* L. Mobutu Sese Seko (L. Albert)
Boyoma Falls Ruwenzori 5109
Elgon 4321 Kenya 5199
L. Turkana (L. Rudolf)
Equator
Bight of Benin Macias Nguema Biyoga
6363 Bight of Bonny
Principe São Tomé
C. Lopez
Pagalu
Gulf of Guinea
Ogoue *Basin*
Zaire (Congo)
L. Idi Amin Dada (L. Edward)
L. Kivu
L. Victoria
Kilimanjaro 5895
A T L A N T I C
Malebo Pool
Kasai Kasai Sankuru Lualaba
INDIAN Pemba Zanzibar
O C E A N
West from Greenwich East from Greenwich
Cuango Cuanza
L. Tanganyika
Lovua
Shaba L. Mweru Bangweulu Luapula Rungwe 2961 L. Nyasa
OCEAN Aldabra Is.
C. Delgado Comoro Is.
Bié Plateau
Cuando Zambezi Malawi Ruvuma
Cubango
Cunene Zambezi
Mulanje 3000
C. Fria
Victoria Falls Matopo
Tropic of Capricorn
Walvis Bay Namib Desert Limpopo
Mozambique Channel Madagascar 2664
Kalahari Delagoa Bay
Orange High Veld Drakensberg 3482
Compass B. 2505 Orange Algoa Bay
Nuweveldberge Gt. Karoo Swartberg
C. of Good Hope C. Agulhas Agulhas Bank

m
4000
3000
2000
1500
1000
400
200
0
0
200
1000
2000
4000
6000
m

Projection: Lambert's Equivalent Azimuthal

ANNUAL RAINFALL
1:80 000 000
mm
3000
2000
1000
500
250

Tropic of Cancer Equator Tropic of Capricorn
Pr. Edward Is.

COPYRIGHT. GEORGE PHILIP & SON

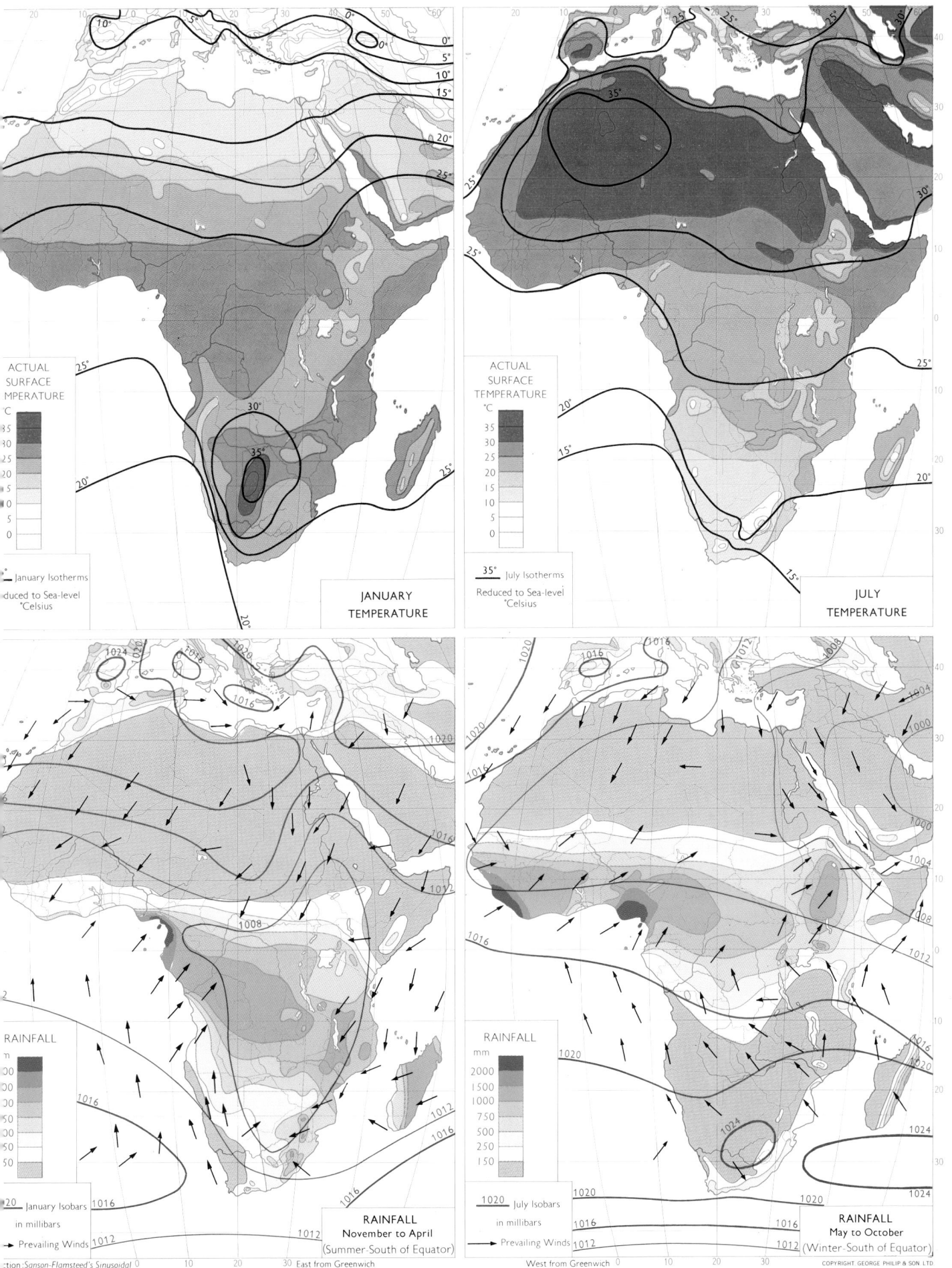

ACTUAL
SURFACE
TEMPERATURE
°C
35
30
25
20
15
10
5
0

January Isotherms
Reduced to Sea-level
°Celsius

JANUARY
TEMPERATURE

ACTUAL
SURFACE
TEMPERATURE
°C
35
30
25
20
15
10
5
0

35° July Isotherms
Reduced to Sea-level
°Celsius

JULY
TEMPERATURE

RAINFALL
mm

1020 January Isobars
in millibars
Prevailing Winds

RAINFALL
November to April
(Summer-South of Equator)

RAINFALL
mm
2000
1500
1000
750
500
250
150

1020 July Isobars
in millibars
Prevailing Winds

RAINFALL
May to October
(Winter-South of Equator)

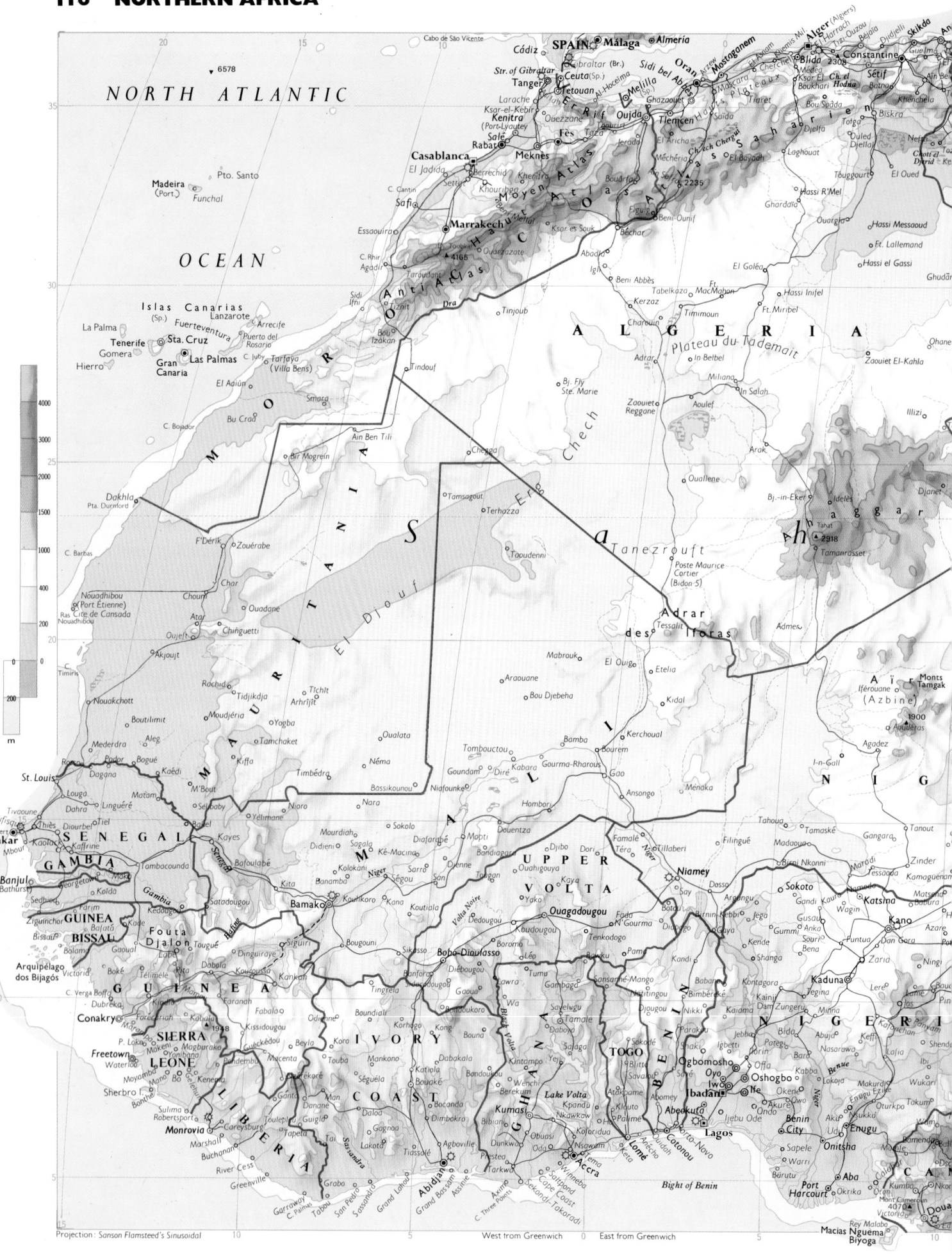

NORTH ATLANTIC

OCEAN

▼ 6578

SPAIN
Cádiz ○ Málaga ● Almería
Cabo de São Vicente
Str. of Gibraltar Gibraltar (Br.)
Ceuta (Sp.)
Tanger Tetouan Al-Hoceima Melilla
Larache Sidi bel Abbès Oran
Ksar-el-Kebir Ghazaouet
Kenitra Ouezzane Taza Tlemcen
(Port-Lyautey) Fès Jerada
Salé Meknès El Aricha
Rabat
El Jadida Berrechid
Casablanca Khouribga Khenifra El Bayadh
Settat Kasba Tadla
Safi Boudfra
Khouribga ▲ 2235
Marrakech Ksar es Souk
Essaouira Ouarzazate Béchar
C. Rhir ▲ 4165 Abadla
Agadir Taroudant Igli Beni Abbès
Sidi Ouarzazate
Ifni Tiznit Dra Tinjoub
Bou Izakan
Tindouf
Madeira Pto. Santo
(Port.) Funchal

Islas Canarias
(Sp.)
La Palma Lanzarote Arrecife
Fuerteventura
Tenerife Sta. Cruz Puerto del Rosario
Gomera Gran Las Palmas
Hierro Canaria
C. Juby Tarfaya
El Aaiún (Villa Bens)
Smara
Bu Craa
C. Bojador
Bir Mogrein
Aïn Ben Tili

Dakhla F'Dérik Zouérate
Pta. Durnford
C. Barbas Char
Nouadhibou Choum Ouadane
(Port Étienne)
Ras Cite de Cansado
Nouadhibou Atar Chinguetti El Djouf
Oujeft
Timiris Akjoujt
Rachid
Nouakchott Tidjikja Tichît
Boutilimit Moudjéria Arhrîjît
Mederdra Aleg Yogba
M'Bout Tamchaket
Kiffa
Rosso Podor Bogué Kaédi
St. Louis Dagana Néma
Louga Matam Timbédra
Tivaoune Dahra Linguère Bassikounou
C. Vert Thiès Diourbel Tiel
Dakar Kaolack Kaffrine
Mbour SENEGAL
GAMBIA
Banjul Georgetown
(Bathurst) Kaur
Sedhiou Kolda
Ziguinchor Farim Kédougou
Bissau Bafatá
GUINEA Fouta
BISSAU Djalon Tougué
Bolama Gaoual
Arquipélago Boké Télimélé
dos Bijagós Dubreka
C. Verga Boffa Télimélé
GUINEA Faranah
Conakry Forécariah
P. Loko ▲ 1948
SIERRA Makeni
Freetown LEONE Bo Kenema
Waterloo
Moyamba Mano
Sherbro I. Pendembu
Bonthe Sulima
LIBERIA Zwedru
Robertsport
Monrovia Careysburg
Marshall Tapeta
Buchanan
River Cess
Greenville
Garraway
C. Palmas Tabou

MOROCCO
ALGERIA
Alger (Algiers) Harrach
Mostaganem Blida Constantine
Tiaret ▲ 2308 Sétif
Saïda Bou Saâda Biskra
Laghouat
Ghardaïa Hassi R'Mel
Ouargla Hassi Messaoud
Ft. Lallemand
Hassi el Gassi
El Goléa
Plateau du Tademaït
Adrar In Belbel In Salah
Timimoun
Zaouiet Aoulef
Reggane Arak
Chech Ouallene
Tanezrouft Bj.-in-Eker Idelès
Poste Maurice Tahat
Cortier ▲ 2918 Tamanrasset
(Bidon 5) Ahaggar
Tessalit Admer
Adrar Aïr
des Iforas (Azbine)
Iférouane Monts
Tamgak
1900
Aguelmes
MALI Agadez
Kidal
Menaka I-n-Gall
Gao NIGER
Bourem
Tombouctou Ansongo Tahoua
Goundam Diré Kabara Tahoua Tamaské
Niafounké Gourma-Rharous Filingué Tanout
Nara Hombori Madaoua Birni Nkonni
Sokolo Douentza Zinder
Diafarabé Mopti Djibo Dori Niamey Dosso Sokoto Katsina
Mourdiah Sagala Bandiagara U P P E R Tillaberi Gaya Gandi Kano
Didiéni Ké-Macina V O L T A Tahoua Azare
M'Bout Sarro Ségou Ouahigouya Filingué Maradi Zaria
Kolokani Niger Kaya Fada Kaduna

A L G E R I A

M A U R I T A N I A

S a h a r a

El Djouf

M A L I

S E N E G A L

SENEGAL
GAMBIA

GUINEA
BISSAU

GUINEA

SIERRA
LEONE

LIBERIA

IVORY
COAST

GHANA

UPPER
VOLTA

TOGO

BENIN

NIGERIA

NIGER

Bamako Koulikoro Kati
Banamba
Siguiri Bougouni Sikasso Bobo-Dioulasso Ouagadougou
Kankan Dabola Kouroussa
Dinguiraye
Bafoulabé Kayes Bamako
Kita
Tambacounda
Bafoulabé
Satadougou
Kédougou
Macenta
Beyla Odienné
Kissidougou Man Korhogo Bouna
Guéckédou Touba Koro Kong
Pendembu Séguéla Katiola Dabakala
Danané Bouaké Bondoukou Kumasi
Kenema Bocanda
Toulepleu Daloa Dimbokro
Guiglo Tai Gagnoa Bibiani Obuasi
Sassandra Lakota Tiassalé Dunkwa
San Pedro Grand Bassam Abidjan Accra
C. Three Points Sekondi-Takoradi
Cape Coast

Bight of Benin

Lagos
Cotonou
Lomé Porto-Novo
Abeokuta Ibadan
Oyo Oshogbo Ife
Ogbomosho Iwo Benin City
Kaduna Zaria
Kano
Port Harcourt

Macias Nguema
Biyogo
Rey Malabo
▲ 4070
Mont Cameroun

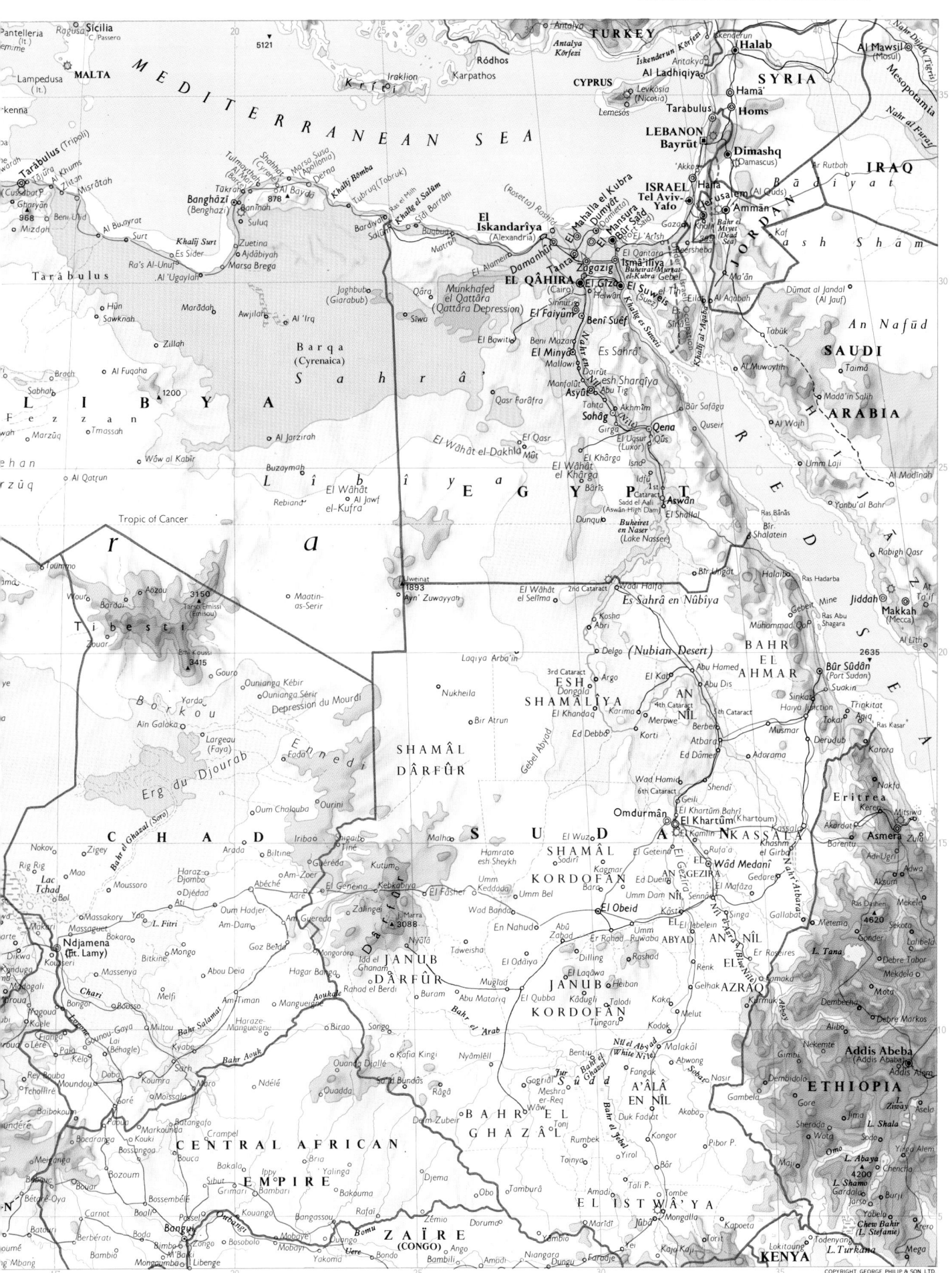

1:15 000 000

100 0 100 200 300 400 500 600 km

COPYRIGHT. GEORGE PHILIP & SON. LTD.

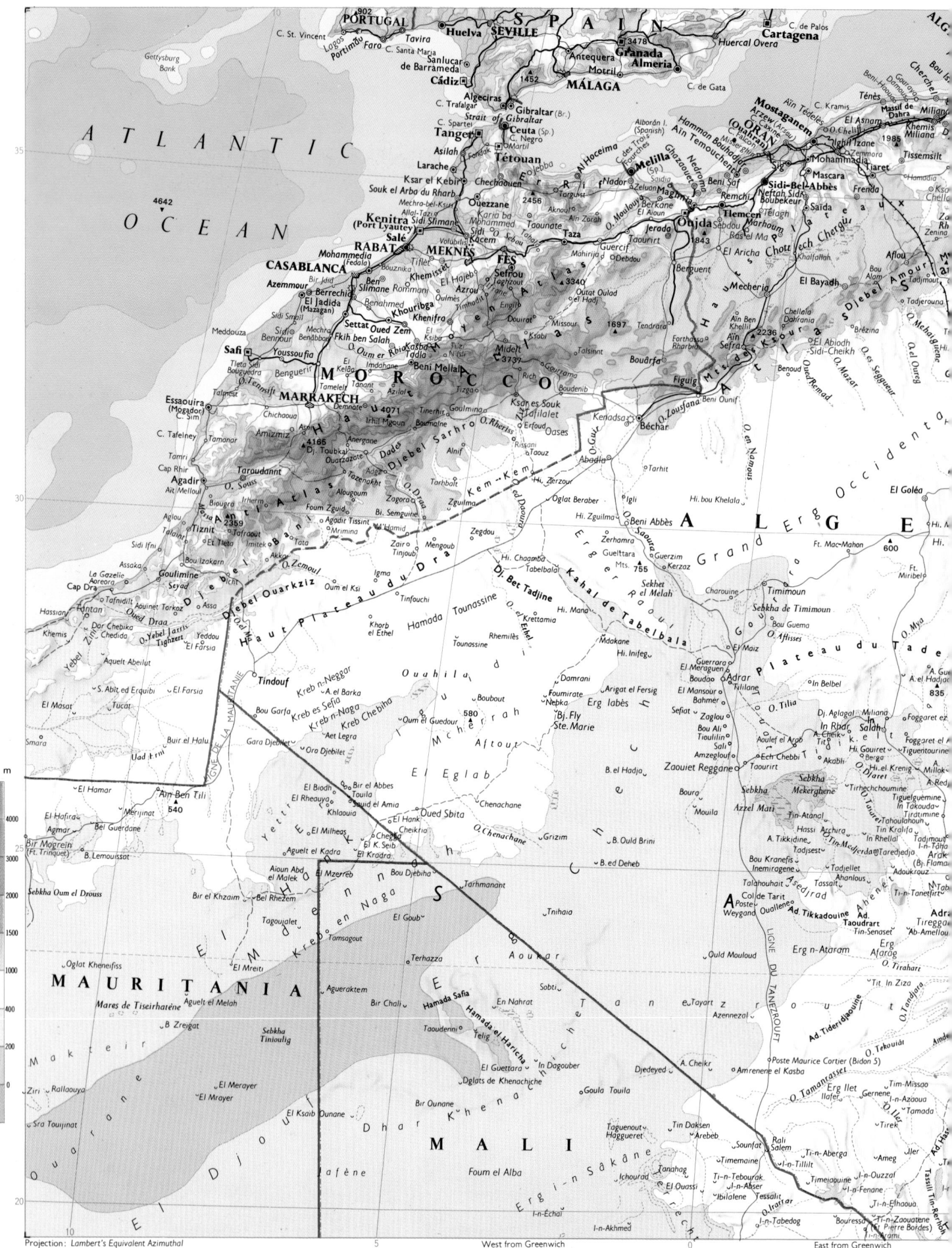

ATLANTIC

OCEAN

PORTUGAL
C. St. Vincent
Lagos
Portimão
Faro
Tavira
C. Santa Maria
Sanlúcar
de Barrameda
Cádiz
C. Trafalgar
Algeciras
Gibraltar (Br.)
C. Spartel
Strait of Gibraltar
Tanger
Asilah
Ceuta (Sp.)
C. Negro
Tétouan
Larache
Fondak
Chechaouen
Ksar el Kebir
Souk el Arba du Rharb
Mechra-bel-Ksur
Ouezzane
Allal-Tazi
Karia ba
Mohammed
Sidi
Kacem
Volubilis
Kenitra
(Port Lyautey)
Salé
RABAT
MEKNES
FES
Sefrou
Mohammedia
(Fedala)
CASABLANCA
Bir Jdid
Tiflet
Bouznika
Khemisset
El Hajeb
Azrou
Azemmour
Berrechid
Ben
Slimane
Rommani
Ifrane
Oulmès
El Jadida
(Mazagan)
Benahmed
Taghzout
Timahdit
Khouribga
Khenifra
Sidi Smail
Mechra
Benâbbou
Settat
Oued Zem
Fkih ben Salah
El
Ksiba
Kasba
Tadla
O. Oum er Rbia
Sidi
Bennour
Safi
Youssoufia
El Kelâa
Imdahane
Tanant
Beni Mellal
Tieta Sidi
Bouguedra
Benguerir
Tizga
Azilal
Meddouza
Sidi
Moussa
Tamelelt
Essaouira
(Mogador)
C. Sim
MARRAKECH
Chichaoua
Demnate
Tinerhir
Amizmiz
Dj. Toubkal
Anergane
Ouarzazate
Agdz
Tazenakht
Irhil Mgoun
Boumalne
Cap Rhir
Tamri
Taroudannt
Aït Melloul
Agadir
O. Souss
Irherm
Alougoum
Foum Zguid
Zagora
Aglou
Biougra
Tiznit
Tafraout
Agadir Tissint
Mrimina
Sidi Ifni
El Tleta
Imitek
Assaka
Goulimine
Seyad
Bou Izakarn
O. Zemoul
Oum el Ksi
La Gazelle
Aoreora
Cap Dra
Tafnidilt
Aouinet Torkoz
Tinfouchi
Hassian
Kantan
Oued Draa
Assa
Igma
Khemis
Dar Chebika
Chedida
O. Yebel Jarris
Yeddou
El Farsia
Tindouf
Khorb
el Ethel
Smara
El Masat
S. Abt ed Erquibi
El Farsia
Kreb n-Neggar
A. el Barka
Tucat
Bou Garfa
Kreb es Sefia
Kreb n-Naga
Bou Chebiha
Oum el Guedour
Buir el Halu
Uad Irni
Aet Legra
Gara Djebilet
Ora Djebilet
El Hamar
Aïn Ben Tili
El Biodh
Bir el Abbes
Touila
El Hafira
Merijinat
El Rheauya
Saguid el Amia
Agmar
Bel Guerdane
Khlaouia
Bir Mogrein
(Ft. Trinquet)
B. Lemouissat
Aguelt el Kadra
El Milheas
El K. Seib
El Kradra
Sebkha Oum el Drouss
Aioun Abd
el Malek
El Mzerreb
Bou Djebiha
Bir el Khzaim
Bel Rhezam
Tagoujalet
El Goub
Tamsagout
Mares de Tiseirhatène
Aguelt el Melah
Bir Chali
El Mreiti
Oglat Kheneifiss
B. Zreigat
Sebkha
Tinioulig
El Merayer
El Mrayer
Ziri
Rallaouya
Sra Tourjinat

MAURITANIA

Maktei

Ouarane

Djouf

MALI

MOROCCO

Haut Atlas
Moyen Atlas
Anti Atlas
Djebel Sarhro
Djebel Bani
Djebel Ouarkziz
Haut Plateau du Dra

Hamada Tounassine
Tounassine
El Ethel
Rhemilès
Ouahila
Boubout
Mcherrah
Aftout
El Eglab

Djebel Achtiane

Yetti

Erg Chech

Hamada Safia
Hamada el Haricha
Taoudenni
Telig
El Guettara
In Dagouber
Dglats de Khenachiche
Bir Ounane
El Ksaib Ounane
Foum el Alba
Dhar Khenachich
Erg i-n Sâkâne

SPAIN
Huelva
SEVILLE
Antequera
Granada
MÁLAGA
Motril
Almería
Huercal Overa
C. de Palos
Cartagena
C. de Gata
Alborán I.
(Spanish)
Al Hoceima
Nador
Melilla
Zeluan
Berkane
Saidia
Beni Saf
Taza
Guercif
Missour
ALGE

Mostaganem
Arzew (Arsaw)
ORAN
(Ouahran)
Aïn Témouchent
Tlemcen
Sidi-Bel-Abbès
Oujda
Figuig
Béchar
Kenadsa
Abadla
Igli
Beni Abbès
Adrar
Reggane
Timimoun
El Goléa

Grand Erg Occidental

Plateau du Tademaït

Tanezrouft

West from Greenwich   East from Greenwich

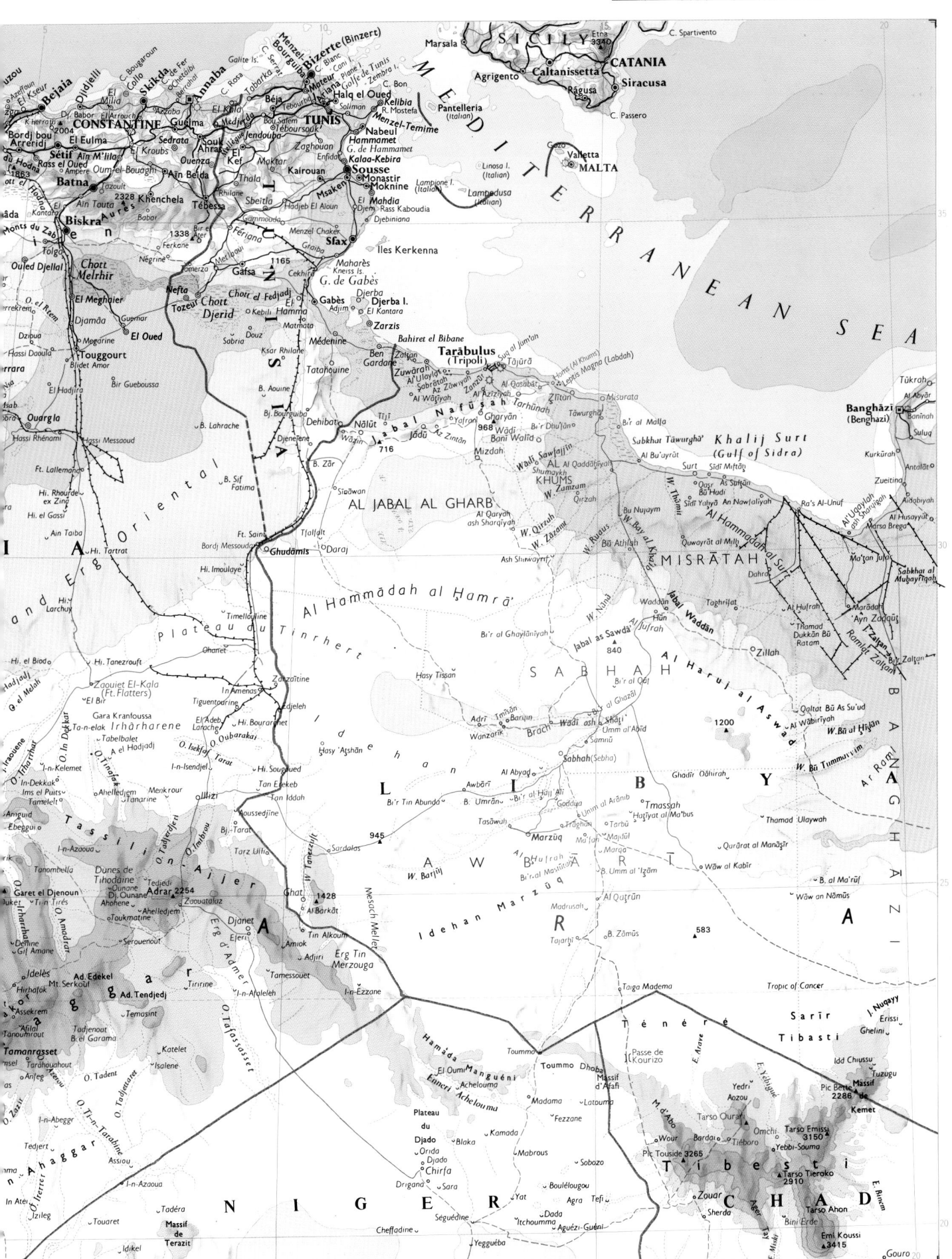

1:8 000 000

50 0 50 100 150 200 250 300 km

MEDITERRANEAN SEA

SICILY
Etna 3340
CATANIA
Marsala   Caltanissetta   Siracusa
Agrigento   Ragusa
C. Spartivento
C. Passero

Pantelleria
(Italian)

Linosa I.
(Italian)

Lampione I.
(Italian)   Lampedusa
(Italian)

Gozo   Valletta
MALTA

Bejaia   El Kseur   Djidjelli   Collo   C. Bougaroun   Skikda   Annaba   Bizerte (Binzert)
Azeffoun   El Milia   C. de Fer   Tabarka   C. Blanc   Menzel-Bourguiba   Mateur
CONSTANTINE   Guelma   El Kala   Béja   Tébourba   Tunis   Menzel-Temime
Bordj bou Arréridj   Sedrata   Souk Ahras   El Kef   Kairouan   Nabeul   Hammamet
Sétif   Aïn M'lila   Aïn Beïda   Maktar   Zaghouan   Kalaa-Kebira
Batna   Khenchela   Tébessa   Sbeitla   Kairouan   Sousse   Monastir   Moknine
Biskra   Aïn Touta   2328   Feriana   Msaken   El Mahdia
Monts du Zab   1338   Gafsa   Sfax   Iles Kerkenna
Chott Melrhir   Nefta   Tozeur   Chott   Gabès   Djerba I.
Ouled Djellal   El Meghaier   Djerid   Kebili   Hamma   Zarzis
El Oued   Douz   Médenine   Bahiret el Bibane
Touggourt   Tataouine   Ben Gardane   Zaltan   Tarābulus (Tripoli)   Tājūrā
Ouargla   Hassi Messaoud   Nālūt   Zuwārah   Az Zāwiyah   Al Qaṣabāt
Ghudāmis   Jabal Nafūsah   Gharyān   Bir Dīu'ib   Misrata
AL JABAL AL GHARB   Mizdah   Banī Walīd   KHUMS   Surt   Banghāzī (Benghazi)

Khalij Surt
(Gulf of Sidra)

Al Hammādah al Ḥamrā'   MISRĀTAH
Plateau du Tinrhert   Jabal Waddān   Waddān   Hūn
SABHAH   Jabal as Sawdā'   Zillah   Al Harūj al Aswad   840
In Amenas   1200   W. Bū Ḥijān
Irhārharene   Sabhah (Sebha)   Awbārī   Marzūq
Tassili n'Ajjer   Adrar 2254   Ghat   Idehan Marzūq   583   Tropic of Cancer
Djanet   Erg Tin Merzouga   Sarīr Tibasti
Tamanrasset   Ténéré   J. Nuqayy 3150
Plateau du Djado   Toummo   Massif d'Afafi   Tibesti   Emi Koussi 3415
Ahaggar   Massif de Terazit   Tarso Emissi 3150
NIGER   CHAD   Gouro

LIBYA

COPYRIGHT. GEORGE PHILIP & SON. LTD.

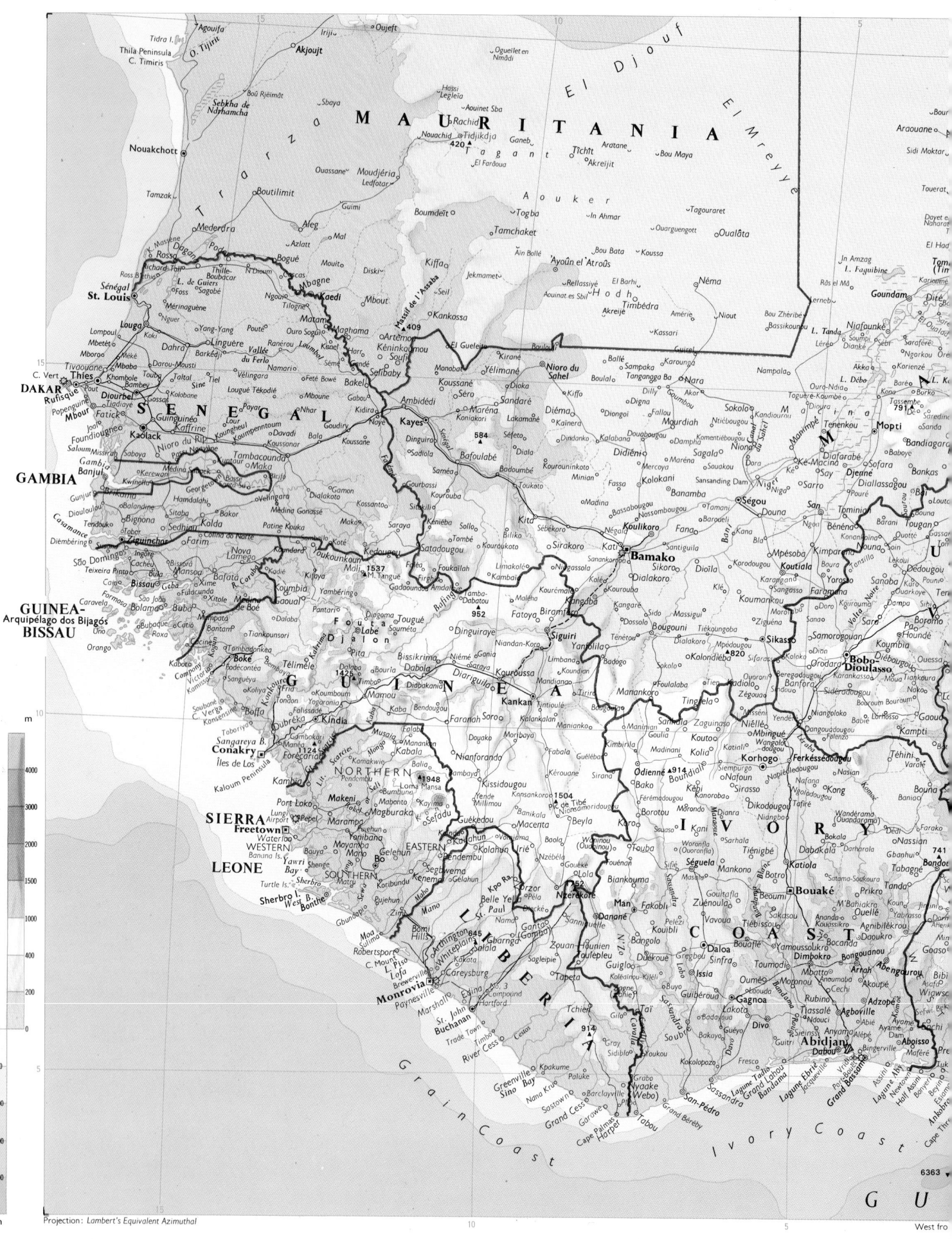

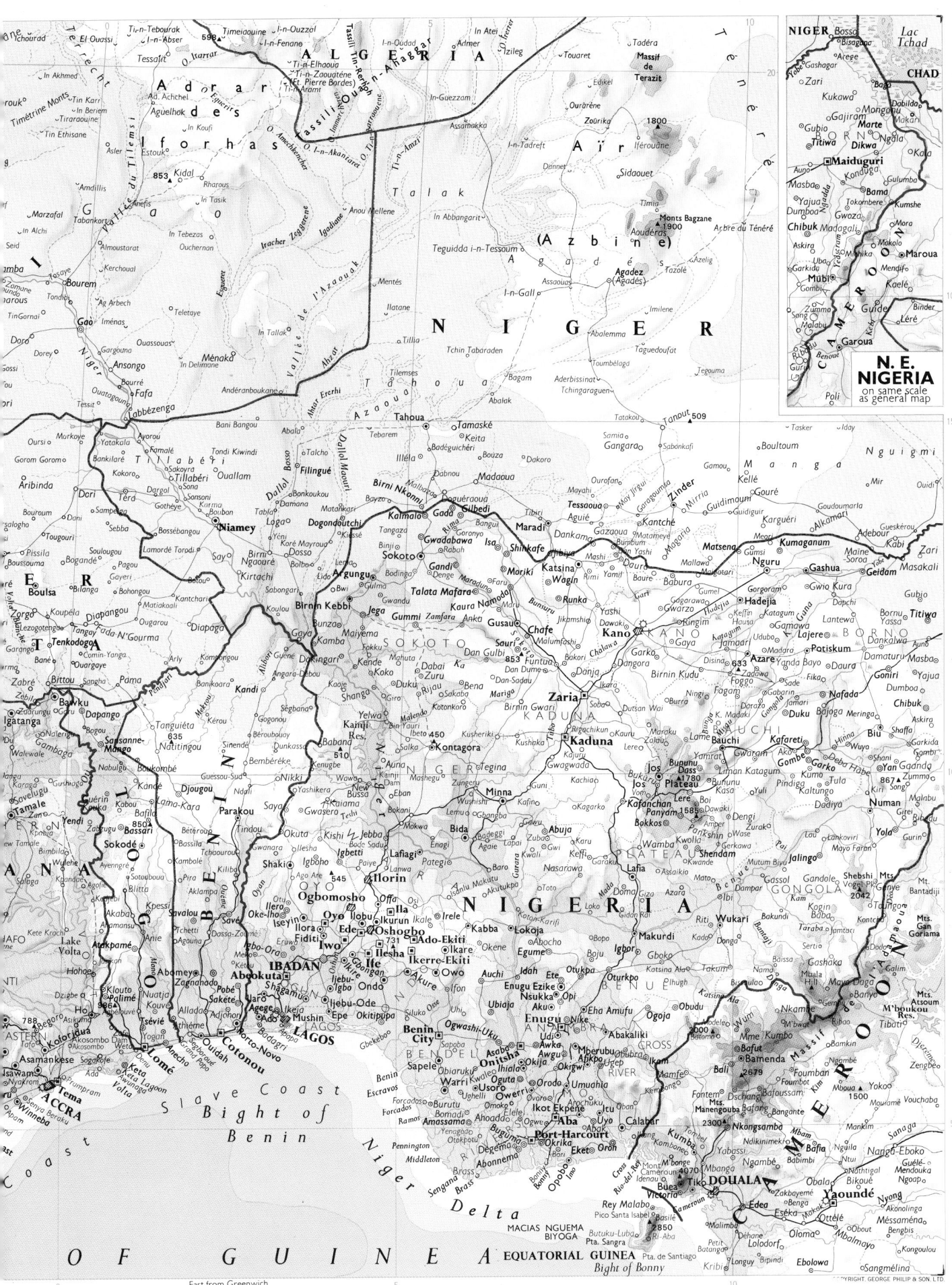

1 : 8 000 000

50 0 50 100 150 200 250 300 km

NIGER

**N. E.
NIGERIA**
on same scale
as general map

ALGERIA

Adrar des Iforhas

Tassili Oua-n-Ahaggar

Aïr

(Azbine)

Agadès

NIGER

Tahoua

Tillabéri

SOKOTO

BENIN

Niamey

Sokoto

Kano

KANO

BORNO

KADUNA

Kaduna

Zaria

BAUCHI

GONGOLA

PLATEAU

N I G E R I A

NIGER

OYO

IBADAN

LAGOS

OGUN

ONDO

BENDEL

Benin
City

ANAMBRA

Onitsha

Enugu

IMO

CROSS
RIVER

RIVERS

Port-Harcourt

C A M E R O O N

Slave Coast

Bight of
Benin

Niger
Delta

MACIAS NGUEMA
BIYOGA

Bight of Bonny

EQUATORIAL GUINEA

O F   G U I N E A

East from Greenwich

COPYRIGHT GEORGE PHILIP & SON LTD.

THE NILE DELTA
1:4 000 000

1 : 8 000 000

50 0 50 100 150 200 250 300 km

123

COPYRIGHT GEORGE PHILIP & SON LTD

Projection: Lambert's Equivalent Azimuthal

East from Greenwich

1:15 000 000

100   0   100 200 300 400 500 600 km

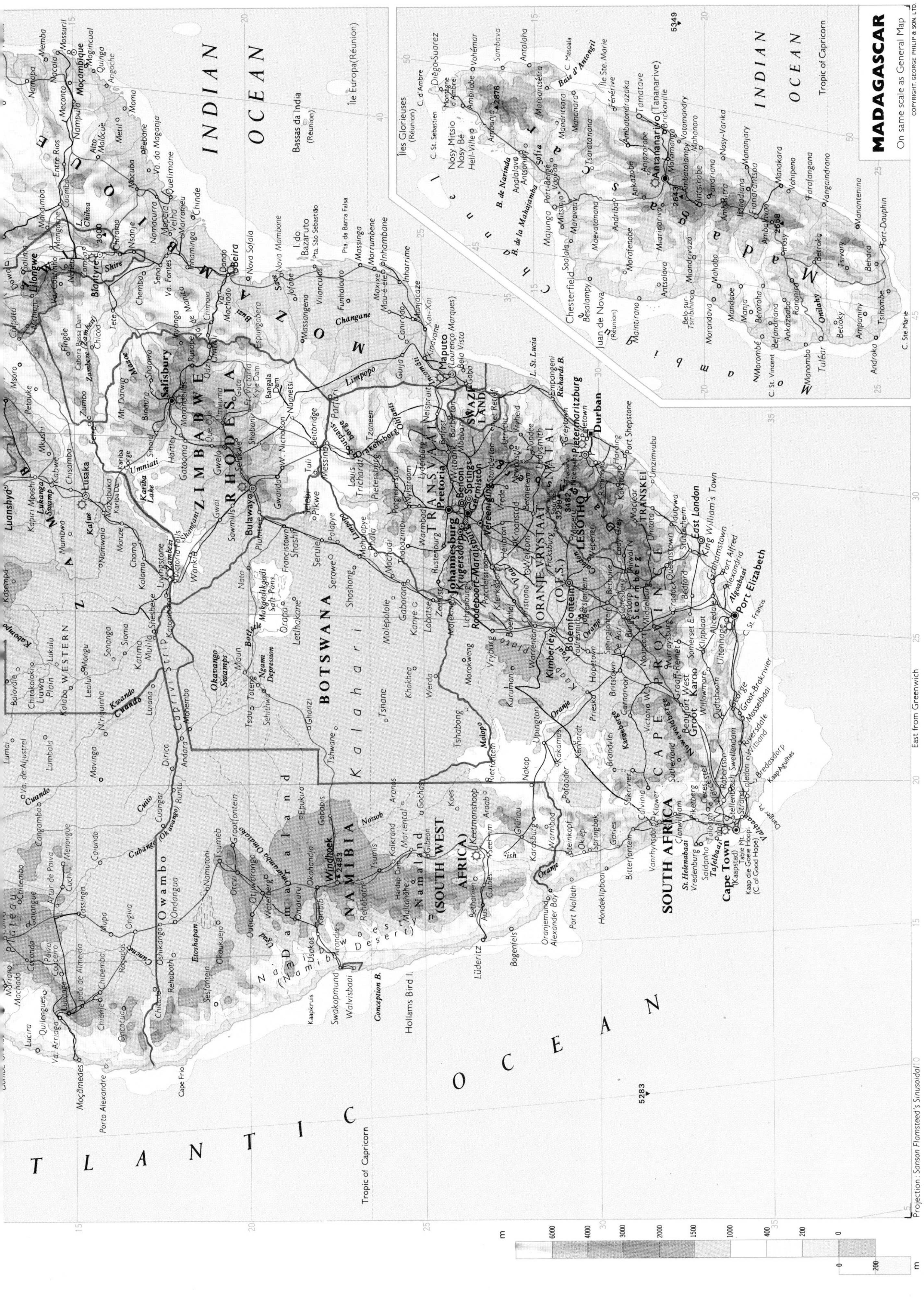

MADAGASCAR
On same scale as General Map

COPYRIGHT. GEORGE PHILIP & SON LTD.

Projection: Sanson Flamsteed's Sinusoidal

East from Greenwich

m 6000 4000 3000 2000 1500 1000 400 200 0

m 0 200

SOMALI REP.

ETHIOPIA

SUDAN

KENYA

UGANDA

ZAIRE

TANZANIA

RWANDA

BURUNDI

CENTRAL AFRICAN EMPIRE

Lake Victoria

L. Turkana (L. Rudolf)

L. Kyoga

L. Albert

L. Edward

Lac Kivu

L. Tanganyika

NAIROBI

MOMBASA

DAR ES SALAAM

Zanzibar

Pemba I.

Kampala

Entebbe

Kisangani (Stanleyville)

Arusha

Moshi

Dodoma

Tabora

Kigoma

Bukavu

Mwanza

EQUATOR

Serengeti Plain

MASAI STEPPE

GREAT RIFT VALLEY

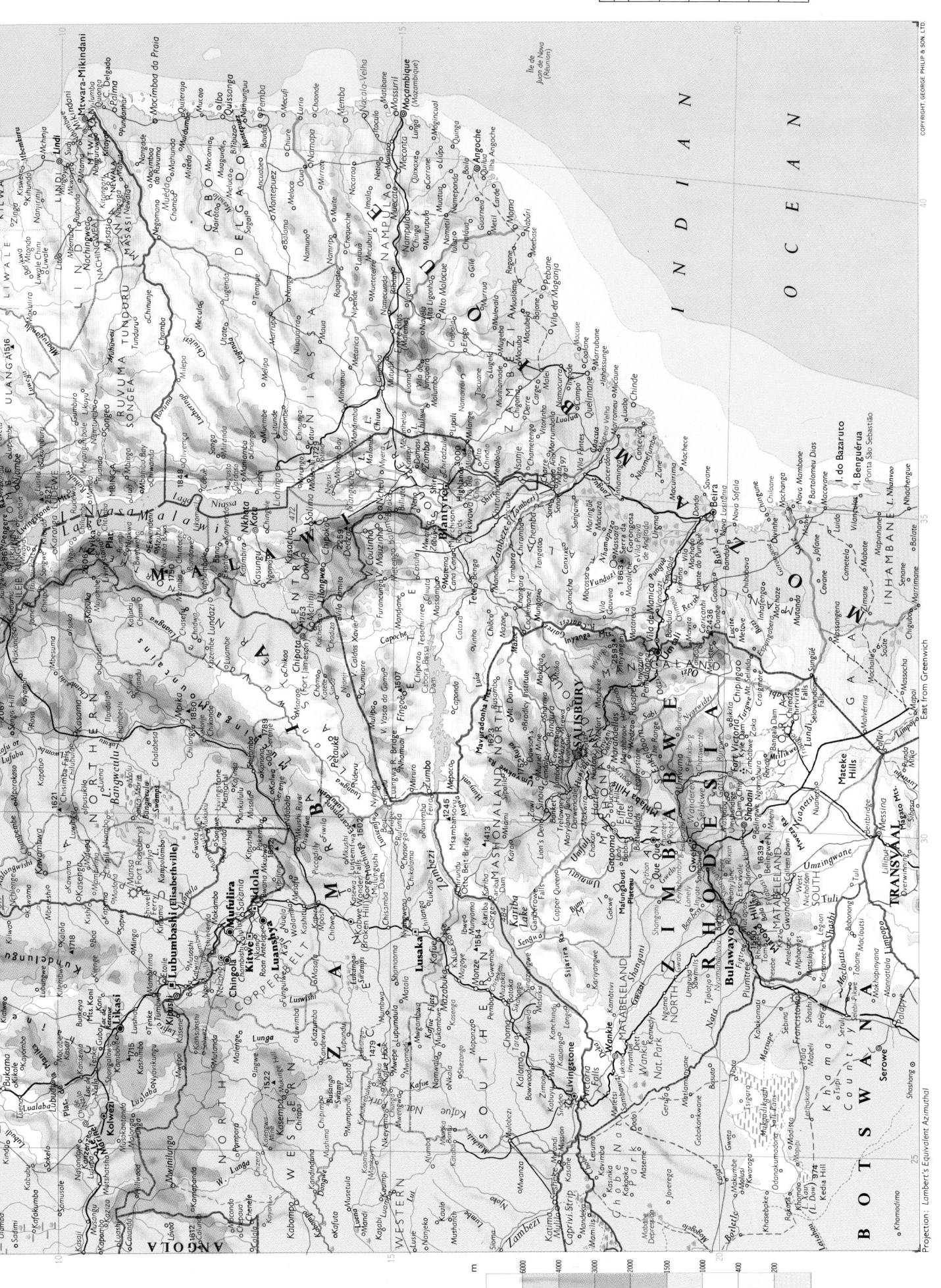

1:8 000 000

50   0   50   100   150   200   250   300 km

127

INDIAN OCEAN

Projection: Lambert's Equivalent Azimuthal

COPYRIGHT GEORGE PHILIP & SON, LTD.

East from Greenwich

ANGOLA

ZAMBIA

ZIMBABWE

MALAWI

MOZAMBIQUE

BOTSWANA

TRANSVAAL

m 6000 4000 3000 2000 1500 1000 400 200

m 0 200 2000

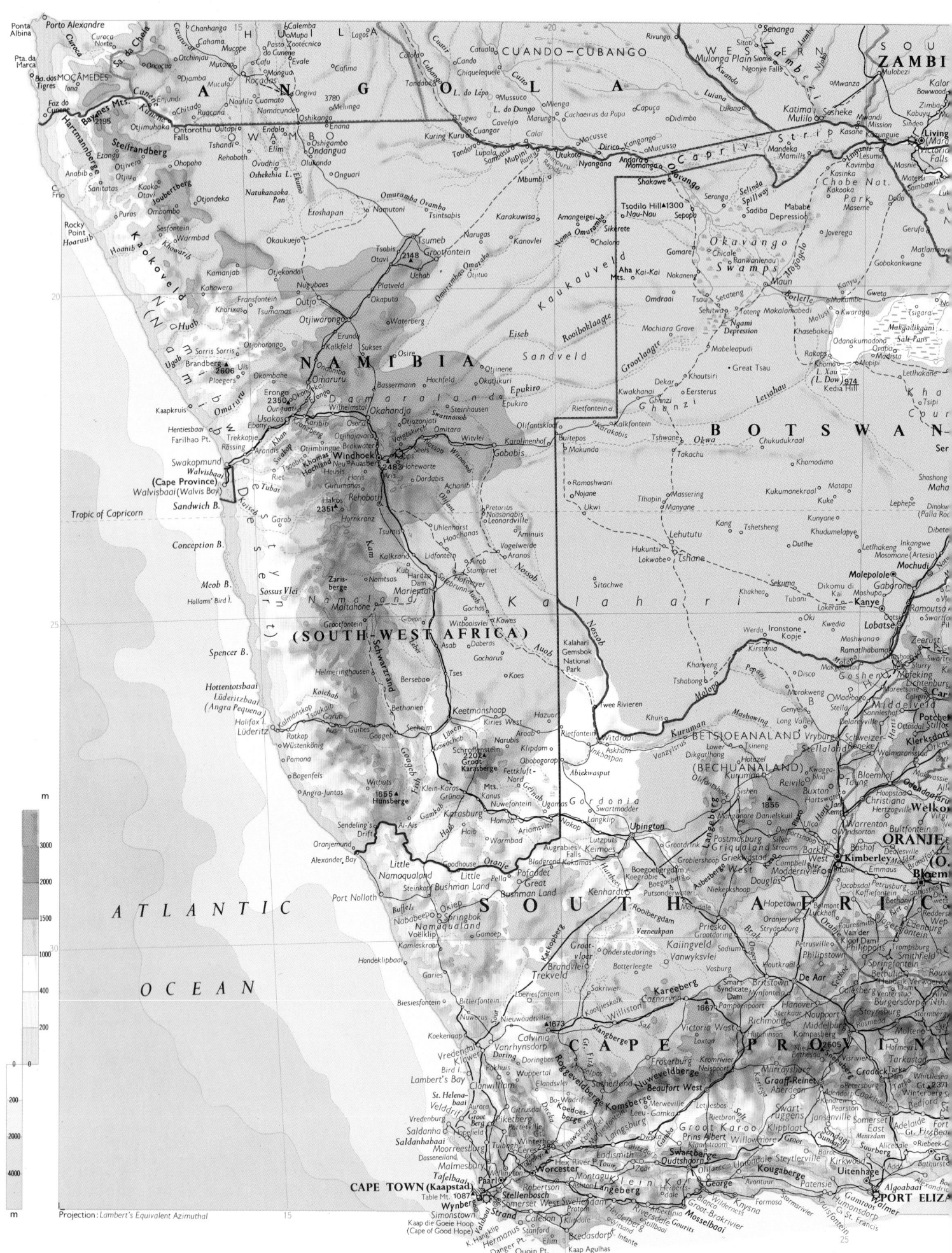

m

3000

2000

1500

1000

400

200

0

200

2000

4000

m

Projection: *Lambert's Equivalent Azimuthal*

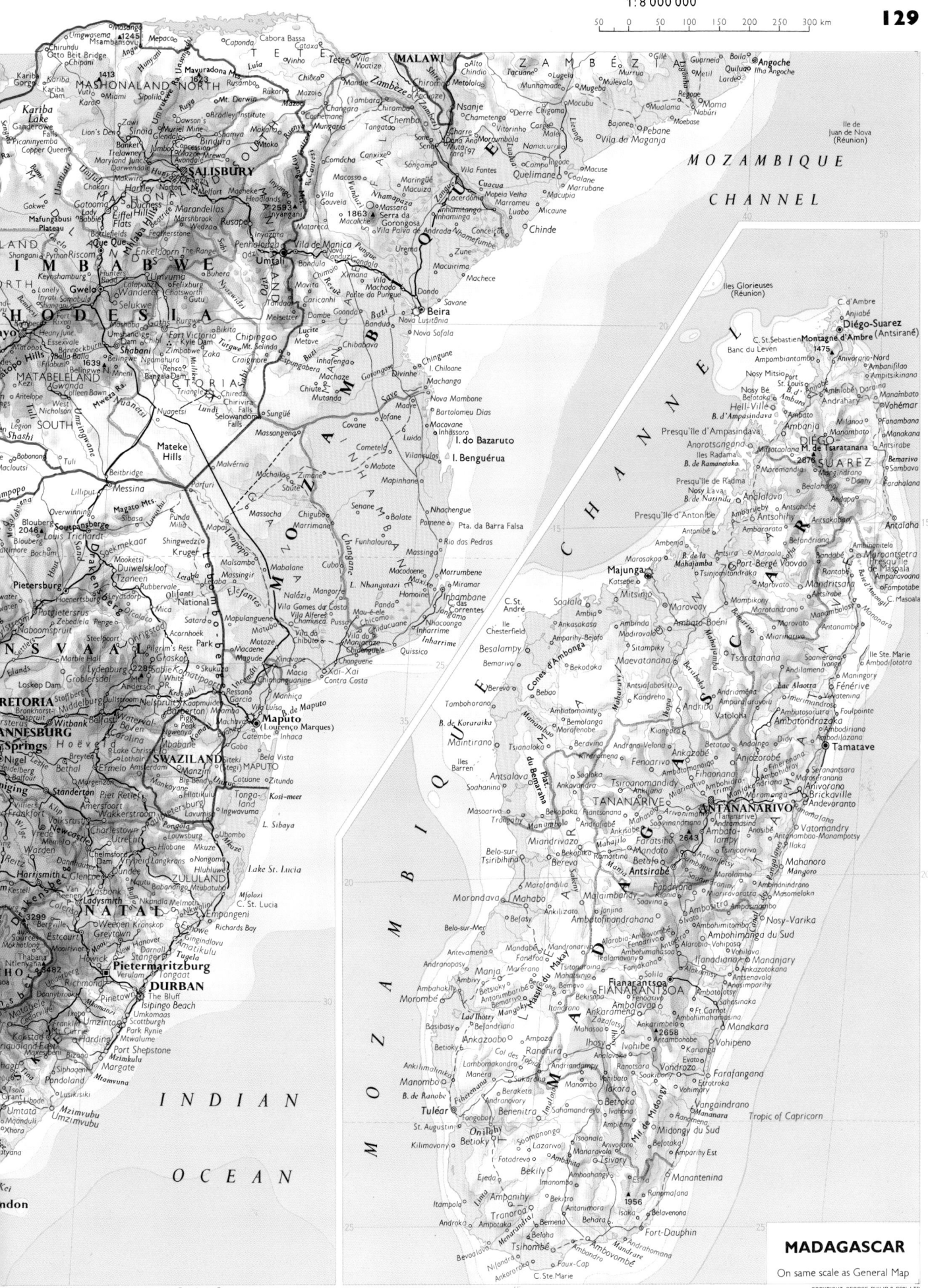

1:8 000 000

50 0 50 100 150 200 250 300 km

MADAGASCAR

On same scale as General Map

COPYRIGHT GEORGE PHILIP & SON LTD.
FHK

East from Greenwich

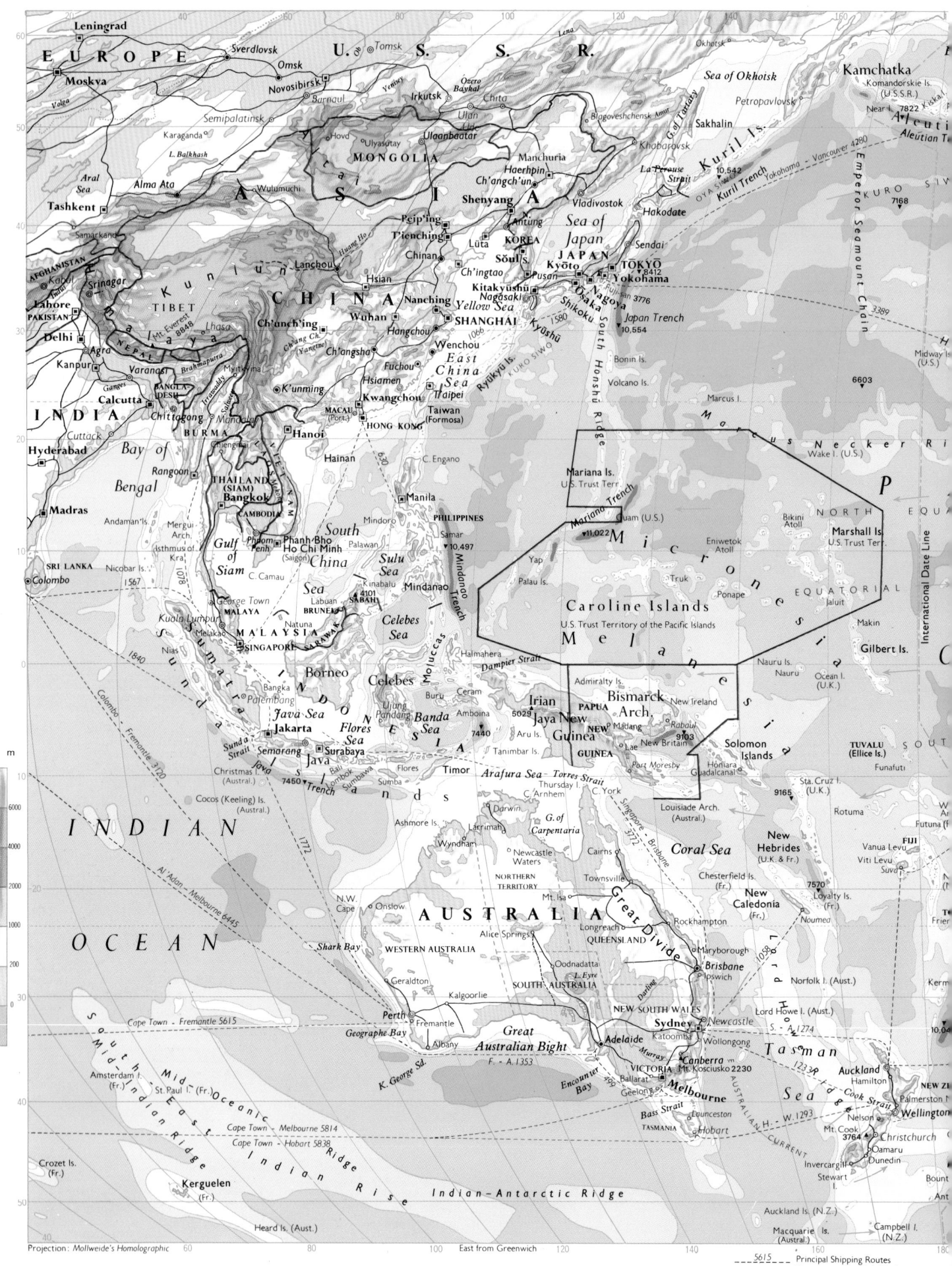

Projection: *Mollweide's Homolographic* East from Greenwich

_ _ _ _ 5615_ _ _ _ Principal Shipping Routes
(Distances in Nautical Miles)

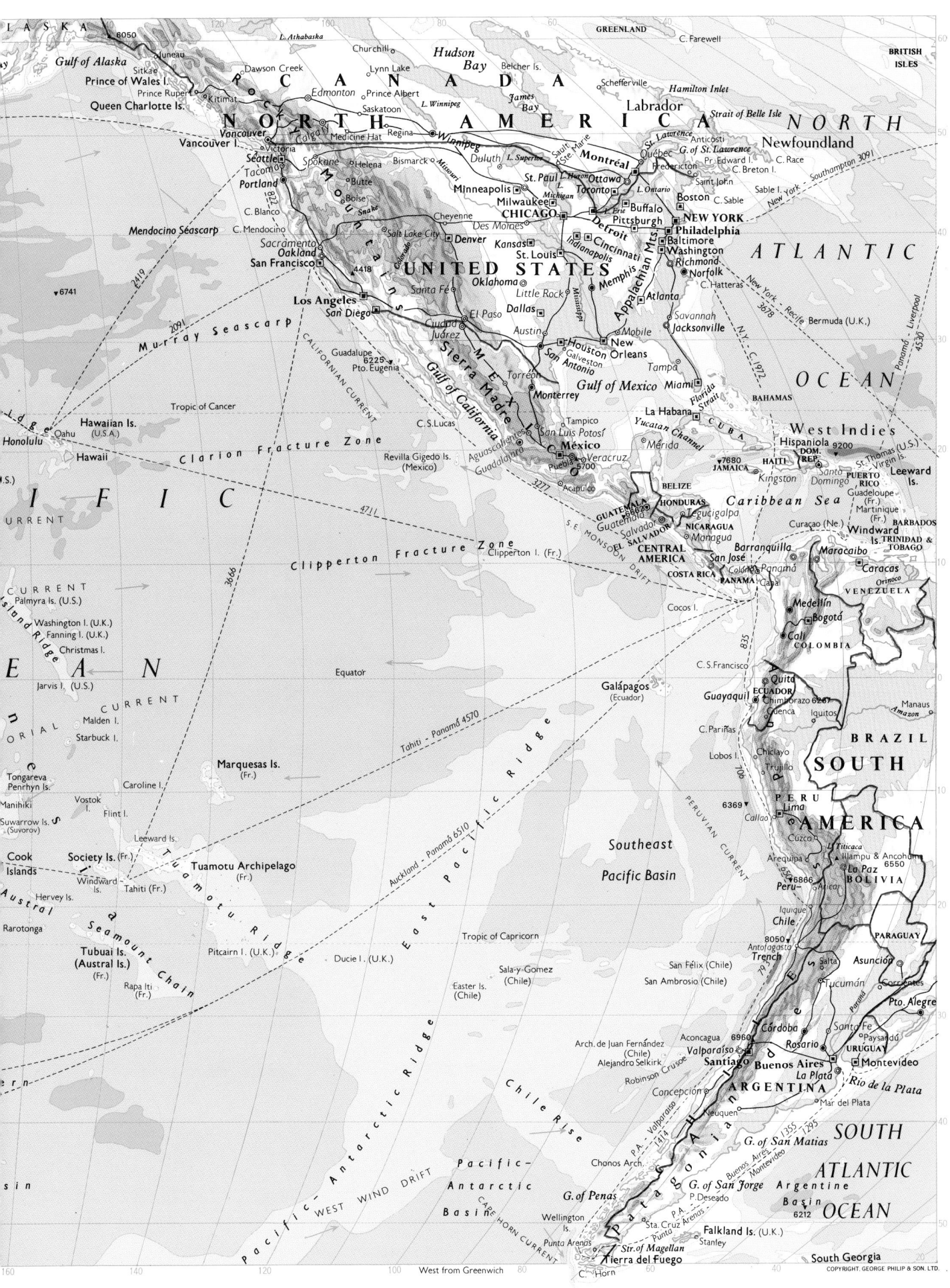

ALASKA
Gulf of Alaska
Sitka
Juneau 6050
Prince of Wales I.
Kitimat
Queen Charlotte Is.
Prince Rupert
Vancouver
Vancouver I.
Victoria
Seattle
Tacoma
Portland
C. Blanco

Dawson Creek
Edmonton
Prince Albert
Saskatoon
Calgary
Medicine Hat
Regina
Spokane
Helena
Butte
Boise
Snake

Churchill
Lynn Lake
L. Athabaska
L. Winnipeg
Winnipeg
Bismarck
Missouri
Cheyenne

Hudson
Bay
James
Bay
Belcher Is.

GREENLAND
C. Farewell

BRITISH
ISLES

Scheffer ville
Hamilton Inlet
Labrador
Strait of Belle Isle
NORTH

ROCKY
NORTH AMERICA
Duluth
L. Superior
Minneapolis
Milwaukee
St. Paul
Michigan
CHICAGO
Des Moines
Salt Lake City
Denver
Kansas
St. Louis
Indianapolis
MOUNTAINS
4418
UNITED STATES
Santa Fe
Oklahoma
Little Rock
Memphis

St. Lawrence
Montréal
Québec
Ottawa
Toronto
L. Ontario
Buffalo
Detroit
Pittsburgh
Cincinnati
Erie
L. Huron
Sault Ste. Marie
Fredericton
Anticosti
G. of St. Lawrence
Pr. Edward I.
C. Breton I.
Newfoundland
C. Race
Sable I.
Southampton 3091
New York

NEW YORK
Philadelphia
Baltimore
Washington
Richmond
Norfolk
C. Hatteras
New York - Recife
Bermuda (U.K.)
ATLANTIC

Mendocino Seascarp
C. Mendocino
Sacramento
Oakland
San Francisco
6741
Los Angeles
San Diego
2419
4418
Salt Lake City
El Paso
Ciudad Juárez
Dallas
Austin
Atlanta
Mobile
Savannah
Jacksonville
3678
N.Y.-C. 1972

Murray Seascarp
2091
CALIFORNIAN CURRENT
Guadalupe 6225
Pto. Eugenia
Sierra Madre
MEXICO
Torreón
Monterrey
Tampico
San Luis Potosí
Houston
San Antonio
New Orleans
Galveston
Gulf of Mexico
Tampa
Miami
Florida Strait
BAHAMAS
La Habana
CUBA
Yucatan Channel
Mérida
OCEAN

Tropic of Cancer
C. S. Lucas
Gulf of California
Aguascalientes
Guadalajara
México
Veracruz
Puebla 5700
Acapulco
3277
BELIZE
GUATEMALA
Guatemala 8862
Salvador
HONDURAS
Tegucigalpa
NICARAGUA
Managua
San José
Barranquilla
West Indies
Hispaniola 9200
HAITI
JAMAICA 7680
Kingston
Santo Domingo
DOM. REP.
PUERTO RICO
St. Thomas (U.S.)
Virgin Is.
Leeward Is.
Guadeloupe (Fr.)
Martinique (Fr.)
BARBADOS
Caribbean Sea
Curaçao (Ne.)
Windward Is.
TRINIDAD & TOBAGO
Maracaibo
Caracas
VENEZUELA

Clarion Fracture Zone
Hawaiian Is. (U.S.A.)
Honolulu
Oahu
Hawaii
Revilla Gigedo Is. (Mexico)
4711
S.E. MONSOON DRIFT
CENTRAL AMERICA
COSTA RICA
PANAMA
Panamá
Panamá Canal
Medellín
Bogotá
Cali
COLOMBIA
Orinoco

PACIFIC
CURRENT
Palmyra Is. (U.S.)
Washington I. (U.K.)
Fanning I. (U.K.)
Christmas I.
Clipperton Fracture Zone
Clipperton I. (Fr.)
3666
Cocos I.
835
C. S. Francisco

EQUATORIAL
CURRENT
Jarvis I. (U.S.)
Equator
Galápagos (Ecuador)
Quito
ECUADOR
Guayaquil
Chimborazo 6267
Cuenca
Iquitos
Manaus
Amazon
BRAZIL
SOUTH

Tongareva
Penrhyn Is.
Malden I.
Starbuck I.
Tahiti - Panamá 4570
C. Pariñas
Lobos I.
Chiclayo
Trujillo
700
AMERICA

Manihiki
Suwarrow Is. (Suvorov)
Vostok I.
Flint I.
Marquesas Is. (Fr.)
Caroline I.
6369
PERU
Lima
Callao
Cuzco

Cook Islands
Society Is. (Fr.)
Leeward Is.
Windward Is.
Tahiti (Fr.)
Tuamotu Archipelago (Fr.)
Auckland - Panamá 6510
Southeast
Pacific Basin
Arequipa
Titicaca
Illampu & Ancohuma 6550
La Paz 6866
BOLIVIA
Peru

Hervey Is.
Rarotonga
Austral
Seamount Chain
Tubuai Is. (Austral Is.) (Fr.)
Rapa Iti (Fr.)
Pitcairn I. (U.K.)
Ducie I. (U.K.)
Tropic of Capricorn
Sala-y-Gomez (Chile)
Easter Is. (Chile)
San Félix (Chile)
San Ambrosio (Chile)
Iquique
Chile
8050
Antofagasta
Trench
Salta
PARAGUAY
Asunción
Tucumán
Corrientes
Pto. Alegre

East Pacific Ridge
Arch. de Juan Fernández (Chile)
Alejandro Selkirk
Robinson Crusoe
Aconcagua 6960
Valparaíso
Santiago
Córdoba
Rosario
Santa Fe
Paysandú
URUGUAY
Montevideo
Río de la Plata
Buenos Aires
La Plata
ARGENTINA
Concepción
Mar del Plata
Neuquen
1355 1295
SOUTH

Pacific - Antarctic Ridge
WEST WIND DRIFT
Pacific - Antarctic Basin
Chile Rise
G. of Penas
Wellington
Chonos Arch.
P.A.
Valparaíso 1414
Buenos Aires - Montevideo
G. of San Matias
G. of San Jorge
P. Deseado
Argentine Basin 6212
SOUTH
ATLANTIC
OCEAN

CAPE HORN CURRENT
Patagonia
Sta. Cruz
Punta Arenas
Str. of Magellan
Tierra del Fuego
C. Horn
Falkland Is. (U.K.)
Stanley
South Georgia

160   140   120   West from Greenwich   80   60   40
COPYRIGHT. GEORGE PHILIP & SON. LTD.

Projection: Bonne

East from Greenwich

m
2000
1500
1000
400
200
0
200
2000
4000
6000
m

1:14 000 000

100   0   100   200   300   400   500   600 km

Wessel
Is.
English Co. Is.
C. Wilberforce
Melville B.
C. Arnhem
P. Bradshaw
Caledon B.
C. Grey
Blue Mud B.
Alyangula
Groote Eylandt
C. Beatrice

Gulf of

Carpentaria

Bight

Thursday I.   Banks I.
Prince of Wales I.   C. York
Endeavour Str.   Newcastle B.
P. Musgrave   Shelburne B.
Cape   C. Grenville
Duifken Pt.   Wenlock   Temple B.
Albatross B.   Weipa   C. Weymouth
York   C. Direction
Archer   C. Direction
Peninsula   Holroyd
C. Keer-Weer
Coleman

C. Flattery
C. Bedford
Cooktown
C. Tribulation
Mossman
Trinity Bay
C. Grafton

Princess Charlotte B.
Bathurst B.
C. Melville Osprey Rf.
Laura
Normanby
Mitchell
Coen

r Edward Pellew Group
Vanderlin I.

rroloola   Mornington   C. van
I.   Diemen
Wellesley Is.
Bentinck I.

Normanton   Burketown
Croydon   Gilbert
Dobbyn   Norman
Camooweal   Kajabbi
Mount Isa   Mary
Kathleen   Cloncurry   Julia Cr.
Duchess   Richmond
Urandangi   Selwyn
Dajarra

Chillagoe Mareeba
Atherton   Cairns
Ravenshoe   Babinda Bartle Frere 1612
Innisfail
Hinchinbrook I.
Ingham   Palm Is.
Halifax B.
C. Cleveland
Townsville   C. Bowling Green

Einasleigh
Forsayth

Newcastle Waters
Gregory Ra.

Leichhardt
Flinders

Pentland   Charters   Ayr
Towers   Home Hill
Bowen   Whitsunday I.
Proserpine   Cumberland Is.
Collinsville   Repulse B.
Netherdale   1274   Mackay
Sarina   Broad Sd.
C. Townshend
Townshend I.

CORAL

SEA

CORAL   SEA   ISLANDS

TERRITORY

Misima I.
Louisiade
Archipelago
Rossel I.
Tagula I.

San Cristóbal

Rennell

Lihou Rfs.
& Cays.

Avon Is.
Chesterfield Is.

P A C I F I C

Selwyn   Range
Winton
Muttaburra
Boulia

QUEENSLAND

Diamantina
Bedourie
Eyre Cr.
L. Machattie
Windorah
Birdsville

Longreach Barcaldine
Ilfracombe   Alpha
Aramac
Clermont   Emerald
Blackall   Springsure
Yaraka
Jundah
Augathella   1312
Adavale

Georgina
Hay
on

L. Eyre
(North)
53—52
L.
Gregory   Cooper   Creek
L. Eyre (South)   L. Blanche

RALIA

Leigh Creek   Copley
Marree
Pimba
L. Torrens
Beltana

Belyando
Blair   Athol
Blackwater
Peak Ra.
Duaringa
Nogoa   Mackenzie
Dawson   Theodore
Expedition Ra.
Injune   Taroom
Wandoan

Rockhampton C. Capricorn
Mt. Morgan   Curtis I.
Gladstone   P. Curtis
Bustard Head
Biloela
Monto   Burnett
Bundaberg
Childers Sandy C.
Gayndah Hervey   Fraser I.
Maryborough   Bay
Murgon   Gympie
Kingaroy   Nambour
Nanango   Bribie I.
Moreton B.
Moreton I.

Bird I.

Saumarez Rf.
Swain   Rfs.

Bellona Rfs.

Cato I.

Tropic of Capricorn

Grey   Range
Warrego   Ra.
Thomson
Barcoo
Quilpie
Charleville
Wyandra
Cunnamulla
Thargomindah

Mitchell
Roma   Miles
WARREGO
Condamine
Balonne
St. George
Moonie
Dirranbandi
Mungindi

Dalby
Toowoomba
Ipswich
Warwick
Goondiwindi

Great   Divide

Brisbane
N. Stradbroke I.
Southport

Moreton B.
Moreton I.

L. Yamma
Yamma

Cooper Creek
Strzelecki Cr.
Warburton

L.
Gregory

Tibooburra

Paroo
Chan.

Bourke
Walgett

Bulloo
Paroo
Warrego

Macintyre
Gwydir
Moree
Warialda
Narrabri
Inverell

Stanthorpe
Tenterfield
Glen
Innes
Casino
Lismore
Ballina

C. Byron

Grafton
Clarence

O C E A N

Leigh Creek
Copley
Beltana

Flinders   Ranges
St. Mary's Pk.
1089
Hawker

Quorn
Mt. Brown
965
Port
Augusta   Orroroo
Peterborough

NEW   SOUTH

Main   Barrier Ra.
Broken Hill
Medium   Hill

Wilcannia
Cobar
Nyngan

Bogan
Gilgandra
Narromine
Dubbo   Wellington

Coonamble
Castlereagh
Gwabegar

Liverpool   Plains

Liverpool Ra.
1505
Muswellbrook
Scone
Singleton

WALES

Gunnedah
Tamworth
1615
Armidale
Walcha
1377

The Round Mountain
1615

N.ENG.
Uralla

Coffs
Harbour
Macleay
Kempsey
Port
Macquarie
Barrington Tops
Sugarloaf Pt.

Pt. Pirie
Jamestown
Burra

Menindee   Ivanhoe
Roto
Hillston   Condobolin
L. Cargelligo
Forbes
Parkes

Newcastle
Stephens

allaroo
P. Pirie
Pinnaroo
Gawler
Elizabeth
ADELAIDE

Murray
Wentworth   Balranald
Mildura
Swan Hill

Hay
Lachlan
Murrumbidgee
Narrandera
Leeton
Griffith

Orange
Bathurst
Cowra
Young
Cootamundra
Junee
Wagga Wagga
Yass

Mudgee
Lithgow
Katoomba

SYDNEY & Port Jackson
Liverpool
Wollongong
Shellharbour
Nowra

Alexandrina
The Coorong
Bordertown

Kerang
Echuca
Bendigo
Shepparton
Benalla

Tumut
Gundagai

Canberra
Queanbeyan
A.C.T.

Jervis B.

Batemans B.

Kingston S.E.
Naracoorte
Penola
Millicent
Mt. Gambier
C. Northumberland
Discovery B.
C. Bridgewater
Portland

Wimmera
Horsham
Stawell
Ararat
Ballarat
Maryborough
Castlemaine
Hamilton

VICTORIA

Australian Alps
Mt. Bogong 1986
Mt.
Kosciusko
2230
Omeo
Bombala
Cooma

Twofold B.
Bega

Eden
C. Everard

Geelong
Colac
C. Otway

MELBOURNE
Dandenong
Yallourn
Moe   Sale
Traralgon
Morwell

Gippsland

Ninety Mile
Beach
Snowy

Disaster B.
Mallacoota Inlet

Port Phillip
Phillip I.
Wonthaggi

Corner Inlet
Wilsons Promontory

T A S M A N

S E A

King I.

Bass   Strait

Hunter I.
C. Grim
Sandy C.
Low Rocky Pt.

Cape Barren I.
C. Portland
Flinders I.
Furneaux
Group
Clarke I.

Devonport
Burnie
Ulverstone
Zeehan   Sheffield   Mt. Ossa 1617
Macquarie Harb.
Strahan
Queenstown   Great L.
New
Norfolk

Scottsdale
Launceston
Beaconsfield
Ben Lomond
St. Marys
Mt. Barrow 1627
Freycinet
Penin.

Lord Howe I.

TASMANIA

Hobart
P. Davey

Bruny I.
Storm B.
Huonville
Tasman Penin.
P. Arthur
S.E. Cape

COPYRIGHT. GEORGE PHILIP & SON. LTD.

1 : 60 000 000

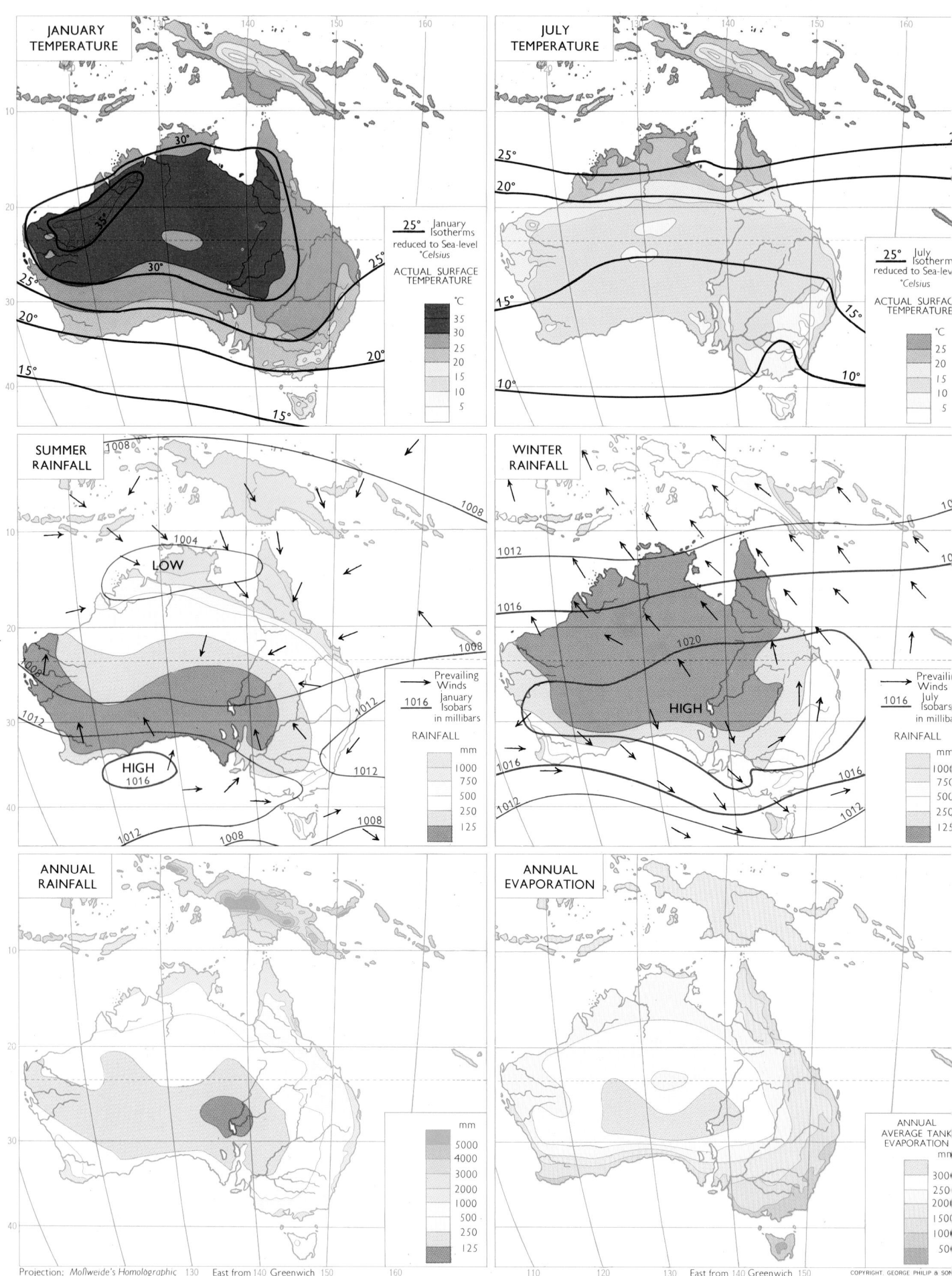

JANUARY
TEMPERATURE

25° January
Isotherms
reduced to Sea-level
°Celsius

ACTUAL SURFACE
TEMPERATURE

°C
35
30
25
20
15
10
5

JULY
TEMPERATURE

25° July
Isotherm
reduced to Sea-lev
°Celsius

ACTUAL SURFAC
TEMPERATURE

°C
25
20
15
10
5

SUMMER
RAINFALL

LOW

HIGH
1016

Prevailing
Winds
January
1016   Isobars
in millibars

RAINFALL
mm
1000
750
500
250
125

WINTER
RAINFALL

HIGH

Prevaili
Winds
July
1016   Isobars
in milliba

RAINFALL
mm
1000
750
500
250
125

ANNUAL
RAINFALL

mm
5000
4000
3000
2000
1000
500
250
125

ANNUAL
EVAPORATION

ANNUAL
AVERAGE TANK
EVAPORATION
mm
3000
2500
2000
1500
1000
500

Projection: Moßweide's Homolographic   130   East from 140 Greenwich   150   160

110   120   130   East from 140 Greenwich   150

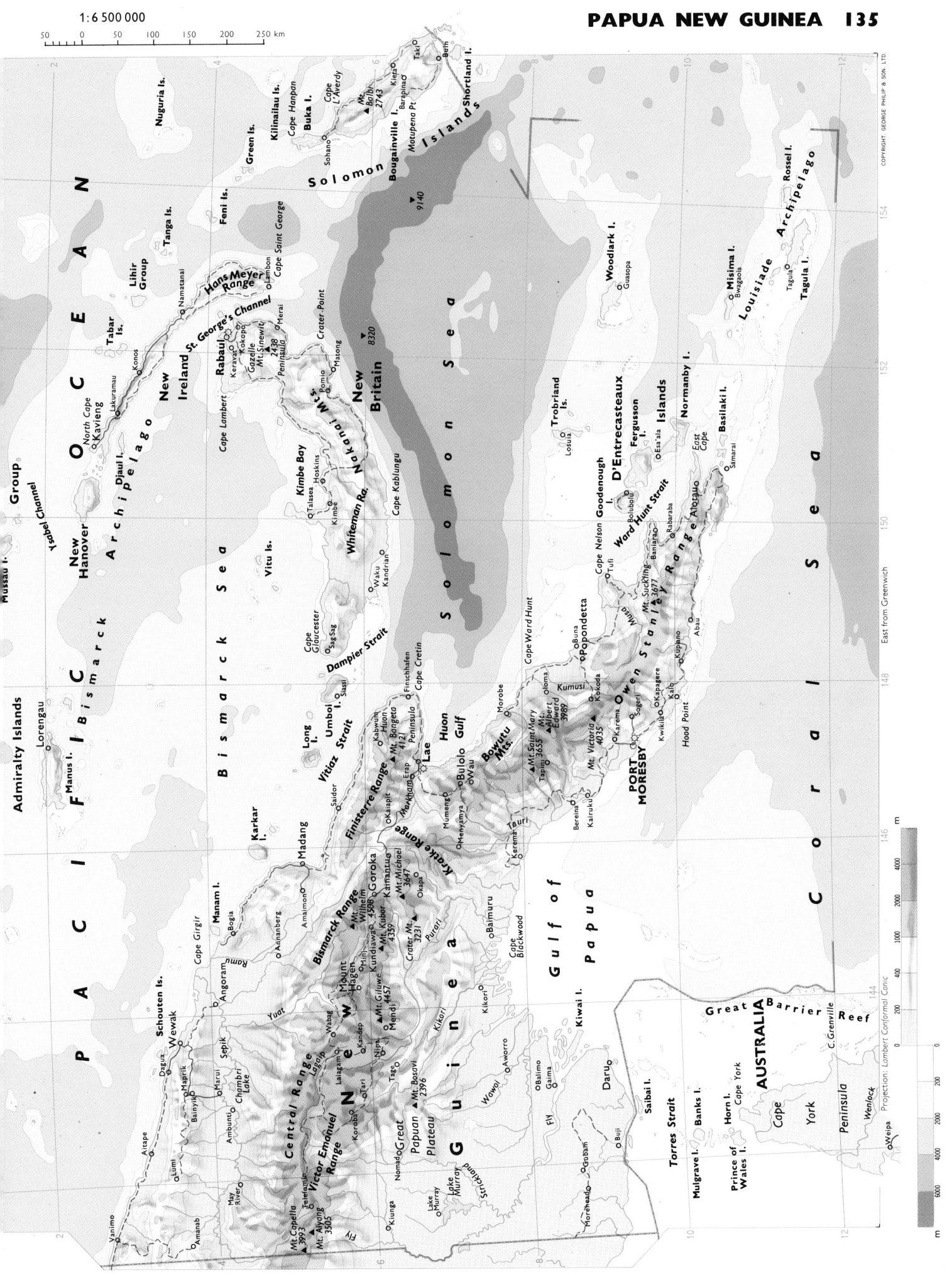

1 : 6 500 000

50   0   50   100   150   200   250 km

COPYRIGHT GEORGE PHILIP & SON, LTD.

P A C I F I C   O C E A N

Nuguria Is.

Mussau I.
Group

Admiralty Islands

Lorengau
Manus I.

Kilinailau Is.
Green Is.
Buka I.
Cape Hanpan
Cape
L'Averdy
Mt.
2743
Taki
Beri
Barapinao
Kieta
Matupena Pt.
Bougainville I.
Sohano

S o l o m o n   I s l a n d s

Shortland I.

Feni Is.
Tanga Is.
Lihir
Group
Namatanai
Lambon
Merai
Cape Saint George

9140

St. George's Channel
Hans Meyer
Range
North Cape
Kavieng
Lakuramau
Konos

New Hanover

Ysabel Channel

Tabar Is.

New
Ireland

Archipelago

Crater Point

Rabaul
Kokopo
Kerava
Mt. Sinewit
2438
Gazelle
Peninsula
Pomio
Matong

Cape Kablungu

New
Britain

8320

S o l o m o n   S e a

Woodlark I.
Guasopa

Misima I.
Bwagaola

Louisiade

Rossel I.

Archipelago

Tagula

Tagula I.

B i s m a r c k   S e a

Cape Lambert

Kimbe Bay
Hoskins
Talasea
Kimbe

Nakanai Mts.
Whiteman Ra.

Trobriand
Is.
Losuia

D'Entrecasteaux

Fergusson
I.
Esa'ala
Rabaraba

Normanby I.

Basilaki I.
Samarai

C o r a l   S e a

Karkar
I.

Cape
Gloucester
Sag Sag
Vitu Is.
Waku
Kandrian

Goodenough
I.
Bolubolu

Islands

East
Cape

Cape Nelson

Madang

Manam I.

Schouten Is.

Wewak

Cape Girgir

Long
I.
Umboi
I.
Siassi
Dampier Strait

Vitiaz Strait

Cape Cretin
Finschhafen

Huon
Peninsula

Morobe

Ward Hunt Strait

Owen

Mt. Suckling
3677

Banjaro

Alotau

Mt. Victoria
4035
Mt.
Albert
Edward
3987
Mt. Saint Mary
Taping 3655

Buna
Popondetta
Kokoda
Oloma
Kumusi
Karema
Sogeri

Stanley

Range

Kwikila
Hood Point
Abau
Kippano
Kalo
Okapagere
Kairuku
Bereina

Saldor

Finisterre Range

Kabwum
Huon
Mt. Bangeta
4121
Erap

Lae
Bulolo
Wau

Huon
Gulf

Bowutu
Mts.

Cape Ward Hunt

Tufi

PORT
MORESBY

Kratke Range

Markham
Okaiapit
Mumeng
Menyamya
Tauri
Kerema

Gulf   of   Papua

Cape
Blackwood

Kikori

Kiwai I.

Torres Strait

Mulgrave I.
Banks I.
Prince of
Wales I.

Horn I.
Cape York

Saibai I.

Daru

AUSTRALIA

Great   Barrier   Reef

Cape
York

Peninsula

C. Grenville

Wenlock

Weipa

East from Greenwich

Projection: Lambert Conformal Conic

Ainanberg
Bogia

Angoram

Sepik

Ramu

Yuat

Bismarck Range

Central   Range

Mt. Gilwe
4508
Mt. Wilhelm
4508
Mt. Michael
3647
Goroka
Kainantu
Kundiawa
4339
Okapa
Crater Mt.
3231
Purari

Mount
Hagen
Wabag
Mendi 4451
Kandep
Nipa
Tari

Victor Emanuel
Range

Mt. Bosavi
2396

Great
Papuan
Plateau

Lake
Murray

Baimuru

Kikori

Kikori

Balimo
Gaima

Fly

N e w   G u i n e a

Mt. Capella
3993
Mt. Aiyang
3505

Telefomin

Kiunga

Nomad

May
River

Vanimo

Aitape

Lumi

Dagua

Maprik

Ambunti

Chambri
Lake

Marui

Bainyik

Amanab

Goban

Wawoi
Wawol
Aworro
Goaribari

Koroba

Tage

Laiagam
Logaip

 Kikori

m
4000
2000
1000
400
200
0
0
200
2000
4000
6000
m

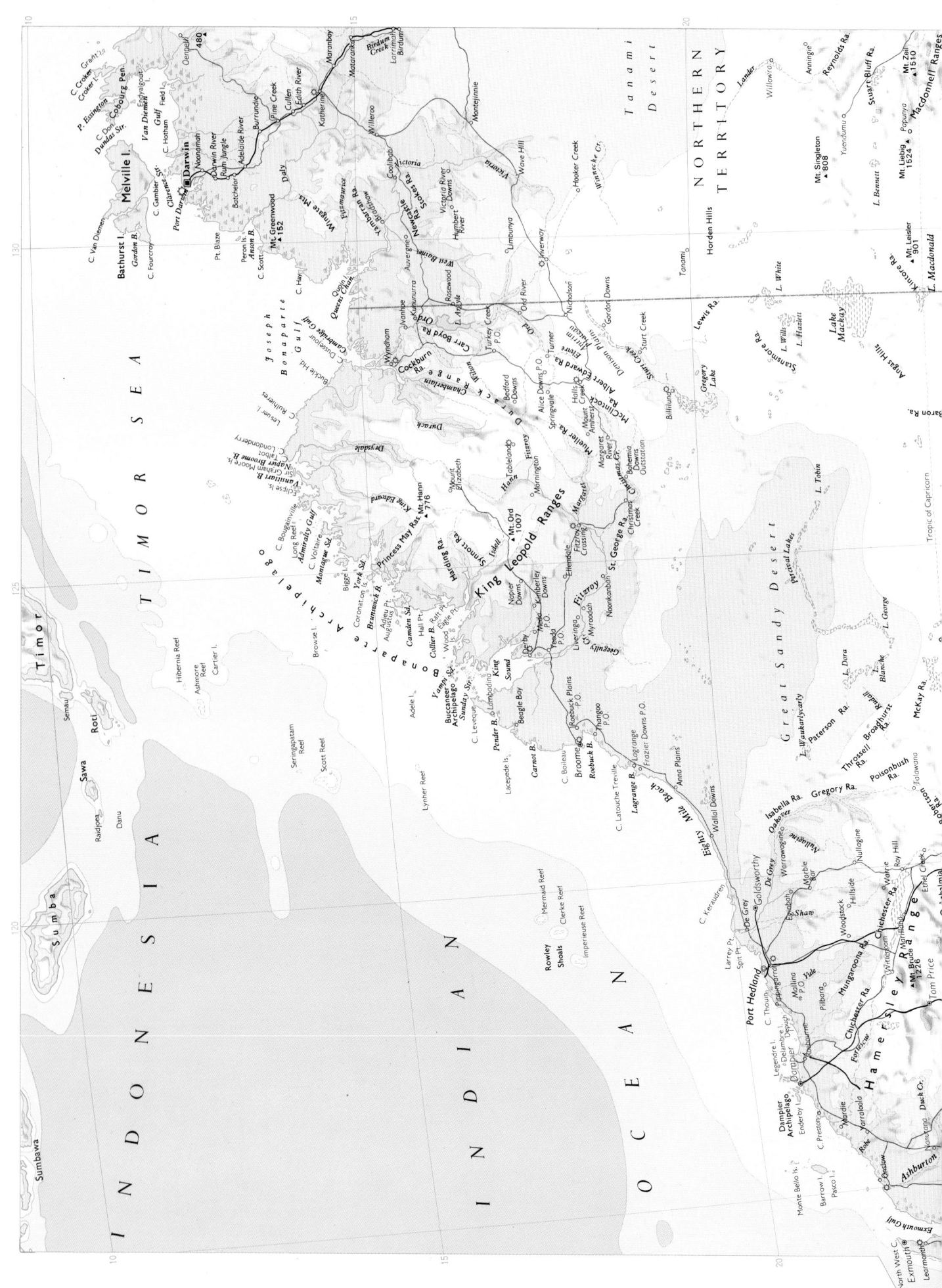

1:8 000 000

50 0 50 100 150 200 250 300 km

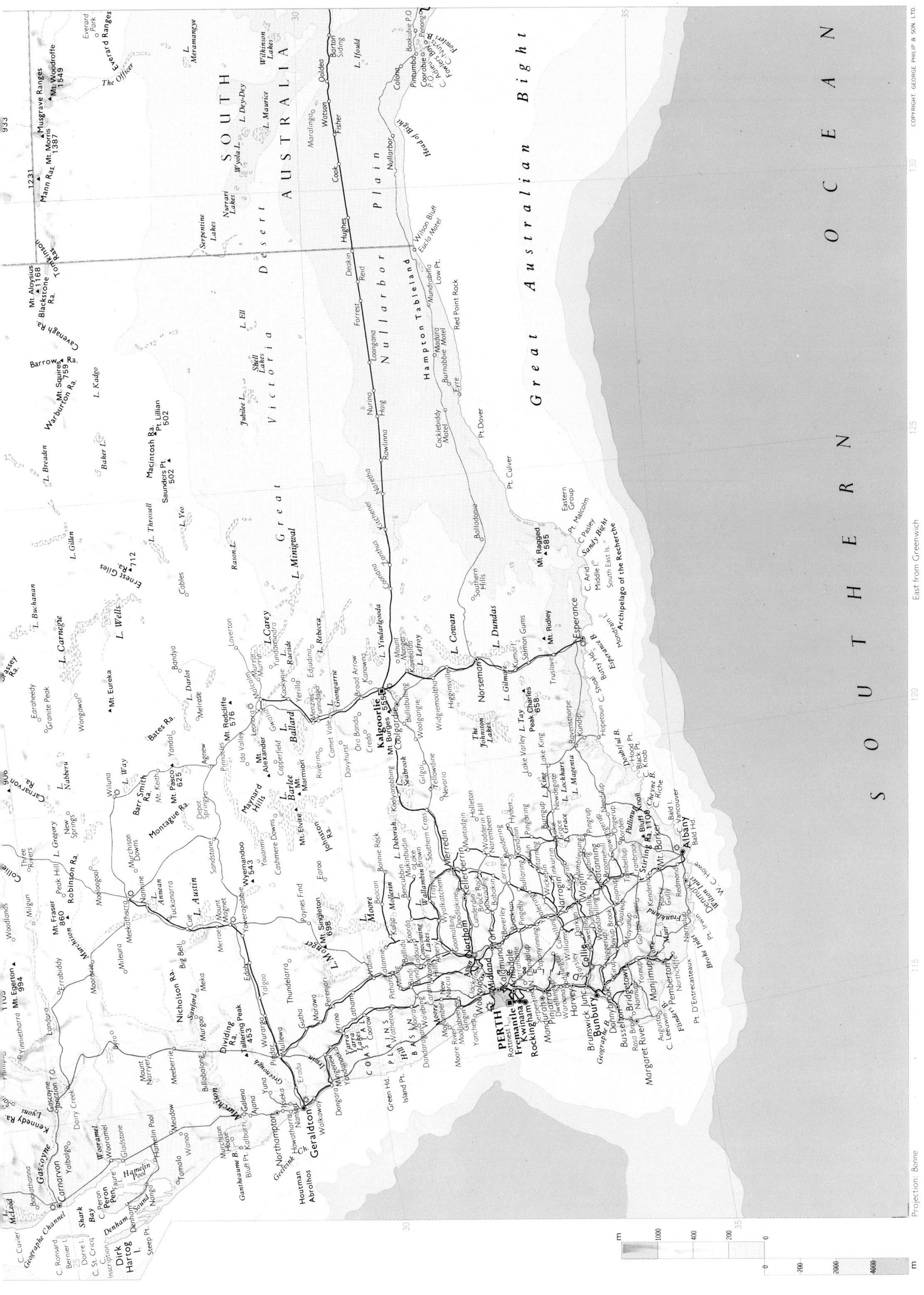

Projection: Bonne

East from Greenwich

S O U T H   A U S T R A L I A

G r e a t   V i c t o r i a   D e s e r t

Nullarbor Plain

Hampton Tableland

G r e a t   A u s t r a l i a n   B i g h t

S O U T H E R N   O C E A N

Musgrave Ranges
Mt. Woodroffe 1549
Mt. Morris 1387
Everard Ranges
Everard Park
The Officer
Mann Ra. 1231
L. Meramangye
L. Dey-Dey
Wynbring L.
Wyola L.
L. Maurice
Narrari Lakes
Serpentine Lakes
Ooldea
Watson
Fisher
Cook
Hughes
Deakin
Reid
Forrest
Nurina
Loongana
Rawlinna
Haig
Nullarbor
Colona
Maralinga
 Mundrabilla
Madura Motel
Mundrabilla
Eucla Motel
Wilson Bluff
Low Pt.
Red Point Rock
Eyre
Burnabbie Motel
Cocklebiddy Motel
Pt. Culver
Pt. Dover

Mt. Aloysius 1168
Blackstone Ra.
Cavenagh Ra.
Barrow Ra.
Warburton Ra.
Mt. Squires 759
L. Kadge
Macintosh Ra. 502
Pt. Lilian 502
Saunders Pt. 502
L. Throssell 712
L. Yeo
L. Minigwal
G r e a t

L. Breaden
Baker L.
L. Gillen
Ernest Giles Ra.
L. Wells
L. Buchanan
L. Carnegie
Mt. Eureka
Earaheedy
Granite Peak
Wongawol

Kennedy Ra.
Lyons R.
C. Cuvier
C. Ronsard
Bernier I.
Dorre I.
Inscription Pt.
Dirk Hartog I.
Steep Pt.
Shark Bay
C. Peron
Peron Peninsula
Denham
Denham Sound
Hamelin Pool
Nanga

Mt. Egerton 994
Mt. Fraser 860
Robinson Ra.
Nicholson Ra.
Dividing Ra.
Tallering Peak 453
Murchison R.
Gascoyne R.
Gascoyne Junction
Carnarvon
Woodlands
Meadow
Billabalong
Meeberrie
Murgoo
Mt. Narryer
Mileura
Milgun
Namure
Murchison Downs
Cue
Mt. Magnet
L. Austin
Sandstone

Yandil
Barr Smith Ra.
Montague Ra.
Bates Ra.
Mt. Keith
Agnew
Wiluna
L. Way
Nabberu
Wongan
Yandal
Leonora
Laverton
L. Carey
L. Rebecca
L. Rason
L. Darlot

Mt. Pesco 625
Maynard Hills
Mt. Alexander
L. Ballard
Copperfield
Mt. Marmion
Mt. Elvire
Johnson Ra.
Mt. Eirie
Menzies
Gwalia
Kookynie
Yerilla
Edjudina
Kalgoorlie
Mt. Burges 556
Coolgardie
Widgiemooltha
Norseman
Balladonia
Mt. Ragged 585
Southern Hills
Salmon Gums
Esperance
C. Arid
C. Pasley
Pt. Malcolm
Eastern Group
Middle I.
Archipelago of the Recherche

PERTH
Fremantle
Rockingham
Mandurah
Pinjarra
Harvey
Bunbury
Brunswick Junct.
Busselton
Donnybrook
Bridgetown
Manjimup
Pemberton
Margaret River
C. Leeuwin
Augusta
Pt. D'Entrecasteaux
Northam
Merredin
Kellerberrin
Narrogin
Katanning
Wagin
Collie
Cranbrook
Mt. Barker
Stirling Ra. 1108
Albany
Bald Hd.
King George Sound
Cheyne B.
Hopetoun
Ravensthorpe
L. King
L. Varley
Lake King
L. Grace
L. Dundas
L. Cowan
L. Lefroy

Geraldton
Northampton
Houtman Abrolhos
Greenough
Dongara
Mingenew
Moora
Gingin
Geographe B.
Bald I.
Bremer B.

1:8 000 000

50   0   50   100   150   200   250   300 km

COPYRIGHT GEORGE PHILIP & SON LTD.

T A S M A N

S E A

NEW SOUTH WALES

SOUTH AUSTRALIA

BRISBANE

SYDNEY

CANBERRA

MELBOURNE

ADELAIDE

Newcastle

Broken Hill

Bass Strait

King Island

Flinders Island

Furneaux Group

Cape Barren

Kangaroo I.

Spencer Gulf

Lake Eyre North

Lake Eyre South

Lake Torrens

Lake Gairdner

Lake Frome

Eyre Peninsula

Yorke Pen.

Darling Downs

Barrier Range

Flinders Range

Grey Range

Projection: Bonne

East from Greenwich

135   140   145   150

m
2000
1500
1000
400
200
0
0
200
2000
4000
m

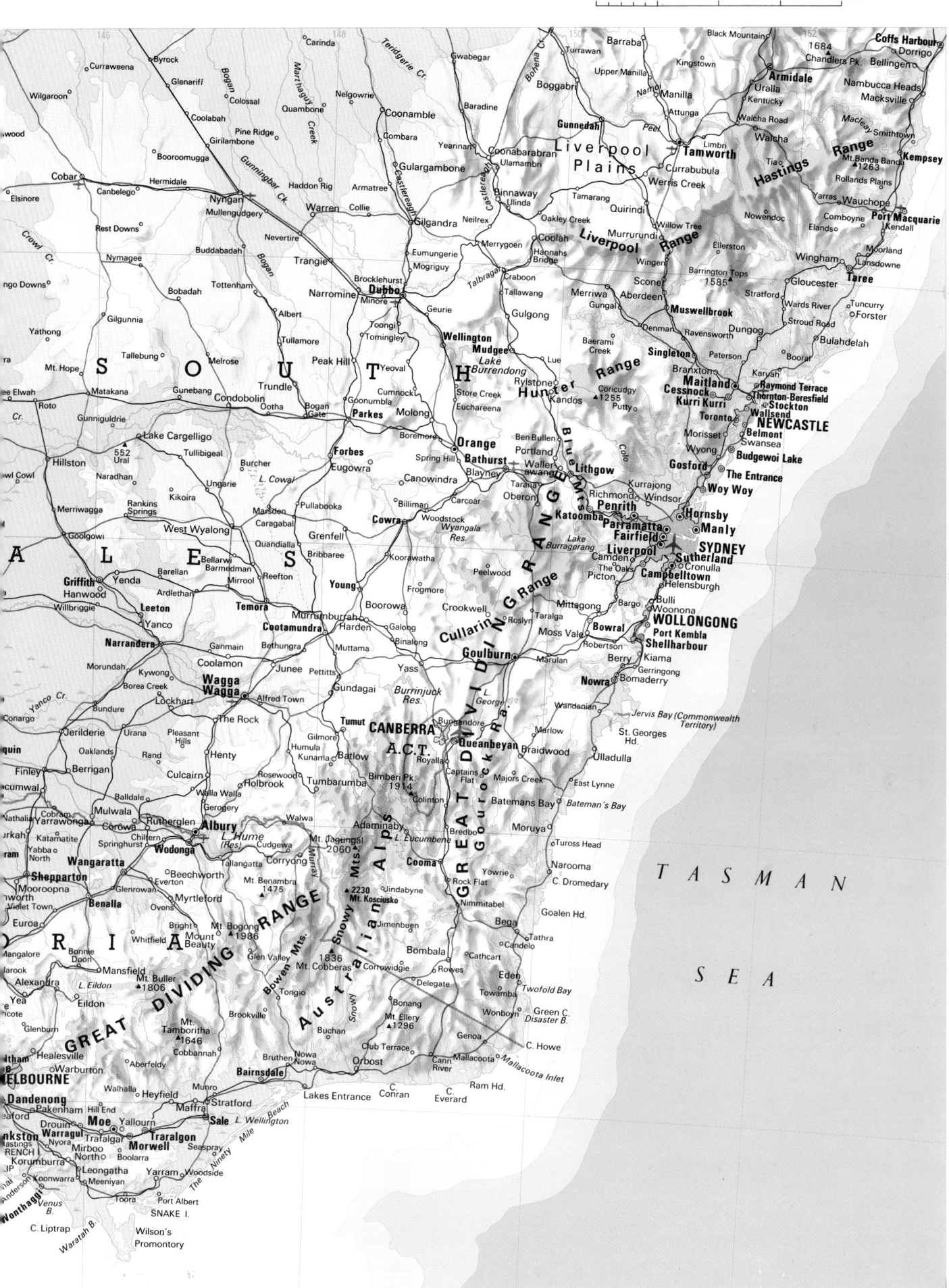

1:4 000 000

50 0 50 100 150 km

141

1:3 500 000

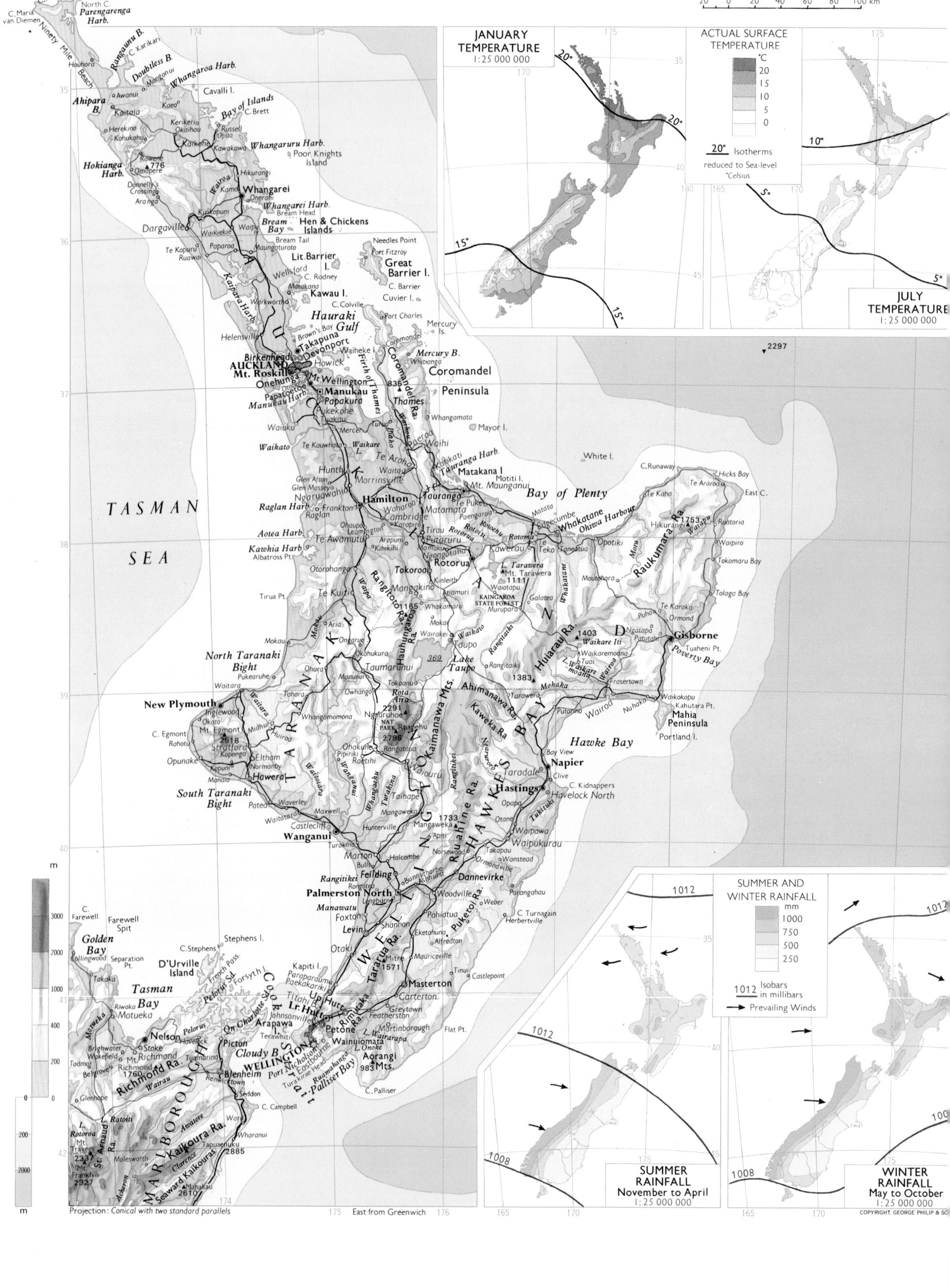
20 0 20 40 60 80 100 km
C. Reinga
North C.
Parengarenga Harb.
C. Maria van Diemen
Ninety Mile Beach
Houhora
Rangaunu B.
C. Karikari
Doubtless B.
Mangonui
Whangaroa Harb.
Ahipara B.
Awanui
Kaitaia
Cavalli I.
Kaeo
Bay of Islands
C. Brett
Kerikeri
Okaihau
Russell
Opua
Herekino
Kohukohu
Kaikohe
Kawakawa
Whangaruru Harb.
Poor Knights Island
Hokianga Harb.
Rawene
Omapere
776
Hikurangi
Donnelly's Crossing
Arango
Wairoa
Kamo
Whangarei
Onerahi
Whangarei Harb.
Bream Head
Bream Bay
Hen & Chickens Islands
Dargaville
Kirikopuni
Waikiekie
Waipu
Bream Tail
Te Kopuru
Ruawai
Paparoa
Maungaturoto
Needles Point
Port Fitzroy
Lit. Barrier I.
Great Barrier I.
Wellsford
C. Rodney
C. Barrier
Matakana
Kawau I.
Cuvier I.
Kaipara Harb.
Warkworth
C. Colville
Hauraki Gulf
Port Charles
Mercury Is.
Helensville
Brown's Bay
Takapuna
Devonport
Coromandel
Waiheke I.
Mercury B.
Whitianga
Birkenhead
AUCKLAND
Mt. Roskill
Howick
Firth of Thames
Coromandel Ra.
Coromandel Peninsula
Onehunga
Otahuhu
Mt. Wellington
Papatoetoe
Manukau Harb.
Manukau
Papakura
835
Thames
Peninsula
Pukekohe
Tuakau
Whangamata
Waiuku
Mercer
Mayor I.
Waikato
Te Kauwhata
Waikare L.
Paeroa
Waihi
Te Aroha
Katikati
Tauranga Harb.
White I.
Huntly
Waitoa
Matakana I.
Motiti I.
C. Runaway
Hicks Bay
Glen Afton
Glen Massey
Morrinsville
Mt. Maunganui
Bay of Plenty
Te Araroa
East C.
Ngaruawahia
Tauranga
Te Kaha
TASMAN
Raglan Harb.
Frankton
Hamilton
Te Puke
Raglan
Cambridge
Matamata
Paengaroa
Matata
Edgecumbe
Whakatane
Ohiwa Harbour
Raukumara Ra.
Hikurangi
1753
Ruatoria
Aotea Harb.
Ohaupo
Leamington
Karapiro
Tirau
Rotoehu
Rotoiti
SEA
Kawhia Harb.
Albatross Pt.
Te Awamutu
Arapuni
Kihikihi
Putaruru
Rotorua
Kawerau
Teko
Opotiki
Waipiro
Tokomaru Bay
Otorohanga
Rotorua
L. Tarawera
Mt. Tarawera
1111
Waiotapu
Tokoroa
Kinleith
Mangakino
Atiamuri
KAINGAROA STATE FOREST
Murupara
Galatea
Whakatane
Motu
Raukumara Ra.
Tirua Pt.
Te Kuiti
Rangitoto Ra.
1165
Whakamaru
Tolaga Bay
Te Karaka
Mokau
Mokau
Aria
Mokai
Waikato
Wairakei
Taupo
Rangitaiki
Puha
1403
Waikare Iti
Ngatapa
Patutahi
Gisborne
Tuaheni Pt.
North Taranaki Bight
Ongarue
Ohakuru
Hauhungaroa Ra.
Lake Taupo
369
Rangitaiki
Waikaremoana
L. Waikaremoana
Tuai
Poverty Bay
Pukearuhe
Ohura
Manunui
Taumarunui
Tokaanu
Huiarau Ra.
1383
Frasertown
Waitara
Tahora
Owhango
Rota Aira
2291
Ngauruhoe
Ahimanawa Ra.
Mohaka
Tarawera
Wairoa
Nuhaka
Waikokopu
Kahutara Pt.
Mahia Peninsula
New Plymouth
Inglewood
Okato
Whangamomona
NAT. PARK
Ruapehu
2796
Kaimanawa Mts.
Kaweka Ra.
Putorino
Mt. Egmont
2518
C. Egmont
Rahotu
Midhurst
Stratford
Kopango
Ohakune
Rangataua
Hawke Bay
Portland I.
Opunake
Kapuni
Eltham
Normanby
Hawera
Manaia
Pipiriki
Raetihi
Waiouru
Bay View
Napier
Taradale
South Taranaki Bight
Patea
Waverley
Waitotara
Maxwell
Taihape
Hastings
Clive
C. Kidnappers
Havelock North
Mangaweka
1733
Hunterville
Opapa
Otane
Castlecliff
Wanganui
Turakina
Waipawa
Waipukurau
Marton
Halcombe
Bulls
Takapau
Wanstead
Rangitikei
Feilding
Norsewood
Ormondville
Ruahine Ra.
HAWKE'S BAY
Rongotea
Bunnythorpe
Ashhurst
Dannevirke
Palmerston North
Longburn
Woodville
Porangahau
Manawatu
Foxton
Pahiatua
Weber
C. Turnagain
Herbertville
Puketoi Ra.
Levin
Shannon
Eketahuna
Alfredton
Otaki
Mitre
1571
Mauriceville
Tararua Ra.
Tinui
Castlepoint
Kapiti I.
Paraparaumu
Paekakariki
Masterton
Carterton
Up. Hutt
Greytown
Featherston
Lr. Hutt
Petone
Martinborough
WELLINGTON
Wainuiomata
L. Wairarapa
Flat Pt.
Port Nicholson
Eastbourne
L. Onoke
Aorangi Mts.
983
Palliser Bay
C. Palliser
Cook Strait
Turakirae Head
WELLINGTON
C. Farewell
Farewell Spit
Golden Bay
Collingwood
Separation Pt.
Stephens I.
C. Stephens
D'Urville Island
French Pass
Pelorus Sd.
Forsyth I.
Takaka
Tasman Bay
Riwaka
Motueka
Nelson
Pelorus
Havelock
Stoke
Mt. Richmond
1760
Richmond
Brightwater
Wakefield
Tadmor
Belgrove
Richmond Ra.
Tuamarina
Picton
Arapawa I.
Terawhiti
Cloudy B.
Blenheim
Renwick
Wairau
Seddon
C. Campbell
Glenhope
L. Rotoiti
L. Rotoroa
Mt. Travers
2337
Mt. Franklyn
2327
St. Arnaud Ra.
MARLBOROUGH
Awatere
Kaikoura Ra.
Tapuaenuku
2885
Ward
Wharanui
Molesworth
Clarence
Seaward Kaikouras
Manakau
2610
Acheron
2297
m
3000
2000
1000
400
200
0
200
2000
m
Projection: Conical with two standard parallels
East from Greenwich
JANUARY TEMPERATURE
1:25 000 000
ACTUAL SURFACE TEMPERATURE
°C
20
15
10
5
0
20° Isotherms reduced to Sea-level °Celsius
JULY TEMPERATURE
1:25 000 000
SUMMER AND WINTER RAINFALL
mm
1000
750
500
250
1012 Isobars in millibars
Prevailing Winds
SUMMER RAINFALL November to April
1:25 000 000
WINTER RAINFALL May to October
1:25 000 000
COPYRIGHT, GEORGE PHILIP & SON

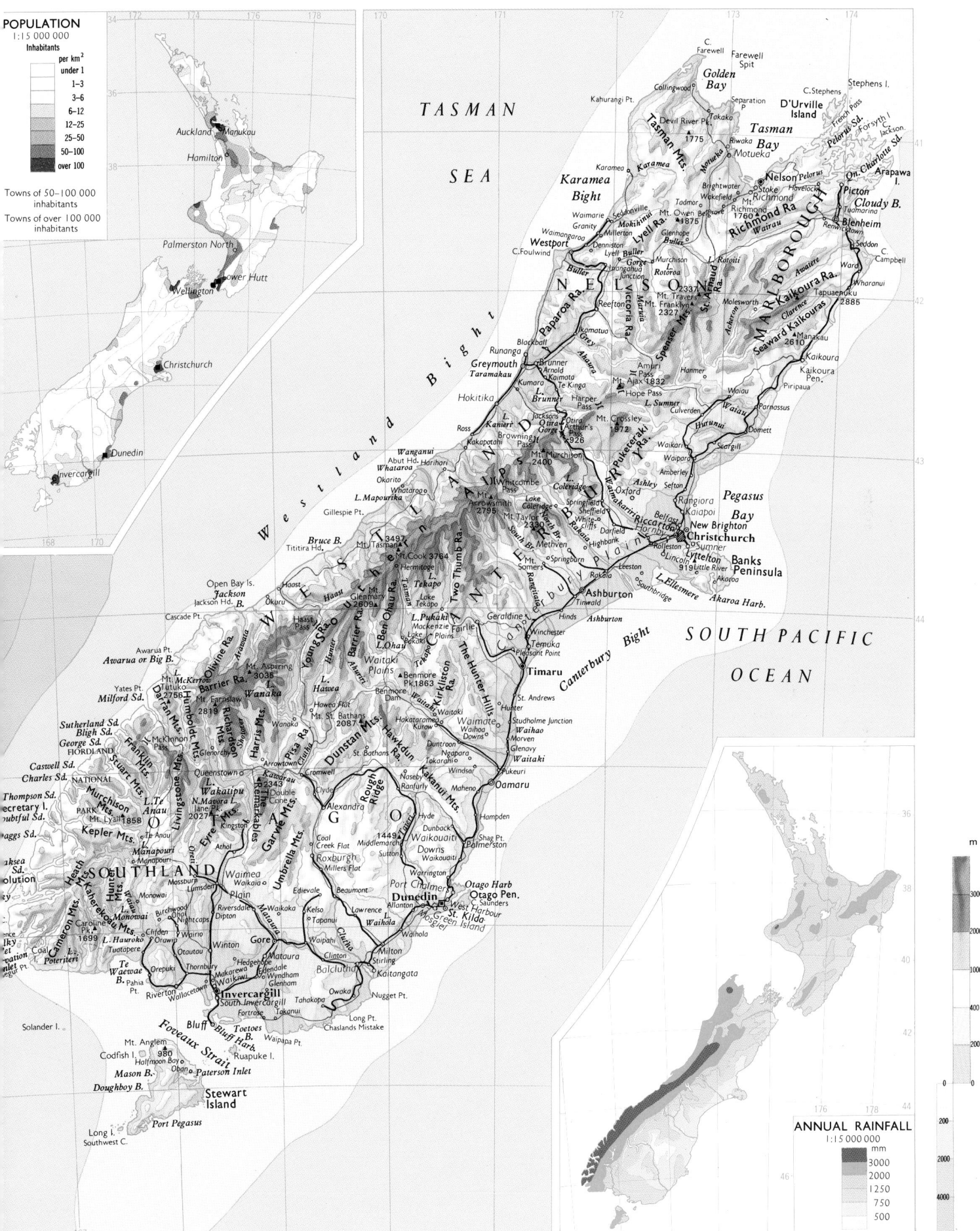

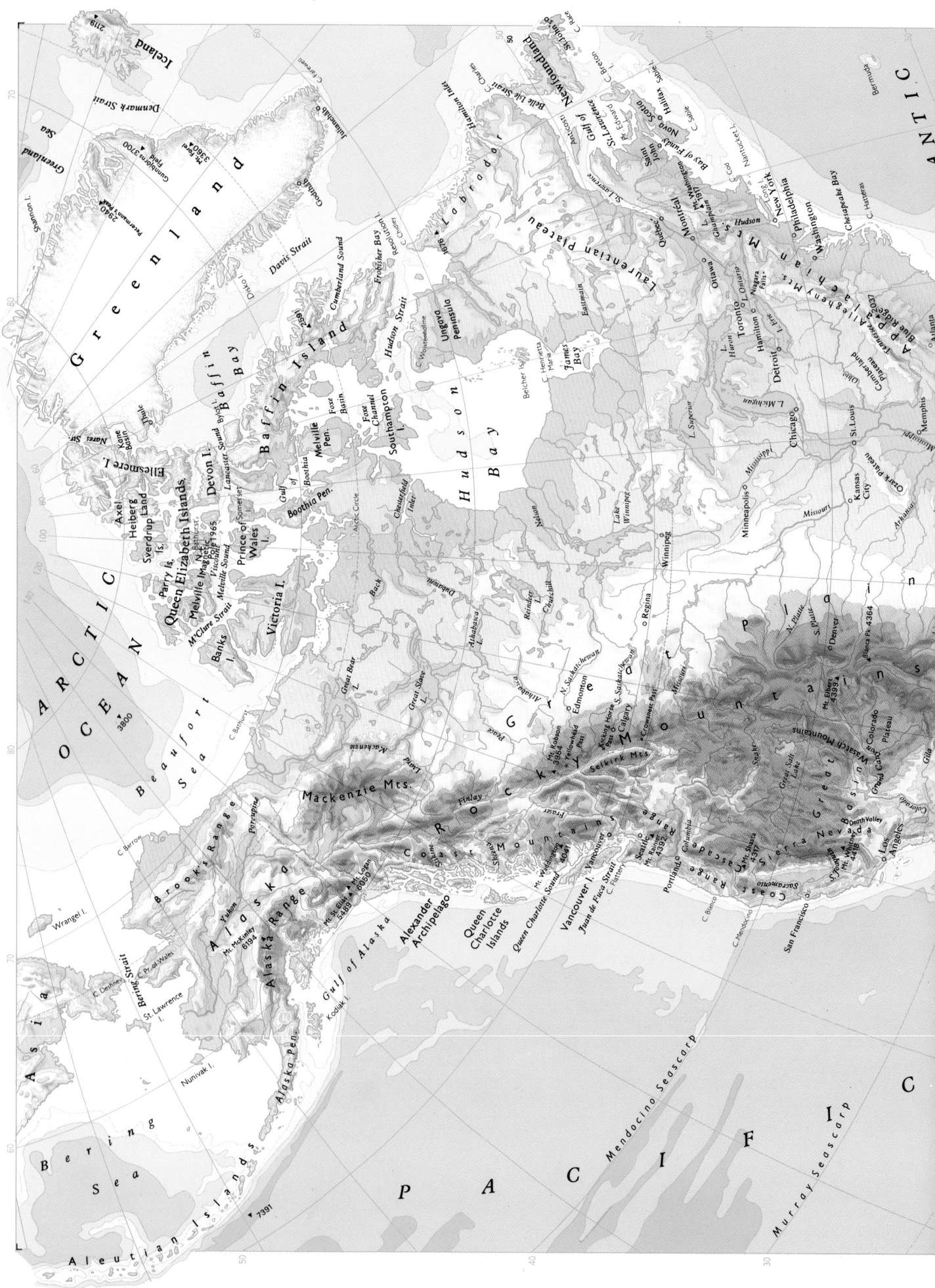

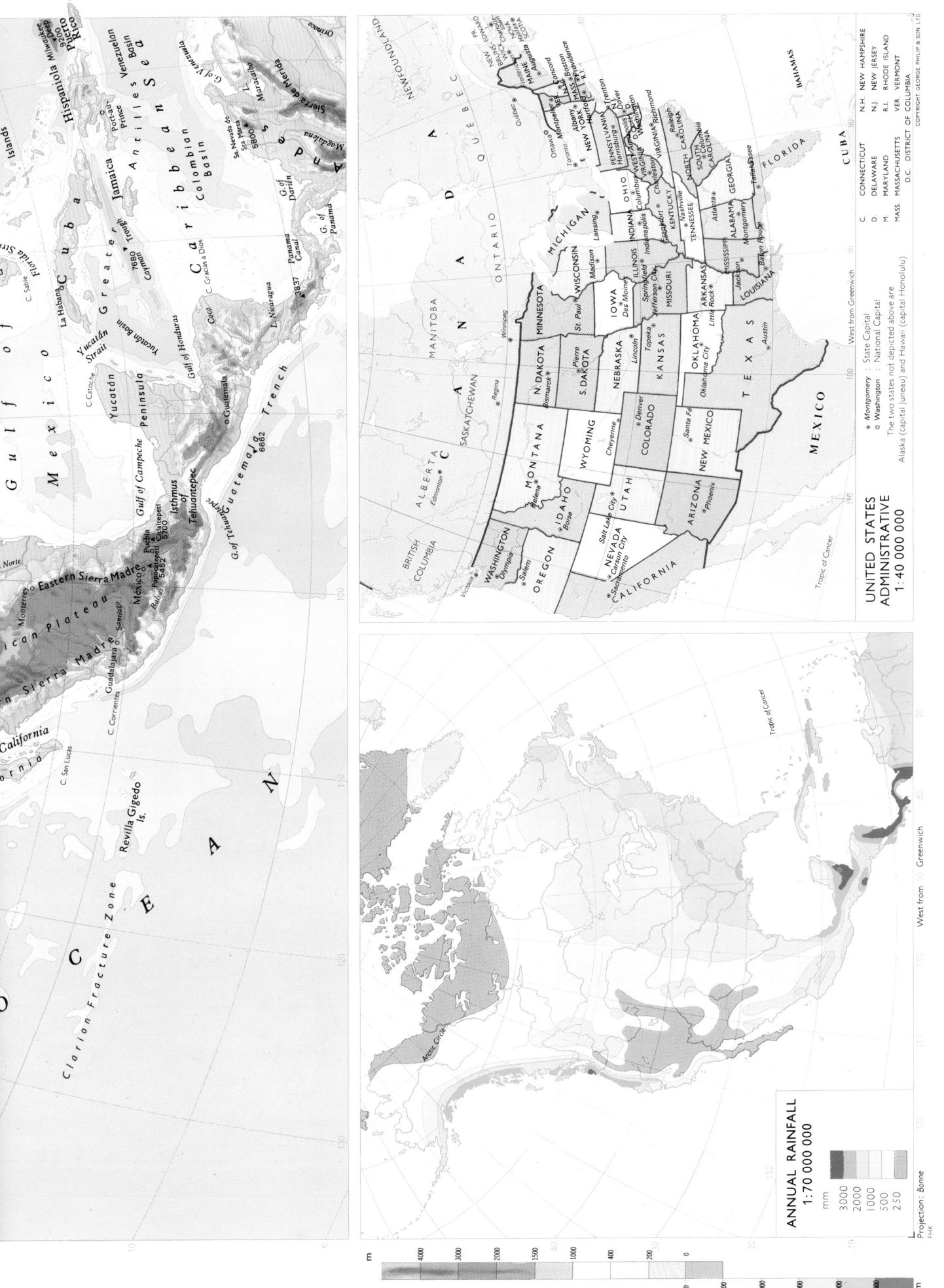

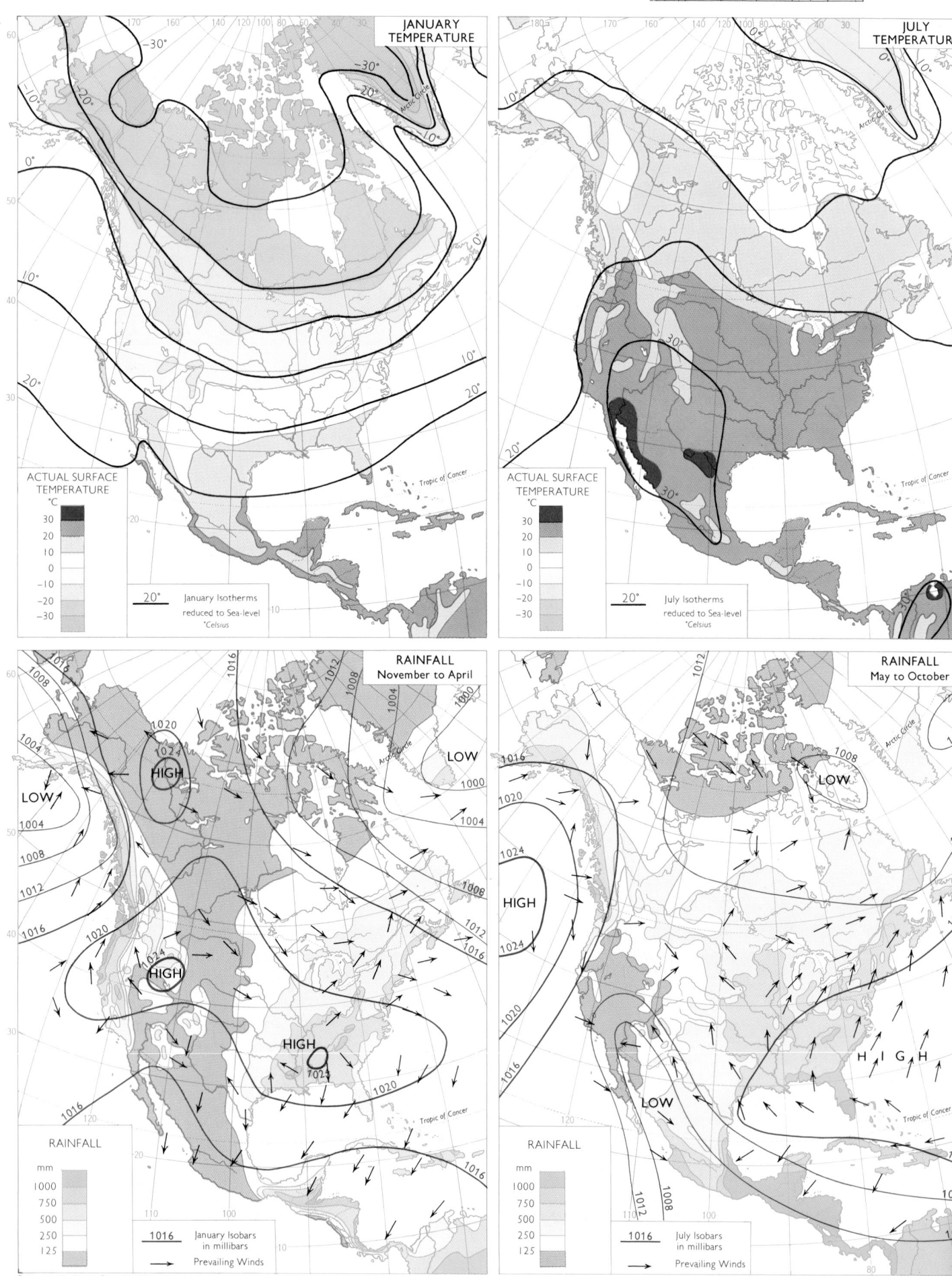

1 : 70 000 000

500   0   500   1000   1500   2000   2500 km

JANUARY
TEMPERATURE

JULY
TEMPERATURE

ACTUAL SURFACE
TEMPERATURE
°C
30
20
10
0
-10
-20
-30

20°   January Isotherms
reduced to Sea-level
°Celsius

ACTUAL SURFACE
TEMPERATURE
°C
30
20
10
0
-10
-20
-30

20°   July Isotherms
reduced to Sea-level
°Celsius

RAINFALL
November to April

RAINFALL
May to October

LOW

HIGH

LOW

HIGH

HIGH

HIGH

LOW

H I G H

LOW

RAINFALL

mm
1000
750
500
250
125

1016   January Isobars
in millibars
→   Prevailing Winds

RAINFALL

mm
1000
750
500
250
125

1016   July Isobars
in millibars
→   Prevailing Winds

Projection: Lambert's Equivalent Azimuthal   West from Greenwich   COPYRIGHT GEORGE PHILIP & S

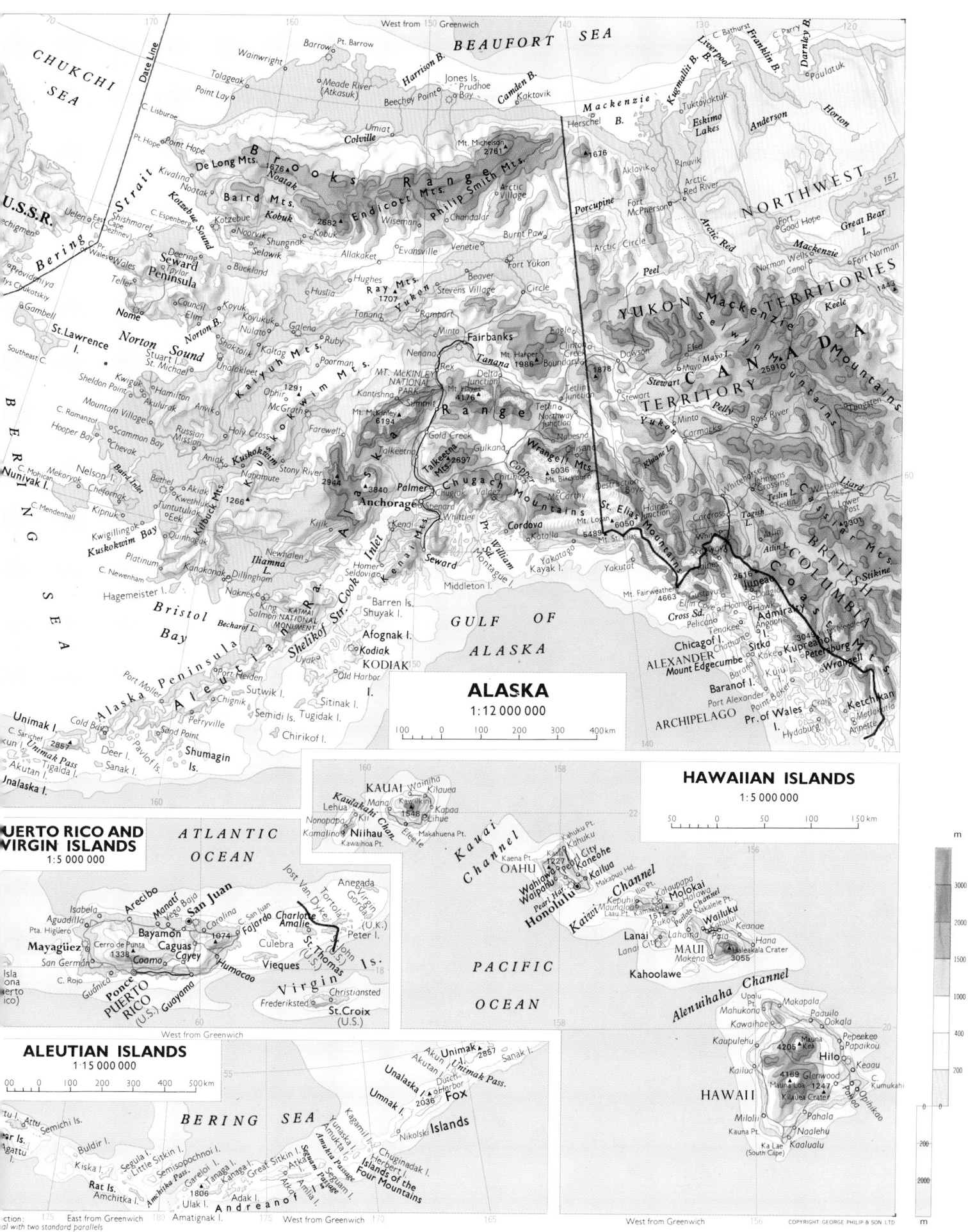

ALASKA
1:12 000 000
100   0   100   200   300   400 km

HAWAIIAN ISLANDS
1:5 000 000
50   0   50   100   150 km

PUERTO RICO AND VIRGIN ISLANDS
1:5 000 000

ALEUTIAN ISLANDS
1:15 000 000
100   0   100   200   300   400   500 km

COPYRIGHT GEORGE PHILIP & SON LTD

1 : 15 000 000

100   0   100   200   300   400   500   600 km

GREENLAND

ATLANTIC

Baffin Bay

Davis Strait

Hudson Strait

Ungava Bay

Ungava Peninsula

COAST OF LABRADOR

NEWFOUNDLAND

St. John's

QUEBEC

James Bay

Gulf of St. Lawrence

St-PIERRE et MIQUELON (Fr.)

PR. EDWARD I.

NEW BRUNSWICK

NOVA SCOTIA

Halifax

MONTRÉAL

Québec

Ottawa

MAINE

TORONTO

NEW YORK

VERMONT

NEW HAMPSHIRE

MASS.

Boston

CONN.

R.I.

NEW YORK

PENNSYLVANIA

NEW JERSEY

DETROIT

OHIO

INDIANA

OCEAN

West from Greenwich

COPYRIGHT. GEORGE PHILIP & SON LTD.

N.W TERRITORIES

MANITOBA

ONTARIO

HUDSON BAY

JAMES BAY

Belcher Islands

North Belcher Is.
Baker's Dozen Is.
Kugong I.
Flaherty I.
Tukarak I.
Innetalling I.
Nastapoka Is.

L. Minto
L. Guillaume-Delisle
L. à l'Eau Claire
Petite Baleine
Grand Baleine
Lac Bie

Akimiski I.
Charlton I.
North Twin I.
South Twin I.
Weston I.
Ekwan Pt.
Trodely I.

Fort George
Nouveau Comptoir
Eastmain
Fort Rupert (Rupert House)

QUÉBEC

Thunder Bay
Duluth
Superior
Sault Ste. Marie
Sudbury
North Bay
Timmins
Kirkland Lake
Rouyn
Noranda
Val d'Or
Cochrane
Kapuskasing
Hearst
Geraldton
Nipigon

LAKE SUPERIOR
LAKE MICHIGAN
LAKE HURON
LAKE ERIE
LAKE ONTARIO

Isle Royale
Manitoulin I.
Georgian Bay
Parry Sound

WISCONSIN
MICHIGAN
INDIANA
OHIO
PENNSYLVANIA

Milwaukee
Madison
Green Bay
Chicago
Rockford
Detroit
Toledo
Cleveland
Grand Rapids
Flint
Saginaw
Bay City
Lansing
Kalamazoo
London
Windsor
Sarnia
Hamilton
Toronto
Buffalo
Rochester
Syracuse
Ottawa
Kingston
Brockville
Cornwall
Niagara Falls
St. Catharines
Peterborough
Barrie
Guelph
Kitchener
Brantford

Lambert's Equivalent Azimuthal

m
1500
1000
400
200
0
0
200
2000
4000
m

1:7 000 000

50   0   50   100   150   200   250   300 km

55

50

NEW FOUNDLAND

COAST OF

LABRADOR

QUEBEC

South Aulatsivik I.
High I.
Nain
Paul I.
Voisey B.
Tunungayualok I.
Davis Inlet
Nunaksaluk I.
Hopedale

Erlandson
Whale
Fraser
George
Kogaluk
L. de la
Hutte
Sauvage
L.
Nachicapau
L.

Fort
McKenzie

Chakonipau L.
Otelnuk L.
Wheeler

Champdoré
L.
Tudor
L.
610
Whitegull
L.
Mistastin
L.
Big Bay
Harp L.

Seal L.
Nipishish
L.
Rigolet
Makkovik
Aillik
Adlavik I.
C. Harrison
Kaipokok B.
Big
Holton
Indian Harbour
Grosswater

Attikamagen L.
Schefferville
Kanairiktok R.
Naskaupi
Smallwood
Reservoir
North-West River
Goose Bay
Happy Valley
Churchill
Churchill Falls
Grand
L. Melville
1128
Mealy Mts.
Paradise
Eagle
Cartwright
Sandwich B.
Island of Ponds
Separation
Point
Table B.
Square Islands

Lac Verneuil
Lac
Clairambault
ac Delorme
L. Bermen
Shabōgamo
L.
Opiskotish L.
Labrador City
Wabush
Lac
Joseph
Ossokmanuan
Lobstick L.
Winokapau
L.
Lac
Atikonak
Minipi
L.
Alexis
St. Lewis
Mary's
Harbour
Red
Bay
Battle Harbour
Belle I.
Str. of Belle Isle
St. Lundaire-
Griquet

Kaniapiskau
L.
L. Naococane
Opiscoteo
L.
1128
Monchalagane
Petit Lac
Manicouagan
Gagnon
Rés.
Manicouagan
Burnt
L.
Little Mecatina
L.
St. Augustin
St-Paul R.
Anse-au-Loup
Forteau
Lourdes-de-
Blanc-Sablon
Bradore Bay
Flower's
Cove
Hare B.
St. Anthony
Groais I.

Pétipi
L.
Nascaupi
Manouane
Ouiards
Betsiamites
Nipissis
1048
Manitou
Moisie
Ste-Marguerite
West Manie
Lac Allard
Natashquan
Nabisipi
Aguanus
Olomane
St-Augustin
Saguenay
Outer I.
I. du
Petit-Mécatina
Harrington Harbour
Daniel's
Harbour
Port
Saunders
Great
Harbour
Deep
Roddickton
Englee
Conche
Bell I.

Péribonca
Rés.
Pipmuacan
Godbout
Clarke
City
Moisie
Port-Cartier
Walker
Rivière-Pentecôte
Pte. Ouest
Port-Menier
Havre-St-Pierre
Mingan
Aguanish
Natashquan
Gethsémoni
Kegaska
Etamamu
Musquaro
L.
White B.
Horse Is.
C. St John
La Scie
Baie
Verte
Notre Dame
Long Range Mts.
Seal Cove
Sop's
Arm
Springdale
South
Brook
Lewisporte
Fogo I.
Fogo
Carmonville
Twillingate

Manouane
Baie-
Comeau
Baie-Trinité
Cap-Chat
Ste-Anne
Mont-Louis
Grande-Vallée
Dét. Sud Ouest
Rivière-
au-Renard
C. de Gaspé
Dét. de Jacques-Cartier
Î. d'Anticosti
Jupiter
Heath Pt.
Trout River
Deer
Lake
Cox's
Bay of Islands
Corner Brook
814
Cow Head
Howley
Windsor
Grand Falls
Badger
Bishop's Falls
Botwood
Gander
Glenwood
Gambo
Dark Cove
Glovertown
Wesleyville
Bonavista
C. Bonavista
Bonavista
Catalina

Forestville
Hauterive
Les Escoumins
Betsiamites
 parc prov.
de la
gaspesie
Mt-Jacques-
Cartier
1310
Mts. Chic-Chocs
Pén. de Gaspé
Gaspé
Percé
Grande-Rivière
Chandler
572
GULF OF
ST. LAWRENCE
Long Pt.
Port au Port B.
Port au Port
Stephenville
St. George's
St. David's
South Branch
Victoria
Res.
Red Indian
Buchans
NEWFOUNDLAND
Grand L.
Grey Res.
Salmon
Res.
381
Blandford
Clarenville
Trinity
Trinity B.
Bay de Verde
Carbonear
Harbour
Grace
Conception B.
Spaniard's Bay
Holyrood
St. John's
Mt.
Pearl
Torbay

Chicoutimi
Bergeronnes
Grandes-
Bergeronnes
Saguenay
Tadoussac
St-Siméon
La Malbaie
Baie-
St-Paul
1190
Mont-
Joli
Matane
Amqui
Causapscal
Matapédia
Bonaventure
Pospébiac
Miscou I.
Grande-Entrée
Îs. de la
Madeleine
(Quebec)
Cap-aux-Meules
Havre-Aubert
St. Paul
C. North
Brion
St. Andrew's
C. Ray
Channel-Port
aux Basques
Isle aux Morts
Rose Blanche
Long Range Mts.
Burgeo
Ramea
François
White
Bear
Res.
St. Alban's
Belleoram
Terrenceville
Bay L'Argent
Marystown
Placentia
Argentia
Placentia B.
St. Bride's
Burin
St. Lawrence
Harbour Breton
Fortune B.
Grand
Bank
Fortune
St-Pierre
Miquelon
Langlade
SAINT-PIERRE
ET MIQUELON
(Fr.)
Cabot
Strait
C. St Mary's
C. Pine
Trepassey
Avalon
Peninsula
Ferryland
C. Race

Rimouski
Bic
Trois-Pistoles
Dalhousie
Chaleur Bay
Campbellton
Atholville
Lamèque
Shippegan
Tracadie
Rivière-du-Loup
Cabano
Édmundston
Kedgwick
St. Arthur
Bathurst
Belledune
Heath Steele
Nepisiguit
819
Miramichi R.
Bellefeuille
Newcastle
Chatham
Tignish
North Pt.
Alberton
PRINCE EDWARD
ISLAND
Summerside
Kensington
Borden
Charlottetown
Georgetown
Souris
East Pt.
Pleasant Bay
NAT.
PARK.
532
Chéticamp
St. Anns B.
Ingonish
Sydney Mines
New Waterford
Glace Bay
N. Sydney
Sydney
Bras d'Or
Cape Breton
Island
Louisbourg
Fourchu

St-Pascal
Cacouna
St-Alexandre
Fort Kent
Van Buren
St. Leonard
Grand Falls
NEW
BRUNSWICK
Plaster
Rock
Blackville
Collette
Richibucto
Buctouche
Shediac
NOVA SCOTIA
Pictou
New Glasgow
Stellarton
Antigonish
Mulgrave
Port
Hawkesbury
Murray Hr.
L'Ardoise
St. Peters
I. Madame
Chedabucto B.
Canso

Lauzon
Lévis
Montmagny
L'Islet
St-Jean-Port-Joli
St-Pacôme
St. John R.
Allagash
Ashland
Caribou
Presque Isle
Houlton
Hartland
Stanley
Woodstock
Minto
Grand
Chipman
Dame
Petitcodiac
Moncton
Amherst
Springhill
Parrsboro
Truro
Upper
Musquodoboit

Beauceville
St-Georges
Thetford Mines
Eagle L.
Island Falls
Patten
1606
Millinocket
Fredericton
Oromocto
Fredericton
Jct.
Gagetown
Minas
Basin
Windsor
Stewiacke
Dartmouth
Halifax

Moosehead
L.
MAINE
Greenville
Mattawamkeag
Lincoln
Chesuncook
L.
St. John R.
Gage
town
Sussex
Elgin
Rothesay
Saint
John
Bay of Fundy
St. Martins
Minas
St. Chignecto
Joggins
Kentville
Annapolis
Royal
Middleton
Bridgetown
Mahone Bay
Lunenburg
Bridgewater
Sheet Hr.
Musquodoboit Hr.

Moosehead
Jackman
St-Angus
Lac-
Mégantic
Dover-Foxcroft
Old Town
Brewer
Bangor
Ellsworth
Machias
Jonesport
Calais
Eastport
Blacks
Hr.
St. Stephen
Grand
Manan I.
Digby
Weymouth
St. Mary's B.
Yarmouth
Wedgeport
Rossignol
Res.
Liverpool
Port Mouton
Shelburne
Lockeport
Clark's Harbour
C. Sable
ATLANTIC
OCEAN
Sable I.
(Nova Scotia)

Bingham
Mooselook
meguntic L.
Rumford
Berlin
Bethel
Waterville
Augusta
Belfast
Camden
Bar Harbor
Mt. Desert I.
Rockland
Freeport
Sebago
Sanford
Saco
Biddeford
Bath
Brunswick
Portland
Auburn
Lewiston
1917
Dover
Portsmouth
Manchester
Haverhill
Lawrence
Lynn
Gloucester
BOSTON
Brockton

West from Greenwich

70   65   60

65   60

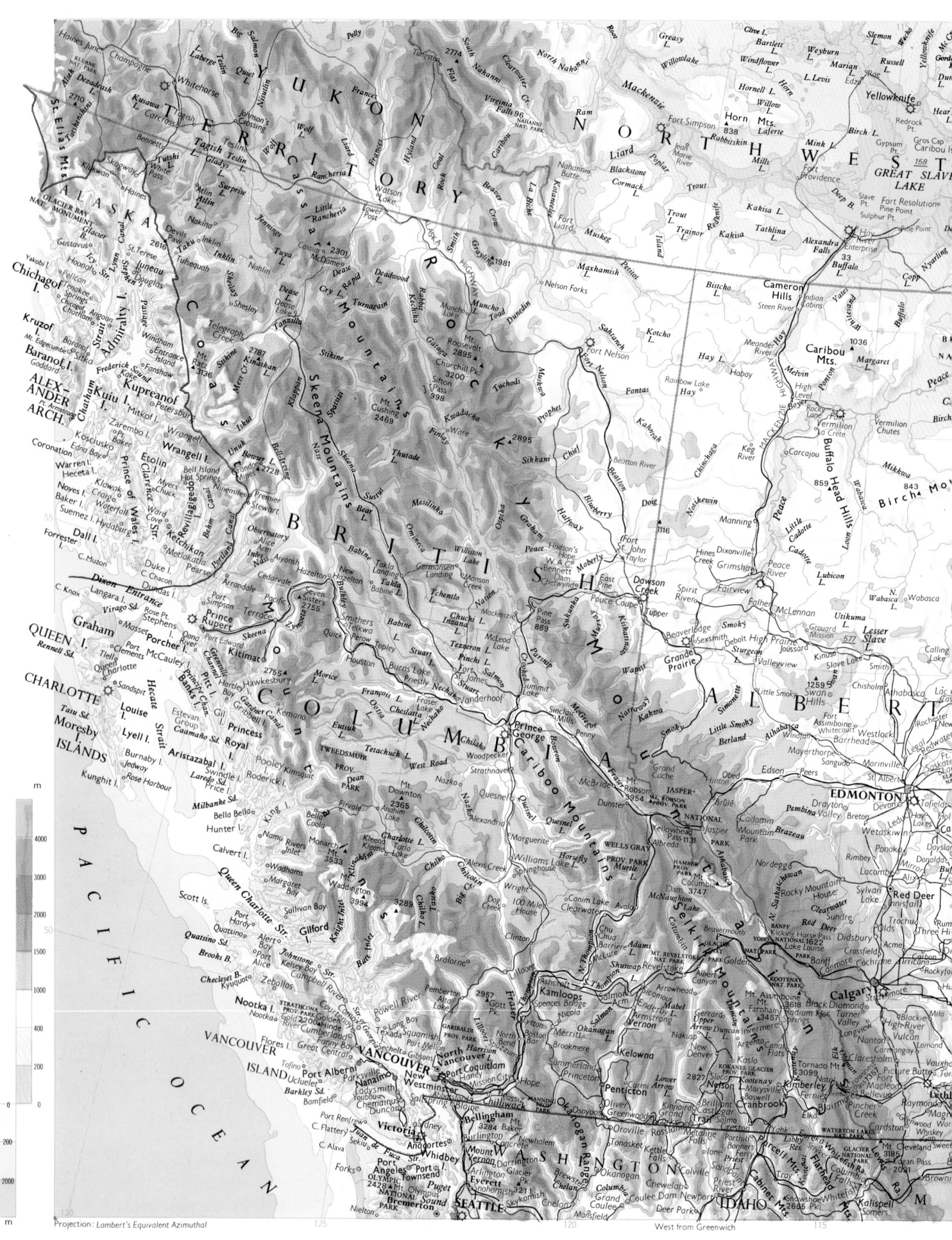

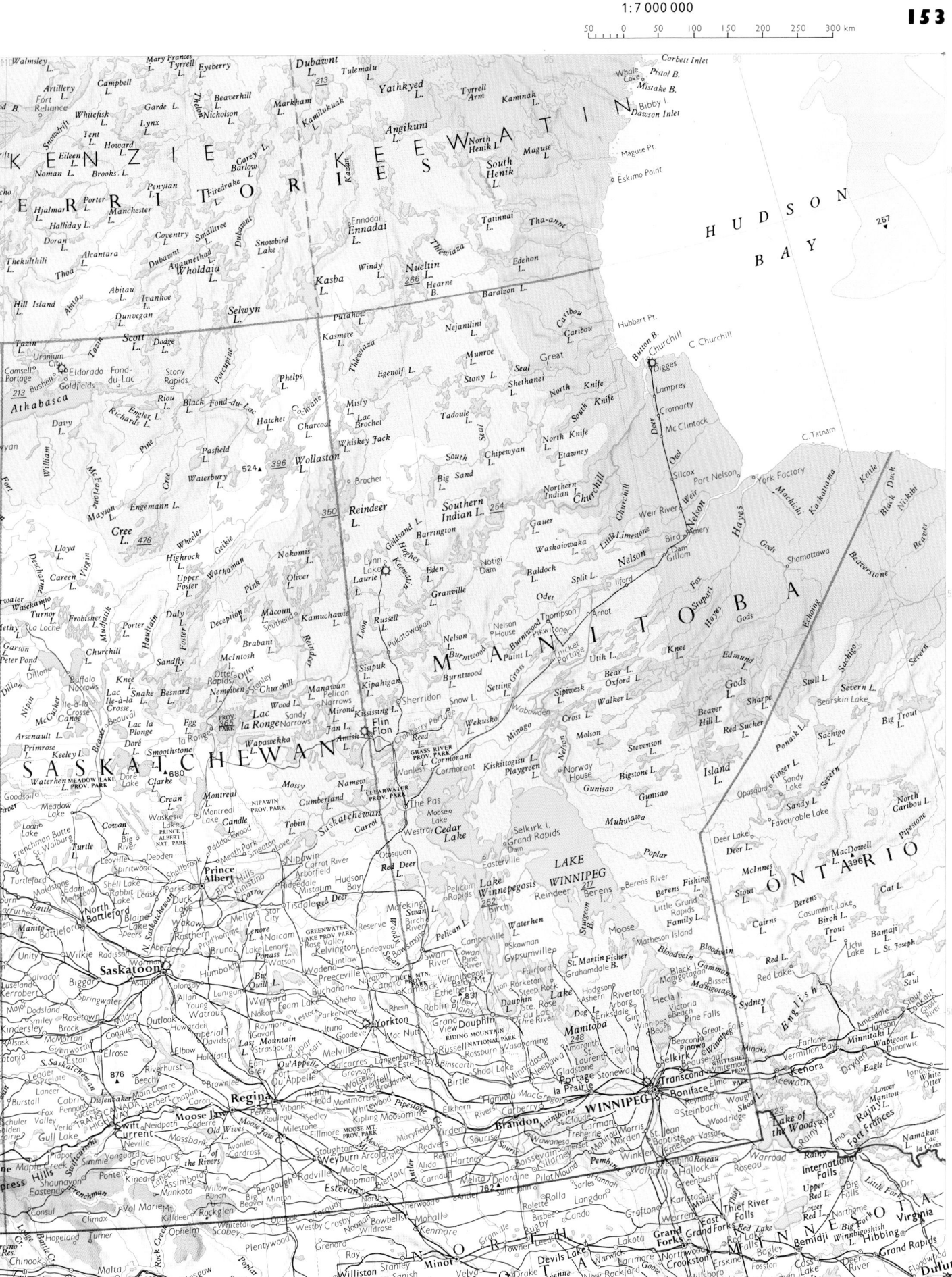

HAWAII
1:10 000 000

0   100   200 km

Projection: Albers' Equal Area with two standard parallels

West from Greenwich

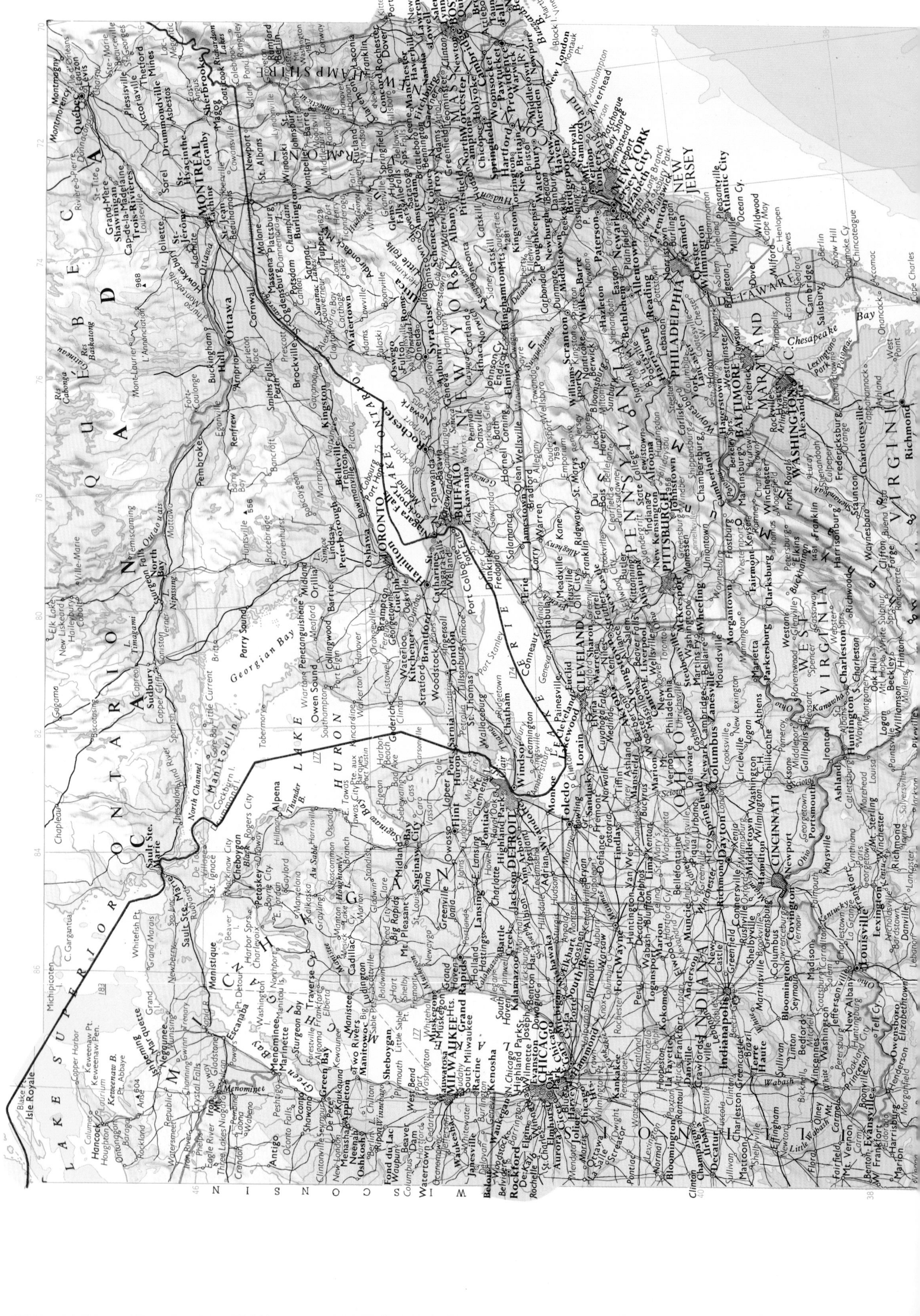

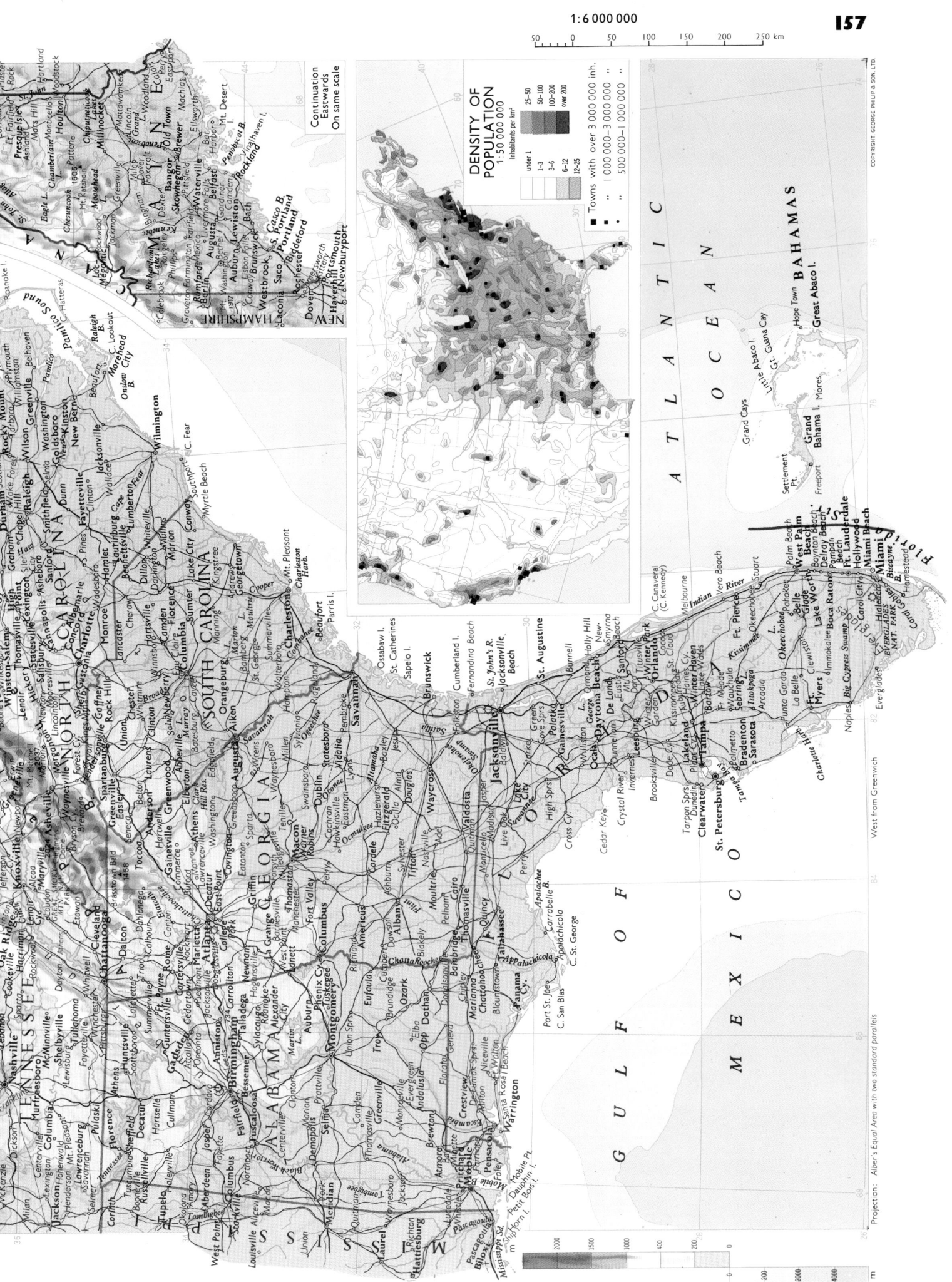

1:6 000 000

50 0 50 100 150 200 250 km

Continuation
Eastwards
On same scale

DENSITY OF
POPULATION
1:50 000 000

inhabitants per km²

under 1
1-3
3-6
6-12
12-25

25-50
50-100
100-200
over 200

■ Towns with over 3 000 000 inh.
  ■ 1 000 000-3 000 000
  ▪ 500 000-1 000 000

ATLANTIC

OCEAN

BAHAMAS

Little Abaco I.
Gt. Guana Cay
Great Abaco I.
Hope Town
Mores

Grand Cays

Settlement
Pt.   Grand
Freeport Bahama I.

COPYRIGHT GEORGE PHILIP & SON LTD.

West from Greenwich

Projection : Alber's Equal Area with two standard parallels

TENNESSEE
NORTH CAROLINA
SOUTH CAROLINA
GEORGIA
ALABAMA
MISSISSIPPI
FLORIDA

GULF OF MEXICO

m
2000
1500
1000
400
200
0

0
200
2000
4000
m

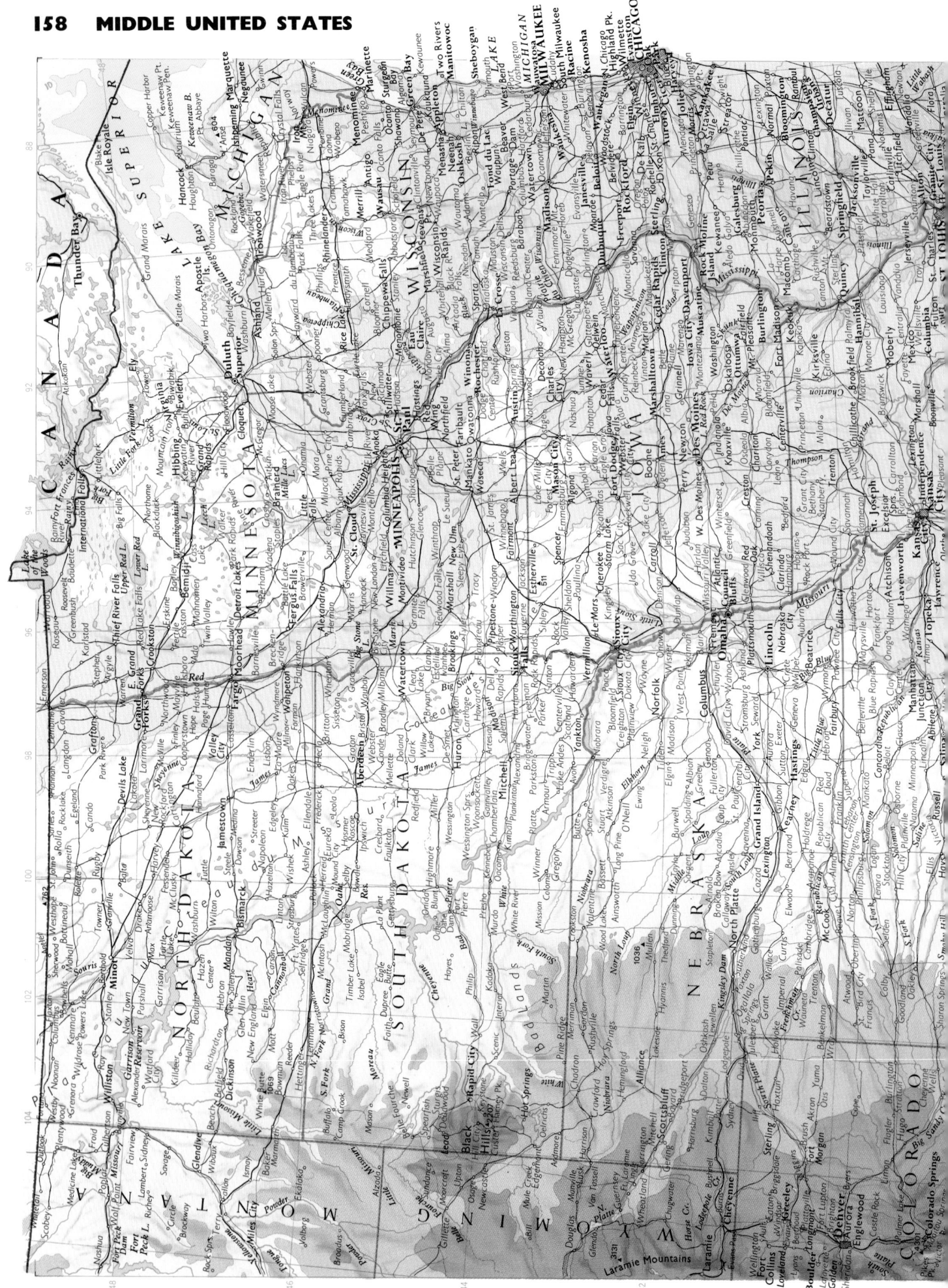

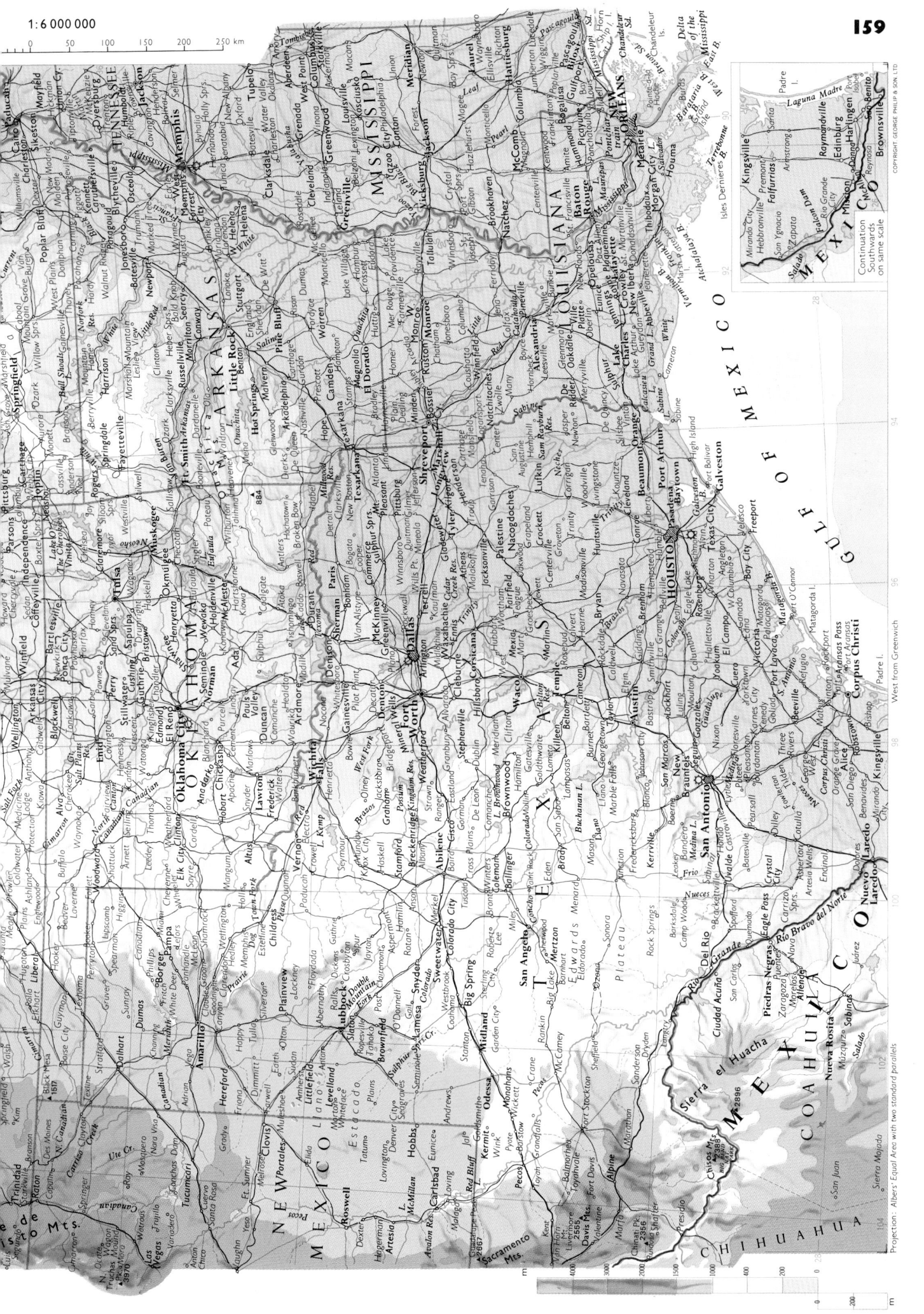

1 : 6 000 000

0 50 100 150 200 250 km

COPYRIGHT GEORGE PHILIP & SON, LTD

Padre I.

Laguna Madre

Continuation
Southwards
on same scale

MEXICO

TENNESSEE

MISSISSIPPI

ARKANSAS

LOUISIANA

OKLAHOMA

T E X A S

NEW MEXICO

COAHUILA

CHIHUAHUA

GULF OF MEXICO

Memphis

New Orleans

Baton Rouge

Jackson

Little Rock

Shreveport

Dallas

Fort Worth

Houston

Galveston

San Antonio

Austin

Waco

Corpus Christi

Oklahoma City

Tulsa

Amarillo

Lubbock

Odessa

El Paso

Laredo

Nuevo Laredo

Piedras Negras

Ciudad Acuña

Del Rio

San Angelo

Abilene

Wichita Falls

Lawton

Springfield

Roswell

Carlsbad

Hobbs

West from Greenwich

Projection: Alber's Equal Area with two standard parallels

1:6 000 000

50   0   50   100   150   200   250 km

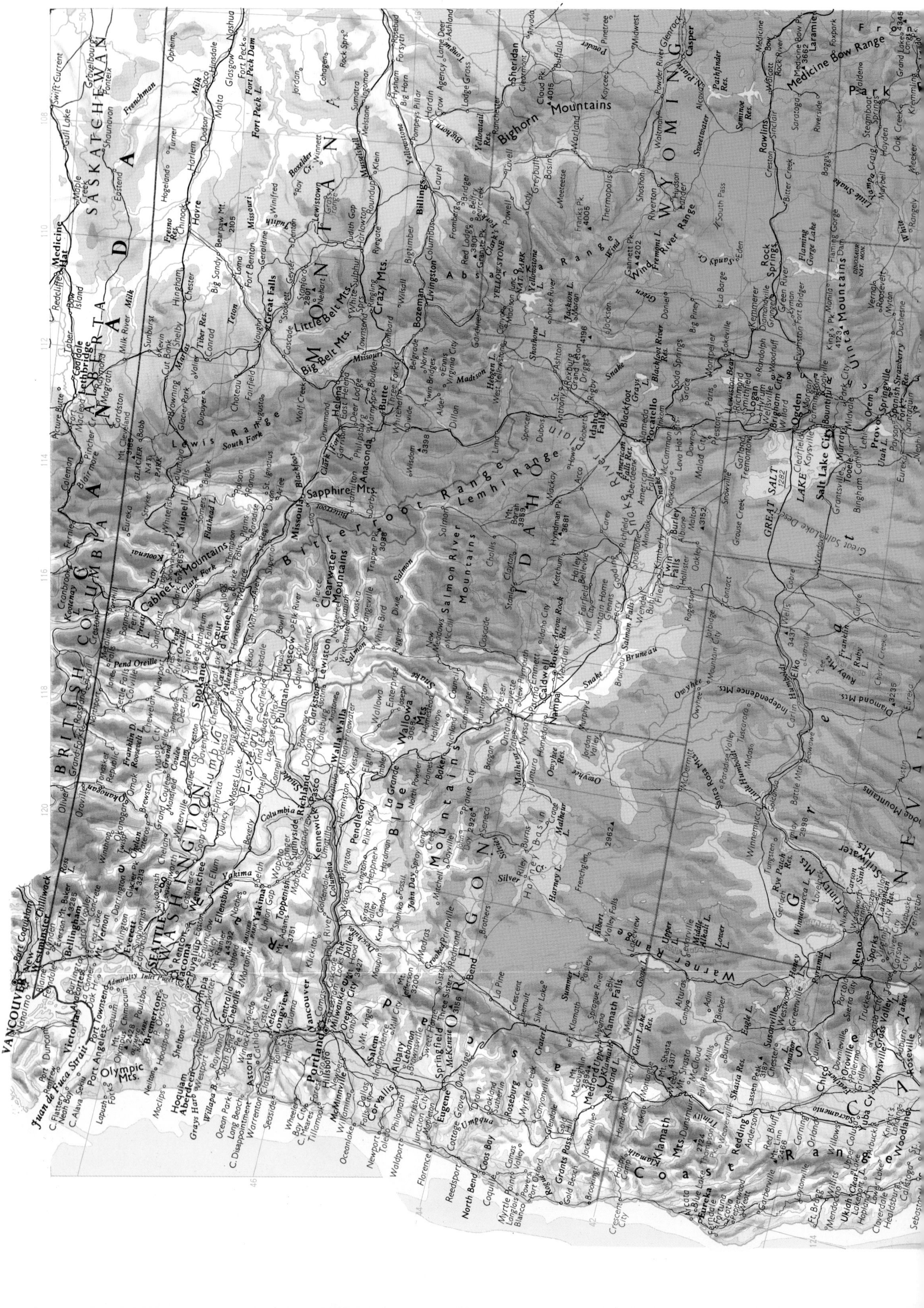

SASKATCHEWAN

ALBERTA

BRITISH COLUMBIA

MONTANA

WYOMING

IDAHO

WASHINGTON

OREGON

NEVADA

UTAH

CALIFORNIA

VANCOUVER

Medicine Hat · Lethbridge · Magrath

Great Falls · Helena · Butte · Bozeman · Billings · Sheridan · Casper

Missoula · Kalispell · Spokane · Lewiston

Seattle · Tacoma · Olympia · Yakima · Wenatchee · Ellensburg

Portland · Salem · Eugene · Corvallis · Bend · Klamath Falls

Boise · Nampa · Caldwell · Twin Falls · Idaho Falls · Pocatello

Salt Lake City · Ogden · Provo

Reno · Redding · Eureka

GREAT SALT LAKE

Bighorn Mountains · Wind River Range · Medicine Bow Range

Bitterroot Range · Salmon River Mountains · Clearwater Mountains

Blue Mountains · Cascade Range · Coast Range

Lewis Range · Little Belt Mts. · Big Belt Mts. · Crazy Mts.

Snake River Plain · Columbia River · Missouri · Yellowstone

Olympic Mts. · Mt. Rainier 4392

YELLOWSTONE NAT. PARK

GLACIER NAT. PARK

Fort Peck Dam · Fort Peck L.

Juan de Fuca Strait

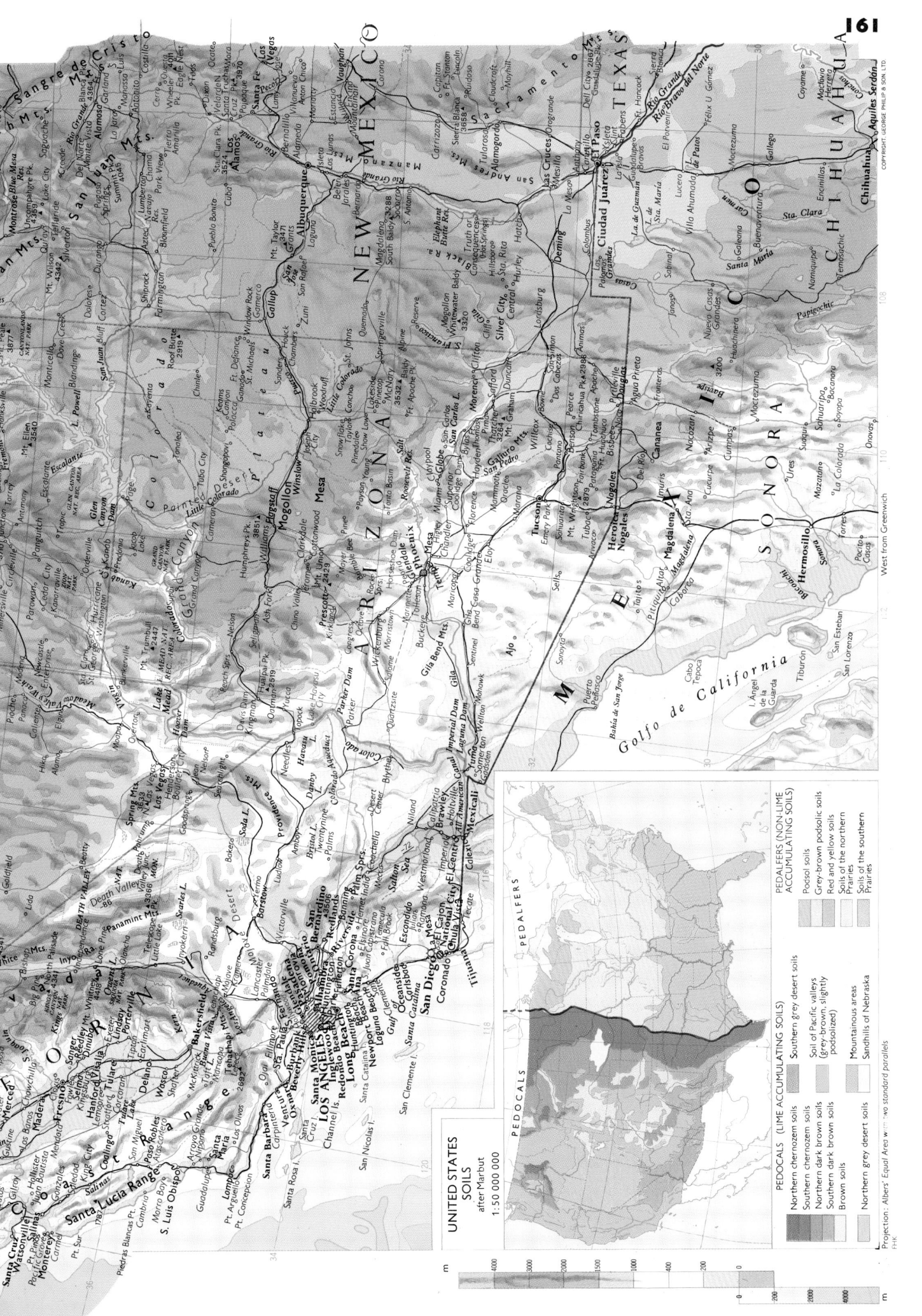

West from Greenwich

COPYRIGHT GEORGE PHILIP & SON LTD

UNITED STATES
SOILS
after Marbut
1 : 50 000 000

PEDOCALS (LIME ACCUMULATING SOILS)

Northern chernozem soils
Southern chernozem soils
Northern dark brown soils
Southern dark brown soils
Brown soils
Northern grey desert soils
Southern grey desert soils
Soil of Pacific valleys
(grey-brown, slightly
podsolized)
Mountainous areas
Sandhills of Nebraska

PEDALFERS (NON-LIME
ACCUMULATING SOILS)

Podsol soils
Grey-brown podsolic soils
Red and yellow soils
Soils of the northern
Prairies
Soils of the southern
Prairies

Projection: Albers' Equal Area with two standard parallels

F.H.K.

m
4000
3000
2000
500
1000
400
200
0

0
200
2000
4000
m

1 : 3 000 000

20 0 20 40 60 80 100 120 km

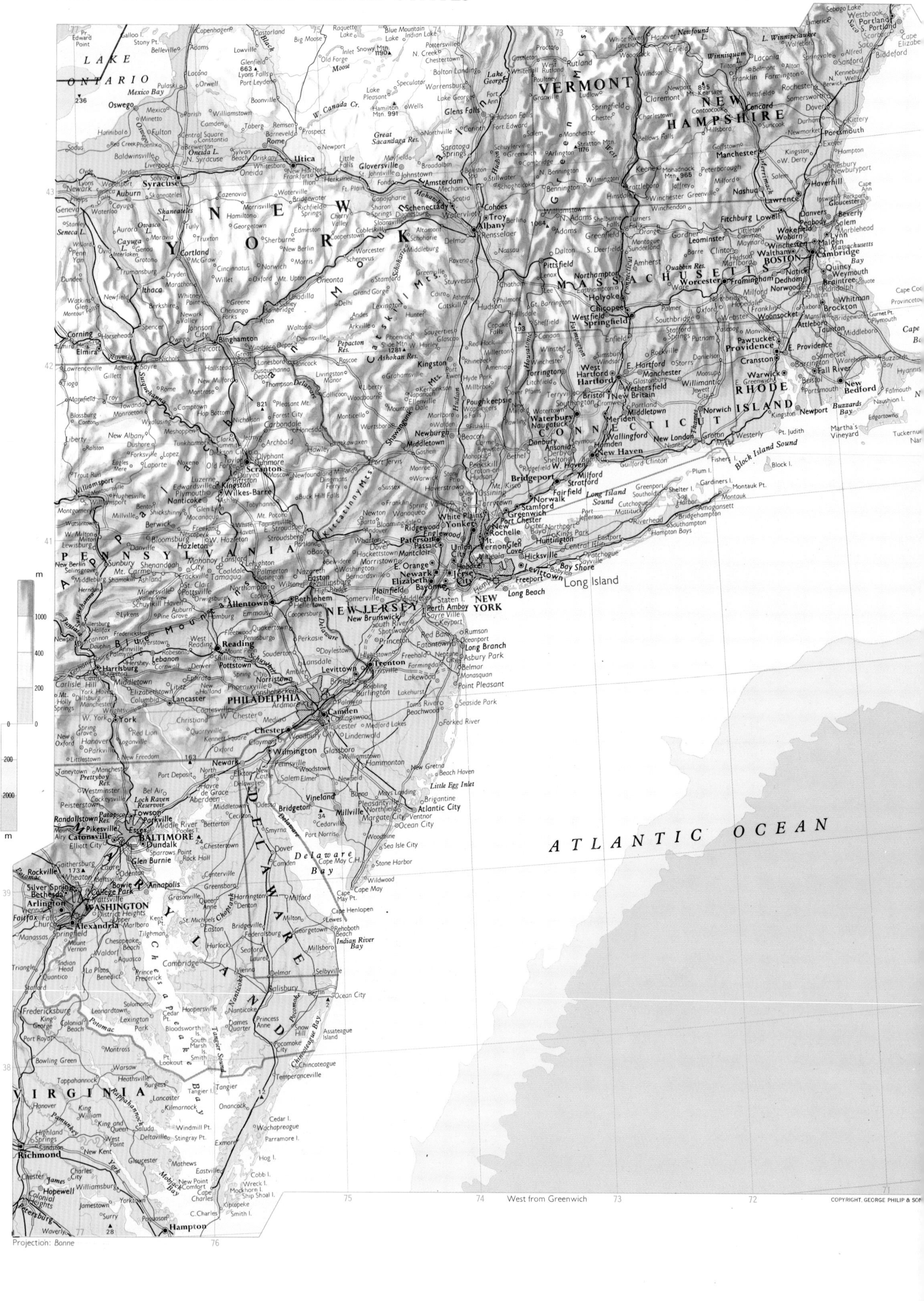

LAKE ONTARIO

VERMONT

NEW HAMPSHIRE

NEW YORK

MASSACHUSETTS

CONNECTICUT

RHODE ISLAND

PENNSYLVANIA

NEW JERSEY

Long Island

NEW YORK

DELAWARE

MARYLAND

VIRGINIA

ATLANTIC OCEAN

Block Island Sound

Delaware Bay

Chesapeake Bay

Oswego Syracuse Utica Rome Albany Schenectady Troy

Binghamton Ithaca Elmira Corning Scranton Wilkes-Barre

Harrisburg Reading Allentown Bethlehem Lancaster York

PHILADELPHIA Camden Trenton Wilmington Chester

BALTIMORE WASHINGTON Alexandria Arlington Annapolis

Richmond Hampton Fredericksburg

Boston Cambridge Worcester Springfield Hartford New Haven

Bridgeport Stamford Providence New Bedford Fall River

Manchester Concord Nashua Lowell Lawrence Portsmouth

Newark Jersey City Elizabeth Paterson Yonkers New Rochelle

Atlantic City Ocean City Cape May

Long Beach Asbury Park Point Pleasant

West from Greenwich

Projection: Bonne

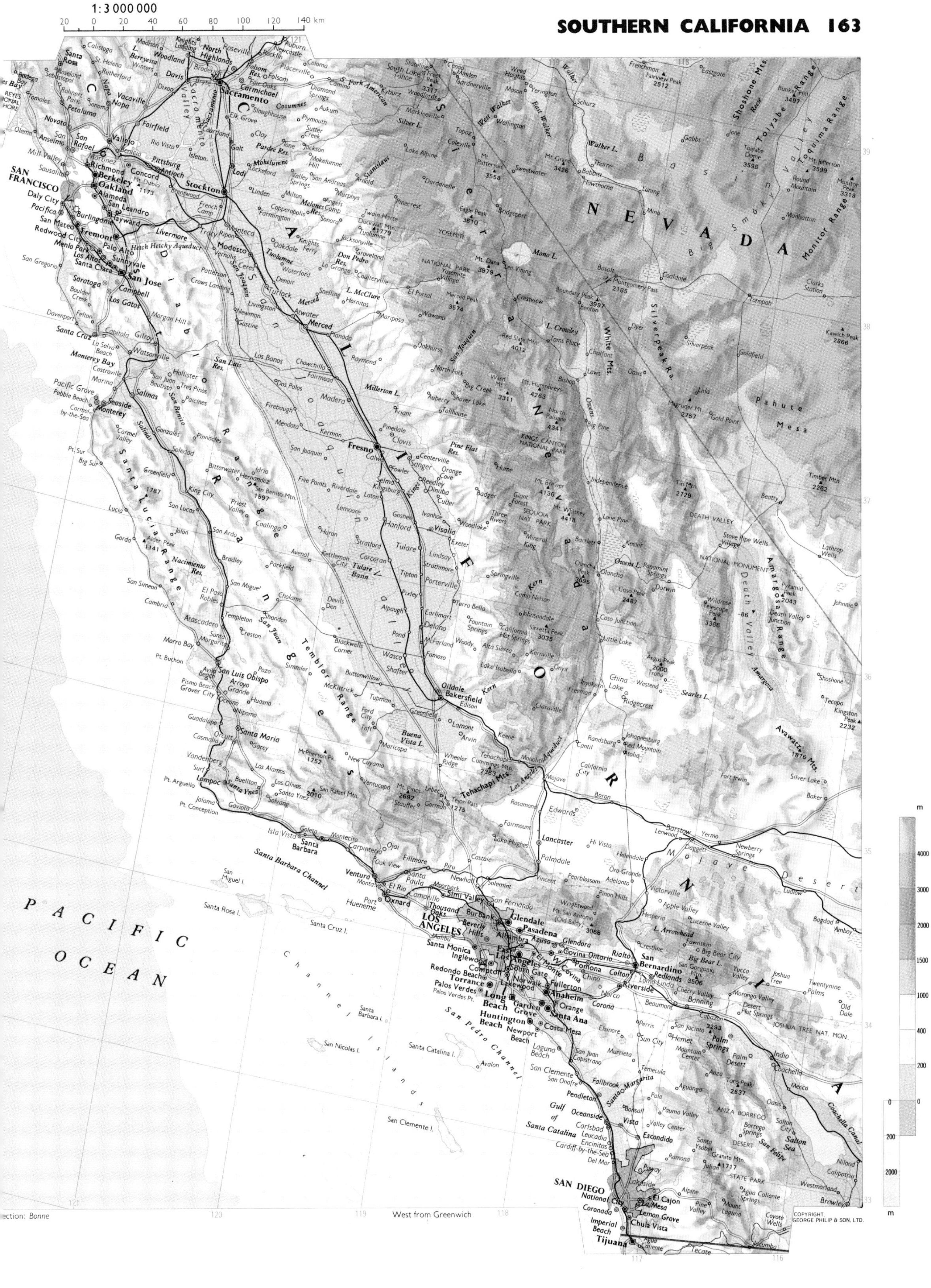

1:3 000 000

20   40   60   80   100   120   140 km

PACIFIC

OCEAN

NEVADA

SAN FRANCISCO
Oakland
Berkeley
Richmond
San Jose
Santa Cruz
Monterey Bay
Monterey
Salinas
Sacramento
Stockton
Modesto
Merced
Fresno
Visalia
Bakersfield
Santa Maria
San Luis Obispo
Santa Barbara
Ventura
Oxnard
LOS ANGELES
Pasadena
Glendale
Long Beach
Anaheim
Santa Ana
San Bernardino
Riverside
Palm Springs
San Diego
Chula Vista
Tijuana

Death Valley
NATIONAL MONUMENT
Mojave Desert
SEQUOIA NAT. PARK
KINGS CANYON NATIONAL PARK
YOSEMITE NATIONAL PARK
Mono L.
JOSHUA TREE NAT. MON.
ANZA BORREGO DESERT STATE PARK
Salton Sea

Projection: Bonne

West from Greenwich

COPYRIGHT.
GEORGE PHILIP & SON. LTD.

REFERENCE TO NUMBERS

1	Federal District	5	México
2	Aguascalientes	6	Morelos
3	Guanajuato	7	Querétaro
4	Hidalgo	8	Tlaxcala

Projection: Bi-polar oblique Conical Orthomorphic

West from Greenwich

1 : 8 000 000

50   0   50   100   150   200   250   300 km

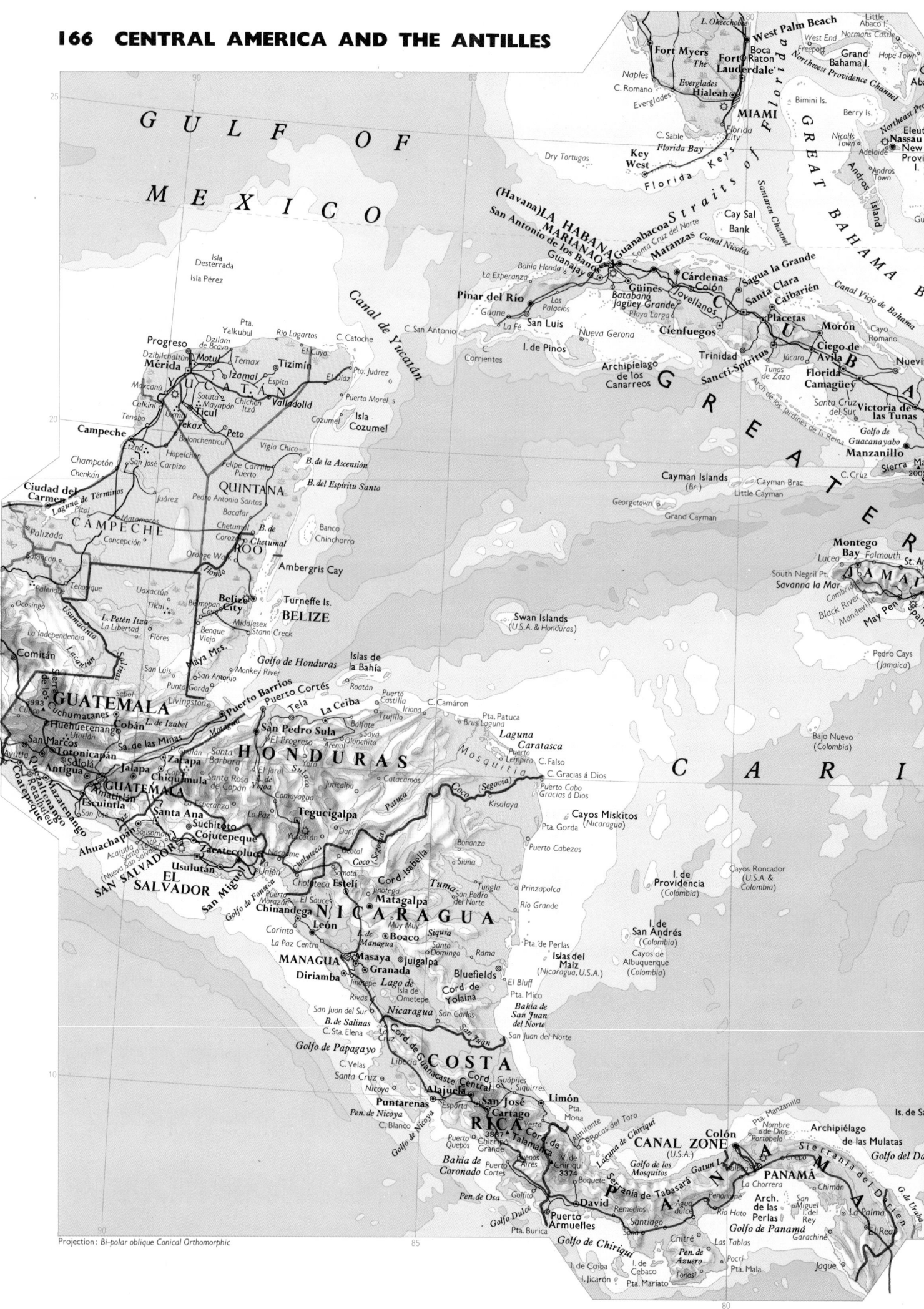

Projection: Bi-polar oblique Conical Orthomorphic

1 : 8 000 000

50   0   50   100   150   200   250   300 km

A T L A N T I C

O C E A N

Tropic of Cancer

San Salvador
(Watling I., Guanahani)
ption I.
um Cay

I.
ence   Atwood or
Crooked I. Passage   Samana Cay
Crooked I.
Plana Cays
Albert   Mayaguana I.
Town   Snug
Corner
Acklins I.
Mira por vos Cay
Hogsty Reef   Caicos Passage
Little Inagua I.   Caicos
Lake Rose   Islands   Turks Islands
(Br.)   (Br.)
Great
Inagua I.

Baracoa
Pta. de
Maisí
Paso de   St.-Marc
los
(Windward) Passage
Cap-à-Foux
Jérémie
Dame
Marie
Massif de la Hotte
Les Cayes   Aquin
Pointe-à-Gravois   I.-à-Vache

Î. de la
Tortue
Port-de-Paix
Cap-Haïtien   Monte Cristi
Fort-Liberté
La Isabela
Santiago de   Puerto Plata
los Cabelleros   La Vega   C. Francés Viejo
Gonaïves   San Francisco de Macorís
HAITI   Hinche   Central   Nagua
DOMINICAN   3175   Sabana de La Mar
Î. de la Gonâve   REP.   Hato Mayor
PORT-   San Juan   C. Engano
AU-PRINCE   San Pedro
2280   Enriquillo   de Macorís   Higüey
Jacmel   Barahona   La Romana
Pedernales   B. de
HISPANIOLA   Compostela   Yuma
SANTO DOMINGO   Saona
I. Beata   C. Beata   San Cristóbal   Isla
A N T I L L E S   Mona
(U.S.A.)

Aguadilla
Arecibo   SAN JUAN
Mayagüez   Bayamón   Fajardo
1338   Ponce   Caguas
B E A N   PUERTO   Guayama
RICO   Charlotte Amalie
(U.S.A.)   Frederiksted   St. Croix
Christiansted

Virgin Gorda   Anegada   Sombrero (Anguilla)
Tortola   Virgin Is.   Anguilla (Br.)
Road Town   (Br.)   St.-Martin (Guad.)
Virgin Is.   St. Maarten   St.-Barthélemy (Fr.)
(U.S.A.)   (Neth.)   Saba (Neth.)   Barbuda (Br.)
St. Eustatius   St. Christopher (St. Kitts)
(Neth.)   Nevis   St. Johns
Basseterre   (Br.)   Antigua (Br.)
Redonda
Montserrat   Guadeloupe Passage
(Br.)
Ste-Rose   Moule   Désirade
(Fr.) GUADELOUPE   Pointe-à-Pitre (Fr.)
Basse-Terre   Marie-Galante   Grand-Bourge
I. des Saintes   (Guad.)
(Guad.)   Dominica Passage
I. de Aves (Bird I.)   Portsmouth   Dominica
(Venezuela)   Roseau   (Br.)
Martinique Passage
Ste-Marie
Mt. Pelée   François
1397   Rivière-Pilot
Fort-de-France   MARTINIQUE
St. Lucia Channel   (Fr.)
Castries   St. Lucia
Soufrière   (Br.)
St. Vincent Passage
Soufrière 1234   St. Vincent
Kingstown   (Br.)   Speightstown
Bridgetown
Hillsborough   BARBADOS
The Grenadines
St. George's   GRENADA

LEEWARD ISLANDS
WINDWARD ISLANDS   LESSER   ANTILLES

S E A

L E S S E R   A N T I L L E S

Aruba   Curaçao
(Neth.)   (Neth.)   Bonaire (Neth.)   I. Blanquilla (Ven.)
Pta. Gallinas   I. Orchila   I. Los Hermanos
Willemstad   (Ven.)   (Ven.)
C. San Román   I. de Aves   I. Los Testigos
Pen. de la   Pta.   Pen. de   (Ven.)   Is. Los Roques   (Ven.)
Guajira   Espada   Paraguaná   (Ven.)   Tobago
Punto Fijo   Scarborough
Ríohacha   Uribia   Puerto   I. Margarita   La Asunción   Galera
Santa   C. San Juan   GUAJIRA   Punta   Cumarebo   NUEVA   Porlamar   Pt.
Marta   de Guía   Cardón   La Vela de Coro   I. La Tortuga   ESPARTA   Pen. de Paria   Port of   Arima
Golfo de   Coro   (Ven.)   Carúpano   Spain   Trinidad
Cienaga   Venezuela   Tucacas   Maiquetía   Río Caribe   Güiria   Río Claro
Soledad   San   FALCÓN   La Guaira   Golfo de Paria   TRINIDAD
Santa   Rafael   Altagracia   Mene de Mauroa   CARACAS   C. Codera   Cumaná   SUCRE   San Fernando   & TOBAGO
Sabanalarga   Nevada de   MARACAIBO   Maracay   Higuerote   Puerto   Caripito   Serpent's Mouth
undación   Santa Marta   La   Baragua   Puerto   Los Teques   Río Chico   La Cruz   Maturin
Calamar   5800   Concepción   Cabimas   San Felipe   Cabello   Ocumare del Tuy   Barcelona   Caripe
Magdalena   Cuidad   Mene   YARACUY   MIRANDA   Aragua de   Anaco   MONAGAS
Plato   Ojeda   Grande   Carora   Villa   Barcelona   DELTA-
Zambrano   CÉSAR   Machiques   BARQUISIMETO   Maritagua de   Villa   Cantaura   Tucupita   AMACUR
Magangué   ZULIA   Lago de   TACHIRA   los Morros   de Cura   El Tigre
Mompós   Maracaibo   La Ceiba   El Tocuyo   San Juan de   Altagracia   Ciudad Guayana
El Banco   TRUJILLO   los Morros de Orituco
NORTE   Betijoque   Acarigua   COJEDES   El Sombrero   Valle de   Sierra Imataca
DE   Trujillo   PORTUGUESA   San Carlos   la Pascua   Soledad
Ocaña   San   Valera   del Zulia   El Baúl   G U A R I C O   Ciudad
SANTANDER   Carlos   MÉRIDA   Barinas   Pariaguán   ANZOÁTEGUI   Bolívar
casia   Cúcuta   TACHIRA   Barbara   Ciudad   Santa María   El Pao
Simití   V E N E Z U E L A   Bolívia   BARINAS   de Ipire   Mapire   Guasipati
MÉRIDA   Libertad   San   Guri   El Callao
Majagual   Pta. de Nutrias   Fernando de   Orinoco   Tumeremo
casia   Achaguas   Apure   APURE   Cáicara
West from Greenwich   Cunaviche

m
4000
3000
2000
1500
1000
400
200
0
m
200
2000
4000
6000
8000
m

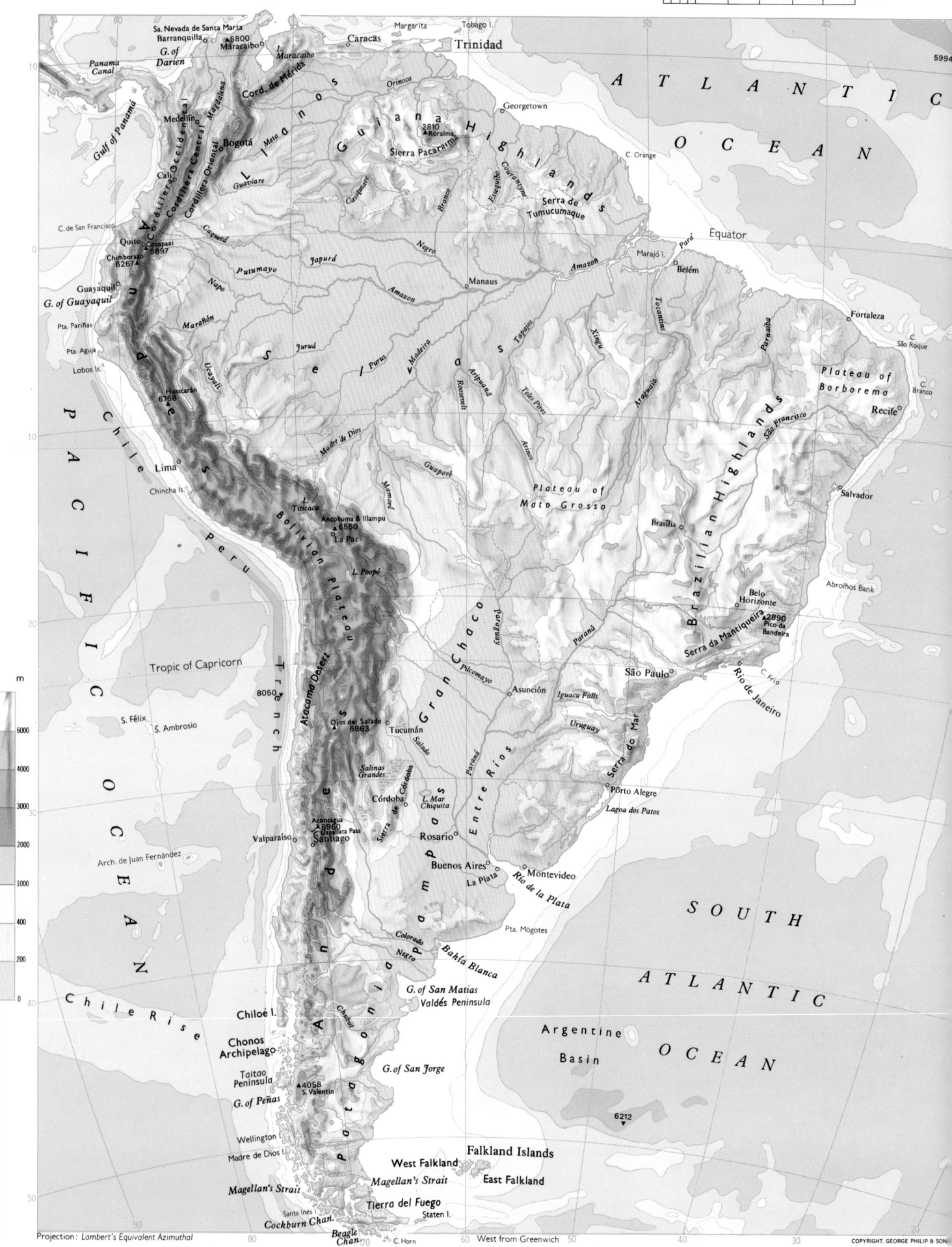

1 : 30 000 000

200   0   200   400   600   800 1000 km

5994

PACIFIC OCEAN

ATLANTIC OCEAN

SOUTH ATLANTIC OCEAN

Panama Canal
Gulf of Darien
Sa. Nevada de Santa Marta
Barranquilla
Maracaibo ▲5800
G. of Darien
L. Maracaibo
Cord. de Mérida
Margarita
Caracas
Tobago I.
Trinidad
Orinoco
Llanos
Georgetown
C. Orange
Medellín
Cordillera Occidental
Cordillera Central
Cordillera Oriental
Magdalena
Bogotá
Cali
Guaviare
Meta
Guiana Highlands
2810 ▲ Roraima
Sierra Pacaraima
Casiquiare
Branco
Essequibo
Serra de Tumucumaque
C. de San Francisco
Quito
Cotopaxi ▲5897
Chimborazo ▲6267
Putumayo
Caquetá
Napo
Japurá
Negro
Amazon
Manaus
Pará
Marajó I.
Belém
Equator
Guayaquil
G. of Guayaquil
Pta. Pariñas
Marañón
Juruá
Purus
Madeira
Tocantins
Fortaleza
S. Roque
Pta. Aguja
Ucayali
Selvas
Xingu
Tapajós
Aripuanã
Roosevelt
Teles Pires
Araguaia
Parnaíba
Plateau of Borborema
Recife
Lobos Is.
Huascarán ▲6768
Madre de Dios
Guaporé
São Francisco
C. Branco
Lima
Chincha Is.
L. Titicaca
Ancohuma & Illampu ▲6550
La Paz
Mamoré
Guaporé
Plateau of Mato Grosso
Brasília
Salvador
Abrolhos Bank
Bolivian Plateau
L. Poopó
Gran Chaco
Paraguay
Paraná
Brazilian Highlands
Belo Horizonte
2890 ▲ Pico da Bandeira
Serra da Mantiqueira
Tropic of Capricorn
8050
Atacama Desert
Ojos del Salado ▲6863
Tucumán
Salado
Pilcomayo
Asunción
Iguacu Falls
Uruguay
São Paulo
Serra do Mar
C. Frio
Rio de Janeiro
S. Félix
S. Ambrosio
Salinas Grandes
Córdoba
Sierra de Córdoba
L. Mar Chiquita
Paraná
Entre Ríos
Pôrto Alegre
Lagoa dos Patos
Aconcagua ▲6960
Uspallata Pass
Santiago
Rosario
Pampas
Valparaíso
Arch. de Juan Fernández
Andes
Buenos Aires
La Plata
Rio de la Plata
Montevideo
Colorado
Negro
Pta. Mogotes
Bahía Blanca
SOUTH
ATLANTIC
OCEAN
Chiloé I.
G. of San Matias
Valdés Peninsula
Argentine Basin
Chonos Archipelago
Chubut
Patagonia
G. of San Jorge
Taitao Peninsula
▲4058
S. Valentin
G. of Peñas
6212 ▼
Wellington I.
Madre de Dios I.
Falkland Islands
West Falkland
Magellan's Strait
Magellan's Strait
East Falkland
Santa Inés I.
Tierra del Fuego
Cockburn Chan.
Beagle Chan.
C. Horn
Staten I.
Chile Rise
Peru Trench
Chile

Projection: Lambert's Equivalent Azimuthal

West from Greenwich

m

6000
4000
3000
2000
1000
400
200
0
0
200
2000
4000
6000
8000

m

1 : 80 000 000

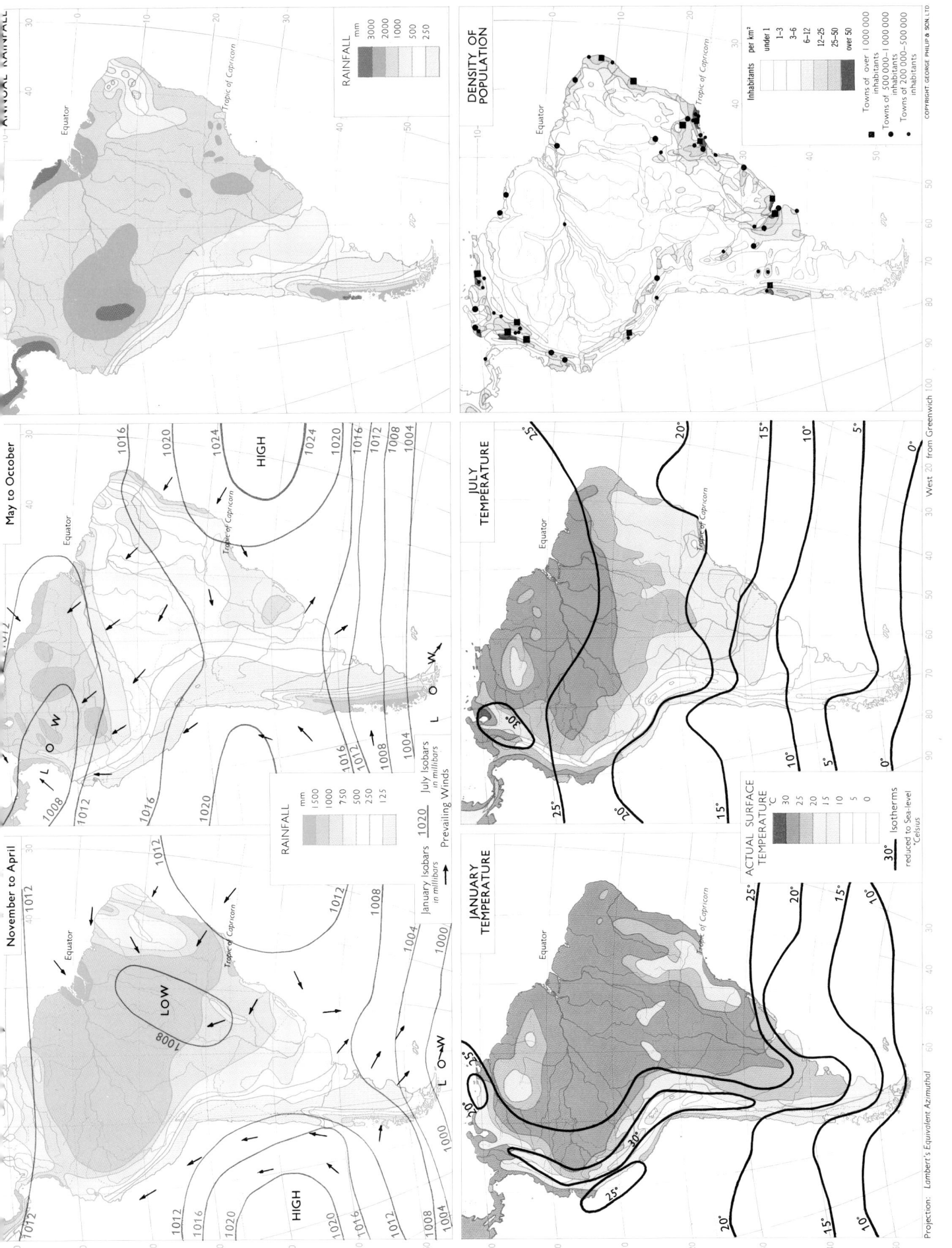

ANNUAL RAINFALL

RAINFALL
mm
3000
2000
1000
500
250

DENSITY OF POPULATION

Inhabitants per km²
under 1
1–3
3–6
6–12
12–25
25–50
over 50

■ Towns of over 1 000 000 inhabitants
■ Towns of 500 000–1 000 000 inhabitants
● Towns of 200 000–500 000 inhabitants

COPYRIGHT GEORGE PHILIP & SON LTD

May to October

HIGH

RAINFALL
mm
1500
1000
750
500
250
125

1020 January Isobars in millibars
1020 July Isobars in millibars
↗ Prevailing Winds

November to April

LOW

HIGH

JULY TEMPERATURE

ACTUAL SURFACE TEMPERATURE
°C
30
25
20
15
10
5
0

30° Isotherms reduced to Sea-level °Celsius

JANUARY TEMPERATURE

Projection : Lambert's Equivalent Azimuthal   West 20 from Greenwich

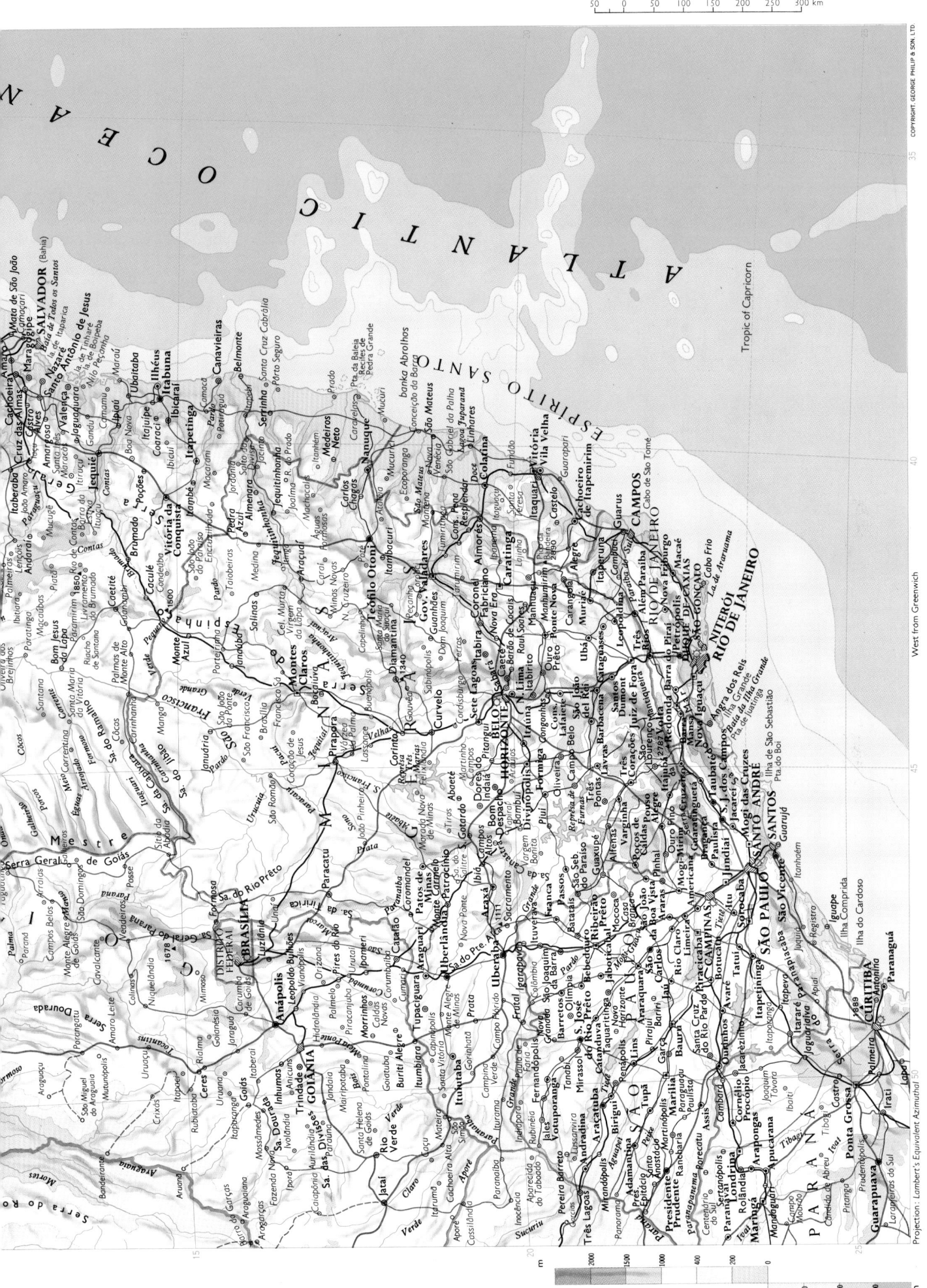

1:8 000 000

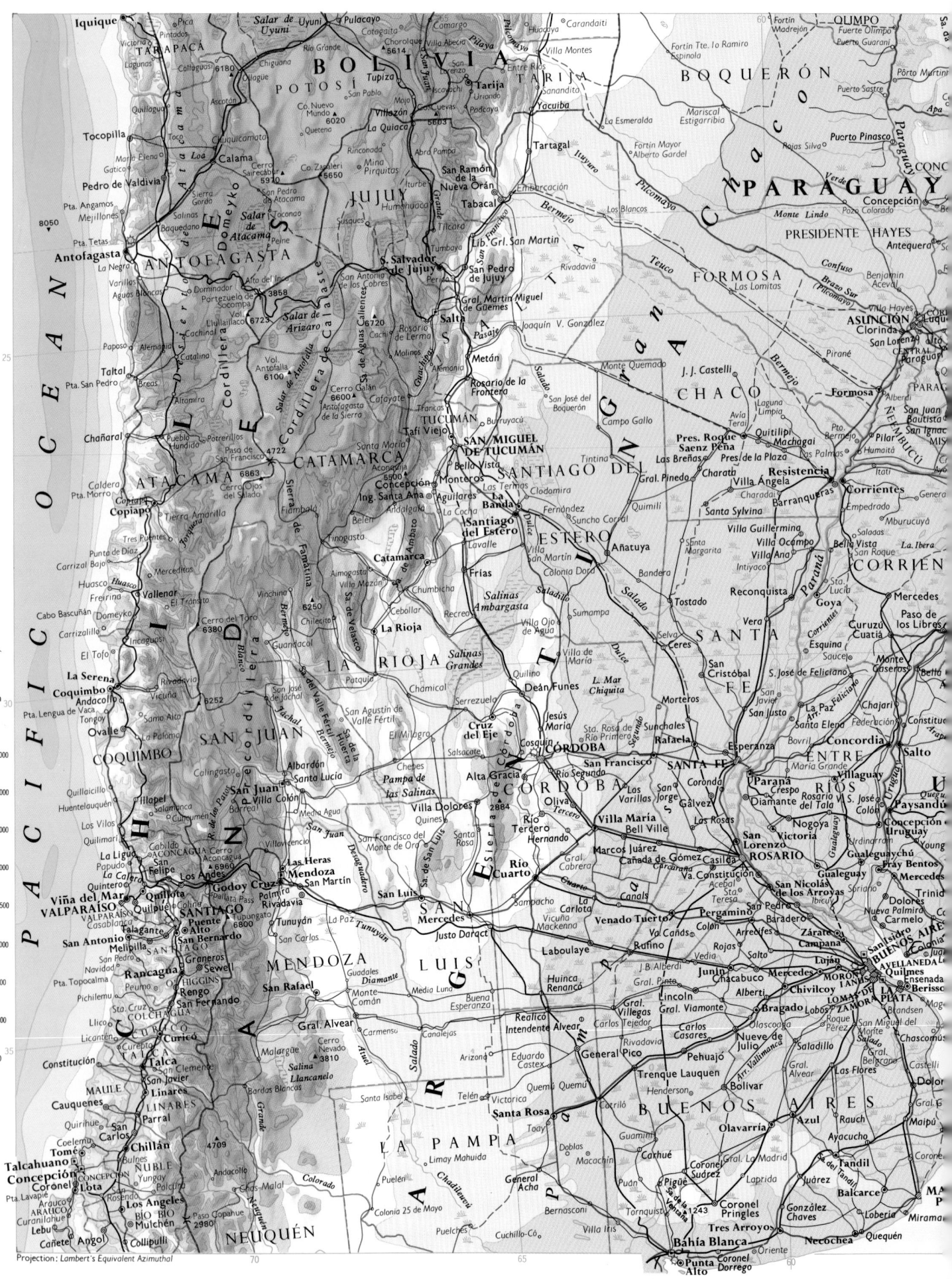

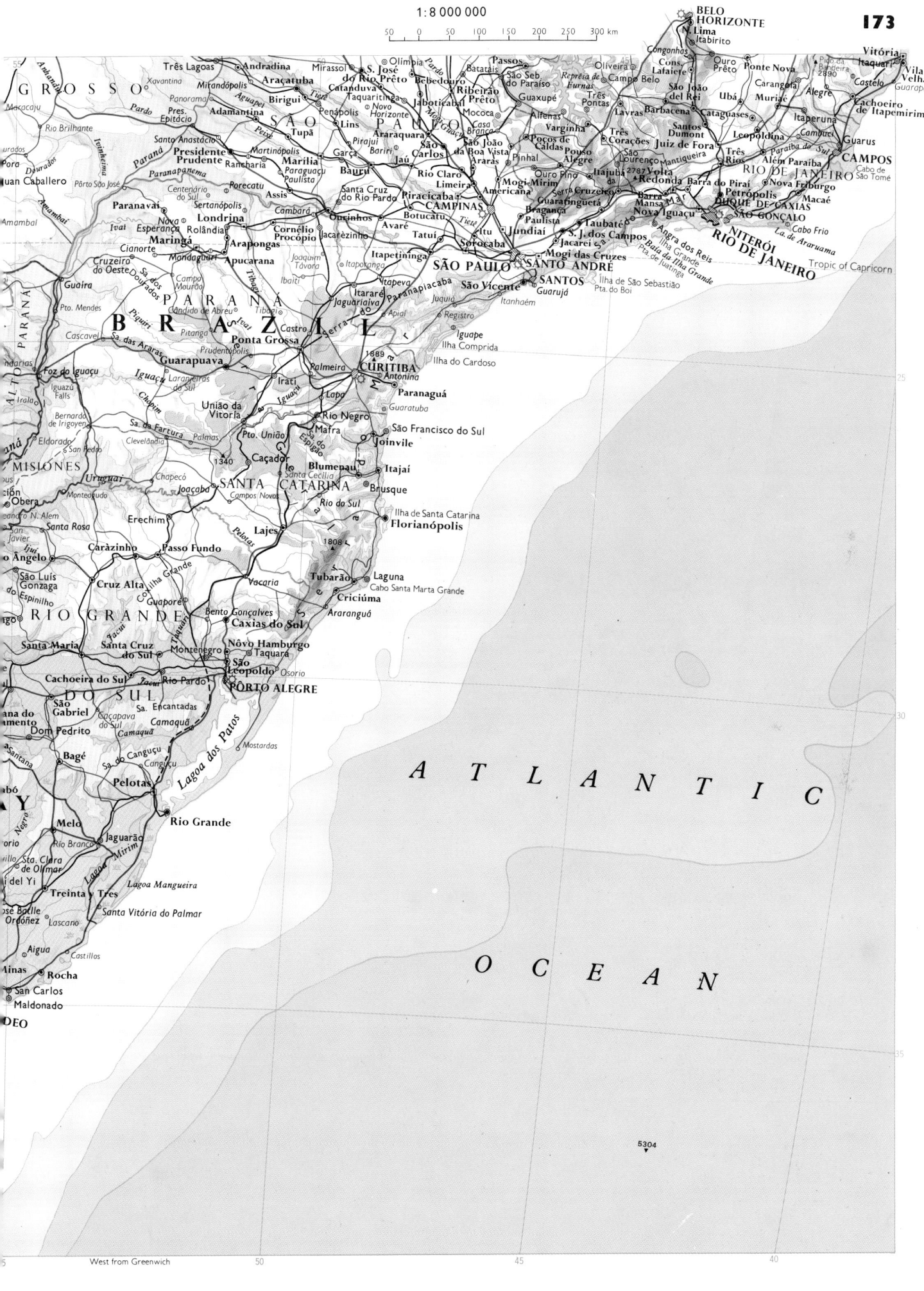

50 0 50 100 150 200 250 300 km

BELO
HORIZONTE
N. Lima
Itabirito
Congonhas Ouro Vitória
Cons. Ponte Nova Itaquari
Lafaiete Prêto Vila
GROSSO Três Lagoas Andradina Mirassol S. José Olímpia Oliveira Campo Belo Carangola Velha
Xavantina Mirandópolis do Rio Prêto Bebedouro Batatais Passos São Seb. São João Muriaé Alegre Guaraparí
Maracaju Panorama Araçatuba Catanduva Taquaritinga Ribeirão do Paraíso Cons. del Rei Ubá Cachoeiro
Adamantina Penápolis Novo Prêto Guaxupé Três Barbacena Cataguases de Itapemirim
Rio Brilhante SÃO Lins Horizonte Jaboticabal Mococa Pontas Santos Leopoldina Itaperuna
Pres. Tupã Pirajuí Casa Alfenas Varginha Dumont Juiz de Fora Cambuci
Presidente Epitácio PAULO Araraquara Branca Poços de Pouso São Três CAMPOS
Prudente Martinópolis Marília Bariri São Caldas Alegre Corações Lourenço Rios Cabo de
Rancharia Paraguaçu Garça Jaú Carlos da Boa Vista Pinhal Mogi-Mirim Itajubá 2787 Volta RIO DE JANEIRO São Tomé
Centenário Paulista Assis Santa Cruz Rio Claro Araras Ouro Fino Americana Cruzeiro da Redonda Barra do Pirai Nova Friburgo
Paranavaí do Sul Sertanópolis Rolândia do Rio Pardo Limeira CAMPINAS Serra Ma Barra Petrópolis Macaé
Nova Piracicaba Mogi das Cruzes Guaratinguetá Mansa Iguaçu DUQUE DE CAXIAS
Esperança Cambará Cornélio Botucatu Bragança Mar Angra dos Reis SÃO GONÇALO
Londrina Maringá Procópio Jacarezinho Avaré Itu Paulista Taubaté Ilha Grande NITERÓI
Cianorte Apucarana Joaquim Itapetininga Tatuí Sorocaba S. J. dos Campos Baia da Ilha Grande RIO DE JANEIRO
Cruzeiro Mondaguaçu Arapongas Távora Jacareí Pta. de Juatinga Cabo Frio
do Oeste Guaira Ibaití Itaporanga SÃO PAULO SANTO ANDRÉ La. de Araruama
Pto. Mendes PARANÁ Itararé Paranapiacaba São Vicente Tropic of Capricorn
BRAZIL Castro Jaguariaíva São Paulo Guarujá Ilha de São Sebastião
Cascavel Sa. das Araras Pitanga Apiaí SANTOS Pta. do Boi
Foz do Iguaçu Guarapuava Ponta Grossa Registro
Iguazú Prudentópolis Itanhaém
Falls Laranjeiras Palmeira CURITIBA Iguape
Bernardo do Sul Irati Antonina Ilha Comprida
de Irigoyen União da Lapa Paranaguá Ilha do Cardoso
Eldorado Vitória Rio Negro Guaratuba
San Pedro Pto. União Mafra São Francisco do Sul
MISIONES Clevelândia Palmas Caçador Joinvile
Obera 1340 Santa Cecília Blumenau Itajaí
Chapecó SANTA Rio do Sul Brusque
N. Alem Uruguai Joaçaba CATARINA Ilha de Santa Catarina
Santa Rosa Erechim Campos Novos Florianópolis
Ijuí 1808
Ângelo Carazinho Passo Fundo Lajes
São Luís Cruz Alta Vacaria Tubarão Laguna
Gonzaga Cabo Santa Marta Grande
Espinilho Guaporé Criciúma
RIO GRANDE Bento Gonçalves Araranguá
Santa Maria Santa Cruz Caxias do Sul
do Sul Montenegro Nôvo Hamburgo
Cachoeira do Sul Taquara
Rio Pardo São
DO SUL Leopoldo Osório
São PÔRTO ALEGRE
ana do Gabriel Sa. Encantadas
amento Dom Pedrito Caçapava Camaquã
do Sul Camaquã
Bagé Cangucu Mostardas
Sa. do Cangucu Lagoa dos Patos
Pelotas
Melo Jaguarão
Rio Branco Rio Grande
Mirim
Sta. Clara Lagoa Mangueira
de Olimar Lagoa
del Yi Santa Vitória do Palmar
José Batlle
Ordóñez Lascano

Aigua Castillos
Minas Rocha
San Carlos
Maldonado
DEO

A T L A N T I C

O C E A N

5304

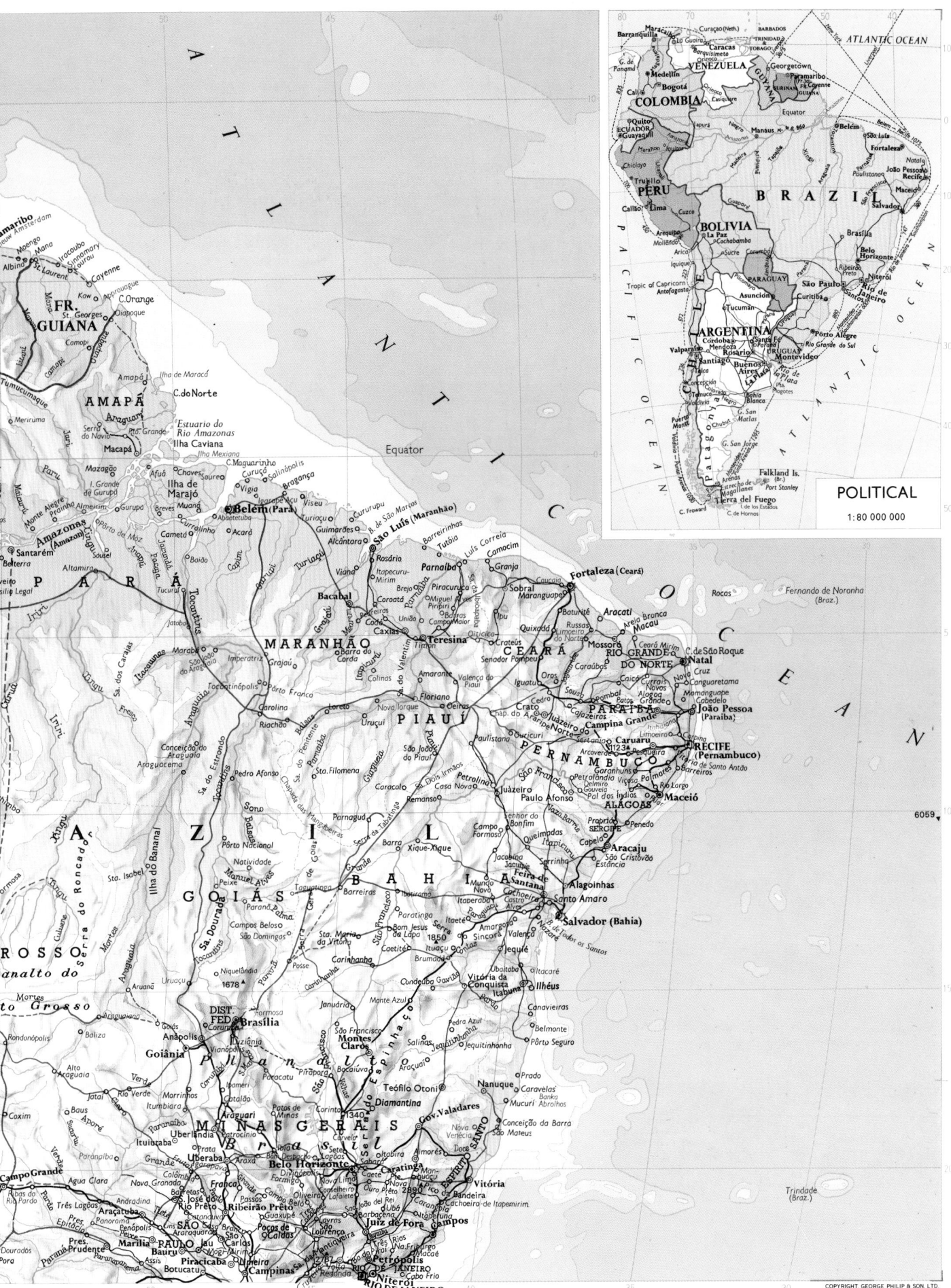

1:16 000 000

200 100 0   200   400   600 km

A T L A N T I C

O C E A N

Equator

FR.
GUIANA

AMAPÁ

Estuario do
Rio Amazonas
Ilha Caviana
Ilha Mexiana

Ilha de
Marajó

Belém (Pará)

Amazonas (Amazonas)

Santarém

PARÁ

B R A Z I L

São Luís (Maranhão)

Parnaíba

Fortaleza (Ceará)

Sobral

MARANHÃO

Teresina

CEARÁ

RIO GRANDE
DO NORTE

Natal

PIAUÍ

PARAÍBA

João Pessoa
(Paraíba)

Campina Grande

PERNAMBUCO

RECIFE
(Pernambuco)

Petrolina

Juàzeiro

Maceió

ALAGOAS

Paulo Afonso

SERGIPE

Aracaju

B A H I A

GOIÁS

Feira de
Santana

Alagoinhas

Salvador (Bahia)

Jequié

Vitória da
Conquista

Ilhéus

Itabuna

DIST.
FED. Brasília

Goiânia

Anápolis

Montes
Claros

Belmonte

Pôrto Seguro

Planalto do
to Grosso

MATO
GROSSO

Diamantina

Teófilo Otoni

Nanuque

Gov.Valadares

MINAS GERAIS

Belo Horizonte

ESPÍRITO
SANTO

Vitória

Uberaba

Campo Grande

Três Lagoas

Ribeirão Prêto

Juiz de Fora

Campos

SÃO
PAULO

Marília

Bauru

Piracicaba

Campinas

PETRÓPOLIS

RIO DE JANEIRO

Niterói

RIO DE JANEIRO

POLITICAL

1:80 000 000

ATLANTIC OCEAN

VENEZUELA

COLOMBIA

GUYANA

Georgetown

Cayenne

Belém

São Luís

Fortaleza

ECUADOR

PERU

B R A Z I L

João Pessoa
Recife
Maceió
Salvador

BOLIVIA

Brasília

PARAGUAY

São Paulo

Rio de
Janeiro

ARGENTINA

URUGUAY

Buenos
Aires

Montevideo

Pôrto Alegre

Rio Grande do Sul

P A C I F I C   O C E A N

A T L A N T I C   O C E A N

Falkland Is.
(Br.)

Port Stanley

Terra del Fuego

1:16 000 000

200 100 0 200 400 600 km

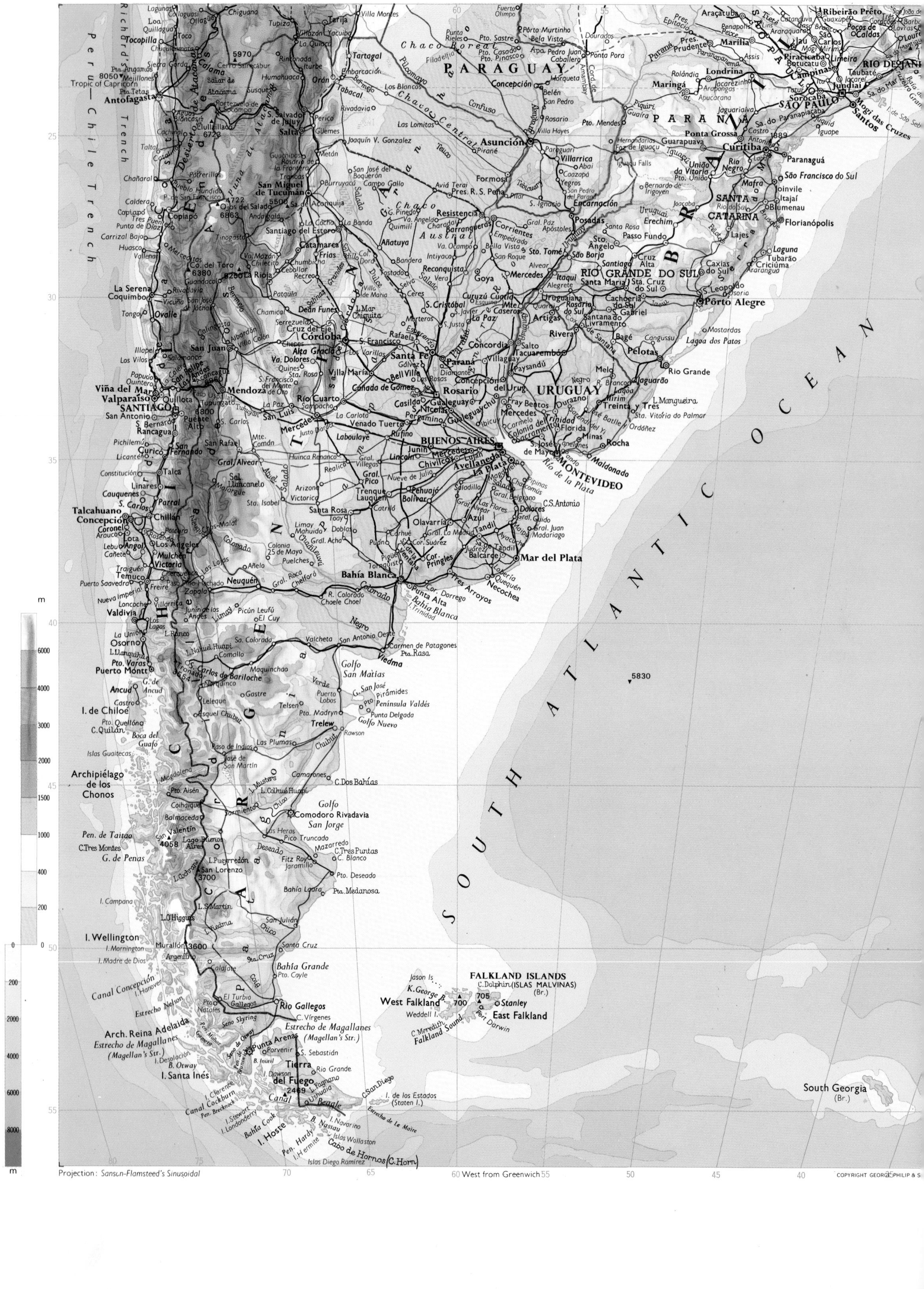

PARAGUAY

Asunción · Concepción · Villarrica · Formosa · Pilar · Encarnación

Chaco Boreal · *Chaco Central* · *Chaco Austral*

BRASIL

São Paulo · Santos · Curitiba · Paranaguá · São Francisco do Sul · Joinville · Blumenau · Florianópolis · Pôrto Alegre · Pelotas · Rio Grande · Ribeirão Prêto · Marília · Londrina · Maringá · Ponta Grossa

PARANÁ · **SANTA CATARINA** · **RIO GRANDE DO SUL** · **RIO DE JANI**

Lagoa dos Patos · *Lagoa Mirim* · *L. Mangueira*

URUGUAY

Montevideo · Salto · Paysandú · Mercedes · Florida · Minas · Rocha · Maldonado · Melo · Treinta y Tres · Rivera · Tacuarembó · Durazno · Artigas

Río de la Plata

ARGENTINA

Buenos Aires · La Plata · Avellaneda · Rosario · Santa Fe · Paraná · Córdoba · Mendoza · San Juan · San Luis · Bahía Blanca · Mar del Plata · Necochea · Santa Rosa · Neuquén · General Pico · Olavarría · Tandil · Azul · Junín · Lincoln · Pergamino · Venado Tuerto · Río Cuarto · Villa María · San Rafael · Catamarca · La Rioja · Santiago del Estero · San Miguel de Tucumán · Salta · Jujuy (S. Salvador de Jujuy) · Metán · Resistencia · Corrientes · Posadas · Goya · Reconquista · Rafaela · Concordia · Gualeguay · Gualeguaychú

Comodoro Rivadavia · Trelew · Rawson · Puerto Madryn · Viedma · Carmen de Patagones · Río Gallegos · San Julián · Santa Cruz · Puerto Deseado · Esquel

Golfo San Matías · *Golfo San Jorge* · *Golfo Nuevo* · *Península Valdés* · *Bahía Grande* · *Tierra del Fuego* · *Estrecho de Magallanes (Magellan's Str.)* · *Cabo de Hornos (C. Horn)* · *Canal Beagle* · *I. de los Estados (Staten I.)*

CHILE

Santiago · Valparaíso · Viña del Mar · San Antonio · Rancagua · San Fernando · Curicó · Talca · Linares · Chillán · Concepción · Talcahuano · Coronel · Los Ángeles · Angol · Temuco · Valdivia · Osorno · Puerto Montt · Ancud · Castro · Coyhaique · Punta Arenas · Porvenir · Antofagasta · Chañaral · Copiapó · Caldera · Vallenar · La Serena · Coquimbo · Ovalle · Tocopilla · Calama · Taltal · Iquique (Pisagua)

Peru–Chile Trench · Tropic of Capricorn · *I. de Chiloé* · *Archipiélago de los Chonos* · *Pen. de Taitao* · *G. de Penas* · *I. Wellington* · *Arch. Reina Adelaida* · *Canal Concepción*

SOUTH ATLANTIC OCEAN

FALKLAND ISLANDS (ISLAS MALVINAS) (Br.)
West Falkland · East Falkland · Stanley · Darwin · Falkland Sound · Weddell I. · Jason Is · K. George · Port Howard

South Georgia (Br.)

·5830

·4058 · 3700 · 3600 · 2469

Projection: Sanson–Flamsteed's Sinusoidal

West from Greenwich

COPYRIGHT GEORGE PHILIP & S

m — 8000 · 6000 · 4000 · 3000 · 2000 · 1500 · 1000 · 400 · 200 · 0 · 200 · 2000 · 4000 · 6000 · 8000 — m

INDEX

The number printed in bold type against each index entry indicates the map page where the feature will be found. The geographical coordinates which follow the name are sometimes only approximate but are close enough for the place name to be located.

An open square □ signifies that the name refers to an administrative subdivision of a country while a solid square ■ follows the name of a country. (□) follows the old county names of the U.K.

The alphabetical order of names composed of two or more words is governed primarily by the first word and then by the second. This rule applies even if the second word is a description or its abbreviation, R.,L.,I. for example. Names composed of a proper name (Gibraltar) and a description (Strait of) are positioned alphabetically by the proper name. If the same place name occurs twice or more times in the index and all are in the same country, each is followed by the name of the administrative subdivision in which it is located. The names are placed in the alphabetical order of the subdivisions. If the same place name occurs twice or more in the index and the places are in different countries they will be followed by their country names, the latter governing the alphabetical order. In a mixture of these situations the primary order is fixed by the alphabetical sequence of the countries and the secondary order by that of the country subdivisions.

A. C. T. – Australian Capital Territory
A. R. – Autonomous Region
A. S. S. R. – Autonomous Soviet Socialist Republic
Afghan. – Afghanistan
Afr. – Africa
Ala. – Alabama
Alas. – Alaska
Alg. – Algeria
Alta. – Alberta
Amer. – America
And. P. – Andhra Pradesh
Ang. – Angola
Arch. – Archipelago
Arg. – Argentina
Ariz. – Arizona
Ark. – Arkansas
Atl. Oc. – Atlantic Ocean
Austral. – Australia
B. – Baie, Bahía, Bay, Bucht, Bugt
B.A. – Buenos Aires
B.C. – British Columbia
Bangla. – Bangladesh
Barr. – Barrage
Bay. – Bayern
Belg. – Belgium
Berks. – Berkshire
Bol. – Bolshoi
Bots. – Botswana
Br. – British
Bri. – Bridge
Bt. – Bight
Bucks. – Buckinghamshire
Bulg. – Bulgaria
C. – Cabo, Cap, Cape
C. Prov. – Cape Province
Calif. – California
Camb. – Cambodia
Cambs. – Cambridgeshire
Can. – Canada
Cat. – Cataract, Cataracta
Cent. – Central
Chan. – Channel
Co. – Country
Colomb. – Colombia
Colo. – Colorado
Conn. – Connecticut
Cord. – Cordillera
Cr.. – Creek
Cumb. – Cumbria
Czech. – Czechoslovakia
D.C. – District of Columbia
Del. – Delaware
Dep. – Dependency
Derby. – Derbyshire
Des. – Desert
Dist. – District
Dj. – Djebel
Dumf. & Gall. – Dumfries and Galloway
E. – East
Eng. – England
Fed. – Federal, Federation
Fla. – Florida

For. – Forest
Fr. – France, French
Fs. – Falls
Ft. – Fort
G. – Golf, Golfo, Gulf, Guba
Ga. – Georgia
Germ. – Germany
Glam. – Glamorgan
Glos. – Gloucestershire
Gr. – Grande, Great, Greater, Group
H.K. – Hong Kong
H.P. – Himachal Pradesh
Hants. – Hampshire
Harb. – Harbor, Harbour
Hd. – Head
Here. & Worcs. – Hereford and Worcester
Herts. – Hertfordshire
Holl. – Holland
Hung. – Hungary
I.o.M. – Isle of Man
I. of W. – Isle of Wight
I.(s). – Île, Ilha, Insel, Isla, Island
Id. – Idaho
Ill. – Illinois
Ind. – Indiana
Ind. Oc. – Indian Ocean
J. – Jabal, Jabel, Jazira
Junc. – Junction
K. – Kap, Kapp
K. – Kuala
Kal. – Kalmyk A.S.S.R.
Kans. – Kansas
Kpl. – Kapell
Ky. – Kentucky
L. – Lac, Lacul, Lago, Lagoa, Lake, Limni, Loch, Lough
La. – Lousiana
Lancs. – Lancashire
Leb. – Lebanon
Leics. – Leicestershire
Lim. – Limerick
Lincs. – Lincolnshire
Lit. – Little
Lr. – Lower
Lt. Ho. – Light House
Mad. P. – Madhya Pradesh
Madag. – Madagascar
Malay. – Malaysia
Man. – Manitoba
Manch. – Manchester
Maran. – Maranhão
Mass. – Massachusetts
Md. – Maryland
Me. – Maine
Mend. – Mendoza
Mer. – Méridionale
Mich. – Michigan
Mid. – Middle
Minn. – Minnesota
Miss. – Mississippi
Mo. – Missouri
Mong. – Mongolia
Mont. – Montana

Moroc. – Morocco
Mozam. – Mozambique
Mt.(e). – Mont, Monte, Monti, Montaña, Mountain
Mys. – Mysore
N. – North, Northern, Nouveau
N.B. – New Brunswick
N.C. – North Carolina
N.D. – North Dakota
N.H. – New Hampshire
N.I. – North Island
N.J. – New Jersey
N. Mex. – New Mexico
N.S. – Nova Scotia
N.S.W. – New South Wales
N.T. – Northern Territory
N.W.T. – North West Territory
N.Y. – New York
N.Z. – New Zealand
Nat. – National
Nat Park. – National Park
Nebr. – Nebraska
Neth. – Netherlands
Nev. – Nevada
Newf. – Newfoundland
Nic. – Nicaragua
Northants. – Northamptonshire
Northumb. – Northumberland
Notts. – Nottinghamshire
O. – Oued, ouadi
O.F.S. – Orange Free State
Okla. – Oklahoma
Ont. – Ontario
Or. – Orientale
Os. – Ostrov
Oxon. – Oxfordshire
Oz. – Ozero
P. – Pass, Passo, Pasul, Pulau
P.E.I. – Prince Edward Island
P.N.G. – Papua New Guinea
P.O. – Post Office
P. Rico. – Puerto Rico
Pa. – Pennsylvania
Pac. Oc. – Pacific Ocean
Pak. – Pakistan
Pass. – Passage
Pen. – Peninsula, Peninsule
Phil. – Philippines
Pk. – Park, Peak
Plat. – Plateau
P-ov. – Poluostrov
Port. – Portugal, Portuguese
Prom. – Promontory
Prov. – Province, Provincial
Pt. – Point
Pta. – Ponta, Punta
Pte. – Pointe
Qué. – Québec
Queens. – Queensland
R. – Rio, River
R.I. – Rhode Island
R.S.F.S.R. – Russian Soviet Federal Socialist Republic
Ra.(s). – Range(s)
Raj. – Rajasthan

Reg. – Region
Rep. – Republic
Res. – Reserve, Reservoir
Rhld. – Pfz. – Rheinland – Pfalz
Rhod. – Rhodesia
S. – San, South
S. Afr. – South Africa
S. Austral. – South Australia
S.D. – South Dakota
S.-Holst. – Schleswig-Holstein
S.I. – South Island
S. Leone – Sierra Leone
S.S.R. – Soviet Socialist Republic
S.-U. – Sinkiang-Uighur
Sa. – Serra, Sierra
Sard. – Sardinia
Sask. – Saskatchewan
Scot. – Scotland
Sd. – Sound
Sept. – Septentrionale
Sib. – Siberia
Som. – Somerset
Span. – Spanish
Sprs. – Springs
St. – Saint
Sta. – Santa, Station
Staffs. – Staffordshire
Ste. – Sainte
Sto. – Santo
Str. – Strait, Stretto
Switz. – Switzerland
T.O. – Telegraph Office
Tas. – Tasmania
Tenn. – Tennessee
Terr. – Territory
Tex. – Texas
Tg. – Tanjung
Thai. – Thailand
Tipp. – Tipperary
Trans. – Transvaal
U.K. – United Kingdom
U.S.A. – United States of America
U.S.S.R. – Union of Soviet Socialist Republics
Ukr. – Ukraine
Ut.P. – Uttar Pradesh
Utd. – United
Va. – Virginia
Vdkhr. – Vodokhranilishche
Venez. – Venezuela
Vic. – Victoria
Viet. – Vietnam
Vol. – Volcano
Vt. – Vermont
W. – Wadi, West
W.A. – Western Australia
W. Isles – Western Isles
Wash. – Washington
Wilts. – Wiltshire
Wis. – Wisconsin
Wlkp. – Wielkopolski
Wyo. – Wyoming
Yorks. – Yorkshire
Yug. – Yugoslavia

FHK

Aabenraa-Sønderborg Amt □ Afognak I

A

Aabenraa-Sønderborg Amt □ 73 55 0N 9 30E
Aachen 48 50 47N 6 4E
Aadorf 15 47 30N 8 55E
Aaiun 116 27 9N 13 12W
Aal 73 55 39N 8 18E
Aâlâ en Nîl □ 123 8 50N 29 55E
Aalen 49 48 49N 10 6E
Aalma ech Chaab 90 33 7N 35 9E
Aalsmeer 46 52 17N 4 43E
Aalsö 73 56 23N 10 52E
Aalst, Belg. 47 50 56N 4 2E
Aalst, Neth. 152 50 57N 4 20E
Aalten 46 51 56N 6 35E
Aalter 47 51 5N 3 28E
Aarau 50 47 23N 8 4E
Aarburg 50 47 2N 7 16E
Aardenburg 47 51 16N 3 28E
Aare, R. 50 47 33N 8 14E
Aareavaara 74 67 27N 23 29E
Aargau □ 50 47 26N 8 10E
Aarhus Amt □ 73 56 15N 10 15E
Aarle 47 51 30N 5 38E
Aarschot 47 50 59N 4 49E
Aarsele 47 51 0N 3 26E
Aartrijke 47 51 7N 3 6E
Aarwangen 50 47 15N 7 46E
Aasleagh 38 53 37N 9 40W
Aastrup 73 55 34N 8 49E
Aba, Congo 126 3 58N 30 17E
Aba, Nigeria 121 5 10N 7 19E
Âbâ, Jazîrat 123 13 30N 32 31E
Abadan 92 30 22N 48 20E
Abade, Ethiopia 123 9 22N 38 3E
Abade, Iran 93 31 8N 52 40E
Abadin 56 43 21N 7 29W
Abadla 118 31 2N 2 45W
Abaeté 171 19 9S 45 27W
Abaeté, R. 171 18 2S 45 12W
Abaetetuba 170 1 40S 48 50W
Abai 173 25 58S 55 54W
Abak 121 4 58N 7 50E
Abakaliki 121 6 22N 8 2E
Abakan 77 53 40N 91 10E
Abal Nam 122 25 20N 38 37E
Abalemma 121 16 12N 7 50E
Aballetuba 170 1 40S 51 15W
Abanilla 59 38 12N 1 3W
Abano Terme 63 45 22N 11 46E
Abarán 59 38 12N 1 23W
Abarqu 93 31 10N 53 20E
Abasan 90 31 19N 34 21E
Abasberes 123 11 33N 35 23E
Abashiri 112 44 0N 144 15E
Abashiri-Wan 112 44 0N 144 30E
Abau 135 10 11S 148 46E
Abaújszántó 53 48 16N 21 12E
Abaya L. 123 6 30N 37 50E
Abbadia San Salvatore 63 42 53N 11 40E
Abbay, R., (Nîl el Azraq) 123 10 17N 35 22E
Abbaye, Pt. 156 46 58N 88 4W
Abbetorp 73 56 57N 16 8E
Abbeville, France 43 50 6N 1 49E
Abbeville, La., U.S.A. 159 30 0N 92 7W
Abbeville, S.C., U.S.A. 157 34 12N 82 21W
Abbey 39 53 7N 8 25W
Abbey Town 32 54 50N 3 18W
Abbeydorney 39 52 21N 9 40W
Abbeyfeale 39 52 23N 9 20W
Abbeyleix 39 52 55N 7 20W
Abbeyside 39 52 5N 7 36W
Abbiategrasso 62 45 23N 8 55E
Abbieglassie 139 27 15S 147 28E
Abbotabad 94 34 10N 73 15E
Abbots Bromley 28 52 50N 1 52W
Abbots Langley 29 51 43N 0 25W
Abbotsbury 28 50 40N 2 36W
Abbotsford, Can. 152 49 0N 122 10W
Abbotsford, U.S.A. 158 44 55N 90 20W
Abcoude 46 52 17N 4 59E
'Abd al Kuri 91 12 5N 52 20E
Abdulino 84 53 42N 53 40E
Abe, L. 123 11 8N 41 47E
Abéché 117 13 50N 20 35E
Abejar 58 41 48N 2 47W
Abekr 123 12 45N 28 50E
Abêlessa 118 22 58N 4 47E
Abelti 123 8 10N 37 30E
Abengourou 120 6 42N 3 27W
Abenrå 73 55 3N 9 25E
Abeokuta 121 7 3N 3 19E
Aber 126 2 12N 32 25E
Aber-soch 31 52 50N 4 31W
Aberaeron 31 52 15N 4 16W
Aberayron = Aberaeron 31 52 15N 4 16W
Abercarn 31 51 39N 3 9W
Aberchirder 37 57 34N 2 40W
Abercorn 139 25 12S 151 5E
Abercorn = Mbala 127 8 46S 31 17E
Abercrave 31 51 48N 3 42W
Aberdare 31 51 43N 3 27W
Aberdare Ra. 126 0 15S 36 50E
Aberdaron 31 52 48N 4 41W
Aberdeen, Austral. 141 32 9S 150 56E
Aberdeen, Can. 153 52 20N 106 8W
Aberdeen, S. Afr. 128 32 28S 24 2E
Aberdeen, U.K. 37 57 9N 2 6W
Aberdeen, Md., U.S.A. 162 39 30N 76 14W
Aberdeen, S.D., U.S.A. 158 45 30N 98 30W
Aberdeen, Wash., U.S.A. 160 47 0N 123 50W
Aberdeen (□) 26 57 18N 2 30W
Aberdour 35 56 2N 3 18W
Aberdovey 31 52 33N 4 3W
Aberdulais 31 51 41N 3 46W
Aberfeldy, Austral. 141 37 42S 146 22E
Aberfeldy, U.K. 37 56 37N 3 50W
Aberffraw 31 53 11N 4 28W
Aberfoyle 34 56 10N 4 23W
Abergaria-a-Velha 56 40 41N 8 32W
Abergavenny 31 51 49N 3 1W
Abergele 31 53 17N 3 35W
Abergwili 31 51 52N 4 18W
Abergynolwyn 31 52 39N 3 58W
Aberkenfig 31 51 33N 3 36W
Aberlady 35 56 0N 2 51W
Abernathy 159 33 49N 101 49W
Abernethy 35 56 19N 3 18W
Aberporth 31 52 8N 4 32W
Abersychan 31 51 44N 3 3W
Abertillery 31 51 44N 3 9W
Aberystwyth 31 52 25N 4 6W
Abha 122 18 0N 42 34E
Abhayapuri 98 26 24N 90 38E
Abidiya 122 18 18N 34 3E
Abidjan 120 5 26N 3 58W
Abilene, Kans., U.S.A. 158 39 0N 97 16W
Abilene, Texas, U.S.A. 159 32 22N 99 40W
Abingdon, U.K. 28 51 40N 1 17W
Abingdon, Ill., U.S.A. 158 40 53N 90 23W
Abingdon, Va., U.S.A. 157 36 46N 81 56W
Abington 35 55 30N 3 42W
Abington Reef 138 18 0S 149 35E
Abitan L. 153 60 27N 107 15W
Abitan, R. 153 59 53N 109 3W
Abitibi L. 150 48 40N 79 40W
Abiy Adi 123 13 39N 39 3E
Abkhaz A.S.S.R. □ 83 43 0N 41 0E
Abkit 77 64 10N 157 10E
Abnûb 122 27 18N 31 4E
Åbo = Turku 75 60 27N 22 14E
Abo, Massif d' 119 21 41N 16 8E
Abocho 121 7 35N 6 56E
Abohar 94 30 10N 74 10E
Aboisso 120 5 30N 3 5W
Abomey 121 7 10N 2 5E
Abondance 45 46 18N 6 42E
Abong Mbang 124 4 0N 13 8E
Abonnema 121 4 41N 6 49E
Abony 53 47 12N 20 3E
Aboso 120 5 23N 1 57W
Abou Deïa 117 11 20N 19 20E
Aboyne 37 57 4N 2 48W
Abqaiq 92 26 0N 49 45E
Abra Pampa 172 22 43S 65 42W
Abrantes 57 39 24N 8 7W
Abraveses 56 40 41N 7 55E
Abreojos, Pta. 164 26 50N 113 40W
Abreschviller 43 48 39N 7 6E
Abrets, Les 45 45 32N 5 35E
Abri, Esh Shimâliya, Sudan 123 20 50N 30 27E
Abri, Kordofân, Sudan 123 11 40N 30 21E
Abrolhos, Arquipélago dos 171 18 0S 38 30W
Abrolhos, banka 171 18 0S 38 0W
Abrud 70 46 19N 23 5E
Abruzzi □ 63 42 15N 14 0E
Absaroka Ra. 160 44 40N 110 0W
Abû al Khasib 92 30 25N 48 0E
Abû 'Ali 92 27 20N 49 27E
Abu Arish 91 16 53N 42 48E
Abû Ballas 122 24 26N 27 36E
Abu Deleiq 123 15 57N 33 48E
Abû Dhabî 93 24 28N 54 36E
Abû Dis 90 31 47N 35 16E
Abu Dis 122 19 12N 33 38E
Abu Dom 123 16 18N 32 25E
Abû Gabra 123 11 2N 26 50E
Abû Ghôsh 90 31 48N 35 6E
Abû Gubeiha 123 11 30N 31 15E
Abu Habl, W. 123 12 37N 31 0E
Abu Hamed 122 19 32N 33 13E
Abû Haraz, Esh Shimâliya, Sudan 122 19 8N 32 18E
Abû Haraz, Nîl el Azraq, Sudan 123 14 35N 34 30E
Abû Higar 123 12 50N 33 59E
Abu Kamal 92 34 30N 41 0E
Abu Markha 92 25 4N 38 22E
Abu Qir 122 31 18N 30 0E
Abu Qireiya 122 24 5N 35 28E
Abu Qurqâs 122 28 1N 30 44E
Abu Salama 122 27 10N 35 51E
Abû Simbel 122 22 18N 31 40E
Abu Tig 122 27 4N 31 15E
Abu Tiga 123 12 47N 34 12E
Abû Zabad 123 12 25N 29 10E
Abu Zenîma 122 29 0N 33 15E
Abuja 121 9 16N 7 2E
Abunã 174 9 40S 65 20W
Abunã, R. 174 9 41S 65 20W
Aburatsu 110 31 34N 131 24E
Aburo, Mt. 126 2 4N 30 53E
Abut Hd. 143 43 7S 170 15E
Abwong 123 9 2N 32 14E
Åby 73 58 40N 16 10E
Aby, Lagune 120 5 15N 3 14W
Acacias 174 3 59N 73 46W
Acajutla 166 13 36N 89 50W
Açallândia 170 5 0S 47 50W
Acámbaro 164 20 0N 100 40W
Acaponeta 164 22 30N 105 20W
Acapulco de Juárez 165 16 51N 99 56W
Acarai, Serra 175 1 50N 57 50W
Acaraú 170 2 53S 40 7W
Acari 170 6 31S 36 38W
Acarigua 174 9 33N 69 12W
Acatlan 165 18 10N 98 3W
Acayucán 165 17 59N 94 58W
Accéglio 62 44 28N 6 59E
Accomac 156 37 43N 75 40W
Accra 121 5 35N 0 6W
Accrington 32 53 46N 2 22W
Acebal 172 33 20S 60 50W
Aceh □ 102 4 0N 97 30E
Acerenza 65 40 50N 15 58E
Acerra 65 40 57N 14 22E
Aceuchal 57 38 39N 6 30W
Achaguas 174 7 46N 68 14W
Achak Gomba 99 33 30N 96 25E
Achalpur 96 21 22N 77 32E
Achavanich 37 58 22N 3 25W
Achel 47 51 15N 5 29E
A'ch'eng 107 45 33N 127 0E
Achenkirch 52 47 32N 11 45E
Achensee 52 47 26N 11 45E
Acher 94 23 10N 72 32E
Achern 49 48 37N 8 5E
Acheron, R. 143 42 16S 173 4E
Achill 38 53 56N 9 55W
Achill Hd. 38 53 59N 10 15W
Achill I. 38 53 58N 10 5W
Achill Sd. 38 53 53N 9 55W
Achillbeg I. 38 53 51N 9 58W
Achim 48 53 1N 9 2E
Achimota 121 5 35N 0 15W
Achinsk 77 56 20N 90 20E
Achisay 85 43 35N 68 53E
Achit 84 56 48N 57 54E
Achnasheen 36 57 35N 5 5W
Achnashellach 36 57 28N 5 20W
Achol 123 6 35N 31 32E
A'Chralaig, Mt. 36 57 11N 5 10W
Acireale 65 37 37N 15 9E
Ackerman 159 33 20N 89 8W
Acklin's I. 167 22 30N 74 0W
Acland, Mt. 133 24 50S 148 20E
Aclare 38 54 4N 8 54W
Acle 29 52 38N 1 32E
Acme 152 51 33N 113 30W
Aconcagua 172 32 50S 70 0W
Aconcagua □ 172 32 15S 70 30W
Aconcagua, Cerro 172 32 39S 70 0W
Aconquija, Mt. 172 27 0S 66 0W
Acopiara 170 6 6S 39 27W
Açores, Is. dos 14 38 44N 29 0W
Acquapendente 63 42 45N 11 50E
Acquasanta 63 42 46N 13 24E
Acquaviva delle Fonti 65 40 53N 16 50E
Acqui 62 44 40N 8 28E
Acre = 'Akko 90 32 35N 35 4E
Acre □ 174 9 1S 71 0W
Acre, R. 174 10 45S 68 25W
Acri 65 39 29N 16 23E
Acs 53 47 42N 18 0E
Acton Burnell 28 52 37N 2 41W
Açu 170 5 34S 36 54W
Ad Dam 91 20 33N 44 45E
Ad Dammam 92 26 20N 50 5E
Ad Dar al Hamra 92 27 20N 37 45E
Ad Dawhah 93 25 15N 51 35E
Ad Dilam 92 23 55N 47 10E
Ada, Ethiopia 123 8 48N 38 51E
Ada, Ghana 121 5 44N 0 40E
Ada, Minn., U.S.A. 158 47 20N 96 30W
Ada, Okla., U.S.A. 159 34 50N 96 45W
Ada, Yugo. 66 45 49N 20 9E
Adair C. 12 71 50N 71 0W
Adaja, R. 56 41 15N 4 50W
Adale 91 2 58N 46 27E
Adalslinden 72 63 27N 16 55E
Adam 93 22 15N 57 28E
Adamantina 171 21 42S 51 4W
Adamaoua, Massif de l' 121 7 20N 12 20E
Adamawa Highlands = Adamaoua 121 7 20N 12 20E
Adamello, Mt. 62 46 10N 10 34E
Adami Tulu 123 7 53N 38 41E
Adaminaby 141 36 0S 148 45E
Adamovka 84 51 32N 59 56E
Adams, Mass., U.S.A. 162 42 38N 73 8W
Adams, N.Y., U.S.A. 162 43 50N 76 3W
Adams, Wis., U.S.A. 158 43 59N 89 50W
Adam's Bridge 97 9 15N 79 40E
Adams L. 152 51 10N 119 40W
Adams Mt. 160 46 10N 121 28W
Adam's Peak 97 6 55N 80 45E
Adamuz 57 38 2N 4 32W
Adana 92 37 0N 35 16E
Adanero 56 40 56N 4 36W
Adapazari 92 40 48N 30 25E
Adarama 123 17 10N 34 52E
Adare 39 52 34N 8 48W
Adare, C. 13 71 0S 171 0E
Adavale 139 25 52S 144 32E
Adayio 123 14 29N 40 50E
Adda, R. 62 45 25N 9 30E
Addis Ababa = Addis Abeba 123 9 2N 38 42E
Addis Abeba 123 9 2N 38 42E
Addis Alem 123 9 0N 38 17E
Addlestone 29 51 22N 0 30W
Addo 29 33 32S 25 44E
Addu Atoll 87 0 30S 73 0E
Adebour 121 13 17N 11 50E
Adel 157 31 10N 83 28W
Adelaide, Austral. 140 34 52S 138 30E
Adelaide, Bahamas 166 25 0N 77 31W
Adelaide I. 13 67 15S 68 30W
Adelaide Pen. 148 68 15N 97 30W
Adelaide River 136 13 15S 131 7E
Adelanto 163 34 35N 117 22W
Adelboden 50 46 29N 7 33E
Adele, I. 136 15 32S 123 9E
Adélie, Terre 13 67 0S 140 0E
Ademuz 58 40 5N 1 13W
Aden 91 12 50N 45 0E
Aden, G. of 91 13 0N 50 0E
Adendorp 128 33 25S 24 30E
Adhoi 94 23 26N 70 32E
Adi 103 4 15S 133 30E
Adi Daro 123 14 20N 38 14E
Adi Keyih 123 14 51N 39 22E
Adi Kwala 123 14 38N 38 48E
Adi Ugri 123 14 58N 38 48E
Adieu, C. 137 32 0S 132 10E
Adieu Pt. 136 15 14S 124 35E
Adigala 123 10 24N 42 15E
Adige, R. 63 45 9N 11 25E
Adigrat 123 14 20N 39 26E
Adilabad 96 19 33N 78 35E
Adin 160 41 10N 121 0W
Adin Khel 93 32 45N 68 5E
Adinkerke 47 51 5N 2 36E
Adirampattinam 97 10 28N 79 20E
Adirondack Mts. 156 44 0N 74 15W
Adis Dera 123 10 12N 38 46E
Adjohon 121 6 41N 2 32E
Adjud 70 46 7N 27 10E
Adjumani 126 3 20N 31 50E
Adlavik Is. 151 55 2N 58 45W
Adler 83 43 28N 39 52E
Adliswil 51 47 19N 8 32E
Admer 119 20 21N 5 27E
Admer, Erg d' 119 24 0N 9 5E
Admiralty B. 13 62 0S 59 0W
Admiralty G. 136 14 20S 125 55E
Admiralty I. 147 57 40N 134 35W
Admiralty Inlet 160 48 0N 122 40W
Admiralty Is. 135 2 0S 147 0E
Admiralty Ra. 13 72 0S 164 0E
Ado 121 6 36N 2 56E
Ado Ekiti 121 7 38N 5 12E
Adok 123 8 10N 30 20E
Adola 123 11 14N 41 44E
Adonara 103 8 15S 123 5E
Adoni 97 15 33N 77 18W
Adony 53 47 6N 18 52E
Adour, R. 44 43 32N 1 32W
Adra, India 95 23 30N 86 42E
Adra, Spain 59 36 43N 3 3W
Adraj 91 20 1N 51 0E
Adrano 65 37 40N 14 49E
Adrar 118 27 51N 0 11W
Adrar des Iforhas 121 19 40N 1 40E
Adrasman 85 40 38N 69 58E
Adré 117 13 40N 22 20E
Adri 119 27 32N 13 2E
Adria 63 45 4N 12 3E
Adrian, Mich., U.S.A. 156 41 55N 84 0W
Adrian, Tex., U.S.A. 159 35 19N 102 37W
Adriatic Sea 60 43 0N 16 0E
Adrigole 39 51 44N 9 42W
Adua 103 1 45S 129 50E
Aduku 126 2 03N 32 45E
Adula 51 46 30N 9 3E
Adung Long 98 28 7N 97 42E
Adur 97 9 8N 76 40E
Adwa, Ethiopia 123 14 15N 38 52E
Adwa, Si Arab. 92 27 15N 42 35E
Adwick le Street 33 53 35N 1 12W
Adzhar A.S.S.R. □ 83 42 0N 42 0E
Adzopé 120 6 7N 3 49W
Æbelø I. 73 55 39N 10 10E
Æbeltoft 73 56 12N 10 41E
Æbeltoft Vig. B. 73 56 9N 10 35E
Ægean Is. 61 38 0N 25 0E
Ægean Sea 61 37 0N 25 0E
Aenemuiden 47 51 30N 3 40E
Ænes 71 60 5N 6 8E
Æolian Is. = Eólie, I. 65 38 40N 15 7E
Aerhchin Shanmo 105 38 0N 88 0E
Aerhshan 105 47 93N 119 59E
Aerht'ai Shan 105 48 0N 90 0E
Æro 73 54 53N 10 20E
Ærø 73 54 52N 10 25E
Ærøskøbing 73 54 53N 10 24E
Aesch 50 47 28N 7 36E
Aëtós 69 37 15N 21 50E
Afafi, Massif d' 119 22 11N 14 48E
Afanasyevo 84 58 52N 53 15E
Afándou 69 36 18N 28 12E
Afarag, Erg 118 23 50N 2 47E
Afdera, Mt. 123 13 16N 41 5E
Affreville = Khemis Miliania 118 36 11N 2 14E
Affric, L. 36 57 15N 5 5W
Affric, R. 37 57 15N 4 50W
Afghanistan ■ 93 33 0N 65 0E
Afgoi 91 2 7N 45 30E
Afif 92 23 53N 42 56E
Afikpo 121 5 53N 7 54E
Aflisses, O. 118 28 30N 0 50E
Aflou 118 34 7N 2 3E
Afodo 123 10 18N 34 49E
Afogados da Ingàzeira 170 7 45S 37 39W
Afognak I. 147 58 10N 152 50W

Afragola 65 40 54N 14 15 E
Africa 114 10 0N 20 0 E
Afton 162 42 14N 75 31W
Aftout 118 26 50N 3 45W
Afuá 170 0 15 S 50 10W
Afula 90 32 37N 35 17 E
Afyon Karahisar 92 38 20N 30 15 E
Agadès 121 16 58N 7 59 E
Agadir 118 30 28N 9 35W
Agadir Tissint 118 29 57N 7 16W
Agano, R. 112 37 50N 139 30 E
Agapa 77 71 27N 89 15 E
Agapovka 84 53 18N 59 8 E
Agar 94 23 40N 76 2 E
Agaro 123 7 50N 36 38 E
Agartala 98 23 50N 91 23 E
Agassiz 152 49 14N 121 46W
Agat 123 15 38N 38 16 E
Agattu I. 147 52 25N 172 30 E
Agbelouvé 121 6 35N 1 14 E
Agboville 120 5 55N 4 15W
Agdam 83 40 0N 46 58 E
Agdash 83 40 44N 47 22 E
Agde 44 43 19N 3 28 E
Agde, C. d' 44 43 16N 3 28 E
Agdz 118 30 47N 6 30W
Agen 44 44 12N 0 38 E
Ageo 111 35 58N 139 36 E
Ager Tay 119 20 0N 17 41 E
Agersø 73 55 13N 11 12 E
Agger 73 56 47N 8 13 E
Aggersborg 73 57 0N 9 16 E
Aggius 64 40 56N 9 4 E
Aghalee 38 54 32N 6 17W
Aghavannagh 39 52 55N 6 25W
Aghern 39 52 5N 8 10W
Aghil Mts. 93 36 0N 77 0 E
Aghil Pass 93 36 15N 76 35 E
Aginskoye 77 51 6N 114 32 E
Agira 65 37 40N 14 30 E
Aglou 118 29 50N 9 50W
Agly, R. 44 42 46N 3 3 E
Agna Branca 170 7 57 S 47 19W
Agnes 137 28 0 S 120 30 E
Agnew 137 28 1 S 120 30 E
Agnews Hill 38 54 51N 5 55W
Agnibilékrou 120 7 10N 3 11W
Agnita 70 45 59N 24 40 E
Agnone 65 41 49N 14 20 E
Ago 111 33 36N 135 29 E
Agofie 121 8 27N 0 15 E
Agogna, R. 62 45 8N 8 42 E
Agogo, Ghana 121 6 50N 1 1W
Agogo, Sudan 123 7 50N 28 45 E
Agon 42 49 2N 1 34W
Agön 72 61 33N 17 25 E
Agon I. 72 61 34N 17 23 E
Agordo 63 46 18N 12 2 E
Agout, R. 44 43 47N 1 41 E
Agra 94 27 17N 77 58 E
Agrado 174 2 15N 75 46W
Agramunt 58 41 48N 1 6 E
Agreda 58 41 51N 1 55W
Agri 73 56 14N 10 32 E
Ağri Daği 92 39 50N 44 15 E
Agri, R. 65 40 17N 16 15 E
Agrigento 64 37 19N 13 33 E
Agrínion 69 38 37N 21 27 E
Agrøpoli 65 40 23N 14 59 E
Agryz 84 56 33N 53 2 E
Agua Caliente, Mexico 164 26 30N 108 20W
Agua Caliente, U.S.A. 163 32 29N 116 59W
Agua Caliente Springs 163 32 56N 116 19W
Agua Clara 175 20 25 S 52 45W
Agua Prieta 164 31 20N 109 32W
Aguadas 174 5 40N 75 38W
Aguadilla 147 18 27N 67 10W
Aguadulce 166 8 15N 80 32W
Aguanaval, R. 164 23 45N 103 10W
Aguanga 163 33 27N 116 51W
Aguanus, R. 151 50 13N 62 5W
Aguapeí, R. 171 21 0 S 51 0W
Aguapey, R. 172 29 7 S 56 36W
Aguaray Guazú, R. 172 24 47 S 57 19W
Aguarico, R. 174 0 0 77 30W
Aguas Blancas 172 24 15 S 69 55W
Aguas Calientes, Sierra de 172 25 26 S 67 27W
Águas Formosas 171 17 5 S 40 57W
Aguas, R. 58 41 20N 0 30W
Aguascalientes 164 22 0N 102 12W
Aguascalientes □ 164 22 0N 102 20W
Agudo 57 38 59N 4 52W
Águeda 56 40 34N 8 27W
Agueda, R. 56 40 45N 6 37W
Aguelt el Kadra 118 25 3N 7 6W
Agueni N'Ikko 118 32 29N 5 47W
Aguié 121 13 31N 7 46 E
Aguilafuente 56 41 13N 4 7W
Aguilar 57 37 31N 4 40W
Aguilar de Campóo 56 42 47N 4 15W
Aguilares 172 27 26 S 65 35W
Aguilas 59 37 23N 1 35W
Aguja, C. de la 174 11 18N 74 12W
Aguja, Pta. 174 6 0 S 81 0W
Agulaa 123 13 40N 39 40 E
Agulhas, Kaap 128 34 52 S 20 0 E
Agung 102 8 20 S 115 28 E
Agur, Israel 90 31 42N 34 55 E
Agur, Uganda 126 2 28N 32 55 E
Agŭš 70 46 28N 26 15 E
Agusan, R. 103 9 20N 125 50 E
Agvali 83 42 36N 46 8 E

Aha Mts. 128 19 45 S 21 0 E
Ahaggar 119 23 0N 6 30 E
Ahamansu 121 7 38N 0 35 E
Ahar 92 38 35N 47 0 E
Ahascragh 38 53 24N 8 20W
Ahaura 143 42 20 S 171 32 E
Ahaura, R. 143 42 21 S 171 34 E
Ahaus 48 52 4N 7 1 E
Ahelledjem 119 26 37N 6 58 E
Ahimanawa Ra. 130 39 5 S 176 30 E
Ahipara B. 142 35 5 S 173 5 E
Ahiri 96 19 30N 80 0 E
Ahlen 48 51 45N 7 52 E
Ahmad Wal 94 29 18N 65 58 E
Ahmadabad (Ahmedabad) 94 23 0N 72 40 E
Ahmadnagar (Ahmednagar) 96 19 7N 74 46 E
Ahmadpur 94 29 12N 71 10 E
Ahmar Mts. 123 9 20N 41 15 E
Ahoada 121 5 8N 6 36 E
Ahoghill 38 54 52N 6 23W
Ahome 164 25 55N 109 11W
Ahr, R. 48 50 25N 6 52 E
Ahrensbök 48 54 0N 10 34 E
Ahrweiler 48 50 31N 7 3 E
Ahsā, Wahatāal 92 25 50N 49 0 E
Ahuachapán 166 13 54N 89 52W
Ahuriri, R. 143 44 31 S 170 12 E
Åhus 73 55 56N 14 18 E
Ahvāz 92 31 20N 48 40 E
Ahvenanmaa 75 60 15N 20 0 E
Ahzar 121 15 30N 3 20 E
Aibaq 93 36 15N 68 5 E
Aichach 49 48 28N 11 9 E
Aichi-ken □ 111 35 0N 137 15 E
Aidone 65 37 26N 14 26 E
Aiello Cálabro 65 39 6N 16 12 E
Aigle 50 46 18N 6 58 E
Aignay-le-Duc 43 47 40N 4 43 E
Aigre 44 45 54N 0 1 E
Aigua 173 34 13 S 54 46W
Aigueperse 44 46 3N 3 13 E
Aigues-Mortes 45 43 35N 4 12 E
Aiguilles 45 44 47N 6 51 E
Aiguillon 44 44 18N 0 21 E
Aiguillon, L' 44 46 20N 1 16W
Aigurande 44 46 27N 1 49 E
Aihui 105 50 16N 127 28 E
Aija 174 9 50 S 77 45W
Aijal 98 23 40N 92 44 E
Aiken 157 33 34N 81 50W
Ailao Shan 108 24 0N 101 30 E
Aillant-sur-Tholon 43 47 52N 3 20 E
Aillik 151 55 11N 59 18W
Ailly-sur-Noye 43 49 45N 2 20 E
Ailsa Craig, I. 34 55 15N 5 7W
Aim 77 59 0N 133 55 E
Aimere 103 8 45 S 121 3 E
Aimogasta 172 28 33 S 66 50W
Aimorés 171 19 30 S 41 4W
Aimorés, Serra dos 171 17 50 S 40 30W
Ain □ 45 46 5N 5 20 E
Ain Banaiyah 93 23 0N 51 0 E
Aïn-Beïda 119 35 50N 7 35 E
Ain ben Khellil 118 33 15N 0 49W
Ain Ben Tili 118 25 59N 9 27W
Aïn Benian 118 36 48N 2 55 E
'Ain Dalla 122 27 20N 27 23 E
Ain Dar 92 25 55N 49 10 E
Ain el Mafki 122 27 30N 28 15 E
Ain Girba 122 29 20N 25 14 E
Aïn M'lila 119 36 2N 6 35 E
Ain Qeiqab 122 29 42N 24 55 E
Ain, R. 45 45 52N 5 11 E
Aïn Rich 118 34 38N 24 55 E
Aïn-Sefra 118 32 47N 0 37W
Ain Sheikh Murzûk 122 26 47N 27 45 E
Ain Sukhna 122 29 32N 32 20 E
Aïn Tédelès 118 36 0N 0 21 E
Aïn-Témouchent 118 35 16N 1 8W
Aïn Touta 119 35 26N 5 54 E
Ain Zeitûn 122 29 10N 25 48 E
Aïn Zorah 118 34 37N 3 32W
Ainabo 91 9 0N 46 25 E
Ainazi 80 57 50N 24 24 E
Aine Galakka 117 18 10N 18 30 E
Aínos Óros 69 38 10N 20 35 E
Ainsdale 32 53 37N 3 2W
Ainsworth 158 42 33N 99 52W
Aioi 110 34 48N 134 28 E
Aion 77 69 50N 169 0 E
Aipe 174 3 13N 75 15W
Aïr 121 18 30N 8 0 E
Airaines 43 49 58N 1 55 E
Aird Brenish, C. 36 58 8N 7 8W
Aird, The, dist. 37 57 26N 4 30W
Airdrie 35 55 53N 3 57W
Aire 43 50 37N 2 22 E
Aire, Isla del 58 39 48N 4 16 E
Aire, R. 43 49 18N 5 0 E
Aire-sur-l'Adour 44 43 42N 0 15W
Aireys Inlet 140 38 29 S 144 5 E
Airolo 51 46 32N 8 37 E
Airvault 42 46 50N 0 8W
Aisgill 32 54 23N 2 21W
Aishihik 147 61 40N 137 46W
Aisne □ 43 49 42N 3 40 E
Aisne, R. 43 49 26N 2 50 E
Aït Melloul 118 30 25N 9 29W
Aitana, Sierra de 59 38 35N 0 24W
Aitape 135 3 11 S 142 22 E
Aith 37 59 8N 2 38W

Aitkin 158 46 32N 93 43W
Aitolía Kai Akarnanía □ 69 38 45N 21 18 E
Aitolikón 69 38 26N 21 21 E
Aitoska Planina 67 42 45N 27 30 E
Aiuaba 170 6 38 S 40 7W
Aiud 70 46 19N 23 44 E
Aix-en-Provence 45 43 32N 5 27 E
Aix-la-Chapelle = Aachen 48 50 47N 6 4 E
Aix-les-Bains 45 45 41N 5 53 E
Aix-les-Thermes 44 42 43N 1 51 E
Aix-sur-Vienne 44 45 48N 1 8 E
Aiyang, Mt. 135 5 10 S 141 20 E
Aiyangpienmen 107 40 55N 124 30 E
Aiyansh 152 55 17N 129 2W
Aiyina 69 37 45N 23 26 E
Aiyínion 68 40 28N 22 28 E
Aiyion 69 38 15N 22 5 E
Aizenay 42 46 44N 1 38W
Aizpute 80 56 43N 21 40 E
Aizuwakamatsu 112 37 30N 139 56 E
Ajaccio 45 41 55N 8 40 E
Ajaccio, G. d' 45 41 52N 8 40 E
Ajalpán 165 18 22N 97 15W
Ajana 137 27 56 S 114 35 E
Ajanta Ra. 96 20 28N 75 50 E
Ajax, Mt. 143 42 35 S 172 5 E
Ajdabiyah 119 30 54N 20 4 E
Ajdīr, Raïs 119 33 4N 11 44 E
AjdovTUina 63 45 54N 13 54 E
Ajibar 123 10 35N 38 36 E
'Ajlun 90 32 18N 35 47 E
Ajman 93 25 25N 55 30 E
Ajmer 94 26 28N 74 37 E
Ajo 161 32 18N 112 54W
Ajoie 50 47 22N 7 0 E
Ajok 123 9 15N 28 28 E
Ajua 120 4 50N 1 55W
Ak Dağ 92 36 30N 30 0 E
Akaba 121 8 10N 1 2 E
Akabli 118 26 49N 1 31 E
Akaishi-Dake 111 35 27N 138 9 E
Akaishi-Sammyaku 111 35 25N 138 10 E
Akaki Beseka 123 8 55N 38 45 E
Akala 123 15 39N 36 13 E
Akaroa 143 43 49 S 172 59 E
Akaroa Harb. 131 43 54 S 172 59 E
Akasha 122 21 10N 30 32 E
Akashi 110 34 45N 135 0 E
Akbou 119 36 31N 4 31 E
Akbulak 84 51 1N 55 37 E
Akdala 85 45 2N 74 35 E
Akechi 111 35 18N 137 23 E
Akegbe 121 6 17N 7 28 E
Akelamo 103 1 35N 129 40 E
Akershus Fylke □ 71 60 10N 11 15 E
Akeru, R. 96 17 25N 80 0 E
Aketi 124 2 38N 23 47 E
Akhaïa □ 69 38 5N 21 45 E
Akhalkalaki 83 41 27N 43 25 E
Akhaltsikhe 83 41 40N 43 0 E
Akharnai 69 38 5N 23 44 E
Akhelóös, R. 69 39 5N 21 25 E
Akhendriá 69 34 58N 25 16 E
Akhéron, R. 68 39 31N 20 29 E
Akhisar 92 38 56N 27 48 E
Akhladhókambos 69 37 31N 22 35 E
Akhmîm 122 26 31N 31 47 E
Akhnur 95 32 52N 74 45 E
Akhtopol 67 42 6N 27 56 E
Akhtubinsk (Petropavlovskiy) 83 48 27N 46 7 E
Akhty 83 41 30N 47 45 E
Akhtyrka 80 50 25N 35 0 E
Aki 110 33 30N 133 54 E
Aki-Nada 110 34 5N 132 40 E
Akiak 147 60 50N 161 12W
Akimiski I. 150 52 50N 81 30W
Akimovka 82 46 44N 35 0 E
Akincilar 69 37 57N 27 25 E
Akinum 138 6 15 S 149 30 E
Åkirkeby 73 55 4N 14 55 E
Akita 112 39 45N 140 0 E
Akita-ken □ 112 39 40N 140 30 E
Akjoujt 120 19 45N 14 15W
Akka 118 29 28N 8 9W
'Akko 90 32 35N 35 4 E
Akkol, Kazakh, U.S.S.R. 85 45 0N 75 39 E
Akkol, Kazakh, U.S.S.R. 85 43 36N 70 45 E
Akköy 69 37 30N 27 18 E
Akkrum 46 53 3N 5 50 E
Aklampa 121 8 15N 2 10 E
Aklavik, Can. 147 68 12N 135 0W
Aklavik, N.W.T., Can. 147 68 12N 135 0W
Akmuz 85 41 15N 76 10 E
Aknoul 118 34 40N 3 55W
Akō 110 34 45N 134 24 E
Ako 121 10 19N 10 48 E
Akobo, R. 123 7 10N 34 25 E
Akola 96 20 42N 77 2 E
Akonolinga 121 3 50N 12 18 E
Akordat 123 15 30N 37 40 E
Akosombo Dam 121 6 20N 0 5 E
Ak'osu 105 41 15N 80 14 E
Akot, India 96 21 10N 77 10 E
Akot, Sudan 123 6 31N 30 9 E
Akpatok I. 149 60 25N 68 8W
Akranes 74 64 19N 22 6W
Åkrehamn 71 59 15N 5 10 E
Akreïjit 120 18 19N 9 11W

Akrítas Venétiko, Ákra 69 36 43N 21 54 E
Akron, Colo., U.S.A. 158 40 13N 103 15W
Akron, Ohio, U.S.A. 156 41 7N 81 31W
Akrotíri, Ákra 68 40 26N 25 27W
Aksai Chih, L. 95 35 15N 79 55 E
Aksaray 92 38 25N 34 2 E
Aksarka 76 66 31N 67 50 E
Aksehir 92 38 18N 31 30 E
Aksenovo Zilovskoye 77 53 20N 117 40 E
Aksuat, Ozero 84 51 32N 64 34 E
Aksum 123 14 5N 38 40 E
Aktash, R.S.F.S.R., U.S.S.R. 84 52 2N 52 7 E
Aktash, Uzbek S.S.R., U.S.S.R. 85 39 55N 65 55 E
Aktobe 84 52 55N 62 22 E
Aktogay 85 44 25N 76 44 E
Aktyubinsk 79 50 17N 57 10 E
Aktyuz 85 42 54N 76 7 E
Aku 121 6 40N 7 18 E
Akulurak 147 62 40N 164 35W
Akun I. 147 54 15N 165 30W
Akune 110 32 1N 130 12 E
Akure 121 7 15N 5 5 E
Akureyri 74 65 40N 18 6W
Akusha 83 42 18N 47 30 E
Akutan I. 147 53 30N 166 0W
Akzhar 85 43 8N 71 37 E
Al Abyâr 119 32 9N 20 29 E
Al Amadiyah 92 37 5N 43 30 E
Al Amārah 92 31 55N 47 15 E
Al Aqabah 92 29 37N 35 0 E
Al Ashkhara 93 21 50N 59 30 E
Al Ayn al Mugshin 91 19 35N 54 40 E
Al 'Azīzīyah 119 32 30N 13 1 E
Al Badi 92 22 0N 46 35 E
Al Barah 90 31 55N 35 12 E
Al Barkāt 119 24 56N 10 14 E
Al Basrah 92 30 30N 47 50 E
Al Baydā 117 32 30N 21 40 E
Al Bu'ayrāt 119 31 24N 15 44 E
Al Buqay'ah 90 32 15N 35 30 E
Al Dīwaniyah 92 32 0N 45 0 E
Al Fallujah 92 33 20N 43 55 E
Al Fāw 92 30 0N 48 30 E
Al Hadithan 92 34 0N 41 13 E
Al Hamad 92 31 30N 39 30 E
Al Hamar 92 22 23N 46 6 E
Al Hariq 92 23 29N 46 27 E
Al Hasakah 92 36 35N 40 45 E
Al Hauta 91 16 5N 48 20 E
Al Havy 92 32 5N 46 5 E
Al Hillah, Iraq 92 32 30N 44 25 E
Al Hillah, Si Arab. 92 23 35N 46 50 E
Al Hilwah 92 23 24N 46 48 E
Al Hindiya 92 32 30N 44 10 E
Al Hoceïma 118 35 8N 3 58W
Al Hufrah, Awbārī, Libya 119 25 32N 14 1 E
Al Hufrah, Misrātah, Libya 119 29 5N 18 3 E
Al Hufuf 92 25 25N 49 45 E
Al Husayyāt 119 30 24N 20 37 E
Al Husn 90 32 29N 35 52 E
Al Irq 117 29 5N 21 35 E
Al Ittihad = Madinat al Shaab 91 12 50N 45 0 E
Al Jahrah 92 29 25N 47 40 E
Al Jalāmid 92 31 20N 39 45 E
Al Jarzirah 117 26 10N 21 20 E
Al Jawf 117 24 10N 23 24 E
Al Jazir 91 18 30N 56 31 E
Al Jubail 92 27 0N 49 50 E
Al Juwara 91 19 0N 57 13 E
Al Khābūrah 93 23 57N 57 5 E
Al Khalih 90 31 32N 35 6 E
Al Khums (Homs) 119 32 40N 14 17 E
Al Kut 92 32 30N 46 0 E
Al Kuwayt 92 29 20N 48 0 E
Al Ladhiqiyah 92 35 30N 35 45 E
Al Līth 122 20 9N 40 15 E
Al Madīnah 92 24 35N 39 52 E
Al-Mafraq 90 32 17N 36 14 E
Al Majma'ah 92 25 57N 45 22 E
Al Manamah 93 26 10N 50 30 E
Al Marj 117 32 25N 20 30 E
Al Masīrah 91 20 25N 58 50 E
Al Mawsil 92 36 15N 43 5 E
Al Miqdadīyah 92 34 0N 45 0 E
Al Mubarraz 92 25 30N 49 40 E
Al Muharraq 93 26 15N 50 40 E
Al Mukha 91 13 18N 43 15 E
Al Musayyib 92 32 40N 44 25 E
Al Muwaylih 92 27 40N 35 30 E
Al Qaddāhīyah 119 31 15N 15 9 E
Al Qamishli 92 37 10N 41 10 E
Al Qaryah ash Sharqīyah 119 30 28N 13 40 E
Al Qaşabāt 119 32 39N 14 1 E
Al Qatif 92 26 35N 50 0 E
Al Qaţrun 119 24 56N 15 3 E
Al Quaisūmah 92 28 10N 46 20 E
Al Quds 90 31 47N 35 10 E
Al Qunfidha 122 19 3N 41 4 E
Al Quraiyat 93 23 17N 58 53 E
Al Qurnah 92 31 1N 47 25 E
Al 'Ula 92 26 35N 38 0 E
Al Uqaylah 119 30 12N 19 10 E
Al Uqayr 92 25 40N 50 15 E
Al' Uwayqilah 92 30 30N 42 10 E
Al 'Uyūn 92 26 30N 43 50 E
Al Wajh 122 26 10N 36 30 E
Al Wakrah 93 25 10N 51 40 E

Al Warīah Almaden

Al Warīah 92 27 50N 47 30E
Al Wātīyah 119 32 28N 11 57E
Ala, Italy 62 45 46N 11 0E
Ala, Sweden 72 61 13N 17 9E
Ala Shan 105 40 0N 104 0E
Alabama □ 157 31 0N 87 0W
Alabama, R. 157 31 30N 87 35W
Alaçati 69 38 16N 26 23E
Alaejos 56 41 18N 5 13W
Alagna Valsésia 62 45 51N 7 56E
Alagôa Grande 170 7 3S 35 35W
Alagôas □ 170 9 0S 36 0W
Alagoinhas 171 12 0S 38 20W
Alagón 58 41 46N 1 12W
Alagón, R. 56 39 50N 6 50W
Alajuela 166 10 2N 84 8W
Alakamisy 129 21 19S 47 14E
Alakurtti 78 67 0N 30 30E
Alam Ajaib 122 25 55N 27 14E
Alameda, Spain 57 37 12N 4 39W
Alameda, Calif., U.S.A. 163 37 46N 122 15W
Alameda, N. Mex., U.S.A. 161 35 10N 106 43W
Alameda, S.D., U.S.A. 160 43 2N 112 30W
Alamitos, Sierra de los 164 26 30N 102 20W
Alamo 161 37 21N 115 10W
Alamogordo 161 32 59N 106 0W
Alamos 164 27 0N 109 0W
Alamosa 161 37 30N 106 0W
Åland 75 60 15N 20 0E
Aland 96 17 36N 76 35E
Alandroal 57 38 41N 7 24W
Ålands hav 75 60 10N 19 30E
Alange, Presa de 57 38 45N 6 18W
Alangouassou 120 7 30N 4 34W
Alanis 57 38 3N 5 43W
Alanya 92 36 38N 32 0E
Alaotra, L. 129 17 30S 48 30E
Alapayevsk 84 57 52N 61 42E
Alar del Rey 56 42 38N 4 20W
Alaraz 56 40 45N 5 17W
Alaşehir 79 38 23N 28 30E
Alashantsoch'i 106 38 59N 105 45E
Alaska □ 147 65 0N 150 0W
Alaska, G. of 147 58 0N 145 0W
Alaska Highway 152 60 0N 130 0W
Alaska Pen. 147 56 0N 160 0W
Alaska Range 147 62 50N 151 0W
Alássio 62 44 1N 8 10E
Alatri 64 41 44N 13 21E
Alatyr 81 54 45N 46 35E
Alatyr, R. 81 54 45N 45 30E
Alausí 174 2 0S 78 50W
Álava □ 58 42 48N 2 28W
Alava, C. 160 48 10N 124 40W
Alaverdi 83 41 2N 44 37E
Alawoona 140 34 45S 140 30E
Alaykel 85 40 15N 74 25E
Alayor 58 39 57N 4 8E
Alayskiy Khrebet 85 39 45N 72 0E
Alazan, R. 83 41 25N 46 35E
Alba 62 44 41N 8 1E
Alba □ 70 46 10N 23 30E
Alba de Tormes 56 40 50N 5 30W
Alba-Iulia 70 46 8N 23 39E
Albac 70 46 28N 23 1E
Albacete 59 39 0N 1 50W
Albacete □ 59 38 50N 2 0W
Albacutya, L. 140 35 45S 141 58E
Albæk 73 57 36N 10 25E
Ålbæk Bugt 73 57 35N 10 40E
Albaida 59 38 51N 0 31W
Albalate de las Nogueras 58 40 22N 2 18W
Albalate del Arzobispo 58 41 6N 0 31W
Albania ■ 68 41 0N 20 0E
Albano Laziale 64 41 44N 12 40E
Albany, Austral. 137 35 1S 117 58E
Albany, Ga., U.S.A. 157 31 40N 84 10W
Albany, Minn., U.S.A. 158 45 37N 94 38W
Albany, N.Y., U.S.A. 162 42 29N 73 47W
Albany, Oreg., U.S.A. 160 44 41N 123 0W
Albany, Tex., U.S.A. 159 32 45N 99 20W
Albany, R. 150 52 17N 81 31W
Albardón 172 31 20S 68 30W
Albarracín 58 40 25N 1 26W
Albarracín, Sierra de 58 40 30N 1 30W
Albatross B. 138 12 45S 141 30E
Albatross Pt. 142 38 7S 174 44E
Albegna, R. 63 42 40N 11 28E
Albemarle 157 35 27N 80 15W
Albemarle Sd. 157 36 0N 76 30W
Albenga 62 44 3N 8 12E
Alberche, R. 56 40 10N 4 30W
Alberdi 172 26 14S 58 20W
Alberes, Mts. 58 42 28N 2 56W
Alberga 139 27 12S 135 28E
Alberga, R. 136 26 50S 133 40E
Alberique 59 39 7N 0 31W
Alberni 152 49 20N 124 50W
Albersdorf 48 54 8N 9 19E
Albert, Austral. 141 32 22S 147 30E
Albert, Can. 151 45 51N 64 38W
Albert, France 43 50 0N 2 38E
Albert Canyon 152 51 8N 117 41W
Albert Edward, Mt. 135 8 20S 147 24E
Albert Edward Ra. 136 18 17S 127 57E
Albert L., Austral. 140 35 30S 139 10E
Albert L., U.S.A. 160 42 40N 120 8W
Albert Lea 158 43 32N 93 20W
Albert, L. = Mobutu Sese Seko, L. 126 1 30N 31 0E
Albert Nile, R. 126 3 16N 31 38E
Albert Town 167 22 37N 74 33E
Alberta □ 152 54 40N 115 0W
Alberti 172 35 1S 60 16W
Albertinia 128 34 11S 21 34E
Albertirsa 53 47 14N 19 37E
Albertkanaal 47 51 14N 4 26E
Alberton 151 46 50N 64 0W
Albertville 45 45 40N 6 22E
Albertville = Kalemie 126 5 55S 29 9E
Albi 44 43 56N 2 9E
Albia 158 41 0N 92 50W
Albina 175 5 37N 54 15W
Albina, Pta. 128 15 52S 11 44E
Albino 62 45 47N 9 48E
Albion, Idaho, U.S.A. 160 42 21N 113 37W
Albion, Mich., U.S.A. 156 42 15N 84 45W
Albion, Nebr., U.S.A. 158 41 47N 98 0W
Alblasserdam 46 51 52N 4 40E
Albocácer 58 40 21N 0 1E
Alböke 73 56 57N 16 47E
Alborán, I. 57 35 57N 3 0W
Alborea 59 39 17N 1 24W
Ålborg 73 57 2N 9 54E
Ålborg Bugt 73 56 50N 10 35E
Alborz, Reshteh-Ye Kūkhā-Ye 93 36 0N 52 0E
Albox 59 37 23N 2 8W
Albreda 152 52 35N 119 10W
Albrighton 28 52 38N 2 17W
Albuera, La 57 38 45N 6 49W
Albufeira 57 37 5N 8 15W
Albula, R. 51 46 38N 9 30E
Albuñol 59 36 48N 3 11W
Albuquerque 161 35 5N 106 47W
Albuquerque, Cayos de 166 12 10N 81 50W
Alburno, Mte. 65 40 32N 15 20E
Alburquerque 57 39 15N 6 59W
Albury 141 36 3S 146 56E
Albuskjell, oilfield 19 56 40N 3 0E
Alby 72 62 30N 15 28E
Alcácer do Sal 57 38 22N 8 33W
Alcalá de Chisvert 58 40 19N 0 13E
Alcalá de Guadaira 57 37 20N 5 50W
Alcalá de Henares 58 40 28N 3 22W
Alcalá de los Gazules 57 36 29N 5 43W
Alcalá la Real 57 37 27N 3 57W
Alcamo 64 37 59N 12 55E
Alcanadre 58 42 24N 2 7W
Alcanadre, R. 58 41 43N 0 12W
Alcanar 58 40 33N 0 28E
Alcanede 57 39 25N 8 49W
Alcanena 57 39 27N 8 40W
Alcañices 57 41 41N 6 21W
Alcaníz 58 41 2N 0 8W
Alcântara 170 2 20S 44 30W
Alcántara 57 39 41N 6 57W
Alcantara L. 153 60 57N 108 9W
Alcantarilla 59 37 59N 1 12W
Alcaracejos 57 38 24N 4 58W
Alcaraz 59 38 40N 2 29W
Alcaraz, Sierra de 59 38 40N 2 20W
AlcáRovas 57 38 23N 8 9W
Alcarria, La 58 40 31N 2 45W
Alcaudete 57 37 35N 4 5W
Alcázar de San Juan 59 39 24N 3 12W
Alcester 28 52 13N 1 52W
Alcira 59 39 9N 0 30W
Alcoa 157 35 50N 84 0W
Alcobaça, Brazil 171 17 30S 39 13W
Alcobaça, Port. 57 39 32N 9 0W
Alcobendas 58 40 32N 3 38W
Alcolea del Pinar 58 41 2N 2 28W
Alcora 58 40 5N 0 14W
Alcoutim 57 37 25N 7 28W
Alcova 160 42 37N 106 52W
Alcoy 59 38 43N 0 30W
Alcubierre, Sierra de 58 41 45N 0 22W
Alcublas 58 39 48N 0 43W
Alcudia 58 39 51N 3 9E
Alcudia, Bahía de 58 39 45N 3 14E
Alcudia, Sierra de la 57 38 34N 4 30W
Aldabra Is. 11 9 22S 46 28E
Aldama 165 22 25N 98 4W
Aldan 77 58 40N 125 30E
Aldan, R. 77 62 30N 135 10E
Aldborough 33 54 6N 1 21W
Aldbourne 28 51 28N 1 38W
Aldbrough 33 53 50N 0 7W
Aldeburgh 29 52 9N 1 35E
Aldeia Nova 57 37 55N 7 24W
Alden I. 71 61 19N 4 45E
Alder 160 45 27N 112 3W
Alder Pk. 163 35 53N 12 22W
Alderbury 28 51 4N 1 45W
Alderley Edge 32 53 18N 2 15W
Aldermaston 28 51 23N 1 9W
Alderney, I. 42 49 42N 2 12W
Aldershot 29 51 15N 0 43W
Aldersyde 152 50 40N 113 53W
Aldingham 32 54 8N 3 3W
Aledo 158 41 10N 90 50W
Alefa 123 11 55N 36 55E
Aleg 120 17 3N 13 55W
Alegre 173 20 50S 41 30W
Alegrete 173 29 40S 56 0W
Aleisk 76 52 40N 83 0E
Alejandro Selkirk, I. 131 33 50S 80 15W
Aleksandriya, U.S.S.R. 79 50 45N 26 22E
Aleksandriya, U.S.S.R. 82 48 42N 33 3E
Aleksandriyskaya 83 43 59N 47 0E
Aleksandrov 81 56 23N 38 44E
Aleksandrov Gay. 81 50 15N 48 35E
Aleksandrovac 66 44 28N 21 13E
Aleksandrovka 82 48 55N 32 20E
Aleksandrovo 67 43 14N 24 51E
Aleksandrovsk 84 59 9N 57 33E
Aleksandrovsk-Sakhaliniskiy 77 50 50N 142 20E
Aleksandrovskiy Zavod 77 50 40N 117 50E
Aleksandrovskoye 76 60 35N 77 50E
Aleksandrów Kujawski 54 52 53N 18 43E
Aleksandrów Łódzki 54 51 49N 19 17E
Alekseyevka, R.S.F.S.R., U.S.S.R. 81 50 43N 38 40E
Alekseyevka, R.S.F.S.R., U.S.S.R. 84 52 35N 51 17E
Aleksin 81 54 31N 37 9E
Aleksinac 66 43 31N 21 42E
Além Paraíba 173 21 52S 42 41W
Alemania, Argent. 172 25 40S 65 30W
Alemania, Chile 172 25 10S 69 55W
Ålen 71 62 51N 11 17E
Alençon 42 48 27N 0 4E
Alentejo, Alto- 55 39 0N 7 40W
Alentejo, Baixo- 55 38 0N 8 30W
Alenuihaha Chan. 147 20 25N 156 0W
Aleppo 92 36 10N 37 15E
Aléria 45 42 5N 9 26E
Alert B. 152 50 30N 127 35W
Alès 45 44 9N 4 5E
Aleşd 70 47 3N 22 22E
Alessándria 62 44 54N 8 37E
Ålestrup 73 56 42N 9 29E
Ålesund 71 62 28N 6 12E
Alet 123 8 14N 29 2E
Alet-les-Bains 44 43 0N 2 14E
Aletschgletscher 50 46 28N 8 2E
Aletschhorn 50 46 28N 8 0E
Aleutian Is. 147 52 0N 175 0W
Aleutian Ra. 147 55 0N 155 0W
Alexander 158 47 51N 103 40W
Alexander Arch. 147 57 0N 135 0W
Alexander B. 128 28 36S 16 33E
Alexander City 157 32 58N 85 57W
Alexander I. 13 69 0S 70 0W
Alexander, Mt. 137 28 58S 120 16E
Alexandra, Austral. 141 37 8S 145 40E
Alexandra, N.Z. 143 45 14S 169 25E
Alexandra Falls 152 60 29N 116 18W
Alexandria, Austral. 138 19 5S 136 40E
Alexandria, Brazil 171 6 25S 38 1W
Alexandria, B.C., Can. 152 52 35N 122 27W
Alexandria, Ont., Can. 150 45 19N 74 38W
Alexandria, Rumania 70 43 57N 25 24E
Alexandria, S. Afr. 128 33 38S 26 28E
Alexandria, U.K. 34 55 59N 4 40W
Alexandria, Ind., U.S.A. 156 40 18N 85 40W
Alexandria, La., U.S.A. 159 31 20N 92 30W
Alexandria, Minn., U.S.A. 158 45 50N 95 20W
Alexandria, S.D., U.S.A. 158 43 40N 97 45W
Alexandria, Va., U.S.A. 162 38 47N 77 1W
Alexandria = El Iskandarîya 122 31 0N 30 0E
Alexandria Bay 156 44 20N 75 52W
Alexandrina, L. 140 35 25S 139 10E
Alexandroúpolis 68 40 50N 25 54E
Alexis Creek 152 52 0N 123 20W
Alexis, R. 151 52 33N 56 8W
Alfambra 58 40 33N 1 5W
Alfândega da Fé 56 41 20N 6 59W
Alfaro 58 42 10N 1 50W
Alfatar 67 43 59N 27 13E
Alfeld 48 52 0N 9 49E
Alfenas 173 21 40S 44 0W
Alfiós, R. 69 37 36N 21 54E
Alfonsine 63 44 30N 12 1E
Alford, Grampian, U.K. 37 57 13N 2 42W
Alford, Lincs., U.K. 33 53 16N 0 10E
Alfred 162 43 28N 70 40W
Alfred Town 141 35 8S 147 30E
Alfredton 142 40 41S 175 54E
Alfreton 33 53 6N 1 22W
Alfriston 29 50 48N 0 10E
Alfta 72 61 21N 16 4E
Alftanes 74 64 29N 22 10W
Alga 84 49 53N 57 20E
Algaba, La 57 37 27N 6 1W
Algar 57 36 40N 5 39W
Ålgård 71 58 46N 5 53E
Ålgård 71 58 46N 5 53E
Algarinejo 57 37 19N 4 9W
Algarve 57 37 15N 8 10W
Algeciras 57 36 9N 5 28W
Algemesí 59 39 11N 0 27W
Alger 118 36 42N 3 8E
Algeria ■ 118 35 10N 3 11E
Alghero 64 40 34N 8 20E
Algiers = Alger 118 36 42N 3 8E
Algoabaai 128 33 50S 25 45E
Algodonales 57 36 54N 5 24W
Algodor, R. 56 39 51N 3 48W
Algoma, Mich., U.S.A. 156 44 35N 87 27W
Algoma, Oreg., U.S.A. 160 42 25N 121 54W
Algonquin Prov. Pk. 150 45 50N 78 30W
Alhama de Almería 59 36 57N 2 34W
Alhama de Aragón 58 41 18N 1 54W
Alhama de Granada 57 37 0N 3 59W
Alhama de Murcia 59 37 51N 1 25W
Alhambra, Spain 59 38 54N 3 4W
Alhambra, U.S.A. 163 34 8N 118 10W
Alhaurín el Grande 57 36 39N 4 41W
Alhucemas = Al-Hoceïma 118 35 8N 3 58W
Ali al Gharbi 92 32 30N 46 45E
Ali Bayramly 83 39 43N 48 52E
Ali Khel 94 33 56N 69 35E
Ali Sabieh 123 11 10N 42 44E
Ália 64 37 47N 13 42E
Aliabad 93 28 10N 57 35E
Aliaga 58 40 40N 0 42W
Aliakmon, R. 68 40 10N 22 0E
Alibag 96 18 38N 72 56E
Alibo 123 9 52N 37 5E
Alibunar 66 45 5N 20 57E
Alicante 59 38 23N 0 30W
Alicante □ 59 38 30N 0 37W
Alice, S. Afr. 128 32 48S 26 55E
Alice, U.S.A. 159 27 47N 98 1W
Alice Arm 152 55 29N 129 31W
Alice Downs 136 17 45S 127 56E
Alice, Punta dell' 65 39 23N 17 10E
Alice, R., Queens., Austral. 138 15 35S 142 20E
Alice, R., Queens., Austral. 138 24 2S 144 50E
Alice Springs 138 23 40S 135 50E
Alicedale 128 33 15S 26 4E
Aliceville 157 33 9N 88 10W
Alick Cr. 138 20 35S 142 10E
Alicudi, I. 65 38 33N 14 20E
Alida 153 49 25N 101 55W
Aligarh, India 93 27 55N 78 10E
Aligarh, Raj., India 94 25 55N 76 15E
Aligarh, Ut. P., India 94 27 55N 78 10E
Aligudarz 92 33 25N 49 45E
Alijó 56 41 16N 7 27W
Alimena 65 37 42N 14 4E
Alimnía 69 36 16N 27 43E
Aling Kangri 99 31 45N 84 45E
Alingaabro 73 56 56N 10 32E
Alingsås 73 57 56N 12 31E
Alipore 95 22 32N 88 24E
Alipur 94 29 25N 70 55E
Alipur Duar 98 26 30N 89 35E
Aliquippa 156 40 38N 80 18W
Aliste, R. 56 41 48N 6 14W
Alivérion 69 38 24N 24 2E
Aliwal North 128 30 45S 26 45E
Alix 152 52 24N 113 11W
Aljezur 57 37 18N 8 49W
Aljustrel 57 37 55N 8 10W
Alkamari 121 13 27N 11 10E
Alken 47 50 53N 5 18E
Alkhalaf 91 20 30N 58 13E
Alkmaar 46 52 37N 4 45E
All American Canal 161 32 45N 115 0W
Allada 121 6 41N 2 9E
Allah Dad 94 25 38N 67 34E
Allahabad 95 25 25N 81 58E
Allakaket 147 66 30N 152 45W
Allakh Yun 77 60 50N 137 5E
Allal Razi 118 34 30N 6 39W
Allan 153 51 53N 106 4W
Allanche 44 45 14N 2 57E
Allanmyo 98 19 16N 95 17E
Allanridge 128 27 45S 26 40E
Allansford 140 38 26S 142 39E
Allanton 143 45 55S 170 15E
Allanwater 150 50 14N 90 10W
Allaqi, Wadi 122 22 15N 34 55E
Allard Lake 151 50 40N 63 10W
Allariz 56 42 11N 7 50W
Allassac 44 45 15N 1 29E
Alle 47 49 51N 4 58E
Allegan 156 42 32N 85 52W
Allegheny Mts. 156 38 0N 80 0W
Allegheny, R. 156 41 14N 79 50W
Allègre 44 45 12N 3 41E
Allen, Bog of 39 53 15N 7 0W
Allen, L. 38 54 30N 8 5W
Allen R. 35 54 53N 2 13W
Allenby (Hussein) Bridge 90 31 53N 35 33E
Allendale 35 54 55N 2 15W
Allende 164 28 20N 100 50W
Allenheads 35 54 49N 2 12W
Allentown 162 40 36N 75 30W
Allentsteig 52 48 41N 15 20E
Allenwood 39 53 16N 6 53W
Alleppey 97 9 30N 76 28E
Alleröd 73 55 54N 12 19E
Alleur 47 50 39N 5 31E
Allevard 45 45 24N 6 5E
Alliance, Nebr., U.S.A. 158 42 10N 102 50W
Alliance, Ohio, U.S.A. 156 40 53N 81 7W
Allier □ 44 46 25N 3 0E
Allier, R. 43 46 57N 3 4E
Alligator Cr., Queens., Austral. 138 21 20S 149 12E
Alligator Cr., Queens., Austral. 138 19 23S 146 58E
Allihies 39 51 39N 10 4W
Allingåbrl 73 56 28N 10 20E
Allingåbro 73 56 28N 10 20E
Allinge 73 55 17N 14 50E
Alliston 150 44 9N 79 52W
Alloa 35 56 7N 3 49W
Allonby 32 54 45N 3 27W
Allos 45 44 15N 6 38E
Alma, Can. 151 48 35N 71 40W
Alma, Kans., U.S.A. 158 39 1N 96 22W
Alma, Mich., U.S.A. 156 43 25N 84 40W
Alma, Nebr., U.S.A. 158 40 10N 99 25W
Alma, Wis., U.S.A. 158 44 19N 91 54W
Alma Ata 85 43 15N 76 57E
Almada 57 38 40N 9 9W
Almaden 138 17 22S 144 40E

Almadén **Amungen**

Almadén 57 38 49N 4 52W
Almagro 57 38 50N 3 45W
Almalyk 85 40 50N 69 35 E
Almanor, L. 160 40 15N 121 11W
Almansa 59 38 51N 1 5W
Almanza 56 42 39N 5 3W
Almanzor, Pico de 56 40 15N 5 18W
Almanzora, R. 59 37 22N 2 21W
Almarcha, La 58 39 41N 2 24W
Almas 171 11 33 S 47 9W
Almaş, Mţii 70 44 49N 22 12 E
Almazán 58 41 30N 2 30W
Almazora 58 39 57N 0 3W
Almeirim, Brazil 175 1 30 S 52 0W
Almeirim, Port. 57 39 12N 8 37W
Almelo 46 52 22N 6 42 E
Almenar 58 41 43N 2 12W
Almenara, Brazil 171 16 11 S 40 42W
Almenara, Spain 58 39 46N 0 14W
Almenara, Sierra de 59 37 34N 1 32W
Almendralejo 57 38 41N 6 26W
Almeria 59 36 52N 2 32W
Almeria □ 59 37 20N 2 20W
Almeria, G. de 59 36 41N 2 28W
Almetyevsk 84 54 53N 52 20 E
Almhult 73 56 32N 14 10 E
Almirante 166 9 10N 82 30W
Almiropótamos 69 38 16N 24 11 E
Almirós 69 39 11N 22 45 E
Almodôvar 57 37 31N 8 2W
Almodóvar del Campo 57 38 43N 4 10W
Almogia 57 36 50N 4 32W
Almonaster la Real 57 37 52N 6 48W
Almond R. 35 56 27N 3 27W
Almondsbury 28 51 33N 2 34W
Almonte, R. 57 39 41N 6 12W
Almora 95 29 38N 79 4 E
Almoradi 59 38 7N 0 46W
Almorox 56 40 14N 4 24W
Almoustarat 121 17 35N 0 8 E
Älmult 73 56 33N 14 8 E
Almuñécar 57 36 43N 3 41W
Almunia, La de Doña Godina 58 41 29N 1 23W
Almvik 73 57 49N 16 30 E
Aln, R. 35 55 24N 1 35W
Alness 37 57 41N 4 15W
Alness R. 37 57 45N 4 20W
Alnif 118 31 10N 5 8W
Alnmouth 35 55 24N 1 37W
Alnön I. 72 62 26N 17 33 E
Alnwick 35 55 25N 1 42W
Aloi 126 2 16N 33 10 E
Alon 98 22 12N 95 5 E
Alonsa 153 50 50N 99 0W
Alor, I. 103 8 15 S 124 30 E
Alor Setar 101 6 7N 100 22 E
Alora 57 36 49N 4 46W
Alosno 57 37 33N 7 7W
Alot'ai 105 47 52N 88 7 E
Alotau 135 10 16 S 150 30 E
Alougoum 118 30 17N 6 56W
Aloysius Mt. 137 26 0 S 128 38 E
Alpaugh 163 35 53N 119 29W
Alpedrinha 56 40 6N 7 27W
Alpena 156 45 6N 83 24W
Alpercatas, R. 170 6 2 S 44 19W
Alpes-de-Haute-Provence □ 45 44 8N 6 10 E
Alpes-Maritimes □ 45 43 55N 7 10 E
Alpes Valaisannes 50 46 4N 7 30 E
Alpha 138 23 39 S 146 37 E
Alphen 47 51 29N 4 58 E
Alphen aan den Rijn 46 52 7N 4 40 E
Alphington 30 50 41N 3 32W
Alpi Apuan 62 44 7N 10 14 E
Alpi Craie 43 45 40N 7 0 E
Alpi Lepontine 51 46 22N 8 27 E
Alpi Orobie 62 46 7N 10 0 E
Alpi Retiche 51 46 45N 10 0 E
Alpiarça 57 39 15N 8 35W
Alpine, Ariz., U.S.A. 161 33 57N 109 4W
Alpine, Calif., U.S.A. 163 32 50N 116 46W
Alpine, Tex., U.S.A. 159 30 35N 103 35W
Alpnach 51 46 57N 8 17 E
Alrewas 28 52 43N 1 44W
Alrø 73 55 52N 10 5 E
Alroy Downs 138 19 20 S 136 5 E
Als 73 56 46N 10 18 E
Alsace 43 48 15N 7 25 E
Alsager 32 53 7N 2 20W
Alsask 153 51 21N 109 59W
Alsásua 58 42 54N 2 10W
Alseda 73 57 27N 15 20 E
Alsen 72 63 23N 13 56 E
Alsfeld 48 50 44N 9 19 E
Alsh, L. 36 57 15N 5 39W
Alsónémedi 53 47 34N 19 15 E
Alsten 74 65 58N 12 40 E
Alston 32 54 48N 2 26W
Alta 74 69 57N 23 10 E
Alta Gracia 172 31 40 S 64 30W
Alta Lake 152 50 10N 123 0W
Alta, Sierra 58 40 31N 1 30W
Alta Sierra 163 35 42N 118 33W
Altaelva 74 69 46N 23 45 E
Altafjorden 74 70 5N 23 5 E
Altagracia 174 10 45N 71 30W
Altai = Aerht'ai Shan 105 48 0N 90 0 E
Altamaha, R. 157 31 50N 82 0W
Altamira, Brazil 175 3 0 S 52 10W
Altamira, Chile 172 25 47 S 69 51W
Altamira, Colomb. 174 2 3N 75 47W
Altamira, Mexico 165 22 24N 97 55W
Altamira, Cuevas de 56 43 20N 4 5W
Altamont 162 42 43N 74 3W
Altamura 65 40 50N 16 33 E
Altanbulag 54 50 19N 106 30 E
Altar 164 30 40N 111 50W
Altarnun 30 50 35N 4 30W
Altata 164 24 30N 108 0W
Altavista 156 37 9N 79 22W
Altdorf 51 46 52N 8 36 E
Altea 59 38 38N 0 2W
Altenberg 48 50 46N 13 47 E
Altenbruch 48 53 48N 8 44 E
Altenburg 48 50 59N 12 28 E
Altenkirchen 48 50 41N 7 38 E
Altenmarkt 52 47 43N 14 39 E
Alter do Chão 57 39 12N 7 40W
Altkirch 43 47 37N 7 15 E
Altnaharra 37 58 17N 4 27W
Alto Adige = Trentino-Alto Adige 62 46 5N 11 0 E
Alto Araguaia 175 17 15 S 53 20W
Alto Chindio 127 16 19 S 35 25 E
Alto Cuchumatanes 164 15 30N 91 10W
Alto del Inca 172 24 10 S 68 10W
Alto Ligonha 127 15 30 S 38 11 E
Alto Molocue 127 15 50 S 37 35 E
Alto Paraná □ 173 25 0 S 54 50W
Alto Parnaíba 170 9 6 S 45 57W
Alto Santo 170 5 31 S 38 15W
Alto Turi 170 2 54 S 45 38W
Alto Uruguay, R. 173 27 0 S 53 30W
Alton, U.K. 29 51 8N 0 59W
Alton, Ill., U.S.A. 158 38 55N 90 5W
Alton, N.H., U.S.A. 162 43 27N 71 13W
Alton Downs 139 26 7 S 138 57 E
Altona 48 53 32N 9 56 E
Altoona 156 40 32N 78 24W
Altopáscio 62 43 50N 10 40 E
Altos 170 5 3 S 42 28W
Altrincham 32 53 25N 2 21W
Altstätten 51 47 22N 9 33 E
Alturas 160 41 36N 120 37W
Altus 159 34 30N 99 25W
Alucra 83 40 22N 38 47 E
Aluksône 80 57 24N 27 3 E
Alula 91 11 50N 50 45 E
Alupka 82 44 23N 34 2 E
Alushta 82 44 40N 34 25 E
Alusi 103 7 35 S 131 40 E
Alustante 58 40 36N 1 40W
Alva, U.K. 35 56 9N 3 49W
Alva, U.S.A. 159 36 50N 98 50W
Alvaiázere 56 39 49N 8 23W
Älvangen 73 58 0N 12 7 E
Alvängen 73 57 58N 12 8 E
Alvarado, Mexico 165 18 40N 95 50W
Alvarado, U.S.A. 159 32 25N 97 15W
Alvaro Obregón, Presa 164 27 55N 109 52W
Alvastra 73 58 20N 14 44 E
Alvdal 71 62 6N 10 37 E
Alvear 172 29 5 S 56 30W
Alvechurch 28 52 22N 1 58W
Alverca 57 38 56N 9 1W
Alveringen 47 51 1N 2 43 E
Alvesta 73 56 54N 14 35 E
Älvho 72 61 30N 14 45 E
Alvie, Austral. 140 38 14 S 143 30 E
Alvie, U.K. 37 57 10N 3 50W
Alvin 159 29 23N 95 12W
Alvito 57 38 15N 8 0W
Älvkarleby 75 60 32N 17 40 E
Alvra, Pic d' 51 46 35N 9 50 E
Älvros 72 62 3N 14 38 E
Älvsborgs län □ 73 58 30N 12 30 E
Älvsby 74 65 42N 20 52 E
Älvsbyn 74 65 40N 20 0 E
Alvsered 73 57 14N 12 51 E
Alwar 94 27 38N 76 34 E
Alwaye 97 10 8N 76 24 E
Alwinton 35 55 20N 2 7W
Alwyn, oilfield 19 60 30N 1 45 E
Alyangula 133 13 55 S 136 30 E
Alyaskitovyy 77 64 45N 141 30 E
Alyata 83 39 58N 49 25 E
Alyth 37 56 38N 3 15W
Alzada 158 45 3N 104 22W
Alzano Lombardo 62 45 44N 9 43 E
Alzette, R. 47 49 45N 6 6 E
Alzey 49 49 48N 8 4 E
Am-Dam 117 12 40N 20 35 E
Am Djeress 117 16 15N 22 50 E
Am Guereda 117 12 53N 21 14 E
Am Timan 117 11 0N 20 10 E
Am-Zoer 124 14 13N 21 23 E
Amadeus, L. 137 24 54 S 131 0 E
Amadi, Congo 126 3 40N 26 40 E
Amadi, Sudan 123 5 29N 30 25 E
Amadi, Zaïre 126 3 40N 26 40 E
Amadia 92 37 6N 43 30 E
Amadjuak 149 64 0N 72 39W
Amadjuak L. 149 65 0N 71 8W
Amadora 57 38 45N 9 13W
Amaga 174 6 3N 75 42W
Amagansett 162 40 58N 72 8W
Amagasaki 111 34 42N 135 20 E
Amager 73 55 37N 12 35 E
Amagi 110 33 25N 130 39 E
Amagunze 121 6 20N 7 40 E
Amaimon 135 5 12 S 145 30 E
Amakusa-Nada 110 32 35N 130 5 E
Amakusa-Shotō 110 32 15N 130 10 E
Amål 72 59 2N 12 40 E
Åmål 72 59 3N 12 42 E
Amalapuram 96 16 35N 81 55 E
Amalfi, Colomb. 174 6 55N 75 4W
Amalfi, Italy 65 40 39N 14 34 E
Amaliás 69 37 47N 21 22 E
Amalner 96 21 5N 75 5 E
Amambaí 173 23 5 S 55 13W
Amambai, R. 173 23 22 S 53 56W
Amambay □ 173 23 0 S 56 0W
Amambay, Cordillera de 173 20 30 S 56 0W
Amami-O-Shima 112 28 0N 129 0 E
Amanab 135 3 40 S 141 14 E
Amandola 63 42 59N 13 21 E
Amanfrom 121 7 20N 0 25 E
Amangeldy 76 50 10N 65 10 E
Amantea 65 39 8N 16 3 E
Amapá 170 2 5N 50 50W
Amapá □ 170 1 40N 52 0W
Amar Gedid 123 14 27N 25 13 E
Amara, Iraq 92 31 57N 47 12 E
Amara, Sudan 123 10 25N 34 10 E
Amarante, Brazil 170 6 14 S 42 50W
Amarante, Port. 56 41 16N 8 5W
Amarante do Maranhão 170 5 36 S 46 45W
Amaranth 153 50 36N 98 43W
Amarapura 98 21 54N 96 3 E
Amaravati, R. 97 10 50N 77 42 E
Amaravati = Amraoti 96 20 55N 77 45 E
Amareleja 57 38 12N 7 13W
Amargosa 171 13 2 S 39 36W
Amargosa, R. 163 36 14N 116 51W
Amargosa Ra., mts 163 36 25N 116 40W
Amarillo 159 35 14N 101 46W
Amaro Leite 171 13 58 S 49 9W
Amaro, Mt. 63 42 5N 14 6 E
Amarpur, India 99 23 30N 91 45 E
Amarpur, Bihar, India 95 25 5N 87 0 E
Amarpur, Tripura, India 99 23 30N 91 45 E
Amasra 92 41 45N 32 30 E
Amassama 121 5 1N 6 2 E
Amasya 92 40 40N 35 50 E
Amatignak I. 147 51 19N 179 10W
Amatikulu 129 29 3 S 31 33 E
Amatitlán 166 14 29N 90 38W
Amatrice 63 42 38N 13 16 E
Amay 47 50 33N 5 19 E
Amazon, R. 175 2 0 S 53 30W
Amazonas □, Brazil 174 4 20 S 64 0W
Amazonas □, Colomb. 174 1 0 S 72 0W
Amazonas □, Venez. 174 3 30N 66 0W
Amazonas, R. 175 2 0 S 53 30W
Ambad 96 19 38N 75 50 E
Ambahakily 129 21 36 S 43 41 E
Ambala 94 30 23N 76 56 E
Ambalangoda 97 6 15N 80 5 E
Ambalapuzha 97 9 25N 76 25 E
Ambalavao 129 21 50 S 46 56 E
Ambalindum 138 23 23 S 134 40 E
Ambam 124 2 20N 11 15 E
Ambanifilao 129 12 48 S 49 47 E
Ambanja 129 13 40 S 48 27 E
Ambararata 129 13 41 S 48 27 E
Ambarchik 77 69 40N 162 20 E
Ambarijeby 129 14 56 S 47 41 E
Ambarnath 96 19 12N 73 22 E
Ambaro, B. d' 129 13 23 S 48 38 E
Ambasamudram 97 8 43N 77 25 E
Ambato 174 1 5 S 78 42W
Ambato-Boéni 129 16 28 S 46 43 E
Ambato, Sierra de 172 28 25N 66 10W
Ambatolampy 129 19 20 S 47 35 E
Ambatondrazaka 129 17 55 S 48 28 E
Ambatosoratra 129 17 37 S 48 31 E
Ambenja 129 15 17 S 46 58 E
Ambeno 103 9 20 S 124 30 E
Amberg 49 49 25N 11 52 E
Ambergris Cay 165 18 0N 88 0W
Ambérieu-en-Bugey 45 45 57N 5 20 E
Amberley 143 43 9 S 172 44 E
Ambert 44 45 33N 3 44 E
Ambevongo 129 15 25 S 42 26 E
Ambia 129 16 11 S 45 33 E
Ambidédi 120 14 35N 11 47W
Ambikapur 95 23 15N 83 15 E
Ambikol 122 21 20N 30 50 E
Ambilobé 125 13 10 S 49 3 E
Ambinanindrano 129 20 5 S 48 23 E
Ambjörnarp 73 57 25N 13 17 E
Amble 35 55 20N 1 36W
Ambler 162 40 9N 75 13W
Ambleside 32 54 26N 2 58W
Amblève 47 50 21N 6 10 E
Amblève, R. 47 50 25N 5 45 E
Ambo, Begemdir & Simen, Ethiopia 123 12 20N 37 30 E
Ambo, Shewa, Ethiopia 123 9 0N 37 48 E
Ambo, Peru 174 10 5 S 76 10W
Ambodifototra 129 16 59 S 49 52 E
Ambodilazana 129 18 6 S 49 10 E
Ambohimahasoa 129 21 7 S 47 13 E
Ambohimanga du Sud 129 20 52 S 47 36 E
Ambon 103 3 35 S 128 20 E
Ambongao, Cones d' 129 17 0 S 45 0 E
Amboseli L. 126 2 40 S 37 10 E
Ambositra 129 20 31 S 47 25 E
Amboy 163 34 33N 115 51W
Ambre, C. d' 129 12 40 S 49 10 E
Ambre, Mt. d' 125 12 30 S 49 10 E
Ambriz 124 7 48 S 13 8 E
Ambrizete 124 7 10 S 12 52 E
Ambunti 135 4 13 S 142 52 E
Ambut 97 12 48N 78 43 E
Amby 139 26 30 S 148 11 E
Amchitka I. 147 51 30N 179 0W
Amchitka P. 147 51 30N 179 0W
Amderma 76 69 45N 61 30 E
Ameca 164 20 30N 104 0W
Ameca, R. 164 20 40N 105 15W
Amecameca 165 19 10N 98 57W
Ameland 46 53 27N 5 45 E
Amélia 63 42 34N 12 25 E
Amèlie-les-Bains-Palalda 44 42 29N 2 41 E
Amen 77 68 45N 180 0 E
Amendolaro 65 39 58N 16 34 E
Amenia 162 41 51N 73 33W
America 47 51 27N 5 59 E
American Falls 160 42 46N 112 56W
American Falls Res. 160 43 0N 112 50W
American Highland 13 73 0 S 75 0 E
Americana 173 22 45 S 47 20W
Americus 157 32 0N 84 10W
Amersfoort, Neth. 46 52 9N 5 23 E
Amersfoort, S. Afr. 129 26 59 S 29 53 E
Amersham 29 51 40N 0 38W
Amery, Austral. 137 31 9 S 117 5 E
Amery, Can. 153 56 34N 94 3W
Ames 158 42 0N 93 40W
Amesbury, U.K. 28 51 10N 1 46W
Amesbury, U.S.A. 162 42 50N 70 52W
Amesdale 153 50 2N 92 55W
Ameson 150 49 50N 84 35W
Amethyst, gasfield 19 53 38N 0 40 E
Amfíklia 69 38 38N 22 35 E
Amfilokhía 69 38 52N 21 9 E
Amfipolis 68 40 48N 23 52 E
Ámfissa 69 38 32N 22 22 E
Amga, R. 77 61 0N 132 0 E
Amgu 77 45 45N 137 15 E
Amherst, Burma 99 16 2N 97 20 E
Amherst, Can. 151 45 48N 64 8W
Amherst, Mass., U.S.A. 162 42 21N 72 30W
Amherst, Tex., U.S.A. 159 34 0N 102 24W
Amherst, Mt. 136 18 11 S 126 59 E
Amherstburg 150 42 6N 83 6W
Amiata Mte. 63 42 54N 11 40 E
Amiens 43 49 54N 2 16 E
Amigdhalokefáli 69 35 23N 23 30 E
Amili 98 28 25N 95 52 E
Amindaion 68 40 42N 21 42 E
Amirante Is. 11 6 0 S 53 0 E
Amisk L. 153 54 35N 102 15W
Amistati, Presa 164 29 24N 101 0W
Amite 159 30 47N 90 31W
Åmli 71 58 45N 8 32 E
Amlia I. 147 52 5N 173 30W
Amlwch 31 53 24N 4 21W
Amm Adam 123 16 20N 36 1 E
'Ammān 90 32 0N 35 52 E
Ammanford 31 51 48N 4 0W
Ammerån 72 63 9N 16 13 E
Ammerån 72 63 9N 16 13 E
Ammersee 49 48 0N 11 7 E
Ammerzoden 46 51 45N 5 13 E
Ammi'ad 90 32 55N 35 32 E
Amnat Charoen 100 15 51N 104 38 E
Amne Machin 105 34 30N 100 0 E
Amnéville 43 49 16N 6 9 E
Amo Chiang, R. 108 22 56N 101 47 E
Amorebieta 58 43 13N 2 44W
Amorgós 69 36 50N 25 57 E
Amory 57 33 59N 88 30W
Amos 150 48 35N 78 5W
Åmot 71 59 54N 9 54 E
Åmot 71 59 34N 8 0 E
Åmotsdal 71 59 37N 8 26 E
Amour, Djebel 118 33 42N 1 37 E
Amoy = Hsiamen 109 24 25N 118 4 E
Amozoc 165 19 2N 98 3W
Ampang 101 3 8N 101 45 E
Ampanihy 129 24 40 S 44 45 E
Amparihy Est. 129 23 57 S 47 20 E
Ampasindava, B. d' 129 13 40 S 48 15 E
Ampasindava, Presqu'île d' 129 13 42 S 47 55W
Amper 121 9 25N 9 40 E
Ampère 119 35 44N 5 27 E
Ampleforth 33 54 13N 1 8W
Ampombiantambo 129 12 42 S 48 57 E
Amposta 58 40 43N 0 34 E
Ampotaka 129 25 3 S 44 41 E
Ampoza 129 22 20 S 44 44 E
Ampthill 29 52 3N 0 30W
Amqa 90 32 59N 35 10 E
Amqui 151 48 28N 67 27W
Amraoti 96 20 55N 77 45 E
Amreli 94 21 35N 71 17 E
Amrenene el Kasba 118 22 10N 0 30 E
Amriswil 51 47 33N 9 18 E
Amritsar 94 31 35N 74 57 E
Amroha 95 28 53N 78 30 E
Amrum 48 54 37N 8 21 E
Amsel 119 22 47N 5 29 E
Amsterdam, Neth. 46 52 23N 4 54 E
Amsterdam, U.S.A. 162 42 58N 74 10W
Amsterdam, I. 11 37 30 S 77 30 E
Amstetten 52 48 7N 14 51 E
Amu Darya, R. 76 37 50N 65 0 E
Amuay 174 11 50N 70 10W
Amukta I. 147 52 29N 171 20W
Amund Ringnes I. 12 78 20N 96 25W
Amundsen Gulf 148 71 0N 124 0W
Amundsen Sea 13 72 0 S 115 0W
Amungen 72 61 10N 15 40 E

Amuntai Anza

Amuntai	**102**	2 28S	115 25E
Amur, R.	**77**	53 30N	122 30E
Amurang	**103**	1 5N	124 40E
Amuri Pass	**143**	42 31S	172 11E
Amurrio	**58**	43 3N	3 0W
Amurzet	**77**	47 50N	131 5E
Amusco	**56**	42 10N	4 28W
Amvrakikós Kólpos	**69**	39 0N	20 55E
Amvrosiyvka	**83**	47 43N	38 30E
Amzeglouf	**118**	26 50N	0 1E
An	**98**	22 29N	96 54E
An Bien	**101**	9 45N	105 0E
An Geata Mór, (Binghamstown)	**38**	54 13N	10 0W
An Hoa	**100**	15 30N	108 20E
An Loc	**101**	11 40N	106 50E
An Nafud	**92**	28 15N	41 0E
An Najaf	**92**	32 3N	44 15E
An-Nāqūrah	**90**	33 7N	35 8E
An Nasiriyah	**92**	31 0N	46 15E
An Nawfaliyah	**119**	30 54N	17 58E
An Nhon (Binh Dinh)	**100**	13 55N	109 7E
An Nîl □	**123**	17 30N	33 0E
An Nîl el Abyad □	**123**	14 0N	32 15E
An Nu'ayriyah	**92**	27 30N	48 30E
An Teallach, Mt.	**36**	57 49N	5 18W
An Thoi, Dao	**101**	9 58N	104 0E
An Tuc	**100**	13 57N	108 39E
An Uaimh	**38**	53 39N	6 40W
Åna-Sira	**71**	58 17N	6 25E
Anabta	**90**	32 19N	35 7E
Anabuki	**110**	34 2N	134 11E
Anaco	**174**	9 27N	64 28W
Anaconda	**160**	46 7N	113 0W
Anacortes	**160**	48 30N	122 40W
Anadarko	**159**	35 4N	98 15W
Anadia, Brazil	**170**	9 42S	36 18W
Anadia, Port.	**56**	40 26N	8 27W
Anadolu	**92**	38 0N	29 0E
Anadyr	**77**	64 35N	177 20E
Anadyr, R.	**77**	66 50N	171 0E
Anadyrskiy Zaliv	**77**	64 0N	180 0E
Anáfi	**69**	36 22N	25 48E
Anafópoulo	**69**	36 17N	25 50E
Anagni	**64**	41 44N	13 8E
Anah	**92**	34 25N	42 0E
Anaheim	**163**	33 50N	118 0W
Anahim Lake	**152**	52 28N	125 18W
Anáhuac	**164**	27 14N	100 9W
Anai Mudi, Mt.	**97**	10 12N	77 20E
Anaimalai Hills	**97**	10 20N	76 40E
Anajás	**170**	0 59S	49 57W
Anajatuba	**170**	3 16S	44 37W
Anakapalle	**96**	17 42N	83 06E
Anakie	**138**	23 32S	147 45E
Anaklia	**83**	42 22N	41 35E
Analalava	**129**	14 35S	48 0E
Analapasy	**129**	25 11S	46 40E
Anam	**121**	6 19N	6 41E
Anambar, R.	**94**	30 10N	68 50E
Anambas, Kepulauan	**102**	3 20N	106 30E
Anamoose	**158**	47 55N	100 7W
Anamosa	**158**	42 7N	91 17W
Anamur	**92**	36 8N	32 58E
Anan	**110**	33 54N	134 40E
Anand	**94**	22 32N	72 59E
Anandpur	**96**	21 16N	86 13E
Anánes	**69**	36 33N	24 9E
Anantapur	**97**	14 39N	77 42E
Anantnag	**95**	33 45N	75 10E
Ananyev	**82**	47 44N	29 57E
Anapa	**82**	44 55N	37 25E
Anápolis	**171**	16 15S	48 50W
Anar	**93**	30 55N	55 13E
Anarak	**93**	33 25N	53 40E
Anatolia = Anadolu	**92**	38 0N	29 0E
Anatone	**160**	46 9N	117 4W
Añatuya	**172**	28 20S	62 50W
Anaunethad L.	**153**	60 55N	104 25W
Anaye	**117**	19 15N	12 50E
Anbyŏn	**107**	39 1N	127 35E
Ancaster	**33**	52 59N	0 32W
Ancenis	**42**	47 21N	1 10W
Anch'i	**109**	25 3N	118 13E
Anch'ing	**109**	30 37N	117 0E
Anch'iu	**107**	36 25N	119 10E
Ancholme, R.	**33**	53 42N	0 32W
Anchorage	**147**	61 10N	149 50W
Ancião	**56**	39 56N	8 27W
Ancohuma, Nevada	**174**	16 0S	68 50W
Ancon	**164**	8 57N	79 33W
Ancón	**174**	11 50S	77 10W
Ancona	**63**	43 37N	13 30E
Ancrum	**35**	55 31N	2 35W
Ancud	**176**	42 0S	73 50W
Ancud, G. de	**176**	42 0S	73 0W
Andacollo, Argent.	**172**	37 10S	70 42W
Andacollo, Chile	**172**	30 15S	71 10W
Andado	**138**	25 25S	135 15E
Andalgalá	**172**	27 40S	66 30W
Åndalsnes	**71**	62 35N	7 43E
Andalucía	**57**	37 35N	5 0W
Andalusia	**157**	31 51N	86 30W
Andalusia = Andalucía	**57**	37 35N	5 0W
Andaman Is.	**101**	12 30N	92 30E
Andaman Sea	**101**	13 0N	96 0E
Andaman Str.	**101**	12 15N	92 20E
Andara	**128**	18 2S	21 9E
Andaraí	**171**	12 48S	41 20W
Andeer	**51**	46 36N	9 26E
Andelfingen	**51**	47 36N	8 41E
Andelot	**43**	46 51N	5 56E
Andelys, Les	**42**	49 15N	1 25E
Andenne	**47**	50 30N	5 5E
Andéranboukane	**121**	15 26N	3 2E
Anderlecht	**47**	50 50N	4 19E
Anderlues	**47**	50 25N	4 16E
Andermatt	**51**	46 38N	8 35E
Andernach	**48**	50 24N	7 25E
Andernos	**44**	44 44N	1 6W
Anderslöv	**73**	55 26N	13 19E
Anderson, Austral.	**141**	38 32S	145 27E
Anderson, Calif., U.S.A.	**160**	40 30N	122 19W
Anderson, Ind., U.S.A.	**156**	40 5N	85 40W
Anderson, Mo., U.S.A.	**159**	36 43N	94 29W
Anderson, S.C., U.S.A.	**157**	34 32N	82 40W
Anderson, Mt.	**129**	25 5S	30 42E
Anderson, R.	**147**	69 42N	129 0W
Anderstorp	**73**	57 19N	13 39E
Andes	**162**	42 12N	74 47W
Andes, mts.	**174**	20 0S	68 0W
Andfjorden	**74**	69 10N	16 20E
Andhra, L.	**96**	18 30N	73 32E
Andhra Pradesh □	**97**	15 0N	80 0E
Andikíthira	**69**	35 52N	23 15E
Andímilos	**69**	36 47N	24 12E
Andíparos	**69**	37 0N	25 3E
Andípaxoi	**69**	39 9N	20 13E
Andípsara	**69**	38 30N	25 29E
Andizhan	**76**	41 10N	72 0E
Andkhui	**93**	36 52N	65 8E
Andohararo	**129**	22 58S	43 45E
Andol	**96**	17 51N	78 4E
Andong	**107**	36 40N	128 43E
Andorra ■	**58**	42 30N	1 30E
Andorra La Vella	**58**	42 31N	1 32E
Andover, U.K.	**28**	51 13N	1 29W
Andover, U.S.A.	**162**	40 59N	74 44W
Andradina	**171**	20 54S	51 23W
Andrahary, Mt.	**129**	13 37S	49 17E
Andraitx	**58**	39 35N	2 25E
Andramasina	**129**	19 11S	47 35E
Andrano-Velona	**129**	18 10S	46 52E
Andranopasy	**129**	21 17S	43 44E
Andreanof Is.	**147**	51 0N	178 0W
Andreapol	**80**	56 40N	32 17E
Andreas	**32**	54 23N	4 25W
Andrespol	**54**	51 45N	19 34E
Andrew, oilfield	**19**	58 4N	1 24E
Andrews, S.C., U.S.A.	**157**	33 29N	79 30W
Andrews, Tex., U.S.A.	**159**	32 18N	102 33W
Andreyevka	**84**	52 19N	51 55E
Ándria	**65**	41 13N	16 17E
Andrian	**65**	46 30N	11 13E
Andriba	**129**	17 30S	46 58E
Andrijevica	**66**	42 45N	19 48E
Andrítsaina	**69**	37 29N	21 52E
Androka	**129**	24 58S	44 2E
Ándros	**69**	37 50N	24 50E
Andros I.	**166**	24 30N	78 0W
Andros Town	**166**	24 43N	77 47W
Andrychów	**54**	49 51N	19 18E
Andújar	**57**	38 3N	4 5W
Aneby	**73**	57 48N	14 49E
Anécho	**121**	6 12N	1 34E
Anegada I.	**147**	18 45N	64 20W
Anergane	**118**	31 4N	7 14W
Aneto, Pico de	**58**	42 37N	0 40E
Anfeg	**119**	22 29N	5 58E
Anfu	**109**	27 23N	114 37E
Ang Thong	**100**	14 35N	100 31E
Anga	**77**	60 35N	132 0E
Angamos, Punta	**172**	23 1S	70 32W
Anganch'i	**98**	47 9N	123 48E
Angara, R.	**77**	58 30N	97 0E
Angarsk	**77**	52 30N	104 0E
Angas Downs	**137**	24 49S	132 14E
Angas Ra.	**137**	23 0S	127 50E
Angaston	**140**	34 30S	139 8E
Ånge	**72**	62 31N	15 35E
Ängebo	**72**	61 58N	16 22E
Angel de la Guarda, I.	**164**	29 30N	113 30W
Ängelholm	**73**	56 15N	12 58E
Angellala	**139**	26 24S	146 54E
Angels Camp	**163**	38 8N	120 30W
Ängelsberg	**72**	59 58N	16 0E
Angenong	**99**	31 57N	94 10E
Anger, R.	**123**	9 30N	36 35E
Angereb	**123**	13 11N	37 7E
Angereb, R.	**123**	14 0N	36 0E
Ångermanälven	**72**	62 40N	18 0E
Angermünde	**48**	53 1N	14 0E
Angers	**42**	47 30N	0 35W
Angerville	**43**	48 19N	2 0E
Ängesån	**74**	66 50N	22 15E
Anghiari	**63**	43 32N	12 3E
Angical	**171**	12 0S	44 42W
Angical do Piauí	**171**	6 5S	42 44W
Angikuni L.	**153**	62 0N	100 0W
Angkor	**100**	13 22N	103 50E
Angle	**31**	51 40N	5 3W
Anglem Mt.	**143**	46 45S	167 53E
Anglés	**58**	41 57N	2 38E
Anglesey (□)	**26**	53 17N	4 20W
Anglesey, I.	**31**	53 17N	4 20W
Anglet	**44**	43 29N	1 31W
Angleton	**159**	29 12N	95 23W
Angleur	**47**	50 36N	5 35E
Anglure	**43**	48 35N	3 50E
Angmagssalik	**12**	65 40N	37 20W
Angmering	**29**	50 48N	0 28W
Ango	**126**	4 10N	26 5E
Angoche	**127**	16 8S	40 0E
Angoche, I.	**127**	16 20S	39 50E
Angol	**172**	37 56S	72 45W
Angola	**156**	41 40N	85 0W
Angola ■	**125**	12 0S	18 0E
Angoon	**147**	57 40N	134 40W
Angoram	**135**	4 4S	144 4E
Angoulême	**44**	45 39N	0 10E
Angoumois	**44**	45 30N	0 25E
Angra dos Reis	**173**	23 0S	44 10W
Angra-Juntas	**128**	27 39S	15 31E
Angran	**76**	80 59N	69 3E
Angren	**85**	41 1N	70 12E
Angtassom	**101**	11 1N	104 41E
Angu	**126**	3 25N	24 28E
Anguilla, I.	**167**	18 14N	63 5W
Angurugu	**138**	14 0S	136 25E
Angus (□)	**26**	56 45N	2 55W
Angus, Braes of	**37**	56 51N	3 0W
Anhanduí, R.	**173**	21 46S	52 9W
Anhée	**47**	50 18N	4 53E
Anholt	**73**	56 42N	11 33E
Anhsi	**105**	40 30N	96 0E
Anhsiang	**109**	29 24N	112 9E
Anhua, Hunan, China	**109**	28 22N	111 10E
Anhua, Kwangsi-Chuang, China	**108**	25 10N	108 21E
Anhwei □	**109**	33 15N	116 50E
Ani, Kiangsi, China	**109**	28 50N	115 32E
Ani, Shansi, China	**106**	35 3N	111 2E
Aniak	**147**	61 58N	159 50W
Anicuns	**171**	16 28S	49 58W
Ánidhros	**69**	36 38N	25 43E
Anié	**121**	7 42N	1 8E
Animas	**161**	31 58N	108 58W
Ånimskog	**73**	58 53N	12 35E
Anin	**101**	15 36N	97 50E
Anivorano	**129**	18 44S	48 58E
Anjangaon	**96**	21 10N	77 20E
Anjar	**94**	23 6N	70 10E
Anjen	**109**	26 42N	113 19E
Anjiabé	**129**	12 7S	49 20E
Anjidiv I.	**97**	14 40N	74 10E
Anjō	**111**	34 57N	137 5E
Anjou	**42**	47 20N	0 15W
Anjozorobe	**129**	18 22S	47 52E
Anju	**107**	39 36N	125 40E
Anka	**121**	12 13N	5 58E
Ank'ang	**108**	32 38N	109 5E
Ankara	**92**	40 0N	32 54E
Ankaramena	**129**	21 57S	46 39E
Ankazoabo	**129**	22 18S	44 31E
Ankazobé	**129**	18 20S	47 10E
Ankazotokana	**129**	21 20S	48 9E
Ankisabé	**129**	19 17S	46 29E
Anklesvar	**96**	21 38N	73 3E
Ankober	**123**	9 35N	39 40E
Ankoro	**126**	6 45S	26 55E
Ankuang	**107**	45 19N	123 40E
Ankuo	**106**	38 25N	115 19E
Anlu	**109**	31 12N	113 38E
Anlung	**108**	25 6N	106 31E
Anmyŏn Do	**107**	36 25N	126 25E
Ånn	**72**	63 19N	12 34E
Ann Arbor	**156**	42 17N	83 45W
Ann C., Antarct.	**13**	66 30S	50 30E
Ann C., U.S.A.	**162**	42 39N	70 37W
Ann, gasfield	**19**	53 40N	2 5E
Ånn L.	**72**	63 15N	12 35E
Anna, U.S.A.	**159**	37 28N	89 10W
Anna, U.S.S.R.	**81**	51 38N	40 23E
Anna Branch, R.	**139**	34 2S	141 50E
Anna Plains	**136**	19 17S	121 37E
Annaba	**119**	36 50N	7 46E
Annaberg-Buchholz	**48**	50 34N	12 58E
Annagassan	**38**	53 53N	6 20W
Annagh Hd.	**38**	54 15N	10 5W
Annaka	**111**	36 19N	138 54E
Annalee, R.	**38**	54 3N	7 15W
Annalong	**38**	54 7N	5 55W
Annam = Trung-Phan	**101**	16 30N	107 30E
Annamitique, Chaîne	**100**	17 0N	106 0E
Annan	**35**	55 0N	3 17W
Annan, R.	**35**	54 58N	3 18W
Annanberg	**135**	4 52S	144 42E
Annandale	**35**	55 10N	3 25W
Annapolis	**162**	39 0N	76 30W
Annapolis Royal	**151**	44 44N	65 32W
Annapurna	**95**	28 34N	83 50E
Annascaul	**39**	52 10N	10 3W
Anne, oilfield	**19**	55 24N	5 7E
Annean, L.	**137**	26 54S	118 14E
Anneberg	**73**	57 32N	12 6E
Annecy	**45**	45 55N	6 8E
Annecy, L. d'	**45**	45 52N	6 10E
Annemasse	**45**	46 12N	6 16E
Annestown	**39**	52 8N	7 18W
Annette	**147**	55 2N	131 35W
Annfield Plain	**33**	54 52N	1 45W
Annie Peak	**137**	33 53S	119 59E
Anning	**108**	24 58N	102 30E
Anningle	**136**	21 50S	133 7E
Anniston	**157**	33 45N	85 50W
Annobón = Pagalu	**114**	1 35S	3 35E
Annonay	**45**	45 15N	4 40E
Annonciation, L'	**150**	46 25N	74 55W
Annot	**45**	43 58N	6 38E
Annotto Bay	**166**	18 17N	77 3W
Annuello	**140**	34 53S	142 55E
Annville	**162**	40 18N	76 32W
Áno Arkhánai	**69**	35 16N	25 11E
Áno Porróia	**68**	41 17N	23 2E
Áno Viánnos	**69**	35 2N	25 21E
Anoka	**158**	45 10N	93 26W
Anorotsangana	**129**	13 56S	47 55E
Anp'ing, Hopei, China	**106**	38 13N	115 31E
Anp'ing, Liaoning, China	**107**	41 10N	123 30E
Ans	**47**	50 39N	5 32E
Ansai	**106**	36 54N	109 10E
Ansbach	**49**	49 17N	10 34E
Anse au Loup, L'	**151**	51 32N	56 50W
Anse, L'	**150**	46 47N	88 28W
Anseba, R.	**123**	16 15N	37 45E
Anserma	**174**	5 13N	75 48W
Anseroeul	**47**	50 43N	3 32E
Anshan	**107**	41 3N	122 58E
Anshun	**105**	26 2N	105 57E
Ansley	**158**	41 19N	99 24W
Ansó	**58**	42 51N	0 48W
Anson	**159**	32 46N	99 54W
Anson B.	**136**	13 20S	130 6E
Ansongo	**121**	15 25N	0 35E
Ansonia	**162**	41 21N	73 6W
Ansonville	**150**	48 46N	80 43W
Anstey	**28**	52 41N	1 14W
Anstey Hill	**109**	34 51S	138 44E
Anstruther	**35**	56 14N	2 40W
Ansudu	**103**	2 11S	139 22E
Antabamba	**174**	14 40S	73 0W
Antakya	**92**	36 14N	36 10E
Antalaha	**129**	14 57S	50 20E
Antalya	**92**	36 52N	30 45E
Antalya Körfezi	**92**	36 15N	31 30E
Antananrivo	**125**	18 55S	47 35E
Antanimbaribé	**129**	21 30S	44 48E
Antarctic Pen.	**13**	67 0S	60 0W
Antarctica	**125**	90 0S	0 0
Antela, Laguna	**56**	42 7N	7 40W
Antelope	**127**	21 2S	28 31E
Anten	**73**	58 5N	12 22E
Antenor Navarro	**170**	6 44S	38 27W
Antequera, Parag.	**172**	24 8S	57 7W
Antequera, Spain	**57**	37 5N	4 33W
Antero Mt.	**161**	38 45N	106 43W
Anthemoús	**68**	40 31N	23 15E
Anthony, Kans., U.S.A.	**159**	37 8N	98 2W
Anthony, N. Mex., U.S.A.	**161**	32 1N	106 37W
Anthony Lagoon	**138**	18 0S	135 30E
Anti Atlas, Mts.	**118**	30 30N	6 30W
Antibes	**45**	43 34N	7 6E
Antibes, C. d'	**45**	43 31N	7 7E
Anticosti, Í. de	**151**	49 30N	63 0W
Antifer, C. d'	**42**	49 41N	0 10E
Antigo	**158**	45 8N	89 5W
Antigonish	**151**	45 38N	61 58W
Antigua	**166**	14 34N	90 41W
Antigua Bahama, Canal de la	**166**	22 10N	77 30W
Antigua, I.	**167**	17 0N	61 50W
Antilla	**166**	20 40N	75 50W
Antimony	**161**	38 7N	112 0W
Antioch	**163**	38 7N	121 45W
Antioquia	**174**	6 40N	75 55W
Antioquia □	**174**	7 0N	75 30W
Antipodes Is.	**130**	49 45S	178 40E
Antler	**158**	48 58N	101 18W
Antler, R.	**153**	49 8N	101 0W
Antlers	**159**	34 15N	95 35W
Antofagasta	**172**	23 50S	70 30W
Antofagasta □	**172**	24 0S	69 0W
Antofagasta de la Sierra	**172**	26 5S	67 20W
Antofallá	**172**	25 30S	68 5W
Antofalla, Salar de	**172**	25 40S	67 45W
Antoing	**47**	50 34N	3 27E
Anton	**159**	33 49N	102 5W
Anton Chico	**161**	35 12N	105 5W
Antongil, B. d'	**129**	15 30S	49 50E
Antonibe	**129**	15 7S	47 24E
Antonibe, Presqu'île d'	**129**	15 30S	49 50E
Antonina	**173**	25 26S	48 42W
Antonito	**161**	37 4N	106 1W
Antonovo	**83**	49 25N	51 42E
Antony	**30**	50 22N	4 13W
Antrain	**42**	48 28N	1 30W
Antrim	**38**	54 43N	6 13W
Antrim □	**38**	54 42N	6 20W
Antrim Co.	**38**	54 58N	6 20W
Antrim, Mts. of	**38**	54 57N	6 8W
Antrim Plateau	**136**	18 8S	128 20E
Antrodoco	**63**	42 25N	13 4E
Antropovo	**81**	58 26N	42 51E
Antsalova	**129**	18 40S	44 37E
Antse	**106**	36 15N	112 15E
Antsirabé	**129**	19 55S	47 2E
Antsohihy	**129**	14 50S	47 50E
Ant'u	**107**	43 6N	128 54E
Antung	**107**	40 10N	124 18E
Antungwei	**107**	35 10N	119 20E
Antwerp	**140**	36 17S	142 4E
Antwerp = Antwerpen	**47**	51 13N	4 25E
Antwerpen	**47**	51 13N	4 25E
Antwerpen □	**47**	51 15N	4 40E
Antz'u	**106**	39 31N	116 41E
Anupgarh	**94**	29 10N	73 10E
Anuradhapura	**97**	8 22N	80 28E
Anvaing	**47**	50 41N	3 34E
Anvers = Antwerp(en)	**47**	51 13N	4 25E
Anvers I.	**13**	64 30S	63 40W
Anvik	**147**	62 37N	160 20W
Anxious B.	**139**	33 24S	134 45E
Anyama	**120**	5 30N	4 3W
Anyang	**106**	36 7N	114 26E
Anyer-Lor	**103**	6 6S	105 56E
Anyüan	**109**	25 9N	115 21E
Anza, Jordan	**90**	32 22N	35 12E
Anza, U.S.A.	**163**	33 35N	116 39W

Anza Borrego Desert State Park Arizpe

Anza Borrego Desert State Park 163 33 0N 116 26W
Anzhero-Sudzhensk 76 56 10N 83 40 E
Ánzio 64 41 28N 12 37 E
Aoga-Shima 111 32 28N 139 46 E
Aoiz 58 42 46N 1 22W
Aomori 112 40 45N 140 45 E
Aomori-ken □ 112 40 45N 140 40 E
Aonla 95 28 16N 79 11 E
Aono-Yama 110 34 28N 131 48 E
Aorangi Mts. 142 41 49 S 175 22 E
Aoreora 118 28 51N 10 53W
Aosta 62 45 43N 7 20 E
Aoudéras 121 17 45N 8 20 E
Aouinet Torkoz 118 28 31N 9 46W
Aoukar □ 118 23 50N 2 45W
Aouker 120 23 48N 4 0W
Aoulef el Arab 118 26 55N 1 2 E
Aoullouz 118 30 44N 8 1W
Apa 108 32 55N 101 40 E
Apa, R. 172 22 6 S 58 2W
Apache, Ariz., U.S.A. 161 31 46N 109 6W
Apache, Okla., U.S.A. 159 34 53N 98 22W
Apahanuerhch'i 106 43 58N 116 2 E
Apalachee B. 157 30 0N 84 0W
Apalachicola 157 29 40N 85 0W
Apalachicola, R. 157 30 0N 85 0W
Apapa 121 6 25N 3 25 E
Apaporis, R. 174 0 30 S 70 30W
Aparecida do Taboado 171 20 5 S 51 5W
Aparri 103 18 22N 121 38 E
Aparurén 174 5 6N 62 8W
Apateu 70 46 36N 21 47 E
Apatin 66 45 40N 19 0 E
Apatzingán 164 19 0N 102 20W
Apeldoorn 46 52 13N 5 57 E
Apeldoornsch Kanal 46 52 29N 6 5 E
Apen 48 53 12N 7 47 E
Apenam 102 8 35 S 116 13 E
Apennines 16 44 20N 10 20 E
Apia 174 5 5N 75 58W
Apiacás, Serra dos 174 9 50 S 57 0W
Apiaí 174 24 31 S 48 50W
Apinajé 171 11 31 S 48 18W
Apiti 142 39 58 S 175 54 E
Apizaco 165 19 26N 98 9W
Aplahoyé 121 6 56N 1 41 E
Aplao 174 16 0 S 72 40W
Apo, Mt. 103 6 53N 125 14 E
Apodi 170 5 39 S 37 48W
Apolda 48 51 1N 11 30 E
Apollo Bay 140 38 45 S 143 40 E
Apollonia, Greece 69 36 58N 24 43 E
Apollonia, Libya 117 32 52N 21 59 E
Apolo 174 14 30 S 68 30W
Aporé, R. 171 19 27 S 50 57W
Aporema 170 1 14N 50 49W
Apostle Is. 158 46 50N 90 30W
Apóstoles 173 28 0 S 56 0W
Apostolovo 82 47 39N 33 39 E
Apoteri 174 4 2N 58 32W
Appalachian Mts. 156 38 0N 80 0W
Appelscha 46 52 57N 6 21 E
Appeninni 65 41 0N 15 0 E
Appeninno Ligure 62 44 30N 9 0 E
Appenzell 51 47 20N 9 25 E
Appenzell-Ausser Rhoden □ 51 47 23N 9 23 E
Appenzell-Inner Rhoden □ 51 47 20N 9 25 E
Appiano 63 46 27N 11 17 E
Appingedam 46 53 19N 6 51 E
Apple Valley 163 34 30N 117 11W
Appleby 32 54 35N 2 29W
Applecross 36 57 26N 5 50W
Applecross For. 36 57 27N 5 40W
Appledore, Devon, U.K. 30 51 3N 4 12W
Appledore, Kent, U.K. 29 51 2N 0 47 E
Appleton 156 44 17N 88 25W
Approuague 170 4 20N 52 0W
Apreivka 81 55 33N 37 4 E
Apricena 65 41 47N 15 25 E
Aprigliano 65 39 17N 16 19 E
Aprília 64 41 38N 12 38 E
Apsheronsk 83 44 28N 39 42 E
Apsley Str. 136 11 35 S 130 28 E
Apt 45 43 53N 5 24 E
Apucarana 173 23 55 S 51 33W
Apulia = Puglia 65 41 0N 16 30 E
Apure □ 174 7 10N 68 50W
Apure, R. 174 8 0N 69 20W
Apurímac, R. 174 12 10 S 73 30W
Apurito, R. 174 7 50N 67 0W
Apuseni, Munţii 70 46 30N 22 45 E
Aq Chah 93 37 0N 66 5 E
'Aqaba 122 29 31N 35 0 E
'Aqaba, Khalīj al 92 28 15N 33 20 E
Aqîq 122 18 14N 38 12 E
Aqîq, Khalîg 122 18 20N 38 10 E
'Aqraba 90 32 9N 35 20 E
'Aqrah 92 36 46N 43 45 E
Aquanish 151 50 14N 62 2W
Aquasco 162 38 35N 76 43W
Aquidaba 171 10 17 S 37 2W
Aquidauana 175 20 30 S 55 50W
Aquila, L' 63 42 21N 13 24 E
Aquiles Serdán 164 28 37N 105 54W
Aquin 167 18 16N 73 24W
Ar Ramadi 92 33 25N 43 20 E
Ar-Ramthā 90 32 34N 36 0 E
Ar Rass 92 25 50N 43 40 E
Ar Rifai 92 31 50N 46 10 E
Ar Riyād 92 24 41N 46 42 E
Ar Rub 'al Khālī 91 21 0N 51 0 E
Ar Rutbah 92 33 0N 40 15 E
Arab, Khalîg el 122 30 55N 29 0 E
Arab, Shott al 92 30 0N 48 31 E
Araba 121 13 7N 5 0 E
Arabatskaya Strelka 82 45 40N 35 0 E
Arabba 63 46 30N 11 51 E
Arabelo 174 4 55N 64 13W
Arabia 86 25 0N 45 0 E
Arabian Desert 122 28 0N 32 20 E
Arabian Sea 86 16 0N 65 0 E
Aracajú 170 10 55 S 37 4W
Aracataca 174 10 38N 74 9W
Aracati 170 4 30 S 37 44W
Araçatuba 173 21 10 S 50 30W
Aracena 57 37 53N 6 38W
Aracruz 171 19 49 S 40 16W
Araçuaí 171 16 52 S 42 4W
Araçuaí, R. 171 16 46 S 42 2W
Arad 66 46 10N 21 20 E
Arada 117 15 0N 20 20 E
Aradu Nou 66 46 8N 21 20 E
Arafura Sea 103 10 0 S 135 0 E
Aragats 83 40 30N 44 15 E
Aragón 58 41 25N 1 0W
Aragón, R. 58 42 35N 0 50W
Aragona 64 37 24N 13 36 E
Aragua □ 174 10 0N 67 10W
Aragua de Barcelona 174 9 28N 64 49W
Araguacema 170 8 50 S 49 20W
Araguaçu 171 12 49 S 49 51W
Araguaia, R. 170 7 0 S 49 15W
Araguaina 170 7 12 S 48 12W
Araguari 171 18 38 S 48 11W
Araguari, R. 170 1 0N 51 40W
Araguatins 170 5 38 S 48 7W
Araioses 170 2 53 S 41 55W
Arak 118 25 20N 3 45 E
Arāk 92 34 0N 49 40 E
Arakan □ 98 19 0N 94 15 E
Arakan Coast 99 19 0N 94 0 E
Arakan Yoma 98 20 0N 94 30 E
Arákhova 69 38 28N 22 35 E
Araks, R. = Aras, Rud-e 92 39 10N 47 10 E
Aral Sea = Aralskoye More 76 44 30N 60 0 E
Aralsk 76 46 50N 61 20 E
Aralskoye More 76 44 30N 60 0 E
Aramac 138 22 58 S 145 14 E
Arambagh 95 22 53N 87 48 E
Aramū, Mţii de 70 47 10N 22 30 E
Aran Fawddwy, Mt. 31 52 48N 3 40W
Aran, I. 38 55 0N 8 30W
Aran Is. 39 53 5N 9 42W
Aranci 64 41 5N 3 40W
Aranci, Golfo 64 41 0N 9 35 E
Aranda de Duero 58 41 39N 3 42W
Arandelovac 66 44 18N 20 37 E
Aranga 142 35 44 S 173 40 E
Aranjuez 56 40 1N 3 40W
Aranos 125 24 9 S 19 7 E
Aransas Pass 159 28 0N 97 9W
Aranyaprathet 101 13 41N 102 30 E
Aranzazu 174 5 16N 75 30W
Arao 110 32 59N 130 25 E
Araouane 120 18 55N 3 30W
Arapahoe 158 40 22N 99 53W
Arapari 170 5 34 S 49 15W
Arapawa I. 131 41 13 S 174 20 E
Arapey Grande, R. 172 30 55 S 57 49W
Arapiraca 170 9 45 S 36 39W
Arapkir 92 39 5N 38 30 E
Arapongas 173 23 29 S 51 28W
Arapuni 130 38 3 S 175 37 E
Araranguá 173 29 0 S 49 30W
Araraquara 171 21 50 S 48 0W
Araras 173 5 15 S 60 35W
Ararás, Serra dos 173 25 0 S 53 10W
Ararat, Austral. 140 37 16 S 143 0 E
Ararat, Turkey 92 39 50N 44 15 E
Ararat, Mt. = Ağri Daği 92 39 50N 44 15 E
Arari 170 3 28 S 44 47W
Araria 95 26 9N 87 33 E
Araripe 171 7 12 S 40 8W
Araripe, Chapada do 170 7 20 S 40 0W
Araripina 170 7 33 S 40 34W
Araro 123 4 41N 38 50 E
Araruama, Lagoa de 173 22 53 S 42 12W
Araruna 170 6 52 S 35 44W
Áras 71 59 42N 10 31 E
Aras, Rud-e 92 39 10N 47 10 E
Araticu 170 1 58 S 49 51W
Arauca 174 7 0N 70 40W
Arauca □ 174 6 40N 71 0W
Arauca, R. 174 7 30N 69 0W
Arauco 172 37 16 S 73 25W
Arauco □ 172 37 40 S 73 25W
Araújos 171 19 56 S 45 14W
Arauquita 174 7 2N 71 25W
Araure 174 9 34N 69 13W
Arawa 123 9 57N 41 58 E
Arawhata 143 43 59 S 168 38 E
Arawhata, R. 143 44 0 S 168 40 E
Araxá 171 19 35 S 46 55W
Araya, Pen. de 174 10 40N 64 0W
Arba 123 9 0N 40 20 E
Arba Jahan 126 2 5N 39 2 E
Arba, L' 118 36 40N 3 9 E
Arba Minch 123 6 0N 37 30 E
Arbah, Wadi al 90 30 30N 35 5 E
Arbatax 64 39 57N 9 42 E
Arbedo 51 46 12N 9 3 E
Arbeláez 174 4 17N 74 26W
Arbīl 92 36 15N 44 5 E
Arboga 72 59 24N 15 52 E
Arbois 43 46 55N 5 46 E
Arbon 51 47 31N 9 26 E
Arbore 123 5 3N 36 50 E
Arborea 64 39 46N 8 34 E
Arborfield 153 53 6N 103 39W
Arborg 153 50 54N 97 13W
Arbrå 72 61 28N 16 22 E
Arbresle, L' 45 45 50N 4 26 E
Arbroath 37 56 34N 2 35W
Arbuckle 160 39 3N 122 2W
Arbus 64 39 30N 8 33 E
Arbuzinka 82 47 52N 31 25 E
Arc 43 47 28N 5 34 E
Arcachon 44 44 40N 1 10W
Arcachon, Bassin d' 44 44 42N 1 10W
Arcadia, Fla., U.S.A. 157 27 20N 81 50W
Arcadia, La., U.S.A. 159 32 34N 92 53W
Arcadia, Nebr., U.S.A. 158 41 29N 99 4W
Arcadia, Wis., U.S.A. 158 44 13N 91 29W
Arcata 160 40 55N 124 4W
Arcévia 63 43 29N 12 58 E
Archangel = Arkhangelsk 78 64 40N 41 0 E
Archar 66 43 50N 22 54 E
Archbald 162 41 30N 75 31W
Archena 59 38 9N 1 16W
Archer B. 138 13 20 S 141 30 E
Archer, R. 138 13 25 S 142 50 E
Archers Post 126 0 35N 37 35 E
Archidona 57 37 6N 4 22W
Archiestown 37 57 28N 3 20W
Arci, Monte 64 39 47N 8 44 E
Arcidosso 63 42 51N 11 30 E
Arcila = Asilah 118 35 29N 6 0W
Arcis-sur-Aube 43 48 32N 4 10 E
Arckaringa 139 27 56 S 134 45 E
Arckaringa Cr. 139 28 10 S 135 22 E
Arco, Italy 62 45 55N 10 54 E
Arco, U.S.A. 160 43 45N 113 16W
Arcola 153 49 40N 102 30W
Arcoona 140 31 2 S 137 1 E
Arcos, Brazil 171 20 17 S 45 32W
Arcos, Spain 58 41 12N 2 16W
Arcos de los Frontera 57 36 45N 5 49W
Arcot 97 12 53N 79 20 E
Arcoverde 170 8 25 S 37 4W
Arctic Ocean 12 78 0N 160 0W
Arctic Red, R. 147 66 0N 132 0W
Arctic Red River 147 67 15N 134 0W
Arctic Village 147 68 5N 145 45W
Arda, R., Bulg. 67 41 40N 25 40 E
Arda, R., Italy 62 44 53N 9 52 E
Ardabil 92 38 15N 48 18 E
Ardagh 39 52 30N 9 5W
Ardakan 93 30 20N 52 5 E
Årdal 71 59 9N 6 13 E
Ardales 57 36 53N 4 51W
Årdalstangen 71 61 14N 7 43 E
Ardara 38 54 47N 8 25W
Ardatov 81 54 51N 46 15 E
Ardavasar 36 57 3N 5 54 E
Ardbeg 34 55 38N 6 6W
Ardcath 38 53 36N 6 21W
Ardcharnich 36 57 52N 5 5W
Ardchyle 34 56 26N 4 24W
Ardèche □ 45 44 42N 4 16 E
Ardee 38 53 51N 6 32W
Arden Stby. 73 56 46N 9 52 E
Ardennes 47 49 30N 5 10 E
Ardennes □ 43 49 35N 4 40 E
Ardentes 43 46 45N 1 50 E
Ardentinny 34 56 3N 4 56 E
Arderin, Mt. 39 53 3N 7 40W
Ardestan 93 33 20N 52 25 E
Ardfert 39 52 20N 9 49W
Ardfinnan 39 52 20N 7 53W
Ardglass 38 54 16N 5 37W
Ardgour 36 56 45N 5 25W
Ardgroom 39 51 44N 9 53W
Ardhas, R. 68 41 36N 26 25 E
Ardhasig 36 57 55N 6 51W
Ardhéa 68 40 58N 22 3 E
Ardila, R. 57 38 10N 7 20W
Ardingly 29 51 3N 0 3W
Ardino 67 41 34N 25 9 E
Ardivachar Pt. 36 57 23N 7 25W
Ardkearagh 39 51 48N 10 11W
Ardkeen 38 54 27N 5 31W
Ardlethan 141 34 22 S 146 53 E
Ardlui 34 56 19N 4 43W
Ardmore, Austral. 138 21 39 S 139 11 E
Ardmore, Okla., U.S.A. 159 34 10N 97 5W
Ardmore, Pa., U.S.A. 162 39 58N 75 18W
Ardmore, S.D., U.S.A. 158 43 0N 103 40W
Ardmore Hd. 39 51 58N 7 43W
Ardmore Pt. 34 55 40N 6 0W
Ardnacrusha 39 52 43N 8 38W
Ardnamurchan, Pen. 36 56 43N 6 0W
Ardnamurchan Pt. 36 56 44N 6 14W
Ardnaree 38 54 6N 9 8W
Ardnave Pt. 34 55 54N 6 20W
Ardooie 47 50 59N 3 13 E
Ardore Marina 65 38 11N 16 10 E
Ardrahan 39 53 10N 8 48W
Ardres 43 50 50N 2 0 E
Ardrishaig 34 56 0N 5 27W
Ardrossan, Austral. 140 34 26 S 137 53 E
Ardrossan, U.K. 34 55 39N 4 50W
Ards □ 38 54 35N 5 30W
Ards Pen. 38 54 30N 5 25W
Ardud 70 47 37N 22 52 E
Ardunac 83 41 8N 42 5 E
Ardvoulie Castle 36 58 0N 6 45W
Ardwell 37 57 20N 3 5W
Åre 72 63 22N 13 15 E
Arecibo 147 18 29N 66 42W
Areia Branca 170 5 0 S 37 0W
Aremark 71 59 15N 11 42 E
Arena de la Ventana, Punta 164 24 4N 109 52W
Arenales, Cerro 176 47 5 S 73 40W
Arenas 56 43 17N 4 50W
Arenas de San Pedro 56 40 12N 5 5W
Arenas, Pta. 174 10 20N 62 39W
Arendal 71 58 28N 8 46 E
Arendonk 47 51 19N 5 5 E
Arendsee 48 52 52N 11 27 E
Arenig Fach, Mt. 31 52 55N 3 45 E
Arenig Fawr, Mt. 31 52 56N 3 45W
Arenys de Mar 58 41 35N 2 33 E
Arenzano 62 44 24N 8 40 E
Areópolis 69 36 40N 22 22 E
Arequipa 174 16 20 S 71 30W
Arero 123 4 41N 38 50 E
Arês 171 6 11 S 35 9W
Arès 44 44 47N 1 8W
Arévalo 56 41 3N 4 43W
Arezzo 63 43 28N 11 50 E
Arga, R. 58 42 30N 1 50W
Argalasti 68 39 13N 23 13 E
Argamasilla de Alba 59 39 8N 3 5W
Arganda 58 40 19N 3 26W
Arganil 56 40 13N 8 3W
Argayash 84 55 29N 60 52 E
Argelès-Gazost 44 43 0N 0 6W
Argelès-sur-Mer 44 42 34N 3 1 E
Argent-sur-Sauldre 43 47 33N 2 25 E
Argenta, Can. 152 50 20N 116 55W
Argenta, Italy 63 44 37N 11 50 E
Argentan 42 48 45N 0 1W
Argentário, Mte. 63 42 23N 11 11 E
Argentat 44 45 6N 1 56 E
Argentera 62 44 23N 6 58 E
Argenteuil 43 48 57N 2 14 E
Argentia 151 47 18N 53 58W
Argentiera, C. dell' 64 40 44N 8 8 E
Argentière, Aiguilles d' 50 45 58N 7 2 E
Argentina 174 0 34N 74 17W
Argentina ■ 176 35 0 S 66 0W
Argentino, L. 176 50 10 S 73 0W
Argenton-sur-Creuse 44 46 36N 1 30 E
Argentré 42 48 5N 0 40W
Argeş □ 70 45 0N 24 45 E
Argeş, R. 70 44 30N 25 50 E
Arghandab, R. 94 32 15N 66 23 E
Argo 122 19 28N 30 30 E
Argo, I. 122 19 28N 30 30 E
Argolikós Kólpos 69 37 20N 22 52 E
Argolis □ 69 37 38N 22 50 E
Argonne 43 49 0N 5 20 E
Árgos 69 37 40N 22 43 E
Árgos Orestikón 68 40 27N 21 26 E
Argostólion 69 38 12N 20 33 E
Arguedas 58 42 11N 1 36W
Arguello, Pt. 163 34 34N 120 40W
Argun, R. 77 53 20N 121 28 E
Argungu 121 12 40N 4 31 E
Argus Pk. 163 35 52N 117 26W
Argyle 158 48 23N 96 49W
Argyle Downs 136 16 17 S 128 47 E
Argyle, L. 136 16 20 S 128 40 E
Argyll (□) 26 56 18N 5 15W
Argyll, Dist. 34 56 14N 5 10W
Argyll, oilfield 19 56 8N 3 5 E
Argyrádhes 68 39 27N 19 58 E
Århus 73 56 8N 10 11 E
Aria 142 38 33 S 175 0 E
Ariamsvlei 128 28 9 S 19 51 E
Ariana 119 36 52N 10 12 E
Ariano Irpino 65 41 10N 15 4 E
Ariano nel Polèsine 63 44 56N 12 5 E
Aribinda 121 14 17N 0 52W
Arica, Chile 174 18 32 S 70 20W
Arica, Colomb. 174 2 0 S 71 50W
Arica, Peru 174 1 30 S 75 30W
Arid, C. 137 34 1 S 123 10 E
Arida 111 33 29N 135 44 E
Ariège □ 44 42 56N 1 30 E
Ariège, R. 44 42 56N 1 25 E
Arieş, R. 70 46 24N 23 20 E
Arilje 66 43 44N 20 7 E
Arima 167 10 38N 61 17W
Arinagour 34 56 38N 6 31W
Arinos, R. 174 11 15 S 57 0W
Ario de Rosales 164 19 12N 101 42W
Aripuanã 174 9 25 S 60 30W
Aripuanã, R. 174 7 30 S 60 25W
Ariquemes 174 9 55 S 63 6W
Arisaig 36 56 55N 5 50W
Arisaig, Sd. of 36 56 50N 5 50W
Arîsh, W. el 122 30 25N 34 52 E
Arismendi 174 8 29N 68 22W
Arissa 123 11 10N 41 35 E
Aristazabal, I. 152 52 40N 129 10W
Arita 110 33 11N 129 54 E
Arivaca 161 31 37N 111 25W
Arivonimamo 129 19 1 S 47 11 E
Ariyalur 97 11 8N 79 8 E
Ariza 58 41 19N 2 3W
Arizaro, Salar de 172 24 40 S 67 50W
Arizona 172 35 45 S 65 25W
Arizona □ 161 34 20N 111 30W
Arizpe 164 30 20N 110 11W

Arjang Atalaia

Arjang **72** 59 24N 12 9E
Arjäng **72** 59 24N 12 8E
Arjeplog **74** 66 3N 18 2E
Arjona, Colomb. **174** 10 14N 75 22W
Arjona, Spain **57** 37 56N 4 4W
Arjuno **103** 7 49S 112 19E
Arka **77** 60 15N 142 0E
Arkadak **81** 51 58N 43 19E
Arkadelphia **159** 34 5N 93 0W
Arkadhia □ **69** 37 30N 22 20E
Arkaig, L. **36** 56 58N 5 10W
Arkansas □ **159** 35 0N 92 30W
Arkansas City **159** 37 4N 97 3W
Arkansas, R. **159** 35 20N 93 30W
Árkathos, R. **68** 39 20N 21 4E
Arkhángelos **69** 36 13N 28 7E
Arkhangelsk **78** 64 40N 41 0E
Arkhangelskoye **81** 51 32N 40 58E
Arkiko **123** 15 33N 39 30E
Arkle R. **32** 54 25N 2 0W
Arklow **39** 52 48N 6 10W
Arklow Hd. **39** 52 46N 6 10W
Árkoi **69** 37 24N 26 44E
Arkona, Kap **48** 54 41N 13 26E
Arkonam **97** 13 7N 79 43E
Arkösund **73** 58 29N 16 56E
Arkoúdhi **69** 38 33N 20 43E
Arkticheskiy, Mys **77** 81 10N 95 0E
Arkul **84** 57 17N 50 3E
Arkville **162** 42 9N 74 37W
Arlanc **44** 45 25N 3 42E
Arlanza, R. **56** 42 6N 4 0W
Arlanzón, R. **56** 42 12N 4 0W
Arlberg Pass **49** 49 9N 10 12E
Arlee **160** 47 10N 114 4W
Arles **45** 43 41N 4 40E
Arlesheim **50** 47 30N 7 37E
Arless **39** 52 53N 7 1W
Arlington, S. Afr. **129** 28 1S 27 53E
Arlington, Oreg., U.S.A. **160** 45 48N 120 6W
Arlington, S.D., U.S.A. **158** 44 25N 97 4W
Arlington, Va., U.S.A. **162** 38 52N 77 5W
Arlington, Vt., U.S.A. **162** 43 5N 73 9W
Arlington, Wash., U.S.A. **160** 48 11N 122 4W
Arlon **47** 49 42N 5 49E
Arlöv **73** 55 38N 13 5E
Arly **121** 11 35N 1 28E
Armadale, Austral. **137** 32 12S 116 0E
Armadale, Lothian, U.K. **35** 55 54N 3 42W
Armadale, Skye, U.K. **36** 57 24N 5 54W
Armagh, Can. **137** 46 41N 70 32W
Armagh, U.K. **38** 54 22N 6 40W
Armagh □ **38** 54 18N 6 37W
Armagh Co. **38** 54 16N 6 35W
Armagnac **44** 43 44N 0 10E
Armançon, R. **43** 47 51N 4 7E
Armavir **83** 45 2N 41 7E
Armenia **174** 4 35N 75 45W
Armenian S.S.R. □ **83** 40 0N 41 0E
Armeniș **70** 45 13N 22 17E
Armentières **43** 50 40N 2 50E
Armero **174** 4 58N 74 54W
Armidale **141** 30 30S 151 40E
Armour **158** 43 20N 98 25W
Armoy **38** 55 8N 6 20W
Arms **150** 49 34N 86 3W
Armstead **160** 45 0N 112 56W
Armstrong, B.C., Can. **152** 50 25N 119 10W
Armstrong, Ont., Can. **150** 50 18N 89 4W
Armstrong, U.S.A. **159** 26 59N 90 48W
Armstrong Cr. **136** 16 35S 131 40E
Armur **96** 18 48N 78 16E
Arnaía **68** 40 30N 23 40E
Arnarfjörður **74** 65 48N 23 40W
Arnay-le-Duc **43** 47 10N 4 27E
Arnedillo **58** 42 13N 2 14W
Arnedo **58** 42 12N 2 5W
Årnes **74** 66 1N 21 31W
Årnes **71** 60 7N 11 28E
Arnett **159** 36 9N 99 44W
Arney **38** 54 17N 7 41W
Arnhem **46** 51 58N 5 55E
Arnhem B. **138** 12 20S 136 10E
Arnhem, C. **138** 12 20S 137 0E
Arnhem Ld. **138** 13 10S 135 0E
Arni **97** 12 43N 79 19E
Árnissa **68** 40 47N 21 49E
Arno Bay **140** 33 54S 136 34E
Arno, R. **62** 43 44N 10 20E
Arnold, N.Z. **143** 42 29S 171 25E
Arnold, U.K. **33** 53 0N 1 8W
Arnold, Calif., U.S.A. **163** 38 15N 120 20W
Arnold, Nebr., U.S.A. **158** 41 29N 100 10W
Arnoldstein **52** 46 33N 13 43E
Arnot **153** 55 46N 96 41W
Arnøy **74** 70 9N 20 40E
Arnprior **150** 45 26N 76 21W
Arnsberg **48** 51 25N 8 10E
Arnside **32** 54 12N 2 49W
Arnstadt **48** 50 50N 10 56E
Aroa **174** 10 26N 68 54W
Aroab **125** 26 41S 19 39E
Aroánia Óri **69** 37 56N 22 12E
Aroche **57** 37 56N 6 57W
Aroeiras **170** 7 31S 35 41W
Arolla **50** 46 2N 7 29E
Arolsen **48** 51 23N 9 1E
Arona **62** 45 45N 8 32E
Arosa **51** 46 47N 9 41E
Arosa, Ría de **56** 42 28N 8 57W
Arpajon, Cantal, France **44** 44 54N 2 28E
Arpajon, Seine et Oise, France **43** 48 37N 2 12E
Arpino **64** 41 40N 13 35E
Arra Mts. **39** 52 50N 8 22W
Arrabury **139** 26 45S 141 0E
Arrah **95** 25 35N 84 32E
Arraias **171** 12 56S 46 57W
Arraias, R. **170** 7 30S 49 20W
Arraiolos **57** 38 44N 7 59W
Arran, I. **34** 55 34N 5 12W
Arrandale **152** 54 57N 130 0W
Arras **43** 50 17N 2 46E
Arreau **44** 42 54N 0 22E
Arrecife **116** 28 59N 13 40W
Arrecifes **172** 34 06S 60 9W
Arrée, Mts. d' **42** 48 26N 3 55W
Arriaga, Chiapas, Mexico **165** 16 15N 93 52W
Arriaga, San Luís de Potosí, Mexico **164** 21 55N 101 23W
Arrild **73** 55 8N 8 58E
Arrilalah P.O. **138** 23 43S 143 54E
Arrino **137** 29 30S 115 40E
Arrochar **34** 56 12N 4 45W
Arrojado, R. **171** 13 24S 44 20W
Arromanches-les-Bains **42** 49 20N 0 38W
Arronches **57** 39 8N 7 16W
Arrou **42** 48 6N 1 8E
Arrow L. **38** 54 3N 8 20W
Arrow Rock Res. **160** 43 45N 115 50W
Arrowhead **152** 50 40N 117 55W
Arrowhead, L. **163** 34 16N 117 10W
Arrowsmith, Mt. **143** 30 7N 141 38E
Arrowtown **143** 44 57S 168 50E
Arroyo de la Luz **57** 39 30N 6 38W
Arroyo Grande **163** 35 9N 120 32W
Års **73** 56 48N 9 30E
Ars **44** 46 13N 1 30W
Ars-sur-Moselle **43** 49 5N 6 4E
Arsenault L. **153** 53 6N 108 32W
Arsiero **63** 45 49N 11 22E
Arsikere **97** 13 15N 76 15E
Arsk **81** 56 10N 49 50E
Årskogen **72** 62 8N 17 20E
Árta **69** 39 8N 21 2E
Artá **58** 39 40N 3 20E
Árta □ **68** 39 15N 26 0E
Arteaga **164** 18 50N 102 20W
Arteijo **56** 43 19N 8 29W
Artem,Os. **83** 40 28N 50 20E
Artémou **120** 15 38N 12 16W
Artemovsk **82** 48 35N 37 55E
Artemovski **83** 54 45N 93 35E
Artemovskiy **84** 57 21N 61 54E
Artenay **43** 48 5N 1 50E
Artern **48** 51 22N 11 18E
Artesa de Segre **58** 41 54N 1 3E
Artesia **159** 32 55N 104 25W
Artesia Wells **159** 28 17N 99 18W
Artesian **158** 44 2N 97 54W
Arth **51** 47 4N 8 31E
Arthez-de-Béarn **44** 43 29N 0 38W
Arthington **120** 6 35N 10 45W
Arthur Cr. **138** 22 30S 136 25E
Arthur Pt. **138** 22 7S 150 3E
Arthur, R. **138** 41 2S 144 40E
Arthur's Pass **143** 42 54S 171 35E
Arthur's Town **167** 24 38N 75 42W
Arthurstown **39** 52 15N 6 58W
Artigas **172** 30 20S 56 30W
Artigavan **38** 54 51N 7 24W
Artik **83** 40 38N 44 50E
Artillery L. **153** 63 9N 107 52W
Artois **43** 50 20N 2 30E
Artotína **69** 38 42N 22 2E
Artvin **92** 41 14N 41 44E
Aru, Kepulauan **103** 6 0S 134 30E
Arua **126** 3 1N 30 58E
Aruanã **171** 15 0S 51 10W
Aruba I. **167** 12 30N 70 0W
Arudy **44** 43 7N 0 28W
Arumpo **140** 33 48S 142 55E
Arun, R. **95** 27 30N 87 15E
Arun R. **29** 50 48N 0 33W
Arunachal Pradesh □ **98** 28 0N 95 0E
Arundel **29** 50 52N 0 32W
Aruppukottai **97** 9 31N 78 8E
Arusha **126** 3 20S 36 40E
Arusha □ **126** 4 0S 36 30E
Arusha Chini **126** 3 32S 37 20E
Arusi □ **123** 7 45N 39 00E
Aruvi,Aru **97** 8 48N 79 53E
Aruwimi, R. **126** 1 30N 25 0E
Arva **38** 53 57N 7 35W
Arvada **160** 44 43N 106 6W
Arvaklu **97** 8 20N 79 58E
Arvayheer **105** 46 15N 102 48E
Arve, R. **45** 46 11N 6 8E
Arvi **96** 20 59N 78 16E
Arvida **151** 48 25N 71 14W
Arvidsjaur **74** 65 35N 19 10E
Arvika **72** 59 40N 12 36E
Arvin **163** 35 12N 118 50W
Arys **85** 42 26N 68 48E
Arys, R. **85** 42 45N 68 15E
Arzachena **64** 41 5N 9 27E
Arzamas **81** 55 27N 43 55E
Arzew **118** 35 50N 0 23W
Arzgir **83** 45 18N 44 23E
Arzignano **63** 45 30N 11 20E
Aš **47** 51 1N 5 35E
Aš **52** 50 13N 12 12E
As Salt **90** 32 2N 35 43E
As Samawah **92** 31 15N 45 15E
As-Samū **90** 31 24N 35 4E
As Sulaimānīyah **92** 35 35N 45 29E
As Sultbn **119** 31 4N 17 8E
As Suwaih **93** 22 10N 59 33E
As Suwayda **92** 32 40N 36 30E
As Suwayrah **92** 32 55N 45 0E
Asab **128** 25 30S 18 0E
Asaba **121** 6 12N 6 38E
Asadabad **92** 34 50N 48 10E
Asafo **120** 6 20N 2 40W
Asahi **111** 35 43N 140 39E
Asahi-Gawa, R. **110** 34 36N 133 58E
Asahikawa **112** 43 45N 142 30E
Asale, L. **123** 14 0N 40 20E
Asama-Yama **111** 36 24N 138 31E
Asamankese **121** 5 50N 0 40W
Asankrangwa **120** 5 45N 2 30W
Asansol **95** 23 40N 87 1E
Åsarna **72** 62 40N 14 20E
Åsarna **72** 62 39N 14 22E
Asbe Teferi **123** 9 4N 40 49E
Asbesberge **128** 29 0S 23 0E
Asbest **84** 57 0N 61 30E
Asbestos **151** 45 47N 71 58W
Asbury Park **162** 40 15N 74 1W
Ascensión **164** 31 6N 107 59W
Ascensión, B. de la **165** 19 50N 87 20W
Ascension, I. **15** 8 0S 14 15W
Aschach **49** 48 23N 14 0E
Aschaffenburg **49** 49 58N 9 8E
Aschendorf **48** 53 2N 7 22E
Aschersleben **48** 51 45N 11 28E
Asciano **63** 43 14N 11 32E
Áscoli Piceno **63** 42 51N 13 34E
Áscoli Satriano **65** 41 11N 15 32E
Ascona **51** 46 9N 8 46E
Ascope **174** 7 46S 79 8W
Ascot **29** 51 24N 0 41W
Ascotán **172** 21 45S 68 17W
Aseb **123** 13 0N 42 40E
Åseda **73** 57 10N 15 20E
Åseda **73** 57 10N 15 20E
Asedjrad **118** 24 51N 1 29E
Asela **123** 8 0N 39 0E
Asenovgrad **67** 42 1N 24 51E
Åseral **71** 58 37N 7 25E
Åseral **71** 58 38N 7 26E
Asfeld **43** 49 27N 4 5E
Asfordby **29** 52 45N 0 57W
Asfûn el Matâ'na **122** 25 26N 32 30E
Åsgårdstrand **71** 59 22N 10 27E
Ash **29** 51 17N 1 16E
Ash Fork **161** 35 14N 112 32W
Ash Grove **159** 37 21N 93 36W
Ash Shām,Bādiyat **92** 31 30N 40 0E
Ash Shāmīyah **92** 31 55N 44 35E
Ash Shatrah **92** 31 30N 46 10E
Ash Shuna **90** 32 32N 35 34E
Asha **84** 55 0N 57 16E
Ashaira **122** 21 40N 40 40E
Ashanti **121** 7 30N 2 0W
Ashau **100** 16 6N 107 22E
Ashbourne, Ireland **38** 53 31N 6 24W
Ashbourne, U.K. **33** 53 2N 1 44W
Ashburn **157** 31 42N 83 40W
Ashburton, N.Z. **143** 43 53S 171 48E
Ashburton, U.K. **30** 50 31N 3 45W
Ashburton Downs **136** 23 25S 117 4E
Ashburton, R., Austral. **136** 21 40S 114 56E
Ashburton, R., N.Z. **131** 44 2S 171 50E
Ashby-de-la-Zouch **28** 52 45N 1 29W
Ashchurch **28** 52 0N 2 7W
Ashcroft **152** 50 40N 121 20W
Ashdod **90** 31 49N 34 35E
Ashdot Ya'aqov **90** 32 39N 35 35E
Ashdown Forest **29** 51 4N 0 2E
Asheboro **157** 35 43N 79 46W
Asherton **159** 28 25N 99 43W
Asheville **157** 35 39N 82 30W
Asheweig, R. **150** 54 17N 87 12W
Ashford, Austral. **139** 29 15S 151 3E
Ashford, Derby., U.K. **33** 53 13N 1 43W
Ashford, Kent, U.K. **29** 51 8N 0 53E
Ashford, U.S.A. **160** 46 45N 122 2W
Ashikaga **111** 36 28N 139 29E
Ashington **35** 55 12N 1 35W
Ashio **111** 36 38N 139 27E
Ashizuri-Zaki **110** 32 35N 132 50E
Ashkarkot **94** 33 3N 67 58E
Ashkhabad **76** 38 0N 57 50E
Ashland, Kans., U.S.A. **159** 37 13N 99 43W
Ashland, Ky., U.S.A. **156** 38 25N 82 40W
Ashland, Me., U.S.A. **151** 46 34N 68 26W
Ashland, Mont., U.S.A. **160** 45 41N 106 12W
Ashland, Nebr., U.S.A. **158** 41 5N 96 27W
Ashland, Ohio, U.S.A. **156** 40 52N 82 20W
Ashland, Oreg., U.S.A. **160** 42 10N 122 38W
Ashland, Pa., U.S.A. **162** 40 45N 76 22W
Ashland, Va., U.S.A. **156** 37 46N 77 30W
Ashland, Wis., U.S.A. **158** 46 40N 90 52W
Ashley, N.D., U.S.A. **158** 46 3N 99 23W
Ashley, Pa., U.S.A. **162** 41 14N 75 53W
Ashmont **152** 54 7N 111 29W
Ashmore Is. **136** 12 14S 123 50E
Ashmore Reef **136** 12 14S 123 5E
Ashmûn **122** 30 18N 30 55E
Ashokan Res. **162** 41 56N 74 13W
Ashquelon **90** 31 42N 34 55E
Ashtabula **156** 41 52N 80 50W
Ashti **96** 18 50N 75 15E
Ashton, S. Afr. **128** 33 50S 20 5E
Ashton, U.S.A. **160** 44 6N 111 30W
Ashton-in-Makerfield **32** 53 29N 2 39W
Ashton-u.-Lyne **32** 53 30N 2 8E
Ashuanipi, L. **151** 52 45N 66 15W
Ashurst **142** 40 16S 175 45E
Ashurstwood **29** 51 6N 0 2E
Ashwater **30** 50 43N 4 18W
Ashwick **28** 51 13N 2 31W
Asia **86** 45 0N 75 0E
Asia, Kepulauan **103** 1 0N 131 13E
Asiago **63** 45 52N 11 30E
Asifabad **96** 19 30N 79 24E
Asilah **118** 35 29N 6 0W
Asinara **64** 41 5N 8 15E
Asinara, G. dell' **64** 41 0N 8 30E
Asinara I. **64** 41 5N 8 15E
Asino **76** 57 0N 86 0E
Asir **91** 18 40N 42 30E
Asir, Ras **91** 11 55N 51 10E
Aska **96** 19 37N 84 42E
Askeaton **39** 52 37N 8 58W
Asker **71** 59 50N 10 26E
Askersund **73** 58 53N 14 55E
Askim **71** 59 35N 11 10E
Askino **84** 56 5N 56 34E
Askja **74** 65 3N 16 48W
Åskloster **73** 57 13N 12 11E
Askrigg **32** 54 19N 2 6W
Asl **122** 29 33N 32 44E
Aslackby **33** 52 53N 0 23W
Asmar **93** 35 10N 71 27E
Asmera (Asmara) **123** 15 19N 38 55E
Asnæs **73** 55 40N 11 0E
Åsnen **73** 56 35N 15 45E
Åsnes **71** 60 37N 11 59E
Asni **118** 31 17N 7 58W
Aso **110** 33 0N 130 42E
Aso-Zan **110** 32 53N 131 6E
Asoa **126** 4 35N 25 48E
Ásola **62** 45 12N 10 25E
Asotin **60** 46 14N 117 2W
Aspatria **32** 54 45N 3 20W
Aspe **59** 38 20N 0 40W
Aspen **161** 39 12N 106 56W
Aspermont **159** 33 11N 100 15W
Aspiring, Mt. **143** 44 23S 168 46E
Aspres **45** 44 32N 5 44E
Aspur **94** 23 58N 74 7E
Asquith **153** 52 8N 107 13W
Assa **118** 28 35N 9 6W
Assaba, Massif de l' **120** 16 10N 11 45W
Assam □ **98** 25 45N 92 30E
Assamakka **121** 19 21N 5 38E
Assateague I. **162** 38 5N 75 6W
Asse **47** 50 54N 4 6E
Assebroek **47** 51 11N 3 17E
Assekrem **119** 23 16N 5 49E
Assémini **64** 39 18N 9 0E
Assen **46** 53 0N 6 35E
Assendelft **46** 52 29N 4 45E
Assenede **47** 51 14N 3 46E
Assens, Odense, Denmark **73** 56 41N 10 3E
Assens, Randers, Denmark **73** 55 16N 9 55E
Assesse **47** 50 22N 5 2E
Assiniboia **153** 49 40N 105 59W
Assiniboine, R. **153** 49 53N 97 8W
Assinica L. **150** 50 30N 75 20W
Assinie **120** 5 9N 3 17W
Assis **173** 22 40S 50 20W
Assisi **63** 43 4N 12 36E
Ássos **69** 38 22N 20 33E
Assynt **36** 58 25N 5 10W
Assynt, L. **36** 58 25N 5 15W
Astakidha **69** 35 53N 26 50E
Astalfort **44** 44 4N 0 40E
Astara **79** 38 30N 48 50E
Astee **39** 52 33N 9 36W
Asten **47** 51 24N 5 45E
Asti **62** 44 54N 8 11E
Astillero **56** 43 24N 3 49W
Astipálaia **69** 36 32N 26 22E
Aston, C. **149** 70 10N 67 40W
Aston Clinton **29** 51 48N 0 44W
Astorga **56** 42 29N 6 8W
Astoria **160** 46 16N 123 50W
Åstorp **73** 56 6N 12 55E
Astrakhan **83** 46 25N 48 5E
Astudillo **56** 42 12N 4 22W
Asturias **56** 43 15N 6 0W
Astwood Bank **28** 52 15N 1 55W
Asunción **172** 25 21S 57 30W
Asunción, La **174** 11 2N 63 53W
Åsunden **73** 57 47N 13 18E
Asutri **123** 15 25N 35 45E
Aswa, R. **126** 2 30N 33 5E
Aswad,Rasal **122** 21 20N 39 0E
Aswân **122** 24 4N 32 57E
Aswân High Dam = Sadd el Aali **122** 24 5N 32 54E
Asyût **122** 27 11N 31 4E
Asyûti, Wadi **122** 27 18N 31 20E
Aszód **53** 47 39N 19 28E
At Tafilah **92** 30 45N 35 30E
At Ta'if **122** 21 5N 40 27E
Atacama **172** 25 40S 67 40W
Atacama □ **172** 27 30S 70 0W
Atacama, Desierto de **176** 24 0S 69 20W
Atacama, Salar de **172** 24 0S 68 20W
Ataco **174** 3 35N 75 23W
Atakor **119** 23 27N 5 31E
Atakpamé **121** 7 31N 1 13E
Atalaia **114** 9 25S 36 0W

Atalándi Ayutla

Atalándi 69 38 39N 22 58 E
Atalaya 174 10 45 S 73 50W
Ataléia 171 18 3 S 41 6W
Atami 111 35 0N 139 55 E
Atankawng 98 25 50N 97 47 E
Atar 116 20 30N 13 5W
Atara 77 63 10N 129 10 E
Ataram, Erg d' 118 23 57N 2 0 E
Atarfe 57 37 13N 3 40W
Atascadero 163 35 32N 120 44W
Atasu 76 48 30N 71 0 E
Atauro 103 8 10 S 125 30 E
Atbara 122 17 42N 33 59 E
Atbara, R. 122 17 40N 33 56 E
Atbashi 85 41 10N 75 48 E
Atbashi, Khrebet 85 40 50N 75 30 E
Atchafalaya B. 159 29 30N 91 20W
Atchison 158 39 40N 95 0W
Atebubu 121 7 47N 1 0W
Ateca 58 41 20N 1 49W
Aterno, R. 63 42 18N 13 45 E
Atesine, Alpi 62 46 55N 11 30 E
Atessa 63 42 5N 14 27 E
Ath 47 50 38N 3 47 E
Ath Thamami 92 27 45N 35 30 E
Athabasca 152 54 45N 113 20W
Athabasca, L. 153 59 15N 109 15W
Athabasca, R. 153 58 40N 110 50W
Athboy 38 53 37N 6 55W
Athea 39 52 27N 9 18W
Athenry 39 53 18N 8 45W
Athens, Ala., U.S.A. 157 34 49N 86 58W
Athens, Ga., U.S.A. 157 33 56N 83 24W
Athens, N.Y., U.S.A. 162 42 15N 73 48W
Athens, Ohio, U.S.A. 156 39 52N 82 6W
Athens, Pa., U.S.A. 162 41 57N 76 36W
Athens, Tex., U.S.A. 159 32 11N 95 48W
Athens = Athínai 69 37 58N 23 46 E
Atherstone 28 52 35N 1 32W
Atherton, Austral. 138 17 17 S 145 30 E
Atherton, U.K. 32 53 32N 2 30W
Athiéme 121 6 37N 1 40 E
Athínai 69 37 58N 23 46 E
Athleague 38 53 34N 8 17W
Athlone 38 53 26N 7 57W
Athni 96 16 44N 75 6 E
Athol 143 45 30 S 168 35 E
Atholl, Forest of 37 56 51N 3 50W
Atholville 151 47 59N 66 43W
Áthos, Mt. 68 40 9N 24 22 E
Athus 47 49 34N 5 50 E
Athy 39 53 0N 7 0W
Ati 123 13 5N 29 2 E
Atiak 126 3 12N 32 2 E
Atiamuri 142 38 24 S 176 5 E
Atico 174 16 14 S 73 40W
Atienza 58 41 12N 2 52W
Atikokan 150 48 45N 91 37W
Atikonak L. 151 52 40N 64 32W
Atka, U.S.A. 147 52 5N 174 40W
Atka, U.S.S.R. 77 60 50N 151 48 E
Atkarsk 81 51 55N 45 2 E
Atkasuk (Meade River) 147 70 30N 157 20W
Atkinson 158 42 35N 98 59W
Atlanta, Ga., U.S.A. 157 33 50N 84 24W
Atlanta, Tex., U.S.A. 159 33 7N 94 8W
Atlantic 158 41 25N 95 0W
Atlantic City 162 39 25N 74 25W
Atlantic Ocean 14 0 0 20 0W
Atlántico □ 174 10 45N 75 0W
Atlas, Great, Mts. 114 33 0N 5 0W
Atlin 147 59 31N 133 41W
Atlin Lake 147 59 26N 133 45W
'Atlit 90 32 42N 34 56 E
Atløy 71 61 21N 4 58 E
Atmakur 97 14 37N 79 40 E
Atmore 157 31 2N 87 30W
Atnarko 152 52 25N 126 0W
Atō 110 34 25N 131 40 E
Atoka 159 34 22N 96 10W
Atokos 69 38 28N 20 49 E
Atolia 163 35 19N 117 37W
Atotonilco el Alto 164 20 20N 98 40W
Atouguia 57 39 20N 9 20W
Atoyac, R. 165 16 30N 97 31W
Åtrafors 73 57 02N 12 40 E
Atrak, R. 93 37 50N 57 0 E
Ätran 73 57 7N 12 57 E
Atrato, R. 174 6 40N 77 0W
Atrauli 94 28 2N 78 20 E
Atri 63 42 35N 14 0 E
Atsbi 122 13 52N 39 50 E
Atsumi 111 34 35N 137 4 E
Atsumi-Wan 111 34 44N 137 13 E
Atsuta 112 43 24N 141 26 E
Attalla 157 34 2N 86 5W
Attawapiskat 150 52 56N 82 24W
Attawapiskat, L. 150 52 18N 87 54W
Attawapiskat, R. 150 52 57N 82 18W
Attendorn 48 51 8N 7 54 E
Attersee 52 47 55N 13 31 E
Attert 47 49 45N 5 47 E
Attica 156 40 20N 87 15W
Attichy 43 49 25N 3 3 E
Attigny 43 49 28N 4 35 E
Attikamagen L. 151 55 0N 66 30W
Attikí Kai Arkhipélagos □ 69 38 10N 23 40 E
Attil 90 32 23N 35 4 E
Attleboro 162 41 56N 71 18W
Attleborough 29 52 32N 1 1 E
Attock 94 33 52N 72 20 E
Attopeu 100 14 48N 106 50 E
Attu 147 52 55N 173 10W
Attunga 141 30 55 S 150 50 E
Attur 97 11 35N 78 30 E
Attymon 39 53 20N 8 37W
Atuel, R. 172 36 17 S 66 50W
Åtvidaberg 73 58 12N 16 0 E
Atwater 163 37 21N 120 37W
Atwood 158 39 52N 101 3W
Au Sable Pt. 150 46 0N 86 0W
Au Sable, R. 156 44 25N 83 20W
Aubagne 45 43 17N 5 37 E
Aubange 47 49 34N 5 48 E
Aubarede Pt. 103 17 15N 122 20 E
Aube □ 43 48 15N 4 0 E
Aubel 47 50 42N 5 51 E
Aubenas 45 44 37N 4 24 E
Aubenton 43 49 50N 4 12 E
Auberry 163 37 7N 119 29W
Aubigny-sur-Nère 43 47 30N 2 24 E
Aubin 44 44 33N 2 15 E
Aubrac, Mts. d' 44 44 38N 2 58 E
Auburn, Ala., U.S.A. 157 32 37N 85 30W
Auburn, Calif., U.S.A. 160 38 50N 121 4W
Auburn, Ind., U.S.A. 156 41 20N 85 0W
Auburn, Nebr., U.S.A. 158 40 25N 95 50W
Auburn, N.Y., U.S.A. 162 42 57N 76 39W
Auburn, Penn., U.S.A. 162 40 36N 76 6W
Auburn Range 139 25 15 S 150 30 E
Auburndale 157 28 5N 81 45W
Aubusson 44 45 57N 2 11 E
Auch 44 43 39N 0 36 E
Auchel 43 50 30N 2 29 E
Auchenblae 37 56 54N 2 26W
Auchencairn 35 54 51N 3 52W
Auchi 121 7 6N 6 13 E
Auchinleck 34 55 28N 4 18W
Auchness 37 58 0N 4 36W
Auchterarder 35 56 18N 3 43W
Auchterderran 35 56 8N 3 16W
Auchtermuchty 35 56 18N 3 15W
Auchtertyre 36 57 17N 5 35W
Auckland 142 36 52 S 174 46 E
Auckland □ 142 38 35 S 177 0 E
Auckland Is. 142 51 0 S 166 0 E
Aude □ 44 43 8N 2 28 E
Aude, R. 44 44 13N 3 15 E
Auden 150 50 14N 87 53W
Auderghem 47 50 49N 4 26 E
Auderville 42 49 43N 1 57W
Audierne 42 48 1N 4 34W
Audincourt 43 47 30N 6 50 E
Audlem 32 52 59N 2 31W
Audo Ra. 123 6 20N 41 50 E
Audrey, gasfield 19 53 35N 2 0 E
Audubon 158 41 43N 94 56W
Aue 48 50 34N 12 43 E
Auerbach 48 50 30N 12 25 E
Auffay 42 49 43N 1 07 E
Augathella 139 25 48 S 146 35 E
Augher 38 54 25N 7 10W
Aughnacloy 38 54 25N 6 58W
Aughrim, Clare, Ireland 39 53 0N 8 57W
Aughrim, Galway, Ireland 39 53 18N 8 19W
Aughrim, Wicklow, Ireland 39 52 52N 6 20W
Aughrus More 38 53 34N 10 10W
Augrabies Falls 128 28 35 S 20 20 E
Augsburg 49 48 22N 10 54 E
Augusta, Italy 65 37 14N 15 12 E
Augusta, Ark., U.S.A. 159 35 17N 91 25W
Augusta, Ga., U.S.A. 157 33 29N 81 59W
Augusta, Kans., U.S.A. 159 37 40N 97 0W
Augusta, Me., U.S.A. 151 44 20N 69 46 E
Augusta, Mont., U.S.A. 160 47 30N 112 29W
Augusta, Wis., U.S.A. 158 44 41N 91 8W
Augustenborg 73 54 57N 9 53 E
Augustine 159 31 30N 94 37W
Augusto Cardosa 127 12 40 S 34 50 E
Augustów 54 53 51N 23 00 E
Augustus Downs 138 18 35 S 139 55 E
Augustus I. 136 15 20 S 124 30 E
Augustus, Mt. 137 24 20 S 116 50 E
Auk, oilfield 19 56 25N 2 15 E
Aukan 123 15 29N 40 50 E
Aukum 163 38 34N 120 43W
Auld, L. 136 22 32 S 123 44 E
Auldearn 37 57 34N 3 50W
Aulla 62 44 12N 9 57 E
Aulnay 44 46 2N 0 22W
Aulne, R. 42 48 17N 4 16W
Ault 158 40 40N 104 42W
Ault-Onival 42 50 5N 1 29 E
Aultbea 36 57 50N 5 36W
Aulus-les-Bains 44 42 49N 1 19 E
Aumale 43 49 46N 1 46 E
Aumont-Aubrac 44 44 43N 3 17 E
Auna 121 10 9N 4 42 E
Aundh 96 17 33N 74 23 E
Aunis 44 46 0N 0 50W
Auponhia 103 1 58 S 125 27 E
Aups 45 43 37N 6 15 E
Aur, P. 101 2 35N 104 10 E
Aura 98 26 59N 97 57 E
Aurahorten, Mt. 71 59 15N 6 53 E
Auraiya 95 26 28N 79 33 E
Aurangabad, Bihar, India 95 24 45N 84 18 E
Aurangabad, Maharashtra, India 96 19 50N 75 23 E
Auray 42 47 40N 3 0W
Aurès 119 35 8N 6 30 E
Aurich 48 53 28N 7 30 E
Aurilândia 171 16 44 S 50 28W
Aurillac 44 44 55N 2 26 E
Aurlandsvangen 71 60 55N 7 12 E
Auronza 63 46 33N 12 27 E
Aurora, Brazil 171 6 57 S 38 58W
Aurora, S. Afr. 128 32 40 S 18 29 E
Aurora, Colo., U.S.A. 158 39 44N 104 55W
Aurora, Ill., U.S.A. 156 41 42N 88 12W
Aurora, Mo., U.S.A. 159 36 58N 93 42W
Aurora, Nebr., U.S.A. 158 40 55N 98 0W
Aurora, N.Y., U.S.A. 162 42 45N 76 42W
Aurskog 71 59 55N 11 26 E
Aurukun Mission 138 13 20 S 141 45 E
Aus 128 26 35 S 16 12 E
Auskerry I. 37 59 2N 2 35W
Aust-Agder fylke □ 75 58 55N 7 40 E
Austad 71 58 58N 7 37 E
Austerlitz = Slavikov 53 49 10N 16 52 E
Austevoll 71 60 5N 5 13 E
Austin, Austral. 137 27 40 S 117 50 E
Austin, Minn., U.S.A. 158 43 37N 92 59W
Austin, Nev., U.S.A. 160 39 30N 117 1W
Austin, Tex., U.S.A. 159 30 20N 97 45W
Austin, L. 137 27 40 S 118 0 E
Austral Downs 138 20 30 S 137 45 E
Austral Is. = Tubuai, Îles 143 25 0 S 150 0 E
Australia ■ 133 23 0 S 135 0 E
Australian Alps 141 36 30 S 148 8 E
Australian Cap. Terr. 139 35 15 S 149 8 E
Australian Dependency 13 73 0 S 90 0 E
Austria ■ 52 47 0N 14 0 E
Austvågøy 74 68 20N 14 40 E
Autelbas 47 49 39N 5 52 E
Auterive 44 43 21N 1 29 E
Authie, R. 43 50 22N 1 38 E
Autlan 164 19 40N 104 30W
Autun 43 46 58N 4 17 E
Auvelais 47 50 27N 4 38 E
Auvergne, Austral. 136 15 39 S 130 1 E
Auvergne, France 44 45 20N 3 0 E
Auxerre 43 47 48N 3 32 E
Auxi-le-Château 43 50 15N 2 8 E
Auxonne 43 47 10N 5 20 E
Auzances 44 46 2N 2 30 E
Avaldsnes 71 59 21N 5 20 E
Avallon 43 47 30N 3 53 E
Avalon 163 33 21N 118 20W
Avalon Pen. 151 47 30N 53 20W
Avalon Res. 159 32 30N 104 30W
Avanigadda 97 16 0N 80 56 E
Avaré 173 23 4 S 48 58W
Avas 68 40 57N 25 56 E
Avawata Mts. 163 35 30N 116 20W
Avebury 28 51 25N 1 52W
Aveh 92 35 40N 49 15 E
Aveiro, Brazil 175 3 10 S 55 5W
Aveiro, Port. 56 40 37N 8 38W
Aveiro □ 56 40 40N 8 35W
Avelgem 47 50 47N 3 27 E
Avellaneda 172 34 50 S 58 10W
Avellino 65 40 54N 14 46 E
Avenal 163 36 0N 120 8W
Avenchen 50 46 53N 7 2 E
Averøya 71 63 0N 7 35 E
Aversa 65 40 58N 14 11 E
Avery 160 47 22N 115 56W
Aves, Islas de 174 12 0N 67 40W
Avesnes-sur-Helpe 43 50 8N 3 55 E
Avesta 72 60 9N 16 10 E
Aveton Gifford 30 50 17N 3 51W
Aveyron □ 44 44 22N 2 45 E
Avezzano 63 42 2N 13 24 E
Avgó 69 35 33N 25 37 E
Aviá Terai 172 26 45 S 60 50W
Aviano 63 46 3N 12 35 E
Avich, L. 34 56 17N 5 25W
Aviemore 37 57 11N 3 50W
Avigliana 62 45 7N 7 13 E
Avigliano 65 40 44N 15 41 E
Avignon 45 43 57N 4 50 E
Ávila 56 40 39N 4 43W
Ávila □ 56 40 30N 5 0W
Avila Beach 163 35 11N 120 44W
Ávila, Sierra de 56 40 40N 5 0W
Avilés 56 43 35N 5 57W
Avionárion 69 38 31N 24 8 E
Avisio, R. 63 46 14N 11 18 E
Aviz 57 39 4N 7 53W
Avize 43 48 59N 4 0 E
Avoca, Austral. 139 37 5 S 143 26 E
Avoca, Ireland 39 52 52N 6 13W
Avoca, R., Austral. 140 35 40 S 143 43 E
Avoca, R., Ireland 39 52 48N 6 10W
Avoch 37 57 34N 4 10W
Avola, Can. 152 51 45N 119 19W
Avola, Italy 65 36 56N 15 7 E
Avon 158 43 0N 98 3W
Avon □ 28 51 30N 2 40W
Avon Downs 133 19 58 S 137 25 E
Avon Is. 133 19 37 S 158 17 E
Avon, R., Austral. 137 31 40 S 116 7 E
Avon, R., Avon, U.K. 28 51 30N 2 43W
Avon, R., Grampian, U.K. 37 57 25N 3 25W
Avon, R., Hants., U.K. 28 50 44N 1 45W
Avon, R., Warwick, U.K. 28 52 0N 2 9W
Avondale, N.Z. 142 36 54 S 174 42 E
Avondale, Rhod. 127 17 43 S 30 58 E
Avonlea 153 50 0N 105 0W
Avonmouth 28 51 30N 2 42W
Avranches 42 48 40N 1 20W
Avrig 70 45 43N 24 21 E
Avrillé 44 46 28N 1 28W
Avtovac 66 43 9N 18 35 E
Avu Meru □ 126 3 20 S 36 50 E
Awag el Baqar 123 10 10N 33 10 E
Awaji 111 34 32N 135 1 E
Awaji-Shima 110 34 30N 134 50 E
Awali 93 26 0N 50 30 E
Awantipur 95 33 55N 75 3 E
Awanui 142 35 4 S 173 17 E
Awarja, R. 96 18 0N 76 15 E
Awarta 90 32 10N 35 17 E
Awarua Pt. 143 44 15 S 168 5 E
Awasa, L. 123 7 0N 38 30 E
Awash 123 9 1N 40 10 E
Awash, R. 123 11 30N 42 0 E
Awaso 120 6 15N 2 22W
Awatere, R. 143 41 37 S 174 10 E
Awbarī 119 26 46N 12 57 E
Awe, L. 34 56 15N 5 15W
Aweil 123 8 42N 27 20 E
Awgu 121 6 4N 7 24 E
Awjilah 117 29 8N 21 7 E
Aworro 135 7 43 S 143 11 E
Ax-les-Thermes 44 42 44N 1 50 E
Axarfjörður 74 66 15N 16 45W
Axbridge 28 51 17N 2 50W
Axe Edge 32 53 14N 2 2W
Axe R. 28 51 17N 2 52W
Axel 47 51 16N 3 55 E
Axel Heiberg I. 12 80 0N 90 0W
Axelfors 73 57 26N 13 7 E
Axholme, Isle of 33 53 30N 1 10 E
Axim 120 4 51N 2 15W
Axintele 70 44 37N 26 47 E
Axiós, R. 68 40 57N 22 35 E
Axmarsbruk 72 61 3N 17 10 E
Axminster 30 50 47N 3 1W
Axmouth 30 50 43N 3 2W
Axstedt 48 53 26N 8 43 E
Axvall 73 58 23N 13 34 E
Ay 43 49 3N 4 0 E
Ay, R. 84 56 8N 57 40 E
Ayabaca 174 4 40 S 79 53W
Ayabe 111 35 20N 135 20 E
Ayacucho, Argent. 172 37 5 S 58 20W
Ayacucho, Peru 174 13 0 S 74 0W
Ayaguz 76 48 10N 80 0 E
Ayakkuduk 85 41 12N 65 12 E
Ayakok'umu Hu 105 37 30N 89 20 E
Ayakudi 97 10 57N 7 6 E
Ayamonte 57 37 12N 7 24W
Ayan 77 56 30N 138 16 E
Ayancık 82 41 57N 34 18 E
Ayapel 174 8 19N 75 9W
Ayapel, Sa. de 174 7 45N 75 30W
Ayaş 82 40 10N 32 14 E
Ayaviri 174 14 50 S 70 35W
Aydın □ 92 37 40N 27 40 E
Aye 47 50 14N 5 18 E
Ayenngré 121 8 40N 1 1 E
Ayer Hitam 101 1 55N 103 11 E
Ayeritam 101 5 24N 100 15 E
Ayers Rock 136 25 23 S 131 5 E
Ayiá 68 39 43N 22 45 E
Ayía Anna 69 38 52N 23 24 E
Ayía Marína, Kásos, Greece 69 35 27N 26 53 E
Ayía Marína, Leros, Greece 69 37 11N 26 48 E
Ayia Paraskeví 68 39 14N 26 16 E
Ayia Rouméli 69 35 14N 23 58 E
Ayiássos 69 39 5N 26 23 E
Áyios Andréas 69 37 21N 22 45 E
Áyios Evstrátios 68 39 34N 24 58 E
Áyios Ioánnis, Ákra 69 35 20N 25 40 E
Áyios Kírikos 69 37 34N 26 17 E
Áyios Matthaíos 68 39 30N 19 47 E
Áyios Míron 69 35 15N 25 1 E
Áyios Nikólaos 69 35 11N 25 41 E
Áyios Pétros 69 38 38N 20 33 E
Áyios Yeóryios 69 37 28N 23 57 E
Aykathonísi 69 37 28N 27 0 E
Ayke, Ozero 84 51 57N 61 36 E
Aylesbury 29 51 48N 0 49W
Aylesford 29 51 18N 0 29 E
Aylmer L. 148 64 0N 108 30W
Aylsham 29 52 48N 1 16 E
Ayn Zālah 92 36 45N 42 35 E
'Ayn Zaqqūt 119 29 0N 19 30 E
Ayna 59 38 34N 2 3W
Aynho 28 51 59N 1 15W
Ayni 85 39 23N 68 32 E
Ayolas 172 27 10 S 56 59W
Ayom 123 7 49N 28 23 E
Ayon, Ostrov 77 69 50N 169 0 E
Ayora 59 39 3N 1 3W
Ayr, Austral. 138 19 35 S 147 25 E
Ayr, U.K. 34 55 28N 4 37W
Ayr (□) 26 55 25N 4 25W
Ayr, Heads of 34 55 25N 4 43W
Ayr, R. 34 55 29N 4 40W
Ayre, Pt. of 37 58 55N 2 43W
Ayre, Pt. of I.o.M. 32 54 27N 4 21W
Aysgarth 32 54 18N 2 0W
Aysha 123 10 50N 42 23 E
Ayton 138 15 45 S 145 25 E
Ayton, Borders, U.K. 35 55 51N 2 6W
Ayton, N. Yorks., U.K. 33 54 15N 0 29W
Aytos 67 42 47N 27 16 E
Aytoska Planina 67 42 45N 27 30 E
Ayu, Kepulauan 103 0 35N 131 5 E
Ayutla, Guat. 166 14 40N 92 10W

Ayutla
Balasore

Ayutla, Mexico 165 16 58N 99 17W
Ayutthaya = Phra Nakhon Si A. 101 14 25N 100 30E
Ayvalık 92 39 20N 26 46E
Aywaille 47 50 28N 5 40E
Az Zahiriya 90 31 25N 34 58E
Az Zahran 92 26 10N 50 7E
Az-Zarqā 90 32 5N 36 4E
Az Zāwiyah 119 32 52N 12 56E
Az-Zilfī 92 26 12N 44 52E
Az Zintān 119 31 59N 12 9E
Az Zubayr 92 30 20N 47 50E
Azambuja 57 39 4N 8 51W
Azamgarh 95 26 35N 83 13E
Azaouak, Vallée de l' 121 15 50N 3 20E
Azārbāijān □ 92 37 0N 44 30E
Azare 121 11 55N 10 10E
Azay-le-Rideau 42 47 16N 0 30E
Azazga 119 36 48N 4 22E
Azbine = Aïr 121 18 0N 8 0E
Azeffoun 119 36 51N 4 26E
Azemmour 118 33 14N 9 20W
Azerbaijan S.S.R. □ 83 40 20N 48 0E
Azezo 123 12 28N 37 15E
Azilal, Beni Mallal 118 32 0N 6 30W
Azimganj 95 24 14N 84 16E
Aznalcóllar 57 37 32N 6 17W
Azogues 174 2 35S 78 0W
Azor 90 32 2N 34 48E
Azores, Is. 14 38 44N 29 0W
Azov 83 47 3N 39 25E
Azov Sea = Azovskoye More 82 46 0N 36 30E
Azovskoye More 82 46 0N 36 30E
Azovy 76 64 55N 64 35E
Azpeitia 58 43 12N 2 19W
Azrou 118 33 28N 5 19W
Aztec 161 36 54N 108 0W
Azúa de Compostela 167 18 25N 70 44W
Azuaga 57 38 16N 5 39W
Azuara 58 41 15N 0 53W
Azuara, R. 58 41 20N 0 55W
Azúcar, Presa del 165 26 0N 99 5W
Azuer, R. 57 38 50N 3 15W
Azuero, Pen. de 166 7 30N 80 30W
Azul 172 36 42S 59 43W
Azusa 163 34 8N 117 52W
Azzaba 119 36 48N 7 6E
Azzano Décimo 63 45 53N 12 46E

B

B. Curri 68 42 22N 20 5E
Ba Don 100 17 45N 106 26E
Ba Dong 101 9 40N 106 33E
Ba Ngoi = Cam Lam 101 11 50N 109 10E
Ba, R. 56 13 5N 109 0E
Ba Tri 101 10 2N 106 36E
Baa 103 10 50S 123 0E
Baamonde 56 43 7N 7 44W
Baar 51 47 12N 8 32E
Baarle Nassau 47 51 27N 4 56E
Baarlo 47 51 20N 6 6E
Baarn 46 52 12N 5 17E
Bāb el Māndeb 91 12 35N 43 25E
Baba Burnu 68 39 29N 26 2E
Baba dag 83 41 0N 48 55E
Baba, Mt. 67 42 44N 23 59E
Babaçulândia 170 7 13S 47 46W
Babadag 70 44 53N 28 44E
Babaeski 67 41 26N 27 6E
Babahoyo 174 1 40S 79 30W
Babakin 137 32 7S 118 1E
Babana 121 10 31N 3 46E
Babar, Alg. 119 35 10N 7 6E
Babar, Pak. 94 31 7N 69 32E
Babar, I. 103 8 0S 129 30E
Babarkach 94 29 45N 68 0E
Babayevo 81 59 24N 35 55E
Babb 160 48 56N 113 27W
Babbitt 163 38 32N 118 39W
Babenhausen 49 49 57N 8 56E
Babi Besar, P. 101 2 25N 103 59E
Babia Gora 54 49 38N 19 38E
Babile 123 9 16N 42 11E
Babinda 138 17 20S 145 56E
Babine 152 55 20N 126 35W
Babine L. 152 54 48N 126 0W
Babine, R. 152 55 45N 127 44W
Babo 103 2 30S 133 30E
Babócsa 53 46 2N 17 21E
Babol 93 36 40N 52 50E
Babol Sar 93 36 45N 52 45E
Baboma 126 2 30N 28 10E
Baborówo Kietrz 53 50 7N 18 1E
Baboua 124 5 49N 14 58E
Babuna, mts. 66 41 30N 21 40E
Babura 121 12 51N 8 59E
Babusar Pass 95 35 12N 73 59E
Babushkin 81 55 45N 37 40E
Babušnica 66 43 7N 22 27E
Babylon, Iraq 92 32 40N 44 30E
Babylon, U.S.A. 162 40 42N 73 20W
Bač 66 45 29N 19 17E
Bac Can 100 22 08N 105 49E
Bac Giang 100 21 16N 106 11E
Bac Kan 101 22 5N 105 50E
Bac Lieu = Vinh Loi 101 9 17N 105 43E
Bac Ninh 100 21 13N 106 4E
Bac Phan 100 22 0N 105 0E
Bac Quang 100 22 30N 104 48E
Bacabal 170 4 15N 44 45W
Bacalar 165 18 12N 87 53W
Bacan, Pulau 103 0 50S 127 30E
Bacarès, Le 44 42 47N 3 3E
Bacarra 103 18 15N 120 37E
Baccarat 43 48 28N 6 42E
Bacchus Marsh 140 37 43S 144 27E
Bacerac 164 30 18N 108 50W
Bach Long Vi, Dao 100 20 10N 107 40E
Bachaquero 174 9 56N 71 8W
Bacharach 49 50 3N 7 46E
Bachclina 76 57 45N 67 20E
Bachok 101 6 4N 102 25E
Bachuma 123 6 31N 36 1E
Bačina 66 43 42N 21 23E
Back 36 58 17N 6 20W
Back, R. 148 65 10N 104 0W
Bačka Palanka 66 45 17N 19 27E
Bačka Topola 66 45 49N 19 39E
Bäckefors 73 58 48N 12 9E
Bački Petrovac 66 45 29N 19 32E
Backnang 49 48 57N 9 26E
Backstairs Passage 133 35 40S 138 5E
Bacolod 103 10 40N 122 57E
Bacqueville 42 49 47N 1 0E
Bacs-Kiskun □ 53 46 43N 19 30E
Bácsalmás 53 46 8N 19 17E
Bacton 29 52 50N 1 29E
Bacuit 103 11 20N 119 20E
Bacup 32 53 42N 2 12W
Bacŭu 70 46 35N 26 55E
Bacŭu □ 70 46 30N 26 45E
Bad Aussee 52 47 43N 13 45E
Bad Axe 150 43 48N 82 59W
Bad Bergzabern 49 49 6N 8 0E
Bad Bramstedt 48 53 56N 9 53E
Bad Doberan 48 54 6N 11 55E
Bad Driburg 48 51 44N 9 0E
Bad Ems 49 50 22N 7 44E
Bad Frankenhausen 48 51 21N 11 3E
Bad Freienwalde 52 52 46N 14 2E
Bad Godesberg 48 50 41N 7 4E
Bad Hersfeld 48 50 52N 9 42E
Bad Hofgastein 52 47 17N 13 6E
Bad Homburg 49 50 17N 8 33E
Bad Honnef 48 50 39N 7 13E
Bad Ischl 52 47 44N 13 38E
Bad Kissingen 49 50 11N 10 5E
Bad Kreuznach 49 49 47N 7 47E
Bad Lands 158 43 40N 102 10W
Bad Lauterberg 48 51 38N 10 29E
Bad Leonfelden 52 48 31N 14 18E
Bad Lippspringe 48 51 47N 8 46E
Bad Mergentheim 49 49 29N 9 47E
Bad Münstereifel 48 50 33N 6 46E
Bad Nauheim 49 50 24N 8 45E
Bad Oeynhausen 48 52 16N 8 45E
Bad Oldesloe 48 53 56N 10 17E
Bad Orb 49 50 16N 9 21E
Bad Pyrmont 48 51 59N 9 5E
Bad, R. 158 44 10N 100 50W
Bad Ragaz 51 47 0N 9 30E
Bad St. Peter 48 54 23N 8 32E
Bad Salzuflen 48 52 8N 8 44E
Bad Segeberg 48 53 58N 10 16E
Bad Tölz 49 47 43N 11 34E
Bad Waldsee 49 47 56N 9 46E
Bad Wildungen 48 51 7N 9 10E
Bad Wimpfen 49 49 12N 9 10E
Bad Windsheim 49 49 29N 10 25E
Badagara 97 11 35N 75 40E
Badagri 121 6 25N 2 55E
Badajoz 57 38 50N 6 59W
Badajoz □ 57 38 40N 6 30W
Badakhshan □ 93 36 30N 71 0E
Badalona 58 41 26N 2 15E
Badalzai 94 29 50N 65 35E
Badampahar 96 22 10N 86 10E
Badanah 92 30 58N 41 30E
Badas 102 4 33N 114 25E
Badas, Kepulauan 102 0 45N 107 5E
Baddo, R. 93 28 15N 65 0E
Bade 103 7 10S 139 35E
Baden, Austria 53 48 1N 16 13E
Baden, Switz. 51 47 28N 8 18E
Baden-Baden 49 48 45N 8 15E
Baden Park 140 32 8S 144 12E
Baden-Württemberg □ 49 48 40N 9 0E
Badenoch 37 58 16N 4 5W
Badenscoth 37 57 27N 2 30W
Badeso 123 9 58N 40 52E
Badgastein 52 47 7N 13 9E
Badger, Can. 151 49 0N 56 4W
Badger, U.S.A. 163 36 38N 119 1W
Badghis □ 93 35 0N 63 0E
Badgom 95 34 1N 74 45E
Badhoevedorp 46 52 20N 4 47E
Badia Polesine 63 45 6N 11 30E
Badin 94 24 38N 68 54E
Badnera 96 20 48N 77 44E
Badogo 120 11 2N 8 13W
Badrinath 95 30 45N 79 30E
Baduen 91 7 15N 47 40E
Badulla 97 7 1N 81 7E
Badupi 98 21 36N 93 27E
Bække 73 55 35N 9 6E
Baena 57 37 37N 4 20W
Baerami Creek 141 32 27S 150 27E
Baetas 174 6 5S 62 15W
Baexem 47 51 13N 5 53E
Baeza, Ecuador 174 0 25S 77 45W
Baeza, Spain 59 37 57N 3 25W
Bafa 93 31 40N 55 25E
Bafa Gölü 69 37 30N 27 29E
Bafatá 120 12 8N 15 20W
Baffin Bay 12 72 0N 64 0W
Baffin I. 149 68 0N 75 0W
Bafia 121 4 40N 11 10E
Bafilo 121 9 22N 1 22E
Bafing, R. 120 11 40N 10 45W
Baflo 46 53 22N 6 31E
Bafoulabé 120 13 50N 10 55W
Bafq 93 31 40N 55 20E
Bafra 82 41 34N 35 54E
Baft 93 29 15N 56 38E
Bafut 121 6 6N 10 2E
Bafwakwandji 126 1 12N 26 52E
Bafwasende 126 1 3N 27 5E
Bagalkot 96 16 10N 75 40E
Bagamoyo 126 6 28S 38 55E
Bagamoyo □ 126 6 20S 38 30E
Bagan Datok 101 3 59N 100 47E
Bagan Serai 101 5 1N 100 32E
Bagan Siapiapi 102 2 12N 100 50E
Baganga 103 7 34N 126 33E
Bagasra 94 21 59N 71 77E
Bagawi 123 12 20N 34 18E
Bagdad 163 34 35N 115 53W
Bagdarin 77 54 26N 113 36E
Bagé 173 31 20S 54 15W
Bagenalstown = Muine Bheag 39 52 42N 6 57W
Baggs 160 41 8N 107 46W
Baggy Pt. 30 51 11N 4 12W
Bagh 95 33 59N 73 45E
Bagh nam Faoileann, B. 36 57 22N 7 13W
Baghdād 92 33 20N 44 30E
Bagherhat 98 22 40N 89 47E
Bagheria 64 38 5N 13 30E
Baghin 93 30 12N 56 45E
Baghlan 93 36 12N 69 0E
Baghlan □ 93 36 0N 68 30E
Baginbun Hd. 39 52 10N 6 50W
Bagley 158 47 30N 95 22W
Bagnacavallo 63 44 25N 11 58E
Bagnara Cálabra 65 38 16N 15 49E
Bagnères-de-Bigorre 44 43 5N 0 9E
Bagnères-de-Luchon 44 42 47N 0 38E
Bagni di Lucca 62 44 1N 10 37E
Bagno di Romagna 63 43 50N 11 59E
Bagnoles-de-l'Orne 42 48 32N 0 25W
Bagnolo Mella 62 45 27N 10 14E
Bagnols-les-Bains 44 44 30N 3 40E
Bagnols-sur-Cèze 45 44 10N 4 36E
Bagnorégio 63 42 38N 12 7E
Bagolino 62 45 49N 10 28E
Bagotville 151 48 22N 70 54W
Bagrdan 66 44 5N 21 11E
Bagshot 29 51 22N 0 41W
Baguio 103 16 26N 120 34E
Bahabón de Esgueva 58 41 52N 3 43W
Bahadurabad 98 25 11N 89 44E
Bahadurgarh 94 28 40N 76 57E
Bahama, Canal Viejo de 166 22 10N 77 30W
Bahama Is. 167 24 40N 74 0W
Bahamas ■ 167 24 0N 74 0W
Baharîya, El Wâhât el 122 28 0N 28 50E
Bahau 101 2 48N 102 26E
Bahawalnagar 94 30 0N 73 15E
Bahawalpur 94 29 37N 71 40E
Bahawalpur □ 94 29 5N 71 3E
Baheri 95 28 45N 79 34E
Baheta 123 13 27N 42 10E
Bahi 126 5 58S 35 21E
Bahi Swamp 126 6 10S 35 0E
Bahia = Salvador 171 13 0S 38 30W
Bahia □ 171 12 0N 42 0W
Bahia Blanca 172 38 35S 62 13W
Bahia de Caráquez 174 0 40S 80 27W
Bahia Honda 166 22 54N 83 10W
Bahia, Islas de la 166 16 45N 86 15W
Bahia Laura 176 48 10S 66 30W
Bahia Negra 174 20 5S 58 5W
Bahir Dar Giyorgis 123 11 33N 37 25E
Bahmer 118 27 32N 0 10W
Bahönye 53 46 25N 17 28E
Bahr Aouk 124 9 20N 20 40E
Bahr Dar 123 11 37N 37 10E
Bahr el Abiad 123 9 30N 31 40E
Bahr el Ahmer □ 122 20 0N 35 0E
Bahr el Arab 123 9 50N 27 10E
Bahr el Azraq 123 10 30N 35 0E
Bahr el Ghazâl □ 123 7 0N 28 0E
Bahr el Ghazâl, R. 123 9 0N 30 0E
Bahr el Jebel 123 7 30N 30 30E
Bahr Salamat 124 10 0N 19 0E
Bahr Yûsef 122 28 25N 30 35E
Bahra 92 21 25N 39 32E
Bahra el Burullus 122 31 28N 30 48E
Bahra el Manzala 122 31 28N 32 01E
Bahraich 95 27 38N 81 50E
Bahrain ■ 93 26 0N 50 35E
Bahramabad 93 30 28N 56 2E
Bahu Kalat 93 25 50N 61 20E
Bai 120 13 35N 3 28W
Bai Bung, Mui 101 8 38N 104 44E
Bai Duc 100 18 3N 105 49E
Bai Thuong 100 19 54N 105 23E
Baia-Mare 70 47 40N 23 17E
Baia-Sprie 70 47 41N 23 43W
Baião 170 2 40S 49 40W
Baïbokoum 117 7 40N 14 45E
Baidoa 91 3 8N 43 30E
Baie Comeau 151 49 12N 68 10W
Baie de l'Abri 151 50 3N 67 0W
Baie Johan Beetz 151 50 18N 62 50W
Baie St. Paul 151 47 28N 70 32W
Baie Trinité 151 49 25N 67 20W
Baie Verte 151 49 55N 56 12W
Baignes 44 45 28N 0 25W
Baigneux-les-Juifs 43 47 31N 4 39E
Ba'ījī 92 35 0N 43 30E
Baikal, L. 77 53 0N 108 0E
Bailadila, Mt. 96 18 43N 81 15E
Baildon 33 53 52N 1 46W
Baile Atha Cliath = Dublin 39 53 20N 6 18W
Bailei 123 6 44N 40 18E
Bailén 57 38 8N 3 48W
Baileux 47 50 2N 4 23E
Bailhongal 97 15 55N 74 53E
Bailique, Ilha 170 1 2N 49 58W
Bailleul 43 50 44N 2 41E
Baillieborough 38 53 55N 7 0W
Baimuru 135 7 35S 144 51E
Bain-de-Bretagne 42 47 50N 1 40W
Bainbridge, U.K. 32 54 18N 2 7W
Bainbridge, Ga., U.S.A. 157 30 53N 84 34W
Bainbridge, N.Y., U.S.A. 162 42 17N 75 29W
Baing 103 10 14S 120 34E
Bainville 158 48 8N 104 10W
Bainyik 135 3 40S 143 4E
Baird 159 32 25N 99 25W
Baird Inlet 147 64 49N 164 18W
Baird Mts. 147 67 10N 160 15W
Bairnsdale 141 37 48S 147 36E
Baissa 121 7 14N 10 38E
Baitadi 95 29 35N 80 25E
Baixa Grande 171 11 57S 40 11W
Baiyuda 122 17 35N 32 07E
Baja 53 46 12N 18 59E
Baja California 164 32 10N 115 12W
Baja, Pta. 164 29 50N 116 0W
Bajah, Wadi 122 23 14N 39 20E
Bajana 94 23 7N 71 49E
Bajimba 139 29 22S 152 0E
Bajimba, Mt. 139 29 17S 152 6E
Bajina Bašta 66 43 58N 19 35E
Bajitpur 95 24 13N 91 0E
Bajmok 66 45 57N 19 24E
Bajo Boquete 167 8 49N 82 27W
Bajoga 121 10 57N 11 20E
Bajool 138 23 40S 150 35E
Bak 53 46 43N 16 51E
Bakal 84 54 56N 58 48E
Bakala 117 6 15N 20 20E
Bakanas 85 44 50N 76 15E
Bakar 63 45 18N 14 32E
Bakel, Neth. 47 51 30N 5 45E
Bakel, Senegal 120 14 56N 12 20W
Baker, Calif., U.S.A. 163 35 16N 116 8W
Baker, Mont., U.S.A. 158 46 22N 104 12W
Baker, Nev., U.S.A. 160 38 59N 114 7W
Baker, Oreg., U.S.A. 160 44 50N 117 55W
Baker Is. 130 0 10N 176 35E
Baker, L., Austral. 137 26 54S 126 5E
Baker, L., Can. 148 64 0N 96 0W
Baker Lake 148 64 20N 96 3W
Baker Mt. 160 48 50N 121 49W
Baker's Dozen Is. 150 56 45N 78 45W
Bakersfield 163 35 25N 119 0W
Bakewell 33 53 13N 1 40W
Bakhchisaray 82 44 40N 33 45E
Bakhmach 80 51 10N 32 45E
Bakhtiari □ 92 32 0N 49 0E
Bakia 123 5 18N 25 45E
Bakinskikh Komissarov 92 39 20N 49 15E
Bakırköy 67 40 59N 28 53E
Bakkafjörðr 74 66 2N 14 48W
Bakkagerði 74 65 31N 13 49W
Bakke 71 58 25N 6 39E
Bakony Forest = Bakony Hegység 53 47 10N 17 30E
Bakony Hegység 53 47 10N 17 30E
Bakony, R. 53 47 35N 17 54E
Bakori 121 11 34N 7 25E
Bakouma 117 5 40N 22 56E
Bakov 52 50 27N 14 55E
Bakpakty 85 44 35N 76 40E
Bakr Uzyak 84 52 59N 58 38E
Baku 83 40 25N 49 45E
Bakwanga = Mbuji Mayi 124 6 9S 23 40E
Bal'a 90 32 20N 35 6E
Bala, L. = Tegid, L. 31 52 53N 3 38W
Balabac I. 102 8 0N 117 0E
Balabac, Selat 102 7 53N 117 5E
Balabagh 94 34 25N 70 12E
Balabakk 92 34 0N 36 10E
Balabalangan, Kepulauan 102 2 20S 117 30E
Balaghat 96 21 49N 80 12E
Balaghat Ra. 96 18 50N 76 30E
Balaguer 58 41 50N 0 50E
Balakhna 81 56 35N 43 32E
Balaklava, Austral. 140 34 7S 138 22E
Balaklava, U.S.S.R. 82 44 30N 33 30E
Balakleya 82 49 28N 36 55E
Balakovo 81 52 4N 47 55E
Balallan 36 58 5N 6 35W
Balancán 165 17 48N 91 32W
Balanda 81 51 30N 44 40E
Balangir 96 20 43N 83 35E
Balapur 96 21 22N 76 45E
Balashikha 81 55 49N 37 59E
Balashov 81 51 30N 43 10E
Balasinor 94 22 57N 73 23E
Balasore 96 21 35N 87 3E

Balassagyarmat **Bangor**

Balassagyarmat	53	48 4N	19 15 E
Balât	122	25 36N	29 19 E
Balaton	53	46 50N	17 40 E
Balatonfüred	53	46 58N	17 54 E
Balatonszentgyörgy	53	46 41N	17 19 E
Balazote	59	38 54N	2 09W
Balbeggie	35	56 26N	3 19W
Balbi, Mt.	135	5 55 S	154 58 E
Balblair	37	57 39N	4 11W
Balboa	166	9 0N	79 30W
Balbriggan	38	53 35N	6 10W
Balcarce	172	38 0 S	58 10W
Balcarres	153	50 50N	103 35W
Balchik	67	43 28N	28 11 E
Balclutha	143	46 15 S	169 45 E
Bald Hd.	137	35 6 S	118 1 E
Bald Hill, W. Australia, Austral.	137	31 36 S	116 13 E
Bald Hill, W. Australia, Austral.	137	24 55 S	119 57 E
Bald I.	137	34 57 S	118 27 E
Bald Knob	159	35 20N	91 35W
Baldegger-See	51	47 12N	8 17 E
Balder, oilfield	19	59 10N	2 20 E
Balderton	33	53 3N	0 46W
Baldock	29	51 59N	0 11W
Baldock L.	153	56 33N	97 57W
Baldoyle	38	53 24N	6 10W
Baldwin, Fla., U.S.A.	156	30 15N	82 10W
Baldwin, Mich., U.S.A.	156	43 54N	85 53W
Baldwinsville	162	43 10N	76 19W
Bale	63	45 4N	13 46 E
Baleares □	58	39 30N	3 0 E
Baleares, Islas	58	39 30N	3 0 E
Balearic Is. = Baleares, Islas	58	39 30N	3 0 E
Baleia, Ponta da	171	17 40 S	39 7W
Balen	47	51 10N	5 10 E
Baler	103	15 46N	121 34 E
Balerna	51	45 52N	9 0 E
Baleshare I.	36	57 30N	7 21W
Balezino	84	58 2N	53 6 E
Balfate	166	15 48N	86 25W
Balfe's Creek	138	20 12 S	145 55 E
Balfour, S. Afr.	129	26 38 S	28 35 E
Balfour, U.K.	37	59 2N	2 54W
Balfour Downs	137	22 45 S	120 50 E
Balfouriyya	90	32 38N	35 18 E
Balfron	34	56 4N	4 20W
Bali	121	5 54N	10 0 E
Bali □	102	8 20 S	115 0 E
Bali, I.	102	8 20 S	115 0 E
Bali, Selat	103	8 30 S	114 35 E
Baligród	54	49 20N	22 17 E
Balikesir	92	39 35N	27 58 E
Balikpapan	102	1 10 S	116 55 E
Balimbing	103	5 10N	120 3 E
Balimo	135	8 6 S	142 57 E
Baling	101	5 41N	100 55 E
Balintore	37	57 45N	3 55W
Balipara	99	26 50N	92 45 E
Balit	95	36 15N	74 40 E
Baliza	175	16 0 S	52 20W
Balk	46	52 54N	5 35 E
Balkan Mts. = Stara Planina	67	43 15N	23 0 E
Balkan Pen.	16	42 0N	22 0 E
Balkh = Wazirabad	93	36 44N	66 47 E
Balkh □	93	36 30N	67 0 E
Balkhash	76	46 50N	74 50 E
Balkhash, Ozero	76	40 0N	74 50 E
Balla, Ireland	38	53 48N	9 7W
Balla, Pak.	99	24 10N	91 35 E
Ballachulish	36	56 40N	5 10W
Balladonia	137	32 27 S	123 51 E
Ballagan Pt.	38	54 0N	6 6W
Ballaghaderreen	38	53 55N	8 35W
Ballantrae	34	55 6N	5 0W
Ballara	140	32 19 S	140 45 E
Ballarat	139	37 33 S	143 50 E
Ballard, L.	137	29 20 S	120 10 E
Ballarpur	96	19 50N	79 23 E
Ballater	37	57 2N	3 2W
Ballaugh	32	54 20N	4 32W
Balldale	141	36 20N	146 33 E
Ballenas, Canal de las	164	29 10N	113 45W
Balleni	70	45 48N	27 51 E
Balleny Is.	13	66 30 S	163 0 E
Ballia	95	25 46N	84 12 E
Ballickmoyler	39	52 54N	7 2W
Ballidu	137	30 35 S	116 45 E
Ballina, Austral.	139	28 50 S	153 31 E
Ballina, Mayo, Ireland	38	54 7N	9 10W
Ballina, Tipp., Ireland	39	52 49N	8 27W
Ballinagar	39	53 15N	7 21W
Ballinagh = Bellananagh	38	53 55N	7 25W
Ballinalack	38	53 38N	7 28W
Ballinalea	39	53 0N	6 8W
Ballinalee	38	53 46N	7 40W
Ballinamallard	38	54 30N	7 36W
Ballinameen	38	53 54N	8 19W
Ballinamore	38	54 3N	7 48W
Ballinamore Bridge	38	53 30N	8 24W
Ballinascarty	39	51 40N	8 52W
Ballinasloe	39	53 20N	8 12W
Ballincollig	39	51 52N	8 35W
Ballindaggin	39	52 33N	6 43W
Ballinderry	38	53 2N	8 13W
Ballinderry R.	38	54 40N	6 32W
Ballindine	38	53 40N	8 57W
Ballineen	39	51 43N	8 57W
Balling	73	56 38N	8 51 E
Ballingarry, Lim., Ireland	39	53 1N	8 3W
Ballingarry, Tipp., Ireland	39	52 29N	8 50W
Ballingarry, Tipp., Ireland	39	52 35N	7 32W
Ballingeary	39	51 51N	9 13W
Ballinger	159	31 45N	99 58W
Ballinhassig	39	51 48N	8 33W
Ballinlough	38	53 45N	8 39W
Ballinluig	37	56 40N	3 40W
Ballinrobe	38	53 36N	9 13W
Ballinskelligs	39	51 50N	10 17W
Ballinskelligs B.	39	51 46N	10 11W
Ballintober	38	53 43N	8 25W
Ballintoy	38	55 13N	6 20W
Ballintra	38	54 35N	8 9W
Ballinunty	39	52 36N	7 40W
Ballinure	39	52 34N	7 46W
Ballivian	172	22 41 S	62 10W
Ballivor	38	53 32N	6 50W
Ballo Pt.	79	8 55N	13 18W
Balloch	34	56 0N	4 35W
Ballon	39	48 10N	0 16 E
Ballston Spa	162	43 0N	73 51W
Ballybay	38	54 8N	6 52W
Ballybofey	38	54 48N	7 47W
Ballyboghil	38	53 32N	6 16W
Ballybogy	38	55 8N	6 33W
Ballybunion	39	52 30N	9 40W
Ballycanew	39	52 37N	6 18W
Ballycarney	39	52 35N	6 44W
Ballycastle	38	55 12N	6 15W
Ballycastle B.	38	55 12N	6 15W
Ballyclare, Ireland	38	53 40N	8 0W
Ballyclare, U.K.	38	54 46N	6 0W
Ballyclerahan	39	52 25N	7 48W
Ballycolla	39	52 53N	7 27W
Ballyconneely	38	53 27N	10 5W
Ballyconneely B.	38	53 23N	10 8W
Ballyconnell	38	54 7N	7 35W
Ballycotton	39	51 50N	8 0W
Ballycroy	38	54 2N	9 49W
Ballydavid	39	53 12N	8 28W
Ballydavid Hd.	39	52 15N	10 20W
Ballydehob	39	51 34N	9 28W
Ballydonegan	39	51 37N	10 12W
Ballydonegan B.	39	51 38N	10 6W
Ballyduff, Kerry, Ireland	39	52 27N	9 40W
Ballyduff, Waterford, Ireland	39	52 9N	8 2W
Ballyforan	38	53 29N	8 18W
Ballygar	38	53 33N	8 20W
Ballygarrett	39	52 34N	6 15W
Ballygawley	38	54 27N	7 2W
Ballyglass	38	53 45N	9 9W
Ballygorman	38	55 23N	7 20W
Ballyhahill	39	52 33N	9 13W
Ballyhaise	38	54 3N	7 20W
Ballyhalbert	38	54 30N	5 28W
Ballyhaunis	38	53 47N	8 47W
Ballyheige I.	39	52 22N	9 51W
Ballyhoura Hills	39	52 18N	8 33W
Ballyjamesduff	38	53 52N	7 11W
Ballylanders	39	52 25N	8 21W
Ballylaneen	39	52 10N	7 25W
Ballylongford	39	52 34N	9 30W
Ballylooby	39	52 20N	7 59W
Ballylynan	39	52 57N	7 02W
Ballymacoda	39	51 53N	7 56W
Ballymagorry	38	54 52N	7 26W
Ballymahon	39	53 35N	7 45W
Ballymena	38	54 53N	6 18W
Ballymena □	38	54 53N	6 18W
Ballymoe	38	53 41N	8 28W
Ballymoney	38	55 5N	6 30W
Ballymoney □	38	55 5N	6 23W
Ballymore	39	53 30N	7 40W
Ballymore Eustace	39	53 8N	6 38W
Ballymote	38	54 5N	8 30W
Ballymurphy	39	52 33N	6 52W
Ballymurray	38	53 36N	8 8W
Ballynabola	39	52 21N	6 50W
Ballynacally	39	52 42N	9 7W
Ballynacargy	38	53 35N	7 32W
Ballynacorra	39	51 53N	8 10W
Ballynagore	38	53 24N	7 29W
Ballynahinch	38	54 24N	5 55W
Ballynahown	38	53 21N	7 52W
Ballynameen	38	54 58N	6 41W
Ballynamona	39	52 5N	8 39W
Ballynure	38	54 47N	5 59W
Ballyquintin, Pt.	38	54 20N	5 30W
Ballyragget	39	52 47N	7 20W
Ballyroan	39	52 57N	7 20W
Ballyronan	38	54 43N	6 32W
Ballyroney	38	54 17N	6 8W
Ballysadare	38	54 12N	8 30W
Ballyshannon	38	54 30N	8 10W
Ballyvaughan	39	53 7N	9 10W
Ballyvourney	39	51 57N	9 10W
Ballyvoy	38	55 11N	6 11W
Ballywalter	38	54 33N	5 30W
Ballywilliam	39	52 27N	6 52W
Balmaceda	176	46 0 S	71 50W
Balmaclellan	35	55 6N	4 5W
Balmazújváros	53	47 37N	21 21 E
Balmedie	37	57 14N	2 4W
Balmhorn	50	46 26N	7 42 E
Balmoral	140	37 15 S	141 48 E
Balmoral For.	37	57 0N	3 15W
Balmorhea	159	31 2N	103 41W
Balnapaling	37	57 42N	4 2W
Balonne, R.	139	28 47 S	147 56 E
Balovale	125	13 30 S	23 15 E
Balquhidder	34	56 22N	4 22W
Balrampur	95	27 30N	82 20 E
Balranald	140	34 38 S	143 33 E
Balş	70	44 22N	24 5 E
Balsas	165	18 0N	99 40W
Balsas, R., Goias, Brazil	170	9 0 S	48 0W
Balsas, R., Maranhão, Brazil	170	7 15 S	44 35W
Balsas, R., Mexico	164	18 30N	101 20W
Bålsta	72	59 35N	17 30 E
Balsthal	50	47 19N	7 41 E
Balta, Rumania	70	44 54N	22 38 E
Balta, U.S.A.	158	48 12N	100 7W
Balta, U.S.S.R.	82	48 2N	29 45 E
Balta, I.	36	60 44N	0 49W
Baltanás	56	41 56N	4 15W
Baltasound	36	60 47N	0 53W
Baltic Sea	75	56 0N	20 0 E
Baltiisk	75	54 38N	19 55 E
Baltim	122	31 35N	31 10 E
Baltimore, Ireland	39	51 29N	9 22W
Baltimore, U.S.A.	162	39 18N	76 37W
Baltinglass	39	52 57N	6 42W
Baltrum	48	53 43N	7 25 E
Baluchistan □	93	27 30N	65 0 E
Balurghat	95	25 15N	88 44 E
Balvicar	34	56 17N	5 38W
Balygychan	77	63 56N	154 12 E
Bam	93	29 7N	58 14 E
Bam La	99	29 25N	98 35 E
Bama	121	11 33N	13 33 E
Bamako	120	12 34N	7 55W
Bamba	121	17 5N	1 0W
Bambari	117	5 40N	20 35 E
Bambaroo	107	18 50 S	146 11 E
Bamberg, Ger.	49	49 54N	10 53 E
Bamberg, U.S.A.	157	33 19N	81 1W
Bambesi	123	9 45N	34 40 E
Bambey	120	14 42N	16 28W
Bambili	126	3 40N	26 0 E
Bamboo	138	14 34 S	143 20 E
Bambouti	126	5 25N	27 12 E
Bambuí	171	20 1 S	45 58W
Bamburgh	35	55 36N	1 42W
Bamenda	121	5 57N	10 11 E
Bamfield	152	48 45N	125 10W
Bamford	33	53 21N	1 41W
Bamian □	93	35 0N	67 0 E
Bamkin	121	6 3N	11 27 E
Bampton, Devon, U.K.	30	50 59N	3 29W
Bampton, Oxon., U.K.	28	51 44N	1 33W
Bampur	93	27 15N	60 21 E
Bampur, R.	93	27 20N	59 30 E
Ban Aranyaprathet	100	13 41N	102 30 E
Ban Ban	100	19 31N	103 15 E
Ban Bang Hin	101	9 32N	98 35 E
Ban Bua Chum	101	15 11N	101 12 E
Ban Bua Yai	100	15 33N	102 26 E
Ban Chiang Klang	100	19 15N	100 55 E
Ban Chik	100	17 15N	102 22 E
Ban Choho	100	15 2N	102 9 E
Ban Dan Lan Hoi	100	17 0N	99 35 E
Ban Don	100	12 53N	107 48 E
Ban Don = Surat Thani	101	9 8N	99 20 E
Ban Don, Go	101	9 20N	99 25 E
Ban Dong	100	19 14N	100 3 E
Ban Hong	100	18 18N	98 50 E
Ban Houei Sai	101	20 22N	100 32 E
Ban Kaeng	100	17 29N	100 7 E
Ban Kantang	101	7 25N	99 31 E
Ban Keun	100	18 22N	102 35 E
Ban Khai	100	12 46N	101 18 E
Ban Khe Bo	101	19 10N	104 39 E
Ban Kheun	100	20 13N	101 7 E
Ban Khlong Kua	101	6 57N	100 8 E
Ban Khuan Mao	101	7 50N	99 37 E
Ban Khun Yuam	100	18 49N	97 57 E
Ban Ko Yai Chim	101	11 17N	99 26 E
Ban Kok	100	16 40N	103 40 E
Ban Laem	100	13 13N	99 59 E
Ban Lao Ngam	100	15 28N	106 10 E
Ban Le Kathe	100	15 49N	98 53 E
Ban Mae Chedi	100	19 11N	99 31 E
Ban Mae Laeng	100	20 1N	99 17 E
Ban Mae Sariang	100	18 0N	97 56 E
Ban Me Thuot	100	12 40N	108 3 E
Ban Mi	100	15 3N	100 32 E
Ban Muong Mo	100	19 4N	103 58 E
Ban Na Mo	100	17 7N	105 40 E
Ban Na San	101	8 33N	99 52 E
Ban Na Tong	100	20 56N	101 47 E
Ban Nam Bac	100	20 38N	102 20 E
Ban Nam Ma	100	22 2N	101 37 E
Ban Ngang	100	15 59N	106 11 E
Ban Nong Bok	100	17 5N	104 48 E
Ban Nong Boua	100	15 40N	106 33 E
Ban Nong Pling	100	15 40N	100 10 E
Ban Pak Chan	101	10 32N	98 51 E
Ban Phai	100	16 4N	102 44 E
Ban Pong	100	13 50N	99 55 E
Ban Ron Phibun	101	8 9N	99 51 E
Ban Sanam Chai	101	7 33N	100 25 E
Ban Sangkha	100	14 37N	103 52 E
Ban Tak	100	17 2N	99 4 E
Ban Tako	100	14 5N	102 40 E
Ban Takua Pa	101	8 55N	98 25 E
Ban Tha Dua	100	17 59N	98 39 E
Ban Tha Li	100	17 37N	101 25 E
Ban Tha Nun	101	8 12N	98 18 E
Ban Thahine	100	14 12N	105 33 E
Ban Thateng	101	15 25N	106 27 E
Ban Xien Kok	100	20 54N	100 39 E
Ban Yen Nhan	100	20 57N	106 2 E
Baña, La, Punta de	58	40 33N	0 40 E
Banadar Daryay Oman □	93	25 30N	56 0 E
Banadia	174	6 54N	71 49W
Banagher	39	53 12N	8 0W
Banalia	126	1 32N	25 5 E
Banam	101	11 20N	105 17 E
Banamba	120	13 29N	7 22W
Banana	138	24 28 S	150 8 E
Bananal, I. do	171	11 30 S	50 30W
Banaras = Varanasi	95	25 22N	83 8 E
Banas, R., Gujarat, India	94	24 25N	72 30 E
Banas, R., Madhya Pradesh, India	95	24 15N	81 30 E
Bânâs, Ras.	122	23 57N	35 50 E
Banat □	66	45 45N	21 15 E
Banbridge	38	54 21N	6 17W
Banbridge □	38	54 21N	6 16W
Banbury	28	52 4N	1 21W
Banchory	37	57 3N	2 30W
Bancroft	150	45 3N	77 51W
Bancroft = Chililabombwe	127	12 18 S	27 43 E
Band	67	46 30N	24 25 E
Band-i-Turkistan, Ra.	93	35 2N	64 0 E
Banda	95	25 30N	80 26 E
Banda Aceh	102	5 35N	95 20 E
Banda Banda, Mt.	141	31 10 S	152 28 E
Banda Elat	103	5 40 S	133 5 E
Banda, Kepulauan	103	4 37 S	129 50 E
Banda, La	172	27 45 S	64 10W
Banda, Punta	164	31 47N	116 50W
Banda Sea	103	6 0 S	130 0 E
Bandama, R.	120	6 32N	5 30W
Bandanwara	94	26 9N	74 38 E
Bandar = Masulipatnam	97	16 12N	81 12 E
Bandar 'Abbâs	93	27 15N	56 15 E
Bandar-e Būshehr	93	28 55N	50 55 E
Bandar-e Chārak	93	26 45N	54 20 E
Bandar-e Deylam	92	30 5N	50 10 E
Bandar-e Lengeh	93	26 35N	54 58 E
Bandar-e Ma'shur	92	30 35N	49 10 E
Bandar-e-Nakhīlu	93	26 58N	53 30 E
Bandar-e Rīg	93	29 30N	50 45 E
Bandar-e Shah	93	37 0N	54 10 E
Bandar-e-Shahpur	92	30 30N	49 5 E
Bandar-i-Pahlavi	92	37 30N	49 30 E
Bandar Maharani = Muar	101	2 3N	102 34 E
Bandar Penggaram = Batu Pahat	101	1 50N	102 56 E
Bandar Seri Begawan	102	4 52N	115 0 E
Bandawe	127	11 58 S	34 5 E
Bande, Belg.	47	50 10N	5 25 E
Bande, Spain	56	42 3N	7 58W
Bandeira, Pico da	173	20 26 S	41 47W
Bandeirante	171	13 41 S	50 48W
Bandera, Argent.	172	28 55 S	62 20W
Bandera, U.S.A.	159	29 45N	99 3W
Banderas, Bahía de	164	20 40N	105 30W
Bandi-San	112	37 36N	140 4 E
Bandia, R.	96	19 30N	80 25 E
Bandiagara	120	14 12N	3 29W
Bandirma	92	40 20N	28 0 E
Bandon	39	51 44N	8 45W
Bandon, R.	39	51 40N	8 11W
Bandula	127	19 0 S	33 7 E
Bandundu	124	3 15 S	17 22 E
Bandung	103	6 36 S	107 48 E
Bandya	137	27 40 S	122 5 E
Bañeres	59	38 44N	0 38W
Banes	167	21 0N	75 42W
Bañeza, La	56	42 17N	5 54W
Banff, Can.	152	51 10N	115 34W
Banff, U.K.	37	57 40N	2 32W
Banff Nat. Park	152	51 30N	116 15W
Banfora	120	10 40N	4 40W
Bang Fai, R.	100	16 57N	104 45 E
Bang Hieng, R.	100	16 24N	105 40 E
Bang Krathum	100	16 34N	100 18 E
Bang Lamung	100	13 3N	100 56 E
Bang Mun Nak	100	16 2N	100 23 E
Bang Pa In	100	14 14N	100 35 E
Bang Rakam	100	16 45N	100 7 E
Bang Saphan	101	11 14N	99 28 E
Bangala Dam	127	21 7 S	31 25 E
Bangalore	97	12 59N	77 40 E
Bangangte	121	5 8N	10 32 E
Bangaon	95	23 0N	88 47 E
Bangassou	124	4 55N	23 55 E
Bangeta, Mt.	135	6 21 S	147 3 E
Banggai	103	1 40 S	123 30 E
Banggi, P.	102	7 50N	117 0 E
Banghāzī	119	32 11N	20 3 E
Bangil	103	7 36 S	112 50 E
Bangjang	123	11 23N	32 41 E
Bangka, Pulau, Celebes, Indon.	103	1 50N	125 5 E
Bangka, Pulau, Sumatera, Indon.	102	2 0 S	105 50 E
Bangka, Selat	102	3 30 S	105 30 E
Bangkalan	103	7 2 S	112 46 E
Bangkinang	102	0 18N	100 5 E
Bangko	102	2 5 S	102 9 E
Bangkok = Krung Thep	100	13 45N	100 31 E
Bangladesh ■	98	24 0N	90 0 E
Bangolo	120	7 1N	7 29W
Bangor, Me., U.S.A.	151	44 48N	68 42W

Bangor Bassevelde

Bangor, Pa., U.S.A. 162 40 51N 75 13W
Bangor, N.I., U.K. 38 54 40N 5 40W
Bangor, Wales, U.K. 31 53 13N 4 9W
Bangued 103 17 40N 120 37 E
Bangui 124 4 23N 18 35 E
Banguru 126 0 30N 27 10 E
Bangweulu, L. 127 11 0S 30 0 E
Bangweulu Swamp 127 11 20S 30 15 E
Banham 29 52 27N 1 3 E
Bani 167 18 16N 70 22W
Bani Bangou 121 15 3N 2 42 E
Bani, Djebel 118 29 16N 8 0W
Bani Na'im 90 31 31N 35 10 E
Bani, R. 120 12 40N 6 30W
Bani Suhayla 90 31 21N 34 19 E
Bania 120 9 4N 3 6W
Baniara 135 9 44S 149 54 E
Banihal Pass 95 33 30N 75 12 E
Baninah 119 32 0N 20 12 E
Baniyas 92 35 10N 36 0 E
Banja Luka 66 44 49N 17 26 E
Banjak, Kepulauan 102 2 10N 97 10 E
Banjar 103 7 24S 108 30 E
Banjarmasin 102 3 20S 114 35 E
Banjarnegara 103 7 24S 109 42 E
Banjul 120 13 28N 16 40W
Banka Banka 138 18 50S 134 0 E
Bankend 35 55 2N 3 31W
Bankeryd 73 57 53N 14 6 E
Banket 127 17 27S 30 19 E
Bankfoot 35 56 30N 3 31W
Bankhead 37 57 11N 2 10W
Bankilaré 121 14 35N 0 44 E
Bankipore 95 25 35N 85 10 E
Banks I., B.C., Can. 152 53 20N 130 0W
Banks I., N. W. Terr., Can. 12 73 15N 121 30W
Banks I., P.N.G. 135 10 10S 142 15 E
Banks Peninsula 143 43 45S 173 15 E
Banks Str. 138 40 40S 148 10 E
Bankura 95 23 11N 87 18 E
Bankya 66 42 43N 23 8 E
Bann R., Down, U.K. 38 54 30N 6 31W
Bann R., Londonderry, U.K. 38 55 10N 6 34W
Bannalec 42 47 57N 3 42W
Bannang Sata 101 6 16N 101 16 E
Bannerton 140 34 42S 142 47 E
Banning, Can. 150 48 44N 91 56W
Banning, U.S.A. 163 33 58N 116 58W
Banningville = Bandundu 124 3 15S 17 22 E
Bannockburn, Rhod. 127 20 17S 29 48 E
Bannockburn, U.K. 35 56 5N 3 55W
Bannow 39 52 12N 6 50W
Bannow B. 39 52 13N 6 48W
Bannu 93 33 0N 70 18 E
Bañolas 58 42 16N 2 44 E
Banon 45 44 2N 5 38 E
Baños de la Encina 57 38 10N 3 46W
Baños de Molgas 56 42 15N 7 40W
Bánovce 53 48 44N 18 16 E
Banská Bystrica 53 48 46N 19 14 E
Banská Stiavnica 53 48 25N 18 55 E
Bansko 67 41 52N 23 28 E
Banswara 94 23 32N 74 24 E
Bantama 121 7 48N 0 42W
Bante 121 8 25N 1 53 E
Banteer 39 52 8N 8 53W
Banten 103 6 5S 106 8 E
Bantry 39 51 40N 9 28W
Bantry, B. 39 51 35N 9 50W
Bantul 103 7 55S 110 19 E
Bantva 94 21 29N 70 12 E
Bantval 97 12 55N 75 0 E
Banu 93 35 35N 69 5 E
Banwell 28 51 19N 2 51W
Banya 67 42 33N 24 50 E
Banyo 121 6 52N 11 45 E
Banyuls 44 42 29N 3 8 E
Banyumas 103 7 32S 109 18 E
Banyuwangi 103 8 13S 114 21 E
Banzare Coast 13 66 30S 125 0 E
Banzyville = Mobayi 124 4 15N 21 8 E
Bao Ha 100 22 11N 104 21 E
Bao Lac 100 22 57N 105 40 E
Bao Loc 101 11 32N 107 48 E
Bap 94 27 23N 72 18 E
Bapatla 97 15 55N 80 30 E
Bapaume 43 50 7N 2 50 E
Bâqa el Gharbiya 90 32 25N 35 2 E
Baqūbah 92 33 45N 44 50 E
Baquedano 172 23 20S 69 52W
Bar, U.S.S.R. 82 49 4N 27 40 E
Bar, Yugo. 66 42 8N 19 8 E
Bar Harbor 151 44 15N 68 20W
Bar-le-Duc 43 48 47N 5 10 E
Bar-sur-Aube 43 48 14N 4 40 E
Bar-sur-Seine 43 48 7N 4 20 E
Barabai 102 2 32S 115 34 E
Barabinsk 76 55 20N 78 20 E
Baraboo 158 43 28N 89 46W
Baracoa 167 20 20N 74 30W
Baradero 172 33 52S 59 29W
Baradine 141 30 56S 149 4 E
Baraga 158 46 49N 88 29W
Barahona, Dom. Rep. 167 18 13N 71 7W
Barahona, Spain 58 41 17N 2 39W
Barail Range 99 25 15N 93 20 E
Barakhola 99 25 0N 92 45 E
Barakot 95 21 33N 84 59 E
Barakula 139 26 30S 150 33 E
Baralaba 138 24 13S 149 50 E
Baralzon L. 153 60 0N 98 3W
Baramati 96 18 11N 74 33 E
Baramba 96 20 25N 85 23 E
Barameiya 122 18 32N 36 38 E
Baramula 95 34 15N 74 20 E
Baran 94 25 9N 76 40 E
Baranoa 174 10 48N 74 55W
Baranof I. 147 57 0N 135 10W
Baranovichi 80 53 10N 26 0 E
Baranów Sandomierski 54 50 29N 21 30 E
Baranya □ 53 46 0N 18 15 E
Barão de Cocais 171 19 56S 43 28W
Barão de Grajaú 170 6 45S 43 1W
Barão de Melgaço 174 11 50S 60 45W
Baraolt 70 46 5N 25 34 E
Barapasi 103 2 15S 137 5 E
Barapina 135 6 21S 155 25 E
Barasat 95 22 46N 88 31 E
Barasoli 123 13 38N 42 0W
Barat Daya, Kepuluan 103 7 30S 128 0 E
Barataria B. 159 29 15N 89 45W
Baraut 94 29 13N 77 7 E
Baraya 174 3 10N 75 4W
Barbacena 173 21 15S 43 56W
Barbacoas, Colomb. 174 1 45N 78 0W
Barbacoas, Venez. 174 9 29N 66 58W
Barbados ■ 167 13 0N 59 30W
Barbalha 170 7 19S 39 17W
Barban 63 45 0N 14 4 E
Barbastro 58 42 2N 0 5 E
Barbate 57 36 13N 5 56W
Barberton, S. Afr. 129 25 42S 31 2 E
Barberton, U.S.A. 156 41 0N 81 40W
Barbigha 95 25 21N 85 47 E
Barbourville 157 36 57N 83 52W
Barbuda I. 167 17 30N 61 40W
Barca d'Alva 56 41 0N 7 0W
Barca, La 164 20 20N 102 40W
Barcaldine 138 23 33S 145 13 E
Barcarrota 57 38 31N 6 51W
Barce = Al Marj 117 32 25N 20 40 E
Barcellona Pozzo di Gotto 65 38 8N 15 15 E
Barcelona, Spain 58 41 21N 2 10 E
Barcelona, Venez. 174 10 10N 64 40W
Barcelona □ 58 41 30N 2 0 E
Barcelonette 45 44 23N 6 40 E
Barcelos 174 1 0S 63 0W
Barcin 54 52 52N 17 55 E
Barcoo, R. 138 28 29S 137 46 E
Barcs 53 45 58N 17 28 E
Barczewo 54 53 50N 20 42 E
Bard, Hd. 36 60 6N 1 5W
Barda 83 40 25N 47 10 E
Bardai 119 21 25N 17 0 E
Bardas Blancas 172 35 49S 69 45W
Bardejov 53 49 18N 21 15 E
Bardera 91 2 20N 42 27 E
Bardi 62 44 38N 9 43 E
Bardiyah 117 31 45N 25 0 E
Bardney 33 53 13N 0 19W
Bardo 54 50 31N 16 42 E
Bardoc 137 30 18S 121 12 E
Bardoli 96 21 12N 73 5 E
Bardsey, I. 31 52 46N 4 47W
Bardsey Sound 31 52 47N 4 46W
Bardstown 156 37 50N 85 29W
Bareilly 95 28 22N 79 27 E
Barellan 141 34 16S 146 24 E
Barengapara 98 25 14N 90 14 E
Barentin 42 49 33N 0 58 E
Barenton 42 48 38N 0 50W
Barents Sea 12 73 0N 39 0 E
Barentu 123 15 2N 37 35 E
Barfleur 42 49 40N 1 17W
Barford 28 52 15N 1 35W
Barga 62 44 5N 10 30 E
Bargal 91 11 25N 51 0 E
Bargara 138 24 50S 152 25 E
Barge 62 44 43N 7 19 E
Barge, La 160 41 12N 110 4W
Bargnop 123 9 32N 28 25 E
Bargo 141 34 18S 150 35 E
Bargoed 31 51 42N 3 22W
Bargteheide 48 53 42N 10 13 E
Barguzin 77 53 37N 109 37 E
Barh 95 25 29N 85 46 E
Barhaj 95 26 18N 83 44 E
Barham 29 51 12N 1 10 E
Barhi 95 24 15N 85 25 E
Bari, India 94 26 39N 77 39 E
Bari, Italy 65 41 6N 16 52 E
Bari Doab 94 30 20N 73 0 E
Baria = Phuoc Le 101 10 39N 107 19 E
Bariadi □ 126 2 45S 34 40 E
Barika 118 35 23N 5 22 E
Barinas 174 8 36N 70 15W
Barinas □ 174 8 10N 69 50W
Baring C. 148 70 0N 117 30W
Baringo 126 0 47N 36 16 E
Baringo □ 126 0 55N 36 0 E
Baringo, L. 126 0 47N 36 16 E
Barinitas 174 8 45N 70 25W
Baripada 96 21 57N 86 45 E
Bariri 171 22 4S 48 44W
Bârîs 122 24 42N 30 31 E
Barisal 98 22 30N 90 20 E
Barisan, Bukit 102 3 30S 102 15 E
Barito, R. 102 2 50S 114 50 E
Barjac 45 44 20N 4 22 E
Barjols 45 43 34N 6 2 E
Barjūji, W. 119 25 26N 12 12 E
Bark L. 150 46 58N 82 25W
Barka 122 17 30N 37 34 E
Barkah 93 23 40N 58 0 E
Barker, Mt. 139 35 4S 138 55 E
Barking 29 51 31N 0 10 E
Barkley Sound 152 48 50N 125 10W
Barkly Downs 138 20 30S 138 30 E
Barkly East 129 30 58S 27 33 E
Barkly Tableland 138 19 50S 138 40 E
Barkly West 128 28 5S 24 31 E
Barkol, Wadi 122 17 40N 32 0 E
Barksdale 159 29 47N 100 2W
Barlborough 33 53 17N 1 17W
Barlby 33 53 48N 1 3W
Barlee, L. 137 29 15S 119 30 E
Barlee, Mt. 137 24 35S 128 10 E
Barlee Ra. 137 23 30S 116 0 E
Barlett 163 36 29N 118 2W
Barletta 65 41 20N 16 17 E
Barlinek 54 53 0N 15 15 E
Barlingbo 73 57 35N 18 27 E
Barlow L. 153 62 00N 103 0W
Barmby Moor 33 53 55N 0 47W
Barmedman 141 34 9S 147 21 E
Barmer 94 25 45N 71 20 E
Barmera 140 34 15S 140 28 E
Barmoor 35 55 38N 2 0W
Barmouth 31 52 44N 4 3W
Barmstedt 48 53 47N 9 46 E
Barna 39 53 14N 9 10W
Barnaderg 38 53 29N 8 43W
Barnagar 94 23 7N 75 19 E
Barnard Castle 32 54 33N 1 55W
Barnato 141 31 38S 145 0 E
Barnaul 76 53 20N 83 40 E
Barnby Moor 33 53 21N 1 0W
Barne Inlet 13 80 15S 160 0 E
Barnes 141 36 2S 144 47 E
Barnesville 157 33 6N 84 9W
Barnet 29 51 37N 0 15W
Barnetby le Wold 33 53 34N 0 24W
Barneveld, Neth. 96 52 7N 5 36 E
Barneveld, U.S.A. 162 43 16N 75 14W
Barneville 42 49 23N 1 46W
Barney, Mt. 133 28 17S 152 44 E
Barngo 138 25 3S 147 20 E
Barnhart 159 31 10N 101 8W
Barnoldswick 32 53 55N 2 11W
Barnsley 33 53 33N 1 29W
Barnstaple 30 51 5N 4 3W
Barnstaple B. 30 51 5N 4 25W
Barnsville 158 46 43N 96 28W
Baro 121 8 35N 6 18 E
Baro, R. 123 8 25N 33 40 E
Baroda 94 25 29N 76 35 E
Baroda = Vadodara, India 93 22 20N 73 10 E
Baroda = Vadodara, Gujarat, India 94 22 20N 73 10 E
Baron Ra. 136 23 30S 127 45 E
Barpali 96 21 11N 83 35 E
Barpathar 98 26 17N 93 53 E
Barpeta 95 26 20N 91 10 E
Barqa 117 27 0N 20 0 E
Barqin 119 27 33N 13 34 E
Barques, Pte. aux 156 44 5N 82 55W
Barquinha 57 39 28N 8 25W
Barquisimeto 174 9 58N 69 13W
Barr, France 43 48 25N 7 28 E
Barr, U.K. 34 55 13N 4 44W
Barr Smith Ra. 137 27 10S 120 15 E
Barra, Brazil 170 11 5S 43 10W
Barra, Gambia 120 13 21N 16 36W
Barra da Estiva 171 13 38S 41 19W
Barra de Navidad 164 19 12N 104 41W
Barra do Corda 170 5 30S 45 10W
Barra do Mendes 171 11 43S 42 4W
Barra do Piraí 173 22 30S 43 50W
Barra Falsa, Pta. da 129 22 58S 35 37 E
Barra Hd. 36 56 47N 7 40W
Barra, I. 36 57 0N 7 30W
Barra Mansa 173 22 35S 44 12W
Barra, Sd. of 36 57 4N 7 25W
Barraba 141 30 21S 150 35 E
Barrackpur 95 22 44N 88 30 E
Barrafranca 65 37 22N 14 10 E
Barranca, Lima, Peru 174 10 45S 77 50W
Barranca, Loreto, Peru 174 4 50S 76 50W
Barrancabermeja 174 7 0N 73 50W
Barrancas, Colomb. 174 10 57N 72 50W
Barrancas, Venez. 174 8 55N 62 5W
Barrancos 57 38 10N 6 58W
Barranqueras 172 27 30S 59 0W
Barranquilla, Atlántico, Colomb. 174 11 0N 74 50W
Barranquilla, Vaupés, Colomb. 174 1 39N 72 19W
Barras, Brazil 170 4 15S 42 18W
Barras, Colomb. 174 1 45S 73 13W
Barraute 150 48 26N 77 38W
Barre, U.S.A. 156 44 15N 72 30W
Barre, U.S.A. 162 42 26N 72 6W
Barreal 172 31 33S 69 28W
Barreiras 171 12 8S 45 0W
Barreirinhas 170 2 30S 42 50W
Barreiro 57 38 40N 9 6W
Barreiros 170 8 49S 35 12W
Barrême 45 43 57N 6 23 E
Barren I. 101 12 17N 95 50 E
Barren Is., Madag. 129 18 25S 43 40 E
Barren Is., U.S.A. 147 58 45N 152 0W
Barren Junc. 139 30 5S 149 0 E
Barretos 171 20 30S 48 35W
Barrhead, Can. 152 54 10N 114 24W
Barrhead, U.K. 34 55 48N 4 23W
Barrhill 34 55 7N 4 46W
Barrie 150 44 24N 79 40W
Barrier, C. 142 36 25S 175 32 E
Barrier Ra., Austral. 140 31 0S 141 30 E
Barrier Ra., N.Z. 143 44 5S 169 42 E
Barrier Rf., Gt. 138 19 0S 149 0 E
Barrière 152 51 12N 120 7W
Barrington, Austral. 133 31 58S 151 55 E
Barrington, Ill., U.S.A. 156 42 8N 88 5W
Barrington, R.I., U.S.A. 162 41 43N 71 20W
Barrington L. 153 56 55N 100 15W
Barrington Tops. 141 32 6S 151 28 E
Barringun 139 29 1S 145 41 E
Barrow 147 71 16N 156 50W
Barrow Creek T.O. 138 21 30S 133 55 E
Barrow I. 136 20 45S 115 20 E
Barrow-in-Furness 32 54 8N 3 15W
Barrow Pt. 138 14 20S 144 40 E
Barrow, Pt. 147 71 22N 156 30W
Barrow, R. 39 52 10N 6 57W
Barrow Ra. 137 26 0S 127 40 E
Barrow Strait 12 74 20N 95 0W
Barrow upon Humber 33 53 41N 0 22W
Barrowford 32 53 51N 2 14W
Barruecopardo 56 41 4N 6 40W
Barruelo 56 42 54N 4 17W
Barry, S. Glam., U.K. 31 51 23N 3 19W
Barry, Tayside, U.K. 35 56 29N 2 45W
Barry I. 31 51 23N 3 17W
Barry's Bay 150 45 29N 77 41W
Barry's Pt. 39 51 36N 8 40W
Barsalogho 121 13 25N 1 3W
Barsat 95 36 10N 72 45 E
Barsi 96 18 10N 75 50 E
Barsø 73 55 7N 9 33 E
Barsoi 99 25 48N 87 57 E
Barstow, Calif., U.S.A. 163 34 58N 117 2W
Barstow, Tex., U.S.A. 170 31 30N 103 25W
Barthélemy, Col 100 19 26N 104 6 E
Bartica 174 6 25N 58 40W
Bartle Frere, Mt. 138 17 27S 145 50 E
Bartlesville 159 36 50N 95 58W
Bartlett 159 30 46N 97 30W
Bartlett, L. 152 63 5N 118 20W
Bartolomeu Dias 127 21 10S 35 8 E
Barton 33 54 28N 1 38W
Barton Siding 137 30 31S 132 39 E
Barton-upon-Humber 33 53 41N 0 27W
Bartoszyce 54 54 15N 20 55 E
Bartow 157 27 53N 81 49W
Barú, I. de 174 10 15N 75 35W
Baruth 48 52 3N 13 31 E
Barvas 36 58 21N 6 31W
Barvaux 47 50 21N 5 29 E
Barvenkovo 82 48 57N 37 0 E
Barwani 94 22 2N 74 57 E
Barwell 28 52 35N 1 22W
Barysh 81 49 2N 25 18 E
Bas-Rhin □ 43 48 40N 7 30 E
Bašaid 66 45 38N 20 25 E
Basa'idu 93 26 35N 55 20 E
Basal 94 33 33N 72 13 E
Basalt 163 38 0N 118 15W
Basankusa 124 1 5N 19 50 E
Basawa 94 34 15N 70 50 E
Bascharage 47 49 34N 5 55 E
Bascuñán, Cabo 172 28 52S 71 35W
Basècles 47 50 32N 3 39 E
Basel (Basle) 50 47 35N 7 35 E
Basel Landschaft □ 50 47 26N 7 45 E
Basel-Stadt □ 50 47 35N 7 35 E
Basento, R. 65 40 35N 16 10 E
Bashi Channel 105 21 15N 122 0 E
Bashkir A.S.S.R. □ 84 54 0N 57 0 E
Basilaki, I. 135 10 35S 151 0 E
Basilan, Selat 103 6 50N 122 0 E
Basilanl, I. 103 6 35N 122 0 E
Basildon 29 51 34N 0 29 E
Basilicata □ 65 40 30N 16 0 E
Basim 96 20 3N 77 0 E
Basin 160 44 22N 108 2W
Basing 28 51 16N 1 3W
Basingstoke 28 51 15N 1 5W
Basirhat 98 22 40N 88 54 E
Baskatong Res. 150 46 46N 75 50W
Baskerville C. 136 17 10S 122 15 E
Basle = Basel 50 47 35N 7 35 E
Basmat 96 19 15N 77 12 E
Basoda 94 23 52N 77 54 E
Basodino 51 46 25N 8 28 E
Basoka 126 1 16N 23 40 E
Basongo 124 4 15S 20 20 E
Basque Provinces = Vascongadas 58 42 50N 2 45W
Basra = Al Basrah 92 30 30N 47 50 E
Bass Rock 35 56 5N 2 40W
Bass Strait 138 39 15S 146 30 E
Bassano, del Grappa 63 45 45N 11 45 E
Bassari 121 9 19N 0 57 E
Bassas da India 125 22 0S 39 0 E
Basse 120 13 13N 14 15W
Basse-Terre, I. 167 16 0N 61 40W
Bassecourt 50 47 20N 7 15 E
Bassée, La 43 50 31N 2 49 E
Bassein, Burma 98 16 30N 94 30 E
Bassein, India 96 19 26N 72 48 E
Bassein Myit 99 16 45N 94 30 E
Bassenthwaite, L. 32 54 40N 3 14W
Basseterre 167 17 17N 62 43W
Bassett, Nebr., U.S.A. 158 42 37N 99 30W
Bassett, Va., U.S.A. 157 36 48N 79 59W
Bassevelde 47 51 15N 3 41 E

Bassi Bekkjarvik

Bassi 94 30 44N 76 21E
Bassigny 43 48 0N 5 10E
Bassikounou 120 15 55N 6 1W
Bassilly 47 50 40N 3 56E
Bassum 48 52 50N 8 42E
Båstad 73 56 25N 12 51E
Båstad 73 56 25N 12 51E
Bastak 93 27 15N 54 25E
Bastar 96 19 25N 81 40E
Basti 95 26 52N 82 55E
Bastia 45 42 40N 9 30E
Bastia Umbra 63 43 4N 12 34E
Bastide, La 44 44 35N 3 55E
Bastogne 47 50 1N 5 43E
Baston 29 52 43N 0 19W
Bastrop 159 30 5N 97 22W
Basuto 128 19 50S 26 25E
Basutoland = Lesotho 129 29 0S 28 0E
Basyanovskiy 84 58 19N 60 44E
Bat Yam 90 32 2N 34 44E
Bata, Eq. Guin. 124 1 57N 9 50E
Bata, Rumania 70 46 1N 22 4E
Bataan 103 14 40N 120 25E
Bataan Pen. 103 14 38N 120 30E
Batabanó 166 22 40N 82 20W
Batabanó, G. de 167 22 30N 82 30W
Batac 103 18 3N 120 34E
Batagoy 77 67 38N 134 38E
Batak 67 41 57N 24 12E
Batalha 57 39 40N 8 50W
Batama 126 0 58N 26 33E
Batamay 77 63 30N 129 15E
Batamshinskiy 84 50 36N 58 16E
Batang 103 6 55S 109 40E
Batangafo 117 7 25N 18 20E
Batangas 103 13 35N 121 10E
Batanta, I. 103 0 55N 130 40E
Bataszék 66 46 10N 18 44E
Batatais 173 20 54S 47 37W
Batavia 156 43 0N 78 10W
Bataysk 83 47 3N 39 45E
Batchelor 136 13 4S 131 1E
Bateman's B. 141 35 40S 150 12E
Batemans Bay 141 35 44S 150 11E
Bates Ra. 137 27 25S 121 0E
Batesburg 157 33 54N 81 32W
Batesville, Ark., U.S.A. 159 35 48N 91 40W
Batesville, Miss., U.S.A. 159 34 17N 89 58W
Batesville, Tex., U.S.A. 159 28 59N 99 38W
Batetski 80 58 47N 30 16E
Bath, U.K. 28 51 22N 2 22W
Bath, Maine, U.S.A. 151 43 50N 69 49W
Bath, N.Y., U.S.A. 156 42 20N 77 17W
Batheay 101 11 59N 104 57E
Bathford 28 51 23N 2 18W
Bathgate 35 55 54N 3 38W
Bâthie, La 46 45 37N 6 28E
Bathmen 46 52 15N 6 29E
Bathurst, Austral. 141 33 25S 149 31E
Bathurst, Can. 151 47 37N 65 43W
Bathurst B. 138 14 16S 144 25E
Bathurst C. 147 70 30N 128 30W
Bathurst, C. 147 70 34N 128 0W
Bathurst, Gambia = Banjul 120 13 28N 16 40W
Bathurst Harb. 138 43 15S 146 10E
Bathurst I., Austral. 136 11 30S 130 10E
Bathurst I., Can. 12 76 30N 130 10W
Bathurst Inlet 148 66 50N 108 1W
Batie 120 9 53N 2 53W
Batley 33 53 43N 1 38W
Batlow 141 35 31S 148 9E
Batman 92 37 55N 41 5E
Batna 119 35 34N 6 15E
Batoka 127 16 45S 27 15E
Baton Rouge 159 30 30N 91 5W
Batong, Ko 101 6 32N 99 12E
Batopilas 164 27 45N 107 45W
Batouri 124 4 30N 14 25E
Battambang 100 13 7N 103 12E
Batticaloa 97 7 43N 81 45E
Battice 47 50 39N 5 50E
Battipáglia 65 40 38N 15 0E
Battir 90 31 44N 35 8E
Battle, Can. 153 52 58N 110 52W
Battle, U.K. 29 50 55N 0 30E
Battle Camp 138 15 20S 144 40E
Battle Creek 156 42 20N 85 36W
Battle Harbour 151 52 16N 55 35W
Battle Lake 158 46 20N 95 43W
Battle Mountain 160 40 45N 117 0W
Battle, R. 153 52 43N 108 15W
Battlefields 127 18 37S 29 47E
Battleford 153 52 45N 108 15W
Battonya 53 46 16N 21 3E
Batu Caves 101 3 15N 101 40E
Batu Gajah 101 4 28N 101 3E
Batu, Kepulauan 102 0 30S 98 25E
Batu, Mt. 123 6 55N 39 45E
Batu Pahat 101 1 50N 102 56E
Batuata, P. 103 6 30S 122 20E
Batulaki 103 5 40N 125 30E
Batumi 83 41 30N 41 30E
Baturadja 102 4 11S 104 15E
Baturité 170 4 28S 38 45W
Baturité, Serra de 170 4 25S 39 0W
Baubau 103 5 25S 123 50E
Bauchi 121 10 22N 9 48E
Bauchi □ 121 10 0N 10 0E
Baud 42 47 52N 3 1W
Baudette 158 48 46N 94 35W
Baudouinville = Moba 126 7 0S 29 48E
Baudour 47 50 29N 3 50E
Bauer, C. 139 32 44S 134 4E
Baugé 42 47 31N 0 8W
Bauhinia Downs 138 24 35S 149 18E
Baule, La 42 47 18N 2 23W
Bauma 51 47 3N 8 53E
Baume les Dames 43 47 22N 6 22E
Baunei 64 40 2N 9 41E
Bauru 173 22 10S 49 0W
Baús 175 18 22S 52 47W
Bauska 80 56 25N 25 15E
Bautzen 48 51 11N 14 25E
Baux, Les 45 43 45N 4 51E
BavaniŠte 66 44 49N 20 53E
Bavaria = Bayern 49 49 7N 11 30E
Båven 72 59 35N 17 30E
Bavispe, R. 164 29 30N 109 11W
Bawdsey 29 52 1N 1 27E
Bawdwin 98 23 5N 97 50E
Bawean 102 5 46S 112 35E
Bawku 121 11 3N 0 19W
Bawlake 98 19 11N 97 21E
Bawnboy 38 54 8N 7 40W
Bawtry 33 53 25N 1 1W
Baxley 157 31 43N 82 23W
Baxter Springs 159 37 3N 94 45W
Bay Bulls 151 47 19N 52 50W
Bay City, Mich., U.S.A. 156 43 35N 83 51W
Bay City, Oreg., U.S.A. 160 45 45N 123 58W
Bay City, Tex., U.S.A. 159 28 59N 95 55W
Bay de Verde 151 48 5N 52 54W
Bay, Laguna de 103 14 20N 121 11E
Bay of Islands 142 35 15S 174 6E
Bay St. Louis 159 30 18N 89 22W
Bay Shore 162 40 44N 73 15W
Bay Springs 159 31 58N 89 18W
Bay View 142 39 25S 176 50E
Baya 127 11 53S 27 25E
Bayamo 166 20 20N 76 40W
Bayamón 147 18 24N 66 10W
Bayan Kara Shan 99 34 0N 98 0E
Bayan-Ovoo 106 47 47N 112 5E
Bayana 94 26 55N 77 18E
Bayanaul 76 50 45N 75 45E
Bayandalay 106 43 30N 103 29E
Bayanga 124 2 53N 16 19E
Bayanhongor 105 46 8N 100 43E
Bayard 158 41 48N 103 17W
Baybay 103 10 40N 124 55E
Bayble 36 58 12N 6 13W
Bayburt 92 40 15N 40 20E
Bayerischer Wald 49 49 0N 13 0E
Bayern □ 49 49 7N 11 30E
Bayeux 42 49 17N 0 42W
Bayfield 158 46 50N 90 48W
Bayir 92 30 45N 36 55E
Baykadam 85 43 48N 69 58E
Baykal, Oz. 77 53 0N 108 0E
Baykit 77 61 50N 95 50E
Baykonur 76 47 48N 65 50E
Baymak 84 52 36N 58 19E
Baynes Mts. 128 17 15S 13 0E
Bayombong 103 16 30N 121 10E
Bayon 43 48 30N 6 20E
Bayona 56 42 6N 8 52W
Bayonne, France 44 43 30N 1 28W
Bayonne, U.S.A. 162 40 41N 74 7W
Bayovar 174 5 50S 81 0W
Baypore, R. 97 11 10N 75 47E
Bayram-Ali 76 37 37N 62 10E
Bayreuth 49 49 56N 11 35E
Bayrischzell 49 47 39N 12 1E
Bayrūt 92 33 53N 35 31E
Baysun 85 38 12N 67 12E
Bayt Aula 90 31 37N 35 2E
Bayt Fajjar 90 31 38N 35 9E
Bayt Fūrīk 90 32 11N 35 20E
Bayt Jala 90 31 43N 35 11E
Bayt Lahm 90 31 43N 35 12E
Bayt Rīma 90 32 2N 35 6E
Bayt Sāhūr 90 31 42N 35 13E
Bayt Ummar 90 31 38N 35 7E
Bayta at Tahtā 90 32 9N 35 18E
Baytin 90 31 56N 35 14E
Baytown 159 29 42N 94 57W
Bayzhansay 85 43 14N 69 54E
Bayzo 121 13 52N 4 35E
Baza 59 37 30N 2 47W
Bazar Dyuzi 83 41 12N 48 10E
Bazarny Karabulak 81 52 30N 46 20E
Bazarny Syzgan 81 53 45N 46 40E
Bazartobe 83 49 26N 51 45E
Bazaruto, I. do 129 21 40S 35 28E
Bazas 44 44 27N 0 13W
Bazuriye 90 33 15N 35 16E
Beabula 141 34 26S 145 9E
Beach 158 46 57N 104 0W
Beach Haven 162 39 34N 74 14W
Beachley 28 51 37N 2 39W
Beachport 140 37 29S 140 0E
Beachwood 162 39 55N 74 8W
Beachy Head 29 50 44N 0 16E
Beacon, Austral. 137 30 26S 117 52E
Beacon, U.S.A. 162 41 32N 73 58W
Beaconia 153 50 25N 96 31W
Beaconsfield, Austral. 133 41 11S 146 48E
Beaconsfield, U.K. 29 51 36N 0 39W
Beadnell 35 55 33N 1 38W
Beagle Bay 136 16 32S 122 54E
Beagle, Canal 176 55 0S 68 30W
Bealanana 129 14 33N 48 44E
Bealey 143 43 2S 171 36E
Beaminster 28 50 48N 2 44W
Bear I. 39 51 38N 9 50W
Bear I. (Nor.) 12 74 30N 19 0E
Bear L., B.C., Can. 152 56 10N 126 52W
Bear L., Man., Can. 153 55 8N 96 0W
Bear L., U.S.A. 160 42 0N 111 20W
Bearcreek 160 45 11N 109 6W
Beardmore 150 49 36N 87 57W
Beardmore Glacier 13 84 30S 170 0E
Beardstown 158 40 0N 90 25W
Bearn 44 43 28N 0 36W
Bearpaw Mt. 160 48 15N 109 55W
Bearsden 34 55 55N 4 21W
Bearskin Lake 150 53 58N 91 2W
Bearsted 29 51 15N 0 35E
Beas de Segura 59 38 15N 2 53W
Beasain 58 43 3N 2 11W
Beata, C. 167 17 40N 71 30W
Beata, I. 167 17 34N 71 31W
Beatrice, Rhod. 127 18 15S 30 55E
Beatrice, U.S.A. 158 40 20N 96 40W
Beatrice, C. 138 14 20S 136 55E
Beatrice, oilfield 19 58 7N 3 6W
Beattock 35 55 19N 3 27W
Beatton, R. 152 56 15N 120 45W
Beatton River 152 57 26N 121 20W
Beatty 163 36 58N 116 46W
Beaucaire 45 43 48N 4 39E
Beauce, Plaines de 43 48 10N 2 0E
Beauceville 151 46 13N 70 46W
Beaudesert 139 27 59S 153 0E
Beaufort, Austral. 140 37 25S 143 25E
Beaufort, Malay. 102 5 30N 115 40E
Beaufort, N.C., U.S.A. 157 34 45N 76 40W
Beaufort, S.C., U.S.A. 157 32 25N 80 40W
Beaufort Sea 12 72 0N 140 0W
Beaufort-West 128 32 18S 22 36E
Beaugency 43 47 47N 1 38E
Beauharnois 150 45 20N 73 52W
Beaujeu 45 46 10N 4 35E
Beaujolais 45 46 0N 4 25E
Beaulieu, Loiret, France 44 47 31N 2 49E
Beaulieu, Vendée, France 45 46 41N 1 37W
Beaulieu, U.K. 28 50 49N 1 27W
Beaulieu, R. 152 62 3N 113 11W
Beauly 37 57 29N 4 27W
Beauly Firth 37 57 30N 4 20W
Beauly, R. 37 57 26N 4 28W
Beaumaris 31 53 16N 4 7W
Beaumetz-les-Loges 43 50 15N 2 40E
Beaumont, Belg. 47 50 15N 4 14E
Beaumont, France 44 44 45N 0 46E
Beaumont, N.Z. 143 45 50S 169 33E
Beaumont, Calif., U.S.A. 163 33 56N 116 58W
Beaumont, Tex., U.S.A. 159 30 5N 94 8W
Beaumont-le-Roger 42 49 4N 0 47E
Beaumont-sur-Oise 43 49 9N 2 17E
Beaune 43 47 2N 4 50E
Beaune-la-Rolande 43 48 4N 2 25E
Beauraing 47 50 7N 4 57E
Beausejour 153 50 5N 96 35E
Beausset, Le 45 43 10N 5 46E
Beauvais 43 49 25N 2 8E
Beauval 153 55 9N 107 37W
Beauvoir, Deux Sèvres, France 44 46 12N 0 30W
Beauvoir, Vendée, France 42 46 55N 2 1W
Beaver, Alaska, U.S.A. 147 66 20N 147 30W
Beaver, Okla., U.S.A. 159 36 52N 100 31W
Beaver, Utah, U.S.A. 161 38 20N 112 45W
Beaver City 158 40 13N 99 50W
Beaver Dam 158 43 28N 88 50W
Beaver Falls 156 40 44N 80 20W
Beaver Hill L. 153 54 16N 94 59W
Beaver I. 150 45 40N 85 31W
Beaver, R. 152 59 52N 124 20W
Beaver, R 150 55 55N 87 48W
Beaver, R. 153 55 26N 107 45W
Beaverhill L., Man., Can. 153 54 5N 94 50W
Beaverhill L., N.W.T., Can. 153 63 2N 111 22W
Beaverhill L., Alb., 152 53 27N 112 32W
Beaverlodge 152 55 11N 119 29W
Beavermouth 152 51 32N 117 23W
Beaverstone, R. 150 54 59N 89 25W
Beawar 94 26 3N 74 18E
Bebedouro 173 21 0S 48 25W
Bebington 32 53 23N 3 1W
Beboa 129 17 22S 44 33E
Bebra 48 50 59N 9 48E
Beccles 29 52 27N 1 33E
Bečej 66 45 36N 20 3E
Beceni 70 45 23N 26 48E
Becerreá 56 42 51N 7 10W
Béchar 118 31 38N 2 18W
Becharof L. 147 58 0N 156 30W
Bechuanaland = Botswana 125 23 0S 24 0E
Bechyně 52 49 17N 14 29E
Beckermet 32 54 26N 3 31W
Beckfoot 32 54 50N 3 25W
Beckingham 33 53 24N 0 49W
Beckley 156 37 50N 81 8W
Bécon 42 47 30N 0 50W
Bečva, R. 53 49 31N 17 40E
Bedale 33 54 18N 1 35W
Bédar 59 37 11N 1 59W
Bédarieux 44 43 37N 3 10E
Bédarrides 45 44 2N 4 54E
Beddone, Mt. 138 25 50S 134 20E
Bedele 123 8 31N 35 44E
Bedel, Pereval 85 41 26N 78 26E
Bederkesa 48 53 37N 8 50E
Bedford, Can. 150 45 7N 72 59W
Bedford, S. Afr. 128 32 40S 26 10E
Bedford, U.K. 29 52 8N 0 29W
Bedford, Ind., U.S.A. 156 38 50N 86 30W
Bedford, Iowa, U.S.A. 158 40 40N 94 41W
Bedford, Ohio, U.S.A. 156 41 23N 81 32W
Bedford, Va., U.S.A. 156 37 25N 79 30W
Bedford □ 29 52 4N 0 28W
Bedford, C. 138 15 14S 145 21E
Bedford Downs 136 17 19S 127 20E
Bedford Level 29 52 25N 0 5E
Bedków 54 51 36N 19 44E
Bedlington 35 55 8N 1 35W
Bednesti 152 53 50N 123 10W
Bednja, R. 63 46 12N 16 25E
Bednodemyanovsk 81 53 55N 43 15E
Bedourie 138 24 30S 139 30E
Bedretto 51 46 31N 8 31E
Bedum 47 53 18N 6 36E
Bedwas 31 51 36N 3 10W
Bedworth 28 52 28N 1 29W
Bedzin 54 50 19N 19 7E
Bee L. 36 57 22N 7 21W
Beebyn 137 27 0S 117 48E
Beech Grove 156 39 40N 86 2W
Beechey Point 147 70 27N 149 18W
Beechworth 141 36 22S 146 43E
Beechy 153 50 53N 107 24W
Beeford 33 53 58N 0 18W
Beek, Gelderland, Neth. 46 51 55N 6 11E
Beek, Limburg, Neth. 47 50 57N 5 48E
Beek, Noord Brabant, Neth. 47 51 32N 5 38E
Beekbergen 46 52 10N 5 58E
Beelitz 48 52 14N 12 58E
Beemem 47 51 9N 3 21E
Beenleigh 139 27 43S 153 10E
Beer 30 50 41N 3 5W
Be'er Sheva' 90 31 15N 34 48E
Be'er Sheva', N. 90 31 12N 34 40E
Be'er Toviyyao 90 31 44N 34 42E
Be'eri 90 31 25N 34 30E
Be'erotayim 90 32 19N 34 59E
Beersheba = Be'er Sheva' 90 31 15N 34 48E
Beerta 46 53 11N 7 6E
Beerze, R. 46 51 39N 5 20E
Beesd 46 51 53N 5 11E
Beesel 47 51 16N 6 2E
Beeskow 48 52 9N 14 14E
Beeston 33 52 55N 1 11W
Beetaloo 138 17 15S 133 50E
Beetsterzwaag 46 53 4N 6 5E
Beetzendorf 48 52 42N 11 6E
Beeville 159 28 27N 97 44W
Befale 124 0 25N 20 45E
Befandriana 125 21 55S 44 0E
Befotaka, Diégo-Suarez, Madag. 129 14 30S 48 0E
Befotaka, Fianarantsoa, Madag. 129 23 49S 47 0E
Beg, L. 38 54 48N 6 28W
Bega 141 36 41S 149 51E
Bega, Canalul 66 45 37N 20 46E
Begelly 31 51 45N 4 44W
Begemdir & Simen □ 123 13 55N 37 30E
Begna 71 60 41N 9 42E
Begonte 56 43 10N 7 40W
Begu-Sarai 95 25 24N 86 9E
Beguildy 31 52 25N 3 11W
Béhagle = Lai 117 9 25N 16 30E
Behara 125 24 55S 46 20E
Behbehan 92 30 30N 50 15E
Behror 94 27 51N 76 20E
Behshahr 93 36 45N 53 35E
Beida (Al Bayda) 117 32 30N 21 40E
Beighton 33 53 21N 1 21W
Beilen 46 52 52N 6 27E
Beilngries 49 49 1N 11 27E
Beilpajah 140 32 54S 143 52E
Beilul 123 13 2N 42 20E
Beinn a' Ghlo, Mt. 37 56 51N 3 42W
Beinn Mhor, Mt. 36 57 59N 6 39W
Beira 127 19 50S 34 52E
Beira-Alta 55 40 35N 7 35W
Beira-Baixa 55 40 2N 7 30W
Beira-Litoral 55 40 5N 8 30W
Beirut = Bayrūt 92 33 53N 35 31E
Beit Bridge 127 14 58S 30 15E
Beit Hanum 90 31 32N 34 32E
Beit Lahiya 90 31 32N 34 30E
Beit 'Ur et Tahta 90 31 54N 35 5E
Beit Yosef 90 32 34N 35 33E
Beitbridge 127 22 12S 30 0E
Beith 34 55 45N 4 38W
Beituniya 90 31 54N 35 10E
Beiuş 70 46 40N 22 21E
Beja 57 38 2N 7 53W
Béja 119 36 43N 9 12E
Beja □ 57 37 55N 7 55W
Béjaïa 119 36 42N 5 2E
Béjar 56 40 23N 5 46W
Bejestan 93 34 30N 58 5E
Bekabad 85 40 13N 69 14E
Bekasi 103 6 20S 107 0E
Békés 53 46 47N 21 9E
Békés □ 53 46 45N 21 0E
Békéscsaba 53 46 40N 21 10E
Bekily 129 24 13S 45 19E
Bekkevoort 47 50 57N 4 58E
Bekkjarvik 71 60 1N 5 13E

Bekoji Berghem

Bekoji 123 7 40N 38 20 E
Bekok 101 2 20N 103 7 E
Bekopaka 129 19 9 S 44 45 E
Bekwai 121 6 30N 1 34W
Bel Air 162 39 32N 76 21W
Bela, India 95 25 50N 82 0 E
Bela, Pak. 94 26 12N 66 20 E
Bela Crkva 66 44 55N 21 27 E
Bela Palanka 66 43 13N 22 17 E
Bela Vista, Brazil 173 22 12 S 56 20W
Bela Vista, Mozam. 129 26 10 S 32 44 E
Bélâbre 44 46 34N 1 8 E
Belaia, Mt. 123 11 25N 36 8 E
Belalcázar 57 38 35N 5 10W
Belanovica 66 44 15N 20 23 E
Belavenona 129 24 50 S 47 4 E
Belawan 102 3 33N 98 32 E
Belaya Glina 83 46 5N 40 48 E
Belaya Kalitva 83 48 13N 40 50 E
Belaya Kholunitsa 84 58 41N 50 13 E
Belaya, R. 84 55 54N 53 33 E
Belaya Tserkov 80 49 45N 30 10 E
Belbroughton 28 52 23N 2 5W
Belceşti 70 47 19N 27 7 E
Bełchatów 54 51 21N 19 22 E
Belcher, C. 12 75 0N 160 0W
Belcher Is. 150 56 15N 78 45W
Belchite 58 41 18N 0 43W
Belclare 38 53 29N 8 55W
Belcoo 38 54 18N 7 52W
Belderg 38 54 18N 9 33W
Beldringe 73 55 28N 10 21 E
Belebey 84 54 7N 54 7 E
Belém de São Francisco 170 8 46 S 38 58W
Belém (Pará) 170 1 20 S 48 30W
Belén, Argent. 172 27 40 S 67 5W
Belén, Colomb. 174 1 26N 75 56W
Belén, Parag. 172 23 30 S 57 6W
Belen 161 34 40N 106 50W
Belene 67 43 39N 25 10 E
Bélesta 44 42 55N 1 56 E
Belet Uen 91 4 30N 45 5 E
Belev 81 53 50N 36 5 E
Belfast, N.Z. 143 43 27 S 172 39 E
Belfast, S. Afr. 129 25 42 S 30 2 E
Belfast, U.K. 38 54 35N 5 56W
Belfast, U.S.A. 151 44 30N 69 0W
Belfast □ 38 54 35N 5 56W
Belfast, L. 38 54 40N 5 50W
Belfeld 47 51 18N 6 6 E
Belfeoram 151 47 32N 55 30W
Belfield 158 46 54N 103 11W
Belford 35 55 36N 1 50W
Belfort 43 47 38N 6 50 E
Belfort □ 43 47 38N 6 52 E
Belfry 160 45 10N 109 2W
Belgaum 97 15 55N 74 35 E
Belgioioso 62 45 9N 9 21 E
Belgium ■ 47 51 30N 5 0 E
Belgooly 138 51 44N 8 30W
Belgorod 82 50 35N 36 35 E
Belgorod Dnestrovskiy 82 46 11N 30 23 E
Belgrade 160 45 50N 111 10W
Belgrade = Beograd 66 44 50N 20 37 E
Belgrove 143 41 27 S 172 59 E
Belhaven 157 35 34N 76 35W
Beli 121 7 52N 10 58 E
Beli Drim, R. 66 42 25N 20 34 E
Beli Manastir 66 45 45N 18 36 E
Beli Timok, R. 66 43 39N 22 14 E
Belice, R. 64 37 44N 12 58 E
Belinga 124 1 10N 13 2 E
Belingwe 127 20 29 S 29 57 E
Belingwe, N., mt. 127 20 37 S 29 55 E
Belinsky (Chembar) 81 53 0N 43 25 E
Belinţ 66 45 48N 21 54 E
Belinyu 102 1 35 S 105 50 E
Beliton, Is. 102 3 10 S 107 50 E
Belitung, I. 102 3 10 S 107 50 E
Beliu 70 46 30N 22 0 E
Belize ■ 165 17 0N 88 30W
Belize City 165 17 25N 88 0W
Beljanica 66 44 08N 21 43 E
Bell 151 53 50N 53 10 E
Bell Bay 138 41 6 S 146 53 E
Bell I. 151 50 46N 55 35W
Bell Irving, R. 152 56 12N 129 5W
Bell Peninsula 149 63 50N 82 0W
Bell, R. 150 49 48N 77 38W
Bell Rock = Inchcape Rock 35 56 26N 2 24W
Bell Ville 172 32 40 S 62 40W
Bella Bella 152 52 10N 128 10W
Bella Coola 152 52 25N 126 40W
Bella Unión 172 30 15 S 57 40W
Bella Vista, Corrientes, Argent. 172 28 33 S 59 0W
Bella Vista, Tucuman, Argent. 172 27 10 S 65 25W
Bella Yella 120 7 24N 10 9W
Bellacorick 38 54 8N 9 35W
Bellaghy 38 54 50N 6 31W
Bellágio 62 45 59N 9 15 E
Bellaire 156 40 1N 80 46W
Bellananagh 38 53 55N 7 25W
Bellarena 38 55 7N 6 57W
Bellarwi 141 34 6 S 147 13 E
Bellary 97 15 10N 76 56 E
Bellata 139 29 53 S 149 46 E
Bellavary 38 53 54N 9 9W
Belle Fourche 158 44 43N 103 52W
Belle Fourche, R. 158 44 25N 105 0W
Belle Glade 157 26 43N 80 38W
Belle Ile 42 47 20N 3 10W
Belle Isle 151 51 57N 55 25W
Belle-Isle-en-Terre 42 48 33N 3 23W
Belle Isle, Str. of 151 51 30N 56 30W
Belle, La 157 26 45N 81 22W
Belle Plaine, Iowa, U.S.A. 158 41 51N 92 18W
Belle Plaine, Minn., U.S.A. 158 44 35N 93 48W
Belledonne 45 45 11N 6 0 E
Belledune 151 47 55N 65 50W
Belleek 38 54 30N 8 6W
Bellefontaine 156 40 20N 83 45W
Bellefonte 156 40 56N 77 45W
Bellegarde, Ain, France 45 46 4N 5 49 E
Bellegarde, Creuse, France 43 45 59N 2 19 E
Bellegarde, Loiret, France 43 48 0N 2 26 E
Belleoram 151 47 31N 55 25W
Belleville, Can. 150 44 10N 77 23W
Belleville, Rhône, France 45 46 7N 4 45 E
Belleville, Vendée, France 42 46 48N 1 28W
Belleville, Ill., U.S.A. 158 38 30N 90 0W
Belleville, Kans., U.S.A. 158 39 51N 97 38W
Belleville, N.Y., U.S.A. 162 43 46N 76 10W
Bellevue, Can. 152 49 35N 114 22W
Bellevue, U.S.A. 160 43 25N 144 23W
Belley 45 45 46N 5 41 E
Bellin (Payne Bay) 149 60 0N 70 0W
Bellingen 141 30 25 S 152 50 E
Bellingham, U.K. 35 55 09N 2 16W
Bellingham, U.S.A. 160 48 45N 122 27W
Bellingshausen Sea 13 66 0 S 80 0W
Bellinzona 51 46 11N 9 1 E
Bello 174 6 20N 75 33W
Bellona Reefs 133 21 26 S 159 0 E
Bellows Falls 162 43 10N 72 30W
Bellpat 94 29 0N 68 5 E
Bellpuig 58 41 37N 1 1 E
Belluno 63 46 8N 12 6 E
Bellville 159 29 58N 96 18W
Belmar 162 40 10N 74 2W
Bélmez 57 38 17N 5 17W
Belmont, Austral. 141 33 4 S 151 42 E
Belmont, U.S.A. 162 43 27N 71 29W
Belmonte, Brazil 171 16 0 S 39 0W
Belmonte, Port. 56 40 21N 7 20W
Belmonte, Spain 58 39 34N 2 43W
Belmopan 165 17 18N 88 30W
Belmore 140 33 34 S 141 13 E
Belmullet 38 54 13N 9 58W
Belo Horizonte 171 19 55 S 43 56W
Belo Jardim 170 8 20 S 36 26W
Belo-sur-Mer 129 20 42 S 44 33 E
Belo-sur-Tsiribihana 129 19 40 S 43 30 E
Belogorsk, R.S.F.S.R., U.S.S.R. 77 51 0N 128 20 E
Belogorsk, Ukraine, U.S.S.R. 82 45 3N 34 35 E
Belogradchik 66 43 37N 22 40 E
Belogradets 67 43 22N 27 18 E
Beloha 129 25 10 S 45 3 E
Beloit, Kans., U.S.A. 158 39 32N 98 9W
Beloit, Wis., U.S.A. 158 42 35N 89 0W
Belokholunitskiy 81 58 55N 50 43 E
Belomorsk 78 64 35N 34 30 E
Belonia 98 23 15N 91 30 E
Belopolye 80 51 14N 34 20 E
Beloretsk 84 53 58N 58 24 E
Belovo 76 54 30N 86 0 E
Beloyarskiy 84 56 45N 61 24 E
Beloye More 78 66 0N 38 0 E
Beloye, Oz. 78 60 10N 37 35 E
Beloye Ozero 83 45 15N 46 50 E
Belozersk 81 60 0N 37 30 E
Belpasso 65 37 37N 15 0 E
Belper 33 53 2N 1 29W
Belsay 35 55 6N 1 53W
Belsele 47 51 9N 4 6 E
Belsito 64 37 50N 13 47 E
Beltana 140 30 48 S 138 25 E
Belterra 175 2 45 S 55 0W
Beltinci 63 46 37N 16 20 E
Belton, Humberside, U.K. 33 53 33N 0 49W
Belton, Norfolk, U.K. 29 52 35N 1 39 E
Belton, S.C., U.S.A. 157 34 31N 82 39W
Belton, Tex., U.S.A. 159 31 4N 97 30W
Beltra, Mayo, Ireland 38 53 57N 9 24W
Beltra, Sligo, Ireland 38 54 12N 8 36W
Beltra L. 38 53 56N 9 28W
Beltsy 82 47 48N 28 0 E
Belturbet 38 54 6N 7 28W
Belukha 76 49 50N 86 50 E
Beluran 102 5 48N 117 35 E
Beluša 53 49 5N 18 27 E
Belušić 66 43 50N 21 10 E
Belvedere Maríttimo 65 39 37N 15 52 E
Belvès 44 44 46N 1 0 E
Belvidere, Ill., U.S.A. 158 42 15N 88 55W
Belvidere, N.J., U.S.A. 162 40 48N 75 5W
Belville 38 54 40N 9 22W
Belvis de la Jara 57 39 45N 4 57W
Belyando, R. 138 21 38 S 146 50 E
Belyj Jar 76 58 26N 84 39 E
Belyy 80 55 48N 32 51 E
Belyy, Ostrov 76 73 30N 71 0 E
Belyye Vody 85 42 25N 69 50 E
Belz 80 50 23N 24 1 E
Belzig 48 52 8N 12 36 E
Belzoni 159 33 12N 90 30W
Bemaraha, Plat. du 129 18 40 S 44 45 E
Bemarivo, Majunga, Madag. 129 17 6 S 44 31 E
Bemarivo, Tuléar, Madag. 129 21 45 S 44 45 E
Bemarivo, R. 129 21 45 S 44 45 E
Bemavo 129 21 33 S 45 25 E
Bembéréke 121 10 11N 2 43 E
Bembesi 127 20 0 S 28 58 E
Bembesi, R. 127 20 0 S 28 58 E
Bembézar, R. 57 38 0N 5 20W
Bembridge 28 50 41N 1 4W
Bemidji 158 47 30N 94 50W
Bemmel 46 51 54N 5 54 E
Ben Alder 37 55 59N 4 30W
Ben Avon 37 57 6N 3 28W
Ben Bheigeir, Mt. 34 55 43N 6 6W
Ben Bullen 141 33 12 S 150 2 E
Ben Chonzine 35 56 27N 4 0W
Ben Cruachan, Mt. 34 56 26N 5 8W
Ben Dearg 37 57 47N 4 58W
Ben Dearg, mt. 37 56 54N 3 49W
Ben Dhorain 37 58 7N 3 50W
Ben Dorian 34 56 30N 4 42W
Ben Gardane 119 33 11N 11 11 E
Ben Hee 37 58 16N 4 43W
Ben Hope, mt. 37 58 24N 4 36W
Ben Klibreck 37 58 14N 4 25W
Ben Lawers, mt. 37 56 33N 4 13W
Ben Lomond, mt. 139 30 1 S 151 43 E
Ben Lomond mt. 138 41 38 S 147 42 E
Ben Lomond, mt. 34 56 12N 4 39W
Ben Loyal 37 58 25N 4 25W
Ben Luc 101 10 39N 106 29 E
Ben Lui, mt. 34 56 24N 4 50W
Ben Macdhui 37 57 4N 3 40W
Ben Mhor 36 57 16N 7 21W
Ben More, Mull, U.K. 34 56 26N 6 2W
Ben More, Perth, U.K. 34 56 23N 4 31W
Ben More Assynt 37 58 7N 4 51W
Ben Nevis, mt., N.Z. 143 45 15 S 169 0 E
Ben Nevis, mt., U.K. 36 56 48N 5 0W
Ben Ohau Ra. 143 44 1 S 170 4 E
Ben Quang 100 17 3N 106 55 E
Ben Stack 36 58 20N 4 58W
Ben Tharsiunn 37 57 47N 4 20W
Ben Venue 34 56 13N 4 28W
Ben Vorlich 34 56 22N 4 15W
Ben Wyvis, mt. 37 57 40N 4 35W
Bena 121 11 20N 5 50 E
Bena Dibele 124 4 4 S 22 50 E
Benagalbón 57 36 45N 4 15W
Benagerie 140 31 25 S 140 22 E
Benahmed 118 33 4N 7 9W
Benalla 141 36 30 S 146 0 E
Benambra, Mt. 141 36 31 S 147 34 E
Benameji 57 37 16N 4 33W
Benanee 140 34 31 S 142 52 E
Benares = Varanasi 95 25 22N 83 8 E
Benavente, Port. 57 38 59N 8 49W
Benavente, Spain 56 42 2N 5 43W
Benavides, Spain 56 42 30N 5 54W
Benavides, U.S.A. 159 27 35N 98 28W
Benbane Hd. 38 55 15N 6 30W
Benbaun, Mt. 38 53 30N 9 50W
Benbecula, I. 36 57 26N 7 21W
Benbonyathe, Mt. 140 30 25 S 139 11 E
Benburb 38 54 25N 6 42W
Bencubbin 137 30 48 S 117 52 E
Bend 160 44 2N 121 15W
Bendel □ 121 6 0N 6 0 E
Bender Beila 91 9 30N 50 48 E
Bender Cassim 91 11 12N 49 18 E
Bendering 137 32 23 S 118 18 E
Bendery 82 46 50N 29 50 E
Bendigo 140 36 40 S 144 15 E
Beneden Knijpe 46 52 58N 5 59 E
Benedick 162 38 31N 76 41W
Beneditinos 170 5 27 S 42 22W
Benedito Leite 170 7 13 S 44 34W
Benei Beraq 129 32 5N 34 50 E
Bénéna 120 13 9N 4 17W
Beneraird, Mt. 34 55 4N 4 57W
Benešov 52 49 46N 14 41 E
Bénestroff 43 48 54N 6 45 E
Benet 44 46 22N 0 35W
Benevento 65 41 7N 14 45 E
Benfeld 43 48 22N 7 34 E
Beng Lovea 100 12 36N 105 34 E
Benga 127 16 11 S 33 40 E
Bengal, Bay of 65 15 0N 00 90 E
Bengawan Solo 103 7 5 S 112 25 E
Benghazi = Banghāzī 119 32 11N 20 3 E
Bengkalis 102 1 30N 102 10 E
Bengkulu 102 3 50 S 102 12 E
Bengkulu □ 102 3 48 S 102 16 E
Bengough 153 49 25N 105 10W
Benguela 125 12 37 S 13 25 E
Benguerir 118 32 16N 7 56W
Benguérua, Î. 129 21 58 S 35 28 E
Benha 122 30 26N 31 8 E
Beni 126 0 30N 29 27 E
Beni Abbès 118 30 5N 2 5W
Beni Haoua 118 36 30N 1 30 E
Benî Mazâr 122 28 32N 30 44 E
Beni Mellal 118 32 21N 6 21W
Beni Ounif 118 32 0N 1 10W
Beni, R. 174 10 30 S 66 0W
Beni Saf 118 35 17N 1 15W
Benî Suêf 122 29 5N 31 6 E
Beniah L. 152 63 23N 112 17W
Benicarló 58 40 23N 0 23 E
Benicia 163 38 3N 122 9W
Benidorm 59 38 33N 0 9W
Benidorm,Islote de 59 38 31N 0 9W
Benin ■ 121 10 0N 2 0 E
Benin, Bight of 121 5 0N 3 0 E
Benin City 121 6 20N 5 31 E
Benington 33 52 59N 0 5 E
Benisa 59 38 43N 0 03 E
Benjamin Aceval 172 24 58 S 57 34W
Benjamin Constant 174 4 40 S 70 15W
Benjamin Hill 164 30 10N 111 10W
Benkelman 158 40 7N 101 32W
Benlidi 138 24 35 S 144 50 E
Benmore Pk. 143 44 25 S 170 8 E
Bennane Hd. 34 55 9N 5 2W
Bennebroek 46 52 19N 4 36 E
Bennekom 46 52 0N 5 41 E
Bennett 147 59 56N 134 53W
Bennettsbridge 39 52 36N 7 12W
Bennettsville 157 34 38N 79 39W
Bennington 162 42 52N 73 12W
Benoa 102 8 50 S 115 20 E
Bénodet 42 47 53N 4 7W
Benoni 129 26 11 S 28 18 E
Benoud 118 32 20N 0 16 E
Benque Viejo 165 17 5N 89 8W
Bensheim 49 49 40N 8 38 E
Benson, U.K. 28 51 37N 1 6W
Benson, U.S.A. 161 31 59N 110 19W
Bent 93 26 20N 59 25 E
Benteng 103 6 10 S 120 30 E
Bentinck I. 138 17 3 S 139 35 E
Bentiu 123 9 10N 29 55 E
Bentley, Hants., U.K. 29 51 12N 0 52W
Bentley, S. Yorks, U.K. 33 53 33N 1 9W
Bento Gonçalves 173 29 10 S 51 31W
Benton, Ark., U.S.A. 159 34 30N 92 35W
Benton, Calif., U.S.A. 163 37 48N 118 32W
Benton, Ill., U.S.A. 158 38 0N 88 55W
Benton, Pa., U.S.A. 162 41 12N 76 23W
Benton Harbor 156 42 10N 86 28W
Bentong 101 3 31N 101 55 E
Bentu Liben 123 8 32N 38 21 E
Benue □ 121 7 30N 7 30 E
Benue Plateau □ 121 8 0N 8 30 E
Benue, R. 121 7 50N 6 30 E
Benwee Hd. 38 54 20N 9 50W
Beo 103 4 25N 126 50 E
Beograd 66 44 50N 20 37 E
Beowawe 160 40 45N 117 0W
Beppu 110 33 15N 131 30 E
Beppu-Wan 110 33 18N 131 34 E
Ber Dagan 90 32 1N 34 49 E
Bera 98 24 5N 89 37 E
Beragh 38 54 34N 7 10W
Berakit 123 14 38N 39 29 E
Berati 68 40 43N 19 59 E
Berber 122 18 0N 34 0 E
Berbéra 117 10 33N 16 35 E
Berbera 91 10 30N 45 2 E
Berbérati 124 4 15N 15 40 E
Berberia, Cabo 59 38 39N 1 24 E
Berbice, R. 174 5 20N 58 10W
Berceto 62 44 30N 10 0 E
Berchtesgaden 49 47 37N 13 1 E
Berck-sur-Mer 43 50 25N 1 36 E
Berdichev 82 49 57N 28 30 E
Berdsk 76 54 47N 83 2 E
Berdyansk 82 46 45N 36 50 E
Berdyaush 84 55 9N 59 9 E
Bere Alston 30 50 29N 4 11W
Bere Regis 28 50 45N 2 13W
Berea 156 37 35N 84 18W
Berebere 103 2 25N 128 45 E
Bereda 91 11 45N 51 0 E
Bereina 135 8 39 S 146 30 E
Berekum 120 7 29N 2 34W
Berenice 122 24 2N 35 25 E
Berens I. 153 52 18N 97 18W
Berens, R. 153 51 21N 97 0W
Berens River 153 52 25N 97 0W
Berestechko 80 50 22N 25 5 E
Bereşti 70 46 6N 27 50 E
Berettyo, R. 53 47 32N 21 47 E
Berettyóújfalu 53 47 13N 21 33 E
Beretău, R. 70 47 30N 22 7 E
Berevo 129 19 44 S 44 58 E
Berevo-sur-Ranobe 129 17 14 S 44 17 E
Bereza 80 52 31N 24 51 E
Berezhany 80 49 26N 24 58 E
Berezina, R. 80 54 10N 28 10 E
Berezna 80 51 35N 30 46 E
Berezniki 84 59 24N 56 46 E
Berezovka 82 47 25N 30 55 E
Berezovo 76 64 0N 65 0 E
Berg 71 59 10N 11 18 E
Berga, Spain 58 42 6N 1 48 E
Berga, Kalmar, Sweden 73 57 14N 16 3 E
Berga, Kronoberg, Sweden 73 56 55N 14 0 E
Bergama 92 39 8N 27 15 E
Bergambacht 46 51 56N 4 48 E
Bérgamo 62 45 42N 9 40 E
Bergantiños 56 43 20N 8 40W
Bergedorf 48 53 28N 10 12 E
Bergeijk 47 51 19N 5 21 E
Bergen, Ger. 48 54 24N 13 26 E
Bergen, Norway 71 60 23N 5 20 E
Bergen-Binnen 46 52 40N 4 43 E
Bergen-op-Zoom 47 51 30N 4 18 E
Bergerac 44 44 51N 0 30 E
Bergheim 48 50 57N 6 38 E
Berghem 46 51 46N 5 33 E

Bergisch-Gladbach **Billesdon**

Bergisch-Gladbach 48 50 59N 7 9E
Bergkvara 73 56 23N 16 5E
Bergschenhoek 46 51 59N 4 30E
Bergsjö 72 61 59N 17 3E
Berguent 118 34 1N 2 0W
Bergues 43 50 58N 2 24E
Bergum 46 53 13N 5 59E
Bergvik 72 61 16N 16 50E
Berhala, Selat 102 1 0S 104 15E
Berhampore 95 24 2N 88 27E
Berhampur 96 19 15N 84 54E
Berheci, R. 70 46 7N 27 19E
Berhungra 139 34 46S 147 52E
Bering Sea 130 58 0N 167 0E
Bering Str. 147 66 0N 170 0W
Beringarra 137 26 0S 116 55E
Beringen, Belg. 47 51 3N 5 14E
Beringen, Switz. 51 47 38N 8 34E
Beringovskiy 77 63 3N 179 19E
Berislav 82 46 50N 33 30E
Berisso 172 34 40S 58 0W
Berja 59 36 50N 2 56W
Berkane 118 34 52N 2 20W
Berkel, R. 46 52 8N 6 12E
Berkeley 163 37 52N 122 20W
Berkeley Springs 156 39 38N 78 12W
Berkhamsted 29 51 45N 0 33W
Berkhout 46 52 38N 4 59E
Berkner I. 13 79 30S 50 0W
Berkovitsa 67 43 16N 23 8E
Berkshire 162 42 19N 76 11W
Berkshire □ 28 51 30N 1 20W
Berkshire Downs 28 51 30N 1 30W
Berkyk 71 62 50N 9 59E
Berlaar 47 51 7N 4 39E
Berland, R. 152 54 0N 116 50W
Berlanga 57 38 17N 5 50W
Berlave 47 51 2N 4 0E
Berleburg 48 51 3N 8 22E
Berlenga, I. 75 39 25N 9 30W
Berlick 47 51 22N 6 9E
Berlin, Ger. 48 52 32N 13 24E
Berlin, Md., U.S.A. 162 38 19N 75 12W
Berlin, N.H., U.S.A. 156 44 29N 71 10W
Berlin, N.Y., U.S.A. 162 42 42N 73 23W
Berlin, E. □ 48 52 30N 13 30E
Berlin, W. □ 48 52 30N 13 20E
Bermeja, Sierra 57 36 45N 5 11W
Bermejo, R., Formosa, Argent. 172 26 30S 58 50W
Bermejo, R., San Juan, Argent. 172 30 0S 68 0W
Bermeo 58 43 25N 2 47W
Bermillo de Sayago 56 41 22N 6 8W
Bermuda, I. 10 32 45N 65 0W
Bern (Berne) 50 46 57N 7 28E
Bern (Berne) □ 50 46 45N 7 40E
Bernalda 65 40 24N 16 44E
Bernalillo 161 35 17N 106 37W
Bernam, R. 101 3 45N 101 5E
Bernardo de Irigoyen 173 26 15S 53 40W
Bernardsville 162 40 43N 74 34W
Bernasconi 172 37 55S 63 44W
Bernau 49 47 53N 12 20E
Bernay 42 49 5N 0 35E
Berndorf 52 47 59N 16 1E
Berne = Bern 50 46 57N 7 28E
Berner Alpen 50 46 27N 7 35E
Berneray, I. 36 56 47N 7 38W
Bernese Oberland = Oberland 50 46 27N 7 35E
Bernier I. 137 24 50S 113 12E
Bernina Pass 51 46 22N 9 54E
Bernina, Piz 51 46 20N 9 54E
Bernissart 47 50 28N 3 39E
Beroroha 125 21 40S 45 10E
Béroubouey 121 10 34N 2 46E
Beroun 52 49 57N 14 5E
Berounka, R. 52 50 0N 13 47E
Berovo 66 41 42N 22 51E
Berrahal 119 36 54N 7 33E
Berre 45 43 28N 5 11E
Berre, Étang de 45 43 27N 5 5E
Berrechid 118 33 18N 7 36W
Berri 140 34 14S 140 35E
Berriedale 37 58 12N 3 30W
Berriew 31 52 36N 3 12W
Berrigan 141 35 38S 145 49E
Berrouaghia 118 36 10N 2 53E
Berrwillock 140 35 36S 142 59E
Berry, Austral. 141 34 46S 150 43E
Berry, France 43 47 0N 2 0E
Berry Hd. 30 50 24N 3 29W
Berry Is. 166 25 40N 77 50W
Berryville 159 36 23N 93 35W
Bersenbrück 48 52 33N 7 56E
Berst Ness 37 59 16N 3 0W
Berthaund 158 40 21N 105 5W
Berthier Is. 136 14 29S 124 59E
Berthold 158 48 19N 101 45W
Bertincourt 43 50 5N 2 58E
Bertoua 124 4 30N 13 45E
Bertraghboy, B. 38 53 22N 9 54W
Bertrand 158 40 35N 99 38W
Bertrange 47 49 37N 6 3E
Bertrix 47 49 51N 5 15E
Beruas 101 4 30N 100 47E
Berufjörður 74 64 48N 14 29W
Berur Hayil 90 31 34N 34 38E
Berwick 162 41 4N 76 17W
Berwick (□) 26 55 46N 2 30W
Berwick-upon-Tweed 35 55 47N 2 0W
Berwyn Mts. 31 52 54N 3 26W
Beryl N., oilfield 19 59 37N 1 30E
Beryl, oilfield 19 59 28N 1 30E
Beryl W., oilfield 19 59 32N 1 20E
Berzasca 66 44 39N 21 58E
Berzence 53 46 12N 17 11E
Besal 95 35 4N 73 56E
Besalampy 129 16 43S 44 29E
Besançon 43 47 9N 6 0E
Besar 102 2 40S 116 0E
Beserah 101 3 50N 103 21E
Beshenkovichi 80 55 2N 29 29E
Beška 66 45 8N 20 6E
Beskids, Mts. 53 49 35N 18 40E
Beslan 83 43 22N 44 28E
Besna Kobila 66 42 31N 22 10E
Besnard L. 153 55 25N 106 0W
Beşparmak Daği 69 37 32N 27 30E
Bessarabiya 70 46 20N 29 0E
Bessarabka 82 46 21N 28 51E
Bessbrook 38 54 12N 6 25W
Bességes 45 44 18N 4 8E
Bessemer 158 46 27N 90 0W
Bessin 42 49 21N 1 0W
Bessines-sur-Gartempe 42 46 6N 1 22E
Best 47 51 31N 5 23E
Bet Alfa 90 32 31N 35 25E
Bet Guvrin 90 31 37N 34 54E
Bet Hashitta 90 32 31N 35 27E
Bet Ha'tmeq 90 32 58N 35 8E
Bet Qeshet 90 32 41N 35 21E
Bet She'an 90 32 30N 35 30E
Bet Tadjine, Djebel 118 29 0N 3 30W
Bet Yosef 90 32 34N 35 33E
Betafo 129 19 50S 46 51E
Betanzos 56 43 15N 8 12W
Bétaré-Oya 124 5 40N 14 5E
Betekom 47 50 59N 4 47E
Bétera 58 39 35N 0 28W
Bethal 129 26 27S 29 28E
Bethanien 125 26 31S 17 8E
Bethany, S. Afr. 128 29 34S 25 59E
Bethany, U.S.A. 158 40 18N 94 0W
Bethany = Eizarilya 90 31 47N 35 15E
Bethel, U.S.A. 147 60 50N 161 50W
Bethel, Conn., U.S.A. 162 41 22N 73 25W
Bethesda, U.K. 31 53 11N 4 3W
Bethesda, U.S.A. 162 38 59N 77 6W
Bethlehem, S. Afr. 129 28 14S 28 18E
Bethlehem, U.S.A. 162 40 39N 75 24W
Bethlehem = Bayt Lahm 90 31 43N 35 12E
Bethulie 128 30 30S 25 59E
Béthune 43 50 30N 2 38E
Béthune, R. 42 49 56N 1 5E
Bethungra 141 34 45S 147 51E
Betijoque 174 9 23N 70 44W
Betim 171 19 58S 44 13W
Betioky 129 23 48S 44 20E
Beton Bazoches 43 48 42N 3 15E
Betong 101 5 45N 101 5E
Betoota 138 25 40S 140 42E
Betroka 129 23 16S 46 0E
Betsiamites 151 48 56N 68 40W
Betsiamites, R. 151 48 56N 68 40W
Betsiboka, R. 129 17 0S 47 0E
Betsjoeanaland 128 26 30S 22 30E
Bettembourg 47 49 31N 6 6E
Betterton 162 39 52N 76 4W
Betteshanger 29 51 14N 1 20E
Bettiah 95 26 48N 84 33E
Bettles 147 66 54N 150 50W
Bèttola 62 44 46N 9 35E
Bettws Bledrws 31 52 9N 4 2W
Bettyhill 37 58 31N 4 12W
Betul 96 21 48N 77 59E
Betung 102 2 0S 103 10E
Betws-y-Coed 31 53 4N 3 49W
Beuca 70 44 14N 24 56E
Beuil 45 44 6N 7 0E
Beulah, Can. 153 50 16N 101 02W
Beulah, U.S.A. 158 47 18N 101 47W
Beuvronne, La 46 48 59N 2 41E
Bevensen 48 53 5N 10 34E
Beveren 47 51 12N 4 16E
Beverley, Austral. 137 32 9S 116 56E
Beverley, U.K. 33 53 52N 0 26W
Beverlo 47 51 7N 5 13E
Beverly, Can. 152 53 36N 113 21W
Beverly, Mass., U.S.A. 162 42 32N 70 50W
Beverly, Wash., U.S.A. 160 46 55N 119 59W
Beverly Hills 163 34 4N 118 29W
Beverwijk 46 52 28N 4 38E
Bewdley 28 52 23N 2 19W
Bex 50 46 15N 7 0E
Bexhill 29 50 51N 0 29E
Bexley 29 51 26N 0 10E
Beyin 120 5 1N 2 41W
Beykoz 67 41 8N 29 7E
Beyla 120 8 30N 8 38W
Beynat 44 45 8N 1 44E
Beyneu 76 45 10N 55 3E
Beypazaı 92 40 10N 31 48E
Beyşehir Gölü 92 37 40N 31 45E
Bezdan 66 45 28N 18 57E
Bezerros 171 8 14S 35 45W
Bezet 90 33 4N 35 8E
Bezhitsa 80 53 19N 34 17E
Béziers 44 43 20N 3 12E
Bezwada = Vijayawada 97 16 31N 80 39E
Bhachau 93 23 20N 70 16E
Bhadarwah 95 32 58N 75 46E
Bhadra, R. 97 13 0N 76 0E
Bhadrakh 96 21 10N 86 30E
Bhadravati 97 13 49N 76 15E
Bhagalpur 95 25 10N 87 0E
Bhairab 98 22 51N 89 34E
Bhairab Bazar 98 24 4N 90 58E
Bhaisa 96 19 10N 77 58E
Bhakkar 94 31 40N 71 5E
Bhakra Dam 95 31 30N 76 45E
Bhamo 98 24 15N 97 15E
Bhamragarh 96 19 30N 80 40E
Bhandara 96 21 5N 79 42E
Bhanrer Ra. 94 23 40N 79 45E
Bharat = India 93 24 0N 78 0E
Bharatpur 94 27 15N 77 30E
Bharuch 96 21 47N 73 0E
Bhatghar L. 96 18 10N 73 48E
Bhatiapara Ghat 98 23 13N 89 42E
Bhatkal 97 13 58N 74 35E
Bhatpara 95 22 50N 88 25E
Bhattiprolu 97 16 7N 80 45E
Bhaun 94 32 55N 72 40E
Bhaunagar = Bhavnagar 94 21 45N 72 10E
Bhavani 97 11 27N 77 43E
Bhavani, R. 97 11 30N 77 15E
Bhavnagar 94 21 45N 72 10E
Bhawanipatna 96 19 55N 83 30E
Bhera 94 32 29N 72 57E
Bhilsa = Vidisha 94 23 28N 77 53E
Bhilwara 94 25 25N 74 38E
Bhima, R. 96 17 20N 76 30E
Bhimber 95 32 59N 74 3E
Bhimvaram 96 16 30N 81 30E
Bhind 95 26 30N 78 46E
Bhir 96 19 4N 75 58E
Bhiwandi 96 19 15N 73 0E
Bhiwani 94 28 50N 76 9E
Bhola 98 22 45N 90 35E
Bhongir 96 17 30N 78 56E
Bhopal 94 23 20N 77 53E
Bhor 96 18 12N 73 53E
Bhubaneswar 96 20 15N 85 50E
Bhuj 94 23 15N 69 49E
Bhumibol Dam 100 17 15N 98 58E
Bhusaval 96 21 15N 69 49E
Bhutan ■ 98 27 25N 89 50E
Biafra, B. of = Bonny, Bight of 121 3 30N 9 20E
Biak 103 1 0S 136 0E
Biała 54 50 24N 17 40E
Biała Piska 54 53 37N 22 5E
Biała Podlaska 54 52 4N 23 6E
Biała Podlaska □ 54 52 0N 23 0E
Biała, R. 54 49 46N 20 53E
Białogard 54 54 2N 15 58E
Biały Bór 54 53 53N 16 51E
Białystok 54 53 10N 23 10E
Białystok □ 54 53 9N 23 10E
Biancavilla 65 37 39N 14 50E
Biano Plateau = Manika Plateau 127 9 55S 26 24E
Biaro 103 2 5N 125 26E
Biarritz 44 43 29N 1 33W
Biasca 51 46 22N 8 58E
Biba 122 28 55N 31 0E
Bibaī 112 43 19N 141 52E
Bibby I. 153 61 55N 93 0W
Biberach 49 48 5N 9 49E
Biberist 50 47 11N 7 34E
Bibey, R. 56 42 24N 7 13W
Bibiani 120 6 30N 2 8W
Bibile 97 7 10N 81 25E
Biboohra 138 16 56S 145 25E
Bibungwa 126 2 40S 28 15E
Bibury 28 51 46N 1 50W
Bic 151 48 20N 68 41W
Bicaj 68 42 0N 20 25E
Bicaz 70 46 53N 26 5E
Biccari 65 41 23N 15 12E
Bicester 28 51 53N 1 9W
Biche, La, R. 152 59 57N 123 50W
Bichena 123 10 28N 38 10E
Bickerton I. 138 13 45S 136 10E
Bicknell, Ind., U.S.A. 156 38 50N 87 20W
Bicknell, Utah, U.S.A. 161 38 16N 111 35W
Bicsad 70 47 56N 23 28E
Bicton 28 52 43N 2 47W
Bida 121 9 3N 5 58E
Bidar 96 17 55N 77 35E
Biddeford 151 43 30N 70 28W
Biddenden 29 51 7N 0 40E
Biddu 90 31 50N 35 8E
Biddulph 32 53 8N 2 11W
Biddwara 123 5 11N 38 34E
Biddya 90 32 7N 35 4E
Bideford 30 51 1N 4 13W
Bideford Bay 30 51 5N 4 20W
Bidford on Avon 28 52 9N 1 53W
Bidor 101 4 6N 101 15E
Bidura 140 34 10S 143 21E
Bié 125 12 22S 16 55E
Bié Plateau 125 12 0S 16 0E
Bieber 160 41 4N 121 6W
Biel (Bienne) 50 47 8N 7 14E
Bielawa 54 50 43N 16 37E
Bielé Karpaty 53 49 5N 18 0E
Bielefeld 48 52 2N 8 31E
Bielersee 50 47 6N 7 5E
Biella 62 45 33N 8 3E
Bielsk Podlaski 54 52 47N 23 12E
Bielsko-Biała 54 49 50N 19 8E
Bielsko-Biała □ 54 49 45N 19 15E
Bien Hoa 101 10 57N 106 49E
Bienfait 153 49 10N 102 50W
Bienne = Biel 50 47 8N 7 14E
Bienvenida 57 38 18N 6 12W
Bienville, L. 150 55 5N 72 40W
Biescas 58 42 37N 0 20W
Biesiesfontein 128 30 57S 17 58E
Bietigheim 49 48 57N 9 8E
Bievre 47 49 57N 5 1E
Biferno, R. 65 41 40N 14 38E
Big B. 151 55 43N 60 35W
Big Bear City 163 34 16N 116 51W
Big Bear L. 163 34 15N 116 56W
Big Beaver 153 49 10N 105 10W
Big Beaver House 150 52 59N 89 50W
Big Bell 137 27 21S 117 40E
Big Belt Mts. 160 46 50N 111 30W
Big Bend 129 26 50S 32 2E
Big Bend Nat. Park 159 29 15N 103 15W
Big Black, R. 159 32 35N 90 30W
Big Blue, R. 158 40 20N 96 40W
Big Cr. 152 51 42N 122 41W
Big Creek 163 37 11N 119 14W
Big Cypress Swamp 157 26 12N 81 10W
Big Delta 147 64 15N 145 0W
Big Falls 158 48 11N 93 48W
Big Horn 160 46 11N 107 25W
Big Horn Mts. = Bighorn Mts. 160 44 30N 107 30W
Big Horn R. 160 45 10N 108 10W
Big Lake 159 31 12N 101 25W
Big Moose 162 43 49N 74 58W
Big Muddy, R. 158 48 25N 104 45W
Big Pine 163 37 12N 118 17W
Big Piney 160 42 32N 110 3W
Big Quill L. 153 51 55N 105 22W
Big, R. 151 54 50N 58 55W
Big Rapids 156 43 42N 85 27W
Big River 153 53 50N 107 0W
Big Sable Pt. 156 44 5N 86 30W
Big Salmon 147 61 50N 136 0W
Big Sand L. 153 57 45N 99 45W
Big Sandy 160 48 12N 110 9W
Big Sandy Cr. 158 38 52N 103 11W
Big Sioux, R. 158 44 20N 96 53W
Big Smoky Valley 163 38 30N 117 15W
Big Snowy Mt. 160 46 50N 109 15W
Big Spring 159 32 10N 101 25W
Big Springs 158 41 4N 102 3W
Big Stone City 158 45 20N 96 30W
Big Stone Gap 157 36 52N 82 45W
Big Stone L. 158 44 25N 96 35W
Big Sur 163 36 15N 121 48W
Big Trout L. 150 53 40N 90 0W
Biganos 44 44 39N 0 59W
Bigbury 30 50 17N 3 52W
Bigbury B. 30 50 18N 3 58W
Bigerymunal, Mt. 137 27 25S 120 40E
Bigfork 160 48 3N 114 2W
Biggar 153 52 4N 108 0W
Bigge I. 136 14 35S 125 10E
Biggenden 139 25 31S 152 4E
Biggleswade 29 52 6N 0 16W
Bighorn Mts. 160 44 30N 107 30W
Bignona 120 12 52N 16 23W
Bigorre 44 43 5N 0 2E
Bigstone L. 153 53 42N 95 44W
Bigtimber 160 45 53N 110 0W
Bigwa 126 7 10S 39 10E
Bihaó 63 44 49N 15 57E
Bihar 95 25 5N 85 40E
Bihar □ 95 25 0N 86 0E
Biharamulo 126 2 25S 31 25E
Biharamulo □ 126 2 30S 31 20E
Biharkeresztes 53 47 8N 21 44E
Bihé Plateau 125 12 0S 16 0E
Bihor □ 70 47 0N 22 10E
Bihor, Munţii 70 46 29N 22 47E
Bijagós, Arquipélago dos 120 11 15N 16 10W
Bijaipur 94 26 2N 77 36E
Bijapur, Mad. P., India 96 18 50N 80 50E
Bijapur, Mysore, India 96 16 50N 75 55E
Bijar 92 35 52N 47 35E
Bijeljina 66 44 46N 19 17E
Bijni 98 26 30N 90 40E
Bijnor 94 29 27N 78 11E
Bikaner 94 28 2N 73 18E
Bikapur 95 26 30N 82 7E
Bikin 77 46 50N 134 20E
Bikini, atoll 130 12 0N 167 30E
Bikoro 124 0 48S 18 15E
Bikoué 121 5 55S 11 50E
Bilād Banī Bū 'Ali 93 22 0N 59 20E
Bilara 94 26 14N 73 53E
Bilaspara 98 26 13N 90 14E
Bilaspur, India 99 22 2N 82 15E
Bilaspur, Mad. P., India 95 22 2N 82 15E
Bilaspur, Punjab, India 94 31 19N 76 50E
Bilauk Taungdan 100 13 0N 99 0E
Bilbao 58 43 16N 2 56W
Bilbor 70 47 18N 25 30E
Bildudalur 74 65 41N 23 36W
Bilecik 92 40 5N 30 5E
Bileóa 66 42 53N 18 27E
Bilibino 77 68 3N 166 20E
Bilibiza 127 12 30S 40 20E
Bilin 98 17 14N 97 15E
Bilir 77 65 40N 131 20E
Bilishti 68 40 37N 20 59E
Bill 158 43 18N 105 18W
Billa 121 8 55N 12 15E
Billabalong 137 27 25S 115 49E
Billericay 29 51 38N 0 25E
Billesdon 29 52 38N 0 56W

Billiluna Blenheim

Billiluna 136 19 37 S 127 41 E
Billimari 71 33 41 S 148 37 E
Billingham 33 54 36N 1 18W
Billinghay 33 53 5N 0 17W
Billings 160 45 43N 108 29W
Billingsfors 72 58 59N 12 15 E
Billingshurst 29 51 2N 0 28W
Billom 44 45 43N 3 20 E
Bilma 117 18 50N 13 30 E
Bilo Gora 66 45 53N 17 15 E
Biloela 138 24 24 S 150 31 E
Biloxi 159 30 30N 89 0W
Bilpa Morea Claypan 138 25 0 S 140 0 E
Bilston 28 52 34N 2 5W
Bilthoven 46 52 8N 5 12 E
Biltine 117 14 40N 20 50 E
Bilugyun 98 16 24N 97 32 E
Bilyana 138 18 5 S 145 50 E
Bilyarsk 84 54 58N 50 22 E
Bilzen 47 50 52N 5 31 E
Bima 103 8 22 S 118 49 E
Bimban 122 24 24N 32 54 E
Bimberi Peak, mt. 141 35 44 S 148 51 E
Bimbila 121 8 54N 0 5 E
Bimbo 124 4 15N 18 33 E
Bina-Etawah 94 24 13N 78 14 E
Binačka Morava, R. 66 42 30N 19 35 E
Binalbagan 103 10 12N 122 50 E
Binalong 141 34 40 S 148 39 E
Binatang 102 2 10N 111 40 E
Binbrook 33 53 26N 0 9W
Binche 47 50 26N 4 10 E
Binda 139 27 52 S 147 21 E
Bindi Bindi 137 30 37 S 116 22 E
Bindle 139 27 40 S 148 45 E
Bindura 127 17 18 S 31 18 E
Bingara, N.S.W., Austral. 139 29 52 S 150 36 E
Bingara, Queens., Austral. 139 28 10 S 144 37 E
Bingen 49 49 57N 7 53 E
Bingerville 120 5 18N 3 49W
Bingham, U.K. 33 52 57N 0 55W
Bingham, U.S.A. 151 45 5N 69 50W
Bingham Canyon 160 40 31N 112 10W
Binghamton 38 42 9N 75 54W
Bingley 32 53 51N 1 50W
Bingöl 92 39 20N 41 0 E
Binh Dinh = An Nhon 100 13 55N 109 7 E
Binh Khe 100 13 57N 108 51 E
Binh Son 100 15 20N 108 40 E
Binjai 102 3 50N 98 30 E
Binnaway 141 31 28 S 149 24 E
Binongko 103 5 55 S 123 55 E
Binscarth 153 50 37N 101 17W
Bint 93 26 22N 59 25 E
Bint Jaibail 90 33 8N 35 25 E
Bintan 102 1 0N 104 0 E
Bintulu 102 3 10N 113 0 E
Binyamina 90 32 32N 34 56 E
Binza 123 5 25N 28 40 E
Binzert = Bizerte 119 37 15N 9 50 E
Bio-Bío □ 172 37 35 S 72 0W
Bio Culma 123 7 20N 42 15 E
Biograd 63 43 56N 15 29 E
Biokovo 66 43 23N 17 0 E
Biougra 118 30 15N 9 14W
Biq'at Bet Netofa 90 32 49N 35 22 E
Bir 93 19 0N 75 54 E
Bîr Abû Hashim 122 23 42N 34 6 E
Bîr Abû M'nqar 122 26 33N 27 33 E
Bir Adal Deib 122 22 35N 36 10 E
Bir al Malfa 119 31 58N 15 18 E
Bir 'Asal 122 25 55N 34 20 E
Bir Autrun 117 18 15N 26 40 E
Bir Dhu'fân 119 31 59N 14 32 E
Bîr Diqnash 122 31 3N 25 23 E
Bir el Abbes 118 26 7N 6 9W
Bir-el-Ater 119 34 46N 8 3 E
Bîr el Basur 122 29 51N 25 49 E
Bîr el Gellaz 122 30 50N 26 40 E
Bîr el Shaqqa 122 30 54N 25 1 E
Bîr Fuad 122 30 35N 26 28 E
Bir Haimur 122 22 45N 33 40 E
Bîr Kanayis 122 24 59N 33 15 E
Bîr Kerawein 122 27 10N 28 25 E
Bir Lemouissat 118 25 0N 10 32W
Bîr Maql 122 23 7N 33 40 E
Bîr Misaha 122 22 13N 27 59 E
Bir Mogreïn, (Fort Trinquet) 116 25 10N 11 25W
Bîr Murr 122 23 28N 30 10 E
Bir Nabala 90 31 52N 35 12 E
Bîr Nakheila 122 24 1N 30 50 E
Bîr Qâtrani 122 30 55N 26 10 E
Bîr Ranga 122 24 25N 35 15 E
Bir Ras 123 12 0N 44 0 E
Bîr Sahara 122 22 54N 28 40 E
Bîr Seiyâla 122 25 10N 34 50 E
Bir Semguine 118 30 1N 5 39W
Bîr Shalatein 122 23 5N 35 25 E
Bîr Shebb 122 22 25N 29 40 E
Bîr Shût 122 23 50N 35 15 E
Bîr Terfawi 122 22 57N 28 55 E
Bîr Umm Qubûr 122 24 35N 34 2 E
Bîr Ungât 122 22 8N 33 48 E
Bîr Za'farâna 122 29 10N 32 40 E
Bîr Zãmus 119 24 16N 15 6 E
Bîr Zeidûn 122 25 45N 34 40 E
Bir Zeit 90 31 59N 35 11 E
Bira 103 2 3 S 132 2 E
Bîra 70 47 2N 27 3 E
Biramfero 120 11 40N 9 10W
Birao 117 10 20N 22 40 E
Birawa 126 2 20 S 28 48 E
Bîrca 70 43 59N 23 36 E
Birch 29 51 50N 0 54 E
Birch Hills 153 52 59N 105 25W
Birch I. 153 52 26N 99 54W
Birch L., N.W.T., Can. 152 62 4N 116 33W
Birch L., Ont., Can. 150 51 23N 92 18W
Birch L., U.S.A. 150 47 48N 91 43W
Birch Mts. 152 57 30N 113 10W
Birch River 153 52 24N 101 6W
Birchington 29 51 22N 1 18 E
Birchip 140 35 56 S 142 55 E
Birchiş 70 45 58N 22 0 E
Birchwood 143 45 55 S 167 53 E
Bird 153 56 30N 94 13W
Bird City 158 39 48N 101 33W
Bird I., Austral. 133 22 10 S 155 28 E
Bird I., S. Afr. 128 32 3 S 18 17 E
Birdaard 46 53 18N 5 53 E
Birdhip 139 35 52 S 142 50 E
Birdlip 28 51 50N 2 7W
Birdsville 138 25 51 S 139 20 E
Birdum 136 15 39 S 133 13 E
Birecik 92 37 0N 38 0 E
Bireuen 102 5 14N 96 39 E
Birhan 123 10 45N 37 55 E
Birifo 120 13 30N 14 0 E
Birigui 173 21 18 S 50 16W
Birimgan 138 22 41 S 147 25 E
Birjand 93 32 57N 59 10 E
Birk 122 18 8N 41 30 E
Birka 122 22 11N 40 38 E
Birkdale 32 53 38N 3 2W
Birkenhead, N.Z. 142 36 49 S 174 46 E
Birkenhead, U.K. 32 53 24N 3 1W
Birket Qârûn 122 29 30N 30 40 E
Birkfeld 52 47 21N 15 45 E
Birkhadem 118 36 43N 3 3 E
Bîrlad 70 46 15N 27 38 E
Birmingham, U.K. 28 52 30N 1 55W
Birmingham, U.S.A. 157 33 31N 86 50W
Birmitrapur 96 22 30N 84 10 E
Birni Ngaouré 121 13 5N 2 51 E
Birni Nkonni 121 13 55N 5 15 E
Birnin Gwari 121 11 0N 6 45 E
Birnin Kebbi 121 12 32N 4 12 E
Birnin Kudu 121 11 30N 9 29 E
Birobidzhan 77 48 50N 132 50 E
Birqin 90 32 23N 35 15 E
Birr 39 53 7N 7 55W
Birrie, R. 139 29 43 S 146 37 E
Birs, R. 50 47 24N 7 32 E
Birsilpur 94 28 11N 72 58 E
Birsk 84 55 25N 55 30 E
Birtin 70 46 59N 22 31 E
Birtle 153 50 30N 101 5W
Birtley, Northumberland, U.K. 35 55 5N 2 12W
Birtley, Tyne & Wear, U.K. 35 54 53N 1 34W
Birur 93 13 30N 75 55 E
Biryuchiy, Ostrov 82 46 10N 35 0 E
Birzai 80 56 11N 24 45 E
Bîrzava 70 46 7N 21 59 E
Bisa 103 1 10 S 127 40 E
Bisáccia 65 41 0N 15 20 E
Bisacquino 64 37 42N 13 13 E
Bisai 111 35 16N 136 44 E
Bisalpur 95 28 14N 79 48 E
Bisbal, La 48 41 58N 3 2 E
Bisbee 161 31 30N 110 0W
Biscay, B. of 14 45 0N 2 0W
Biscayne B. 157 25 40N 80 12W
Biscéglie 65 41 14N 16 30 E
Bischofshofen 52 47 26N 13 14 E
Bischofswerda 48 51 8N 14 11 E
Bischofszell 51 47 29N 9 15 E
Bischwiller 43 48 41N 7 50 E
Biscoe I. 13 66 0 S 67 0W
Biscostasing 150 47 18N 82 9W
Biscucuy 174 9 22N 69 59W
Biševo, I. 63 42 57N 16 3 E
Bisha 123 15 30N 37 31 E
Bisha, Wadi 122 20 30N 43 0 E
Bishop, Calif., U.S.A. 163 37 20N 118 26W
Bishop, Tex., U.S.A. 159 27 35N 97 49W
Bishop Auckland 33 54 40N 1 40W
Bishop's Castle 28 52 29N 3 0W
Bishop's Cleeve 28 51 56N 2 3W
Bishop's Falls 151 49 2N 55 30W
Bishop's Frome 28 52 8N 2 29W
Bishops Lydeard 28 51 4N 3 12W
Bishop's Nympton 30 50 58N 3 44W
Bishop's Stortford 29 51 52N 0 11 E
Bishop's Waltham 28 50 57N 1 13W
Bishopsteignton 30 50 32N 3 32W
Bishopstoke 28 50 58N 1 19W
Bisignano 65 30 30N 16 17 E
Bisina, L. 126 1 38N 33 56 E
Biskra 119 34 50N 5 44 E
Biskupiec 54 53 53N 20 58 E
Bislig 103 8 15N 126 27 E
Bismarck 158 46 49N 100 49W
Bismarck Arch. 135 2 30 S 150 0 E
Bismarck Ra. 135 5 35 S 145 0 E
Bismarck Sea 135 4 10 S 146 50 E
Bismark 48 52 39N 11 31 E
Biso 126 1 44N 31 26 E
Bison 158 45 34N 102 28W
Bispfors 74 63 1N 16 39 E
Bispgarden 72 63 2N 16 40 E
Bissagos = Bijagós 120 11 15N 16 10W
Bissau 120 11 45N 15 45W
Bissett 153 51 2N 95 41W
Bissikrima 120 10 50N 10 58W
Bistcho L. 152 59 45N 118 50W
Bistreţu 70 43 54N 23 23 E
Bistrica = Ilirska Bistrica 63 45 34N 14 14 E
Bistriţa 70 47 9N 24 35 E
Bistriţa Năsăud □ 70 47 15N 24 30 E
Bistriţa, R. 70 47 10N 24 30 E
Bistriţei, Munţii 70 47 15N 25 40 E
Biswan 95 27 29N 81 2 E
Bisztynek 54 54 8N 20 53 E
Bitam 124 2 5N 11 25 E
Bitche 43 48 58N 7 25 E
Bitkine 124 11 59N 18 13 E
Bitlis 92 38 20N 42 3 E
Bitola (Bitolj) 66 41 5N 21 21 E
Bitonto 65 41 7N 16 40 E
Bitter Creek 160 41 39N 108 36W
Bitter L., Gt. 122 30 15N 32 40 E
Bitter L. = Buheirat-Murrat el Kubra 122 30 15N 32 40 E
Bitterfeld 48 51 36N 12 20 E
Bitterfontein 128 31 0 S 18 32 E
Bitteroot, R. 160 46 30N 114 20W
Bitterroot Range 160 46 0N 114 20W
Bitterwater 163 36 23N 121 0W
Bitti 64 40 29N 9 20 E
Bitton 28 51 25N 2 27W
Bittou 121 11 17N 0 18W
Bitumount 152 57 26N 112 40W
Biu 121 10 40N 12 3 E
Bivolari 70 47 31N 27 27 E
Bivolu 70 47 16N 25 58 E
Biwa-Ko 111 35 15N 135 45 E
Biwabik 158 47 33N 92 19W
Biylikol, Ozero 85 43 5N 70 45 E
Biysk 76 52 40N 85 0 E
Bizana 129 30 50 S 29 52 E
Bizen 110 34 43N 134 8 E
Bizerte (Binzert) 119 37 15N 9 50 E
Bjandovan, Mys 83 39 45N 49 28 E
Bjargtangar 74 65 30N 24 30W
Bjärka-Säby 73 58 16N 15 44 E
Bjarnanes 74 64 20N 15 6W
Bjelasica 66 42 50N 19 40 E
Bjelo Polje 66 43 1N 19 45 E
Bjelovar 66 45 56N 16 49 E
Bjerringbro 73 56 23N 9 39 E
Bjórbo 72 60 27N 14 44 E
Björkhamre 72 61 24N 16 25 E
Björkhult 73 57 50N 15 40 E
Björneborg 72 59 14N 14 16 E
Bjuv 73 56 5N 12 55 E
Bla Bheinn 36 57 14N 6 7W
Blaby 28 52 34N 1 10W
Blace 66 43 18N 21 17 E
Blachownia 54 50 49N 18 56 E
Black Combe, mt. 32 54 16N 3 20W
Black Diamond 152 50 45N 114 14W
Black Esk R. 35 55 14N 3 13W
Black Forest = Schwarzwald 49 48 0N 8 0 E
Black Hd., Ireland 39 53 9N 9 18W
Black Hd., Antrim, U.K. 38 54 56N 5 42W
Black Hd., Cornwall, U.K. 30 50 1N 5 6W
Black Hills 158 44 0N 103 50W
Black I. 153 51 12N 96 30W
Black Island Sd. 162 41 10N 71 45W
Black Isle, Reg. 37 57 35N 4 15W
Black L., Can. 153 59 12N 105 15W
Black L., U.S.A. 156 45 28N 84 15W
Black Mesa, Mt. 159 36 57N 102 55W
Black Mt. = Mynydd Du 31 51 45N 3 45W
Black Mountain 141 30 18 S 151 39 E
Black Mts. 31 51 52N 3 5W
Black Pt. 137 34 30 S 119 25 E
Black R. 38 53 54N 7 42W
Black, R., Ark., U.S.A. 159 36 15N 90 45W
Black, R., N.Y., U.S.A. 162 43 59N 76 40W
Black, R., Wis., U.S.A. 158 44 18N 90 52W
Black, R., Vietnam = Da, R. 100 21 15N 105 20 E
Black Range, Mts. 161 33 30N 107 55W
Black River 166 18 0N 77 50W
Black Rock 140 32 50 S 138 44 E
Black Sea 21 43 30N 35 0 E
Black Volta, R. 120 9 0N 2 40W
Black Warrior, R. 157 33 0N 87 45W
Blackall 138 24 25 S 145 45 E
Blackball 143 42 22 S 171 26 E
Blackbull 138 17 55 S 141 45 E
Blackburn 32 53 44N 2 30W
Blackburn, Mt. 147 61 5N 142 3W
Blackbutt 139 26 51 S 152 6 E
Blackdown Hills 28 50 57N 3 15W
Blackduck 158 47 43N 94 32W
Blackfoot 160 43 13N 112 12W
Blackfoot, R. 160 47 0N 113 35W
Blackford 35 56 15N 3 48W
Blackie 152 50 36N 113 37W
Blackmoor Gate 30 51 9N 3 55W
Blackmoor Vale 28 50 54N 2 28W
Blackpool 32 53 48N 3 3W
Blackridge 138 22 35 S 147 35 E
Blackrock 39 53 18N 6 11W
Blacks Harbour 151 45 3N 66 49W
Blacksburg 156 37 17N 80 23W
Blacksod B. 38 54 6N 10 0W
Blacksod Pt. 38 54 7N 10 5W
Blackstairs Mt. 39 52 33N 6 50W
Blackstone 156 37 6N 78 0W
Blackstone, R. 152 61 5N 122 55W
Blackstone Ra. 137 26 00 S 129 00 E
Blackville 151 46 44N 65 50W
Blackwater, Austral. 138 23 35 S 148 53 E
Blackwater, Can. 152 53 20N 123 0W
Blackwater, Ireland 39 52 26N 6 20W
Blackwater Cr. 139 25 56 S 144 30 E
Blackwater, R., Limerick, Ireland 39 51 55N 7 50W
Blackwater, R., Meath, Ireland 38 53 40N 6 40W
Blackwater, R., Essex, U.K. 29 51 44N 0 53 E
Blackwater, R., Ulster, U.K. 38 54 31N 6 35W
Blackwater Res. 37 56 42N 4 45W
Blackwell 159 36 55N 97 20W
Blackwells Corner 163 35 37N 119 47W
Blackwood 35 55 40N 3 56W
Blackwood, C. 135 7 49 S 144 31 E
Bladel 47 51 22N 5 13 E
Blading 73 56 52N 14 29 E
Blädinge 73 56 52N 14 29 E
Blaenau Ffestiniog 31 53 0N 3 57W
Blaenavon 31 51 46N 3 5W
Blagaj 66 43 16N 17 55 E
Blagdon 28 51 19N 2 42W
Blagnac 44 43 38N 1 24 E
Blagodarnoye 83 45 7N 43 37 E
Blagoevgrad (Gorna Dzhumayo) 66 42 2N 23 5 E
Blagoveshchensk, Amur, U.S.S.R. 77 50 20N 127 30 E
Blagoveshchensk, Urals, U.S.S.R. 84 55 1N 55 59 E
Blagoveshchenskoye 85 43 18N 74 12 E
Blaina 31 51 46N 3 10W
Blaine 160 48 59N 122 43W
Blaine Lake 153 52 51N 106 52W
Blainville 43 48 33N 6 23 E
Blair 158 41 38N 96 10W
Blair Athol 138 22 42 S 147 31 E
Blair Atholl 37 56 46N 3 50W
Blairgowrie 37 56 36N 3 20W
Blairmore 152 49 40N 114 25W
Blaj 70 46 10N 23 57 E
Blake Pt. 158 48 12N 88 27W
Blakely 157 31 22N 85 0W
Blakeney, Glos., U.K. 28 51 45N 2 29W
Blakeney, Norfolk, U.K. 29 52 57N 1 1 E
Blâmont 43 48 35N 6 50 E
Blanc, C., Maurit. 116 20 50N 17 0W
Blanc, C., Tunisia 119 37 15N 9 56 E
Blanc, Le 44 46 37N 1 3 E
Blanc, Mont 45 45 48N 6 50 E
Blanc Sablon 151 51 24N 57 8W
Blanca, Bahía 176 39 10 S 61 30W
Blanca Peak 161 37 35N 105 29W
Blanchard 159 35 8N 97 40W
Blanche, C. 139 33 1 S 134 9 E
Blanche L., S. Austral., Austral. 139 29 15 S 139 40 E
Blanche L., W. Austral., Austral. 136 22 25 S 123 17 E
Blanco, S. Afr. 128 33 55 S 22 23 E
Blanco, U.S.A. 159 30 7N 98 30W
Blanco, C., C. Rica 166 9 34N 85 8W
Blanco, C., Peru 174 4 10 S 81 10W
Blanco, C., Spain 59 39 21N 2 51 E
Blanco, C., U.S.A. 160 42 50N 124 40W
Blanco, R. 172 31 54 S 69 42W
Blanda 74 65 20N 19 40W
Blandford Forum 28 50 52N 2 10W
Blanding 161 37 35N 109 30W
Blanes 58 41 40N 2 48 E
Blangy 43 49 14N 0 17 E
Blanice, R. 52 49 10N 14 5 E
Blankenberge 47 51 20N 3 9 E
Blankenburg 48 51 46N 10 56 E
Blanquefort 44 44 55N 0 38W
Blanquilla, La 174 11 51N 64 37W
Blanquillo 173 32 53 S 55 37W
Blansko 53 49 22N 16 40 E
Blantyre 127 15 45 S 35 0 E
Blaricum 46 52 16N 5 14 E
Blarney 39 51 57N 8 35W
Błaski 54 51 38N 18 30 E
Blatná 52 49 25N 13 52 E
Blatnitsa 67 43 41N 28 32 E
Blatten 50 46 16N 8 0 E
Blåvands Huk 75 55 33N 8 4 E
Blaydon 35 54 56N 1 47W
Blaye 44 45 8N 0 40W
Blaye-les-Mines 44 44 1N 2 8 E
Blayney 141 33 32 S 149 14 E
Blaze, Pt. 136 12 56 S 130 11 E
Błazowa 54 49 53N 22 7 E
Bleadon 28 51 18N 2 57W
Blean 29 51 18N 1 3 E
Bleasdale Moors 32 53 57N 2 40W
Bleckede 48 53 18N 10 43 E
Bled 63 46 27N 14 7 E
Blednaya, Gora 76 65 50N 65 30 E
Bléharis 47 50 31N 3 25 E
Bleiburg 52 46 35N 14 49 E
Blejeşti 70 44 19N 25 27 E
Blekinge län □ 73 56 20N 15 20 E
Blenheim 143 41 38 S 174 5 E

Bléone, R Booral

Bléone, R. 45 44 5N 6 0E
Bletchingdon 28 51 51N 1 16W
Bletchley 29 51 59N 0 44W
Bleymard, Le 44 44 30N 3 42E
Blidet Amor 119 32 59N 5 58E
Blidö 72 59 37N 18 53E
Blidsberg 73 57 56N 13 30E
Bligh Sound 143 44 47S 167 32E
Blind River 150 46 10N 82 58W
Blinishti 68 41 52N 19 58E
Blinnenhorn 51 46 26N 8 19E
Blisworth 29 52 11N 0 56W
Blitar 103 8 5S 112 11E
Blitta 121 8 23N 1 6E
Block I. 162 41 11N 71 35W
Blockley 28 52 1N 1 45W
Bloemendaal 46 52 24N 4 39E
Bloemfontein 128 29 6S 26 14E
Bloemhof 128 27 38S 25 32E
Blofield 29 52 38N 1 25E
Blois 42 47 35N 1 20E
Blokziji 46 52 43N 5 58E
Blomskog 72 59 16N 12 2E
Blonduös 74 65 40N 20 12W
Bloodsworth Is. 162 38 9N 76 3W
Bloodvein, R. 153 51 47N 96 43W
Bloody Foreland 38 55 10N 8 18W
Bloomer 158 45 8N 91 30W
Bloomfield, Iowa, U.S.A. 158 40 44N 92 26W
Bloomfield, N. Mexico, U.S.A. 161 36 46N 107 59W
Bloomfield, Nebr., U.S.A. 158 42 38N 97 15W
Bloomfield R. 138 15 56S 145 22E
Bloomingdale 162 41 33N 74 26W
Bloomington, Ill., U.S.A. 158 40 49N 89 0W
Bloomington, Ind., U.S.A. 156 39 10N 86 30W
Bloomsburg 162 41 0N 76 30W
Blora 103 6 57S 111 25E
Blossburg 162 41 40N 77 4W
Blouberg 129 23 8S 29 0E
Blountstown 157 30 28N 85 5W
Bloxham 28 52 1N 1 22W
Bludenz 52 47 10N 9 50E
Blue I. 156 41 40N 87 40W
Blue Lake 160 40 53N 124 0W
Blue Mesa Res. 161 38 30N 107 15W
Blue Mountain Lake 162 43 52N 74 30W
Blue Mountain Peak 167 18 0N 76 40W
Blue Mts., Austral. 133 33 40S 150 0E
Blue Mts., Jamaica 167 18 0N 76 40W
Blue Mts., Ore., U.S.A. 160 45 15N 119 0W
Blue Mts., Pa., U.S.A. 156 40 30N 76 0W
Blue Mud B. 138 13 30S 136 0E
Blue Nile = Nîl el Azraq 123 12 30N 34 30E
Blue Nile □ = An Nîl el Azraq □ 123 12 30N 34 30E
Blue Nile, R. = Nîl el Azraq 123 10 30N 35 0E
Blue Ridge, Mts. 157 36 30N 80 15W
Blue Stack Mts. 38 54 46N 8 5W
Blueberry, R. 152 56 45N 120 49W
Bluefield 156 37 18N 81 14W
Bluefields 166 12 0N 83 50W
Bluemull Sd. 36 60 45N 1 0W
Blueskin B. 143 45 44S 170 38E
Bluff, Austral. 138 23 35S 149 4E
Bluff, N.Z. 143 46 37S 168 20E
Bluff, U.S.A. 147 64 50N 147 15W
Bluff Downs 138 19 37S 145 30E
Bluff Harbour 143 46 36S 168 21E
Bluff Knoll, Mt. 137 34 24S 118 15E
Bluff Pt. 137 27 50S 114 5E
Bluffton 156 40 43N 85 9W
Blumenau 173 27 0S 49 0W
Blumenthal 48 53 5N 12 20E
Blümisalphorn 50 46 30N 7 47E
Blundeston 29 52 33N 1 42E
Blunt 158 44 32N 100 0W
Bly 160 42 23N 121 0W
Blyberg 72 61 9N 14 11E
Blyth, Austral. 140 33 49S 138 28E
Blyth, Northumberland, U.K. 35 55 8N 1 32W
Blyth, Notts., U.K. 33 53 22N 1 2W
Blyth Bridge 35 55 41N 3 22W
Blyth, R. 35 55 8N 1 30W
Blythburgh 29 52 19N 1 36E
Blythe 161 33 40N 114 33W
Blyton 33 53 25N 0 42W
Bo, Norway 71 59 25N 9 3E
Bo, S. Leone 120 7 55N 11 50W
Bo Duc 101 11 58N 106 50E
Bō-no-Misaki 110 31 15N 130 13E
Boa I. 38 54 30N 7 50W
Boa Nova 171 14 22S 40 10W
Boa Viagem 170 5 7S 39 44W
Boa Vista 174 2 48N 60 30W
Boaco 166 12 29N 85 35W
Boal 56 43 25N 6 49W
Boat of Garten 37 57 15N 3 45W
Boatman 139 27 16S 146 55E
Bobadah 141 32 19S 146 41E
Bobbili 96 18 35N 83 30E
Bòbbio 62 44 47N 9 22E
Bobcaygeon 150 44 33N 78 33W
Böblingen 57 48 41N 9 1E
Bobo-Dioulasso 120 11 8N 4 13W
Boboc 67 45 13N 26 59E
Bobolice 54 53 58N 16 37E
Boboshevo 66 42 9N 23 0E
Bobov Dol 66 42 20N 23 0E
Bóbr, R. 54 51 50N 15 15E
Bobrinets 82 48 4N 32 5E
Bobrov 81 51 5N 40 2E
Bobruysk 80 53 10N 29 15E
Bobures 174 9 15N 71 11W
Boca de Uracoa 174 9 8N 62 20W
Bôca do Acre 174 8 50S 67 27W
Bocage 41 49 0N 1 0W
Bocaiúva 171 17 7S 43 49W
Bocanda 120 7 5N 4 31W
Bocaranga 117 7 0N 15 35E
Bocas del Dragon 174 11 0N 61 50W
Bocas del Toro 166 9 15N 82 20W
Bocdam 36 59 55N 1 16W
Boceguillas 58 41 20N 3 39W
Bochnia 54 49 58N 20 27E
Bocholt, Belg. 47 51 10N 5 35E
Bocholt, Ger. 48 51 50N 6 35E
Bochov 52 50 9N 13 3E
Bochum 48 51 28N 7 12E
Bockenem 48 52 1N 10 8E
Bocoyna 164 27 52N 107 35W
Bocq, R. 47 50 20N 4 55E
Boçsa Montanǔ 66 45 21N 21 47E
Boda 124 4 19N 17 26E
Böda 73 57 15N 17 3E
Boda 74 57 15N 17 0E
Bodaybo 77 57 50N 114 0E
Boddam 37 57 28N 1 46W
Boddington 137 32 50S 116 30E
Bodedern 31 53 17N 4 29W
Bodegraven 46 52 5N 4 46E
Boden 74 65 50N 21 42E
Bodenham 28 52 9N 2 41W
Bodensee 51 47 35N 9 25E
Bodenteich 48 52 49N 10 41E
Boderg, L. 38 53 52N 8 0W
Bodhan 96 18 40N 77 55E
Bodiam 29 51 1N 0 33E
Bodinayakkanur 97 10 2N 77 10E
Bodinga 121 12 58N 5 10E
Bodinnick 30 50 20N 4 37W
Bodio 51 46 23N 8 55E
Bodmin 30 50 28N 4 44W
Bodmin Moor 30 50 33N 4 36W
Bodø 74 67 17N 14 24E
Bodrog, R. 53 48 15N 21 35E
Bodrum 92 37 5N 27 30E
Bódva, R. 53 48 19N 20 45E
Bodyke 39 52 53N 8 38W
Boechout 47 51 10N 4 30E
Boegoebergdam 128 29 7S 22 9E
Boekelo 46 52 12N 6 49E
Boelenslaan 46 53 10N 6 10E
Boën 45 45 44N 4 0E
Boende 124 0 24S 21 12E
Boerne 159 29 48N 98 41W
Boertange 46 53 1N 7 12E
Boezinge 47 50 54N 2 52E
Boffa 120 10 16N 14 3W
Bofin L. 38 53 51N 7 55W
Bofors 72 59 19N 14 34E
Bogale 98 21 16N 92 24E
Bogalusa 159 30 50N 89 55W
Bogan Gate 141 33 7S 147 49E
Bogan, R. 141 32 45S 148 8E
Bogantungan 138 23 41S 147 17E
Bogata 159 33 26N 95 10W
Bogatió 66 44 51N 19 30E
Bogdan, Mt. 67 42 37N 24 20E
Bogdanovitch 84 56 47N 62 1E
Bogenfels 125 27 25S 15 25E
Bogense 73 55 34N 10 5E
Boggabilla 139 28 36S 150 24E
Boggabri 141 30 45S 150 0E
Boggeragh Mts. 39 52 2N 8 55W
Boghari = Ksar el Boukhari 118 35 51N 2 52E
Bogia 135 4 9S 145 0E
Bognor Regis 29 50 47N 0 40W
Bogø 73 54 55N 12 2E
Bogo 103 11 3N 124 0E
Bogodukhov 80 50 9N 35 33E
Bogong, Mt. 141 36 47S 147 17E
Bogor 103 6 36S 106 48E
Bogoro 121 9 37N 9 29E
Bogoroditsk 81 53 47N 38 8E
Bogorodsk 81 56 4N 43 30E
Bogorodskoye 77 52 22N 140 30E
Bogoso 120 5 38N 2 3W
Bogotá 174 4 34N 74 0W
Bogotol 76 56 15N 89 50E
Bogra 98 24 51N 89 22E
Boguchany 77 58 40N 97 30E
Boguchar 83 49 55N 40 32E
Bogué 120 16 45N 14 10W
Boguslav 82 49 47N 30 53E
Boguszów Lubawka 54 50 43N 15 56E
Bohain 43 49 59N 3 28E
Bohemia 52 50 0N 14 0E
Bohemia Downs 136 18 53S 126 14E
Bohemian Forest = Böhmerwald 49 49 30N 12 40E
Bohena Cr. 139 30 17S 149 42E
Boheraphuca 39 53 1N 7 45W
Bohinjska Bistrica 63 46 17N 14 1E
Böhmerwald 49 49 30N 12 40E
Bohmte 48 52 24N 8 20E
Bohola 38 53 54N 9 4W
Boholl, I. 103 9 50N 124 10E
Bohotleh 91 8 20N 46 25E
Boi 121 9 35N 9 27E
Boi, Pta. de 173 23 55S 45 15W
Boiano 65 41 28N 14 29E
Boiestown 151 46 27N 66 26W
Boigu I. 138 9 15S 143 30E
Boileau, C. 136 17 40S 122 7E
Boipeba, I. de 171 13 39S 38 55W
Bois, Les 50 47 11N 6 50E
Bois, R. 171 18 35S 50 2W
Boischot 47 51 3N 4 47E
Boisdale L. 36 57 9N 7 19W
Boise 160 43 43N 116 9W
Boise City 159 36 45N 102 30W
Boissevain 153 49 15N 100 0W
Boite, R. 63 46 24N 12 13E
Boitzenburg 48 55 16N 13 36E
Boizenburg 48 53 22N 10 42E
Bojador C. 116 26 0N 14 30W
Bojanow 54 51 43N 16 42E
Bøjden 73 55 6N 10 7E
Bojnurd 93 37 30N 57 20E
Bojonegoro 103 7 11S 111 54E
Boju 121 7 22N 7 55E
Boka 66 45 22N 20 52E
Boka Kotorska 66 42 23N 18 32E
Bokala 120 8 31N 4 33W
Boké 120 10 56N 14 17W
Bokhara, R. 139 29 55S 146 42E
Bokkos 121 9 17N 9 1E
Boknafjorden 71 59 14N 5 40E
Bokombayevskoye 85 47 7N 77 0E
Bokoro 117 12 25N 17 14E
Bokote 124 0 12S 21 8E
Bokpyin 101 11 18N 98 42E
Boksitogorsk 80 59 32N 33 56E
Bokungu 124 0 35S 22 50E
Bol, Chad 124 13 30N 15 0E
Bol, Yugo. 63 43 18N 16 38E
Bolama 120 11 30N 15 30W
Bolan Pass 93 29 50N 67 20E
Bolangum 140 36 42S 142 54E
Bolaños, R. 164 22 0N 104 10W
Bolbec 42 49 30N 0 30E
Bolchereche 76 56 4N 74 45E
Boldeşti 70 45 3N 26 2E
Bole 123 6 36N 37 20E
Bolekhov 80 49 0N 24 0E
Bolesławiec 54 51 17N 15 37E
Bolgary 78 55 3N 48 50E
Bolgatanga 121 10 44N 0 53W
Bolgrad 82 45 40N 28 32E
Boli 123 6 2N 28 48E
Bolinao C. 103 16 30N 119 55E
Bolívar, Argent. 172 36 15S 60 53W
Bolívar, Antioquia, Colomb. 174 5 50N 76 1W
Bolívar, Cauca, Colomb. 174 2 0N 77 0W
Bolivar, Mo., U.S.A. 159 37 38N 93 22W
Bolivar, Tenn., U.S.A. 159 35 14N 89 0W
Bolívar □ 174 9 0N 74 40W
Bolivia ■ 174 17 6S 64 0W
Boljevac 66 43 51N 21 58E
Bolkhov 81 53 25N 36 0E
Bollène 45 44 18N 4 45E
Bollington 32 53 18N 2 8W
Bollnäs 72 61 21N 16 24E
Bollon 139 28 2S 147 29E
Bollstabruk 72 63 1N 17 40E
Bollullos 57 37 19N 6 32W
Bolmen 73 56 55N 13 40E
Bolney 29 50 59N 0 11W
Bolo Silase 123 8 51N 39 27E
Bolobo 124 2 6S 16 20E
Bologna 63 44 30N 11 20E
Bologne 43 48 10N 5 8E
Bologoye 80 57 55N 34 0E
Bolomba 124 0 35N 19 0E
Bolonchenticul 165 20 0N 89 49W
Bolong 103 6 6N 122 16E
Bolotovskoye 84 58 31N 62 28E
Boloven, Cao Nguyen 100 15 10N 106 30E
Bolpur 95 23 40N 87 45E
Bolsena 63 42 40N 11 58E
Bolsena, L. di 63 42 35N 11 55E
Bolshaya Glushitsa 81 52 24N 50 29E
Bolshaya Khobda, R. 84 50 50N 54 53E
Bolshaya Kinel, R. 84 53 14N 50 30E
Bolshaya Lepetrikha 82 47 11N 33 57E
Bolshaya Martynovka 83 47 12N 41 46E
Bolshaya Shatan, Gora 84 53 37N 58 3E
Bolshevik, Ostrov 77 78 30N 102 0E
Bolshezemelskaya Tundra 78 67 0N 56 0E
Bolshoi Kavkas 83 42 50N 44 0E
Bolshoi Tuters, O. 80 59 44N 26 57E
Bolshoy Atlym 76 62 25N 66 50E
Bolshoy Tokmak 82 47 16N 35 42E
Bol'soj T'uters, O. 80 59 44N 26 57E
Bolsover 33 53 14N 1 18W
Bolsward 46 53 3N 5 32E
Bolt Head 30 50 13N 3 48W
Bolt Tail 30 50 13N 3 55W
Boltaña 58 42 28N 0 4E
Boltigen 50 46 38N 7 24E
Bolton 32 53 35N 2 26W
Bolton Abbey 32 53 59N 1 53W
Bolton by Bowland 32 53 56N 2 21W
Bolton Landing 162 43 32N 73 35W
Bolton le Sands 32 54 7N 2 49W
Bolton-on-Dearne 33 53 31N 1 19W
Bolu 92 40 45N 31 35E
Bolubolu 135 9 21S 150 20E
Bolus Hd. 39 51 48N 10 20W
Bolvadin 92 38 45N 31 57E
Bolzano (Bozen) 63 46 30N 11 20E
Bom Conselho 170 9 42S 37 26W
Bom Despacho 171 19 43S 45 15W
Bom Jardim 171 7 47S 35 35W
Bom Jesus 170 9 4S 44 22W
Bom Jesus da Gurguéia, Serra 170 9 0S 43 0W
Bom Jesus da Lapa 171 13 15S 43 25W
Boma 124 5 50S 13 4E
Bomaderry 141 34 52S 150 37E
Bōmba, Khalīj 117 32 20N 23 15E
Bomba, La 164 31 53N 115 2W
Bombala 141 36 56S 149 15E
Bombarral 57 39 15N 9 9W
Bombay 96 18 55N 72 50E
Bomboma 124 2 25N 18 55E
Bombombwa 126 2 18N 19 3E
Bomi Hills 120 7 1N 10 38E
Bomili 126 1 45N 27 5E
Bomokandi, R. 126 3 10N 28 15E
Bomongo 124 1 27N 18 21E
Bomu, R. 124 4 40N 23 30E
Bon C. 119 37 1N 11 2E
Bon Sar Pa 100 12 24N 107 35E
Bonaduz 15 46 49N 9 25E
Bonaire, I. 167 12 10N 68 15W
Bonang 141 37 11S 148 41E
Bonanza 166 13 54N 84 35W
Bonaparte Archipelago 136 14 0S 124 30E
Boñar 56 42 52N 5 19W
Bonarbridge 37 57 53N 4 20W
Bonäset 72 63 16N 18 45E
Bonaventure 151 48 5N 65 32W
Bonavista 151 48 40N 53 5W
Bonavista, C. 151 48 42N 53 5W
Bonchester Bri. 35 55 23N 2 36W
Bonchurch 28 50 36N 1 11W
Bondeno 63 44 53N 11 22E
Bondo 124 3 55N 23 53E
Bondoukoro 120 9 51N 4 25W
Bondoukou 120 8 2N 2 47W
Bondowoso 120 7 56S 113 49E
Bondyug 84 60 29N 55 56E
Bone Rate, I. 103 7 25S 121 5E
Bone Rate, Kepulauan 103 6 30S 121 10E
Bone, Teluk 103 4 10S 120 50E
Bonefro 65 41 42N 14 55E
Bo'ness 35 56 0N 3 38W
Bong Son = Hoai Nhon 100 14 26N 109 1E
Bongandanga 124 1 24N 21 3E
Bonge 123 6 5N 37 16E
Bongor 117 10 35N 15 20E
Bongouanou 120 6 42N 4 15W
Bonham 159 33 30N 96 10W
Bonherden 47 51 1N 4 32E
Bonifacio 45 41 24N 9 10E
Bonifacio, Bouches de 64 41 12N 9 15E
Bonin Is. 130 27 0N 142 0E
Bonito de Santa Fé 171 7 19S 38 31W
Bonn 48 50 43N 7 6E
Bonnat 44 46 20N 1 53E
Bonne B. 151 40 31N 58 0W
Bonne Espérance, I. 151 51 24N 57 40W
Bonne Terre 159 37 55N 90 38W
Bonners Ferry 160 48 38N 116 21W
Bonnert 47 49 43N 5 49E
Bonnétable 42 48 11N 0 25E
Bonneuil Matours 42 46 41N 0 34E
Bonneville 45 46 5N 6 24E
Bonney, L. 140 37 50S 140 20E
Bonnie Doon 141 37 2S 145 53E
Bonnie Rock 137 30 29S 118 22E
Bonny, France 43 47 34N 2 50E
Bonny, Nigeria 121 4 25N 7 13E
Bonny, Bight of 121 3 30N 9 20E
Bonny, R. 121 4 20N 7 14E
Bonnyrigg 35 55 52N 3 8W
Bonnyville 153 54 20N 110 45W
Bonoi 103 1 45S 137 41E
Bonorva 64 40 25N 8 47E
Bonsall 163 33 16N 117 14W
Bontang 102 0 10N 117 30E
Bonthain 103 5 34S 119 56E
Bonthe 120 7 30N 12 33W
Bonyeri 120 5 1N 2 46W
Bonyhád 53 46 18N 18 32E
Bonython Ra. 136 23 40S 128 45E
Boogardie 137 28 2S 117 45E
Bookabie P.O. 137 31 50S 132 41E
Booker 159 36 29N 100 30W
Boolaboolka, L. 140 32 38S 143 10E
Boolarra 141 38 20S 146 20E
Boolathanna 137 21 40S 113 41E
Boolcoomata 140 31 57S 140 33E
Booleroo Centre 140 32 53S 138 21E
Booligal 141 33 58S 144 53E
Booloo Downs 137 23 52S 119 33E
Boom 47 51 6N 4 20E
Boonah 139 27 58S 152 41E
Boondall 108 27 20S 153 4E
Boone, Iowa, U.S.A. 158 42 5N 93 53W
Boone, N.C., U.S.A. 157 36 14N 81 43W
Booneville, Ark., U.S.A. 159 35 10N 93 54W
Booneville, Miss., U.S.A. 157 34 39N 88 34W
Boongoondoo 138 22 55S 145 55E
Boonville, Ind., U.S.A. 156 38 3N 87 13W
Boonville, Mo., U.S.A. 158 38 57N 92 45W
Boonville, N.Y., U.S.A. 162 43 31N 75 20W
Booral 141 32 30S 151 56E

Boorindal Bramminge

Boorindal 139 30 22 S 146 11 E
Booroomugga 141 31 17 S 146 27 E
Boorowa 141 34 28 S 148 44 E
Boot 32 54 24N 3 18W
Boothia, Gulf of 149 71 0N 91 0W
Boothia Pen. 148 71 0N 94 0W
Bootle, Cumb., U.K. 32 54 17N 3 24W
Bootle, Merseysude, U.K. 32 53 28N 3 1W
Booué 124 0 5 S 11 55 E
Bopeechee 139 29 36 S 137 22 E
Bophuthatswana □ 126 26 0 S 26 0 E
Bopo 79 7 33N 7 50 E
Boppard 49 50 13N 7 36 E
Boquete 166 8 46N 82 27W
Boquillas 164 29 17N 102 53W
Bor 52 49 41N 12 45 E
Bôr 123 6 10N 31 40 E
Bor, Sweden 73 57 9N 14 10 E
Bor, Yugo. 66 44 8N 22 7 E
Borah, Mt. 160 44 19N 113 46W
Borang 123 4 50N 30 59 E
Borås 73 57 43N 12 56 E
Borås 73 57 43N 12 56 E
Borazjan 93 29 22N 51 10 E
Borba, Brazil 174 4 12 S 59 34W
Borba, Port. 57 38 50N 7 26W
Borborema, Planalto da 170 7 0 S 37 0W
Borçka 83 41 25N 41 41 E
Borculo 46 52 7N 6 31 E
Borda, C. 140 35 45 S 136 34 E
Bordeaux 44 44 50N 0 36W
Borden, Austral. 137 34 3 S 118 12 E
Borden, Can. 151 46 18N 63 47W
Borden I. 12 78 30N 111 30W
Borders □ 35 55 45N 2 50W
Bordertown 140 36 19 S 140 45 E
Borðeyri 74 65 12N 21 6W
Bordighera 62 43 47N 7 40 E
Bordj bou Arridj 119 36 4N 4 45 E
Bordj Djeneiene 119 31 47N 10 3 E
Bordj el Hobra 119 32 9N 4 51 E
Bordj Fly Ste. Marie 118 27 19N 2 32W
Bordj-in-Eker 119 24 9N 5 3 E
Bordj Ménaiel 119 36 46N 3 43 E
Bordj Nili 118 33 28N 3 2 E
Bordj Zelfana 119 32 27N 4 15 E
Bordoba 85 39 31N 73 16 E
Bordon Camp 29 51 6N 0 52W
Borea Creek 141 35 5 S 146 35 E
Borehamwood 29 51 40N 0 15W
Borek Wlkp. 54 51 54N 17 11 E
Boreland 35 55 12N 3 16W
Boremore 141 33 15 S 149 0 E
Borensberg 73 58 34N 15 17 E
Borgarnes 74 64 32N 21 55W
Borgefjellet 74 65 20N 13 45 E
Borger, Neth. 46 52 54N 6 33 E
Borger, U.S.A. 159 35 40N 101 20W
Borgerhout 47 51 12N 4 28 E
Borghamn 73 58 23N 14 41 E
Borgholm 73 56 52N 16 39 E
Bórgia 65 38 50N 16 30 E
Borgie R. 37 58 28N 4 20W
Borgo San Dalmazzo 62 44 19N 7 29 E
Borgo San Lorenzo 63 43 57N 11 21 E
Borgo Val di Taro 62 44 29N 9 47 E
Borgomanero 62 45 41N 8 28 E
Borgonovo Val Tidone 62 45 1N 9 28 E
Borgorose 63 42 12N 13 14 E
Borgosésia 62 45 43N 8 17 E
Borgvattnet 72 63 26N 15 48 E
Borhaug 71 58 6N 6 33 E
Borikhane 100 18 33N 103 43 E
Borisoglebsk 81 51 27N 42 5 E
Borisoglebskiy 81 56 28N 43 59 E
Borisov 80 54 17N 28 28 E
Borisovka 85 43 15N 68 10 E
Borisovo-Sudskoye 81 59 58N 35 57 E
Borispol 80 50 21N 30 59 E
Borja, Peru 174 4 20 S 77 40W
Borja, Spain 58 41 48N 1 34W
Borjas Blancas 58 41 31N 0 52 E
Borkou 117 18 15N 18 50 E
Borlänge 72 60 29N 15 26 E
Borley, C. 13 66 15 S 52 30 E
Bormida, R. 62 44 35N 8 10 E
Bórmio 62 46 28N 10 22 E
Born 47 51 2N 5 49 E
Borna 48 51 8N 12 31 E
Borndiep, Str. 46 53 27N 5 35 E
Borne 46 52 18N 6 46 E
Bornem 47 51 6N 4 14 E
Borneo, I. 102 1 0N 115 0 E
Bornholm, I. 73 55 10N 15 0 E
Bornholmsgattet 73 55 15N 14 20 E
Borno □ 121 12 30N 12 30 E
Bornos 57 36 48N 5 42W
Bornu Yassa 121 12 14N 12 25 E
Borodino 80 55 31N 35 40 E
Borogontsy 77 62 42N 131 8 E
Boromo 120 11 45N 2 58W
Boron 163 35 0N 117 39W
Boronga Is. 98 19 58N 93 6 E
Borongan 103 11 37N 125 26 E
Bororen 138 24 13 S 151 33 E
Borotangba Mts. 123 6 30N 25 0 E
Boroughbridge 33 54 6N 1 23W
Borovan 67 43 27N 23 45 E
Borovichi 80 58 25N 33 55 E
Borovsk, Moscow, U.S.S.R. 81 55 12N 36 24 E
Borovsk, Urals, U.S.S.R. 84 59 43N 56 40 E
Borovskoye 84 53 48N 64 12 E
Borradaile, Mt. 136 12 5 S 132 51 E
Borrby 73 55 27N 14 10 E
Borrego Springs 163 33 15N 116 23W
Borriol 58 40 4N 0 4W
Borris 39 52 36N 6 57W
Borris-in-Ossory 39 52 57N 7 40W
Borrisokane 39 53 0N 8 8W
Borrisoleigh 39 52 48N 7 58W
Borroloola 138 16 4 S 136 17 E
Borrowdale 32 54 31N 3 10W
Borsa 70 47 41N 24 50 E
Borsod-Abaúj-Zemplén □ 53 48 20N 21 0 E
Borssele 47 51 26N 3 45 E
Bort-les-Orgues 44 45 24N 2 29 E
Borth 31 52 29N 4 3W
Borujerd 92 33 55N 48 50 E
Borve 36 58 25N 6 28W
Borzhomi 83 41 48N 43 28 E
Borzna 80 51 18N 32 26 E
Borzya 77 50 24N 116 31 E
Bos. Dubica 63 45 10N 16 50 E
Bos. Gradiška 66 45 10N 17 15 E
Bos. Grahovo 63 44 12N 16 26 E
Bos. Kostajnica 63 45 11N 16 33 E
Bos. Krupa 63 44 53N 16 10 E
Bos. Novi 63 45 2N 16 22 E
Bos. Petrovac 63 44 35N 16 21 E
Bos. Samac 66 45 3N 18 29 E
Bosa 64 40 17N 8 32 E
Bosaga 85 37 33N 65 41 E
Bosanska Brod 66 45 10N 18 0 E
Bosanski Novi 63 45 2N 16 22 E
Bosavi, Mt. 135 6 30 S 142 49 E
Bosbury 28 52 5N 2 27W
Boscastle 30 50 42N 4 42W
Boscotrecase 65 40 46N 14 28 E
Bosham 29 50 50N 0 51W
Boshoek 128 25 30 S 27 9 E
Boshof 128 28 31 S 25 13 E
Boshrūyeh 93 33 50N 57 30 E
Bosilegrad 66 42 30N 22 27 E
Boskoop 46 52 4N 4 40 E
Boskovice 53 49 29N 16 40 E
Bosna i Hercegovina □ 66 44 0N 18 0 E
Bosna, R. 66 44 50N 18 10 E
Bosnia = Bosna 66 44 0N 18 0 E
Bosnik 103 1 5 S 136 10 E
Bōsō-Hantō 111 35 20N 140 20 E
Bosobolo 124 4 15N 19 50 E
Bosporus = Karadeniz Boğazı 92 41 10N 29 10 E
Bossangoa 117 6 35N 17 30 E
Bossekop 74 69 57N 23 15 E
Bossembélé 117 5 25N 17 40 E
Bossier City 159 32 28N 93 38W
Bosso 121 13 43N 13 19 E
Bossut C. 136 18 42 S 121 35 E
Boston, U.K. 33 52 59N 0 2W
Boston, U.S.A. 162 42 20N 71 0W
Boston Bar 152 49 52N 121 22W
Bosut, R. 66 45 5N 19 2 E
Boswell, Can. 152 49 28N 116 45W
Boswell, U.S.A. 159 34 1N 95 30W
Botad 94 22 15N 71 40 E
Botany Bay 139 34 0 S 151 14 E
Botene 100 17 35N 101 12 E
Botevgrad 67 42 55N 23 47 E
Bothaville 128 27 23 S 26 34 E
Bothel 32 54 43N 3 16W
Bothnia, G. of 74 63 0N 21 0 E
Bothwell 138 42 20 S 147 1 E
Boticas 56 41 41N 7 40W
Botletle R. 128 20 10 S 24 10 E
Botoroaga 70 44 8N 25 32 E
Botoşani 70 47 42N 26 41 E
Botoşani □ 70 47 50N 26 50 E
Botro 120 7 51N 5 19W
Botswana ■ 125 22 0 S 24 0 E
Bottesford 33 52 57N 0 48W
Bottineau 158 48 49N 100 25W
Bottrop 48 51 34N 6 59 E
Botucatu 173 22 55 S 48 30W
Botwood 151 49 6N 55 23W
Bou Alam 118 33 50N 1 26 E
Bou Ali 118 27 11N 0 4W
Bou Djébéha 120 18 25N 2 45W
Bou Garfa 118 27 4N 7 59W
Bou Guema 118 28 49N 0 19 E
Bou Iblane, Djebel 118 33 50N 4 0W
Bou Ismail 118 36 38N 2 42 E
Bou Izakarn 118 29 12N 6 46W
Bou Kahil, Djebel 118 34 22N 9 23 E
Bou Saâda 119 35 11N 4 9 E
Bou Salem 119 36 45N 9 2 E
Bouaké 120 7 40N 5 2W
Bouar 124 6 0N 15 40 E
Bouârfa 118 32 32N 1 58 E
Bouca 117 6 45N 18 25 E
Boucau 44 43 32N 1 29W
Boucaut B. 138 12 0 S 134 25 E
Bouches-du-Rhône □ 45 43 37N 5 2 E
Bouda 118 27 50N 0 27W
Boudenib 118 31 59N 3 31W
Boudry 50 46 57N 6 50 E
Boufarik 118 36 34N 2 58 E
Bougainville C. 136 13 57 S 126 4 E
Bougainville I. 135 6 0 S 155 0 E
Bougainville Reef 138 15 30 S 147 5 E
Bougaroun, C. 119 37 6N 6 30 E
Bougie = Béjaïa 119 36 42N 5 2 E
Bougouni 120 11 30N 7 20W
Bouillon 47 49 44N 5 3 E
Bouïra 119 36 20N 3 59 E
Boujad 118 32 46N 6 24W
Bouladuff 39 52 42N 7 55W
Boulder, Austral. 132 30 46 S 121 30 E
Boulder, Colo., U.S.A. 158 40 3N 105 10W
Boulder, Mont., U.S.A. 160 46 14N 112 4W
Boulder City 161 36 0N 114 50W
Boulder Creek 163 37 7N 122 7W
Boulder Dam = Hoover Dam 161 36 0N 114 45W
Bouleau, Lac au 150 47 40N 77 35W
Boulhaut 118 33 30N 7 1W
Boulia 138 22 52 S 139 51 E
Bouligny 43 49 17N 5 45 E
Boulogne, R. 42 46 50N 1 25W
Boulogne-sur-Gesse 44 43 18N 0 38 E
Boulogne-sur-Mer 43 50 42N 1 36 E
Boulsa 121 12 39N 0 34W
Boultoum 121 14 45N 10 25 E
Boumalne 118 31 25N 6 0W
Boun Neua 100 21 38N 101 54 E
Boun Tai 100 21 23N 101 58 E
Bouna 120 9 10N 3 0W
Boundary 147 64 11N 141 2W
Boundary Pk. 163 37 51N 118 21W
Boundiali 120 9 30N 6 20W
Bountiful 160 40 57N 111 58W
Bounty I. 130 46 0 S 180 0 E
Bour Khaya 77 71 50N 133 10 E
Bourbon-l'Archambault 44 46 36N 3 4 E
Bourbon-Lancy 44 46 37N 3 45 E
Bourbonnais 44 46 28N 3 0 E
Bourbonne 43 47 59N 5 45 E
Bourem 121 17 0N 0 24W
Bourg 44 45 3N 0 34W
Bourg-Argental 45 45 18N 4 32 E
Bourg-de-Péage 45 45 2N 5 3 E
Bourg-en-Bresse 45 46 13N 5 12 E
Bourg-St.-Andéol 45 44 23N 4 39 E
Bourg-St.-Maurice 45 45 35N 6 46 E
Bourg-St.-Pierre 50 45 57N 7 12 E
Bourganeuf 44 45 57N 1 45 E
Bourges 43 47 9N 2 25 E
Bourget, L. du 45 45 44N 5 52 E
Bourgneuf 42 47 2N 1 58W
Bourgneuf, B. de 42 47 3N 2 10W
Bourgneuf, Le 42 48 10N 0 59W
Bourgogne 43 47 0N 4 30 E
Bourgoin-Jallieu 45 45 36N 5 17 E
Bourke 139 30 8 S 145 55 E
Bourlamaque 150 48 5N 77 56W
Bourne 29 52 46N 0 22W
Bournemouth 28 50 43N 1 53W
Bourriot-Bergonce 44 44 7N 0 14W
Bourton-on-the-Water 28 51 53N 1 45W
Bouscat, Le 44 44 53N 0 32W
Boussac 44 46 22N 2 13 E
Boussens 44 43 12N 0 58 E
Bousso 117 10 34N 16 52 E
Boussu 47 50 26N 3 48 E
Bouthillier, Le 151 47 47N 64 55W
Boutilimit 120 17 45N 14 40W
Bouvet I. 15 55 0 S 3 30 E
Bouznika 118 33 46N 7 6W
Bouzonville 43 49 17N 6 32 E
Bova Marina 65 37 59N 15 56 E
Bovalino Marina 65 38 9N 16 10 E
Bovec 63 46 20N 13 33 E
Bovenkarspel 46 52 41N 5 14 E
Bóves 62 44 19N 7 29 E
Boves 62 44 19N 7 33 E
Bovey Tracey 30 50 36N 3 40W
Bovigny 47 50 12N 5 55 E
Bovill 160 46 58N 116 27W
Bovino 65 41 15N 15 20 E
Bow Island 152 49 50N 111 23W
Bow, R. 152 51 10N 115 0W
Bowbells 158 48 47N 102 19W
Bowdle 158 45 30N 100 2W
Bowelling 137 33 25 S 116 30 E
Bowen 138 20 0 S 148 16 E
Bowen Mts. 141 37 0 S 148 0 E
Bowen, R. 138 20 24 S 147 20 E
Bowes 32 54 31N 1 59W
Bowie, U.S.A. 162 39 0N 76 47W
Bowie, Ariz., U.S.A. 161 32 15N 109 30W
Bowie, Tex., U.S.A. 159 33 33N 97 50W
Bowland, Forest of 32 54 0N 2 30W
Bowling Green, Ky., U.S.A. 156 37 0N 86 25W
Bowling Green, Ohio, U.S.A. 156 41 22N 83 40W
Bowling Green, Va., U.S.A. 162 38 3N 77 21W
Bowling Green, C. 138 19 19 S 147 25 E
Bowman 158 46 12N 103 21W
Bowman, I. 13 65 0 S 104 0 E
Bowmans 140 34 10 S 138 17 E
Bowmanville 150 43 55N 78 41W
Bowmore 34 55 45N 6 18W
Bowness, Can. 152 50 55N 114 25W
Bowness, Solway, U.K. 32 54 57N 3 13W
Bowness, Windermere, U.K. 32 54 22N 2 56W
Bowral 141 34 26 S 150 27 E
Bowraville 139 30 37 S 152 52 E
Bowron, R. 152 54 3N 121 50W
Bowser L. 152 56 30N 129 30W
Bowsman 153 52 14N 101 12W
Bowutu Mts. 135 7 45 S 147 10 E
Bowwood 127 17 5 S 26 20 E
Box 28 51 24N 2 16W
Box Hill 29 51 16N 0 16W
Boxelder Creek 160 47 20N 108 30W
Boxholm 73 58 12N 15 3 E
Boxley 29 51 17N 0 34 E
Boxmeer 47 51 38N 5 56 E
Boxtel 47 51 36N 5 9 E
Boyabat 82 41 28N 34 42 E
Boyacá □ 174 5 30N 72 30W
Boyanup 137 33 30 S 115 40 E
Boyce 159 31 25N 92 39W
Boyd L. 150 61 30N 103 20W
Boyer, R. 152 58 27N 115 57W
Boyle 38 53 58N 8 19W
Boyne City 156 45 13N 85 1W
Boyne, R. 38 53 40N 6 34W
Boynton Beach 157 26 31N 80 3W
Boyoma, Chutes 124 0 12N 25 25 E
Boyup Brook 137 33 50 S 116 23 E
Bozburun 69 36 43N 28 8 E
Bozcaada 68 39 49N 26 3 E
Bozeat 29 52 14N 0 41W
Bozeman 160 45 40N 111 0W
Bozepole Wlk. 54 54 33N 17 56 E
Bozevac 66 44 32N 21 24 E
Bozouls 44 44 28N 2 43 E
Bozoum 117 6 25N 16 35 E
Bozovici 70 44 56N 22 1 E
Bra 62 44 41N 7 50 E
Brabant □ 47 50 46N 4 30 E
Brabant L. 153 54 18N 108 5W
Brabrand 73 56 9N 10 7 E
BraC 63 43 20N 16 40 E
Bracadale 36 57 22N 6 24W
Bracadale, L. 36 57 20N 6 30W
Bracciano 63 42 6N 12 10 E
Bracciano, L. di 63 42 8N 12 11 E
Bracebridge 150 45 2N 79 19W
Bracebridge Heath 33 53 13N 0 32W
Brach 119 27 31N 14 20 E
Bracieux 43 47 30N 1 30 E
Bräcke 72 62 45N 15 26 E
Brackettville 159 29 21N 100 20W
Brackley 28 52 3N 1 9W
Bracknell 29 51 24N 0 45W
Braco 35 56 16N 3 55W
Brad 70 46 10N 22 50 E
Brădano, R. 65 40 41N 16 20 E
Bradda Hd. 32 54 6N 4 46W
Bradenton 157 27 25N 82 35W
Bradford, U.K. 33 53 47N 1 45W
Bradford, Pa., U.S.A. 156 41 58N 78 41W
Bradford, Vt., U.S.A. 162 43 59N 72 9W
Bradford-on-Avon 28 51 20N 2 15W
Brading 28 50 41N 1 9W
Bradley, Ark., U.S.A. 159 33 7N 93 39W
Bradley, Calif., U.S.A. 163 35 52N 120 48W
Bradley, S.D., U.S.A. 158 45 10N 97 40W
Bradley Institute 127 17 7 S 31 25 E
Bradore Bay 151 51 27N 57 18W
Bradshaw 136 15 21 S 130 16 E
Bradwell-on-Sea 29 51 44N 0 55 E
Bradworthy 30 50 54N 4 22W
Brady 159 31 8N 99 25W
Brae 36 60 23N 1 20W
Brae, oilfield 19 58 45N 1 18 E
Brædstrup 73 55 58N 9 37 E
Braemar, Queens., Austral. 139 25 35 S 152 20 E
Braemar, S. Austral., Austral. 140 33 12 S 139 35 E
Braemar, U.K. 37 57 2N 3 20W
Braemar, dist. 37 57 2N 3 20W
Braemore, Grampian, U.K. 37 58 16N 3 33W
Braemore, Highland, U.K. 36 57 45N 5 2W
Braeriach Mt. 37 57 4N 3 44W
Braga 56 41 35N 8 25W
Braga □ 56 41 30N 8 30W
Bragado 172 35 2 S 60 27W
Bragança, Brazil 170 1 0 S 47 2W
Bragança, Port. 56 41 48N 6 50W
Bragança □ 56 41 30N 6 45W
Bragança Paulista 173 22 55 S 46 32W
Brahmanbaria 98 23 50N 91 15 E
Brahmani, R. 96 21 0N 85 15 E
Brahmaputra, R. 98 26 30N 93 30 E
Brahmaur 93 32 28N 76 32 E
Braich-y-Pwll 31 52 47N 4 46W
Braidwood 141 35 27 S 149 49 E
Brailsford 33 52 58N 1 35W
Braine-l'Alleud 47 50 42N 4 23 E
Braine-le-Comte 47 50 37N 4 8 E
Brainerd 158 46 20N 94 10W
Braintree, U.K. 29 51 53N 0 34 E
Braintree, U.S.A. 162 42 11N 71 0W
Braithwaite Pt. 138 12 5 S 133 50 E
Brak, R. 128 29 50 S 23 10 E
Brake 48 53 19N 8 30 E
Brakel 46 51 49N 5 5 E
Bräkne-Hoby 73 56 12N 15 8 E
Bräkne-Hoby 73 56 14N 15 6 E
Brakpan 129 26 13 S 28 20 E
Brakwater 128 22 28 S 17 3 E
Brålanda 73 58 34N 12 21 E
Brålanda 73 58 34N 12 21 E
Brăila 70 45 19N 27 59 E
Brăila □ 70 45 5N 27 30 E
Bralorne 152 50 50N 123 15W
Bramford 29 52 5N 1 6 E
Bramminge 73 55 28N 8 42 E

Bramon Brøttum

Bramon	72	62 14N	17 40 E
Brampton, Can.	150	43 45N	79 45W
Brampton, Cambs., U.K.	29	52 19N	0 13W
Brampton, Cumb., U.K.	32	54 56N	2 43W
Bramsche	48	52 25N	7 58 E
Bramshott	29	51 5N	0 47W
Bramwell	138	12 8 S	142 37 E
Brancaster	29	52 58N	0 40 E
Branco, Cabo	170	7 9 S	34 47W
Branco, R.	174	0 0	61 15W
Brande	73	55 57N	9 8 E
Brandenburg	48	52 24N	12 33 E
Brander, Pass of	34	56 25N	5 10W
Branderburgh	37	57 43N	3 17W
Brandfort	128	28 40 S	26 30 E
Brandon, Can.	153	49 50N	99 57W
Brandon, Durham, U.K.	33	54 46N	1 37W
Brandon, Suffolk, U.K.	29	52 27N	0 37 E
Brandon, U.S.A.	156	43 48N	73 4W
Brandon, U.S.A.	162	44 2N	73 5W
Brandon B.	39	52 17N	10 8W
Brandon, Mt.	39	52 15N	10 15W
Brandon Pt.	39	52 18N	10 10W
Brandsen	172	35 10 S	58 15W
Brandval	71	60 19N	12 1 E
Brandvlei	128	30 25 S	20 30 E
Brandýs	52	50 10N	14 40 E
Branford	162	41 15N	72 48W
Braniewo	54	54 25N	19 50 E
Brännarp	73	56 46N	12 38 E
Bransby	139	28 10 S	142 0 E
Bransfield Str.	13	63 0 S	59 0W
Branson, Colo., U.S.A.	159	37 4N	103 53W
Branson, Mo., U.S.A.	159	36 40N	93 18W
Branston	33	53 13N	0 28W
Brantford	150	43 15N	80 15W
Brantôme	44	45 22N	0 39 E
Branxholme	140	37 52 S	141 49 E
Branxton	141	32 38 S	151 21 E
Branzi	62	46 0N	9 46 E
Bras d'or, L.	151	45 50N	60 50W
Brasiléia	174	11 0 S	68 45W
Brasília	171	15 47 S	47 55 E
Braslav	80	55 38N	27 0 E
Braslovče	63	46 21N	15 3 E
Braşov	70	45 38N	25 35 E
Braşov □	70	45 45N	25 15 E
Brass	121	4 35N	6 14 E
Brass, R.	121	4 15N	6 13 E
Brasschaat	47	51 19N	4 27 E
Brassey, Barisan	102	5 0N	117 15 E
Brassey Ra.	137	25 8 S	122 15 E
Brasstown Bald, Mt.	157	34 54N	83 45W
Brassus, Le	50	46 35N	6 13 E
Brasted	29	51 16N	0 8 E
Bratislava	53	48 10N	17 7 E
Bratsk	77	56 10N	101 30 E
Bratteborg	73	57 37N	14 4 E
Brattleboro	162	42 53N	72 37W
Brattvær	71	63 25N	7 48 E
Braţul Chilia, R.	70	45 25N	29 20 E
Braţul Sfîntu Gheorghe, R.	70	45 0N	29 20 E
Braţul Sulina, R.	70	45 10N	29 20 E
Bratunac	66	44 13N	19 21 E
Braunau	52	48 15N	13 3 E
Braunschweig	48	52 17N	10 28 E
Braunton	30	51 6N	4 9W
Brava	91	1 20N	44 8 E
Bråvikeh	72	58 38N	16 32 E
Bravo del Norte, R.	164	30 30N	105 0W
Brawley	163	32 58N	115 30W
Bray, France	43	49 15N	1 40 E
Bray, Ireland	39	53 12N	6 6W
Bray, U.K.	29	51 30N	0 42W
Bray Hd.	39	51 52N	10 26W
Bray, Mt.	138	14 0N	134 30 E
Bray-sur-Seine	43	48 25N	3 14 E
Brazeau, R.	152	52 55N	115 14W
Brazil	156	39 30N	87 8W
Brazil ■	174	5 0N	20 0W
Brazilian Highlands	170	18 0 S	46 30W
Brazo Sur, R.	172	25 30 S	58 0W
Brazos, R.	159	30 30N	96 20W
Brazzaville	124	4 9 S	15 12 E
Brčko	66	44 54N	18 46 E
Breadalbane, Austral.	138	23 50 S	139 35 E
Breadalbane, U.K.	34	56 30N	4 15W
Breaden, L.	137	25 51 S	125 28 E
Breage	30	50 6N	5 17W
Breaksea Sd.	143	45 35 S	166 35 E
Bream Bay	142	35 56 S	174 28 E
Bream Head	142	35 51 S	174 36 E
Bream Tail	142	36 3 S	174 36 E
Breamish, R.	35	55 30N	1 55W
Breas	172	25 29 S	70 24W
Brebes	103	6 52 S	109 3 E
Brechin	37	56 44N	2 40W
Brecht	47	51 21N	4 38 E
Breckenridge, Colo., U.S.A.	160	39 30N	106 2W
Breckenridge, Minn., U.S.A.	158	46 20N	96 36W
Breckenridge, Tex., U.S.A.	159	32 48N	98 55W
Breckland	23	52 30N	0 40 E
Brecknock (□)	26	51 58N	3 25W
Břeclav	53	48 46N	16 53 E
Brecon	31	51 57N	3 23W
Brecon Beacons	31	51 53N	3 27W
Breda	47	51 35N	4 45 E
Bredaryd	73	57 10N	13 45 E
Bredasdorp	128	34 33 S	20 2 E
Bredbo	141	35 58 S	149 10 E
Brede	29	50 56N	0 37 E
Bredene	47	51 14N	2 59 E
Bredon Hill	28	52 3N	2 2W
Bredy	84	52 26N	60 21 E
Bree	47	51 8N	5 35 E
Breezand	46	52 53N	4 49 E
Bregalnica, R.	66	41 50N	22 20 E
Bregenz	52	47 30N	9 45 E
Bregning	73	56 8N	8 30 E
Bréhal	42	48 53N	1 30W
Bréhat, I. de	42	48 51N	3 0W
Breiðafjörður	74	65 15N	23 15W
Breil	45	43 56N	7 31 E
Breisach	49	48 2N	7 37 E
Brejinho de Nazaré	170	11 1 S	48 34W
Brejo	170	3 41 S	42 47W
Brekke	71	61 1N	5 26 E
Bremangerlandet	71	61 51N	5 0 E
Bremangerpollen	71	61 51N	5 0 E
Bremen	48	53 4N	8 47 E
Bremen □	48	53 6N	8 46 E
Bremer I.	138	12 5 S	136 45 E
Bremerhaven	48	53 34N	8 35 E
Bremerton	160	47 30N	122 38W
Bremervörde	48	53 28N	9 10 E
Bremgarten	51	47 21N	8 21 E
Bremnes	71	59 47N	5 8 E
Bremsnes	71	63 6N	7 40 E
Brendon Hills	28	51 6N	3 25W
Brenes	57	37 32N	5 54W
Brenham	159	30 5N	96 27W
Brenner Pass	52	47 0N	11 30 E
Breno	62	45 57N	10 20 E
Brent, Can.	150	46 2N	78 29W
Brent, U.K.	29	51 33N	0 18W
Brent, oil and gasfield	19	61 0N	1 45 E
Brenta, R.	63	45 11N	12 18 E
Brentwood, U.K.	29	51 37N	0 19W
Brentwood, U.S.A.	163	37 55N	121 42W
Bréscia	65	45 33N	10 13 E
Breskens	47	51 23N	3 33 E
Breslau = Wrocław.	54	51 5N	17 5 E
Bresle, R.	43	50 4N	1 21 E
Bresles	43	49 25N	2 13 E
Bressanone	63	46 43N	11 40 E
Bressay	36	60 10N	1 6W
Bressay I.	36	60 10N	1 5W
Bressay Sd.	36	60 8N	1 10W
Bresse, La	43	48 0N	6 53 E
Bresse, Plaine de	43	46 20N	5 10 E
Bressuire	42	46 51N	0 30W
Brest, France	42	48 24N	4 31W
Brest, U.S.S.R.	80	52 10N	23 40 E
Bretagne	42	48 0N	3 0W
Bretçu	70	46 7N	26 18 E
Breteuil	43	49 38N	2 18 E
Breton	152	53 7N	114 28W
Breton Sd.	159	29 40N	89 12W
Brett, C.	142	35 10 S	174 20 E
Bretten	49	49 2N	8 43 E
Bretuil	42	48 50N	0 53 E
Breukelen	46	52 10N	5 0 E
Brevard	157	35 19N	82 42W
Breves	170	1 40 S	50 29W
Brevik	71	59 4N	9 42 E
Brewarrina	139	30 0 S	146 51 E
Brewer	151	44 43N	68 50W
Brewer, Mt.	163	36 44N	118 28W
Brewerton	162	43 14N	76 9W
Brewood	28	52 41N	2 10W
Brewster, N.Y., U.S.A.	162	41 23N	73 37W
Brewster, Wash., U.S.A.	160	48 10N	119 51W
Brewster, Kap	12	70 7N	22 0W
Brewton	157	31 9N	87 2W
Breyten	129	26 16 S	30 0 E
Breytovo	81	58 18N	37 50 E
Brézina	118	33 4N	1 14 E
Březnice	52	49 32N	13 57 E
Breznik	66	42 44N	22 50 E
Brezno	53	48 50N	19 40 E
Bria	117	6 30N	21 58 E
Briançon	45	44 54N	6 39 E
Briare	43	47 38N	2 45 E
Bribbaree	141	34 10 S	147 51 E
Bribie I.	139	27 0 S	152 58 E
Brickaville	129	18 49 S	49 4 E
Bricon	43	48 5N	5 0 E
Bricquebec	42	49 29N	1 39W
Bride	32	54 24N	4 23W
Bridestowe	30	50 41N	4 7W
Bridge	29	51 14N	1 8 E
Bridge of Allan	35	56 9N	3 57W
Bridge of Don	37	57 10N	2 8W
Bridge of Earn	35	56 20N	3 25W
Bridge of Orchy	34	56 29N	4 48W
Bridge of Weir	34	55 51N	4 35W
Bridge, R.	152	50 50N	122 40W
Bridgehampton	162	40 56N	72 18W
Bridgend, Islay, U.K.	34	55 46N	6 15W
Bridgend, Mid Glam., U.K.	31	51 30N	3 35W
Bridgeport, Calif., U.S.A.	163	38 14N	119 15W
Bridgeport, Conn., U.S.A.	162	41 12N	73 12W
Bridgeport, Nebr., U.S.A.	158	41 42N	103 10W
Bridgeport, Tex., U.S.A.	159	33 15N	97 45W
Bridger	160	45 20N	108 58W
Bridgeton	162	39 29N	75 10W
Bridgetown, Austral.	137	33 58 S	116 7 E
Bridgetown, Barbados	167	13 0N	59 30W
Bridgetown, Can.	151	44 55N	65 18W
Bridgetown, Ireland	39	52 13N	6 33W
Bridgeville	162	38 45N	75 36W
Bridgewater, Austral.	140	36 36 S	143 59 E
Bridgewater, Can.	151	44 25N	64 31W
Bridgewater, Mass., U.S.A.	162	41 59N	70 56W
Bridgewater, N.Y., U.S.A.	162	42 58N	75 15W
Bridgewater, S.D., U.S.A.	158	43 34N	97 29W
Bridgewater, C.	140	38 23 S	141 23 E
Bridgnorth	28	52 33N	2 25W
Bridgwater	28	51 7N	3 0W
Bridgwater B.	28	51 15N	3 15W
Bridlington	33	54 6N	0 11W
Bridlington B.	33	54 4N	0 10W
Bridport, Austral.	138	40 59 S	147 23 E
Bridport, U.K.	28	50 43N	2 45W
Brie-Comte-Robert	43	48 40N	2 35 E
Brie, Plaine de	43	48 35N	3 10 E
Briec	42	48 6N	4 0W
Brielle	46	51 54N	4 10 E
Brienne-le-Château	43	48 24N	4 30 E
Brienon	43	48 0N	3 35 E
Brienz	50	46 46N	8 2 E
Brienzersee	50	46 44N	7 53 E
Brierfield	32	53 49N	2 15W
Brierley Hill	28	52 29N	2 7W
Briey	43	49 14N	5 57 E
Brig	50	46 18N	7 59 E
Brigantine	162	39 24N	74 22W
Brigg	33	53 33N	0 30W
Briggsdale	158	40 40N	104 20W
Brigham City	160	41 30N	112 1W
Brighouse	33	53 42N	1 47W
Brighstone	29	50 38N	1 36W
Bright	141	36 42 S	146 56 E
Brightlingsea	29	51 49N	1 1 E
Brighton, Austral.	140	35 5 S	138 30 E
Brighton, Can.	150	44 2N	77 44W
Brighton, U.K.	29	50 50N	0 9W
Brighton, U.S.A.	158	39 59N	104 50W
Brightstone	28	50 38N	1 23W
Brightwater	143	41 22 S	173 9 E
Brignogan-Plage	42	48 40N	4 20W
Brignoles	45	43 25N	6 5 E
Brigstock	29	52 27N	0 38W
Brihuega	58	40 45N	2 52W
Brikama	120	13 15N	16 45W
Brill	28	51 49N	1 3W
Brilliant	152	49 19N	117 38W
Brilon	48	51 23N	8 32 E
Brim	140	36 3 S	142 27 E
Brimfield	28	52 18N	2 42W
Brindisi	65	40 39N	17 55 E
Brinkley	159	34 55N	91 15W
Brinklow	28	52 25N	1 22W
Brinkworth, Austral.	140	33 42 S	138 26 E
Brinkworth, U.K.	28	51 33N	1 59W
Brinyan	37	59 8N	3 0W
Brion I.	151	47 46N	61 26W
Brionne	42	49 11N	0 43 E
Brionski, I.	63	44 55N	13 45 E
Brioude	44	45 18N	3 23 E
Briouze	42	48 42N	0 23W
Brisbane	139	27 25 S	153 2 E
Brisbane, R.	139	27 24 S	153 9 E
Brisignella	63	44 14N	11 46 E
Bristol, U.K.	28	51 26N	2 35W
Bristol, Conn., U.S.A.	162	41 44N	72 57W
Bristol, Pa., U.S.A.	162	40 6N	74 52W
Bristol, R.I., U.S.A.	162	41 40N	71 15W
Bristol, S.D., U.S.A.	158	45 25N	97 43W
Bristol B.	147	58 0N	160 0W
Bristol Channel	30	51 18N	4 30W
Bristol I.	13	58 45 S	28 0W
Bristol L.	161	34 23N	116 0W
Briston	29	52 52N	1 4 E
Bristow	159	35 5N	96 28W
British Antarctic Territory	13	66 0 S	45 0W
British Columbia □	152	55 0N	125 15W
British Guiana = Guyana	174	5 0N	59 0W
British Honduras = Belize	165	17 0N	88 30W
British Isles	16	55 0N	4 0W
Briton Ferry	31	51 37N	3 50W
Brits	129	25 37 S	27 48 E
Britstown	128	30 37 S	23 30 E
Britt	150	45 46N	80 34W
Brittany = Bretagne	42	48 0N	3 0W
Brittas	39	53 14N	6 29W
Brittatorp	73	57 3N	14 58 E
Britton	158	45 50N	97 47W
Brive-la-Gaillarde	44	45 10N	1 32 E
Briviesca	58	42 32N	3 19W
Brixham	30	50 24N	3 31W
Brixton	138	23 32 S	144 57 E
Brixworth	29	52 20N	0 54W
Brize Norton	28	51 46N	1 35W
Brlik, U.S.S.R.	76	44 0N	74 5 E
Brlik, Kazakh S.S.R., U.S.S.R.	85	44 5N	73 31 E
Brlik, Kazakh S.S.R., U.S.S.R.	85	43 40N	73 49 E
Brno	53	49 10N	16 35 E
Bro	72	59 13N	13 2 E
Broach = Bharuch	96	21 47N	73 0 E
Broad Arrow	137	30 23 S	121 15 E
Broad B.	36	58 14N	6 16W
Broad Chalke	28	51 2N	1 54W
Broad Clyst	30	50 46N	3 27W
Broad Haven, Ireland	38	54 20N	9 55W
Broad Haven, U.K.	31	51 46N	5 6W
Broad Law, Mt.	35	55 30N	3 22W
Broad, R.	157	34 30N	81 26W
Broad Sd., Austral.	138	22 0 S	149 45 E
Broad Sd., U.K.	30	49 56N	6 19W
Broadalbin	162	43 3N	74 12W
Broadford, Austral.	141	37 14 S	145 4 E
Broadford, Clare, Ireland	39	52 48N	8 38W
Broadford, Limerick, Ireland	39	52 21N	8 59W
Broadford, U.K.	36	57 14N	5 55W
Broadhembury	30	50 49N	3 16W
Broadhurst Ra.	136	22 30 S	122 30 E
Broads, The	29	52 45N	1 30 E
Broadsound Ra.	133	22 50 S	149 30 E
Broadstairs	29	51 21N	1 28 E
Broadus	158	45 28N	105 27W
Broadview	153	50 22N	102 35W
Broadway, Ireland	39	52 13N	6 23W
Broadway, U.K.	28	52 2N	1 51W
Broadwindsor	28	50 49N	2 49W
Broager	73	54 53N	9 40 E
Broaryd	73	57 7N	13 15 E
Brochet, Man., Can.	153	57 53N	101 40W
Brochet, Manitoba, Can.	153	57 55N	101 40W
Brochet, Québec, Can.	150	47 12N	72 42W
Brochet, L.	153	58 36N	101 35W
Brock	153	51 26N	108 43W
Brocken	48	51 48N	10 40 E
Brockenhurst	28	50 49N	1 34W
Brocklehurst	141	32 9 S	148 38 E
Brockman Mt.	137	22 25 S	117 15 E
Brockville	150	44 35N	75 41W
Brockway	158	47 18N	105 46W
Brockworth	28	51 51N	2 9W
Brod	66	41 35N	21 17 E
Brodarevo	66	43 14N	19 44 E
Brodeur Pen.	149	72 30N	88 10W
Brodick	34	55 34N	5 9W
Brodnica	54	53 15N	19 25 E
Brodokalmak	84	55 35N	62 6 E
Brody	80	50 5N	25 10 E
Broechem	47	51 11N	4 38 E
Broek	46	52 26N	5 0 E
Broek op Langedijk	46	52 41N	4 49 E
Brogan	160	44 14N	117 32W
Broglie	42	49 0N	0 30 E
Brok	54	52 43N	21 52 E
Broke Inlet	137	34 55 S	116 25 E
Broken Bank, gasfield	19	53 20N	2 4 E
Broken Bow, Nebr., U.S.A.	158	41 25N	99 35W
Broken Bow, Okla., U.S.A.	159	34 2N	94 43W
Broken Hill	140	31 58 S	141 29 E
Broken Hill = Kabwe	127	14 27 S	28 28 E
Brokind	73	58 13N	15 42 E
Bromborough	32	53 20N	3 0W
Bromham	28	51 23N	2 3W
Bromhead	153	49 18N	103 40W
Bromley	29	51 20N	0 5 E
Bromölla	73	56 5N	14 28 E
Brompton	33	54 22N	1 25W
Bromsgrove	28	52 20N	2 3W
Bromyard	28	52 12N	2 30W
Brønderslev	73	57 16N	9 57 E
Brong Ahafo	120	7 50N	2 0 E
Bronkhorstspruit	129	25 46 S	28 45 E
Bronnitsy	81	55 27N	38 10 E
Bronte, Italy	65	37 48N	14 49 E
Bronte, U.S.A.	159	31 54N	100 18W
Bronte Park	138	42 8 S	146 30 E
Brookeborough	38	54 19N	7 23W
Brookfield	158	39 50N	93 4W
Brookhaven	159	31 40N	90 25W
Brookings, Oreg., U.S.A.	160	42 4N	124 10W
Brookings, S.D., U.S.A.	158	44 20N	96 45W
Brooklands	138	18 5 S	144 0 E
Brookmere	152	49 52N	120 53W
Brooks	152	50 35N	111 55W
Brooks B.	152	50 15N	127 55W
Brooks L.	153	61 55N	106 35W
Brooks Ra.	147	68 40N	147 0W
Brooksville	157	28 32N	82 21W
Brookton	137	32 22 S	116 57 E
Brookville	156	39 25N	85 0W
Brooloo	139	26 30 S	152 43 E
Broom, L.	36	57 55N	5 15W
Broome	136	18 0 S	122 15 E
Broomehill	137	31 51 S	117 39 E
Broomfield	28	51 46N	0 28 E
Broomhill	35	55 19N	1 36W
Broons	42	48 20N	2 16W
Brora	37	58 0N	3 50W
Brora L.	37	58 3N	3 58W
Brora, R.	37	58 4N	3 52W
Brosarp	73	55 44N	14 8 E
Brösarp	73	55 43N	14 6 E
Broseley	28	52 36N	2 30W
Brosna, R.	39	53 8N	8 0W
Broşteni	70	47 14N	25 43 E
Brotas de Macaúbas	171	12 0 S	42 38W
Brothers	160	43 56N	120 39W
Brothertoft	33	53 0N	0 5W
Brotton	33	54 34N	0 55W
Brøttum	71	61 2N	10 34 E

Brough **Bura**

Brough, Cumbria, U.K. 32 54 32N 2 19W
Brough, Humberside, U.K. 33 53 44N 0 35W
Brough Hd. 37 59 8N 3 20W
Broughams Gate 140 30 51S 140 59E
Broughshane 38 54 54N 6 12W
Broughton, Austral. 138 20 10S 146 20E
Broughton, Borders, U.K. 35 55 37N 3 25W
Broughton, Humberside, U.K. 33 53 33N 0 36W
Broughton, Northampton, U.K. 29 52 22N 0 45W
Broughton, Yorkshire, U.K. 33 54 26N 1 8W
Broughton-in-Furness 32 54 17N 3 12W
Broughty Ferry 35 56 29N 2 50W
Broumov 53 50 35N 16 20E
Brouwershaven 46 51 45N 3 55E
Brouwershavensche Gat 46 51 46N 3 50E
Brovary 80 50 34N 30 48E
Brovst 73 57 6N 9 31E
Browerville 158 46 3N 94 50W
Brown, Mt. 140 32 30S 138 0E
Brown, Pt. 139 32 32S 133 50E
Brown Willy, Mt. 30 50 35N 4 34W
Brownfield 159 33 10N 102 15W
Browngrove 38 53 33N 8 49W
Brownhills 28 52 38N 1 57W
Browning 160 48 35N 113 10W
Brownlee 153 50 43N 106 1W
Browns Bay 142 36 40S 174 40E
Brownstown Hd. 39 52 8N 7 8W
Brownsville, Oreg., U.S.A. 160 44 29N 123 0W
Brownsville, Tenn., U.S.A. 159 35 35N 89 15W
Brownsville, Tex., U.S.A. 159 25 56N 97 25W
Brownwood 159 31 45N 99 0W
Brownwood, L. 159 31 51N 98 35W
Browse I. 136 14 7S 123 33E
Broxburn 35 55 56N 3 23W
Broye, R. 50 46 52N 6 58E
Brozas 57 39 37N 6 47W
Bruas 101 4 31N 100 46E
Bruay-en-Artois 43 50 29N 2 33E
Bruce Bay 143 43 35S 169 42E
Bruce, gasfield 19 59 45N 1 32E
Bruce Mines 150 46 20N 83 45W
Bruce, Mt. 136 22 37S 118 8E
Bruce Rock 137 31 52S 118 8E
Bruchsal 49 49 9N 8 39E
Bruck a.d. Leitha 53 48 1N 16 47E
Bruck a.d. Mur 52 47 24N 15 16E
Brückenau 49 50 17N 9 48E
Brǎdiceni 70 45 3N 23 4E
Brue, R. 28 51 10N 2 59W
Bruernish Pt. 36 57 0N 7 22W
Bruff 39 52 29N 8 35W
Brugelette 47 50 35N 3 52E
Bruges = Brugge 47 51 13N 3 13E
Brugg 50 47 29N 8 11E
Brugge 47 51 13N 3 13E
Brühl 48 50 49N 6 51E
Bruinisse 47 51 40N 4 5E
Brûlé 152 53 15N 117 58W
Brûlon 42 47 58N 0 15W
Brûly 47 49 58N 4 32E
Brumado 171 14 14S 41 40W
Brumado, R. 171 14 13S 41 40W
Brumath 43 48 43N 7 40E
Brummen 46 52 5N 6 10E
Brumunddal 71 60 53N 10 56E
Brunchilly 138 18 50S 134 30E
Brundidge 157 31 43N 85 45W
Bruneau 160 42 57N 115 55W
Bruneau, R. 160 42 45N 115 50W
Brunei = Bandar Seri Begawan 102 4 52N 115 0E
Brunei ■ 102 4 50N 115 0E
Brunette Downs 138 18 40S 135 55E
Brunflo 72 63 5N 14 50E
Brunico 63 46 50N 11 55E
Brünig, Col de 50 46 46N 8 8E
Brunkeberg 71 59 26N 8 28E
Brunna 72 59 52N 17 25E
Brunnen 51 46 59N 8 37E
Brunner 143 42 27S 171 20E
Brunner, L. 143 42 27S 171 20E
Brunnsvik 72 60 12N 15 8E
Bruno 153 52 20N 105 30W
Brunsberg 72 59 38N 12 52E
Brunsbüttelkoog 48 53 52N 9 13E
Brunssum 47 50 57N 5 59E
Brunswick, Ga., U.S.A. 157 31 10N 81 30W
Brunswick, Md., U.S.A. 156 39 20N 77 38W
Brunswick, Me., U.S.A. 151 43 53N 69 50W
Brunswick, Mo., U.S.A. 158 39 26N 93 10W
Brunswick = Braunschweig 48 52 17N 10 28E
Brunswick B. 136 15 15S 124 50E
Brunswick Junction 137 33 15S 115 50E
Brunswick, Pen. de 176 53 30S 71 30W
Bruntál 53 50 0N 17 27E
Brunton 35 55 2N 2 6W
Bruny I. 138 43 20S 147 15E
Bruree 39 52 25N 8 40W
Brus Laguna 166 15 47N 84 35W
Brusartsi 66 43 40N 23 5E
Brush 158 40 17N 103 33W
Brusio 51 46 14N 10 8E
Brusque 173 27 5S 49 0W
Brussel 47 50 51N 4 21E
Brussels = Bruxelles 47 50 51N 4 21E
Brustem 47 50 48N 5 14E
Bruthen 141 37 42S 147 50E
Bruton 28 51 6N 2 28W
Bruvik 71 60 29N 5 40E
Bruxelles 47 50 51N 4 21E
Bruyères 43 48 10N 6 40E
Brwinow 54 52 9N 20 40E
Bryagovo 67 41 58N 25 8E
Bryan, Ohio, U.S.A. 156 41 30N 84 30W
Bryan, Texas, U.S.A. 159 30 40N 96 27W
Bryan, Mt. 140 33 30S 139 0E
Bryansk 80 53 13N 34 25E
Bryanskoye 83 44 9N 47 10E
Bryant 58 44 39N 97 26W
Bryggja 71 61 56N 5 27E
Bryher I. 30 49 57N 6 21W
Brymbo 31 53 4N 3 5W
Brynamman 31 51 49N 3 52W
Bryncethin 31 51 33N 3 34W
Bryne 71 58 44N 5 38E
Brynmawr 31 51 48N 3 11W
Bryrup 73 56 2N 9 30E
Bryson City 157 35 28N 83 25W
Bryte 163 38 35N 121 33W
Brza Palanka 66 44 28N 22 37E
Brzava, R. 66 45 21N 20 45E
Brzeg 54 50 52N 17 30E
Brzeg Dln 54 51 16N 16 41E
Brzesko 54 49 59N 20 34E
Brześć Kujawski 54 52 36N 18 55E
Brzeszcze 54 49 59N 19 10E
Brzeziny 54 51 49N 19 42E
Brzozów 54 49 41N 22 3E
Bu Athiah 119 30 1N 15 30E
Bu Craa 116 26 45N 17 2E
Buapinang 103 4 40S 121 30E
Buayan 103 5 3N 125 28E
Buba 120 11 40N 14 59W
Bubanza 126 3 6S 29 23E
Bucaramanga 174 7 0N 73 0W
Buccaneer Arch. 136 16 7S 123 20E
Bucchiánico 63 42 20N 14 10E
Bucecea 70 47 47N 26 28E
Bǔceşti 70 46 50N 27 11E
Buchach 80 49 5N 25 25E
Buchan, Austral. 141 37 30S 148 12E
Buchan, U.K. 37 57 32N 2 8W
Buchan Ness 37 57 29N 1 48W
Buchan, oilfield 19 57 55N 0 0
Buchanan, Can. 153 51 40N 102 45W
Buchanan, Liberia 120 5 57N 10 2W
Buchanan Cr. 138 17 10S 138 6E
Buchanan, L., Queens., Austral. 138 21 35S 145 52E
Buchanan, L., W. Australia, Austral. 137 25 33S 123 2E
Buchanan, L., U.S.A. 159 30 50N 98 25W
Buchans 151 49 50N 56 52W
Bucharest = Bucureşti 70 44 27N 26 10E
Buchholz 48 53 19N 9 51E
Buchloe 49 48 3N 10 45E
Buchlyvie 34 56 7N 4 20W
Buchon, Pt. 163 35 15N 120 54W
Buchs 51 47 10N 9 28E
Buck Hill Falls 162 41 11N 75 16W
Buck, The, mt. 37 57 19N 3 0W
Buckden 29 52 17N 0 16W
Bückeburg 48 52 16N 9 2E
Buckeye 161 33 28N 112 40W
Buckfastleigh 30 50 28N 3 47W
Buckhannon 156 39 2N 80 10W
Buckhaven 35 56 10N 3 2W
Buckie 37 57 40N 2 58W
Buckingham, Can. 150 45 37N 75 24W
Buckingham, U.K. 29 52 0N 0 59W
Buckingham □ 29 51 50N 0 55W
Buckingham B. 138 12 10S 135 40E
Buckingham Can. 97 14 0N 80 5E
Buckinguy 139 31 3S 147 30E
Buckland 147 66 0N 161 5W
Buckland Brewer 30 50 56N 4 14W
Buckle Hd. 136 14 26S 127 52E
Buckleboo 140 32 54S 136 12E
Buckley, U.K. 31 53 10N 3 5W
Buckley, U.S.A. 160 47 10N 122 2W
Bucklin 159 37 37N 99 40W
Bucksburn 37 57 10N 2 10W
Bucquoy 43 50 9N 2 43E
Buctouche 151 46 30N 64 45W
Bucureşti 70 44 27N 26 10E
Bucyrus 156 40 48N 83 0W
Budacul, Munte 41 47 5N 25 40E
Budafok 53 47 26N 19 2E
Budalin 98 22 20N 95 10E
Budapest 53 47 29N 19 5E
Budaun 95 28 5N 79 10E
Budd Coast 13 67 0S 112 0E
Buddabadah 141 31 56S 147 14E
Buddon Ness 35 56 29N 2 42W
Buddusò 64 40 35N 9 18E
Bude 30 50 49N 4 33W
Bude Bay 30 50 50N 4 40W
Budel 47 51 17N 5 34E
Budeşti 70 44 13N 26 30E
Budge Budge 95 22 30N 88 25E
Budgewoi Lake 141 33 13S 151 34E
Budia 58 40 38N 2 46W
Búdir 74 64 49N 23 23W
Budjala 124 2 50N 19 40E
Budle B. 35 55 37N 1 45W
Budleigh Salterton 30 50 37N 3 19W
Búdrio 63 44 31N 11 31E
Budva 66 42 17N 18 50E
Budzyn 54 52 54N 16 59E
Buea 121 4 10N 9 9E
Buellton 163 34 37N 120 12W
Buena 162 39 31N 74 56W
Buena Vista, Colo., U.S.A. 161 38 56N 106 6W
Buena Vista, Va., U.S.A. 156 37 47N 79 23W
Buena Vista L. 163 35 15N 119 21W
Buenaventura 164 29 50N 107 30W
Buenaventura, B. de 174 3 48N 77 17W
Buendia, Pantano de 58 40 25N 2 43W
Buenópolis 171 17 54S 44 11W
Buenos Aires, Argent. 172 34 30S 58 20W
Buenos Aires, Colomb. 174 1 36N 73 18W
Buenos Aires, C. Rica 166 9 10N 83 20W
Buenos Aires □ 172 36 30S 60 0W
Buenos Aires, Lago 176 46 35S 72 30W
Buesaco 174 1 23N 77 9W
Buffalo, Can. 153 50 49N 110 42W
Buffalo, Mo., U.S.A. 159 37 40N 93 5W
Buffalo, Okla., U.S.A. 159 36 55N 99 42W
Buffalo, S.D., U.S.A. 159 45 39N 103 31W
Buffalo, Wyo., U.S.A. 160 44 25N 106 50W
Buffalo Center 147 64 2N 145 50W
Buffalo Head Hills 152 57 25N 115 55W
Buffalo L. 152 52 27N 112 54W
Buffalo Narrows 153 55 51N 108 29W
Buffalo, R. 152 57 50N 117 1W
Buffels, R. 129 29 36S 17 15E
Buford 157 34 5N 84 0W
Bug, R., Poland 54 51 20N 23 40E
Bug, R., U.S.S.R. 82 48 0N 31 0E
Buga 174 4 0N 77 0W
Buganda □ 126 0 0N 31 30E
Buganga 126 0 25N 32 0E
Bugeat 44 45 36N 1 55E
Buggenhout 47 51 1N 4 12E
Buggs I. L. 157 36 20N 78 30W
Buglawton 32 53 12N 2 11W
Bugle 30 50 23N 4 46W
Bugojno 66 44 2N 17 25E
Bugsuk, I. 102 8 15N 117 15E
Bugue, Le 44 44 55N 0 56E
Bugulma 84 54 33N 52 48E
Buguma 121 4 42N 6 55E
Bugun Shara 105 49 0N 104 0E
Buguruslan 84 53 39N 52 26E
Buheirat-Murrat-el-Kubra 122 30 15N 32 40E
Buhl, Idaho, U.S.A. 160 42 35N 114 54W
Buhl, Minn., U.S.A. 158 47 30N 92 46W
Buhǔeşti 70 46 47N 27 32E
Buhuşi 70 46 41N 26 45E
Buick 159 37 8N 91 2W
Bǔicoi 70 45 3N 25 52E
Buie L. 34 56 20N 5 55W
Bǔileşti 70 44 01N 23 20E
Builth Wells 31 52 10N 3 26W
Buina Qara 93 36 20N 67 0E
Buinsk 81 55 0N 48 18E
Buíque 170 8 37S 37 9W
Buis-les-Baronnies 45 44 17N 5 16E
Buit, L. 151 50 59N 63 13W
Buitenpost 46 53 15N 6 9E
Buitrago 56 41 0N 3 38W
Bujalance 57 37 54N 4 23W
Buján 56 42 59N 8 36W
Bujaraloz 58 41 29N 0 10W
Buje 63 45 24N 13 39E
Buji 135 9 8S 142 11E
Bujnurd 93 37 35N 57 15E
Bujumbura (Usumbura) 126 3 16S 29 18E
Bük 53 47 22N 16 45E
Buk 54 52 21N 16 17E
Buka I. 135 5 10S 154 35E
Bukachacha 77 52 55N 116 50E
Bukama 127 9 10S 25 50E
Bukandula 126 0 13N 31 50E
Bukavu 126 2 20S 28 52E
Bukene 126 4 15S 32 48E
Bukhara 85 39 48N 64 25E
Bukima 126 1 50S 33 25E
Bukit Mertajam 101 5 22N 100 28E
Bukittinggi 102 0 20S 100 20E
Bukkapatnam 97 14 14N 77 46E
Buklyan 84 55 42N 52 10E
Bukoba 126 1 20S 31 49E
Bukoba □ 126 1 30S 32 0E
Bukowno 54 50 17N 19 35E
Bukrale 123 4 32N 42 0E
Bukuru 121 9 42N 8 48E
Bukuya 126 0 40N 31 52E
Bula 120 12 7N 15 43W
Bülach 51 47 31N 8 32E
Bulahdelah 141 32 23S 152 13E
Bulan 103 12 40N 123 52E
Bulanash 84 57 16N 62 0E
Bulandshahr 94 28 28N 77 58E
Bulanovo 84 52 27N 55 10E
Bulantai 99 36 33N 92 18E
Bûlâq 122 25 10N 30 38E
Bulawayo 127 20 7S 28 32E
Buldana 96 20 30N 76 18E
Buldir I. 147 52 20N 175 55E
Bulford 28 51 11N 1 45W
Bulgan 105 48 45N 103 34E
Bulgaria ■ 67 42 35N 25 30E
Bulgroo 138 25 47S 143 58E
Bulgunnia 139 30 10S 134 53E
Bulhar 91 10 25N 44 30E
Buli, Teluk 103 1 5N 128 25E
Buliluyan, C. 102 8 20N 117 15E
Bulki 123 6 11N 36 31E
Bulkington 163 52 29N 1 25W
Bulkley, R. 152 55 15N 127 40W
Bulkur 77 71 50N 126 30E
Bull Shoals L. 159 36 40N 93 5W
Bullabulling 137 31 1S 120 32E
Bullange 47 50 24N 6 15E
Bullaque, R. 57 39 20N 4 13W
Bullara 136 22 40S 114 3E
Bullaring 137 32 30S 117 45E
Bullas 59 38 2N 1 40W
Bulle 50 46 37N 7 3E
Buller Gorge 143 41 40S 172 10E
Buller, Mt. 141 37 10S 146 28E
Buller, R. 143 41 44S 171 36E
Bullfinch 137 30 58S 119 3E
Bulli 141 34 15S 150 57E
Bullock Cr. 138 17 51S 143 45E
Bulloo Downs, Queens., Austral. 139 28 31S 142 57E
Bulloo Downs, W.A., Austral. 137 24 0S 119 32E
Bulloo L. 139 28 43S 142 25E
Bulloo, R. 139 28 43S 142 30E
Bulls 142 40 10S 175 24E
Bully-les-Mines 43 50 27N 2 44E
Bulnes 172 36 42S 72 19W
Bulo Burti 91 3 50N 45 33E
Bulolo 135 7 10S 146 40E
Bulpunga 140 33 47S 141 45E
Bulqiza 68 40 30N 20 21E
Bulsar 96 20 40N 72 58E
Bultfontein 128 28 18S 26 10E
Bulu Karakelong 103 4 35N 126 50E
Buluan 103 9 0N 125 30E
Bǔlǔciţa 70 44 23N 23 8E
Bulukumba 103 5 33S 120 11E
Bulun 77 70 37N 127 30E
Bulwell 33 53 1N 1 12W
Bumba 124 2 13N 22 30E
Bumbiri I. 126 1 40S 31 55E
Bumble Bee 161 34 8N 112 18W
Bumbum 121 14 10N 8 10E
Bumhkang 98 26 51N 97 40E
Bumhpa Bum 98 26 51N 97 14E
Bumi, R. 127 17 30S 28 30E
Bumtang, R. 98 26 56N 90 53E
Buna, Kenya 124 2 58N 39 30E
Buna, P.N.G. 135 8 42S 148 27E
Bunaiyin 92 23 10N 51 8E
Bunaw 39 51 47N 9 50W
Bunazi 126 1 3S 31 23E
Bunbeg 38 55 4N 8 18W
Bunbury 132 33 20S 115 35E
Bunclody 39 52 40N 6 40W
Buncrana 38 55 8N 7 28W
Bundaberg 139 24 54S 152 22E
Bünde 48 52 11N 8 33E
Bundey, R. 138 21 46S 135 37E
Bundi 94 25 30N 75 35E
Bundooma 138 24 54S 134 16E
Bundoran 38 54 24N 8 17W
Bundukia 123 5 14N 30 55E
Bundure 141 35 10S 146 1E
Bǔneasa 70 45 56N 27 55E
Bunessan 34 56 18N 6 15W
Bung Kan 100 18 23N 103 37E
Bungay 29 52 27N 1 26E
Bungendore 141 35 14S 149 30E
Bungil Cr. 138 27 5S 149 5E
Bungō-Suidō 110 33 0N 132 15E
Bungoma 126 0 34N 34 34E
Bungotakada 110 33 35N 131 25E
Bungu 126 7 35S 39 0E
Bunguran N. Is. 102 4 45N 108 0E
Bunia 126 1 35N 30 20E
Bunji 95 35 45N 74 40E
Bunju 102 3 35N 117 50E
Bunker Hill 163 39 15N 117 8W
Bunkerville 161 36 47N 114 6W
Bunkie 159 31 1N 92 12W
Bunmahon 39 52 8N 7 22W
Bunnanaddan 38 54 3N 8 35W
Bunnell 157 29 28N 81 12W
Bunnik 46 52 4N 5 12E
Bunnyconnellan 38 54 7N 9 1W
Bunnythorpe 142 40 16S 175 39E
Buñol 59 39 25N 0 47W
Bunsbeek 47 50 50N 4 56E
Bunschoten 46 52 14N 5 22E
Buntingford 29 51 57N 0 1W
Buntok 102 1 40S 114 58E
Bununu 121 9 51N 9 32E
Bununu Doss 121 10 6N 9 25E
Bunwell 29 52 30N 1 9E
Bunyoro □ = Western □ 126 1 45N 31 30E
Bunza 121 12 8N 4 0E
Búoareyri 74 65 2N 14 13W
Buol 103 1 15N 121 32E
Buon Brieng 100 13 9N 108 12E
Buong Long 100 13 44N 106 59E
Buorkhaya, Mys 77 71 50N 133 10E
Buqbuq 122 31 29N 25 29E
Buqei'a 90 32 58N 35 20E
Bur Acaba 91 3 12N 44 20E
Bûr Fuad 122 31 15N 32 20E
Bûr Safâga 122 26 43N 33 57E
Bûr Sa'îd 122 31 16N 32 18E
Bûr Sûdân 122 19 32N 37 9E
Bûr Taufiq 122 29 54N 32 32E
Bura 126 1 4S 39 58E

Buraidah **Caithness, Ord of, C**

Buraidah 92 26 20N 44 8 E
Buraimī, Al Wāhāt al 93 24 15N 55 43 E
Burak Sulayman 90 31 42N 35 7 E
Burama 91 9 55N 43 7 E
Burao 91 9 32N 45 32 E
Buras 159 29 20N 89 33W
Burayevo 84 55 50N 55 24 E
Burbage, Derby, U.K. 32 53 15N 1 55W
Burbage, Leics., U.K. 28 52 31N 1 20W
Burbage, Wilts., U.K. 28 51 21N 1 40W
Burbank 163 34 9N 118 23W
Burcher 141 33 30 S 147 16 E
Burdekin, R. 138 19 38 S 147 25 E
Burdett 152 49 50N 111 32W
Burdur 92 37 45N 30 22 E
Burdwan 95 23 16N 87 54 E
Bure 123 10 40N 37 4 E
Bure, R. 29 52 38N 1 45 E
Bureba, La 58 42 36N 3 24W
Buren 46 51 55N 5 20 E
Burfell 74 64 5N 20 56W
Burford 28 51 48N 1 38W
Burg, Magdeburg, Ger. 48 52 16N 11 50 E
Burg, Schleswig-Holstein, Ger. 48 54 25N 11 10 E
Burg el Arab 122 30 54N 29 32 E
Burg et Tuyur 122 20 55N 27 56 E
Burgan 92 29 0N 47 57 E
Burgas 67 42 33N 27 29 E
Burgaski Zaliv 67 42 30N 27 39 E
Burgdorf, Ger. 48 52 27N 10 0 E
Burgdorf, Switz. 50 47 3N 7 37 E
Burgenland □ 53 47 20N 16 20 E
Burgeo 151 47 37N 57 38W
Burgersdorp 128 31 0 S 26 20 E
Burges, Mt. 137 30 50 S 121 5 E
Burgess 162 37 53N 76 21W
Burgess Hill 29 50 57N 0 7W
Burgh-le-Marsh 33 53 10N 0 15 E
Burghclere 28 51 19N 1 20W
Burghead 37 57 42N 3 30W
Burghead B. 37 57 40N 3 33W
Búrgio 64 37 35N 13 18 E
Bürglen 51 46 53N 8 40 E
Burglengenfeld 49 49 11N 12 2 E
Burgo de Osma 58 41 35N 3 4W
Burgohondo 56 40 26N 4 47W
Burgos 58 42 21N 3 41W
Burgos □ 58 42 21N 3 42W
Burgstädt 48 50 55N 12 49 E
Burgsteinfurt 48 52 9N 7 23 E
Burgsvik 73 57 3N 18 19 E
Burguillos del Cerro 57 38 23N 6 35W
Burgundy = Bourgogne 43 47 0N 4 30 E
Burhanpur 96 21 18N 76 20 E
Burhou Rocks 42 49 45N 2 15W
Buri Pen. 123 15 25N 39 55 E
Burias, I. 103 12 55N 123 5 E
Buribay 84 51 57N 58 10 E
Burica, Punta 166 8 3N 82 51W
Burigi, L. 126 2 2 S 31 22 E
Burin, Can. 151 47 1N 55 14W
Burin, Jordan 90 32 11N 35 15 E
Buriram 100 15 0N 103 0 E
Buriti Alegre 171 18 9 S 49 3W
Buriti Bravo 170 5 50 S 43 50W
Buriti dos Lopes 170 3 10 S 41 52W
Burji 123 5 29N 37 51 E
Burkburnett 159 34 7N 98 35W
Burke 160 47 31N 115 56W
Burke, R. 138 23 12 S 139 33 E
Burketown 138 17 45 S 139 33 E
Burk's Falls 150 45 37N 79 24W
Burley, Hants, U.K. 28 50 49N 1 41W
Burley, N. Yorks., U.K. 33 53 55N 1 46W
Burley, U.S.A. 160 42 37N 113 55W
Burlingame 163 37 35N 122 21W
Burlington, Colo., U.S.A. 158 39 21N 102 18W
Burlington, Iowa, U.S.A. 158 40 50N 91 5W
Burlington, Kans., U.S.A. 158 38 15N 95 47W
Burlington, N.C., U.S.A. 157 36 7N 79 27W
Burlington, N.J., U.S.A. 162 40 5N 74 50W
Burlington, Wash., U.S.A. 160 48 29N 122 19W
Burlington, Wis., U.S.A. 156 42 41N 88 18W
Burlyu-Tyube 76 46 30N 79 10 E
Burma ■ 98 21 0N 96 30 E
Burnabbie 137 32 7 S 126 21 E
Burnaby I. 152 52 25N 131 19W
Burnamwood 141 31 7 S 144 53 E
Burnet 159 30 45N 98 11W
Burnett, R. 133 24 45 S 152 23 E
Burney 160 40 56N 121 41W
Burnfoot 38 55 4N 7 15W
Burngup 137 33 2 S 118 42 E
Burnham, Essex, U.K. 29 51 37N 0 50 E
Burnham, Somerset, U.K. 28 51 14N 3 0W
Burnham Market 29 52 57N 0 43 E
Burnie 138 41 4 S 145 56 E
Burnley 32 53 47N 2 15W
Burnmouth 35 55 50N 2 4W
Burnoye 85 42 36N 70 47 E
Burns, Oreg., U.S.A. 160 43 40N 119 4W
Burns, Wyo., U.S.A. 158 41 13N 104 18W
Burns Lake 152 54 20N 125 45W
Burnside, L. 137 25 25 S 123 0 E
Burnt Paw 147 67 2N 142 43W
Burntisland 35 56 4N 3 14W
Burntwood L. 153 55 22N 100 26W
Burntwood, R. 153 56 8N 96 34W
Burqa 90 32 18N 35 11 E
Burra 140 33 40 S 138 55 E
Burragorang, L. 141 33 52 S 150 37 E
Burramurra 138 20 25N 137 15 E
Burravoe 36 60 30N 1 3W
Burray I. 37 58 50N 2 54W
Burreli 68 41 36N 20 1 E
Burrelton 35 56 30N 3 16W
Burren 39 53 9N 9 5W
Burren Junction 139 30 7 S 148 59 E
Burrendong Dam 139 32 39 S 149 6 E
Burrendong Res. 141 32 45 S 149 10 E
Burriana 58 39 50N 0 4W
Burrinjuck Res. 141 35 0 S 148 36 E
Burro, Serranías del 164 29 0N 102 0W
Burrow Hd. 34 54 40N 4 23W
Burrundie 136 13 32 S 131 42 E
Burruyacú 172 26 30 S 64 40W
Burry Port 31 51 41N 4 17W
Bursa 92 40 15N 29 5 E
Burseryd 73 57 12N 13 17 E
Burstall 153 50 39N 109 54W
Burstwick 33 53 43N 0 6W
Burton 32 54 10N 2 43W
Burton Agnes 33 54 4N 0 18W
Burton Bradstock 28 50 41N 2 43W
Burton Fleming 33 54 8N 0 20W
Burton L. 150 54 45N 78 20W
Burton Latimer 29 52 23N 0 41W
Burton upon Stather 33 53 39N 0 41W
Burton-upon-Trent 28 52 48N 1 39W
Burtonport 38 54 59N 8 26W
Burtundy 140 33 45 S 142 15 E
Burtville 137 28 42 S 122 33 E
Buru, I. 103 3 30 S 126 30 E
Burufu 120 10 25N 2 50W
Burujird 92 33 58N 48 41 E
Burullus, Bahra el 122 31 25N 31 0 E
Burunday 85 43 20N 76 51 E
Burundi ■ 126 3 15 S 30 0 E
Burung 102 0 21N 108 25 E
Bururi 126 3 57 S 29 37 E
Burutu 121 5 20N 5 29 E
Burwash 29 50 59N 0 24 E
Burwash Landing 147 61 21N 139 0W
Burwell, U.K. 29 52 17N 0 20 E
Burwell, U.S.A. 158 41 49N 99 8W
Bury 32 53 36N 2 19W
Bury St. Edmunds 29 52 15N 0 42 E
Buryat A.S.S.R. □ 77 53 0N 110 0 E
Burzenin 54 51 28N 18 47 E
Busalla 62 44 34N 8 58 E
Busango Swamp 127 14 15 S 25 45 E
Busayyah 92 30 0N 46 10 E
Busby 152 53 55N 114 0W
Bushati 68 41 58N 19 34 E
Bushell 153 59 31N 108 45W
Bushenyi 126 0 35 S 30 10 E
Bushey 29 51 38N 0 20W
Bushman Land 128 29 30 S 19 30 E
Bushmills 38 55 14N 6 32W
Bushnell, Ill., U.S.A. 158 40 32N 90 30W
Bushnell, Nebr., U.S.A. 158 41 18N 103 50W
Busia □ 126 0 25N 34 6 E
Busie 120 10 29N 2 22W
Businga 124 3 16N 20 59 E
Buskerud fylke □ 75 60 13N 9 0 E
Busko Zdrój 54 50 28N 20 42 E
Busovača 66 44 6N 17 53 E
Busra 92 32 30N 36 25 E
Bussa 121 10 11N 4 32 E
Bussang 43 47 50N 6 50 E
Busselton 137 33 42 S 115 15 E
Bussigny 50 46 33N 6 33 E
Bussum 46 52 16N 5 10 E
Bustard Hd. 133 24 0 S 151 48 E
Busto Arsizio 62 45 40N 8 50 E
Busto, C. 56 43 34N 6 28W
Busu-Djanoa 124 1 50N 21 5 E
Busuangal, I. 103 12 10N 120 0 E
Büsum 48 54 7N 8 50 E
Buta 126 2 50N 24 53 E
Butare 126 2 31 S 29 52 E
Bute 140 33 51 S 138 2 E
Bute (□) 26 55 40N 5 10W
Bute, I. 34 55 48N 5 2W
Bute Inlet 152 50 40N 124 53W
Bute, Kyles of 34 55 55N 5 10W
Bute, Sd. of 34 55 43N 5 8W
Butemba 126 1 9N 31 37 E
Butembo 126 0 9N 29 18 E
Butera 65 37 10N 14 10 E
Bütgenbach 47 50 26N 6 12 E
Buthidaung 98 20 52N 92 32 E
Butiaba 126 1 50N 31 20 E
Butler 158 38 17N 94 18W
Bütschwil 51 47 23N 9 5 E
Butte, Mont., U.S.A. 160 46 0N 112 31W
Butte, Nebr., U.S.A. 158 42 56N 98 54W
Butterfield, Mt. 137 24 45 S 128 7 E
Buttermere 32 54 32N 3 17W
Butterworth 101 5 24N 100 23 E
Buttevant 39 52 14N 8 40 E
Buttfield, Mt. 137 24 45 S 128 9 E
Button B. 153 58 45N 94 23W
Buttonwillow 163 35 24N 119 28W
Butty Hd. 137 33 54 S 121 39 E
Butuan 103 8 57N 125 33 E
Butuku-Luba 121 3 29N 8 33 E
Butung, I. 103 5 0 S 122 45 E
Buturlinovka 81 50 50N 40 35 E
Butzbach 48 50 24N 8 40 E
Buxar 95 25 34N 83 58 E
Buxton, S. Afr. 128 27 38 S 24 42 E
Buxton, U.K. 32 53 16N 1 54W
Buxy 43 46 44N 4 40 E
Buyaga 77 59 50N 127 0 E
Buynaksk 83 42 36N 47 42 E
Buyr Nuur 105 47 50N 117 42 E
Büyük çekmece 67 41 2N 28 35 E
Büyük Kemikli Burun 68 40 20N 26 15 E
Büyük Menderes, R. 79 37 45N 27 40 E
Buzançais 42 46 54N 1 25 E
Buzau, Pasul 70 45 35N 26 12 E
Buzaymah 117 24 35N 22 0 E
Buzen 110 33 35N 131 5 E
Buzet 63 45 24N 13 58 E
Buzi, R. 127 19 52 S 34 30 E
Buziaş 66 45 38N 21 36 E
Buzuluk 84 52 48N 52 12 E
Buzuluk, R. 81 50 50N 52 12 E
Buzŭu 70 45 10N 26 50 E
Buzŭu □ 70 45 20N 26 30 E
Buzŭu, R. 70 45 10N 27 20 E
Buzzards Bay 162 41 45N 70 38W
Bwagaoia 135 10 40 S 152 52 E
Bwana Mkubwe 127 13 8 S 28 38 E
Byala, Ruse, Bulg. 67 43 28N 25 44 E
Byala, Varna, Bulg. 67 42 53N 27 55 E
Byala Slatina 67 43 26N 23 55 E
Byandovan, Mys 83 39 45N 49 28 E
Bychawa 54 51 1N 22 36 E
Byczyha 54 51 7N 18 12 E
Bydgoszcz 54 53 10N 18 0 E
Bydgoszcz □ 54 53 16N 17 33 E
Byelorussian S.S.R. □ 80 53 30N 27 0 E
Byers 158 39 46N 104 13W
Byfield 28 52 10N 1 15W
Bygland 71 58 50N 7 48 E
Byglandsfjord 71 58 40N 7 50 E
Byglandsfjorden 71 58 44N 7 50 E
Byhalia 159 34 53N 89 41W
Bykhov 80 53 31N 30 14 E
Bykle 71 59 20N 7 22 E
Bykovo 83 49 50N 45 25 E
Bylas 161 33 11N 110 9W
Bylchau 31 53 9N 3 32W
Bylderup 73 54 57N 9 6 E
Bylot I. 149 73 13N 78 34W
Byrd Land = Marie Byrd Land 13 79 30 S 125 0W
Byrd Sub-Glacial Basin 13 82 0 S 120 0W
Byro 137 26 5 S 116 11 E
Byrock 141 30 40 S 146 27 E
Byron B. 151 54 42N 57 40W
Byron, C. 133 28 38 S 153 40W
Byrranga, Gory 77 75 0N 100 0 E
Byrum 73 57 16N 11 0 E
Byske 74 64 57N 21 11 E
Byske, R. 74 65 20N 20 0 E
Bystrovka 85 42 47N 75 42 E
Bystrzyca Kłodzka 54 50 19N 16 39 E
Byten 80 52 50N 25 27 E
Bytom 54 50 25N 19 0 E
Bytom Ordz. 54 51 44N 15 48 E
Bytów 54 54 10N 17 30 E
Byumba 126 1 35 S 30 4 E
Byvalla 72 61 22N 16 27 E
Bzéma 117 24 50N 22 20 E
Bzenec 53 48 58N 17 18 E

C

Ca Mau = Quan Long 101 9 7N 105 8 E
Ca Mau, Mui = Bai Bung 101 8 35N 104 42 E
Ca Na 101 11 20N 108 54 E
Ca, R. 100 18 45N 105 45 E
Caacupé 172 25 23N 57 5W
Caamano Sd. 152 52 55N 129 25W
Caatingas 170 7 0 S 52 30W
Caazapá 172 26 8 S 56 19W
Caazapá □ 173 26 10 S 56 0W
Caballería, Cabo de 58 40 5N 4 5 E
Cabañaquinta 56 43 10N 5 38W
Cabanatuan 103 15 30N 121 5 E
Cabanes 58 40 9N 0 2 E
Cabano 151 47 40N 68 56 E
Cabazon 163 33 55N 116 47W
Cabbage Tree Hd. 108 27 20 S 153 5 E
Cabedelo 170 7 0 S 34 50W
Cabeza del Buey 57 38 44N 5 13W
Cabildo 172 32 30 S 71 5W
Cabimas 174 10 30N 71 25W
Cabinda 124 5 40 S 12 11 E
Cabinda □ 124 5 0 S 12 30 E
Cabinet Mts. 160 48 0N 115 30W
Cables 137 27 55 S 123 25 E
Cableskill 162 42 39N 74 30W
Cabo Blanco 176 47 56 S 65 47W
Cabo Delgado □ 127 10 35 S 40 35 E
Cabo Frio 173 22 51 S 42 3W
Cabo Pantoja 174 1 0 S 75 10W
Cabonga Reservoir 150 47 20N 76 40W
Cabool 159 37 10N 92 8W
Caboolture 139 27 5 S 152 58 E
Cabora Bassa Dam 127 15 20 S 32 50 E
Caborca (Heroica) 164 30 40N 112 10W
Cabot Strait 151 47 15N 59 40W
Cabra 57 37 30N 4 28W
Cabra del Santo Cristo 59 37 42N 3 16W
Cabrach 37 57 20N 3 0W
Cabras 64 39 57N 8 30 E
Cabrera, I. 59 39 6N 2 59 E
Cabrera, Sierra 56 42 12N 6 40W
Cabri 153 50 35N 108 25W
Cabriel, R. 59 39 20N 1 20W
Cabruta 174 7 50N 66 10W
Caburan 103 6 3N 125 45 E
Cabuyaro 174 4 18N 72 49W
Çacabelos 56 42 36N 6 44W
ČaCak 66 43 54N 20 20 E
Cáceres, Brazil 174 16 5 S 57 40W
Cáceres, Colomb. 174 7 35N 75 20W
Cáceres, Spain 57 39 26N 6 23W
Cáceres □ 57 39 45N 6 0W
Cache B. 150 46 26N 80 1W
Cache Bay 150 46 22N 80 0W
Cachepo 57 37 20N 7 49W
Cacheu 120 12 10N 16 8W
Cachi 172 25 5 S 66 10W
Cachimbo, Serra do 175 9 30 S 55 0W
Cáchira 174 7 21N 73 17W
Cachoeira 171 12 30 S 39 0W
Cachoeira Alta 171 18 48 S 50 58W
Cachoeira de Itapemirim 173 20 51 S 41 7W
Cachoeira do Sul 173 30 3 S 52 53W
Cachoeiro do Arari 170 1 1 S 48 58W
Cachopo 57 37 20N 7 49W
Cacolo 124 10 9 S 19 21 E
Caconda 125 13 48 S 15 8 E
Caçu 171 18 37 S 51 4W
Caculé 171 14 30 S 42 13W
Cadamstown 39 53 7N 7 39W
Cadarga 139 26 8 S 150 58 E
Çadaux 137 30 48 S 117 15 E
Čadca 53 49 26N 18 45 E
Caddo 159 34 8N 96 18W
Cadenazzo 51 46 9N 8 57 E
Cader Idris 31 52 43N 3 56W
Cadereyta Jiménez 165 25 40N 100 0W
Cadí, Sierra del 58 42 17N 1 42 E
Cadibarrawirracanna, L. 139 28 52 S 135 27 E
Cadillac, Can. 150 48 14N 78 23W
Cadillac, France 44 44 38N 0 20W
Cadillac, U.S.A. 156 44 16N 85 25W
Cadiz 103 11 30N 123 15 E
Cádiz 57 36 30N 6 20W
Cádiz □ 57 36 36N 5 45W
Cádiz, G. de 57 36 40N 7 0W
Cadomin 152 53 2N 117 20W
Cadotte, R. 152 56 43N 117 10W
Cadours 44 43 44N 1 2 E
Cadoux 137 30 46 S 117 7 E
Caen 42 49 10N 0 22W
Caenby Corner 33 53 23N 0 32W
Caergwrle 29 53 6N 3 3W
Caerhun 31 53 14N 3 50W
Caerleon 31 51 37N 2 57W
Caernarfon 31 53 8N 4 17W
Caernarfon B. 31 53 4N 4 40W
Caernarvon = Caernarfon 31 53 8N 4 17W
Caernarvon (□) 26 53 8N 4 17W
Caerphilly 31 51 34N 3 13W
Caersws 31 52 32N 3 27W
Caerwent 31 51 37N 2 47W
Cæsarea = Qesari 90 32 30N 34 53 E
Caeté 171 20 0 S 43 40W
Caetité 171 13 50 S 42 50W
Cafayate 172 26 2 S 66 0W
Cafu 128 16 30 S 15 8 E
Cagayan de Oro 103 8 30N 124 40 E
Cagayan, R. 103 18 25N 121 42 E
Cagli 63 43 32N 12 38 E
Cágliari 64 39 15N 9 6 E
Cágliari, G. di 64 39 8N 9 10 E
Cagnano Varano 65 41 49N 15 47 E
Cagnes-sur-Mer 45 43 40N 7 9 E
Caguas 147 18 14N 66 4W
Caha Mts. 39 51 45N 9 40W
Caher I. 38 53 44N 10 1W
Caherconlish 39 52 36N 8 30W
Cahermore 39 51 35N 10 2W
Cahir 39 52 23N 7 56W
Cahirciveen 39 51 57N 10 13W
Cahore Pt. 39 52 34N 6 11W
Cahors 44 44 27N 1 27 E
Cahuapanas 174 5 15 S 77 0W
Cai Ban, Dao 100 21 10N 107 27 E
Cai Nuoc 101 8 56N 105 1 E
Caianda 127 11 29 S 23 31 E
Caibarién 166 22 30N 79 30W
Caicara 174 7 38N 66 10W
Caicó 170 6 20 S 37 0W
Caicos Is. 167 21 40N 71 40W
Caicos Passage 167 22 45N 72 45W
Caihaique 176 45 30 S 71 45W
Caird Coast 13 75 0 S 25 0W
Cairn Gorm 37 57 7N 3 40W
Cairn Table 35 55 30N 4 0W
Cairngorm Mts. 37 57 6N 3 42W
Cairnryan 34 54 59N 5 0W
Cairns 138 16 57 S 145 45 E
Cairo, Ga., U.S.A. 157 30 52N 84 12W
Cairo, Illinois, U.S.A. 159 37 0N 89 10W
Cairo, N.Y., U.S.A. 162 42 18N 74 0W
Cairo = El Qâhira 122 30 1N 31 14 E
Cairo Montenotte 62 44 23N 8 16 E
Caister-on-Sea 29 52 38N 1 43 E
Caistor 33 53 29N 0 20W
Caithness (□) 26 58 25N 3 25W
Caithness, Ord of, C. 37 58 35N 3 37W

Caiundo Canton

Caiundo 125 15 50 S 17 52 E
Caiza 174 20 2 S 65 40 W
Cajamarca 174 7 5 S 78 28 W
Cajapió 170 2 58 S 44 48 W
Cajarc 44 44 29 N 1 50 E
Çajàzeiros 170 7 0 S 38 30 W
Çajetina 66 43 47 N 19 42 E
Čajniče 66 43 34 N 19 5 E
Çakirgöl 83 40 33 N 39 40 E
Cala 57 37 59 N 6 21 W
Cala Cadolar 59 38 38 N 1 35 E
Cala, R. 57 37 50 N 6 8 W
Calabar 121 4 57 N 8 20 E
Calabozo 174 9 0 N 67 20 W
Calábria □ 65 39 24 N 16 30 E
Calaburras, Pta. de 57 36 30 N 4 38 W
Calaceite 58 41 1 N 0 11 E
Calafat 70 43 58 N 22 59 E
Calafate 176 50 25 S 72 25 W
Calahorra 58 42 18 N 1 59 W
Calais, France 43 50 57 N 1 56 E
Calais, U.S.A. 151 45 5 N 67 20 W
Calais, Pas de 160 50 57 N 1 20 E
Calalaste, Sierra de 172 25 0 S 67 0 W
Calama, Brazil 174 8 0 S 62 50 W
Calama, Chile 172 22 30 S 68 55 W
Calamar, Bolívar, Colomb. 174 10 15 N 74 55 W
Calamar, Vaupés, Colomb. 174 1 58 N 72 32 W
Calamian Group 103 11 50 N 119 55 E
Calamocha 58 40 50 N 1 17 W
Calanaque 174 0 5 S 64 0 W
Calañas 57 37 40 N 6 53 W
Calanda 58 40 56 N 0 15 W
Calang 102 4 30 N 95 43 E
Calangiánus 64 40 56 N 9 12 E
Calapan 103 13 25 N 121 7 E
Calasparra 59 38 14 N 1 41 W
Calatafimi 64 37 56 N 12 50 E
Calatayud 58 41 20 N 1 40 W
Calauag 103 13 55 N 122 15 E
Calavà, C. 65 38 11 N 14 55 E
Calavite, Cape 103 13 26 N 120 10 E
Calbe 48 51 57 N 11 47 E
Calca 174 13 10 S 72 0 W
Calci 62 43 44 N 10 31 E
Calcidica = Khalkidhikí □ 170 40 25 N 23 40 E
Calcutta 95 22 36 N 88 24 E
Caldaro 63 46 23 N 11 15 E
Caldas □ 174 5 15 N 75 30 W
Caldas da Rainha 57 39 24 N 9 8 W
Caldas de Reyes 56 42 36 N 8 39 W
Caldas Novas 171 17 45 S 48 38 W
Caldbeck 32 54 45 N 3 3 W
Calder Bridge 32 54 27 N 3 31 W
Calder Hall 32 54 26 N 3 31 W
Calder, R. 33 53 44 N 1 21 W
Caldera 172 27 5 S 70 55 W
Caldew R. 32 54 54 N 2 59 W
Caldiran 92 39 7 N 44 0 E
Caldwell, Idaho, U.S.A. 160 43 45 N 116 42 W
Caldwell, Kans., U.S.A. 159 37 5 N 97 37 W
Caldwell, Texas, U.S.A. 159 30 30 N 96 42 W
Caldy I. 31 51 38 N 4 42 W
Caledon, S. Afr. 128 34 14 S 19 26 E
Caledon, U.K. 38 54 22 N 6 50 W
Caledon B. 138 12 45 S 137 0 E
Caledon, R. 128 30 0 S 26 46 E
Caledonian Can. 37 56 50 N 5 6 W
Calella 58 41 37 N 2 40 E
Calemba 128 16 0 S 15 38 E
Calera, La 172 32 50 S 71 10 W
Calexico 161 32 40 N 115 33 W
Calf of Man 32 54 4 N 4 48 W
Calgary, Can. 152 51 0 N 114 10 W
Calgary, U.K. 34 56 34 N 6 17 W
Calhoun 157 34 30 N 84 55 W
Cali 174 3 25 N 76 35 W
Caliach Pt. 34 56 37 N 6 20 W
Calicoan, I. 103 10 59 N 125 50 E
Calicut 93 11 15 N 75 43 E
Calicut, (Kozhikode) 97 11 15 N 75 43 E
Caliente 161 37 43 N 114 34 W
California 158 38 37 N 92 30 W
California □ 160 37 25 N 120 0 W
California, Baja 164 32 10 N 115 12 W
California, Baja, T.N. □ 164 30 0 N 115 0 W
California, Baja, T.S. □ 164 25 50 N 111 50 W
California City 163 35 7 N 117 57 W
California, Golfo de 164 27 0 N 111 0 W
California Hot Springs 163 35 51 N 118 41 W
California, Lr. = California, Baja 164 25 50 N 111 50 W
Calilegua 172 23 45 S 64 42 W
Călimăneşti 70 45 14 N 24 20 E
Calingasta 172 31 15 S 69 30 W
Calipatria 161 33 8 N 115 30 W
Calistoga 160 38 36 N 122 32 W
Calitri 65 40 54 N 15 25 E
Calkiní 165 20 21 N 90 3 W
Callabonna, L. 139 29 40 S 140 5 E
Callac 42 48 25 N 3 27 W
Callafo 91 · 6 48 N 43 47 E
Callan 39 52 33 N 7 25 W
Callanish 36 58 12 N 6 43 W
Callantsoog 46 52 50 N 4 42 E
Callao 174 12 0 S 77 0 W
Callaway 158 41 20 N 99 56 W
Calles 165 23 2 N 98 42 W
Callicoon 162 41 46 N 75 3 W
Callide 138 24 18 S 150 28 E
Calling Lake 152 55 15 N 113 12 W
Callington 30 56 30 N 4 19 W
Calliope 138 24 0 S 151 16 E
Callosa de Ensarriá 59 38 40 N 0 8 W
Callosa de Segura 59 38 1 N 0 53 W
Callow 38 53 58 N 9 2 W
Calne 28 51 26 N 2 0 W
Calola 128 16 25 S 17 48 E
Calore, R. 65 41 8 N 14 45 E
Caloundra 139 26 45 S 153 10 E
Calpe 59 38 39 N 0 3 E
Calshot 28 50 49 N 1 18 W
Calstock, Can. 150 49 47 N 84 9 W
Calstock, U.K. 30 50 30 N 4 13 W
Caltabellotta 64 37 36 N 13 11 E
Caltagirone 65 37 13 N 14 30 E
Caltanissetta 65 37 30 N 14 3 E
Caluire-et-Cuire 45 45 49 N 4 51 E
Calulo 124 10 1 S 14 56 E
Calumbo 124 9 0 S 13 20 E
Caluso 62 45 18 N 7 52 E
Calvados □ 42 49 5 N 0 15 W
Calvert 159 30 59 N 96 50 W
Calvert Hills 138 17 15 S 137 20 E
Calvert I. 152 51 30 N 128 0 W
Calvert, R. 138 16 17 S 137 44 E
Calvert Ra. 136 24 0 S 122 30 E
Calvillo 164 21 51 N 102 43 W
Calvinia 128 31 28 S 19 45 E
Calwa 163 36 42 N 119 46 W
Calzada Almuradiel 59 38 32 N 3 28 W
Calzada de Calatrava 57 38 42 N 3 46 W
Cam Lam 101 11 54 N 109 10 E
Cam Pha 100 21 1 N 107 18 E
Cam, R. 29 52 21 N 0 16 E
Cam Ranh 101 11 54 N 109 12 E
Cam Xuyen 100 18 15 N 106 0 E
Camabatela 124 8 20 S 15 26 E
Camacã 171 15 24 S 39 30 W
Camaçari 171 12 41 S 38 18 W
Camacho 164 24 25 N 102 18 W
Camaguán 174 8 6 N 67 36 W
Camagüey 166 21 20 N 78 0 W
Camaiore 62 43 57 N 10 18 E
Camamu 171 13 57 S 39 7 W
Camaná 174 16 30 S 72 50 W
Camaquã, R. 173 30 50 S 52 50 W
Camaret 42 48 16 N 4 37 W
Camargo 174 20 38 S 65 15 E
Camargue 45 43 34 N 4 34 E
Camarillo 163 34 13 N 119 2 W
Camariñas 56 43 8 N 9 12 W
Camarón, C. 166 16 0 N 85 0 W
Camarones, Argent. 176 44 50 S 65 40 W
Camarones, Chile 174 19 0 S 69 58 W
Camas 160 45 35 N 122 24 W
Camas Valley 160 43 0 N 123 46 W
Cambados 56 42 31 N 8 49 W
Cambará 173 23 2 S 50 5 W
Cambay 94 22 23 N 72 33 E
Cambay, G. of 94 20 45 N 72 30 E
Camberley 29 51 20 N 0 44 W
Cambil 59 37 40 N 3 33 W
Cambo 35 55 9 N 1 57 W
Cambo-les-Bains 44 43 22 N 1 23 W
Cambodia ■ 100 12 15 N 105 0 E
Camborne 30 50 13 N 5 18 W
Cambrai 43 50 11 N 3 14 E
Cambria 163 35 44 N 121 6 W
Cambrian Mts. 31 52 25 N 3 52 W
Cambridge, Can. 150 43 23 N 80 15 W
Cambridge, Jamaica 166 18 18 N 77 54 W
Cambridge, N.Z. 142 37 54 S 175 29 E
Cambridge, U.K. 29 52 13 N 0 8 E
Cambridge, Idaho, U.S.A. 160 44 36 N 116 52 W
Cambridge, Mass., U.S.A. 162 42 20 N 71 8 W
Cambridge, Md., U.S.A. 162 38 33 N 76 2 W
Cambridge, Minn., U.S.A. 158 45 34 N 93 15 W
Cambridge, Nebr., U.S.A. 158 40 20 N 100 12 W
Cambridge, N.Y., U.S.A. 162 43 2 N 73 22 W
Cambridge, Ohio, U.S.A. 156 40 1 N 81 22 W
Cambridge Bay 148 69 10 N 105 0 W
Cambridge Gulf 136 14 45 S 128 0 E
Cambridgeshire □ 29 52 12 N 0 7 E
Cambrils 58 41 8 N 1 3 E
Cambuci 173 21 35 S 41 55 W
Camden, Austral. 141 34 1 S 150 43 E
Camden, U.K. 29 51 33 N 0 10 W
Camden, Ala., U.S.A. 157 31 59 N 87 15 W
Camden, Ark., U.S.A. 159 33 30 N 92 50 W
Camden, Del., U.S.A. 162 39 7 N 75 33 W
Camden, Me., U.S.A. 151 44 14 N 69 6 W
Camden, N.J., U.S.A. 162 39 57 N 75 1 W
Camden, N.Y., U.S.A. 162 43 20 N 75 45 W
Camden, S.C., U.S.A. 157 34 17 N 80 34 W
Camden, B. 147 71 0 N 145 0 W
Camden Sound 136 15 27 S 124 25 E
Camel R. 30 50 28 N 4 49 W
Camelford 30 50 37 N 4 41 W
Camembert 42 48 53 N 0 10 E
Cámeri 62 45 30 N 8 40 E
Camerino 63 43 10 N 13 4 E
Cameron, Ariz., U.S.A. 161 35 55 N 111 31 W
Cameron, La., U.S.A. 159 29 50 N 93 18 W
Cameron, Mo., U.S.A. 158 39 42 N 94 14 W
Cameron, Tex., U.S.A. 159 30 53 N 97 0 W
Cameron Falls 150 49 8 N 88 19 W
Cameron Highlands 101 4 27 N 101 22 E
Cameron Hills 152 59 48 N 118 0 W
Cameron Mts. 143 46 1 S 167 0 E
Cameroon ■ 124 3 30 N 12 30 E
Camerota 65 40 2 N 15 21 E
Cameroun, Mt. 121 4 45 N 8 55 E
Cameroun, R. 121 4 0 N 9 35 E
Camerton 28 51 18 N 2 27 W
Cametá 170 2 0 S 49 30 W
Caminha 56 41 50 N 8 50 W
Camino 163 38 47 N 120 40 W
Camira Creek 139 29 15 S 152 58 E
Camiranga 170 1 48 S 46 17 W
Cammachmore 37 57 2 N 2 9 W
Camocim 170 2 55 S 40 50 W
Camogli 62 44 21 N 9 9 E
Camolin 39 52 37 N 6 26 W
Camooweal 138 19 56 S 138 7 E
Camopi, R. 175 3 12 N 52 17 W
Camp Crook 158 45 36 N 103 59 W
Camp Hill 162 40 15 N 76 56 W
Camp Nelson 163 36 8 N 118 39 W
Camp Wood 159 29 47 N 100 0 W
Campagna 65 40 40 N 15 5 E
Campana 172 34 10 S 58 55 W
Campana, I. 176 48 20 S 75 10 W
Campanario 57 38 52 N 5 36 W
Campania □ 65 40 50 N 14 45 E
Campbell 163 37 17 N 121 57 W
Campbell, C. 143 41 47 S 174 18 E
Campbell I. 142 52 30 S 169 0 E
Campbell L. 153 63 14 N 106 55 W
Campbell River 152 50 5 N 125 20 W
Campbell Town 138 41 52 S 147 30 E
Campbellpur 94 33 46 N 72 20 E
Campbellsville 156 37 23 N 85 12 W
Campbellton, Alta., Can. 152 53 32 N 113 15 W
Campbellton, N.B., Can. 151 47 57 N 66 43 W
Campbelltown, Austral. 141 34 4 S 150 49 E
Campbelltown, U.K. 37 57 34 N 4 2 W
Campbeltown 34 55 25 N 5 36 W
Campeche 165 19 50 N 90 32 W
Campeche □ 165 19 50 N 90 32 W
Campeche, Golfo de 165 19 30 N 93 0 W
Camperdown 140 38 14 S 143 9 E
Camperville 153 51 59 N 100 9 W
Campi Salentina 65 40 22 N 18 2 E
Campidano 64 39 30 N 8 40 E
Campillo de Altobuey 58 39 36 N 1 49 W
Campillo de Llerena 57 38 30 N 5 50 W
Campillos 57 37 4 N 4 51 W
Campina Grande 170 7 20 S 35 47 W
Campiña, La 57 37 45 N 4 45 W
Campina Verde 171 19 31 S 49 28 W
Campinas 173 22 50 S 47 0 W
Campine 47 51 8 N 5 20 E
Campinho 170 14 30 S 39 10 W
Campli 63 42 44 N 13 40 E
Campo 124 2 15 N 9 58 E
Campo Beló 171 21 0 S 45 30 W
Campo de Criptana 59 39 25 N 3 7 W
Campo de Gibraltar 57 36 15 N 5 25 W
Campo Flórido 171 19 47 S 48 35 W
Campo Formoso 170 10 30 S 40 20 W
Campo Grande 175 20 25 S 54 40 W
Campo Maior, Brazil 170 4 50 S 42 12 W
Campo Maior, Port. 57 38 59 N 7 7 W
Campo Mourão 171 24 3 S 52 22 W
Campo Tencia 51 46 26 N 8 43 E
Campo Túres 63 46 53 N 11 55 E
Campoalegre 174 2 41 N 75 20 W
Campobasso 65 41 34 N 14 40 E
Campobello di Licata 64 37 16 N 13 55 E
Campobello di Mazara 64 37 38 N 12 45 E
Campofelice 64 37 54 N 13 53 E
Camporeale 64 37 53 N 13 3 E
Campos 173 21 50 S 41 20 W
Campos Altos 171 19 41 S 46 10 W
Campos Belos 171 13 10 S 46 45 W
Campos del Puerto 59 39 26 N 3 1 E
Campos Novos 173 27 21 S 51 20 W
Campos Sales 170 7 4 S 40 23 W
Camprodón 58 42 19 N 2 23 E
Campsie Fells 23 56 2 N 4 20 W
Camptown 162 41 44 N 76 14 W
Campuya, R. 174 1 10 S 74 0 W
Camrose, Can. 152 53 0 N 112 50 W
Camrose, U.K. 31 51 50 N 5 2 W
Camsall L. 153 72 32 N 106 47 W
Camsell Portage 153 59 37 N 109 15 W
Camurra 139 29 21 S 149 52 E
Can Gio 101 10 25 N 106 58 E
Can Tho 101 10 2 N 105 46 E
Canada ■ 148 60 0 N 100 0 W
Cañada de Gómez 73 32 55 S 61 30 W
Canadian 159 35 56 N 100 25 W
Canadian, R. 159 36 0 N 98 45 W
Canairiktok, R. 151 54 30 N 62 30 W
Canajoharie 162 42 54 N 74 35 W
Çanakkale 68 40 8 N 26 30 E
Çanakkale Boğazi 68 40 0 N 26 0 E
Canal de l'Est 43 48 45 N 5 35 E
Canal Flats 152 50 10 N 115 48 W
Canal latéral à la Garonne 44 44 25 N 0 15 E
Canalejas 172 35 15 S 66 34 W
Canals 172 33 35 S 62 40 W
Canáls 59 38 58 N 0 35 W
Canandaigua 156 42 55 N 77 18 W
Cananea 164 31 0 N 110 20 W
Canarias, Islas 116 29 30 N 17 0 W
Canarreos, Arch. de los 166 21 35 N 81 40 W
Canary Is. = Canarias, Islas 116 29 30 N 17 0 W
Canastra, Serra da 171 20 0 S 46 20 W
Canatlán 164 24 31 N 104 47 W
Canaveral, C. 157 28 28 N 80 31 W
Cañaveras 58 40 27 N 2 14 W
Canavieiras 171 15 39 S 39 0 W
Canbelego 141 31 32 S 146 18 E
Canberra 141 35 15 S 149 8 E
Canby, Calif., U.S.A. 160 41 26 N 120 58 W
Canby, Minn., U.S.A. 158 44 44 N 96 15 W
Canby, Oregon, U.S.A. 160 45 24 N 122 45 W
Cancale 42 48 40 N 1 50 W
Candala 91 11 30 N 49 58 E
Candas 56 43 35 N 5 45 W
Candé 42 47 34 N 1 0 W
Candea = Iráklion 69 35 20 N 25 12 E
Candela 65 41 8 N 15 31 E
Candelaria 173 27 29 S 55 44 W
Candelaria, Pta. de la 56 43 45 N 8 0 W
Candeleda 56 40 10 N 5 14 W
Candelo 141 36 47 S 149 43 E
Candia = Iráklion 69 35 20 N 25 12 E
Cândido de Abreu 171 24 35 S 51 20 W
Cândido Mendes 170 1 27 S 45 43 W
Candle L. 153 53 50 N 105 18 W
Cando 158 48 30 N 99 14 W
Canea = Khaniá 69 35 30 N 24 4 E
Canela 170 10 15 S 48 25 W
Canelli 62 44 44 N 8 18 E
Canelones 172 34 32 S 56 10 W
Canet-Plage 44 42 41 N 3 2 E
Cañete, Chile 172 37 50 S 73 30 W
Cañete, Cuba 167 20 36 N 74 43 W
Cañete, Peru 174 13 0 S 76 30 W
Cañete, Spain 58 40 3 N 1 54 W
Cañete de las Torres 57 37 53 N 4 19 W
Canfranc 58 42 42 N 0 31 W
Cangamba 125 13 40 S 19 54 E
Cangas 56 42 16 N 8 47 W
Cangas de Narcea 56 43 10 N 6 32 W
Cangas de Onís 56 43 21 N 5 8 W
Canguaretama 170 6 20 S 35 5 W
Canguçu 173 31 22 S 52 43 W
Canhotinho 171 8 53 S 36 12 W
Cani, Is. 119 36 21 N 10 5 E
Canicado 125 24 2 S 33 2 E
Canicatti 64 37 21 N 13 50 E
Canicattini 65 37 1 N 15 3 E
Canim, L. 152 51 45 N 120 50 W
Canim Lake 152 51 17 N 120 54 W
Canindé 170 4 22 S 39 19 W
Canindé, R. 170 6 15 S 42 52 W
Canipaan 102 8 33 N 117 15 E
Canisbay 37 58 38 N 3 6 W
Canisp Mt. 36 58 8 N 5 5 W
Cañitas 164 23 36 N 102 43 W
Cañiza, La 56 42 13 N 8 16 W
Cañizal 56 41 20 N 5 22 W
Canjáyar 59 37 1 N 2 44 W
Cankırı 92 40 40 N 33 30 E
Cankuzo 126 3 10 S 30 31 E
Canlaon, Mt. 103 9 27 N 118 25 E
Canmore 152 51 7 N 115 18 W
Cann River 141 37 35 S 149 7 E
Canna I. 36 57 3 N 6 33 W
Canna, Sd. of 36 57 1 N 6 30 W
Cannanore 97 11 53 N 75 27 E
Cannes 45 43 32 N 7 0 E
Cannich 37 57 20 N 4 48 W
Canning Basin 136 19 50 S 124 0 E
Canning Town 95 22 23 N 88 40 E
Cannington 28 51 8 N 3 4 W
Cannock 28 52 42 N 2 2 W
Cannock Chase, hills 23 52 43 N 2 0 W
Cannon Ball, R. 158 46 20 N 101 20 W
Cannondale, Mt. 138 25 13 S 148 57 E
Caño Colorado 174 2 18 N 68 22 W
Canoe L. 153 55 10 N 108 15 W
Canol 147 65 15 N 126 50 W
Canon City 158 39 30 N 105 20 W
Canonbie 35 55 4 N 2 58 W
Canopus 140 33 29 S 140 42 E
Canora 153 51 40 N 102 30 W
Canosa di Púglia 65 41 13 N 16 4 E
Canourgue, Le 44 44 26 N 3 13 E
Canowindra 141 33 35 S 148 38 E
Canso 151 45 20 N 61 0 W
Cantabria, Sierra de 58 42 40 N 2 30 W
Cantabrian Mts. = Cantábrica 56 43 0 N 5 10 W
Cantábrica, Cordillera 56 43 0 N 5 10 W
Cantal □ 44 45 4 N 2 45 E
Cantanhede 56 40 20 N 8 36 W
Cantaura 174 9 19 N 64 21 W
Çantavieja 58 40 31 N 0 25 W
Čantavir 66 45 55 N 19 46 E
Canterbury, Austral. 138 25 23 S 141 53 E
Canterbury, U.K. 29 51 17 N 1 5 E
Canterbury □ 143 43 45 S 171 19 E
Canterbury Bight 143 44 16 S 171 55 E
Canterbury Plains 143 43 55 S 171 22 E
Cantil 163 35 18 N 117 58 W
Cantillana 57 37 36 N 5 50 W
Canto do Buriti 170 8 7 S 42 58 W
Canton, Ga., U.S.A. 157 34 13 N 84 29 W
Canton, Ill., U.S.A. 158 40 32 N 90 0 W
Canton, Mass., U.S.A. 162 42 9 N 71 9 W
Canton, Miss., U.S.A. 159 32 40 N 90 1 W
Canton, Mo., U.S.A. 158 40 10 N 91 33 W
Canton, Ohio, U.S.A. 156 40 47 N 81 22 W
Canton, Okla., U.S.A. 159 36 5 N 98 36 W

Canton **Cascade**

Canton, Pa., U.S.A. 162 41 39N 76 51W
Canton, S.D., U.S.A. 158 43 20N 96 35W
Canton = Kuangchou 109 23 10N 113 10 E
Canton I. 130 2 30 S 172 0W
Canton L. 159 36 12N 98 40W
Cantù 62 45 44N 9 8 E
Canudos 174 7 13 S 58 5W
Canulloit 161 31 58N 106 36W
Canutama 174 6 30 S 64 20W
Canvey 29 51 32N 0 35 E
Canyon, Can. 147 47 25N 84 36W
Canyon, Texas, U.S.A. 159 35 0N 101 57W
Canyon, Wyo., U.S.A. 160 44 43N 110 36W
Canyonlands Nat. Park 161 38 25N 109 30W
Canyonville 160 42 55N 123 14W
Canzo 62 45 54N 9 18 E
Cao Bang 100 22 40N 106 15 E
Cao Lanh 101 10 27N 105 38 E
Caoles 34 56 32N 6 43W
Caolisport, Loch 34 55 54N 5 40W
Cáorle 63 45 36N 12 51 E
Cap-aux-Meules 151 47 23N 61 52W
Cap Chat 151 49 6N 66 40W
Cap-de-la-Madeleine 150 46 22N 72 31W
Cap Haïtien 167 19 40N 72 20W
Cap St.-Jacques = Vung Tau 101 10 21N 107 4 E
Capa Stilo 65 38 25N 16 25 E
Capáccio 65 40 26N 15 4 E
Capaia 124 8 27 S 20 13 E
Capanaparo, R. 174 7 0N 67 30W
Capanema 170 1 12 S 47 11W
Caparo, R. 174 7 30N 70 30W
Capatárida 174 11 11N 70 37W
Capbreton 44 43 39N 1 26W
Capdenac 44 44 34N 2 5 E
Cape Barren I. 138 40 25 S 148 15 E
Cape Breton Highlands Nat. Park 151 46 50N 60 40W
Cape Breton I. 151 46 0N 60 30W
Cape Charles 162 37 15N 75 59W
Cape Coast 121 5 5N 1 15W
Cape Cod B. 162 41 50N 70 18W
Cape Dorset 149 64 14N 76 32W
Cape Dyer 149 66 40N 61 22W
Cape Fear, R. 157 34 30N 78 25W
Cape Girardeau 159 37 20N 89 30W
Cape Jervis 140 35 40 S 138 5 E
Cape May 162 39 1N 74 53W
Cape May C.H. 162 39 5N 74 50W
Cape May Pt. 162 38 56N 74 56W
Cape Montague 151 46 5N 62 25W
Cape Palmas 120 4 25N 7 49W
Cape Preston 136 20 51 S 116 12 E
Cape Province □ 128 32 0 S 23 0 E
Cape, R. 138 20 37 S 147 1 E
Cape Tormentine 151 46 8N 63 47W
Cape Town (Kaapstad) 128 33 55 S 18 22 E
Cape Verde Is. 14 17 10N 25 20W
Cape York Peninsula 138 33 34 S 115 33 E
Capel 29 51 8N 0 18W
Capel Curig 31 53 6N 3 55W
Capela 170 10 30 S 37 0W
Capela de Campo 170 4 40 S 41 55W
Capelinha 171 17 42 S 42 31W
Capella 138 23 2 S 148 1 E
Capella, G. 138 4 45 S 140 50 E
Capella, Mt. 135 5 4 S 141 8 E
Capelle, La 43 49 59N 3 50 E
Capendu 44 43 11N 2 31 E
Capernaum = Kefar Nahum 90 32 54N 35 32 E
Capestang 44 43 20N 3 2 E
Capim 170 1 41 S 47 47W
Capim, R. 170 3 0 S 48 0W
Capinópolis 171 18 41 S 49 35W
Capitan 161 33 40N 105 41W
Capitola 163 36 59N 121 57W
Capivara, Serra da 171 14 35 S 45 0W
Capizzi 65 37 50N 14 26 E
Čapljina 66 43 35N 17 43 E
Capoche, R. 127 15 0 S 32 45 E
Cappamore 39 52 38N 8 20W
Cappoquin 39 52 9N 7 46W
Capraia, I. 62 43 2N 9 50 E
Caprarola 63 42 21N 12 11 E
Capreol 150 46 43N 80 56W
Caprera, I. 64 41 12N 9 28 E
Capri, I. 65 40 34N 14 15 E
Capricorn, C. 133 23 30 S 151 13 E
Capricorn Group 138 23 30 S 151 55 E
Capricorn Ra. 136 23 20 S 117 0 E
Caprino Veronese 62 45 37N 10 47 E
Caprivi Strip 128 18 0 S 23 0 E
Captainganj 95 26 55N 83 45 E
Captain's Flat 141 35 35 S 149 27 E
Captieux 44 44 18N 0 16W
Cápua 65 41 7N 14 15 E
Capulin 159 36 48N 103 59W
Caquetá □ 174 1 0N 74 0W
Caquetá, R. 174 1 0N 76 20W
Cáqueza 174 4 25N 73 57W
Carabobo 174 10 10N 68 5W
Caracal 70 44 8N 24 22 E
Caracaraí 174 1 50N 61 8W
Caracas 174 10 30N 66 55W
Caracol, Piaui, Brazil 170 9 15 S 43 45W
Caracol, Rondonia, Brazil 174 9 15 S 64 20W
Caradoc 140 30 35 S 143 5 E
Caragabal 141 33 49 S 147 45 E
Caragh L. 39 52 3N 9 50W
Caráglio 62 44 25N 7 25 E
Caraí 171 17 12 S 41 42W
Carajás, Serra dos 170 6 0 S 51 30W
Caramanta 174 5 33N 75 38W
Carangola 173 20 50 S 42 5W
Carani 137 30 57 S 116 28 E
Caransebeş 70 45 28N 22 18 E
Carapelle, R. 65 41 20N 15 35 E
Caraş Severin □ 66 45 10N 22 10 E
Caraşova 66 45 11N 21 51 E
Caratasca, Laguna 166 15 30N 83 40W
Caratec 42 48 40N 3 55W
Caratinga 171 19 50 S 42 10W
Caratunk 151 45 13N 69 55W
Caraúbas 170 7 43 S 36 31W
Caravaca 59 38 8N 1 52W
Caravággio 62 45 30N 9 39 E
Caravelas 171 17 45 S 39 15W
Caraveli 174 15 45 S 73 25W
Caràzinho 173 28 0 S 53 0W
Carballino 56 42 26N 8 5W
Carballo 56 43 13N 8 41W
Carberry 153 49 50N 99 25W
Carbia 56 42 48N 8 14W
Carbó 164 29 42N 110 58W
Carbon 152 51 30N 113 9W
Carbonara, C. 64 39 8N 9 30 E
Carbondale, Colo, U.S.A. 160 39 30N 107 10W
Carbondale, Ill., U.S.A. 159 37 45N 89 10W
Carbondale, Pa., U.S.A. 162 41 37N 75 30W
Carbonear 151 47 42N 53 13W
Carboneras 59 37 0N 1 53W
Carboneras de Guadazaón 58 39 54N 1 50W
Carbonia 64 39 10N 8 30 E
Carbost 36 57 19N 6 21W
Carbury 38 53 22N 6 58W
Carcabuey 57 37 27N 4 17W
Carcagente 59 39 8N 0 28W
Carcajou 152 57 47N 117 6W
Carcasse, C. 167 18 30N 74 28W
Carcassonne 44 43 13N 2 20 E
Carche 59 38 26N 1 9W
Carcoar 141 33 36 S 149 8 E
Carcross 147 60 13N 134 45W
Cardabia 136 23 2 S 113 55 E
Cardamom Hills 97 9 30N 77 15 E
Cárdenas, Cuba 166 23 0N 81 30W
Cárdenas, San Luis Potosí, Mexico 166 22 0N 99 41W
Cárdenas, Tabasco, Mexico 165 17 59N 93 21W
Cardenete 58 39 46N 1 41W
Cardiff 31 51 28N 3 11W
Cardiff-by-the-Sea 163 33 1N 117 17W
Cardigan 31 52 6N 4 41W
Cardigan (□) 26 52 6N 4 41W
Cardigan B. 31 52 30N 4 30W
Cardington 29 52 7N 0 23W
Cardón 174 11 37N 70 14W
Cardona, Spain 58 41 56N 1 40 E
Cardona, Uruguay 172 33 53 S 57 18W
Cardoner, R. 58 42 0N 1 33 E
Cardross 153 49 50N 105 40W
Cardston 152 49 15N 113 20W
Cardwell 138 18 14 S 146 2 E
Careen L. 153 57 0N 108 11W
Carei 70 47 40N 22 29 E
Carentan 42 49 19N 1 15W
Carey, Idaho, U.S.A. 160 43 19N 113 58W
Carey, Ohio, U.S.A. 156 40 58N 83 22W
Carey, L. 137 29 0 S 122 15 E
Carey L. 153 62 12N 102 55W
Careysburg 120 6 34N 10 30W
Cargados Garajos, Is. 11 17 0 S 59 0 E
Cargelligo, L. 139 33 17 S 146 24 E
Cargèse 45 42 7N 8 35 E
Carhaix-Plouguer 42 48 18N 3 36W
Carhué 172 37 10 S 62 50W
Cariacica 171 20 16 S 40 25W
Cariaco 174 10 29N 63 33W
Caribaná, Pta. 174 8 37N 76 52W
Caribbean Sea 167 15 0N 75 0W
Cariboo Mts. 152 53 0N 121 0W
Caribou, Can. 153 53 15N 121 55W
Caribou, U.S.A. 151 46 55N 68 0W
Caribou I. 150 47 22N 85 49W
Caribou Is. 152 61 55N 113 15W
Caribou L., Man., Can. 153 59 21N 96 10W
Caribou L., Ont., Can. 150 50 25N 89 5W
Caribou Mts. 152 59 12N 115 40W
Caribou, R., Man., Can. 153 59 20N 94 44W
Caribou, R., N.W.T., Can. 152 61 27N 125 45W
Carichic 164 27 56N 107 3W
Carignan 43 49 38N 5 10 E
Carignano 62 44 55N 7 40 E
Carillo 164 26 50N 103 55W
Carinda 141 30 28 S 147 41 E
Cariñena 58 41 20N 1 13W
Carinhanha 171 14 15 S 44 0W
Carinhanha, R. 171 14 20 S 43 47W
Carini 64 38 9N 13 10 E
Carinish 36 57 31N 7 20W
Carinola 64 41 11N 13 58 E
Carinthia □ = Kärnten 52 46 52N 13 30 E
Caripito 174 10 8N 63 6W
Cariríacu 171 7 2 S 39 17W
Carisbrooke 28 50 42N 1 19W
Caritianas 174 9 20 S 63 0W
Cark 32 54 11N 2 59W
Carlentini 65 37 15N 15 2 E
Carleton Place 150 45 8N 76 9W
Carleton Rode 29 52 30N 1 6 E
Carletonville 128 26 23 S 27 22 E
Carlin 160 40 50N 116 5W
Carlingford 38 54 3N 6 10W
Carlingford, L. 38 54 0N 6 5W
Carlinville 158 39 20N 89 55W
Carlisle, U.K. 32 54 54N 2 55W
Carlisle, U.S.A. 162 40 12N 77 10W
Carlitte, Pic 44 42 35N 1 43 E
Carloforte 64 39 10N 8 18 E
Carlops 35 55 47N 3 20W
Carlos Casares 172 35 53 S 61 20W
Carlos Chagas 171 17 43 S 40 45W
Carlos Tejedor 172 35 25 S 62 25W
Carlota, La 172 33 30 S 63 20W
Carlow 39 52 50N 6 58W
Carlow □ 39 52 43N 6 50W
Carloway 36 58 17N 6 48W
Carlsbad, Calif., U.S.A. 163 33 11N 117 25W
Carlsbad, N. Mex., U.S.A. 159 32 20N 104 7W
Carlton 33 52 58N 1 6W
Carlton Colville 29 52 27N 1 41 E
Carlton Miniott 33 54 13N 1 22W
Carluke 35 55 44N 3 50W
Carlyle, Can. 153 49 40N 102 20W
Carlyle, U.S.A. 158 38 38N 89 23W
Carmacks 147 62 5N 136 16W
Carmagnola 62 44 50N 7 42 E
Carman 153 49 30N 98 0W
Carmangay 152 50 10N 113 10W
Carmanville 151 49 23N 54 19W
Carmarthen 31 51 52N 4 20W
Carmarthen (□) 26 53 40N 4 18W
Carmarthen B. 31 51 40N 4 30W
Carmaux 44 44 3N 2 10 E
Carmel, Calif., U.S.A. 163 36 38N 121 55W
Carmel, N.Y., U.S.A. 162 41 25N 73 38W
Carmel Hd. 31 53 24N 4 34W
Carmel Mt. 90 32 45N 35 3 E
Carmel Valley 163 36 29N 121 43W
Carmelo 172 34 0 S 58 10W
Carmen, Colomb. 174 9 43N 75 8W
Carmen, Parag. 173 27 13 S 56 12W
Carmen de Patagones 176 40 50 S 63 0W
Carmen, I. 164 26 0N 111 20W
Carmen, R. 164 30 42N 106 29W
Cármenes 56 42 58N 5 34W
Carmensa 172 35 15 S 67 40W
Carmi 156 38 6N 88 10W
Carmichael 163 38 38N 121 19W
Carmila 138 21 55 S 149 24 E
Carmo do Paranaiba 171 18 59 S 46 21W
Carmona 57 37 28N 5 42W
Carmyllie 37 56 36N 2 41W
Carn Ban 37 57 6N 4 15W
Carn Eige 36 57 17N 5 9W
Carn Glas Chorie 37 57 20N 3 50W
Carn Mor 37 57 14N 3 13W
Carn na Saobhaidh 37 57 12N 4 20W
Carna 39 53 20N 9 50W
Carnarvon, Queens., Austral. 138 24 48 S 147 45 E
Carnarvon, W. Austral., Austral. 137 24 51 S 113 42 E
Carnarvon, S. Afr. 128 30 56 S 22 8 E
Carnarvon Ra., Queensland, Austral. 138 25 15 S 148 30 E
Carnarvon Ra., W.A., Austral. 137 25 0 S 120 45 E
Carnaxide 57 38 43N 9 14W
Carncastle 38 54 55N 5 52W
Carndonagh 38 55 15N 7 16W
Carnduff 153 49 10N 101 50W
Carnedd Llewelyn, Mt. 31 53 9N 3 58W
Carnegie, L. 137 26 5 S 122 30 E
Carnew 39 52 43N 6 30W
Carney 38 54 20N 8 30W
Carnforth 32 54 8N 2 47W
Carnic Alps = Karnische Alpen 63 46 34N 12 50 E
Carnlough 38 55 0N 6 0W
Carno 31 52 34N 3 31W
Carnon 44 43 32N 3 59 E
Carnot 124 4 59N 15 56 E
Carnot B. 136 17 20 S 121 30 E
Carnoustie 35 56 30N 2 41W
Carnsore Pt. 39 52 10N 6 20W
Carnwath 35 55 42N 3 38W
Caro 156 43 29N 83 27W
Carolina, Brazil 170 7 10 S 47 30W
Carolina, S. Afr. 129 26 5 S 30 6 E
Carolina, La 57 38 17N 3 38W
Caroline I. 131 9 15 S 150 3W
Caroline Is. 130 8 0N 150 0 E
Caroline Pk. 143 45 57 S 167 15 E
Carolside 152 51 20N 111 40W
Caron 153 50 30N 105 50W
Caroni, R. 174 6 0N 62 40W
Carora 174 10 11N 70 5W
Carovigno 65 40 42N 17 40 E
Carpathians, Mts. 53 46 20N 26 0 E
Carpaţii Meridionali 70 45 30N 25 0 E
Carpenèdolo 62 45 22N 10 25 E
Carpentaria Downs 138 18 44 S 144 20 E
Carpentaria, G. of 133 14 0 S 139 0 E
Carpentras 45 44 3N 5 2 E
Carpi 62 44 47N 10 52 E
Carpina 170 7 51 S 35 15W
Carpino 65 41 50N 15 51 E
Carpinteria 163 34 25N 119 31W
Carpio 56 41 13N 5 7W
Carpolac = Morea 140 36 45 S 141 18 E
Carr Boyd Ra. 136 16 15 S 128 35 E
Carra L. 38 53 41N 9 12W
Carrabelle 157 29 52N 84 40W
Carracastle 38 53 57N 8 42W
Carradale 34 55 35N 5 30W
Carraipia 174 11 16N 72 22W
Carrara 62 44 5N 10 7 E
Carrascosa del Campo 58 40 2N 2 45W
Carrauntohill, Mt. 39 52 0N 9 49W
Carraweena 139 29 10 S 140 0 E
Carrbridge 37 57 17N 3 50W
Carriacou, I. 167 12 30N 61 28W
Carribee 140 35 7 S 136 57 E
Carrick 38 54 40N 8 39W
Carrick, dist. 34 55 12N 4 38W
Carrick-on-Shannon 38 53 57N 8 7W
Carrick-on-Suir 39 52 22N 7 30W
Carrick Ra. 143 45 15 S 169 8 E
Carrickart 38 55 10N 7 47W
Carrickbeg 39 52 20N 7 25W
Carrickboy 38 53 36N 7 40W
Carrickfergus 36 54 43N 5 50W
Carrickfergus □ 38 54 43N 5 49W
Carrickmacross 38 54 0N 6 43W
Carrieton 140 32 25 S 138 31 E
Carrigaholt 39 52 37N 9 42W
Carrigahorig 39 53 4N 8 10W
Carrigaline 39 51 49N 8 22W
Carrigallen 38 53 59N 7 40W
Carrigan Hd. 38 54 38N 8 40W
Carrignavar 39 52 0N 8 29W
Carrigtwohill 39 51 55N 8 15W
Carrington 158 47 30N 99 7W
Carrión de los Condes 56 42 20N 4 37W
Carrión, R. 56 42 42N 4 47W
Carrizal 174 12 1N 72 11W
Carrizal Bajo 172 28 5 S 71 20W
Carrizalillo 172 29 0 S 71 30W
Carrizo Cr. 159 36 30N 103 40W
Carrizo Springs 159 28 28N 99 50W
Carrizozo 161 33 40N 105 57W
Carroll 158 42 2N 94 55W
Carrollton, Ga., U.S.A. 157 33 36N 85 5W
Carrollton, Ill., U.S.A. 158 39 20N 90 25W
Carrollton, Ky., U.S.A. 156 38 40N 85 10W
Carrollton, Mo., U.S.A. 158 39 19N 93 24W
Carron L. 36 57 22N 5 35W
Carron R., U.K. 36 57 30N 5 30W
Carron R., U.K. 37 57 51N 4 21W
Carrot, R. 153 53 50N 101 17W
Carrot River 153 53 17N 103 35W
Carrouges 42 48 34N 0 10W
Carrowkeel 38 55 7N 7 12W
Carrowmore L. 38 54 12N 9 48W
Carruthers 153 52 52N 109 16W
Carryduff 38 54 32N 5 52W
Çarşamba 92 41 15N 36 45 E
Carsoli 63 42 7N 13 3 E
Carson 158 46 27N 101 29W
Carson City 160 39 12N 119 46W
Carson Sink 160 39 50N 118 40W
Carsonville 156 43 25N 82 39W
Carsphairn 34 55 13N 4 15W
Carstairs 35 55 42N 3 41W
Cartagena, Colomb. 174 10 25N 75 33W
Cartagena, Spain 59 37 38N 0 59W
Cartago, Colomb. 174 4 45N 75 55W
Cartago, C. Rica 166 9 50N 84 0W
Cartaret 42 49 23N 1 47W
Cartaxo 57 39 10N 8 47W
Cartaya 57 37 16N 7 9W
Cartersville 157 34 11N 84 48W
Carterton 142 41 2 S 175 31 E
Carthage, Ark., U.S.A. 159 34 4N 92 32W
Carthage, Ill., U.S.A. 158 40 25N 91 10W
Carthage, Mo., U.S.A. 159 37 10N 94 20W
Carthage, N.Y., U.S.A. 156 43 59N 75 37W
Carthage, S.D., U.S.A. 158 44 14N 97 38W
Carthage, Texas, U.S.A. 159 32 8N 94 20W
Cartier I. 136 12 31 S 123 29 E
Cartmel 32 54 13N 2 57W
Cartwright 151 53 41N 56 58W
Caruaru 170 8 15 S 35 55W
Carúpano 174 10 45N 63 15W
Carutapera 170 1 13 S 46 1W
Caruthersville 159 36 10N 89 40W
Carvarzere 63 45 8N 12 7 E
Carvin 43 50 30N 2 57 E
Carvoeiro 174 1 30 S 61 59W
Carvoeiro, Cabo 57 39 21N 9 24W
Casa Agapito 174 2 3N 73 58W
Casa Branca, Brazil 171 21 46 S 47 4W
Casa Branca, Port. 57 38 29N 8 12W
Casa Grande 161 32 53N 111 51W
Casa Nova 170 9 10 S 41 5W
Casablanca, Chile 172 33 20 S 71 25W
Casablanca, Moroc. 118 33 36N 7 36W
Casacalenda 65 41 45N 14 50 E
Casalbordino 63 42 10N 14 34 E
Casale Monferrato 62 45 8N 8 28 E
Casalmaggiore 62 44 59N 10 25 E
Casalpusterlengo 62 45 10N 9 40 E
Casamance, R. 120 12 54N 15 0W
Casamássima 65 40 58N 16 55 E
Casanare, R. 174 6 30N 71 20W
Casarano 65 40 0N 18 10 E
Casares 57 36 27N 5 16W
Casas Grandes 164 30 22N 108 0W
Casas IbáPez 59 39 17N 1 30W
Casasimarro 59 39 22N 2 3W
Casatejada 56 39 54N 5 40W
Casavieja 56 40 17N 4 46W
Cascade, Idaho, U.S.A. 160 44 30N 116 2W

Cascade **Cepin**

Cascade, Mont., U.S.A. **160** 47 16N 111 46W
Cascade Locks **160** 45 44N 121 54W
Cascade Pt. **143** 44 1S 168 20E
Cascade Ra. **160** 45 0N 121 30W
Cascais **57** 38 41N 9 25W
Cascina **62** 43 40N 10 32E
Caselle Torinese **62** 45 12N 7 39E
Caserta **65** 41 5N 14 20E
Cashel **39** 52 31N 7 53W
Cashla B. **39** 53 12N 9 37W
Cashmere **160** 47 31N 120 30W
Cashmere Downs **137** 28 57S 119 35E
Casigua **174** 11 2N 71 1W
Casiguran **103** 16 15N 122 15E
Casilda **172** 33 10S 61 10W
Casimcea **70** 44 45N 28 23E
Casino **139** 28 52S 153 3E
Casiquiare, R. **174** 2 45N 66 20W
Caslan **152** 54 38N 112 31W
Casma **174** 9 30S 78 20W
Casmalia **163** 34 50N 120 32W
Casola Valsenio **63** 44 12N 11 40E
Cásoli **63** 42 7N 14 18E
Caspe **58** 41 14N 0 1W
Casper **160** 42 52N 106 27W
Caspian Sea **79** 43 0N 50 0E
Casquets **42** 49 46N 2 15W
Cass City **156** 43 34N 83 15W
Cass Lake **158** 47 23N 94 38W
Cassá de la Selva **58** 41 53N 2 52E
Cassano Iónio **65** 39 47N 16 20E
Cassel **43** 50 48N 2 30E
Casselton **158** 47 0N 97 15W
Cássia **171** 20 36S 46 56W
Cassiar **152** 59 16N 129 40W
Cassiar Mts. **152** 59 30N 130 30W
Cassils **152** 50 29N 112 15W
Cassinga **125** 15 5S 16 23E
Cassino **64** 41 30N 13 50E
Cassiporé, C. **170** 3 50N 51 5W
Cassis **45** 43 14N 5 32E
Cassville **159** 36 45N 93 59W
Cástagneto Carducci **62** 43 9N 10 36E
Castaic **163** 34 30N 118 38W
Castanhal **170** 1 18S 47 55W
Castanheiro **174** 0 17S 65 38W
Casteau **47** 50 32N 4 2E
Castéggio **62** 45 1N 9 8E
Castejón de Monegros **58** 41 37N 0 15W
Castel di Sangro **65** 41 41N 14 5E
Castel San Giovanni **62** 45 4N 9 25E
Castel San Pietro **63** 44 23N 11 30E
Castelbuono **65** 37 56N 14 4E
Casteldelfino **62** 44 35N 7 4E
Castelfiorentino **62** 43 36N 10 58E
Castelfranco Emília **62** 44 37N 11 2E
Castelfranco Veneto **63** 45 40N 11 56E
Casteljaloux **44** 44 19N 0 6E
Castellabate **65** 40 18N 14 55E
Castellammare del Golfo **64** 38 2N 12 53E
Castellammare di Stábia **65** 40 47N 14 29E
Castellammare, G. di **64** 38 5N 12 55E
Castellamonte **62** 45 23N 7 42E
Castellana Grotte **65** 40 53N 17 10E
Castellane **45** 43 50N 6 31E
Castellaneta **65** 40 40N 16 57E
Castellar de Santisteban **59** 38 16N 3 8W
Castelleone **62** 45 19N 9 47E
Castelli **172** 36 7S 57 47W
Castelló de Ampurias **58** 42 15N 3 4E
Castellón □ **58** 40 15N 0 5W
Castellón de la Plana **58** 39 58N 0 3W
Castellote **58** 40 48N 0 15W
Castelltersol **58** 41 45N 2 8E
Castelmáuro **65** 41 50N 14 40E
Castelnau-de-Médoc **44** 45 2N 0 48W
Castelnaudary **44** 43 20N 1 58E
Castelnovo ne' Monti **62** 44 27N 10 26E
Castelnuovo di Val di Cécina **62** 43 12N 10 54E
Castelo **173** 20 53S 41 42E
Castelo Branco **56** 39 50N 7 31W
Castelo Branco □ **56** 39 52N 7 45W
Castelo de Paiva **56** 41 2N 8 16W
Castelo de Vide **57** 39 25N 7 27W
Castelo do Piauí **170** 5 20S 41 33W
Castelsarrasin **44** 44 2N 1 7E
Casteltérmini **64** 37 32N 13 38E
Castelvetrano **64** 37 40N 12 46E
Casterton **140** 37 30S 141 30E
Castets **44** 43 52N 1 6W
Castiglione del Lago **63** 43 7N 12 3E
Castiglione della Pescáia **62** 42 46N 10 53E
Castiglione della Stiviere **62** 45 23N 10 30E
Castiglione Fiorentino **63** 43 20N 11 55E
Castilblanco **57** 39 17N 5 5W
Castilla La Nueva **57** 39 45N 3 20W
Castilla La Vieja **56** 41 55N 4 0W
Castilla, Playa de **57** 37 0N 6 33W
Castille = Castilla **56** 40 0N 3 30W
Castilletes **174** 11 51N 71 19W
Castillón **164** 28 20N 103 38W
Castillon-en-Couserans **44** 42 56N 1 1E
Castillon-la-Bataille **44** 44 51N 0 2W
Castillonès **44** 44 39N 0 37E
Castillos **173** 34 12S 53 52W
Castle Acre **29** 52 42N 0 42W
Castle Cary **28** 51 5N 2 32W
Castle Dale **160** 39 11N 111 1W
Castle Donington **28** 52 50N 1 20W
Castle Douglas **35** 54 57N 3 57W
Castle Eden **54** 54 45N 1 20W
Castle Point **142** 40 54N 176 15E
Castle Rock, Colo., U.S.A. **158** 39 26N 104 50W
Castle Rock, Wash., U.S.A. **160** 46 20N 122 58W
Castlebar **38** 53 52N 9 17W
Castlebay **36** 56 57N 7 30W
Castlebellingham **38** 53 53N 6 22W
Castleblakeney **38** 53 26N 8 28W
Castleblayney **38** 54 7N 6 44W
Castlebridge **39** 52 23N 6 28W
Castlecliff **142** 39 57S 174 59E
Castlecomer **39** 52 49N 7 13W
Castleconnell **39** 52 44N 8 30W
Castledawson **38** 54 47N 6 35W
Castlederg **38** 54 43N 7 35W
Castledermot **39** 52 55N 6 50W
Castlefinn **38** 54 47N 7 35W
Castleford **33** 53 43N 1 21W
Castlegar **152** 49 20N 117 40W
Castlegate **160** 39 45N 110 57W
Castlegregory **39** 52 16N 10 0W
Castlehill **38** 51 1N 9 49W
Castleisland **39** 52 14N 9 28W
Castlemaine, Austral. **140** 37 2S 144 12E
Castlemaine, Ireland **39** 52 10N 9 42W
Castlemaine Harb. **39** 52 8N 9 50W
Castlemartyr **39** 51 54N 8 3W
Castlepollard **38** 53 40N 7 20W
Castlereagh **38** 53 47N 8 30W
Castlereagh □ **38** 54 33N 5 33W
Castlereagh B. **138** 12 10S 135 10E
Castlereagh, R. **141** 30 12S 147 32E
Castleside **32** 54 50N 1 52W
Castleton, Derby., U.K. **33** 53 20N 1 47W
Castleton, N. Yorks., U.K. **33** 54 27N 0 57W
Castleton, U.S.A. **162** 43 37N 73 11W
Castletown, Geoghegan, Ireland **38** 53 27N 7 30W
Castletown, Laois, Ireland **38** 52 58N 7 31W
Castletown, Meath, Ireland **39** 53 47N 6 41W
Castletown, I. of Man **32** 54 4N 4 40W
Castletown, U.K. **37** 58 35N 3 22W
Castletown Bearhaven **39** 51 40N 9 54W
Castletownroche **39** 52 10N 8 28W
Castletownshend **39** 51 31N 9 11W
Castlevale **138** 24 30S 146 48E
Castlewellan **38** 54 16N 5 57W
Castor **152** 52 15N 111 50W
Castorland **162** 43 53N 75 31W
Castres **44** 43 37N 2 13E
Castricum **46** 52 33N 4 40E
Castries **167** 14 0N 60 50W
Castril **59** 37 48N 2 46W
Castro, Brazil **173** 24 45S 50 0W
Castro, Chile **176** 42 30S 73 50W
Castro Alves **171** 12 46S 39 26W
Castro del Río **57** 37 41N 4 29W
Castro Marim **57** 37 13N 7 26W
Castro Urdiales **58** 43 23N 3 19W
Castro Verde **57** 37 41N 8 4W
Castrojeriz **56** 42 17N 4 9W
Castropol **56** 43 32N 7 0W
Castroreale **65** 38 5N 15 15E
Castrovillari **65** 39 49N 16 11E
Castroville, Calif., U.S.A. **163** 36 46N 121 45W
Castroville, Tex, U.S.A. **159** 29 20N 98 53W
Castuera **57** 38 43N 5 37W
Casummit L. **150** 51 29N 92 22W
Cat Ba **100** 20 50N 107 0E
Cat I., Bahamas **167** 24 30N 75 30W
Cat I., U.S.A. **159** 30 15N 89 7W
Cat L. **150** 51 40N 91 50W
Čata **53** 47 58N 18 38E
Catacamas **166** 14 54N 85 56W
Catacaos **174** 5 20S 80 45W
Cataguases **173** 21 23S 42 39W
Catahoula L. **159** 31 30N 92 5W
Catalão **171** 18 10S 47 57W
Çatalca **92** 41 9N 28 28E
Catalina **151** 48 31N 53 4W
Catalonia = Cataluña **58** 41 40N 1 15E
Cataluña **58** 41 40N 1 15E
Catamarca **172** 28 30S 65 50W
Catamarca □ **172** 28 30S 65 50W
Catanduanas, Is. **103** 13 50N 124 20E
Catanduva **173** 21 5S 48 58W
Catánia **65** 37 31N 15 4E
Catánia, G. di **65** 37 25N 15 8E
Catanzaro **65** 38 54N 16 38E
Catarman **103** 12 28N 124 1E
Catastrophe C. **136** 34 59S 136 0E
Catcleugh **35** 55 19N 2 22W
Cateau, Le **43** 50 6N 3 30E
Cateel **103** 7 47N 126 24E
Catende **170** 8 40S 35 43W
Caterham **29** 51 16N 0 4W
Cathcart, Austral. **141** 36 2S 149 24E
Cathcart, S. Afr. **128** 32 18S 27 10E
Catine **41** 46 30N 0 15W
Catio **120** 11 17N 15 15W
Catismiña **174** 4 5N 63 52W
Catita **170** 9 31S 43 1W
Catlettsburg **156** 38 23N 82 38W
Cato I. **133** 23 15S 155 32E
Catoche, C. **165** 21 40N 87 0W
Catolé **171** 7 19S 36 1W
Catolé do Rocha **170** 6 21S 37 45W
Caton **32** 54 5N 2 41W
Catonsville **162** 39 16N 76 44W
Catral **59** 38 10N 0 47W
Catria, Mt. **63** 43 28N 12 42E
Catrimani **174** 0 27N 61 41W
Catrine **34** 55 30N 4 20W
Catsfield **29** 50 53N 0 28E
Catskill **162** 42 14N 73 52W
Catskill Mts. **162** 42 15N 74 15W
Catt, Mt. **138** 13 49S 134 23E
Catterick **33** 54 23N 1 38W
Cattólica **63** 43 58N 12 43E
Cattólica Eraclea **64** 37 27N 13 24E
Catton **35** 54 56N 2 16W
Catu **171** 12 21S 38 23W
Catuala **128** 16 25S 19 2E
Catur **127** 13 45S 35 30E
Catwick Is. **101** 10 0N 109 0E
Cauca □ **174** 2 30N 76 50W
Cauca, R. **174** 7 25N 75 30W
Caucasia **174** 8 0N 75 12W
Caucasus Mts. = Bolshoi Kavkas **83** 42 50N 44 0E
Cauccaia **170** 3 40S 38 35W
Caudebec-en-Caux **42** 49 30N 0 42E
Caudete **59** 38 42N 1 2W
Caudry **43** 50 7N 3 22E
Caulkerbush **35** 54 54N 3 40W
Caulnes **42** 48 18N 2 10W
Caulónia **65** 38 23N 16 25E
Caungula **124** 8 15S 18 50E
Cáuquenes **172** 36 0S 72 30W
Caura, R. **174** 6 20N 64 30W
Cauresi, R. **127** 17 40S 33 10E
Causapscal **151** 48 19N 67 12W
Causeway **39** 52 25N 9 45W
Caussade **44** 44 10N 1 33E
Cauterets **44** 42 52N 0 8W
Cauvery, R. **93** 12 0N 77 45E
Caux **42** 49 38N 0 35E
Cava dei Tirreni **65** 40 42N 14 42E
Cávado, R. **56** 41 37N 8 15W
Cavaillon **45** 43 50N 5 2E
Cavalaire-sur-Mer **45** 43 10N 6 33E
Cavalcante **171** 13 48S 47 30W
Cavalerie, La **44** 44 0N 3 10E
Cavalese **63** 46 17N 11 29E
Cavalier **158** 48 50N 97 39W
Cavalli Is. **142** 35 0S 173 58E
Cavallo, I. **45** 41 22N 9 16E
Cavally, R. **120** 5 0N 7 40W
Cavan **38** 54 0N 7 22W
Cavan □ **38** 53 58N 7 10W
Cavanagh Ra. **137** 26 10S 122 50E
Cavárzere **63** 45 8N 12 6E
Cave City **156** 37 13N 85 57W
Cavenagh Range **137** 26 12S 127 55E
Cavendish **140** 37 31S 142 2E
Cavers **150** 48 55N 87 41W
Caviana, Ilha **170** 0 15N 50 0W
Cavite **103** 14 20N 120 55E
Cavour **62** 44 47N 7 22E
Cavtat **66** 42 35N 18 13E
Cawdor **37** 57 31N 3 56W
Cawkers Well **140** 31 41S 142 57E
Cawndilla, L. **140** 32 30S 142 15E
Cawnpore = Kanpur **95** 26 35N 80 20E
Cawood **33** 53 50N 1 7W
Cawston **29** 52 47N 1 10E
Caxias **174** 5 0S 43 27W
Caxias do Sul **173** 29 10S 51 10W
Caxine, C. **118** 35 56N 0 27W
Caxito **124** 8 30S 13 30E
Cay Sal Bank **166** 23 45N 80 0W
Cayambe **174** 0 3N 78 22W
Cayce **157** 33 59N 81 2W
Cayenne **175** 5 0N 52 18W
Cayes, Les **167** 18 15N 73 46W
Cayeux-sur-Mer. **43** 50 10N 1 30E
Cayey **147** 18 7N 66 10W
Caylus **44** 44 15N 1 47E
Cayman Brac, I. **166** 19 43N 79 49W
Cayman Is. **166** 19 40N 79 50W
Cayo **165** 17 10N 89 0W
Cayo Romano, I. **167** 22 0N 73 30W
Cayuga **162** 42 28N 76 30W
Cayuga L. **162** 42 45N 76 45W
Cazalla de la Sierra **57** 37 56N 5 45W
Cazaux et de Sanguinet, Étang de **44** 44 29N 1 10W
Cazenovia **162** 42 56N 75 51W
Cazères **44** 43 13N 1 5E
Čazin **63** 44 57N 15 57E
Čazma **63** 45 45N 16 39E
Cazombo **125** 12 0S 22 48E
Cazorla, Spain **59** 37 55N 3 2W
Cazorla, Venez. **174** 8 1N 67 0W
Cazorla, Sierra de **59** 38 5N 2 55W
Cea, R. **56** 42 40N 5 5W
Ceamurlia de Jos **67** 44 43N 28 47E
Ceanannas Mor **38** 53 42N 6 53W
Ceará = Fortaleza **170** 3 35S 38 35W
Ceará □ **170** 5 0S 40 0W
Ceará Mirim **170** 5 38S 35 25W
Ceauru, L. **70** 44 58N 23 11E
Cebaco, I. **166** 7 33N 81 9W
Cebollar **172** 29 10S 66 35W
Cebollera, Sierra de **58** 42 0N 2 30W
Cebreros **56** 40 27N 4 28W
Cebú **103** 10 18N 123 54E
Cebú, I. **103** 10 15N 123 40E
Ceccano **64** 41 34N 13 18E
Cece **53** 46 46N 18 39E
Cechi **120** 6 15N 4 25W
Cecil Plains **139** 27 30S 151 11E
Cecilton **162** 39 24N 75 52W
Cécina **62** 43 19N 10 33E
Cécina, R. **62** 43 19N 10 40E
Ceclavin **56** 39 50N 6 45W
Cedar City **161** 37 41N 113 3W
Cedar Creek Res. **159** 32 15N 96 0W
Cedar Falls **158** 42 39N 92 29W
Cedar I. **162** 37 35N 75 32W
Cedar Key **157** 29 9N 83 5W
Cedar L. **153** 53 20N 100 10W
Cedar Pt. **162** 38 18N 76 25W
Cedar, R. **158** 41 50N 91 20W
Cedar Rapids **158** 42 0N 91 38W
Cedarburg **156** 43 18N 87 55W
Cedartown **157** 34 1N 85 15W
Cedarvale **152** 55 1N 128 22W
Cedarville **160** 41 37N 120 13W
Cedeira **56** 43 39N 8 2W
Cedral **164** 23 50N 100 42W
Cedrino, R. **64** 40 8N 9 25E
Cedro **170** 6 34S 39 3W
Cedros, I. de **164** 28 10N 115 20W
Ceduna **139** 32 7S 133 46E
Cedynia **54** 52 53N 14 12E
Ceepeecee **152** 49 52N 126 42W
Cefalù **65** 38 3N 14 1E
Cega, R. **56** 41 17N 4 10W
Cegléd **53** 47 11N 19 47E
Céglie Messápico **65** 40 39N 17 31E
Cehegín **59** 38 6N 1 48W
Cehu-Silvaniei **70** 47 24N 23 9E
Ceiba, La **166** 15 40N 86 50W
Ceica **70** 46 53N 22 10E
Ceira, R. **56** 40 15N 7 55W
Cekhira **119** 34 20N 10 5E
Celano **63** 42 6N 13 30E
Celanova **56** 42 9N 7 58W
Celaya **164** 20 31N 100 37W
Celbridge **39** 53 20N 6 33W
Celebes I. = Sulawesi **103** 2 0S 120 0E
Celebes Sea **103** 3 0N 123 0E
Celga **123** 12 38N 37 3E
Çelina **156** 40 32N 84 31W
Čelić **66** 44 43N 18 47E
Celje **63** 46 16N 15 18E
Cellar Hd. **36** 58 25N 6 10W
Celldömölk **53** 47 16N 17 10E
Celle **48** 52 37N 10 4E
Celles **47** 50 42N 3 28E
Celorica da Beira **56** 40 38N 7 24W
Cemaes Bay **31** 53 24N 4 27W
Cemaes Hd. **31** 52 7N 4 44W
Çement **159** 34 56N 98 8W
Čemerno **66** 43 26N 20 26E
Cemmaes Road **31** 52 39N 3 41W
Cenarth **31** 52 3N 4 32W
Cenis, Col du Mt. **45** 45 15N 6 55E
Ceno, R. **62** 44 40N 9 52E
Cenon **44** 44 50N 0 33W
Centallo **62** 44 30N 7 35E
Centenário do Sul **171** 22 48S 51 57W
Center, N.D., U.S.A. **158** 47 9N 101 17W
Center, Texas, U.S.A. **159** 31 50N 94 10W
Centerfield **160** 39 9N 111 56W
Centerville, Ala., U.S.A. **157** 32 55N 87 7W
Centerville, Calif., U.S.A. **163** 36 44N 119 30W
Centerville, Iowa, U.S.A. **158** 40 45N 92 57W
Centerville, Miss., U.S.A. **159** 31 10N 91 3W
Centerville, S.D., U.S.A. **158** 43 10N 96 58W
Centerville, Tenn., U.S.A. **157** 35 46N 87 29W
Centerville, Tex., U.S.A. **159** 31 15N 95 56W
Cento **63** 44 43N 11 16E
Central **170** 11 8S 42 8W
Central □, Kenya **126** 0 30S 33 30E
Central □, Malawi **126** 13 30S 33 30E
Central □, U.K. **34** 56 0N 4 30W
Central □, Zambia **127** 14 25S 28 50E
Central African Empire ■ **124** 7 0N 20 0E
Central Auckland □ **142** 37 30S 175 30E
Central City, Ky., U.S.A. **156** 37 20N 87 7W
Central City, Nebr., U.S.A. **158** 41 8N 98 0W
Central, Cordillera, C. Rica **166** 10 10N 84 5W
Central, Cordillera, Dom. Rep. **167** 19 15N 71 0W
Central I., L. Turkana **126** 3 30N 36 0E
Central Islip **162** 40 49N 73 13W
Central Makran Range **93** 26 30N 64 15E
Central Patricia **150** 51 30N 90 9W
Central Ra. **135** 5 0S 143 0E
Central Russian Uplands **16** 54 0N 36 0E
Central Siberian Plateau **77** 65 0N 105 0E
Central Square **162** 43 17N 76 9W
Centralia, Ill., U.S.A. **158** 38 32N 89 5W
Centralia, Mo., U.S.A. **158** 39 12N 92 6W
Centralia, Wash., U.S.A. **160** 46 46N 122 59W
Centúripe **65** 37 37N 14 41E
Cephalonia = Kefallinia **69** 38 28N 20 30E
Cepin **66** 45 32N 18 34E

Ceprano
Château d'Oex

Ceprano 64 41 33N 13 30 E
Ceptura 70 45 1N 26 21 E
Ceram I. = Seram I. 103 3 10S 129 0 E
Ceram Sea 103 2 30S 128 30 E
Cerbère 44 42 26N 3 10 E
Cerbicales, Îles 45 41 33N 9 22 E
Cerbu 70 44 46N 24 46 E
Cercal 57 37 48N 8 40W
Cercemaggiore 65 41 27N 14 43 E
Cerdaña 58 42 22N 1 35 E
Cerdedo 56 42 33N 8 23W
Cerea 63 45 12N 11 13 E
Ceres, Argent. 172 29 55S 61 55W
Ceres, Brazil 171 15 17S 49 35W
Ceres, Italy 62 45 19N 7 22 E
Ceres, S. Afr. 128 33 21S 19 18 E
Ceres, U.K. 35 56 18N 2 57W
Ceres, U.S.A. 163 37 35N 120 57W
Céret 44 42 30N 2 42 E
Cereté 174 8 53N 75 48W
Cerfontaine 47 50 11N 4 26 E
Cerignola 65 41 17N 15 53 E
Cerigo = Kíthira 69 36 9N 23 0 E
Cérilly 44 46 37N 2 50 E
Cerisiers 43 48 8N 3 30 E
Cerizay 42 46 50N 0 40W
Çerkeş 92 40 40N 32 58 E
Cerknica 63 45 48N 14 21 E
Çermerno 66 43 35N 20 25 E
Cerna 70 44 4N 28 17 E
Cerna, R. 70 44 45N 24 0 E
Cernavodŭ 70 44 22N 28 3 E
Cernay 43 47 44N 7 10 E
Cerne Abbas 28 50 49N 2 29W
Cernik 66 45 17N 17 22 E
Cerralvo, I. 164 24 20N 109 45 E
Cerreto Sannita 65 41 17N 14 34 E
Cerrig-y-druidion 31 53 2N 3 34W
Cerritos 164 22 20N 100 20W
Cerro 161 36 47N 105 36W
Cêrro Corá 171 6 3S 36 21W
Cerro de Punta, Mt. 147 18 10N 67 0W
Certaldo 62 43 32N 11 2 E
Cervaro, R. 65 41 21N 15 30 E
Cervera 58 41 40N 1 16 E
Cervera de Pisuerga 56 42 51N 4 30W
Cervera del Rio Alhama 58 42 2N 1 58W
Cérvia 63 44 15N 12 20 E
Cervignano del Friuli 63 45 49N 13 20 E
Cervinara 65 41 2N 14 36 E
Cervo 56 43 40N 7 24W
Cervoine 45 42 20N 9 29 E
Cesanâtico 63 44 12N 12 22 E
César □ 174 9 0N 73 30W
Cesaro 65 37 50N 14 38 E
Cesena 63 44 9N 12 14 E
Cesenático 63 44 12N 12 22 E
Cēsis 80 57 17N 25 28 E
Česká Třebová 53 49 54N 16 27 E
Česke Budějovice 52 48 55N 14 25 E
České Velenice 52 48 45N 15 1 E
Českézemě 52 50 0N 14 0 E
Ceskomoravská Vrchovina 52 49 20N 15 45 E
Český Brod 52 50 4N 14 52 E
Český Krumlov 52 48 43N 14 21 E
Český Těšin 53 49 45N 18 39 E
Çeşme 69 38 20N 26 23 E
Cess, R. 120 5 25N 9 35W
Cessnock 141 32 50S 151 21 E
Cestos, R. 120 5 30N 9 30W
Cetate 70 44 7N 23 2 E
Cetina, R. 63 43 50N 16 30 E
Cetinje 66 42 23N 18 59 E
Cetraro 65 39 30N 15 56 E
Ceuta 118 35 52N 5 18W
Ceva 62 44 23N 8 0 E
Cévennes, mts. 44 44 10N 3 50 E
Ceylon = Sri Lanka ■ 97 7 30N 80 50 E
Cha-am 100 12 48N 99 58 E
Cha Pa 100 22 21N 103 50 E
Chaam 47 51 30N 4 52 E
Chabeuil 45 44 54N 5 1 E
Chabjuwardoo B. 137 23 0S 113 30 E
Chablais 45 46 20N 6 36 E
Chablis 43 47 47N 3 48 E
Chabounia 118 35 30N 2 38 E
Chacabuco 172 34 40S 60 27W
Chacewater 30 50 15N 5 8W
Chachapoyas 174 6 15S 77 50W
Chachoengsao 100 13 42N 101 5 E
Chachran 93 28 55N 70 30 E
Chachro 94 25 5N 70 15 E
Chaco □ 172 25 0S 61 0W
Chaco Austral 176 27 30S 61 40W
Chaco Boreal 172 22 30S 60 10W
Chaco Central 176 24 0S 61 0W
Chad ■ 117 12 30N 17 15 E
Chadan 77 51 17N 91 35 E
Chadileuvú, R. 172 37 0S 65 55W
Chadiza 127 14 10S 33 34 E
Chadron 158 42 50N 103 0W
Chadyr-Lunga 82 46 3N 28 51 E
Chae Hom 100 18 43N 99 35 E
Chaem, R. 100 18 11N 98 38 E
Chaeryŏng 107 38 24N 125 36 E
Chafurray 174 3 10N 73 14W
Chagai 93 29 30N 63 0 E
Chagai Hills 93 29 30N 63 0 E
Chagda 77 58 45N 130 30 E
Chagford 30 50 40N 3 50W
Chagny 43 46 57N 4 45 E
Chagoda 80 59 10N 35 25 E
Chagos Arch. 86 6 0S 72 0 E
Chāh Bahār 93 25 20N 60 40 E
Ch'ahaerhyuichungch'i 106 41 18N 112 48 E
Ch'ahanch'elo 106 41 41N 114 15 E
Chahar Buriak 93 30 15N 62 0 E
Chāhr-e Babak 93 30 10N 55 20 E
Chahsikiang 105 32 32N 79 41 E
Chahtung 98 26 41N 98 10 E
Chai-nat 100 15 11N 100 8 E
Chaibasa 99 22 42N 85 49 E
Chaillé-les-Marais 44 46 25N 1 2W
Chaise Dieu, La 44 45 20N 3 40 E
Chaiya 101 9 23N 99 14 E
Chaiyaphum 100 15 48N 102 2 E
Chaize-le-Vicomté, La 42 46 40N 1 18W
Chaj Doab 94 32 0N 73 0 E
Chajari 172 30 42N 58 0W
Chakaria 98 21 45N 92 5 E
Chake Chake 126 5 15S 39 45 E
Chakhansur 93 31 10N 62 0 E
Chaklashi 94 22 40N 72 52 E
Chakonipau, L. 151 56 18N 68 30W
Chakradharpur 95 22 45N 85 40 E
Chakwadam 98 27 29N 98 31 E
Chakwal 94 32 50N 72 45 E
Chala 174 15 48S 74 20W
Chalais 44 45 16N 0 3 E
Chalakudi 97 10 18N 76 20 E
Chalcatongo 165 17 4N 97 34W
Chalchihuites 164 23 29N 103 53W
Chalcis = Khalkis 69 38 27N 23 42 E
Chale 28 50 35N 1 19W
Chaleur B. 151 47 55N 65 30W
Chalfant 163 37 32N 118 21W
Chalfont St. Peter 29 51 36N 0 33W
Chalhuanca 174 14 15S 73 5W
Ch'aling 109 26 47N 113 45 E
Chaling Hu 105 34 55N 98 0 E
Chalisgaon 96 20 30N 75 10 E
Chalkar 83 50 35N 51 52 E
Chalkar Oz. 83 50 33N 51 45 E
Chalky Inlet 143 46 3S 166 31 E
Challans 42 46 50N 1 52W
Challapata 174 19 0S 66 50W
Challerange 43 49 18N 4 46 E
Challis 160 44 32N 114 25W
Chalna 95 22 36N 89 35 E
Chalon-sur-Saône 43 46 48N 4 50 E
Chalonnes 42 47 20N 0 45W
Châlons-sur-Marne 43 48 58N 4 20 E
Châlus 44 45 39N 0 58 E
Cham, Ger. 49 49 12N 12 40 E
Cham, Switz. 51 47 11N 8 28 E
Cham, Cu Lao 100 15 57N 108 30 E
Chama, R. 127 36 57N 106 37W
Chaman 93 30 58N 66 25 E
Chamarajanagar-Ramasamudram 97 11 52N 76 52 E
Chamartín de la Rosa 58 40 28N 3 40W
Chamba, India 94 32 35N 76 10 E
Chamba, Tanz. 125 11 37S 37 0 E
Chambal, R. 94 26 0N 76 55 E
Chamberlain, Austral. 136 15 58S 127 54 E
Chamberlain, U.S.A. 158 43 50N 99 21W
Chambers 161 35 13N 109 30W
Chambersburg 156 39 53N 77 41W
Chambéry 45 45 34N 5 55 E
Chambeshi 127 12 39S 28 1 E
Chambeshi, R. 124 10 20S 31 58 E
Chambois 42 48 48N 0 6 E
Chambon-Feugerolles, Le 45 45 24N 4 18 E
Châmbon, Le 45 45 35N 4 26 E
Chambord 151 48 25N 72 6W
Chamboulive 44 45 26N 1 42 E
Chambri L. 135 4 15S 143 10 E
Chamela 164 19 32N 105 5W
Chamical 172 30 22S 66 27W
Chamkar Luong 101 11 0N 103 45 E
Chamonix 45 45 55N 6 51 E
Champa 95 22 2N 82 43 E
Champagne, Can. 152 60 49N 136 30W
Champagne, France 43 49 0N 4 40 E
Champagnole 43 46 45N 5 55 E
Champaign 156 40 8N 88 14W
Champassak 100 14 53N 105 52 E
Champaubert 43 48 50N 3 45 E
Champdeniers 44 46 29N 0 25W
Champeix 44 45 37N 3 8 E
Champerico 166 14 18N 91 55W
Champier 50 45 27N 5 17 E
Champion B. 137 28 44S 114 36 E
Champlain 151 46 27N 72 24W
Champotón 165 19 20N 90 50W
Chamusca 57 39 21N 8 29W
Chana 101 6 55N 100 44 E
Chañaral 172 26 15S 70 50W
Chanasma 94 23 44N 72 5 E
Chanca, R. 57 37 49N 7 15W
Chanchiang 109 21 15N 110 20 E
Chancy 50 46 8N 6 0 E
Chanda 96 19 57N 79 25 E
Chandalar 147 67 30N 148 35W
Chandausi 95 28 27N 78 49 E
Chandeleur Is. 59 29 45N 88 53W
Chandeleur Sd. 159 29 58N 88 40W
Chandernagore 95 22 52N 88 24 E
Chandigarh 94 30 30N 76 58 E
Chandler, Can. 151 48 18N 64 46W
Chandler, Ariz., U.S.A. 161 33 20N 111 56W
Chandler, Okla., U.S.A. 159 35 43N 97 20W
Chandler's Ford 28 50 59N 1 23W
Chandlers Peak 141 30 24S 152 10 E
Chandmani 105 45 20N 97 59 E
Chandpur, Bangla. 98 22 8N 90 55 E
Chandpur, India 94 29 8N 78 19 E
Chang 94 26 59N 68 30 E
Ch'ang Chiang, R. 109 31 40N 121 50 E
Chang, Ko 101 12 0N 102 23 E
Changa 95 33 53N 77 35 E
Changanacheri 97 9 25N 76 31 E
Changane, R. 125 23 30S 33 50 E
Ch'anganpao 108 26 9N 109 42 E
Changchiak'ou 106 40 50N 114 53 E
Ch'angchiang 100 19 19N 108 43 E
Ch'angchih 106 36 11N 113 6 E
Ch'angchou 109 31 47N 119 58 E
Changchou 109 24 31N 117 40 E
Ch'angch'un 107 43 58N 125 19 E
Ch'angch'unling 107 45 22N 125 28 E
Changdori 107 38 30N 127 40 E
Ch'angfeng 109 32 27N 117 9 E
Changhsing 109 31 0N 119 56 E
Ch'anghua 109 30 10N 119 15 E
Changhua 109 24 2N 120 30 E
Changhŭng 107 34 41N 126 52 E
Changhŭngni 107 40 24N 128 19 E
Ch'angi 107 36 51N 119 23 E
Changjin 107 40 23N 127 15 E
Changjin-chŏsuji 107 40 30N 127 15 E
Changkuangts'ai Ling 107 45 50N 128 50 E
Changli 107 39 40N 119 19 E
Ch'angling 107 44 16N 123 57 E
Ch'anglo, Fukien, China 109 25 58N 119 31 E
Ch'anglo, Fukien, China 109 26 40N 117 20 E
Ch'anglo, Kwangtung, China 109 24 4N 115 37 E
Changlun 101 6 25N 100 26 E
Changming 108 31 44N 104 44 E
Ch'angning, Hunan, China 109 26 25N 112 15 E
Ch'angning, Szechwan, China 108 28 38N 104 57 E
Ch'angning, Yunnan, China 108 24 50N 99 36 E
Ch'angpai 107 41 26N 128 0 E
Ch'angpai Shan 107 42 25N 129 0 E
Changpei 106 41 7N 114 51 E
Ch'angp'ing 106 40 12N 116 12 E
Changp'ing 109 25 18N 117 24 E
Changpu 109 24 2N 117 31 E
Ch'angsha 109 28 15N 113 0 E
Ch'angshan 109 28 57N 118 31 E
Ch'angshou 108 29 50N 107 2 E
Ch'angshu 109 31 33N 120 45 E
Ch'angshun 108 25 59N 106 25 E
Ch'angt'ai 109 24 34N 117 50 E
Ch'angte 109 29 5N 111 42 E
Ch'angt'ing 109 25 52N 116 20 E
Ch'angt'u 107 42 47N 124 0 E
Ch'angtu 108 31 10N 97 14 E
Ch'angt'u Shan 109 30 15N 122 20 E
Ch'angwu 106 35 9N 107 42 E
Changwu 107 42 24N 122 30 E
Ch'angyang 109 30 28N 111 9 E
Ch'angyatien 106 40 18N 108 46 E
Changyeh 105 38 56N 100 37 E
Changyŏn 107 38 15N 125 6 E
Ch'angyüan 106 35 17N 114 50 E
Chanhanga 128 16 0S 14 8 E
Chanhua 107 37 42N 118 8 E
Chani 108 25 36N 103 49 E
Channapatna 97 12 40N 77 15 E
Channel Is. 42 49 30N 2 40W
Channel Islands 163 33 30N 119 0W
Channing, Mich., U.S.A. 156 46 9N 88 1W
Channing, Tex., U.S.A. 159 35 45N 102 20W
Chantada 56 42 36N 7 46W
Chanthaburi 100 12 38N 102 12 E
Chantilly 43 49 12N 2 29 E
Chantonnay 42 46 40N 1 3W
Chantrey Inlet 148 67 48N 96 20W
Chanute 159 37 45N 85 25W
Chanyü 107 44 39N 122 45 E
Chanza, R. 57 37 49N 7 15W
Ch'ao Hu 109 31 40N 117 30 E
Chao Phraya Lowlands 100 15 30N 100 0 E
Chao Phraya, R. 100 13 32N 100 36 E
Ch'aoan 109 23 41N 116 33 E
Chaoan 109 23 47N 117 5 E
Chaoch'eng, Shansi, China 106 36 26N 111 43 E
Chaoch'eng, Shantung, China 106 36 3N 115 35 E
Chaochiao 108 28 1N 102 49 E
Chaoch'ing 109 23 7N 112 24 E
Chaohsien 106 37 45N 114 46 E
Ch'aohsien 109 31 41N 117 49 E
Chaop'ing 109 24 1N 110 59 E
Chaot'ung 108 27 19N 103 42 E
Ch'aoyang, Kwangtung, China 109 23 10N 116 30 E
Ch'aoyang, Liaoning, China 107 41 46N 120 16 E
Chaoyüan, Heilungkiang, China 107 45 30N 125 8 E
Chaoyüan, Shantung, China 107 37 22N 120 24 E
Chap Kuduk 76 48 45N 55 5 E
Chapala 127 15 50S 37 35 E
Chapala, Lago de 164 20 10N 103 20W
Chaparmukh 98 26 12N 92 31 E
Chapayevo 83 50 25N 51 10 E
Chapayevsk 81 53 0N 49 40 E
Chapecó 173 27 14S 52 41W
Chapel-en-le-Frith 32 53 19N 1 54W
Chapel Hill 157 35 53N 79 3W
Chapelle-d'Angillon, La 43 47 21N 2 25 E
Chapelle Glain, La 42 47 38N 1 11W
Chapeyevo 84 50 12N 51 10 E
Chapleau 150 47 50N 83 24W
Chaplin 153 50 28N 106 40W
Chaplino 82 48 8N 36 15 E
Chaplygin 81 53 15N 39 55 E
Chapra 95 25 48N 84 50 E
Char 116 21 40N 12 45W
Chara 77 56 54N 118 12 E
Charadai 172 27 35S 60 0W
Charagua 174 19 45S 63 10W
Charak 93 26 46N 54 18 E
Charalá 174 6 17N 73 10W
Charaña 174 17 30S 69 35W
Charapita 174 0 37S 74 21W
Charata 172 27 13S 61 14W
Charcas 164 23 10N 101 20W
Charcoal L. 153 58 49N 102 22W
Charcot I. 13 70 0S 75 0W
Chard, Can. 153 55 55N 111 10W
Chard, U.K. 28 50 52N 2 59W
Chardara 76 41 16N 67 59 E
Chardara, Step 85 42 20N 68 0 E
Charduar 98 26 51N 92 46 E
Chardzhou 85 39 6N 63 34 E
Charente-Maritime □ 44 45 50N 0 35W
Charente □ 44 45 50N 0 16W
Charente, R. 44 45 41N 0 30W
Charentsavan 83 40 35N 44 41 E
Chârib, G. 122 28 6N 32 54 E
Charikar 93 35 0N 69 10 E
Charing 29 51 12N 0 49 E
Charité, La 43 47 10N 3 0 E
Chariton R. 158 39 19N 92 58W
Charkhari 95 25 24N 79 45 E
Charkhi Dadri 94 28 37N 76 17 E
Charlbury 28 51 52N 1 29W
Charlemont 38 54 26N 6 40W
Charleroi 47 50 24N 4 27 E
Charles, C. 162 37 10N 75 52W
Charles City, Iowa, U.S.A. 158 43 2N 92 41W
Charles City, Va., U.S.A. 162 37 20N 77 4W
Charles L. 153 59 50N 110 33W
Charles, Pk. 137 32 53S 121 8 E
Charles Town 156 39 20N 77 50W
Charleston, Miss., U.S.A. 159 34 2N 90 3W
Charleston, Mo., U.S.A. 159 36 52N 89 20W
Charleston, S.C., U.S.A. 157 32 47N 79 56W
Charleston, W. Va., U.S.A. 157 38 24N 81 36W
Charlestown, Ireland 38 53 58N 8 48W
Charlestown, S. Afr. 129 27 26S 29 53 E
Charlestown, Ind., U.S.A. 156 38 29N 85 40W
Charlestown, N.H., U.S.A. 162 43 14N 72 24W
Charlestown of Aberlour 37 57 27N 3 13W
Charlesville 124 5 27S 20 59 E
Charleville 139 26 24S 146 15 E
Charleville-Mézières 43 49 44N 4 40 E
Charleville = Rath Luirc 39 52 21N 8 40W
Charlevoix 156 45 19N 85 14W
Charlieu 45 46 10N 4 10 E
Charlotte, Mich., U.S.A. 156 42 36N 84 48W
Charlotte, N.C., U.S.A. 157 35 16N 80 46W
Charlotte Amalie 147 18 22N 64 56W
Charlotte Harb. 157 26 45N 82 10W
Charlotte Waters 136 25 56N 134 54 E
Charlottenberg 72 59 54N 12 17 E
Charlottesville 156 38 1N 78 30W
Charlottetown 151 46 14N 63 8W
Charlton, Austral. 140 36 16S 143 24 E
Charlton, U.S.A. 158 40 59N 93 20W
Charlton I. 150 52 0N 79 20W
Charlton Kings 28 51 52N 2 3W
Charlwood 29 51 8N 0 12W
Charmes 43 48 22N 6 17 E
Charminster 28 50 43N 2 28W
Charmouth 28 50 45N 2 54W
Charnwood Forest 23 52 43N 1 18W
Charny 151 46 43N 71 15W
Charolles 45 46 27N 4 16 E
Charost 43 47 0N 2 7 E
Charouïne 118 29 0N 0 15W
Charre 127 17 19S 35 10 E
Charroux 44 46 9N 0 25 E
Charsadda 94 34 7N 71 45 E
Charters Towers 138 20 5S 146 13 E
Chartham 29 51 14N 1 1 E
Chartre, La 42 47 42N 0 34 E
Chartres 42 48 29N 1 30 E
Chascomús 172 35 30S 58 0W
Chasefu 127 11 55N 32 58 E
Chaslands Mistake 143 46 38S 169 22 E
Chasseneuil-sur-Bonnieure 44 45 52N 0 29 E
Chata 94 27 42N 77 30 E
Châtaigneraie, La 42 46 38N 0 45W
Chatal Balkan = Udvoy Balkan 67 42 50N 26 50 E
Château-Chinon 43 47 4N 3 56 E
Château d'Oex 50 46 28N 7 8 E

Château-du-Loir 42 47 40N 0 25 E
Château Gontier 42 47 50N 0 42W
Château-la-Vallière 42 47 30N 0 20 E
Château-Landon 43 48 8N 2 40 E
Château, Le 44 45 52N 1 12W
Château Porcien 43 49 31N 4 13 E
Château Renault 42 47 36N 0 56 E
Château-Salins 43 48 50N 6 30 E
Château-Thierry 43 49 3N 3 20 E
Châteaubourg 43 48 7N 1 25W
Châteaubriant 42 47 43N 1 23W
Châteaudun 42 48 3N 1 20 E
Châteaugiron 42 48 3N 1 30W
Châteaulin 42 48 11N 4 8W
Châteaumeillant 44 46 35N 2 12 E
Châteauneuf 42 48 35N 1 15 E
Châteauneuf-du-Faou 42 48 11N 3 50W
Châteauneuf-sur-Charente 44 45 36N 0 3W
Châteauneuf-sur-Cher 43 46 52N 2 18 E
Châteauneuf-sur-Loire 43 47 52N 2 13 E
Châteaurenard 45 43 53N 4 51 E
Châteauroux 43 46 50N 1 40 E
Châtel-Guyon 44 45 55N 3 4 E
Châtel St. Denis 50 46 32N 6 54 E
Châtelaillon-Plage 44 46 5N 1 5W
Châtelard, Le 50 46 4N 6 57 E
Châtelaudren 42 48 33N 2 59W
Chatelet 47 50 24N 4 32 E
Châtelet, Le, Cher, France 44 46 40N 2 20 E
Châtelet, Le, Seine et Marne, France 43 48 30N 2 47 E
Châtellerault 42 46 50N 0 30 E
Châtelus-Malvaleix 44 46 18N 2 1 E
Chatham, N.B., Can. 151 47 2N 65 28W
Chatham, Ont., Can. 150 42 24N 82 11W
Chatham, U.K. 29 51 22N 0 32 E
Chatham, Alaska, U.S.A. 147 57 30N 135 0W
Chatham, La., U.S.A. 159 32 22N 92 26W
Chatham, N.Y., U.S.A. 162 42 21N 73 32W
Chatham Is. 130 44 0 S 176 40W
Chatham Str. 152 57 0N 134 40W
Châtillon, Loiret, France 43 47 36N 2 44 E
Châtillon, Marne, France 43 49 5N 3 43 E
Chatillon 62 45 45N 7 40 E
Châtillon-Coligny 43 47 50N 2 51 E
Châtillon-en-Bazois 43 47 3N 3 39 E
Châtillon-en-Diois 45 44 41N 5 29 E
Châtillon-sur-Seine 43 47 50N 4 33 E
Châtillon-sur-Sèvre 42 46 56N 0 45W
Chatkal, R. 85 41 38N 70 1 E
Chatkalskiy Khrebet 85 41 30N 70 45 E
Chatmohar 95 24 15N 89 26 E
Chatra 95 24 12N 84 56 E
Chatrapur 96 19 22N 85 2 E
Châtre, La 44 46 35N 1 59 E
Chatsworth 127 19 32 S 30 46 E
Chatta-Hantō 111 34 45N 136 55 E
Chattahoochee 157 30 43N 84 51W
Chattanooga 157 35 2N 85 17W
Chatteris 29 52 27N 0 3 E
Chatton 35 55 34N 1 55W
Chaturat 100 15 34N 101 51 E
Chatyrkel, Ozero 85 40 40N 75 18 E
Chatyrtash 85 40 55N 76 25 E
Chau Phu 101 10 42N 105 7 E
Chaudes-Aigues 44 44 51N 3 1 E
Chauffailles 44 46 13N 4 20 E
Chauk 98 20 53N 94 49 E
Chaukan La 99 27 0N 97 15 E
Chaukan Pass 98 27 8N 97 10 E
Chaulnes 43 49 48N 2 47 E
Chaumont 43 48 7N 5 8 E
Chaumont-en-Vexin 43 49 16N 1 53 E
Chaumont-sur-Loire 42 47 29N 1 11 E
Chaunay 44 46 13N 0 9 E
Chauny 43 49 37N 3 12 E
Chausey, Îs. 42 48 52N 1 49W
Chaussin 43 46 59N 5 22 E
Chauvin 153 52 45N 110 10W
Chaux de Fonds, La 50 47 7N 6 50 E
Chaves, Brazil 170 0 15 S 49 55W
Chaves, Port. 56 41 45N 7 32W
Chavuma 125 13 10 S 22 55 E
Chawang 101 8 25N 99 30 E
Ch'aya 108 30 35N 98 3 E
Chayan 85 43 5N 69 25 E
Chayek 85 41 55N 74 30 E
Chaykovskiy 84 56 47N 54 9 E
Chazelles-sur-Lyon 45 45 39N 4 22 E
Cheadle, Gr. Manchester, U.K. 32 53 23N 2 14W
Cheadle, Staffs., U.K. 32 52 59N 1 59W
Cheadle Hulme 32 53 22N 2 12W
Cheb (Eger) 52 50 9N 12 20 E
Chebarkul 84 55 0N 60 25 E
Cheboksary 81 56 8N 47 30 E
Cheboygan 156 45 38N 84 29W
Chebsara 81 59 10N 38 45 E
Chech, Erg 118 25 0N 2 15W
Chechaouen 118 35 9N 5 15W
Chechen 83 43 59N 47 40 E
Chech'eng 106 34 4N 115 13 E
Checheno-Ingush, A.S.S.R. □ 83 43 30N 45 29 E
Chechon 107 37 8N 128 12 E
Checiny 54 50 46N 20 37 E
Checleset B. 152 50 5N 127 35W
Checotah 159 35 31N 95 30W

Chedabucto B. 151 45 25N 61 8W
Cheddar 28 51 16N 2 47W
Cheddleton 32 53 5N 2 2W
Cheduba I. 98 18 45N 93 40 E
Cheepie 139 26 43 S 144 59 E
Ch'eerhch'en Ho, R. 105 39 30N 88 15 E
Chef-Boutonne 44 46 7N 0 4W
Chefoo = Yent'ai 107 37 30N 121 12 E
Chefornak 147 60 10N 164 15W
Chegdomyn 77 51 7N 132 52 E
Chegga 118 25 15N 5 40W
Chehalis 160 46 44N 122 59W
Cheju 107 33 28N 126 30 E
Cheju Do 107 33 29N 126 34 E
Chejung 109 27 13N 119 52 E
Chekalin 81 54 10N 36 10 E
Chekao 109 31 46N 117 45 E
Chekiang □ 109 29 30N 120 0 E
Chela, Sa. da 128 16 20 S 13 20 E
Chelan, Can. 153 52 38N 103 22 E
Chelan, U.S.A. 160 47 49N 120 0W
Chelan, L. 152 48 5N 120 30W
Cheleken 76 39 26N 53 7 E
Chelforó 176 39 0 S 66 40W
Chéliff, O. 118 36 0N 0 8 E
Chelkar 76 47 40N 59 32 E
Chelkar Tengiz, Solonchak 76 48 0N 62 30 E
Chellala Dahrania 118 33 2N 0 1 E
Chelles 43 48 52N 2 33 E
Chelm 54 51 8N 23 30 E
Chelm □ 54 51 15N 23 30 E
Chelmarsh 28 52 29N 2 25W
Chelmek 54 50 6N 19 16 E
Chelmer, R. 29 51 45N 0 42 E
Chelmno 54 53 20N 18 30 E
Chelmsford 29 51 44N 0 29 E
Chelmza 54 53 10N 18 39 E
Chelsea, Austral. 141 38 5 S 145 8 E
Chelsea, Okla., U.S.A. 159 36 35N 95 25W
Chelsea, Vermont, U.S.A. 162 43 59N 72 27W
Cheltenham 28 51 55N 2 5W
Chelva 58 39 45N 1 0W
Chelyabinsk 84 55 10N 61 24 E
Chelyuskin, C. 86 77 30N 103 0 E
Chemainus 152 48 55N 123 48W
Chemikovsk 78 56 31N 58 11 E
Chemillé 42 47 14N 0 45W
Chemnitz = Karl-Marx-Stadt 48 50 50N 12 55 E
Chemor 101 4 44N 101 6 E
Chemult 160 43 14N 121 54W
Chen, Gora 77 65 10N 141 20 E
Chenab, R. 94 30 40N 73 30 E
Chenachane, O. 118 25 30N 3 30W
Chenan 106 33 16N 109 1 E
Chenango Forks 162 42 15N 75 51W
Chencha 123 6 15N 37 32 E
Ch'ench'i 109 28 1N 110 13 E
Ch'enchiachiang 107 34 25N 119 50 E
Chenchiang 109 32 12N 119 27 E
Chenchieh 108 23 15N 107 9 E
Chênée 47 50 37N 5 37 E
Cheney 160 47 38N 117 34W
Chenfeng 108 25 25N 105 51 E
Chengan 108 28 30N 107 30 E
Ch'engch'eng 106 35 6N 109 52 E
Ch'engchiang 108 24 40N 102 55 E
Chengchou 106 34 38N 113 43 E
Chengchow = Chengchou 106 34 38N 113 43 E
Chengelee 98 28 47N 96 16 E
Chengho 109 27 25N 118 46 E
Ch'enghsi Hu 109 32 22N 116 12 E
Ch'enghsien, Chekiang, China 109 29 30N 120 48 E
Ch'enghsien, Kansu, China 106 33 42N 105 36 E
Ch'engk'ou 108 31 58N 108 48 E
Ch'engku 106 33 9N 107 22 E
Ch'engkung 108 24 53N 102 45 E
Ch'engmai 100 19 44N 109 59 E
Ch'engpu 109 26 12N 110 5 E
Ch'engte 107 41 0N 117 58 E
Chengting 106 38 8N 114 37 E
Ch'engtu 108 30 45N 104 0 E
Ch'engtung Hu 109 32 17N 116 23 E
Ch'engtzut'uan 107 39 30N 122 30 E
Ch'engwu 106 35 0N 115 56 E
Ch'engyang 107 36 20N 120 16 E
Chengyang 109 32 36N 114 23 E
Chengyangkuan 109 32 29N 116 37 E
Chenhai 109 29 57N 121 42 E
Ch'enhsien 109 25 48N 113 2 E
Chenhsiung 108 27 27N 104 50 E
Chenhsü 109 27 6N 120 16 E
Chenkán 165 19 8N 90 58W
Chenk'ang 108 24 4N 99 18 E
Chenlai 107 45 52N 123 12 E
Chenning 108 25 57N 105 51 E
Chenp'ing 106 33 2N 112 14 E
Ch'enp'ing 108 31 52N 109 31 E
Chenyüan, Kansu, China 106 35 59N 107 2 E
Chenyüan, Kweichow, China 108 27 0N 108 20 E
Cheo Reo = Hau Bon 101 13 25N 108 28 E
Cheom Ksan 107 36 13N 104 56 E
Chepelare 67 41 44N 24 40 E
Chepén 174 7 10 S 79 15W
Chepes 172 31 20 S 66 35W
Chepo 166 9 10N 79 6W

Chepstow 31 51 38N 2 40W
Cheptsa, R. 81 58 36N 50 4 E
Cheptulil, Mt. 126 1 25N 35 35 E
Chequamegon B. 158 46 40N 90 30W
Chequeche 127 14 13 S 38 30 E
Cher □ 43 47 10N 2 30 E
Chér, R. 43 47 10N 2 10 E
Cheran 98 25 45N 90 44 E
Cherasco 62 44 39N 7 50 E
Cheratte 47 50 40N 5 41 E
Cheraw 157 34 42N 79 54W
Cherbourg 42 49 39N 1 40W
Cherchell 118 36 35N 2 12 E
Cherdakly 81 54 25N 48 50 E
Cherdyn 84 60 24N 56 29 E
Cheremkhovo 77 53 32N 102 40 E
Cherepanovo 76 54 15N 83 30 E
Cherepovets 81 59 5N 37 55 E
Chergui, Chott Ech 118 34 10N 0 25 E
Cheri 121 13 26N 11 21 E
Cherikov 80 53 32N 31 20 E
Cheriton 28 51 3N 1 9W
Cheriton Fitzpaine 30 50 51N 3 38W
Cherkessk 83 44 25N 42 10 E
Cherlak 76 54 15N 74 55 E
Chermoz 84 58 46N 56 10 E
Chernak 85 43 24N 68 2 E
Chernaya Kholunitsa 84 58 51N 51 52 E
Cherni, Mt. 67 42 35N 23 18 E
Chernigov 80 51 28N 31 20 E
Chernikovsk 84 54 48N 56 8 E
Chernobyl 80 51 13N 30 15 E
Chernogorsk 77 54 5N 91 10 E
Chernomorskoye 82 45 31N 32 46 E
Chernovskoye 81 58 48N 47 20 E
Chernovtsy 82 48 0N 26 0 E
Chernoye 77 70 30N 89 10 E
Chernushka 84 56 29N 56 3 E
Chernyakhovsk 80 54 29N 21 48 E
Chernyshevskiy 77 62 40N 112 30 E
Chernyshkovskiy 83 48 30N 42 28 E
Cherokee, Iowa, U.S.A. 158 42 40N 95 30W
Cherokee, Okla., U.S.A. 159 36 45N 98 25W
Cherokees, L. of the 159 36 50N 95 12W
Cherquenco 176 38 35 S 72 0W
Cherrapunji 99 25 17N 91 47 E
Cherry Creek 160 39 50N 114 58W
Cherry Valley, U.S.A. 162 42 48N 74 45W
Cherry Valley, U.S.A. 163 33 59N 116 57W
Cherryvale 159 37 20N 95 33W
Cherskiy 77 68 45N 161 18 E
Cherskogo Khrebet 77 65 0N 143 0 E
Chertkovo 83 49 25N 40 19 E
Chertsey 29 51 23N 0 30W
Cherven 80 53 45N 28 13 E
Cherven-Bryag 67 43 17N 24 7 E
Cherwell, R. 28 51 46N 1 18W
Chesapeake Bay 162 38 0N 76 12W
Chesapeake Beach 162 38 41N 76 32W
Chesha B. = Cheshskaya G. 78 67 20N 47 0 E
Chesham 29 51 42N 0 36W
Cheshire □ 32 53 14N 2 30W
Cheshunt 29 51 42N 0 1W
Chesil Beach 23 50 37N 2 33W
Cheslatta L. 152 53 49N 125 20W
Chesne, Le 43 49 30N 4 45 E
Cheste 59 39 30N 0 41W
Chester, U.K. 32 53 12N 2 53W
Chester, Calif., U.S.A. 160 40 22N 121 22W
Chester, Ill., U.S.A. 158 37 58N 89 50W
Chester, Mont., U.S.A. 160 48 31N 111 0W
Chester, Pa., U.S.A. 162 39 54N 75 20W
Chester, S.C., U.S.A. 157 34 44N 81 13W
Chester, Va., U.S.A. 162 37 21N 77 27W
Chester, Vt., U.S.A. 162 43 16N 72 36W
Chester-le-Street 33 54 53N 1 34W
Chesterfield, Can. 148 63 0N 91 0W
Chesterfield, U.K. 33 53 14N 1 26W
Chesterfield, U.S.A. 162 37 23N 77 31W
Chesterfield I. 129 16 20 S 43 58 E
Chesterfield, Îles 133 19 52 S 158 15 E
Chesterfield Inlet 148 63 30N 90 45W
Chesterton Range 138 25 30 S 147 27 E
Chestertown 162 39 13N 76 4W
Chesuncook L. 151 46 0N 69 10W
Chetaibi 119 37 1N 7 20 E
Cheticamp 151 46 37N 60 59W
Chetumal 165 18 30N 88 20W
Chetumal, Bahía de 165 18 40N 88 10W
Chetwynd 152 55 45N 121 45W
Chevanceaux 44 45 18N 0 14W
Cheviot Hills 35 55 20N 2 30W
Cheviot Ra. 138 25 20 S 143 45 E
Cheviot, The 35 55 29N 2 8W
Chew Bahir 123 4 40N 36 50 E
Chew Magna 28 51 21N 2 37W
Chewelah 160 48 17N 117 43W
Cheyenne, Okla., U.S.A. 159 35 40N 99 40W
Cheyenne, Wyo., U.S.A. 158 41 9N 104 49W
Cheyenne, R. 158 44 50N 101 0W
Cheyenne Wells 158 38 51N 102 23W
Cheylard, Le 45 44 55N 4 25 E
Cheyne B. 137 34 35 S 118 50 E
Chhabra 94 24 40N 76 54 E
Chhang 102 12 15N 104 14 E
Chhatak 95 25 5N 91 37 E
Chhatarpur 95 24 55N 79 43 E
Chhep 100 13 45N 105 24 E
Chhindwara 95 22 2N 78 59 E
Chhlong 101 12 15N 105 58 E

Chhuk 101 10 46N 104 8 E
Chi, R. 100 15 11N 104 43 E
Chiaho 109 25 33N 112 15 E
Chiahsiang 106 35 25N 116 21 E
Chiahsien, Hensi, China 106 38 6N 110 28 E
Chiahsien, Honan, China 106 33 58N 113 13 E
Chiahsing 109 30 45N 120 43 E
Chiai 109 23 29N 120 25 E
Chiali 109 23 10N 120 11 E
Chialing Chiang, R. 108 30 2N 106 19 E
Chiamussu 105 46 50N 130 21 E
Chian, Kiangsi, China 109 27 8N 115 0 E
Chian, Kirin, China 107 41 6N 126 10 E
Chiang Dao 100 19 22N 98 58 E
Chiang Kham 100 19 32N 100 18 E
Chiang Khan 100 17 52N 101 36 E
Chiang Khong 100 20 17N 100 24 E
Chiang Mai 100 18 47N 98 59 E
Chiang Saen 100 20 16N 100 5 E
Chiangch'eng 108 22 36N 101 50 E
Chiangchiat'un 107 40 54N 120 36 E
Chiangching 108 29 13N 106 15 E
Chiangchun 109 23 5N 120 5 E
Chianghua 109 25 2N 111 45 E
Chiangk'ou 108 27 42N 108 50 E
Chiangling 109 30 21N 112 5 E
Chiangmen 109 22 37N 113 3 E
Chiangpei 108 29 47N 106 29 E
Chiangp'ing 108 21 36N 108 8 E
Chiangshan 109 28 45N 118 37 E
Chiangta 108 31 28N 99 12 E
Chiangti 108 27 1N 103 37 E
Chiangyin 109 31 50N 120 18 E
Chiangyü 108 31 47N 104 45 E
Chiangyung 109 25 16N 111 20 E
Chianie 125 15 35 S 13 40 E
Ch'iaochia 108 26 57N 103 3 E
Chiaochou Wan 107 36 10N 120 15 E
Chiaoho, Hopei, China 106 38 1N 116 17 E
Chiaoho, Kirin, China 107 43 42N 127 19 E
Chiaohsien 107 36 20N 120 0 E
Chiaoling 109 24 40N 117 10 E
Chiaotso 106 35 17N 113 18 E
Chiapa de Corzo 165 16 42N 93 0W
Chiapa, R. 165 16 42N 93 0W
Chiapas □ 165 17 0N 92 45W
Chiaramonte Gulfi 65 37 1N 14 41 E
Chiaravalle 63 38 41N 16 24 E
Chiaravalle Centrale 65 38 41N 16 25 E
Chiari 62 45 31N 9 55 E
Chiashan 109 32 37N 118 8 E
Chiasso 51 45 50N 9 0 E
Chiating 109 31 21N 121 15 E
Chiautla 165 18 18N 98 34W
Chiávari 62 44 20N 9 20 E
Chiavenna 62 46 18N 9 23 E
Chiawang 107 34 30N 117 22 E
Chiayü 109 29 59N 113 54 E
Chiba 111 35 30N 140 7 E
Chiba-ken □ 111 35 30N 140 20 E
Chibabava 129 20 35 S 33 35 E
Chibemba 125 15 48 S 14 8 E
Chibougamau 150 49 56N 74 24W
Chibougamau L. 150 49 50N 74 20W
Chibougamau, R. 150 49 50N 75 40W
Chibuk 121 10 52N 12 50 E
Chibuto 129 24 40 S 33 33 E
Chic-Chocs, Mts. 151 48 55N 66 0W
Chic-Chocs, Parc Prov. des 151 48 55N 66 20W
Chicacole = Srikakulam 97 18 14N 84 4 E
Chicago 156 41 53N 87 40W
Chicago Heights 156 41 29N 87 37W
Chicago North 156 42 20N 87 50W
Chichagof I. 152 58 0N 136 0W
Chichaoua 118 31 32N 8 44W
Chichén Itzá 165 20 40N 88 32W
Chichester 29 50 50N 0 47W
Chichester Ra. 136 21 35 S 117 45 E
Chich'i 109 30 4N 118 34 E
Ch'ichiang 108 29 0N 106 40 E
Chichibu 111 36 5N 139 10 E
Ch'ich'ihaerh 105 47 22N 123 57 E
Chichiriviche 174 10 56N 68 16W
Ch'ich'un 109 30 14N 115 25 E
Chickasha 159 35 0N 98 0W
Chicken Hd. 31 58 10N 6 15W
Chiclana de la Frontera 57 36 26N 6 9W
Chiclayo 174 6 42 S 79 50W
Chico 160 39 45N 121 54W
Chico, R., Chubut, Argent. 160 44 0 S 67 0W
Chico, R., Santa Cruz, Argent. 176 49 30 S 69 30W
Chicoa 125 15 35 S 32 20 E
Chicomo 129 24 31 S 34 6 E
Chicontepec 165 20 58N 98 10W
Chicopee 162 42 6N 72 37W
Chicoutimi 151 48 28N 71 5W
Chidambaram 97 11 20N 79 45 E
Chiddingfold 29 51 6N 0 37W
Chidenguele 129 24 55 S 34 2 E
Chidley C. 149 60 23N 64 26W
Chiehhsiu 106 37 0N 111 55 E
Ch'iehmo 105 38 8N 85 32 E
Chiehshou 109 33 19N 115 22 E
Chiehyang 109 23 37N 116 19 E
Chiem Hoa 100 22 12N 105 17 E
Chiemsee 49 47 53N 12 27 E
Chiench'ang 107 41 16N 124 28 E
Chiench'angying 107 40 8N 118 50 E
Ch'iench'engchen 108 27 12N 109 50 E

Ch'ienchiang

Chomen Swamp

Ch'ienchiang, Hupeh, China **109** 30 25N 112 51 E
Ch'ienchiang, Kwangsi-Chuang, China **108** 23 40N 108 58 E
Ch'ienchiang, Szechwan, China **108** 29 31N 108 46 E
Chiench'uan **108** 26 28N 99 52 E
Chiengi **124** 8 45 S 29 10 E
Chienho **108** 26 39N 108 35 E
Ch'ienhsi **108** 27 3N 106 0 E
Ch'ienhsien **106** 34 30N 108 10 E
Chienko **108** 32 0N 105 23 E
Chienli **109** 29 49N 112 53 E
Chienou **109** 27 5N 118 20 E
Ch'ienshan, Anhwei, China **109** 30 41N 116 35 E
Ch'ienshan, Kiangsi, China **109** 28 18N 117 40 E
Chienshih **108** 30 40N 109 43 E
Chienshui **108** 23 37N 102 49 E
Chiente **109** 29 29N 119 16 E
Chienti, R. **63** 43 15N 13 30 E
Chienwei **108** 29 13N 103 56 E
Chienyang **109** 27 21N 118 5 E
Ch'ienyang, Hunan, China **109** 27 18N 110 10 E
Ch'ienyang, Kansu, China **106** 34 35N 107 2 E
Chienyang **108** 30 24N 104 33 E
Chierhkalang **107** 43 6N 122 54 E
Chieri **62** 45 0N 7 50 E
Chiese, R. **62** 45 45N 10 35 E
Chieti **63** 42 22N 14 10 E
Chièvres **47** 50 35N 3 48 E
Chigasaki **111** 35 19N 139 24 E
Chignecto B. **151** 45 48N 64 40W
Chignik **147** 56 15N 158 27W
Chigorodó **174** 7 41N 76 42W
Chiguana **172** 21 0 S 67 50W
Chihari **107** 38 40N 126 30 E
Ch'ihch'i **109** 21 59N 112 58 E
Chihchiang, Hunan, China **108** 27 27N 109 41 E
Chihchiang, Hupei, China **109** 30 19N 111 30 E
Chihchin **108** 26 42N 105 45 E
Ch'ihfeng **107** 42 18N 118 57 E
Chihkou **107** 35 55N 119 13 E
Chihli, G. of = Po Hai **107** 38 40N 119 0 E
Ch'ihshui **108** 29 29N 105 38 E
Ch'ihshui Ho, R. **108** 28 53N 105 48 E
Chihsi **107** 45 20N 130 55 E
Ch'ihsien **106** 34 33N 114 47 E
Chihsien, Honan, China **106** 35 25N 114 5 E
Chihsien, Hopei, China **106** 37 34N 115 34 E
Chihsien, Shansi, China **106** 36 8N 110 39 E
Chihtan **106** 36 56N 108 47 E
Chihte **109** 30 9N 117 0 E
Chihuahua **164** 28 40N 106 3W
Chihuahua □ **164** 28 40N 106 3W
Chihuatlán **164** 19 14N 104 35W
Chiili **85** 44 20N 66 15 E
Chik Ballapur **97** 13 25N 77 45 E
Chikawawa **127** 16 2 S 34 50 E
Chikhli **96** 20 20N 76 18 E
Chikmagalur **97** 13 15N 75 45 E
Chikodi **96** 16 26N 74 38 E
Chikonde **127** 12 16 S 31 38 E
Ch'ik'ou **107** 38 37N 117 35 E
Chikugo **110** 33 14N 130 28 E
Chikuma-Gawa, R. **111** 36 59N 138 35 E
Chilac **165** 18 20N 97 24W
Chilako, R. **152** 53 53N 122 57W
Chilam Chavki **95** 35 5N 75 5 E
Chilanga **127** 15 33 S 28 16 E
Chilant'ai **106** 39 45N 105 45 E
Chilapa **165** 17 40N 99 20W
Chilas **95** 35 25N 74 5 E
Chilaw **93** 7 30N 79 50 E
Chilcotin, R. **152** 51 44N 122 23W
Childers **139** 25 15 S 152 17 E
Childress **159** 34 30N 100 50W
Chile ■ **176** 35 0 S 71 15W
Chilecito **172** 29 0 S 67 40W
Chilete **174** 7 10 S 78 50W
Chilham **29** 51 15N 0 59 E
Chilik, Kazakh S.S.R., U.S.S.R. **84** 51 7N 53 55 E
Chilik, Kirgiz S.S.R., U.S.S.R. **85** 43 33N 78 17 E
Chililabombwe (Bancroft) **125** 12 18 S 27 43 E
Chilin **105** 43 53N 126 38 E
Ch'ilin Hu **105** 31 50N 89 0 E
Chilka L. **96** 19 40N 85 25 E
Chilko, L. **152** 52 60N 124 10W
Chilko, R. **152** 52 6N 124 9W
Chillagoe **138** 17 14 S 144 33 E
Chillán **172** 36 40 S 72 10W
Chillicothe, Ill., U.S.A. **158** 40 55N 89 32W
Chillicothe, Mo., U.S.A. **158** 39 45N 93 30W
Chillicothe, Ohio, U.S.A. **156** 39 53N 82 58W
Chilliwack **152** 49 10N 122 0W
Chilo **94** 27 12N 73 32 E
Chiloane, I. **129** 20 40 S 34 55 E
Chiloé, I. de **176** 42 50 S 73 45W
Chilpancingo **165** 17 30N 99 40W
Chiltern **141** 36 10 S 146 36 E
Chiltern Hills **29** 51 44N 0 42W
Chilton **156** 44 1N 88 12W
Chiluage **124** 9 15 S 21 42 E
Chilubula **127** 10 14 S 30 51 E
Chilumba **127** 10 28 S 34 12 E
Chilung **109** 25 3N 121 45 E
Chilwa, L. (Shirwa) **127** 15 15 S 35 40 E
Chimacum **160** 48 1N 122 53W
Chimaltitán **164** 21 46N 103 50W
Chimán **166** 8 45N 78 40W
Chimay **47** 50 3N 4 20 E
Chimbay **76** 42 57N 59 47 E
Chimborazo **174** 1 20 S 78 55W
Chimbote **174** 9 0 S 78 35W
Ch'imen **109** 29 56N 117 47 E
Chimion **85** 40 15N 71 32 E
Chimishliya **70** 46 34N 28 44 E
Chimkent **85** 42 18N 69 36 E
Chimo **107** 36 23N 120 27 E
Chimpembe **127** 9 31 S 29 33 E
Chin □ **98** 22 0N 93 0 E
Chin Chiang, R. **109** 28 23N 115 48 E
Chin Hills **98** 22 30N 93 30 E
Chin Ho, R. **106** 35 2N 113 25 E
Chin Ling Shan **106** 34 0N 107 0 E
Ch'in Shui, R. **109** 26 13N 115 15 E
China **164** 25 40N 99 20W
China ■ **105** 30 0N 110 0 E
China Lake **163** 35 44N 117 37W
Chinacates **164** 25 0N 105 14W
Chinacota **174** 7 37N 72 36W
Ch'inan **106** 34 50N 105 35 E
Chinan **106** 36 32N 117 0 E
Chinandega **166** 12 30N 87 0W
Chinati Pk. **159** 30 0N 104 25W
Chincha Alta **174** 13 20 S 76 0W
Chinch'eng **106** 35 30N 112 50 E
Chinchi **106** 37 57N 106 6 E
Chinch'i **109** 27 54N 116 44 E
Chinchiang, Fukien, China **109** 24 54N 118 35 E
Chinchiang, Kiangsi, China **109** 29 44N 115 59 E
Chinchiang, Yunnan, China **108** 26 14N 100 34 E
Chinchilla **139** 26 45 S 150 38 E
Chinchilla de Monte Aragón **59** 38 53N 1 40W
Chinchón **58** 40 9N 3 26W
Chinchorro, Banco **165** 18 35N 87 20W
Ch'inchou **108** 21 58N 108 35 E
Chinchou **107** 41 8N 121 6 E
Chinch'uan **108** 31 30N 101 55 E
Chincoteague **162** 37 58N 75 21W
Chincoteague B. **162** 38 5N 75 8W
Chinde **127** 18 45 S 36 30 E
Chindo **107** 34 28N 126 15 E
Chindwin, R. **98** 21 26N 95 15 E
Chineni **95** 33 2N 75 15 E
Ch'ing Chiang, R. **109** 29 51N 112 22 E
Ch'ing Hai **105** 37 0N 100 20 E
Ching Ho, R. **106** 34 29N 109 5 E
Ching Shan **109** 31 40N 111 30 E
Chinga **127** 15 13 S 38 35 E
Chingan **109** 28 52N 115 22 E
Ch'ingchen **108** 26 32N 106 30 E
Ch'ingch'eng **107** 37 11N 117 42 E
Chingchiang **109** 32 2N 120 16 E
Ch'ingchiang, Kiangsi, China **109** 28 5N 115 30 E
Ch'ingchiang, Kiangsu, China **107** 33 33N 119 4 E
Ch'ingchien **106** 37 12N 110 6 E
Chingch'uan **106** 35 15N 107 22 E
Ch'ingfeng **106** 35 54N 115 7 E
Chinghai **106** 38 56N 116 55 E
Ch'inghomen **107** 41 45N 121 25 E
Chinghsi **108** 23 8N 106 25 E
Ch'inghsien **106** 38 35N 116 48 E
Chinghsien **109** 30 42N 118 23 E
Ch'inghsü **106** 37 40N 112 20 E
Chinghung **108** 22 0N 100 49 E
Chingi Chiang, R. **108** 29 32N 103 44 E
Chingku **108** 23 28N 100 42 E
Chingleput **97** 12 42N 79 58 E
Ch'ingliu **109** 26 12N 116 48 E
Chinglo **106** 38 24N 111 54 E
Ch'inglung **108** 25 48N 105 14 E
Chingmen **109** 30 58N 112 6 E
Chingning, Chekiang, China **109** 27 58N 119 38 E
Chingning, Kansu, China **106** 35 30N 105 45 E
Chingola **127** 12 31 S 27 53 E
Chingole **127** 13 4 S 34 17 E
Chingpien **106** 37 24N 108 36 E
Chingpo Hu **107** 43 50N 128 50 E
Ch'ingp'u **109** 31 9N 121 6 E
Chingshan **109** 31 2N 113 3 E
Chingshih **109** 29 40N 111 50 E
Ch'ingshui **106** 34 44N 106 2 E
Chingsing **106** 38 5N 114 8 E
Chingt'ai **106** 37 10N 104 8 E
Ch'ingtao **107** 36 5N 120 25 E
Chingte **109** 30 19N 118 31 E
Chingtechen **109** 29 19N 117 15 E
Ch'ingt'ien **109** 28 9N 120 17 E
Chingtung **108** 24 22N 100 50 E
Chingtzukuan **106** 33 13N 111 2 E
Chinguar **125** 12 18 S 16 45 E
Chinguetti **116** 20 25N 12 15W
Chingune **129** 20 33 S 35 0 E
Ch'ingyang **105** 36 5N 107 40 E
Chingyang **106** 34 32N 108 52 E
Ch'ingyang, Anhwei, China **109** 30 38N 117 50 E
Ch'ingyang, Ningsia Hui, China **106** 36 5N 107 40 E
Chingyü **107** 42 22N 126 45 E
Chingyüan **106** 36 35N 104 40 E
Ch'ingyüan, Chekiang, China **109** 27 37N 119 3 E
Ch'ingyüan, Kwangtung, China **109** 23 42N 112 58 E
Ch'ingyüan, Liaoning, China **107** 42 6N 124 55 E
Ch'ingyün **107** 37 53N 117 23 E
Chinhae **107** 35 9N 128 40 E
Chinhanguanine **129** 25 21 S 32 30 E
Chinhsi **107** 40 49N 120 55 E
Chinhsiang **106** 35 5N 116 18 E
Chinhsien, Hopei, China **106** 38 2N 115 2 E
Chinhsien, Kiangsi, China **109** 28 22N 116 14 E
Chinhsien, Liaoning, China **107** 39 6N 121 3 E
Chinhua **109** 29 9N 119 41 E
Ch'inhuangtao **107** 39 57N 119 40 E
Chining, Inner Mongolia, China **106** 41 2N 113 8 E
Chining, Shantung, China **106** 35 19N 116 36 E
Chiniot **94** 31 45N 73 0 E
Chinipas **164** 27 22N 108 32W
Chinju **107** 35 12N 128 2 E
Chink'ou **109** 30 20N 114 7 E
Chinle **161** 36 14N 109 38W
Chinmen **109** 24 27N 118 21 E
Chinmen Tao, I. **109** 24 25N 118 25 E
Chinnamanur **97** 9 50N 77 16 E
Chinnampo **107** 38 52N 125 28 E
Chinning **108** 24 40N 102 35 E
Chinnur **96** 18 57N 79 43 E
Chino, Japan **111** 35 59N 138 9 E
Chino, U.S.A. **163** 34 1N 117 41W
Chino Valley **161** 34 54N 112 28W
Chinon **42** 47 10N 0 15 E
Chinook, Can. **153** 51 28N 110 59W
Chinook, U.S.A. **160** 48 35N 109 19W
Chinp'ing, Kweichow, China **108** 26 40N 109 7 E
Chinp'ing, Yunnan, China **108** 22 46N 103 15 E
Chinsali **124** 10 30 S 32 2 E
Chinsha **108** 27 29N 106 15 E
Chinsha Chiang, R. = Yangtze Chiang, R. **108** 27 30N 99 30 E
Chinshan **109** 30 3N 121 13 E
Ch'inshui **106** 35 41N 112 11 E
Chintamani **97** 13 26N 78 3 E
Chint'an **109** 31 45N 119 35 E
Chint'ang **108** 30 51N 104 27 E
Chinwangtao = Ch'inhuangtao **107** 39 57N 119 40 E
Ch'inyang **106** 35 5N 112 55 E
Ch'inyüan **106** 36 31N 112 15 E
Chióggia **63** 45 13N 12 15 E
Chíos = Khíos **69** 38 27N 26 9 E
Chip Lake **152** 53 35N 115 35W
Chipai L. **150** 52 56N 87 53W
Chipata (Ft . Jameson) **127** 13 38 S 32 28 E
Chipewyan L. **153** 58 0N 98 27W
Chipinga **127** 20 13 S 32 36 E
Chipiona **57** 36 44N 6 26W
Chipley **157** 30 45N 85 32W
Chiplun **96** 17 31N 73 34 E
Chipman **151** 46 6N 65 53W
Chipoka **127** 13 57 S 34 28 E
Chiporovtsi **66** 43 24N 22 52 E
Chippenham **28** 51 27N 2 7W
Chippewa Falls **158** 44 55N 91 22W
Chippewa, R. **158** 44 45N 91 55W
Chipping Campden **28** 52 4N 1 48W
Chipping Norton **28** 51 56N 1 32W
Chipping Ongar **29** 51 43N 0 15 E
Chipping Sodbury **28** 51 31N 2 23W
Chiquian **174** 10 10 S 77 0W
Chiquimula **166** 14 51N 89 37W
Chiquinquirá **174** 5 37N 73 50W
Chir, R. **83** 48 45N 42 10 E
Chirala **97** 15 50N 80 20 E
Chiramba **127** 16 55 S 34 39 E
Chiran **110** 31 22N 130 27 E
Chiras **93** 35 14N 65 40 E
Chirawa **94** 28 14N 75 42 E
Chirayinkil **97** 8 41N 76 49 E
Chirbury **28** 52 35N 3 6W
Chirchik **85** 41 29N 69 35 E
Chirfa **117** 20 55N 12 14 E
Chiricahua Pk. **161** 31 53N 109 14W
Chirikof I. **147** 55 50N 155 40W
Chiriquí, Golfo de **166** 8 0N 82 10W
Chiriquí, Lago de **166** 9 10N 82 0W
Chiriquí, Vol. **166** 8 55N 82 35W
Chirivira Falls **127** 21 10 S 32 12 E
Chirk **31** 52 57N 3 4W
Chirmiri **99** 23 15N 82 20 E
Chirnogi **70** 44 7N 26 32 E
Chirnside **35** 55 47N 2 11W
Chiromo **125** 16 30 S 35 7 E
Chirpan **67** 42 10N 25 19 E
Chirripó Grande, cerro **166** 9 29N 83 29W
Chisamba **127** 14 55 S 28 20 E
Chisapani Garhi **99** 27 30N 84 2 E
Ch'ishan **106** 34 28N 107 35 E
Chishan **106** 35 36N 110 59 E
Ch'ishan **109** 22 44N 120 31 E
Chishmy **84** 54 35N 55 23 E
Chisholm **152** 54 55N 114 10W
Chishou **108** 28 12N 109 43 E
Chishui **109** 27 14N 115 10 E
Chisimba Falls **127** 10 12 S 30 56 E
Chisineu Criş **66** 46 32N 21 37 E
Chisledon **28** 51 30N 1 44W
Chisone, R. **62** 45 0N 7 5 E
Chisos Mts. **159** 29 20N 103 15W
Chistian Mandi **94** 29 50N 72 55 E
Chistopol **81** 55 25N 50 38 E
Chita, Colomb. **174** 6 11N 72 28W
Chita, U.S.S.R. **77** 52 0N 113 25 E
Chitado **125** 17 10 S 14 8 E
Ch'it'ai **105** 44 1N 89 28 E
Chitapur **96** 17 10N 76 50 E
Chitembo **125** 13 30 S 16 50 E
Chitina **147** 61 30N 144 30W
Chitinghsilin **105** 32 51N 92 28 E
Chitipa **127** 9 41 S 33 19 E
Chitokoloki **125** 13 43 S 23 4 E
Chitorgarh **94** 24 52N 74 43 E
Chitrakot **96** 19 20N 81 40 E
Chitral **93** 35 50N 71 56 E
Chitravati, R. **97** 14 30N 78 0 E
Chitré **167** 7 59N 80 27W
Chitse **106** 36 54N 114 52 E
Chittagong **98** 22 19N 91 55 E
Chittagong □ **98** 24 5N 91 25 E
Chittoor **97** 13 15N 79 5 E
Chittur **97** 10 40N 76 45 E
Chitu **123** 8 38N 37 58 E
Ch'itung, Hunan, China **109** 26 47N 112 7 E
Ch'itung, Kiangsu, China **109** 31 49N 121 40 E
Chiuant'u **107** 42 33N 128 19 E
Chiuchaohua **108** 32 20N 105 45 E
Chiuch'engch'i **108** 27 10N 108 42 E
Chiuchiang, Kiangsi, China **109** 29 43N 115 55 E
Chiuchiang, Kwangtung, China **109** 22 50N 112 50 E
Chiuch'üan **105** 39 46N 98 34 E
Chiuhsiangch'eng **109** 33 13N 114 50 E
Chiukuanch'eng **106** 35 50N 115 22 E
Chiuling Shan **109** 28 50N 114 20 E
Chiuliuch'eng **108** 24 32N 109 15 E
Chiulung **108** 28 59N 101 32 E
Ch'iungchou Haihsia **100** 20 10N 110 15 E
Ch'iunghai **100** 19 15N 110 26 E
Chiunglai **108** 30 25N 103 30 E
Chiunglai Shan **108** 31 20N 102 50 E
Ch'iungshan **100** 19 51N 110 26 E
Chiuningkang **109** 26 48N 114 6 E
Ch'iupei **108** 24 3N 104 12 E
Chiushench'iu **106** 33 10N 115 8 E
Chiushengch'i **108** 27 31N 109 12 E
Chiusi **63** 43 1N 11 58 E
Chiut'ai **107** 44 10N 125 49 E
Chiutaosha **106** 35 39N 103 45 E
Chiuwuch'ing **106** 39 23N 116 53 E
Chiva **59** 39 27N 0 41W
Chivasso **62** 45 10N 7 52 E
Chivilcoy **172** 35 0 S 60 0W
Chiwanda **127** 11 23 S 34 55 E
Chiwefwe **127** 13 37 S 29 31 E
Chiyang **107** 37 0N 117 13 E
Ch'iyang **109** 26 35N 111 52 E
Chiyüan **106** 35 5N 112 39 E
Chiyün **109** 28 35N 120 2 E
Chizera **127** 13 10 S 25 0 E
Chkalov = Orenburg **78** 52 0N 55 5 E
Chkolovsk **81** 56 50N 43 10 E
Chlumec **52** 50 9N 15 29 E
Chmielnik **54** 50 37N 20 43 E
Cho Bo **100** 20 46N 105 10 E
Cho Do **107** 38 30N 124 40 E
Cho Phuoc **101** 10 26N 107 18 E
Choba **126** 2 30N 38 5 E
Chobe National Park **128** 21 30 S 25 0 E
Chobe, R. **128** 18 10 S 24 10 E
Chobol **121** 11 53N 13 1 E
Chochiwŏn **107** 36 37N 127 18 E
Chocianów **54** 51 35N 15 33 E
Chociwel **54** 53 29N 15 21 E
Chocó □ **174** 6 0N 77 0W
Chocontá **174** 5 9N 73 41W
Chodaków **54** 52 16N 20 18 E
Chodavaram **96** 17 40N 82 50 E
Chodecz **54** 52 56N 19 2 E
Chodziez **54** 52 58N 17 0 E
Choele Choel **176** 39 11 S 65 40W
Chōfu **111** 35 39N 139 33 E
Chohsien **106** 39 30N 116 0 E
Choiseul I. **130** 7 0 S 156 40 E
Choisy-le-Roi **43** 48 45N 2 24 E
Choix **164** 26 40N 108 10W
Chojna **54** 52 58N 14 25 E
Chojnice **54** 53 42N 17 40 E
Chojnów **54** 51 25N 15 58 E
Choke Mts. **123** 11 18N 37 15 E
Chokurdakh **77** 70 38N 147 55 E
Cholame **163** 35 44N 120 18W
Cholet **42** 47 4N 0 52W
Chollerton **35** 55 4N 2 7W
Cholpon-Ata **85** 42 40N 77 6 E
Cholsey **28** 51 34N 1 10W
Cholu **106** 40 19N 115 5 E
Choluteca **166** 13 20N 87 14W
Choluteca, R. **166** 13 5N 87 20W
Chom Bung **100** 13 37N 99 36 E
Chom Thong **100** 18 25N 98 41 E
Choma **127** 16 48 S 26 59 E
Chomen Swamp **123** 9 20N 37 10 E

Chomu Clee Hills

Chomu 94 27 15N 75 40 E
Chomutov 52 50 28N 13 23 E
Chon Buri 100 13 22N 100 59 E
Chon Thanh 101 11 24N 106 36 E
Chŏnan 107 36 48N 127 9 E
Chonburi 101 13 21N 101 1 E
Chone 174 0 40 S 80 0W
Chong Kai 100 13 57N 103 35 E
Chong Mek 100 15 10N 105 27 E
Chŏngdo 107 35 38N 128 42 E
Chŏngha 107 36 12N 129 21 E
Chŏngjin 107 41 47N 129 50 E
Chŏngju 107 39 40N 125 5 E
Chŏngup 107 35 35N 126 50 E
Chŏnju 107 35 50N 127 4 E
Chonos, Arch. de los 176 45 0 S 75 0W
Chopda 96 21 20N 75 15 E
Chopim, R. 173 25 35 S 53 5W
Choptank, R. 162 38 41N 76 0W
Chorbat La 95 34 42N 76 37 E
Chorley 32 53 39N 2 39W
Chormet el Melah 119 30 11N 16 29 E
Chorolque, Cerro 172 20 59 S 66 5W
Choroszcz 54 53 10N 22 59 E
Chortkov 80 49 2N 25 46 E
Chorul Tso 95 32 30N 82 30 E
Chŏrwŏn 107 38 15N 127 10 E
Chorzele 54 53 15N 21 2 E
Chorzów 54 50 18N 19 0 E
Chos-Malal 172 37 15 S 70 5W
Chosan 107 40 50N 125 47 E
Choshi 111 35 45N 140 45 E
Choszczno 54 53 7N 15 25 E
Choteau 160 47 50N 112 10W
Chotila 94 22 30N 71 15 E
Chotzu 106 40 52N 112 33 E
Chou Shan 109 30 2N 122 6 E
Chouchih 106 34 8N 108 14 E
Chouch'ü 106 33 46N 104 18 E
Chouning 109 27 15N 119 13 E
Chouts'un 107 36 48N 117 52 E
Ch'ouyang 108 23 14N 104 35 E
Chowchilla 163 37 11N 120 12W
Chowkham 98 20 52N 97 28 E
Choybalsan 105 48 4N 114 30 E
Christchurch, N.Z. 143 43 33 S 172 47 E
Christchurch, U.K. 28 50 44N 1 47W
Christiana, S. Afr. 128 27 52 S 25 8 E
Christiana, U.S.A. 162 39 40N 75 40W
Christiansfeld 73 55 21N 9 29 E
Christiansö, I. 73 55 19N 15 12 E
Christiansted 147 17 45N 64 42W
Christie B. 153 62 32N 111 10W
Christina, R. 153 56 40N 111 3W
Christmas Cr. 136 18 53 S 125 55 E
Christmas Creek 136 18 29 S 125 23 E
Christmas I., Ind. Oc. 142 10 0 S 105 40 E
Christmas I., Pac. Oc. 131 1 58N 157 27W
Christopher L. 137 24 49 S 127 42 E
Chrudim 52 49 58N 15 43 E
Chrzanów 54 50 10N 19 21 E
Chtimba 127 10 35 S 34 13 E
Chu 85 43 36N 73 42 E
Ch'u Chiang, R. 108 30 2N 106 19 E
Chu Chua 152 51 22N 120 10W
Chu Lai 100 15 28N 108 45 E
Chu, R., U.S.S.R. 85 45 0N 67 44 E
Chu, R., Viet. 100 19 53N 105 45 E
Chuadanga 98 23 38N 88 51 E
Ch'üanchou, Fukien, China 109 24 56N 118 35 E
Ch'üanchou, Kwangsi-Chuang, China 109 25 59N 111 4 E
Chuangho 107 39 42N 123 0 E
Chüannan 109 24 50N 114 40 E
Chūbu □ 112 36 45N 137 30 E
Chubut, R. 176 43 0 S 70 0W
Chuch'eng 107 36 0N 119 16 E
Chuch'i 108 32 19N 109 52 E
Chuchi, Chekiang, China 109 29 43N 120 14 E
Chuchi, Honan, China 106 34 27N 115 39 E
Chuchi L. 152 55 12N 124 30W
Ch'uching 108 25 34N 103 45 E
Chuchou 109 27 50N 113 10 E
Chudleigh 30 50 35N 3 36W
Chudovo 80 59 10N 31 30 E
Chudskoye, Oz. 80 58 13N 27 30 E
Ch'üehshan 109 32 48N 114 1 E
Chugach Mts. 147 62 0N 146 0W
Chugiak 147 61 7N 149 10W
Chuginadak I. 147 52 50N 169 45W
Chūgoku □ 110 35 0N 133 0 E
Chūgoku-Sanchi 110 35 0N 133 0 E
Chuguyev 82 49 55N 36 45 E
Chugwater 158 41 48N 104 47W
Chuhai 109 22 17N 113 34 E
Chühsien 107 35 35N 118 49 E
Ch'uhsien, China 109 28 57N 118 58 E
Ch'uhsien, China 109 32 18N 118 18 E
Chuhsien 105 28 57N 118 58 E
Ch'ühsien 108 30 51N 107 1 E
Ch'uhsiung 108 25 2N 101 32 E
Chüjung 109 31 56N 119 10 E
Chukai 101 4 13N 103 25 E
Chukhloma 81 58 45N 42 40 E
Chūko 111 36 44N 139 27 E
Chukotskiy Khrebet 77 68 0N 175 0 E
Chukotskiy, Mys 77 66 10N 169 3 E
Chukotskoye More 77 68 0N 175 0W
Chula Vista 163 32 39N 117 8W
Chulak-Kurgan 85 43 46N 69 9 E
Chülu 106 37 13N 115 1 E
Chulucanas 174 5 0 S 80 0W
Chum Phae 100 16 32N 102 6 E
Chum Saeng 100 15 55N 100 15 E
Chumar 95 32 40N 78 35 E
Chumatien 109 33 0N 114 4 E
Chumbicha 172 29 0 S 66 10W
Chumerna 67 42 45N 25 55 E
Chumikan 77 54 40N 135 10 E
Chumphon 101 10 35N 99 14 E
Chumuare 127 14 31 S 31 50 E
Chumunjin 107 37 55N 127 44 E
Chunchŏn 107 37 58N 127 44 E
Chunga 127 15 0 S 26 2 E
Ch'ungan 109 27 45N 118 0 E
Ch'ungch'ing, Szechwan, China 108 29 30N 106 30 E
Ch'ungch'ing, Szechwan, China 108 30 27N 103 43 E
Chungch'üantzu 106 39 22N 102 42 E
Chunggang ŭp 107 41 48N 126 48 E
Chunghsiang 109 31 10N 112 35 E
Chunghsien 108 30 17N 108 4 E
Chunghwa 107 38 52N 125 47 E
Ch'ungi 109 25 42N 114 19 E
Ch'ungjen 109 27 44N 116 2 E
Chungju 107 36 58N 127 58 E
Chungkang 107 43 42N 127 37 E
Chungking = Ch'ungch'ing 108 29 30N 106 30 E
Ch'ungli 106 40 5N 115 12 E
Chungli 109 24 57N 121 13 E
Ch'ungming 109 31 27N 121 24 E
Ch'ungming Tao, I. 109 31 35N 121 40 E
Chungmu 107 34 50N 128 20 E
Chungning 106 35 22N 105 40 E
Chungshan, Kwangsi-Chuang, China 109 24 30N 111 17 E
Chungshan, Kwangtung, China 109 22 31N 113 20 E
Ch'ungshuiho 106 39 54N 111 34 E
Ch'ungte 109 30 32N 120 26 E
Chungt'iaoshan 106 35 0N 111 30 E
Chungtien 108 27 51N 99 42 E
Ch'ungtso 108 22 20N 107 20 E
Chungtu 108 24 41N 109 42 E
Chungwei 106 37 35N 105 10 E
Chungyang 106 37 24N 111 10 E
Chungyang Shanmo 109 23 10N 121 0 E
Chungyüan 100 19 9N 110 28 E
Chünhsien 109 32 40N 111 15 E
Chunian 94 31 10N 74 0 E
Chunya 127 8 30 S 33 27 E
Chunya □ 126 7 48 S 33 0 E
Ch'unyang 107 43 42N 129 26 E
Chuquibamba 174 15 47N 72 44W
Chuquicamata 172 22 15 S 69 0W
Chuquisaca □ 172 23 30 S 63 30W
Chur 51 46 52N 9 32 E
Churachandpur 98 24 20N 93 40 E
Church Hill 38 55 0N 7 53W
Church House 152 50 20N 125 10W
Church Stretton 28 52 32N 2 49W
Churchdown 28 51 53N 2 9W
Churchill 153 58 47N 94 11W
Churchill, C. 153 58 46N 93 12W
Churchill Falls 151 53 36N 64 19W
Churchill L. 153 55 55N 108 20W
Churchill Pk. 152 58 10N 125 10W
Churchill, R., Man., Can. 153 58 47N 94 12W
Churchill, R., Newf., Can. 151 53 19N 60 10W
Churchill, R., Sask., Can. 153 58 47N 94 12W
Churchtown 39 52 12N 6 20W
Churfisten 51 47 8N 9 17 E
Churston Ferrers 30 50 23N 3 32W
Churu 94 28 20N 75 0 E
Churuguaro 174 10 49N 69 32W
Churwalden 51 46 47N 9 33 E
Chusan 109 32 13N 110 24 E
Chushul 95 33 40N 78 40 E
Chusovaya, R. 84 58 18N 56 22 E
Chusovoy 84 58 15N 57 40 E
Chust 85 41 0N 71 13 E
Ch'ützu 106 36 24N 107 27 E
Chuuronjang 107 41 35N 129 40 E
Chuvash A.S.S.R. □ 81 55 30N 48 0 E
Chuwassu 108 28 48N 97 27 E
Ch'üwu 106 35 35N 111 23 E
Ch'üyang 106 38 37N 114 41 E
Chüyeh 106 35 23N 116 6 E
Ciacova 66 45 35N 21 10 E
Cicero 156 41 48N 87 48W
Cícero Dantas 170 10 36 S 38 23W
Cidacos, R. 58 42 15N 2 10W
Cide 82 41 40N 32 50 E
Ciechanów 54 52 52N 20 38 E
Ciechanów □ 54 53 0N 20 30 E
Ciechocinek 54 52 53N 18 45 E
Ciego de Avila 166 21 50N 78 50W
Ciénaga 174 11 1N 74 15W
Ciénaga de Oro 174 8 53N 75 37W
Cienfuegos 166 22 10N 80 30W
Cieplice Slaskie Zdrój 54 50 50N 15 40 E
Cierp 44 42 55N 0 40 E
Cies, Islas 56 42 12N 8 55W
Cieszyn 54 49 45N 18 35 E
Cieza 59 38 17N 1 23W
Cifuentes 58 40 47N 2 37W
Ciha Pa. 101 22 20N 103 47 E
Cijara, Pantano de 57 39 18N 4 52W
Cijulang 103 7 42 S 108 27 E
Cikampek 103 6 23 S 107 28 E
Cilacap 103 7 43 S 109 0 E
Cıldır 83 41 10N 43 20 E
Cilgerran 31 52 4N 4 39W
Cilician Gates P. 92 37 20N 34 52 E
Cilician Taurus 92 36 40N 34 0 E
Cîlnicu 70 44 54N 23 4 E
Cimarron, Kans., U.S.A. 159 37 50N 100 20W
Cimarron, N. Mex., U.S.A. 159 36 30N 104 52W
Cimarron, R. 159 37 10N 102 10W
Cîmpia Turzii 70 46 34N 23 53 E
Cîmpina 70 45 10N 25 45 E
Cîmpulung, Argeş, Rumania 70 45 17N 25 3 E
Cîmpulung, Suceava, Rumania 70 47 32N 25 30 E
Cîmpuri 67 46 0N 26 50 E
Cinca, R. 58 42 20N 0 9 E
Cincer 66 43 55N 17 5 E
Cinch, R. 157 36 0N 84 15W
Cincinnati 156 39 10N 84 26W
Cincinnatus 162 42 33N 75 54W
Cinderford 28 51 49N 2 30W
Cîndeşti 70 45 15N 26 42 E
Ciney 47 50 18N 5 5 E
Cinigiano 63 42 53N 11 23 E
Cinogli 63 43 23N 13 10 E
Cinto, Mt. 45 42 24N 8 54 E
Cioranii 70 44 45N 26 25 E
Ciotat, La 45 43 12N 5 36 E
Čiovo 63 43 30N 16 17 E
Cipó 171 11 6 S 38 31W
Circle, Alaska, U.S.A. 147 65 50N 144 10W
Circle, Montana, U.S.A. 158 47 26N 105 35W
Circleville, Ohio, U.S.A. 156 39 35N 82 57W
Circleville, Utah, U.S.A. 161 38 12N 112 24W
Cirebon 103 6 45 S 108 32 E
Cirencester 28 51 43N 1 59W
Cireşu 70 44 47N 22 31 E
Cirey-sur-Vezouze 43 48 35N 6 57 E
Ciriè 62 45 14N 7 35 E
Cirò 65 39 23N 17 3 E
Cisco 159 32 25N 99 0W
Cislău 70 45 14N 26 33 E
Cisna 54 49 12N 22 20 E
Cisneros 174 6 33N 75 4W
Cisnădie 70 45 42N 24 9 E
Cisterna di Latina 64 41 35N 12 50 E
Cisternino 65 40 45N 17 26 E
Cité de Cansado 116 20 51N 17 0W
Citega (Kitega) 126 3 30 S 29 58 E
Citeli-Ckaro 83 41 33N 46 0 E
Citlaltépetl, mt. 165 19 0N 97 20W
Citrusdal 128 32 35 S 19 0 E
Città della Pieve 63 42 57N 12 0 E
Città di Castello 63 43 27N 12 14 E
Città Sant' Angelo 63 42 32N 14 5 E
Cittadella 63 45 39N 11 48 E
Cittaducale 63 42 24N 12 58 E
Cittanova 65 38 22N 16 0 E
Ciucaş, mt. 70 45 31N 25 56 E
Ciudad Acuña 164 29 20N 101 10W
Ciudad Altamirano 164 18 20N 100 40W
Ciudad Bolívar 174 8 5N 63 30W
Ciudad Camargo 164 27 41N 105 10W
Ciudad de Valles 165 22 0N 98 30W
Ciudad del Carmen 165 18 20N 97 50W
Ciudad Delicias = Delicias 164 28 10N 105 30W
Ciudad Guerrero 164 28 33N 107 28W
Ciudad Guzmán 164 19 40N 103 30W
Ciudad Juárez 164 31 40N 106 28W
Ciudad Madero 165 22 19N 97 50W
Ciudad Mante 165 22 50N 99 0W
Ciudad Obregón 164 27 28N 109 59W
Ciudad Piar 174 7 27N 63 19W
Ciudad Real 57 38 59N 3 55W
Ciudad Real □ 57 38 50N 4 0W
Ciudad Rodrigo 56 40 35N 6 32W
Ciudad Trujillo = Sto. Domingo 167 18 30N 70 0W
Ciudad Victoria 165 23 41N 99 9W
Ciudadela 58 40 0N 3 50 E
Ciulnița 70 44 26N 27 22 E
Civa, B. 82 41 20N 36 40 E
Cividale del Friuli 63 46 6N 13 25 E
Civita Castellana 63 42 18N 12 24 E
Civitanova Marche 63 43 18N 13 41 E
Civitavécchia 63 42 6N 11 46 E
Civitella del Tronto 63 42 48N 13 40 E
Civray 44 46 10N 0 17 E
Çivril 92 38 20N 29 55 E
Cixerri, R. 64 39 45N 8 40 E
Cizre 92 37 19N 42 10 E
Clabach 34 56 38N 6 36W
Clabby 38 54 24N 7 22W
Clach Leathad 34 56 36N 7 52W
Clachan, N. Uist., U.K. 36 57 33N 7 20W
Clachan, Strathclyde, U.K. 34 55 45N 5 35W
Clackline 137 31 40 S 116 32 E
Clackmannan 35 56 10N 3 50W
Clackmannan (□) 26 56 10N 3 47W
Clacton-on-Sea 29 51 47N 1 10 E
Cladich 34 56 21N 5 5W
Claire, L. 152 58 35N 112 5W
Clairemont 159 33 9N 100 44W
Clairvaux-les-Laes 45 46 35N 5 45 E
Clamecy 43 47 28N 3 30 E
Clane 39 53 18N 6 40W
Clanfield 29 50 56N 1 0W
Clanton 157 32 48N 86 36W
Clanwilliam 128 32 11 S 18 52 E
Clar, L. nan 37 58 17N 4 8W
Clara 39 53 20N 7 38W
Clara, R. 138 19 8 S 142 30 E
Claraville 163 35 24N 118 20W
Clare, N.S.W., Austral. 140 33 24 S 143 54 E
Clare, S. Austral., Austral. 140 33 50 S 138 37 E
Clare, N. Ireland, U.K. 38 54 25N 6 19W
Clare, Suffolk, U.K. 29 52 5N 0 36 E
Clare, U.S.A. 156 43 47N 84 45W
Clare □ 39 52 20N 7 38W
Clare I. 38 53 48N 10 0W
Clare, R. 38 53 20N 9 0W
Clarecastle 39 52 50N 8 58W
Clareen 39 53 4N 7 49W
Claregalaway 39 53 20N 8 57W
Claremont 162 43 23N 72 20W
Claremont Pt. 138 14 1 S 143 41 E
Claremore 159 36 20N 95 20W
Claremorris 38 53 45N 9 0W
Clarence I. 13 61 30 S 53 50W
Clarence, I. 176 54 0 S 72 0W
Clarence, R., Austral. 139 29 25 S 153 22 E
Clarence, R., N.Z. 143 42 10 S 173 56 E
Clarence Str., Austral. 136 12 0 S 131 0 E
Clarence Str., U.S.A. 152 55 40N 132 10W
Clarence Town 167 23 6N 74 59W
Clarendon, Ark., U.S.A. 159 34 41N 91 20W
Clarendon, Tex., U.S.A. 159 34 58N 100 54W
Clarenville 151 48 10N 54 1W
Claresholm 152 50 0N 113 45W
Clarie Coast 13 67 0 S 135 0 E
Clarinbridge 39 53 13N 8 55W
Clarinda 158 40 45N 95 0W
Clarion 158 42 41N 93 46W
Clark 158 44 55N 97 45W
Clark Fork 160 48 9N 116 9W
Clark Fork, R. 160 48 0N 115 40W
Clark Hill Res. 157 33 45N 82 20W
Clarkdale 161 34 53N 112 3W
Clarke City 151 50 12N 66 38W
Clarke, I. 138 40 32 S 148 10 E
Clarke L. 153 54 24N 106 54W
Clarke Ra. 138 20 45 S 148 20 E
Clarks Fork, R. 160 45 0N 109 30W
Clark's Harbour 151 43 25N 65 38W
Clarks Station 163 38 8N 116 42W
Clarks Summit 162 41 31N 75 44W
Clarksburg 156 39 18N 80 21W
Clarksdale 159 34 12N 90 33W
Clarkston 160 46 28N 117 2W
Clarksville, Ark., U.S.A. 159 35 29N 93 27W
Clarksville, Tenn., U.S.A. 157 36 32N 87 20W
Clarksville, Tex., U.S.A. 159 33 37N 94 59W
Claro, R. 171 19 8 S 50 40W
Clashmore 37 57 53N 4 8W
Clatskanie 160 46 9N 123 12W
Clatteringshaws L. 34 55 3N 4 17W
Claude 159 35 8N 101 22W
Claudio 171 20 26 S 44 46W
Claudy 38 54 55N 7 10W
Claunie L. 36 57 8N 5 6W
Claveria 103 18 37N 121 15 E
Claverley 28 52 32N 2 19W
Clay 163 38 17N 121 10W
Clay Center 158 39 27N 97 9W
Clay Cross 33 53 11N 1 26W
Clay Hd. 32 54 13N 4 23W
Claydon 29 52 6N 1 7 E
Clayette, La 45 46 17N 4 19 E
Claymont 162 39 48N 75 28W
Claymore, oilfield 19 58 30N 0 15W
Claypool 161 33 27N 110 55W
Clayton, Idaho, U.S.A. 160 44 12N 114 31W
Clayton, N. Mex., U.S.A. 159 36 30N 103 10W
Cle Elum 160 47 15N 120 57W
Cleady 39 51 53N 9 32W
Clear C. 39 51 26N 9 30W
Clear I. 39 51 26N 9 30W
Clear Lake, Calif., U.S.A. 160 39 5N 122 47W
Clear Lake, S.D., U.S.A. 158 44 48N 96 41W
Clear Lake, Wash., U.S.A. 160 48 27N 122 15W
Clear Lake Res. 160 41 55N 121 10W
Clearfield, Pa., U.S.A. 156 41 0N 78 27W
Clearfield, Utah, U.S.A. 160 41 10N 112 0W
Clearmont 160 44 43N 106 29W
Clearwater, Can. 152 51 38N 120 2W
Clearwater, U.S.A. 157 27 58N 82 45W
Clearwater Cr. 152 61 36N 125 30W
Clearwater L. 150 56 10N 75 0W
Clearwater, Mts. 160 46 20N 115 30W
Clearwater Prov. Park 153 54 0N 101 0W
Clearwater, R., Alta., Can. 152 52 22N 114 57W
Clearwater, R., Alta., Can. 153 56 44N 111 23W
Clearwater, R., B.C., Can. 152 51 38N 120 3W
Cleat 37 58 45N 2 56W
Cleator Moor 32 54 30N 3 32W
Cleburne 159 32 18N 97 25W
Cleddau R. 31 51 46N 4 44W
Clee Hills 23 52 26N 2 35W

Cleethorpes Columbia

Cleethorpes	33	53 33N	0 2W
Cleeve Cloud	28	51 56N	2 0W
Cleggan	38	53 33N	10 7W
Clelles	45	44 50N	5 38E
Clemency	47	49 35N	5 53E
Clent	28	52 25N	2 6W
Cleobury Mortimer	28	52 23N	2 28W
Clerke Reef	136	17 22S	119 20E
Clerks Rocks	13	56 0S	36 30W
Clermont	133	22 49S	147 39E
Clermont-en-Argonne	43	49 5N	5 4E
Clermont-Ferrand	44	45 46N	3 4E
Clermont-l'Hérault	44	43 38N	3 26E
Clerval	43	47 25N	6 30E
Cléry-Saint-André	43	47 50N	1 46E
Cles	62	46 21N	11 4E
Clevedon	28	51 26N	2 52W
Cleveland, Austral.	139	27 30S	153 15E
Cleveland, Miss., U.S.A.	159	33 43N	90 43W
Cleveland, Ohio, U.S.A.	156	41 28N	81 43W
Cleveland, Okla., U.S.A.	159	36 21N	96 33W
Cleveland, Tenn., U.S.A.	157	35 9N	84 52W
Cleveland, Tex., U.S.A.	159	30 18N	95 0W
Cleveland □	33	54 35N	1 8E
Cleveland, C.	138	19 11S	147 1E
Cleveland Hills	33	54 25N	1 11W
Clevelândia	173	26 24S	52 23W
Clevvaux	47	50 4N	6 2E
Clew Bay	38	53 54N	9 50W
Clewiston	157	26 44N	80 50W
Cley	29	52 57N	1 3E
Clifden, Ireland	38	53 30N	10 2W
Clifden, N.Z.	143	46 1S	167 42E
Clifden B.	38	53 29N	10 5W
Cliff	161	33 0N	108 44W
Cliffe	29	51 27N	0 31E
Cliffony	38	54 25N	8 28W
Clifford	28	52 6N	3 6W
Clift Sound	36	60 4N	1 17W
Clifton, Austral.	139	27 59S	151 53E
Clifton, Ariz., U.S.A.	161	33 8N	109 23W
Clifton, Tex., U.S.A.	159	31 46N	97 35W
Clifton Forge	156	37 49N	79 51W
Climax	153	49 10N	108 20W
Clingmans Dome	157	35 35N	83 30W
Clint	161	31 37N	106 11W
Clinton, B.C., Can.	152	51 6N	121 35W
Clinton, Ont., Can.	150	43 37N	81 32W
Clinton, N.Z.	143	46 12S	169 23E
Clinton, Ark., U.S.A.	159	35 37N	92 30W
Clinton, Conn., U.S.A.	162	41 17N	72 32W
Clinton, Ill., U.S.A.	158	40 8N	89 0W
Clinton, Ind., U.S.A.	156	39 40N	87 22W
Clinton, Iowa, U.S.A.	158	41 50N	90 12W
Clinton, Mass., U.S.A.	162	42 26N	71 40W
Clinton, Mo., U.S.A.	158	38 20N	93 46W
Clinton, N.C., U.S.A.	157	35 5N	78 15W
Clinton, Okla., U.S.A.	159	35 30N	99 0W
Clinton, S.C., U.S.A.	157	34 30N	81 54W
Clinton, Tenn., U.S.A.	157	36 6N	84 10W
Clinton C.	138	22 30S	150 45E
Clinton Colden L.	148	64 58N	107 27W
Clintonville	158	44 35N	88 46W
Clipperton, I.	143	10 18N	109 13W
Clipston	29	52 26N	0 58W
Clisson	42	47 5N	1 16W
Clitheroe	32	53 52N	2 23W
Clive	142	39 36S	176 58E
Clive L.	152	63 13N	118 54W
Cloates, Pt.	136	22 43S	113 40E
Clocolan	129	28 55S	27 34E
Clodomira	172	27 35S	64 14W
Clogh	39	52 51N	7 11W
Cloghan, Donegal, Ireland	38	54 50N	7 56W
Cloghan, Offaly, Ireland	39	53 13N	7 53W
Cloghan, W'meath, Ireland	38	53 33N	7 15W
Clogheen	39	52 17N	8 0W
Clogher	38	54 25N	7 10W
Clogher Hd.	38	53 48N	6 15W
Cloghjordan	39	52 57N	8 2W
Cloghran	38	53 26N	6 14W
Clonakilty	39	51 37N	8 53W
Clonakilty B.	39	51 33N	8 50W
Clonbur	38	53 32N	9 21W
Cloncurry, Austral.	138	20 40S	140 28E
Cloncurry, Ireland	38	53 26N	6 47W
Cloncurry, R.	138	18 37S	140 40E
Clondalkin	39	53 20N	6 25W
Clonee	38	53 25N	6 28W
Cloneen	39	52 28N	7 36W
Clones	38	54 10N	7 13W
Clonkeen	39	51 59N	9 20W
Clonmany	38	55 16N	7 24W
Clonmel	39	52 22N	7 42W
Clonmore	39	52 49N	6 35W
Clonroche	39	52 27N	6 42W
Clontarf	38	53 22N	6 10W
Cloonakool	38	54 6N	8 47W
Cloone	38	53 57N	7 47W
Cloonfad	38	53 41N	8 45W
Cloppenburg	48	52 50N	8 3E
Cloquet	158	46 40N	92 30W
Clorinda	172	25 16S	57 45W
Closeburn	35	55 13N	3 45W
Cloud Peak	160	44 30N	107 10W
Cloudcroft	161	33 0N	105 48W
Cloudy B.	143	41 25S	174 10E
Clough, Ballymena, U.K.	38	54 58N	6 16W
Clough, Down, U.K.	38	54 18N	5 50W
Cloughton	33	54 20N	0 27W
Clova	37	56 50N	3 4W
Clovelly	30	51 0N	4 25W
Cloverdale	160	38 49N	123 0W
Clovis, Calif., U.S.A.	163	36 54N	119 45W
Clovis, N. Mex., U.S.A.	159	34 20N	103 10W
Clowne	33	53 18N	1 16W
Cloyne	39	51 52N	8 7W
Club Terrace	141	37 35S	148 58E
Cluj	70	46 47N	23 38E
Cluj □	70	46 45N	23 30E
Clun	28	52 26N	3 2W
Clun Forest	28	52 27N	3 7W
Clunbury	28	52 25N	2 55W
Clunes, Austral.	140	37 20S	143 45E
Clunes, U.K.	36	56 57N	4 58W
Cluny	45	46 26N	4 38E
Cluses	45	46 5N	6 35E
Clusone	62	45 54N	9 58E
Clutha, R.	143	46 20S	169 49E
Clwyd □	31	53 5N	3 20W
Clwyd, R.	31	53 12N	3 30W
Clwydian Ra.	31	53 10N	3 15W
Clydach	31	51 42N	3 54W
Clyde, Austral.	139	28 48S	143 40E
Clyde, Can.	149	70 30N	68 30W
Clyde, N.Z.	143	45 12S	169 20E
Clyde, Firth of	34	55 20N	5 0W
Clyde, R.	34	55 46N	4 58W
Clydebank	34	55 54N	4 25W
Clydesdale	35	55 42N	3 50W
Clynnog-fawr	31	53 2N	4 22W
Cõa, R.	56	40 45N	7 0W
Coachella	163	33 44N	116 13W
Coachella Canal	163	32 43N	114 57W
Coachford	39	51 54N	8 48W
Coachman's Cove	151	50 6N	56 20W
Coagh	38	54 39N	6 37W
Coahoma	159	32 17N	101 20W
Coahuayana, R.	164	18 41N	103 45W
Coahuayutla	164	18 19N	101 42W
Coahuila □	164	27 0N	112 30W
Coal Creek Flat	143	45 27S	169 19E
Coal I.	143	46 8S	166 40E
Coal, R.	152	59 39N	126 57W
Coalane	127	17 48S	37 2E
Coalbrookdale	28	52 38N	2 30W
Coalburn	35	55 35N	3 55W
Coalcomán	164	18 40N	103 10W
Coaldale, Can.	152	49 45N	112 35W
Coaldale, U.S.A.	163	38 2N	117 55W
Coaldale, Pa., U.S.A.	162	40 50N	75 54W
Coalgate	159	34 35N	96 13W
Coalinga	163	36 10N	120 21W
Coalisland	38	54 33N	6 42W
Coalspur	152	53 15N	117 0W
Coalville, U.K.	28	52 43N	1 21W
Coalville, U.S.A.	160	40 58N	111 24W
Coamo	147	18 5N	66 22W
Coaraci	171	14 38S	39 32W
Coari	174	4 8S	63 7W
Coast □	126	2 40S	39 45E
Coast Mts.	152	52 0N	126 0W
Coast Range	163	40 0N	124 0W
Coastal Plains Basin	137	30 10S	115 30E
Coatbridge	35	55 52N	4 2W
Coatepec	165	19 27N	96 58W
Coatepeque	166	14 46N	91 55W
Coatesville	162	39 59N	75 30W
Coaticook	151	45 10N	71 46W
Coats I.	149	62 30N	83 0W
Coats Land	13	77 0S	25 0W
Coatzacoalcos	165	18 7N	94 35W
Cobadin	70	44 5N	28 13E
Cobalt	150	47 25N	79 42W
Cobán	166	15 30N	90 21W
Cobar	141	31 27S	145 48E
Cobb I.	162	37 17N	75 42W
Cobbannah	141	37 37S	147 12E
Cobberas, Mt.	141	36 53S	148 12E
Cobden	140	38 20S	143 3E
Cóbh	39	51 50N	8 18W
Cobija	174	11 0S	68 50W
Cobourg	150	43 58N	78 10W
Cobourg Pen.	136	11 20S	132 15E
Cobram	141	35 54S	145 40E
Cobre	160	41 6N	114 25W
Cóbué	125	12 0S	34 58E
Coburg	49	50 15N	10 58E
Coca	56	41 13N	4 32W
Coca, R.	174	0 25S	77 5W
Cocal	170	3 28S	41 34W
Cocanada = Kakinada	96	16 55N	82 20E
Cocentaina	59	38 45N	0 27W
Cocha, La	172	27 50S	65 40W
Cochabamba	174	17 15S	66 20W
Coche, I.	174	10 47N	63 56W
Cochem	49	50 8N	7 7E
Cochemane	127	17 0S	32 54E
Cochilha Grande de Albardão	173	28 30S	51 30W
Cochin	97	9 55N	76 22E
Cochin China	101	10 30N	106 0E
Cochin China = Nam-Phan	101	10 30N	106 0E
Cochise	161	32 6N	109 58W
Cochran	157	32 25N	83 23W
Cochrane, Alta., Can.	152	51 11N	114 30W
Cochrane, Ont., Can.	150	49 0N	81 0W
Cochrane, L.	176	47 10S	72 0W
Cochrane, R.	153	57 53N	101 34W
Cockatoo I.	136	16 6S	123 37E
Cockburn	140	32 5S	141 0E
Cockburn, Canal	176	54 30S	72 0W
Cockburn, C.	136	11 20S	132 52E
Cockburn I.	150	45 55N	83 22W
Cockburn Ra.	136	15 46S	128 0E
Cockburnspath	35	55 56N	2 23W
Cockenzie	35	55 58N	2 59W
Cockerham	32	53 58N	2 49W
Cockermouth	32	54 40N	3 22W
Cockeysville	162	39 29N	76 39W
Cockfield	29	52 8N	0 47E
Cocklebiddy	137	32 0S	126 3E
Coco Chan.	101	13 50N	93 25E
Coco Is.	101	14 0N	93 12E
Coco, Pta.	174	2 58N	77 43W
Coco, R. (Wanks)	166	14 10N	85 0W
Cocoa	157	28 22N	80 40W
Cocobeach	124	0 59N	9 34E
Cocoli, R.	120	12 0N	14 0W
Cocora	70	44 45N	27 3E
Côcos	171	14 10S	44 33W
Cocos (Keeling) Is.	11	12 12S	96 54E
Côcos, R.	171	12 44S	44 48W
Cod, C.	162	42 8N	70 10W
Cod, gasfield	19	57 8N	2 35E
Codajás	174	3 40S	62 0W
Coddenham	29	52 8N	1 8E
Codera, C.	174	10 35N	66 4W
Coderre	153	50 11N	106 31W
Codigoro	63	44 50N	12 5E
Codó	170	4 30S	43 55W
Codogno	62	45 10N	9 42E
Codróipo	63	45 57N	13 0E
Codru, Munţii	70	46 30N	22 15E
Cods Hd.	39	51 40N	10 7W
Cody	160	44 35N	109 0W
Coe Hill	150	44 52N	77 50W
Coelemu	172	36 30S	72 48W
Coelho Neto	170	4 15S	43 0W
Coen	138	13 52S	143 12E
Coesfeld	48	51 56N	7 10E
Coeur d'Alene	160	47 45N	116 51W
Coevorden	46	52 40N	6 44E
Coffeyville	159	37 0N	95 40W
Coffin B. Pen.	136	34 20S	135 10E
Coffs Harbour	141	30 16S	153 5E
Cofre de Perote, Cerro	165	19 30N	97 10W
Cofrentes	59	39 13N	1 5W
Cogealac	70	44 36N	28 36E
Coggeshall	29	51 53N	0 41E
Coghinas, R.	64	40 55N	8 48E
Cognac	44	45 41N	0 20W
Cogne	62	45 37N	7 21E
Cogolludo	58	40 59N	3 10W
Cohagen	160	47 2N	106 45W
Cohoes	162	42 47N	73 42W
Cohuna	140	35 45S	144 15E
Coiba I.	166	7 30N	81 40W
Coig, R.	176	51 0S	70 20W
Coigach, dist.	36	58 0N	5 10W
Coillore	36	57 21N	6 23W
Coimbatore	97	11 2N	76 59E
Coimbra	56	40 15N	8 27W
Coimbra □	56	40 12N	8 25W
Coin	57	36 40N	4 48W
Cojedes □	174	9 20N	68 20W
Cojimies	174	0 20N	80 0W
Cojocna	70	46 45N	23 50E
Cojutepequé	166	13 41N	88 54W
Čoka	66	45 57N	20 12E
Cokeville	160	42 4N	111 0W
Col di Tenda	62	44 7N	7 36E
Colaba Pt.	96	18 54N	72 47E
Colac	140	38 21S	143 35E
Colachel	97	8 10N	77 15E
Colares	57	38 48N	9 30W
Colatina	171	19 32S	40 37W
Colbinabbin	141	36 38S	144 48E
Colby, U.K.	32	54 6N	4 42W
Colby, U.S.A.	158	39 27N	101 2W
Colchagua □	172	34 30S	71 0W
Colchester	29	51 54N	0 55E
Cold Fell	32	54 54N	2 40W
Coldingham	35	55 53N	2 10W
Coldstream	35	55 39N	2 14W
Coldwater	159	37 18N	99 24W
Coldwell	150	48 45N	86 30W
Colebrook	138	42 31S	147 12E
Colebrooke	30	50 45N	3 44W
Coleford	28	51 46N	2 38W
Coleman, Can.	152	49 40N	114 30W
Coleman, U.S.A.	159	31 52N	99 30W
Coleman, R.	138	15 6S	141 38E
Colenso	129	28 44S	29 50E
Coleraine, Austral.	140	37 36S	141 40E
Coleraine, U.K.	38	55 8N	6 40E
Coleraine □	38	55 8N	6 40E
Coleridge, L.	143	43 17S	171 30E
Coleroon, R.	97	11 0N	79 0E
Colesberg	128	30 45S	25 5E
Coleshill	28	52 30N	1 42W
Coleville	163	38 44N	119 30W
Colfax, La., U.S.A.	159	31 35N	92 39W
Colfax, Wash., U.S.A.	160	46 57N	117 28W
Colgrave Sd.	36	60 35N	1 0W
Colhué Huapi, L.	176	45 30S	69 0W
Cólico	62	46 8N	9 22E
Coligny	128	46 24N	5 21E
Colima	164	19 10N	103 40W
Colima □	164	19 10N	103 40W
Colima, Nevado de	164	19 30N	103 40W
Colina	172	33 13S	70 45W
Colina do Norte	120	12 28N	15 0W
Colinas, Goiás, Brazil	171	14 15S	48 2W
Colinas, Maranhão, Brazil	170	6 0S	44 10W
Colinton, Austral.	141	35 50S	149 10E
Colinton, U.K.	35	55 54N	3 17W
Coll, I.	34	56 40N	6 35W
Collaguasi	172	21 5S	68 45W
Collarada, Peña	58	42 43N	0 29W
Collarenebri	139	29 33S	148 36E
Collbran	161	39 16N	107 58W
Colle Salvetti	62	43 34N	10 27E
Colle Sannita	65	41 22N	14 48E
Colléchio	62	44 23N	10 10E
Colleen Bawn	127	21 0S	29 12E
College Park, Ga., U.S.A.	157	33 42N	84 27W
College Park, Md., U.S.A.	162	39 0N	76 55W
Collette	151	46 40N	65 30W
Collie, N.S.W., Austral.	141	31 41S	148 18E
Collie, W. Austral., Austral.	137	33 22S	116 8E
Collier B.	136	16 10S	124 15E
Collier Law Pk.	32	54 47N	1 59W
Collier Ra.	137	24 45S	119 10E
Collin	35	55 4N	3 30W
Colline Metallifere	62	43 10N	11 0E
Collingbourne	28	51 16N	1 39W
Collingswood	162	39 55N	75 4W
Collingwood, Austral.	138	22 20S	142 31E
Collingwood, Can.	150	44 29N	80 13W
Collingwood, N.Z.	143	40 25S	172 40E
Collingwood B.	138	9 30S	149 30E
Collins	150	50 17N	89 27W
Collinsville	138	20 30S	147 56E
Collipulli	172	37 55S	72 30W
Collison Ra.	136	14 49S	127 25E
Collo	119	36 58N	6 37E
Collon	38	53 46N	6 29W
Collonges	45	46 9N	5 52E
Collooney	38	54 11N	8 28W
Colmar	43	48 5N	7 20E
Colmars	45	44 11N	6 39E
Colmenar	57	36 54N	4 20W
Colmenar de Oreja	58	40 6N	3 25W
Colmenar Viejo	56	40 39N	3 47W
Colmor	159	36 18N	104 36W
Colne	32	53 51N	2 11W
Colne, R., Essex, U.K.	29	51 55N	0 50E
Colne, R., Herts., U.K.	29	51 36N	0 30W
Colnett, Cabo	164	31 0N	116 20W
Colo, R.	141	33 25S	150 52E
Cologna Véneta	63	45 19N	11 21E
Colomb-Béchar = Béchar	118	31 38N	2 18E
Colombey-les-Belles	43	48 32N	5 54E
Colombey-les-deux Églises	43	48 20N	4 50E
Colômbia	171	20 10S	48 40W
Colombia	174	3 24N	79 49W
Colombia ■	174	3 45N	73 0W
Colombier	50	46 58N	6 53E
Colombo	97	6 56N	79 58E
Colombus, Kans., U.S.A.	159	37 15N	94 30W
Colombus, Nebr., U.S.A.	158	41 30N	97 25W
Colombus, N.Mex., U.S.A.	161	31 54N	107 43W
Colome	158	43 20N	99 44W
Colón, Argent.	172	32 12S	58 30W
Colón, Cuba	166	22 42N	80 54W
Colón, Panama	166	9 20N	80 0W
Colonel Hill	167	22 50N	74 21W
Colonella	63	42 52N	13 50E
Colonia del Sacramento	173	34 25S	57 50W
Colonia Dora	172	28 34S	62 59W
Colonia Las Heras	176	46 30S	69 0W
Colonia Sarmiento	176	45 30S	68 15W
Colonial Hts.	162	37 15N	77 25W
Colonne, C. delle	65	39 2N	17 11E
Colonsay	153	51 59N	105 52W
Colonsay, I.	34	56 4N	6 12W
Colorado □	154	37 40N	106 0W
Colorado Aqueduct	161	34 17N	114 10W
Colorado City	159	32 25N	100 50W
Colorado Desert	154	34 20N	116 0W
Colorado Plateau	161	36 40N	110 30W
Colorado, R., Argent.	172	37 30S	69 0W
Colorado, R., Ariz., U.S.A.	161	33 30N	114 30W
Colorado, R., Calif., U.S.A.	161	34 0N	114 33W
Colorado, R., Tex., U.S.A.	159	29 40N	96 30W
Colorado Springs	158	38 55N	104 50W
Colorno	62	44 55N	10 21E
Colossal	141	30 52S	147 3E
Colotepec	165	15 47N	97 3W
Colotlán	164	22 6N	103 16W
Colpy	37	57 23N	2 35W
Colsterworth	29	52 48N	0 37W
Coltishall	29	52 44N	1 21E
Colton, Calif., U.S.A.	163	34 4N	117 20W
Colton, Wash., U.S.A.	160	46 41N	117 6W
Columbia, La., U.S.A.	159	32 7N	92 5W
Columbia, Miss., U.S.A.	159	31 16N	89 50W
Columbia, Mo., U.S.A.	158	38 58N	92 20W
Columbia, Pa., U.S.A.	162	40 2N	76 30W
Columbia, S.C., U.S.A.	157	34 0N	81 0W

Columbia Coroaci

Columbia, Tenn., U.S.A. 157 35 40N 87 0W
Columbia, C. 12 83 0N 70 0W
Columbia City 156 41 8N 85 30W
Columbia, District of □ 156 38 55N 77 0W
Columbia Falls 160 48 25N 114 16W
Columbia Heights 158 45 5N 93 10W
Columbia, Mt. 152 52 8N 117 20W
Columbia Plateau 160 47 30N 118 30W
Columbia, R. 160 45 49N 120 0W
Columbretes, Is. 58 39 50N 0 50 E
Columbus, Ga., U.S.A. 157 32 30N 84 58W
Columbus, Ind., U.S.A. 156 39 14N 85 55W
Columbus, Miss., U.S.A. 157 33 30N 88 26W
Columbus, Mont., U.S.A. 160 45 45N 109 14W
Columbus, N.D., U.S.A. 158 48 52N 102 48W
Columbus, Ohio, U.S.A. 156 39 57N 83 1W
Columbus, Tex., U.S.A. 159 29 42N 96 33W
Columbus, Wis., U.S.A. 158 43 20N 89 2W
Colunda 125 12 7 S 23 36 E
Colunga 56 43 29N 5 16W
Colusa 160 39 15N 122 1W
Colville 160 48 33N 117 54W
Colville, C. 142 36 29 S 175 21 E
Colville, R. 147 69 15N 152 0W
Colwell 35 55 4N 2 4W
Colwich 28 52 48N 1 58W
Colwyn 31 53 17N 3 43W
Colwyn Bay 31 53 17N 3 44W
Colyton 30 50 44N 3 4W
Comácchio 63 44 41N 12 10 E
Comalcalco 165 18 16N 93 13W
Comallo 176 41 0 S 70 5W
Comana 70 44 10N 26 10 E
Comanche, Okla., U.S.A. 159 34 27N 97 58W
Comanche, Tex., U.S.A. 159 31 55N 98 35W
Comăneşti 70 46 25N 26 26 E
Comayagua 166 14 25N 87 37W
Combahee, R. 157 32 45N 80 50W
Combara 141 31 10 S 148 22 E
Combe Martin 30 51 12N 4 2W
Combeaufontaine 43 47 38N 5 54 E
Comber 38 54 33N 5 45W
Combermere Bay 98 19 37N 93 34 E
Comblain 47 50 29N 5 35 E
Combles 43 50 0N 2 50 E
Combourg 42 48 25N 1 46W
Comboyne 141 31 34 S 152 34 E
Combronde 44 45 58N 3 5 E
Comeragh Mts. 39 52 17N 7 35W
Comercinho 171 16 19 S 41 47W
Comet 138 23 36 S 148 38 E
Comet Vale 137 29 55 S 121 4 E
Comilla 98 23 28N 91 10 E
Comines 47 50 46N 3 0 E
Comino, C. 64 40 28N 9 47 E
Cómiso 65 36 57N 14 35 E
Comitán 165 16 18N 92 9W
Commentry 44 46 20N 2 46 E
Commerce, Ga., U.S.A. 157 34 10N 83 25W
Commerce, Tex., U.S.A. 159 33 15N 95 50W
Commercy 43 48 40N 5 34 E
Committee B. 149 68 30N 86 30W
Commonwealth B. 13 67 0 S 144 0 E
Commoron Cr., R. 139 28 22 S 150 8 E
Communism Pk. = Kommunizma, Pk. 93 38 40N 72 20 E
Como 62 45 48N 9 5 E
Como, L. di 62 46 5N 9 17 E
Comodoro Rivadavia 176 45 50 S 67 40W
Comores, Arch. des 11 10 0 S 50 0 E
Comores, Is. 11 12 10 S 44 15 E
Comorin, C. 97 8 3N 77 40 E
Comorişte 70 45 10N 21 35 E
Comoro Is. 11 12 10 S 44 15 E
Comox 152 49 42N 124 55W
Compiègne 43 49 24N 2 50 E
Compíglia Maríttima 62 43 4N 10 37 E
Comporta 57 38 22N 8 46W
Compostela 164 21 15N 104 53W
Comprida, I. 173 24 50 S 47 42W
Compton, U.K. 28 51 2N 1 19W
Compton, U.S.A. 163 33 54N 118 13W
Compton Downs 139 30 28 S 146 30 E
Comrie 35 56 22N 4 0W
Con Cuong 100 19 2N 104 54 E
Côn Dao 101 8 45N 106 45 E
Con Son, Is. 101 8 41N 106 37 E
Conakry 120 9 29N 13 49W
Conara Junction 138 41 50 S 147 26 E
Conargo 141 35 16 S 145 10 E
Conatlán 164 24 30N 104 42W
Concarneau 42 47 52N 3 56W
Conceição, Brazil 170 7 33 S 38 31W
Conceição, Mozam. 127 18 47 S 36 7 E
Conceição da Barra 171 18 35 S 39 45W
Conceição do Araguaia 170 8 0 S 49 2W
Conceição do Canindé 170 7 54 S 41 34W
Conceição do Mato Dentro 171 19 1 S 43 25W
Concepcián 165 18 15N 90 5W
Concepción, Argent. 172 27 20 S 65 35W
Concepción, Boliv. 174 15 50 S 61 40W
Concepción, Chile 172 36 50 S 73 0W
Concepción, Colomb. 174 0 5N 75 37W
Concepción, Parag. 172 23 30 S 57 20W
Concepción, Venez. 174 10 48N 71 46W
Concepción □ 172 37 0 S 72 30W
Concepcion, C. 154 34 30N 120 34W
Concepción del Oro 164 24 40N 101 30W
Concepción del Uruguay 172 32 35 S 58 20W
Concepción, L. 174 17 20 S 61 10W
Concepción, La = Ri-Aba 121 3 28N 84 0 E
Concepción, Punta 164 26 55N 111 50W
Concepción, R. 164 30 32N 113 2W
Conception B. 128 23 55 S 14 22 E
Conception I. 167 23 52N 75 9W
Conception, Pt. 163 34 27N 120 28W
Concession 127 17 27 S 30 56 E
Conchas Dam 159 35 25N 104 10W
Conche 151 50 48N 55 58W
Conches-en-Ouche 50 48 58N 0 58 E
Concho 161 34 32N 109 43W
Concho, R. 159 31 30N 100 8W
Conchos, R., Chihnahua, Mexico 164 29 20N 105 0W
Conchos, R., Tamaulipas, Mexico 165 25 0N 97 32W
Concon 172 32 56 S 71 33W
Concord, Calif., U.S.A. 163 37 59N 122 2W
Concord, N.C., U.S.A. 157 35 28N 80 35W
Concord, N.H., U.S.A. 162 43 12N 71 30W
Concórdia, Argent. 172 31 20 S 58 2W
Concórdia, Brazil 174 4 36 S 66 36W
Concordia, Colomb. 174 2 39N 72 47W
Concordia, Mexico 164 23 18N 106 2W
Concordia, U.S.A. 158 39 35N 97 40W
Concordia, La 165 16 8N 92 38W
Concots 44 44 26N 1 40 E
Concrete 160 48 35N 121 49W
Condah 140 37 57 S 141 44 E
Condamine, R. 133 27 7 S 149 48 E
Condat 44 45 21N 2 46 E
Conde 171 11 49 S 37 37W
Condé 43 50 26N 3 34 E
Conde 158 45 13N 98 5W
Condé-sur-Noireau 42 48 51N 0 33W
Condeúba 171 15 0 S 42 0W
Condobolin 141 33 4 S 147 6 E
Condom 44 43 57N 0 22 E
Condon 160 45 15N 120 8W
Condove 62 45 8N 7 19 E
Condover 28 52 39N 2 46W
Conegliano 63 45 53N 12 18 E
Conejera, I. 59 39 11N 2 58 E
Conejos 164 26 14N 103 53W
Conflans-en-Jarnisy 43 49 10N 5 52 E
Confolens 44 46 2N 0 40 E
Confuso, R. 172 24 10 S 59 0W
Congleton 32 53 10N 2 12W
Congo 170 7 48 S 36 40W
Congo ■ 124 1 0 S 16 0 E
Congo Basin 114 0 10 S 24 30 E
Congo, Democratic Rep. of = Zaïre ■ 124 3 0 S 22 0 E
Congo (Kinshasa) ■ = Zaïre ■ 124 1 0 S 16 0 E
Congo, R. = Zaïre, R. 124 1 30N 28 0 E
Congonhas 173 20 30 S 43 52W
Congresbury 28 51 20N 2 49W
Congress 161 34 11N 112 56W
Congucu 113 31 25 S 52 30W
Conil 57 36 17N 6 10W
Coningsby 33 53 7N 0 9W
Conisbrough 33 53 29N 1 12W
Coniston, Can. 150 46 29N 80 51W
Coniston, U.K. 32 54 22N 3 6W
Coniston Water 32 54 20N 3 5W
Conjeevaram = Kancheepuram 97 12 52N 79 45 E
Conjuboy 138 18 35 S 144 45 E
Conklin 153 55 38N 111 5W
Conlea 139 30 7 S 144 35 E
Conn, L. 38 54 3N 9 15W
Conna 39 52 5N 8 8W
Connacht 38 53 23N 8 40W
Connah's Quay 31 53 13N 3 6W
Conneaut 156 41 55N 80 32W
Connecticut □ 162 41 40N 72 40W
Connecticut, R. 162 41 17N 72 21W
Connel 34 56 27N 5 24W
Connel Park 34 55 22N 4 15W
Connell 160 46 45N 118 58W
Connemara 38 53 29N 9 45W
Conner, La 160 48 22N 122 27W
Connersville 156 39 40N 85 10W
Connonagh 39 51 35N 9 8W
Connor, Mt. 136 14 34 S 126 4 E
Connors Ra. 138 21 40 S 149 10 E
Conoble 141 32 55 S 144 42 E
Cononaco, R. 174 1 20 S 76 30W
Conquest 153 51 32N 107 14W
Conquet, Le 42 48 21N 4 46W
Conrad 160 48 11N 112 0W
Conran, C. 141 37 49 S 148 44 E
Conroe 159 30 15N 95 28W
Conselheiro Lafaiete 173 20 40 S 43 48W
Conselheiro Pena 171 19 10 S 41 30W
Consett 32 54 52N 1 50W
Conshohocken 162 40 5N 75 18W
Consort 153 52 1N 110 46W
Constance = Konstanz 49 47 39N 9 10 E
Constance, L. = Bodensee 51 47 35N 9 25 E
Constanţa 70 44 14N 28 38 E
Constanţa □ 70 44 15N 28 15 E
Constantia 162 43 15N 76 1W
Constantina 57 37 51N 5 40W
Constantine 119 36 25N 6 42 E
Constitución, Chile 172 35 20 S 72 30W
Constitución, Uruguay 172 31 0 S 58 10W
Consuegra 57 39 28N 3 43W
Consul 153 49 20N 109 30W
Contact 160 41 50N 114 56W
Contai 95 21 54N 87 55 E
Contamana 174 7 10 S 74 55W
Contarina 63 45 2N 12 13 E
Contas, R. 171 13 5 S 41 53W
Contes 45 43 49N 7 19 E
Conthey 50 46 14N 7 28 E
Contin 37 57 34N 4 35W
Contoocook 162 43 13N 71 45W
Contra Costa 129 25 9 S 33 30 E
Contres 43 47 24N 1 26 E
Contrexéville 43 48 6N 5 53 E
Convención 174 8 28N 73 21W
Conversano 65 40 57N 17 8 E
Convoy 38 54 52N 7 40W
Conway, Ark., U.S.A. 159 35 5N 92 30W
Conway, N.H., U.S.A. 162 43 58N 71 8W
Conway, S.C., U.S.A. 157 33 49N 79 2W
Conway = Conwy 31 53 17N 3 50W
Conway, L. 139 28 17 S 135 35 E
Conwy 31 53 17N 3 50W
Conwy Bay 31 53 17N 3 57W
Conwy, R. 31 53 18N 3 50W
Coober Pedy 136 29 1 S 134 43 E
Coobina 137 23 22 S 120 10 E
Cooch Behar 98 26 22N 89 29 E
Cook, Austral. 137 30 37 S 130 25 E
Cook, U.S.A. 158 47 49N 92 39W
Cook, Bahía 176 55 10 S 70 0W
Cook Inlet 147 59 0N 151 0W
Cook Is. 131 20 0 S 160 0W
Cook, Mount 143 43 36 S 170 9 E
Cook Strait 143 41 15 S 174 29 E
Cooke Plains 140 35 23 S 139 34 E
Cookeville 157 36 12N 85 30W
Cookham 29 51 33N 0 42W
Cookhouse 128 32 44 S 25 47 E
Cookstown 38 54 40N 6 43W
Cookstown □ 38 54 40N 6 43W
Cooktown 138 15 30 S 145 16 E
Coolabah 141 31 1 S 146 43 E
Cooladdi 139 26 37 S 145 23 E
Coolah 141 31 48 S 149 41 E
Coolamon 141 34 46 S 147 8 E
Coolaney 38 54 10N 8 36W
Coolangatta 139 28 11 S 153 29 E
Coole 38 53 42N 7 23W
Coolgardie 137 30 55 S 121 8 E
Coolgreany 39 52 46N 6 14W
Coolibah 136 15 33 S 130 56 E
Coolidge 161 33 1N 111 35W
Coolidge Dam 161 33 10N 110 30W
Coolmore 38 54 33N 8 12W
Cooma 141 36 12 S 149 8 E
Coomacarrea Mts. 39 51 59N 10 0W
Coonabarabran 141 31 14 S 149 18 E
Coonalpyn 140 35 43 S 139 52 E
Coonamble 141 30 56 S 148 27 E
Coonana 137 31 0 S 123 0 E
Coondapoor 97 13 42N 74 40 E
Coongie 139 27 9 S 140 8 E
Coongoola 139 27 43 S 145 47 E
Cooninie, L. 139 26 4 S 139 59 E
Coonoor 97 11 10N 76 45 E
Cooper 159 33 20N 95 40W
Cooper Cr. 139 28 29 S 137 46 E
Cooper, R. 157 33 0N 79 55W
Coopersburg 162 40 31N 75 23W
Cooperstown, N.D., U.S.A. 158 47 30N 98 14W
Cooperstown, New York, U.S.A. 162 42 42N 74 57W
Coorabie P.O. 137 31 54 S 132 18 E
Coorabulka 138 23 41 S 140 20 E
Coorong, The 133 35 50 S 139 20 E
Coorow 137 29 53 S 116 2 E
Cooroy 139 26 22 S 152 54 E
Coos Bay 160 43 26N 124 7W
Cootamundra 141 34 36 S 148 1 E
Cootehill 38 54 5N 7 5W
Cooyar 139 26 59 S 151 51 E
Cooyeana 138 24 29 S 138 45 E
Copahué, Paso 172 37 49 S 71 8W
Copainalá 165 17 8N 93 11W
Copake Falls 162 42 7N 73 31W
Copán 166 14 50N 89 9W
Cope 158 39 44N 102 50W
Cope, Cabo 59 37 26N 1 28W
Cope Cope 140 36 27 S 143 5 E
Copeland I. 38 54 38N 5 33W
Copenhagen 162 43 54N 75 41W
Copenhagen = København 73 55 41N 12 34 E
Copertino 65 40 17N 18 2W
Copeville 140 34 47 S 139 51 E
Copiapó 172 27 15 S 70 20 E
Copiapó, R. 172 27 19 S 70 56W
Copinsay I. 37 58 54N 2 40W
Coplay 162 40 44N 75 29W
Copley 140 30 24 S 138 26 E
Copp L. 152 60 14N 114 40W
Copparo 63 44 52N 11 49 E
Copper Center 147 62 10N 145 25W
Copper Cliff 150 46 28N 81 4W
Copper Harbor 156 47 31N 87 55W
Copper Mountain 152 49 20N 120 30W
Copper Queen 127 17 29 S 29 18 E
Copper R. 147 61 30N 144 30W
Copperbelt □ 127 13 15N 27 30 E
Copperfield 137 29 1 S 120 26 E
Coppermine 148 67 50N 115 5W
Coppermine, R. 148 67 49N 115 4W
Copperopolis 163 37 58N 120 38W
Cöppingen 49 48 42N 9 40 E
Copythorne 28 50 56N 1 34W
Coquet, I. 35 55 21N 1 30W
Coquet, R. 35 55 18N 1 45W
Coquilhatville = Mbandaka 124 0 1N 18 18 E
Coquille 160 43 15N 124 6W
Coquimbo 172 30 0 S 71 20W
Coquimbo □ 172 31 0 S 71 0W
Cora, oilfield 19 55 45N 4 45 E
Corabia 70 43 48N 24 30 E
Coraçáo de Jesus 171 11 39 S 39 56W
Coracora 174 15 5 S 73 45W
Coradi, Is. 65 40 27N 17 10 E
Coral Harbour 149 64 8N 83 10W
Coral Rapids 150 50 20N 81 40W
Coral Sea 142 15 0 S 150 0 E
Coral Sea Islands Terr. 133 20 0 S 155 0 E
Corato 65 41 12N 16 22 E
Corbeil-Essonnes 43 48 36N 2 26 E
Corbie 43 49 54N 2 30 E
Corbières, mts. 44 42 55N 2 35 E
Corbigny 43 47 16N 3 40 E
Corbin 156 37 0N 84 3W
Corbion 47 49 48N 5 0 E
Corbones, R. 57 37 25N 5 35W
Corbridge 35 54 58N 2 0W
Corby, Lincs., U.K. 29 52 49N 0 31W
Corby, Northants., U.K. 29 52 29N 0 41W
Corcoles, R. 59 39 12N 2 40W
Corcoran 163 36 6N 119 35W
Corcubión 56 42 56N 9 12W
Cord. de Caravaya 174 14 0 S 70 30W
Cordele 157 31 55N 83 49W
Cordell 159 35 18N 99 0W
Cordenons 63 45 59N 12 42 E
Cordes 44 44 5N 1 57 E
Cordillera Oriental 174 5 0N 74 0W
Cordisburgo 171 19 7 S 44 21W
Córdoba 172 31 20 S 64 10W
Córdoba 164 26 20N 103 20W
Córdoba, Mexico 165 18 50N 97 0W
Córdoba, Spain 57 37 50N 4 50W
Córdoba □, Argent. 172 31 22 S 64 15W
Córdoba □, Colomb. 174 8 20N 75 40W
Córdoba □, Spain 57 38 5N 5 0W
Córdoba, Sierra de 172 31 10 S 64 25W
Cordon 103 16 42N 121 32 E
Cordova, Ala., U.S.A. 157 33 45N 87 12W
Cordova, Alaska, U.S.A. 147 60 36N 145 45W
Corella 58 42 7N 1 48W
Corella, R. 138 19 34 S 140 47 E
Coremas 170 7 1 S 37 58W
Corfe Castle 28 50 58N 2 3W
Corfe Mullen 28 50 45N 2 0W
Corfield 138 21 40 S 143 21 E
Corfu = Kerkira 68 39 38N 19 50 E
Corgo 56 42 56N 7 25W
Cori 64 41 39N 12 53 E
Coria 56 40 0N 6 33W
Coricudgy, Mt. 141 32 51 S 150 24 E
Corigliano Cálabro 65 39 36N 16 31 E
Coringa Is. 138 16 58 S 149 58 E
Corinna 138 41 35 S 145 10 E
Corinth, Miss., U.S.A. 157 34 54N 88 30W
Corinth, N.Y., U.S.A. 162 43 15N 73 50W
Corinth = Korinthos 69 37 56N 22 55 E
Corinth Canal 69 37 48N 23 0 E
Corinth, G. of = Korinthiakós 69 38 16N 22 30 E
Corinto, Brazil 171 18 20 S 44 30W
Corinto, Nic. 166 12 30N 87 10W
Corj □ 70 45 5N 23 25 E
Cork 39 51 54N 8 30W
Cork □ 39 51 50N 8 50W
Cork Harbour 39 51 46N 8 16W
Corlay 42 48 20N 3 5W
Corleone 64 37 48N 13 16 E
Corleto Perticara 65 40 23N 16 2 E
Çorlu 67 41 11N 27 49 E
Cormack L. 152 60 56N 121 37W
Cormóns 63 45 58N 13 29 E
Cormorant 153 54 14N 100 35W
Cormorant L. 153 54 15N 100 50W
Cormorant, oilfield 19 61 0N 1 0 E
Corn Hill, Mt. 38 53 48N 7 43W
Corn Is. 167 12 0N 83 0W
Cornelio 164 29 55N 111 8W
Cornélio Procópio 173 23 7 S 50 40W
Cornell 158 45 10N 91 8W
Corner Brook 151 48 57N 57 58W
Corner Inlet 133 38 45 S 146 20 E
Cornforth 33 54 42N 1 28W
Corniglio 62 44 29N 10 5 E
Corning, Ark., U.S.A. 159 36 27N 90 34W
Corning, Calif., U.S.A. 160 39 56N 122 9W
Corning, Iowa, U.S.A. 158 40 57N 94 40W
Corning, N.Y., U.S.A. 162 42 10N 77 3W
Cornwall, Austral. 138 41 33 S 148 7 E
Cornwall, Can. 150 45 2N 74 44W
Cornwall, U.S.A. 162 40 17N 76 25W
Cornwall □ 30 50 26N 4 40W
Cornwall, C. 30 50 8N 5 42W
Cornwallis I. 12 75 8N 95 0W
Corny Pt. 140 34 55 S 137 0 E
Coro 174 11 25N 69 41W
Coroaci 171 18 35 S 42 17W

Coroatá Crooksville

Coroatá 170 4 20S 44 0W
Corocoro 174 17 15S 69 19W
Corofin 39 53 27N 8 50W
Coroico 174 16 0S 67 50W
Coromandel, Brazil 171 18 28S 47 13W
Coromandel, N.Z. 142 36 45S 175 31E
Coromandel Coast 97 12 30N 81 0E
Coromandel Pen. 142 37 0S 175 45E
Coromandel Ra. 142 37 0S 175 40E
Coromorant, L. 153 54 20N 100 50W
Corona, Austral. 139 31 16S 141 24E
Corona, Calif., U.S.A. 163 33 49N 117 36W
Corona, N. Mex., U.S.A. 161 34 15N 105 32W
Coronada B. 166 9 0N 83 40W
Coronado 163 32 45N 117 9W
Coronado, Bahía de 166 9 0N 83 40W
Coronation 152 52 5N 111 27W
Coronation Gulf 148 68 25N 112 0W
Coronation I., Antarct. 13 60 45S 46 0W
Coronation I., U.S.A. 152 55 52N 134 20W
Coronation Is. 136 14 57S 124 55E
Coronda 172 31 58S 60 56W
Coronel 172 37 0S 73 10W
Coronel Bogado 172 27 11S 56 18W
Coronel Dorrego 172 38 40S 61 10W
Coronel Fabriciano 171 19 31S 42 38W
Coronel Murta 171 16 37S 42 11W
Coronel Oviedo 172 25 24S 56 30W
Coronel Pringles 172 38 0S 61 30W
Coronel Suárez 172 37 30S 62 0W
Coronel Vidal 172 37 28S 57 45W
Coronie 170 5 55N 56 25W
Corovoda 68 40 31N 20 14E
Corowa 141 35 58S 146 21E
Corozal, Belize 165 18 30N 88 30W
Corozal, Colomb. 174 9 19N 75 18W
Corpach 36 56 50N 5 9W
Corps 45 44 50N 5 56E
Corpus 173 27 10S 55 30W
Corpus Christi 159 27 50N 97 28W
Corpus Christi L. 159 28 5N 97 54W
Corque 174 18 10S 67 50W
Corral de Almaguer 58 39 45N 3 10W
Corran 36 56 44N 5 14W
Corrandibby Ra. 137 26 0S 115 20E
Corraun Pen. 38 53 58N 10 15W
Corrégio 62 44 46N 10 47E
Corrente 170 10 27S 45 10W
Corrente, R. 170 13 8S 43 28W
Correntes, C. das 129 24 6S 35 34E
Correntina 171 13 20S 44 39W
Corrèze □ 44 45 20N 1 45E
Corrib, L. 38 53 25N 9 10W
Corrie 34 55 39N 5 10W
Corrientes 172 27 30S 58 45W
Corrientes □ 172 28 0S 57 0W
Corrientes, C., Colomb. 174 5 30N 77 34W
Corrientes, C., Cuba 166 21 43N 84 30W
Corrientes, C., Mexico 164 20 25N 105 42W
Corrientes, R., Argent. 172 30 21S 59 33W
Corrientes, R., Colomb. 174 3 15S 75 58W
Corrigan 159 31 0N 94 48W
Corrigin 137 32 20S 117 53E
Corringham 33 53 25N 0 42W
Corris 31 52 41N 3 49W
Corrowidgie 141 36 56S 148 50E
Corry 156 41 55N 79 39W
Corryong 141 36 12S 147 53E
Corryvrecken, G. of 34 56 10N 5 44W
Corse, C. 45 43 1N 9 25E
Corse-du-Sud □ 45 41 45N 9 0E
Corse, Î 45 42 0N 9 0E
Corsewall Pt. 34 55 0N 5 10W
Corsham 28 51 25N 2 11W
Corsica = Corse 45 42 0N 9 0E
Corsicana 159 32 5N 96 30W
Corsley 28 51 12N 2 14W
Corsock 35 55 54N 3 56W
Corté 45 42 19N 9 11E
Corte do Pinto 57 37 42N 7 29W
Cortegana 57 37 52N 6 49W
Cortez 161 37 24N 108 35W
Cortina d'Ampezzo 63 46 32N 12 9E
Cortland 162 42 35N 76 11W
Corton 29 52 31N 1 46E
Cortona 63 43 16N 12 0E
Coruche 57 38 57N 8 30W
Çorum 92 40 30N 35 5E
Corumbá, Goias, Brazil 171 16 0S 48 50W
Corumbá, Mato Grosso, Brazil 174 19 0S 57 30W
Corumbá R. 171 17 25S 48 30W
Corumbaíba 171 18 9S 48 34W
Coruña □ 56 43 0N 8 37E
Coruña, La 56 43 20N 8 25W
Coruña, La □ 56 43 10N 8 30W
Corund 70 46 30N 25 13E
Corunna = La Coruña 56 43 20N 8 25W
Coruripe 171 10 5S 36 10W
Corvallis 160 44 36N 123 15W
Corve, R. 28 52 22N 2 43W
Corvette, L. de la 150 53 25N 73 55W
Corwen 31 52 59N 3 23W
Corydon 158 40 42N 93 22W
Cosalá 164 24 28N 106 40W
Cosamaloapán 165 18 23N 95 50W
Coseley 28 52 33N 2 6W
Cosenza 65 39 17N 16 14E
Coşereni 70 44 38N 26 35E
Cosham 28 50 51N 1 3W
Coshocton 156 40 17N 81 51W
Cosne-s.-Loire 43 47 24N 2 54E
Coso Junction 163 36 3N 117 57W
Coso Pk. 163 36 13N 117 44W
Cospeito 56 43 12N 7 34W
Cosquín 172 31 15S 64 30W
Cossato 62 45 34N 8 10E
Cossé-le-Vivien 42 47 57N 0 54W
Costa Azul 50 43 25N 6 50E
Costa Blanca 59 38 25N 0 10W
Costa Brava 58 41 30N 3 0E
Costa del Sol 57 36 30N 4 30W
Costa Dorada 58 40 45N 1 15E
Costa Mesa 163 33 39N 117 55W
Costa Rica 164 31 20N 112 40W
Costa Rica ■ 166 10 0N 84 0W
Costa Smeralda 64 41 5N 9 35E
Costelloe 39 53 20N 9 33W
Costessey 29 52 40N 1 11E
Costigliole d'Asti 62 44 48N 8 11E
Costilla 161 37 0N 105 30W
Coştiui 70 47 53N 24 2E
Cosumnes, R. 163 38 14N 121 25W
Coswig 48 51 52N 12 31E
Cotabato 103 7 14N 124 15E
Cotabena 140 31 42S 138 11E
Cotagaita 172 20 45S 65 30W
Côte d'Azur 45 43 25N 6 50E
Côte d'Or 43 47 10N 4 50E
Côte d'Or □ 43 47 30N 4 50E
Côte, La 50 46 25N 6 15E
Côte-St. André, La 45 45 24N 5 15E
Coteau des Prairies 158 44 30N 97 0W
Coteau du Missouri, Plat. du 154 47 0N 101 0W
Cotegipe 171 12 2S 44 15W
Cotentin 42 49 30N 1 30W
Côtes de Meuse 43 49 15N 5 22E
Côtes-du-Nord □ 42 48 25N 2 40W
Cotherstone 32 54 34N 1 59W
Cotiella 58 42 31N 0 19E
Cotina, R. 66 43 36N 19 9E
Cotonou 121 6 20N 2 25E
Cotopaxi, Vol. 174 0 30S 78 30W
Cotronei 65 39 9N 16 27E
Cotswold Hills 28 51 42N 2 10W
Cottage Grove 160 43 48N 123 2W
Cottbus 48 51 44N 14 20E
Cottbus □ 48 51 43N 13 30E
Cottenham 29 52 18N 0 8E
Cottingham 36 53 47N 0 23W
Cottonwood, Can. 152 53 5N 121 50W
Cottonwood, U.S.A. 161 34 48N 112 1W
Coubre, Pte. de la 44 45 42N 1 15W
Couches 43 46 53N 4 30E
Couço 57 38 59N 8 17W
Coudersport 156 41 45N 78 1W
Couedic, C. du 140 36 5S 136 40E
Couëron 42 47 13N 1 44W
Coueson, R. 42 48 20N 1 15W
Couhé-Vérac 44 46 18N 0 12E
Couillet 47 50 23N 4 28E
Coulags 36 57 26N 5 24W
Coulanges, Deux Sèvres, France 44 46 58N 0 35W
Coulanges, Yonne, France 43 47 30N 3 30E
Coulee City 160 47 44N 119 12W
Coulman I. 13 73 35S 170 0E
Coulommiers 43 48 50N 3 3E
Coulonge, R. 150 45 52N 76 46W
Coulport 34 56 3N 4 53W
Coulterville 163 37 42N 120 12W
Council 147 64 55N 163 45W
Council Bluffs 158 41 20N 95 50W
Council Grove 158 38 41N 96 30W
Coupar Angus 35 56 33N 3 17W
Courantyne, R. 174 5 0N 57 45W
Courçon 44 46 15N 0 50W
Cours 45 46 7N 4 19E
Courseulles 42 49 20N 0 29W
Court-St.-Etienne 47 50 38N 4 34E
Courtenay 152 49 45N 125 0W
Courtine, La 44 45 43N 2 16E
Courtland 163 38 20N 121 34W
Courtmacsherry 39 51 38N 8 43W
Courtmacsherry B. 39 51 37N 8 37W
Courtown 39 52 39N 6 14W
Courtrai = Kortrijk 47 50 50N 3 17E
Courville 42 48 28N 1 15E
Coutances 42 49 3N 1 28W
Couterne 42 48 30N 0 25W
Coutras 44 45 3N 0 8W
Coutts 152 49 0N 111 57W
Couvet 50 46 57N 6 38E
Couvin 47 50 3N 4 29E
Covarrubias 58 42 4N 3 31W
Covasna 70 45 50N 26 10E
Covasna □ 70 45 50N 26 0E
Cove Bay 37 57 5N 2 5W
Coventry 28 52 25N 1 31W
Coventry L. 153 61 15N 106 15W
Cover R. 32 54 14N 1 45W
Coverack 30 50 2N 5 6W
Covilhã 56 40 17N 7 31W
Covina 163 34 5N 117 52W
Covington, Ga., U.S.A. 157 33 36N 83 50W
Covington, Ky., U.S.A. 156 39 5N 84 30W
Covington, Okla., U.S.A. 159 36 21N 97 36W
Covington, Tenn., U.S.A. 159 35 34N 89 39W
Cowal Creek Settlement 138 10 54S 142 20E
Cowal, dist. 34 56 5N 5 8W
Cowal, L. 141 33 40S 147 25E
Cowan 153 52 5N 100 45W
Cowan, L. 137 31 45S 121 45E
Cowan L. 153 54 0N 107 15W
Cowangie 140 35 12S 141 26E
Coward Springs 139 29 24S 136 48E
Cowarie 139 27 45S 138 15E
Cowarna 137 30 55S 122 40E
Cowbridge 31 51 28N 3 28W
Cowcowing Lakes 137 30 55S 117 20E
Cowdenbeath 35 56 7N 3 20W
Cowell 140 33 39S 136 56E
Cowes 28 50 45N 1 18W
Cowfold 29 50 58N 0 16W
Cowl Cowl 141 33 36S 145 18E
Cowley 28 51 43N 1 12W
Cowpen 35 55 8N 1 34W
Cowra 141 33 49S 148 42E
Coxim 175 18 30S 54 55W
Cox's Bazar 98 21 26N 91 59E
Cox's Cove 151 49 7N 58 5W
Coyame 164 29 28N 105 6W
Coylton 34 55 26N 4 31W
Coyuca de Benitez 165 17 1N 100 8W
Coyuca de Catalán 164 18 58N 100 41W
Cozad 158 40 55N 99 57W
Cozie, Alpi 62 44 50N 6 59E
Cozumel 165 20 31N 86 55W
Cozumel, Isla de 165 20 30N 86 40W
Craanford 39 52 40N 6 23W
Craboon 141 32 3S 149 30E
Cracow 139 25 17S 150 17E
Cradock 128 32 8S 25 36E
Craggie 37 57 25N 4 6W
Craig, Alaska, U.S.A. 147 55 30N 133 5W
Craig, Colo., U.S.A. 160 40 32N 107 44W
Craigavon = Portadown 38 54 27N 6 26W
Craigavon = Lurgan 38 54 28N 6 20W
Craigellachie 37 57 29N 3 9W
Craighouse 34 55 50N 5 58W
Craigmore 127 20 28S 32 30E
Craignish, L. 34 56 11N 5 32W
Craigtown 37 58 30N 3 53W
Crail 35 56 16N 2 38W
Crailsheim 49 49 7N 10 5E
Craiova 70 44 21N 23 48E
Cramlington 35 55 5N 1 36W
Crampel 117 7 8N 19 81E
Cramsie 138 23 20S 144 15E
Cranberry Portage 153 54 35N 101 23W
Cranborne 28 50 55N 1 55W
Cranborne Chase 29 50 56N 2 6W
Cranbrook, Tas., Austral. 138 42 0S 148 5E
Cranbrook, W. Austral., Austral. 137 34 18S 117 33E
Cranbrook, Can. 152 49 30N 115 46W
Cranbrook, U.K. 29 51 6N 0 33E
Crandon 158 45 32N 88 52W
Crane, Oregon, U.S.A. 160 43 21N 118 39W
Crane, Texas, U.S.A. 159 31 26N 102 27W
Cranfield Pt. 38 54 1N 6 3W
Cranleigh 29 51 8N 0 29W
Cranshaws 35 55 51N 2 30W
Cranston 162 41 47N 71 27W
Cranwell 33 53 4N 0 29W
Craon 42 47 50N 0 58W
Craonne 43 49 27N 3 46E
Crasna 70 46 32N 27 51E
Crasna, R. 70 47 44N 22 35E
Crater Lake 160 42 55N 122 3W
Crater Mt. 135 6 37S 145 7E
Crater Pt. 135 5 25S 152 9E
Crateús 170 5 10S 40 50W
Crathie 37 57 3N 3 12W
Crati, R. 65 39 41N 16 30E
Crato, Brazil 171 7 10S 39 25W
Crato, Port. 57 39 16N 7 39W
Crau 45 43 32N 4 40E
Craughwell 39 53 15N 8 44W
Craven Arms 28 52 27N 2 49W
Crawford, U.K. 35 55 28N 3 40W
Crawford, U.S.A. 158 42 40N 103 25W
Crawford, oilfield 19 59 7N 1 30E
Crawfordsville 156 40 2N 86 51W
Crawley 29 51 7N 0 10W
Cray 31 51 55N 3 38W
Crazy Mts. 160 46 14N 110 30W
Creag Meagaidh, mt. 37 56 57N 4 38W
Crean L. 153 54 5N 106 9W
Crèche, La 44 46 23N 0 19W
Crécy-en-Brie 43 48 50N 2 53E
Crécy-en-Ponthieu 43 50 15N 1 53E
Crécy-sur-Serre 43 49 40N 3 32E
Credenhill 28 52 6N 2 49W
Crediton 30 50 47N 3 39W
Credo 137 30 28S 120 45E
Cree L. 153 57 30N 106 30W
Cree, R., Can. 153 58 57N 105 47W
Cree, R., U.K. 34 54 51N 4 24W
Creede 161 37 56N 106 59W
Creegh 39 52 45N 9 25W
Creel 164 27 45N 107 38W
Creeside 34 55 4N 4 41W
Creeslough 38 55 8N 7 55W
Creetown 34 54 54N 4 23W
Creeves 39 52 33N 9 3W
Creggan 38 54 39N 7 0W
Cregganbaun 38 53 42N 9 48W
Creighton 158 42 30N 97 52W
Creil 43 49 15N 2 34E
Crema 62 45 21N 9 40E
Cremona 62 45 8N 10 2E
Crepaja 66 45 1N 20 38E
Crépy 43 49 37N 3 32E
Crépy-en-Valois 43 49 14N 2 54E
Cres 63 44 58N 14 25E
Cresbard 158 45 13N 98 57W
Crescent, Okla., U.S.A. 159 35 38N 97 36W
Crescent, Oreg., U.S.A. 160 43 30N 121 37W
Crescent City 160 41 45N 124 12W
Crescentino 62 45 11N 8 7E
Crespino 63 44 59N 11 51E
Crespo 172 32 2S 60 19W
Cressman 150 47 40N 72 55W
Cressy 140 38 2S 143 40E
Crest 45 44 44N 5 2E
Crested Butte 161 38 57N 107 0W
Crestline 163 34 14N 117 18W
Creston, Can. 152 49 10N 116 31W
Creston, Calif., U.S.A. 163 35 32N 120 33W
Creston, Iowa, U.S.A. 158 41 0N 94 20W
Creston, Wash., U.S.A. 160 47 47N 118 36W
Creston, Wyo., U.S.A. 160 41 46N 107 50W
Crestone 161 35 2N 106 0W
Crestview, Calif., U.S.A. 163 37 46N 118 58W
Crestview, Fla., U.S.A. 157 30 45N 86 35W
Creswick 140 37 25S 143 51E
Crete 158 40 38N 96 58W
Crete = Kriti 69 35 15N 25 0E
Crete, La, Can. 152 58 10N 116 29W
Crete, La, Alta., Can. 152 58 11N 116 24W
Crete, Sea of 69 26 0N 25 0E
Cretin, C. 135 6 40S 147 53E
Creus, C. 58 42 20N 3 19E
Creuse □ 44 46 0N 2 0E
Creuse, R. 44 47 0N 0 34E
Creusot, Le 43 46 50N 4 24E
Creuzburg 48 51 3N 10 15E
Crevalcore 63 44 41N 11 10E
Crèvecœur-le-Grand 43 49 37N 2 5E
Crevillente 59 38 12N 0 48W
Crewe 32 53 6N 2 28W
Crewkerne 28 50 53N 2 48W
Crianlarich 34 56 24N 4 37W
Crib Point 139 38 22S 145 13E
Criccieth 31 52 55N 4 15W
Criciúma 173 28 40S 49 23W
Crick 28 52 22N 1 9W
Crickhowell 31 51 52N 3 8W
Cricklade 28 51 38N 1 50W
Crieff 35 56 22N 3 50W
Criffell Mt. 35 54 56N 3 38W
Crikvenica 63 45 11N 14 40E
Crillon, Mt. 152 58 39N 137 14W
Crimea = Krymskaya 82 45 0N 34 0E
Crimmitschau 48 50 48N 12 23E
Crimond 37 57 35N 1 53W
Crinan Canal 34 56 4N 5 30W
Crinkill 39 53 5N 7 55E
Cristalândia 170 10 36S 49 11W
Cristeşti 70 47 15N 26 33E
Cristino Castro 170 8 49S 44 13W
Crişul Alb, R. 66 46 25N 21 40E
Crişul Negru, R. 70 46 38N 22 26E
Crişul Repede, R. 70 47 20N 22 25E
Crivitz 48 53 35N 11 39E
Crixás 171 14 27S 49 58W
Crna Gora □ 66 42 40N 19 20E
Crna Trava 66 42 49N 22 19E
Crni Drim, R. 66 41 17N 20 40E
Crni Timok, R. 66 43 53N 22 0E
Crnoljeva Planina 66 42 20N 21 0E
Črnomelj 63 45 33N 15 10E
Croagh Patrick, mt. 38 53 46N 9 40W
Croatia = Hrvatska 63 45 20N 16 0E
Crocker, Barisan 102 5 0N 116 30E
Crocketford 35 55 3N 3 49W
Crockets Town 38 54 8N 9 7W
Crockett 159 31 20N 95 30W
Crocodile Is. 138 11 43S 135 8E
Crocodile, R. 129 25 30S 31 15E
Crocq 44 45 52N 2 21E
Croghan 38 53 55N 8 13W
Croglin 32 54 50N 2 37W
Crohy Hd. 38 54 55N 8 28W
Croisic, Le 42 47 18N 2 30W
Croisic, Pte. du. 42 47 19N 2 31W
Croix, La, L. 150 48 20N 92 15W
Croker, C. 136 10 58S 132 35E
Croker, I. 136 11 12N 132 32E
Crolly 38 55 2N 8 16W
Cromalt Hills 36 58 0N 5 2W
Cromarty, Can. 153 58 3N 94 9W
Cromarty, U.K. 37 57 40N 4 2W
Cromarty Firth 37 57 40N 4 15W
Cromdale, Hills of 37 57 20N 3 28W
Cromer 29 52 56N 1 18E
Cromore 36 58 6N 6 23W
Cromwell, N.Z. 143 45 3S 169 14E
Cromwell, U.S.A. 162 41 36N 72 39W
Cronat 43 46 43N 3 40E
Crondall 29 51 13N 0 51W
Cronulla 141 34 3S 151 8E
Crook 33 54 43N 1 45W
Crooked I. 167 22 50N 74 10W
Crooked Island Passage 167 23 0N 74 30W
Crooked, R., Can. 152 54 10N 122 35W
Crooked, R., U.S.A. 160 44 30N 121 0W
Crooklands 32 54 16N 2 43W
Crookston, Minn., U.S.A. 158 47 50N 96 40W
Crookston, Nebr., U.S.A. 158 42 56N 100 45W
Crookstown 39 51 50N 8 50W
Crooksville 156 39 45N 82 8W

Dalarö Degeh-Bur

Dalarö 75 59 8N 18 24 E
Dalat 101 12 3N 108 32 E
Dalbandin 93 29 0N 4 23 E
Dalbeattie 35 54 55N 3 50W
Dalbosjön, L. 73 58 40N 12 45 E
Dalby, Austral. 139 27 10 S 151 17 E
Dalby, Sweden 73 55 42N 13 22 E
Dale, Sogn og Fjordane, Norway 71 61 27N 7 28 E
Dale, Sogn og Fjordane, Norway 71 61 22N 5 23 E
Dale, U.K. 31 51 42N 5 11W
Dalen, Neth. 46 52 42N 6 46 E
Dalen, Norway 71 59 26N 8 0 E
Dalet 98 19 59N 93 51 E
Daletme 98 21 36N 92 46 E
Dalfsen 46 52 31N 6 16 E
Dalga 122 27 39N 30 41 E
Dalgaranger, Mt. 137 27 50 S 117 5 E
Dalhalvaig 37 58 28N 3 53W
Dalhart 159 36 0N 102 30W
Dalhousie, Can. 151 48 0N 66 26W
Dalhousie, India 94 32 38N 76 0 E
Daliburgh 36 57 10N 7 23W
Dalj 174 45 28N 18 58 E
Dalkeith 35 55 54N 3 5W
Dalkey 39 53 16N 6 7W
Dall I. 152 54 59N 133 25W
Dallarnil 139 25 19 S 152 2 E
Dallas, U.K. 37 57 33N 3 32W
Dallas, Oregon, U.S.A. 160 45 0N 123 15W
Dallas, Texas, U.S.A. 159 32 50N 96 50W
Dallol 123 14 14N 40 17 E
Dalmacija 66 43 20N 17 0 E
Dalmally 34 56 25N 5 0W
Dalmatia = Dalmacija 66 43 20N 17 0 E
Dalmatovo 84 56 16N 62 56 E
Dalmellington 34 55 20N 4 25W
Dalneretchensk 77 45 50N 133 40 E
Daloa 120 7 0N 6 30W
Dalry 34 55 44N 4 42W
Dalrymple, Mt. 133 21 1 S 148 39 E
Dalsjöfors 73 57 46N 18 5 E
Dalskog 73 58 44N 12 18 E
Dalton, Can. 150 48 11N 84 1W
Dalton, Cumbria, U.K. 33 54 9N 3 11W
Dalton, Dumfries, U.K. 35 55 3N 3 22W
Dalton, N. Yorks., U.K. 33 54 28N 1 32W
Dalton, Ga., U.S.A. 103 34 45N 85 0W
Dalton, Mass., U.S.A. 162 42 28N 73 11W
Dalton, Nebr., U.S.A. 158 41 27N 103 0W
Dalton Post 152 66 42N 137 0W
Daltonganj 95 24 0N 84 4 E
Dalvík 74 65 58N 18 32W
Dalwhinnie 37 56 56N 4 14W
Daly City 163 37 42N 122 28W
Daly L. 153 56 32N 105 39W
Daly, R. 136 13 21 S 130 18 E
Daly Waters 138 16 15 S 133 24 E
Dalystown 38 53 26N 7 23W
Dam 170 4 45N 55 0W
Dam Doi 101 8 59N 105 12 E
Dam Gillan 153 56 20N 94 40W
Dam Ha 100 21 21N 107 36 E
Dama, Wadi 122 27 12N 35 50 E
Daman 96 20 25N 72 57 E
Daman □ 96 20 25N 72 58 E
Damanhûr 122 31 0N 30 30 E
Damar, I. 103 7 15 S 128 30 E
Damaraland 128 21 0 S 17 0 E
Damascus = Dimashq 92 33 30N 36 18 E
Damaturu 121 11 45N 11 55 E
Damāvand 93 36 0N 52 0 E
Damāvand, Qolleh-ye 93 35 45N 52 10 E
Damba, Angola 124 6 44 S 15 29 E
Damba, Ethiopia 123 15 10N 38 47 E
Dâmbovnic, R. 70 44 28N 25 18 E
Dame Marie 167 18 36N 74 26W
Damerham 28 50 57N 1 52W
Dames Quarter 162 38 11N 75 54W
Damghan 93 36 10N 54 17 E
Damietta = Dumyât 122 31 24N 31 48 E
Damin 93 27 30N 60 40 E
Damiya 90 32 6N 35 34 E
Damman 92 26 25N 50 2 E
Dammarie 43 48 20N 1 30 E
Dammartin 43 49 3N 2 41 E
Dammastock 51 46 38N 8 24 E
Damme 48 52 32N 8 12 E
Damodar, R. 95 23 17N 87 35 E
Damoh 95 23 50N 79 28 E
Dampier 136 20 41 S 116 42 E
Dampier Arch. 136 20 38 S 116 32 E
Dampier Downs 136 18 24 S 123 5 E
Dampier, Selat 103 0 40 S 131 0 E
Dampier Str. 135 5 50 S 148 0 E
Damrei, Chuor Phnum 101 12 30N 103 0 E
Damville 42 48 51N 1 5 E
Damvillers 43 49 20N 5 21 E
Dan Chadi 121 12 47N 5 17 E
Dan Dume 121 11 28N 7 8 E
Dan Gora 121 11 30N 8 7 E
Dan Gulbi 121 11 40N 6 15 E
Dan, oilfield 19 55 30N 5 10 E
Dan Sadau 121 11 25N 6 20 E
Dana 103 11 0 S 122 52 E
Dana, Lac 150 50 53N 77 20W
Dana, Mt 163 37 54N 119 12W
Danakil Depression 123 12 45N 41 0 E
Danao 103 10 31N 124 1 E
Danbury 162 41 23N 73 29W
Danby L. 161 34 17N 115 0W
Dand 94 31 28N 65 32 E
Dandaragan 137 30 40 S 115 40 E
Dandeldhura 95 29 20N 80 35 E
Dandeli 93 15 5N 74 30 E
Dandenong 141 38 0 S 145 15 E
Dandkandi 98 23 32N 90 43 E
Danforth 151 45 39N 67 57W
Dang Raek 101 14 40N 104 0 E
Dangara 85 38 6N 69 22 E
Danger Is. 131 10 53 S 165 49W
Danger Pt. 128 34 40 S 19 17 E
Dangla 123 11 18N 36 56 E
Dangora 121 11 30N 8 7 E
Dangrek, Phnom 100 14 15N 105 0 E
Daniel 160 42 56N 110 2W
Daniel's Harbour 151 50 13N 57 35W
Danielskull 128 28 11 S 23 33 E
Danielson 162 41 50N 71 52W
Danilov 81 58 16N 40 13 E
Danilovgrad 66 42 38N 19 9 E
Danilovka 81 50 25N 44 12 E
Danissa 126 3 15N 40 58 E
Danja 121 11 29N 7 30 E
Dankalwa 121 11 52N 12 12 E
Dankama 121 13 20N 7 44 E
Dankhar Gompa 93 32 10N 78 10 E
Dankov 81 53 20N 39 5 E
Danlí 166 14 4N 86 35W
Dannemora 75 60 12N 17 51 E
Dannenberg 48 53 7N 11 4 E
Dannevirke 142 40 12 S 176 8 E
Dannhauser 129 28 0 S 30 3 E
Dansalan 103 8 2N 124 30 E
Dansville 156 42 32N 77 41W
Dantan 95 21 57N 87 20 E
Danube, R. 53 45 0N 28 20W
Danubyo 98 17 15N 95 35 E
Danvers 162 42 34N 70 55 E
Danville, Ill., U.S.A. 156 40 10N 87 40W
Danville, Ky., U.S.A. 156 37 40N 84 45W
Danville, Pa., U.S.A. 162 40 58N 76 37W
Danville, Va., U.S.A. 157 36 40N 79 20W
Danzig = Gdansk 54 54 22N 18 40 E
Dão 103 10 30N 122 6 E
Dão, R. 56 40 28N 8 0W
Daosa 94 26 52N 76 20 E
Daoud = Aïn Beida 119 35 50N 7 29 E
Daoulas 42 48 22N 4 17W
Dapango 121 10 55N 0 16 E
Dar al Hamra, Ad 92 27 22N 37 43 E
Dar es Salaam 126 6 50 S 39 12 E
Dar'á 90 32 36N 36 7 E
Darab 93 28 50N 54 30 E
Darabani 70 48 10N 26 39 E
Daraj 119 30 10N 10 28 E
Daraut Kurgan 85 39 33N 72 11 E
Daravica 66 42 32N 20 8 E
Daraw 121 24 22N 32 51 E
Darazo 121 11 1N 10 24W
Darband 94 34 30N 72 50 E
Darbhanga 95 26 15N 86 8 E
Darby 160 46 2N 114 7W
D'Arcy 152 50 35N 122 30W
Darda 66 45 40N 18 41 E
Dardanelle 163 38 2N 119 50W
Dardanelles = Canakkale Boğlazi 92 40 0N 26 20 E
Dardenelle 159 35 12N 93 9W
Darent, R. 29 51 22N 0 12 E
Darfield 143 43 29 S 172 7 E
Darfo 62 45 43N 10 11 E
Dargai 94 34 25N 71 45 E
Dargan Ata 76 40 40N 62 20 E
Dargaville 142 35 57 S 173 52 E
Darharala 120 8 23N 4 20W
Dari 123 5 48N 30 26 E
Darién, G. del 174 9 0N 77 0W
Darién, Serranía del 174 8 30N 77 30W
Dariganga 106 45 5N 113 45 E
Darinskoye 84 51 20N 51 44 E
Darjeeling 95 27 3N 88 18 E
Dark Cove 151 48 47N 54 13W
Darkan 137 33 20 S 116 43 E
Darke Peak 140 33 27 S 136 12 E
Darkot Pass 95 36 45N 73 26 E
Darlaston 28 52 35N 2 1W
Darling Downs 139 28 30 S 152 0 E
Darling, R. 140 34 4 S 141 54 E
Darling Ra. 137 32 30 S 116 0 E
Darlington, U.K. 33 54 33N 1 33W
Darlington, S.C., U.S.A. 157 34 18N 79 50W
Darlington, Wis., U.S.A. 158 42 43N 90 7W
Darlot, L. 137 27 48 S 121 35 E
Darłowo 54 54 25N 16 25 E
Darmstadt 49 49 51N 8 40 E
Darnall 129 29 23 S 31 18 E
Darnétal 42 49 25N 1 10 E
Darney 43 48 5N 6 0 E
Darnick 140 32 48 S 143 38 E
Darnley B. 147 69 30N 123 30W
Darnley, C. 13 68 0 S 69 0 E
Daroca 58 41 9N 1 25W
Darr 138 23 13 S 144 7 E
Darr, R. 138 23 39 S 143 50 E
Darragh 39 52 47N 9 7W
Darran Mts. 143 44 37 S 167 59 E
Darrington 160 48 14N 121 37W
Darror, R. 91 10 30N 50 0 E
Darsana 98 23 35N 88 48 E
Darsi 97 15 46N 79 44 E
Darsser Ort 48 54 27N 12 30 E
Dart, R., N.Z. 143 44 20 S 168 20 E
Dart, R., U.K. 30 50 24N 3 36W
Dartford 29 51 26N 0 15 E
Dartington 30 50 26N 3 42W
Dartmoor, Austral. 140 37 56N 141 19 E
Dartmoor, U.K. 30 50 36N 4 0W
Dartmouth, Austral. 138 23 31 S 144 44 E
Dartmouth, Can. 151 44 40N 63 30W
Dartmouth, U.K. 30 50 21N 3 35W
Dartmouth, L. 139 26 4 S 145 18 E
Darton 33 53 36N 1 32W
Dartuch, C. 58 39 55N 3 49 E
Daru, P.N.G. 135 9 3 S 143 13 E
Daru, S. Leone 120 8 0N 10 52W
Darvel 34 55 37N 4 20W
Darvel Bay 103 4 50N 118 20 E
Darwen 32 53 42N 2 29W
Darwha 96 20 15N 77 45 E
Darwin, Austral. 136 12 25 S 130 51 E
Darwin, U.S.A. 163 36 15N 117 35W
Darwin, Mt. 127 16 45 S 31 33 E
Darwin River 136 12 50 S 130 58 E
Daryacheh-ye-Sistan 93 31 0N 61 0 E
Daryapur 96 20 55N 77 20 E
Dase 123 14 53N 37 15 E
Dashato, R. 123 7 25N 42 40 E
Dashkesan 83 40 40N 46 0 E
Dasht-e Kavīr 93 34 30N 55 0 E
Dasht-e Lut 93 31 30N 58 0 E
Dasht-i-Khash 93 32 0N 62 0 E
Dasht-i-Margo 93 30 40N 62 30 E
Dasht-i-Nawar 94 33 52N 68 0 E
Dasht, R. 93 25 40N 62 20 E
Daska 94 32 20N 74 20 E
Dassa-Zoume 121 7 46N 2 14 E
Dasseneiland 128 33 37 S 18 3 E
Datça 69 36 46N 27 40 E
Datia 95 25 39N 78 27 E
Dattapur 96 20 45N 78 15 E
Daugava 80 57 0N 24 0 E
Daugavpils 80 55 53N 26 32 E
Daulat Yar 93 34 30N 65 45 E
Daulatabad 96 19 57N 75 15 E
Daun 49 50 5N 6 53 E
Dauphin, Can. 153 51 9N 100 5W
Dauphin, U.S.A. 162 40 22N 76 56W
Dauphin I. 157 30 16N 88 10W
Dauphin L. 153 51 20N 99 45W
Dauphiné 45 45 15N 5 25 E
Dauqa 122 19 30N 41 0 E
Daura, Kano, Nigeria 121 13 2N 8 21 E
Daura, N.-E., Nigeria 121 11 31N 11 24 E
Davadi 120 14 10N 16 3W
Davangere 97 14 25N 75 50 E
Davao 103 7 0N 125 40 E
Davao, G. of 103 6 30N 125 48 E
Davar Panab 93 27 25N 62 15 E
Dave 74 52 55N 1 50W
Davenport, Calif., U.S.A. 163 37 1N 122 12W
Davenport, Iowa, U.S.A. 158 41 30N 90 40W
Davenport, Wash., U.S.A. 160 47 40N 118 5W
Davenport Downs 138 24 8 S 141 7 E
Davenport Ra. 138 20 28 S 134 0 E
Daventry 28 52 16N 1 10W
David 166 8 30N 82 30W
David City 158 41 18N 97 10W
David Gorodok 80 52 4N 27 8 E
Davidson 153 51 16N 105 59W
Davik 71 61 53N 5 33 E
Davis 163 38 33N 121 45W
Davis Dam 161 35 11N 114 35W
Davis Inlet 151 55 50N 60 45W
Davis Mts. 159 30 42N 104 15W
Davis Str. 149 65 0N 58 0W
Davlekanovo 84 54 13N 55 3 E
Davos 51 46 48N 9 49 E
Davy L. 153 58 53N 108 18W
Davyhurst 137 30 2 S 120 40 E
Dawa, R. 123 5 0N 39 5 E
Dawaki, Jos, Nigeria 121 9 25N 9 33 E
Dawaki, Kano, Nigeria 121 12 5N 8 23 E
Dawayima 90 31 33N 34 55 E
Dawes Ra. 138 24 40 S 150 40 E
Dawley 28 52 40N 2 29W
Dawlish 30 50 34N 3 28W
Dawna Range 98 16 30N 98 30 E
Dawnyein 98 15 54N 95 36 E
Dawros Hd. 38 54 48N 8 32W
Dawson, Can. 147 64 10N 139 30W
Dawson, Ga., U.S.A. 157 31 45N 84 28W
Dawson, N.D., U.S.A. 158 46 56N 99 45W
Dawson Creek 152 55 45N 120 15W
Dawson, I. 176 53 50 S 70 50W
Dawson Inlet 153 61 50N 93 25W
Dawson, R. 133 23 25 S 150 10 E
Dawson Range 138 24 30 S 149 48 E
Dawson's 127 17 0 S 30 57 E
Daylesford 140 37 21 S 144 9 E
Dayr al-Ghusūn 90 32 21N 35 4 E
Dayr az Zawr 92 35 20N 40 5 E
Daysland 152 52 50N 112 20W
Dayton, Ohio, U.S.A. 156 39 45N 84 10W
Dayton, Tenn., U.S.A. 157 35 30N 85 1W
Dayton, Wash., U.S.A. 160 46 20N 118 0W
Daytona Beach 157 29 14N 81 0W
Dayville 160 44 33N 119 37W
De Aar 128 30 39 S 24 0 E
De Bilt 46 52 6N 5 11 E
De Funiak Springs 157 30 42N 86 10W
De Grey 136 20 12 S 119 12 E
De Grey, R. 136 20 0 S 119 13 E
De Kalb 158 41 55N 88 45W
De Koog 46 53 6N 4 46 E
De Land 157 29 1N 81 19W
De Leon 159 32 9N 98 35W
De Long Mts. 147 68 10N 163 0W
De Long, Ostrova 77 76 40N 149 20 E
De Panne 47 51 6N 2 34 E
De Pere 156 44 28N 88 1W
De Queen 159 34 3N 94 24W
De Quincy 159 30 30N 93 27W
De Ridder 159 30 48N 93 15W
De Rijp 46 52 33N 4 51 E
De Smet 158 44 25N 97 35W
De Tour Village 156 45 49N 83 56W
De Witt 159 34 19N 91 20W
Dead Sea = Miyet, Bahr el 92 31 30N 35 30 E
Deadwood 58 44 25N 103 43W
Deadwood L. 152 59 10N 128 30W
Deaf Adder Cr. 136 13 0 S 132 47 E
Deakin 137 30 46 S 129 58 E
Deal 29 51 13N 1 25 E
Dealesville 128 28 41 S 25 44 E
Dean, Forest of 28 51 50N 2 35W
Deán Funes 172 30 20 S 64 20W
Dearborn 150 42 18N 83 15W
Dearham 32 54 43N 3 28W
Dease L. 152 58 40N 130 5W
Dease Lake 152 58 25N 130 6W
Dease, R. 152 59 56N 128 32W
Death Valley 163 36 27N 116 52W
Death Valley Junc. 163 36 21N 116 30W
Death Valley Nat. Monument 163 36 30N 117 0W
Deauville 42 49 23N 0 2 E
Deba Habe 121 10 14N 11 20 E
Debaltsevo 82 48 22N 38 26 E
Debar 66 41 21N 20 37 E
Debba 123 14 20N 41 18 E
Debden 153 53 30N 106 50W
Debdou 118 33 59N 3 0W
Debeeti 128 23 45 S 26 32 E
Deben, R. 29 52 4N 1 19 E
Debenham 29 52 14N 1 10 E
Debessy 84 57 39N 53 49 E
Dębica 54 50 2N 21 25 E
Dęblin 54 51 34N 21 50 E
Debo, L. 120 15 14N 3 57W
Debolt 152 55 12N 118 1W
Deborah, gasfield 19 53 4N 1 50 E
Deborah, L. 137 30 45 S 119 0 E
Debrc 66 44 38N 19 53 E
Debre Birhan 123 9 41N 39 31 E
Debre Markos 123 10 20N 37 40 E
Debre May 123 11 20N 37 25 E
Debre Sina 123 9 51N 39 50 E
Debre Tabor 123 11 50N 38 26 E
Debrecen 53 47 33N 21 42 E
Dečani 66 42 30N 20 10 E
Decatur, Ala., U.S.A. 157 34 35N 87 0W
Decatur, Ga., U.S.A. 157 33 47N 84 17W
Decatur, Ill., U.S.A. 158 39 50N 89 0W
Decatur, Ind., U.S.A. 156 40 52N 85 28W
Decatur, Texas, U.S.A. 159 33 15N 97 35W
Decazeville 44 44 34N 2 15 E
Deccan 97 14 0N 77 0 E
Deception I. 13 63 0 S 60 15W
Deception L. 153 56 33N 104 13W
Deception, Mt. 140 30 42 S 138 16 E
Decize 43 46 50N 3 28 E
Decollatura 65 39 2N 16 21 E
Decorah 158 43 20N 91 50W
Deda 70 46 56N 24 50 E
Dedaye 98 16 24N 95 53 E
Deddington 28 51 58N 1 19W
Dedemsvaavt 46 52 36N 6 28 E
Dedham 162 42 14N 71 10W
Dedilovo 81 53 59N 37 50 E
Dédougou 120 12 30N 3 35W
Deduru Oya 97 7 32N 81 45 E
Dedza 127 14 20 S 34 20 E
Dee, R., Eng.-Wales, U.K. 31 53 15N 3 7W
Dee, R., Scot., U.K. 37 57 4N 2 7W
Deel R. 38 53 35N 7 9W
Deelish 39 51 41N 9 18W
Deep B. 152 61 15N 116 35W
Deep Lead 140 37 0 S 142 43 E
Deep Well 138 24 20 S 134 0 E
Deepdale 136 26 22 S 114 20 E
Deeping Fen 29 52 45N 0 15W
Deeping, St. Nicholas 29 52 44N 0 11W
Deepwater 139 29 25 S 151 51 E
Deer I. 147 54 55N 162 20W
Deer Lake, Newf., Can. 151 49 11N 57 27W
Deer Lake, Ontario, Can. 153 52 36N 94 20W
Deer Lodge 160 46 25N 112 40W
Deer Park 160 47 55N 117 21W
Deer, R. 153 58 23N 94 13W
Deer River 158 47 21N 93 44W
Deer Sound 37 58 58N 2 50W
Deeral 138 17 14 S 145 55 E
Deerdepoort 128 24 37 S 26 27 E
Deering 147 66 5N 162 50W
Deerlijk 47 50 51N 3 22 E
Deerness 37 58 57N 2 44W
Deesa 94 24 18N 72 10 E
Deferiet 162 44 2N 75 41W
Defiance 156 41 20N 84 20W
Deganwy 31 53 18N 3 49W
Deganya 90 32 43N 35 34 E
Degebe, R. 57 38 21N 7 37W
Degeh-Bur 91 8 11N 43 31 E

Degema Dieuze

Degema 121 4 50N 6 48 E
Degerfors 74 64 16N 19 46 E
Degersfor 73 59 20N 14 28 E
Degersheim 51 47 23N 9 12 E
Degersiö 72 63 13N 18 3 E
Deggendorf 49 48 49N 12 59 E
Degloor 96 18 34N 77 33 E
Deh Bīd 93 30 39N 53 11 E
Deh Kheyr 93 28 45N 54 40 E
Deh Titan 93 33 45N 63 50 E
Dehibat 119 32 0N 10 47 E
Dehiwala 97 6 50N 79 51 E
Dehkhvareqan 92 37 50N 45 55 E
Dehra Dun 94 30 20N 78 4 E
Dehri 95 24 50N 84 15 E
Deinze 47 50 59N 3 32 E
Deir Abu Sa'id 90 32 30N 38 42 E
Deir Dibwan 90 31 55N 35 15 E
Dej 70 47 10N 23 52 E
Deje 72 59 35N 13 29 E
Dekar 128 18 30 S 23 10 E
Dekemhare 123 15 6N 39 0 E
Dekese 124 3 24 S 21 24 E
Dekhkanabad 85 38 21N 66 30 E
Del Mar 163 32 58N 117 16W
Del Norte 161 37 47N 106 27W
Del Rey, Rio 121 4 30N 8 48 E
Del Rio, Mexico 164 29 22N 100 54W
Del Rio, U.S.A. 159 29 15N 100 50W
Delabole 30 50 37N 4 45W
Delagoa B. 129 25 50 S 32 45 E
Delagua 159 32 35N 104 40W
Delai 122 17 21N 36 6 E
Delambre I. 136 20 27 S 117 4 E
Delano 163 35 48N 119 13W
Delareyville 128 26 41 S 25 26 E
Delavan 158 42 40N 88 39W
Delaware 156 40 20N 83 0W
Delaware □ 162 39 0N 75 40W
Delaware B. 162 38 50N 75 0W
Delaware City 162 39 34N 75 36W
Delaware, R. 162 39 20N 75 25W
Delčevo 66 41 58N 22 46 E
Delchirach 37 57 23N 3 20W
Delegate 141 37 4 S 148 56 E
Delémont 50 47 22N 7 20 E
Delft 46 52 1N 4 22 E
Delft I. 97 9 30N 79 40 E
Delfzijl 46 53 20N 6 55 E
Delgado, C. 127 10 45 S 40 40 E
Delgerhet 106 45 50N 110 30 E
Delgo 122 20 6N 30 40 E
Delhi, India 94 28 38N 77 17 E
Delhi, U.S.A. 162 42 17N 74 56W
Deli Jovan 66 44 13N 22 9 E
Delia 152 51 38N 112 23W
Delice, R. 92 39 45N 34 15 E
Delicias 164 28 10N 105 30W
Delicias, Laguna 164 28 7N 105 40W
Delimiro Gouveia 170 9 23 S 37 59W
Delitzsch 48 51 32N 12 22 E
Dell City 161 31 58N 105 19W
Dell Rapids 158 43 53N 96 44W
Delle 43 47 30N 7 2 E
Dellys 119 36 50N 3 57 E
Delmar, Del., U.S.A. 162 38 27N 75 34W
Delmar, N.Y., U.S.A. 162 42 5N 73 50W
Delmenhorst 48 53 3N 8 37 E
Delmiro 170 9 24 S 38 6W
Delnice 63 45 23N 14 50 E
Deloraine, Austral. 138 41 30 S 146 40 E
Deloraine, Can. 153 49 15N 100 29W
Delorme, L. 151 54 31N 69 52W
Delovo 66 44 55N 20 52 E
Delphi 156 40 37N 86 40W
Delphos 156 40 51N 84 17W
Delportshoop 128 28 22 S 24 20 E
Delray Beach 157 26 27N 80 4W
Delsbo 72 61 48N 16 32 E
Delta, Colo., U.S.A. 161 38 44N 108 5W
Delta, Utah, U.S.A. 160 39 21N 112 29W
Delta Amacuro □ 174 8 30N 61 30W
Deltaville 162 37 33N 76 20W
Delungra 139 29 39 S 150 51 E
Delvin 38 53 37N 7 8W
Delvina 68 39 59N 20 4 E
Delvinákion 68 39 57N 20 32 E
Demak 103 6 50 S 110 40 E
Demanda, Sierra de la 58 42 15N 3 0W
Demba 124 5 28 S 22 15 E
Dembecha 123 10 32N 37 30 E
Dembi 123 8 5N 36 25 E
Dembia 126 3 33N 25 48 E
Dembidolo 123 8 34N 34 50 E
Demchok 93 32 40N 79 29 E
Demer, R. 47 51 0N 5 8 E
Demerais, L. 150 47 35N 77 0W
Demerara, R. 174 7 0N 58 0W
Demidov 80 55 10N 31 30 E
Deming 161 32 10N 107 50W
Demini, R. 174 0 46N 62 56W
Demmin 48 53 54N 13 2 E
Demmit 152 55 20N 119 50W
Demnate 118 31 44N 6 59W
Demonte 62 44 18N 7 18 E
Demopolis 157 32 30N 87 48W
Dempo, Mt. 102 4 10 S 103 15 E
Demyansk 80 57 30N 32 27 E
Den Bemmel 46 51 43N 4 26 E
Den Burg 46 53 3N 4 47 E
Den Chai 100 17 59N 100 4 E
Den Dungen 47 51 41N 5 22 E
Den Haag = 's Gravenhage 46 52 7N 4 17 E
Den Ham 46 52 28N 6 30 E
Den Helder 46 52 57N 4 45 E
Den Hulst 46 52 36N 6 16 E
Den Oever 46 52 56N 5 2 E
Denain 43 50 20N 3 22 E
Denair 163 37 32N 120 48W
Denau 85 38 16N 67 54 E
Denbigh 31 53 12N 3 26W
Denbigh (□) 26 53 8N 3 30W
Denby Dale 33 53 35N 1 40W
Denchin 99 31 35N 95 15 E
Dendang 102 3 7 S 107 56 E
Dender, R. 47 51 2N 4 6 E
Denderhoutem 47 50 53N 4 2 E
Denderleeuw 47 50 54N 4 5 E
Dendermonde 47 51 2N 4 5 E
Deneba 123 9 47N 39 10 E
Denekamp 46 52 22N 7 1 E
Denezhkin Kamen, Gora 84 60 25N 59 32 E
Denge 121 12 52N 5 21 E
Dengi 121 9 25N 9 55 E
Denham 137 25 56 S 113 31 E
Denham Ra. 138 21 55 S 147 46 E
Denham Sd. 137 25 45 S 113 15 E
Denholm 153 52 40N 108 0W
Denia 59 38 49N 0 8 E
Denial B. 139 32 14 S 133 32 E
Deniliquin 141 35 30 S 144 58 E
Denison, Iowa, U.S.A. 158 42 0N 95 18W
Denison, Texas, U.S.A. 159 33 50N 96 40W
Denison Plains 136 18 35 S 128 0 E
Denison Range 136 28 30 S 136 5 E
Denisovka 84 52 28N 61 46 E
Denizli 92 37 42N 29 2 E
Denkez Iyesus 123 12 27N 37 43 E
Denman 141 32 24 S 150 42 E
Denmark 137 34 59 S 117 18 E
Denmark ■ 73 55 30N 9 0 E
Denmark Str. 14 66 0N 30 0W
Dennis Hd. 37 59 23N 2 26W
Denniston 143 41 45 S 171 49 E
Denny 35 56 1N 3 55W
Denpasar 102 8 45 S 115 5 E
Dent 32 54 17N 2 28W
Denton, E. Sussex, U.K. 29 50 48N 0 5 E
Denton, Gr. Manchester, U.K. 32 53 26N 2 10W
Denton, Lincs., U.K. 33 52 52N 0 42W
Denton, Md., U.S.A. 162 38 53N 75 50W
Denton, Mont., U.S.A. 160 47 25N 109 56W
Denton, Texas, U.S.A. 159 33 12N 97 10W
D'Entrecasteaux, C. 137 34 50 S 115 59 E
D'Entrecasteaux Is. 135 9 0 S 151 0 E
D'Entrecasteaux Pt. 137 34 50 S 115 57 E
Dents du Midi 50 46 10N 6 56 E
Denu 121 6 4N 1 8 E
Denver, Colo., U.S.A. 158 39 45N 105 0W
Denver, Pa., U.S.A. 162 40 14N 76 8W
Denver City 159 32 58N 102 48W
Deoband 94 29 42N 77 43 E
Deobhog 96 19 53N 82 44 E
Deogarh 96 21 32N 84 45 E
Deoghar 95 24 30N 86 59 E
Deolali 96 19 50N 73 50 E
Deoli 94 25 50N 75 50 E
Deoria 95 26 31N 83 48 E
Deosai, Mts. 95 35 40N 75 0 E
Deposit 162 42 5N 75 23W
Depot Spring 137 27 55 S 120 3 E
Depuch I. 136 20 35 S 117 44 E
Deputatskiy 77 69 18N 139 54 E
Dera Ghazi Khan 94 30 5N 70 43 E
Dera Ismail Khan 94 31 50N 70 50 E
Dera Ismail Khan □ 94 32 30N 70 0 E
Derati Wells 126 3 52N 36 37 E
Derbent 74 42 5N 48 15 E
Derby, Austral. 136 17 18 S 123 38 E
Derby, U.K. 33 52 55N 1 28W
Derby, U.S.A. 162 41 20N 73 5W
Derby □ 33 52 55N 1 28W
Derecske 53 47 20N 21 33 E
Derg, L. 39 53 0N 8 20W
Derg, R. 38 54 42N 7 26W
Dergachi 81 50 3N 36 3 E
Dergaon 99 26 45N 94 0 E
Dermantsi 67 43 8N 24 17 E
Derna 117 32 40N 22 35 E
Dernieres Isles 159 29 0N 90 45W
Derriana, L. 39 51 54N 10 1W
Derrinallum 140 37 57 S 143 15 E
Derry R. 39 52 43N 6 35W
Derrybrien 39 53 4N 8 38W
Derrygonnelly 38 54 25N 7 50W
Derrygrogan 39 53 19N 7 23W
Derrykeighan 38 55 8N 6 30W
Derrylin 38 54 12N 7 34W
Derry = Londonderry 38 55 0N 7 19W
Derrynasaggart Mts. 39 51 58N 9 15W
Derryrush 38 53 23N 9 40W
Derryveagh Mts. 38 55 0N 8 40W
Derudub 122 17 31N 36 7 E
Dervaig 34 56 35N 6 13W
Derval 42 47 40N 1 41W
Dervéni 69 38 8N 22 25 E
Derwent 153 53 41N 110 58W
Derwent, R., Derby, U.K. 33 52 53N 1 17W
Derwent, R., N. Yorks., U.K. 33 53 45N 0 57W
Derwent, R., Tyne & Wear, U.K. 35 54 58N 1 40W
Derwentwater, L. 32 53 34N 3 9W
Des Moines, Iowa, U.S.A. 158 41 35N 93 37W
Des Moines, N. Mex., U.S.A. 159 36 50N 103 51W
Des Moines, R. 158 40 23N 91 25W
Desaguadero, R., Argent. 172 33 28 S 67 15W
Desaguadero, R., Boliv. 174 17 30 S 68 0W
Desborough 29 52 27N 0 50W
Deschaillons 151 46 32N 72 7W
Descharme, R. 153 56 51N 109 13W
Deschutes, R. 160 45 30N 121 0W
Dese 123 11 5N 39 40 E
Deseado, R. 176 40 0 S 69 0W
Desemboque 164 30 30N 112 27W
Desenzano del Gardo 62 45 28N 10 32 E
Desert Center 161 33 45N 115 27W
Desert Hot Springs 163 33 58N 116 30W
Desertmartin 38 54 47N 6 40W
Desford 28 52 38N 1 19W
Désirade, I. 167 16 18N 61 3W
Deskenatlata L. 152 60 55N 112 3W
Desna, R. 80 52 0N 33 15 E
Desnŭtui, R. 70 44 15N 23 27 E
Desolación, I. 176 53 0 S 74 0W
Despeñaperros, Paso 59 38 24N 3 30W
Despotovac 66 44 6N 21 30 E
Dessa 121 14 44N 1 6 E
Dessau 48 51 49N 12 15 E
Dessel 47 51 15N 5 7 E
Dessye = Dese 123 11 5N 39 40 E
D'Estress B. 140 35 55 S 137 45 E
Desuri 94 25 18N 73 35 E
Desvrès 43 50 40N 1 48 E
Det Udom 100 14 54N 105 5 E
Detinjá, R. 66 43 51N 19 45 E
Detmold 48 51 55N 8 50 E
Detour Pt. 156 45 37N 86 35W
Detroit, Mich., U.S.A. 150 42 13N 83 22W
Detroit, Tex., U.S.A. 159 33 40N 95 10W
Detroit Lakes 158 46 50N 95 50W
Dett 127 18 32 S 26 57 E
Dettifoss 74 65 49N 16 24W
Děčín 52 50 47N 14 12 E
Deurne, Belg. 47 51 12N 4 24 E
Deurne, Neth. 47 51 27N 5 49 E
Deutsche Bucht 48 54 10N 7 51 E
Deutschlandsberg 52 46 49N 15 14 E
Deux-Acren, Les 47 50 44N 3 51 E
Deux-Sèvres □ 42 46 35N 0 20W
Deva 70 45 53N 22 55 E
Devakottai 97 9 55N 78 45 E
Devaprayag 95 30 13N 78 35 E
Dévaványa 53 47 2N 20 59 E
Deveci Daği 82 40 10N 36 0 E
Devecser 53 47 6N 17 26 E
Deventer 46 52 15N 6 10 E
Deveron, R. 37 57 40N 2 31W
Devesel 70 44 28N 22 41 E
Devgad, I. 97 14 48N 74 5 E
Devil R., Pk. 143 40 56 S 172 37 E
Devils Bridge 31 52 23N 3 50W
Devils Den 163 35 46N 119 58W
Devils Lake 158 48 5N 98 50W
Devils Paw, mt. 152 58 47N 134 0W
Devils Pt. 97 9 26N 80 6 E
Devilsbit Mt. 39 52 50N 7 58W
Devin 67 41 44N 24 24 E
Devizes 28 51 21N 2 0W
Devnya 67 43 13N 27 33 E
Devolli, R. 68 40 57N 20 15 E
Devon 152 53 24N 113 44W
Devon I. 12 75 47N 88 0W
Devonport, Austral. 138 41 10 S 146 22 E
Devonport, N.Z. 142 36 49 S 174 49 E
Devonport, U.K. 30 50 23N 4 11W
Devonshire □ 30 50 50N 3 40W
Dewas 94 22 59N 76 3 E
Dewetsdorp 128 29 33 S 26 39 E
Dewgad Baria 94 22 40N 73 55 E
Dewsbury 33 53 42N 1 38W
Dexter, Mo., U.S.A. 159 36 50N 90 0W
Dexter, N. Mex., U.S.A. 159 33 15N 104 25W
Dey-Dey, L. 137 29 12 S 131 4 E
Deyhuk 93 33 15N 104 25W
Deyyer 93 27 55N 51 55 E
Dezadeash L. 152 60 28N 136 58W
Dezfūl 92 32 20N 48 30 E
Dezh Shanpur 92 35 30N 46 25 E
Dezhneva, Mys 77 66 10N 169 3 E
Dhaba 92 27 25N 35 40 E
Dháfni 69 37 48N 22 1 E
Dhahaban 122 21 58N 39 3 E
Dhahiriya = Qz Zahiriya 90 31 25N 34 58 E
Dhahran 92 26 9N 50 10 E
Dhama Dzong 99 28 15N 91 15 E
Dhamási 68 39 43N 22 11 E
Dhampur 95 29 19N 78 33 E
Dhamtari 96 20 42N 81 35 E
Dhanbad 95 23 50N 86 30 E
Dhangarhi 99 28 55N 80 40 E
Dhankuta 95 26 55N 87 20 E
Dhanora 96 20 20N 80 22 E
Dhar 94 22 35N 75 26 E
Dharampur, Mad. P., India 94 22 13N 75 18 E
Dharampur, Maharashtra, India 96 20 32N 73 17 E
Dharapuram 97 10 45N 77 34 E
Dharmapuri 97 12 10N 78 10 E
Dharmavaram 97 14 29N 77 44 E
Dharmsala, (Dharamsala) 94 32 16N 73 23 E
Dhaulagiri Mt. 95 28 45N 83 45 E
Dhebar, L. 94 24 10N 74 0 E
Dhenkanal 96 20 45N 85 35 E
Dhenoúsa 69 37 8N 25 48 E
Dhesfina 69 38 25N 22 31 E
Dheskáti 68 39 55N 21 49 E
Dhespotikó 69 36 57N 24 58 E
Dhidhimótikhon 68 41 22N 26 29 E
Dhikti, Mt. 69 35 8N 25 29 E
Dhilianáta 69 38 15N 20 34 E
Dhílos 69 37 23N 25 15 E
Dhimitsána 69 37 36N 22 3 E
Dhirfis, Mt. 69 38 40N 23 54 E
Dhodhekánisos 69 36 35N 27 0 E
Dhofar 91 17 0N 54 10 E
Dhokós 69 37 20N 23 20 E
Dholiana 68 39 54N 20 32 E
Dholka 94 22 44N 72 29 E
Dholpur 94 26 45N 77 59 E
Dhomokós 69 39 10N 22 18 E
Dhond 96 18 26N 74 40 E
Dhoraji 94 21 45N 70 37 E
Dhoxáthon 68 41 9N 24 16 E
Dhragonisi 69 37 27N 25 29 E
Dhrangadhra 94 22 59N 71 31 E
Dhriopós 69 37 35N 24 35 E
Dhrol 94 22 40N 70 25 E
Dhubaibah 93 23 25N 54 35 E
Dhubri 98 26 2N 90 2 E
Dhulasar 98 21 52N 90 14 E
Dhulia 96 20 58N 74 50 E
Dhupdhara 98 25 58N 91 4 E
Dhurm 122 20 18N 42 53 E
Di Linh 101 11 35N 108 4 E
Di Linh, Cao Nguyen 101 11 30N 108 0 E
Dia, I. 69 35 26N 25 13 E
Diable, Mt. 163 37 53N 121 56W
Diablerets, Les 50 46 22N 7 10 E
Diablo Range 163 37 0N 121 5W
Diafarabé 120 14 17N 4 57W
Diala 120 13 59N 10 0W
Dialakoro 120 12 18N 7 54W
Diallassagou 120 13 47N 3 41W
Diamante 172 32 5 S 60 40W
Diamante, R. 172 34 31 S 66 56W
Diamantina 171 18 5 S 43 40W
Diamantina, R. 138 22 25 S 142 20 E
Diamantino 175 14 30 S 56 30W
Diamond Harbour 95 22 11N 88 14 E
Diamond Is. 138 17 25 S 151 5 E
Diamond Mts. 160 40 0N 115 58W
Diamond Springs 163 38 42N 120 49W
Diamondville 160 41 51N 110 30W
Diano Marina 62 43 55N 8 3 E
Dianópolis 171 11 38 S 46 50W
Dianra 120 8 45N 6 14W
Diaole, Î. du. 170 5 15N 52 45W
Diapaga 121 12 5N 1 46 E
Diapangou 121 12 5N 0 10 E
Diapur 140 36 19 S 141 29 E
Diariguila 120 10 35N 10 2W
Dibai (Dubai) 93 25 15N 55 20 E
Dibaya 124 6 20 S 22 0 E
Dibaya Lubue 124 4 12 S 19 54 E
Dibba 93 25 45N 56 16 E
Dibbi 123 4 10N 41 52 E
Dibden 28 50 53N 1 24W
Dibega 92 35 50N 43 46 E
Dibër 68 41 38N 20 15 E
Dibete 128 23 45 S 26 32 E
Dibi 123 4 10N 41 52 E
Dibrugarh 98 27 29N 94 55 E
Dibulla 174 11 17N 73 19W
Dickinson 158 46 50N 102 40W
Dickson 157 36 5N 87 22W
Dickson City 162 41 29N 75 40W
Dicomano 63 43 53 S 11 30 E
Didam 46 51 57N 6 8 E
Didcot 28 51 36N 1 14W
Didesa, W. 123 9 40N 35 50 E
Didiéni 120 14 5N 7 50W
Didsbury 152 51 35N 114 10W
Didwana 94 27 17N 74 25 E
Die 45 44 47N 5 22 E
Diébougou 120 11 0N 3 15W
Diefenbaker L. 153 51 0N 106 55W
Diego Garcia, I. 11 9 50 S 75 0 E
Diégo Suarez 129 12 25 S 49 20 E
Diekirch 47 49 52N 6 10 E
Diélette 42 49 33N 1 52W
Diéma 120 14 32N 9 3W
Diemen 46 52 21N 4 58 E
Dieméring 120 12 29N 16 47W
Dien Ban 100 15 53N 108 16 E
Diên Biên Phu 100 21 20N 103 0 E
Dien Khanh 101 12 15N 109 6 E
Diepenheim 46 52 12N 6 33 E
Diepenveen 46 52 18N 6 9 E
Diepholz 48 52 37N 8 22 E
Diepoldsau 51 47 23N 9 40 E
Dieppe 42 49 54N 1 4 E
Dieren 46 52 3N 6 6 E
Dierks 159 34 9N 94 0W
Diessen 47 51 29N 5 10 E
Diessenhofen 51 47 42N 8 46 E
Diest 47 50 58N 5 4 E
Dietikon 51 47 24N 8 24 E
Dieulefit 45 44 32N 5 4 E
Dieuze 43 48 30N 6 40 E

Donya Lendava **Duncan Town**

Donya Lendava 63 46 35N 16 25E
Donzère 45 44 28N 4 43E
Donzy 43 47 20N 3 6E
Dooagh 38 53 59N 10 7W
Doochary 38 54 54N 8 10W
Doodlakine 137 31 34S 117 51E
Dooega Hd. 38 53 54N 10 3W
Doon L. 34 55 15N 4 22W
Doon, R. 34 55 26N 4 41W
Doonbeg 39 52 44N 9 31W
Doonbeg R. 39 52 42N 9 20W
Doorn 46 52 2N 5 20E
Dor (Tantura) 90 32 37N 34 55E
Dora Báltea, R. 62 45 42N 7 25E
Dora, L. 136 22 0S 123 0E
Dora Riparia, R. 62 45 7N 7 24E
Dorada, La 174 5 30N 74 40W
Dorading 123 8 30N 33 5E
Doran L. 153 61 13N 108 6W
Dorat, Le 44 46 14N 1 5E
Dörby 73 56 20N 16 12E
Dorchester, Dorset, U.K. 28 50 42N 2 28W
Dorchester, Oxon., U.K. 28 51 38N 1 10W
Dorchester, C. 149 65 27N 77 27W
Dordogne □ 44 45 5N 0 40E
Dordogne, R. 44 45 2N 0 36W
Dordrecht, Neth. 46 51 48N 4 39E
Dordrecht, S. Afr. 128 31 20S 27 3E
Doré L. 153 54 46N 107 17W
Doré Lake 153 54 38N 107 54W
Dore, Mt. 44 45 32N 2 50E
Dore, R. 44 45 59N 3 28E
Dores 37 57 22N 4 20W
Dores do Indaiá 171 19 27S 45 36W
Dorfen 49 48 16N 12 10E
Dorgali 64 40 18N 9 35E
Dori 121 14 3N 0 2W
Doring, R. 128 32 30S 19 30E
Dorion 150 45 23N 74 3W
Dorking 29 51 14N 0 20W
Dormaa-Ahenkro 120 7 15N 2 52W
Dormo, Ras 123 13 14N 42 35E
Dornach 50 47 29N 7 37E
Dornberg 63 45 45N 13 50E
Dornbirn 52 47 25N 9 45E
Dornes 43 46 48N 3 18E
Dornie 36 57 17N 5 30W
Dornoch 37 57 52N 4 0W
Dornoch, Firth of 37 57 52N 4 0W
Dornogovi □ 106 44 0N 110 0E
Doro 121 16 9N 0 51W
Dorog 53 47 42N 18 45E
Dorogobuzh 80 54 50N 33 10E
Dorohoi 70 47 56N 26 30E
Döröö Nuur 105 47 40N 93 30E
Dorre I. 137 25 13S 113 12E
Dorrigo 141 30 20S 152 44E
Dorris 160 41 59N 121 58W
Dorset □ 28 50 48N 2 25W
Dorsten 48 51 40N 6 55E
Dorstone 28 52 4N 3 0W
Dortmund 48 51 32N 7 28E
Dörtyol 92 36 52N 36 12E
Dorum 48 53 40N 8 33E
Doruma 126 4 42N 27 33E
Dorya, W. 123 5 15N 41 30E
Dos Bahías, C. 176 44 58S 65 32W
Dos Cabezas 161 32 1N 109 37W
Dos Hermanas 57 37 16N 5 55W
Dos Palos 163 36 59N 120 37W
Dosara 121 12 20N 6 5E
Doshi 93 35 35N 68 50E
Dosso 121 13 0N 3 13E
Döstrup 73 56 41N 9 42E
Dot 152 50 12N 121 25W
Dothan 157 31 10N 85 25W
Dottignies 47 50 44N 3 19E
Dotty, gasfield 19 53 3N 1 48E
Douai 43 50 21N 3 4E
Douala 121 4 0N 9 45E
Douarnenez 42 48 6N 4 21W
Double Island Pt. 139 25 56S 153 11E
Doubrava, R. 52 49 40N 15 30E
Doubs □ 43 47 10N 6 20E
Doubs, R. 43 46 53N 5 1E
Doubtful B. 137 34 15S 119 28E
Doubtful Sd. 143 45 20S 166 49E
Doubtless B. 142 34 55S 173 26E
Doucet 150 48 15N 76 35W
Doudeville 42 49 43N 0 47E
Doué 42 47 11N 0 20W
Douentza 120 14 58N 2 48W
Douglas, S. Afr. 128 29 4S 23 46E
Douglas, U.K. 32 54 9N 4 29W
Douglas, U.K. 35 55 33N 3 50W
Douglas, Alaska, U.S.A. 147 58 23N 134 32W
Douglas, Ariz., U.S.A. 161 31 21N 109 30W
Douglas, Ga., U.S.A. 157 31 32N 82 52W
Douglas, Wyo., U.S.A. 158 42 45N 105 20W
Douglas Hd. 32 54 9N 4 28W
Douglastown 151 48 46N 64 24W
Douglasville 157 33 46N 84 43W
Douirat 118 33 2N 4 11W
Doukáton, Ákra 69 38 34N 20 30E
Doulevant 43 48 22N 4 53E
Doullens 43 50 10N 2 20E
Doulus Hd. 39 51 57N 10 19W
Doumé 124 4 15N 13 25E
Douna 120 12 40N 6 0W
Dounby 37 59 4N 3 13W
Doune 35 56 12N 4 3W
Dounreay 37 58 40N 3 28W
Dour 47 50 24N 3 46E
Dourada, Serra 171 13 10S 48 45W
Dourados 173 22 9S 54 50W
Dourados, R. 173 21 58S 54 18W
Dourdan 43 48 30N 2 0E
Douro Litoral □ 55 41 10N 8 20W
Douro, R. 56 41 1N 8 16W
Douŭzeci Si Trei August 70 43 50N 28 40E
Douvaine 45 46 19N 6 16E
Douz 119 33 25N 9 0E
Dove 32 52 51N 1 36W
Dove Brook 151 53 40N 57 40W
Dove Creek 161 37 53N 108 59W
Dove Dale 33 53 10N 1 47W
Dove, R. 33 54 20N 0 55W
Dover, Austral. 138 43 18S 147 2E
Dover, U.K. 29 51 7N 1 19E
Dover, Del., U.S.A. 162 39 10N 75 31W
Dover, N.H., U.S.A. 162 43 5N 70 51W
Dover, N.J., U.S.A. 162 40 53N 74 34W
Dover, Ohio, U.S.A. 156 40 32N 81 30W
Dover-Foxcroft 151 45 14N 69 14W
Dover Plains 162 41 43N 73 35W
Dover, Pt. 137 32 32S 125 32E
Dover, Str. of 16 51 0N 1 30E
Doveridge 32 52 54N 1 49E
Dovey, R. 31 52 32N 4 0W
Dovre 71 62 0N 9 15E
Dovrefjell 71 62 15N 9 33E
Dowa 127 13 38S 33 58E
Dowagiac 156 42 0N 86 8W
Dowlatabad 93 28 20N 50 40E
Down □ 38 54 20N 5 50W
Down, Co. 38 54 20N 6 0W
Downey 160 42 29N 112 3W
Downham 29 52 26N 0 15E
Downham Market 29 52 36N 0 22E
Downhill 38 55 10N 6 48W
Downieville 160 39 34N 120 50W
Downpatrick 38 54 20N 5 43W
Downpatrick Hd. 38 54 20N 9 21W
Downs Division 139 27 10S 150 44E
Downs, The 38 53 30N 7 15W
Downsville 162 42 5N 74 60W
Downton 28 51 0N 1 44W
Dowra 38 54 11N 8 2W
Doylestown 162 40 21N 75 10W
Doyung 99 33 40N 99 25E
Dra, Cap 118 28 58N 11 0W
Draa, O. 118 30 29N 6 1W
Drachten 46 53 7N 6 5E
Drăgăneşti 70 44 9N 24 32E
Drăgăneşti-Viaşca 70 44 5N 25 33E
Dragaš 66 42 5N 20 35E
Drăgăsani 70 44 39N 24 17E
Dragina 66 44 30N 19 25E
Dragocvet 66 44 0N 21 15E
Dragonera, I. 58 39 35N 2 19E
Dragon's Mouth 174 11 0N 61 50W
Dragovistica, (Berivol) 66 42 22N 22 39E
Draguignan 45 43 30N 6 27E
Drain 160 43 45N 123 17W
Drake, Austral. 139 28 55S 152 25E
Drake, U.S.A. 158 47 56N 100 31W
Drake Passage 13 58 0S 68 0W
Drakensberg 129 31 0S 25 0E
Dráma 68 41 9N 24 10E
Dráma □ 68 41 10N 24 0E
Drammen 71 59 42N 10 12E
Drangajökull 74 66 9N 22 15W
Drangan 39 52 32N 7 36W
Drangedal 71 59 6N 9 3E
Dranov, Ostrov 70 44 55N 29 30E
Draperstown 38 54 48N 6 47E
Dras 95 34 25N 75 48E
Drau, R. 52 47 46N 13 33E
Drava, R. 66 45 50N 18 0W
Draveil 43 48 41N 2 25E
Dravograd 63 46 36N 15 5E
Drawa, R. 54 53 6N 15 56E
Drawno 54 53 13N 15 46E
Drawsko Pom 54 53 35N 15 50E
Drayton Valley 152 53 25N 114 58W
Dreghorn 34 55 36N 4 30W
Dreibergen 46 52 3N 5 17E
Drejö 73 54 58N 10 25E
Dren 66 43 8N 20 44E
Drenagh 38 55 3N 6 55W
Drenthe □ 54 52 52N 6 40E
Drentsche Hoofdvaart 46 52 39N 6 4E
Dresden 48 51 2N 13 45E
Dresden □ 48 51 12N 14 0E
Dreumel 47 51 51N 5 26E
Dreux 42 48 44N 1 23E
Drezdenko 54 52 50N 15 49E
Driel 46 51 57N 5 49E
Driffield 33 54 0N 0 25W
Driftwood 150 49 8N 81 23E
Drigana 119 20 51N 12 17E
Driggs 160 43 50N 111 8W
Drimnin 36 56 36N 6 0W
Drimoleague 39 51 40N 9 15W
Drin-i-zi, R. 68 41 37N 20 28E
Drina, R. 66 44 30N 19 10E
Drincea, R. 70 44 20N 22 55E
Drînceni 70 46 49N 28 10E
Drini, R. 68 42 20N 20 0E
Drinjača, R. 66 44 20N 19 0E
Driva 71 62 33N 9 38E
Driva, R. 71 62 34N 9 33E
Drivstua 71 62 26N 9 37E
Drniš 63 43 51N 16 10E
Drøbak 71 59 39N 10 39E
Dröbak 75 59 39N 10 48E
Drobbakk 71 59 39N 10 39E
Drobin 54 52 42N 19 58E
Drogheda 38 53 45N 6 20W
Drogichin 80 52 15N 25 8E
Drogobych 80 49 20N 23 30E
Droichead Nua 39 53 11N 6 50W
Droitwich 28 52 16N 2 10W
Dromahair 38 54 13N 8 18W
Dromara 38 54 21N 6 1W
Dromard 38 54 14N 8 40W
Drôme □ 45 44 38N 5 15E
Drôme, R. 45 44 46N 4 46E
Dromedary, C. 141 36 17S 150 10E
Dromiskin 38 53 56N 6 25W
Dromod 38 53 52N 7 55W
Dromore, Down, U.K. 38 54 24N 6 10W
Dromore, Tyrone, U.K. 38 54 31N 7 28W
Dromore West 38 54 15N 8 50W
Dronero 62 44 29N 7 22E
Dronfield, Austral. 138 21 12S 140 3E
Dronfield, U.K. 33 53 18N 1 29W
Dronninglund 73 57 10N 10 19E
Dronrijp 46 53 11N 5 39E
Drosendorf 52 48 52N 15 37E
Drouin 141 38 10S 145 53E
Drouzhba 67 43 22N 28 0E
Drum 38 54 6N 7 9W
Drumbeg, N. Ire., U.K. 38 54 33N 6 0W
Drumbeg, Scot., U.K. 36 58 15N 5 12W
Drumcard 38 54 14N 7 42W
Drumcliffe 38 54 20N 8 30W
Drumcondra 38 53 50N 6 40W
Drumheller 152 51 25N 112 40W
Drumjohn 34 55 14N 4 15W
Drumkeerin 38 54 10N 8 8W
Drumlish 38 53 50N 7 47W
Drummond 160 46 46N 113 4W
Drummond I. 150 46 0N 83 40W
Drummond Pt. 139 34 9S 135 16E
Drummond Ra. 138 23 45S 147 10E
Drummondville 150 45 55N 72 25W
Drummore 34 54 41N 4 53W
Drumquin 38 54 38N 7 30W
Drumright 159 35 59N 96 38W
Drumshanbo 38 54 2N 8 4W
Drumsna 38 53 57N 8 0W
Drunen 47 51 41N 5 8E
Druridge B. 35 55 16N 1 32W
Druskinankaj 80 54 3N 23 58E
Drut, R. 80 52 32N 30 0E
Druten 46 51 53N 5 36E
Druya 80 55 45N 27 15E
Druzhina 77 68 14N 145 18E
Drvar 63 44 21N 16 2E
Drvenik 63 43 27N 16 3E
Dry Tortugas 166 24 38N 82 55W
Dryanovo 67 42 59N 25 28E
Dryden, Can. 153 49 50N 92 50W
Dryden, N.Y., U.S.A. 162 42 30N 76 18W
Dryden, Tex., U.S.A. 159 30 3N 102 3W
Drygalski I. 13 66 0S 92 0E
Drygarn Fawr 31 52 13N 3 39W
Drymen 70 56 4N 4 28W
Drynoch 36 57 17N 6 18W
Drysdale I. 138 11 41S 136 0E
Drysdale, R. 136 13 59S 126 51E
Dschang 121 5 32N 10 3E
Du 121 10 26N 1 34W
Du Bois 156 41 8N 78 46W
Du Quoin 158 38 0N 89 10W
Duanesburg 162 42 45N 74 11W
Duaringa 138 23 42S 149 42E
Duba 92 27 10N 35 40E
Dubai = Dubayy 93 24 10N 55 20E
Dubawnt, L. 153 63 4N 101 42W
Dubawnt, R. 153 64 33N 100 6W
Dubbayy 93 24 10N 55 20E
Dubbeldam 46 51 47N 4 43E
Dubbo 141 32 11S 148 35E
Dubele 126 2 56N 29 35E
Dübendorf 51 47 24N 8 37E
Dubenskiy 84 51 27N 56 38E
Dubh Artach 34 56 8N 6 40W
Dubica 63 45 17N 16 48E
Dublin, Ireland 38 53 20N 6 18W
Dublin, Ga., U.S.A. 157 32 30N 83 0W
Dublin, Tex., U.S.A. 159 32 0N 98 20W
Dublin □ 38 53 24N 6 20W
Dublin, B. 39 53 24N 6 20W
Dubna 81 54 8N 36 52E
Dubno 80 50 25N 25 45E
Dubois 160 44 7N 112 9W
Dubossary 82 47 15N 29 10E
Dubossasy Vdkhr. 82 47 30N 29 0E
Dubovka 83 49 5N 44 50E
Dubovskoye 83 47 28N 42 40E
Dubrajpur 95 23 48N 87 25E
Dubrékah 120 9 46N 13 31W
Dubrovitsa 80 51 31N 26 35E
Dubrovnik 66 42 39N 18 6E
Dubrovskoye 77 58 55N 111 0E
Dubuque 158 42 30N 90 41W
Duchesne 160 40 14N 110 22W
Duchess 138 21 20S 139 50E
Ducie I. 131 24 47S 124 40W
Duck Cr., N.S.W., Austral. 139 31 4S 147 6E
Duck Cr., W. Australia, Austral. 136 22 37S 116 53E
Duck Lake 153 52 50N 106 16W
Duck, Mt. 153 51 27N 100 35W
Duck Mt. Prov. Parks 153 51 45N 101 0W
Duckwall Mtn. 163 37 58N 120 7W
Duddington 29 52 36N 0 32W
Duddon R. 32 54 12N 3 15W
Düdelange 47 49 29N 6 5E
Duderstadt 48 51 30N 10 15E
Dudhi 99 24 15N 83 10E
Dudhnai 98 25 59N 90 47E
Düdingen 50 46 52N 7 12E
Dudinka 77 69 30N 86 0E
Dudley 28 52 30N 2 5W
Dudna, R. 96 19 36N 76 20E
Dueñas 56 41 52N 4 33W
Dūeni 70 44 51N 28 10E
Dueodde 73 54 59N 15 4E
Dueré 171 11 20S 49 17W
Duero, R. 56 41 37N 4 25W
Duff Is. 142 9 0S 167 0E
Duffel 47 51 6N 4 30E
Duffield 33 52 59N 1 30W
Dufftown 37 57 26N 3 9W
Dufourspitz 50 45 56N 7 52E
Dugi, I. 63 44 0N 15 0E
Dugo Selo 63 45 51N 16 18E
Duhak 93 33 20N 57 30E
Duifken Pt. 138 12 33S 141 38E
Duisburg 48 51 27N 6 42E
Duitama 174 5 50N 73 2W
Duiveland 47 51 38N 4 0E
Duiwelskloof 129 23 42S 30 10E
Dukana 126 3 59N 37 20E
Dukati 68 40 16N 19 32E
Duke I. 152 54 50N 131 20W
Dukhan 93 25 25N 50 50E
Dukhovshchina 80 55 15N 32 27E
Duki 93 30 14N 68 25E
Dukla 54 49 30N 21 35E
Duku, North-Eastern, Nigeria 121 10 43N 10 43E
Duku, North-Western, Nigeria 121 11 11N 4 55E
Dulas B. 31 53 22N 4 16W
Dulawan 103 7 5N 124 20E
Dulce, Golfo 166 8 40N 83 20W
Dulce, R. 172 29 30S 63 0W
Duleek 38 53 40N 6 24W
Dŭlgopol 67 43 3N 27 22E
Dullewala 94 31 50N 71 25E
Dülmen 48 51 49N 7 18E
Dulnain Bridge 37 57 19N 3 40W
Dulovo 67 43 48N 27 9E
Dululu 138 23 48S 150 15E
Duluth 158 46 48N 92 10W
Dulverton 28 51 2N 3 33W
Dum Dum 95 22 39N 88 26E
Dum Duma 99 27 40N 95 40E
Dumaguete 103 9 17N 123 15E
Dumai 102 1 35N 101 20E
Dumaran I. 103 10 33N 119 50E
Dumaring 103 1 46N 118 10E
Dumas, Ark., U.S.A. 159 33 52N 91 30W
Dumas, Okla., U.S.A. 159 35 50N 101 58W
Dūmat al Jandal 92 29 55N 39 40E
Dumba I. 71 61 43N 4 50E
Dumbarton 34 55 58N 4 35W
Dumbleyung 137 33 17S 117 42E
Dumbrăveni 70 46 14N 24 34E
Dumfries 35 55 4N 3 37W
Dumfries & Galloway □ 35 54 30N 4 0W
Dumfries (□) 26 55 0N 3 30W
Dŭmienesti 70 46 44N 27 1E
Dumka 95 24 0N 87 22E
Dumoine L. 150 46 55N 77 55W
Dumoine, R. 150 46 13N 77 51W
Dumraon 95 25 33N 84 8E
Dumyât 122 31 24N 31 48E
Dumyât, Masabb 122 31 28N 32 0E
Dun Laoghaire, (Dunleary) 39 53 17N 6 9W
Dun-le-Palestel 44 46 18N 1 39E
Dun-sur-Auron 43 46 53N 2 33E
Duna, R. 53 45 51N 18 48E
Dunaff Hd. 38 55 18N 7 30W
Dunaföldvár 53 46 50N 18 57E
Dunai, R. 53 47 50N 18 52E
Dunaj, R. 67 45 17N 29 32E
Dunajec, R. 54 50 12N 20 52E
Dunajska Streda 53 48 0N 17 37E
Dunamanagh 38 54 53N 7 20W
Dunans 34 56 4N 5 9W
Dunany Pt. 38 53 51N 6 15W
Dunapatai 53 46 39N 19 4E
Dunaszekcsö 53 46 22N 18 45E
Dunaújváros 53 47 0N 18 57E
Dunav, R. 66 45 0N 20 21E
Dunavtsi 66 43 57N 22 53E
Dunback 143 45 23S 170 36E
Dunbar, Austral. 138 16 0S 142 22E
Dunbar, U.K. 35 56 0N 2 32W
Dunbarton (□) 26 56 4N 4 42W
Dunbeath 37 58 15N 3 25W
Dunblane 35 56 10N 3 58W
Dunboyne 38 53 25N 6 30W
Duncan, Can. 152 48 45N 123 40W
Duncan, Ariz., U.S.A. 161 32 46N 109 6W
Duncan, Okla., U.S.A. 159 34 25N 98 0W
Duncan L. 152 62 51N 113 58W
Duncan, L., Brit. Col., Can. 150 50 20N 117 0W
Duncan, L., Qué., Can. 152 53 29N 77 58W
Duncan Pass. 101 11 0N 92 30E
Duncan Town 166 22 15N 75 45W

Duncansby Ecoporanga

Duncansby 37 58 37N 3 3W
Duncansby Head 37 58 39N 3 0W
Dunchurch 28 52 21N 1 19W
Duncormick 39 53 14N 6 40W
Dundalk, Ireland 38 53 55N 6 45W
Dundalk, U.S.A. 162 39 15N 76 31W
Dundalk, B. 38 53 55N 6 15W
Dundas 150 43 17N 79 59W
Dundas I. 152 54 30N 130 50W
Dundas, L. 137 32 35 S 121 50 E
Dundas Str. 136 11 15 S 131 35 E
Dundee, S. Afr. 129 28 11 S 30 15 E
Dundee, U.K. 35 56 29N 3 0W
Dundee, U.S.A. 162 42 32N 76 59W
Dundgovi □ 106 45 10N 106 0 E
Dundo 124 7 23 S 20 48 E
Dundonald 38 54 37N 5 50W
Dundoo 139 27 40 S 144 37 E
Dundrennan 35 54 49N 3 56W
Dundrum, Ireland 39 53 17N 6 15W
Dundrum, U.K. 38 54 17N 5 50W
Dundwara 95 27 48N 79 9 E
Dunedin, N.Z. 143 45 50 S 170 33 E
Dunedin, U.S.A. 157 28 1N 82 45W
Dunedin, R. 152 59 30N 124 5W
Dunfanaghy 38 55 10N 7 59W
Dunfermline 35 56 5N 3 28W
Dungannon 38 54 30N 6 47W
Dungannon □ 38 54 30N 6 55W
Dungarpur 94 23 52N 73 45 E
Dungarvan 39 52 6N 7 40W
Dungarvan Harb. 39 52 5N 7 35W
Dungas 121 13 4N 9 20 E
Dungavel 35 55 37N 4 7W
Dungbura La 99 34 41N 93 18 E
Dungeness 29 50 54N 0 59 E
Dungiven 38 54 55N 6 56W
Dunglow 38 54 57N 8 20W
Dungo, L. do 128 17 15 S 19 0 E
Dungog 141 32 22 S 151 40 E
Dungourney 39 51 58N 8 5W
Dungu 124 2 32N 28 22 E
Dungunâb 122 21 10N 37 9 E
Dungunâb, Khalîg 122 21 5N 37 12 E
Dunhinda Falls 97 7 5N 81 6 E
Dunières 45 45 13N 4 20 E
Dunk I. 138 17 59 S 146 14 E
Dunkeld, Austral. 140 37 40 S 142 22 E
Dunkeld, U.K. 37 56 34N 3 36W
Dunkerque 43 51 2N 2 20 E
Dunkery Beacon 28 51 15N 3 37W
Dunkineely 38 54 38N 8 22W
Dunkirk 156 42 30N 79 18W
Dunkirk = Dunkerque 43 51 2N 2 20 E
Dunkuj 123 11 15N 33 0 E
Dunkur 123 11 58N 35 58 E
Dunkwa, Central, Ghana 120 6 0N 1 47W
Dunkwa, Central, Ghana 121 5 30N 1 0W
Dunlap 158 41 50N 95 30W
Dunlavin 39 53 3N 6 40W
Dunleary = Dun Laoghaire 39 53 17N 6 8W
Dunleer 38 53 50N 6 23W
Dunlin, oilfield 19 61 12N 1 40 E
Dunloe, Gap of 39 52 2N 9 40W
Dunlop 34 55 43N 4 32W
Dunloy 38 55 1N 6 25W
Dunmanus B. 39 51 31N 9 50W
Dunmanway 39 51 43N 9 8W
Dunmara 138 16 42 S 133 25 E
Dunmod 105 47 45N 106 58 E
Dunmore, Ireland 38 53 37N 8 44W
Dunmore, U.S.A. 162 41 27N 75 38W
Dunmore East 39 52 9N 7 0W
Dunmore Town 166 25 30N 76 39W
Dunmurry 38 54 33N 6 0W
Dunn 157 35 18N 78 36W
Dunnellon 157 29 4N 82 28W
Dunnet 37 58 37N 3 20W
Dunnet B. 37 58 37N 3 23W
Dunnet Hd. 37 58 38N 3 22W
Dunning, U.K. 35 56 18N 3 37W
Dunning, U.S.A. 158 41 52N 100 4W
Dunolly 140 36 51 S 143 44 E
Dunoon 34 55 57N 4 56W
Dunqul 122 23 40N 31 10 E
Duns 35 55 47N 2 20W
Dunscore 35 55 8N 3 48W
Dunseith 158 48 49N 100 2W
Dunsford 30 50 41N 3 40W
Dunshaughlin 38 53 31N 6 32W
Dunsmuir 160 41 0N 122 10W
Dunstable 29 51 53N 0 31W
Dunstan Mts. 143 44 53 S 169 35 E
Dunster, Can. 152 53 8N 119 50W
Dunster, U.K. 28 51 11N 3 28W
Dunston 28 52 46N 2 7W
Duntelchaig, L. 37 57 20N 4 18W
Dunton Green 29 51 17N 0 11 E
Duntroon 143 44 51 S 170 40 E
Dunûrea, R. 70 45 0N 29 40 E
Dunvegan 36 57 26N 6 35W
Dunvegan Hd. 36 57 30N 6 42W
Dunvegan L. 153 60 8N 107 10W
Duong Dong 101 10 13N 103 58 E
Dupree 158 45 4N 101 35W
Dupuyer 160 48 11N 112 31W
Duque de Caxias 173 22 45 S 43 19W
Dura 90 31 31N 35 1 E
Durack 136 15 33 S 127 52 E
Durack Ra. 136 16 50 S 127 40 E
Durance, R. 45 43 55N 4 45 E
Durand 156 42 54N 83 58W
Durango, Mexico 164 24 3N 104 39W
Durango, Spain 58 43 13N 2 40W
Durango, U.S.A. 161 37 10N 107 50W
Durango □ 164 25 0N 105 0W
Duranillin 137 33 30 S 116 45 E
Durant 159 34 0N 96 25W
Duratón, R. 56 41 27N 4 0W
Durazno 172 33 25 S 56 38W
Durazzo = Durrësi 68 41 19N 19 28 E
Durban, France 44 43 0N 2 49W
Durban, S. Afr. 129 29 49 S 31 1 E
Dúrcal 57 37 0N 3 34W
Đurđevac 66 46 2N 17 3 E
Düren 48 50 48N 6 30 E
Durg 96 21 15N 81 22 E
Durgapur 95 23 30N 87 9 E
Durham, Can. 150 44 10N 80 49W
Durham, U.K. 33 54 47N 1 34W
Durham, N.C., U.S.A. 157 36 0N 78 55W
Durham, N.H., U.S.A. 162 43 8N 70 56W
Durham □ 32 54 42N 1 45W
Durham Downs 139 26 6 S 149 3 E
Durlstone Hd. 28 50 35N 1 58W
Durmitor Mt. 66 43 18N 19 0 E
Dûrmûneşti 70 46 21N 26 33 E
Durness 37 58 34N 4 45W
Durness, Kyle of 37 58 35N 4 55W
Durrandella 138 24 3 S 146 35 E
Durrësi 68 41 19N 19 28 E
Durrie 138 25 40 S 140 15 E
Durrington 28 51 12N 1 47W
Durrow 39 53 20N 7 31W
Durrus 39 51 37N 9 32W
Dursey Hd. 39 51 34N 10 41W
Dursey I. 39 51 36N 10 12W
Dursley 28 51 41N 2 21W
Durtal 42 47 40N 0 18W
Duru 126 4 20N 28 50 E
Durup 73 56 45N 8 57 E
D'Urville Island 143 40 50 S 173 55 E
Duryea 162 41 20N 75 45W
Dusa Mareb 91 5 40N 46 33 E
Dûsh 122 24 35N 30 41 E
Dushak 76 37 20N 60 10 E
Dushanbe 85 38 33N 68 48 E
Dusheti 83 42 0N 44 55 E
Dushore 162 41 31N 76 24W
Dusky Sd. 143 45 47 S 166 30 E
Dussejour, C. 136 14 45 S 128 13 E
Düsseldorf 48 51 15N 6 46 E
Dussen 46 51 44N 4 59 E
Duszniki Zdrój 54 51 26N 16 22 E
Dutch Harbour 147 53 54N 166 35W
Dutlhe 128 23 58 S 23 46 E
Dutsan Wai 121 10 50N 8 10 E
Dutton, R. 138 20 44 S 143 10 E
Duvan 84 55 42N 57 54 E
Duved 72 63 24N 12 55 E
Duvno 66 43 42N 17 13 E
Duwadami 92 24 35N 44 15 E
Duzdab = Zāhedān 93 29 30N 60 50 E
Dve Mogili 67 43 47N 25 55 E
Dvina, Sev. 78 56 30N 24 0 E
Dvina, Zap. 80 61 40N 45 30 E
Dvinsk = Daugavpils 80 55 33N 26 32 E
Dvinskaya Guba 78 65 0N 39 0 E
Dvor 63 45 4N 16 22 E
Dvorce 53 49 50N 17 34 E
Dvur Králové 52 50 27N 15 50 E
Dwarka 94 22 18N 69 8 E
Dwellingup 137 32 43 S 116 4 E
Dwight 156 41 5N 88 25W
Dyakovskoya 81 60 5N 41 12 E
Dyatkovo 80 53 48N 34 27 E
Dyaul, I. 138 3 0 S 150 55 E
Dyce 37 57 12N 2 11W
Dyer 163 37 40N 118 5W
Dyer, C. 149 67 0N 61 0W
Dyerbeldzhin 85 41 13N 74 54 E
Dyersburg 159 36 2N 89 20W
Dyfed □ 31 52 0N 4 30W
Dyje, R. 53 48 50N 16 45 E
Dyke Acland Bay 138 8 45 S 148 45 E
Dykehead 37 56 43N 3 0W
Dyle, R. 47 50 58N 4 41 E
Dymchurch 29 51 2N 1 0 E
Dymock 28 51 58N 2 27W
Dynevor Downs 139 28 10 S 144 20 E
Dynów 54 49 50N 22 11 E
Dypvag 71 79 40N 9 8 E
Dyrnes 71 63 25N 7 52 E
Dysart, Can. 153 50 57N 104 2W
Dysart, U.K. 35 56 8N 3 8W
Dysjön 72 62 38N 15 31 E
Dyulgeri 67 42 18N 27 23 E
Dyurtyuli 84 55 9N 54 4 E
Dzambeyty 83 50 15N 52 30 E
Dzaudzhikau = Ordzhonikidze 83 43 0N 44 35 E
Dzerzhinsk 80 53 40N 27 7 E
Dzhailma 76 51 30N 61 50 E
Dzhalal-Abad 84 40 56N 73 0 E
Dzhalinda 77 53 40N 124 0 E
Dzhambeyty 84 50 16N 52 35 E
Dzhambul 85 42 54N 71 22 E
Dzhambul, Gora 85 44 54N 73 0 E
Dzhankoi 82 45 40N 34 30 E
Dzhanybek 83 49 25N 46 50 E
Dzhardzhan 77 68 10N 123 5 E
Dzharkurgan 85 37 31N 67 25 E
Dzhelinde 77 70 0N 114 20 E
Dzherzhinsk 80 53 48N 27 19 E
Dzhetygara 84 52 11N 61 12 E
Dzhetym, Khrebet 85 41 30N 77 0 E
Dzhezkazgan 76 47 10N 67 40 E
Dzhizak 85 40 6N 67 50 E
Dzhugdzur, Khrebet 77 57 30N 138 0 E
Dzhuma 85 39 42N 66 40 E
Dzhumgoltau, Khrebet 85 42 15N 74 30 E
Dzhungarskiye Vorota 76 45 0N 82 0 E
Dzhvari 83 42 42N 42 4 E
Działdowo 54 53 15N 20 15 E
Działoszyce 54 50 22N 20 20 E
Działoszyn 54 51 6N 18 50 E
Dzibilchaltún 165 21 5N 89 36W
Dzierzgon 54 53 58N 19 20 E
Dzierzoniow 54 50 45N 16 39 E
Dzilam de Bravo 165 21 24N 88 53W
Dzioua 119 33 14N 5 14 E
Dziwnów 54 54 2N 14 45 E
Dzungaria 105 44 10N 88 0 E
Dzungarian Gates = Dzhungarskiye V. 105 45 0N 82 0 E

E

Eabamet, L. 150 51 30N 87 46W
Eads 158 38 30N 102 46W
Eagle, Alaska, U.S.A. 147 64 44N 141 29W
Eagle, Colo., U.S.A. 160 39 45N 106 55W
Eagle Butt 158 45 1N 101 12W
Eagle Grove 158 42 37N 93 53W
Eagle L., Calif., U.S.A. 160 40 35N 120 50W
Eagle L., Me., U.S.A. 151 46 23N 69 22W
Eagle Lake 159 29 35N 96 21W
Eagle Nest 161 36 33N 105 13W
Eagle Pass 159 28 45N 100 35W
Eagle Pk. 163 38 10N 119 25W
Eagle Pt. 136 16 11 S 124 23 E
Eagle, R. 151 53 36N 57 26W
Eagle River 158 45 55N 89 17W
Eaglehawk 140 36 43 S 144 16 E
Eagles Mere 162 41 25N 76 33W
Eaglesfield 35 55 3N 3 12W
Eagleshan 34 55 44N 4 18W
Eakring 33 53 9N 0 59W
Ealing 29 51 30N 0 19W
Earaheedy 137 25 34 S 121 29 E
Earby 32 53 55N 2 8W
Eardisland 28 52 14N 2 50W
Eardisley 28 52 8N 3 0W
Earith 29 52 21N 0 1 E
Earl Grey 153 50 57N 104 43W
Earl Shilton 28 52 35N 1 20W
Earl Soham 29 52 14N 1 15 E
Earle 159 35 18N 90 26W
Earlimart 163 35 53N 119 16W
Earls Barton 29 52 16N 0 44W
Earl's Colne 29 51 56N 0 43 E
Earlsferry 35 56 11N 2 50W
Earlston 35 55 39N 2 40W
Earn, L. 34 56 23N 4 14W
Earn, R. 35 56 20N 3 19W
Earnslaw, Mt. 143 44 32 S 168 27 E
Earoo 137 29 34 S 118 22 E
Earsdon 35 55 4N 1 30W
Earth 159 34 18N 102 30W
Easebourne 29 51 0N 0 42W
Easington, Durham, U.K. 33 54 50N 1 24W
Easington, Yorks., U.K. 33 54 40N 0 7W
Easington Colliery 33 54 49N 1 19W
Easingwold 33 54 8N 1 11W
Easky 38 54 17N 8 58W
Easley 157 34 52N 82 35W
East Aberthaw 31 51 23N 3 23W
East Anglian Hts. 29 52 10N 0 17 E
East Angus 151 45 30N 71 40W
East, B. 159 29 2N 89 16W
East Barming 29 51 15N 0 29 E
East Bathurst 151 47 35N 65 40W
East Bengal 99 24 0N 90 0 E
East Bergholt 29 51 58N 1 2 E
East Beskids, mts. 53 49 30N 18 45 E
East Brent 28 51 14N 2 55W
East C., N.Z. 142 37 42 S 178 35 E
East C., P.N.G. 135 10 13 S 150 53 E
East Chicago 156 41 40N 87 30W
East China Sea 105 30 5N 126 0 E
East Coulee 152 51 23N 112 27W
East Cowes 28 50 45N 1 17W
East Dereham 29 52 40N 0 57 E
East Falkland 176 51 30 S 58 30W
East Fen 33 53 4N 0 5 E
East Florenceville 151 46 26N 67 36W
East Grand Forks 158 47 55N 97 5W
East Greenwich 162 41 40N 71 27W
East Grinstead 29 51 8N 0 1W
East Harling 29 52 26N 0 55 E
East Hartford 162 41 46N 72 39W
East Helena 160 46 37N 111 58W
East Ilsley 28 51 33N 1 15W
East Indies 102 0 0 120 0 E
East Jordan 156 45 10N 85 7W
East Kilbride 35 55 46N 4 10W
East Kirkby 33 53 5N 1 15W
East Lansing 156 42 44N 84 37W
East Linton 35 56 0N 2 40W
East Liverpool 156 40 39N 80 35W
East London 129 33 0 S 27 55 E
East Looe 30 50 22N 4 28W
East Los Angeles 163 34 1N 118 9W
East Lynne 141 35 35 S 150 16 E
East Main (Eastmain) 151 52 20N 78 30W
East Markham 33 53 15N 0 53W
East Midlands, oilfield 19 53 20N 0 45W
East Moor 33 53 15N 1 30W
East, Mt. 137 29 0 S 122 30 E
East Orange 162 40 46N 74 13W
East P. 151 46 27N 61 58W
East Pakistan = Bangladesh 99 24 0N 90 0 E
East Pine 152 55 48N 120 5W
East Point 157 33 40N 84 28W
East Providence 162 41 49N 71 23W
East Retford 33 53 19N 0 55W
East St. Louis 158 38 36N 90 10W
East Schelde, R. 47 51 38N 3 40 E
E. Siberian Sea 77 73 0N 160 0 E
East Stroudsburg 162 41 0N 75 11W
East Sussex □ 29 50 55N 0 20 E
East Tawas 156 44 17N 83 31W
East Toorale 139 30 27 S 145 28 E
East Walker, R. 163 38 52N 119 10W
East Wemyss 35 56 8N 3 5W
East Woodhay 28 51 21N 1 26W
Eastbourne, N.Z. 142 41 19 S 174 55 E
Eastbourne, U.K. 29 50 46N 0 18 E
Eastchurch 29 51 23N 0 53 E
Eastend 153 49 32N 108 50W
Easter Islands 143 27 0 S 109 0W
Easter Ross, dist. 37 57 50N 4 35W
Easter Skeld 36 60 12N 1 27W
Eastern □ 126 0 0 S 38 30 E
Eastern Cr. 138 20 40 S 141 35 E
Eastern Ghats 97 15 0N 80 0 E
Eastern Group, Is. 137 33 30 S 124 30 E
Eastern Province □ 120 8 15N 11 0W
Easterville 153 53 8N 99 49W
Easthampton 162 42 16N 72 40W
Eastland 159 32 26N 98 45W
Eastleigh 28 50 58N 1 21W
Eastmain (East Main) 150 52 20N 78 30W
Eastmain, R. 150 52 27N 72 26W
Eastman 157 32 13N 83 41W
Eastnor 28 52 2N 2 22W
Easton, Dorset, U.K. 28 50 32N 2 27W
Easton, Northants., U.K. 29 52 37N 0 31W
Easton, Somerset, U.K. 28 51 28N 2 42W
Easton, Md., U.S.A. 162 38 47N 76 7W
Easton, Pa., U.S.A. 162 40 41N 75 15W
Easton, Wash., U.S.A. 160 47 14N 121 8W
Eastport, Maine, U.S.A. 151 44 57N 67 0W
Eastport, N.Y., U.S.A. 162 40 50N 72 44W
Eastry 29 51 15N 1 19 E
Eastview 150 45 27N 75 40W
Eastville 162 37 21N 75 57W
Eastwood 33 53 2N 1 17W
Eaton, U.K. 29 52 52N 0 46W
Eaton, U.S.A. 158 40 35N 104 42W
Eaton, L. 136 22 55 S 130 57 E
Eaton Socon 29 52 13N 0 18W
Eatonia 153 51 13N 109 25W
Eatonton 157 33 22N 83 24W
Eatontown 162 40 18N 74 7W
Eau Claire, S.C., U.S.A. 157 34 5N 81 2W
Eau Claire, Wis., U.S.A. 158 44 46N 91 30W
Eauze 44 43 53N 0 7 E
Eaval, Mt. 36 57 33N 7 12W
Ebagoola 138 14 15 S 143 12 E
Eban 121 9 40N 4 50 E
Ebberston 33 54 14N 0 35W
Ebbw Vale 31 51 47N 3 12W
Ebeggui 119 26 2N 6 0 E
Ebeltoft 75 56 12N 10 41 E
Ebensee 52 47 48N 13 46 E
Eberbach 49 49 27N 8 59 E
Eberswalde 48 52 49N 13 50 E
Ebikon 51 47 5N 8 21 E
Ebingen 49 48 13N 9 1 E
Ebino 110 32 2N 130 48 E
Ebnat-Kappel 51 47 16N 9 7 E
Eboli 65 40 39N 15 2 E
Ebolowa 121 2 55N 11 10 E
Ebony 128 22 6 S 15 15 E
Ébrié, Lagune 120 5 12N 4 40W
Ebro, Pantano del 56 43 0N 3 58W
Ebro, R. 58 41 49N 1 5W
Ebstorf 48 53 2N 10 23 E
Ecaussines-d' Enghien 47 50 35N 4 11 E
Ecclefechan 35 55 3N 3 18W
Eccleshall 28 52 52N 2 14W
Eceabat 68 40 11N 26 21 E
Éceuillé 42 47 10N 1 19 E
Ech Chebbi 118 26 41N 0 29 E
Echallens 50 46 38N 6 38 E
Echaneni 77 27 33 S 32 6 E
Echelles, Les 45 45 27N 5 45 E
Echizen-Misaki 111 35 59N 135 57 E
Echmiadzin 83 40 12N 44 19 E
Echo Bay, N.W.T., Can. 148 66 10N 117 40W
Echo Bay, Ont., Can. 150 46 29N 84 4W
Echoing, R. 153 55 51N 92 5W
Echt, Neth. 47 51 7N 5 52 E
Echt, U.K. 37 57 8N 2 26W
Echternach 47 49 49N 6 3 E
Echuca 141 36 3 S 144 46 E
Ecija 57 37 30N 5 10W
Eck L. 34 56 5N 5 0W
Eckernförde 48 54 26N 9 50 E
Eckington 33 53 19N 1 21W
Eclipse Is. 136 13 54 S 126 19 E
Écommoy 42 47 50N 0 17 E
Ecoporanga 171 18 23 S 40 50W

Écos Eldorado

Écos 43 49 9N 1 35 E
Écouché 42 48 42N 0 10W
Ecuador ■ 174 2 0S 78 0W
Ed 73 58 55N 11 55 E
Ed Dabbura 122 17 40N 34 15 E
Ed Damer 122 17 27N 34 0 E
Ed Debba 122 18 0N 30 51 E
Ed-Déffa 122 30 40N 26 30 E
Ed Deim 123 10 10N 28 20 E
Ed Dueim 123 14 0N 32 10 E
Ed Dzong 99 32 11N 90 12 E
Edah 137 28 16S 117 10 E
Edam, Can. 153 53 11N 108 46W
Edam, Neth. 46 52 31N 5 3 E
Edapally 97 11 19N 78 3 E
Eday, I. 37 59 11N 2 47W
Eday Sd. 37 59 12N 2 45W
Edd 123 14 0N 41 30 E
Edda, oilfield 19 56 25N 3 15 E
Edderton 37 57 50N 4 10W
Eddrachillis B. 36 58 16N 5 10W
Eddystone 30 50 11N 4 16W
Eddystone Pt. 138 40 59S 148 20 E
Ede, Neth. 46 52 4N 5 40 E
Ede, Nigeria 121 7 45N 4 29 E
Ede, Sweden 72 62 10N 16 50 E
Édea 121 3 51N 10 9 E
Edegem 47 51 10N 4 27 E
Edehon L. 153 60 25N 97 15W
Edekel, Adrar 119 23 56N 6 47 E
Eden, Austral. 141 37 3S 149 55 E
Eden, U.K. 38 54 44N 5 47W
Eden, Tex., U.S.A. 159 31 16N 99 50W
Eden, Wyo., U.S.A. 160 42 2N 109 27W
Eden L. 153 56 38N 100 15W
Eden, R. 32 54 57N 3 2W
Edenbridge 29 51 12N 0 4 E
Edenburg 128 29 43S 25 58 E
Edendale 143 46 19S 168 48 E
Edenderry 39 53 21N 7 3W
Edenton 157 36 5N 76 36W
Edenville 129 27 37S 27 34 E
Ederny 38 54 32N 7 40W
Edgar 158 40 25N 98 0W
Edgartown 162 41 22N 70 28W
Edge Hill 28 52 7N 1 28W
Edge I. 12 77 45N 22 30 E
Edgecumbe 142 37 59S 176 47 E
Edgefield 157 33 43N 81 59W
Edgeley 158 46 27N 98 41W
Edgemont 158 43 15N 103 53W
Edgeøya 12 77 45N 22 30 E
Edgeworthstown = Mostrim 38 53 42N 7 36W
Edhessa 68 40 48N 22 5 E
Edievale 143 45 49S 169 22 E
Edina, Liberia 120 6 0N 10 19W
Edina, U.S.A. 158 40 6N 92 10W
Edinburg 159 26 22N 98 10W
Edinburgh 35 55 57N 3 12W
Edington 28 51 17N 2 6W
Edirne 67 41 40N 26 45 E
Edison 163 35 21N 118 52W
Edithburgh 140 35 5S 137 43 E
Edjeleh 119 28 25N 9 40 E
Edjudina 137 29 48S 122 23 E
Edmeston 162 42 42N 75 15W
Edmond 159 35 37N 97 30W
Edmondbyers 32 54 50N 1 59W
Edmonds 160 47 47N 122 22W
Edmonton, Austral. 138 17 2S 145 46 E
Edmonton, Can. 152 53 30N 113 30W
Edmund L. 153 54 45N 93 17W
Edmundston 151 47 23N 68 20W
Edna 159 29 0N 96 40W
Edna Bay 152 55 55N 133 40W
Edolo 62 46 10N 10 21 E
Edouard, L. 126 0 25S 29 40 E
Edremit 92 39 40N 27 0 E
Edsbyn 72 61 23N 15 49 E
Edsel Ford Ra. 13 77 0S 143 0W
Edsele 72 63 25N 16 32 E
Edson 152 53 40N 116 28W
Eduardo Castex 172 35 50S 64 25W
Edward I. 150 48 22N 88 37W
Edward, L. = Idi Amin Dada, L. 126 0 25S 29 40 E
Edward, R. 140 35 0S 143 30 E
Edward VII Pen. 13 80 0S 160 0W
Edwards 163 34 55N 117 51W
Edwards Plat. 159 30 30N 101 5W
Edwardsville 162 41 15N 75 56W
Edzell 37 56 49N 2 40W
Edzo 152 62 49N 116 4W
Eefde 46 52 10N 6 13 E
Eek 147 60 10N 162 0W
Eekloo 47 51 11N 3 33 E
Eelde 46 53 8N 6 34 E
Eem, R. 46 52 16N 5 20 E
Eems Kanaal 46 53 18N 6 46 E
Eems, R. 46 53 26N 6 57 E
Eenrum 46 53 22N 6 28 E
Eernegem 47 51 8N 3 2 E
Eerste Valthermond 46 52 53N 6 58 E
Eersterivier 128 34 0S 18 45 E
Efate, I. (Vate) 46 17 40S 168 25 E
Eferding 52 48 18N 14 1 E
Eferi 119 24 30N 9 28 E
Effingham 156 39 8N 88 30W
Effiums 121 6 35N 8 0 E
Effretikon 51 47 25N 8 42 E
Efiduasi 121 6 45N 1 25W
Eforie Sud 70 44 1N 28 37 E
Ega, R. 58 42 32N 1 58W
Égadi, Ísole 64 37 55N 12 10 E
Eganville 150 45 32N 77 5W
Egeland 158 48 42N 99 6W
Egenolf L. 153 59 3N 100 0W
Eger 53 47 53N 20 27 E
Eger, R. 53 47 43N 20 32 E
Egersund = Eigersund 75 58 26N 6 1 E
Egerton, Mt. 137 24 42S 117 44 E
Egg L. 153 55 5N 105 30W
Eggenburg 52 48 38N 15 50 E
Eggiwil 50 46 52N 7 47 E
Egham 29 51 25N 0 33W
Egilsay I. 37 59 10N 2 56W
Eginbah 136 20 53S 119 47 E
Egletons 44 45 24N 2 3 E
Eglisau 51 47 35N 8 31 E
Egmond-aan-Zee 46 52 37N 4 38 E
Egmont, C. 142 39 16S 173 45 E
Egmont, Mt. 142 39 17S 174 5 E
Egogi Bad 123 13 10N 41 30 E
Egremont 32 54 28N 3 33W
Eğridir Gölü 92 37 53N 30 50 E
Egton 33 54 27N 0 45W
Egtved 73 55 38N 9 18 E
Egua 174 5 5N 68 0W
Éguas, R. 171 13 26S 44 14W
Egume 121 7 30N 7 14 E
Éguzon 44 46 27N 1 33 E
Egvekinot 77 66 19N 179 50W
Egyek 53 47 39N 20 52 E
Egypt ■ 122 28 0N 31 0 E
Eha Amufu 121 6 30N 7 40 E
Ehime-ken □ 110 33 30N 132 40 E
Ehingen 49 48 16N 9 43 E
Ehrwald 52 47 24N 10 56 E
Eibar 58 43 11N 2 28W
Eibergen 46 52 6N 6 39 E
Eichstätt 49 48 53N 11 12 E
Eidanger 71 59 7N 9 43 E
Eide 71 60 31N 6 44 E
Eider, R. 48 54 15N 8 50 E
Eidsberg 71 59 32N 11 16 E
Eidsfoss 71 59 36N 10 2 E
Eidsvold 139 25 25S 151 12 E
Eidsvoll 75 60 19N 11 14 E
Eifel 49 50 10N 6 45 E
Eiffel Flats 127 18 20S 30 0 E
Eigersund 71 58 26N 6 1 E
Eigg, I. 36 56 54N 6 10W
Eigg, Sd. of 36 56 52N 6 15W
Eighty Mile Beach 136 19 30S 120 40 E
Eil 91 8 0N 49 50 E
Eil, L. 36 56 50N 5 15W
Eilat 90 29 30N 34 56 E
Eildon 141 37 14S 145 55 E
Eildon, L. 139 37 10S 146 0 E
Eileen L. 153 62 16N 107 37W
Eilenburg 48 51 28N 12 38 E
Ein 'Arik 90 31 54N 35 8 E
Ein el Luweiqa 123 14 5N 33 50 E
Einasleigh 138 18 32S 144 5 E
Einasleigh, R. 138 17 30S 142 17 E
Einbeck 48 51 48N 9 50 E
Eindhoven 47 51 26N 5 30 E
Einsiedeln 51 47 7N 8 46 E
Eiríksjökull 74 64 46N 20 24W
Eirlandsche Gat 46 53 12N 4 54 E
Eirunepé 174 6 35S 70 0W
Eisden 47 50 59N 5 42 E
Eisenach 48 50 58N 10 18 E
Eisenberg 48 50 59N 11 50 E
Eisenerz 52 47 32N 15 54 E
Eisenhüttenstadt 48 52 9N 14 41 E
Eisenkappel 52 46 29N 14 36 E
Eisenstadt 53 47 51N 16 31 E
Eiserfeld 47 50 50N 8 0 E
Eisfeld 49 50 25N 10 54 E
Eishort, L. 36 57 9N 6 0W
Eisleben 48 51 31N 11 31 E
Eizariya (Bethany) 90 31 47N 35 15 E
Ejby 73 55 25N 9 56 E
Eje, Sierra del 56 42 24N 6 54W
Ejea de los Caballeros 58 42 7N 1 9W
Ejido 174 8 33N 71 14W
Ejura 121 7 25N 1 25 E
Ejutla 165 16 34N 96 44W
Ekalaka 158 45 55N 104 30 E
Ekawasaki 110 33 13N 132 46 E
Ekeryd 73 57 37N 14 6 E
Eket 121 4 38N 7 56W
Eketahuna 142 40 38S 175 43 E
Ekhinos 68 41 16N 25 1W
Ekibastuz 76 51 40N 75 22 E
Ekimchan 77 53 0N 133 0W
Ekofisk, oilfield 19 56 35N 3 30 E
Ekofisk, W., oilfield 19 56 35N 3 5 E
Ekoli 126 0 23S 24 13 E
Ekoln, I. 72 59 45N 17 40 E
Eksjö 73 57 40N 14 58W
Ekwan Pt. 150 53 16N 82 7W
Ekwan, R. 150 53 12N 82 15W
El Abiodh 118 32 53N 0 31 E
El Aïoun 118 34 33N 2 30W
El 'Aiyat 122 29 36N 31 15 E
El Alamein 122 30 48N 28 58 E
El Aqaba 90 29 31N 35 0 E
El Arahal 57 37 15N 5 33W
El Araq 122 28 40N 26 20 E
El Arba 118 36 28N 3 12 E
El Arba du Rharb 118 34 50N 5 59W
El Aricha 118 34 13N 1 16W
El Arīhā 90 31 52N 35 27 E
El Arish 138 17 49S 146 1 E
El 'Arîsh 122 31 8N 33 50 E
El Arnaud 119 36 7N 5 49 E
El Arrouch 119 36 37N 6 53 E
El Asnam 118 36 10N 1 20 E
El Astillero 56 43 24N 3 49W
El Badâri 122 27 4N 31 25 E
El Bahrein 122 28 30N 26 25 E
El Ballâs 122 26 2N 32 43 E
El Balyana 122 26 10N 32 3 E
El Baqeir 122 18 40N 33 40 E
El Barco de Ávila 56 40 21N 5 31W
El Barco de Valdeorras 56 42 23N 7 0W
El Bauga 122 18 18N 33 52 E
El Baúl 174 8 57N 68 17W
El Bawiti 122 28 25N 28 45 E
El Bayadh 118 33 40N 1 1 E
El Bierzo 56 42 45N 6 30W
El Biodh 118 26 0N 6 32W
El Bluff 166 11 59N 83 40W
El Bonillo 59 38 57N 2 35W
El Cajon 163 32 49N 117 0W
El Callao 174 7 25N 61 50W
El Camp 58 41 5N 1 10 E
El Campo 159 29 10N 96 20W
El Carmen 174 1 16N 66 52W
El Castillo 57 37 41N 6 19W
El Centro 161 32 50N 115 40W
El Cerro, Boliv. 174 17 30S 61 40W
El Cerro, Spain 57 37 45N 6 57W
El Cocuy 174 6 25N 72 27W
El Coronil 57 37 5N 5 38W
El Cuy 176 39 55S 68 25W
El Cuyo 165 21 30N 87 40W
El Dab'a 122 31 0N 28 27 E
El Dátil 164 30 7N 112 15W
El Deir 122 25 25N 32 20 E
El Dere 91 3 50N 47 8 E
El Díaz 165 21 1N 87 17W
El Dificul 174 9 51N 74 14W
El Díos 164 20 40N 87 20W
El Diviso 174 1 22N 78 14W
El Djouf 120 20 0N 11 30 E
El Dorado, Colomb. 174 1 11N 71 52W
El Dorado, Ark., U.S.A. 159 33 10N 92 40W
El Dorado, Kans., U.S.A. 159 37 55N 96 56W
El Dorado, Venez. 174 6 55N 61 30W
El Dorado Springs 159 37 54N 93 59W
El Eglab 118 26 20N 4 30W
El Escorial 56 40 35N 4 7W
El Faiyûm 122 29 19N 30 50 E
El Fâsher 123 13 33N 25 26 E
El Fashn 122 28 50N 30 54 E
El Ferrol 56 43 29N 3 14W
El Fifi 123 10 4N 25 0 E
El Fuerte 164 26 30N 108 40W
El Gal 91 10 58N 50 20 E
El Gebir 123 13 40N 29 40 E
El Gedida 122 25 40N 28 30 E
El Geneina 117 13 27N 22 45 E
El Geteina 123 14 50N 32 27 E
El Gezira 123 14 0N 33 0 E
El Gezira □ 123 15 0N 33 0 E
El Gîza 122 30 0N 31 10 E
El Goléa 118 30 30N 2 50 E
El Guettar 119 34 5N 4 38 E
El Hadjire 119 32 36N 5 30 E
El Hagiz 123 15 15N 35 50 E
El Hajeb 118 33 41N 5 23W
El Hammâm 122 30 52N 29 25 E
El Hank, Alg. 118 25 38N 5 29W
El Hank, Maurit. 118 24 37N 7 0W
El Haql 122 29 15N 34 59 E
El Hawata 123 13 25N 34 42 E
El Heiz 122 27 50N 28 40 E
El 'Idisât 122 25 30N 32 35 E
El Iskandarîya 122 31 0N 30 0 E
El Istwâ'ya □ 123 5 0N 30 0 E
El Jadida 118 33 16N 9 31W
El Jorf Lasfar, C. 118 33 5N 8 54W
El Kab 122 19 27N 32 46 E
El Kala 119 36 50N 8 30 E
El Kamlin 123 15 3N 33 11 E
El Kantara, Alg. 119 35 14N 5 45 E
El Kantara, Tunisia 119 33 45N 10 58 E
El Karaba 123 18 32N 33 41 E
El Kef 119 36 12N 8 47 E
El Kelâa des Srarhna 118 32 4N 7 27W
El Khandaq 122 18 30N 30 30 E
El Khârga 122 25 30N 30 33 E
El Khartûm 123 15 31N 32 35 E
El Khartûm Bahrî 123 15 40N 32 31 E
El-Khroubs 119 36 10N 6 55 E
El Khureiba 122 28 3N 35 10 E
El Kseur 119 36 46N 4 49 E
El Ksiba 118 32 45N 6 1W
El Kuntilla 122 30 1N 34 45 E
El Ladhiqiya 92 35 20N 35 30 E
El Laqeita 122 25 50N 33 15 E
El Leiya 123 16 15N 35 28 E
El Mafâza 123 13 38N 34 30 E
El Mahalla el Kubra 122 31 0N 31 0 E
El Mahârîq 122 25 35N 30 35 E
El Maiz 118 28 19N 0 9W
El-Maks el-Bahari 122 24 30N 30 40 E
El Manshâh 122 26 26N 31 50 E
El Mansour 118 27 47N 0 14W
El Mansûra 122 31 0N 31 19 E
El Mantico 174 7 27N 62 32W
El Manzala 122 31 10N 31 50 E
El Marâgha 122 26 35N 31 10 E
El Masid 123 15 15N 33 0 E
El Matariya 122 31 15N 32 0 E
El Meghaier 119 33 55N 5 58 E
El Melfa 119 31 58N 15 18 E
El Meraguen 118 28 0N 0 7W
El Metemma 123 16 50N 33 10 E
El Miamo 174 7 39N 61 46W
El Milagro 172 30 59S 65 59W
El Milheas 118 25 27N 6 57W
El Milia 119 36 51N 6 13 E
El Minyâ 122 28 7N 30 33 E
El Molar 58 40 42N 3 45W
El Monte 163 34 4N 118 2W
El Mreyye 120 18 0N 6 0W
El Obeid 123 13 8N 30 10 E
El Oro = Sta. María del Oro 164 25 50N 105 20W
El Oro de Hidalgo 165 19 48N 100 8W
El Oued 119 33 20N 6 58 E
El Ouig 120 19 31N 0 27 E
El Palmar 174 7 58N 61 53W
El Palmito, Presa 164 25 40N 105 3W
El Panadés 58 41 10N 1 30 E
El Pao 174 9 38N 68 8W
El Pardo 56 40 31N 3 47W
El Paso 161 31 50N 106 30W
El Paso Robles 163 35 38N 120 41W
El Pedernoso 59 39 29N 2 45W
El Pedroso 57 37 51N 5 45W
El Pilar 174 10 32N 63 9W
El Pobo de Dueñas 58 40 46N 1 39W
El Portal 163 37 44N 119 49W
El Porvenir, Mexico 164 31 15N 105 51W
El Porvenir, Venez. 174 4 42N 71 19W
El Prat de Llobregat 58 41 18N 2 3 E
El Progreso 166 15 26N 87 51W
El Provencío 59 39 23N 2 35W
El Pueblito 164 29 3N 105 4W
El Qahîra 122 30 1N 31 14 E
El Qantara 122 30 51N 32 20 E
El Qasr 122 25 44N 28 42 E
El Qubba 123 11 10N 27 5 E
El Quseima 122 30 40N 34 15 E
El Qusîya 122 27 29N 30 44 E
El Râshda 122 25 36N 28 57 E
El Reno 159 35 30N 98 0W
El Rheauya 118 25 52N 6 30W
El Ribero 56 42 30N 8 30W
El Rîdisiya 122 24 56N 32 51 E
El Rio 163 34 14N 119 10W
El Ronquillo 57 37 44N 6 10W
El Rubio 57 37 22N 5 0W
El Saff 122 29 34N 31 16 E
El Salado 174 8 56N 73 55W
El Salto 164 23 47N 105 22W
El Salvador ■ 166 13 50N 89 0W
El Sancejo 57 37 4N 5 6W
El Sauce 166 13 0N 86 40W
El Shallal 122 24 0N 32 53 E
El Suweis 122 29 58N 32 31 E
El Temblador 174 8 59N 62 44W
El Thamad 122 29 40N 34 28 E
El Tigre 174 8 55N 64 15W
El Tocuyo 174 9 47N 69 48W
El Tofo 172 29 22S 71 18W
El Tránsito 172 28 52S 70 17W
El Tûr 122 28 14N 33 36 E
El Turbio 176 51 30S 72 40W
El Uqsur 122 25 41N 32 38 E
El Vado 58 41 2N 3 18W
El Vallés 58 41 35N 2 20 E
El Vigía 174 8 38N 71 39W
El Wak 124 2 49N 40 56 E
El Waqf 122 25 45N 32 15 E
El Wâsta 122 29 19N 31 12 E
El Weguet 123 5 28N 42 17 E
Ela 123 12 50N 42 20 E
Elafónisos 69 36 29N 22 56 E
Elaine 140 37 44S 144 2 E
Elamanchili = Yellamanchilli 96 17 26N 82 50 E
Elan R. 31 52 17N 3 40W
Elan Village 31 52 18N 3 34W
Elands 141 31 37S 152 20 E
Elandsvlei 128 32 19S 19 31 E
Élassa 69 35 18N 26 21 E
Elassón 68 39 53N 22 12 E
Elat 103 5 40S 133 5 E
Elateia 69 38 37N 22 46 E
Elâziğ 92 38 37N 39 22 E
Elba 157 31 27N 86 4W
Elba, I. 62 42 48N 10 15 E
Elbasani 68 41 9N 20 9 E
Elbasani-Berati 68 40 58N 20 0 E
Elbe, R. 48 53 15N 10 7 E
Elbert, Mt. 161 39 12N 106 36W
Elberta 156 44 35N 86 14W
Elberton 157 34 7N 82 51W
Elbeuf 42 49 17N 1 2 E
Elbląg □ 54 54 15N 19 30 E
Elblag (Elbing) 54 54 10N 19 25 E
Elbow 153 51 7N 106 35W
Elbrus, Mt. 83 43 30N 42 30 E
Elburg 46 52 26N 5 50 E
Elburz Mts. = Alborz 93 36 0N 52 0 E
Elche 59 38 15N 0 42W
Elche de la Sierra 59 38 27N 2 3W
Elcho I. 138 11 55S 135 45 E
Elda 59 38 29N 0 47W
Eldfisk, oilfield 19 56 25N 3 30 E
Eldon, Iowa, U.S.A. 97 40 50N 92 12W
Eldon, Mo., U.S.A. 158 38 20N 92 38W
Eldora 158 42 20N 93 5W
Eldorado, Argent. 173 26 28S 54 43W

Eldorado
Ermelo

Eldorado, Ont., Can. 97 44 40N 77 32W
Eldorado, Sask., Can. 153 59 35N 108 30W
Eldorado, Mexico 164 24 0N 107 30W
Eldorado, Ill., U.S.A. 156 37 50N 88 25W
Eldorado, Tex., U.S.A. 159 30 52N 100 35W
Eldoret 126 0 30N 35 25E
Electra 159 34 0N 99 0W
Eleele 147 21 54N 159 35W
Elefantes, R. 129 24 0S 32 30E
Elektrogorsk 81 55 56N 38 50E
Elektrostal 81 55 41N 38 32E
Elele 121 5 5N 6 50E
Elena 67 42 55N 25 53E
Elephant Butte Res. 161 33 45N 107 30W
Elephant I. 13 61 0S 55 0W
Elephant Pass 97 9 35N 80 25E
Elesbão Veloso 170 6 13S 42 8W
Eleshnitsa 67 41 52N 23 36E
Eleuthera I. 166 25 0N 76 20W
Elevsís 69 38 4N 23 26E
Elevtheroúpolis 68 40 52N 24 20E
Elfin Cove 147 58 11N 136 20W
Elgåhogna, Mt. 72 62 7N 12 7E
Elgepiggen 71 62 10N 11 21E
Elgeyo-Marakwet □ 126 0 45N 35 30E
Elgg 51 47 29N 8 52E
Elgin, Can. 151 45 48N 65 10W
Elgin, U.K. 37 57 39N 3 20W
Elgin, Ill., U.S.A. 156 42 0N 88 20W
Elgin, N.D., U.S.A. 158 46 24N 101 46W
Elgin, Nebr., U.S.A. 158 41 58N 98 3W
Elgin, Nev., U.S.A. 161 37 27N 114 36W
Elgin, Oreg., U.S.A. 160 45 37N 118 0W
Elgin, Texas, U.S.A. 159 30 21N 97 22W
Elgol 36 57 9N 6 6W
Elgon, Mt. 126 1 10N 34 30E
Elham 29 51 9N 1 7E
Eliase 103 8 10S 130 55E
Elida 159 33 56N 103 41W
Elie 153 49 48N 97 52W
Elie de Beaumont, Mt. 143 43 30S 170 20E
Elikón, Mt. 69 38 18N 22 45E
Elim 147 64 35N 162 20W
Elin Pelin 126 42 40N 23 38E
Elisabethville = Lubumbashi 127 11 32S 27 38E
Eliseu Martins 170 8 13S 43 42W
Elishaw 35 55 16N 2 14W
Elista 83 46 16N 44 14E
Elit 123 15 10N 37 0E
Elizabeth, Austral. 140 34 42S 138 41E
Elizabeth, U.S.A. 162 40 37N 74 12W
Elizabeth City 157 36 18N 76 16W
Elizabetha 126 1 3N 23 37E
Elizabethton 157 36 20N 82 13W
Elizabethtown, Ky., U.S.A. 156 37 40N 85 54W
Elizabethtown, Pa., U.S.A. 162 40 8N 76 36W
Elizondo 58 43 12N 1 30W
Elk City 159 35 25N 99 25W
Elk Grove 163 38 25N 121 22W
Elk Island Nat. Park 152 53 47N 112 59W
Elk Lake 150 47 40N 80 25W
Elk Point 153 53 54N 110 55W
Elk River, Idaho, U.S.A. 160 46 50N 116 8W
Elk River, Minn., U.S.A. 158 45 17N 93 34W
Elkedra 138 21 9S 135 26E
Elkedra, R. 138 21 8S 136 22E
Elkhart, Ind., U.S.A. 156 41 42N 85 55W
Elkhart, Kans., U.S.A. 159 37 3N 101 54W
Elkhorn 153 49 59N 101 14W
Elkhorn, R. 158 42 0N 98 15W
Elkhotovo 83 43 19N 44 15E
Elkhovo 67 42 10N 26 40E
Elkin 157 36 17N 80 50W
Elkins 156 38 53N 79 53W
Elko, Can. 152 49 20N 115 10W
Elko, U.S.A. 160 40 40N 115 50W
Elkton 162 39 36N 75 50W
Ell, L. 137 29 13S 127 46E
Elland 33 53 41N 1 49W
Ellecom 46 52 2N 6 6E
Ellef Ringnes I. 12 78 30N 102 2W
Ellen, Mt. 161 38 4N 110 56W
Ellen R. 32 54 44N 3 24W
Ellendale, Austral. 136 17 56S 124 48E
Ellendale, U.S.A. 158 46 3N 98 30W
Ellensburg 160 47 0N 120 30W
Ellenville 162 41 42N 74 23W
Eller Beck Bri. 33 54 23N 0 40W
Ellerston 141 31 49S 151 20E
Ellery, Mt. 141 37 28S 148 40E
Ellesmere 32 52 55N 2 53W
Ellesmere I. 12 79 30N 80 0W
Ellesmere, L. 131 43 46S 172 27E
Ellesmere Port 32 53 17N 2 55W
Ellesworth Land 13 74 0S 85 0W
Ellezelles 47 50 44N 3 42E
Ellice Is. 130 8 0S 176 0E
Ellicott City 162 39 16N 76 48W
Ellington 35 55 14N 1 34W
Ellinwood 158 38 27N 98 37W
Elliot, Austral. 138 17 33S 133 32E
Elliot, S. Afr. 129 31 22S 27 48E
Elliot Lake 150 46 35N 82 35W
Ellis 158 39 0N 99 39W
Ellisville 157 31 38N 89 12W
Ellon 37 57 21N 2 5W
Ellore = Eluru 96 16 48N 81 8E
Ells, R. 152 57 18N 111 40W
Ellsworth 158 38 47N 98 15W
Ellsworth Land 13 76 0S 89 0W
Ellwangen 49 48 57N 10 9E
Ellwood City 156 40 52N 80 19W
Elm 51 46 54N 9 10E
Elma, Can. 153 49 52N 95 55W
Elma, U.S.A. 160 47 0N 123 30E
Elmer 162 39 36N 75 10W
Elmhurst 156 41 52N 87 58W
Elmina 121 5 5N 1 21W
Elmira, Can. 151 46 30N 61 59W
Elmira, U.S.A. 162 42 8N 76 49W
Elmira Heights 162 42 8N 76 50W
Elmore, Austral. 140 36 30S 144 37E
Elmore, U.S.A. 163 33 7N 115 49W
Elmshorn 48 53 44N 9 40E
Elmswell 29 52 14N 0 53E
Elorza 174 7 3N 69 31W
Eloy 161 32 46N 111 46W
Éloyes 43 48 6N 6 36E
Elphin, Ireland 38 53 50N 8 11W
Elphin, U.K. 36 58 4N 5 3W
Elphinstone 138 21 30S 148 17E
Elrose 153 51 12N 108 0W
Elsas 150 48 32N 82 55W
Elsinore, Austral. 141 31 35S 145 11E
Elsinore, Cal., U.S.A. 163 33 40N 117 15W
Elsinore, Utah, U.S.A. 161 38 40N 112 2W
Elsinore = Helsingor 73 56 2N 12 35E
Elspe 48 51 10N 8 1E
Elspeet 46 52 17N 5 48E
Elst 46 51 55N 5 51E
Elsterwerda 48 51 27N 13 32E
Elstree 29 51 38N 0 16W
Elten 46 51 52N 6 9E
Eltham, Austral. 141 37 43S 145 12E
Eltham, N.Z. 142 39 26S 174 19E
Elton 83 49 5N 46 52E
Eluru 96 16 48N 81 8E
Elvas 57 38 50N 7 17W
Elven 42 47 44N 2 36W
Elverum 71 60 53N 11 34E
Elvire, Mt. 137 21 52S 116 50E
Elvire, R. 136 17 51S 128 11E
Elvo, R. 62 45 32N 8 14E
Elvran 71 63 24N 11 3E
Elwood, Ind., U.S.A. 156 40 20N 85 50W
Elwood, Nebr., U.S.A. 158 40 38N 99 51W
Ely, U.K. 29 52 24N 0 16E
Ely, Minn., U.S.A. 158 47 54N 91 52W
Ely, Nev., U.S.A. 160 39 10N 114 50W
Elyashiv 90 32 23N 34 55E
Elyria 156 41 22N 82 8W
Emådalen 72 61 20N 14 44E
Emaiygi, R. 80 58 30N 26 30E
Emba 76 48 50N 58 8E
Embarcación 172 23 10S 64 0W
Embarras Portage 153 58 27N 111 28W
Embleton 35 55 30N 1 38W
Embo 37 57 55N 4 0W
Embóna 69 36 13N 27 51E
Embrach 51 47 30N 8 36E
Embrun 45 44 34N 6 30E
Embu 126 0 32S 37 38E
Embu □ 126 0 30S 37 35E
Emden 48 53 22N 7 12E
Emeq Hula 90 33 5N 35 8E
'Emeq Yizre'el 90 32 35N 35 12E
Emerald 138 23 32S 148 10E
Emerson 153 49 0N 97 10W
Emery 161 38 59N 111 17W
Emery Park 161 32 10N 110 59W
Emi Koussi, Mt. 117 20 0N 18 55E
Emilia-Romagna □ 62 44 33N 10 40E
Emilius, Mt. 62 45 41N 7 23E
Eminabad 94 32 2N 74 8E
Emine 67 42 40N 27 56E
Emlichheim 48 52 37N 6 51E
Emly 39 52 28N 8 20W
Emmaboda 73 56 37N 15 32E
Emmaus 162 40 32N 75 30W
Emme, R. 50 47 0N 7 42E
Emmeloord 46 52 44N 5 46E
Emmen, Neth. 47 52 48N 6 57E
Emmen, Switz. 51 47 4N 8 17E
Emmendingen 49 48 7N 7 51E
Emmental 50 47 0N 7 35E
Emmer-Compascum 46 52 49N 7 2E
Emmerich 48 51 50N 6 12E
Emmet 138 24 45S 144 30E
Emmetsburg 158 43 3N 94 40W
Emmett 160 43 51N 116 33W
Emöd 53 47 57N 20 47E
Emona 67 42 43N 27 53E
Empalme 164 28 1N 110 49W
Empangeni 129 28 50S 31 52E
Empedrado 172 28 0S 58 46W
Empoli 62 43 43N 10 57E
Emporia, Kans., U.S.A. 158 38 25N 96 16W
Emporia, Va., U.S.A. 157 36 41N 77 32W
Emporium 156 41 30N 78 17W
Empress 153 50 57N 110 0W
Emptinne 47 50 19N 5 8E
Ems, R. 48 52 37N 7 16E
Emsdetten 48 52 11N 7 31E
Emsworth 29 50 51N 0 56E
Emu 140 36 44S 143 26E
Emu Park 138 23 13S 150 50E
Emu Ra. 136 23 0S 122 0E
Emyvale 38 54 20N 6 57W
En Gedi 90 31 28N 35 25E
En Harod 90 32 33N 35 22E
'En Kerem 90 31 47N 35 6E
En Nahud 123 12 45N 28 25E
en Namous, O. 118 31 15N 0 10W
Ena 111 35 25N 137 25E
Ena-San 111 35 26N 137 36E
Enafors 72 63 17N 12 20E
Enambú 174 1 1N 70 17W
Enana 128 17 30S 16 23E
Enånger 72 61 30N 17 9E
Enard B. 36 58 5N 5 20W
Enbetsu 112 44 44N 141 47E
Encantadas, Serra 173 30 40S 53 0W
Encanto, Cape 103 20 20N 121 40E
Encarnación 173 27 15S 56 0W
Encarnación de Diaz 164 21 30N 102 20W
Ench'eng 106 37 9N 116 16E
Enchi 120 5 53N 2 48W
Encinal 159 28 3N 99 25W
Encinillas 164 33 3N 117 17W
Encinitas 163 33 3N 117 17W
Encino 161 34 46N 106 16W
Encounter B. 140 35 45S 138 45E
Encruzilhada 171 15 31S 40 54W
Endau 101 2 40N 103 38E
Endau, R. 101 2 30N 103 30E
Ende 103 8 45S 121 30E
Endeavour 153 52 10N 102 39W
Endeavour Str. 138 10 45S 142 0E
Endelave 73 55 46N 10 18E
Enderbury I. 131 3 8S 171 5W
Enderby, Can. 152 50 35N 119 10W
Enderby, U.K. 28 52 35N 1 15W
Enderby I. 136 20 35S 116 30E
Enderby Land 13 66 0S 53 0E
Enderlin 158 46 45N 97 41W
Endicott, N.Y., U.S.A. 162 42 6N 76 2W
Endicott, Wash., U.S.A. 160 47 0N 117 45W
Endicott Mts. 147 68 0N 152 30W
Endröd 53 46 55N 20 47E
Endyalgout I. 136 11 40S 132 35E
Enebakk 71 59 46N 11 9E
Enez 68 40 45N 26 5E
Enfida 119 36 6N 10 28E
Enfield, U.K. 29 51 39N 0 4W
Enfield, U.S.A. 162 43 34N 71 57W
Engadin 51 46 45N 10 10E
Engadine, Lower = Engiadina Bassa 51 46 51N 10 18E
Engadine, Upper = Engiadin 'Ota 51 46 38N 10 0E
Engano, C. 167 18 30N 68 20W
Engaño, C. 103 18 35N 122 23E
Engeddi 90 31 28N 35 25E
Engelberg 51 46 48N 8 26E
Engels 81 51 28N 46 6E
Engemann L. 153 55 55N 106 55W
Enger 71 60 35N 10 20E
Enggano, I. 102 5 20S 102 40E
Enghien 47 50 37N 4 2E
Engiadin 'Ota 51 46 38N 10 0E
Engiadina Bassa 51 46 51N 10 18E
Engkilili 102 1 3N 111 42E
England 159 34 30N 91 58W
England □ 27 53 0N 2 0W
Englee 151 50 45N 56 5W
Englefield 140 37 21S 141 48E
Englehart 150 47 49N 79 52W
Engler L. 153 59 8N 106 52W
Englewood, Colo., U.S.A. 158 39 40N 105 0W
Englewood, Kans., U.S.A. 159 37 7N 99 59W
Englewood, N.J., U.S.A. 162 40 54N 73 59W
English Bazar 95 24 58N 88 21E
English Channel 42 50 0N 2 0W
English Company Is. 133 12 0S 137 0E
English, R. 153 50 30N 93 50W
English River 150 49 20N 91 0W
Enid 159 36 26N 97 52W
Enipévs, R. 68 39 22N 22 17E
Eniwetok 131 11 30N 152 16E
Enjil 118 33 12N 4 32W
Enkeldoorn 127 19 2S 30 52E
Enkhuizen 46 52 42N 5 17E
Enköping 72 59 37N 17 4E
Enlo 108 24 0N 107 7E
Enna 65 37 34N 14 15E
Ennadai 153 61 8N 100 53W
Ennadai L. 153 61 0N 101 0W
Ennedi 117 17 15N 22 0E
Ennell L. 38 53 29N 7 25W
Ennerdale Water 32 54 32N 3 24W
Enngonia 139 29 21S 145 50E
Enningdal 71 58 59N 11 33E
Ennis, Ireland 39 52 51N 8 59W
Ennis, Mont., U.S.A. 160 45 27N 111 48W
Ennis, Texas, U.S.A. 159 32 15N 96 40W
Enniscorthy 39 52 30N 6 35W
Enniskean 39 51 44N 8 56W
Enniskerry 39 53 12N 6 10W
Enniskillen 38 54 20N 7 40W
Ennistimon 39 52 56N 9 18W
Enns 52 48 12N 14 28E
Enns, R. 52 48 8N 14 27E
Enoggera Range 108 27 26S 152 56E
Enoggera Res. 109 27 27S 152 55E
Enontekiö 74 68 23N 23 37E
Enp'ing 109 22 11N 112 18E
Enriquillo, L. 167 18 20N 72 5W
Ens 46 52 38N 5 50E
Enschede 46 52 13N 6 53E
Ensenada, Argent. 172 34 55S 57 55W
Ensenada, Mexico 164 31 50N 116 50W
Enshih 108 30 18N 109 27E
Enshū-Nada 111 34 27N 137 38E
Ensisheim 43 47 50N 7 20E
Enstone 28 51 55N 1 25W
Entebbe 126 0 4N 32 28E
Enter 46 52 17N 6 35E
Enterprise, Can. 152 60 47N 115 45W
Enterprise, Oreg., U.S.A. 160 45 30N 117 11W
Enterprise, Utah, U.S.A. 161 37 37N 113 36W
Entlebuch 50 46 59N 8 4E
Entrance 152 53 25N 117 50W
Entre Rios, Boliv. 172 21 30S 64 25W
Entre Rios, Mozam. 127 14 57S 37 20E
Entre Rios □ 172 30 30S 58 30W
Entre Rios, Bahia 171 11 56S 38 5W
Entrecasteaux, Pt. d' 137 34 50S 115 56E
Entrepeñas, Pantano de 58 40 34N 2 42W
Entwistle 152 53 30N 115 0W
Enugu 121 6 30N 7 30E
Enugu Ezike 121 7 0N 7 29E
Enumclaw 160 47 12N 122 0W
Envermeu 42 49 53N 1 15E
Envigado 174 6 10N 75 35W
Enza, R. 62 44 33N 10 22E
Enzan 111 35 42N 138 44E
Eólie o Lípari, Is. 65 38 30N 14 50E
Epa 138 8 28S 146 52E
Epanomí 68 40 25N 22 59E
Epe, Neth. 47 52 21N 5 59E
Epe, Nigeria 121 6 36N 3 59E
Épernay 43 49 3N 3 56E
Épernon 43 48 35N 1 40E
Ephesus 92 38 0N 27 30E
Ephraim 160 39 30N 111 37W
Ephrata, Pa., U.S.A. 162 40 11N 76 11W
Ephrata, Wash., U.S.A. 160 47 28N 119 32W
Épila 58 41 36N 1 17W
Épinac-les-Mines 43 46 59N 4 31E
Épinal 43 48 19N 6 27E
Episcopia Bihorului 70 47 12N 21 55E
Epitálion 69 37 37N 21 30E
Eport L. 36 57 33N 7 10W
Epping 29 51 42N 0 8E
Epping Forest 29 51 40N 0 5E
Epsom 29 51 19N 0 16W
Epukiro 125 21 30S 19 0E
Epworth 33 53 30N 0 50W
Equatorial Guinea ■ 124 2 0S 78 0W
Equeurdreville-Hainneville 42 49 40N 1 40W
Er Rahad 123 12 45N 30 32E
Er Rif 118 35 1N 4 1W
Er Roseires 123 11 55N 34 30E
Er Rumman 90 32 9N 35 48E
Eradu 137 28 40S 115 2E
Erandol 96 20 56N 75 20E
Erap 135 6 37S 146 51E
Erāwadī Myit, R. = Irrawaddy, R. 98 19 30N 95 15E
Erba, Italy 62 45 49N 9 12E
Erba, Sudan 122 19 5N 36 40E
Ercha 77 69 45N 147 20E
Erciyas Daği 92 38 30N 35 30E
Erdene 106 44 30N 111 10E
Erding 49 48 18N 11 55E
Erebus, Mt. 13 77 35S 167 0E
Erechim 173 27 35S 52 15W
Ereğli 92 41 15N 31 30E
Erei, Monti 65 37 20N 14 20E
Erembodegem 47 50 56N 4 4E
Eresma, R. 56 41 13N 4 30W
Eressós 69 39 11N 25 57E
Erewadi Myitwanya 99 15 30N 95 0E
Erfenis Dam 128 28 30S 26 50E
Erfjord 71 59 20N 6 14E
Erfoud 118 31 30N 4 15W
Erfurt 48 50 58N 11 2E
Erfurt □ 48 51 10N 10 30E
Ergani 92 38 26N 39 49E
Ergene, R. 67 41 20N 27 0E
Ergeni Vozyshennost 83 47 0N 44 0E
Erhlien 106 43 42N 112 2E
Erhlin 109 23 54N 120 22E
Erhtao Chiang, R. 107 42 35N 128 10E
Erhyüan 108 26 7N 99 57E
Eria, R. 56 42 10N 6 8W
Eriba 123 16 40N 36 10E
Eriboll, L. 37 58 28N 4 41W
Erica 46 52 43N 6 56E
Érice 64 38 4N 12 34E
Ericht, L. 37 56 50N 4 25W
Erie 156 42 10N 80 7W
Erigavo 91 10 35N 47 35E
Erikoúsa 68 39 55N 19 14E
Eriksdale 153 50 52N 98 7W
Erikslund 72 62 31N 15 54E
Erímanthos 69 37 57N 21 50E
Erimo-misaki 112 41 50N 143 15E
Eriskay I. 36 57 4N 7 18W
Eriskay, Sd. of 36 57 5N 7 20W
Erisort L. 36 58 5N 6 30W
Eriswil 50 47 5N 7 46E
Erith 152 53 25N 116 46W
Erithraí 69 38 13N 23 20E
Eritrea □ 123 14 0N 41 0E
Erjas, R. 56 39 45N 6 52W
Erker, L. 72 59 51N 18 29E
Erlangen 49 49 35N 11 0E
Erldunda 138 25 14S 133 12E
Ermelo, Neth. 46 52 35N 5 35E
Ermelo, S. Afr. 129 26 31S 29 59E

Ermenak **Fairmount**

Ermenak	**92**	36 44N	33 0E
Ermióni	**69**	37 23N	23 15E
Ermoúpolis = Siros	**69**	37 28N	24 57E
Ernakulam	**97**	9 59N	76 19E
Erne, Lough	**38**	54 26N	7 46W
Erne, R.	**38**	54 30N	8 16W
Ernée	**42**	48 18N	0 56W
Ernest Giles Ra.	**137**	27 0S	123 45E
Erode	**97**	11 24N	77 45E
Eromanga	**139**	26 40S	143 11E
Erongo	**128**	21 39S	15 58E
Erongoberg	**128**	21 45S	15 32E
Erp	**47**	51 36N	5 37E
Erquelinnes	**47**	50 19N	4 8E
Erquy	**42**	48 38N	2 29W
Erquy, Cap d'	**42**	48 39N	2 29W
Err, Piz d'	**51**	46 34N	9 43E
Errabiddy	**137**	25 25S	117 5E
Erramala Hills	**97**	15 30N	78 15E
Errer, R.	**123**	42 35N	8 40E
Errigal, Mt.	**38**	55 2N	8 8W
Errill	**39**	52 52N	7 40W
Erris Hd.	**38**	54 19N	10 0W
Errochty, L.	**37**	56 45N	4 10W
Errogie	**37**	57 16N	4 23W
Errol	**35**	56 24N	3 13W
Erseka	**68**	40 22N	20 40E
Erskine	**158**	47 37N	96 0W
Erstein	**43**	48 25N	7 38E
Erstfeld	**51**	46 50N	8 38E
Ertil	**81**	51 55N	40 50E
Ertvågøy	**71**	63 12N	8 25E
Ertvelde	**47**	51 11N	3 45E
Erundu	**128**	20 39S	16 26E
Eruwa	**121**	7 33N	3 26E
Ervalla	**72**	59 28N	15 16E
Ervy-le-Châtel	**43**	48 2N	3 55E
Erwin	**157**	36 10N	82 28W
Erzgebirge	**48**	50 25N	13 0E
Erzin	**77**	50 15N	95 10E
Erzincan	**92**	39 46N	39 30E
Erzurum	**92**	39 57N	41 15E
Es Sahrâ' Esh Sharqîya	**122**	26 0N	33 30E
Es Sider	**119**	30 50N	18 21E
Es Sînâ'	**122**	29 0N	34 0E
Es Souk	**121**	18 48N	1 2E
Es Sûkî	**123**	13 20N	34 58E
Esa'ala	**135**	9 45S	150 49E
Esambo	**126**	3 48S	23 30E
Esan-misaki	**112**	41 40N	141 10E
Esbjerg	**73**	55 29N	8 29E
Escada	**170**	8 22S	35 14W
Escalante	**161**	37 47N	111 37W
Escalante, R.	**161**	37 45N	111 0W
Escalón	**164**	26 40N	104 20W
Escalona	**56**	40 9N	4 29W
Escambia, R.	**157**	30 45N	87 15W
Escanaba	**156**	45 44N	87 5W
Escant, R.	**47**	51 2N	3 45E
Esch-sur-Alzette	**47**	49 32N	6 0E
Eschallens	**50**	46 39N	6 38E
Eschede	**48**	52 44N	10 13E
Escholzmatt	**50**	46 55N	7 56E
Eschwege	**48**	51 10N	10 3E
Eschweiler	**48**	50 49N	6 14E
Escondida, La	**164**	24 6N	99 55W
Escondido	**163**	33 9N	117 4W
Escrick	**33**	53 53N	1 3W
Escuinapa	**164**	22 50N	105 50W
Escuintla	**166**	14 20N	90 48W
Escuminac	**151**	48 0N	67 0W
Escutillas = Ceba	**174**	6 33N	70 24W
Eséka	**121**	3 41N	10 44E
Esens	**48**	53 40N	7 35E
Esera, R.	**58**	42 24N	0 22E
Esfahan □	**93**	33 0N	53 0E
Esgueva, R.	**56**	41 46N	4 14W
Esh Sham = Dimashq	**92**	33 30N	36 18E
Esh Shamâlîya □	**122**	19 0N	31 0E
Esha Ness	**36**	60 30N	1 36W
Eshowe	**129**	28 50S	31 30E
Eshta' ol	**90**	31 47N	35 0E
Esiama	**120**	4 48N	2 25W
Esino, R.	**63**	43 28N	13 8E
Esk R.	**32**	54 23N	3 21W
Esk, R., Dumfries, U.K.	**35**	54 58N	3 4W
Esk, R., N. Yorks., U.K.	**33**	54 27N	0 36W
Eskdale	**35**	55 12N	3 4W
Eskifjördur	**74**	65 3N	13 55W
Eskilstuna	**72**	59 22N	16 32E
Eskimo Ls.	**147**	69 15N	132 17W
Eskimo Pt.	**153**	61 10N	94 3W
Eskişehir	**92**	39 50N	30 35E
Esla, R.	**56**	41 45N	5 50W
Eslöv	**73**	55 50N	13 20E
Esmeralda, La	**172**	22 16S	62 33W
Esmeraldas	**174**	1 0N	79 40W
Esneux	**47**	50 32N	5 33E
Espa	**71**	60 35N	11 15E
Espada, Pta.	**174**	12 5N	71 7W
Espalion	**44**	44 32N	2 47E
Espalmador, I.	**59**	38 48N	1 26E
Espanola	**150**	46 15N	81 46W
Espardell, I. del	**59**	38 47N	1 25E
Esparraguera	**58**	41 33N	1 52E
Esparta	**166**	9 59N	84 40W
Espejo	**57**	37 40N	4 34W
Espenberg, C.	**147**	66 35N	163 40W
Esperança	**170**	7 1S	35 51W
Esperance	**137**	33 45S	121 55E
Esperance B.	**137**	33 48S	121 55E
Esperantinópolis	**170**	4 53S	44 53W
Esperanza	**172**	31 29S	61 3W
Esperanza, La, Argent.	**172**	24 9S	64 52W
Esperanza, La, Boliv.	**174**	14 20S	62 0W
Esperanza, La, Cuba	**166**	22 46N	83 44W
Esperanza, La, Hond.	**166**	14 15N	88 10W
Espéraza	**44**	42 56N	2 14E
Espevær Lt. Ho.	**71**	59 35N	5 7E
Espichel, C.	**57**	38 22N	9 16W
Espiel	**57**	38 11N	5 1W
Espigão, Serra do	**173**	26 35S	50 30W
Espinal	**174**	4 9N	74 53W
Espinazo, Sierra del = Espinhaço, Serra do	**171**	17 30S	43 30W
Espinhaço, Serra do	**171**	17 30S	43 30W
Espinho	**56**	41 1N	8 38W
Espinilho, Serra do	**173**	28 30S	55 0W
Espino	**174**	8 34N	66 1W
Espinosa de los Monteros	**56**	43 5N	3 34W
Espírito Santo □	**171**	20 0S	40 45W
Espíritu Santo, B. del	**165**	19 15N	79 40W
Espíritu Santo, I.	**164**	24 30N	110 23W
Espita	**165**	21 1N	88 19W
Esplanada	**171**	11 47S	37 57W
Espluga de Francolí	**58**	41 24N	1 7E
Espuña, Sierra de	**59**	37 51N	1 35W
Espungabera	**129**	20 29S	32 45E
Esquel	**176**	42 40S	71 20W
Esquimalt	**148**	48 30N	123 23W
Esquina	**172**	30 0S	59 30W
Essaouira (Mogador)	**118**	31 32N	9 42W
Essarts, Les	**42**	46 47N	1 12W
Essebie	**126**	2 58N	30 40E
Essen, Belg.	**47**	51 28N	4 28E
Essen, Ger.	**48**	51 28N	6 59E
Essendon, Mt.	**137**	25 0S	120 30E
Essequibo, R.	**174**	5 45N	58 50W
Essex	**162**	39 18N	76 29W
Essex □	**29**	51 48N	0 30E
Esslingen	**49**	48 43N	9 19E
Essonne □	**43**	48 30N	2 20E
Essvik	**72**	62 18N	17 24E
Estadilla	**58**	42 4N	0 16E
Estados, I. de los	**176**	54 40S	64 30W
Estagel	**44**	42 47N	2 40E
Estância	**170**	11 16S	37 26W
Estancia	**161**	34 50N	106 1W
Estarreja	**56**	40 45N	8 35W
Estats, P. d'	**44**	42 40N	1 40E
Estavayer le Lac	**50**	46 51N	6 51E
Estcourt	**129**	28 58S	29 53E
Este	**63**	45 12N	11 40E
Esteban	**56**	43 33N	6 5W
Estelí	**166**	13 9N	86 22W
Estella	**58**	42 40N	2 0W
Estelline, S.D., U.S.A.	**158**	44 39N	96 52W
Estelline, Texas, U.S.A.	**159**	34 35N	100 27W
Estena, R.	**57**	39 23N	4 44W
Estepa	**57**	37 17N	4 52W
Estepona	**57**	36 24N	5 7W
Esterhazy	**153**	50 37N	102 5W
Esternay	**43**	48 44N	3 33E
Esterri de Aneu	**58**	42 38N	1 5E
Estevan	**153**	49 10N	102 59W
Estevan Group	**152**	53 3N	129 38W
Estherville	**158**	43 25N	94 50W
Estissac	**43**	48 16N	3 48E
Eston, Can.	**153**	51 8N	108 40W
Eston, U.K.	**33**	54 33N	1 6W
Estonian S.S.R. □	**80**	48 30N	25 30E
Estoril	**57**	38 42N	9 23W
Estrada, La	**56**	42 43N	8 27W
Estrêla, Serra da	**56**	40 10N	7 45W
Estrella	**59**	38 25N	3 35W
Estremadura	**57**	39 0N	9 0W
Estremoz	**57**	38 51N	7 39W
Estrondo, Serra do	**170**	7 20S	48 0W
Esztergom	**53**	47 47N	18 44E
Et Tieta	**118**	29 37N	9 15W
Et Turra	**90**	32 39N	35 39E
Étables-sur-Mer	**42**	48 38N	2 51W
Etah	**95**	27 35N	78 40E
Étain	**43**	49 13N	5 38E
Etalle	**47**	49 40N	5 36E
Etamamu	**151**	50 18N	59 59W
Étampes	**43**	48 26N	2 10E
Étang	**43**	46 52N	4 10E
Etanga	**128**	17 55S	13 00E
Étaples	**43**	50 30N	1 39E
Etawah	**95**	26 48N	79 6E
Etawah, R.	**157**	34 20N	84 15W
Etawney L.	**153**	57 50N	96 50W
Etchingham	**29**	51 0N	0 27E
Eteh	**121**	7 2N	7 28E
Etelia	**121**	19 10N	0 55E
Éthe	**47**	49 35N	5 35E
Ethel Creek	**136**	22 55S	120 11E
Ethel, Oued el	**118**	28 31N	3 37W
Ethelbert	**153**	51 32N	100 25W
Ethiopia ■	**91**	8 0N	40 0E
Ethiopian Highlands	**114**	10 0N	37 0E
Etive, L.	**34**	56 30N	5 12W
Etna, Mt.	**65**	37 45N	15 0E
Etne	**71**	59 40N	5 56E
Etoile	**127**	11 33S	27 30E
Etolin I.	**152**	56 5N	132 20W
Eton	**29**	51 29N	0 37W
Etoshapan	**128**	18 40S	16 30E
Etowah	**157**	35 20N	84 30W
Étrépagny	**42**	49 18N	1 36E
Étretat	**42**	49 42N	0 12E
Etroits, Les	**151**	47 24N	68 54W
Etropole	**68**	43 50N	24 0E
Ettelbrüch	**47**	49 50N	6 5E
Ettelbruck	**47**	49 51N	6 5E
Etten	**47**	51 34N	4 38E
Ettington	**28**	52 8N	1 38W
Ettlingen	**49**	48 58N	8 25E
Ettrick Forest	**35**	55 30N	3 0W
Ettrick Water	**35**	55 31N	2 55W
Etuku	**126**	3 42S	25 45E
Etzatlán	**164**	20 48N	104 5W
Etzna	**165**	19 35N	90 15W
Eu	**42**	50 3N	1 26E
Euboea = Évvoia	**69**	38 40N	23 40E
Euchareena	**141**	32 57S	149 6E
Eucla Basin	**137**	31 19S	126 9E
Euclid	**156**	41 32N	81 31W
Euclides da Cunha	**170**	10 31S	39 1W
Eucumbene, L.	**141**	36 2S	148 40E
Eudora	**159**	33 5N	91 17W
Eudunda	**140**	34 12S	139 7E
Eufaula, Ala., U.S.A.	**157**	31 55N	85 11W
Eufaula, Okla., U.S.A.	**159**	35 20N	95 33W
Eufaula, L.	**159**	35 15N	95 28W
Eugene	**160**	44 0N	123 8W
Eugenia, Punta	**164**	27 50N	115 5W
Eugowra	**141**	33 22S	148 24E
Eulo	**139**	28 10S	145 3E
Eumungerie	**141**	31 56N	148 36E
Eunice, La., U.S.A.	**159**	30 35N	92 28W
Eunice, N. Mex., U.S.A.	**159**	32 30N	103 10W
Eupen	**47**	50 37N	6 3E
Euphrates = Furat, Nahr al	**92**	33 30N	43 0E
Eure □	**42**	49 6N	1 0E
Eure-et-Loir □	**42**	48 22N	1 30E
Eureka, Can.	**12**	80 0N	85 56W
Eureka, Calif., U.S.A.	**160**	40 50N	124 0W
Eureka, Kans., U.S.A.	**159**	37 50N	96 20W
Eureka, Mont., U.S.A.	**160**	48 53N	115 6W
Eureka, Nev., U.S.A.	**160**	39 32N	116 2W
Eureka, S.D., U.S.A.	**158**	45 49N	99 38W
Eureka, Utah, U.S.A.	**160**	40 0N	112 0W
Eureka, Mt.	**137**	26 35S	121 35E
Eurelia	**140**	32 33S	138 35E
Euroa	**141**	36 44S	145 35E
Europa, Île	**125**	22 20S	40 22E
Europa, Picos de	**56**	43 10N	5 0W
Europa Pt.	**55**	36 2N	6 32W
Europa Pt. = Europa, Pta. de	**57**	36 3N	5 21W
Europa, Pta. de	**57**	36 3N	5 21W
Europe	**16**	20 0N	20 0E
Europoort	**46**	51 57N	4 10E
Euskirchen	**48**	50 40N	6 45E
Eustis	**157**	28 54N	81 36W
Eutin	**48**	54 7N	10 38E
Eutsuk L.	**152**	53 20N	126 45W
Euxton	**32**	53 41N	2 42W
Eva Downs	**138**	18 1S	134 52E
Eval, Mt.	**90**	32 15N	35 15E
Evanger	**71**	60 39N	6 7E
Evans	**158**	40 25N	104 43W
Evans Head	**139**	29 7S	153 27E
Evans L.	**150**	50 50N	77 0W
Evans P.	**158**	41 0N	105 35W
Evanston, Ill., U.S.A.	**156**	42 0N	87 40W
Evanston, Wy., U.S.A.	**160**	41 10N	111 0W
Evansville, Ind., U.S.A.	**156**	38 0N	87 35W
Evansville, Wis., U.S.A.	**158**	42 47N	89 18W
Evanton	**37**	57 40N	4 20W
Evato	**129**	20 37S	47 10E
Évaux-les-Bains	**44**	46 12N	2 29E
Eveleth	**158**	47 35N	92 40W
Even Yahuda	**90**	32 16N	34 53E
Evensk	**77**	61 57N	159 14E
Evenstad	**71**	61 25N	11 7E
Everard, C.	**141**	37 49S	149 17E
Everard, L.	**139**	31 30S	135 0E
Everard Ras.	**137**	27 5S	132 28E
Evercreech	**28**	51 8N	2 30W
Everdale	**141**	31 52S	144 46E
Evere	**47**	50 52N	4 25E
Everest, Mt.	**95**	28 5N	86 58E
Everett	**160**	48 0N	122 10W
Evergem	**47**	51 7N	3 43E
Everglades	**157**	26 0N	80 30W
Evergreen	**157**	31 28N	86 55W
Everöd	**73**	55 53N	14 5E
Everson	**160**	48 57N	122 22W
Everton	**141**	36 25S	146 33E
Evesham	**28**	52 6N	1 57W
Evian-les-Bains	**45**	46 24N	6 35E
Evinayong	**124**	1 50N	10 35E
Évinos, R.	**69**	38 27N	21 40E
Evisa	**45**	42 15N	8 48E
Évora	**57**	38 33N	7 57W
Évora □	**57**	38 33N	7 50W
Évreux	**42**	49 0N	1 8E
Évritania □	**69**	39 5N	21 30E
Évron	**42**	48 23N	1 58W
Évros □	**68**	41 10N	26 0E
Evrótas, R.	**69**	36 50N	22 40E
Évvoia	**69**	38 30N	24 0E
Évvoia □	**69**	38 40N	23 40E
Ewe, L.	**36**	57 49N	5 38W
Ewell	**29**	51 20N	0 15W
Ewhurst	**29**	51 9N	0 25W
Ewing	**158**	42 18N	98 22W
Ewo	**124**	0 48S	14 45E
Exaltación	**174**	13 10S	65 20W
Excelsior	**139**	33 6S	149 59W
Excelsior Springs	**158**	39 20N	94 10W
Excideuil	**44**	45 20N	1 4E
Exe, R.	**30**	50 38N	3 27W
Exeter, U.K.	**30**	50 43N	3 31W
Exeter, Calif., U.S.A.	**163**	36 17N	119 9W
Exeter, Nebr., U.S.A.	**158**	40 43N	97 30W
Exeter, N.H., U.S.A.	**162**	43 0N	70 58W
Exford	**28**	51 8N	3 39W
Exloo	**46**	52 53N	6 52E
Exmes	**42**	48 45N	0 10E
Exminster	**30**	50 40N	3 29W
Exmoor	**30**	51 10N	3 59W
Exmore	**162**	37 32N	75 50W
Exmouth, Austral.	**136**	22 6S	114 0E
Exmouth, U.K.	**30**	50 37N	3 26W
Exmouth G.	**136**	22 15S	114 15E
Expedition Range	**138**	24 30S	149 12E
Exton	**29**	52 42N	0 38W
Extremadura	**57**	39 30N	6 5W
Exu	**171**	7 31S	39 43W
Exuma Sound	**166**	24 30N	76 20W
Eyam	**33**	53 17N	1 40W
Eyasi, L.	**126**	3 30S	35 0E
Eyawaddi Myii	**98**	15 50N	95 6E
Eye, Camb., U.K.	**29**	52 36N	0 11W
Eye, Norfolk, U.K.	**29**	52 19N	1 9E
Eye Pen.	**36**	58 13N	6 10W
Eyeberry L.	**153**	63 8N	104 43W
Eyemouth	**35**	55 53N	2 5W
Eygurande	**44**	45 40N	2 26E
Eyhatten	**47**	50 43N	6 1E
Eyisen	**82**	41 0N	36 50E
Eyjafjorður	**74**	66 15N	18 30W
Eymet	**44**	44 40N	0 25E
Eymoutiers	**44**	45 40N	1 45E
Eynhallow Sd.	**37**	59 8N	3 7W
Eynort, L.	**36**	57 13N	7 18W
Eynsham	**28**	51 47N	1 21W
Eyrarbakki	**74**	63 52N	21 9W
Eyre	**137**	32 15S	126 18E
Eyre Cr.	**138**	26 40S	139 0E
Eyre, L.	**133**	29 30S	137 26E
Eyre L., (North)	**139**	28 30S	137 20E
Eyre L., (South)	**139**	29 18S	137 25E
Eyre Mts.	**143**	45 25S	168 25E
Eyre Pen.	**139**	33 30S	137 17E
Eyrecourt	**39**	53 12N	8 8W
Ez Zeidab	**122**	17 25N	33 55E
Ez Zergoun, W.	**118**	32 45N	2 25E
Ezcaray	**58**	42 19N	3 0W
Ezine	**68**	39 48N	26 12E

F

Fabens	**161**	31 30N	106 8W
Fåborg	**73**	55 6N	10 15E
Fabriano	**63**	43 20N	12 52E
Fabrizia	**43**	38 29N	16 19E
Făcăeni	**70**	44 32N	27 53E
Facatativá	**174**	4 49N	74 22W
Facture	**44**	44 39N	0 58W
Fada	**117**	17 13N	21 34E
Fada-n-Gourma	**121**	12 10N	0 30E
Fadd	**53**	46 28N	18 49E
Faddeyevski, Ostrov	**77**	76 0N	150 0E
Fadhili	**92**	26 55N	49 10E
Fadlab	**122**	17 42N	34 2E
Faenza	**63**	44 17N	11 53E
Fafa	**121**	15 22N	0 48E
Fafe	**56**	41 27N	8 11W
Fagam	**121**	11 1N	10 1E
Fågelsjö	**72**	61 50N	14 35E
Fagerhult	**73**	57 8N	15 40E
Fagernes	**75**	60 59N	9 14E
Fagersta	**72**	60 1N	15 46E
Fåglavik	**73**	58 6N	13 6E
Fagnano Castello	**65**	39 31N	16 4E
Fagnano, L.	**176**	54 30S	68 0W
Fagnières	**43**	48 58N	4 20E
Fahral	**93**	29 0N	59 0E
Fahūd	**93**	22 18N	56 28E
Faid	**92**	27 1N	42 52E
Faido	**51**	46 29N	8 48E
Fair, C.	**138**	12 24S	143 16E
Fair Hd.	**38**	55 14N	6 10W
Fair Isle	**23**	59 30N	1 40W
Fair Oaks	**163**	38 39N	121 16W
Fairbank	**161**	31 44N	110 12W
Fairbanks	**147**	64 59N	147 40W
Fairbourne	**31**	52 42N	4 3W
Fairbury	**158**	40 5N	97 5W
Fairfax, Okla., U.S.A.	**159**	36 37N	96 45W
Fairfax, Va., U.S.A.	**162**	38 51N	77 18W
Fairfield, Austral.	**141**	33 53S	150 57E
Fairfield, Ala., U.S.A.	**157**	33 30N	87 0W
Fairfield, Calif., U.S.A.	**163**	38 14N	122 1W
Fairfield, Conn., U.S.A.	**162**	41 8N	73 16W
Fairfield, Idaho, U.S.A.	**160**	43 27N	114 52W
Fairfield, Ill., U.S.A.	**156**	38 20N	88 20W
Fairfield, Iowa, U.S.A.	**158**	41 0N	91 58W
Fairfield, Mont., U.S.A.	**160**	47 40N	112 0W
Fairfield, Texas, U.S.A.	**159**	31 40N	96 0W
Fairford, Can.	**153**	51 37N	98 38W
Fairford, U.K.	**28**	51 42N	1 48W
Fairhope	**157**	30 35N	87 50W
Fairlie, N.Z.	**143**	44 5S	170 49E
Fairlie, U.K.	**34**	55 44N	4 52W
Fairlight	**29**	50 53N	0 40E
Fairmead	**163**	37 5N	120 10W
Fairmont, Minn., U.S.A.	**158**	43 37N	94 30W
Fairmont, W. Va., U.S.A.	**156**	39 29N	80 10W
Fairmont Hot Springs	**152**	50 20N	115 56W
Fairmount	**163**	34 45N	118 26W

Fairplay Field

Fairplay	**161**	39 9N	107 0W
Fairport	**156**	43 8N	77 29W
Fairview, Austral.	**138**	15 31S	144 17E
Fairview, Can.	**152**	56 5N	118 25W
Fairview, N. Dak., U.S.A.	**158**	47 49N	104 7W
Fairview, Okla., U.S.A.	**159**	36 19N	98 30W
Fairview, Utah, U.S.A.	**160**	39 50N	111 0W
Fairweather, Mt.	**147**	58 55N	137 45W
Faith	**158**	45 2N	102 4W
Faither, The, C.	**36**	60 34N	1 30W
Faizabad, Afghan.	**93**	37 7N	70 33E
Faizabad, India	**95**	26 45N	82 10E
Faizpur	**96**	21 14N	75 49E
Fajardo	**147**	18 20N	65 39W
Fakenham	**29**	52 50N	0 51E
Fakfak	**103**	3 0S	132 15E
Fakiya	**170**	42 10N	27 4E
Fakobli	**120**	7 23N	7 23W
Fakse	**73**	55 15N	12 8E
Fakse B.	**73**	55 11N	12 15E
Fakse Ladeplads	**73**	55 16N	12 9E
Fak'u	**107**	42 31N	123 26E
Falaise	**42**	48 54N	0 12W
Falaise, Mui	**100**	19 6N	105 45E
Falakrón Óros	**68**	41 15N	23 58E
Falam	**98**	23 0N	93 45E
Falcarragh	**38**	55 8N	8 8W
Falces	**58**	42 24N	1 48W
Falcón □	**174**	11 0N	69 50W
Falcon, C.	**118**	35 50N	0 50W
Falcón Dam	**159**	26 50N	99 20W
Falconara Marittima	**63**	43 37N	13 23E
Faldingworth	**33**	53 21N	0 22W
Faléa	**120**	12 16N	11 17W
Falelatai	**84**	13 55S	171 59W
Falenki	**84**	58 22N	51 35E
Faleshty	**82**	47 32N	27 44E
Falfurrias	**159**	27 8N	98 8W
Falher	**152**	55 44N	117 15W
Falkenberg, Ger.	**48**	51 34N	13 13E
Falkenberg, Sweden	**73**	56 54N	12 30E
Falkensee	**48**	52 35N	13 6E
Falkenstein	**48**	50 27N	12 24E
Falkirk	**35**	56 0N	3 47W
Falkland	**35**	56 15N	3 13W
Falkland Is.	**176**	51 30S	59 0W
Falkland Is. Dep.	**13**	57 0S	40 0W
Falkland Sd.	**176**	52 0S	60 0W
Falkonéra	**69**	36 50N	23 52E
Falköping	**73**	58 12N	13 33E
Fall Brook	**161**	33 25N	117 12W
Fall River	**162**	41 45N	71 5W
Fall River Mills	**160**	41 1N	121 30W
Fallbrook	**163**	33 23N	117 15W
Fallmore	**38**	54 6N	10 5W
Fallon, Mont., U.S.A.	**158**	46 52N	105 8W
Fallon, Nev., U.S.A.	**160**	39 31N	118 51W
Falls Church	**162**	38 53N	77 11W
Falls City, Nebr., U.S.A.	**158**	40 0N	95 40W
Falls City, Oreg., U.S.A.	**160**	44 54N	123 29W
Falmey	**121**	12 36N	2 51E
Falmouth, Jamaica	**166**	18 30N	77 40W
Falmouth, U.K.	**30**	50 9N	5 5W
Falmouth, Ky., U.S.A.	**156**	38 40N	84 20W
Falmouth, Mass., U.S.A.	**162**	41 34N	70 38W
Falmouth B.	**30**	50 7N	5 3E
False B.	**128**	34 15S	18 40E
False Divi Pt.	**97**	15 35N	80 50E
Falset	**58**	41 7N	0 50E
Falso, C.	**166**	15 12N	83 21W
Falster	**73**	54 45N	11 55E
Falsterbo	**73**	55 23N	12 50E
Falsterbokanalen	**73**	55 25N	12 56E
Falstone	**35**	55 10N	2 26W
Faluja	**90**	31 48N	31 37E
Falun	**72**	60 37N	15 37E
Famagusta	**92**	35 8N	33 55E
Famaka	**123**	11 24N	34 52E
Famatina, Sierra, de	**172**	29 5S	68 0W
Family L.	**153**	51 54N	95 27W
Famoso	**163**	35 37N	119 12W
Fampotabe	**129**	15 56S	50 8E
Fan i Madh, R.	**68**	41 56N	20 16E
Fana, Mali	**120**	13 0N	6 56W
Fana, Norway	**71**	60 16N	5 20E
Fanad Hd.	**38**	55 17N	7 40W
Fanambana	**129**	13 34S	50 0E
Fanárion	**68**	39 24N	21 47E
Fanch'ang	**109**	31 2N	118 13E
Fanchiat'un	**107**	43 42N	125 5E
Fanchih	**106**	39 14N	113 19E
Fandriana	**129**	20 14S	47 21E
Fang	**100**	19 55N	99 13E
Fangch'eng, Honan, China	**106**	33 16N	112 59E
Fangch'eng, Kwangsi-Chuang, China	**108**	21 46N	108 21E
Fanghsien	**109**	32 0N	111 0E
Fangliao	**109**	22 22N	130 35E
Fangshan	**106**	38 0N	111 16E
Fangtzu	**107**	36 39N	119 15E
Fannich, L.	**36**	57 40N	5 0W
Fanning I.	**131**	3 51N	159 22W
Fanny Bay	**152**	49 27N	124 48W
Fanø	**73**	55 25N	8 25E
Fano	**63**	43 50N	13 0E
Fanø, I.	**73**	55 25N	8 25E
Fanshaw	**152**	57 11N	133 30W
Fao (Al Fāw)	**92**	30 0N	48 30E
Faqirwali	**94**	29 27N	73 0E
Fara in Sabina	**63**	42 13N	12 44E
Farab	**85**	39 9N	63 36E
Faraday Seamount Group	**14**	50 0N	27 0W
Faradje	**126**	3 50N	29 45E
Farafangana	**129**	22 49S	47 50E
Farâfra, El Wâhât el-	**122**	27 15N	28 20E
Farah	**93**	32 20N	62 7E
Farah □	**93**	32 25N	62 10E
Farahalana	**129**	14 26S	50 10E
Faraid, Gebel	**122**	23 33N	35 19E
Faraid Hd.	**37**	58 35N	4 48W
Faramana	**120**	11 56N	4 45W
Faranah	**120**	10 3N	10 45W
Farasān, Jazā'ir	**91**	16 45N	41 55E
Farasan Kebir	**91**	16 40N	42 0E
Faratsiho	**129**	19 24S	46 57E
Fardes, R.	**59**	37 25N	3 10W
Fareham	**28**	50 52N	1 11W
Farewell	**147**	62 30N	154 0W
Farewell, C.	**143**	40 29S	172 43E
Farewell C. = Farvel, K.	**12**	59 48N	43 55W
Farewell Spit	**143**	40 35S	173 0E
Farfán	**174**	0 16N	76 41W
Fargo	**158**	47 0N	97 0W
Faria, R.	**90**	32 12N	35 27E
Faribault	**158**	44 15N	93 19W
Faridkot	**94**	30 44N	74 45E
Faridpur, Bangla.	**98**	23 15N	90 0E
Faridpur, India	**95**	18 14N	79 34E
Farila	**72**	61 48N	15 50E
Färila	**72**	61 48N	15 50E
Farim	**120**	12 27N	15 17W
Farimān	**93**	35 40N	60 0E
Farina	**139**	30 3S	138 15E
Faringdon	**28**	51 39N	1 34W
Faringe	**72**	59 55N	18 7E
Farinha, R.	**170**	6 15S	47 30W
Färjestaden	**73**	56 38N	16 25E
Farmakonisi	**69**	37 17N	27 8E
Farmerville	**159**	32 48N	92 23W
Farmingdale	**162**	40 12N	74 10W
Farmington, Calif., U.S.A.	**163**	37 56N	121 0W
Farmington, N. Mex., U.S.A.	**161**	36 45N	108 28W
Farmington, N.H., U.S.A.	**162**	43 25N	71 3W
Farmington, Utah, U.S.A.	**160**	41 0N	111 58W
Farmington, R.	**162**	41 51N	72 38W
Farmville	**156**	37 19N	78 22W
Farnborough	**29**	51 17N	0 46W
Farne Is.	**35**	55 38N	1 37W
Farnham	**29**	51 13N	0 49W
Farnham, Mt.	**152**	45 20N	72 55W
Farnworth	**32**	53 33N	2 24W
Faro, Brazil	**175**	2 0S	56 45W
Faro, Port.	**57**	37 2N	7 55W
Fårö	**75**	58 0N	19 10E
Faro □	**57**	37 12N	8 10W
Faroe Is.	**16**	62 0N	7 0W
Farquhar, C.	**137**	23 38S	113 36E
Farquhar, Mt.	**136**	22 18S	116 53E
Farr	**37**	57 21N	4 13W
Farranfore	**39**	52 10N	9 32W
Farrars, Cr.	**138**	25 35S	140 43E
Farrashband	**93**	28 57N	52 5E
Farrell	**156**	41 13N	80 29W
Farrell Flat	**140**	33 48S	138 48E
Farrukhabad	**95**	27 30N	79 32E
Fars □	**93**	29 30N	55 0E
Fársala	**68**	39 17N	22 23E
Farsø	**73**	56 46N	9 19E
Farsö	**73**	56 48N	9 20E
Farstrup	**73**	56 59N	9 28E
Farsund	**71**	58 5N	6 55E
Fartura, Serra da	**173**	26 21S	52 52W
Faru	**121**	12 48N	6 12E
Farum	**73**	55 49N	12 21E
Farvel, Kap	**12**	59 48N	43 55W
Farwell	**159**	34 25N	103 0W
Faryab	**93**	28 7N	57 14E
Fasa	**93**	29 0N	53 32E
Fasag	**36**	57 33N	5 32W
Fasano	**65**	40 50N	17 20E
Fashoda	**123**	9 50N	32 2E
Faskari	**79**	11 42N	6 58E
Faslane	**34**	56 3N	4 49W
Fastnet Rock	**39**	51 22N	9 37W
Fastov	**80**	50 7N	29 57E
Fatehgarh	**95**	27 25N	79 35E
Fatehpur, Raj., India	**94**	28 0N	75 4E
Fatehpur, Ut. P., India	**95**	27 8N	81 7E
Fatick	**120**	14 19N	16 27W
Fatima	**151**	47 24N	61 53W
Fátima	**57**	39 37N	8 39W
Fatoya	**120**	11 37N	9 10W
Faucilles, Monts	**43**	48 5N	5 50E
Fauldhouse	**35**	55 50N	3 44W
Faulkton	**158**	45 4N	99 8W
Faulquemont	**43**	49 3N	6 36E
Fauquembergues	**43**	50 36N	2 5E
Faure I.	**137**	25 52S	113 50E
Fauresmith	**128**	29 44S	25 17E
Fauske	**74**	67 17N	15 25E
Fauvillers	**47**	49 51N	5 40E
Faux-Cap	**129**	25 33S	45 32E
Favara	**64**	37 19N	13 39E
Faversham	**29**	51 18N	0 54E
Favignana	**64**	37 56N	12 18E
Favone	**45**	41 47N	9 26E
Favourable Lake	**150**	52 50N	93 39W
Fawley	**28**	50 49N	1 20W
Fawn, R.	**150**	52 22N	88 20W
Fawnskin	**163**	34 16N	116 56W
Faxaflói	**74**	64 29N	23 0W
Faxälven	**72**	63 13N	17 13E
Faya = Largeau	**117**	17 58N	19 6E
Fayence	**45**	43 38N	6 42E
Fayette, Ala., U.S.A.	**157**	33 40N	87 50W
Fayette, La., U.S.A.	**156**	40 22N	86 52W
Fayette, Mo., U.S.A.	**158**	39 10N	92 40W
Fayetteville, Ark., U.S.A.	**159**	36 0N	94 5W
Fayetteville, N.C., U.S.A.	**157**	35 0N	78 58W
Fayetteville, Tenn., U.S.A.	**157**	35 0N	86 30W
Fayón	**58**	41 15N	0 20E
Fazeley	**28**	52 36N	1 42W
Fazenda Nova	**171**	16 11S	50 48W
Fazilka	**94**	30 27N	74 2E
Fazilpur	**94**	29 18N	70 29E
F'Derik	**116**	22 40N	12 45W
Fé, La	**166**	22 2N	84 15W
Feakle	**39**	52 56N	8 41W
Feale, R.	**39**	52 26N	9 28W
Fear, C.	**157**	33 45N	78 0W
Fearn	**37**	57 47N	4 0W
Fearnan	**37**	56 34N	4 6W
Feather, R.	**160**	39 30N	121 20W
Featherston	**142**	41 6S	175 20E
Featherstone	**127**	18 42S	30 55E
Fécamp	**42**	49 45N	0 22E
Fedala = Mohammeda	**118**	33 44N	7 21W
Fedamore	**39**	52 33N	8 36W
Federación	**172**	31 0S	57 55W
Federalsburg	**162**	38 42N	75 47W
Fedjadj, Chott el	**119**	33 52N	9 14E
Fedje	**71**	60 47N	4 43E
Fedorovka	**84**	53 38N	62 42E
Feeagh L.	**38**	53 56N	9 35W
Feeny	**38**	54 54N	7 0W
Fehérgyarmat	**53**	48 0N	22 30E
Fehmarn	**48**	54 26N	11 10E
Fehmarn Bælt	**73**	54 35N	11 20E
Feihsiang	**106**	36 32N	114 47E
Feihsien	**107**	35 12N	118 0E
Feilding	**142**	40 13S	175 35E
Feira	**65**	15 35S	30 16E
Feira de Santana	**171**	12 15S	38 57W
Fejér □	**53**	47 9N	18 30E
Fejø	**73**	54 55N	11 30E
Felanitx	**59**	39 27N	3 7E
Feldbach	**52**	46 57N	15 52E
Feldberg	**48**	53 20N	13 26E
Feldberg, mt.	**49**	47 51N	7 58E
Feldis	**51**	46 48N	9 26E
Feldkirch	**52**	47 15N	9 37E
Feldkirchen	**52**	46 44N	14 6E
Felhit	**123**	16 40N	38 1E
Felipe Carrillo Puerto	**165**	19 38N	88 3W
Felixlândia	**171**	18 47S	44 55W
Felixstowe	**29**	51 58N	1 22W
Felletin	**44**	45 53N	2 11E
Felpham	**29**	50 47N	0 38W
Felton, U.K.	**35**	55 18N	1 42W
Felton, U.S.A.	**163**	37 3N	122 4W
Feltre	**63**	46 1N	11 55E
Feltwell	**29**	52 29N	0 32E
Femø	**73**	54 58N	11 53E
Femunden	**71**	62 10N	11 53E
Fen Ho, R.	**106**	35 36N	110 42E
Fench'ing	**108**	24 35N	99 54E
Fénérive	**129**	17 22S	49 25E
Fenerwa	**123**	13 5N	39 3E
Fengári	**68**	40 25N	25 32E
Fengchen	**106**	40 30N	113 0E
Fengch'eng, Kiangsi, China	**109**	28 10N	115 43E
Fengch'eng, Liaoning, China	**107**	40 30N	124 2E
Fengchieh	**108**	31 3N	109 28E
Fengch'iu	**106**	35 2N	114 24E
Fenghsiang	**106**	34 26N	107 18E
Fenghsien, Kiangsu, China	**106**	34 42N	116 34E
Fenghsien, Shanghai, China	**109**	30 55N	121 27E
Fenghsien, Shensi, China	**106**	33 56N	106 41E
Fenghsin	**109**	28 42N	115 23E
Fenghua	**109**	29 40N	121 24E
Fenghuang	**108**	27 58N	109 19E
Fenghuangtsui	**106**	33 30N	109 27E
Fengi	**108**	25 35N	100 18E
Fengjun	**107**	39 51N	118 8E
Fengk'ai	**109**	23 26N	111 30E
Fengkang	**108**	27 58N	107 47E
Fengloho	**109**	31 29N	112 29E
Fengning	**106**	41 12N	116 32E
Fengshan, Hopei, China	**107**	41 13N	117 6E
Fengshan, Kwangsi-Chuang, China	**108**	24 32N	107 3E
Fengt'ai, Anhwei, China	**109**	32 44N	116 43E
Fengt'ai, Peip'ing, China	**106**	39 51N	116 17E
Fengteng	**106**	36 25N	114 14E
Fengtu	**108**	29 58N	107 59E
Fengyuang	**109**	32 52N	117 32E
Fenhsi	**106**	36 38N	111 31E
Feni	**109**	27 48N	114 41E
Feni Is.	**135**	4 0S	153 40E
Fenit	**39**	52 17N	9 51W
Fennagh	**39**	52 42N	6 50W
Fennimore	**158**	42 58N	90 41W
Fenny	**98**	22 55N	91 32E
Fenny Bentley	**33**	53 4N	1 43W
Fenny Compton	**28**	52 9N	1 20W
Fenny Stratford	**29**	51 59N	0 42W
Feno, C. de	**45**	41 58N	8 33E
Fenoarivo	**129**	18 26S	46 34E
Fens, The	**29**	52 45N	0 2E
Fenton, Can.	**153**	53 0N	105 35W
Fenton, U.S.A.	**156**	42 47N	83 44W
Fenwick	**34**	55 38N	4 25W
Fenyang	**106**	37 19N	111 46E
Feodosiya	**82**	45 2N	35 28E
Fer, C. de	**119**	37 3N	7 10E
Ferbane	**39**	53 17N	7 50W
Ferdows	**93**	33 58N	58 2E
Fère-Champenoise	**43**	48 45N	4 0E
Fère-en-Tardenois	**43**	49 10N	3 30E
Fère, La	**43**	49 40N	3 20E
Ferentino	**64**	41 42N	13 14E
Ferfer	**91**	5 18N	45 20E
Fergana	**85**	40 23N	71 46E
Ferganskaya Dolina	**85**	40 50N	71 30E
Ferganskiy Khrebet	**85**	41 0N	73 50E
Fergus	**150**	43 43N	80 24W
Fergus Falls	**158**	46 25N	96 0W
Fergus, R.	**39**	52 45N	9 0W
Ferguson	**150**	47 50N	73 30W
Fergusson I.	**135**	9 30S	150 45E
Fériana	**119**	34 59N	8 33E
FeriCanci	**66**	45 32N	18 0E
Ferkane	**119**	34 37N	7 26E
Ferkéssédougou	**120**	9 35N	5 6W
Ferlach	**52**	46 32N	14 18E
Ferland	**150**	50 19N	88 27W
Ferlo, Vallée du	**120**	15 15N	14 15W
Fermanagh (□)	**38**	54 21N	7 40W
Fermo	**63**	43 10N	13 42E
Fermoselle	**56**	41 19N	6 27W
Fermoy	**39**	52 4N	8 18W
Fernagh	**38**	54 2N	7 51W
Fernan Nuñ,z	**57**	37 40N	4 44W
Fernández	**172**	27 55S	63 50W
Fernandina	**157**	30 40N	81 30W
Fernando de Noronha, I.	**170**	4 0S	33 10W
Fernando do Noronho □	**170**	4 0S	33 10W
Fernando Póo = Macias Nguema Biyoga	**113**	3 30N	8 40E
Fernandópolis	**171**	20 16S	50 14W
Ferndale, Calif., U.S.A.	**160**	40 37N	124 12W
Ferndale, Wash., U.S.A.	**160**	48 51N	122 41W
Ferness	**37**	57 28N	3 44W
Fernhurst	**29**	51 3N	0 43W
Fernie	**152**	49 30N	115 5W
Fernilea	**36**	57 18N	6 24W
Fernlees	**138**	23 51S	148 7E
Fernley	**160**	39 42N	119 20W
Feroke	**97**	11 9N	75 46E
Ferozepore	**94**	30 55N	74 40E
Férrai	**68**	40 53N	26 10E
Ferrandina	**65**	40 30N	16 28E
Ferrara	**63**	44 50N	11 36E
Ferrato, C.	**64**	39 18N	9 39E
Ferreira do Alentejo	**57**	38 4N	8 6W
Ferreñafe	**174**	6 35S	79 50W
Ferret, C.	**44**	44 38N	1 15W
Ferrette	**43**	47 30N	7 20E
Ferriday	**159**	31 35N	91 33W
Ferrières	**43**	48 5N	2 48E
Ferriete	**62**	44 40N	9 30E
Ferrol	**56**	43 29N	8 15W
Ferron	**160**	39 3N	111 3W
Ferros	**171**	19 14S	43 2W
Ferryhill	**33**	54 42N	1 32W
Ferryland	**151**	47 2N	52 53W
Ferté Bernard, La	**42**	48 10N	0 40E
Ferté, La	**43**	48 57N	3 6E
Ferté-Mace, La	**42**	48 35N	0 21W
Ferté-St. Aubin, La	**43**	47 42N	1 57E
Ferté-Vidame, La	**42**	48 37N	0 53E
Fertile	**158**	47 37N	96 18W
Fertília	**64**	40 37N	8 13E
Fertöszentmiklós	**53**	47 35N	16 53E
Fès	**118**	34 0N	5 0W
Feschaux	**47**	50 9N	4 54E
Feshi	**124**	6 0S	18 10E
Fessenden	**158**	47 42N	99 44W
Fet	**71**	59 57N	11 12E
Feteşti	**70**	44 22N	27 51E
Fethaland, Pt.	**36**	60 39N	1 20W
Fethard	**39**	52 29N	7 42W
Fethiye	**92**	36 36N	29 10E
Fetlar, I.	**36**	60 36N	0 52W
Fettercairn	**37**	56 50N	2 33W
Feuerthalen	**51**	47 32N	8 38E
Feurs	**45**	45 45N	4 13E
Fezzan	**117**	27 0N	15 0E
Ffestiniog	**31**	52 58N	3 56W
Fforest Fawr, mt.	**31**	51 52N	3 35W
Fiambalá	**172**	27 45S	67 37W
Fianarantsoa	**125**	21 20S	46 45E
Fianarantsoa □	**129**	19 30S	47 0E
Fianga	**117**	9 55N	15 20E
Fibiş	**66**	45 57N	21 26E
Fichot, I.	**151**	51 12N	55 40W
Fichtelgebirge	**49**	50 10N	12 0E
Ficksburg	**129**	28 51S	27 53E
Fiddown	**39**	52 20N	7 20W
Fidenza	**62**	44 51N	10 3E
Field	**150**	46 31N	80 1W

Field I Fort Garland

Field I.	136	12 5 S	132 23 E
Field, R.	138	23 48 S	138 0 E
Fields Finds	137	29 0 S	117 10 E
Fierenana	129	18 29 S	48 24 E
Fiéri	68	40 43 N	19 33 E
Fiesch	50	46 25 N	8 12 E
Fife □	35	56 13 N	3 2 W
Fife Ness	35	56 17 N	2 35 W
Fifth Cataract	123	18 15 N	33 50 E
Figeac	44	44 37 N	2 2 E
Figline Valdarno	63	43 37 N	11 28 E
Figtree	127	20 22 S	28 20 E
Figueira da Foz	56	40 7 N	8 54 W
Figueiró dos Vinhos	56	39 55 N	8 16 W
Figueras	58	42 18 N	2 58 E
Figuig	118	32 5 N	1 11 W
Fihaonana	129	18 36 S	47 12 E
Fiherenana, R.	129	22 50 S	44 0 E
Fiji ■	142	17 20 S	179 0 E
Fiji Is.	130	17 20 S	179 0 E
Fik	90	32 46 N	35 41 E
Fika	121	11 15 N	11 13 E
Filabres, Sierra de los	59	37 13 N	2 20 W
Filadélfia, Brazil	170	7 21 S	47 30 W
Filadélfia, Italy	65	38 47 N	16 17 E
Filadelfia	172	22 25 S	60 0 W
Fil'akovo	53	48 17 N	19 50 E
Filby	29	52 40 N	1 39 E
Filchner Ice Shelf	13	78 0 S	60 0 W
Filer	160	42 30 N	114 35 W
Filey	33	54 13 N	0 18 W
Filey B.	33	54 12 N	0 15 W
Filiaşi	70	44 32 N	23 31 E
Filiátes	68	39 38 N	20 16 E
Filiatrá	69	37 9 N	21 35 E
Filicudi, I.	65	38 35 N	14 33 E
Filiourí, R.	68	41 15 N	25 40 E
Filipstad	72	59 43 N	14 9 E
Filisur	51	46 41 N	9 40 E
Fillmore, Can.	153	49 50 N	103 25 W
Fillmore, U.S.A.	163	34 23 N	118 58 W
Filottrano	63	43 28 N	13 20 E
Filton	28	51 29 N	2 34 E
Filyos	82	41 34 N	32 4 E
Filyos çayi	92	41 35 N	32 10 E
Finale Ligure	62	44 10 N	8 21 E
Finale nell' Emília	63	44 50 N	11 18 E
Fiñana	59	37 10 N	2 50 W
Fincham	29	52 38 N	0 30 E
Findhorn	37	57 39 N	3 36 W
Findhorn, R.	37	57 38 N	3 38 W
Findlay	156	41 0 N	83 41 W
Findon	29	50 53 N	0 24 W
Finea	38	53 46 N	7 23 W
Finedon	29	52 20 N	0 40 W
Finger L.	153	53 9 N	93 30 W
Fingest	29	51 35 N	0 52 W
Finglas	38	53 22 N	6 18 W
Fingõe	127	15 12 S	31 50 E
Finike	92	36 21 N	30 10 E
Finistère □	42	48 20 N	4 0 W
Finisterre	56	42 54 N	9 16 W
Finisterre, C.	56	42 50 N	9 19 W
Finisterre Ra.	135	6 0 S	146 30 E
Finke	138	25 34 S	134 35 E
Finke, R.	138	24 54 S	134 16 E
Finland ■	78	70 0 N	27 0 E
Finland, G. of	78	60 0 N	26 0 E
Finlay, R.	152	55 50 N	125 10 W
Finley, Austral.	141	35 38 S	145 35 E
Finley, U.S.A.	158	47 35 N	97 50 W
Finn, R.	38	54 50 N	7 55 W
Finnart	34	56 7 N	4 48 W
Finnigan, Mt.	138	15 49 S	145 17 E
Finniss	140	35 24 S	138 48 E
Finniss, C.	139	33 38 S	134 51 E
Finnmark fylke □	74	69 30 N	25 0 E
Finschhafen	135	6 33 S	147 50 E
Finse	71	60 36 N	7 30 E
Finspång	73	58 45 N	15 43 E
Finsta	72	59 45 N	18 34 E
Finsteraarhorn	50	46 31 N	8 10 E
Finsterwalde	48	51 37 N	13 42 E
Finsterwolde	46	53 12 N	7 6 E
Finstown	37	59 0 N	3 8 W
Fintona	38	54 30 N	7 20 W
Fintown	38	54 52 N	8 8 W
Finucanel I.	132	20 19 S	118 30 E
Finvoy	38	55 0 N	6 29 W
Fionn L.	36	57 46 N	5 30 W
Fionnphort	34	56 19 N	6 23 W
Fiora, R.	63	42 25 N	11 35 E
Fiordland National Park	143	45 0 S	167 50 E
Fiorenzuola d'Arda	62	44 56 N	9 54 E
Fiq	90	32 46 N	35 41 E
Fire River	150	48 47 N	83 36 W
Firebag, R.	153	57 45 N	111 21 W
Firebaugh	163	36 52 N	120 27 W
Firedrake L.	153	61 25 N	104 30 W
Firenze	63	43 47 N	11 15 E
Firkessédougou	120	9 35 N	5 6 W
Firmi	44	44 32 N	2 19 E
Firminy	45	45 23 N	4 18 E
Firoz Kohi	93	34 45 N	63 0 E
Firozabad	95	27 10 N	78 25 E
First Cataract	122	24 1 N	32 51 E
Fīrūzābād	93	28 52 N	52 35 E
Firuzkuh	93	35 50 N	52 40 E
Firvale	152	52 27 N	126 13 W
Fish, R.	128	27 40 S	17 30 E
Fisher	137	30 30 S	131 0 E
Fisher B.	153	51 35 N	97 13 W
Fishguard	31	51 59 N	4 59 W
Fishguard B.	31	52 2 N	4 58 W
Fishing L.	153	52 10 N	95 24 W
Fishkill	162	41 32 N	73 53 W
Fishtoft	33	52 27 N	0 2 E
Fishtown	120	4 24 N	7 45 E
Fiskivötn	74	64 50 N	20 45 W
Fiskum	71	59 42 N	9 46 E
Fismes	43	49 20 N	3 40 E
Fister	71	59 10 N	6 5 E
Fitchburg	162	42 35 N	71 47 W
Fitero	58	42 4 N	1 52 W
Fitful Hd.	36	59 54 N	1 20 W
Fitjar	71	59 55 N	5 17 E
Fitri, L.	124	12 50 N	17 28 E
Fitz Roy	176	47 10 S	67 0 W
Fitzgerald, Can.	152	59 51 N	111 36 W
Fitzgerald, U.S.A.	157	31 45 N	83 10 W
Fitzmaurice, R.	136	14 50 S	129 50 E
Fitzpatrick	150	47 29 N	72 46 W
Fitzroy Crossing	136	18 9 S	125 38 E
Fitzroy, R., Queens., Austral.	138	23 32 S	150 52 E
Fitzroy, R., W. Australia, Austral.	136	17 25 S	124 0 E
Fiume = Rijeka	63	45 20 N	14 21 E
Fiumefreddo Brúzio	65	39 14 N	16 4 E
Five Alley	39	53 9 N	7 51 W
Five Points	163	36 26 N	120 6 W
Fivemiletown	38	54 23 N	7 20 W
Fizi	126	4 17 S	28 55 E
Fjæra	71	59 52 N	6 22 E
Fjaere	71	58 23 N	8 36 E
Fjellerup	73	56 29 N	10 34 E
Fjerritslev	73	57 5 N	9 15 E
Fkih ben Salah	118	32 45 N	6 45 W
Fla	71	60 25 N	9 26 E
Flå	71	63 13 N	10 18 E
Flagler	158	39 20 N	103 4 W
Flagstaff	161	35 10 N	111 40 W
Flagstone	152	49 4 N	115 10 W
Flaherty, I.	150	56 15 N	79 15 W
Flåm	75	60 52 N	7 14 E
Flambeau, R.	158	45 40 N	90 50 W
Flamborough	33	54 7 N	0 7 W
Flamborough Hd.	33	54 8 N	0 4 W
Flaming Gorge Dam	160	40 50 N	109 25 W
Flaming Gorge L.	160	41 15 N	109 30 W
Flamingo, Teluk	103	5 30 S	138 0 E
Flanders = Flandres	47	51 10 N	3 15 E
Flandre Occidental □	47	51 0 N	3 0 E
Flandre Orientale □	47	51 0 N	4 0 E
Flandreau	158	44 5 N	96 38 W
Flandres, Plaines des	47	51 10 N	3 15 E
Flannan Is.	23	58 9 N	7 52 W
Flaren L.	73	57 2 N	14 5 E
Flåsjön	74	64 5 N	15 50 E
Flat, R.	152	61 51 N	128 0 W
Flat River	159	37 50 N	90 30 W
Flatey, Barðastrandarsýsla, Iceland	74	66 10 N	17 52 W
Flatey, Suður-þingeyjarsýsla, Iceland	74	65 22 N	22 56 W
Flathead L.	160	47 50 N	114 0 W
Flattery, C., Austral.	138	14 58 S	145 21 E
Flattery, C., U.S.A.	160	48 21 N	124 43 W
Flavy-le-Martel	43	49 43 N	3 12 E
Flawil	51	47 26 N	9 11 E
Flaxton	158	48 52 N	102 24 W
Flèche, La	42	47 42 N	0 5 W
Fleeming, C.	136	11 15 S	131 21 E
Fleet	29	51 16 N	0 50 W
Fleetwood, U.K.	32	53 55 N	3 1 W
Fleetwood, U.S.A.	162	40 27 N	75 49 W
Flekkefjord	71	58 18 N	6 39 E
Flémalle	47	50 36 N	5 28 E
Flensborg Fjord	73	54 50 N	9 40 E
Flensburg	48	54 46 N	9 28 E
Flers	42	48 47 N	0 33 W
Flesberg	71	59 51 N	9 22 E
Fletton	29	52 34 N	0 13 W
Fleurance	44	43 52 N	0 40 E
Fleurier	50	46 54 N	6 35 E
Fleurus	47	50 29 N	4 32 E
Flickerbäcken	72	61 47 N	12 34 E
Flims	51	46 50 N	9 17 E
Flin Flon	153	54 46 N	101 53 W
Flinders B.	137	34 19 S	115 9 E
Flinders Group, Is.	138	14 11 S	144 15 E
Flinders I.	138	40 0 S	148 0 E
Flinders, R.	138	17 36 S	140 36 E
Flinders Ranges	140	31 30 S	138 30 E
Flinders Reefs	138	17 37 S	148 31 E
Flint	156	43 5 N	83 19 W
Flint (□)	26	53 15 N	3 12 W
Flint, I.	131	11 26 S	151 48 W
Flint, R.	157	31 20 N	84 10 W
Flinton	139	27 55 S	149 32 E
Fliseryd	73	57 6 N	16 15 E
Flitwick	29	51 59 N	0 30 W
Flix	58	41 14 N	0 32 E
Flixecourt	43	50 0 N	2 5 E
Flobecq	47	50 44 N	3 45 E
Floda	72	60 30 N	14 53 E
Flodden	35	55 37 N	2 8 W
Floodwood	158	46 55 N	92 55 W
Flora, N. Tröndelag, Norway	71	63 27 N	11 22 E
Flora, Sogn & Fjordane, Norway	71	61 35 N	5 1 E
Flora, U.S.A.	156	38 40 N	88 30 W
Florac	44	44 20 N	3 37 E
Florala	157	31 0 N	86 20 W
Florânia	170	6 8 S	36 49 W
Floreffe	47	50 26 N	4 46 E
Florence, Ala., U.S.A.	157	34 50 N	87 50 W
Florence, Ariz., U.S.A.	161	33 0 N	111 25 W
Florence, Colo., U.S.A.	158	38 26 N	105 0 W
Florence, Oreg., U.S.A.	160	44 0 N	124 3 W
Florence, S.C., U.S.A.	157	34 5 N	79 50 W
Florence = Firenze	63	43 47 N	11 15 E
Florence, L.	139	28 53 S	138 9 E
Florennes	47	50 15 N	4 35 E
Florensac	44	43 23 N	3 28 E
Florenville	47	49 40 N	5 19 E
Flores, Azores	16	39 13 N	31 13 W
Flores, Brazil	170	7 51 S	37 59 W
Flores, Guat.	166	16 50 N	89 40 W
Flores I.	152	49 20 N	126 10 W
Flores, I.	103	8 35 S	121 0 E
Flores Sea	102	6 30 S	124 0 E
Floresta	170	9 46 S	37 26 W
Floresville	159	29 10 N	98 10 W
Floriano	170	6 50 S	43 0 W
Florianópolis	173	27 30 S	48 30 W
Florida, Cuba	166	21 32 N	78 14 W
Florida, Uruguay	173	34 7 S	56 10 W
Florida □	157	28 30 N	82 0 W
Florida B.	167	25 0 N	81 20 W
Florida Keys	167	25 0 N	80 40 W
Florida, Strait of	167	25 0 N	80 0 W
Florídia	65	37 6 N	15 9 E
Flórina	68	40 48 N	21 26 E
Flórina □	68	40 45 N	21 20 E
Florningen	72	61 50 N	12 16 E
Florø	71	61 35 N	5 1 E
Flosta	71	58 32 N	8 56 E
Flower's Cove	151	51 14 N	56 46 W
Floydada	159	33 58 N	101 18 W
Flüela Pass	51	46 45 N	9 57 E
Fluk	103	1 42 S	127 38 E
Flumen, R.	58	41 50 N	0 25 W
Flumendosa, R.	64	39 30 N	9 25 E
Fluminimaggiore	64	39 25 N	8 30 E
Flums	51	47 6 N	9 21 E
Flushing = Vlissingen	47	51 26 N	3 34 E
Fluviá, R.	58	42 12 N	3 7 E
Fly, R.	135	8 25 S	143 0 E
Foam Lake	153	51 40 N	103 32 W
Foča	66	43 31 N	18 47 E
Focşani	70	45 41 N	27 15 E
Fofo Fofo	138	8 9 S	147 6 E
Foggaret el Arab	118	27 3 N	2 59 E
Foggaret ez Zoua	118	27 20 N	3 0 E
Fóggia	65	41 28 N	15 31 E
Foggo	121	11 21 N	9 57 E
Foglia, R.	63	43 50 N	12 32 E
Fogo	151	49 43 N	54 17 W
Fogo I.	151	49 40 N	54 5 W
Fohnsdorf	52	47 12 N	14 40 E
Föhr	48	54 40 N	8 30 E
Foia, Cerro da	57	37 19 N	8 10 W
Foix	44	42 58 N	1 38 E
Fojnica	66	43 59 N	17 51 E
Fokang	109	23 52 N	113 31 E
Fokino	80	53 30 N	34 10 E
Fokís □	69	38 30 N	22 15 E
Fokstua	71	62 8 N	9 16 E
Folda, Nord-Trøndelag, Norway	74	64 41 N	10 50 E
Folda, Nordland, Norway	74	67 38 N	14 50 E
Földeák	53	46 19 N	20 30 E
Folette, La	157	36 23 N	84 9 W
Foley	128	30 25 N	87 40 W
Foleyet	150	48 15 N	82 25 W
Folgefonni	71	60 23 N	6 34 E
Foligno	63	42 58 N	12 40 E
Folkestone	29	51 5 N	1 11 E
Folkston	157	30 55 N	82 0 W
Follett	159	36 30 N	100 12 W
Follónica	62	42 55 N	10 45 E
Folsom	160	38 41 N	121 7 W
Fond-du-Lac	153	59 19 N	107 12 W
Fond du lac	158	43 46 N	88 26 W
Fond-du-Lac, R.	153	59 17 N	106 0 W
Fondak	118	35 34 N	5 35 W
Fondi	64	41 21 N	13 25 E
Fonfría	56	41 37 N	6 9 W
Fongen	71	63 11 N	11 38 E
Fonni	64	40 5 N	9 16 E
Fonsagrada	56	43 8 N	7 4 W
Fonseca, G. de	166	13 10 N	87 40 W
Fontaine-Française	43	47 32 N	5 21 E
Fontainebleau	43	48 24 N	2 40 E
Fontas, R.	152	58 14 N	121 48 W
Fonte Boa	174	2 25 S	66 0 W
Fontem	121	5 32 N	9 52 E
Fontenay-le-Comte	44	46 28 N	0 48 W
Fontenelle	151	48 54 N	64 33 W
Fontur	74	66 23 N	14 32 W
Fonyód	53	46 44 N	17 33 E
Foochow = Fuchou	109	26 5 N	119 18 E
Foping	106	33 22 N	108 19 E
Foppiano	62	46 21 N	8 24 E
Föra	73	57 1 N	16 51 E
Forbach	43	49 10 N	6 52 E
Forbes	141	33 22 S	148 0 E
Forbesganj	95	26 17 N	87 18 E
Forcados	121	5 26 N	5 26 E
Forcados, R.	121	5 25 N	5 20 E
Forcall, R.	58	40 40 N	0 12 W
Forcalquier	45	43 58 N	5 47 E
Forchheim	49	49 42 N	11 4 E
Forclaz, Col de la	50	46 3 N	7 1 E
Ford City	163	35 9 N	119 27 W
Førde	71	61 27 N	5 53 E
Fordingbridge	28	50 56 N	1 48 W
Fordongianus	44	40 0 N	8 50 E
Fords Bridge	139	29 41 S	145 29 E
Fordyce	159	33 50 N	92 20 W
Forécariah	120	9 20 N	13 10 W
Forel	12	66 52 N	36 55 W
Foremost	152	49 26 N	111 25 W
Forenza	65	40 50 N	15 50 E
Forest, Belg.	47	50 49 N	4 20 E
Forest, U.S.A.	159	32 21 N	89 27 W
Forest City, Ark., U.S.A.	159	35 0 N	90 50 W
Forest City, Iowa, U.S.A.	158	43 12 N	93 39 W
Forest City, N.C., U.S.A.	157	35 23 N	81 50 W
Forest Grove	160	45 31 N	123 4 W
Forest Lawn	152	51 4 N	114 0 W
Forest Row	29	51 6 N	0 3 E
Forestburg	152	52 35 N	112 1 W
Forestier Pen.	138	43 0 S	148 0 E
Forestville, Can.	151	48 48 N	69 20 W
Forestville, U.S.A.	156	44 41 N	87 29 W
Forez, Mts. du	44	45 40 N	3 50 E
Forfar	37	56 40 N	2 53 W
Forges-les-Eaux	43	49 37 N	1 30 E
Forget	150	49 40 N	102 50 W
Forked River	162	39 50 N	74 12 W
Forks	160	47 56 N	124 23 W
Forksville	162	41 29 N	76 35 W
Forlì	63	44 14 N	12 2 E
Forman	158	46 9 N	97 43 W
Formazza	62	46 23 N	8 26 E
Formby Pt.	32	53 33 N	3 7 W
Formentera, I.	59	38 40 N	1 30 E
Formentor, C. de	58	39 58 N	3 13 E
Fórmia	64	41 15 N	13 34 E
Formiga	171	20 27 S	45 25 W
Formigine	62	44 37 N	10 51 E
Formiguères	44	42 37 N	2 5 E
Formosa, Argent.	172	26 15 S	58 10 W
Formosa, Brazil	171	15 32 S	47 20 W
Formosa = Taiwan ■	109	24 0 N	121 0 E
Formosa □	172	26 5 S	58 10 W
Formosa Bay	126	2 40 S	40 20 E
Formosa Strait	109	24 40 N	120 0 E
Formoso, R.	171	10 34 S	49 56 W
Fornaes, C.	73	56 27 N	10 58 E
Fornells	58	40 4 N	4 4 E
Fornos de Algodres	56	40 38 N	7 32 W
Fornovo di Taro	62	44 42 N	10 7 E
Forres	37	57 37 N	3 38 W
Forrest, Vic., Austral.	140	38 22 S	143 40 E
Forrest, W. Australia, Austral.	137	30 51 S	128 6 E
Forrest Lakes	137	29 12 S	128 46 E
Forrest, Mt.	137	24 48 S	127 45 E
Forrières	47	50 8 N	5 17 E
Fors, Jämtland, Sweden	72	63 0 N	16 40 E
Fors, Kopparberg, Sweden	72	60 14 N	16 20 E
Forsa	72	61 44 N	16 55 E
Forsand	71	58 54 N	6 5 E
Forsayth	138	18 33 S	143 34 E
Forsbacka	72	60 39 N	16 54 E
Forse	72	63 8 N	17 1 E
Forserum	73	57 42 N	14 30 E
Forshaga	72	59 33 N	13 29 E
Forshem	73	58 38 N	13 30 E
Forsmo	72	63 16 N	17 11 E
Forst	48	51 43 N	14 37 E
Forster	141	32 12 S	152 31 E
Forsyth, Ga., U.S.A.	157	33 4 N	83 55 W
Forsyth, Mont., U.S.A.	160	46 14 N	106 37 W
Forsyth I.	143	40 58 S	174 5 E
Fort Albany	150	52 15 N	81 35 W
Fort Ann	162	43 25 N	73 30 W
Fort Apache	161	33 50 N	110 0 W
Fort Archambault = Sarh	117	9 5 N	18 23 E
Fort Assiniboine	152	54 20 N	114 45 W
Fort Augustus	37	57 9 N	4 40 W
Fort Babine	152	55 22 N	126 37 W
Fort Beaufort	128	32 46 S	26 40 E
Fort Benton	160	47 50 N	110 40 W
Fort Bragg	160	39 28 N	123 50 W
Fort Bretonnet = Bousso	117	10 34 N	16 52 E
Fort Bridger	160	41 22 N	110 20 W
Fort Charlet = Djanet	121	24 35 N	9 32 E
Fort Chimo	149	58 6 N	68 25 W
Fort Chipewyan	153	58 42 N	111 8 W
Fort Collins	158	40 30 N	105 4 W
Fort Coulonge	150	45 50 N	76 45 W
Fort Crampel = Crampel	117	7 8 N	19 18 E
Fort-Dauphin	129	25 2 S	47 0 E
Fort Davis	159	30 38 N	103 53 W
Fort-de-France	167	14 36 N	61 2 W
Fort de Polignac = Illizi	119	26 31 N	8 32 E
Fort de Possel = Possel	124	5 5 N	19 10 E
Fort Defiance	161	35 47 N	109 4 W
Fort Dodge	158	42 29 N	94 10 W
Fort Flatters = Zaouiet El-Khala	119	27 10 N	6 40 E
Fort Foureau = Kousseri	117	12 0 N	14 55 E
Fort Frances	153	48 35 N	93 25 W
Fort Franklin	148	65 30 N	123 45 W
Fort Garland	161	37 28 N	105 30 W

Fort George Frýdek-Místek

Fort George 151 53 50N 79 0W
Fort George, R. 150 53 50N 77 0W
Fort Good-Hope 147 66 14N 128 40W
Fort Gouraud = F'Dérik 116 22 40N 12 45W
Fort Grahame 152 56 30N 124 35W
Fort Hancock 161 31 19N 105 56W
Fort Hauchuca 161 31 32N 110 30W
Fort Hertz (Putao) 99 27 28N 97 30 E
Fort Hope 150 51 30N 88 10W
Fort Irwin 163 35 16N 116 34W
Fort Jameson = Chipata 127 13 38 S 32 38 E
Fort Johnston 127 14 25 S 35 16 E
Fort Kent 151 47 12N 68 30W
Fort Klamath 160 42 45N 122 0W
Fort Lallemand 119 31 13N 6 17 E
Fort-Lamy = Ndjamena 117 12 4N 15 8 E
Fort Lapperrine = Tamanrasset 119 22 56N 5 30 E
Fort Laramie 158 42 15N 104 30W
Fort Lauderdale 157 26 10N 80 5W
Fort Liard 152 60 20N 123 30W
Fort Liberté 167 19 42N 71 51W
Fort Lupton 158 40 8N 104 48W
Fort Mackay 152 57 12N 111 41W
Fort McKenzie 151 57 20N 69 0W
Fort Macleod 152 49 45N 113 30W
Fort MacMahon 118 29 51N 1 45 E
Fort McMurray 152 56 44N 111 23W
Fort McPherson 147 67 30N 134 55W
Fort Madison 158 40 39N 91 20W
Fort Meade 157 27 45N 81 45W
Fort Miribel 118 29 31N 2 55 E
Fort Morgan 158 40 10N 103 50W
Fort Myers 157 26 30N 82 0W
Fort Nelson 152 58 50N 122 38W
Fort Nelson, R. 152 59 32N 124 0W
Fort Norman 147 64 57N 125 30W
Fort Pacot (Chirfa) 119 20 55N 12 14 E
Fort Payne 157 34 25N 85 44W
Fort Peck 160 47 1N 105 30W
Fort Peck Dam 160 48 0N 106 20W
Fort Peck Res. 160 47 40N 107 0W
Fort Pierce 158 27 29N 80 19W
Fort Pierre 158 44 25N 100 25W
Fort Pierre Bordes 118 20 0N 2 55 E
Fort Portal 126 0 40N 30 20 E
Fort Providence 152 61 21N 117 40W
Fort Qu'Appelle 153 50 45N 103 50W
Fort Randall 147 55 10N 162 48W
Fort Reliance 153 63 0N 109 20W
Fort Resolution 152 61 10N 113 40W
Fort Rixon 127 20 2 S 29 17 E
Fort Roseberry = Mansa 127 11 10 S 28 50 E
Fort Rupert (Rupert House) 150 51 30N 78 40W
Fort Saint 119 30 13N 9 31 E
Fort St. James 152 54 30N 124 10W
Fort St. John 152 56 15N 120 50W
Fort Sandeman 94 31 20N 69 25 E
Fort Saskatchewan 152 53 40N 113 15W
Fort Scott 159 38 0N 94 40W
Fort Selkirk 147 62 43N 137 22W
Fort Severn 150 56 0N 87 40W
Fort Shevchenko 83 44 30N 50 10W
Fort Sibut = Sibut 117 5 52N 19 10 E
Fort Simpson 152 61 45N 121 23W
Fort Smith, Can. 152 60 0N 111 51W
Fort Smith, U.S.A. 159 35 25N 94 25W
Fort Stanton 161 33 33N 105 36W
Fort Stockton 159 30 48N 103 2W
Fort Sumner 159 34 24N 104 8W
Fort Thomas 161 33 2N 109 59W
Fort Trinquet = Bir Mogrein 116 25 10N 11 25W
Fort Valley 157 32 33N 83 52W
Fort Vermilion 152 58 24N 116 0W
Fort Victoria 127 20 8 S 30 55 E
Ft. Walton Beach 157 30 25N 86 40W
Fort Wayne 156 41 5N 85 10W
Fort William 36 56 48N 5 8W
Fort William = Thunder Bay 150 48 20N 89 10W
Fort Worth 159 32 45N 97 25W
Fort Yates 158 46 8N 100 38W
Fort Yukon 147 66 35N 145 12W
Fortaleza 170 3 35 S 38 35W
Forte Coimbra 174 19 55 S 57 48W
Forte Rocadas 125 16 38 S 15 22 E
Forteau 151 51 28N 57 1W
Fortescue 136 21 4 S 116 4 E
Fortescue, R. 136 21 20 S 116 5 E
Forth, Firth of 35 56 5N 2 55W
Forthassa Rharbia 118 32 52N 1 11W
Forties, oilfield 19 57 40N 1 0 E
Fortín Corrales 174 22 21 S 60 35W
Fortín Guachalla 174 22 22 S 62 23W
Fortín Rojas Silva 172 22 40 S 59 3W
Fortín Siracuas 174 21 3 S 61 46W
Fortín Teniente Montania 172 22 1 S 59 45W
Fortore, R. 63 41 40N 15 0 E
Fortrose 143 46 38 S 168 45 E
Fortuna, Spain 59 38 11N 1 7W
Fortuna, Cal., U.S.A. 160 48 38N 124 8W
Fortuna, N.D., U.S.A. 158 48 55N 103 48W
Fortune Bay 151 47 30N 55 22W
Forty Mile 147 64 20N 140 30W
Forūr 93 26 20N 54 30 E
Fos 62 43 20N 4 57 E
Fos do Jordâo 174 9 30 S 72 14W
Fos-sur-Mer 45 43 26N 4 56 E
Foshan 109 23 4N 113 5 E
Fossacesia 63 42 15N 14 30 E
Fossano 62 44 39N 7 40 E
Fosses-la-Ville 47 50 24N 4 41 E
Fossil 160 45 0N 120 9W
Fossilbrook 138 17 47 S 144 29 E
Fossombrone 63 43 41N 12 49 E
Fosston 158 47 33N 95 39W
Foster, R. 153 55 47N 105 49W
Fosters Ra. 138 21 35 S 133 48 E
Fostoria 156 41 8N 83 25W
Fou Chiang, R. 108 30 3N 106 21 E
Fouch'eng 106 37 52N 116 8 E
Fougamou 124 1 38 S 11 39 E
Fougéres 42 48 21N 1 14W
Fouhsinshih 107 42 13N 121 51 E
Foul Pt. 97 8 35N 81 25 E
Foula, I. 23 60 10N 2 5W
Fouling 108 29 40N 107 20 E
Foulpointe 129 17 41 S 49 31 E
Foum el Alba 118 20 45N 3 0W
Foum el Kreneg 118 29 0N 0 58W
Foum Tatahouine 119 32 57N 10 29 E
Foum Zguid 118 30 2N 6 59W
Foumban 121 5 45N 10 50 E
Foundiougne 120 14 5N 16 32W
Founing 107 33 47N 119 48 E
Fountain, Colo., U.S.A. 158 38 42N 104 40W
Fountain, Utah, U.S.A. 160 39 41N 111 50W
Fountain Springs 163 35 54N 118 51W
Foup'ing 106 38 55N 114 13 E
Four Mts., Is. of the 147 52 0N 170 30W
Fourchambault 43 47 0N 3 3 E
Fourchu 151 45 43N 60 17W
Fourcroy, C. 136 11 45 S 130 2 E
Fourmies 43 50 1N 4 2 E
Fournás 69 39 3N 21 52 E
Foúrnoi 69 37 36N 26 32 E
Fours 43 46 50N 3 42 E
Foushan 106 35 58N 111 51 E
Fouta Djalon 120 11 20N 12 10W
Foux, Cap-à- 167 19 43N 73 27W
Fouyang 109 32 55N 115 52 E
Foveaux Str. 143 46 42 S 168 10 E
Fowler, Calif., U.S.A. 163 36 41N 119 41W
Fowler, Colo., U.S.A. 158 38 10N 104 0W
Fowler, Kans., U.S.A. 159 37 28N 100 7W
Fowlers B. 137 31 59 S 132 34 E
Fowlers Bay 137 32 0 S 132 29 E
Fowlerton 159 28 26N 98 50W
Fox Is. 147 52 30N 166 0W
Fox, R. 153 56 3N 93 18W
Fox Valley 153 50 30N 109 25W
Foxboro 162 42 4N 71 16W
Foxe Basin 149 68 30N 77 0W
Foxe Channel 149 66 0N 80 0W
Foxe Pen. 149 65 0N 76 0W
Foxen, L. 72 59 25N 11 55 E
Foxhol 46 53 10N 6 43 E
Foxpark 160 41 4N 106 6W
Foxton 142 40 29 S 175 18 E
Foyle, Lough 38 55 6N 7 8W
Foynes 38 52 30N 9 5W
Foz 56 43 33N 7 20W
Foz do Cunene 128 17 15 S 11 55 E
Foz do Gregório 174 6 47 S 71 0W
Foz do Iguaçu 173 25 30 S 54 30W
Frackville 162 40 46N 76 15W
Fraga 58 41 32N 0 21 E
Fraire 47 50 16N 4 31 E
Frameries 47 50 24N 3 54 E
Framlingham 29 52 14N 1 20 E
Franca 171 20 25 S 47 30W
Francavilla al Mare 63 42 25N 14 16 E
Francavilla Fontana 65 40 32N 17 35 E
France ■ 41 47 0N 3 0 E
Frances 140 36 41 S 140 55 E
Frances Creek 136 13 25 S 132 3 E
Frances L. 152 61 23N 129 30W
Frances, R. 152 60 16N 129 10W
Francés Viejo, C. 167 19 40N 70 0W
Franceville 124 1 40 S 13 32 E
Franche Comté □ 43 46 30N 5 50 E
Franches Montagnes 50 47 10N 7 0 E
Francis-Garnier 118 36 30N 1 30 E
Francis Harbour 151 52 34N 55 44W
Francisco I. Madero, Coahuila, Mexico 164 25 48N 103 18W
Francisco I. Madero, Durango, Mexico 164 24 32N 104 22W
Francisco Sá 171 16 28 S 43 30W
Francistown 125 21 7 S 27 33 E
Francofonte 65 37 13N 14 50 E
François 151 47 35N 56 45W
Francois L. 152 54 0N 125 30W
François, Le 167 14 38N 60 57W
Francorchamps 47 50 27N 5 57 E
Franeker 46 53 12N 5 33 E
Frankado 123 12 30N 43 12 E
Frankenberg 48 51 3N 8 47 E
Frankenthal 49 49 32N 8 21 E
Frankford = Kilcormac 39 53 10N 7 43W
Frankfort, Ind., U.S.A. 156 40 20N 86 33W
Frankfort, Kans., U.S.A. 158 39 42N 96 26W
Frankfort, Ky., U.S.A. 156 38 12N 84 52W
Frankfort, Mich., U.S.A. 156 44 38N 86 14W
Frankfort, N.Y., U.S.A. 162 43 2N 75 4W
Frankfurt □ 48 52 30N 14 0 E
Frankfurt am Main 49 50 7N 8 40 E
Frankfurt an der Oder 48 52 50N 14 31 E
Fränkische Alb 49 49 20N 11 30 E
Fränkische Saale 49 50 7N 9 49 E
Fränkische Saale, R. 49 50 7N 9 49 E
Fränkische Schweiz 49 49 45N 11 10 E
Frankland, R. 137 35 0 S 116 48 E
Franklin, Ky., U.S.A. 157 36 40N 86 30W
Franklin, La., U.S.A. 159 29 45N 91 30W
Franklin, Mass., U.S.A. 162 42 4N 71 23W
Franklin, Nebr., U.S.A. 158 40 9N 98 55W
Franklin, N.H., U.S.A. 162 43 28N 71 39W
Franklin, N.J., U.S.A. 162 41 9N 74 38W
Franklin, Pa., U.S.A. 156 41 22N 79 45W
Franklin, Tenn., U.S.A. 157 35 54N 86 53W
Franklin, Va., U.S.A. 157 36 40N 76 58W
Franklin, W. Va., U.S.A. 156 38 38N 79 21W
Franklin □ 149 71 0N 99 0W
Franklin B. 147 69 45N 126 0W
Franklin D. Roosevelt L. 160 48 30N 118 16W
Franklin I. 13 76 10 S 168 30 E
Franklin, L. 160 40 20N 115 26W
Franklin Mts., Can. 148 66 0N 125 0W
Franklin Mts., N.Z. 143 44 55 S 167 45 E
Franklin Str. 148 72 0N 96 0W
Franklinton 159 30 53N 90 10W
Franklyn Mt. 143 42 4 S 172 42 E
Franks Peak 160 43 50N 109 5W
Frankston 141 38 8 S 145 8 E
Frankton Junc. 142 37 47 S 175 16 E
Fränsta 72 62 30N 16 11 E
Frant 29 51 5N 0 17 E
Frantsa Josifa, Zemlya 76 76 0N 62 0 E
Franz 150 48 25N 84 30W
Franz Josef Fd. 12 73 20N 22 0 E
Franz Josef Land = Frantsa Josifa 76 76 0N 62 0 E
Franzburg 48 54 9N 12 52 E
Frascati 64 41 48N 12 41 E
Fraser I. 139 25 15 S 153 10 E
Fraser L. 152 54 0N 124 50W
Fraser, Mt. 137 25 35 S 118 20 E
Fraser, R., B.C., Can. 152 49 7N 123 11W
Fraser, R., Newf., Can. 151 56 39N 63 10W
Fraserburg 128 31 55 S 21 30 E
Fraserburgh 37 57 41N 2 0W
Fraserdale 150 49 55N 81 37W
Frasertown 142 38 58 S 177 28 E
Frashëri 68 40 23N 20 26 E
Frasne 43 46 50N 6 10 E
Frater 150 47 20N 84 25W
Frauenfeld 51 47 34N 8 54 E
Fray Bentos 172 33 10 S 58 15W
Frazier Downs P.O. 136 18 48 S 121 42 E
Frechilla 56 42 8N 4 50W
Fredericia 73 55 34N 9 45 E
Frederick, Md., U.S.A. 162 39 25N 77 23W
Frederick, Okla., U.S.A. 159 34 22N 99 0W
Frederick, S.D., U.S.A. 158 45 55N 98 29W
Frederick Reef 133 20 58 S 154 23 E
Frederick Sd. 153 57 10N 134 0W
Fredericksburg, Tex., U.S.A. 159 30 17N 98 55W
Fredericksburg, Va., U.S.A. 162 38 16N 77 29W
Frederickstown 159 37 35N 90 15W
Fredericton 151 45 57N 66 40W
Fredericton Junc. 151 45 41N 66 40W
Frederiksberg 72 60 12N 14 25 E
Frederiksborg Amt □ 73 55 50N 12 10 E
Frederikshåb 12 62 0N 49 30W
Frederikshavn 73 57 28N 10 31 E
Frederikssund 73 55 50N 12 3 E
Frederiksted 147 17 43N 64 53W
Fredonia, Ariz., U.S.A. 161 36 59N 112 36W
Fredonia, Kans., U.S.A. 159 37 34N 95 50W
Fredonia, N.Y., U.S.A. 156 42 26N 79 20W
Fredrikstad 71 59 13N 10 57 E
Freehold 162 40 15N 74 18W
Freel Pk. 163 38 52N 119 53W
Freeland 162 41 3N 75 48W
Freeling, Mt. 136 22 35 S 133 06 E
Freels, C. 151 49 15N 53 30W
Freeman, Calif., U.S.A. 163 35 35N 117 53W
Freeman, S.D., U.S.A. 158 43 25N 97 20W
Freeport, Bahamas 167 25 45N 88 30 E
Freeport, Can. 151 44 15N 66 20W
Freeport, Ill., U.S.A. 158 42 18N 89 40W
Freeport, N.Y., U.S.A. 162 40 39N 73 35W
Freeport, Tex., U.S.A. 159 28 55N 95 22W
Freetown 120 8 30N 13 10W
Freevater Forest 37 57 51N 4 45W
Fregenal de la Sierra 57 38 10N 6 39W
Fregene 64 41 50N 12 12 E
Fregeneda, La 56 40 58N 6 54W
Fréhel C. 42 48 40N 2 20W
Freiberg 48 50 55N 13 20 E
Freibourg = Fribourg 50 46 49N 7 9 E
Freiburg, Baden, Ger. 49 48 0N 7 52 E
Freiburg, Sachsen, Ger. 48 53 49N 9 17 E
Freiburger Alpen 50 46 37N 7 10 E
Freire 176 39 0 S 72 50W
Freirina 172 28 30 S 71 10W
Freising 49 48 24N 11 47 E
Freistadt 52 48 30N 14 30 E
Freital 48 51 0N 13 40 E
Fréjus 45 43 25N 6 44 E
Fremantle 137 32 1 S 115 47 E
Fremont, Calif., U.S.A. 163 37 32N 122 57W
Fremont, Mich., U.S.A. 156 43 29N 85 59W
Fremont, Nebr., U.S.A. 158 41 30N 96 30W
Fremont, Ohio, U.S.A. 156 41 20N 83 5W
Fremont, L. 160 43 0N 109 50W
Fremont, R. 161 38 15N 110 20W
French Camp 163 37 53N 121 16W
French Cr. 156 41 30N 80 2W
French Guiana ■ 175 4 0N 53 0W
French I. 141 38 20 S 145 22 E
French Terr. of Afars & Issas □ = Djibouti 123 11 30N 42 15 E
Frenchglen 160 42 56N 119 0W
Frenchman Butte 153 53 36N 109 36W
Frenchman Creek, R. 158 40 34N 101 35W
Frenchman, R. 160 49 25N 108 20W
Frenchpark 38 53 53N 8 25W
Frenda 118 35 2N 1 1 E
Fresco, R. 175 7 15 S 51 30W
Freshfield, C. 13 68 25 S 151 10 E
Freshford 39 52 45N 7 25W
Freshwater 28 50 42N 1 31W
Fresnillo 164 23 10N 103 0W
Fresno 163 36 47N 119 50W
Fresno Alhandiga 56 40 42N 5 37W
Fresno Res. 160 48 47N 110 0W
Freswick 37 58 35N 3 5W
Freuchie 35 56 14N 3 8W
Freudenstadt 49 48 27N 8 25 E
Freux 47 49 59N 5 27 E
Frévent 43 50 15N 2 17 E
Frew, R. 138 20 0 S 135 38 E
Frewena 138 19 50 S 135 50 E
Freycinet, C. 137 34 9 S 115 0 E
Freycinet Pen. 138 42 10 S 148 25 E
Fria 120 10 27N 13 32W
Fria, La 174 8 13N 72 15W
Friant 163 36 59N 119 43W
Frias 172 28 40 S 65 5W
Fribourg 50 46 49N 7 9 E
Fribourg □ 50 45 40N 7 0 E
Frick 50 47 31N 8 1 E
Fridafors 73 56 25N 14 39 E
Fridaythorpe 33 54 2N 0 40W
Friedberg, Bayern, Ger. 49 48 21N 10 59 E
Friedberg, Hessen, Ger. 10 50 19N 8 45 E
Friedland 49 53 40N 13 33 E
Friedrichshafen 49 47 39N 9 29 E
Friedrichskoog 48 54 1N 8 52 E
Friedrichsort 48 54 24N 10 11 E
Friedrichstadt 48 54 23N 9 6 E
Friendly (Tonga) Is. 130 19 50 S 174 30W
Friesach 52 46 57N 14 24 E
Friesack 48 52 43N 12 35 E
Friesche Wad 46 53 22N 5 44 E
Friesland □ 46 53 5N 5 50 E
Friesoythe 48 53 1N 7 51 E
Frigate, L. 150 53 15N 74 45W
Frigg E., gasfield 19 59 50N 2 20 E
Frigg, gasfield 19 59 50N 2 15 E
Frigg N.E., gasfield 19 60 0N 2 17 E
Frillesås 73 57 20N 12 12 E
Frimley 29 51 18N 0 43W
Frinnaryd 73 57 55N 14 50 E
Frinton-on-Sea 29 51 50N 1 16 E
Frio, C. 128 18 0 S 12 0 E
Frio, R. 159 29 40N 99 40W
Friockheim 37 56 39N 2 40W
Friona 159 34 40N 102 42W
Frisa, Loch 34 56 34N 6 5W
Frisian Is. 48 53 30N 6 0 E
Fristad 73 57 50N 13 0 E
Fritch 159 35 40N 101 35W
Fritsla 73 57 33N 12 47 E
Fritzlar 48 51 8N 9 19 E
Friuli-Venezia-Giulia □ 63 46 0N 13 0 E
Frizington 32 54 33N 3 30W
Frobisher B. 149 63 0N 67 0W
Frobisher L. 153 56 20N 108 15W
Frobisher Sd. 149 62 30N 66 0W
Frodsham 32 53 17N 2 45W
Frogmore 141 34 15 S 148 52 E
Frohavet 74 64 5N 9 35 E
Froid 158 48 20N 104 29W
Froid-Chapelle 47 50 9N 4 19 E
Frolovo 83 49 45N 43 30 E
Fromberg 160 45 19N 108 58W
Frombork 54 54 21N 19 41 E
Frome 28 51 16N 2 17W
Frome Downs 140 31 13 S 139 46 E
Frome, L. 140 30 45 S 139 45 E
Frome, R. 28 50 44N 2 5W
Fromentine 42 46 53N 2 9W
Frómista 56 42 16N 4 25W
Front Range 160 40 0N 105 10W
Front Royal 156 38 55N 78 10W
Fronteira 57 39 3N 7 39W
Fronteiras 170 7 5 S 40 37W
Frontera 165 18 30N 92 40W
Frontignan 44 43 27N 3 45 E
Frosinone 64 41 38N 13 20 E
Frosolone 65 41 34N 14 27 E
Frostburg 156 39 43N 78 57W
Frostisen 74 68 14N 17 10 E
Frouard 43 48 47N 6 8 E
Frövi 72 59 28N 15 24 E
Frower Pt. 39 51 40N 8 30W
Froya 71 63 43N 8 40 E
Frøya 71 63 43N 8 40 E
Fröya I. 74 63 45N 8 45 E
Fruges 43 50 30N 2 8 E
Frumoasa 70 46 28N 25 48 E
Frunze 85 42 54N 74 36 E
Fruška Gora 66 45 7N 19 30 E
Frutal 171 20 0 S 49 0W
Frutigen 50 46 35N 7 38 E
Frýdek-Místek 53 49 40N 18 20 E

Frýdlant **Garibaldi Prov. Park**

Frýdlant, Severočeský, Czech. 52 50 56N 15 9E
Frýdlant, Severomoravsky, Czech. 53 49 35N 18 20E
Fryvaldov = Jesenik 53 50 0N 17 8E
Fthiótis □ 69 38 50N 22 25E
Fu 72 60 57N 14 44E
Fuan 109 27 9N 119 38E
Fucécchio 62 43 44N 10 51E
Fuch'ing 109 25 43N 119 22E
Fuchou, Fukien, China 109 26 5N 119 18E
Fuchou, Liaoning, China 107 39 45N 121 45E
Fuchü 110 34 34N 133 14E
Fūchū 111 35 40N 139 29E
Fuch'üan 108 26 42N 107 33E
Fuch'uan 109 24 50N 111 16E
Fucino, L. 44 42 0N 13 30E
Fuencaliente 57 38 25N 4 18W
Fuengirola 57 36 32N 4 41W
Fuente-Alamo 59 38 44N 1 24W
Fuente de Cantos 57 38 15N 6 18W
Fuente de San Esteban, La 56 40 49N 6 15W
Fuente del Maestre 57 38 31N 6 28W
Fuente el Fresno 57 39 14N 3 46W
Fuente Ovejuna 57 38 15N 5 25W
Fuentes de Andalucía 57 37 28N 5 20W
Fuentes de Ebro 58 41 31N 0 38W
Fuentes de León 57 38 5N 6 32W
Fuentes de Oñoro 56 40 33N 6 52W
Fuentesaúco 56 41 15N 5 30W
Fuerte Olimpo 172 21 0S 58 0W
Fuerte, R. 164 26 0N 109 0W
Fuerteventura, I. 116 28 30N 14 0W
Fuertey 38 53 37N 8 16W
Fufeng 106 34 20N 107 51E
Fŭget 70 45 52N 22 10E
Fŭget, Munţii 70 45 50N 22 9E
Fugløysund 74 70 15N 20 20E
Fŭgŭraş 70 45 48N 24 58E
Fŭgŭraş, Munţii 70 45 40N 24 40E
Fuhai 105 47 6N 87 23E
Fuhsien, Liaoning, China 107 39 38N 122 0E
Fuhsien, Shensi, China 106 36 2N 109 20E
Fuhsingchen 108 22 47N 101 5E
Fujaira 93 25 7N 56 18E
Fuji 111 35 9N 138 39E
Fuji-no-miya 111 35 20N 138 40E
Fuji-San 111 35 22N 138 44E
Fuji-yoshida 111 35 30N 138 46E
Fujieda 111 34 52N 138 16E
Fujioka 111 36 15N 139 5E
Fujisawa 111 35 22N 139 29E
Fukien □ 109 26 0N 117 30E
Fukou 106 34 3N 114 27E
Fuku 106 39 2N 111 3E
Fukuchiyama 111 35 25N 135 9E
Fukui 111 36 0N 136 10E
Fukui-ken □ 111 36 0N 136 12E
Fukuma 110 33 46N 130 28E
Fukung 108 26 58N 98 54E
Fukuoka 110 33 30N 130 30E
Fukuoka-ken □ 110 33 30N 131 0E
Fukuroi 111 34 45N 137 55E
Fukushima 112 37 30N 140 15E
Fukushima-ken □ 112 37 30N 140 15E
Fukuyama 110 34 35N 133 20E
Fŭlciu 70 46 17N 28 7E
Fulda 48 50 32N 9 41E
Fullerton, Calif., U.S.A. 163 33 52N 117 58W
Fullerton, Nebr., U.S.A. 158 41 25N 98 0W
Fulmar, oilfield 19 56 30N 2 8E
Fülöpszállás 53 46 49N 19 16E
Fŭlticeni 70 47 21N 26 20W
Fulton, Mo., U.S.A. 158 38 50N 91 55W
Fulton, N.Y., U.S.A. 162 43 20N 76 22W
Fuluälven 72 61 18N 13 4E
Fulufjället 72 61 32N 12 41E
Fulungch'üan 107 44 24N 124 37E
Fülüpszállás 53 46 49N 19 16E
Fumay 43 50 0N 4 40E
Fumbusi 121 10 25N 1 20W
Fumel 44 44 30N 0 58E
Fumin 108 25 14N 102 29E
Funabashi 111 35 45N 140 0E
Funafuti, I. 130 8 30S 179 0E
Funchal 116 32 45N 16 55W
Fundación 174 10 31N 74 11W
Fundão, Brazil 171 19 55S 40 24W
Fundão, Port. 56 40 8N 7 30W
Fundu 127 14 58S 30 14E
Fundy, B. of 151 45 0N 56 0W
Funes 174 1 0N 77 28W
Funing, Hopei, China 107 39 54N 119 12E
Funing, Yunnan, China 108 23 37N 105 36E
Funiu Shan 106 33 40N 112 30E
Funsi 120 10 21N 1 54W
Funtua 121 11 30N 7 18E
Fupien 108 31 18N 102 27E
Fup'ing 106 34 47N 109 7E
Fur 73 56 50N 9 0E
Furat, Nahr al 92 33 30N 43 0E
Furbero 165 20 22N 97 31W
Furka Pass 51 46 34N 8 35E
Furmanov 81 57 25N 41 3E
Furmanovka 85 44 17N 72 57E
Furmanovo 83 49 42N 49 25E
Furnas, Reprêsa de 173 20 50S 45 0W
Furneaux Group 138 40 10S 147 50E
Furness, Pen. 32 54 12N 3 10W
Fürstenau 48 52 32N 7 40E
Fürstenfeld 52 47 3N 16 3E
Fürstenfeldbruck 49 48 10N 11 15E
Fürstenwalde 48 52 20N 14 3E
Fürth 49 49 29N 11 0E
Fürth i. Wald 49 49 19N 12 51E
Furtwangen 49 48 3N 8 14E
Furudal 72 61 10N 15 11E
Furukawa 111 36 14N 137 11E
Furusund 72 59 40N 18 55E
Fury and Hecla Str. 149 69 56N 84 0W
Fusa 71 60 12N 5 37E
Fusagasugá 174 4 21N 74 22W
Fuscaldo 65 39 25N 16 1E
Fushan 107 37 30N 121 5E
Fushë Arrëzi 68 42 4N 20 2E
Fushun, Liaoning, China 107 41 50N 123 55E
Fushun, Szechwan, China 108 29 13N 105 0E
Fush'un Chiang, R. 109 30 5N 120 5E
Fusio 51 46 27N 8 40E
Füssen 49 47 35N 10 43E
Fusui 108 22 35N 107 58E
Fusung 107 42 15N 127 20E
Futago-Yama 110 33 35N 131 36E
Futing 109 27 15N 120 10E
Futuk 121 9 45N 10 56E
Futuna I. 130 14 25S 178 20E
Fŭurei 70 45 6N 27 19E
Fuwa 122 31 12N 30 33E
Fuyang 109 30 5N 119 56E
Fuyang Ho, R. 106 38 14N 116 5E
Fuyü 107 45 10N 124 50E
Fuyüan 105 47 40N 132 30E
Füzesgyarmat 53 47 6N 21 14E
Fwaka 125 12 5S 29 25E
Fylde 32 53 50N 2 58W
Fylingdales Moor 33 54 22N 0 32W
Fyn 73 55 20N 10 30E
Fyne, L. 34 56 0N 5 20W
Fyns Amt □ 73 55 15N 10 30E
Fynshav 73 54 59N 9 59E
Fyresvatn 71 59 6N 8 10E
Fyvie 37 57 26N 2 24W

G

Gaanda 121 10 10N 12 27E
Gaba 123 6 20N 35 7E
Gaba Tula 82 0 20N 38 35E
Gabah, C. 91 8 0N 50 0E
Gabarin 121 11 8N 10 27E
Gabbs 163 38 52N 117 55W
Gabela 124 11 0S 14 37E
Gaberones = Gaborone 128 24 37S 25 57E
Gabès 119 33 53N 10 2E
Gabès, Golfe de 119 34 0N 10 30E
Gabgaba, W. 122 22 10N 33 5E
Gabin 54 52 23N 19 41E
Gabon ■ 124 0 10S 10 0E
Gaborone 128 24 37S 25 57E
Gabrovo 67 42 52N 25 27E
Gacé 42 48 49N 0 20E
Gach Saran 93 30 15N 50 45E
Gacko 66 43 10N 18 33E
Gada 121 13 38N 5 36E
Gadag 97 15 30N 75 45E
Gadamai 123 17 11N 36 10E
Gadap 94 25 5N 67 28E
Gadarwara 95 22 50N 78 50E
Gäddede 74 64 30N 14 15E
Gadebusch 48 53 41N 11 6E
Gadein 123 8 10N 28 45E
Gadhada 94 22 0N 71 35E
Gadmen 51 46 45N 8 16E
Gádor, Sierra de 59 36 57N 2 45W
Gadsden, Ala., U.S.A. 157 34 1N 86 0W
Gadsden, Ariz., U.S.A. 161 32 35N 114 47W
Gadwal 96 16 10N 77 50E
Gaerwen 31 53 13N 4 17W
Gaeta 64 41 12N 13 35E
Gaeta, G. di 64 41 0N 13 25E
Gaffney 157 35 10N 81 31W
Gafsa 119 34 24N 8 51E
Gagarin (Gzhatsk) 80 55 30N 35 0E
Gagetown 151 45 46N 66 29W
Gagino 81 55 15N 45 10E
Gagliano del Capo 65 39 50N 18 23E
Gagnef 72 60 36N 15 5E
Gagnoa 120 6 4N 5 55W
Gagnon 151 51 50N 68 5W
Gagnon, L. 153 62 3N 110 27W
Gagra 83 43 20N 40 10E
Gah 44 43 12N 0 27W
Gahini 126 1 50S 30 30E
Gahmar 95 25 27N 83 55E
Gaibandha 98 25 20N 89 36E
Gaïdhouronísi 69 34 53N 25 41E
Gail 159 32 48N 101 25W
Gail, R. 52 46 37N 13 15E
Gaillac 44 43 54N 1 54E
Gaillon 42 49 10N 1 20E
Gaima 135 8 9S 142 59E
Gainesville, Fla., U.S.A. 157 29 38N 82 20W
Gainesville, Ga., U.S.A. 157 34 17N 83 47W
Gainesville, Mo., U.S.A. 159 36 35N 92 26W
Gainesville, Tex., U.S.A. 159 33 40N 97 10W
Gainford 33 54 34N 1 44W
Gainsborough 33 53 23N 0 46W
Gairdner L. 140 31 30S 136 0E
Gairloch 36 57 42N 5 40W
Gairloch L. 36 57 43N 5 45W
Gairlochy 36 56 55N 5 0W
Gairsay, I. 37 59 4N 2 59W
Gais 51 47 22N 9 27E
Gaithersburg 162 39 9N 77 12W
Gaj 66 45 28N 17 3E
Gajale 121 11 25N 8 10E
Gajiram 121 12 29N 13 9E
Gakuch 95 36 7N 73 45E
Gal Oya Res. 97 8 5N 80 55E
Galachipa 98 22 8N 90 26E
Galadi 121 13 5N 6 20E
Galán, Cerro 172 25 55S 66 52W
Galana, R. 126 3 0S 39 10E
Galangue 125 13 48S 16 3E
Galanta 53 48 11N 17 45E
Galápagos, Is. 131 0 0 89 0W
Galas, R. 101 4 55N 101 57E
Galashiels 35 55 37N 2 50W
Galatás 69 37 30N 23 26E
Galatea 142 38 24S 176 45E
Galaţi 70 45 27N 28 2E
Galaţi □ 70 45 45N 27 30E
Galatina 65 40 10N 18 10E
Galátone 65 40 8N 18 3E
Galax 157 36 42N 80 57W
Galaxídhion 69 38 22N 22 23E
Galbally 39 52 24N 8 17W
Galbraith 138 16 25S 141 30E
Galdhøpiggen 71 61 38N 8 18E
Galeana 164 24 50N 100 4W
Galela 103 1 50N 127 55E
Galena, Austral. 137 27 48S 114 42E
Galena, U.S.A. 147 64 42N 157 0W
Galeota Point 167 10 8N 61 0W
Galera 59 37 45N 2 33W
Galera, Pta. de la 174 10 48N 75 16W
Galesburg 158 40 57N 90 23W
Galey R. 39 52 30N 9 23W
Galgate 32 53 59N 2 47W
Galheirão, R. 171 12 23S 45 5W
Galheiros 171 13 18S 46 25W
Galicea Mare 70 44 4N 23 19E
Galich, R.S.F.S.R., U.S.S.R. 81 58 23N 42 18E
Galich, Uk., U.S.S.R. 80 49 10N 24 40E
Galiche 67 43 34N 23 50E
Galicia 56 42 43N 8 0W
Galijp 46 53 10N 5 58E
Galilee = Hagalil 90 32 53N 35 18E
Galilee, L. 138 22 20S 145 50E
Galite, Is. de la 119 37 30N 8 59E
Galivro Mts. 161 32 40N 110 30W
Gallan Hd. 36 58 14N 7 0W
Gallarate 62 45 40N 8 48E
Gallatin 157 36 24N 86 27W
Galle 97 6 5N 80 10E
Gallego 164 29 49N 106 22W
Gállego, R. 58 42 23N 0 30W
Gallegos, R. 176 51 50S 71 0W
Galley Hd. 39 51 32N 8 56W
Galliate 62 45 27N 8 44E
Gallinas, Pta. 174 12 28N 71 40W
Gallipoli 65 40 8N 18 0E
Gallipoli = Gelibolu 68 40 28N 26 43E
Gallipolis 156 38 50N 82 10W
Gällivare 74 67 9N 20 40E
Gällö 72 62 56N 15 15E
Gallo, C. di 64 38 13N 13 19E
Gallocanta, Laguna de 58 40 58N 1 30W
Galloway 34 55 0N 4 25W
Galloway, Mull of 34 54 38N 4 50W
Gallup 161 35 30N 108 54W
Gallur 58 41 52N 1 19W
Gallyaaral 85 40 2N 67 35E
Galmi 121 13 58N 5 41E
Gal'on 90 31 38N 34 51E
Galong 141 34 37S 148 34E
Galoya 93 8 10N 80 55E
Galston 34 55 36N 4 22W
Galt, Can. 150 43 21N 80 19W
Galt, U.S.A. 163 38 15N 121 18W
Galtström 72 62 10N 17 30E
Galtür 52 46 58N 10 11E
Galty Mts. 39 52 22N 8 10W
Galtymore, Mt. 39 52 22N 8 12W
Galva 158 41 10N 90 0W
Galve de Sorbe 58 41 13N 3 10W
Galveston 159 29 15N 94 48W
Galveston B. 159 29 30N 94 50W
Gálvez, Argent. 172 32 0S 61 20W
Gálvez, Spain 57 39 42N 4 16W
Galway 39 53 16N 9 4W
Galway □ 38 53 16N 9 3W
Galway B. 39 53 10N 9 20W
Gam, R. 100 21 55N 105 12E
Gamagōri 111 34 50N 137 14E
Gamare, L. 123 11 32N 41 40E
Gamarra 174 8 20N 73 45W
Gamawa 121 12 10N 10 31E
Gambaga 121 10 30N 0 28W
Gambat 94 27 17N 68 26E
Gambela 123 8 14N 34 38E
Gambell 147 63 55N 171 50W
Gambia ■ 120 13 25N 16 0W
Gambia, R. 120 13 20N 15 45W
Gambier, C. 136 11 56S 130 57E
Gambier Is. 140 35 3S 136 30E
Gamboli 94 29 53N 68 24E
Gamboma 124 1 55S 15 52E
Gamboola 138 16 29S 143 43E
Gameleira 170 7 50S 50 0W
Gamerco 161 35 33N 108 56W
Gamleby 73 57 54N 16 20W
Gamlingay 29 52 9N 0 11W
Gammelgarn 171 57 24N 18 49E
Gammon, R. 153 51 24N 95 44W
Gamōda-Saki 110 33 50N 134 45E
Gan (Addu Atoll) 87 0 10S 71 10E
Gan Shemu'el 90 32 28N 34 56E
Gan Yavne 90 31 48N 34 42E
Ganado, Ariz., U.S.A. 161 35 46N 109 41W
Ganado, Tex., U.S.A. 159 29 4N 96 31W
Gananoque 150 44 20N 76 10W
Ganaveh 93 29 35N 50 35E
Gand 47 51 2N 3 37E
Gandak, R. 95 27 0N 84 8E
Gandava 94 28 32N 67 32E
Gander 151 48 18N 54 29W
Gander L. 151 48 58N 54 35W
Ganderowe Falls 127 17 20S 29 10E
Gandesa 58 41 3N 0 26E
Gand = Gent 47 51 2N 3 37E
Gandhi Sagar 94 24 40N 75 40E
Gandi 121 12 55N 5 49E
Gandia 59 38 58N 0 9W
Gandino 62 45 50N 9 52E
Gandole 121 8 28N 11 35E
Gandu 171 13 45S 39 30W
Ganedidalem = Gani 103 0 48S 128 14E
Ganetti 122 18 0N 31 10E
Ganga, Mouths of the 95 21 30N 90 0E
Ganga, R. 95 25 0N 88 0E
Ganganagar 94 29 56N 73 56E
Gangapur 94 26 32N 76 37E
Gangara 121 14 35N 8 40E
Gangavati 97 15 30N 76 36E
Gangaw 98 22 5N 94 15E
Ganges 44 43 56N 3 42E
Ganges = Ganga, R. 95 25 0N 88 0E
Gangoh 94 29 46N 77 18E
Gangtok 98 27 20N 88 37E
Ganj 95 27 45N 78 47E
Ganmain 141 34 47S 147 1E
Gannat 44 46 7N 3 11E
Gannett Pk. 160 43 15N 109 47W
Gannvalley 158 44 3N 98 57W
Ganserdorf 53 48 20N 16 43E
Ganta (Gompa) 120 7 15N 8 59W
Gantheaume B. 137 27 40S 114 10E
Gantheaume, C. 140 36 4S 137 25E
Gantsevichi 80 52 42N 26 30E
Ganyushkino 83 46 35N 49 20E
Ganzi 123 4 30N 31 15E
Gao □ 121 18 0N 1 0E
Gao Bang 101 22 37N 106 18E
Gaoua 120 10 20N 3 8W
Gaoual 120 11 45N 13 25W
Gaouz 118 31 52N 4 20W
Gap 45 44 33N 6 5E
Gar Dzong 93 32 20N 79 55E
Gara, L. 38 53 57N 8 26W
Garachiné 166 8 0N 78 12W
Garanhuns 170 8 50S 36 30W
Garawe 120 4 35N 8 0W
Garba Tula 126 0 30N 38 32E
Garber 159 36 30N 97 36W
Garberville 160 40 11N 123 50W
Garboldisham 29 52 24N 0 57E
Garça 171 22 14S 49 37W
Garças, R. 170 8 43S 39 41W
Gard □ 45 44 2N 4 10E
Garda, L. di 62 45 40N 10 40E
Gardanne 45 43 27N 5 27E
Garde L. 153 62 50N 106 13W
Gardelegen 48 52 32N 11 21E
Garden City, Kans., U.S.A. 159 38 0N 100 45W
Garden City, Tex., U.S.A. 159 31 52N 101 28W
Garden Grove 163 33 47N 117 55W
Gardenstown 37 57 40N 2 20W
Gardez 94 33 31N 68 59E
Gardhiki 69 38 50N 21 55E
Gardian 117 15 45N 19 40E
Gardiner, Can. 150 49 19N 81 2W
Gardiner, Mont., U.S.A. 160 45 3N 110 53W
Gardiner, New Mexico, U.S.A. 159 36 55N 104 29W
Gardiners I. 162 41 4N 72 5W
Gardner 162 42 35N 72 0W
Gardner Canal 152 53 27N 128 8W
Gardnerville 160 38 59N 119 47W
Gardo 91 9 18N 49 20E
Gare, L. 34 56 1N 4 50W
Garelochhead 34 56 7N 4 50W
Gareloi I. 147 51 49N 178 50W
Garešnica 66 45 36N 16 56E
Garéssio 62 44 12N 8 1E
Garey 163 34 53N 120 19W
Garfield, Utah, U.S.A. 160 40 45N 112 15W
Garfield, Wash., U.S.A. 160 47 3N 117 8W
Garforth 33 53 48N 1 22W
Gargaliánoi 69 37 4N 21 38E
Gargano, Mte. 65 41 43N 15 43E
Gargans, Mt. 145 45 37N 1 39E
Gargantua, C. 150 47 35N 85 0W
Gargouna 121 15 56N 0 13E
Gargrave 32 53 58N 2 7W
Garhshankar 94 31 13N 76 11E
Gari 84 59 26N 62 21E
Garibaldi 152 49 56N 123 15W
Garibaldi Prov. Park 152 49 50N 122 40W

Garies **Ghent**

Garies	**125**	30 32S	17 59E
Garigliano, R.	**64**	41 13N	13 44E
Garissa	**126**	0 25S	39 40E
Garissa □	**126**	0 20S	40 0E
Garkida	**121**	10 27N	12 36E
Garko	**121**	11 45N	8 53E
Garland	**160**	41 47N	112 10W
Garlasco	**62**	45 11N	8 55E
Garlieston	**34**	54 47N	4 22W
Garm	**85**	39 0N	70 20E
Garmab	**94**	32 50N	65 30E
Garmisch-Partenkirchen	**49**	47 30N	11 5E
Garmo	**126**	61 51N	8 48E
Garmouth	**37**	57 40N	3 8W
Garmsar	**93**	35 20N	52 25E
Garner	**158**	43 4N	93 37W
Garnett	**158**	38 18N	95 12W
Garo Hills	**95**	25 30N	90 30E
Garoe	**91**	8 35N	48 40E
Garoke	**139**	36 45S	141 30E
Garona, R.	**58**	42 55N	0 45E
Garonne, R.	**44**	45 2N	0 36W
Garoua (Garwa)	**121**	9 19N	13 21E
Garraway	**120**	4 35N	8 0W
Garrel	**48**	52 58N	7 59E
Garrigues	**44**	43 40N	3 30E
Garrison, Ireland	**38**	54 25N	8 5W
Garrison, Mont., U.S.A.	**160**	46 37N	112 56W
Garrison, N.D., U.S.A.	**158**	31 50N	94 28W
Garrison, Tex., U.S.A.	**159**	47 39N	101 27W
Garrison Res.	**158**	47 30N	102 0W
Garron Pt.	**38**	55 3N	6 0W
Garrovillas	**57**	39 40N	6 33W
Garrucha	**59**	37 11N	1 49W
Garry L., Can.	**148**	65 58N	100 18W
Garry L., U.K.	**37**	57 5N	4 52W
Garry, R.	**37**	56 47N	3 47W
Garsdale Head	**32**	54 19N	2 19W
Garsen	**124**	2 20S	40 5E
Garson L., Alta., Can.	**153**	56 19N	110 2W
Garson L., Sask., Can.	**153**	56 20N	110 1W
Garstang	**32**	53 53N	2 47W
Garston	**32**	53 21N	2 55W
Gartempe, R.	**44**	46 47N	0 49E
Gartok	**93**	31 59N	80 30E
Gartz	**48**	54 17N	13 21E
Garu, Ghana	**121**	10 55N	0 20W
Garu, Nigeria	**121**	13 35N	5 25E
Garub	**128**	26 37S	16 0E
Garupá	**170**	1 25S	51 35W
Garut	**103**	7 14S	107 53E
Garvagh	**38**	55 0N	6 41W
Garvaghey	**38**	54 29N	7 8W
Garvald	**35**	55 55N	2 39W
Garváo	**57**	37 42N	8 21W
Garvellachs, Is.	**34**	56 14N	5 48W
Garvie Mts.	**143**	45 30S	168 50E
Garwa	**95**	24 11N	83 47E
Garwolin	**54**	51 55N	21 38E
Gary	**156**	41 35N	87 20W
Garzón	**174**	2 10N	75 40W
Gasan Kuli	**76**	37 40N	54 20E
Gascogne	**44**	43 45N	0 20E
Gascogne, G. de	**58**	44 0N	2 0W
Gascony = Gascogne	**44**	43 45N	0 20E
Gascoyne Junc. Teleg. Off.	**137**	25 2S	115 17E
Gascoyne, R.	**137**	24 52S	113 37E
Gascueña	**58**	40 18N	2 31W
Gash, W.	**123**	15 0N	37 15E
Gashaka	**121**	7 20N	11 29E
Gasherbrum	**95**	35 40N	76 40E
Gashua	**121**	12 54N	11 0E
Gasmata	**138**	6 15S	150 30E
Gaspé	**151**	48 52N	64 30W
Gaspé, C.	**151**	48 48N	64 7W
Gaspé Pass.	**151**	49 10N	64 0W
Gaspé Pen.	**151**	48 45N	65 40W
Gaspésie, Parc Prov. de la	**151**	48 55N	65 50W
Gaspesian Prov. Park	**151**	49 0N	66 45W
Gassaway	**156**	38 42N	80 43W
Gasselte	**46**	52 58N	6 48E
Gasselternijveen	**46**	52 59N	6 51E
Gàssino Torinese	**62**	45 8N	7 50E
Gassol	**121**	8 34N	10 25E
Gastonia	**157**	35 17N	81 10W
Gastoúni	**69**	37 51N	21 15E
Gastoúri	**68**	39 34N	19 54E
Gastre	**176**	42 10S	69 15W
Gata, C. de	**59**	36 41N	2 13W
Gata, Sierra de	**56**	40 20N	6 20W
Gataga, R.	**152**	58 35N	126 59W
Gatchina	**80**	59 35N	30 0E
Gatehouse of Fleet	**34**	54 53N	4 10W
Gateshead	**35**	54 57N	1 37W
Gatesville	**159**	31 29N	97 45W
Gaths	**127**	26 2S	30 32E
Gatico	**172**	22 40S	70 20W
Gatinais	**43**	48 5N	2 40E
Gâtine, Hauteurs de	**44**	46 35N	0 45W
Gatineau, Parc de la	**150**	45 20N	76 0W
Gatineau, R.	**150**	45 27N	75 42W
Gatley	**32**	53 25N	2 15W
Gatooma	**125**	18 20S	29 52E
Gattinara	**62**	45 37N	8 22E
Gatun, L.	**166**	9 7N	79 56W
Gaucín	**57**	36 31N	5 19W
Gaud-i-Zirreh	**93**	29 45N	62 0E
Gauer L.	**153**	57 0N	97 50W
Gauhati	**98**	26 10N	91 45E
Gauja, R.	**80**	57 10N	24 45E
Gaula, R.	**71**	62 57N	11 0E
Gaurain-Ramecroix	**47**	50 36N	3 30E
Gaurdak	**85**	37 50N	66 4E
Gaussberg, Mt.	**13**	66 45S	89 0E
Gausta	**71**	59 50N	8 37E
Gausta, Mt.	**75**	59 48N	8 40E
Gavá	**58**	41 18N	2 0E
Gavarnie	**44**	42 44N	0 3W
Gavater	**93**	25 10N	61 23E
Gavdhopoúla	**69**	34 56N	24 0E
Gávdhos	**69**	34 50N	24 5E
Gavere	**47**	50 55N	3 40E
Gavião	**57**	39 28N	7 50W
Gaviota	**163**	34 29N	120 13W
Gavle	**72**	60 41N	17 13E
Gävle	**72**	60 40N	17 9E
Gävleborgs Lan □	**72**	61 20N	16 15E
Gavorrano	**62**	42 55N	10 55E
Gavray	**42**	49 55N	1 20W
Gavrilov Yam	**81**	57 10N	39 37E
Gávrion	**69**	37 54N	24 44E
Gawachab	**128**	27 4S	17 55E
Gawai	**98**	27 56N	97 40E
Gawilgarh Hills	**96**	21 15N	76 45E
Gawler	**140**	34 30S	138 42E
Gawler Ranges	**136**	32 30S	135 45E
Gawthwaite	**32**	54 16N	3 6W
Gay	**84**	51 27N	58 27E
Gaya, India	**95**	24 47N	85 4E
Gaya, Niger	**121**	11 58N	3 28E
Gaya, Nigeria	**121**	11 57N	9 0E
Gaylord	**156**	45 1N	84 35W
Gayndah	**139**	25 35S	151 39E
Gayny	**84**	60 18N	54 19E
Gaysin	**82**	48 57N	28 25E
Gayton	**29**	52 45N	0 35E
Gayvoron	**82**	48 22N	29 45E
Gaywood	**29**	52 46N	0 26E
Gaza	**90**	31 30N	34 28E
Gaza □	**129**	23 10S	32 45E
Gaza Strip	**90**	31 29N	34 25E
Gazaoua	**121**	13 32N	7 55E
Gazelle Pen.	**135**	4 40S	152 0E
Gazi	**126**	1 3N	24 30E
Gaziantep	**92**	37 6N	37 23E
Gbanga	**120**	7 19N	9 13W
Gbekebo	**121**	6 26N	4 48E
Gboko	**121**	7 17N	9 4E
Gbongan	**121**	7 28N	4 20E
Gcuwa	**129**	32 20S	28 11E
Gdansk	**54**	54 22N	18 40E
Gdansk □	**54**	54 10N	18 30E
Gdanska, Zatoka	**54**	54 30N	19 20E
Gdov	**80**	58 40N	27 55E
Gdynia	**54**	54 35N	18 33E
Geashill	**39**	53 14N	7 20W
Gebe, I.	**103**	0 5N	129 25E
Gebeit Mine	**122**	21 3N	36 29E
Gecoa	**123**	7 30N	35 18E
Gedaref	**123**	14 2N	35 28E
Gedera	**90**	31 49N	34 46E
Gedinne	**47**	49 59N	4 56E
Gedney	**29**	52 47N	0 5W
Gedo	**123**	9 2N	37 25E
Gèdre	**44**	42 47N	0 2E
Gedser	**73**	54 35N	11 55E
Gedser Odde, C.	**73**	54 30N	12 5E
Geel	**47**	51 10N	4 59E
Geelong	**140**	38 10S	144 22E
Geelvink Chan.	**137**	28 30S	114 0E
Geer, R.	**47**	50 51N	5 42E
Geestenseth	**48**	53 31N	8 51E
Geesthacht	**48**	53 25N	10 20E
Geffen	**46**	51 44N	5 28E
Geh	**126**	26 10N	60 0E
Geia	**90**	31 38N	34 37E
Geidam	**121**	12 57N	11 57E
Geikie, R.	**153**	57 45N	103 52W
Geilenkirchen	**48**	50 58N	6 8E
Geili	**123**	16 1N	32 37E
Geilo	**71**	60 32N	8 14E
Geinica	**53**	48 51N	20 55E
Geisingen	**49**	47 55N	8 37E
Geita	**126**	2 48S	32 12E
Geita □	**126**	2 50S	32 10E
Gel, R.	**123**	7 5N	29 10E
Gel River	**123**	7 5N	29 10E
Gela, Golfo di	**65**	37 0N	14 8E
Geladi	**91**	6 59N	46 30E
Gelderland □	**46**	52 5N	6 10E
Geldermalsen	**46**	51 53N	5 17E
Geldern	**48**	51 32N	6 18E
Geldrop	**47**	51 25N	5 32E
Geleen	**47**	50 57N	5 49E
Gelehun	**120**	8 20N	11 40W
Gelendzhik	**82**	44 33N	38 17E
Gelibolu	**68**	40 28N	26 43E
Gelnhausen	**49**	50 12N	9 12E
Gelsenkirchen	**48**	51 30N	7 5E
Gelting	**48**	54 43N	9 53E
Gemas	**101**	2 37N	102 36E
Gembloux	**47**	50 34N	4 43E
Gembu	**121**	8 58N	12 31E
Gemena	**124**	3 20N	19 40E
Gemerek	**92**	39 15N	36 10E
Gemert	**47**	51 33N	5 41E
Gemiston	**128**	26 15S	28 10E
Gemlik	**92**	40 28N	29 13E
Gemmi	**50**	46 25N	7 37E
Gemona del Friuli	**63**	46 16N	13 7E
Gemsa	**122**	27 39N	33 35E
Gemu-Gofa □	**123**	5 40N	36 40E
Gemünden	**49**	50 3N	9 43E
Genale	**123**	6 0N	39 30E
Genappe	**47**	50 37N	4 27E
Gençay	**44**	46 23N	0 23E
Gendringen	**46**	51 52N	6 21E
Gendt	**46**	51 53N	5 59E
Geneina, Gebel	**122**	29 2N	33 55E
Genemuiden	**46**	52 38N	6 2E
General Acha	**172**	37 20S	64 38W
General Alvear, B. A., Argent.	**172**	36 0S	60 0W
General Alvear, Mend., Argent.	**172**	35 0S	67 40W
General Artigas	**172**	26 52S	56 16W
General Belgrano	**172**	36 0S	58 30W
General Cabrera	**172**	32 53S	63 58W
General Cepeda	**164**	25 23N	101 27W
General Guido	**172**	36 40S	57 50W
General Juan Madariaga	**172**	37 0S	57 0W
General La Madrid	**172**	37 30S	61 10W
General MacArthur	**103**	11 18N	125 28E
General Martin Mignuel de Güemes	**172**	24 50S	65 0W
General Paz	**172**	27 45S	57 36W
General Paz, L.	**176**	44 0S	72 0W
General Pico	**172**	35 45S	63 50W
General Pinedo	**172**	27 15S	61 30W
General Pinto	**172**	34 45S	61 50W
General Roca	**176**	30 0S	67 40W
General Sampaio	**170**	4 2S	39 29W
General Santos	**103**	6 12N	125 14E
General Toshevo	**67**	43 42N	28 6E
General Treviño	**165**	26 14N	99 29W
General Trías	**164**	28 21N	106 22W
General Viamonte	**172**	35 1S	61 3W
General Villegas	**172**	35 0S	63 0W
Generoso, Mte.	**51**	45 56N	9 2E
Genesee	**160**	46 31N	116 59W
Genesee, R.	**156**	41 35N	78 0W
Geneseo, Ill., U.S.A.	**158**	41 25N	90 10W
Geneseo, Kans., U.S.A.	**158**	38 32N	98 8W
Geneva, Ala., U.S.A.	**157**	31 2N	85 52W
Geneva, Nebr., U.S.A.	**158**	40 35N	97 35W
Geneva, N.Y., U.S.A.	**162**	42 53N	77 0W
Geneva, Ohio, U.S.A.	**156**	41 49N	80 58W
Geneva = Genève	**50**	46 12N	6 9E
Geneva, L.	**156**	42 38N	88 30W
Geneva, L. = Léman, Lac	**50**	46 26N	6 30E
Genève	**50**	46 12N	6 9E
Genève □	**50**	46 10N	6 10E
Gengenbach	**49**	48 25N	8 0E
Genichesk	**82**	46 12N	34 50E
Genil, R.	**57**	37 12N	3 50W
Génissiat, Barrage de	**45**	46 1N	5 48E
Genk	**47**	50 58N	5 32E
Genkai-Nada	**110**	34 0N	130 0E
Genlis	**43**	47 15N	5 12E
Gennargentu, Mt. del	**64**	40 0N	9 10E
Gennep	**47**	51 41N	5 59E
Gennes	**42**	47 20N	0 17W
Genoa, Austral.	**141**	37 29S	149 35E
Genoa, Nebr., U.S.A.	**158**	41 31N	97 44W
Genoa, N.Y., U.S.A.	**162**	42 40N	76 32W
Genoa = Génova	**62**	44 24N	8 57E
Génova	**62**	44 24N	8 56E
Génova, Golfo di	**62**	44 0N	9 0E
Gent	**47**	51 2N	3 37E
Gentbrugge	**47**	51 3N	3 47E
Genteng	**103**	7 25S	106 23E
Genthin	**48**	52 24N	12 10E
Gentio do Ouro	**170**	11 25S	42 30W
Geographe B.	**137**	33 30S	113 20E
Geographe Chan.	**137**	24 30S	113 0E
Geokchay	**83**	40 42N	47 43E
George, Can.	**151**	46 12N	62 32W
George, S. Afr.	**128**	33 58S	22 29E
George, L., New South Wales, Austral.	**141**	35 10S	149 25E
George, L., S. Austral., Austral.	**140**	37 25S	140 0E
George, L., W. A., Austral.	**137**	22 45S	123 40E
George, L., Uganda	**126**	0 5N	30 10E
George, L., Fla., U.S.A.	**157**	29 15N	81 35W
George, L., N.Y., U.S.A.	**162**	43 30N	73 30W
George, Mt.	**137**	25 17S	119 0E
George, R.	**151**	58 49N	66 10W
George River = Port Nouveau	**149**	58 30N	65 50W
George Sound	**143**	44 52S	167 25E
George Town, Austral.	**138**	41 5S	146 49E
George Town, Bahamas	**166**	23 33N	75 47W
George Town, Malay.	**101**	5 25N	100 19E
George V Coast	**13**	67 0S	148 0E
George West	**159**	28 18N	98 5W
Georgetown, Austral.	**133**	18 17S	143 33E
Georgetown, Ont., Can.	**150**	43 40N	80 0W
Georgetown, P.E.I., Can.	**151**	46 13N	62 24W
Georgetown, Cay. Is.	**166**	19 20N	81 24W
Georgetown, Gambia	**120**	13 30N	14 47W
Georgetown, Guyana	**174**	6 50N	58 12W
Georgetown, Colo., U.S.A.	**160**	39 46N	105 49W
Georgetown, Del., U.S.A.	**162**	38 42N	75 23W
Georgetown, N.Y., U.S.A.	**162**	42 46N	75 44W
Georgetown, Ohio, U.S.A.	**156**	38 50N	83 50W
Georgetown, S.C., U.S.A.	**157**	33 22N	79 15W
Georgetown, Tex., U.S.A.	**159**	30 45N	98 10W
Georgi Dimitrov	**67**	42 15N	23 54E
Georgia □	**156**	32 0N	82 0W
Georgia, Str. of	**152**	49 25N	124 0W
Georgian B.	**150**	45 15N	81 0W
Georgian S.S.R. □	**83**	41 0N	45 0E
Georgievsk	**83**	44 12N	43 28E
Georgina Downs	**138**	21 10S	137 40E
Georgina, R.	**138**	23 30S	139 47E
Georgiu-Dezh	**81**	51 3N	39 20E
Georgiyevka	**85**	43 3N	74 43E
Gera	**48**	50 53N	12 5E
Gera □	**48**	50 45N	11 30E
Geraardsbergen	**47**	50 45N	3 53E
Geral de Goias, Serra	**171**	12 0S	46 0W
Geral do Paranã Serra	**171**	15 0S	47 0W
Geral, Serra, Bahia, Brazil	**171**	14 0S	41 0W
Geral, Serra, Goiás, Brazil	**170**	11 15S	46 30W
Geral, Serra, Santa Catarina, Brazil	**173**	26 25S	50 0W
Geraldine, N.Z.	**143**	44 5S	171 15E
Geraldine, U.S.A.	**160**	47 45N	110 18W
Geraldton, Austral.	**137**	28 48S	114 32E
Geraldton, Can.	**150**	49 44N	86 59W
Geranium	**140**	35 23S	140 11E
Gerardmer	**43**	48 3N	6 50E
Gerdine, Mt.	**147**	61 32N	152 30W
Gerede	**82**	40 45N	32 10E
Gérgal	**59**	37 7N	2 31W
Geriban	**91**	7 10N	48 55E
Gerik	**101**	5 25N	100 8E
Gering	**158**	41 51N	103 40W
Gerizim	**90**	32 13N	35 15E
Gerlach	**160**	40 43N	119 27W
Gerlachovka, Mt.	**53**	49 11N	20 7E
Gerlafingen	**50**	47 10N	7 34E
Gerlev	**73**	56 36N	10 9E
Gerlogubi	**91**	6 53N	45 3E
German Planina	**66**	42 33N	22 0E
Germansen Landing	**152**	55 43N	124 40W
Germany, East ■	**48**	52 0N	12 0E
Germany, West ■	**48**	52 0N	9 0E
Germersheim	**49**	49 13N	8 0E
Germiston	**125**	26 11S	28 10E
Gernsheim	**49**	49 44N	8 29E
Gero	**111**	35 48N	137 14E
Gerogery	**141**	35 50S	147 1E
Gerolstein	**49**	50 12N	6 24E
Gerona	**58**	41 58N	2 46E
Gerona □	**58**	42 11N	2 30E
Gérouville	**47**	49 37N	5 26E
Gerrans B.	**30**	50 12N	4 57W
Gerrard	**152**	50 30N	117 17W
Gerrards Cross	**29**	51 35N	0 32W
Gerrild	**73**	56 30N	10 50E
Gerringong	**141**	34 46S	150 47E
Gers □	**44**	43 35N	0 38E
Gersau	**51**	47 0N	8 32E
Gersoppa Falls	**97**	14 12N	74 46E
Gerufa	**128**	19 8S	26 0E
Gerze	**92**	41 45N	35 10E
Geseke	**48**	51 38N	8 29E
Geser	**103**	3 50N	130 35E
Gesso, R.	**62**	44 21N	7 20E
Gesves	**47**	50 24N	5 4E
Getafe	**56**	40 18N	3 44W
Gethsémani	**151**	50 13N	60 40W
Gettysburg, Pa., U.S.A.	**156**	39 47N	77 18W
Gettysburg, S.D., U.S.A.	**158**	45 3N	99 56W
Getz Ice Shelf	**13**	75 0S	130 0W
Geul, R.	**47**	50 53N	5 43E
Geurie	**141**	32 22S	148 50E
Gevaudan	**44**	44 40N	3 40E
Gevgelija	**66**	41 9N	22 30E
Gévora, R.	**57**	38 53N	6 57W
Gex	**45**	46 21N	6 3E
Geyikli	**68**	39 50N	26 12E
Geyser	**160**	47 17N	110 30W
Geysir	**74**	64 19N	20 18W
Geyve	**82**	40 32N	30 18E
Ghaghara, R.	**95**	26 0N	84 20E
Ghail	**92**	21 40N	46 20E
Ghalla, Wadi el	**123**	12 0N	28 58E
Ghana ■	**121**	6 0N	1 0W
Ghandhi Dam	**93**	24 30N	75 35E
Ghansor	**95**	22 39N	80 1E
Ghanzi	**128**	21 50S	21 45E
Ghanzi □	**128**	21 50S	21 45E
Gharbîya, Es Sahrâ el	**122**	27 40N	26 30E
Ghard Abû Muharik	**122**	26 50N	30 0E
Ghardaïa	**118**	32 31N	3 37E
Gharyān	**119**	32 10N	13 0E
Ghāt	**119**	24 59N	10 19E
Ghat Ghat	**92**	26 0N	45 5E
Ghatal	**95**	22 40N	87 46E
Ghatampur	**95**	26 8N	80 13E
Ghatprabha, R.	**96**	16 15N	75 20E
Ghazal, Bahr el	**117**	15 0N	17 0E
Ghazaouet	**118**	35 8N	1 50W
Ghaziabad	**94**	28 42N	77 35E
Ghazipur	**95**	25 38N	83 35E
Ghazni	**94**	33 30N	68 17E
Ghazni □	**93**	33 0N	68 0E
Ghedi	**62**	45 24N	10 16E
Ghelari	**70**	45 42N	22 45E
Ghelinsor	**91**	6 35N	46 55E
Ghent = Gand	**47**	51 4N	3 43E

Gheorghe Gheorghiu-Dej Gobo

Gheorghe Gheorghiu-Dej	70	46 17N	26 47 E
Gheorgheni	70	46 43N	25 41 E
Ghergani	70	44 37N	25 37 E
Gherla	70	47 0N	23 57 E
Ghilarza	64	40 8N	8 50 E
Ghisonaccia	45	42 1N	9 26 E
Ghizao	94	33 30N	65 59 E
Ghizar, R.	95	36 10N	73 4 E
Ghod, R.	96	18 40N	74 15 E
Ghorat □	93	34 0N	64 20 E
Ghost River, Can.	150	50 10N	91 27W
Ghost River, Ont., Can.	150	51 25N	83 20W
Ghot Ogrein	122	31 10N	25 20 E
Ghotaru	94	27 20N	70 1 E
Ghotki	94	28 5N	69 30 E
Ghudāmis	119	30 11N	9 29 E
Ghugri	95	22 39N	80 41 E
Ghugus	96	20 0N	79 0 E
Ghulam Mohammad Barrage	94	25 30N	67 0 E
Ghuriān	93	34 17N	61 25 E
Gia Dinh	101	10 49N	106 42 E
Gia Lai = Pleiku	101	14 3N	108 0 E
Gia Nghia	101	12 0N	107 42 E
Gia Ngoc	100	14 50N	108 58 E
Gia Vuc	100	14 42N	108 34 E
Giamda Dzong	99	30 3N	93 2 E
Giannutri, I.	62	42 16N	11 5 E
Giant Forest	163	36 36N	118 43W
Giant Mts. = Krkonose	52	50 50N	16 10 E
Giant's Causeway	38	55 15N	6 30W
Giarabub = Jaghbub	117	29 42N	24 38 E
Giarre	65	37 44N	15 10 E
Giaveno	62	45 3N	7 20 E
Gibara	166	21 0N	76 20W
Gibbon	158	40 49N	98 45W
Gibe, R.	123	6 25N	36 10 E
Gibellina	64	37 48N	13 0 E
Gibeon	128	25 7 S	17 45 E
Gibraléon	57	37 23N	6 58W
Gibraltar	57	36 7N	5 22W
Gibraltar Pt.	33	53 6N	0 20 E
Gibraltar, Str. of	57	35 55N	5 40W
Gibson Des.	136	24 0 S	126 0 E
Gibsons	152	49 24N	123 32W
Gida. G.	12	72 30N	77 0 E
Giddalur	97	15 20N	78 57 E
Gidde	123	5 40N	37 25 E
Giddings	159	30 11N	96 58W
Gide	123	9 52N	35 5 E
Gien	43	47 40N	2 36 E
Giessen	48	50 34N	8 40 E
Gieten	46	53 0N	6 46 E
Gif-sur-Yvette	46	48 42N	2 8 E
Gifatin, Geziret	122	27 10N	33 50 E
Gifford	35	55 54N	2 45W
Gifford Creek	137	24 3 S	116 16 E
Gifhorn	48	52 29N	10 32 E
Gifu	111	35 30N	136 45 E
Gifu-ken □	111	36 0N	137 0 E
Gigant	83	46 28N	41 30 E
Giganta, Sa. de la	164	25 30N	111 30W
Gigen	67	43 40N	24 28 E
Giggleswick	32	54 5N	2 19W
Gigha, I.	39	55 42N	5 45W
Giglio, I.	62	42 20N	10 52 E
Gignac	44	43 39N	3 32 E
Gigüela, R.	58	39 47N	3 0W
Gijón	56	43 32N	5 42W
Gil I.	152	53 12N	129 15W
Gila Bend	161	33 0N	112 46W
Gila Bend Mts.	161	33 15N	113 0W
Gila, R.	161	33 5N	108 40W
Gilau	138	5 38 S	149 3 E
Gilbedi	121	13 40N	5 45 E
Gilbert Is.	130	1 0 S	176 0 E
Gilbert Plains	153	51 9N	100 28W
Gilbert, R.	138	16 35 S	141 15 E
Gilbert River	138	18 9 S	142 52 E
Gilberton	138	19 16 S	143 35 E
Gilbués	170	9 50 S	45 21W
Gilford	38	54 23N	6 20W
Gilford I.	152	50 40N	126 30W
Gilgai	137	31 15 S	119 56 E
Gilgandra	141	31 43 S	148 39 E
Gilgil	126	0 30 S	36 20 E
Gilgit	95	35 50N	74 15 E
Gilgit, R.	95	35 50N	74 25 E
Gilgunnia	141	32 26 S	146 2 E
Giligulgul	139	26 26 S	150 0 E
Gilima	126	3 53N	28 15 E
Giljeva Planina	66	43 9N	20 0 E
Gill L.	38	54 15N	8 25W
Gillam	153	56 20N	94 40W
Gilleleje	73	56 8N	12 19 E
Gillen, L.	137	26 11 S	124 38 E
Gilles, L.	140	32 50 S	136 45 E
Gillespie Pt.	143	43 24 S	169 49 E
Gillett	162	41 57N	76 48W
Gillette	158	44 20N	105 38W
Gilliat	138	20 40 S	141 28 E
Gillingham, Dorset, U.K.	28	51 2N	2 15W
Gillingham, Kent, U.K.	29	51 23N	0 34 E
Gilmer	159	32 44N	94 55W
Gilmore	141	35 14 S	148 12 E
Gilmore, L.	137	32 29 S	121 37 E
Gilmour	150	44 48N	77 37W
Gilo	123	7 35N	34 30 E
Gilo, R.	161	33 5N	108 40W
Gilort, R.	70	44 38N	23 32 E
Gilroy	163	37 1N	121 37W
Gilsland	32	55 0N	2 34W
Gilău	70	46 45N	23 23W
Giluwe, Mt.	135	6 8 S	143 52 E
Gilwern	31	51 49N	3 5W
Gilze	47	51 32N	4 57 E
Gimåfors	72	62 40N	16 25 E
Gimbi	123	9 3N	35 42 E
Gimigliano	65	38 53N	16 32 E
Gimli	153	50 40N	97 10W
Gimmi	123	9 0N	37 20 E
Gimo	72	60 11N	18 12 E
Gimont	44	43 38N	0 52 E
Gimzo	90	31 56N	34 56 E
Gin Ganga	97	6 5N	80 7 E
Gin Gin	139	25 0 S	151 44 E
Ginâh	122	25 21N	30 30 E
Gindie	138	23 44 S	148 8 E
Gineta, La	59	39 8N	2 1W
Gingin	137	31 22 S	115 54 E
Gîngiova	70	43 54N	23 50 E
Ginir	123	7 12N	40 40 E
Ginosa	65	40 35N	16 45 E
Ginowan	112	26 15N	127 47 E
Ginzo de Limia	56	42 3N	7 47W
Giohar	91	2 20N	45 15 E
Gióia del Colle	65	40 49N	16 55 E
Gióia, G. di	65	38 30N	15 50 E
Gióia Táuro	65	38 26N	15 53 E
Gioiosa Jónica	65	38 20N	16 19 E
Gióna, Óros	69	38 38N	22 14 E
Giong, Teluk	103	4 50N	118 20 E
Giovi, P. dei	45	44 30N	8 55 E
Giovinazzo	65	41 10N	16 40 E
Gippsland	133	37 45 S	147 15 E
Gir Hills	94	21 0N	71 0 E
Girab	94	26 2N	70 38 E
Giralla	136	22 31 S	114 15 E
Giraltovce	53	49 7N	21 32 E
Girard	159	37 30N	94 50W
Girardot	174	4 18N	74 48W
Girdle Ness	37	57 9N	2 2W
Giresun	92	40 45N	38 30 E
Girga	122	26 17N	31 55 E
Girgir, C.	135	3 50 S	144 35 E
Giridih	95	24 10N	86 21 E
Girifalco	65	38 49N	16 25 E
Girilambone	141	31 16 S	146 57 E
Girishk	93	31 47N	64 24 E
Giro	121	11 7N	4 42 E
Giromagny	43	47 44N	6 50 E
Gironde □	44	44 45N	0 30W
Gironde, R.	44	45 27N	0 53W
Gironella	58	42 2N	1 53 E
Giru	138	19 30 S	147 5 E
Girvan	34	55 15N	4 50W
Girvan R.	34	55 18N	4 51W
Gisborne	142	38 39 S	178 5 E
Gisburn	32	53 56N	2 16W
Gisenyi	126	1 41 S	29 30 E
Giske	71	62 30N	6 3 E
Gisla	36	58 7N	6 53W
Gislaved	73	57 19N	13 32 E
Gisors	43	49 15N	1 40 E
Gissarskiy, Khrebet	85	39 0N	69 0 E
Gistel	47	51 9N	2 59 E
Giswil	50	46 50N	8 11 E
Gitega (Kitega)	126	3 26 S	29 56 E
Gits	47	51 0N	3 6 E
Giubiasco	51	46 11N	9 1 E
Giugliano in Campania	65	40 55N	14 12 E
Giulianova	63	42 45N	13 58 E
Giurgeni	70	44 45N	27 38 E
Giurgiu	70	43 52N	25 57 E
Giv'at Brenner	90	31 52N	34 47 E
Give	73	55 51N	9 13 E
Givet	43	50 8N	4 49 E
Givors	45	45 35N	4 45 E
Givry, Belg.	47	50 23N	4 2 E
Givry, France	43	46 41N	4 46 E
Giza (El Giza)	122	30 1N	31 11 E
Gizhduvan	85	40 6N	64 41 E
Gizhiga	77	62 0N	150 27 E
Gizhiginskaya, Guba	77	61 0N	158 0 E
Gizycko	54	54 2N	21 48 E
Gizzeria	65	38 57N	16 10 E
Gjegjan	68	41 58N	20 3 E
Gjerpen	71	59 15N	9 33 E
Gjerstad	71	58 54N	9 0 E
Gjiri-i-Vlorës	68	40 29N	19 27 E
Gjirokastër	68	40 7N	20 16 E
Gjoa Haven	148	68 20N	96 0W
Gjovdal	71	58 52N	8 19 E
Gjøvik	71	60 47N	10 43 E
Glace Bay	151	46 11N	59 58W
Glacier B.	152	58 30N	136 10W
Glacier Nat. Park	152	51 15N	117 30W
Glacier National Park	160	48 35N	113 40W
Glacier Peak Mt.	160	48 7N	121 7W
Gladewater	159	32 30N	94 58W
Gladstone, Queens., Austral.	74	23 52 S	151 16 E
Gladstone, S.A., Austral.	140	33 15 S	138 22 E
Gladstone, W. Australia, Austral.	137	25 57 S	114 17 E
Gladstone, Can.	153	50 13N	98 57W
Gladstone, U.S.A.	156	45 52N	87 1W
Gladwin	156	43 59N	84 29W
Gladys L.	152	59 50N	133 0W
Glafsfjorden	72	59 30N	12 45 E
Głagów Małapolski	53	50 10N	21 56 E
Glåma	74	65 48N	23 0W
Glåma, R.	71	60 30N	12 8 E
Glamis	37	56 37N	3 0W
Glamorgan (□)	26	51 37N	3 35W
Glamorgan, Vale of	23	50 45N	3 15W
Glan, Phil.	103	5 45N	125 20 E
Glan, Sweden	73	58 37N	16 0 E
Glanaman	31	51 48N	3 56W
Glanaruddery Mts.	39	52 20N	9 27W
Glandore	39	51 33N	9 7W
Glandore Harb.	39	51 33N	9 8W
Glanerbrug	46	52 13N	6 58 E
Glanton	35	55 25N	1 54W
Glanworth	39	52 10N	8 25W
Glarner Alpen	51	46 50N	9 0 E
Glärnisch	51	47 0N	9 0 E
Glarus	51	47 3N	9 4 E
Glarus □	51	47 0N	9 5 E
Glas Maol	37	56 52N	3 20W
Glasco, Kans., U.S.A.	158	39 25N	97 50W
Glasco, N.Y., U.S.A.	162	42 3N	73 57W
Glasgow, U.K.	34	55 52N	4 14W
Glasgow, Ky., U.S.A.	156	37 2N	85 55W
Glasgow, Mont., U.S.A.	160	48 12N	106 35W
Glasnevin	38	53 22N	6 18W
Glassboro	162	39 42N	75 7W
Glasslough	38	54 20N	6 53W
Glastonbury, U.K.	28	51 9N	2 42W
Glastonbury, U.S.A.	162	41 42N	72 27W
Glatt, R.	51	47 28N	8 32 E
Glattfelden	51	47 33N	8 30 E
Glauchau	48	50 50N	12 33 E
Glazov	81	58 9N	52 40 E
Glbovo	67	42 1N	24 43 E
Gleichen	152	50 50N	113 0W
Gleisdorf	52	47 6N	15 44 E
Glemsford	29	52 6N	0 41 E
Glen Affric	36	57 15N	5 0W
Glen Afton	142	37 46 S	175 4 E
Glen Almond	35	56 28N	3 50W
Glen B.	38	54 43N	8 45W
Glen Burnie	162	39 10N	76 37W
Glen Canyon Dam	161	37 0N	111 25W
Glen Canyon Nat. Recreation Area	161	37 30N	111 0W
Glen Coe	23	56 40N	5 0W
Glen Cove	162	40 51N	73 37W
Glen Esk	37	56 53N	2 50W
Glen Etive	34	56 37N	5 0W
Glen Florrie	136	22 55 S	115 59 E
Glen Garry, Inv., U.K.	36	57 3N	5 7W
Glen Garry, Per., U.K.	37	56 47N	4 5W
Glen Gowrie	140	31 4 S	143 10 E
Glen Helen	32	54 14N	4 35W
Glen Innes	139	29 40 S	151 39 E
Glen Lyon, U.K.	37	56 35N	4 20W
Glen Lyon, U.S.A.	162	41 10N	76 7W
Glen Massey	142	37 38 S	175 2 E
Glen Mor	37	57 12N	4 37 E
Glen Moriston	36	57 10N	4 58W
Glen Orchy	34	56 27N	4 52W
Glen Orrin	37	57 30N	4 45W
Glen Oykel	37	58 5N	4 50W
Glen, R.	29	52 50N	0 7W
Glen Shee	37	56 45N	3 25W
Glen Shiel	36	57 8N	5 20W
Glen Spean	37	56 53N	4 40W
Glen Trool Lodge	34	55 5N	4 30W
Glen Ullin	158	46 48N	101 46W
Glen Valley	141	36 54 S	147 28 E
Glenade	38	54 22N	8 17W
Glenamoy	38	54 14N	9 40W
Glénans, Is. de	42	47 42N	4 0W
Glenariff	141	30 50 S	146 33 E
Glenarm	38	54 58N	5 58W
Glenart Castle	39	52 48N	6 12W
Glenavy, N.Z.	143	44 54 S	171 7 E
Glenavy, U.K.	38	54 36N	6 12W
Glenbarr	34	55 34N	5 40W
Glenbeigh	39	52 3N	9 57W
Glenbrittle	36	57 13N	6 18W
Glenbrook	142	33 46 S	150 37 E
Glenburn	141	37 37 S	145 26 E
Glencoe, S. Afr.	129	28 11 S	30 11 E
Glencoe, U.S.A.	158	44 45N	94 10W
Glencolumbkille	38	54 43N	8 41W
Glendale, Can.	150	46 45N	84 2W
Glendale, Rhod.	127	17 22 S	31 5 E
Glendale, Ariz., U.S.A.	161	33 40N	112 8W
Glendale, Calif., U.S.A.	163	34 7N	118 18W
Glendale, Oreg., U.S.A.	160	42 44N	123 29W
Glendive	158	47 7N	104 40W
Glendo	158	42 30N	105 0W
Glendora	163	34 8N	117 52W
Gleneagles	35	56 16N	3 44W
Glenealy	39	52 59N	6 10W
Gleneely	38	52 14N	7 8W
Glenelg, Austral.	140	34 58 S	138 31 E
Glenelg, U.K.	36	57 13N	5 37W
Glenelg, R.	140	38 4 S	140 59 E
Glenfarne	38	54 17N	8 0W
Glenfield	162	43 43N	75 24W
Glenfinnan	36	56 52N	5 28W
Glengad Hd.	38	55 19N	7 11W
Glengariff	39	51 45N	9 33W
Glengormley	38	54 41N	5 57W
Glengyle	138	24 48 S	139 37 E
Glenham	143	46 26 S	168 52 E
Glenhope	143	41 40 S	172 39 E
Glenisland	38	53 54N	9 24W
Glenkens, The	34	55 10N	4 15W
Glenluce	34	54 53N	4 50W
Glenmary, Mt.	143	44 0 S	169 55 E
Glenmaye	32	54 11N	4 42W
Glenmora	159	31 1N	92 34W
Glenmorgan	139	27 14 S	149 42 E
Glenn, oilfield	19	57 55N	0 15 E
Glennagevlagh	38	53 36N	9 41W
Glennamaddy	38	53 37N	8 33W
Glenn's Ferry	160	43 0N	115 15W
Glenoe	38	54 47N	5 50W
Glenorchy, S. Austral., Austral.	140	31 55 S	139 46 E
Glenorchy, Tas., Austral.	138	42 49 S	147 18 E
Glenorchy, Vic., Austral.	140	36 55 S	142 41 E
Glenore	138	17 50 S	141 12 E
Glenormiston	138	22 55 S	138 50 E
Glenreagh	139	30 2 S	153 1 E
Glenrock	160	42 53N	105 55W
Glenrothes	35	56 12N	3 11W
Glenrowan	141	36 29 S	146 13 E
Glenroy, S. Australia, Austral.	140	37 13 S	140 48 E
Glenroy, W. Australia, Austral.	136	17 16 S	126 14 E
Glenroy, S. Afr.	132	26 23 S	28 17 E
Glens Falls	162	43 19N	73 39W
Glentane	38	53 25N	8 30W
Glenties	38	54 48N	8 18W
Glenville	156	38 56N	80 50W
Glenwood, Alta., Can.	152	49 21N	113 31W
Glenwood, Newf., Can.	151	49 0N	54 47W
Glenwood, Ark., U.S.A.	159	34 20N	93 30W
Glenwood, Hawaii, U.S.A.	147	19 29N	155 10W
Glenwood, Iowa, U.S.A.	158	41 7N	95 41W
Glenwood, Minn., U.S.A.	158	45 38N	95 21W
Glenwood Sprs.	160	39 39N	107 15W
Gletsch	51	46 34N	8 22 E
Glettinganes	51	65 30N	13 37W
Glin	39	52 34N	9 17W
Glina	63	45 20N	16 6 E
Glinojeck	54	52 49N	20 21 E
Glinsk	39	53 23N	9 49W
Glittertind	71	61 40N	8 32 E
Gliwice (Gleiwitz)	54	50 22N	18 41 E
Globe	161	33 25N	110 53W
Glodeanu-Siliştea	70	44 50N	26 48 E
Glödnitz	52	46 53N	14 7 E
Glodyany	70	47 45N	27 31 E
Gloggnitz	52	47 41N	15 56 E
Głogów	54	51 37N	16 5 E
Głogowek	54	50 21N	17 53 E
Gloria, La	174	8 37N	73 48W
Glorieuses, Îs.	129	11 30 S	47 20 E
Glossop	32	53 27N	1 56W
Gloucester, Austral.	141	32 0 S	151 59 E
Gloucester, U.K.	28	51 52N	2 15W
Gloucester, U.S.A.	162	42 38N	70 39W
Gloucester, Va., U.S.A.	162	37 25N	76 32W
Gloucester, C.	135	5 26 S	148 21 E
Gloucester City	162	39 54N	75 8W
Gloucester, I.	138	20 0 S	148 30 E
Gloucestershire □	28	51 44N	2 10W
Gloversville	162	43 5N	74 18W
Glovertown	151	48 40N	54 03W
Głubczyce	54	50 13N	17 52 E
Glubokiy	83	48 35N	40 25 E
Glubokoye	80	55 10N	27 45 E
Głucholazy	54	50 19N	17 24 E
Glücksburg	48	54 48N	9 34 E
Glückstadt	48	53 46N	9 28 E
Gluepot	140	33 45 S	140 0 E
Glukhov	80	51 40N	33 50 E
Glussk	80	52 53N	28 41 E
Gł ó wno	54	51 59N	19 42 E
Glyn-ceiriog	31	52 56N	3 12W
Glyn Neath	31	51 45N	3 37W
Glyncorrwg	31	51 40N	3 39W
Glyngøre	73	56 46N	8 52 E
Glynn	39	52 29N	6 55W
Gmünd, Kärnten, Austria	52	46 54N	13 31 E
Gmünd, Niederösterreich, Austria	52	48 45N	15 0 E
Gmunden	52	47 55N	13 48 E
Gnarp	72	62 3N	17 16 E
Gnesta	72	59 3N	17 17 E
Gniew	54	53 50N	18 50 E
Gniewkowo	54	52 54N	18 25 E
Gniezno	54	52 30N	17 35 E
Gnoien	48	53 58N	12 41 E
Gnopp	123	8 47N	29 50 E
Gnosall	28	52 48N	2 15W
Gnosjö	73	57 22N	13 43 E
Gnowangerup	137	33 58 S	117 59 E
Go Cong	101	10 22N	106 40 E
Gō-no-ura	110	33 44N	129 40 E
Goa	97	15 33N	73 59 E
Goa □	97	15 33N	73 59 E
Goageb	128	26 49 S	17 15 E
Goalen Hd.	141	36 33 S	150 4 E
Goalpara	98	26 10N	90 40 E
Goalundo	95	23 50N	89 47 E
Goaso	120	6 48N	2 30W
Goat Fell	34	55 37N	5 11W
Goba, Ethiopia	123	7 1N	39 59 E
Goba, Mozam.	125	26 15 S	32 13 E
Gobabis	128	22 16 S	19 0 E
Gobi, desert	105	44 0N	111 0 E
Gobichettipalayam	97	11 31N	77 21 E
Gobō	111	33 53N	135 10 E
Gobo	123	5 40N	30 10 E

Goch Grand Bassa

Goch 48 51 40N 6 9E
Gochas 125 24 59S 19 25E
Godalming 29 51 12N 0 37W
Godavari Point 96 17 0N 82 20E
Godavari, R. 96 19 5N 79 0E
Godbout 151 49 20N 67 38W
Godda 95 24 50N 87 20E
Goddua 119 26 26N 14 19E
Godech 66 43 1N 23 4E
Godegård 73 58 43N 15 8E
Goderich 150 43 45N 81 41W
Goderville 42 49 38N 0 22E
Godhavn 12 69 15N 53 38W
Godhra 94 22 49N 73 40E
Godmanchester 29 52 19N 0 11W
Gödöllö 53 47 38N 19 25E
Godoy Cruz 172 32 56S 68 52W
Godrevy Pt. 30 50 15N 5 24W
Gods L. 153 54 40N 94 15W
Gods, R. 153 56 22N 92 51W
Godshill 28 50 38N 1 13W
Godstone 29 51 15N 0 3W
Godthåb 12 64 10N 51 46W
Godwin Austen (K2) 93 36 0N 77 0E
Goeie Hoop, Kaap die 128 34 24S 18 30E
Goeland, L. 150 49 50N 76 48W
Goeree 46 51 50N 4 0E
Goes 47 51 30N 3 55E
Goffstown 162 43 1N 71 36W
Gogama 150 47 35N 81 43W
Gogango 138 23 40S 150 2E
Gogebic, L. 158 46 30N 89 34W
Gogha 94 21 32N 72 9E
Gogolin 54 50 30N 18 0E
Gogra, R. = Ghaghara 99 26 0N 84 20E
Gogriâl 123 8 30N 28 0E
Goiana 170 7 33S 34 59W
Goiandira 171 11 46S 46 40W
Goianésia 171 15 18S 49 7W
Goiânia 171 16 35S 49 20W
Goiás 171 15 55S 50 10W
Goiás □ 170 12 10S 48 0W
Goiatuba 171 18 1S 49 23W
Goil L. 34 56 8N 4 52W
Goirle 47 51 31N 5 4E
Góis 56 40 10N 8 6W
Goisern 52 47 38N 13 38E
Gojam □ 123 10 55N 36 30E
Gojeb, W. 123 7 12N 36 40E
Gojō 111 34 21N 135 42E
Gojra 94 31 10N 72 40E
Gokak 97 16 11N 74 52E
Gokarannath 95 27 57N 80 39E
Gokarn 97 14 33N 74 17E
Gökçeada 68 40 10N 26 0E
Gokteik 99 22 26N 97 0E
Gokurt 94 29 47N 67 26E
Gøl 73 57 4N 9 42E
Gola 95 28 3N 80 32E
Gola I. 38 55 4N 8 20W
Golaghat 98 26 30N 94 0E
Golakganj 95 26 8N 89 52E
Golaya Pristen 82 46 29N 32 23E
Golchikha 12 71 45N 84 0E
Golconda 160 40 58N 117 32W
Gold Beach 160 42 25N 124 25W
Gold Coast, Austral. 139 28 0S 153 25E
Gold Coast, W. Afr. 121 4 0N 1 40W
Gold Creek 147 62 45N 149 45W
Gold Hill 160 42 28N 123 2W
Gold Point 163 37 21N 117 21W
Gold River 152 49 40N 126 10E
Goldach 51 47 28N 9 28E
Goldau 51 47 3N 8 33E
Goldberg 48 53 34N 12 6E
Golden, Can. 152 51 20N 117 0W
Golden, Ireland 39 52 30N 8 0W
Golden, U.S.A. 158 39 42N 105 30W
Golden Bay 143 40 40S 172 50E
Golden Gate 160 37 54N 122 30W
Golden Hinde, mt. 152 49 40N 125 44W
Golden Prairie 153 50 13N 109 37W
Golden Rock 97 10 45N 78 48E
Golden Vale 39 52 33N 8 17W
Goldendale 160 45 53N 120 48W
Goldfield 163 37 45N 117 13W
Goldfields 153 59 28N 108 29W
Goldpines 153 50 45N 93 05W
Goldsand L. 153 57 2N 101 8W
Goldsboro 157 35 24N 77 59W
Goldsmith 159 32 0N 102 40W
Goldsworthy 136 20 21S 119 30E
Goldsworthy, Mt. 136 20 23S 119 31E
Goldthwaite 159 31 25N 98 32W
Goleen 39 51 30N 9 43W
Golegã 57 39 24N 8 29W
Goleniów 54 53 35N 14 50E
Goleta 163 34 27N 119 50W
Golfito 166 8 41N 83 5W
Golfo degli Aranci 65 41 0N 9 38E
Goliad 159 28 40N 97 22W
Golija 66 43 22N 20 15E
Golija, Mts. 66 43 5N 18 45E
Golina 54 52 15N 18 4E
Golo, R. 45 42 31N 9 32E
Golovanesvsk 82 48 25N 30 30E
Gölpazari 82 40 17N 30 17E
Golra 94 33 37N 72 56E
Golspie 37 57 58N 3 58W
Golub Dobrzyn 54 53 7N 19 2E
Golubac 66 44 38N 21 38E
Golyama Kamchiya, R. 67 43 2N 27 18E
Goma, Ethiopia 123 8 29N 36 53E
Goma, Rwanda 126 2 11S 29 18E
Goma, Zaïre 126 1 37S 29 10E
Gomare 128 19 25S 22 8E
Gomati, R. 95 26 30N 81 50E
Gombari 126 2 45N 29 3E
Gombe 121 10 19N 11 2E
Gombe, R. 126 4 30S 32 50E
Gombi 121 10 12N 12 45E
Gomel 80 52 28N 31 0E
Gomera, I. 116 28 10N 17 5W
Gometra I. 34 56 30N 6 18W
Gómez Palacio 164 25 40N 104 40W
Gommern 48 52 54N 11 47E
Gomogomo 103 6 25S 134 53E
Gomoh 99 23 52N 86 10E
Gomotartsi 66 44 6N 22 57E
Goms 50 46 30N 8 15E
Gonābād 93 34 15N 58 45E
Gonaïves 167 19 20N 72 50W
Gonâve, G. de la 167 19 29N 72 42W
Gonâve, I. de la 167 18 45N 73 0W
Gönc 53 48 28N 21 14E
Gonda 95 27 9N 81 58E
Gondab-e Kāvūs 93 37 20N 55 25E
Gondal 94 21 58N 70 52E
Gonder 123 12 23N 37 30E
Gondia 96 21 30N 80 10E
Gondola 127 19 4S 33 37E
Gondomar, Port. 56 41 10N 8 35W
Gondomar, Spain 56 42 7N 8 45W
Gondrecourt-le-Château 43 48 26N 5 30E
Gongola □ 121 8 0N 12 0E
Gongola, R. 121 10 30N 10 22E
Goniadz 54 53 30N 22 44E
Goniri 121 11 30N 12 15E
Gonnesa 64 39 17N 8 27E
Gonno-Altaysk 76 51 50N 86 5E
Gonnos 68 39 52N 22 29E
Gonnosfanadiga 64 39 30N 8 39E
Gonzales, Calif., U.S.A. 163 36 35N 121 30W
Gonzales, Tex., U.S.A. 159 29 30N 97 30W
González Chaves 172 38 02S 60 05W
Good Hope, C. of = Goeie Hoop 128 34 24S 18 30E
Goode 139 31 58S 133 45E
Goodenough I. 135 9 20S 150 15E
Gooderham 150 44 54N 78 21W
Goodeve 153 51 4N 103 10W
Gooding 160 43 0N 114 50W
Goodland 158 39 22N 101 44W
Goodnight 159 35 4N 101 13W
Goodooga 139 29 1S 147 28E
Goodrich 28 51 52N 2 38W
Goodsoil 153 54 24N 109 13W
Goodsprings 161 35 51N 115 30W
Goodwick 31 52 0N 5 0W
Goodwin, Mt. 136 14 13S 129 32E
Goodwood 29 50 53N 0 44W
Goole 33 53 42N 0 52W
Goolgowi 141 33 58S 145 41E
Goolwa 140 35 30S 138 47E
Goomalling 137 31 15S 116 42E
Goombalie 139 29 59S 145 26E
Goonalga 140 31 45S 143 37E
Goonda 127 19 48S 33 57E
Goondiwindi 139 28 30S 150 21E
Goongarrie 137 30 2S 121 8E
Goonumbla 141 32 59S 148 11E
Goonyella 138 21 47S 147 58E
Goor 46 52 13N 6 33E
Gooray 139 28 25S 150 2E
Goose Bay 151 53 15N 60 20W
Goose L. 160 42 0N 120 30W
Goose R. 151 53 20N 60 35W
Goothinga 138 17 36S 140 50E
Gooty 97 15 7N 77 41E
Gop 93 22 5N 69 50E
Gopalganj, Bangla. 98 23 1N 89 50E
Gopalganj, India 95 26 28N 84 30E
Goppenstein 50 46 23N 7 46E
Göppingen 49 48 42N 9 40E
Gor 59 37 23N 2 58W
Góra 54 51 40N 16 31E
Gorakhpur 95 26 47N 83 32E
Gorbatov 81 56 12N 43 2E
Gorbea, Peña 58 43 1N 2 50W
Gorda 163 35 53N 121 26W
Gorda, Punta 166 14 10N 83 10W
Gordon, Austral. 140 32 7S 138 20E
Gordon, U.K. 35 55 41N 2 32W
Gordon, U.S.A. 158 42 49N 102 6W
Gordon B. 136 11 35S 130 10E
Gordon Downs 136 18 48S 128 40E
Gordon L., Alta., Can. 153 56 30N 110 25W
Gordon L., N.W.T., Can. 152 63 5N 113 11W
Gordon, R. 138 42 27S 145 30E
Gordon River 137 34 10S 117 15E
Gordonia 128 28 13S 21 10E
Gordonvale 138 17 5S 145 50E
Gore 139 28 17S 151 30E
Goré 117 7 59N 16 49E
Gore, Ethiopia 123 8 12N 35 32E
Gore, N.Z. 143 46 5S 168 58E
Gore B. 150 45 57N 82 28W
Gorebridge 35 55 51N 3 2W
Goresbridge 39 52 38N 7 0W
Gorey 39 52 41N 6 18W
Gorgan 93 36 55N 54 30E
Gorge, The 138 18 27S 145 30E
Gorgona, I. 174 3 0N 78 10W
Gorgona I. 62 43 27N 9 52E
Gorgora 123 12 15N 37 17E
Gori 83 42 0N 44 7E
Gorinchem 46 51 50N 4 59E
Goring, Oxon, U.K. 28 51 31N 1 8W
Goring, Sussex, U.K. 29 50 49N 0 26W
Gorinhatã 171 19 15S 49 45W
Goritsy 81 57 4N 36 43E
Gorízia 63 45 56N 13 37E
Gorka 54 51 39N 16 58E
Gorki = Gorkiy 81 56 20N 44 0E
Gorkiy 81 57 20N 44 0E
Gorkovskoye Vdkhr. 81 57 2N 43 4E
Gorleston 29 52 35N 1 44E
Gorlev 73 55 30N 11 15E
Gorlice 54 49 35N 21 11E
Görlitz 54 51 10N 14 59E
Gorlovka 81 48 25N 37 58E
Gorman, Calif., U.S.A. 163 34 47N 118 51W
Gorman, Tex., U.S.A. 159 32 15N 98 43W
Gorna Oryakhovitsa 67 43 7N 25 40E
Gorna Radgona 63 46 40N 16 2E
Gornja Tuzla 66 44 35N 18 46E
Gornji Grad 63 46 20N 14 52E
Gornji Milanovac 66 44 00N 20 29E
Gornji Vafuk 66 43 57N 17 34E
Gorno Ablanovo 67 43 37N 25 43E
Gorno Filinskoye 76 60 5N 70 0E
Gornyy 81 51 50N 48 30E
Gorodenka 82 48 41N 25 29E
Gorodets 81 56 38N 43 28E
Gorodische 81 53 13N 45 40E
Gorodnitsa 80 50 46N 27 26E
Gorodnya 80 51 55N 31 33E
Gorodok, Byelorussia, U.S.S.R. 80 55 30N 30 3E
Gorodok, Ukraine, U.S.S.R. 80 49 46N 23 32E
Goroka 135 6 7S 145 25E
Goroke 140 36 43S 141 29E
Gorokhov 80 50 15N 24 45E
Gorokhovets 81 56 13N 42 39E
Gorom Gorom 121 14 26N 0 14W
Goromonzi 127 17 52S 31 22E
Gorong, Kepulauan 103 4 5S 131 15E
Gorongosa, Sa. da 127 18 27S 32 2E
Gorongose, R. 129 20 40S 34 30E
Gorontalo 103 0 35N 123 13E
Goronyo 121 13 29N 5 39E
Gorredijk 46 53 0N 6 3E
Gorron 42 48 25N 0 50W
Gorseinon 31 51 40N 4 2W
Gorssel 46 52 12N 6 12E
Gort 39 53 4N 8 50W
Gortin 38 54 43N 7 13W
Gorumahisani 96 22 20N 86 24E
Gorumna I. 39 53 15N 9 44W
Gorzkowice 54 51 13N 19 36E
Gorzno 54 53 12N 19 38E
Gorzów Slaski 54 51 3N 18 22E
Gorzów Wielkopolski 54 52 43N 15 15E
Gorzów Wielkopolski □ 54 52 45N 15 30E
Gosainthan, Mt. 99 28 20N 85 45E
Gosberton 33 52 52N 0 10W
Göschenen 51 46 40N 8 36E
Gōse 111 34 27N 135 44E
Gosford 141 33 23N 151 18E
Gosforth 32 54 24N 3 27W
Goshen, S. Afr. 128 25 50S 25 0E
Goshen, Calif., U.S.A. 163 36 21N 119 25W
Goshen, Ind., U.S.A. 156 41 36N 85 46W
Goshen, N.Y., U.S.A. 162 41 23N 74 21W
Goslar 48 51 55N 10 23E
Gospič 63 44 35N 15 23E
Gosport 28 50 48N 1 8W
Gossa, I. 71 62 52N 6 50E
Gossau 51 47 25N 9 15E
Gosse, R. 138 19 32S 134 37E
Gostivar 66 41 48N 20 57E
Gostyn 54 51 50N 17 3E
Gostynin 54 52 26N 19 29E
Göta 73 58 6N 12 10E
Göta älv 73 57 42N 11 54E
Göta Kanal 73 58 35N 14 15E
Götaland, reg. 73 58 0N 14 0E
Göteborg 73 57 43N 11 59E
Göteborg & Bohus □ 75 58 20N 11 50E
Gotemba 111 35 18N 138 56E
Götene 73 58 32N 13 30E
Gotha 48 50 56N 10 42E
Gothenburg 158 40 58N 100 8W
Gothenburg = Göteborg 73 57 43N 11 59E
Gotse Delchev (Nevrokop) 67 41 43N 23 46E
Gotska Sandön 75 58 24N 19 15E
Gōtsu 110 35 0N 132 14E
Göttingen 48 51 31N 9 55E
Gottwaldov (Zlin) 53 49 14N 17 40E
Gouda 46 52 1N 4 42E
Goudhurst 29 51 7N 0 28E
Goudiry 120 14 15N 12 45E
Gough I. 15 40 10S 9 45W
Gouin Res. 150 48 35N 74 40W
Gouitafla 120 7 30N 5 53W
Goula Touila 118 21 50N 1 57E
Goulburn 141 34 44S 149 44E
Goulburn Is. 138 11 40S 133 20E
Gould, mt. 137 25 46S 117 18E
Goulia 120 10 1N 7 11W
Goulimine 118 28 50N 10 0W
Goulmima 118 31 41N 4 57W
Gouménissa 68 40 56N 22 37E
Goumeur 119 20 40N 18 30E
Goundam 135 16 25N 3 45W
Gounou-Gaya 124 9 38N 15 31E
Goúra 69 37 56N 22 20E
Gourara 118 29 0N 0 30E
Gouraya 118 36 31N 1 56E
Gourdon, France 44 44 44N 1 23E
Gourdon, U.K. 37 56 50N 2 15W
Gouré 121 14 0N 10 10E
Gourits, R. 128 34 15S 21 45E
Gourma Rharous 121 16 55N 2 5W
Gournay-en-Bray 43 49 29N 1 44E
Gouro 117 19 30N 19 30E
Gourock 34 55 58N 4 49W
Gourock Ra. 141 36 0S 149 25E
Gourselik 121 13 31N 10 52E
Goursi 120 12 42N 2 37W
Gouvêa 171 18 27S 43 44W
Gouzon 44 46 12N 2 14E
Govan 153 51 20N 105 0W
Gove 133 12 25S 136 55E
Goverla 82 49 9N 24 30E
Governador Valadares 171 18 15S 41 57W
Governor's Harbour 166 25 10N 76 14W
Gowan 138 25 0S 145 0E
Gowanda 156 42 29N 78 58W
Gower, The 31 51 35N 4 10W
Gowerton 31 51 38N 4 2W
Gowna, L. 38 53 52N 7 35W
Gowran 39 52 38N 7 5W
Goya 172 29 10S 59 10W
Goyder's Lagoon 139 27 3S 139 58E
Goyllarisquizga 174 10 19S 76 31W
Goz Beîda 117 12 20N 21 30E
Goz Regeb 123 16 3N 35 33E
Gozdnica 54 51 28N 15 4E
Gozo (Ghaudex) 60 36 0N 14 13E
Graaff-Reinet 128 32 13S 24 32E
Graasten 73 54 57N 9 34E
Grabow 48 53 17N 11 31E
Grabów 54 51 31N 18 7E
Grabs 51 47 11N 9 27E
Gračac 63 44 18N 15 57E
Gračanica 66 44 43N 18 18E
Graçay 43 47 10N 1 50E
Grace 160 42 38N 111 46W
Grace, L., (North) 137 33 10S 118 20E
Grace, L., (South) 137 33 15S 118 25E
Graceville 158 45 36N 96 23W
Grachevka 84 52 55N 52 52E
Gracias a Dios, C. 166 15 0N 83 20W
Gradačac 66 44 52N 18 26E
Gradaús 170 7 43S 51 11W
Gradaús, Serra dos 170 8 0S 50 45W
Gradeska Planina 66 41 30N 22 15E
Gradets 67 42 46N 26 30E
Gradignan 66 44 47N 0 36W
Gradnitsa 67 42 57N 24 58E
Grado, Italy 63 45 40N 13 20E
Grado, Spain 56 43 23N 6 4W
Gradule 139 28 32S 149 15E
Grady 159 34 52N 103 15W
Graeca, Lacul 70 44 5N 26 10E
Graemsay I. 37 58 56N 3 17W
Graénalon, L. 74 64 10N 17 20W
Grafham Water 29 52 18N 0 17W
Grafton, Austral. 139 29 38S 152 58E
Grafton, U.S.A. 158 48 30N 97 25W
Grafton, C. 133 16 51S 146 0E
Gragnano 65 40 42N 14 30E
Graham, Can. 150 49 20N 90 30W
Graham, N.C., U.S.A. 157 36 5N 79 22W
Graham, Tex., U.S.A. 159 33 7N 98 38W
Graham Bell, Os. 76 80 5N 70 0E
Graham I. 152 53 40N 132 30W
Graham Land 13 65 0S 64 0W
Graham Mt. 161 32 46N 109 58W
Graham, R. 152 56 31N 122 17W
Grahamdale 153 51 23N 98 30W
Grahamstown 128 33 19S 26 31E
Grahamsville 162 41 51N 74 33W
Grahovo 66 42 40N 18 4E
Graïba 119 34 30N 10 13E
Graide 47 49 58N 5 4E
Graigue 39 52 51N 6 56W
Graiguenamanagh 39 52 32N 6 58W
Grain Coast 120 4 20N 10 0W
Grainthorpe 33 53 27N 0 5E
Graivoron 80 50 29N 35 39E
Grajaú 170 5 50S 46 30W
Grajaú, R. 170 3 41S 44 48W
Grajewo 54 53 39N 22 30E
Gramada 66 43 49N 22 39E
Gramat 44 44 48N 1 43E
Gramisdale 36 57 29N 7 18W
Grammichele 65 37 12N 14 37E
Grampian □ 37 57 0N 3 0W
Grampians, Mts. 140 37 0S 142 20E
Gran Canaria 116 27 55N 15 35W
Gran Chaco 156 25 0S 61 0W
Gran Paradiso 62 49 33N 7 17E
Gran Sabana, La 174 5 30N 61 30W
Gran Sasso d'Italia, Mt. 44 42 25N 13 30E
Granada, Nic. 166 11 58N 86 0W
Granada, Spain 59 37 10N 3 35W
Granada, U.S.A. 158 38 5N 102 13W
Granada □ 57 37 5N 4 30W
Granard 38 53 47N 7 30W
Granbo 72 61 16N 16 33E
Granbury 159 32 28N 97 48W
Granby 150 45 25N 72 45W
Grand Bahama I. 166 26 40N 78 30W
Grand Bank 151 47 6N 55 48W
Grand Bassa 120 6 0N 10 2W

Grand Bassam Grillby

Grand Bassam 120 5 10N 3 49W
Grand Béréby 120 4 38N 6 55W
Grand-Bourg 167 15 53N 61 19W
Grand Canal 39 53 15N 8 10W
Grand Canyon National Park 161 36 15N 112 20W
Grand Cayman 166 19 20N 81 20W
Grand Cess 120 4 40N 8 12W
Grand 'Combe, La 45 44 13N 4 2E
Grand Coulee 160 47 48N 119 1W
Grand Coulee Dam 160 48 0N 118 50W
Grand Erg Occidental 118 30 20N 1 0E
Grand Erg Oriental 119 30 0N 6 30E
Grand Falls 151 47 2N 67 46W
Grand Forks, Can. 152 49 0N 118 30W
Grand Forks, U.S.A. 158 48 0N 97 3W
Grand-Fougeray 42 47 43N 1 44W
Grand Fougeray, Le 42 47 44N 1 43W
Grand Haven 156 43 3N 86 13W
Grand I. 150 46 30N 86 40W
Grand Island 158 40 59N 98 25W
Grand Isle 159 29 15N 89 58W
Grand Junction 161 39 0N 108 30W
Grand L., N.B., Can. 151 45 57N 66 7W
Grand L., Newf., Can. 151 48 45N 57 45W
Grand L., Newf., Can. 151 53 40N 60 30W
Grand L., Newf., Can. 151 49 0N 57 30W
Grand L., U.S.A. 159 29 55N 92 45W
Grand Lac 150 47 35N 77 35W
Grand Lahou 120 5 10N 5 0W
Grand Lake 160 40 20N 105 54W
Grand-Leez 47 50 35N 4 45E
Grand Lieu, Lac de 42 47 6N 1 40W
Grand Manan I. 151 44 45N 66 52W
Grand Marais, Can. 158 47 45N 90 25W
Grand Marais, U.S.A. 156 46 39N 85 59W
Grand Mère 150 46 36N 72 40W
Grand Motte, La 45 48 35N 1 4E
Grand Popo 121 6 15N 1 44E
Grand Portage 150 47 58N 89 41W
Grand Pressigny, Le 42 46 55N 0 48E
Grand, R., Mo., U.S.A. 160 39 23N 93 27W
Grand, R., S.D., U.S.A. 160 45 45N 101 30W
Grand Rapids, Can. 153 53 12N 99 19W
Grand Rapids, Mich., U.S.A. 156 42 57N 85 40W
Grand Rapids, Minn., U.S.A. 158 47 19N 93 29W
Grand St.-Bernard, Col. du 50 45 53N 7 11E
Grand Teton 160 43 45N 110 57W
Grand Valley 160 39 30N 108 2W
Grand View 153 51 11N 100 51W
Grandas de Salime 56 43 13N 6 53W
Grande 170 11 30S 44 30W
Grande, B. 176 50 30S 68 20W
Grande Baie 151 48 19N 70 52W
Grande Cache 152 53 53N 119 8W
Grande, Coxilha 173 28 18S 51 30W
Grande de Santiago, R. 164 21 20N 105 50W
Grande Dixence, Barr. de la 50 46 5N 7 23E
Grande-Entrée 151 47 30N 61 40W
Grande, I. 171 23 9S 44 14W
Grande, La 160 45 15N 118 0W
Grande Prairie 152 55 15N 118 50W
Grande, R., Jujuy, Argent. 172 23 9S 65 52W
Grande, R., Mendoza, Argent. 172 36 52S 69 45W
Grande R. 174 18 35S 63 0W
Grande, R., Brazil 171 20 0S 50 0W
Grande, R., Spain 59 39 6N 0 48W
Grande, R., U.S.A. 159 29 20N 100 40W
Grande Rivière 151 48 26N 64 30W
Grande, Serra, Goiás, Brazil 170 11 15S 46 30W
Grande, Serra, Maranhao, Brazil 170 4 30S 41 20W
Grande, Serra, Piauí, Brazil 170 8 0S 45 0W
Grande Vallée 151 49 14N 65 8W
Grandes Bergeronnes 151 48 16N 69 35W
Grandfalls 159 31 21N 102 51W
Grandglise 47 50 30N 3 42E
Grandoe Mines 152 56 29N 129 54W
Grândola 57 38 12N 8 35W
Grandpré 43 49 20N 4 50E
Grandson 50 46 49N 6 39E
Grandview, Can. 153 51 10N 100 42W
Grandview, U.S.A. 160 46 13N 119 58W
Grandvilliers 43 49 40N 1 57E
Graneros 172 34 5S 70 45W
Graney L. 39 53 0N 8 40W
Grange 38 54 24N 8 32W
Grange, La, Austral. 136 18 45S 121 43E
Grange, La, U.S.A. 163 37 42N 120 27W
Grange, La, Ga., U.S.A. 157 33 4N 85 0W
Grange, La, Ky., U.S.A. 156 38 20N 85 20W
Grange, La, Tex., U.S.A. 159 29 54N 96 52W
Grange-over-Sands 32 54 12N 2 55W
Grangemouth 35 56 1N 3 43W
Granger 160 46 25N 120 5W
Grangesberg 72 60 6N 15 1E
Grängesberg 72 60 6N 15 1E
Grangetown 33 54 36N 1 7W
Grangeville 160 45 57N 116 4W
Granite City 158 38 45N 90 3W
Granite Falls 158 44 45N 95 35W
Granite Mtn. 163 33 5N 116 28W
Granite Peak 137 25 40S 121 20E
Granite Pk., mt. 160 45 8N 109 52W
Granitnyy, Pik 85 39 32N 70 20E
Granity 143 41 39S 171 51E
Granja 170 3 17S 40 50W
Granja de Moreruela 56 41 48N 5 44W
Granja de Torrehermosa 57 38 19N 5 35W
Gränna 73 58 1N 14 28E
Granollers 58 41 39N 2 18E
Gransee 48 53 0N 13 10E
Grant, Can. 150 50 6N 86 18W
Grant, U.S.A. 158 40 53N 101 42W
Grant City 158 40 30N 94 25W
Grant, I. 136 11 10S 132 52E
Grant, Mt. 163 38 34N 118 48W
Grant Range Mts. 161 38 30N 115 30W
Grantham 33 52 55N 0 39W
Grantown-on-Spey 37 57 19N 3 36W
Grants 161 35 14N 107 57W
Grant's Pass 160 42 30N 123 22W
Grantsburg 158 45 46N 92 44W
Grantshouse 35 55 53N 2 17W
Grantsville 160 40 35N 112 32W
Granville, France 42 48 50N 1 35W
Granville, U.K. 38 54 30N 6 47W
Granville, N.D., U.S.A. 158 48 18N 100 48W
Granville, N.Y., U.S.A. 162 43 24N 73 16W
Granville L. 153 56 18N 100 30W
Grao de Gandía 59 39 0N 0 27W
Grapeland 159 31 30N 95 25W
Gras, L. de 148 64 30N 110 30W
Graskop 129 24 56S 30 49E
Gräsmark 72 59 58N 12 44E
Grasmere, Austral. 139 35 1S 117 45E
Grasmere, U.K. 32 54 28N 3 2W
Gräsö 72 60 21N 18 28E
Graso 72 60 28N 18 35E
Grasonville 162 38 57N 76 13W
Grass, R. 153 56 3N 96 33W
Grass Range 160 47 0N 109 0W
Grass River Prov. Park 153 54 40N 100 50W
Grass Valley, Calif., U.S.A. 160 39 18N 121 0W
Grass Valley, Oreg., U.S.A. 160 45 28N 120 48W
Grassano 65 40 38N 16 17E
Grasse 45 43 38N 6 56E
Grassington 32 54 5N 2 0W
Grassmere 140 31 24S 142 38E
Grate's Cove 151 48 8N 53 0W
Graubünden (Grisons) □ 51 46 45N 9 30E
Graulhet 44 43 45N 1 58E
Graus 58 42 11N 0 20E
Gravatá 170 6 59S 35 29W
Grave 46 51 46N 5 44E
Grave, Pte. de 44 45 34N 1 4W
's-Graveland 46 52 15N 5 7E
Gravelbourg 153 49 50N 106 35W
Gravelines 43 51 0N 2 10E
's-Gravendeel 46 51 47N 4 37E
's-Gravenhage 46 52 7N 4 17E
's-Gravenpolder 47 51 28N 3 54E
's-Gravensande 46 52 0N 4 9E
Graversfors 73 58 42N 16 8E
Gravesend, Austral. 139 29 35S 150 20E
Gravesend, U.K. 29 51 25N 0 22E
Gravina di Púglia 65 40 48N 16 25E
Gravir 36 58 2N 6 25W
Gravois, Pointe-à 167 16 15N 73 45W
Gravone, R. 45 42 3N 8 54E
Grävsnäs 73 58 5N 12 29E
Gray 43 47 27N 5 35E
Grayling 156 44 40N 84 42W
Grayling, R. 152 59 21N 125 0W
Grayrigg 32 54 22N 2 40W
Grays Harbor 160 46 55N 124 8W
Grays L. 160 43 8N 111 30W
Grays Thurrock 29 51 28N 0 23E
Grayson 153 50 45N 102 40W
Grayvoron 80 50 29N 35 39E
Graz 52 47 4N 15 27E
Grazalema 57 36 46N 5 23W
Grdelica 66 42 55N 22 3E
Greasy L. 152 62 55N 122 12W
Great Abaco I. 166 26 15N 77 10W
Great Australia Basin 133 26 0S 140 0E
Great Australian Bight 137 33 30S 130 0E
Great Ayton 33 54 29N 1 8W
Great Baddow 29 51 43N 0 31E
Great Bahama Bank 166 23 15N 78 0W
Great Barrier I. 142 36 11S 175 25E
Great Barrier Reef 138 19 0S 149 0E
Great Barrington 162 42 11N 73 22W
Great Basin 154 40 0N 146 30W
Great Bear L. 148 65 0N 120 0W
Great Bear, R. 148 65 0N 124 0W
Great Belt 73 55 20N 11 0E
Great Bena 162 41 57N 75 45W
Great Bend 158 38 25N 98 55W
Great Bentley 29 51 51N 1 5E
Great Bernera, I. 137 58 15N 6 50W
Great Bitter Lake 122 30 15N 32 40E
Great Blasket, I. 39 52 5N 10 30W
Great Britain 16 54 0N 2 15W
Great Bushman Land 128 29 20S 19 20E
Great Central 152 49 20N 125 10W
Great Chesterford 29 52 4N 0 11E
Great Clifton 32 54 39N 3 29W
Great Coco I. 101 14 10N 93 25E
Great Divide 141 23 0S 146 0E
Great Dunmow 29 51 52N 0 22E
Great Exuma I. 166 23 30N 75 50W
Great Falls, Can. 153 50 27N 96 1W
Great Falls, U.S.A. 160 47 27N 111 12W
Great Fish R., S. Afr. 128 33 28S 27 5E
Great Fish R., S. Afr. 128 31 30S 20 16E
Great Gonerby 33 52 56N 0 40W
Great Guana Cay 166 24 0N 76 20W
Great Hanish 123 13 40N 43 0E
Great Harbour Deep 151 50 35N 56 25W
Great Harwood 32 52 41N 2 49W
Great I., Can. 153 58 53N 96 35W
Great I., Ireland 39 51 52N 8 15W
Great Inagua I. 167 21 0N 73 20W
Gt. Indian Desert = Thar Desert 94 28 0N 72 0E
Great Jarvis 151 47 39N 57 12W
Great Karoo = Groot Karoo 128 32 30S 23 0E
Great Lake 138 41 50S 146 30E
Great Lakes 153 44 0N 82 0W
Great Malvern 28 52 7N 2 19W
Great Massingham 29 52 47N 0 41E
Great Missenden 29 51 42N 0 42W
Gt. Namaqualand = Groot Namakwaland 128 26 0S 18 0E
Great Orme's Head 31 53 20N 3 52W
Great Ouse, R. 29 52 20N 0 8E
Great Palm I. 138 18 45S 146 40E
Great Papuan Plateau 135 6 30S 142 25E
Great Plains 50 45 0N 100 0W
Great Ruaha, R. 126 7 30S 35 0E
Great Salt Lake 160 41 0N 112 30W
Great Salt Lake Desert 160 40 20N 113 50W
Great Salt Plains Res. 159 36 40N 98 15W
Great Sandy Desert 136 21 0S 124 0E
Great Sandy I. = Fraser I. 139 25 15S 153 0E
Great Scarcies, R. 120 9 30N 12 40W
Great Shefford 28 51 29N 1 27W
Great Shelford 29 52 9N 0 9E
Great Shunner Fell 32 54 22N 2 16W
Great Sitkin I. 147 52 0N 176 10W
Great Slave L. 152 61 23N 115 38W
Great Stour, R. 29 51 21N 1 15E
Gt. Sugar Loaf, mt. 39 53 10N 6 10W
Great Torrington 30 50 57N 4 9W
Gt. Victoria Des. 137 29 30S 126 30E
Great Wall 106 38 30N 109 30E
Gt. Waltham 29 51 47N 0 29E
Great Whale, R. 150 55 20N 75 30W
Great Whernside, mt. 147 54 9N 1 59W
Great Winterhoek, mt. 128 33 07S 19 10E
Great Wyrley 28 52 40N 2 1W
Great Yarmouth 29 52 40N 1 45E
Great Yeldham 29 52 1N 0 33E
Greater Antilles 167 17 40N 74 0W
Greater Manchester □ 32 53 30N 2 15W
Greatham 33 54 38N 1 14W
Grebbestad 73 58 42N 11 15E
Grebenka 80 50 9N 32 22E
Greco, Mt. 64 41 48N 14 0E
Gredos, Sierra de 56 40 20N 5 0W
Greece ■ 68 40 0N 23 0E
Greeley, Colo., U.S.A. 158 40 30N 104 40W
Greeley, Nebr., U.S.A. 158 41 36N 98 32W
Green B. 156 45 0N 87 30W
Green Bay 156 44 30N 88 0W
Green C. 141 37 13S 150 1E
Green Cove Springs 157 29 59N 81 40W
Green Hammerton 33 54 2N 1 17W
Green Hd. 137 30 5S 114 56E
Green Is. 135 4 35S 154 10E
Green Island 143 45 55S 170 26E
Green Lowther, Mt. 35 55 22N 3 44W
Green R., Ky., U.S.A. 156 37 54N 87 30W
Green R., Utah, U.S.A. 161 39 0N 110 6W
Green R., Wyo., U.S.A. 160 43 2N 110 2W
Green R., Wyo., U.S.A. 160 41 44N 109 28W
Greenbush 158 48 46N 96 10W
Greencastle, U.K. 38 54 2N 6 5W
Greencastle, U.S.A. 156 39 40N 86 48W
Greene 162 42 20N 75 45W
Greenfield, Calif., U.S.A. 163 35 15N 119 0W
Greenfield, Calif., U.S.A. 163 36 19N 121 15W
Greenfield, Ind., U.S.A. 156 39 47N 85 51W
Greenfield, Iowa, U.S.A. 158 41 18N 94 28W
Greenfield, Mass., U.S.A. 162 42 38N 72 38W
Greenfield, Miss., U.S.A. 159 37 28N 93 50W
Greenhead 35 54 58N 2 31W
Greening 150 48 10N 74 55W
Greenisland 38 54 42N 5 50W
Greenland 12 66 0N 45 0W
Greenland Sea 12 73 0N 10 0W
Greenlaw 35 55 42N 2 28W
Greenock 34 55 57N 4 46W
Greenodd 32 54 14N 3 3W
Greenore 38 54 2N 6 8W
Greenore Pt. 39 52 15N 6 20W
Greenough, R. 137 28 54S 115 36E
Greenport 162 41 5N 72 23W
Greensboro, Ga., U.S.A. 157 33 34N 83 12W
Greensboro, Md., U.S.A. 162 38 59N 75 48W
Greensboro, N.C., U.S.A. 157 36 7N 79 46W
Greensburg, Ind., U.S.A. 156 39 20N 85 30W
Greensburg, Kans., U.S.A. 159 37 38N 99 20W
Greensburg, Pa., U.S.A. 156 40 18N 79 31W
Greenstone Pt. 36 57 55N 5 38W
Greenville, Liberia 120 5 7N 9 6W
Greenville, Ala., U.S.A. 157 31 50N 86 37W
Greenville, Calif., U.S.A. 160 40 8N 121 0W
Greenville, Ill., U.S.A. 158 38 53N 89 22W
Greenville, Me., U.S.A. 151 45 30N 69 32W
Greenville, Mich., U.S.A. 156 43 12N 85 14W
Greenville, Miss., U.S.A. 159 33 25N 91 0W
Greenville, N.C., U.S.A. 157 35 37N 77 26W
Greenville, N.H., U.S.A. 162 42 46N 71 49W
Greenville, N.Y., U.S.A. 162 42 25N 74 1W
Greenville, Ohio, U.S.A. 156 40 5N 84 38W
Greenville, Pa., U.S.A. 156 41 23N 80 22W
Greenville, S.C., U.S.A. 157 34 54N 82 24W
Greenville, Tenn., U.S.A. 157 36 13N 82 51W
Greenville, Tex., U.S.A. 159 33 5N 96 5W
Greenwater Lake Prov. Park 153 52 32N 103 30W
Greenway 31 51 56N 4 49W
Greenwich, U.K. 29 51 28N 0 0
Greenwich, Conn., U.S.A. 162 41 1N 73 38W
Greenwich, N.Y., U.S.A. 162 43 2N 73 36W
Greenwood, Can. 152 49 10N 118 40W
Greenwood, Miss., U.S.A. 159 33 30N 90 4W
Greenwood, S.C., U.S.A. 157 34 13N 82 13W
Greenwood, Mt. 136 13 48S 130 4E
Gregory 158 43 14N 99 20W
Gregory Downs 138 18 35S 138 45E
Gregory, L. 139 28 55S 139 0E
Gregory L. 136 20 5S 127 0E
Gregory, L. 137 25 38S 119 58E
Gregory Lake 136 20 10S 127 30E
Gregory, R. 138 17 53S 139 17E
Gregory Ra., Queens., Austral. 138 19 30S 143 40E
Gregory Ra., W. Austral., Austral. 136 21 20S 121 12E
Greian Hd. 36 57 1N 7 30W
Greiffenberg 48 53 6N 13 57E
Greifswald 48 54 6N 13 23E
Greifswalder Bodden 48 54 12N 13 35E
Greifswalder Oie 48 54 15N 13 55E
Grein 52 48 14N 14 51E
Greiner Wald 52 48 30N 15 0E
Greiz 48 50 39N 12 12E
Gremikha 78 67 50N 39 40E
Grenå 73 56 25N 10 53E
Grenada 159 33 45N 89 50W
Grenada I. ■ 167 12 10N 61 40W
Grenade 44 43 47N 1 17E
Grenadines 167 12 40N 61 20W
Grenchen 50 47 12N 7 24E
Grenen 73 57 44N 10 40E
Grenfell, Austral. 141 33 52S 148 8E
Grenfell, Can. 153 50 30N 102 56W
Grenoble 45 45 12N 5 42E
Grenora 158 48 38N 103 54W
Grenville, C. 138 12 0S 143 13E
Grenville Chan. 152 53 40N 129 46W
Gréoux-les-Bains 45 43 55N 5 52E
Gresham 160 45 30N 122 31W
Gresik 103 9 13S 112 38E
Gressoney St. Jean 62 45 49N 7 47E
Greta 32 54 9N 2 36W
Greta R. 32 54 36N 3 5W
Gretna, U.K. 35 54 59N 3 4W
Gretna, U.S.A. 159 30 0N 90 2W
Gretna Green 35 55 0N 3 3W
Gretton 29 52 33N 0 40W
Grevelingen Krammer 46 51 44N 4 0E
Greven 48 52 7N 7 36E
Grevená 68 40 4N 21 25E
Grevená □ 68 40 2N 21 25E
Grevenbroich 48 51 6N 6 32E
Grevenmacher 47 49 41N 6 26E
Grevesmühlen 48 53 51N 11 10E
Grevie 73 56 22N 12 46E
Grevinge 73 55 48N 11 34E
Grey, C. 138 13 0S 136 35E
Grey, R. 143 42 27S 171 12E
Grey Range 133 27 0S 143 30E
Grey Res. 151 48 20N 56 30W
Greyabbey 38 54 32N 5 35W
Greybull 160 44 30N 108 3W
Greystone 32 54 39N 2 52W
Greystones 39 53 9N 6 4W
Greytown, N.Z. 142 41 5S 175 29E
Greytown, S. Afr. 129 29 1S 30 36E
Gribanovskiy 81 51 28N 41 50E
Gribbell I. 152 53 23N 129 0W
Gribbin Head 30 50 18N 4 41W
Gridley 160 39 27N 121 47W
Griekwastad 128 28 49S 23 15E
Griffin 157 33 17N 84 14W
Griffith 141 34 18S 146 2E
Griffith Mine 153 50 47N 93 25W
Grigoryevka 84 50 48N 58 18E
Grijalva, R. 164 16 20N 92 20W
Grijpskerk 46 53 16N 6 18E
Grillby 72 59 38N 17 15E

Grim, C
Gus

Grim, C. **133** 40 45 S 144 45 E
Grimaïlov **80** 49 20N 26 5 E
Grimari **117** 5 43N 20 0 E
Grimbergen **47** 50 56N 4 22 E
Grimeton **73** 57 6N 12 25 E
Griminish Pt. **36** 57 40N 7 30W
Grimma **48** 51 14N 12 44 E
Grimmen **48** 54 6N 13 2 E
Grimsay I. **36** 57 29N 7 12W
Grimsby **33** 53 35N 0 5W
Grimsel Pass **51** 46 34N 8 23 E
Grímsey **74** 66 33N 18 0W
Grimshaw **152** 56 10N 117 40W
Grimstad **71** 58 22N 8 35 E
Grindelwald **50** 46 38N 8 2 E
Grindsted **73** 55 46N 8 55 E
Grindstone Island **151** 47 25N 62 0W
Grindu **70** 44 44N 26 50 E
Grinduşul, Mt. **70** 46 40N 26 7 E
Griñón **56** 40 13N 3 51W
Grinnell **158** 41 45N 92 43W
Grip **71** 63 16N 7 37 E
Griqualand East **129** 30 30 S 29 0 E
Griqualand West **128** 28 40 S 23 30 E
Griquet **151** 51 30N 55 35W
Grisolles **44** 43 49N 1 19 E
Grisons ☐ **49** 46 40N 9 30 E
Grisslehamm **72** 60 5N 18 49 E
Grita, La **174** 8 8N 71 59W
Gritley **37** 58 56N 2 45W
Grivegnée **47** 50 37N 5 36 E
Griz Nez **43** 50 50N 1 35 E
Grizebeck **32** 54 16N 3 10W
Grmeč Planina **63** 44 43N 16 16 E
Groais I. **151** 50 55N 55 35W
Groblersdal **129** 25 15 S 29 25 E
Grobming **52** 47 27N 13 54 E
Grocka **66** 44 40N 20 42 E
Grodek **80** 52 46N 23 38 E
Grodkow **54** 50 43N 17 40 E
Grodno **80** 53 42N 23 52 E
Grodzisk Mazowiecki **54** 52 7N 20 37 E
Grodzisk Wlkp. **54** 52 15N 16 22 E
Grodzyanka **80** 53 31N 28 42 E
Groenlo **46** 52 2N 6 37 E
Groesbeck **159** 31 32N 96 34W
Groesbeek **46** 51 47N 5 58 E
Groix **42** 47 38N 3 29W
Groix, I. de **42** 47 38N 3 28W
Grójec **54** 51 50N 20 58 E
Grolloo **46** 52 56N 6 41 E
Gronau **48** 52 13N 7 2 E
Grong **74** 64 25N 12 8 E
Groningen **46** 53 15N 6 35 E
Groningen ☐ **46** 53 16N 6 40 E
Groninger Wad **46** 53 27N 6 30 E
Grönskåra **73** 57 5N 15 43 E
Gronsveld **47** 50 49N 5 44 E
Groom **159** 35 12N 100 59W
Groomsport **38** 54 41N 5 37W
Groot Berg, R. **128** 32 50 S 18 20 E
Groot-Brakrivier **128** 34 2 S 22 18 E
Groot Karoo **128** 32 35 S 23 0 E
Groot Namakwaland = Namaland **128** 26 0 S 18 0 E
Groot, R. **128** 33 10 S 23 35 E
Groote Eylandt **138** 14 0 S 136 50 E
Grootebroek **46** 52 41N 5 13 E
Grootfontein **128** 19 31 S 18 6 E
Grootlaagte, R. **128** 21 10 S 21 20 E
Gros C. **152** 61 59N 113 32W
Grosa, Punta **59** 39 6N 1 36 E
Grósio **62** 46 18N 10 17 E
Grosne, R. **45** 46 30N 4 40 E
Gross Glockner **52** 47 5N 12 40 E
Gross Ottersleben **48** 52 5N 11 33 E
Grossa, Pta. **170** 1 20N 50 0W
Grossenbrode **48** 54 21N 11 4 E
Grossenhain **48** 51 17N 13 32 E
Grosseto **62** 42 45N 11 7 E
Grossgerungs **52** 48 34N 14 57 E
Grosswater B. **151** 54 20N 57 40W
Grote Gette, R. **47** 50 51N 5 6 E
Grote Nete, R. **47** 51 8N 4 34 E
Groton, U.S.A. **162** 41 22N 72 12W
Groton, U.S.A. **162** 42 36N 76 22W
Grottaglie **65** 40 32N 17 25 E
Grottaminarda **65** 41 5N 15 4 E
Grouard Mission **152** 55 33N 116 9W
Grouin, Pointe du **42** 48 43N 1 51W
Groundhog, R. **150** 48 45N 82 20W
Grouse Creek **160** 41 51N 113 57W
Grouw **46** 53 5N 5 51 E
Groveland **163** 37 50N 120 14W
Grovelsjön **72** 62 6N 12 16 E
Grover City **163** 35 7N 120 37W
Groveton **159** 31 5N 95 4W
Groznjan **63** 45 22N 13 43 E
Groznyy **83** 43 20N 45 45 E
Grubbenvorst **47** 51 25N 6 9 E
Grubišno Polje **66** 45 44N 17 12 E
Grudusk **54** 53 3N 20 38 E
Grudziadz **54** 53 30N 18 47 E
Gruinard B. **36** 57 56N 5 35W
Gruissan **44** 43 8N 3 7 E
Grumo Áppula **65** 41 2N 16 43 E
Grums **72** 59 22N 13 5 E
Grünau **125** 27 45 S 18 26 E
Grünberg **48** 50 37N 8 55 E
Grundy Center **158** 42 22N 92 45W
Grungedal **71** 59 44N 7 43 E
Gruting Voe **36** 60 12N 1 32W
Gruver **159** 36 19N 101 20W
Gruyères **50** 46 35N 7 4 E
Gruza **66** 43 54N 20 46 E
Gryazi **81** 52 30N 39 58 E
Gryazovets **81** 58 50N 40 20 E
Grybów **54** 49 36N 20 55 E
Grycksbo **72** 60 40N 15 29 E
Gryfice **54** 53 55N 15 13 E
Gryfino **54** 53 16N 14 29 E
Grytgöl **73** 58 49N 15 33 E
Grythyttan **72** 59 41N 14 32 E
Grytviken **13** 53 50 S 37 10W
Gstaad **50** 46 28N 7 18 E
Gua **99** 22 18N 85 20 E
Gua Musang **101** 4 53N 101 58 E
Guacanayabo, Golfo de **166** 20 40N 77 20W
Guacara **174** 10 14N 67 53W
Guachípas **172** 25 40 S 65 30W
Guachiría, R. **174** 5 30N 71 30W
Guadajoz, R. **57** 37 50N 4 51W
Guadalajara, Mexico **164** 20 40N 103 20W
Guadalajara, Spain **58** 40 37N 3 12W
Guadalajara ☐ **58** 40 47N 3 0W
Guadalcanal **57** 38 5N 5 52W
Guadalcanal, I. **130** 9 32 S 160 12 E
Guadalén, R. **59** 38 30N 3 7W
Guadales **172** 34 30 S 67 55W
Guadalete, R. **57** 36 45N 5 47W
Guadalhorce, R. **57** 36 50N 4 42W
Guadalimar, R. **59** 38 10N 2 53W
Guadalmena, R. **59** 38 31N 2 50W
Guadalmez, R. **57** 38 33N 4 42W
Guadalope, R. **58** 41 0N 0 13W
Guadalquivir, R. **57** 38 0N 4 0W
Guadalupe, Brazil **170** 6 44 S 43 47W
Guadalupe, Spain **57** 39 27N 5 17W
Guadalupe, U.S.A. **163** 34 59N 120 33W
Guadalupe Bravos **164** 31 20N 106 10W
Guadalupe de los Reyes **164** 25 23N 104 15W
Guadalupe I. **143** 21 20N 118 50W
Guadalupe Pk. **161** 31 50N 105 30W
Guadalupe, R. **159** 29 25N 97 30W
Guadalupe, Sierra de **55** 39 28N 5 30W
Guadalupe y Calvo **164** 26 6N 106 58W
Guadarrama, Sierra de **56** 41 0N 4 0W
Guadeloupe, I. **167** 16 20N 61 40W
Guadeloupe Passage **167** 16 50N 68 15W
Guadiamar, R. **57** 37 9N 6 20W
Guadiana Menor, R. **59** 37 45N 3 7W
Guadiana, R. **57** 37 45N 7 35W
Guadiaro, R. **57** 36 39N 5 17W
Guadiato, R. **57** 37 55N 4 53W
Guadiela, R. **58** 40 30N 2 23W
Guadix **59** 37 18N 3 11W
Guafo, Boca del **176** 43 35 S 74 0W
Guaina **174** 5 9N 63 36W
Guainía ☐ **174** 2 30N 69 00W
Guaíra **173** 24 5 S 54 10W
Guaira, La **174** 10 36N 66 56W
Guaitecas, Islas **176** 44 0 S 74 30W
Guajará-Mirim **174** 10 50 S 65 20W
Guajira, La ☐ **174** 11 30N 72 30W
Guajira, Pen. de la **167** 12 0N 72 0W
Gualan **166** 15 8N 89 22W
Gualdo Tadino **63** 43 14N 12 46 E
Gualeguay **172** 33 10 S 59 20W
Gualeguaychú **172** 33 3 S 58 31W
Guam I. **130** 13 27N 144 45 E
Guamá **170** 1 37 S 47 29W
Guama **174** 10 16N 68 49W
Guamá, R. **170** 1 29 S 48 30W
Guamareyes **174** 0 30 S 73 0W
Guaminí **172** 37 1 S 62 28W
Guampí, Sierra de **174** 6 0N 65 35W
Guamuchil **164** 25 25N 108 3W
Guanabacoa **166** 23 8N 82 18W
Guanabara ☐ **173** 23 0 S 43 25W
Guanacaste **166** 10 40N 85 30W
Guanacaste, Cordillera del **166** 10 40N 85 4W
Guanacevío **164** 25 40N 106 0W
Guanajay **166** 22 56N 82 42W
Guanajuato **164** 21 0N 101 20W
Guanajuato ☐ **164** 20 40N 101 20W
Guanambi **171** 14 13 S 42 47W
Guanare **174** 8 42N 69 12W
Guanare, R. **174** 8 50N 68 50W
Guandacol **172** 29 30 S 68 40W
Guane **166** 22 10N 84 0W
Guanhães **171** 18 47 S 42 57W
Guanica **147** 17 58N 66 55W
Guanipa, R. **174** 9 20N 63 30W
Guanta **174** 10 14N 64 36W
Guantánamo **167** 20 10N 75 20W
Guapí **174** 2 36N 77 54W
Guápiles **166** 10 10N 83 46W
Guaporé **173** 12 0 S 64 0W
Guaporé, R. **174** 13 0 S 63 0W
Guaqui **174** 16 41 S 68 54W
Guara, Sierra de **58** 42 19N 0 15W
Guarabira **170** 6 51 S 35 29W
Guarapari **173** 20 40 S 40 30W
Guarapuava **171** 25 20 S 51 30W
Guaratinguetá **173** 22 49 S 45 9W
Guaratuba **173** 25 53 S 48 38W
Guard Bridge **35** 56 21N 2 52W
Guarda **56** 40 32N 7 20W
Guarda ☐ **56** 40 40N 7 20W
Guardafui, C. = Asir, Ras **91** 11 55N 51 10 E
Guardamar del Segura **59** 38 5N 0 39W
Guardavalle **65** 38 31N 16 30 E
Guardia, La **56** 41 56N 8 52W
Guardiagrele **63** 42 11N 14 11 E
Guardo **56** 42 47N 4 50W
Guareña **57** 38 51N 6 6W
Guareña, R. **56** 41 25N 5 25W
Guaria ☐ **172** 25 45N 56 30W
Guárico ☐ **174** 8 40N 66 35W
Guarujá **173** 24 2 S 46 25W
Guarus **173** 21 30 S 41 20W
Guasave **164** 25 34N 108 27W
Guasdualito **174** 7 15N 70 44W
Guasipati **174** 7 28N 61 54W
Guasopa **135** 9 12 S 152 56 E
Guastalla **62** 44 55N 10 40 E
Guatemala **166** 14 40N 90 30W
Guatemala ■ **166** 15 40N 90 30W
Guatire **174** 10 28N 66 32W
Guaviare, R. **174** 3 30N 71 0W
Guaxupé **173** 21 10 S 47 5W
Guayabal **174** 4 43N 71 37W
Guayama **147** 17 59N 66 7W
Guayaquil **174** 2 15 S 79 52W
Guayaquil, Golfo de **174** 3 10 S 81 0W
Guaymallen **172** 32 50 S 68 45W
Guaymas **164** 27 50N 111 0W
Guba, Ethiopia **123** 4 52N 39 18 E
Guba, Zaïre **127** 10 38 S 26 27 E
Gubakha **84** 58 52N 57 36 E
Gubam **135** 8 39 S 141 53 E
Gúbbio **63** 43 20N 12 34 E
Gubio **121** 12 30N 12 42 E
Gubkin **81** 51 17N 37 32 E
Guča **66** 43 46N 20 15 E
Guchil **101** 5 35N 102 10 E
Gudalur **97** 11 30N 76 29 E
Gudata **83** 43 7N 40 32 E
Gudbransdal **75** 61 33N 10 0 E
Guddu Barrage **93** 28 30N 69 50 E
Gudenå **73** 56 27N 9 40 E
Gudermes **83** 43 24N 46 20 E
Gudhjem **73** 55 12N 14 58 E
Gudiña, La **56** 42 4N 7 8W
Gudivada **96** 16 30N 81 15 E
Gudiyatam **97** 12 57N 78 55 E
Gudmundra **72** 62 56N 17 47 E
Gudrun, gasfield **19** 58 50N 1 48 E
Gudur **97** 14 12N 79 55 E
Guebwiller **43** 47 55N 7 12 E
Guecho **58** 43 21N 2 59W
Guéckédou **120** 8 40N 10 5W
Guelma **119** 36 25N 7 29 E
Guelph **150** 43 35N 80 20W
Guelt es Stel **118** 35 12N 3 1 E
Guelttara **118** 29 23N 2 10W
Guemar **119** 33 30N 6 57 E
Guéméné-Penfao **42** 47 38N 1 50W
Guéméné-sur-Scorff **42** 48 4N 3 13W
Güemes **172** 24 50 S 65 0W
Guéné **121** 11 44N 3 16 E
Guer **42** 47 54N 2 8W
Guérande **42** 47 20N 2 26W
Guerche, La **42** 47 57N 1 16W
Guerche-sur-l'Aubois, La **43** 46 58N 2 56 E
Guercif **118** 34 14N 3 21W
Guéréda **124** 14 31N 22 5 E
Guéret **44** 46 11N 1 51 E
Guérigny **43** 47 6N 3 10 E
Guernica **58** 43 19N 2 40W
Guernsey **158** 42 19N 104 45W
Guernsey I. **42** 49 30N 2 35W
Guerrara, Oasis, Alg. **119** 32 51N 4 35 E
Guerrara, Saoura, Alg. **118** 28 5N 0 8W
Guerrero ☐ **165** 17 30N 100 0W
Guerzim **118** 29 45N 1 47W
Güeş ti **70** 44 48N 25 19 E
Guestling Green **29** 50 53N 0 40 E
Gueugnon **45** 45 36N 4 3 E
Gueydan **159** 30 3N 92 30W
Guezendi = Ghesendor **119** 21 14N 18 14 E
Guglia, P. dal **51** 46 28N 9 45 E
Guglionesi **63** 51 55N 14 54 E
Guhra **93** 27 36N 56 8 E
Guia Lopes da Laguna **173** 21 26 S 56 7W
Guiana Highlands **174** 5 0N 60 0W
Guibes **128** 26 41 S 16 49 E
Guider **121** 9 55N 13 59 E
Guidimouni **121** 13 42N 9 31 E
Guiglo **120** 6 45N 7 30W
Guija **125** 34 35 S 33 15 E
Guijo de Coria **56** 40 6N 6 28W
Guildford **29** 51 14N 0 34W
Guilford, Conn., U.S.A. **162** 41 15N 72 40W
Guilford, Me., U.S.A. **151** 45 12N 69 25W
Guillaumes **45** 44 5N 6 52 E
Guillestre **45** 44 39N 6 40 E
Guilsfield **31** 52 42N 3 9W
Guilvinec **42** 47 48N 4 17W
Guimarães **170** 2 9 S 44 35W
Guimarãis **56** 41 28N 8 24W
Guimaras I. **103** 10 35N 122 37 E
Guinea ■ **120** 10 20N 10 0W
Guinea Bissau ■ **120** 12 0N 15 0W
Guinea, Gulf of **121** 3 0N 2 30 E
Guinea, Port. = Guinea Bissau **120** 12 0N 15 0W
Güines **166** 22 50N 82 0W
Guingamp **42** 48 34N 3 10W
Guipavas **42** 48 26N 4 29W
Guipúzcoa ☐ **58** 43 12N 2 15W
Guir, O. **118** 39 29N 2 58W
Guirgo **121** 11 54N 1 21W
Güiria **174** 10 32N 62 18W
Guisborough **33** 54 32N 1 2W
Guiscard **43** 49 40N 3 0 E
Guise **43** 49 52N 3 35 E
Guitiriz **56** 43 11N 7 50W
Guivan **103** 11 5N 125 55 E
Gujan-Mestras **44** 44 38N 1 4W
Gujar Khan **84** 33 15N 73 21 E
Gujarat ☐ **94** 23 20N 71 0 E
Gujranwala **94** 32 10N 74 12 E
Gujrat **94** 32 40N 74 2 E
Gukhothae **101** 17 2N 99 50 E
Gukovo **83** 48 1N 39 58 E
Gulak **121** 10 50N 13 30 E
Gulargambone **141** 31 20 S 148 30 E
Gulbahar **93** 35 5N 69 10 E
Gulbargâ **96** 17 20N 76 50 E
Gulbene **80** 57 8N 26 52 E
Gulcha **85** 40 19N 73 26 E
Guldborg Sd. **73** 54 39N 11 50 E
Guledgud **97** 16 3N 75 48 E
Gulf Basin **136** 15 20 S 129 0 E
Gulfport **159** 30 28N 89 3W
Gulgong **141** 32 20 S 149 30 E
Gulistan, Pak. **94** 30 36N 66 35 E
Gulistan, U.S.S.R. **85** 40 29N 68 46 E
Gulkana **147** 62 15N 145 48W
Gull Lake **153** 50 10N 108 29W
Gullane **35** 56 2N 2 50W
Gullegem **47** 50 51N 3 13 E
Gullringen **73** 57 48N 15 44 E
Güllük **69** 37 12N 27 36 E
Gulma **121** 12 40N 4 23 E
Gulmarg **95** 34 3N 74 25 E
Gulnam **123** 6 55N 29 30 E
Gulnare **140** 33 27 S 138 27 E
Gulpaigan **92** 33 26N 50 20 E
Gulpen **47** 50 49N 5 53 E
Gülpinar **68** 39 32N 26 10 E
Gulshad **76** 46 45N 74 25 E
Gulsvik **71** 60 24N 9 38 E
Gulu **126** 2 48N 32 17 E
Gulwe **126** 6 30 S 36 25 E
Gulyaypole **82** 47 45N 36 21 E
Gum Lake **140** 32 42 S 143 9 E
Gumal, R. **94** 32 5N 70 5 E
Gumbaz **94** 30 2N 69 0 E
Gumel **121** 12 39N 9 22 E
Gumiel de Hizán **58** 41 46N 3 41W
Gumlu **138** 19 53 S 147 41 E
Gumma-ken ☐ **111** 36 30N 138 20 E
Gummersbach **48** 51 2N 7 32 E
Gummi **121** 12 4N 5 9 E
Gümüsane **92** 40 30N 39 30 E
Gümuşhaciköy **82** 40 50N 35 18 E
Gumzai **103** 5 28 S 134 42 E
Guna **94** 24 40N 77 19 E
Guna Mt. **123** 11 50N 37 40 E
Gundagai **141** 35 3 S 148 6 E
Gundih **103** 7 10 S 110 56 E
Gundlakamma, R. **97** 15 30N 80 15 E
Gunebang **141** 33 5 S 146 38 E
Gungal **141** 32 17 S 150 32 E
Gungi **123** 10 20N 38 3 E
Gungu **124** 5 43 S 19 20 E
Gunisao L. **153** 53 33N 96 15W
Gunisao, R. **153** 53 56N 97 53W
Gunnedah **141** 30 59 S 150 15 E
Gunniguldrie **141** 33 12 S 146 8 E
Gunningbar Cr. **141** 31 14 S 147 6 E
Gunnison, Colo., U.S.A. **161** 38 32N 106 56W
Gunnison, Utah, U.S.A. **160** 39 11N 111 48W
Gunnison, R. **161** 38 50N 108 30W
Gunnworth **153** 51 20N 108 9W
Guntakal **97** 15 11N 77 27 E
Guntersville **157** 34 18N 86 16W
Guntong **101** 4 36N 101 3 E
Guntur **96** 16 23N 80 30 E
Gunungapi **103** 6 45 S 126 30 E
Gunungsitoli **102** 1 15N 97 30 E
Gunungsugih **102** 4 58 S 105 7 E
Gunupur **96** 19 5N 83 50 E
Gunworth **153** 51 20N 108 10W
Gunza **124** 10 50 S 13 50 E
Gunzenhausen **49** 49 6N 10 45 E
Gupis **95** 36 15N 73 20 E
Gura **94** 25 12N 71 39 E
Gura Humorului **70** 47 35N 25 53 E
Gura Teghii **70** 45 30N 26 25 E
Gurage, mt. **123** 8 20N 38 20 E
Gurchan **92** 34 55N 49 25 E
Gurdaspur **94** 32 5N 75 25 E
Gurdon **159** 33 55N 93 10W
Gurdzhaani **83** 41 43N 45 52 E
Gurgan **93** 36 51N 54 25 E
Gurgaon **94** 28 33N 77 10 E
Gurghiu, Munţii **70** 46 41N 25 15 E
Gurguéia, R. **170** 6 50 S 43 24W
Guria **62** 44 30N 9 0 E
Gurk, R. **52** 46 48N 14 20 E
Gurkha **95** 28 5N 84 40 E
Gurla Mandhata **95** 30 30N 81 10 E
Gurley **139** 29 45 S 149 48 E
Gurnard's Head **30** 50 12N 5 37W
Gurnet Pt. **162** 42 1N 70 34W
Gurrumbah **138** 17 30 S 144 55 E
Gurun **101** 5 49N 100 27 E
Gürün **92** 38 41N 37 22 E
Gurupá **175** 1 20 S 51 45W
Gurupá, I. Grande de **175** 1 0 S 51 45W
Gurupi **171** 11 43 S 49 4W
Gurupi, R. **170** 3 20 S 47 20W
Gurupi, Serra do **170** 5 0 S 47 30W
Guryev **83** 47 5N 52 0 E
Gus **126** 3 2N 36 57 E

Gus-Khrsutalnyy Han Chiang, R

Gus-Khrsutalnyy 81 55 42N 40 35 E
Gusau 121 12 18N 6 31 E
Gusev 80 54 35N 22 20 E
Gushiago 121 9 55N 0 15W
Gusinje 66 42 35N 19 50 E
Gúspini 64 39 32N 8 38 E
Gusselby 72 59 38N 15 14 E
Güssing 53 47 3N 16 20 E
Gustanj 63 46 36N 14 49 E
Gustavus 147 58 25N 135 58W
Gustine 163 37 21N 121 0W
Güstrow 48 53 47N 12 12 E
Gusum 73 58 16N 16 30 E
Gûtaia 70 45 26N 21 30 E
Gütersloh 48 51 54N 8 25 E
Gutha 137 28 58 S 115 55 E
Guthalungra 138 19 52 S 147 50 E
Guthrie 159 35 55N 97 30W
Guttannen 51 46 38N 8 18 E
Guttenberg 158 42 46N 91 10W
Guyana ■ 174 5 0N 59 0W
Guyenne 44 44 30N 0 40 E
Guyman 159 36 45N 101 30W
Guyra 139 30 15 S 151 40 E
Guzar 85 38 36N 66 15 E
Guzmán, Laguna de 164 31 25N 107 25W
Gwa 98 17 30N 94 40 E
Gwaai 127 19 15 S 27 45 E
Gwabegar 141 30 31 S 149 0 E
Gwadabawa 121 13 20N 5 15 E
Gwâdar 93 25 10N 62 18 E
Gwagwada 121 10 15N 7 15 E
Gwalchmai 31 53 16N 4 23W
Gwalia 137 28 54 S 121 20 E
Gwalior 94 26 12N 78 10 E
Gwanara 121 18 55N 3 10 E
Gwanda 127 20 55 S 29 0 E
Gwandu 121 12 30N 4 41 E
Gwane 126 4 45N 25 48 E
Gwaram 121 11 15N 9 51 E
Gwarzo 121 12 20N 8 55 E
Gwasero 121 9 30N 8 30 E
Gwaun-Cae-Gurwen 31 51 46N 3 51W
Gweebarra B. 38 54 52N 8 21W
Gweedore 38 55 4N 8 15W
Gweek 30 50 6N 5 12W
Gwelo 125 19 28 S 29 45 E
Gwennap 30 50 12N 5 9W
Gwent □ 31 51 45N 2 55W
Gweta 128 20 12 S 25 17 E
Gwi 121 9 0N 7 10 E
Gwinn 156 46 15N 87 29W
Gwio Kura 121 12 40N 11 2 E
Gwolu 120 10 58N 1 59W
Gwoza 121 11 12N 13 40 E
Gwyddelwern 31 53 2N 3 23W
Gwydir, R. 139 29 27 S 149 48 E
Gwynedd □ 31 53 0N 4 0W
Gya La 95 28 45N 84 45 E
Gyangtse 99 28 50N 89 33 E
Gydanskiy P-ov. 76 70 0N 78 0 E
Gyland 71 58 24N 6 45 E
Gympie 139 26 11 S 152 38 E
Gyobingauk 98 18 13N 95 39 E
Gyoda 111 36 10N 139 30 E
Gyoma 53 46 56N 20 58 E
Gyöngyös 53 47 48N 20 15 E
Györ 53 47 41N 17 40 E
Györ-Sopron □ 53 47 40N 17 20 E
Gypsum Palace 140 32 37 S 144 9 E
Gypsum Pt. 152 61 53N 114 35W
Gypsumville 153 51 45N 98 40W
Gyttorp 72 59 31N 14 58 E
Gyula 53 46 38N 21 17 E
Gzhatsk = Gagarin 80 55 30N 35 0 E

H

Ha Coi 100 21 26N 107 46 E
Ha Dong 100 20 58N 105 46 E
Ha Giang 100 22 50N 104 59 E
Ha Nam = Phu-Ly 100 20 35N 105 50 E
Ha Tien 101 10 23N 104 29 E
Ha Tinh 100 18 20N 105 54 E
Ha Trung 100 20 0N 105 50 E
Haa, The 36 60 20N 1 0 E
Haacht 47 50 59N 4 37 E
Haag 49 48 11N 12 12 E
Haaksbergen 46 52 9N 6 45 E
Haaltert 47 50 55N 4 1 E
Haamstede 47 51 42N 3 45 E
Haapamäki 74 62 18N 24 28 E
Haapsalu 80 58 56N 23 30 E
Haarby 73 55 13N 10 8 E
Haarlem 46 52 23N 4 39 E
Haast 143 43 51 S 169 1 E
Haast P. 143 44 6 S 169 21 E
Haast, R. 143 43 50 S 169 2 E
Haastrecht 46 52 0N 4 47 E
Hab Nadi Chauki 94 25 0N 66 50 E
Hab, R. 93 25 15N 67 8 E
Haba 92 27 10N 47 0 E
Habana, La 166 23 8N 82 22W
Habaswein 126 1 2N 39 30 E
Habay 152 58 50N 118 44W
Habay-la-Neuve 47 49 44N 5 38 E
Habiganj 98 24 24N 91 30 E
Hablingbo 73 57 12N 18 16 E
Habo 73 57 55N 14 6 E
Haccourt 47 50 44N 5 40 E
Hachenburg 48 50 40N 7 49 E
Hachijō-Jima 111 33 5N 139 45 E
Hachinohe 112 40 30N 141 29 E
Hachiōji 111 35 30N 139 30 E
Hachŏn 107 40 29N 129 2 E
Hachy 47 49 42N 5 41 E
Hacketstown 39 52 52N 6 35W
Hackett 152 52 9N 112 28W
Hackettstown 162 40 51N 74 50W
Hackney 29 51 33N 0 2W
Hackthorpe 32 54 37N 2 42W
Hadali 94 32 16N 72 11 E
Hadarba, Ras 122 22 4N 36 51 E
Hadd, Ras al 93 22 35N 59 50 E
Haddenham 29 51 46N 0 56W
Haddington 35 55 57N 2 48W
Haddon Rig 141 31 27 S 147 52 E
Hadeija 121 12 30N 10 5 E
Hadeija, R. 121 12 20N 9 30W
Haden 139 27 13 S 151 54 E
Hadera 90 32 27N 34 55 E
Haderslev 73 55 15N 9 30 E
Hadhra 122 20 10N 41 5 E
Hadhramaut = Hadramawt 91 15 30N 49 30 E
Hadibu 91 12 35N 54 2 E
Hadjeb el Aïoun 119 35 21N 9 32 E
Hadleigh 29 52 3N 0 58 E
Hadley 28 52 42N 2 28W
Hadlow 29 51 12N 0 20 E
Hadong 107 35 5N 127 44 E
Hadramawt 91 15 30N 49 30 E
Hadrians Wall 35 55 0N 2 30W
Hadsten 73 56 19N 10 3 E
Hadsund 73 56 44N 10 8 E
Haeju 107 38 3N 125 45 E
Haenam 107 34 34N 126 15 E
Haerhpin 107 45 45N 126 45 E
Hafar al Batin 92 28 25N 46 50 E
Hafizabad 94 32 5N 73 40 E
Haflong 98 25 10N 93 5 E
Hafnarfjörður 74 64 4N 21 57W
Haft-Gel 92 31 30N 49 32 E
Hafun 91 10 25N 51 16 E
Hafun, Ras 91 10 29N 51 20 E
Hagalil 90 32 53N 35 18 E
Hagar Banga 117 10 40N 22 45 E
Hagari, R. 97 14 0N 76 45 E
Hagemeister I. 147 58 42N 161 0W
Hagen 48 51 21N 7 29 E
Hagenow 48 53 25N 11 10 E
Hagerman 159 33 5N 104 22W
Hagerstown 156 39 39N 77 46W
Hagetmau 44 43 39N 0 37W
Hagfors 72 60 3N 13 45 E
Häggenås 72 63 24N 14 55 E
Hagi, Iceland 74 65 28N 23 25W
Hagi, Japan 110 34 30N 131 30 E
Hagion Evstratios 68 39 30N 25 0 E
Hagion Oros 68 40 37N 24 6 E
Hags Hd. 39 52 57N 9 30W
Hague, C. de la 42 49 44N 1 56W
Hague, The = s'-Gravenhage 47 52 7N 4 17 E
Haguenau 43 48 49N 7 47 E
Hai □ 126 3 10 S 37 10 E
Hai Duong 100 20 56N 106 19 E
Haian, Kiangsu, China 109 32 37N 120 33 E
Haian, Kwangtung, China 109 20 18N 110 11 E
Haich'eng, Fukien, China 109 24 24N 117 51 E
Haich'eng, Liaoning, China 107 40 52N 122 45 E
Haichou 107 34 34N 119 6 E
Haichou Wan 107 35 0N 119 30 E
Haidar Khel 94 33 58N 68 38 E
Haifa 90 32 46N 35 0 E
Haifeng 109 22 59N 115 21 E
Haig 137 30 55 S 126 10 E
Haiger 48 50 44N 8 12 E
Haik'ang 109 20 56N 110 4 E
Haik'ou 100 20 5N 110 20 E
Hā'il 92 27 28N 42 2 E
Hailaerh 105 49 12N 119 42 E
Hailakandi 98 24 42N 92 34 E
Hailey 160 43 30N 114 15W
Haileybury 150 47 30N 79 38W
Hailin 107 44 32N 129 24 E
Hailing Tao 109 21 37N 111 65 E
Hailsham 29 50 52N 0 17 E
Hailun 105 47 27N 126 56 E
Hailung 107 42 30N 125 40 E
Hailuoto 74 65 3N 24 45 E
Haimen, Chekiang, China 109 28 39N 121 25 E
Haimen, Kwangtung, China 109 23 15N 116 35 E
Hainan 100 19 0N 110 0 E
Hainan Str. = Ch'iungcho Haihsia 100 20 10N 110 15 E
Hainaut □ 47 50 30N 4 0 E
Hainburg 53 48 9N 16 56 E
Haines, Alaska, U.S.A. 147 59 20N 135 36W
Haines, Oreg., U.S.A. 160 44 51N 117 59W
Haines City 157 28 6N 81 35W
Haines Junction 147 60 45N 137 30W
Hainfeld 52 48 3N 15 48 E
Haining 109 30 23N 120 30 E
Hainton 33 53 21N 0 13W
Haiphong 100 20 47N 106 35 E
Hait'an Tao 109 25 35N 119 45 E
Haiti ■ 167 19 0N 72 30W
Haiya Junc. 122 18 20N 36 40 E
Haiyang 107 36 45N 121 15 E
Haiyen 109 30 28N 120 57 E
Haiyüan, Kwangsi-Chuang, China 108 22 6N 107 25 E
Haiyüan, Ningsia Hui, China 106 36 32N 105 40 E
Haja 103 3 19 S 129 37 E
Hajdú-Bihar □ 53 47 30N 21 30 E
Hajdúböszörmény 53 47 40N 21 30 E
Hajdúdurog 53 47 48N 21 30 E
Hajdúhadház 53 47 40N 21 40 E
Hajdúnánás 53 47 50N 21 26 E
Hajdúsámson 53 47 37N 21 42 E
Hajdúszoboszló 53 47 27N 21 22 E
Haji Langar 93 35 50N 79 20 E
Hajiganj 98 23 15N 90 50 E
Hajipur 95 25 45N 85 20 E
Hajr 93 24 0N 56 34 E
Haka 98 22 39N 93 37 E
Hakansson, Mts. 127 8 40 S 25 45 E
Hakantorp 73 58 18N 12 55 E
Håkantorp 73 58 18N 12 55 E
Hakataramea 143 44 30 S 170 30 E
Hakataramea, R. 143 44 35 S 170 40 E
Hakken-Zan 111 34 10N 135 54 E
Hakodate 112 41 45N 140 44 E
Hakota 111 36 5N 140 30 E
Haku-San 111 36 9N 136 46 E
Hakun 98 26 46N 95 42 E
Hala 93 25 43N 68 20 E
Hala Hu 105 38 15N 97 40 E
Halab = Aleppo 92 36 10N 37 15 E
Halabjah 92 35 10N 45 58 E
Halaib 122 22 5N 36 30 E
Halanzy 47 49 33N 5 44 E
Halawa 147 21 9N 156 47W
Halbe 122 19 40N 42 15 E
Halberstadt 48 51 53N 11 2 E
Halberton 30 50 55N 3 24W
Halcombe 142 40 8 S 175 30 E
Halcyon, Mt. 103 13 0N 121 30 E
Halden 72 59 7N 11 23 E
Haldensleben 48 52 17N 11 30 E
Haldia 99 22 5N 88 3 E
Haldwani 95 29 25N 79 30 E
Hale 32 53 24N 2 21W
Hale, R. 138 24 56 S 135 53 E
Haleakala Crater 147 20 43N 156 12W
Halen 47 50 57N 5 6 E
Halesowen 28 52 27N 2 2W
Halesworth 29 52 21N 1 30 E
Haleyville 157 34 15N 87 40W
Half Assini 120 5 1N 2 50W
Halfmoon B. 143 46 50 S 168 5 E
Halfway 160 44 56N 117 8W
Halfway, R. 152 56 12N 121 32W
Halhul 90 31 35N 35 7 E
Hali 122 18 40N 41 15 E
Haliburton 150 45 3N 78 30W
Halibut, oilfield 19 61 20N 1 36 E
Halifax, Austral. 138 18 32 S 146 22 E
Halifax, Can. 151 44 38N 63 35W
Halifax, U.K. 32 53 43N 1 51W
Halifax, U.S.A. 162 40 25N 76 55W
Halifax B. 138 18 50 S 147 0 E
Halifax I. 128 26 38 S 15 4 E
Halil, R. 93 27 40N 58 30 E
Halkirk 37 58 30N 3 30W
Hall 52 47 17N 11 30 E
Hall Land 12 81 20N 60 0W
Hall Pt. 136 15 40 S 124 23 E
Hallabro 73 56 22N 15 5 E
Halland 73 56 55N 12 50 E
Hallands län □ 73 56 50N 12 50 E
Hallands Väderö 73 56 27N 12 34 E
Hallandsås 73 56 22N 13 0 E
Halle, Belg. 47 50 44N 4 13W
Halle, Nordrhein-Westfalen, Ger. 48 52 4N 8 20 E
Halle, Sachsen-Anhalt, Ger. 48 51 29N 12 0 E
Halle □ 48 51 28N 11 58 E
Hällefors 72 59 47N 14 31 E
Hallein 52 47 40N 13 5 E
Hällekis 73 58 38N 13 27 E
Hallett 140 33 25 S 138 55 E
Hallettsville 159 29 28N 96 57W
Hallevadsholm 73 58 37N 11 33 E
Hällevadsholm 73 58 35N 11 33 E
Halley Bay 13 75 31 S 26 36W
Hallia, R. 96 16 55N 79 10 E
Halliday 158 47 20N 102 25W
Halliday L. 153 61 21N 108 56W
Hallim 107 33 24N 126 15 E
Hallingdal, R. 75 60 34N 9 12 E
Hallingskeid 71 60 40N 7 17 E
Hällnäs 74 64 19N 19 36 E
Hallock 153 48 47N 97 57W
Hallow 28 52 14N 2 15W
Hall's Creek 136 18 16 S 127 46 E
Hallsberg 72 59 5N 15 7 E
Hallstahammar 72 59 38N 16 15 E
Hallstatt 52 47 33N 13 38 E
Hallstavik 72 60 5N 18 37 E
Hallstead 162 41 56N 75 45W
Hallwiler See 50 47 16N 8 12 E
Hallworthy 30 50 38N 4 34W
Halmahera, I. 103 0 40N 128 0 E
Halmeu 70 47 57N 23 2 E
Halmstad 73 56 41N 12 52 E
Halq el Oued 119 36 53N 10 10 E
Hals 73 56 59N 10 18 E
Halsa 71 63 3N 8 14 E
Halsafjorden 71 63 5N 8 10 E
Hälsingborg = Helsingborg 73 56 3N 12 42 E
Halstad 158 47 21N 96 41W
Halstead 29 51 59N 0 39 E
Haltdalen 71 62 56N 11 8 E
Haltern 48 51 44N 7 10 E
Haltwhistle 35 54 58N 2 27W
Ham 128 49 44N 3 3 E
Ham Tan 101 10 40N 107 45 E
Ham Yen 100 22 4N 105 3 E
Hamā 92 35 5N 36 40 E
Hamab 128 28 7 S 19 16 E
Hamad 123 15 20N 33 32 E
Hamada 110 34 50N 132 10 E
Hamadān 92 34 52N 48 32 E
Hamadān □ 92 35 0N 49 0 E
Hamadh 122 24 55N 39 3 E
Hamadia 118 35 28N 1 57 E
Hamakita 111 34 45N 137 47 E
Hamale 120 10 56N 2 45W
Hamamatsu 111 34 45N 137 45 E
Hamar 71 60 48N 11 7 E
Hamar Koke 123 51 5N 36 45 E
Hamarøy 74 68 5N 15 38 E
Hamâta, Gebel 122 24 17N 35 0 E
Hambantota 93 6 10N 81 10 E
Hamber Prov. Park 152 52 20N 118 0W
Hambledon 28 50 56N 1 6W
Hambleton Hills 33 54 17N 1 12W
Hamburg, Ger. 48 53 32N 9 59 E
Hamburg, Ark., U.S.A. 159 33 15N 91 47W
Hamburg, Iowa, U.S.A. 158 40 37N 95 38W
Hamburg, Pa., U.S.A. 162 40 33N 76 0W
Hamburg □ 48 53 30N 10 0 E
Hamden 162 41 21N 72 56W
Hame 75 61 30N 24 0 E
Hämeen Lääni 75 61 24N 24 10 E
Hämeenlinna 75 61 0N 24 28 E
Hamelin Pool 137 26 22 S 114 20 E
Hamelin Pool Bay 137 26 10 S 114 5 E
Hameln 48 52 7N 9 24 E
Hamersley 136 22 20 S 117 37 E
Hamersley Ra. 136 22 0 S 117 45 E
Hamhung 107 40 0N 127 30 E
Hami 105 42 47N 93 32 E
Hamilton, Austral. 140 37 45 S 142 2 E
Hamilton, Can. 150 43 20N 79 50W
Hamilton, N.Z. 142 37 47 S 175 19 E
Hamilton, U.K. 35 55 47N 4 2W
Hamilton, Alas., U.S.A. 147 62 55N 164 0W
Hamilton, Mont., U.S.A. 160 46 20N 114 6W
Hamilton, N.Y., U.S.A. 162 42 49N 75 31W
Hamilton, Ohio, U.S.A. 156 39 20N 84 35W
Hamilton, Tex., U.S.A. 159 31 40N 98 5W
Hamilton Downs 106 21 25 S 142 23 E
Hamilton, gasfield 19 56 54N 2 13 E
Hamilton Hotel 138 22 45 S 140 40 E
Hamilton Inlet 151 54 0N 57 30W
Hamilton Mt. 162 43 25N 74 22W
Hamilton, R., Queens., Austral. 138 23 30 S 139 47 E
Hamilton, R., S. Austral., Austral. 136 26 40 S 134 20 E
Hamiota 153 50 11N 100 38W
Hamlet 157 34 56N 79 40W
Hamley Bridge 140 34 17 S 138 35 E
Hamlin 159 32 58N 100 8W
Hamm 48 51 40N 7 58 E
Hammam bou Hadjar 118 35 23N 0 58W
Hammamet 119 36 24N 10 38 E
Hammamet, G. de 119 36 10N 10 48 E
Hammarö, I. 72 59 20N 13 30 E
Hammarstrand 72 63 7N 16 20 E
Hamme 47 51 6N 4 8 E
Hamme-Mille 47 50 47N 4 43 E
Hammel 73 56 16N 9 52 E
Hammelburg 49 50 7N 9 54 E
Hammenton 156 39 40N 74 47W
Hammeren 73 55 18N 14 47 E
Hammerfest 74 70 39N 23 41 E
Hammersmith 29 51 30N 0 15W
Hammond, Ind., U.S.A. 156 41 40N 87 30W
Hammond, La., U.S.A. 159 30 32N 90 30W
Hammonton 162 39 38N 74 48W
Hamnavoe 36 60 25N 1 5W
Hamneda 73 56 41N 13 51 E
Hamoir 47 50 25N 5 32 E
Hamont 47 51 15N 5 32 E
Hampden 143 45 18 S 170 50 E
Hampshire □ 28 51 3N 1 20W
Hampshire Downs 28 51 10N 1 10W
Hampton, Ark., U.S.A. 159 33 35N 92 29W
Hampton, Iowa, U.S.A. 158 42 42N 93 12W
Hampton, N.H., U.S.A. 162 42 56N 70 48W
Hampton, S.C., U.S.A. 157 32 52N 81 2W
Hampton, Va., U.S.A. 162 37 4N 76 18W
Hampton Bays 162 40 53N 72 31W
Hampton Harbour 136 20 30 S 116 30 E
Hampton in Arden 28 52 26N 1 42W
Hampton Tableland 137 32 0N 127 0 E
Hamra 92 24 2N 38 55 E
Hamrange 72 60 59N 17 5 E
Hamrat esh Sheykh 123 14 45N 27 55 E
Hamre 71 60 33N 5 20 E
Hamun Helmand 93 31 15N 61 15 E
Hamun-i-Lora, Pak. 93 29 38N 64 58 E
Hamun-i-Lora, Pak. 93 29 38N 64 58 E
Hamun-i-Mashkel 93 28 30N 63 0 E
Hamyang 107 35 32N 127 42 E
Han Chiang, R., Hupeh, China 109 30 35N 114 15 E

Han Chiang, R **Hawzen**

Han Chiang, R.,
Kwangtung, China 109 23 30N 116 48 E
Hana 147 20 45N 155 59W
Hanak 122 25 32N 37 0 E
Hanamaki 112 39 23N 141 7 E
Hanang □ 126 4 10 S 35 40 E
Hanang, mt. 126 4 30 S 35 25 E
Hanau 49 50 8N 8 56 E
Hanbogd 106 43 11N 107 10 E
Hanch'eng 106 35 30N 110 30 E
Hanchiang 109 25 29N 119 5 E
Hanch'uan 109 30 39N 113 46 E
Hanchuang 107 34 36N 117 22 E
Hanchung 106 33 10N 107 2 E
Hancock, Mich., U.S.A. 158 47 10N 88 35W
Hancock, Minn., U.S.A. 158 45 26N 95 46W
Hancock, Pa., U.S.A. 162 41 57N 75 19W
Handa, Japan 111 34 53N 137 0 E
Handa, Somalia 91 10 37N 51 2 E
Handa I. 36 58 23N 5 10W
Handen 72 59 12N 18 12 E
Handeni 124 5 25 S 38 2 E
Handeni □ 126 5 30 S 38 0 E
Handlová 155 48 45N 18 35 E
Handub 122 19 15N 37 25 E
Handwara 95 34 21N 74 20 E
Handzame 47 51 2N 3 0 E
Hanegev 90 30 50N 35 0 E
Haney 152 49 12N 122 40W
Hanford 163 36 25N 119 39W
Hang Chat 100 18 20N 99 21 E
Hang Dong 100 18 41N 98 55 E
Hangang, R. 107 37 50N 126 30 E
Hangayn Nuruu 105 47 30N 100 0 E
Hangchinch'i 106 39 54N 108 56 E
Hangchinhouch'i 106 41 55N 107 15 E
Hangchou 109 30 15N 120 8 E
Hangchou Wan 109 30 30N 121 30 E
Hanger 73 57 6N 13 58 E
Hangklip, K. 128 34 26 S 18 48 E
Hangö (Hanko) 75 59 59N 22 57 E
Hanhongor 106 43 55N 104 28 E
Hanish J. 91 13 45N 42 46 E
Hanita 90 33 5N 35 10 E
Hankinson 158 46 9N 96 58W
Hanko = Hangö 75 59 59N 22 57 E
Hank'ou 109 30 40N 114 18 E
Hankow = Hank'ou 109 30 40N 114 18 E
Hanksville 161 38 19N 110 45W
Hanku 107 39 16N 117 50 E
Hanle 95 32 42N 79 4 E
Hanmer 143 42 32 S 172 50 E
Hann, Mt. 136 16 0 S 126 0 E
Hann, R. 136 17 26 S 126 17 E
Hanna 152 51 40N 111 54W
Hannaford 158 47 23N 98 18W
Hannah 158 48 58N 98 42W
Hannah B. 150 51 40N 80 0W
Hannahs Bridge 141 31 55 S 149 41 E
Hannibal, Mo., U.S.A. 158 39 42N 91 22W
Hannibal, N.Y., U.S.A. 162 43 19N 76 35W
Hannik 122 18 12N 32 20 E
Hanningfield Water 29 51 40N 0 30 E
Hannover 48 52 23N 9 43 E
Hannut 47 50 40N 5 4 E
Hanö 73 56 0N 14 50 E
Hanö, I. 73 56 2N 14 50 E
Hanöbukten 73 55 35N 14 30 E
Hanoi 100 21 5N 105 55 E
Hanover, S. Afr. 128 31 4 S 24 29 E
Hanover, N.H., U.S.A. 162 43 43N 72 17W
Hanover, Pa., U.S.A. 162 39 46N 76 59W
Hanover, Va., U.S.A. 162 37 46N 77 22W
Hanover = Hannover 48 52 23N 9 43 E
Hanover, I. 176 51 0 S 74 50W
Hanpan, C. 135 5 0 S 154 35 E
Hans Meyer Ra. 135 4 20 S 152 55 E
Hansholm 73 57 8N 8 38 E
Hanshou 109 28 55N 111 58 E
Hansi 94 29 10N 75 57 E
Hansjö 72 61 10N 14 40 E
Hanson, L. 140 31 0 S 136 15 E
Hanson Range 136 27 0 S 136 30 E
Hansted 73 57 8N 8 36 E
Hantan 105 36 42N 114 30 E
Hante 47 50 19N 4 11 E
Hanton 106 36 42N 114 30 E
Hanwood 141 34 26 S 146 3 E
Hanyang 109 30 35N 114 0 E
Hanyin 108 32 53N 108 37 E
Hanyū 111 36 10N 139 32 E
Hanyüan 108 29 21N 102 43 E
Haoch'ing 108 26 34N 100 12 E
Haokang 105 47 25N 132 8 E
Haopi 106 35 57N 114 13 E
Haparanda 74 65 52N 24 8 E
Hapert 47 51 22N 5 15 E
Happy 159 34 47N 101 50W
Happy Camp 160 41 52N 123 30W
Happy Valley 151 53 15N 60 20W
Hapsu 107 41 13N 128 51 E
Hapur 94 28 45N 77 45 E
Haql 92 29 10N 35 0 E
Har 103 5 16 S 133 14 E
Har-Ayrag 106 45 47N 109 16 E
Har Tuv 90 31 46N 35 0 E
Har Us Nuur 105 48 0N 92 10 E
Har Yehuda 90 31 35N 34 57 E
Harad 92 24 15N 49 0 E
Haradera 91 4 33N 47 38 E
Haradh 92 24 15N 49 0 E
Haramsøya 71 62 39N 6 12 E
Haran 92 36 48N 39 0 E
Harat 123 16 5N 39 26 E
Haraze 117 14 20N 19 12 E
Haraze-Mangueigne 117 7 22N 17 3 E
Harbin = Haerhpin 107 45 45N 126 45 E
Harboør 73 56 38N 8 10 E
Harbor Beach 156 43 50N 82 38W
Harbor Springs 156 45 28N 85 0W
Harbour Breton 151 47 29N 55 50W
Harbour Deep 151 50 25N 56 30W
Harbour Grace 151 47 40N 53 22W
Harburg 48 53 27N 9 58 E
Hårby 73 55 13N 10 7 E
Harcourt 138 24 17 S 149 55 E
Harda 94 22 27N 77 5 E
Hardangerfjorden. 71 60 15N 6 0 E
Hardangerjøkulen 71 60 30N 7 0 E
Hardangervidda 71 60 20N 7 20 E
Hardap Dam 128 24 32 S 17 50 E
Hardegarijp 46 53 13N 5 57 E
Harden 141 34 32 S 148 24 E
Hardenberg 46 52 34N 6 37 E
Harderwijk 46 52 21N 5 38 E
Hardey, R. 136 22 45 S 116 8 E
Hardin 160 45 50N 107 35W
Harding 129 30 22 S 29 55 E
Harding Ra. 136 16 17 S 124 55 E
Hardisty 152 52 40N 111 18W
Hardman 160 45 12N 119 49W
Hardoi 95 27 26N 80 15 E
Hardwar 94 29 58N 78 16 E
Hardy 159 36 20N 91 30W
Hardy, Pen. 176 55 30 S 68 20W
Hare B. 151 51 15N 55 45W
Hare Gilboa 90 32 31N 35 25 E
Hare Meron 90 32 59N 35 24 E
Harelbeke 47 50 52N 3 20 E
Haren, Ger. 48 52 47N 7 18 E
Haren, Neth. 46 53 11N 6 36 E
Harer 123 9 20N 42 8 E
Harer □ 123 7 12N 42 0 E
Hareto 123 9 23N 37 6 E
Harfleur 42 49 30N 0 10 E
Hargeisa 91 9 30N 44 2 E
Hargshamn 72 60 12N 18 30 E
Hari, R., Afghan. 93 34 20N 64 30 E
Hari, R., Indon. 102 1 10 S 101 50 E
Haricha, Hamada el 118 22 40N 3 15W
Harihar 97 14 32N 75 44 E
Harim, J. al 60 26 0N 56 10 E
Harima-Nada 110 34 30N 134 35 E
Haringey 29 51 35N 0 7W
Haringhata, R. 98 22 0N 89 58 E
Haringvliet 46 51 48N 4 10 E
Haripad 97 9 14N 76 28 E
Harirúd 93 35 0N 61 0 E
Harkat 122 20 25N 39 40 E
Harlan, Iowa, U.S.A. 158 41 37N 95 20W
Harlan, Tenn., U.S.A. 157 36 58N 83 20W
Harlech 31 52 52N 4 7W
Harlem 160 48 29N 108 39W
Harleston 29 52 25N 1 18 E
Harlingen, Neth. 46 53 11N 5 25 E
Harlingen, U.S.A. 159 26 30N 97 50W
Harlow 29 51 47N 0 9 E
Harlowton 160 46 30N 109 54W
Harmånger 72 61 55N 17 20 E
Harmil 123 16 30N 40 10 E
Harney Basin 160 43 30N 119 0W
Harney L. 160 43 0N 119 0W
Harney Pk. 158 43 52N 103 33W
Härnön 72 62 36N 18 0 E
Härnösand 72 62 38N 18 5 E
Haro 58 42 35N 2 55W
Haro, C. 164 27 50N 110 55W
Haroldswick 36 60 48N 0 50W
Håroy 73 55 13N 10 8 E
Harp L. 151 55 5N 61 50W
Harpe, La 158 40 30N 91 0W
Harpenden 29 51 48N 0 20W
Harpenhalli 97 14 47N 76 2 E
Harper 120 4 25N 7 43 E
Harper Mt. 147 64 15N 143 57W
Harplinge 73 56 45N 12 45 E
Harport L. 36 57 20N 6 20W
Harput 92 38 48N 39 15 E
Harrand 94 29 28N 70 3 E
Harrat al Kishb 92 22 30N 40 15 E
Harrat al Umuirid 92 26 50N 38 0 E
Harrat Khaibar 122 25 45N 40 0 E
Harrat Nawāsīf 122 21 30N 42 0 E
Harray, L. of 37 59 0N 3 15W
Harricana, R. 150 50 30N 79 10W
Harrietsham 29 51 15N 0 41 E
Harriman 157 36 0N 84 35W
Harrington, U.K. 32 54 37N 3 55W
Harrington, U.S.A. 162 38 56N 75 35W
Harrington Harbour 151 50 31N 59 30W
Harris 36 57 50N 6 55W
Harris L. 136 31 10 S 135 10 E
Harris Mts. 143 44 49 S 168 49 E
Harris, Sd. of 36 57 44N 7 6W
Harrisburg, Ill., U.S.A. 159 37 42N 88 30W
Harrisburg, Nebr.,
U.S.A. 158 41 36N 103 46W
Harrisburg, Oreg.,
U.S.A. 160 44 25N 123 10W
Harrisburg, Pa., U.S.A. 162 40 18N 76 52W
Harrismith 129 28 15 S 29 8 E
Harrison, Ark., U.S.A. 159 36 10N 93 4W
Harrison, Idaho, U.S.A. 160 47 30N 116 51W
Harrison, Nebr., U.S.A. 158 42 42N 103 52W
Harrison B. 147 70 25N 151 0W
Harrison, C. 151 55 0N 58 0W
Harrison L. 152 49 33N 121 50W
Harrisonburg 156 38 28N 78 52W
Harrisonville 158 38 45N 93 45W
Harriston 150 43 57N 80 53W
Harrisville 150 44 40N 83 19W
Harrogate 33 53 59N 1 32W
Harrow 29 51 35N 0 15W
Harry, L. 139 29 23 S 138 19 E
Harsefeld 48 53 26N 9 31 E
Harskamp 46 52 8N 5 46 E
Harstad 74 68 48N 16 30 E
Hart 156 43 42N 86 21W
Hart, L. 140 31 10 S 136 25 E
Hartbees, R. 128 29 8 S 20 48 E
Hartberg 52 47 17N 15 58 E
Harteigen, Mt. 71 60 11N 7 5 E
Hartest 29 52 7N 0 41 E
Hartford, Conn., U.S.A. 162 41 47N 72 41W
Hartford, Ky., U.S.A. 156 37 26N 86 50W
Hartford, S.D., U.S.A. 158 43 40N 96 58W
Hartford, Wis., U.S.A. 158 43 18N 88 25W
Hartford City 156 40 22N 85 20W
Harthill 35 55 52N 3 45W
Hartland, Can. 151 46 20N 67 32W
Hartland, U.K. 30 50 59N 4 29W
Hartland Pt. 30 51 2N 4 32W
Hartlebury 28 52 20N 2 13W
Hartlepool 33 54 42N 1 11W
Hartley, Rhod. 127 18 10 S 30 7 E
Hartley, U.K. 35 55 5N 1 27W
Hartley Bay 152 53 25N 129 15W
Hartmannberge 128 17 0 S 13 0 E
Hartney 153 49 30N 100 35W
Hartpury 28 51 55N 2 18W
Hartselle 157 34 25N 86 55W
Hartshorne 159 34 51N 95 30W
Hartsville 157 34 23N 80 2W
Hartwell 157 34 21N 82 52W
Harunabad 94 29 35N 73 2 E
Harur 97 12 3N 78 29 E
Harvard, Mt. 161 39 0N 106 5W
Harvey, Austral. 137 33 5 S 115 54 E
Harvey, Ill., U.S.A. 156 41 40N 87 50W
Harvey, N.D., U.S.A. 158 47 50N 99 58W
Harwell 28 51 40N 1 17W
Harwich 29 51 56N 1 18 E
Harwood 33 53 54N 1 30W
Haryana □ 94 29 0N 76 10 E
Harz 48 51 40N 10 40 E
Harzé 47 50 27N 5 40 E
Harzgerode 48 51 38N 11 8 E
Hasa 92 26 0N 49 0 E
Hasaheisa 123 14 25N 33 20 E
Hasani 122 25 0N 37 8 E
Hasanpur 94 28 51N 78 9 E
Haselünne 48 52 40N 7 30 E
Hasharon 90 32 12N 34 49 E
Hashefela 90 31 30N 34 43 E
Hashima 111 35 20N 136 40 E
Hashimoto 111 34 19N 135 37 E
Hasjö 72 63 1N 16 20 E
Håsjö 72 63 1N 16 5 E
Haskell, Kans., U.S.A. 159 35 51N 95 40W
Haskell, Tex., U.S.A. 159 33 10N 99 45W
Haskier Is. 36 57 42N 7 40W
Haslach 49 48 16N 8 7 E
Hasle 73 55 11N 14 44 E
Haslemere 29 51 5N 0 41W
Haslev 73 55 18N 11 57 E
Haslingden 32 53 43N 2 20W
Hasparren 44 43 24N 1 18W
Hassan 92 13 0N 76 5 E
Hasselt, Belg. 47 50 56N 5 21 E
Hasselt, Neth. 46 52 36N 6 6 E
Hassene, Ad. 118 21 0N 4 0 E
Hassfurt 49 50 2N 10 30 E
Hassi Berrekrem 119 33 45N 5 16 E
Hassi Daoula 119 33 4N 5 38 E
Hassi el Biod 119 28 30N 6 0 E
Hassi el Heïda 74 29 34N 0 14W
Hassi Inifel 118 29 50N 3 41 E
Hassi Marroket 119 30 10N 3 0 E
Hassi Messaoud 119 31 43N 6 8 E
Hassi Taguenza 172 29 8N 0 23W
Hassi Zerzour 118 30 51N 3 56W
Hässleby 73 57 37N 15 30 E
Hässleholmen 73 56 9N 13 45 E
Hastière-Lavaux 47 50 13N 4 49 E
Hastigrow 37 58 32N 3 15W
Hastings, Austral. 141 38 18 S 145 12 E
Hastings, N.Z. 142 39 39 S 176 52 E
Hastings, U.K. 29 50 51N 0 36 E
Hastings, Mich., U.S.A. 156 42 40N 82 20W
Hastings, Minn., U.S.A. 158 44 41N 92 51W
Hastings, Nebr., U.S.A. 158 40 34N 98 22W
Hastings Ra. 141 31 15 S 152 14 E
Hästveda 73 56 17N 13 55 E
Hat Nhao 101 14 46N 106 32 E
Hat Yai 101 7 1N 100 27 E
Hatanbulag 106 43 8N 109 14 E
Hatano 111 35 22N 139 14 E
Hatch 161 32 45N 107 8W
Hatches Creek 138 20 56 S 135 12 E
Hatchet L. 153 58 36N 103 40W
Haţeg 70 45 36N 22 55 E
Haţeg, Mţii 70 45 25N 23 0 E
Hatert 46 51 49N 5 50 E
Hatfield 29 51 46N 0 11W
Hatfield Broad Oak 29 51 48N 0 16 E
Hatfield Post Office 140 33 54N 143 49 E
Hatgal 105 50 26N 100 9 E
Hatherleigh 30 50 49N 4 4W
Hathersage 33 53 20N 1 39W
Hathras 94 27 36N 78 6 E
Hatia 99 22 30N 91 5 E
Hato de Corozal 174 6 11N 71 45W
Hato Mayor 167 18 46N 69 15W
Hattah 140 34 48N 142 17 E
Hattem 46 52 28N 6 4 E
Hatteras, C. 157 35 10N 75 30W
Hattiesburg 159 31 20N 89 20W
Hatton, Can. 153 50 2N 109 50W
Hatton, U.K. 37 57 24N 1 57W
Hatvan 53 47 40N 19 45 E
Hau Bon (Cheo Reo) 100 13 25N 108 28 E
Hau Duc 100 15 20N 108 13 E
Hauchinango 164 20 12N 97 45W
Haug 71 60 23N 10 26 E
Haugastøl 71 60 30N 7 50 E
Haugesund 71 59 23N 5 13 E
Haugh of Urr 35 55 0N 3 51W
Haughangaroa Ra. 142 38 42 S 175 40 E
Haughley 29 52 13N 0 59 E
Haukelisæter 71 59 51N 7 9 E
Haulerwijk 46 53 4N 6 20 E
Haultain, R. 153 55 51N 106 46W
Haungpa 98 25 29N 96 7 E
Haura 91 13 50N 47 35 E
Hauraki Gulf 142 36 35 S 175 5 E
Hausruck 52 48 6N 13 30 E
Haut Atlas 118 32 0N 7 0W
Haut-Rhin □ 43 48 0N 7 15 E
Haut Zaïre □ 126 2 20N 26 0 E
Hauta Oasis 92 23 40N 47 0 E
Hautah, Wahât al 92 23 40N 47 0 E
Haute-Corse □ 45 42 30N 9 30 E
Haute-Garonne □ 44 43 28N 1 30 E
Haute-Loire □ 44 45 5N 3 50 E
Haute-Marne □ 43 48 10N 5 20 E
Haute-Saône □ 43 47 45N 6 10 E
Haute-Savoie □ 45 46 0N 6 20 E
Haute-Vienne □ 44 45 50N 1 10 E
Hauterive 151 49 10N 68 16W
Hautes-Alpes □ 45 44 42N 6 20 E
Hautes Fagnes 47 50 34N 6 6 E
Hautes-Pyrénées □ 44 43 0N 0 10 E
Hauteville-Lompnes 45 45 59N 5 35 E
Hautmont 43 50 15N 3 55 E
Hautrage 47 50 29N 3 46 E
Hauts-de-Seine □ 43 48 52N 2 15 E
Hauts Plateaux 118 34 14N 1 0 E
Hauxley 35 55 21N 1 35W
Havana 158 40 19N 90 3W
Havana = La Habana 166 23 8N 82 22W
Havant 29 50 51N 0 59W
Havasu, L. 161 34 18N 114 8W
Havdhem 73 57 10N 18 20 E
Havelange 47 50 23N 5 15 E
Havelian 94 34 2N 73 10 E
Havelock, N.B., Can. 151 46 2N 65 24W
Havelock, Ont., Can. 150 44 26N 77 53W
Havelock, N.Z. 143 41 17 S 173 48 E
Havelock I. 101 11 55N 93 2 E
Havelte 46 52 46N 6 14 E
Haverfordwest 31 51 48N 4 59W
Haverhill, U.K. 29 52 6N 0 27 E
Haverhill, U.S.A. 162 42 50N 71 2W
Haveri 97 14 53N 75 24 E
Haverigg 32 54 12N 3 16W
Havering 29 51 33N 0 20 E
Haverstraw 162 41 12N 73 58W
Håverud 73 58 50N 12 28 E
Havîrna 70 48 4N 26 43 E
Havlíčkuv Brod 52 49 36N 15 33 E
Havnby 73 55 5N 8 34 E
Havre 160 48 40N 109 34W
Havre-Aubert 151 47 12N 62 0W
Havre de Grace 162 39 33N 76 6W
Havre, Le 42 49 30N 0 5 E
Havre St. Pierre 151 50 18N 63 33W
Havza 92 41 0N 35 35 E
Haw, R. 157 37 43N 80 52W
Hawaii □ 147 20 30N 157 0W
Hawaii I. 147 20 0N 155 0W
Hawaiian Is. 147 20 30N 156 0W
Hawarden, Can. 153 51 25N 106 36W
Hawarden, U.K. 31 53 11N 3 2W
Hawarden, U.S.A. 158 43 2N 96 28W
Hawea Flat 143 44 40 S 169 19 E
Hawea Lake 143 44 28 S 169 19 E
Hawera 142 39 35 S 174 19 E
Hawes 32 54 18N 2 12W
Hawes Water, L. 32 54 32N 2 48W
Hawick 35 55 25N 2 48W
Hawk Junction 150 48 30N 84 38W
Hawkchurch 30 50 47N 2 56W
Hawkdun Ra. 143 44 53 S 170 5 E
Hawke B. 142 39 25N 177 20 E
Hawker 28 31 59 S 138 22 E
Hawke's Bay □ 142 39 45 S 176 35 E
Hawke's Harbour 151 53 2N 55 50W
Hawkesbury 150 45 35N 74 40W
Hawkesbury I. 152 53 37N 129 3W
Hawkesbury Pt. 138 11 55 S 134 5 E
Hawkesbury River 133 33 50 S 151 44W
Hawkesbury Upton 28 51 34N 2 19W
Hawkhurst 29 51 2N 0 31 E
Hawkinsville 157 32 17N 83 30W
Hawkshead 32 54 23N 3 0W
Hawkwood 139 25 45 S 150 50 E
Hawley, Minn., U.S.A. 158 46 58N 96 20W
Hawley, Pa., U.S.A. 162 41 28N 75 11W
Haworth 32 53 50N 1 57W
Hawsker 33 54 27N 0 34W
Hawthorne 163 38 31N 118 37W
Hawzen 123 13 58N 39 28 E

Haxby
Higashiōsaka

Haxby 33 54 1N 1 4W
Haxtun 158 40 40N 102 39W
Hay, Austral. 141 34 30S 144 51E
Hay, U.K. 31 52 4N 3 9W
Hay, C. 136 14 5S 129 29E
Hay L. 152 58 50N 118 50W
Hay Lakes 152 53 12N 113 2W
Hay, R., Austral. 138 24 10S 137 20E
Hay, R., Can. 152 60 0N 116 56W
Hay River 152 60 51N 115 44W
Hay Springs 158 42 40N 102 38W
Hayange 43 49 20N 6 2E
Hayato 110 31 40N 130 43E
Hayburn Wyke 33 54 22N 0 28W
Haycock 147 65 10N 161 20W
Hayden, Ariz., U.S.A. 161 33 2N 110 54W
Hayden, Wyo., U.S.A. 160 40 30N 107 22W
Haydenville 162 42 22N 72 42W
Haydon 138 18 0S 141 30E
Haydon Bridge 35 54 58N 2 15W
Haye Descartes, La 42 46 58N 0 42E
Haye-du-Puits, La 42 49 17N 1 33W
Hayes 158 44 22N 101 1W
Hayes Pen. 12 75 30N 65 0W
Hayes, R. 153 57 3N 92 12W
Hayle 30 50 12N 5 25W
Haymana 92 39 30N 32 35E
Haynesville 159 33 0N 93 7W
Hays, Can. 152 50 6N 111 48W
Hays, U.S.A. 158 38 55N 99 25W
Hayton 32 54 55N 2 45W
Hayward, Calif., U.S.A. 163 37 40N 122 5W
Hayward, Wis., U.S.A. 158 46 2N 91 30W
Hayward's Heath 29 51 0N 0 5W
Hazard 156 37 18N 83 10W
Hazaribagh 95 23 58N 85 26E
Hazaribagh Road 95 24 12N 85 57E
Hazebrouck 43 50 42N 2 31E
Hazelton, Can. 152 55 20N 127 42W
Hazelton, U.S.A. 158 46 30N 100 15W
Hazen 160 39 37N 119 2W
Hazerswoude 46 52 5N 4 36E
Hazlehurst 157 31 50N 82 35W
Hazleton 156 40 58N 76 0W
Hazlett, L. 136 21 30S 128 48E
Hazrat Imam 93 37 15N 68 50E
Heacham 29 52 55N 0 30E
Head of Bight 137 31 30S 131 25E
Headcorn 29 51 10N 0 39E
Headford 38 53 28N 9 6W
Headington 28 51 46N 1 13W
Headlands 127 18 15S 32 2E
Healdsburg 160 38 33N 122 51W
Healdton 159 34 16N 97 31W
Healesville 141 37 35S 145 30E
Heanor 33 53 1N 1 20W
Heard I. 11 53 0S 74 0E
Hearne 159 30 54N 96 35W
Hearne B. 153 60 10N 99 10W
Hearne L. 152 62 20N 113 10W
Hearst 150 49 40N 83 41W
Heart, R. 158 46 40N 101 30W
Heart's Content 151 47 54N 53 27W
Heath Mts. 143 45 39S 167 9E
Heath Pt. 151 49 8N 61 40W
Heath Steele 151 47 17N 66 5W
Heathcote 141 36 56S 144 45E
Heather, oilfield 19 60 55N 0 50E
Heathfield 29 50 58N 0 18E
Heathsville 162 37 55N 76 28W
Heavener 159 34 54N 94 36W
Hebbronville 159 27 20N 98 40W
Hebburn 35 54 59N 1 30W
Hebden Bridge 32 53 45N 2 0W
Hebel 139 28 58S 147 47E
Heber Springs 159 35 29N 91 39W
Hebgen, L. 160 44 50N 111 15W
Hebrides, U.K. 36 57 30N 7 0W
Hebrides, Inner Is., U.K. 36 57 20N 6 40W
Hebrides, Outer Is., U.K. 36 57 50N 7 25W
Hebron, Can. 149 58 12N 62 38W
Hebron, N.D., U.S.A. 158 46 56N 102 2W
Hebron, Nebr., U.S.A. 158 40 15N 97 33W
Hebron (Al Khalil) 90 31 32N 35 6E
Heby 72 59 56N 16 53E
Hecate Str. 152 53 10N 130 30W
Hechingen 49 48 20N 8 58E
Hechtel 47 51 8N 5 22E
Heckington 33 52 59N 0 17W
Hecla 158 45 56N 98 8W
Hecla I. 153 51 10N 96 43W
Hecla Mt. 36 57 18N 7 15W
Heddal 71 59 36N 9 20E
Heddon 35 55 0N 1 47W
Hédé 42 48 18N 1 49W
Hede 72 62 23N 13 30E
Hedemora 72 60 18N 15 58E
Hedgehope 143 46 12S 168 34E
Hedley 159 34 53N 100 39W
Hedmark □ 75 61 17N 11 40E
Hedmark fylke □ 71 61 17N 11 40E
Hednesford 28 52 43N 2 0W
Hedon 33 53 44N 0 11W
Hedrum 71 59 7N 10 5E
Heeg 46 52 58N 5 37E
Heegermeer 46 52 56N 5 32E
Heemskerk 46 52 31N 4 40E
Heemstede 46 52 22N 4 37E
Heer 47 50 50N 5 43E
Heerde 46 52 24N 6 2E
's Heerenburg 46 51 53N 6 16E
's Heerenloo 46 52 19N 5 36E
Heerenveen 46 52 57N 5 55E
Heerhugowaard 46 52 40N 4 51E
Heerlen 47 50 55N 6 0E
Heerlerheide 47 50 54N 5 58E
Heers 47 50 45N 5 18E
Heesch 46 51 44N 5 32E
Heestert 47 50 47N 3 25E
Heeze 47 51 23N 5 35E
Hegyalja, Mts. 53 48 25N 21 25E
Heich'engchen 106 36 16N 106 19E
Heide 48 54 10N 9 7E
Heide, oilfield 19 54 5N 9 5E
Heidelberg, Ger. 49 49 23N 8 41E
Heidelberg, C. Prov., S. Afr. 128 34 6S 20 59E
Heidelberg, Trans., S. Afr. 129 26 30S 28 23E
Heidenheim 49 48 40N 10 10E
Heigun-To 110 33 47N 132 14E
Heikant 47 51 15N 4 1E
Heilam 37 58 31N 4 40W
Heilbron 129 27 16S 27 59E
Heilbronn 49 49 8N 9 13E
Heiligenblut 52 47 2N 12 51E
Heiligenhafen 48 54 21N 10 58E
Heiligenstadt 48 51 22N 10 9E
Heilungkiang □ 46 48 0N 128 0E
Heim 71 63 26N 9 5E
Heimdal, gasfield 19 59 35N 2 15E
Heino 46 52 26N 6 14E
Heinola 75 61 13N 26 24E
Heinsburg 153 53 50N 110 30W
Heinsch 47 49 42N 5 44E
Heinsun 98 25 52N 95 35E
Heinze Is. 101 14 25N 97 45E
Heirnkut 98 25 14N 94 44E
Heishan 107 41 40N 122 3E
Heishui, Liaoning, China 107 42 6N 119 22E
Heishui, Szechwan, China 108 32 15N 103 0E
Heist 47 51 20N 3 15E
Heist-op-den-Berg 47 51 5N 4 44E
Heistad 71 59 35N 9 40E
Hejaz = Hijāz 92 26 0N 37 30E
Hekelegem 47 50 55N 4 7E
Hekimhan 92 38 50N 38 0E
Hekinan 111 34 52N 137 0E
Hekla 74 63 56N 19 35W
Hel 60 54 38N 18 50E
Helagsfjället 72 62 54N 12 25E
Helchteren 47 51 4N 5 22E
Helden 47 51 19N 6 0E
Helechosa 57 39 22N 4 53W
Helena, Ark., U.S.A. 159 34 30N 90 35W
Helena, Mont., U.S.A. 160 46 40N 112 0W
Helendale 163 34 45N 117 19W
Helensburgh, Austral. 141 34 11S 151 1E
Helensburgh, U.K. 34 56 0N 4 44W
Helensville 142 36 41S 174 29E
Helets 90 31 36N 34 39E
Helgasjön 73 57 0N 14 50E
Helgeland 74 66 20N 13 30E
Helgeroa 71 59 0N 9 45E
Helgoland, I. 48 54 10N 7 51E
Helgum 72 63 25N 16 50E
Heligoland = Helgoland 48 54 10N 7 51E
Heliopolis 122 30 6N 31 17E
Hell-Ville 129 13 25S 48 16E
Hellebæk 73 56 4N 12 32E
Helleland 71 58 33N 6 7E
Hellendoorn 46 52 24N 6 27E
Hellertown 162 40 35N 75 21W
Hellevoetsluis 46 51 50N 4 8E
Helli Ness 36 60 3N 1 10W
Hellick Kenyon Plateau 13 82 0S 110 0W
Hellifield 32 54 0N 2 13W
Hellín 59 38 31N 1 40W
Hellum 73 57 16N 10 10E
Helmand □ 93 31 20N 64 0E
Helmand, R. 94 34 0N 67 0E
Helmond 47 51 29N 5 41E
Helmsdale 37 58 7N 3 40W
Helmsley 33 54 15N 1 2W
Helmstedt 48 52 16N 11 0E
Helnæs 73 55 9N 10 0E
Helper 160 39 44N 110 56W
Helperby 33 54 8N 1 20W
Helsby 32 53 16N 2 47W
Helsingborg 73 56 3N 12 42E
Helsinge 73 56 2N 12 12E
Helsingfors = Helsinki 75 60 15N 25 3E
Helsingør 73 56 2N 12 35E
Helsinki (Helsingfors) 75 60 15N 25 3E
Helston 30 50 7N 5 17W
Helvick Hd. 39 52 3N 7 33W
Helvoirt 47 51 38N 5 14E
Helwân 122 29 50N 31 20E
Hem 71 59 26N 10 0E
Hemavati, R. 97 12 50N 67 0E
Hemel Hempstead 29 51 45N 0 28W
Hemet 163 33 45N 116 59W
Hemingford 158 42 21N 103 4W
Hemphill 159 31 21N 93 49W
Hempstead 159 30 5N 96 5W
Hempton 29 52 50N 0 49E
Hemse 73 57 15N 18 22E
Hemsö, I. 72 62 43N 18 5E
Hemsön 72 62 42N 18 5E
Hemsworth 33 53 37N 1 21W
Hemyock 30 50 55N 1 13W
Hen & Chicken Is. 142 35 58S 174 45E
Henares, R. 58 40 55N 3 0W
Hendaye 44 43 23N 1 47W
Henderson, Argent. 172 36 18S 61 43W
Henderson, U.K. 36 57 42N 5 47W
Henderson, Ky., U.S.A. 156 37 50N 87 38W
Henderson, Nev., U.S.A. 161 36 2N 115 0W
Henderson, Pa., U.S.A. 157 35 25N 88 40W
Henderson, Tex., U.S.A. 159 32 5N 94 49W
Hendersonville 157 35 21N 82 28W
Hendon 139 28 5S 151 50E
Hendorf 70 46 4N 24 5E
Henfield 29 50 56N 0 17W
Hengch'eng 106 38 26N 106 26E
Hengelo, Gelderland, Neth. 46 52 3N 6 19E
Hengelo, Overijssel, Neth. 46 52 16N 6 48E
Hengfeng 109 28 25N 117 35E
Henghsien 108 22 36N 109 16E
Hengoed 31 51 39N 3 14W
Hengshan, Hunan, China 109 27 15N 112 51E
Hengshan, Shansi, China 106 37 56N 108 53E
Hengshui 106 37 43N 115 42E
Hengtaohotze 107 44 55N 129 3E
Hengyang 109 26 51N 112 30E
Hengyanghsien 109 26 58N 112 21E
Hénin-Beaumont 43 50 25N 2 58E
Henley 29 51 32N 0 53W
Henley-in-Arden 28 52 18N 1 47W
Henllan 31 53 13N 3 29W
Henlopen, C. 162 38 48N 75 5W
Henlow 29 51 2N 0 18W
Hennan, L. 72 62 3N 15 55E
Henne 73 55 44N 8 11E
Hennebont 42 47 49N 3 19W
Hennenman 128 27 59S 27 1E
Hennessy 159 36 8N 97 53W
Hennigsdorf 48 52 38N 13 13E
Henribourg 153 53 25N 105 38W
Henrichemont 43 47 20N 2 21E
Henrietta 159 33 50N 98 15W
Henrietta Maria C. 150 55 9N 82 20W
Henry 158 41 5N 89 20W
Henryetta 159 35 2N 96 0W
Henstridge 28 50 59N 2 24W
Hentiyn Nuruu 105 48 30N 108 30E
Henty 141 35 30N 147 0E
Henzada 98 17 38N 95 35E
Heppner 160 45 27N 119 34W
Herad 71 58 5N 6 47E
Héraðsflói 74 65 42N 14 12W
Héraðsvötn 74 65 25N 19 5W
Herald Cays 138 16 58S 149 9E
Herāt 93 34 20N 62 7E
Herāt □ 93 35 0N 62 0E
Hérault □ 44 43 34N 3 15E
Hérault, R. 44 43 20N 3 32E
Herbert 153 50 30N 107 10W
Herbert Downs 138 23 7S 139 9E
Herbert I. 147 52 49N 170 10W
Herbert, R. 138 18 31S 146 17E
Herberton 138 17 28S 145 25E
Herbertstown 39 52 32N 8 29W
Herbiers, Les 42 46 52N 1 0W
Herbignac 42 47 27N 2 18W
Herborn 48 50 40N 8 19E
Herby 54 50 45N 18 50E
Hercegnovi 66 42 30N 18 33E
Herðubreið 74 65 11N 16 21W
Herdla 71 60 34N 4 56E
Hereford, U.K. 28 52 4N 2 42W
Hereford, U.S.A. 159 34 50N 102 28W
Hereford and Worcester □ 28 52 10N 2 30W
Herefordshire □ 26 52 15N 2 50W
Herefoss 71 58 32N 8 32E
Herekino 142 35 18S 173 11E
Herent 47 50 54N 4 40E
Herentals 47 51 12N 4 51E
Herenthout 47 51 8N 4 45E
Herfølge 73 55 26N 12 9E
Herford 48 52 7N 8 40E
Héricourt 43 47 32N 6 55E
Herington 158 38 43N 97 0W
Herisau 51 47 22N 9 17E
Hérisson 44 46 32N 2 42E
Herjehogna 75 61 43N 12 7E
Herk, R. 47 50 56N 5 12E
Herkenbosch 47 51 9N 6 4E
Herkimer 162 43 0N 74 59W
Herm I. 42 49 30N 2 28W
Herma Ness 36 60 50N 0 54W
Hermagor 52 46 38N 13 23E
Herman 158 45 51N 96 8W
Hermandez 163 36 24N 120 46W
Hermann 158 38 40N 91 25W
Hermannsburg 48 52 49N 10 6E
Hermannsburg Mission 136 23 57S 132 45E
Hermanus 128 34 27S 19 12E
Herment 44 45 45N 2 24E
Hermidale 141 31 30S 146 42E
Hermiston 160 45 50N 119 16W
Hermitage 143 43 44S 170 5E
Hermitage B. 151 47 33N 56 10W
Hermite, Is. 176 55 50S 68 0W
Hermon, Mt. = Sheikh, J. ash 92 33 20N 36 0E
Hermosillo 164 29 10N 111 0W
Hernad, R. 53 48 20N 21 15E
Hernandarias 173 25 20S 54 40W
Hernando, Argent. 172 32 28S 63 40W
Hernando, U.S.A. 159 34 50N 89 59W
Herndon 162 40 43N 76 51W
Herne, Belg. 47 50 44N 4 2E
Herne, Ger. 48 51 33N 7 12E
Herne Bay 29 51 22N 1 8E
Herne Hill 137 31 45S 116 5E
Herning 73 56 8N 8 58E
Heroica Nogales 164 31 14N 110 56W
Heron Bay 150 48 40N 85 25W
Heröy 71 62 18N 5 45E
Herreid 158 45 53N 100 5W
's Herrenbroek 46 52 32N 6 1E
Herrera 57 39 12N 4 50W
Herrera de Alcántar 57 39 39N 7 25W
Herrera de Pisuerga 56 42 35N 4 20W
Herrera del Duque 57 39 10N 5 3W
Herrero, Punta 165 19 17N 87 27W
Herrick 138 41 5S 147 55E
Herrin 159 37 50N 89 0W
Herrljunga 73 58 5N 13 1E
Hersbruck 49 49 30N 11 25E
Herschel I. 147 69 35N 139 5W
Herseaux 47 50 43N 3 15E
Herselt 47 51 3N 4 53E
Herserange 47 49 30N 5 48E
Hershey 162 40 17N 76 39W
Herstal 47 50 40N 5 38E
Herstmonceux 29 50 53N 0 21E
Hersvik 71 61 10N 4 53E
Hertford 29 51 47N 0 4W
Hertford □ 29 51 51N 0 5W
's Hertogenbosch 47 51 42N 5 18E
Hertzogville 128 28 9S 25 30E
Hervás 56 40 16N 5 52W
Herve 47 50 38N 5 48E
Hervey B. 133 25 0S 152 52E
Hervey Is. 131 19 30S 159 0W
Hervey Junction 150 46 50N 72 29W
Herwijnen 46 51 50N 5 7E
Herzberg, Cottbus, Ger. 48 51 40N 13 13E
Herzberg, Niedersachsen, Ger. 48 51 38N 10 20E
Herzele 47 50 53N 3 53E
Herzliyya 90 32 10N 34 50E
Herzogenbuchsee 50 47 11N 7 42E
Herzogenburg 52 48 17N 15 41E
Hesdin 43 50 21N 2 0E
Hesel 48 53 18N 7 36E
Heskestad 71 58 28N 6 22E
Hesperange 47 49 35N 6 10E
Hesperia 163 34 25N 117 18W
Hesse = Hessen 48 50 57N 9 20E
Hessen □ 48 50 57N 9 20E
Hessle 33 53 44N 0 28E
Hetch Hetchy Aqueduct 163 37 36N 121 25W
Heteren 46 51 58N 5 46E
Hethersett 29 52 35N 1 10E
Hettinger 158 46 8N 102 38W
Hetton-le-Hole 35 54 49N 1 26W
Hettstedt 48 51 39N 11 30E
Heugem 47 50 49N 5 42E
Heule 47 50 51N 3 15E
Heusden, Belg. 47 51 2N 5 17E
Heusden, Neth. 46 51 44N 5 8E
Hève, C. de la 42 49 30N 0 5E
Heverlee 47 50 52N 4 42E
Heves □ 53 47 50N 20 0E
Hevron, N. 90 31 28N 34 52E
Hewett, C. 149 70 16N 67 45W
Hewett, gasfield 19 53 5N 1 50E
Hex River 128 33 30S 19 35E
Hexham 35 54 58N 2 7W
Heybridge 29 51 44N 0 42E
Heyfield 141 37 59S 146 47E
Heysham 32 54 5N 2 53W
Heytesbury 28 51 11N 2 7W
Heythuysen 47 51 15N 5 55E
Heywood, Austral. 140 38 8S 141 37E
Heywood, U.K. 32 53 36N 2 13W
Hi-no-Misaki 110 35 26N 132 38E
Hi Vista 163 34 44N 117 46W
Hiamen 109 31 52N 121 15E
Hiawatha, Kans., U.S.A. 158 39 55N 95 33W
Hiawatha, Utah, U.S.A. 160 39 37N 111 1W
Hibbing 158 47 30N 93 0W
Hibbs B. 138 42 35S 145 15E
Hibbs, Pt. 138 42 38S 145 15E
Hibernia Reef 136 12 0S 123 23E
Hibiki-Nada 110 34 0N 130 0E
Hickman 159 36 35N 89 8W
Hickory 157 35 46N 81 17W
Hicks Bay 142 37 34S 178 21E
Hicksville 162 40 46N 73 30W
Hida-Gawa 70 47 10N 23 9E
Hida-Gawa, R. 111 35 26N 137 3E
Hida-Sammyaku 111 36 30N 137 40E
Hida-Sanchi 111 36 10N 137 0E
Hidaka 110 35 30N 134 44E
Hidalgo □ 164 20 30N 99 10W
Hidalgo del Parral 164 26 58N 105 40W
Hidalgo, Presa M. 164 26 30N 108 35W
Hiddensee 48 54 30N 13 6E
Hidrolândia 171 17 0S 49 15W
Hieflau 52 47 36N 14 46E
Hiendelaencina 58 41 5N 3 0W
Hierro I. 116 27 57N 17 56E
Higashi-matsuyama 111 36 2N 139 25E
Higashiōsaka 111 34 40N 135 37E

Higasi-Suidō Hong Kong ■

Higasi-Suidō 110 34 0N 129 30 E
Higgins 159 36 9N 100 1W
Higginsville 137 31 42S 121 38 E
Higgs I. L. 157 36 20N 78 30W
High Atlas = Haut Atlas 118 32 30N 5 0W
High Bentham 32 54 8N 2 31W
High Borrow Bri. 32 54 26N 2 43W
High Bridge 162 40 40N 74 54W
High Ercall 28 52 46N 2 37W
High Hesket 32 54 47N 2 49W
High I. 151 56 40N 61 10W
High Island 159 29 32N 94 22W
High Level 152 58 31N 117 8W
High Pike, mt. 32 54 43N 3 4W
High Point 157 35 57N 79 58W
High Prairie 152 55 30N 116 30W
High River 152 50 30N 113 50W
High Springs 157 29 50N 82 40W
High Tatra 53 49 30N 20 00 E
High Veld = Hoëveld 129 26 30S 30 0 E
High Willhays, hill 30 50 41N 3 59W
High Wycombe 29 51 37N 0 45W
Higham Ferrers 29 52 18N 0 36W
Highbank 138 47 34S 171 45 E
Highbridge 28 51 13N 2 59W
Highbury 138 16 25S 143 9 E
Highclere 28 51 20N 1 22W
Highland □ 36 57 30N 5 0W
Highland Pk. 156 42 10N 87 50W
Highland Springs 162 37 33N 77 20W
Highley 28 52 25N 2 23W
Highmore 158 44 35N 99 26W
Highrock L. 153 57 5N 105 32W
Hightae 35 55 5N 3 27W
Hightstown 162 40 16N 74 31W
Highworth 28 51 38N 1 42W
Higley 161 33 27N 111 46W
Higüay 167 18 37N 68 42W
Higüero, Pta. 147 18 22N 67 16W
Hiiumaa 80 58 50N 22 45 E
Híjar 58 41 10N 0 27W
Hijāz 91 26 0N 37 30 E
Hiji 110 33 22N 131 32 E
Hijken 46 52 54N 6 30 E
Hikari 110 33 58N 131 58 E
Hiketa 110 34 13N 134 24 E
Hiko 161 37 30N 115 13W
Hikone 111 35 15N 136 10 E
Hikurangi, East Court 142 37 55S 178 4 E
Hikurangi, Mt. 142 37 55S 178 4 E
Hilawng 98 21 23N 93 48 E
Hildburghhausen 49 50 24N 10 43 E
Hildesheim 48 52 9N 9 55 E
Hilgay 29 52 34N 0 23 E
Hill 150 45 40N 74 45W
Hill City, Idaho, U.S.A. 160 43 20N 115 2W
Hill City, Kans., U.S.A. 158 39 25N 99 51W
Hill City, Minn., U.S.A. 158 46 57N 93 35W
Hill City, S.D., U.S.A. 158 43 58N 103 35W
Hill End 141 38 1S 146 9 E
Hill Island L. 153 60 30N 109 50W
Hill, R. 137 30 23S 115 3 E
Hilla, Iraq 92 32 30N 44 27 E
Hilla, Si Arab. 92 23 35N 46 50 E
Hillared 73 57 37N 13 10 E
Hillegom 46 52 18N 4 35 E
Hillerød 73 55 56N 12 19 E
Hillerstorp 73 57 20N 13 52 E
Hilli 98 25 17N 89 1 E
Hillingdon 29 51 33N 0 29W
Hillman 156 45 5N 83 52W
Hillmond 153 53 26N 109 41W
Hillsboro, Kans., U.S.A. 158 38 28N 97 10W
Hillsboro, N. Mex., U.S.A. 161 33 0N 107 35W
Hillsboro, N. Mex., U.S.A. 161 33 0N 107 35W
Hillsboro, N.D., U.S.A. 158 47 23N 97 9W
Hillsboro, N.H., U.S.A. 156 43 8N 71 56W
Hillsboro, Oreg., U.S.A. 160 45 31N 123 0W
Hillsboro, Tex., U.S.A. 159 32 0N 97 10W
Hillsborough, U.K. 38 54 28N 6 6W
Hillsborough, W. Indies 167 12 28N 61 28W
Hillsdale, Mich., U.S.A. 156 41 55N 84 40W
Hillsdale, N.Y., U.S.A. 162 42 11N 73 30W
Hillside 136 21 45S 119 23 E
Hillsport 150 49 27N 85 34W
Hillston 141 33 30S 145 31 E
Hillswick 36 60 29N 1 28W
Hilltown 38 54 12N 6 8W
Hilo 147 19 44N 155 5W
Hilonghilong, mt. 103 9 10N 125 45 E
Hilpsford Pt. 32 54 4N 3 12W
Hilvarenbeek 47 51 29N 5 8 E
Hilversum 46 52 14N 5 10 E
Himachal Pradesh □ 94 31 30N 77 0 E
Himalaya 99 29 0N 84 0 E
Himara 68 40 8N 19 43 E
Himatnagar 93 23 37N 72 57 E
Hime-Jima 110 33 43N 131 40 E
Himeji 110 34 50N 134 40 E
Himi 111 36 50N 137 0 E
Himmerland 73 56 45N 9 30 E
Hims = Homs 92 34 40N 36 45 E
Hinako, Kepulauan 102 0 50N 97 20 E
Hinche 167 19 9N 72 1W
Hinchinbrook I. 138 18 20S 146 15 E
Hinckley, U.K. 28 52 33N 1 21W
Hinckley, U.S.A. 160 39 18N 112 41W
Hindås 73 57 42N 12 27 E
Hindaun 94 26 44N 77 5 E
Hinde Rapids (Hells Gate) 126 5 25S 27 3 E
Hinderwell 33 54 32N 0 45W
Hindhead 29 51 6N 0 42W
Hindley 32 53 32N 2 35W
Hindmarsh L. 140 36 5S 141 55 E
Hindol 95 20 40N 85 10 E
Hinds 143 43 59S 171 36 E
Hindsholm 73 55 30N 10 40 E
Hindu Bagh 94 30 56N 67 57 E
Hindu Kush 93 36 0N 71 0 E
Hindubagh 93 30 56N 67 57 E
Hindupur 97 13 49N 77 32 E
Hines Creek 152 56 20N 118 40W
Hinganghat 96 20 30N 78 59 E
Hingeon 47 50 32N 4 59 E
Hingham, U.K. 29 52 35N 0 59 E
Hingham, U.S.A. 160 48 40N 110 29W
Hingol, R. 93 25 30N 65 30 E
Hingoli 96 19 41N 77 15 E
Hinkley Pt. 28 50 59N 3 32W
Hinlopenstretet 12 79 35N 18 40 E
Hinna 121 10 25N 11 28 E
Hinnøy 74 68 40N 16 28 E
Hino 111 35 0N 136 15 E
Hinojosa 55 38 30N 5 17W
Hinojosa del Duque 57 38 30N 5 17W
Hinokage 110 32 39N 131 24 E
Hinsdale 160 48 26N 107 2W
Hinstock 28 52 50N 2 28W
Hinterrhein, R. 51 46 40N 9 25 E
Hinton, Can. 152 53 26N 117 34W
Hinton, U.S.A. 156 37 40N 80 51W
Hinwil 51 47 18N 8 51 E
Hippolytushoef 46 52 54N 4 58 E
Hirado 110 33 22N 129 33 E
Hirado-Shima 110 33 20N 129 30 E
Hirakarta 111 34 48N 135 40 E
Hirakud 96 21 32N 83 51 E
Hirakud Dam 96 21 32N 83 45 E
Hirara 112 24 48N 125 17 E
Hirata 110 35 24N 132 49 E
Hiratsuka 111 35 19N 139 21 E
Hirhafok 119 23 49N 5 45 E
Hirlŭu 70 47 23N 27 0 E
Hiromi 110 33 13N 132 36 E
Hirosaki 112 40 34N 140 28 E
Hiroshima 110 34 30N 132 30 E
Hiroshima-ken □ 112 34 50N 133 0 E
Hiroshima-Wan 110 34 5N 132 20 E
Hirsoholmene 73 57 30N 10 36 E
Hirson 43 49 55N 4 4 E
Hîrşova 70 44 40N 27 59 E
Hirtshals 73 57 36N 9 57 E
Hirwaun 31 51 43N 3 30W
Hisoy 71 58 26N 8 44 E
Hispaniola, I. 165 19 0N 71 0W
Hissar 94 29 12N 75 45 E
Histon 29 52 15N 0 6 E
Hita 110 33 20N 130 58 E
Hitachi 111 36 36N 140 39 E
Hitachiota 111 36 30N 140 30 E
Hitchin 29 51 57N 0 16W
Hitoyoshi 110 32 13N 130 45 E
Hitra 71 63 30N 8 45 E
Hitzacker 48 53 9N 11 1 E
Hiuchi-Nada 110 34 5N 133 20 E
Hjalmar L. 153 61 33N 109 25W
Hjälmare Kanal 72 59 20N 15 59 E
Hjälmaren 72 59 18N 15 40 E
Hjartdal 71 59 37N 8 41 E
Hjärtsäter 73 58 35N 12 3 E
Hjerkinn 71 62 13N 9 33 E
Hjerpsted 73 55 2N 8 39 E
Hjo 73 58 22N 4 17 E
Hjørring 73 57 29N 9 59 E
Hjorted 73 57 37N 16 19 E
Hjortkvarn 73 58 54N 15 26 E
Hko-ut 98 21 40N 97 46 E
Hkyenhpa 98 27 43N 97 25 E
Hlaingbwe 98 17 8N 97 50 E
Hlinsko 52 49 45N 15 54 E
Hlohovec 53 48 26N 17 49 E
Hlwaze 98 18 54N 96 37 E
Ho 121 6 37N 0 27 E
Ho Chi Minh, Phanh Bho 101 10 58N 106 40 E
Ho Thuong 100 19 32N 105 48 E
Hoa Binh 100 20 50N 105 20 E
Hoa Da (Phan Ri) 100 11 16N 108 40 E
Hoa Hiep 101 11 34N 105 51 E
Hoadley 152 52 45N 114 30W
Hoai Nhon (Bon Son) 100 14 28N 109 1 E
Hoare B. 149 65 17N 62 55W
Hobart, Austral. 138 42 50S 147 21 E
Hobart, U.S.A. 159 35 0N 99 5W
Hobbs 159 32 40N 103 3W
Hobjærg 73 56 19N 9 32 E
Hobo 174 2 35N 75 30W
Hoboken, Belg. 47 51 11N 4 21 E
Hoboken, U.S.A. 162 40 45N 74 4W
Hobro 73 56 39N 9 46 E
Hobscheid 47 49 42N 5 57 E
Hoburg C. 73 56 54N 18 8 E
Hoburgen 73 56 55N 18 7 E
Hochang 108 27 8N 104 45 E
Hochatown 159 34 11N 94 39W
Hochdorf 51 47 10N 8 17 E
Hochiang 108 28 48N 105 48 E
Hochien 106 38 26N 116 5 E
Hoch'ih 108 24 43N 108 2 E
Hoching 106 35 37N 110 43 E
Hoch'iu 109 32 21N 116 13 E
Höchst 49 50 6N 8 33 E
Hoch'ü 106 39 26N 111 8 E
Hoch'uan 108 30 2N 106 18 E
Hockenheim 49 49 18N 8 33 E
Hod, oilfield 19 56 10N 3 25 E
Hodaka-Dake 111 36 17N 137 39 E
Hodde 73 55 42N 8 39 E
Hodder R. 32 53 57N 2 27W
Hoddesdon 29 51 45N 0 1W
Hodeïda 91 14 50N 43 0 E
Hodge, R. 33 54 14N 0 55W
Hodgson 153 51 13N 97 36W
Hódmezóvásárhely 53 46 28N 20 22 E
Hodna, Chott el 119 35 30N 5 0 E
Hodonín 53 48 50N 17 0 E
Hodsager 73 56 19N 8 51 E
Hoeamdong 107 42 30N 130 16 E
Hoëdic, I. 42 47 21N 2 52W
Hoegaarden 47 50 47N 4 53 E
Hoek van Holland 46 52 0N 4 7 E
Hoeksche Waard 46 51 46N 4 25 E
Hoenderloo 46 52 7N 5 52 E
Hoengsŏng 107 37 29N 127 59 E
Hoensbroek 47 50 55N 5 55 E
Hoeryong 107 42 30N 129 58 E
Hoeselt 47 50 51N 5 29 E
Hoëveld 129 26 30S 30 0 E
Hoeven 47 51 35N 4 35 E
Hoeyang 107 38 43N 127 36 E
Hof, Ger. 49 50 18N 11 55 E
Hof, Iceland 74 64 33N 14 40W
Höfðakaupstaður 74 65 50N 20 19W
Hofei 109 31 52N 117 15 E
Hoff 32 54 34N 2 31W
Hofgeismar 48 51 29N 9 23 E
Hofors 72 60 35N 16 15 E
Hofsjökull 74 64 49N 18 48W
Hofsós 74 65 53N 19 26W
Hōfu 110 34 3N 131 34 E
Hofuf 92 25 20N 49 40 E
Hög-Gia, Mt. 71 62 23N 10 7 E
Hog I. 162 37 26N 75 42W
Hogan Group 139 39 13S 147 1 E
Höganäs 73 56 13N 12 34 E
Hogansville 157 33 14N 84 50W
Hogarth, Mt. 138 21 50S 137 0 E
Hogeland 160 48 51N 108 40W
Högen 72 61 47N 14 11 E
Hogenaki Falls 97 12 6N 77 50 E
Högfors, Örebro, Sweden 72 59 58N 15 3 E
Högfors, Västmanlands, Sweden 72 60 2N 16 3 E
Hoggar = Ahaggar 119 23 0N 6 30 E
Högo-Kaikyo 110 33 20N 131 58 E
Hog's Back, hill 29 51 13N 0 40W
Hogs Hd. 39 51 46N 10 13W
Högsäter 73 58 38N 12 5 E
Högsby 73 57 10N 16 1 E
Högsjo 73 59 4N 15 44 E
Hogsthorpe 33 53 13N 0 19 E
Hogsty Reef 167 21 41N 73 48W
Hohe Rhön 49 50 24N 9 58 E
Hohe Tauern 52 47 11N 12 40 E
Hohenau 53 48 36N 16 55 E
Hohenems 52 47 22N 9 42 E
Hohenstein Ernstthal 48 50 48N 12 43 E
Hohenwald 157 35 35N 87 30W
Hohenwestedt 48 54 6N 9 40 E
Hohoe 121 7 8N 0 32 E
Hohsi 108 24 9N 102 38 E
Hohsien, Anhwei, China 109 31 43N 118 22 E
Hohsien, Kwangsi-Chuang, China 109 24 25N 111 31 E
Hohsüeh 109 30 2N 112 25 E
Hôi An 100 15 30N 108 19 E
Hoi Xuan 100 20 25N 105 9 E
Hoisington 158 38 33N 98 50W
Højer 73 54 58N 8 42 E
Hōjō 110 33 58N 132 46 E
Hok 73 57 31N 14 16 E
Hokensås 73 58 0N 14 5 E
Hökensås 73 58 0N 14 5 E
Hökerum 73 57 51N 13 16 E
Hokianga Harbour 142 35 31S 173 22 E
Hokitika 143 42 42S 171 0 E
Hokkaidō 112 43 30N 143 0 E
Hokkaidō □ 112 43 30N 143 0 E
Hokksund 71 59 44N 9 59 E
Hok'ou, Kansu, China 106 36 9N 103 29 E
Hok'ou, Kwantang, China 109 23 13N 112 45 E
Hok'ou, Yunnan, China 108 22 39N 103 57 E
Hokow 101 22 39N 103 57 E
Hol-Hol. 123 11 20N 42 50 E
Holan Shan 106 38 50N 105 50 E
Holbæk 73 55 43N 11 43 E
Holbeach 29 52 48N 0 1 E
Holbeach Marsh 29 52 52N 0 5 E
Holborn Hd. 37 58 37N 3 30W
Holbrook, Austral. 141 35 42S 147 18 E
Holbrook, U.S.A. 161 35 0N 110 0W
Holden 152 53 13N 112 11W
Holden Fillmore 160 39 0N 112 26W
Holdenville 159 35 5N 96 25W
Holder 140 34 21S 140 0 E
Holderness 33 53 45N 0 5W
Holdfast 153 50 58N 105 25W
Holdrege 153 40 25N 99 30W
Hole 71 60 6N 10 12 E
Hole-Narsipur 97 12 48N 76 16 E
Holešov 53 49 20N 17 35 E
Holguin 166 20 50N 76 20W
Holinkoerh 106 40 23N 111 53 E
Holič 53 48 49N 17 10 E
Holkham 29 52 57N 0 48 E
Holla, Mt. 123 7 5N 36 35 E
Hollabrunn 52 48 34N 16 5 E
Hollams Bird I. 128 24 40S 14 30 E
Holland 156 42 47N 86 7W
Holland Fen 33 53 0N 0 8W
Holland-on-Sea 29 51 48N 1 12 E
Hollandia = Jajapura 103 2 28S 140 38 E
Hollands Bird I. 128 24 40S 14 30 E
Hollandsch Diep 47 51 41N 4 30 E
Hollandsch IJssel, R. 46 51 55N 4 34 E
Hollandstoun 37 59 22N 2 25W
Höllen 71 58 6N 7 49 E
Holleton 137 31 55S 119 0 E
Hollidaysburg 156 40 26N 78 25W
Hollis 159 34 45N 99 55W
Hollister 161 36 51N 121 24W
Hollum 46 53 26N 5 38 E
Holly 158 38 7N 102 7W
Holly Hill 157 29 15N 81 3W
Holly Springs 159 34 45N 89 25W
Hollymount 38 53 40N 9 7W
Hollywood, Ireland 39 53 6N 6 35W
Hollywood, Calif., U.S.A. 154 34 7N 118 25W
Hollywood, Fla., U.S.A. 157 26 0N 80 9W
Holm 72 62 40N 16 40 E
Holman Island 148 71 0N 118 0W
Hólmavik 74 65 42N 21 40W
Holme, Humberside,, U.K. 33 53 50N 0 48W
Holme, N. Yorks., U.K. 32 53 34N 1 50W
Holmedal 71 59 46N 5 50 E
Holmedal, Fjordane 71 61 22N 5 11 E
Holmegil 72 59 10N 11 44 E
Holmes Chapel 32 53 13N 2 21W
Holmes Reefs 138 16 27S 148 0 E
Holmestrand 71 59 31N 10 14 E
Holmfirth 33 53 34N 1 48W
Holmsbu 71 59 32N 10 27 E
Holmsjön 72 62 26N 15 20 E
Holmsland Klit 73 56 0N 8 5 E
Holmsund 74 63 41N 20 20 E
Holmwood 29 51 12N 0 19W
Hölö 72 59 3N 17 36 E
Holo Ho, R. 107 44 54N 122 22 E
Holod 70 46 49N 22 8 E
Holon 90 32 2N 34 47 E
Holroyd, R. 138 14 10S 141 36 E
Holsen 71 61 25N 6 8 E
Holstebro 73 56 22N 8 37 E
Holsworthy 30 50 48N 4 21W
Holt, Iceland 74 63 33N 19 48W
Holt, Clwyd, U.K. 31 53 4N 2 52W
Holt, Norfolk, U.K. 29 52 55N 1 4 E
Holte 73 55 50N 12 29 E
Holten 46 52 17N 6 26 E
Holton Harbour 151 54 31N 57 12W
Holton le Clay 33 53 29N 0 3W
Holtville 161 32 50N 115 27W
Holum 71 58 6N 7 32 E
Holwerd 46 53 22N 5 54 E
Holy Cross 147 62 10N 159 52W
Holy I., England, U.K. 35 55 42N 1 48W
Holy I., Scotland, U.K. 34 55 31N 5 4W
Holy I., Wales, U.K. 31 53 17N 4 37W
Holyhead 31 53 18N 4 38W
Holyhead B. 31 53 20N 4 35W
Holyoke, Mass., U.S.A. 162 42 14N 72 37W
Holyoke, Nebr., U.S.A. 158 40 39N 102 18W
Holyrood 151 47 27N 53 8W
Holywell 31 53 16N 3 14W
Holywood 38 54 38N 5 50W
Holzminden 48 51 49N 9 31 E
Homa Bay 126 0 36S 34 22 E
Homa Bay □ 126 0 50S 34 30 E
Homalin 98 24 55N 95 0 E
Homberg 48 51 2N 9 20 E
Hombori 121 15 20N 1 38W
Homburg 49 49 19N 7 21 E
Home B. 149 68 40N 67 10W
Home Hill 138 19 43S 147 25 E
Homedale 160 43 42N 116 59W
Homer, Alaska, U.S.A. 147 59 40N 151 35W
Homer, La., U.S.A. 159 32 50N 93 4W
Homestead, Austral. 138 20 20S 145 40 E
Homestead, U.S.A. 157 25 29N 80 27W
Hominy 159 36 26N 96 24W
Homnabad 96 17 45N 77 5 E
Homoine 129 23 55S 35 8 E
Homorod 70 46 5N 25 15 E
Homs = Al Khums 119 32 40N 14 17 E
Homs (Hims) 92 34 40N 36 45 E
Hon Chong 101 10 16N 104 38 E
Hon Me 100 19 23N 105 56 E
Honan □ 106 34 10N 113 10 E
Honbetsu 112 43 7N 143 37 E
Honda 174 5 12N 74 45W
Hondeklipbaai 125 30 19S 17 17 E
Hondo, Japan 110 32 27N 130 12 E
Hondo, U.S.A. 159 29 22N 99 6W
Hondo, R. 165 18 25N 88 21W
Honduras ■ 166 14 40N 86 30W
Honduras, Golfo de 166 16 50N 87 0W
Hönefoss 71 60 10N 10 12 E
Honey L. 160 40 13N 120 14W
Honfleur 42 49 25N 0 13 E
Hōng 73 55 30N 11 14 E
Hong Gai 100 20 57N 107 5 E
Hong Kong ■ 109 22 11N 114 14 E

Hong, R.	100	20 17N	106 34 E
Hongchŏn	107	37 44N	127 53 E
Hongha, R.	101	22 0N	104 0 E
Hongor	106	45 56N	112 50 E
Hongsa	100	19 43N	101 20 E
Hongsŏng	107	36 37N	126 38 E
Honguedo, Détroit d'	151	49 15N	64 0W
Hongwon	107	40 0N	127 56 E
Honiara	142	9 30S	160 0 E
Honington	33	52 58N	0 35W
Honiton	30	50 48N	3 11W
Honjo, Akita, Japan	112	39 23N	140 3 E
Honjo, Gumma, Japan	111	36 14N	139 11 E
Honkawane	111	35 5N	138 5 E
Honkorâb, Ras	122	24 35N	35 10 E
Honolulu	147	21 19N	157 52W
Honshū	112	36 0N	138 0 E
Hontoria del Pinar	58	41 50N	3 10W
Hoo	29	51 25N	0 33 E
Hood Mt.	160	45 15N	122 0W
Hood, Pt.	137	34 23S	119 34 E
Hood Pt.	135	10 4S	147 45 E
Hood River	160	45 45N	121 37W
Hoodsport	160	47 24N	123 7W
Hooge	48	54 31N	8 36 E
Hoogerheide	47	51 26N	4 20 E
Hoogeveen	46	52 44N	6 30 E
Hoogeveensche Vaart	46	52 42N	6 12 E
Hoogezand	46	53 11N	6 45 E
Hooghly-Chinsura	95	22 53N	88 27 E
Hooghly, R.	95	21 59N	88 10 E
Hoogkerk	46	53 13N	6 30 E
Hooglede	47	50 59N	3 5 E
Hoogstraten	47	51 24N	4 46 E
Hoogvliet	46	51 52N	4 21 E
Hook	29	51 17N	0 55W
Hook Hd.	39	52 8N	6 57W
Hook I.	138	20 4S	149 0 E
Hook of Holland = Hoek v. Holland	47	52 0N	4 7 E
Hooker	159	36 55N	101 10W
Hooker Cr.	136	18 23S	130 50 E
Hoonah	147	58 15N	135 30W
Hooper Bay	147	61 30N	166 10W
Hoopersville	162	38 16N	76 11W
Hoopeston	156	40 30N	87 40W
Hoopstad	128	27 50S	25 55 E
Höör	73	55 55N	13 33 E
Hoorn	46	52 38N	5 4 E
Hoover Dam	161	36 0N	114 45W
Hop Bottom	162	41 41N	75 47W
Hopà	83	41 28N	41 30 E
Hope, Can.	152	49 25N	121 25 E
Hope, U.K.	31	53 7N	3 2W
Hope, Ark., U.S.A.	159	33 40N	93 30W
Hope, N.D., U.S.A.	158	47 21N	97 42W
Hope Bay	13	65 0S	55 0W
Hope, L.	139	28 24S	139 18 E
Hope L.	37	58 24N	4 38W
Hope Pt.	147	68 20N	166 50W
Hope Town	157	26 30N	76 30W
Hopedale, Can.	151	55 28N	60 13W
Hopedale, U.S.A.	162	42 8N	71 33W
Hopefield	128	33 3S	18 22 E
Hopei □	107	39 25N	116 45 E
Hopelchén	165	19 46N	89 50W
Hopeman	37	57 42N	3 26W
Hopen	71	63 27N	8 2 E
Hopetoun	137	33 57S	120 7 E
Hopetown, Austral.	140	35 42S	142 22 E
Hopetown, S. Afr.	128	29 34S	24 3 E
Hopewell	162	37 18N	77 17W
Hopien-Ts'un	108	27 40N	101 55 E
Hopin	98	21 14N	96 53 E
Hop'ing	109	24 26N	114 56 E
Hopkins	158	40 31N	94 45W
Hopkins, L.	136	24 15S	128 35 E
Hopkinsville	157	36 52N	87 26W
Hopland	160	39 0N	123 7W
Hopo	108	31 24N	99 0 E
Hoptrup	73	55 11N	9 28 E
Hop'u	108	21 41N	109 10 E
Hoquiam	160	46 50N	123 55W
Hōrai	111	34 58N	137 32 E
Horazdovice	52	49 19N	13 42 E
Hörby	73	55 50N	13 44 E
Horcajo de Santiago	58	39 50N	3 1W
Hordaland fylke □	71	60 25N	6 15 E
Horden	33	54 45N	1 17W
Hordern Hills	136	20 40S	130 20 E
Hordio	91	10 36N	51 8 E
Horezu	70	45 6N	24 0 E
Horgen	51	47 15N	8 35 E
Horgoš	66	46 10N	20 0 E
Horice	52	50 21N	15 39 E
Horley	29	51 10N	0 10W
Horlick Mts.	13	84 0S	102 0W
Hormoz	93	27 35N	55 0 E
Hormuz, I.	93	27 8N	56 28 E
Hormuz Str.	93	26 30N	56 30 E
Horn, Austria	52	48 39N	15 40 E
Horn, Isafjarðarsýsla, Iceland	74	66 28N	22 28W
Horn, Suður-Múlasýsla, Iceland	74	65 10N	13 31W
Horn, Neth.	47	51 12N	5 57 E
Horn, Cape = Hornos, C. de	176	55 50S	67 30W
Horn Head	38	55 13N	8 0W
Horn I., Austral.	138	10 37S	142 17 E
Horn I., P.N.G.	135	10 35S	142 20 E
Horn, I.	157	30 17N	88 40W
Horn Mts.	152	62 15N	119 15W
Horn, R.	152	61 30N	118 1W
Hornachuelos	57	37 50N	5 14W
Hornavan	74	66 15N	17 30 E
Hornbæk, Frederiksborg, Denmark	73	56 5N	12 26 E
Hornbæk, Viborg, Denmark	73	56 28N	9 58 E
Hornbeck	159	31 22N	93 20W
Hornbrook	160	41 58N	122 37W
Hornburg	48	52 2N	10 36 E
Hornby	143	43 33S	172 33 E
Horncastle	33	53 13N	0 8W
Horndal	72	60 18N	16 23 E
Horndean	29	50 56N	1 5W
Hornell	156	42 23N	77 41W
Hornell L.	152	62 20N	119 25W
Hornepayne	150	49 14N	84 48W
Hornindal	71	61 58N	6 30 E
Horningsham	28	51 11N	2 16W
Hornitos	163	37 30N	120 14W
Hornnes	71	58 34N	7 45 E
Hornos, Cabo de	176	55 50S	67 30W
Hornoy	43	49 50N	1 54 E
Hornsberg, Jamtland, Sweden	72	63 14N	14 40 E
Hornsberg, Kronobergs, Sweden	72	56 37N	13 47 E
Hornsby	141	33 42S	151 2 E
Hornsea	33	53 55N	0 10W
Hornslandet Pen.	72	61 35N	17 37 E
Hornslet	73	56 18N	10 19 E
Hornu	47	50 26N	3 50 E
Hörnum	73	54 44N	8 18 E
Horovice	52	49 48N	13 53 E
Horqueta	172	23 15S	56 55W
Horra, La	56	41 44N	3 53W
Horred	73	57 22N	12 28 E
Horse Cr.	158	41 33N	104 45W
Horse Is.	151	50 15N	55 50W
Horsefly L.	152	52 25N	121 0W
Horseheads	162	42 10N	76 49W
Horseleap	38	53 25N	7 34W
Horsens	73	55 52N	9 51 E
Horsens Fjord	73	55 50N	10 0 E
Horseshoe	137	25 27S	118 31 E
Horseshoe Dam	161	33 45N	111 35W
Horsforth	33	53 50N	1 39W
Horsham, Austral.	140	36 44S	142 13 E
Horsham, U.K.	29	51 4N	0 20W
Horsham St. Faith	29	52 41N	1 15 E
Horsovsky Tyn	52	49 31N	12 58 E
Horst	47	51 27N	6 3 E
Horsted Keynes	29	51 2N	0 1W
Horten	71	59 25N	10 32 E
Hortobágy, R.	53	47 30N	21 6 E
Horton	158	39 42N	95 30W
Horton-in-Ribblesdale	32	54 9N	2 19W
Horton, R.	147	69 56N	126 52W
Hörvik	73	56 2N	14 45 E
Horw	51	47 1N	8 19 E
Horwich	32	53 37N	2 33W
Horwood, L.	150	48 10N	82 20W
Hosaina	123	7 30N	37 47 E
Hosdurga	97	13 40N	76 17 E
Hose, Pegunungan	102	2 5N	114 6 E
Hoshan	109	31 24N	116 20 E
Hoshangabad	94	22 45N	77 45 E
Hoshiarpur	94	31 30N	75 58 E
Hoshui	106	36 0N	107 59 E
Hoshun	106	37 19N	113 34 E
Hosingen	47	50 1N	6 6 E
Hoskins	135	5 29S	150 27 E
Hosmer	158	45 36N	99 29W
Hososhima	110	32 26N	131 40 E
Hospental	51	46 37N	8 34 E
Hospet	97	15 15N	76 20 E
Hospital	39	52 30N	8 28W
Hospitalet de Llobregat	58	41 21N	2 6 E
Hospitalet, L'	44	42 36N	1 47 E
Hoste, I.	176	55 0S	69 0W
Hostens	44	44 30N	0 40W
Hoswick	36	60 0N	1 15W
Hot	100	18 8N	98 29 E
Hot Creek Ra.	160	39 0N	116 0W
Hot Springs, Ark, U.S.A.	159	34 30N	93 0W
Hot Springs, S.D., U.S.A.	158	43 25N	103 30W
Hotagen, L.	74	63 50N	14 30 E
Hotazel	128	27 17S	23 00 E
Hotchkiss	161	38 55N	107 47W
Hotham, C.	136	12 2S	131 18 E
Hot'ien	105	37 7N	79 55 E
Hoting	74	64 8N	16 15 E
Hotolishti	68	41 10N	20 25 E
Hotse	106	35 14N	115 27 E
Hotte, Massif de la	167	18 30N	73 45W
Hottentotsbaai	128	26 8S	14 59 E
Hotton	47	50 16N	5 26 E
Houat, I.	42	47 24N	2 58W
Houck	161	35 15N	109 15W
Houdan	43	48 48N	1 35 E
Houdeng-Goegnies	47	50 29N	4 10 E
Houei Sai	100	20 18N	100 26 E
Houffalize	47	50 8N	5 48 E
Houghton	158	47 9N	88 39W
Houghton L.	156	44 20N	84 40W
Houghton-le-Spring	35	54 51N	1 28W
Houghton Regis	29	51 54N	0 32W
Houhora	142	34 49S	173 9 E
Houille, R.	47	50 8N	4 50 E
Houlton	151	46 5N	68 0W
Houma	159	29 35N	90 50W
Houmt Souk = Djerba	119	33 53N	10 37 E
Houndé	120	11 34N	3 31W
Hounslow	29	51 29N	0 20W
Hourn L.	36	57 7N	5 35W
Hourtin	44	45 11N	1 4W
Housatonic, R.	162	41 10N	73 7W
Houston, Can.	152	54 25N	126 30W
Houston, Mo., U.S.A.	159	37 20N	92 0W
Houston, Tex., U.S.A.	159	29 50N	95 20W
Houten	46	52 2N	5 10 E
Houthalen	47	51 2N	5 23 E
Houthem	47	50 48N	2 57 E
Houthulst	47	50 59N	2 57 E
Houtman Abrolhos	137	28 43S	113 48 E
Houyet	47	50 11N	5 1 E
Hova	73	58 53N	14 14 E
Høvag	71	58 10N	8 15 E
Hövåg	71	58 10N	8 16 E
Hovd	105	48 1N	91 39 E
Hovden	71	59 33N	7 22 E
Hove	29	50 50N	0 10W
Hoveton	29	52 45N	1 23 E
Hovingham	33	54 10N	0 59W
Hovmantorp	73	56 47N	15 7 E
Hövsgöl	106	43 37N	109 39 E
Hovsta	72	59 22N	15 15 E
Howakil	123	15 10N	40 16 E
Howar, W., (Shau)	123	17 0N	25 30 E
Howard, Austral.	139	25 16S	152 32 E
Howard, Kans., U.S.A.	159	37 30N	96 16W
Howard, S.D., U.S.A.	158	44 2N	97 30W
Howard I.	138	12 10S	135 24 E
Howard L.	153	62 15N	105 57W
Howatharra	137	28 29S	114 33 E
Howden	33	53 45N	0 52W
Howe	160	43 48N	113 0W
Howe, C.	141	37 30S	150 0 E
Howell	156	42 38N	84 0W
Howick, N.Z.	142	36 54S	174 48 E
Howick, S. Afr.	129	29 28S	30 14 E
Howick Group	138	14 20S	145 30 E
Howitt, L.	139	27 40S	138 40 E
Howley	151	49 12N	57 2W
Howmore	36	57 18N	7 23W
Howrah	95	22 37N	88 27 E
Howth	38	53 23N	6 3W
Howth Hd.	38	53 21N	6 0W
Hoxne	29	52 22N	1 11 E
Höxter	48	51 45N	9 26 E
Hoy I.	37	58 50N	3 15W
Hoy Sd.	37	58 57N	3 20W
Hoya	48	52 47N	9 10 E
Høyanger	71	61 25N	6 50 E
Höydalsmo	71	59 30N	8 15 E
Hoyerswerda	48	51 26N	14 14 E
Hoylake	32	53 24N	3 11W
Höyland	71	58 50N	5 43 E
Hoyleton	140	34 2S	138 34 E
Hoyos	56	40 9N	6 45W
Hoyüan	109	23 50N	114 40 E
Hpawlum	98	27 12N	98 12 E
Hpettintha	98	24 14N	95 23 E
Hpizow	98	26 57N	98 24 E
Hpungan Pass	99	27 30N	96 55 E
Hrádec Králové	52	50 15N	15 50 E
Hrádek	53	48 46N	16 16 E
Hranice	53	49 34N	17 45 E
Hron, R.	53	48 0N	18 4 E
Hrubieszów	54	50 49N	23 51 E
Hrubý Nizký Jeseník	53	50 7N	17 10 E
Hrvatska	63	45 20N	16 0 E
Hsenwi	98	23 22N	97 55 E
Hsi Chiang, R.	109	22 20N	113 20 E
Hsiach'engtzu, Heilungkiang, China	107	44 41N	130 27 E
Hsiach'engtzu, Schechwan, China	108	29 24N	101 46 E
Hsiachiang	109	27 33N	115 10 E
Hsiaching	106	36 57N	115 59 E
Hsiach'uan Shan	109	21 40N	112 37 E
Hsiahsien	106	35 12N	111 11 E
Hsiai	106	34 17N	116 11 E
Hsiakuan	108	25 39N	100 9 E
Hsiamen	109	24 30N	118 7 E
Hsian	106	34 17N	109 0 E
Hsiang Chiang, R.	109	29 30N	113 10 E
Hsiangch'eng, Honan, China	106	33 50N	113 29 E
Hsiangch'eng, Honan, China	106	33 13N	114 50 E
Hsiangch'eng, Szechwan, China	108	29 0N	99 46 E
Hsiangchou	108	23 58N	109 41 E
Hsiangfan	109	32 7N	112 9 E
Hsianghsiang	109	27 46N	112 30 E
Hsiangning	106	36 1N	110 47 E
Hsiangshan	109	29 18N	121 37 E
Hsiangshuik'ou	107	34 12N	119 34 E
Hsiangt'an	109	27 55N	112 52 E
Hsiangtu	108	23 14N	106 57 E
Hsiangyang	109	32 2N	112 6 E
Hsiangyin	109	28 40N	112 53 E
Hsiangyüan	106	36 32N	113 2 E
Hsiangyün	108	25 29N	100 35 E
Hsiaochin	108	31 1N	102 23 E
Hsiaofeng	109	30 36N	119 33 E
Hsiaohsien	106	34 2N	116 56 E
Hsiaohsinganling Shanmo	105	48 45N	127 0 E
Hsiaoi	106	37 7N	111 46 E
Hsiaokan	109	30 57N	113 53 E
Hsiaoshan	109	30 10N	120 15 E
Hsiaot'ai Shan	107	36 18N	116 38 E
Hsiap'u	109	26 58N	119 57 E
Hsiawa	107	42 38N	120 31 E
Hsich'ang	108	27 50N	102 18 E
Hsichieht'o	108	30 24N	108 13 E
Hsich'uan	109	33 0N	111 24 E
Hsich'ung	108	31 0N	105 48 E
Hsiehch'eng	107	34 48N	117 15 E
Hsiehmaho	109	31 38N	111 12 E
Hsienchü	109	28 51N	120 44 E
Hsienfeng	108	29 40N	109 7 E
Hsienhsien	106	38 2N	116 12 E
Hsienning	109	29 51N	114 15 E
Hsienshui Ho, R.	108	30 5N	101 5 E
Hsienyang	106	34 22N	108 48 E
Hsienyu	109	25 24N	118 40 E
Hsifei Ho, R.	109	32 38N	116 39 E
Hsifeng, Kweichow, China	108	27 5N	106 42 E
Hsifeng, Liaoning, China	107	42 44N	124 42 E
Hsifengchen	106	35 40N	107 42 E
Hsifengk'ou	107	40 24N	118 19 E
Hsiho	106	34 2N	105 12 E
Hsihsia, Honan, China	106	33 30N	111 30 E
Hsihsia, Shantung, China	107	37 25N	120 48 E
Hsihsiang	108	33 1N	107 40 E
Hsihsien, Honan, China	109	32 24N	114 52 E
Hsihsien, Shensi, China	106	36 41N	110 56 E
Hsihua	106	33 47N	114 31 E
Hsilamunlun Ho, R.	107	43 24N	123 42 E
Hsiliao Ho, R.	107	43 24N	123 42 E
Hsilin	108	24 30N	105 3 E
Hsin Chiang, R.	109	28 50N	116 40 E
Hsin Ho, R.	107	43 33N	123 31 E
Hsinchan	107	43 52N	127 20 E
Hsinch'ang	109	29 30N	120 54 E
Hsincheng	106	34 25N	113 46 E
Hsinch'eng, Hopei, China	106	39 15N	115 59 E
Hsinch'eng, Kwangsi-Chuang, China	108	24 4N	108 40 E
Hsinchiang	106	35 40N	111 15 E
Hsinchien	109	28 58N	102 47 E
Hsinchin	107	39 25N	121 59 E
Hsinching	108	30 25N	103 49 E
Hsinchi'u	107	41 53N	119 40 E
Hsinchou	109	30 52N	114 48 E
Hsinchu	109	24 48N	120 58 E
Hsinfeng, Kiangsi, China	109	25 27N	114 58 E
Hsinfeng, Kiangsi, China	109	26 7N	116 11 E
Hsinfeng, Kwangtung, China	109	24 4N	114 12 E
Hsingan	109	25 39N	110 39 E
Hsingch'eng	107	40 40N	120 48 E
Hsingho	106	40 52N	113 58 E
Hsinghsien	106	38 31N	111 4 E
Hsinghua	107	32 55N	119 52 E
Hsinghua Wan	109	25 20N	119 20 E
Hsingi	108	25 5N	104 55 E
Hsinging	109	26 25N	110 44 E
Hsingjen	108	25 25N	105 13 E
Hsingjenp'ao	106	37 0N	105 0 E
Hsingkuo	109	26 26N	115 16 E
Hsinglung	107	40 29N	117 32 E
Hsingning	109	24 8N	115 43 E
Hsingp'ing	106	34 18N	108 26 E
Hsingshan	109	31 10N	110 51 E
Hsingt'ai	106	37 5N	114 38 E
Hsingyeh	108	22 45N	109 52 E
Hsinhailien = Lienyünchiangshih	107	34 37N	119 13 E
Hsinhsiang	106	35 15N	113 54 E
Hsinhsien, Shansi, China	106	38 24N	112 47 E
Hsinhsien, Shantung, China	106	36 15N	115 40 E
Hsinhsing	109	22 45N	112 11 E
Hsinhua	109	27 43N	111 18 E
Hsinhui	109	22 32N	113 0 E
Hsini	109	22 12N	110 53 E
Hsining	105	36 37N	101 46 E
Hsink'ai Ho, R.	107	41 10N	122 5 E
Hsinkan	109	27 45N	115 21 E
Hsinkao Shan	109	23 25N	120 52 E
Hsinlit'un	107	42 2N	122 19 E
Hsinlo	106	38 15N	114 50 E
Hsinmin	107	42 0N	122 52 E
Hsinpaoan	106	40 27N	115 23 E
Hsinpin	107	41 43N	125 2 E
Hsinp'ing	108	24 6N	101 58 E
Hsinshao	109	27 20N	111 26 E
Hsint'ai	107	35 54N	117 44 E
Hsint'ien	109	25 56N	112 13 E
Hsints'ai	109	32 44N	114 59 E
Hsinyang	109	32 10N	114 6 E
Hsinyeh	109	37 31N	112 21 E
Hsinyü	109	27 48N	114 56 E
Hsipaw	98	22 37N	97 18 E
Hsip'ing, Honan, China	106	33 34N	110 45 E
Hsip'ing, Honan, China	106	33 23N	114 2 E
Hsishni	109	30 27N	115 15 E
Hsitalahai	106	40 38N	109 38 E
Hsiu Shui, R.	109	29 13N	116 0 E
Hsiujen	109	24 26N	110 14 E
Hsiunghsien	106	38 50N	116 11 E
Hsiungyüeh	107	40 12N	122 12 E
Hsiuning	109	29 51N	118 15 E
Hsiushan	108	28 27N	108 59 E
Hsiushui	109	29 2N	114 34 E

Hsiuwen **Ibara**

Hsiuwen	**108**	26 52N	106 35 E
Hsiuyen	**107**	40 19N	123 15 E
Hsiyang	**106**	37 27N	113 46 E
Hsüanch'eng	**109**	30 54N	118 41 E
Hsüanen	**108**	29 59N	109 24 E
Hsüanhan	**108**	31 25N	107 38 E
Hsüanhua	**106**	40 38N	115 5 E
Hsüanwei	**108**	26 13N	104 5 E
Hsüch'ang	**106**	34 1N	113 53 E
Hsüchou	**107**	34 15N	117 10 E
Hsüehfeng Shan	**109**	27 0N	110 30 E
Hsüehweng Shan	**109**	24 24N	121 12 E
Hsun Chiang, R.	**109**	23 30N	111 30 E
Hsünhsien	**106**	35 40N	114 32 E
Hsüni	**106**	35 6N	108 20 E
Hsüntien	**108**	25 33N	103 15 E
Hsünwu	**109**	24 57N	115 28 E
Hsünyang	**108**	32 48N	109 27 E
Hsüp'u	**109**	27 56N	110 36 E
Hsüshui	**106**	39 1N	115 39 E
Hsüwen	**109**	20 20N	110 9 E
Hsüyung	**108**	28 6N	105 21 E
Htawgaw	**98**	25 57N	98 23 E
Hua Hin	**100**	12 34N	99 58 E
Huaan	**109**	25 1N	117 33 E
Huachacalla	**164**	18 45 S	68 17W
Huachinera	**164**	30 9N	108 55W
Huachipato	**172**	36 45 S	73 09W
Huacho	**174**	11 10 S	77 35W
Huachón	**174**	10 35 S	76 0W
Huachou	**109**	21 38N	110 35 E
Huacrachuco	**174**	8 35 S	76 50W
Huahsien, Honan, China	**106**	35 33N	114 34 E
Huahsien, Shensi, China	**106**	34 31N	109 46 E
Huai Yot	**101**	7 45N	99 37 E
Huaiachen	**106**	40 33N	114 30 E
Huaian, Hopei, China	**106**	40 33N	114 30 E
Huaian, Kiangsu, China	**107**	33 31N	119 8 E
Huaichi	**109**	24 0N	112 8 E
Huaihua	**109**	27 34N	109 56 E
Huaijen	**106**	39 50N	113 7 E
Huaijou	**106**	40 20N	116 37 E
Huainan	**109**	32 39N	117 2 E
Huaining	**109**	30 21N	116 42 E
Huaite	**107**	43 30N	124 50 E
Huaitechen	**107**	43 52N	124 45 E
Huaiyang	**106**	33 50N	115 2 E
Huaiyüan, Anhwei, China	**109**	32 58N	117 13 E
Huaiyüan, Kwangsi-Chuang, China	**108**	24 36N	108 27 E
Huajuapan	**165**	17 50N	98 0W
Huajung	**109**	29 34N	112 34 E
Hualien	**109**	24 0N	121 30 E
Huallaga, R.	**174**	5 30 S	76 10W
Hualpai Pk.	**161**	35 8N	113 58W
Huan Chiang, R.	**106**	36 4N	107 40 E
Huancabamba	**174**	5 10 S	79 15W
Huancané	**174**	15 10 S	69 50W
Huancapi	**174**	13 25 S	74 0W
Huancavelica	**174**	12 50 S	75 5W
Huancayo	**174**	12 5 S	75 0W
Huanchiang	**108**	24 50N	108 15 E
Huang Ho, R.	**107**	36 50N	118 20 E
Huangchiakopa	**106**	40 20N	109 18 E
Huangch'uan	**109**	32 8N	115 4 E
Huanghsien, Hunen, China	**108**	27 22N	109 10 E
Huanghsien, Shantung, China	**107**	37 38N	120 30 E
Huangkang	**109**	30 27N	114 50 E
Huanglienp'u	**108**	25 32N	99 44 E
Huangling	**106**	35 36N	109 17 E
Huangliu	**105**	18 20N	108 50 E
Huanglung	**106**	35 37N	109 58 E
Huanglungt'an	**109**	32 38N	110 33 E
Huangmei	**109**	30 4N	115 56 E
Huangshih	**109**	30 10N	115 2 E
Huangt'uan	**107**	36 55N	121 41 E
Huangyang	**106**	37 27N	111 42 E
Huangyen	**109**	28 37N	121 12 E
Huanhsien	**106**	36 32N	107 10 E
Huaning	**108**	24 12N	102 55 E
Huanjen	**107**	41 16N	125 21 E
Huanp'ing	**108**	26 54N	107 55 E
Huant'ai	**107**	36 57N	118 5 E
Huánuco	**174**	9 55 S	76 15W
Huap'ing	**108**	26 37N	101 13 E
Huap'itientzu	**107**	43 30N	130 2 E
Huaraz	**174**	9 30 S	77 32W
Huarmey	**174**	10 5 S	78 5W
Huasamota	**164**	22 30N	104 30W
Huascarán	**174**	9 0 S	77 30W
Huasco	**172**	28 24 S	71 15W
Huasco, R.	**172**	28 27 S	71 13W
Huasna	**163**	35 6N	120 24W
Huatabampo	**164**	26 50N	109 50W
Huate	**106**	41 57N	114 4 E
Huatien	**107**	42 58N	126 50 E
Huauchinango	**165**	20 11N	98 3W
Huautla	**164**	18 20N	96 50W
Huautla de Jiménez	**165**	18 8N	96 51W
Huay Namota	**164**	21 56N	104 30W
Huayin	**106**	34 36N	110 2 E
Huayllay	**174**	11 03 S	76 21W
Huayüan	**108**	28 30N	109 25 E
Hubbard	**159**	31 50N	96 50W
Hubbart Pt.	**153**	59 21N	94 41W
Hubli-Dharwar	**97**	15 22N	75 15 E
Huchang	**107**	41 25N	127 2 E
Huchuetenango	**164**	15 25N	91 30W
Hückelhoven-Ratheim	**48**	51 6N	6 3 E
Hucknall	**33**	53 3N	1 12W
Huddersfield	**33**	53 38N	1 49W
Hudi	**122**	17 43N	34 28 E
Hudiksvall	**72**	61 43N	17 10 E
Hudson, Can.	**153**	50 6N	92 09W
Hudson, Mich., U.S.A.	**156**	41 50N	84 20W
Hudson, N.H., U.S.A.	**162**	42 46N	71 26W
Hudson, N.Y., U.S.A.	**162**	42 15N	73 46W
Hudson, Wis., U.S.A.	**158**	44 57N	92 45W
Hudson, Wyo., U.S.A.	**160**	42 54N	108 37W
Hudson B.	**153**	59 0N	91 0W
Hudson Bay, Can.	**149**	60 0N	86 0W
Hudson Bay, Sask., Can.	**153**	52 51N	102 23W
Hudson Falls	**162**	43 18N	73 34W
Hudson, R.	**162**	40 42N	74 2W
Hudson Str.	**148**	62 0N	70 0W
Hudson's Hope	**152**	56 0N	121 54W
Hué	**100**	16 30N	107 35 E
Huebra, R.	**56**	40 54N	6 28W
Huedin	**70**	46 52N	23 2 E
Huehuetenango	**166**	15 20N	91 28W
Huejúcar	**164**	22 21N	103 13W
Huelgoat	**42**	48 22N	3 46W
Huelma	**59**	37 39N	3 28W
Huelva	**57**	37 18N	6 57W
Huelva □	**57**	37 40N	7 0W
Huelva, R.	**57**	37 46N	6 15W
Huentelauquén	**172**	31 38 S	71 33W
Huércal Overa	**59**	37 23N	1 57W
Huerta, Sa. de la	**172**	31 10 S	67 30W
Huertas, C. de las	**59**	38 21N	0 24W
Huerva, R.	**58**	41 13N	1 15W
Huesca	**58**	42 8N	0 25W
Huesca □	**58**	42 20N	0 1 E
Huéscar	**59**	37 44N	2 35W
Huétamo	**164**	18 36N	100 54W
Huete	**58**	40 10N	2 43W
Hugh, R.	**138**	25 1 S	134 10 E
Hugh Town	**30**	49 55N	6 19W
Hughenden	**138**	20 52 S	144 10 E
Hughes, Austral.	**137**	30 42 S	129 31 E
Hughes, U.S.A.	**147**	66 0N	154 20W
Hughesville	**162**	41 14N	76 44W
Hugo, Colo., U.S.A.	**158**	39 12N	103 27W
Hugo, Okla., U.S.A.	**159**	34 0N	95 30W
Hugoton	**159**	37 18N	101 22W
Huhehot = Huhohaot'e	**106**	40 50N	110 39 E
Huhohaot'e	**106**	40 50N	110 39 E
Huhsien	**106**	34 8N	108 34 E
Huian	**109**	25 4N	118 47 E
Huianp'u	**106**	37 30N	106 40 E
Huiarau Ra.	**142**	38 45 S	176 55 E
Huich'ang	**109**	25 32N	115 45 E
Huichapán	**165**	20 24N	99 40W
Huichou	**109**	23 5N	114 24 E
Huifa Ho, R.	**107**	43 6N	126 53 E
Huihsien, Honan, China	**106**	35 32N	113 54 E
Huihsien, Kansu, China	**106**	33 46N	106 6 E
Huila	**128**	15 30 S	15 0 E
Huila □	**174**	2 30N	75 45W
Huila, Nevado del	**174**	3 0N	76 0W
Huilai	**109**	23 4N	116 18 E
Huili	**108**	26 39N	102 11 E
Huimin	**107**	37 29N	117 29 E
Huinan	**107**	42 40N	126 5 E
Huinca Renancó	**172**	34 51 S	64 22W
Huining	**106**	35 41N	105 8 E
Huinung	**106**	39 0N	106 45 E
Huiroa	**142**	39 15 S	174 30 E
Huise	**47**	50 54N	3 36 E
Huishui	**108**	26 8N	106 35 E
Huissen	**46**	51 57N	5 57 E
Huiting	**106**	34 6N	116 4 E
Huitse	**108**	26 22N	103 15 E
Huit'ung	**108**	26 56N	109 36 E
Huixtla	**165**	15 9N	92 28W
Huiya	**92**	24 40N	49 15 E
Huizen	**46**	52 18N	5 14 E
Hukawng Valley	**99**	26 30N	96 30 E
Hukou	**109**	29 45N	116 13 E
Hukuma	**123**	14 55N	36 2 E
Hukuntsi	**128**	23 58 S	21 45 E
Hula	**123**	6 33N	38 30 E
Hulaifa	**92**	25 58N	41 0 E
Hulan	**105**	46 0N	126 44 E
Huld	**106**	45 5N	105 30 E
Hülda	**90**	31 50N	34 51 E
Hull, Can.	**150**	45 20N	75 40W
Hull, U.K.	**33**	53 45N	0 20W
Hullavington	**28**	51 31N	2 9W
Hulme End	**32**	53 8N	1 51W
Hulst	**47**	51 17N	4 2 E
Hultsfred	**73**	57 30N	15 52 E
Hulun Ch'ih	**105**	49 1N	117 32 E
Humacao	**147**	18 9N	65 50W
Humahuaca	**172**	23 10 S	65 25W
Humaitá	**174**	7 35 S	62 40W
Humaita	**172**	27 2 S	58 31W
Humansdorp	**128**	34 2 S	24 46 E
Humber, Mouth of	**33**	53 32N	0 8 E
Humber, R.	**33**	53 40N	0 10W
Humberside □	**33**	53 50N	0 30W
Humbert River	**136**	16 30 S	130 45 E
Humble	**159**	29 59N	95 10W
Humboldt, Can.	**153**	52 15N	105 9W
Humboldt, Iowa, U.S.A.	**158**	42 42N	94 15W
Humboldt, Tenn., U.S.A.	**157**	35 50N	88 55W
Humboldt Gletscher	**12**	79 30N	62 0W
Humboldt, R.	**160**	40 55N	116 0W
Humbolt Mts.	**143**	44 30 S	168 15 E
Hume	**163**	36 48N	118 54W
Hume, L.	**141**	36 0 S	147 0 E
Humenné	**53**	48 55N	21 50 E
Humphreys, Mt.	**163**	37 17N	118 40W
Humphreys Pk.	**161**	35 24N	111 38W
Humpolec	**52**	49 31N	15 20 E
Humshaugh	**35**	55 3N	2 8W
Humula	**141**	35 30 S	147 46 E
Hün	**119**	29 2N	16 0 E
Hun Chiang, R.	**107**	40 52N	125 42 E
Huna Floi	**74**	65 50N	20 50W
Hunan □	**109**	27 30N	111 30 E
Hunch'un	**107**	42 52N	130 21 E
Hundested	**73**	55 58N	11 52 E
Hundred House	**31**	52 11N	3 17W
Hundred Mile House	**152**	51 38N	121 18W
Hundshögen, mt.	**72**	62 57N	13 46 E
Hunedoara	**70**	45 40N	22 50 E
Hunedoara □	**70**	45 45N	22 54 E
Hünfeld	**48**	50 40N	9 47 E
Hung Chiang, R.	**108**	27 7N	109 57 E
Hung Ho, R.	**109**	32 24N	115 32 E
Hung Liu Ho, R.	**106**	38 3N	109 10 E
Hung Yen	**100**	20 39N	106 4 E
Hungan	**109**	31 18N	114 33 E
Hungary ■	**53**	47 20N	19 20 E
Hungary, Plain of	**16**	47 0N	20 0 E
Hungchiang	**109**	27 6N	110 0 E
Hungerford, Austral.	**139**	28 58 S	144 24 E
Hungerford, U.K.	**28**	51 25N	1 30W
Hunghai Wan	**109**	22 45N	115 15 E
Hunghu	**109**	29 49N	113 30 E
Hüngnam	**107**	39 55N	127 45 E
Hungshui Ho, R.	**108**	23 24N	110 12 E
Hungtech'eng	**106**	36 48N	107 6 E
Hungt'ou Hsü	**109**	22 4N	121 25 E
Hungt'se Hu	**107**	33 15N	118 45 E
Hungtung	**106**	36 15N	111 37 E
Hungya	**108**	29 56N	103 25 E
Hungyüan	**108**	32 46N	102 42 E
Huni Valley	**120**	5 33N	1 56W
Hunmanby	**33**	54 12N	0 19W
Hunsberge	**128**	27 58 S	17 5 E
Hunsrück, mts.	**49**	50 0N	7 30 E
Hunstanton	**29**	52 57N	0 30 E
Hunsur	**97**	12 16N	76 16 E
Hunte, R.	**48**	52 47N	8 28 E
Hunter, N.Z.	**143**	44 36 S	171 2 E
Hunter, N.D., U.S.A.	**158**	47 12N	97 17W
Hunter, N.Y., U.S.A.	**162**	42 13N	74 13W
Hunter Hills, The	**143**	44 26 S	170 46 E
Hunter, I.	**138**	40 30 S	144 54 E
Hunter I.	**152**	51 55N	128 0W
Hunter Mts.	**143**	45 43 S	167 25 E
Hunter, R.	**143**	44 21 S	169 27 E
Hunter Ra.	**141**	32 45 S	150 15 E
Hunters Road	**127**	19 9 S	29 49 E
Hunterston	**34**	55 43N	4 55W
Hunterton	**139**	26 12 S	148 30 E
Hunterville	**142**	39 56 S	175 35 E
Huntingburg	**156**	38 20N	86 58W
Huntingdon, Can.	**150**	45 10N	74 10W
Huntingdon, U.K.	**29**	52 20N	0 11W
Huntingdon, N.Y., U.S.A.	**162**	40 52N	73 25W
Huntingdon, Pa., U.S.A.	**156**	40 28N	78 1W
Huntingdon & Peterborough (□)	**26**	52 23N	0 10W
Huntingdon I.	**151**	53 48N	56 45W
Huntington, U.K.	**33**	54 0N	1 4W
Huntington, Id., U.S.A.	**160**	44 22N	117 21W
Huntington, Ind., U.S.A.	**156**	40 52N	85 30W
Huntington, Ut., U.S.A.	**160**	39 24N	111 1W
Huntington, W. Va., U.S.A.	**156**	38 20N	82 30W
Huntington Beach	**163**	33 40N	118 0W
Huntington Park	**161**	34 58N	118 15W
Huntly, N.Z.	**142**	37 34 S	175 11 E
Huntly, U.K.	**37**	57 27N	2 48W
Huntsville, Can.	**150**	45 20N	79 14W
Huntsville, Ala., U.S.A.	**157**	34 45N	86 35W
Huntsville, Tex., U.S.A.	**159**	30 50N	95 35W
Hunyani Dams.	**127**	18 0 S	31 10 E
Hunyani, R.	**127**	18 0 S	31 10 E
Hunyüan	**106**	39 44N	113 42 E
Hunza, R.	**95**	36 24N	75 12 E
Huohsien	**106**	36 38N	111 43 E
Huon, G.	**135**	7 0 S	147 30 E
Huon Pen.	**135**	6 20 S	147 30 E
Huong Hoa	**100**	16 37N	106 45 E
Huong Khe	**100**	18 13N	105 41 E
Huonville	**138**	43 0 S	147 5 E
Huoshaop'u	**107**	43 23N	130 26 E
Hupei □	**109**	31 5N	113 5 E
Hurbanovo	**53**	47 51N	18 11 E
Hurezani	**70**	44 49N	23 40 E
Hurghada	**122**	27 15N	33 50 E
Hŭrghita □	**70**	46 30N	25 30 E
Hŭrghita Mţii	**70**	46 25N	25 35 E
Hurley, N. Mex., U.S.A.	**161**	32 45N	108 7W
Hurley, Wis., U.S.A.	**158**	46 26N	90 10W
Hurlford	**34**	55 35N	4 29W
Hurliness	**37**	58 47N	3 15W
Hurlock	**162**	38 38N	75 52W
Huron, Calif., U.S.A.	**163**	36 12N	120 6W
Huron, S.D., U.S.A.	**158**	44 30N	98 20W
Hurricane	**161**	37 10N	113 12W
Hursley	**28**	51 1N	1 23W
Hurso	**123**	9 35N	41 33 E
Hurstbourne Tarrant	**28**	51 17N	1 27W
Hurstpierpoint	**29**	50 56N	0 11W
Hurum, Buskerud, Norway	**71**	59 36N	10 23 E
Hurum, Oppland, Norway	**71**	61 9N	8 46 E
Hurunui, R.	**143**	42 54 S	173 18 E
Hurup	**73**	56 46N	8 25 E
Husaby	**73**	58 35N	13 25 E
Húsavík	**74**	66 3N	17 21W
Husband's Bosworth	**28**	52 27N	1 3W
Husi	**70**	46 41N	28 7 E
Husinish Pt.	**36**	57 59N	7 6W
Huskvarna	**73**	57 47N	14 15 E
Huslia	**147**	65 40N	156 30W
Husøy	**71**	61 3N	4 44 E
Hussar	**152**	51 3N	112 41W
Hussein (Allenby) Br.	**90**	31 53N	35 33 E
Hustopéce	**53**	48 57N	16 43 E
Husum, Ger.	**48**	54 27N	9 3 E
Husum, Sweden	**72**	63 21N	19 12 E
Hutchinson, Kans., U.S.A.	**159**	38 3N	97 59W
Hutchinson, Minn, U.S.A.	**158**	44 50N	94 22W
Huttenberg	**52**	46 56N	14 33 E
Hüttental	**47**	50 53N	8 1 E
Huttig	**159**	33 5N	92 10W
Hutton, Mt.	**139**	25 51 S	148 20 E
Hutton, oilfield	**19**	61 0N	1 30 E
Hutton Ra.	**137**	24 45 S	124 30 E
Huttwil	**50**	47 7N	7 50 E
Huwarā	**90**	32 9N	35 15 E
Huwun	**123**	4 23N	40 6 E
Huy	**47**	50 31N	5 15 E
Huyton	**32**	53 25N	2 52W
Hvaler	**71**	59 4N	11 1 E
Hvammsfjörður	**74**	65 4N	22 5W
Hvammur	**74**	65 13N	21 49W
Hvar	**63**	43 10N	16 45 E
Hvar, I.	**63**	43 11N	16 28 E
Hvarski Kanal	**63**	43 15N	16 35 E
Hvítá, Arnessýsla, Iceland	**74**	64 0N	20 58W
Hvítá, Mýrasýsla, Iceland	**74**	64 40N	21 5W
Hvítárvatn	**74**	63 37N	19 50W
Hvitsten	**71**	59 35N	10 42 E
Hwachon-chŏsuji	**107**	38 5N	127 50 E
Hwang Ho = Huang Ho, R.	**107**	36 50N	118 20 E
Hwekum	**98**	26 7N	95 22 E
Hyannis, Mass., U.S.A.	**162**	41 39N	70 17W
Hyannis, Nebr., U.S.A.	**158**	41 60N	101 45W
Hyargas Nuur	**105**	49 12N	93 34 E
Hyattsville	**162**	38 59N	76 55W
Hybo	**72**	61 49N	16 15 E
Hydaburg	**147**	55 15N	132 45W
Hyde, N.Z.	**143**	45 18 S	170 16 E
Hyde, U.K.	**32**	53 26N	2 6W
Hyde Park	**162**	41 47N	73 56W
Hyden	**137**	32 24 S	118 46 E
Hyderabad, India	**96**	17 10N	78 29 E
Hyderabad, Pak.	**94**	25 23N	68 36 E
Hyderabad □	**94**	25 3N	68 24 E
Hyères	**45**	43 8N	6 9 E
Hyères, Is. d'	**45**	43 0N	6 28 E
Hyesan	**107**	41 20N	128 10 E
Hyland Post	**139**	57 40N	128 10W
Hyland, R.	**152**	59 52N	128 12W
Hylestad	**71**	59 6N	7 29 E
Hyllested	**71**	56 17N	10 46 E
Hyltebruk	**73**	56 59N	13 15 E
Hymia	**95**	33 40N	78 2 E
Hyndman Pk.	**160**	44 4N	114 0W
Hynish	**34**	56 27N	6 54W
Hynish B.	**34**	56 29N	6 40W
Hyōgo-ken □	**110**	35 15N	135 0 E
Hyrum	**160**	41 35N	111 56W
Hysham	**160**	46 21N	107 11W
Hythe	**29**	51 4N	1 5 E
Hyūga	**110**	32 25N	131 35 E
Hyvinkä	**75**	60 38N	24 50 E

I

I Ho, R.	**107**	34 10N	118 4 E
I-n-Azaoua	**119**	20 45N	7 31 E
I-n-Échaïe	**118**	20 10N	2 5W
I-n-Gall	**121**	6 51N	7 1 E
I-n-Tabedog	**118**	19 54N	1 3 E
Iabès, Erg	**118**	27 30N	2 2W
Iaco, R.	**174**	10 25 S	70 30W
Iaçu	**171**	12 45 S	40 13W
Iakora	**129**	23 6 S	46 40 E
Ialomiţa □	**70**	44 30N	27 30 E
Ianca	**70**	45 6N	27 29 E
Iar Connacht	**39**	53 20N	9 20W
Iara	**70**	46 31N	23 35 E
Iaşi □	**70**	47 20N	27 0 E
Iaşi (Jassy)	**70**	47 10N	27 40 E
Iauaretê	**174**	0 30N	69 5W
Iaucdjovac, (Port Harrison)	**149**	58 25N	78 15W
Iba	**103**	15 22N	120 0 E
Ibadan	**121**	7 22N	3 58 E
Ibagué	**174**	4 27N	73 14W
Ibaiti	**171**	23 50 S	50 10W
Iballja	**68**	42 12N	20 0 E
Ibar, R.	**66**	43 15N	20 40 E
Ibara	**110**	34 36N	133 28 E

Ibaraki-ken □ Inhambane

Ibaraki-ken □ 111 36 10N 140 10E
Ibararaki 111 34 49N 135 34E
Ibarra 174 0 21N 78 7W
Ibba 123 4 49N 29 2E
Ibba, Bahr el 123 5 30N 28 55E
Ibbenbüren 48 52 16N 7 41E
Ibembo 126 2 35N 23 35E
Ibera, Laguna 172 28 30S 57 9W
Iberian Peninsula 16 40 0N 5 0W
Iberville 150 45 19N 73 17W
Iberville, Lac d' 150 55 55N 73 15W
Ibi 121 8 15N 9 50E
Ibiá 171 19 30S 46 30W
Ibicaraí 171 14 51S 39 36W
Ibicuí 171 14 51S 39 59W
Ibicuy 172 33 55S 59 10W
Ibioapaba, Serra da 170 20 14S 40 25W
Ibipetuba 171 11 0S 44 32W
Ibiracu 171 19 50S 40 30W
Ibitiara 171 12 39S 42 13W
Ibiza 59 38 54N 1 26E
Ibiza, I. 59 39 0N 1 30E
Iblei, Monti 65 37 15N 14 45E
Ibo 127 12 22S 40 32E
Ibonma 103 3 22S 133 31E
Ibotirama 171 12 13S 43 12W
Ibriktepe 68 41 2N 26 33E
Ibshawâi 122 29 21N 30 40E
Ibstock 28 52 42N 1 23W
Ibu 103 1 35N 127 25E
Ibuki-Sanchi 111 35 25N 136 34E
Ibŭneşti 70 46 45N 24 50E
Iburg 48 52 10N 8 3E
Ibusuki 110 31 12N 130 32E
Ibwe Munyama 127 16 5S 28 31E
Ica 174 14 0S 75 30W
Ica, R. 174 2 55S 69 0W
Icabarú 174 4 20N 61 45W
Içana 174 1 21N 69 0W
Icatu 170 2 46S 44 4W
Iceland, I. ■ 74 65 0N 19 0W
Icha 77 55 30N 156 0E
Ichang 109 25 25N 112 55E
Ich'ang 109 30 40N 111 20E
Ichchapuram 96 19 10N 84 40E
Icheng 109 32 16N 119 12E
Ich'eng, Hupeh, China 109 31 43N 112 12E
Ich'eng, Shansi, China 106 35 42N 111 40E
Ichihara 111 35 28N 140 5E
Ichikawa 111 35 44N 139 55E
Ichilo, R. 174 16 30S 64 45W
Ichinomiya, Gifu, Japan 111 35 18N 136 48E
Ichinomiya, Kumamoto, Japan 110 32 58N 131 5E
Ichinoseki 112 38 55N 141 8E
Ichŏn 107 37 17N 127 27E
Icht 118 29 6N 8 54W
Ichtegem 47 51 5N 3 1E
Ich'uan 106 36 4N 110 6E
Ich'un 105 47 42N 128 54E
Ichün 106 35 23N 109 7E
Ich'un, Heilungkiang, China 105 47 42N 128 54E
Ich'un, Kiangsi, China 109 27 47N 114 22E
Icó 170 6 24S 38 51W
Icoraci 170 1 18S 48 28W
Icy C. 12 70 25N 162 0W
Icy Str. 153 58 20N 135 30W
Ida Grove 158 42 20N 95 25W
Ida Valley 137 28 42S 120 29E
Idabel 159 33 53N 94 50W
Idaga Hamus 123 14 13N 39 35E
Idah 121 6 10N 6 40E
Idaho □ 160 44 10N 114 0W
Idaho City 160 43 50N 115 52W
Idaho Falls 160 43 30N 112 10W
Idaho Springs 160 39 49N 105 30W
Idanha-a-Nova 56 39 50N 7 15W
Idanre 121 7 8N 5 5E
Idar-Oberstein 49 49 43N 7 19E
Idd el Ghanam 117 11 30N 24 25E
Iddan 91 6 10N 49 5E
Idehan 119 27 10N 11 30E
Idehan Marzūq 119 24 50N 13 51E
Idelès 119 23 58N 5 53E
Idfû 122 25 0N 32 49E
Idhi Oros 69 35 15N 24 45E
Idhra 69 37 20N 23 28E
Idi 102 4 55N 97 45E
Idi Amin Dada, L. 93 0 25S 29 40E
Idiofa 124 4 55S 19 42E
Idkerberget 72 60 22N 15 15E
Idle 33 53 50N 1 45W
Idle, R. 33 53 27N 0 49W
Idmiston 28 51 8N 1 43W
Idna 90 31 34N 34 58E
Idria 163 36 25N 120 41W
Idrija 63 46 0N 14 5E
Idritsa 80 56 25N 28 57E
Idstein 49 50 13N 8 17E
Idsworth 29 50 56N 0 56W
Idutywa 125 32 8S 28 18E
Ieper 47 50 51N 2 53E
Ierápetra 69 35 0N 25 44E
Ierissós 68 40 22N 23 52E
Ierissóu Kólpos 68 40 27N 23 57E
Ierzu 64 39 48N 9 32E
Ieshima-Shotō 110 34 40N 134 32E
Iesi 63 43 32N 13 12E
Ifach, Punta 59 38 38N 0 5E
Ifanadiana 129 21 29S 47 39E
Ife 121 7 30N 4 31E
Iférouâne 121 19 5N 8 35E
Ifni 118 29 25N 10 10W
Ifon 121 6 58N 5 40E
Iga 111 34 45N 136 10E
Iganga 126 0 30N 33 28E
Igarapava 171 20 3S 47 47W
Igarapé Açu 170 1 4S 47 33W
Igarapé-Mirim 170 1 59S 48 58W
Igarka 77 67 30N 87 20E
Igatimi 173 24 5S 55 30W
Igatpuri 96 19 40N 73 35E
Igbetti 121 8 44N 4 8E
Igbo-Ora 121 7 10N 3 15E
Igboho 121 8 40N 3 50E
Iggesund 72 61 39N 17 10E
Igherm 118 30 7N 8 18W
Ighil Izane 118 35 44N 0 31E
Iglene 118 22 57N 4 58E
Iglésias 64 39 19N 8 27E
Igli 118 30 25N 2 12W
Iglino 84 54 50N 56 26E
Igloolik Island 149 69 20N 81 30W
Igma 118 29 9N 6 11W
Igma, Gebel el 122 28 55N 34 0E
Ignace 150 49 30N 91 40W
Igoshevo 81 59 25N 42 35E
Igoumenítsa 68 39 32N 20 18E
Igra 84 57 33N 53 7E
Iguaçu, Cat. del 173 25 41N 54 26W
Iguaçu, R. 173 25 30S 53 10W
Iguala 165 18 20N 99 40W
Igualada 58 41 37N 1 37E
Iguape 171 24 43S 47 33W
Iguape, R. 173 24 40S 48 0W
Iguassu = Iguaçu 173 25 41N 54 26W
Iguatu 170 6 20S 39 18W
Iguéla 124 2 0S 9 16E
Igumale 121 6 47N 7 55E
Igunga □ 126 4 20S 33 45E
Ihiala 121 5 40N 6 55E
Ihosy 129 22 24S 46 8E
Ihotry, L. 129 21 56S 43 41E
Ihsien, Anwhei, China 109 29 53N 117 57E
Ihsien, Hopeh, China 106 39 21N 115 29E
Ihsien, Liaoning, China 107 41 34N 121 15E
Ihsien, Shantung, China 107 37 11N 119 55E
Ihuang 109 27 32N 115 57E
Ii 74 65 15N 25 30E
Iida 111 35 35N 138 0E
Iiey 138 18 53S 141 12E
Iijoki 74 65 20N 26 15E
Iisalmi 74 63 32N 27 10E
Iizuka 110 33 38N 130 42E
Ijebu-Igbo 121 6 56N 4 1E
Ijebu-Ode 121 6 47N 3 52E
IJmuiden 46 52 28N 4 35E
IJssel, R. 46 52 35N 5 50E
IJsselmeer 46 52 45N 5 20E
IJsselmuiden 46 52 34N 5 57E
IJsselstein 46 52 1N 5 2E
Ijuí, R. 173 27 58S 55 20W
Ijūin 110 31 37N 130 24E
IJzendijke 47 51 19N 3 37E
IJzer, R. 47 51 9N 2 44E
Ik, R. 84 55 55N 52 36E
Ikamatua 41 42 15S 171 41E
Ikare 121 7 18N 5 40E
Ikaria, I. 69 37 35N 26 10E
Ikast 73 56 8N 9 10E
Ikawa 111 35 13N 138 15E
Ikeda 111 34 1N 133 48E
Ikeja 121 6 28N 3 45E
Ikela 124 1 0S 23 35E
Ikerre 121 7 25N 5 19E
Ikhtiman 67 42 27N 23 48E
Iki 110 33 45N 129 42E
Iki-Kaikyō 110 33 40N 129 42E
Ikimba L. 126 1 30S 31 20E
Ikire 121 7 10N 4 15E
Ikirun 121 7 54N 4 40E
Ikitsuki-Shima 110 33 23N 129 26E
Ikole 121 7 40N 5 37E
Ikom 121 6 0N 8 42E
Ikopa, R. 129 17 45S 46 40E
Ikot Ekpene 121 5 12N 7 40E
Ikungu 126 1 33S 33 42E
Ikuno 110 35 10N 134 48E
Ila 121 8 0N 4 51E
Ilam 95 26 58N 87 58E
Ilan, China 105 46 14N 129 33E
Ilan, Taiwan 109 24 45N 121 44E
Ilanskiy 77 56 14N 96 3E
Ilanz 51 46 46N 9 12E
Ilaomita, R. 47 44 47N 27 0E
Ilaro Agege 121 6 53N 3 3E
Ilayangudi 97 9 34N 78 37E
Ilbilbie 138 21 45S 149 20E
Ilchester 28 51 0N 2 41W
Ile-à-la Crosse 153 55 27N 107 53W
Ile-à-la-Crosse, Lac 153 55 40N 107 45W
Ile Bouchard, L' 42 47 7N 0 26E
Ile de France □ 43 49 0N 2 20E
Ilebo 124 4 17S 20 47E
Ileje □ 127 9 30S 33 25E
Ilek 84 51 32N 53 21E
Ilek, R. 84 51 30N 53 22E
Ilen R. 39 51 38N 9 19W
Ilero 121 8 0N 3 20E
Ilesha, West-Central, Nigeria 121 7 37N 4 40E
Ilesha, Western, Nigeria 121 8 57N 3 28E
Ilford 153 56 4N 95 35W
Ilfov □ 70 44 20N 26 0E
Ilfracombe, Austral. 138 23 30S 144 30E
Ilfracombe, U.K. 30 51 13N 4 8W
Ilha Grande, Baia da 171 23 9S 44 30W
Ílhavo 56 40 33N 8 43W
Ilheus 171 14 49S 39 2W
Ili 85 45 53N 77 10E
Ilia 70 45 57N 22 40E
Ilia □ 69 37 45N 21 35E
Iliamna L. 147 59 35N 155 30W
Iliang, Yunnan, China 108 24 54N 103 9E
Iliang, Yunnan, China 108 27 35N 104 1E
Ilich 85 40 50N 68 27E
Ilico 172 34 50S 72 20W
Iliff 158 40 50N 103 3W
Ilíki 69 38 24N 23 15E
Ilio Pt. 147 21 13N 157 16W
Iliodhrómia 68 39 12N 23 50E
Ilion 162 43 0N 75 3W
Ilirska Bistrica 63 45 34N 14 14E
Iliysk 76 44 10N 77 20E
Ilkal 97 15 57N 76 8E
Ilkeston 33 52 59N 1 19W
Ilkley 21 53 56N 1 49W
Illana B. 103 7 35N 123 45E
Illapel 172 32 0S 71 10W
'Illar 90 32 23N 35 7E
Ille 44 42 40N 2 37E
Ille-et-Vilaine □ 42 48 10N 1 30W
Iller, R. 49 47 53N 10 10E
Illescás 56 40 8N 3 51W
Illig 91 7 47N 49 45E
Illimani, Mte. 174 16 30S 67 50W
Illinois □ 155 40 15N 89 30W
Illinois, R. 155 40 10N 90 20W
Illizi 119 26 31N 8 32E
Illora 57 37 17N 3 53W
Ilmen, Oz. 80 58 15N 31 10E
Ilmenau 48 50 41N 10 55E
Ilminster 28 50 55N 2 56W
Ilo 174 17 40S 71 20W
Ilobu 121 7 45N 4 25E
Ilohuli Shan 105 51 20N 124 20E
Iloilo 103 10 45N 122 33E
Ilok 66 45 15N 19 20E
Ilora 121 7 45N 3 50E
Ilorin 121 8 30N 4 35E
Ilovatka 81 50 30N 46 50E
Ilovlya 83 49 15N 44 2E
Ilovlya, R. 83 49 38N 44 20E
Iłowa 54 51 30N 15 10E
Ilubabor □ 123 7 25N 35 0E
Ilukste 80 55 55N 26 20E
Ilung 108 31 34N 106 24E
Ilva Micá 70 47 17N 24 40E
Ilwaki 103 7 55S 126 30E
Ilyichevsk 82 46 10N 30 35E
Imabari 110 34 4N 133 0E
Imadahane 118 32 8N 7 0W
Imaichi 111 36 6N 139 16E
Imaloto, R. 129 23 10S 45 15E
Iman = Dalneretchensk 77 45 50N 133 40E
Imari 110 33 15N 129 52E
Imasa 122 18 0N 36 12E
Imathía □ 68 40 30N 22 15E
Imbâbah 122 30 5N 31 12E
Imbler 160 45 31N 118 0W
Imbros = Imroz 68 40 10N 26 0E
Imen 108 24 40N 102 9E
Imeni Panfilova 85 43 23N 77 7E
Imeni Poliny Osipenko 77 55 25N 136 29E
Imeri, Serra 174 0 50N 65 25W
Imerimandroso 129 17 26S 48 35E
Imi (Hinna) 123 6 35N 42 30E
Imi n'Tanoute 118 31 13N 8 51E
Imienp'o 107 45 0N 128 16E
Imishly 83 39 49N 48 4E
Imiteg 118 29 43N 8 10W
Imlay 160 40 45N 118 9W
Immingham 33 53 37N 0 12W
Immokalee 157 26 25N 81 20W
Imo □ 121 5 15N 7 20E
Imola 63 44 20N 11 42E
Imotski 66 43 27N 17 21E
Imperatriz 170 5 30S 47 29W
Impéria 62 43 52N 8 0E
Imperial, Can. 153 51 21N 105 28W
Imperial, Calif., U.S.A. 161 32 52N 115 34W
Imperial, Nebr., U.S.A. 158 40 38N 101 39W
Imperial Beach 163 32 35N 117 8W
Imperial Dam 161 32 50N 114 30W
Imperial Valley 163 32 55N 115 30W
Imperieuse Reef 136 17 36S 118 50E
Impfondo 124 1 40N 18 0E
Imphal 98 24 48N 93 56E
Imphy 43 46 56N 3 15E
Imroz = Gökçeada 68 40 10N 26 0E
Imst 52 47 15N 10 44E
Imuruan B. 103 10 40N 119 10E
In Belbel 118 27 55N 1 12E
In Delimane 121 15 52N 1 31E
In-Gall 121 16 51N 7 1E
In Rhar 118 27 10N 1 59E
In Salah 118 27 10N 2 32E
In Tallak 121 16 19N 3 15E
Ina 111 35 50N 138 0E
Ina-Bonchi 111 35 45N 137 58E
Inagh 39 52 53N 9 11W
Inajá 170 8 54S 37 49W
Inangahua Junc. 143 41 52S 171 59E
Inanwatan 103 2 10S 132 5E
Iñapari 174 11 0S 69 40W
Inari 74 68 54N 27 5E
Inari, L. 74 69 0N 28 0E
Inazawa 111 35 15N 136 47E
Inca 58 39 43N 2 54E
Incaguasi 172 29 12S 71 5W
Ince 32 53 32N 2 38W
İnce Burnu 92 42 2N 35 0E
Inch 39 52 42N 8 8W
Inch Br. 39 52 49N 9 6W
Inchard, Loch 36 58 28N 5 2W
Inchcape Rock 35 56 26N 2 24W
Inchigeelagh 39 51 50N 9 8W
Inchini 123 8 55N 37 37E
Inchkeith, I. 35 56 2N 3 8W
Inchnadamph 36 58 9N 5 0W
Inch'ŏn 107 37 27N 126 40E
Inchture 35 56 26N 3 8W
Incio 56 42 39N 7 21W
Incomáti, R. 129 25 15S 32 35E
Incudine, Mte. l' 45 41 50N 9 12E
Inda Silase 123 14 10N 38 15E
Indaal L. 34 55 44N 6 20W
Indalsälven 72 62 36N 17 30E
Indaw 98 24 15N 96 5E
Indbir 123 8 7N 37 52E
Indefatigable, gasfield 19 53 20N 2 40E
Independence, Calif., U.S.A. 163 36 51N 118 7W
Independence, Iowa, U.S.A. 158 42 27N 91 52W
Independence, Kans., U.S.A. 159 37 10N 95 50W
Independence, Mo., U.S.A. 158 39 3N 94 25W
Independence, Oreg., U.S.A. 160 44 53N 123 6W
Independence Fjord 12 82 10N 29 0W
Independence Mts. 160 41 30N 116 2W
Independência 170 5 23S 40 19W
Independencia, La 165 16 31N 91 47W
Independenta 70 45 25N 27 42E
Inderborskly 83 48 30N 51 42E
India ■ 87 20 0N 80 0E
Indian Cabins 152 59 52N 117 2W
Indian Harbour 151 54 27N 57 13W
Indian Head 153 50 30N 103 35W
Indian House L. 151 56 30N 64 30W
Indian Lake 162 43 47N 74 16W
Indian Ocean 11 5 0S 75 0E
Indian River B. 162 38 36N 75 4W
Indiana 156 40 38N 79 9W
Indiana □ 156 40 0N 86 0W
Indianapolis 156 39 42N 86 10W
Indianola, Iowa, U.S.A. 158 41 20N 93 38W
Indianola, Miss., U.S.A. 159 33 27N 90 40W
Indianópolis 171 19 2S 47 55E
Indiapora 171 19 57S 50 17W
Indiaroba 171 11 32S 37 31W
Indiga 78 67 50N 48 50E
Indigirka, R. 77 69 0N 147 0E
Indija 66 45 6N 20 7E
Indio 163 33 46N 116 15W
Indonesia ■ 102 5 0S 115 0E
Indore 94 22 42N 75 53E
Indramaju 103 6 21S 108 20E
Indramaju, Tg. 103 6 20S 108 20E
Indravati, R. 96 19 0N 81 15E
Indre □ 43 47 12N 1 39E
Indre-et-Loire □ 42 47 12N 0 40E
Indre, R. 42 47 2N 1 8E
Indre Söndeled 71 58 46N 9 5E
Indus, Mouth of the 94 24 00N 68 00E
Indus, R. 94 28 40N 70 10E
İnebolu 92 41 55N 33 40E
Infante, Kaap 128 34 27S 20 51E
Infantes 59 38 43N 3 1W
Infiernillo, Presa del 164 18 9N 102 0W
Infiesto 56 43 21N 5 21W
Ingá 171 7 17S 35 36W
Ingatestone 29 51 40N 0 23W
Ingelmunster 47 50 56N 3 16E
Ingende 124 0 12S 18 57E
Ingenio Santa Ana 172 27 25S 65 40W
Ingesvang 73 56 10N 9 20E
Ingham 138 18 43S 146 10E
Ingichka 85 39 47N 65 58E
Ingleborough, mt. 32 54 11N 2 23W
Inglefield Land 143 78 30N 70 0W
Ingleton 32 54 9N 2 29W
Inglewood, Queensland, Austral. 139 28 25S 151 8E
Inglewood, Vic., Austral. 140 36 29S 143 53E
Inglewood, N.Z. 142 39 9S 174 14E
Inglewood, U.S.A. 163 33 58N 118 21W
Ingoldmells, Pt. 33 53 11N 0 21E
Ingólfshöfði 74 63 48N 16 39W
Ingolstadt 49 48 45N 11 26E
Ingomar 160 46 43N 107 37W
Ingonish 151 46 42N 60 18W
Ingore 120 12 24N 15 48W
Ingul, R. 82 47 30N 32 15E
Ingulec 82 47 42N 33 4E
Ingulets, R. 82 47 20N 33 20E
Inguri, R. 83 42 58N 42 17E
Inhaca, I. 129 26 1S 32 57E
Inhafenga 129 20 36S 33 47E
Inhambane 125 23 54S 35 30E

Inhambane □ Itaueira

Inhambane □ 129 22 30S 34 20E
Inhambupe 171 11 47S 38 21W
Inhaminga 127 18 26S 35 0E
Inharrime 129 24 30S 35 0E
Inharrime, R. 129 24 30S 35 0E
Inhassoro 127 21 50S 35 15E
Inhuma 170 6 40S 41 42W
Inhumas 171 16 22S 49 30W
Iniesta 59 39 27N 1 45W
Ining, Kwangsi-Chuang, China 109 25 8N 109 57E
Ining, Sinkiang-Uigur, China 105 43 54N 81 21E
Inírida, R. 174 3 0N 68 40W
Inishark 38 53 36N 10 17W
Inishark I. 38 53 38N 10 17W
Inishbofin I., Donegal, Ireland 38 55 10N 8 10W
Inishbofin I., Galway, Ireland 38 53 35N 10 12W
Inisheer 39 53 3N 9 32W
Inishfree B. 38 55 4N 8 20W
Inishkea Is. 38 54 8N 10 10W
Inishmaan I. 39 53 5N 9 35W
Inishmore, I. 39 53 8N 9 45W
Inishmurray I. 38 54 26N 8 40W
Inishowen Hd. 38 55 14N 6 56W
Inishowen, Pen. 38 55 14N 7 15W
Inishrush 38 54 52N 6 32W
Inishtooskert I. 39 52 10N 10 35W
Inishturk I. 38 53 42N 10 8W
Inishvickillane 39 52 3N 10 37W
Inistioge 39 52 30N 7 5W
Injune 139 25 46S 148 32E
Inkberrow 28 52 13N 1 59W
Inklin 152 58 56N 133 5W
Inklin, R. 152 58 50N 133 10W
Inkom 160 42 51N 112 7W
Inkpen Beacon 28 51 22N 1 28W
Inle Aing 98 20 30N 96 58E
Inn, R. 49 48 35N 13 28E
Innamincka 139 27 44S 140 46E
Innellan 34 55 54N 4 58W
Inner Mongolia □ 106 44 50N 117 40E
Inner Sound 36 57 30N 5 55W
Innerleithen 35 55 37N 3 4W
Innertkirchen 50 46 43N 8 14E
Innetalling I. 150 56 0N 79 0W
Innfield 38 53 25N 6 50W
Inniscrone 38 54 13N 9 0W
Innisfail, Austral. 138 17 33S 146 5E
Innisfail, Can. 152 52 0N 113 57W
Innishannon 39 51 45N 8 40W
Inniskeen 38 54 0N 6 35W
In'no-shima 110 34 19N 133 10E
Innsbruck 52 47 16N 11 23E
Ino 110 33 33N 133 26E
Inocência 171 19 47S 51 48W
Inongo 124 1 35S 18 30E
Inosu 174 12 22N 71 38W
Inoucdjouac (Port Harrison) 149 58 27N 78 6W
Inowrocław 54 52 50N 18 20E
Inpundong 107 41 25N 126 34E
Inquisivi 174 16 50S 66 45W
Ins 50 47 1N 7 7E
Insch 37 57 20N 2 39W
Inscription, C. 137 25 29S 112 59E
Insein 98 17 15N 96 0E
Însurăţei 70 44 50N 27 40E
Intendente Alvear 172 35 12S 63 32W
Interior 158 43 46N 101 59W
Interlaken, Switz. 50 46 41N 7 50E
Interlaken, U.S.A. 162 42 37N 76 43W
International Falls 158 48 36N 93 25W
Interview I. 101 12 55N 92 42E
Inthanon, Mt. 101 18 35N 98 29E
Intiyaco 172 28 50S 60 0W
Intragna 51 46 11N 8 42E
Inubō-Zaki 111 35 42N 140 52E
Inútil, B. 176 53 30S 70 15W
Inuvik 147 68 16N 133 40W
Inuyama 111 35 23N 136 56E
Inver B. 38 54 35N 8 28W
Inverallochy 37 57 40N 1 56W
Inveran, Ireland 39 53 14N 9 28W
Inveran, U.K. 37 57 58N 4 26W
Inveraray 34 56 13N 5 5W
Inverbervie 37 56 50N 2 17W
Invercargill 143 46 24S 168 24E
Inverell 139 29 45S 151 8E
Invergarry 37 57 5N 4 48W
Invergordon 37 57 41N 4 10W
Invergowrie 35 56 29N 3 5W
Inverie 36 57 2N 5 40W
Inverkeilor 37 56 38N 2 33W
Inverkeithing 35 56 2N 3 24W
Inverleigh 140 38 6S 144 3E
Invermere 152 50 30N 116 2W
Invermoriston 37 57 13N 4 38W
Inverness, Can. 151 46 15N 61 19W
Inverness, U.K. 37 57 29N 4 12W
Inverness, U.S.A. 157 28 50N 82 20W
Inverness (□) 26 57 6N 4 40W
Invershiel 36 57 13N 5 25W
Inverurie 37 57 15N 2 21W
Inverway 136 17 50S 129 38E
Investigator Group 136 34 45S 134 20E
Investigator Str. 140 35 30S 137 0E
Inyanga 127 18 12S 32 40E
Inyangahi, mt. 127 18 20S 32 20E
Inyantue 127 18 30S 26 40E
Inyazura 127 18 40S 31 40E
Inyo Range 161 37 0N 118 0W
Inyokern 163 35 37N 117 54W
Inywa 98 22 4N 94 44E
Inza 81 53 55N 46 25E
Inzell 49 47 48N 12 15E
Inzer 84 54 14N 57 34E
Inzhavino 81 52 22N 42 23E
Ioánnina (Janinà) □ 68 39 39N 20 57E
Iōhen 110 32 58N 132 32E
Iola 159 38 0N 95 20W
Ioma 135 8 19S 147 52E
Ion Corvin 70 44 7N 27 50E
Iona I. 34 56 20N 6 25W
Ionava 80 55 8N 24 12E
Ione, Calif., U.S.A. 163 38 20N 121 0W
Ione, Wash., U.S.A. 160 48 44N 117 29W
Ionia 156 42 59N 85 7W
Ionian Is. = Ionioi Nisoi 69 38 40N 20 0E
Ionian Sea 61 37 30N 17 30E
Iónioi Nisoi 69 38 40N 20 8E
Ioniškis 80 56 13N 23 35E
Iori, R. 83 41 12N 46 10E
Íos, I. 69 36 41N 25 20E
Iowa □ 158 42 18N 93 30W
Iowa City 158 41 40N 91 35W
Iowa Falls 158 42 30N 93 15W
Ipala 126 4 30S 33 5E
Ipameri 171 17 44S 48 9W
Ipanema 75 9 48S 41 45W
Ipáti 69 38 52N 22 14E
Ipatovo 83 45 45N 42 50E
Ipel, R. 53 48 10N 19 35E
Ipiales 174 0 50N 77 37W
Ipiaú 171 14 8S 39 44W
Ipin 108 28 48N 104 33E
Ipinlang 108 25 5N 101 58E
Ipirá 171 12 10S 39 44W
Ipiros □ 68 39 30N 20 30E
Ipixuna 174 7 0S 71 40W
Ipoh 101 4 35N 101 5E
Iporá 171 16 28S 51 7W
Ippy 117 6 5N 21 7E
Ipsárion Óros 68 40 40N 24 40E
Ipswich, Austral. 139 27 35S 152 46E
Ipswich, U.K. 29 52 4N 1 9E
Ipswich, N.H., U.S.A. 162 42 40N 70 50W
Ipswich, S.D., U.S.A. 158 45 28N 99 20W
Ipu 170 4 23S 40 44W
Ipueiras 170 4 33S 40 43W
Ipupiara 171 11 49S 42 37W
Iput, R. 80 53 0N 32 10E
Iquique 174 20 19S 70 5W
Iquitos 174 3 45S 73 10W
Iracoubo 175 5 30N 53 10W
Iráklia, I. 69 36 50N 25 28E
Iráklion 69 35 20N 25 12E
Iráklion □ 69 35 10N 25 10E
Irako-Zaki 111 34 35N 137 1E
Irala 173 25 55S 54 35W
Iramba □ 126 4 30S 34 30E
Iran ■ 93 33 0N 53 0E
Iran, Pegunungan 102 2 20N 114 50E
Iran, Plateau of 43 33 00N 55 0E
Iranamadu Tank 97 9 23N 80 29E
Iranshahr 93 27 75N 60 40E
Irapa 174 10 34N 62 35W
Irapuato 164 20 40N 101 40W
Iraq ■ 92 33 0N 44 0E
Irarrar, W. 118 20 10N 1 30E
Irati 173 25 25S 50 38W
Irbid 90 32 35N 35 48E
Irbit 84 57 41N 63 3E
Irchester 29 52 17N 0 40W
Irebu 124 0 40S 17 55E
Irecê 170 11 18S 41 52W
Iregua, R. 58 42 22N 2 24E
Ireland ■ 38 53 0N 8 0W
Ireland's Eye 38 53 25N 6 4W
Irele 121 7 40N 5 40E
Iremel, Gora 84 54 33N 58 50E
Iret 77 60 10N 154 5E
Irgiz, Bol. 81 52 10N 49 10E
Irharharene 119 27 37N 7 30E
Irharrhar, O. 119 27 30N 6 0E
Irhyangdong 107 41 15N 129 30E
Iri 107 35 59N 127 0E
Irian Jaya □ 103 4 0S 137 0E
Iriba 124 15 7N 22 15E
Irié 120 8 15N 9 10W
Iriklinskiy 84 51 39N 58 38E
Iringa 126 7 48S 35 43E
Iringa □, Tanz. 126 7 48S 35 43E
Iringa □, Tanz. 127 9 0S 35 0E
Irinjalakuda 97 10 21N 76 14E
Iriomote-Jima 112 24 19N 123 48E
Iriona 166 15 57N 85 11W
Irish Sea 32 54 0N 5 0W
Irish Town 93 40 55S 145 9E
Irkeshtam 85 39 41N 73 55E
Irkutsk 77 52 10N 104 20E
Irlam 32 53 26N 2 27W
Irma 153 52 55N 111 14W
Irmak 92 39 58N 33 25E
Irō-Zaki 111 34 36N 138 51E
Iroise 42 48 15N 4 45W
Iron Baron 140 33 3S 137 11E
Iron Gate = Porţile de Fier 70 44 42N 22 30E
Iron Knob 140 32 46S 137 8E
Iron, L. 38 53 37N 7 34W
Iron Mountain 156 45 49N 88 4W
Iron River 158 46 6N 88 40W
Ironbridge 28 52 38N 2 29W
Ironhurst 138 18 5S 143 28E
Ironstone Kopje, Mt. 128 25 17S 24 5E
Ironton, Mo., U.S.A. 159 37 40N 90 40W
Ironton, Ohio, U.S.A. 156 38 35N 82 40W
Ironwood 158 46 30N 90 10W
Iroquois Falls 150 48 46N 80 41W
Irpen 80 50 30N 30 8E
Irrara Cr. 139 29 35S 145 31E
Irrawaddy 98 17 0N 95 0E
Irrawaddy □ 98 17 0N 95 0E
Irrawaddy, R. 98 15 50N 95 6E
Irsina 65 40 45N 16 15E
Irt R. 32 54 24N 3 25W
Irthing R. 35 54 25N 2 48W
Irthlingborough 29 52 20N 0 37W
Irtysh, R. 76 53 36N 75 30E
Irumu 126 1 32N 29 53E
Irún 58 43 20N 1 52W
Irurzun 58 42 55N 1 50W
Irvine, Can. 153 49 57N 110 16W
Irvine, U.K. 34 55 37N 4 40W
Irvine, U.S.A. 156 37 42N 83 58W
Irvinestown 38 54 28N 7 38W
Irwin, Pt. 137 35 5S 116 55E
Irwin, R. 137 29 15S 114 54E
Irymple 140 34 14S 142 8E
Is-sur-Tille 43 47 30N 5 10E
Isa 121 13 14N 6 24E
Isaac, R. 138 22 55S 149 20E
Isabel 158 45 27N 101 22W
Isabela, Dom. Rep. 167 19 58N 71 2W
Isabela, Pto Rico 147 18 30N 67 01W
Isabela, Cord. 166 13 30N 85 25W
Isabela, I. 164 21 51N 105 55W
Isabella Ra. 136 21 0S 121 4E
Ísafjarðardjúp 74 66 10N 23 0W
Ísafjörður 74 66 5N 23 9W
Isagarh 94 24 48N 77 51E
Isahaya 110 32 52N 130 2E
Isaka 126 3 56S 32 59E
Isakly 84 54 8N 51 32E
Isangi 124 0 52N 24 10E
Isar, R. 49 48 40N 12 30E
Isarco, R. 63 46 40N 11 30E
Isari 69 37 22N 22 0E
Isbergues 43 50 36N 2 24E
Isbiceni 70 43 45N 24 40E
Ischia, I. 64 40 45N 13 51E
Iscuandé 174 2 28N 77 59W
Isdell, R. 136 16 27S 124 51E
Ise 111 34 25N 136 45E
Ise-Heiya 111 34 40N 136 30E
Ise-Wan 111 34 43N 136 43E
Isefjord 73 55 53N 11 50E
Iseltwald 50 46 43N 7 58E
Isenthal 51 46 55N 8 34E
Iseo 62 45 40N 10 3E
Iseo, L. di 62 45 45N 10 3E
Iseramagazi 126 4 37S 32 10E
Isère □ 45 45 15N 5 40E
Isère, R. 44 45 15N 5 30E
Iserlohn 48 51 22N 7 40E
Isérnia 65 41 35N 14 12E
Isesaki 111 36 19N 139 12E
Iset, R. 84 56 36N 66 24E
Iseyin 121 8 0N 3 36E
Isfara 85 40 7N 70 38E
Ishan 108 24 30N 108 41E
Ishara 121 6 40N 3 40E
Ishigaki 112 24 20N 124 10E
Ishikari-Wan 112 43 20N 141 20E
Ishikawa 112 26 25N 127 48E
Ishikawa-ken □ 111 36 30N 136 30E
Ishim 76 56 10N 69 18E
Ishim, R. 76 57 45N 71 10E
Ishimbay 84 53 28N 56 2E
Ishinomaki 112 38 32N 141 20E
Ishioka 111 36 11N 140 16E
Ishizuchi-Yama 110 33 45N 133 6E
Ishkashim 85 36 44N 71 37E
Ishkuman 95 36 30N 73 50E
Ishmi 68 41 33N 19 34E
Ishpeming 156 46 30N 87 40W
Ishua 121 7 15N 5 50E
Ishui 107 35 50N 118 32E
Ishurdi 98 24 9N 89 3E
Isigny-sur-Mer 42 49 19N 1 6W
Işik 82 40 40N 32 35E
Isil Kul 76 54 55N 71 16E
Isili 44 39 45N 9 6E
Isiolo 126 0 24N 37 33E
Isipingo 129 30 00S 30 57E
Isipingo Beach 129 30 00S 30 57E
Isiro 126 2 53N 27 58E
Iskander 85 41 36N 69 41E
İskenderun 92 36 32N 36 10E
İskilip 82 40 50N 34 20E
Iskut, R. 152 56 45N 131 49W
Iskyr, R. 67 43 35N 24 20E
Isla Cristina 57 37 13N 7 17W
Isla, La 174 6 51N 76 56W
Isla, R. 37 56 32N 3 20W
Islamabad 94 33 40N 73 0E
Islamkot 94 24 42N 70 13E
Islampur 96 17 2N 72 9E
Island Falls, Can. 150 49 35N 81 20W
Island Falls, U.S.A. 151 46 0N 68 25W
Island L. 153 53 47N 94 25W
Island Lagoon 140 31 30S 136 40E
Island Pt. 137 30 20S 115 1E
Island Pond 156 44 50N 71 50W
Island, R. 152 60 25N 121 12W
Islands, B. of, Can. 151 49 11N 58 15W
Islands, B. of, N.Z. 142 35 20S 174 20E
Islay, I. 34 55 46N 6 10W
Islay Sound 34 55 45N 6 5W
Isle-Adam, L' 43 49 6N 2 14E
Isle aux Morts 151 47 35N 59 0W
Isle-Jourdain, L', Gers, France 44 43 36N 1 5E
Isle-Jourdain, L', Vienne, France 42 46 13N 0 31E
Isle, L', Tarn, France 44 43 52N 1 49E
Isle, L', Vaucluse, France 45 43 55N 5 3E
Isle of Whithorn 34 54 42N 4 22W
Isle of Wight □ 28 50 40N 1 20W
Isle Ornsay 36 57 9N 5 50W
Isle Royale 158 48 0N 88 50W
Isle-sur-la-Sorgue, L' 45 43 55N 5 2E
Isle-sur-le-Doubs, L' 43 47 26N 6 34E
Isle Vista 163 34 27N 119 52W
Isleham 29 52 21N 0 24E
Islet, L' 151 47 4N 70 23W
Isleta 161 34 58N 106 46W
Isleton 163 38 10N 121 37W
Islip 28 51 49N 1 12W
Ismail 82 45 22N 28 46E
Ismâ'ilîya 122 30 37N 32 18E
Ismay 158 46 33N 104 44W
Isna 122 25 17N 32 30E
Isogstalo 95 34 15N 78 46E
Isola del Liri 64 41 39N 13 32E
Isola della Scala 62 45 16N 11 0E
Isola di Capo Rizzuto 65 38 56N 17 5E
Isparta 92 37 47N 30 30E
Isperikh 67 43 43N 26 50E
Ispica 65 36 47N 14 53E
Israel ■ 90 32 0N 34 50E
Isseka 137 28 22S 114 35E
Issia 120 6 33N 6 33W
Issoire 44 45 32N 3 15E
Issoudun 43 46 57N 2 0E
Issyk-Kul, Ozero 85 42 25N 77 15E
İstanbul 92 41 0N 29 0E
Istmina 174 5 10N 76 39W
Istok 66 42 45N 20 24E
Istokpoga, L. 157 27 22N 81 14W
Istra, U.S.S.R. 81 55 55N 36 50E
Istra, Yugo. 63 45 10N 14 0E
Istranca Dağlari 67 41 48N 27 30E
Istres 45 43 31N 4 59E
Istria = Istra 63 45 10N 14 0E
Itá 172 25 29N 57 21W
Itabaiana, Paraíba, Brazil 170 7 18S 35 19W
Itabaiana, Sergipe, Brazil 170 10 41S 37 26W
Itabaianinha 170 11 16S 37 47W
Itaberaba 171 12 32S 40 18W
Itaberaí 171 16 2S 49 48W
Itabira 171 19 37S 43 13W
Itabirito 173 20 15S 43 48W
Itabuna 171 14 48S 39 16W
Itacaiunas, R. 170 5 21S 49 8W
Itacajá 170 8 19S 47 46W
Itaete 171 13 0S 41 5W
Itaguaçu 171 19 48S 40 51W
Itaguari, R. 171 14 11S 44 40W
Itaguatins 170 5 47S 47 29W
Itaim, R. 170 7 2S 42 2W
Itainópolis 170 7 24S 41 31W
Itaituba 175 4 10S 55 50W
Itajaí 173 27 0S 48 45W
Itajubá 173 22 24S 45 30W
Itajuípe 171 14 41S 39 22W
Itaka 127 8 50S 32 49E
Itako 111 35 56N 140 33E
Italy ■ 60 42 0N 13 0E
Itamataré 170 2 16S 46 24W
Itambacuri 171 18 1S 41 42W
Itambé 171 15 15S 40 37W
Itambe, mt. 170 18 30S 43 15W
Itampolo 129 24 41S 43 57E
Itanhaém 121 24 9S 46 47W
Itanhém 171 17 9S 40 20W
Itano 110 34 1N 134 28E
Itapaci 171 14 57S 49 34W
Itapagé 170 3 41S 39 34W
Itaparica, I. de 171 12 54S 38 42W
Itapebi 171 15 56S 39 32W
Itapecerica 171 20 28S 45 7W
Itapecuru-Mirim 170 3 24S 44 20W
Itapecuru, R. 170 3 20S 44 15W
Itaperuna 171 21 10S 42 0W
Itapetinga 171 15 15S 40 15W
Itapetininga 173 23 36S 48 7W
Itapeva 173 23 59S 48 59W
Itapicuru 170 10 50S 38 40W
Itapicuru, R. 170 5 40S 44 30W
Itapipoca 170 3 30S 39 35W
Itapiúna 170 4 33S 38 57W
Itaporanga 171 7 18S 38 10W
Itapuá □ 173 26 40S 55 40W
Itapuranga 171 15 35S 49 59W
Itaquari 173 20 12S 40 25W
Itaquatiana 174 2 58S 58 30W
Itaquí 172 29 0S 56 30W
Itararé 173 24 6S 49 23W
Itarsi 94 22 36N 77 51E
Itarumã 171 18 42S 51 25W
Itatí 172 27 16S 58 15W
Itatira 170 4 30S 39 37W
Itatuba 174 5 40S 63 20W
Itaueira 170 7 36S 43 2W

Itaueira, R Jedrzejów

Itaueira, R. 170 6 41S 42 55W
Itaúna 171 20 4S 44 34W
Itchen, R. 28 50 57N 1 20W
Itéa 69 38 25N 22 25E
Ithaca 162 42 25N 76 30W
Ithaca = Itháki 69 38 25N 20 43E
Itháki, I. 69 38 25N 20 40E
Ithon R. 31 52 16N 3 23W
It'iaoshan 106 37 10N 104 2E
Itinga 171 16 36S 41 47W
Itiruçu 171 13 31S 40 9W
Itiúba 171 10 43S 39 51W
Ito 111 34 58N 139 5E
Itonamas, R. 174 13 0S 64 25W
Itsa 122 29 15N 30 40E
Itsukaichi 110 34 22N 132 8E
Itsuki 110 32 24N 130 50E
Itteville 46 48 31N 2 21E
Ittiri 64 40 38N 8 32E
Itu, Brazil 173 23 10S 47 15W
Itu, Hupeh, China 109 30 24N 111 26E
Itu, Shantung, China 107 36 41N 118 28E
Itu, Nigeria 121 5 10N 7 58E
Ituaçu 171 13 50S 41 18W
Ituango 174 7 4N 75 45W
Ituiutaba 171 19 0S 49 25W
Itumbiara 171 18 20S 49 10W
Ituna 153 51 10N 103 30W
It'ung 107 43 20N 125 17E
Itunge Port 127 9 40S 33 55E
Itupiranga 170 5 9S 49 20W
Iturama 171 19 44S 50 11W
Iturbe 172 23 0S 65 25W
Ituri, R. 126 1 45N 26 45E
Iturup, Ostrov 77 45 0N 148 0E
Ituverava 171 20 20S 47 47W
Ituyuro, R. 172 22 40S 63 50W
Itzehoe 48 53 56N 9 31E
Ivalo 74 68 38N 27 35E
Ivalojoki 74 68 30N 27 0E
Ivanaj 68 42 17N 19 25E
Ivanhoe, N.S.W., Austral. 140 32 56S 144 20E
Ivanhoe, N.T., Austral. 136 15 41S 128 41E
Ivanhoe, U.S.A. 163 36 23N 119 13W
Ivanhoe L. 153 60 25N 106 30W
Ivanió Grad 63 45 41N 16 25E
Ivanjica 66 43 35N 20 12E
Ivanjscie 63 46 12N 16 13E
Ivankovskoye Vdkhr. 81 56 48N 36 55E
Ivano-Frankovsk, (Stanislav) 80 49 0N 24 40E
Ivanovka 84 52 34N 53 23E
Ivanovo, Byelorussia, U.S.S.R. 80 52 7N 25 29E
Ivanovo, R.S.F.S.R., U.S.S.R. 81 57 5N 41 0E
Ivato 129 20 37S 47 10E
Ivaylovgrad 67 41 32N 26 8E
Ivinghoe 29 51 50N 0 38W
Ivinheima, R. 173 21 48S 54 15W
Iviza = Ibiza 59 39 0N 1 30E
Ivohibe 129 22 31S 46 57E
Ivolândia 171 16 34S 50 51W
Ivory Coast ■ 120 7 30N 5 0W
Ivösjön 73 56 8N 14 25E
Ivrea 62 45 30N 7 52E
Ivugivik, (N.D. d'Ivugivic) 149 62 24N 77 55W
Ivybridge 30 50 24N 3 56W
Iwahig 102 8 35N 117 32E
Iwai-Jima 110 33 47N 131 58E
Iwaki 112 37 3N 140 55E
Iwakuni 110 34 15N 132 8E
Iwami 110 35 32N 134 15E
Iwamisawa 112 43 12N 141 46E
Iwanai 112 42 58N 140 30E
Iwanuma 112 38 7N 140 58E
Iwase 110 36 21N 140 6E
Iwata 111 34 49N 137 59E
Iwate-ken □ 112 39 30N 141 30E
Iwate-San 112 39 51N 141 0E
Iwo 121 7 39N 4 9E
Iwonicz-Zdroj 54 49 37N 21 47E
Ixiamas 174 13 50S 68 5W
Ixopo 129 30 11S 30 5E
Ixtepec 165 16 40N 95 10W
Ixtlán de Juárez 165 17 23N 96 28W
Ixtlán del Rio 164 21 5N 104 28W
Ixworth 29 52 18N 0 50E
Iyang, Honan, China 106 34 9N 112 25E
Iyang, Hunan, China 109 28 36N 112 20E
Iyang, Kiangsi, China 109 28 23N 117 25E
Iyo 110 33 45N 132 45E
Iyo-mishima 110 33 58N 133 30E
Iyo-Nada 110 33 40N 132 20E
Izabal, L. 166 15 30N 89 10W
Izamal 165 20 56N 89 1W
Izberbash 83 42 35N 47 45E
Izbica Kujawski 54 52 25N 18 30E
Izegem 47 50 55N 3 12E
Izgrev 67 43 36N 26 58E
Izh, R. 84 55 58N 52 38E
Izhevsk 84 56 51N 53 14E
Izmail 82 45 22N 28 46E
Izmir (Smyrna) 79 38 25N 27 8E
Izmit 92 40 45N 29 50E
Izola 63 45 32N 13 39E
Izu-Hantō 111 34 45N 139 0E
Izuhara 110 34 12N 129 17E
Izumi 110 32 5N 130 22E
Izumiotsu 111 34 30N 135 24E
Izumisano 111 34 40N 135 43E
Izumo 110 35 20N 132 55E
Izyaslav 80 50 5N 25 50E
Izyum 82 49 12N 37 28E

J

Jaba 123 6 20N 35 7E
Jaba' 90 32 20N 35 13E
Jabaliya 90 31 32N 34 27E
Jabalón, R. 59 38 45N 3 35W
Jabalpur 95 23 9N 79 58E
Jablah 92 35 20N 36 0E
Jablanac 63 44 42N 14 56E
Jablonec 52 50 43N 15 10E
Jablonica 53 48 37N 17 26E
Jabłonowo 54 53 23N 19 10E
Jaboatão 170 8 7S 35 1W
Jaboticabal 173 21 15S 48 17W
Jabukovac 66 44 22N 22 21E
Jaburu 174 5 30S 64 0W
Jaca 58 42 35N 0 33W
Jacala 165 21 1N 99 11W
Jacaré, R. 170 10 3S 42 13W
Jacareí 173 23 20S 46 0W
Jacarèzinho 173 23 5S 50 0W
Jáchal 172 30 5S 69 0W
Jáchymov 52 50 22N 12 55E
Jacinto 171 16 10S 40 17W
Jack Lane B. 151 55 45N 60 35W
Jackfish 150 48 45N 87 0W
Jackman 151 45 35N 70 17W
Jacksboro 159 33 14N 98 15W
Jackson, Austral. 139 26 39S 149 39E
Jackson, Ala., U.S.A. 157 31 32N 87 53W
Jackson, Calif., U.S.A. 159 37 25N 89 42W
Jackson, Ill., U.S.A. 163 38 25N 120 47W
Jackson, Ky., U.S.A. 156 37 35N 83 22W
Jackson, Mich., U.S.A. 156 42 18N 84 25W
Jackson, Minn., U.S.A. 158 43 35N 95 30W
Jackson, Miss., U.S.A. 159 32 20N 90 10W
Jackson, Ohio, U.S.A. 156 39 0N 82 40W
Jackson, Tenn., U.S.A. 157 35 40N 88 50W
Jackson, Wyo., U.S.A. 160 43 30N 110 49W
Jackson Bay, Can. 152 50 32N 125 57W
Jackson Bay, N.Z. 143 43 58S 168 42E
Jackson, C. 143 40 59S 174 20E
Jackson, L. 160 43 55N 110 40W
Jacksons 143 42 46S 171 32E
Jacksonville, Ala., U.S.A. 157 33 49N 85 45W
Jacksonville, Calif., U.S.A. 163 37 52N 120 24W
Jacksonville, Fla., U.S.A. 157 30 15N 81 38W
Jacksonville, Ill., U.S.A. 158 39 42N 90 15W
Jacksonville, N.C., U.S.A. 157 34 50N 77 29W
Jacksonville, Oreg., U.S.A. 160 42 13N 122 56W
Jacksonville, Tex., U.S.A. 159 31 58N 95 12W
Jacksonville Beach 157 30 19N 81 26W
Jacmel 167 18 20N 72 40W
Jacob Lake 161 36 45N 112 12W
Jacobabad 94 28 20N 68 29E
Jacobeni 70 47 25N 25 20E
Jacobina 170 11 11S 40 30W
Jacob's Well 90 32 13N 35 13E
Jacques Cartier, Mt. 151 48 57N 66 0W
Jacques Cartier Pass 151 49 50N 62 30W
Jacqueville 120 5 12N 4 25W
Jacuí, R. 173 30 2S 51 15W
Jacuipe, R. 171 12 30S 39 5W
Jacundá, R. 170 1 57S 50 26W
Jade 48 53 22N 8 14E
Jadebusen, B. 48 53 30N 8 15E
Jadoigne 47 50 43N 4 52E
Jadotville = Likasi 127 10 55S 26 48E
Jadovnik 66 43 20N 19 45E
Jadraque 58 40 55N 2 55W
Jādū 119 32 0N 12 0E
Jaén, Peru 174 5 25S 78 40W
Jaén, Spain 57 37 44N 3 43W
Jaén □ 57 37 50N 3 30W
Jafène 118 20 35N 5 30W
Jaffa = Tel Aviv-Yafo 90 32 4N 34 48E
Jaffa, C. 140 36 58S 139 40E
Jaffna 97 9 45N 80 2E
Jaffrey 162 42 50N 72 4W
Jagadhri 94 30 10N 77 20E
Jagadishpur 95 25 30N 84 21E
Jagdalpur 96 19 3N 82 6E
Jagersfontein 128 29 44S 25 27E
Jaghbub 117 29 42N 24 38E
Jagraon 93 30 50N 75 25E
Jagst, R. 49 49 13N 10 0E
Jagtial 96 18 50N 79 0E
Jaguaquara 171 13 32S 39 58W
Jaguariaíva 173 24 10S 49 50W
Jaguaribe 170 5 53S 38 37W
Jaguaribe, R. 170 6 0S 38 35W
Jaguaruana 170 4 50S 37 47W
Jagüey 166 22 35N 81 7W
Jagungal, Mt. 141 36 8S 148 22E
Jahangirabad 94 28 19N 78 4E
Jahrom 92 28 30N 53 31E
Jaicós 170 7 21S 41 8W
Jainti 98 26 45N 89 40E
Jaintiapur 98 25 8N 92 7E
Jaipur 94 27 0N 76 10E
Jajarm 93 37 5N 56 20E
Jajce 66 44 19N 17 17E
Jajere 121 11 58N 11 25E
Jajpur 96 20 53N 86 22E
Jakarta 103 6 9S 106 49E
Jakobstad (Pietarsaari) 74 63 40N 22 43E
Jakupica 66 41 45N 21 22E
Jal 159 32 8N 103 8W
Jala 93 27 30N 62 40E
Jalalabad, Afghan. 94 34 30N 70 29E
Jalalabad, India 95 26 41N 79 42E
Jalalpur Jattan 94 32 38N 74 19E
Jalama 163 34 29N 120 29W
Jalapa, Guat. 166 14 45N 89 59W
Jalapa, Mexico 165 19 30N 96 50W
Jalas, Jabal al 92 27 30N 36 30E
Jalaun 95 26 8N 79 25E
Jales 171 20 16S 50 33W
Jaleswar 95 26 38N 85 48E
Jalgaon, Maharashtra, India 96 21 2N 76 31E
Jalgaon, Maharashtra, India 96 21 0N 75 42E
Jalhay 47 50 33N 5 58E
Jalingo 121 8 55N 11 25E
Jalisco □ 164 20 0N 104 0W
Jalkot 95 35 20N 73 24E
Jallas, R. 56 42 57N 9 0W
Jallumba 140 36 55N 141 57E
Jalna 96 19 48N 75 57E
Jalón, R. 58 41 20N 1 40W
Jalpa 164 21 38N 102 58W
Jalpaiguri 98 26 32N 88 46E
Jalq 93 27 35N 62 33E
Jaluit I. 130 6 0N 169 30E
Jamaari 121 11 44N 9 53E
Jamaica, I. ■ 166 18 10N 77 30W
Jamalpur, Bangla. 98 24 52N 90 2E
Jamalpur, India 95 25 18N 86 28E
Jamalpurganj 95 23 2N 88 1E
Jamanxim, R. 175 6 30S 55 50W
Jambe 103 1 15S 132 10E
Jambes 47 50 27N 4 52E
Jambi 102 1 38S 103 30E
Jambusar 94 22 3N 72 51E
Jamdena, I. = Yamdena 103 7 45S 131 20E
James B. 150 53 30N 80 0W
James, R., Dak., U.S.A. 158 44 50N 98 0W
James, R., Va., U.S.A. 162 37 0N 76 27W
James Ranges 136 24 10S 132 0E
James Ross I. 13 63 58S 50 94W
Jamestown, Austral. 140 33 10S 138 32E
Jamestown, S. Afr. 128 31 6S 26 45E
Jamestown, Ky., U.S.A. 156 37 0N 85 5W
Jamestown, N.D., U.S.A. 158 47 0N 98 30W
Jamestown, N.Y., U.S.A. 156 42 5N 79 18W
Jamestown, Tenn., U.S.A. 157 36 25N 85 0W
Jamestown, Va., U.S.A. 162 37 12N 76 46W
Jamiltepec 165 16 17N 97 49W
Jamkhandi 97 16 30N 75 15E
Jamma'in 90 32 8N 35 12E
Jammalamadugu 97 14 51N 78 25E
Jammerbugt 73 57 15N 9 20E
Jammu 94 32 43N 74 54E
Jammu & Kashmir □ 95 34 25N 77 0E
Jamnagar 94 22 30N 70 0E
Jamner 96 20 45N 75 45E
Jamoigne 47 49 41N 5 24E
Jampur 94 29 39N 70 32E
Jamrud 94 34 2N 71 24E
Jamshedpur 95 22 44N 86 20E
Jamtara 95 23 59N 86 41E
Jämtlands län □ 72 62 40N 13 50E
Jamuna, R. 98 23 51N 89 45E
Jamurki 98 24 9N 90 2E
Jan Kemp 128 27 55S 24 51E
Jan L. 153 54 56N 102 55W
Jan Mayen Is. 12 71 0N 11 0W
Janaúba 171 15 48S 43 19W
Janaucu, I. 170 0 30N 50 10W
Jand 94 33 30N 72 0E
Janda, Laguna de la 57 36 15N 5 45W
Jandaia 171 17 6S 50 7W
Jandaq 92 34 3N 54 22E
Jandola 94 32 20N 70 9E
Jandowae 139 26 45S 151 7E
Jandrain-Jandrenouilles 47 50 40N 4 58E
Jándula, R. 57 38 25N 3 55W
Jane Pk. 142 45 15S 168 20E
Janesville 158 42 39N 89 1W
Janga 121 10 5N 1 0W
Jangaon 96 17 44N 79 5E
Janhtang Ga 98 26 32N 96 38E
Jani Khel 93 32 45N 68 25E
Janja 66 44 40N 19 17E
Janjevo 66 42 35N 21 19E
Janjina 66 42 58N 17 25E
Janos 164 30 45N 108 10W
Jánoshalma 53 46 18N 19 21E
Jánosháza 53 47 8N 17 12E
Jánossomorja 53 47 47N 17 11E
Janów 54 50 43N 22 30E
Janów Lubelski 54 50 48N 22 23E
Janów Podlaski 54 52 11N 23 11E
Janowiec Wlkp. 54 52 45N 17 30E
Januária 171 15 25S 44 25W
Janub Dârfûr □ 123 11 0N 25 0E
Janub Kordofân □ 123 12 0N 30 0E
Janville 43 48 10N 1 50E
Janzé 42 47 55N 1 28W
Jaop'ing 109 23 43N 117 0E
Jaora 94 23 40N 75 10E
Jaoyang 106 38 14N 115 44E
Japan ■ 112 36 0N 136 0E
Japan, Sea of 112 40 0N 135 0E
Japan Trench 142 28 0N 145 0E
Japara 103 6 30S 110 40E
Japen, I. = Yapen 103 1 50S 136 0E
Japero 103 4 59S 137 11E
Japurá 174 1 48S 66 30W
Japurá, R. 174 3 8S 64 46W
Jaque 174 7 27N 78 15W
Jaques Cartier, Détroit de 151 50 0N 63 30W
Jara, La 161 37 16N 106 0W
Jaraguá 171 15 45S 49 20W
Jaraicejo 57 39 40N 5 49W
Jaraiz 56 40 4N 5 45W
Jarales 161 34 44N 106 51W
Jarama, R. 58 40 50N 3 20W
Jarandilla 56 40 8N 5 39W
Jaranwala 94 31 15N 73 20E
Jarash 90 32 17N 35 54E
Järbo 72 60 42N 16 38E
Jarbridge 160 41 56N 115 27W
Jardim 172 21 28S 56 9W
Jardín, R. 59 38 50N 2 10W
Jardines de la Reina, Is. 166 20 50N 78 50W
Jargalant = Hovd 105 48 1N 91 38E
Jargeau 43 47 50N 2 7E
Jarmen 48 53 56N 13 20E
Järna, Kopp., Sweden 72 60 33N 14 26E
Järna, Stockholm, Sweden 72 59 7N 17 35E
Jarnac 44 45 40N 0 11W
Jarny 43 49 9N 5 53E
Jarocin 54 51 59N 17 29E
Jaroměr 52 50 22N 15 52E
Jarosław 54 50 2N 22 42E
Järpås 73 58 23N 12 57E
Järpås 73 58 23N 12 57E
Järpen 72 63 21N 13 26E
Jarrahdale 137 32 24S 116 5E
Jarres, Plaine des 100 19 27N 103 10E
Jarrow 35 54 58N 1 28W
Jarso 123 5 15N 37 30E
Järved 72 63 16N 18 43E
Jarvis I. 131 0 15S 159 55W
Jarvornik 53 50 23N 17 2E
Jarwa 95 27 45N 82 30E
Jaša Tomió 66 45 26N 20 50E
Jasien 54 51 46N 15 0E
Jasin 101 2 20N 102 26E
Jāsk 93 25 38N 57 45E
Jasło 54 49 45N 21 30E
Jasper, Can. 152 52 55N 118 5W
Jasper, Ala., U.S.A. 157 33 48N 87 16W
Jasper, Ark., U.S.A. 97 36 0N 93 10W
Jasper, Fla., U.S.A. 157 30 31N 82 58W
Jasper, La., U.S.A. 159 30 59N 93 58W
Jasper, S.D., U.S.A. 158 43 52N 96 22W
Jasper Nat. Park 152 52 50N 118 8W
Jasper Place 152 53 33N 113 25W
Jastrebarsko 63 45 41N 15 39E
Jastrowie 54 53 26N 16 49E
Jastrzebie Zdroj 54 49 57N 18 35E
Jászapáti 53 47 32N 20 10E
Jászárokszállás 53 47 39N 20 1E
Jászberény 53 47 30N 19 55E
Jászkiser 53 47 27N 20 20E
Jászladány 53 47 23N 20 18E
Jataí 171 17 50S 51 45W
Jati 94 24 27N 68 19E
Jatibarang 103 6 28S 108 18E
Jatinegara 103 6 13S 106 52E
Játiva 59 39 0N 0 32W
Jatobal 170 4 35S 49 33W
Jatt 90 32 24N 35 2E
Jaú 173 22 10S 48 30W
Jau al Milah 91 15 15N 45 40E
Jauche 47 50 41N 4 57E
Jauja 174 11 45S 75 30W
Jaunelgava 80 56 35N 25 0E
Jaunpur 95 25 46N 82 44E
Java = Jawa 103 7 0S 110 0E
Java Sea 102 4 35S 107 15E
Javadi Hills 97 12 40N 78 40E
Jávea 59 38 48N 0 10E
Javhlant = Ulyasutay 105 47 45N 96 49E
Javla 96 17 18N 75 9E
Javron 42 48 25N 0 25W
Jawa 103 7 0S 110 0E
Jawor 54 51 4N 16 11E
Jaworzno 54 50 13N 19 22E
Jay 159 33 17N 94 46W
Jayawijaya, Pengunungan 103 7 0S 139 0E
Jaydot 153 49 15N 110 15W
Jaynagar 99 26 43N 86 9E
Jayton 159 33 17N 100 35W
Jazminal 164 24 56N 101 25W
Jean 161 35 47N 115 20W
Jean Marie River 152 61 32N 120 38W
Jean Rabel 167 19 50N 73 30W
Jeanerette 159 29 52N 91 38W
Jebba, Moroc. 118 35 11N 4 43W
Jebba, Nigeria 121 9 9N 4 48E
Jebel 66 40 35N 21 15E
Jebel Aulia 123 15 10N 32 31E
Jebel Qerri 123 16 16N 32 50E
Jedburgh 35 55 28N 2 33W
Jedlicze 54 49 43N 21 40E
Jedlnia-Letnisko 54 51 25N 21 19E
Jedrzejów 54 50 35N 20 15E

Jedway
Kaboudia, Rass

Jedway 152 52 17N 131 14W
Jeetze, R. 48 52 58N 11 6 E
Jefferson, Iowa, U.S.A. 158 42 3N 94 25W
Jefferson, Tex., U.S.A. 159 32 45N 94 23W
Jefferson, Wis., U.S.A. 158 43 0N 88 49W
Jefferson City 157 36 8N 83 30W
Jefferson, Mt., Calif., U.S.A. 163 38 51N 117 0W
Jefferson, Mt., Oreg., U.S.A. 160 44 45N 121 50W
Jeffersonville 156 38 20N 85 42W
Jega 121 12 15N 4 23 E
Jekabpils 80 56 29N 25 57 E
Jelenia Góra 54 50 50N 15 45 E
Jelenia Góra □ 54 51 0N 15 30 E
Jelgava 80 56 41N 22 49 E
Jelica 66 43 50N 20 17 E
Jelli 123 5 25N 31 45 E
Jellicoe 150 49 40N 87 30W
Jelšava 53 48 37N 20 15 E
Jemaja 103 3 5N 105 45 E
Jemaluang 101 2 16N 103 52 E
Jemappes 47 50 27N 3 54 E
Jember 103 8 11 S 113 41 E
Jembongan, I. 102 6 45N 117 20 E
Jemmapes = Azzaba 119 36 48N 7 6 E
Jemnice 52 49 1N 15 34 E
Jena, Ger. 48 50 56N 11 33 E
Jena, U.S.A. 159 31 41N 92 7W
Jench'iu 106 38 43N 116 5 E
Jendouba 119 36 29N 8 47 E
Jenhochieh 108 26 29N 101 45 E
Jenhsien 106 37 8N 114 37 E
Jenhua 109 25 5N 113 45 E
Jenhuai 108 27 53N 106 17 E
Jenin 90 32 28N 35 18 E
Jenkins 156 37 13N 82 41W
Jennings 159 30 10N 92 45W
Jennings, R. 152 59 38N 132 5W
Jenny 73 57 47N 16 35 E
Jeparit 140 36 8 S 142 1 E
Jequié 171 13 51 S 40 5W
Jequitaí, R. 171 17 4 S 44 50W
Jequitinhonha 171 16 30 S 41 0W
Jequitinhonha, R. 171 15 51 S 38 53W
Jerada 118 34 40N 2 10W
Jerantut 101 3 56N 102 22 E
Jérémie 167 18 40N 74 10W
Jeremoabo 170 10 4 S 38 21W
Jerez de García Salinas 164 22 39N 103 0W
Jerez de la Frontera 57 36 41N 6 7W
Jerez de los Caballeros 57 38 20N 6 45W
Jerez, Punta 165 22 58N 97 40W
Jericho 138 23 38 S 146 6 E
Jericho = El Arīhā 90 31 52N 35 27 E
Jerichow 48 52 30N 12 2 E
Jerilderie 141 35 20 S 145 41 E
Jermyn 162 41 31N 75 31W
Jerome 161 34 50N 112 0W
Jersey City 162 40 41N 74 8W
Jersey, I. 42 49 13N 2 7W
Jersey Shore 156 41 17N 77 18W
Jerseyville 158 39 5N 90 20W
Jerumenha 171 7 5 S 43 30W
Jerusalem 90 31 47N 35 10 E
Jervaulx 33 54 19N 1 41W
Jervis B. 141 35 8 S 150 46 E
Jervis, C. 139 35 38 S 138 6 E
Jesenice 63 46 28N 14 3 E
Jesenik 53 50 0N 17 8 E
Jeseník (Frývaldov) 53 50 15N 17 11 E
Jesenske 53 48 20N 20 10 E
Jesselton = Kota Kinabalu 102 6 0N 116 12 E
Jessnitz 48 51 42N 12 19 E
Jessore 98 23 10N 89 10 E
Jesup 157 31 30N 82 0W
Jesús Carranza 165 17 28N 95 1W
Jesús María 172 30 59 S 64 5W
Jetmore 159 38 10N 99 57W
Jetpur 94 21 45N 70 10 E
Jette 47 50 53N 4 20 E
Jevnaker 71 60 15N 10 26 E
Jewett 159 31 20N 96 8W
Jewett City 162 41 36N 72 0W
Jeypore 96 18 50N 82 38 E
Jeziorany 54 53 58N 20 46 E
J.F. Rodrigues 170 2 55 S 50 20W
Jhajjar 94 28 37N 76 14 E
Jhal Jhao 93 26 20N 65 35 E
Jhalakati 98 22 39N 90 12 E
Jhalawar 94 24 35N 76 10 E
Jhang Maghiana 94 31 15N 72 15 E
Jhansi 95 25 30N 78 36 E
Jharia 95 23 45N 86 18 E
Jharsaguda 99 21 50N 84 5 E
Jharsuguda 96 21 50N 84 5 E
Jhelum 94 33 0N 73 45 E
Jhelum, R. 95 31 50N 72 10 E
Jhunjhunu 94 28 10N 75 20 E
Jiangshan 95 28 45N 118 37 E
Jibão, Serra do 171 14 48 S 45 0W
Jibiya 121 13 5N 7 12 E
Jibou 70 47 15N 23 17 E
Jicín 52 50 25N 15 20 E
Jicarón, I. 166 7 10N 81 50W
Jiddah 92 21 29N 39 16 E
Jido 99 29 2N 94 58 E
Jifna 90 31 58N 35 13 E
Jiggalong 136 23 24 S 120 47 E
Jihk'atse 107 29 15N 88 53 E
Jihlava 52 49 28N 15 35 E
Jihočeský □ 52 49 8N 14 35 E
Jihomoravský □ 53 49 5N 16 30 E
Jiht'u 105 33 27N 79 42 E
Jijiga 91 9 20N 42 50 E
Jijona 59 38 34N 0 30W
Jikamshi 121 12 12N 7 45 E
Jiloca, R. 58 41 0N 1 20W
Jílové 52 49 52N 14 29 E
Jim Jim Cr. 136 12 50 S 132 32 E
Jima 123 7 40N 36 55 E
Jimbolia 66 45 47N 20 57 E
Jimena de la Frontera 57 36 27N 5 24W
Jimenbuen 141 36 42 S 148 53 E
Jiménez 164 27 10N 105 0W
Jind 94 29 19N 76 16 E
Jindabyne 141 36 25 S 148 35 E
Jindrichuv Hradeç 52 49 10N 15 2 E
Jinja 126 0 25N 33 12 E
Jinjang 101 3 13N 101 39 E
Jinjini 120 7 20N 3 42W
Jinnah Barrage 93 32 58N 71 33 E
Jinotega 166 13 6N 85 59W
Jinotepe 166 11 50N 86 10W
Jiparaná (Machado), R. 174 8 45 S 62 20W
Jipijapa 174 1 0 S 80 40W
Jiquilpán 164 19 57N 102 42W
Jisresh Shughur 92 35 49N 36 18 E
Jitarning 137 32 48 S 117 57 E
Jitra 101 6 16N 100 25 E
Jiu, R. 70 44 50N 23 20 E
Jiuchin 109 25 53N 116 0 E
Jiuli 108 24 6N 97 54 E
Jizera, R. 52 50 21N 14 48 E
Jizl Wadi 122 26 30N 38 0 E
Jizō-zaki 110 35 34N 133 20 E
Joaçaba 173 27 5 S 51 31W
Joaíma 171 16 39 S 41 2W
João 170 2 46 S 50 59W
João Amaro 171 12 46 S 40 22W
João Câmara 170 5 32 S 35 48W
João de Almeida 125 15 10 S 13 50 E
João Pessoa 170 7 10 S 34 52W
João Pinheiro 171 17 45 S 46 10W
Joaquim Távora 171 23 30 S 49 58W
Joaquín V. González 172 25 10 S 64 0W
Jobourg, Nez de 42 49 41N 1 57W
Joch'iang 105 39 2N 88 0 E
Jódar 59 37 50N 3 21W
Jodhpur 94 26 23N 73 2 E
Joe Batt's Arm 151 49 44N 54 10W
Joensuu 78 62 37N 29 49 E
Joeuf 43 49 12N 6 1 E
Jofane 125 21 15 S 34 18 E
Joggins 151 45 42N 64 27W
Jogjakarta = Yogyakarta 103 7 49 S 110 22 E
Jōhana 111 36 37N 136 57 E
Johannesburg, S. Afr. 129 26 10 S 28 8 E
Johannesburg, U.S.A. 163 35 22N 117 38W
Johannisnäs 72 62 45N 16 15 E
Johansfors, Halland, Sweden 73 56 50N 12 58 E
Johansfors, Kronoberg, Sweden 73 56 42N 15 32 E
John Days, R. 160 45 0N 120 0W
John o' Groats 37 58 39N 3 3W
Johnshaven 37 56 48N 2 20W
Johnson 159 37 35N 101 48W
Johnson City, N.Y., U.S.A. 162 42 7N 75 57W
Johnson City, Tenn., U.S.A. 157 36 18N 82 21W
Johnson City, Tex., U.S.A. 159 30 15N 98 24W
Johnson Cy. 156 42 9N 67 0W
Johnson Ra. 137 29 40 S 119 15 E
Johnsondale 163 35 58N 118 32W
Johnsons Crossing 152 60 29N 133 18W
Johnsonville 142 41 13 S 174 48 E
Johnston 31 51 45N 5 5W
Johnston Falls = Mambilima Falls 127 10 31 S 28 45 E
Johnston I. 131 17 10N 169 8 E
Johnston Lakes 137 32 20 S 120 45 E
Johnston Ra. 137 29 40 S 119 20 E
Johnstone 34 55 50N 4 31W
Johnstone Str. 152 50 28N 126 0W
Johnstown, Ireland 39 52 46N 7 34W
Johnstown, N.Y., U.S.A. 162 43 1N 74 20W
Johnstown, Pa., U.S.A. 156 40 19N 78 53W
Johnstown Bridge 38 53 23N 6 53W
Johor □ 101 2 5N 103 20 E
Johor Baharu 101 1 28N 103 46 E
Johor, S. 101 1 45N 103 47 E
Joigny 43 48 0N 3 20 E
Joinvile 173 26 15 S 48 55 E
Joinville 43 48 27N 5 10 E
Joinville I. 13 63 15N 55 30W
Jojutla 165 18 37N 99 11W
Jokkmokk 74 66 35N 19 50 E
Jökulsá á Brú 74 65 40N 14 16W
Jökulsá Fjöllum 74 65 30N 16 15W
Jökulsa R. 74 65 30N 16 15W
Jolan 163 35 58N 121 9W
Joliet 156 41 30N 88 0W
Joliette 150 46 3N 73 24W
Jolo I. 103 6 0N 121 0 E
Jome, I. 103 1 16 S 127 30 E
Jönåker 73 58 44N 16 40 E
Jönaker 73 58 44N 16 43 E
Jones C. 150 54 33N 79 35W
Jones Sound 12 76 0N 89 0W
Jonesboro, Ark., U.S.A. 159 35 50N 90 45W
Jonesboro, Ill., U.S.A. 159 37 26N 89 18W
Jonesboro, La., U.S.A. 159 32 15N 92 41W
Jonesport 151 44 32N 67 38W
Jönköping 73 57 45N 14 10 E
Jönköpings län □ 75 57 30N 14 30 E
Jonquière 151 48 27N 71 14W
Jonsberg 73 58 30N 16 48 E
Jonsered 73 57 45N 12 10 E
Jonzac 44 45 27N 0 28W
Joplin 159 37 0N 94 25W
Jordan, Phil. 103 10 41N 122 38 E
Jordan, Mont., U.S.A. 160 47 25N 106 58W
Jordan, N.Y., U.S.A. 162 43 4N 76 29W
Jordan ■ 92 31 0N 36 0 E
Jordan, R. 90 32 10N 35 32 E
Jordan Valley 160 43 0N 117 2W
Jordânia 171 15 45 S 40 11W
Jordanów 54 49 41N 19 49 E
Jorhat 98 26 45N 94 20 E
Jörn 74 65 4N 20 1 E
Jørpeland 71 59 3N 6 1 E
Jorquera, R. 172 28 3 S 69 58W
Jos 121 9 53N 8 51 E
Jošanička Banja 66 43 24N 20 47 E
José Batlle y OrdóPez 173 33 20 S 55 10W
Josefow 54 52 10N 21 11 E
Joseni 70 47 42N 25 29 E
Joseph 160 45 27N 117 13W
Joseph Bonaparte G. 136 14 35 S 128 50 E
Joseph City 161 35 0N 110 16W
Joseph, Lac 151 52 45N 65 18W
Josephine, oilfield 19 58 35N 2 45 E
Joshua Tree 163 34 8N 116 19W
Joshua Tree Nat. Mon. 163 33 56N 116 5W
Josselin 42 47 57N 2 33W
Jostedal 71 61 35N 7 15 E
Jostedalsbre, Mt. 71 61 45N 7 0 E
Jotunheimen 71 61 35N 8 25 E
Jounieh 92 33 59N 35 30 E
Jourdanton 159 28 54N 98 32W
Journe 46 52 58N 5 48 E
Joussard 152 55 22N 115 57W
Joux, Lac de 50 46 39N 6 18 E
Jouzjan □ 93 36 10N 66 0 E
Jovellanos 166 22 40N 81 10W
Jowai 98 25 26N 92 12 E
Joyce's Country, dist. 38 53 32N 9 30W
Joyeuse 45 44 29N 4 16 E
Jozini Dam 129 27 27 S 32 7 E
Ju Shui, R. 109 28 36N 116 4 E
Juan Aldama 164 24 20N 103 23W
Juan Bautista 161 36 55N 121 33W
Juan Bautista Alberdi 172 34 26 S 61 48W
Juan de Fuca Str. 160 48 15N 124 0W
Juan de Nova, I. 129 17 3 S 42 45 E
Juan Fernández, Arch. de 131 33 50 S 80 0W
Juan José Castelli 172 25 57 S 60 37W
Juan L. Lacaze 172 34 26 S 57 25W
Juárez, Argent. 172 37 40 S 59 43W
Juárez, Mexico 164 27 37N 100 44W
Juárez, Sierra de 164 32 0N 116 0W
Juatinga, Ponta de 171 23 17 S 44 30W
Juàzeiro 170 9 30 S 40 30W
Juàzeiro do Norte 170 7 10 S 39 18W
Jûbâ 123 4 57N 31 35 E
Juba, R. 91 1 30N 42 35 E
Jubaila 92 24 55N 46 25 E
Jûbâl 122 27 30N 34 0 E
Jubbulpore = Jabalpur 95 23 9N 79 58 E
Jübek 48 54 31N 9 24 E
Jubga 83 44 19N 38 48 E
Jubilee L. 137 29 0 S 126 50 E
Juby, C. 116 28 0N 12 59W
Júcar, R. 58 40 8N 2 13W
Júcaro 166 21 37N 78 51W
Juch'eng 109 25 32N 113 39 E
Juchitán 165 16 27N 95 5W
Judaea = Yehuda 90 31 35N 34 57 E
Judenburg 52 47 12N 14 38 E
Judith Gap 160 46 48N 109 46W
Judith Pt. 162 41 20N 71 30W
Judith, R. 160 47 30N 109 30W
Juian 109 27 45N 120 38 E
Juich'ang 109 29 40N 115 39 E
Juigalpa 166 12 6N 85 26W
Juillac 44 45 20N 1 19 E
Juist, I. 48 53 40N 7 0 E
Juiz de Fora 171 21 43 S 43 19W
Jujuy 172 24 10 S 65 25W
Jujuy □ 172 23 20 S 65 40W
Jukao 109 32 24N 120 35 E
Julesberg 158 41 0N 102 20W
Juli 174 16 10 S 69 25W
Julia Cr. 138 20 0 S 141 11 E
Julia Creek 138 20 39 S 141 44 E
Juliaca 174 15 25 S 70 10W
Julian 163 33 4N 116 38W
Julian Alps = Julijske Alpe 63 46 15N 14 1 E
Julianakanaal 47 51 6N 5 52 E
Julianehåb 12 60 43N 46 0W
Julianstown 38 53 40N 6 16W
Jülich 48 50 55N 6 20 E
Julier P. 51 46 28N 9 32 E
Julijske Alpe 63 46 15N 14 1 E
Julimes 164 28 25N 105 27W
Jullundur 94 31 20N 75 40 E
Jumbo 127 17 30 S 30 58 E
Jumento, Cayos 167 23 0N 75 40 E
Jumet 47 50 27N 4 25 E
Jumilla 59 38 28N 1 19W
Jumla 95 29 15N 82 13 E
Jumna, R. = Yamuna 94 27 0N 78 30 E
Junagadh 94 21 30N 70 30 E
Junan 109 32 58N 114 31 E
Junction, Tex., U.S.A. 159 30 29N 99 48W
Junction, Utah, U.S.A. 161 38 10N 112 15W
Junction B. 138 11 52 S 133 55 E
Junction City, Kans., U.S.A. 158 39 4N 96 55W
Junction City, Oreg., U.S.A. 160 44 20N 123 12W
Jundah 138 24 46 S 143 2 E
Jundiaí 173 23 10 S 47 0W
Juneau 147 58 26N 134 30W
Junee 141 34 53 S 147 35 E
Jung Chiang, R. 108 23 25N 110 0 E
Jungan 108 25 14N 109 23 E
Jungch'ang 108 29 27N 105 33 E
Jungch'eng 107 37 9N 122 23 E
Jungchiang 108 25 56N 108 31 E
Jungching 108 29 49N 102 55 E
Jungfrau 50 46 32N 7 58 E
Jungho 106 35 21N 110 32 E
Junghsien, Kwangsi-Chuang, China 109 22 52N 110 33 E
Junghsien, Szechwan, China 108 29 29N 104 22 E
Junglinster 47 49 43N 6 15 E
Jungshahi 94 24 52N 67 44 E
Jungshui 108 24 14N 109 23 E
Juniata, R. 162 40 30N 77 40W
Junín 172 34 33 S 60 57W
Junín de los Andes 176 39 45 S 71 0W
Junnar 96 19 12N 73 58 E
Junquera, La 58 42 25N 2 53 E
Junta, La 159 38 0N 103 30W
Juntura 160 43 44N 119 4W
Juparanã, Lagoa 171 19 35 S 40 18W
Jupiter, R. 151 49 29N 63 37W
Juquiá 171 24 19 S 47 38W
Jur, Nahr el 123 8 45N 29 0 E
Jura 43 46 35N 6 5 E
Jura □ 43 46 47N 5 45 E
Jura, I. 34 56 0N 5 50W
Jura, Paps of, mts. 34 55 55N 6 0W
Jura, Sd. of 34 55 57N 5 45W
Jura Suisse 50 47 10N 7 0 E
Jurado 174 7 7N 77 46W
Jurby Hd. 32 54 23N 4 31W
Jurien B. 132 30 17 S 115 0 E
Jurilovca 70 44 46N 28 52W
Jurm 93 36 50N 70 45 E
Juruá, R. 174 2 30 S 66 0W
Juruena, R. 174 7 20 S 58 3W
Juruti 175 2 9 S 56 4W
Jushan 107 36 54N 121 30 E
Jussey 43 47 50N 5 55 E
Justo Daract 172 33 52 S 65 12W
Jüterbog 48 51 59N 13 6 E
Juticalpa 166 14 40N 85 50W
Jutland 16 56 0N 8 0 E
Jutphaas 46 52 2N 5 6 E
Jutung 109 32 19N 121 14 E
Juvigny-sous-Andaine 42 48 32N 0 30W
Juvisy 43 48 43N 2 23 E
Juwain 93 31 45N 61 30 E
Juyüan 109 24 46N 113 16 E
Juzennecourt 43 48 10N 5 0 E
Jye-kundo 99 33 0N 96 50 E
Jylhama 74 64 34N 26 40 E
Jylland 73 56 15N 9 20 E
Jylland (Jutland) 73 56 25N 9 30 E
Jyväskylä 74 62 14N 25 44 E

K

K. Sedili Besar 101 1 55N 104 5 E
K2, Mt. 95 36 0N 77 0 E
Ka Lae (South C.) 147 18 55N 155 41W
Kaaia, Mt. 147 21 31N 158 9W
Kaap die Goeie Hoop 128 34 24 S 18 30 E
Kaap Plato 128 28 30 S 24 0 E
Kaapkruis 128 21 43 S 14 0 E
Kaapstad = Cape Town 125 33 56 S 18 27 E
Kaatsheuvel 47 51 39N 5 2 E
Kabaena, I. 103 5 15 S 122 0 E
Kabala 120 9 38N 11 37W
Kabale 126 1 15 S 30 0 E
Kabalo 126 6 0 S 27 0 E
Kabambare 126 4 41 S 27 39 E
Kabango 127 8 35 S 28 30 E
Kabanjahe 102 8 2N 98 27 E
Kabara 120 16 40N 2 50W
Kabardinka 82 44 40N 37 57 E
Kabardino-Balkar, A.S.S.R. □ 83 43 30N 43 30 E
Kabarega Falls 126 2 15N 31 38 E
Kabasalan 103 7 47N 122 44 E
Kabba 121 7 57N 6 3 E
Kabe 110 34 31N 132 31 E
Kabi 121 13 30N 12 35 E
Kabin Buri 100 13 57N 101 43 E
Kabinakagami L. 150 48 54N 84 25W
Kabinda 126 6 23 S 24 28 E
Kablungu, C. 135 6 20 S 150 1 E
Kabna 122 19 6N 32 40 E
Kabompo 127 13 30 S 24 14 E
Kabompo, R. 127 13 50 S 24 10 E
Kabondo 127 8 58 S 25 40 E
Kabongo 126 7 22 S 25 33 E
Kabou 121 9 28N 0 55 E
Kaboudia, Rass 119 35 13N 11 10 E

Kabra **Kandalakshkiyzaliv**

Kabra	**138**	23 25 S	150 25 E
Kabūd Gonbad	**93**	37 5N	59 45 E
Kabuiri	**121**	11 30N	13 30 E
Kabul	**94**	34 28N	69 18 E
Kabul □	**93**	34 0N	68 30 E
Kabul, R.	**94**	34 30N	69 13 E
Kabunga	**126**	1 38 S	28 3 E
Kaburuang	**103**	3 50N	126 30 E
Kabushiya	**123**	16 54N	33 41 E
Kabwe	**127**	14 30 S	28 29 E
Kabwum	**135**	6 11 S	147 15 E
Kačanik	**66**	42 13N	21 12 E
Kachanovo	**80**	57 25N	27 38 E
Kachebera	**127**	13 56 S	32 50 E
Kachin □	**98**	26 0N	97 0 E
Kachira, Lake	**126**	0 40 S	31 0 E
Kachiry	**76**	53 10N	75 50 E
Kachisi	**123**	9 40N	37 57 E
Kachkanar	**84**	58 42N	59 33 E
Kachot	**101**	11 30N	103 3 E
Kaçkar	**83**	40 45N	41 30 E
Kadaingti	**98**	17 37N	97 32 E
Kadan Kyun, I.	**101**	12 30N	98 20 E
Kadanai, R.	**94**	32 0N	66 10 E
Kadarkút	**53**	46 13N	17 39 E
Kadayanallur	**97**	9 3N	77 22 E
Kaddi	**121**	13 40N	5 40 E
Kade	**121**	6 7N	0 56W
Kadgo, L.	**137**	25 30 S	125 30 E
Kadi	**94**	23 18N	72 23 E
Kadina	**140**	34 0 S	137 43 E
Kadiri	**97**	14 12N	78 13 E
Kadiyevka	**83**	48 35N	38 30 E
Kadoka	**158**	43 50N	101 31W
Kadom	**81**	54 37N	42 24 E
Kaduna	**121**	10 30N	7 21 E
Kaduna □	**121**	11 0N	7 30 E
Kaduna, R.	**121**	10 5N	8 10 E
Kadyoha	**120**	8 58N	5 53W
Kadzhi-Say	**85**	42 8N	77 10 E
Kaedi	**120**	16 9N	13 28W
Kaelé	**121**	10 15N	14 15 E
Kaena Pt.	**147**	21 35N	158 17W
Kaeng Khoï	**100**	14 35N	101 0 E
Kaeo	**142**	35 6 S	173 49 E
Kaerh, China	**105**	31 45N	80 22 E
Kaerh, Sudan	**123**	5 35N	31 20 E
Kaesŏng	**107**	37 58N	126 35 E
Kaf	**92**	31 25N	37 20 E
Kafakumba	**124**	9 38 S	23 46 E
Kafan	**79**	39 18N	46 15 E
Kafanchan	**121**	9 40N	8 20 E
Kafareti	**121**	10 25N	11 12 E
Kaffrine	**120**	14 8N	15 36W
Kafia Kingi	**117**	9 20N	24 25 E
Kafinda	**127**	12 32 S	30 20 E
Kafirévs, Ákra	**69**	38 9N	24 8 E
Kafiristan	**93**	35 0N	70 30 E
Kafr Ana	**70**	32 2N	34 48 E
Kafr 'Ein	**90**	32 3N	35 7 E
Kafr el Dauwâr	**122**	31 8N	30 8 E
Kafr Kama	**90**	32 44N	35 26 E
Kafr Kannã	**90**	32 45N	35 20 E
Kafr Malik	**90**	32 0N	35 18 E
Kafr Mandã	**90**	32 49N	35 15 E
Kafr Quaddum	**90**	32 14N	35 7 E
Kafr Ra'i	**90**	32 23N	35 9 E
Kafr Sir	**90**	33 19N	35 23 E
Kafr Yasif	**90**	32 58N	35 10 E
Kafue	**127**	15 46 S	28 9 E
Kafue Flats	**127**	15 32 S	27 0 E
Kafue Gorge	**127**	16 0 S	28 0 E
Kafue Hook	**127**	14 58 S	26 0 E
Kafue Nat. Park	**65**	15 30 S	25 40 E
Kafue, R.	**125**	15 30 S	26 0 E
Kafulwe	**127**	9 0 S	29 1 E
Kaga, Afghan.	**94**	34 14N	70 10 E
Kaga, Japan	**111**	36 16N	136 15 E
Kagamil I.	**147**	53 0N	169 40W
Kagan	**85**	39 43N	64 33 E
Kagawa-ken □	**110**	34 15N	134 0 E
Kagera R.	**126**	1 15 S	31 20 E
Kagoshima	**110**	31 36N	130 40 E
Kagoshima-ken □	**110**	30 0N	130 0 E
Kagoshima-Wan	**110**	31 0N	130 40 E
Kagul	**82**	45 50N	28 15 E
Kahajan, R.	**102**	2 10 S	114 0 E
Kahama	**126**	4 8 S	32 30 E
Kahama □	**126**	3 40 S	32 0 E
Kahang	**101**	2 12N	103 32 E
Kahe	**126**	3 30 S	37 25 E
Kahemba	**124**	7 18 S	18 55 E
Kaherekoua Mts.	**143**	45 45 S	167 15 E
Kahniah, R.	**152**	58 15N	120 55W
Kahnuj	**93**	27 55N	57 40 E
Kahoka	**158**	40 25N	91 42W
Kahoolawe, I.	**147**	20 33N	156 35W
Kahuku & Pt.	**147**	21 41N	157 57W
Kahulai	**147**	20 54N	156 28W
Kahurangi, Pt.	**143**	40 50 S	172 10 E
Kahuta	**94**	33 35N	73 24 E
Kai Kai	**128**	19 52 S	21 15 E
Kai, Kepulauan	**103**	5 55 S	132 45W
Kaiama	**121**	9 36N	4 1 E
Kaiapit	**135**	6 18 S	146 18 E
Kaiapoi	**143**	42 24 S	172 40 E
Kaibara	**111**	35 8N	135 5 E
K'aichien	**109**	23 45N	111 47 E
K'aifeng	**106**	34 50N	114 27 E
Kaihsien	**107**	40 25N	122 25 E
K'aihsien	**108**	31 12N	108 25 E
K'aihua	**109**	29 9N	118 24 E
Kaiingveld	**128**	30 0 S	22 0 E
Kaikohe	**142**	35 25 S	173 49 E
Kaikoura	**143**	42 25 S	173 43 E
Kaikoura Pen.	**143**	42 25 S	173 43 E
Kaikoura Ra.	**143**	41 59 S	173 41 E
Kailahun	**120**	8 18N	10 39W
Kailashahar	**98**	25 19N	92 0 E
Kaili	**108**	26 32N	107 57 E
K'ailu	**107**	43 35N	121 12 E
Kailua	**147**	19 39N	156 0W
Kaimana	**103**	3 30 S	133 45 E
Kaimanawa Mts.	**142**	39 15 S	175 56 E
Kaimata	**143**	42 34 S	171 28 E
Kaimganj	**95**	27 33N	79 24 E
Kaimon-Dake	**110**	31 11N	130 32 E
Kaimur Hill	**95**	24 30N	82 0 E
Kainan	**110**	34 9N	135 12 E
Kainantu	**135**	6 18 S	145 52 E
Kaingaroa Forest	**142**	38 30 S	176 30 E
Kainji Res.	**121**	10 1N	4 40 E
Kaipara Harb.	**142**	36 25 S	174 14 E
K'aip'ing	**109**	22 31N	112 32 E
Kaipokok B.	**151**	54 54N	59 47W
Kairana	**94**	29 33N	77 15 E
Kairiru, I.	**138**	3 20 S	143 20 E
Kaironi	**103**	0 47 S	133 40 E
Kairouan	**119**	35 45N	10 5 E
Kairuku	**135**	8 51 S	146 35 E
Kaiserslautern	**49**	49 30N	7 43 E
Kaitaia	**142**	35 8 S	173 17 E
Kaitangata	**143**	46 17 S	169 51 E
Kaithal	**94**	29 48N	76 26 E
Kaitu, R.	**94**	33 20N	70 20 E
Kaiwi Channel	**147**	21 13N	157 30W
K'aiyang	**108**	27 4N	106 55 E
K'aiyüan, Liaoning, China	**107**	42 33N	124 4 E
K'aiyüan, Yunnan, China	**108**	23 47N	103 10 E
Kaiyuh Mts.	**147**	63 40N	159 0W
Kajaani	**74**	64 17N	27 46 E
Kajabbi	**138**	20 0 S	140 1 E
Kajan, R.	**102**	2 40N	116 40 E
Kajang	**101**	2 59N	101 48 E
Kajeli	**103**	3 20 S	127 10 E
Kajiado	**126**	1 53 S	36 48 E
Kajiki	**110**	31 44N	130 40 E
Kajo Kaji	**123**	3 58N	31 40 E
Kajoa, I.	**103**	0 1N	127 28 E
Kajuagung	**102**	32 8 S	104 46 E
Kakabeka Falls	**150**	48 24N	89 37W
Kakamas	**125**	28 45 S	20 33 E
Kakamega	**126**	0 20N	34 46 E
Kakamega □	**126**	0 20N	34 46 E
Kakamigahara	**111**	35 28N	136 48 E
Kakanj	**66**	44 9N	18 7 E
Kakanui Mts.	**143**	45 10 S	170 30 E
Kakapotahi	**143**	43 0 S	170 45 E
Kake, Japan	**110**	34 36N	132 19 E
Kake, U.S.A.	**147**	57 0N	134 0W
Kakegawa	**111**	34 45N	138 1 E
Kakhib	**83**	42 28N	46 34 E
Kakhovskoye Vdkhr.	**82**	47 5N	34 16 E
Kakia	**125**	24 48 S	23 22 E
Kakinada = Cocanada	**99**	16 50N	82 11 E
Kakinada (Cocanada)	**96**	16 50N	82 11 E
Kakisa L.	**152**	60 56N	117 43W
Kakisa, R.	**152**	61 3N	117 10W
Kakogawa	**110**	34 46N	134 51 E
Kaktovik	**147**	70 8N	143 50W
Kakwa, R.	**152**	54 37N	118 28W
Kala	**121**	12 2N	14 40 E
Kala Oya.	**97**	8 15N	80 0 E
Kala Shank'ou	**95**	35 42N	78 20 E
Kalaa-Kebira	**119**	35 59N	10 32 E
Kalabagh	**94**	33 0N	71 28 E
Kalabáka	**68**	39 42N	21 39 E
Kalabo	**125**	14 58 S	22 33 E
Kalach	**81**	50 22N	41 0 E
Kaladan, R.	**99**	21 30N	92 45 E
Kalahari, Des.	**128**	24 0 S	22 0 E
Kalahari Gemsbok Nat. Pk.	**128**	26 0 S	20 30 E
Kalahasti	**97**	13 45N	79 44 E
Kalai-Khumb	**85**	38 28N	70 46 E
Kalaja e Turrës	**68**	41 10N	19 28 E
Kalakamati	**129**	20 40 S	27 25 E
Kalakan	**77**	55 15N	116 45 E
K'alak'unlun Shank'ou	**95**	35 33N	77 46 E
Kalam	**95**	35 34N	72 30 E
Kalama, U.S.A.	**160**	46 0N	122 55W
Kalama, Zaîre	**126**	2 52 S	28 35 E
Kalamariá	**68**	40 33N	22 55 E
Kalamata	**69**	37 3N	22 10 E
Kalamazoo	**156**	42 20N	85 35W
Kalamazoo, R.	**156**	42 40N	86 12W
Kalamb	**96**	18 3N	74 48 E
Kalambo Falls	**127**	8 37 S	31 35 E
Kálamos, I.	**69**	38 37N	20 55 E
Kalamoti	**69**	38 15N	26 4 E
Kalamunda	**137**	32 0 S	116 0 E
Kalangadoo	**140**	37 34 S	140 41 E
Kalannie	**137**	30 22 S	117 5 E
Kalao, I.	**103**	7 21 S	121 0 E
Kalaotoa, I.	**103**	7 20 S	121 50 E
Kälarne	**72**	62 59N	16 8 E
Kalárovo	**53**	47 54N	18 0 E
Kalasin	**100**	16 26N	103 30 E
Kalat	**93**	29 8N	66 31 E
Kalat □	**93**	27 0N	64 30 E
Kalat-i-Ghilzai	**93**	32 15N	66 58 E
Kálathos (Calato)	**69**	36 9N	28 8 E
Kalaupapa	**147**	21 12N	156 59W
Kalaus, R.	**83**	45 40N	43 30 E
Kalávrita	**69**	38 3N	22 8 E
Kalaw	**98**	16 24N	97 30 E
Kalba	**120**	9 30N	2 42W
Kalbarri	**137**	27 40 S	114 10 E
Kaldhovd	**71**	60 5N	8 20 E
Kalecik	**82**	40 4N	33 26 E
Kalegauk Kyun	**99**	15 33N	97 35 E
Kalehe	**126**	2 6 S	28 50 E
Kalema	**126**	1 12 S	31 55 E
Kalemie	**124**	5 55 S	29 9 E
Kalemyo	**98**	23 11N	94 4 E
Kalety	**54**	50 35N	18 52 E
Kalewa	**98**	22 41N	95 32 E
Kálfafellsstaður	**74**	64 11N	15 53W
Kalgan = Changchiak'ou	**106**	40 50N	114 53 E
Kalgoorlie	**137**	30 40 S	121 22 E
Kaliakra, Nos	**67**	43 21N	28 30 E
Kalianda	**102**	5 50 S	105 45 E
Kalibo	**103**	11 43N	122 22 E
Kaliganj Town	**98**	23 25N	89 8 E
Kalima	**126**	2 33 S	26 32 E
Kalimantan Barat □	**102**	0 0	110 30 E
Kalimantan Selatan □	**102**	4 10 S	115 30 E
Kalimantan Tengah □	**102**	2 0 S	113 30 E
Kalimantan Timor □	**102**	1 30N	116 30 E
Kálimnos, I.	**69**	37 0N	27 0 E
Kalimpong	**95**	27 4N	88 35 E
Kalinadi, R.	**97**	14 50N	74 20 E
Kalinin	**81**	56 55N	35 55 E
Kaliningrad	**80**	54 42N	20 32 E
Kalinino	**83**	45 12N	38 59 E
Kalininskoye	**85**	42 50N	73 49 E
Kalinkovichi	**80**	52 12N	29 20 E
Kalinovik	**66**	43 31N	18 29 E
Kalipetrovo (Starčevo)	**67**	44 5N	27 14 E
Kaliro	**126**	0 56N	33 30 E
Kalirrákhi	**68**	40 40N	24 35 E
Kalispell	**160**	48 10N	114 22W
Kalisz	**54**	51 45N	18 8 E
Kalisz □	**54**	51 30N	18 0 E
Kalisz Pom	**54**	53 17N	15 55 E
Kaliua	**126**	5 5 S	31 48 E
Kaliveli Tank	**97**	12 5N	79 50 E
Kalix R.	**74**	67 0N	22 0 E
Kalka	**94**	30 56N	76 57 E
Kalkaroo	**140**	31 12 S	143 54 E
Kalkaska	**150**	44 44N	85 11W
Kalkfeld	**128**	20 57 S	16 14 E
Kalkfontein	**128**	22 4 S	20 57 E
Kalkfontein Dam	**128**	29 30 S	24 15 E
Kalkrand	**128**	24 1 S	17 35 E
Kall L.	**72**	63 35N	13 10 E
Kallakurichi	**97**	11 44N	79 1 E
Kållandsö	**73**	58 40N	13 5 E
Källby	**73**	58 30N	13 8 E
Kallia	**86**	31 46N	35 30 E
Kallidaikurichi	**97**	8 38N	77 31 E
Kallinge	**73**	56 15N	15 18 E
Kallithéa	**69**	37 55N	23 41 E
Kallmeti	**68**	41 51N	19 41 E
Kallonís, Kólpos	**69**	39 10N	26 10 E
Kallsjön	**74**	63 38N	13 0 E
Kalltorp	**73**	58 23N	13 20 E
Kalmalo	**121**	13 40N	5 20 E
Kalmar	**73**	56 40N	16 20 E
Kalmar län □	**73**	57 25N	16 15 E
Kalmar sund	**73**	56 40N	16 25 E
Kalmthout	**47**	51 23N	4 29 E
Kalmyk A.S.S.R. □	**83**	46 5N	46 1 E
Kalmykovo	**83**	49 0N	51 35 E
Kalna	**95**	23 13N	88 25 E
Kalo	**135**	10 1 S	147 48 E
Kalocsa	**53**	46 32N	19 0 E
Kalofer	**67**	42 37N	24 59 E
Kalol, Gujarat, India	**94**	23 15N	72 33 E
Kalol, Gujarat, India	**94**	22 37N	73 31 E
Kalola	**127**	10 0 S	28 0 E
Kalolímnos	**69**	37 4N	27 8 E
Kalomo	**127**	17 0 S	26 30 E
Kaloнerón	**69**	37 20N	21 38 E
Kalpi	**95**	26 8N	79 47 E
Kalrayan Hills	**97**	11 45N	78 40 E
Kalsubai, Mt.	**96**	17 35N	73 45 E
Kaltbrunn	**51**	47 13N	9 2 E
Kaltungo	**121**	9 48N	11 19 E
Kalu	**94**	25 5N	67 39 E
Kaluga	**81**	54 35N	36 10 E
Kalulushi	**127**	12 50 S	28 3 E
Kalundborg	**73**	55 41N	11 5 E
Kalush	**80**	42 9N	24 12 E
Kałuszyn	**54**	52 13N	21 52 E
Kalutara	**97**	6 35N	80 0 E
Kalwaria	**54**	49 53N	19 41 E
Kalya	**84**	60 15N	59 59 E
Kalyan, Austral.	**140**	34 55 S	139 49 E
Kalyan, India	**96**	20 30N	74 3 E
Kalyani	**174**	17 53N	76 59 E
Kalyazin	**81**	57 15N	37 45 E
Kam Keut	**101**	18 20N	104 48 E
Kama, Burma	**98**	22 10N	95 10 E
Kama, Zaîre	**126**	3 30 S	27 5 E
Kama, R.	**84**	60 0N	53 0 E
Kamachumu	**126**	1 37 S	31 37 E
Kamae	**110**	32 48N	131 56 E
Kamaguenam	**121**	13 36N	10 30 E
Kamaing	**98**	24 26N	94 55 E
Kamaishi	**112**	39 20N	142 0 E
Kamakura	**111**	35 19N	139 33 E
Kamalia	**94**	30 44N	72 42 E
Kamalino	**147**	21 50N	160 14W
Kamamaung	**98**	17 21N	97 40 E
Kamango	**126**	0 40N	29 52 E
Kamapanda	**127**	12 5 S	24 0 E
Kamaran	**91**	15 28N	42 35 E
Kamashi	**85**	38 51N	65 23 E
Kamativi	**127**	18 15 S	0 27 E
Kamba	**121**	11 50N	3 45 E
Kambalda	**137**	31 10 S	121 37 E
Kambam	**97**	9 45N	77 16 E
Kambar	**94**	27 37N	68 1 E
Kambarka	**84**	56 15N	54 11 E
Kambia	**120**	9 3N	12 53W
Kambolé	**127**	8 47 S	30 48 E
Kambove	**127**	10 51 S	26 33 E
Kamchatka, P-ov.	**77**	57 0N	160 0 E
Kamde	**138**	8 0 S	140 58 E
Kamen	**76**	53 50N	81 30 E
Kamen Kashirskiy	**80**	51 39N	24 56 E
Kamenica	**66**	44 25N	19 40 E
Kamenice	**52**	49 18N	15 2 E
Kamenjak, Rt.	**63**	44 47N	13 55 E
Kamenka, R.S.F.S.R., U.S.S.R.	**78**	65 58N	44 0 E
Kamenka, R.S.F.S.R., U.S.S.R.	**81**	50 47N	39 20 E
Kamenka Bugskaya	**80**	50 8N	24 16 E
Kamenka Dneprovskaya	**82**	47 29N	34 14 E
Kamensk	**76**	56 25N	62 45 E
Kamensk Shakhtinskiy	**83**	48 23N	40 20 E
Kamensk-Uralskiy	**84**	56 25N	62 2 E
Kamenskiy	**81**	50 48N	45 25 E
Kamenskoye	**77**	62 45N	165 30 E
Kamenyak	**67**	43 24N	26 57 E
Kamenz	**48**	51 17N	14 7 E
Kameoka	**111**	35 0N	135 35 E
Kames	**34**	55 53N	5 15W
Kameyama	**111**	34 51N	126 27 E
Kami	**68**	42 17N	20 18 E
Kami-Jima	**110**	32 27N	130 20 E
Kami-koshiki-Jima	**110**	31 50N	129 52 E
Kamiah	**160**	46 12N	116 2W
Kamien Krajenskie	**54**	53 32N	17 32 E
Kamien Pomorski	**54**	53 57N	14 43 E
Kamiensk	**54**	51 12N	19 29 E
Kamiita	**110**	34 6N	134 22 E
Kamilonísion	**69**	35 50N	26 15 E
Kamilukuak, L.	**153**	62 22N	101 40W
Kamina	**127**	8 45 S	25 0 E
Kaminak L.	**153**	62 10N	95 0W
Kamioka	**111**	36 25N	137 15 E
Kamituga Mungombe	**126**	3 2 S	28 10 E
Kamiyaku	**112**	30 25N	130 30 E
Kamloops	**152**	50 40N	120 20W
Kamo	**143**	35 42 S	174 20 E
Kamogawa	**111**	35 5N	140 5 E
Kamoke	**94**	32 4N	74 4 E
Kamono	**124**	3 10 S	13 20 E
Kamp, R.	**52**	48 35N	15 26 E
Kampala	**126**	0 20N	32 30 E
Kampar	**101**	4 18N	101 9 E
Kampar, R.	**102**	0 30N	102 0 E
Kampen	**46**	52 33N	5 53 E
Kamperland	**47**	51 34N	3 43 E
Kamphaeng Phet	**100**	16 28N	99 30 E
Kampolombo, L.	**127**	11 30 S	29 35 E
Kampong Ayer Puteh	**101**	4 15N	103 10 E
Kampong Jerangau	**101**	4 50N	103 10 E
Kampong Raja	**101**	5 45N	102 35 E
Kampong Sedili Besar	**101**	1 56N	104 8 E
Kampong To	**101**	6 3N	101 13 E
Kampot	**101**	10 36N	104 10 E
Kamptee	**94**	21 9N	79 19 E
Kampti	**120**	10 7N	3 25W
Kampuchea ■ = Cambodia	**100**	12 15N	105 0 E
Kamrau, Teluk	**103**	3 30 S	133 45 E
Kamsack	**153**	51 34N	101 54W
Kamskove Ustye	**81**	55 10N	49 20 E
Kamskoye Vdkhr.	**78**	58 0N	56 0 E
Kamuchawie L.	**153**	56 18N	101 59W
Kamui-Misaki	**112**	45 3N	142 30 E
Kamyshin	**81**	50 10N	45 30 E
Kamyshlov	**84**	56 50N	62 43 E
Kamyzyak	**83**	46 4N	48 10 E
Kan	**98**	20 53N	93 49 E
Kan Chiang, R.	**109**	29 45N	116 10 E
Kanaaupscow	**150**	54 2N	76 30W
Kanab	**161**	37 3N	112 29W
Kanab Creek	**161**	37 0N	112 40W
Kanaga I.	**147**	51 45N	177 22W
Kanagawa-ken □	**111**	35 20N	139 20 E
Kanairiktok, R.	**151**	55 2N	60 18W
Kanakanak	**147**	59 0N	158 58W
Kanakapura	**97**	12 33N	77 28 E
Kanália	**68**	39 30N	22 53 E
Kananga	**124**	5 55 S	22 18 E
Kanarraville	**161**	37 34N	113 12W
Kanash	**81**	55 48N	47 32 E
Kanawha, R.	**156**	39 40N	82 0W
Kanayis, Ras el	**122**	31 30N	28 5 E
Kanazawa	**111**	36 30N	136 38 E
Kanbalu	**98**	17 55N	85 24 E
Kanchanaburi	**100**	14 8N	99 31 E
Kanchenjunga, Mt.	**95**	27 50N	88 10 E
Kanchipuram (Conjeeveram)	**97**	12 52N	79 45 E
Kanchou	**109**	25 51N	114 59 E
Kanch'üan	**106**	36 19N	109 19 E
Kanda Kanda	**124**	6 52 S	23 48 E
Kandagach	**79**	49 20N	57 15 E
Kandahar	**94**	31 32N	65 30 E
Kandahar □	**94**	31 0N	65 0 E
Kandalaksha	**78**	67 9N	32 30 E
Kandalakshkiyzaliv	**78**	66 0N	35 0 E

Kandalu Kástron

Kandalu 93 29 55N 63 20 E
Kandangan 102 2 50S 115 20 E
Kandanos 69 35 19N 23 44 E
Kandé 121 9 57N 1 53 E
Kandep 135 5 54S 143 32 E
Kander, R. 50 46 33N 7 38 E
Kandersteg 50 46 30N 7 40 E
Kandewu 127 14 1S 26 16 E
Kandhila 69 37 46N 22 22 E
Kandhkot 94 28 16N 69 8 E
Kandhla 94 29 18N 77 19 E
Kandi, Benin 121 11 7N 2 55 E
Kandi, India 95 23 58N 88 5 E
Kandinduna 127 13 58S 24 19 E
Kandira 92 41 5N 30 10 E
Kandla 94 23 0N 70 10 E
Kandos 141 32 45S 149 58 E
Kandrach 93 25 30N 65 30 E
Kandrian 135 6 14S 149 37 E
Kandukur 95 15 12N 79 57 E
Kandy 97 7 18N 80 43 E
Kane 156 41 39N 78 53W
Kane Bassin 12 79 30N 68 0W
Kanel 120 13 18N 14 35W
Kaneohe 147 21 25N 157 48W
Kanevskaya 83 46 3N 39 3 E
Kanfanar 63 45 7N 13 50 E
Kang 93 30 55N 61 55 E
Kangaba 120 11 56N 8 25W
Kangar 101 6 27N 100 12 E
Kangaroo I. 140 35 45S 137 0 E
Kangaroo Mts. 138 23 25S 142 0 E
Kangavar 92 34 40N 48 0 E
Kangean, Kepulauan 102 6 55S 115 23 E
Kangerdlugsuaé 12 68 10N 32 20W
Kanggye 107 41 0N 126 35 E
Kanggyŏng 107 36 10N 126 0 E
Kanghwa 107 37 45N 126 30 E
K'angkang 108 32 46N 101 3 E
Kangnŭng 107 37 45N 128 54 E
Kango 124 0 11N 10 5 E
K'angp'ing 107 43 45N 123 20 E
Kangpokpi 98 25 8N 93 58 E
K'angting 108 30 2N 102 0 E
Kangtissu Shan 95 31 0N 82 0 E
Kangto, Mt. 99 27 50N 92 35 E
Kangyao 107 44 15N 126 40 E
Kangyidaung 98 16 56N 94 54 E
Kanhangad 97 12 21N 74 58 E
Kanheri 96 19 13N 72 50 E
Kani, China 99 29 25N 95 25 E
Kani, Ivory C. 120 8 29N 6 36W
Kaniama 126 7 30S 24 12 E
Kaniapiskau L. 151 54 10N 69 55W
Kaniapiskau, R. 151 57 40N 69 30 E
Kanibadam 85 40 17N 70 25 E
Kanin Nos, Mys 78 68 45N 43 20 E
Kanin, P-ov. 78 68 0N 45 0 E
Kanina 68 40 23N 19 30 E
Kaniva 140 36 22S 141 18 E
Kanjiza 66 46 3N 20 4 E
Kanjut Sar 95 36 15N 75 25 E
Kankakee 156 41 6N 87 50W
Kankakee, R. 156 41 13N 87 0W
Kankan 120 10 30N 9 15W
Kanker 96 20 10N 81 40 E
Kankouchen 107 40 30N 119 27 E
Kanku 106 34 45N 105 12 E
Kankunskiy 77 57 37N 126 8 E
Kanmuri-Yama 110 34 30N 132 4 E
Kannabe 110 34 32N 133 23 E
Kannapolis 157 35 32N 80 37W
Kannauj 95 27 3N 79 26 E
Kannod 93 22 45N 76 40 E
Kano 121 12 2N 8 30 E
Kano □ 121 12 30N 9 0 E
Kan'onji 110 34 7N 133 39 E
Kanoroba 120 9 7N 6 8W
Kanowit 102 2 14N 112 20 E
Kanowna 137 30 32S 121 31 E
Kanoya 110 31 25N 130 50 E
Kanózuga 54 49 58N 22 25 E
Kanpetlet 98 21 10N 93 59 E
Kanpur 95 26 35N 80 20 E
Kansas □ 158 38 40N 98 0W
Kansas City, Kans., U.S.A. 158 39 0N 94 40W
Kansas City, Mo., U.S.A. 158 39 3N 94 30W
Kansas, R. 158 39 15N 96 20W
Kansenia 127 10 20S 26 0 E
Kansk 77 56 20N 95 37 E
Kansŏng 107 38 24N 128 30 E
Kansu □ 105 35 30N 104 30 E
Kant 85 42 53N 74 51 E
Kant'angtzu 106 37 28N 104 33 E
Kantché 121 13 31N 8 30 E
Kantemirovka 83 49 43N 39 55 E
Kantharalak 100 14 39N 104 39 E
Kantishna 147 63 31N 151 5W
Kantō □ 111 36 0N 140 0 E
Kantō-Heiya 111 36 0N 139 30 E
Kantō-Sanchi 111 35 50N 138 50 E
Kantu-long 98 19 57N 97 36 E
Kanturk 39 52 10N 8 55W
Kantzu 108 31 37N 100 0 E
Kanuma 111 36 44N 139 42 E
Kanus 128 27 50S 18 39 E
Kanye 128 25 0S 25 28 E
Kanyu 128 20 7S 24 37 E
Kanyŭ 107 34 53N 119 9 E
Kanzene 127 10 30S 25 12 E
Kanzi, Ras 126 7 1S 39 33 E
Kaoan 109 28 25N 115 22 E
Kaochou 109 21 55N 110 52 E
Kaohofu 109 30 43N 116 49 E
Kaohsien 108 28 21N 104 31 E
Kaohsiung 109 22 35N 120 16 E
Kaok'eng 109 27 39N 114 4 E
Kaoko Otavi 125 18 12S 13 45 E
Kaokoveld 128 19 0S 13 0 E
Kaolack 120 14 5N 16 8W
Kaolan Shan 109 21 55N 113 15 E
Kaolikung Shan 108 26 0N 98 55 E
Kaomi 107 36 25N 119 45 E
Kaopao Hu 109 32 50N 119 15 E
Kaop'ing 106 35 48N 112 55 E
K'aoshant'un 107 44 25N 124 27 E
Kaot'ang 106 36 51N 116 13 E
Kaoyang 106 38 42N 115 47 E
Kaoyu 109 32 46N 119 32 E
Kaoyüan 107 37 7N 118 0 E
Kapaa 147 22 5N 159 19W
Kapadvanj 94 23 5N 73 0 E
Kapagere 135 9 46S 147 42 E
Kapanga 124 8 30S 22 40 E
Kapanovka 83 47 28N 46 50 E
Kapata 127 14 16S 26 15 E
Kapellen 47 51 19N 4 25 E
Kapello, Ákra 69 36 9N 23 3 E
Kapema 127 10 45S 28 22 E
Kapfenberg 52 47 26N 15 18 E
Kapiri Mposhi 127 13 59S 28 43 E
Kapiskau 150 52 50N 82 1W
Kapiskau, R. 150 52 47N 81 55W
Kapit 102 2 0N 113 5 E
Kapiti I. 142 40 50S 174 56 E
Kaplice 52 48 42N 14 30 E
Kapoe 101 9 34N 98 32 E
Kapoeta 123 4 50N 33 35 E
Kápolnásnyék 53 47 16N 18 41 E
Kaponga 143 39 29S 174 9 E
Kapos, R. 53 46 30N 18 20 E
Kaposvár 53 46 25N 17 47 E
Kappeln 48 54 37N 9 56 E
Kapps 128 22 32S 17 18 E
Kaprije 63 43 42N 15 43 E
Kaprijke 47 51 13N 3 38 E
Kapsan 107 41 4N 128 19 E
Kapsukas 80 54 33N 23 19 E
Kapuas Hulu, Pegunungan 102 1 30N 113 30 E
Kapuas, R. 102 0 20N 111 40 E
Kapuka 127 10 30S 32 55 E
Kapulo 127 8 18S 29 15 E
Kapunda 140 34 20S 138 56 E
Kapurthala 94 31 23N 75 25 E
Kapuskasing 150 49 25N 82 30W
Kapuskasing, R. 150 49 49N 82 0W
Kapustin Yar 83 48 37N 45 40 E
Kaputar, Mt. 139 30 15S 150 10 E
Kaputir 126 2 5N 35 28 E
Kapuvár 53 47 36N 17 1 E
Kara, Turkey 69 38 29N 26 19 E
Kara, U.S.S.R. 76 69 10N 65 25 E
Kara Bogaz Gol, Zaliv 76 41 0N 53 30 E
Kara Burun 69 38 41N 26 28 E
Kara, I. 69 36 58N 27 30 E
Kara Kalpak A.S.S.R. □ 76 43 0N 60 0 E
Kara Kum 76 39 30N 60 0 E
Kara-Saki 110 34 41N 129 30 E
Kara Sea 76 75 0N 70 0 E
Kara Su 85 40 44N 72 53 E
Kara, Wadi 122 20 40N 42 0 E
Karabash 84 55 29N 60 14 E
Karabekaul 85 38 30N 64 8 E
Karabük 82 41 10N 32 30 E
Karabulak 85 44 54N 78 30 E
Karaburuni 68 40 25N 19 20 E
Karabutak 84 49 59N 60 14 E
Karachala 83 39 45N 48 53 E
Karachayevsk 83 43 50N 42 0 E
Karachev 80 53 10N 35 5 E
Karachi 94 24 53N 67 0 E
Karachi □ 94 25 30N 67 0 E
Karad 96 17 15N 74 10 E
Karadeniz Boğazı 92 41 10N 29 5 E
Karadeniz Dağlari 92 41 30N 35 0 E
Karaga 121 9 58N 0 28W
Karagajly 76 49 26N 76 0 E
Karaganda 76 49 50N 73 0 E
Karaginskiy, Ostrov 77 58 45N 164 0 E
Karagwe □ 126 2 0S 31 0 E
Karaikal 97 10 59N 79 50 E
Karaikkudi 97 10 0N 78 45 E
Karaitivu I. 97 9 45N 79 52 E
Karaj 93 35 4N 51 0 E
Karak, Jordan 90 31 14N 35 40 E
Karak, Malay. 101 3 25N 102 2 E
Karakas 76 48 20N 83 30 E
Karakitang 103 3 14N 125 28 E
Karakobis 128 22 3S 20 37 E
Karakoram 95 35 20N 76 0 E
Karakoram P. = K'alak'unlun Shank'ou 95 35 33N 77 46 E
Karakoram Pass 93 35 20N 78 0 E
Karakul, Tadzhik, S.S.R., U.S.S.R. 85 39 2N 73 33 E
Karakul, Uzbek S.S.R., U.S.S.R. 85 39 22N 63 50 E
Karakuldzha 85 40 39N 73 26 E
Karakulino 84 56 1N 53 43 E
Karalon 77 57 5N 115 50 E
Karaman 92 37 14N 33 13 E
Karambu 102 3 53S 116 6 E
Karamea 143 41 14S 172 6 E
Karamea Bight 143 41 22S 171 40 E
Karamea, R. 143 41 13S 172 26 E
Karamet Niyaz 85 37 45N 64 34 E
Karamoja □ 126 3 0N 34 15 E
Karamsad 94 22 35N 72 50 E
Karanganjar 103 7 38S 109 37 E
Karanja 96 20 29N 77 31 E
Karapoit 142 37 53S 175 32 E
Karaşar 82 40 21N 31 55 E
Karasburg 128 28 0S 18 44 E
Karasino 76 66 50N 86 50 E
Karasjok 74 69 27N 25 30 E
Karasuk 76 53 44N 78 2 E
Karasuk □ 126 2 12N 35 15 E
Karasuyama 111 36 39N 140 9 E
Karatau 85 43 10N 70 28 E
Karatau, Khrebet 85 43 30N 69 30 E
Karativu, I. 97 8 22N 79 52 E
Karatiya 90 31 39N 34 43 E
Karatobe 84 49 44N 53 30 E
Karatoya, R. 98 24 7N 89 36 E
Karaturuk 85 43 35N 78 0 E
Karaul-Bazar 85 39 30N 64 48 E
Karauli 94 26 30N 77 4 E
Karavasta 68 40 53N 19 28 E
Karawa 124 3 18N 20 17 E
Karawanken 52 46 30N 14 40 E
Karazhal 76 48 2N 70 49 E
Karbala 92 32 47N 44 3 E
Kårböle 72 61 59N 15 22 E
Karcag 53 47 19N 21 1 E
Karcha, R. 95 34 15N 75 57 E
Kärda 73 57 10N 13 49 E
Kardeljevo 66 43 2N 17 27 E
Kardhámila 69 38 35N 26 5 E
Kardhítsa 68 39 23N 21 54 E
Kardhitsa □ 68 39 15N 21 50 E
Kärdla 80 58 50N 22 40 E
Kareeberge 128 30 50S 22 0 E
Kareima 122 18 30N 31 49 E
Karelian A.S.S.R. □ 78 65 30N 32 30 E
Karema, P.N.G. 135 9 12S 147 18 E
Karema, Tanz. 126 6 49S 30 24 E
Karen 101 12 49N 92 53 E
Karganrud 92 37 55N 49 0 E
Kargapolye 84 55 57N 64 24 E
Kargasok 76 59 3N 80 53 E
Kargat 76 55 10N 80 15 E
Kargı 82 41 11N 34 30 E
Kargil 95 34 32N 76 12 E
Kargowa 54 52 5N 15 51 E
Karguéri 121 13 36N 10 30 E
Kariai 69 40 14N 24 19 E
Kariba 127 16 28S 28 36 E
Kariba Dam 125 16 30S 28 35 E
Kariba Gorge 127 16 30S 28 35 E
Kariba Lake 127 16 40S 28 25 E
Karibib 128 21 0S 15 56 E
Karikal 97 10 59N 79 50 E
Karikkale 92 39 55N 33 30 E
Karimata, Kepulauan 102 1 40S 109 0 E
Karimata, Selat 102 2 0S 108 20 E
Karimnagar 96 18 26N 79 10 E
Karimundjawa, Kepulauan 102 5 50S 110 30 E
Karin 91 10 50N 45 52 E
Káristos 69 38 1N 24 29 E
Karitane 51 45 38S 170 39 E
Kariya 111 34 58N 137 1 E
Karkal 97 13 15N 74 56 E
Karkar I. 135 4 40S 146 0 E
Karkinitskiy Zaliv 82 45 36N 32 35 E
Karkur 90 32 29N 34 57 E
Karkur Tohl 122 22 5N 25 5 E
Karl Libknekht 80 51 40N 35 45 E
Karl-Marx-Stadt 48 50 50N 12 55 E
Karl-Marx-Stadt □ 48 50 45N 13 0 E
Karla, L = Voiviis, Limni 68 39 35N 22 45 E
Karlino 54 54 3N 15 53 E
Karlobag 63 44 32N 15 5 E
Karlovac 63 45 31N 15 36 E
Karlovka 82 49 29N 35 8 E
Karlovy Vary 52 50 13N 12 51 E
Karlsborg 73 58 33N 14 33 E
Karlshamn 73 56 10N 14 51 E
Karlskoga 72 59 22N 14 33 E
Karlskrona 73 56 10N 15 35 E
Karlsruhe 49 49 3N 8 23 E
Karlstad, Sweden 72 59 23N 13 30 E
Karlstad, U.S.A. 158 48 38N 96 30W
Karmøy 71 59 15N 5 15 E
Karnal 94 29 42N 77 2 E
Karnali, R. 95 29 0N 82 0 E
Karnaphuli Res. 98 22 40N 92 20 E
Karnataka □ 97 13 15N 77 0 E
Karnes City 159 28 53N 97 53W
Karni 120 10 45N 2 40W
Karnische Alpen 52 46 36N 13 0 E
Karnobat 67 42 40N 27 0 E
Kärnten □ 52 46 52N 13 30 E
Karo 120 12 16N 2 22W
Karoi 127 16 48S 29 45 E
Karonga 127 9 57S 33 55 E
Karoonda 140 35 1S 139 59 E
Karos, Is. 69 36 54N 25 40 E
Karousâdhes 68 39 47N 19 45 E
Karpalund 73 56 4N 14 5 E
Kárpathos, I. 69 35 37N 27 10 E
Kárpathos, Stenón 69 36 0N 27 30 E
Karpinsk 84 59 45N 60 1 E
Karpogory 78 63 59N 44 27 E
Karrebaek 73 55 12N 11 39 E
Kars 92 40 40N 43 5 E
Karsakpay 76 47 55N 66 40 E
Karsha 83 49 45N 51 35 E
Karshi 85 38 53N 65 48 E
Karsun 81 54 14N 46 57 E
Kartál Óros 68 41 15N 25 13 E
Kartaly 84 53 3N 60 40 E
Kartapur 94 31 27N 75 32 E
Kartuzy 54 54 22N 18 10 E
Karuah 141 32 37S 151 56 E
Karufa 103 3 50S 133 20 E
Karumba 138 17 31S 140 50 E
Karumo 126 2 25S 32 50 E
Karumwa 126 3 12S 32 38 E
Karungu 126 0 50S 34 10 E
Karunjie 136 16 18S 127 12 E
Karup 73 56 19N 9 10 E
Karur 97 10 59N 78 2 E
Karviná 53 49 53N 18 25 E
Karwar 93 14 55N 74 13 E
Karwi 95 25 12N 80 57 E
Kas Kong 101 11 27N 102 12 E
Kasache 127 13 25S 34 20 E
Kasai 110 34 55N 134 52 E
Kasai Occidental □ 127 6 30S 22 30 E
Kasai Oriental □ 126 5 0S 24 30 E
Kasai, R. 124 8 20S 22 0 E
Kasaji 127 10 25S 23 27 E
Kasama, Japan 111 36 23N 140 16 E
Kasama, Zambia 127 10 16S 31 9 E
Kasandong 107 41 18N 126 55 E
Kasane 128 17 34S 24 50 E
Kasanga 127 8 30S 31 10 E
Kasangulu 124 4 15S 15 15 E
Kasaoka 110 34 30N 133 30 E
Kasaragod 97 12 30N 74 58 E
Kasat 98 15 56N 98 13 E
Kasba 98 25 51N 87 37 E
Kasba L. 153 60 20N 102 10W
Kasba Tadla 118 32 36N 6 17W
Kaschmar 93 35 16N 58 26 E
Kaseberga 73 55 24N 14 8 E
Kaseda 110 31 25N 130 19 E
Kasempa 127 13 30S 25 44 E
Kasenga 127 10 20S 28 45 E
Kasese 126 0 13N 30 3 E
Kasewa 127 14 28S 28 53 E
Kasganj 95 27 48N 78 42 E
Kashabowie 150 48 40N 90 26W
Kashan 93 34 5N 51 30 E
Kashgar = K'oshin 105 39 29N 75 58 E
Kashihara 111 34 35N 135 37 E
Kashima, Ibaraki, Japan 111 35 58N 140 38 E
Kashima, Saga, Japan 110 33 7N 130 6 E
Kashima-Nada 111 36 0N 140 45 E
Kashimbo 127 11 12S 26 19 E
Kashin 81 57 20N 37 36 E
Kashipur, Orissa, India 96 19 16N 83 3 E
Kashipur, Ut. P., India 95 29 15N 79 0 E
Kashira 81 54 45N 38 10 E
Kashiwa 111 35 52N 139 59 E
Kashiwazaki 112 37 22N 138 33 E
Kashkasu 85 39 54N 72 44 E
Kashmir □ 95 32 44N 74 54 E
Kashmor 94 28 28N 69 32 E
Kashpirovka 81 53 0N 48 30 E
Kashum Tso 99 34 45N 86 0 E
Kashun Noerh 105 42 25N 101 0 E
Kasimov 81 54 55N 41 20 E
Kasing 126 6 15S 26 58 E
Kaskaskia, R. 158 37 58N 89 57W
Kaskattama, R. 153 57 3N 90 4W
Kaskelan 85 43 20N 76 35 E
Kaskinen (Kaskö) 74 62 22N 21 15 E
Kaskö (Kaskinen) 74 62 22N 21 15 E
Kasli 84 55 53N 60 46 E
Kaslo 152 49 55N 117 0W
Kasmere L. 153 59 34N 101 10W
Kasonawedjo 127 1 50S 137 41 E
Kasongo 126 4 30S 26 33 E
Kasongo Lunda 124 6 35S 17 0 E
Kásos, I. 69 35 20N 26 55 E
Kásos, Stenón 69 35 30N 26 30 E
Kaspi 83 41 54N 44 17 E
Kaspiysk 83 42 45N 47 40 E
Kaspiyskiy 83 45 22N 47 23 E
Kassab ed Doleib 123 13 30N 33 35 E
Kassaba 122 22 40N 29 55 E
Kassala 123 15 20N 36 26 E
Kassala □ 123 15 20N 36 26 E
Kassan 85 39 2N 65 35 E
Kassandra 68 40 0N 23 30 E
Kassansay 85 41 15N 71 31 E
Kassel 48 51 19N 9 32 E
Kassinger 122 18 46N 31 51 E
Kassiopi 80 39 48N 19 55 E
Kassue 103 6 58S 139 21 E
Kastamonu 92 41 25N 33 43 E
Kastav 63 45 22N 14 20 E
Kastélli 69 35 29N 23 38 E
Kastéllion 69 35 12N 25 20 E
Kastellorizon = Megiste 61 36 8N 29 34 E
Kastellou, Ákra 69 35 30N 27 15 E
Kasterlee 47 51 15N 4 59 E
Kastlösa 73 56 26N 16 25 E
Kastó, I. 69 38 35N 20 55 E
Kastóri 69 37 10N 22 17 E
Kastoría 68 40 30N 21 19 E
Kastoría □ 68 40 30N 21 15 E
Kastorías 68 40 30N 21 20 E
Kastornoye 81 51 55N 38 2 E
Kástron 68 39 53N 25 8 E

Kastrosikiá | Kerman

Place	Page	Lat.	Long.
Kastrosikiá	**69**	39 6N	20 36 E
Kasugai	**111**	35 12N	136 59 E
Kasukabe	**111**	35 58N	139 49 E
Kasulu	**126**	4 37 S	30 5 E
Kasulu □	**126**	4 37 S	30 5 E
Kasumi	**110**	35 38N	134 38 E
Kasumiga-Ura	**111**	36 0N	140 25 E
Kasumkent	**83**	41 47N	48 15 E
Kasungu	**127**	13 0 S	33 29 E
Kasur	**94**	31 5N	74 25 E
Kata	**77**	58 46N	102 40 E
Kataba	**127**	16 10 S	25 10 E
Katako Kombe	**126**	3 25 S	24 20 E
Katákolon	**69**	37 38N	21 19 E
Katale	**126**	4 52 S	31 7 E
Katalla	**147**	60 10N	144 35W
Katama	**123**	9 35N	38 36 E
Katamatite	**141**	36 6 S	145 41 E
Katanda	**126**	0 55 S	29 21 E
Katanga = Shaba	**126**	8 0 S	25 0 E
Katanghan □	**93**	36 0N	69 0 E
Katangi	**96**	21 56N	79 50 E
Katangli	**77**	51 42N	143 14 E
Katanich	**123**	6 0N	33 40 E
Katanning	**132**	33 40 S	117 33 E
Katastári	**69**	37 50N	20 45 E
Katav Ivanovsk	**84**	54 45N	58 12 E
Katavi Swamps	**126**	6 50 S	31 10 E
Katerini	**68**	40 18N	22 37 E
Katesbridge	**38**	54 18N	6 8W
Katha	**99**	24 10N	96 30 E
Katherina, Gebel	**122**	28 30N	33 57 E
Katherine	**136**	14 27 S	132 20 E
Kathiawar, dist.	**93**	22 20N	71 0 E
Kathua	**95**	32 23N	75 30 E
Kati	**120**	12 41N	8 4W
Katiet	**102**	2 21 S	99 44 E
Katihar	**95**	25 34N	87 36 E
Katima Mulilo	**125**	17 28 S	24 13 E
Katima Mulilo Rapids	**128**	17 28 S	24 13 E
Katimbira	**127**	12 40 S	34 0 E
Katiola	**120**	8 10N	5 10W
Katkopberg	**128**	30 0 S	20 0 E
Katlanovo	**66**	41 52N	21 40 E
Katmai Nat. Monument	**147**	58 30N	155 0W
Katmai, vol.	**147**	58 20N	154 59W
Katmandu	**95**	27 45N	85 12 E
Kato Akhaïa	**69**	38 8N	21 33 E
Kato Stazros	**68**	40 39N	23 43 E
Katol	**96**	21 17N	78 38 E
Katompi	**124**	6 2 S	26 23 E
Katonga, R.	**126**	0 15N	31 50 E
Katoomba	**141**	33 41 S	150 19 E
Katowice	**54**	50 17N	19 5 E
Katowice □	**53**	50 15N	19 0 E
Katrine L.	**34**	56 15N	4 30W
Katrineholm	**72**	59 9N	16 12 E
Katsepe	**129**	15 45 S	46 15 E
Katsina	**121**	7 10N	9 20 E
Katsina Ala, R.	**121**	6 52N	9 40 E
Katsumoto	**110**	33 51N	129 42 E
Katsuta	**111**	36 25N	140 31 E
Katsuura	**111**	35 15N	140 20 E
Katsuyama	**111**	36 3N	136 30 E
Kattakurgan	**85**	39 55N	66 15 E
Kattawaz	**93**	32 48N	68 23 E
Kattawaz-Urgun □	**93**	32 10N	62 20 E
Kattegat	**73**	57 0N	11 20 E
Katumba	**126**	7 40 S	25 17 E
Katungu	**126**	2 55 S	40 3 E
Katwa	**95**	23 30N	89 25 E
Katwijk-aan-Zee	**46**	52 12N	4 24 E
Katy	**54**	51 2N	16 45 E
Kau Tao	**101**	10 6N	99 48 E
Kauai Chan.	**147**	21 45N	158 50W
Kauai, I.	**147**	19 30N	155 30W
Kaufakha	**90**	31 29N	34 40 E
Kaufbeuren	**49**	47 42N	10 37 E
Kaufman	**159**	32 35N	96 20W
Kaukauna	**156**	44 20N	88 13W
Kaukauveld	**128**	20 0 S	20 15 E
Kaukonen	**74**	67 31N	24 53 E
Kaulille	**47**	51 11N	5 31 E
Kauliranta	**74**	66 27N	23 41 E
Kaunas	**80**	54 54N	23 54 E
Kaunghein	**98**	25 41N	95 26 E
Kaupulehu	**147**	19 43N	155 53W
Kaura Namoda	**121**	12 37N	6 33 E
Kautokeino	**74**	69 0N	23 4 E
Kavacha	**77**	60 16N	169 51 E
Kavadarci	**66**	41 26N	22 3 E
Kavaja	**68**	41 11N	19 33 E
Kavali	**97**	14 55N	80 1 E
Kaválla	**68**	40 57N	24 28 E
Kaválla □	**68**	41 05N	24 30 E
Kaválla Kólpos	**68**	40 50N	24 25 E
Kavanayén	**174**	5 38N	61 48W
Kavarna	**67**	43 26N	28 22 E
Kavieng	**135**	2 36 S	150 51 E
Kavkaz, Bolshoi	**83**	42 50N	44 0 E
Kavousi	**69**	35 7N	25 51 E
Kaw = Caux	**175**	4 30N	52 15W
Kawa	**123**	13 42N	32 34 E
Kawachi-Nagano	**111**	34 28N	135 31 E
Kawagoe	**111**	35 55N	139 29 E
Kawaguchi	**111**	35 52N	138 45 E
Kawaihae	**147**	20 3N	155 50W
Kawaihoa Pt.	**147**	21 47N	160 12W
Kawaikini, Mt.	**147**	22 0N	159 30W
Kawakawa	**142**	35 23 S	174 6 E
Kawama	**127**	9 30 S	28 30 E
Kawambwa	**127**	9 48 S	29 3 E
Kawanoe	**110**	34 1N	133 34 E
Kawarau	**143**	45 3 S	169 0 E
Kawardha	**95**	22 0N	81 17 E
Kawasaki	**111**	35 35N	138 42 E
Kawau I.	**142**	36 25 S	174 52 E
Kawene	**150**	48 45N	91 15W
Kawerau	**142**	38 7 S	176 42 E
Kawhia Harbour	**142**	38 5 S	174 51 E
Kawick Peak	**163**	37 58N	116 57W
Kawkareik	**98**	16 33N	98 14 E
Kawlin	**98**	23 47N	95 41 E
Kawnro	**99**	22 48N	99 8 E
Kawthaung	**101**	10 5N	98 36 E
Kawthoolei □ = Kawthuk	**98**	18 0N	97 30 E
Kawthuk □	**98**	18 0N	97 30 E
Kawya	**98**	16 40N	97 50 E
Kay	**84**	59 57N	52 59 E
Kaya	**121**	13 25N	1 10W
Kayah □	**98**	19 15N	97 15 E
Kayaho	**107**	43 5N	129 46 E
Kayak I.	**147**	60 0N	144 30W
Kayan	**98**	16 54N	96 34 E
Kayangulam	**97**	9 10N	76 33 E
Kaycee	**160**	43 45N	106 46W
Kayenta	**161**	36 46N	110 15W
Kayes	**120**	14 25N	11 30W
Kayima	**120**	8 54N	11 15W
Kayl	**47**	49 29N	6 2 E
Kayomba	**127**	13 11 S	24 2 E
Kayoro	**121**	11 0N	1 28W
Kayrakkumskoye Vdkhr.	**85**	40 20N	70 0 E
Kayrunnera	**139**	30 40 S	142 30 E
Kaysatskoye	**83**	49 47N	46 49 E
Kayseri	**92**	38 45N	35 30 E
Kaysville	**160**	41 2N	111 58W
Kazachinskoye	**77**	56 16N	107 36 E
Kazachye	**77**	70 52N	135 58 E
Kazakh S.S.R. □	**85**	50 0N	58 0 E
Kazakhstan	**84**	51 11N	53 0 E
Kazan	**81**	55 48N	49 3 E
Kazan, R.	**153**	64 2N	95 30W
Kazanluk	**67**	42 38N	25 35 E
Kazanskaya	**83**	49 50N	40 30 E
Kazarman	**85**	41 24N	73 59 E
Kazatin	**82**	49 45N	28 50 E
Kazerun	**93**	29 38N	51 40 E
Kazhim	**84**	60 21N	51 33 E
Kazi Magomed	**83**	40 3N	49 0 E
Kazimierza Wielki	**54**	50 15N	20 30 E
Kazincbarcika	**53**	48 17N	20 36 E
Kazo	**111**	36 7N	139 36 E
Kaztalovka	**83**	49 47N	48 43 E
Kazu	**98**	25 27N	97 46 E
Kazumba	**124**	6 25 S	22 5 E
Kazvin	**92**	36 15N	50 0 E
Kazym, R.	**76**	63 40N	68 30 E
Kcynia	**54**	53 0N	17 30 E
Ké	**120**	13 58N	5 18W
Ke-hsi Mansam	**98**	21 56N	97 50 E
Ke-Macina	**120**	14 5N	5 20W
Kéa	**69**	37 35N	24 22 E
Kea	**30**	50 13N	5 4W
Kéa, I.	**69**	37 30N	24 22 E
Keaau	**147**	19 37N	155 3W
Keady	**38**	54 15N	6 42W
Keal, Loch na	**34**	56 30N	6 5W
Kealkill	**39**	51 45N	9 20W
Keams Canyon	**161**	35 53N	110 9W
Keanae	**147**	20 52N	156 9W
Kearney	**158**	40 45N	99 3W
Kearsage, Mt.	**162**	43 25N	71 51W
Keban	**92**	38 50N	38 50 E
Kebele	**123**	12 52N	40 40 E
Kebi	**120**	9 18N	6 37W
Kebili	**119**	33 47N	9 0 E
Kebkabiya	**117**	13 50N	24 0 E
Kebnekaise, mt.	**74**	67 54N	18 33 E
Kebock Hd.	**36**	58 1N	6 20W
Kebri Dehar	**91**	6 45N	44 17 E
Kebumen	**103**	7 42 S	109 40 E
Kecel	**53**	46 31N	19 16 E
Kechika, R.	**152**	59 41N	127 12W
Kecskemét	**53**	46 57N	19 35 E
Kedada	**123**	5 30N	35 58 E
Kedah □	**101**	5 50N	100 40 E
Kedainiai	**80**	55 15N	23 57 E
Kedgwick	**151**	47 40N	67 20W
Kedia Hill	**128**	21 28 S	24 37 E
Kediri	**103**	7 51 S	112 1 E
Kédougou	**120**	12 35N	12 10W
Kedzierzyn	**54**	50 20N	18 12 E
Keefers	**152**	50 0N	121 40W
Keel	**38**	53 59N	10 2W
Keelby	**33**	53 34N	0 15W
Keele	**32**	53 0N	2 17W
Keele, R.	**147**	64 15N	127 0W
Keeler	**163**	36 29N	117 52W
Keeley L.	**153**	54 54N	108 8W
Keeling Is. = Cocos Is.	**142**	12 12 S	96 54 E
Keelung = Chilung	**109**	25 3N	121 45 E
Keen, Mt.	**37**	56 58N	2 54W
Keenagh	**38**	53 36N	7 50W
Keene, Calif., U.S.A.	**163**	35 13N	118 33W
Keene, N.H., U.S.A.	**162**	42 57N	72 17W
Keeper, Mt.	**39**	52 46N	8 17W
Keer-Weer, C.	**138**	14 0 S	141 32 E
Keerbergen	**47**	51 1N	4 38 E
Keeten Mastgat	**47**	51 36N	4 0 E
Keetmanshoop	**128**	26 35 S	18 8 E
Keewatin	**158**	47 23N	93 0W
Keewatin □	**153**	63 20N	94 40W
Keewatin, R.	**153**	56 29N	100 46W
Kefa □	**123**	6 55N	36 30 E
Kefallinía, I.	**69**	38 28N	20 30 E
Kefamenanu	**103**	9 28 S	124 38 E
Kefar Ata	**90**	32 48N	35 7 E
Kefar Etsyon	**90**	31 39N	35 7 E
Kefar Hasidim	**90**	32 47N	35 5 E
Kefar Hittim B.	**90**	32 48N	35 27 E
Kefar Nahum	**90**	32 54N	35 22 E
Kefar Sava	**90**	32 11N	34 54 E
Kefar Szold	**90**	33 11N	35 34 E
Kefar Vitkin	**90**	32 22N	34 53 E
Kefar Yehezqel	**90**	32 34N	35 22 E
Kefar Yona	**90**	32 20N	34 54 E
Kefar Zekharya	**90**	31 43N	34 57 E
Keffi	**121**	8 55N	7 43 E
Keflavík	**74**	64 2N	22 35W
Keg River	**152**	57 54N	117 7W
Kegalla	**97**	7 15N	80 21 E
Kegashka	**151**	50 14N	61 18W
Kegworth	**28**	52 50N	1 17W
Kehl	**49**	48 34N	7 50 E
Keighley	**32**	53 52N	1 54W
Keimaneigh, P. of	**39**	51 49N	9 17W
Keimoes	**128**	28 41 S	21 0 E
Keiss	**37**	58 33N	3 6W
Keïta	**121**	14 46N	5 56 E
Keith, Austral.	**140**	36 0 S	140 20 E
Keith, U.K.	**37**	57 33N	2 58W
Keith Arm	**148**	65 20N	122 15W
Kekaygyr	**85**	40 42N	75 32 E
Kekri	**94**	26 0N	75 10 E
Kël	**77**	69 30N	124 10 E
Kelamet	**123**	16 0N	38 20 E
Kelang	**101**	3 2N	101 26 E
Kelani Ganga, R.	**97**	6 58N	79 50 E
Kelantan □	**101**	5 10N	102 0 E
Kelantan, R.	**101**	6 13N	102 14 E
Këlcyra	**68**	40 22N	20 12 E
Keld	**32**	54 24N	2 11W
Keles, R.	**85**	41 1N	68 37 E
Kelheim	**49**	48 58N	11 57 E
Kelibia	**119**	36 50N	11 3 E
Kellas	**37**	57 33N	3 23W
Kellé, Congo	**124**	0 8 S	14 38 E
Kellé, Niger	**121**	14 18N	10 10 E
Keller	**160**	48 2N	118 44W
Kellerberrin	**137**	31 36 S	117 38 E
Kellett C.	**12**	72 0N	126 0W
Kellogg	**160**	47 30N	116 5W
Kelloselkä	**74**	66 56N	28 53 E
Kells, Ireland	**39**	52 33N	7 18W
Kells, U.K.	**38**	54 48N	6 13W
Kells = Ceanannas Mor	**38**	53 42N	6 53W
Kells, Rhinns of	**34**	55 9N	4 22W
Kelmentsy	**80**	48 30N	26 50 E
Kélo	**124**	9 10N	15 45 E
Kelowna	**152**	49 50N	119 25W
Kelsale	**29**	52 15N	1 30 E
Kelsall	**32**	53 14N	2 44W
Kelsey Bay	**152**	50 25N	126 0W
Kelso, N.Z.	**143**	45 54 S	169 15 E
Kelso, U.K.	**35**	55 36N	2 27W
Kelso, U.S.A.	**160**	46 10N	122 57W
Keltemashat	**85**	42 25N	70 8 E
Keluang	**101**	2 3N	103 18 E
Kelvedon	**29**	51 50N	0 43 E
Kelvington	**153**	52 10N	103 30W
Kem	**78**	65 0N	34 38 E
Kem-Kem	**118**	30 40N	4 30W
Kem, R.	**78**	64 45N	32 20 E
Kema	**103**	1 22N	125 8 E
Kemah	**92**	39 32N	39 5 E
Kemano	**152**	53 35N	128 0W
Kemapyu	**98**	18 49N	97 19 E
Kemasik	**101**	4 25N	103 25 E
Kembolcha	**123**	11 29N	39 42 E
Kemenets-Podolskiy	**82**	48 40N	26 30 E
Kemerovo	**76**	55 20N	85 50 E
Kemi	**74**	65 44N	24 34 E
Kemi älv = Kemijoki	**74**	65 47N	24 32 E
Kemijärvi	**74**	66 43N	27 22 E
Kemijoki	**74**	65 47N	24 32 E
Kemmel	**47**	50 47N	2 50 E
Kemmerer	**160**	41 52N	110 30W
Kemnay	**37**	57 14N	2 28W
Kemp Coast	**13**	69 0 S	55 0 E
Kemp L.	**159**	33 45N	99 15W
Kempsey, Austral.	**141**	31 1 S	152 50 E
Kempsey, U.K.	**28**	52 8N	2 11W
Kempston	**29**	52 7N	0 30W
Kempt, L.	**150**	47 25N	74 22W
Kempten	**49**	47 42N	10 18 E
Kemptville	**150**	45 0N	75 38W
Ken L.	**35**	55 0N	4 8W
Kenadsa	**118**	31 48N	2 26W
Kenai	**147**	60 35N	151 20W
Kenai Mts.	**147**	60 0N	150 0W
Kendal, Indon.	**103**	6 56 S	110 14 E
Kendal, U.K.	**32**	54 19N	2 44W
Kendall	**141**	31 35 S	152 44 E
Kendall, R.	**138**	14 4 S	141 35 E
Kendallville	**156**	41 25N	85 15W
Kendari	**103**	3 50 S	122 30 E
Kendawangan	**102**	2 32 S	110 17 E
Kende	**121**	11 30N	4 12 E
Kendenup	**137**	34 30 S	117 38 E
Kendrapara	**96**	20 35N	86 30 E
Kendrick	**160**	46 43N	116 41W
Kendriki Kai Dhitiki Makedhonia □	**68**	40 30N	22 0 E
Kene Thao	**100**	17 44N	101 25 E
Kenema	**120**	7 50N	11 14W
Keng Kok	**100**	16 26N	105 12 E
Keng Tawng	**98**	20 45N	98 18 E
Keng Tung, Burma	**99**	21 0N	99 30 E
Keng Tung, Burma	**99**	21 0N	99 30 E
Kenge	**124**	4 50 S	16 55 E
Kengeja	**126**	5 26 S	39 45 E
Kengma	**108**	23 34N	99 24 E
Kenhardt	**128**	29 19 S	21 12 E
Kenilworth	**28**	52 22N	1 35W
Kenimekh	**85**	40 16N	65 7 E
Kéninkoumou	**120**	15 17N	12 18W
Kénitra (Port Lyautey)	**118**	34 15N	6 40W
Kenmare, Ireland	**39**	51 52N	9 35W
Kenmare, U.S.A.	**158**	48 40N	102 4W
Kenmare, R.	**39**	51 40N	10 0W
Kenmore	**37**	56 35N	4 0W
Kenn Reef	**133**	21 12 S	155 46 E
Kennebec	**158**	43 56N	99 54W
Kennedy	**127**	18 52 S	27 10 E
Kennedy, C. = Canaveral, C.	**157**	28 28N	80 31W
Kennedy, Mt.	**148**	60 19N	139 0W
Kennedy Ra.	**137**	24 45 S	115 10 E
Kennedy Taungdeik	**99**	23 35N	94 4 E
Kennet, R.	**28**	51 24N	1 7W
Kenneth Ra.	**137**	23 50 S	117 8 E
Kennett	**159**	36 7N	90 0W
Kennett Square	**162**	39 51N	75 43W
Kennewick	**160**	46 11N	119 2W
Kenninghall	**29**	52 26N	1 0 E
Kénogami	**151**	48 25N	71 15W
Kenogami, R.	**150**	51 6N	84 28W
Kenora	**153**	49 50N	94 35W
Kenosha	**156**	42 33N	87 48W
Kensington, Can.	**151**	46 28N	63 34W
Kensington, U.S.A.	**158**	39 48N	99 2W
Kensington Downs	**138**	22 31 S	144 19 E
Kent, Ohio, U.S.A.	**156**	41 8N	81 20W
Kent, Oreg., U.S.A.	**160**	45 11N	120 45W
Kent, Tex., U.S.A.	**159**	31 5N	104 12W
Kent □	**29**	51 12N	0 40 E
Kent Gr.	**138**	39 30 S	147 20 E
Kent Pen.	**148**	68 30N	107 0W
Kent Pt.	**162**	38 50N	76 22W
Kent, Vale of	**23**	51 12N	0 30 E
Kentau	**85**	43 32N	68 36 E
Kentdale	**137**	34 54 S	117 3 E
Kentisbeare	**30**	50 51N	3 18W
Kentland	**156**	40 45N	87 25W
Kenton, U.K.	**30**	50 37N	3 28W
Kenton, U.S.A.	**156**	40 40N	83 35W
Kentucky	**141**	30 45 S	151 28 E
Kentucky □	**156**	37 20N	85 0W
Kentucky Dam	**156**	37 2N	88 15W
Kentucky L.	**157**	36 0N	88 0W
Kentucky, R.	**156**	38 41N	85 11W
Kentville	**151**	45 6N	64 29W
Kentwood	**159**	31 0N	90 30W
Kenya ■	**126**	2 20N	38 0 E
Kenya, Mt.	**126**	0 10 S	37 18 E
Keo Nena, Deo	**100**	18 23N	105 10 E
Keokuk	**158**	40 25N	91 24W
Kep, Camb.	**101**	10 29N	104 19 E
Kep, Viet.	**100**	21 24N	106 16 E
Kep-i-Gjuhëzës	**68**	40 28N	19 15 E
Kep-i-Palit	**68**	41 25N	19 21 E
Kep-i-Rodonit	**68**	41 32N	19 30 E
Kepi	**103**	6 32 S	139 19 E
Kepice	**54**	54 16N	16 51 E
Kepler Mts.	**143**	45 25 S	167 20 E
Kepno	**54**	51 18N	17 58 E
Keppel B.	**133**	23 21 S	150 55 E
Kepsut	**92**	39 40N	28 15 E
Kepuhi	**147**	22 13N	159 21W
Kepulauan, R.	**103**	5 30 S	139 0 E
Kepulauan Sunda, Ketjil Barat □	**102**	8 50 S	117 30 E
Kepulauan Sunda, Ketjil Timor □	**103**	9 30 S	122 0 E
Kerala □	**97**	11 0N	76 15 E
Kerama-Shotō	**112**	26 12N	127 22 E
Keran	**95**	34 35N	73 59 E
Kerang	**140**	35 40 S	143 55 E
Keratéa	**69**	37 48N	23 58 E
Keraudren, C., Tas., Austral.	**136**	40 22 S	144 47 E
Keraudren, C., W. Austral., Austral.	**138**	19 58 S	119 45 E
Keravat	**135**	4 17 S	152 2 E
Keray	**93**	26 15N	57 30 E
Kerch	**82**	45 20N	36 20 E
Kerchinskiy Proliv	**82**	45 10N	36 30 E
Kerchoual	**121**	17 20N	0 20 E
Kerem Maharal	**90**	32 39N	34 59 E
Kerema	**135**	7 58 S	145 50 E
Keren	**123**	15 45N	38 28 E
Kerewan	**120**	13 35N	16 10W
Kerguelen I.	**11**	48 15 S	69 10 E
Kerhonkson	**162**	41 46N	74 11W
Keri	**69**	37 40N	20 49 E
Keri Kera	**123**	12 21N	32 37 E
Kericho	**126**	0 22 S	35 15 E
Kericho □	**126**	0 30 S	35 15 E
Kerikeri	**143**	35 12 S	173 59 E
Kerinci	**102**	2 5 S	101 0 E
Kerkdriel	**46**	51 47N	5 20 E
Kerkenna, Iles	**119**	34 48N	11 1 E
Kerki	**85**	37 50N	65 12 E
Kérkira	**68**	39 38N	19 50 E
Kerkrade	**47**	50 53N	6 4 E
Kerma	**122**	19 33N	30 32 E
Kermadec Is.	**130**	31 8 S	175 16W
Kermān	**93**	30 15N	57 1 E
Kerman	**163**	36 43N	120 4W

Kermãn □ **Killavullen**

Kermãn □ **93** 30 0N 57 0E
Kermanshah **92** 34 23N 47 0E
Kermanshah □ **92** 34 0N 46 30E
Kerme Körfezi **69** 36 55N 27 50E
Kermen **67** 42 30N 26 16E
Kermit **159** 31 56N 103 3W
Kern, R. **163** 35 16N 119 18W
Kerns **51** 46 54N 8 17E
Kernville **163** 35 45N 118 26W
Keroh **101** 5 43N 101 1E
Kerr, Pt. **142** 34 25S 173 5E
Kerrera I. **34** 56 24N 5 32W
Kerrobert **157** 52 0N 109 11W
Kerrville **159** 30 1N 99 8W
Kerry **31** 52 28N 3 16W
Kerry □ **39** 52 7N 9 35W
Kerry Hd. **39** 52 26N 9 56W
Kerrysdale **36** 57 41N 5 39W
Kersa **123** 9 28N 41 48E
Kerstinbo **72** 60 16N 16 58E
Kerteminde **73** 55 28N 10 39E
Kertosono **103** 7 38S 112 9E
Keru **123** 15 40N 37 5E
Kerulen, R. **105** 48 48N 117 0E
Kerzaz **118** 29 29N 1 25W
Kerzers **50** 46 59N 7 12E
Kesagami L. **150** 50 23N 80 15W
Kesagami, R. **150** 51 4N 79 45W
Kesan **68** 41 49N 26 38E
Kesch, Piz **51** 46 38N 9 53E
Kesh **38** 54 31N 7 43W
Keski Suomen □ **74** 62 45N 25 15E
Kessel, Belg. **47** 51 8N 4 38E
Kessel, Neth. **47** 51 17N 6 3E
Kessel-Lo **47** 50 53N 4 43E
Kessingland **29** 52 25N 1 41E
Kestell **129** 28 17S 28 42E
Kestenga **78** 66 0N 31 50E
Kesteren **46** 51 56N 5 34E
Keswick **32** 54 35N 3 9W
Keszthely **53** 46 50N 17 15E
Keta **121** 5 49N 1 0E
Ketapang **102** 1 55S 110 0E
Ketchikan **147** 55 25N 131 40W
Ketchum **160** 43 50N 114 27W
Kete Krachi **121** 7 55N 0 1W
Ketef, Khalîg Umm el **122** 23 40N 35 35E
Ketelmeer **46** 32 36N 5 46E
Keti Bandar **94** 24 8N 67 27E
Ketri **94** 28 1N 75 50E
Kętrzyn **54** 54 7N 21 22E
Kettering **29** 52 24N 0 44W
Kettla, Ness **36** 60 3N 1 20W
Kettle Falls **160** 48 41N 118 2W
Kettle Ness **33** 54 32N 0 41W
Kettle, R. **153** 56 23N 94 34W
Kettleman City **163** 36 1N 119 58W
Kettlewell **32** 54 8N 2 2W
Kety **54** 49 51N 19 16E
Kevin **160** 48 45N 111 58W
Kewanee **158** 41 18N 90 0W
Kewaunee **156** 44 27N 87 30W
Keweenaw B. **156** 46 56N 88 23W
Keweenaw Pen. **156** 47 30N 88 0W
Keweenaw Pt. **156** 47 26N 87 40W
Kexby **33** 53 21N 0 41W
Key Harbour **150** 45 50N 80 45W
Key, L. **38** 54 0N 8 15W
Key West **166** 24 40N 82 0W
Keyingham **33** 53 42N 0 7W
Keyling Inlet **136** 14 50S 129 40E
Keymer **29** 50 55N 0 5W
Keynsham **28** 51 25N 2 30W
Keynshamburg **127** 19 15S 29 40E
Keyport **162** 40 26N 74 12W
Keyser **156** 39 26N 79 0W
Keystone, S.D., U.S.A. **158** 43 54N 103 27W
Keystone, W. Va., U.S.A. **156** 37 30N 81 30W
Keyworth **28** 52 52N 1 8W
Kez **84** 57 55N 53 46E
Kezhma **77** 59 15N 100 57E
Kezmarok **53** 49 10N 20 28E
Khabarovo **76** 69 30N 60 30E
Khabarovsk **77** 48 20N 135 0E
Khachmas **83** 41 31N 48 42E
Khachraud **94** 23 25N 75 20E
Khadari, W. el **123** 10 35N 26 16E
Khadro **94** 26 11N 68 50E
Khadyzhensk **83** 44 26N 39 32E
Khadzhilyangar **95** 35 45N 79 20E
Khagaria **95** 25 18N 86 32E
Khaibar **92** 25 38N 39 28E
Khaibor **122** 25 49N 39 16E
Khaipur, Bahawalpur, Pak. **94** 29 34N 72 17E
Khaipur, Hyderabad, Pak. **94** 27 32N 68 49E
Khair **94** 27 57N 77 46E
Khairabad **95** 27 33N 80 47E
Khairagarh **95** 21 27N 81 2E
Khairpur **93** 27 32N 68 49E
Khairpur □ **94** 23 30N 69 8E
Khakhea **125** 24 48S 23 22E
Khalach **85** 38 4N 64 52E
Khalfallah **118** 34 33N 0 16E
Khalij-e-Fars □ **93** 28 20N 51 45E
Khalilabad **95** 26 48N 83 5E
Khálki **68** 39 36N 22 30E
Khálki, I. **69** 36 15N 27 35E
Khalkidhikí □ **68** 40 25N 23 20E
Khalkís **69** 38 27N 23 42E
Khalmer-Sede = Tazovskiy **76** 67 30N 78 30E
Khalmer Yu **76** 67 58N 65 1E
Khalturin **81** 58 40N 48 50E
Kham Kent **100** 18 15N 104 43E
Khamaria **96** 23 10N 80 52E
Khama's Country **128** 21 45S 26 30E
Khamba Dzong **99** 28 25N 88 30W
Khambhalia **94** 22 14N 69 41E
Khamgaon **96** 20 42N 76 37E
Khammam **96** 17 11N 80 6E
Khān Yūnis **90** 31 21N 34 18E
Khan Yunus **90** 31 21N 34 18E
Khanabad, Afghan. **93** 36 45N 69 5E
Khanabad, U.S.S.R. **85** 40 59N 70 38E
Khānaqin **92** 34 23N 45 25E
Khandrá **69** 35 3N 26 8E
Khandwa **96** 21 49N 76 22E
Khandyga **77** 62 30N 134 50E
Khanewal **94** 30 20N 71 55E
Khanga Sidi Nadji **119** 34 50N 6 50E
Khanh Duong **100** 12 44N 108 44E
Khanh Hung **101** 9 36N 105 58E
Khaniá **69** 35 30N 24 4E
Khaniá □ **69** 35 0N 24 0E
Khanion Kólpos **69** 35 33N 23 55E
Khanka, Oz. **76** 45 0N 132 30E
Khanna **94** 30 42N 76 16E
Khanpur **94** 28 42N 70 35E
Khantau **85** 44 13N 73 48E
Khanty-Mansiysk **76** 61 0N 69 0E
Khapalu **95** 35 10N 76 20E
Kharagpur **95** 22 20N 87 25E
Kharaij **122** 21 25N 41 0E
Kharan Kalat **93** 28 34N 65 21E
Kharanaq **93** 32 20N 54 45E
Kharda **96** 18 40N 75 40E
Khardung La **95** 34 20N 77 43E
Kharfa **92** 22 0N 46 35E
Kharg, Jazireh **92** 29 15N 50 28E
Khârga, El Wâhât el **122** 25 0N 30 0E
Khargon, India **93** 21 45N 75 35E
Khargon, India **96** 21 45N 75 40E
Kharit, Wadi el **122** 24 5N 34 10E
Kharkov **82** 49 58N 36 20E
Kharmanli **67** 41 55N 25 55E
Kharovsk **81** 59 56N 40 13E
Kharsaniya **92** 27 10N 49 10E
Khartoum = El Khartûm **123** 15 31N 32 35E
Khartoum □ **123** 16 0N 33 0E
Khasab **93** 26 14N 56 15E
Khasavyurt **83** 43 30N 46 40E
Khasebake **128** 20 42S 24 29E
Khash **93** 28 15N 61 5E
Khashm el Girba **123** 14 59N 35 58E
Khasi Hills **98** 25 30N 91 30E
Khaskovo **67** 41 56N 25 30E
Khatanga **77** 72 0N 102 20E
Khatanga, Zaliv **12** 66 0N 112 0E
Khatauli **94** 29 17N 77 43E
Khatyrchi **85** 40 2N 65 58E
Khatyrka **77** 62 3N 175 15E
Khavar □ **92** 37 20N 46 0E
Khavast **85** 40 10N 68 49E
Khawa **122** 29 45N 40 25E
Khaydarken **85** 39 57N 71 20E
Khazzân Jabal el Awliyâ **123** 15 24N 32 20E
Khe Bo **100** 19 8N 104 41E
Khe Long **100** 21 29N 104 46E
Khed, Maharashtra, India **96** 18 51N 73 56E
Khed, Maharashtra, India **96** 17 43N 73 27E
Khed Brahma **93** 24 7N 73 5E
Khekra **94** 28 52N 77 20E
Khemarak Phouminville **101** 11 37N 102 59E
Khemis Miliana **118** 36 11N 2 14E
Khemisset **118** 33 50N 6 1W
Khemmarat **100** 16 10N 105 15E
Khenchela **119** 35 28N 7 11E
Khenifra **118** 32 58N 5 46W
Khenmarak Phouminville **102** 11 40N 102 58E
Kherrata **119** 36 27N 5 13E
Kherson **82** 46 35N 32 35E
Khersónisos Akrotíri **69** 35 30N 24 10E
Khetinsiring **99** 32 54N 92 50E
Khiliomódhion **69** 37 48N 22 51E
Khilok **77** 51 30N 110 45E
Khimki **81** 55 50N 37 20E
Khingan, mts. **86** 47 0N 119 30E
Khíos **69** 38 27N 26 9E
Khisar-Momina Banya **67** 42 30N 24 44E
Khiuma = Hiiumaa **80** 58 50N 22 45E
Khiva **76** 41 30N 60 18E
Khiyav **92** 38 30N 47 45E
Khlaoula **118** 25 50N 6 32W
Khlong Khlung **100** 16 12N 99 43E
Khlong, R. **101** 15 30N 98 50E
Khmelnitsky **82** 49 23N 27 0E
Khmer Republic ■ = Cambodia **100** 12 15N 105 0E
Khoai, Hon **101** 8 26N 104 50E
Khodzhent **85** 40 14N 69 37E
Khoi **92** 38 40N 45 0E
Khojak P. **93** 30 55N 66 30E
Khok Kloi **101** 8 17N 98 19E
Khok Pho **101** 6 43N 101 6E
Khokholskiy **81** 51 35N 38 50E
Kholm **80** 57 10N 31 15E
Kholmsk **77** 35 5N 139 48E
Khomas Hochland **128** 22 40S 16 0E
Khomayn **92** 33 40N 50 7E
Khomo **128** 21 7S 24 35E
Khon Kaen **100** 16 30N 102 47E
Khong, Camb. **101** 13 55N 105 56E
Khong, Laos **100** 14 7N 105 51E
Khong, R., Laos **101** 15 0N 106 50E
Khong, R., Thai. **101** 17 45N 104 20E
Khong Sedone **100** 15 34N 105 49E
Khonh Hung (Soc Trang) **101** 9 37N 105 50E
Khonu **77** 66 30N 143 25E
Khoper, R. **81** 52 0N 43 20E
Khor el 'Atash **123** 13 20N 34 15E
Khóra **69** 37 3N 21 42E
Khóra Sfákion **69** 35 15N 24 9E
Khorasan □ **93** 34 0N 58 0E
Khorat = Nakhon Ratchasima **100** 14 59N 102 12E
Khorat, Cao Nguyen **100** 15 30N 102 50E
Khorat Plat. **101** 15 30N 102 50E
Khorb el Ethel **118** 28 44N 6 11W
Khorog **85** 37 30N 71 36E
Khorol **82** 49 48N 33 15E
Khorramabad **92** 33 30N 48 25E
Khorramshahr **92** 30 29N 48 15E
Khota Kota **127** 12 55S 34 15E
Khotan = Hot'ien **105** 37 7N 79 55E
Khotin **82** 48 31N 26 27E
Khouribga **118** 32 58N 6 50W
Khowai **98** 24 5N 91 40E
Khoyniki **80** 51 54N 29 55E
Khrami, R. **83** 41 30N 44 30E
Khrenovoye **81** 51 4N 40 6E
Khristianá, I. **69** 36 14N 25 13E
Khromtau **84** 50 17N 58 27E
Khtapodhiá, I. **69** 37 24N 25 34E
Khu Khan **100** 14 42N 104 12E
Khufaifiya **92** 24 50N 44 35E
Khugiani **94** 31 28N 66 14E
Khulna **98** 22 45N 89 34E
Khulna □ **98** 22 45N 89 35E
Khulo **83** 41 33N 42 19E
Khunzakh **83** 42 35N 46 42E
Khur **93** 32 55N 58 18E
Khurai **94** 24 3N 78 23E
Khurais **92** 24 55N 48 5E
Khurja **94** 28 15N 77 58E
Khurma **92** 21 58N 42 3E
Khūryān Mūryān, Jazā 'ir **91** 17 30N 55 58E
Khush **93** 32 55N 62 10E
Khushab **94** 32 20N 72 20E
Khuzdar **94** 27 52N 66 30E
Khuzestan □ **92** 31 0N 50 0E
Khvalynsk **81** 52 30N 48 2E
Khvatovka **81** 52 24N 46 32E
Khvor **93** 33 45N 55 0E
Khvormuj **93** 28 40N 51 30E
Khvoy **92** 38 35N 45 0E
Khvoynaya **80** 58 49N 34 28E
Khwaja Muhammad **93** 36 0N 70 0E
Khyber Pass **94** 34 10N 71 8E
Kiabukwa **127** 8 40S 24 48E
Kiadho, R. **96** 19 50N 76 55E
Kiama **141** 34 40S 150 50E
Kiamba **126** 6 0N 124 40E
Kiambi **126** 7 15S 28 0E
Kiambu **126** 1 8S 36 50E
Kiangsi □ **109** 27 20N 115 40E
Kiangsu □ **109** 33 0N 119 50E
Kiania **126** 10 18S 47 8E
Kiaohsien = Chiaohsien **107** 36 20N 120 0E
Kibæk **73** 56 2N 8 51E
Kibanga Port **126** 0 10S 32 58E
Kibangou **124** 3 18S 12 22E
Kibara **126** 2 8S 33 30E
Kibara, Mts. **126** 8 25S 27 10E
Kibombo **126** 3 57S 25 53E
Kibondo **126** 3 35S 30 45E
Kibondo □ **126** 4 0S 30 55E
Kibumbu **126** 3 32S 29 45E
Kibungu **126** 2 10S 30 32E
Kibuye, Burundi **126** 3 39S 29 59E
Kibuye, Rwanda **126** 2 3S 29 21E
Kibwesa **126** 6 30S 29 58E
Kibwezi **124** 2 27S 37 57E
Kibworth Beauchamp **29** 52 33N 0 59W
Kičevo **66** 41 34N 20 59E
Kichiga **77** 59 50N 163 5E
Kicking Horse Pass **152** 51 27N 116 25W
Kidal **121** 17 50N 1 22E
Kidderminster **28** 52 24N 2 13W
Kidete **126** 6 25S 37 17E
Kidira **120** 14 28N 12 13W
Kidlington **28** 51 49N 1 18W
Kidnappers, C. **142** 39 38S 177 5E
Kidsgrove **32** 53 6N 2 15W
Kidston **138** 18 52S 144 8E
Kidstones **32** 54 15N 2 2W
Kidugalle **126** 6 49S 38 15E
Kidwelly **31** 51 44N 4 20W
Kiel **48** 54 16N 10 8E
Kiel Canal = Nord-Ostee-Kanal **48** 54 15N 9 40E
Kielce **54** 50 58N 20 42E
Kielce □ **54** 51 0N 20 40E
Kielder **35** 55 14N 2 35W
Kieldrecht **47** 51 17N 4 11E
Kieler Bucht **48** 54 30N 10 30E
Kien Binh **101** 9 55N 105 19E
Kien Hung **101** 9 43N 105 17E
Kien Tan **101** 10 7N 105 17E
Kienchwan **99** 26 30N 99 45E
Kienge **127** 10 30S 27 30E
Kiessé **121** 13 29N 4 1E
Kieta **135** 6 12S 155 36E
Kiev = Kiyev **80** 50 30N 30 28E
Kiffa **120** 16 50N 11 15W
Kifisiá **69** 38 4N 23 49E
Kifissós, R. **69** 38 30N 23 0E
Kifri **92** 34 45N 45 0E
Kigali **126** 1 5S 30 4E
Kigarama **126** 1 1S 31 50E
Kigoma □ **126** 5 0S 30 0E
Kigoma-Ujiji **126** 5 30S 30 0E
Kigomasha, Ras **126** 4 58S 38 58E
Kihee **139** 27 23S 142 37E
Kihikihi **142** 38 2S 175 22E
Kii-Hantō **111** 34 0N 135 45E
Kii-Sanchi **111** 34 20N 136 0E
Kijik **147** 60 20N 154 20W
Kikai-Jima **112** 28 19N 129 58E
Kikinda **66** 45 50N 20 30E
Kikládhes □ **69** 37 0N 25 0E
Kikládhes, Is. **69** 37 20N 24 30E
Kikoira **141** 33 59S 146 40E
Kikori **135** 7 13S 144 15E
Kikori, R. **135** 7 5S 144 0E
Kikuchi **110** 32 59N 130 47E
Kikwit **124** 5 5S 18 45E
Kil **72** 59 30N 13 20E
Kilafors **72** 61 14N 16 36E
Kilakarai **97** 9 12N 78 47E
Kilauea **147** 22 13N 159 25W
Kilauea Crater **147** 19 24N 155 17W
Kilbaha **39** 52 35N 9 51W
Kilbeggan **38** 53 22N 7 30W
Kilbeheny **39** 52 18N 8 13W
Kilbennan **38** 53 33N 8 54W
Kilbirnie **34** 55 46N 4 42W
Kilbrannan Sd. **34** 55 40N 5 23W
Kilbride **39** 52 56N 6 5W
Kilbrien **39** 52 12N 7 40W
Kilbrittain **39** 51 40N 8 42W
Kilbuck Mts. **147** 60 30N 160 0W
Kilchberg **51** 47 18N 8 33E
Kilchoan **36** 56 42N 6 8W
Kilcock **38** 53 24N 6 40W
Kilcoe **39** 51 33N 9 26W
Kilcogan **39** 53 13N 8 52W
Kilconnell **39** 53 20N 8 25W
Kilcoo **38** 54 14N 6 1W
Kilcormac **39** 53 11N 7 44W
Kilcoy **139** 26 59S 152 30E
Kilcreggan **34** 55 59N 4 50W
Kilcrohane **39** 51 35N 9 44W
Kilcullen **39** 53 8N 6 45W
Kilcurry **38** 54 3N 6 26W
Kildare **39** 53 10N 6 50W
Kildare □ **39** 53 10N 6 50W
Kildavin **39** 52 41N 6 42W
Kildemo **39** 52 37N 8 50W
Kildonan **37** 58 10N 3 50W
Kildorrery **39** 52 15N 8 25W
Kilembe **126** 0 15N 30 3E
Kilfenora **39** 53 0N 9 13W
Kilfinan **34** 55 57N 5 19W
Kilfinnane **39** 52 21N 8 30W
Kilgarvan **39** 51 54N 9 28W
Kilgore **159** 32 22N 94 40W
Kilham **33** 54 4N 0 22W
Kilian Qurghan **93** 36 52N 78 3E
Kilifi **126** 3 40S 39 48E
Kilifi □ **126** 3 30S 39 40E
Kilimanjaro □ **126** 4 0S 38 0E
Kilimanjaro, Mt. **126** 3 7S 37 20E
Kilinailau, Is. **135** 4 45S 155 20E
Kilindini **126** 4 4S 39 40E
Kilis **92** 36 50N 37 10E
Kiliya **82** 45 28N 29 16E
Kilju **107** 40 57N 129 25E
Kilkea **39** 52 57N 6 55W
Kilkee **39** 52 41N 9 40W
Kilkeel **38** 54 4N 6 0W
Kilkelly **38** 53 53N 8 50W
Kilkenny **39** 52 40N 7 17W
Kilkenny □ **39** 52 35N 7 15W
Kilkerrin **38** 52 32N 8 36W
Kilkhampton **30** 50 53N 4 30W
Kilkieran **39** 53 20N 9 45W
Kilkieran B. **38** 53 18N 9 45W
Kilkis **68** 40 58N 22 57E
Kilkís □ **68** 41 5N 22 50E
Kilkishen **39** 52 49N 8 45W
Kilknock **38** 53 42N 8 53W
Kill **39** 52 11N 7 20W
Killadoon **38** 53 44N 9 53W
Killadysert **39** 52 40N 9 7W
Killala **38** 54 13N 9 12W
Killala B. **38** 54 20N 9 12W
Killaloe **39** 52 48N 8 28W
Killam **152** 52 47N 111 51W
Killane **39** 53 20N 7 6W
Killard, Pt. **38** 54 18N 5 31W
Killare **38** 53 28N 7 34W
Killarney, Man., Can. **150** 49 10N 99 40W
Killarney, Ont., Can. **153** 45 55N 81 30W
Killarney, Ireland **39** 52 2N 9 30W
Killarney, L's. of **39** 52 0N 9 30W
Killary Harb. **38** 53 38N 9 52W
Killashandra **38** 54 1N 7 32W
Killashee **38** 53 40N 7 52W
Killavally **38** 53 22N 7 23W
Killavullen **39** 52 8N 8 32W

Killchianaig Kíthnos

Killchianaig 34 56 2N 5 48W
Killdeer, Can. 153 49 6N 106 22W
Killdeer, U.S.A. 158 47 26N 102 48W
Killeagh 39 51 56N 8 0W
Killean 34 55 38N 5 40W
Killeen 159 31 7N 97 45W
Killeenleigh 39 51 58N 8 49W
Killeigh 39 53 14N 7 27W
Killenaule 39 52 35N 7 40W
Killianspick 39 52 21N 7 18W
Killiecrankie P. 37 56 44N 3 46W
Killimor 39 53 10N 8 17W
Killin 34 56 28N 4 20W
Killiney 39 53 15N 6 8W
Killingdal 71 62 47N 11 26 E
Killinghall 33 54 1N 1 33W
Killini 69 37 55N 21 8 E
Killini, Mts. 69 37 54N 22 25 E
Killinick 39 52 15N 6 29W
Killorglin 39 52 6N 9 48W
Killough 38 54 16N 5 40W
Killtullagh 39 53 17N 8 37W
Killucan 38 53 30N 7 10W
Killurin 39 52 23N 6 35W
Killybegs 38 54 38N 8 26W
Killyleagh 38 54 24N 5 40W
Kilmacolm 34 55 54N 4 39W
Kilmacthomas 39 52 13N 7 27W
Kilmaganny 39 52 26N 7 20W
Kilmaine 38 53 33N 9 10W
Kilmaley 39 52 50N 9 11W
Kilmallock 39 52 22N 8 35W
Kilmaluag 36 57 40N 6 18W
Kilmanagh 39 52 38N 7 28W
Kilmarnock, U.K. 34 55 36N 4 30W
Kilmarnock, U.S.A. 162 37 43N 76 23W
Kilmartin 34 56 8N 5 29W
Kilmaurs 34 55 37N 4 33W
Kilmeaden 39 52 15N 7 15W
Kilmeedy 39 52 25N 8 55W
Kilmelford 34 56 16N 5 30W
Kilmez 84 56 58N 50 55 E
Kilmez, R. 84 56 58N 50 28 E
Kilmichael 39 51 49N 9 4W
Kilmichael Pt. 39 52 44N 6 8W
Kilmihill 39 52 44N 9 18W
Kilmore, Austral. 141 37 25 S 144 53 E
Kilmore, Ireland 39 52 12N 6 35W
Kilmore Quay 39 52 10N 6 36W
Kilmuir 37 57 44N 4 7W
Kilmurry 39 52 47N 9 30W
Kilmurvy 39 53 9N 9 46W
Kilnaleck 38 53 52N 7 21W
Kilninver 34 56 20N 5 30W
Kilombero □ 127 8 0 S 37 0 E
Kilondo 127 9 45 S 34 20 E
Kilosa 126 6 48 S 37 0 E
Kilosa □ 126 6 48 S 37 0 E
Kilpatrick 39 51 46N 8 42W
Kilrea 38 54 58N 6 34W
Kilrenny 35 56 15N 2 40W
Kilronan 39 53 8N 9 40W
Kilrush 39 52 39N 9 30W
Kilsby 28 52 20N 1 11W
Kilsheelan 39 52 23N 7 37W
Kilsmo 72 59 6N 15 35 E
Kilsyth 35 55 58N 4 3W
Kiltamagh 38 53 52N 9 0W
Kiltealy 39 52 34N 6 45W
Kiltegan 39 52 53N 6 35W
Kiltoom 38 53 30N 8 0W
Kilwa □ 127 9 0 S 39 0 E
Kilwa Kisiwani 127 8 58 S 39 32 E
Kilwa Kivinje 127 8 45 S 39 25 E
Kilwa Masoko 127 8 55 S 39 30 E
Kilwinning 34 55 40N 4 41W
Kilworth 39 52 10N 8 15W
Kilworth, mts. 39 52 10N 8 15W
Kim 159 37 18N 103 20W
Kimamba 126 6 45 S 37 10 E
Kimba 140 33 8 S 136 23 E
Kimball, Nebr., U.S.A. 158 41 17N 103 20W
Kimball, S.D., U.S.A. 158 43 47N 98 57W
Kimbe 135 5 33 S 150 11 E
Kimbe B. 135 5 15 S 150 30 E
Kimberley, N.S.W., Austral. 140 32 50 S 141 4 E
Kimberley, W. Australia, Austral. 136 16 20 S 127 0 E
Kimberley, Can. 152 49 40N 115 59W
Kimberley, S. Afr. 128 28 43 S 24 46 E
Kimberley, dist. 132 16 20 S 127 0 E
Kimberley Downs 136 17 24 S 124 22 E
Kimberly 160 42 33N 114 25W
Kimbolton 29 52 17N 0 23W
Kimchŏn 107 36 11N 128 4 E
Kimi 69 38 38N 24 6 E
Kimje 107 35 48N 126 45 E
Kimmeridge, oilfield 19 50 36N 2 6W
Kímolos 69 36 48N 24 37 E
Kímolos, I. 69 36 48N 24 35 E
Kimovsk 81 54 0N 38 29 E
Kimparana 120 12 48N 5 0W
Kimry 81 56 55N 37 15 E
Kimsquit 152 52 45N 126 57W
Kimstad 73 58 35N 15 58 E
Kinabalu, mt. 102 6 0N 116 0 E
Kínaros, I. 69 36 59N 26 15 E
Kinaskan L. 152 57 38N 130 8W
Kinawley 38 54 14N 7 40W
Kinbrace 37 58 16N 3 56W
Kincaid 153 49 40N 107 0W
Kincardine, Can. 150 44 10N 81 40W
Kincardine, Fife, U.K. 35 56 4N 3 43W
Kincardine, Highland, U.K. 37 57 52N 4 20W
Kincardine (□) 26 56 56N 2 28W
Kincraig 37 57 8N 3 57W
Kindersley 153 51 30N 109 10W
Kindia 120 10 0N 12 52W
Kindu 126 2 55 S 25 50 E
Kinel 84 53 15N 50 40 E
Kineshma 81 57 30N 42 5 E
Kinesi 126 1 25 S 33 50 E
Kineton 28 52 10N 1 30W
King and Queen 162 37 42N 76 50W
King City 163 36 11N 121 8W
King Cr. 138 24 35 S 139 30 E
King Edward, R. 136 14 14 S 126 35 E
King Frederick VI Land 12 63 0N 43 0W
King Frederick VIII Land 12 77 30N 25 0W
King George 162 38 15N 77 10W
King George B. 176 51 30 S 60 30W
King George I. 13 60 0 S 60 0W
King George Is. 149 53 40N 80 30W
King George Sd. 132 35 5 S 118 0 E
King I., Austral. 138 39 50 S 144 0 E
King I., Can. 152 52 10N 127 40W
King I. = Kadah Kyun 101 12 30N 98 20 E
King, L. 137 33 10 S 119 35 E
King Leopold Ranges 136 17 20 S 124 20 E
King, Mt. 138 25 10 S 147 30 E
King Sd. 136 16 50 S 123 20 E
King William I. 148 69 10N 97 25W
King William, L. 50 42 14 S 146 15 E
King William's Town 128 32 51 S 27 22 E
Kingairloch, dist. 36 56 37N 5 30W
Kingaroy 139 26 32 S 151 51 E
Kingarrow 38 54 55N 8 5W
Kingarth 34 55 45N 5 2W
Kingfisher 159 35 50N 97 55W
Kinghorn 35 56 4N 3 10W
Kingisepp 80 59 25N 28 40 E
Kingisepp (Kuressaare) 80 58 15N 22 15 E
Kingman, Ariz., U.S.A. 161 35 12N 114 2W
Kingman, Kans., U.S.A. 159 37 41N 96 9W
Kings B. 12 78 0N 15 0 E
Kings Canyon National Park 163 37 0N 118 35W
King's Lynn 29 52 45N 0 25 E
Kings Mountain 157 35 13N 81 20W
Kings Park 162 40 53N 73 16W
King's Peak 160 40 46N 110 27W
King's, R. 39 52 32N 7 12W
Kings, R. 163 36 10N 119 50W
King's Sutton 28 52 1N 1 16W
King's Worthy 28 51 6N 1 18W
Kingsbarns 35 56 18N 2 40W
Kingsbridge 30 50 17N 3 46W
Kingsburg 163 36 35N 119 36W
Kingsbury 28 52 33N 1 41W
Kingscote 140 35 33 S 137 31 E
Kingscourt 38 53 55N 6 48W
Kingskerswell 30 50 30N 3 34W
Kingsland 28 52 15N 2 49W
Kingsley 158 42 37N 95 58W
Kingsley Dam 158 41 20N 101 40W
Kingsport 157 36 33N 82 36W
Kingsteignton 30 50 32N 3 35W
Kingston, Can. 150 44 14N 76 30W
Kingston, Jamaica 166 18 0N 76 50W
Kingston, N.Z. 143 45 20 S 168 43 E
Kingston, U.K. 28 51 23N 1 40W
Kingston, N.Y., U.S.A. 162 41 55N 74 0W
Kingston, Pa., U.S.A. 162 41 19N 75 58W
Kingston, R.I., U.S.A. 162 41 29N 71 30W
Kingston South East 140 36 51 S 139 55 E
Kingston-upon-Thames 29 51 23N 0 20W
Kingstown, Austral. 141 30 29 S 151 6 E
Kingstown, St. Vinc. 167 13 10N 61 10W
Kingstree 157 33 40N 79 48W
Kingsville, Can. 150 42 2N 82 45W
Kingsville, U.S.A. 159 27 30N 97 53W
Kingswear 30 50 21N 3 33W
Kingswood 28 51 26N 2 31W
Kington 28 52 12N 3 2W
Kingtung 99 24 30N 100 50 E
Kingussie 37 47 5N 4 2W
Kinistino 153 52 57N 105 2W
Kinkala 124 4 18 S 14 49 E
Kinki □ 111 35 0N 135 30 E
Kinleith 142 38 20 S 175 56 E
Kinloch, N.Z. 143 44 51 S 168 20 E
Kinloch, L. More, U.K. 37 58 17N 4 50W
Kinloch, Rhum, U.K. 36 57 0N 6 18W
Kinloch Rannoch 37 56 41N 4 12W
Kinlochbervie 36 58 28N 5 5W
Kinlochewe 36 57 37N 5 20W
Kinlochiel 36 56 52N 5 20W
Kinlochleven 36 56 42N 4 59W
Kinlochmoidart 36 56 47N 5 43W
Kinloss 37 57 38N 3 37W
Kinlough 38 54 27N 8 16W
Kinn 71 61 34N 4 45 E
Kinna 73 57 32N 12 42 E
Kinnaird 152 49 17N 117 39W
Kinnaird's Hd. 37 57 40N 2 0W
Kinnared 73 57 2N 13 7 E
Kinnegad 38 53 28N 7 8W
Kinneret 90 32 44N 35 34 E
Kinneret, Yam 90 32 45N 35 35 E
Kinneviken, B. 73 58 38N 18 20 E
Kinnitty 39 53 6N 7 44W
Kino 164 28 45N 111 59W
Kinoje, R. 150 52 8N 81 25W
Kinomoto 111 35 30N 136 13 E
Kinoni, C. Afr. Emp. 123 5 40N 26 10 E
Kinoni, Uganda 126 0 41 S 30 28 E
Kinping 101 22 56N 103 15 E
Kinrooi 47 51 9N 5 45 E
Kinross 35 56 13N 3 25W
Kinross (□) 26 56 13N 3 25W
Kinsale 39 51 42N 8 31W
Kinsale Harbour 39 51 40N 8 30W
Kinsale Head, gasfield 19 51 20N 8 0W
Kinsale Old Hd. 39 51 37N 8 32W
Kinsarvik 71 60 22N 6 43 E
Kinshasa 124 4 20 S 15 15 E
Kinsley 159 37 57N 99 30W
Kinston 157 35 18N 77 35W
Kintampo 121 8 5N 1 41W
Kintap 102 3 51 S 115 13 E
Kintaravay 36 58 4N 6 42W
Kintore 37 57 14N 2 20W
Kintore Ra. 137 23 15 S 128 47 E
Kintyre, Mull of 34 55 17N 5 4W
Kintyre, pen. 34 55 30N 5 35W
Kinu 98 22 46N 95 37 E
Kinu-Gawa, R. 111 35 36N 139 57 E
Kinushseo, R. 150 55 15N 83 45W
Kinuso 152 55 25N 115 25W
Kinvara 39 53 8N 8 57W
Kinyangiri 126 4 35 S 34 37 E
Kióni 69 38 27N 20 41 E
Kiosk 150 46 6N 78 53W
Kiowa, Kans., U.S.A. 159 37 3N 98 30W
Kiowa, Okla., U.S.A. 159 34 45N 95 50W
Kipahigan L. 153 55 20N 101 55W
Kipanga 126 6 15 S 35 20 E
Kiparissia 69 37 15N 21 40 E
Kiparissiakós Kólpos 69 37 25N 21 25 E
Kipawa Res. Prov. Park 150 47 0N 78 30W
Kipembawe 124 7 38 S 33 27 E
Kipengere Ra. 127 9 12 S 34 15 E
Kipili 126 7 28 S 30 32 E
Kipini 126 2 30 S 40 32 E
Kipling 153 50 6N 102 38W
Kipnuk 147 59 55N 164 7W
Kippen 34 56 8N 4 12W
Kippure, Mt. 39 53 11N 6 23W
Kipushi 127 11 48 S 27 12 E
Kir 124 1 29 S 19 25 E
Kirandul 96 18 33N 81 10 E
Kiratpur 94 29 32N 78 12 E
Kirchberg 50 47 5N 7 35 E
Kirchhain 48 50 49N 8 54 E
Kirchheim 49 48 38N 9 20 E
Kirchheim Bolanden 49 49 40N 8 0 E
Kirchschlag 53 47 30N 16 19 E
Kircubbin 38 54 30N 5 33W
Kirensk 77 57 50N 107 55 E
Kirgiz S.S.R. □ 85 42 0N 75 0 E
Kirgiziya Steppe 79 50 0N 55 0 E
Kiri 124 1 29 S 19 25 E
Kiriburu 96 22 0N 85 0 E
Kirikkale 92 39 51N 33 32 E
Kirikopuni 142 35 50 S 174 1 E
Kirillov 81 59 51N 38 14 E
Kirin □ 107 43 50N 125 45 E
Kirindi, R. 97 6 15N 81 20 E
Kirishi 80 51 28N 31 59 E
Kirishima-Yama 110 31 58N 130 55 E
Kiriwina Is. = Trobriand Is. 138 8 40 S 151 0 E
Kirk Michael 32 54 17N 4 35W
Kirkbean 35 54 56N 3 35W
Kirkbride 32 54 54N 3 13W
Kirkburton 33 53 36N 1 42W
Kirkby 32 53 29N 2 54W
Kirkby-in-Ashfield 33 53 6N 1 15W
Kirkby Lonsdale 32 54 13N 2 36W
Kirkby Malzeard 33 54 10N 1 38W
Kirkby Moorside 33 54 16N 0 56W
Kirkby Steven 32 54 27N 2 23W
Kirkby Thore 32 54 38N 2 34W
Kirkcaldy 35 56 7N 3 10W
Kirkcolm 34 54 59N 5 4W
Kirkconnel 35 55 23N 4 0W
Kirkcowan 34 54 53N 4 38W
Kirkcudbright 35 54 50N 4 3W
Kirkcudbright (□) 26 55 4N 4 0W
Kirkcudbright B. 35 54 46N 4 0W
Kirkeby 73 55 7N 8 33 E
Kirkee 96 18 34N 73 56 E
Kirkenær 71 60 27N 12 3 E
Kirkenes 74 69 40N 30 5 E
Kirkham 32 53 47N 2 52W
Kirkinner 34 54 59N 4 28W
Kirkintilloch 35 55 57N 4 10W
Kirkjubæjarklaustur 74 63 47N 18 4W
Kirkland, Ariz., U.S.A. 161 34 29N 112 46W
Kirkland, Wash., U.S.A. 160 47 40N 122 10W
Kirkland Lake 150 48 9N 80 2W
Kırklareli 67 41 44N 27 15 E
Kirkliston 35 55 55N 3 27W
Kirkliston Ra. 143 44 25 S 170 34 E
Kirkmichael 37 56 43N 3 31W
Kirkoswald 32 54 46N 2 41W
Kirkoswold 34 55 19N 4 48W
Kirkstone P. 32 54 29N 2 55W
Kirksville 158 40 8N 92 35W
Kirkuk 92 35 30N 44 21 E
Kirkwall 37 58 59N 2 59W
Kirkwhelpington 35 55 9N 2 0W
Kirkwood 128 33 22 S 25 15 E
Kirlampudi 96 17 12N 82 12 E
Kirn 49 49 46N 7 29 E
Kirov, R.S.F.S.R., U.S.S.R. 81 54 3N 34 12 E
Kirov, R.S.F.S.R., U.S.S.R. 84 58 35N 49 40 E
Kirovabad 83 40 45N 46 10 E
Kirovakan 83 41 0N 44 0 E
Kirovo 85 40 26N 70 36 E
Kirovo-Chepetsk 81 58 28N 50 0 E
Kirovograd 82 48 35N 32 20 E
Kirovsk, R.S.F.S.R., U.S.S.R. 78 67 48N 33 50 E
Kirovsk, Ukraine, U.S.S.R. 83 48 35N 38 30 E
Kirovski 83 45 51N 48 11 E
Kirovskiy 85 44 52N 78 12 E
Kirovskoye 85 42 39N 71 35 E
Kirriemuir, Can. 153 51 56N 110 20W
Kirriemuir, U.K. 37 56 41N 3 0W
Kirs 84 59 21N 52 14 E
Kirsanov 81 52 35N 42 40 E
Kirşehir 92 39 14N 34 5 E
Kirstonia 128 25 30 S 23 45 E
Kirtachi 121 12 52N 2 30 E
Kirthar Range 93 27 0N 67 0 E
Kirtling 29 52 11N 0 27 E
Kirtlington 28 51 54N 1 9W
Kirton 39 52 56N 0 3W
Kirton-in-Lindsey 33 53 29N 0 35W
Kiruna 74 67 52N 20 15 E
Kirundu 124 0 50 S 25 35 E
Kirup 137 33 40 S 115 50 E
Kiryū 111 36 24N 139 20 E
Kiryu 81 55 5N 46 45 E
Kirzhach 81 56 12N 38 50 E
Kisa 73 58 0N 15 39 E
Kisaga 126 4 30 S 34 23 E
Kisalaya 166 14 40N 84 3W
Kisámou, Kólpos 69 35 30N 23 38 E
Kisanga 126 2 30N 26 35 E
Kisangani 126 0 35N 25 15 E
Kisar, I. 103 8 5 S 127 10 E
Kisaran 102 2 47N 99 29 E
Kisarawe 126 6 53 S 39 0 E
Kisarawe □ 126 7 3 S 39 0 E
Kisarazu 111 35 23N 139 55 E
Kisbér 53 47 30N 18 0 E
Kiselevsk 76 54 5N 86 6 E
Kishanganga, R. 95 34 50N 74 15 E
Kishanganj 95 26 3N 88 14 E
Kishangarh 94 27 50N 70 30 E
Kishi 121 9 1N 3 45 E
Kishinev 82 47 0N 28 50 E
Kishinoi 82 47 1N 28 50 E
Kishiwada 111 34 28N 135 22 E
Kishkeam 39 52 15N 9 12 E
Kishon 90 32 33N 35 12 E
Kishorganj 98 24 26N 90 40 E
Kishorn L. 36 57 22N 5 40W
Kishtwar 95 33 20N 75 48 E
Kisii 126 0 40 S 34 45 E
Kisii □ 126 0 40 S 34 45 E
Kisiju 124 7 23 S 39 19 E
Kısır, Dağ 83 41 0N 43 5 E
Kisizi 126 1 0 S 29 58 E
Kiska I. 147 52 0N 177 30 E
Kiskatinaw, R. 152 56 8N 120 10W
Kiskittogisu L. 153 54 13N 98 20W
Kiskomárom = Zalakomár 53 46 33N 17 10 E
Kiskőrös 53 46 37N 19 20 E
Kiskundorozsma 53 46 16N 20 5 E
Kiskunfelégyháza 53 46 42N 19 53 E
Kiskunhalas 53 46 28N 19 37 E
Kiskunmajsa 53 46 30N 19 48 E
Kislovodsk 83 43 50N 42 45 E
Kismayu 113 0 20 S 42 30 E
Kiso-Gawa, R. 111 35 2N 136 45 E
Kiso-Sammyaku 111 35 30N 137 45 E
Kisofukushima 111 35 52N 137 43 E
Kisoro 126 1 17 S 29 48 E
Kispest 53 47 27N 19 9 E
Kissidougou 120 9 5N 10 0W
Kissimmee 157 28 18N 81 22W
Kissimmee, R. 157 27 20N 81 0W
Kississing L. 153 55 34N 100 47W
Kistanje 63 43 58N 15 55 E
Kisterenye 53 48 3N 19 50 E
Kisújszállás 53 47 12N 20 50 E
Kisuki 110 35 17N 132 54 E
Kisumu 126 0 3 S 34 45 E
Kisvárda 53 48 14N 22 4 E
Kiswani 126 4 5 S 37 57 E
Kiswere 127 9 27 S 39 30 E
Kit Carson 158 38 48N 102 45W
Kita 120 13 5N 9 25W
Kita-Ura 111 36 0N 140 34 E
Kitab 85 39 7N 66 52 E
Kitakami, R. 112 38 25N 141 19 E
Kitakyūshū 110 33 50N 130 50 E
Kitale 126 1 0N 35 12 E
Kitami 112 43 48N 143 54 E
Kitangiri, L. 126 4 5 S 34 20 E
Kitano-Kaikyō 110 34 17N 134 58 E
Kitaya 127 10 38 S 40 8 E
Kitchener, Austral. 137 30 55 S 124 8 E
Kitchener, Can. 150 43 27N 80 29W
Kitchigami, R. 150 50 35N 78 5W
Kitega = Citega 126 3 30 S 29 58 E
Kiteto □ 126 5 0 S 37 0 E
Kitgum Matidi 126 3 17N 32 52 E
Kíthira 69 36 9N 23 0 E
Kíthira, I. 69 36 15N 23 0 E
Kíthnos 69 37 26N 24 27 E

Kíthnos, I Konstantinovski

Kíthnos, I. **69** 37 25N 24 25 E
Kitimat **152** 54 3N 128 38W
Kitinen, R. **74** 67 34N 26 40 E
Kitiyab **123** 17 13N 33 35 E
Kítros **68** 40 22N 22 34 E
Kitsuki **110** 33 35N 131 37 E
Kittakittaooloo, L. **139** 28 3 S 138 14 E
Kittanning **156** 40 49N 79 30W
Kittatinny Mts. **162** 41 0N 75 0W
Kittery **162** 43 7N 70 42W
Kitui **126** 1 17 S 38 0 E
Kitui □ **126** 1 30 S 38 25 E
Kitwe **127** 12 54 S 28 7 E
Kitzbühel **52** 47 27N 12 24 E
Kitzingen **49** 49 44N 10 9 E
Kivalina **147** 67 45N 164 40W
Kivalo **74** 66 18N 26 0 E
Kivarli **94** 24 33N 72 46 E
Kivotós **68** 40 13N 21 26 E
Kivu □ **126** 3 10 S 27 0 E
Kivu, L. **126** 1 48 S 29 0 E
Kiwai I. **135** 8 35 S 143 30 E
Kiyev **80** 50 30N 30 28 E
Kiyevskoye Vdkhr. **80** 51 0N 30 0 E
Kizel **84** 59 3N 57 40 E
Kiziguru **126** 1 46 S 30 23 E
Kizil Jilga **95** 35 26N 79 50 E
Kizil Kiya **76** 40 20N 72 35 E
Kızılcahaman **82** 40 30N 32 30 E
Kızılırmak **83** 39 15N 36 0 E
Kizilskoye **84** 52 44N 58 54 E
Kizimkazi **126** 6 28 S 39 30 E
Kizlyar **83** 43 51N 46 40 E
Kizyl-Arvat **76** 38 58N 56 15 E
Kjellerup **73** 56 17N 9 25 E
Klabat, Teluk **102** 1 30 S 105 40 E
Kladanj **66** 44 14N 18 42 E
Kladnica **66** 43 23N 20 2 E
Kladno **52** 50 10N 14 7 E
Kladovo **66** 44 36N 22 33 E
Klaeng **100** 12 47N 101 39 E
Klagenfurt **52** 46 38N 14 20 E
Klagerup **73** 55 36N 13 17 E
Klagshamn **73** 55 32N 12 53 E
Klagstorp **73** 55 22N 13 23 E
Klaipeda **80** 55 43N 21 10 E
Klakring **73** 55 42N 9 59 E
Klamath Falls **160** 42 20N 121 50W
Klamath Mts. **160** 41 20N 123 0W
Klamath, R. **160** 41 40N 123 30W
Klang = Kelang **101** 3 1N 101 33 E
Klangklang **98** 22 41N 93 26 E
Klanjec **63** 46 3N 15 45 E
Klappan, R. **152** 58 0N 129 43W
Klarälven **72** 60 32N 13 15 E
Klaten **103** 7 43 S 110 36 E
Klatovy **52** 49 23N 13 18 E
Klawak **152** 55 35N 133 0W
Klawer **128** 31 44 S 18 36 E
Klazienaveen **46** 52 44N 7 0 E
Kłecko **54** 52 38N 17 25 E
Kleczew **54** 52 22N 18 9 E
Kleena Kleene **152** 52 0N 124 50W
Klein **160** 46 26N 108 31W
Klein-Karas **128** 27 33 S 18 7 E
Klein Karoo **128** 33 45 S 21 30 E
Kleine Gette, R. **47** 50 51N 5 6 E
Kleine Nete, R. **47** 51 12N 4 46 E
KlekovaCa, mt. **63** 44 25N 16 32 E
Klemtu **152** 52 35N 128 55W
Klenovec, Czech. **53** 48 36N 19 54 E
Klenovec, Yugo. **66** 31 32N 20 49 E
Klepp **71** 59 48N 5 36 E
Klerksdorp **128** 26 51 S 26 38 E
Kletnya **80** 53 30N 33 2 E
Kletsk **80** 53 5N 26 45 E
Kletskiy **83** 49 20N 43 0 E
Kleve **48** 51 46N 6 10 E
Klickitat **160** 45 50N 12 10W
Klimovichi **80** 53 36N 32 0 E
Klin **81** 56 28N 36 48 E
Klinaklini, R. **152** 51 21N 125 40W
Klinte **73** 53 35N 10 12 E
Klintehamn **73** 57 22N 18 12 E
Klintsey **80** 52 50N 32 10 E
Klipplaat **128** 33 0 S 24 22 E
Klisura **67** 42 40N 24 28 E
Klitmøller **73** 57 3N 8 30 E
Kljajićevo **66** 45 45N 19 17 E
Ključ **63** 44 32N 16 48 E
Kłobuck **54** 50 55N 19 5 E
Kłodzko **54** 50 28N 16 38 E
Kloetinge **47** 51 30N 3 56 E
Klondike **147** 64 0N 139 26W
Kloosterzande **47** 51 22N 4 1 E
Klosi **68** 41 28N 20 10 E
Klosterneuburg **53** 48 18N 16 19 E
Klosters **51** 46 52N 9 52 E
Kloten, Sweden **72** 59 54N 15 19 E
Kloten, Switz. **51** 47 27N 8 35 E
Klötze **48** 52 38N 11 9 E
Klouto **121** 6 57N 0 44 E
Klovborg **73** 55 56N 9 30 E
Klövsjöfj, mt. **72** 62 36N 13 57 E
Kluane, L. **147** 61 15N 138 40W
Kluang = Keluang **101** 1 59N 103 20 E
Kluczbork **54** 50 58N 18 12 E
Klundert **47** 51 40N 4 32 E
Klyuchevskaya, Guba **83** 55 50N 160 30 E
Kmelnitski **80** 49 23N 27 0 E
Knapdale, dist. **34** 55 55N 5 30W
Knaresborough **33** 54 1N 1 29W
Knebworth **29** 51 52N 0 11W
Knee L., Man., Can. **153** 55 3N 94 45W
Knee L., Sask., Can. **153** 55 51N 107 0W
Knesselare **47** 51 9N 3 26 E
Knezha **67** 43 30N 23 56 E
Knic **66** 43 53N 20 45 E
Knight Inlet **152** 50 45N 125 40W
Knighton **31** 52 21N 3 2W
Knights Ferry **163** 37 50N 120 40W
Knight's Landing **160** 38 50N 121 43W
Knin **63** 44 1N 16 17 E
Knittelfeld **52** 47 13N 14 51 E
Knjazevac **66** 43 35N 22 18 E
Knob, C. **137** 34 32 S 119 16 E
Knock **38** 53 48N 8 55W
Knockananna **39** 52 52N 6 34W
Knockhoy Mt. **39** 51 49N 9 27W
Knocklayd Mt. **38** 55 10N 6 15W
Knocklofty **39** 52 20N 7 49W
Knockmahon **39** 52 8N 7 21W
Knockmealdown Mts. **39** 52 16N 8 0W
Knocknaskagh Mt. **39** 52 7N 8 25W
Knokke **47** 51 20N 3 17 E
Knott End **32** 53 55N 3 0W
Knottingley **33** 53 42N 1 15W
Knowle **28** 52 23N 1 43W
Knox **156** 41 18N 86 36W
Knox, C. **152** 54 11N 133 5W
Knox City **159** 33 26N 99 38W
Knox Coast **13** 66 30 S 108 0 E
Knoxville, Iowa, U.S.A. **158** 41 20N 93 5W
Knoxville, Pa., U.S.A. **157** 41 57N 77 26W
Knoxville, Tenn., U.S.A. **157** 35 58N 83 57W
Knoydart, dist. **36** 57 3N 5 33W
Knurów **54** 50 13N 18 38 E
Knutsford **32** 53 18N 2 22W
Knutshø **71** 62 18N 9 41 E
Knysna **128** 34 2 S 23 2 E
Knyszyn **54** 53 20N 22 56 E
Ko Chang **101** 12 0N 102 20 E
Ko Ho, R. **109** 32 58N 117 13 E
Ko Kha **100** 18 11N 99 24 E
Ko Kut **101** 11 40N 102 32 E
Ko Phangan **101** 9 45N 100 10 E
Ko Phra Thong **101** 9 6N 98 15 E
Kō-Saki **110** 34 5N 129 13 E
Ko Samui **101** 9 30N 100 0 E
Koartac (Notre Dame de Koartac) **149** 61 5N 69 36 E
Koba, Aru, Indon. **103** 6 37 S 134 37 E
Koba, Bangka, Indon. **102** 2 26 S 106 14 E
Kobarid **63** 46 15N 13 30 E
Kobayashi **110** 31 56N 130 59 E
Kōbe **111** 34 45N 135 10 E
Kobelyaki **82** 49 11N 34 9 E
København **73** 55 41N 12 34 E
Koblenz, Ger. **49** 50 21N 7 36 E
Koblenz, Switz. **50** 47 37N 8 14 E
Kobo **123** 12 2N 39 56 E
Kobrin **80** 52 15N 24 22 E
Kobroor, Kepulauan **103** 6 10 S 134 30 E
Kobuchizawa **111** 35 52N 138 19 E
Kobuk **147** 66 55N 157 0W
Kobuk, R. **147** 66 55N 157 0W
Kobuleti **83** 41 55N 41 45 E
Kobylin **54** 51 43N 17 12 E
Kobyłka **54** 52 21N 21 10 E
Kobylkino **81** 54 8N 43 46 E
Kobylnik **80** 54 58N 26 39 E
Kočani **66** 41 55N 22 25 E
Koçarli **69** 37 45N 27 43 E
Koceljevo **66** 44 28N 19 50 E
Kočevje **63** 45 39N 14 50 E
Kochang **107** 35 41N 127 55 E
Kochas **95** 25 15N 83 56 E
Kōchi **110** 33 30N 133 35 E
Kōchi-Heiya **110** 33 28N 133 30 E
Kōchi-ken □ **110** 33 40N 133 30 E
Kochiu **108** 23 25N 103 7 E
Kochkor-Ata **85** 41 1N 72 29 E
Kochkorka **85** 42 13N 75 46 E
Kodaikanai **97** 10 13N 77 32 E
Kodaira **111** 35 44N 139 29 E
Koddiyar Bay **97** 8 33N 81 15 E
Kodiak **147** 57 30N 152 45W
Kodiak I. **147** 57 30N 152 45W
Kodiang **101** 6 21N 100 18 E
Kodinar **94** 20 46N 70 46 E
Kodori, R. **83** 43 0N 41 40 E
Koekelare **47** 51 5N 2 59 E
K'oerch'inyuich-'iench'i **107** 46 5N 122 5 E
Koerhmu **105** 36 22N 94 55 E
Koersel **47** 51 3N 5 17 E
Koes **125** 26 0 S 19 15 E
Köflach **13** 47 4N 15 4 E
Koforidua **121** 6 3N 0 17W
Kōfu **111** 35 40N 138 30 E
Koga **111** 36 11N 139 43 E
Kogaluk, R. **151** 56 12N 61 44W
Kogan **139** 27 2 S 150 40 E
Kogin Baba **121** 7 55N 11 35 E
Kogizman **92** 40 5N 43 10 E
Kogon **121** 11 20N 14 32W
Kogota **112** 38 33N 141 3 E
Koh-i-Bab, mts. **93** 34 30N 67 0 E
Koh-i-Khurd **94** 33 30N 65 59 E
Koh-i-Mazar **94** 32 30N 66 25 E
Kohat **94** 33 40N 71 29 E
Kohima **98** 25 35N 94 10 E
Kohler Ra. **13** 77 0N 110 0W
Kohtla-Järve **80** 59 20N 27 20 E
Kohukohu **142** 36 31 S 173 38 E
Koindong **107** 40 28N 126 18 E
Kojabuti **103** 2 36 S 140 37 E
Kojetin **53** 49 21N 17 20 E
Kojima **110** 34 20N 133 38 E
Kōjo **110** 34 33N 133 55 E
Kojō **107** 38 58N 127 58 E
Kojonup **137** 33 48 S 117 10 E
Kok Yangak **85** 41 2N 73 12 E
Koka **122** 20 5N 30 35 E
Kokand **85** 40 30N 70 57 E
Kokanee Glacier Prov. Park **152** 49 47N 117 10W
Kokas **103** 2 42 S 132 26 E
Kokava **53** 48 35N 19 50 E
Kokchetav **76** 53 20N 69 10 E
Kokemäenjoki **75** 61 32N 21 44 E
Kokemäenjoki = Kumo älv **75** 61 32N 21 44 E
Kokhma **81** 56 55N 41 18 E
Kokkola (Gamlakarleby) **74** 63 50N 23 8 E
Koko, Mid-Western, Nigeria **121** 6 5N 5 28 E
Koko, North-Western, Nigeria **121** 11 28N 4 29 E
Koko Kyunzu **101** 14 10N 93 25 E
Koko-Nor = Ch'ing Hai **105** 37 0N 100 20 E
Koko Shili **99** 35 20N 91 0 E
Kokoda **135** 8 54 S 147 47 E
Kokolopozo **120** 5 8N 6 5W
Kokomo **156** 40 30N 86 6W
Kokopo **135** 4 22 S 152 19 E
Kokoro **121** 14 12N 0 55 E
Kokoura **77** 71 35N 144 50 E
Koksan **107** 38 46N 126 40 E
Koksengir, Gora **85** 44 21N 65 6 E
Koksoak, R. **149** 54 5N 64 10W
Kokstad **125** 30 32 S 29 29 E
Kokubu **110** 31 44N 130 46 E
Kola **78** 68 45N 33 8 E
Kola, I. **103** 5 35 S 134 30 E
Kola Pen. = Kolskiy P-ov. **78** 67 30N 38 0 E
Kolagede **103** 7 54 S 110 26 E
Kolahoi **95** 34 12N 75 22 E
Kolahun **120** 8 15N 10 4W
Kolaka **103** 4 3 S 121 46 E
K'olamai **105** 45 30N 84 55 E
K'olan **106** 38 43N 111 32 E
Kolar **97** 13 12N 78 15 E
Kolar Gold Fields **97** 12 58N 78 16 E
Kolari **74** 67 20N 23 48 E
Kolarovgrad **67** 43 27N 26 42 E
Kolarovo **53** 47 56N 18 0 E
Kolašin **66** 42 50N 19 31 E
Kolayat **93** 27 50N 72 50 E
Kolby **73** 55 49N 10 33 E
Kolby Kås **73** 55 48N 10 32 E
Kolchugino **81** 56 17N 39 22 E
Kolda **120** 12 55N 14 50W
Koldewey I. **12** 77 0N 18 0W
Kolding **73** 55 30N 9 29 E
Kole **124** 3 16 S 22 42 E
Koléa **118** 36 38N 2 46 E
Kolepom, Pulau **103** 8 0 S 138 30 E
Kölfors **72** 62 9N 16 30 E
Kolguyev, Ostrov **78** 69 20N 48 30 E
Kolham **46** 53 11N 6 44 E
Kolhapur **96** 16 43N 74 15 E
Kolia **120** 9 46N 6 28W
Kolín **52** 50 2N 15 9 E
Kolind **73** 56 21N 10 34 E
Kölleda **48** 51 11N 11 14 E
Kollegal **97** 12 9N 77 9 E
Kolleru L. **96** 16 40N 81 10 E
Kollum **46** 53 17N 6 10 E
Kolmanskop **128** 26 45 S 15 14 E
Köln **48** 50 56N 9 58 E
Koło **54** 52 14N 18 40 E
Kołobrzeg **54** 54 10N 15 35 E
Kologriv **81** 58 48N 44 25 E
Kolokani **120** 13 35N 7 45W
Kolomna **81** 55 8N 38 45 E
Kolomyya **82** 48 31N 25 2 E
Kolondiéba **120** 11 5N 6 54W
Kolonodale **103** 2 3 S 121 25 E
Kolosib **98** 24 15N 92 45 E
Kolpashevo **76** 58 20N 83 5 E
Kolpino **80** 59 44N 30 39 E
Kolpny **81** 52 12N 37 10 E
Kolskiy Poluostrov **78** 67 30N 38 0 E
Kolskiy Zaliv **78** 69 23N 34 0 E
Koltubanovskiy **84** 52 57N 52 2 E
Kolubara, R. **66** 44 35N 20 15 E
Kolumna **54** 51 36N 19 14 E
Koluszki **54** 51 45N 19 46 E
Kolwezi **124** 10 40 S 25 25 E
Kolyberovo **81** 55 15N 38 40 E
Kolyma, R. **77** 64 40N 153 0 E
Kolymskoye, Okhotsko **77** 63 0N 157 0 E
Kôm Ombo **122** 24 25N 32 52 E
Komagene **111** 35 44N 137 58 E
Komaki **111** 35 17N 136 55 E
Komandorskiye Ostrava **77** 55 0N 167 0 E
Komárno **53** 47 49N 18 5 E
Komárom **53** 47 43N 18 7 E
Komárom □ **53** 47 35N 18 20 E
Komarovo **80** 58 38N 33 40 E
Komatsu **111** 36 25 S 136 30 E
Komatsukima **110** 34 0N 134 35 E
Kombissiri **121** 12 4N 1 20W
Kombori **120** 13 26N 3 56W
Kombóti **69** 39 6N 21 5 E
Komen **63** 45 49N 13 45 E
Komenda **121** 5 4N 1 28W
Komi, A.S.S.R. □ **84** 64 0N 55 0 E
Komiza **63** 43 3N 16 11 E
Komló **53** 46 15N 18 16 E
Kommamur Canal **97** 16 0N 80 25 E
Kommunarsk **83** 48 30N 38 45 E
Kommunizma, Pik **85** 39 0N 72 2 E
Komnes **71** 59 30N 9 55 E
Komodo **103** 8 37 S 119 20 E
Komoé **120** 5 12N 3 44W
Komono **124** 3 15 S 13 20 E
Komoran, Pulau **103** 8 18 S 138 45 E
Komoro **111** 36 19N 138 26 E
Komorze **54** 62 8N 17 38 E
Komotiri **68** 41 9N 25 26 E
Kompong Bang **101** 12 24N 104 40 E
Kompong Cham **101** 11 54N 105 30 E
Kompong Chhnang **101** 12 20N 104 35 E
Kompong Chikreng **100** 13 5N 104 18 E
Kompong Kleang **101** 13 6N 104 8 E
Kompong Luong **101** 11 49N 104 48 E
Kompong Pranak **101** 13 35N 104 55 E
Kompong Som **101** 10 38N 103 30 E
Kompong Som, Chhung **101** 10 50N 103 32 E
Kompong Speu **101** 11 26N 104 32 E
Kompong Sralao **100** 14 5N 105 46 E
Kompong Thom **100** 12 35N 104 51 E
Kompong Trabeck, Camb. **100** 13 6N 105 14 E
Kompong Trabeck, Camb. **101** 11 9N 105 28 E
Kompong Trach, Camb. **101** 11 25N 105 48 E
Kompong Trach, Camb. **118** 10 34N 104 28 E
Kompong Tralach **101** 11 54N 104 47 E
Komrat **82** 46 18N 28 40 E
Komsberge **128** 32 40 S 20 45 E
Komsomolabad **85** 38 50N 69 55 E
Komsomolets **84** 53 45N 62 2 E
Komsomolets, Ostrov **77** 80 30N 95 0 E
Komsomolsk, R.S.F.S.R., U.S.S.R. **77** 50 30N 137 0 E
Komsomolsk, Turkmen S.S.R., U.S.S.R. **85** 39 2N 63 36 E
Komsomolskiy **81** 53 30N 49 40 E
Kona, Niger **121** 13 33N 8 3 E
Kona, Nigeria **121** 8 58N 11 15 E
Konakovo **81** 56 52N 36 45 E
Konam Dzong **99** 29 5N 93 0 E
Konawa **159** 34 59N 96 46W
Kondagaon **96** 19 35N 81 35 E
Konde **126** 4 57 S 39 45 E
Kondiá **68** 39 52N 25 10 E
Kondinin **137** 32 34 S 118 8 E
Kondoa **126** 4 55 S 35 50 E
Kondoa □ **126** 5 0 S 36 0 E
Kondratyevo **77** 57 30N 98 30 E
Konduga **121** 11 35N 13 26 E
Kong **120** 8 54N 4 36W
Kong Christian IX.s Land **12** 68 0N 36 0W
Kong Christian X.s Land **12** 74 0N 29 0W
Kong Frederik VIII.s Land **12** 78 30N 26 0W
Kong Frederik VI.s Kyst **12** 63 0N 43 0W
Kong, Koh **101** 11 20N 103 0 E
Kong Oscar Fjord **12** 72 20N 24 0W
Kong, R. **100** 13 32N 105 58 E
Konga **73** 56 30N 15 6 E
Kongeå **73** 55 24N 8 39 E
Kongju **107** 36 30N 127 0 E
Konglu **98** 27 13N 97 57 E
Kongolo **126** 5 22 S 27 0 E
Kongoussi **121** 13 19N 1 32W
Kongsberg **71** 59 39N 9 39 E
Kongsvinger **71** 60 12N 12 2 E
Kongsvoll **71** 62 20N 9 36 E
Kongwa **126** 6 11 S 36 26 E
Koni **127** 10 40 S 27 11 E
Koni, Mts. **127** 10 36 S 27 10 E
Koniecpol **54** 50 46N 19 40 E
Königsberg = Kaliningrad **80** 54 42N 20 32 E
Königslutter **48** 52 14N 10 50 E
Königswusterhausen **48** 52 19N 13 38 E
Konin **54** 52 12N 18 15 E
Konin □ **54** 52 15N 18 30 E
Konispol **68** 39 42N 20 10 E
Kónitsa **68** 40 5N 20 48 E
Köniz **50** 46 56N 7 25 E
Konjic **66** 43 42N 17 58 E
Konjice **63** 46 20N 15 28 E
Konkouré, R. **120** 10 30N 13 40W
Könnern **48** 51 40N 11 45 E
Konnur **96** 16 14N 74 49 E
Kono **120** 8 30N 11 5W
Konoğlu **82** 40 35N 31 50 E
Konolfingen **50** 46 54N 7 38 E
Konongo **121** 6 40N 1 15W
Konos **135** 3 10 S 151 44 E
Konosha **78** 61 0N 40 5 E
Kōnosu **111** 36 3N 139 31 E
Konotop **80** 51 12N 33 7 E
Konskaya, R. **82** 47 30N 35 0 E
Konskie **54** 51 15N 20 23 E
Konsmo **71** 58 16N 7 23 E
Konstantinovka **82** 48 32N 37 39 E
Konstantinovski, R.S.F.S.R., U.S.S.R. **81** 57 45N 39 35 E

FHK

Konstantinovski **Krokom**

Konstantinovski, R.S.F.S.R., U.S.S.R.	**83**	47 33N	41 10 E
Konstantynów Łódzki	**54**	51 45N	19 20 E
Konstanz	**49**	47 39N	9 10 E
Kontagora	**121**	10 23N	5 27 E
Kontich	**47**	51 8N	4 26 E
Kontum	**100**	14 24N	108 0 E
Kontum, Plat. du	**100**	14 30N	108 0 E
Konya	**92**	37 52N	32 35 E
Konyin	**98**	22 58N	94 42 E
Konz Karthaus	**49**	49 41N	6 36 E
Konza	**124**	1 45 S	37 0 E
Konzhakovskiy Kamen, Gora	**84**	59 38N	59 8 E
Koog	**12**	52 27N	4 49 E
Kookynie	**137**	29 17 S	121 22 E
Koolan I.	**136**	16 0 S	123 45 E
Kooline	**136**	22 57 S	116 20 E
Kooloonong	**140**	34 48 S	143 10 E
Koolyanobbing	**137**	30 48 S	119 36 E
Koolymilka P.O.	**140**	30 58 S	136 32 E
Koondrook	**140**	35 33 S	144 8 E
Koorawatha	**141**	34 2 S	148 33 E
Koorda	**137**	30 48 S	117 35 E
Kooskia	**160**	46 9N	115 59W
Koostatak	**153**	51 26N	97 26W
Kootenai, R.	**160**	48 30N	115 30W
Kootenay L.	**153**	49 45N	117 0W
Kootenay Nat. Park	**152**	51 0N	116 0W
Kootingal	**173**	31 1 S	151 3 E
Kopa	**85**	43 31N	75 50 E
Kopaonik Planina	**66**	43 10N	21 0 E
Kopargaon	**96**	19 51N	74 28 E
Kópavogur	**74**	64 6N	21 55W
Koper	**63**	45 31N	13 44 E
Kopervik	**71**	59 17N	5 17 E
Kopeysk	**84**	55 7N	61 37 E
Kopi	**139**	33 24 S	135 40 E
Köping	**72**	59 31N	16 3 E
Kopiste	**63**	42 48N	16 42 E
Kopliku	**68**	42 15N	19 25 E
Köpmanholmen	**72**	63 10N	18 35 E
Köpmannebro	**73**	58 45N	12 30 E
Koppal	**97**	15 23N	76 5 E
Koppang	**71**	61 34N	11 3 E
Kopparberg	**75**	59 52N	15 0 E
Kopparbergs län □	**147**	61 20N	14 15 E
Koppeh Dāgh	**93**	38 0N	58 0 E
Kopperå	**71**	63 24N	11 50 E
Kopperå	**71**	63 24N	11 52 E
Koppio	**140**	34 26 S	135 51 E
Koppom	**72**	59 43N	12 10 E
Koprivlen	**67**	41 36N	23 53 E
Koprivnica	**63**	46 12N	16 45 E
Koprivshtitsa	**67**	42 40N	24 19 E
Kopychintsy	**80**	49 7N	25 58 E
Korab, mt.	**66**	41 44N	20 40 E
Korakiána	**68**	39 42N	19 45 E
Koraput	**96**	18 50N	82 40 E
Korba	**95**	22 20N	82 45 E
Korbach	**48**	51 17N	8 50 E
Korbu, G.	**101**	4 41N	101 18 E
Korça	**68**	40 37N	20 50 E
Korça □	**68**	40 40N	20 50 E
Korčula	**63**	42 57N	17 8 E
Korčula, I.	**63**	42 57N	17 0 E
Korčulanski Kanal	**63**	43 3N	16 40 E
Kordestān □	**92**	36 0N	47 0 E
Korea	**107**	40 0N	127 0 E
Korea Bay	**107**	39 0N	124 0 E
Korea, South ■	**107**	36 0N	128 0 E
Korea Strait	**107**	34 0N	129 30 E
Koregaon	**96**	17 40N	74 10 E
Korenevo	**80**	51 27N	34 55 E
Korenovsk	**83**	45 12N	39 22 E
Korets	**80**	50 40N	27 5 E
Korgus	**122**	19 16N	33 48 E
Korhogo	**120**	9 29N	5 28W
Koribundu	**120**	7 41N	11 46W
Koridina	**139**	29 42 S	143 25 E
Korim	**103**	0 58 S	136 10 E
Korinthía □	**69**	37 50N	22 35 E
Korinthiakós Kólpos	**69**	38 16N	22 30 E
Kórinthos	**69**	37 56N	22 55 E
Korioumé	**120**	16 35N	3 0W
Kōriyama	**112**	37 24N	140 23 E
Korkino	**84**	54 54N	61 23 E
Körmend	**53**	47 5N	16 35 E
Kornat, I.	**63**	43 50N	15 20 E
Korneshty	**82**	47 21N	28 1 E
Korneuburg	**53**	48 20N	16 20 E
Korning	**73**	56 30N	9 44 E
Kornsjø	**71**	58 57N	11 39 E
Kornstad	**71**	62 59N	7 27 E
Koro, Ivory C.	**120**	8 32N	7 30W
Koro, Mali	**120**	14 1N	2 58W
Koroba	**135**	5 44 S	142 47 E
Korocha	**81**	50 55N	37 30 E
Korogwe	**124**	5 5 S	38 25 E
Korogwe □	**126**	5 0 S	38 20 E
Koroit	**140**	38 18 S	142 24 E
Korong Vale	**140**	36 22 S	143 45 E
Koróni	**69**	36 48N	21 57 E
Korónia, Limni	**68**	40 47N	23 37 E
Koronis	**69**	37 12N	25 35 E
Koronowo	**54**	53 19N	17 55 E
Koror	**103**	7 20N	134 28 E
Körös, R.	**53**	46 45N	20 20 E
Köröstarcsa	**53**	46 53N	21 3 E
Korosten	**80**	50 57N	28 25 E
Korotoyak	**81**	51 1N	39 2 E
Korraraika, B. de	**129**	17 45 S	43 57 E
Korsakov	**77**	46 30N	142 42 E
Korshavn	**71**	58 2N	7 0 E
Korshunovo	**77**	58 37N	110 10 E
Korsör	**73**	55 20N	11 9 E
Korsze	**54**	54 11N	21 9 E
Kortemark	**47**	51 2N	3 3 E
Kortessem	**47**	50 52N	5 23 E
Korti	**122**	18 0N	31 40 E
Kortrijk	**47**	50 50N	3 17 E
Korumburra	**141**	38 26 S	145 50 E
Korwai	**94**	24 7N	78 5 E
Koryakskiy Khrebet	**77**	61 0N	171 0 E
Koryŏng	**107**	35 44N	128 15 E
Kos	**69**	36 52N	27 19 E
Kos, I.	**69**	36 50N	27 15 E
Kosa, Ethiopia	**123**	7 50N	36 50 E
Kosa, U.S.S.R.	**84**	59 56N	55 0 E
Kosa, R.	**84**	60 11N	55 10 E
Kosaya Gora	**81**	54 10N	37 30 E
Koschagy	**79**	46 40N	54 0 E
Kosciusko	**159**	33 3N	89 34W
Kosciusko, I.	**152**	56 0N	133 40W
Kosciusko, Mt.	**141**	36 27 S	148 16 E
Kösély, R.	**53**	47 25N	21 30 E
Kosgi	**96**	16 58N	77 43 E
Kosha	**122**	20 50N	30 30 E
Koshigaya	**111**	35 54N	139 48 E
K'oshih	**105**	39 29N	75 58 E
K'oshihk'ot'engch'i	**107**	43 17N	117 24 E
Koshiki-Rettō	**110**	31 45N	129 49 E
Kōshoku	**111**	36 38N	138 6 E
Koshtëbë	**85**	41 5N	74 15 E
Kosi	**94**	27 48N	77 29 E
Kosi-meer	**129**	27 0 S	32 50 E
Košice	**53**	48 42N	21 15 E
Kosjerič	**66**	44 0N	19 55 E
Koslan	**78**	63 28N	48 52 E
Kosŏng	**107**	38 48N	128 24 E
Kosovska-Mitrovica	**66**	42 54N	20 52 E
Kosścian	**54**	52 5N	16 40 E
Kosścierzyna	**54**	54 8N	17 59 E
Kosso	**120**	5 3N	5 47W
Kostajnica	**63**	45 17N	16 30 E
Kostanjevica	**63**	45 51N	15 27 E
Kostelec	**53**	50 14N	16 35 E
Kostenets	**67**	42 15N	23 52 E
Koster	**128**	25 52 S	26 54 E
Kôstî	**123**	13 8N	32 43 E
Kostolac	**66**	44 43N	21 15 E
Kostroma	**81**	57 50N	41 58 E
Kostromskoye Vdkhr.	**81**	57 52N	40 49 E
Kostrzyn	**54**	52 24N	17 14 E
Kostyukovichi	**80**	53 10N	32 4 E
Koszalin	**54**	54 12N	16 8 E
Koszalin □	**54**	54 10N	16 10 E
Kószeg	**53**	47 23N	16 33 E
Kot Adu	**94**	30 30N	71 0 E
Kot Moman	**94**	32 13N	73 0 E
Kota	**94**	25 14N	75 49 E
Kota Baharu	**101**	6 7N	102 14 E
Kota Kinabalu	**102**	6 0N	116 12 E
Kota-Kota = Khota Kota	**127**	12 55 S	34 15 E
Kota Tinggi	**101**	1 44N	103 53 E
Kotaagung	**102**	5 38 S	104 29 E
Kotabaru	**102**	3 20 S	116 20 E
Kotabumi	**102**	4 49 S	104 46 E
Kotamobagu	**103**	0 57N	124 31 E
Kotaneelee, R.	**152**	60 11N	123 42W
Kotawaringin	**102**	2 28 S	111 27 E
Kotchandpur	**98**	23 24N	89 1 E
Kotcho L.	**152**	59 7N	121 12W
Kotel	**67**	42 52N	26 26 E
Kotelnich	**81**	58 20N	48 10 E
Kotelnikovo	**83**	47 45N	43 15 E
Kotelnyy, Ostrov	**77**	75 10N	139 0 E
Kothagudam	**96**	17 30N	80 40 E
Kothapet	**96**	19 21N	79 28 E
Köthen	**48**	51 44N	11 59 E
Kothi	**95**	24 45N	80 40 E
Kotiro	**94**	26 17N	67 13 E
Kotka	**75**	60 28N	26 58 E
Kotlas	**78**	61 15N	47 0 E
Kotlenska Planina	**67**	42 56N	26 30 E
Kotli	**94**	33 30N	73 55 E
Kotmul	**95**	35 32N	75 10 E
Kotohira	**110**	34 11N	133 49 E
Kotonkoro	**121**	11 3N	5 58 E
Kotor	**66**	42 25N	18 47 E
Kotor Varoš	**66**	44 38N	17 22 E
Kotoriba	**63**	46 23N	16 48 E
Kotovo	**81**	50 22N	44 45 E
Kotovsk	**82**	47 55N	29 35 E
Kotputli	**94**	27 43N	76 12 E
Kotri	**94**	25 22N	68 22 E
Kotri, R.	**96**	19 45N	80 35 E
Kótronas	**69**	36 38N	22 29 E
Kötschach-Mauthern	**52**	46 41N	13 1 E
Kottayam	**97**	9 35N	76 33 E
Kottur	**97**	10 34N	76 56 E
Kotturu	**93**	14 45N	76 10 E
Kotuy, R.	**77**	70 30N	103 0 E
Kotzebue	**147**	66 50N	162 40W
Kotzebue Sd.	**147**	66 30N	164 0W
Kouango	**124**	5 0N	20 10 E
Koudekerke	**47**	51 29N	3 33 E
Koudougou	**120**	12 10N	2 20W
Koufonísi, I.	**69**	34 56N	26 8 E
Koufonísia, I.	**69**	36 57N	25 35 E
Kougaberge	**128**	33 48 S	24 20 E
Kouibli	**120**	7 15N	7 14W
Kouilou, R.	**124**	4 10 S	12 5 E
Kouki	**124**	7 22N	17 3 E
Koula Moutou	**124**	1 15 S	12 25 E
Koulen	**100**	13 50N	104 40 E
Koulikoro	**120**	12 40N	7 50W
Koumala	**138**	21 38 S	149 15 E
Koumankoun	**120**	11 58N	6 6W
Koumbia, Guin.	**120**	11 54N	13 40W
Koumbia, Upp. Vol.	**120**	11 10N	3 50W
Koumboum	**120**	10 25N	13 0W
Koumpenntoum	**120**	13 59N	14 34W
Koumra	**117**	8 50N	17 35 E
Koumradskiy	**76**	47 20N	75 0 E
Koundara	**120**	12 29N	13 18W
Kountze	**159**	30 20N	94 22W
Koupangtzu	**107**	41 22N	121 46 E
Koupéla	**121**	12 11N	0 21 E
Kourizo, Passe de	**119**	22 28N	15 27 E
Kouroussa	**120**	10 45N	9 45W
Koussané	**120**	14 53N	11 14W
Kousseri	**117**	12 0N	14 55 E
Koutiala	**120**	12 25N	5 35W
Kouto	**120**	9 53N	6 25W
Kouvé	**121**	6 25N	0 59 E
KovaCica	**66**	45 5N	20 38 E
Kovel	**80**	51 10N	24 20 E
Kovilpatti	**97**	9 10N	77 50 E
Kovin	**66**	44 44N	20 59 E
Kovrov	**81**	56 25N	41 25 E
Kovur, Andhra Pradesh, India	**96**	17 3N	81 39 E
Kovur, Andhra Pradesh, India	**97**	14 30N	80 1 E
Kowal	**54**	52 32N	19 7 E
Kowalewo Pomorskie	**54**	53 10N	18 52 E
Kowkash	**150**	50 20N	87 20W
Kowloon	**109**	22 20N	114 15 E
Kowŏn	**107**	39 26N	127 14 E
Kōyama	**110**	31 20N	130 56 E
Koyan, Pegunungan	**102**	3 15N	114 30 E
Koyang	**106**	33 31N	116 11 E
Koytash	**85**	40 11N	67 19 E
Koyuk	**147**	64 55N	161 20W
Koyukuk, R.	**147**	65 45N	156 30W
Koyulhisar	**82**	40 20N	37 52 E
Koza	**112**	26 19N	127 46 E
Kozan	**92**	37 35N	35 50 E
Kozàni	**68**	40 19N	21 47 E
Kozàni □	**68**	40 18N	21 45 E
Kozara, Mts.	**63**	45 0N	17 0 E
Kozarac	**63**	44 58N	16 48 E
Kozelsk	**80**	54 2N	35 38 E
Kozhikode = Calicut	**97**	11 15N	75 43 E
Kozhva	**78**	65 10N	57 0 E
Koziegłowy	**54**	50 37N	19 8 E
Kozje	**63**	46 5N	15 35 E
Kozle	**54**	50 20N	18 8 E
Kozlodui	**67**	43 45N	23 42 E
Kozlovets	**67**	43 30N	25 20 E
Kozmin	**54**	51 48N	17 27 E
Kōzu-Shima	**111**	34 13N	139 10 E
Kozuchów	**54**	51 45N	15 31 E
Kpabia	**121**	9 10N	0 20W
Kpandae	**121**	8 30N	0 2W
Kpandu	**121**	7 2N	0 18 E
Kpessi	**121**	8 4N	1 16 E
Kra Buri	**101**	10 22N	98 46 E
Kra, Isthmus of = Kra, Kho Khot	**101**	10 15N	99 30 E
Kra, Kho Khot	**101**	10 15N	99 30 E
Krabbendijke	**47**	51 26N	4 7 E
Krabi	**101**	8 4N	98 55 E
Kragan	**103**	6 43 S	111 38 E
Kragerø	**71**	58 52N	9 25 E
Kragujevac	**66**	44 2N	20 56 E
Krajenka	**54**	53 18N	16 59 E
Krakatau = Rakata, Pulau	**102**	6 10 S	105 20 E
Krakor	**100**	12 32N	104 12 E
Kraków	**54**	50 4N	19 57 E
Kraków □	**53**	50 0N	20 0 E
Kraksaan	**103**	7 43 S	113 23 E
Kraksmala	**73**	57 2N	15 20 E
Kråkstad	**71**	59 40N	10 50 E
Kråkstad	**71**	59 39N	10 55 E
Kralanh	**100**	13 35N	103 25 E
Králiky	**53**	50 6N	16 45 E
Kraljevo	**66**	43 44N	20 41 E
Kralovice	**52**	49 59N	13 29 E
Královsky Chlmec	**53**	48 27N	22 0 E
Kralupy	**52**	50 13N	14 20 E
Kramatorsk	**82**	48 50N	37 30 E
Kramer	**161**	35 0N	117 38W
Kramfors	**72**	62 55N	17 48 E
Kramis, C.	**118**	36 26N	0 45 E
Krångede	**72**	63 9N	16 10 E
Krångede	**72**	63 9N	16 6 E
Kraniá	**68**	39 53N	21 18 E
Kranidhion	**69**	37 20N	23 10 E
Kranj	**63**	46 16N	14 22 E
Kranjska Gora	**63**	46 29N	13 48 E
Kranzberg	**128**	21 59 S	15 37 E
Krapina	**63**	46 10N	15 52 E
Krapina, R.	**63**	46 0N	15 55 E
Krapivna	**81**	53 58N	37 10 E
Krapkowice	**54**	50 29N	17 56 E
Kras Polyana	**83**	43 40N	40 25 E
Krashyy Klyuch	**84**	55 23N	56 39 E
Kraskino	**77**	42 44N	130 48 E
Krāslāva	**80**	55 52N	27 12 E
Kraslice	**52**	50 19N	12 31 E
Krasnaya Gorbatka	**81**	55 52N	41 45 E
Krasnik Fabryezny	**54**	50 58N	22 11 E
Krasnoarmeisk	**82**	48 18N	37 11 E
Krasnoarmeysk, R.S.F.S.R., U.S.S.R.	**81**	50 32N	45 50 E
Krasnoarmeysk, R.S.F.S.R., U.S.S.R.	**83**	48 30N	44 25 E
Krasnodar	**83**	45 5N	38 50 E
Krasnodonetskaya	**83**	48 5N	40 50 E
Krasnog Dardeiskoye	**82**	45 32N	34 16 E
Krasnogorskiy	**81**	56 10N	48 28 E
Krasnograd	**82**	49 27N	35 27 E
Krasnogvardeysk	**85**	39 46N	67 16 E
Krasnogvardeyskoye	**83**	45 52N	41 33 E
Krasnoïarsk	**77**	56 8N	93 0 E
Krasnokamsk	**84**	58 4N	55 48 E
Krasnokutsk	**80**	50 10N	34 50 E
Krasnoperekopsk	**82**	46 0N	33 54 E
Krasnoselkupsk	**76**	65 20N	82 10 E
Krasnoslobodsk	**83**	48 42N	44 33 E
Krasnoturinsk	**84**	59 46N	60 12 E
Krasnoufimsk	**84**	56 57N	57 46 E
Krasnouralsk	**84**	58 21N	60 3 E
Krasnousolskiy	**84**	53 54N	56 27 E
Krasnovishersk	**84**	60 23N	57 3 E
Krasnovodsk	**79**	40 0N	52 52 E
Krasnoyarsk	**77**	56 8N	93 0 E
Krasnoyarskiy	**84**	51 58N	59 55 E
Krasnoye, Kal., U.S.S.R.	**83**	46 16N	45 0 E
Krasnoye, R.S.F.S.R., U.S.S.R.	**81**	59 15N	47 40 E
Krasnoye, Ukr., U.S.S.R.	**80**	49 56N	24 42 E
Krasnozavodsk	**81**	56 38N	38 16 E
Krasny Liman	**82**	48 58N	37 50 E
Krasny Sulin	**83**	47 52N	40 8 E
Krasnystaw	**54**	50 57N	23 5 E
Krasnyy	**80**	49 56N	24 42 E
Krasnyy Kholm, R.S.F.S.R., U.S.S.R.	**81**	58 10N	37 10 E
Krasnyy Kholm, R.S.F.S.R., U.S.S.R.	**84**	51 35N	54 9 E
Krasnyy Kut	**81**	50 50N	47 0 E
Krasnyy Luch	**83**	48 13N	39 0 E
Krasnyy Yar, Kal., U.S.S.R.	**83**	46 43N	48 23 E
Krasnyy Yar, R.S.F.S.R., U.S.S.R.	**81**	50 42N	44 45 E
Krasnyy Yar, R.S.F.S.R., U.S.S.R.	**81**	53 30N	50 22 E
Krasnyyoskolskoye, Vdkhr.	**82**	49 30N	37 30 E
Kraśnik	**54**	50 55N	22 5 E
Kraszna, R.	**53**	48 0N	22 20 E
Kratie	**100**	12 32N	106 10 E
Kratke Ra.	**135**	6 45 S	146 0 E
Kratovo	**66**	42 6N	22 10 E
Kravanh, Chuor Phnum	**101**	12 0N	103 32 E
Krawang	**103**	6 19N	107 18 E
Krefeld	**48**	51 20N	6 22 E
Kremaston, Límni	**69**	38 52N	21 30 E
Kremenchug	**82**	49 5N	33 25 E
Kremenchugskoye Vdkhr.	**82**	49 20N	32 30 E
Kremenets	**82**	50 8N	25 43 E
Kremenica	**66**	40 55N	21 25 E
Kremennaya	**82**	49 1N	38 10 E
Kremikovtsi	**67**	42 46N	23 28 E
Kremmen	**48**	52 45N	13 1 E
Kremmling	**160**	40 10N	106 30W
Kremnica	**53**	48 45N	18 50 E
Krems	**52**	48 25N	15 36 E
Kremsmünster	**52**	48 3N	14 8 E
Kretinga	**80**	55 53N	21 15 E
Krettamia	**118**	28 47N	3 27W
Krettsy	**80**	58 15N	32 30 E
Kreuzlingen	**51**	47 38N	9 10 E
Kribi	**121**	2 57N	9 56 E
Krichem	**67**	46 16N	24 28 E
Krichev	**80**	53 45N	31 50 E
Kriens	**51**	47 2N	8 17 E
Krim, mt.	**63**	45 53N	14 30 E
Krimpen	**46**	51 55N	4 34 E
Krionéri	**69**	38 20N	21 35 E
Krishna, R.	**96**	16 30N	77 0 E
Krishnagiri	**97**	12 32N	78 16 E
Krishnanagar	**95**	23 24N	88 33 E
Krishnaraja Sagara	**97**	12 20N	76 30 E
Kristianopel	**73**	56 12N	16 0 E
Kristiansand	**71**	58 9N	8 1 E
Kristianstad	**73**	56 2N	14 9 E
Kristianstad □	**75**	56 15N	14 0 E
Kristiansund	**71**	63 7N	7 45 E
Kristiinankaupunki	**74**	62 16N	21 21 E
Kristinehamn	**72**	59 18N	14 13 E
Kristinestad	**74**	62 16N	21 21 E
Kríti, I.	**69**	35 15N	25 0 E
Kritsá	**69**	35 10N	25 41 E
Kriva Palanka	**66**	42 11N	22 19 E
Kriva, R.	**66**	42 12N	22 18 E
Krivaja, R.	**66**	44 15N	18 22 E
Krivelj	**66**	44 8N	22 5 E
Krivoy Rog	**82**	47 51N	33 20 E
Krizevci	**63**	46 3N	16 32 E
Krk	**63**	45 5N	14 36 E
Krk, I.	**63**	45 8N	14 40 E
Krka, R.	**63**	45 50N	15 30 E
Krkonoše	**52**	50 50N	16 10 E
Krnov	**53**	50 5N	17 40 E
Krobia	**54**	51 47N	16 59 E
Kročehlavy	**52**	50 8N	14 9 E
Kroeng Krai	**101**	14 55N	98 30 E
Krokawo	**54**	54 47N	18 9 E
Krokeaí	**69**	36 53N	22 32 E
Kroken, Norway	**71**	58 57N	9 8 E
Kroken, Sweden	**71**	59 2N	11 23 E
Krokom	**72**	63 20N	14 30 E

Krolevets Kuybyshevskoye Vdkhr

Krolevets 80 51 35N 33 20 E
Kroměříz 53 49 18N 17 21 E
Krommenie 46 52 30N 4 46 E
Krompachy 53 48 54N 20 52 E
Kromy 80 52 40N 35 48 E
Kronobergs län □ 73 56 45N 14 30 E
Kronprins Harald Kyst 13 70 0 S 35 1 E
Kronprins Olav Kyst 13 69 0 S 42 0 E
Kronprinsesse Märtha Kyst 13 73 30 S 10 0W
Kronshtadt 80 60 5N 29 35 E
Kroonstad 125 27 43 S 27 19 E
Kröpelin 48 54 4N 11 48 E
Kropotkin 77 45 25N 40 35 E
Kropp 48 54 24N 9 32 E
Krósniewice 54 52 15N 19 11 E
Krosno 54 49 35N 21 56 E
Krosno □ 54 49 30N 22 0 E
Krosno Odrz 54 52 3N 15 7 E
Krosścienko 54 49 29N 20 25 E
Krotoszyn 54 51 42N 17 23 E
Krotovka 84 53 18N 51 10 E
Krraba 68 41 13N 20 0 E
Krško 63 45 57N 15 30 E
Krstača, mt. 66 42 57N 20 8 E
Kruger Nat. Pk. 129 24 0 S 31 40 E
Krugersdorp 129 26 5 S 27 46 E
Kruidfontein 128 32 48 S 21 59 E
Kruiningen 47 51 27N 4 2 E
Kruis, Kaap 128 21 55 S 13 57 E
Kruishoutem 47 50 54N 3 32 E
Kruisland 47 51 34N 4 25 E
Kruja 68 41 32N 19 46 E
Krulevshchina 80 55 5N 27 45 E
Kruma 68 42 37N 20 28 E
Krumovgrad 67 41 29N 25 38 E
Krung Thep 100 13 45N 100 35 E
Krupanj 66 44 25N 19 22 E
Krupina 53 48 22N 19 5 E
Krupinica, R. 53 48 15N 19 5 E
Kruševac 66 43 35N 21 28 E
Krušovo 66 41 23N 21 19 E
Kruszwica 54 52 40N 18 20 E
Kruzof I. 152 57 10N 135 40W
Krylbo 72 60 7N 16 15 E
Krymsk Abinsk 82 44 50N 38 0 E
Krymskaya 82 45 0N 34 0 E
Krynica 54 49 25N 20 57 E
Krynica Morska 54 54 23N 19 28 E
Krynki 54 53 17N 23 43 E
Kryulyany 70 47 12N 29 9 E
Krzepice 54 50 58N 18 50 E
Krzeszowice 54 50 8N 19 37 E
Krzywin 54 51 58N 16 50 E
Krzyz 54 52 52N 16 0 E
Ksabi, Alg. 118 29 8N 0 58W
Ksabi, Moroc. 118 32 51N 4 13W
Ksar Chellala 118 35 13N 2 19 E
Ksar el Boukhari 118 35 51N 2 52 E
Ksar el Kebir 118 35 0N 6 0W
Ksar es Souk 118 31 58N 4 20W
Ksar Rhilane 119 33 0N 9 39 E
Ksiba 118 32 46N 6 0W
Ksour, Mts. des 118 32 45N 0 30W
Kstovo 81 56 12N 44 13 E
Kuachou 109 32 14N 119 24 E
Kuala 102 2 46N 105 47 E
Kuala Berang 101 5 5N 103 1 E
Kuala Dungun 101 4 45N 103 25 E
Kuala Kangsar 101 4 46N 100 56 E
Kuala Kerai 101 5 30N 102 12 E
Kuala Klawang 101 2 56N 102 5 E
Kuala Kubu Baharu 101 3 34N 101 39 E
Kuala Lipis 101 4 10N 102 3 E
Kuala Lumpur 101 3 9N 101 41 E
Kuala Marang 101 5 12N 103 13 E
Kuala Nerang 101 6 16N 100 37 E
Kuala Pilah 101 2 45N 102 15 E
Kuala Rompin 101 2 49N 103 29 E
Kuala Selangor 101 3 20N 101 15 E
Kuala Terengganu 101 5 20N 103 8 E
Kuala Trengganu 101 5 20N 103 8 E
Kualakahi Chan 147 22 2N 159 53W
Kualakapuas 102 2 55 S 114 20 E
Kualakurun 102 1 10 S 113 50 E
Kualapembuang, Indon. 102 3 14 S 112 38 E
Kualapembuang, Indon. 102 2 52 S 111 45 E
Kuanaan 107 34 8N 119 24 E
Kuanch'eng 107 40 39N 118 32 E
Kuandang 103 0 56N 123 1 E
Kuangan 108 30 30N 106 35 E
Kuangch'ang 109 26 50N 116 15 E
Kuangchou 109 23 12N 113 12 E
Kuangfeng 109 28 26N 118 12 E
Kuanghan 108 30 56N 104 15 E
Kuanghua 109 32 22N 111 43 E
Kuangjao 107 37 5N 118 25 E
Kuangling 106 39 47N 114 10 E
Kuangnan 108 24 3N 105 3 E
Kuangning 109 23 40N 112 23 E
Kuangshi 109 29 55N 115 25 E
Kuangshun 108 26 5N 106 16 E
Kuangte 109 30 54N 119 26 E
Kuangtse 109 27 30N 117 24 E
Kuangwuch'eng 106 37 49N 108 51 E
Kuangyüan 108 32 22N 105 50 E
Kuanhsien 108 31 0N 103 40 E
Kuanling 108 25 55N 105 35 E
Kuanp'ing 109 31 39N 110 16 E
Kuantan 101 3 49N 103 20 E
Kuant'ao 106 36 31N 115 16 E
Kuantaok'ou 106 34 18N 111 1 E
K'uantien 107 40 47N 124 43 E
Kuanyang 109 25 29N 111 9 E
Kuanyün 107 34 17N 119 15 E
Kuaram 123 12 25N 39 30 E
Kuba 83 41 21N 48 32 E
Kubak 93 27 10N 63 10 E
Kuban, R. 82 45 5N 38 0 E
Kubenskoye, Oz. 81 59 40N 39 25 E
Kuberle 83 47 0N 42 20 E
Kubokawa 110 33 12N 133 8 E
Kubor 135 6 10 S 144 44 E
Kubrat 67 43 49N 26 31 E
Kučevo 66 44 30N 21 40 E
Kucha Gompa 95 34 25N 76 56 E
Kuchaman 94 27 13N 74 47 E
Kuch'ang 108 24 58N 102 45 E
Kuchang 109 28 37N 109 56 E
K'uche K'uerhlo 105 41 43N 82 54 E
Kuchenspitze 49 47 3N 10 14 E
Kuchiang 109 27 11N 114 47 E
Kuching 102 1 33N 110 25 E
Kuchinoerabu-Jima 112 30 28N 130 11 E
Kuchinotsu 110 32 36N 130 11 E
Kuçove = Qytet Stalin 68 40 47N 19 57 E
Kud, R. 94 26 30N 66 12 E
Kuda 93 23 10N 71 15 E
Kudalier, R. 96 18 20N 78 40 E
Kudamatsu 110 34 0N 131 52 E
Kudara 85 38 25N 72 39 E
Kudat 102 6 55N 116 55 E
Kudremukh, Mt. 97 13 15N 75 20 E
Kuduarra Well 136 20 38 S 126 20 E
Kudus 103 6 48 S 110 51 E
Kudymkar 84 59 1N 54 39 E
Kuei Chiang, R. 109 23 33N 111 18 E
Kueich'i 109 28 17N 117 11 E
Kueich'ih 109 30 42N 117 30 E
Kueichu 108 26 25N 106 40 E
Kueihsien 108 23 6N 109 36 E
Kueilin 109 25 20N 110 18 E
Kueip'ing 108 23 24N 110 5 E
Kueiting 108 26 30N 107 17 E
Kueitung 109 26 12N 114 0 E
Kueiyang, Hunan, China 109 25 44N 112 43 E
Kueiyang, Kweichow, China 108 26 35N 106 43 E
K'uerhlo 105 41 44N 86 9 E
Kufra, El Wâhât el 117 24 17N 23 15 E
Kufrinja 90 32 20N 35 41 E
Kufstein 52 47 35N 12 11 E
Kugmallit B. 147 29 0N 134 0W
Kugong, I. 150 56 18N 79 50W
Kūh-e-Alijuq 93 31 30N 51 41 E
Kūh-e-Dinar 93 30 10N 51 0 E
Kūh-e-Hazaran 93 29 35N 57 20 E
Kūh-e-Jebel Barez 93 29 0N 58 0 E
Kūh-e-Sorkh 93 35 30N 58 45 E
Kūh-e-Taftan 93 28 40N 61 0 E
Kūhak 93 27 12N 63 10 E
Kūhha-ye-Bashakerd 93 26 45N 59 0 E
Kūhha-ye Sabalān 93 38 15N 47 45 E
Kuhnsdorf 52 46 37N 14 38 E
Kuhpayeh 93 32 44N 52 20 E
Kui Buri 101 12 3N 99 52 E
Kuinre 46 52 47N 5 51 E
Kuiseb, R. 125 23 40 S 15 30 E
Kuiu I. 147 56 40N 134 15W
Kujangdong 107 39 57N 126 1 E
Kuji 112 40 11N 141 46 E
Kujū-San 110 33 5N 131 15 E
Kujukuri-Heiya 111 35 45N 140 30 E
Kukavica, mt. 66 42 48N 21 57 E
Kukawa 121 12 58N 13 27 E
Kukerin 137 33 13 S 118 0 E
Kukësi 68 42 5N 20 20 E
Kukësi □ 68 42 25N 20 15 E
Kukko 123 8 26N 41 35 E
Kukmor 84 56 11N 50 54 E
Kukup 101 1 20N 103 27 E
K'uk'ushihli Shanmo 105 35 20N 91 0 E
Kukvidze 81 50 40N 43 15 E
Kula, Bulg. 66 43 52N 22 36 E
Kula, Yugo. 66 45 37N 19 32 E
Kulai 101 1 44N 103 35 E
Kulal, Mt. 126 2 42N 36 57 E
Kulaly, O. 83 45 0N 50 0 E
Kulanak 85 41 22N 75 30 E
Kulasekharapattanam 97 8 20N 78 0 E
Kuldiga 80 56 58N 21 59 E
Kuldja = Ining 105 43 54N 81 21 E
Kuldu 123 12 50N 28 30 E
Kulebaki 81 55 22N 42 25 E
Kulen Vakuf 63 44 35N 16 2 E
Kulgam 95 33 36N 75 2 E
Kuli 83 42 2N 46 12 E
Kulim 101 5 22N 100 34 E
Kulin 137 32 40 S 118 2 E
Kulja 137 30 28 S 117 18 E
Küllük 69 37 12N 27 36 E
Kulm 158 46 22N 98 58W
K'uloch'akonnoerh 106 43 40N 114 50 E
Kulsary 76 46 59N 54 1 E
Kultay 83 45 5N 51 40 E
Kulti 95 23 43N 86 50 E
Kulu 93 37 12N 115 2 E
Kulumadau 138 9 15 S 152 50 E
K'ulunch'i 107 42 44N 121 44 E
Kulunda 76 52 45N 79 15 E
Kulungar 94 34 0N 69 2 E
Kulwin 140 35 0 S 142 42 E
Kulyab 85 37 55N 69 50 E
Kum Tekei 76 43 10N 79 30 E
Kuma 110 33 39N 132 54 E
Kuma, R. 83 44 55N 45 57 E
Kumaganum 121 13 8N 10 38 E
Kumagaya 111 36 9N 139 22 E
Kumak 84 51 10N 60 8 E
Kumamoto 110 32 45N 130 45 E
Kumamoto-ken □ 110 32 30N 130 40 E
Kumano 111 33 54N 136 5 E
Kumano-Nada 111 33 47N 136 20 E
Kumanovo 66 42 9N 21 42 E
Kumara 143 42 37 S 171 12 E
Kumarkhali 98 23 51N 89 15 E
Kumarl 137 32 47 S 121 33 E
Kumasi 120 6 41N 1 38W
Kumba 121 4 36N 9 24 E
Kumbakonam 97 10 58N 79 25 E
Kumbarilla 139 27 15 S 150 55 E
Kumbo 121 6 15N 10 36 E
Kumbukkan Oya 97 6 35N 81 40 E
Kŭmchŏn 107 38 10N 126 29 E
Kumdok 95 33 32N 78 10 E
Kumeny 81 58 10N 49 47 E
Kŭmhwa 107 38 17N 127 28 E
Kumi 126 1 30N 33 58 E
Kumkale 68 40 30N 26 13 E
Kumla 72 59 8N 15 10 E
Kumo 121 10 1N 11 12 E
Kumon Bum 98 26 30N 97 15 E
Kumotori-Yama 111 35 51N 138 57 E
Kumta 97 14 29N 74 32 E
Kumtorkala 83 43 2N 46 50 E
Kumukahi, C. 147 19 31N 154 49W
Kumusi, R. 135 8 16 S 148 13 E
Kumylzhenskaya 83 49 51N 42 38 E
Kunágota 53 46 26N 21 3 E
Kunama 141 35 35 S 148 4 E
Kunar 93 34 30N 71 3 E
Kunashir, Ostrov 77 44 0N 146 0 E
Kunch 95 26 0N 79 10 E
Kunda 80 59 30N 26 34 E
Kundiawa 135 6 2 S 145 1 E
Kundip 137 33 42 S 120 10 E
Kundla 94 21 21N 71 25 E
Kunduz 93 36 50N 68 50 E
Kunduz □ 93 36 50N 68 50 E
Kunene, R. 128 17 15 S 13 40 E
Kungala 139 29 58 S 153 7 E
Kungälv 73 57 53N 11 59 E
Kungan 109 30 1N 112 12 E
Kungch'eng 109 24 50N 110 49 E
K'ungch'iao Ho 105 41 48N 86 47 E
Kŭngdong 107 39 9N 126 5 E
Kungey Alatau, Khrebet 85 42 50N 77 0 E
Kunghit I. 152 52 6N 131 3W
Kungho 105 36 28N 100 45 E
Kungka 108 28 44N 100 22 E
Kungkuan 108 21 51N 109 33 E
Kungrad 76 43 6N 58 54 E
Kungsbacka 73 57 30N 12 5 E
Kungshan 108 27 41N 97 37 E
Kungt'an 108 28 49N 108 38 E
Kungur 84 57 25N 56 57 E
Kungurri 138 21 3 S 148 46 E
Kungyangon 98 16 27N 96 1 E
Kungyingtzu 107 43 38N 121 0 E
Kunhar, R. 95 35 0N 73 40 E
Kunhegyes 53 47 22N 20 36 E
Kunimi-Dake 110 32 33N 131 1 E
Kuningan 103 6 59 S 108 29 E
Kunisaki 110 33 33N 131 45 E
Kunlara 140 34 54 S 139 55 E
Kunlong 98 23 20N 98 50 E
Kunlun Shan 105 36 0N 86 30 E
Kunmadaras 53 47 28N 20 45 E
K'unming 108 25 5N 102 40 E
Kunnamkulam 97 10 38N 76 7 E
Kunrade 47 50 53N 5 57 E
Kunsan 107 35 59N 126 45 E
K'unshan 109 31 22N 121 0 E
Kunszentmárton 53 46 50N 20 20 E
Kununurra 136 15 40 S 128 39 E
Kunwarara 138 22 55 S 150 9 E
Kuohsien 106 38 57N 112 46 E
Kuopio 74 62 53N 27 35 E
Kuopion Lääni □ 74 63 25N 27 10 E
Kupa, R. 63 45 30N 16 10 E
Kupang 103 10 19 S 123 39 E
Kupeik'ou 107 40 42N 117 9 E
Kupiano 135 10 4 S 148 14 E
Kupreanof I. 147 56 50N 133 30W
Kupres 66 44 1N 17 15 E
Kupyansk 82 49 45N 37 35 E
Kupyansk-Uzlovoi 82 49 52N 37 34 E
Kur, R. 98 26 50N 91 0 E
Kura, R. 83 40 20N 47 30 E
Kurahashi-Jima 110 34 8N 132 31 E
Kuranda 138 16 48 S 145 35 E
Kurandvad 96 16 45N 74 39 E
Kurashiki 110 34 40N 133 50 E
Kurayoshi 110 35 26N 133 50 E
Kurday 85 43 21N 74 59 E
Kurdistan, reg. 92 37 30N 42 0 E
Kurduvadi 96 18 8N 75 29 E
Kure 110 34 14N 132 32 E
Kuressaare = Kingisepp 80 58 15N 22 15 E
Kurgaldzhino 76 50 35N 70 20 E
Kurgan, R.S.F.S.R., U.S.S.R. 77 64 5N 172 50W
Kurgan, R.S.F.S.R., U.S.S.R. 84 55 26N 65 18 E
Kurgan-Tyube 85 37 50N 68 47 E
Kuria Muria I = Khy ryān Muryān J. 91 17 30N 55 58 E
Kurichchi 97 11 36N 77 35 E
Kuridala 138 21 16 S 140 29 E
Kurigram 98 25 49N 89 39 E
Kurihashi 111 36 8N 139 42 E
Kuril Trench 142 44 0N 153 0 E
Kurilskiye Ostrova 77 45 0N 150 0 E
Kuring Kuru 128 17 42 S 18 32 E
Kuringen 47 50 56N 5 18 E
Kurino 110 31 57N 130 43 E
KüRKkkuyu 68 39 35N 26 27 E
Kurkur 122 23 50N 32 0 E
Kurkûrah 119 31 30N 20 1 E
Kurla 96 19 5N 72 52 E
Kurlovski 81 55 25N 40 40 E
Kurma 123 13 55N 24 40 E
Kurmuk 123 10 33N 34 21 E
Kurnalpi 137 30 29 S 122 16 E
Kurnool 97 15 45N 78 0 E
Kurobe-Gawe, R. 111 36 55N 137 25 E
Kurogi 110 33 12N 130 40 E
Kurovskoye 81 55 35N 38 55 E
Kurow 143 44 4 S 170 29 E
Kurrajong, N.S.W., Austral. 141 33 33 S 150 42 E
Kurrajong, W.A., Austral. 137 28 39 S 120 59 E
Kurram, R. 94 33 30N 70 15 E
Kurri Kurri 141 32 50 S 151 28 E
Kuršenai 80 56 1N 23 3 E
Kurseong 95 26 56N 88 18 E
Kursk 81 51 42N 36 11 E
Kuršumlija 66 43 9N 21 19 E
Kuršumlijska Banja 66 43 3N 21 11 E
Kurtalon 92 37 55N 41 40 E
Kurtamysh 84 54 55N 64 27 E
Kurty, R. 85 44 16N 76 42 E
Kuru (Chel), Bahr el 123 8 10N 26 50 E
Kuruman 128 27 28 S 23 28 E
Kurume 110 33 15N 130 30 E
Kurunegala 97 7 30N 80 18 E
Kurya 77 61 15N 108 10 E
Kusa 84 55 20N 59 29 E
Kuşadası 69 37 52N 27 15 E
Kuşadası Körfezı 69 37 56N 27 0 E
Kusatsu, Gumma, Japan 111 36 37N 138 36 E
Kusatsu, Shiga, Japan 111 34 58N 136 5 E
Kusawa L. 152 60 20N 136 13W
Kusel 49 49 31N 7 25 E
Kushchevskaya 83 46 33N 39 35 E
Kushikino 110 31 44N 130 16 E
Kushima 110 31 29N 131 14 E
Kushimoto 111 33 28N 135 47 E
Kushin 109 32 12N 115 48 E
Kushiro 112 43 0N 144 25 E
Kushiro, R. 112 42 59N 144 23 E
Kushk 93 34 55N 62 30 E
Kushka 76 35 20N 62 18 E
Kushmurun 84 52 27N 64 36 E
Kushmurun, Ozero 84 52 40N 64 48 E
Kushnarenkovo 84 55 6N 55 22 E
Kushol 95 33 40N 76 36 E
Kushrabat 85 40 18N 66 32 E
Kushtia 98 23 55N 89 5 E
Kushum, R. 83 50 40N 50 20 E
Kushva 84 58 18N 59 45 E
Kuskokwim Bay 147 59 50N 162 56W
Kuskokwim Mts. 147 63 0N 156 0W
Kuskokwim, R. 147 61 48N 157 0W
Küsnacht 51 47 19N 8 15 E
Kussa 123 4 9N 38 58 E
Küssnacht 51 47 5N 8 26 E
Kustanay 84 53 10N 63 35 E
Kusu 110 33 16N 131 9 E
Kusung 108 28 25N 105 12 E
Kut, Ko 101 11 40N 102 35 E
Kutá Horq 52 49 57N 15 16 E
Kutahya 92 39 30N 30 2 E
Kutaisi 83 42 19N 42 40 E
Kutaradja = Banda Aceh 102 5 35N 95 20 E
Kutatjane 102 3 45N 97 50 E
Kutch, G. of 94 22 50N 69 15 E
Kutch, Rann of 94 24 0N 70 0 E
Kut'ien 109 26 36N 118 48 E
Kutina 63 45 29N 16 48 E
Kutiyana 94 21 36N 70 2 E
Kutjevo 66 45 23N 17 55 E
Kutkai 98 23 27N 97 56 E
Kutkashen 83 40 58N 47 47 E
Kutná Hora 52 49 57N 15 16 E
Kutno 54 52 15N 19 23 E
Kuttabul 138 21 5 S 148 48 E
Kutu 124 2 40 S 18 11 E
Kutum 123 14 20N 24 10 E
Kúty 53 48 40N 17 3 E
Kuŭptong 107 40 45N 126 1 E
Kuurne 47 50 51N 3 18 E
Kuvandyk 84 51 28N 57 21 E
Kuvasay 85 40 18N 71 59 E
Kuvshinovo 80 57 2N 34 11 E
Kuwait = Al Kuwayt 92 29 30N 47 30 E
Kuwait ■ 92 29 30N 47 30 E
Kuwana 111 35 0N 136 43 E
Kuyang 106 41 8N 110 1 E
Kuybyshev 81 55 27N 78 19 E
Kuybyshevo, Ukraine S.S.R., U.S.S.R. 82 47 25N 36 40 E
Kuybyshevo, Uzbek S.S.R., U.S.S.R. 85 40 20N 71 15 E
Kuybyshevskiy 85 37 52N 68 44 E
Kuybyshevskoye Vdkhr. 81 55 2N 49 30 E

Kuyeh Ho, R **Lambay I**

Kuyeh Ho, R.	**106**	38 30N	110 44 E
Kuylyuk	**85**	41 14N	69 17 E
Kuyto, Oz.	**78**	64 40N	31 0 E
Kuyüan, Hopeh, China	**106**	41 34N	115 38 E
Kuyüan, Ningsia Hui, China	**106**	36 1N	106 17 E
Kuzhithura	**97**	8 18N	77 11 E
Kuzino	**84**	57 1N	59 27 E
Kuzmin	**66**	45 2N	19 25 E
Kuznetsk	**81**	53 12N	46 40 E
Kuzomen	**78**	66 22N	36 50 E
Kvænangen	**74**	69 55N	21 15 E
Kvam	**71**	61 40N	9 42 E
Kvamsøy	**71**	61 7N	6 28 E
Kvarken	**74**	63 30N	21 0 E
Kvarner	**63**	44 50N	14 10 E
Kvarnerič	**63**	44 43N	14 37 E
Kvarnsveden	**72**	60 32N	15 25 E
Kvarntorp	**72**	59 8N	15 17 E
Kvås	**71**	58 16N	7 14 E
Kvernes	**71**	63 1N	7 44 E
Kvillsfors	**73**	57 24N	15 29 E
Kvina, R.	**71**	58 43N	6 52 E
Kvinesdal	**71**	58 18N	6 59 E
Kviteseid	**71**	59 24N	8 29 E
Kwabhaca	**129**	30 51 S	29 0 E
Kwadacha, R.	**152**	57 28N	125 38W
Kwakhanai	**128**	21 39 S	21 16 E
Kwakoegron	**175**	5 25N	55 25W
Kwale, Kenya	**126**	4 15 S	39 31 E
Kwale, Nigeria	**121**	6 18N	5 28 E
Kwale □	**126**	4 15 S	39 10 E
Kwamouth	**124**	3 9 S	16 20 E
Kwando, R.	**128**	16 48 S	22 45 E
Kwangdaeri	**107**	40 31N	127 32 E
Kwangju	**107**	35 9N	126 54 E
Kwangsi-Chuang A.R. □	**109**	24 0N	109 0 E
Kwangtung □	**109**	23 45N	114 0 E
Kwara □	**121**	8 0N	5 0 E
Kwaraga	**128**	20 26 S	24 32 E
Kwataboahegan, R.	**150**	51 9N	80 50W
Kwatisore	**103**	3 7 S	139 59 E
Kweichow □	**108**	27 20N	107 0 E
Kweiyang = Kueiyang	**108**	26 35N	106 43 E
Kwethluk	**147**	60 45N	161 34W
Kwidzyn	**54**	54 45N	18 58 E
Kwigillingok	**147**	59 50N	163 10W
Kwiguk	**147**	63 45N	164 35W
Kwikila	**135**	9 49 S	147 38 E
Kwimba □	**126**	3 0 S	33 0 E
Kwinana	**137**	32 15 S	115 47 E
Kwitaba	**126**	3 56 S	29 39 E
Kya-in-Seikkyi	**98**	16 2N	98 8 E
Kyabe	**117**	9 30N	19 0 E
Kyabra Cr.	**139**	25 36 S	142 55 E
Kyabram	**139**	36 19 S	145 4 E
Kyaiklat	**98**	16 46N	96 52 E
Kyaikmaraw	**98**	16 23N	97 44 E
Kyaikthin	**98**	23 32N	95 40 E
Kyaikto	**100**	17 20N	97 3 E
Kyakhta	**77**	50 30N	106 25 E
Kyangin	**98**	18 20N	95 20 E
Kyaring Tso	**99**	31 5N	88 25 E
Kyaukhnyat	**98**	18 15N	97 31 E
Kyaukpadaung	**99**	20 52N	95 8 E
Kyaukpyu	**99**	19 28N	93 30 E
Kyaukse	**98**	21 36N	96 10 E
Kyauktaw	**98**	21 16N	96 44 E
Kyawkku	**98**	21 48N	96 56 E
Kyburz	**163**	38 47N	120 18W
Kybybolite	**140**	36 53 S	140 55 E
Kyegegwa	**126**	0 30N	31 0 E
Kyeintali	**98**	18 0N	94 29 E
Kyela □	**127**	9 45 S	34 0 E
Kyenjojo	**126**	0 40N	30 37 E
Kyidaunggan	**98**	19 53N	96 12 E
Kyle Dam	**127**	20 15 S	31 0 E
Kyle, dist.	**34**	55 32N	4 25W
Kyle of Lochalsh	**36**	57 17N	5 43W
Kyleakin	**36**	57 16N	5 44W
Kyneton	**140**	37 10 S	144 29 E
Kynuna	**138**	21 37 S	141 55 E
Kyō-ga-Saki	**111**	35 45N	135 15 E
Kyoga, L.	**126**	1 35N	33 0 E
Kyogle	**139**	28 40 S	153 0 E
Kyongju	**107**	35 51N	129 14 E
Kyongpyaw	**99**	17 12N	95 10 E
Kyŏngsŏng	**107**	41 35N	129 36 E
Kyōto	**111**	35 0N	135 45 E
Kyōto-fu □	**111**	35 15N	135 30 E
Kyrínia	**92**	35 20N	33 20 E
Kyritz	**48**	52 57N	12 25 E
Kyrkebyn	**72**	59 18N	13 3 E
Kyrping	**71**	59 45N	6 5 E
Kyshtym	**84**	55 42N	60 34 E
Kystatyam	**77**	67 20N	123 10 E
Kytalktakh	**77**	65 30N	123 40 E
Kytlym	**84**	59 30N	59 12 E
Kyu-hkok	**98**	24 4N	98 4 E
Kyulyunken	**77**	64 10N	137 5 E
Kyunhla	**98**	23 25N	95 15 E
Kyuquot	**152**	50 3N	127 25W
Kyuquot Sd.	**83**	50 0N	127 25W
Kyurdamir	**83**	40 25N	48 3 E
Kyūshū	**110**	33 0N	131 0 E
Kyūshū □	**110**	33 0N	131 0 E
Kyūshū-Sanchi	**110**	32 45N	131 40 E
Kyustendil	**66**	42 25N	22 41 E
Kyusyur	**77**	70 39N	127 15 E
Kywong	**141**	34 58 S	146 44 E
Kyzyl	**77**	51 50N	94 30 E
Kyzyl-Kiya	**85**	40 16N	72 8 E
Kyzyl Orda	**85**	44 56N	65 30 E
Kyzyl Rabat	**76**	37 45N	74 55 E
Kyzylkum	**84**	42 30N	65 0 E
Kyzylsu, R.	**85**	39 11N	72 2 E
Kzyl-orda	**85**	44 48N	65 28 E

L

Laa	**53**	48 43N	16 23 E
Laage	**48**	53 55N	12 21 E
Laasphe	**48**	50 56N	8 23 E
Laau Pt.	**147**	21 57N	159 40W
Laba, R.	**83**	45 0N	40 30 E
Laban, Burma	**98**	25 52N	96 40 E
Laban, Ireland	**39**	53 8N	8 50W
Labasheeda	**39**	52 37N	9 15W
Labastide	**44**	43 28N	2 39 E
Labastide-Murat	**44**	44 39N	1 33 E
Labbézenga	**121**	15 2N	0 48 E
Labdah = Leptis Magna	**119**	32 40N	14 12 E
Labé	**120**	11 24N	12 16W
Labe, R.	**52**	50 3N	15 20 E
Laberec, R.	**53**	21 57N	49 7 E
Laberge, L.	**152**	61 11N	135 12W
Labin	**63**	45 5N	14 8 E
Labinsk	**83**	44 40N	40 48W
Labis	**101**	2 22N	103 2 E
Labiszyn	**54**	52 57N	17 54 E
Laboa	**103**	8 6 S	122 50 E
Laboe	**48**	54 25N	10 13 E
Labouheyre	**44**	44 13N	0 55W
Laboulaye	**172**	34 10 S	63 30W
Labrador City	**151**	52 57N	66 55W
Labrador, Coast of ■	**149**	53 20N	61 0W
Labranzagrande	**174**	5 33N	72 34W
Lábrea	**174**	7 15 S	64 51W
Labrède	**44**	44 41N	0 32W
Labuan, I.	**102**	5 15N	115 38W
Labuha	**103**	0 30 S	127 30 E
Labuhan	**103**	6 26 S	105 50 E
Labuhanbajo	**103**	8 28 S	120 1 E
Labuissière	**47**	50 19N	4 11 E
Labuk, Telok	**102**	6 10N	117 50 E
Labutta	**98**	16 9N	94 46 E
Labytnangi	**78**	66 29N	66 40 E
Lac Allard	**151**	50 33N	63 24W
Lac Bouchette	**151**	48 16N	72 11W
Lac du Flambeau	**158**	46 1N	89 51W
Lac Édouard	**151**	47 40N	72 16W
Lac la Biche	**152**	54 45N	111 58W
Lac-Mégantic	**151**	45 35N	70 53W
Lac Seul	**153**	50 28N	92 0W
Lac Thien	**100**	12 25N	108 11 E
Lacanau, Étang de	**44**	44 58N	1 7W
Lacanau Médoc	**44**	44 59N	1 5W
Lacantum, R.	**165**	16 36N	90 40W
Lacara, R.	**57**	39 7N	6 25W
Lacaune	**44**	43 43N	2 40 E
Lacaune, Mts. de	**44**	43 43N	2 50 E
Laccadive Is. = Lakshadweep Is.	**86**	10 0N	72 30 E
Laceby	**33**	53 32N	0 10W
Lacepede B.	**140**	36 40 S	139 40 E
Lacepede Is.	**136**	16 55 S	122 0 E
Lacerdónia	**127**	18 3 S	35 35 E
Lachen, Sikkim	**98**	47 12N	8 51 E
Lachen, Switz.	**51**	47 12N	8 51 E
Lachi	**94**	33 25N	71 20 E
Lachine	**150**	45 30N	73 40W
Lachlan	**139**	42 50 S	147 3 E
Lachlan, R.	**140**	34 22 S	143 55 E
Lachmangarh	**94**	27 50N	75 4 E
Lachute	**150**	45 39N	74 21 E
Lackagh Hills	**38**	54 14N	8 0W
Lackawanna	**156**	42 49N	78 50W
Lackawaxen	**162**	41 29N	74 59W
Lacock	**28**	51 24N	2 8W
Lacombe	**152**	52 30N	113 44W
Lacona	**162**	43 37N	76 5W
Láconi	**64**	39 54N	9 4 E
Laconia	**162**	43 32N	71 30W
Lacq	**44**	43 25N	0 35W
Lacrosse	**160**	46 51N	117 58W
Ladainha	**171**	17 39 S	41 44W
Ladakh Ra.	**95**	34 0N	78 0 E
Ladder Hills	**37**	57 14N	3 13W
Ladhar Bheinn	**36**	57 5N	5 37W
Ladhon, R.	**69**	37 40N	21 50 E
Lâdik	**82**	40 57N	35 58 E
Ladismith	**128**	33 28 S	21 15 E
Lādiz	**93**	28 55N	61 15 E
Ladnun	**94**	27 38N	74 25 E
Ladock	**30**	50 19N	4 58W
Ladoga, L. = Ladozhskoye Oz.	**78**	61 15N	30 30 E
Ladon	**43**	48 0N	2 30 E
Ladozhskoye Ozero	**76**	61 15N	30 30 E
Ladrone Is. = Mariana Is.	**130**	17 0N	145 0 E
Lady Babbie	**127**	18 30 S	29 20 E
Lady Beatrix L.	**150**	5 20N	76 50W
Lady Edith Lagoon	**136**	20 36 S	126 47 E
Lady Grey	**128**	30 43 S	27 13 E
Ladybank	**35**	56 16N	3 8W
Ladybrand	**128**	29 9 S	27 29 E
Lady's I. Lake	**39**	52 12N	6 23W
Ladysmith, Can.	**152**	49 0N	123 49W
Ladysmith, S. Afr.	**129**	28 32 S	29 46 E
Ladysmith, U.S.A.	**158**	45 27N	91 4W
Lae	**135**	6 40 S	147 2 E
Laem Ngop	**101**	12 10N	102 26 E
Laem Pho	**101**	6 55N	101 19 E
Læsø	**73**	57 15N	10 53 E
Læsø Rende	**73**	57 20N	10 45 E
Lafayette, Colo., U.S.A.	**158**	40 0N	105 2W
Lafayette, Ga., U.S.A.	**157**	34 44N	85 15W
Lafayette, La., U.S.A.	**159**	30 18N	92 0W
Lafayette, Tenn., U.S.A.	**157**	36 35N	86 0W
Laferté	**150**	48 37N	78 48W
Laferte, R.	**152**	61 53N	117 44W
Laffan's Bridge	**39**	52 36N	7 45W
Lafia	**121**	8 30N	8 34 E
Lafiagi	**121**	8 52N	5 20 E
Lafleche	**153**	49 45N	106 40W
Lafon	**123**	5 5N	32 29 E
Laforest	**150**	47 4N	81 12W
Laforsen	**72**	61 56N	15 3 E
Lagaip, R.	**135**	5 4 S	141 52 E
Lagan	**73**	56 32N	12 58 E
Lagan, R.	**38**	54 35N	5 55W
Lagarfljót	**74**	65 40N	14 18W
Lagarto	**170**	10 54 S	37 41W
Lagarto, Serra do	**173**	23 0 S	57 15W
Lage, Ger.	**48**	52 0N	8 47 E
Lage, Spain	**56**	43 13N	9 0W
Lage-Mierde	**47**	51 25N	5 9 E
Lågen	**71**	61 29N	10 2 E
Lågen, R.	**75**	61 30N	10 20 E
Lägerdorf	**48**	53 53N	9 35 E
Lagg	**34**	56 57N	5 50W
Laggan, Grampian, U.K.	**37**	57 24N	3 6W
Laggan, Highland, U.K.	**37**	57 3N	4 48W
Laggan B.	**34**	55 40N	6 20W
Laggan L.	**37**	56 57N	4 30W
Laggers Pt.	**139**	30 52 S	153 4 E
Laghman □	**93**	34 20N	70 0 E
Laghouat	**118**	33 50N	2 59 E
Laghy	**38**	54 37N	8 7W
Lagnieu	**45**	45 55N	5 20 E
Lagny	**43**	48 52N	2 40 E
Lago	**65**	39 9N	16 8 E
Lagôa	**57**	37 8N	8 27W
Lagoaça	**56**	41 11N	6 44W
Lagodekhi	**83**	41 50N	46 22 E
Lagónegro	**65**	40 8N	15 45 E
Lagonoy Gulf	**103**	13 50N	123 50 E
Lagos, Nigeria	**121**	6 25N	3 27 E
Lagos, Port.	**57**	37 5N	8 41W
Lagos de Moreno	**164**	21 21N	101 55W
Lagrange	**136**	14 13 S	125 46 E
Lagrange B.	**136**	18 38 S	121 42 E
Laguardia	**58**	42 33N	2 35W
Laguépie	**44**	44 8N	1 57 E
Laguna, Brazil	**173**	28 30 S	48 50W
Laguna, U.S.A.	**161**	35 3N	107 28W
Laguna Beach	**163**	33 31N	117 52W
Laguna Dam	**161**	32 55N	114 30W
Laguna de la Janda	**57**	36 15N	5 45W
Laguna Limpia	**172**	26 32 S	59 45W
Laguna Madre	**165**	27 0N	97 20W
Laguna Veneta	**63**	45 23N	12 25 E
Lagunas, Chile	**172**	21 0 S	69 45W
Lagunas, Peru	**174**	5 10 S	75 35W
Lagunillas	**174**	10 8N	71 16W
Lahad Datu	**103**	5 0N	118 30 E
Lahaina	**147**	20 52N	156 41W
Lahan Sai	**100**	14 25N	102 52 E
Lahanam	**100**	16 16N	105 16 E
Lahardaun	**38**	54 2N	9 20W
Laharpur	**95**	27 43N	80 56 E
Lahat	**102**	3 45 S	103 30 E
Lahe	**98**	19 18N	93 36 E
Lahewa	**102**	1 22N	97 12 E
Lahijan	**93**	37 10N	50 6 E
Lahn, R.	**48**	50 52N	8 35 E
Laholm	**73**	56 30N	13 2 E
Laholmsbukten	**73**	56 30N	12 45 E
Lahontan Res.	**160**	39 28N	118 58W
Lahore	**94**	31 32N	74 22 E
Lahore □	**94**	31 55N	74 5 E
Lahpongsel	**98**	27 7N	98 25 E
Lahr	**49**	48 20N	7 52 E
Lahti	**75**	60 58N	25 40 E
Lai (Béhagle)	**117**	9 25N	16 30 E
Lai Chau	**100**	22 5N	103 3 E
Lai-hka	**98**	21 16N	97 40 E
Laiagam	**135**	5 33 S	143 30 E
Laian	**109**	32 27N	118 25 E
Laichou Wan	**107**	37 30N	119 30 E
Laidley	**139**	27 39 S	152 20 E
Laidon L.	**37**	56 40N	4 40W
Laifeng	**108**	29 31N	109 18 E
Laigle	**42**	48 46N	0 38 E
Laignes	**43**	47 50N	4 20 E
Laihsi	**107**	36 51N	120 30 E
Laikipia □	**126**	0 30N	36 30 E
Laila	**92**	22 10N	46 40 E
Laillahue, Mt.	**174**	17 0 S	69 30W
Laingsburg	**128**	33 9 S	20 52 E
Laipin	**108**	23 42N	109 16 E
Lairg	**37**	58 1N	4 24W
Lais	**102**	3 35 S	102 0 E
Laishui	**106**	39 23N	115 42 E
Laiwu	**107**	36 12N	117 38 E
Laiyang	**107**	36 58N	120 41 E
Laiyüan	**106**	39 19N	114 41 E
Laja, R.	**164**	20 55N	100 46W
Lajes, Rio Grande d. N., Brazil	**170**	5 41 S	36 14W
Lajes, Sta. Catarina, Brazil	**173**	27 48 S	50 20W
Lajinha	**171**	20 9 S	41 37W
Lajkovac	**66**	44 27N	20 14 E
Lajosmizse	**53**	47 3N	19 32 E
Lak Sao	**100**	18 11N	104 59 E
Laka Chih	**95**	30 40N	81 10 E
Lakaband	**94**	31 2N	69 15 E
Lakar	**103**	8 15 S	128 17 E
Lake Alpine	**163**	38 29N	120 0W
Lake Andes	**158**	43 10N	98 32W
Lake Anse	**156**	46 42N	88 25W
Lake Arthur	**159**	30 8N	92 40W
Lake Brown	**137**	30 56 S	118 20 E
Lake Cargelligo	**141**	33 15 S	146 22 E
Lake Charles	**159**	31 10N	93 10W
Lake City, Colo, U.S.A.	**161**	38 3N	107 27W
Lake City, Fla., U.S.A.	**157**	30 10N	82 40W
Lake City, Iowa, U.S.A.	**158**	42 12N	94 42W
Lake City, Mich., U.S.A.	**156**	44 20N	85 10W
Lake City, Minn., U.S.A.	**158**	44 28N	92 21W
Lake City, S.C., U.S.A.	**157**	33 51N	79 44W
Lake Coleridge	**143**	43 17 S	171 30 E
Lake District	**23**	54 30N	3 10W
Lake George	**162**	43 25N	73 43W
Lake Grace	**137**	33 7 S	118 28 E
Lake Harbour	**149**	62 30N	69 50W
Lake Havasu City	**161**	34 25N	114 29W
Lake Hughes	**163**	34 41N	118 26W
Lake Isabella	**163**	35 38N	118 28W
Lake King	**137**	33 5 S	119 45 E
Lake Lenore	**153**	52 24N	104 59W
Lake Louise	**152**	51 30N	116 10W
Lake Mason	**137**	27 30 S	119 30 E
Lake Mead Nat. Rec. Area	**161**	36 0N	114 30W
Lake Mills	**158**	43 23N	93 33W
Lake Murray	**135**	6 48 S	141 29 E
Lake Nash	**138**	20 57 S	138 0 E
Lake of the Woods	**155**	49 0N	95 0W
Lake Pleasant	**162**	43 28N	74 25W
Lake Providence	**159**	32 49N	91 12W
Lake River	**150**	54 22N	82 31W
Lake Superior Prov. Park	**150**	47 45N	84 45W
Lake Tekapo	**143**	43 55 S	170 30 E
Lake Traverse	**150**	45 56N	78 4W
Lake Varley	**137**	32 48 S	119 30 E
Lake Village	**159**	33 20N	91 19W
Lake Wales	**157**	27 55N	81 32W
Lake Worth	**157**	26 36N	80 3W
Lakefield	**150**	44 25N	78 16W
Lakehurst	**162**	40 1N	74 19W
Lakeland	**157**	28 0N	82 0W
Lakenheath	**29**	52 25N	0 30 E
Lakes Entrance	**141**	37 50 S	148 0 E
Lakeside, Ariz., U.S.A.	**161**	34 12N	109 59W
Lakeside, Calif., U.S.A.	**163**	32 52N	116 55W
Lakeside, Nebr., U.S.A.	**158**	42 5N	102 24W
Lakeview, N.Y., U.S.A.	**156**	42 43N	78 57W
Lakeview, Oreg., U.S.A.	**160**	42 15N	120 22W
Lakewood, Calif., U.S.A.	**163**	33 51N	118 8W
Lakewood, N.J., U.S.A.	**162**	40 5N	74 13W
Lakhaniá	**69**	35 58N	27 54 E
Lákhi	**69**	35 24N	23 27 E
Lakhimpur	**95**	27 14N	94 7 E
Lakhipur, Assam, India	**98**	24 48N	93 0 E
Lakhipur, Assam, India	**98**	26 2N	90 18 E
Lakhonpheng	**100**	15 54N	105 34 E
Lakhpat	**94**	23 48N	68 47 E
Laki	**74**	64 4N	18 14W
Lakin	**159**	37 58N	101 18W
Lakitusaki, R.	**150**	54 21N	82 25W
Lakki	**93**	32 38N	70 50 E
Lakonia □	**69**	36 55N	22 30 E
Lakonikós Kólpos	**69**	36 40N	22 40 E
Lakor, I.	**103**	8 15 S	128 17 E
Lakota, Ivory C.	**120**	5 50N	5 30W
Lakota, U.S.A.	**158**	48 0N	98 22W
Laksefjorden	**74**	70 45N	26 50 E
Lakselv	**74**	70 2N	24 56 E
Lakselvbukt	**74**	69 26N	19 40 E
Lakshadweep Is.	**86**	10 0N	72 30 E
Laksham	**98**	23 14N	91 8 E
Lakshmi Kantapur	**95**	22 5N	88 20 E
Lakshmipur	**98**	22 38N	88 16 E
Lakuramau	**135**	2 54 S	151 15 E
Lala Ghat	**99**	24 30N	92 40 E
Lala Musa	**94**	32 40N	73 57 E
Lalago	**126**	3 28 S	33 58 E
Lalapanzi	**127**	19 20 S	30 15 E
Lalganj	**95**	25 52N	85 13 E
Lalibala	**123**	12 8N	39 10 E
Lalin	**107**	45 14N	126 52 E
Lalín	**56**	42 40N	8 5W
Lalin Ho, R.	**107**	45 28N	125 43 E
Lalinde	**44**	44 50N	0 44 E
Lalitapur	**99**	26 36N	85 32 E
Lalitpur	**95**	24 42N	78 28 E
Lam	**100**	21 21N	106 31 E
Lam Pao Res.	**100**	16 50N	103 15 E
Lama Kara	**121**	9 30N	1 15 E
Lamaing	**99**	15 25N	97 53 E
Lamaipum	**98**	25 40N	97 57 E
Lamar, Colo., U.S.A.	**158**	38 9N	102 35W
Lamar, Mo., U.S.A.	**159**	37 30N	94 20W
Lamas	**174**	6 28 S	76 31W
Lamastre	**45**	44 59N	4 35 E
Lamaya	**108**	29 50N	99 56 E
Lamb Hd.	**37**	59 5N	2 32W
Lambach	**52**	48 6N	13 51 E
Lamballe	**42**	48 29N	2 31W
Lambaréné	**124**	0 20 S	10 12 E
Lambay I.	**38**	53 30N	6 0W

Lambayeque □ Lawrenceville

Lambayeque □	174	6 45S	80 0W
Lamberhurst	29	51 5N	0 21E
Lambert	158	47 44N	104 39W
Lambert, C.	135	4 11S	151 31E
Lambert Land	12	79 12N	20 30W
Lambesc	45	43 39N	5 16E
Lambeth	29	51 27N	0 7W
Lambi Kyun, (Sullivan I.)	101	10 50N	98 20E
Lámbia	69	37 52N	21 53E
Lambley	35	54 56N	2 30W
Lambon	135	4 45S	152 48E
Lambourn	28	51 31N	1 31W
Lambro, R.	62	45 18N	9 20E
Lambs Hd.	39	51 44N	10 10W
Lame	121	10 27N	9 12E
Lame Deer	160	45 45N	106 40W
Lamego	56	41 5N	7 52W
Lameque	151	47 45N	64 38W
Lameroo	140	35 19S	140 33E
Lamesa	159	32 45N	101 57W
Lamhult	73	57 12N	14 36E
Lamia	69	38 55N	22 41E
Lamitan	103	6 40N	122 10E
Lammermuir	35	55 50N	2 25W
Lammermuir Hills	35	55 50N	2 40W
Lamoille	160	40 47N	115 31W
Lamon Bay	103	14 30N	122 20E
Lamont, Can.	152	53 46N	112 50W
Lamont, U.S.A.	163	35 15N	118 55W
Lampa	174	15 10S	70 30W
Lampang	100	18 18N	99 31E
Lampasas	159	31 5N	98 10W
Lampaul	42	48 28N	5 7W
Lampazos de Naranjo	164	27 2N	100 32W
Lampedusa, I.	60	35 36N	12 40E
Lampeter	31	52 6N	4 6W
Lampione, I.	119	35 33N	12 20E
Lampman	153	49 25N	102 50W
Lamprechtshausen	52	48 0N	12 58E
Lampung	102	1 48S	115 0E
Lamu, Burma	98	19 14N	94 10E
Lamu, Kenya	126	2 10S	40 55E
Lamy	161	35 30N	105 58W
Lan Tsan Kiang (Mekong)	87	18 0N	104 15E
Lanai City	147	20 50N	156 56W
Lanai I.	147	20 50N	156 55W
Lanak La	95	34 27N	79 32E
Lanaken	47	50 53N	5 39E
Lanak'o Shank'ou = Lanak La	95	34 27N	79 32E
Lanao, L.	103	7 52N	124 15E
Lanark	35	55 40N	3 48W
Lanark (□)	26	55 37N	3 50W
Lancashire □	32	53 40N	2 30W
Lancaster, Can.	151	45 17N	66 10W
Lancaster, U.K.	32	54 3N	2 48W
Lancaster, Calif., U.S.A.	163	34 47N	118 8W
Lancaster, Ky., U.S.A.	156	37 40N	84 40W
Lancaster, Pa., U.S.A.	162	40 4N	76 19W
Lancaster, S.C., U.S.A.	157	34 45N	80 47W
Lancaster, Va., U.S.A.	162	37 46N	76 28W
Lancaster, Wis., U.S.A.	158	42 48N	90 43W
Lancaster Sd.	12	74 13N	84 0W
Lancer	153	50 48N	108 53W
Lanchester	33	54 50N	1 44W
Lanch'i	109	29 11N	119 30E
Lanchou	106	36 5N	103 55E
Lanciano	63	42 15N	14 22E
Lancing	29	50 49N	0 19W
Łancut	54	50 10N	22 20E
Lancy	50	46 12N	6 8E
Lándana	124	5 11S	12 5E
Landau	49	49 12N	8 7E
Landeck	52	47 9N	10 34E
Landen	47	50 45N	5 3E
Lander, Austral.	136	20 25S	132 0E
Lander, U.S.A.	160	42 50N	108 49W
Landerneau	42	48 28N	4 17W
Landeryd	73	57 7N	13 15E
Landes □	44	43 57N	0 48W
Landes, Les	44	44 20N	1 0W
Landete	58	39 56N	1 25W
Landi Kotal	94	34 7N	71 6E
Landivisiau	42	48 31N	4 6W
Landkey	30	51 2N	4 0W
Landor	137	25 10S	117 0E
Landquart	51	46 58N	9 32E
Landquart, R.	51	46 50N	9 47E
Landrecies	43	50 7N	3 40E
Land's End, Can.	12	76 10N	123 0W
Land's End, U.K.	30	50 4N	5 43W
Landsberg	49	48 3N	10 52E
Landsborough Cr.	138	22 28S	144 35E
Landsbro	73	57 24N	14 56E
Landschaft	50	47 28N	7 40E
Landshut	48	48 31N	12 10E
Landskrona	73	56 53N	12 50E
Landvetter	73	57 41N	12 17E
Lane	73	58 25N	12 3E
Laneffe	47	50 17N	4 35E
Lanesboro	162	41 57N	75 34W
Lanesborough	38	53 40N	8 0W
Lanett	157	33 0N	85 15W
Lang Bay	152	49 17N	124 21W
Lang Qua	100	22 16N	104 27E
Lang Shan	106	41 0N	106 20E
Lang Suan	101	9 57N	99 4E
Langaa	73	56 23N	9 51E
Långadhás	68	40 46N	23 2E
Langádhia	69	37 43N	22 1E
Långan	72	63 19N	14 44E
Langara I.	152	54 14N	133 1W
Langavat L.	36	58 4N	6 48W
Langchen Khambah (Sutlej)	95	31 25N	80 0E
Langch'i	109	31 10N	119 10E
Langchung	108	31 31N	105 58E
Langdon	158	48 47N	98 24W
Langdorp	47	50 59N	4 52E
Langeac	44	45 7N	3 29E
Langeb, R.	122	17 28N	36 50E
Langeberge, C. Prov., S. Afr.	128	28 15S	22 33E
Langeberge, C. Prov., S. Afr.	128	33 55S	21 20E
Langeland	73	54 56N	10 48E
Langelands Bælt	73	54 55N	10 56E
Langemark	47	50 55N	2 55E
Langen	49	53 36N	8 36E
Langenburg	153	50 51N	101 43W
Langeness	48	54 34N	8 35E
Langenlois	52	48 29N	15 40E
Langensalza	48	51 6N	10 40E
Langenthal	50	47 13N	7 47E
Langeoog	48	53 44N	7 33E
Langeskov	73	55 22N	10 35E
Langesund	71	59 0N	9 45E
Langhem	73	57 36N	13 14E
Länghem	73	57 36N	13 14E
Langhirano	62	44 39N	10 16E
Langholm	35	55 9N	2 59W
Langidoon	140	31 36S	142 2E
Langjökull	74	64 39N	20 12W
Langkawi I.	101	6 20N	99 45E
Langkawi, P.	101	6 25N	99 45E
Langkon	102	6 30N	116 40E
Langk'ouhsü	109	26 8N	115 10E
Langlade, Can.	150	48 14N	76 10W
Langlade, St. P. & M.	151	46 50N	56 20W
Langlo	139	26 26S	146 5E
Langlois	160	42 54N	124 26W
Langnau	50	46 56N	7 47E
Langness	32	54 3N	4 37W
Langogne	44	44 43N	3 50E
Langon	44	44 33N	0 16W
Langøya	74	68 45N	15 10E
Langport	28	51 2N	2 51W
Langres	43	47 52N	5 20E
Langres, Plateau de	43	47 45N	5 20E
Langsa	102	4 30N	97 57E
Långsele	72	63 12N	17 4E
Långshyttan	72	60 27N	16 2E
Langson	100	21 52N	106 42E
Langstrothdale Chase	32	54 14N	2 13W
Langtai	108	26 6N	105 20E
Langtao	98	27 15N	97 34E
Langting	98	25 31N	93 7E
Langtoft	29	52 42N	0 19W
Langtree	30	50 55N	4 11W
Langtry	159	29 50N	101 33W
Langu	101	6 53N	99 47E
Languedoc □	44	43 58N	3 22E
Langwies	51	46 50N	9 44E
Lanhsien	106	38 17N	111 38E
Lanigan	153	51 51N	105 2W
Lank'ao	106	34 50N	114 49E
Lanna	72	59 16N	14 56E
Lannemezan	44	43 8N	0 23E
Lannercost	138	18 35S	146 0E
Lannilis	42	48 35N	4 32W
Lannion	42	48 46N	3 29W
Lanouaille	44	45 24N	1 9E
Lanp'ing	108	26 25N	99 24E
Lansdale	162	40 14N	75 18W
Lansdowne	141	31 48S	152 30E
Lansdowne House	150	52 14N	87 53W
Lansford	162	40 48N	75 55W
Lanshan	109	25 18N	112 6E
Lansing	156	42 47N	84 32W
Lanslebourg-Mont-Cenis	45	45 17N	6 52E
Lanta Yai, Ko	101	7 35N	99 3E
Lant'ien	106	34 3N	109 20E
Lants'ang	108	22 40N	99 58E
Lants'ang Chiang, R.	108	30 0N	98 0E
Lantsien	99	32 4N	96 6E
Lants'un	107	36 24N	120 10E
Lantuna	103	8 19S	124 8E
Lanus	172	34 44S	58 27W
Lanusei	64	39 53N	9 31E
Lanzarote, I.	116	29 0N	13 40W
Lanzo Torinese	62	45 16N	7 29E
Lao Bao	100	16 35N	106 30E
Lao Cai	100	22 30N	103 57E
Lao, R.	65	39 45N	15 45E
Laoag	103	18 7N	120 34E
Laoang	103	12 32N	125 8E
Laoha Ho, R.	107	43 24N	120 39E
Laois □	39	53 0N	7 20W
Laon	43	49 33N	3 35E
Laona	156	45 32N	88 41W
Laos ■	100	17 45N	105 0E
Lapa	173	25 46S	49 44W
Lapalisse	44	46 15N	3 44E
Laparan Cap, I.	103	6 0N	120 0E
Lapeer	156	43 3N	83 20W
Lapford	30	50 52N	3 49W
Lapi □	74	67 0N	27 0E
Lapland = Lappland	74	68 7N	24 0E
Laporte	162	41 27N	76 30W
Lapovo	66	44 10N	21 2E
Lappland	74	68 7N	24 0E
Laprida	172	37 34S	60 45W
Laptev Sea	77	76 0N	125 0E
Lapush	160	47 56N	124 33W
Lăpuşu, R.	70	47 25N	23 40E
Lar	93	27 40N	54 14E
Lara	140	38 2S	144 26E
Lara □	174	10 10N	69 50W
Larabanga	120	9 16N	1 56W
Laracha	56	43 15N	8 35W
Larache	118	35 10N	6 5W
Laragh	39	53 0N	6 20W
Laragne-Montéglin	45	44 18N	5 49E
Laramie	158	41 15N	105 29W
Laramie Mts.	158	42 0N	105 30W
Laranjeiras	170	10 48S	37 10W
Laranjeiras do Sul	173	25 23S	52 23W
Larantuka	103	8 5S	122 55E
Larap	103	14 18N	122 39E
Larat, I.	103	7 0S	132 0E
Larbert	35	56 2N	3 50W
Lärbro	73	57 47N	18 50E
Larch, R.	149	57 30N	71 0W
Lårdal	71	59 20N	8 25E
Lårdal	71	59 25N	8 10E
Larde	127	16 28S	39 43E
Larder Lake	150	48 5N	79 40W
Lárdhos, Akra	69	36 4N	28 10E
Laredo, Spain	58	43 26N	3 28W
Laredo, U.S.A.	159	27 34N	99 29W
Laredo Sd.	152	52 30N	128 53W
Laren	46	52 16N	5 14E
Largeau (Faya)	117	17 58N	19 6E
Largentière	45	44 34N	4 18E
Largs	34	55 48N	4 51W
Lari	62	43 34N	10 35E
Lariang	103	1 35S	119 25E
Larimore	158	47 55N	97 35W
Larino	65	41 48N	14 54E
Lárisa	68	39 38N	22 28E
Lárisa □	68	39 39N	22 24E
Larkana	94	27 32N	68 2E
Larkollen	71	59 20N	10 41E
Larnaca	92	35 0N	33 35E
Lárnax	92	35 0N	33 35E
Larne	38	54 52N	5 50W
Larne L.	38	54 52N	5 50W
Larned	158	38 15N	99 10W
Laroch	36	56 40N	5 9W
Larochette	47	49 47N	6 13E
Laroquebrou	44	44 58N	2 12E
Larrey, Pt.	136	19 55S	119 7E
Larrimah	136	15 35S	133 12E
Larsen Ice Shelf	13	67 0S	62 0W
Larteh	121	5 50N	0 5W
Laru	126	2 54N	24 25E
Larvik	71	59 4N	10 0E
Laryak	76	61 15N	80 0E
Larzac, Causse du	44	44 0N	3 17E
Las Animas	159	38 8N	103 18W
Las Anod	91	8 26N	47 19E
Las Blancos	59	37 38N	0 49W
Las Bonitas	174	7 50N	65 40W
Las Brenãs	172	27 5S	61 7W
Las Cabezas de San Juan	57	37 0N	5 58W
Las Cruces	161	32 25N	106 50W
Las Flores	172	36 0S	59 0W
Las Heras, Mendoza, Argent.	173	32 51S	68 49W
Las Heras, Santa Cruz, Argent.	176	46 30S	69 0W
Las Huertas, Cabo de	59	38 22N	0 24W
Las Khoreh	91	11 4N	48 20E
Las Lajas	176	38 30S	70 25W
Las Lajitas	174	6 55N	65 39W
Las Lomitas	172	24 35S	60 50W
Las Marismas	57	37 5N	6 20W
Las Mercedes	174	9 7N	66 24W
Las Navas de la Concepción	57	37 56N	5 30W
Las Navas de Tolosa	57	38 18N	3 38W
Las Palmas, Argent.	172	27 8S	58 45W
Las Palmas, Canary Is.	116	28 10N	15 28W
Las Palmas □	116	28 10N	15 28W
Las Piedras	173	34 35S	56 20W
Las Plumas	176	43 40S	67 15W
Las Rosas	172	32 30S	61 40W
Las Tablas	166	7 49N	80 14W
Las Termas	172	27 29S	64 52W
Las Tres Marías, Is.	164	20 12N	106 30W
Las Varillas	172	32 0S	62 50W
Las Vegas, Nev., U.S.A.	161	36 10N	115 5W
Las Vegas, N.M., U.S.A.	161	35 35N	105 10W
Lascano	173	33 35S	54 18W
Lascaux	44	45 5N	1 10E
Lashburn	153	53 10N	109 40W
Lashio	98	22 56N	97 45E
Lashkar	94	26 10N	78 10E
Łasin	54	53 30N	19 2E
Lasithi □	69	35 5N	25 50E
Lask	54	51 34N	19 8E
Laskill	33	54 19N	1 6W
Laško	63	46 10N	15 16E
Lassance	171	17 54S	44 34W
Lassay	42	48 27N	0 30W
Lassen, Pk.	160	40 20N	121 0W
Lasswade	35	55 53N	3 8W
Last Mountain L.	153	51 5N	105 14W
Lastoursville	124	0 55S	12 38E
Lastovo	63	42 46N	16 55E
Lastovo, I.	63	42 46N	16 55E
Lastovski Kanal	63	42 50N	17 0E
Lat Yao	100	15 45N	99 48E
Latacunga	174	0 50S	78 35W
Latakia = Al Ladhiqiya	92	35 30N	35 45E
Latchford	150	47 20N	79 50W
Laterza	65	40 38N	16 47E
Latham	137	29 44S	116 20E
Lathen	48	52 51N	7 21E
Latheron	37	58 17N	3 20W
Lathrop Wells	163	36 39N	116 24W
Latiano	65	40 33N	17 43E
Latina	64	41 26N	12 53E
Latisana	63	45 47N	13 1E
Latium = Lazio	63	42 0N	12 30E
Laton	163	36 26N	119 41W
Latorica, R.	53	48 31N	22 0E
Latouche	147	60 0N	148 0W
Latouche Treville, C.	136	18 27S	121 49E
Latrobe	138	38 8S	146 44E
Latrobe, Mt.	139	39 0S	146 23E
Latrónico	65	40 5N	16 0E
Latrun	90	31 50N	34 58E
Latur	96	18 25N	76 40E
Latvia, S.S.R. □	80	56 50N	24 0E
Latzu	105	29 10N	87 45E
Lauchhammer	48	51 35N	13 40E
Laudal	71	58 15N	7 30E
Lauder	35	55 43N	2 45W
Lauderdale	35	55 43N	2 44W
Lauenburg	48	53 23N	10 33E
Läufelfingen	50	47 24N	7 52E
Laufen	50	47 25N	7 30E
Laugarbakki	74	65 20N	20 55W
Laugharne	31	51 45N	4 28W
Laujar	59	37 0N	2 54W
Launceston, Austral.	138	41 24S	147 8E
Launceston, U.K.	30	50 38N	4 21W
Laune, R.	39	52 5N	9 40W
Launglon Bok	101	13 50N	97 54E
Laupheim	49	48 13N	9 53E
Laura, Queens., Austral.	133	15 32S	144 32E
Laura, S.A., Austral.	140	33 10S	138 18E
Lauragh	39	51 46N	9 46W
Laureana di Borrello	65	38 28N	16 5E
Laurel, Del., U.S.A.	162	38 33N	75 34W
Laurel, Md., U.S.A.	162	39 6N	76 51W
Laurel, Miss., U.S.A.	159	31 50N	89 0W
Laurel, Mont., U.S.A.	160	45 46N	108 49W
Laurencekirk	37	56 50N	2 30W
Laurencetown	39	53 14N	8 11W
Laurens	157	34 32N	82 2W
Laurentian Plat.	151	52 0N	70 0W
Laurentides, Parc Prov. des	151	47 45N	71 15W
Lauria	65	40 3N	15 50E
Laurie I.	13	60 0S	46 0W
Laurie L.	153	56 35N	101 57W
Laurieston	35	54 57N	4 2W
Laurinburg	157	34 50N	79 25W
Laurium	156	47 14N	88 26W
Lausanne	50	46 32N	6 38E
Laut Kecil, Kepulauan	102	4 45S	115 40E
Laut, Kepulauan	102	4 45N	108 0E
Lauterbach	48	50 39N	9 23E
Lauterbrunnen	50	46 36N	7 55E
Lauterecken	49	49 38N	7 35E
Lauwe	47	50 47N	3 12E
Lauwers	46	53 32N	6 23E
Lauwers Zee	46	53 21N	6 13E
Lauzon	151	46 48N	71 10W
Lava Hot Springs	160	42 38N	112 1W
Lavadores	56	42 14N	8 41W
Lavagna	62	44 18N	9 22E
Laval	42	48 4N	0 48W
Lavalle	172	28 15S	65 15W
Lavandou, Le	45	43 8N	6 22E
Lâvara	68	41 19N	26 22E
Lavardac	44	44 12N	0 20E
Lavaur	44	43 42N	1 49E
Lavaux	50	46 30N	6 45E
Lavaveix	44	46 5N	2 8E
Lavelanet	44	42 57N	1 51E
Lavello	65	41 4N	15 47E
Lavendon	29	52 11N	0 39W
Lavenham	29	52 7N	0 48E
Laverendrye Prov. Park	150	46 15N	17 15W
Laverne	159	36 43N	99 58W
Lavers Hill	140	38 40S	143 25E
Laverton	137	28 44S	122 29E
Lavi	90	32 47N	35 25E
Lavik	71	61 6N	5 25E
Lávkos	69	39 9N	23 14E
Lavos	56	40 6N	8 49W
Lavras	173	21 20S	45 0W
Lavre	57	38 46N	8 22W
Lavrentiya	77	65 35N	171 0W
Lávrion	69	37 40N	24 4E
Lavumisa	129	27 20S	31 55E
Lawas	102	4 55N	115 40E
Lawele	103	5 16S	123 3E
Lawers	35	56 31N	4 9W
Lawksawk	98	21 15N	96 52E
Lawn Hill	138	18 36S	138 33E
Lawng Pit	99	26 45N	98 35E
Lawra	120	10 39N	2 51W
Lawrence, Austral.	173	29 30S	153 8E
Lawrence, Kans., U.S.A.	158	39 0N	95 10W
Lawrence, Mass., U.S.A.	162	42 40N	71 9W
Lawrenceburg, Ind., U.S.A.	156	39 5N	84 50W
Lawrenceburg, Tenn., U.S.A.	157	35 12N	87 19W
Lawrenceville, Ga., U.S.A.	157	33 55N	83 59W

Lawrenceville Lexington

Lawrenceville, Pa., U.S.A. **162** 42 0N 77 8W
Laws **163** 37 24N 118 20W
Lawton **159** 34 33N 98 25W
Lawu Mt. **103** 7 40S 111 13E
Laxa **72** 59 0N 14 37E
Laxey **32** 54 15N 4 23W
Laxfield **29** 52 18N 1 23E
Laxford, L. **36** 58 25N 5 10W
Laxmeshwar **97** 15 9N 75 28E
Laysan I. **143** 25 30N 167 0W
Laytonville **160** 39 44N 123 29W
Laytown **38** 53 40N 6 15W
Laza **98** 26 30N 97 38E
Lazarevac **66** 44 23N 20 17E
Lazio □ **63** 42 10N 12 30E
Lazonby **32** 54 45N 2 42W
Łazy **54** 50 27N 19 24E
Łbzenica **54** 53 18N 17 15E
Lea **33** 53 22N 0 45W
Lea, R. **29** 51 40N 0 3W
Leach **101** 12 21N 103 46E
Lead **158** 44 20N 103 40W
Leadenham **33** 53 5N 0 33W
Leader **153** 50 50N 109 30W
Leadhills **35** 55 25N 3 47W
Leadville **161** 39 17N 106 23W
Leaf, R., Can. **149** 58 47N 70 4W
Leaf, R., U.S.A. **159** 31 45N 89 20W
Leakey **159** 29 45N 99 45W
Leaksville **157** 36 30N 79 49W
Lealui **125** 15 10S 23 2E
Leamington, Can. **150** 42 3N 82 36W
Leamington, N.Z. **130** 37 55S 175 29E
Leamington, U.K. **28** 52 18N 1 32W
Leamington, U.S.A. **160** 39 37N 112 17W
Leandro Norte Alem **173** 27 34S 55 15W
Leane L. **39** 52 2N 9 32W
Leaoto, Mt. **70** 45 20N 25 20E
Leap **39** 51 34N 9 11W
Learmonth **136** 22 40S 114 10E
Leask **153** 53 5N 106 45W
Leatherhead **29** 51 18N 0 20W
Leavenworth, Mo., U.S.A. **158** 39 25N 95 0W
Leavenworth, Wash., U.S.A. **160** 47 44N 120 37W
Łeba **54** 54 45N 17 32E
Lebak **103** 6 32N 124 5E
Lebane **66** 42 56N 21 44E
Lebanon, Ind., U.S.A. **156** 40 3N 86 55W
Lebanon, Kans., U.S.A. **158** 39 50N 98 35W
Lebanon, Ky., U.S.A. **156** 37 35N 85 15W
Lebanon, Mo., U.S.A. **159** 37 40N 92 40W
Lebanon, Oreg., U.S.A. **160** 44 31N 122 57W
Lebanon, Pa., U.S.A. **162** 40 20N 76 28W
Lebanon, Tenn., U.S.A. **157** 36 15N 86 20W
Lebanon ■ **92** 34 0N 36 0E
Lebbeke **47** 51 0N 4 8E
Lebec **163** 34 36N 118 59W
Lebedin **80** 50 35N 34 30E
Lebedyan **81** 53 0N 39 10E
Lebomboberge **129** 24 30S 32 0E
Łebork **54** 54 33N 17 46E
Lebrija **57** 36 53N 6 5W
Lebu **172** 37 40S 73 47W
Lecce **65** 40 20N 18 10E
Lecco **62** 45 50N 9 27E
Lecco, L. di. **62** 45 51N 9 22E
Lécera **58** 41 13N 0 43W
Lech **52** 47 13N 10 9E
Lech, R. **49** 48 45N 10 45E
Lechlade **28** 51 42N 1 40W
Lechtaler Alpen **52** 47 15N 10 30E
Lectoure **44** 43 56N 0 38E
Łeczyca **54** 52 5N 19 45E
Ledbury **28** 52 3N 2 25W
Lede **47** 50 58N 3 59E
Ledeberg **47** 51 2N 3 45E
Ledec **52** 49 41N 15 18E
Ledesma **56** 41 6N 5 59W
Leduc **152** 53 20N 113 30W
Ledyczek **54** 53 33N 16 59E
Lee, U.K. **28** 50 47N 1 11W
Lee, U.S.A. **160** 40 35N 115 36W
Lee Vining **163** 37 58N 119 7W
Leech L. **158** 47 9N 94 23W
Leedey **159** 35 53N 99 24W
Leeds, U.K. **33** 53 48N 1 34W
Leeds, U.S.A. **157** 33 32N 86 30W
Leek, Neth. **46** 53 10N 6 24E
Leek, U.K. **32** 53 7N 2 2W
Leende **47** 51 21N 5 33E
Leer **48** 53 13N 7 29E
Leerdam **46** 51 54N 5 6E
Leersum **46** 52 0N 5 26E
Leesburg **157** 28 47N 81 52W
Leeston **143** 43 45N 172 19E
Leesville **159** 31 12N 93 15W
Leeton **141** 34 23S 146 23E
Leeuwarden **46** 53 15N 5 48E
Leeuwin, C. **137** 34 20S 115 9E
Leeward Is. **167** 16 30N 63 30W
Lefors **159** 35 30N 100 50W
Lefroy, L. **137** 31 21S 121 40E
Legal **152** 53 55N 113 45W
Legendre I. **136** 20 22S 116 55E
Leghorn = Livorno **62** 43 32N 10 18E
Legion **127** 21 25S 28 30E
Legionowo **54** 52 25N 20 50E
Léglise **47** 49 48N 5 32E
Legnago **63** 45 10N 11 19E
Legnano **62** 45 35N 8 55E
Legnica **54** 51 12N 16 10E
Legnica □ **54** 51 30N 16 0E
Legoniel **38** 54 38N 6 0W
Legrad **63** 46 17N 16 51E
Legume **139** 28 20S 152 12E
Leh **95** 34 15N 77 35E
Lehi **160** 40 20N 112 0W
Lehighton **162** 40 50N 75 44W
Lehinch **39** 52 56N 9 21E
Lehliu **70** 44 29N 26 20E
Lehrte **48** 52 22N 9 58E
Lehua, I. **147** 22 1N 160 6W
Lehututu **128** 23 54S 21 55E
Lei Shui, R. **109** 26 56N 112 39E
Leiah **94** 30 58N 70 58E
Leibnitz **52** 46 47N 15 34E
Leicester **28** 52 39N 1 9W
Leicester □ **28** 52 40N 1 10W
Leichhardt, R. **133** 17 50S 139 49E
Leichhardt Ra. **138** 20 46S 147 40E
Leichou Chiang, R. **109** 20 52N 110 10E
Leichou Pantao **108** 20 40N 110 10E
Leiden **46** 52 9N 4 30E
Leiderdorp **46** 52 9N 4 32E
Leidschendam **46** 52 5N 4 24E
Leie, R. **47** 51 2N 3 45E
Leigh, Gr. Manch., U.K. **32** 53 29N 2 31W
Leigh, Here. & Worcs., U.K. **28** 52 10N 2 21W
Leigh Creek **140** 30 28S 138 24E
Leighlinbridge **39** 52 45N 7 2W
Leighton Buzzard **29** 51 55N 0 39W
Leignon **47** 50 16N 5 7E
Leiktho **98** 19 13N 96 35E
Leinster, Mt. **39** 52 38N 6 47W
Leinster, prov. **39** 53 0N 7 10W
Leintwardine **28** 52 22N 2 51W
Leipo **108** 28 15N 103 34E
Leipzig **48** 51 20N 12 23E
Leipzig □ **48** 51 20N 12 30E
Leiria **57** 39 46N 8 53W
Leiria □ **57** 39 46N 8 53W
Leisler, Mt. **136** 23 23S 129 30E
Leiston **29** 52 13N 1 35E
Leith **35** 55 59N 3 10W
Leith Hill **29** 51 10N 0 23W
Leitha, R. **53** 47 57N 17 5E
Leitholm **35** 55 42N 2 16W
Leitrim **38** 54 0N 8 5W
Leitrim □ **38** 54 8N 8 0W
Leiyang **109** 26 24N 112 51E
Leiza **58** 43 5N 1 55W
Lek, R. **46** 51 54N 4 38E
Lekáni **68** 41 10N 24 35E
Leke **47** 51 6N 2 54E
Lekhainá **69** 37 57N 21 16E
Lekkerkerk **46** 51 54N 4 41E
Leknice **61** 51 34N 14 45E
Leksula **103** 3 46S 126 31E
Leland **159** 33 25N 90 52W
Leland Lakes **153** 60 0N 110 59W
Lelant **30** 50 11N 5 26W
Leleque **176** 42 15S 71 0W
Lelu **98** 19 4N 95 30E
Lelystad **46** 52 30N 5 25E
Lema **121** 12 58N 4 13E
Lemagrut, mt. **123** 3 9S 35 22E
Leman Bank, gasfield **19** 53 5N 2 20E
Léman, Lac **50** 46 26N 6 30E
Lemelerveld **46** 52 26N 6 20E
Lemera **126** 3 0S 28 55E
Lemery **103** 13 58N 120 56E
Lemesós **92** 34 42N 33 1E
Lemgo **48** 52 2N 8 52E
Lemhi Ra. **160** 44 30N 113 30W
Lemmer **46** 52 51N 5 43E
Lemmon **158** 45 59N 102 10W
Lemon Grove **163** 32 45N 117 2W
Lemoore **163** 36 23N 119 46W
Lempdes **44** 45 22N 3 17E
Lemvig **73** 56 33N 8 20E
Lemyethna **98** 21 10N 95 52E
Lena, R. **77** 64 30N 127 0E
Lenadoon Pt. **38** 54 19N 9 3W
Lencloître **42** 46 50N 0 20E
Lençóis **171** 12 35S 41 43W
Lendalfoot **34** 55 12N 4 55W
Lendelede **47** 50 53N 3 16E
Lendinara **63** 45 4N 11 37E
Lene L. **38** 53 40N 7 12W
Lengau de Vaca, Punta **172** 30 14S 71 38W
Lenger **85** 42 12N 69 54E
Lengerich **48** 52 12N 7 50E
Lenggong **101** 5 6N 100 58E
Lengyeltóti **53** 46 40N 17 40E
Lenham **29** 51 14N 0 44E
Lenhovda **73** 57 0N 15 16E
Lenia **123** 4 10N 37 25E
Lenin **83** 48 20N 40 56E
Lenina, Pik **85** 39 20N 72 55E
Leninabad **85** 40 17N 69 37E
Leninakan **83** 41 0N 42 50E
Leningrad **80** 59 55N 30 20E
Leninogorsk, Kazakh S.S.R., U.S.S.R. **76** 50 20N 83 30E
Leninogorsk, R.S.F.S.R., U.S.S.R. **84** 54 36N 52 30E
Leninpol **85** 42 29N 71 55E
Leninsk, R.S.F.S.R., U.S.S.R. **83** 48 40N 45 15E
Leninsk, Uzbek S.S.R., U.S.S.R. **85** 40 38N 72 15E
Leninsk-Kuznetskiy **76** 55 10N 86 10E
Leninskaya **81** 56 7N 44 29E
Leninskoye, R.S.F.S.R., U.S.S.R. **77** 47 56N 132 38E
Leninskoye, R.S.F.S.R., U.S.S.R. **81** 58 23N 47 3E
Leninskoye, Uzbek S.S.R., U.S.S.R. **85** 41 45N 69 23E
Lenk **50** 46 27N 7 28E
Lenkoran **79** 39 45N 48 50E
Lenmalu **103** 1 58S 130 0E
Lennard, R. **136** 17 22S 124 20E
Lennox Hills **34** 56 3N 4 12W
Lennoxtown **34** 55 58N 4 14W
Leno **62** 45 24N 10 14E
Lenoir **157** 35 55N 81 36W
Lenoir City **157** 35 40N 84 20W
Lenora **158** 39 39N 100 1W
Lenore L. **153** 52 30N 104 59W
Lenox **162** 42 20N 73 18W
Lens, Belg. **47** 50 33N 3 54E
Lens, France **43** 50 26N 2 50E
Lens St. Remy **47** 50 39N 5 7E
Lensk (Mukhtuya) **77** 60 48N 114 55E
Lenskoye **82** 45 3N 34 1E
Lent **46** 51 52N 5 52E
Lentini **65** 37 18N 15 0E
Lenwood **163** 34 53N 117 7W
Lenzburg **50** 47 23N 8 11E
Lenzen **48** 53 6N 11 26E
Lenzerheide **51** 46 44N 9 34E
Léo **120** 11 3N 2 2W
Leoben **52** 47 22N 15 5E
Leola **158** 45 47N 98 58W
Leominster, U.K. **28** 52 15N 2 43W
Leominster, U.S.A. **162** 42 32N 71 45W
Léon **44** 43 53N 1 18W
León, Mexico **164** 21 7N 101 30W
León, Nic. **166** 12 20N 86 51W
León, Spain **56** 42 38N 5 34W
Leon **158** 40 40N 93 40W
León □ **56** 42 40N 5 55W
León, Montañas de **56** 42 30N 6 18W
Leonardtown **162** 38 19N 76 39W
Leonel, Mte. **50** 46 15N 8 5E
Leonforte **65** 37 39N 14 22E
Leongatha **141** 38 30S 145 58E
Leonídhion **69** 37 9N 22 52E
Leonora **137** 28 49S 121 19E
Leonora Downs **140** 32 29S 142 5E
Léopold II, Lac = Mai-Ndombe **124** 2 0S 18 0E
Leopoldina **173** 21 28S 42 40W
Leopoldo Bulhões **171** 16 37S 48 46W
Leopoldsburg **47** 51 7N 5 13E
Léopoldville = Kinshasa **124** 4 20S 15 15E
Leoti **158** 38 31N 101 19W
Leoville **153** 53 39N 107 33W
Lépa, L. do **128** 17 0S 19 0E
Lepe **57** 37 15N 7 12W
Lepel **80** 54 50N 28 40E
Lephin **36** 57 26N 6 43W
Lepikha **77** 64 45N 125 55E
Lépo, L. do **128** 17 0S 19 0E
Lepontine Alps **62** 46 22N 8 27E
Lepsény **53** 47 0N 18 15E
Leptis Magna **119** 32 40N 14 12E
Lequeitio **58** 43 20N 2 32W
Lerbäck **72** 58 56N 15 2E
Lercara Friddi **64** 37 42N 13 36E
Lerdo **164** 25 32N 103 32W
Léré **124** 9 39N 14 13E
Lere **121** 9 43N 9 18E
Leribe **129** 28 51S 28 3E
Lérici **62** 44 4N 9 48E
Lérida **58** 41 37N 0 39E
Lérida □ **58** 42 6N 1 0E
Lérins, Is. de **45** 43 31N 7 3E
Lerma **56** 42 0N 3 47W
Léros, I. **69** 37 10N 26 50E
Lérouville **43** 48 50N 5 30E
Lerrig **39** 52 22N 9 47W
Lerwick **36** 60 10N 1 10W
Les **70** 46 58N 21 50E
Lesbos, I. = Lésvos **69** 39 0N 26 20E
Lesbury **35** 55 25N 1 37W
Lésina, L. di **63** 41 53N 15 25E
Lesja **71** 62 7N 8 51E
Lesjaverk **71** 62 12N 8 34E
Lesko **54** 49 30N 22 23E
Leskov, I. **13** 56 0S 28 0W
Leskovac **68** 43 0N 21 58E
Leskovec **68** 40 10N 20 34E
Leslie, U.K. **35** 56 12N 3 12W
Leslie, U.S.A. **159** 35 50N 92 35W
Lesmahagow **35** 55 38N 3 55W
Lesna **54** 51 0N 15 15E
Lesneven **42** 48 35N 4 20W
Lesnič a **66** 44 39N 19 20E
Lesnoy **84** 59 47N 52 9E
Lesnoye **80** 58 15N 35 31E
Lesotho ■ **129** 29 40S 28 0E
Lesozavodsk **77** 45 30N 133 20E
Lesparre-Médoc **44** 45 18N 0 57W
Lessay **42** 49 14N 1 30W
Lesse, R. **47** 50 15N 4 54E
Lesser Antilles **167** 12 30N 61 0W
Lesser Slave L. **152** 55 30N 115 25W
Lessines **47** 50 42N 3 50E
Lestock **153** 51 19N 103 59W
Lesuer I. **136** 13 50S 127 17E
Lesuma **128** 17 58S 25 12E
Lésvos, I. **69** 39 0N 26 20E
Leswalt **34** 54 56N 5 6W
Leszno **54** 51 50N 16 30E
Leszno □ **54** 51 45N 16 30E
Letchworth **29** 51 58N 0 13W
Letea, Ostrov **70** 45 18N 29 20E
Lethbridge **152** 49 45N 112 45W
Lethero **140** 33 33S 142 30E
Lethlhakeng **128** 24 0S 24 59E
Leti **103** 8 10S 127 40E
Leti, Kepulauan **103** 8 10S 128 0E
Letiahau, R. **128** 21 40S 23 30E
Leticia **174** 4 0S 70 0W
Letpadan **98** 17 45N 96 0E
Letpan **98** 19 28N 93 52E
Letsôk-aw-Kyun (Domel I.) **101** 11 30N 98 25E
Letterbreen **38** 54 18N 7 43W
Letterfrack **38** 53 33N 9 58W
Letterkenny **38** 54 57N 7 42W
Lettermacaward **38** 54 51N 8 18W
Lettermore I. **39** 53 18N 9 40W
Lettermullan **39** 53 15N 9 44W
Letterston **31** 51 56N 5 0W
Lettoch **37** 57 22N 3 30W
Leu **70** 44 10N 24 0E
Leucadia **163** 33 4N 117 18W
Leucate **44** 42 56N 3 3E
Leucate, Étang de **44** 42 50N 3 0E
Leuchars **35** 56 23N 2 53W
Leuk **50** 46 19N 7 37E
Leukerbad **50** 46 24N 7 36E
Leupegem **47** 50 50N 3 36E
Leuser, G. **102** 4 0N 96 51E
Leutkirch **49** 47 49N 10 1E
Leuven (Louvain) **47** 50 52N 4 42E
Leuze, Hainaut, Belg. **47** 50 36N 3 37E
Leuze, Namur, Belg. **47** 50 33N 4 54E
Lev Tolstoy **81** 53 13N 39 29E
Levádhia **69** 38 27N 22 54E
Levan **160** 39 37N 111 32W
Levanger **74** 63 45N 11 19E
Levani **68** 40 40N 19 28E
Lévanto **62** 44 10N 9 37E
Levanzo, I. **64** 38 0N 12 19E
Levelland **159** 33 38N 102 17W
Leven, Fife, U.K. **35** 56 12N 3 0W
Leven, Humb., U.K. **33** 53 54N 0 18W
Leven, Banc du **129** 12 30S 47 45E
Leven, L. **35** 56 12N 3 22W
Leven R. **33** 54 27N 1 15W
Levens **45** 43 50N 7 12E
Leveque C. **136** 16 20S 123 0E
Leverano **65** 40 16N 18 0E
Leverburgh **36** 57 46N 7 0W
Leverkusen **48** 51 2N 6 59E
Levet **43** 46 56N 2 22E
Levice **53** 48 13N 18 35E
Levick, Mt. **13** 75 0S 164 0E
Levico **63** 46 0N 11 18E
Levie **45** 41 40N 9 7E
Levier **43** 46 58N 6 8E
Levin **142** 40 37S 175 18E
Levis **151** 46 48N 71 9W
Levis, L. **152** 62 37N 117 58W
Levítha, I. **69** 37 0N 26 28E
Levittown, N.Y., U.S.A. **162** 40 41N 73 31W
Levittown, Pa., U.S.A. **162** 40 10N 74 51W
Levka **67** 41 52N 26 15E
Lévka, Mt. **69** 35 18N 24 3E
Levkás **69** 38 48N 20 43E
Levkás, I. **69** 38 40N 20 43E
Levkimmi **68** 39 25N 20 3E
Levkôsia = Nicosia **92** 35 10N 33 25E
Levoča **53** 48 59N 20 35E
Levroux **43** 47 0N 1 38E
Levski **67** 43 21N 25 10E
Levskigrad **67** 42 38N 24 47E
Lewe **98** 19 38N 96 7E
Lewellen **158** 41 22N 102 5W
Lewes, U.K. **29** 50 53N 0 2E
Lewes, U.S.A. **156** 38 45N 75 8W
Lewes, L. **148** 60 30N 134 20W
Lewin Brzeski **54** 50 45N 17 37E
Lewis, Butt of **36** 58 30N 6 12W
Lewis, I. **36** 58 10N 6 40W
Lewis, R. **160** 48 0N 113 15W
Lewis Ra. **136** 20 3S 128 50E
Lewisburg, Pa., U.S.A. **162** 40 57N 76 57W
Lewisburg, Tenn., U.S.A. **157** 35 29N 86 46W
Lewisham **29** 51 27N 0 1W
Lewisporte **151** 49 15N 55 3W
Lewiston, U.K. **37** 57 19N 4 30W
Lewiston, Idaho, U.S.A. **160** 45 58N 117 0W
Lewiston, Utah, U.S.A. **160** 42 0N 111 56W
Lewistown, Mont., U.S.A. **160** 47 0N 109 25W
Lewistown, Pa., U.S.A. **156** 40 37N 77 33W
Lexington, Ill., U.S.A. **158** 40 37N 88 47W
Lexington, Ky., U.S.A. **156** 38 6N 84 30W
Lexington, Md., U.S.A. **162** 38 16N 76 27W
Lexington, Miss., U.S.A. **159** 33 8N 90 2W
Lexington, Mo., U.S.A. **158** 39 7N 93 55W
Lexington, N.C., U.S.A. **157** 35 50N 80 13W
Lexington, Nebr., U.S.A. **158** 40 48N 99 45W
Lexington, N.Y., U.S.A. **162** 42 15N 74 22W
Lexington, Oreg., U.S.A. **160** 45 29N 119 46W

Lexington Litija

Lexington, Tenn., U.S.A. 157 35 38N 88 25W
Leyburn 33 54 19N 1 50W
Leyland 32 53 41N 2 42W
Leysdown on Sea 29 51 23N 0 57E
Leysin 50 46 21N 7 0E
Leyte, I. 103 11 0N 125 0E
Lezay 44 46 17N 0 0E
Lèze, R. 44 43 28N 1 25E
Lezha 68 41 47N 19 42E
Lézignan-Corbières 44 43 13N 2 43E
Lezoux 44 45 49N 3 21E
Lgov 80 51 42N 35 10E
Lhanbryde 37 57 38N 3 12W
Lhariguo 99 30 29N 93 4E
Lhasa 105 29 39N 91 6E
Lhokseumawe 102 5 20N 97 10E
Lhuntsi Dzong 98 27 39N 91 10E
Li, Finland 74 65 20N 25 20E
Li, Thai. 100 17 48N 98 57E
Li Shui, R. 109 29 24N 112 1E
Liádhoi, I. 69 36 50N 26 11E
Liang Liang 103 5 58N 121 30E
Liang Shan 108 23 42N 99 48E
Lianga 103 8 38N 126 6E
Liangch'eng, Inner Mongolia, China 106 40 26N 112 14E
Liangch'eng, Shantung, China 107 35 35N 119 32E
Lianghok'ou 108 29 10N 108 44E
Lianghsiang 106 39 44N 116 8E
Liangp'ing 108 30 41N 107 49E
Liangpran, Gunong 102 1 0N 114 23E
Liangtang 106 33 56N 106 12E
Liao Ho, R. 107 40 39N 122 12E
Liaoch'eng 106 36 26N 115 58E
Liaochung 107 41 30N 122 42E
Liaoning □ 107 41 15N 122 0E
Liaotung Pantao 107 40 0N 122 22E
Liaotung Wan 107 40 30N 121 30E
Liaoyang 107 41 17N 123 11E
Liaoyüan 107 42 55N 125 10E
Liapádhes 68 39 42N 19 40E
Liard, R. 152 61 51N 121 18W
Liari 94 25 37N 66 30E
Libau = Liepaja 80 56 30N 21 0E
Libby 160 48 20N 115 10W
Libenge 124 3 40N 18 55E
Liberal, Kans., U.S.A. 159 37 4N 101 0W
Liberal, Mo., U.S.A. 159 37 35N 94 30W
Liberec 52 50 47N 15 7E
Liberia 166 10 40N 85 30W
Liberia ■ 120 6 30N 9 30W
Libertad 174 8 20N 69 37W
Libertad, La 166 16 47N 90 7W
Liberty, Mo., U.S.A. 158 39 15N 94 24W
Liberty, N.Y., U.S.A. 162 41 48N 74 45W
Liberty, Pa., U.S.A. 162 41 34N 77 6W
Liberty, Tex., U.S.A. 159 30 5N 94 50W
Libiaz 53 50 7N 19 21E
Libin 47 49 59N 5 15E
Lîbîya, Sahrâ' 114 27 35N 25 0E
Libohava 68 40 3N 20 10E
Libourne 44 44 55N 0 14W
Libramont 47 49 55N 5 23E
Librazhdi 68 41 12N 20 22E
Libreville 124 0 25N 9 26E
Libya ■ 117 28 30N 17 30E
Libyan Plateau = Ed-Déffa 122 30 40N 26 30E
Licantén 172 34 55S 72 0W
Licata 64 37 6N 13 55E
Lich'eng 106 36 59N 113 31E
Lichfield 28 52 40N 1 50W
Lichiang 108 26 54N 100 12E
Lichin 107 37 32N 118 20E
Lichtaart 47 51 13N 4 55E
Lichtenburg 128 26 8S 26 8E
Lichtenfels 49 50 7N 11 4E
Lichtenvoorde 46 51 59N 6 34E
Lichtervelde 47 51 2N 3 9E
Lich'uan, Hupeh, China 109 30 18N 108 51E
Lich'uan, Kiangsi, China 109 27 14N 116 51E
Licosa, Punta 65 40 15N 14 53E
Lida, U.S.A. 163 37 30N 117 30W
Lida, U.S.S.R. 80 53 53N 25 15E
Lidhult 73 56 50N 13 27E
Lidingö 73 59 22N 18 8E
Lidköping 73 58 31N 13 14E
Lido, Italy 63 45 25N 12 23E
Lido, Niger 121 12 54N 3 44E
Lido di Ostia 64 41 44N 12 14E
Lidzbark 54 53 15N 19 49E
Lidzbark Warminski 54 54 7N 20 34E
Liebenwalde 48 52 51N 13 23E
Lieberose 48 51 59N 14 18E
Liebling 66 45 36N 21 20E
Liechtenstein ■ 49 47 8N 9 35E
Liederkerke 47 50 52N 4 5E
Liège 47 50 38N 5 35E
Liège □ 47 50 32N 5 35E
Liegnitz = Legnica 54 51 12N 16 10E
Liempde 47 51 35N 5 23E
Lienart 126 3 3N 25 31E
Lienartville 126 3 3N 25 31E
Liench'eng 109 25 47N 116 48E
Lienchiang, Fukien, China 109 26 11N 119 32E
Lienchiang, Kwangtung, China 109 21 36N 110 16E
Lienhsien 109 24 50N 112 23E
Lienp'ing 109 24 22N 114 30E
Lienshan, Kwangtung, China 109 24 37N 112 2E
Lienshan, Yunnan, China 108 24 48N 97 54E
Lienshankuan 107 40 58N 123 46E
Lienshui 107 33 46N 119 18E
Lienyüan 109 27 41N 111 40E
Lienyünchiang 107 34 47N 119 30E
Lienyünchiangshih 107 34 37N 119 13E
Lienz 52 46 50N 12 46E
Liepāja 80 56 30N 21 0E
Lier 47 51 7N 4 34E
Lierneux 47 50 17N 5 47E
Lieshout 47 51 31N 5 36E
Lieşta 70 45 38N 27 34E
Liestal 50 47 29N 7 44E
Lieşti 70 45 38N 27 34E
Liévin 43 50 24N 2 47E
Lièvre, R. 150 45 31N 75 26W
Liezen 52 47 34N 14 15E
Liffey, R. 39 53 21N 6 20W
Lifford 38 54 50N 7 30W
Liffré 42 48 12N 1 30W
Lifjell 71 59 27N 8 45E
Lightning Ridge 139 29 22S 148 0E
Lignano 63 45 42N 13 8E
Ligny-er-Barrois 43 48 36N 5 20E
Ligny-le-Châtel 43 47 54N 3 45E
Ligoúrion 69 37 37N 23 2E
Ligua, La 172 32 30S 71 16W
Liguria □ 62 44 30N 9 0E
Ligurian Sea 62 43 20N 9 0E
Lihir Group 135 3 0S 152 35E
Lihou Reefs and Cays 138 17 25S 151 40E
Lihsien, Hopeh, China 106 38 29N 115 34E
Lihsien, Hunan, China 109 29 38N 111 45E
Lihsien, Kansu, China 106 34 11N 105 2E
Lihsien, Szechwan, China 108 31 28N 103 17E
Lihue 147 21 59N 159 24W
Lihwa 99 30 4N 100 18E
Likasi 127 10 55S 26 48E
Likati 124 3 20N 24 0E
Likhoslavl 80 57 12N 35 30E
Likhovski 83 48 10N 40 10E
Likoma I. 127 12 3S 34 45E
Likumburu 127 9 43S 35 8E
Liling 109 27 40N 113 30E
Lill 47 51 15N 4 50E
Lille 43 50 38N 3 3E
Lille Bælt 73 55 30N 9 45E
Lillebonne 42 49 30N 0 32E
Lillehammer 71 61 8N 10 30E
Lillers 43 50 35N 2 28E
Lillesand 71 58 15N 8 23E
Lillestrøm 71 59 58N 11 5E
Lillian Point, Mt. 137 27 40S 126 6E
Lillo 58 39 45N 3 20W
Lillooet, R. 152 49 15N 121 57W
Lilongwe 127 14 0S 33 48E
Liloy 103 8 4N 122 39E
Lilun 108 28 3N 100 27E
Lim, R. 66 43 0N 19 40E
Lima, Indon. 103 3 37S 128 4E
Lima, Peru 174 12 0S 77 0W
Lima, Sweden 72 60 55N 13 20E
Lima, Mont., U.S.A. 160 44 41N 112 38W
Lima, Ohio, U.S.A. 156 40 42N 84 5W
Lima, R. 56 41 50N 8 18W
Limanowa 54 49 42N 20 22E
Limassol 92 34 42N 33 1E
Limavady 38 55 3N 6 58W
Limavady □ 38 55 0N 6 55W
Limay Mahuida 172 37 10S 66 45W
Limay, R. 176 39 40S 69 45W
Limbang 102 4 42N 115 6E
Limbara, Monti 64 40 50N 9 10E
Limbdi 94 22 34N 71 51E
Limbourg 47 50 37N 5 56E
Limbourg □ 47 51 2N 5 25E
Limbri 141 31 3S 151 5E
Limbunya 136 17 14S 129 50E
Limburg 49 50 22N 8 4E
Limburg □ 47 51 20N 5 55E
Limedsforsen 72 60 52N 13 25E
Limeira 173 22 35S 47 28W
Limenária 68 40 38N 24 32E
Limerick 39 52 40N 8 38W
Limerick □ 39 52 30N 8 50W
Limerick Junction 39 52 30N 8 12W
Limestone, R. 153 56 31N 94 7W
Limfjorden 73 56 55N 9 0E
Limia, R. 56 41 55N 8 8W
Limmared 73 57 34N 13 20E
Limmat, R. 51 47 26N 8 20E
Limmen 46 52 34N 4 42E
Limmen Bight 138 14 40S 135 35E
Limmen Bight R. 138 15 7S 135 44E
Límni 69 38 43N 23 18E
Límnos, I. 68 39 50N 25 5E
Limoeiro 170 7 52S 25 27W
Limoeiro do Norte 170 5 5S 38 0W
Limoges 44 45 50N 1 15E
Limón 167 10 0N 83 2W
Limon 158 39 18N 103 38W
Limone 62 44 12N 7 32E
Limousin 44 46 0N 1 0E
Limousin, Plateau de 44 46 0N 1 0E
Limoux 44 43 4N 2 12E
Limpopo, R. 129 23 15S 32 5E
Limpsfield 29 51 15N 0 1E
Limu Ling, mts. 100 19 0N 109 20E
Limuru 126 1 2S 36 35E
Lin 68 41 4N 20 38E
Linan 109 30 13N 119 40E
Linares 172 35 50S 71 40W
Linàres 174 1 23N 77 31W
Linares, Mexico 165 24 50N 99 40W
Linares, Spain 59 38 10N 3 40W
Linares □ 172 36 0S 71 0W
Línas Mte. 64 39 25N 8 38E
Linchenchen 106 36 28N 110 0E
Linch'eng 106 37 26N 114 34E
Linch'i 106 35 46N 113 53E
Linchiang 107 41 50N 126 55E
Linchin 106 35 6N 110 33E
Linch'ing 106 36 56N 115 45E
Linch'ü 107 36 30N 118 32E
Linch'uan 109 28 0N 116 20E
Lincluden 35 55 5N 3 40W
Lincoln, Argent. 172 34 55N 61 30W
Lincoln, N.Z. 143 43 38S 172 30E
Lincoln, U.K. 33 53 14N 0 32W
Lincoln, Ill., U.S.A. 158 40 10N 89 20W
Lincoln, Kans., U.S.A. 158 39 6N 98 9W
Lincoln, Maine, U.S.A. 151 45 27N 68 29W
Lincoln, N. Mex., U.S.A. 161 33 30N 105 26W
Lincoln, Nebr., U.S.A. 158 40 50N 96 42W
Lincoln, N.H., U.S.A. 162 44 3N 71 40W
Lincoln □ 33 53 14N 0 32W
Lincoln Sea 12 84 0N 55 0W
Lincoln Wolds 33 53 20N 0 5W
Lincolnton 157 35 30N 81 15W
Lind, Austral. 138 18 58S 144 30E
Lind, U.S.A. 160 47 0N 118 33W
Lindale 32 54 14N 2 54W
Lindås 71 60 44N 5 10E
Lindås, Norway 71 60 44N 5 9E
Lindås, Sweden 73 56 38N 15 35E
Lindau 49 47 33N 9 41E
Linde 46 52 50N 6 57E
Linden, Guyana 174 6 0N 58 10W
Linden, Calif., U.S.A. 163 38 1N 121 5W
Linden, Tex., U.S.A. 159 33 0N 94 20W
Lindenheuvel 47 50 59N 5 48E
Lindenwold 162 39 49N 72 59W
Linderöd 73 55 56N 13 47E
Linderödsåsen 73 55 53N 13 53E
Lindesberg 72 59 36N 15 15E
Lindesnes 71 57 58N 7 3E
Lindfield 29 51 2N 0 5W
Lindi 127 9 58S 39 38E
Lindi □ 127 9 40S 38 30E
Lindi, R. 126 1 25N 25 50E
Lindoso 56 41 52N 8 11W
Lindow 48 52 58N 12 58E
Lindsay, Can. 150 44 22N 78 43W
Lindsay, Calif., U.S.A. 163 36 14N 119 6W
Lindsay, Okla., U.S.A. 159 34 51N 97 37W
Lindsborg 158 38 35N 97 40W
Línea de la Concepción, La 55 36 15N 5 23W
Línea de la Concepción, La 57 36 15N 5 23W
Linfen 106 36 5N 111 32E
Lingakok 99 29 55N 87 38E
Lingayer 103 16 1N 120 14E
Lingayer G. 103 16 10N 120 15E
Lingch'iu 106 39 28N 114 10E
Lingch'uan, Kwangsi Chuang, China 109 25 25N 110 20E
Lingch'uan, Shansi, China 106 35 46N 113 26E
Lingen 48 52 32N 7 21E
Lingfield 29 51 11N 0 1W
Lingga, Kepulauan 102 0 10S 104 30E
Linghed 72 60 48N 15 55E
Linghsien, Hunan, China 109 26 26N 113 45E
Linghsien, Shantung, China 106 37 21N 116 34E
Lingle 158 42 10N 104 18W
Lingling 109 26 13N 111 37E
Lingpi 107 33 33N 117 33E
Lingshan 108 22 26N 109 17E
Lingshih 106 36 51N 111 47E
Lingshou 106 38 18N 114 22E
Lingshui 100 18 27N 110 0E
Lingt'ai 106 35 4N 107 37E
Linguéré 120 15 25N 15 5W
Lingwu 106 38 5N 106 20E
Lingyün 108 24 24N 106 31E
Linh Cam 100 18 31N 105 31E
Linhai 109 28 51N 121 7E
Linhares 171 19 25S 40 4W
Linho 106 40 50N 107 30E
Linhsi 107 43 37N 118 8E
Linhsia 105 35 36N 103 5E
Linhsiang 109 29 29N 113 30E
Linhsien 106 37 57N 110 57E
Lini 107 35 5N 118 20E
Linju 106 34 14N 112 45E
Link 68 41 4N 20 38E
Linkao 100 19 56N 109 42E
Linkinhorne 30 50 31N 4 22W
Linköping 73 58 28N 15 36E
Link'ou 107 45 18N 130 15E
Linli 109 29 27N 111 39E
Linlithgow 35 55 58N 3 38W
Linn, Mt. 160 40 0N 123 0W
Linney Head 31 51 37N 5 4W
Linnhe, L. 34 56 36N 5 25W
Linosa 119 35 51N 12 50E
Lins 173 21 40S 49 44W
Linshui 108 30 18N 106 55E
Linslade 29 51 55N 0 40W
Lint'ao 106 35 20N 104 0E
Linth, R. 49 46 54N 9 0E
Linthal 51 46 54N 9 0E
Lintlaw 153 52 4N 103 14W
Linton, Can. 151 47 15N 72 16W
Linton, U.K. 29 52 6N 0 19E
Linton, Ind., U.S.A. 156 39 0N 87 10W
Linton, N. Dak., U.S.A. 158 46 21N 100 12W
Lints'ang 108 23 54N 100 0E
Lint'ung 106 34 24N 109 13E
Linville 139 26 50S 152 11E
Linwu 109 25 17N 112 33E
Linxe 44 43 56N 1 13W
Linyanti, R. 128 18 10S 24 10E
Linyüan 107 41 18N 119 15E
Linz, Austria 52 48 18N 14 18E
Linz, Ger. 48 50 33N 7 18E
Lion-d'Angers, Le 42 47 37N 0 43W
Lion, G. du 44 43 0N 4 0E
Lioni 65 40 52N 15 10E
Lion's Den 127 17 15S 30 5E
Lion's Head 150 44 58N 81 15W
Liozno 80 55 0N 30 50E
Lipali 127 15 50S 35 50E
Lípari 65 38 26N 14 58E
Lípari, Is. 65 38 40N 15 0E
Lipetsk 81 52 45N 39 35E
Lipiany 54 53 2N 14 58E
Lip'ing 108 26 16N 109 8E
Lipkany 82 48 14N 26 25E
Lipljan 66 42 31N 21 7E
Lipnik 53 49 32N 17 36E
Lipno 54 52 49N 19 15E
Lipo 108 25 25N 107 53E
Lipova 66 46 8N 21 42E
Lipovets 82 49 12N 29 1E
Lippstadt 48 51 40N 8 19E
Lipsco 54 51 10N 21 36E
Lipscomb 159 36 16N 100 28W
Lipsko 54 51 9N 21 40E
Lipsói, I. 69 37 19N 26 50E
Liptovsky Svaty Milkula 53 49 6N 19 35E
Liptrap C. 141 38 50S 145 55E
Lip'u 109 24 30N 110 23E
Lira 126 2 17N 32 57E
Liri, R. 64 41 25N 13 45E
Liria 58 39 37N 0 35W
Lisala 124 2 12N 21 38E
Lisbellaw 38 54 20N 7 32W
Lisboa 57 38 42N 9 10W
Lisboa □ 57 39 0N 9 12W
Lisbon 158 46 30N 97 46W
Lisbon = Lisboa 57 38 42N 9 10W
Lisburn 38 54 30N 6 9W
Lisburne, C. 147 68 50N 166 0W
Liscannor 39 52 57N 9 24W
Liscannor, B. 39 52 57N 9 24W
Liscarroll 39 52 15N 8 44W
Liscia, R. 64 41 5N 9 17E
Liscomb 151 45 2N 62 0W
Lisdoonvarna 39 53 2N 9 18W
Lishe Ho, R. 108 24 18N 101 32E
Lishih 106 37 30N 111 7E
Lishu 107 43 20N 124 37E
Lishuchen 107 45 5N 130 40E
Lishui, Chekiang, China 109 28 27N 119 54E
Lishui, Kiangsu, China 109 31 38N 119 2E
Lisianski I. 130 25 30N 174 0W
Lisieux 42 49 10N 0 12E
Lisichansk 83 48 55N 38 30E
Liskeard 30 50 27N 4 29W
Lismore, N.S.W., Austral. 139 28 44S 153 21E
Lismore, Vic., Austral. 133 37 58S 143 21E
Lismore, Ireland 39 52 8N 7 58W
Lismore I. 34 56 30N 5 30W
Lisnacree 38 54 4N 6 5W
Lisnaskea 38 54 15N 7 27W
Liss 29 51 3N 0 53W
Lissatinning Bri. 39 51 55N 10 1W
Lisse 46 52 16N 4 33E
Lisselton 39 52 30N 9 34W
Lissycasey 39 52 44N 9 12W
List 48 55 1N 8 26E
Lista, Norway 71 58 7N 6 39E
Lista, Sweden 75 59 19N 16 16E
Lister, Mt. 13 78 0S 162 0E
Liston 139 28 39S 152 6E
Listowel, Can. 150 43 44N 80 58W
Listowel, Ireland 39 52 27N 9 30W
Listowel Dns. 139 25 10S 145 12E
Lit-et-Mixe 44 44 2N 1 15W
Lit'ang, Kwangsi-Chuang, China 108 23 11N 109 5E
Lit'ang, Szechwan, China 108 30 4N 100 18E
Litang 103 5 27N 118 31E
Lit'ang Ho, R. 108 28 5N 101 28E
Litcham 29 52 43N 0 49E
Litchfield, Austral. 140 36 18S 142 52E
Litchfield, Conn., U.S.A. 162 41 44N 73 12W
Litchfield, Ill., U.S.A. 158 39 10N 89 40W
Litchfield, Minn., U.S.A. 158 45 5N 95 0W
Liteni 70 47 32N 26 32E
Litherland 32 53 29N 3 0W
Lithgow 141 33 25S 150 8E
Líthinon, Ákra 69 34 55N 24 44E
Lithuania S.S.R. □ 80 55 30N 24 0E
Litija 63 46 3N 14 50E

Lititz Londonderry

Lititz	**162**	40 9N	76 18W
Litókhoron	**68**	40 8N	22 34E
Litoměrice	**52**	50 33N	14 10E
Litomysl	**53**	49 52N	16 20E
Litschau	**52**	48 58N	15 4E
Little Abaco I.	**157**	26 50N	77 30W
Little Aden	**91**	12 41N	45 6E
Little America	**13**	79 0N	160 0W
Little Andaman I.	**101**	10 40N	92 15E
Little Barrier I.	**142**	36 12S	175 8E
Little Belt	**72**	55 8N	9 55E
Little Belt Mts.	**160**	46 50N	111 0W
Little Blue, R.	**158**	40 18N	97 45W
Little Bushman Land	**128**	29 10S	18 10E
Little Cadotte, R.	**152**	56 41N	117 6W
Little Cayman, I.	**166**	19 41N	80 3W
Little Churchill, R.	**153**	57 30N	95 22W
Little Coco I.	**101**	14 0N	93 15E
Little Colorado, R.	**161**	36 0N	111 31W
Little Current	**150**	45 55N	82 0W
Little Current, R.	**150**	50 57N	84 36W
Little Egg Inlet	**162**	39 30N	74 20W
Little Falls, Minn., U.S.A.	**158**	45 58N	94 19W
Little Falls, N.Y., U.S.A.	**162**	43 3N	74 50W
Lit. Grand Rapids	**153**	52 0N	95 29W
Lit. Humbaldt, R.	**160**	41 20N	117 27W
Lit. Inagua I.	**167**	21 40N	73 50W
Little Lake	**163**	35 58N	117 58W
Little Longlac	**150**	49 42N	86 58W
Little Marais	**158**	47 24N	91 8W
Little Mecatina I.	**151**	50 30N	59 25W
Little Minch	**36**	57 35N	6 45W
Lit. Miquelon I.	**151**	46 45N	56 25W
Lit. Missouri R.	**158**	46 40N	103 50W
Little Namaqualand	**128**	29 0S	17 9E
Little Ormes Hd.	**31**	53 19N	3 47W
Little Ouse, R.	**29**	52 25N	0 50E
Little Para, R.	**109**	34 47S	138 25E
Little Rann of Kutch	**94**	23 25N	71 25E
Little Red, R.	**159**	35 40N	92 15W
Little River	**143**	43 45S	172 49E
Little Rock	**159**	34 41N	92 10W
Little Ruaha, R.	**126**	7 50S	35 30E
Little Sable Pt.	**156**	43 40N	86 32W
Little Scarcies, R.	**125**	9 30N	12 25W
Little Sioux, R.	**147**	42 20N	95 55W
Little Smoky	**152**	54 44N	117 11W
Little Smoky River	**152**	55 40N	117 38W
Little Snake, R.	**160**	40 45N	108 15W
Little Wabash, R.	**156**	38 40N	88 20W
Little Walsingham	**29**	52 53N	0 51E
Little Whale, R.	**150**	55 50N	75 0W
Littleborough	**32**	53 38N	2 8W
Littlefield	**159**	33 57N	102 17W
Littlefork	**158**	48 24N	93 35W
Littlehampton, Austral.	**109**	35 3S	138 52E
Littlehampton, U.K.	**29**	50 48N	0 32W
Littlemill	**37**	57 31N	3 49W
Littleport	**29**	52 27N	0 18E
Littlestone-on-Sea	**29**	50 59N	0 59E
Littlestown	**162**	39 45N	77 3W
Littleton Common	**162**	42 32N	71 28W
Litu	**108**	28 24N	101 16E
Liuan	**109**	31 45N	116 30E
Liuch'eng	**108**	24 39N	109 14E
Liuchou	**108**	24 15N	109 22E
Liuchuang	**107**	33 9N	120 18E
Liuheng Tao	**109**	29 43N	122 8E
Liuho, Kiangsu, China	**109**	32 20N	118 51E
Liuho, Kirin, China	**107**	42 16N	125 42E
Liukou	**107**	40 57N	118 18E
Liuli	**127**	11 3S	34 38E
Liupa	**106**	33 40N	107 0E
Liuwa Plain	**125**	14 20S	22 30E
Liuyang	**109**	28 9N	113 38E
Livada	**70**	47 52N	23 5E
Livadherón	**68**	40 2N	21 57E
Livanovka	**84**	52 6N	61 59E
Livarot	**42**	49 0N	0 9E
Live Oak	**157**	30 17N	83 0W
Liveringa	**136**	18 3S	124 10E
Livermore	**163**	37 41N	121 47W
Livermore, Mt.	**159**	30 45N	104 8W
Liverpool, Austral.	**141**	33 54S	150 58E
Liverpool, Can.	**151**	44 5N	64 41W
Liverpool, U.K.	**32**	53 25N	3 0W
Liverpool, U.S.A.	**162**	43 6N	76 13W
Liverpool Bay, Can.	**147**	70 0N	128 0W
Liverpool Bay, U.K.	**23**	53 30N	3 20W
Liverpool Plains	**141**	31 15S	150 15E
Liverpool Ra.	**141**	31 50S	150 30E
Livingston, Guat.	**166**	15 50N	88 50W
Livingston, U.K.	**45**	55 52N	3 33W
Livingston, Calif., U.S.A.	**163**	37 23N	120 43W
Livingston, Mont., U.S.A.	**160**	45 40N	110 40W
Livingstone	**159**	30 44N	94 54W
Livingstone Falls	**126**	5 25S	13 35E
Livingstone I.	**13**	63 0S	60 15W
Livingstone (Maramba)	**127**	17 46S	25 52E
Livingstone Memorial	**127**	12 20S	30 18E
Livingstone Mts., N.Z.	**143**	45 15S	168 9E
Livingstone Mts., Tanz.	**127**	9 40S	34 20E
Livingstonia	**127**	10 38S	34 5E
Livno	**66**	43 50N	17 0E
Livny	**81**	52 30N	37 30E
Livorno	**62**	43 32N	10 18E
Livramento	**173**	30 55S	55 30W
Livramento do Brumado	**171**	13 39S	41 50W
Livron-sur-Drôme	**45**	44 46N	4 51E
Liwale	**127**	9 48S	37 58E
Liwale □	**127**	9 0S	38 0E
Liwale Chini	**127**	9 40S	38 0E
Lixnaw	**39**	52 24N	9 37W
Lixoúrion	**69**	38 14N	20 24E
Liyang	**109**	31 22N	119 30E
Lizard	**30**	49 58N	5 10W
Lizard I.	**138**	14 42S	145 30E
Lizard Pt.	**30**	49 57N	5 11W
Lizarda	**170**	9 36S	46 41W
Lizzano	**65**	40 23N	17 25E
Ljig	**66**	44 13N	20 18E
Ljubija	**63**	44 55N	16 35E
Ljubinje	**66**	42 58N	18 5E
Ljubljana	**63**	46 4N	14 33E
Ljubno	**63**	46 25N	14 46E
Ljubovija	**66**	44 11N	19 22E
Ljubuški	**66**	43 12N	17 34E
Ljung	**73**	58 1N	13 3E
Ljungan	**72**	62 18N	17 23E
Ljungan, R.	**74**	62 30N	14 30E
Ljungaverk	**72**	62 30N	16 5E
Ljungby	**73**	56 49N	13 55E
Ljusdal	**72**	61 46N	16 3E
Ljusnan	**72**	61 12N	17 8E
Ljusnan, R.	**75**	62 0N	15 20E
Ljusne	**72**	61 13N	17 7E
Ljutomer	**63**	46 31N	16 11E
Lki	**67**	41 28N	23 43E
Llagostera	**58**	41 50N	2 54E
Llanaber	**31**	52 45N	4 5W
Llanaelhaiarn	**31**	52 59N	4 24W
Llanafan-fawr	**31**	52 12N	3 29W
Llanarmon Dyffryn Ceiriog	**31**	52 53N	3 15W
Llanarth	**31**	52 12N	4 19W
Llanarthney	**31**	51 51N	4 9W
Llanbedr	**31**	52 40N	4 7W
Llanbedrog	**31**	52 52N	4 29W
Llanberis	**31**	53 7N	4 7W
Llanbister	**31**	52 22N	3 19W
Llanbrynmair	**31**	52 36N	3 19W
Llancanelo, Salina	**172**	35 40S	69 8W
Llandaff	**31**	51 29N	3 13W
Llanddewi-Brefi	**31**	52 11N	3 57W
Llandilo	**31**	51 45N	4 0W
Llandogo	**31**	51 44N	2 40W
Llandovery	**31**	51 59N	3 49W
Llandrillo	**31**	52 56N	3 27W
Llandrindod Wells	**31**	52 15N	3 23W
Llandudno	**31**	53 19N	3 51W
Llandybie	**31**	51 49N	4 0W
Llandyfriog	**31**	52 2N	4 26W
Llandygwydd	**31**	52 3N	4 33W
Llandyrnog	**31**	53 10N	3 19W
Llandyssul	**31**	52 3N	4 20W
Llanelli	**31**	51 41N	4 11W
Llanelltyd	**31**	52 45N	3 54W
Llanenddwyn	**31**	52 48N	4 7W
Llanerchymedd	**31**	53 20N	4 22W
Llanes	**56**	43 25N	4 50W
Llanfaelog	**31**	53 13N	4 29W
Llanfair Caereinion	**31**	52 39N	3 20W
Llanfair Talhaiarn	**31**	53 13N	3 37W
Llanfairfechan	**31**	53 15N	3 58W
Llanfechell	**31**	52 23N	4 25W
Llanfyllin	**31**	52 47N	3 17W
Llangadog	**31**	51 56N	3 53W
Llangefni	**31**	53 15N	4 20W
Llangelynin	**31**	52 39N	4 7W
Llangennech	**31**	51 41N	4 10W
Llangerniew	**31**	53 12N	3 41W
Llangollen	**31**	52 58N	3 10W
Llangranog	**31**	52 11N	4 29W
Llangurig	**31**	52 25N	3 36W
Llangynog	**31**	52 50N	3 24W
Llanharan	**31**	51 32N	3 28W
Llanidloes	**31**	52 28N	3 31W
Llanilar	**31**	52 22N	4 2W
Llanllyfni	**31**	53 2N	4 18W
Llannor	**31**	52 55N	4 25W
Llano Estacado	**154**	34 0N	103 0W
Llano R.	**159**	30 50N	99 0W
Llanon	**31**	52 17N	4 9W
Llanos	**174**	3 25N	71 35W
Llanpumpsaint	**31**	51 56N	4 19W
Llanrhaedr-ym-Mochnant	**31**	52 50N	3 18W
Llanrhidian	**31**	51 36N	4 11W
Llanrhystyd	**31**	52 19N	4 9W
Llanrwst	**31**	53 8N	3 49W
Llansannan	**31**	53 10N	3 35W
Llansawel	**31**	52 0N	4 1W
Llanstephan	**31**	51 46N	4 24W
Llanthony	**31**	51 57N	3 2W
Llantrisant	**31**	51 33N	3 22W
Llanuwchllyn	**31**	52 52N	3 41W
Llanvihangel Crucorney	**31**	51 53N	2 58W
Llanwenog	**31**	52 6N	4 11W
Llanwrda	**31**	51 58N	3 52W
Llanwrtyd Wells	**31**	52 6N	3 39W
Llanyblodwel	**28**	52 47N	3 8W
Llanybyther	**31**	52 4N	4 10W
Llanymynech	**28**	52 48N	3 6W
Llanystymdwy	**31**	52 56N	4 17W
Llera	**165**	23 19N	99 1W
Llerena	**57**	38 17N	6 0W
Llethr Mt.	**31**	52 47N	3 58W
Lleyn Peninsula	**31**	52 55N	4 35W
Llico	**172**	34 46S	72 5W
Llobregat, R.	**58**	41 19N	2 9E
Lloret de Mar	**58**	41 41N	2 53E
Lloyd B.	**138**	12 45S	143 27E
Lloyd Barrage	**95**	27 46N	68 50E
Lloyd L.	**153**	57 22N	108 57W
Lloydminster	**153**	53 20N	110 0W
Lluchmayor	**59**	39 29N	2 53E
Llullaillaco, volcán	**172**	24 30S	68 30W
Llwyngwril	**31**	52 41N	4 6W
Llyswen	**31**	52 2N	3 18W
Lo	**47**	50 59N	2 45E
Lo Ho, Honan, China	**106**	34 48N	113 4E
Lo Ho, Shensi, China	**106**	34 41N	110 6E
Lo, R.	**100**	21 18N	105 25E
Loa	**161**	38 18N	111 46W
Loa, R.	**172**	21 30S	70 0W
Loan	**109**	27 24N	115 49E
Loanhead	**35**	55 53N	3 10W
Loano	**62**	44 8N	8 14E
Loans	**34**	55 33N	4 39W
Lobatse	**125**	25 12S	25 40E
Löbau	**48**	51 5N	14 42E
Lobaye, R.	**128**	4 30N	17 0E
Lobbes	**47**	50 21N	4 16E
Lobenstein	**48**	50 25N	11 39E
Lobería	**172**	38 10S	58 40W
Łobez	**54**	53 38N	15 39E
Lobito	**125**	12 18S	13 35E
Lobón, Canal de	**57**	38 50N	6 55W
Lobos	**172**	35 2S	59 0W
Lobos, I.	**164**	21 27N	97 13W
Lobos, Is.	**168**	6 35S	80 45W
Lobstick L.	**151**	54 0N	65 12W
Lobva	**84**	59 10N	60 30E
Lobva, R.	**84**	59 8N	60 48E
Loc Binh	**100**	21 46N	106 54E
Loc Ninh	**101**	11 50N	106 34E
Locarno	**51**	46 10N	8 47E
Loch Raven Res.	**162**	39 26N	76 33W
Lochaber	**36**	56 55N	5 0W
Lochailort	**36**	56 53N	5 40W
Lochaline	**36**	56 32N	5 47W
Loch'ang	**109**	25 10N	113 20E
Lochans	**34**	54 52N	5 1W
Lochboisdale	**36**	57 10N	7 20W
Lochbuie	**34**	56 21N	5 52W
Lochcarron	**36**	57 25N	5 30W
Lochdonhead	**34**	56 27N	5 40W
Loche L., La	**153**	56 40N	109 30W
Loche, La	**153**	56 29N	109 26W
Lochearnhead	**34**	56 24N	4 19W
Lochem	**46**	52 9N	6 26E
Loch'eng	**108**	24 47N	108 54E
Loches	**42**	47 7N	1 0E
Lochgelly	**35**	56 7N	3 18W
Lochgilphead	**34**	56 2N	5 37W
Lochgoilhead	**34**	56 10N	4 54W
Lochiang	**108**	31 21N	104 28E
Lochih	**108**	30 18N	105 0E
Loch'ing	**109**	28 8N	120 57E
Loch'ing Wan	**109**	28 4N	121 5E
Lochinver	**36**	58 9N	5 15W
Lochlaggan Hotel	**37**	56 59N	4 25W
Lochmaben	**35**	55 8N	3 27W
Lochmaddy	**36**	57 36N	7 10W
Lochnagar, Queens., Austral.	**138**	24 34S	144 52E
Lochnagar, Queens., Austral.	**138**	23 33S	145 38E
Lochnagar, Mt.	**37**	56 57N	3 14W
Łochow	**54**	52 33N	21 42E
Lochranza	**34**	55 42N	5 18W
Lochs Park, Reg.	**36**	58 7N	6 33W
Loch'uan	**106**	35 48N	109 35E
Lochwinnoch	**34**	55 47N	4 39W
Lochy, L.	**37**	56 58N	4 55W
Lochy, R.	**36**	56 52N	5 3W
Lock	**139**	33 34S	135 46E
Lock Haven	**156**	41 7N	77 31W
Lockeford	**163**	38 10N	121 9W
Lockeport	**151**	43 47N	65 4W
Lockerbie	**35**	55 7N	3 21W
Lockhart, Austral.	**141**	35 14S	146 40E
Lockhart, U.S.A.	**159**	29 55N	97 40W
Lockhart, L.	**137**	33 15S	119 3E
Lockington	**140**	36 16S	144 34E
Lockport	**156**	43 12N	78 42W
Locle, Le	**50**	47 3N	6 44E
Locminé	**42**	47 54N	2 51W
Locri	**65**	38 14N	16 14E
Locronan	**42**	48 7N	4 15W
Loctudy	**42**	47 50N	4 12W
Lod	**90**	31 57N	34 54E
Lodalskåpa	**71**	61 47N	7 13E
Loddon	**29**	52 32N	1 29E
Lodève	**44**	43 44N	3 19E
Lodge Grass	**160**	45 21N	107 27W
Lodgepole	**158**	41 12N	102 40W
Lodgepole Cr.	**158**	41 20N	104 30W
Lodhran	**94**	29 32N	71 30E
Lodi, Italy	**62**	45 19N	9 30E
Lodi, U.S.A.	**163**	38 12N	121 16W
Lodja	**124**	3 30S	23 23E
Lodji	**103**	1 38S	127 28E
Lodosa	**58**	42 25N	2 4W
Lodose	**73**	58 5N	12 10E
Lödöse	**73**	58 2N	12 9E
Lodwar	**126**	3 10N	35 40E
Łodz	**54**	51 45N	19 27E
Łodz □	**54**	51 45N	19 27E
Loengo	**126**	4 48S	26 30E
Lofer	**52**	47 35N	12 41E
Lofoten	**74**	68 10N	13 0E
Lofoten Is.	**74**	68 30N	15 0E
Lofsen	**72**	62 7N	13 57E
Loftahammar	**73**	57 54N	16 41E
Loftsdalen	**72**	62 10N	13 20E
Loftus	**33**	54 33N	0 52W
Lofty Ra.	**136**	24 15S	119 30E
Loga	**121**	13 37N	3 14E
Logan, Kans., U.S.A.	**158**	39 23N	99 35W
Logan, Ohio, U.S.A.	**156**	39 25N	82 22E
Logan, Utah, U.S.A.	**160**	41 45N	111 50W
Logan, Mt.	**147**	60 41N	140 22W
Logan Pass	**152**	48 41N	113 44W
Logansport	**156**	31 58N	93 58W
Loganville	**162**	39 51N	76 42W
Logo	**123**	5 20N	30 18E
Logo Dergo	**123**	6 10N	29 18E
Logroño	**58**	42 28N	2 32W
Logroño □	**58**	42 28N	2 27W
Logrosán	**57**	39 20N	5 32W
Løgstør	**73**	56 58N	9 14E
Lohardaga	**95**	23 27N	84 45E
Loheia	**91**	15 45N	42 40E
Lohja	**75**	60 12N	24 5E
Loho	**106**	33 33N	114 5E
Lohr	**49**	50 0N	9 35E
Loikaw	**98**	19 40N	97 17E
Loimaa	**75**	60 50N	23 5E
Loir-et-Cher □	**43**	47 40N	1 20E
Loire □	**45**	45 40N	4 5E
Loire-Atlantique □	**42**	47 25N	1 40W
Loire, R.	**42**	47 16N	2 10W
Loiret □	**43**	47 58N	2 10E
Loitz	**48**	53 58N	13 8E
Loja, Ecuador	**174**	3 59S	79 16W
Loja, Spain	**57**	37 10N	4 10W
Lojung	**108**	24 27N	109 36E
Loka	**123**	4 13N	31 0E
Lokandu	**124**	2 30S	25 45E
Løken	**71**	59 48N	11 29E
Lokerane	**128**	24 54S	24 42E
Lokeren	**47**	51 6N	3 59E
Lokhvitsa	**80**	50 25N	33 18E
Lokichokio	**126**	4 19N	34 13E
Lokitaung	**124**	4 12N	35 48E
Lokka	**74**	67 49N	27 45E
Løkken, Denmark	**73**	57 22N	9 41E
Løkken, Norway	**71**	63 8N	9 45E
Loknya	**80**	56 49N	30 4E
Lokobo	**123**	4 20N	30 30E
Lokoja	**121**	7 47N	6 45E
Lokolama	**124**	2 35S	19 50E
Loktung	**100**	18 41N	109 5E
Lokuti	**123**	4 21N	33 15E
Lokwei	**100**	19 12N	110 30E
Lol	**123**	5 28N	29 36E
Lol, R.	**123**	9 0N	28 10E
Lola	**120**	7 52N	8 29W
Lolibai, Gebel	**123**	3 50N	33 50E
Lolimi	**123**	4 35N	34 0E
Loliondo	**124**	2 2S	35 39E
Lolland	**73**	54 45N	11 30E
Lollar	**48**	50 39N	8 43E
Lolo	**160**	46 50N	114 8W
Lolodorf	**121**	3 16N	10 49E
Lolungchung	**126**	30 43N	96 7E
Lom	**67**	43 48N	23 20E
Lom Kao	**100**	16 53N	101 14E
Lom, R.	**66**	43 45N	23 7E
Lom Sak	**100**	16 47N	101 15E
Loma	**160**	47 59N	110 29W
Loma Linda	**163**	34 3N	117 16W
Lomami, R.	**126**	1 0S	24 40E
Lomas de Zamóra	**172**	34 45S	58 25W
Lombadria	**136**	16 31S	122 54E
Lombard	**160**	46 7N	111 28W
Lombardia □	**62**	45 35N	9 45E
Lombardy = Lombardia	**62**	45 35N	9 45E
Lombez	**44**	43 29N	0 55E
Lomblen, I.	**103**	8 30S	123 32E
Lombok, I.	**102**	8 35S	116 20E
Lomé	**121**	6 9N	1 20E
Lomela	**124**	2 5S	23 52E
Lomela, R.	**124**	1 30S	22 50E
Lomello	**62**	45 11N	8 46E
Lometa	**159**	31 15N	98 25W
Lomie	**124**	3 13N	13 38E
Loming	**123**	4 27N	33 40W
Lomma	**73**	55 43N	13 6E
Lomme, R.	**47**	50 8N	5 10E
Lommel	**47**	51 14N	5 19E
Lomond	**152**	50 24N	112 36W
Lomond, gasfield	**19**	57 18N	1 12E
Lomond, L.	**34**	56 8N	4 38W
Lomond, mt.	**139**	30 0S	151 45E
Lomphat	**101**	13 30N	106 59E
Lompobatang, mt.	**103**	5 24S	119 56E
Lompoc	**163**	34 41N	120 32W
Lomsegga	**71**	61 49N	8 21E
Łomza	**54**	53 10N	22 2E
Łomza □	**54**	53 0N	22 30E
Lonan	**106**	34 6N	110 10E
Lonavla	**96**	18 46N	73 29E
Loncoche	**176**	39 20S	72 50W
Londa	**97**	15 30N	74 30E
Londe, La	**45**	43 8N	6 14E
Londerzeel	**47**	51 0N	4 19E
Londiani	**126**	0 10S	35 33E
Londinières	**42**	49 50N	1 25E
London, Can.	**150**	43 0N	81 15W
London, U.K.	**29**	51 30N	0 5W
London, Ky., U.S.A.	**156**	37 11N	84 5W
London, Ohio, U.S.A.	**156**	39 54N	83 28W
London □	**29**	51 30N	0 5W
Londonderry	**38**	55 0N	7 20W

Londonderry, C — Lugano, L. di

Londonderry, C. 136 13 45 S 126 55 E
Londonderry, Co. 38 55 0N 7 20W
Londonderry, I. 176 55 0 S 71 0W
Londrina 173 23 0 S 51 10W
Lone Pine 163 36 35N 118 2W
Long Beach, Calif., U.S.A. 163 33 46N 118 12W
Long Beach, N.Y., U.S.A. 162 40 35N 73 40W
Long Beach, Wash., U.S.A. 160 46 20N 124 1W
Long Bennington 33 52 59N 0 45W
Long Branch 162 40 19N 74 0W
Long Clawson 29 52 51N 0 56W
Long Crendon 29 51 47N 1 0W
Long Eaton 33 52 54N 1 16W
Long Gully 109 35 1 S 138 40 E
Long I., Austral. 138 22 8 S 149 53 E
Long I., Bahamas 167 23 20N 75 10W
Long I., Can. 150 44 23N 66 19W
Long I., Ireland 39 51 30N 9 35W
Long I., P.N.G. 135 5 20 S 147 5 E
Long I., U.S.A. 162 40 50N 73 20W
Long I. Sd. 162 41 10N 73 0W
Long Itchington 28 52 16N 1 24W
Long L. 150 49 30N 86 50W
Long, L. 34 56 4N 4 50W
Long L. 162 43 57N 74 25W
Long Melford 29 52 5N 0 44 E
Long Mt. 31 52 38N 3 7W
Long Mynd 23 52 35N 2 50W
Long Pine 158 43 33N 99 50W
Long Pocket 138 18 30 S 146 0 E
Long Pt., Can. 151 48 47N 58 46W
Long Pt., N.Z. 143 46 34 S 169 36 E
Long Preston 32 54 0N 2 16W
Long Ra. 151 49 30N 57 30W
Long Range Mts 151 48 0N 58 30W
Long Reef 136 13 55 S 125 45 E
Long Str. 12 70 0N 175 0 E
Long Sutton 29 52 47N 0 9 E
Long Thanh 101 10 47N 106 57 E
Long Xuyen 101 10 19N 105 28 E
Longá 69 36 53N 21 55 E
Longa I. 36 57 45N 5 50W
Longarone 63 46 15N 12 18 E
Longburn 142 40 23 S 175 35 E
Longdam 99 28 12N 98 16 E
Longeau 43 47 47N 5 20 E
Longford, Austral. 138 41 32 S 147 3 E
Longford, Ireland 38 53 43N 7 50W
Longford, U.K. 28 51 53N 2 14W
Longford □ 38 53 42N 7 45W
Longforgan 35 56 28N 3 8W
Longframlington 35 55 18N 1 47W
Longhawan 102 2 15N 114 55 E
Longhorsley 35 55 15N 1 46W
Longhoughton 35 55 26N 1 38W
Longido 126 2 43 S 36 35 E
Longiram 102 0 5 S 115 45 E
Longkin 98 25 39N 96 22 E
Longlac 150 49 45N 86 25W
Longlier 47 49 52N 5 27 E
Longling 99 24 42N 98 58 E
Longmont 158 40 10N 105 4W
Longnawan 102 21 50N 114 55 E
Longobucco 65 39 27N 16 37 E
Longone, R. 117 10 0N 15 40 E
Longreach 138 23 28 S 144 14 E
Longridge 32 53 50N 2 37W
Long's Peak 160 40 20N 105 50W
Longside 37 57 30N 1 57W
Longton, Austral. 138 21 0 S 145 55 E
Longton, Lancs., U.K. 32 53 43N 2 48W
Longton, Stafford, U.K. 32 53 00N 2 8W
Longtown 32 55 1N 2 59W
Longué 42 47 22N 0 8W
Longueau 42 49 52N 2 22 E
Longuyon 43 49 27N 5 35 E
Longview, Can. 152 50 32N 114 10W
Longview, Tex., U.S.A. 159 32 30N 94 45W
Longview, Wash., U.S.A. 160 46 9N 122 58W
Longvilly 47 50 2N 5 50 E
Longwy 43 49 30N 5 45 E
Lonigo 63 45 23N 11 22 E
Loning 106 34 28N 111 42 E
Löningen 48 54 43N 7 44 E
Lonja, R. 63 45 30N 16 40 E
Lonkor Tso 95 32 40N 83 15 E
Lonoke 159 34 48N 91 57W
Lonouaille 44 46 30N 1 35 E
Lons-le-Saunier 43 46 40N 5 31 E
Lønsdal 74 66 46N 15 26 E
Lønstrup 73 57 29N 9 47 E
Looc 103 12 20N 112 5 E
Lookout, C., Can. 150 55 18N 83 56W
Lookout, C., U.S.A. 157 34 30N 76 30W
Lookout, Pt. 162 38 2N 76 21W
Loolmalasin, mt. 126 3 0 S 35 53 E
Loomis 153 49 15N 108 45W
Loon L. 153 44 50N 77 15W
Loon Lake 153 54 2N 109 10W
Loon-op-Zand 47 51 38N 5 5 E
Loon, R., Alta., Can. 152 57 8N 115 3W
Loon, R., Man., Can. 153 55 53N 101 59W
Loongana 137 30 52 S 127 5 E
Loop Hd. 39 52 34N 9 55W
Loosduinen 46 52 3N 4 14 E
Lop Buri 100 14 48N 100 37 E
Lop Nor 105 40 20N 90 10 E
Lopare 66 44 39N 18 46 E
Lopatin 83 43 50N 47 35 E
Lopatina, G. 77 50 0N 143 30 E
Lopaye 123 6 37N 33 40 E
Lopera 57 37 56N 4 14W
Lopez 162 41 27N 76 20W
Lopez C. 124 0 47 S 8 40 E
Lop'ing, Kiangsi, China 109 28 57N 117 5 E
Lop'ing, Yunnan, China 108 24 56N 104 20 E
Lopodi 123 5 5N 33 15 E
Loppem 47 51 9N 3 12 E
Loppersum 46 53 20N 6 44 E
Lopphavet 74 70 27N 21 15 E
Lora Cr. 139 28 10 S 135 22 E
Lora del Río 57 37 39N 5 33W
Lora, La 56 42 45N 4 0W
Lora, R. 93 32 0N 67 15 E
Lorain 156 41 20N 82 5W
Loralai 94 30 29N 68 30 E
Lorca 59 37 41N 1 42W
Lord Howe I. 130 31 33 S 159 6 E
Lordsburg 161 32 15N 108 45W
Lorengau 135 2 1 S 147 15 E
Loreto, Brazil 170 7 5 S 45 30W
Loreto, Italy 63 43 26N 13 36 E
Loreto, Mexico 164 26 1N 111 21W
Loreto Aprutina 63 42 24N 13 59 E
Lorgues 45 43 28N 6 22 E
Lorica 174 9 14N 75 49W
Lorient 42 47 45N 3 23W
Lorne, Austral. 140 38 33 S 143 59 E
Lorne, U.K. 34 56 26N 5 10W
Lorne, Firth of 34 56 20N 5 40W
Lörrach 49 47 36N 7 38 E
Lorraine 43 49 0N 6 0 E
Lorrainville 150 47 21N 79 23W
Los Alamos, Calif., U.S.A. 163 34 44N 120 17W
Los Alamos, N. Mex., U.S.A. 161 35 57N 106 17W
Los Altos 163 37 23N 122 7W
Los Andes 172 32 50 S 70 40W
Los Angeles 172 37 28 S 72 23W
Los Angeles 163 34 0N 118 10W
Los Angeles Aqueduct 163 35 25N 118 0W
Los Banos 163 37 8N 120 56W
Los Barrios 57 36 11N 5 30W
Los Blancos, Argent. 172 23 45 S 62 30W
Los Blancos, Spain 59 37 38N 0 49W
Los Gatos 163 37 15N 121 59W
Los, Îles de 120 9 30N 13 50W
Los Lamentos 164 30 36N 105 50W
Los Lunas 161 34 55N 106 47W
Los Mochis 164 25 45N 109 5W
Los Monegros 58 41 29N 0 3W
Los Muertos, Punta de 59 36 57N 1 54W
Los Olivos 163 34 40N 120 7W
Los Palacios 166 22 35N 83 15W
Los Palacios y Villafranca 57 37 10N 5 55W
Los Reyes 164 19 21N 99 7W
Los Roques, Is. 167 11 50N 66 45W
Los Santos de Maimona 57 38 37N 6 22W
Los Testigos, Is. 174 11 23N 63 6W
Los Vilos 172 32 0 S 71 30W
Los Yébenes 57 39 36N 3 55W
Loshan, Honan, China 109 32 12N 114 32 E
Loshan, Szechwan, China 108 29 34N 103 44 E
Loshkalakh 77 62 45N 147 20 E
Lošinj, I. 63 44 55N 14 45 E
Losser 46 52 16N 7 1 E
Lossiemouth 37 57 43N 3 17W
Lostwithiel 30 50 24N 4 41W
Losuia 135 8 30 S 151 4 E
Lot □ 44 44 39N 1 40 E
Lot-et-Garonne □ 44 44 22N 0 30 E
Lot, R. 44 44 18N 0 20 E
Lota, Austral. 108 27 28 S 153 11 E
Lota, Chile 172 37 5 S 73 10W
Løten 71 60 51N 11 21 E
Lothian, (□) 26 55 55N 3 35W
Lothiers 43 46 42N 1 33 E
Lotien 108 25 29N 106 39 E
Lot'ien 109 30 47N 115 20 E
Lot'ing 107 39 26N 118 56 E
Loting 109 22 46N 111 34 E
Lötschberg 49 46 25N 7 53 E
Lotschbergtunnel 50 46 26N 7 43 E
Lottefors 72 61 25N 16 24 E
Lotung, China 100 18 44N 109 9 E
Lotung, Taiwan 109 24 41N 121 46 E
Lotz'u 108 25 19N 102 18 E
Lotzukou 107 43 44N 130 20 E
Lotzwil 50 47 12N 7 48 E
Loudéac 42 48 11N 2 47W
Loudon 157 35 41N 84 22W
Loudun 42 47 0N 0 5 E
Loué 42 47 59N 0 9W
Loue, R. 42 47 4N 6 10 E
Louga 120 15 45N 16 5W
Loughborough 28 52 46N 1 11W
Loughbrickland 38 54 19N 6 19W
Loughmore 39 52 45N 7 50W
Loughor 31 51 39N 4 5W
Loughrea 39 53 11N 8 33W
Loughros More, B. 38 54 48N 8 30W
Louhans 45 46 38N 5 12 E
Louis Gentil 118 32 16N 8 31W
Louis Trichardt 125 23 0 S 29 55 E
Louis XIV, Pte. 150 54 37N 79 45W
Louisa 156 38 5N 82 40W
Louisbourg 151 45 55N 60 0W
Louisbourg Nat. Historic Park 151 45 58N 60 20W
Louisburgh 38 53 46N 9 49W
Louise I. 152 52 55N 131 40W
Louiseville 150 46 20N 73 0W
Louisiade Arch. 135 11 10 S 153 0 E
Louisiana 158 39 25N 91 0W
Louisiana □ 159 30 50N 92 0W
Louisville, Ky., U.S.A. 156 38 15N 85 45W
Louisville, Miss., U.S.A. 159 33 7N 89 3W
Loulay 44 46 3N 0 30W
Loulé 57 37 9N 8 0W
Lount L. 153 50 10N 94 20W
Louny 52 50 20N 13 48 E
Loup City 158 41 19N 98 57W
Loupe, La 42 48 29N 1 1 E
Lourdes 44 43 6N 0 3W
Lourdes-de-Blanc-Sablon 151 51 24N 57 12W
Lourenço-Marques, B. de 129 25 50 S 32 45 E
Lourenço-Marques = Maputo 129 25 58 S 32 32 E
Loures 57 38 50N 9 9W
Lourinhã 57 39 14N 9 17W
Louroux Béconnais, Le 42 47 30N 0 55W
Lousã 56 40 7N 8 14W
Louth, Austral. 141 30 30 S 145 8 E
Louth, Ireland 38 53 47N 6 33W
Louth, U.K. 33 53 23N 0 0W
Louth □ 38 53 55N 6 30W
Louti 109 27 45N 111 58 E
Loutrá Aidhipsoú 69 38 54N 23 2 E
Loutráki 69 38 0N 22 57 E
Louveigné 47 50 32N 5 42 E
Louvière, La 47 50 27N 4 10 E
Louviers 42 49 12N 1 10 E
Lovat, R. 80 56 30N 31 20 E
Love 153 53 29N 104 10W
Loveland 158 40 27N 105 4W
Lovell 160 44 51N 108 20W
Lovelock 160 40 17N 118 25W
Lóvere 62 45 50N 10 4 E
Loviisa = Lovisa 75 60 31N 26 20 E
Loving 159 32 17N 104 4W
Lovington 159 33 0N 103 20W
Lovios 56 41 55N 8 4W
Lovisa (Loviisa) 75 60 28N 26 12 E
Lovosice 52 50 30N 14 2 E
Lovran 63 45 18N 14 15 E
Lovrin 66 45 58N 20 48 E
Lövstabukten 72 60 35N 17 45 E
Low Pt. 137 32 25 S 127 25 E
Low Rocky Pt. 133 42 59 S 145 29 E
Lowa 124 1 25 S 25 47 E
Lowa, R. 126 1 15 S 27 40 E
Lowell 162 42 38N 71 19W
Lower Arrow L. 152 49 40N 118 5W
Lower Austria = Niederösterreich 52 48 25N 15 40 E
Lower Beeding 29 51 2N 0 15W
Lower Hermitage 109 34 49 S 138 46 E
Lower Hutt 142 41 10 S 174 55 E
Lower L. 160 41 17N 120 3W
Lower Lake 160 38 56N 122 36W
Lower Neguac 151 47 20N 65 10W
Lower Post 152 59 58N 128 30W
Lower Sackville 151 44 45N 63 43W
Lower Saxony = Niedersachsen 48 52 45N 9 0 E
Lower Seal, L. 150 56 30N 74 23W
Lower Woolgar 138 19 47 S 143 27 E
Lowes Water L. 32 54 35N 3 23W
Lowestoft 29 52 29N 1 44 E
Lowick 35 55 38N 1 57W
Łowicz 54 52 6N 19 55 E
Lowther Hills 35 55 20N 3 40W
Lowville 162 43 48N 75 30W
Loxton 140 34 28 S 140 31 E
Loyal L. 37 58 24N 4 20W
Loyalty Is. 130 21 0 S 167 30 E
Loyang 106 34 41N 112 28 E
Loyauté, Îles 130 21 0 S 167 30 E
Loyeh 108 24 48N 106 34 E
Loyev 80 57 7N 30 40 E
Loyoro 126 3 22N 34 14 E
Loyüan 109 26 30N 119 33 E
Loz 63 45 43N 14 14 E
Lozère □ 44 44 35N 3 30 E
Loznica 66 44 32N 19 14 E
Lozovaya 82 49 0N 36 27 E
Lozva, R. 84 59 36N 62 20 E
Lu 98 45 0N 8 29 E
Lü-Tao 109 22 47N 121 20 E
Luabo 147 18 30 S 36 10 E
Luacano 124 11 15 S 21 37 E
Lualaba, R. 126 5 45 S 26 50 E
Luampa 127 15 4 S 24 20 E
Luan 103 6 10N 124 25 E
Luan Chau 100 21 38N 103 24 E
Luan Ho, R. 107 39 25N 119 15 E
Luanch'eng 106 37 53N 114 39 E
Luanda 124 8 58 S 13 9 E
Luang Doi 100 18 30N 101 0 E
Luang Prabang 100 19 45N 102 10 E
Luang Thale 101 7 30N 100 15 E
Luangwa, R. 125 14 25 S 30 25 E
Luangwa Val. 127 13 30 S 31 30 E
Luanho 107 40 56N 117 42 E
Luanhsien 107 39 45N 118 44 E
Luanping 107 40 56N 117 42 E
Luanshya 127 13 3 S 28 28 E
Luapula □ 127 11 0 S 29 0 E
Luapula, R. 127 12 0 S 28 50 E
Luarca 56 43 32N 6 32W
Luashi 127 10 50 S 23 36 E
Lubalo 124 9 10 S 19 15 E
Luban 54 51 5N 15 15 E
Lubana, Osero 80 56 45N 27 0 E
Lubang Is. 103 13 50N 120 12 E
Lubartów 54 51 28N 22 42 E
Lubawa 54 53 30N 19 48 E
Lubban 90 32 9N 35 14 E
Lubbeek 47 50 54N 4 50 E
Lübben 48 51 56N 13 54 E
Lübbenau 48 51 49N 13 59 E
Lubbock 159 33 40N 102 0W
Lubcroy 37 57 58N 4 47W
Lübeck 48 53 52N 10 41 E
Lübecker Bucht 48 54 3N 11 0 E
Lubefu 126 4 47 S 24 27 E
Lubefu, R. 126 4 47 S 24 27 E
Lubero = Luofu 126 0 1 S 29 15 E
Lubicon L. 152 56 23N 115 56W
Lubien Kujawski 54 52 23N 19 9 E
Lubin 54 51 24N 16 11 E
Lublin 54 51 12N 22 38 E
Lublin □ 54 51 5N 22 30 E
Lubliniec 54 50 43N 18 45 E
Lubny 80 50 3N 32 58 E
Lubok Antu 102 1 3N 111 50 E
Lubon 54 52 21N 16 51 E
Lubongola 126 2 35 S 27 50 E
Lubotin 53 49 17N 20 53 E
Lubraniec 54 52 33N 18 50 E
Lubsko 54 51 45N 14 57 E
Lübtheen 48 53 18N 11 4 E
Lubuagan 103 17 21N 121 10 E
Lubudi 124 6 50 S 21 20 E
Lubudi, R. 127 9 30 S 25 0 E
Lubuhanbilik 102 2 33N 100 14 E
Lubuk Linggau 102 3 15 S 102 55 E
Lubuk Sikaping 102 0 10N 100 15 E
Lubumbashi 127 11 32 S 27 28 E
Lubunda 126 5 12 S 26 41 E
Lubungu 127 14 35 S 26 24 E
Lubutu 126 0 45 S 26 30 E
Luc An Chau 100 22 6N 104 43 E
Luc-en-Diois 45 44 36N 5 28 E
Luc, Le 45 43 23N 6 21 E
Lucan 38 53 21N 6 27W
Lucania, Mt. 147 60 48N 141 25W
Lucca 62 43 50N 10 30 E
Luccens 50 46 43N 6 51 E
Luce Bay 138 54 45N 4 48W
Lucea 166 18 25N 78 10W
Lucedale 157 30 55N 88 34W
Lucena, Phil. 103 13 56N 121 37 E
Lucena, Spain 57 37 27N 4 31W
Lucena del Cid 58 40 9N 0 17W
Lučenec 53 48 18N 19 42 E
Lucera 65 41 30N 15 20 E
Lucerne = Luzern 51 47 3N 8 18 E
Lucerne Valley 163 34 27N 116 57W
Lucero 164 30 49N 106 30W
Luchai 108 24 33N 109 48 E
Luchena, R. 59 37 50N 2 0W
Luch'eng 106 36 18N 113 15 E
Lucheringo, R. 127 12 0 S 36 5 E
Luch'i 109 28 17N 110 10 E
Luchiang, China 109 31 14N 117 17 E
Luchiang, Taiwan 109 24 1N 120 22 E
Luchou 108 28 53N 105 22 E
Lüchow 48 52 58N 11 8 E
Luch'uan 109 22 20N 110 14 E
Lucindale 93 36 59 S 140 23 E
Lucira 125 14 0 S 12 35 E
Luckau 48 51 50N 13 43 E
Luckenwalde 48 52 5N 13 11 E
Lucknow 95 26 50N 81 0 E
Lucomagno, Paso del 51 46 34N 8 49 E
Luçon 44 46 28N 1 10W
Luda Kamchiya, R. 67 42 50N 27 0 E
Ludbreg 63 46 15N 16 38 E
Lüdenscheid 48 51 13N 7 37 E
Lüderitz 128 26 41 S 15 8 E
Ludewa □ 127 10 0 S 34 50 E
Ludgershall 28 51 15N 1 38W
Ludgvan 30 50 9N 5 30W
Ludhiana 94 30 57N 75 56 E
Lüdinghausen 48 51 46N 7 28 E
Ludington 156 43 58N 86 27W
Ludlow, U.K. 28 52 23N 2 42W
Ludlow, Calif., U.S.A. 163 34 43N 116 10W
Ludlow, Vt., U.S.A. 162 43 25N 72 40W
Luduş 70 46 29N 24 5 E
Ludvika 72 60 8N 15 14 E
Ludwigsburg 49 48 53N 9 11 E
Ludwigshafen 49 49 27N 8 27 E
Ludwigslust 48 53 19N 11 28 E
Ludza 80 56 32N 27 43 E
Lue 141 32 38 S 149 50 E
Luebo 124 5 21 S 21 17 E
Lüehyang 106 33 20N 106 3 E
Lueki 126 3 20 S 25 48 E
Luena, Zaïre 127 9 28 S 25 43 E
Luena, Zambia 127 10 40 S 30 25 E
Luepa 174 5 43N 61 31W
Lufeng, Kwangtung, China 109 23 2N 115 37 E
Lufeng, Yunnan, China 108 25 10N 102 5 E
Lufira R. 124 9 30 S 27 0 E
Lufkin 159 31 25N 94 40W
Lufupa 127 10 32 S 24 50 E
Luga 80 58 40N 29 55 E
Luga, R. 80 59 5N 28 30 E
Lugano 51 46 0N 8 57 E
Lugano, L. di 51 46 0N 9 0 E

Lugansk McIlwraith Ra

Lugansk = Voroshilovgrad 83 48 35N 39 29 E
Lugard's Falls 126 3 6S 38 41 E
Lugela 127 16 25S 36 43 E
Lugenda, R. 127 12 35S 36 50 E
Lugh Ganana 91 3 48N 42 40 E
Lugnaquilla, Mt. 39 52 48N 6 28W
Lugnvik 72 62 56N 17 55 E
Lugo, Italy 63 44 25N 11 53 E
Lugo, Spain 56 43 2N 7 35W
Lugo □ 56 43 0N 7 30W
Lugoj 66 45 42N 21 57 E
Lugones 56 43 26N 5 50W
Lugovoy 76 43 0N 72 20 E
Lugovoye 85 42 55N 72 43 E
Lugwardine 28 52 4N 2 38W
Luhe, R. 48 53 7N 10 0 E
Luhsi, Yunan, China 108 24 31N 103 46 E
Luhsi, Yunnan, China 108 24 27N 98 36 E
Luhuo 108 31 24N 100 41 E
Lui 106 33 52N 115 28 E
Luiana 125 17 25S 22 30W
Luichart L. 37 57 36N 4 43W
Luichow Pen. = Leichou Pantao 108 20 40N 110 5 E
Luing I. 34 56 15N 5 40W
Luino 62 46 0N 8 42 E
Luis 164 26 36N 109 11W
Luís Correia 170 3 0S 41 35W
Luís Gomes 171 6 25S 38 23W
Luís Gonçalves 170 5 37S 50 25W
Luisa 124 7 40S 22 30 E
Luiza 124 7 40S 22 30 E
Luizi 126 6 0S 27 25 E
Luján 172 34 45S 59 5W
Lukanga Swamp 127 14 30S 27 40 E
Lukenie, R. 124 3 0S 18 50 E
Lukhisaral 95 27 11N 86 5 E
Lukolela 124 1 10S 17 12 E
Lukosi 127 18 30S 26 30 E
Lukovit 67 43 13N 24 11 E
Lukoyanov 81 55 2N 44 20 E
Lukuhu 108 27 46N 100 50 E
Lukulu 125 14 35S 23 25 E
Lula 126 0 30N 25 10 E
Lule, R. 74 65 35N 22 10 E
Luleå 74 65 35N 22 10 E
Lüleburgaz 67 41 23N 27 28 E
Luliang 108 25 3N 103 39 E
Luling 159 29 45N 97 40W
Lulonga, R. 124 1 0N 19 0 E
Lulua, R. 124 6 30S 22 50 E
Luluabourg = Kananga 124 5 55S 22 18 E
Lulung 107 39 55N 118 57 E
Lumai 125 13 20S 21 25 E
Lumajang 103 8 8S 113 16 E
Lumbala, Angola 125 12 36S 22 30 E
Lumbala, Angola 125 14 18S 21 18 E
Lumberton, Miss., U.S.A. 159 31 4N 89 28W
Lumberton, N. Mex., U.S.A. 161 36 58N 106 57W
Lumberton, N.C., U.S.A. 157 34 37N 78 59W
Lumbres 43 50 40N 2 5 E
Lumbwa 126 0 12S 35 28 E
Lumby 152 50 10N 118 50W
Lumding 98 25 46N 93 10 E
Lumege 125 11 45S 20 50 E
Lumeyen 123 4 55N 33 28 E
Lumi 135 3 30S 142 2 E
Lummen 47 50 59N 5 12 E
Lumphanan 37 57 8N 2 41W
Lumsden, N.Z. 143 45 44S 168 27 E
Lumsden, U.K. 37 57 16N 2 51W
Lumut 101 4 13N 100 37 E
Lumut, Tg. 102 3 50S 105 58 E
Lunan 108 24 47N 103 16 E
Lunan B. 37 56 40N 2 25W
Lunavada 94 23 8N 73 37 E
Lunca 70 47 22N 25 1 E
Lund, Norway 74 68 42N 18 9 E
Lund, Sweden 73 55 41N 13 12 E
Lund, U.S.A. 160 38 53N 115 0W
Lunda 124 9 40S 20 12 E
Lundazi 125 12 20S 33 7 E
Lunde 71 59 17N 9 5 E
Lunderskov 73 55 29N 9 19 E
Lundi, R. 127 21 15S 31 25 E
Lundu 102 1 40N 109 50 E
Lundy, I. 30 51 10N 4 41W
Lune, R. 32 54 0N 2 51W
Lüneburg 48 53 15N 10 23 E
Lüneburg Heath = Lüneburger Heide 48 53 0N 10 0 E
Lüneburger Heide 48 53 0N 10 0 E
Lunel 45 43 39N 4 9 E
Lünen 48 51 36N 7 31 E
Lunenburg 151 44 22N 64 18W
Lunéville 43 48 36N 6 30 E
Lung Chiang, R. 108 24 30N 109 15 E
Lunga, R. 127 13 0S 26 33 E
Lungan 108 23 11N 107 41 E
Lungch'ang 108 29 20N 105 19 E
Lungch'ih 108 29 25N 103 24 E
Lungchou 108 22 24N 106 50 E
Lungch'üan 109 28 5N 119 7 E
Lungch'uan, Kwangtung, China 109 24 6N 115 15 E
Lungch'uan, Yunnan, China 108 24 16N 97 58 E
Lungern 50 46 48N 8 10 E
Lungholt 74 63 35N 18 10 E
Lunghsi 106 35 3N 104 38 E
Lunghsien 106 34 47N 107 0 E
Lunghua 107 41 18N 117 42 E
Lunghui 109 27 18N 110 52 E
Lungi Airport 120 8 40N 16 47 E
Lungk'ou 107 37 42N 120 21 E
Lungkuan 106 40 45N 115 43 E
Lungkukang 108 32 18N 99 7 E
Lungleh 98 22 55N 92 45 E
Lungli 108 26 27N 106 58 E
Lunglin 108 24 43N 105 26 E
Lungling 108 24 38N 98 35 E
Lungmen 109 23 44N 114 15 E
Lungming 108 23 4N 107 14 E
Lungnan 109 24 54N 114 47 E
Lungngo 98 21 57N 93 36 E
Lungshan 108 29 27N 109 23 E
Lungsheng 109 25 48N 110 0 E
Lungte 106 35 38N 106 6 E
Lungyen 109 25 9N 117 0 E
Lungyu 109 29 2N 119 10 E
Luni 94 26 0N 73 6 E
Luni, R. 94 25 40N 72 20 E
Luninets 80 52 15N 27 0 E
Luning 163 38 30N 118 10W
Lunino 81 53 35N 45 6 E
Lunna Ness 36 60 27N 1 4W
Lunner 71 60 19N 10 35 E
Lunsemfwa Falls 127 14 30S 29 6 E
Lunsemfwa, R. 127 14 50S 30 10 E
Lunteren 46 52 5N 5 38 E
Luofu 126 0 1S 29 15 E
Luozi 124 4 54S 14 0 E
Lupeni 70 45 21N 23 13 E
Łupków 53 49 15N 22 4 E
Lupundu 127 14 18S 26 45 E
Luque, Parag. 172 25 19S 57 25W
Luque, Spain 57 37 35N 4 16W
Luray 156 38 39N 78 26W
Lure 43 47 40N 6 30 E
Luremo 124 8 30S 17 50 E
Lurgainn L. 36 58 1N 5 15W
Lurgan 38 54 28N 6 20W
Luristan 92 33 20N 47 0 E
Lusaka 127 15 28S 28 16 E
Lusambo 126 4 58S 23 28 E
Luseland 153 52 5N 109 24W
Lushan, Honan, China 106 33 45N 113 10 E
Lushan, Kweichow, China 108 26 33N 107 58 E
Lushan, Szechwan, China 108 30 10N 102 59 E
Lushih 106 34 4N 110 2 E
Lushnja 68 40 55N 19 41 E
Lushoto 126 4 47S 38 20 E
Lushoto □ 126 4 45S 38 20 E
Lushui 108 25 51N 98 55 E
Lüshun 107 38 48N 121 16 E
Lusignan 44 46 26N 0 8 E
Lusigny-sur-Barse 43 48 16N 4 15 E
Lusk, Ireland 38 53 32N 6 10W
Lusk, U.S.A. 158 42 47N 104 27W
Luss 34 56 6N 4 40W
Lussac-les-Châteaux 44 46 24N 0 43 E
Lussanvira 171 20 42S 51 7W
Lüta 107 38 55N 121 40 E
Luti 108 7 14S 157 0 E
Luting 108 29 56N 102 12 E
Luton 29 51 53N 0 24W
Lutong 102 4 30N 114 0 E
Lutry 50 46 31N 6 42 E
Lutsk 80 50 50N 25 15 E
Lutterworth 28 52 28N 1 12W
Luverne 158 43 35N 96 12W
Luvua 127 8 48S 25 17 E
Luwegu, R. 127 9 30S 36 20 E
Luwingu, Mt. 124 10 15S 30 2 E
Luwuk 103 10 0S 122 40 E
Luxembourg 47 49 37N 6 9 E
Luxembourg □ 47 49 58N 5 30 E
Luxembourg ■ 47 50 0N 6 0 E
Luxeuil-les-Bains 43 47 49N 6 24 E
Luxor = El Uqsur 122 25 41N 32 38 E
Luy de Béarn, R. 44 43 39N 0 48W
Luy de France, R. 44 43 39N 0 48W
Luy, R. 44 43 39N 1 9W
Luyksgestel 47 51 17N 5 20 E
Luz, Brazil 171 19 48S 45 40W
Luz, France 44 42 53N 0 1 E
Luzern 51 47 3N 8 18 E
Luzern □ 50 47 2N 7 55 E
Luzerne 162 41 17N 75 54W
Luziânia 171 16 20S 48 0W
Luzilândia 170 3 28S 42 22W
Luzon, I. 103 16 0N 121 0 E
Luzy 43 46 47N 3 58 E
Luzzi 65 39 28N 16 17 E
Lvov 80 49 40N 24 0 E
Lwówek 54 52 28N 16 10 E
Lwówek Ślaşki 54 51 7N 15 38 E
Lyakhovichi 80 53 2N 26 32 E
Lyakhovskiye, Ostrova 77 73 40N 141 0 E
Lyaki 83 40 34N 47 22 E
Lyall Mt. 142 45 16S 167 32 E
* Lyallpur 94 31 30N 73 5 E
Lyalya, R. 84 59 9N 61 29 E
Lyaskovets 67 43 6N 25 44 E
Lybster 37 58 18N 3 16W
Lychen 48 53 13N 13 20 E
Lyckeby 73 56 12N 15 37 E
Lycksele 74 64 38N 18 40 E
Lydd 29 50 57N 0 56 E
Lydda = Lod 90 31 57N 34 54 E
Lydenburg 129 25 10S 30 29 E
Lydford 30 50 38N 4 7W
Lydham 28 52 31N 2 59W
Lyell 143 41 48S 172 4 E
Lyell I. 152 52 40N 131 35W
Lyell, oilfield 19 60 55N 1 12 E
Lyell Range 143 41 38S 172 20 E
Lygnern 73 57 30N 12 15 E
Lykens 162 40 34N 76 42W
Lykling 71 59 42N 5 12 E
Lyman 160 41 24N 110 15W
Lyme Bay 23 50 36N 2 55W
Lyme Regis 30 50 44N 2 57W
Lyminge 29 51 7N 1 6 E
Lymington 28 50 46N 1 32W
Lymm 32 53 23N 2 30W
Lympne 29 51 4N 1 2 E
Lynchburg 156 37 23N 79 10W
Lynd, R. 138 16 28S 143 18 E
Lynd Ra. 139 25 30S 149 20 E
Lynden 160 48 56N 122 32W
Lyndhurst, N.S.W., Austral. 138 33 41S 149 2 E
Lyndhurst, Queens., Austral. 138 19 12S 144 20 E
Lyndhurst, S. Australia, Austral. 139 30 15S 138 18 E
Lyndhurst, U.K. 28 50 53N 1 33W
Lyndon, R. 137 23 29S 114 6 E
Lyneham 28 51 30N 1 57W
Lyngdal, Agder, Norway 71 58 8N 7 7 E
Lyngdal, Buskerud, Norway 71 59 54N 9 32 E
Lynher Reef 136 15 27S 121 55 E
Lynmouth 30 51 14N 3 50W
Lynn 162 42 28N 70 57W
Lynn Canal 152 58 50N 135 20W
Lynn L. 153 56 30N 101 40W
Lynn Lake 153 56 51N 101 3W
Lynton 30 51 14N 3 50W
Lyntupy 80 55 4N 26 23 E
Lynx L. 153 62 25N 106 15W
Lyø 73 55 3N 10 9 E
Lyon 45 45 46N 4 50 E
Lyonnais 45 45 45N 4 15 E
Lyons, Colo., U.S.A. 158 40 17N 105 15W
Lyons, Ga., U.S.A. 157 32 10N 82 15W
Lyons, Kans., U.S.A. 158 38 24N 98 13W
Lyons, N.Y., U.S.A. 162 43 3N 77 0W
Lyons = Lyon 45 45 46N 4 50 E
Lyons Falls 162 43 37N 75 22W
Lyons, R. 137 25 2S 115 9 E
Lyrestad 73 58 48N 14 4 E
Lysá 52 50 11N 14 51 E
Lysekil 73 58 17N 11 26 E
Lyskovo 81 56 0N 45 3 E
Lyss 50 47 4N 7 19 E
Lysva 84 58 07N 57 49 E
Lysvik 72 60 1N 13 9 E
Lytchett Minster 28 50 44N 2 3W
Lytham St. Anne's 32 53 45N 2 58W
Lythe 33 54 30N 0 40W
Lytle 159 29 14N 98 46W
Lyttelton 143 43 35S 172 44 E
Lytton 152 50 13N 121 31W
Lyuban 80 59 16N 31 18 E
Lyubim 81 58 20N 40 50 E
Lyubimets 67 41 50N 26 5 E
Lyubomi 81 51 10N 24 2 E
Lyubotin 82 50 0N 36 4 E
Lyubytino 80 58 50N 33 16 E
Lyudinovo 80 53 52N 34 28 E

M

Ma, R. 100 19 47N 105 56 E
Ma'ad 90 32 37N 35 36 E
Maam Cross 38 53 28N 9 32W
Maamba 128 17 17S 26 28 E
Ma'an 92 30 12N 35 44 E
Maanshan 109 31 40N 118 30 E
Maarheeze 47 51 19N 5 36 E
Maarianhamina 75 60 5N 19 55 E
Maarn 47 52 3N 5 22 E
Maarssen 46 52 9N 5 2 E
Maartensdijk 46 52 9N 5 10 E
Maas 38 54 49N 8 21W
Maas, R. 47 51 48N 4 55 E
Maasbracht 47 51 9N 5 54 E
Maasbree 47 51 22N 6 3 E
Maasdan 46 51 48N 4 34 E
Maasdijk 46 51 58N 4 13 E
Maaseik 47 51 6N 5 45 E
Maasin 102 10 5N 124 55 E
Maasland 46 51 57N 4 16 E
Maasniel 47 51 12N 6 1 E
Maassluis 47 51 56N 4 16 E
Maastricht 47 50 50N 5 40 E
Maatin-es-Sarra 117 21 45N 22 0 E
Maave 129 21 4S 34 47 E
Mabein 98 23 29N 96 37 E
Mabel L. 152 50 35N 118 43W
Mabel, oilfield 19 58 6N 1 36 E
Mabenge 126 4 15N 24 12 E
Mablethorpe 33 53 21N 0 14 E
Mabrouk 121 19 29N 1 15W
Mabton 127 46 13N 120 1W
Mac Bac 101 9 46N 106 7 E
Mc Grath 147 62 58N 155 40W
Macachín 172 37 10S 63 43W
Macadam Ra. 136 14 40S 129 50 E
Macaé 173 22 20S 41 55W
Macaguane 174 6 35N 71 43W
Macaíba 170 5 15S 35 21W
Macajuba 171 12 9S 40 22W
McAlester 159 34 57N 95 40W
Macamic 150 48 45N 79 0W
Macão 57 39 35N 7 59W
Macao = Macau ■ 109 22 16N 113 35 E
Macapá 175 0 5N 51 10W
Macarani 171 15 33S 40 24W
Macarena, Serranía de la 174 2 45N 73 55W
Macarthur 140 38 5S 142 0 E
McArthur, R. 136 16 45S 136 0 E
McArthur River 138 16 27S 137 7 E
Macau 170 5 0S 36 40W
Macau ■ 109 22 16N 113 35 E
Macaúbas 171 13 2S 42 42W
McBride 152 53 20N 120 10W
McCamey 159 31 8N 102 15W
McCammon 160 42 41N 112 11W
McCarthy 147 61 25N 143 0W
McCauley I. 152 53 40N 130 15W
Macclesfield 32 53 16N 2 9W
McClintock 153 57 50N 94 10W
McClintock Chan. 148 72 0N 102 0W
McClintock Ra., Mts. 136 18 44S 127 38 E
McCloud 160 41 14N 122 5W
McCluer Gulf 103 2 20S 133 0 E
McCluer I. 136 11 5S 133 0 E
McClure, L. 163 37 35N 120 16W
McClusky 158 47 30N 100 31W
McComb 159 31 20N 90 30W
McConnell Creek 152 56 53N 126 30W
McCook 158 40 15N 100 35W
McCulloch 152 49 45N 119 15W
McCusker, R. 153 55 32N 108 39W
McDame 152 59 44N 128 59W
McDermitt 160 42 0N 117 45W
McDonald I. 11 54 0S 73 0 E
Macdonald L. 137 23 30S 129 0 E
Macdonald Ra. 136 15 35S 124 50 E
Macdonnell Ranges 136 23 40S 133 0 E
McDouall Peak 139 29 51S 134 55 E
Macdougall L. 148 66 00N 98 27W
McDougalls Well 140 31 8S 141 15 E
MacDowell L. 150 52 15N 92 45W
Macduff 37 57 40N 2 30W
Mace 150 48 55N 80 0W
Maceda 56 42 16N 7 39W
Macedo da Cavaleiros 124 11 25S 16 45 E
Macedo de Cavaleiros 56 41 31N 6 57W
Macedonia = Makedonija 66 41 53N 21 40 E
Macedonia = Makhedonia 68 40 39N 22 0 E
Maceió 170 9 40S 35 41W
Maceira 57 39 41N 8 55W
Macenta 120 8 35N 9 20W
Macerata 63 43 19N 13 28 E
McFarland 163 35 41N 119 14W
Macfarlane, L. 140 32 0S 136 40 E
McFarlane, R. 153 59 12N 107 58W
McGehee 159 33 40N 91 25W
McGill 160 39 27N 114 50W
Macgillycuddy's Reeks, mts. 39 52 2N 9 45W
McGraw 162 42 35N 76 4W
MacGregor 153 49 57N 98 48W
McGregor, Iowa, U.S.A. 158 42 58N 91 15W
McGregor, Minn., U.S.A. 158 46 37N 93 17W
McGregor, R. 152 55 10N 122 0W
McGregor Ra. 139 27 0S 142 45 E
Mach 93 29 50N 67 20 E
Machacalis 171 17 5S 40 45W
Machachi 174 0 30S 78 15W
Machado, R. = Jiparana 174 8 45S 62 20W
Machagai 172 26 56S 60 2W
Machakos 126 1 30S 37 15 E
Machakos □ 126 1 30S 37 15 E
Machala 174 3 10S 79 50W
Machanga 129 20 59S 35 0 E
Machar Marshes 123 9 28N 33 21 E
Machattie, L. 138 24 50S 139 48 E
Machava 129 25 54S 32 28 E
Machece 127 19 15S 35 32 E
Machecoul 42 47 0N 1 49W
Machelen 47 50 55N 4 26 E
Mach'eng 109 31 11N 115 2 E
Mcherrah 118 27 0N 4 30W
Machevna 77 61 20N 172 20 E
Machezo, mt. 57 39 21N 4 20W
Machiang 108 26 30N 107 35 E
Mach'iaoho 107 44 41N 130 32 E
Machias 151 44 40N 67 34W
Machichaco, Cabo 58 43 28N 2 47W
Machichi, R. 153 57 3N 92 6W
Machida 111 35 28N 139 23 E
Machilipatnam 99 16 12N 81 12 E
Machilipatnam = Masulipatnam 96 16 12N 131 15 E
Machine, La 43 46 54N 3 27 E
Mchinja 127 9 44S 39 45 E
Mchinji 127 13 47S 32 58 E
Machiques 174 10 4N 72 34W
Machrihanish 34 55 25N 5 42W
Machupicchu 174 13 8S 72 30W
Machynlleth 31 52 36N 3 51W
Macias Nguema Biyoga 113 3 30N 8 40 E
McIlwraith Ra. 138 13 50S 143 20 E

* Renamed Shah Faisalabad

Macina
Makgobistad

Macina 120 14 40N 4 50W
Macina, Canal de 120 13 50N 5 40W
McIntosh 158 45 57N 101 20W
McIntosh L. 153 55 11N 104 41W
MacIntosh Range, Mts. 137 24 45S 121 33E
Macintyre, R. 139 28 37S 149 40E
Macizo Galaico 56 42 30N 7 30W
Mackay, Austral. 138 21 8S 149 11E
Mackay, U.S.A. 160 43 58N 113 37W
Mackay, L. 136 22 30S 129 0E
Mackay, R. 152 57 10N 111 38W
McKay Ra. 137 23 0S 122 30E
McKeesport 156 40 21N 79 50W
Mackenzie 152 55 20N 123 05W
McKenzie 157 36 10N 88 31W
Mackenzie Bay 147 69 0N 137 30W
Mackenzie City = Linden 174 6 0N 58 10W
Mackenzie Highway 152 58 0N 117 15W
Mackenzie Mts. 147 64 0N 128 0W
Mackenzie Plains 143 44 10S 170 25W
Mackenzie, R., Austral. 138 23 38S 149 46E
Mackenzie, R., Can. 148 69 10N 134 20W
McKenzie, R. 160 44 2N 122 30W
Mackenzie, Terr. 149 61 30N 144 30W
McKerrow L. 143 44 25S 168 5E
Mackinaw City 156 45 47N 84 44W
McKinlay 138 21 16S 141 18E
McKinlay, R. 138 20 50S 141 28E
McKinley, Mt. 147 63 10N 151 0W
McKinley Sea 12 84 0N 10 0W
McKinney 159 33 10N 96 40W
Mackinnon Road 126 3 40S 39 1E
Mackintosh Ra. 137 27 39S 125 32E
McKittrick 163 35 18N 119 39W
Mackmyra 72 60 40N 17 3E
Macksville 141 30 40S 152 56E
McLaren Vale 140 35 13S 138 31E
McLaughlin 158 45 50N 100 50W
Maclean 139 29 26S 153 16E
McLean 159 35 15N 100 35W
McLeansboro 158 38 5N 88 30W
Maclear 129 31 2S 28 23E
Macleay, R. 141 30 56S 153 0E
McLennan 152 55 42N 116 50W
MacLeod, B. 152 62 53N 110 0W
McLeod L. 137 24 9S 113 47E
McLeod, L. 137 24 50S 114 0E
MacLeod Lake 152 54 58N 123 0W
McIlwraith Ra., Mts. 138 13 43S 143 23E
McLoughlin, Mt. 160 42 30N 122 30W
McLure 152 51 2N 120 13W
McMillan L. 159 32 40N 104 20W
McMinnville, Oreg., U.S.A. 160 45 16N 123 11W
McMinnville, Tenn., U.S.A. 157 35 43N 85 45W
McMorran 153 51 19N 108 42W
McMurdo Sd. 13 77 0S 170 0E
McMurray = Fort McMurray 152 56 45N 111 27W
McNary 161 34 4N 109 53W
McNaughton L. 152 52 0N 118 10W
Macnean L. 38 54 19N 7 52W
MacNutt 153 51 5N 101 36W
Macodoene 129 23 32S 35 5E
Macomb 158 40 25N 90 40W
Macomer 64 40 16N 8 48E
Mâcon 45 46 19N 4 50E
Macon, Ga., U.S.A. 157 32 50N 83 37W
Macon, Miss., U.S.A. 157 33 7N 88 31W
Macon, Mo., U.S.A. 158 39 40N 92 26W
Macondo 125 12 37S 23 46E
Macosquink 38 55 5N 6 43W
Macossa 127 17 55S 33 56E
Macoun L. 153 56 32N 103 50W
Macovane 129 21 30S 35 0E
McPherson 158 38 25N 97 40W
McPherson Pk. 163 34 53N 119 53W
Macpherson Ra. 139 28 15S 153 15E
Macquarie Harbour 138 42 15S 145 15E
Macquarie Is. 130 50 0S 160 0E
Macquarie, R. 139 30 50S 147 30E
McRae, Mt. 136 22 17S 117 35E
MacRobertson Coast 13 68 30S 63 0E
Macroom 39 51 54N 8 57W
McSwyne's B. 38 54 37N 8 25W
Macu 174 0 25N 69 15W
Macugnaga 62 45 57N 7 58E
Macuirima 127 19 14S 35 5E
Macuiza 127 8 7S 34 29E
Macujer 174 0 24N 73 0W
Macumba, R. 133 27 11S 136 0E
Macuse 127 17 45S 37 17E
Macuspana 165 17 46N 92 36W
Macusse 128 17 48S 20 23E
Mácuzari, Presa 164 27 10N 109 10W
Macuze 127 17 45S 37 17E
Madā 'in Sālih 122 26 51N 37 58E
Madagali 121 10 56N 13 33E
Madagascar ■ 129 20 0S 47 0E
Madagascar, I. 129 20 0S 47 0E
Madam 120 7 58N 3 32W
Madama 119 22 0N 14 0E
Madame I. 151 45 30N 60 58W
Madanapalle 97 13 33N 78 28E
Madang 135 5 12S 145 49E
Madaoua 121 14 5N 6 27E
Madara 121 11 45N 10 35E
Madaripur 98 23 2N 90 15E
Madauk 98 17 56N 96 52E
Madawaska 150 45 30N 77 55W
Madawaska, R. 150 45 27N 76 21W
Madaya 98 22 20N 96 10E
Madbar 123 6 17N 30 45E
Maddalena, I. 64 41 15N 9 23E
Maddalena, La 64 41 13N 9 25E
Maddaloni 65 41 4N 14 23E
Maddy, L. 36 57 36N 7 8W
Made 47 51 41N 4 49E
Madebele 123 12 30N 41 10E
Madeira, Is. 116 32 50N 17 0W
Madeira, R. 174 5 30S 61 20W
Madeleine, Is. de la 151 47 30N 61 40W
Madeley 28 52 38N 2 28W
Madely 32 52 59N 2 20W
Madenda 127 13 42S 35 1W
Madera 163 37 0N 120 1W
Madha 96 18 0N 75 55E
Madhubani 95 26 21N 86 7E
Madhumati, R. 98 22 53N 89 52E
Madhupur 126 24 18N 86 37E
Madhya Pradesh □ 94 21 50N 81 0E
Madi Opei 126 3 47N 33 5E
Madill 159 34 5N 96 49W
Madimba, Mozam. 127 4 58S 15 6E
Madimba, Zaïre 124 5 0S 15 0E
Madinat al Shaab 91 12 50N 45 0E
Madingou 124 4 10S 13 33E
Madirovalo 129 16 26S 46 32E
Madison, Fla., U.S.A. 157 30 29N 83 26W
Madison, Ind., U.S.A. 156 38 42N 85 20W
Madison, Nebr., U.S.A. 158 41 53N 97 25W
Madison, S.D., U.S.A. 158 44 0N 97 8W
Madison, Wis., U.S.A. 158 43 5N 89 25W
Madison City 158 43 5N 93 10W
Madison Junc. 160 44 42N 110 56W
Madison, R. 160 45 0N 111 48W
Madisonville 156 37 42N 87 30W
Madista 128 21 15S 25 6E
Madiun 103 7 38S 111 32E
Madol 123 9 3N 27 45E
Madona 80 56 53N 26 5E
Madonie, Le, Mts. 64 37 50N 13 50E
Madoonga 174 26 56S 117 35E
Madras, India 97 13 8N 80 19E
Madras, U.S.A. 160 44 40N 121 10W
Madras = Tamil Nadu □ 97 11 0N 77 0E
Madre de Dios, I. 176 50 20N 75 10W
Madre de Dios, R. 174 11 30S 67 30W
Madre del Sur, Sierra 165 17 30N 100 0W
Madre, Laguna 165 25 0N 97 30W
Madre Occidental, Sierra 164 27 0N 107 0W
Madre Oriental, Sierra 164 25 0N 100 0W
Madre, Sierra, Mexico 165 16 0N 93 0W
Madre, Sierra, Phil. 103 17 0N 122 0E
Madri 94 24 16N 73 32E
Madrid 56 40 25N 3 45W
Madrid □ 56 40 30N 3 45W
Madridejos 57 39 28N 3 33W
Madrigal de las Altas Torres 56 41 5N 5 0W
Madrona, Sierra 57 38 27N 4 16W
Madroñera 57 39 26N 5 42W
Madu 123 14 37N 26 4E
Madura Motel 137 31 55S 127 0E
Madura, Selat 103 7 30S 113 20E
Madurai 97 9 55N 78 10E
Madurantakam 97 12 30N 79 50E
Madurta 109 35 1S 138 44E
Maduru Oya 97 7 40N 81 7E
Madzhalis 83 42 9N 47 47E
Mae Chan 100 20 9N 99 52E
Mae Hong Son 100 19 16N 98 8E
Mae Khlong, R. 100 13 24N 100 0E
Mae Phrik 100 17 27N 99 7E
Mae Ramat 100 16 58N 98 31E
Mae Rim 100 18 54N 98 57E
Mae Sot 100 16 43N 98 34E
Mae Suai 100 19 39N 99 33E
Mae Tha 100 18 28N 99 8E
Maebaru 110 33 33N 130 12E
Maebashi 111 36 24N 139 4E
Maella 58 41 8N 0 7E
Maentwrog 31 52 57N 4 0W
Maerhk'ang 108 31 51N 102 28E
Mâeruş 70 45 53N 25 31E
Maesteg 31 51 36N 3 40W
Maestra, Sierra 166 20 15N 77 0W
Maestrazgo, Mts. del 58 40 30N 0 25W
Maevatanana 125 16 56N 46 49E
Ma'fan 119 25 56N 14 56E
Mafeking, Can. 153 52 40N 101 10W
Mafeking, S. Afr. 128 25 50S 25 38E
Maféré 120 5 30N 3 2W
Mafeteng 128 29 51S 27 15E
Maffe 47 50 21N 5 19E
Maffra 141 37 53S 146 58E
Mafia □ 126 7 50S 39 45E
Mafia I. 126 7 45S 39 50E
Mafou 109 31 34N 115 15E
Mafra, Brazil 173 26 10N 50 0W
Mafra, Port. 57 38 55N 9 20W
Mafungabusi Plateau 127 18 30S 29 8E
Magadan 77 59 30N 151 0E
Magadi 126 1 54S 36 19E
Magadi, L. 126 1 54S 36 19E
Magaliesburg 129 26 1S 27 32E
Magallanes, Estrecho de 176 52 30S 75 0W
Magangué 174 9 14N 74 45W
Magaria 121 13 4N 9 5W
Magburaka 120 8 47N 12 0W
Magdal 90 32 51N 35 30E
Magdalen Is. = Madeleine, Is. de la 151 47 30N 61 40W
Magdalena, Argent. 172 35 5S 57 30W
Magdalena, Boliv. 174 13 13S 63 57W
Magdalena, Mexico 164 30 50N 112 0W
Magdalena, U.S.A. 161 34 10N 107 20W
Magdalena □ 174 10 0N 74 0W
Magdalena, B. 164 24 30N 112 10W
Magdalena, I. 164 24 40N 112 15W
Magdalena, Llano de la 164 25 0N 111 30W
Magdalena, mt. 102 4 25N 117 55E
Magdalena, R., Colomb. 174 8 30N 74 0W
Magdalena, R., Mexico 164 30 50N 112 0W
Magdeburg 48 52 8N 11 36E
Magdeburg □ 48 52 20N 11 40E
Magdelaine Cays 138 16 33S 150 18E
Magdiel 90 32 10N 34 54E
Magdub 123 13 42N 25 5E
Magee 159 31 53N 89 45W
Magee, I. 38 54 48N 5 44W
Magelang 103 7 29S 110 13E
Magellan's Str. 176 52 30S 75 0W
Magellan's Str. = Magallanes, Est. de 176 52 30S 75 0W
Magenta, Austral. 140 33 51S 143 34E
Magenta, Italy 62 45 28N 8 53E
Magenta, L. 137 33 30S 119 10E
Maggea 140 34 28S 140 2E
Maggia 51 46 15N 8 42E
Maggia, R. 51 46 18N 8 36E
Maggiorasca, Mt. 62 44 33N 9 29E
Maggiore, L. 62 46 0N 8 35E
Maghama 120 15 32N 12 57W
Maghar 90 32 54N 35 24E
Maghera 38 54 51N 6 40W
Magherafelt 38 54 44N 6 37W
Maghnia 118 34 50N 1 43W
Maghull 32 53 31N 2 56W
Magilligan 38 55 10N 6 53W
Magilligan Pt. 38 55 10N 6 58W
Magione 63 43 10N 12 12E
Maglaj 66 44 33N 18 7E
Magliano in Toscana 63 42 36N 11 18E
Máglie 65 40 8N 18 17E
Magnac-Laval 44 46 13N 1 11E
Magnetic Pole, 1976, (South) 13 68 48S 139 30E
Magnetic Pole, 1976(North) 12 76 12N 100 12W
Magnisia □ 69 39 24N 22 46E
Magnitogorsk 84 53 27N 59 4E
Magnolia, Ark., U.S.A. 159 33 18N 93 12W
Magnolia, Miss., U.S.A. 159 31 8N 90 28W
Magnor 71 59 56N 12 15E
Magnus, oilfield 19 61 40N 1 20E
Magny-en-Vexin 43 49 9N 1 47E
Mâgoé 127 15 45S 31 42E
Magog 151 45 18N 72 9W
Magoro 126 1 45N 34 12E
Magosta = Famagusta 92 35 8N 33 55E
Magoye 127 16 1S 27 30E
Magpie L. 151 51 0N 64 40W
Magrath 152 49 25N 112 50W
Magro, R. 59 39 20N 0 45W
Magruder Mt. 163 37 25N 117 33W
Magrur, W. 123 16 5N 26 30E
Magu □ 126 2 45S 33 15E
Maguarinho, C. 170 0 15S 48 30W
Maguire's Bri. 38 54 18N 7 28W
Maguse L. 153 61 40N 95 10W
Maguse Pt. 153 61 20N 93 50W
Maguse River 153 61 20N 94 25W
Magwe 98 20 10N 95 0E
Maha Sarakham 100 16 12N 103 16E
Mahābād 92 36 50N 45 45E
Mahabaleshwar 96 17 58N 73 50E
Mahabarat Lekh 95 28 30N 82 0E
Mahabo 129 20 23S 44 40E
Mahad 96 18 6N 73 29E
Mahadeo Hills 94 22 20N 78 30E
Mahadeopur 96 18 48N 80 0E
Mahagi 126 2 20N 31 0E
Mahajamba, B. de la 129 15 24S 47 5E
Mahajamba, R. 129 17 0S 47 30E
Mahajan 94 28 48N 73 56E
Mahajilo, R. 129 19 30S 46 0E
Mahakam, R. 102 1 0N 114 40E
Mahalapye 128 23 1S 26 51E
Mahalla el Kubra 122 31 10N 31 0E
Mahallāt 93 33 55N 50 30E
Mahanadi R. 96 20 33N 85 0E
Mahanagh 38 53 31N 8 42W
Mahanoro 129 19 54S 48 48E
Mahanoy City 162 40 48N 76 10W
Maharashtra □ 96 19 30N 75 30E
Maharès 119 34 32N 10 29E
Mahari Mts. 126 6 20S 30 0E
Mahasolo 129 19 7S 46 22E
Mahaweli Ganga 97 8 0N 81 10E
Mahaxay 100 17 22N 105 48E
Mahboobabad 96 17 42N 80 2E
Mahbubnagar 96 16 45N 77 59E
Mahd Dhahab 92 25 55N 45 30E
Mahdia 119 35 28N 11 0E
Mahé 97 11 42N 75 34E
Mahe 95 33 10N 78 32E
Mahendra Giri, mt. 97 8 20N 77 30E
Mahendraganj 98 25 20N 89 45E
Mahenge 127 8 45S 36 35E
Maheno 143 45 10S 170 50E
Mahia Pen. 142 39 9S 177 55E
Mahirija 118 34 0N 3 16W
Mahlaing 98 21 6N 95 39E
Mahmiya 123 17 5N 33 50E
Mahmud Kot 94 30 16N 71 0E
Mahmudia 70 45 5N 29 5E
Mahnomen 158 47 22N 95 57W
Mahoba 95 25 15N 79 55E
Mahón 58 39 50N 4 18E
Mahone Bay 151 44 30N 64 20W
Mahopac 162 41 22N 73 45W
Mahsū 108 30 31N 100 19E
Mahukona 147 20 11N 155 52W
Mahuta 121 11 32N 4 58E
Mai-Ndombe, L. 124 2 0S 18 0E
Mai-Sai 100 20 20N 99 55E
Maibara 111 35 19N 136 17E
Maîche 43 47 16N 6 48E
Maicuru, R. 175 1 0S 54 30W
Máida 65 38 51N 16 21E
Maidan Khula 94 33 36N 69 50E
Maiden Bradley 28 51 9N 2 18W
Maiden Newton 28 50 46N 2 35W
Maidenhead 29 51 31N 0 42W
Maidi 123 16 20N 42 45E
Maidstone, Can. 153 53 5N 109 20W
Maidstone, U.K. 29 51 16N 0 31E
Maiduguri 121 12 0N 13 20E
Maignelay 43 49 32N 2 30E
Maigualida, Sierra 174 5 30N 65 10W
Maijdi 98 22 48N 91 10E
Maikala Ra. 96 22 0N 81 0E
Mailly-le-Camp 43 48 41N 4 12E
Mailsi 94 29 48N 72 15E
Maimana 93 35 53N 64 38E
Main Barrier Ra. 133 31 10S 141 20E
Main Centre 153 50 35N 107 21W
Main Coast Ra. 138 16 22S 145 10E
Main, R., Ger. 49 50 13N 11 0E
Main, R., U.K. 38 54 49N 6 20W
Mainburg 49 48 37N 11 49E
Maindargi 96 17 33N 74 21E
Maine 42 48 0N 0 0E
Maine □ 151 45 20N 69 0W
Maine-et-Loire □ 42 47 31N 0 30W
Maine, R. 39 52 10N 9 40W
Maïne-Soroa 121 13 13N 12 2E
Maingkwan 98 26 15N 96 45E
Mainit, L. 103 9 31N 125 30E
Mainkaing 98 24 48N 95 16E
Mainland, I., Orkneys, U.K. 37 59 0N 3 10W
Mainland, I., Shetlands, U.K. 36 60 15N 1 22W
Mainpuri 95 27 18N 79 4E
Maintenon 43 48 35N 1 35E
Maintirano 129 18 3S 44 1E
Mainvault 47 50 39N 3 43E
Mainz 49 50 0N 8 17E
Maipú 172 37 0S 58 0W
Maipures 174 5 11N 67 49W
Maiquetía 174 10 36N 66 57W
Maira, R. 62 44 29N 7 15E
Mairabari 98 26 30N 92 30E
Mairipotaba 171 17 18S 49 28W
Maisi 167 20 17N 74 9W
Maisi, C. 167 20 10N 74 10W
Maisse 43 48 24N 2 21E
Maissin 47 49 58N 5 10E
Maitland, N.S.W., Austral. 141 32 44S 151 36E
Maitland, S. Australia, Austral. 140 34 23S 137 40E
Maitland, L. 137 27 11S 121 3E
Maiyema 121 12 5N 4 25E
Maiz, Islas del 166 12 15N 83 4W
Maizuru 111 35 25N 135 22E
Majagual 174 8 33N 74 38W
Majalengka 103 6 55S 108 14E
Majd el Kurum 90 32 56N 35 15E
Majene 103 3 27S 118 57E
Majevica Planina 66 44 45N 18 50E
Maji 123 6 20N 35 30E
Major 153 51 52N 109 37W
Majorca, I. = Mallorca, I. 58 39 30N 3 0E
Majors Creek 141 35 33S 149 45E
Majunga 125 15 40S 46 25E
Majunga □ 129 17 0S 47 0E
Maka 120 13 40N 14 10W
Makak 121 3 36N 11 0E
Makale 103 3 6S 119 51E
Makamba 126 4 8S 29 49E
Makamik 150 48 45N 79 0W
Makapuu Hd. 147 21 19N 157 39W
Makarewa 143 46 20S 168 21E
Makari 124 12 35N 14 28E
Makarikari = Makgadikgadi 128 20 40S 25 45E
Makarovo 77 57 40N 107 45E
Makarska 66 43 20N 17 2E
Makaryev 81 57 52N 43 50E
Makasar = Ujung Pandang 103 5 10S 119 20E
Makasar, Selat 103 1 0S 118 20E
Makat 76 47 39N 53 19E
Makedhonia □ 68 40 39N 22 0E
Makedonija □ 66 41 53N 21 40E
Makena 147 20 39N 156 27W
Makeni 120 8 55N 12 5W
Maker 30 50 20N 4 10W
Makeyevka 82 48 0N 38 0E
Makgadikgadi 128 20 40S 25 45E
Makgadikgadi Salt Pans 128 20 40S 25 45E
Makgobistad 128 25 45S 25 12E

Makhachkala Manitou I

Makhachkala	**83**	43 0N	47 15 E
Makharadze	**83**	41 55N	42 2 E
Makian, I.	**103**	0 12N	127 20 E
Makin, I.	**130**	3 30N	174 0 E
Makindu	**124**	2 7S	37 40 E
Makinsk	**76**	52 37N	70 26 E
Makkah	**122**	21 30N	39 54 E
Makkovik	**151**	55 0N	59 10W
Makkum	**46**	53 3N	5 25 E
Maklakovo	**77**	58 16N	92 29 E
Makó	**53**	46 14N	20 33 E
Makokou	**124**	0 40N	12 50 E
Makongo	**126**	3 15N	26 17 E
Makoro	**126**	3 10N	29 59 E
Makoua	**124**	0 5S	15 50 E
Maków Podhal	**54**	49 43N	19 45 E
Makrá, I.	**69**	36 15N	25 54 E
Makrai	**93**	22 2N	77 0 E
Makran	**93**	26 13N	61 30 E
Makran Coast Range	**93**	25 40N	4 0 E
Makrana	**94**	27 2N	74 46 E
Mákri	**68**	40 52N	25 40 E
Maksimkin Yar	**76**	58 58N	86 50 E
Maktar	**119**	35 48N	9 12 E
Mākū	**92**	39 15N	44 31 E
Makuan	**108**	23 2N	104 24 E
Makum	**98**	27 30N	95 23 E
Makumbe	**128**	20 15S	24 26 E
Makumbi	**124**	5 50S	20 43 E
Makunda	**128**	22 30S	20 7 E
Makurazaki	**110**	31 15N	130 20 E
Makurdi	**120**	7 43N	8 28 E
Makwassie	**128**	27 17S	26 0 E
Mal	**98**	26 51N	86 45 E
Mal B.	**39**	52 50N	9 30W
Mal-i-Gjalicës së Lumës	**68**	42 2N	20 25 E
Mal i Gribës	**68**	40 17N	9 45 E
Mal i Nemërçkës	**68**	40 15N	20 15 E
Mal i Tomorit	**68**	40 42N	20 11 E
Mala Kapela	**63**	44 45N	15 30 E
Mala, Pta.	**166**	7 28N	80 2W
Malabang	**103**	7 36N	124 3 E
Malabar Coast	**97**	11 0N	75 0 E
Malacca = Melaka	**101**	2 15N	102 15 E
Malacca, Str. of	**101**	3 0N	101 0 E
Malacky	**53**	48 27N	17 0 E
Malad City	**160**	41 10N	112 20 E
Maladetta, Mt.	**59**	42 40N	0 30 E
Malafaburi	**123**	10 37N	40 30 E
Málaga, Colomb.	**174**	6 42N	72 44W
Málaga, Spain	**57**	36 43N	4 23W
Malaga	**159**	32 12N	104 2W
Málaga □	**57**	36 38N	4 58W
Malagarasi	**126**	5 5S	30 50 E
Malagarasi, R.	**126**	3 50S	30 30 E
Malagasy Rep. ■ = Madagascar ■	**129**	20 0S	47 0 E
Malagón	**57**	39 11N	3 52W
Malagón, R.	**57**	37 40N	7 20W
Malahide	**38**	53 26N	6 10W
Malaimbandy	**129**	20 20S	45 36 E
Malakâl	**123**	9 33N	31 50 E
Malakand	**94**	34 40N	71 55 E
Malakoff	**159**	32 10N	95 55W
Malakwa	**152**	50 55N	118 50W
Malamyzh	**77**	50 0N	136 50 E
Malang	**103**	7 59S	112 35 E
Malanje	**124**	9 30S	16 17 E
Mälaren	**72**	59 30N	17 10 E
Malargüe	**172**	35 40S	69 30W
Malartic	**150**	48 9N	78 9W
Malatya	**92**	38 25N	38 20 E
Malawi ■	**127**	13 0S	34 0 E
Malawi, L. (Lago Niassa)	**127**	12 30S	34 30 E
Malay Pen.	**101**	7 25N	100 0 E
Malaya □	**101**	4 0N	102 0 E
Malaya Belözerka	**82**	47 12N	34 56 E
Malaya Vishera	**80**	58 55N	32 25 E
Malaybalay	**103**	8 5N	125 15 E
Malayer	**92**	34 19N	48 51 E
Malaysia ■	**102**	5 0N	110 0 E
Malaysia, Western □	**101**	5 0N	102 0 E
Malazgirt	**92**	39 10N	42 33 E
Malbaie, La	**151**	47 40N	70 10W
Malbon	**138**	21 5S	140 17 E
Malbooma	**139**	30 41S	134 11 E
Malbork	**54**	54 3N	19 10 E
Malca Dube	**123**	6 40N	41 52 E
Malchin	**48**	53 43N	12 44 E
Malchow	**48**	53 29N	12 25 E
Malcolm	**137**	28 51S	121 25 E
Malcolm, Pt., S. Australia, Austral.	**109**	34 52S	138 29 E
Malcolm, Pt., W. Australia, Austral.	**137**	33 48S	123 45 E
Malczyce	**54**	51 14N	16 29 E
Maldegem	**47**	51 14N	3 26 E
Malden, Mass., U.S.A.	**162**	42 26N	71 5W
Malden, Mo., U.S.A.	**159**	36 35N	90 0W
Malden I.	**143**	4 3S	155 1W
Maldive Is. ■	**86**	2 0N	73 0W
Maldon, Austral.	**140**	37 0S	144 6 E
Maldon, U.K.	**29**	51 43N	0 41 E
Maldonado	**173**	35 0S	55 0W
Maldonado, Punta	**165**	16 19N	98 35W
Malé	**62**	46 20N	10 55 E
Malé Karpaty	**53**	48 30N	17 20 E
Malea, Akra	**69**	36 28N	23 7 E
Malegaon	**96**	20 30N	74 30 E
Malei	**127**	17 12S	36 58 E
Malela	**126**	4 22S	26 8 E
Malenge	**127**	12 40S	26 42 E
Målerås	**73**	56 54N	15 34 E
Malerkotla	**94**	30 32N	75 58 E
Måles	**69**	36 6N	25 35 E
Malesherbes	**43**	48 15N	2 24 E
Maleske Planina	**66**	41 38N	23 7 E
Malestroit	**42**	47 49N	2 25W
Malfa	**65**	38 35N	14 50 E
Malgobek	**83**	43 30N	44 52 E
Malgomaj L.	**74**	64 40N	16 30 E
Malgrat	**58**	41 39N	2 46 E
Malham Tarn	**32**	54 6N	2 11W
Malhão, Sa. do	**55**	37 25N	8 0W
Malheur L.	**160**	43 19N	118 42W
Malheur, R.	**160**	43 55N	117 55W
Mali	**120**	12 10N	12 20W
Mali ■	**121**	15 0N	10 0W
Mali H Ka R.	**98**	25 42N	97 30 E
Mali Kanal	**66**	45 36N	19 24 E
Mali Kyun, I.	**101**	13 0N	98 20 E
Mali, R.	**99**	26 20N	97 40 E
Malibu	**163**	34 2N	118 41W
Malih, Nahr al	**90**	32 20N	35 29 E
Malik	**103**	0 39S	123 16 E
Malili	**103**	2 42S	121 23 E
Malimba, Mts.	**126**	7 30S	29 30 E
Malin, Ireland	**38**	55 18N	7 16W
Malin, U.S.S.R.	**80**	50 46N	29 15 E
Malin Hd.	**38**	55 18N	7 16W
Malin Pen.	**38**	55 20N	7 17W
Malinau	**102**	3 35N	116 30 E
Malindi	**126**	3 12S	40 5 E
Maling, Mt.	**103**	1 0N	121 0 E
Malingping	**103**	6 45S	106 2 E
Malinyi	**127**	8 56S	36 0 E
Maliqi	**68**	40 45N	20 48 E
Malita	**103**	6 19N	125 39 E
Malkapur, Maharashtra, India	**96**	16 57N	74 0W
Malkapur, Maharashtra, India	**96**	20 53N	76 17 E
Małkinia Grn.	**54**	52 42N	21 58 E
Malko Turnovo	**67**	41 59N	27 31 E
Mallacoota	**141**	37 40S	149 40 E
Mallacoota Inlet	**141**	37 40S	149 40 E
Mallaha	**90**	33 6N	35 35 E
Mallaig	**36**	57 0N	5 50W
Mallala	**140**	34 26S	138 30 E
Mallawan	**95**	27 4N	80 12 E
Mallawi	**122**	27 44N	30 44 E
Mallemort	**45**	43 44N	5 11 E
Málles Venosta	**62**	46 42N	10 32 E
Mállia	**69**	35 17N	25 27 E
Mallina P.O.	**136**	20 53S	118 2 E
Mallorca, I.	**58**	39 30N	3 0 E
Mallow	**39**	52 8N	8 40W
Malltraeth B.	**31**	53 7N	4 30W
Mallwyd	**31**	52 43N	3 41W
Malmbäck	**73**	57 34N	14 28 E
Malmberget	**74**	67 11N	20 40 E
Malmédy	**47**	50 25N	6 2 E
Malmesbury, S. Afr.	**128**	33 28S	18 41 E
Malmesbury, U.K.	**28**	51 35N	2 5W
Malmö	**75**	55 36N	12 59 E
Malmöhus län □	**73**	55 45N	13 30 E
Malmslätt	**73**	58 27N	15 33 E
Malmyzh	**84**	56 31N	50 41 E
Malmyzh Mozhga	**81**	56 35N	50 30 E
Malnaş	**70**	46 2N	25 49 E
Malo Konare	**67**	42 12N	24 24 E
Maloarkhangelsk	**81**	52 28N	36 30 E
Maloja	**51**	46 25N	9 35 E
Maloja Pass	**51**	46 23N	9 42 E
Malolos	**103**	14 50N	121 2 E
Malomalsk	**84**	58 45N	59 53 E
Malombe L.	**127**	14 40S	35 15 E
Malomir	**67**	42 16N	26 30 E
Malone	**156**	44 50N	74 19W
Malorad	**67**	43 28N	23 41 E
Malorita	**80**	51 41N	24 3 E
Maloyaroslovets	**81**	55 2N	36 20 E
Malozemelskaya Tundra	**78**	67 0N	50 0 E
Malpartida	**57**	39 26N	6 30W
Malpas	**32**	53 3N	2 47W
Malpelo I.	**174**	4 3N	80 35W
Malpica	**56**	43 19N	8 50W
Malprabha, R.	**97**	15 40N	74 50 E
Malta, Brazil	**170**	6 54S	37 31W
Malta, Idaho, U.S.A.	**160**	42 15N	113 50W
Malta, Mont., U.S.A.	**160**	48 20N	107 55W
Malta Channel	**64**	36 40N	14 0 E
Maltahöhe	**125**	24 55S	17 0 E
Maltby	**33**	53 25N	1 12W
Malters	**50**	47 3N	8 11 E
Malton	**33**	54 9N	0 48W
Maluku □	**103**	3 0S	128 0 E
Maluku, Kepulauan	**103**	3 0S	128 0 E
Malumfashi	**121**	11 48N	7 39 E
Malung, China	**108**	25 18N	103 20 E
Malung, Sweden	**72**	60 42N	13 44 E
Malvalli	**97**	12 28N	77 8 E
Malvan	**97**	16 2N	73 30 E
Malvern, U.K.	**28**	52 7N	2 19W
Malvern, U.S.A.	**159**	34 22N	92 50W
Malvern Hills	**28**	52 0N	2 19W
Malvern Wells	**28**	52 4N	2 19W
Malvérnia	**129**	22 6S	31 42 E
Malvik	**71**	63 25N	10 40 E
Malvinas Is. = Falkland Is.	**174**	51 30S	59 0W
Malya	**126**	3 5S	33 38 E
Malybay	**85**	43 30N	78 25 E
Mama	**77**	58 18N	112 54 E
Mamadysh	**81**	55 44N	51 23 E
Mamaia	**70**	44 18N	28 37 E
Mamaku	**142**	38 5S	176 8 E
Mamanguape	**170**	6 50S	35 4W
Mamasa	**103**	2 55S	119 20 E
Mambasa	**126**	1 22N	29 3 E
Mamberamo, R.	**103**	2 0S	137 50 E
Mambilima Falls	**127**	10 31S	28 45 E
Mambirima	**127**	11 25S	27 33 E
Mambo	**126**	4 52S	38 22 E
Mambrui	**126**	3 5S	40 5 E
Mameigwess L.	**150**	52 35N	87 50W
Mamer	**47**	49 38N	6 2 E
Mamers	**42**	48 21N	0 22 E
Mamfe	**121**	5 50N	9 15 E
Mammamattawa	**150**	50 25N	84 23W
Mámmola	**65**	38 23N	16 13 E
Mammoth	**161**	32 46N	110 43W
Mamoré, R.	**175**	9 55S	65 20W
Mamou	**120**	10 15N	12 0W
Mampatá	**120**	11 54N	14 53W
Mampawah	**102**	0 30N	109 5 E
Mampong	**121**	7 6N	1 26W
Mamuju	**103**	2 50S	118 50 E
Man	**120**	7 30N	7 40W
Man, I. of	**32**	54 15N	4 30W
Man Na	**98**	23 27N	97 19 E
Man O' War Peak	**151**	56 58N	61 40W
Man, R.	**96**	17 20N	75 0 E
Man Tun	**98**	23 2N	98 38 E
Mana, Fr. Gui.	**175**	5 45N	53 55W
Mana, U.S.A.	**147**	22 3N	159 45W
Mana, R.	**123**	6 20N	40 41 E
Måna, R.	**71**	59 55N	8 50 E
Manaar, Gulf of	**97**	8 30N	79 0 E
Manacacías, R.	**174**	4 23N	72 4W
Manacapuru	**174**	3 10S	60 50W
Manacles, The	**30**	50 3N	5 5W
Manacor	**58**	39 32N	3 12 E
Manage	**47**	50 31N	4 15 E
Managua	**166**	12 0N	86 20W
Managua, L.	**166**	12 20N	86 30W
Manaia	**142**	39 33S	174 8 E
Manakana	**129**	13 45S	50 4 E
Manakara	**129**	22 8S	48 1 E
Manakau Mt.	**143**	42 15S	173 42 E
Manam I.	**135**	4 5S	145 0 E
Manamāh, Al	**93**	26 11N	50 35 E
Manambao, R.	**129**	17 35S	44 45 E
Manambato	**129**	13 43S	49 7 E
Manambolo, R.	**129**	19 20S	45 0 E
Manambolosy	**129**	16 2S	49 40 E
Mananara	**129**	16 10S	49 30 E
Mananara, R.	**129**	23 25S	48 10 E
Mananjary	**129**	21 13S	48 20 E
Manantenina	**129**	24 17S	47 19 E
Manaos = Manaus	**174**	3 0S	60 0W
Manapouri	**143**	45 34S	167 39 E
Manapouri, L.	**143**	45 32S	167 32 E
Manar, R.	**96**	18 50N	77 20 E
Manas, Gora	**85**	42 22N	71 2 E
Manas, R.	**99**	26 12N	90 40 E
Manasarowar, L.	**105**	30 45N	81 20 E
Manasarowar L.	**105**	30 45N	81 20 E
Manasir	**93**	24 30N	51 10 E
Manaslu, Mt.	**95**	28 33N	84 33 E
Manasquan	**162**	40 7N	74 3W
Manassa	**161**	37 12N	105 58W
Manassas	**162**	38 45N	77 28W
Manassu	**105**	44 18N	86 13 E
Manati	**147**	18 26N	66 29W
Manaung Kyun	**98**	18 45N	93 40 E
Manaus	**174**	3 0S	60 0W
Manawan L.	**153**	55 24N	103 14W
Manawatu, R.	**142**	40 28S	175 12 E
Manay	**103**	7 17N	126 33 E
Manby	**33**	53 22N	0 6 E
Mancelona	**156**	44 54N	85 5W
Mancha, La	**59**	39 10N	2 54W
Mancha Real	**57**	37 48N	3 39W
Manchaster, L.	**108**	27 29S	152 46 E
Manche □	**42**	49 10N	1 20W
Manchester, U.K.	**32**	53 30N	2 15W
Manchester, Conn., U.S.A.	**162**	41 47N	72 30W
Manchester, Ga., U.S.A.	**157**	32 53N	84 32W
Manchester, Iowa, U.S.A.	**158**	42 28N	91 27W
Manchester, Ky., U.S.A.	**156**	38 40N	83 45W
Manchester, N.H., U.S.A.	**162**	42 58N	71 29W
Manchester, Pa., U.S.A.	**162**	40 4N	76 43W
Manchester, Vt., U.S.A.	**162**	43 10N	73 5W
Manchester L.	**153**	61 28N	107 29W
Manchouli	**105**	49 46N	117 24 E
Manchuria = Tung Pei	**107**	44 0N	126 0 E
Manciano	**63**	42 35N	11 30 E
Mancifa	**123**	6 53N	41 50 E
Mand, R.	**93**	28 20N	52 30 E
Manda, Chunya, Tanz.	**127**	6 51S	32 29 E
Manda, Jombe, Tanz.	**127**	10 30S	34 40 E
Mandabé	**125**	21 0S	44 55 E
Mandaguari	**173**	23 32S	51 42W
Mandah	**106**	44 27N	108 20 E
Mandal	**71**	58 2N	7 25 E
Mandalay	**99**	22 0N	96 10 E
Mandalay = Mandale	**98**	22 0N	96 10 E
Mandale	**99**	22 0N	96 10 E
Mandalgovi	**106**	45 45N	106 20 E
Mandali	**92**	33 52N	45 28 E
Mandalya Körfezi	**69**	37 15N	27 20 E
Mandan	**158**	46 50N	101 0W
Mandapeta	**96**	16 47N	81 56 E
Mandar, Teluk	**103**	3 35S	119 4 E
Mandas	**64**	39 40N	9 8 E
Mandasaur	**93**	24 3N	75 8 E
Mandasor (Mandsaur)	**94**	24 3N	75 8 E
Mandawai (Katingan), R.	**102**	1 30S	113 0 E
Mandelieu-la-Napoule	**45**	43 34N	6 57 E
Mandera	**126**	3 55N	41 42 E
Mandera □	**126**	3 30N	41 0 E
Manderfeld	**47**	50 20N	6 20 E
Mandi, India	**94**	31 39N	76 58 E
Mandi, Zambia	**127**	14 30S	23 45 E
Mandimba	**125**	14 20S	35 40 E
Mandioli	**103**	0 40S	127 20 E
Mandla	**95**	22 39N	80 30 E
Mandø	**73**	55 18N	8 33 E
Mandoto	**129**	19 34S	46 17 E
Mandoúdhion	**69**	38 48N	23 29 E
Mandra	**94**	33 23N	73 12 E
Mandráki	**69**	36 36N	27 11 E
Mandrase, R.	**129**	25 10S	46 30 E
Mandritsara	**129**	15 50S	48 49 E
Mandsaur (Mandasor)	**94**	24 3N	75 8 E
Mandurah	**137**	32 36S	115 48 E
Mandúria	**65**	40 25N	17 38 E
Mandvi	**96**	22 51N	69 22 E
Mandya	**97**	12 30N	77 0 E
Mandzai	**94**	30 55N	67 6 E
Mané	**121**	12 59N	1 21W
Manea	**29**	52 29N	0 10 E
Maner, R.	**97**	18 30N	79 40 E
Maneroo	**138**	23 22S	143 53 E
Maneroo Cr.	**138**	23 21S	143 53 E
Manfalût	**122**	27 20N	30 52 E
Manfred	**140**	33 19S	143 45 E
Manfredónia	**65**	41 40N	15 55 E
Manfredónia, G. di	**65**	41 30N	16 10 E
Manga, Brazil	**171**	14 46S	43 56W
Manga, Upp. Vol.	**121**	11 40N	1 4W
Mangabeiras, Chapada das	**170**	10 0S	46 30W
Mangahan	**142**	40 26S	175 48 E
Mangalagiri	**96**	16 26N	80 36 E
Mangaldai	**98**	26 26N	92 2 E
Mangalia	**70**	43 50N	28 35 E
Mangalore, Austral.	**141**	36 56S	145 10 E
Mangalore, India	**97**	12 55N	74 47 E
Manganeses	**56**	41 45N	5 43W
Mangaon	**96**	18 15N	73 20 E
Manger	**71**	60 38N	5 3W
Mangerton Mt.	**39**	51 59N	9 30W
Manggar	**102**	2 50S	108 10 E
Manggawitu	**103**	4 8S	133 32 E
Mangin Range	**98**	24 15N	95 45 E
Mangla Dam	**95**	33 32N	73 50 E
Manglaur	**94**	29 44N	77 49 E
Mangoche	**125**	14 25S	35 16 E
Mangoky, R.	**129**	21 55S	44 40 E
Mangole I.	**103**	1 50S	125 55 E
Mangombe	**126**	1 20S	26 48 E
Mangonui	**142**	35 1S	173 32 E
Mangotsfield	**28**	51 29N	2 29W
Mangualde	**56**	40 38N	7 48W
Mangueigne	**117**	10 40N	21 5 E
Mangueira, Lagoa da	**173**	33 0S	52 50W
Manguéni, Hamada	**119**	22 47N	12 56 E
Mangum	**159**	34 50N	99 30W
Mangyai	**105**	37 50N	91 38 E
Mangyshlak P-ov.	**83**	43 40N	52 30 E
Manhattan, Kans., U.S.A.	**158**	39 10N	96 40W
Manhattan, Nev., U.S.A.	**163**	38 31N	117 3W
Manhiça	**129**	25 23S	32 49 E
Manhuaçu	**171**	20 15S	42 2W
Manhui	**106**	41 1N	107 14 E
Manhumirim	**171**	20 22S	41 57W
Mani	**99**	34 52N	87 11 E
Maní	**174**	4 49N	72 17W
Mania, R.	**129**	19 55S	46 10 E
Maniago	**63**	46 11N	12 40 E
Manica	**127**	18 58S	32 59 E
Manica e Sofala □	**129**	19 10S	33 45 E
Manicaland □	**127**	19 0S	32 30 E
Manicoré	**174**	6 0S	61 10W
Manicouagan L.	**151**	51 25N	68 15W
Manicouagan, R.	**151**	49 30N	68 30W
Manifah	**92**	27 30N	49 0 E
Manifold	**138**	22 41S	150 40 E
Manigotagan	**153**	51 6N	96 8W
Manigotagan L.	**153**	50 52N	95 37W
Manihiki I.	**131**	10 24S	161 1W
Manika, Plat. de	**127**	10 0S	25 5 E
Manikganj	**98**	23 52N	90 0 E
Manila, Phil.	**103**	14 40N	121 3 E
Manila, U.S.A.	**160**	41 0N	109 44W
Manila B.	**103**	14 0N	120 0 E
Manilla	**141**	30 45S	150 43 E
Manimpé	**120**	14 11N	5 28W
Maningory	**129**	17 9S	49 30 E
Manipur □	**98**	24 30N	94 0 E
Manipur, R.	**98**	23 45N	93 40 E
Manisa	**92**	38 38N	27 30 E
Manistee	**156**	44 15N	86 20W
Manistee, R.	**156**	44 15N	86 21W
Manistique	**156**	45 59N	86 18W
Manito L.	**153**	52 43N	109 43W
Manitoba □	**153**	55 30N	97 0W
Manitoba, L.	**153**	51 0N	98 45W
Manitou	**153**	49 15N	98 32W
Manitou I.	**150**	47 22N	87 30W

Manitou Is Marosakoa

Manitou Is. 156 45 8N 86 0W
Manitou L., Ont., Can. 153 49 15N 93 0W
Manitou L., Qué., Can. 151 50 55N 65 17W
Manitoulin I. 150 45 40N 82 30W
Manitowaning 150 45 46N 81 49W
Manitowoc 156 44 8N 87 40W
Manizales 174 5 5N 75 32W
Manja 129 21 26S 44 20E
Manjacaze 125 24 45S 34 0E
Manjakandriana 129 18 55S 47 47E
Manjeri 97 11 7N 76 11E
Manjhand 94 25 50N 68 10E
Manjil 92 36 46N 49 30E
Manjimup 137 34 15S 116 6E
Manjra, R. 96 18 20N 77 20E
Mankaiana 129 26 38S 31 6E
Mankato, Kans., U.S.A. 158 39 49N 98 11W
Mankato, Minn., U.S.A. 158 44 8N 93 59W
Mankono 120 8 10N 6 10W
Mankota 153 49 25N 107 5W
Manlay 106 44 9N 106 50E
Manlleu 58 42 2N 2 17E
Manly, N.S.W., Austral. 141 33 48S 151 17E
Manly, Queens., Austral. 108 27 27S 153 11E
Manmad 96 20 18N 74 28E
Mann Ranges, Mts. 137 26 6S 130 5E
Manna 102 4 25S 102 55E
Mannahill 140 32 25S 140 0E
Mannar 97 9 1N 79 54E
Mannar, G. of 97 8 30N 79 0E
Mannar I. 97 9 5N 79 45E
Mannargudi 97 10 45N 79 32E
Männedorf 51 47 15N 8 43E
Mannheim 49 49 28N 8 29E
Manning, Can. 152 56 53N 117 39W
Manning, U.S.A. 157 33 40N 80 9W
Manning Prov. Park 152 49 5N 120 45W
Mannington 156 39 35N 80 25W
Manningtree 29 51 56N 1 3E
Mannu, C. 64 40 2N 8 24E
Mannu, R. 64 39 35N 8 56E
Mannum 140 34 57S 139 12E
Mano 120 8 3N 12 12W
Manokwari 103 0 54S 134 0E
Manolás 69 38 4N 21 21E
Manombo 129 22 57S 43 28E
Manono 124 7 15S 27 25E
Manorbier 31 51 38N 4 48W
Manorhamilton 38 54 19N 8 11W
Manosque 45 43 49N 5 47E
Manouane L. 151 50 45N 70 45W
Manpojin 107 41 6N 126 24E
Manresa 58 41 48N 1 50E
Mans, Le 42 48 0N 0 10E
Mansa, Gujarat, India 94 23 27N 72 45E
Mansa, Punjab, India 94 30 0N 75 27E
Mansa, Zambia 127 11 13S 28 55E
Mansel I. 149 62 0N 79 50W
Mansenra 94 34 20N 73 11E
Mansfield, Austral. 141 37 4S 146 6E
Mansfield, U.K. 33 53 8N 1 12W
Mansfield, La., U.S.A. 159 32 2N 93 40W
Mansfield, Mass., U.S.A. 162 42 2N 71 12W
Mansfield, Ohio, U.S.A. 156 40 45N 82 30W
Mansfield, Pa., U.S.A. 162 41 48N 77 4W
Mansfield, Wash., U.S.A. 160 47 51N 119 44W
Mansfield Woodhouse 33 53 11N 1 11W
Mansi 98 24 40N 95 44E
Mansidão 170 10 43S 44 2W
Mansilla de las Mulas 56 42 30N 5 25W
Mansle 44 45 52N 0 9E
Manso, R. 171 14 0S 52 0W
Mansôa 120 12 0N 15 20W
Manson Cr. 152 55 37N 124 25W
Mansoura, Djebel 119 36 1N 4 31E
Manta 174 1 0S 80 40W
Mantalingajan, Mt. 102 8 55N 117 45E
Mantare 126 2 42S 33 13E
Manteca 163 37 50N 121 12W
Mantecal 174 7 34N 69 17W
Mantekomu Hu 99 34 40N 89 0E
Mantena 171 18 47S 40 59W
Manteo 157 35 55N 75 41W
Mantes-la-Jolie 43 49 0N 1 41E
Manthani 96 18 40N 79 35E
Manthelan 42 47 9N 0 47E
Manti 160 39 23N 111 32W
Mantiqueira, Serra da 173 22 0S 44 0W
Manton, U.K. 29 52 37N 0 41W
Manton, U.S.A. 156 44 23N 85 25W
Mantorp 73 58 21N 15 20E
Mántova 62 45 10N 10 47E
Mänttä 74 62 0N 24 40E
Mantua = Mántova 62 45 10N 10 47E
Mantung 140 34 35S 140 3E
Manturova 81 58 10N 44 30E
Manu 174 12 10S 71 0W
Manucan 103 8 14N 123 3E
Manuel Alves Grande, R. 170 7 27S 47 35W
Manuel Alves, R. 171 11 19S 48 28W
Manui I. 103 3 35S 123 5E
Manukau 142 37 1S 174 55E
Manukau Harbour 142 37 3S 174 45E
Manunui 142 38 54S 175 21E
Manus I. 135 2 0S 147 0E
Manvi 97 15 57N 76 59E
Manville, R.I., U.S.A. 162 41 58N 71 28W
Manville, Wyo., U.S.A. 158 42 48N 104 36W
Manwath 96 19 19N 76 32E
Many 159 31 36N 93 28W
Manyane 128 23 21S 21 42E
Manyara L. 126 3 40S 35 50E
Manych-Gudilo, Oz. 83 46 24N 42 38E
Manych, R. 83 47 0N 41 15E
Manyonga, R. 126 4 5S 34 0E
Manyoni 126 5 45S 34 55E
Manyoni □ 126 6 30S 34 30E
Manzai 94 32 20N 70 15E
Manzala, Bahra el 122 31 10N 31 56E
Manzanares 59 39 0N 3 22W
Manzaneda, Cabeza de 56 42 12N 7 15W
Manzanillo, Cuba 166 20 20N 77 10W
Manzanillo, Mexico 164 19 0N 104 20W
Manzanillo, Pta. 166 9 30N 79 40W
Manzano Mts. 161 34 30N 106 45W
Manzini 129 26 30S 31 25E
Mao 117 14 4N 15 19E
Maohsing 107 45 31N 124 32E
Maoke, Pengunungan 102 3 40S 137 30E
Maolin 107 43 55N 123 25E
Maoming 109 21 39N 110 54E
Maopi T'ou 109 21 56N 120 43E
Maoping 109 30 51N 110 54E
Maowen 108 31 41N 103 52E
Mapastepec 165 15 26N 92 54W
Mapia, Kepulauan 103 0 50N 134 20E
Mapien 108 28 48N 103 39E
Mapimí 164 25 50N 103 31W
Mapimí, Bolsón de 164 27 30N 103 15W
Map'ing 109 31 36N 113 33E
Mapinga 126 6 40S 39 12E
Mapinhane 129 22 20S 35 0E
Maple Creek 153 49 55N 109 29W
Mapleton 160 44 4N 123 58W
Maplewood 158 38 33N 90 18W
Mappinga 109 34 58S 138 52E
Maprik 135 3 44S 143 3E
Mapuca 97 15 36N 73 46E
Mapuera, R. 174 0 30S 58 25W
Maputo 129 25 58S 32 32E
Maqnã 92 28 25N 34 50E
Maquela do Zombo 124 6 0S 15 15E
Maquinchao 176 41 15S 68 50W
Maquoketa 158 42 4N 90 40W
Mar Chiquita, L. 172 30 40S 62 50W
Mar del Plata 172 38 0S 57 30W
Mar Menor, L. 59 37 40N 0 45W
Mar, Reg. 37 57 11N 2 53W
Mar, Serra do 173 25 30S 49 0W
Mara, Bangla. 98 28 11N 94 7E
Mara, Tanz. 126 1 30S 34 32E
Mara □, Tanz. 126 1 45S 34 20E
Mara □, Tanz. 126 1 30S 34 32E
Maraã 174 1 43S 65 25W
Marabá 170 5 20S 49 5W
Maracá, I. de 170 2 10N 50 30W
Maracaibo 174 10 40N 71 37W
Maracaibo, Lago de 174 9 40N 71 30W
Maracaju 173 21 38S 55 9W
Maracanã 170 0 46S 47 27W
Maracás 171 13 26S 40 27W
Maracay 174 10 15N 67 36W
Marādah 119 29 4N 19 4E
Maradi 121 13 35N 8 10E
Maradun 121 12 35N 6 18E
Marāgheh 92 37 30N 46 12E
Maragogipe 171 12 46S 38 55W
Marajó, B. de 170 1 0S 48 30W
Marajó, Ilha de 170 1 0S 49 30W
Maralal 124 1 0N 36 38E
Maralinga 137 29 45S 131 15E
Marama 140 35 10S 140 10E
Marampa 120 8 45N 10 28W
Maramureş □ 70 47 45N 24 0E
Maran 101 3 35N 102 45E
Marana 161 32 30N 111 9W
Maranboy 136 14 40S 132 40E
Maranchón 58 41 6N 2 15W
Marand 92 38 30N 45 45E
Marandellas 127 18 5S 31 42E
Maranguape 170 3 55S 38 50W
Maranhão = São Luis 170 2 31S 44 16W
Maranhão □ 170 5 0S 46 0W
Marañón, R. 174 4 50S 75 35W
Marano, L. di 63 45 42N 13 13E
Maranoa R. 139 27 50S 148 37E
Maraş 92 37 37N 36 53E
Maraşeşti 70 45 52N 27 5E
Maratea 65 39 59N 15 43E
Marateca 57 38 34N 8 40W
Marathókambos 69 37 43N 26 42E
Marathon, Austral. 138 20 51S 143 32E
Marathon, Can. 150 48 44N 86 23W
Marathón 69 38 11N 23 58E
Marathon, N.Y., U.S.A. 162 42 25N 76 3W
Marathon, Tex., U.S.A. 159 30 15N 103 15W
Maratua, I. 103 2 10N 118 35E
Maraú 171 14 6S 39 0W
Marazion 30 50 8N 5 29W
Marbat 91 17 0N 54 45E
Marbella 57 36 30N 4 57W
Marble Bar 136 21 9S 119 44E
Marble Falls 159 30 30N 98 15W
Marblehead 162 42 29N 70 51W
Marburg 48 50 49N 8 44E
Marby 72 63 7N 14 18E
Marcal, R. 53 47 21N 17 15E
Marcali 53 46 35N 17 25E
Marcaria 62 45 7N 10 34E
March 29 52 33N 0 5E
Marchand = Rommani 118 33 20N 6 40W
Marché 44 46 0N 1 20E
Marche □ 63 43 22N 13 10E
Marche-en-Famenne 47 50 14N 5 19E
Marchena 57 37 18N 5 23W
Marches = Marche 63 43 22N 13 10E
Marciana Marina 62 42 44N 10 12E
Marcianise 65 41 3N 14 16E
Marcigny 45 46 17N 4 2E
Marcillac-Vallon 44 44 29N 2 27E
Marcillat 44 46 12N 2 38E
Marcinelle 47 50 24N 4 26E
Marck 43 50 57N 1 57E
Marckolsheim 43 48 10N 7 30E
Marcos Juárez 172 32 42S 62 5W
Marcus I. 130 24 0N 153 45E
Mardan 94 34 20N 72 0E
Marden 28 52 7N 2 42W
Mardie 136 21 12S 115 59E
Mardin 92 37 20N 40 36E
Marechal Deodoro 170 9 43S 35 54W
Maree L. 36 57 40N 5 30W
Mareeba 138 16 59S 145 28E
Mareham le Fen 33 53 7N 0 3W
Marek 103 4 41S 120 24E
Marek = Stanke Dimitrov 66 42 27N 23 9E
Maremma 62 42 45N 11 15E
Maréna 120 14 0N 7 30W
Marenberg 63 46 38N 15 13E
Marengo 158 41 42N 92 5W
Marennes 126 45 49N 1 5W
Marenyi 126 4 22S 39 8E
Marerano 129 21 23S 44 52E
Maréttimo, I. 64 37 58N 12 5E
Mareuil-sur-Lay 44 46 32N 1 14W
Marfa 159 30 15N 104 0W
Marfleet 33 53 45N 0 15W
Margable 123 12 54N 42 38E
Margam 31 51 33N 3 45W
Marganets 82 47 40N 34 40E
Margao 97 14 12N 73 58E
Margaree Harbour 151 46 26N 61 8W
Margaret Bay 152 51 20N 127 20W
Margaret L. 152 58 56N 115 25W
Margaret, R. 136 12 57S 131 16E
Margaret River 137 33 57S 115 7E
Margarita, Isla de 174 11 0N 64 0W
Margarition 68 39 22N 20 26E
Margate, S. Afr. 129 30 50S 30 20E
Margate, U.K. 29 51 23N 1 24E
Margate City 162 39 20N 74 31W
Margelan 85 40 27N 71 42E
Margeride, Mts. de la 44 44 43N 3 38E
Margherita 98 27 16N 95 40E
Margherita di Savola 65 41 25N 16 5E
Marghita 70 47 22N 22 22E
Margonin 54 52 58N 17 5E
Margreten 47 50 49N 5 49E
Marguerite 152 52 30N 122 25W
Marhoum 118 34 27N 0 11W
Mari, A.S.S.R. □ 81 56 30N 48 0E
Maria Elena 172 22 18S 69 40W
Maria Grande 172 31 45S 59 55W
Maria, I. 138 14 52S 135 45E
Maria I. 138 42 35S 148 0E
Maria van Diemen, C. 142 34 29S 172 40E
Mariager 73 56 40N 10 0E
Mariager Fjord 73 56 42N 10 19E
Mariakani 126 3 50S 39 27E
Marian L. 152 63 0N 116 15W
Mariana 171 20 23S 43 25W
Mariana Is. 130 17 0N 145 0E
Mariana Trench 130 13 0N 145 0E
Marianao 166 23 8N 82 24W
Mariani 98 26 39N 94 19E
Marianna, Ark., U.S.A. 159 34 48N 90 48W
Marianna, Fla., U.S.A. 157 30 45N 85 15W
Mariannelund 73 57 37N 15 35E
Mariánské Lázně 52 49 57N 12 41E
Marias, R. 160 48 26N 111 40W
Mariato, Punta 166 7 12N 80 52W
Mariazell 52 47 47N 15 19E
Marib 91 15 25N 45 20E
Maribo 73 54 48N 11 30E
Maribor 63 46 36N 15 40E
Marico, R. 128 24 25S 26 30E
Maricopa, Ariz., U.S.A. 161 33 5N 112 2W
Maricopa, Calif., U.S.A. 163 35 7N 119 27W
Marîdî 123 4 55N 29 25E
Marîdî, W. 123 5 25N 29 21E
Marie Galante, I. 167 15 56N 61 16W
Mariecourt 149 61 30N 72 0W
Mariefred 72 59 15N 17 12E
Mariehamn (Maarianhamina) 75 60 5N 19 57E
Marienberg, Ger. 48 50 40N 13 10E
Marienberg, Neth. 47 52 30N 6 35E
Marienberg, P.N.G. 138 3 54S 144 10E
Marienbourg 47 50 6N 4 31E
Mariental 128 24 36S 18 0E
Mariestad 73 58 43N 13 50E
Marietta, Ga., U.S.A. 157 34 0N 84 30W
Marietta, Ohio, U.S.A. 156 39 27N 81 27W
Marignane 45 43 25N 5 13E
Mariinsk 76 56 10N 87 20E
Mariinskiy Posad 81 56 10N 47 45E
Marilia 173 22 0S 50 0W
Marillana 136 22 37S 119 24E
Marin 56 42 23N 8 42W
Marina 163 36 41N 121 48W
Marina di Cirò 65 39 22N 17 8E
Mariña, La 56 43 30N 7 40W
Marina Plains 138 14 37S 143 57E
Marinduque, I. 103 13 25N 122 0E
Marine City 156 42 45N 82 29W
Marinel, Le 127 10 25S 25 17E
Marineo 64 37 57N 13 23E
Marinette, Ariz., U.S.A. 161 33 41N 112 16W
Marinette, Wis., U.S.A. 156 45 4N 87 40W
Maringá 173 23 35S 51 50W
Marinha Grande 57 39 45N 8 56W
Marino 109 35 3S 138 31E
Marino Rocks 109 35 3S 138 31E
Marion, Austral. 109 34 59S 138 33E
Marion, Ala., U.S.A. 157 32 33N 87 20W
Marion, Ill., U.S.A. 159 37 45N 88 55W
Marion, Ind., U.S.A. 156 40 35N 85 40W
Marion, Iowa, U.S.A. 158 42 2N 91 36W
Marion, Kans., U.S.A. 158 38 25N 97 2W
Marion, Mich., U.S.A. 156 44 7N 85 8W
Marion, N.C., U.S.A. 157 35 42N 82 0W
Marion, Ohio, U.S.A. 156 40 38N 83 8W
Marion, S.C., U.S.A. 157 34 11N 79 22W
Marion, Va., U.S.A. 157 36 51N 81 29W
Marion Bay 140 35 12S 136 59E
Marion, L. 157 33 30N 80 15W
Marion Reef 138 19 10S 152 17E
Maripa 174 7 26N 65 9W
Mariposa 163 37 31N 119 59W
Mariscal Estigarribia 172 22 3S 60 40W
Maritime Alps = Alpes Maritimes 62 44 10N 7 10E
Maritsa 67 42 1N 25 50E
Maritsá 69 36 22N 28 10E
Maritsa, R. 67 42 15N 24 0E
Mariyampole = Kapsukas 80 54 33N 23 19E
Marjan 93 32 5N 68 20E
Mark 34 55 2N 5 1W
Marka 122 18 14N 41 19E
Markapur 97 15 44N 79 19E
Markaryd 73 56 28N 13 35E
Marke 47 50 48N 3 14E
Marked Tree 159 35 35N 90 24W
Markelo 46 52 14N 6 30E
Markelsdorfer Huk 48 54 33N 11 0E
Marken 46 52 26N 5 12E
Markerwaard 46 52 33N 5 15E
Market Bosworth 28 52 37N 1 24W
Market Deeping 29 52 40N 0 20W
Market Drayton 32 52 55N 2 30W
Market Harborough 29 52 29N 0 55W
Market Lavington 28 51 17N 1 59W
Market Rasen 33 53 24N 0 20W
Market Weighton 33 53 52N 0 40W
Markethill 38 54 18N 6 31W
Markfield 28 52 42N 1 18W
Markham I. 12 84 0N 0 45W
Markham L. 153 62 30N 102 35W
Markham Mts. 13 83 0S 164 0E
Markham, R. 135 6 41S 147 2E
Marki 54 52 20N 21 2E
Markinch 35 56 12N 3 9W
Markleeville 163 38 42N 119 47W
Markoupoulon 69 37 53N 23 57E
Markovac 66 44 14N 21 7E
Markovo 77 64 40N 169 40E
Markoye 121 14 39N 0 2E
Marks 81 51 45N 46 50E
Marks Tey 29 51 53N 0 48E
Marksville 159 31 10N 92 2W
Markt Schwaben 49 48 14N 11 49E
Marktredwitz 49 50 1N 12 2E
Marlboro, Can. 152 53 30N 116 50W
Marlboro, U.S.A. 162 42 19N 71 33W
Marlboro, N.Y., U.S.A. 162 41 36N 73 58W
Marlborough, Austral. 138 22 46S 149 52E
Marlborough, U.K. 28 51 26N 1 44W
Marlborough □ 143 41 45S 173 33E
Marlborough Downs 28 51 25N 1 55W
Marle 43 49 43N 3 47E
Marlin 159 31 25N 96 50W
Marlow, Austral. 141 35 17S 149 55E
Marlow, Ger. 48 54 8N 12 34E
Marlow, U.K. 29 51 34N 0 47W
Marlow, U.S.A. 159 34 40N 97 58W
Marly-le-Grand 50 46 47N 7 10E
Marmagao 97 15 25N 73 56E
Marmande 44 44 30N 0 10E
Marmara denizi 92 40 45N 28 15E
Marmara, I. 82 40 35N 27 38E
Marmara, Sea of = Marmara denizi 92 40 45N 28 15E
Marmaris 92 36 50N 28 14E
Marmarth 158 46 21N 103 52W
Marmion L. 150 48 55N 91 30W
Marmion Mt. 137 29 16S 119 50E
Marmolada, Mte. 63 46 25N 11 55E
Marmolejo 57 38 3N 4 13W
Marmora 150 44 28N 77 41W
Marnay 43 47 20N 5 48E
Marne 48 53 57N 9 1E
Marne □ 43 49 0N 4 10E
Marne, R. 43 48 53N 4 25E
Marnhull 28 50 58N 2 20W
Maro 124 8 30N 19 0E
Maroa 174 2 43N 67 33W
Maroala 129 15 23S 47 59E
Maroantsetra 129 15 26S 49 44E
Marocco ■ 129 32 0N 5 50W
Maromandia 129 14 13S 48 5E
Maroni, R. 175 4 0N 52 0W
Marónia 68 40 53N 25 24E
Maroochydore 139 26 29S 153 5E
Maroona 140 37 27S 142 54E
Maros, R. 53 46 25N 20 20E
Marosakoa 129 15 26S 46 38E

Marostica Maya, R

Marostica 63 45 44N 11 40 E
Maroua 121 10 40N 14 20 E
Marovoay 129 16 6 S 46 39 E
Marple 32 53 23N 2 5W
Marquard 128 28 40 S 27 28 E
Marqueira 57 38 41N 9 9W
Marquesas Is. = Marquises 131 9 30 S 140 0W
Marquette 156 46 30N 87 21W
Marquise 43 50 50N 1 40 E
Marquises, Is. 131 9 30 S 140 0W
Marra 139 31 12 S 144 10 E
Marra, Gebet 123 7 20N 27 35 E
Marradi 63 44 5N 11 37 E
Marrakech 118 31 40N 8 0W
Marrat 92 25 0N 45 35 E
Marrawah 138 40 55 S 144 42 E
Marrecas, Serra das 170 9 0 S 41 0W
Marree 139 29 39 S 138 1 E
Marrimane 129 22 58 S 33 34 E
Marromeu 125 18 40 S 36 25 E
Marroqui, Punta 56 36 0N 5 37W
Marrowie Creek 141 33 23 S 145 40 E
Marrubane 127 18 0 S 37 0 E
Marrum 46 53 19N 5 48 E
Marrupa 127 13 8 S 37 30 E
Mars, Le 158 43 0N 96 0W
Marsa Susa (Apollonia) 117 32 52N 21 59 E
Marsabit 126 2 18N 38 0 E
Marsabit □ 126 2 45N 37 45 E
Marsala 64 37 48N 12 25 E
Marsciano 63 42 54N 12 20 E
Marsden 141 33 47N 147 32 E
Marsdiep 46 52 58N 4 46 E
Marseillan 44 43 23N 3 31 E
Marseille 45 43 18N 5 23 E
Marseilles = Marseille 45 43 18N 5 23 E
Marsh I. 159 29 35N 91 50W
Marshall, Liberia 120 6 8N 10 22W
Marshall, Ark., U.S.A. 159 35 58N 92 40W
Marshall, Mich., U.S.A. 156 42 17N 84 59W
Marshall, Minn., U.S.A. 158 44 25N 95 45W
Marshall, Mo., U.S.A. 158 39 8N 93 15W
Marshall, Tex., U.S.A. 159 32 29N 94 20W
Marshall Is. 130 9 0N 171 0 E
Marshall, R. 138 22 59 S 136 59 E
Marshalltown 158 42 0N 93 0W
Marshfield, U.K. 28 51 27N 2 18W
Marshfield, Mo., U.S.A. 159 37 20N 92 58W
Marshfield, Wis., U.S.A. 158 44 42N 90 10W
Mársico Nuovo 65 40 26N 15 43 E
Marske by the sea 33 54 35N 1 0W
Märsta 72 59 37N 17 52 E
Marstal 73 54 51N 10 30 E
Marston Moor 33 53 58N 1 17W
Marstrand 73 57 53N 11 35 E
Mart 159 31 34N 96 51W
Marta, R. 63 42 18N 11 47 E
Martaban 98 16 30N 97 35 E
Martaban, G. of 98 15 40N 96 30 E
Martano 65 40 14N 18 18 E
Martapura 102 3 22 S 114 56 E
Marte 121 12 23N 13 46 E
Martebo 73 57 45N 18 30 E
Martelange 47 49 49N 5 43 E
Martés, Sierra 59 39 20N 1 0W
Marthaguy Creek 141 30 50 S 147 45 E
Martham 29 52 42N 1 38 E
Martha's Vineyard 162 41 25N 70 35W
Martigné Ferchaud 42 47 50N 1 20W
Martigny 50 46 6N 7 3 E
Martigues 45 43 24N 5 4 E
Martil 118 35 36N 5 15W
Martin, Czech. 53 49 6N 18 48 E
Martin, S.D., U.S.A. 158 43 11N 101 45W
Martin, Tenn., U.S.A. 159 36 23N 88 51W
Martin, L. 157 32 45N 85 50W
Martin, R. 58 41 2N 0 43W
Martina 51 46 53N 10 28 E
Martina Franca 65 40 42N 17 20 E
Martinborough 142 41 14 S 175 29 E
Martinez 163 38 1N 122 8W
Martinho Campos 171 19 20 S 45 13W
Martinique, I. 167 14 40N 61 0W
Martinique Passage 167 15 15N 61 0W
Martínon 69 38 25N 23 15 E
Martinópolis 173 22 11 S 51 12W
Martins 171 6 5 S 37 55W
Martinsberg 52 48 22N 15 9 E
Martinsburg 156 39 30N 77 57W
Martinsville, Ind., U.S.A. 156 39 29N 86 23W
Martinsville, Va., U.S.A. 157 36 41N 79 52W
Martley 28 52 14N 2 22W
Martock 28 50 58N 2 47W
Marton 142 40 4 S 175 23 E
Martorell 58 41 28N 1 56 E
Martos 57 37 44N 3 58W
Martre, La, L. 148 63 8N 117 16W
Martre, La, R. 148 63 0N 118 0W
Martuk 84 50 46N 56 31 E
Martuni 83 40 9N 45 10 E
Maru 121 12 22N 6 22 E
Marudi 102 4 10N 114 25 E
Maruf 93 31 30N 67 0 E
Marugame 110 34 15N 133 55 E
Maruggio 65 40 20N 17 33 E
Marui 135 4 4 S 143 2 E
Maruim 170 10 45 S 37 5W
Marulan 141 34 43 S 150 3 E
Marum 46 53 9N 6 16 E
Marunga 128 17 20 S 20 2 E
Marungu, Mts. 126 7 30 S 30 0 E
Maruoka 111 36 9N 136 16 E
Marvejols 44 44 33N 3 19 E
Marvine Mt. 161 38 44N 111 40W
Marwar 94 25 43N 73 45 E
Mary 76 37 40N 61 50 E
Mary Frances L. 153 63 19N 106 13W
Mary Kathleen 138 20 35 S 139 48 E
Maryborough, Queens., Austral. 139 25 31 S 152 37 E
Maryborough, Vic., Austral. 140 37 0 S 143 44 E
Maryets 81 56 17N 49 47 E
Maryfield 153 49 50N 101 35W
Marykirk 37 56 47N 2 30W
Maryland □ 156 39 10N 76 40W
Maryland Jc. 127 12 45 S 30 31 E
Maryport 32 54 43N 3 30W
Mary's Harbour 151 52 18N 55 51W
Marystown 151 47 10N 55 10W
Marysvale 161 38 25N 112 17W
Marysville, Can. 152 49 35N 116 0W
Marysville, Calif., U.S.A. 160 39 14N 121 40W
Marysville, Kans., U.S.A. 158 39 50N 96 38W
Marysville, Ohio, U.S.A. 156 40 15N 83 20W
Marytavy 30 50 34N 4 6W
Maryvale 139 28 4 S 152 12 E
Maryville 157 35 50N 84 0W
Marywell 37 56 35N 2 31W
Marzo, Punta 174 6 50N 77 42W
Marzuq 119 25 53N 14 10 E
Masada = Mesada 90 31 20N 35 19 E
Masafa 127 13 50 S 27 30 E
Masai 101 1 29N 103 55 E
Masai Steppe 126 4 30 S 36 30 E
Masaka 126 0 21 S 31 45 E
Masakali 121 13 2N 12 32 E
Masalima, Kepulauan 102 5 10 S 116 50 E
Masamba 103 2 30 S 120 15 E
Masan 107 35 11N 128 32 E
Masanasa 59 39 25N 0 25W
Masandam, Ras 93 26 30N 56 30 E
Masasi 127 10 45 S 38 52 E
Masasi □ 127 10 45 S 38 50 E
Masaya 166 12 0N 86 7W
Masba 121 10 35N 13 1 E
Mascara 118 35 26N 0 6 E
Mascota 164 20 30N 104 50W
Masela 103 8 9 S 129 51 E
Maseme 147 18 46 S 25 3 E
Maseru 128 29 18 S 27 30 E
Mashaba 127 20 2 S 30 29 E
Mashabih 92 25 35N 36 30 E
Masham 33 54 15N 1 40W
Mashan 108 23 44N 108 14 E
Masherbrum, mt. 95 35 38N 76 18 E
Mashhad 93 36 20N 59 35 E
Mashi 121 13 0N 7 54 E
Mashiki 110 32 51N 130 53 E
Mashki Chah 93 29 5N 62 30 E
Mashkode 150 47 2N 84 7W
Mashonaland, North, □ 127 16 30 S 30 0 E
Mashonaland, South, □ 127 18 0 S 31 30 E
Mashtagi 83 40 35N 50 0 E
Masi 74 69 26N 23 50 E
Masi-Manimba 124 4 40 S 18 5 E
Masindi 126 1 40N 31 43 E
Masindi Port 126 1 43N 32 2 E
Masirah 91 20 25N 58 50 E
Masisea 174 8 35 S 74 15W
Masisi 126 1 23 S 28 49 E
Masjed Solyman 92 31 55N 49 25 E
Mask, L. 38 53 36N 9 24W
Maski 97 15 56N 76 46 E
Maslen Nos 67 42 18N 27 48 E
Maslinica 63 43 24N 16 13 E
Masnou 58 41 28N 2 20 E
Masoala, C. 129 15 59 S 50 13 E
Masoarivo 129 19 3 S 44 19 E
Masohi 103 3 2 S 128 15 E
Masomeloka 129 20 17 S 48 37 E
Mason, Nev., U.S.A. 163 38 56N 119 8W
Mason, S.D., U.S.A. 158 45 12N 103 27W
Mason, Tex., U.S.A. 159 30 45N 99 15W
Mason B. 143 46 55 S 167 45 E
Mason City 160 48 0N 119 0W
Masqat 93 23 37N 58 36 E
Massa 62 44 2N 10 7 E
Massa Marittima 62 43 3N 10 52 E
Massa, O. 118 30 0N 9 30W
Massachusetts □ 162 42 25N 72 0W
Massachusetts B. 162 42 30N 70 0W
Massada 90 33 12N 35 45 E
Massafra 65 40 35N 17 8 E
Massaguet 124 12 28N 15 26 E
Massakory 117 13 0N 15 49 E
Massangena 129 21 34 S 33 0 E
Massapê 170 3 31 S 40 19W
Massarosa 62 43 53N 10 17 E
Massat 44 42 53N 1 21 E
Massava 84 60 40N 62 6 E
Massawa = Mitsiwa 123 15 35N 39 25 E
Massena 156 44 52N 74 55W
Massenya 117 11 30N 16 25 E
Masset 152 54 0N 132 0W
Massiac 44 45 15N 3 11 E
Massif Central 44 45 30N 2 21 E
Massillon 156 40 47N 81 30W
Massinga 125 23 15 S 35 22 E
Massingir 129 23 46 S 32 4 E
Mässlingen 98 62 42N 12 48 E
Massman 138 16 25 S 145 25 E
Masson I. 13 66 10 S 93 20 E
Mastaba 122 20 52N 39 30 E
Mastanli = Momchilgrad 21 41 33N 25 23 E
Masterton 142 40 56 S 175 39 E
Mástikho, Ákra 68 38 10N 26 2 E
Mastuj 95 36 20N 72 36 E
Mastung 93 29 50N 66 42 E
Mastura 122 23 7N 38 52 E
Masuda 110 34 40N 131 51 E
Masulipatam 96 16 12N 81 12 E
Maswa □ 126 1 20 S 34 0 E
Mat, R. 68 41 40N 20 0 E
Mata de São João 171 12 31 S 38 17W
Matabeleland North □ 127 20 0 S 28 0 E
Matabeleland South □ 127 19 0 S 29 0 E
Mataboor 103 1 41 S 138 3 E
Matachel, R. 57 38 32N 6 0W
Matachewan 150 47 56N 80 39W
Matad 105 47 12N 115 29 E
Matadi 124 5 52 S 13 31 E
Matador 153 50 49N 107 56W
Matagalpa 166 13 10N 85 40W
Matagami 150 49 45N 77 34W
Matagami, L. 150 49 50N 77 40W
Matagorda 159 28 43N 96 0W
Matagorda, B. 159 28 30N 96 15W
Matagorda I. 159 28 10N 96 40W
Matak, P. 101 3 18N 106 16 E
Matakana 141 32 59 S 145 54 E
Matale 97 7 30N 80 44 E
Matam 120 15 34N 13 17W
Matamata 142 37 48 S 175 47 E
Matameye 121 13 26N 8 28 E
Matamoros, Campeche, Mexico 165 25 53N 97 30W
Matamoros, Coahuila, Mexico 164 25 45N 103 1W
Matamoros, Puebla, Mexico 165 18 2N 98 17W
Matamoros, Tamaulipas, Mexico 165 25 50N 97 30W
Matana, D. 103 2 30 S 121 25 E
Matandu, R. 127 8 35 S 39 40 E
Matane 151 48 50N 67 33W
Mat'ang, Szechwan, China 108 31 54N 102 55 E
Mat'ang, Yunnan, China 108 23 30N 104 4 E
Matankari 121 13 46N 4 1 E
Matanuska 148 61 38N 149 0W
Matanzá 174 7 22N 73 2W
Matanzas 166 23 0N 81 40W
Matapá, Ákra 69 36 22N 22 27 E
Matapedia 151 48 0N 66 59W
Matara 97 5 58N 80 30 E
Mataram 102 8 41 S 116 10 E
Matarani 174 16 50 S 72 10W
Mataranka 136 14 55 S 133 4 E
Mataró 58 41 32N 2 29 E
Matarraña, R. 58 40 55N 0 8 E
Mataruška Banja 66 43 40N 20 45 E
Matata 142 37 54 S 176 48 E
Matatiele 129 30 20 S 28 49 E
Mataura 143 46 11 S 168 51 E
Mataura, R. 143 45 49 S 168 44 E
Matehuala 164 23 40N 100 50W
Mateira 171 18 54 S 50 30W
Mateke Hills 127 21 48 S 31 0 E
Matélica 63 43 15N 13 0 E
Matera 65 40 40N 16 37 E
Mátészalka 53 47 58N 22 20 E
Matetsi 127 18 12 S 26 0 E
Mateur 119 37 0N 9 48 E
Mateyev Kurgan 83 47 35N 38 47 E
Matfors 72 62 21N 17 2 E
Matha 44 45 52N 0 20W
Matheson I. 153 51 45N 96 56W
Mathews 162 37 26N 76 19W
Mathias Pass 143 43 7 S 171 6 E
Mathis 159 28 4N 97 48W
Mathoura 141 35 50 S 144 55 E
Mathry 31 51 56N 5 6W
Mathura 94 27 30N 77 48 E
Mati 103 6 55N 126 15 E
Mati, R. 68 41 40N 20 0 E
Matías Romero 165 16 53N 95 2W
Matibane 127 14 49 S 40 45 E
Matien 109 32 55N 116 26 E
Matlock 33 53 8N 1 32W
Matmata 119 33 30N 9 59 E
Matna 123 13 49N 35 10 E
Mato Grosso □ 175 14 0 S 55 0W
Mato Grosso, Planalto do 174 15 0 S 54 0W
Mato Verde 171 15 23 S 42 52W
Matochkin Shar 76 73 10N 56 40 E
Matong 135 5 36 S 151 50 E
Matopo Hills 127 20 36 S 28 20 E
Matopos 127 20 20 S 28 29 E
Matour 45 46 19N 4 29 E
Matozinhos 56 41 11N 8 42W
Matrah 93 23 37N 58 30 E
Matrûh 122 31 19N 27 9 E
Matsang Tsangpo (Brahmaputra), R. 99 29 25N 88 0 E
Matsena 121 13 5N 10 5 E
Matsesta 83 43 34N 39 44 E
Matsu Tao 109 26 9N 119 56 E
Matsubara 111 34 33N 135 34 E
Matsudo 111 35 47N 139 54 E
Matsue 110 35 25N 133 10 E
Matsumae 112 41 26N 140 7 E
Matsumoto 111 36 15N 138 0 E
Matsusaka 111 34 34N 136 32 E
Matsutō 111 36 31N 136 34 E
Matsuura 110 33 20N 129 49 E
Matsuyama 110 33 45N 132 45 E
Mattagami, R. 150 50 43N 81 29W
Mattancheri 97 9 50N 76 15 E
Mattawa 150 46 20N 78 45W
Mattawamkeag 151 45 30N 68 30W
Matterhorn, mt. 50 45 58N 7 39 E
Mattersburg 53 47 44N 16 24 E
Matthew Town 167 20 57N 73 40W
Matthew's Ridge 174 7 37N 60 10W
Mattice 150 49 40N 83 20W
Mattituck 162 40 58N 72 32W
Mattmar 72 63 18N 13 54 E
Mattoon 156 39 30N 88 20W
Matua 102 2 58 S 110 52 E
Matuba 129 24 28 S 32 49 E
Matucana 174 11 55 S 76 15W
Matun 94 33 22N 69 58 E
Maturín 174 9 45N 63 11W
Matutina 171 19 13 S 45 58W
Matzuzaki 111 34 43N 138 50 E
Mau-é-ele 129 24 18 S 34 2 E
Mau Escarpment 126 0 40 S 36 0 E
Mau Ranipur 95 25 16N 79 8 E
Mauagami, R. 150 49 30N 82 0W
Maubeuge 43 50 17N 3 57 E
Maubourguet 44 43 29N 0 1 E
Mauchline 34 55 31N 4 23W
Maud 37 57 30N 2 8W
Maud, Pt. 137 23 6 S 113 45 E
Maude 140 34 29 S 144 18 E
Maudheim 13 71 5 S 11 0W
Maudin Sun 99 16 0N 94 30 E
Maués 174 3 20 S 57 45W
Mauganj 99 24 50N 81 55 E
Maughold 32 54 18N 4 17W
Maughold Hd. 32 54 18N 4 17W
Maui I. 147 20 45N 156 20 E
Maulamyaing 99 16 30N 97 40 E
Maule □ 172 36 5 S 72 30W
Mauleon 44 43 14N 0 54W
Maulvibazar 98 24 29N 91 42 E
Maum 38 53 31N 9 35W
Maumee 156 41 35N 83 40W
Maumee, R. 156 41 42N 83 28W
Maumere 103 8 38 S 122 13 E
Maumturk Mts. 38 53 32N 9 42W
Maun 128 20 0 S 23 26 E
Mauna Kea, Mt. 147 19 50N 155 28W
Mauna Loa, Mt. 147 19 50N 155 28W
Maunath Bhanjan 95 25 56N 83 33 E
Maungaturoto 142 36 6 S 174 23 E
Maungdow 98 21 14N 94 5 E
Maungmagan Is. 99 14 0 S 97 48 E
Maungmagan Kyunzu 101 14 0N 97 48 E
Maupin 160 45 12N 121 9W
Maure-de-Bretagne 42 47 53N 2 0W
Maureen, oilfield 19 58 5N 1 45 E
Maurepas L. 159 30 18N 90 35W
Maures, mts. 45 43 15N 6 15 E
Mauriac 44 45 13N 2 19 E
Maurice L. 137 29 30 S 131 0 E
Mauriceville 142 40 45 S 175 35 E
Maurienne 45 45 15N 6 20 E
Mauritania ■ 116 20 50N 10 0W
Mauritius ■ 11 20 0 S 57 0 E
Mauron 42 48 9N 2 18W
Maurs 44 44 43N 2 12 E
Maurthe, R. 43 48 47N 6 9 E
Mauston 158 43 48N 90 5W
Mauterndorf 52 47 9N 13 40 E
Mauvezin 44 43 44N 0 53 E
Mauzé-sur le Mignon 44 46 12N 0 41W
Mavelikara 97 9 14N 76 32 E
Mavinga 125 15 50 S 20 10 E
Mavli 94 24 45N 73 55 E
Mavqi'im 90 31 38N 34 32 E
Mavrova 68 40 26N 19 32 E
Mavuradonha Mts. 127 16 30 S 31 30 E
Mawa 126 2 45N 26 33 E
Mawana 94 29 6N 77 58 E
Mawand 94 29 33N 68 38 E
Mawer 153 50 46N 106 22W
Mawgan 30 50 4N 5 10W
Mawkmai 98 20 14N 97 50 E
Mawlaik 98 23 40N 94 26 E
Mawlawkho 98 17 50N 97 38 E
Mawson Base 13 67 30 S 65 0 E
Max 158 47 50N 101 20W
Maxcanú 165 20 40N 90 10W
Maxhamish L. 152 59 50N 123 17W
Maxixe 129 23 54 S 35 17 E
Maxwellheugh 35 55 35N 2 23W
Maxwelltown 142 39 51 S 174 49 E
Maxwelton, Queens., Austral. 138 15 45 S 142 30 E
Maxwelton, Queens., Austral. 138 20 43 S 142 41 E
May Downs 138 22 38 S 148 55 E
May, I. of 35 56 11N 2 32W
May Nefalis 123 15 0N 38 12 E
May Pen 166 17 58N 77 15W
May River 135 4 19 S 141 58 E
Maya 58 43 12N 1 29W
Maya Gudo, Mt. 123 7 30N 37 8 E
Maya Mts. 165 16 30N 89 0W
Maya, R. 77 58 20N 135 0 E

Mayaguana Island Menglien

Mayaguana Island 167 21 30N 72 44W
Mayagüez 147 18 12N 67 9W
Mayahi 121 13 58N 7 40E
Mayals 58 41 22N 0 30E
Mayang 108 27 53N 109 48E
Mayanup 137 33 58S 116 25E
Mayapán 165 20 38N 89 27W
Mayarf 167 20 40N 75 39W
Mayarí 167 20 40N 75 41W
Mayavaram = Mayuram 97 11 3N 79 42E
Maybell 160 40 30N 108 4W
Maybole 34 55 21N 4 41W
Maychew 123 12 50N 39 42E
Maydena 138 42 45S 146 39E
Maydos 68 40 13N 26 20E
Mayen 49 50 18N 7 10E
Mayenne 42 48 20N 0 38W
Mayenne □ 42 48 10N 0 40W
Mayer 161 34 28N 112 17W
Mayerthorpe 152 53 57N 115 8W
Mayfield, Derby., U.K. 33 53 1N 1 47W
Mayfield, E. Sussex, U.K. 29 51 1N 0 17E
Mayfield, Ky., U.S.A. 157 36 45N 88 40W
Mayfield, N.Y., U.S.A. 162 43 6N 74 16W
Mayhill 161 32 58N 105 30W
Maykop 83 44 35N 40 25E
Mayli-Say 85 41 17N 72 24E
Maymyo 100 22 2N 96 28E
Maynard 162 42 30N 71 33W
Maynard Hills 137 28 35S 119 50E
Mayne, Le, L. 151 57 5N 68 30W
Mayne, R. 138 23 40S 142 10E
Maynooth, Can. 150 45 14N 77 56W
Maynooth, Ireland 38 53 22N 6 38W
Mayo 147 63 38N 135 57W
Mayo □ 139 53 47N 9 7W
Mayo Bridge 38 54 11N 6 13W
Mayo L. 147 63 45N 135 0W
Mayo, R. 164 26 45N 109 47W
Mayon, Mt. 103 13 15N 123 42E
Mayor I. 142 37 16S 176 17E
Mayorga 56 42 10N 5 16W
Mays Landing 162 39 27N 74 44W
Mayskiy 83 43 47N 43 59E
Mayson L. 153 57 55N 107 10W
Maysville 156 38 43N 84 16W
Mayu, I. 103 1 30N 126 30E
Mayuram 97 11 3N 79 42E
Mayville 158 47 30N 97 23W
Mayya 77 61 44N 130 18E
Mazabuka 127 15 52S 27 44E
Mazagán = El Jadida 118 33 11N 8 17W
Mazagão 175 0 20S 51 50W
Mazama 152 49 43N 120 8W
Mazamet 44 43 30N 2 20E
Mazán 174 3 15S 73 0W
Mazapil 164 24 38N 101 34W
Mazar-i-Sharif 93 36 41N 67 0E
Mazar, O. 118 32 0N 1 38E
Mazara del Vallo 64 37 40N 12 34E
Mazarredo 176 47 10S 66 50W
Mazarrón 59 37 38N 1 19W
Mazarrón, Golfo de 59 37 27N 1 19W
Mazaruni, R. 174 6 15N 60 0W
Mazatán 164 29 0N 110 8W
Mazatenango 166 14 35N 91 30W
Mazatlán 164 23 10N 106 30W
Māzhān 93 32 30N 59 0E
Mazheikyai 80 56 20N 22 20E
Mazinān 93 36 25N 56 48E
Mazoe 127 17 28S 30 58E
Mazoe R. 125 16 45S 32 30E
Mazoi 127 16 42S 33 7E
Mazrûb 123 14 0N 29 20E
Mazurian Lakes = Mazurski, Pojezierze 54 53 50N 21 0E
Mazurski, Pojezierze 54 53 50N 21 0E
Mazzarino 65 37 19N 14 12E
Mbaba 120 14 59N 16 44W
Mbabane 129 26 18S 31 6E
Mbagne 120 16 6N 14 47W
M'bahiakro 120 7 33N 4 19W
M'Baiki 124 3 53N 18 1E
Mbala 127 8 46S 31 17E
Mbale 126 1 8N 34 12E
Mbalmayo 121 3 33N 11 33E
Mbamba Bay 127 11 13S 34 49E
Mbandaka 124 0 1S 18 18E
Mbanga 121 4 30N 9 33E
Mbanza Congo 124 6 18S 14 16E
Mbanza Ngungu 124 5 12S 14 53E
Mbarara 126 0 35S 30 25E
Mbatto 120 6 28N 4 22W
Mbenkuru, R. 127 9 25S 39 50E
Mberubu 121 6 10N 7 38E
Mbesuma 127 10 0S 32 2E
Mbeya 127 8 54S 33 29E
Mbeya □ 126 8 15S 33 30E
Mbia 123 6 15N 29 18E
Mbimbi 127 13 25S 23 2E
Mbinga 127 10 50S 35 0E
Mbinga □ 127 10 50S 35 0E
Mbini □ 124 1 30N 10 0E
Mbiti 123 5 42N 28 3E
Mboki 123 5 19N 25 58E
Mboro 120 15 9N 16 54W
Mboune 120 14 42N 13 34W
Mbour 120 14 22N 16 54W
Mbout 120 16 1N 12 38W
Mbozi □ 127 9 0S 32 50E
Mbuji-Mayi 126 6 9S 23 40E
Mbulu 124 3 45S 35 30E
Mbulu □ 126 3 52S 35 33E
Mbumbi 128 18 26S 19 59E
Mburucuyá 172 28 1S 58 14W
M'chounech 119 34 57N 6 1E
M'Clure Str., Can. 10 75 0N 118 0W
M'Clure Str., Can. 12 74 0N 120 0W
Mdennah 118 24 37N 6 0W
Mead L. 161 36 1N 114 44W
Meade, Can. 150 49 26N 83 51W
Meade, U.S.A. 159 37 18N 100 25W
Meadow 137 26 35S 114 40E
Meadow Lake 153 54 10N 108 26W
Meadow Lake Prov. Park 153 54 27N 109 0W
Meadville 156 41 39N 80 9W
Meaford 150 44 36N 80 35W
Mealfuarvonie, Mt. 37 57 15N 4 34W
Mealhada 56 40 22N 8 27W
Mealsgate 32 54 46N 3 14W
Mealy Mts. 151 53 10N 60 0W
Meander, R. = Menderes, Büyük 92 37 45N 27 40E
Meander River 152 59 2N 117 42W
Meare's, C. 160 45 37N 124 0W
Mearim, R. 170 3 4S 44 35W
Mearns, Howe of the 37 56 52N 2 26W
Measham 28 52 43N 1 30W
Meath □ 38 53 32N 6 40W
Meath Park 153 53 27N 105 22W
Meatian 140 35 34S 143 21E
Meaulne 44 46 36N 2 28E
Meaux 43 48 58N 2 50E
Mecanhelas 127 15 12S 35 54E
Mecca 163 33 37N 116 3W
Mecca = Makkah 122 21 30N 39 54E
Mechanicsburg 162 40 12N 77 0W
Mechanicville 162 42 54N 73 41W
Mechara 123 8 36N 40 20E
Mechelen, Anvers, Belg. 47 51 2N 4 29E
Mechelen, Limbourg, Belg. 47 50 58N 5 41E
Méchéria 118 33 35N 0 18W
Mechernich 48 50 35N 6 39E
Mechetinskaya 83 46 45N 40 32E
Mecidiye 68 40 38N 26 32E
Mecitözü 82 40 32N 35 25E
Mecklenburg B. 48 54 20N 11 40E
Meconta 127 14 59S 39 50E
Meda 56 40 57N 7 18W
Meda P.O. 136 17 22S 123 59E
Meda, R. 136 17 20S 124 30E
Medaguine 118 33 41N 3 26E
Medak 96 18 1N 78 15E
Medan 102 3 40N 98 38E
Medanosa, Pta. 176 48 0S 66 0W
Medawachchiya 97 8 30N 80 30E
Meddouza, cap 118 32 33N 9 9W
Médéa 118 36 12N 2 50E
Mededa 66 43 44N 19 15E
Medeiros Neto 171 17 20S 40 14W
Medel, Pic 51 46 37N 8 55E
Medellín 174 6 15N 75 35W
Medemblik 46 52 46N 5 8E
Meder 123 14 42N 40 44E
Mederdra 120 17 0N 15 38W
Medford, Oreg., U.S.A. 160 42 20N 122 52W
Medford, Wis., U.S.A. 158 45 9N 90 21W
Medford Lakes 162 39 52N 74 48W
Medgidia 70 44 15N 28 19E
Medi 123 5 4N 30 42E
Media 162 39 55N 75 23W
Media Agua 172 31 58S 68 25W
Media Luna 172 34 45S 66 44W
Mediaş 70 46 9N 24 22E
Medical Lake 160 47 41N 117 42W
Medicina 63 44 29N 11 38E
Medicine Bow 160 41 56N 106 11W
Medicine Hat 153 50 0N 110 45W
Medicine Lake 158 48 30N 104 30W
Medicine Lodge 159 37 20N 98 37W
Medina, Brazil 171 16 15S 41 29W
Medina, Colomb. 174 4 30N 73 21W
Medina, N.D., U.S.A. 158 46 57N 99 20W
Medina, N.Y., U.S.A. 156 43 15N 78 27W
Medina, Ohio, U.S.A. 156 41 9N 81 50W
Medina = Al Madīnah 92 24 35N 39 52E
Medina de Rioseco 56 41 53N 5 3W
Medina del Campo 56 41 18N 4 55W
Medina L. 159 29 35N 98 58W
Medina, R. 159 29 10N 98 20W
Medina-Sidonia 57 36 28N 5 57W
Medinaceli 58 41 12N 2 30W
Mediterranean Sea 60 35 0N 15 0E
Medjerda, O. 119 36 35N 8 30E
Medkovets 67 43 37N 23 10E
Medley 153 54 25N 110 16W
Mednogorsk 84 51 24N 57 37E
Médoc 44 45 10N 0 56W
Medstead, Can. 153 53 19N 108 5W
Medstead, U.K. 28 51 7N 1 4W
Medulin 63 44 49N 13 55E
Medveda 66 42 50N 21 32E
Medveditsa, R. 81 50 30N 44 0E
Medvedok 81 57 20N 50 1E
Medvezhi, Ostrava 77 71 0N 161 0E
Medvezhyegorsk 78 63 0N 34 25E
Medway, R. 29 51 12N 0 23E
Medyn 81 54 59N 35 56E
Medzev 53 48 43N 20 55E
Medzilaborce 53 49 17N 21 52E
Meeandh 108 27 26S 153 6E
Meeberrie 137 26 57S 116 0E
Meekatharra 137 26 32S 118 29E
Meeker 160 40 1N 107 58W
Meelpaeg L. 151 48 18N 56 35W
Meeniyan 141 38 35S 146 0E
Meer 47 51 27N 4 45E
Meerane 48 50 51N 12 30E
Meerbeke 47 50 50N 4 3E
Meerle 47 51 29N 4 48E
Meerssen 47 50 53N 5 50E
Meerut 94 29 1N 77 50E
Meeteetsa 160 44 10N 108 56W
Meeuwen 47 51 6N 5 31E
Mega 123 3 57N 38 30E
Megálo Khorío 69 36 27N 27 24E
Megálo Petalí, I. 69 38 0N 24 15E
Megalópolis 69 37 25N 22 7E
Meganísi, I. 69 38 39N 20 48E
Mégantic 151 45 35N 70 56W
Mégara 69 37 58N 23 22E
Megarine 119 33 14N 6 2E
Megdhova, R. 69 39 10N 21 45E
Megen 46 51 49N 5 34E
Mégève 45 45 51N 6 37E
Meghalaya □ 98 25 50N 91 0E
Meghalayap 99 25 40N 89 55E
Meghezez, Mt. 123 9 18N 39 26E
Meghna, R. 98 23 45N 90 40E
Megiddo 90 32 36N 35 11E
Mégiscane, L. 150 48 35N 75 55W
Megiste 61 36 8N 29 34E
Mehadia 70 44 56N 22 23E
Mehaigne, R. 47 50 32N 5 13E
Mehaïguene, O. 118 32 20N 2 45E
Meharry, Mt. 132 22 59S 118 35E
Mehedinti □ 70 44 40N 22 45E
Meheisa 122 19 38N 32 57E
Mehndawal 95 26 58N 83 5E
Mehsana 94 23 39N 72 26E
Mehun-sur-Yèvre 43 47 10N 2 13E
Mei Chiang, R. 109 24 24N 116 35E
Meia Ponte, R. 171 18 32S 49 36W
Meichuan 109 30 9N 115 33E
Meidrim 31 51 51N 4 3W
Meiganga 124 6 20N 14 10E
Meigh 38 54 8N 6 22W
Meihsien, Kwangtung, China 109 24 18N 116 7E
Meihsien, Shensi, China 106 34 16N 107 42E
Meijel 47 51 21N 5 53E
Meiktila 98 21 0N 96 0E
Meilen 51 47 16N 8 39E
Meiningen 48 50 32N 10 25E
Meio, R. 171 13 36S 49 7W
Meira, Sierra de 56 43 15N 7 15W
Meiringen 50 46 43N 8 12E
Meishan 108 30 3N 103 51E
Meissen 48 51 10N 13 29E
Meit'an 108 27 48N 107 28E
Meithalun 90 32 21N 35 16E
Méjean 44 44 15N 3 30E
Mejillones 172 23 10S 70 30W
Meka 137 27 25S 116 48E
Mekambo 124 1 2N 14 5E
Mekdela 123 11 24N 39 10E
Mekhtar 93 30 30N 69 15E
Meklong = Samut Songkhram 101 13 24N 100 1E
Meknès 118 33 57N 5 33W
Meko 121 7 27N 2 52E
Mekong, R. 101 18 0N 104 15E
Mekongga 103 3 50S 121 30E
Mekoryok 147 60 20N 166 20W
Melagiri Hills 97 12 20N 77 30E
Melah, Sebkhet el 118 29 20N 1 30W
Melaka 101 2 15N 102 15E
Melaka □ 101 2 20N 102 15E
Melalap 102 5 10N 116 5E
Mélambes 69 35 8N 24 40E
Melanesia 130 4 0S 155 0E
Melapalaiyam 97 8 39N 77 44E
Melbost 36 58 12N 6 20W
Melbourn 29 52 5N 0 1E
Melbourne, Austral. 141 37 50S 145 0E
Melbourne, U.K. 28 52 50N 1 25W
Melbourne, U.S.A. 157 28 13N 80 14W
Melcésine 62 45 46N 10 48E
Melchor Múzquiz 164 27 50N 101 40W
Melchor Ocampo (San Pedro Ocampo) 164 24 52N 101 40W
Méldola 63 44 7N 12 3E
Meldorf 48 54 5N 9 5E
Mêle-sur-Sarthe, Le 42 48 31N 0 22E
Melegnano 62 45 21N 9 20E
Melekess = Dimitrovgrad 81 54 25N 49 33E
Melenci 66 45 32N 20 20E
Melenki 81 55 20N 41 37E
Meleuz 84 52 58N 55 55E
Melfi, Chad 117 11 0N 17 59E
Melfi, Italy 65 41 0N 15 40E
Melfort, Can. 153 52 50N 104 37W
Melfort, Rhod. 127 18 0S 31 25E
Melfort, Loch 34 56 13N 5 33W
Melgaço 56 42 7N 8 15W
Melgar de Fernamental 56 42 27N 4 17W
Melhus 71 63 17N 10 18E
Melick 47 51 10N 6 1E
Melide 51 45 57N 8 57E
Meligalá 69 37 15N 21 59E
Melilla 118 35 21N 2 57W
Melilot 42 31 22N 34 37E
Melipilla 172 33 42S 71 15W
Mélissa Óros 69 37 32N 26 4E
Melita 153 49 15N 101 5W
Mélito di Porto Salvo 65 37 55N 15 47E
Melitopol 82 46 50N 35 22E
Melk 52 48 13N 15 20E
Melksham 28 51 22N 2 9W
Mellan-Fryken 72 59 45N 13 10E
Mellansel 74 63 25N 18 17E
Melle, Belg. 47 51 0N 3 49E
Melle, France 44 46 14N 0 10W
Melle, Ger. 48 52 12N 8 20E
Mellégue, O. 119 36 32N 8 51E
Mellen 158 46 19N 90 36W
Mellerud 73 58 41N 12 28E
Mellette 158 45 11N 98 29W
Mellid 56 42 55N 8 1W
Mellish Reef 133 17 25S 155 50E
Mellit 123 14 15N 25 40E
Mellon Charles 36 57 52N 5 37W
Melmerby 32 54 44N 2 35W
Melnik 67 40 58N 23 25E
Mělník 52 50 22N 14 23E
Melo 173 32 20S 54 10W
Melolo 103 9 53S 120 40E
Melones Res. 163 37 57N 120 31W
Melouprey 100 13 48N 105 16E
Melovoye 83 49 25N 40 5E
Melrhir, Chott 119 34 25N 6 24E
Melrose, N.S.W., Austral. 141 32 42S 146 57E
Melrose, W. Australia, Austral. 137 27 50S 121 15E
Melrose, U.K. 35 55 35N 2 44W
Melrose, U.S.A. 159 34 27N 103 33W
Mels 51 47 3N 9 25E
Melsele 47 51 13N 4 17E
Melsonby 33 54 28N 1 41W
Melstone 160 46 45N 108 0W
Melsungen 48 51 8N 9 34E
Melton 29 52 51N 1 1E
Melton Constable 29 52 52N 1 1E
Melton Mowbray 29 52 46N 0 52W
Melun 43 48 32N 2 39E
Melunga 128 17 15S 16 22E
Melur 97 10 2N 78 23E
Melut 123 10 30N 32 20E
Melvaig 36 57 48N 5 49W
Melvich 37 58 33N 3 55W
Melville 153 50 55N 102 50W
Melville B. 138 12 0S 136 45E
Melville, C. 138 14 11S 144 30E
Melville I., Austral. 136 11 30S 131 0E
Melville I., Can. 12 75 30N 111 0W
Melville, L., Newf., Can. 151 53 45N 59 40W
Melville, L., Newf., Can. 151 59 30N 53 40W
Melville Pen. 149 68 0N 84 0W
Melvin L. 38 54 26N 8 10W
Melvin, R. 152 59 11N 117 31W
Mélykút 53 46 11N 19 25E
Memaliaj 68 40 25N 19 58E
Memba 127 14 11S 40 30E
Memboro 103 9 30S 119 30E
Membrilla 59 38 59N 3 21W
Memel 129 27 38S 29 36E
Memel = Klaipeda 80 55 43N 21 10E
Memmingen 49 47 59N 10 12E
Memphis, Tenn., U.S.A. 159 35 7N 90 0W
Memphis, Tex., U.S.A. 159 34 45N 100 30W
Mena 159 34 40N 94 15W
Menai Bridge 31 53 14N 4 11W
Menai Strait 31 53 7N 4 20W
Ménaka 121 15 59N 2 18E
Menaldum 46 53 13N 5 40E
Menamurtee 140 31 25S 143 11E
Menarandra, R. 129 25 0S 44 50E
Menard 159 30 57N 99 58W
Menasha 156 44 13N 88 27W
Menate 102 0 12S 112 47E
Mendawai, R. 102 1 30S 113 0E
Mende 44 44 31N 3 30E
Mendebo Mts. 123 7 0N 39 22E
Mendenhall, C. 147 59 44N 166 10W
Menderes, R. 92 37 25N 28 45E
Mendez 165 25 7N 98 34W
Mendhar 95 33 35N 74 10E
Mendi, Ethiopia 123 9 47N 35 4E
Mendi, P.N.G. 135 6 11S 143 47E
Mendip Hills 28 51 17N 2 40W
Mendlesham 29 52 15N 1 4E
Mendocino 160 39 26N 123 50W
Mendong Gompa 95 31 16N 85 11E
Mendota, Calif., U.S.A. 163 36 46N 120 24W
Mendota, Ill., U.S.A. 158 41 35N 89 5W
Mendoza 172 32 50S 68 52W
Mendoza □ 172 33 0S 69 0W
Mendrisio 51 45 52N 8 59E
Mene Grande 174 9 49N 70 56W
Menemen 92 38 18N 27 10E
Menen 47 50 47N 3 7E
Menfi 64 37 36N 12 57E
Meng-pan 99 23 5N 100 19E
Meng-so 101 22 33N 99 31E
Meng-wang 99 22 17N 100 32E
Meng Wang 101 22 18N 100 31E
Mengch'eng 106 33 17N 116 34E
Mengeš 63 46 24N 14 35E
Menggala 102 4 20S 105 15E
Menghai 108 21 58N 100 28E
Menghsien 106 34 54N 112 47E
Mengíbar 57 37 58N 3 48W
Mengla 108 21 28N 101 35E
Menglien 108 22 21N 99 36E

Mengoub Mikołajki

Mengoub 118 29 49N 5 26W
Mengpolo 108 24 24N 99 14E
Mengshan 109 24 12N 110 31E
Mengting 108 23 33N 98 5E
Mengtz = Mengtzu 108 23 25N 103 20E
Mengtzu 108 23 25N 103 20E
Mengyin 107 35 40N 117 55E
Menihek L. 151 54 0N 67 0W
Menin 47 50 47N 3 7E
Menindee 140 32 20N 142 25E
Menindee, L. 140 32 20N 142 25E
Meningie 140 35 43S 139 20E
Menkúng 99 28 38N 98 24E
Menlo Park 163 37 27N 122 12W
Menominee 156 45 9N 87 39W
Menominee, R. 156 45 30N 87 50W
Menomonie 158 44 50N 91 54W
Menor, Mar 59 37 43N 0 48W
Menorca, I. 58 40 0N 4 0E
Mentawai, Kepulauan 102 2 0S 99 0E
Mentekab 101 3 29N 102 21E
Menton 45 43 50N 7 29E
Menyamya 135 7 10S 145 59E
Menzel-Bourguiba 119 39 9N 9 49E
Menzel Chaker 119 35 0N 10 26E
Menzelinsk 84 55 53N 53 1E
Menzies 137 29 40S 120 58E
Me'ona (Tarshiha) 90 33 1N 35 15E
Meoqui 164 28 17N 105 29W
Mepaco 127 15 57S 30 48E
Meppel 47 52 42N 6 12E
Meppen 48 52 41N 7 20E
Mequinenza 58 41 22N 0 17E
Mer Rouge 159 32 47N 91 48W
Merabéllou, Kólpos 69 35 10N 25 50E
Merai 135 4 52S 152 19E
Merak 103 5 55S 106 1E
Meramangye, L. 137 28 25S 132 13E
Merano (Meran) 63 46 40N 11 10E
Merate 62 45 42N 9 23E
Merauke 103 8 29S 140 24E
Merbabu, Mt. 103 7 30S 110 40E
Merbein 140 34 10S 142 2E
Merca 91 1 48N 44 50E
Mercadal 58 39 59N 4 5E
Mercara 97 12 30N 75 45E
Mercato Saraceno 63 43 57N 12 11E
Merced 163 37 18N 120 30W
Merced Pk. 163 37 36N 119 24W
Merced, R. 163 37 21N 120 58W
Mercedes, Buenos Aires, Argent. 172 34 40S 59 30W
Mercedes, Corrientes, Argent. 172 29 10S 58 5W
Mercedes, San Luis, Argent. 172 33 5S 65 21W
Mercedes, Uruguay 172 33 12S 58 0W
Merceditas 172 28 20S 70 35W
Mercer 142 37 16S 175 5E
Merchtem 47 50 58N 4 14E
Mercy C. 149 65 0N 62 30W
Merdrignac 42 48 11N 2 27W
Mere, Belg. 47 50 55N 3 58E
Mere, U.K. 28 51 5N 2 16W
Meredith C. 176 52 15S 60 40W
Meredith, L. 159 35 30N 101 35W
Merei 70 45 7N 26 43E
Merelbeke 47 51 0N 3 45E
Méréville 43 48 20N 2 5E
Merewa 123 7 40N 36 54E
Mergenevo 84 49 56N 51 18E
Mergenevskiy 83 49 59N 51 15E
Mergui 101 12 30N 98 35E
Mergui Arch. = Myeik Kyunzu 101 11 30N 97 30E
Meribah 140 34 43S 140 51E
Mérida, Mexico 165 20 50N 89 40W
Mérida, Spain 57 38 55N 6 25W
Mérida, Venez. 174 8 36N 71 8W
Mérida □ 174 8 30N 71 10W
Mérida, Cord. de 174 9 0N 71 0W
Meriden, U.K. 28 52 27N 1 36W
Meriden, U.S.A. 162 41 33N 72 47W
Meridian, Idaho, U.S.A. 160 43 41N 116 25W
Meridian, Miss., U.S.A. 157 32 20N 88 42W
Meridian, Tex., U.S.A. 159 31 55N 97 37W
Mering 49 48 15N 11 0E
Merioneth (□) 26 52 49N 3 55W
Merirumã 175 1 15N 54 50W
Merke 85 42 52N 73 11E
Merkel 159 32 30N 100 0W
Merkem 47 50 57N 2 51E
Merksem 47 51 16N 4 25E
Merksplas 47 51 22N 4 52E
Merlebach 43 49 5N 6 52E
Merlerault, Le 42 48 41N 0 16E
Mermaid Mt. 108 27 29S 152 49E
Mermaid Reef 136 17 6S 119 36E
Mern 73 55 3N 12 3E
Merowe 122 18 29N 31 46E
Merredin 137 31 28S 118 18E
Merrick, Mt. 34 55 8N 4 30W
Merrill, Oregon, U.S.A. 160 42 2N 121 37W
Merrill, Wis., U.S.A. 158 45 11N 89 41W
Merrimack, R. 162 42 49N 70 49W
Merritt 152 50 10N 120 45W
Merriwa 141 32 6S 150 22E
Merriwagga 141 33 47S 145 43E
Merroe 137 27 53S 117 50E
Merry I. 150 55 29N 77 31W
Merrygoen 141 31 51S 149 12E
Merryville 159 30 47N 93 31W
Mersa Fatma 123 14 57N 40 17E
Mersch 47 49 44N 6 7E
Merse, dist. 35 55 40N 2 30W
Mersea I. 29 51 48N 0 55E
Merseburg 48 51 20N 12 0E
Mersey, R. 32 53 20N 2 56W
Merseyside □ 32 53 25N 2 55W
Mersin 92 36 51N 34 36E
Mersing 101 2 25N 103 50E
Merta 94 26 39N 74 4E
Mertert 47 49 43N 6 29E
Merthyr Tydfil 31 51 45N 3 23W
Mértola 57 37 40N 7 40E
Merton 29 51 25N 0 13W
Mertzig 47 49 51N 6 1E
Mertzon 159 31 17N 100 48W
Méru 43 49 13N 2 8E
Meru 126 0 3N 37 40E
Meru □ 126 0 3N 37 46E
Meru, mt. 126 3 15S 36 46E
Merville 43 50 38N 2 38E
Méry-sur-Seine 43 48 31N 3 54E
Merzifon 82 40 53N 35 32E
Merzig 49 49 26N 6 37E
Merzouga, Erg Tin 119 24 0N 11 4E
Mesa 161 33 20N 111 56W
Mesa, La, Colomb. 174 4 38N 74 28W
Mesa, La, Calif., U.S.A. 163 32 48N 117 5W
Mesa, La, N. Mex., U.S.A. 161 32 6N 106 48W
Mesach Mellet 119 24 30N 11 30E
Mesada 90 31 20N 35 19E
Mesagne 65 40 34N 17 48E
Mesaras, Kólpos 69 35 6N 24 47E
Meschede 48 51 20N 8 17E
Mesfinto 123 13 30N 37 22E
Mesgouez, L. 150 51 20N 75 0W
Meshchovsk 80 54 22N 35 17E
Meshed = Mashhad 93 36 20N 59 35E
Meshoppen 162 41 36N 76 3W
Mesick 156 44 24N 85 42W
Mesilinka, R. 152 56 6N 124 30W
Mesilla 161 32 20N 107 0W
Meslay-du-Maine 42 47 58N 0 33W
Mesocco 51 46 23N 9 12E
Mesolóngion 69 38 27N 21 28E
Mesopotamia, reg. 69 33 30N 44 0E
Mesoraca 65 39 5N 16 47E
Mésou Volímais 69 37 53N 27 35E
Mess Cr. 152 57 55N 131 14W
Messac 42 47 49N 1 50W
Messad 118 34 8N 3 30E
Méssaména 121 3 48N 12 49E
Messancy 47 49 36N 5 49E
Messeix 44 45 37N 2 33E
Messina, Italy 65 38 10N 15 32E
Messina, S. Afr. 129 22 20S 30 12E
Messina, Str. di 65 38 5N 15 35E
Messini 69 37 4N 22 1E
Messínia □ 69 37 10N 22 0E
Messiniakós, Kólpos 69 36 45N 22 5E
Mestà, Ákra 69 38 16N 25 53E
Mesta, R. 67 41 30N 24 0E
Mestanza 57 38 35N 4 4W
Město Teplá 52 49 59N 12 52E
Mestre 63 45 30N 12 13E
Mestre, Espigão 171 12 30S 46 10W
Městys Zelezná Ruda 52 49 8N 13 15E
Meta □ 174 3 30N 73 0W
Meta, R. 174 6 20N 68 5W
Metagama 150 47 0N 81 55W
Metaline Falls 160 48 52N 117 22W
Metán 172 25 30S 65 0W
Metauro, R. 63 43 45N 12 59E
Metchosin 152 48 15N 123 37W
Metehara 123 8 58N 39 57E
Metema 123 12 56N 36 13E
Metengobalame 127 14 49S 34 30E
Méthana 69 37 35N 23 23E
Metheringham 33 53 9N 0 22W
Methlick 37 57 26N 2 13W
Methóni 69 36 49N 21 42E
Methuen, Mt. 136 15 54S 124 44E
Methven, N.Z. 143 43 38S 171 40E
Methven, U.K. 35 56 25N 3 35W
Methwin, Mt. 137 25 3S 120 45E
Methwold 29 52 30N 0 33E
Methy L. 153 56 28N 109 30W
Metil 125 16 24S 39 0E
Metkovets 67 43 37N 23 10E
Metkovió 66 43 6N 17 39E
Metlakatla 147 55 10N 131 33W
Metlaoui 119 34 24N 8 24E
Metlika 63 45 40N 15 20E
Metowra 139 25 3S 146 15E
Metropolis 159 37 10N 88 47W
Métsovon 68 39 48N 21 12E
Mettet 47 50 19N 4 41E
Mettuppalaiyam 97 11 18N 76 59E
Mettur 97 11 48N 77 47E
Mettur Dam 95 11 45N 77 45E
Metulla 90 33 17N 35 34E
Metz 43 49 8N 6 10E
Meulaboh 102 4 11N 96 3E
Meulan 43 49 0N 1 52E
Meung-sur-Loire 43 47 50N 1 40E
Meureudu 102 5 19N 96 10E
Meurthe-et-Moselle □ 43 48 52N 6 0E
Meuse □ 43 49 8N 5 25E
Meuse, R. 47 50 45N 5 41E
Meuselwitz 48 51 3N 12 18E
Mevagissey 30 50 16N 4 48W
Mevagissey Bay 30 50 15N 4 40W
Mexborough 33 53 29N 1 18W
Mexia 159 31 38N 96 32W
Mexiana, I. 170 0 0 49 30W
Mexicali 164 32 40N 115 30W
México 165 19 20N 99 10W
Mexico, Me., U.S.A. 156 44 35N 70 30W
Mexico, Mo., U.S.A. 158 39 10N 91 55W
Mexico, N.Y., U.S.A. 162 43 28N 76 18W
Mexico ■ 164 20 0N 100 0W
México □ 164 19 20N 99 10W
Mexico, G. of 165 25 0N 90 0W
Mey 37 58 38N 3 14W
Meyenburg 48 53 19N 12 15E
Meymac 44 45 32N 2 10E
Meyrargues 45 43 38N 5 32E
Meyrueis 44 44 12N 3 27E
Meyssac 44 45 3N 1 40E
Mezdra 67 43 12N 23 35E
Mèze 44 43 27N 3 36E
Mezen 78 65 50N 44 20E
Mezha, R. 80 55 50N 31 45E
Mezhdurechenskiy 84 59 36N 65 56E
Mezidon 42 49 5N 0 1W
Mézières 43 49 45N 4 42E
Mézilhac 45 44 49N 4 21E
Mézin 44 44 4N 0 16E
Mezöberény 53 46 49N 21 3E
Mezöfalva 53 46 55N 18 49E
Mezöhegyes 53 46 19N 20 49E
Mezokövácsháza 53 46 25N 20 57E
Mezökövesd 53 47 49N 20 35E
Mézos 44 44 5N 1 10W
Mezötúr 53 47 0N 20 41E
Mezquital 164 23 29N 104 23W
Mezzolombardo 62 46 13N 11 5E
Mgeta 127 8 22S 38 6E
Mglin 80 53 2N 32 50E
Mhlaba Hills 127 18 30S 30 30E
Mhow 94 22 33N 75 50E
Mi-Shima 110 34 46N 131 9E
Miahuatlán 165 16 21N 96 36W
Miajadas 57 39 9N 5 54W
Mialar 94 26 15N 70 20E
Miallo 138 16 28S 145 22E
Miami, Ariz., U.S.A. 161 33 25N 111 0W
Miami, Fla., U.S.A. 157 25 52N 80 15W
Miami, Tex., U.S.A. 159 35 44N 100 38W
Miami Beach 157 25 49N 80 6W
Miami, R. 156 39 20N 84 40W
Miamisburg 156 39 40N 84 11W
Miandowãb 92 37 0N 46 5E
Miandrivazo 125 19 50S 45 56E
Miãneh 92 37 30N 47 40E
Mianwali 94 32 38N 71 28E
Miaoli 109 24 34N 120 48E
Miarinarivo 129 18 57S 46 55E
Miass 84 54 59N 60 6E
Miass, R. 84 56 6N 64 30E
Miasteczko Kraj 54 53 7N 17 1E
Miastko 54 54 0N 16 58E
Mica Dam 152 52 5N 118 32W
Mica Res. 152 51 55N 118 00W
Michael, Mt. 135 6 27S 145 22E
Michalovce 29 48 44N 21 54E
Micheldever 28 51 7N 1 17W
Michelson, Mt. 147 69 20N 144 20W
Michelstadt 49 49 40N 9 0E
Michigan □ 155 44 40N 85 40W
Michigan City 156 41 42N 86 56W
Michigan, L. 156 44 0N 87 0W
Michih 106 37 49N 110 7E
Michikamau L. 151 54 0N 64 0W
Michipicoten 150 47 55N 84 55W
Michipicoten I. 150 47 40N 85 40W
Michoacan □ 164 19 0N 102 0W
Michurin 67 42 9N 27 51E
Michurinsk 81 52 58N 40 27E
Mickle Fell 32 54 38N 2 16W
Mickleover 33 52 55N 1 32W
Mickleton, Oxon., U.K. 28 52 5N 1 45W
Mickleton, Yorks., U.K. 32 54 36N 2 3W
Miclere 138 22 34S 147 32E
Micronesia 130 17 0N 160 0E
Micûsasa 70 46 7N 24 7E
Mid Calder 35 55 53N 3 23W
Mid Glamorgan □ 31 51 40N 3 25W
Mid Yell 36 60 36N 1 5W
Midai, P. 101 3 0N 107 47E
Midale 153 49 25N 103 20W
Midas 160 41 14N 116 56W
Middagsfjället 72 63 27N 12 19E
Middelbeers 47 51 28N 5 15E
Middelburg, Neth. 47 51 30N 3 36E
Middelburg, C. Prov., S. Afr. 128 31 30S 25 0E
Middelburg, Trans., S. Afr. 129 25 49N 29 28E
Middelfart 73 55 30N 9 43E
Middelharnis 46 51 46N 4 10E
Middelkerke 47 51 11N 2 49E
Middelrode 47 51 41N 5 26E
Middelveld 128 29 45S 22 30E
Middle Alkali L. 160 41 30N 120 3W
Middle Andaman I. 101 12 30N 92 30E
Middle Brook 151 48 40N 54 20W
Middle I. 137 28 55S 113 55E
Middle River 162 39 19N 76 25W
Middle Zoy 28 51 5N 2 54W
Middleboro 162 41 49N 70 55W
Middleburg, N.Y., U.S.A. 162 42 36N 74 19W
Middleburg, Pa., U.S.A. 162 40 47N 77 3W
Middlebury 162 44 0N 73 9W
Middleham 33 54 17N 1 49W
Middlemarch 143 45 30S 170 9E
Middlemarsh 28 50 51N 2 29W
Middleport 156 39 0N 82 5W
Middlesbrough 33 54 35N 1 14W
Middlesex, Belize 165 17 2N 88 31W
Middlesex, U.S.A. 162 40 36N 74 30W
Middleton, Can. 151 44 57N 65 4W
Middleton, Gr. Manchester, U.K. 32 53 33N 2 12W
Middleton, Norfolk, U.K. 29 52 43N 0 29E
Middleton Cheney 28 52 4N 1 17W
Middleton Cr. 138 22 35S 141 51E
Middleton I. 147 59 30N 146 28W
Middleton-in-Teesdale 32 54 38N 2 5W
Middleton in the Wolds 33 53 56N 0 35W
Middleton P.O. 138 22 22S 141 32E
Middletown, U.K. 38 54 18N 6 50W
Middletown, Conn., U.S.A. 162 41 37N 72 40W
Middletown, Del., U.S.A. 162 39 30N 84 21W
Middletown, N.Y., U.S.A. 162 41 28N 74 28W
Middletown, Pa., U.S.A. 162 40 12N 76 44W
Middlewich 32 53 12N 2 28W
Midelt 118 32 46N 4 44W
Midhurst, N.Z. 142 39 17S 174 18E
Midhurst, U.K. 29 50 59N 0 44W
Midi, Canal du 44 43 45N 1 21E
Midi d'Ossau 58 42 50N 0 25W
Midland, Austral. 137 31 54S 115 59E
Midland, Can. 150 44 45N 79 50W
Midland, Mich., U.S.A. 156 43 37N 84 17W
Midland, Tex., U.S.A. 159 32 0N 102 3W
Midland Junc. 137 31 50S 115 58E
Midlands □ 127 19 40S 29 0E
Midleton 39 51 52N 8 12W
Midlothian, Austral. 138 17 10S 141 12E
Midlothian, U.S.A. 159 32 30N 97 0W
Midlothian (□) 26 55 45N 3 15W
Midnapore 95 22 25N 87 21E
Midongy du Sud 129 23 35S 47 1E
Midongy, Massif de 129 23 30S 47 0E
Midskog 73 58 56N 14 5E
Midsomer Norton 28 51 17N 2 29W
Midvale 160 40 39N 111 58W
Midway Is. 130 28 13N 177 22W
Midwest 160 43 27N 106 11W
Midwolda 46 53 12N 6 52E
Midzur 66 43 24N 22 40E
Mie-ken □ 111 34 30N 136 10E
Miechów 54 50 21N 20 5E
Miedzyborz 54 51 39N 17 24E
Miedzychód 54 52 35N 15 53E
Miedzylesie 54 50 41N 16 40E
Miedzyrzec Podlaski 54 51 58N 22 45E
Miedzyrzecz 54 52 26N 15 35E
Miedzyzdroje 54 53 56N 14 26E
Miejska Górka 54 51 39N 16 58E
Miélan 44 43 27N 0 19E
Mielelek 138 6 1S 148 58E
Mianch'ih 106 34 48N 111 40E
Mienchu 108 31 22N 104 7E
Mienga 128 17 12S 19 48E
Mienhsien 106 33 11N 106 36E
Mienning 108 28 30N 102 10E
Mienyang, Hupei, China 109 30 10N 113 20E
Mienyang, Szechwan, China 108 31 28N 104 46E
Miercurea Ciuc 70 46 21N 25 48E
Mieres 56 43 18N 5 48W
Mierlo 47 51 27N 5 37E
Mieso 123 9 15N 40 43E
Mieszkowice 54 52 47N 14 30E
Migdal 90 32 51N 35 30E
Migdal Afeq 90 32 5N 34 58E
Migennes 43 47 58N 3 31E
Migliarino 63 44 54N 11 56E
Miguel Alemán, Presa 165 18 15N 96 40W
Miguel Alves 170 4 11S 42 55W
Miguel Calmon 170 11 26S 40 36W
Mihara 110 34 24N 133 5E
Mihara-Yama 111 34 43N 139 23E
Mihsien 106 34 31N 113 22E
Mii 108 26 50N 102 3E
Mijares, R. 58 40 15N 0 50W
Mijas 57 36 36N 4 40W
Mijdrecht 46 52 13N 4 53E
Mijilu 121 10 22N 13 19E
Mikese 126 6 48S 37 55E
Mikha Tskhakaya 83 42 15N 42 7E
Mikhailovgrad 67 43 27N 23 16E
Mikhailovka 82 47 16N 35 27E
Mikhaylov 81 54 20N 39 0E
Mikhaylovka, Azerbaijan, U.S.S.R. 83 41 31N 48 52E
Mikhaylovka, R.S.F.S.R., U.S.S.R. 81 50 3N 43 5E
Mikhaylovski 84 56 27N 59 7E
Mikhnevo 81 55 4N 37 59E
Miki, Hyōgō, Japan 110 34 48N 134 59E
Miki, Kagawa, Japan 110 34 12N 134 7E
Mikinai 69 37 43N 22 46E
Mikindani 127 10 15S 40 2E
Mikkeli 75 61 43N 27 25E
Mikkeli □ 74 62 0N 28 0E
Mikkelin Lääni □ 74 61 56N 28 0E
Mikkwa, R. 152 58 25N 114 46W
Mikniya 123 17 0N 33 45E
Mikołajki 54 53 49N 21 37E

Mikol Mjømna

Mikołów	**53**	50 10N	18 50 E
Míkonos, I.	**69**	37 30N	25 25 E
Mikrón Dhérion	**68**	41 19N	26 6 E
Mikulov	**53**	48 48N	16 39 E
Mikumi	**126**	7 26 S	37 9 E
Mikun	**78**	62 20N	50 0 E
Mikuni	**111**	36 13N	136 9 E
Mikuni-Tōge	**111**	36 50N	138 40 E
Mikura-Jima	**111**	33 52N	139 36 E
Mila	**119**	36 27N	6 16 E
Milaca	**158**	45 45N	93 40W
Milagro	**174**	2 0 S	79 30W
Milan, Mo., U.S.A.	**158**	40 10N	93 5W
Milan, Tenn., U.S.A.	**157**	35 55N	88 45W
Milan = Milano	**62**	45 28N	9 10 E
Milang, S. Australia, Austral.	**139**	32 2 S	139 10 E
Milang, S. Australia, Austral.	**140**	35 24 S	138 58 E
Milange	**127**	16 3 S	35 45 E
Milano	**62**	45 28N	9 10 E
Milâs	**92**	37 20N	27 50 E
Milazzo	**65**	38 13N	15 13 E
Milbank	**158**	45 17N	96 38W
Milborne Port	**28**	50 58N	2 28W
Milden	**153**	51 29N	107 32W
Mildenhall	**29**	52 20N	0 30 E
Mildura	**140**	34 13 S	142 9 E
Miléai	**68**	39 20N	23 9 E
Miles, Austral.	**139**	26 40 S	150 23 E
Miles, U.S.A.	**159**	31 39N	100 11W
Miles City	**158**	46 30N	105 50W
Milestone	**153**	49 59N	104 31W
Mileto	**65**	38 37N	16 3 E
Miletto, Mte.	**65**	41 26N	14 23 E
Mileurà	**137**	26 22 S	117 20 E
Milevsko	**52**	49 27N	14 21 E
Milford, Ireland	**39**	52 20N	8 52W
Milford, Conn., U.S.A.	**162**	41 13N	73 4W
Milford, Del., U.S.A.	**162**	38 52N	75 27W
Milford, Mass., U.S.A.	**162**	42 8N	71 30W
Milford, N.H., U.S.A.	**162**	42 50N	71 39W
Milford, Pa., U.S.A.	**162**	41 20N	74 47W
Milford, Utah, U.S.A.	**161**	38 20N	113 0W
Milford Haven	**31**	51 43N	5 2W
Milford Haven, B.	**31**	51 40N	5 10W
Milford on Sea	**28**	50 44N	1 36W
Milford Sd.	**143**	44 34 S	167 47 E
Milgun	**137**	25 6 S	118 18 E
Milh, Ras el	**117**	32 0N	24 55 E
Miliana, Aïn Salah, Alg.	**118**	27 20N	2 32 E
Miliana, Médéa, Alg.	**118**	36 12N	2 15 E
Milicz	**54**	51 31N	17 19 E
Miling	**137**	30 30 S	116 17 E
Militello in Val di Catánia	**65**	37 16N	14 46 E
Milk, R.	**160**	48 40N	107 15W
Milk River	**152**	49 10N	112 5W
Mill	**47**	51 41N	5 48 E
Mill City	**160**	44 45N	122 28W
Mill, I.	**13**	66 0 S	101 30 E
Mill Valley	**163**	37 54N	122 32W
Millau	**44**	44 8N	3 4 E
Millbrook, U.K.	**30**	50 19N	4 12W
Millbrook, U.S.A.	**162**	41 47N	73 42W
Millbrook Res.	**109**	34 50 S	138 49 E
Mille Lacs, L.	**158**	46 10N	93 30W
Mille Lacs, L. des	**150**	48 45N	90 35W
Milledgeville	**157**	33 7N	83 15W
Millen	**157**	32 50N	81 57W
Miller	**158**	44 35N	98 59W
Millerovo	**82**	48 57N	40 28 E
Miller's Flat	**143**	45 39 S	169 23 E
Millersburg	**162**	40 32N	76 58W
Millerton, N.Z.	**143**	41 39 S	171 54 E
Millerton, U.S.A.	**162**	41 57N	73 32W
Millerton, L.	**163**	37 0N	119 42W
Milleur Pt.	**34**	55 2N	5 5W
Millevaches, Plat. de	**44**	45 45N	2 0 E
Millicent	**140**	37 34 S	140 21 E
Millingen	**46**	51 52N	6 2 E
Millinocket	**151**	45 45N	68 45W
Millisle	**38**	54 38N	5 33W
Millmerran	**139**	27 53 S	151 16 E
Millom	**32**	54 13N	3 16W
Millport	**34**	55 45N	4 55W
Mills L.	**152**	61 30N	118 20W
Millsboro	**162**	38 36N	75 17W
Millstreet	**39**	52 4N	9 5W
Milltown, Galway, Ireland	**38**	53 37N	8 54W
Milltown, Kerry, Ireland	**39**	52 9N	9 42W
Milltown, U.K.	**37**	57 33N	4 48W
Milltown Malbay	**39**	52 51N	9 25W
Millville, N.J., U.S.A.	**162**	39 22N	75 0W
Millville, Pa., U.S.A.	**162**	41 7N	76 32W
Millwood Res.	**159**	33 45N	94 0W
Milly	**43**	48 24N	2 20 E
Milly Milly	**137**	26 4 S	116 43 E
Milna	**63**	43 20N	16 28 E
Milnathort	**35**	56 14N	3 25W
Milne Inlet	**149**	72 30N	80 0W
Milne, R.	**138**	21 10 S	137 33 E
Milngavie	**34**	55 57N	4 20W
Milnor	**158**	46 19N	97 29W
Milnthorpe	**32**	54 14N	2 47W
Milo, Can.	**152**	50 34N	112 53W
Milo, China	**108**	24 28N	103 23 E
Milolii	**147**	22 8N	159 42W
Mílos	**69**	36 44N	24 25 E
Mílos, I.	**69**	36 44N	24 25 E
Miloševo	**66**	45 42N	20 20 E
Miłoslaw	**54**	52 12N	17 32 E
Milovaig	**36**	57 27N	6 45W
Milparinka P.O.	**139**	29 46 S	141 57 E
Miltenberg	**49**	49 41N	9 13 E
Milton, N.Z.	**143**	46 7 S	169 59 E
Milton, Dumf. & Gall., U.K.	**34**	55 18N	4 50W
Milton, Hants., U.K.	**28**	50 45N	1 40W
Milton, Northants, U.K.	**29**	52 12N	0 55W
Milton, Calif., U.S.A.	**163**	38 3N	120 51W
Milton, Del., U.S.A.	**162**	38 47N	75 19W
Milton, Fla., U.S.A.	**157**	30 38N	87 0W
Milton, Pa., U.S.A.	**162**	41 0N	76 53W
Milton Abbot	**30**	50 35N	4 16W
Milton-Freewater	**160**	45 57N	118 24W
Milton Keynes	**29**	52 3N	0 42W
Milverton	**28**	51 2N	3 15W
Milwaukee	**156**	43 9N	87 58W
Milwaukie	**160**	45 27N	122 39W
Mim	**120**	6 57N	2 33W
Mimizan	**44**	44 12N	1 13W
Mimon	**52**	50 38N	14 43 E
Mimoso	**171**	15 10 S	48 5W
Min Chiang, R., China	**105**	28 48N	104 33 E
Min Chiang, R., Fukien, China	**109**	26 5N	119 37 E
Min Chiang, R., Szechwan, China	**108**	28 48N	104 33 E
Min-Kush	**85**	41 4N	74 28 E
Mina	**161**	38 21N	118 9W
Mina Pirquitas	**172**	22 40 S	66 40W
Mina Saud	**92**	28 45N	48 20 E
Minā'al Ahmadī	**92**	29 5N	48 10 E
Mīnāb	**93**	27 10N	57 1 E
Minago, R.	**153**	54 33N	98 13W
Minakami	**111**	36 49N	138 59 E
Minaki	**153**	50 0N	94 40W
Minakuchi	**111**	34 58N	136 10 E
Minamata	**110**	32 10N	130 30 E
Minamitane	**112**	30 25N	130 54 E
Minas Basin	**151**	45 20N	64 12W
Minas de Rio Tinto	**57**	37 42N	6 22W
Minas de San Quintín	**57**	38 49N	4 23W
Minas Gerais □	**171**	18 50 S	46 0W
Minas Novas	**171**	17 15 S	42 36W
Minas, Sierra de las	**166**	15 9N	89 31W
Minatitlán	**165**	17 58N	94 35W
Minbu	**98**	20 10N	95 0 E
Minbya	**98**	20 22N	93 16 E
Mincha	**140**	36 1 S	144 6 E
Minch'in	**106**	38 42N	103 11 E
Minch'ing	**109**	26 13N	118 51 E
Minchinhampton	**28**	51 42N	2 10W
Mincio, R.	**62**	45 8N	10 55 E
Mindanao, I.	**103**	8 0N	125 0 E
Mindanao Sea	**103**	9 0N	124 0 E
Mindanao Trench	**103**	8 0N	128 0 E
Mindelheim	**49**	48 4N	10 30 E
Minden, Ger.	**48**	52 18N	8 54 E
Minden, U.S.A.	**159**	32 40N	93 20W
Mindiptana	**103**	5 45 S	140 22 E
Mindon	**98**	19 21N	94 44 E
Mindoro, I.	**103**	13 0N	121 0 E
Mindoro Strait	**103**	12 30N	120 30 E
Mindouli	**124**	4 12 S	14 28 E
Mine	**110**	34 12N	131 7 E
Mine Hd.	**39**	52 0N	7 37W
Minehead	**28**	51 12N	3 29W
Mineola, N.Y., U.S.A.	**162**	40 45N	73 38W
Mineola, Tex., U.S.A.	**159**	32 40N	95 30W
Minera	**31**	53 3N	3 7W
Mineral King	**163**	36 27N	118 36W
Mineral Wells	**159**	32 50N	98 5W
Mineralnyye Vody	**83**	44 18N	43 15 E
Minersville, Pa., U.S.A.	**162**	40 40N	76 17W
Minersville, Utah, U.S.A.	**161**	38 14N	112 58W
Minervino Murge	**65**	41 6N	16 4 E
Minette	**157**	30 54N	87 43W
Minetto	**162**	43 24N	76 28W
Mingan	**151**	50 20N	64 0W
Mingary, Austral.	**140**	32 8 S	140 45 E
Mingary, U.K.	**36**	56 42N	6 5W
Mingch'i	**109**	26 24N	117 12 E
Mingchiang	**109**	32 28N	114 8 E
Mingechaur	**83**	40 52N	47 0 E
Mingechaurskoye Vdkhr.	**83**	40 56N	47 20 E
Mingela	**138**	19 52 S	146 38 E
Mingenew	**137**	29 12 S	115 21 E
Mingera Cr.	**138**	20 38 S	138 10 E
Mingin	**98**	22 50N	94 30 E
Minginish, Dist.	**36**	57 14N	6 15W
Minglanilla	**58**	39 34N	1 38W
Mingulay I.	**36**	56 50N	7 40W
Minho □	**55**	41 25N	8 20W
Minho, R.	**55**	41 58N	8 40W
Minhou	**109**	26 0N	119 18 E
Minhow = Fuchou	**109**	26 5N	119 18 E
Minhsien	**106**	34 26N	104 2 E
Minidoka	**160**	42 47N	113 34W
Minigwal L.	**137**	29 31 S	123 14 E
Minilya	**137**	23 55 S	114 0 E
Minilya, R.	**137**	23 45 S	114 0 E
Mininera	**140**	37 37 S	142 58 E
Minióevo	**66**	43 42N	22 18 E
Minipi, L.	**151**	52 25N	60 45W
Minj	**135**	5 54 S	144 30 E
Mink L.	**152**	61 54N	117 40W
Minlaton	**140**	34 45 S	137 35 E
Minna	**121**	9 37N	6 30 E
Minneapolis, Kans., U.S.A.	**158**	39 11N	97 40W
Minneapolis, Minn., U.S.A.	**158**	44 58N	93 20W
Minnesota □	**158**	46 40N	94 0W
Minnesund	**71**	60 23N	11 14 E
Minnie Creek	**137**	24 3 S	115 42 E
Minnigaff	**34**	54 58N	4 30W
Minnitaki L.	**150**	49 47N	91 5W
Mino	**111**	35 32N	136 55 E
Mino-Kamo	**111**	35 23N	137 2 E
Mino-Mikawą-Kōgen	**111**	35 10N	137 30 E
Miño, R.	**56**	41 58N	8 40W
Minobu	**111**	35 22N	138 26 E
Minobu-Sanchi	**111**	35 14N	138 20 E
Minorca = Menorca	**58**	40 0N	4 0 E
Minore	**141**	32 14 S	148 27 E
Minot	**158**	48 10N	101 15W
Minquiers, Les	**42**	48 58N	2 8W
Minsen	**48**	53 43N	7 58 E
Minsk	**80**	53 52N	27 30 E
Minsk Mazowiecki	**54**	52 10N	21 33 E
Minster	**29**	51 20N	1 20 E
Minster-on-Sea	**29**	51 25N	0 50 E
Minsterley	**28**	52 38N	2 56W
Mintaka Pass	**93**	37 0N	74 58 E
Minthami	**98**	23 55N	94 16 E
Mintlaw	**37**	57 32N	1 59W
Minto	**147**	64 55N	149 20W
Minto L.	**150**	48 0N	84 45W
Minton	**153**	49 10N	104 35W
Minturn	**160**	39 45N	106 25W
Minturno	**64**	41 15N	13 43 E
Minûf	**122**	30 26N	30 52 E
Minusinsk	**77**	53 50N	91 20 E
Minutang	**98**	28 15N	96 30 E
Minvoul	**124**	2 9N	12 8 E
Minya Konka	**108**	29 34N	101 53 E
Minyar	**84**	55 4N	57 33 E
Minyip	**140**	36 29 S	142 36 E
Mionica	**66**	44 14N	20 6 E
Mios Num, I.	**103**	1 30 S	135 10 E
Miquelon	**151**	47 3N	56 20W
Miquelon, St. Pierre et, □	**151**	47 8N	56 24W
Mir-Bashir	**83**	40 11N	46 58 E
Mira, Italy	**63**	45 26N	12 9 E
Mira, Port.	**56**	40 26N	8 44W
Mira, R.	**57**	37 30N	8 30W
Mirabella Eclano	**65**	41 3N	14 59 E
Miracema do Norte	**170**	9 33 S	48 24W
Mirador	**170**	6 22 S	44 22W
Miraflores	**164**	23 21N	109 45W
Miraj	**96**	16 50N	74 45 E
Miram	**138**	21 15 S	148 55 E
Miram Shah	**94**	33 0N	70 0 E
Miramar, Argent.	**172**	38 15 S	57 50W
Miramar, Mozam.	**129**	23 50 S	35 35 E
Miramas	**45**	43 33N	4 59 E
Mirambeau	**44**	45 23N	0 35W
Miramichi B.	**151**	47 15N	65 0W
Miramont-de-Guyenne	**44**	44 37N	0 21 E
Miranda	**175**	20 10 S	56 15W
Miranda de Ebro	**58**	42 41N	2 57W
Miranda do Corvo	**56**	40 6N	8 20W
Miranda do Douro	**56**	41 30N	6 16W
Mirando City	**159**	27 28N	98 59W
Mirandola	**62**	44 53N	11 2 E
Mirandópolis	**173**	21 9 S	51 6W
Mirango	**127**	13 32 S	34 58 E
Mirano	**63**	45 29N	12 6 E
Miraporvos, I.	**167**	22 9N	74 30W
Mirassol	**173**	20 46 S	49 28W
Mirboo North	**141**	38 24 S	146 10 E
Mirear, I.	**122**	23 15N	35 41 E
Mirebeau, Côte d'Or, France	**43**	47 25N	5 20 E
Mirebeau, Vienne, France	**42**	46 49N	0 10 E
Mirecourt	**43**	48 20N	6 10 E
Mirgorod	**80**	49 58N	33 50 E
Miri	**102**	4 18N	114 0 E
Miriam Vale	**138**	24 20 S	151 33 E
Mirim, Lagoa	**173**	32 45 S	52 50W
Mirimire	**174**	11 10N	68 43W
Mirny	**13**	66 0 S	95 0 E
Mirnyy	**77**	62 33N	113 53 E
Mirond L.	**153**	55 6N	102 47W
Mirosławiec	**54**	53 20N	16 5 E
Mirpur	**95**	33 15N	73 50 E
Mirpur Bibiwari	**94**	28 33N	67 44 E
Mirpur Khas	**94**	25 30N	69 0 E
Mirpur Sakro	**94**	24 33N	67 41 E
Mirrool	**141**	34 19 S	147 10 E
Mirror	**152**	52 30N	113 7W
Mirsani	**70**	44 1N	23 59 E
Mirsk	**54**	50 58N	15 23 E
Miryang	**107**	35 31N	128 44 E
Mirzaani	**83**	41 24N	46 5 E
Mirzapur	**95**	25 10N	82 45 E
Misantla	**165**	19 56N	96 50W
Miscou I.	**151**	47 57N	64 31W
Misery, Mt.	**108**	34 52 S	138 48 E
Mish'ab, Ra'as al	**92**	28 15N	48 43 E
Mishan	**105**	45 31N	132 2 E
Mishawaka	**156**	41 40N	86 8W
Mishbih, Gebel	**122**	22 48N	34 38 E
Mishima	**111**	35 10N	138 52 E
Mishkino	**84**	55 20N	63 55 E
Mishmar Aiyalon	**90**	31 52N	34 57 E
Mishmar Ha' Emeq	**90**	32 37N	35 7 E
Mishmar Ha Negev	**90**	31 22N	34 48 E
Mishmar Ha Yarden	**90**	33 0N	35 56 E
Mishmi Hills	**98**	29 0N	96 0 E
Misilmeri	**64**	38 2N	13 25 E
Misima I.	**135**	10 40 S	152 45 E
Misión, La	**164**	32 5N	116 50W
Misiones □, Argent.	**173**	27 0 S	55 0W
Misiones □, Parag.	**172**	27 0 S	56 0W
Miskin	**93**	23 44N	56 52 E
Miskitos, Cayos	**166**	14 26N	82 50W
Miskolc	**53**	48 7N	20 50 E
Misoke	**126**	0 42 S	28 2 E
Misoöl, I.	**103**	2 0 S	130 0 E
Misrātah	**119**	32 18N	15 3 E
Missanabie	**150**	48 20N	84 6W
Missão Velha	**170**	7 15 S	39 10W
Misserghin	**118**	35 44N	0 49W
Missinaibi L.	**150**	48 23N	83 40W
Missinaibi, R.	**150**	50 30N	82 40W
Mission, S.D., U.S.A.	**158**	43 21N	100 36W
Mission, Tex., U.S.A.	**159**	26 15N	98 30W
Mission City	**152**	49 10N	122 15W
Missisa L.	**150**	52 20N	85 7W
Mississagi	**150**	46 15N	83 9W
Mississippi, R.	**159**	35 30N	90 0W
Mississippi Sd.	**159**	30 25N	89 0W
Missoula	**160**	47 0N	114 0W
Missouri □	**158**	38 25N	92 30W
Missouri, Little, R.	**160**	46 0N	111 35W
Missouri, R.	**158**	40 20N	95 40W
Mistake B.	**153**	62 8N	93 0W
Mistassini L.	**150**	51 0N	73 40W
Mistassini, R.	**151**	48 42N	72 20W
Mistastin L.	**151**	55 57N	63 20W
Mistatim	**153**	52 52N	103 22W
Mistelbach	**53**	48 34N	16 34 E
Misterbianco	**65**	37 32N	15 0 E
Misterton, Notts., U.K.	**33**	53 27N	0 49W
Misterton, Som., U.K.	**28**	50 51N	2 46W
Mistretta	**65**	37 56N	14 20 E
Misty L.	**153**	58 53N	101 40W
Misugi	**111**	34 31N	136 16 E
Misumi	**110**	32 37N	130 27 E
Mît Ghamr	**122**	30 42N	31 12 E
Mitaka	**111**	35 40N	139 33 E
Mitan	**85**	40 0N	66 35 E
Mitatib	**123**	15 59N	36 12 E
Mitcham	**109**	34 59 S	138 37 E
Mitchel Troy	**31**	51 46N	2 45W
Mitcheldean	**28**	51 51N	2 29W
Mitchell, Austral.	**139**	26 29 S	147 58 E
Mitchell, Ind., U.S.A.	**156**	38 42N	86 25W
Mitchell, Nebr., U.S.A.	**158**	41 58N	103 45W
Mitchell, Oreg., U.S.A.	**160**	44 31N	120 8W
Mitchell, S.D., U.S.A.	**158**	43 40N	98 0W
Mitchell, Mt.	**157**	35 40N	82 20W
Mitchell, R.	**138**	15 12 S	141 35 E
Mitchelstown	**39**	52 16N	8 18W
Mitchelton	**108**	27 25 S	152 59 E
Mitha Tiwana	**94**	32 13N	72 6 E
Mithimna	**68**	39 20N	26 12 E
Mitiamo	**140**	36 12 S	144 15 E
Mitilini	**69**	39 6N	26 35 E
Mitilíni = Lesvos	**68**	39 0N	26 20 E
Mitilinoi	**69**	37 42N	26 56 E
Mitla	**165**	16 55N	96 24W
Mito	**111**	36 20N	140 30 E
Mitsinjo	**129**	16 1 S	45 52 E
Mitsiwa	**123**	15 35N	39 25 E
Mitsiwa Channel	**123**	15 30N	40 0 E
Mitsukaidō	**111**	36 1N	139 59 E
Mittagong	**141**	34 28 S	150 29 E
Mittelland	**50**	46 50N	7 23 E
Mittelland Kanal	**48**	52 23N	7 45 E
Mittenwalde	**48**	52 16N	13 33 E
Mittweida	**48**	50 59N	13 0 E
Mitu	**108**	25 21N	100 32 E
Mitú	**174**	1 8N	70 3W
Mituas	**174**	3 52N	68 49W
Mitumba	**126**	7 8 S	31 2 E
Mitumba, Chaîne des	**126**	10 0 S	26 20 E
Mitwaba	**127**	8 2N	27 17 E
Mityana	**126**	0 23N	32 2 E
Mitzick	**124**	0 45N	11 40 E
Miura	**111**	35 12N	139 40 E
Mius, R.	**83**	47 30N	39 0 E
Mixteco, R.	**165**	18 11N	98 30W
Miyagi-Ken □	**112**	38 15N	140 45 E
Miyâh, W. el	**122**	25 10N	33 30 E
Miyake-Jima	**111**	34 0N	139 30 E
Miyako	**112**	39 40N	141 75 E
Miyako-Jima	**112**	24 45N	125 20 E
Miyakonojō	**110**	31 32N	131 5 E
Miyanojō	**110**	31 54N	130 27 E
Miyanoura-Dake	**112**	30 20N	130 26 E
Miyata	**110**	33 49N	130 42 E
Miyazaki	**110**	31 56N	131 30 E
Miyazaki-ken □	**110**	32 0N	131 30 E
Miyazu	**110**	35 35N	135 10 E
Miyet, Bahr el	**92**	31 30N	35 30 E
Miyoshi	**110**	34 48N	132 51 E
Miyün	**106**	40 22N	116 49 E
Mizamis = Ozamiz	**103**	8 15N	123 50 E
Mizdah	**119**	31 30N	13 0 E
Mizen Hd., Cork, Ireland	**39**	51 27N	9 50W
Mizen Hd., Wick., Ireland	**39**	52 52N	6 4W
Mizil	**70**	44 59N	26 29 E
Mizoram □	**98**	23 0N	92 40 E
Mizuho	**111**	35 6N	135 17 E
Mizunami	**111**	35 22N	137 15 E
Mjöbäck	**73**	57 28N	12 53 E
Mjölby	**73**	58 20N	15 10 E
Mjømna	**71**	60 55N	4 55 E

Mjörn Montcornet

Mjörn 73 57 55N 12 25 E
Mjøsa 71 60 40N 11 0 E
Mkata 126 5 45 S 38 20 E
Mkokotoni 126 5 55 S 39 15 E
Mkomazi 126 4 40 S 38 7 E
Mkulwe 127 8 37 S 32 20 E
Mkumbi, Ras 126 7 38 S 39 55 E
Mkushi 127 14 25 S 29 15 E
Mkushi River 127 13 40 S 29 30 E
Mkuze, R. 129 27 45 S 32 30 E
Mkwaya 126 6 17 S 35 40 E
Mladá Boleslav 52 50 27N 14 53 E
Mladenovac 66 44 28N 20 44 E
Mlala Hills 126 6 50 S 31 40 E
Mlange 127 16 2 S 35 33 E
Mlava, R. 66 44 35N 21 18 E
Mława 54 53 9N 20 25 E
Mlinište 63 44 15N 16 50 E
Mljet, I. 66 42 43N 17 30 E
Młynary 54 54 12N 19 46 E
Mme 121 6 18N 10 14 E
Mo, Hordaland, Norway 71 60 49N 5 48 E
Mo, Telemark, Norway 71 59 28N 7 50 E
Mo, Sweden 72 61 19N 16 47 E
Mo i Rana 74 66 15N 14 7 E
Moa, I. 103 8 0 S 128 0 E
Moa, R. 120 7 0N 11 40W
Moab 161 38 40N 109 35W
Moabi 124 2 24 S 10 59 E
Moalie Park 139 29 42 S 143 3 E
Moaña 56 42 18N 8 43W
Moanda 124 1 28 S 13 21 E
Moapo 161 36 45N 114 37W
Moate 39 53 25N 7 43W
Moba 126 7 0 S 29 48 E
Mobara 111 35 25N 140 18 E
Mobaye 124 4 25N 21 5 E
Mobayi 124 4 15N 21 8 E
Moberley 158 39 25N 92 25W
Moberly, R. 152 56 12N 120 55W
Mobert 150 48 41N 85 40W
Mobile 157 30 41N 88 3W
Mobile B. 157 30 30N 88 0W
Mobile, Pt. 157 30 15N 88 0W
Mobjack B. 162 37 16N 76 22W
Möborg 73 56 24N 8 21 E
Mobridge 158 45 40N 100 28W
Mobutu Sese Seko, L. 126 1 30N 31 0 E
Moc Chav 100 20 50N 104 38 E
Moc Hoa 101 10 46N 105 56 E
Mocabe Kasari 127 9 58 S 26 12 E
Mocajuba 170 2 35 S 49 30W
Moçambique 127 15 3 S 40 42 E
Moçambique □ 127 14 45 S 38 30 E
Mocanaqua 162 41 9N 76 8W
Mochiang 108 23 25N 101 44 E
Mochiara Grove 128 20 43 S 21 50 E
Mochudi 128 24 27 S 26 7 E
Mocimboa da Praia 127 11 25 S 40 20 E
Mociu 70 46 46N 24 3 E
Möckeln 73 56 40N 14 15 E
Mockhorn I. 162 37 10N 75 52W
Moclips 160 47 14N 124 10W
Moçâmedes □ 128 16 35 S 12 30 E
Mocoa 174 1 15N 76 45W
Mococa 173 21 28 S 47 0W
Mocorito 164 25 20N 108 0W
Moctezuma 164 30 12N 106 26W
Moctezuma, R. 165 21 59N 98 34W
Mocuba 125 16 54 S 37 25 E
Moda 98 24 22N 96 29 E
Modane 45 45 12N 6 40 E
Modasa 94 23 30N 73 21 E
Modave 47 50 27N 5 18 E
Modbury, Austral. 109 34 50 S 138 41 E
Modbury, U.K. 30 50 21N 3 53W
Modder, R. 128 28 50 S 24 50 E
Modderrivier 128 29 2 S 24 38 E
Módena 62 44 39N 10 55 E
Modena 161 37 55N 113 56W
Modesto 163 37 43N 121 0W
Módica 65 36 52N 14 45 E
Modigliana 63 44 9N 11 48 E
Modjokerto 103 7 29 S 112 25 E
Modlin 54 52 24N 20 41 E
Mödling 53 48 5N 16 17 E
Modo 123 5 31N 30 33 E
Modra 53 48 19N 17 20 E
Modreeny 39 52 57N 8 6W
Modriča 66 44 57N 18 17 E
Moe 141 38 12 S 146 19 E
Moebase 127 17 3 S 38 41 E
Moei, R. 101 17 25N 98 10 E
Moëlan-s-Mer 42 47 49N 3 38W
Moelfre 31 53 21N 4 15W
Moengo 175 5 45N 54 20W
Moergestel 47 51 33N 5 11 E
Moësa, R. 51 46 12N 9 10 E
Moffat 35 55 20N 3 27W
Moga 94 30 48N 75 8 E
Mogadiscio = Mogadishu 91 2 2N 45 25 E
Mogadishu 91 2 2N 45 25 E
Mogador = Essaouira 118 31 32N 9 42W
Mogadouro 56 41 22N 6 47W
Mogami-gawa, R. 112 38 45N 140 0 E
Mogaung 98 25 20N 97 0 E
Møgeltønder 73 54 57N 8 48 E
Mogente 59 38 52N 0 45W
Moggil 108 27 34 S 152 52 E
Mogho 123 4 54N 40 16 E
Mogi das Cruzes 173 23 45 S 46 20W
Mogi-Guaçu, R. 173 20 53 S 48 10W
Mogi-Mirim 173 22 20 S 47 0W
Mogielnica 54 51 42N 20 41 E
Mogilev 80 53 55N 30 18 E
Mogilev Podolskiy 82 48 20N 27 40 E
Mogilno 54 52 39N 17 55 E
Mogincual 125 15 35 S 40 25 E
Mogliano Veneto 63 45 33N 12 15 E
Mogocha 77 53 40N 119 50 E
Mogoi 103 1 55 S 133 10 E
Mogok 98 23 0N 96 40 E
Mogollon 161 33 25N 108 55W
Mogollon Mesa 161 43 40N 111 0W
Mogriguy 141 32 3 S 148 40 E
Moguer 57 37 15N 6 52W
Mogumber 137 31 2 S 116 3 E
Mohács 53 45 58N 18 41 E
Mohaka, R. 142 39 7 S 177 12 E
Mohall 158 48 46N 101 30W
Mohammadābād 93 37 30N 59 5 E
Mohammedia 118 33 44N 7 21W
Mohave Desert 161 35 0N 117 30W
Mohawk 161 32 45N 113 50W
Mohawk, R. 162 42 47N 73 42W
Moheda 73 57 1N 14 35 E
Mohembo 125 18 15 S 21 43 E
Moher, Cliffs of 39 52 58N 9 30W
Mohican, C. 147 60 10N 167 30W
Mohill 38 53 57N 7 52W
Möhne, R. 48 51 29N 8 10 E
Mohnyin 98 24 47N 96 22 E
Moholm 73 58 37N 14 5 E
Mohon 43 49 45N 4 44 E
Mohoro 126 8 6 S 39 8 E
Moia 123 5 3N 28 2 E
Moidart, L. 36 56 47N 5 40W
Moinabad 96 17 44N 77 16 E
Moineşti 70 46 28N 26 21 E
Mointy 76 47 40N 73 45 E
Moira 38 54 28N 6 16W
Moirais 69 35 4N 24 56 E
Moirans 45 45 20N 5 33 E
Moirans-en-Montagne 45 46 26N 5 43 E
Moisäkula 80 58 3N 24 38 E
Moisie 151 50 7N 66 1W
Moisie, R. 151 50 6N 66 5W
Moissac 44 44 7N 1 5 E
Moita 57 38 38N 8 58W
Mojácar 59 37 6N 1 55W
Mojados 56 41 26N 4 40W
Mojave 163 35 8N 118 8W
Mojave Desert 163 35 0N 116 30W
Mojo, Boliv. 172 21 48 S 65 33W
Mojo, Ethiopia 123 8 35N 39 5 E
Mojo, I. 102 8 10 S 117 40 E
Moju, R. 170 1 40 S 48 25W
Mokai 142 38 32 S 175 56 E
Mokambo 127 12 25 S 28 20 E
Mokameh 95 25 24N 85 55 E
Mokau, R. 142 38 35 S 174 55 E
Mokelumne Hill 163 38 18N 120 43W
Mokelumne, R. 163 38 23N 121 25W
Mokhós 69 35 16N 25 27 E
Mokhotlong 126 29 22 S 29 2 E
Mokihinui 143 41 33 S 171 58 E
Moknine 119 35 35N 10 58 E
Mokokchung 99 26 15N 94 30 E
Mokpalin 98 17 26N 96 53 E
Mokpo 107 34 50N 126 30 E
Mokra Gora 66 42 50N 20 30 E
Mokronog 63 45 57N 15 9 E
Moksha, R. 81 54 45N 43 40 E
Mokshan 81 53 25N 44 35 E
Mokta Spera 120 16 38N 9 6W
Moktama Kwe 99 15 40N 96 30 E
Mol 47 51 11N 5 5 E
Mola, C. de la 58 39 53N 4 20 E
Mola di Bari 65 41 3N 17 5 E
Moland 71 59 11N 8 6 E
Moláoi 69 36 49N 22 56 E
Molat, I. 63 44 15N 14 50 E
Molchanovo 76 57 40N 83 50 E
Mold 31 53 10N 3 10W
Moldava nad Bodvou 53 48 38N 21 0 E
Moldavia = Moldova 70 46 30N 27 0 E
Moldavian S.S.R. □ 82 47 0N 28 0 E
Molde 71 62 45N 7 9 E
Moldotau, Khrebet 85 41 35N 75 0 E
Moldova 70 46 30N 27 0 E
Moldova Nouă 70 44 45N 21 41 E
Moldoveanu, mt. 67 45 36N 24 45 E
Mole Creek 138 41 32 S 146 24 E
Mole, R. 29 51 13N 0 15W
Molepolole 125 24 28 S 25 28 E
Moléson 50 46 33N 7 1 E
Molesworth 143 42 5 S 173 16 E
Molfetta 65 41 12N 16 35 E
Molina de Aragón 58 40 46N 1 52W
Moline 158 41 30N 90 30W
Molinella 63 44 38N 11 40 E
Molinos 172 25 28 S 66 15W
Moliro 126 8 12 S 30 30 E
Molise □ 63 41 45N 14 30 E
Moliterno 65 40 14N 15 50 E
Mollahat 98 22 56N 89 48 E
Mölle 73 56 17N 12 31 E
Molledo 56 43 8N 4 6W
Mollendo 174 17 0 S 72 0W
Mollerin, L. 137 30 30 S 117 35 E
Mollerusa 58 41 37N 0 54 E
Mollina 57 37 8N 4 38W
Mölln 48 53 37N 10 41 E
Mollösund 73 58 4N 11 30 E
Mölltorp 73 58 30N 14 26 E
Mölndal 73 57 40N 12 3 E
Mölnlycke 73 57 40N 12 8 E
Molo 98 23 22N 96 53 E
Molochansk 82 47 15N 35 23 E
Molochaya, R. 82 47 0N 35 30 E
Molodechno 80 54 20N 26 50 E
Molokai, I. 147 21 8N 157 0W
Moloma, R. 81 59 0N 48 15 E
Molong 141 33 5 S 148 54 E
Molopo, R. 125 25 40 S 24 30 E
Mólos 69 38 47N 22 37 E
Molotov, Mys 77 81 10N 95 0 E
Moloundou 124 2 8N 15 15 E
Molsheim 43 48 33N 7 29 E
Molson L. 153 54 22N 95 32W
Molteno 128 31 22 S 26 22 E
Molu, I. 103 6 45 S 131 40 E
Molucca Sea 103 4 0 S 124 0 E
Moluccas = Maluku, Is. 103 1 0 S 127 0 E
Molusi 128 20 21 S 24 29 E
Moma, Mozam. 127 16 47 S 39 4 E
Moma, Zaïre 126 1 35 S 23 52 E
Momanga 128 18 7 S 21 41 E
Momba 140 30 58 S 143 30 E
Mombaça 170 15 43 S 48 43W
Mombasa 126 4 2 S 39 43 E
Mombetsu, Hokkaido, Japan 112 42 27N 142 4 E
Mombetsu, Hokkaido, Japan 112 44 21N 143 22 E
Mombuey 56 42 3N 6 20W
Momchilgrad 67 41 33N 25 23 E
Momi 126 1 42 S 27 0 E
Momignies 47 50 2N 4 10 E
Mompós 174 9 14N 74 26W
Møn 73 54 57N 12 15 E
Mon, R. 99 20 25N 94 30 E
Mona, Canal de la 167 18 30N 67 45W
Mona, I. 167 18 5N 67 54W
Mona Passage 167 18 0N 67 40W
Mona, Punta, C. Rica 166 9 37N 82 36W
Mona, Punta, Spain 57 36 43N 3 45W
Monach Is. 36 57 32N 7 40W
Monach, Sd. of 36 57 34N 7 26W
Monaco ■ 44 43 46N 7 23 E
Monadhliath Mts. 37 57 10N 4 4W
Monadnock Mt. 162 42 52N 72 7W
Monagas □ 174 9 20N 63 0W
Monaghan 38 54 15N 6 58W
Monaghan □ 38 54 10N 7 0W
Monahans 159 31 35N 102 50W
Monapo 127 14 50 S 40 12 E
Monar For. 36 57 27N 5 10W
Monar L. 36 57 26N 5 8W
Monarch Mt. 152 51 55N 125 57W
Monasterevan 39 53 10N 7 5W
Monastier-sur-Gazeille, Le 44 44 57N 3 59 E
Monastir 119 35 50N 10 49 E
Monastyriska 80 49 8N 25 14 E
Monavullagh Mts. 39 52 14N 7 35W
Moncada 58 39 30N 0 24W
Moncalieri 62 45 0N 7 40 E
Moncalvo 62 45 3N 8 15 E
Moncarapacho 57 37 5N 7 46W
Moncayo, Sierra del 58 41 48N 1 50W
Mönchengladbach 48 51 12N 6 23 E
Monchique 57 37 19N 8 38W
Monchique, Sa. de, 55 37 18N 8 39W
Monclova 164 26 50N 101 30W
Monção 56 42 4N 8 27W
Moncontant 42 46 43N 0 36W
Moncontour 42 48 22N 2 38W
Moncton 151 46 7N 64 51W
Mondego, Cabo 56 40 11N 8 54W
Mondego, R. 56 40 28N 8 0W
Mondeodo 103 3 21 S 122 9 E
Mondolfo 63 43 45N 13 8 E
Mondoñedo 56 43 25N 7 23W
Mondovi 62 44 23N 7 56 E
Mondovi 158 44 37N 91 40W
Mondragon 45 44 13N 4 44 E
Mondragone 64 41 8N 13 52 E
Mondrain I. 137 34 9 S 122 14 E
Monduli □ 126 3 0 S 36 0 E
Monemvasía 69 36 41N 23 3 E
Monessen 156 40 9N 79 50W
Monesterio 57 38 6N 6 15W
Monestier-de-Clermont 45 44 55N 5 38 E
Monet 150 48 10N 75 40W
Monêtier-les-Bains, Le 45 44 58N 6 30 E
Monett 159 36 55N 93 56W
Moneygall 39 52 54N 7 59W
Moneymore 38 54 42N 6 40W
Monfalcone 63 45 49N 13 32 E
Monflanquin 44 44 32N 0 47 E
Monforte 57 39 6N 7 25W
Monforte de Lemos 56 42 31N 7 33W
Mong Cai 101 21 27N 107 54 E
Möng Hsu 99 21 54N 98 30 E
Mong Hta 98 19 50N 98 35 E
Mong Ket 98 23 8N 98 22 E
Möng Kung 98 21 35N 97 35 E
Mong Kyawt 98 19 56N 98 45 E
Mong Lang 101 20 29N 97 52 E
Möng Nai 98 20 32N 97 55 E
Möng Pai 98 19 40N 97 15 E
Mong Pawk 99 22 4N 99 16 E
Mong Ping 98 21 22N 99 2 E
Mong Pu 98 20 55N 98 44 E
Mong Ton 98 20 25N 98 45 E
Mong Tung 98 22 2N 97 41 E
Mong Wa 99 21 26N 100 27 E
Mong Yai 98 22 28N 98 3 E
Mongalla 123 5 8N 31 55 E
Monger, L. 137 29 25 S 117 5 E
Monghyr 95 25 23N 86 30 E
Mongla 98 22 8N 89 35 E
Mongngaw 98 22 47N 96 59 E
Mongo 117 12 14N 18 43 E
Mongolia ■ 105 47 0N 103 0 E
Mongonu 121 12 40N 13 32 E
Mongororo 124 12 22N 22 26 E
Mongoumba 124 3 33N 18 40 E
Mongpang 101 23 5N 100 25 E
Mongu 125 15 16 S 23 12 E
Mongua 128 16 43 S 15 20 E
Moniaive 35 55 11N 3 55W
Monifieth 35 56 30N 2 48W
Monistral-St.-Loire 45 45 17N 4 11 E
Monitor, Pk. 163 38 52N 116 35W
Monitor, Ra. 163 38 30N 116 45W
Monivea 38 53 22N 8 42W
Monk 153 47 7N 69 59W
Monkey Bay 127 14 7 S 35 1 E
Monkey River 165 16 22N 88 29W
Monki 54 53 23N 22 48 E
Monkira 138 24 46 S 140 30 E
Monkoto 124 1 38 S 20 35 E
Monmouth, U.K. 31 51 48N 2 43W
Monmouth, U.S.A. 158 40 50N 90 40W
Monmouth (□) 26 51 34N 3 5W
Monnow R. 28 51 54N 2 48W
Mono, L. 163 38 0N 119 9W
Mono, Punta del 166 12 0N 83 30W
Monolith 163 35 7N 118 22W
Monópoli 65 40 57N 17 18 E
Monor 53 47 21N 19 27 E
Monóvar 59 38 28N 0 53W
Monowai 143 45 53 S 167 25 E
Monowai, L. 143 45 53 S 167 25 E
Monreal del Campo 58 40 47N 1 20W
Monreale 64 38 6N 13 16 E
Monroe, La., U.S.A. 159 32 32N 92 4W
Monroe, Mich., U.S.A. 156 41 55N 83 26W
Monroe, N.C., U.S.A. 157 35 2N 80 37W
Monroe, Utah, U.S.A. 161 38 45N 111 39W
Monroe, Wis., U.S.A. 158 42 38N 89 40W
Monroe City 158 39 40N 91 40W
Monroeton 162 41 43N 76 29W
Monroeville 157 31 33N 87 15W
Monrovia, Liberia 120 6 18N 10 47W
Monrovia, U.S.A. 161 34 7N 118 1W
Mons 47 50 27N 3 58 E
Møns Klint 73 54 57N 12 33 E
Monsaraz 57 38 28N 7 22W
Monse 103 4 0 S 123 10 E
Monségur 44 44 38N 0 4 E
Monsélice 63 43 13N 11 45 E
Monster 46 52 1N 4 10 E
Mont-aux-Sources 129 28 44 S 28 52 E
Mont-de-Marsin 44 43 54N 0 31W
Mont d'Or, Tunnel 43 46 45N 6 18 E
Mont-Dore, Le 44 45 35N 2 50 E
Mont Joli 151 48 37N 68 10W
Mont Laurier 150 46 35N 75 30W
Mont Luis 151 42 31N 2 6 E
Mont St. Michel 42 48 40N 1 30W
Mont-sur-Marchienne 47 50 23N 4 24 E
Mont Tremblant Prov. Park 150 46 30N 74 30W
Montabaur 48 50 26N 7 49 E
Montacute 109 34 53 S 138 45 E
Montagnac 44 43 29N 3 28 E
Montagnana 63 45 13N 11 29 E
Montagu 128 33 45 S 20 8 E
Montagu, I. 164 58 30 S 26 15W
Montague, Can. 151 46 10N 62 39W
Montague, Calif., U.S.A. 160 41 47N 122 30W
Montague, Mass., U.S.A. 162 42 31N 72 33W
Montague, I. 164 31 40N 144 46W
Montague I. 147 60 0N 147 0W
Montague Ra. 137 29 15 S 119 30 E
Montague Sd. 136 14 28 S 125 20 E
Montaigu 42 46 59N 1 18W
Montalbán 58 40 50N 0 45W
Montalbano di Elicona 65 38 1N 15 0 E
Montalbano Iónico 65 40 17N 16 33 E
Montalbo 58 39 53N 2 42W
Montalcino 63 43 4N 11 30 E
Montalegre 56 41 49N 7 47W
Montalto di Castro 63 42 20N 11 36 E
Montalto Uffugo 65 39 25N 16 9 E
Montalvo 163 34 15N 119 12W
Montamarta 56 41 39N 5 49W
Montaña 174 6 0 S 73 0W
Montana 50 46 19N 7 29 E
Montana □ 154 47 0N 110 0W
Montánchez 57 39 15N 6 8W
Montañita 174 1 30N 75 28W
Montargis 43 48 0N 2 43 E
Montauban 44 44 0N 1 21 E
Montauk 162 41 3N 71 57W
Montauk Pt. 162 41 4N 71 52W
Montbard 43 47 38N 4 20 E
Montbéliard 43 47 31N 6 48 E
Montblanch 58 41 23N 1 4 E
Montbrison 45 45 36N 4 3 E
Montcalm, Pic de 44 42 40N 1 25 E
Montceau-les-Mines 43 46 40N 4 23 E
Montchanin 62 46 47N 4 30 E
Montclair 162 40 53N 74 49W
Montcornet 43 49 40N 4 0 E

Montcuq **Morvan, Mts. du**

Montcuq	**44**	44 21N	1 13 E
Montdidier	**43**	49 38N	2 35 E
Monte Albán	**165**	17 2N	96 45W
Monte Alegre	**175**	2 0 S	54 0W
Monte Alegre de Goiás	**171**	13 14 S	47 10W
Monte Alegre de Minas	**171**	18 52 S	48 52W
Monte Azul	**171**	15 9 S	42 53W
Monte Bello Is.	**136**	20 30 S	115 45 E
Monte Carlo	**45**	43 46N	7 23 E
Monte Carmelo	**171**	18 43 S	47 29W
Monte Caseros	**172**	30 10 S	57 50W
Monte Comán	**172**	34 40 S	68 0W
Monte Cristi	**167**	19 52N	71 39W
Monte Libano	**16**	8 5N	75 29W
Monte Lindo, R.	**172**	25 30 S	58 40W
Monte Quemado	**172**	25 53 S	62 41W
Monte Redondo	**56**	39 53N	8 50W
Monte San Savino	**63**	43 20N	11 42 E
Monte Sant' Angelo	**65**	41 42N	15 59 E
Monte Santo, C. di	**64**	40 5N	9 42 E
Monte Visto	**161**	37 40N	106 8W
Monteagudo	**173**	27 14 S	54 8W
Montealegre	**59**	38 48N	1 17W
Montebello	**150**	45 40N	74 55W
Montebelluna	**63**	45 47N	12 3 E
Montebourg	**42**	49 30N	1 20W
Montecastrilli	**63**	42 40N	12 30 E
Montecatini Terme	**62**	43 55N	10 48 E
Montecito	**163**	34 26N	119 40W
Montecristi	**174**	1 0 S	80 40W
Montecristo, I.	**62**	42 20N	10 20 E
Montefalco	**63**	42 53N	12 38 E
Montefiascone	**63**	42 31N	12 2 E
Montefrío	**57**	37 20N	3 39W
Montegnée	**47**	50 38N	5 31 E
Montego B.	**166**	18 30N	78 0W
Montegranaro	**63**	43 13N	13 38 E
Monteiro	**170**	7 22 S	37 38W
Monteith	**140**	35 11 S	139 23 E
Montejicar	**59**	37 33N	3 30W
Montejinnie	**136**	16 40 S	131 45 E
Montekomu Hu	**99**	34 40N	89 0 E
Montelibano	**174**	8 5N	75 29W
Montélimar	**45**	44 33N	4 45 E
Montella	**65**	40 50N	15 0 E
Montellano	**57**	36 59N	5 36W
Montello	**158**	43 49N	89 21W
Montelupo Fiorentino	**62**	43 44N	11 2 E
Montemór-o-Novo	**57**	38 38N	8 12W
Montemór-o-Velho	**56**	40 11N	8 40W
Montemorelos	**165**	25 11N	99 42W
Montendre	**44**	45 16N	0 26W
Montenegro	**173**	29 39 S	51 29W
Montenegro □	**66**	42 40N	19 20 E
Montenero di Bisaccia	**63**	42 0N	14 47 E
Montepuez	**127**	13 8 S	38 59 E
Montepuez, R.	**127**	12 40 S	40 15 E
Montepulciano	**63**	43 5N	11 46 E
Montereale	**63**	42 31N	13 13 E
Montereau	**43**	48 22N	2 57 E
Monterey	**163**	36 35N	121 57W
Monterey, B.	**163**	36 50N	121 55W
Montería	**174**	8 46N	75 53W
Monteros	**172**	27 11 S	65 30W
Monterotondo	**63**	42 3N	12 36 E
Monterrey	**164**	25 40N	100 30W
Montes Altos	**170**	5 50 S	47 4W
Montes Claros	**171**	16 30 S	43 50W
Montes de Toledo	**57**	39 35N	4 30W
Montesano	**160**	47 0N	123 39W
Montesárchio	**65**	41 5N	14 37 E
Montescaglioso	**65**	40 34N	16 40 E
Montesilvano	**63**	42 30N	14 8 E
Montevarchi	**63**	43 30N	11 32 E
Monteverde	**124**	8 45 S	16 45 E
Montevideo	**173**	34 50 S	56 11W
Montezuma	**158**	41 32N	92 35W
Montfaucon, Haute-Loire, France	**45**	45 11N	4 20 E
Montfaucon, Meuse, France	**43**	49 16N	5 8 E
Montfort	**47**	51 7N	5 58 E
Montfort-l'Amaury	**43**	48 47N	1 49 E
Montfort-sur-Meu	**42**	48 8N	1 58W
Montgenèvre	**45**	44 56N	6 42 E
Montgomery, U.K.	**31**	52 34N	3 9W
Montgomery, Ala., U.S.A.	**157**	32 20N	86 20W
Montgomery, Pa., U.S.A.	**162**	41 10N	76 53W
Montgomery, W. Va., U.S.A.	**156**	38 9N	81 21W
Montgomery = Sahiwal	**94**	30 45N	73 8 E
Montgomery (□)	**26**	52 34N	3 9W
Montgomery Pass	**163**	37 58N	118 20W
Montguyon	**44**	45 12N	0 12W
Monthey	**50**	46 15N	6 56 E
Monticelli d'Ongina	**62**	45 3N	9 56 E
Monticello, Ark., U.S.A.	**159**	33 40N	91 48W
Monticello, Fla., U.S.A.	**157**	30 35N	83 50W
Monticello, Ind., U.S.A.	**156**	40 40N	86 45W
Monticello, Iowa, U.S.A.	**158**	42 18N	91 18W
Monticello, Ky., U.S.A.	**157**	36 52N	84 50W
Monticello, Minn., U.S.A.	**158**	45 17N	93 52W
Monticello, Miss., U.S.A.	**159**	31 35N	90 8W
Monticello, N.Y., U.S.A.	**162**	41 37N	74 42W
Monticello, Utah, U.S.A.	**161**	37 55N	109 27W

Montichiari	**62**	45 28N	10 29 E
Montieri	**43**	48 30N	4 45 E
Montignac	**44**	45 4N	1 10 E
Montignies-sur-Sambre	**47**	50 24N	4 29 E
Montigny-les-Metz	**43**	49 7N	6 10 E
Montigny-sur-Aube	**43**	47 57N	4 45 E
Montijo	**57**	38 52N	6 39W
Montijo, Presa de	**57**	38 55N	6 26W
Montilla	**57**	37 36N	4 40W
Montivideo	**158**	44 55N	95 40W
Montlhéry	**43**	48 39N	2 15 E
Montluçon	**44**	46 22N	2 36 E
Montmagny	**151**	46 58N	70 34W
Montmarault	**53**	46 11N	2 54 E
Montmartre	**153**	50 14N	103 27W
Montmédy	**43**	49 30N	5 20 E
Montmélian	**45**	45 30N	6 4 E
Montmirail	**43**	48 51N	3 30 E
Montmoreau-St.-Cybard	**44**	45 23N	0 8 E
Montmorency	**151**	46 53N	71 11W
Montmorillon	**44**	46 26N	0 50 E
Montmort	**43**	48 55N	3 49 E
Monto	**138**	24 52 S	151 12 E
Montório al Vomano	**63**	42 35N	13 38 E
Montoro	**57**	38 1N	4 27W
Montour Falls	**162**	42 20N	76 51W
Montpelier, Idaho, U.S.A.	**160**	42 15N	111 29W
Montpelier, Ohio, U.S.A.	**156**	41 34N	84 40W
Montpelier, Vt., U.S.A.	**156**	44 15N	72 38W
Montpellier	**44**	43 37N	3 52 E
Montpezat-de-Quercy	**44**	44 15N	1 30 E
Montpon-Ménestrol	**44**	45 2N	0 11 E
Montréal, Can.	**150**	45 31N	73 34W
Montréal, France	**44**	43 13N	2 8 E
Montréal L.	**153**	54 20N	105 45W
Montreal Lake	**153**	54 3N	105 46W
Montredon-Labessonnié	**44**	43 45N	2 18 E
Montréjeau	**44**	43 6N	0 35 E
Montrésor	**42**	47 10N	1 10 E
Montreuil	**43**	50 27N	1 45 E
Montreuil-Bellay	**42**	47 8N	0 9W
Montreux	**50**	46 26N	6 55 E
Montrevault	**42**	47 17N	1 2W
Montrevel-en-Bresse	**45**	46 21N	5 8 E
Montrichard	**42**	47 20N	1 10 E
Montrose, U.K.	**37**	56 43N	2 28W
Montrose, Col., U.S.A.	**161**	38 30N	107 52W
Montrose, Pa., U.S.A.	**162**	41 50N	75 55W
Montrose, oilfield	**19**	57 20N	1 35 E
Montross	**162**	38 6N	76 50W
Monts, Pte des	**151**	49 27N	67 12W
Montsalvy	**44**	44 41N	2 30 E
Montsant, Sierra de	**58**	41 17N	0 1 E
Montsauche	**43**	47 13N	4 0 E
Montsech, Sierra del	**58**	42 0N	0 45 E
Montseny	**58**	42 29N	1 2 E
Montserrat, I.	**167**	16 40N	62 10W
Montserrat, mt.	**58**	41 36N	1 49 E
Montuenga	**56**	41 3N	4 38W
Montuiri	**58**	39 34N	2 59 E
Monveda	**124**	2 52N	21 30 E
Monymusk	**37**	57 13N	2 32W
Monyo	**98**	17 59N	95 30 E
Mônywa	**98**	22 7N	95 11 E
Monza	**62**	45 35N	9 15 E
Monze	**127**	16 17 S	27 29 E
Monze, C.	**94**	24 47N	66 37 E
Monzón	**58**	41 52N	0 10 E
Mook	**46**	51 46N	5 54 E
Mo'oka	**111**	36 26N	140 1 E
Moolawatana	**139**	29 55 S	139 45 E
Mooleulooloo	**140**	31 36 S	140 32 E
Mooliabeenee	**137**	31 20 S	116 2 E
Mooloogool	**137**	26 2 S	119 5 E
Moomin, Cr.	**139**	29 44 S	149 20 E
Moonah, R.	**138**	22 3 S	138 33 E
Moonbeam	**150**	49 20N	82 10W
Mooncoin	**39**	52 18N	7 17W
Moonie	**139**	27 46 S	150 20 E
Moonie, R.	**139**	27 45 S	150 0 E
Moonta	**140**	34 6 S	137 32 E
Moora	**137**	30 37 S	115 58 E
Mooraberree	**138**	25 13 S	140 54 E
Moorarie	**137**	25 56 S	117 35 E
Moorcroft	**158**	44 17N	104 58W
Moore, L.	**137**	29 50 S	117 35 E
Moore, R.	**137**	31 22 S	115 30 E
Moore Reefs	**138**	16 0 S	149 5 E
Moore River Native Settlement	**137**	31 1 S	115 56 E
Moorebank	**47**	33 56 S	150 56 E
Moorefield	**156**	39 5N	78 59W
Mooresville	**157**	35 36N	80 45W
Moorfoot Hills	**35**	55 44N	3 8W
Moorhead	**158**	47 0N	97 0W
Moorland	**141**	31 46 S	152 38 E
Mooroopna	**141**	36 25 S	145 22 E
Moorpark	**163**	34 17N	118 53W
Moorreesburg	**128**	33 6 S	18 38 E
Moorslede	**47**	50 54N	3 4 E
Moosburg	**49**	48 28N	11 57 E
Moose Factory	**150**	51 20N	80 40W
Moose I.	**153**	51 42N	97 10W
Moose Jaw	**153**	50 24N	105 30W
Moose Jaw R.	**153**	50 34N	105 18W
Moose Lake, Can.	**153**	53 43N	100 20W
Moose Lake, U.S.A.	**158**	46 27N	92 48W
Moose Mountain Cr.	**153**	49 13N	102 12W
Moose Mtn. Prov. Park	**153**	49 48N	102 25W

Moose, R.	**150**	51 20N	80 25W
Moose River	**150**	50 48N	81 17W
Moosehead L.	**151**	45 40N	69 40W
Moosomin	**153**	50 9N	101 40W
Moosonee	**150**	51 17N	80 39W
Moosup	**162**	41 44N	71 52W
Mopeia	**125**	17 30 S	35 40 E
Mopipi	**128**	21 6 S	24 55 E
Mopoi	**123**	5 6N	26 54 E
Moppin	**139**	29 12 S	146 45 E
Mopti	**120**	14 30N	4 0W
Moqatta	**123**	14 38N	35 50 E
Moquegua	**174**	17 15 S	70 46W
Mór	**53**	47 25N	18 12 E
Móra	**57**	38 55N	8 10W
Mora, Sweden	**72**	61 2N	14 38 E
Mora, Minn., U.S.A.	**158**	45 52N	93 19W
Mora, N. Mex., U.S.A.	**161**	35 58N	105 21W
Mora de Ebro	**58**	41 6N	0 38 E
Mora de Rubielos	**58**	40 15N	0 45W
Mora la Nueva	**58**	41 7N	0 39 E
Morača, R.	**66**	42 40N	19 20 E
Morada Nova	**170**	5 7 S	38 23W
Morada Nova de Minas	**171**	18 37 S	45 22W
Moradabad	**94**	28 50N	78 50 E
Morafenobe	**129**	17 50 S	44 53 E
Morag	**54**	53 55N	19 56 E
Moral de Calatrava	**59**	38 51N	3 33W
Moraleja	**56**	40 6N	6 43W
Morales	**174**	2 45N	76 38W
Moramanga	**125**	18 56 S	48 12 E
Moran, Kans., U.S.A.	**159**	37 53N	94 35W
Moran, Wyo., U.S.A.	**160**	43 53N	110 37W
Morano Cálabro	**65**	39 51N	16 8 E
Morant Cays	**166**	17 22N	76 0W
Morant Pt.	**166**	17 55N	76 12W
Morar	**36**	56 58N	5 49W
Morar L.	**36**	56 57N	5 40W
Moratalla	**59**	38 14N	1 49W
Moratuwa	**97**	6 45N	79 55 E
Morava, R.	**53**	49 50N	16 50 E
Moravatio	**164**	19 51N	100 25W
Moravia, Iowa, U.S.A.	**158**	40 50N	92 50W
Moravia, N.Y., U.S.A.	**162**	42 43N	76 25W
Moravian Hts. = Ceskemoravská V.	**52**	49 30N	15 40 E
Moravica, R.	**66**	43 40N	20 8 E
Moravice, R.	**53**	49 50N	17 43 E
Moravita	**66**	45 17N	21 14 E
Moravska Trebová	**53**	49 45N	16 40 E
Moravské Budějovice	**52**	49 4N	15 49 E
Morawa	**137**	29 13 S	116 0 E
Morawhanna	**174**	8 30N	59 40W
Moray (□)	**26**	57 32N	3 25W
Moray Firth	**37**	57 50N	3 30W
Morbach	**49**	49 48N	7 7 E
Morbegno	**62**	46 8N	9 34 E
Morbihan □	**42**	47 55N	2 50W
Morcenx	**44**	44 0N	0 55W
Mordelles	**42**	48 5N	1 52W
Morden	**153**	49 15N	98 10W
Mordovian S.S.R. □	**81**	54 20N	44 30 E
Mordovo	**81**	52 13N	40 50 E
More L.	**37**	58 18N	4 52W
Møre og Romsdal □	**71**	63 0N	9 0 E
Morea	**140**	36 45 S	141 18 E
Moreau, R.	**158**	45 15N	102 45W
Morebattle	**35**	55 30N	2 20W
Morecambe	**32**	54 5N	2 52W
Morecambe B.	**32**	54 7N	3 0W
Morecambe, gasfield	**19**	53 57N	3 40W
Moree	**139**	29 28 S	149 54 E
Morehead, P.N.G.	**135**	8 41 S	141 41 E
Morehead, U.S.A.	**156**	38 12N	83 22W
Morehead City	**157**	34 46N	76 44W
Moreira	**174**	0 34 S	63 26W
Morelia	**164**	19 40N	101 11W
Morella, Austral.	**138**	23 0 S	143 47 E
Morella, Spain	**58**	40 35N	0 2 E
Morelos	**164**	26 42N	107 40W
Morelos □	**165**	18 40N	99 10W
Morena, Sierra	**57**	38 20N	4 0W
Morenci	**161**	33 7N	109 20W
Moreni	**70**	44 59N	25 36 E
Moreno	**171**	8 7 S	35 6W
Mores, I.	**157**	26 15N	77 35W
Moresby I.	**152**	52 30N	131 40W
Morestel	**45**	45 40N	5 28 E
Moret	**43**	48 22N	2 48 E
Moreton B.	**133**	27 10 S	153 10 E
Moreton, I.	**139**	27 10 S	153 25 E
Moreton-in-Marsh	**28**	51 59N	1 42W
Moreton Telegraph Office	**138**	12 22 S	142 30 E
Moretonhampstead	**30**	50 39N	3 45W
Moreuil	**43**	49 46N	2 30 E
Morez	**45**	46 31N	6 2 E
Morgan, Austral.	**140**	34 0 S	139 35 E
Morgan, U.S.A.	**160**	41 3N	111 44W
Morgan City	**159**	29 40N	91 15W
Morgan Hill	**163**	37 8N	121 39W
Morganfield	**156**	37 40N	87 55W
Morganton	**157**	35 46N	81 48W
Morgantown	**156**	39 39N	79 58W
Morganville, Queens., Austral.	**139**	25 10 S	152 0 E
Morganville, S. Australia, Austral.	**140**	33 10 S	140 32 E
Morgat	**42**	48 15N	4 32 E
Morgenzon	**129**	26 45 S	29 36 E
Morges	**50**	46 31N	6 29 E
Morhange	**43**	48 55N	6 38 E
Mori	**62**	45 51N	10 59 E

Morialmée	**47**	50 17N	4 30 E
Morialta Falls Reserve	**109**	34 54 S	138 43 E
Moriarty	**161**	35 3N	106 2W
Morice L.	**152**	53 50N	127 40W
Morichal	**174**	2 10N	70 34W
Morichal Largo, R.	**174**	8 55N	63 0W
Moriguchi	**111**	34 44N	135 34 E
Moriki	**121**	12 52N	6 30 E
Morinville	**152**	53 49N	113 41W
Morioka	**112**	39 45N	141 8 E
Moris	**164**	28 8N	108 32W
Morisset	**141**	33 6 S	151 30 E
Morkalla	**140**	34 23 S	141 10 E
Morlaàs	**44**	43 21N	0 18W
Morlaix	**42**	48 36N	3 52W
Morlanwelz	**47**	50 28N	4 15 E
Morley	**33**	53 45N	1 36W
Mormanno	**65**	39 53N	15 59 E
Mormant	**43**	48 37N	2 52 E
Morney	**139**	25 22 S	141 23 E
Morningside	**108**	27 28 S	153 4 E
Mornington, Victoria, Austral.	**141**	38 15 S	145 5 E
Mornington, W. Australia, Austral.	**136**	17 31 S	126 6 E
Mornington, Ireland	**38**	53 42N	6 17W
Mornington I.	**138**	16 30 S	139 30 E
Mornington, I.	**176**	49 50 S	75 30W
Mórnos, R.	**69**	38 30N	22 0 E
Moro	**123**	10 50N	30 9 E
Moro G.	**103**	6 30N	123 0 E
Morobe	**135**	7 49 S	147 38 E
Morocco ■	**118**	32 0N	5 50W
Morococha	**174**	11 40 S	76 5W
Morogoro	**126**	6 50 S	37 40 E
Morogoro □	**126**	8 0 S	37 0 E
Morokweng	**125**	26 12 S	23 45 E
Moroleón	**164**	20 8N	101 32W
Morombé	**129**	21 45 S	43 22 E
Moron	**172**	34 39 S	58 37W
Morón	**166**	22 0N	78 30W
Morón de Almazán	**58**	41 29N	2 27W
Morón de la Frontera	**57**	37 6N	5 28W
Morondava	**129**	20 17 S	44 17 E
Morondo	**120**	8 57N	6 47W
Morongo Valley	**163**	34 3N	116 37W
Moronou	**120**	6 16N	4 59W
Morotai, I.	**103**	2 10N	128 30 E
Moroto	**124**	2 28N	34 42 E
Moroto Summit, Mt.	**126**	2 30N	34 43 E
Morozov (Bratan), mt.	**67**	42 30N	25 10 E
Morozovsk	**83**	48 25N	41 50 E
Morpeth	**35**	55 11N	1 41W
Morrelganj	**98**	22 28N	89 51 E
Morrilton	**159**	35 10N	92 45W
Morrinhos, Ceara, Brazil	**170**	3 14 S	40 7W
Morrinhos, Minas Gerais, Brazil	**171**	17 45 S	49 10W
Morrinsville	**142**	37 40 S	175 32 E
Morris, Can.	**153**	49 25N	97 22W
Morris, Ill., U.S.A.	**156**	41 20N	88 20W
Morris, Minn., U.S.A.	**158**	45 33N	95 56W
Morris, N.Y., U.S.A.	**162**	42 33N	75 15W
Morris, Mt.	**137**	26 9 S	131 4 E
Morrisburg	**150**	44 55N	75 7W
Morrison	**158**	41 47N	90 0W
Morristown, Ariz., U.S.A.	**161**	33 54N	112 45W
Morristown, N.J., U.S.A.	**162**	40 48N	74 30W
Morristown, S.D., U.S.A.	**158**	45 57N	101 44W
Morristown, Tenn., U.S.A.	**157**	36 18N	83 20W
Morrisville, N.Y., U.S.A.	**162**	42 54N	75 39W
Morrisville, Pa., U.S.A.	**162**	40 13N	74 47W
Morro Agudo	**171**	20 44 S	48 4W
Morro Bay	**163**	35 27N	120 54W
Morro do Chapéu	**171**	11 33 S	41 9W
Morro, Pta.	**172**	27 6 S	71 0W
Morros	**170**	2 52 S	44 3W
Morrosquillo, Golfo de	**167**	9 35N	75 40W
Morrum	**73**	56 12N	14 45 E
Morrumbene	**125**	23 31 S	35 16 E
Mors	**73**	56 50N	8 45 E
Morshank	**81**	53 28N	41 50 E
Mörsil	**72**	63 19N	13 40 E
Mortagne, Charente Maritime, France	**44**	45 28N	0 49W
Mortagne, Orne, France	**42**	48 30N	0 32 E
Mortagne, Vendée, France	**42**	46 59N	0 57W
Mortagne-au-Perche	**42**	48 31N	0 33 E
Mortagne, R.	**43**	48 30N	6 30 E
Mortain	**42**	48 40N	0 57W
Mortara	**62**	45 15N	8 43 E
Morte Bay	**30**	51 10N	4 13W
Morte Pt.	**30**	51 13N	4 14W
Morteau	**43**	47 3N	6 35 E
Mortehoe	**30**	51 21N	4 12W
Morteros	**172**	30 50 S	62 0W
Mortes, R. das	**171**	11 45 S	50 44W
Mortimer's Cross	**28**	52 17N	2 50W
Mortlake	**140**	38 5 S	142 50 E
Morton, Tex., U.S.A.	**159**	33 39N	102 49W
Morton, Wash., U.S.A.	**160**	46 33N	122 17W
Morton Fen	**29**	52 45N	0 23W
Mortsel	**47**	51 11N	4 27 E
Morundah	**141**	34 57 S	146 19 E
Moruya	**141**	35 58N	150 3 E
Morvan, Mts. du	**43**	47 5N	4 0 E

Morven Mukden

Morven, Austral. 139 26 22S 147 5E
Morven, N.Z. 143 44 50S 171 6E
Morven, dist. 34 56 38N 5 44W
Morven, mt., Grampian, U.K. 37 57 8N 3 1W
Morven, mt., Highland, U.K. 37 58 15N 3 40W
Morvern 36 56 38N 5 44W
Morwell 141 38 10S 146 22E
Moryn 54 52 51N 14 22E
Mosalsk 80 54 30N 34 55E
Mosbach 49 49 21N 9 9E
Mosciano Sant' Ángelo 63 42 42N 13 52E
Moscos Is. 101 14 0N 97 30E
Moscow, Idaho, U.S.A. 160 46 45N 116 59W
Moscow, Pa., U.S.A. 162 41 20N 75 31W
Moscow = Moskva 81 55 45N 37 35E
Mosel, R. 49 50 22N 7 36E
Moselle □ 43 48 59N 6 33E
Moselle, R. 47 50 22N 7 36E
Moses Lake 160 47 16N 119 17W
Mosgiel 143 45 53S 170 21E
Moshi 126 3 22S 37 18E
Moshi □ 126 3 22S 37 18E
Moshupa 128 24 46S 25 29E
Mósina 54 52 15N 16 50E
Mosjøen 74 65 51N 13 12E
Moskenesøya 74 67 58N 13 0E
Moskenstraumen 74 67 47N 13 0E
Moskva 81 55 45N 37 35E
Moskva, R. 81 55 5N 38 51E
Moslavačka Gora 63 45 40N 16 37E
Mošćenice 63 45 17N 14 16E
Mosomane (Artesia) 128 24 2S 26 19E
Mosonmagyaróvár 53 47 52N 17 18E
Mo orin 66 45 19N 20 4E
Mospino 82 47 52N 38 0E
Mosquera 174 2 35N 78 30W
Mosquero 159 35 48N 103 57W
Mosqueruela 58 40 21N 0 27W
Mosquitia 166 15 20N 84 10W
Mosquitos, Golfo de los 166 9 15N 81 10W
Moss 71 59 27N 10 40E
Moss Vale 141 34 32S 150 25E
Mossaka 124 1 15S 16 45E
Mossâmedes, Angola 125 15 7S 12 11E
Mossâmedes, Brazil 171 16 7S 50 11W
Mossbank 153 49 56N 105 56W
Mossburn 143 45 41S 168 15E
Mosselbaai 128 34 11S 22 8E
Mossendjo 124 2 55S 12 42E
Mosses, Col des 50 46 25N 7 7E
Mossgiel 140 33 15S 144 30E
Mossley 32 53 31N 2 1W
Mossman 138 16 28S 145 23E
Mossoró 170 5 10S 37 15W
Mossuril 127 14 58S 40 42E
Mossy, R. 153 54 5N 102 58W
Most 52 50 31N 13 38E
Mostar 66 43 22N 17 50E
Mostardas 173 31 2S 50 51W
Mostefa, Rass 119 36 55N 11 3E
Mosterøy 71 59 5N 5 37E
Mostiska 80 49 48N 23 4E
Mostrim 38 53 42N 7 38W
Mosty 80 53 27N 24 38E
Mostyn 31 53 18N 3 14W
Mosul = Al Mawsil 92 36 20N 43 5E
Mosulpo 107 33 20N 126 17E
Mosvatn, L. 71 59 52N 8 5E
Mota del Cuervo 58 39 30N 2 52W
Mota del Marqués 56 41 38N 5 11W
Motagua, R. 166 15 44N 88 14W
Motala 73 58 32N 15 1E
Motcombe 28 51 1N 2 12W
Motegi 111 36 32N 140 11E
Mothe-Achard, La 42 46 37N 1 40W
Motherwell 35 55 48N 4 0W
Motihari 95 26 37N 85 1E
Motilla del Palancar 58 39 34N 1 55W
Motnik 63 46 14N 14 54E
Motocurunya 174 4 24N 64 5W
Motovun 63 45 20N 13 50E
Motozintea de Mendoza 165 15 21N 92 14W
Motril 59 36 44N 3 37W
Motrul, R. 70 44 44N 22 59E
Mott 158 46 25N 102 14W
Motte-Chalançon, La 45 44 30N 5 21E
Motte, La 45 44 20N 6 3E
Mottisfont 28 51 22N 1 32W
Mottola 65 40 38N 17 0E
Motueka 143 41 7S 173 1E
Motul 165 21 0N 89 20W
Motupena Pt. 135 6 30S 155 10E
Mouchalagane, R. 151 50 56N 68 41W
Moúdhros 68 39 50N 25 18E
Moudjeria 120 17 50N 12 15W
Moudon 50 46 40N 6 49E
Mouila 124 1 50S 11 0E
Moulamein 140 35 3S 144 1E
Moule, Le 167 16 20N 61 22W
Moulins 44 46 35N 3 19E
Moulmein 98 16 30N 97 40E
Moulmeingyun 98 16 23N 95 16E
Moulouya, O. 118 35 8N 2 22W
Moulton, U.K. 29 52 17N 0 51W
Moulton, U.S.A. 159 29 35N 97 8W
Moultrie 157 31 11N 83 47W
Moultrie, L. 157 33 25N 80 10W
Mound City, Mo., U.S.A. 158 40 2N 95 25W
Mound City, S.D., U.S.A. 158 45 46N 100 3W
Moúnda, Ákra 69 38 5N 20 45E
Moundou 117 8 40N 16 10E
Moundsville 156 39 53N 80 43W
Moung 100 12 46N 103 27E
Mount Airy 162 36 31N 80 37W
Mount Amherst 136 18 24S 126 58E
Mount Angel 160 45 4N 122 46W
Mount Augustus 137 24 20S 116 56E
Mount Barker, S.A., Austral. 140 35 5S 138 52E
Mount Barker, W.A., Austral. 137 34 38S 117 40E
Mount Barker Junc. 109 35 1S 138 52E
Mount Beauty 141 36 47S 147 10E
Mount Bellew Bridge 38 53 28N 8 30W
Mount Buckley 138 20 6S 148 0E
Mount Carmel, Ill., U.S.A. 156 38 20N 87 48W
Mount Carmel, Pa., U.S.A. 162 40 46N 76 25W
Mount Clemens 150 42 35N 82 50W
Mount Coolon 138 21 25S 147 25E
Mount Cootatha Park 108 27 29S 152 57E
Mount Crosby 108 27 32S 152 48E
Mount Darwin 125 16 47S 31 38E
Mount Desert I. 151 44 25N 68 25W
Mount Dora 157 28 49N 81 32W
Mount Douglas 138 21 35S 146 50E
Mount Edgecumbe 147 57 8N 135 22W
Mount Elizabeth 136 16 0S 125 50E
Mount Enid 136 21 42S 116 26E
Mount Forest 150 43 59N 80 43W
Mount Fox 138 18 45S 145 45E
Mount Gambier 140 37 50S 140 46E
Mount Garnet 138 17 37S 145 6E
Mount Goldsworthy 132 20 25S 119 39E
Mount Gravatt 108 27 32S 153 5E
Mount Hagen 135 5 52S 144 16E
Mount Hope, N.S.W., Austral. 141 32 51S 145 51E
Mount Hope, S.A., Austral. 139 34 7S 135 23E
Mount Hope, U.S.A. 156 37 52N 81 9W
Mount Horeb 158 43 0N 89 42W
Mount Howitt 139 26 31S 142 16E
Mount Isa 138 20 42S 139 26E
Mount Ive 140 32 25S 136 5E
Mount Keith 137 27 15S 120 30E
Mount Kisco 162 41 12N 73 44W
Mount Laguna 163 32 52N 116 25W
Mount Larcom 138 23 48S 150 59E
Mount Lavinia 93 6 50N 79 50E
Mount Lofty Ra. 133 34 35S 139 5E
Mount McKinley Nat. Pk. 147 64 0N 150 0W
Mount Magnet 137 28 2S 117 47E
Mount Manara 140 32 29S 143 58E
Mount Margaret 139 26 54S 143 21E
Mount Maunganui 142 37 40S 176 14E
Mount Monger 137 31 0S 122 0E
Mount Morgan 138 23 40S 150 25E
Mount Morris 156 42 43N 77 50W
Mount Mulligan 138 16 45S 144 47E
Mount Narryer 137 26 30S 115 55E
Mount Newman 136 23 18S 119 45E
Mount Nicholas 137 22 54S 120 27E
Mount Oxide 138 19 30S 139 29E
Mount Pearl 151 47 31N 52 47W
Mount Penn 162 40 20N 75 54W
Mount Perry 139 25 13S 151 42E
Mount Phillips 137 24 25S 116 15E
Mount Pleasant, Iowa, U.S.A. 158 41 0N 91 35W
Mount Pleasant, Mich., U.S.A. 156 43 35N 84 47W
Mount Pleasant, S.C., U.S.A. 157 32 45N 79 48W
Mount Pleasant, Tenn., U.S.A. 157 35 31N 87 11W
Mount Pleasant, Tex., U.S.A. 159 33 5N 95 0W
Mount Pleasant, Ut., U.S.A. 160 39 40N 111 29W
Mount Pocono 162 41 8N 75 21W
Mount Rainier Nat. Park. 160 46 50N 121 43W
Mount Revelstoke Nat. Park 152 51 5N 118 30W
Mount Robson 152 52 56N 119 15W
Mount Robson Prov. Park 152 53 0N 119 0W
Mount Samson 108 27 18S 152 51E
Mount Sandiman 137 24 25S 115 30E
Mount Shasta 160 41 20N 122 18W
Mount Somers 143 43 45S 171 27E
Mount Sterling, Ill., U.S.A. 158 40 0N 90 40W
Mount Sterling, Ky., U.S.A. 158 38 0N 84 0W
Mount Surprise 138 18 10S 144 17E
Mount Talbot 38 53 31N 8 18W
Mount Tom Price 137 22 50S 117 40E
Mount Upton 162 42 26N 75 23W
Mount Vernon, Austral. 137 24 15S 118 15E
Mount Vernon, D.C., U.S.A. 162 38 47N 77 10W
Mount Vernon, Ill., U.S.A. 162 38 17N 88 57W
Mount Vernon, Ind., U.S.A. 158 38 17N 88 57W
Mount Vernon, N.Y., U.S.A. 156 40 57N 73 49W
Mount Vernon, Ohio, U.S.A. 156 40 20N 82 30W
Mount Vernon, Wash., U.S.A. 160 48 27N 122 18W
Mount Victor 140 32 11S 139 44E
Mount Whaleback 132 23 18S 119 44E
Mount Willoughby 139 27 58S 134 8E
Mountain Ash 31 51 42N 3 22W
Mountain Center 163 33 42N 116 44W
Mountain City, Nev., U.S.A. 160 41 54N 116 0W
Mountain City, Tenn., U.S.A. 157 36 30N 81 50W
Mountain Dale 162 41 41N 74 32W
Mountain Grove 159 37 5N 92 20W
Mountain Home, Ark., U.S.A. 159 36 20N 92 25W
Mountain Home, Idaho, U.S.A. 160 43 11N 115 45W
Mountain Iron 158 47 30N 92 87W
Mountain Park. 152 52 50N 117 15W
Mountain View, Ark., U.S.A. 159 35 52N 92 10W
Mountain View, Calif., U.S.A. 161 37 26N 122 5W
Mountain Village 147 62 10N 163 50W
Mountainair 161 34 35N 106 15W
Mountcharles 38 54 37N 8 12W
Mountfield 38 54 34N 7 10W
Mountmellick 39 53 7N 7 20W
Mountnorris 38 54 15N 6 29W
Mountnorris B. 136 11 25S 132 45E
Mountrath 39 53 0N 7 30W
Mounts Bay 30 50 3N 5 27W
Mountsorrel 28 52 43N 1 9W
Mountvernon 152 48 25N 122 20W
Mouping 107 37 24N 121 35E
Moura, Austral. 138 24 35S 149 58E
Moura, Brazil 174 1 25S 61 45W
Moura, Port. 57 38 7N 7 30W
Mourão 57 38 22N 7 22W
Mourdi, Depression du 117 18 10N 23 0E
Mourdiah 120 14 35N 7 25W
Moure, La 158 46 27N 98 17W
Mourenx 44 43 23N 0 36W
Mouri 121 5 6N 1 14W
Mourilyan 138 17 35S 146 3E
Mourmelon-le-Grand 43 49 8N 4 22E
Mourne Mts. 38 54 10N 6 0W
Mourne, R. 38 54 45N 7 39W
Mouroubra 137 29 42S 117 52E
Mourzouq 119 25 53N 14 10W
Mousa I. 36 60 0N 1 10W
Mouscron 47 50 45N 3 12E
Moussoro 117 13 50N 16 35E
Mouthe 43 46 44N 6 12E
Moutier 50 47 16N 7 21E
Moûtiers 45 45 29N 6 31E
Mouting 108 25 22N 101 32E
Moutong 103 0 28N 121 13E
Mouy 43 49 18N 2 20E
Mouzáki 68 39 25N 21 37E
Movas 164 28 10N 109 25W
Moville 38 55 11N 7 3W
Moxhe 47 50 38N 5 5E
Moxotó, R. 170 9 19S 38 14W
Moy, Inverness, U.K. 37 57 22N 4 3W
Moy, Ulster, U.K. 38 54 27N 6 40W
Moy, R. 38 54 5N 8 50W
Moyagee 137 27 48S 117 48E
Moyahua 164 21 16N 103 10W
Moyale, Ethiopia 123 3 34N 39 4E
Moyale, Kenya 126 3 30N 39 0E
Moyamba 120 8 15N 12 30W
Moyasta 39 52 40N 9 31W
Moycullen 39 53 20N 9 10W
Moyie 152 49 17N 115 50W
Moyle □ 38 55 10N 6 15W
Moylett 38 53 57N 7 7W
Moynalty 38 53 48N 6 52W
Moyne 39 52 45N 7 43W
Moyobamba 174 6 0S 77 0W
Moyvalley 38 53 26N 6 55W
Moza 90 31 48N 35 8E
Mozambique = Moçambique 125 15 3S 40 42E
Mozambique ■ 129 19 0S 35 0E
Mozambique Chan. 129 20 0S 39 0E
Mozdok 83 43 45N 44 48E
Mozhaisk 81 55 30N 36 2E
Mozhga 84 56 26N 52 15E
Mozirje 63 46 22N 14 58E
Mozua 126 3 57N 24 2E
Mozyr 80 52 0N 29 15E
Mpanda 126 6 23S 31 40E
Mpanda □ 126 6 23S 31 40E
Mpésoba 120 12 31N 5 39W
Mpika 127 11 51S 31 25E
Mpraeso 121 6 50N 0 50W
Mpulungu 127 8 51S 31 5E
Mpwapwa 124 6 30S 36 30E
Mpwapwa □ 126 6 30S 36 20E
Mragowo 54 53 57N 21 18E
Mrakovo 84 52 43N 56 38E
Mramor 66 43 20N 21 45E
Mrhaïer 119 33 55N 5 58E
Mrimina 118 29 50N 7 9W
Mrkonjió Grad 66 44 26N 17 4E
Mrkopalj 63 45 21N 14 52E
Mrocza 54 53 16N 17 35E
Msab, Oued en 119 32 35N 5 20E
Msaken 119 35 49N 10 33E
M'Salu, R. 127 12 25S 39 15E
Msambansovu, mt. 127 15 50S 30 3E
M'sila 119 35 46N 4 30E
Msoro 125 13 35S 31 50E
Msta, R. 80 58 30N 33 30E
Mstislavl 80 54 0N 31 50E
Mszana Dolna 54 49 41N 20 5E
Mszczonów 54 51 58N 20 33E
Mtama 127 10 17S 39 21E
Mtilikwe, R. 127 21 0S 31 12E
Mtsensk 81 53 25N 36 30E
Mtskheta 83 41 52N 44 45E
Mtwara 124 10 20S 40 20E
Mtwara □ 126 1 0S 39 0E
Mtwara-Mikindani 127 10 20S 40 20E
Mu Gia, Deo 100 17 40N 105 47E
Mu Ness 36 60 41N 0 50W
Mu, R. 98 21 56N 95 38E
Muaná 170 1 25S 49 15W
Muanda 124 6 0S 12 20E
Muang Chiang Rai 100 19 52N 99 50E
Muang Kalasin 101 16 26N 103 30E
Muang Lampang 101 18 16N 99 32E
Muang Lamphun 100 18 40N 98 53E
Muang Nan 101 18 52N 100 42E
Muang Phetchabun 101 16 23N 101 12E
Muang Phichit 101 16 29N 100 21E
Muang Ubon 101 15 15N 104 50E
Muang Yasothon 101 15 50N 104 10E
Muar 101 2 3N 102 34E
Muar, R. 101 2 15N 102 48E
Muarabungo 102 1 40S 101 10E
Muaradjuloi 102 0 12S 114 3E
Muaraenim 102 3 40S 103 50E
Muarakaman 102 0 2S 116 45E
Muaratebo 102 1 30S 102 26E
Muaratembesi 102 1 42S 103 2E
Muaratewe 102 0 50S 115 0E
Mubairik 92 23 22N 39 8E
Mubarakpur 95 26 12N 83 24E
Mubende 126 0 33N 31 22E
Mubi 121 10 18N 13 16E
Mubur, P. 101 3 20N 106 12E
Mucajaí, Serra do 174 2 23N 61 10W
Much Dewchurch 28 51 58N 2 45W
Much Marcle 28 51 59N 2 27W
Much Wenlock 28 52 36N 2 34W
Muchalls 37 57 2N 2 10W
Mücheln 48 51 18N 11 49E
Muchinga Mts. 127 11 30S 31 30E
Muchkapskiy 81 51 52N 42 28E
Mûcin 70 45 16N 28 8E
Muck, I. 36 56 50N 6 15W
Muckadilla 139 26 35S 148 23E
Muckle Roe I. 36 60 22N 1 22W
Muckross Hd. 38 54 37N 8 35W
Mucubela 129 16 53S 37 49E
Mucugê 171 13 5S 37 49E
Mucuri 171 18 0S 40 0W
Mucurici 171 18 6S 40 31W
Mud I. 108 27 20S 153 14E
Mud L. 160 40 15N 120 15W
Mudanya 82 40 25N 28 50E
Muddy, R. 161 38 30N 110 55W
Mudgee 141 32 32S 149 31E
Mudhnib 92 25 50N 44 18E
Mudjatik, R. 153 56 1N 107 36W
Mudon 98 16 15N 97 44E
Muecate 127 14 55S 39 34E
Muêda 127 11 36S 39 28E
Muela, La 58 41 36N 1 7W
Mueller Ra., Mts. 136 18 18S 126 46E
Muerto, Mar 165 16 10N 94 10W
Muff 38 55 4N 7 16W
Mufindi □ 127 8 30S 35 20E
Mufou Shan 109 29 15N 114 20E
Mufulira 127 12 32S 28 15E
Mufumbiro Range 126 1 25S 29 30E
Mugardos 56 43 27N 8 15W
Muge 57 39 3N 8 40W
Muge, R. 57 39 15N 8 18W
Múggia 63 45 36N 13 47E
Mugi 110 33 40N 134 25E
Mugia 56 43 3N 9 17W
Mugila, Mts. 126 7 0S 28 50E
Muğla 92 37 15N 28 28E
Müglizh 67 42 37N 25 32E
Mugu 95 29 45N 82 30E
Muhammad Qol 122 20 53N 37 9E
Muhammad Râs 122 27 50N 34 0E
Muhammadabad 95 26 4N 83 25E
Muharraqa = Sa'ad 90 31 28N 34 33E
Muhesi, R. 126 6 40S 35 5E
Muheza □ 126 5 0S 39 0E
Mühldorf 49 48 14N 12 23E
Mühlhausen 48 51 12N 10 29E
Mühlig-Hofmann-fjella 13 72 30S 5 0E
Muhutwe 126 1 35S 31 45E
Mui Bai Bung 101 8 35N 104 42E
Mui Ron 101 18 7N 106 27E
Muiden 46 52 20N 5 4E
Muine Bheag 39 52 42N 6 59W
Muiños 56 41 58N 7 59W
Muir, L. 137 34 30S 116 40E
Muir of Ord 37 57 30N 4 35W
Muirdrum 35 56 31N 2 40W
Muirkirk 35 55 31N 4 6W
Muja 123 12 2N 39 30E
Mukachevo 80 48 27N 22 45E
Mukah 102 2 55N 112 5E
Mukalla 91 14 33N 49 2E
Mukawwa, Geziret 122 23 55N 35 53E
Mukdahan 100 16 32N 104 43E
Mukden = Shenyang 107 41 48N 123 27E

Mukeiras Nabari

Mukeiras **91** 13 59N 45 52 E
Mukhtolovo **81** 55 29N 43 15 E
Mukinbudin **137** 30 55 S 118 5 E
Mukombwe **127** 15 48 S 26 32 E
Mukomuko **102** 2 20 S 101 10 E
Mukomwenze **126** 6 49 S 27 15 E
Mukry **85** 37 54N 65 12 E
Muktsar **94** 30 30N 74 30 E
Muktsar Bhatinda **94** 30 15N 74 57 E
Mukur **94** 32 50N 67 50 E
Mukutawa, R. **153** 53 10N 97 24W
Mukwela **127** 17 0 S 26 40 E
Mula **59** 38 3N 1 33W
Mula, R. **96** 19 16N 74 20 E
Mulanay **103** 13 30N 122 30 E
Mulange **126** 3 40 S 27 10 E
Mulatas, Arch. de las **166** 6 51N 78 31W
Mulchén **172** 37 45 S 72 20W
Mulde, R. **48** 50 55N 12 42 E
Mule Creek **158** 43 19N 104 8W
Muleba **126** 1 50 S 31 37 E
Muleba □ **126** 2 0 S 31 30 E
Mulegé **164** 26 53N 112 1W
Mulegns **51** 46 32N 9 38 E
Mulengchen **107** 44 32N 130 14 E
Muleshoe **159** 34 17N 102 42W
Mulga Valley **140** 31 8 S 141 3 E
Mulgathing **139** 30 15 S 134 0 E
Mulgrave **151** 45 38N 61 31W
Mulgrave I. **135** 10 5 S 142 10 E
Mulhacén **59** 37 4N 3 20W
Mülheim **48** 51 26N 6 53W
Mulhouse **43** 47 40N 7 20 E
Muli, China **99** 28 21N 100 40 E
Muli, China **108** 27 50N 101 15 E
Mull Head **37** 59 23N 2 53W
Mull I. **34** 56 27N 6 0W
Mull, Ross of, dist. **34** 56 20N 6 15W
Mull, Sound of **34** 56 30N 5 50W
Mullagh **39** 53 13N 8 25W
Mullaghareirk Mts. **39** 52 20N 9 10W
Mullaittvu **97** 9 15N 80 55 E
Mullardoch L. **36** 57 30N 5 0W
Mullen **158** 42 5N 101 0W
Mullengudgery **141** 31 43 S 147 29 E
Mullens **156** 37 34N 81 22W
Muller, Pegunungan **102** 0 30N 113 30 E
Muller Ra. **138** 5 30 S 143 0 E
Mullet Pen. **38** 54 10N 10 2W
Mullewa **137** 28 29 S 115 30 E
Mullheim **49** 47 48N 7 37 E
Mulligan, R. **138** 26 40 S 139 0 E
Mullin **159** 31 33N 98 38W
Mullinahone **39** 52 30N 7 31W
Mullinavat **39** 52 23N 7 10W
Mullingar **38** 53 31N 7 20W
Mullins **157** 34 12N 79 15W
Mullion **30** 50 1N 5 15W
Mullsjö **73** 57 56N 13 55 E
Mullumbimby **139** 28 30 S 153 30 E
Mulobezi **127** 16 45 S 25 7 E
Mulrany **38** 53 54N 9 47W
Mulroy B. **38** 55 15N 7 45W
Mulshi L. **96** 18 30N 73 20 E
Multai **96** 21 39N 78 15 E
Multan **94** 30 15N 71 30 E
Multan □ **94** 30 29N 72 29 E
Multrå **72** 63 10N 17 24 E
Mulumbe, Mts. **127** 8 40 S 27 30 E
Mulungushi Dam **127** 14 48 S 28 48 E
Mulvane **159** 37 30N 97 15W
Mulwad **122** 18 45N 30 39 E
Mulwala **141** 35 59 S 146 0 E
Mumbles **31** 51 34N 4 0W
Mumbles Hd. **31** 51 33N 4 0W
Mumbwa **125** 15 0 S 27 0 E
Mumeng **135** 7 1 S 146 37 E
Mumra **83** 45 45N 47 41 E
Mun **101** 15 17N 103 0 E
Mun, R. **100** 15 19N 105 30 E
Muna, I. **103** 5 0 S 122 30 E
Muna Sotuta **165** 20 29N 89 43W
Munawwar **95** 32 47N 74 27 E
Münchberg **49** 50 11N 11 48 E
Müncheberg **48** 52 30N 14 9 E
München **49** 48 8N 11 33 E
Munchen-Gladbach = Mönchengladbach **48** 51 12N 6 23 E
Muncho Lake **152** 59 0N 125 50W
Munchŏn **107** 39 14N 127 19 E
Münchwilen **51** 47 38N 8 59 E
Muncie **156** 40 10N 85 20W
Mundakayam **97** 9 30N 76 32 E
Mundala, Puncak **103** 4 30 S 141 0 E
Mundare **152** 53 35N 112 20W
Munday **159** 33 26N 99 39W
Münden **48** 51 25N 9 42 E
Mundesley **29** 52 53N 1 24 E
Mundiwindi **136** 23 47 S 120 9 E
Mundo Novo **171** 11 50 S 40 29W
Mundo, R. **59** 38 30N 2 15W
Mundra **94** 22 54N 69 26 E
Mundrabilla **137** 31 52 S 127 51 E
Munera **59** 39 2N 2 29W
Muneru, R. **96** 16 45N 80 3 E
Mungallala **139** 26 25 S 147 34 E
Mungallala Cr. **139** 28 53 S 147 5 E
Mungana **138** 17 8 S 144 27 E
Mungaoli **94** 24 24N 78 7 E
Mungari **127** 17 12 S 33 42 E
Mungbere **124** 2 36N 28 28 E
Mungindi **139** 28 58 S 149 1 E
Munhango **125** 12 10 S 18 38 E
Munhango R. **125** 11 30 S 19 30 E
Munich = München **49** 48 8N 11 35 E
Munising **156** 46 25N 86 39W
Munjiye **122** 18 47N 41 20W
Munka-Ljungby **73** 56 16N 12 58 E
Munkedal **73** 58 28N 11 40 E
Munkfors **72** 59 50N 13 30 E
Muñoz Gamero, Pen. **176** 52 30 S 73 5 E
Munro **141** 37 56 S 147 11 E
Munroe L. **153** 59 13N 98 35W
Munsan **107** 37 51N 126 48 E
Munshiganj **98** 23 33N 90 32 E
Münsingen **50** 46 52N 7 32 E
Munster **43** 48 2N 7 8 E
Münster, Niedersachsen, Ger. **48** 52 59N 10 5 E
Münster, Nordrhein-Westfalen, Ger. **48** 51 58N 7 37 E
Münster, Switz. **51** 46 30N 8 17 E
Munster □ **39** 52 20N 8 40W
Muntadgin **137** 31 45 S 118 33 E
Muntele Mare **70** 46 30N 23 12 E
Muntok **102** 2 5 S 105 10 E
Muon Pak Beng **101** 19 51N 101 4 E
Muong Beng **100** 20 23N 101 46 E
Muong Boum **100** 22 24N 102 49 E
Muong Er **100** 20 49N 104 1 E
Muong Hai **100** 21 3N 101 49 E
Muong Hiem **100** 20 5N 103 22 E
Muong Houn **100** 20 8N 101 23 E
Muong Hung **100** 20 56N 103 53 E
Muong Kau **100** 15 6N 105 47 E
Muong Khao **100** 19 47N 103 29 E
Muong Khoua **100** 21 5N 102 31 E
Muong La **101** 20 52N 102 5 E
Muong Liep **100** 18 29N 101 40 E
Muong May **100** 14 49N 106 56 E
Muong Ngeun **100** 20 36N 101 3 E
Muong Ngoi **100** 20 43N 102 41 E
Muong Nhie **100** 22 12N 102 28 E
Muong Nong **100** 16 22N 106 30 E
Muong Ou Tay **100** 22 7N 101 48 E
Muong Oua **100** 18 18N 101 20 E
Muong Pak Bang **100** 19 54N 101 8 E
Muong Penn **100** 20 13N 103 52 E
Muong Phalane **100** 16 39N 105 34 E
Muong Phieng **100** 19 6N 101 32 E
Muong Phine **100** 16 32N 106 2 E
Muong Sai **100** 20 42N 101 59 E
Muong Saiapoun **100** 18 24N 101 31 E
Muong Sen **100** 19 24N 104 8 E
Muong Sing **100** 21 11N 101 9 E
Muong Son **100** 20 27N 103 19 E
Muong Soui **100** 19 33N 102 52 E
Muong Va **100** 21 53N 102 19 E
Muong Xia **100** 20 19N 104 50 E
Muonio **74** 67 57N 23 40 E
Muonio älv **74** 67 48N 23 25 E
Muotathal **51** 46 58N 8 46 E
Muotohora **142** 38 18 S 177 40 E
Mupa **125** 16 5 S 15 50 E
Muqaddam, Wadi **123** 17 0N 32 0 E
Mur-de-Bretagne **42** 48 12N 3 0W
Mur, R. **52** 47 7N 13 55 E
Mura, R. **63** 46 37N 16 9 E
Murallón, Cuerro **176** 49 55 S 73 30W
Muralto **51** 46 11N 8 49 E
Muranda **126** 1 52 S 29 20 E
Murang'a **126** 0 45 S 37 9 E
Murashi **81** 59 30N 49 0 E
Murat **44** 45 7N 2 53 E
Murau **52** 47 6N 14 10 E
Muravera **64** 39 25N 9 35 E
Murça **56** 41 24N 7 28W
Murchison **143** 41 49 S 172 21 E
Murchison Downs **137** 26 45 S 118 55 E
Murchison Falls = Kabarega Falls **126** 2 15N 31 38 E
Murchison House **137** 27 39 S 114 14 E
Murchison Mts. **143** 45 13 S 167 23 E
Murchison, oilfield **19** 61 25N 1 40 E
Murchison, R. **137** 26 45 S 116 15 E
Murchison Ra. **138** 20 0 S 134 10 E
Murchison Rapids **127** 15 55 S 34 35 E
Murcia **59** 38 2N 1 10W
Murcia □ **59** 37 50N 1 30W
Murdo **158** 43 56N 100 43W
Murdoch Pt. **138** 14 37 S 144 55 E
Murdock Hill **109** 34 59 S 138 55 E
Mure, La **45** 44 55N 5 48 E
Mureş □ **70** 46 45N 24 40 E
Mureşul, R. **70** 46 15N 20 13 E
Muret **44** 43 30N 1 20 E
Murfatlar **70** 44 10N 28 26 E
Murfreesboro **157** 35 50N 86 21W
Murg **51** 47 8N 9 13 E
Murgab **85** 38 10N 73 59 E
Murgeni **70** 46 12N 28 1 E
Murgenthal **50** 47 16N 7 50 E
Murgon **139** 26 15 S 151 54 E
Murgoo **137** 27 24 S 116 28 E
Muri **51** 47 17N 8 21 E
Muriaé **173** 21 8 S 42 23W
Murias de Paredes **56** 42 52N 6 19W
Murici **170** 9 19 S 35 56W
Muriel Mine **127** 17 14 S 30 40 E
Muritiba **171** 12 55 S 39 15W
Murits see **48** 53 25N 12 40 E
Murjo Mt. **103** 6 36 S 110 53 E
Murka **126** 3 27 S 38 0 E
Murmansk **78** 68 57N 33 10 E
Murmerwoude **46** 53 18N 6 0 E
Murnau **49** 47 40N 11 11 E
Muro, France **45** 42 34N 8 54 E
Muro, Spain **58** 39 45N 3 3 E
Muro, C. di **45** 41 44N 8 37 E
Muro Lucano **65** 40 45N 15 30 E
Murom **81** 55 35N 42 3 E
Muroran **112** 42 25N 141 0 E
Muros **56** 42 45N 9 5W
Muros y de Noya, Ria de **56** 42 45N 9 0W
Muroto **110** 33 18N 134 9 E
Muroto-Misaki **110** 33 15N 134 10 E
Murowana Gośślina **54** 52 35N 17 0 E
Murphy **160** 43 11N 116 33W
Murphys **163** 38 8N 120 28W
Murphysboro **159** 37 50N 89 20W
Murrat **122** 18 51N 29 33 E
Murray, Ky., U.S.A. **157** 36 40N 88 20W
Murray, Utah, U.S.A. **160** 40 41N 111 58W
Murray Bridge **140** 35 6 S 139 14 E
Murray Downs **138** 21 4 S 134 40 E
Murray Harb. **151** 46 0N 62 28W
Murray, L., P.N.G. **135** 7 0 S 141 35 E
Murray, L., U.S.A. **157** 34 8N 81 30W
Murray, R., S. Australia, Austral. **140** 35 20 S 139 22 E
Murray, R., W. Australia, Austral. **133** 32 33 S 115 45 E
Murray, R., Can. **152** 56 11N 120 45W
Murraysburg **128** 31 58 S 23 47 E
Murree **94** 33 56N 73 28 E
Murrieta **163** 33 33N 117 13W
Murrin Murrin **137** 28 50 S 121 45 E
Murrough **39** 53 7N 9 18W
Murrumbidgee, R. **140** 34 40 S 143 0 E
Murrumburrah **141** 34 32 S 148 22 E
Murrurundi **141** 31 42 S 150 51 E
Murshid **122** 21 40N 31 10 E
Murshidabad **95** 24 11N 88 19 E
Murska Sobota **63** 46 39N 16 12 E
Murtazapur **96** 20 40N 77 25 E
Murten **50** 46 56N 6 7 E
Murten-see **50** 46 56N 7 4 E
Murtle L. **152** 52 8N 119 38W
Murtoa **140** 36 35 S 142 28 E
Murton **33** 54 51N 1 22W
Murtosa **56** 40 44N 8 40W
Muru **123** 6 36N 29 16 E
Murungu **126** 4 12 S 31 10 E
Murupara **142** 38 28 S 176 42 E
Murwara **95** 23 46N 80 28 E
Murwillumbah **139** 28 18 S 153 27 E
Mürz, R. **52** 47 30N 15 25 E
Mürzzuschlag **52** 47 36N 15 41 E
Muş **92** 38 45N 41 30 E
Musa, Gebel (Sinai) **122** 28 32N 33 59 E
Musa Khel **94** 30 29N 69 52 E
Musa Qala (Musa Kala) **93** 32 20N 64 50 E
Musa, R. **135** 9 3 S 148 55 E
Musaffargarh **93** 30 10N 71 10 E
Musairik, Wadi **122** 19 30N 43 10 E
Musala, I. **102** 1 41N 98 28 E
Musalla, mt. **67** 42 13N 23 37 E
Musan **107** 42 12N 129 12 E
Musangu **127** 10 28 S 23 55 E
Musasa **126** 3 25 S 31 30 E
Musashino **111** 35 42N 139 34 E
Muscat = Masqat **93** 23 37N 58 36 E
Muscat & Oman = Oman **91** 23 0N 58 0 E
Muscatine **158** 41 25N 91 5W
Musel **56** 43 34N 5 42W
Musetula **127** 14 28 S 24 1 E
Musgrave Ras. **137** 26 0 S 132 0 E
Mushie **124** 2 56 S 17 4 E
Mushin **121** 6 32N 3 21 E
Musi, R., India **96** 17 10N 79 25 E
Musi, R., Indon. **102** 2 55 S 103 40 E
Muskeg, R. **152** 60 20N 123 20W
Muskegon **156** 43 15N 86 17W
Muskegon Hts. **156** 43 12N 86 17W
Muskegon, R. **156** 43 25N 86 0W
Muskogee **159** 35 50N 95 25W
Muskwa, R. **152** 58 47N 122 48W
Musmar **122** 18 6N 35 40 E
Musofu **127** 13 30 S 29 0 E
Musoma **126** 1 30 S 33 48 E
Musoma □ **126** 1 50 S 34 30 E
Musquaro, L. **151** 50 38N 61 5W
Musquodoboit Harbour **151** 44 50N 63 9W
Mussau I. **135** 1 30 S 149 40 E
Musselburgh **35** 55 57N 3 3W
Musselkanaal **46** 52 57N 7 0 E
Musselshell, R. **160** 46 30N 108 15W
Mussidan **44** 45 2N 0 22 E
Mussomeli **64** 37 35N 13 43 E
Musson **47** 49 33N 5 42 E
Mussooree **94** 30 27N 78 6 E
Mussuco **128** 17 2 S 19 3 E
Mustafa Kemalpaşa **92** 40 3N 28 25 E
Mustajidda **92** 26 30N 41 50 E
Mustang **95** 29 10N 83 55 E
Mustapha, C. **119** 36 55N 11 3 E
Musters, L. **176** 45 20 S 69 25W
Musudan **107** 40 50N 129 43 E
Muswellbrook **141** 32 16 S 150 56 E
Muszyna **53** 49 22N 20 55 E
Mût **122** 25 28N 28 58 E
Mut **92** 36 40N 33 28 E
Mutan Chiang, R. **107** 46 18N 129 31 E
Mutanchiang **107** 44 40N 129 35 E
Mutanda, Mozam. **129** 21 0 S 33 34 E
Mutanda, Zambia **127** 12 15 S 26 13 E
Muthill **35** 56 20N 3 50W
Mutis **174** 1 4N 77 25W
Mutooroo **140** 32 26 S 140 55 E
Mutshatsha **127** 10 35 S 24 20 E
Mutsu-Wan **112** 41 5N 140 55 E
Muttaburra **138** 22 38 S 144 29 E
Muttama **141** 34 46 S 148 8 E
Mutton Bay **151** 50 50N 59 2W
Mutton I. **39** 52 50N 9 31W
Mutuáli **127** 14 55 S 37 0 E
Mutung **108** 29 35N 106 51 E
Mutunópolis **171** 13 40 S 49 15W
Muvatupusha **97** 9 53N 76 35 E
Muxima **124** 9 25 S 13 52 E
Muy, Le **45** 43 28N 6 34 E
Muy Muy **166** 12 39N 85 36W
Muya **77** 56 27N 115 39 E
Muyaga **126** 3 14 S 30 33 E
Muyunkum, Peski **85** 44 12N 71 0 E
Muzaffarabad **95** 34 25N 73 30 E
Muzaffargarh **94** 30 5N 71 14 E
Muzaffarnagar **94** 29 26N 77 40 E
Muzaffarpur **95** 26 7N 85 32 E
Muzhi **76** 65 25N 64 40 E
Muzillac **42** 47 35N 2 30W
Muzkol, Khrebet **85** 38 22N 73 20 E
Muzo **174** 5 32N 74 6W
Muzon C. **152** 54 40N 132 40W
Mvôlô **123** 6 10N 29 53 E
Mwadui **126** 3 35 S 33 40 E
Mwandi Mission **127** 17 30 S 24 51 E
Mwango **126** 6 48 S 24 12 E
Mwanza, Katanga, Congo **126** 7 55 S 26 43 E
Mwanza, Kwango, Congo **127** 5 29 S 17 43 E
Mwanza, Malawi **126** 16 58 S 24 28 E
Mwanza, Tanz. **126** 2 30 S 32 58 E
Mwanza □ **126** 2 0 S 33 0 E
Mwaya **126** 9 32 S 33 55 E
Mweelrea, Mt. **38** 53 37N 9 48W
Mweka **124** 4 50 S 21 40 E
Mwenga **126** 3 1 S 28 21 E
Mwepo **127** 11 50 S 26 10 E
Mweru, L. **127** 9 0 S 29 0 E
Mweza Range **127** 21 0 S 30 0 E
Mwimbi **127** 8 38 S 31 39 E
Mwinilunga **127** 11 43 S 24 25 E
Mwinilunga, Mt. **127** 11 43 S 24 25 E
My Tho **101** 10 29N 106 23 E
Mya, O. **119** 30 46N 4 44 E
Myadh **124** 1 16N 13 10 E
Myanaung **98** 18 25N 95 10 E
Myaungmya **98** 16 30N 95 0 E
Mybster **37** 58 27N 3 24W
Myddfai **31** 51 59N 3 47W
Myddle **28** 52 49N 2 47W
Myerstown **162** 40 22N 76 18W
Myingyan **98** 21 30N 95 30 E
Myitkyina **98** 25 30N 97 26 E
Myittha, R. **98** 16 15N 94 34 E
Myjava **53** 48 41N 17 37 E
Mylor **109** 35 3 S 138 46 E
Mymensingh **98** 24 45N 90 24 E
Myndmere **158** 46 23N 97 7W
Mynydd Bach, Hills **31** 52 16N 4 6W
Mynydd Eppynt, Mts. **31** 52 4N 3 30W
Mynydd Prescelly, mt. **31** 51 57N 4 48W
Mynzhilgi, Gora **85** 43 48N 68 51 E
Myogi **101** 21 24N 96 28 E
Myrdal **71** 60 43N 7 10 E
Mýrdalsjökull **74** 63 40N 19 6W
Myrrhee **136** 36 46 S 146 17 E
Myrtle Beach **157** 33 43N 78 50W
Myrtle Creek **160** 43 0N 123 19W
Myrtle Point **160** 43 0N 124 4W
Myrtleford **141** 36 34 S 146 44 E
Myrtletown **108** 27 23 S 153 8 E
Mysen **71** 59 33N 11 20 E
Myslenice **54** 49 51N 19 57 E
Myslibórz **54** 52 55N 14 50 E
Mysłowice **54** 50 15N 19 12 E
Mysore **97** 12 17N 76 41 E
Mysore □ = Karnataka **142** 13 15N 77 0 E
Mystic **162** 41 21N 71 58W
Mystishchi **81** 55 50N 37 50 E
Myszkow **54** 50 45N 19 22 E
Mythen **51** 47 2N 8 42 E
Myton **160** 40 10N 110 2W
Mývatn **74** 65 36N 17 0W
Mze, R. **52** 49 47N 12 50 E
Mzimba **127** 11 48 S 33 33 E
Mzuzu **127** 11 30 S 33 55 E

N

N' Dioum **120** 16 31N 14 39W
Na-lang **98** 22 42N 97 33 E
Na Noi **100** 18 19N 100 43 E
Na Phao **100** 17 35N 105 44 E
Na Sam **100** 22 3N 106 37 E
Na San **100** 21 12N 104 2 E
Naaldwijk **46** 51 59N 4 13 E
Naalehu **147** 19 4N 155 35W
Na'am **123** 9 42N 28 27 E
Na'an **90** 31 53N 34 52 E
Naantali **75** 60 29N 22 2 E
Naarden **46** 52 18N 5 9 E
Naas **39** 53 12N 6 40W
Nababeep **128** 29 36 S 17 46 E
Nabadwip **95** 23 34N 88 20 E
Nabari **111** 34 37N 136 5 E

Nabas Nashville

Nabas 103 11 47N 122 6 E
Nabberu, L. 137 25 30S 120 30 E
Naberezhnyye Chelny 84 55 42N 52 19 E
Nabesna 147 62 33N 143 10W
Nabeul 119 36 30N 10 51 E
Nabha 94 30 26N 76 14 E
Nabi Rubin 90 31 56N 34 44 E
Nabire 103 3 15S 136 27 E
Nabisar 94 25 8N 69 40 E
Nabispi, R. 151 50 14N 62 13W
Nabiswera 126 1 27N 32 15 E
Nablus = Nābulus 90 32 14N 35 15 E
Naboomspruit 129 24 32S 28 40 E
Nābulus 90 32 14N 35 15 E
Nabúri 127 16 53S 38 59 E
Nacala-Velha 127 14 32S 40 34 E
Nacaome 166 13 31N 87 30W
Nacaroa 127 14 22S 39 56 E
Naches 160 46 48N 120 49W
Nachikatsuura 111 33 33N 135 58 E
Nachingwea 127 10 49S 38 49 E
Nachingwea □ 127 10 30S 38 30 E
Nachna 94 27 34N 71 41 E
Náchod 53 50 25N 16 8 E
Nacimento Res. 163 35 46N 120 53W
Nacka 72 59 17N 18 12 E
Nackara 140 32 48S 139 12 E
Naco, Mexico 164 31 20N 109 56W
Naco, U.S.A. 161 31 24N 109 58W
Nacogdoches 159 31 33N 95 30W
Nácori Chico 164 29 39N 109 1W
Nacozari 164 30 30N 109 50W
Nadi 122 18 40N 33 41 E
Nadiad 94 22 41N 72 56 E
Nador 118 35 14N 2 58W
Nadushan 93 32 2N 53 35 E
Nadvornaya 80 48 40N 24 35 E
Nadym 76 63 35N 72 42 E
Nadym, R. 76 65 30N 73 0 E
Nærbø 71 58 40N 5 39 E
Næstved 73 55 13N 11 44 E
Nafada 121 11 8N 11 20 E
Näfels 51 47 6N 9 4 E
Nafferton 33 54 1N 0 24W
Naft Shāh 92 34 0N 45 30 E
Nafūd ad Dahy 92 22 0N 45 0 E
Nafūsah, Jabal 119 32 12N 12 30 E
Nag Hammâdi 122 26 2N 32 18 E
Naga 103 13 38N 123 15 E
Naga Hills 99 26 0N 94 30 E
Naga, Kreb en 118 24 12N 6 0W
Naga-Shima, Kagoshima, Japan 110 32 10N 130 9 E
Naga-Shima, Yamaguchi, Japan 110 33 55N 132 5 E
Nagagami, R. 150 49 40N 84 40W
Nagahama, Ehime, Japan 111 33 36N 132 29 E
Nagahama, Shiga, Japan 111 35 23N 136 16 E
Nagai Parkar 94 24 28N 70 46 E
Nagaland □ 98 26 0N 94 30 E
Nagambie 141 36 47S 145 10 E
Nagano 111 36 40N 138 10 E
Nagano-ken □ 111 36 15N 138 0 E
Nagaoka 112 37 27N 138 50 E
Nagappattinam 97 10 46N 79 51 E
Nagar Parkar 93 24 30N 70 35 E
Nagara-Gawa, R. 111 35 1N 136 43 E
Nagari Hills 97 15 30N 79 45 E
Nagarjuna Sagar 96 16 35N 79 17 E
Nagasaki 110 32 47N 129 50 E
Nagasaki-ken □ 110 32 50N 129 40 E
Nagato 110 34 19N 131 5 E
Nagaur 94 27 15N 73 45 E
Nagbhir 96 20 34N 79 42 E
Nagchu Dzong 99 31 22N 91 54 E
Nagercoil 97 8 12N 77 33 E
Nagina 95 29 30N 78 30 E
Nagineh 93 34 20N 57 15 E
Nagold 49 48 38N 8 40 E
Nagoorin 138 24 17S 151 15 E
Nagorsk 81 59 18N 50 48 E
Nagorum 126 4 1N 34 33 E
Nagoya 111 35 10N 136 50 E
Nagpur 96 21 8N 79 10 E
Nagrong 99 32 46N 84 16 E
Nagua 167 19 23N 69 50W
Nagyatád 53 46 14N 17 22 E
Nagyecsed 53 47 53N 22 24 E
Nagykanizsa 53 46 28N 17 0 E
Nagykörös 53 46 55N 19 48 E
Nagyléta 53 47 23N 21 55 E
Naha 112 26 13N 127 42 E
Nahalal 90 32 41N 35 12 E
Nahanni Butte 152 61 2N 123 20W
Nahanni Nat. Pk. 152 61 15N 125 0W
Naharayim 90 32 28N 35 33 E
Nahariyya 90 33 1N 35 5 E
Nahāvand 92 34 10N 48 30 E
Nahe, R. 49 49 48N 7 33 E
Nahf 90 32 56N 35 18 E
Nahīya, Wadi 122 27 37N 32 0 E
Nahlin 152 58 55N 131 38W
Nahud 122 18 12N 41 40 E
Naiapu 70 44 12N 25 47 E
Naicá 164 27 53N 105 31W
Naicam 153 52 30N 104 30W
Na'ifah 91 19 59N 50 46 E
Naila 49 50 19N 11 43 E
Nailsea 28 51 25N 2 44W
Nailsworth 28 51 41N 2 12W
Nain 151 56 34N 61 40W
Na'in 93 32 54N 53 0 E
Naini Tal 95 29 23N 79 30 E
Nainpur 93 22 30N 80 10 E
Naintré 42 46 46N 0 29 E
Naira, I. 103 4 28S 130 0 E
Nairn 37 57 35N 3 54W
Nairn (□) 26 57 28N 3 52W
Nairn R. 37 57 32N 3 58W
Nairobi 126 1 17S 36 48 E
Naivasha 126 0 40S 36 30 E
Naivasha □ 126 0 40S 36 30 E
Naivasha L. 126 0 48S 36 20 E
Najac 44 44 14N 1 58 E
Najafābād 93 32 40N 51 15 E
Najd 92 26 30N 42 0 E
Nájera 58 42 26N 2 48W
Najerilla, R. 58 42 15N 2 45W
Najibabad 94 29 40N 78 20 E
Najin 107 42 12N 130 15 E
Naju 107 35 3N 126 43 E
Naka-Gawa, R. 111 36 20N 140 36 E
Naka-no-Shima 112 29 51N 129 46 E
Nakalagba 126 2 50N 27 58 E
Nakama 110 33 56N 130 43 E
Nakaminato 111 36 21N 140 36 E
Nakamura 110 33 0N 133 0 E
Nakanai Mts. 135 5 40S 151 0 E
Nakano 111 36 45N 138 22 E
Nakanojō 111 36 35N 138 51 E
Nakatane 112 30 31N 130 57 E
Nakatsu 110 33 40N 131 15 E
Nakatsugawa 111 35 29N 137 30 E
Nakelele Pt. 147 21 2N 156 35W
Nakfa 123 16 40N 38 25 E
Nakhichevan, A.S.S.R. □ 79 39 14N 45 30 E
Nakhl 122 29 55N 33 43 E
Nakhl Mubarak 92 24 10N 38 10 E
Nakhodka 77 43 10N 132 45 E
Nakhon Nayok 100 14 12N 101 13 E
Nakhon Pathom 100 13 49N 100 3 E
Nakhon Phanom 100 17 23N 104 43 E
Nakhon Ratchasima (Khorat) 100 14 59N 102 12 E
Nakhon Sawan 100 15 35N 100 10 E
Nakhon Si Thammarat 100 8 29N 100 0 E
Nakhon Thai 100 17 17N 100 50 E
Nakina, B.C., Can. 152 59 12N 132 52W
Nakina, Ont., Can. 150 50 10N 86 40W
Nakło n. Noteoja 54 53 9N 17 38 E
Naknek 147 58 45N 157 0W
Nakodar 94 31 8N 75 31 E
Nakomis 127 39 19N 89 19W
Nakskov 73 54 50N 11 8 E
Näkten 72 62 48N 14 38 E
Naktong, R. 107 35 7N 128 57 E
Nakur 94 30 2N 77 32 E
Nakuru 126 0 15S 35 5 E
Nakuru □ 126 0 15S 35 5 E
Nakuru, L. 126 0 23S 36 5 E
Nakusp 152 50 20N 117 45W
Nal, R. 94 27 0N 65 50 E
Nalchik 83 43 30N 43 33 E
Nälden 72 63 21N 14 14 E
Näldsjön 72 63 25N 14 15 E
Nalerigu 121 10 35N 0 25W
Nalgonda 96 17 6N 79 15 E
Nalhati 95 24 17N 87 52 E
Nalinnes 47 50 19N 4 27 E
Nallamalai Hills 97 15 30N 78 50 E
Nalón, R. 56 43 35N 6 10W
Nālūt 119 31 54N 11 0 E
Nam Can 101 8 46N 104 59 E
Nam Dinh 100 20 25N 106 5 E
Nam Du, Hon 101 9 41N 104 21 E
'Nam', gasfields 19 53 17N 3 36 E
Nam Ngum 100 18 35N 102 34 E
'Nam', oilfield 19 54 50N 4 40 E
Nam-Phan 101 10 30N 106 0 E
Nam Phong 100 16 42N 102 52 E
Nam Tha 100 20 58N 101 30 E
Nam Tok 100 14 14N 99 4 E
Nam Tso = Namu Hu 105 30 45N 90 30 E
Namacurra 125 17 30S 36 50 E
Namakkal 97 11 13N 78 13 E
Namaland, Africa 128 26 0S 18 0 E
Namaland, S. Afr. 128 30 0S 18 0 E
Namangan 85 41 0N 71 40 E
Namapa 127 13 43S 39 50 E
Namasagali 126 1 2N 33 0 E
Namatanai 135 3 40S 152 29 E
Nambala 120 14 1N 5 58W
Namber 103 1 2S 134 57 E
Nambour 139 26 32S 152 58 E
Nambucca Heads 141 30 37S 153 0 E
Namcha Barwa 105 29 40N 95 10 E
Namche Bazar 95 27 51N 86 47 E
Namchonjŏm 107 38 15N 126 26 E
Namêche 47 50 28N 5 0 E
Namecund 127 14 54S 37 37 E
Nameh 102 2 34N 116 21 E
Nameponda 127 15 50S 39 50 E
Namerikawa 111 36 46N 137 20 E
Námestovo 53 49 24N 19 25 E
Nametil 127 15 40S 39 15 E
Náměšt nad Oslavou 53 49 12N 16 10 E
Namew L. 153 54 14N 101 56W
Namhsan 98 22 48N 97 42 E
Nami 101 6 2N 100 46 E
Namib Desert = Namib Woestyn 128 22 30S 15 0 E
Namib-Woestyn 128 22 30S 15 0 E
Namibia □ 128 22 0S 18 9 E
Namiquipa 164 29 15N 107 25W
Namja Pass 95 30 0N 82 25 E
Namkhan 98 23 50N 97 41 E
Namlea 103 3 10S 127 5 E
Namoi, R. 141 30 12S 149 30 E
Namous, O. 118 30 44N 0 18W
Nampa 160 43 40N 116 40W
Nampula 127 15 6S 39 7 E
Namrole 103 3 46S 126 46 E
Namsen 74 64 27N 11 42 E
Namsen, R. 74 64 40N 12 45 E
Namsos 74 64 28N 11 0 E
Namtu 98 23 5N 97 28 E
Namtumbo 127 10 30S 36 4 E
Namu 152 51 52N 127 41W
Namu Hu 105 30 45N 90 30 E
Namur 47 50 27N 4 52 E
Namur □ 47 50 17N 5 0 E
Namutoni 128 18 49S 16 55 E
Namwala 127 15 44S 26 30 E
Namwŏn 107 35 23N 127 23 E
Namysłow 54 51 6N 17 42 E
Nan 100 18 48N 100 46 E
Nan Ling 109 25 0N 112 30 E
Nan, R. 100 15 42N 100 9 E
Nan Shan 105 38 30N 99 0 E
Nana 70 44 17N 26 34 E
Nānā, W. 119 30 0N 15 24 E
Nanaimo 152 49 10N 124 0W
Nanam 107 41 44N 129 40 E
Nan'an 109 24 58N 118 23 E
Nanango 139 26 40S 152 0 E
Nanao 109 23 26N 117 1 E
Nanch'ang 109 28 40N 115 50 E
Nanchang, Fukien, China 109 24 26N 117 18 E
Nanchang, Hupei, China 109 31 47N 111 42 E
Nanch'eng 109 27 33N 116 35 E
Nancheng = Hanchung 106 33 10N 107 2 E
Nanchiang 108 32 21N 106 50 E
Nanchiao 108 22 2N 100 15 E
Nanchien 106 25 5N 100 30 E
Nanching 109 32 3N 118 47 E
Nanchishan Liehtao 108 27 28N 121 4 E
Nanch'uan 108 29 7N 107 16 E
Nanch'ung 108 30 50N 106 4 E
Nancy 43 48 42N 6 12 E
Nanda Devi, Mt. 95 30 30N 80 30 E
Nandan 110 34 10N 134 42 E
Nander 96 19 10N 77 20 E
Nandewar Ra. 139 30 15S 150 35 E
Nandi □ 126 0 15N 35 0 E
Nandikotkur 97 15 52N 78 18 E
Nandura 96 20 52N 76 25 E
Nandurbar 96 21 20N 74 15 E
Nandyal 97 15 30N 78 30 E
Nanfeng 109 27 10N 116 24 E
Nanga 137 26 7S 113 45 E
Nanga Eboko 121 4 41N 12 22 E
Nanga Parbat, mt. 95 35 10N 74 35 E
Nangade 127 11 5S 39 36 E
Nangapinoh 102 0 20S 111 14 E
Nangarhar □ 93 34 20N 70 0 E
Nangatajap 102 1 32S 110 34 E
Nangeya Mts. 126 3 30N 33 30 E
Nangis 43 48 33N 3 0 E
Nangodi 121 10 58N 0 42W
Nangola 120 12 41N 6 35W
Nangwarry 140 37 33S 140 48 E
Nanhsien 109 29 22N 112 25 E
Nanhsiung 109 25 10N 114 18 E
Nanhua 108 25 10N 101 20 E
Nanhui 109 31 3N 121 46 E
Nani Hu 109 31 10N 118 55 E
Nanjangud 97 12 6N 76 43 E
Nanjeko 127 5 31S 23 30 E
Nanjirinji 127 9 41S 39 5 E
Nankana Sahib 94 31 27N 73 38 E
Nank'ang 109 25 38N 114 45 E
Nanking = Nanching 109 32 5N 118 45 E
Nankoku 110 33 29N 133 38 E
Nankung 106 37 22N 115 20 E
Nanling 109 30 56N 118 19 E
Nannine 137 26 51S 118 18 E
Nanning 108 22 48N 108 20 E
Nannup 137 33 59S 115 48 E
Nanpa 108 32 13N 104 51 E
Nanp'an Chiang, R. 108 25 0N 106 11 E
Nanpara 95 27 52N 81 33 E
Nanp'i 106 38 4N 116 34 E
Nanp'ing, Fukien, China 109 26 38N 118 10 E
Nanp'ing, Hupeh, China 109 29 55N 112 2 E
Nanpu 108 31 19N 106 2 E
Nanripe 127 13 52S 38 52 E
Nansei-Shotō 112 26 0N 128 0 E
Nansen Sd. 12 81 0N 91 0W
Nansio 126 2 3S 33 4 E
Nanson 137 28 35S 114 45 E
Nant 44 44 1N 3 18 E
Nantes 42 47 12N 1 33W
Nanteuil-le-Haudouin 43 49 9N 2 48 E
Nantiat 44 46 1N 1 11 E
Nanticoke 162 41 12N 76 1W
Nanticoke, R. 162 38 16N 75 56W
Nanton, Can. 152 50 21N 113 46W
Nanton, China 108 24 59N 107 32 E
Nantua 45 46 10N 5 35 E
Nantucket 162 41 17N 70 6W
Nantucket I. 155 41 16N 70 3W
Nantucket Sd. 162 41 30N 70 15W
Nant'ung 109 32 0N 120 55 E
Nantwich 32 53 5N 2 31W
Nanuque 171 17 50S 40 21W
Nanutarra 136 22 32S 115 30 E
Nanyang 106 33 0N 112 32 E
Nan'yō 110 34 3N 131 49 E
Nanyüan 106 39 48N 116 24 E
Nanyuki 126 0 2N 37 4 E
Nao, C. de la 59 38 44N 0 14 E
Nao Chou Tao 109 20 55N 110 35 E
Nao, La, Cabo de 59 38 44N 0 14 E
Naococane L. 151 52 50N 70 45W
Naogaon 98 24 52N 88 52 E
Napa 163 38 18N 122 17W
Napa, R. 163 38 10N 122 19W
Napamute 147 61 30N 158 45W
Napanee 150 44 15N 77 0W
Napanoch 162 41 44N 74 2W
Nape 100 18 18N 105 6 E
Nape Pass = Keo Neua, Deo 100 18 23N 105 10 E
Napf 50 47 1N 7 56 E
Napiéolédougou 120 9 18N 5 35W
Napier 142 39 30S 176 56 E
Napier Broome B. 136 14 2S 126 37 E
Napier Downs 136 17 11S 124 36 E
Napier Pen. 138 12 4S 135 43 E
Naples 157 26 10N 81 45W
Naples = Nápoli 65 40 50N 14 5 E
Nap'o 108 23 44N 106 49 E
Napo □ 174 0 30S 77 0W
Napo, R. 174 3 5S 73 0W
Napoleon, N. Dak., U.S.A. 158 46 32N 99 49W
Napoleon, Ohio, U.S.A. 156 41 24N 84 7W
Nápoli 65 40 50N 14 5 E
Nápoli, G. di 65 40 40N 14 10 E
Napopo 126 4 15N 28 0 E
Napoule, La 45 43 31N 6 56 E
Nappa 32 53 58N 2 14W
Nappa Merrie 139 27 36S 141 7 E
Naqâda 122 25 53N 32 42 E
Nara, Japan 111 34 40N 135 49 E
Nara, Mali 120 15 25N 7 20W
Nara, Canal 94 26 0N 69 20 E
Nara-ken □ 111 34 30N 136 0 E
Nara Visa 159 35 39N 103 10W
Naracoorte 140 36 58S 140 45 E
Naradhan 141 33 34S 146 17 E
Narasapur 96 16 26N 81 50 E
Narasaropet 96 16 14N 80 4 E
Narathiwat 101 6 40N 101 55 E
Narayanganj 98 23 31N 90 33 E
Narayanpet 96 16 45N 77 30 E
Narberth 31 51 48N 4 45W
Narbonne 44 43 11N 3 0 E
Narborough 28 52 34N 1 12W
Narcea, R. 56 43 15N 6 30W
Nardò 65 40 10N 18 0 E
Nare Head 30 50 12N 4 55W
Narembeen 137 32 7S 118 17 E
Naretha 137 31 0S 124 45 E
Nari, R. 94 29 10N 67 50 E
Narin 93 36 5N 69 0 E
Narinda, B. de 129 14 55S 47 30 E
Narino □ 174 1 30N 78 0W
Narita 111 35 47N 140 19 E
Narmada, R. 94 22 40N 77 30 E
Narnaul 94 28 5N 76 11 E
Narni 63 42 30N 12 30 E
Naro, Ghana 120 10 22N 2 27W
Naro, Italy 64 37 18N 13 48 E
Naro Fominsk 81 55 23N 36 32 E
Narodnaya, G. 78 65 5N 60 0 E
Narok 126 1 20S 33 30 E
Narok □ 126 1 20S 33 30 E
Narón 56 43 32N 8 9W
Narooma 141 36 14S 150 4 E
Narowal 94 32 6N 74 52 E
Narrabri 139 30 19S 149 46 E
Narran, R. 139 28 37S 148 12 E
Narrandera 141 34 42S 146 31 E
Narraway, R. 152 55 44N 119 55W
Narrogin 137 32 58S 117 14 E
Narromine 141 32 12S 148 12 E
Narrows, str. 36 57 20N 6 5W
Narsampet 96 17 57N 79 58 E
Narsinghpur 95 22 54N 79 14 E
Naruto 110 34 11N 134 37 E
Narutō 111 35 36N 140 25 E
Naruto-Kaikyō 110 34 14N 134 39 E
Narva 80 59 10N 28 5 E
Narva, R. 80 59 10N 27 50 E
Narvik 74 68 28N 17 26 E
Narvskoye Vdkhr. 80 59 10N 28 5 E
Narwana 94 29 39N 76 6 E
Naryan-Mar 78 68 0N 53 0 E
Naryilco 139 28 37S 141 53 E
Narym 76 59 0N 81 58 E
Narymskoye 76 49 10N 84 15 E
Naryn 85 41 26N 75 58 E
Naryn, R. 85 40 52N 71 36 E
Nasa 74 66 29N 15 23 E
Nasa, mt. 74 66 32N 15 23 E
Nasarawa 121 8 32N 7 41 E
Naseby, N.Z. 143 45 1S 170 10 E
Naseby, U.K. 29 52 24N 0 59W
Naser, Buheirat en 122 23 0N 32 30 E
Nash Pt. 31 51 24N 3 34W
Nashua, Iowa, U.S.A. 158 42 55N 92 34W
Nashua, Mont., U.S.A. 160 48 10N 106 25W
Nashua, N.H., U.S.A. 162 42 45N 71 25W
Nashville, Ark., U.S.A. 159 33 56N 93 50W

Nashville **Nevillé-Pont-Pierre**

Nashville, Ga., U.S.A.	157	31 13N	83 15W
Nashville, Tenn., U.S.A.	157	36 12N	86 46W
Našice	66	45 32N	18 4 E
Nasielsk	54	52 35N	20 50 E
Nasik	96	20 2N	73 50 E
Nasirabad, Bangla.	95	24 42N	90 30 E
Nasirabad, India	94	26 15N	74 45 E
Nasirabad, Pak.	96	28 25N	68 25 E
Naskaupi, R.	151	53 47N	60 51W
Naso	65	38 8N	14 46 E
Nass, R.	152	55 0N	129 40W
Nassau, Bahamas	166	25 0N	77 30W
Nassau, U.S.A.	162	42 30N	73 34W
Nassau, Bahia	176	55 20 S	68 0W
Nasser City = Kôm Ombo	122	24 25N	32 52 E
Nasser, L. = Naser, Buheiret en	122	23 0N	32 30 E
Nassian	120	7 58N	2 57W
Nässjö	73	57 38N	14 45 E
Nastopoka Is.	150	57 0N	77 0W
Näsum	73	56 10N	14 29 E
Näsviken	72	61 46N	16 52 E
Nata, Bots.	128	20 7 S	26 4 E
Nata, China	100	19 37N	109 17 E
Nata, Si Arab.	92	27 15N	48 35 E
Nata, Tanz.	125	2 0 S	34 25 E
Natagaima	174	3 37N	75 6W
Natal, Brazil	170	5 47 S	35 13W
Natal, Can.	152	49 43N	114 51W
Natal, Indon.	102	0 35N	99 0 E
Natal □	129	28 30 S	30 30 E
Natalinci	66	44 15N	20 49 E
Natanz	93	33 30N	51 55 E
Natashquan	151	50 14N	61 46W
Natashquan Pt.	151	50 8N	61 40W
Natashquan, R.	151	50 7N	61 50W
Natchez	159	31 35N	91 25W
Natchitoches	159	31 47N	93 4W
Naters	50	46 19N	8 0 E
Nathalia	141	36 1 S	145 7 E
Nathdwara	94	24 55N	73 50 E
Natick	162	42 16N	71 19W
Natih	93	22 25N	56 30 E
Natimuk	140	36 42 S	142 0 E
Nation, R.	152	55 30N	123 32W
National City	163	32 45N	117 7W
National Mills	153	52 52N	101 40W
Natitingou	121	10 20N	1 26 E
Natividad, I. de	164	27 50N	115 10W
Natkyizin	101	14 57N	97 59 E
Natogyi	98	21 25N	95 39 E
Natoma	158	39 14N	99 0W
Natron L.	126	2 20 S	36 0 E
Natrûn, W. el.	122	30 25N	30 0 E
Natuna Besar, Kepulauan	101	4 0N	108 15 E
Natuna Selatan, Kepulauan	101	2 45N	109 0 E
Naturaliste, C.	132	33 32 S	115 0 E
Naturaliste C.	138	40 50 S	148 15 E
Naturaliste Channel	137	25 20 S	113 0 E
Natya	140	34 57 S	143 13 E
Nau	85	40 9N	69 22 E
Nau-Nau	128	18 57 S	21 4 E
Nau Qala	94	34 5N	68 5 E
Naubinway	150	46 7N	85 27W
Naucelle	44	44 13N	2 20 E
Nauders	52	46 54N	10 30 E
Nauen	48	52 36N	12 52 E
Naujoji Vilnia	80	54 48N	25 27 E
Naumburg	48	51 10N	11 48 E
Nauru I.	130	0 25N	166 0 E
Naurzum	84	51 32N	64 34 E
Naushahra	93	34 0N	72 0 E
Nauta	174	4 20 S	73 35W
Nautanwa	99	27 20N	83 25 E
Nautla	165	20 20N	96 50W
Nava	164	28 25N	100 46W
Nava del Rey	56	41 22N	5 6W
Navacerrada, Puerto de	56	40 47N	4 0W
Navahermosa	57	39 41N	4 28W
Navalcarnero	56	40 17N	4 5W
Navalmoral de la Mata	56	39 52N	5 16W
Navalvillar de Pela	57	39 9N	5 24W
Navan = An Uaimh	38	53 39N	6 40W
Navarino, I.	176	55 0 S	67 30W
Navarra □	58	42 40N	1 40W
Navarre	44	43 15N	1 20 E
Navarreux	44	43 20N	0 47W
Navasota	159	30 20N	96 5W
Navassa I.	167	18 30N	75 0W
Nave	62	45 35N	10 17 E
Navenby	33	53 7N	0 32W
Naver L.	37	58 18N	4 20W
Naver, R.	37	58 34N	4 15W
Navia	56	43 24N	6 42W
Navia de Suarna	56	42 58N	6 59W
Navia, R.	56	43 15N	6 50W
Navidad	172	33 57 S	71 50W
Navlya	80	52 53N	34 15 E
Navoi	85	40 9N	65 22 E
Navojoa	164	27 0N	109 30W
Navolato	164	24 47N	107 42W
Navolok	78	62 33N	39 57 E
Návpaktos	69	38 23N	21 42 E
Návplion	69	37 33N	22 50 E
Navrongo	121	10 57N	0 58W
Navsari	96	20 57N	72 59 E
Nawa Kot	94	28 21N	71 24 E
Nawabganj	98	24 35N	81 14 E
Nawabganj, Bara Banki	95	26 56N	81 14 E
Nawabganj, Bareilly	95	28 32N	79 40 E
Nawabshah	94	26 15N	68 25 E
Nawada	95	24 50N	85 25 E
Nawakot	95	28 0N	85 10 E
Nawalgarh	96	27 50N	75 15 E
Nawansnahr	95	32 33N	74 48 E
Nawapara	95	20 52N	82 33 E
Nawi	122	18 32N	30 50 E
Nawng Hpa	98	21 52N	97 52 E
Náxos	69	37 8N	25 25 E
Náxos, I.	69	37 5N	25 30 E
Nay	44	43 10N	0 18W
Nay Band	93	27 20N	52 40 E
Naya	174	3 13N	77 22W
Naya, R.	174	3 13N	77 22W
Nayakhan	77	62 10N	159 0 E
Nayarit □	164	22 0N	105 0W
Nayé	120	14 28N	12 12W
Nayung	108	26 50N	105 17 E
Nazaré, Bahia, Brazil	171	13 0 S	39 0W
Nazaré, Goiás, Brazil	170	6 23 S	47 40W
Nazaré, Port.	57	39 36N	9 4W
Nazaré Antônio de Jesus	171	13 2 S	39 0W
Nazaré da Mata	171	7 44 S	35 14W
Nazareth, Israel	90	32 42N	35 17 E
Nazareth, U.S.A.	162	40 44N	75 19W
Nazas	164	25 10N	104 0W
Nazas, R.	164	25 20N	104 4W
Naze	112	28 22N	129 27 E
Naze, The	29	51 43N	1 19 E
Nazeret	123	8 45N	39 15 E
Nazir Hat	98	22 35N	91 55 E
Nazko	152	53 1N	123 37W
Nazko, R.	152	53 7N	123 34W
Nchacoongo	129	24 20 S	35 9 E
Nchanga	127	12 30 S	27 49 E
Ncheu	127	14 50 S	34 37 E
Ndala	126	4 45 S	33 23 E
Ndali	121	9 50N	2 46 E
Ndareda	126	4 12 S	35 30 E
Ndélé	117	8 25N	20 36 E
Ndendeé	124	2 29 S	10 46 E
Ndjamena	117	12 4N	15 8 E
Ndjolé	124	0 10 S	10 45 E
Ndola	127	13 0 S	28 34 E
Ndoto Mts.	126	2 0N	37 0 E
Ndrhamcha, Sebkra de	120	18 30N	15 55W
Nduguti	126	4 18 S	34 41 E
NE Frt. Agency = Arun. Pradesh □	98	28 0N	95 0 E
Nea	71	63 15N	11 0 E
Néa Epidhavros	69	37 40N	23 7 E
Néa Filippiás	68	39 12N	20 53W
Néa Kallikrátiá	68	40 21N	23 1 E
Néa Vissi	68	41 34N	26 33 E
Neagari	111	36 26N	136 25 E
Neagh, Lough	38	54 35N	6 25W
Neah Bay	160	48 25N	124 40W
Neale L.	137	24 15 S	130 0 E
Neamarrói	127	15 58 S	36 50 E
Neamţ □	70	47 0N	26 20 E
Neápolis, Kozan, Greece	68	40 20N	21 24 E
Neápolis, Kriti, Greece	69	35 15N	25 36 E
Neápolis, Lakonia, Greece	69	36 27N	23 8 E
Near Is.	147	53 0N	172 0W
Neath	31	51 39N	3 49W
Neath, R.	23	51 46N	3 35W
Nebbou	121	11 9N	1 51W
Nebine Cr.	139	29 7 S	146 56 E
Nebo	138	21 42 S	148 42 E
Nebolchy	81	59 12N	32 58 E
Nebraska □	158	41 30N	100 0W
Nebraska City	158	40 40N	95 52W
Necedah	158	44 2N	90 7W
Nechako, R.	152	53 30N	122 44W
Neches, R.	159	31 80N	94 20W
Neckar, R.	49	48 43N	9 15 E
Necochea	172	38 30 S	58 50W
Nectar Brook	140	32 43 S	137 57 E
Nedelišće	63	46 23N	16 22 E
Neder Rijn, R.	46	51 57N	6 2 E
Nederbrakel	47	50 48N	3 46 E
Nederlandsöy I.	71	62 20N	5 35 E
Nederweert	47	51 17N	5 45 E
Nedha, R.	69	37 25N	21 45 E
Nedroma	118	35 1N	1 45W
Nedstrand	71	59 21N	5 49 E
Neede	46	52 8N	6 37 E
Needham Market	29	52 9N	1 2 E
Needilup	137	33 55 S	118 45 E
Needles	161	34 50N	114 35W
Needles, Pt.	142	36 3 S	175 25 E
Needles, The	28	50 48N	1 19W
Ñeembucú □	172	27 0 S	58 0W
Neemuch (Nimach)	94	24 30N	74 50 E
Neenah	156	44 10N	88 30W
Neepawa	153	50 20N	99 30W
Neer	47	51 16N	5 59 E
Neerheylissem	47	51 5N	5 42 E
Neeroeteren	47	50 44N	4 58 E
Neerpelt	47	51 13N	5 26 E
Nefta	119	33 53N	7 58 E
Neftah Sidi Boubekeur	118	35 1N	0 4 E
Neftegorsk	83	44 25N	39 45 E
Neftenbach	51	47 32N	8 41 E
Neftyannye Kamni	79	40 20N	50 55 E
Nefyn	31	52 57N	4 29W
Negapatam = Nagappattinam	97	10 46N	79 38 E
Negaunee	156	46 30N	87 36W
Negba	90	31 40N	34 41 E
Negele	123	5 20N	39 30 E
Negeri Sembilan □	101	2 50N	102 10 E
Negev = Hanegev	90	30 50N	35 0 E
Negolu	70	45 48N	24 32 E
Negombo	97	7 12N	79 50 E
Negotin	66	44 16N	22 37 E
Negotino	66	41 29N	22 9 E
Negra, La	172	23 46 S	70 18W
Negra, Peña	56	42 11N	6 30W
Negra Pt.	103	18 40N	120 50 E
Negrais C.	98	16 0N	94 30 E
Negreira	56	42 54N	8 45W
Negreşti	70	46 50N	27 30 E
Négrine	119	34 30N	7 30 E
Negro, C.	118	35 40N	5 11W
Negro, R., Argent.	176	40 0 S	64 0W
Negro, R., Brazil	174	0 25 S	64 0W
Negro, R., Uruguay	173	32 30 S	55 30W
Negros, I.	103	10 0N	123 0 E
Negru Vodǔ	70	43 47N	28 21 E
Nehbandān	93	31 35N	60 5 E
Neheim-Hüsten	48	51 27N	7 58 E
Nehoiaşu	70	45 24N	26 20 E
Neichiang	108	29 35N	105 0 E
Neich'iu	106	37 17N	114 31 E
Neidpath	153	50 12N	107 20W
Neihart	160	47 0N	110 52W
Neihsiang	106	33 3N	111 53 E
Neilrex	141	31 44 S	149 20 E
Neilston	34	55 47N	4 27W
Neilton	160	47 24N	123 59W
Neira de Jusá	56	42 53N	7 14W
Neisse, R.	48	51 0N	15 0 E
Neiva	174	2 56N	75 18W
Nejanilini L.	153	59 33N	97 48W
Nejo	123	9 30N	35 28 E
Nekemte	123	9 4N	36 30 E
Nêkheb	122	25 10N	33 0 E
Neksø	73	55 4N	15 8 E
Nelas	56	40 32N	7 52W
Nelaug	71	58 39N	8 40 E
Nelgowrie	141	30 54 S	148 7 E
Nelia	138	20 39 S	142 12 E
Nelidovo	80	56 13N	32 49 E
Neligh	158	42 11N	98 2W
Nelkan	77	57 50N	136 15 E
Nellikuppam	97	11 46N	79 43 E
Nellore	97	14 27N	79 59 E
Nelma	77	47 30N	139 0 E
Nelson, Can.	152	49 30N	117 20W
Nelson, N.Z.	143	41 18 S	173 16 E
Nelson, U.K.	32	53 50N	2 14W
Nelson, Ariz., U.S.A.	161	35 35N	113 24W
Nelson, Nev., U.S.A.	161	35 46N	114 55W
Nelson □	143	42 11 S	172 15 E
Nelson, C., Austral.	140	38 26 S	141 32 E
Nelson, C., P.N.G.	135	9 0 S	149 20 E
Nelson, Estrecho	176	51 30 S	75 0W
Nelson Forks	152	59 30N	124 0W
Nelson House	153	55 47N	98 51W
Nelson I.	147	60 40N	164 40W
Nelson L.	153	55 48N	100 7W
Nelson, R.	153	54 33N	98 2W
Nelspruit	126	25 29 S	30 59 E
Néma	120	16 40N	7 15W
Neman (Nemunas), R.	80	53 30N	25 10 E
Neméa	69	37 49N	22 40 E
Nemegos	150	47 40N	83 15W
Nemeiben L.	153	55 20N	105 20W
Nemira, Mt.	70	46 17N	26 19 E
Nemiscau	150	49 30N	111 15W
Nemours	43	48 16N	2 40 E
Nemunas, R.	80	55 25N	21 10 E
Nemuro	112	43 20N	145 35 E
Nemuro-Kaikyō	112	43 30N	145 30 E
Nemuy	77	55 40N	135 55 E
Nenagh	39	52 52N	8 11W
Nenana	147	64 30N	149 0W
Nenasi	101	3 9N	103 23 E
Nenchiang	105	49 11N	125 13 E
Nene, R.	29	52 38N	0 7 E
Neno	127	15 25 S	34 40 E
Nenusa, Kepulauan	103	4 45N	127 1 E
Neodesha	159	37 30N	95 37W
Néon Petrítsi	68	41 16N	23 15 E
Neópolis	170	10 18 S	36 35W
Neosho	159	36 56N	94 28W
Neosho, R.	159	35 59N	95 10W
Nepal ■	95	28 0N	84 30 E
Nepalganj	95	28 0N	81 40 E
Nephi	160	39 43N	111 52W
Nephin Beg Ra.	38	54 0N	9 40W
Nephin, Mt.	38	54 1N	9 21W
Nepomuk	52	49 29N	13 35 E
Neptune City	162	40 13N	74 4W
Néra, R.	66	44 52N	21 45 E
Nerac	44	44 19N	0 20 E
Nerchinsk	77	52 0N	116 39 E
Nerchinskiy Zavod	77	51 10N	119 30 E
Nereju	70	45 43N	26 43 E
Nerekhta	81	57 26N	40 38 E
Neret L.	151	54 45N	70 44W
Neretva, R.	66	43 30N	17 50 E
Neretvanski	66	43 7N	17 10 E
Neringa	80	55 21N	21 5 E
Nerja	57	36 43N	3 55W
Nerl, R.	81	56 30N	40 30 E
Nerokoúrou	69	35 29N	24 3 E
Nerpio	59	38 11N	2 16W
Nerva	57	37 42N	6 30W
Nes, Iceland	74	65 53N	17 24W
Nes, Neth.	46	53 26N	5 47 E
Nes Ziyyona	90	31 56N	34 48W
Nesbyen	71	60 34N	9 6 E
Nescopeck	162	41 3N	76 12W
Nesebyr	67	42 41N	27 46 E
Nesflaten	71	59 38N	6 48 E
Neskaupstaður	74	65 9N	13 42W
Nesland	71	59 31N	7 59 E
Neslandsvatn	71	58 57N	9 10 E
Nesle	43	49 45N	2 53 E
Nesodden	71	59 48N	10 40 E
Ness, dist.	36	58 27N	6 20W
Ness, Loch	37	57 15N	4 30W
Nesslau	51	47 14N	9 13 E
Neston	32	53 17N	3 3W
Nestórion Óros	68	40 24N	21 16 E
Néstos, R.	68	41 20N	24 35 E
Nesttun	71	60 19N	5 21 E
Nesvizh	80	53 14N	26 38 E
Netanya	90	32 20N	34 51 E
Nĕthe, R.	47	51 5N	4 55 E
Netherdale	138	21 10 S	148 33 E
Netherlands ■	47	52 0N	5 30 E
Netherlands Guiana = Surinam	170	4 0N	56 0W
Nethy Bridge	37	57 15N	3 40W
Netley	28	50 53N	1 21W
Netley Gap	28	32 43 S	139 59 E
Netley Marsh	28	50 55N	1 32W
Neto, R.	65	39 10N	16 58 E
Netrakong	98	24 53N	90 47 E
Nettancourt	43	48 51N	4 57 E
Nettilling L.	149	66 30N	71 0W
Nettlebed	29	51 34N	0 54W
Nettleham	33	53 15N	0 28W
Nettuno	64	41 29N	12 40 E
Netzahualcoyotl, Presa	165	17 10N	93 30W
Neu-Isenburg	49	50 3N	8 42 E
Neu Ulm	49	48 23N	10 2 E
Neubrandenburg	48	53 33N	13 17 E
Neubrandenburg □	48	53 30N	13 20 E
Neubukow	48	54 1N	11 40 E
Neuburg	49	48 43N	11 11 E
Neuchâtel	50	47 0N	6 55 E
Neuchâtel □	50	47 0N	6 55 E
Neuchâtel, Lac de	50	46 53N	6 50 E
Neudau	52	47 11N	16 6 E
Neuenegg	50	46 54N	7 18 E
Neuenhaus	48	52 30N	6 55 E
Neuf-Brisach	43	48 0N	7 30 E
Neufchâteau, Belg.	47	49 50N	5 25 E
Neufchâteau, France	43	48 21N	5 40 E
Neufchâtel	43	49 43N	1 30 E
Neufchâtel-sur-Aisne	43	49 26N	4 0 E
Neuhaus	48	53 16N	10 54 E
Neuhausen	51	47 41N	8 37 E
Neuilly-St. Front	43	49 10N	3 15 E
Neukalen	49	53 49N	12 48 E
Neumarkt	49	49 16N	11 28 E
Neumünster	48	54 4N	9 58 E
Neung-sur-Beuvron	43	47 30N	1 50 E
Neunkirchen, Austria	52	47 43N	16 4 E
Neunkirchen, Ger.	49	49 23N	7 6 E
Neuquén	176	38 0 S	68 0 E
Neuquén □	172	38 0 S	69 50W
Neuruppin	48	52 56N	12 48 E
Neuse, R.	157	35 5N	77 40W
Neusiedl	53	47 57N	16 50 E
Neusiedler See	53	47 50N	16 47 E
Neuss	48	51 12N	6 39 E
Neussargues-Moissac	44	45 9N	3 1 E
Neustadt, Bay., Ger.	49	49 42N	12 10 E
Neustadt, Bay., Ger.	49	48 48N	11 47 E
Neustadt, Bay., Ger.	49	49 34N	10 37 E
Neustadt, Bay., Ger.	49	50 23N	11 0 E
Neustadt, Gera, Ger.	48	50 45N	11 43 E
Neustadt, Hessen, Ger.	48	50 51N	9 9 E
Neustadt, Niedersachsen, Ger.	48	52 30N	9 30 E
Neustadt, Potsdam, Ger.	48	52 50N	12 27 E
Neustadt, Rhld-Pfz., Ger.	49	49 21N	8 10 E
Neustadt, S.-Holst., Ger.	48	54 6N	10 49 E
Neustrelitz	48	53 22N	13 4 E
Neuveville, La	50	47 4N	7 6 E
Neuvic	44	45 23N	2 16 E
Neuville, Belg.	95	50 11N	4 32 E
Neuville, France	43	45 52N	4 51 E
Neuville-aux-Bois	43	48 4N	2 3 E
Neuvy-St.-Sépulchure	44	46 35N	1 48 E
Neuvy-sur-Barangeon	43	47 20N	2 15 E
Neuwerk, I.	48	53 55N	8 30 E
Neuwied	48	50 26N	7 29 E
Neva, R.	78	59 50N	30 30 E
Nevada	159	37 20N	94 40W
Nevada □	160	39 20N	117 0W
Nevada City	163	39 20N	121 0W
Nevada de Sta. Marta, Sa.	174	10 55N	73 50W
Nevada, Sierra, Spain	59	37 3N	3 15W
Nevada, Sierra, U.S.A.	160	39 0N	120 30W
Nevado, Cerro	172	35 30 S	68 20W
Nevado de Colima, Mt.	164	19 35N	103 45W
Nevanka	77	56 45N	98 55 E
Nevasa	94	19 34N	75 0 E
Nevel	80	56 0N	29 55 E
Nevele	47	51 3N	3 28 E
Nevern	31	52 2N	4 49W
Nevers	43	47 0N	3 9 E
Nevertire	141	31 50 S	147 44 E
Neville	153	49 58N	107 39W
Nevillé-Pont-Pierre	42	47 33N	0 33 E

Nevinnomyssk Nîl el Abyad, Bahr

Nevinnomyssk 83 44 40N 42 0 E
Nevis I. 167 17 0N 62 30W
Nevis, L. 36 57 0N 5 43W
Nevlunghavn 71 58 58N 9 53 E
Nevoria 137 31 25 S 119 25 E
Nevrokop = Gotse Delchev 67 41 43N 23 46 E
Nevşehir 92 38 33N 34 40 E
Nevyansk 84 57 30N 60 13 E
New Abbey 35 54 59N 3 38W
New Aberdour 37 57 39N 2 12W
New Adawso 121 6 50N 0 2W
New Albany, Ind., U.S.A. 156 38 20N 85 50W
New Albany, Miss., U.S.A. 159 34 30N 89 0W
New Albany, Pa., U.S.A. 162 41 35N 76 28W
New Alresford 28 51 6N 1 10W
New Amsterdam 174 6 15N 57 30W
New Angledool 139 29 10 S 147 55 E
New Bedford 162 41 40N 70 52W
New Berlin, N.Y., U.S.A. 162 42 38N 75 20W
New Berlin, Pa., U.S.A. 162 40 50N 76 57W
New Bern 157 35 8N 77 3W
New Birmingham 39 52 36N 7 38W
New Boston 159 33 27N 94 21W
New Braunfels 159 29 43N 98 9W
New Brighton, N.Z. 143 43 29 S 172 43 E
New Brighton, U.K. 32 53 27N 3 2W
New Britain 162 41 41N 72 47W
New Britain, I. 135 5 50 S 150 20 E
New Brunswick 162 40 30N 74 28W
New Brunswick □ 151 46 50N 66 30W
New Buildings 38 54 57N 7 21W
New Bussa 121 9 53N 4 31 E
New Byrd 13 80 0 S 120 0W
New Caledonia, I. 130 21 0 S 165 0 E
New Castile = Castilla La Neuva 57 39 45N 3 20W
New Castle, Del., U.S.A. 162 39 40N 75 34W
New Castle, Ind., U.S.A. 156 39 55N 85 23W
New Castle, Pa., U.S.A. 156 41 0N 80 20W
New Chapel Cross 39 51 51N 10 12W
New City 162 41 8N 74 0W
New Cumnock 34 55 24N 4 13W
New Cuyama 163 34 57N 119 38W
New Deer 37 57 30N 2 10W
New Delhi 94 28 37N 77 13 E
New Denver 152 50 0N 117 25W
New England 158 46 36N 102 47W
New England Ra. 139 30 20 S 151 45 E
New Forest 28 50 53N 1 40W
New Freedom 162 39 44N 76 42W
New Galloway 35 55 4N 4 10W
New Glasgow 151 45 35N 62 36W
New Gretna 162 39 35N 74 28W
New Guinea, I. 135 4 0 S 136 0 E
New Hampshire □ 156 43 40N 71 40W
New Hampton 158 43 2N 92 20W
New Hanover 129 29 22 S 30 31 E
New Hanover I. 135 2 30 S 150 10 E
New Hartford 162 43 4N 75 18W
New Haven 162 41 20N 72 54W
New Hazelton 152 55 20N 127 30W
New Hebrides, Is. 130 15 0 S 168 0 E
New Holland, U.K. 33 53 42N 0 22W
New Holland, U.S.A. 162 40 6N 76 5W
New Iberia 159 30 2N 91 54W
New Inn 39 53 5N 7 10W
New Ireland, I. 135 3 20 S 151 50 E
New Jersey □ 162 39 50N 74 10W
New Kensington 156 40 36N 79 43W
New Kent 162 37 31N 76 59W
New Lexington 156 39 40N 82 15W
New Liskeard 150 47 31N 79 41W
New London, Conn., U.S.A. 162 41 23N 72 8W
New London, Minn., U.S.A. 158 45 17N 94 55W
New London, Wis., U.S.A. 158 44 23N 88 43W
New Luce 34 54 57N 4 50W
New Madrid 159 36 40N 89 30W
New Meadows 160 45 0N 116 10W
New Mexico □ 154 34 30N 106 0W
New Milford, Conn., U.S.A. 162 41 35N 73 25W
New Milford, Pa., U.S.A. 162 41 50N 75 45W
New Mills 32 53 22N 2 0W
New Norcia 137 30 57 S 116 13 E
New Norfolk 138 42 46 S 147 2 E
New Orleans 159 30 0N 90 5W
New Oxford 162 39 52N 77 4W
New Philadelphia 156 40 29N 81 25W
New Pitsligo 37 57 35N 2 11W
New Plymouth, Bahamas 166 26 56N 77 20W
New Plymouth, N.Z. 142 39 4 S 174 5 E
New Point Comfort 162 37 18N 76 15W
New Providence I. 166 25 0N 77 30W
New Quay 31 52 13N 4 21W
New Radnor 31 52 15N 3 10W
New Richmond 158 45 6N 92 34W
New Roads 159 30 43N 91 30W
New Rockford 158 47 44N 99 7W
New Romney 29 50 59N 0 57 E
New Ross 39 52 24N 6 58W
New Rossington 33 53 30N 1 4W
New Salem 158 46 51N 101 25W
New Siberian Is. = Novosibirskiye Os. 77 75 0N 140 0 E
New Smyrna Beach 157 29 0N 80 50W
New South Wales □ 139 33 0 S 146 0 E
New Springs 137 25 49 S 120 1 E
New Tamale 121 9 10N 1 10W
New Tredegar 31 51 43N 3 15W
New Ulm 158 44 15N 94 30W
New Waterford 151 46 13N 60 4W
New Westminster 152 49 10N 122 52W
New York □ 156 42 40N 76 0W
New York City 162 40 45N 74 0W
New Zealand ■ 143 40 0 S 176 0 E
Newala 127 10 58 S 39 10 E
Newala □ 127 10 46 S 39 20 E
Newark, U.K. 33 53 6N 0 48W
Newark, Del., U.S.A. 162 39 42N 75 45W
Newark, N.J., U.S.A. 162 40 41N 74 12W
Newark, N.Y., U.S.A. 162 43 2N 77 10W
Newark, Ohio, U.S.A. 156 40 5N 82 30W
Newark Valley 162 42 14N 76 11W
Newberg 160 45 22N 123 0W
Newberry 156 46 20N 85 32W
Newberry Springs 163 34 50N 116 41W
Newbiggin-by-the-Sea 35 55 12N 1 31W
Newbigging 35 55 42N 3 33W
Newbliss 38 54 10N 7 8W
Newborough 31 53 10N 4 22W
Newbridge, Kildare, Ireland 39 53 11N 6 50W
Newbridge, Limerick, Ireland 38 52 33N 9 0W
Newbridge-on-Wye 31 52 13N 3 27W
Newbrook 152 54 24N 112 57W
Newburgh, Fife, U.K. 35 56 21N 3 15W
Newburgh, Grampian, U.K. 37 57 19N 2 0W
Newburgh, U.S.A. 162 41 30N 74 1W
Newburn 35 54 57N 1 45W
Newbury 28 51 24N 1 19W
Newburyport 162 42 48N 70 50W
Newby Bridge 32 54 16N 2 59W
Newbyth 37 57 35N 2 17W
Newcastle, Austral. 141 33 0 S 151 40 E
Newcastle, Can. 151 47 1N 65 38W
Newcastle, Ireland 39 53 5N 6 4W
Newcastle, S. Afr. 125 27 45 S 29 58 E
Newcastle, U.K. 38 54 13N 5 54W
Newcastle, U.S.A. 158 43 50N 104 12W
Newcastle Emlyn 31 52 2N 4 29W
Newcastle Ra. 136 15 45 S 130 15 E
Newcastle-under-Lyme 32 53 2N 2 15W
Newcastle-upon-Tyne 35 54 59N 1 37W
Newcastle Waters 136 17 30 S 133 28 E
Newcastle West 38 52 27N 9 3W
Newcastleton 35 55 10N 2 50W
Newchurch 31 52 9N 3 10W
Newdegate 137 33 6 S 119 0 E
Newe Etan 90 32 30N 35 32 E
Newe Sha'anan 90 32 47N 34 59 E
Newe Zohar 90 31 9N 35 21 E
Newell 158 44 48N 103 25W
Newenham, C. 147 58 40N 162 15W
Newent 28 51 56N 2 24W
Newfield, N.J., U.S.A. 162 39 33N 75 1W
Newfield, N.Y., U.S.A. 162 42 18N 76 33W
Newfound L. 162 43 40N 71 47W
Newfoundland 151 48 30N 56 0W
Newfoundland □ 151 48 28N 56 0W
Newhalem 152 48 41N 121 16W
Newhalen 147 59 40N 155 0W
Newhall 163 34 23N 118 32W
Newham 29 51 31N 0 2 E
Newhaven 29 50 47N 0 4 E
Newington, N. Kent, U.K. 29 51 21N 0 40 E
Newington, S. Kent, U.K. 29 51 5N 1 8 E
Newinn 39 52 28N 7 54W
Newkirk 159 36 52N 97 3W
Newlyn 30 50 6N 5 33W
Newlyn East 30 50 22N 5 3W
Newmachar 37 57 16N 2 11W
Newman 163 37 19N 121 1W
Newman, Mt. 137 23 20 S 119 34 E
Newmarket, Ireland 39 52 13N 9 0W
Newmarket, Lewis, U.K. 36 58 14N 6 24W
Newmarket, Norfolk, U.K. 29 52 15N 0 23 E
Newmarket, U.S.A. 162 43 4N 70 57W
Newmarket-on-Fergus 39 52 46N 8 54W
Newmill 37 57 34N 2 58W
Newmills 38 54 56N 7 49W
Newmilns 34 55 36N 4 20W
Newnan 157 33 22N 84 48W
Newnes 139 33 9 S 150 16 E
Newnham 28 51 48N 2 27W
Newport, Essex, U.K. 29 51 58N 0 13 E
Newport, Gwent, U.K. 31 51 35N 3 0W
Newport, I. of W., U.K. 28 50 42N 1 18W
Newport, Salop, U.K. 28 52 47N 2 22W
Newport, Ark., U.S.A. 159 35 38N 91 15W
Newport, Ky., U.S.A. 156 39 5N 84 23W
Newport, N.H., U.S.A. 162 43 23N 72 8W
Newport, Oreg., U.S.A. 160 44 41N 124 2W
Newport, R.I., U.S.A. 162 41 30N 71 19W
Newport, Tenn., U.S.A. 157 35 39N 83 12W
Newport, Wash., U.S.A. 160 48 11N 117 2W
Newport B. 38 53 52N 9 38W
Newport Beach 163 33 40N 117 58W
Newport News 162 37 2N 76 54W
Newport on Tay 35 56 27N 2 56W
Newport Pagnell 29 52 5N 0 42W
Newquay 30 50 24N 5 6W
Newry 38 54 10N 6 20W
Newry & Mourne □ 38 54 10N 6 15W
Newton, Iowa, U.S.A. 158 41 40N 93 3W
Newton, Kans., U.S.A. 159 38 2N 97 30W
Newton, Mass., U.S.A. 156 42 21N 71 10W
Newton, N.C., U.S.A. 157 35 42N 81 10W
Newton, N.J., U.S.A. 162 41 3N 74 46W
Newton, Texas, U.S.A. 159 30 54N 93 42W
Newton Abbot 30 50 32N 3 37W
Newton Arlosh 32 54 53N 3 15W
Newton-Aycliffe 33 54 36N 1 33W
Newton Boyd 139 29 45 S 152 16 E
Newton Ferrers 30 50 19N 4 3W
Newton le Willows 32 53 28N 3 27W
Newton St. Cyres 30 50 46N 3 35W
Newton Stewart 34 54 57N 4 30W
Newtonabbey □ 38 54 45N 6 0W
Newtongrange 35 55 52N 3 4W
Newtonhill 37 57 1N 20 52 E
Newtonmore 37 57 4N 4 7W
Newtown, Ireland 39 52 20N 8 47W
Newtown, Scot, U.K. 35 55 34N 2 38W
Newtown, Wales, U.K. 31 52 31N 3 19W
Newtown Crommelin 38 54 59N 6 13W
Newtown Cunningham 38 55 0N 7 32W
Newtown Forbes 38 53 46N 7 50W
Newtown Gore 38 54 3N 7 41W
Newtown Hamilton 38 54 12N 6 35W
Newtownabbey 38 54 40N 5 55W
Newtownards 38 54 37N 5 40W
Newtownbutler 38 54 12N 7 22W
39 53 5N 6 7W
Newtownstewart 38 54 43N 7 22W
Nexon 48 45 41N 1 10 E
Neya 81 58 21N 43 49 E
Neyland 31 51 43N 4 58W
Neyrīz 93 29 15N 54 55 E
Neyshābūr 93 36 10N 58 20 E
Neyyattinkara 97 8 26N 77 5 E
Nezhin 80 51 5N 31 55 E
Nezperce 160 46 13N 116 15W
Ngabang 102 0 30N 109 55 E
Ngaiphaipi 98 22 14N 93 15 E
Ngambé 121 5 48N 11 29 E
Ngami Depression 128 20 30 S 22 46 E
Ngamo 127 19 3 S 27 25 E
Ngandjuk 103 7 32 S 111 55 E
Ngao 100 18 46N 99 59 E
Ngaoundéré 124 7 15N 13 35 E
Ngapara 143 44 57 S 170 46 E
Ngara 126 2 29 S 30 40 E
Ngara □ 126 2 29 S 30 40 E
Ngaruawahia 142 37 42 S 175 11 E
Ngatapa 142 38 32 S 177 45 E
Ngathainggyaung 98 17 24N 95 5 E
Ngauruhoe, Mt. 142 39 13 S 175 45 E
Ngawi 103 7 24 S 111 26 E
Ngetera 121 12 40 S 12 46 E
Ngha Lo 101 21 33N 104 28 E
Nghia Lo 100 21 33N 104 28 E
Ngoma 127 13 8 S 33 45 E
Ngomahura 127 20 33 S 30 57 E
Ngomba 127 8 20 S 32 53 E
Ngonye Falls 128 16 35 S 23 30 E
Ngop 123 6 17N 30 9 E
Ngorkou 120 15 40N 3 41W
Ngorongoro 126 3 11 S 35 32 E
Ngozi 126 2 54 S 29 50 E
Ngudu 126 2 58 S 33 25 E
N'Guigrai 117 14 20N 13 20 E
Nguna, I. 100 17 26 S 168 21 E
Ngunga 126 3 37 S 33 37 E
Ngungu 143 6 15N 28 16 E
Ngunguru 94 35 37 S 174 30 E
Nguru 121 12 56N 10 29 E
Nguru Mts. 126 6 0 S 37 30 E
Nguyen Binh 100 22 39N 105 56 E
Ngwenya 129 26 5 S 31 7 E
Nha Trang 101 12 16N 109 10 E
Nhacoongo 129 24 18 S 35 14 E
Nhangutazi, Lago 129 24 0 S 34 30 E
Nhill 140 36 18 S 141 40 E
Nho Quan 100 20 18N 105 45 E
Nhulunbuy 138 12 10 S 136 45 E
Nia-nia 126 1 30N 27 40 E
Niafounké 120 16 0N 4 5W
Niagara 156 45 45N 88 0W
Niagara Falls, Can. 150 43 7N 79 5W
Niagara Falls, N. Amer. 150 43 5N 79 5W
Niah 102 3 58N 113 46 E
Niamey 121 13 27N 2 6 E
Nianforando 120 9 37N 10 36W
Nianfors 72 61 36N 16 46 E
Niangara 126 3 50N 27 50 E
Niantic 162 41 19N 72 12W
Nias, I. 102 1 0N 97 40 E
Niassa □ 127 13 30 S 36 0 E
Niassa, Lago 127 12 30 S 34 30 E
Nibbiano 62 44 54N 9 20 E
Nibe 73 56 59N 9 38 E
Nibong Tebal 101 5 10N 100 29 E
Nicaragua ■ 166 11 40N 85 30W
Nicaragua, Lago de 166 12 50N 85 30W
Nicastro 65 39 0N 16 18 E
Nice 45 43 42N 7 14 E
Niceville 157 30 30N 86 30W
Nichinan 110 31 38N 131 23 E
Nicholas, Chan. 166 23 30N 80 30W
Nicholasville 156 37 54N 84 31W
Nichols 162 42 1N 76 22W
Nicholson, Austral. 136 18 2 S 128 54 E
Nicholson, Can. 150 47 58N 83 47W
Nicholson, U.S.A. 162 41 37N 75 47W
Nicholson, R. 138 17 31 S 139 36 E
Nicholson Ra. 137 27 15 S 116 30 E
Nicobar Is. 86 9 0N 93 0 E
Nicoclí 174 8 26N 76 48W
Nicola 152 50 8N 120 40W
Nicolet 150 46 17N 72 35W
Nicolls Town 166 25 8N 78 0W
Nicosia, Cyprus 92 35 10N 33 25 E
Nicosia, Italy 65 37 45N 14 22 E
Nicótera 65 38 33N 15 57 E
Nicoya 166 10 9N 85 27W
Nicoya, Golfo de 166 10 0N 85 0W
Nicoya, Pen. de 166 9 45N 85 40W
Nidau 50 47 7N 7 15 E
Nidd, R. 33 54 1N 1 32W
Nidda 48 50 24N 9 2 E
Nidda, R. 49 50 25N 9 2 E
Nidderdale 33 54 5N 1 46W
Nidzica 54 53 25N 20 28 E
Niebüll 48 54 47N 8 49 E
Niederaula 48 50 48N 9 37 E
Niederbipp 50 47 16N 7 42 E
Niederbronn 43 48 57N 7 39 E
Niedere Tauern 93 47 18N 14 0 E
Niedermarsberg 48 51 28N 8 52 E
Niederösterreich □ 52 48 25N 15 40 E
Niedersachsen □ 48 54 45N 9 0 E
Niel 47 51 7N 4 20 E
Niellé 120 10 5N 5 38W
Niemba 126 5 58 S 28 24 E
Niemcza 54 50 42N 16 47 E
Niemodlin 54 50 38N 17 38 E
Niemur 140 35 17 S 144 9 E
Nienburg 48 52 38N 9 15 E
Niench'ing'angkula Shan 105 30 10N 90 0 E
Niepołomice 54 50 3N 20 13 E
Niesen 50 46 38N 7 39 E
Niesky 48 51 18N 14 48 E
Nieszawa 54 52 52N 18 42 E
Nieuw Amsterdam 46 52 43N 6 52 E
Nieuw Beijerland 46 51 49N 4 20 E
Nieuw-Buinen 46 52 58N 6 56 E
Nieuw-Dordrecht 46 52 45N 6 59 E
Nieuw Hellevoet 46 51 51N 4 8 E
Nieuw Loosdrecht 46 52 12N 5 8 E
Nieuw Nickerie 175 6 0N 57 10W
Nieuw-Schoonebeek 46 52 39N 7 0 E
Nieuw-Vassemeer 47 51 34N 4 12 E
Nieuw-Vennep 46 52 16N 4 38 E
Nieuw-Weerdinge 46 52 51N 6 59 E
Nieuwe-Niedorp 46 52 44N 4 54 E
Nieuwe-Pekela 46 53 5N 6 58 E
Nieuwe-Schans 46 53 11N 7 12 E
Nieuwe-Tonge 47 51 43N 4 10 E
Nieuwendijk 46 51 46N 4 55 E
Nieuwerkerken 47 50 52N 5 12 E
Nieuwkoop 46 52 9N 4 48 E
Nieuwleusen 46 52 34N 6 17 E
Nieuwnamen 47 51 18N 4 9 E
Nieuwolda 46 53 15N 6 58 E
Nieuwpoort 47 51 8N 2 45 E
Nieuwveen 46 52 12N 4 46 E
Nieves 56 42 7N 8 26W
Nièvre □ 43 47 10N 3 40 E
Nigata 110 34 13N 132 39 E
Nigde 92 38 0N 34 40 E
Nigel 129 26 27 S 28 25 E
Niger □ 121 10 0N 5 0 E
Niger ■ 121 13 30N 10 0 E
Niger, R. 121 10 0N 4 40 E
Nigeria ■ 121 8 30N 8 0 E
Nigg B. 37 57 41N 4 5W
Nightcaps 143 45 57 S 168 14 E
Nigrita 68 40 56N 23 29 E
Nihtaur 94 29 27N 78 23 E
Nii-Jima 111 34 20N 139 15 E
Niigata 112 37 58N 139 0 E
Niigata-ken □ 112 37 15N 138 45 E
Niihama 110 33 55N 133 10 E
Niihau, I. 147 21 55N 160 10W
Niimi 110 34 59N 133 28 E
Nijar 59 36 53N 2 15W
Nijkerk 47 52 13N 5 30 E
Nijlen 47 51 10N 4 40 E
Nijmegen 47 51 50N 5 52 E
Nijverdal 46 52 22N 6 28 E
Nike 121 6 26N 7 29 E
Nikel 74 69 30N 30 5 E
Nikiniki 103 9 40 S 124 30 E
Nikitas 68 40 17N 23 34 E
Nikki 121 9 58N 3 21 E
Nikkō 111 36 45N 139 35 E
Nikolayev 82 46 58N 32 7 E
Nikolayevsk-na-Amur 77 53 40N 140 50 E
Nikolayevski 81 50 10N 45 35 E
Nikolsk 81 59 30N 45 28 E
Nikolski 147 53 0N 168 50W
Nikolskoye, Amur, U.S.S.R. 77 47 50N 131 5 E
Nikolskoye, Kamandorskiye, U.S.S.R. 77 55 12N 166 0 E
Nikopol, Bulg. 67 43 43N 24 54 E
Nikopol, U.S.S.R. 82 47 35N 34 25 E
Niksar 82 40 31N 37 2 E
Nikshah 93 26 15N 60 10 E
Nikšić 66 42 50N 18 57 E
Nîl el Abyad, Bahr 123 9 30N 31 40 E

Nîl el Azraq □ N. Taranaki Bt

Nîl el Azraq □ 123 12 30N 34 30 E
Nîl el Azraq, Bahr 123 10 30N 35 0 E
Nîl, Nahr el 122 27 30N 30 30 E
Nila 103 8 24 S 120 29 E
Niland 161 33 16N 115 30W
Nile □ 126 2 0N 31 30 E
Nile Delta 122 31 40N 31 0 E
Nile, R. = Nîl, Nahr el 122 27 30N 30 30 E
Niles 156 41 8N 80 40W
Nilgiri Hills 97 11 30N 76 30 E
Nilo Peçanha 171 13 37 S 39 6W
Nilpena 140 30 58 S 138 20 E
Nimach = Neemuch 94 24 30N 74 50 E
Nimar 96 21 49N 76 22 E
Nimba, Mt. 120 7 39N 8 30W
Nimbahera 94 24 37N 74 45 E
Nîmes 45 43 50N 4 23 E
Nimfaíon, Ákra 68 40 5N 24 20 E
Nimingarra 132 20 31 S 119 55 E
Nimmitabel 141 36 29 S 149 15 E
Nimneryskiy 77 58 0N 125 10 E
Nimule 123 3 32N 32 3 E
Nimy 47 50 28N 3 57 E
Nin 63 44 16N 15 12 E
Nindigully 139 28 21 S 148 50 E
Ninemile 152 56 0N 130 7W
Ninemilehouse 39 52 28N 7 29W
Ninety Mile Beach 130 34 45 S 173 0 E
Ninety Mile Beach, The 133 38 15 S 147 24 E
Nineveh 92 36 25N 43 10 E
Ninfield 29 50 53N 0 26 E
Ningaloo 136 22 41 S 113 41 E
Ningan 107 44 23N 129 26 E
Ningch'eng 107 41 34N 119 20 E
Ningch'iang 106 32 49N 106 13 E
Ningchin 106 37 37N 114 55 E
Ningching Shan 108 31 45N 97 15 E
Ninghai 109 29 18N 121 25 E
Ninghsiang 109 28 15N 112 30 E
Ninghsien 106 35 35N 107 58 E
Ninghua 109 26 14N 116 36 E
Ningkang 109 26 45N 113 58 E
Ningkuo 109 30 38N 118 58 E
Ninglang 108 27 19N 100 53 E
Ningling 106 34 27N 115 19 E
Ningming 108 22 12N 107 5 E
Ningnan 108 27 7N 102 42 E
Ningpo 109 29 53N 121 33 E
Ningshan 106 33 12N 108 29 E
Ningsia Hui A.R. □ 106 37 45N 106 0 E
Ningte 109 26 45N 120 0 E
Ningtsin 99 29 44N 98 28 E
Ningtu 109 26 22N 115 48 E
Ningwu 106 29 2N 112 15 E
Ningyang, Fukien, China 109 25 44N 117 8 E
Ningyang, Shantung, China 106 35 46N 116 47 E
Ningyüan 109 25 36N 111 54 E
Ninh Binh 100 20 15N 105 55 E
Ninh Giang 100 20 44N 106 24 E
Ninh Hoa 100 12 30N 109 7 E
Ninh Ma 100 12 48N 109 21 E
Ninian, oilfield 19 60 42N 1 30 E
Ninove 47 50 51N 4 2 E
Nioaque 173 21 5 S 55 50W
Niobrara 158 42 48N 97 59W
Niobrara R. 158 42 30N 103 0W
Nioki 124 2 47 S 17 40 E
Niono 120 14 15N 6 0W
Nioro 120 15 30N 9 30W
Nioro du Rip 120 13 40N 15 50W
Nioro du Sahel 120 15 30N 9 30W
Niort 44 46 19N 0 29W
Niou 121 12 42N 2 1W
Nipa 135 6 9 S 143 29 E
Nipan 138 24 45 S 150 0 E
Nipani 96 16 20N 74 25 E
Nipawin 153 53 20N 104 0W
Nipawin Prov. Park 153 54 0N 104 37W
Nipigon 150 49 0N 88 17W
Nipigon, L. 150 49 50N 88 30W
Nipin, R. 153 55 46N 109 2W
Nipishish L. 151 54 12N 60 45W
Nipissing L. 150 46 20N 80 0W
Nipomo 163 35 4N 120 29W
Niquelândia 171 14 33 S 48 23W
Nira, R. 96 18 5N 74 25 E
Nirasaki 111 35 42N 138 27 E
Nirmal 96 19 3N 78 20 E
Nirmali 95 26 20N 86 35 E
Niš 66 43 19N 21 58 E
Nisa 57 39 30N 7 41W
Nisab 91 14 25N 46 29 E
Nišava, R. 66 43 20N 22 10 E
Niscemi 65 37 8N 14 21 E
Nishi-Sonogi-Hantō 110 32 55N 129 45 E
Nishinomiya 111 34 45N 135 20 E
Nishinoomote 112 30 43N 130 59 E
Nishio 111 34 52N 137 3 E
Nishiwaki 110 34 59N 134 48 E
Nísiros, I. 69 36 35N 27 12 E
Niskibi, R. 150 56 29N 88 9W
Nisko 54 50 35N 22 7 E
Nispen 47 51 29N 4 28 E
Nisporeny 70 47 4N 28 10 E
Nissafors 73 57 25N 13 37 E
Nissan 73 56 40N 12 51 E
Nissan I. 138 4 30 S 154 10 E
Nissedal 71 59 10N 8 30 E
Nisser 71 59 7N 8 28 E
Nissum Fjord 73 56 20N 8 11 E
Nistelrode 47 51 42N 5 34 E
Nisutlin, R. 152 60 14N 132 34W
Nitchequon 151 53 10N 70 58W
Niterói 173 22 52 S 43 0W
Nith, R. 35 55 20N 3 5W
Nithsdale 35 55 14N 3 50W
Niton 28 50 35N 1 14W
Nitra 53 48 19N 18 4 E
Nitra, R. 53 48 30N 18 7 E
Nitsa, R. 84 57 29N 64 33 E
Nittedal 71 60 1N 10 57 E
Niuchieh 108 27 47N 104 16 E
Niuchuang 107 40 58N 122 38 E
Niue I. (Savage I.) 130 19 2 S 169 54W
Niulan Chiang, R. 108 27 24N 103 9 E
Niut, Mt. 102 0 55N 109 30 E
Nivelles 47 50 35N 4 20 E
Nivernais 43 47 0N 3 40 E
Nixon, Nev., U.S.A. 160 39 54N 119 22W
Nixon, Tex., U.S.A. 159 29 17N 97 45W
Nizam Sagar 96 18 10N 77 58 E
Nizamabad 96 18 45N 78 7 E
Nizamghat 98 28 20N 95 45 E
Nizhanaya Tunguska 77 64 20N 93 0 E
Nizhiye Sergi 84 56 40N 59 18 E
Nizhne Kolymsk 77 68 40N 160 55 E
Nizhne-Vartovskoye 76 60 56N 76 38 E
Nizhneangarsk 77 56 0N 109 30 E
Nizhnegorskiy 82 45 27N 34 38 E
Nizhneudinsk 77 55 0N 99 20 E
Nizhniy Lomov 81 53 34N 43 38 E
Nizhniy Novgorod = Gorkiy 81 56 20N 44 0 E
Nizhniy Pyandzh 85 37 12N 68 35 E
Nizhniy Tagil 84 57 55N 59 57 E
Nizhny Salda 84 58 8N 60 42 E
Nizké Tatry 53 48 55N 20 0 E
Nizza Monferrato 62 44 46N 8 22 E
Njakwa 127 11 1 S 33 56 E
Njinjo 127 8 34 S 38 44 E
Njombe 124 9 20 S 34 50 E
Njombe □ 127 9 20 S 34 49 E
Njombe, R. 126 7 15 S 34 30 E
Nkambe 121 6 35N 10 40 E
Nkana 127 13 0 S 28 8 E
Nkawkaw 121 6 36N 0 49W
Nkhata Bay 124 11 33 S 34 16 E
Nkhota Kota 127 12 56 S 34 15 E
Nkongsamba 121 4 55N 9 55 E
Nkunka 127 14 57 S 25 58 E
Nkwanta 120 6 10N 2 10W
Nmai Pit, R. 99 25 30N 98 0 E
Nmai, R. 99 25 30N 98 0 E
Nmaushahra 95 33 11N 74 15 E
Nnewi 121 6 0N 6 59 E
Noakhali = Maijdi 98 22 50N 90 45 E
Noatak 147 67 32N 163 10W
Noatak, R. 147 68 0N 161 0W
Nobber 38 53 49N 6 45W
Nobeoka 110 32 36N 131 41 E
Nōbi-Heiya 111 35 15N 136 45 E
Noblejas 58 39 58N 3 26W
Noblesville 156 40 1N 85 59W
Noce, R. 62 46 22N 11 0 E
Nocera Inferiore 65 40 45N 14 37 E
Nocera Terinese 65 39 2N 16 9 E
Nocera Umbra 63 43 8N 12 47 E
Nochixtlán 165 17 28N 97 14W
Noci 65 40 47N 17 7 E
Nockatunga 139 27 42 S 142 42 E
Nocona 159 33 48N 97 45W
Nocrich 70 45 55N 24 26 E
Noda, Japan 111 35 56N 139 52 E
Noda, U.S.S.R. 77 47 30N 142 5 E
Noel 159 36 36N 94 29W
Nogales, Mexico 164 31 36N 94 29W
Nogales, U.S.A. 161 31 33N 115 50W
Nōgata 110 33 48N 130 54 E
Nogent-en-Bassigny 43 48 0N 5 20 E
Nogent-le-Rotrou 42 48 20N 0 50 E
Nogent-sur-Seine 43 48 30N 3 30 E
Noggerup 137 33 32 S 116 5 E
Noginsk, Moskva, U.S.S.R. 81 55 50N 38 25 E
Noginsk, Sib., U.S.S.R. 77 64 30N 90 50 E
Nogoa, R. 138 23 33 S 148 32 E
Nogoyá 172 32 24 S 59 48W
Nógrád □ 53 48 0N 19 30 E
Nogueira de Ramuin 56 42 21N 7 43W
Noguera Pallaresa, R. 58 42 15N 1 0 E
Noguera Ribagorzana, R. 58 42 15N 0 45 E
Nohar 94 29 11N 74 49 E
Noi, R. 101 14 50N 100 15 E
Noire, Mts. 42 48 11N 3 40W
Noirétable 44 45 48N 3 46 E
Noirmoutier 42 47 0N 2 15W
Noirmoutier, Î. de 42 46 58N 2 10W
Nojane 128 23 15 S 20 14 E
Nojima-Zaki 111 34 54N 139 53 E
Nok Kundi 93 28 50N 62 45 E
Nokaneng 128 19 47 S 22 17 E
Nokhtuysk 77 60 0N 117 45 E
Nokomis 153 51 35N 105 0W
Nokomis L. 153 57 0N 103 0W
Nokou 124 14 35N 14 47 E
Nol 73 57 56N 12 5 E
Nola, C. Afr. Emp. 124 3 35N 16 10 E
Nola, Italy 65 40 54N 14 29 E
Nolay 43 46 58N 4 35 E
Nolby 72 62 17N 17 26 E
Noli, C. di 62 44 12N 8 26 E
Nolinsk 84 57 28N 49 57 E
Noma Omuramba, R. 128 19 6 S 20 30 E
Noma-Saki 110 31 25N 130 7 E
Nomad 135 6 19 S 142 13 E
Noman L. 153 62 15N 108 55W
Nombre de Dios 166 9 34N 79 28W
Nome 147 64 30N 165 30W
Nomo-Zaki 110 32 35N 129 44 E
Nonacho L. 153 61 57N 109 28W
Nonancourt 42 48 47N 1 11 E
Nonant-le-Pin 42 48 42N 0 12 E
Nonda 138 20 40 S 142 28 E
Nong Chang 100 15 23N 99 51 E
Nong Het 100 19 29N 103 59 E
Nong Khae 101 14 29N 100 53 E
Nong Khai 100 17 50N 102 46 E
Nonoava 164 27 22N 106 38W
Nonopapa 147 21 50N 160 15W
Nonthaburi 100 13 51N 100 34 E
Nontron 44 45 31N 0 40 E
Noonamah 136 12 40 S 131 4 E
Noonan 158 48 51N 102 59W
Noondoo 139 28 35 S 148 30 E
Noonkanbah 102 18 30 S 124 50 E
Noord-Bergum 46 53 14N 6 1 E
Noord Brabant □ 47 51 40N 5 0 E
Noord Holland □ 46 52 30N 4 45 E
Noordbeveland 47 51 45N 3 50 E
Noordeloos 46 51 55N 4 56 E
Noordhollandsch Kanaal 46 52 55N 4 48 E
Noordhorn 46 53 16N 6 24 E
Noordoostpolder 46 52 45N 5 45 E
Noordwijk aan Zee 46 52 14N 4 26 E
Noordwijk-Binnen 46 52 14N 4 27 E
Noordwijkerhout 46 52 16N 4 30 E
'Noordwinning', gasfield 19 53 13N 3 10 E
Noordzee Kanaal 46 52 28N 4 35 E
Noorvik 147 66 50N 161 14W
Noorwolde 46 52 54N 6 8 E
Nootka 152 49 38N 126 38W
Nootka I. 152 49 40N 126 50W
Noqui 124 5 55 S 13 30 E
Nora, Ethiopia 123 16 6N 40 4 E
Nora, Sweden 72 59 32N 15 2 E
Noranda 150 48 20N 79 0W
Norberg 72 60 4N 15 56 E
Norbottens län □ 74 66 58N 20 0 E
Nórcia 63 42 50N 13 5 E
Norco 163 33 56N 117 33W
Nord □ 43 50 15N 3 30 E
Nord-Ostee Kanal 48 54 5N 9 15 E
Nord-Süd Kanal 48 53 0N 10 32 E
Nord-Trondelag Fylke □ 74 64 20N 12 0 E
Nordagutu 71 59 25N 9 20 E
Nordaustlandet 12 79 55N 23 0 E
Nordborg 73 55 5N 9 50 E
Nordby, Fanø, Denmark 73 55 27N 8 24 E
Nordby, Samsø, Denmark 73 55 58N 10 32 E
Norddal 71 62 15N 7 14 E
Norddalsfjord kpl. 71 61 39N 5 23 E
Norddeich 48 53 37N 7 10 E
Nordegg 152 52 29N 116 5W
Nordelph 29 52 34N 0 18 E
Norden 48 53 35N 7 12 E
Nordenham 48 53 29N 8 28 E
Norderhov 71 60 7N 10 17 E
Norderney 48 53 42N 7 9 E
Norderney, I. 48 53 42N 7 15 E
Nordfjord 71 61 55N 5 30 E
Nordfriesische Inseln 48 54 40N 8 20 E
Nordhausen 48 51 29N 10 47 E
Nordhorn 48 52 27N 7 4 E
Nordjyllands Amt □ 73 57 0N 10 0 E
Nordkapp, Norway 74 71 10N 25 44 E
Nordkapp, Svalb. 12 80 31N 20 0 E
Nordkinn 16 71 3N 28 0 E
Nordland Fylke □ 74 65 40N 13 0 E
Nördlingen 49 48 50N 10 30 E
Nordrhein-Westfalen □ 48 51 45N 7 30 E
Nordstrand, I. 48 54 27N 8 50 E
Nordvik 77 73 40N 110 57 E
Nore 71 60 10N 9 0 E
Nore R. 39 52 40N 7 20W
Noreena Cr. 136 22 20 S 120 25 E
Norefjell 71 60 16N 9 29 E
Norembega 150 48 59N 80 43W
Noresund 71 60 11N 9 37 E
Norfolk, Nebr., U.S.A. 158 42 3N 97 25W
Norfolk, Va., U.S.A. 156 36 52N 76 15W
Norfolk □ 29 52 39N 1 0 E
Norfolk Broads 29 52 30N 1 15 E
Norfolk I. 130 28 58 S 168 3 E
Norfork Res. 159 36 25N 92 0W
Norg 46 53 4N 6 28 E
Norham 35 55 44N 2 9W
Norilsk 77 69 20N 88 0 E
Norley 139 27 45 S 143 48 E
Normal 158 40 30N 89 0W
Norman 159 35 12N 97 30W
Norman, R. 138 19 20 S 142 35 E
Norman Wells 147 65 17N 126 45W
Normanby 142 39 32 S 174 18 E
Normanby I. 135 10 55 S 151 5 E
Normanby, R. 138 14 23 S 144 10 E
Normandie 42 48 45N 0 10 E
Normandie, Collines de 42 48 55N 0 45W
Normandin 150 48 49N 72 31W
Normandy = Normandie 42 48 45N 0 10 E
Normanhurst, Mt. 137 25 13 S 122 30 E
Normanton, Austral. 138 17 40 S 141 10 E
Normanton, U.K. 33 53 41N 1 26W
Normanville 140 35 27 S 138 18 E
Norna, Mt. 138 20 55 S 140 42 E
Nornalup 137 35 0 S 116 48 E
Norquay 153 51 53N 102 5W
Ñorquinco 176 41 51 S 70 55W
Norrahammar 73 57 43N 14 7 E
Norrbottens län □ 74 66 50N 18 0 E
Norrby 74 64 55N 18 15 E
Nørre Åby 73 55 27N 9 52 E
Nørre Nebel 73 55 47N 8 17 E
Nørresundby 73 57 5N 9 52 E
Norris 160 45 40N 111 48W
Norristown 162 40 9N 75 15W
Norrköping 73 58 37N 16 11 E
Norrland □ 74 66 50N 18 0 E
Norrtälje 72 59 46N 18 42 E
Norseman 137 32 8 S 121 43 E
Norsholm 73 58 31N 15 59 E
Norsk 77 52 30N 130 0 E
Norte de Santander □ 174 8 0N 73 0W
North Adams 162 42 42N 73 6W
North America 50 40 0N 70 0W
North Andaman I. 101 13 15N 92 40 E
North Atlantic Ocean 14 30 0N 50 0W
North Ballachulish 36 56 42N 5 9W
North Battleford 153 52 50N 108 17W
North Bay 150 46 20N 79 30W
North Belcher Is. 150 56 50N 79 50W
North Bend, Can. 152 49 50N 121 35W
North Bend, U.S.A. 160 43 28N 124 7W
North Bennington 162 42 56N 73 15W
North Berwick, U.K. 35 56 4N 2 44W
North Berwick, U.S.A. 162 43 18N 70 43W
North Br., Ashburton R. 143 43 30 S 171 30 E
North Buganda □ 126 1 0N 32 0 E
North Canadian, R. 159 36 48N 103 0W
North C., Antarct. 13 71 0N 166 0 E
North C., Can. 151 47 2N 60 20W
North, Cape 151 47 2N 60 25W
North C., N.Z. 142 34 23 S 173 4 E
North C., P.N.G. 135 2 32 S 150 50 E
North C., Spitsbergen 12 80 40N 20 0 E
North Caribou L. 150 52 50N 90 40W
North Carolina □ 157 35 30N 80 0W
North Cerney 28 51 45N 1 58W
North Channel, Br. Is. 34 55 0N 5 30W
North Channel, Can. 150 46 0N 83 0W
North Chicago 156 42 19N 87 50W
North Collingham 33 53 8N 0 46W
North Dakota □ 158 47 30N 100 0W
North Dandalup 137 32 30 S 116 2 E
N. Dorset Downs 28 50 50N 2 30W
North Down □ 38 54 40N 5 45W
North Downs 29 51 17N 0 30W
North East 162 39 36N 75 56W
North Eastern □ 126 1 30N 40 0 E
North Esk, R. 37 56 44N 2 25W
North European Plain 16 55 0N 20 0 E
N. Foreland, Pt. 29 51 22N 1 28 E
North Fork 163 37 14N 119 29W
N. Frisian Is. = Nordfr'sche Inseln 48 54 50N 8 20 E
N. Harris, dist. 36 58 0N 6 55W
North Henik L. 153 61 45N 97 40W
North Hill 30 50 33N 4 26W
North Horr 126 3 20N 37 8 E
North Hykeham 33 53 10N 0 35W
North I., Kenya 126 4 5N 36 5 E
North I., N.Z. 143 38 0 S 175 0 E
North Kamloops 152 50 40N 120 25W
North Kessock 37 57 30N 4 15W
North Knife L., Can. 153 58 0N 97 0W
North Knife L., Man., Can. 153 58 5N 97 5W
North Knife, R. 153 58 53N 94 45W
North Koel, R. 95 23 50N 84 5 E
North Korea ■ 105 40 0N 127 0 E
N. Lakhimpur 99 27 15N 94 10 E
N. Las Vegas 161 36 15N 115 6W
North Mara □ 126 1 20 S 34 20 E
North Minch 36 58 5N 5 55W
North Molton 30 51 3N 3 48W
North Nahanni, R. 152 62 15N 123 20W
North Ossetian A.S.S.R. □ 83 43 30N 44 30 E
North Palisade 163 37 6N 118 32W
North Petherton 28 51 6N 3 1W
North Platte 158 41 10N 100 50W
North Platte, R. 160 42 50N 106 50W
North Pt., Austral. 108 27 23 S 153 14 E
North Pt., Can. 151 47 5N 65 0W
North Pole 12 90 0N 0 0 E
North Portal 153 49 0N 102 33W
North Powder 160 45 2N 117 59W
North Queensferry 35 56 1N 3 22W
North Riding (□) 26 54 22N 1 30W
North Roe, dist. 36 60 40N 1 22W
North Ronaldsay, I. 37 59 20N 2 30W
North Sea 19 56 0N 4 0 E
North Sentinel, I. 101 11 35N 92 15 E
North Somercotes 33 53 28N 0 9 E
North Sound 39 53 10N 9 48W
North Sound, The 37 59 18N 2 45W
North Sporades = Voríai Sporádhes 69 39 0N 24 10 E
North Stradbroke I. 133 27 35 S 153 28 E
North Sunderland 35 55 35N 1 40W
North Sydney 151 46 12N 60 21W
North Syracuse 162 43 8N 76 7W
N. Taranaki Bt. 82 38 45 S 174 20 E

North Tawton Nyirbátor

North Tawton	30	50 48N	3 55W
North Thompson, R.	152	50 40N	120 20W
North Thoresby	33	53 27N	0 3W
North Tidworth	28	51 14N	1 40W
North Tolsta	36	58 21N	6 13W
N. Tonawanda	156	43 5N	78 50W
N. Truchas Pk.	161	36 0N	105 30W
North Twin I.	150	53 20N	80 0W
North Tyne, R.	35	54 59N	2 7W
North Uist I.	36	57 40N	7 15W
North Vancouver	152	49 25N	123 20W
North Vermilion	152	58 25N	116 0W
North Vernon	156	39 0N	85 35W
North Vietnam ■	100	22 0N	105 0E
North Wabasca L.	152	56 0N	113 55W
North Walsham	29	52 49N	1 22E
North West C.	136	21 45S	114 9E
North West Highlands	36	57 35N	5 2W
North West River	151	53 30N	60 10W
North Western □	127	13 30S	25 30E
North York Moors	33	54 25N	0 50W
North Yorkshire □	33	54 15N	1 25W
Northallerton	33	54 20N	1 26W
Northam, Austral.	132	31 35S	116 42E
Northam, S. Afr.	137	24 55S	27 15E
Northam, U.K.	30	51 2N	4 13W
Northampton, Austral.	137	28 21S	114 33E
Northampton, U.K.	29	52 14N	0 54W
Northampton, Mass., U.S.A.	162	42 22N	72 39W
Northampton, Pa., U.S.A.	162	40 38N	75 24W
Northampton □	29	52 16N	0 55W
Northampton Downs	138	24 35S	145 48E
Northbridge	162	42 12N	71 40W
Northcliffe	137	34 39S	116 7E
N.E. Land	12	80 0N	24 0E
N.E. Providence Chan.	166	26 0N	76 0W
Northeast Providence Channel	166	26 0N	76 0W
Northeim	48	51 42N	10 0E
Northern □, Malawi	127	11 0S	34 0E
Northern □, Uganda	126	3 5N	32 30E
Northern □, Zambia	127	10 30S	31 0E
Northern Circars	96	17 30N	82 30E
Northern Indian L.	153	57 20N	97 20W
Northern Ireland □	38	54 45N	7 0W
Northern Light, L.	150	48 15N	90 39W
Northern Province □	120	9 0S	11 30W
Northern Territory □	136	16 0S	133 0E
Northfield, Minn., U.S.A.	158	44 37N	93 10W
Northfield, N.J., U.S.A.	162	39 22N	74 33W
Northfleet	29	51 26N	0 20E
Northiam	29	50 59N	0 39E
Northland □	143	35 30S	173 30E
Northleach	28	51 49N	1 50W
Northome	158	47 53N	94 15W
Northop	31	53 13N	3 8W
Northport, Ala., U.S.A.	157	33 15N	87 35W
Northport, Mich., U.S.A.	156	45 8N	85 39W
Northport, N.Y., U.S.A.	162	40 53N	73 20W
Northport, Wash., U.S.A.	160	48 55N	117 48W
Northrepps	29	52 53N	1 20E
Northumberland □	35	55 12N	2 0W
Northumberland, C.	140	38 5S	140 40E
Northumberland Is.	138	21 30S	149 50E
Northumberland Str.	151	46 20N	64 0W
Northville	162	43 13N	74 11W
Northway Junction	147	63 0N	141 55W
N.W. Providence Chan.	166	26 0N	78 0W
Northwest Terr.	148	65 0N	100 0W
N.W.Basin	137	25 45S	115 0E
Northwich	32	53 16N	2 30W
Northwold	29	52 33N	0 37E
Northwood, Iowa, U.S.A.	158	43 27N	93 12W
Northwood, N.D., U.S.A.	158	47 44N	97 30W
Norton, Rhod.	127	17 52S	30 40E
Norton, N. Yorks., U.K.	33	54 9N	0 48W
Norton, Suffolk, U.K.	29	52 15N	0 52E
Norton, U.S.A.	158	39 50N	100 0W
Norton B.	147	64 40N	162 0W
Norton Fitzwarren	28	51 1N	3 10W
Norton Sd.	147	64 0N	165 0W
Norton Summit	109	34 56S	138 43E
Nortorf	48	54 14N	9 47E
Norwalk, Calif., U.S.A.	163	33 54N	118 5W
Norwalk, Conn., U.S.A.	162	41 9N	73 25W
Norwalk, Ohio, U.S.A.	156	41 13N	82 38W
Norway	156	45 46N	87 57W
Norway ■	74	67 0N	11 0E
Norway House	153	53 59N	97 50W
Norwegian Dependency	13	66 0N	15 0E
Norwegian Sea	14	66 0N	1 0E
Norwich, U.K.	29	52 38N	1 17E
Norwich, Conn., U.S.A.	162	41 33N	72 5W
Norwich, N.Y., U.S.A.	162	42 32N	75 30W
Norwood, Austral.	109	34 56S	138 39E
Norwood, U.S.A.	162	42 10N	71 10W
Noshiro	112	40 12N	140 0E
Noshiro, R.	112	40 15N	140 15E
Nosok	76	70 10N	82 20E
Nosovka	80	50 50N	31 30E
Nosratābād	93	29 55N	60 0E
Noss Hd.	37	58 29N	3 4W
Noss, I. of	36	60 8N	1 1W
Nossa Senhora da Glória	170	10 14S	37 25W
Nossa Senhora das Dores	170	10 29S	37 13W
Nossebro	73	58 12N	12 43E
Nossob	128	22 15S	17 48E
Nossob, R.	128	25 15S	20 30E
Nosy Bé, I.	125	13 25S	48 15E
Nosy Mitsio, I.	125	12 54S	48 36E
Nosy Varika	125	20 35S	48 32E
Notigi Dam	153	56 40N	99 10W
Notikewin	152	56 55N	117 50W
Notikewin, R.	152	56 59N	117 38W
Notios Evvoïkós Kólpos	69	38 20N	24 0E
Noto	65	36 52N	15 4E
Noto, G. di	65	36 50N	15 10E
Notodden	71	59 35N	9 17E
Notre Dame	151	46 18N	64 46W
Notre Dame B.	151	49 45N	55 30W
Notre Dame de Koartac	149	60 55N	69 40W
Notre Dame d'Ivugivic	149	62 20N	78 0W
Nottaway, R.	150	51 22N	78 55W
Nøtterøy	71	59 14N	10 24E
Nottingham	33	52 57N	1 10W
Nottingham □	33	53 10N	1 0W
Nottoway, R.	156	37 0N	77 45W
Notwani, R.	128	24 14S	26 20E
Nouadhibou	116	21 0N	17 0W
Nouakchott	120	18 20N	15 50W
Nouméa	130	22 17S	166 30E
Noup Hd.	37	59 20N	3 2W
Noupoort	128	31 10S	24 57E
Nouveau Comptoir (Paint Hills)	150	53 0N	78 49W
Nouvelle Calédonie	142	21 0S	165 0E
Nouzonville	43	49 48N	4 44E
Nova-Annenskiy	81	50 32N	42 39E
Nová Bana	53	48 28N	18 39E
Nová Bystrice	52	49 2N	15 8E
Nova Chaves	124	10 50S	21 15E
Nova Cruz	170	6 28S	35 25W
Nova Era	171	19 45S	43 3W
Nova Esperança	173	23 8S	52 13W
Nova Friburgo	173	22 10S	42 30W
Nova Gaia	124	10 10S	17 35E
Nova Gradiška	66	45 17N	17 28E
Nova Granada	171	20 30S	49 20W
Nova Iguaçu	173	22 45S	43 28W
Nova Iorque	170	7 0S	44 5W
Nova Lamego	120	12 19N	14 11W
Nova Lima	173	19 59S	43 51W
Nova Lisboa = Huambo	125	12 42S	15 54E
Nova Lusitânia	127	19 50S	34 34E
Nova Mambone	129	21 0S	35 3E
Nova Mesto	63	45 47N	15 12E
Nova Paka	52	50 29N	15 30E
Nova Ponte	171	19 8S	47 41W
Nova Preixo	127	14 45S	36 22E
Nova Scotia □	151	45 10N	63 0W
Nova Sofala	129	20 7S	34 48E
Nova Varoš	66	43 29N	19 48E
Nova Venécia	171	18 45S	40 24W
Nova Zagora	67	42 32N	25 59E
Novaci, Rumania	70	45 10N	23 42E
Novaci, Yugo.	66	41 5N	21 29E
Novaleksandrovskaya	83	45 29N	41 17E
Novalorque	171	6 48S	44 0W
Novara	62	45 27N	8 36E
Novato	163	38 6N	122 35W
Novaya Kakhovka	82	46 42N	33 27E
Novaya Ladoga	78	60 7N	32 16E
Novaya Lyalya	84	58 50N	60 35E
Novaya Sibir, O.	77	75 10N	150 0E
Novaya Zemlya	76	75 0N	56 0E
Novelda	59	38 24N	0 45W
Novellara	62	44 50N	10 43E
Noventa Vicentina	63	45 18N	11 30E
Novgorod	80	58 30N	31 25E
Novgorod Severskiy	80	52 2N	33 10E
Novgorod Volynski	80	50 38N	27 47E
Novi Bečej.	66	45 36N	20 10E
Novi Grad	63	45 19N	13 33E
Novi Knezeva	66	46 4N	20 8E
Novi Krichim	67	42 22N	24 31E
Novi Lígure	62	44 45N	8 47E
Novi-Pazar	67	43 25N	27 15E
Novi Pazar	66	43 12N	20 28E
Novi Sad	66	45 18N	19 52E
Novi Vinodolski	63	45 10N	14 48E
Novigrad	63	44 10N	15 32E
Noville	47	50 4N	5 46E
Novo Acôrdo	170	13 10S	46 48W
Nôvo Cruzeiro	171	17 29S	41 53W
Novo Freixo	127	14 49S	36 30E
Nôvo Hamburgo	173	29 37S	51 7W
Novo Horizonte	171	21 25S	49 10W
Novo Luso	103	4 3S	126 6E
Novo Redondo	124	11 10S	13 48E
Novo Selo	66	44 11N	22 47E
Novo-Sergiyevskiy	84	52 5N	53 38E
Novo-Zavidovskiy	81	56 32N	36 29E
Novoalekseyevka	84	50 8N	55 39E
Novoataysk	76	53 30N	84 0E
Novoazovsk	82	47 15N	38 4E
Novobelitsa	80	52 27N	31 2E
Novobogatinskoye	83	47 26N	51 17E
Novocherkassk	83	47 27N	40 5E
Novodevichye	81	53 37N	48 58E
Novograd Volynskiy	80	50 40N	27 35E
Novogrudok	80	53 40N	25 50E
Novokayakent	83	42 45N	42 52E
Novokazalinsk	76	45 40N	61 40E
Novokhopersk	81	51 5N	41 50E
Novokuybyshevsk	84	53 7N	49 58E
Novokuznetsk	76	54 0N	87 10E
Novomirgorod	82	48 57N	31 33E
Novomoskovsk, R.S.F.S.R., U.S.S.R.	81	54 5N	38 15E
Novomoskovsk, Ukrainian S.S.R., U.S.S.R.	81	48 33N	35 17E
Novoorsk	84	51 21N	59 2E
Novopolotsk	80	55 38N	28 37E
Novorossiysk	82	44 43N	37 52E
Novorzhev	80	57 3N	29 25E
Novoselitsa	82	48 14N	26 15E
Novoshakhtinsk	83	47 39N	39 58E
Novosibirsk	76	55 0N	83 5E
Novosibirskiye Ostrava	77	75 0N	140 0E
Novosil	81	52 58N	36 58E
Novosokolniki	80	56 33N	28 42E
Novotroitsk	84	51 10N	58 15E
Novotroitskoye	85	43 42N	73 46E
Novotulskiy	81	54 10N	37 36E
Novoukrainka	82	48 25N	31 30E
Novouzensk	81	50 32N	48 17E
Novovolynsk	80	50 45N	24 4E
Novovyatsk	84	58 24N	49 45E
Novozybkov	80	52 30N	32 0E
Novska	66	45 19N	17 0E
Novy Bug	82	47 34N	34 29E
Nový Bydzov	52	50 14N	15 29E
Novy Dwór Mazowiecki	54	52 26N	20 44E
Nový Jičin	53	49 15N	18 0E
Novyy Oskol	81	50 44N	37 55E
Novyy Port	76	67 40N	72 30E
Novyye Aneny	70	46 51N	29 13E
Now Shahr	93	36 40N	51 40E
Nowa Deba	54	50 26N	21 41E
Nowa Nowa	141	37 44S	148 3E
Nowa Skalmierzyce	54	51 43N	18 0E
Nowa Sól	54	51 48N	15 44E
Nowe	54	53 41N	18 44E
Nowe Miasteczko	54	51 42N	15 42E
Nowe Miasto	54	51 38N	20 34E
Nowe Miasto Lubawskie	54	53 27N	19 33E
Nowe Warpno	54	53 42N	14 18E
Nowen Hill	39	51 42N	9 15W
Nowendoc	141	31 32S	151 44E
Nowgong	98	26 20N	92 50E
Nowingi	140	34 33S	142 15E
Nowogard	54	53 41N	15 10E
Nowogród	54	53 14N	21 53E
Nowra	141	34 53S	150 35E
Nowthanna Mt.	137	27 0S	118 40E
Nowy Dwór	54	53 40N	23 0E
Nowy Korczyn	54	50 19N	20 48E
Nowy Sącz	54	49 40N	20 41E
Nowy Sącz □	54	49 30N	20 30E
Nowy Staw	54	54 13N	19 2E
Nowy Targ	53	49 30N	20 2E
Nowy Tomyssl	54	52 19N	16 10E
Noxen	162	41 25N	76 4W
Noxon	160	48 0N	115 54W
Noya	56	42 48N	8 53W
Noyant	42	47 30N	0 6E
Noyers	43	47 40N	4 0E
Noyes, I.	152	55 30N	133 40W
Noyon	43	49 34N	3 0E
Nriquinha	125	16 0S	21 25E
Nsa, O. en	119	32 23N	5 20E
Nsanje	127	16 55S	35 12E
Nsawam	121	5 50N	0 24W
Nsomba	127	10 45S	29 59E
Nsopzup	98	25 51N	97 30E
Nsukka	121	7 0N	7 50E
Nuanetsi	125	21 15S	30 48E
Nuanetsi, R.	127	21 10S	31 20E
Nuatja	121	7 0N	1 10E
Nuba Mts. = Nubāh, Jibālan	123	12 0N	31 0E
Nubāh, Jibālan	123	12 0N	31 0E
Nûbîya, Es Sahrâ En	122	21 30N	33 30E
Nuble □	172	37 0S	72 0W
Nuboai	103	2 10S	136 30E
Nubra, R.	95	34 50N	77 25E
Nudgee	108	27 22S	153 5E
Nudgee Beach	108	27 21S	153 6E
Nûdlac	66	46 10N	20 50E
Nudo Ausangate, Mt.	174	13 45S	71 10W
Nudo de Vilcanota	174	14 30S	70 0W
Nueces, R.	159	28 18N	98 39W
Nueltin L.	153	60 30N	99 30W
Nuenen	47	51 29N	5 33E
Nueva Antioquia	174	6 5N	69 26W
Nueva Casas Grandes	164	30 25N	107 55W
Nueva Esparta □	174	11 0N	64 0W
Nueva Gerona	166	21 53N	82 49W
Nueva Imperial	176	38 45S	72 58W
Nueva Palmira	172	33 52S	58 20W
Nueva Rosita	164	28 0N	101 20W
Nueva San Salvador	166	13 40N	89 25W
Nuéve de Julio	172	35 30S	61 0W
Nuevitas	166	21 30N	77 20W
Nuevo, Golfo	176	43 0S	64 30W
Nuevo Guerrero	165	26 34N	99 15W
Nuevo Laredo	165	27 30N	99 40W
Nuevo León □	164	25 0N	100 0W
Nuevo Rocafuerte	174	0 55S	76 50W
Nugget Pt.	143	46 27S	169 50E
Nugrus Gebel	122	24 58N	39 34E
Nuhaka	142	39 3S	177 45E
Nuhurowa, I.	103	5 30S	132 45E
Nuits	43	47 10N	4 56E
Nuits-St.-Georges	43	47 10N	4 56E
Nukey Bluff, Mt.	132	32 32S	135 40E
Nukheila (Merga)	122	19 1N	26 21E
Nukus	76	42 20N	59 40E
Nuland	46	51 44N	5 26E
Nulato	147	64 40N	158 10W
Nules	58	39 51N	0 9W
Nullagine	136	21 53S	120 6E
Nullagine, R.	136	21 20S	120 20E
Nullarbor	137	31 28S	130 55E
Nullarbor Plain	137	30 45S	129 0E
Numalla, L.	139	28 43S	144 20E
Numan	121	9 29N	12 3E
Numansdorp	46	51 43N	4 26E
Numata	111	36 45N	139 4E
Numatinna, W.	123	6 38N	27 15E
Numazu	111	35 7N	138 51E
Numbulwar	138	14 15S	135 45E
Numfoor, I.	103	1 0S	134 50E
Numurkah	141	36 0S	145 26E
Nun, R.	105	47 30N	124 40E
Nunaksaluk, I.	151	55 49N	60 20W
Nundah	108	27 24S	152 54E
Nuneaton	28	52 32N	1 29W
Nungo	127	13 23S	37 43E
Nungwe	126	2 48S	32 2E
Nunivak I.	147	60 0N	166 0W
Nunkun, Mt.	95	33 57N	76 8E
Nunney	28	51 13N	2 20W
Nunspeet	46	52 21N	5 45E
Nuoro	64	40 20N	9 20E
Nûousa	68	40 42N	22 9E
Nuqayy, Jabal	119	23 11N	19 30E
Nuqui	174	5 42N	77 17W
Nurata	85	40 33N	65 41E
Nuratau, Khrebet	85	40 40N	66 30E
Nure, R.	62	44 40N	9 32E
Nuremburg = Nürnberg	49	49 26N	11 5E
Nuri	164	28 2N	109 22W
Nurina	137	30 44S	126 23E
Nuriootpa	140	34 27S	139 0E
Nurlat	84	54 29N	50 45E
Nürnberg	49	49 26N	11 5E
Nurrari Lakes	137	29 1S	130 5E
Nurri	64	39 43N	9 13E
Nusa Barung	103	8 22S	113 20E
Nusa Kambangan	103	7 47S	109 0E
Nusa Tenggara □	102	7 30S	117 0E
Nusa Tenggara Barat	102	8 50S	117 30E
Nusa Tenggara Timur	103	9 30S	122 0E
Nushki	94	29 35N	65 65E
Nûsûud	70	47 19N	24 29E
Nutak	149	57 28N	61 52W
Nuth	47	50 55N	5 53E
Nutwood Downs	138	15 49S	134 10E
Nuwaiba	122	28 58N	34 40E
Nuwakot	95	28 10N	83 55E
Nuwara Eliya	97	6 58N	80 55E
Nuwefontein	128	28 1S	19 6E
Nuweveldberge	128	32 10S	21 45E
Nuyts Arch.	139	32 12S	133 20E
Nuyts, C.	137	32 2S	132 21E
Nuyts, Pt.	132	35 4S	116 38E
Nuzvid	96	16 47N	80 53E
NW Tor, oilfield	19	56 42N	3 13E
Nyaake (Webo)	120	4 52N	7 37W
Nyabing	137	33 30S	118 7E
Nyack	162	41 5N	73 57W
Nyadal	72	62 48N	17 59E
Nyagyn	76	62 8N	63 36E
Nyah West	140	35 11S	143 21E
Nyahanga	126	2 20S	33 37E
Nyahua	126	5 25S	33 23E
Nyahururu	126	0 2N	36 27E
Nyahururu Falls	126	0 2N	36 27E
Nyakanazi	126	3 2S	31 10E
Nyakasu	126	3 58S	30 6E
Nyakrom	121	5 40N	0 50W
Nyâlâ	123	12 2N	24 58E
Nyamandhlovu	127	19 55S	28 16E
Nyambiti	126	2 48S	33 27E
Nyamwaga	126	1 27S	34 33E
Nyandekwa	126	3 57S	32 32E
Nyanga, L.	137	29 57S	126 10E
Nyangana	128	18 0S	20 40E
Nyanguge	126	2 30S	33 12E
Nyangwena	127	15 18S	28 45E
Nyanji	127	14 25S	31 46E
Nyankpala	121	9 21N	0 58W
Nyanza, Burundi	126	4 21S	29 36E
Nyanza, Rwanda	126	2 20S	29 42E
Nyanza □	126	0 10S	34 15E
Nyarling, R.	152	60 41N	113 23W
Nyasa, L. = Malawi, L.	127	12 0S	34 30E
Nyaunglebin	98	17 52N	96 42E
Nyazepetrovsk	84	56 3N	59 36E
Nyazwidzi, R.	127	19 35S	32 0E
Nyborg	73	55 18N	10 47E
Nybro	73	56 44N	15 55E
Nybster	37	58 34N	3 6W
Nyda	76	66 40N	73 10E
Nyenchen Tanglha Shan	99	30 30N	95 0E
Nyeri	126	0 23S	36 56E
Nyeri □	126	0 25S	36 55E
Nyerol	123	8 41N	32 1E
Nyhem	72	62 54N	15 37E
Nyiel	123	6 9N	31 4E
Nyika Plat.	127	10 30S	36 0E
Nyilumba	127	10 30S	40 22E
Nyinahin	120	6 43N	2 3W
Nyirbátor	53	47 49N	22 9E

Nyíregyháza
Oldmeldrum

Nyíregyháza 53 48 0N 21 47 E
Nykarleby (Uusikaarlepyy) 74 63 32N 22 31 E
Nykobing 73 54 56N 11 52 E
Nykøbing, Falster, Denmark 73 54 56N 11 52 E
Nykøbing, Mors, Denmark 73 56 48N 8 51 E
Nykøbing, Sjælland, Denmark 73 55 55N 11 40 E
Nyköbing 73 56 49N 8 50 E
Nyköping 73 58 45N 17 0 E
Nykroppa 72 59 37N 14 18 E
Nykvarn 72 59 11N 17 25 E
Nyland 72 63 1N 17 45 E
Nylstroom 129 24 42 S 28 22 E
Nymagee 141 32 7 S 146 20 E
Nymburk 52 50 10N 15 1 E
Nymindegab 73 55 50N 8 12 E
Nynäshamn 72 58 54N 17 57 E
Nyngan 141 31 30 S 147 8 E
Nyon 50 46 23N 6 14 E
Nyons 45 44 22N 5 10 E
Nyora 141 38 20 S 145 41 E
Nyord 73 55 4N 12 13 E
Nysa 54 50 40N 17 22 E
Nysa, R. 54 52 4N 14 46 E
Nyssa 160 43 56N 117 2W
Nysted 73 54 40N 11 44 E
Nytva 84 57 56N 55 20 E
Nyūgawa 110 33 56N 133 5 E
Nyunzu 126 5 57 S 27 58 E
Nyurba 77 63 17N 118 20 E
Nzega 126 4 10 S 33 12 E
Nzega □ 126 4 10 S 33 10 E
N'Zérékoré 120 7 49N 8 48W
Nzilo, Chutes de 127 10 18 S 25 27 E
Nzubuka 126 4 45 S 32 50 E

O

O-Shima, Fukuoka, Japan 110 33 54N 130 25 E
O-Shima, Nagasaki, Japan 110 33 29N 129 33 E
O-Shima, Shizuoka, Japan 111 34 44N 139 24 E
Oa, Mull of 34 55 35N 6 20W
Oa, The, Pen. 34 55 36N 6 17W
Oacoma 158 43 50N 99 26W
Oadby 28 52 37N 1 7W
Oahe 158 44 33N 100 29W
Oahe Dam 158 44 28N 100 25W
Oahe Res 158 45 30N 100 15W
Oahu I. 147 21 30N 158 0W
Oak Creek 160 40 15N 106 59W
Oak Harb. 160 48 20N 122 38W
Oak Lake 153 49 45N 100 45W
Oak Park 156 41 55N 87 45W
Oak Ridge 157 36 1N 84 5W
Oak View 163 34 24N 119 18W
Oakbank, S. Australia, Austral. 109 34 59 S 138 51 E
Oakbank, S. Australia, Austral. 140 33 4 S 140 33 E
Oakdale, Calif., U.S.A. 163 37 49N 120 56W
Oakdale, La., U.S.A. 159 30 50N 92 38W
Oakengates 28 52 42N 2 29W
Oakes 158 46 14N 98 4W
Oakesdale 160 47 11N 117 9W
Oakey 139 27 25 S 151 43 E
Oakham 29 52 40N 0 43W
Oakhill 156 38 0N 81 7W
Oakhurst 163 37 19N 119 40W
Oakland 163 37 50N 122 18W
Oakland City 156 38 20N 87 20W
Oaklands, N.S.W., Austral. 141 35 34 S 146 10 E
Oaklands, S. Australia, Austral. 109 35 1 S 138 32 E
Oakley 160 42 14N 113 55W
Oakley Creek 141 31 37 S 149 46 E
Oakover, R. 136 20 43 S 120 33 E
Oakridge 160 43 47N 122 31W
Oakwood 159 31 35N 95 47W
Oamaru 143 45 5 S 170 59 E
Oamishirasato 111 35 23N 140 18 E
Oarai 111 36 21N 140 40 E
Oasis, Calif., U.S.A. 163 33 28N 116 6W
Oasis, Nev., U.S.A. 163 37 29N 117 55W
Oates Coast 13 69 0 S 160 0 E
Oatman 161 35 1N 114 19W
Oaxaca 165 17 2N 96 40W
Oaxaca □ 165 17 0N 97 0W
Ob, R. 76 62 40N 66 0 E
Oba 150 49 4N 84 7W
Obala 121 4 9N 11 32 E
Obama, Eukui, Japan 111 35 30N 135 45 E
Obama, Nagasaki, Japan 110 32 43N 130 13 E
Oban, N.Z. 143 46 55 S 168 10 E
Oban, U.K. 34 56 25N 5 30W
Obatogamau L. 150 49 34N 74 26W
Obbia 91 5 25N 48 30 E
Obdam 46 52 41N 4 55 E
Obed 152 53 30N 117 10W
Obeh 93 34 28N 63 10 E
Ober-Aagau 50 47 10N 7 45 E
Obera 173 27 21 S 55 2W
Oberalppass 51 46 39N 8 35 E
Oberalpstock 51 46 45N 8 47 E
Oberammergau 49 47 35N 11 3 E
Oberdrauburg 52 46 44N 12 58 E
Oberengadin 51 46 35N 9 55 E
Oberentfelden 50 47 21N 8 2 E
Oberhausen 48 51 28N 6 50 E
Oberkirch 49 48 31N 8 5 E
Oberland 50 46 30N 7 30 E
Oberlin, Kans., U.S.A. 158 39 52N 100 31W
Oberlin, La., U.S.A. 159 30 42N 92 42W
Obernai 43 48 28N 7 30 E
Oberndorf 49 48 17N 8 35 E
Oberon 141 33 45 S 149 52 E
Oberösterreich □ 52 48 10N 14 0 E
Oberpfalzer Wald 49 49 30N 12 25 E
Oberseebach 51 48 53N 7 58 E
Obersiggenthal 51 47 29N 8 18 E
Oberstdorf 49 47 25N 10 16 E
Oberwil 50 47 32N 7 33 E
Obi, Kepulauan 103 1 30 S 127 30 E
Obiaruku 121 5 51N 6 9 E
Óbidos, Brazil 175 1 50 S 55 30W
Óbidos, Port. 57 39 19N 9 10W
Obihiro 112 42 25N 143 12 E
Obilnoye 83 47 32N 44 30 E
Obisfelde 48 52 27N 10 57 E
Objat 44 45 16N 1 24 E
Obluchye 77 49 10N 130 50 E
Obninsk 81 55 8N 36 13 E
Obo, C. Afr. Emp. 123 5 20N 26 32 E
Obo, Ethiopia 123 3 34N 38 52 E
Oboa, Mt. 126 1 45N 34 45 E
Obock 123 12 0N 43 20 E
Oborniki 54 52 39N 16 59 E
Oborniki Śl. 54 51 17N 16 53 E
Obot 123 4 32N 37 13 E
Obout 121 3 28N 11 47 E
Oboyan 81 51 20N 36 28 E
Obrenovac 66 44 40N 20 11 E
O'Briensbridge 39 52 46N 8 30W
Obrovac 63 44 11N 15 41 E
Observatory Inlet 152 55 25N 129 45W
Obshchi Syrt 16 52 0N 53 0 E
Obskaya Guba 76 70 0N 73 0 E
Obuasi 121 6 17N 1 40W
Obubra 121 6 8N 8 20 E
Obyachevo 84 60 20N 49 37 E
Obzor 67 42 50N 27 52 E
Ocala 157 29 11N 82 5W
Ocampo 164 28 9N 108 8W
Ocaña 58 39 55N 3 30W
Ocanomowoc 158 43 7N 88 30W
Ocate 159 36 12N 104 59W
Occidental, Cordillera 174 5 0N 76 0W
Ocean City, Md., U.S.A. 162 38 20N 75 5W
Ocean City, N.J., U.S.A. 162 39 18N 74 34W
Ocean Falls 152 52 25N 127 40W
Ocean I. 130 0 45 S 169 50 E
Ocean Park 160 46 30N 124 2W
Oceanlake 160 45 0N 124 0W
Oceano 163 35 6N 120 37W
Oceanside 163 33 13N 117 26W
Ochagavia 58 42 55N 1 5W
Ochakov 82 46 35N 31 30 E
Ochamchire 83 42 46N 41 32 E
Ochamps 47 49 56N 5 16 E
Och'eng 109 30 20N 114 51 E
Ocher 84 57 53N 54 42 E
Ochiai 110 35 1N 133 45 E
Ochil Hills 35 56 14N 3 40W
Ochiltree 34 55 26N 4 23W
Ochre River 153 51 4N 99 47W
Ochsenfurt 49 49 38N 10 3 E
Ocilla 157 31 35N 83 12W
Ockelbo 72 60 54N 16 45 E
Ocmulgee, R. 157 32 0N 83 19W
Ocna Mureş 70 46 23N 23 49 E
Ocna-Sibiului 70 45 52N 24 2 E
Ocnele Mari 70 45 8N 24 18 E
Oconee, R. 157 32 30N 82 55W
Oconto 156 44 52N 87 53W
Oconto Falls 156 44 52N 88 10W
Ocós 166 14 31N 92 11W
Ocosingo 165 18 4N 92 15W
Ocotal 166 13 41N 86 41W
Ocotlán 164 20 21N 102 42W
Ocquier 47 50 24N 5 24 E
Ocreza, R. 56 39 50N 7 35W
Ocsa 53 47 17N 19 15 E
Octave 161 34 10N 112 43W
Octeville 42 49 38N 1 40W
Octyabrskoy Revolyutsii, Os. 77 79 30N 97 0 E
Ocumare del Tuy 174 10 7N 66 46W
Ocussi 103 9 20 S 124 30 E
Oda, Ghana 121 5 50N 1 5W
Oda, Ehime, Japan 110 33 36N 132 53 E
Oda, Shimane, Japan 110 35 11N 132 30 E
Ödåkra 73 56 9N 12 45 E
Ödåkra 73 56 7N 12 45 E
Odanakumadona 128 20 55 S 24 46 E
Ódáoahraun 74 65 5N 17 0W
Odate 112 40 16N 140 34 E
Odawara 111 35 20N 139 6 E
Odda 71 60 3N 6 35 E
Odder 73 55 58N 10 10 E
Oddobo 123 12 21N 42 6 E
Oddur 91 4 0N 43 35 E
Ödeborg 73 58 32N 11 58 E
Odei, R. 153 56 6N 96 54W
Ödemira 57 37 35N 8 40W
Ödemiş 92 38 15N 28 0 E
Odense 73 55 22N 10 23 E
Odenton 162 39 5N 76 42W
Odenwald 48 49 18N 9 0 E
Oder, R. 48 53 0N 14 12 E
Oderzo 63 45 47N 12 29 E
Odessa, Del., U.S.A. 162 39 27N 75 40W
Odessa, Tex., U.S.A. 159 31 51N 102 23W
Odessa, Wash., U.S.A. 160 47 25N 118 35W
Odessa, U.S.S.R. 82 46 30N 30 45 E
Odiel, R. 57 37 30N 6 55W
Odienné 120 9 30N 7 34W
Odiham 29 51 16N 0 56W
Odin, gasfield 19 60 5N 2 10 E
Odoben 121 5 38N 0 56W
Odobeşti 70 45 43N 27 4 E
Odolanów 54 51 34N 17 40 E
O'Donnell 159 33 0N 101 48W
Odoorn 46 52 51N 6 51 E
Odorheiul Secuiesc 70 46 21N 25 21 E
Odoyevo 81 53 56N 36 42 E
Odra, R., Czech. 53 49 43N 17 47 E
Odra, R., Poland 54 52 40N 14 28 E
Odra, R., Spain 56 42 30N 4 15W
Odzaci 66 45 30N 19 17 E
Odzak 66 45 3N 18 18 E
Odzi 125 19 0 S 32 20 E
Oedelem 47 51 10N 3 21 E
Oegstgeest 46 52 11N 4 29 E
Oeiras, Brazil 170 7 0 S 42 8W
Oeiras, Port. 57 38 41N 9 18W
Oelrichs 158 43 11N 103 14W
Oelsnitz 48 50 24N 12 11 E
Oenpelli 136 12 20 S 133 4 E
Oensingen 50 47 17N 7 43 E
Oerhtossu, reg. 106 39 20N 108 30 E
Ofanto, R. 65 41 8N 15 50 E
Ofen Pass 51 46 37N 10 17 E
Offa 121 8 13N 4 42 E
Offaly □ 39 53 15N 7 30W
Offenbach 49 50 6N 8 46 E
Offenbeek 47 51 17N 6 5 E
Offenburg 126 48 27N 7 56 E
Offerdal 72 63 28N 14 0 E
Offida 63 42 56N 13 40 E
Offranville 42 49 52N 1 0 E
Ofidhousa, I. 69 36 33N 26 8 E
Ofotfjorden 74 68 27N 16 40 E
Oga-Hantō 111 39 58N 139 59 E
Ogahalla 150 50 6N 85 51W
Ōgaki 111 35 21N 136 37 E
Ogallala 158 41 12N 101 40W
Ogbomosho 121 8 1N 3 29 E
Ogden, Iowa, U.S.A. 158 42 3N 94 0W
Ogden, Utah, U.S.A. 160 41 13N 112 1W
Ogdensburg 156 44 40N 75 27W
Ogeechee, R. 157 32 30N 81 32W
Oglio, R. 62 45 15N 10 15 E
Ogmore 138 22 37 S 149 35 E
Ogmore, R. 31 51 29N 3 37W
Ogmore Vale 30 51 35N 3 32W
Ogna 71 58 31N 5 48 E
Ognon, R. 43 47 43N 6 32 E
Ogoja 121 6 38N 8 39 E
Ogoki 150 51 35N 86 0W
Ogoki L. 150 50 50N 87 10W
Ogoki, R. 150 51 38N 85 57W
Ogoki Res. 150 50 45N 88 15W
Ogooué, R. 124 1 0 S 10 0 E
Ogori 110 34 6N 131 24 E
Ogosta, R. 67 43 35N 23 35 E
Ogowe, R. = Ogooué, R. 124 1 0 S 10 0 E
Ograzden 66 41 30N 22 50 E
Ogrein 122 17 55N 34 50 E
Ogulin 63 45 16N 15 16 E
Ogun □ 121 7 0N 3 0 E
Oguni 110 33 4N 131 2 E
Oguta 121 5 44N 6 44 E
Ogwashi-Uku 121 6 15N 6 30 E
Ogwe 121 5 0N 7 14 E
Ohai 143 44 55 S 168 0 E
Ohakune 142 39 24 S 175 24 E
Ohara 111 35 15N 140 23 E
Ohau, L. 143 44 15 S 169 53 E
Ohaupo 142 37 56 S 175 20 E
Ohey 47 50 26N 5 8 E
O'Higgins □ 172 34 15 S 71 1W
Ohio □ 156 40 20N 83 0W
Ohio, R. 156 38 0N 86 0W
Ohiwa Harbour 142 37 59 S 177 10 E
Ohre, R. 52 50 10N 12 30 E
Ohrid 66 41 8N 20 52 E
Ohridsko, Jezero 66 41 8N 20 52 E
Ohrigstad 129 24 41 S 30 36 E
Öhringen 49 49 11N 9 31 E
Oi Ho 108 28 37N 98 16 E
Oignies 47 50 28N 3 0 E
Oil City 156 41 26N 79 40W
Oildale 163 35 25N 119 1W
Oilgate 39 52 25N 6 30W
Oinousa, I. 69 38 33N 26 14 E
Oirschot 47 51 30N 5 18 E
Oise □ 43 49 28N 2 30 E
Oise, R. 43 49 53N 3 50 E
Oisterwijk 47 51 35N 5 12 E
Oita 110 33 14N 131 36 E
Oita-ken □ 110 33 15N 131 30 E
Oiticica 170 5 3 S 41 5W
Ojai 163 34 28N 119 16W
Ojinaga 164 29 34N 104 25W
Ojocaliente 164 30 25N 106 30W
Ojos del Salado 172 27 0 S 68 40W
Oka, R. 81 56 20N 43 59 E
Okahandja 128 22 0 S 16 59 E
Okahukura 142 38 48N 175 14 E
Okaihau 142 35 19 S 173 36 E
Okakune 142 39 26 S 175 24 E
Okanagan L. 152 50 0N 119 30W
Okanogan 160 48 22N 119 35W
Okanogan, R. 160 48 40N 119 24W
Okány 53 46 52N 21 21 E
Okapa 135 6 38 S 145 39 E
Okaputa 128 20 5 S 17 0 E
Okara 94 30 50N 73 25 E
Okarito 143 43 15 S 170 9 E
Okato 142 39 12 S 173 53 E
Okaukuejo 125 19 10 S 16 0 E
Okavango, R. = Cubango, R. 125 16 15 S 18 0 E
Okavango Swamp 128 19 30 S 23 0 E
Okawa 110 33 9N 130 21 E
Okaya 111 36 0N 138 10 E
Okayama 110 34 40N 133 54 E
Okayama-ken □ 110 35 0N 133 50 E
Okazaki 111 34 57N 137 10 E
Oke-Iho 121 8 1N 3 18 E
Okeechobee 157 27 16N 80 46W
Okeechobee L. 157 27 0N 80 50W
Okefenokee Swamp 157 30 50N 82 15W
Okehampton 30 50 44N 4 1W
Okene 121 7 32N 6 11 E
Oker, R. 48 52 7N 10 34 E
Okha 77 53 40N 143 0 E
Ókhi Óros 69 38 5N 24 25 E
Okhotsk 77 59 20N 143 10 E
Okhotsk, Sea of 77 55 0N 145 0 E
Okhotskiy Perevoz 77 61 52N 135 35 E
Okhotsko Kolymskoy 77 63 0N 157 0 E
Oki-no-Shima 110 32 44N 132 33 E
Oki-Shotō 110 36 15N 133 15 E
Okiep 128 29 39 S 17 53 E
Okigwi 121 5 52N 7 20 E
Okija 121 5 54N 6 55 E
Okinawa-Jima 112 26 32N 128 0 E
Okinawa-Shotō 112 27 0N 128 0 E
Okinoerabu-Jima 112 27 21N 128 33 E
Okitipupa 121 6 31N 4 50 E
Oklahoma □ 159 35 20N 97 30W
Oklahoma City 159 35 25N 97 30W
Okmulgee 159 35 38N 96 0W
Oknitsa 82 48 25N 27 20 E
Okolo 126 2 37N 31 8 E
Okondeka 128 21 38 S 15 37 E
Okondja 124 0 35 S 13 45 E
Okonek 54 53 32N 16 51 E
Okrika 121 4 47N 7 4 E
Oksby 73 55 33N 8 8 E
Oktyabr 85 43 41N 77 12 E
Oktyabrskiy 84 54 28N 53 28 E
Okuchi 110 32 4N 130 37 E
Okulovka 80 58 19N 33 28 E
Okuru 143 43 55 S 168 55 E
Okushiri-Tō 112 42 15N 139 30 E
Okuta 121 9 14N 3 12 E
Okwa, R. 128 22 25 S 22 30 E
Okwoga 121 7 3N 7 42 E
Ola 159 35 2N 93 10W
Ólafsfjörður 74 66 4N 18 39W
Ólafsvík 74 64 53N 23 43W
Olancha 163 36 15N 118 1W
Olancha Pk. 163 36 15N 118 7W
Olanchito 167 15 30N 86 30W
Öland 73 56 45N 16 50 E
Olargues 44 43 34N 2 53 E
Olary 140 32 18 S 140 19 E
Olascoaga 172 35 15 S 60 39W
Olathe 158 38 50N 94 50W
Olavarría 172 36 55 S 60 20W
Oława 54 50 57N 17 20 E
Olbia 64 40 55N 9 30 E
Olbia, G. di 64 40 55N 9 35 E
Old Bahama Chan. 166 22 10N 77 30W
Old Baldy Pk = San Antonio, Mt. 163 34 17N 117 38W
Old Castile = Castilla la Vieja 56 41 55N 4 0W
Old Castle 38 53 46N 7 10W
Old Cork 138 22 57 S 142 0 E
Old Dale 163 34 8N 115 47W
Old Deer 37 57 30N 2 3W
Old Dongola 122 18 11N 30 44 E
Old Factory 150 52 36N 78 43W
Old Forge, N.J., U.S.A. 162 43 43N 74 58W
Old Forge, N.Y., U.S.A. 162 43 43N 74 58W
Old Forge, Pa., U.S.A. 162 41 20N 75 46W
Old Fort, R. 153 58 36N 110 24W
Old Harbor 147 57 12N 153 22W
Old Kilpatrick 34 55 56N 4 34W
Old Leake 33 53 2N 0 6 E
Old Leighlin 39 52 46N 7 2W
Old Man of Hoy 37 58 53N 3 25W
Old Point Comfort 162 37 0N 76 20W
Old Radnor 31 52 14N 3 7W
Old Serenje 127 13 7 S 30 45 E
Old Shinyanga 126 3 33 S 33 27 E
Old Town 151 45 0N 68 50W
Old Wives L. 153 50 5N 106 0W
Oldbury 28 52 33N 2 0W
Oldeani 126 3 22 S 35 35 E
Oldenburg, Niedersachsen, Ger. 48 53 10N 8 10 E
Oldenburg, S.-Holst, Ger. 48 54 16N 10 53 E
Oldenzaal 46 52 19N 6 53 E
Oldham 32 53 33N 2 8W
Oldman, R. 152 49 57N 111 42W
Oldmeldrum 37 57 20N 2 19W

Olds Örken, L

Name	Page	Lat.	Long.
Olds	152	51 50N	114 10W
Olean	156	42 8N	78 25W
Oléggio	62	45 36N	8 38E
Oleiros	56	39 56N	7 56W
Olekma, R.	77	58 0N	121 30E
Olekminsk	77	60 40N	120 30E
Olema	163	38 3N	122 47W
Olen	47	51 9N	4 52E
Olenek	77	68 20N	112 30E
Olenek, R.	77	71 0N	123 50E
Olenino	80	56 15N	33 20E
Oléron, I. d'	44	45 55N	1 15W
Olesno	54	50 51N	18 26E
Oleśnica	54	51 13N	17 22E
Olevsk	80	51 18N	27 39E
Olga	77	43 50N	135 0E
Olga, L.	150	49 47N	77 15W
Olga, Mt.	137	25 20S	130 40E
Olgastretet	12	78 35N	25 0E
Ølgod	73	55 49N	8 36E
Olgrinmole	37	58 29N	3 33W
Olhão	57	37 3N	7 48W
Olib	63	44 23N	14 44E
Olib, I.	63	44 23N	14 44E
Oliena	64	40 18N	9 22E
Oliete	58	41 1N	0 41W
Olifants, R.	125	24 5S	31 20E
Olifantshoek	128	27 57S	22 42E
Ólimbos	69	35 44N	27 11E
Ólimbos, Óros	68	40 6N	22 23E
Olímpia	173	20 44S	48 54W
Olimpo□	172	20 30S	58 45W
Olinda	170	8 1S	34 51W
Olindiná	170	11 22S	38 21W
Oling Hu	105	34 52N	97 30E
Olite	58	42 29N	1 40W
Oliva, Argent.	172	32 0S	63 38W
Oliva, Spain	59	38 58N	0 15W
Oliva de la Frontera	57	38 17N	6 54W
Oliva, Punta del	56	43 37N	5 28W
Olivares	58	39 46N	2 20W
Oliveira, Bahia, Brazil	171	12 23S	38 35W
Oliveira, Minas Gerais, Brazil	171	20 50S	44 50W
Oliveira de Azemeis	56	40 49N	8 29W
Oliveira dos Brejinhos	171	12 19S	42 54W
Olivença	127	11 47S	35 13E
Olivenza	57	38 41N	7 9W
Oliver	152	49 20N	119 30W
Oliver L.	153	56 56N	103 22W
Olivine Ra.	143	44 15S	168 30E
Olivone	51	46 32N	8 57E
Olkhovka	83	49 48N	44 32E
Olkusz	54	50 18N	19 33E
Ollagüe	172	21 15S	68 10W
Ollerton	33	53 12N	1 1W
Olloy	47	50 5N	4 36E
Olmedo	56	41 20N	4 43W
Olmos, L.	172	33 25S	63 19W
Olney, U.K.	29	52 9N	0 42W
Olney, Ill., U.S.A.	156	38 40N	88 0W
Olney, Tex., U.S.A.	159	33 25N	98 45W
Olofström	73	56 17N	14 32E
Oloma	121	3 29N	11 19E
Olomane, R.	151	50 14N	60 37W
Olomouc	53	49 38N	17 12E
Olonets	78	61 10N	33 0E
Olongapo	103	14 50N	120 18E
Oloron-Ste.-Marie	44	43 11N	0 38W
Olot	58	42 11N	2 30E
Olovo	66	44 8N	18 35E
Olovyannaya	77	50 50N	115 10E
Olpe	48	51 2N	7 50E
Olsene	47	50 58N	3 28E
Olshanka	82	48 16N	30 58E
Olst	46	52 20N	6 7E
Olsztyn	54	53 48N	20 29E
Olsztyn□	54	54 0N	21 0E
Olsztynek	54	53 34N	20 19E
Olt□	70	44 20N	24 30E
Olt, R.	70	43 50N	24 40E
Olten	50	47 21N	7 53E
Oltenita	70	44 7N	26 42E
Olton	159	34 16N	102 7W
Oltu	92	40 35N	41 50E
Oluanpi	109	21 54N	120 51E
Oluego	58	41 47N	2 0W
Olvera	57	36 55N	5 18W
Olympia, Greece	69	37 39N	21 39E
Olympia, U.S.A.	160	47 0N	122 58W
Olympic Mts.	160	47 50N	123 45W
Olympic Nat. Park	160	47 48N	123 30W
Olympus, Mt.	160	47 52N	123 40W
Olympus, Mt. = Olimbos, Oros	68	40 6N	22 23E
Olyphant	162	41 28N	75 37W
Om Hajer	123	14 20N	36 41E
Om Koï	100	17 48N	98 22E
Omachi	111	36 30N	137 50E
Omae-Zaki	111	34 36N	138 14E
Omagh	38	54 36N	7 20W
Omagh□	38	54 35N	7 15W
Omaha	158	41 15N	96 0W
Omak	160	48 24N	119 31W
Oman■	92	23 0N	58 0E
Oman, G. of	93	24 30N	58 30E
Omaruru	128	21 26S	16 0E
Omaruru, R.	128	21 44S	14 30E
Omate	174	16 45S	71 0W
Ombai, Selat	103	8 30S	124 50E
Ombersley	28	52 17N	2 12W
Ombo	71	59 18N	6 0E
Ombombo	128	18 43S	13 57E
Omboué	124	1 35S	9 15E
Ombrone, R.	62	42 48N	11 15E
Omchi	119	21 22N	17 53E
Omdraai	128	20 5S	21 56E
Omdurmân	121	15 40N	32 28E
Ome	111	35 47N	139 15E
Omegna	62	45 52N	8 23E
Omeonga	126	3 40S	24 22E
Ometepe, Isla de	166	11 32N	85 35W
Ometepec	165	16 39N	98 23W
Omez	90	32 22N	35 0E
Omi-Shima, Ehime, Japan	110	34 15N	133 0E
Omi-Shima, Yamaguchi, Japan	110	34 15N	131 9E
Omihachiman	111	35 7N	136 3E
Omineca, R.	152	56 3N	124 16W
Omiš	63	43 28N	16 40E
Omisalj	63	45 13N	14 32E
Omitara	128	22 16S	18 2E
Ōmiya	111	35 54N	139 38E
Omme	73	55 56N	8 32E
Ommen	46	52 31N	6 26E
Ömnöovi□	106	43 15N	104 0E
Omono, R.	112	39 46N	140 3E
Omsk	76	55 0N	73 38E
Omsukchan	77	62 32N	155 48E
Omul, Mt.	70	45 27N	25 29E
Omura	110	33 8N	130 0E
Omura-Wan	110	32 57N	129 52E
Omuramba, R.	125	19 10S	19 20E
Omurtag	67	43 8N	26 26E
Ōmuta	110	33 0N	130 26E
Omutninsk	84	58 45N	52 4E
On	47	50 11N	5 18E
On-Take	110	31 35N	130 39E
Oña	58	42 43N	3 25W
Onaga	158	39 32N	96 12W
Onalaska	158	43 53N	91 14W
Onamia	158	46 4N	93 38W
Onancock	162	37 42N	75 49W
Onang	103	3 2S	118 55E
Onaping L.	150	47 3N	81 30W
Onarheim	71	59 57N	5 35E
Oñate	58	43 3N	2 25W
Onavas	164	28 28N	109 30W
Onawa	158	42 2N	96 2W
Onaway	156	45 21N	84 11W
Oncesti	70	43 56N	25 52E
Onchan	32	54 11N	4 27W
Oncocua	128	16 30S	13 40E
Onda	58	39 55N	0 17W
Ondaejin	107	41 34N	129 40E
Ondangua	128	17 57S	16 4E
Ondárroa	58	43 19N	2 25W
Ondas, R.	171	12 8S	45 0W
Ondava, R.	53	48 50N	21 40E
Onderdijk	46	52 45N	5 8E
Ondo, Japan	110	24 11N	132 32E
Ondo, Nigeria	121	7 4N	4 47E
Ondo□	121	7 0N	5 0E
Ondombo	128	21 3S	16 5E
Öndörhaan	105	47 19N	110 39E
Öndörshil	106	45 33N	108 5E
Ondverdarnes	74	64 52N	24 0W
One Tree Hill	109	34 43S	138 46E
Onega	78	64 0N	38 10E
Onega, G. of = Onezhskaya G.	78	64 30N	37 0E
Onega, L. = Onezhskoye Oz.	78	62 0N	35 30E
Onega, R.	78	63 0N	39 0E
Onehunga	142	36 55N	174 30E
Oneida	162	43 5N	75 40W
Oneida L.	162	43 12N	76 0W
O'Neill	158	42 30N	98 38W
Onekotan, Ostrov	77	49 59N	154 0E
Onema	126	4 35S	24 30E
Oneonta, Ala., U.S.A.	157	33 58N	86 29W
Oneonta, N.Y., U.S.A.	162	42 26N	75 5W
Onerahi	142	35 45S	174 22E
Onezhskaya Guba	78	64 30N	37 0E
Onezhskoye Ozero	78	62 0N	35 30E
Ongarue	142	38 42S	175 19E
Ongerup	137	33 58S	118 28E
Ongjin	107	37 56N	125 21E
Ongkharak	100	14 8N	101 1E
Ongoka	126	1 20S	26 0E
Ongole	97	15 33N	80 2E
Ongon	106	45 41N	113 5E
Onhaye	47	50 15N	4 50E
Oni	83	42 33N	43 26E
Onida	158	44 42N	100 5W
Onilahy, R.	129	23 30S	44 0E
Onitsha	121	6 6N	6 42E
Onkaparinga, R.	109	35 2S	138 47E
Onmaka	98	22 17N	96 41E
Onny, R.	28	52 30N	2 50W
Ono, Japan	110	34 51N	134 56E
Ono, Japan	111	35 59N	136 29E
Onoda	110	33 59N	131 11E
Onomichi	110	34 25N	133 12E
Onpyŏngni	107	33 25N	126 55E
Ons, Islas de	56	42 23N	8 55W
Onsala	73	57 26N	12 0E
Onslow	136	21 40S	115 0E
Onslow B.	157	34 10N	77 0W
Onstwedde	46	52 2N	7 4E
Ontake-San	111	35 53N	137 29E
Ontaneda	56	43 12N	3 57W
Ontario, Calif., U.S.A.	163	34 2N	117 40W
Ontario, Oreg., U.S.A.	160	44 1N	117 1W
Ontario□	150	52 0N	88 10W
Ontario, L.	150	43 40N	78 0W
Onteniente	59	38 50N	0 35W
Ontonagon	158	46 52N	89 19W
Ontur	59	38 38N	1 29W
Onyx	163	35 41N	118 14W
Oodnadatta	139	27 33S	135 30E
Ooglaamie	12	72 1N	157 0W
Ookala	147	20 1N	155 17W
Ooldea	137	30 27S	131 50E
Ooltgensplaat	47	51 41N	4 21E
Oona River	152	53 57N	130 16W
Oordegem	47	50 58N	3 54E
Oorindi	138	20 40S	141 1E
Oost-Vlaanderen□	47	51 5N	3 50E
Oost-Vlieland	46	53 18N	5 4E
Oostakker	47	51 6N	3 46E
Oostburg	47	51 19N	3 30E
Oostduinkerke	47	51 7N	2 41E
Oostelijk-Flevoland	46	52 31N	5 38E
Oostende	47	51 15N	2 50E
Oosterbeek	46	51 59N	5 51E
Oosterdijk	46	52 44N	5 14E
Oosterend, Frise, Neth.	46	53 24N	5 23E
Oosterend, Holl. Sept., Neth.	46	53 5N	4 52E
Oosterhout, Brabank, Neth.	47	51 39N	4 52E
Oosterhout, Gueldre, Neth.	46	51 53N	5 50E
Oosterschelde	47	51 33N	4 0E
Oosterwolde	46	53 0N	6 17E
Oosterzele	47	50 57N	3 48E
Oostkamp	47	51 9N	3 14E
Oostmalle	47	51 18N	4 44E
Oostrozebekke	47	50 55N	3 21E
Oostvleteven	47	50 56N	2 45E
Oostvoorne	46	51 55N	4 5E
Oostzaan	46	52 26N	4 52E
Ootacamund	97	11 30N	76 44E
Ootha	141	33 6S	147 29E
Ootmarsum	46	52 24N	6 54E
Ootsa L.	152	53 50N	126 20W
Ootsi	128	25 2S	25 45E
Opaka	67	43 28N	26 10E
Opala, U.S.S.R.	77	52 15N	156 15E
Opala, Zaïre	124	1 11S	24 45E
Opalenica	54	52 18N	16 24E
Opalton	138	23 15S	142 46E
Opan	67	42 13N	25 41E
Opanake	97	6 35N	80 40E
Opapa	142	39 47S	176 42E
Opasatika	150	49 30N	82 50W
Opasquia	153	53 16N	93 34W
Opatija	63	45 21N	14 17E
Opatów	54	50 50N	21 27E
Opava	53	49 57N	17 58E
Opawica, L.	150	49 35N	75 55W
Opeinde	46	53 8N	6 4E
Opelousas	159	30 35N	92 0W
Opémisca L.	150	50 0N	75 0W
Open Bay Is.	143	43 51S	168 51E
Opglabbeek	47	51 3N	5 35E
Opheim	160	48 52N	106 30W
Ophir, U.K.	147	58 56N	3 11W
Ophir, U.S.A.	147	63 10N	156 40W
Ophthalmia Ra.	136	23 15S	119 30E
Opi	121	6 36N	7 28E
Opien	108	29 15N	103 24E
Opinaca L.	150	52 39N	76 20W
Opinaca, R.	150	52 15N	78 2W
Opioo	47	51 37N	5 54E
Opiskotish, L.	151	53 10N	67 50W
Opmeer	46	52 42N	4 57E
Opobo	121	4 35N	7 34E
Opochka	80	56 42N	28 45E
Opoczno	54	51 22N	20 18E
Opole	54	50 42N	17 58E
Opole□	54	50 40N	17 56E
Oporto = Porto	56	41 8N	8 40W
Opotiki	142	38 1S	177 19E
Opp	157	31 19N	86 13W
Oppegård	71	59 48N	10 48E
Oppenheim	49	49 50N	8 22E
Opperdoes	46	52 45N	5 4E
Óppido Mamertina	65	38 16N	15 59E
Oppland fylke□	71	61 15N	9 30E
Oppstad	71	60 17N	11 40E
Opua	142	35 19S	174 9E
Opunake	142	39 26S	173 52E
Opuzen	66	43 1N	17 34E
Or Yehuda	90	32 2N	34 50E
Ora	63	46 20N	11 19E
Ora Banda	137	30 20S	121 0E
Oracle	161	32 45N	110 46W
Oradea	70	47 2N	21 58E
Öræfajökull	74	64 2N	16 39W
Orahovac	66	42 24N	20 40E
Orahovica	66	45 35N	17 52E
Orai	95	25 58N	79 30E
Oraison	45	43 55N	5 55E
Oran, Alg.	118	35 37N	0 39W
Oran, Argent.	172	23 10S	64 20W
Oran, Ireland	38	53 40N	8 20W
Orange, Austral.	141	33 15S	149 7E
Orange, France	45	44 8N	4 47E
Orange, Calif., U.S.A.	163	33 47N	117 51W
Orange, Mass., U.S.A.	162	42 35N	72 15W
Orange, Tex., U.S.A.	159	30 0N	93 40W
Orange, Va., U.S.A.	156	38 17N	78 5W
Orange, C.	175	4 20N	51 30W
Orange Cove	163	36 38N	119 19W
Orange Free State = Oranje Vrystaat	128	28 30S	27 0E
Orange Free State□	128	28 30S	27 0E
Orange Grove	159	27 57N	97 57W
Orange, R. = Oranje, R.	128	28 30S	18 0E
Orange Walk	165	18 6N	88 33W
Orangeburg	157	33 27N	80 53W
Orangerie B.	138	10 30S	149 30E
Orangeville	150	43 55N	80 5W
Oranienburg	48	52 45N	13 15E
Oranje, R.	128	28 30S	18 0E
Oranje Vrystaat□	128	28 30S	27 0E
Oranjemund (Orange Mouth)	128	28 32S	16 29E
Oranmore	39	53 16N	8 57W
Orapa	128	21 13S	25 25E
Oras	103	12 9N	125 22E
Orašje	66	45 1N	18 42E
Oraşul Stalin = Braşov	70	45 7N	25 39E
Orava, R.	53	49 24N	19 20E
Oravita	66	45 6N	21 43E
Orb, R.	44	43 28N	3 5E
Orba, R.	62	44 45N	8 40E
Ørbæk	73	55 17N	10 39E
Orbe	50	46 43N	6 32E
Orbec	42	49 1N	0 23E
Orbetello	63	42 26N	11 11E
Órbigo, R.	56	42 40N	5 45W
Orbost	141	37 40S	148 29E
Örbyhus	72	60 15N	17 43E
Orbyhus	72	60 13N	17 43E
Orce	59	37 44N	2 28W
Orce, R.	59	37 45N	2 30W
Orchies	43	50 28N	3 14E
Orchila, Isla	167	11 48N	66 10W
Orco, R.	62	45 20N	7 45E
Orcutt	163	34 52N	120 27W
Ord	136	17 23S	128 51E
Ord, Mt.	136	17 20S	125 34E
Ord, R.	136	15 33S	128 35E
Ordenes	56	43 5N	8 29W
Orderville	161	37 18N	112 43W
Ordhead	37	57 10N	2 31W
Ordie	37	57 6N	2 54W
Ordos (Oerhtossu)	106	39 0N	108 0E
Ordu	92	40 55N	37 53E
Orduña	58	42 58N	2 58W
Orduña, Mte.	59	37 20N	3 30W
Ordway	158	38 15N	103 42W
Ordzhonikidze, R.S.F.S.R., U.S.S.R.	83	43 0N	44 35E
Ordzhonikidze, Ukraine S.S.R., U.S.S.R.	82	47 32N	34 3E
Ordzhonikidze, Uzbek S.S.R., U.S.S.R.	85	41 21N	69 22E
Ordzhonikidzeabad	85	38 34N	69 1E
Ore, Sweden	72	61 8N	15 10E
Ore, Zaïre	126	3 17N	29 30E
Ore Mts. = Erzgebirge	49	50 25N	13 0E
Örebic	66	43 0N	17 11E
Örebro	72	59 20N	15 18E
Örebro län□	72	59 27N	15 0E
Oregon	158	42 1N	89 20W
Oregon□	160	44 0N	120 0W
Oregon City	160	45 21N	122 35W
Öregrund	72	60 21N	18 30E
Öregrundsgrepen	72	60 25N	18 15E
Orekhov	82	47 30N	35 32E
Orekhovo-Zuyevo	81	55 50N	38 55E
Orel	81	52 57N	36 3E
Orel, R.	82	49 5N	35 25E
Orellana, Canal de	57	39 2N	6 0W
Orellana la Vieja	57	39 1N	5 32W
Orellana, Pantano de	57	39 5N	5 10W
Orem	160	40 27N	111 45W
Oren	69	37 3N	27 57E
Orenburg	84	51 45N	55 6E
Orense	56	42 19N	7 55W
Orense□	56	42 15N	7 30W
Orepuki	143	46 19S	167 46E
Orestiás	68	41 30N	26 33E
Øresund	73	55 45N	12 45E
Oreti, R.	143	45 39S	168 14E
Orford	29	52 6N	1 31E
Orford Ness	29	52 6N	1 31E
Orgañá	58	42 13N	1 20E
Orgaz	57	39 39N	3 53W
Orgeyev	82	47 9N	29 10E
Orgon	45	43 47N	5 3E
Orhon Gol, R.	105	50 21N	106 5E
Oria	65	40 30N	17 38E
Orient	139	28 7S	143 3E
Orient Bay	150	49 20N	88 10W
Oriente	172	38 44S	60 37W
Origny	43	49 50N	3 30E
Origny-Ste.-Benoîte	43	49 50N	3 30E
Orihuela	59	38 7N	0 55W
Orihuela del Tremedal	58	40 33N	1 39W
Oriku	68	40 20N	19 30E
Orinoco, Delta del	167	8 30N	61 0W
Orinoco, R.	174	5 45N	67 40W
Orion	153	49 28N	110 49W
Oriskany	162	43 9N	75 20W
Orissa□	96	21 0N	85 0E
Oristano	64	39 54N	8 35E
Oristano, Golfo di	64	39 50N	8 22E
Orizaba	165	18 50N	97 10W
Orizare	67	42 44N	27 39E
Orizona	171	17 3S	48 18W
Ørje	71	59 29N	11 39E
Orjen, mt.	66	42 35N	18 34E
Orjiva	59	36 53N	3 24W
Orkanger	71	63 18N	9 52E
Orkelljunga	73	56 17N	13 17E
Örken, L.	73	57 11N	15 0E

Örkény Owen

Örkény 53 47 9N 19 26 E
Orkla 71 63 18N 9 51 E
Orkla, R. 74 63 18N 9 51 E
Orkney 128 26 42 S 26 40 E
Orkney □ 37 59 0N 3 0W
Orkney Is. 37 59 0N 3 0W
Orland 160 39 46N 122 12W
Orlando 157 28 30N 81 25W
Orlando, C.d' 65 38 10N 14 43 E
Orléanais 43 48 0N 2 0 E
Orléans 43 47 54N 1 52 E
Orleans, I. d' 156 46 54N 70 58W
Orlice, R. 52 50 5N 16 10 E
Orlické Hory 53 50 15N 16 30 E
Orlov 53 49 17N 20 51 E
Orlov Gay 81 51 4N 48 19 E
Orlovat 66 45 14N 20 33 E
Ormara 93 25 16N 64 33 E
Ormea 62 44 9N 7 54 E
Ormesby St. Margaret 29 52 39N 1 42 E
Ormília 68 40 16N 23 33 E
Ormoc 103 11 0N 124 37 E
Ormond, N.Z. 142 38 33 S 177 56 E
Ormond, U.S.A. 157 29 13N 81 5W
Ormondville 142 40 5 S 176 19 E
Ormoz 63 46 25N 16 10 E
Ormskirk 32 53 35N 2 53W
Ornans 43 47 7N 6 10 E
Orne □ 42 48 40N 0 0 E
Orneta 54 54 8N 20 9 E
Ørnhøj 73 56 13N 8 34 E
Ornö 72 59 4N 18 24 E
Örnsköldsvik 72 63 17N 18 40 E
Oro Grande 163 34 36N 117 20W
Oro, R. 164 26 8N 105 58W
Orocué 174 4 48N 71 20W
Orodo 121 5 34N 7 4 E
Orogrande 161 32 20N 106 4W
Orol 56 43 34N 7 39W
Oromocto 151 45 54N 66 29W
Oron, Israel 90 30 55N 35 1 E
Oron, Nigeria 121 4 48N 8 14 E
Oron, Switz. 50 46 34N 6 50 E
Oron, R. 77 69 21N 95 43 E
Oronsay I. 34 56 0N 6 14W
Oronsay, Pass of 34 56 0N 6 10W
Oropesa 56 39 57N 5 10W
Oroquieta 103 8 32N 123 44 E
Orori 107 40 1N 127 27 E
Orós 170 6 15 S 38 55W
Orosei, G. di 64 40 15N 9 40 E
Orosháza 53 46 32N 20 42 E
Orotukan 77 62 16N 151 42 E
Oroville, Calif., U.S.A. 160 39 31N 121 30W
Oroville, Wash., U.S.A. 160 48 58N 119 30W
Orowia 143 46 1 S 167 50 E
Orphir 37 58 56N 3 8W
Orrefors 73 56 50N 15 45 E
Orroroo 140 32 43 S 138 38 E
Orsa 72 61 7N 14 37 E
Orsara di Puglia 65 41 17N 15 16 E
Orsasjön 72 61 7N 14 37 E
Orsha 80 54 30N 30 25 E
Orsières 50 46 2N 7 9 E
Orsk 84 51 12N 58 34 E
Ørslev 73 55 23N 11 56 E
Orsogna 63 42 13N 14 17 E
Orşova 70 44 41N 22 25 E
Ørsted 73 56 30N 10 20 E
Orta, L. d' 62 45 48N 8 21 E
Orta Nova 65 41 20N 15 40 E
Orte 63 42 28N 12 23 E
Ortegal, C. 56 43 43N 7 52W
Orthez 44 43 29N 0 48W
Ortho 47 50 8N 5 37 E
Ortigueira 56 43 40N 7 50W
Ortles, mt. 62 46 31N 10 33 E
Orto, Tokay 85 42 20N 76 1 E
Ortón, R. 174 10 50 S 67 0W
Orton Tebay 32 54 28N 2 35W
Ortona 63 42 21N 14 24 E
Orune 64 40 25N 9 20 E
Oruro 174 18 0 S 67 19W
Orust 73 58 10N 11 40 E
Orūştie 70 45 50N 23 10 E
Oruzgan 94 32 30N 66 35 E
Orvault 42 47 17N 1 38 E
Orvieto 63 42 43N 12 8 E
Orwell 162 43 35N 75 60W
Orwell, R. 29 52 2N 1 12 E
Orwigsburg 162 40 38N 76 6W
Oryakhovo 66 43 40N 23 57 E
Orzinuovi 62 45 24N 9 55 E
Orzysz 54 53 50N 21 58 E
Os 71 60 9N 5 30 E
Osa 84 57 17N 55 26 E
Osa, Pen. de 166 8 0N 84 0W
Osage, Iowa, U.S.A. 158 43 15N 92 50W
Osage, Wyo., U.S.A. 158 43 59N 104 25W
Osage City 158 38 43N 95 51W
Osage, R. 158 38 15N 92 30W
Osaka 111 34 30N 135 30 E
Osaka-fu □ 111 34 40N 135 30 E
Osaka-Wan 111 34 30N 135 18 E
Osan 107 37 11N 127 4 E
Osawatomie 158 38 30N 94 55W
Osborne 158 39 30N 98 45W
Osby 73 56 23N 13 59 E
Osceola, Ark., U.S.A. 159 35 40N 90 0W
Osceola, Iowa, U.S.A. 158 41 0N 93 20W
Oschatz 48 51 17N 13 8 E
Oschersleben 48 52 2N 11 13 E
Oschiri 64 40 43N 9 7 E
Osečina 66 44 23N 19 34 E
Ösel = Saaremaa 80 58 30N 22 30W
Osenovka 66 70 40N 120 50 E
Osëry 81 54 52N 38 28 E
Osh 85 40 37N 72 49 E
Oshan 108 24 11N 102 24 E
Oshawa 150 43 50N 78 45W
Oshikango 128 17 9 S 16 10 E
Oshima 110 33 11N 132 24 E
Oshkosh, Nebr., U.S.A. 156 41 27N 102 20W
Oshkosh, Wis., U.S.A. 156 44 3N 88 35W
Oshmyany 80 54 26N 25 58 E
Oshogbo 121 7 48N 4 37 E
Oshwe 124 3 25 S 19 28 E
Osica de Jos 70 44 14N 24 20 E
Osieczna 54 51 55N 16 40 E
Osijek 66 45 34N 18 41 E
Osilo 64 40 45N 8 41 E
Osimo 63 43 40N 13 30 E
Osintorf 80 54 34N 30 31 E
Osipovichi 80 53 25N 28 33 E
Oskaloosa 158 41 18N 92 40W
Oskarshamn 73 57 15N 16 27 E
Oskelaneo 150 48 5N 75 15W
Oskol, R. 81 50 20N 38 0 E
Oslo 71 59 55N 10 45 E
Oslob 103 9 31N 123 26 E
Oslofjorden 71 59 20N 10 35 E
Osmanabad 96 18 5N 76 10 E
Osmancık 82 40 45N 34 47 E
Osmand Ra. 136 17 10 S 128 45 E
Osmaniye 92 37 5N 36 10 E
Osmo 72 58 58N 17 55 E
Osmotherley 33 54 22N 1 18W
Osnabrück 48 52 16N 8 2 E
Osobláha 53 50 17N 17 44 E
Osolo 71 59 53N 10 52 E
Osona 128 22 3 S 16 59 E
Osorio 173 29 53 S 50 17W
Osorno, Chile 176 40 25 S 73 0W
Osorno, Spain 56 42 24N 4 22W
Osorno, Vol. 176 41 0N 72 30W
Osoyoos 152 49 0N 119 30W
Ospika, R. 152 56 20N 124 0W
Osprey Reef 138 13 52 S 146 36 E
Oss 46 51 46N 5 32 E
Ossa de Montiel 59 38 58N 2 45W
Ossa, Mt. 138 41 52 S 146 3 E
Ossa, Oros 68 39 47N 22 42 E
Ossabaw I. 157 31 45N 81 8W
Ossendrecht 47 51 24N 4 20 E
Ossett 33 53 40N 1 35W
Ossining 162 41 9N 73 50W
Ossipee 162 43 41N 71 9W
Osśno Lubuskie 54 52 28N 14 51 E
Ossokmanuan L. 151 53 25N 65 0W
Ossora 77 59 20N 163 13 E
Osświecim 54 50 2N 19 11 E
Ostashkov 80 57 4N 33 2 E
Oste, R. 48 53 30N 9 12 E
Ostend = Oostende 47 51 15N 2 50 E
Oster 80 50 57N 30 46 E
Österburg 48 52 47N 11 44 E
Österby 72 60 13N 17 55 E
Österbymo 73 57 49N 15 15 E
Österdalälven 72 61 30N 13 45 E
Östergötlands Län □ 73 58 35N 15 45 E
Osterholz-Scharmbeck 48 53 14N 8 48 E
Østerild 73 57 3N 8 50 E
Østerild 73 57 2N 8 51 E
Österkorsberga 73 57 18N 15 6 E
Ostermundigen 50 46 58N 7 30 E
Østerøya 71 60 32N 5 30 E
Östersund 72 63 10N 14 38 E
Østfold fylke □ 71 59 25N 11 25 E
Ostfriesische Inseln 48 53 45N 7 15 E
Ostia Lido (Lido di Roma) 64 41 43N 12 17 E
Ostiglía 63 45 4N 11 9 E
Ostrava 53 49 51N 18 18 E
Ostrgrog 54 52 37N 16 33 E
Ostróda 54 53 42N 19 58 E
Ostrog 80 50 20N 26 30 E
Ostrogozhsk 81 50 55N 39 7 E
Ostrołeka 54 53 4N 21 38 E
Ostrołeka □ 54 53 0N 21 30 E
Ostrov, Bulg. 67 43 40N 24 9 E
Ostrov, Rumania 70 44 6N 27 24 E
Ostrov, U.S.S.R. 80 57 25N 28 20 E
Ostrów Mazowiecka 54 52 50N 21 51 E
Ostrów Wielkopolski 54 51 36N 17 44 E
Ostrowiec-Swietokrzyski 54 50 55N 21 22 E
Ostrozac 66 43 43N 17 49 E
Ostrzeszów 54 51 25N 17 52 E
Ostseebad-Kühlungsborn 48 54 10N 11 40 E
Östsinni 71 60 53N 10 3 E
Ostuni 65 40 44N 17 34 E
Osum, R. 67 43 35N 25 0 E
Osumi-Hanto 110 31 20N 130 55 E
Osumi-Kaikyō 112 30 55N 130 50 E
Osumi, R. 68 40 40N 20 10 E
Osumi-Shoto 112 30 30N 130 40 E
Osuna 57 37 14N 5 8W
Oswaldtwistle 32 53 44N 2 27W
Oswego 162 43 29N 76 30W
Oswestry 28 52 52N 3 3W
Ota, Japan 111 35 11N 136 38 E
Ota, Japan 111 36 18N 139 22 E
Ota-Gawa 110 34 21N 132 18 E
Otago □ 143 45 20 S 169 20 E
Otago Harb. 143 45 47 S 170 42 E
Otago Pen. 143 45 48 S 170 45 E
Otahuhu 142 36 56 S 174 51 E
Otake 110 34 12N 132 13 E
Otaki, Japan 111 35 17N 140 15 E
Otaki, N.Z. 142 40 45 S 175 10 E
Otane 142 39 54 S 176 39 E
Otar 85 43 32N 75 12 E
Otaru 112 43 10N 141 0 E
Otaru-Wan 112 43 25N 141 1 E
Otautau 143 46 9 S 168 1 E
Otava, R. 52 49 16N 13 32 E
Otavalo 174 0 20N 78 20W
Otavi 128 19 40 S 17 24 E
Otchinjau 128 16 30 S 13 56 E
Otelec 66 45 36N 20 50 E
Otero de Rey 56 43 6N 7 36W
Othello 160 46 53N 119 8W
Othonoí, I. 68 39 52N 19 22 E
Othris, Mt. 69 39 4N 22 42 E
Otira 143 42 49 S 171 35 E
Otira Gorge 143 42 53 S 171 33 E
Otis 158 40 12N 102 58W
Otjiwarongo 128 20 30 S 16 33 E
Otley 33 53 54N 1 41W
Otmuchow 54 50 28N 17 10 E
Otočac 63 44 53N 15 12 E
Otoineppu 112 44 44N 142 16 E
Otorohanga 142 38 12 S 175 14 E
Otoskwin, R. 150 52 13N 88 6W
Otosquen 153 53 17N 102 1W
Otoyo 110 33 43N 133 45 E
Otra 71 58 8N 8 1 E
Otranto 65 40 9N 18 28 E
Otranto, C.d' 65 40 7N 18 30 E
Otranto, Str. of 65 40 15N 18 40 E
Otrøy 71 62 43N 6 50 E
Otsuki 111 35 36N 138 57 E
Otta 71 61 46N 9 32 E
Ottapalam 97 10 46N 76 23 E
Ottawa, Can. 150 45 27N 75 42W
Ottawa, Ill., U.S.A. 156 41 20N 88 55W
Ottawa, Kans., U.S.A. 158 38 40N 95 10W
Ottawa Is. 149 59 35N 80 16W
Ottawa, R. 150 47 45N 78 35W
Ottélé 121 3 38N 11 19 E
Ottenby 73 56 15N 16 24 E
Otter L. 153 55 35N 104 39W
Otter R. 30 50 47N 3 12W
Otter Rapids, Ont., Can. 150 50 11N 81 39W
Otter Rapids, Sask., Can. 153 55 38N 104 44W
Otterburn 35 55 14N 2 12W
Otterndorf 48 53 47N 8 52 E
Otteröy, I. 71 62 45N 6 50 E
Ottersheim 52 48 21N 14 12 E
Otterup 73 55 30N 10 22 E
Ottery St. Mary 30 50 45N 3 16W
Ottignies 47 50 40N 4 33 E
Otto Beit Bridge 127 15 59 S 28 56 E
Ottosdal 128 26 46 S 25 59 E
Ottoshoop 128 25 45 S 26 58 E
Ottsjö 72 63 13N 13 2 E
Ottter Ferry 34 56 1N 5 20W
Ottumwa 158 41 0N 92 25W
Otu 121 8 14N 3 22 E
Otukpa (Al Owuho) 121 7 9N 7 41 E
Oturkpo 121 7 10N 8 15 E
Otway, Bahía 176 53 30 S 74 0W
Otway, C. 140 38 52 S 143 30 E
Otwock 54 52 5N 21 20 E
Ötz 52 47 13N 10 53 E
Ötz, Fl. 52 47 13N 10 53 E
Ötz, R. 52 47 14N 10 50 E
Ötztaler Alpen 52 46 58N 11 0 E
Ou, Neua 100 22 18N 101 48 E
Ou, R. 100 20 4N 102 13 E
Ouachita Mts. 159 34 50N 94 30W
Ouachita, R. 159 33 0N 92 15W
Ouadane 116 20 50N 11 40W
Ouadda 117 8 15N 22 20 E
Ouagadougou 121 12 25N 1 30W
Ouahigouya 120 13 40N 2 25W
Ouahila 118 27 50N 5 0W
Ouahran = Oran 118 35 37N 0 39W
Oualâta 121 17 20N 6 55W
Ouallene 118 24 41N 1 11 E
Ouanda Djallé 117 8 55N 22 53 E
Ouango 124 4 19N 22 30 E
Ouargla 119 31 59N 5 25 E
Ouarkziz, Djebel 118 28 50N 8 0W
Ouarzazate 118 30 55N 6 55W
Ouatagouna 121 15 11N 0 43 E
Oubangi, R. 124 1 0N 17 50 E
Oubarakai, O. 119 27 20N 9 0 E
Ouche, R. 43 47 11N 5 10 E
Oud-Gastel 47 51 35N 4 28 E
Oud Turnhout 47 51 19N 5 0 E
Ouddorp 46 51 50N 3 57 E
Oude-Pekela 46 53 6N 7 0 E
Oude Rijn, R. 46 52 12N 4 24 E
Oudega 46 53 8N 6 0 E
Oudenaarde 47 50 50N 3 37 E
Oudenbosch 47 51 35N 4 32 E
Oudenburg 47 51 11N 3 1 E
Ouderkerk, Holl. Mérid., Neth. 46 51 56N 4 38 E
Ouderkerk, Utrecht, Neth. 46 52 18N 4 55 E
Oudeschild 46 53 2N 4 50 E
Oudewater 46 52 2N 4 52 E
Oudkarspel 46 52 43N 4 49 E
Oudon 42 47 22N 1 19W
Oudon, R. 42 47 47N 1 2W
Oudtshoorn 128 33 35 S 22 14 E
Oued Sbita 118 25 50N 5 2W
Ouellé 120 7 26N 4 1W
Ouessa 120 11 4N 2 47W
Ouessant, Île d' 42 48 28N 5 6W
Ouesso 124 1 37N 16 5 E
Ouezzane 118 34 51N 5 42W
Ouffet 47 50 26N 5 28 E
Oughter L. 38 54 2N 7 30W
Oughterard 38 53 26N 9 20W
Ougrée 47 50 36N 5 32 E
Ouidah 121 6 25N 2 0 E
Ouimet 150 48 43N 88 35W
Ouistreham 42 49 17N 0 18W
Ouj, R. 118 51 15N 29 45 E
Oujda □ 118 33 18N 1 25W
Oujeft 116 20 2N 13 0W
Oulad Naïl, Mts. des 118 34 30N 3 30 E
Ouled Djellal 119 34 28N 5 2 E
Oulmès 118 33 17N 6 0W
Oulton 29 52 29N 1 40 E
Oulton Broad 29 52 28N 1 43 E
Oulu 74 65 1N 25 29 E
Oulu □ 74 65 10N 27 20 E
Oulujärvi 74 64 25N 27 0 E
Oulujoki 74 64 45N 26 30 E
Oulun Lääni □ 74 64 36N 27 20 E
Oulx 62 45 2N 6 49 E
Oum el Bouaghi 119 35 55N 7 6 E
Oum el Ksi 118 29 4N 6 59W
Oum-er-Rbia 118 32 30N 6 30W
Oum-er-Rbia, O. 118 32 30N 6 30W
Oumè 120 5 21N 5 27W
Ounane, Dj. 119 25 4N 7 10 E
Ounasjoki 74 66 31N 25 44 E
Oundle 29 52 28N 0 28W
Ounguati 128 21 54 S 15 46 E
Ounianga Kébir 117 19 4N 20 29 E
Ounlivou 121 7 20N 1 34 E
Our, R. 47 49 55N 6 5 E
Ouray 161 38 3N 107 48W
Oureg, Oued el 118 32 34N 2 10 E
Ourém 170 1 33 S 47 6W
Ouricuri 170 7 53 S 40 5W
Ourinhos 173 23 0 S 49 54W
Ourini 117 16 7N 22 25 E
Ourique 57 37 38N 8 16W
Ouro Fino 173 22 16 S 46 25W
Ouro Prêto 173 20 20 S 43 30W
Ouro Sogui 120 15 36N 13 19W
Oursi 121 14 41N 0 27W
Ourthe, R. 47 50 29N 5 35 E
Ouse 138 42 25 S 146 42 E
Ouse, R., Sussex, U.K. 29 50 58N 0 3 E
Ouse, R., Yorks., U.K. 33 54 3N 0 7 E
Oust 44 42 52N 1 13 E
Oust, R. 42 48 8N 2 49W
Out Skerries, Is. 36 60 25N 0 50W
Outardes, R. 151 50 0N 69 4W
Outer Hebrides, Is. 36 57 30N 7 40W
Outer I. 151 51 10N 58 35W
Outes 56 42 52N 8 55W
Outjo 128 20 5 S 16 7 E
Outlook, Can. 153 51 30N 107 0W
Outlook, U.S.A. 158 48 53N 104 46W
Outreau 43 50 40N 1 36 E
Outwell 29 52 36N 0 14 E
Ouyen 140 35 1 S 142 22 E
Ouzouer-le-Marché 42 47 54N 1 32 E
Ovada 62 44 39N 8 40 E
Ovalle 172 30 33 S 71 18W
Ovamboland = Owambo 128 17 20 S 16 30 E
Ovar 56 40 51N 8 40W
Ovejas 174 9 32N 75 14W
Ovens 141 36 35 S 146 46 E
Over Flakkee, I. 47 51 45N 4 5 E
Over Wallop 28 51 9N 1 35W
Overbister 37 59 16N 2 33W
Overdinkel 46 52 14N 7 2 E
Overflakkee 46 51 44N 4 10 E
Overijse 47 50 47N 4 32 E
Overijssel 46 50 46N 4 32 E
Overijssel □ 46 52 25N 6 35 E
Overijsselsch Kanaal 46 52 31N 6 6 E
Överkalix 74 66 19N 22 50 E
Overpelt 47 51 12N 5 20 E
Overstand 29 52 55N 1 20W
Overton, Clwyd, U.K. 31 52 58N 2 56W
Overton, Hants, U.K. 28 51 14N 1 16W
Overton, U.S.A. 161 36 32N 114 31W
Övertorneå 74 66 23N 23 40 E
Overum 73 58 0N 16 20 E
Ovid, Colo., U.S.A. 158 41 0N 102 17W
Ovid, N.Y., U.S.A. 162 42 41N 76 49W
Ovidiopol 82 46 15N 30 30 E
Oviedo 56 43 25N 5 50W
Oviedo □ 56 43 20N 6 0W
Oviken 72 63 0N 14 23 E
Oviksfjällen 72 63 0N 13 49 E
Övör Hangay □ 106 45 0N 102 30 E
Ovoro 121 5 26N 7 16 E
Övre Sirdal 71 58 48N 6 43 E
Øvre Sirdal 71 58 48N 6 47 E
Ovruch 80 51 25N 28 45 E
Owaka 143 46 27 S 169 40 E
Owambo 128 17 20 S 16 30 E
Owasco L. 162 42 50N 76 31W
Owase 111 34 7N 136 5 E
Owatonna 158 44 3N 93 17W
Owego 162 42 6N 76 17W
Owel, L. 38 53 34N 7 24W
Owen 140 34 15 S 138 32 E

Owen Falls **Pang-Yang**

Owen Falls **126** 0 30N 33 5E
Owen Mt. **143** 41 35S 152 33E
Owen Sound **150** 44 35N 80 55W
Owen Stanley Range **135** 8 30S 147 0E
Owendo **124** 0 17N 9 30E
Oweniny R. **38** 54 13N 9 32W
Owenkillew R. **38** 54 44N 7 15W
Owens L. **163** 36 20N 118 0W
Owens, R. **163** 36 32N 117 59W
Owensboro **156** 37 40N 87 5W
Owensville **158** 38 20N 91 30W
Owerri **121** 5 29N 7 0E
Owhango **142** 39 51S 175 20E
Owl, R. **153** 57 51N 92 44W
Owo **121** 7 18N 5 30E
Owosso **156** 43 0N 84 10W
Owston Ferry **33** 53 28N 0 47W
Owyhee **160** 42 0N 116 3W
Owyhee, R. **160** 43 10N 117 37W
Owyhee Res. **160** 43 30N 117 30W
Ox Mts. **38** 54 6N 9 0W
Oxberg **72** 61 7N 14 11E
Oxelösund **73** 58 43N 17 15E
Oxford, N.Z. **143** 43 18S 172 11E
Oxford, U.K. **28** 51 45N 1 15W
Oxford, Mass., U.S.A. **162** 42 7N 71 52W
Oxford, Miss., U.S.A. **159** 34 22N 89 30W
Oxford, N.C., U.S.A. **157** 36 19N 78 36W
Oxford, N.Y., U.S.A. **162** 42 27N 75 36W
Oxford, Ohio, U.S.A. **156** 39 30N 84 40W
Oxford, Pa., U.S.A. **162** 39 47N 75 59W
Oxford □ **28** 51 45N 1 15W
Oxford L. **153** 54 51N 95 37W
Oxilíthos **69** 38 35N 24 7E
Oxley **140** 34 11S 144 6E
Oxley Cr. **108** 27 35S 153 0E
Oxnard **163** 34 10N 119 14W
Oya **102** 2 55N 111 55E
Oyabe **111** 36 47N 136 56E
Oyama **111** 36 18N 139 48E
Oyana **110** 32 32N 130 18E
Oyem **124** 1 42N 11 43E
Oyen **153** 51 22N 110 28W
Øyeren **71** 59 48N 11 14E
Öyeren **71** 59 50N 11 15E
Oykel Bridge **37** 57 58N 4 45W
Oykell, R. **37** 57 55N 4 26W
Oymyakon **77** 63 25N 143 10E
Oyo **121** 7 46N 3 56E
Oyo □ **121** 8 0N 3 30E
Oyonnax **45** 46 16N 5 40E
Oyster B. **138** 42 15S 148 5E
Øystese **71** 60 22N 6 9E
Øystese **71** 60 24N 6 12E
Oytal **85** 42 54N 73 17E
Ozamis (Mizamis) **103** 8 15N 123 50E
Ozark, Ala., U.S.A. **157** 31 29N 85 39W
Ozark, Ark., U.S.A. **159** 35 30N 93 50W
Ozark, Mo., U.S.A. **159** 37 0N 93 15W
Ozark Plateau **159** 37 20N 91 40W
Ozarks, L. of **158** 38 10N 93 0W
Ózd **53** 48 14N 20 15E
Ozerhinsk **80** 53 40N 27 7E
Ozërnyy **84** 51 8N 60 50E
Ozieri **64** 40 35N 9 0E
Ozimek **54** 50 41N 18 11E
Ozona **159** 30 43N 101 11W
Ozorków **54** 51 57N 19 16E
Ozren, Mt. **66** 43 55N 18 29E
Ozu **110** 33 30N 132 33E
Ozu Kumamoto **110** 32 52N 130 52E
Ozuluama **165** 21 40N 97 50W
Ozun **70** 45 47N 25 50E

P

Pa **120** 11 33N 3 19W
Pa-an **98** 16 45N 97 40E
Pa Mong Dam **100** 18 0N 102 22E
Pa Sak, R. **101** 15 30N 101 0E
Paal **47** 51 2N 5 10E
Paar, R. **49** 48 42N 11 27E
Paarl **128** 33 45S 18 56E
Paatsi, R. **74** 68 55N 29 0E
Paauilo **147** 20 3N 155 22W
Pab Hills **94** 26 30N 66 45E
Pabbay I. **36** 57 46N 7 12W
Pabbay, Sd. of **36** 57 45N 7 4W
Pabianice **54** 51 40N 19 20E
Pabna **98** 24 1N 89 18E
Pabo **126** 2 56N 32 3E
Pacajá, R. **170** 1 56S 50 50W
Pacajus **170** 4 10S 38 38W
Pacasmayo **174** 7 20S 79 35W
Pacaudière, La **43** 46 11N 3 52E
Paceco **64** 37 59N 12 32E
Pachhar **94** 24 40N 77 42E
Pachino **65** 36 43N 15 4E
Pacho **174** 5 8N 74 10W
Pachora **96** 20 38N 75 29E
Pachpadra **93** 25 58N 72 10E
Pachuca **165** 20 10N 98 40W
Pachung **108** 31 58N 106 40E
Pacific **152** 54 48N 128 28W
Pacific Grove **163** 36 38N 121 58W
Pacific Ocean **143** 10 0N 140 0W
Pacifica **163** 37 36N 122 30W
Packsaddle **140** 30 36S 141 58E
Pacoh **152** 53 0N 132 30W
Pacov **52** 49 27N 15 0E
Pacsa **53** 46 44N 17 2E
Pacuí, R. **171** 16 46S 45 1W
Pacy-sur-Eure **171** 49 1N 1 23E
Paczkow **54** 50 28N 17 0E
Padaido, Kepulauan **103** 1 5S 138 0E
Padalarang **103** 7 50S 107 30E
Padang **102** 1 0S 100 20E
Padang, I. **102** 1 0S 100 10E
Padangpanjang **102** 0 30S 100 20E
Padangsidimpuan **102** 1 30N 99 15E
Padatchuang **98** 19 41N 96 35E
Padborg **73** 54 49N 9 21E
Paddock Wood **29** 51 13N 0 24E
Paddockwood **153** 53 30N 105 30W
Paderborn **48** 51 42N 8 44E
Padesul **70** 45 40N 22 22E
Padiham **32** 53 48N 2 20W
Padina **70** 44 50N 27 8E
Padlei **153** 62 10N 97 5W
Padloping Island **149** 67 0N 63 0W
Padma, R. **98** 23 22N 90 32E
Padmanabhapuram **97** 8 16N 77 17E
Pádova **63** 45 24N 11 52E
Padra **94** 22 15N 73 7E
Padrauna **95** 26 54N 83 59E
Padre I. **159** 27 0N 97 20W
Padrón **56** 42 41N 8 39W
Padstow **32** 50 33N 4 57W
Padstow Bay **30** 50 35N 4 58W
Padua = Pádova **63** 45 24N 11 52E
Paducah, Ky., U.S.A. **156** 37 0N 88 40W
Paducah, Tex., U.S.A. **159** 34 3N 100 16W
Padul **57** 37 1N 3 38W
Padula **65** 40 20N 15 40E
Padwa **96** 18 27N 82 37E
Paekakariki **142** 40 59S 174 58E
Paektu-san **107** 42 0N 128 3E
Paengaroa **142** 37 49S 176 29E
Paengnyŏng Do **107** 37 57N 124 40E
Paeroa **142** 37 23S 175 41E
Paesana **62** 44 40N 7 18E
Pag **63** 44 27N 15 5E
Pag, I. **63** 44 50N 15 0E
Paga **121** 11 1N 1 8W
Pagadian **103** 7 55N 123 30E
Pagai Selatan, I. **102** 3 0S 100 15W
Pagai Utara, I. **102** 2 35S 100 0E
Pagalu, I. **114** 1 35S 3 35E
Pagaralam **102** 4 0S 103 17E
Pagastikós Kólpos **68** 39 15N 23 12E
Pagatan **102** 3 33S 115 59E
Page **158** 47 11N 97 37W
Paglieta **63** 42 10N 14 30E
Pagnau **123** 8 15N 34 7E
Pagny-sur-Moselle **43** 48 59N 6 2E
Pagosa Springs **161** 37 16N 107 4W
Pagwa River **150** 50 2N 85 14W
Pahala **147** 20 25N 156 0W
Pahang □ **101** 3 40N 102 20E
Pahang, R. **101** 3 30N 103 9E
Pahang, st. **101** 3 30N 103 9E
Pahiatua **142** 40 27S 175 50E
Pahoa **147** 19 30N 154 57W
Pahokee **157** 26 50N 80 30W
Pahrump **161** 36 15N 116 0W
Pahsien **106** 39 10N 116 20E
Pahsientung **107** 43 11N 120 57E
Pai **100** 19 19N 98 27E
Paia **147** 20 54N 156 22W
Paible **36** 57 35N 7 30W
Paich'eng **105** 45 40N 122 52E
Paich'i **109** 28 2N 111 18E
P'aichou **109** 30 12N 113 56E
Paicines **163** 36 44N 121 17W
Paide **80** 58 57N 25 31E
Paignton **30** 50 26N 3 33W
Paiho, China **109** 32 49N 110 3E
Paiho, Taiwan **109** 23 21N 120 25E
Paihok'ou **109** 31 46N 110 13E
Päijänne **75** 61 30N 25 30E
Pailin **101** 12 46N 102 36E
Pailolo Chan. **147** 21 5N 156 42W
Paimbœuf **42** 47 17N 2 0W
Paimboeuf **44** 47 17N 2 2W
Paimpol **42** 48 48N 3 4W
Painan **102** 1 15S 100 40E
Painesville **156** 41 42N 81 18W
Painiu **109** 32 51N 112 10E
Painscastle **31** 52 7N 3 13W
Painswick **28** 51 47N 2 11W
Paint I. **153** 55 28N 97 57W
Painted Desert **161** 36 40N 112 0W
Paintsville **156** 37 50N 82 50W
Paipa **174** 5 47N 73 7W
Paise **108** 23 55N 106 28E
Paisha **106** 34 23N 112 32E
Paisley, U.K. **34** 55 51N 4 27W
Paisley, U.S.A. **160** 42 43N 120 40W
Paita **174** 5 5S 81 0W
Paiva, R. **56** 40 50N 7 55W
Paiyin **105** 36 45N 104 4E
Paiyü **99** 31 12N 98 45E
Paiyunopo **106** 41 46N 109 58E
Pajares **56** 39 57N 1 48W
Pak Lay **100** 18 15N 101 27E
Pak Phanang **101** 8 21N 100 12E
Pak Sane **100** 18 22N 103 39E
Pak Song **100** 15 11N 106 14E
Pak Suong **100** 19 58N 102 15E
Pakala **97** 13 29N 79 8E
Pakanbaru **102** 0 30N 101 15E
Pakaraima, Sierra **174** 6 0N 60 0W
Pakemba **127** 13 3S 29 58E
Pakenham **141** 38 6S 145 30E
Pakhoi = Peihai **108** 21 30N 109 5E
Pakhtakor **85** 40 2N 65 46E
Pakistan ■ **93** 30 0N 70 0E
Pakistan, East = Bangladesh ■ **99** 24 0N 90 0E
Pakkading **100** 18 19N 103 59E
Paknam = Samut Prakan **100** 13 36N 100 36E
P'ako **105** 30 52N 81 19E
Pakokku **98** 21 30N 95 0E
Pakpattan **94** 30 25N 73 16E
Pakrac **66** 45 27N 17 12E
Paks **53** 46 38N 18 55E
Pakse **100** 15 5N 105 52E
Paksikori **107** 42 27N 130 31E
Paktya □ **93** 33 0N 69 15E
Pakwach **126** 2 28N 31 27E
Pal **93** 33 45N 79 33E
Pala, Chad **117** 9 25N 15 5E
Pala, U.S.A. **163** 33 22N 117 5W
Pala, Zaïre **126** 6 45S 29 30E
Palabek **126** 3 22N 32 33E
Palacious **159** 28 44N 96 12W
Palafrugell **58** 41 55N 3 10E
Palagiano **65** 40 35N 17 0E
Palagonía **65** 37 20N 14 43E
Palagruza **63** 42 24N 16 15E
Palaiókastron **69** 35 12N 26 18E
Palaiokhora **69** 35 16N 23 39E
Pálairos **69** 38 45N 20 51E
Palais, Le **42** 47 20N 3 10W
Palakol **96** 16 31N 81 46E
Palam **96** 19 0N 77 0E
Palamás **68** 39 26N 22 4E
Palamós **58** 41 50N 3 10E
Palampur **94** 32 10N 76 30E
Palana, Austral. **138** 39 45S 147 55E
Palana, U.S.S.R. **77** 59 10N 160 10E
Palanan **103** 17 8N 122 29E
Palandri **95** 33 42N 73 40E
Palanpur **94** 24 10N 72 25E
Palapye **128** 22 30S 27 7E
Palar, R. **97** 12 27N 80 13E
Palas **95** 35 4N 73 4E
Palatka **157** 29 40N 81 40W
Palau Is. **130** 7 30N 134 30E
Palauig **103** 15 26N 119 54E
Palauk **101** 13 10N 98 40E
Palavas **44** 43 32N 3 56E
Palawan, I. **102** 10 0N 119 0E
Palayancottai **97** 8 45N 77 45E
Palazzo San Gervásio **65** 40 53N 15 58E
Palazzolo Acreide **65** 37 4N 14 43E
Paldiski **80** 59 23N 24 9E
Pale **66** 43 50N 18 38E
Palel **98** 24 27N 94 2E
Paleleh **103** 1 10N 121 50E
Palembang **102** 3 0S 104 50E
Palencia **56** 42 1N 4 34W
Palencia □ **56** 42 31N 4 33W
Palermo, Colomb. **174** 2 54N 75 26W
Palermo, Italy **64** 38 8N 13 20E
Palermo, U.S.A. **160** 39 30N 121 37W
Palestine, Asia **90** 32 0N 35 0E
Palestine, U.S.A. **159** 31 42N 95 35W
Palestrina **64** 41 50N 12 52E
Paletwa **98** 21 30N 92 50E
Palghat **97** 10 46N 76 42E
Palgrave **29** 52 22N 1 7E
Palgrave, Mt. **136** 23 22S 115 58E
P'ali **105** 27 45N 89 10E
Pali **94** 25 50N 73 20E
Palik'un **105** 43 35N 92 51E
Palimé **121** 6 57N 0 37E
Palintaoch'i **107** 43 59N 119 20E
Palinuro, C. **65** 40 1N 15 14E
Palinyuch'i (Tapanshang) **107** 43 40N 118 20E
Palisade **158** 40 35N 101 10W
Paliseul **47** 49 54N 5 8E
Palitana **94** 21 32N 71 49E
Palizada **165** 18 18N 92 8W
Palizzi **65** 37 58N 15 59E
Palk Bay **97** 9 30N 79 30E
Palk Strait **97** 10 0N 80 0E
Palkonda **96** 18 36N 83 48E
Palkonda Ra. **97** 13 50N 79 20E
Pallasgreen **39** 52 35N 8 22W
Pallaskenry **39** 52 39N 8 53W
Pallasovka **81** 50 4N 47 0E
Palleru, R. **96** 17 30N 79 40E
Pallinup **137** 34 0S 117 55E
Pallisa **126** 1 12N 33 43E
Palliser Bay **142** 41 26S 175 5E
Palliser, C. **142** 41 37S 175 14E
Pallu **94** 28 59N 74 14E
Palm Beach **157** 26 46N 80 0W
Palm Desert **163** 33 43N 116 22W
Palm Is. **138** 18 40S 146 35E
Palm Springs **163** 33 51N 116 35W
Palma, Canary Is. **16** 28 40N 17 50W
Palma, Mozam. **127** 10 46S 40 29E
Palma, Spain **58** 39 33N 2 39E
Palma, Bahía de **59** 39 30N 2 39E
Palma del Río **57** 37 43N 5 17W
Palma di Montechiaro **64** 37 12N 13 46E
Palma, I. **116** 28 45N 17 50W
Palma, La, Panama **166** 8 15N 78 0W
Palma, La, Spain **57** 37 21N 6 38W
Palma, R. **171** 10 10N 71 50W
Palma Soriano **166** 20 15N 76 0W
Palmanova **63** 45 54N 13 18E
Palmares **170** 8 41S 35 36W
Palmarito **174** 7 37N 70 10W
Palmarola, I. **64** 40 57N 12 50E
Palmas **173** 26 29S 52 0W
Palmas, C. **120** 4 27N 7 46W
Palmas de Monte Alto **171** 14 16S 43 10W
Pálmas, G. di **64** 39 0N 8 30E
Palmdale **163** 34 36N 118 7W
Palmeira **171** 25 25S 50 0W
Palmeira dos Índios **170** 9 25S 36 37W
Palmeirais **170** 12 31S 41 34W
Palmeiras, R. **171** 12 22S 47 8W
Palmeirinhas, Pta. das **124** 9 2S 12 57E
Palmela **57** 38 32N 8 57W
Palmelo **171** 17 20S 48 27W
Palmer, Alaska, U.S.A. **147** 61 35N 149 10W
Palmer, Mass., U.S.A. **162** 42 9N 72 21W
Palmer Arch **13** 64 15S 65 0W
Palmer Lake **158** 39 10N 104 52W
Palmer Pen. **13** 73 0S 60 0W
Palmer, R., N. Terr., Austral. **138** 24 30S 133 0E
Palmer, R., Queens., Austral. **138** 16 5S 142 43E
Palmerston **142** 45 29S 170 43E
Palmerston, C. **133** 21 32S 149 29E
Palmerston North **143** 40 21S 175 39E
Palmerton **162** 40 47N 75 36W
Palmetto **157** 27 33N 82 33W
Palmi **65** 38 21N 15 51E
Palmira, Argent. **172** 32 59S 68 25W
Palmira, Colomb. **174** 3 32N 76 16W
Palmyra, Mo., U.S.A. **158** 39 45N 91 30W
Palmyra, N.J., U.S.A. **162** 40 0N 75 1W
Palmyra, Pa., U.S.A. **162** 40 18N 76 36W
Palmyra = Tadmor **92** 34 30N 37 55E
Palni **97** 10 30N 77 30E
Palni Hills **97** 10 14N 77 33E
Palo Alto **163** 37 25N 122 8W
Palo del Colle **65** 41 4N 16 43E
Paloe **103** 8 20S 121 43E
Paloma, La **172** 30 35S 71 0W
Palombara Sabina **63** 42 4N 12 45E
Palopo **103** 3 0S 120 16E
Palos, Cabo de **59** 37 38N 0 40W
Palos Verdes **163** 33 48N 118 23W
Palos Verdes, Pt. **163** 33 43N 118 26W
Palouse **160** 46 59N 117 5W
Palparara **138** 24 47S 141 22E
Pålsboda **73** 59 3N 15 22E
Palu, Indon. **103** 1 0S 119 59E
Palu, Turkey **92** 38 45N 40 0E
Paluan **103** 13 35N 120 29E
Palwal **94** 28 8N 77 19E
Pama, China **108** 24 9N 107 15E
Pama, Upp. Vol. **121** 11 19N 0 44E
Pamanukan **103** 6 16S 107 49E
Pamban I. **97** 9 24N 79 35E
Pamekasan **103** 7 10S 113 29E
Pameungpeuk **103** 7 38S 107 44E
Pamiench'eng **107** 43 13N 124 2E
Pamiers **44** 43 7N 1 39E
Pamir, R. **85** 37 1N 72 41E
Pamirs, Ra. **85** 37 40N 73 0E
Pamlico, R. **157** 35 25N 76 40W
Pamlico Sd. **157** 35 20N 76 0W
Pampa **159** 35 35N 100 58W
Pampa de las Salinas **172** 32 1S 66 58W
Pampa, La □ **172** 36 50S 66 0W
Pampanua **103** 4 22S 120 14E
Pamparato **62** 44 16N 7 54E
Pampas, Argent. **172** 34 0S 64 0W
Pampas, Peru **174** 12 20S 74 50W
Pamplona, Colomb. **174** 7 23N 72 39W
Pamplona, Spain **58** 42 48N 1 38W
Pampoenpoort **128** 31 3S 22 40E
Pamunkey, R. **162** 37 32N 76 50W
Pana **158** 39 25N 89 0W
Panaca **161** 37 51N 114 50W
Panagyurishte **67** 42 49N 24 15E
Panaitan, I. **103** 6 35S 105 10E
Panaji (Panjim) **97** 15 25N 73 50E
Panamá **166** 9 0N 79 25W
Panama ■ **166** 8 48N 79 55W
Panama Canal **166** 9 10N 79 56W
Panama Canal Zone **166** 9 10N 79 56W
Panama City **157** 30 10N 85 41W
Panamá, Golfo de **166** 8 4N 79 20W
Panamint Mts. **161** 36 15N 117 20W
Panamint Springs **163** 36 20N 117 28W
Panão **174** 9 55S 75 55W
Panare **101** 6 51N 101 30E
Panarea, I. **65** 38 38N 15 3E
Panaro, R. **62** 44 48N 11 5E
Panarukan **103** 7 40S 113 52E
Panay, G. **103** 11 0N 122 30E
Panay I. **103** 11 10N 122 30E
Pancake Ra. **161** 38 30N 116 0W
Pančevo **66** 44 52N 20 41E
Panciu **70** 45 54N 27 8E
Pancorbo, Paso **58** 42 32N 3 5W
Pandan **103** 11 45N 122 10E
Pandangpanjang **102** 0 40S 100 20E
Pandeglang **103** 6 25S 106 0E
Pandharpur **96** 17 41N 75 20E
Pandhurna **96** 21 36N 78 35E
Pandilla **58** 41 32N 3 43W
Pando **173** 34 30S 56 0W
Pando, L. = Hope L. **139** 28 24S 139 18E
Panevėžys **80** 55 42N 24 25E
Panfilov **76** 44 30N 80 0E
Panfilovo **81** 50 25N 42 46E
Pang-Long **99** 23 11N 98 45E
Pang-Yang **99** 22 7N 98 48E

Panga Paulista

Panga 126 1 52N 26 18 E
Pangaion Óros 68 40 50N 24 0 E
Pangalanes, Canal des 129 22 48 S 47 50 E
Pangani 126 5 25 S 38 58 E
Pangani □ 126 5 25 S 39 0 E
Pangani, R. 126 4 40 S 37 50 E
Pangbourne 28 51 28N 1 5W
P'angchiang 106 42 50N 113 1 E
Pangfou 109 32 55N 117 25 E
Pangi 126 3 10 S 26 35 E
Pangkai 98 22 40N 97 31 E
Pangkalanberandan 102 4 1N 98 20 E
Pangkalansusu 102 4 2N 98 42 E
Pangkoh 102 3 5 S 114 8 E
Pangnirtung 149 66 0N 66 0W
Pangong Tso, L. 95 34 0N 78 20 E
Pangrango 103 6 46 S 107 1 E
Pangsau Pass 98 27 15N 96 10 E
Pangta 105 30 14N 97 24 E
Pangtara 98 20 57N 96 40 E
Panguitch 161 37 55N 112 30W
Pangutaran Group 103 6 18N 120 34 E
Panhandle 159 35 23N 101 23W
P'anhsien 108 25 46N 104 39 E
Pani Mines 94 22 29N 73 50 E
Panipat 94 29 25N 77 2 E
Panjal Range 94 32 30N 76 50 E
Panjgur 93 27 0N 64 5 E
Panjim = Panaji 93 15 25N 73 50 E
Panjinad Barrage 93 29 22N 71 15 E
Panjwai 94 31 26N 65 27 E
Pankadjene 103 4 46 S 119 34 E
Pankal Pinang 102 2 0 S 106 0 E
Pankshin 121 9 25N 9 25 E
P'anlung Chiang, R. 108 21 18N 105 25 E
Panmunjŏm 107 37 59N 126 38 E
Panna 95 24 40N 80 15 E
Panna Hills 95 24 40N 81 15 E
Pannuru 97 16 5N 80 34 E
Panorama 173 21 21 S 51 51W
Panruti 97 11 46N 79 35 E
P'anshan 107 41 12N 122 4 E
P'anshih 107 42 55N 126 3 E
Pant'anching 106 39 7N 103 52 E
Pantano 161 32 0N 110 32W
Pantar, I. 103 8 28 S 124 10 E
Pantelleria 64 36 52N 12 0 E
Pantelleria, I. 64 36 52N 12 0 E
Pantha 98 24 7N 94 17 E
Pantin Sakan 98 18 38N 97 33 E
Pantjo 103 8 42 S 118 40 E
Pantón 56 42 31N 7 37W
Pantukan 103 7 17N 125 58 E
Panuco 165 22 0N 98 25W
Panyam 121 9 27N 9 8 E
P'anyü 109 23 2N 113 20 E
Pão de AçIcar 171 9 45 S 37 26W
Paoan 109 22 32N 114 8 E
Paoch'eng 106 33 14N 106 56 E
Paochi 106 34 25N 107 11 E
Paochiatun 107 33 56N 120 12 E
Paoching 108 28 41N 109 35 E
Paok'ang 109 31 57N 111 20 E
Paokuot'u 107 42 20N 120 42 E
Páola 65 39 21N 16 2 E
Paola 158 38 36N 94 50W
Paonia 161 38 56N 107 37W
Paoshan, Shanghai, China 109 31 25N 121 29 E
Paoshan, Yunnan, China 105 25 7N 99 9 E
Paote 106 39 7N 111 13 E
Paoti 107 39 44N 117 18 E
Paoting 106 38 50N 115 30 E
Paot'ou 106 40 35N 110 3 E
Paoua 117 7 25N 16 30 E
Paoying 107 33 15N 119 20 E
Papá 53 47 22N 17 30 E
Papa Sd. 37 59 20N 2 56W
Papa, Sd. of 36 60 19N 1 40W
Papa Stour I. 36 60 20N 1 40W
Papa Stronsay I. 37 59 10N 2 37W
Papa Westray I. 37 59 20N 2 55W
Papagayo, Golfo de 166 10 4N 85 50W
Papagayo, R., Brazil 164 12 30 S 58 10W
Papagayo, R., Mexico 165 16 36N 99 43W
Papagni R. 97 14 10N 78 30 E
Papaikou 147 19 47N 155 6W
Papakura 142 37 4 S 174 59 E
Papaloapan, R. 164 18 2N 96 51W
Papantla 165 20 45N 97 21W
Papar 102 5 45N 116 0 E
Paparoa 142 36 6 S 174 16 E
Paparoa Range 143 42 5 S 171 35 E
Pápas, Ákra 69 38 13N 21 6 E
Papatoetoe 142 36 59 S 174 51 E
Papenburg 48 53 7N 7 25 E
Papien Chiang, R. (Da) 108 22 56N 101 47 E
Papigochic, R. 164 29 9N 109 40W
Paposo 172 25 0 S 70 30W
Paps, The, mts. 39 52 0N 9 15W
Papua, Gulf of 135 9 0 S 144 50 E
Papua New Guinea ■ 135 8 0 S 145 0 E
PapuCa 63 44 22N 15 30 E
Papudo 172 32 29 S 71 27W
Papuk, mts. 66 45 30N 17 30 E
Papun 98 18 0N 97 30 E
Pará = Belém 170 1 20 S 48 30W
Pará □ 175 3 20 S 52 0W
Parábita 65 40 3N 18 8 E
Paracatú 171 17 10 S 46 50W
Paracatu, R. 171 16 30 S 45 4W
Paracel Is. 102 16 49N 111 2 E
Parachilna 140 31 10 S 138 21 E
Parachinar 94 34 0N 70 5 E
Paracombe 109 34 51 S 138 47 E
Paracuru 170 3 24 S 39 4W
Paradas 57 37 18N 5 29W
Paradela 56 42 44N 7 37W
Paradip 95 20 15N 86 35 E
Paradise 160 47 27N 114 54W
Paradise, R. 151 53 27N 57 19W
Paradise Valley 160 41 30N 117 28W
Parado 103 8 42 S 118 30 E
Paradyz 54 51 19N 20 2 E
Parafield 109 34 47 S 138 38 E
Parafield Airport 109 34 48 S 138 38 E
Paragould 159 36 5N 90 30W
Paragua, La 174 6 50N 63 20W
Paragua, R. 174 6 30N 63 30W
Paraguaçu Paulista 173 22 22 S 50 35W
Paraguaçu, R. 171 12 45 S 38 54W
Paraguai, R. 174 16 0 S 57 52W
Paraguaipoa 174 11 21N 71 57W
Paraguana, Pen. de 174 12 0N 70 0W
Paraguarí 172 25 36 S 57 0W
Paraguarí □ 172 26 0 S 57 10W
Paraguay ■ 172 23 0 S 57 0W
Paraguay, R. 172 27 18 S 58 38W
Paraíba = Joéo Pessoa 164 7 10 S 35 0W
Paraíba □ 170 7 0 S 36 0W
Paraíba do Sul, R. 173 21 37 S 41 3W
Paraibano 171 6 30 S 44 1W
Parainen 75 60 18N 22 18 E
Paraiso 165 19 3 S 52 59W
Paraiso 165 18 24N 93 14W
Parakhino Paddubye 80 58 46N 33 10 E
Parakou 121 9 25N 2 40 E
Parakylia 140 30 24 S 136 25 E
Paralion-Astrous 69 37 25N 22 45 E
Paramagudi 97 9 31N 78 39 E
Paramaribo 175 5 50N 55 10W
Parambu 170 6 13 S 40 43W
Paramillo, Nudo del 174 7 4N 75 55W
Paramirim 171 13 26 S 42 15W
Paramirim, R. 171 11 34 S 43 18W
Paramithiá 68 39 30N 20 35 E
Paramushir, Ostrov 77 40 24N 156 0 E
Paran, N. 90 30 14N 34 48 E
Paraná 172 32 0 S 60 30W
Paranã 171 12 30 S 47 40W
Paraná □ 173 24 30 S 51 0W
Paraná, R. 172 33 43 S 59 15W
Paranã, R. 171 22 25 S 53 1W
Paranaguá 173 25 30 S 48 30W
Paranaíba, R. 171 18 0 S 49 12W
Paranapanema, R. 173 22 40 S 53 9W
Paranapiacaba, Serra do 173 24 31 S 48 35W
Paranavaí 173 23 4 S 52 28W
Parang, Jolo, Phil. 103 5 55N 120 54 E
Parang, Mindanao, Phil. 103 7 23N 124 16 E
Parangaba 170 3 45 S 38 33W
Paraóin 66 43 54N 21 27 E
Paraparanma 143 40 57 S 175 3 E
Parapóla, I. 69 36 55N 23 27 E
Paraspóri, Ákra 69 35 55N 27 15 E
Paratinga 171 12 40 S 43 10W
Paratoo 140 32 42 S 139 22 E
Parattah 138 42 22 S 147 23 E
Paraúna 171 17 2 S 50 26W
Paray-le-Monial 45 46 27N 4 7 E
Parbati, R. 94 25 51N 76 34 E
Parbatipur 98 25 39N 88 55 E
Parbhani 96 19 8N 76 52 E
Parchim 48 53 25N 11 50 E
Parczew 54 51 9N 22 52 E
Pardee Res. 163 38 16N 120 51W
Pardes Hanna 90 32 28N 34 57 E
Pardilla 56 41 33N 3 43W
Pardo, R., Bahia, Brazil 171 15 40 S 39 0W
Pardo, R., Mato Grosso, Brazil 171 21 0 S 53 25W
Pardo, R., Minas Gerais, Brazil 171 15 48 S 44 48W
Pardo, R., São Paulo, Brazil 171 20 45 S 48 0W
Pardubice 52 50 3N 15 45 E
Pare 103 7 43 S 112 12 E
Pare □ 126 4 10 S 38 0 E
Pare Mts. 126 4 0 S 37 45 E
Pare Pare 103 4 0 S 119 45 E
Parecis, Serra dos 174 13 0 S 60 0W
Paredes de Nava 56 42 9N 4 42W
Parelhas 170 6 41 S 36 39W
Paren 77 62 45N 163 0 E
Parengarenga Harbour 142 34 31 S 173 0 E
Parent 150 47 55N 74 35W
Parent, Lac. 150 48 31N 77 1W
Parentis-en-Born 44 44 21N 1 4W
Parepare 103 4 0 S 119 40 E
Parfino 80 57 59N 31 34 E
Parfuri 129 22 28 S 31 17 E
Paria, Golfo de 174 10 20N 62 0W
Paria, Pen. de 174 10 50N 62 30W
Pariaguán 174 8 51N 64 43W
Pariaman 102 0 47 S 100 11 E
Paricutín, Cerro 164 19 28N 102 15W
Parigi 103 0 50 S 120 5 E
Parika 174 6 50N 58 20W
Parima, Serra 174 2 30N 64 0W
Parinari 174 4 35 S 74 25W
Parincea 70 46 27N 27 9 E
Paring, mt. 70 45 20N 23 37 E
Parintins 175 2 40 S 56 50W
Pariparit Kyun 99 14 55 S 93 45 E
Paris, Can. 150 43 12N 80 25W
Paris, France 43 48 50N 2 20 E
Paris, Idaho, U.S.A. 160 42 13N 111 30W
Paris, Ky., U.S.A. 156 38 12N 84 12W
Paris, Tenn., U.S.A. 157 36 20N 88 20W
Paris, Tex., U.S.A. 159 33 40N 95 30W
Parish 162 43 24N 76 9W
Pariti 103 9 55 S 123 30 E
Park City 160 40 42N 111 35W
Park Falls 158 45 58N 90 27 E
Park Range 160 40 0N 106 30W
Park Rapids 158 46 56N 95 0W
Park River 158 48 25N 97 17W
Park Rynie 129 30 25 S 30 35 E
Park View 161 36 45N 106 37W
Parkent 85 41 18N 69 40 E
Parker, Ariz., U.S.A. 161 34 8N 114 16W
Parker, S.D., U.S.A. 158 43 25N 97 7W
Parker Dam 161 34 13N 114 5W
Parkersburg 156 39 18N 81 31W
Parkerview 153 51 21N 103 18W
Parkes, A.C.T., Austral. 133 35 18 S 149 8 E
Parkes, N.S.W., Austral. 141 33 9 S 148 11 E
Parkfield 163 35 54N 120 26W
Parkhar 85 37 30N 69 34 E
Parknasilla 39 51 49N 9 50W
Parkside 153 53 10N 106 33W
Parkston 158 43 25N 98 0W
Parksville 152 49 20N 124 21W
Parkville 162 39 23N 76 33W
Parlakimedi 96 18 45N 84 5 E
Parma, Italy 62 44 50N 10 20 E
Parma, U.S.A. 160 43 49N 116 59W
Parna, R. 62 44 27N 10 3 E
Parnaguá 170 10 10 S 44 10W
Parnaíba, Piauí, Brazil 170 3 0 S 41 40W
Parnaíba, São Paulo, Brazil 170 19 34 S 51 14W
Parnaíba, R. 170 3 35 S 43 0W
Parnamirim 170 8 5 S 39 34W
Parnarama 170 5 41 S 43 6W
Parnassós, mt. 69 38 17N 21 30 E
Parnassus 143 42 42 S 173 23 E
Párnis, mt. 69 38 14N 23 45 E
Párnon Óros 69 37 15N 22 45 E
Pärnu 80 58 12N 24 33 E
Parola 96 20 47N 75 7 E
Paroo Chan. 133 30 50 S 143 35 E
Paroo, R. 139 30 0 S 144 5 E
Paropamisus Range = Fīroz Kohi 93 34 45N 63 0 E
Páros 69 37 5N 25 9 E
Páros, I. 69 37 5N 25 12 E
Parowan 161 37 54N 112 56W
Parpaillon, mts. 45 44 30N 6 40 E
Parracombe 30 51 11N 3 55W
Parral 172 36 10 S 72 0W
Parramatta 141 33 48 S 151 1 E
Parramore I. 162 37 32N 75 39W
Parras 164 25 30N 102 20W
Parrett, R. 28 51 7N 2 58W
Parris I. 157 32 20N 80 30W
Parrsboro 151 45 30N 64 10W
Parry 153 49 47N 104 41W
Parry, C. 147 70 20N 123 38W
Parry Is. 12 77 0N 110 0W
Parry Sound 150 45 20N 80 0W
Parshall 158 47 56N 102 11W
Parsnip, R. 152 55 10N 123 2W
Parsons 159 37 20N 95 10W
Parsons Ra., Mts. 138 13 30 S 135 15 E
Partabpur 96 20 0N 80 42 E
Partanna 64 37 43N 12 51 E
Partapgarh 94 24 2N 74 40 E
Parthenay 42 46 38N 0 16W
Partille 73 57 48N 12 18 E
Partinico 64 38 3N 13 6 E
Partney 33 53 12N 0 7 E
Parton 32 54 34N 3 35W
Partry Mts. 38 53 40N 9 28W
Partur 96 19 40N 76 14 E
Paru, R. 175 0 20 S 53 30W
Parur 97 10 13N 76 14 E
Paruro 174 13 45 S 71 50W
Parvatipuram 96 18 50N 83 25 E
Parwan □ 93 35 0N 69 0 E
Påryd 73 56 34N 15 55 E
Parys 128 26 52 S 27 29 E
Parys, Mt. 31 53 23N 4 18W
Pas-de-Calais □ 43 50 30N 2 30 E
Pasadena, Calif., U.S.A. 163 34 5N 118 9W
Pasadena, Tex., U.S.A. 159 29 45N 95 14W
Pasaje 174 3 10 S 79 40W
Pasaje, R. 172 25 35 S 64 57W
Pascagoula 159 30 30N 88 30W
Pascagoula, R. 159 30 40N 88 35W
Paşcani 70 47 14N 26 45 E
Pasco 160 46 10N 119 0W
Pasco, Cerro de 174 10 45 S 76 10W
Pascoag 162 41 57N 71 42W
Pascoe, Mt. 137 27 25 S 120 40 E
Pasewalk 48 53 30N 14 0 E
Pasfield L. 153 58 24N 105 20W
Pasha, R. 80 60 20N 33 0 E
Pashiwari 95 34 40N 75 10 E
Pashiya 84 58 33N 58 26 E
Pashmakli = Smolyan 67 41 36N 24 38 E
Pasighat 98 28 4N 95 21 E
Pasir Mas 101 6 2N 102 8 E
Pasir Puteh 101 5 50N 102 24 E
Pasirian 103 8 13 S 113 8 E
Pasley, C. 137 33 52 S 123 35 E
Pasman I. 63 43 58N 15 20 E
Pasmore, R. 140 31 5 S 139 49 E
Pasni 93 25 15N 63 27 E
Paso de Indios 176 43 55 S 69 0W
Paso de los Libres 172 29 44 S 57 10W
Paso de los Toros 172 32 36 S 56 37W
Paso Robles 161 35 40N 120 45W
Paspebiac 151 48 3N 65 17W
Pasrur 94 32 16N 74 43 E
Passage East 39 52 15N 7 0W
Passage West 39 51 52N 8 20W
Passaic 162 40 50N 74 8W
Passau 49 48 34N 13 27 E
Passendale 47 50 54N 3 2 E
Passero, C. 65 36 42N 15 8 E
Passo Fundo 173 28 10 S 52 30W
Passos 171 20 45 S 46 37W
Passow 48 53 13N 14 3 E
Passwang 50 47 22N 7 41 E
Passy 43 45 55N 6 41 E
Pastaza, R. 174 2 45 S 76 50W
Pastek 54 54 3N 19 41 E
Pasto 174 1 13N 77 17W
Pasto Zootécnico do Cunene 128 16 20 S 15 20 E
Pastos Bons 170 6 36 S 44 5W
Pastrana 58 40 27N 2 53W
Pasuruan 103 7 40 S 112 53 E
Pasym 54 53 48N 20 49 E
Pásztó 53 47 52N 19 43 E
Patagonia, Argent. 176 45 0 S 69 0W
Patagonia, U.S.A. 161 31 35N 110 45W
Patan, India 93 23 54N 72 14 E
Patan, Gujarat, India 96 17 22N 73 48 E
Patan, Maharashtra, India 94 23 54N 72 14 E
Patan (Lalitapur) 99 27 40N 85 20 E
Pat'ang Szechwan 105 30 2N 98 58 E
Patani 103 0 20N 128 50 E
Pataohotzu 107 43 5N 127 33 E
Patapsco Res. 162 39 27N 76 55W
Pataudi 94 28 18N 76 48 E
Patay 43 48 2N 1 40 E
Patcham 29 50 52N 0 9W
Patchewollock 140 35 22 S 142 12 E
Patchogue 162 40 46N 73 1W
Patea 142 39 45 S 174 30 E
Pategi 121 8 50N 5 45 E
Pateley Bridge 33 54 5N 1 45W
Patensie 128 33 46 S 24 49 E
Paternò 65 37 34N 14 53 E
Paternoster, Kepulauan 102 7 5 S 118 15 E
Pateros 160 48 4N 119 58W
Paterson, Austral. 141 32 37 S 151 39 E
Paterson, U.S.A. 162 40 55N 74 10W
Paterson Inlet 143 46 56 S 168 12 E
Paterson Ra. 136 21 45 S 122 10 E
Paterswolde 46 53 9N 6 34 E
Pathankot 94 32 18N 75 45 E
Patharghata 98 22 2N 89 58 E
Pathfinder Res. 160 42 0N 107 0W
Pathiu 101 10 42N 99 19 E
Pathum Thani 100 14 1N 100 32 E
Páti 103 6 45 S 111 3 E
Patiala 94 30 23N 76 26 E
Patine Kouta 120 12 45N 13 45W
Patjitan 103 8 12 S 111 8 E
Patkai Bum 98 27 0N 95 30 E
Pátmos 69 37 21N 26 36 E
Pátmos, I. 69 37 21N 26 36 E
Patna, India 95 25 35N 85 18 E
Patna, U.K. 34 55 21N 4 30W
Patonga 126 2 45N 33 15 E
Patos 170 7 1 S 37 16W
Patos de Minas 171 18 35 S 46 32W
Patos, Lag. dos 173 31 20 S 51 0 E
Patosi 68 40 42N 19 38 E
Patquía 172 30 0 S 66 55W
Pátrai 69 38 14N 21 47 E
Pátraikos, Kólpos 69 38 17N 21 30 E
Patrick 32 54 13N 4 41W
Patrocínio 171 18 57 S 47 0W
Patta 126 2 10 S 41 0 E
Patta, I. 126 2 10 S 41 0 E
Pattada 64 40 35N 9 7 E
Pattanapuram 97 9 6N 76 33 E
Pattani 101 6 48N 101 15 E
Patten 151 45 59N 68 28W
Patterdale 32 54 33N 2 55W
Patterson, Calif., U.S.A. 163 37 30N 121 9W
Patterson, La., U.S.A. 159 29 44N 91 20W
Patterson, Mt. 163 38 29N 119 20W
Patti 94 31 17N 74 54 E
Patti Castroreale 65 38 8N 14 57 E
Pattoki 94 31 5N 73 52 E
Pattukkottai 97 10 25N 79 20 E
Patu 170 6 6 S 37 38W
Patuakhali 98 22 20N 90 25 E
Patuca, Punta 166 15 49N 84 14W
Patuca, R. 166 15 20N 84 40W
Patung 109 31 0N 110 30 E
Pâturages 47 50 25N 3 52 E
Patutahi 142 38 38 S 177 55 E
Pátzcuaro 164 19 30N 101 40W
Pau 44 43 19N 0 25W
Pau d'Arco 170 7 30 S 49 22W
Pau dos Ferros 170 6 7 S 38 10W
Pauillac 44 45 11N 0 46W
Pauini, R. 174 1 42 S 62 50W
Pauk 98 21 55N 94 30 E
Paul I. 151 56 30N 61 20W
Paulatuk 147 69 25N 124 0W
Paulhan 44 43 33N 3 28 E
Paulis = Isiro 126 2 53N 27 58 E
Paulista 170 7 57 S 34 53W

Paulistana Perryton

Paulistana 170 8 9S 41 9W
Paull 33 53 42N 0 12W
Paullina 158 42 55N 95 40W
Paulo Afonso 170 9 21S 38 15W
Paulo de Faria 171 20 2S 49 24W
Paulpietersburg 129 27 23S 30 50E
Paul's Valley 159 34 40N 97 17W
Pauma Valley 163 33 16N 116 58W
Paungde 98 18 29N 95 30E
Pauni 96 20 48N 79 40E
Pavelets 81 53 49N 39 14E
Pavia 62 45 10N 9 10E
Pavlikeni 67 43 14N 25 20E
Pavlodar 76 52 33N 77 0E
Pavlof Is. 147 55 30N 161 30W
Pavlograd 82 48 30N 35 52E
Pavlovo, Gorkiy, U.S.S.R. 81 55 58N 43 5E
Pavlovo, Yakut A.S.S.R., U.S.S.R. 77 63 5N 115 25E
Pavlovsk 81 50 26N 40 5E
Pavlovskaya 83 46 17N 39 47E
Pavlovskiy Posad 81 55 37N 38 42E
Pavullo nel Frignano 62 44 20N 10 50E
Pawahku 98 26 11N 98 40E
Pawhuska 159 36 40N 96 25W
Pawling 162 41 35N 73 37W
Pawnee 159 36 24N 96 50W
Pawnee City 158 40 8N 96 10W
Pawtucket 162 41 51N 71 22W
Paximádhia 69 35 0N 24 35E
Paxoi, I. 68 39 14N 20 12E
Paxton, Ill., U.S.A. 156 40 25N 88 0W
Paxton, Nebr., U.S.A. 158 41 12N 101 27W
Paya Bakri 101 2 3N 102 44E
Payakumbah 102 0 20S 100 35E
Payenhaot'e (Alashantsoch'i) 106 38 50N 105 32E
Payenk'ala Shan 105 34 20N 97 0E
Payerne 50 46 49N 6 56E
Payette 160 44 0N 117 0W
Paymogo 57 37 44N 7 21W
Payne L. 149 59 30N 74 30W
Payne, R. 149 60 0N 70 0W
Payneham 109 34 54S 138 39E
Paynes Find 137 29 15S 117 42E
Paynesville, Liberia 120 6 20N 10 45W
Paynesville, U.S.A. 158 45 21N 94 44W
Paysandú 172 32 19S 58 8W
Payson, Ariz., U.S.A. 161 34 17N 111 15W
Payson, Utah, U.S.A. 160 40 8N 111 41W
Paz, Bahía de la 164 24 15N 110 25W
Paz Centro, La 166 12 20N 86 41W
Paz, La, Entre Ríos, Argent. 172 30 50S 59 45W
Paz, La, San Luis, Argent. 172 33 30S 67 20W
Paz, La, Boliv. 174 16 20S 68 10W
Paz, La, Hond. 166 14 20N 87 47W
Paz, La, Mexico 164 24 10N 110 20W
Paz, La, Bahía de 164 24 20N 110 40W
Paz, R. 166 13 44N 90 10W
Pazar 92 41 10N 40 50E
Pazardzhik 67 42 12N 24 20E
Pazin 63 45 14N 13 56E
Pčinja, R. 66 42 0N 21 45E
Pe Ell 160 46 30N 123 18W
Peabody 162 42 31N 70 56W
Peace Point 152 59 7N 112 27W
Peace, R. 152 59 0N 111 25W
Peace River 152 56 15N 117 18W
Peace River Res. 152 55 40N 123 40W
Peacehaven 29 50 47N 0 1E
Peach Springs 161 35 36N 113 30W
Peak Downs 138 22 55S 148 0E
Peak Downs Mine 138 22 17S 148 11E
Peak Hill, N.S.W., Austral. 141 32 39S 148 11E
Peak Hill, W. A., Austral. 137 25 35S 118 43E
Peak Range 138 22 50S 148 20E
Peak, The 32 53 24N 1 53W
Peake 140 35 25S 140 0E
Peake Cr. 139 28 2S 136 7E
Peale Mt. 161 38 25N 109 12W
Pearblossom 163 34 30N 117 55W
Pearce 161 31 57N 109 56W
Pearl Banks 97 8 45N 79 45E
Pearl City 147 2 21N 158 0W
Pearl Harbor 147 21 20N 158 0W
Pearl, R. 159 31 50N 90 0W
Pearsall 159 28 55N 99 8W
Pearse I. 152 54 52N 130 14W
Peary Land 12 82 40N 33 0W
Pease, R. 159 34 18N 100 15W
Peasenhall 29 52 17N 1 24E
Pebane 127 17 10S 38 8E
Pebas 174 3 10S 71 55W
Pebble Beach 163 36 34N 121 57W
Peçanha 171 18 33S 42 34W
Péccioli 62 43 32N 10 43E
Pechea 70 45 36N 27 49E
Pechenezhin 82 48 30N 24 48E
Pechenga 78 69 30N 31 25E
Pechnezhskoye Vdkhr. 81 50 0N 36 50E
Pechora, R. 78 62 30N 56 30E
Pechorskaya Guba 78 68 40N 54 0E
Pechory 80 57 48N 27 40E
Pecica 66 46 10N 21 3E
Pečka 66 44 18N 19 33E
Pécora, C. 64 39 28N 8 23E
Pecos 159 31 25N 103 35W
Pecos, R. 159 31 22N 102 30W
Pecqueuse 47 48 39N 2 3E
Pécs 53 46 5N 18 15E
Pedasí 166 7 32N 80 3W
Peddapalli 96 18 40N 79 24E
Peddapuram 96 17 6N 82 5E
Peddavagu, R. 96 16 33N 79 8E
Pedder, L. 138 42 55S 146 10E
Pedernales 167 18 2N 71 44W
Pedirka 139 26 40S 135 14E
Pedjantan, I. 102 0 5S 106 15E
Pedra Azul 171 16 2S 41 17W
Pedra Grande, Recifes do 171 17 45S 38 58W
Pedras, Pta. de 171 7 38S 34 47W
Pedreiras 170 4 32S 44 40W
Pedrera, La 174 1 18S 69 43W
Pedro Afonso 170 9 0S 48 10W
Pedro Antonio Santos 165 18 54N 88 15W
Pedro Cays 166 17 5N 77 48W
Pedro Chico 174 1 4N 70 25W
Pedro de Valdivia 172 22 33S 69 38W
Pedro Juan Caballero 173 22 30S 55 40W
Pedro Muñoz 59 39 25N 2 56W
Pedrógão Grande 56 39 55N 8 0W
Peebinga 140 34 52S 140 57E
Peebles 35 55 40N 3 12W
Peebles (□) 26 55 37N 3 4W
Peekshill 162 41 18N 73 57W
Peel, Austral. 139 33 20S 149 38E
Peel, I. of Man 32 54 14N 4 40W
Peel Fell, mt. 35 55 17N 2 35W
Peel, R., Austral. 141 30 50S 150 29E
Peel, R., Can. 147 67 0N 135 0W
Peelwood 141 34 7S 149 27E
Peene, R. 48 53 53N 13 53E
Peera Peera Poolanna L. 139 26 30S 138 0E
Peers 152 53 40N 116 0W
Pegasus Bay 143 43 20S 173 10E
Peggau 52 47 12N 15 21E
Pego 59 38 51N 0 8W
Pegswood 35 55 12N 1 38W
Pegu 99 17 20N 96 29E
Pegu Yoma, mts. 98 19 0N 96 0E
Pegwell Bay 29 51 18N 1 22E
Pehčevo 66 41 41N 22 55E
Pehuajó 172 36 0S 62 0W
Pei Chiang, R. 109 23 12N 112 45E
Pei Wan 107 36 25N 120 45E
Peian 105 48 16N 126 36E
Peichen 107 41 38N 121 50E
Peichengchen 107 44 30N 123 27E
Peichiang 109 23 0N 120 0E
Peihai 108 21 30N 109 5E
P'eihsien, Kiangsu, China 106 34 44N 116 55E
P'eihsien, Kiangsu, China 107 34 20N 117 57E
Peiliu 109 22 45N 110 20E
Peine, Chile 172 23 45S 68 8W
Peine, Ger. 48 52 19N 10 12E
Peip'an Chiang, R. 108 25 0N 106 11E
Peip'ei 105 29 49N 106 27E
Peip'iao 107 41 48N 120 44E
Peip'ing 106 39 45N 116 25E
Peissenberg 49 47 48N 11 4E
Peitz 48 51 50N 14 23E
Peixe 171 12 0S 48 40W
Peixe, R. 171 21 31S 51 58W
Peize 46 53 9N 6 30E
Pek, R. 66 44 58N 21 55E
Pekalongan 103 6 53S 109 40E
Pekan 101 3 30N 103 25E
Pekin 158 40 35N 89 40W
Peking = Peip'ing 106 39 45N 116 25E
Pelabuhan Ratu, Teluk 103 7 5S 106 30E
Pelabuhanratu 103 7 0S 106 32E
Pélagos, I. 68 39 17N 24 4E
Pelagruza, Is. 63 42 24N 16 15E
Pelaihari 102 3 55S 114 45E
Pełczyce 54 53 3N 15 16E
Peleaga, mt. 70 45 22N 22 55E
Pelee I. 150 41 47N 82 40W
Pelée, Mt. 167 14 40N 61 0W
Pelee, Pt. 150 41 54N 82 31W
Pelekech, mt. 126 3 52N 35 8E
Peleng, I. 103 1 20S 123 30E
Pelham 157 31 5N 84 6W
Pelhrimov 52 49 24N 15 12E
Pelican 147 58 12N 136 28W
Pelican L. 153 52 28N 100 20W
Pelican Narrows 153 55 10N 102 56W
Pelican Portage 152 55 51N 113 0W
Pelican Rapids 153 52 45N 100 42W
Peligre, L. de 167 19 1N 71 58W
Pelkosenniemi 74 67 6N 27 28E
Pella 158 41 20N 93 0W
Pélla □ 68 40 52N 22 0E
Péllaro 65 38 1N 15 40E
Pellworm, I. 48 54 30N 8 40E
Pelly Bay 149 68 0N 89 50W
Pelly L. 148 66 0N 102 0W
Pelly, R. 147 62 15N 133 30W
Peloponnese = Pelóponnisos 69 37 10N 22 0E
Pelopónnisos Kai Dhitikí Iprotikí Ellas □ 69 37 10N 22 0E
Peloritani, Monti 65 38 2N 15 15E
Peloro, C. 65 38 15N 15 40E
Pelorus Sound 143 40 59S 173 59E
Pelotas 173 31 42S 52 23W
Pelòvo 67 43 26N 24 17E
Pelvoux, Massif de 45 44 52N 6 20E
Pelym R. 84 59 39N 63 6E
Pemalang 103 6 53S 109 23E
Pematang Siantar 102 2 57N 99 5E
Pemba, Mozam. 127 12 58S 40 30E
Pemba, Zambia 127 16 30S 27 28E
Pemba Channel 126 5 0S 39 37E
Pemba, I. 126 5 0S 39 45E
Pemberton, Austral. 137 34 30S 116 0E
Pemberton, Can. 152 50 25N 122 50W
Pembina 153 48 58N 97 15W
Pembina, R. 153 49 0N 98 12W
Pembine 156 45 38N 87 59W
Pembrey 31 51 42N 4 17W
Pembroke, Can. 150 45 50N 77 7W
Pembroke, N.Z. 143 44 33S 169 9E
Pembroke, U.K. 31 51 41N 4 57W
Pembroke, U.S.A. 157 32 5N 81 32W
Pembroke (□) 26 51 40N 5 0W
Pembroke Dock 31 51 41N 4 57W
Pembury 29 51 8N 0 20E
Pen-y-Ghent 32 54 10N 2 15W
Pen-y-groes, Dyfed, U.K. 31 51 48N 4 3W
Pen-y-groes, Gwynedd, U.K. 31 53 3N 4 18W
Peñíscola 58 40 22N 0 24E
Peña de Francia, Sierra de 56 40 32N 6 10W
Peña Roya, mt. 58 40 24N 0 40W
Peña, Sierra de la 58 42 32N 0 45W
Penafiel 56 41 12N 8 17W
Peñafiel 56 41 35N 4 7W
Peñaflor 57 37 43N 5 21W
Peñalara, Pico 56 40 51N 3 57W
Penally 31 51 39N 4 44W
Penalva 170 3 18S 45 10W
Penamacôr 56 40 10N 7 10W
Penang = Pinang 101 5 25N 100 15E
Penápolis 173 21 30S 50 0W
Peñaranda de Bracamonte 56 40 53N 5 13W
Peñarroya-Pueblonuevo 57 38 19N 5 16W
Penarth 31 51 26N 3 11W
Peñas, C. de 56 43 42N 5 52W
Peñas de San Pedro 59 38 44N 2 0W
Peñas, G. de 176 47 0S 75 0W
Peñas, Pta. 174 11 17N 70 28W
Pench'i 107 41 20N 123 48E
Pencoed 31 51 31N 3 30W
Pend Oreille, L. 160 48 0N 116 30W
Pend Oreille, R. 160 49 4N 117 37W
Pendálofon 68 40 14N 21 12E
Pendeen 30 50 11N 5 39W
Pendelikón 69 38 5N 23 53E
Pendembu 120 9 7N 12 14W
Pendências 170 5 15S 36 43W
Pender B. 136 16 45S 122 42E
Pendine 31 51 44N 4 33W
Pendle Hill 32 53 53N 2 18W
Pendleton, Calif., U.S.A. 163 33 16N 117 23W
Pendleton, Oreg., U.S.A. 160 45 35N 118 50W
Pendzhikent 85 39 29N 67 37E
Penedo 170 10 15S 36 36W
Penetanguishene 150 44 50N 79 55W
Penfield 109 34 44S 138 38E
Pengalengan 103 7 9S 107 30E
P'engch'i 108 30 50N 105 42E
Penge, Kasai, Congo 126 5 30S 24 33E
Penge, Kivu, Congo 126 4 27S 28 25E
P'enghsien 108 30 59N 103 56E
P'enghu Liehtao 109 22 30N 119 30E
P'englai 107 37 49N 120 47E
P'engshui 108 29 19N 108 12E
P'engtse 109 29 53N 116 32E
Penguin 138 41 8S 146 6E
Penhalonga 127 18 52S 32 40E
Peniche 57 39 19N 9 22W
Penicuik 35 55 50N 3 14W
Penida, I. 102 8 45S 115 30E
Penistone 33 53 31N 1 38W
Penitentes, Serra dos 170 8 45S 46 20W
Penkridge 28 52 44N 2 8W
Penmachno 31 53 2N 3 47W
Penmaenmawr 31 53 16N 3 55W
Penmarch 42 47 49N 4 21W
Penmarch, Pte. de 42 47 48N 4 22W
Penn Yan 162 42 39N 77 7W
Pennabilli 63 43 50N 12 17E
Pennant 153 50 32N 108 14W
Penne 63 42 28N 13 56E
Penner, R. 97 14 50N 78 20E
Penneshaw 140 35 44S 137 56E
Pennines 32 54 50N 2 20W
Pennino, Mte. 63 43 6N 12 54E
Pennsburg 162 40 23N 75 30W
Pennsville 162 39 39N 75 31W
Pennsylvania □ 156 40 50N 78 0W
Penny 152 53 51N 121 48W
Peno 80 57 2N 32 33E
Penola 140 37 25S 140 47E
Penong 139 31 59S 133 5E
Penonomé 166 8 31N 80 21W
Penpont 35 55 14N 3 49W
Penrhyn Is. 131 9 0S 150 30W
Penrith, Austral. 141 33 43S 150 38E
Penrith, U.K. 32 54 40N 2 45W
Penryn 30 50 10N 5 7W
Pensacola 157 30 30N 87 10W
Pensacola Mts. 13 84 0S 40 0W
Pense 153 50 25N 104 59W
Penshurst, Austral. 140 37 49S 142 20W
Penshurst, U.K. 29 51 10N 0 12E
Pentecoste 170 3 48S 37 17W
Penticton 152 49 30N 119 30W
Pentire Pt. 30 50 35N 4 57W
Pentland 138 20 32S 145 25E
Pentland Firth 37 58 43N 3 10W
Pentland Hills 35 55 48N 3 25W
Pentland Skerries 37 58 41N 2 53W
Pentraeth 31 53 17N 4 13W
Pentre Foelas 31 53 2N 3 41W
Penukonda 97 14 5N 77 38E
Penwortham 32 53 45N 2 44W
Penybont 31 52 17N 3 18W
Penylan L. 153 61 50N 106 20W
Penza 81 53 15N 45 5E
Penzance 30 50 7N 5 32W
Penzberg 49 47 46N 11 23E
Penzhinskaya Guba 77 61 30N 163 0E
Penzlin 48 53 32N 13 6E
Peó 66 42 40N 20 17E
Peoria, Ariz., U.S.A. 161 33 40N 112 15W
Peoria, Ill., U.S.A. 158 40 40N 89 40W
Pepacton Res. 162 42 5N 74 58W
Pepingen 47 50 46N 4 10E
Pepinster 47 50 34N 5 47E
Pepmbridge 28 52 13N 2 54W
Pepperwood 160 40 23N 124 0W
Peqini 68 41 4N 19 44E
Pera Hd. 138 12 55S 141 37E
Perabumilih 102 3 27S 104 15E
Perakhóra 69 38 2N 22 56E
Peraki, R. 101 5 10N 101 4E
Perales de Alfambra 58 40 38N 1 0W
Perales del Puerto 56 40 10N 6 40W
Peralta 58 42 21N 1 49W
Pérama 69 35 20N 24 22E
Perast 66 42 31N 18 47E
Percé 151 48 31N 64 13W
Perche 42 48 31N 1 1E
Perche, Collines de la 42 42 30N 2 5E
Percival Lakes 136 21 25S 125 0E
Percy 42 48 55N 1 11W
Percy Is. 138 21 39S 150 16E
Percyville 138 19 2S 143 45E
Perdido, Mte. 58 42 40N 0 50E
Pereira 174 4 49N 75 43W
Pereira Barreto 171 20 38S 51 7W
Pereira de Eóa 128 16 48S 15 50E
Perekerten 140 34 55S 143 40E
Perenjori 137 29 26S 116 16E
Pereslavi-Zelesskiy 80 56 45N 38 58E
Pereyaslav-Khmelnitskiy 80 50 3N 31 28E
Perez, I. 165 22 24N 89 42W
Perg 52 48 15N 14 38E
Pergamino 172 33 52S 60 30W
Pergine Valsugano 63 46 4N 11 15E
Pérgola 63 43 35N 12 50E
Perham 158 46 36N 95 36W
Perham Down Camp 28 51 14N 1 38W
Perhentian, Kepulauan 101 5 54N 102 42E
Peri, L. 140 30 45S 143 35E
Periam 66 46 2N 20 59E
Peribonca, L. 151 50 1N 71 10W
Péribonca, R. 151 48 45N 72 5W
Perico 172 24 20S 65 5W
Pericos 164 25 3N 107 42W
Périers 42 49 11N 1 25W
Périgord 44 45 0N 0 40E
Périgueux 44 45 10N 0 42E
Perija, Sierra de 174 9 30N 73 3W
Perim, I. 91 12 39N 43 25E
Peristera, I. 69 39 15N 23 58E
Peritoró 170 4 20S 44 18W
Periyakulam 97 10 5N 77 30E
Periyar, L. 97 9 25N 77 10E
Periyar, R. 97 10 15N 76 10E
Perkam, Tg. 103 1 35S 137 50E
Perkasie 162 40 22N 75 18W
Perkovió 63 43 41N 16 10E
Perlas, Arch. de las 166 8 41N 79 7W
Perlas, Punta de 166 11 30N 83 30W
Perleberg 48 53 5N 11 50E
Perlevka 81 51 56N 38 57E
Perlez 66 45 11N 20 22E
Perlis □ 101 6 30N 100 15E
Perm (Molotov) 84 58 0N 57 10E
Përmeti 68 40 15N 20 21E
Pernambuco = Recife 170 8 0S 35 0W
Pernambuco □ 170 8 0S 37 0W
Pernatty Lagoon 140 31 30S 137 12E
Peron, C. 137 25 30S 113 30E
Peron Is. 136 13 9S 130 4E
Peron Pen. 137 26 0S 113 10E
Péronne 43 49 55N 2 57E
Péronnes 47 50 27N 4 9E
Perosa Argentina 62 44 57N 7 11E
Perouse Str., La 86 45 40N 142 0E
Perow 152 54 35N 126 10W
Perpendicular Pt. 139 31 37S 152 52E
Perpignan 44 42 42N 2 53E
Perranporth 30 50 21N 5 9W
Perranzabuloe 30 50 18N 5 7W
Perris 163 33 47N 117 14W
Perros-Guirec 42 48 49N 3 28W
Perry, Fla., U.S.A. 157 30 9N 83 10W
Perry, Ga., U.S.A. 157 32 25N 83 41W
Perry, Iowa, U.S.A. 158 41 48N 94 5W
Perry, Maine, U.S.A. 157 44 59N 67 20W
Perry, Okla., U.S.A. 159 36 20N 97 20W
Perry, Mt. 139 25 12S 151 41E
Perryton 159 36 28N 100 48W

Perryville Ping, R

Perryville, Alas., U.S.A. **147** 55 54N 159 10W
Perryville, Mo., U.S.A. **159** 37 42N 89 50W
Persberg **72** 59 47N 14 15E
Persepolis **93** 29 55N 52 50E
Pershore **28** 52 7N 2 4W
Persia = Iran **93** 35 0N 50 0E
Persian Gulf **93** 27 0N 50 0E
Perstorp **73** 56 10N 13 25E
Perth, Austral. **137** 31 57S 115 52E
Perth, N.B., Can. **150** 46 43N 67 42W
Perth, Ont., Can. **150** 44 55N 76 15W
Perth, U.K. **35** 56 24N 3 27W
Perth (□) **26** 56 30N 4 0W
Perth Amboy **162** 40 30N 74 25W
Perthus, Le **44** 42 30N 2 53E
Pertuis **45** 43 42N 5 30E
Pertuis Breton **44** 46 17N 1 25W
Pertuis d'Antioche **44** 46 6N 1 20W
Peru, Ill., U.S.A. **158** 41 18N 89 12W
Peru, Ind., U.S.A. **156** 40 42N 86 0W
Peru ■ **174** 8 0S 75 0W
Perúgia **63** 43 6N 12 24E
Perušić **63** 44 40N 15 22E
Péruwelz **47** 50 31N 3 36E
Pervomayskiy **81** 53 20N 40 10E
Pervouralsk **84** 56 55N 60 0E
Perwez **47** 50 38N 4 48E
Pésaro **63** 43 55N 12 53E
Pesca, La **165** 23 46N 97 47W
Pescadores Is. (P'enghu Liehtao) **109** 23 30N 119 30E
Pescara **63** 42 28N 14 13E
Peschanokopskoye **83** 46 14N 41 4E
Péscia **62** 43 54N 10 40E
Pescina **63** 42 0N 13 39E
Peseux **50** 46 59N 6 53E
Peshawar **94** 34 2N 71 37E
Peshawar □ **94** 35 0N 72 50E
Peshkopia **68** 41 41N 20 25E
Peshovka **84** 59 4N 52 22E
Peshtera **67** 42 2N 24 18E
Peshtigo **156** 45 4N 87 46W
Peski **81** 51 14N 42 12E
Peskovka **81** 59 9N 52 28E
Pêso da Régua **56** 41 10N 7 47W
Pesqueira **170** 8 20S 36 42W
Pesqueria **164** 29 23N 110 54W
Pesquieria, R. **164** 25 54N 99 11W
Pessac **44** 44 48N 0 37W
Pessoux **47** 50 17N 5 11E
Pest □ **53** 47 29N 19 5E
Pestovo **80** 58 33N 35 18E
Pestravka **81** 52 28N 49 57E
Péta **69** 39 10N 21 2E
Petah Tiqwa **90** 32 6N 34 53E
Petalídhion, Khóra **69** 36 57N 21 55E
Petaling Jaya **101** 3 4N 101 42E
Petaluma **163** 38 13N 122 39W
Petange **47** 49 33N 5 55E
Petatlán **164** 17 31N 101 16W
Petauke **127** 14 14S 31 12E
Petawawa **150** 45 54N 77 17W
Petegem **47** 50 59N 3 32E
Petén Itza, Lago **166** 16 58N 89 50W
Peter 1st, I. **13** 69 0S 91 0W
Peter Pond L. **153** 55 55N 108 44W
Peterbell **150** 48 36N 83 21W
Peterboro **162** 42 55N 71 59W
Peterborough, S. Australia, Austral. **140** 32 58S 138 51E
Peterborough, Victoria, Austral. **133** 38 37S 142 50E
Peterborough, U.K. **29** 52 35N 0 14W
Peterchurch **28** 52 3N 2 57W
Peterculter **37** 57 5N 2 18W
Peterhead **37** 57 30N 1 49W
Peterlee **33** 54 45N 1 18W
Petersburg, Alas., U.S.A. **152** 56 50N 133 0W
Petersburg, Ind., U.S.A. **156** 38 30N 87 15W
Petersburg, Va., U.S.A. **162** 37 17N 77 26W
Petersburg, W. Va., U.S.A. **156** 38 59N 79 10W
Petersfield **29** 51 0N 0 56W
Peterswell **39** 53 7N 8 46W
Petford **138** 17 20S 144 50E
Petilia Policastro **65** 39 7N 16 48E
Petit Bois I. **157** 30 16N 88 25W
Petit Cap **151** 48 58N 63 58W
Petit Goâve **167** 18 27N 72 51W
Petit-Quevilly, Le **42** 49 26N 1 0E
Petitcodiac **151** 45 57N 65 11W
Petite Saguenay **151** 47 59N 70 1W
Petitsikapau, L. **151** 54 37N 66 25W
Petlad **94** 22 30N 72 45E
Peto **165** 20 10N 89 0W
Petone **142** 41 13S 174 53E
Petoskey **150** 45 22N 84 57W
Petra, Jordan **90** 30 20N 35 22E
Petra, Spain **58** 39 37N 3 6E
Petra, Ostrova **12** 76 15N 118 30E
Petralia **65** 37 49N 14 4E
Petrel **59** 38 30N 0 46W
Petrich **67** 41 24N 23 13E
Petrijanec **63** 46 23N 16 17E
Petrikov **80** 52 11N 28 29E
Petrila **70** 45 29N 23 29E
Petrinja **63** 45 28N 16 18E
'Petroland', gasfield **19** 53 35N 4 15E
Petrolândia **170** 9 5S 38 20W
Petrolia **150** 42 54N 82 9W
Petrolina **170** 9 24S 40 30W
Petropavlovsk **76** 55 0N 69 0E
Petropavlovsk-Kamchatskiy **77** 53 16N 159 0E
Petrópolis **173** 22 33S 43 9W
Petroşeni **70** 45 28N 23 20E
Petrova Gora **63** 45 15N 15 45E
Petrovac **66** 42 13N 18 57E
Petrovaradin **66** 45 16N 19 55E
Petrovsk **81** 52 22N 45 19E
Petrovsk-Zabaykalskiy **77** 51 26N 108 30E
Petrovskoye, R.S.F.S.R., U.S.S.R. **83** 45 25N 42 58E
Petrovskoye, R.S.F.S.R., U.S.S.R. **84** 53 37N 56 23E
Petrozavodsk **78** 61 41N 34 20E
Petrus Steyn **129** 27 38S 28 8E
Petrusburg **128** 29 4S 25 26E
Pettigo **38** 54 32N 7 49W
Pettitts **141** 34 56S 148 10E
Petworth **29** 50 59N 0 37W
Peumo **172** 34 21S 71 19W
Peureulak **102** 4 48N 97 45E
Pevek **77** 69 15N 171 0E
Pevensey **29** 50 49N 0 20E
Pevensey Levels **29** 50 50N 0 20E
Peveragno **62** 44 20N 7 37E
Pewsey **28** 51 20N 1 46W
Pewsey, Vale of **28** 51 20N 1 46W
Peyrehorade **44** 43 34N 1 7W
Peyruis **45** 44 1N 5 56E
Pézenas **44** 43 28N 3 24E
Pezinok **53** 48 17N 17 17E
Pfaffenhofen **49** 48 31N 11 31E
Pfäffikon **51** 47 13N 8 46E
Pfarrkirchen **49** 48 25N 12 57E
Pforzheim **49** 48 53N 8 43E
Pfungstadt **49** 49 47N 8 36E
Phagwara **93** 31 10N 75 40E
Phala **128** 23 45S 26 50E
Phalodi **94** 27 12N 72 24E
Phalsbourg **43** 48 46N 7 15E
Phan **100** 19 28N 99 43E
Phan Rang **101** 11 40N 109 9E
Phan Thiet **101** 11 1N 108 9E
Phanat Nikhom **100** 13 27N 101 11E
Phangan, Ko **101** 9 45N 100 0E
Phangnga **101** 8 28N 98 30E
Phanh Bho Ho Chi Minh **101** 10 58N 106 40E
Phanom Dang Raek, mts. **100** 14 45N 104 0E
Phanom Sarakham **100** 13 45N 101 21E
Pharenda **95** 27 5N 83 17E
Phatthalung **101** 7 39N 100 6E
Phayao **100** 19 11N 99 55E
Phelps, N.Y., U.S.A. **162** 42 57N 77 5W
Phelps, Wis., U.S.A. **158** 46 2N 89 2W
Phelps L. **153** 59 15N 103 15W
Phenix City **157** 32 30N 85 0W
Phet Buri **100** 13 1N 99 55E
Phetchabun **100** 16 25N 101 8E
Phetchabun, Thiu Khao **100** 16 0N 101 20E
Phetchaburi **101** 13 1N 99 55E
Phi Phi, Ko **101** 7 45N 98 46E
Phiafay **100** 14 48N 106 0E
Phibun Mangsahan **100** 15 14N 105 14E
Phichai **100** 17 22N 100 10E
Phichit **100** 16 26N 100 22E
Philadelphia, Miss., U.S.A. **159** 32 47N 89 5W
Philadelphia, Pa., U.S.A. **162** 40 0N 75 10W
Philip **158** 44 4N 101 42W
Philip Smith Mts. **147** 68 0N 146 0W
Philippeville **47** 50 12N 4 33E
Philippi L. **138** 24 20S 138 55E
Philippines ■ **103** 12 0N 123 0E
Philippolis **128** 30 15S 25 16E
Philippopolis = Plovdiv **67** 42 8N 24 44E
Philipsburg **160** 46 20N 113 21W
Philipstown **128** 30 28S 24 30E
Phillip, I. **141** 38 30S 145 12E
Phillips, Texas, U.S.A. **159** 35 48N 101 17W
Phillips, Wis., U.S.A. **158** 45 41N 90 22W
Phillips Ra. **136** 16 53S 125 50E
Phillipsburg, Kans., U.S.A. **158** 39 48N 99 20W
Phillipsburg, Penn., U.S.A. **162** 40 43N 75 12W
Phillott **139** 27 53S 145 50E
Philmont **162** 42 14N 73 37W
Philomath **160** 44 28N 123 21W
Phimai **100** 15 13N 102 30E
Phitsanulok **100** 16 50N 100 12E
Phnom Penh **101** 11 33N 104 55E
Phnom Thbeng **100** 13 50N 104 56E
Phoenicia **162** 42 5N 74 14W
Phoenix, Ariz., U.S.A. **161** 33 30N 112 10W
Phoenix, N.Y., U.S.A. **162** 43 13N 76 18W
Phoenix Is. **130** 3 30S 172 0W
Phoenixville **162** 40 12N 75 29W
Phon **100** 15 49N 102 36E
Phon Tiou **100** 17 53N 104 37E
Phong, R. **100** 16 23N 102 56E
Phong Saly **100** 21 42N 102 9E
Phong Tho **100** 22 32N 103 21E
Phongdo **99** 30 14N 91 14E
Phonhong **100** 18 30N 102 25E
Phonum **101** 8 49N 98 48E
Photharam **100** 13 41N 99 51E
Phra Chedi Sam Ong **100** 15 16N 98 23E
Phra Nakhon Si Ayutthaya **100** 14 25N 100 30E
Phra Thong, Ko **101** 9 5N 98 17E
Phrae **100** 18 7N 100 9E
Phrao **101** 19 23N 99 15E
Phrom Phiram **100** 17 2N 100 12E
Phu Dien **100** 18 58N 105 31E
Phu Doan **101** 21 40N 105 10E
Phu Loi **100** 20 14N 103 14E
Phu Ly (Ha Nam) **100** 20 35N 105 50E
Phu Qui **100** 19 20N 105 20E
Phu Tho **100** 21 24N 105 13E
Phuc Yen **100** 21 16N 105 45E
Phuket **100** 8 0N 98 28E
Phuket, Ko, I. **101** 8 0N 98 22E
Phulbari **98** 21 52N 88 8E
Phulera (Phalera) **94** 26 52N 75 16E
Phun Phin **101** 9 7N 99 12E
Phuoc Le (Baria) **101** 10 39N 107 19E
Piabia **138** 25 12S 152 45E
Piacá **170** 7 42S 47 18W
Piacenza **62** 45 2N 9 42E
Piaçubaçu **170** 10 24S 36 25W
Piádena **62** 45 8N 10 22E
Pialba **139** 25 20S 152 45E
Pian, Cr. **139** 30 2S 148 12E
Piancó **171** 7 12S 37 57W
Pianella **63** 42 24N 14 5E
Piangil **140** 35 5S 143 20E
Pianoro **63** 44 20N 11 20E
Pianosa, I., Puglia, Italy **63** 42 12N 15 44E
Pianosa, I., Toscana, Italy **62** 42 36N 10 4E
Piapot **153** 49 59N 109 8W
Pias **57** 38 1N 7 29W
Piaseczno **54** 52 5N 21 2E
Piassabussu **171** 10 24S 36 25W
Piastow **54** 52 12N 20 48E
Piatá **171** 13 9S 41 48W
Piatra Neamţ **70** 46 56N 26 21E
Piatra Olt **70** 43 51N 25 9E
Piauí □ **170** 7 0S 43 0W
Piaui, R. **170** 6 38S 42 42W
Piave, R. **63** 45 50N 13 9E
Piazza Ármerina **65** 37 21N 14 20E
Pibor Post **123** 6 47N 33 3E
Pibor, R. **123** 7 1N 33 0E
Pica **174** 20 35S 69 25W
Picard, Plaine de **43** 50 0N 2 0E
Picardie **43** 50 0N 2 15E
Picardy = Picardie **43** 50 0N 2 15E
Picayune **159** 30 40N 89 40W
Piccadilly, Austral. **109** 34 59S 138 44E
Piccadilly, Zambia **127** 14 0S 29 30E
Picerno **65** 40 40N 15 37E
Pichiang **108** 26 40N 98 53E
Pichieh **108** 27 20N 105 20E
Pichilemu **172** 34 22S 72 9W
Pickerel L. **150** 48 40N 91 25W
Pickering **33** 54 15N 0 46W
Pickering, Vale of **33** 54 0N 0 45W
Pickle Lake **150** 51 30N 90 12W
Pico **16** 38 28N 28 18W
Pico Truncado **176** 46 40S 68 10W
Picos **170** 7 5S 41 28W
Picos Ancares, Sierra de **56** 42 51N 6 52W
Picquigny **43** 49 56N 2 10E
Picton, Austral. **141** 34 12S 150 34E
Picton, Can. **150** 44 1N 77 9W
Picton, N.Z. **143** 41 18S 174 3E
Pictou **151** 45 41N 62 42W
Picture Butte **152** 49 55N 112 45W
Picuí **170** 6 31S 36 21W
Picún-Leufú **176** 39 30S 69 5W
Pidley **29** 52 33N 0 4W
Pidurutalagala, mt. **97** 7 10N 80 50E
Piedad, La **164** 20 20N 102 1W
Piedecuesta **174** 6 59N 73 3W
Piedicavallo **62** 45 41N 7 57E
Piedmont **157** 33 55N 85 39W
Piedmont = Piemonte **62** 45 0N 7 30E
Piedmont Plat. **157** 34 0N 81 30W
Piedmonte d'Alife **65** 41 22N 14 22E
Piedra, R. **58** 41 10N 1 45W
Piedrabuena **57** 39 0N 4 10W
Piedrahita **56** 40 28N 5 23W
Piedras Blancas Pt. **161** 35 45N 121 18W
Piedras Negras **164** 28 35N 100 35W
Piedras, R. de las **174** 11 40S 70 50W
Piemonte **62** 45 0N 7 30E
Piena **45** 42 15N 8 34E
Piensk **54** 51 16N 15 2E
Pier Millan **140** 35 14S 142 40E
Pierce **160** 46 46N 115 53W
Piería □ **68** 40 13N 22 25E
Pierowall **37** 59 20N 3 0W
Pierre, France **43** 46 54N 5 13E
Pierre, U.S.A. **158** 44 23N 100 20W
Pierrefeu **45** 43 8N 6 9E
Pierrefonds **43** 49 20N 3 0E
Pierrefontaine **43** 47 14N 6 32E
Pierrefort **44** 44 55N 2 50E
Pierrelatte **45** 44 23N 4 43E
Pieštany **155** 48 35N 17 50E
Piesting, R. **53** 48 0N 16 19E
Pieszyce **54** 50 43N 16 33E
Piet Retief **129** 27 1S 30 50E
Pietarsaari **74** 63 41N 22 40E
Pietermaritzburg **129** 29 35S 30 25E
Pietersburg **129** 23 54S 29 25E
Pietraperzia **65** 37 26N 14 8E
Pietrasanta **62** 43 57N 10 12E
Pietrosu **70** 47 12N 25 8E
Pietrosul **70** 47 35N 24 43E
Pieve di Cadore **63** 46 25N 12 22E
Pieve di Teco **62** 44 3N 7 54E
Pievepélago **62** 44 12N 10 35E
Pigadhítsa **68** 39 59N 21 23E
Pigadia **69** 35 30N 27 12E
Pigeon I. **97** 14 2N 74 20E
Pigeon, R. **150** 48 1N 89 42W
Piggott **159** 36 20N 90 10W
Pigna **62** 43 57N 7 40E
Pigü **172** 37 36S 62 25W
Pihani **95** 27 36N 80 15E
Pijnacker **46** 52 1N 4 26E
Pikalevo **80** 59 37N 34 0E
Pikes Peak **158** 38 50N 105 10W
Pikesville **162** 39 23N 76 44W
Piketberg **128** 32 55S 18 40E
Pikeville **156** 37 30N 82 30W
Pik'ochi **106** 40 45N 111 17E
Pikou **106** 32 45N 105 22E
Pikwitonei **153** 55 35N 97 9W
Piła **54** 53 10N 16 48E
Piła □ **54** 53 0N 17 0E
Pila, mte. **59** 38 16N 1 11W
Pilaia **68** 40 32N 22 59E
Pilani **94** 28 22N 75 33E
Pilão Arcado **170** 10 9S 42 26W
Pilar, Brazil **170** 9 36S 35 56W
Pilar, Parag. **172** 26 50S 58 10W
Pilas, I. **103** 6 39N 121 37E
Pilatus **51** 46 59N 8 15E
Pilbara Cr. **132** 21 15S 118 22E
Pilbara Mining Centre **136** 21 15S 118 16E
Pilcomayo, R. **172** 25 21S 57 42W
Pili **69** 36 50N 27 15E
Pilibhit **95** 28 40N 79 50E
Pilion, mt. **68** 39 27N 23 7E
Pilis **53** 47 17N 19 35E
Pilisvörösvár **53** 47 38N 18 56E
Pilkhawa **94** 28 43N 77 42E
Pilling **32** 53 55N 2 54W
Pilltown **39** 51 59N 7 49W
Pílos **69** 36 55N 21 42E
Pilot Mound **153** 49 15N 98 54W
Pilot Point **159** 33 26N 97 0W
Pilot Rock **160** 45 30N 118 58W
Pilsen = Plzen **52** 49 45N 13 22E
Pilštanj **63** 46 8N 15 39E
Pilton **28** 51 0N 2 35W
Piltown **39** 52 22N 7 18W
Pilzno **54** 50 0N 21 16E
Pimba **140** 31 18S 136 46E
Pimenta Bueno **174** 11 35S 61 10W
Pimentel **174** 6 45S 79 55W
Pimuacan, Rés. **151** 49 45N 70 30W
Pina **58** 41 29N 0 33W
Pinang, I. **101** 5 25N 100 15E
Pinar del Río **166** 22 26N 83 40W
Pinawa **149** 50 9N 95 50W
Pince C. **151** 46 38N 53 45W
Pinchbeck **29** 52 48N 0 9W
Pincher Creek **152** 49 30N 113 57W
Pinchi L. **152** 54 38N 124 30W
Pinch'uan **108** 25 51N 100 34E
Pinckneyville **158** 38 5N 89 20W
Pîncota **66** 46 20N 21 45E
Pind Dadan Khan **94** 32 55N 73 47E
Pindar **137** 28 30S 115 47E
Pindaré Mirim **170** 3 37S 45 21W
Pindaré, R. **170** 3 17S 44 47W
Pindi Gheb **94** 33 14N 72 12E
Pindiga **121** 9 58N 10 53E
Pindobal **170** 3 16S 48 25W
Pindos Óros **68** 40 0N 21 0E
Pindus Mts. = Pindos Óros **68** 40 0N 21 0E
Pine **161** 34 27N 111 30W
Pine Bluff **159** 34 10N 92 0W
Pine, C. **151** 46 37N 53 32W
Pine City **158** 45 46N 93 0W
Pine Creek, N.T., Austral. **132** 13 50S 131 49E
Pine Creek, Queens., Austral. **138** 13 13S 142 47E
Pine Dock **153** 51 38N 96 48W
Pine Falls **153** 50 34N 96 11W
Pine Flat Res. **163** 36 50N 119 20W
Pine Grove **162** 40 33N 76 23W
Pine Hill **138** 23 42S 147 0E
Pine, La **160** 40 53N 80 45W
Pine Pass **152** 55 25N 122 42W
Pine Point **152** 60 50N 114 28W
Pine, R., Austral. **108** 27 18S 153 2E
Pine, R., Can. **153** 55 20N 107 38W
Pine Ridge, Austral. **141** 31 10S 147 30E
Pine Ridge, U.S.A. **158** 42 2N 102 35W
Pine River, Can. **153** 51 45N 100 30W
Pine River, U.S.A. **158** 46 40N 94 20W
Pine Valley **163** 32 50N 116 32W
Pinecrest **163** 38 12N 120 1W
Pinedale, Ariz., U.S.A. **161** 34 23N 110 16W
Pinedale, Calif., U.S.A. **163** 36 50N 119 48W
Pinega **52** 64 45N 43 40E
Pinega, R. **78** 64 20N 43 0E
Pinehill **138** 23 38S 146 57E
Pinerolo **62** 44 47N 7 21E
Pineto **63** 42 36N 14 4E
Pinetop **161** 34 10N 109 57W
Pinetown **129** 29 48S 30 54E
Pinetree **158** 43 42N 105 52W
Pineville, Ky., U.S.A. **157** 36 42N 83 42W
Pineville, La., U.S.A. **159** 31 22N 92 30W
Pinewood **153** 48 45N 94 10W
Piney, Can. **153** 49 5N 96 10W
Piney, France **43** 48 22N 4 21E
Ping, R. **100** 15 42N 100 9E

Pingaring **Polcura**

Pingaring **137** 32 40S 118 32E
P'ingch'ang **108** 31 33N 107 6E
P'ingchiang **109** 28 42N 113 35E
P'ingch'uan **107** 41 0N 118 36E
Pingelly **137** 32 29S 116 59E
P'ingho **109** 24 18N 117 2E
P'inghsiang, Kiangsi, China **109** 27 39N 113 50E
P'inghsiang, Kwangsi Chuang, China **108** 22 6N 106 44E
P'inghu **109** 30 38N 121 0E
P'ingi, Shantung, China **107** 35 30N 117 36E
P'ingi, Yünnan, China **108** 25 40N 104 14E
P'ingkuo **108** 23 20N 107 34E
P'ingli **108** 32 26N 109 22E
P'ingliang **105** 35 32N 106 50E
Pinglo, Kwangsi-Chuang, China **109** 24 30N 110 45E
Pinglo, Ningsia Hui, China **106** 38 58N 106 30E
P'inglu **106** 37 32N 112 14E
P'ingluch'eng **106** 39 46N 112 6E
P'ingnan, Fukien, China **109** 26 56N 119 3E
P'ingnan, Kwangsi-Chiang, China **109** 23 33N 110 23E
P'ingpa **108** 26 25N 106 15E
P'ingpien **108** 22 54N 103 40E
Pingrup **137** 33 32S 118 29E
P'ingt'an **109** 25 31N 119 47E
P'ingt'ang **108** 25 50N 107 19E
P'ingting **106** 37 48N 113 37E
P'ingt'ingshan **106** 33 43N 113 28E
P'ingtu **107** 36 47N 119 56E
P'ingtung **105** 22 38N 120 30E
Pingwu **105** 32 27N 104 25E
P'ingwu **108** 32 25N 104 36E
P'ingyang **109** 27 40N 120 33E
P'ingyangchen **107** 45 11N 131 15E
P'ingyao **106** 37 12N 112 10E
P'ingyin **106** 36 18N 116 26E
P'ingyüan, Kwangtung, China **109** 24 34N 115 54E
P'ingyüan, Ningsia Hui, China **106** 37 9N 116 25E
Pinhai **107** 34 0N 119 50E
Pinhal **173** 22 10S 46 46W
Pinheiro **170** 2 31S 45 5W
Pinhel **56** 40 18N 7 0W
Pinhoe **30** 50 44N 3 29W
Pinhsien, Heilung Kiang, China **107** 45 44N 127 27E
Pinhsien, Shensi, China **106** 35 10N 108 10E
Pini, I. **102** 0 10N 98 40E
Piniós, R., Ilia, Greece **69** 37 38N 21 20E
Piniós, R., Trikkala, Greece **68** 39 55N 22 10E
Pinjarra **137** 32 37S 115 52E
Pink, R. **153** 56 50N 103 50W
Pinkafeld **53** 47 22N 16 9E
Pinlebu **98** 24 5N 95 22E
Pinnacles, Austral. **137** 28 12S 120 26E
Pinnacles, U.S.A. **163** 36 33N 121 8W
Pinnaroo **140** 35 13S 140 56E
Pinon Hills **163** 34 26N 117 39W
Pinos **164** 22 20N 101 40W
Pinos, I. de **166** 21 40N 82 40W
Pinos, Mt **163** 34 49N 119 8W
Pinos Pt. **161** 36 50N 121 57W
Pinos Puente **57** 37 15N 3 45W
Pinotepa Nacional **165** 16 25N 97 55W
Pinrang **103** 3 46S 119 34E
Pinsk **80** 52 10N 26 8E
Pintados **174** 20 35S 69 40W
Pinto Butte Mt. **153** 49 22N 107 27W
Pintumba **137** 31 50S 132 18E
Pinwherry **34** 55 9N 4 50W
Pinyang **108** 23 17N 108 47E
Pinyug **78** 60 5N 48 0E
Pinzolo **62** 46 9N 10 45E
Pio XII **170** 3 53S 45 17W
Pioche **161** 38 0N 114 35W
Piombino **62** 42 54N 10 30E
Pioner, I. **77** 79 50N 92 0E
Pionki **54** 51 29N 21 28E
Piorini, L. **174** 3 15S 62 35W
Piotrków Trybunalski **54** 51 23N 19 43E
Piotrków Trybunalski □ **54** 51 30N 19 45E
Piove di Sacco **63** 45 18N 12 1E
Pip **93** 26 45N 60 10E
Pipar **94** 26 25N 73 31E
Pipariya **96** 22 45N 78 23E
Piper, oilfield **19** 58 30N 0 15E
Pipéri, I. **68** 39 20N 24 19E
Pipestone **158** 44 0N 96 20W
Pipestone Cr. **153** 53 37N 109 46W
Pipestone, R. **150** 52 53N 89 23W
Pipinas **172** 35 30S 57 19W
Pipiriki **142** 38 28S 175 5E
Pipmuacan Res. **151** 49 40N 70 25W
Pippingarra **136** 20 27S 118 42E
Pipriac **42** 47 49N 1 58W
Piqua **156** 40 10N 84 10W
Piquet Carneiro **171** 5 48S 39 25W
Piquiri, R. **173** 24 3S 54 14W
Piracanjuba **171** 17 18S 49 1W
Piracicaba **173** 22 45S 47 30W
Piracuruca **170** 3 50S 41 50W
Piræus = Piraiévs **69** 37 57N 23 42E
Piraiévs **69** 37 57N 23 42E
Piraiévs □ **69** 37 0N 23 30E
Piráino **65** 38 10N 14 52E
Pirajuí **173** 21 59S 49 29W
Piran (Pirano) **63** 45 31N 13 33E
Pirane **172** 25 25S 59 30W
Piranhas **170** 9 27S 37 46W
Pirapemas **170** 3 43S 44 14W
Pirapora **171** 17 20S 44 56W
Piratyin **80** 50 15N 32 25E
Pirbright **29** 51 17N 0 40W
Pirdop **67** 42 40N 24 10E
Pires do Rio **171** 17 18S 48 17W
Pirganj **98** 25 51S 88 24E
Pirgos, Ilia, Greece **69** 37 40N 21 27E
Pirgos, Messinia, Greece **69** 36 50N 22 16E
Pirgovo **67** 43 44N 25 43E
Piriac-sur-Mer **42** 47 22N 2 33W
Piribebuy **172** 25 26S 57 2W
Pirin Planina **67** 41 40N 23 30E
Pirineos, mts. **58** 42 40N 1 0E
Piripiri **170** 4 15S 41 46W
Piritu **174** 9 23N 69 12W
Pirmasens **49** 49 12N 7 30E
Pirna **48** 50 57N 13 57E
Pirojpur **98** 22 35N 90 1E
Pirot **66** 43 9N 22 39E
Pirsagat, R. **83** 40 15N 48 45E
Pirtleville **161** 31 25N 109 35W
Piru **163** 34 25N 118 48W
Piryí **69** 38 13N 25 59E
Pisa **62** 43 43N 10 23E
Pisa Ra. **143** 44 52S 169 12E
Pisagua **174** 19 40S 70 15W
Pisarovina **63** 45 35N 15 50E
Pisciotta **65** 40 7N 15 12E
Pisco **174** 13 50S 76 5W
Piscu **70** 45 30N 27 43E
Pisek **52** 49 19N 14 10E
Pisham **108** 29 37N 106 13E
P'ishan **105** 37 38N 78 19E
Pishin Lora, R. **94** 30 15N 66 5E
Pising **103** 5 8S 121 53E
Pismo Beach **163** 35 9N 120 38W
Pissos **44** 44 19N 0 49W
Pisticci **65** 40 24N 16 33E
Pistoia **62** 43 57N 10 53E
Pistol B. **153** 62 25N 92 37W
Pisuerga, R. **56** 42 10N 4 15W
Pisz **54** 53 38N 21 49E
Pitalito **174** 1 51N 76 2W
Pitanga **171** 24 46S 51 44W
Pitangui **171** 19 40S 44 54E
Pitarpunga, L. **140** 34 24S 143 30E
Pitcairn I. **131** 25 5S 130 5W
Pite älv **74** 65 44N 20 50W
Piteå **74** 65 20N 21 25E
Piteşti **70** 44 52N 24 54E
Pithapuram **96** 17 10N 82 15E
Pithara **137** 30 20S 116 35E
Pithion **68** 41 24N 26 40W
Pithiviers **43** 48 10N 2 13E
Pitigliano **63** 42 38N 11 40E
Pitiquito **164** 30 42N 112 2W
Pitlochry **37** 56 43N 3 43W
Pitt I. **152** 53 30N 129 50W
Pittem **47** 51 1N 3 13E
Pittenweem **35** 56 13N 2 43W
Pittsburg, Calif., U.S.A. **163** 38 1N 121 50W
Pittsburg, Kans., U.S.A. **159** 37 21N 94 43W
Pittsburg, Tex., U.S.A. **159** 32 59N 94 58W
Pittsburgh **156** 40 25N 79 55W
Pittsfield, Ill., U.S.A. **158** 39 35N 90 46W
Pittsfield, N.H., U.S.A. **162** 43 17N 71 18W
Pittston **162** 41 19N 75 50W
Pittsworth **139** 27 41S 151 37E
Pituri, R. **138** 22 35S 138 30E
Pitzewo **107** 39 28N 122 30E
Piuí **171** 20 28S 45 58W
Pium **170** 10 27S 49 11W
Piura **174** 5 5S 80 45W
Piva, R. **66** 43 15N 18 50E
Pivijay **174** 10 28N 74 37W
Piwniczna **54** 49 27N 20 42E
Pixariá Óros **69** 38 42N 23 39E
Pixley **163** 35 58N 119 18W
Piyai **68** 39 17N 21 25E
Piyang **109** 32 50N 113 30E
Piz Bernina **49** 46 23N 9 45E
Pizarro **174** 4 58N 77 22W
Pizol **51** 46 57N 9 23E
Pizzo **65** 38 44N 16 10E
Placentia **151** 47 20N 54 0W
Placentia B. **151** 47 0N 54 40W
Placerville **160** 38 47N 120 51W
Placetas **166** 22 15N 79 44W
'Placid', gasfield **19** 53 25N 4 20E
Plač kovica, mts. **66** 41 45N 22 30E
Pladda, I. **34** 55 25N 5 7W
Plaffein **50** 46 45N 7 17E
Plain Dealing **159** 32 56N 93 41W
Plainfield **162** 40 37N 74 28W
Plains, Kans., U.S.A. **159** 37 20N 100 35W
Plains, Mont., U.S.A. **160** 47 27N 114 57W
Plains, Tex., U.S.A. **159** 33 11N 102 50W
Plainview, Nebr., U.S.A. **158** 42 25N 97 48W
Plainview, Tex., U.S.A. **159** 34 10N 101 40W
Plainville **158** 39 18N 99 19W
Plainwell **156** 42 28N 85 40W
Plaisance **44** 43 36N 0 3E
Pláka **68** 36 45N 24 26E
Plakhino **76** 67 45N 86 5E
Planá **52** 49 50N 12 44E
Plana Cays **167** 22 38N 73 30W
Planada **163** 37 18N 120 19W
Planaltina **171** 15 30S 47 45W
Plancoët **42** 48 32N 2 13W
Plandište **66** 45 16N 21 10E
Planeta Rica **174** 8 25N 75 36W
Planina, Slovenija, Yugo. **63** 45 47N 14 19E
Planina, Slovenija, Yugo. **63** 46 10N 15 12E
Plankinton **158** 43 45N 98 27W
Plano **159** 33 0N 96 45W
Plant City **157** 28 0N 82 15W
Plant, La **158** 45 11N 100 40W
Plaquemine **159** 30 20N 91 15W
Plasencia **56** 40 3N 6 8W
Plaški **63** 45 4N 15 22E
Plassen **72** 61 9N 12 30E
Plast **84** 54 22N 60 50E
Plaster Rock **151** 46 53N 67 22W
Plata, La, Argent. **172** 35 0S 57 55W
Plata, La, U.S.A. **162** 38 32N 76 59W
Plata, La, Río de **172** 35 0S 56 40W
Platani, R. **64** 37 28N 13 23E
Plateau **13** 70 55S 40 0E
Plateau □ **121** 9 0N 9 0E
Plateau du Coteau du Missouri **158** 47 9N 101 5W
Plati, Ákra **68** 40 27N 24 0E
Platinum **147** 59 2N 161 50W
Plato **174** 9 47N 74 47W
Platte **158** 43 28N 98 50W
Platte, Piz **51** 46 30N 9 35E
Platte, R. **158** 41 0N 98 0W
Platteville **158** 40 18N 104 47W
Plattling **49** 48 46N 12 53E
Plattsburgh **156** 44 41N 73 30W
Plattsmouth **158** 41 0N 96 0W
Plau **48** 53 27N 12 16E
Plauen **48** 50 29N 12 9E
Plav **66** 42 38N 19 57E
Plavnica **66** 42 10N 19 20E
Plavsk **81** 53 40N 37 18E
Playa Azul **164** 17 59N 102 24W
Playa de Castilla **57** 41 25N 0 12W
Playgreen L. **153** 54 0N 98 15W
Pleasant Bay **151** 46 51N 60 48W
Pleasant Hill **158** 38 48N 94 14W
Pleasant Hills **141** 35 28S 146 50E
Pleasant Mount **162** 41 44N 75 26W
Pleasant Pt. **143** 44 16S 171 9E
Pleasanton **159** 29 0N 98 30W
Pleasantville **162** 39 25N 74 30W
Pléaux **44** 45 8N 2 13E
Pleiku (Gia Lai) **101** 14 3N 108 0E
Plélan-le-Grand **42** 48 0N 2 7W
Plémet **42** 48 11N 2 36W
Pléneuf-Val-André **42** 48 35N 2 32W
Pleniţa **70** 44 14N 23 10E
Plenty, Bay of **142** 37 45S 177 0E
Plenty, R. **138** 23 25S 136 31E
Plentywood **158** 48 45N 104 35W
Plesetsk **78** 62 40N 40 10E
Plessisville **151** 46 14N 71 47W
Plestin-les-Grèves **42** 48 40N 3 39W
Pleszew **54** 51 53N 17 47E
Pleternica **66** 45 17N 17 48E
Pletipi L. **151** 51 44N 70 6W
Pleven **67** 43 26N 24 37E
Plevlja **66** 43 21N 19 21E
Płock **54** 52 32N 19 40E
Płock □ **54** 52 30N 19 45E
Plöcken Passo **63** 46 37N 12 57E
Plockton **36** 57 20N 5 40W
Ploegsteert **47** 50 44N 2 53E
Ploëmeur **42** 47 44N 3 26W
Ploërmel **42** 47 55N 2 26W
Ploieşti **70** 44 57N 26 5E
Plomárion **69** 38 58N 26 24E
Plomb du Cantal **44** 45 2N 2 48E
Plombières **43** 47 59N 6 27E
Plomin **63** 45 8N 14 10E
Plön **48** 54 8N 10 22E
Plöner See **48** 53 9N 15 5E
Plonge, Lac La **153** 55 8N 107 20W
Płonsk **54** 52 37N 20 21E
Płoty **54** 53 48N 15 18E
Plouay **42** 47 55N 3 21W
Ploudalmézeau **42** 48 34N 4 41W
Plougasnou **42** 48 42N 3 49W
Plouha **42** 48 41N 2 57W
Plouhinec **42** 48 0N 4 29W
Plovdiv **67** 42 8N 24 44E
Plum I. **162** 41 10N 72 12W
Plumbridge **38** 54 46N 7 15W
Plummer **160** 47 21N 116 59W
Plumtree **127** 20 27S 27 55E
Plunge **80** 55 53N 21 51E
Pluvigner **42** 47 46N 3 1W
Plymouth, U.K. **30** 50 23N 4 9W
Plymouth, Calif., U.S.A. **163** 38 29N 120 51W
Plymouth, Ind., U.S.A. **156** 41 20N 86 19W
Plymouth, Mass., U.S.A. **162** 41 58N 70 40W
Plymouth, N.C., U.S.A. **157** 35 54N 76 55W
Plymouth, N.H., U.S.A. **162** 43 44N 71 41W
Plymouth, Pa., U.S.A. **162** 41 17N 76 0W
Plymouth, Wis., U.S.A. **156** 43 42N 87 58W
Plymouth Sd. **30** 50 20N 4 10W
Plympton **30** 50 24N 4 2W
Plymstock **30** 50 22N 4 6W
Plynlimon = Pumlumon Fawr **31** 52 29N 3 47W
Plyussa **80** 47 40N 29 0E
Plyussa, R. **80** 58 40N 28 30E
Plzen **52** 49 45N 13 22E
Pniewy **54** 52 31N 16 16E
Pô **121** 11 14N 1 5W
Po Hai **107** 38 30N 119 0E
Po, R. **62** 45 0N 10 45E
Poai **106** 35 10N 113 4E
Pobé **121** 7 0N 2 38E
Pobedino **76** 49 51N 142 49E
Pobedy Pik **76** 40 45N 79 58E
Pobiedziska **54** 52 29N 17 19E
Pobla de Lillet, La **58** 42 16N 1 59E
Pobla de Segur **58** 42 15N 0 58E
Pobladura de Valle **56** 42 6N 5 44W
Pocahontas, Arkansas, U.S.A. **159** 37 18N 81 20W
Pocahontas, Iowa, U.S.A. **158** 42 41N 94 42W
Pocatello **160** 42 50N 112 25W
Pochep **80** 52 58N 33 15E
Pochinki **81** 54 41N 44 59E
Pochinok **80** 54 28N 32 29E
Pöchlarn **52** 48 12N 15 12E
Pochontas **152** 53 0N 117 51W
Pochutla **165** 15 50N 96 31W
Pocinhos **170** 7 4S 36 3W
Pocita Casas **164** 28 32N 111 6W
Pocklington **33** 53 56N 0 48W
Poções **171** 14 31S 40 21W
Pocomoke City **162** 38 4N 75 32W
Pocomoke, R. **162** 38 5N 75 34W
Poços de Caldas **173** 21 50S 46 45W
Pocrane **171** 19 37S 41 37W
PoC!tky **52** 49 15N 15 14E
Poddebice **54** 51 54N 18 58E
Podĕbrady **52** 50 9N 15 8E
Podensac **44** 44 40N 0 22W
Podgorica = Titograd **66** 42 30N 19 19E
Podkamennaya Tunguska **77** 61 50N 90 26E
Podlapac **63** 44 45N 15 47E
Podmokly **52** 50 48N 14 10E
Podoleni **70** 46 46N 26 39E
Podolínec **53** 49 16N 20 31E
Podolsk **81** 55 25N 37 30E
Podor **120** 16 40N 14 50W
Podporozhy **78** 60 55N 34 2E
Podravska Slatina **66** 45 42N 17 45E
Podsreda **63** 45 42N 17 41E
Podu Turcului **70** 46 11N 27 25E
Podujevo **66** 42 54N 21 10E
Poel, I. **48** 54 0N 11 25E
Pofadder **128** 29 10S 19 22E
Pogamasing **150** 46 55N 81 50W
Poggiardo **65** 40 3N 18 21E
Poggibonsi **63** 43 27N 11 8E
Pogoanele **70** 44 55N 27 0E
Pogorzela **54** 51 50N 17 12E
Pogradeci **68** 40 57N 20 48E
Poh **103** 0 46S 122 51E
Pohang **107** 36 1N 129 23E
Pohorelá **53** 48 50N 20 2E
Pohorelice **53** 48 59N 16 31E
Pohorje, mts. **63** 46 30N 15 7E
Poiana Mare **70** 43 57N 23 5E
Poiana Ruscăi, Munţii **70** 45 45N 22 25E
Pt. Augusta **140** 32 30S 137 50E
Point Baker **147** 56 20N 133 35W
Point Cloates **137** 22 40S 113 45E
Point Edward **150** 43 10N 82 30W
Point Fortin **167** 10 9N 61 46W
Point Hope **147** 68 20N 166 50W
Point Lay **147** 69 45N 163 10W
Point Pass **140** 34 5S 139 5E
Point Pedro **97** 9 50N 80 15E
Point Pleasant, N.J., U.S.A. **162** 40 5N 74 4W
Point Pleasant, W. Va., U.S.A. **156** 38 50N 82 7W
Point Reyes Nat. Seashore **163** 38 0N 122 58W
Point Rock **159** 31 30N 99 56W
Pointe-à-la Hache **159** 29 35N 89 55W
Pointe-à-Pitre **167** 16 10N 61 30W
Pointe-Noire **124** 4 48S 12 0E
Poirino **62** 44 55N 7 50E
Poisonbush Ra. **136** 22 30S 121 30E
Poissy **43** 48 55N 2 0E
Poitiers **42** 46 35N 0 20W
Poitou, Plaines du **44** 46 30N 0 1W
Poix **43** 49 47N 2 0E
Poix-Terron **43** 49 38N 4 38E
Pojoaque **161** 35 55N 106 0W
Pojuca **171** 12 21S 38 20W
Pokaran **93** 27 0N 71 50E
Pokataroo **139** 29 30S 148 34E
Poko, Sudan **123** 5 41N 31 55E
Poko, Zaïre **126** 3 7N 26 52E
Pok'ot'u **105** 48 46N 121 54E
Pokrovka **85** 42 20N 78 0E
Pokrovsk **77** 61 29N 129 6E
Pokrovsk-Uralskiy **84** 60 10N 59 49E
Pol **56** 43 9N 7 20W
Pola **80** 57 30N 32 0E
Pola de Allande **56** 43 16N 6 37W
Pola de Gordón, La **56** 42 51N 5 41W
Pola de Lena **56** 43 10N 5 49W
Pola de Siero **56** 43 24N 5 39W
Pola de Somiedo **56** 43 5N 6 15W
Polacca **161** 35 52N 110 25W
Polan **93** 25 30N 61 10E
Poland ■ **54** 52 0N 20 0E
Polanów **54** 54 7N 16 41E
Polar Bear Prov. Park **150** 54 30N 83 20W
Polcura **172** 37 10S 71 50W

Połcyn Zdrój

Portel

Połcyn Zdrój 54 53 47N 16 5 E
Polden Hills 28 51 7N 2 50W
Polegate 29 50 49N 0 15 E
Polessk 80 54 50N 21 8 E
Polesworth 28 52 37N 1 37W
Polevskoy 84 56 26N 60 11 E
Polewali, Sulawesi, Indon. 103 4 8 S 119 43 E
Polewali, Sulawesi, Indon. 103 3 21 S 119 31 E
Polgar 53 47 54N 21 6 E
Pŏlgyo-ri 107 34 51N 127 21 E
Poli 124 8 34N 12 54 E
Políaigos, I. 69 36 45N 24 38 E
Policastro, Golfo di 65 39 55N 15 35 E
Police 54 53 33N 14 33 E
Polička 53 49 43N 16 15 E
Polignano a Mare 65 41 0N 17 12 E
Poligny 43 46 50N 5 42 E
Políkhnitas 69 39 4N 26 10 E
Polillo I. 103 14 56N 122 0 E
Polis 92 35 3N 32 30 E
Polístena 65 38 25N 16 4 E
Políyiros 68 40 23N 23 25 E
Polkowice 54 51 29N 16 3 E
Polla 65 40 31N 15 27 E
Pollachi 97 10 35N 77 0 E
Pollensa 58 39 54N 3 2 E
Pollensa, B. de 58 39 55N 3 5 E
Póllica 65 40 13N 15 3 E
Pollino, Mte. 65 39 54N 16 13 E
Pollock 158 45 58N 100 18W
Pollremon 38 53 40N 8 38W
Polna 80 58 31N 28 0 E
Polnovat 76 63 50N 66 5 E
Polo, Kwangtung, China 109 23 9N 114 17 E
Polo, S.-U., China 105 44 59N 81 57 E
Polo, U.S.A. 158 42 0N 89 38W
Pologi 82 47 29N 36 15 E
Polonnoye 80 50 6N 27 30 E
Polossu 108 31 12N 98 36 E
Polotsk 80 55 30N 28 50 E
Polperro 30 50 19N 4 31W
Polruan 30 50 17N 4 36W
Polski Trmbesh 67 43 20N 25 38 E
Polsko Kosovo 67 43 23N 25 38 E
Polson 160 47 45N 114 12W
Poltava 82 49 35N 34 35 E
Polur 97 12 32N 79 11 E
Polyarny 78 69 8N 33 20 E
Pomarance 62 43 18N 10 51 E
Pomarico 65 40 31N 16 33 E
Pomaro 164 18 20N 103 18W
Pombal, Brazil 170 6 55 S 37 50W
Pombal, Port. 56 39 55N 8 40W
Pómbia 69 35 0N 24 51 E
Pomeroy, U.K. 38 54 36N 6 56W
Pomeroy, Ohio, U.S.A. 156 39 0N 82 0W
Pomeroy, Wash., U.S.A. 160 46 30N 117 33W
Pomio 135 5 32 S 151 33 E
Pomona 163 34 2N 117 49W
Pomorie 67 42 26N 27 41 E
Pompano 157 26 12N 80 6W
Pompei 65 40 45N 14 30 E
Pompey 43 48 50N 6 2 E
Pompeys Pillar 160 46 0N 108 0W
Ponape I. 130 6 55N 158 10 E
Ponask, L. 150 54 0N 92 41W
Ponass L. 153 52 16N 103 58W
Ponca 158 42 38N 96 41W
Ponca City 159 36 40N 97 5W
Ponce 147 18 1N 66 37W
Ponchatoula 159 30 27N 90 25W
Poncheville, L. 150 50 10N 76 55W
Poncin 45 46 6N 5 25 E
Pond 163 35 43N 119 20W
Pond Inlet 149 72 30N 75 0W
Pondicherry 97 11 59N 79 50 E
Pondoland 129 31 10 S 29 30W
Pondooma 140 33 29 S 136 59 E
Pondrôme 47 50 6N 5 0 E
Ponds, I. of 151 53 27N 55 52W
Ponferrada 56 42 32N 6 35W
Pongaroa 142 40 33 S 176 15 E
Póngo , Ponte de 127 19 0 S 34 0 E
Pongo, W. 123 8 0N 27 20 E
Poniatowa 54 51 11N 22 3 E
Poniec 54 51 48N 16 50 E
Ponnaiyar, R. 97 11 50N 79 45 E
Ponnani 97 10 45N 75 59 E
Ponnani, R. 97 10 45N 75 59 E
Ponneri 97 13 20N 80 15 E
Ponnyadaung 99 22 0N 94 10 E
Ponoi 78 67 0N 41 0 E
Ponoi, R. 78 67 10N 39 0 E
Ponoka 152 52 42N 113 40W
Ponomarevka 84 53 19N 54 8 E
Ponorogo 103 7 52 S 111 29 E
Pons, France 44 45 35N 0 34W
Pons, Spain 58 41 55N 1 12 E
Ponsul, R. 57 39 54N 8 45 E
Pont-à-Celles 47 50 30N 4 22 E
Pont-à-Mousson 43 45 54N 6 1 E
Pont Audemer 42 49 21N 0 30 E
Pont Aven 42 47 51N 3 47W
Pont Canavese 62 45 24N 7 33 E
Pont Château 42 47 26N 2 8W
Pont-de-Roide 43 47 23N 6 45 E
Pont-de-Salars 44 44 18N 2 44 E
Pont-de-Vaux 43 46 26N 4 56 E
Pont-de-Veyle 45 46 17N 4 53 E
Pont-l'Abbé 42 47 52N 4 15W
Pont Lafrance 151 47 40N 64 58W
Pont, Le 50 46 41N 6 20 E
Pont-l'Eveque 42 49 18N 0 11 E
Pont-St.-Esprit 45 44 16N 4 40 E
Pont-sur-Yonne 43 48 18N 3 10 E
Ponta de Pedras 170 1 23 S 48 52W
Ponta Grossa 173 25 0 S 50 10W
Ponta Pora 173 22 20 S 55 35W
Ponta São Sebastião 129 22 2 S 35 25 E
Pontacq 44 43 11N 0 8W
Pontailler 43 47 18N 5 24 E
Pontal, R. 170 9 8 S 40 12W
Pontalina 171 17 31 S 49 27W
Pontardawe 31 51 43N 3 51W
Pontardulais 31 51 42N 4 3W
Pontarlier 43 46 54N 6 20 E
Pontassieve 63 43 47N 11 25 E
Pontaubault 42 48 40N 1 20W
Pontaumur 44 45 52N 2 40 E
Pontcharra 45 45 26N 6 1 E
Pontchartrain, L. 159 30 12N 90 0W
Pontchâteau 42 47 25N 2 5W
Ponte Alta do Norte 170 10 45 S 47 34W
Ponte Alta, Serra do 171 19 42 S 47 40W
Ponte da Barca 56 41 48N 8 25W
Ponte de Sor 57 39 17N 7 57W
Ponte dell 'Olio 62 44 52N 9 39 E
Ponte di Legno 62 46 15N 10 30 E
Ponte do Lima 56 41 46N 8 35W
Ponte do Pungué 127 19 30 S 34 33 E
Ponte Leccia 45 42 28N 9 13 E
Ponte nell' Alpi 63 46 10N 12 18 E
Ponte Nova 173 20 25 S 42 54W
Ponte San Martino 62 45 36N 7 47 E
Ponte San Pietro 62 45 42N 9 35 E
Pontebba 63 46 30N 13 17 E
Pontecorvo 64 41 28N 13 40 E
Pontedera 62 43 40N 10 37 E
Pontefract 33 53 42N 1 19W
Ponteix 153 49 46N 107 29W
Ponteland 35 53 3N 1 45W
Pontelandolfo 65 41 17N 14 41 E
Pontemacassar Naikliu 103 9 30 S 123 58 E
Pontevedra 56 42 26N 8 40W
Pontevedra □ 56 42 25N 8 39W
Pontevedra, R. de 56 42 22N 8 45W
Pontevico 62 45 16N 10 6 E
Ponthierville = Ubundi 126 0 22 S 25 30 E
Pontiac, Ill., U.S.A. 158 40 50N 88 40W
Pontiac, Mich., U.S.A. 156 42 40N 83 20W
Pontian Kechil 101 1 29N 103 23 E
Pontianak 102 0 3 S 109 15 E
Pontine Is. = Ponziane, Isole 64 40 55N 13 0 E
Pontine Mts. = Karadeniz D. 92 41 30N 35 0 E
Pontínia 64 41 25N 13 2 E
Pontivy 42 48 5N 3 0W
Pontoise 43 49 3N 2 5 E
Ponton, R. 152 58 27N 116 11W
Pontorson 42 48 34N 1 30W
Pontrémoli 62 44 22N 9 52 E
Pontresina 51 46 29N 9 48 E
Pontrhydfendigaid 31 52 17N 3 50W
Pontrieux 28 48 42N 3 10W
Pontrilas 28 51 56N 2 53W
Ponts-de Cé, Les 42 47 25N 0 30W
Pontypool 31 51 42N 3 1W
Pontypridd 31 51 36N 3 21W
Ponza, I. 64 40 55N 12 57 E
Ponziane, Isole 64 40 55N 13 0 E
Poochera 139 32 43 S 134 51 E
Poole 28 50 42N 2 2W
Poole Harb. 28 50 41N 2 0W
Poolewe 36 57 45N 5 38W
Pooley Bridge 32 54 37N 2 49W
Pooley I. 152 52 45N 128 15W
Poonamallee 97 13 3N 80 10 E
Poona = Pune 96 18 29N 73 57 E
Pooncarie 140 33 22 S 142 31 E
Poonindie 140 34 34 S 135 54 E
Poopelloe, L. 140 31 40 S 144 0 E
Poopó, Lago de 174 18 30 S 67 35W
Poor Knights Is. 142 35 29 S 174 43 E
Pooraka 109 34 50 S 138 38 E
Poorman 147 64 5N 155 48W
Popai 108 22 13N 109 55 E
Popak 101 22 15N 109 56 E
Popakai, Austral. 170 32 12 S 141 46 E
Popakai, Surinam 170 3 20N 55 30W
Popanyinning 137 32 40 S 117 2 E
Popayán 174 2 27N 76 36W
Poperinge 47 50 51N 2 42 E
Popigay 77 71 55N 110 47 E
Popilta, L. 140 33 10 S 141 42 E
Popio, L. 140 33 10 S 141 52 E
Poplar 158 48 3N 105 9W
Poplar Bluff 159 36 45N 90 22W
Poplar, R., Man., Can. 153 53 0N 97 19W
Poplar, R., N.W.T., Can. 152 61 22N 121 52W
Poplarville 159 30 55N 89 30W
Popocatepetl, vol. 165 19 10N 98 40W
Popokabaka 124 5 49 S 16 40 E
Pópoli 63 42 12N 13 50 E
Popondetta 135 8 48 S 148 17 E
Popovača 63 45 30N 16 41 E
Popovo 67 43 21N 26 18 E
Poppel 47 51 27N 5 2 E
Poprád 53 49 3N 20 18 E
Poprád, R. 53 49 15N 20 30 E
Poquoson 162 37 7N 76 21W
Poradaha 98 23 51N 89 1 E
Porali, R. 94 27 15N 66 24 E
Porangahau 142 40 17 S 176 37 E
Porangatu 171 13 26 S 49 10W
Porbandar 94 21 44N 69 43 E
Porcher I. 152 53 50N 130 30W
Porcos, R. 171 12 42 S 45 7W
Porcuna 57 37 52N 4 11W
Porcupine, R., Can. 153 59 11N 104 46W
Porcupine, R., U.S.A. 147 67 0N 143 0W
Pordenone 63 45 58N 12 40 E
Pordim 67 43 23N 24 51 E
Pore 174 5 43N 72 0W
Poreč 63 45 14N 13 36 E
Porecatu 171 22 43 S 51 24W
Poretskoye 81 55 9N 46 21 E
Pori 75 61 29N 21 48 E
Porirua 142 41 8 S 174 52 E
Porjus 74 66 57N 19 50 E
Porkhov 80 57 45N 29 38 E
Porkkala 75 59 59N 24 26 E
Porlamar 174 10 57N 63 51W
Porlezza 62 46 2N 9 8 E
Porlock 28 51 13N 3 36W
Porlock B. 28 51 14N 3 37W
Porlock Hill 28 51 12N 3 40W
Porma, R. 56 42 45N 5 21W
Pornic 42 47 7N 2 5W
Poronaysk 77 49 20N 143 0 E
Póros 69 37 30N 23 30 E
Póros, I. 69 37 30N 23 30 E
Poroshiri-Dake 112 42 41N 142 52 E
Poroszló 53 47 39N 20 40 E
Poroto Mts. 127 9 0 S 33 30 E
Porraburdoo 137 23 15 S 117 28 E
Porrentruy 50 47 25N 7 6 E
Porreras 58 39 29N 3 2 E
Porsangen 74 70 40N 25 40 E
Porsgrunn 71 59 10N 9 40 E
Port 43 47 43N 6 4 E
Port Adelaide 140 34 46 S 138 30 E
Port Alberni 152 49 15N 124 50W
Port Albert 141 38 42 S 146 42 E
Port Albert Victor 94 21 0N 71 30 E
Port Alexander 147 56 13N 134 40W
Port Alfred, Can. 151 48 18N 70 53W
Port Alfred, S. Afr. 125 33 36 S 26 55 E
Port Alice 152 50 25N 127 25W
Port Allegany 156 41 49N 78 17W
Port Allen 159 30 30N 91 15W
Port Alma 138 23 38 S 150 53 E
Port Angeles 160 48 7N 123 30W
Port Antonio 166 18 10N 76 30W
Port Aransas 159 27 49N 97 4W
Port Arthur, Austral. 138 43 7 S 147 50 E
Port Arthur, U.S.A. 159 30 0N 94 0W
Port Arthur = Lüshun 107 38 51N 121 20 E
Port Arthur = Thunder Bay 150 48 25N 89 10W
Port Askaig 34 55 51N 6 8W
Port au Port B. 151 48 40N 58 50W
Port-au-Prince 167 18 40N 72 20W
Port Augusta West 140 32 29 S 137 47 E
Port Austin 150 44 3N 82 59W
Port aux Basques 151 47 32N 59 8W
Port Awanui 142 37 50 S 178 29 E
Port Bannatyne 34 55 51N 5 4W
Port Bell 126 0 18N 32 35 E
Port Bergé Vaovao 129 15 33 S 47 40 E
Port Blair 101 11 40N 92 30 E
Port Blandford 151 48 30N 53 50W
Port Bolivar 159 29 20N 94 40W
Port Bou 58 42 25N 3 9 E
Port Bouet 120 5 16N 4 57W
Port Bradshaw 138 12 30 S 137 0 E
Port Broughton 140 33 37 S 137 56 E
Port Burwell 150 42 40N 80 48W
Port Campbell 140 35 37 S 143 1 E
Port Canning 95 22 17N 88 48 E
Port Carlisle 32 54 56N 3 12W
Port-Cartier 151 50 10N 66 50W
Port Chalmers 143 45 49 S 170 30 E
Port Charlotte 34 55 44N 6 22W
Port Chester 162 41 0N 73 41W
Port Clements 152 53 40N 132 10W
Port Clinton 156 41 30N 83 0W
Port Colborne 150 42 50N 79 10W
Port Coquitlam 152 49 20N 122 45W
Port Curtis 138 24 0 S 151 34 E
Port Darwin, Austral. 136 12 24 S 130 45 E
Port Darwin, Falk. Is. 176 51 50 S 59 0W
Port Davey 138 43 16 S 145 55 E
Port-de-Bouc 45 43 24N 4 59 E
Port de Paix 167 19 50N 72 50W
Port Deposit 162 39 37N 76 5W
Port Dickson 101 2 30N 101 49 E
Port Dinorwic 31 53 11N 4 12W
Port Douglas 138 16 30 S 145 30 E
Port Edward 152 54 12N 130 10W
Port Elgin 150 44 25N 81 25W
Port Elizabeth 128 33 58 S 25 40 E
Port Ellen 34 55 38N 6 10W
Port Erin 32 54 5N 4 45W
Port Erroll 37 57 25N 1 50W
Port Essington 136 11 15 S 132 10 E
Port Étienne = Nouadhibou 116 21 0N 17 0W
Port Ewen 162 41 54N 73 59W
Port Fairy 140 38 22 S 142 12 E
Port Fitzroy 142 36 8 S 175 20 E
Port Fouâd = Bûr Fuad 122 31 15N 32 20 E
Port Francqui 124 4 17 S 20 47 E
Port-Gentil 124 0 47 S 8 40 E
Port Gibson 159 31 57N 91 0W
Port Glasgow 34 55 57N 4 40W
Port Gregory 137 27 40 S 114 0 E
Port Harcourt 121 4 40N 7 10 E
Port Hardy 152 50 41N 127 30W
Port Harrison 149 58 25N 78 15W
Port Hawkesbury 151 45 36N 61 22W
Port Hedland 136 20 25 S 118 35 E
Port Heiden 147 57 0N 158 40W
Port Hood 151 46 0N 61 32W
Port Hope 150 44 0N 78 20W
Port Hueneme 163 34 7N 119 12W
Port Huron 156 43 0N 82 28W
Port Isaac 30 50 35N 4 50W
Port Isaac B. 30 50 36N 4 50W
Port Isabel 159 26 12N 97 9W
Port Jackson 133 33 50 S 151 18 E
Port Jefferson 162 40 58N 73 5W
Port Jervis 162 41 22N 74 42W
Port Joinville 42 46 45N 2 23W
Port Kaituma 174 8 3N 59 58W
Port Katon 83 46 27N 38 56 E
Port Kelang 101 3 0N 101 23 E
Port Kembla 141 34 29 S 150 56 E
Port La Nouvelle 44 43 1N 3 3 E
Port Laoise 39 53 2N 7 20W
Port Lavaca 159 28 38N 96 38W
Port Leyden 162 43 35N 75 21W
Port Lincoln 140 34 42 S 135 52 E
Port Logan 34 54 42N 4 57W
Port Loko 120 8 48N 12 46W
Port Louis 42 47 42N 3 22W
Port Lyautey = Kenitra 118 34 15N 6 40W
Port Lyttelton 143 43 37N 172 50 E
Port Macdonnell 140 38 0 S 140 39 E
Port Macquarie 141 31 25 S 152 54 E
Port Maitland 151 44 0N 66 2W
Port Maria 166 18 25N 76 55W
Port Mellon 152 49 32N 123 31W
Port Menier 151 49 51N 64 15W
Port Morant 166 17 54N 76 19W
Port Moresby 135 9 24 S 147 8 E
Port Mouton 151 43 58N 64 50W
Port Musgrave 138 11 55 S 141 50 E
Port Navalo 42 47 34N 2 54W
Port Nelson 153 57 3N 92 36W
Port Nicholson 142 41 20 S 174 52 E
Port Nolloth 128 29 17 S 16 52 E
Port Norris 162 39 15N 75 2W
Port Nouveau-Quebec (George R.) 149 58 30N 65 50W
Port O'Connor 159 28 26N 96 24W
Port of Ness 36 58 29N 6 13W
Port of Spain 167 10 40N 61 20W
Port Orchard 160 47 31N 122 38W
Port Oxford 160 42 45N 124 28W
Port Pegasus 143 47 12 S 167 41 E
Port Perry 150 44 6N 78 56W
Port Phillip B. 139 38 10 S 144 50 E
Port Pirie 140 33 10 S 137 58 E
Port Pólnocny □ 54 54 25N 18 42 E
Port Radium = Echo Bay 148 66 10N 117 40W
Port Renfrew 152 48 30N 124 20W
Port Roper 138 14 45 S 134 47 E
Port Rowan 150 42 40N 80 30W
Port Royal 162 38 10N 77 12W
Port Safaga = Bûr Safâga 122 26 43N 33 57 E
Port Said = Bûr Sa'îd 122 31 16N 32 18 E
Port St. Joe 157 29 49N 85 20W
Port St. Johns = Umzimvubu 129 31 38 S 29 33 E
Port-St. Louis 45 43 23N 4 50 E
Port St. Louis 129 13 7 S 48 48 E
Port-St.-Louis-du-Rhône 45 43 23N 4 49 E
Port St. Mary 32 54 5N 4 45W
Port St. Servain 151 51 21N 58 0W
Port Sanilac 150 43 26N 82 33W
Port Saunders 151 50 40N 57 18W
Port Shepstone 129 30 44 S 30 28 E
Port Simpson 152 54 30N 130 20W
Port Stanley 150 42 40N 81 10W
Port Sudan = Bôr Sôdân 122 19 32N 37 9 E
Port Sunlight 32 53 22N 3 0W
Port Talbot 31 51 35N 3 48W
Port Taufîq = Bûr Taufiq 122 29 54N 32 32 E
Port Townsend 160 48 7N 122 50W
Port-Vendres 44 42 32N 3 8 E
Port Victoria 140 34 30 S 137 29 E
Port Wakefield 140 34 12 S 138 10 E
Port Washington 156 43 25N 87 52W
Port Weld 101 4 50N 100 38 E
Port William 34 54 46N 4 35W
Portachuelo 174 17 10 S 63 20W
Portacloy 38 54 20N 9 48W
Portadown (Craigavon) 38 54 27N 6 26W
Portaferry 38 54 23N 5 32W
Portage, Can. 151 46 40N 64 5W
Portage, U.S.A. 158 43 31N 89 25W
Portage la Prairie 153 49 58N 98 18W
Portage Mt. Dam 152 56 0N 122 0W
Portageville 159 36 25N 89 40W
Portaguiran 36 58 15N 6 10W
Portalegre 57 39 19N 7 25W
Portalegre □ 57 39 20N 7 40W
Portales 159 34 12N 103 25W
Portarlington 39 53 10N 7 10W
Porte, La 156 41 40N 86 40W
Porteirinha 171 15 44 S 43 2W
Portel, Brazil 170 1 57 S 50 49W

Portel Prochowice

Portel, Port. 57 38 19N 7 41W
Porter L., N.W.T., Can. 153 61 41N 108 5W
Porter L., Sask., Can. 153 56 20N 107 20W
Porterville, S. Afr. 128 33 0S 18 57E
Porterville, U.S.A. 163 36 5N 119 0W
Portet 44 43 34N 0 11W
Porteynon 31 51 33N 4 13W
Portglenone 38 54 53N 6 30W
Portgordon 37 57 40N 3 1W
Porth Neigwl 31 52 48N 4 35W
Porth Neigwl, B. 31 52 48N 4 33W
Porthcawl 31 51 28N 3 42W
Porthill 160 49 0N 116 30W
Porthleven 30 50 5N 5 19W
Porthmadog 31 52 55N 4 13W
Portile de Fier 70 44 42N 22 30E
Portimão 57 37 8N 8 32W
Portishead 28 51 29N 2 46W
Portknockle 37 57 40N 2 52W
Portland, N.S.W., Austral. 141 33 20S 150 0E
Portland, Victoria, Austral. 140 38 20S 141 35E
Portland, Conn., U.S.A. 162 41 34N 72 39W
Portland, Me., U.S.A. 151 43 40N 70 15W
Portland, Mich., U.S.A. 156 42 52N 84 58W
Portland, Oreg., U.S.A. 160 45 35N 122 40W
Portland B. 140 38 15S 141 45E
Portland Bill 28 50 31N 2 27W
Portland, C. 133 40 46S 148 0E
Portland I. 142 39 20S 177 51E
Portland, I. of 28 50 32N 2 25W
Portland, Pa. 162 40 55N 75 6W
Portland Prom. 149 58 40N 78 33W
Portlaw 39 52 18N 7 20W
Portmagee 39 51 53N 10 22W
Portmahomack 37 57 50N 3 50W
Portmarnock 38 53 25N 6 10W
Portnacroish 34 56 34N 5 24W
Portnahaven 34 55 40N 6 30W
Portneuf 151 46 43N 71 55W
Pôrto, Brazil 170 3 54S 42 42W
Pôrto, Port. 56 41 8N 8 40W
Pôrto □ 56 41 8N 8 20W
Pôrto Alegre, Mato Grosso, Brazil 170 21 40S 53 30W
Pôrto Alegre, Rio Grande do Sul, Brazil 173 30 5S 51 3W
Porto Alexandre 128 15 55S 11 55E
Porto Amboim = Gunza 124 10 50S 13 50E
Porto Amelia = Pemba 127 12 58S 40 30E
Porto Argentera 62 44 15N 7 27E
Porto Azzurro 62 42 46N 10 24E
Porto Botte 64 39 3N 8 33E
Pôrto Calvo 171 9 4S 35 24W
Porto Civitanova 63 43 19N 13 44E
Pôrto da Fôlha 170 9 55S 37 17W
Pôrto de Moz 170 1 41S 52 22W
Pôrto de Pedras 170 9 10S 35 17W
Porto Empédocle 64 37 18N 13 30E
Pôrto Esperança 174 19 37S 57 29W
Pôrto Franco 170 6 20S 47 24W
Porto Garibaldi 63 44 41N 12 14E
Porto, G. de 45 42 17N 8 34E
Pórto Lago 68 41 1N 25 6E
Porto Mendes 173 24 30S 54 15W
Porto Murtinho 174 21 45S 57 55W
Pôrto Nacional 170 10 40S 48 30W
Porto Novo, Benin 121 6 23N 2 42E
Porto Novo, India 97 11 30N 79 38E
Porto Recanati 63 43 26N 13 40E
Porto San Giorgio 63 43 11N 13 49E
Porto San Stéfano 68 42 26N 11 6E
Porto Santo, I. 116 33 45S 16 25W
Pôrto São José 173 22 43S 53 10W
Pôrto Seguro 171 16 26S 39 5W
Porto Tolle 63 44 57N 12 20E
Porto Tórres 64 40 50N 8 23E
Pôrto União 173 26 10S 51 10W
Pôrto Válter 174 8 5S 72 40W
Porto-Vecchio 45 41 35N 9 16E
Pôrto Velho 174 8 46S 63 54W
Portobelo 166 9 35N 79 42W
Portoferráio 62 42 50N 10 20E
Portogruaro 63 45 47N 12 50E
Portola 160 39 49N 120 28W
Portomaggiore 63 44 41N 11 47E
Porton Camp 28 51 8N 1 42W
Portoscuso 64 39 12N 8 22E
Portovénere 62 44 2N 9 50E
Portoviejo 174 1 0S 80 20W
Portpatrick 34 54 50N 5 7W
Portree 36 57 25N 6 11W
Portroe 39 52 53N 8 20W
Portrush 38 55 13N 6 40W
Portsall 42 48 37N 4 45W
Portsalon 38 55 12N 7 37W
Portskerra 37 58 35N 3 55W
Portslade 29 50 50N 0 11W
Portsmouth, Domin. 167 15 34N 61 27W
Portsmouth, U.K. 28 50 48N 1 6W
Portsmouth, N.H., U.S.A. 162 43 5N 70 45W
Portsmouth, Ohio, U.S.A. 156 38 45N 83 0W
Portsmouth, R.I., U.S.A. 162 41 35N 71 44W
Portsmouth, Va., U.S.A. 156 36 50N 76 20W
Portsoy 37 57 41N 2 41W
Portstewart 38 55 12N 6 43W
Porttipahta 74 68 5N 26 30E
Portugal ■ 56 40 0N 7 0W
Portugalete 58 43 19N 3 4W
Portuguesa □ 174 9 10N 69 15W
Portuguese Guinea = Guinea Bissau 120 12 0N 15 0W
Portuguese Timor ■ = Timor 103 8 0S 126 30E
Portumna 39 53 5N 8 12W
Porvenir 176 53 10S 70 30W
Porvoo 75 60 24N 25 40E
Porzuna 57 39 9N 4 9W
Posada, R. 64 40 40N 9 35E
Posadas, Argent. 173 27 30S 56 0W
Posadas, Spain 57 37 47N 5 11W
Poschiavo 51 46 19N 10 4E
Posets, mt. 58 42 39N 0 25E
Poshan 107 36 30N 117 50E
Posídhio, Ákra 68 39 57N 23 30E
Poso 103 1 20S 120 55E
Poso Colorado 172 23 30S 58 45W
Poso, D. 103 1 20S 120 55E
Posong 107 34 46N 129 5E
Posse 171 14 4S 46 18W
Possel 124 5 5N 19 10E
Possession I. 13 72 4S 172 0E
Pössneck 48 50 42N 11 34E
Possut'eng Hu 105 42 0N 87 0E
Post 159 33 13N 101 21W
Post Falls 160 47 50N 116 59W
Postavy 80 55 4N 26 58E
Postbridge 30 50 36N 3 54W
Poste-de-la-Baleine 30 50 36N 3 54W
Poste Maurice Cortier (Bidon 5) 118 22 14N 1 2E
Postiljon, Kepulauan 103 6 30S 118 50E
Postmasburg 128 28 18S 23 5E
Postojna 63 45 46N 14 12E
Potamós 69 39 38N 19 53E
Potchefstroom 125 26 41S 27 7E
Potcoava 70 44 30N 24 39E
Poté 171 17 49S 41 49W
Poteau 159 35 5N 94 37W
Poteet 159 29 4N 98 35W
Potelu, Lacul 70 43 44N 24 20E
Potenza 65 40 40N 15 50E
Potenza Picena 63 43 22N 13 37E
Poteriteri, L. 143 46 5S 167 10E
Potes 56 43 15N 4 42W
Potgietersrus 129 24 10S 29 3E
Poti 83 42 10N 41 38E
Potiraguá 171 15 36S 39 53W
Potiskum 121 11 39N 11 2E
Potlogi 70 44 34N 25 34E
Potomac, R. 162 38 0N 76 23W
Potosí 174 19 38S 65 50W
Potosí □ 174 20 31S 67 0W
Pot'ou 106 37 57N 116 39E
Potrerillos 172 26 20S 69 30W
Potros, Cerro del 172 28 32S 69 0W
Potsdam, Ger. 48 52 23N 13 4E
Potsdam, U.S.A. 156 44 40N 74 59W
Potsdam □ 48 52 40N 12 50E
Potter 158 41 15N 103 20W
Potter Heigham 29 52 44N 1 33E
Potterne 28 51 19N 2 0W
Potters Bar 29 51 42N 0 11W
Potterspury 29 52 5N 0 52W
Pottery Hill = Abu Ballas 122 24 26N 27 36E
Pottstown 162 40 17N 75 40W
Pottsville 162 40 39N 76 12W
Pottuvil 93 6 55N 81 50E
P'otzu 109 23 30N 120 25E
Pouancé 42 47 44N 1 10W
Pouce Coupé 152 55 40N 120 10W
Poughkeepsie 162 41 40N 73 57W
Pouilly 43 47 18N 2 57E
Poulaphouca Res. 39 53 8N 6 30W
Pouldu, Le 42 47 41N 3 36W
Poulsbo 160 47 45N 122 39W
Poultney 162 43 31N 73 14W
Poulton le Fylde 32 53 51N 2 59W
Poundstock 30 50 44N 4 34W
Pouso Alegre, Mato Grosso, Brazil 175 11 55S 57 0W
Pouso Alegre, Minas Gerais, Brazil 173 22 14S 45 57W
Pouzages 44 46 40N 0 50W
Povenets 78 62 50N 34 50E
Poverty Bay 142 38 43S 178 2E
Póvoa de Lanhosa 56 41 33N 8 15W
Póvoa de Varzim 56 41 25N 8 46W
Povorino 81 51 12N 42 28E
Powassan 150 46 5N 79 25W
Poway 163 32 58N 117 2W
Powder, R. 158 46 47N 105 12W
Powell 160 44 45N 108 45W
Powell Creek 136 18 6S 133 46E
Powell River 152 49 22N 125 31W
Powers, Mich., U.S.A. 156 45 40N 87 32W
Powers, Oreg., U.S.A. 160 42 53N 124 2W
Powers Lake 158 48 37N 102 38W
Powick 28 52 9N 2 15W
Powis, Vale of 23 52 40N 3 10W
Powys □ 31 52 20N 3 20W
P'oyang 109 29 1N 116 38E
Poyang Hu 109 29 10N 116 10E
Poyarkovo 77 49 36N 128 41E
Poyntzpass 38 54 17N 6 22W
Poysdorf 53 48 40N 16 37E
Poza de la Sal 58 42 35N 3 31W
Poza Rica 165 20 33N 97 27W
Pozarevac 66 44 35N 21 18E
Pozega 66 45 21N 17 41E
Pozhva 84 59 5N 56 5E
Poznan 54 52 25N 17 0E
Pozo 163 35 20N 120 24W
Pozo Alcón 59 37 42N 2 56W
Pozo Almonte 174 20 10S 69 50W
Pozoblanco 57 38 23N 4 51W
Pozzallo 65 36 44N 15 40E
Pra, R. 121 5 30N 1 38W
Prabuty 54 53 47N 19 15E
Prača 66 43 47N 18 43E
Prachatice 52 49 1N 14 0E
Prachin Buri 100 14 0N 101 25E
Prachuap Khiri Khan 101 11 49N 99 48E
Pradelles 44 44 46N 3 52E
Pradera 174 3 25N 76 15W
Prades 44 42 38N 2 23E
Prado 171 17 20S 39 13W
Prado del Rey 57 36 48N 5 33W
Præstø 73 55 8N 12 2E
Pragersko 63 46 27N 15 42E
Prague = Praha 52 50 5N 14 22E
Praha 52 50 5N 14 22E
Prahecq 44 46 19N 0 26W
Prahita, R. 97 19 0N 79 55E
Prahova □ 70 44 50N 25 50E
Prahova, R. 70 44 50N 25 50E
Prahova, Reg. 70 44 50N 25 50E
Prahovo 66 44 18N 22 39E
Praid 70 46 32N 25 10E
Prainha, Amazonas, Brazil 174 7 10S 60 30W
Prainha, Pará, Brazil 175 1 45S 53 30W
Prairie, Queens., Austral. 138 20 50S 144 35E
Prairie, S. Australia, Austral. 109 34 51S 138 49E
Prairie City 160 45 27N 118 44W
Prairie du Chien 158 43 1N 91 9W
Prairie, R. 159 34 45N 101 15W
Praja 102 8 39S 116 27E
Prajeczno 54 51 10N 19 0E
Pramánda 68 39 32N 21 8E
Pran Buri 100 12 23N 99 55E
Prang 121 8 1N 0 56W
Prapat 102 2 41N 98 58E
Praszka 54 51 32N 18 31E
Prata, Minas Gerais, Brazil 171 19 25S 49 0W
Prata, Pará, Brazil 170 1 10S 47 35W
Prática di Mare 64 41 40N 12 26E
Prato 62 43 53N 11 5E
Prátola Peligna 63 42 7N 13 51E
Pratovécchio 63 43 44N 11 43E
Prats-de-Molló 44 42 25N 2 27E
Pratt 159 37 40N 98 45W
Pratteln 50 47 31N 7 41E
Prättigau 51 46 56N 9 44E
Prattville 157 32 30N 86 28W
Pravara, R. 96 19 30N 74 28E
Pravdinsk 81 56 29N 43 28E
Pravia 56 43 30N 6 12W
Prawle Pt. 30 50 13N 3 41W
Pré-en-Pail 42 48 28N 0 12W
Pré St. Didier 62 45 45N 7 0E
Precordillera 172 30 0S 69 1W
Predáppio 63 44 7N 11 58E
Predazzo 63 46 19N 11 37E
Predejane 66 42 51N 22 9E
Preeceville 153 51 57N 102 40W
Prees 32 52 54N 2 40W
Preesall 32 53 55N 2 58W
Préfailles 42 47 9N 2 11W
Pregonero 174 8 1N 71 46W
Pregrada 63 46 11N 15 45E
Preko 63 44 7N 15 14E
Prelate 153 50 51N 109 24W
Prelog 63 46 18N 16 32E
Premier 152 56 4N 129 56W
Premier Downs 137 30 30S 126 30E
Premont 159 27 19N 91 8W
Premuda, I. 63 44 20N 14 36E
Prenj, mt. 66 43 33N 17 53E
Prenjasi 68 41 6N 20 32E
Prentice 158 45 31N 90 19W
Prenzlau 48 53 19N 13 51E
Prepansko Jezero 68 40 45N 21 0E
Preparis I. 99 14 55N 93 45E
Preparis North Channel 101 15 12N 93 40E
Preparis South Channel 101 14 36N 93 40E
Prerov 53 49 28N 17 27E
Prescot 32 53 27N 2 49W
Prescott, Can. 150 44 45N 75 30W
Prescott, Ariz., U.S.A. 161 34 35N 112 30W
Prescott, Ark., U.S.A. 159 33 49N 93 22W
Preservation Inlet 143 46 8S 166 35E
Preševo 66 42 19N 21 39E
Presho 158 43 56N 100 4W
Preshute 28 51 24N 1 45W
Presicce 65 39 53N 18 13E
Presidencia de la Plaza 172 27 0S 60 0W
Presidencia Roque Sáenz Peña 172 26 45S 60 30W
Presidente Dutra 164 5 15S 44 30W
Presidente Epitácio 171 21 46S 52 6W
Presidente Hayes □ 172 24 0S 59 0W
Presidente Hermes 174 11 0S 61 55W
Presidente Prudente 173 22 5S 51 25W
Presidente Rogue Saena Peña 172 34 33S 58 30W
Presidio, Mexico 164 29 29N 104 23W
Presidio, U.S.A. 159 29 30N 104 20W
Preslav 67 43 10N 26 52E
Prespa, L. = Prepansko Jezero 68 40 45N 21 0E
Prespa, mt. 67 41 44N 25 0E
Presque Isle 151 46 40N 68 0W
Prestatyn 31 53 20N 3 24W
Prestea 120 5 22N 2 7W
Presteigne 31 52 17N 3 0W
Preštice 52 49 34N 13 20E
Preston, Borders, U.K. 35 55 48N 2 18W
Preston, Dorset, U.K. 28 50 38N 2 26W
Preston, Lancs., U.K. 32 53 46N 2 42W
Preston, Idaho, U.S.A. 160 42 0N 112 0W
Preston, Minn., U.S.A. 158 43 39N 92 3W
Preston, Nev., U.S.A. 160 38 59N 115 2W
Preston, C. 136 20 51S 116 12E
Prestonpans 35 55 58N 3 0W
Prestwich 32 53 32N 2 18W
Prestwick 34 55 30N 4 38W
Prêto, R., Bahia 170 11 21S 43 52W
Pretoria 129 25 44S 28 12E
Prettyboy Res. 162 39 37N 76 43W
Preuilly-sur-Claise 42 46 51N 0 56E
Préveza 69 38 57N 20 47E
Préveza □ 68 39 20N 20 40E
Prey-Veng 101 11 35N 105 29E
Priazovskoye 82 46 22N 35 28E
Pribilov Is. 12 56 0N 170 0W
Priboj 66 43 35N 19 32E
Pribram 52 49 41N 14 2E
Price 160 39 40N 110 48W
Price I. 152 52 23N 128 41W
Prichalnaya 83 48 57N 44 33E
Priego 58 40 38N 2 21W
Priego de Córdoba 57 37 27N 4 12W
Priekule 80 57 27N 21 45E
Prieska 128 29 40S 22 42E
Priest Gully Cr. 108 27 29S 153 11E
Priest L. 160 48 30N 116 55W
Priest River 160 48 11N 117 0W
Priest Valley 163 36 10N 120 39W
Priestly 152 54 8N 125 20W
Prievidza 53 48 46N 18 36E
Prijedor 63 44 58N 16 41E
Prijepolje 66 43 27N 19 40E
Prilep 66 41 21N 21 37E
Priluki 80 50 30N 32 15E
Prime Seal I. 138 40 3S 147 43E
Primeira Cruz 170 2 30S 43 26W
Primorsko 67 42 15N 27 44E
Primorsko-Akhtarsk 82 46 2N 38 10E
Primrose L. 153 54 55N 109 45W
Prince Albert 153 53 15N 105 50W
Prince Albert Nat. Park 153 54 0N 106 25W
Prince Albert Pen. 148 72 30N 116 0W
Prince Alfred C. 12 74 20N 124 40W
Prince Charles I. 149 67 47N 76 12W
Prince Edward I. □. 151 44 2N 77 20W
Prince Edward Is. 11 45 15S 39 0E
Prince Frederick 162 38 33N 76 35W
Prince George 152 53 50N 122 50W
Prince of Wales, C. 147 65 50N 168 0W
Prince of Wales I. 147 73 0N 99 0W
Prince of Wales, I. 147 53 30N 131 30W
Prince of Wales Is. 135 10 40S 142 10E
Prince Patrick I. 12 77 0N 120 0W
Prince Regent Inlet 12 73 0N 90 0W
Prince Rupert 152 54 20N 130 20W
Prince William Sd. 147 60 20N 146 30W
Princenhage 47 51 9N 4 45E
Princes Risborough 29 51 43N 0 50W
Princesa Isabel 170 7 44S 38 0W
Princess Anne 162 38 12N 75 41W
Princess Charlotte B. 138 14 25S 144 0E
Princess Mary Ranges 136 15 30S 125 30E
Princess Royal I. 152 53 0N 128 40W
Princeton, Can. 152 49 27N 120 30W
Princeton, Ill., U.S.A. 158 41 25N 89 25W
Princeton, Ind., U.S.A. 156 38 20N 87 35W
Princeton, Ky., U.S.A. 156 37 6N 87 55W
Princeton, Mo., U.S.A. 158 40 23N 93 35W
Princeton, N.J., U.S.A. 162 40 18N 74 40W
Princeton, W. Va., U.S.A. 156 37 21N 81 8W
Princetown 30 50 33N 4 0W
Principe Chan. 152 53 28N 130 0W
Principe da Beira 174 12 20S 64 30W
Principe, I. de 114 1 37N 7 27E
Prineville 160 44 17N 120 57W
Prins Albert 128 33 12S 22 2E
Prins Harald Kyst 13 70 0S 35 1E
Prinzapolca 166 13 20N 83 35W
Prior, C. 56 43 34N 8 17W
Pripet Marshes = Polesye 80 52 0N 28 10E
Pripet, R. = Pripyat, R. 80 51 30N 30 0E
Pripyat, R. 80 51 30N 30 0E
Prislop, Pasul 70 47 37N 25 15E
Pristen 81 51 15N 12 40E
Priština 66 42 40N 21 13E
Pritchard 157 30 47N 88 5W
Pritzwalk 48 53 10N 12 11E
Privas 45 44 45N 4 37E
Priverno 64 41 29N 13 10E
Privolzhsk 81 57 9N 14 9E
Privolzhskaya Vozvyshennest 81 51 0N 46 0E
Privolzhskiy 81 51 25N 46 3E
Privolzhye 81 52 52N 48 33E
Privutnoye 83 47 12N 43 30E
Prizren 66 42 13N 20 45E
Prizzi 64 37 44N 13 24E
Prnjavor 66 44 52N 17 43E
Probolinggo 103 7 46S 113 13E
Probus 30 50 17N 4 55W
Prochowice 54 51 17N 16 20E

Procida, I
Qattâra, Munkhafed el

Procida, I. 64 40 46N 14 0E
Proctor 162 43 40N 73 2W
Proddatur 97 14 45N 78 30E
Proença-a-Nova 57 39 45N 7 54W
Profondeville 47 50 23N 4 52E
Progreso 165 21 20N 89 40W
Prokhladnyy 83 43 50N 44 2E
Prokletije 68 42 30N 19 45E
Prokopyevsk 76 54 0N 87 3E
Prokuplje 66 43 16N 21 36E
Proletarskaya 83 46 42N 41 50E
Prome = Pyè 99 18 45N 95 30E
Prophet, R. 152 58 48N 122 40W
Propriá 170 10 13S 36 51W
Propriano 45 41 41N 8 52E
Proserpine 138 20 21S 148 36E
Prospect, Austral. 109 34 53S 138 36E
Prospect, U.S.A. 162 43 18N 75 9W
Prosser 160 46 11N 119 52W
•Prostějov 53 49 30N 17 9E
Proston 139 26 14S 151 32E
Proszowice 54 50 13N 20 16E
Protection 159 37 16N 99 30W
Próti, I. 69 37 5N 21 32E
Provadija 67 43 12N 27 30E
Proven 47 50 54N 2 40E
Provence 45 43 40N 5 46E
Providence, Ky., U.S.A. 156 37 25N 87 46W
Providence, R.I., U.S.A. 162 41 41N 71 15W
Providence Bay 150 45 41N 82 15W
Providence C. 143 45 59S 166 29E
Providence Mts. 161 35 0N 115 30W
Providencia 174 0 28S 76 28W
Providencia, I. de 166 13 25N 81 26W
Provideniya 77 64 23N 173 18E
Province Wellesley 101 5 15N 100 20E
Provincetown 162 42 5N 70 11W
Provins 43 48 33N 3 15E
Provo 160 40 16N 111 37W
Provost 153 52 25N 110 20W
Prozor 66 43 50N 17 34E
Prudentópolis 171 25 12S 50 57W
Prudhoe 35 54 57N 1 52W
Prudhoe Bay, Austral. 138 21 30S 149 30W
Prudhoe Bay, U.S.A. 147 70 20N 148 20W
Prudhoe I. 138 21 23S 149 45E
Prudhoe Land 12 78 1N 65 0W
Prud'homme 153 52 20N 105 54W
Prudnik 54 50 20N 17 38E
Prüm 49 50 14N 6 22E
Pruszcz 54 54 17N 19 40E
Pruszków 54 52 9N 20 49E
Prut, R. 70 46 3N 28 10E
Prvič, I. 63 44 55N 14 47E
Prvomay 67 42 8N 25 17E
Prydz B. 13 69 0S 74 0E
Pryor 159 36 17N 95 20W
Przasnysz 54 53 2N 20 45E
Przedbórz 54 51 6N 19 53E
Przedecz 54 52 20N 18 53E
Przemyśl 54 49 50N 22 45E
Przemyśl □ 54 80 0N 23 0E
Przeworsk 54 50 6N 22 32E
Przewóz 54 51 28N 14 57E
Przhevalsk 85 42 30N 78 20E
Przysucha 54 51 22N 20 38E
Psakhná 69 38 34N 23 35E
Psarà, I. 69 38 37N 25 38E
Psathoúra, I. 68 39 30N 24 12E
Psel, R. 82 49 25N 33 50E
Pserimos, I. 69 36 56N 27 12E
Pskem, R. 85 41 38N 70 1E
Pskemskiy Khrebet 85 42 0N 70 45E
Pskent 85 40 54N 69 20E
Pskov 80 57 50N 28 25E
Psunj, mt. 66 45 25N 17 19E
Pszczyna 54 49 59N 18 58E
Pteleón 69 39 3N 22 57E
Ptich, R. 80 52 30N 28 45E
Ptolemais 68 40 30N 21 43E
Ptuj 63 46 28N 15 50E
Ptujska Gora 63 46 23N 15 47E
Pua 100 19 11N 100 55E
Puán 172 37 30S 63 0W
P'uan 108 25 47N 104 57E
Puan 107 35 44N 126 7E
Pubnico 151 43 47N 65 50W
Pucallpa 174 8 25S 74 30W
P'uchen 107 37 21N 118 1E
P'uch'eng 109 27 45N 118 47E
Pucheni 70 45 12N 25 17E
P'uch'i 109 29 43N 113 53E
Pucisce 63 43 22N 16 43E
Puck 54 54 45N 18 23E
Puddletown 28 50 45N 2 21W
Pudsey 33 53 47N 1 40W
Pudukkottai 97 10 28N 78 47E
Puebla 165 19 0N 98 10W
Puebla □ 165 18 30N 98 0W
Puebla de Alcocer 57 38 59N 5 14W
Puebla de Don Fadrique 59 37 58N 2 25W
Puebla de Don Rodrigo 57 39 5N 4 37W
Puebla de Guzmán 57 37 37N 7 15W
Puebla de los Infantes, La 57 37 47N 5 24W
Puebla de Montalbán, La 56 39 52N 4 22W
Puebla de Sanabria 56 42 4N 6 38W
Puebla de Trives 56 42 20N 7 10W
Puebla del Caramiñal 56 42 37N 8 56W
Puebla, La 58 39 50N 3 0E
Pueblo 158 38 20N 104 40W
Pueblo Bonito 161 36 4N 107 57W
Pueblo Hundido 172 26 20S 69 30W
Pueblo Nuevo 174 8 26N 71 26W
Pueblonuevo 55 38 16N 5 16W
Puelches 172 38 5S 66 0W
Puelén 172 37 32S 67 38W
Puente Alto 172 33 32S 70 35W
Puente del Arzobispo 56 39 48N 5 10W
Puente Genil 57 37 22N 4 47W
Puente la Reina 58 42 40N 1 49W
Puentearas 56 42 10N 8 28W
Puentedeume 56 43 24N 8 10W
Puentes de García Rodríguez 56 43 27N 7 51W
Puerco, R. 161 35 10N 109 45W
Puerh 105 23 11N 100 56E
P'uerh 108 23 5N 101 5E
Puerhching 105 47 43N 86 53E
Puerta, La 59 38 22N 2 45W
Puerto Aisén 176 45 10S 73 0W
Puerto Angel 165 15 40N 96 29W
Puerto Arista 165 15 56N 93 48W
Puerto Armuelles 166 8 20N 83 10W
Puerto Ayacucho 174 5 40N 67 35W
Puerto Barrios 166 15 40N 88 40W
Puerto Bermejo 172 26 55S 58 34W
Puerto Bermúdez 174 10 20S 75 0W
Puerto Bolívar 174 3 10S 79 55W
Puerto Cabello 174 10 28N 68 1W
Puerto Cabezas 166 14 0N 83 30W
Puerto Cabo Gracias a Dios 166 15 0N 83 10W
Puerto Capaz = Jebba 118 35 11N 4 43W
Puerto Carreño 174 6 12N 67 22W
Puerto Casado 172 22 19S 57 56W
Puerto Castilla 166 16 0N 86 0W
Puerto Chicama 174 7 45S 79 20W
Puerto Coig 176 50 54S 69 15W
Puerto Columbia 174 10 59N 74 58W
Puerto Cortés, C. Rica 166 8 20N 82 20W
Puerto Cortés, Hond. 166 15 51N 88 0W
Puerto Cuemani 174 0 5N 73 21W
Puerto Cumarebo 174 11 29N 69 21W
Puerto de Cabras 116 28 40N 13 30W
Puerto de Morelos 165 20 49N 86 52W
Puerto de Santa María 57 36 36N 6 13W
Puerto Deseado 176 47 45S 66 0W
Puerto Heath 174 12 25S 68 45W
Puerto Huitoto 174 0 18N 74 3W
Puerto Juárez 165 21 11N 86 49W
Puerto La Cruz 174 10 13N 64 38W
Puerto Leguízamo 174 0 12S 74 46W
Puerto Libertad 164 29 55N 112 41W
Puerto Limón, Meta, Colomb. 174 3 23N 73 30W
Puerto Limón, Putumayo, Colomb. 174 1 3N 76 30W
Puerto Lobos 176 42 0S 65 3W
Puerto López 174 4 5N 72 58W
Puerto Lumbreras 59 37 34N 1 48W
Puerto Madryn 176 42 48S 65 4W
Puerto Maldonado 174 12 30S 69 10W
Puerto Manotí 166 21 22N 76 50W
Puerto Mazarrón 59 37 34N 1 15W
Puerto Mercedes 174 1 11N 72 53W
Puerto Montt 176 41 22S 72 40W
Puerto Natales 176 51 45S 72 25W
Puerto Nuevo 174 5 53N 69 56W
Puerto Ordaz 174 8 16N 62 44W
Puerto Padre 166 21 13N 76 35W
Puerto Páez 174 6 13N 67 28W
Puerto Peñasco 164 31 20N 113 33W
Puerto Pinasco 172 22 43S 57 50W
Puerto Pirámides 176 42 35S 64 20W
Puerto Plata 167 19 40N 70 45W
Puerto Princesa 94 9 44N 118 44E
Puerto Quellón 176 43 7S 73 37W
Puerto Quepos 166 9 29N 84 6W
Puerto Real 57 36 33N 6 12W
Puerto Rico 174 1 54N 75 10W
Puerto Rico ■ 147 18 15N 66 45W
Puerto Rico Trough 14 20 0N 63 0W
Puerto Sastre 172 22 25S 57 55W
Puerto Suárez 174 18 58S 57 52W
Puerto Tejada 174 3 14N 76 24W
Puerto Umbria 174 0 52N 76 33W
Puerto Vallarta 164 20 26N 105 15W
Puerto Villamizar 174 8 25N 72 30W
Puerto Wilches 174 7 21N 73 54W
Puertollano 57 38 43N 4 7W
Puertomarín 56 42 48N 7 37W
Pueyrredón, L. 176 47 20S 72 0W
Puffin I., Ireland 39 51 50N 10 25W
Puffin I., U.K. 31 53 19N 4 1W
Pugachev 81 52 0N 48 55E
Puge 126 4 45S 33 11E
Puget Sd. 160 47 15N 123 30W
Puget-Théniers 45 43 58N 6 53E
Púglia 65 41 0N 16 30E
Pugŏdong 107 42 5N 130 0E
Pugu 126 6 55S 39 4E
Puha 142 38 30S 177 50E
P'uhsien 106 36 25N 110 4E
Puhute Mesa 163 37 25N 116 50W
Pui 70 45 30N 23 4E
Puieşti 70 46 25N 27 33E
Puig Mayor, Mte. 58 39 49N 2 47E
Puigcerdá 58 42 24N 1 50E
Puigmal, Mt. 58 42 23N 2 7E
Puisaye, Collines de 43 47 34N 3 28E
Puiseaux 43 48 11N 2 30E
Pujon-chosuji 107 40 35N 127 35E
Puka 68 42 2N 19 53E
Pukaki L. 143 44 4S 170 1E
Pukatawagan 153 55 45N 101 20W
Pukchin 107 40 12N 125 45E
Pukchŏng 107 40 14N 128 18E
Pukearuhe 142 38 55S 174 31E
Pukekohe 142 37 12S 174 55E
Puketeraki Ra. 143 42 58S 172 13E
Pukeuri 143 45 4S 171 2E
P'uko 108 27 27N 102 34E
Pukoo 147 21 4N 156 48W
P'uk'ou 109 32 7N 118 43E
Pula 64 39 0N 9 0E
Pula (Pola) 63 44 54N 13 57E
Pulaski, N.Y., U.S.A. 162 43 32N 76 9W
Pulaski, Tenn., U.S.A. 157 35 10N 87 0W
Pulaski, Va., U.S.A. 156 37 4N 80 49W
Pulawy 54 51 23N 21 59E
Pulborough 29 50 58N 0 30W
Pulgaon 96 20 44N 78 21E
Pulham Market 29 52 25N 1 15E
Pulham St. Mary 29 52 25N 1 14E
Pulicat, L. 97 13 40N 80 15E
Puliyangudi 97 9 11N 77 24E
Pullabooka 141 33 44S 147 46E
Pullen Cr. 108 27 33S 152 54E
Pullman 160 46 49N 117 10W
Pulmakong 121 11 2N 0 2E
Pulog, Mt. 103 16 40N 120 50E
Puloraja 102 4 55N 95 24E
Pułtusk 54 52 43N 21 6E
Pumlumon Fawr 31 52 29N 3 47W
Pumpsaint 31 52 3N 3 58W
Puna 174 19 45S 65 28W
Puna de Atacama 172 25 0S 67 0W
Puná, I. 174 2 55S 80 5W
Punakha 98 27 42N 89 52E
Punalur 97 9 0N 76 56E
Punasar 94 27 6N 73 6E
Punata 174 17 25S 65 50W
Punch 95 33 48N 74 4E
Pune 96 18 29N 73 57E
Pungsan 107 40 50N 128 9E
P'uning 109 23 19N 116 9E
Punjab □ 94 31 0N 76 0E
Punkatawagon 153 55 44N 101 20W
Puno 174 15 55S 70 3W
Punt, La 51 46 35N 9 56E
Punta Alta 176 38 53S 62 4W
Punta Arenas 176 53 0S 71 0W
Punta de Díaz 172 28 0S 70 45W
Punta de Piedras 174 10 54N 64 6W
Punta del Lago Viedma 176 49 45S 72 0W
Punta Gorda, Belize 165 16 10N 88 45W
Punta Gorda, U.S.A. 157 26 55N 82 0W
Punta Prieta 164 28 58N 114 17W
Puntabie 139 32 12S 134 5E
Puntarenas 166 10 0N 84 50W
Puntes de García Rodríguez 56 43 27N 7 50W
Punto Fijo 174 11 42N 70 13W
Punxsutawney 156 40 56N 79 0W
P'upei 108 22 16N 109 33E
Puquio 174 14 45S 74 10W
Pur, R. 76 65 30N 77 40E
Purace, vol. 174 2 21N 76 23W
Puračió 66 44 33N 18 28E
Purari, R. 135 7 49S 145 0E
Purbeck, Isle of 28 50 40N 2 5W
Purcell 159 35 0N 97 25W
Purchena Tetica 59 37 21N 2 21W
Purdy Is. 138 3 0S 146 0E
Purfleet 29 51 29N 0 15E
Puri 96 19 50N 85 58E
Purificación 174 3 51N 74 55W
Purísima, La 164 26 10N 112 4W
Purley 28 51 29N 1 4W
Purli 96 18 50N 76 35E
Purmerend 47 52 30N 4 58E
Purna, R. 96 19 55N 76 20E
Purnea 95 25 45N 87 31E
Pursat 101 12 34N 103 50E
Puruey 174 7 35N 64 48W
Purukcahu 102 0 35S 114 35E
Purulia 95 23 17N 86 33E
Purus, R. 174 5 25S 64 0W
Purwakarta 103 6 35S 107 29E
Purwodadi, Jawa, Indon. 103 7 7S 110 55E
Purwodadi, Jawa, Indon. 103 7 51S 110 0E
Purworejo 103 7 43S 110 2E
Puryŏng 107 42 0N 129 43E
Pus, R. 96 19 50N 77 45E
Pusad 96 19 56N 77 36E
Pusan 107 35 5N 129 0E
Pushchino 77 54 20N 158 10E
Pushkin 80 59 45N 30 25E
Pushkino 81 51 16N 47 9E
Puskitamika L. 150 49 20N 76 30W
Püspökladány 53 47 19N 21 6E
Pussa 129 24 30S 33 55E
Pustoshka 80 56 11N 29 30E
Puszczykowo 54 52 18N 16 49E
Putahow L. 153 59 54N 100 40W
Putao 98 27 28N 97 30E
Putaruru 142 38 2S 175 50E
Putbus 48 54 19N 13 29E
Put'ehach'i 105 48 0N 122 43E
Puţeni 70 45 49N 27 42E
Puthein Myit, R. 99 15 56N 94 18E
P'ut'ien 109 25 27N 118 59E
Putignano 65 40 50N 17 5E
P'uting 108 26 19N 105 45E
Putlitz 48 53 15N 12 3E
Putna 70 47 50N 25 33E
Putna, R. 70 45 42N 27 26E
Putnam 162 41 55N 71 55W
Putnok 53 48 18N 20 26E
P'ut'o 109 29 58N 122 15E
Putorana, Gory 77 69 0N 95 0E
Putorino 142 39 4S 177 9E
Putta 47 51 4N 4 38E
Puttalam 93 8 1N 79 55E
Puttalam Lagoon 97 8 15N 79 45E
Putte 47 51 22N 4 24E
Putten 46 52 16N 5 36E
Puttgarden 48 54 28N 11 15E
Puttur 97 12 46N 75 12E
Putty 141 32 57S 150 42E
Putumayo □ 174 1 30S 70 0W
Putumayo, R. 174 1 30S 70 0W
Putussibau, G. 102 0 45N 113 50E
Pututahi 142 38 39S 177 53E
Puurs 47 51 5N 4 17E
Puy-de-Dôme 44 45 46N 2 57E
Puy-de-Dôme □ 44 45 47N 3 0E
Puy-de-Sancy 44 45 32N 2 41E
Puy Guillaume 44 45 57N 3 28E
Puy, Le 44 45 3N 3 52E
Puy l'Evêque 44 44 31N 1 9E
Puyallup 160 47 10N 122 22W
P'uyang 106 35 41N 115 0E
Puylaurens 44 43 35N 2 0E
Puyôo 44 43 33N 0 56W
Pwalagu 121 10 38N 0 50W
Pwani □, Tanz. 126 7 0S 39 0E
Pwani □, Tanz. 126 7 0S 39 30E
Pweto 127 8 25S 28 51E
Pwinbyu 98 20 23N 94 40E
Pwllheli 31 52 54N 4 26W
Pya Ozero 78 66 8N 31 22E
Pyana, R. 81 55 30N 45 0E
Pyandzh 85 37 14N 69 6E
Pyandzh, R. 85 37 6N 68 20E
Pyapon 98 16 5N 95 50E
Pyasina, R. 77 72 30N 90 30E
Pyatigorsk 83 44 2N 43 0E
Pyatikhatki 82 48 28N 33 38E
Pyaye 98 19 12N 95 10E
Pyè 98 18 49N 95 13E
Pyinbauk 98 19 10N 95 12E
Pyinmana 98 19 45N 96 20E
Pyŏktong 107 40 37N 125 26E
Pyŏnggang 107 38 24N 127 17E
Pyŏngtaek 107 37 1N 127 4E
P'yŏngyang 107 39 0N 125 45E
Pyote 159 31 34N 103 5W
Pyramid L. 160 40 0N 119 30W
Pyramid Pk. 163 36 25N 116 37W
Pyramids 122 29 58N 31 9E
Pyrenees 44 42 45N 0 18E
Pyrénées-Atlantiques □ 44 43 15N 1 0W
Pyrénées-Orientales □ 44 42 35N 2 26E
Pyrzyce 54 53 10N 14 55E
Pyshchug 81 58 57N 45 27E
Pyshma, R. 84 57 8N 66 18E
Pytalovo 80 57 5N 27 55E
Python 127 17 56S 29 10E
Pyttegga 71 62 13N 7 42E
Pyu 98 18 30N 96 35E
Pyzdry 54 52 11N 17 42E

Q

Qaar Zeitun 122 29 10N 25 48E
Qabalon 90 32 8N 35 17E
Qabatiya 90 32 25N 35 16E
Qadam 93 32 55N 66 45E
Qadhimah 92 22 20N 39 13E
Qadian 94 31 51N 74 19E
Qal at Shajwa 122 25 2N 38 57E
Qala-i-Jadid (Spin Baldak) 94 31 1N 66 25E
Qala-i-Kirta 93 32 15N 63 0E
Qala Nau 93 35 0N 63 5E
Qala Punja 93 37 0N 72 40E
Qala Yangi 94 34 20N 66 30E
Qal'at al Akhdhar 92 28 0N 37 10E
Qal'at Saura 122 26 10N 38 40E
Qal'eh Shaharak 93 34 10N 64 20E
Qalqīlya 90 32 12N 34 58E
Qalyûb 122 30 12N 31 11E
Qam 90 32 36N 35 43E
Qamar, Ghubbat al 91 16 20N 52 30E
Qamruddin Karez 94 31 45N 68 20E
Qana 90 33 12N 35 17E
Qâra 122 29 38N 26 30E
Qara Qash, R. 95 35 45N 78 45E
Qara Tagh La = Kala Shank'ou 95 35 42N 78 20E
Qarachuk 92 37 0N 42 2E
Qarah 92 29 55N 40 3E
Qardud 123 10 20N 29 56E
Qarrasa 123 14 38N 32 5E
Qarsa 123 9 28N 41 48E
Qaşr Bū Hadi 119 31 1N 16 45E
Qasr-e-Qand 93 26 15N 60 45E
Qasr Farâfra 122 27 0N 28 1E
Qastina 90 31 44N 34 45E
Qatar ■ 93 25 30N 51 15E
Qattâra 122 30 12N 27 3E
Qattara Depression = Q. Munkhafed el 122 29 30N 27 30E
Qattâra, Munkhafed el 122 29 30N 27 30E

Qayen Rancharia

Qayen 93 33 40N 59 10 E
Qazvin 92 36 15N 50 0 E
Qena 122 26 10N 32 43 E
Qena, Wadi 122 26 57N 32 50 E
Qendrevca 68 40 20N 19 48 E
Qesari 90 32 30N 34 53 E
Qeshm 93 26 55N 56 10 E
Qeshm, I. 93 26 50N 56 0 E
Qila Safed 93 29 0N 61 30 E
Qila Saifulla 94 30 45N 68 17 E
Qiryat 'Anivim 90 31 49N 35 7 E
Qiryat Bialik 90 32 50N 35 5 E
Qiryat 'Eqron 90 31 52N 34 49 E
Qiryat Hayyim 90 32 49N 35 4 E
Qiryat Shemona 90 33 13N 35 35 E
Qiryat Yam 90 32 51N 35 4 E
Qishon, R. 90 32 42N 35 7 E
Qishran 122 20 14N 40 2 E
Qizan 123 16 57N 42 34 E
Qom 93 34 40N 51 0 E
Quabbin Res. 162 42 17N 72 21W
Quabbo 123 12 2N 39 56 E
Quackenbrück 48 52 40N 7 59 E
Quadring 33 52 53N 0 9W
Quainton 29 51 51N 0 53W
Quairading 137 32 0 S 117 21 E
Quakerstown 162 40 27N 75 20W
Qualeup 137 33 48 S 116 48 E
Quambatook 138 35 49 S 143 34 E
Quambone 141 30 57 S 147 53 E
Quan Long 101 9 7N 105 8 E
Quanan 159 34 20N 99 45W
Quandialla 141 34 1 S 147 47 E
Quang Nam 101 15 55N 108 15 E
Quang Ngai 101 15 13N 108 58 E
Quang Yen 100 21 3N 106 52 E
Quantock Hills, The 28 51 8N 3 10W
Quaraí 172 30 15 S 56 20W
Quarré les Tombes 43 47 21N 4 0 E
Quarryville 162 39 54N 76 10W
Quartu Sant' Elena 64 39 15N 9 10 E
Quartzsite 161 33 44N 114 16W
Quatsino 152 50 30N 127 40W
Quatsino Sd. 152 50 42N 127 58W
Qubab = Mishmar Aiyalon 90 31 52N 34 57 E
Qūchān 93 37 10N 58 27 E
Que Que 127 18 58 S 29 48 E
Queanbeyan 141 35 17 S 149 14 E
Québec 151 46 52N 71 13W
Québec □ 151 50 0N 70 0W
Quedlinburg 48 51 47N 11 9 E
Queen Alexandra Ra. 13 85 0 S 170 0 E
Queen Anne 162 38 55N 75 57W
Queen Bess Mt. 152 51 13N 124 35W
Queen Charlotte 152 53 15N 132 2W
Queen Charlotte Is. 152 53 20N 132 10W
Queen Charlotte Sd. 143 41 10 S 174 15 E
Queen Charlotte Str. 152 51 0N 128 0W
Queen Elizabeth Is. 10 78 0N 95 0W
Queen Elizabeth Nat. Pk. 126 0 0 S 30 0 E
Queen Mary Coast 13 70 0 S 95 0 E
Queen Maud G. 148 68 15N 102 30W
Queenborough 29 51 24N 0 46 E
Queen's Chan. 136 15 0 S 129 30 E
Queensbury 32 53 46N 1 50W
Queenscliff 138 38 16 S 144 39 E
Queensferry 35 56 0N 3 25W
Queensland □ 138 15 0 S 142 0 E
Queenstown, Austral. 138 42 4 S 145 35 E
Queenstown, N.Z. 143 45 1 S 168 40 E
Queenstown, S. Afr. 125 31 52 S 26 52 E
Queguay Grande, R. 172 32 9 S 58 9W
Queimadas 170 11 0 S 39 38W
Quela 124 9 10 S 16 56 E
Quelimane 127 17 53 S 36 58 E
Quemado, N. Mex., U.S.A. 161 34 17N 108 28W
Quemado, Tex., U.S.A. 159 28 58N 100 35W
Quemoy, I. = Chinmen Tao, I. 109 24 25N 118 25 E
Quemú-Quemú 172 36 3 S 63 36W
Quendale, B. of 36 59 53N 1 20W
Quequén 172 38 30 S 58 30W
Querein 123 13 30N 34 50 E
Querétaro 164 20 40N 100 23W
Querétaro □ 164 20 30N 100 30W
Querfurt 48 51 22N 11 33 E
Quesada 59 37 51N 3 4W
Quesnel 152 53 5N 122 30W
Quesnel L. 152 52 30N 121 20W
Quesnel, R. 152 52 58N 122 29W
Quest, Pte. 151 49 52N 64 40W
Questa 161 36 45N 105 35W
Questembert 42 47 40N 2 28W
Quetico 150 48 45N 90 55W
Quetico Prov. Park 150 48 30N 91 45W
Quetta 93 30 15N 66 55 E
Quetta □ 93 30 15N 66 55 E
Quezaltenango 166 14 40N 91 30W
Quezon City 103 14 38N 121 0 E
Qui Nhon 101 13 40N 109 13 E
Quiaca, La 172 22 5 S 65 35W
Quibaxi 124 8 24 S 14 27 E
Quibdó 174 5 42N 76 40W
Quiberon 42 47 29N 3 9W
Quibor 174 9 56N 69 37W
Quick 152 54 36N 126 54W
Quickborn 48 53 42N 9 52 E
Quiet L. 152 61 5N 133 5W
Quiévrain 47 50 24N 3 41 E
Quiindy 172 25 58 S 57 14W
Quila 164 24 23N 107 13W
Quilán, C. 176 43 15 S 74 30W
Quilengues 125 14 12 S 14 12 E
Quilimarí 172 32 5 S 70 30W
Quilino 172 30 14 S 64 29W
Quillabamba 174 12 50 S 72 50W
Quillagua 172 21 40 S 69 40W
Quillaicillo 172 31 17 S 71 40W
Quillan 44 42 53N 2 10 E
Quillebeuf 42 49 28N 0 30 E
Quillota 172 32 54 S 71 16W
Quilmes 172 34 43 S 58 15W
Quilon 97 8 50N 76 38 E
Quilpie 139 26 35 S 144 11 E
Quilpué 172 33 5 S 71 33W
Quilty 39 52 50N 9 27W
Quilua 127 16 17 S 39 54 E
Quimili 172 27 40 S 62 30W
Quimper 42 48 0N 4 9W
Quimperlé 42 47 53N 3 33W
Quin 39 52 50N 8 52W
Quinag 36 58 13N 5 5W
Quincy, Calif., U.S.A. 160 39 56N 121 0W
Quincy, Fla., U.S.A. 157 30 34N 84 34W
Quincy, Ill., U.S.A. 158 39 55N 91 20W
Quincy, Mass., U.S.A. 162 42 14N 71 0W
Quincy, Wash., U.S.A. 160 47 22N 119 56W
Quines 172 32 13 S 65 48W
Quinga 127 15 49 S 40 15 E
Quingey 43 47 7N 5 52 E
Quinhagak 147 59 45N 162 0W
Quintana de la Serena 57 38 45N 5 40W
Quintana Roo □ 165 19 0N 88 0W
Quintanar de la Orden 58 39 36N 3 5W
Quintanar de la Sierra 58 41 57N 2 55W
Quintanar del Rey 59 39 21N 1 56W
Quintero 172 32 45 S 71 30W
Quintin 42 48 26N 2 56W
Quinto 58 41 25N 0 32W
Quinyambie 139 30 15 S 141 0 E
Quipar, R. 59 37 58N 2 3W
Quirihue 172 36 15 S 72 35W
Quirindi 141 31 28 S 150 40 E
Quiriquire 174 9 59N 63 13W
Quiroga 56 42 28N 7 18W
Quirpon I. 151 51 32N 55 28W
Quisiro 174 10 53N 71 17W
Quissac 45 43 55N 4 0 E
Quissanga 127 12 24 S 40 28 E
Quitilipi 172 26 50 S 60 13W
Quitman, Ga., U.S.A. 157 30 49N 83 35W
Quitman, Miss., U.S.A. 157 32 2N 88 42W
Quitman, Tex., U.S.A. 159 32 48N 95 25W
Quito 174 0 15 S 78 35W
Quixadá 170 4 55 S 39 0W
Quixaxe 127 15 17 S 40 4 E
Quixeramobim 170 5 12 S 39 17W
Qul'ân, Jazâ'ir 122 24 22N 35 31 E
Qumran 90 31 43N 35 27 E
Quneitra 90 33 7N 35 48 E
Quoich L. 36 57 4N 5 20W
Quoile, R. 38 54 21N 5 40W
Quoin I. 136 14 54 S 129 32 E
Quoin Pt., N.Z. 143 46 19 S 170 11 E
Quoin Pt., S. Afr. 128 34 46 S 19 37 E
Quondong 140 33 6 S 140 18 E
Quorn, Austral. 140 32 25 S 138 0 E
Quorn, Can. 150 49 25N 90 55W
Quorndon 28 52 45N 1 10W
Qûs 122 25 55N 32 50 E
Quseir 122 26 7N 34 16 E
Qusra 90 32 5N 35 20 E
Quthing 129 30 25 S 27 36 E
Quynh Nhai 100 21 49N 103 33 E
Qytet Stalin (Kuçove) 68 40 47N 19 57 E

R

Ra, Ko 101 9 13N 98 16 E
Raa. 73 56 0N 12 45 E
Råa 73 56 0N 12 45 E
Raahana 90 32 12N 34 52 E
Raahe 74 64 40N 24 28 E
Raalte 46 52 23N 6 16 E
Raamsdonksveer 47 51 43N 4 52 E
Raasay I. 36 57 25N 6 4W
Raasay, Sd. of 36 57 30N 6 8W
Rab 63 44 45N 14 45 E
Rab, I. 63 44 45N 14 45 E
Raba 103 8 36 S 118 55 E
Rába, R. 54 47 38N 17 38 E
Rabaçal, R. 56 41 41N 7 15W
Rabah 121 13 5N 5 30 E
Rabai 126 3 50 S 39 31 E
Rabaraba 135 9 58 S 149 49 E
Rabastens 44 43 50N 1 43 E
Rabastens, Hautes Pyrénées 44 43 25N 0 10 E
Rabat 118 34 2N 6 48W
Rabaul 135 4 24 S 152 18 E
Rabbalshede 73 58 40N 11 27 E
Rabbit L. 153 47 0N 79 38W
Rabbit Lake 153 53 8N 107 46W
Rabbit, R. 152 59 41N 127 12W
Rabbitskin, R. 152 61 47N 120 42W
Rabigh 92 22 50N 39 5 E
Rabka 54 49 37N 19 59 E
Rača 66 44 14N 21 0 E
Răcale 65 39 57N 18 6 E
Racalmuto 64 37 25N 13 41 E
Racconigi 62 44 47N 7 41 E
Race, C. 151 46 40N 53 5W
Raceview 108 27 38 S 152 47 E
Rach Gia 101 10 5N 105 5 E
Raciaz 54 52 46N 20 10 E
Racibórz (Ratibor) 54 50 7N 18 18 E
Racine 156 42 41N 87 51W
Rackheath 29 52 41N 1 22 E
Rackwick 37 58 52N 3 23W
Radama, Îs. 129 14 0 S 47 47 E
Radama, Presqu'île d' 129 14 16 S 47 53 E
Radan, mt. 66 42 59N 21 29 E
Radbuza, R. 52 49 35N 13 5 E
Radcliffe, Gr. Manch., U.K. 32 53 35N 2 19W
Radcliffe, Notts., U.K. 33 52 57N 1 3W
Rade 71 59 21N 10 53 E
Radeburg 48 51 6N 13 45 E
Radeče 63 46 5N 15 14 E
Radekhov 80 50 25N 24 32 E
Radford 156 37 8N 80 32W
Radhanpur 94 23 50N 71 38 E
Radika, R. 66 41 38N 20 37 E
Radisson 153 52 30N 107 20W
Radium Hill 133 32 30 S 140 42 E
Radium Hot Springs 152 50 48N 116 12W
Radkow 54 50 30N 16 24 E
Radley 28 51 42N 1 14W
Radlin 54 50 3N 18 29 E
Radna 66 46 7N 21 41 E
Radnevo 67 42 17N 25 58 E
Radnice 52 49 51N 13 35 E
Radnor (□) 26 52 20N 3 20W
Radnor Forest 31 52 17N 3 10W
Radom 54 51 23N 21 12 E
Radom □ 54 51 30N 21 0 E
Radomir 66 42 37N 23 4 E
Radomsko 54 51 5N 19 28 E
Radomyshl 80 50 30N 29 12 E
Radomysl Wielki 54 50 14N 21 15 E
Radoszyce 54 51 4N 20 15 E
Radoviš 66 41 38N 22 28 E
Radovljica 63 46 22N 14 12 E
Radöy I. 71 60 40N 4 55 E
Radstadt 52 47 24N 13 28 E
Radstock 28 51 17N 2 25W
Radstock, C. 139 33 12 S 134 20 E
Raduša 66 42 7N 21 15 E
Radviliškis 80 55 49N 23 33 E
Radville 153 49 30N 104 15W
Radymno 54 49 59N 22 52 E
Radyr 31 51 32N 3 16W
Radzanów 54 52 56N 20 8 E
Radziejów 54 52 40N 18 30 E
Radzyn Chełminski 54 53 23N 18 55 E
Rae 152 62 50N 116 3W
Rae Bareli 95 26 18N 81 20 E
Rae Isthmus 149 66 40N 87 30W
Raeside, L. 137 29 20 S 122 0 E
Raetihi 142 39 25 S 175 17 E
Rafaela 172 31 10 S 61 30W
Rafah 122 31 18N 34 14 E
Rafai 126 4 59N 23 58 E
Raffadali 64 37 23N 13 29 E
Rafhā 92 29 35N 43 35 E
Rafid 90 32 57N 35 52 E
Rafsanjān 93 30 30N 56 5 E
Raft Pt. 136 16 4 S 124 26 E
Ragag 123 10 59N 24 40 E
Ragama 93 7 0N 79 50 E
Ragged Mt. 137 33 27 S 123 25 E
Raglan, Austral. 138 23 42 S 150 49 E
Raglan, N.Z. 142 37 55 S 174 55 E
Raglan, U.K. 31 51 46N 2 51W
Ragueneau 151 49 11N 68 18W
Ragunda 72 63 6N 16 23 E
Ragusa 65 36 56N 14 42 E
Raha 103 8 20 S 118 40 E
Rahad el Berdi 117 11 20N 23 40 E
Rahad, Nahr er 123 12 40N 35 30 E
Rahden 48 52 26N 8 36 E
Raheita 123 12 46N 43 4 E
Raheng = Tak 100 17 5N 99 10 E
Rahimyar Khan 94 28 30N 70 25 E
Rahotu 142 39 20 S 173 49 E
Raichur 96 16 10N 77 20 E
Raiganj 95 25 37N 88 10 E
Raigarh, Madhya Pradesh, India 96 21 56N 83 25 E
Raigarh, Orissa, India 96 19 51N 82 6 E
Raiis 92 23 33N 38 43 E
Raijua 103 10 37 S 121 36 E
Railton 138 41 25 S 146 28 E
Rainbow 140 35 55 S 142 0 E
Rainbow Lake 152 58 30N 119 23W
Rainham 29 51 22N 0 36 E
Rainier 160 46 4N 123 0W
Rainier, Mt. 160 46 50N 121 50W
Rainworth 33 53 8N 1 6W
Rainy L. 153 48 30N 92 30W
Rainy River 153 48 50N 94 30W
Raipur 96 21 17N 81 45 E
Raith 150 48 50N 90 0W
Raj Nandgaon 99 21 0N 81 0 E
Raja Empat, Kepulauan 103 0 30 S 129 40 E
Raja-Jooseppi 74 68 28N 28 29 E
Raja, Ujung 102 3 40N 96 25 E
Rajahmundry 96 17 1N 81 48 E
Rajang, R. 102 2 30N 113 30 E
Rajapalaiyarm 97 9 25N 77 35 E
Rajasthan □ 94 26 45N 73 30 E
Rajasthan Canal 94 30 31N 71 0 E
Rajauri 95 33 25N 74 21 E
Rajbari 98 23 47N 89 41 E
Rajgarh, Mad. P., India 94 24 2N 76 45 E
Rajgarh, Raj., India 94 28 40N 75 25 E
Rajgród 54 53 42N 22 42 E
Rajhenburg 63 46 1N 15 29 E
Rajkot 94 22 15N 70 56 E
Rajmahal Hills 95 24 30N 87 30 E
Rajnandgaon 96 21 5N 81 5 E
Rajojooseppi 74 68 25N 28 30 E
Rajpipla 96 21 50N 73 30 E
Rajpura 94 30 32N 76 32 E
Rajshahi 98 24 22N 88 39 E
Rajshahi □ 95 25 0N 89 0 E
Rakaia 143 43 45 S 172 1 E
Rakaia, R. 143 43 26 S 171 47 E
Rakan, Ras 93 26 10N 51 20 E
Rakaposhi 95 36 10N 74 0 E
Rakaposhi, mt. 93 36 20N 74 30 E
Rakha 122 18 25N 41 30 E
Rakhni 94 30 4N 69 56 E
Rakitovo 67 41 59N 24 5 E
Rakkestad 71 59 25N 11 21 E
Rakoniewice 54 52 10N 16 16 E
Rakops 128 21 1 S 24 28 E
Rákospalota 53 47 30N 19 5 E
Rakovica 63 44 59N 15 38 E
Rakovník 52 50 6N 13 42 E
Rakovski 67 42 21N 24 57 E
Raleigh, Can. 150 49 30N 92 5W
Raleigh, U.S.A. 150 35 46N 78 38W
Raleigh B. 157 34 50N 76 15W
Ralja 66 44 33N 20 34 E
Ralls 159 33 40N 101 20W
Ralston 162 41 30N 76 57W
Rām Allāh 90 31 55N 35 10 E
Ram Hd. 141 37 47 S 149 30 E
Ram, R. 152 62 1N 123 41W
Rama, Israel 90 32 56N 35 21 E
Rama, Nic. 166 12 9N 84 15W
Ramacca 65 37 24N 14 40 E
Ramachandrapuram 96 16 50N 82 4 E
Ramadi 92 33 28N 43 15 E
Ramales de la Victoria 58 43 15N 3 28W
Ramalho, Serra do 171 13 45 S 44 0W
Raman 101 6 29N 101 18 E
Ramanathapuram 97 9 25N 78 55 E
Ramanetaka, B. de 129 14 13 S 47 52 E
Ramas C. 97 15 5N 73 55 E
Ramat Gan 90 32 4N 34 48 E
Ramatlhabama 128 25 37 S 25 33 E
Ramban 95 33 14N 75 12 E
Rambervillers 43 48 20N 6 38 E
Rambipudji 103 8 12 S 113 37 E
Rambla, La 57 37 37N 4 45W
Rambouillet 43 48 40N 1 48 E
Rambre Kyun 98 19 0N 94 0 E
Ramdurg 97 15 58N 75 22 E
Rame Head 30 50 19N 4 14W
Ramechhap 95 27 25N 86 10 E
Ramelau, Mte. 103 8 55 S 126 22 E
Ramenskoye 81 55 32N 38 15 E
Ramgarh, Bihar, India 95 23 40N 85 35 E
Ramgarh, Rajasthan, India 94 27 16N 75 14 E
Ramgarh, Rajasthan, India 94 27 30N 70 36 E
Ramhormoz 92 31 15N 49 35 E
Ramla 90 31 55N 34 52 E
Ramlat Zaltan 119 28 30N 19 30 E
Ramlu Mt. 123 13 32N 41 40 E
Ramme 73 56 30N 8 11 E
Rammun 90 31 55N 35 17 E
Ramna Stacks, Is. 36 60 40N 1 20W
Ramnad = Ramanathapuram 97 9 25N 78 55 E
Ramnagar 95 32 47N 75 18 E
Ramnäs 72 59 46N 16 12 E
Ramon 81 52 8N 39 21 E
Ramona 163 33 1N 116 56W
Ramor L. 38 53 50N 7 5W
Ramore 150 48 30N 80 25W
Ramos Arizpe 164 23 35N 100 59W
Ramos, R. 164 25 35N 105 3W
Ramoutsa 128 24 50 S 25 52 E
Rampart 147 65 0N 150 15W
Rampside 32 54 6N 3 10W
Rampur, H.P., India 94 31 26N 77 43 E
Rampur, M.P., India 94 23 25N 73 53 E
Rampur, Orissa, India 96 21 48N 83 58 E
Rampur, U.P., India 94 28 50N 79 5 E
Rampura 94 24 30N 75 27 E
Rampurhat 95 24 10N 87 50 E
Ramsbottom 32 53 36N 2 20W
Ramsbury 28 51 26N 1 37W
Ramsel 47 51 2N 4 50 E
Ramsele 74 63 31N 16 27 E
Ramsey, Can. 150 47 25N 82 20W
Ramsey, Cambs., U.K. 29 52 27N 0 6W
Ramsey, Essex, U.K. 29 51 55N 1 12 E
Ramsey, I. of M., U.K. 32 54 20N 4 21W
Ramsgate 29 51 20N 1 25 E
Ramshai 98 26 44N 88 51 E
Rämshyttan 72 60 17N 15 15 E
Ramsjö 72 62 11N 15 37 E
Ramtek 96 21 20N 79 15 E
Ramu, R. 135 4 0 S 144 41 E
Ramvik 72 62 49N 17 51 E
Ranaghat 95 23 15N 88 35 E
Ranahu 94 25 55N 69 45 E
Ranau 102 6 2N 116 40 E
Rancagua 172 34 10 S 70 50W
Rance 47 50 9N 4 16 E
Rance, R. 42 48 34N 1 59W
Rancharia 171 22 15 S 50 55W

Rancheria, R **Rennell Sd**

Rancheria, R. 152 60 13N 129 7W
Ranchester 160 44 57N 107 12W
Ranchi 95 23 19N 85 27 E
Rancu 70 44 32N 24 15 E
Rand 141 35 33 S 146 32 E
Randallstown 162 39 22N 76 48W
Randalstown 38 54 45N 6 20W
Randan 44 46 2N 3 21 E
Randazzo 65 37 53N 14 56 E
Randböl 73 55 43N 9 17 E
Randers 73 56 29N 10 1 E
Randers Fjord 73 56 37N 10 20 E
Randfontein 129 26 8 S 27 45 E
Randolph, Mass., U.S.A. 162 42 10N 71 3W
Randolph, Utah, U.S.A. 160 41 43N 111 10W
Randolph, Vt., U.S.A. 162 43 55N 72 39W
Randsburg 163 35 26N 117 44W
Randsfjord 71 60 15N 10 25 E
Råne älv 74 66 26N 21 10 E
Råneå 74 65 53N 22 18 E
Ranfurly 143 45 7 S 170 6 E
Rangae 101 6 19N 101 44 E
Rangamati 98 22 38 S 92 12 E
Rangataua 142 39 26 S 175 28 E
Rangaunu B. 142 34 51 S 173 15 E
Rångedala 73 57 47N 13 9 E
Rangeley 156 44 58N 70 33W
Rangely 160 40 3N 108 53W
Ranger 159 32 30N 98 42W
Rangia 98 26 15N 91 20 E
Rangiora 143 43 19 S 172 36 E
Rangitaiki 130 38 52 S 176 23 E
Rangitaiki, R. 142 37 54 S 176 49 E
Rangitata, R. 143 43 45 S 171 15 E
Rangitikei, R. 142 40 17 S 175 15 E
Rangitoto Range 142 38 25 S 175 35 E
Rangkasbitung 103 6 22 S 106 16 E
Rangon 99 16 45N 96 20 E
Rangon, R. 99 16 28N 96 40 E
Rangoon 98 16 45N 96 20 E
Rangpur 98 25 42N 89 22 E
Rangsit 100 13 59N 100 37 E
Ranibennur 97 14 35N 75 30 E
Raniganj 95 23 40N 87 15 E
Ranipet 97 12 56N 79 23 E
Raniwara 93 24 50N 72 10 E
Ranken, R. 138 20 31 S 137 36 E
Rankin 159 31 16N 101 56W
Rankin Inlet 148 62 30N 93 0W
Rankin's Springs 141 33 49 S 146 14 E
Rannes 138 24 6 S 150 11 E
Rannoch L. 37 56 41N 4 20W
Rannoch Moor 34 56 38N 4 48W
Rannoch Sta. 37 56 40N 4 32W
Ranobe, B. de 129 23 3 S 43 33 E
Ranohira 129 22 29 S 45 24 E
Ranomafana, Tamatave, Madag. 129 18 57 S 48 50 E
Ranomafana, Tuléar, Madag. 129 24 34 S 47 0 E
Ranong 101 9 56N 98 40 E
Rantau 102 4 15N 98 5 E
Rantauprapat 102 2 15N 99 50 E
Rantemario 103 3 15 S 119 57 E
Rantis 90 32 4N 35 3 E
Rantoul 156 40 18N 88 10W
Ranum 73 56 54N 9 14 E
Ranwanlenau 128 19 37 S 22 49 E
Raon-l' Étape 43 48 24N 6 50 E
Raoui, Erg er 118 29 0N 2 0W
Rapa Iti, I. 131 27 35 S 144 20W
Rapallo 62 44 21N 9 12 E
Rapang 103 3 45 S 119 55 E
Râpch 93 25 40N 59 15 E
Raphoe 38 54 52N 7 36W
Rapid City 158 44 0N 103 0W
Rapid, R. 152 59 15N 129 5W
Rapid River 156 45 55N 87 0W
Rapides des Joachims 150 46 13N 77 43W
Rapla 80 58 88N 24 52 E
Rapness 37 59 15N 2 51W
Raposos 171 19 57 S 43 48W
Rappahannock, R. 162 37 35N 76 17W
Rapperswil 51 47 14N 8 45 E
Raqqa 92 36 0N 38 55 E
Raquete 127 14 8 S 38 13 E
Raquette Lake 162 43 49N 74 40W
Rareagh 38 53 37N 8 37W
Rarotonga, I. 131 21 30 S 160 0W
Ras al Khaima 93 25 50N 56 5 E
Ra's Al-Unūf 119 30 25N 18 15 E
Ra's at Tannurah 92 26 40N 50 10 E
Ras Dashan, mt. 123 13 8N 37 45 E
Ras el Ma 118 34 26N 0 50W
Ras Gharib 122 28 6N 33 18 E
Ras Mallap 122 29 18N 32 50 E
Rasa, Punta 176 40 50 S 62 15W
Rasboda 72 60 8N 16 58 E
Raseiniai 80 55 25N 23 5 E
Rashad 123 11 55N 31 0 E
Rashîd 122 31 21N 30 22 E
Rashîd, Masabb 122 31 22N 30 17 E
Rasht 92 37 20N 49 40 E
Rasi Salai 100 15 20N 104 9 E
Rasipuram 97 11 30N 78 25 E
Raška 66 43 19N 20 39 E
Raso, C. 170 1 50N 50 0W
Rason, L. 137 28 45 S 124 25 E
Raşova 70 44 15N 27 55 E
Rasovo 67 43 42N 23 17 E
Rasra 95 25 50N 83 50 E
Rass el Oued 119 35 57N 5 2 E
Rasskazovo 81 52 35N 41 50 E
Rastatt 49 48 50N 8 12 E
Rastu 70 43 53N 23 16 E
Raszków 54 51 43N 17 40 E
Rat Buri 100 13 30N 99 54 E
Rat, Is. 147 51 50N 178 15 E
Rat, R. 152 56 0N 99 30W
Rat River 152 61 7N 112 36W
Rätan 72 62 27N 14 33 E
Ratangarh 94 28 5N 74 35 E
Rath 95 25 36N 79 37 E
Rath Luirc (Charleville) 39 52 21N 8 40W
Rathangan 39 53 13N 7 0W
Rathconrah 38 53 30N 7 32W
Rathcoole 39 53 17N 6 29W
Rathcormack 39 52 5N 8 19W
Rathdowney 39 52 52N 7 36W
Rathdrum, Ireland 39 52 57N 6 13W
Rathdrum, U.S.A. 160 47 50N 116 58W
Ratheclaung 98 20 29N 92 45 E
Rathen 37 57 38N 1 58W
Rathenow 48 52 38N 12 23 E
Rathfriland 38 54 12N 6 12W
Rathkeale 39 52 32N 8 57W
Rathkenny 38 53 45N 6 39W
Rathlin I. 38 55 18N 6 14W
Rathlin O'Birne I. 38 54 40N 8 50W
Rathmelton 38 55 3N 7 35W
Rathmolyon 38 53 30N 6 49W
Rathmore, Cork, Ireland 39 51 30N 9 21W
Rathmore, Kerry, Ireland 39 52 5N 9 12W
Rathmore, Kildare, Ireland 39 53 13N 6 35W
Rathmullen 38 55 6N 7 32W
Rathnure 39 52 30N 6 47W
Rathvilly 72 52 54N 6 42W
Ratlam 94 23 20N 75 0 E
Ratnagiri 96 16 57N 73 18 E
Ratnapura 97 6 40N 80 20 E
Ratoath 38 53 30N 6 27W
Raton 159 37 0N 104 30W
Rattaphum 101 7 8N 100 16 E
Ratten 52 47 28N 15 44 E
Rattray 37 56 36N 3 20W
Rattray Hd. 37 57 38N 1 50W
Rättvik 72 60 52N 15 7 E
Ratz, Mt. 152 57 23N 132 12W
Ratzeburg 48 53 41N 10 46 E
Raub 101 3 47N 101 52 E
Rauch 172 36 45 S 59 5W
Raufarhöfn 74 66 27N 15 57W
Raufoss 71 60 44N 10 37 E
Raukumara Ra. 142 38 5 S 177 55 E
Raul Soares 171 20 5 S 42 22W
Rauland 71 59 43N 8 0 E
Rauma 75 61 10N 21 30 E
Rauma, R. 71 62 34N 7 43 E
Raundal 71 60 40N 6 37 E
Raunds 29 52 20N 0 32W
Raung, Mt. 103 8 8 S 114 4 E
Raurkela 96 22 14N 84 50 E
Rava Russkaya 80 50 15N 23 42 E
Ravanusa 64 37 16N 13 58 E
Ravar 93 31 20N 56 51 E
Ravels 47 51 22N 5 0 E
Ravena 162 42 28N 73 49W
Ravenglass 32 54 21N 3 25W
Ravenna, Italy 63 44 28N 12 15 E
Ravenna, U.S.A. 158 41 3N 98 58W
Ravensburg 49 47 48N 9 38 E
Ravenshoe 138 17 37 S 145 29 E
Ravenstein 46 51 47N 5 39 E
Ravensthorpe 137 33 35 S 120 2 E
Ravenstonedale 32 54 26N 2 26W
Ravenswood, Austral. 138 20 6 S 146 54 E
Ravenswood, U.S.A. 156 38 58N 81 47W
Ravensworth 141 32 26 S 151 4 E
Raventasón 174 6 10 S 81 0W
Ravi, R. 94 31 0N 73 0 E
Ravna Gora 63 45 24N 14 50 E
Ravna Reka 66 43 59N 21 35 E
Ravnstrup 73 56 27N 9 17 E
Rawa Mazowiecka 54 51 46N 20 12 E
Rawalpindi 94 33 38N 73 8 E
Rawalpindi □ 93 33 10N 72 50 E
Rawāndūz 92 36 40N 44 30 E
Rawang 101 3 20N 101 35 E
Rawdon 150 46 3N 73 40W
Rawene 142 35 25 S 173 32 E
Rawicz 54 51 36N 16 52 E
Rawlinna 137 30 58 S 125 28 E
Rawlins 160 41 50N 107 20W
Rawlinson Range 137 24 40 S 128 30 E
Rawmarsh 33 53 27N 1 20W
Rawson 176 43 15 S 65 0W
Rawtenstall 32 53 42N 2 18W
Rawuya 121 12 10N 6 50 E
Ray, N. Mex., U.S.A. 159 35 57N 104 8W
Ray, N.D., U.S.A. 158 48 21N 103 6W
Ray, C. 151 47 33N 59 15W
Ray Mts. 147 66 0N 152 10W
Rayachoti 97 14 4N 78 50 E
Rayadrug 97 14 40N 76 50 E
Rayagada 96 19 15N 83 20 E
Raychikhinsk 77 49 46N 129 25 E
Rayevskiy 84 54 4N 54 56 E
Rayin 93 29 40N 57 22 E
Rayleigh 29 51 36N 0 38 E
Raymond, Can. 152 49 30N 112 35W
Raymond, Calif., U.S.A. 163 37 13N 119 54W
Raymond, Wash., U.S.A. 160 46 45N 123 48W
Raymond Terrace 141 32 45 S 151 44 E
Raymondville 159 26 30N 97 50W
Raymore 153 51 25N 104 31W
Rayne 159 30 16N 92 16W
Rayón 164 29 43N 110 35W
Rayong 100 12 40N 101 20 E
Rayville 159 32 30N 91 45W
Raz, Pte. du 42 48 2N 4 47W
Razana 66 44 6N 19 55 E
Razanj 66 43 40N 21 31 E
Razdelna 67 43 13N 27 41 E
Razelm, Lacul 70 44 50N 29 0 E
Razgrad 67 43 33N 26 34 E
Razlog 67 41 53N 23 28 E
Razmak 94 32 45N 69 50 E
Razole 96 16 56N 81 48 E
Razor Back Mt. 152 51 32N 125 0W
Ré, Île de 44 46 12N 1 30W
Rea, L. 39 53 10N 8 32W
Reading, U.K. 29 51 27N 0 57W
Reading, U.S.A. 162 40 20N 75 53W
Realicó 172 35 0 S 64 15W
Réalmont 44 43 48N 2 10 E
Ream 101 10 34N 103 39 E
Reata 164 26 8N 101 5W
Reay 37 58 33N 3 48W
Rebais 43 48 50N 3 10 E
Rebecca L. 137 30 0 S 122 30 E
Rebi 103 5 30 S 134 7 E
Rebiana 117 24 12N 22 10 E
Rebun-Tō 112 45 23N 141 2 E
Recanati 63 43 24N 13 32 E
Recaş 66 45 46N 21 30 E
Recess 38 53 29N 9 4W
Recherche, Arch. of the 137 34 15 S 122 50 E
Rechitsa 80 52 13N 30 15 E
Recht 47 50 20N 6 3 E
Recife 170 8 0 S 35 0W
Recklinghausen 48 51 36N 7 10 E
Reconquista 172 29 10 S 59 45W
Recreo 172 29 25 S 65 10W
Reculver 29 51 22N 1 12 E
Recz 54 53 16N 15 31 E
Red B. 38 55 4N 6 2W
Red Bank 162 40 21N 74 4W
Red Bay 151 51 44N 56 25W
Red Bluff 160 40 11N 122 11W
Red Bluff L. 159 31 59N 103 58W
Red Cliffs 140 34 19 S 142 11 E
Red Cloud 158 40 8N 98 33W
Red Creek 162 43 14N 76 45W
Red Deer 152 52 20N 113 50W
Red Deer L. 153 52 55N 101 20W
Red Deer, R. 152 50 58N 110 0W
Red Deer R. 153 52 53N 101 1W
Red Dial 32 54 48N 3 9W
Red Hook 162 41 55N 73 53W
Red Indian L. 151 48 35N 57 0W
Red L. 158 48 0N 95 0W
Red Lake 153 51 1N 94 1W
Red Lake Falls 158 47 54N 96 30W
Red Lion 162 39 54N 76 36W
Red Lodge 160 45 10N 109 10W
Red Mountain 163 35 37N 117 38W
Red Oak 158 41 0N 95 10W
Red Point Rock 137 32 13 S 127 32 E
Red, R., Can. 153 50 24N 96 48W
Red, R., Minn., U.S.A. 158 48 10N 97 0W
Red, R., Tex., U.S.A. 159 33 57N 95 30W
Red, R. = Hong, R. 100 20 17N 106 34 E
Red Rock 150 48 55N 88 15W
Red Rock, L. 158 41 30N 93 15W
Red Sea 91 25 0N 36 0 E
Red Slate Mtn. 163 37 31N 118 52W
Red Sucker L 153 54 9N 93 40W
Red Tower Pass = Turnu Rosu P. 70 45 33N 24 17 E
Red Wharf Bay 31 53 18N 4 10W
Red Wing 158 44 32N 92 35W
Reda 54 54 40N 18 19 E
Rédange 47 49 46N 5 52 E
Redbank 108 27 36 S 152 52 E
Redbridge 29 51 35N 0 7 E
Redcar 33 54 37N 1 4W
Redcliff 153 50 10N 110 50W
Redcliffe 139 27 12 S 153 0 E
Redcliffe, Mt. 137 28 30 S 121 30 E
Redcliffs 139 34 16 S 142 10 E
Reddersburg 128 29 41 S 26 10 E
Redding 160 40 30N 122 25W
Redditch 28 52 18N 1 57W
Rede, R. 35 55 8N 2 12W
Redenção 170 4 13 S 38 43W
Redesmouth 35 55 7N 2 12W
Redfield 158 45 0N 98 30W
Redhill 29 51 14N 0 10W
Redknife, R. 152 61 14N 119 22W
Redland 37 59 6N 3 4W
Redlands 163 34 0N 117 11W
Redlynch 28 50 59N 1 42W
Redmile 33 52 54N 0 48W
Redmire 32 54 19N 1 55W
Redmond, Austral. 137 34 55 S 117 40 E
Redmond, U.S.A. 160 44 19N 121 11W
Redon 42 47 40N 2 6W
Redonda, I. 167 16 58N 62 19W
Redondela 56 42 15N 8 38W
Redondo 57 38 39N 7 37W
Redondo Beach 163 33 52N 118 26W
Redrock Pt. 152 62 11N 115 2W
Redruth 30 50 14N 5 14W
Redvers 153 49 35N 101 40W
Redwater 152 53 55N 113 6W
Redwood City 163 37 30N 122 15W
Redwood Falls 158 44 30N 95 2W
Ree, L. 38 53 35N 8 0W
Reed City 156 43 52N 85 30W
Reed L. 153 54 38N 100 30W
Reed, Mt. 151 52 5N 68 5W
Reeder 158 47 7N 102 52W
Reedham 29 52 34N 1 33 E
Reedley 163 36 36N 119 27W
Reedsburg 158 43 34N 90 5W
Reedsport 160 43 45N 124 4W
Reedy Creek 140 36 58 S 140 2 E
Reef Pt. 142 35 10 S 173 5 E
Reefton, N.S.W., Austral. 141 34 15 S 147 27 E
Reefton, S. Australia, Austral. 109 34 57 S 138 55 E
Reefton, N.Z. 143 42 6 S 171 51 E
Reepham 29 52 46N 1 6 E
Reeth 32 54 23N 1 56W
Refsnes 71 61 9N 7 14 E
Reftele 73 57 11N 13 35 E
Refugio 159 28 18N 97 17W
Rega, R. 54 53 52N 15 16 E
Regalbuto 65 37 40N 14 38 E
Regar 85 38 30N 68 14 E
Regavim 90 32 32N 35 2 E
Regen 49 48 58N 13 9 E
Regeneração 170 6 15 S 42 41W
Regensburg 49 49 1N 12 7 E
Regensdorf 51 47 26N 8 28 E
Réggio di Calábria 65 38 7N 15 38 E
Réggio nell' Emilia 62 44 42N 10 38 E
Regina 153 50 30N 104 35W
Registan □ 93 30 15N 65 0 E
Registro 173 24 29 S 47 49W
Reguengos de Monsaraz 57 38 25N 7 32W
Rehar 95 23 36N 82 52 E
Rehoboth, Damaraland, Namibia 128 23 15 S 17 4 E
Rehoboth, Ovamboland, Namibia 128 17 55 S 15 5 E
Rehoboth Beach 162 38 43N 75 5W
Rehovot 90 31 54N 34 48 E
Reichenbach, Ger. 48 50 36N 12 19 E
Reichenbach, Switz. 50 46 38N 7 42 E
Reid 137 30 49 S 128 26 E
Reid River 138 19 40 S 146 48 E
Reiden 50 47 14N 7 59 E
Reidsville 157 36 21N 79 40W
Reigate 29 51 14N 0 11W
Reillo 58 39 54N 1 53W
Reims 43 49 15N 4 0 E
Reina 90 32 43N 35 18 E
Reina Adelaida, Arch. 176 52 20 S 74 0W
Reinach, Aargau, Switz. 50 47 14N 8 11 E
Reinach, Basel, Switz. 50 47 29N 7 35 E
Reinbeck 158 42 18N 92 40W
Reindeer I. 153 52 30N 98 0W
Reindeer L. 153 57 15N 102 15W
Reindeer, R. 153 55 36N 103 11W
Reine, La 150 48 50N 79 30W
Reinga, C. 142 34 25 S 172 43 E
Reinosa 56 43 2N 4 15W
Reinosa, Paso 56 42 56N 4 10W
Reira 123 15 25N 34 50 E
Reiss 37 58 29N 3 7W
Reisterstown 162 39 28N 76 50W
Reitdiep 46 53 20N 6 20 E
Reitz 129 27 48 S 28 29 E
Reivilo 128 27 36 S 24 8 E
Rejmyra 73 58 50N 15 55 E
Reka, R. 63 45 40N 14 0 E
Rekovac 66 43 51N 21 3 E
Remad, Ouedber 118 33 28N 1 20W
Remanso 170 9 41 S 42 4W
Remarkable, Mt. 140 32 48 S 138 10 E
Rembang 103 6 42 S 111 21 E
Remchi 118 35 2N 1 26W
Remedios, Colomb. 174 7 2N 74 41W
Remedios, Panama 166 8 15N 81 50W
Remeshk 93 26 55N 58 50 E
Remetea 70 46 45N 29 29 E
Remich 47 49 32N 6 22 E
Remiremont 43 48 0N 6 36 E
Remo 123 6 48N 41 20 E
Remontnoye 83 47 44N 43 37 E
Remoulins 45 43 55N 4 35 E
Remscheid 48 51 11N 7 12 E
Remsen 162 43 19N 75 11W
Rena 71 61 8N 11 20 E
Renda 123 14 30N 40 0 E
Rende 65 39 19N 16 11 E
Rendeux 47 50 14N 5 30 E
Rendína 69 39 4N 21 58 E
Rendsburg 48 54 18N 9 41 E
Rene 77 66 2N 179 25W
Renee, oilfield 19 58 4N 0 16 E
Renens 50 46 31N 6 34 E
Renfrew, Can. 150 45 30N 76 40W
Renfrew, U.K. 34 55 52N 4 24W
Renfrew (□) 26 55 50N 4 30W
Rengat 102 0 30 S 102 45 E
Rengo 172 34 24 S 70 50W
Reni 82 45 28N 28 15 E
Renigunta 97 13 38N 79 30 E
Renish Pt. 36 57 44N 6 59W
Renkum 46 51 58N 5 43 E
Renmark 140 34 11 S 140 43 E
Rennell Sd. 152 53 23N 132 35W

Renner Springs Teleg. Off **Riverton**

Renner Springs Teleg. Off. 138 18 20 S 133 47 E
Rennes 42 48 7N 1 41W
Rennesøy 71 59 6N 5 43 E
Reno 160 39 30N 119 50W
Reno, R. 63 44 45N 11 40 E
Renovo 156 41 20N 77 47W
Rens 55 54 54N 9 5 E
Rensselaer, Ind., U.S.A. 156 41 0N 87 10W
Rensselaer, N.Y., U.S.A. 162 42 38N 73 41W
Renteria 58 43 19N 1 54W
Renton 160 47 30N 122 9W
Renwicktown 143 41 30 S 173 51 E
Réo 120 12 28N 2 35 E
Réole, La 44 44 35N 0 1W
Reotipur 95 25 33N 83 45 E
Repalle 97 16 2N 80 45 E
Répcelak 53 47 24N 17 1 E
Repton 28 52 50N 1 32W
Republic, Mich., U.S.A. 156 46 25N 87 59W
Republic, Wash., U.S.A. 160 48 38N 118 42W
Republican City 158 40 9N 99 20W
Republican, R. 158 40 0N 98 30W
Repulse B., Antarct. 13 64 30 S 99 30 E
Repulse B., Austral. 133 20 31 S 148 45 E
Repulse Bay 149 66 30N 86 30W
Requena, Peru 174 5 5 S 73 52W
Requena, Spain 59 39 30N 1 4W
Resele 72 63 20N 17 5 E
Resen 66 41 5N 21 0 E
Reserve, Can. 153 52 28N 102 39W
Reserve, U.S.A. 161 33 50N 108 54W
Resht = Rasht 92 37 20N 49 40 E
Resistencia 172 27 30 S 59 0W
Reşiţa 66 45 18N 21 53 E
Resko 54 53 47N 15 25 E
Resolution I., Can. 149 61 30N 65 0W
Resolution I., N.Z. 143 45 40 S 166 40 E
Resolven 31 51 43N 3 42W
Resplandes 170 6 17 S 45 13W
Resplendor 171 19 20 S 41 15W
Ressano Garcia 129 25 25 S 32 0 E
Rest Downs 141 31 48 S 146 21 E
Reston, Can. 153 49 33N 101 6W
Reston, U.K. 35 55 51N 2 11W
Restrepo 174 4 15N 73 33W
Reszel 54 54 4N 21 10 E
Retalhuleu 166 14 33N 91 46W
Reteag 70 47 10N 24 0 E
Retem, O. el 119 33 40N 0 40 E
Retenue, Lac de 127 11 0 S 27 0 E
Rethel 43 49 30N 4 20 E
Rethem 48 52 47N 9 25 E
Réthimnon 69 35 15N 24 40 E
Réthimnon □ 69 35 23N 24 28 E
Retie 47 51 16N 5 5 E
Rétiers 42 47 55N 1 25W
Retiro 172 35 59 S 71 47W
Retortillo 56 40 48N 6 21W
Rétság 53 47 58N 19 10 E
Reuland 47 50 12N 6 8 E
Réunion, Î. 11 22 0 S 56 0 E
Reus 58 41 10N 1 5 E
Reusel 47 51 21N 5 9 E
Reuss, R. 51 47 16N 8 24 E
Reuterstadt-Stavenhagen 48 53 41N 12 54 E
Reutlingen 49 48 28N 9 13 E
Reutte 52 47 29N 10 42 E
Reuver 47 51 17N 6 5 E
Revda 84 56 48N 59 57 E
Revel 44 43 28N 2 0 E
Revelganj 95 25 50N 84 40 E
Revelstoke 152 51 0N 118 0W
Revigny 43 48 50N 5 0 E
Revilla Gigedo, Is. de 131 18 40N 112 0W
Revillagigedo I. 152 55 50N 131 20W
Revin 43 49 55N 4 39 E
Revolyutsii, Pix 85 38 31N 72 21 E
Revué, R. 127 19 30 S 33 35 E
Rewa 95 24 33N 81 25 E
Rewari 94 28 15N 76 40 E
Rex 147 64 10N 149 20W
Rexburg 160 43 45N 111 50W
Rey Bouba 117 8 40N 14 15 E
Rey Malabo 121 3 45N 8 50 E
Reyes, Pt. 163 37 59N 123 2W
Reykjahlið 74 65 40N 16 55W
Reykjanes 74 63 48N 22 40W
Reykjavík 74 64 10N 21 57 E
Reynolds 153 49 40N 95 55W
Reynolds Ra. 136 22 30 S 133 0 E
Reynosa 165 26 5N 98 18W
Reza'iyeh 92 37 40N 45 0 E
Rezā'iyeh, Daryāchech-ye 92 37 30N 45 30 E
Rēzekne 80 56 30N 27 17 E
Rezh 84 57 23N 61 24 E
Rezina 70 47 45N 29 0 E
Rezovo 67 42 0N 28 0 E
Rgotina 67 44 1N 22 18 E
Rhaeadr Ogwen 31 53 8N 4 0W
Rharis, O. 119 26 30N 5 4 E
Rhayader 31 52 19N 3 30W
Rheden 46 52 0N 6 3 E
Rheidol, R. 31 52 25N 3 57W
Rhein 153 51 25N 102 15W
Rhein, R. 48 51 42N 6 20 E
Rheinbach 48 50 38N 6 54 E
Rheine 48 52 17N 7 25 E
Rheineck 51 47 28N 9 31 E
Rheinfelden 50 47 32N 7 47 E
Rheinland-Pfalz □ 49 50 50N 7 0 E
Rheinsberg 48 53 6N 12 52 E
Rheinwaldhorn 51 46 30N 9 3 E
Rhenen 46 51 58N 5 33 E
Rheydt 48 51 10N 6 24 E
Rhin, R. 48 51 42N 6 20 E
Rhinau 43 48 19N 7 43 E
Rhine, R. = Rhein 47 51 42N 6 20 E
Rhinebeck 162 41 56N 73 55W
Rhinelander 158 45 38N 89 29W
Rhino Camp 126 3 0N 31 22 E
Rhisnes 47 50 31N 4 48 E
Rhiw 31 52 49N 4 37W
Rho 62 45 31N 9 2 E
Rhode Island □ 162 41 38N 71 37W
Rhodes = Ródhos 69 36 15N 28 10 E
Rhodes' Tomb 127 20 30 S 28 30 E
* Rhodesia ■ 127 20 0 S 30 0 E
Rhodope Mts. = Rhodopi Planina 67 41 40N 24 20 E
Rhodopi Planina 67 41 40N 24 20 E
Rhondda 31 51 39N 3 30W
Rhône □ 45 45 54N 4 35 E
Rhône, R. 45 43 28N 4 42 E
Rhos-on-Sea 31 53 18N 3 46W
Rhosllanerchrugog 31 53 3N 3 4W
Rhossilli 31 51 34N 4 18W
Rhu Coigach, C. 36 58 6N 5 27W
Rhuddlan 31 53 17N 3 28W
Rhum, I. 36 57 0N 6 20W
Rhyl 31 53 19N 3 29W
Rhymney 31 51 45N 3 17W
Rhynie 37 57 20N 2 50W
Ri-Aba 121 3 28N 8 40 E
Riachão 170 7 20 S 46 37W
Riachão do Jacuípe 171 11 48 S 39 21W
Riacho de Santana 171 13 37 S 42 57W
Rialma 171 15 18 S 49 34W
Rialto 163 34 6N 117 22W
Riang 98 27 31N 92 56 E
Riaño 56 42 59N 5 0W
Rians 45 43 37N 5 44 E
Riansares, R. 58 40 0N 3 0W
Riasi 95 33 10N 74 50 E
Riau □ 102 0 0 102 35 E
Riau, Kepulauan 102 0 30N 104 20 E
Riaza 58 41 18N 3 30W
Riaza, R. 58 41 16N 3 29W
Riba de Saelices 58 40 55N 2 18 E
Ribadavia 56 42 17N 8 8W
Ribadeo 56 43 35N 7 5W
Ribadesella 56 43 30N 5 7W
Ribamar 170 2 33 S 44 3W
Ribas 58 42 19N 2 15 E
Ribat 125 29 50N 60 55 E
Ribatejo □ 55 39 15N 8 30W
Ribble, R. 32 54 13N 2 20W
Ribe 73 55 19N 8 44 E
Ribe Amt □ 73 55 34N 8 30 E
Ribeauvillé 43 48 10N 7 20 E
Ribécourt 43 49 30N 2 55 E
Ribeira 56 42 36N 8 58W
Ribeira do Pombal 170 10 50 S 38 32W
Ribeirão Prêto 173 21 10 S 47 50W
Ribeiro Gonçalves 170 7 32 S 45 14W
Ribémont 43 49 47N 3 27 E
Ribera 64 37 30N 13 13 E
Ribérac 44 45 15N 0 20 E
Riberalta 174 11 0 S 66 0W
Ribnica 63 45 45N 14 45 E
Ribnitz-Dangarten 48 54 14N 12 24 E
Říčany 52 50 0N 14 40 E
Riccall 33 53 50N 1 4W
Riccarton 143 43 32 S 172 37 E
Riccia 65 41 30N 14 50 E
Riccione 63 44 0N 12 39 E
Rice Lake 158 45 30N 91 42W
Rich 118 32 16N 4 30W
Rich Hill 159 38 5N 94 22W
Richards B. 129 28 48 S 32 6 E
Richards Deep 15 25 0 S 73 0W
Richards L. 153 59 10N 107 10W
Richardson Mts. 143 44 49 S 168 34 E
Richardson, R. 153 58 25N 111 14W
Richardton 158 46 56N 102 22W
Riche, C. 137 34 36 S 118 47 E
Richelieu 42 47 0N 0 20 E
Richey 158 47 42N 105 5W
Richfield, Idaho, U.S.A. 160 43 2N 114 5W
Richfield, Utah, U.S.A. 161 38 50N 112 0W
Richfield Springs 162 42 51N 74 59W
Richibucto 151 46 42N 64 54W
Richland, Ga., U.S.A. 157 32 7N 84 40W
Richland, Oreg., U.S.A. 160 44 49N 117 9W
Richland, Wash., U.S.A. 160 46 15N 119 15W
Richland Center 158 43 21N 90 22W
Richlands 156 37 7N 81 49W
Richmond, N.S.W., Austral. 141 33 35 S 150 42 E
Richmond, Queens., Austral. 138 20 43 S 143 8 E
Richmond, N.Z. 143 41 4 S 173 12 E
Richmond, S. Afr. 125 29 51 S 30 18 E
Richmond, N. Yorks., U.K. 33 54 24N 1 43W
Richmond, Surrey, U.K. 29 51 28N 0 18W
Richmond, Calif., U.S.A. 163 38 0N 122 21W
Richmond, Ind., U.S.A. 156 39 50N 84 50W
Richmond, Ky., U.S.A. 156 37 40N 84 20W
Richmond, Mo., U.S.A. 158 39 15N 93 58W
Richmond, Tex., U.S.A. 159 29 32N 95 42W
Richmond, Va., U.S.A. 162 37 33N 77 27W
Richmond Gulf 150 56 20N 75 50W
Richmond, Mt. 143 41 32 S 173 22 E
Richmond, Ra. 139 29 0 S 152 45 E
Richmond Ra. 143 41 32 S 173 22 E
Richterswil 51 47 13N 8 43 E
Richton 157 31 23N 88 58W
Richwood 156 38 17N 80 32W
Rickmansworth 29 51 38N 0 28W
Ricla 58 41 31N 1 24W
Riddarhyttan 72 59 49N 15 33 E
Ridderkerk 46 51 52N 4 35 E
Riddes 50 46 11N 7 14 E
Ridgecrest 163 35 38N 117 40W
Ridgedale 153 53 0N 104 10W
Ridgefield 162 41 17N 73 30W
Ridgeland 157 32 30N 80 58W
Ridgelands 138 23 16 S 150 17 E
Ridgetown 150 42 26N 81 52W
Ridgewood 162 40 59N 74 7W
Ridgway 156 41 25N 78 43W
Riding Mt. Nat. Park 153 50 50N 100 0W
Ridley Mt. 137 33 12 S 122 7 E
Ridsdale 35 55 9N 2 8W
Ried 52 48 14N 13 30 E
Riehen 50 47 35N 7 39 E
Riel 47 51 31N 5 1 E
Rienne 47 50 0N 4 53 E
Rienza, R. 63 46 49N 11 47 E
Riesa 48 51 19N 13 19 E
Riesi 65 37 16N 14 4 E
Rietfontein 128 26 44 S 20 1 E
Rieti 63 42 23N 12 50 E
Rieupeyroux 44 44 19N 2 12 E
Rievaulx 33 54 16N 1 7W
Riez 45 43 49N 6 6 E
Rifle 160 39 40N 107 50W
Rifstangi 74 66 32N 16 12W
Rift Valley 126 0 20N 36 0 E
Rig Rig 117 14 13N 14 25 E
Riga 80 56 53N 24 8 E
Riga, G. of = Rīgas Jūras Līcis 80 57 40N 23 45 E
Rīgas Jūras Līcis 80 57 40N 23 45 E
Rigby 160 43 41N 111 58W
Riggins 160 45 29N 116 26W
Rignac 44 44 25N 2 16 E
Rigo 138 9 41 S 147 31 E
Rigolet 151 54 10N 58 23W
Riihimäki 75 60 45N 24 48 E
Riiser-Larsen halvøya 13 68 0 S 35 0 E
Riishiri-Tō 112 45 11N 141 15 E
Rijau 121 11 8N 5 17 E
Rijeka Crnojevica 66 42 24N 19 1 E
Rijeka (Fiume) 63 45 20N 14 21 E
Rijen 47 51 35N 4 55 E
Rijkevorsel 47 51 21N 4 46 E
Rijn, R. 47 52 5N 4 50 E
Rijnsberg 46 52 11N 4 27 E
Rijsbergen 47 51 31N 4 41 E
Rijssen 46 52 19N 6 30 E
Rijswijk 46 52 4N 4 22 E
Rike 123 10 50N 39 53 E
Rikita 123 5 5N 28 29 E
Rila 67 42 7N 23 7 E
Rila Planina 66 42 10N 23 30 E
Rillington 33 54 10N 0 41W
Rilly 43 49 11N 4 3 E
Rima 99 28 35N 97 5 E
Rima, R. 121 13 15N 5 15 E
Rimavská Sobota 53 48 22N 20 2 E
Rimbey 152 52 35N 114 15W
Rimbo 72 59 44N 18 21 E
Rimforsa 73 58 8N 15 42 E
Rimi 121 12 58N 7 43 E
Rimini 63 44 3N 12 33 E
Rîmna, R. 70 45 36N 27 3 E
Rîmnicu Sûrat 70 45 26N 27 3 E
Rîmnicu Vîlcece 70 45 9N 24 21 E
Rimouski 151 48 27N 68 30W
Rinca 103 8 45 S 119 35 E
Rincón de Romos 164 22 14N 102 18W
Rinconada 172 22 26 S 66 10W
Ringarum 73 58 21N 16 26 E
Ringe 73 55 13N 10 28 E
Ringel Spitz 51 46 53N 9 19 E
Ringford 35 54 55N 4 3W
Ringim 121 12 13N 9 10 E
Ringkøbing 73 56 5N 8 15 E
Ringkøbing Amt □ 73 56 15N 8 30 E
Ringling 160 46 16N 110 56W
Ringmer 29 50 53N 0 5 E
Ringmoen 71 60 21N 10 6 E
Ringsaker 71 60 54N 10 45 E
Ringsend 38 55 2N 6 45W
Ringsjön L. 73 55 55N 13 30 E
Ringsted 73 55 25N 11 46 E
Ringvassøy 74 69 36N 19 15 E
Ringville 39 52 3N 7 37W
Ringwood 28 50 50N 1 48W
Rinia, I. 69 37 23N 25 13 E
Rinjani 65 8 20 S 116 30 E
Rinns, The, Reg. 34 54 52N 5 3W
Rintein 48 52 11N 9 3 E
Rio Arica 174 1 35 S 75 30W
Rio Branco 174 9 58 S 67 49W
Rio Branco 173 32 40 S 53 40W
Rio Brilhante 173 21 48 S 54 33W
Rio Chico 174 10 19N 65 59W
Rio Claro, Brazil 173 22 19 S 47 35W
Rio Claro, Trin 167 10 20N 61 25W
Rio Colorado 176 39 0 S 64 0W
Rio Cuarto 172 33 10 S 64 25W
Rio das Pedras 129 23 8 S 35 28 E
Rio de Contas 171 13 36 S 41 48W
Rio de Janeiro 173 23 0 S 43 12W
Rio de Janeiro □ 173 22 50 S 43 0W
Rio del Rey 121 4 42N 8 37 E
Rio do Prado 171 16 35 S 40 34W
Rio do Sul 173 27 95 S 49 37W
Rio Gallegos 176 51 35 S 69 15W
Rio Grande 176 53 50 S 67 45W
Rio Grande 173 32 0 S 52 20W
Rio Grande, Mexico 164 23 50N 103 2W
Rio Grande, Nic. 166 12 54N 83 33W
Rio Grande City 159 26 30N 91 55W
Rio Grande del Norte, R. 154 26 0N 97 0W
Rio Grande do Norte □ 170 5 40 S 36 0W
Rio Grande do Sul □ 173 30 0 S 53 0W
Rio Grande, R. 161 37 47N 106 15W
Rio Hato 166 8 22N 80 10W
Rio Lagartos 165 21 36N 88 10W
Rio Largo 171 9 28 S 35 50W
Rio Maior 57 39 19N 8 57W
Rio Marina 62 42 48N 10 25 E
Rio Mulatos 174 19 40 S 66 50W
Rio Muni □ = Mbini □ 124 1 30N 10 0 E
Rio Negro 173 26 0 S 50 0W
Rio Oriente 166 22 17N 81 13W
Rio Pardo, Minas Gerais, Brazil 171 15 55 S 42 30W
Rio Pardo, Rio Grande do Sul, Brazil 173 30 0 S 52 30W
Rio Prêto, Serra do 171 13 29 S 39 55W
Rio, Punta del 59 36 49N 2 24W
Rio Real 171 11 28 S 37 56W
Rio Segundo 172 31 40 S 63 59W
Rio Tercero 172 32 15 S 64 8W
Rio Tinto, Brazil 170 6 48 S 35 5W
Rio Tinto, Port. 56 41 11N 8 34W
Rio Verde 170 17 50 S 51 0W
Rio Verde 165 21 56N 99 59W
Rio Vista 163 38 11N 121 44W
Riobamba 174 1 50 S 78 45W
Riohacha 174 11 33N 72 55W
Rioja, La, Argent. 172 29 20 S 67 0W
Rioja, La, Spain 58 42 20N 2 20W
Rioja, La □ 172 29 30 S 67 0W
Riom 44 45 54N 3 7 E
Riom-ès-Montagnes 44 45 17N 2 39 E
Rion-des-Landes 44 43 55N 0 56W
Rionegro 174 6 9N 75 22W
Rionero in Vúlture 65 40 55N 15 40 E
Rios 56 41 58N 7 16W
Riosucio, Caldas, Colomb. 174 5 30N 75 40W
Riosucio, Choco, Colomb. 174 7 27N 77 7W
Riou L. 153 59 7N 106 25W
Riparia, Dora, R. 62 45 7N 7 24 E
Ripatransone 63 43 0N 13 45 E
Ripley, Derby, U.K. 33 53 3N 1 24W
Ripley, N. Yorks, U.K. 33 54 3N 1 34W
Ripley, U.S.A. 159 35 43N 89 34W
Ripoll 58 42 15N 2 13 E
Ripon, Calif., U.S.A. 163 37 44N 121 7W
Ripon, Wis., U.S.A. 156 43 51N 88 50W
Riposto 65 37 44N 15 12 E
Risalpur 94 34 3N 71 59 E
Risan 66 42 32N 18 42 E
Risca 31 51 36N 3 6W
Riscle 44 43 39N 0 5W
Rishon Le Zion 90 31 58N 34 48 E
Rishpon 90 32 12N 34 49 E
Rishton 32 53 46N 2 26W
Riska 71 58 56N 5 52 E
Risle, R. 42 48 55N 0 41 E
Rîsnov 70 45 35N 25 27 E
Rison 159 33 57N 92 11W
Risør 71 58 43N 9 13 E
Ritchie's Archipelago 101 12 5N 94 0 E
Riti 121 7 57N 9 41 E
Ritzville 160 47 10N 118 21W
Riu 98 28 19N 95 3 E
Riva Bella Ouistreham 42 49 17N 0 18W
Riva del Garda 62 45 53N 10 50 E
Rivadavia, Buenos Aires, Argent. 172 35 29 S 62 59W
Rivadavia, Mendoza, Argent. 172 33 13 S 68 30W
Rivadavia, Salta, Argent. 172 24 5 S 63 0W
Rivadavia, Chile 172 29 50 S 70 35W
Rivarolo Canavese 62 45 20N 7 42 E
Rivas 166 11 30N 85 50W
Rive-de-Gier 45 45 32N 4 37 E
River Cess 120 5 30N 9 25W
Rivera 173 31 0 S 55 50W
Riverchapel 39 52 38N 6 14W
Riverdale 163 36 26N 119 52W
Riverhead 162 40 53N 72 40W
Riverhurst 153 50 55N 106 50W
Riverina 136 29 45 S 120 40 E
Riverina, dist. 133 35 30 S 145 20 E
Rivers 153 50 2N 100 14W
Rivers □ 121 5 0N 6 30 E
Rivers Inlet 152 51 40N 127 20W
Rivers, L. of the 153 49 49N 105 44W
Riversdal 128 34 7 S 21 15 E
Riverside, Calif., U.S.A. 163 34 0N 117 22W
Riverside, Wyo., U.S.A. 160 41 12N 106 57W
Riversleigh 138 19 5 S 138 48 E
Riverton, Austral. 140 34 10 S 138 46 E

* *Renamed Zimbabwe Rhodesia*

Riverton

Ross and Cromarty (□)

Riverton, Can.	153	51 5N	97 0W
Riverton, N.Z.	143	46 21S	168 0E
Riverton, U.S.A.	160	43 1N	108 27W
Riverview	108	27 36S	152 51E
Rives	45	45 21N	5 31E
Rivesaltes	44	42 47N	2 50E
Riviera	62	44 0N	8 30E
Rivière à Pierre	151	46 57N	72 12W
Rivière-au-Renard	151	48 59N	64 23W
Rivière Bleue	151	47 26N	69 2W
Rivière-du-Loup	151	47 50N	69 30W
Rivière Pontecôte	151	49 57N	67 1W
Rívoli	62	45 3N	7 31E
Rivoli B.	140	37 32S	140 3E
Rivungo	128	16 9S	21 51E
Riwaka	143	41 5S	172 59E
Rixensart	47	50 43N	4 32E
Riyadh = Ar Riyad	92	24 41N	46 42E
Rize	92	41 0N	40 30E
Rizzuto, C.	65	38 54N	17 5E
Rjukan	71	59 54N	8 33E
Roa, Norway	71	60 17N	10 37E
Roa, Spain	56	41 41N	3 56W
Road Town	167	18 27N	64 37W
Road Weedon	28	52 14N	1 6W
Roade	29	52 10N	0 53W
Roadhead	32	55 4N	2 44W
Roag, L.	36	58 10N	6 55W
Roan Antelope	127	13 2S	28 19E
Roanne	45	46 3N	4 4E
Roanoke, Ala., U.S.A.	157	33 9N	85 23W
Roanoke, Va., U.S.A.	156	37 19N	79 55W
Roanoke I.	157	35 55N	75 40W
Roanoke, R.	157	36 15N	77 20W
Roanoke Rapids	157	36 36N	77 42W
Roaringwater B.	39	51 30N	9 30W
Roatán	166	16 18N	86 35W
Robbins I.	138	40 42S	145 0E
Robe, R., Austral.	136	21 42S	116 15E
Robe, R., Ireland	38	53 38N	9 10W
Röbel	48	53 24N	12 37E
Robert Lee	159	31 55N	100 26W
Robert Pt.	137	32 34S	115 40E
Roberton	35	55 24N	2 53W
Roberts	160	43 44N	112 8W
Robertsganj	95	24 44N	83 12E
Robertson, Austral.	132	34 37S	150 36E
Robertson, S. Afr.	128	33 46S	19 50E
Robertson I.	13	68 0S	75 0W
Robertson Ra.	136	23 15S	121 0E
Robertsport	120	6 45N	11 26W
Robertstown, Austral.	140	33 58S	139 5E
Robertstown, Ireland	39	53 16N	6 50W
Roberval	150	48 32N	72 15W
Robeson Kanal	12	82 0N	61 30W
Robesonia	162	40 21N	76 8W
Robin Hood's B.	33	54 26N	0 31W
Robinson Crusoe I.	143	33 50S	78 30W
Robinson, R.	138	16 3S	137 16E
Robinson Ranges	137	25 40S	118 0E
Robinson River	138	16 45S	136 58E
Robinvale	140	34 40S	142 45E
Robla, La	56	42 50N	5 41W
Roblin	153	51 14N	101 21W
Roboré	174	18 10S	59 45W
Robson, Mt.	152	53 10N	119 10W
Robstown	159	27 47N	97 40W
Roca, C. da	57	38 40N	9 31W
Roca Partida, I.	164	19 1N	112 2W
Roçadas	128	16 45S	15 0E
Rocas, I.	170	4 0S	34 1W
Rocca d'Aspidé	65	40 27N	15 10E
Rocca San Casciano	63	44 3N	11 30E
Roccalbegna	63	42 47N	11 30E
Roccastrada	63	43 0N	11 10E
Rocella Iónica	65	38 20N	16 24E
Rocester	32	52 56N	1 50W
Rocha	173	34 30S	54 25W
Rochdale	32	53 36N	2 10W
Roche	30	50 24N	4 50W
Roche-Bernard, La	42	47 31N	2 19W
Roche-Canillac, La	44	45 12N	1 57E
Roche-en-Ardenne, La	47	50 11N	5 35E
Roche, La, France	45	46 4N	6 19E
Roche, La, Switz.	50	46 42N	7 7E
Roche-sur-Yon, La	42	46 40N	1 25W
Rochechouart	44	45 50N	0 49E
Rochefort, Belg.	47	50 9N	5 12E
Rochefort, France	44	45 56N	0 57W
Rochefort-en-Terre	42	47 42N	2 22W
Rochefoucauld, La	44	45 44N	0 24E
Rochelle	158	41 55N	89 5W
Rochelle, La	44	46 10N	1 9W
Rocher River	152	61 23N	112 44W
Rocherath	47	50 26N	6 18E
Rocheservière	42	46 57N	1 30W
Rochester, Austral.	140	36 22S	144 41E
Rochester, Can.	152	54 22N	113 27W
Rochester, Kent, U.K.	29	51 22N	0 30E
Rochester, Northum., U.K.	35	55 16N	2 16W
Rochester, Ind., U.S.A.	156	41 5N	86 15W
Rochester, Minn., U.S.A.	158	44 1N	92 28W
Rochester, N.H., U.S.A.	162	43 19N	70 57W
Rochester, N.Y., U.S.A.	156	43 10N	77 40W
Rochford	29	51 36N	0 42E
Rochfortbridge	38	53 25N	7 19W
Rociana	57	37 19N	6 35W
Rociu	70	44 43N	25 2E
Rock Flat	141	36 21S	149 13E
Rock Hall	162	39 8N	76 14W
Rock Hill	157	34 55N	81 2W
Rock Island	158	41 30N	90 35W
Rock Lake	158	48 50N	99 13W
Rock, R.	152	60 7N	127 7W
Rock Rapids	158	43 25N	96 10W
Rock River	160	41 49N	106 0W
Rock Sound	166	24 54N	76 12W
Rock Sprs., Ariz., U.S.A.	161	34 2N	112 11W
Rock Sprs., Mont., U.S.A.	160	46 55N	106 11W
Rock Sprs., Tex., U.S.A.	159	30 2N	100 11W
Rock Sprs., Wyo., U.S.A.	160	41 40N	109 10W
Rock Valley	158	43 10N	96 17W
Rockall I.	16	57 37N	13 42W
Rockanje	46	51 52N	4 4E
Rockcliffe	32	54 58N	3 0W
Rockcorry	38	54 7N	7 0W
Rockdale	159	30 40N	97 0W
Rockefeller Plat.	13	84 0S	130 0W
Rockford	158	42 20N	89 0W
Rockglen	153	49 11N	105 57W
Rockhampton	138	23 22S	150 32E
Rockhampton Downs	138	18 57S	135 10E
Rockhill	39	52 25N	8 44W
Rockingham, Austral.	137	32 15S	115 38E
Rockingham, U.K.	29	52 32N	0 43W
Rockingham B.	138	18 5S	146 10E
Rockingham For.	29	52 28N	0 42W
Rockland, Idaho, U.S.A.	160	42 37N	112 57W
Rockland, Me., U.S.A.	151	44 0N	69 0W
Rockland, Mich., U.S.A.	158	46 40N	89 10W
Rockmart	157	34 1N	85 2W
Rockmills	39	52 13N	8 25W
Rockport, Mass., U.S.A.	162	42 39N	70 36W
Rockport, Mo., U.S.A.	158	40 26N	95 30W
Rockport, Tex., U.S.A.	159	28 2N	97 3W
Rockville, Conn., U.S.A.	162	41 51N	72 27W
Rockville, Md., U.S.A.	162	39 7N	77 10W
Rockwall	159	32 55N	96 30W
Rockwell City	158	42 20N	94 35W
Rockwood	157	35 52N	84 40W
Rocky Ford	158	38 7N	103 45W
Rocky Gully	137	34 30S	117 0E
Rocky Lane	152	58 31N	116 22W
Rocky Mount	157	35 55N	77 48W
Rocky Mountain House	152	52 22N	114 55W
Rocky Mts.	152	55 0N	121 0W
Rocky Pt.	137	33 30S	123 57E
Rockyford	152	51 14N	113 10W
Rocroi	43	49 55N	4 30E
Rod	93	28 10N	63 5E
Roda, La, Albacete, Spain	59	39 13N	2 15W
Roda, La, Sevilla, Spain	57	37 12N	4 46W
Rødberg	71	60 17N	8 56E
Rødby	73	54 41N	11 23E
Rødby Havn	73	54 39N	11 22E
Roddickton	151	50 51N	56 8W
Rødding	73	55 23N	9 3E
Rødekro	73	55 4N	9 20E
Rodel	36	57 45N	6 57W
Roden	46	53 8N	6 26E
Rødenes	71	59 35N	11 34E
Rodenkirchen	48	53 24N	8 26E
Roderick I.	152	52 38N	128 22W
Rodez	44	44 21N	2 33E
Rodholívas	68	40 55N	24 0E
Rodhópi □	68	41 10N	25 30E
Ródhos	69	36 15N	28 10E
Ródhos, I.	69	36 15N	28 10E
Roding R.	29	51 31N	0 7E
Rödjenäs	73	57 33N	14 50E
Rodna	70	47 25N	24 50E
Rodney, C.	142	36 17S	174 50E
Rodniki	81	57 7N	41 37E
Rodriguez, I.	11	20 0S	65 0E
Roe, R.	38	55 0N	6 56W
Roebling	162	40 7N	74 45W
Roebourne	136	20 44S	117 9E
Roebuck B.	136	18 5S	122 20E
Roebuck Plains P.O.	136	17 56S	122 28E
Roelofarendsveen	46	52 12N	4 38E
Roer, R.	47	51 12N	5 59E
Roermond	47	51 12N	6 0E
Roes Welcome Sd.	149	65 0N	87 0W
Roeselare	47	50 57N	3 7E
Rœulx	47	50 31N	4 7E
Rogachev	80	53 8N	30 5E
Rogagua, L.	174	14 0S	66 50W
Rogaland fylke □	75	59 12N	6 20E
Rogans Seat, Mt.	32	54 25N	2 10W
Rogaóica	66	44 4N	19 40E
Rogaška Slatina	63	46 15N	15 42E
Rogate	29	51 0N	0 51W
Rogatec	63	46 15N	21 46E
Rogatin	80	29 24N	24 36E
Rogers	159	36 20N	94 0W
Rogers City	156	45 25N	83 49W
Rogerson	160	42 10N	114 40W
Rogersville	157	36 27N	83 1W
Roggan River	151	54 25N	79 32W
Roggel	47	51 16N	5 56E
Roggeveldberge	128	32 10S	20 10E
Roggiano Gravina	65	39 37N	16 9E
Rogliano, France	45	42 57N	9 30E
Rogliano, Italy	65	39 11N	16 20E
Rogoaguado, L.	174	13 0S	65 30W
Rogowo	54	52 43N	17 38E
Rogozno	54	52 45N	16 59E
Rogue, R.	160	42 30N	124 0W
Rohan	42	48 4N	2 45W
Rohnert Park	163	38 16N	122 40W
Rohrbach	43	49 3N	7 15E
Rohri	94	27 45N	68 51E
Rohri Canal	94	26 15N	68 27E
Rohtak	94	28 55N	76 43E
Roi Et	100	15 56N	103 40E
Roisel	43	49 58N	3 6E
Rojas	172	34 10S	60 45W
Rojo, C., Mexico	165	21 33N	97 20W
Rojo, C., W. Indies	147	17 56N	67 11W
Rokan, R.	102	1 30N	100 50E
Rokeby	138	13 39S	142 40E
Rokiskis	80	55 55N	25 35E
Rokitnoye	81	50 57N	35 56E
Rokycany	52	49 43N	13 35E
Rolândia	173	23 5S	52 0W
Røldal	71	59 47N	6 50E
Rolde	46	52 59N	6 39E
Rolette	158	48 42N	99 50W
Rolfstorp	73	57 11N	12 27E
Rolla, Kansas, U.S.A.	159	37 10N	101 40W
Rolla, Missouri, U.S.A.	159	38 0N	91 42W
Rolla, N. Dak., U.S.A.	158	48 50N	99 36W
Rollag	71	60 2N	9 18E
Rollands Plains	141	31 17S	152 42E
Rolle	50	46 28N	6 20E
Rolleston, Austral.	138	24 28S	148 35E
Rolleston, N.Z.	143	43 35S	172 24E
Rollingstone	138	19 2S	146 24E
Rom	123	9 54N	32 16E
Roma, Austral.	139	26 32S	148 49E
Roma, Italy	64	41 54N	12 30E
Roma, Sweden	73	57 32N	18 26E
Roman, Bulg.	67	43 8N	23 54E
Roman, Rumania	70	46 57N	26 55E
Romana, La	167	18 27N	68 57W
Romang, I.	103	7 30S	127 20E
Rômani	122	30 59N	32 38E
Romanija planina	66	43 50N	18 45E
Romano, Cayo	166	22 0N	77 30W
Romano di Lombardía	62	45 32N	9 45E
Romanovka = Bessarabka	82	46 21N	28 51E
Romans	62	45 3N	5 3E
Romanshorn	51	47 33N	9 22E
Romanzof, C.	147	62 0N	165 50W
Rombo □	126	3 10S	37 30E
Rome, U.S.A.	162	41 51N	76 21W
Rome, Ga., U.S.A.	157	34 20N	85 0W
Rome, N.Y., U.S.A.	162	43 14N	75 29W
Rome = Roma	64	41 54N	12 30E
Romeleåsen	73	55 34N	13 33E
Romenây	45	46 30N	5 1E
Romeo	151	47 28N	57 4W
Romerike	71	60 7N	11 10E
Romilly	43	48 31N	3 44E
Romíni	70	44 59N	24 11E
Rommani	118	33 31N	6 40W
Romney	156	39 21N	78 45W
Romney Marsh	29	51 0N	1 0E
Romny	80	50 48N	33 28E
Rømø	73	55 10N	8 30E
Romodan	80	50 0N	33 15E
Romodanovo	81	54 26N	45 23E
Romont	50	46 42N	6 54E
Romorantin-Lanthenay	43	47 21N	1 45E
Romsdal, R.	71	62 25N	8 0E
Romsdalen	74	62 25N	7 50E
Romsey	28	51 0N	1 29W
Ron	100	17 53N	106 27E
Rona I.	36	57 33N	6 0W
Ronan	160	47 30N	114 11W
Ronas Hill	36	60 33N	1 25W
Ronay I.	36	57 30N	7 10W
Roncador Cay	166	13 40N	80 4W
Roncador, Serra do	171	12 30S	52 30W
Roncesvalles, Paso	58	43 1N	1 19W
Ronceverte	156	37 45N	80 28W
Ronciglione	63	42 18N	12 12E
Ronco, R.	63	44 26N	12 15E
Ronda	57	36 46N	5 12W
Ronda, Serranía de	57	36 44N	5 3W
Rondane	71	61 57N	9 50E
Rondón	174	6 17N	71 6W
Rondônia □	174	11 0S	63 0W
Rong, Koh	101	10 45N	103 15E
Ronge, La, Can.	153	55 5N	105 20W
Ronge, La, Sask., Can.	153	55 6N	105 17W
Ronge, Lac La	153	55 10N	105 0W
Rongotea	142	40 19S	175 25E
Rønne	73	55 6N	14 44E
Ronne Land	13	83 0S	70 0W
Ronneby	73	56 12N	15 17E
Ronsard, C.	137	24 46S	113 10E
Ronse	47	50 45N	3 35E
Roodepoort-Maraisburg	125	26 8S	27 52E
Roodeschool	46	53 25N	6 46E
Roof Butte	161	36 29N	109 5W
Roompot	47	51 37N	3 44E
Roorkee	94	29 52N	77 59E
Roosendaal	47	51 32N	4 29E
Roosevelt, Minn., U.S.A.	158	48 51N	95 2W
Roosevelt, Utah, U.S.A.	160	40 19N	110 1W
Roosevelt I.	13	79 0S	161 0W
Roosevelt, Mt.	152	58 20N	125 20W
Roosevelt Res.	161	33 46N	111 0W
Roosky	38	53 50N	7 55W
Ropczyce	54	50 4N	21 38E
Roper, R.	138	14 43S	135 27E
Ropesville	159	33 25N	102 10W
Ropsley	33	52 53N	0 31W
Roque Pérez	172	35 25S	59 24W
Roquefort	44	44 2N	0 20W
Roquefort-sur-Souizon	44	43 58N	2 59E
Roquemaure	45	44 3N	4 48E
Roquetas	58	40 50N	0 30E
Roquevaire	45	43 20N	5 36E
Roraima □	174	2 0N	61 30W
Roraima, Mt.	174	5 10N	60 40W
Rorketon	153	51 24N	99 35W
Røros	71	62 35N	11 23E
Rorschach	51	47 28N	9 30E
Rørvik	74	64 54N	11 15E
Rosa, U.S.A.	160	38 15N	122 16W
Rosa, Zambia	127	9 33S	31 15E
Rosa Brook	137	33 57S	115 10E
Rosa, C.	119	37 0N	8 16E
Rosa, Monte	50	45 57N	7 53E
Rosal	56	41 57N	8 51W
Rosal de la Frontera	57	37 59N	7 13W
Rosalia	160	47 26N	117 25W
Rosamund	163	34 52N	118 10W
Rosans	45	44 24N	5 29E
Rosario	172	33 0S	60 50W
Rosário, Maran., Brazil	170	3 0S	44 15W
Rosário, Rio Grande do Sul, Brazil	176	30 15S	55 0W
Rosario, Baja California, Mexico	164	30 0N	116 0W
Rosario, Durango, Mexico	164	26 30N	105 35W
Rosario, Sinaloa, Mexico	164	23 0N	106 0W
Rosario, Venez.	174	10 19N	72 19W
Rosario de la Frontera	172	25 50S	65 0W
Rosario de Lerma	172	24 59S	65 35W
Rosario del Tala	172	32 20S	59 10W
Rosário do Sul	173	30 15S	54 55W
Rosarito	164	28 38N	114 4W
Rosarno	65	38 29N	15 59E
Rosas	58	42 19N	3 10E
Rosas, G. de,	55	42 10N	3 15E
Rosburgh	143	45 33S	169 19E
Roscoe	162	41 56N	74 55W
Roscoff	42	48 44N	4 0W
Roscommon, Ireland	38	53 38N	8 11W
Roscommon, U.S.A.	156	44 27N	84 35W
Roscommon □	38	53 40N	8 15W
Roscrea	39	52 58N	7 50W
Rose Blanche	151	47 38N	58 45W
Rose Harbour	152	52 15N	131 10W
Rose Ness	37	58 52N	2 50W
Rose Pt.	152	54 11N	131 39W
Rose, R.	138	14 16S	135 45E
Rose Valley	153	52 19N	103 49W
Roseau, Domin.	167	15 20N	61 30W
Roseau, U.S.A.	158	48 51N	95 46W
Rosebery	138	41 46S	145 33E
Rosebud, Austral.	141	38 21S	144 54E
Rosebud, U.S.A.	159	31 5N	97 0W
Roseburg	160	43 10N	123 10W
Rosedale, Austral.	138	24 38S	151 53E
Rosedale, U.S.A.	159	33 51N	91 0W
Rosedale Abbey	33	54 22N	0 51W
Rosée	47	50 14N	4 41E
Rosegreen	39	52 28N	7 51W
Rosehall	37	57 59N	4 36W
Rosehearty	37	57 42N	2 8W
Rosemarkie	37	57 35N	4 8W
Rosemary	152	50 46N	112 5W
Rosenallis	39	53 10N	7 25W
Rosenberg	159	29 30N	95 48W
Rosendaël	43	51 3N	2 24E
Rosenheim	49	47 51N	12 9E
Roseto degli Abruzzi	63	42 40N	14 2E
Rosetown	153	51 35N	108 3W
Rosetta = Rashîd	122	31 21N	30 22E
Roseville	160	38 46N	121 17W
Rosewood, N.S.W., Austral.	141	35 38S	147 52E
Rosewood, N.T., Austral.	136	16 28S	128 58E
Rosewood, Queens., Austral.	139	27 38S	152 36E
Rosh Haniqra, Kefar	90	33 5N	35 5E
Rosh Pinna	90	32 58N	35 32E
Rosh Ze'ira	90	31 14N	35 15E
Roshage C.	73	57 7N	8 35E
Rosières	43	48 36N	6 20E
Rosignano Marittimo	62	43 23N	10 28E
Rosignol	174	6 15N	57 30W
Roşiori-de-Vede	70	44 9N	25 0E
Rositsa	67	43 57N	27 57E
Rositsa, R.	67	43 10N	25 30E
Roskeeragh Pt.	38	54 22N	8 40W
Roskhill	36	57 24N	6 31W
Roskilde	73	55 38N	12 3E
Roskilde Amt □	73	55 35N	12 5E
Roskilde Fjord	73	55 50N	12 2E
Roskill, Mt.	142	36 55S	174 45E
Roslavl	80	53 57N	32 55E
Roslyn	141	34 29S	149 37E
Rosmaninhal	57	39 44N	7 5W
Røsnæs	73	55 44N	10 55E
Rosneath	34	56 1N	4 49W
Rosolini	65	36 49N	14 58E
Rosporden	42	47 57N	3 50W
Ross, Austral.	138	42 2S	147 30E
Ross, N.Z.	143	42 53S	170 49E
Ross, U.K.	28	51 55N	2 34W
Ross and Cromarty (□)	26	57 43N	4 50W

Ross Dependency **Sabang, O**

Place	Page	Lat.	Long.
Ross Dependency	**13**	70 0S	170 5W
Ross I.	**13**	77 30S	168 0E
Ross Ice Shelf	**13**	80 0S	180 0W
Ross L.	**160**	48 50N	121 0W
Ross on Wye	**28**	51 55N	2 34W
Ross River, Austral.	**138**	19 15S	146 51E
Ross River, Can.	**147**	62 30N	131 30W
Ross Sea	**13**	74 0S	178 0E
Rossa	**51**	46 23N	9 8E
Rossall Pt.	**32**	53 55N	3 2W
Rossan Pt.	**38**	54 42N	8 47W
Rossano Cálabro	**65**	39 36N	16 39E
Rossburn	**153**	50 40N	100 49W
Rosscahill	**38**	53 23N	9 15W
Rosscarbery	**39**	51 39N	9 1W
Rosscarbery B.	**39**	51 32N	9 0W
Rossel I.	**138**	11 30S	154 30E
Rosses B.	**38**	55 2N	8 30W
Rosses Point	**38**	54 17N	8 34W
Rosses, The	**38**	55 2N	8 20W
Rossignol, L., N.S., Can.	**151**	44 12N	65 0W
Rossignol, L., Qué., Can.	**150**	52 43N	73 40W
Rossing	**128**	22 30S	14 50E
Rossland	**152**	49 6N	117 50W
Rosslare	**39**	52 17N	6 23W
Rosslau	**48**	51 52N	12 15E
Rosslea	**38**	54 15N	7 11W
Rosso	**120**	16 40N	15 45W
Rossosh	**83**	50 15N	39 20E
Rossport	**150**	48 50N	87 30W
Rossum	**46**	51 48N	5 20E
Røssvatnet	**74**	65 45N	14 5E
Rossville	**138**	15 48S	145 15E
Rosthern	**153**	52 40N	106 20W
Rostock	**48**	54 4N	12 9E
Rostock □	**48**	54 10N	12 30E
Rostov, Don, U.S.S.R.	**83**	47 15N	39 45E
Rostov, Moskva, U.S.S.R.	**81**	57 14N	39 25E
Rostrenen	**42**	48 14N	3 21W
Rostrevor	**38**	54 7N	6 12W
Roswell	**159**	33 26N	104 32W
Rosyth	**35**	56 2N	3 26W
Rota	**57**	36 37N	6 20W
Rotälven	**72**	61 30N	14 10E
Rotan	**159**	32 52N	100 30W
Rotem	**47**	51 3N	5 45E
Rotenburg	**48**	53 6N	9 24E
Rothbury	**35**	55 19N	1 55W
Rothbury Forest	**35**	55 19N	1 50W
Rothenburg	**51**	47 6N	8 16E
Rothenburg ob der Tauber	**49**	49 21N	10 11E
Rother, R.	**29**	50 59N	0 40W
Rotherham	**33**	53 26N	1 21W
Rothes	**37**	57 31N	3 12W
Rothesay, Can.	**151**	45 23N	66 0W
Rothesay, U.K.	**34**	55 50N	5 3W
Rothhaar G., mts.	**50**	51 6N	8 10E
Rothienorman	**37**	57 24N	2 28W
Rothrist	**50**	47 18N	8 54E
Rothwell, Northants, U.K.	**29**	52 25N	0 48W
Rothwell, W. Yorks., U.K.	**33**	53 46N	1 29W
Roti, I.	**103**	10 50S	123 0E
Rotkop	**128**	26 44S	15 27E
Roto	**141**	33 0S	145 30E
Roto Aira L.	**142**	39 3S	175 55E
Rotoehu L.	**142**	38 1S	176 32E
Rotoiti L.	**142**	41 51S	172 49E
Rotoma L.	**142**	38 2S	176 35E
Rotondella	**65**	40 10N	16 30E
Rotoroa Lake	**143**	41 55S	172 39E
Rotorua	**142**	38 9S	176 16E
Rotorua, L.	**142**	38 5S	176 18E
Rotselaar	**47**	50 57N	4 42E
Rottal	**37**	56 48N	3 1W
Rotten, R.	**50**	46 18N	7 36E
Rottenburg	**49**	48 28N	8 56E
Rottenmann	**52**	47 31N	14 22E
Rotterdam	**46**	51 55N	4 30E
Rottingdean	**29**	50 48N	0 3W
Rottnest I.	**137**	32 0S	115 27E
Rottumeroog	**46**	53 33N	6 34E
Rottweil	**49**	48 9N	8 38E
Rotuma, I.	**130**	12 25S	177 5E
Roubaix	**43**	50 40N	3 10E
Roudnice	**52**	50 25N	14 15E
Rouen	**42**	49 27N	1 4E
Rouergue	**45**	44 20N	2 20E
Rough, gasfield	**19**	53 50N	0 27E
Rough Pt.	**39**	52 19N	10 0W
Rough Ridge	**143**	45 10S	169 55E
Rouillac	**44**	45 47N	0 4W
Rouleau	**153**	50 10N	104 56W
Round Mt.	**139**	30 26S	152 16E
Round Mountain	**163**	38 46N	117 3W
Roundstone	**38**	53 24N	9 55W
Roundup	**160**	46 25N	108 35W
Roundwood	**39**	53 4N	6 14W
Rourkela	**95**	22 14N	84 50E
Rousay, I.	**37**	59 10N	3 2W
Rousky	**38**	54 44N	7 10E
Rousse, L'Île	**45**	43 27N	8 57E
Roussillon	**45**	45 24N	4 49E
Rouveen	**46**	52 37N	6 11E
Rouxville	**128**	30 11S	26 50E
Rouyn	**150**	48 20N	79 0W
Rovaniemi	**74**	66 29N	25 41E
Rovato	**62**	45 34N	10 0E
Rovenki	**83**	48 5N	39 27E
Rovereto	**62**	45 53N	11 3E
Rovigo	**63**	45 4N	11 48E
Rovinari	**70**	46 56N	23 10E
Rovinj	**63**	45 18N	13 40E
Rovira	**174**	4 15N	75 20W
Rovno	**80**	50 40N	26 10E
Rovnoye	**81**	50 52N	46 3E
Rovuma, R.	**127**	11 30S	36 10E
Rowanburn	**35**	55 5N	2 54W
Rowena	**139**	29 48S	148 55E
Rowes	**141**	37 0S	149 6E
Rowley Shoals	**136**	17 40S	119 20E
Rowood	**161**	32 18N	112 54W
Rowrah	**32**	54 34N	3 26W
Roxa	**120**	11 15N	15 45W
Roxas	**103**	11 36N	122 49E
Roxboro	**157**	36 24N	78 59W
Roxborough Downs	**138**	22 20S	138 45E
Roxburgh, N.Z.	**143**	45 33S	169 19E
Roxburgh, U.K.	**35**	55 34N	2 30W
Roxburgh (□)	**26**	55 30N	2 30W
Roxby	**33**	53 38N	0 37W
Roxen	**73**	58 30N	15 40E
Roy	**160**	47 17N	109 0W
Roy Hill	**136**	22 37S	119 58E
Roy, Le	**159**	38 8N	95 35W
Roya, Peña	**58**	40 25N	0 40W
Royal Canal	**38**	53 29N	7 0W
Royal Oak	**156**	42 30N	83 5W
Royalla	**141**	35 30S	149 9E
Royan	**44**	45 37N	1 2W
Roybridge	**37**	56 53N	4 50W
Roye	**43**	47 40N	6 31E
Røyken	**71**	59 45N	10 23E
Royston	**29**	52 3N	0 1W
Royton	**32**	53 34N	2 7W
Rozaj	**66**	42 50N	20 15E
Rozan	**54**	52 52N	21 25E
Rozdol	**80**	49 30N	24 1E
Rozier, Le	**44**	44 13N	3 12E
Roznava	**53**	48 37N	20 35E
Rozoy	**43**	48 40N	2 56E
Rozoy-sur-Serre	**43**	49 40N	4 8E
Rozwadów	**54**	50 37N	22 2E
Rrësheni	**68**	41 47N	19 49E
Rtanj, mt.	**66**	43 45N	21 50W
Rtem, Oued el	**119**	33 40N	5 34E
Rtishchevo	**81**	52 35N	43 50E
Rúa	**56**	42 24N	7 6W
Ruacaná	**128**	17 20S	14 12E
Ruahine Ra.	**142**	39 55S	176 2E
Ruamahanga, R.	**142**	41 24S	175 8E
Ruapehu	**142**	39 17S	175 35E
Ruapuke I.	**143**	46 46S	168 31E
Ruatoria	**142**	37 55S	178 20E
Ruãus, W.	**119**	30 14N	15 0E
Ruawai	**142**	36 15S	173 59E
Rub 'al Khali	**91**	21 0N	51 0E
Rubeho, mts.	**126**	6 50S	36 25E
Rubery	**28**	52 24N	1 59W
Rubezhnoye	**82**	49 6N	38 25E
Rubha Ardvule C.	**36**	57 17N	7 32W
Rubha Hunish, C.	**36**	57 42N	6 20W
Rubh'an Dunain, C.	**36**	57 10N	6 20W
Rubiataba	**171**	15 8S	49 48W
Rubicone, R.	**63**	44 0N	12 20E
Rubim	**171**	16 23S	40 32W
Rubinéia	**171**	20 13S	51 2W
Rubino	**120**	6 4N	4 18W
Rubio	**174**	7 43N	72 22W
Rubona	**126**	0 29N	30 9E
Rubtsovsk	**76**	51 30N	80 50E
Ruby	**147**	64 40N	155 35W
Ruby L.	**160**	40 10N	115 28W
Ruby Mts.	**160**	40 30N	115 30W
Rubyvale	**138**	23 25S	147 45E
Rucava	**80**	56 9N	20 32E
Ruciane-Nida	**54**	53 40N	21 32E
RûcûSdia	**66**	44 59N	21 36E
Rud	**71**	60 1N	10 1E
Ruda	**73**	57 6N	16 7E
Ruda Slaska	**53**	50 16N	18 50E
Rudall	**140**	33 43S	136 17E
Rudbar	**93**	30 0N	62 30E
Ruden, I.	**48**	54 13N	13 47E
Rüdersdorf	**48**	52 28N	13 48E
Rudewa	**127**	10 7S	34 47E
Rudgwick	**29**	51 7N	0 54W
Rudkøbing	**73**	54 56N	10 41E
Rudna	**54**	51 30N	16 17E
Rudnichnyy	**84**	59 38N	52 26E
Rudnik, Bulg.	**67**	42 36N	27 30E
Rudnik, Yugo.	**67**	44 7N	20 35E
Rudnik, mt.	**67**	44 7N	20 35E
Rudnogorsk	**77**	57 15N	103 42E
Rudnya	**80**	54 55N	31 13E
Rudnyy	**84**	52 57N	63 7E
Rudo	**66**	43 41N	19 23E
Rudolstadt	**48**	50 44N	11 20E
Rudozem	**67**	41 29N	24 51E
Rudston	**33**	54 6N	0 19W
Rŭducaneni	**70**	46 58N	27 54E
Rŭdŭuţi	**70**	47 50N	25 59E
Rudyard	**156**	46 14N	84 35E
Rue	**43**	50 15N	1 40E
Ruelle	**44**	45 41N	0 14E
Rufa'a	**123**	14 44N	33 32E
Ruffec Charente	**44**	46 2N	0 12W
Rufi	**123**	5 58N	30 18E
Rufiji □	**126**	8 0S	38 30E
Rufiji, R.	**124**	7 50S	38 15E
Rufino	**172**	34 20S	62 50W
Rufisque	**120**	14 40N	17 15W
Rufunsa	**127**	15 4S	29 34E
Rugby, U.K.	**28**	52 23N	1 16W
Rugby, U.S.A.	**158**	48 21N	100 0W
Rugeley	**28**	52 47N	1 56W
Rügen, I.	**48**	54 22N	13 25E
Rugezi	**126**	2 6S	33 18E
Rugles	**42**	48 50N	0 40E
Ruhāma	**90**	31 31N	34 43E
Ruhea	**98**	26 10N	88 25E
Ruhengeri	**126**	1 30S	29 36E
Ruhla	**48**	50 53N	10 21E
Ruhland	**48**	51 27N	13 52E
Ruhr, R.	**48**	51 25N	7 15E
Ruhuhu, R.	**127**	10 15S	34 55E
Rui Barbosa	**171**	12 18S	40 27W
Ruidosa	**159**	29 59N	104 39W
Ruidoso	**161**	33 19N	105 39W
Ruinen	**46**	52 46N	6 21E
Ruinen A Kanaal	**46**	52 54N	7 8E
Ruinerwold	**46**	52 44N	6 15E
Ruj, mt.	**66**	42 52N	22 42E
Rujen, mt.	**66**	42 9N	22 30E
Ruk	**94**	27 50N	68 42E
Rukwa □, Tanz.	**126**	7 0S	31 30E
Rukwa □, Tanz.	**126**	7 0S	31 30E
Rukwa L.	**126**	7 50S	32 10E
Rulhieres, C.	**136**	13 56S	127 22E
Rulles	**47**	49 43N	5 32E
Rully	**167**	46 52N	4 44E
Rum Jungle	**136**	13 0S	130 59E
Ruma	**66**	45 8N	19 50E
Rumah	**92**	25 35N	47 10E
Rumania ■	**61**	46 0N	25 0E
Rumbalara	**138**	25 20S	134 29E
Rumbek	**123**	6 54N	29 37E
Rumbeke	**47**	50 56N	3 10E
Rumburk	**52**	50 57N	14 32E
Rumelange	**47**	49 27N	6 2E
Rumford	**156**	44 30N	70 30W
Rumia	**54**	54 37N	18 25E
Rumilly	**45**	45 53N	5 56E
Rumney	**31**	51 32N	3 7W
Rumoi	**112**	43 56N	141 39W
Rumonge	**126**	3 59S	29 26E
Rumsey	**152**	51 51N	112 48W
Rumson	**162**	40 23N	74 0W
Rumula	**138**	16 35S	145 20E
Rumuruti	**126**	0 17N	36 32E
Runabay Hd.	**38**	55 10N	6 2W
Runanga	**143**	42 25S	171 15E
Runaway, C.	**142**	37 32S	178 2E
Runcorn, Austral.	**108**	27 36S	153 4E
Runcorn, U.K.	**32**	53 20N	2 44W
Rungwa	**126**	6 55S	33 32E
Rungwa, R.	**126**	7 15S	33 10E
Rungwe	**127**	9 11S	33 32E
Rungwe □	**127**	9 25S	33 32E
Runka	**121**	12 28N	7 20E
Runn	**72**	60 30N	15 40E
Rupa	**98**	27 15N	92 30E
Rupar	**94**	31 2N	76 38E
Rupat, I.	**102**	1 45N	101 40E
Rupea	**61**	46 2N	25 13E
Rupert House = Fort Rupert	**150**	51 30N	78 40W
Rupert, R.	**150**	51 29N	78 45W
Rupsa	**98**	21 44N	87 20E
Rupununi, R.	**175**	3 30N	59 30W
Ruquka Gie La	**99**	31 35N	97 55E
Rurrenabaque	**174**	14 30S	67 32W
Rus, R.	**58**	39 30N	2 30W
Rusambo	**127**	16 30S	32 4E
Rusape	**125**	18 35S	32 8E
Ruschuk = Ruse	**67**	43 48N	25 59E
Ruse	**67**	43 48N	25 59E
Rusetu	**70**	44 57N	27 14E
Rush	**38**	53 31N	6 7W
Rushden	**29**	52 17N	0 37W
Rushford	**158**	43 48N	91 46W
Rushville, Ill., U.S.A.	**158**	40 6N	90 35W
Rushville, Ind., U.S.A.	**156**	39 38N	85 22W
Rushville, Nebr., U.S.A.	**158**	42 43N	102 35W
Rushworth	**141**	36 32S	145 1E
Rusken	**73**	57 15N	14 20E
Ruskington	**33**	53 5N	0 23W
Russas	**171**	4 56S	38 2W
Russell, Can.	**153**	50 50N	101 20W
Russell, N.Z.	**142**	35 16S	174 10E
Russell, U.S.A.	**158**	38 56N	98 55W
Russell L., Man., Can.	**153**	56 15N	101 30W
Russell L., N.W.T., Can.	**152**	63 5N	115 44W
Russellkonda	**96**	19 57N	84 42E
Russellville, Ala., U.S.A.	**157**	34 30N	87 44W
Russellville, Ark., U.S.A.	**159**	35 15N	93 0W
Russellville, Ky., U.S.A.	**157**	36 50N	86 50W
Russi	**63**	44 21N	12 1E
Russian Mission	**147**	61 45N	161 25W
Russian S.F.S.R. □	**77**	62 0N	105 0E
Russkoye Ustie	**12**	71 0N	149 0E
Rust	**53**	47 49N	16 42E
Rustam	**94**	34 25N	72 13E
Rustam Shahr	**94**	26 58N	66 6E
Rustavi	**83**	40 45N	44 30E
Rustenburg	**128**	25 41S	27 14E
Ruston	**159**	32 30N	92 40W
Ruswil	**50**	47 5N	8 8E
Rutana	**126**	3 55S	30 0E
Rutba	**92**	33 4N	40 15E
Rute	**57**	37 19N	4 29W
Ruteng	**103**	8 26S	120 30E
Ruth	**160**	39 15N	115 1W
Ruth, oilfield	**19**	55 33N	4 55E
Rutherglen, Austral.	**141**	36 5S	146 29E
Rutherglen, U.K.	**34**	55 50N	4 11W
Ruthin	**31**	53 7N	3 20W
Ruthven	**37**	57 4N	4 2W
Ruthwell	**35**	55 0N	3 24W
Rüti	**51**	47 16N	8 51E
Rutigliano	**65**	41 1N	17 0E
Rutland	**162**	43 38N	73 0W
Rutland (□)	**26**	52 38N	0 40W
Rutland I.	**101**	11 25N	92 40E
Rutland Plains	**138**	15 38S	141 49E
Rutledge L.	**153**	61 33N	110 47W
Rutledge, R.	**153**	61 4N	112 0W
Rutshuru	**126**	1 13S	29 25E
Ruurlo	**46**	52 5N	6 24E
Ruvo di Púglia	**65**	41 7N	16 27E
Ruvu	**126**	6 49S	38 43E
Ruvu, R.	**126**	7 25S	38 15E
Ruvuma □	**127**	10 20S	36 0E
Ruvuma, R.	**127**	11 30S	36 10E
Ruwaidha	**92**	23 40N	44 40E
Ruwandiz	**92**	36 40N	44 32E
Ruwenzori Mts.	**126**	0 30N	29 55E
Ruwenzori, mt.	**126**	0 30N	29 55E
Ruyigi	**126**	3 29S	30 15E
Ruzayevka	**81**	54 10N	45 0E
Ruzhevo Konare	**67**	42 23N	24 46E
Ruzomberok	**53**	49 3N	19 17E
Rwanda ■	**126**	2 0S	30 0E
Ryaberg	**73**	56 47N	13 15E
Ryakhovo	**67**	44 0N	26 18E
Ryan, L.	**34**	55 0N	5 2W
Ryazan	**81**	54 50N	39 40E
Ryazhsk	**81**	53 45N	40 3E
Rybache	**76**	46 40N	81 20E
Rybachi Poluostrov	**78**	69 43N	32 0E
Rybachye	**85**	42 26N	76 12E
Rybinsk (Shcherbakov)	**81**	58 5N	38 50E
Rybinsk Vdkhr.	**81**	58 30N	38 0E
Rybnik	**54**	50 6N	18 32E
Rybnitsa	**82**	47 45N	29 0E
Rychwał	**54**	52 4N	18 10E
Ryd	**73**	56 27N	14 42E
Rydal	**32**	54 28N	2 59W
Ryde	**28**	50 44N	1 9W
Rydö	**73**	56 58N	13 10E
Rydsnäs	**73**	57 47N	15 9E
Rydułtowy	**54**	50 4N	18 23E
Rydzyna	**54**	51 47N	16 39E
Rye, Denmark	**73**	56 5N	9 45E
Rye, U.K.	**29**	50 57N	0 46E
Rye Patch Res.	**160**	40 45N	118 20W
Rye, R.	**33**	54 12N	0 53W
Ryegate	**160**	46 21N	109 27W
Ryhope	**35**	54 52N	1 22W
Rylsk	**80**	51 30N	34 51E
Rylstone	**141**	32 46S	149 58E
Rymanów	**54**	49 35N	21 51E
Ryn	**54**	53 57N	21 34E
Ryningsnäs	**73**	57 17N	15 58E
Ryōhaku-Sanchi	**111**	36 0N	136 49E
Rypin	**54**	53 3N	19 32E
Ryton, Tyne & Wear, U.K.	**35**	54 58N	1 44W
Ryton, Warwick, U.K.	**28**	52 23N	1 25W
Ryūgasaki	**111**	35 54N	140 11E
Ryūkyū Is. = Nansei-Shotō	**112**	26 0N	128 0E
Rzepin	**54**	52 20N	14 49E
Rzeszów	**54**	50 5N	21 58E
Rzeszów □	**54**	50 0N	22 0E
Rzhev	**80**	56 20N	34 20E

S

Place	Page	Lat.	Long.
s'-Hertogenbosch	**47**	51 42N	5 17E
Sa	**100**	18 34N	100 45E
Sa. da Canastra	**125**	19 30S	46 5W
Sa Dec	**101**	10 20N	105 46E
Sa-Koi	**98**	19 54N	97 3E
Sa'ad (Muharraga)	**90**	31 28N	34 33E
Sa'ādatabād	**93**	30 10N	53 5E
Saale, R.	**48**	51 25N	11 56E
Saaler Bodden	**48**	54 20N	12 25E
Saalfelden	**70**	47 26N	12 51E
Saalfield	**48**	50 39N	11 21E
Saane, R.	**50**	46 23N	7 18E
Saanen	**50**	46 29N	7 15E
Saar (Sarre), □	**43**	49 20N	6 45E
Saarbrücken	**49**	49 15N	6 58E
Saarburg	**49**	49 36N	6 32E
Saaremaa	**80**	58 30N	22 30E
Saariselkä	**74**	68 16N	28 15E
Saarland □	**131**	49 20N	6 45E
Saarlouis	**49**	49 19N	6 45E
Saas Fee	**50**	46 7N	7 56E
Saas-Grund	**50**	46 7N	7 57E
Saba I.	**167**	17 30N	63 10W
Sabac	**66**	44 48N	19 42E
Sabadell	**58**	41 28N	2 7E
Sabae	**111**	35 57N	136 11E
Sabagalel	**102**	1 36S	98 40E
Sabah □	**102**	6 0N	117 0E
Sabak	**100**	3 46N	100 58E
Sábana de la Mar	**167**	19 7N	69 40W
Sábanalarga	**174**	10 38N	74 55W
Sabang, O.	**102**	5 50N	95 15E

Sabará St. Lawrence

Sabará 171 19 55 S 43 55 W
Sabarania 103 2 5 S 138 18 E
Sabari, R. 96 18 0 N 81 25 E
Sabastiya 90 32 17 N 35 12 E
Sabaudia 64 41 17 N 13 2 E
Sabderat 123 15 26 N 36 42 E
Sabhah 119 27 9 N 14 29 E
Sabie 129 25 4 S 30 48 E
Sabinal, Mexico 164 30 50 N 107 25 W
Sabinal, U.S.A. 159 29 20 N 99 27 W
Sabinal, Punta del 59 36 43 N 2 44 W
Sabinas 164 27 50 N 101 10 W
Sabinas Hidalgo 164 26 40 N 100 10 W
Sabinas, R. 164 27 37 N 100 42 W
Sabine 159 29 42 N 93 54 W
Sabine, R. 159 31 30 N 93 35 W
Sabinópolis 171 18 40 S 43 6 W
Sabinov 53 49 6 N 21 5 E
Sabirabad 83 40 0 N 48 30 E
Sabkhat Tawurgha 119 31 48 N 15 30 E
Sablayan 103 12 5 N 120 50 E
Sable 42 47 50 N 0 21 W
Sable, C., Can. 151 43 29 N 65 38 W
Sable, C., U.S.A. 166 25 5 N 81 0 W
Sable I. 151 44 0 N 60 0 W
Sablé-sur-Sarthe 42 47 50 N 0 20 W
Sables-D'Olonne, Les 44 46 30 N 1 45 W
Saboeiro 170 6 32 S 39 54 W
Sabor, R. 56 41 16 N 7 10 W
Sabou 120 12 1 N 2 28 W
Sabrātah 119 32 47 N 12 29 E
Sabrina Coast 13 67 0 S 120 0 E
Sabugal 56 40 20 N 7 5 W
Sabzevar 93 36 15 N 57 40 E
Sabzvaran 93 28 45 N 57 50 E
Sac City 158 42 26 N 95 0 W
Sacandaga Res. 162 43 6 N 74 16 W
Sacedón 58 40 29 N 2 41 W
Sachigo, L. 150 53 50 N 92 12 W
Sachigo, R. 150 55 6 N 88 58 W
Sachinbulako 106 43 5 N 111 47 E
Sachkhere 83 42 25 N 43 28 E
Sachseln 51 46 52 N 8 15 E
Sacile 63 45 58 N 16 7 E
Säckingen 49 47 34 N 7 56 E
Saco, Me., U.S.A. 162 43 30 N 70 27 W
Saco, Mont., U.S.A. 160 48 28 N 107 19 W
Sacquoy Hd. 37 59 12 N 3 5 W
Sacramento, Brazil 171 19 53 S 47 27 W
Sacramento, U.S.A. 163 38 39 N 121 30 E
Sacramento Mts. 161 32 30 N 105 30 W
Sacramento, R. 163 38 3 N 121 56 W
Sacratif, Cabo 59 36 42 N 3 28 W
Sacriston 33 54 49 N 1 38 W
Sada 56 43 22 N 8 15 W
Sada-Misaki-Hantō 110 33 22 N 132 1 E
Sadaba 58 2 19 N 1 12 W
Sa'dani 124 5 58 S 38 35 E
Sadao 101 6 38 N 100 26 E
Sadasivpet 96 17 38 N 77 50 E
Sadberge 33 54 32 N 1 30 W
Sadd el Aali 122 24 5 N 32 54 E
Saddell 34 55 31 N 5 30 W
Saddle, Hd. 38 54 0 N 10 10 W
Saddle, The 36 57 10 N 5 27 W
Sade 121 11 22 N 10 45 E
Sadiba 128 18 53 S 23 1 E
Sadimi 127 9 25 S 23 32 E
Sado 112 38 0 N 138 25 E
Sado, R. 57 38 10 N 8 22 W
Sadon, Burma 99 25 28 N 98 0 E
Sadon, U.S.S.R. 83 42 52 N 43 58 E
Sadri 94 24 28 N 74 30 E
Saduya 98 27 50 N 95 40 E
Sæby 73 57 21 N 10 30 E
Saelices 58 39 55 N 2 49 W
Safâga 122 26 42 N 34 0 E
Safaha 122 26 25 N 39 0 E
Safaniya 92 28 5 N 48 42 E
Safárikovo 53 48 25 N 20 20 E
Safed Koh, Mts. 94 34 15 N 64 0 E
Safford 61 32 54 N 109 52 W
Saffron Walden 29 52 2 N 0 15 E
Safi, Jordan 90 31 2 N 35 28 E
Safi, Moroc. 118 32 18 N 9 14 W
Safiah 42 31 27 N 34 46 E
Safonovo 80 65 40 N 47 50 E
Safranbolu 82 41 15 N 32 34 E
Sag Harbor 162 40 59 N 72 17 W
Sag Sag 135 5 32 S 148 23 E
Saga, Indon. 103 2 40 S 132 55 E
Saga, Kōchi, Japan 110 33 5 N 133 6 E
Saga, Saga, Japan 110 33 15 N 130 16 E
Saga-ken □ 110 33 15 N 130 20 E
Sagåg 71 59 46 N 5 25 E
Sagaing 98 23 30 N 95 30 E
Sagaing □ 98 22 0 N 95 30 E
Sagala 120 14 9 N 6 38 W
Sagami-Nada 111 34 58 N 139 23 E
Sagami-Wan 111 35 15 N 139 25 E
Sagamihara 111 35 33 N 139 25 E
Saganoseki 110 33 15 N 131 53 E
Sagar 93 23 50 N 78 50 E
Sagara, India 97 14 14 N 75 6 E
Sagara, Japan 111 34 41 N 138 12 E
Sagara, L. 126 5 20 S 31 0 E
Sagawa 110 33 28 N 133 11 E
Sågen 72 60 17 N 14 10 E
Sagil 105 50 20 N 91 40 E
Saginaw 156 43 26 N 83 55 W
Saginaw B. 150 43 50 N 83 40 W
Sagleipie 45 45 25 N 7 0 E
Saglouc (Sugluk) 149 62 30 N 74 15 W
Sagone 45 42 7 N 8 42 E
Sagone, G. de 45 42 4 N 8 40 E
Sagori 107 35 25 N 126 49 E
Sagra, La, Mt. 59 38 0 N 2 35 W
Sagres 57 37 0 N 8 58 W
Sagu 98 20 13 N 94 46 E
Sagua la Grande 166 22 50 N 80 10 W
Saguache 161 38 10 N 106 4 W
Saguenay, R. 151 48 22 N 71 0 W
Sagunto 58 39 42 N 0 18 W
Sahaba 122 18 57 N 30 25 E
Sahagún, Colomb. 174 8 57 N 75 27 W
Sahagún, Spain 56 42 18 N 5 2 W
Saham 90 32 42 N 35 46 E
Sahara 118 23 0 N 5 0 W
Saharanpur 94 29 58 N 77 33 E
Saharien Atlas 118 34 9 N 3 29 E
Sahasinaka 129 21 49 S 47 49 E
Sahaswan 95 28 5 N 78 45 E
Sahel, Canal du 120 14 20 N 6 0 W
Sahibganj 95 25 12 N 87 55 E
Sahiwal 94 30 45 N 73 8 E
Sahl Arraba 90 37 26 N 35 12 E
Sahtaneh, R. 152 59 2 N 122 28 W
Sahuaripa 164 29 30 N 109 0 W
Sahuarita 161 31 58 N 110 59 W
Sahuayo 164 20 4 N 102 43 W
Sahy 53 48 4 N 18 55 E
Sai Buri 101 6 43 N 101 39 E
Saibai I. 135 9 25 S 142 40 E
Sa'id Bundas 117 8 24 N 24 48 E
Saïda 118 34 50 N 0 11 E
Sa'idabad 93 29 30 N 55 45 E
Saidapet 97 13 0 N 80 15 E
Saidor 135 5 40 S 146 29 E
Saidu 95 34 50 N 72 15 E
Säle 72 59 8 N 12 55 E
Saighan 93 35 10 N 67 55 E
Saignelégier 50 47 15 N 7 0 E
Saignes 44 45 20 N 2 31 E
Saigō 110 36 12 N 133 20 E
Saigon = Phanh Bho Ho Chi Minh 101 10 58 N 106 40 E
Saih-al-Malih 93 23 37 N 58 31 E
Saihut 91 15 12 N 51 10 E
Saijō, Ehima, Japan 110 33 55 N 133 11 E
Saijō, Hiroshima, Japan 110 34 25 N 132 45 E
Saikhoa Ghat 99 27 50 N 95 40 E
Saiki 110 32 58 N 131 57 E
Saillans 45 44 42 N 5 12 E
Sailolof 103 1 7 S 130 46 E
Saima 107 40 59 N 124 15 E
Saimaa, L. 78 61 15 N 28 15 E
St. Abbs 35 55 54 N 2 7 W
St. Abb's Head 35 55 55 N 2 10 W
St. Aegyd 52 47 52 N 15 33 E
St. Affrique 44 43 57 N 2 53 E
St. Agnes 30 50 18 N 5 13 W
St. Agnes Hd. 30 50 19 N 5 14 W
St. Agnes I. 30 49 53 N 6 20 W
St.-Agrève 45 45 0 N 4 23 E
St.-Aignan 42 47 16 N 1 22 E
St. Albans, Austral. 138 24 43 S 139 56 E
St. Albans, Can. 151 47 51 N 55 50 W
St. Albans, U.K. 29 51 44 N 0 19 W
St. Albans, Vt., U.S.A. 156 44 49 N 73 7 W
St. Albans, W. Va., U.S.A. 156 38 21 N 81 50 W
St. Alban's Head 28 50 34 N 2 3 W
St. Albert 152 53 37 N 113 40 W
St. Amand 43 50 25 N 3 6 E
St.-Amand-en-Puisaye 43 47 32 N 3 5 E
St.-Amand-Mont-Rond 43 46 43 N 2 30 E
St.-Amarin 43 47 54 N 7 0 E
St.-Amour 45 46 26 N 5 21 E
St. Andrä 52 46 46 N 14 50 E
St. André, C. 129 16 11 S 44 27 E
St.-André-de-Cubzac 44 44 59 N 0 26 W
St. André de l'Eure 42 48 54 N 1 16 E
St.-André-les-Alpes 45 43 58 N 6 30 E
St. Andrews, Can. 151 47 45 N 59 15 W
St. Andrews, N.Z. 143 44 33 S 171 10 E
St. Andrews, U.K. 35 56 20 N 2 48 W
St. Ann B. 151 46 22 N 60 25 W
St. Anne 42 49 43 N 2 11 W
St. Anne's 32 53 45 N 3 2 W
St. Ann's 35 55 14 N 3 28 W
St. Ann's Bay 166 18 26 N 77 15 W
St. Ann's Hd. 31 51 41 N 5 11 W
St. Anthony, Can. 151 51 22 N 55 35 W
St. Anthony, U.S.A. 160 44 0 N 111 49 W
St.-Antonin-Noble-Val 44 44 10 N 1 45 E
St. Arnaud 140 36 32 S 143 16 E
St. Arnaud Ra. 143 42 1 S 172 53 E
St. Arthur 151 47 47 N 67 46 W
St. Asaph 32 53 15 N 3 27 W
St. Astier 44 45 8 N 0 31 E
St.-Aubin 50 46 54 N 6 47 E
St.-Aubin-du-Cormier 42 48 15 N 1 26 W
St. Augustin 129 23 33 S 43 46 E
St-Augustin-Saguenay 151 51 13 N 58 38 W
St. Augustine 157 29 52 N 81 20 W
St. Austell 30 50 20 N 4 48 W
St.-Avold 43 49 6 N 6 43 E
St. Barthélemy, I. 167 17 50 N 62 50 W
St. Bathans 143 44 53 S 170 0 E
St. Bathan's Mt. 143 44 45 S 169 45 E
St. Bees 32 54 29 N 3 36 W
St. Bee's Hd. 32 54 30 N 3 38 E
St.-Benoît-du-Sault 44 46 26 N 1 24 E
St. Bernard, Col du Grand 50 45 53 N 7 11 E
St.-Blaise 50 47 1 N 6 59 E
St. Blazey 32 50 22 N 4 48 W
St. Boniface 153 49 50 N 97 10 W
St. Bonnet 45 44 40 N 6 5 E
St. Boswells 35 55 34 N 2 39 W
St.-Brévin-les-Pins 42 47 14 N 2 10 W
St. Briavels 28 51 44 N 2 39 W
St.-Brice-en-Coglès 42 48 25 N 1 22 W
St. Bride's 151 46 56 N 54 10 W
St. Bride's B. 31 51 48 N 5 15 W
St.-Brieuc 42 48 30 N 2 46 W
St. Budeaux 30 50 23 N 4 10 W
St. Buryan 30 50 4 N 5 34 W
St.-Calais 42 47 55 N 0 45 E
St.-Cast 42 48 37 N 2 18 W
St. Catharines 150 43 10 N 79 15 W
St. Catherine's I. 157 31 35 N 81 10 W
St. Catherine's Pt. 28 50 34 N 1 18 W
St.-Céré 44 44 51 N 1 54 E
St. Cergue 50 46 27 N 6 10 E
St. Cernin 44 45 5 N 2 25 E
St.-Chamond 45 45 28 N 4 31 E
St. Charles, Ill., U.S.A. 156 41 55 N 88 21 W
St. Charles, Mo., U.S.A. 158 38 46 N 90 30 W
St.-Chély-d'Apcher 44 44 48 N 3 17 E
St.-Chinian 44 43 25 N 2 56 E
St. Christopher (St. Kitts) 167 17 20 N 62 40 W
St.-Ciers-sur-Gironde 44 45 17 N 0 37 W
St. Clair 162 40 42 N 76 12 W
St. Clair, L. 150 42 30 N 82 45 W
St.-Claud 44 45 54 N 0 28 E
St. Claude 153 49 40 N 98 20 W
St.-Claude 45 46 22 N 5 52 E
St. Clears 31 51 48 N 4 30 W
St.-Cloud 42 48 51 N 2 12 E
St. Cloud, Fla., U.S.A. 157 28 15 N 81 15 W
St. Cloud, Minn., U.S.A. 158 45 30 N 94 11 W
St. Coeur de Marie 151 48 39 N 71 43 W
St. Columb Major 30 50 26 N 4 56 W
St. Combs 37 57 40 N 1 55 W
St. Cricq, C. 137 25 17 S 113 6 E
St. Croix Falls 158 45 18 N 92 22 W
St. Croix, I. 147 17 45 N 64 45 W
St. Croix, R. 158 45 20 N 92 50 W
St. Cyprien 44 42 37 N 3 0 E
St.-Cyr 45 43 11 N 5 43 E
St. Cyrus 36 56 47 N 2 25 W
St. David's, Can. 151 48 12 N 58 52 W
St. David's, U.K. 31 51 54 N 5 16 W
St. David's Head 31 51 54 N 5 16 W
St.-Denis 43 48 56 N 2 22 E
St.-Denis-d'Orques 42 48 2 N 0 17 W
St. Dennis 30 50 23 N 4 53 W
St.-Dié 43 48 17 N 6 56 E
St. Dizier 43 48 40 N 5 0 E
St. Dogmaels 31 52 6 N 4 42 W
St. Dominick 30 50 28 N 4 15 W
St. Donats 31 51 23 N 3 32 W
St.-Egrève 45 45 14 N 5 41 E
St. Elias, Mt. 147 60 20 N 141 59 W
St. Elias Mts. 147 59 30 N 137 30 W
St. Eloy 44 46 10 N 2 51 E
St. Emilon 44 44 53 N 0 9 W
St. Endellion 30 50 33 N 4 49 W
St. Enoder 30 50 22 N 4 57 W
St. Erth 30 50 10 N 5 26 W
St. Etienne 45 45 27 N 4 22 E
St.-Étienne-de-Tinée 45 44 16 N 6 56 E
St. Eustatius I. 167 17 20 N 63 0 W
St. Félicien 150 48 40 N 72 25 W
St. Fergus 37 57 33 N 1 50 W
St. Fillans 35 56 25 N 4 7 W
St. Finian's B. 39 51 50 N 10 22 W
St. Fintan's 151 48 10 N 58 50 W
St.-Florent 45 42 41 N 9 18 E
St.-Florent-sur-Cher 43 46 59 N 2 15 E
St.-Florentin 43 48 0 N 3 45 E
St.-Flour 44 45 2 N 3 6 E
St.-Fons 45 45 42 N 4 52 E
St. Francis 158 39 48 N 101 47 W
St. Francis C. 128 34 14 S 24 49 E
St. Francis, R. 159 32 25 N 90 36 W
St.-Fulgent 42 46 50 N 1 10 W
St. Gabriel de Brandon 150 46 17 N 73 24 W
St.-Gengoux-le-National 45 46 37 N 4 40 E
St.-Geniez-d'Olt 44 44 27 N 2 58 E
St. George, Austral. 139 28 1 S 148 41 E
St. George, Can. 151 45 11 N 66 50 W
St. George, P.N.G. 135 4 10 S 152 20 E
St. George, S.C., U.S.A. 157 33 13 N 80 37 W
St. George, Utah, U.S.A. 161 37 10 N 113 35 W
St. George, C., Can. 151 48 30 N 59 16 W
St. George, C., P.N.G. 135 4 49 S 152 53 E
St. George, C., U.S.A. 157 29 36 N 85 2 W
St. George Hd. 139 35 11 S 150 45 E
St. George Ra., Mts. 136 18 40 S 125 0 E
St. George West 153 50 33 N 96 7 W
St.-Georges 47 50 37 N 4 20 E
St. George's 151 48 26 N 58 31 W
St. Georges, Qué., Can. 151 46 8 N 70 40 W
St. Georges, Quebec, Can. 150 46 42 N 72 35 W
St. Georges, Fr. Gui. 175 4 0 N 52 0 W
St. George's 167 12 5 N 61 43 W
St. George's B. 151 48 24 N 58 53 W
St. George's Channel 147 52 0 N 6 0 W
St. Georges-de-Didonne 44 45 36 N 1 0 W
St. Georges Head 141 35 12 S 150 42 E
St.-Gérard 47 50 21 N 4 44 E
St. Germain 43 48 53 N 2 5 E
St.-Germain-Lembron 44 45 27 N 3 14 E
St.-Germain-de-Calberte 44 44 13 N 3 48 E
St.-Germain-des-Fossés 44 46 12 N 3 26 E
St.-Germain-du-Plain 43 46 42 N 4 58 E
St.-Germain-Laval 45 45 50 N 4 1 E
St. Germans 30 50 24 N 4 19 W
St. Gervais, Haute Savoie, France 45 45 53 N 6 42 E
St. Gervais, Puy de Dôme, France 44 46 4 N 2 50 E
St.-Gervais-les-Bains 43 45 53 N 6 41 E
St.-Gildas, Pte. de 42 47 8 N 2 14 W
St.-Gilles 45 43 40 N 4 26 E
St. Gilles Croix-de-Vie 42 46 41 N 1 55 W
St.-Gingolph 50 46 24 N 6 48 E
St.-Girons 44 42 59 N 1 8 E
St. Gla, L. 72 59 35 N 12 30 E
St. Goar 49 50 31 N 7 43 E
St. Gotthard P. = San Gottardo 51 46 33 N 8 33 E
St. Govan's Hd. 31 51 35 N 4 56 W
St.-Guadens 44 43 6 N 0 44 E
St.-Gualtier 42 46 39 N 1 26 E
St.-Guénolé 42 47 49 N 4 23 W
St. Harmon 31 52 21 N 3 29 W
St. Heddinge 73 55 9 N 12 26 E
St. Helena 160 38 29 N 122 30 W
St. Helena, I. 15 15 55 S 5 44 W
St. Helenabaai 128 32 40 S 18 10 E
St. Helens, Austral. 138 41 20 S 148 15 E
St. Helens, I.o.W., U.K. 28 50 42 N 1 6 W
St. Helens, Merseyside, U.K. 32 53 28 N 2 44 W
St. Helens, U.S.A. 160 45 55 N 122 50 W
St. Helier 42 49 11 N 2 6 W
St. Hilaire 42 48 35 N 1 7 W
St. Hippolyte 43 47 20 N 6 50 E
St. Hippolyte-du-Fort 44 43 58 N 3 52 E
St.-Honoré 43 46 54 N 3 50 E
St.-Hubert 47 50 2 N 5 23 E
St. Hyacinthe 150 45 40 N 72 58 W
St. Ignace 156 45 53 N 84 43 W
St. Ignace I. 150 48 45 N 88 0 W
St. Ignatius 160 47 25 N 114 2 W
St.-Imier 50 47 9 N 6 58 E
St. Issey 30 50 30 N 4 55 W
St. Ives, Cambs., U.K. 29 52 20 N 0 5 W
St. Ives, Cornwall, U.K. 30 50 13 N 5 29 W
St. Ives Bay 30 50 15 N 5 27 W
St.-James 42 48 31 N 1 20 W
St. James 158 43 57 N 94 40 W
St. James C. 152 51 55 N 131 0 W
St. Jean 150 45 20 N 73 50 W
St.-Jean 45 48 57 N 3 1 E
St. Jean Baptiste 153 49 15 N 97 20 W
St. Jean, C. 124 1 5 N 9 20 E
St.-Jean-de-Maurienne 45 45 16 N 6 28 E
St.-Jean-de-Luz 44 43 23 N 1 39 W
St.-Jean-de-Monts 42 46 47 N 2 4 W
St. Jean-du-Gard 44 47 7 N 3 52 E
St.-Jean-en-Royans 45 45 1 N 5 18 E
St.-Jean, L. 151 48 40 N 72 0 W
St. Jean-Port-Joli 151 47 15 N 70 13 W
St.-Jean, R. 151 50 17 N 64 20 W
St. Jérôme, Qué., Can. 150 45 47 N 74 0 W
St. Jérôme, Qué., Can. 151 48 26 N 71 53 W
St. John, Can. 151 45 20 N 66 8 W
St. John, Kans., U.S.A. 159 37 59 N 98 45 W
St. John, N.D., U.S.A. 158 48 58 N 99 40 W
St. John, C. 151 50 0 N 55 32 W
St. John, I. 147 18 20 N 64 45 W
St. John, R. 151 45 15 N 66 4 W
St. Johns 167 17 6 N 61 51 W
St. John's, Can. 151 47 35 N 52 40 W
St. John's, U.K. 32 54 13 N 4 38 W
St. Johns, Ariz., U.S.A. 161 34 31 N 109 26 W
St. Johns, Mich., U.S.A. 156 43 0 N 84 38 W
St. Johns Chapel 32 54 43 N 2 10 W
St. John's Pt., Ireland 38 54 35 N 8 26 W
St. John's Pt., U.K. 38 54 14 N 5 40 W
St. Johns, R. 157 30 20 N 81 30 W
St. Johnsbury 156 44 25 N 72 1 W
St. Johnston 38 54 56 N 7 29 W
St. Johnsville 162 43 0 N 74 43 W
St. Joseph, La., U.S.A. 159 31 55 N 91 15 W
St. Joseph, Mo., U.S.A. 158 39 40 N 94 50 W
St. Joseph, I. 150 46 12 N 83 58 W
St. Joseph, L. 150 51 10 N 90 35 W
St. Joseph, R. 156 42 7 N 86 30 W
St. Joseph's 156 42 5 N 86 30 W
St. Jovite 150 46 8 N 74 38 W
St. Juéry 44 43 55 N 2 42 E
St. Julien 45 46 8 N 6 5 E
St.-Julien-Chapteuil 45 45 2 N 4 4 E
St. Julien du Sault 43 48 1 N 3 17 E
St.-Junien 44 45 53 N 0 55 E
St. Just 30 50 7 N 5 41 W
St.-Just-en-Chaussée 43 49 30 N 2 25 E
St.-Just-en-Chevalet 44 45 55 N 3 50 E
St.-Justin 44 43 59 N 0 14 W
St. Karlsö, I. 73 57 17 N 17 58 E
St. Keverne 30 50 3 N 5 5 W
St. Kew 30 50 34 N 4 48 W
St. Kilda 143 45 53 S 170 31 E
St. Kilda, I. 23 57 40 N 8 50 W
St. Kitts, I. 167 17 20 N 62 40 W
St. Laurent 153 50 25 N 97 58 W
St.-Laurent-du-Pont 45 45 23 N 5 45 E
St.-Laurent-en-Grandvaux 45 46 35 N 5 45 E
St. Lawrence, Austral. 138 22 16 S 149 31 E
St. Lawrence, Can. 151 46 54 N 55 23 W

St. Lawrence, Gulf of
Sam Ngao

St. Lawrence, Gulf of 151 48 25N 62 0W
St. Lawrence, I. 147 63 0N 170 0W
St. Lawrence, R. 151 49 30N 66 0W
St.-Léger 47 49 37N 5 39E
St. Leonard 151 47 12N 67 58W
St.-Léonard-de-Noblat 44 45 49N 1 29E
St. Leonards 29 50 51N 0 34E
St. Levan 30 50 3N 5 36W
St Lewis, R. 151 52 26N 56 11W
St. Lin 150 45 44N 73 46W
St.-Lô 42 49 7N 1 5W
St. Louis, Senegal 120 16 8N 16 27W
St. Louis, Mich., U.S.A. 156 43 27N 84 38W
St. Louis, Mo., U.S.A. 158 38 40N 90 12W
St. Louis R. 158 47 15N 92 45W
St.-Loup-sur-Semouse 43 47 53N 6 16E
St. Lucia, C. 129 28 32S 32 29E
St. Lucia Channel 167 14 15N 61 0W
St. Lucia I. 167 14 0N 60 50W
St. Lucia, Lake 129 28 5S 32 30E
St. Lunaire-Griquet 151 51 31N 55 28W
St. Maarten, I. 167 18 0N 63 5W
St. Mabyn 30 50 30N 4 45W
St. Magnus B. 36 60 25N 1 35W
St.-Maixent-l'École 44 46 24N 0 12W
St.-Malo 42 48 39N 2 1W
St. Malo, G. de 42 48 50N 2 30W
St. Mandrier 45 43 4N 5 56E
St. Marc 167 19 10N 72 50W
St.-Marcellin 45 45 9N 5 20E
St. Marcouf, Îs. 42 49 30N 1 10W
St.-Mard 47 49 2N 2 42E
St. Margaret's-at-Cliffe 29 51 10N 1 23E
St. Margaret's Hope 37 58 49N 2 58W
St. Maries 160 47 17N 116 34W
St. Martin 43 50 42N 1 38E
St.-Martin, I. 167 18 0N 63 0W
St. Martin L. 153 51 40N 98 30W
St. Martin-Tende-Vésubie 45 44 4N 7 15E
St. Martins 151 45 22N 65 25W
St. Martin's I. 30 49 58N 6 16W
St. Martinsville 159 30 10N 91 50W
St.-Martory 44 43 9N 0 56E
St. Mary B. 151 46 50N 53 50W
St. Mary Bourne 28 51 16N 1 24W
St. Mary C. 120 13 24N 13 10E
St. Mary Is. 97 13 20N 74 35E
St. Mary, Mt. 135 8 8S 146 54E
St. Mary Pk. 140 31 32S 138 34E
St. Marys, N.S.W., Austral. 133 33 44S 150 49E
St. Marys, Tas., Austral. 138 41 32S 148 11E
St. Mary's, Can. 151 46 56N 53 34W
St. Mary's, U.K. 37 58 53N 2 55W
St. Mary's, Ohio, U.S.A. 156 40 33N 84 20W
St. Mary's, Pa., U.S.A. 156 41 30N 78 33W
St Marys Bay 151 44 25N 66 10W
St. Mary's, C. 151 46 50N 54 12W
St. Mary's I. 30 49 55N 6 17W
St. Mary's Pk. 133 31 30S 138 33E
St. Mary's Sd. 30 49 53N 6 19W
St. Mathews I. = Zadetkyi Kyun 101 10 0N 48 25E
St.-Mathieu, Pte. de 42 48 20N 4 45W
St. Matthias Grp. 135 1 30S 150 0E
St.-Maur-des-Fosses 43 48 48N 2 30E
St. Maurice 50 46 13N 7 0E
St. Maurice R. 150 47 20N 72 50W
St. Mawes 30 50 10N 5 1W
St.-Médard-de-Guizières 44 45 1N 0 4W
St.-Méen-le-Grand 42 48 11N 2 12W
St. Merryn 30 50 31N 4 58W
St. Michael 147 63 30N 162 30W
St. Michaels, Arizona, U.S.A. 161 35 45N 109 5W
St. Michaels, Maryland, U.S.A. 162 38 47N 76 14W
St. Michael's Mt. 30 50 7N 5 30W
St. Michel 45 45 15N 6 29E
St. Mihiel 43 48 54N 5 30E
St. Minver 30 50 34N 4 52W
St. Monans 35 56 13N 2 46W
St.-Nazaire 42 47 17N 2 12W
St. Neots 29 52 14N 0 16W
St.-Nicholas-de-Port 43 48 38N 6 18E
St. Niklaus 50 46 10N 7 49E
St. Ninian's, I. 36 59 59N 1 20W
St. Olaf 73 55 40N 14 12E
St.-Omer 43 50 45N 2 15E
St. Osyth 29 51 47N 1 4E
St. Ouen 43 48 50N 2 20E
St. Pacome 151 47 24N 69 58W
St. Palais 44 45 40N 1 8W
St. Pamphile 151 46 58N 69 48W
St.-Pardoux-la-Rivière 44 45 29N 0 45E
St. Pascal 151 47 32N 69 48W
St. Patrickswell 39 52 36N 8 43W
St. Paul, Can. 152 54 59N 111 17W
St. Paul, France 44 43 44N 1 3W
St. Paul, Minn., U.S.A. 158 44 54N 93 5W
St. Paul, Nebr., U.S.A. 158 41 15N 98 30W
St. Paul-de-Fenouillet 44 42 50N 2 28E
St. Paul, I., Atl. Oc. 14 0 50N 31 40W
St. Paul, I., Can. 151 47 12N 60 9W
St. Paul, I., Ind. Oc. 11 30 40S 77 34E
St. Paul's B. 151 49 48N 57 58W
St.-Peray 45 44 57N 4 50E
St.-Père-en-Retz 42 47 11N 2 2W
St. Peter 158 44 15N 93 57W
St. Peter Port 42 49 27N 2 31W
St. Peters, N.S., Can. 151 45 40N 60 53W
St. Peters, P.E.I., Can. 151 46 25N 62 35W
St. Petersburg 157 27 45N 82 40W
St.-Philbert-de-Grand-Lieu 42 47 2N 1 39W
St Pierre 151 46 40N 56 0W
St.-Pierre-d'Oleron 44 45 57N 1 19W
St.-Pierre-Église 42 49 40N 1 24W
St.-Pierre-en-Port 42 49 48N 0 30E
Saint-Pierre et Miquelon □ 151 46 55N 56 10W
St-Pierre, L. 150 46 12N 72 52W
St.-Pierre-le-Moûtier 43 46 47N 3 7E
St. Pierre-sur-Dives 42 49 2N 0 1W
St.-Pieters Leew 47 50 47N 4 16E
St. Pol 43 50 21N 2 20E
St.-Pol-de-Léon 42 48 41N 4 0W
St.-Pol-sur-Mer 43 51 1N 2 20E
St. Pons 44 43 30N 2 45E
St.-Pourçain-sur-Sioule 43 46 18N 3 18E
St.-Quay-Portrieux 42 48 39N 2 51W
St.-Quentin 43 49 50N 3 16E
St. Rambert-d'Albon 45 45 17N 1 35E
St.-Raphaël 45 43 25N 6 46E
St. Regis 160 47 20N 115 3W
St.-Rémy-de-Provence 45 43 48N 4 50E
St.-Renan 42 48 26N 4 37W
St.-Saëns 42 49 41N 1 16E
St.-Sauveur-en-Puisaye 43 47 37N 3 12E
St.-Sauveur-le-Vicomte 42 49 23N 1 32W
St. Savin 44 46 34N 0 50E
St.-Savinien 44 45 53N 0 42W
St. Sebastien, C. 129 12 26S 48 44E
St.-Seine-l'Abbaye 43 47 26N 4 47E
St. Sernin 44 43 54N 2 35E
St.-Servan-sur-Mer 42 48 38N 2 0E
St.-Sever-Calvados 42 48 50N 1 3W
St. Simeon 151 47 51N 69 54W
St. Stephen, Can. 151 45 16N 67 17W
St. Stephen, U.K. 30 50 20N 4 52W
St.-Sulpice 44 43 46N 1 41E
St.-Sulpice-Laurière 44 46 3N 1 29E
St. Teath 30 50 34N 4 45W
St.-Thegonnec 42 48 31N 3 57W
St. Thomas 150 42 45N 81 10W
St. Thomas, I. 147 18 21N 64 55W
St. Tite 150 46 45N 72 40W
St. Tropez 45 43 17N 6 38E
St. Troud 47 50 48N 5 10E
St. Tudwal's Is. 31 52 48N 4 28W
St. Tudy 30 50 33N 4 45W
St.-Vaast-la-Hougue 42 49 35N 1 17W
St. Valéry 43 50 10N 1 38E
St.-Valéry-en-Caux 42 49 52N 0 43E
St.-Vallier 45 45 11N 4 50E
St.-Vallier-de-Thiey 45 43 42N 6 51E
St.-Varent 42 46 53N 0 13W
St. Vincent 14 18 0N 26 1W
St. Vincent C. 125 21 58S 43 20E
St. Vincent, C. = São Vincente 57 37 0N 9 0W
St. Vincent-de-Tyrosse 44 43 39N 1 18W
St. Vincent, G. 140 35 0S 138 0E
St. Vincent, I. 167 13 10N 61 10W
St. Vincent Passage 167 13 30N 61 0W
St.-Vith 47 50 17N 6 9E
St.-Yrieux-la-Perche 44 45 31N 1 12E
Ste.-Adresse 42 49 31N 0 5E
Ste.-Agathe-des-Monts 150 46 3N 74 17W
Ste. Anne 167 14 26N 60 53W
Ste. Anne de Beaupré 151 47 2N 70 58W
Ste. Anne de Portneuf 151 48 38N 69 8W
Ste.-Anne-des-Monts 151 49 8N 66 30W
Ste. Benoîte 43 49 47N 3 30E
Ste. Cecile 151 47 56N 64 34W
Ste.-Croix 43 46 49N 6 34W
Ste.-Enimie 44 44 22N 3 26E
Ste.-Foy-la-Grande 44 44 50N 0 13E
Ste. Genevieve 158 37 59N 90 2W
Ste. Germaine 151 46 24N 70 24W
Ste.-Hermine 44 46 32N 1 4W
Ste.-Livrade-sur-Lot 44 44 24N 0 36E
Ste. Marguerite, R. 151 50 9N 66 36W
Ste. Marie 167 14 48N 61 1W
Ste.-Marie-aux-Mines 43 48 10N 7 12E
Ste. Marie, C. 129 25 36S 45 8E
Ste. Marie de la Madeleine 151 46 26N 71 0W
Ste. Marie, I. 129 16 50S 49 55E
Ste.-Maure-de-Touraine 42 47 7N 0 37E
Ste.-Maxime 45 43 19N 6 39E
Ste.-Menehould 43 49 5N 4 54E
Ste.-Mère-Église 42 49 24N 1 19W
Ste. Rose 167 16 20N 61 45W
Ste. Rose du lac 153 51 41N 99 30W
Ste. Teresa 172 33 33S 60 54W
Saintes 44 45 45N 0 37W
Saintes, I. des 167 15 50N 61 35W
Saintes-Maries-de-la-Mer 45 43 26N 4 26E
Saintes Maries, Les 45 43 27N 4 25E
Saintfield 38 54 28N 5 50W
Saintonge 44 45 40N 0 50W
Sairang 99 23 50N 92 45E
Sairecábur, Cerro 172 22 43S 67 54W
Saitama-ken □ 111 36 25N 137 0E
Saito 110 32 3N 131 18E
Sajama, Nevada 174 18 0S 68 55W
Sajan 66 45 50N 20 58E
Sajószentpéter 53 48 12N 20 44E
Sajum, mt. 95 33 20N 79 0E
Saka Ilkalat 93 27 20N 64 7E
Sakai 111 34 30N 135 30E
Sakaide 110 34 15N 133 56E
Sakaiminato 110 35 38N 133 11E
Sakaka 92 30 0N 40 8E
Sakami, L. 150 53 15N 76 45W
Sâkâne, 'Erg i-n 118 20 30N 1 30W
Sakania 127 12 43S 28 30E
Sakar, I. 138 5 30S 148 0E
Sakarya, R. 82 40 5N 31 0E
Sakata 112 36 38N 138 19E
Sakchu 107 40 23N 125 2E
Sakeny, R. 129 20 0S 45 25E
Sakété 121 6 40N 2 32E
Sakhalin, Ostrov 77 51 0N 143 0E
Sakhi Gopal 96 19 58N 85 50E
Sakhnin 90 32 52N 35 12E
Saki 82 45 16N 33 34E
Sakiai 80 54 59N 23 0E
Sakmara 84 52 0N 55 20E
Sakmara, R. 84 51 46N 55 1E
Sakołow Małopolski 54 50 10N 22 9E
Sakon Nakhon 100 17 10N 104 9E
Sakrand 94 26 10N 68 15E
Sakri 96 21 2N 74 40E
Sakskøbing 73 54 49N 11 39E
Saku 111 36 11N 138 31E
Sakuma 111 35 3N 137 56E
Sakurai 111 34 30N 135 51E
Sakuru 111 35 43N 140 14E
Säkylä 75 61 4N 22 20E
Sal, R. 83 47 25N 42 20E
Sal'a 53 48 10N 17 50E
Sala 72 59 58N 16 35E
Sala Consilina 65 40 23N 15 35E
Sala-y-Gomez, I. 131 26 28S 105 28W
Salaberry-de-Valleyfield 150 45 15N 74 8W
Salada, La 164 24 30N 111 30W
Saladas 172 28 15S 58 40W
Saladillo 172 35 40S 59 55W
Salado, R., Buenos Aires, Argent. 172 35 40S 58 10W
Salado, R., Santa Fe, Argent. 172 27 0S 63 40W
Salado, R., Mexico 164 26 52N 99 19W
Salaga 121 8 31N 0 31W
Salala, Liberia 120 6 42N 10 7W
Salala, Sudan 122 21 17N 36 16E
Salalah 91 16 56N 53 59E
Salama 90 32 3N 34 48E
Salamanca, Chile 172 32 0S 71 25W
Salamanca, Spain 56 40 58N 5 39W
Salamanca, U.S.A. 156 42 10N 78 42W
Salamanca □ 56 40 57N 5 40W
Salamaua 138 7 10S 147 0E
Salamina 174 5 25N 75 29W
Sałamis 69 37 56N 23 30E
Salar de Atacama 176 23 30S 68 25W
Salar de Uyuni 174 20 30S 67 45W
Salard 70 47 12N 22 3E
Salas 56 43 25N 6 15W
Salas de los Infantes 58 42 2N 3 17W
Salavat 84 53 21N 55 55E
Salaverry 174 8 15S 79 0W
Salawe 126 3 17S 32 56E
Salayar, I. 103 6 15S 120 30E
Salazar, R. 58 42 45N 1 8W
Salbohed 72 59 55N 16 22E
Salbris 43 47 25N 2 3E
Salcia 70 43 56N 24 55E
Salcombe 30 50 14N 3 47W
Salcombe Regis 30 50 41N 3 11W
Saldaña 56 42 32N 4 48W
Saldanha 128 33 0S 17 58E
Saldanhabaai 128 33 6S 18 0E
Saldus 80 56 45N 22 37E
Sale 141 38 6S 147 6E
Salé 118 34 3N 6 48W
Sale 32 53 26N 2 19W
Saléa-koïra 121 16 54N 0 46W
Salebabu 103 3 45N 125 55E
Salehabad 93 35 40N 61 2E
Salekhard 76 66 30N 66 25E
Salem, India 97 11 40N 78 11E
Salem, Ind., U.S.A. 156 38 38N 86 16W
Salem, Mass., U.S.A. 162 42 29N 70 53W
Salem, Mo., U.S.A. 159 37 40N 91 30W
Salem, N.H., U.S.A. 162 42 47N 71 12W
Salem, N.J., U.S.A. 162 39 34N 75 29W
Salem, N.Y., U.S.A. 162 43 10N 73 20W
Salem, Ohio, U.S.A. 156 40 52N 80 50W
Salem, Oreg., U.S.A. 160 45 0N 123 0W
Salem, Va., U.S.A. 156 37 19N 80 8W
Salembu, Kepulauan 102 5 35S 114 30E
Salemi 64 37 49N 12 47E
Salen, Norway 75 64 41N 11 27E
Salen, Highland, U.K. 36 56 42N 5 48W
Salen, Strathclyde, U.K. 34 56 31N 5 57W
Salernes 45 43 34N 6 15E
Salerno 65 40 40N 14 44E
Salerno, G. di 65 40 35N 14 45E
Salfit 90 32 5N 35 11E
Salford 32 53 30N 2 17W
Salford Priors 28 52 10N 1 52W
Salgir, R. 82 45 30N 34 30E
Salgótarján 53 48 5N 19 47E
Salgueiro 170 8 4S 39 6W
Salies-de-Béarn 44 43 28N 0 56W
Salima 125 13 47S 34 28E
Salin 98 20 35N 94 40E
Salina 158 38 50N 97 40W
Salina Cruz 165 16 10N 95 10W
Salina, I. 65 38 35N 14 50E
Salina, La 174 10 22N 71 27W
Salinas, Brazil 171 16 20S 42 10W
Salinas, Chile 172 23 31S 69 29W
Salinas, Ecuador 174 2 10S 80 50W
Salinas, Mexico 164 23 37N 106 8W
Salinas, U.S.A. 163 36 40N 121 31W
Salinas Ambargasta 172 29 0S 65 30W
Salinas, B. de 166 11 4N 85 45W
Salinas, Cabo de 59 39 16N 3 4E
Salinas (de Hidalgo) 164 22 30N 101 40W
Salinas Grandes 172 30 0S 65 0W
Salinas, Pampa de las 172 31 58S 66 42W
Salinas, R., Mexico 165 16 28N 90 31W
Salinas, R., U.S.A. 163 36 45N 121 48W
Saline, R. 158 39 10N 99 5W
Salines-les-Bains 43 46 58N 5 52E
Salinópolis 170 0 40S 47 20W
Salir 57 37 14N 8 2W
Salisbury, Austral. 140 34 46S 138 40E
Salisbury, Rhod. 127 17 50S 31 2E
Salisbury, U.K. 28 51 4N 1 48W
Salisbury, Md., U.S.A. 162 38 20N 75 38W
Salisbury, N.C., U.S.A. 157 35 42N 80 29W
Salisbury Plain 28 51 13N 1 50W
Salitre, R. 170 9 29S 40 39W
Salka 121 10 20N 4 58E
Salle, La 158 41 20N 89 5W
Sallent 58 41 49N 1 54E
Salles-Curan 44 44 11N 2 48E
Salling 73 56 40N 8 55E
Sallisaw 159 35 26N 94 45W
Sallom Junc. 122 19 23N 37 6E
Sally Gap, Mt. 39 53 7N 6 18W
Salmerón 58 40 33N 2 29W
Salmo 152 49 10N 117 20W
Salmon 160 45 12N 113 56W
Salmon Arm 152 50 40N 119 15W
Salmon Falls 160 42 55N 114 59W
Salmon Gums 137 32 59S 121 38E
Salmon, R., Can. 152 54 3N 122 40W
Salmon, R., U.S.A. 160 46 0N 116 30W
Salmon Res. 151 48 05N 56 00W
Salmon River Mts. 160 45 0N 114 30W
Salo 75 60 22N 23 3E
Salò 62 45 37N 10 32E
Salobreña 57 36 44N 3 35W
Salome 161 33 51N 113 37W
Salon-de-Provence 45 43 39N 5 6E
Salonica = Thessaloníki 68 40 38N 22 58E
Salonta 70 46 49N 21 42E
Salop □ 28 52 36N 2 45W
Salor, R. 57 39 39N 7 3W
Salou, Cabo 58 41 3N 1 10E
Salsacate 172 31 20S 65 5W
Salsaker 72 62 59N 18 20E
Salses 44 42 50N 2 55E
Salsette I. 96 19 5N 72 50E
Salsk 83 46 28N 41 30E
Salso, R. 65 37 6N 13 55E
Salsomaggiore 62 44 48N 9 59E
Salt 90 32 2N 35 43E
Salt Creek 140 36 8S 139 38E
Salt Creek Telegraph Office 139 36 0S 139 35E
Salt Fork R. 159 37 25N 98 40W
Salt Lake City 160 40 45N 111 58W
Salt, R., Can. 152 60 0N 112 25W
Salt, R., U.S.A. 161 33 50N 110 25W
Salt Range 94 32 30N 72 25E
Salta 172 24 47S 65 25W
Salta □ 172 24 48S 65 30W
Saltash 30 50 25N 4 13W
Saltburn by Sea 33 54 35N 0 58W
Saltcoats 34 55 38N 4 47W
Saltee Is. 39 52 7N 6 37W
Saltergate 33 54 20N 0 40W
Saltfjorden 74 67 15N 14 20E
Saltfleet 33 53 25N 0 11E
Saltfleetby 33 53 23N 0 10E
Salthill 39 53 15N 9 6W
Saltholm 73 55 38N 12 43E
Salthólmavík 74 65 24N 21 57W
Saltillo 164 25 30N 100 57W
Salto, Argent. 172 34 20S 60 15W
Salto, Uruguay 172 31 20S 57 59W
Salto □ 172 31 20S 57 59W
Salto Augusto, falls 172 8 30S 58 0W
Salto da Divisa 171 16 0S 39 57W
Salton City 163 33 21N 115 59W
Salton Sea 163 33 20N 115 50W
Saltpond 121 5 15N 1 3W
Saltsjöbaden 73 59 15N 18 20E
Saltspring 152 48 54N 123 37W
Saltwood 29 51 4N 1 5E
Saluda 162 37 36N 76 36W
Salula, R. 157 34 12N 81 45W
Salûm 122 31 31N 25 7E
Salûm, Khâlig el 122 31 30N 25 9E
Salur 96 18 27N 83 18E
Saluzzo 62 44 39N 7 29E
Salvador, Brazil 171 13 0S 38 30W
Salvador, Can. 153 52 10N 109 25W
Salvador ■ 164 13 50N 89 0W
Salvador, L. 159 29 46N 90 16W
Salvaterra 170 0 46S 48 31W
Salvaterra de Magos 57 39 1N 8 47W
Sálvora, Isla 56 42 30N 8 58W
Salwa 93 24 45N 50 55E
Salween, R. 98 16 31N 97 37E
Salza, R. 52 47 43N 15 0E
Salzach, R. 52 47 15N 12 25E
Salzburg 52 47 48N 13 2E
Salzgitter 48 52 2N 10 22E
Salzwedel 48 52 50N 11 11E
Sam Neua 100 20 29N 104 0E
Sam Ngao 100 17 18N 99 0E

Sam Rayburn Res San Quintín

Sam Rayburn Res. 159 31 15N 94 20W
Sam Son 100 19 44N 105 54 E
Sam Ten 100 19 59N 104 38 E
Sama 84 60 12N 60 22 E
Sama de Langreo 56 43 18N 5 40W
Samales Group 103 6 0N 122 0 E
Samalkot 96 17 3N 82 13 E
Samâlût 122 28 20N 30 42 E
Samana 94 30 10N 76 13 E
Samana Cay 167 23 3N 73 45W
Samanco 174 9 10 S 78 30W
Samanga 127 8 20 S 39 13 E
Samangan 93 36 15N 67 40 E
Samangwa 126 4 23 S 24 10 E
Samani 112 42 7N 142 56 E
Samar, I. 103 12 0N 125 0 E
Samara, R. 84 53 10N 50 4 E
Samaria 135 10 39 S 150 41 E
Samaria = Shomron 90 32 15N 35 13 E
Samarkand 85 39 40N 67 0 E
Samarra 92 34 16N 43 55 E
Samastipur 95 25 50N 85 50 E
Samatan 44 43 29N 0 55 E
Samba, Kashmir 95 32 32N 75 10 E
Samba, Zaïre 126 4 38 S 26 22 E
Sambaiba 170 7 8 S 45 21W
Sambaina 129 19 37 S 47 8 E
Sambaise 65 38 58N 16 16 E
Sambalpur 96 21 28N 83 58 E
Sambas, S. 102 1 20N 109 20 E
Sambava 129 14 16 S 50 10 E
Sambawizi 127 18 24 S 26 13 E
Sambhal 95 28 35N 78 37 E
Sambhar 94 26 52N 75 10 E
Sambonifacio 62 45 24N 11 16 E
Sambor, Camb. 100 12 46N 106 0 E
Sambor, U.S.S.R. 80 49 30N 23 10 E
Sambre, R. 47 50 27N 4 52 E
Sambuca 64 37 39N 13 6 E
Samburu □ 126 1 10N 37 0 E
Sambusu 128 17 55 S 19 21 E
Samchök 107 37 30N 129 10 E
Samchonpo 107 34 54N 128 6 E
Same 126 4 2 S 37 38 E
Samedan 51 46 32N 9 52 E
Samer 43 50 38N 1 44 E
Samfya 127 11 16 S 29 31 E
Sámi 69 38 15N 20 39 E
Samna 122 25 12N 37 17 E
Samnager 71 60 23N 5 39 E
Samnaun 51 46 57N 10 22 E
Samnu 119 27 15N 14 55 E
Samo Alto 172 30 22 S 71 0W
Samoan Is. 10 14 0 S 171 0W
Samobor 63 45 47N 15 44 E
Samoëns 45 46 5N 6 45 E
Samoorombón, Bahía 172 36 5 S 57 20W
Samorogouan 120 11 21N 4 57W
Samos 56 42 44N 7 20W
Samoš 66 45 13N 20 49 E
Sámos, I. 69 37 45N 26 50 E
Samosir, P. 102 2 35N 98 50 E
Samothráki 68 40 28N 25 38 E
Samothráki, I. 68 40 25N 25 40 E
Sampa 120 8 0N 2 36W
Sampacho 172 33 20 S 64 50W
Sampang 103 7 11 S 113 13 E
Samper de Calanda 58 41 11N 04 2W
Sampford Courtenay 30 50 47N 3 58W
Sampit 102 2 20 S 113 0 E
Samra 92 25 35N 41 0 E
Samreboi 120 5 34N 7 28 E
Samrée 47 50 13N 5 39 E
Samrong, Camb. 100 14 15N 103 30 E
Samrong, Thai. 100 15 10N 100 40 E
Samsø 73 55 50N 10 35 E
Samsø Bælt 73 55 45N 10 45 E
Samsonovo 85 37 53N 65 15 E
Samsun 92 41 15N 36 15 E
Samsun Daği 69 37 45N 27 10 E
Samtredia 83 42 7N 42 24 E
Samui, Ko 101 9 30N 100 0 E
Samur, R. 83 41 30N 48 0 E
Samusole 127 10 2 S 24 0 E
Samut Prakan 100 13 32N 100 40 E
Samut Sakhon 100 13 31N 100 20 E
Samut Songkhram (Mekong) 100 13 24N 100 1 E
Samwari 94 28 5N 66 46 E
Samyo La 99 29 55N 84 46 E
San 120 13 15N 4 45W
San Adrián, C. de 56 43 21N 8 50W
San Adrián, G. de 56 43 21N 8 50W
San Agustin 174 1 53N 76 16W
San Agustin, C. 103 6 20N 126 13 E
San Agustín de Valle Fértil 172 30 35 S 67 30W
San Ambrosio, I. 131 26 35 S 79 30W
San Andreas 163 38 17N 120 39W
San Andrés, I. de 166 12 42N 81 46W
San Andres Mts. 161 33 0N 106 45W
San Andrés Tuxtla 165 18 30N 95 20W
San Angelo 159 31 30N 100 30W
San Anselmo 163 37 49N 122 34W
San Antonio, Belize 165 16 15N 89 2W
San Antonio, Chile 172 33 40 S 71 40W
San Antonio, N. Mex., U.S.A. 161 33 58N 106 57W
San Antonio, Tex., U.S.A. 159 29 30N 98 30W
San Antonio, Venez. 174 3 30N 66 44W
San Antonio Abad 59 38 59N 1 19 E
San Antonio, C., Argent. 172 36 15 S 56 40W
San Antonio, C., Cuba 166 21 50N 84 57W
San Antonio, C. de 59 38 48N 0 12 E
San Antonio de Caparo 174 7 35N 71 27W
San Antonio de los Baños 166 22 54N 82 31W
San Antonio de los Cobres 172 24 16 S 66 2W
San Antonio do Zaire 124 6 8 S 12 11 E
San Antonio, Mt. (Old Baldy Pk.) 163 34 17N 117 38W
San Antonio Oeste 176 40 40 S 65 0W
San Antonio, R. 159 28 30N 97 14W
San Ardo 163 36 1N 120 54W
San Bartolomeo in Galdo 65 41 23N 15 2 E
San Benedetto 62 45 2N 10 57 E
San Benedetto del Tronto 63 42 57N 13 52 E
San Benedicto, I. 164 19 18N 110 49W
San Benito 159 26 5N 97 32W
San Benito Mtn. 163 36 22N 120 37W
San Benito, R. 163 36 53N 121 50W
San Bernardino 163 34 7N 117 18W
San Bernardino, Paso del 51 46 28N 9 11 E
San Bernardo 172 33 40 S 70 50W
San Bernardo, I. de 174 9 45N 75 50W
San Blas 164 26 10N 108 40W
San Blas, C. 157 29 40N 85 25W
San Blas, Cord. de 166 9 15N 78 30W
San Borja 174 15 0 S 67 12W
San Buenaventura 164 27 5N 101 32W
San Buenaventura = Ventura 163 34 17N 119 18W
San Carlos, Argent. 172 33 50 S 69 0W
San Carlos, Mexico 164 29 0N 101 10W
San Carlos, Nic. 166 11 12N 84 50W
San Carlos, Phil. 103 10 29N 123 25 E
San Carlos, Uruguay 173 34 46 S 54 58W
San Carlos, U.S.A. 161 33 24N 110 27W
San Carlos, Amazonas, Venez. 174 1 55N 67 4W
San Carlos, Cojedes, Venez. 174 9 40N 68 36W
San Carlos de Bariloche 176 41 10 S 71 25W
San Carlos de la Rápita 58 40 37N 0 35 E
San Carlos del Zulia 174 9 1N 71 55W
San Carlos L. 161 33 20N 110 10W
San Carlos = Butuku-Luba 121 3 29N 8 33 E
San Cataldo 64 37 30N 13 58 E
San Celoni 58 41 42N 2 30 E
San Clemente, Chile 172 35 30 S 71 39W
San Clemente, Spain 59 39 24N 2 25W
San Clemente, U.S.A. 163 33 29N 117 45W
San Clemente I. 163 32 53N 118 30W
San Constanzo 63 43 46N 13 5 E
San Cristóbal, Argent. 172 30 20 S 61 10W
San Cristóbal, Dom. Rep. 167 18 25N 70 6W
San Cristóbal, Venez. 174 7 46N 72 14W
San Cristóbal de las Casas 165 16 50N 92 33W
San Damiano d'Asti 62 44 51N 8 4 E
San Daniel del Friuli 63 46 10N 13 0 E
San Demétrio Corone 65 39 34N 16 22 E
San Diego, Calif., U.S.A. 163 32 43N 117 10W
San Diego, Tex., U.S.A. 159 27 47N 98 15W
San Diego, C. 176 54 40 S 65 10W
San Diego de la Unión 164 21 28N 100 52W
San Donà di Piave 63 45 38N 12 34 E
San Elpídio a Mare 63 43 16N 13 41 E
San Estanislao 172 24 39 S 56 26W
San Esteban de Gormaz 58 41 34N 3 13W
San Felice sul Panaro 62 44 51N 11 9 E
San Felipe, Chile 172 32 43 S 70 50W
San Felipe, Mexico 164 31 0N 114 52W
San Felipe, Venez. 174 10 20N 68 44W
San Felipe, R. 163 33 12N 115 49W
San Feliu de Guixols 58 41 45N 3 1 E
San Feliu de Llobregat 58 41 23N 2 2 E
San Félix 174 8 20N 62 35W
San Felix, I. 131 26 30 S 80 0W
San Fernando, Chile 172 34 30 S 71 0W
San Fernando, Mexico 164 30 0N 115 10W
San Fernando, Luzon, Phil. 103 15 5N 120 37 E
San Fernando, Luzon, Phil. 103 16 40N 120 23 E
San Fernando, Spain 57 36 22N 6 17W
San Fernando, Trin 167 10 20N 61 30W
San Fernando, U.S.A. 163 34 15N 118 29W
San Fernando de Apure 174 7 54N 67 28W
San Fernando de Atabapo 174 4 3N 67 42W
San Fernando di Puglia 65 41 18N 16 5 E
San Fernando, R. 164 25 0N 99 0W
San Francisco, Córdoba, Argent. 172 31 30 S 62 5W
San Francisco, San Luis, Argent. 172 32 45 S 66 10W
San Francisco, U.S.A. 163 37 47N 122 30W
San Francisco de Macoris 167 19 19N 70 15W
San Francisco del Monte de Oro 172 32 36 S 66 8W
San Francisco del Oro 164 26 52N 105 50W
San Francisco Javier 59 38 40N 1 25 E
San Francisco, Paso de 172 35 40 S 70 24W
San Francisco, R. 161 33 30N 109 0W
San Francisco Solano, Pta. 174 6 18N 77 29W
San Francisville 159 30 48N 91 22W
San Fratello 65 38 1N 14 33 E
San Gabriel 174 0 36N 77 49W
San Gavino Monreale 64 39 33N 8 47 E
San German 147 18 5N 67 3W
San Gil 174 6 33N 73 8W
San Gimignano 62 43 28N 11 3 E
San Giórgio di Nogaro 63 45 50N 13 13 E
San Giórgio Iónico 65 40 27N 17 23 E
San Giovanni Bianco 62 45 52N 9 40 E
San Giovanni in Fiore 65 39 16N 16 42 E
San Giovanni in Persieceto 63 44 39N 11 12 E
San Giovanni Rotondo 65 41 41N 15 42 E
San Giovanni Valdarno 63 43 32N 11 30 E
San Giuliano Terme 62 43 45N 10 26 E
San Gorgonio Mtn. 163 34 7N 116 51W
San Gottardo, Paso del 51 46 33N 8 33 E
San Gregorio, Uruguay 173 32 37 S 55 40W
San Gregorio, U.S.A. 163 37 20N 122 23W
San Guiseppe Iato 64 37 37N 13 11 E
San Ignacio, Boliv. 174 16 20 S 60 55W
San Ignacio, Mexico 164 27 27N 112 51W
San Ignacio, Parag. 172 26 52 S 57 3W
San Ignacio, Laguna 164 26 50N 113 11W
San Ildefonso, C. 103 16 0N 122 10 E
San Isidro 172 34 29 S 58 31W
San Jacinto, Colomb. 174 9 50N 75 8W
San Jacinto, U.S.A. 163 33 47N 116 57W
San Javier, Misiones, Argent. 173 27 55 S 55 5W
San Javier, Santa Fe, Argent. 172 30 40 S 59 55W
San Javier, Boliv. 174 16 18 S 62 30W
San Javier, Chile 172 35 40 S 71 45W
San Javier, Spain 59 37 49N 0 50W
San Jerónimo, Sa. de 174 8 0N 75 50W
San Joaquin 163 36 36N 120 11W
San Joaquin 174 10 16N 67 47W
San Joaquin R. 163 38 4N 121 51W
San Joaquin Valley 163 37 0N 120 30W
San Jorge 172 31 54 S 61 50W
San Jorge, Bahía de 164 31 20N 113 20W
San Jorge, Golfo de 176 46 0 S 66 0W
San Jorge, G. de 58 40 50N 0 55W
San José, Boliv. 174 17 45 S 60 50W
San José, C. Rica 166 10 0N 84 2W
San José, Guat. 164 14 0N 90 50W
San José, Luzon, Phil. 103 15 45N 120 55 E
San José, Mindoro, Phil. 103 10 50N 122 5 E
San José, Spain 59 38 55N 1 18 E
San Jose, Calif., U.S.A. 163 37 20N 121 53W
San Jose, N. Mex., U.S.A. 159 35 26N 105 30W
San José Carpizo 165 19 26N 90 32W
San José de Feliciano 172 30 26 S 58 46W
San José de Jáchal 172 30 5 S 69 0W
San José de Mayo 172 34 27 S 56 27W
San José de Ocuné 174 4 15N 70 20W
San José del Cabo 164 23 0N 109 50W
San José del Guaviare 174 2 35N 72 38W
San José, I. 164 25 0N 110 50W
San Juan, Argent. 172 31 30 S 68 30W
San Juan, Antioquía, Colomb. 174 8 46N 76 32W
San Juan, Meta, Colomb. 174 3 26N 73 50W
San Juan, Dom. Rep. 147 18 49N 71 12W
San Juan, Coahuila, Mexico 164 29 34N 101 53W
San Juan, Jalisco, Mexico 164 21 20N 102 50W
San Juan, Querétaro, Mexico 164 20 25N 100 0W
San Juan, Phil. 103 8 35N 126 20 E
San Juan, Pto Rico 147 18 28N 66 37W
San Juan □ 172 31 9 S 69 0W
San Juan Bautista, Parag. 172 26 37 S 57 6W
San Juan Bautista, Spain 59 39 5N 1 31 E
San Juan Bautista, U.S.A. 163 36 51N 121 32W
San Juan, C. 147 18 23N 65 37W
San Juan Capistrano 163 33 29N 117 40W
San Juan de Guadalupe 164 24 38N 102 44W
San Juan de los Cayos 174 11 10N 68 25W
San Juan de los Morros 174 9 55N 67 21W
San Juan de Norte, B. de 166 11 30N 83 40W
San Juan del Norte 166 10 58N 83 40W
San Juan del Puerto 57 37 20N 6 50W
San Juan del Rio 165 24 47N 104 27W
San Juan del Sur 166 11 20N 86 0W
San Juan Mts. 161 38 30N 108 30W
San Juan, Presa de 164 17 45N 95 15W
San Juan, R., Argent. 172 32 20 S 67 25W
San Juan, R., Colomb. 174 4 0N 77 20W
San Juan, R., Nic. 166 11 0N 84 30W
San Juan, R., Calif., U.S.A. 163 36 14N 121 9W
San Juan, R., Utah, U.S.A. 161 37 20N 110 20W
San Julián 176 49 15 S 68 0W
San Just, Sierra de 58 40 45N 0 41W
San Justo 172 30 55 S 60 30W
San Kamphaeng 100 18 45N 99 8 E
San Lázaro, C. 164 24 50N 112 18W
San Lázaro, Sa. de 164 23 25N 110 0W
San Leandro 163 37 40N 122 6W
San Leonardo 58 41 51N 3 5W
San Lorenzo, Argent. 172 32 45 S 60 45W
San Lorenzo, Ecuador 174 1 15N 78 50W
San Lorenzo, Parag. 172 25 20 S 57 32W
San Lorenzo, Venez. 174 9 47N 71 4W
San Lorenzo de la Parilla 58 39 51N 2 22W
San Lorenzo de Morunys 58 42 8N 1 35 E
San Lorenzo, I., Mexico 164 28 35N 112 50W
San Lorenzo, I., Peru 174 12 20 S 77 35W
San Lorenzo, Mt. 176 47 40 S 72 20W
San Lorenzo, R. 164 24 15N 107 24W
San Lucas, Boliv. 174 20 5 S 65 0W
San Lucas, Baja California S., Mexico 164 27 10N 112 14W
San Lucas, Baja California S., Mexico 164 22 53N 109 54W
San Lucas, U.S.A. 163 36 8N 121 1W
San Lucas, C. de 164 22 50N 110 0W
San Lucido 65 39 18N 16 3 E
San Luis, Argent. 172 33 20 S 66 20W
San Luis, Cuba 166 22 17N 83 46W
San Luis, Guat. 166 16 14N 89 27W
San Luis, U.S.A. 161 37 14N 105 26W
San Luis, Venez. 174 11 7N 69 42W
San Luis □ 172 34 0 S 66 0W
San Luis de la Loma 164 17 18N 100 55W
San Luis de la Paz 164 21 19N 100 32W
San Luis de Potosí 164 22 9N 100 59W
San Luis de Potosí □ 164 22 10N 101 0W
San Luis, I. 164 29 58N 114 26W
San Luis Obispo 161 35 21N 120 38W
San Luis Res. 163 37 4N 121 5W
San Luis Río Colorado 164 32 29N 114 48W
San Luis, Sierra de 172 37 25N 66 10W
San Marco Argentano 65 39 34N 16 8 E
San Marco dei Cavoti 65 41 20N 14 50 E
San Marco in Lámis 65 41 43N 15 38 E
San Marcos, Guat. 166 14 59N 91 52W
San Marcos, U.S.A. 159 29 53N 98 0W
San Marcos, I. 164 27 13N 112 6W
San Marino 63 43 56N 12 25 E
San Marino ■ 63 43 56N 12 25 E
San Martín, Argent. 172 33 5 S 68 28W
San Martín, Colomb. 174 3 42N 73 42W
San Martín de Valdeiglesias 56 40 21N 4 24W
San Martín, L. 176 48 50 S 72 50W
San Martino de Calvi 62 45 57N 9 41 E
San Mateo, Spain 58 40 28N 0 10 E
San Mateo, U.S.A. 163 37 32N 122 19W
San Matías 174 16 25 S 58 20W
San Matías, Golfo de 176 41 30 S 64 0W
San Miguel, El Sal. 166 13 30N 88 12W
San Miguel, Panama 166 8 27N 78 55W
San Miguel, Spain 59 39 3N 1 26 E
San Miguel, U.S.A. 163 35 45N 120 42W
San Miguel, Venez. 174 9 40N 65 11W
San Miguel de Salinas 59 37 59N 0 47W
San Miguel de Tucumán 172 26 50 S 65 20W
San Miguel del Monte 172 35 23 S 58 50W
San Miguel I. 163 34 2N 120 23W
San Miguel, R., Boliv. 174 16 0 S 62 45W
San Miguel, R., Ecuador/Ecuador 174 0 25N 76 30W
San Miniato 62 43 40N 10 50 E
San Narcisco 103 15 2N 120 3 E
San Nicolás de los Arroyas 172 33 17 S 60 10W
San Nicolas I. 154 33 16N 119 30W
San Onfare 163 33 22N 117 34W
San Onofre 174 9 44N 75 32W
San Pablo, Boliv. 172 21 43 S 66 38W
San Pablo, Colomb. 174 5 27N 70 56W
San Paolo di Civitate 65 41 44N 15 16 E
San Pedro, Buenos Aires, Argent. 173 33 43 S 59 45W
San Pedro, Jujuy, Argent. 172 24 12 S 64 55W
San Pedro, Chile 172 21 58 S 68 30W
San Pedro, Colomb. 174 4 56N 71 53W
San Pedro, Dom. Rep. 167 18 30N 69 18W
San Pedro, Ivory C. 120 4 50N 6 33W
San Pedro, Mexico 164 23 55N 110 17W
San Pedro □ 172 24 0 S 57 0W
San Pedro Channel 163 33 35N 118 25W
San Pedro de Arimena 174 4 37N 71 42W
San Pedro de Atacama 172 22 55 S 68 15W
San Pedro de Jujuy 172 24 12 S 64 55W
San Pedro de las Colonias 164 25 50N 102 59W
San Pedro de Lloc 174 7 15 S 79 28W
San Pedro del Norte 166 13 4N 84 33W
San Pedro del Paraná 172 26 43 S 56 13W
San Pedro del Pinatar 59 37 50N 0 50W
San Pedro Mártir, Sierra 164 31 0N 115 30W
San Pedro Mixtepec 165 16 2N 97 0W
San Pedro Ocampo = Melchor Ocampo 164 24 52N 101 40W
San Pedro, Pta. 172 25 30 S 70 38W
San Pedro, R., Chihuahua, Mexico 164 28 20N 106 10W
San Pedro, R., Michoacan, Mexico 164 19 23N 103 51W
San Pedro, R., Nayarit, Mexico 164 21 45N 105 30W
San Pedro, R., U.S.A. 161 32 45N 110 35W
San Pedro, Sierra de 57 39 18N 6 40W
San Pedro Sula 166 15 30N 88 0W
San Pedro Tututepec 165 16 9N 97 38W
San Pedro,Pta. 172 25 30 S 70 38W
San Pietro, I. 64 39 9N 8 17 E
San Pietro Vernotico 65 40 28N 18 0 E
San Quintín, Mexico 164 30 29N 115 57W

San Quintín, Phil.	103	16 1N	120 56 E
San, R.	54	50 25N	22 20 E
San Rafael, Argent.	172	34 40 s	68 30W
San Rafael, Colomb.	174	6 2N	69 45W
San Rafael, Calif., U.S.A.	163	38 0N	122 32W
San Rafael, N. Mex., U.S.A.	161	35 6N	107 58W
San Rafael, Venez.	174	10 42N	71 46W
San Rafael Mtn.	163	34 41N	119 52W
San Ramón de la Nueva Orán	172	23 10 s	64 20W
San Remo	62	43 48N	7 47 E
San Román, C.	174	12 12N	70 0W
San Roque, Argent.	172	28 15 s	58 45W
San Roque, Spain	57	36 17N	5 21W
San Rosendo	172	37 10 s	72 50W
San Saba	159	31 12N	98 45W
San Salvador	166	13 40N	89 20W
San Salvador de Jujuy	172	23 30 s	65 40W
San Salvador (Watlings) I.	167	24 0N	74 40W
San Sebastián, Argent.	176	53 10 s	68 30W
San Sebastián, Spain	58	43 17N	1 58W
San Sebastián, Venez.	174	9 57N	67 11W
San Serverino	63	43 13N	13 10 E
San Severo	63	41 41N	15 23 E
San Simeon	163	35 39N	121 11W
San Simon	161	32 14N	109 16W
San Stéfano di Cadore	63	46 34N	12 33 E
San Telmo	164	30 58N	116 6W
San Tiburcio	164	24 8N	101 32W
San Valentin, Mte.	176	46 30 s	73 30W
San Vicente de Alcántara	57	39 22N	7 8W
San Vicente de la Barquera	56	43 30N	4 29W
San Vicente del Caguán	174	2 7N	74 46W
San Vicenzo	93	43 9N	10 32 E
San Vito al Tagliamento	63	45 55N	12 50 E
San Vito, C.	64	38 11N	12 41 E
San Vito Chietino	63	42 19N	14 27 E
San Vito dei Normanni	65	40 40N	17 40 E
San Yanaro	174	2 47N	69 42W
San Ygnacio	159	27 6N	92 24W
San Ysidro	161	32 33N	117 5W
San'a	91	15 27N	44 12 E
Sana, R.	63	44 40N	16 43 E
Sanaba	120	12 25N	3 47W
Sanabria, La	56	42 0N	6 30W
Sanâfir	122	27 49N	34 37 E
Sanaga, R.	121	3 35N	9 38 E
Sanak I	147	53 30N	162 30W
Sanaloa, Presa	164	24 50N	107 20W
Sanana	103	2 5 s	125 50 E
Sanand	94	22 59N	72 25 E
Sanandaj	92	35 25N	47 7 E
Sanandita	172	21 40 s	63 35W
Sanary	45	43 7N	5 48 E
Sanawad	94	22 11N	76 5 E
Sanbe-San	110	35 6N	132 38 E
Sancergues	43	47 10N	2 54 E
Sancerre	43	47 20N	2 50 E
Sanch'a Ho	108	26 55N	106 6 E
Sanch'aho	107	44 59N	126 1 E
Sánchez	167	19 15N	69 36W
Sanchiang	108	25 22N	109 26 E
Sanchor	94	24 52N	71 49 E
Sanco, Pt.	103	8 15N	126 24 E
Sancoins	43	46 47N	2 55 E
Sancti-Spíritus	166	21 52N	79 33W
Sand Lake	150	47 46N	84 31W
Sand Point	147	55 20N	160 32W
Sand, R.	129	22 25 s	30 5 E
Sand Springs	159	36 12N	96 5W
Sanda	111	34 53N	135 14 E
Sanda I.	34	55 17N	5 35W
Sandah	122	20 35N	39 32 E
Sandakan	102	5 53N	118 10 E
Sandalwood	140	34 55 s	140 9 E
Sandan	101	12 46N	106 0 E
Sandanski	67	41 35N	23 16 E
Sandaré	120	14 40N	10 15W
Sanday I.	36	57 2N	6 30W
Sanday, I.	37	59 15N	2 30W
Sanday Sd.	37	59 11N	2 31W
Sandbach	32	53 9N	2 23W
Sandbank	34	55 58N	4 57W
Sande, Möre og Romsdal, Norway	71	62 15N	5 27 E
Sande, Sogn og Fjordane, Norway	71	61 20N	5 47 E
Sandefjord	71	59 10N	10 15 E
Sandeid	71	59 33N	5 52 E
Sanders	161	35 12N	109 25W
Sanderson	159	30 5N	102 30W
Sanderston	140	34 46 s	139 15 E
Sandfell	74	63 57N	16 48W
Sandfly L.	153	55 43N	106 6W
Sandgate, Austral.	139	27 18 s	153 3 E
Sandgate, U.K.	29	51 5N	1 9 E
Sandhammaren, C.	73	55 23N	14 14 E
Sandhead	34	54 48N	4 58W
Sandhurst	29	51 21N	0 48W
Sandia	174	14 10 s	69 30W
Sandikli	92	38 30N	30 20 E
Sandiman, Mt.	137	24 21 s	115 20 E
Sandnes	71	58 50N	5 45 E
Sandness	37	60 18N	1 38W
Sandoa	124	9 48 s	23 0 E
Sandomierz	54	50 40N	21 43 E
Sandona	174	1 17N	77 28W
Sandover, R.	138	21 43 s	136 32 E

Sandoway	99	18 20N	94 30 E
Sandown	28	50 39N	1 9W
Sandpoint	160	48 20N	116 40W
Sandray, I.	36	56 53N	7 30W
Sandringham	29	52 50N	0 30 E
Sandslån	72	63 2N	17 49 E
Sandspit	152	53 14N	131 49W
Sandston	162	37 31N	77 19W
Sandstone	137	27 59 s	119 16 E
Sandusky, Mich., U.S.A.	150	43 26N	82 50W
Sandusky, Ohio, U.S.A.	156	41 25N	82 40W
Sandveld	128	32 0 s	18 15 E
Sandvig, Denmark	73	55 18N	14 48 E
Sandvig, Sweden	72	55 32N	14 47 E
Sandvika	71	59 54N	10 29 E
Sandviken	72	60 38N	16 46 E
Sandwich	29	51 16N	1 21 E
Sandwich B., Can.	151	53 40N	57 15W
Sandwich B., S. Afr.	128	23 25 s	14 20 E
Sandwich, C.	138	18 14 s	146 18 E
Sandwich Group	13	57 0 s	27 0W
Sandwip Chan.	99	22 35N	91 35 E
Sandy	29	53 8N	0 18W
Sandy Bight	137	33 50 s	123 20 E
Sandy C., Queens., Austral.	139	24 42 s	153 15 E
Sandy C., Tas., Austral.	138	41 25 s	144 45 E
Sandy Cay	167	23 13N	75 18W
Sandy Cr.	160	42 20N	109 30W
Sandy L.	150	53 2N	93 0W
Sandy Lake	150	53 0N	93 15W
Sandy Narrows	153	55 5N	103 4W
Sanford, Fla., U.S.A.	157	28 45N	81 20W
Sanford, Me., U.S.A.	162	43 28N	70 47W
Sanford, N.C., U.S.A.	157	35 30N	79 10W
Sanford, Mt.	136	16 58 s	130 32 E
Sanford Mt.	148	62 30N	143 0W
Sanford, R.	137	27 22 s	115 53 E
Sang-i-Masha	94	33 16N	67 5 E
Sanga	127	12 22 s	35 21 E
Sanga, R.	124	1 0N	16 30 E
Sanga Tolon	77	61 50N	149 40 E
Sangamner	96	19 30N	74 15 E
Sangar, Afghan.	94	32 56N	65 30 E
Sangar, U.S.S.R.	77	63 55N	127 31 E
Sangar Sarcai	94	34 27N	70 35 E
Sangasanga	102	0 29 s	117 13 E
Sangchen La	99	31 30N	84 40 E
Sangchih	109	29 25N	109 30 E
Sange	126	6 58 s	84 40 E
Sangeang, I.	103	8 12 s	119 6 E
Sanger	163	36 47N	119 35W
Sangerhausen	48	51 28N	11 18 E
Sanggau	102	0 5N	110 30 E
Sangihe, Kep.	103	3 0N	126 0 E
Sangihe, P.	103	3 45N	125 30 E
Sangju	107	36 25N	128 10 E
Sangkan Ho	106	40 24N	115 19 E
Sangkapura	102	5 52 s	112 40 E
Sangkhla	100	15 7N	98 28 E
Sangli	96	16 55N	74 33 E
Sangmélima	121	2 57N	12 1 E
Sangonera, R.	59	37 39N	2 0W
Sangpang Bum	98	26 30N	95 50 E
Sangre de Cristo Mts.	159	37 0N	105 0W
Sangro, R.	63	42 10N	14 30 E
Sangudo	152	53 50N	114 54W
Sangüesa	58	42 37N	1 17W
Sanguinaires, I.	45	41 51N	8 36 E
Sanhala	120	10 3N	6 51W
Sanho	107	39 59N	117 4 E
Sani R.	100	13 32N	105 57 E
Sanish	158	48 0N	102 30W
Sanje	126	0 49 s	31 30 E
Sankaranayinarkovil	97	9 10N	77 35 E
Sankeshwar	96	16 23N	74 23 E
Sankosh, R.	98	26 24N	89 47 E
Sankt Andra	52	46 46N	14 50 E
Sankt Antönien	51	46 58N	9 48 E
Sankt Blasien	49	47 47N	8 7 E
Sankt Gallen	51	47 26N	9 22 E
Sankt Gallen □	51	47 25N	9 22 E
Sankt Ingbert	49	49 16N	7 6 E
Sankt Johann	52	47 22N	13 12 E
Sankt Margrethen	51	47 28N	9 37 E
Sankt Moritz	51	46 30N	9 50 E
Sankt Olof	73	55 37N	14 8 E
Sankt Pölten	52	48 12N	15 38 E
Sankt Valentin	52	48 11N	14 33 E
Sankt Veit	52	46 54N	14 22 E
Sankt Wendel	49	49 27N	7 9 E
Sankt Wolfgang	52	47 43N	13 27 E
Sankuru, R.	124	4 17 s	20 25 E
Sanlúcar de Barrameda	57	36 46N	6 21W
Sanlúcar la Mayor	57	37 26N	6 18W
Sanluri	64	39 35N	8 55 E
Sanmártin	70	46 19N	25 58 E
Sanmen	109	29 5N	121 35 E
Sanmenhsia	106	34 46N	111 30 E
Sanming	109	26 13N	117 35 E
Sannan	111	35 2N	135 1 E
Sannaspos	129	29 6 s	26 34 E
Sannicandro Gargánico	65	41 50N	15 34 E
Sânnicolaul-Maré	66	46 5N	20 39 E
Sannidal	71	58 55N	9 15 E
Sannieshof	128	26 30 s	25 47 E
Sano	111	36 19N	139 35 E
Sanok	54	49 35N	22 10 E
Sanokwelle	120	7 19N	8 38W
Sanpa	108	29 43N	99 33 E
Sanpah	139	30 32 s	141 12 E
Sanquhar	35	55 21N	3 56W

Sansanding Dam	120	13 37N	6 0W
Sansanné-Mango	121	10 20N	0 30 E
Sansepolcro	63	43 34N	12 8 E
Sanshui	109	23 11N	112 53 E
Sanski Most	63	44 46N	16 40 E
Sansui	108	26 57N	108 37 E
Sant' Agata de Gati	65	41 6N	14 30 E
Sant' Agata di Militello	65	38 2N	14 40 E
Santa Ana, Ecuador	174	1 10 s	80 20W
Santa Ana, El Sal.	166	14 0N	89 40W
Santa Ana, Mexico	164	30 31N	111 8W
Santa Ana, U.S.A.	163	33 48N	117 55W
Santa Ana, El Beni	174	13 50 s	65 40W
Sant' Angelo Lodigiano	62	45 14N	9 25 E
Sant' Antíoco	64	39 2N	8 30 E
Sant' Antíoco, I.	64	39 2N	8 30 E
Sant' Arcángelo di Romagna	63	44 4N	12 26 E
Santa Bárbara, Brazil	171	16 0 s	59 0W
Santa Bárbara, Colomb.	174	5 53N	75 35W
Santa Barbara	166	14 53N	88 14W
Santa Bárbara, Mexico	164	26 48N	105 50W
Santa Bárbara, Spain	58	40 42N	0 29 E
Santa Bárbara	163	34 25N	119 40W
Santa Bárbara	174	7 47N	71 10W
Santa Barbara Channel	163	34 20N	120 0W
Santa Barbara I.	163	33 29N	119 2W
Santa Barbara Is.	161	33 31N	119 0W
Santa Bárbara, Mt.	59	37 23N	2 50W
Santa Catalina	174	10 36N	75 17W
Santa Catalina, G. of	163	33 0N	118 0W
Santa Catalina, I., Mexico	164	25 40N	110 50W
Santa Catalina, I., U.S.A.	163	33 20N	118 30W
Santa Catarina □	173	27 25 s	48 30W
Santa Catarina, I. de	173	27 30 s	48 40W
Santa Caterina	65	37 37N	14 1 E
Santa Cecilia	173	26 56 s	50 27W
Santa Clara, Cuba	166	22 20N	80 0W
Santa Clara, Calif., U.S.A.	163	37 21N	122 0W
Santa Clara, Utah, U.S.A.	161	37 10N	113 38W
Santa Clara de Olimar	173	32 50 s	54 54W
Santa Clotilde	174	2 25 s	73 45W
Santa Coloma de Farnés	58	41 50N	2 39 E
Santa Coloma de Gramanet	58	41 27N	2 13 E
Santa Comba	56	43 2N	8 49W
Santa Croce Camerina	65	36 50N	14 30 E
Santa Cruz, Argent.	176	50 0 s	68 50W
Santa Cruz, Boliv.	174	17 43 s	63 10W
Santa Cruz, Brazil	170	7 57 s	36 12W
Santa Cruz, Canary Is.	116	28 29N	16 26W
Santa Cruz, Chile	172	34 38 s	71 27W
Santa Cruz, C. Rica	166	10 15N	85 41W
Santa Cruz, Phil.	103	14 20N	121 30 E
Santa Cruz, Calif., U.S.A.	163	36 55N	122 1W
Santa Cruz, N. Mexico, U.S.A.	161	35 59N	106 1W
Santa Cruz □	174	17 43 s	63 10W
Santa Cruz Cabrália	171	16 17 s	39 2W
Santa Cruz de Barahona	167	18 12N	71 6W
Santa Cruz de Mudela	59	38 39N	3 28W
Santa Cruz de Tenerife □	72	28 10N	17 20W
Santa Cruz del Norte	166	23 9N	81 55W
Santa Cruz del Retamar	56	40 8N	4 14W
Santa Cruz del Sur	166	20 50N	78 0W
Santa Cruz do Río Pardo	173	22 54 s	49 37W
Santa Cruz do Sul	173	29 42 s	52 25W
Santa Cruz I.	154	34 0N	119 45W
Santa Cruz, Is.	130	10 30 s	166 0 E
Santa Cruz, R.	176	50 10 s	70 0W
Santa Elena, Argent.	172	30 58 s	59 47W
Santa Elena, Ecuador	174	2 16 s	80 52W
Santa Elena C.	167	10 54N	85 56W
Santa Enimie	44	44 24N	3 26 E
Sant' Eufémia, Golfo di	65	38 50N	16 10 E
Santa Eulalia	59	40 34N	1 20W
Santa Fe, Argent.	172	31 35 s	60 41W
Santa Fe, Spain	57	37 11N	3 43W
Santa Fe, U.S.A.	161	35 40N	106 0W
Santa Fé □	172	31 50 s	60 55W
Santa Filomena	170	9 6 s	45 50W
Santa Genoveva, Mt.	164	23 18N	109 52W
Santa Groce di Magliano	65	41 43N	14 59 E
Santa Helena	170	2 14 s	45 18W
Santa Helena de Goiás	171	17 43 s	50 35W
Santa Inês	171	13 17 s	39 48W
Santa Inés, I.	176	54 0 s	73 0W
Santa Inés, Mt.	57	38 32N	5 37W
Santa Isabel, Argent.	172	36 10 s	67 0W
Santa Isabel, Brazil	171	13 45 s	56 30W
Santa Isabel = Rey Malabo	121	3 45N	8 50 E
Santa Isabel do Araguaia	170	6 7 s	48 19W
Santa Isabel, Pico	121	4 43N	8 49 E
Santa Juliana	171	19 19 s	47 32W
Santa Lucía, Corrientes, Argent.	172	28 58 s	59 5W
Santa Lucía, San Juan, Argent.	172	31 30 s	68 45W
Santa Lucía, Spain	59	37 35N	0 58W
Santa Lucia	172	34 27 s	56 24W
Santa Lucia Range	163	36 0N	121 20W
Santa Luzia	170	6 53 s	36 56W
Santa Magdalena, I.	164	24 50N	112 15W

Santa Margarita, Argent.	172	38 18 s	61 35W
Santa Margarita, U.S.A.	163	35 23N	120 37W
Santa Margarita, I.	164	24 30N	112 0W
Santa Margarita, R.	163	33 13N	117 23W
Santa Margherita	62	44 20N	9 11 E
Santa María, Argent.	172	26 40 s	66 0W
Santa María, Brazil	173	29 40 s	53 40W
Santa Maria	65	41 3N	14 29 E
Santa María	164	27 40N	114 40W
Santa María, Spain	58	39 39N	2 45 E
Santa Maria, Switz.	51	46 36N	10 25 E
Santa María, U.S.A.	163	34 58N	120 29W
Santa María, Zambia	127	11 5 s	29 58 E
Santa María, Bahía de	164	25 10N	108 40W
Santa María, Cabo de	57	36 39N	7 53W
Santa María da Vitória	171	13 24 s	44 12W
Santa María del Oro	164	25 30N	105 20W
Santa Maria di Leuca, C.	65	39 48N	18 20 E
Santa María do Suaçuí	171	18 12 s	42 25W
Santa María la Real de Nieva	56	41 4N	4 24W
Santa María, R.	164	31 0N	107 14W
Santa Marta, Colomb.	174	11 15N	74 13W
Santa Marta, Spain	57	38 37N	6 39W
Santa Marta Grande, C.	173	28 43 s	48 50W
Santa Marta, Ría de	56	43 44N	7 45W
Santa Marta, Sierra Nevada de	147	10 55N	73 50W
Santa Monica	163	34 0N	118 30W
Santa Napa	160	38 28N	122 45W
Santa Olalla, Huelva, Spain	57	37 54N	6 14W
Santa Olalla, Toledo, Spain	56	40 2N	4 25W
Sant' Onofrio	65	38 42N	16 10 E
Santa Paula	163	34 20N	119 2W
Santa Pola	59	38 13N	0 35W
Santa Quitéria	170	4 20 s	40 10W
Santa Rita, U.S.A.	161	32 50N	108 0W
Santa Rita, Guarico, Venez.	174	8 8N	66 16W
Santa Rita, Zulia, Venez.	174	10 32N	71 32W
Santa Rosa, La Pampa, Argent.	172	36 40 s	64 30W
Santa Rosa, San Luis, Argent.	172	32 30 s	65 10W
Santa Rosa, Boliv.	174	10 25 s	67 20W
Santa Rosa, Brazil	173	27 52 s	54 29W
Santa Rosa, Colomb.	174	3 32N	69 48W
Santa Rosa, Hond.	164	14 40N	89 0W
Santa Rosa, Calif., U.S.A.	163	38 26N	122 43W
Santa Rosa, N. Mexico, U.S.A.	159	34 58N	104 40W
Santa Rosa, Amazonas, Venez.	174	1 29N	66 55W
Santa Rosa, Apure, Venez.	174	6 37N	67 57W
Santa Rosa de Cabal	174	4 52N	75 38W
Santa Rosa de Copán	166	14 47N	88 46W
Santa Rosa de Osos	174	6 39N	75 28W
Santa Rosa de Río Primero	172	31 8 s	63 20W
Santa Rosa de Viterbo	174	5 53N	72 59W
Santa Rosa I., Calif., U.S.A.	163	34 0N	120 6W
Santa Rosa I., Fla., U.S.A.	157	30 23N	87 0W
Santa Rosa Mts.	160	41 45N	117 30W
Santa Rosalia	164	27 20N	112 30W
Santa Sofia	63	43 57N	11 55 E
Santa Sylvina	172	27 50 s	61 10W
Santa Tecla = Nueva San Salvador	164	13 40N	89 25W
Santa Teresa, Argent.	172	33 25 s	60 47W
Santa Teresa, Brazil	171	19 55 s	40 36W
Santa Teresa, Mexico	165	25 17N	97 51W
Santa Teresa, Venez.	174	4 43N	61 4W
Santa Teresa di Riva	63	37 58N	15 21 E
Santa Teresa Gallura	64	41 14N	9 12 E
Santa Teresinha	170	12 45 s	39 32W
Santa Vitória	171	18 50 s	50 8W
Santa Vitória do Palmar	173	33 32 s	53 25W
Santa Ynez	163	34 37N	120 5W
Santa Ynez, R.	163	34 37N	120 41W
Santa Ysabel	163	33 7N	116 40W
Sant'ai	108	31 5N	105 2 E
Santadi	64	39 5N	8 42 E
Santahar	98	24 48N	88 59 E
Santaluz	171	11 15 s	39 22W
Santana	171	13 2 s	44 5W
Santana, Coxilha de	173	30 50 s	55 35W
Santana do Ipanema	170	9 22 s	37 14W
Santana do Livramento	173	30 55 s	55 30W
Santander, Colomb.	174	3 1N	76 28W
Santander, Spain	56	43 27N	3 51W
Santander □	56	43 25N	4 0W
Santander Jiménez	165	24 11N	98 29W
Santañy	59	39 20N	3 5 E
Santaquin	160	40 0N	111 51W
Santarém, Brazil	175	2 25 s	54 42W
Santarém, Port.	57	39 12N	8 42W
Santarém □	57	39 10N	8 40W
Santaren Channel	166	24 0N	79 30W
Santèramo in Colle	65	40 48N	16 45 E
Santerno, R.	63	44 10N	11 38 E
Santhia	62	45 20N	8 10 E
Santiago, Brazil	173	29 11 s	54 52W
Santiago, Chile	172	33 24 s	70 50W
Santiago, Dom. Rep.	167	19 30N	70 40W

Santiago Sayville

Santiago, Panama 166 8 0N 81 0W
Santiago □ 172 33 30S 70 50W
Santiago de Compostela 56 42 52N 8 37W
Santiago de Cuba 166 20 0N 75 49W
Santiago del Estero 172 27 50S 64 15W
Santiago del Estero □ 172 27 50S 64 20W
Santiago do Cacém 57 38 1N 8 42W
Santiago Ixcuintla 164 21 50N 105 11W
Santiago Papasquiaro 164 25 0N 105 20W
Santiago, Punta de 121 3 12N 8 40E
Santiaguillo, L. de 164 24 50N 104 50W
Santillana del Mar 56 43 24N 4 6W
Santipur 95 23 17N 88 25E
Säntis 51 47 15N 9 22E
Santisteban del Puerto 59 38 17N 3 15W
Santo Amaro 171 12 30S 38 50W
Santo Anastácio 173 21 58S 51 39W
Santo André 173 23 39S 46 29W
Santo Ângelo 173 28 15S 54 15W
Santo Antonio 170 15 50S 56 0W
Santo Antônio de Jesus 171 12 58S 39 16W
Santo Antonio do Zaire 124 6 7S 12 20E
Santo Corazón 174 18 0S 58 45W
Santo Domingo, Dom. Rep. 167 18 30N 70 0W
Santo Domingo, Baja Calif. N., Mexico 164 30 43N 115 56W
Santo Domingo, Baja Calif. S., Mexico 164 25 32N 112 2W
Santo Domingo, Nic. 166 12 14N 84 59W
Santo Domingo de la Calzada 58 42 26N 2 27W
Santo Isabel do Morro 171 11 34S 50 40W
Santo Stéfano di Camastro 65 38 1N 14 22E
Santo Stino di Livenza 63 45 45N 12 40E
Santo Tirso 56 41 29N 8 18W
Santo Tomas 164 31 33N 116 24W
Santo Tomás 174 14 34S 72 30W
Santo Tomé 173 28 40S 56 5W
Santoña 56 43 29N 3 20W
Santos 173 24 0S 46 20W
Santos Dumont 173 22 55S 43 10W
Santos, Sierra de los 57 38 7N 5 12W
Santport 46 52 26N 4 39E
Santu 108 25 59N 107 52E
Sanur 90 32 22N 35 15E
Sanvignes-les-Mines 43 46 40N 4 18E
San'yō 110 34 2N 131 5E
Sanyuki-Sammyaku 110 34 5N 133 0E
Sanza Pombo 124 7 18S 15 56E
São Anastacio 173 22 0S 51 40W
São Bartolomeu de Messines 57 37 15N 8 17W
São Benedito 170 4 3S 40 53W
São Bento 170 2 42S 44 50W
São Bento do Norte 170 5 4S 36 2W
São Borja 173 28 45S 56 0W
São Bras d'Alportel 57 37 8N 7 58W
São Caitano 170 8 21S 36 6W
São Carlos 173 22 0S 47 50W
São Cristóvão 170 11 15S 37 15W
São Domingos, Brazil 171 13 25S 46 10W
São Domingos, Guin.-Biss. 170 12 22N 16 8W
São Domingos do Maranhão 170 5 42S 44 22W
São Félix, Bahia, Brazil 171 12 38S 38 58W
São Félix, Mato Grosso, Brazil 171 11 36S 50 39W
Sao Francisco 171 16 0S 44 50W
São Francisco do Maranhão 170 6 15S 42 52W
São Francisco do Sul 173 26 15S 48 36W
São Francisco, R. 170 10 30S 36 24W
São Gabriel 173 30 10S 54 30W
São Gabriel da Palha 171 18 47S 40 59W
São Gonçalo 173 22 48S 43 5W
Sao Gotardo 171 19 19S 46 3W
Sao Hill 127 8 20S 35 18E
São João da Boa Vista 173 22 0S 46 52W
São João da Pesqueira 56 41 8N 7 24W
São João da Ponte 171 15 56S 44 1W
São João del Rei 173 21 8S 44 15W
São João do Araguaia 170 5 23S 48 46W
São João do Paraíso 171 15 19S 42 1W
São João do Piauí 170 8 10S 42 15W
São João dos Patos 170 6 30S 43 42W
São João Evangelista 171 18 32S 42 45W
São Joaquim da Barra 171 20 35S 47 53W
São José, B. de 170 2 38S 44 4W
São José da Laje 170 9 1S 36 3W
São José de Mipibu 170 6 5S 35 15W
São José do Peixe 170 7 24S 42 34W
São José do Rio Prêto 173 20 50S 49 20W
São José dos Campos 173 23 7S 45 52W
São Leopoldo 173 29 50S 51 10W
São Lourenço, Mato Grosso, Brazil 173 16 30S 55 5W
São Lourenço, Minas Gerais, Brazil 171 22 7S 45 3W
São Lourenço, R. 175 16 40S 56 0W
São Luís do Curu 170 3 40S 39 14W
São Luís Gonzaga 173 28 25S 55 0W
São Luís (Maranhão) 170 2 39S 44 15W
Sao Marcelino 174 1 0N 67 12W
São Marcelino 174 1 0N 67 12W
São Marcos, B. de 170 2 0S 44 0W
São Marcos, R. 171 18 15S 47 37W
São Martinho 56 39 30N 9 8W
São Mateus 171 18 44S 39 50W
São Mateus, R. 171 18 35S 39 44W
São Miguel 16 37 33N 25 27W
São Miguel do Araguaia 171 13 19S 50 13W
São Miguel dos Campos 170 9 47S 36 5W
São Nicolau, R. 170 5 45S 42 2W
São Paulo 173 23 40S 46 50W
São Paulo □ 173 22 0S 49 0W
São Pedro do Piaui 171 5 56S 42 43W
São Pedro do Sul 56 40 46N 8 4W
São Rafael 170 5 47S 36 55W
São Raimundo das Mangabeiras 170 7 1S 45 29W
São Raimundo Nonato 170 9 1S 42 42W
São Romão, Amazonas, Brazil 174 5 53S 67 50W
São Romão, Minas Gerais, Brazil 171 16 22S 45 4W
São Roque, C. de 170 5 30S 35 10W
São Sebastião do Paraíso 173 20 54S 46 59W
São Sebastião, I. 173 23 50S 45 18W
São Simão 171 18 56S 50 30W
São Teotónio 57 37 30N 8 42W
São Tomé 170 5 58S 36 4W
São Tomé, C. de 173 22 0S 41 10W
São Tomé, I. 114 0 10N 7 0E
São Vicente 173 23 57S 46 23W
São Vicente, Cabo de 57 37 0N 9 0W
Saona, I. 167 18 10N 68 40W
Saône-et-Loire □ 43 46 25N 4 50E
Saône, R. 43 46 25N 4 50E
Saonek 103 0 28S 130 47E
Saoura, O. 118 29 55N 1 50W
Sapai 68 41 2N 25 43E
Sapão, R. 170 11 1S 45 32W
Saparua, I. 103 3 33S 128 40E
Sapé 170 7 6S 35 13W
Sapele 121 5 50N 5 40E
Sapelo I. 157 31 28N 81 15W
Sapiéntza I. 69 36 33N 21 43E
Sapodnyy Sayan 77 52 30N 94 0E
Sapone 121 12 3N 1 35W
Saposoa 174 6 55S 76 30W
Sapozhok 81 53 59N 40 51E
Sappemeer 46 53 10N 6 48E
Sapporo 112 43 0N 141 15E
Sapri 65 40 5N 15 37E
Sapudi, I. 103 7 2S 114 17E
Sapulpa 159 36 0N 96 40W
Sapur 95 34 18N 74 27E
Saqota 123 12 40N 39 1E
Saqqez 92 36 15N 46 20E
Sar-i-Pul 93 36 10N 66 0E
Sar Planina 66 42 10N 21 0E
Sara 120 11 40N 3 53W
Sara Buri 100 14 30N 100 55E
Sarab 92 38 0N 47 30E
Sarada, R. 99 28 15N 80 30E
Saragossa = Zaragoza 58 41 39N 0 53W
Saraguro 174 3 35S 79 16W
Sarai 70 44 43N 28 10E
Saraipalli 96 21 20N 82 59E
Sarajevo 66 43 52N 18 26E
Saraktash 84 51 47N 56 22E
Saramati 98 25 44N 95 2E
Saran 122 19 35N 40 30E
Saran, G. 102 0 30S 111 25E
Saranac Lake 156 44 20N 74 10W
Saranda, Alb. 68 39 59N 19 55E
Saranda, Tanz. 126 5 45S 34 59E
Sarandí del Yi 173 33 18S 55 38W
Sarandí Grande 172 33 20S 55 50W
Sarangani B. 103 6 0N 125 13E
Sarangani Is. 103 5 25N 125 25E
Sarangarh 96 21 30N 82 57E
Saransk 81 54 10N 45 10E
Sarapul 84 56 28N 53 48E
Sarasota 157 27 10N 82 30W
Saratoga, Calif., U.S.A. 163 37 16N 122 2W
Saratoga, Wyo., U.S.A. 160 41 30N 106 56W
Saratoga Springs 162 43 5N 73 47W
Saratok 102 3 5S 110 50E
Saratov 81 51 30N 46 2E
Saravane 100 15 43N 106 25E
Sarawak □ 102 2 0N 113 0E
Saraya 120 12 50N 11 45W
Sarbaz 93 26 38N 61 19E
Sarbisheh 93 32 30N 59 40E
Sârbogârd 53 46 55N 18 40E
Sarca, R. 62 46 5N 10 45E
Sardalas 119 25 50N 10 54E
Sardarshahr 94 28 30N 74 29E
Sardegna, I. 64 39 57N 9 0E
Sardhana 94 29 9N 77 39E
Sardinata 174 8 5N 72 48W
Sardinia = Sardegna 64 39 57N 9 0E
Sardo 123 11 56N 41 14E
Sarektjåkkå 74 67 27N 17 43E
Sarengrad 66 45 14N 19 16E
Saréyamou 120 16 25N 3 10W
Sargasso Sea 14 27 0N 72 0W
Sargent 158 41 42N 99 24W
Sargodha 94 32 10N 72 40E
Sargodha □ 94 31 50N 72 0E
Sarh 117 9 5N 18 23E
Sarhro, Jebel 118 31 6N 5 0W
Sári 93 36 30N 53 11E
Sária, I. 69 35 54N 27 17E
Sarichef C. 147 54 38N 164 59W
Sarida, R. 90 32 4N 35 3E
Sarikamiş 92 40 22N 42 35E
Sarikei 102 2 8N 111 30E
Sarina 138 21 22S 149 13E
Sarine, R. 50 46 32N 7 4E
Sariñena 58 41 47N 0 10W
Sarír Tibasti 119 22 50N 18 30E
Sarita 159 27 14N 90 49W
Sariwołn 107 38 31N 125 46E
Sariyer 67 41 10N 29 3E
Sark, I. 42 49 25N 2 20W
Sarkad 53 46 47N 21 17E
Sarlat-la-Canéda 44 44 54N 1 13E
Sarles 158 48 58N 98 57W
Sarmi 103 1 49S 138 38E
Särna 72 61 41N 12 58E
Sarnano 63 43 2N 13 17E
Sarnen 50 46 53N 8 13E
Sarnia 150 42 58N 82 23W
Sarno 65 40 48N 14 35E
Sarnowa 54 51 39N 16 53E
Sarny 80 51 17N 26 40E
Särö 73 57 31N 11 57E
Sarolangun 102 2 30S 102 30E
Saronikós Kólpos 69 37 45N 23 45E
Saros Körfezi 68 40 30N 26 15E
Sárospatak 53 48 18N 21 33E
Sarosul Romanesc 66 45 34N 21 43E
Sarpsborg 71 59 16N 11 12E
Sarracín 58 42 15N 3 45W
Sarralbe 43 48 55N 7 1E
Sarraz, La 50 46 38N 6 30E
Sarre, La 150 48 45N 79 15W
Sarre, R. 43 48 49N 7 0E
Sarre-Union 43 48 55N 7 4E
Sarrebourg 43 48 43N 7 3E
Sarreguemines 43 49 1N 7 4E
Sarriá 56 42 41N 7 29W
Sarrión 58 40 9N 0 49W
Sarro 120 13 40N 5 5W
Sarstedt 48 52 13N 9 50E
Sartène 45 41 38N 9 0E
Sarthe □ 42 47 58N 0 10E
Sarthe, R. 42 47 33N 0 31W
Sartilly 42 48 45N 1 28W
Sartynya 76 63 30N 62 50E
Sarum 122 21 11N 39 10E
Sarúr 93 23 17N 58 4E
Sárvár 53 47 15N 16 56E
Sarveston 93 29 20N 53 10E
Särvfjället 72 62 42N 13 30E
Sárviz, R. 53 46 40N 18 40E
Sary Ozek 85 44 22N 77 59E
Sary-Tash 85 39 44N 73 15E
Saryagach 85 41 27N 69 9E
Sarych, Mys. 82 44 25N 33 25E
Sarykolskiy Khrebet 85 38 30N 74 30E
Sarykopa, Ozero 84 50 22N 64 6E
Sarymoin, Ozero 84 51 36N 64 30E
Saryshagan 76 46 12N 73 48E
Sarzana 70 44 7N 9 57E
Sarzeau 42 47 31N 2 48W
Sas van Gent 47 51 14N 3 48E
Sasa 90 33 2N 35 23E
Sasabeneh 91 7 59N 44 43E
Sasaram 95 24 57N 84 5E
Sasayama 111 35 4N 135 13E
Sasca Montanů 66 44 41N 21 45E
Sasebo 110 33 10N 129 43E
Saser Mt. 95 34 50N 77 50E
Saskatchewan □ 153 54 40N 106 0W
Saskatchewan, R. 153 53 12N 99 16W
Saskatoon 153 52 10N 106 38W
Sasolburg 129 26 46S 27 49E
Sasovo 81 54 25N 41 55E
Sassandra 120 5 0N 6 8W
Sassandra, R. 120 5 0N 6 8W
Sássari 64 40 44N 8 33E
Sassenheim 46 52 14N 4 31E
Sassnitz 48 54 29N 13 39E
Sasso Marconi 63 44 22N 11 12E
Sassocorvaro 63 43 47N 12 30E
Sassoferrato 63 43 26N 12 51E
Sassuolo 62 44 31N 10 47E
Sástago 58 41 19N 0 21W
Sastown 120 4 45N 8 27W
Sasumua Dam 126 0 54S 36 46E
Sasyk, Ozero 70 45 45N 30 0E
Sasykkul 85 37 41N 73 11E
Sata-Misaki 110 30 59N 130 40E
Satadougou 120 12 40N 11 25W
Satanta 159 37 30N 101 0W
Satara 96 17 44N 73 58E
Satilla, R. 157 31 15N 81 50W
Satka 84 55 3N 59 1E
Satkania 98 22 4N 92 3E
Satkhira 98 22 43N 89 8E
Satmala Hills 96 20 15N 74 40E
Satna 95 24 35N 80 50E
Sator, mt. 63 44 11N 16 43E
Sátoraljaújhely 53 48 25N 21 41E
Satpura Ra. 94 21 40N 75 0E
Satrup 48 54 39N 9 38E
Satsuma-Hantō 110 31 25N 130 25E
Satsuna-Shotō 112 30 0N 130 0E
Sattahip 100 12 41N 100 54E
Sattenpalle 96 16 25N 80 6E
Satu Mare 70 47 46N 22 55E
Satui 102 3 50S 115 20E
Satumare □ 70 47 45N 23 0E
Satun 101 6 43N 100 2E
Saturnina, R. 174 12 15S 58 10W
Sauce 172 30 5S 58 46W
Sauceda 164 25 46N 101 19W
Saucillo 164 28 1N 105 17W
Sauda 71 59 38N 6 21E
Saúde 170 10 56S 40 24W
Sauðarkrókur 74 65 45N 19 40W
Saudi Arabia ■ 92 26 0N 44 0E
Sauerland 48 51 0N 8 0E
Saugerties 162 42 4N 73 58W
Saugues 44 44 58N 3 32E
Sauherad 71 59 25N 9 15E
Sauid el Amia 118 25 57N 6 8W
Saujon 44 45 41N 0 55W
Sauk Center 158 45 42N 94 56W
Sauk Rapids 158 45 35N 94 10W
Saulgau 49 48 4N 9 32E
Saulieu 43 47 17N 4 14E
Sault 45 44 6N 5 24E
Sault Ste. Marie, Can. 150 46 30N 84 20W
Sault Ste. Marie, U.S.A. 156 46 27N 84 22W
Saumlaki 103 7 55S 131 20E
Saumur 42 47 15N 0 5W
Saunders 152 52 58N 115 40W
Saunders C. 143 45 53S 170 45E
Saunders I. 13 57 30S 27 30W
Saunders Point, Mt. 137 27 52S 125 38E
Saundersfoot 31 51 43N 4 42W
Saurbær, Borgarfjarðarsýsla, Iceland 74 64 24N 21 35W
Saurbær, Eyjafjarðarsýsla, Iceland 74 65 27N 18 13W
Sauri 121 11 50N 6 44E
Sausalito 163 37 51N 122 29W
Sautatá 174 7 50N 77 4W
Sauveterre, B. 44 43 25N 0 57W
Sauzé-Vaussais 44 46 8N 0 8E
Savá 166 15 32N 86 15W
Sava 65 40 28N 17 32E
Sava, R. 63 44 40N 19 50E
Savage 158 47 43N 104 20W
Savalou 121 7 57N 2 4E
Savanah Downs 138 19 30S 141 30E
Savane 127 19 37S 35 8E
Savanna 158 42 5N 90 10W
Savanna la Mar 166 18 10N 78 10W
Savannah, Ga., U.S.A. 157 32 4N 81 4W
Savannah, Mo., U.S.A. 158 39 55N 94 46W
Savannah, Tenn., U.S.A. 157 35 12N 88 18W
Savannah Downs 138 19 28S 141 47E
Savannah, R. 157 33 0N 81 30W
Savannakhet 100 16 30N 104 49E
Savant L. 150 50 14N 90 6W
Savant Lake 150 50 30N 90 25W
Savantvadi 97 15 55N 73 54E
Savanur 97 14 59N 75 28E
Savda 96 21 9N 75 56E
Savé 121 8 2N 2 17E
Save R. 125 21 16S 34 0E
Saveh 92 35 2N 50 20E
Savelovo 81 56 51N 37 20E
Savelugu 121 9 38N 0 54W
Savenay 42 47 20N 1 55W
Saverdun 44 43 14N 1 34E
Saverne 43 48 39N 7 20E
Savièse 50 46 17N 7 22E
Savigliano 62 44 39N 7 40E
Savigny-sur-Braye 44 47 53N 0 49E
Saviñao 56 42 35N 7 38W
Savio, R. 63 43 58N 12 10E
Savnik 66 42 59N 19 10E
Savognin 51 46 36N 9 37E
Savoie □ 45 45 26N 6 35E
Savona 62 44 19N 8 29E
Savonlinna 78 61 55N 28 55E
Sävsjö 73 57 20N 14 40E
Sävsjøström 73 57 1N 15 25E
Sawahlunto 102 0 52S 100 52E
Sawai 103 3 0S 129 5E
Sawai Madhopur 94 26 0N 76 25E
Sawang Daen Din 100 17 28N 103 28E
Sawankhalok 100 17 19N 99 50E
Sawara 111 35 55N 140 30E
Sawatch Mts. 161 38 30N 106 30W
Sawbridgeworth 29 51 49N 0 10E
Sawdā, Jabal as 119 28 51N 15 12E
Sawel, Mt. 38 54 48N 7 5W
Sawfajjin, W. 119 31 46N 14 30E
Sawi 101 10 14N 99 5E
Sawmills 127 19 30S 28 2E
Sawston 29 52 7N 0 11E
Sawtry 29 52 26N 0 17W
Sawu, I. 103 10 35S 121 50E
Sawu Sea 103 9 30S 121 50E
Saxby, R. 138 18 25S 140 53E
Saxilby 33 53 16N 0 40W
Saxlingham Nethergate 29 52 33N 1 16E
Saxmundham 29 52 13N 1 29E
Saxon 50 46 9N 7 11E
Saxony, Lower = Niedersachsen 48 52 45N 9 0E
Say 121 13 8N 2 22E
Saya 121 9 30N 3 18E
Sayabec 151 48 35N 67 41W
Sayaboury 100 19 15N 101 45E
Sayán 174 11 0S 77 25W
Sayan, Vostochnyy 77 54 0N 96 0E
Sayan, Zapadnyy 77 52 30N 94 0E
Sayasan 83 42 56N 46 15E
Sayda 92 33 35N 35 25E
Sayhan Ovoo 106 45 27N 103 54E
Sayhandulaan 106 44 40N 109 1E
Saynshand 106 44 55N 110 11E
Sayō 110 34 59N 134 22E
Sayre, Okla., U.S.A. 159 35 20N 99 40W
Sayre, Pa., U.S.A. 162 42 0N 76 30W
Sayula 164 19 50N 103 40W
Sayville 162 40 45N 73 7W

Semisopochnoi I **Shawbost**

Semisopochnoi I.	147	52 0N	179 40W
Semitau	102	0 29N	111 57 E
Semiyarskoye	76	50 55N	78 30 E
Semmering Pass.	52	47 41N	15 45 E
Semnan	93	35 55N	53 25 E
Semnan □	93	36 0N	54 0 E
Semois, R.	47	49 53N	4 44 E
Semporna	103	4 30N	118 33 E
Semuda	102	2 51 S	112 58 E
Semur-en-Auxois	43	47 30N	4 20 E
Sen. R.	101	13 45N	105 12 E
Sena Madureira	174	9 5 S	68 45W
Senador Pompeu	170	5 40 S	39 20W
Senai	101	1 38N	103 38 E
Senaja	102	6 49 S	117 2 E
Senanga	128	16 2 S	23 14 E
Senatobia	159	34 38N	89 57W
Sendafa	123	9 11N	39 3 E
Sendai, Kagoshima, Japan	110	31 50N	130 20 E
Sendai, Miyagi, Japan	112	38 15N	141 0 E
Sendamangalam	97	11 17N	78 17 E
Sendeling's Drift	128	28 12 S	16 52 E
Sendenhorst	48	51 50N	7 49 E
Sendurjana	96	21 32N	78 24 E
Senec	53	48 12N	17 23 E
Seneca, Oreg., U.S.A.	160	44 10N	119 2W
Seneca, S.C., U.S.A.	157	34 43N	82 59W
Seneca Falls	162	42 55N	76 50W
Seneca L.	162	42 40N	76 58W
Seneffe	47	50 32N	4 16 E
Senegal ■	120	14 30N	14 30W
Senegal, R.	120	16 30N	15 30W
Senekal	129	28 18 S	27 36 E
Senftenberg	48	51 30N	13 51 E
Senga Hill	127	9 19 S	31 11 E
Senge Khambab (Indus), R.	94	28 40N	70 10 E
Sengerema □	126	2 10 S	32 20 E
Sengiley	81	53 58N	48 54 E
Sengwa, R.	127	17 10 S	28 15 E
Senhor-do-Bonfim	170	10 30 S	40 10W
Senica	53	48 41N	17 25 E
Senigállia	63	43 42N	13 12 E
Seniku	98	25 32N	97 48 E
Senio, R.	63	44 18N	11 47 E
Senj	63	45 0N	14 58 E
Senja	74	69 25N	17 20 E
Senlis	43	49 13N	2 35 E
Senmonorom	100	12 27N	107 12 E
Sennâr	123	13 30N	33 35 E
Senne, R.	47	50 42N	4 13 E
Sennen	30	50 4N	5 42W
Senneterre	150	48 25N	77 15W
Senno	80	54 45N	29 58 E
Sennori	64	40 49N	8 36 E
Senny Bridge	31	51 57N	3 35W
Seno	100	16 41N	105 1 E
Senonches	42	48 34N	1 2 E
Senorbi	64	39 33N	9 8 E
Senožeče	63	45 43N	14 3 E
Sens	43	48 11N	3 15 E
Senta	66	45 55N	20 3 E
Sentein	44	42 53N	0 58 E
Senteny	126	5 17 S	25 42 E
Sentier, Le	51	46 37N	6 15 E
Sentinel	161	32 56N	113 13W
Sento Sé	170	9 40 S	41 18W
Sentolo	103	7 55 S	110 13 E
Senya Beraku	121	5 28N	0 31W
Seo de Urgel	58	42 22N	1 23 E
Seohara	95	29 15N	78 33 E
Seoni	95	22 5N	79 30 E
Seorinayan	96	21 45N	82 34 E
Separation Point	151	53 37N	57 25W
Seph, R.	33	54 17N	1 9W
Sepik, R.	135	3 49 S	144 30 E
Sepólno Krajenskie	54	53 26N	17 30 E
Sepone	100	16 45N	106 13 E
Sepopa	128	18 49 S	22 12 E
Sepopol	54	54 16N	21 2 E
Sepori	107	38 57N	127 25 E
Sept Îles	151	50 13N	66 22W
Septemvri	67	42 13N	24 6 E
Septimus	138	21 13 S	148 47 E
Sepúlveda	56	41 18N	3 45W
Sequeros	56	40 31N	6 2W
Sequim	160	48 3N	123 9W
Sequoia Nat. Park	163	36 30N	118 30W
Serafimovich	83	49 30N	42 50 E
Seraing	47	50 35N	5 32 E
Seraja	101	2 41N	108 35 E
Seram, I.	103	3 10 S	129 0 E
Serampore	95	22 44N	88 30 E
Serang	103	6 8 S	106 10 E
Serasan	101	2 31N	109 2 E
Serasan, I.	102	2 29N	109 4 E
Seravezza	62	43 59N	10 13 E
Serbia = Srbija	66	43 30N	21 0 E
Sercaia	70	45 49N	25 9 E
Serdo	123	11 56N	41 14 E
Serdobsk	81	52 28N	44 10 E
Seredka	80	58 12N	28 3 E
Seregno	62	45 40N	9 12 E
Seremban	101	2 43N	101 53 E
Serena, La, Chile	172	29 55 S	71 10W
Serena, La, Spain	57	38 45N	5 40W
Serengeti □	126	2 0 S	34 30 E
Serengeti Plain	126	2 40 S	35 0 E
Serenje	125	13 14 S	30 15 E
Sergach	81	55 30N	45 30 E
Serge, R.	58	42 5N	1 21 E
Sergievsk	81	54 0N	51 10 E
Sergipe □	170	10 30 S	37 30W
Seria	102	4 37N	114 30 E
Serian	102	1 10N	110 40 E
Seriate	62	45 42N	9 43 E
Sérifontaine	43	49 20N	1 45 E
Sérifos, I.	69	37 9N	24 30 E
Sérignan	44	43 17N	3 17 E
Serik	92	36 55N	31 10 E
Seringapatam Reef	136	13 38 S	122 5 E
Sermaize-les-Bains	43	48 47N	4 54 E
Sermata, I.	103	8 15 S	128 50 E
Sérmide	63	45 0N	11 17 E
Sernovdsk	76	61 20N	73 28 E
Sernovodsk	84	53 54N	51 16 E
Sero	120	14 42N	10 59W
Serón	59	37 20N	2 29W
Serós	58	41 27N	0 24 E
Serov	84	59 36N	60 35 E
Serowe	128	22 25 S	26 43 E
Serpa	57	37 57N	7 38 E
Serpeddi, Punta	64	39 19N	9 28 E
Serpentara	64	39 8N	9 38 E
Serpentine	137	32 23 S	115 58 E
Serpentine L.	137	28 30 S	129 10 E
Serpent's Mouth	174	10 0N	61 30W
Serpis, R.	59	38 45N	0 21W
Serpukhov	81	54 55N	37 28 E
Serra	171	20 7 S	40 18W
Serra Capriola	65	41 47N	15 12 E
Serra do Salitre	74	19 6 S	46 41W
Serra Talhada	170	7 59 S	38 18W
Serradilla	56	39 50N	6 9W
Sérrai □	68	41 5N	23 37 E
Serramanna	64	39 26N	8 56 E
Serrania de Cuenca	58	40 10N	1 50W
Serrat, C.	119	37 14N	9 10 E
Serres	45	44 26N	5 43 E
Serrezuela	172	30 40 S	65 20W
Serrinha	171	11 39 S	39 0W
Serrita	170	7 56 S	39 19W
Serro	171	18 37 S	43 23W
Sersale	65	39 1N	16 44 E
Sertã	56	39 48N	8 6W
Sertânia	170	8 5 S	37 20W
Sertanópolis	173	23 4 S	51 2W
Sertão	170	10 0 S	40 20W
Sertig	51	46 44N	9 52 E
Serua, P.	103	6 18 S	130 1 E
Serui	103	1 45 S	136 10 E
Serule	128	21 57 S	27 11 E
Sérvia	68	40 9N	21 58 E
Sesajap Lama	102	3 32N	117 11 E
Sese Is.	126	0 30 S	32 30 E
Sesepe	103	1 30 S	127 59 E
Sesfontein	128	19 7 S	13 39 E
Sesheke	128	17 29 S	24 13 E
Sesia, R.	62	45 35N	8 23 E
Sesimbra	57	38 28N	9 20W
Seskanore	38	54 31N	7 15W
Sessa Aurunca	64	41 14N	13 55 E
Sestao	58	43 18N	3 0W
Sesto S. Giovanni	62	45 32N	9 14 E
Sestri Levante	62	44 17N	9 22 E
Sestrières	62	44 58N	6 56 E
Sestrunj, I.	63	44 10N	15 0 E
Sestu	64	39 18N	9 6 E
Sesvenna	51	46 42N	10 25 E
Seta	108	32 20N	100 41 E
Setaka	110	33 9N	130 28 E
Setana	112	42 26N	139 51 E
Sète	44	43 25N	3 42 E
Sete Lagoas	171	19 27 S	44 16W
Sétif	119	36 9N	5 26 E
Seto	111	35 14N	137 6 E
Seto Naikai	110	34 20N	133 30 E
Setouchi	112	28 8N	129 19 E
Setsan	98	16 3N	95 23 E
Settat	118	33 0N	7 40W
Setté Cama	124	2 32 S	9 57 E
Séttimo Tor	62	45 9N	7 46 E
Setting L.	153	55 0N	98 38W
Settle	32	54 5N	2 18W
Settlement Pt.	157	26 40N	79 0W
Setto Calende	62	45 44N	8 37 E
Setúbal	57	38 30N	8 58W
Setúbal □	57	38 25N	8 35W
Setúbal, B. de	57	38 40N	8 56W
Seul L.	150	50 25N	92 30W
Seul Reservoir, Lac	150	50 25N	92 30W
Seulimeum	102	5 27N	95 15 E
Seuzach	51	47 32N	8 49 E
Sevastopol	82	44 35N	33 30 E
Sevelen	51	47 7N	9 30 E
Seven Emu	138	16 20 S	137 8 E
Seven Heads	39	51 35N	8 43W
Seven Hogs, Is.	39	52 20N	10 0W
Seven, R.	33	54 11N	0 51W
Seven Sisters	31	51 46N	3 43W
Seven Sisters, mt	152	54 56N	128 10W
Sevenoaks	29	51 16N	0 11 E
Sevenum	47	51 25N	6 2 E
Sever, R.	57	39 40N	7 32W
Sévérac-le-Chateau	44	44 20N	3 5 E
Severn Beach	28	51 34N	2 39W
Severn L.	150	53 54N	90 48W
Severn, R., Can.	150	56 2N	87 36W
Severn, R., U.K.	28	51 35N	2 38W
Severn Stoke	28	52 5N	2 13W
Severnaya Zemlya	77	79 0N	100 0 E
Severnyye Uvaly	78	58 0N	48 0 E
Severo-Kurilsk	77	50 40N	156 8 E
Severodonetsk	83	48 50N	38 30 E
Severodvinsk	78	64 27N	39 58 E
Severomoravsky □	53	49 38N	17 40 E
Severouralsk	84	60 9N	59 57 E
Sevier	161	38 39N	112 11W
Sevier L.	160	39 0N	113 20W
Sevier, R.	161	39 10N	112 50W
Sevilla, Colomb.	174	4 16N	75 57W
Sevilla, Spain	57	37 23N	6 0W
Sevilla □	57	37 0N	6 0W
Seville = Sevilla	57	37 23N	6 0W
Sevnica	63	46 2N	15 19 E
Sevsk	80	52 10N	34 30 E
Seward	147	60 0N	149 40W
Seward Pen.	147	65 0N	164 0W
Sewell	172	34 10 S	70 45W
Sewer	103	5 46 S	134 40 E
Sexbierum	46	53 13N	5 29 E
Sexsmith	152	55 21N	118 47W
Seychelles, Is.	11	5 0 S	56 0 E
Seyðisfjörður	74	65 16N	14 0W
Seym, R.	80	51 45N	35 0 E
Seymchan	77	62 40N	152 30 E
Seymour, Austral.	141	37 0 S	145 10 E
Seymour, Conn., U.S.A.	162	41 23N	73 5W
Seymour, Ind., U.S.A.	156	39 0N	85 50W
Seymour, Tex., U.S.A.	159	33 35N	99 18W
Seymour, Wis., U.S.A.	156	44 30N	88 20W
Seyne	45	44 21N	6 22 E
Seyne-sur-Mer, La	45	43 7N	5 52 E
Sezana	63	45 43N	13 41 E
Sézanne	43	48 40N	3 40 E
Sezze	64	41 30N	13 3 E
Sfântu Gheorghe	70	45 52N	25 48 E
Sfax	119	34 49N	10 48 E
Sgurr Mor	36	57 42N	5 0W
Sgurr na Ciche	36	57 0N	5 29W
Sgurr na Lapaich	36	57 23N	5 5W
Sha Ch'i, R.	109	26 35N	118 8 E
Shaartuz	85	37 16N	68 8 E
Shaba	126	8 0 S	25 0 E
Shaba Gamba	99	32 8N	88 55 E
Shaballe, R.	123	5 0N	44 0 E
Shabani	127	20 17 S	30 2 E
Shabbear	30	50 52N	4 12W
Shabla	67	43 31N	28 32 E
Shabogamo L.	151	48 40N	77 0W
Shabunda	126	2 40 S	27 16 E
Shackleton	13	78 30 S	36 1W
Shackleton Inlet	13	83 0 S	160 0 E
Shaddad	122	21 25N	40 2 E
Shadi	95	33 24N	77 14 E
Shadrinsk	84	56 5N	63 58 E
Shadwân	122	27 30N	34 0 E
Shaffa	121	10 30N	12 6 E
Shafter	163	35 32N	119 14W
Shaftesbury	28	51 0N	2 12W
Shag Pt.	143	45 29 S	170 52 E
Shagamu	121	6 51N	3 39 E
Shagram	95	36 24N	72 20 E
Shah Bunder	94	24 13N	67 50 E
Shahabad, And. P., India	96	17 10N	78 11 E
Shahabad, Punjab, India	94	30 10N	76 55 E
Shahabad, Raj., India	94	25 15N	77 11 E
Shahabad, Uttar Pradesh, India	95	27 36N	79 56 E
Shāhābād	93	37 40N	56 50 E
Shahada	96	21 33N	74 30 E
Shahapur	96	15 50N	74 34 E
Shāhbād	92	34 10N	46 30 E
Shahdād	93	30 30N	57 40 E
Shahdadkot	94	27 50N	67 55 E
Shahddpur	94	25 55N	68 35 E
Shahganj	95	26 3N	82 44 E
Shahgarh	93	27 15N	69 50 E
Shahhat (Cyrene)	117	32 40N	21 35 E
Shāhī	93	36 30N	52 55 E
Shahjahanpur	95	27 54N	79 57 E
Shaho	106	36 31N	114 35 E
Shahpur, Mad. P., India	94	22 12N	77 58 E
Shahpur, Mysore, India	97	16 40N	76 48 E
Shahpur, Iran	92	38 12N	44 45 E
Shahpur, Pak.	94	28 46N	68 27 E
Shahpura	95	23 10N	80 45 E
Shahr-e Babak	93	30 10N	55 20 E
Shahr Kord	93	32 15N	50 55 E
Shahraban	92	34 0N	45 0 E
Shahreza	93	32 0N	51 55 E
Shahrig	94	30 15N	67 40 E
Shahriza	93	32 0N	51 50 E
Shahrud	93	36 30N	55 0 E
Shahrukh	93	33 50N	60 10 E
Shahsavar	93	36 45N	51 12 E
Shahsien	109	26 25N	117 50 E
Shahuk'ou	106	40 20N	112 18 E
Shaibâra	123	25 26N	36 47 E
Shaikhabad	94	34 0N	68 45 E
Shaim	84	60 21N	64 10 E
Shajapur	94	23 20N	76 15 E
Shakargarh	94	32 17N	75 43 E
Shakawe	128	18 28 S	21 49 E
Shakhristan	85	39 47N	68 49 E
Shakhrisyabz	85	39 3N	66 50 E
Shakhty	83	47 40N	40 10 E
Shakhunya	81	57 40N	47 0 E
Shaki	121	8 41N	3 21 E
Shakopee	158	44 45N	93 30W
Shaktolik	147	64 30N	161 15W
Shala Lake	123	7 30N	38 30 E
Shaldon	30	50 32N	3 31W
Shalkar Karashatau, Ozero	84	50 26N	61 12 E
Shalkar Yega Kara, Ozero	84	50 45N	60 54 E
Sham, J. ash	93	23 10N	57 5 E
Shama	121	5 1N	1 42W
Shamâl Dâfû □	123	15 0N	25 0 E
Shamâl Kordofân □	123	15 0N	30 0 E
Shamar, Jabal	92	27 40N	41 0 E
Shamattawa	153	55 51N	92 5W
Shamattawa, R.	150	55 1N	85 23W
Shambe	123	7 2N	30 46 E
Shambu	123	9 32N	37 3 E
Shamgong Dzong	98	27 19N	90 35 E
Shamil, India	94	29 32N	77 18 E
Shamil, Iran	93	27 30N	56 55 E
Shamkhor	83	40 56N	46 0 E
Shamo, L.	123	5 45N	37 30 E
Shamokin	162	40 47N	76 33W
Shamrock	159	35 15N	100 15W
Shamva	125	17 20 S	31 32 E
Shan □	98	21 30N	98 30 E
Shanagolden	39	52 35N	9 6W
Shanan, R.	123	8 0N	40 20 E
Shanch'eng	109	31 45N	115 30 E
Shandon	163	35 39N	120 23W
Shandon Downs	138	17 45 S	134 50 E
Shanga	121	9 1N	5 2 E
Shangalowe	127	10 50 S	26 30 E
Shangani	127	19 1 S	28 51 E
Shangani, R.	127	18 35 S	27 45 E
Shangchih, (Chuho)	107	45 10N	127 59 E
Shangching	106	33 9N	110 2 E
Shangch'iu	105	34 26N	115 40 E
Shangch'uan Shan, I.	109	21 45N	112 45 E
Shanghai	109	31 10N	121 25 E
Shanghang	109	25 5N	116 30 E
Shangho	107	37 19N	117 9 E
Shanghsien	106	33 30N	109 58 E
Shangjao	109	28 25N	117 57 E
Shangkao	109	28 16N	114 50 E
Shanglin	108	23 26N	108 36 E
Shangnan	106	33 35N	110 49 E
Shangpanch'eng	107	40 50N	118 0 E
Shangshui	106	33 42N	114 34 E
Shangssu	108	22 10N	108 0 E
Shangtsai	106	33 15N	114 20 E
Shangtu	106	41 31N	113 35 E
Shangyu	109	25 59N	114 29 E
Shanhaikuan	107	40 2N	119 48 E
Shanhot'un	107	44 42N	127 12 E
Shanhsien	106	34 51N	116 9 E
Shani	121	10 14N	12 2 E
Shaniko	160	45 0N	120 15W
Shanklin	28	50 39N	1 9W
Shannon, Greenl.	12	75 10N	18 30W
Shannon, N.Z.	142	40 33 S	175 25 E
Shannon Airport	39	52 42N	8 57W
Shannon Bridge	39	53 17N	8 2W
Shannon I.	12	75 0N	18 0W
Shannon, Mouth of the	39	52 30N	9 55W
Shannon, R.	39	53 10N	8 10W
Shansi □	106	37 30N	112 15 E
Shantar, Ostrov Bolshoi	77	55 9N	137 40 E
Shant'ou	109	23 28N	116 40 E
Shantung □	105	36 0N	117 30 E
Shantung Pantao	107	37 5N	121 0 E
Shanyang	106	33 39N	110 2 E
Shanyin	106	39 34N	112 50 E
Shaohing	109	30 0N	120 32 E
Shaokuan	109	24 50N	113 35 E
Shaowu	109	27 25N	117 30 E
Shaoyang	109	27 10N	111 30 E
Shap	32	54 32N	2 40W
Shap'ing	109	22 46N	112 57 E
Shapinsay, I.	37	59 2N	2 50W
Shapinsay Sd.	37	59 0N	2 51W
Shaqra	92	25 15N	45 16 E
Sharafa (Ogr)	123	11 59N	27 7 E
Sharavati, R.	97	14 32N	74 0 E
Sharhjui	93	32 30N	67 22 E
Shari	92	27 20N	43 45 E
Sharjah	93	25 23N	55 26 E
Shark B., N. Territory, Austral.	132	11 20 S	130 35 E
Shark B., W. Australia, Austral.	137	25 55 S	113 32 E
Sharm el Sheikh	122	27 53N	34 15 E
Sharon, Mass., U.S.A.	162	42 5N	71 11W
Sharon, Pa., U.S.A.	156	41 18N	80 30W
Sharon, Plain of = Hasharon	90	32 12N	34 49 E
Sharon Springs	162	42 48N	74 37W
Sharp Pt.	138	10 58 S	142 43 E
Sharpe, L.	150	54 10N	93 21W
Sharpe L.	153	50 23N	95 30W
Sharpness	28	51 43N	2 28W
Sharya	81	58 12N	45 40 E
Shasha	123	6 29N	35 59 E
Shashemene	123	7 13N	38 33 E
Shashi	125	21 15 S	27 27 E
Shashi, R.	127	21 40 S	28 40 E
Shashih	109	30 19N	112 14 E
Shasta, Mt.	160	41 45N	122 0W
Shasta Res.	160	40 50N	122 15W
Shati	109	26 6N	114 51 E
Shatsk	81	54 0N	41 45 E
Shattuck	159	36 17N	99 55W
Shaumyani	83	41 13N	44 45 E
Shaunavon	153	49 35N	108 25W
Shaver Lake	163	37 9N	119 18W
Shaw I.	138	20 30 S	149 2 E
Shaw, R.	136	20 21 S	119 17 E
Shawan	105	44 21N	85 37 E
Shawangunk Mts.	162	41 40N	74 25W
Shawano	156	44 45N	88 38W
Shawbost	36	58 20N	6 40W

Shawbury **Siddeburen**

Shawbury 28 52 48N 2 40W
Shawinigan 150 46 35N 72 50W
Shawnee 159 35 15N 97 0W
Shaymak 85 37 33N 74 50 E
Shaziz 99 33 10N 82 43 E
Shchëkino 81 54 1N 37 28 E
Shcherbakov = Rybinsk 81 58 5N 38 50 E
Shchigri 81 51 55N 36 58 E
Shchuchinsk 76 52 56N 70 12 E
Shchuchye 84 55 12N 62 46 E
Shchurovo 81 55 0N 38 51 E
Shebekino 81 50 28N 37 0 E
Shebele, Wabi 123 2 0N 44 0 E
Sheboygan 156 43 46N 87 45W
Shechem 90 32 13N 35 21 E
Shech'i 106 33 3N 112 57 E
Shediac 151 46 14N 64 32W
Sheefry Hills 38 53 40N 9 40W
Sheelin, Lough 38 53 48N 7 20W
Sheep Haven 38 55 12N 7 55W
Sheeps Hd. 39 51 32N 9 50W
Sheerness 29 51 26N 0 47 E
Sheet Harbour 151 44 56N 62 31W
Shefar'am 90 32 48N 35 10 E
Shefeiya 90 32 35N 34 58 E
Sheffield, U.K. 33 53 23N 1 28W
Sheffield, Ala., U.S.A. 157 34 45N 87 42W
Sheffield, Mass., U.S.A. 162 42 6N 73 23W
Sheffield, Tex., U.S.A. 159 30 42N 101 49W
Shefford 29 52 2N 0 20W
Shegaon 96 20 48N 76 59 E
Sheho 153 51 35N 103 13W
Shehojele 123 10 40N 35 27 E
Shehsien, Anhwei, China 109 29 52N 118 26 E
Shehsien, Hopeh, China 106 36 33N 113 40 E
Shehung 108 31 0N 105 12 E
Shehy Mts. 39 51 47N 9 15W
Sheikhpura 95 25 9N 85 53 E
Shek Hasan 123 13 5N 35 58 E
Shekar Dzong 95 28 45N 87 0 E
Shekhupura 94 31 42N 73 58 E
Sheki 83 41 10N 47 5 E
Sheksna, R. 81 59 30N 38 30 E
Shelburne, N.S., Can. 151 43 47N 65 20W
Shelburne, Ont., Can. 150 44 4N 80 15W
Shelburne B. 133 11 50 S 143 0 E
Shelburne Falls 162 42 36N 72 45W
Shelby, Mich., U.S.A. 156 43 34N 86 27W
Shelby, Mont., U.S.A. 160 48 30N 111 59W
Shelby, N.C., U.S.A. 157 35 18N 81 34W
Shelbyville, Ill., U.S.A. 158 39 25N 88 45W
Shelbyville, Ind., U.S.A. 156 39 30N 85 42W
Shelbyville, Tenn., U.S.A. 157 35 30N 86 25W
Sheldon 158 43 6N 95 51W
Sheldon Point 147 62 30N 165 0W
Sheldrake 151 50 20N 64 51W
Shelikef, Str. 147 58 0N 154 0W
Shelikhova, Zaliv 77 59 30N 157 0 E
Shell, L. 36 58 0N 6 28W
Shell Lake 153 53 19N 107 14W
Shell Lakes 137 29 20 S 127 30 E
Shellbrook 153 53 13N 106 24W
Shellharbour 141 34 31 S 150 51 E
Shelon, R. 80 58 10N 30 30 E
Shelter Bay 151 50 30N 67 20W
Shelter I 162 41 5N 72 21W
Shelton, Conn., U.S.A. 162 41 18N 73 7W
Shelton, Wash., U.S.A. 160 47 15N 123 6W
Shemakha 83 40 50N 48 28 E
Shenandoah, Iowa, U.S.A. 158 40 50N 95 25W
Shenandoah, Pa., U.S.A. 162 40 49N 76 13W
Shenandoah, Va., U.S.A. 156 38 30N 78 38W
Shenandoah, R. 156 38 30N 78 38W
Shencha 105 30 56N 88 38 E
Shench'ih 106 39 8N 112 10 E
Shenchingtzu 107 44 48N 124 32 E
Shench'iu 106 33 26N 115 2 E
Shencottah 97 8 59N 77 18 E
Shendam 121 9 10N 9 30 E
Shendî 123 16 46N 33 33 E
Shendurni 96 20 39N 75 36 E
Shenfield 29 51 39N 0 21 E
Shengfang 106 39 5N 116 42 E
Shëngjergji 68 41 2N 20 10 E
Shëngjini 68 41 50N 19 35 E
Shenmëria 68 42 7N 20 13 E
Shenmu 106 38 54N 110 24 E
Shensi □ 106 34 50N 109 25 E
Shenton, Mt. 137 27 57 S 123 22 E
Shenyang 107 42 50N 123 25 E
Sheopur Kalan 93 25 40N 76 40 E
Shepetovka 80 50 10N 27 0 E
Shephelah = Hashefela 90 31 30N 34 43 E
Shepparton 141 36 23 S 145 26 E
Sheppey, I. of 29 51 23N 0 50 E
Shepshed 28 52 47N 1 18W
Shepton Mallet 28 51 11N 2 31W
Sher Khan Qala 94 29 55N 66 10 E
Sher Qila 95 36 7N 74 2 E
Sherada 123 7 25N 36 30 E
Sherborne 28 50 56N 2 31W
Sherborne St. John 28 51 18N 1 7W
Sherbro I. 120 7 30N 12 40W
Sherbrooke 151 45 8N 81 57W
Sherburn, N. Yorks., U.K. 33 54 12N 0 32W
Sherburn, N. Yorks., U.K. 33 53 47N 1 15W
Sherburne 162 42 41N 75 30W
Shercock 38 54 0N 6 54W
Sherda 119 20 7N 16 46 E
Shere 29 51 13N 0 28W
Shereik 122 18 52N 33 40 E
Sherfield English 28 51 1N 1 35W
Sheridan, Ark., U.S.A. 159 34 20N 92 25W
Sheridan, Col., U.S.A. 158 39 44N 105 3W
Sheridan, Wyo., U.S.A. 160 44 50N 107 0W
Sheriff Hutton 33 54 5N 1 0W
Sheriff Muir 35 56 12N 3 53W
Sheringham 29 52 56N 1 11 E
Sherkin I. 39 51 38N 9 25W
Sherkot 95 29 22N 78 35 E
Sherman 159 33 40N 96 35W
Sherpur 98 24 41N 89 25 E
Sherridon 153 55 8N 101 5W
Sherston 28 51 35N 2 13W
Sherwood, N.D., U.S.A. 158 48 59N 101 36W
Sherwood, Tex., U.S.A. 159 31 18N 100 45W
Sherwood For. 33 53 5N 1 5W
Shesheke 125 17 14 S 24 22 E
Sheslay 152 58 17N 131 45W
Sheslay, R. 152 58 48N 132 5W
Shethanei L. 153 58 48N 97 50W
Shetland □ 36 60 30N 1 30W
Shetland Is. 36 60 30N 1 30W
Shevaroy Hills 97 11 58N 78 12 E
Shevchenko 83 44 25N 51 20 E
Shewa □ 123 9 33N 38 10 E
Sheyenne 159 47 52N 99 8W
Sheyenne, R. 158 47 40N 98 15W
Shiant Is. 36 57 54N 6 20W
Shiant, Sd. of Scot. 36 57 54N 6 30W
Shibam 91 16 0N 48 36 E
Shibata 112 37 57N 139 20 E
Shiberghan □ 93 35 45N 66 0 E
Shibetsu 112 44 10N 142 23 E
Shibîn El Kôm 122 30 31N 30 55 E
Shibogama L. 150 53 35N 88 15W
Shibukawa 111 36 29N 139 0 E
Shibushi 110 31 25N 131 0 E
Shibushi-Wan 110 31 24N 131 8 E
Shickshinny 162 41 9N 76 9W
Shido 110 34 19N 134 10 E
Shiel, L. 36 56 48N 5 32W
Shield, C. 138 13 20 S 136 20 E
Shieldaig 36 57 31N 5 39W
Shifnal 28 52 40N 2 23W
Shiga-ken □ 111 35 20N 136 0 E
Shigaib 117 15 5N 23 35 E
Shigaraki 111 34 57N 136 2 E
Shihch'eng 109 26 19N 116 15 E
Shihchiachuangi 106 38 2N 114 30 E
Shihch'ien 108 27 30N 108 14 E
Shihchiu Hu 109 31 28N 118 53 E
Shihchu 108 30 4N 108 10 E
Shihch'üan 106 33 3N 108 17 E
Shihhsing 109 24 57N 114 4 E
Shihku 108 26 52N 99 56 E
Shihkuaikou 106 40 42N 110 20 E
Shihlung 109 23 55N 113 35 E
Shihmen 109 29 36N 111 23 E
Shihmenchien 109 29 33N 116 47 E
Shihmien 108 29 20N 102 28 E
Shihping 108 27 2N 108 7 E
Shihp'ing 108 23 43N 102 30 E
Shihshou 109 29 43N 112 26 E
Shihtai 109 30 22N 117 57 E
Shihtien 108 24 44N 99 11 E
Shiht'ouhotzu 107 44 25N 128 41 E
Shihtsuishan 106 39 15N 106 50 E
Shihtsung 108 24 51N 103 59 E
Shiiba 110 32 29N 131 4 E
Shijaku 68 41 21N 19 33 E
Shikarpur, India 94 28 17N 78 7 E
Shikarpur, Pak. 94 27 57N 68 39 E
Shikine-Jima 111 34 19N 139 13 E
Shikohabad 93 27 6N 78 38 E
Shikoku 110 33 30N 133 30 E
Shikoku □ 110 33 30N 133 30 E
Shikoku-Sanchi 110 33 30N 133 30 E
Shilbottle 35 55 23N 1 42W
Shilda 84 51 49N 59 47 E
Shildon 33 54 37N 1 39W
Shilka 77 52 0N 115 55 E
Shilka, R. 77 57 30N 93 18 E
Shillelagh 39 52 46N 6 32W
Shillingstone 28 50 54N 2 15W
Shillington 162 40 18N 75 58W
Shillong 98 25 35N 91 53 E
Shiloh 90 32 4N 35 10 E
Shilovo 81 54 25N 40 57 E
Shima-Hantō 111 34 22N 136 45 E
Shimabara 110 32 48N 130 20 E
Shimada 111 34 49N 138 19 E
Shimane-Hantō 110 35 30N 133 0 E
Shimane-ken □ 110 35 0N 132 30 E
Shimenovsk 77 52 15N 127 30 E
Shimizu 111 35 0N 138 30 E
Shimo-Jima 110 32 15N 130 7 E
Shimo-Koshiki-Jima 110 31 40N 129 43 E
Shimoda 111 34 40N 138 57 E
Shimodate 111 36 20N 139 55 E
Shimoga 97 13 57N 75 32 E
Shimoni 126 4 38 S 39 20 E
Shimonita 111 36 13N 138 47 E
Shimonoseki 110 33 58N 131 0 E
Shimotsuma 111 36 11N 139 58 E
Shimpuru Rapids 128 17 45 S 19 55 E
Shimsha, R. 97 13 15N 76 54 E
Shimsk 80 58 15N 30 50 E
Shin Dand 93 33 12N 62 8 E
Shin, L. 37 58 7N 4 30W
Shin, R. 37 58 0N 4 26W
Shin-Tone-Gawa 111 35 57N 140 27 E
Shingbwiyang 98 26 41N 96 13 E
Shingleton 150 46 33N 86 33W
Shingu 111 33 40N 135 55 E
Shinji 110 35 24N 132 54 E
Shinji Ko 110 35 26N 132 57 E
Shinjō 112 38 46N 140 18 E
Shinkafe 121 13 8N 6 29 E
Shinminato 111 36 47N 137 4 E
Shinonoi 111 36 35N 138 9 E
Shinrone 39 53 0N 7 58W
Shinshiro 111 34 54N 137 30 E
Shinyanga 126 3 45 S 33 27 E
Shinyanga □ 126 3 30 S 33 30 E
Shio-no-Misaki 111 33 25N 135 45 E
Shiogama 112 38 19N 141 1 E
Shiojiri 111 36 6N 137 58 E
Ship I. 159 30 16N 88 55W
Ship Shoal I. 162 37 10N 75 45W
Shipbourne 29 51 13N 0 19 E
Shipdham 29 52 38N 0 53 E
Shipehenski Prokhod 67 42 39N 25 28 E
Shipki La 93 31 45N 78 40 E
Shipley 33 53 50N 1 47W
Shippegan 151 47 45N 64 45W
Shippensburg 156 40 4N 77 32W
Shiprock 161 36 51N 108 45W
Shipston-on-Stour 28 52 4N 1 38W
Shipton-under-Wychwood 28 51 51N 1 35W
Shir Kūh 93 31 45N 53 30 E
Shirabad 85 37 40N 67 1 E
Shirahama 111 33 41N 135 20 E
Shirakawa 111 36 17N 136 56 E
Shirane-San, Gumma, Japan 111 36 48N 139 22 E
Shirane-San, Yamanashi, Japan 111 35 34N 138 9 E
Shiraoi 112 42 33N 141 21 E
Shirati 126 1 10 S 34 0 E
Shiraz 93 29 42N 52 30 E
Shire, R. 127 16 30 S 35 0 E
Shirebrook 33 53 13N 1 11W
Shiresh 85 39 58N 70 59 E
Shirinab, R. 94 29 30N 66 30 E
Shiringushi 81 42 54N 53 56W
Shiriya-Zaki 112 41 25N 141 30 E
Shirol 96 16 47N 74 41 E
Shirpur 96 21 21N 74 57 E
Shirvan 93 37 30N 57 50 E
Shirwa L. = Chilwa L. 127 15 15 S 35 40 E
Shishmanova 67 42 58N 23 12 E
Shishmaref 147 66 15N 166 10W
Shivali, (Sirkall) 97 11 15N 79 41 E
Shivpuri 94 25 18N 77 42 E
Shivta 90 30 53N 34 40 E
Shiwele Ferry 127 11 25 S 28 31 E
Shiyata 122 29 25N 25 7 E
Shizuoka 111 35 0N 138 30 E
Shizuoka-ken □ 111 35 15N 138 40 E
Shklov 80 54 10N 30 15 E
Shkoder = Shkodra 68 42 6N 19 20 E
Shkodra 68 42 6N 19 20 E
Shkodra □ 68 42 5N 19 20 E
Shkumbini, R. 68 41 5N 19 50 E
Shmidt, O. 77 81 0N 91 0 E
Shō Gawa, R. 111 36 47N 137 4 E
Shoa Ghimirra, (Wota) 123 7 4N 35 51 E
Shoal, C. 137 33 52 S 121 10 E
Shoal Lake 153 50 30N 100 35W
Shōbara 110 34 51N 133 1 E
Shōdo-Shima 110 34 30N 134 15 E
Shoeburyness 29 51 31N 0 49 E
Shokpar 85 43 49N 74 21 E
Sholapur 96 17 43N 75 56 E
Shologontsy 77 66 13N 114 14 E
Shomera 90 33 4N 35 17 E
Shōmrōn 90 32 15N 35 13 E
Shona I. 36 56 48N 5 50W
Shongopovi 161 35 49N 110 37W
Shoranur 97 10 46N 76 19 E
Shorapur 96 16 31N 76 48 E
Shoreham-by-Sea 29 50 50N 0 17W
Shortland I. 135 7 0 S 155 45 E
Shoshone, Calif., U.S.A. 163 35 58N 116 16W
Shoshone, Idaho, U.S.A. 160 43 0N 114 27W
Shoshone L. 160 44 0N 111 0W
Shoshone Mts. 160 39 30N 117 30W
Shoshong 125 22 56 S 26 31 E
Shoshoni 160 43 13N 108 5W
Shostka 80 51 57N 33 32 E
Shotts 35 55 49N 3 47W
Shouch'ang 109 29 22N 119 13 E
Shouhsien 109 32 35N 116 48 E
Shoukuang 107 36 53N 118 42 E
Shouning 109 27 26N 119 27 E
Shouyang 106 37 59N 113 9 E
Show Low 161 34 16N 110 0W
Shpola 82 49 1N 31 30 E
Shreveport 159 32 30N 93 50W
Shrewsbury 28 52 42N 2 45W
Shrewton 28 51 11N 1 55W
Shrivardhan 96 18 10N 73 3 E
Shrivenham 28 51 36N 1 39W
Shropshire (□) = Salop 28 52 36N 2 45W
Shrule 38 53 32N 9 7W
Shuangch'eng 107 45 25N 126 20 E
Shuangchiang 108 23 33N 99 45 E
Shuangfeng 109 27 26N 112 10 E
Shuangfeng Tao 109 26 35N 120 8 E
Shuangkou 107 34 3N 117 34 E
Shuangliao 105 43 31N 123 30 E
Shuangpai 108 24 50N 101 36 E
Shuangshantzu 107 40 21N 119 12 E
Shuangyang 107 43 32N 125 40 E
Shuangyashan 105 46 37N 131 22 E
Shuch'eng 109 31 27N 116 57 E
Shugden Gomba 99 29 35N 96 55 E
Shuguri Falls 127 8 33 S 37 22 E
Shuich'eng 108 26 35N 104 54 E
Shuichi 109 27 28N 118 21 E
Shuiyeh 106 36 8N 114 6 E
Shujalpur 94 23 43N 76 40 E
Shulan 107 44 27N 126 57 E
Shumagin Is. 147 55 0N 159 0W
Shumerlya 81 55 30N 46 10 E
Shumikha 84 55 10N 63 15 E
Shunan 109 29 37N 119 0 E
Shunch'ang 109 26 48N 117 47 E
Shungay 83 48 30N 46 45 E
Shungnak 147 66 55N 157 10W
Shunning 99 24 35N 99 50 E
Shunte 109 22 48N 113 17 E
Shuohsien 106 39 19N 112 25 E
Shupka Kunzang 95 34 22N 78 22 E
Shuqra 91 13 22N 45 34 E
Shur, R. 93 28 30N 55 0 E
Shurab 85 40 3N 70 33 E
Shurchi 85 37 59N 67 47 E
Shurkhua 98 22 15N 93 38 E
Shurma 84 56 58N 50 21 E
Shusf 93 31 50N 60 5 E
Shūshtar 92 32 0N 48 50 E
Shuswap L. 152 50 55N 119 3W
Shuweika 90 32 20N 35 1 E
Shuya 81 56 50N 41 28 E
Shuyak I. 147 58 35N 152 30W
Shuzenji 111 34 58N 138 56 E
Shwebo 98 22 30N 95 45 E
Shwegu 98 18 49N 95 26 E
Shwegun 98 17 9N 97 39 E
Shweli Myit 99 23 45N 96 45 E
Shweli, R. 99 23 45N 96 45 E
Shwenyaung 98 20 46N 96 57 E
Shyok 95 34 15N 78 5 E
Shyok, R. 95 34 30N 78 15 E
Si Chon 101 9 0N 99 54 E
Si Kiang = Hsi Chiang, R. 39 22 20N 113 20 E
Si Prachan 100 14 37N 100 9 E
Si Racha 101 13 10N 100 56 E
Siah 92 22 0N 47 0 E
Siahan Range 93 27 30N 64 40 E
Siaksriinderapura 102 0 51N 102 0 E
Sialkot 94 32 32N 74 30 E
Sialsuk 98 23 24N 92 45 E
Siam 140 32 35 S 136 41 E
Siam, G. of 101 11 30N 101 0 E
Siam = Thailand ■ 100 16 0N 102 0 E
Sian = Hsian 106 34 17N 109 0 E
Siantan, P. 101 3 10N 106 15 E
Siareh 93 28 5N 60 20 E
Siargao, I. 103 9 52N 126 3 E
Siari 95 34 55N 76 40 E
Siasi 103 5 34N 120 50 E
Siassi 135 5 40 S 147 51 E
Siátista 68 40 15N 21 33 E
Siau, I. 103 2 50N 125 25 E
Siauliai 80 55 56N 23 15 E
Siaya □ 126 0 0N 34 20 E
Siazan 83 41 3N 48 7 E
Sibâi, Gebel el 122 25 45N 34 10 E
Sibari 65 39 47N 16 27 E
Sibay 84 52 42N 58 39 E
Sibaya, L. 129 27 20 S 32 45 E
Sibbald 153 51 24N 110 10W
Sibenik 63 43 48N 15 54 E
Siberia 77 60 0N 100 0 E
Siberut, I. 102 1 30 S 99 0 E
Sibi 94 29 30N 67 48 E
Sibil 103 4 59 S 140 35 E
Sibiti 124 3 38 S 13 19 E
Sibiu 70 45 45N 24 9 E
Sibiu □ 70 45 50N 24 15 E
Sible Hedingham 29 51 58N 0 37 E
Sibley, Iowa, U.S.A. 158 43 21N 95 43W
Sibley, La., U.S.A. 159 32 34N 93 16W
Sibolga 102 1 50N 98 45 E
Sibret 47 49 58N 5 38 E
Sibsagar 98 27 0N 94 36 E
Sibsey 33 53 3N 0 1 E
Sibuco 103 7 20N 122 10 E
Sibuguey B. 103 7 50N 122 45 E
Sibuko 103 7 20N 122 10 E
Sibut 117 5 52N 19 10 E
Sibutu, I. 102 4 45N 119 30 E
Sibutu Passage 103 4 50N 120 0 E
Sibuyan, I. 103 12 25N 122 40 E
Sicamous 152 50 49N 119 0W
Sicapoo 103 18 9N 121 34 E
Sicasica 154 17 20 S 67 45W
Siccus, R. 140 31 42 S 139 25 E
Sicilia, Canale di 64 37 25N 12 30 E
Sicilia, I. 65 37 30N 14 30 E
Sicily = Sicilia 65 37 30N 14 30 E
Sicuani 174 14 10 S 71 10W
Siculiana 64 37 20N 13 23 E
Sid 63 45 6N 19 16 E
Sidamo □ 123 5 0N 37 50 E
Sidaouet 121 18 34N 8 3 E
Sidaradougou 120 10 42N 4 12W
Sidbury 30 50 43N 3 12W
Siddeburen 46 53 15N 6 52 E

Siddipet	**96**	18 0N	79 0E
Sidensjo	**72**	63 20N	18 20E
Sidéradougou	**120**	10 42N	4 12W
Siderno Marina	**65**	38 16N	16 17E
Sidheros, Ákra	**69**	35 19N	26 19E
Sidhirókastron	**68**	37 20N	21 46E
Sidhpur	**94**	23 56N	71 25E
Sîdi Abd el Rahman	**122**	30 55N	28 41E
Sîdi Barrâni	**122**	31 32N	25 58E
Sidi-Bel-Abbès	**118**	35 13N	0 10W
Sidi Bennour	**118**	32 40N	9 26W
Sidi Haneish	**122**	31 10N	27 35E
Sidi Ifni	**118**	29 29N	10 3W
Sidi Kacem	**118**	34 11N	5 40W
Sīdī Miftāh	**119**	31 8N	16 58E
Sidi Moussa, O.	**118**	33 0N	8 50W
Sidi Omar	**122**	31 24N	24 57E
Sīdī Yahya	**119**	30 55N	16 30E
Sidlaw Hills	**35**	56 32N	3 10W
Sidlesham	**29**	50 46N	0 46W
Sidmouth	**30**	50 40N	3 13W
Sidmouth, C.	**138**	13 25S	143 36E
Sidney, Can.	**152**	48 39N	123 24W
Sidney, Mont., U.S.A.	**158**	47 51N	104 7W
Sidney, N.Y., U.S.A.	**162**	42 18N	75 20W
Sidney, Ohio, U.S.A.	**156**	40 18N	84 6W
Sidoardjo	**103**	7 30S	112 46E
Sidoktaya	**98**	20 27N	94 15E
Sidon, (Saida)	**92**	33 38N	35 28E
Sidra, G. of = Khalīj Surt	**61**	31 40N	18 30E
Siedlce	**54**	52 10N	22 20E
Siedlce □	**54**	52 0N	22 0E
Siegburg	**48**	50 48N	7 12E
Siegen	**48**	50 52N	8 2E
Siem Pang	**100**	14 7N	106 23E
Siem Reap	**100**	13 20N	103 52E
Siena	**63**	43 20N	11 20E
Sieniawa	**54**	50 11N	22 38E
Sieradź	**54**	51 37N	18 41E
Sieradź □	**54**	51 30N	19 0E
Sieraków	**54**	52 39N	16 2E
Sierck-les-Bains	**43**	49 26N	6 20E
Sierpc	**54**	52 55N	19 43E
Sierpe, Bocas de la	**174**	10 0N	61 30W
Sierra Alta	**58**	40 31N	1 30W
Sierra Blanca	**161**	31 11N	105 17W
Sierra Blanca, mt.	**161**	33 20N	105 54W
Sierra City	**160**	39 34N	120 42W
Sierra Colorado	**176**	40 35S	67 50W
Sierra de Gádor	**59**	36 57N	2 45W
Sierra de Yeguas	**57**	37 7N	4 52W
Sierra Gorda	**172**	23 0S	69 15W
Sierra Leone ■	**120**	9 0N	12 0W
Sierra Majada	**164**	27 19N	103 42W
Sierre	**50**	46 17N	7 31E
Sífnos	**69**	37 0N	24 45E
Sifton	**153**	51 21N	100 8W
Sifton Pass	**152**	57 52N	126 15W
Sig	**118**	35 32N	0 12W
Sigaboy	**103**	6 39N	126 10E
Sigdal	**71**	60 4N	9 38E
Sigean	**44**	43 2N	2 58E
Sighetul Marmatiei	**70**	47 57N	23 52E
Sighişoara	**70**	46 12N	24 50E
Sighty Crag	**35**	55 8N	2 37W
Sigli	**102**	5 25N	96 0E
Siglufjörður	**74**	66 12N	18 55W
Sigma	**103**	11 29N	122 40E
Sigmaringen	**49**	48 5N	9 13E
Signakhi	**83**	40 52N	45 57E
Signau	**50**	46 56N	7 45E
Signy I.	**13**	60 45S	46 30W
Signy-l'Abbaye	**43**	49 40N	4 25E
Sigsig	**174**	3 0S	78 50W
Sigtuna	**72**	59 36N	17 44E
Sigüenza	**58**	41 3N	2 40W
Siguiri	**120**	11 31N	9 10W
Sigulda	**80**	57 10N	24 55E
Sigurd	**161**	38 57N	112 0W
Sihanoukville = Kompong Som	**101**	10 40N	103 30E
Si'ir	**90**	31 35N	35 9E
Siirt	**92**	37 57N	41 55E
Sijarira, Ra.	**127**	17 36S	27 45E
Sijsele	**13**	51 12N	3 20E
Sikandarabad	**94**	28 30N	77 39E
Sikandra Rao	**93**	27 43N	78 24E
Sikar	**94**	27 39N	75 10E
Sikasso	**120**	11 7N	5 35W
Sikerete	**128**	19 0S	20 48E
Sikeston	**159**	36 52N	89 35W
Sikhote Alin, Khrebet	**77**	46 0N	136 0E
Sikiá.	**68**	40 2N	23 56E
Sikinos, I.	**69**	36 40N	25 8E
Sikionia	**69**	38 0N	22 44E
Sikkani Chief, R.	**152**	57 47N	122 15W
Sikkim ■	**98**	27 50N	88 50E
Siklós	**53**	45 50N	18 19E
Sikoro	**120**	12 19N	7 8W
Sikqo	**101**	7 34N	99 21E
Sil, R.	**56**	42 23N	7 30W
Sila, La, Mts.	**65**	39 15N	16 35E
Silacayoapán	**165**	17 30N	98 9W
Silandro	**62**	46 38N	10 48E
Sîlat adh Dhahr	**90**	32 19N	35 11E
Silba	**63**	44 24N	14 41E
Silba, I.	**63**	44 24N	14 41E
Silchar	**98**	24 49N	92 48E
Silcox	**153**	57 12N	94 10W
Silenrieux	**47**	50 14N	4 27E
Siler City	**157**	35 44N	79 30W
Sileru, R.	**96**	18 0N	82 0E
Silesia = Slask	**54**	51 0N	16 30E
Silet	**118**	22 44N	4 37E
Silgarhi Doti	**95**	29 15N	82 0E
Silghat	**98**	26 35N	93 0E
Silifke	**92**	36 22N	33 58E
Siliguri	**98**	26 45N	88 25E
Silíqua	**64**	39 20N	8 49E
Silistra	**67**	44 6N	27 19E
Siljan, L.	**72**	60 55N	14 45E
Silkeborg	**73**	56 10N	9 32E
Sillajhuay, Cordillera	**174**	19 40S	68 40W
Sillé-le Guillaume	**42**	48 10N	0 8W
Silloth	**32**	54 53N	3 25W
Siloam Springs	**159**	36 15N	94 31W
Silogui	**102**	1 10S	98 46E
Silsbee	**159**	30 20N	94 8W
Silsden	**32**	53 55N	1 55W
Silute	**80**	55 21N	21 33E
Silva Porto = Bié	**125**	12 22S	16 55E
Silvaplana	**51**	46 28N	9 48E
Silver City, Calif., U.S.A.	**160**	36 19N	119 44W
Silver City, N. Mex., U.S.A.	**161**	32 50N	108 18W
Silver Cr., R.	**160**	43 30N	119 30W
Silver Creek	**156**	42 33N	79 9W
Silver L.	**163**	38 39N	120 6W
Silver Lake, Calif., U.S.A.	**163**	35 21N	116 7W
Silver Lake, Oreg., U.S.A.	**160**	43 9N	121 4W
Silver Springs	**162**	39 2N	77 3W
Silverhojden	**72**	60 2N	15 0E
Silvermine, Mts.	**39**	52 47N	8 15W
Silvermines	**39**	52 48N	8 15W
Silverpeak, Ra.	**163**	37 35N	117 45W
Silverstone	**28**	52 5N	1 3W
Silverton, Austral.	**140**	31 52S	141 10E
Silverton, U.K.	**30**	50 49N	3 29W
Silverton, Colo., U.S.A.	**161**	37 51N	107 45W
Silverton, Tex., U.S.A.	**159**	34 30N	101 16W
Silves	**57**	37 11N	8 26W
Silvia	**174**	2 37N	76 21W
Silvies, R.	**160**	43 57N	119 5W
Silvolde	**46**	51 55N	6 23E
Silvretta Gruppe	**51**	46 50N	10 6E
Silwa Bahari	**122**	24 45N	32 55E
Silwan	**90**	31 59N	35 15E
Silwani	**93**	23 18N	78 27E
Silz	**52**	47 16N	10 56E
Sim, C.	**118**	31 26N	9 51W
Simanggang	**102**	1 15N	111 25E
Simão Dias	**170**	10 44S	37 49W
Simard, L.	**150**	47 40N	78 40W
Simarun	**93**	31 16N	51 40E
Simba	**126**	1 41S	34 12E
Simbach	**49**	48 16N	13 3E
Simbo	**126**	4 51S	29 41E
Simcoe	**150**	42 50N	80 20W
Simcoe, L.	**150**	44 25N	79 20W
Simenga	**77**	62 50N	107 55E
Simeon	**47**	50 45N	5 36E
Simeulue, I.	**102**	2 45N	95 45E
Simferopol	**82**	44 55N	34 3E
Sími	**69**	36 35N	27 50E
Simi, I.	**69**	36 35N	27 50E
Simi Valley	**163**	34 16N	118 47W
Simikot	**95**	30 0N	81 50E
Simití	**174**	7 58N	73 57W
Simitli	**66**	41 52N	23 7E
Simla	**94**	31 2N	77 15E
Simleu-Silvaniei	**70**	47 17N	22 50E
Simme, R.	**50**	46 38N	7 25E
Simmern	**48**	49 59N	7 32E
Simmie	**153**	49 56N	108 6W
Simmler	**163**	35 21N	119 59W
Simões	**170**	7 30S	40 49W
Simojärvi	**74**	66 5N	27 10E
Simojoki	**74**	65 46N	25 15E
Simojovel	**165**	17 12N	92 38W
Simonette, R.	**152**	55 9N	118 15W
Simonsbath	**28**	51 8N	3 45W
Simonside, Mt.	**35**	55 17N	2 0W
Simonstown	**128**	34 14S	18 26E
Simontornya	**53**	46 45N	18 33E
Simpang	**101**	4 50N	100 40E
Simpleveld	**47**	50 50N	5 58E
Simplício Mendes	**170**	7 51S	41 54W
Simplon	**50**	46 12N	8 4E
Simplon Pass	**50**	46 15N	8 0E
Simplon Tunnel	**50**	46 15N	8 7E
Simpson Des.	**138**	25 0S	137 0E
Simpungdong	**107**	41 56N	129 29E
Simrishamn	**73**	55 33N	14 22E
Simsbury	**162**	41 52N	72 48W
Simunjan	**102**	1 25N	110 45E
Sîmŭrtin	**70**	46 19N	25 58E
Simushir, Ostrov	**77**	46 50N	152 30E
Sina, R.	**97**	18 25N	75 28E
Sinaai	**47**	51 9N	4 2E
Sinabang	**102**	2 30N	46 30E
Sinai = Es Sînâ'	**122**	29 0N	34 0E
Sinai, Mt. = Musa, G.	**122**	28 32N	33 59E
Sinaia	**70**	45 21N	25 38E
Sinaloa	**164**	25 50N	108 20W
Sinaloa □	**164**	25 0N	107 30W
Sinalunga	**63**	43 12N	11 43E
Sinamaica	**174**	11 5N	71 51W
Sînandrei	**70**	45 52N	21 13E
Sīnāwan	**119**	31 0N	10 30E
Sinbaung we	**98**	19 43N	95 10E
Sinbo	**98**	24 46N	97 3E
Sincé	**174**	9 15N	75 9W
Sincelejo	**174**	9 18N	75 24W
Sinchangni, Kor., N.	**107**	40 7N	128 28E
Sinchangni, Kor., N.	**107**	39 24N	126 8E
Sinclair	**160**	41 47N	107 35W
Sinclair Mills	**152**	54 5N	121 40W
Sinclair's B.	**37**	58 30N	3 0W
Sincorá, Serra do	**171**	13 30S	41 0W
Sind, R.	**95**	34 18N	75 0E
Sind Sagar Doab	**94**	32 0N	71 30E
Sinda	**127**	17 28S	25 51E
Sindal	**73**	57 28N	10 10E
Sindangan	**103**	8 10N	123 5E
Sindangbarang	**103**	7 27S	107 9E
Sindjai	**103**	5 0S	120 20E
Sinelnikovo	**82**	48 25N	35 30E
Sines	**57**	37 56N	8 51W
Sines, Cabo de	**57**	37 58N	8 53W
Sineu	**58**	39 39N	3 0E
Sinewit, Mt.	**135**	4 44S	152 2E
Sinfra	**120**	6 35N	5 56W
Sing Buri	**100**	14 53N	100 25E
Singa	**123**	13 10N	33 57E
Singanallurt	**97**	11 2N	77 1E
Singaparna	**103**	7 23S	108 4E
Singapore ■	**101**	1 17N	103 51E
Singapore, Straits of	**101**	1 15N	104 0E
Singaraja	**102**	8 15S	115 10E
Singen	**49**	47 45N	8 50E
Singida	**126**	4 49S	34 48E
Singida □	**126**	6 0S	34 30E
Singitikós, Kólpos	**68**	40 6N	24 0E
Singkaling Hkamti	**98**	26 0N	95 45E
Singkang	**103**	4 8S	120 1E
Singkawang	**102**	1 0N	109 5E
Singkep, I.	**102**	0 30S	104 20E
Singleton, Austral.	**141**	32 33S	151 10E
Singleton, U.K.	**29**	50 55N	0 45W
Singleton, Mt.	**137**	29 27S	117 15E
Singö	**72**	60 12N	18 45E
Singoli	**94**	25 0N	75 16E
Singora = Songkhla	**101**	7 12N	100 36E
Singosan	**107**	38 52N	127 25E
Sinhailian (Lienyünchiangshih)	**107**	34 31N	118 15E
Sinhung	**107**	40 11N	127 34E
Siniatsikon, Óros	**68**	40 25N	21 35E
Siniscóla	**64**	40 35N	9 40E
Sinj	**63**	43 42N	16 39E
Sinjajevina, Planina	**66**	42 57N	19 22E
Sinjil	**90**	32 3N	35 15E
Sinkat	**122**	18 55N	36 49E
Sinkiang-Uighur □	**105**	42 0N	86 0E
Sinmark	**107**	38 25N	126 14E
Sinnai Sardinia	**64**	39 18N	9 13E
Sinnar	**96**	19 48N	74 0E
Sinni, R.	**65**	40 6N	16 15E
Sinnicolau-Maré	**70**	46 5N	20 39E
Sinnûris	**122**	29 26N	30 31E
Sinoe, L.	**70**	44 35N	28 50E
Sinoia	**127**	17 20S	30 8E
Sinop	**92**	42 1N	35 11E
Sinop, R.	**82**	42 1N	35 2E
Sinpo	**107**	40 0N	128 13E
Sins	**51**	47 12N	8 24E
Sinskoye	**77**	61 8N	126 48E
Sint Annaland	**47**	51 36N	4 6E
Sint Annaparochie	**46**	53 16N	5 40E
Sint-Denijs	**47**	50 45N	3 23E
Sint Eustatius, I.	**167**	17 30N	62 59W
Sint-Genesius-Rode	**47**	50 45N	4 22E
Sint-Gillis-Waas	**47**	51 13N	4 6E
Sint-Huibrechts-Lille	**47**	51 13N	5 29E
Sint-Katelinje-Waver	**47**	51 5N	4 32E
Sint-Kruis	**47**	51 13N	3 15E
Sint-Laureins	**47**	51 14N	3 32E
Sint Maarten, I.	**167**	18 4N	63 4W
Sint-Michiels	**47**	51 11N	3 15E
Sint Nicolaasga	**46**	52 55N	5 45E
Sint Niklaas	**47**	51 10N	4 9E
Sint Oedenrode	**47**	51 35N	5 29E
Sint Pancras	**46**	52 40N	4 48E
Sint-Pauwels	**47**	51 11N	3 57E
Sint Philipsland	**47**	51 37N	4 10E
Sint Truiden	**47**	50 48N	5 12E
Sint Willebroad	**47**	51 33N	4 33E
Sîntana Ano	**70**	46 20N	21 30E
Sintang	**102**	0 5N	111 35E
Sintjohannesga	**46**	52 55N	5 52E
Sinton	**159**	28 1N	97 30W
Sintra	**57**	38 47N	9 25W
Sinŭiju	**107**	40 5N	124 24E
Sinuk	**147**	64 42N	166 22W
Sinyang = Hsinyang	**109**	32 10N	114 6E
Sinyukha, R.	**82**	48 31N	30 31E
Siófok	**53**	46 54N	18 4E
Sióma	**128**	16 25S	23 28E
Sion	**50**	46 14N	7 20E
Sion Mills	**38**	54 47N	7 29W
Sioua, El Wâhât es	**122**	29 10N	25 30E
Sioux City	**158**	42 32N	96 25W
Sioux Falls	**158**	43 35N	96 40W
Sioux Lookout	**150**	50 10N	91 50W
Sip Song Chaw Thai, reg.	**100**	21 30N	103 30E
Sipan	**66**	42 45N	17 52E
Sipera, I.	**102**	2 18S	99 40E
Sipiwesk L.	**153**	55 5N	97 35W
Sipul	**138**	5 50S	148 28E
Siquia, R.	**166**	12 30N	84 30W
Siquijor, I.	**103**	9 12N	123 45E
Siquirres	**166**	10 6N	83 30W
Siquisique	**174**	10 34N	69 42W
Sir Edward Pellew Group	**138**	15 40S	137 10E
Sir Graham Moore Is.	**136**	13 53S	126 34E
Sir Samuel Mt.	**137**	27 45S	120 40E
Sir Thomas, Mt.	**137**	27 10S	129 45E
Sira	**97**	13 41N	76 49E
Sira, R.	**71**	58 43N	6 40E
Siracusa	**65**	37 4N	15 17E
Sirajganj	**95**	24 25N	89 47E
Sirake	**138**	9 1S	141 2E
Sirakoro	**120**	12 41N	9 14W
Sirasso	**120**	9 16N	6 6W
Siret	**70**	47 55N	26 5E
Siret, R.	**70**	47 58N	26 5E
Siria	**66**	46 16N	21 38E
Sirinhaém	**171**	8 35S	35 7W
Sirkall (Shivali)	**97**	11 15N	79 41E
Sirna, I.	**69**	36 22N	26 42E
Sirnach	**51**	47 28N	8 59E
Sirohi	**94**	24 52N	72 53E
Siroki Brijeg	**66**	43 21N	17 36E
Sironj	**94**	24 5N	77 45E
Siros	**69**	37 28N	24 57E
Siros, I.	**69**	37 28N	24 57E
Sirretta Pk.	**163**	35 56N	118 19W
Sirsa	**94**	29 33N	75 4E
Sirsi	**97**	14 40N	74 49E
Siruela	**57**	38 58N	5 3W
Sisak	**63**	45 30N	16 21E
Sisaket	**100**	15 8N	104 23E
Sisante	**59**	39 25N	2 12W
Sisargas, Islas	**56**	43 21N	8 50W
Sishen	**128**	27 55S	22 59E
Sisipuk I.	**153**	55 40N	102 0W
Sisipuk L.	**153**	55 45N	101 50W
Sisophon	**100**	13 31N	102 59E
Sissach	**50**	47 27N	7 48E
Sisseton	**158**	45 43N	97 3W
Sissonne	**43**	49 34N	3 51E
Sistan-Baluchistan □	**93**	27 0N	62 0E
Sistema Central	**56**	40 40N	5 55W
Sistema Ibérico	**58**	41 0N	2 10W
Sisteron	**45**	44 12N	5 57E
Sisters	**160**	44 21N	121 32W
Sitamarhi	**95**	26 37N	85 30E
Sitapur	**95**	27 38N	80 45E
Siteki	**129**	26 32S	31 58E
Sitges	**58**	41 17N	1 47E
Sithoniá	**68**	40 0N	23 45E
Sitía	**69**	35 13N	26 6E
Sítio da Abadia	**171**	14 48S	46 16W
Sitka	**147**	57 9N	134 58W
Sitona	**123**	14 25N	37 23E
Sitoti	**128**	23 15S	23 40E
Sitra	**122**	28 40N	26 53E
Sittang Myit, R.	**99**	18 20N	96 45E
Sittang, R.	**98**	17 10N	96 58E
Sittard	**47**	51 0N	5 52E
Sittaung	**98**	24 10N	94 35E
Sittensen	**48**	53 17N	9 32E
Sittingbourne	**29**	51 20N	0 43E
Sittwe	**99**	20 15N	92 45E
Situbondo	**103**	7 45S	114 0E
Siuch'uan	**109**	26 20N	114 30E
Siuna	**166**	13 37N	84 45W
Sivaganga	**97**	9 50N	78 28E
Sivagiri	**97**	9 16N	77 26E
Sivakasi	**97**	9 24N	77 47E
Sivand	**93**	30 5N	52 55E
Sivas	**92**	39 43N	36 58E
Siverek	**92**	37 50N	39 25E
Sivrihisar	**92**	39 30N	31 35E
Sivry	**47**	50 10N	4 12E
Siwa	**122**	29 11N	25 31E
Siwalik Range	**95**	28 0N	83 0E
Siwan	**95**	26 13N	84 27E
Sixmile Cross	**38**	54 34N	7 7W
Sixmilebridge	**39**	52 45N	8 46W
Siyâl, Jazâ'ir	**122**	22 49N	36 6E
Siyana	**94**	28 37N	78 6E
Sizewell	**29**	52 13N	1 38E
Sjaelland	**73**	55 30N	11 30E
Sjaellands Odde	**73**	56 0N	11 15E
Själevad	**72**	63 18N	18 36E
Sjarinska Banja	**66**	42 45N	21 38E
Sjenica	**66**	43 16N	20 0E
Sjernaröy	**71**	59 15N	5 50E
Sjoa	**71**	61 41N	9 40E
Sjöbo	**73**	55 37N	13 45E
Sjöholt	**71**	62 27N	6 52E
Sjönsta	**74**	67 10N	16 3E
Sjösa	**73**	58 47N	17 4E
Skadovsk	**82**	46 17N	32 52E
Skælskör	**73**	55 16N	11 18E
Skagafjörður	**74**	65 54N	19 35W
Skagastölstindane, mt.	**75**	61 25N	8 10E
Skagen	**75**	68 37N	14 27E
Skagen, pt.	**73**	57 43N	10 35E
Skagern	**72**	59 0N	14 20E
Skagerrak	**73**	57 30N	9 0E
Skagway	**147**	59 30N	135 20W
Skaidi	**74**	70 26N	24 30E
Skala Podolskaya	**82**	48 50N	26 15E
Skalat	**80**	49 23N	25 55E
Skalbmierz	**54**	56 22N	12 30E
Skalderviken	**73**	56 22N	12 30E
Skalicd	**53**	48 50N	17 15E
Skallingen, Odde	**73**	55 32N	8 13E
Skalni Dol = Kamenyak	**67**	43 24N	26 57E
Skals	**73**	56 34N	9 24E
Skanderborg	**73**	56 2N	9 55E
Skaneateles	**162**	42 57N	76 26W

Skaneateles L **Sollentuna**

Skaneateles L.	**162**	42 51N	76 22W
Skånevik	**71**	59 43N	5 53 E
Skanninge	**73**	58 24N	15 5 E
Skanör	**73**	55 24N	12 50 E
Skanor	**73**	55 24N	12 50 E
Skantzoúra I.	**69**	39 5N	24 6 E
Skara	**73**	58 25N	13 30 E
Skaraborgs län □	**73**	58 20N	13 30 E
Skarblacka	**73**	58 36N	15 50 E
Skardhö	**71**	62 30N	8 47 E
Skardu	**95**	35 20N	75 35 E
Skaresta	**73**	58 26N	16 22 E
Skarszewy	**54**	54 4N	18 25 E
Skarvane, Mt.	**71**	63 18N	11 27 E
Skarzysko Kamienna	**54**	51 7N	20 52 E
Skatöy	**71**	50 50N	9 30 E
Skattungbyn	**72**	61 10N	14 56 E
Skaw (Grenen)	**73**	57 46N	10 34 E
Skaw Taing	**36**	60 23N	0 57W
Skebo	**72**	59 58N	18 37 E
Skebokvarn	**72**	59 7N	16 45 E
Skeena Mts.	**152**	56 40N	128 30W
Skeena, R.	**152**	54 9N	130 5W
Skeggjastadir	**74**	66 3N	14 50W
Skegness	**33**	53 9N	0 20 E
Skeldon	**174**	6 0N	57 20W
Skellefte älv	**74**	65 30N	18 30 E
Skellefteå	**74**	64 45N	20 58 E
Skelleftehamn	**74**	64 41N	21 14 E
Skellig Rocks	**39**	51 47N	10 32W
Skellingthorpe	**33**	53 14N	0 37W
Skelmersdale	**32**	53 34N	2 49W
Skelmorlie	**34**	55 52N	4 53W
Skelton, Cleveland., U.K.	**33**	54 33N	0 59W
Skelton, Cumb., U.K.	**32**	54 42N	2 50W
Skender Vakuf	**66**	44 29N	17 22 E
Skene	**73**	57 30N	12 37 E
Skerries, Rks.	**38**	55 14N	6 40W
Skerries, The	**31**	53 27N	4 40W
Skhirra, La = Cekhira	**119**	34 20N	10 5 E
Skhíza, I.	**69**	36 41N	20 40 E
Skhoinoúsa, I.	**69**	36 53N	25 31 E
Ski	**71**	59 43N	10 52 E
Skíathos, I.	**69**	39 12N	23 30 E
Skibbereen	**39**	51 33N	9 16W
Skiddaw, Mt.	**32**	54 39N	3 9W
Skidegate, Inlet	**48**	53 20N	132 0W
Skien	**71**	59 12N	9 35 E
Skierniewice	**54**	51 58N	20 19 E
Skikda	**119**	36 50N	6 58 E
Skillingaryd	**73**	57 27N	14 5 E
Skillinge	**73**	55 30N	14 16 E
Skillingmark	**72**	59 48N	120 1 E
Skinari, Ákra	**69**	37 56N	20 40 E
Skipness	**34**	55 46N	5 20W
Skipsea	**33**	53 58N	0 13W
Skipton, Austral.	**140**	37 39 S	143 21 E
Skipton, U.K.	**32**	53 57N	2 1W
Skirild	**73**	55 58N	8 53 E
Skirmish Pt.	**138**	11 59 S	134 17 E
Skiropoúla, I.	**69**	38 50N	24 21 E
Skíros	**69**	38 55N	24 34 E
Skíros, I.	**69**	38 55N	24 34 E
Skivarp	**73**	55 26N	13 34 E
Skive	**73**	56 33N	9 2 E
Skjåk	**71**	61 52N	8 22 E
Skjálfandafljót	**74**	65 15N	17 25W
Skjálfandi	**74**	66 5N	17 30W
Skjeberg	**71**	59 12N	11 12 E
Skjern	**73**	55 57N	8 30 E
Skjönne	**71**	60 16N	9 1 E
Skoczów	**54**	49 49N	18 45 E
Skodje	**71**	62 30N	6 43 E
Skofja Loka	**63**	46 9N	14 19 E
Skoger	**71**	59 42N	10 16 E
Skoghall	**72**	59 20N	13 30 E
Skoghult	**73**	56 59N	15 55 E
Skokholm, I.	**31**	51 42N	5 16W
Skoki	**54**	52 40N	17 11 E
Skole	**80**	49 3N	23 30 E
Skomer, I.	**31**	51 44N	5 19W
Skonsberg	**72**	62 25N	17 21 E
Skópelos	**69**	39 9N	23 47 E
Skópelos, I.	**69**	39 9N	23 47 E
Skopin	**81**	53 55N	39 32 E
Skopje	**66**	42 1N	21 32 E
Skorcz	**54**	43 47N	18 30 E
Skorped	**72**	63 23N	17 55 E
Skotfoss	**71**	59 12N	9 30 E
Skoudas	**80**	56 21N	21 45 E
Skövde	**75**	58 15N	13 59 E
Skovorodino	**77**	54 0N	125 0 E
Skowhegan	**151**	44 49N	69 40W
Skowman	**153**	51 58N	99 35W
Skradin	**63**	43 52N	15 53 E
Skreanäs	**73**	56 52N	12 35 E
Skudeneshavn	**71**	59 10N	5 10 E
Skull	**39**	51 32N	9 40W
Skultorp	**73**	58 24N	13 51 E
Skulyany	**82**	47 19N	27 39 E
Skunk, R.	**158**	40 42N	91 7W
Skurup	**73**	55 28N	13 30 E
Skutskär	**73**	60 37N	17 25 E
Skvira	**82**	49 44N	29 32 E
Skwaner, Pegunungan	**102**	1 0 S	112 30 E
Skwierzyna	**54**	52 46N	15 30 E
Skye, I.	**36**	57 15N	6 10W
Skykomish	**160**	47 43N	121 16W
Skyros (Skiros), L.	**69**	38 52N	24 37 E
Slagelse	**73**	55 23N	11 19 E
Slagharen	**46**	52 37N	6 34 E
Slaidburn	**32**	53 57N	2 28W
Slaley	**35**	54 55N	2 4W
Slamannon	**140**	32 1 S	143 41 E
Slamet, G.	**102**	7 16 S	109 8 E
Slane	**38**	53 42N	6 32W
Slaney, R.	**39**	52 52N	6 45W
Slangerup	**73**	55 50N	12 11 E
Slănic	**70**	45 14N	25 58 E
Slankamen	**66**	45 8N	20 15 E
Slano	**66**	42 48N	17 53 E
Slantsy	**80**	59 7N	28 5 E
Slany	**52**	50 13N	14 6 E
Slask	**54**	51 25N	16 0 E
Slatbaken	**73**	58 28N	16 30 E
Slate Is.	**150**	48 40N	87 0W
Slatina	**70**	44 28N	24 22 E
Slatington	**162**	40 45N	75 37W
Slaton	**159**	33 27N	101 38W
Slave Coast	**121**	6 0N	2 30 E
Slave Lake	**152**	55 17N	114 50W
Slave Pt.	**152**	61 11N	114 56W
Slave, R.	**152**	61 18N	113 39W
Slavgorod	**76**	53 10N	78 50 E
Slavinja	**66**	43 14N	22 50 E
Slavkov (Austerlitz)	**53**	49 10N	16 52 E
Slavnoye	**80**	54 24N	29 15 E
Slavonski Brod	**66**	45 11N	18 0 E
Slavonski Pozega	**66**	45 20N	17 40 E
Slavuta	**80**	50 15N	27 2 E
Slavyans	**82**	48 55N	37 30 E
Slavyansk	**82**	45 15N	38 11 E
Sława	**54**	51 52N	16 2 E
Sławno	**54**	54 20N	16 41 E
Sławoborze	**54**	53 55N	15 42 E
Slea Hd.	**39**	52 7N	10 30W
Sleaford	**33**	53 0N	0 22W
Sleaford B.	**139**	34 55 S	135 45 E
Sleat, Pt. of	**36**	57 1N	6 0W
Sleat, Sd. of	**36**	57 5N	5 47W
Sledmere	**33**	54 4N	0 35W
Sleeper, Is.	**149**	56 50N	80 30W
Sleepers, The	**149**	58 30N	81 0W
Sleepy Eye	**158**	44 15N	94 45W
Sleidinge	**47**	51 8N	3 41 E
Sleights	**33**	54 27N	0 40W
Sleipner, gasfield	**19**	58 30N	1 48 E
Sleman	**103**	7 40 S	110 20 E
Slemmestad	**71**	59 47N	10 30 E
Slemon L.	**152**	63 13N	116 4W
Slesin	**54**	52 22N	18 14 E
Sletterhage, Kap	**73**	56 7N	10 31 E
Slide Mt.	**162**	42 0N	74 23W
Slidell	**159**	30 20N	89 48W
Sliedrecht	**46**	51 50N	4 45 E
Slieve Anierin	**38**	54 5N	7 58W
Slieve Aughty	**39**	53 4N	8 30W
Slieve Bernagh	**39**	52 50N	8 30W
Slieve Bloom	**39**	53 4N	7 40W
Slieve Callan	**39**	52 51N	9 16W
Slieve Donard	**38**	54 10N	5 57W
Slieve Felim	**39**	52 40N	8 20W
Slieve Gamph	**38**	54 6N	9 0W
Slieve Gullion	**38**	54 8N	6 26W
Slieve League	**38**	54 40N	8 42W
Slieve Mish	**39**	52 12N	9 50W
Slieve Miskish	**39**	51 40N	10 10W
Slieve More	**38**	54 1N	10 3W
Slieve Snaght	**38**	54 59N	8 7W
Slieve Tooey	**38**	54 46N	8 39W
Slievenamon Mt.	**39**	52 25N	7 37W
Sligachan	**36**	57 17N	6 10W
Sligo	**38**	54 17N	8 28W
Sligo □	**38**	54 10N	8 35W
Sligo B.	**38**	54 20N	8 40W
Slikkerveer	**46**	51 53N	4 36 E
Slioch, mt.	**36**	57 40N	5 20W
Slipje	**47**	51 9N	2 51 E
Slite	**75**	57 42N	18 48 E
Sliven	**67**	42 42N	26 19 E
Slivnitsa	**66**	42 50N	23 0 E
Sljeme, mt.	**63**	45 57N	15 58 E
Słupsk □	**54**	54 15N	17 30 E
Sloansville	**162**	42 45N	74 22W
Slobodskoy	**84**	58 40N	50 6 E
Slobozia, Ialomiţa, Rumania	**70**	44 34N	27 23 E
Slobozia, Valahia, Rumania	**70**	44 30N	25 14 E
Slocan	**152**	49 48N	117 28W
Slochteren	**46**	53 12N	6 48 E
Slochteren-Groningen, gasfield	**19**	53 10N	6 45 E
Slöinge	**73**	56 51N	12 42 E
Słomniki	**54**	50 16N	20 4 E
Slonim	**80**	53 4N	25 19 E
Slotermeer	**46**	52 55N	5 38 E
Slough	**29**	51 30N	0 35W
Sloughhouse	**163**	38 26N	121 12W
Slovakia □	**53**	48 30N	19 0 E
Slovenia = Slovenija	**63**	45 58N	14 30 E
Slovenija □	**63**	45 58N	14 30 E
Slovenska Bistrica	**63**	46 24N	15 35 E
Slovenske Krusnohorie	**53**	48 45N	20 0 E
Slovenské Rhudhorie	**52**	48 45N	19 0 E
Slubice	**54**	52 22N	14 35 E
Sluis	**47**	51 18N	3 23 E
Slunchev Bryag	**67**	42 40N	27 41 E
Slunj	**63**	45 6N	15 33 E
Słupca	**54**	52 15N	17 52 E
Słupsk	**54**	54 30N	17 3 E
Slurry	**128**	25 49 S	25 42 E
Slyne Hd.	**38**	53 25N	10 10W
Slyudyanka	**77**	51 40N	103 30 E
Smål-Taberg	**73**	57 42N	14 5 E
Smålandsfarvandet	**73**	55 10N	11 20 E
Smalandsstenar	**73**	57 9N	13 24 E
Smålandstarvandet	**73**	55 10N	11 20 E
Smalltree L.	**153**	61 0N	105 0W
Smallwood Reservoir	**151**	54 20N	63 10W
Smara	**118**	26 48N	11 31W
Smarje	**63**	46 15N	15 34 E
Smart Syndicate Dam	**128**	30 45 S	23 10 E
Smeaton	**153**	53 30N	105 49W
Smedberg	**73**	58 35N	12 0 E
Smederevo	**66**	44 40N	20 57 E
Smedstorp	**73**	55 38N	13 58 E
Smela	**82**	49 30N	32 0 E
Smerwick Harb.	**39**	52 12N	10 23W
Smethwick	**28**	52 29N	1 58W
Smidovich	**77**	48 36N	133 49 E
Smilde	**46**	52 58N	6 28 E
Smiley	**153**	51 38N	109 29W
Smilyan	**67**	41 29N	24 46 E
Smith	**152**	55 10N	114 0W
Smith Arm	**152**	66 15N	123 0W
Smith Center	**158**	39 50N	98 50W
Smith I.	**162**	38 0N	76 0W
Smith, R.	**152**	59 34N	126 30W
Smith Sund	**12**	78 30N	74 0W
Smithborough	**38**	54 13N	7 8W
Smithburne, R.	**138**	17 3 S	140 57 E
Smithers	**152**	54 45N	127 10W
Smithfield, U.K.	**32**	54 59N	2 51W
Smithfield, U.S.A.	**157**	35 31N	78 16W
Smith's Falls	**150**	44 55N	76 0W
Smithton, N.S.W., Austral.	**139**	31 0 S	152 48 E
Smithton, Tas., Austral.	**138**	40 53 S	145 6 E
Smithtown	**141**	30 58 S	152 56 E
Smithville	**159**	30 2N	97 12W
Smjörfjöll	**74**	65 30N	15 42W
Smoky Bay	**139**	32 22 S	133 56 E
Smoky Falls	**150**	50 4N	82 10W
Smoky Hill, R.	**158**	38 45N	98 0W
Smoky Lake	**152**	54 10N	112 30W
Smola	**71**	63 23N	8 3 E
Smolensk	**80**	54 45N	32 0 E
Smolikas, Óros	**68**	40 9N	20 58 E
Smolnik	**53**	48 43N	20 44 E
Smolyan	**67**	41 36N	24 38 E
Smooth Rock Falls	**150**	49 17N	81 37W
Smoothstone L.	**153**	54 40N	106 50W
Smorgon	**80**	54 28N	26 24 E
Smulţi	**70**	45 57N	27 44 E
Smyadovo	**67**	43 2N	27 1 E
Smyrna	**162**	39 18N	75 36W
Smyrna = Izmir	**92**	38 25N	27 8 E
Snaefell	**30**	54 18N	4 26W
Snaefells Jökull	**74**	64 45N	23 25W
Snainton	**33**	54 14N	0 33W
Snaith	**33**	53 42N	1 1W
Snake I.	**141**	38 47 S	146 33 E
Snake L.	**153**	55 32N	106 35W
Snake, R.	**160**	46 31N	118 50W
Snake Ra., Mts.	**160**	39 0N	114 30W
Snake River Plain	**160**	43 13N	113 0W
Snap, The	**36**	60 35N	0 50W
Snape	**29**	52 11N	1 29 E
Snarum	**71**	60 1N	9 54 E
Snasahogarha	**72**	63 10N	12 20 E
Snedsted	**73**	56 55N	8 32 E
Sneek	**46**	53 2N	5 40 E
Sneeker-meer	**46**	53 2N	5 45 E
Sneem	**39**	51 50N	9 55W
Snejbjerg	**73**	56 8N	8 54 E
Snĕka	**52**	50 41N	15 50 E
Snelling	**163**	37 31N	120 26W
Snettisham	**29**	52 52N	0 30 E
Snezhnoye	**83**	48 0N	38 58 E
Sneznik, mt.	**63**	45 36N	14 35 E
Snigirevka	**82**	47 2N	32 35 E
Snina	**53**	49 0N	22 9 E
Snizort, L.	**36**	57 33N	6 28W
Snohetta	**71**	62 19N	9 16 E
Snohomish	**160**	47 53N	122 6W
Snonuten	**71**	59 31N	6 50 E
Snoul	**101**	12 4N	106 26 E
Snow Hill	**162**	38 10N	75 21W
Snow L.	**153**	54 52N	100 3W
Snowbird L.	**153**	60 45N	103 0W
Snowdon, Mt.	**31**	53 4N	4 8W
Snowdrift	**153**	62 24N	110 44W
Snowdrift, R.	**153**	62 24N	110 44W
Snowflake	**161**	34 30N	110 4W
Snowshoe	**152**	53 43N	121 0W
Snowtown	**140**	33 46 S	138 14 E
Snowville	**160**	41 59N	112 47W
Snowy Mt.	**162**	43 45N	74 26W
Snowy Mts.	**141**	36 30 S	148 20 E
Snowy, R.	**141**	37 46 S	148 30 E
Snug Corner	**167**	22 33N	73 52W
Snyder, Okla., U.S.A.	**159**	34 4N	99 0W
Snyder, Tex., U.S.A.	**159**	32 45N	100 57W
Soacha	**174**	4 35N	74 13W
Soahanina	**129**	18 42 S	44 13 E
Soalala	**129**	16 6 S	45 20 E
Soan, R.	**94**	33 20N	72 40 E
Soanierana-Ivongo	**129**	16 55 S	49 35 E
Soap Lake	**160**	47 29N	119 31W
Soay, I.	**36**	57 9N	6 13W
Soay Sd.	**36**	57 10N	6 15W
Sobat, Nahr	**123**	8 32N	32 40 E
Soběslav	**52**	49 16N	14 45 E
Sobhapur	**94**	22 47N	78 17 E
Sobinka	**81**	56 0N	40 0 E
Sobo-Yama	**110**	32 51N	131 16 E
Sobótka	**54**	50 54N	16 44 E
Sobrado	**56**	43 2N	8 2W
Sobral	**170**	3 50 S	40 30W
Sobreira Formosa	**57**	39 46N	7 51W
Soc Giang	**100**	22 54N	106 1 E
Soc Trang = Khonh Hung	**101**	9 37N	105 50 E
Soča, R.	**63**	46 20N	13 40 E
Socha	**174**	6 0N	72 41W
Sochaczew	**54**	52 15N	20 13 E
Soch'e	**105**	38 24N	37 20 E
Sochi	**83**	43 35N	39 40 E
Société, Is. de la	**131**	17 0 S	151 0W
Socompa, Portezuelo de	**172**	24 27 S	68 18W
Socorro	**174**	6 29N	73 16W
Socorro, I.	**164**	18 45N	110 58W
Socotra, I.	**91**	12 30N	54 0 E
Socúellmos	**59**	39 16N	2 47W
Soda Creek	**152**	52 25N	122 10W
Soda L.	**161**	35 7N	116 2W
Soda Plains	**94**	35 30N	79 0 E
Soda Springs	**160**	42 4N	111 40W
Sodankylä	**74**	67 29N	26 40 E
Söderfjärden	**72**	62 3N	17 25 E
Söderfors	**72**	60 23N	17 25 E
Söderhamn	**72**	61 18N	17 10 E
Söderköping	**72**	58 31N	16 35 E
Södermanlands län □	**72**	59 10N	16 30 E
Södertälje	**72**	59 12N	17 50 E
Sodium	**128**	30 15 S	15 45 E
Sodo	**123**	7 0N	37 57 E
Södra Vi	**73**	57 45N	15 45 E
Sodrazica	**63**	45 45N	14 39 E
Sodus	**162**	43 13N	77 5W
Soekmekaar	**129**	23 30 S	29 55 E
Soest, Ger.	**48**	51 34N	8 7 E
Soest, Neth.	**46**	52 9N	5 19 E
Soestdijk	**46**	52 11N	5 17 E
Sofádhes	**68**	39 28N	22 4 E
Sofara	**120**	13 59N	4 9W
Sofia = Sofiya	**67**	42 45N	23 20 E
Sofia, R.	**129**	15 25 S	48 40 E
Sofievka	**82**	47 58N	34 14 E
Sofikón	**69**	37 47N	23 3 E
Sofila	**67**	42 45N	23 20 E
Sofiya	**67**	42 45N	23 20 E
Sogad	**103**	10 30N	125 0 E
Sogakofe	**121**	6 2N	0 39 E
Sogamoso	**174**	5 43N	72 56W
Sögel	**48**	52 50N	7 32 E
Sogeri	**135**	9 26 S	147 35 E
Sogipo	**107**	33 13N	126 34 E
Sogn og Fjordane fylke □	**71**	61 40N	6 0 E
Sogndal	**71**	58 20N	6 15 E
Sogndalsfjøra	**75**	61 14N	7 5 E
Sognefjorden	**71**	61 10N	5 50 E
Sohâg	**122**	26 27N	31 43 E
Soham	**29**	52 20N	0 20 E
Sohano	**135**	5 22 S	154 37 E
Sŏhori	**107**	40 7N	128 23 E
Soignies	**47**	50 35N	4 5 E
Soira, Mt.	**123**	14 45N	39 30 E
Soissons	**43**	49 25N	3 19 E
Soitava, R.	**53**	49 30N	16 37 E
Sojat	**94**	25 55N	73 38 E
Sok, R.	**84**	53 24N	50 8 E
Sokal	**80**	50 31N	24 15 E
Söke	**69**	37 48N	27 28 E
Sokhós	**68**	40 48N	23 22 E
Sokhta Chinar	**93**	35 5N	67 35 E
Sokna	**71**	60 16N	9 50 E
Soknedal	**71**	62 57N	10 13 E
Soko Banja	**66**	43 40N	21 51 E
Sokodé	**121**	9 0N	1 11 E
Sokó'ka	**54**	53 25N	23 30 E
Sokol	**81**	59 30N	40 5 E
Sokolo	**120**	14 42N	6 8W
Sokolov	**52**	50 12N	12 40 E
Sokoł ó w Matopolski	**53**	50 12N	22 7 E
Sokoł ó w Podlaski	**54**	52 25N	22 15 E
Sokoto	**121**	13 2N	5 16 E
Sokoto □	**121**	12 30N	5 0 E
Sokoto, R.	**121**	12 30N	6 10 E
Sokuluk	**85**	42 52N	74 18 E
Sol Iletsk	**84**	51 10N	55 0 E
Sola	**71**	58 53N	5 36 E
Sola, R.	**126**	49 38N	19 8 E
Solai	**126**	0 2N	36 12 E
Solana, La	**59**	38 59N	3 14W
Solano	**103**	16 25N	121 15 E
Solares	**56**	43 23N	3 43W
Solberga	**73**	57 45N	14 43 E
Solca	**70**	47 40N	25 50 E
Solec Kujawski	**54**	53 5N	18 14 E
Soledad, Colomb.	**174**	10 55N	74 46W
Soledad, U.S.A.	**163**	36 27N	121 16W
Soledad, Venez.	**174**	8 10N	63 34W
Solemint	**163**	34 25N	118 27W
Solent, The	**28**	50 45N	1 25W
Solenzara	**45**	41 53N	9 23 E
Solesmes	**43**	50 10N	3 30 E
Solfonn, Mt.	**71**	60 2N	6 57 E
Soligalich	**81**	59 5N	42 10 E
Solihull	**28**	52 26N	1 47W
Solikamsk	**84**	59 38N	56 50 E
Solila	**129**	21 25 S	46 37 E
Soliman	**119**	36 42N	10 30 E
Solimões, R.	**174**	2 15 S	66 30W
Solingen	**48**	51 10N	7 4 E
Sollas	**36**	57 39N	7 20W
Sollebrunn	**73**	58 8N	12 32 E
Sollefteå	**72**	63 12N	17 20 E
Sollentuna	**72**	59 26N	17 56 E

Soller Speer

Soller 58 39 43N 2 45 E
Sollerön 72 60 54N 14 38 E
Solna 72 59 22N 18 1 E
Solnechnogorsk 81 56 10N 36 57 E
Sölnkletten, Mt. 71 61 55N 10 18 E
Sologne 59 47 40N 2 0 E
Solojärg 73 56 50N 10 8 E
Solok 102 0 55 S 100 40 E
Sololá 166 14 49N 91 10 E
Solomon Is. 135 6 0 S 155 0 E
Solomon, N. Fork, R. 158 39 45N 99 0W
Solomon Sea 135 7 0 S 150 0 E
Solomon, S. Fork, R. 158 39 25N 99 12W
Solomon's Pools = Burak Sulayman 90 31 42N 35 7 E
Solon Springs 158 46 19N 91 47W
Solonópole 170 5 44 S 39 1W
Solor, I. 103 8 27 S 123 0 E
Solotcha 81 54 48N 39 53 E
Solothurn 50 47 13N 7 32 E
Solothurn □ 50 47 18N 7 40 E
Solotobe 85 44 37N 66 3 E
Solsona 58 42 0N 1 31 E
Solt 53 46 45N 19 1 E
Solta, I. 63 43 24N 16 15 E
Soltanabad 93 36 29N 58 5 E
Soltaniyeh 92 36 20N 48 55 E
Soltau 48 52 59N 9 50 E
Soltsy 80 58 10N 30 10 E
Solun 105 46 40N 120 40 E
Solund 71 61 5N 4 50 E
Solund I. 71 61 7N 4 50 E
Solunska Glava 66 41 44N 21 31 E
Solva 31 51 52N 5 12W
Solvang 163 34 36N 120 8W
Solvay 162 43 5N 76 17W
Solvesborg 73 56 5N 14 35 E
Sölvesborg 73 56 5N 14 35 E
Solway Firth 32 54 45N 3 38W
Solwezi 127 12 20 S 26 21 E
Somali Rep. ■ 91 7 0N 47 0 E
Somaliland 123 12 0N 43 0 E
Sombe Dzong 98 27 13N 89 8 E
Sombernon 43 47 20N 4 40 E
Sombor 66 45 46N 19 17 E
Sombrerete 164 23 40N 103 40W
Sombrero I. 167 18 30N 63 30W
Somerby 29 52 42N 0 49W
Someren 47 51 23N 5 42 E
Somers 160 48 4N 114 18W
Somerset, Austral. 138 10 45 S 142 25 E
Somerset, Can. 153 49 25N 98 39W
Somerset, Colo., U.S.A. 161 38 55N 107 30W
Somerset, Ky., U.S.A. 156 37 5N 84 40W
Somerset, Mass., U.S.A. 162 41 45N 71 10W
Somerset □ 28 51 9N 3 0W
Somerset East 128 32 42 S 25 35 E
Somerset, I. 148 73 30N 93 0W
Somerset West 128 34 8 S 18 50 E
Somersham 29 52 24N 0 0W
Somersworth 162 43 15N 70 51W
Somerton, U.K. 28 51 3N 2 45W
Somerton, U.S.A. 161 32 41N 114 47W
Somerville 162 40 34N 74 36W
Someş, R. 70 47 15N 23 45 E
Someşul Mare, R. 70 47 18N 24 30 E
Somma Lombardo 62 45 41N 8 42 E
Somma Vesuviana 65 40 52N 14 23 E
Sommariva 139 26 24 S 146 36 E
Sommatino 65 37 20N 14 0 E
Somme □ 43 50 0N 2 20 E
Somme, B. de la 42 5 22N 1 30 E
Sommelsdijk 46 51 46N 4 9 E
Sommen 73 58 12N 15 0 E
Sommen, L. 73 58 0N 15 15 E
Sommepy-Tahure 43 49 15N 4 31 E
Sömmerda 48 51 10N 11 8 E
Sommersted 73 55 19N 9 18 E
Sommesous 43 48 44N 4 12 E
Sommières 45 43 47N 4 6 E
Somogy □ 53 46 19N 17 30 E
Somogyszob 53 46 18N 17 20 E
Somoto 166 13 28N 86 37W
Sompolno 54 52 26N 18 45 E
Somport, Paso 58 42 48N 0 31W
Somport, Puerto de 58 42 48N 0 31W
Sompting 29 50 51N 0 20W
Son, Neth. 47 51 31N 5 30 E
Son, Norway 71 59 32N 10 42 E
Son, Spain 56 42 43N 8 58W
Son Hoa 100 13 2N 108 58 E
Son La 100 21 20N 103 50 E
Son Ma 100 15 3N 108 34 E
Son Tay 100 21 8N 105 30 E
Soná 166 8 0N 81 10W
Sonamarg 95 34 18N 75 21 E
Sonamukhi 95 23 18N 87 27 E
Sonamura 98 23 29N 91 15 E
Sŏnchŏn 107 39 48N 124 55 E
Soncino 62 45 24N 9 52 E
Sondags, R. 128 32 10N 24 40 E
Sóndala 62 46 20N 10 20 E
Sondar 95 33 28N 75 56 E
Sönder Hornum 73 56 32N 9 38 E
Sønder Omme 73 55 50N 8 54 E
Sønderborg 73 54 55N 9 49 E
Sonderhausen 48 51 22N 10 50 E
Sonderjyllands Amt □ 73 55 10N 9 10 E
Sondre Höland 71 59 44N 11 30 E
Sondre Land 71 60 44N 10 21 E
Söndre Stromfjord 12 66 30N 50 52W
Sóndrio 62 46 10N 9 53 E
Sone 127 17 23 S 34 55 E
Sonepat 94 29 0N 77 5 E
Sonepur 96 20 55N 83 50 E
Song 100 18 28N 100 11 E
Song Cau 100 13 20N 109 18 E
Songa, R. 71 59 57N 7 30 E
Sŏngchŏn 107 39 12N 126 15 E
Songea 127 10 40 S 35 40 E
Songea □ 127 10 30 S 36 0 E
Songeons 43 49 32N 1 50 E
Songjin 107 40 40N 129 10 E
Songjŏngni 107 35 8N 126 47 E
Songkhla 101 7 13N 100 37 E
Songnim 107 38 45N 125 39 E
Songwe, Malawi 127 9 44 S 33 58 E
Songwe, Zaïre 127 3 20 S 26 16 E
Sonkel, Ozero 85 41 50N 75 12 E
Sonkovo 81 57 50N 37 5 E
Sonmiani 94 25 25N 66 40 E
Sonning 29 51 28N 0 53W
Sonnino 64 41 25N 13 13 E
Sono, R., Goias, Brazil 170 8 58 S 48 11W
Sono, R., Minas Gerais, Brazil 171 17 2 S 45 32W
Sonobe 111 35 6N 135 28 E
Sonogno 51 46 22N 8 47 E
Sonoma 163 38 17N 122 27W
Sonora, Calif., U.S.A. 163 37 59N 120 27W
Sonora, Texas, U.S.A. 159 30 33N 100 37W
Sonora □ 164 28 0N 111 0W
Sonora P. 160 38 17N 119 35W
Sonora, R. 164 28 30N 111 33W
Sonoyta 164 31 51N 112 50W
Sŏnsan 107 36 14N 128 17 E
Sonskyn 128 30 47 S 26 28 E
Sonsonate 166 13 43N 89 44W
Sonthofen 49 47 31N 10 16 E
Soo Junction 156 46 20N 85 14W
Soochow = Suchou 109 31 15N 120 40 E
Söonder Nissum 73 56 19N 8 11 E
Sop Hao 100 20 33N 104 27 E
Sop Prap 100 17 53N 99 20 E
Sopi 103 2 40N 128 28 E
Sopo, Nahr 123 8 40N 26 30 E
Sopot, Poland 54 54 27N 18 31 E
Sopot, Yugo. 66 44 29N 20 30 E
Sopotnica 66 41 23N 21 13 E
Sopron 49 47 41N 16 37 E
Sop's Arm 151 49 46N 56 56W
Sör-Fron 71 61 35N 9 59 E
Sor, R. 57 39 7N 9 52 E
Sør-Rondane 13 72 0 S 25 0 E
Sør Trøndelag fylke □ 71 63 0N 11 0 E
Sora 64 41 45N 13 36 E
Sorada 96 19 32N 84 45 E
Sorah 94 27 13N 68 56 E
Söråker 72 62 30N 17 32 E
Sorano 63 42 40N 11 42 E
Sorata 174 15 50 S 68 50W
Sorbas 59 37 6N 2 7W
Sorbie 34 54 46N 4 26W
Sordale 37 58 33N 3 26W
Sordeval 42 48 44N 0 55W
Sorel 150 46 0N 73 10W
Sörenberg 50 46 50N 8 2 E
Soresina 62 45 17N 9 51 E
Sörfold 74 67 5N 14 20 E
Sorgues 45 44 1N 4 53 E
Soria 58 41 43N 2 32W
Soria □ 58 41 46N 2 28W
Soriano 172 33 24 S 58 19W
Soriano □ 176 33 30 S 58 0W
Sorisdale 34 56 40N 6 28W
Sorn 34 55 31N 4 18W
Sorø 73 55 26N 11 32 E
Soro 120 10 9N 9 48W
Sorocaba 173 23 31 S 47 35W
Sorochinsk 84 52 26N 53 10 E
Soroki 82 48 8N 28 12 E
Soroksár 53 47 24N 19 9 E
Soron 94 27 55N 78 45 E
Sorong 103 0 55 S 131 15 E
Sororoca 174 0 43N 61 31W
Soroti 126 1 43N 33 35 E
Soröy Sundet 74 70 25N 23 0 E
Soröya 74 70 35N 22 45 E
Soroyane 71 62 25N 5 32 E
Sorraia, R. 57 38 55N 8 35W
Sorrento, Austral. 139 38 22 S 144 47 E
Sorrento, Italy 65 40 38N 14 23 E
Sorris Sorris 128 21 0 S 14 46 E
Sorsele 74 65 31N 17 30 E
Sorso 64 40 50N 8 34 E
Sorsogon 103 13 0N 124 0 E
Sortat 37 58 32N 3 12W
Sortino 65 37 9N 15 1 E
Sos 58 42 30N 1 13W
Sŏsan 107 36 47N 126 27 E
Soscumica, L. 150 50 15N 77 27W
Sosdala 73 56 2N 13 41 E
Sosna, R. 81 52 30N 38 0 E
Sosnowiec 54 50 20N 19 10 E
Sospel 45 43 52N 7 27 E
Soštanj 63 46 23N 15 4 E
Sŏsura 107 42 16N 130 36 E
Sosva 84 59 10N 61 50 E
Sosva, R. 84 59 32N 62 20 E
Soto la Marina, R. 165 23 40N 97 40W
Soto y Amío 56 42 46N 5 53W
Sotra I. 71 60 15N 5 0 E
Sotteville 42 49 24N 1 5 E
Souanké 124 2 10N 14 10 E
Souderton 162 40 19N 75 19W
Soufi 120 15 13N 12 17W
Souflíon 68 41 12N 26 18 E
Soufrière 167 13 51N 61 4W
Soufrière, vol. 167 13 10N 61 10W
Sougne-Remouchamps 47 50 29N 5 42 E
Souillac 44 44 53N 1 29 E
Souk-Ahras 119 36 17N 7 57 E
Souk el Arba du Rharb 118 34 50N 5 59W
Souk el Khemis 119 36 36N 8 58 E
Soukhouma 100 14 38N 105 48 E
Sŏul 105 37 31N 127 6 E
Soulac-sur-Mer 44 45 30N 1 7W
Soultz 43 48 57N 7 52 E
Soumagne 47 50 37N 5 44 E
Sound, The 75 56 7N 12 30 E
Soúnion, Ákra 69 37 37N 24 1 E
Sour el Ghozlane 119 36 10N 3 45 E
Sources, Mt. aux 129 28 45 S 28 50 E
Sourdeval 42 48 43N 0 55W
Soure, Brazil 170 0 35 S 48 30W
Soure, Port. 56 40 4N 8 38W
Souris, Man., Can. 153 49 40N 100 20W
Souris, P.E.I., Can. 151 46 21N 62 15W
Souris, R. 153 49 40N 99 34W
Soúrpi 69 39 6N 22 54 E
Sous, R. 118 30 31N 9 27W
Sousa 170 6 45 S 38 10W
Sousel, Brazil 170 2 38 S 52 29W
Sousel, Port. 57 38 57N 7 40W
Souss, O. 118 30 23N 8 24W
Sousse 119 35 50N 10 38 E
Soustons 44 43 45N 1 19W
Souterraine, La 44 46 15N 1 30 E
South Africa, Rep. of, ■ 125 30 0 S 25 0 E
South Amboy 162 40 29N 74 17W
South America 168 10 0 S 60 0W
South Auckland & Bay of Plenty □ 142 38 30 S 177 0 E
South Aulatsivik I. 151 56 45N 61 30W
South Australia □ 136 32 0 S 139 0 E
South Baldy, Mt. 161 34 6N 107 27W
South Bend, Indiana, U.S.A. 156 41 38N 86 20W
South Bend, Wash., U.S.A. 160 46 44N 123 52W
South Benfleet 29 51 33N 0 34 E
South Blackwater 138 24 00 S 148 35 E
South Boston 157 36 42N 78 58W
South Br. Ashburton, R. 143 43 30 S 171 15 E
South Branch, Can. 151 47 55N 59 2W
South Branch, U.S.A. 151 44 30N 83 55W
South Brent 30 50 26N 3 50W
South Brook 151 49 26N 56 5W
South Buganda □ 126 0 15 S 31 30 E
South Cape 147 18 58N 155 24 E
South Carolina □ 157 33 45N 81 0W
South Cave 33 53 46N 0 37W
South Charleston 156 38 20N 81 40W
South China Sea 101 7 0N 107 0 E
South Dakota □ 158 45 0N 100 0W
South Dell 36 58 28N 6 20W
South Dorset Downs 28 50 40N 2 26W
South Downs 29 50 53N 0 10W
South East C. 138 43 40 S 146 50 E
South East Is. 137 34 17 S 123 30 E
South Elkington 33 53 22N 0 5W
South Esk, R. 37 56 44N 3 3W
South Foreland 29 51 7N 1 23 E
S. Fork, American, R. 163 38 45N 121 5W
South Fork, R. 160 47 54N 113 15W
South Gamboa 164 9 4N 79 40W
South Gate 163 33 57N 118 12W
South Georgia 13 54 30 S 37 0W
South Glamorgan □ 31 51 30N 3 20W
South Grafton 139 29 41 S 152 47 E
South Harris, district 36 56 51N 3 10W
South Haven 156 42 22N 86 20W
South Hayling 29 50 47N 0 56W
South Henik, L. 153 61 30N 97 30W
South Horr 126 2 12N 36 56 E
South I., Kenya 126 2 35N 36 35 E
South I., N.Z. 143 43 0 S 170 0 E
South Invercargill 143 46 26N 168 23 E
South Kirby 33 53 35N 1 25W
South Knife, R. 153 58 55N 94 37W
S. Kolok 101 6 2N 101 58 E
South Korea ■ 107 36 0N 128 0 E
S. Lembing 101 3 55N 103 3 E
South Magnetic Pole 13 66 30 S 139 30 E
South Marsh Is. 162 38 6N 76 1W
South Milwaukee 156 42 50N 87 52W
South Molton 30 51 1N 3 50W
South Nahanni, R. 152 61 3N 123 21W
South Nesting B. 36 60 18N 1 5W
South Orkney Is. 13 63 0 S 45 0W
South Pass 160 42 20N 108 58W
South Passage 137 26 07 S 113 09 E
S. Petani 101 5 37N 100 30 E
South Petherton 28 50 57N 2 49W
South Petherwin 30 50 35N 4 22W
South Pines 157 35 10N 79 25W
South Platte, R. 158 40 50N 102 45W
South Pt. 151 49 6N 62 11W
South Pole 13 90 0 S 0 0 E
South Porcupine 150 48 30N 81 12W
South Portland 162 43 38N 70 15W
South River, Can. 150 45 52N 79 29W
South River, U.S.A. 162 40 27N 74 23W
South Ronaldsay, I. 37 58 46N 2 58W
S. Sandwich Is. 15 57 0 S 27 0W
South Saskatchewan, R. 153 53 15N 105 5W
South Sd. 39 53 4N 9 28W
South Seal, R. 153 58 48N 98 8W
South Sentinel, I. 101 11 1N 92 16 E
South Shetland Is. 13 62 0 S 59 0W
South Shields 35 54 59N 1 26W
South Sioux City 158 42 30N 96 30W
South Taranaki Bight 142 39 40 S 174 5 E
South Tawton 30 50 44N 3 55W
South Thompson, R. 152 50 40N 120 20W
South Twin I. 150 53 7N 79 52W
South Tyne, R. 35 54 46N 2 25W
South Uist, I. 37 57 4N 7 21W
South Ulvön, I. 72 63 0N 18 45 E
South Walls, I. 37 58 45N 3 7W
South West Africa ■ = Namibia 128 22 0 S 18 9 E
South West C. 138 43 34 S 146 3 E
South West Cape 143 47 16 S 167 31 E
South Williamsport 162 41 14N 77 0W
South Yarmouth 162 41 35N 70 10W
South Yemen ■ 91 15 0N 48 0 E
South Yorkshire □ 33 53 30N 1 20W
Southam 28 52 16N 1 24W
Southampton, Can. 150 44 30N 81 25W
Southampton, U.K. 28 50 54N 1 23W
Southampton, U.S.A. 162 40 54N 72 22W
Southampton I. 149 64 30N 84 0W
Southampton Water 28 50 52N 1 21W
Southborough 29 51 10N 0 15 E
Southbridge, N.Z. 143 43 48 S 172 16 E
Southbridge, U.S.A. 162 42 4N 72 2W
Southeast C. 147 62 55N 169 40W
Southend, Can. 153 56 19N 103 14W
Southend, U.K. 34 55 18N 5 38W
Southend-on-Sea 29 51 32N 0 42 E
Southern □, Malawi 127 15 0 S 35 0 E
Southern □, S. Leone 120 0 8N 12 30 E
Southern □, Uganda 122 0 30 S 30 30 E
Southern □, Zambia 127 16 20 S 26 20 E
Southern Alps 143 43 41 S 170 11 E
Southern Cross 137 31 12 S 119 15 E
Southern Hills 137 32 15 S 122 40 E
Southern Indian L. 153 57 10N 98 30W
Southern Indian Lake 153 57 0N 99 0W
Southern Ocean 13 62 0 S 160 0W
Southern Uplands 35 55 30N 3 3W
Southery 29 52 32N 0 23 E
Southington 162 41 37N 72 53W
Southland □ 143 45 51 S 168 13 E
Southminster 29 51 40N 0 51 E
Southold 162 41 4N 72 26W
Southport, Austral. 139 27 58 S 153 25 E
Southport, U.K. 32 53 38N 3 1W
Southport, U.S.A. 157 33 55N 78 0W
Southwark 29 51 29N 0 5W
Southwell 33 53 4N 0 57W
Southwick 29 50 50N 0 14W
Southwold 29 52 19N 1 41 E
Soutpansberge 129 23 0 S 29 30 E
Souvigny 44 46 33N 3 10 E
Sovata 70 46 35N 25 3 E
Sovetsk, Lithuania, U.S.S.R. 80 55 6N 21 50 E
Sovetsk, R.S.F.S.R., U.S.S.R. 81 57 38N 48 53 E
Sovetskaya Gavan 77 48 50N 140 0 E
Sovicille 63 43 16N 11 12 E
Sovra 66 42 44N 17 34 E
Sowerby 33 54 13N 1 19W
Sōya-Misaki 112 45 30N 142 0 E
Soyopa 164 28 41N 109 37W
Sozh, R. 80 53 50N 31 50 E
Sozopol 67 42 23N 27 42 E
Spa 47 50 29N 5 53 E
Spain ■ 55 40 0N 5 0W
Spakenburg 46 52 15N 5 22 E
Spalding, Austral. 140 33 30 S 138 37 E
Spalding, U.K. 29 52 47N 0 9W
Spalding, U.S.A. 158 41 45N 98 27W
Spandet 73 55 15N 8 54 E
Spånga 72 59 23N 17 55 E
Spångenäs 73 57 36N 16 7 E
Spangereid 71 58 3N 7 9 E
Spaniard's Bay 151 47 38N 53 20W
Spanish 150 46 12N 82 20W
Spanish Fork 160 40 10N 111 37W
Spanish Pt. 39 52 51N 9 27W
Spanish Sahara □ = Western Sahara 116 25 0N 13 0W
Spanish Town 166 18 0N 77 20W
Sparkford 28 51 2N 2 33W
Sparrows Point 162 39 13N 76 29W
Sparta, Ga., U.S.A. 157 33 18N 82 59W
Sparta, N.J., U.S.A. 162 41 2N 74 38W
Sparta, Wis., U.S.A. 158 43 55N 91 10W
Sparta = Spárti 69 37 5N 22 25 E
Spartanburg 157 35 0N 82 0W
Spartel, C. 118 35 47N 5 56W
Spárti 69 37 5N 22 25 E
Spartivento, C., Calabria, Italy 65 37 56N 16 4 E
Spartivento, C., Sard., Italy 65 38 52N 8 50 E
Spas-Demensk 80 54 20N 34 0 E
Spas-Klepiki 81 54 34N 40 2 E
Spassk-Dalniy 77 44 40N 132 40 E
Spassk-Ryazanskiy 81 54 30N 40 25 E
Spatha Ákra. 69 35 42N 23 43 E
Spatsizi, R. 152 57 42N 128 7W
Spean Bridge 36 56 53N 4 55W
Spearfish 158 44 32N 103 52W
Spearman 159 36 15N 101 10W
Speculator 162 43 30N 74 25W
Speed 140 35 21 S 142 27 E
Speer 51 47 12N 9 8 E

Speers Stíra

Speers 153 52 43N 107 34W
Speightstown 167 13 15N 59 39W
Speke 32 53 21N 2 51W
Speke Gulf, L. Victoria 126 2 20S 32 50E
Spekholzerheide 47 50 51N 6 2E
Spelve, L. 34 56 22N 5 45W
Spenard 147 61 5N 149 50W
Spencer, Idaho, U.S.A. 160 44 18N 112 8W
Spencer, Iowa, U.S.A. 158 43 5N 95 3W
Spencer, Nebr., U.S.A. 158 42 52N 98 43W
Spencer, N.Y., U.S.A. 162 42 14N 76 30W
Spencer, W. Va., U.S.A. 156 38 47N 81 24W
Spencer B. 128 25 30S 14 47E
Spencer Bay 148 69 32N 93 32W
Spencer, C. 140 35 20S 136 45E
Spencer G. 140 34 0S 137 20E
Spences Bridge 152 50 25N 121 20W
Spennymoor 33 54 43N 1 35W
Spenser Mts. 143 42 15S 172 45E
Sperkhiós, R. 69 38 57N 22 3E
Sperrin Mts. 38 54 50N 7 0W
Spessart 49 50 0N 9 20E
Spetsai 69 37 16N 23 9E
Spétsai, I. 69 37 15N 23 10E
Spey B. 37 57 41N 3 0W
Spey Bay 37 57 39N 3 4W
Spey, R. 37 57 26N 3 25W
Speyer 49 49 19N 8 26E
Speyer, R. 41 49 18N 7 52E
Spezia = La Spézia 62 44 7N 9 49E
Spézia, La 62 44 8N 9 50E
Spezzano Albanese 65 39 41N 16 19E
Spiddal 39 53 14N 9 19W
Spiekeroog, I. 48 53 45N 7 42E
Spielfeld 63 46 43N 15 38E
Spiez 50 46 40N 7 40E
Spijk 46 53 24N 6 50E
Spijkenisse 46 51 51N 4 20E
Spili 69 35 13N 24 31E
Spilimbergo 63 46 7N 12 53E
Spillimacheen 152 51 6N 117 0W
Spilsby 33 53 10N 0 6E
Spin Baldak 93 31 3N 66 16E
Spinazzola 65 40 58N 16 5E
Spincourt 43 49 20N 5 39E
Spind 71 58 6N 6 53E
Spineni 70 44 43N 24 37E
Spirit Lake 160 47 56N 116 56W
Spirit River 152 55 45N 118 50W
Spiritwood 153 53 24N 107 33W
Spišská Nová Ves 53 48 58N 20 34E
Spišské Podhradie 53 49 0N 20 48E
Spit Pt. 136 20 4S 118 59E
Spithead 29 50 43N 0 56W
Spittal 52 46 48N 13 31E
Spitzbergen (Svalbard) 12 78 0N 17 0E
Split 63 43 31N 16 26E
Split L. 153 56 8N 96 15W
Splitski Kan 63 43 31N 16 20E
Splügen 51 46 34N 9 21E
Splügenpass 51 46 30N 9 20E
Spoffard 159 29 10N 100 27W
Spofforth 33 53 57N 1 28W
Spokane 160 47 45N 117 25W
Sponvika 71 59 7N 11 15E
Spooner 158 45 49N 91 51W
Sporádhes 69 37 0N 27 0E
Sporyy Navolok, M. 76 75 50N 68 40E
Spotswood 162 40 23N 74 23W
Spragge 150 46 15N 82 40W
Sprague 160 47 25N 117 59W
Sprague River 160 42 49N 121 31W
Spratly, I. 102 8 20N 112 0E
Spray 160 44 56N 119 46W
Spree, R. 48 52 23N 13 52E
Sprimont 47 50 30N 5 40E
Spring City, Pa., U.S.A. 162 40 11N 75 33W
Spring City, Utah, U.S.A. 160 39 31N 111 28W
Spring Grove 162 39 55N 76 56W
Spring Hill 141 33 23S 149 9E
Spring Mts. 161 36 20N 115 43W
Spring Valley, Minn., U.S.A. 158 43 40N 92 30W
Spring Valley, N.Y., U.S.A. 162 41 7N 74 4W
Springbok 128 29 42S 17 54E
Springburn 143 43 40S 171 32E
Springdale, Can. 151 49 30N 56 6W
Springdale, Ark., U.S.A. 159 36 10N 94 5W
Springdale, Wash., U.S.A. 160 48 1N 117 50W
Springe 48 52 12N 9 35E
Springerville 161 34 10N 109 16W
Springfield, N.Z. 143 43 19S 171 56E
Springfield, Colo., U.S.A. 159 37 26N 102 40W
Springfield, Ill., U.S.A. 158 39 48N 89 40W
Springfield, Mass., U.S.A. 162 42 8N 72 37W
Springfield, Mo., U.S.A. 159 37 15N 93 20W
Springfield, Ohio, U.S.A. 156 39 50N 83 48W
Springfield, Oreg., U.S.A. 160 44 2N 123 0W
Springfield, Tenn., U.S.A. 157 36 35N 86 55W
Springfield, Va., U.S.A. 162 38 45N 77 13W
Springfield, Vt., U.S.A. 162 43 20N 72 30W
Springfontein 128 30 15S 25 40E
Springhill 151 45 40N 64 4W
Springhouse 152 51 56N 122 7W
Springhurst 141 36 10S 146 31E
Springs 129 26 13S 28 25E
Springsure 138 24 8S 148 6E
Springvale, Queens., Austral. 138 23 33S 140 42E
Springvale, W. Australia, Austral. 136 17 48S 127 41E
Springvale, U.S.A. 162 43 28N 70 48W
Springville, Calif., U.S.A. 163 36 8N 118 49W
Springville, N.Y., U.S.A. 156 42 31N 78 41W
Springville, Utah, U.S.A. 160 40 14N 111 35W
Springwater 153 51 58N 108 23W
Sproatley 33 53 46N 0 9W
Spur 159 33 28N 100 50W
Spurn Hd. 33 53 34N 0 8E
Spuz 66 42 32N 19 10E
Spuzzum 152 49 37N 121 23W
Spydeberg 71 59 37N 11 4E
Squam L. 162 43 45N 71 32W
Squamish 152 49 45N 123 10W
Square Islands 151 52 47N 55 47W
Squillace, Golfo di 65 38 43N 16 35E
Squinzano 65 40 27N 18 1E
Squires, Mt. 137 26 14S 127 46E
Sragen 103 7 28S 110 59E
Srbac 66 45 7N 17 30E
Srbija □ 66 43 30N 21 0E
Srbobran 66 45 32N 19 48E
Sre Khtum 101 12 10N 106 52E
Sre Umbell 101 11 8N 103 46E
Srebrnica 66 44 10N 19 18E
Sredinyy Khrebet 77 57 0N 160 0E
Središce 63 46 24N 16 17E
Sredna Gora 67 42 40N 25 0E
Sredne Tambovskoye 77 50 55N 137 45E
Srednekolymsk 77 67 20N 154 40E
Srednevilyuysk 77 63 50N 123 5E
Sredni Rodopi 67 41 40N 24 45E
Sredniy Ural, mts. 166 59 0N 59 0E
Srem 54 52 6N 17 2E
Srepok, R. 100 13 33N 106 16E
Sretensk 77 52 10N 117 40E
Sri Lanka ■ 97 7 30N 80 50E
Sriharikota, I. 97 13 40N 81 30E
Srikakulam 96 18 14N 84 4E
Srinagar 95 34 12N 74 50E
Sripur 98 24 14N 90 30E
Srirangam 97 10 54N 78 42E
Srirangapatnam 97 12 26N 76 43E
Srivilliputtur 97 9 31N 77 40E
Sroda Wlkp. 54 52 15N 17 19E
Srpska Crnja 66 45 38N 20 44E
Srpska Itabej 66 45 35N 20 44E
Ssu Chiao 109 30 43N 122 28E
Ssuhsien 107 33 25N 117 54E
Ssuhui 109 23 20N 112 41E
Ssunan 108 27 56N 108 14E
Ssup'ing 105 43 10N 124 25E
Ssushui, Honan, China 106 34 51N 113 12E
Ssushui, Shantung, China 107 35 39N 117 15E
Ssutzuwangch'i 106 41 30N 111 37E
Staaten, R. 138 16 24S 141 17E
Stabroek 47 51 20N 4 22E
Stack's Mts. 39 52 20N 9 34W
Stad Delden 46 52 16N 6 43E
Stade 48 53 35N 9 31E
Staden 47 50 59N 3 1E
Staðarhólskirkja 74 65 23N 21 58W
Stadil 73 56 12N 8 12E
Städjan 72 61 56N 12 30E
Stadlandet 72 62 10N 5 10E
Stadsforsen 72 63 0N 16 45E
Stadskanaal 46 53 4N 6 48E
Stadthagen 48 52 20N 9 14E
Stadtlohn 48 51 59N 6 52E
Stadtroda 48 50 51N 11 44E
Stäfa 51 47 14N 8 45E
Stafafell 74 64 25N 14 52W
Staffa, I. 34 56 26N 6 21W
Stafford, U.K. 28 52 49N 2 9W
Stafford, Kansas, U.S.A. 159 38 0N 98 35W
Stafford, Va., U.S.A. 162 38 2S 77 30W
Stafford □ 28 52 53N 2 10W
Stafford Springs 162 41 58N 72 20W
Stagnone, I. 64 37 50N 12 28E
Staindrop 33 54 35N 1 49W
Staines 29 51 26N 0 30W
Stainforth 33 53 37N 0 59W
Stainmore For. 32 54 29N 2 5W
Stainton 33 53 17N 0 23W
Stainz 52 46 53N 15 17E
Staithes 33 54 33N 0 47W
Stakkroge 73 55 53N 8 51E
Stalač 66 43 43N 21 28E
Stalbridge 28 50 57N 2 22W
Stalden 50 46 14N 7 52E
Stalham 29 52 46N 1 31E
Stalingrad = Volgograd 83 48 40N 44 25E
Staliniri = Tskhinvali 83 42 14N 44 1E
Stalino = Donetsky 82 48 0N 37 45E
Stalinogorsk = Novomoskovsk 81 54 5N 38 15E
Stallingborough 33 53 36N 0 11W
Stalowa Wola 54 50 34N 22 3E
Stalybridge 32 53 29N 1 56W
Stamford, Austral. 138 21 15S 143 46E
Stamford, U.K. 29 52 39N 0 29W
Stamford, Conn., U.S.A. 162 41 5N 73 30W
Stamford, N.Y., U.S.A. 162 42 25N 74 37W
Stamford, Tex., U.S.A. 159 32 58N 99 50W
Stamford Bridge 33 53 59N 0 53W
Stamfordham 35 55 3N 1 53W
Stampersgat 47 51 37N 4 26E
Stamps 159 33 22N 93 30W
Stanberry 158 40 12N 94 32W
Standerton 129 26 55S 29 13E
Standish, U.K. 32 53 35N 2 39W
Standish, U.S.A. 156 43 58N 83 57W
Standon 29 51 53N 0 2E
Stanford 160 47 11N 110 10W
Stanford on Teme 28 52 17N 2 26W
Stange Hedmark 71 60 43N 11 11E
Stanger 129 29 18S 31 21E
Stanhope, Austral. 141 36 27S 144 59E
Stanhope, U.K. 32 54 45N 2 0W
Stanišic 53 45 53N 19 12E
Stanislaus, R. 163 37 40N 121 15W
Stanislav = Ivano-Frankovsk 80 49 0N 24 40E
Stanke Dimitrov 66 42 27N 23 9E
Stanley, Austral. 138 40 46S 145 19E
Stanley, N.B., Can. 151 46 20N 66 50W
Stanley, Sask., Can. 153 55 24N 104 22W
Stanley, Falk. Is. 176 51 40S 58 0W
Stanley, Durham, U.K. 33 54 53N 1 42W
Stanley, Tayside, U.K. 35 56 29N 3 28W
Stanley, Idaho, U.S.A. 160 44 10N 114 59W
Stanley, N.D., U.S.A. 158 48 20N 102 23W
Stanley, Wis., U.S.A. 158 44 57N 91 0W
Stanley Res. 97 11 50N 77 40E
Stanleyville = Kisangani 126 0 35N 25 15E
Stanlow 32 53 17N 2 52W
Stann Creek 165 17 0N 88 20W
Stannington 35 55 7N 1 41W
Stanovoy Khrebet 77 55 0N 130 0E
Stans 51 46 58N 8 21E
Stansmore Ra. 136 21 23S 128 33E
Stansted Mountfitchet 29 51 54N 0 13E
Stanthorpe 139 28 36S 151 59E
Stanton, Can. 147 69 45N 128 52W
Stanton, U.S.A. 159 32 8N 101 45W
Stantsiya Karshi 85 38 49N 65 47E
Stanwix 32 54 54N 2 56W
Staphorst 46 52 39N 6 12E
Stapleford 33 52 56N 1 16W
Staplehurst 29 51 9N 0 35E
Stapleton 158 41 30N 100 31W
Staporkow 54 51 9N 20 31E
Star City 153 52 55N 104 20W
Stara-minskaya 83 46 33N 39 0E
Stara Moravica 66 45 50N 19 30E
Stara Pazova 66 45 0N 20 10E
Stara Planina 67 43 15N 23 0E
Stara Zagora 67 42 26N 25 39E
Starachowice-Wierzbnik 54 51 3N 21 2E
Staraya Russa 80 57 58N 31 10E
Starbuck I. 131 5 37S 155 55W
Stargard 48 53 29N 13 19E
Stargard Szczecinski 54 53 20N 15 0E
Stari Bar 66 42 7N 19 13E
Stari Trg. 63 45 29N 15 7E
Staritsa 80 56 33N 35 0E
Starke 157 30 0N 82 10W
Starkville, Colo., U.S.A. 159 37 10N 104 31W
Starkville, Miss., U.S.A. 157 33 26N 88 48W
Starnberg 49 48 0N 11 20E
Starnberger See 49 48 0N 11 0E
Starobelsk 83 49 27N 39 0E
Starodub 80 52 30N 32 50E
Starogard 54 53 55N 18 30E
Start Bay 30 50 15N 3 35W
Start Pt., Devon, U.K. 30 50 13N 3 38W
Start Pt., Orkney, U.K. 37 59 17N 2 25W
Stary Sacz 54 49 33N 30 26E
Staryy Biryuzyak 83 44 46N 46 50E
Staryy Kheydzhan 77 60 0N 144 50E
Staryy Krym 82 44 48N 35 8E
Staryy Oskol 81 51 12N 37 55E
Stassfurt 48 51 51N 11 34E
State College 156 40 47N 77 49W
State Is. 150 48 40N 87 0W
Staten I. 162 40 35N 74 10W
Staten, I. = Los Estados, I. de 176 54 40S 64 0W
Statesboro 157 32 26N 81 46W
Statesville 157 35 48N 80 51W
Statfjord, oilfield 19 61 15N 1 50E
Stathelle 71 59 3N 9 41E
Stauffer 163 34 45N 119 3W
Staunton, U.K. 28 51 58N 2 19W
Staunton, Ill., U.S.A. 158 39 0N 89 49W
Staunton, Va., U.S.A. 156 38 7N 79 4W
Stavanger 159 58 57N 5 40E
Staveley, Cumbria, U.K. 32 54 24N 2 49W
Staveley, Derby, U.K. 33 53 16N 1 20W
Stavelot 47 50 23N 5 55E
Stavenisse 47 51 35N 4 1E
Staveren 46 52 53N 5 22E
Stavern 71 59 0N 10 1E
Stavfjord 71 61 30N 5 0E
Stavre 72 62 51N 15 19E
Stavropol 83 45 5N 42 0E
Stavroúpolis 68 41 12N 24 45E
Stavsjö 73 48 42N 16 30E
Stawell 140 37 5S 142 47E
Stawell, R. 138 20 38S 142 55E
Stawiszyn 54 51 56N 18 4E
Staxigoe 37 58 28N 3 2W
Steamboat Springs 160 40 30N 106 58W
Stebark 54 53 30N 20 10E
Stebleva 68 41 18N 20 33E
Steckborn 51 47 44N 8 59E
Steele 158 46 56N 99 52W
Steelton 162 40 17N 76 50W
Steelville 159 37 57N 91 21W
Steen, R. 152 59 35N 117 10W
Steen River 152 59 40N 117 12W
Steenbergen 47 51 35N 4 19E
Steenvoorde 43 50 48N 2 33E
Steenwijk 46 52 47N 6 7E
Steep Pt. 137 26 08S 113 8E
Steep Rock 153 51 30N 98 48W
Steep Rock Lake 150 48 50N 91 38W
Stefânesti 70 47 44N 27 15E
Stefanie L. = Chew Bahir 123 4 40N 30 50E
Steffisburg 50 46 47N 7 38E
Stefûnesti 70 47 44N 27 15E
Stege 73 55 0N 12 18E
Steierdorf Anina 66 45 6N 21 51E
Steiermark □ 52 47 26N 15 0E
Steigerwald 49 49 45N 10 30E
Stein, Neth. 47 50 58N 5 45E
Stein, Switz. 51 47 40N 8 50E
Stein, U.K. 36 57 30N 6 35W
Steinbach 153 49 32N 96 40W
Steinfort 47 49 39N 5 55E
Steinheim 48 51 50N 9 6E
Steinkjer 74 63 59N 11 31E
Steinkopf 125 29 15S 17 48E
Stekene 47 51 12N 4 2E
Stella Land 128 26 45S 24 50E
Stellarton 151 45 32N 62 45W
Stellenbosch 128 33 58S 18 50E
Stellendam 46 51 49N 4 1E
Stelvio, Paso dello 51 46 32N 10 27E
Stemshaug 71 63 19N 8 44E
Stendal 48 52 36N 11 50E
Stene 47 51 12N 2 56E
Stenhousemuir 35 56 2N 3 46W
Stenmagle 73 55 49N 11 39E
Stenness, L., of 37 59 0N 3 15W
Stensele 74 65 3N 17 8E
Stenstorp 73 58 17N 13 45E
Stenungsund 73 58 6N 11 50E
Stepanakert 79 40 0N 46 25E
Stephan 158 48 30N 96 53W
Stephens Cr. 140 32 15S 141 55E
Stephens I., Can. 152 54 10N 130 45W
Stephens I., N.Z. 143 40 40S 174 1E
Stephenville, Can. 151 48 31N 58 30W
Stephenville, U.S.A. 159 32 12N 98 12W
Stepnica 54 53 38N 14 36E
Stepnoi = Elista 83 46 25N 44 17E
Stepnoye 84 54 4N 60 26E
Sterkstroom 128 31 32S 26 32E
Sterlego, Mys 12 80 30N 90 0E
Sterling, Colo., U.S.A. 158 40 40N 103 15W
Sterling, Ill., U.S.A. 158 41 45N 89 45W
Sterling, Kans., U.S.A. 158 38 17N 98 13W
Sterling City 159 31 50N 100 59W
Sterlitamak 84 53 40N 56 0E
Sternberg 48 53 42N 11 48E
Sternberk 53 49 45N 17 15E
Stettin = Szczecin 54 53 27N 14 27E
Stettiner Haff 48 53 50N 14 25E
Stettler 152 52 19N 112 40W
Steubenville 156 40 21N 80 39W
Stevenage 29 51 54N 0 11W
Stevens Port 158 44 32N 89 34W
Stevens Village 147 66 0N 149 10W
Stevenson L. 153 53 55N 95 9W
Stevenson, R. 136 46 15S 134 10E
Stevenston 34 55 38N 4 46W
Stevns Klint 73 55 17N 12 28E
Stewart 152 55 56N 129 57W
Stewart, C. 138 11 57S 134 45E
Stewart, I. 176 54 50S 71 30W
Stewart I. 143 46 58S 167 54E
Stewart River 147 63 19N 139 26W
Stewarton 34 55 40N 4 30W
Stewartstown 38 54 35N 6 40W
Stewiacke 151 45 9N 63 22W
Steyning 29 50 54N 0 19W
Steynsburg 128 31 15S 25 49E
Steyr 52 48 3N 14 25E
Steyr, R. 52 48 57N 14 15E
Steytlerville 128 33 17S 24 19E
Stia 63 43 48N 11 41E
Stiens 46 53 16N 5 46E
Stigler 159 35 19N 95 6W
Stigliano 65 40 24N 16 13E
Stigsnæs 73 55 13N 11 18E
Stigtomta 73 58 47N 16 48E
Stikine Mts. 148 59 30N 129 30W
Stikine, R. 147 58 0N 131 12W
Stilfontein 128 26 50S 26 50E
Stilis 69 38 55N 22 37E
Stillington 33 54 7N 1 5W
Stillwater, Minn., U.S.A. 158 45 3N 92 47W
Stillwater, N.Y., U.S.A. 162 42 55N 73 41W
Stillwater, Okla., U.S.A. 159 36 5N 97 3W
Stillwater Mts. 160 39 45N 118 6W
Stilwell 159 35 52N 94 36W
Stimfalias, L. 69 37 51N 22 27E
Stimson 150 48 58N 80 30W
Stinchar, R. 34 55 10N 4 50W
Stingray Pt. 162 37 35N 76 15W
Stip 66 41 42N 22 10E
Stiperstones Mt. 28 52 36N 2 57W
Stira 69 38 9N 24 14E

Stiring Wendel **Sukkur**

Stiring Wendel **43** 49 12N 6 57 E
Stirling, Austral. **138** 17 12S 141 35 E
Stirling, Can. **152** 49 30N 112 30W
Stirling, N.Z. **143** 46 14S 169 49 E
Stirling, U.K. **35** 56 17N 3 57W
Stirling (□) **26** 56 3N 4 10W
Stirling Ra. **137** 34 0S 118 0 E
Stjärneborg **73** 57 53N 14 45 E
Stjarnsfors **72** 60 2N 13 45 E
Stjördalshalsen **71** 63 29N 10 51 E
Stobo **35** 55 38N 3 18W
Stoborough, oilfield **19** 50 38N 2 8W
Stockaryd **73** 57 19N 14 36 E
Stockbridge **28** 51 7N 1 30W
Stockerau **53** 48 24N 16 12 E
Stockett **160** 47 23N 111 7W
Stockholm **72** 59 20N 18 3 E
Stockholms län □ **72** 59 30N 18 20 E
Stockhorn **50** 46 42N 7 33 E
Stockport **32** 53 25N 2 11W
Stocksbridge **33** 53 30N 1 36W
Stockton, Austral. **141** 32 56S 151 47 E
Stockton, Calif., U.S.A. **163** 38 0N 121 20W
Stockton, Kans., U.S.A. **158** 39 30N 99 20W
Stockton, Mo., U.S.A. **159** 37 40N 93 48W
Stockton-on-Tees **33** 54 34N 1 20W
Stockvik **72** 62 17N 17 23 E
Stoczek Łukowski **54** 51 58N 22 22 E
Stode **72** 62 28N 16 35 E
Stoer **36** 58 12N 5 20W
Stogovo, mts. **66** 41 31N 20 38 E
Stoke, N.Z. **143** 41 19N 173 14 E
Stoke, U.K. **29** 51 26N 0 41 E
Stoke Ferry **29** 52 34N 0 31 E
Stoke Fleming **30** 50 19N 3 36W
Stoke Mandeville **29** 51 46N 0 47W
Stoke Prior **28** 52 18N 2 5W
Stokenham **30** 50 15N 3 40W
Stokes Bay **150** 45 0N 81 22W
Stokes Pt. **138** 40 10S 143 56 E
Stokes Ra. **136** 15 50S 130 50 E
Stokesley **33** 54 27N 1 12W
Stokke **71** 59 13N 10 17 E
Stokkem **47** 51 1N 5 45 E
Stokken **71** 58 31N 8 53 E
Stokkseyri **74** 63 50N 20 58W
Stokksnes **74** 64 14N 14 58W
Stolac **66** 43 8N 17 59 E
Stolberg, Germ., E. **48** 51 33N 11 0 E
Stolberg, Germ., W. **48** 50 48N 6 13 E
Stolbovaya, R.S.F.S.R., U.S.S.R. **77** 64 50N 153 50 E
Stolbovaya, R.S.F.S.R., U.S.S.R. **81** 55 10N 37 32 E
Stolbtsy **80** 53 22N 26 43 E
Stolin **80** 51 53N 26 50 E
Stolnici **70** 44 31N 24 48 E
Stolwijk **46** 51 59N 4 47 E
Ston **66** 42 51N 17 43 E
Stone, Bucks., U.K. **29** 51 48N 0 52W
Stone, Stafford, U.K. **32** 52 55N 2 10W
Stone Harbor **162** 39 3N 74 45W
Stonecliffe **150** 46 13N 77 56W
Stonehaven **37** 56 58N 2 11W
Stonehenge, Austral. **138** 24 22S 143 17 E
Stonehenge, U.K. **28** 51 9N 1 45W
Stonehouse, Glous., U.K. **28** 51 45N 2 18W
Stonehouse, Strathclyde, U.K. **35** 55 42N 4 0W
Stonewall **153** 50 10N 97 19W
Stongfjord **71** 61 28N 14 0 E
Stonham Aspall **29** 52 11N 1 7 E
Stony L. **153** 58 51N 98 40W
Stony Point **162** 41 14N 73 59W
Stony Rapids **153** 59 16N 105 50W
Stony River **147** 61 48N 156 48W
Stony Stratford **29** 52 4N 0 51W
Stony Tunguska = Tunguska, Nizhmaya **77** 64 0N 95 0 E
Stopnica **54** 50 27N 20 57 E
Stor Elvdal **71** 61 30N 11 1 E
Stora Borge Fjell, Mt. **48** 65 12N 14 0 E
Stora Gla **72** 59 30N 12 30 E
Stora Karlsö **73** 57 17N 17 59 E
Stora Lulevatten **74** 67 10N 19 30 E
Stora Sjøfallet **74** 67 29N 18 40 E
Storavan **74** 65 45N 18 10 E
Stord Leirvik, I. **71** 59 48N 5 27 E
Store Bælt **73** 55 20N 11 0 E
Store Creek **141** 32 54S 149 6 E
Store Heddinge **73** 55 18N 12 23 E
Storen **71** 63 3N 10 18 E
Storfjorden **71** 62 25N 6 30 E
Storm B. **138** 43 10S 147 30 E
Storm Lake **158** 42 35N 95 5W
Stormberg **125** 31 16S 26 17 E
Stormsrivier **128** 33 59S 23 52 E
Stornoway **36** 58 12N 6 23W
Storozhinets **82** 48 14S 25 45 E
Storr, The, mt. **36** 57 30N 6 12W
Storrs **162** 41 48N 72 15W
Storsjö **72** 62 49N 13 5 E
Storsjöen, Hedmark, Norway **71** 60 20N 11 40 E
Storsjöen, Hedmark, Norway **71** 61 30N 11 14 E
Storsjön, Gavleborg, Sweden **72** 60 35N 16 45 E
Storsjön, Jämtland, Sweden **72** 62 50N 13 8 E
Storstroms Amt □ **73** 49 50N 11 45 E
Stort, R. **29** 51 50N 0 7 E
Storuman **74** 65 5N 17 10 E
Storuman, L. **74** 65 5N 17 10 E
Storvätteshagna, Mt. **72** 62 6N 12 30 E
Storvik **72** 60 35N 16 33 E
Stotfold **29** 52 2N 0 13W
Stoughton **153** 49 40N 103 0W
Stour, R., Dorset, U.K. **28** 50 48N 2 7W
Stour, R., Heref. & Worcs., U.K. **28** 52 25N 2 13W
Stour, R., Kent, U.K. **29** 51 15N 0 57 E
Stour, R., Suffolk, U.K. **29** 51 55N 1 5 E
Stourbridge **28** 52 28N 2 8W
Stourport **28** 52 21N 2 18W
Stout, L. **153** 52 0N 94 40W
Stove Pipe Wells Village **163** 36 35N 117 11W
Stow **35** 55 41N 2 50W
Stow Bardolph **29** 52 38N 0 24 E
Stow-on-the-Wold **28** 51 55N 1 42W
Stowmarket **29** 52 11N 1 0 E
Stowupland **29** 52 12N 1 3 E
Strabane **38** 54 50N 7 28W
Strabane □ **38** 54 45N 7 25W
Strachan **37** 57 1N 2 31W
Strachur **34** 56 10N 5 5W
Stracin **66** 42 13N 22 2 E
Stradbally, Kerry, Ireland **39** 52 15N 10 4W
Stradbally, Laoighis, Ireland **39** 53 2N 7 10W
Stradbally, Waterford, Ireland **39** 52 7N 7 28W
Stradbroke **29** 52 19N 1 16 E
Strade **38** 53 56N 9 8W
Stradella **62** 45 4N 9 20 E
Stradone **38** 54 0N 7 12W
Strahan **138** 42 9S 145 20 E
Straldzha **67** 42 35N 26 40 E
Stralkonice **52** 49 15N 13 53 E
Stralsund **48** 54 17N 13 5 E
Strand, Hedmark, Norway **71** 61 18N 11 15 E
Strand, Rogaland, Norway **71** 59 3N 5 56 E
Strand, S. Afr. **128** 34 9S 18 48 E
Stranda **71** 62 19N 6 58 E
Strandby **73** 56 47N 9 13 E
Strandebarm **71** 60 17N 6 0 E
Strandhill **38** 54 16N 8 34W
Strandvik **71** 60 9N 5 41 E
Strangford **38** 54 23N 5 34W
Strängnäs **72** 59 23N 17 8 E
Stranorlar **38** 54 58N 7 47W
Stranraer **34** 54 54N 5 0W
Strasbourg, Can. **153** 51 4N 104 55W
Strasbourg, France **43** 48 35N 7 42 E
Strasburg, Ger. **48** 53 30N 13 44 E
Strasburg, U.S.A. **158** 46 12N 101 9W
Strassen **47** 49 37N 6 4 E
Stratford, N.S.W., Austral. **141** 32 7S 151 55 E
Stratford, Vic., Austral. **141** 37 59S 147 7 E
Stratford, Can. **150** 43 23N 81 0W
Stratford, N.Z. **142** 39 20S 174 19 E
Stratford, Calif., U.S.A. **163** 36 10N 119 49W
Stratford, Conn., U.S.A. **162** 41 13N 73 8W
Stratford, Tex., U.S.A. **159** 36 20N 102 3W
Stratford-on-Avon **28** 52 12N 1 42W
Stratford St. Mary **29** 51 58N 0 59 E
Strath Avon **37** 57 19N 3 23W
Strath Dearn **37** 57 20N 4 0W
Strath Earn **35** 56 20N 3 50W
Strath Glass **37** 57 20N 4 40W
Strath Naver **37** 58 24N 4 12W
Strath Spey **37** 57 15N 3 40W
Strathalbyn **140** 35 13S 138 53 E
Strathaven **35** 55 40N 4 4W
Strathbogie, Dist. **37** 57 25N 2 45W
Strathclyde □ **34** 56 0N 4 50W
Strathcona Prov. Park **152** 49 38N 125 40W
Strathdon **37** 57 12N 3 4W
Strathkanaird **36** 57 58N 5 5W
Strathmore, Austral. **138** 17 50S 142 35 E
Strathmore, Can. **152** 51 5N 113 25W
Strathmore, Highland, U.K. **37** 58 20N 4 40W
Strathmore, Tayside, U.K. **37** 56 40N 3 4W
Strathmore, U.S.A. **163** 36 9N 119 4W
Strathnaver **152** 53 20N 122 33W
Strathpeffer **37** 57 35N 4 32W
Strathroy **150** 42 58N 81 38W
Strathy **37** 58 30N 4 0W
Strathy Pt. **37** 58 35N 4 0W
Strathyre **34** 56 14N 4 20W
Stratmiglo Scot. **35** 56 16N 3 15W
Stratton, U.K. **30** 50 49N 4 31W
Stratton, U.S.A. **158** 39 20N 102 36W
Stratton St. Margaret **28** 51 35N 1 45W
Straubing **49** 48 53N 12 35 E
Straumnes **74** 66 26N 23 8W
Straumsnes Åsskard **71** 63 4N 8 2 E
Strausberg **48** 52 40N 13 52 E
Strawberry Res. **160** 40 0N 111 0W
Strawn **159** 32 36N 98 30W
Strážnice **53** 48 54N 17 19 E
Streaky B. **139** 32 51S 134 18 E
Streaky Bay **139** 32 48S 134 13 E
Streatley **28** 51 31N 1 9W
Streator **158** 41 9N 88 52W
Stredočeský □ **52** 49 55N 14 30 E
Stredoslovenský □ **53** 48 30N 19 15 E
Streé **47** 50 17N 4 18 E
Street **28** 51 7N 2 43W
Strehaia **70** 44 37N 23 10 E
Strelcha **67** 42 30N 24 19 E
Strelka **77** 58 5N 93 10 E
Streng, R. **100** 13 12N 103 37 E
Strengelvåg **74** 68 58N 15 11 E
Strensall **33** 54 3N 1 2W
Stretford **32** 53 27N 2 19W
Stretton **32** 53 21N 2 34W
Strezhevoy **76** 60 42N 77 34 E
Strezhnoye **76** 57 45N 84 2 E
Stribro **52** 49 44N 13 0 E
Strichen **37** 57 35N 2 5W
Strickland, R. **135** 7 35S 141 36 E
Strijen **46** 51 45N 4 33 E
Strimón, R. **68** 41 0N 23 30 E
Strimonikós Kólpos **68** 40 33N 24 0 E
Striven, L. **34** 55 58N 5 9W
Strofadhes, I. **69** 37 15N 21 0 E
Strokestown **38** 53 47N 8 6W
Strom **71** 60 17N 11 44 E
Ström **72** 61 52N 17 20 E
Stroma, I. of **37** 58 40N 3 8W
Strombacka **72** 61 58N 16 44 E
Strómboli, I. **65** 38 48N 15 12 E
Stromeferry **36** 57 20N 5 33W
Stromemore **36** 57 22N 5 33W
Stromness **37** 58 58N 3 18W
Ströms Vattudal L. **74** 64 0N 15 30 E
Stromsberg **72** 60 28N 17 44 E
Strömsnäsbruk **73** 56 35N 13 45 E
Strömstad **72** 58 55N 11 15 E
Stromsund **74** 63 51N 15 35 E
Stronachlachar **34** 56 15N 4 35W
Strone **34** 55 59N 4 54W
Stróngoli **65** 39 16N 17 2 E
Stronsay Firth **37** 59 4N 2 50W
Stronsay, I. **37** 59 8N 2 38W
Strontian **36** 56 42N 5 32W
Strood **29** 51 23N 0 30 E
Stroove **38** 55 13N 6 57W
Stropkov **53** 49 13N 21 39 E
Stroud **28** 51 44N 2 12W
Stroud Road **141** 32 18S 151 57 E
Stroudsberg **162** 40 59N 75 15W
Struer **73** 56 30N 8 35 E
Struga **66** 41 13N 20 44 E
Strugi Krasnye **80** 58 21N 28 51 E
Struma, R. **67** 41 50N 23 18 E
Strumble Hd. **31** 52 3N 5 6W
Strumica **66** 41 28N 22 41 E
Strumica, R. **66** 41 26N 27 46 E
Strusshamn **71** 60 24N 5 10 E
Struthers **150** 48 41N 85 51W
Struy **37** 57 25N 4 40W
Stryama **67** 42 16N 24 54 E
Stryi **80** 49 16N 23 48 E
Stryker **152** 48 40N 114 44W
Stryków **54** 51 55N 19 33 E
Strzegom **54** 50 58N 16 20 E
Strzelce Krajenskie **54** 52 52N 15 33 E
Strzelecki Creek **139** 29 37S 139 59 E
Strzelin **54** 50 46N 17 2 E
Strzelno **54** 52 35N 18 9 E
Strzyzów **54** 49 52N 21 47 E
Stuart, Fla., U.S.A. **157** 27 11N 80 12W
Stuart, Nebr., U.S.A. **158** 42 39N 99 8W
Stuart I. **147** 63 55N 164 50W
Stuart L. **152** 54 30N 124 30W
Stuart Mts. **143** 45 2S 167 39 E
Stuart, R. **152** 54 0N 123 35W
Stuart Range **139** 29 10S 134 56 E
Stuart's Ra. **136** 29 10S 135 0 E
Stubbekøbing **73** 54 53N 12 9 E
Stuben **52** 46 58N 10 31 E
Stuberhuk **48** 54 23N 11 18 E
Studholme Junc. **143** 44 42S 171 9 E
Studland **28** 50 39N 1 58W
Studley **28** 52 16N 1 54W
Stugsund **72** 61 16N 17 18 E
Stugun **72** 63 10N 15 40 E
Stull, L. **153** 54 24N 92 34W
Stung-Treng **100** 13 31N 105 58 E
Stupart, R. **153** 56 0N 93 25W
Stupino **81** 54 57N 38 2 E
Sturgeon B. **153** 52 0N 97 50W
Sturgeon Bay **156** 44 52N 87 20W
Sturgeon Falls **150** 46 25N 79 57W
Sturgeon L., Alta., Can. **152** 55 6N 117 32W
Sturgeon L., Ont., Can. **150** 50 0N 90 45W
Sturgis, Mich., U.S.A. **156** 41 50N 85 25W
Sturgis, S.D., U.S.A. **158** 44 25N 103 30W
Sturko, I. **73** 56 5N 15 42 E
Sturminster Marshall **28** 50 48N 2 4W
Sturminster Newton **28** 50 56N 2 18W
Stúrovo **53** 47 48N 18 41 E
Sturt Cr. **136** 19 0S 128 15 E
Sturt Creek **136** 19 0S 128 15 E
Sturt, R. **136** 34 58S 138 31 E
Sturton **33** 53 22N 0 39W
Sturts Meadows **140** 31 18S 141 42 E
Stutterheim **128** 32 33S 27 28 E
Stuttgart, Ger. **49** 48 46N 9 10 E
Stuttgart, U.S.A. **159** 34 30N 91 33W
Stuyvesant **162** 42 23N 73 45W
Stykkishólmur **74** 65 2N 22 40W
Styr, R. **80** 51 4N 25 20 E
Styria = Steiermark **52** 47 26N 15 0 E
Su-no-Saki **111** 34 58N 139 45 E
Suakin **122** 19 0N 37 20 E
Suan **107** 38 42N 126 22 E
Suaqui **164** 29 12N 109 41W
Suay Rieng **101** 11 9N 105 45 E
Subang **103** 7 30S 107 45 E
Subansiri, R. **98** 26 48N 93 50 E
Subi **101** 2 55N 108 50 E
Subi, I. **102** 2 58N 108 50 E
Subiaco **63** 41 56N 13 5 E
Subotica **66** 46 6N 19 29 E
Success **153** 50 28N 108 6W
Suceava **70** 47 38N 26 16 E
Suceava □ **70** 47 37N 26 18 E
Suceava, R. **70** 47 38N 26 16 E
Sucha-Beskidzka **54** 49 44N 19 35 E
Suchan **54** 53 18N 15 18 E
Suchedniów **54** 51 3N 20 49 E
Such'i **109** 21 23N 110 16 E
Suchien **107** 33 58N 118 17 E
Suchil **164** 23 38N 103 55W
Suchitoto **166** 13 56N 89 0W
Suchou **109** 31 15N 120 40 E
Süchow = Hsüchou **107** 34 15N 117 10 E
Suchowola **54** 53 33N 23 3 E
Sucio, R. **174** 6 40N 77 0W
Suck, R. **39** 53 17N 8 10W
Suckling, Mt. **135** 9 43S 148 59 E
Sucre, Boliv. **174** 19 0S 65 15W
Sucre, Venez. **174** 10 25N 64 5W
Sucre □, Colomb. **174** 8 50N 75 40W
Sucre □, Venez. **174** 10 25N 63 30W
Sůcueni **70** 47 20N 22 5 E
Sucunduri, R. **174** 6 20N 58 35W
SuCuraj **63** 43 10N 17 8 E
Sucuriju **170** 1 39N 49 57W
Sud-Ouest, Pte. du **151** 49 23N 63 36W
Sud, Pte. **151** 49 3N 62 14W
Suda, R. **81** 59 40N 36 30 E
Sudak **82** 44 51N 34 57 E
Sudan ■ **117** 15 0N 30 0 E
Sudan, The **114** 11 0N 9 0 E
Suday **81** 59 0N 43 15 E
Sudbury, Can. **150** 46 30N 81 0W
Sudbury, Derby, U.K. **33** 52 53N 1 43W
Sudbury, Suffolk, U.K. **29** 52 2N 0 44 E
Sûdd **123** 8 20N 29 30 E
Süderbrarup **48** 54 38N 9 47 E
Süderlügum **48** 54 50N 8 46 E
Sudetan Mts. = Sudety **53** 50 20N 16 45 E
Sudety **53** 50 20N 16 45 E
Sudi **127** 10 11S 39 57 E
Sudirman, Pengunungan **103** 4 30N 137 0 E
Sudiţi **70** 44 35N 27 38 E
Sudogda **81** 55 55N 40 50 E
Sudr **122** 29 40N 32 42 E
Sudzha **80** 51 14N 35 25 E
Sueca **59** 39 12N 0 21W
Sueur, Le **158** 44 25N 93 52W
Suez = Suweis **122** 28 40N 33 0 E
Suf **90** 32 19N 35 49 E
Sufaina **92** 23 6N 40 44 E
Suffield **153** 50 12N 111 10W
Suffolk **156** 36 47N 76 33W
Suffolk □ **29** 52 16N 1 0 E
Suffolk, East, □ **29** 52 16N 1 10 E
Suffolk, West, □ **29** 52 16N 0 45 E
Sufi-Kurgan **85** 40 2N 73 30 E
Sufuk **93** 23 50N 51 50 E
Suga no-Sen **110** 35 25N 134 25 E
Sugag **70** 45 47N 23 37 E
Sugar City **158** 38 18N 103 38W
Sugarloaf Pt. **126** 32 22S 152 30 E
Sugluk = Sagloue **149** 62 10N 75 40W
Sugny **47** 49 49N 4 54 E
Suhaia, L. **70** 43 45N 25 15 E
Suhār **93** 24 20N 56 40 E
Suhbaatar **105** 46 54N 113 25 E
Suhl **48** 50 35N 10 40 E
Suhl □ **48** 50 37N 10 43 E
Suhr **50** 47 22N 8 5 E
Suhsien **106** 33 40N 117 0 E
Suhum **121** 6 5N 0 27W
Suian **109** 29 28N 118 44 E
Suica **66** 43 52N 17 11 E
Suich'ang **109** 28 36N 119 16 E
Suichiang **108** 28 40N 103 58 E
Suifenho **107** 44 30N 131 2 E
Suihsien **109** 31 41N 113 20 E
Suihua **98** 46 37N 127 0 E
Suilu **108** 22 20N 107 48 E
Suining, Hunan, China **108** 26 21N 110 0 E
Suining, Kiangsu, China **107** 33 54N 117 56 E
Suining, Szechwan, China **108** 30 31N 105 34 E
Suippes **43** 49 8N 4 30 E
Suir, R. **39** 52 31N 7 59W
Suita **111** 34 45N 135 32 E
Suiteh **106** 37 35N 110 5 E
Suiyang, Heilungkiang, China **107** 44 26N 130 51 E
Suiyang, Kweichow, China **108** 27 57N 107 11 E
Sujangarh **94** 27 42N 74 31 E
Sukabumi **103** 6 56S 106 57 E
Sukadana **102** 1 10S 110 0 E
Sukandja **102** 2 28S 110 25 E
Sukarnapura = Jajapura **103** 2 28N 140 38 E
Sukarno, G. = Jaja, Puncak **103** 3 57S 137 17 E
Sukchŏn **107** 39 22N 125 35 E
Sukhinichi **80** 54 8N 35 10 E
Sukhona, R. **78** 60 30N 45 0 E
Sukhothai **100** 17 1N 99 49 E
Sukhoy Log **84** 56 55N 62 1 E
Sukhumi **83** 43 0N 41 0 E
Sukkur **94** 27 50N 68 46 E

Sukkur Barrage **Sydra, G. of**

Sukkur Barrage **93** 27 50N 68 45 E
Sukma **96** 18 24N 81 37 E
Sukovo **66** 43 4N 22 37 E
Sukumo **110** 32 56N 132 44 E
Sukunka, R. **152** 55 45N 121 15W
Sul, Canal do **170** 0 10 S 48 30W
Sula, Kepulauan **103** 1 45 S 125 0 E
Sula, R. **80** 50 0N 33 0 E
Sulaco, R. **166** 15 2N 87 44W
Sulaiman Range **94** 30 30N 69 50 E
Sulaimanke Headworks **94** 30 27N 73 55 E
Sălaj □ **70** 47 15N 23 0 E
Sulak, R. **83** 43 20N 47 20 E
Sulam Tsor **90** 33 4N 35 6 E
Sulawesi □ **103** 2 0 S 120 0 E
Sulawesi, I. **103** 2 0 S 120 0 E
Sulby **32** 54 18N 4 29W
Sulechów **54** 52 5N 15 40 E
Sulecin **54** 52 26N 15 10 E
Sulejów **54** 51 26N 19 53 E
Sulejówek **54** 52 13N 21 17 E
Sulgen **51** 47 33N 9 7 E
Sulima **120** 6 58N 11 32W
Sulina **70** 45 10N 29 40 E
Sulingen **48** 52 41N 8 47 E
Sülişte **70** 45 45N 23 56 E
Suliţa **70** 47 39N 20 59 E
Sulitälma **74** 67 17N 17 28 E
Sulitjelma **74** 61 7N 16 8 E
Sułkowice **54** 49 50N 19 49 E
Sullana **174** 5 0 S 80 45W
Sullivan, Ill., U.S.A. **158** 39 40N 88 40W
Sullivan, Ind., U.S.A. **156** 39 5N 87 26W
Sullivan, Mo., U.S.A. **158** 38 10N 91 10W
Sullivan Bay **152** 50 55N 126 50W
Sullom Voe **36** 60 30N 1 20W
Sully-sur-Loire **43** 47 45N 2 20 E
Sulmierzyce **57** 51 36N 17 30 E
Sulmona **63** 42 3N 13 55 E
Sulo **105** 39 25N 76 6 E
Sulphur, La., U.S.A. **159** 30 20N 93 22W
Sulphur, Okla., U.S.A. **159** 34 35N 97 0W
Sulphur Pt. **152** 60 56N 114 48W
Sulphur Springs **159** 33 5N 95 30W
Sulphur Springs, Cr. **159** 32 50N 102 8W
Sultan **150** 47 36N 82 47W
Sultanpur **95** 26 18N 82 10 E
Sulu Arch. **103** 6 0N 121 0 E
Sulu Sea **103** 8 0N 120 0 E
Sululta **123** 9 10N 38 43 E
Sulung Shan **108** 31 30N 99 30 E
Suluq **119** 31 44N 20 14 E
Sulyukta **85** 39 56N 69 34 E
Sulzbach-Rosenburg **49** 49 30N 11 46 E
Sumalata **103** 1 0N 122 37 E
Sumampa **172** 29 25 S 63 29W
Sumatera, I. **102** 0 40N 100 20 E
Sumatera Selatan □ **102** 3 30 S 104 0 E
Sumatera Tengah □ **102** 1 0 S 100 0 E
Sumatera Utara □ **102** 2 0N 99 0 E
Sumatra **160** 46 45N 107 37W
Sumatra = Sumatera **102** 0 40N 100 20 E
Sumba, I. **103** 9 45 S 119 35 E
Sumba, Selat **103** 9 0 S 118 40 E
Sumbawa **102** 8 26 S 117 30 E
Sumbawa, I. **103** 8 34 S 117 17 E
Sumbawanga □ **126** 8 0 S 31 30 E
Sumbing, mt. **103** 7 19 S 110 3 E
Sumburgh Hd. **36** 59 52N 1 17W
Sumdo **95** 35 6N 79 43 E
Sumé **170** 7 39 S 36 55W
Sumedang **103** 6 49 S 107 56 E
Sümeg **53** 46 59N 17 20 E
Sumenep **103** 7 3 S 113 51 E
Sumgait **83** 40 34N 49 10 E
Sumisu-Jima **111** 31 27N 140 3 E
Sumiswald **50** 47 2N 7 44 E
Summer Is. **36** 58 0N 5 27W
Summer L. **160** 42 50N 120 50W
Summerhill **38** 53 30N 6 44W
Summerland **152** 49 32N 119 41W
Summerside **151** 46 24N 63 47W
Summerville, Ga., U.S.A. **157** 34 30N 85 20W
Summerville, S.C., U.S.A. **157** 33 2N 80 11W
Summit, Can. **150** 47 50N 72 20W
Summit, U.S.A. **147** 63 20N 149 20W
Summit L. **152** 54 20N 122 40W
Summit Pk. **161** 37 20N 106 48W
Sumner, N.Z. **143** 43 35 S 172 48 E
Sumner, U.S.A. **158** 42 49N 92 7W
Sumner L. **143** 42 42 S 172 15 E
Sumoto **110** 34 21N 134 54 E
Sumperk **53** 49 59N 17 0 E
Sumprabum **98** 26 33N 97 4 E
Sumter **157** 33 55N 80 10W
Sumy **80** 50 57N 34 50 E
Sun City **163** 33 41N 117 11W
Suna **126** 5 23 S 34 48 E
Sunan **107** 39 15N 125 40 E
Sunart, dist. **36** 56 40N 5 40W
Sunart, L. **36** 56 42N 5 43W
Sunburst **160** 48 56N 111 59W
Sunbury, Austral. **141** 37 35 S 144 44 E
Sunbury, U.S.A. **162** 40 50N 76 46W
Sunchales **172** 30 58 S 61 35W
Suncho Corral **172** 27 55 S 63 14W
Sunchŏn **107** 34 52N 127 31 E
Suncook **162** 43 8N 71 27W
Sund **71** 60 13N 5 10 E
Sunda Ketjil, Kepulauan **102** 7 30 S 117 0 E
Sunda, Selat **102** 6 20 S 105 30 E
Sundalsöra **71** 62 40N 8 36 E
Sundance **158** 44 27N 104 27W
Sundarbans, The **98** 22 0N 89 0 E
Sundargarh **96** 22 10N 84 5 E
Sunday Str. **136** 16 25 S 123 18 E
Sundays, R. **128** 32 10 S 24 40 E
Sundby **73** 56 53N 8 40 E
Sundbyberg **72** 59 22N 17 58 E
Sunderland, U.K. **35** 54 54N 1 22W
Sunderland, U.S.A. **162** 42 27N 72 36W
Sundre **152** 51 49N 114 38W
Sundridge, Can. **150** 45 45N 79 25W
Sundridge, U.K. **29** 51 15N 0 10 E
Sunds **73** 56 13N 9 1 E
Sundsjö **72** 62 59N 15 9 E
Sundsvall **72** 62 23N 17 17 E
Sung Hei **101** 10 20N 106 2 E
Sungaipakning **102** 1 19N 102 0 E
Sungaipenuh **102** 2 1 S 101 20 E
Sungaitiram **102** 0 45 S 117 8 E
Sungari, R. = Sunghua Chiang **107** 44 30N 126 20 E
Sungch'i **109** 27 2N 118 19 E
Sungchiang **109** 31 2N 121 14 E
Sungei Lembing **101** 2 53N 103 4 E
Sungei Patani **101** 5 38N 100 29 E
Sungei Siput **101** 4 51N 101 6 E
Sungfou **109** 31 5N 114 42 E
Sungguminasa **103** 5 17 S 119 30 E
Sunghsien **106** 34 10N 112 10 E
Sunghua Chiang, R. **105** 47 42N 132 30 E
Sungikai **123** 12 20N 29 51 E
Sungk'an **108** 28 33N 106 52 E
Sungming **108** 25 22N 103 2 E
Sungpan **105** 32 50N 103 20 E
Sungp'an **108** 32 36N 103 36 E
Sungt'ao **108** 28 12N 109 12 E
Sungtzu Hu **109** 30 10N 111 45 E
Sungü **129** 21 18 S 32 28 E
Sungurlu **82** 40 12N 34 21 E
Sungyang **109** 28 16N 119 29 E
Sunja **63** 45 21N 16 35 E
Sunk Island **33** 53 38N 0 7W
Sunkar, Gora **85** 44 15N 73 50 E
Sunnäsbruk **72** 61 10N 7 12 E
Sunne, Jamtland, Sweden **72** 63 7N 14 25 E
Sunne, Varmland, Sweden **72** 59 52N 13 12 E
Sunnfjord **71** 61 25N 5 18 E
Sunnhordland **71** 59 50N 5 30 E
Sunninghill **29** 51 25N 0 40W
Sunnmöre **71** 62 15N 6 30 E
Sunnyside, Utah, U.S.A. **160** 39 40N 110 24W
Sunnyside, Wash., U.S.A. **160** 46 24N 120 2W
Sunnyvale **163** 37 23N 122 2W
Sunray **159** 36 1N 101 47W
Sunshine **141** 37 48 S 144 52 E
Sunson **121** 9 35N 0 2W
Suntar **77** 62 15N 117 30 E
Sunyani **120** 7 21N 2 22W
Suō-Nada **110** 33 50N 131 30 E
Suolahti **74** 62 34N 25 52 E
Suonenjoki **74** 62 37N 27 7 E
Supai **161** 36 14N 112 44W
Supaul **95** 26 10N 86 40 E
Supe **123** 8 34N 35 35 E
Superior, Ariz., U.S.A. **161** 33 19N 111 9W
Superior, Mont., U.S.A. **160** 47 15N 114 57W
Superior, Nebr., U.S.A. **158** 40 3N 98 2W
Superior, Wis., U.S.A. **158** 46 45N 92 0W
Superior, L. **155** 47 40N 87 0W
Supetar **63** 43 25N 16 32 E
Suphan Buri **100** 14 30N 100 10 E
Suprasśl **54** 53 13N 23 19 E
Suq al Jumah **119** 32 58N 13 12 E
Sūr, Leb. **90** 33 19N 35 16 E
Sūr, Oman **93** 22 34N 59 32 E
Sur, Pt. **163** 36 18N 121 54W
Sura, R. **81** 55 30N 46 20 E
Surab **94** 28 25N 66 15 E
Surabaja = Surabaya **103** 7 17 S 112 45 E
Surabaya **103** 7 17 S 112 45 E
Surahammar **72** 59 43N 16 13 E
Suraia **70** 45 40N 27 25 E
Surakarta **103** 7 35 S 110 48 E
Surakhany **83** 40 13N 50 1 E
Surandai **97** 8 58N 77 26 E
Surany **53** 48 6N 18 10 E
Surat, Austral. **139** 27 10 S 149 6 E
Surat, India **96** 21 12N 72 55 E
Surat, Khalīj **119** 31 40N 18 30 E
Surat Thani **101** 9 6N 99 14 E
Suratgarh **94** 29 18N 73 55 E
Surazh **80** 53 5N 32 27 E
Surduc **70** 47 15N 23 25 E
Surduc Pasul **70** 45 21N 23 23 E
Surdulica **66** 42 41N 22 11 E
Sûre, R. **47** 49 51N 6 6 E
Surendranagar **94** 22 45N 71 40 E
Surf **163** 34 41N 120 36W
Surf Inlet **152** 53 8N 128 50W
Surgères **44** 46 7N 0 47W
Surhuisterveen **46** 53 11N 6 10 E
Suri **95** 23 50N 87 34 E
Surianu, mt. **70** 45 33N 23 31 E
Suriapet **96** 17 10N 79 40 E
Surif **90** 31 40N 35 4 E
Surin **100** 14 50N 103 34 E
Surin Nua, Ko **101** 9 30N 97 55 E
Surinam ■ **175** 4 0N 56 15W
Suriname, R. **170** 4 30N 55 30W
Surkhandarya, R. **85** 37 12N 67 20 E
Sŭrmasu **70** 46 45N 25 13 E
Sürmene **83** 41 0N 40 1 E
Surovikino **83** 48 32N 42 55 E
Surprise L. **152** 59 40N 133 15W
Surrey □ **29** 51 16N 0 30W
Surry **162** 37 8N 76 50W
Sursee **50** 47 11N 8 6 E
Sursk **81** 53 3N 45 40W
Surt **119** 31 11N 16 46 E
Surt, Al Hammādah al **119** 30 0N 17 50 E
Surtsey **74** 63 20N 20 30W
Surubim **170** 7 50 S 35 45W
Suruga-Wan **111** 34 45N 138 30 E
Surup **103** 6 27N 126 17 E
Surur **93** 23 20N 58 10 E
Susa **62** 45 8N 7 3 E
Susaa, R. **73** 55 20N 11 42 E
Sušac, I. **63** 42 46N 16 30 E
Susak, I. **63** 44 30N 14 28 E
Susaki **110** 33 22N 133 17 E
Susamyr **85** 42 12N 73 58 E
Susamyrtau, Khrebet **85** 42 8N 73 15 E
Susangerd **92** 31 35N 48 20 E
Susanino **77** 52 50N 140 14 E
Susanville **160** 40 28N 120 40W
Susch **51** 46 46N 10 5 E
Sušice **52** 49 17N 13 30 E
Susquehanna Depot **162** 41 55N 75 36W
Susquehanna, R. **156** 41 50N 76 20W
Susques **172** 23 35 S 66 25W
Sussex, Can. **151** 45 45N 65 37W
Sussex, U.S.A. **162** 41 12N 74 38W
Sussex (□) **26** 50 55N 0 20W
Sussex, E. □ **29** 51 0N 0 0 E
Sussex, W. □ **29** 51 0N 0 30W
Susten Pass **51** 46 43N 8 26 E
Susteren **47** 51 4N 5 51 E
Sustut, R. **152** 56 20N 127 30W
Susuman **77** 62 47N 148 10 E
Susuna **103** 3 20 S 133 25 E
Susung **109** 30 9N 116 6 E
Susz **54** 53 44N 19 20 E
Suţeşti **70** 45 13N 27 27 E
Sutherland, Austral. **141** 34 2 S 151 4 E
Sutherland, Can. **153** 52 15N 106 40W
Sutherland, S. Afr. **125** 32 33 S 20 40 E
Sutherland, U.S.A. **158** 41 12N 101 11W
Sutherland (□) **26** 58 10N 4 30W
Sutherland Falls **143** 44 48 S 167 46 E
Sutherland Pt. **133** 28 15 S 153 35 E
Sutherland Ra. **137** 25 42 S 125 21 E
Sutherlin **160** 43 28N 123 16W
Sutivan **63** 43 23N 16 30 E
Sutlej, R. **94** 30 0N 73 0 E
Sutter Creek **163** 38 24N 120 48W
Sutterton **33** 52 54N 0 8W
Sutton, N.Z. **143** 45 34 S 170 8 E
Sutton, U.K. **29** 51 22N 0 13W
Sutton, U.S.A. **158** 40 40N 97 50W
Sutton Bridge **29** 52 46N 0 12 E
Sutton Coldfield **28** 52 33N 1 50W
Sutton Courtenay **28** 51 39N 1 16W
Sutton-in-Ashfield **33** 52 8N 1 16W
Sutton-on-Sea **33** 53 18N 0 18 E
Sutton, R. **150** 55 15N 83 45W
Sutton Scotney **28** 51 9N 1 20W
Suttor, R. **138** 20 36 S 147 2 E
Sutwik I. **147** 56 35N 157 10W
Suva **143** 17 40 S 178 8 E
Suva Gora **66** 41 45N 21 3 E
Suva Planina **66** 43 10N 22 5 E
Suva Reka **66** 42 21N 20 50 E
Suvarov Is. **131** 13 15 S 163 30W
Suvo Rudĭste **66** 43 17N 20 49 E
Suvorovo **67** 43 20N 27 35 E
Suwa **111** 36 2N 138 8 E
Suwa-Ko **111** 36 3N 138 5 E
Suwałki **54** 54 8N 22 59 E
Suwałki □ **54** 54 0N 22 30 E
Suwannaphum **100** 15 33N 105 47 E
Suwannee, R. **157** 30 0N 83 0W
Suwanose-Jima **112** 29 38N 129 38 E
Suweis, El **122** 29 58N 32 31 E
Suweis, Khalîg es **122** 28 40N 33 0 E
Suweis, Qanâl es **122** 31 0N 32 20 E
Suwŏn **107** 37 17N 127 1 E
Suykbulak **84** 50 25N 62 33 E
Suzak **85** 44 9N 68 27 E
Suzaka **111** 36 39N 138 19 E
Sŭzava, R. **52** 49 50N 15 0 E
Suzdal **81** 56 29N 40 26 E
Suze, La **42** 47 54N 0 2 E
Suzuka **111** 34 55N 136 36 E
Suzuka-Sam **111** 35 5N 136 30 E
Suzzara **62** 45 0N 10 45 E
Svalbard, Arctica **12** 78 0N 17 0 E
Svalbard, Iceland **74** 66 12N 15 43W
Svalöv **73** 55 57N 13 8 E
Svanå **72** 59 46N 15 23 E
Svanvik **74** 69 38N 30 3 E
Svappavaari **74** 67 40N 21 03 E
Svarstad **71** 59 27N 9 56 E
Svartisen **74** 66 40N 14 16 E
Svartvik **72** 62 19N 17 24 E
Svatovo **82** 49 35N 38 5 E
Svay Chek **100** 13 48N 102 58 E
Svay Rieng **101** 11 5N 105 48 E
Svealand □ **75** 59 55N 15 0 E
Svedala **73** 55 30N 13 15 E
Sveg **72** 62 2N 14 21 E
Sveio **71** 59 33N 5 23 E
Svelvik **71** 59 37N 10 24 E
Svendborg **73** 55 4N 10 35 E
Svene **71** 59 45N 9 31 E
Svenljunga **73** 57 29N 13 29 E
Svensbro **73** 58 15N 13 52 E
Svenstavik **72** 62 45N 14 26 E
Svenstrup **73** 56 58N 9 50 E
Sverdlovsk **84** 56 50N 60 30 E
Sverdrup Is. **12** 79 0N 97 0W
Svetac **63** 43 3N 15 43 E
Sveti Ivan Zelina **63** 45 57N 16 16 E
Sveti Jurij **63** 46 14N 15 24 E
Sveti Lenart **63** 46 36N 15 48 E
Sveti Nikola **66** 41 51N 21 56 E
Sveti Trojica **63** 46 37N 15 33 E
Svetlogorsk **80** 52 38N 29 46 E
Svetlograd **83** 45 25N 42 58 E
Svetlovodsk **80** 49 2N 33 13 E
Svetlyy **84** 50 48N 60 51 E
Svetozarevo **66** 44 0N 21 15 E
Svidník **53** 49 20N 21 37 E
Svilaja Pl. **63** 43 49N 16 31 E
Svilajnac **66** 44 15N 21 11 E
Svilengrad **67** 41 49N 26 12 E
Svinö **73** 55 6N 11 44 E
Svir, R. **78** 61 2N 34 50 E
Svishov **67** 43 36N 25 23 E
Svisloch **80** 53 26N 24 2 E
Svitavy **53** 49 47N 16 28 E
Svobodnyy **77** 51 20N 128 0 E
Svoge **67** 42 59N 23 23 E
Svolvær **74** 68 15N 14 34 E
Svratka, R. **53** 49 27N 16 12 E
Svrljig **66** 43 25N 22 6 E
Swa **98** 19 15N 96 17 E
Swabian Alps **49** 48 30N 9 30 E
Swadlincote **28** 52 47N 1 34W
Swaffham **29** 52 38N 0 42 E
Swain Reefs **138** 21 45 S 152 20 E
Swainsboro **157** 32 38N 82 22W
Swakopmund **128** 22 37 S 14 30 E
Swale, R. **34** 54 18N 1 20W
Swallowfield **29** 51 23N 0 56W
Swalmen **47** 51 13N 6 2 E
Swan Hill **140** 35 20 S 143 33 E
Swan Hills **152** 54 42N 115 24W
Swan Islands **166** 17 22N 83 57W
Swan L. **153** 52 30N 100 50W
Swan Pt. **136** 16 22 S 123 1 E
Swan, R. **132** 32 3 S 115 35 E
Swan Reach **140** 34 35 S 139 37 E
Swan River **153** 52 10N 101 16W
Swanage **28** 50 36N 1 59W
Swanlinbar **38** 54 11N 7 42W
Swansea, Austral. **141** 33 3 S 151 35 E
Swansea, U.K. **31** 51 37N 3 57W
Swansea Bay **31** 51 34N 3 55W
Swar, R. **95** 35 15N 72 24 E
Swartberg **128** 30 15 S 29 23 E
Swartberge **128** 33 20 S 22 0 E
Swarte Bank, gasfield **19** 53 27N 2 10 E
Swartruggens **128** 25 39 S 26 42 E
Swarzedz **54** 52 25N 17 4 E
Swastika **150** 48 7N 80 6W
Swatow = Shant'ou **109** 23 28N 116 40 E
Swatragh **38** 54 55N 6 40W
Swaziland ■ **129** 26 30 S 31 30 E
Sweden ■ **74** 67 0N 15 0 E
Swedru **121** 5 32N 0 41W
Sweet Home **160** 44 26N 122 38W
Sweetwater, Nev., U.S.A. **163** 38 27N 119 9W
Sweetwater, Tex., U.S.A. **159** 32 30N 100 28W
Sweetwater, R. **160** 42 31N 107 30W
Swellendam **128** 34 1 S 20 26 E
Świdin **54** 53 47N 15 49 E
Swidnica **54** 50 50N 16 30 E
Świdnik **54** 51 13N 22 39 E
Świebodzice **54** 50 51N 16 20 E
Swiebodzin **54** 52 15N 15 37 E
Swiecie **54** 53 25N 18 30 E
Swietorkrzyskie, Góry **54** 51 0N 20 30 E
Swift Current **153** 50 20N 107 45W
Swiftcurrent Cr. **153** 50 38N 107 44W
Swilly L. **38** 55 12N 7 35W
Swilly, R. **38** 54 56N 7 50W
Swindle, I. **152** 52 30N 128 35W
Swindon **28** 51 33N 1 47W
Swinemünde = Świnoujście **54** 53 54N 14 16 E
Swineshead **33** 57 57N 0 9W
Swinford **38** 53 57N 8 57W
Świnoujście **54** 53 54N 14 16 E
Swinton, Borders, U.K. **35** 55 43N 2 14W
Swinton, Gr. Manch., U.K. **32** 53 31N 2 21W
Swinton, S. Yorks., U.K. **33** 53 28N 1 20W
Switzerland ■ **49** 46 30N 8 0 E
Swona, I. **37** 58 30N 3 3W
Swords **38** 53 27N 6 15W
Syasstroy **80** 60 5N 32 15 E
Sybil Pt. **39** 52 12N 10 28W
Sychevka **80** 55 45N 34 10 E
Syców **54** 51 19N 17 40 E
Sydney, Austral. **141** 33 53 S 151 10 E
Sydney, Can. **151** 46 7N 60 7W
Sydney, U.S.A. **158** 41 12N 103 0W
Sydney Mines **151** 46 18N 60 15W
Sydproven **12** 60 30N 45 35W
Sydra, G. of = Surt **61** 31 40N 18 30 E

Syke Tambelan, Kepulauan

Syke 48 52 55N 8 50 E
Syktyvkar 78 61 45N 50 40 E
Sylacauga 157 33 10N 86 15W
Sylarna, Mt. 72 63 2N 12 11 E
Sylhet 98 24 54N 91 52 E
Sylt, I. 48 54 50N 8 20 E
Sylva, R. 84 58 0N 56 54 E
Sylvan Beach 162 43 12N 75 44W
Sylvan Lake 152 52 20N 114 10W
Sylvania 157 32 45N 81 37W
Sylvester 157 31 31N 83 50W
Sym 76 60 20N 87 50 E
Symington 35 55 35N 3 36W
Symón 164 24 42N 102 35W
Symonds Yat 28 51 50N 2 38W
Synnott Ra. 136 16 30 S 125 20 E
Syr Darya 76 45 0N 65 0 E
Syracuse, Kans., U.S.A. 159 38 0N 101 40W
Syracuse, N.Y., U.S.A. 162 43 4N 76 11W
Syrdarya 85 40 50N 68 40 E
Syria ■ 92 35 0N 38 0 E
Syriam 98 16 44N 96 19 E
Syrian Des. 92 31 30N 40 0 E
Sysert 84 56 29N 60 49 E
Syston 28 52 42N 1 5W
Syuldzhyukyor 77 63 25N 113 40 E
Syutkya, mt. 67 41 50N 24 16 E
Syzran 81 53 12N 48 30 E
Szabolcs-Szatmár □ 53 48 2N 21 45 E
Szamocin 54 53 2N 17 7 E
Szamotuły 54 52 35N 16 34 E
Szaraz, R. 53 46 28N 20 44 E
Szazhalombatta 53 47 20N 18 58 E
Szczara, R. 53 53 15N 25 10 E
Szczebrzeszyn 54 50 42N 22 59 E
Szczecin 54 53 27N 14 27 E
Szczecin □ 54 53 25N 14 32 E
Szczecinek 54 53 43N 16 41 E
Szczekocimy 54 50 38N 19 48 E
Szczrk 53 49 42N 19 1 E
Szczuczyn 54 53 36N 22 19 E
Szczytno 54 53 33N 21 0 E
Szechwan □ 109 30 15N 103 15 E
Szécsény 53 48 7N 19 30 E
Szeged 53 46 16N 20 10 E
Szeghalom 53 47 1N 21 10 E
Székesfehérvár 53 47 15N 18 25 E
Szekszárd 53 46 22N 18 42 E
Szendrö 53 48 24N 20 41 E
Szentendre 53 47 39N 19 4 E
Szentes 53 46 39N 20 21 E
Szentgotthárd 53 46 58N 16 19 E
Szentlörinc 53 46 3N 18 1 E
Szerencs 53 48 10N 21 12 E
Szeshui 33 34 50N 113 20 E
Szigetvár 53 46 3N 17 46 E
Szlichtyogowa 54 51 42N 16 15 E
Szob 53 47 48N 18 53 E
Szolnok 53 47 10N 20 15 E
Szolnok □ 53 47 15N 20 30 E
Szombathely 53 47 14N 16 38 E
Szprotawa 54 51 33N 15 35 E
Sztum 54 53 55N 19 1 E
Sztuto 54 54 20N 19 15 E
Sztutowo 54 54 20N 19 15 E
Szûrvas 53 46 50N 20 38 E
Szydłowiec 54 51 15N 20 51 E
Szypliszki 54 54 17N 23 2 E

T

't Harde 46 52 24N 5 54 E
't Zandt 46 53 22N 6 46 E
Ta-erh Po, L. 106 43 15N 116 35 E
Ta Khli Khok 100 15 18N 100 20 E
Ta Lai 101 11 24N 107 23 E
Taalintehdas 74 60 2N 22 30 E
Taan 107 45 30N 124 18 E
Taavetti 75 60 56N 27 32 E
Taba 92 26 55N 42 30 E
Tabacal 172 23 15 S 64 15W
Tabaco 103 13 22N 123 44 E
Tabagné 120 7 59N 3 4W
Tabar Is. 135 2 50 S 152 0 E
Tabarca, Isla de 59 38 17N 0 30W
Tabarka 119 36 56N 8 46 E
Tabarra 59 38 37N 1 44 E
Tabas, Khorasan, Iran 93 33 35N 56 55 E
Tabas, Khorasan, Iran 93 32 48N 60 12 E
Tabasará, Serranía de 166 8 35N 81 40W
Tabasco □ 165 17 45N 93 30W
Tabatinga 174 4 11 S 69 58W
Tabatinga, Serra da 170 10 30 S 44 0W
Tabayin 98 22 42N 95 20 E
Tabelbala, Kahal de 118 28 47N 2 0W
Taber 152 49 47N 112 8W
Taberg 162 43 18N 75 37W
Tabernas 59 37 4N 2 26W
Tabernas de Valldigna 59 39 5N 0 13W
Tabigha 90 32 53N 35 33 E
Tabira 170 7 35 S 37 33W
Tablas, I. 103 12 25N 122 2 E
Table B. 151 53 40N 56 25W
Table Mt. 128 34 0 S 18 22 E
Table Top, Mt. 138 23 24 S 147 11 E
Tableland 136 17 16 S 126 51 E
Tabletop, mt. 137 22 32 S 123 50 E
Tábor 52 49 25N 14 39 E
Tabor 90 32 42N 35 24 E
Tabora 126 5 2 S 32 57 E
Tabora □ 126 5 0 S 33 0 E
Tabory 84 58 31N 64 33 E
Tabou 120 4 30N 7 20W
Tabouda 118 34 44N 5 14W
Tabrīz 92 38 7N 46 20 E
Tabūk 92 28 30N 36 25 E
Täby 72 59 29N 18 4 E
Tacámbaro 164 19 14N 101 28W
Tacarigua, L. de 174 11 3N 68 25W
Tach'aitan 105 37 50N 95 18 E
T'ach'eng 105 46 45N 82 57 E
Tach'eng 106 38 35N 116 39 E
Tach'engtzu 107 41 44N 118 52 E
Tach'i 109 24 51N 121 14 E
Tachia 109 24 25N 120 28 E
Tachiai 108 23 44N 103 57 E
Tachibana-Wan 110 32 45N 130 7 E
Tachikawa 111 35 42N 139 25 E
Tach'in Ch'uan, R. 108 31 57N 102 11 E
Tach'ing Shan, mts. 106 40 50N 111 0 E
Tachira 174 8 7N 72 21W
Tachira □ 174 8 7N 72 15W
Tachov 52 49 47N 12 39 E
Tachu 108 30 45N 107 13 E
Tacina, R. 65 39 5N 16 51 E
Tacloban 103 11 15N 124 58 E
Tacna 174 18 0 S 70 20W
Tacoma 160 47 15N 122 30W
Tacuarembó 173 31 45 S 56 0W
Tacumshin L. 39 52 12N 6 28W
Tadcaster 33 53 53N 1 16W
Tademaït, Plateau du 118 28 30N 2 30 E
Tadent, O. 119 22 30N 7 0 E
Tadjerdjert, O. 119 26 0N 8 0W
Tadjerouna 118 33 31N 2 3 E
Tadjettaret, O. 119 22 0N 7 30W
Tadjmout, O. 118 25 37N 3 48 E
Tadjoura 123 11 50N 42 55 E
Tadjoura, Golfe de 123 11 50N 43 0 E
Tadley 28 51 21N 1 8W
Tadmor, N.Z. 143 41 27 S 172 45 E
Tadmor, Syria 92 34 30N 37 55 E
Tado 174 5 16N 76 32W
Tadotsu 110 34 16N 133 45 E
Tadoule L 153 58 36N 98 20W
Tadoussac 151 48 11N 69 42W
Tadzhik S.S.R. □ 85 35 30N 70 0 E
Taechŏnni 107 36 21N 126 36 E
Taegu 107 35 50N 128 37 E
Taegwandong 107 40 13N 125 12 E
Taejŏn 107 36 20N 127 28 E
Taerhhanmaoming-anlienhoch'i 106 41 50N 110 27 E
Taerhting 105 37 15N 92 36 E
Taf, R. 31 51 55N 4 36W
Tafalla 58 42 30N 1 41W
Tafang 108 27 10N 105 39 E
Tafar 123 6 52N 28 15 E
Tafas 90 32 44N 36 5 E
Tafassasset, O. 119 23 0N 9 11 E
Tafelbaai 128 33 35 S 18 25 E
Tafelney, C. 118 31 3N 9 51W
Tafermaar 103 6 47 S 134 10 E
Tafí Viejo 172 26 43 S 65 17W
Tafiré 120 9 4N 5 10W
Tafnidilt 118 28 47N 10 58W
Tafraout 118 29 50N 8 58W
Taft, Phil. 103 11 57N 125 30 E
Taft, Ala., U.S.A. 163 35 10N 119 28W
Taft, Tex., U.S.A. 159 27 58N 97 23W
Taga Dzong 98 27 5N 90 0 E
Taganrog 83 47 12N 38 50 E
Taganrogskiy Zaliv 82 47 0N 38 30 E
Tagant 120 18 20N 11 0W
Tagap Ga 98 26 56N 96 13 E
Tagbilaran 103 9 39N 123 51 E
Tage 135 6 19 S 143 20 E
Tággia 62 43 52N 7 50 E
Taghmon 39 52 19N 6 40W
Taghrīfat 119 29 5N 17 26 E
Taghzout 118 33 30N 4 49W
Tagish 152 60 19N 134 16W
Tagish L. 147 60 10N 134 20W
Tagliacozzo 63 42 4N 13 13 E
Tagliamento, R. 63 45 38N 13 5 E
Táglio di Po 63 45 0N 12 12 E
Tagomago, Isla de 59 39 2N 1 39 E
Tagua, La 174 0 3N 74 40W
Taguatinga 171 12 26 S 46 26W
Tagula 135 11 22 S 153 15 E
Tagula I. 135 11 30 S 153 30 E
Tagum (Hijo) 103 7 33N 125 53 E
Tagus = Tajo, R. 55 39 44N 5 50W
Tahahbala, I. 102 0 30 S 98 30 E
Tahakopa 143 46 30 S 169 23 E
Tahala 118 34 0N 4 28W
Tahan, Gunong 101 4 45N 102 25 E
Tahara 111 34 40N 137 16 E
Tahat Mt. 119 23 18N 5 21 E
Tāherī 93 27 43N 52 20 E
Tahiti, I. 131 17 37 S 149 27W
Tahoe 160 39 12N 120 9W
Tahoe, L. 160 39 0N 120 9W
Tahora 142 39 2 S 174 49 E
Tahoua 121 14 57N 5 16 E
Tahsien 108 31 17N 107 30 E
Tahsin 108 22 48N 107 23 E
Tahsinganling Shanmo 105 49 0N 122 0 E
Tahsingkou 107 43 23N 129 39 E
Tahsintien 107 37 37N 120 50 E
Tahsüeh Shan, mts. 108 31 15N 101 20 E
Tahta 122 26 44N 31 32 E
Tahulandang, I. 103 2 27N 125 23 E
Tahuna 103 3 45N 125 30 E
Tahung Shan, mts. 109 31 30N 112 50 E
Tai 108 30 41N 103 29 E
Taï 120 5 55N 7 30W
T'ai Hu 105 31 10N 120 0 E
Tai Shan 109 30 17N 122 10 E
T'aian 107 36 12N 117 7 E
T'aichiang 108 26 40N 108 19 E
T'aichou 109 32 22N 119 45 E
T'aichou Liehtao 109 28 30N 121 53 E
T'aichung 105 24 9N 120 37 E
T'aichunghsien 109 24 15N 120 35 E
Taieri, R. 143 46 3 S 170 12 E
Taiga Madema 119 23 46N 15 25 E
T'aihang Shan, mts. 106 35 40N 113 20 E
Taihape 142 39 41 S 175 48 E
T'aiho, Anhwei, China 109 33 10N 115 36 E
T'aiho, Kiangsi, China 109 26 50N 114 53 E
T'aihsien 109 32 17N 120 10 E
T'aihsing 109 32 10N 120 4 E
Taihu 109 30 30N 116 25 E
T'aik'ang 106 34 4N 114 52 E
Taikkyi 98 17 20N 96 0 E
T'aiku 106 37 23N 112 34 E
Tailem Bend 140 35 12 S 139 29 E
Tailfingen 49 48 15N 9 1 E
Taïma 92 27 35N 38 45 E
Taimyr = Taymyr 77 75 0N 100 0 E
Taimyr, Oz. 77 74 20N 102 0 E
Tain 37 57 49N 4 4W
T'ainan 109 23 0N 120 10 E
T'ainanhsien 109 23 21N 120 17 E
Taínaron, Ákra 69 36 22N 22 27 E
Tainggya 98 17 49N 94 29 E
T'aining 109 26 55N 117 12 E
Taintignies 47 50 33N 3 22 E
Taiobeiras 171 15 49 S 42 14W
T'aipei 109 25 2N 121 30 E
T'aip'ing 109 30 18N 118 6 E
Taiping 101 4 51N 100 44 E
Taipu 170 5 37 S 35 36W
T'aip'ussuchi 106 41 55N 115 23 E
Taisha 110 35 24N 132 40 E
T'aishan 109 22 17N 112 43 E
Taishun 109 27 33N 119 43 E
Taita □ 126 4 0 S 38 30 E
Taita Hills 126 3 25 S 38 15 E
Taitao, Pen. de 176 46 30 S 75 0W
T'aitung 105 22 43N 121 4 E
Taivalkoski 74 65 33N 28 12 E
Taiwan (Formosa) ■ 109 23 30N 121 0 E
Taiwara 93 33 30N 64 24 E
Taïyetos Óros 69 37 0N 22 23 E
Taiyiba, Israel 90 32 36N 35 27 E
Taiyiba, Jordan 90 31 55N 35 17 E
T'aiyüan 106 37 55N 112 40 E
Ta'izz 91 13 43N 44 7 E
Tajapuru, Furo do 170 1 50 S 50 25W
Tajarhī 119 24 15N 14 46 E
Tajicaringa 164 23 15N 104 44W
Tajima 112 35 19N 135 8 E
Tajimi 111 35 19N 137 8 E
Tajimi Gifu 55 35 25N 137 5 E
Tajitos 164 30 58N 112 18W
Tajo, R. 57 40 35N 1 52W
Tajumulco, Volcán de 165 15 20N 91 50W
Tājūrā 119 32 51N 13 27 E
Tak 100 16 52N 99 8 E
Takachiho 110 32 42N 131 18 E
Takahashi 110 34 51N 133 39 E
Takaka 143 40 51N 172 50 E
Takamatsu 110 34 20N 134 5 E
Takanabe 110 32 8N 131 30 E
Takaoka 111 36 40N 137 0 E
Takapau 142 40 2 S 176 21 E
Takapuna 142 36 47 S 174 47 E
Takasago 110 34 45N 134 48 E
Takasaki 111 36 20N 139 0 E
Takase 110 34 7N 133 48 E
Takatsuki 111 34 51N 135 37 E
Takaungu 126 3 38 S 39 52 E
Takawa 110 33 47N 130 51 E
Takayama 111 36 18N 137 11 E
Takayama-Bonchi 111 36 0N 137 18 E
Takefu 111 35 50N 136 10 E
Takehara 110 34 21N 132 55 E
Takeley 29 51 52N 0 16 E
Takeo, Camb. 101 10 59N 104 47 E
Takeo, Japan 110 33 12N 130 1 E
Tåkern 73 58 22N 14 45 E
Takestan 92 36 0N 49 50 E
Taketa 110 32 58N 131 24 E
Takh 95 33 6N 77 32 E
Takhman 101 11 29N 104 57 E
Taki 135 6 29 S 155 52 E
Takingeun 102 4 45N 96 50 E
Takla L. 152 55 15N 125 45W
Takla Landing 152 55 30N 125 50W
Takla Makan 105 39 0N 83 0 E
Takoradi 120 4 58N 1 55W
Taku, China 107 38 59N 117 41 E
Taku, Japan 110 33 18N 130 3 E
Taku, R. 152 58 30N 133 50W
Takuan 108 27 44N 103 53 E
Takum 121 7 18N 9 36 E
Takuma 110 34 13N 133 40 E
Takushan 107 39 55N 123 30 E
Tal-y-llyn 31 52 40N 3 44W
Tal-y-sarn 31 53 3N 4 12W
Tala, Uruguay 173 34 21 S 55 46W
Tala, U.S.S.R. 77 72 40N 113 30 E
Talach'in 106 36 42N 104 54 E
Talagante 172 33 40 S 70 50W
Talaint 118 29 37N 9 45W
Talak 121 18 0N 5 0 E
Talamanca, Cordillera de 166 9 20N 83 20W
Talara 174 4 30 S 81 10 E
Talas 85 42 45N 72 0 E
Talas, R. 85 44 0N 70 20 E
Talasea 135 5 20 S 150 2 E
Talasskiy, Khrebet 85 42 15N 72 0 E
Talata Mafara 121 12 38N 6 4 E
Talaud, Kepulauan 103 4 30N 127 10 E
Talavera de la Reina 56 39 55N 4 46W
Talawana 136 22 51 S 121 9 E
Talawgyi 98 25 4N 97 19 E
Talayan 103 6 52N 124 24 E
Talbot, C. 136 13 48 S 126 43 E
Talbragar, R. 141 32 5 S 149 15 E
Talca 172 35 20 S 71 46W
Talca □ 172 35 20 S 71 46W
Talcahuano 172 36 40 S 73 10W
Talcher 96 20 55N 85 3 E
Talcho 121 14 35N 3 22 E
Taldom 81 56 45N 37 29 E
Taldy Kurgan 76 45 10N 78 45 E
Taleqan □ 93 36 40N 69 30 E
Talesh, Kūlhā-Ye 92 39 0N 48 30 E
Talfit 90 32 5N 35 17 E
Talga, R. 136 21 2 S 119 51 E
Talgar 85 43 19N 77 15 E
Talgar, Pic 85 43 5N 77 20 E
Talgarth 31 51 59N 3 15W
Talguharai 122 18 19N 35 56 E
Talguppa 93 14 10N 74 45 E
Tali, Shensi, China 106 34 48N 109 48 E
Tali, Yunnan, China 108 25 45N 100 5 E
Tali Post 123 5 55N 30 44 E
Taliabu, I. 103 1 45 S 125 0 E
Taliang Shan 108 28 0N 103 0 E
Talibong, Ko 101 7 15N 99 23 E
Talihina 159 34 45N 95 1W
Talikoti 96 16 29N 76 17 E
Talimardzhan 85 38 23N 65 37 E
Taling Ho, R. 107 40 54N 121 38 E
Taling Sung 101 15 5N 99 11 E
Talitsa 84 57 0N 63 43 E
Taliwang 102 8 50 S 116 55 E
Talkeetna 147 62 20N 150 0W
Talkeetna Mts. 147 62 20N 149 0W
Tall 'Asūr 90 31 59N 35 17 E
Talla 122 28 5N 30 43 E
Talladale 36 57 41N 5 20W
Talladega 157 33 28N 86 2W
Tallahassee 157 30 25N 84 15W
Tallangatta 141 36 15 S 147 10 E
Tallarook 141 37 5 S 145 6 E
Tallåsen 72 61 52N 16 2 E
Tallawang 141 32 12 S 149 28 E
Tällberg 72 60 51N 15 2 E
Tallebung 141 32 42 S 146 34 E
Tallering Pk 137 28 6 S 115 37 E
Tallinn (Reval) 80 59 29N 24 58 E
Tallow 39 52 6N 8 0W
Tallowbridge 39 52 6N 8 1W
Tallulah 159 32 25N 91 12W
Talluza 90 32 17N 35 18 E
Talmage 153 49 46N 103 40W
Talmest 118 31 48N 9 21W
Talmont 44 46 27N 1 37W
Talnoye 82 48 57N 30 35 E
Taloda 96 21 34N 74 19 E
Talodi 123 10 35N 30 22 E
Talou Shan, mts. 108 28 20N 107 10 E
Talovaya 81 51 13N 40 38 E
Talpa de Allende 164 20 23N 104 51W
Talsarnau 31 52 54N 4 4W
Talsinnt 118 32 33N 3 27W
Taltal 172 25 23 S 70 40W
Taltson L. 153 61 30N 110 15W
Taltson R. 152 61 24N 112 46W
Talwood 139 28 29 S 149 29 E
Talyawalka Cr. 140 32 28 S 142 22 E
Talybont 31 52 29N 3 59W
Tam Chau 101 10 48N 105 12 E
Tam Ky 100 15 34N 108 29 E
Tam Quan 100 14 35N 109 3 E
Tama 158 41 56N 92 37W
Tama Abu, Pegunungan 102 3 50N 115 0 E
Tamala 137 26 35 S 113 40 E
Tamalameque 174 8 52N 73 49W
Tamale 121 9 22N 0 50W
Taman 82 45 14N 36 41 E
Tamana 110 32 58N 130 32 E
Tamanar 118 31 1N 9 46W
Tamano 110 34 35N 133 59 E
Tamanrasset 119 22 56N 5 30 E
Tamanrasset, O. 118 22 0N 2 0 E
Tamanthi 98 25 19N 95 17 E
Tamaqua 162 40 46N 75 58W
Tamar, R. 30 50 33N 4 15W
Tamara 174 5 50N 72 10W
Tamarang 141 31 27 S 150 5 E
Tamarite de Litera 58 41 52N 0 25 E
Tamashima 110 34 32N 133 40 E
Tamási 53 46 40N 18 18 E
Tamaské 121 14 55N 5 55 E
Tamatave 129 18 10 S 49 25 E
Tamatave □ 129 18 0 S 49 0 E
Tamaulipas □ 165 24 0N 99 0W
Tamaulipas, Sierra de 165 23 30N 98 20W
Tamazula 164 24 55N 106 58W
Tamazunchale 165 21 16N 98 47W
Tambacounda 120 13 55N 13 45W
Tambai 123 16 32N 37 13 E
Tambelan, Kepulauan 102 1 0N 107 30 E

Tambellup **Taunton**

Tambellup	**137**	34 4S	117 37E
Tambo	**138**	24 54S	146 14E
Tambo de Mora	**174**	13 30S	76 20W
Tambohorano	**129**	17 30S	43 58E
Tambora, G.	**102**	8 12S	118 5E
Tamboritha, Mt.	**141**	37 31S	146 51E
Tambov	**81**	52 45N	41 20E
Tambre, R.	**56**	42 55N	8 30W
Tambuku, G.	**103**	7 8S	113 40E
Tamburâ	**123**	5 40N	27 25E
Tamchaket	**120**	17 25N	10 40W
Tamchok Khambab (Brahmaputra)	**99**	29 25N	88 0E
Tamdybulak	**85**	41 46N	64 36E
Tame	**174**	6 28N	71 44W
Tame, R.	**28**	52 43N	1 45W
Tamega, R.	**56**	41 12N	8 5W
Tamelelt	**119**	26 30N	6 14E
Tamenglong	**98**	25 0N	93 35E
Tamerfors	**75**	61 30N	23 50E
Tamerlanovka	**85**	42 36N	69 17E
Tamerton Foliot	**30**	50 25N	4 10W
Tamerza	**119**	34 23N	7 58E
Tamgak, Mts.	**121**	19 12N	8 35E
Tamiahua, Laguna de	**165**	21 30N	97 30W
Tamil Nadu □	**97**	11 0N	77 0E
Tamines	**47**	50 26N	4 36E
Taming	**106**	36 20N	115 10E
Tamins	**51**	46 50N	9 24E
Tamluk	**95**	22 18N	87 58E
Tammisaari (Ekenäs)	**75**	60 0N	23 26E
Tammun'	**90**	32 18N	35 23E
Tamnaren	**72**	60 10N	17 25E
Tamou	**121**	12 45N	2 11E
Tampa	**157**	27 57N	82 30W
Tampa B.	**157**	27 40N	82 40W
Tampere	**75**	61 30N	23 50E
Tampico	**165**	22 20N	97 50W
Tampin	**101**	2 28N	102 13E
Tamri	**118**	30 49N	9 50W
Tamrida = Hadibu	**91**	12 35N	54 2E
Tamsagbulag	**105**	47 14N	117 21E
Tamsagout	**118**	24 5N	6 35W
Tamsalu	**80**	59 11N	26 8E
Tamsweg	**52**	47 7N	13 49E
Tamu	**99**	24 13N	94 12E
Tamuja, R.	**57**	39 33N	6 8W
Tamworth, Austral.	**141**	31 0S	150 58E
Tamworth, U.K.	**28**	52 38N	1 41W
Tamyang	**107**	35 19N	126 59E
Tan An	**101**	10 32N	106 25E
Tana	**74**	70 7N	28 5E
Tana Fd.	**74**	70 35N	28 30E
Tana, L.	**123**	13 5N	37 30E
Tana, R., Kenya	**126**	0 50S	39 45E
Tana, R., Norway	**48**	69 50N	26 0E
Tanabe	**111**	33 44N	135 22E
Tanabi	**171**	20 37S	49 37W
Tanacross	**147**	63 40N	143 30W
Tanafjorden	**74**	70 45N	28 25E
Tanagro, R.	**65**	40 35N	15 25E
Tanahdjampea, I.	**103**	7 10S	120 35E
Tanahgrogot	**102**	1 55S	116 15E
Tanahmasa, I.	**102**	0 5S	98 29E
Tanahmerah	**103**	6 0S	140 7E
Tanami	**136**	19 59S	129 43E
Tanami Des.	**136**	18 50S	132 0E
Tanana	**147**	65 10N	152 15W
Tanana, R.	**147**	64 25N	145 30W
Tananarive	**129**	18 55S	47 31E
Tananarive □	**129**	19 0S	47 0E
Tananarive = Antananarivo	**125**	18 55S	47 31E
Tananger	**71**	58 57N	5 37E
Tanant	**118**	31 54N	6 56W
Tánaro, R.	**62**	44 9N	7 50E
Tanaunelia	**64**	40 42N	9 45E
Tanba-Sanchi	**111**	35 7N	135 48E
Tanbar	**97**	25 55S	142 0E
Tancarville	**42**	49 29N	0 28E
Tanchai	**108**	25 58N	107 49E
T'anch'eng	**107**	34 38N	118 21E
Tanda, U.P., India	**95**	26 33N	82 35E
Tanda, U.P., India	**95**	28 57N	78 56E
Tanda, Ivory C.	**120**	7 48N	3 10W
Tandag	**103**	9 4N	126 9E
Tandala	**127**	9 25S	34 15E
Tândârei	**70**	44 39N	27 40E
Tandil	**172**	37 15S	59 6W
Tandjungpandan	**102**	2 43S	107 38E
Tandlianwald	**94**	31 3N	73 9E
Tando Adam	**94**	25 45N	68 40E
Tandou L.	**140**	32 40S	142 5E
Tandragee	**38**	54 22N	6 23W
Tandsbyn	**72**	63 0N	14 45W
Tandur	**96**	19 11N	79 30E
Tane-ga-Shima	**112**	30 35N	130 59E
Taneatua	**142**	38 4S	177 1E
Tanen Range	**101**	19 40N	99 0E
Tanen Tong Dan, Burma	**99**	16 30N	98 30E
Tanen Tong Dan, Thai.	**100**	19 43N	98 30E
Taneytown	**162**	39 40N	77 10W
Tanezrouft	**118**	23 9N	0 11E
Tanfeng	**106**	33 45N	110 18E
Tang	**38**	53 31N	7 49W
Tang, Koh	**101**	10 16N	103 7E
Tang Krasang	**101**	12 34N	105 3E
Tang La	**99**	32 59N	92 17E
Tang Pass	**99**	32 59N	92 17E
Tanga	**99**	5 5S	39 2E
Tanga □	**126**	5 20S	38 0E
Tanga Is.	**135**	3 20S	153 15E
Tangail	**98**	24 15N	89 55E
Tanganyika, L.	**126**	6 40S	30 0E
T'angch'i	**109**	29 3N	119 24E
Tanger	**118**	35 50N	5 49W
Tangerang	**103**	6 12S	106 39E
Tangerhütte	**48**	52 26N	11 50E
Tangermünde	**48**	52 32N	11 57E
T'angho	**109**	32 10N	112 20E
Tangier	**162**	37 49N	75 59W
Tangier = Tanger	**118**	35 50N	5 49W
Tangier I.	**162**	37 50N	76 0W
Tangier Sd.	**162**	38 3N	75 5W
Tangkak	**101**	2 18N	102 34E
T'angku	**107**	39 4N	117 45E
T'angkula Shanmo	**98**	33 0N	92 0E
Tanglha Shan	**99**	33 0N	90 0E
Tangorin P.O.	**138**	21 47S	144 12E
Tangra Tso	**99**	31 25N	85 30E
Tangshan	**106**	34 25N	116 24E
T'angshan	**107**	39 40N	118 10E
T'angt'ang	**108**	26 29N	104 12E
T'angt'ou	**107**	35 21N	118 32E
Tangt'u	**109**	31 34N	118 29E
Tanguiéta	**121**	10 40N	1 21E
Tangyang, Chekiang, China	**109**	29 17N	120 14E
Tangyang, Hupeh, China	**109**	30 50N	111 45E
Tangyen Ho, R.	**108**	28 55N	108 36E
Tanimbar, Kepulauan	**103**	7 30S	131 30E
Taning	**106**	36 32N	110 47E
Taniyama	**110**	31 31N	130 31E
Tanjay	**103**	9 30N	123 5E
Tanjore = Thanjavur	**97**	10 48N	79 12E
Tanjung	**102**	2 10S	115 25E
Tanjung Malim	**101**	3 42N	101 31E
Tanjungbalai	**102**	2 55N	99 44E
Tanjungbatu	**102**	2 23N	118 3E
Tanjungkarang	**102**	5 20S	105 10E
Tanjungpinang	**102**	1 5N	104 30E
Tanjungpriok	**103**	6 8S	106 55E
Tanjungredeb	**102**	2 9N	117 29E
Tanjungselor	**102**	2 55N	117 25E
Tank	**94**	32 14N	70 25E
Tankan Shan	**109**	22 3N	114 16E
Tanleng	**108**	30 2N	103 33E
Tanndalen	**72**	62 33N	12 18E
Tannin	**150**	49 40N	91 0W
Tannis B.	**73**	57 40N	10 15E
Tano, R.	**120**	6 0N	2 30W
Tanoumrout	**119**	23 2N	5 31E
Tanout	**121**	14 50N	8 55E
Tanquinho	**171**	12 42S	39 43W
Tanshui	**109**	25 10N	121 28E
Tanta	**122**	30 45N	30 57E
Tantan	**118**	28 29N	11 1W
Tantoyuca	**165**	21 21N	98 10W
Tantung	**107**	40 10N	124 23E
Tantura = Dor	**90**	32 37N	34 55E
Tanuku	**96**	16 45N	81 44E
Tanum	**73**	58 42N	11 20E
Tanunda	**140**	34 30S	139 0E
Tanur	**97**	11 1N	75 46E
Tanus	**44**	44 8N	2 19E
Tanworth	**28**	52 20N	1 50W
Tanzania ■	**126**	6 40S	34 0E
Tanzawa-Sanchi	**111**	35 27N	139 0E
Tanzilla, R.	**152**	58 8N	130 43W
T'aoan	**107**	45 20N	122 50E
Taoch'eng	**108**	29 3N	100 10E
Taoerh Ho	**107**	45 42N	124 5E
Taofu	**108**	31 0N	101 9E
Taohsien	**109**	25 37N	111 24E
T'aohua Tao	**109**	29 48N	122 17E
T'aolo	**106**	38 45N	106 40E
Taormina	**65**	37 52N	15 16E
Taos	**161**	36 28N	105 35W
Taoudenni	**118**	22 40N	3 55W
Taoudrart, Adrar	**118**	24 25N	2 24E
Taounate	**118**	34 32N	4 41W
Taourirt, Alg.	**118**	26 37N	0 8E
Taourirt, Moroc.	**118**	34 20N	2 47W
Taouz	**118**	31 2N	4 0W
T'aoyüan, China	**109**	28 54N	111 29E
T'aoyüan, Taiwan	**109**	25 0N	121 4E
Tapa	**80**	59 15N	26 0E
Tapa Shan	**108**	31 45N	109 30E
Tapachula	**165**	14 54N	92 17W
Tapah	**101**	4 12N	101 15E
Tapajós, R.	**175**	4 30S	56 10W
Tapaktuan	**102**	3 30N	97 10E
Tapanui	**143**	45 56S	169 18E
Tapauá	**174**	5 40S	64 20W
Tapauá, R.	**174**	6 0S	65 40W
Tapeta	**120**	6 36N	8 52W
Taphan Hin	**100**	16 13N	100 16E
Tapia	**56**	43 34N	6 56W
Tapieh Shan, mts.	**109**	31 20N	115 30E
T'ap'ingchen	**106**	33 42N	111 44E
Tapini	**135**	8 19S	147 0E
Tápiószele	**53**	47 45N	19 55E
Tapiraí	**171**	19 52S	46 1W
Tapirapé, R.	**170**	10 41S	50 38W
Tapirapecó, Serra	**174**	1 10N	65 0W
Taplan	**140**	34 33S	140 52E
Tapolca	**53**	46 53N	17 29E
Tappahannock	**162**	37 56N	76 50W
Tapsing	**99**	30 22N	96 25E
Tapti, R.	**96**	21 25N	75 0E
Tapu	**109**	24 31N	116 41E
Tapuaenuku, Mt.	**143**	41 55S	173 50E
Tapul Group, Is.	**103**	5 35N	120 50E
Tapun	**98**	18 22N	95 27E
Taquara	**173**	29 36N	50 46W
Taquari, R.	**173**	18 10S	56 0W
Taquaritinga	**171**	21 24S	48 30W
Tara, Austral.	**139**	27 17S	150 31E
Tara, Japan	**110**	33 2N	130 11E
Tara, U.S.S.R.	**76**	56 55N	74 30E
Tara, Zambia	**127**	16 58S	26 45E
Tara-Dake	**110**	32 58N	130 6E
Tara, R.	**66**	43 10N	19 20E
Tarabagatay, Khrebet	**77**	48 0N	83 0E
Tarãbulus, Leb.	**92**	34 31N	33 52E
Tarãbulus, Libya	**119**	32 49N	13 7E
Taradale	**142**	39 33S	176 53E
Tarahouahout	**119**	22 47N	5 59E
Tarakan	**102**	3 20N	117 35E
Tarakit, Mt.	**126**	2 2N	35 10E
Taralga	**141**	34 26S	149 52E
Taramakau, R.	**143**	42 34S	171 8E
Tarana	**141**	33 31S	149 52E
Taranagar	**94**	28 43N	75 9E
Taranaki □	**142**	39 5S	174 51E
Tarancón	**58**	40 1N	3 1W
Taranga	**94**	23 56N	72 43E
Taranga Hill	**94**	24 0N	72 40E
Taranșay, I.	**36**	57 54N	7 0W
Taransay, Sd. of	**36**	57 52N	7 0W
Táranto	**65**	40 30N	17 11E
Táranto, G. di	**65**	40 0N	17 15E
Tarapacá	**174**	2 56S	69 46W
Tarapacá □	**172**	20 45S	69 30W
Tarare	**45**	45 54N	4 26E
Tararua Range	**142**	40 45S	175 25E
Tarascon, Ariège, France	**44**	42 50N	1 37E
Tarascon, Bouches-du-Rhône, France	**45**	43 48N	4 39E
Tarashcha	**82**	49 30N	30 31E
Tarat, Bj.	**119**	26 4N	9 7E
Tarauacá	**174**	8 6S	70 48W
Tarauacá, R.	**174**	7 30S	70 30W
Taravo, R.	**45**	41 48N	8 52E
Tarawera	**142**	39 2S	176 36E
Tarawera L.	**142**	38 13S	176 27E
Tarawera Mt.	**142**	38 14S	176 32E
Tarazat, Massif de	**119**	20 2N	8 30E
Tarazona	**58**	41 55N	1 43W
Tarazona de la Mancha	**59**	39 16N	1 55W
Tarbat Ness	**37**	57 52N	3 48W
Tarbela Dam	**94**	34 0N	72 52E
Tarbert, Ireland	**39**	52 34N	9 22W
Tarbert, Strathclyde, U.K.	**34**	55 55N	5 25W
Tarbert, W. Isles, U.K.	**36**	57 54N	6 49W
Tarbert, L. E.	**36**	57 50N	6 45W
Tarbert, L. W., Strathclyde, U.K.	**34**	55 58N	5 30W
Tarbert, L. W., W. Isles, U.K.	**36**	57 55N	6 56W
Tarbes	**44**	43 15N	0 3E
Tarbet, Highland, U.K.	**36**	56 58N	5 38W
Tarbet, Strathclyde, U.K.	**34**	56 13N	4 44W
Tarbolton	**34**	55 30N	4 30W
Tarboro	**157**	35 55N	77 3W
Tarbrax	**138**	21 7S	142 26E
Tarbū	**119**	26 0N	15 5E
Tarcento	**63**	46 12N	13 12E
Tarcoola	**139**	30 44S	134 36E
Tarcoon	**139**	30 15S	146 35E
Tarcǔu, Munţii	**70**	46 39N	26 7E
Tardets-Sorholus	**44**	43 17N	0 52W
Taree	**141**	31 50S	152 30E
Tarentaise	**45**	45 30N	6 35E
Tarf Shaqq al Abd	**122**	26 50N	36 6E
Tarfa, Wadi el	**122**	28 16N	31 15E
Tarfaya	**116**	27 55N	12 55W
Targon	**44**	44 44N	0 16W
Targuist	**118**	34 59N	4 14W
Tarhbalt	**118**	30 48N	5 10W
Tarhit	**118**	30 58N	2 0W
Tarhūnah	**119**	32 15N	13 28E
Tari	**135**	5 54S	142 59E
Tarib, Wadi	**122**	18 30N	43 23E
Táriba	**174**	7 49N	72 13W
Tarifa	**57**	36 1N	5 36W
Tarija	**172**	21 30S	64 40W
Tarija □	**172**	21 30S	63 30W
Tarim, R.	**105**	41 5N	86 40E
Tarime □	**126**	1 15S	34 0E
Taringo Downs	**141**	32 13S	145 33E
Taritoe, R.	**103**	3 0S	138 5E
Tarka, R.	**128**	32 10S	26 0E
Tarkastad	**128**	32 0S	26 16E
Tarkhankut, Mys	**82**	45 25N	32 30E
Tarko Sale	**76**	64 55N	77 50E
Tarkwa	**120**	5 20N	2 0W
Tarlac	**103**	15 29N	120 35E
Tarland	**37**	57 8N	2 51W
Tarleton	**32**	53 41N	2 50W
Tarlsland	**152**	57 03N	111 40W
Tarlton Downs	**138**	22 40S	136 45E
Tarm	**73**	55 56N	8 31E
Tarma	**174**	11 25S	75 45W
Tarn □	**44**	43 49N	2 8E
Tarn-et-Garonne □	**44**	44 8N	1 20E
Tarn, R.	**44**	44 5N	1 2E
Tärna	**74**	65 45N	15 10E
Tarna, R.	**53**	48 0N	20 5E
Tårnby	**73**	55 37N	12 36E
Tarnobrzeg □	**54**	50 40N	22 0E
Tarnów	**54**	50 3N	21 0E
Tarnów □	**54**	50 0N	21 0E
Tarnowskie Góry	**54**	50 27N	18 54E
Táro, R.	**62**	44 37N	9 58E
Tarong	**139**	26 47S	151 51E
Taroom	**139**	25 36S	149 48E
Taroudannt	**118**	30 30N	8 52W
Tarp	**48**	54 40N	9 25E
Tarpon Springs	**157**	28 8N	82 42W
Tarporley	**32**	53 10N	2 42W
Tarquínia	**63**	42 15N	11 45E
Tarqumiyah	**90**	31 35N	35 1E
Tarragona	**58**	41 5N	1 17E
Tarragona □	**58**	41 0N	1 0E
Tarrasa	**58**	41 26N	2 1E
Tárrega	**58**	41 39N	1 9E
Tarrytown	**162**	41 5N	73 52W
Tarshiha = Me'ona	**90**	33 1N	35 15E
Tarso Emissi	**119**	21 27N	18 36E
Tarso Ovrari	**119**	21 27N	17 27E
Tarsus	**92**	36 58N	34 55E
Tartagal	**172**	22 30S	63 50W
Tartan, oilfield	**19**	58 22N	0 5E
Tartas	**44**	43 50N	0 49W
Tartna Point	**140**	32 54S	142 24E
Tartu	**80**	58 25N	26 58E
Tartus	**92**	34 55N	35 55E
Tarumirim	**171**	19 16S	41 59W
Tarumizu	**110**	31 29N	130 42E
Tarussa	**81**	54 44N	37 10E
Tarutao, Ko	**101**	6 33N	99 40E
Tarutung	**102**	2 0N	99 0E
Tarves	**37**	57 22N	2 13W
Tarvisio	**63**	46 31N	13 35E
Tarz Ulli	**119**	25 46N	9 44E
Tas-Buget	**85**	44 46N	65 33E
Tasahku	**98**	27 33N	97 52E
Tasãwah	**119**	26 0N	13 37E
Taschereau	**150**	48 40N	78 40W
Taseko, R.	**152**	52 4N	123 9W
Tasgaon	**96**	17 2N	74 39E
Ta'shan	**123**	16 31N	42 33E
Tashauz	**76**	42 0N	59 20E
Tashet'ai	**106**	41 0N	109 21E
Tashi Chho Dzong	**98**	27 31N	89 45E
Tashihch'iao (Yingk'ou)	**107**	40 38N	122 30E
T'ashihk'uerhkan	**85**	37 47N	75 14E
Tashkent	**85**	41 20N	69 10E
Tashkumyr	**85**	41 40N	72 10E
Tashkurghan	**93**	36 45N	67 40E
Tashtagol	**76**	52 47N	87 53E
Tasikmalaya	**103**	7 18S	108 12E
Tasjön	**74**	64 15N	15 45E
Taşköpru	**82**	41 30N	34 15E
Tasman Bay	**143**	40 59S	173 25E
Tasman Glacier	**143**	43 45S	170 20E
Tasman, Mt.	**143**	43 34S	170 12E
Tasman Mts.	**143**	41 3S	172 25E
Tasman Pen.	**138**	43 10S	148 0E
Tasman, R.	**143**	43 48S	170 8E
Tasman Sea	**142**	36 0S	160 0E
Tasmania, I., □	**138**	49 0S	146 30E
Tassil Tin-Rerhoh	**118**	20 5N	3 55E
Tassili n-Ajjer	**119**	25 47N	8 1E
Tassili-Oua-Ahaggar	**119**	20 41N	5 30E
Tasty	**85**	44 47N	69 7E
Tasu Sd.	**152**	52 47N	132 2W
Tata, Hung.	**53**	47 37N	18 19E
Tata, Moroc.	**118**	29 46N	7 50W
Tatabánya	**53**	47 32N	18 25E
Tatar A.S.S.R. □	**84**	55 30N	51 30E
Tatarsk	**76**	55 20N	75 50E
Tatarskiy Proliv	**77**	54 0N	141 0E
Tatebayashi	**111**	36 15N	139 32E
Tateshina-Yama	**111**	36 8N	138 11E
Tateyama	**111**	35 0N	139 50E
Tathlina L.	**152**	60 33N	117 39W
Tathra	**141**	36 44S	149 59E
Tat'ien, Fukien, China	**109**	25 42N	117 50E
Tat'ien, Szechwan, China	**108**	26 18N	101 45E
Tatinnai L.	**153**	60 55N	97 40W
Tatlayoka Lake	**152**	51 35N	124 24W
Tatnam, C.	**153**	57 16N	91 0W
Tato Ho, R.	**108**	31 25N	100 42E
Tatra = Tatry	**54**	49 20N	20 0E
Tatry	**54**	49 20N	20 0E
Tatsu	**108**	29 40N	105 45E
Tatsuno	**110**	34 52N	134 33E
Tatta	**94**	24 42N	67 55E
Tattenhall	**32**	53 7N	2 47W
Tatu Ho, R.	**108**	29 35N	103 47E
Tatuī	**173**	23 25S	48 0W
Tatum	**159**	33 16N	103 16W
Tat'ung, Anhwei, China	**109**	30 48N	117 44E
Tat'ung, Shansi, China	**106**	40 9N	113 19E
Tatura	**141**	36 29S	145 16E
Tatvan	**92**	37 28N	42 27E
Tauá	**170**	6 1S	40 26W
Taubaté	**173**	23 5S	45 30W
Tauberbischofsheim	**49**	49 37N	9 40E
Taucha	**48**	51 22N	12 31E
Tauern, mts.	**52**	47 15N	12 40E
Tauern-tunnel	**52**	47 0N	13 12E
Taufikia	**123**	9 24N	31 37E
Taumarunui	**142**	38 53S	175 15E
Taumaturgo	**174**	9 0S	73 50W
Taung	**128**	27 33S	24 47E
Taungdwingyi	**98**	20 1N	95 40E
Taunggyi	**98**	20 50N	97 0E
Taungtha	**98**	20 45N	94 50E
Taungup	**98**	18 51N	94 14E
Taungup Pass	**98**	18 40N	94 45E
Taungup Taunggya	**99**	18 20N	93 40E
Taunsa Barrage	**95**	31 0N	71 0E
Taunton, U.K.	**28**	51 1N	3 7W

Taunton Tetbury

Taunton, U.S.A. 162 41 54N 71 6W
Taunus 49 50 15N 8 20 E
Taupo 142 38 41 S 176 7 E
Taupo, L. 142 38 46 S 175 55 E
Tauq 92 35 12N 44 29 E
Taurage 80 55 14N 22 28 E
Tauramena 174 5 1N 72 45W
Tauranga 142 37 35 S 176 11 E
Tauranga Harb. 142 37 30 S 176 5 E
Taureau, Lac 150 46 50N 73 40W
Tauri, R. 135 8 8 S 146 8 E
Taurianova 65 38 22N 16 1 E
Taurus Mts. = Toros Dağlari 92 37 0N 35 0 E
Táuste 58 41 58N 1 18W
Tauz 83 41 0N 45 40 E
Tavani 153 62 10N 93 30W
Tavannes 50 47 13N 7 12 E
Tavas 92 37 35N 29 8 E
Tavda 84 58 7N 65 8 E
Tavda, R. 84 59 30N 63 0 E
Taverny 43 49 2N 2 13 E
Taveta 124 3 31N 37 37 E
Taviche 165 16 38N 96 32W
Tavignano, R. 45 42 7N 9 33 E
Tavira 57 37 8N 7 40W
Tavistock 30 50 33N 4 9W
Tavolara, I. 64 40 55N 9 40 E
Távora, R. 56 41 0N 7 30W
Tavoy 101 14 7N 98 18 E
Tavoy, I. = Mali Kyun 99 13 0N 98 20 E
Taw, R. 30 50 58N 3 58W
Tawang 99 27 37N 91 50 E
Tawas City 156 44 16N 83 31W
Tawau 102 4 20N 117 55 E
Tawngche 98 26 34N 95 38 E
Tawnyinah 38 53 55N 8 45W
Tāworgha' 119 32 1N 15 2 E
Taxila 94 33 42N 72 52 E
Tay Bridge 35 56 28N 3 0W
Tay, Firth of 35 56 25N 3 8W
Tay, L., Austral. 137 32 55 S 120 48 E
Tay, L., U.K. 35 56 30N 4 10W
Tay Ninh 101 11 20N 106 5 E
Tay, R. 35 56 37N 3 38W
Tay Strath 37 56 38N 3 40W
Tayabamba 174 8 15 S 77 10W
Tayao 108 25 41N 101 18 E
Tayaparva La 95 31 35N 83 20 E
Tayeh 109 30 5N 114 57 E
Taylor, Can. 152 56 13N 120 40W
Taylor, Alaska, U.S.A. 147 65 40N 164 50W
Taylor, Pa., U.S.A. 162 41 23N 75 43W
Taylor, Tex., U.S.A. 159 30 30N 97 30W
Taylor, Mt. 143 43 30 S 171 20 E
Taylor Mt. 161 35 16N 107 50W
Taylorville 158 39 32N 89 20W
Taymyr, Oz. 77 74 50N 102 0 E
Taymyr, P-ov. 77 75 0N 100 0 E
Taynuilt 34 56 25N 5 15W
Tayport 34 56 27N 2 52W
Tayr Zebna 90 33 14N 35 23 E
Tayshet 77 55 58N 97 25 E
Tayside □ 35 56 25N 3 30W
Taytay 103 10 45N 119 30 E
Tayu 109 25 38N 114 9 E
Tayülo 105 29 13N 98 13 E
Tayung 109 29 8N 110 30 E
Taz, R. 76 65 40N 82 0 E
Taza 118 34 10N 4 0W
Taze 98 22 57N 95 24 E
Tazenakht 118 30 46N 7 3W
Tazin L. 153 59 44N 108 42W
Tazin, R. 153 60 26N 110 45W
Tazoult 119 35 29N 6 11 E
Tazovskiy 76 67 30N 78 30 E
Tbilisi (Tiflis) 83 41 50N 44 50 E
Tchad (Chad) ■ 117 12 30N 17 15 E
Tchad, Lac 117 13 30N 14 30 E
Tchaourou 121 8 58N 2 40 E
Tchentlo L. 152 55 15N 125 0W
Tchibanga 124 2 45 S 11 12 E
Tchin Tabaraden 121 15 58N 5 50 E
Tczew 54 54 8N 18 50 E
Te Anau L. 143 45 15 S 167 45 E
Te Araroa 142 37 39 S 178 25 E
Te Aroha 142 37 32 S 175 44 E
Te Awamutu 142 38 1 S 175 20 E
Te Horo 142 40 48 S 175 6 E
Te Kaha 142 37 44 S 177 44 E
Te Karaka 142 38 26 S 177 53 E
Te Kauwhata 142 37 25 S 175 9 E
Te Kinga 143 42 35 S 171 31 E
Te Kopuru 142 36 2 S 173 56 E
Te Kuiti 142 38 20 S 175 11 E
Te Puke 142 37 46 S 176 22 E
Te Waewae B. 143 46 13 S 167 33 E
Tea Tree 136 22 11 S 133 17 E
Teaca 70 46 55N 24 30 E
Teague 159 31 40N 96 20W
Tean 109 29 21N 115 42 E
Teangue 36 57 7N 5 52W
Teano 65 41 15N 14 1 E
Teapa 165 17 35N 92 56W
Teba 57 36 59N 4 55W
Tebay 32 54 25N 2 35W
Teberda 83 43 30N 43 54 E
Tébessa 119 35 22N 8 8 E
Tebicuary, R. 172 26 36 S 58 16W
Tebing Tinggi 102 3 38 S 102 1 E
Tébourba 119 36 49N 9 51 E
Téboursouk 119 36 29N 9 10 E
Tebulos 83 42 36N 45 25 E
Tecapa 163 35 51N 116 14W
Tecate 164 32 34N 116 38W
Techa, R. 84 56 13N 62 58 E
Tech'ang 108 27 22N 102 10 E
Techiang 108 28 19N 108 5 E
Techiman 120 7 35N 1 58W
Tech'in 108 28 30N 98 52 E
Tech'ing 109 23 8N 111 46 E
Techirghiol 70 44 4N 28 32 E
Techou 106 37 19N 116 19 E
Tecomán 164 18 55N 103 53W
Tecoripa 164 28 37N 109 57W
Tecuci 70 45 51N 27 27 E
Tecumseh 156 42 1N 83 59W
Tedavnet 38 54 19N 7 2W
Tedesa 123 5 10N 37 40 E
Tedzhen 76 37 23N 60 31 E
Tees B. 72 54 37N 1 10W
Tees, R. 33 54 36N 1 25W
Teesdale 32 54 37N 2 10W
Teesside 33 54 37N 1 13W
Tefé 174 3 25 S 64 50W
Tegal 103 6 52 S 109 8 E
Tegelen 47 51 20N 6 9 E
Teggiano 65 40 24N 15 32 E
Teghra 95 25 30N 85 34 E
Tegid, L. 31 52 53N 3 38W
Tegina 121 10 5N 6 11 E
Tegucigalpa 166 14 10N 87 0W
Tehachapi 163 35 11N 118 29W
Tehachapi Mts. 163 35 0N 118 40W
Tehamiyam 122 18 26N 36 45 E
Tehilla 122 17 42N 36 6 E
Têhini 120 9 39N 3 32W
Tehrān 93 35 44N 51 30 E
Tehrān □ 93 35 0N 49 30 E
Tehsing 109 28 54N 117 34 E
Tehua 109 25 30N 118 14 E
Tehuacán 165 18 20N 97 30W
Tehuantepec 165 16 10N 95 19W
Tehuantepec, Golfo de 165 15 50N 95 0W
Tehuantepec, Istmo de 165 17 0N 94 30W
Tehui 107 44 32N 125 42 E
Teich, Le 44 44 38N 0 59W
Teifi, R. 31 52 4N 4 14W
Teign, R. 30 50 41N 3 42W
Teignmouth 30 50 33N 3 30W
Teikovo 81 56 55N 40 30 E
Teil, Le 45 44 33N 4 40 E
Teilleul, Le 42 48 32N 0 53W
Teishyai 80 55 59N 22 14 E
Teiuş 70 46 12N 23 40 E
Teixeira 170 7 13 S 37 15W
Teixeira de Sousa = Luau 124 10 40 S 22 10 E
Teixeira Pinto 120 12 10N 13 55 E
Tejo, R. 57 39 15N 8 35W
Tejon Pass 163 34 49N 118 53W
Tejung 108 28 46N 99 19 E
Tekamah 158 41 48N 96 14W
Tekapo, L. 143 43 53 S 170 33 E
Tekax 165 20 20N 89 30W
Tekeli 85 44 50N 79 0 E
Tekeze, W. 123 13 50N 37 50 E
Tekija 66 44 42N 22 26 E
Tekirdağ 92 40 58N 27 30 E
Tekkali 96 18 43N 84 24 E
Teko 108 31 49N 98 40 E
Tekoa 160 47 19N 117 4W
Tekoulât, O. 118 22 30N 2 20 E
Tel Adashim 90 32 39N 35 17 E
Tel Aviv-Yafo 90 32 4N 34 48 E
Tel Hanan 90 32 47N 35 3 E
Tel Hazor 90 33 2N 35 2 E
Tel Lakhish 90 31 34N 34 51 E
Tel Malhata 90 31 13N 35 2 E
Tel Megiddo 90 32 35N 38 11 E
Tel Mond 90 32 15N 34 56 E
Tela 166 15 40N 87 28W
Télagh 118 34 51N 0 32W
Telanaipura = Jambi 102 1 38 S 103 30 E
Telavi 83 42 0N 45 30 E
Telciu 70 47 25N 24 24 E
Telefomin 135 5 10 S 141 40 E
Telega = Doftana 70 45 17N 25 45 E
Telegraph Cr. 152 58 0N 131 10W
Telekhany 80 52 30N 25 46 E
Telemark fylke □ 71 59 25N 8 30 E
Telén 172 36 15 S 65 31W
Teleneshty 70 47 35N 28 24 E
Teleño 56 42 23N 6 22W
Teleorman □ 70 44 0N 25 0 E
Teleorman, R. 70 44 15N 25 20 E
Teles Pires (São Manuel), R. 174 8 40 S 57 0W
Telescope Peak, Mt. 163 36 6N 117 7W
Teletaye 121 16 31N 1 30 E
Telford 28 52 42N 2 31W
Telfs 52 47 19N 11 4 E
Telgte 48 51 59N 7 46 E
Telichie 139 31 45 S 139 59 E
Télimélé 120 10 54N 13 2W
Telkwa 152 54 41N 126 56W
Tell 90 32 12N 35 12 E
Tell City 156 38 0N 86 44W
Teller 147 65 12N 166 24W
Tellicherry 97 11 45N 75 30 E
Tellin 47 50 5N 5 13 E
Telluride 161 37 58N 107 54W
Telok Anson 101 4 3N 101 0 E
Teloloapán 165 18 21N 99 51W
Telom, R. 101 4 20N 101 46 E
Telpos Iz. 78 63 35N 57 30 E
Telsen 176 42 30 S 66 50W
Teltow 48 52 24N 13 15 E
Telukbetung 102 5 29 S 105 17 E
Telukbutun 101 4 5N 108 7 E
Telukdalem 102 0 45N 97 50 E
Tema 121 5 41N 0 0 E
Temagami L. 150 47 0N 80 10W
Temanggung 103 7 18 S 110 10 E
Temapache 165 21 4N 97 38W
Temax 165 21 10N 88 50W
Tembe 126 0 30 S 28 25 E
Tembeling, R. 101 4 20N 102 23 E
Tembleque 58 39 41N 3 30W
Temblor Ra, mts. 163 35 30N 120 0W
Tembuland □ 129 31 35 S 28 0 E
Teme, R. 28 52 23N 2 15W
Temecula 163 33 26N 117 6W
Temelelt 118 31 50N 7 32W
Temerloh 101 3 27N 102 25 E
Temir Tau 76 53 10N 87 20 E
Temirtau 76 50 5N 72 56 E
Témiscaming 150 46 44N 79 5W
Temma 138 41 12 S 144 42 E
Temnikov 81 54 40N 43 11 E
Temo, R. 64 40 20N 8 30 E
Temora 141 34 30 S 147 30 E
Temosachic 164 28 58N 107 50W
Tempe, S. Afr. 161 29 1 S 26 13 E
Tempe, U.S.A. 161 33 26N 111 59W
Tempe Downs 136 24 22 S 132 24 E
Temperanceville 162 37 54N 75 33W
Tempestad 174 1 20 S 74 56W
Tempino 102 1 55 S 103 23 E
Tëmpio Pausania 64 40 53N 9 6 E
Temple 159 31 5N 97 28W
Temple B. 138 12 15 S 143 3 E
Temple Combe 28 51 0N 2 25W
Temple Ewell 29 51 9N 1 16W
Temple Sowerby 30 54 38N 2 33W
Templemore 39 52 48N 7 50W
Templenoe 39 51 52N 9 40W
Templeton, Austral. 138 18 30 S 142 30 E
Templeton, U.K. 31 51 46N 4 45W
Templeton, U.S.A. 163 35 33N 120 42W
Templeton, R. 138 21 0 S 138 40 E
Templeuve 47 50 39N 3 17 E
Templin 48 53 8N 13 31 E
Tempo 38 54 23N 7 28W
Tempoal 165 21 31N 98 23W
Temryuk 82 45 15N 37 11 E
Temse 47 51 7N 4 13 E
Temska, R. 66 43 17N 22 33 E
Temuco 176 38 50 S 72 50W
Temuka 143 44 14 S 171 17 E
Ten Boer 46 53 16N 6 42 E
Tena 174 0 59 S 77 49W
Tenabo 165 20 2N 90 12W
Tenaha 159 31 57N 94 15W
Tenali 96 16 15N 80 35 E
Tenancingo 165 19 0N 99 33W
Tenango 165 19 0N 99 40W
Tenasserim 100 12 6N 99 3 E
Tenasserim □ 100 14 0N 98 30 E
Tenay 45 45 55N 5 30 E
Tenbury 28 52 18N 2 35W
Tenby 31 51 40N 4 42W
Tenda 45 44 5N 7 34 E
Tenda, Col de 45 44 9N 7 32 E
Tendaho 123 11 39N 40 54 E
Tende 45 44 5N 7 35 E
Tendelti 123 13 1N 31 55 E
Tendjedi, Adrar 119 23 41N 7 32 E
Tendrara 118 33 3N 1 58W
Tendre, Mt. 50 46 35N 6 18 E
Teneida 122 25 30N 29 19 E
Ténéré 119 23 2N 16 0 E
Tenerife, I. 116 28 20N 16 40W
Ténès 118 36 31N 1 14 E
T'eng Ch'ung 99 25 9N 98 22 E
Teng, R. 101 20 30N 98 10 E
Tengah □ 103 2 0 S 122 0 E
Tengah Kepulauan 102 7 5 S 118 15 E
Tengchow = P'englai 107 37 49N 120 47 E
Tengch'uan 108 26 0N 100 4 E
Tengch'ung 108 25 2N 98 28 E
Tengfeng 106 34 27N 113 2 E
Tenggara □ 103 3 0 S 122 0 E
Tenggol, P. 101 4 48N 103 41 E
T'enghsien, Honan, China 109 32 41N 112 5 E
T'enghsien, Kwangsi Chuang, China 109 23 23N 110 54 E
T'enghsien, Shantung, China 105 35 8N 117 9 E
Tengiz, Ozero 76 50 30N 69 0 E
Tengko 99 32 30N 98 0 E
Tengk'o 108 32 32N 97 35 E
Tengk'ou 106 40 18N 106 59 E
Tenigerbad 51 46 42N 8 57 E
Tenille 157 32 58N 82 50W
Tenindewa 137 28 30 S 115 20 E
Tenkasi 97 8 55N 77 20 E
Tenke, Congo 127 11 22 S 26 40 E
Tenke, Zaîre 127 10 32 S 26 7 E
Tenkodogo 121 12 0N 0 10W
Tenna, R. 63 43 12N 13 43 E
Tennant Creek 136 19 30 S 134 0 E
'Tenneco', oilfield 19 54 6N 4 42 E
Tennessee □ 155 36 0N 86 30W
Tenneville 47 50 6N 5 32 E
Tennsift, Oued 118 32 3N 9 28W
Tenom 102 5 4N 115 38 E
Tenosique 165 17 30N 91 24W
Tenri 111 34 46N 135 55 E
Tenryū 111 34 52N 137 55 E
Tent L. 153 62 25N 107 54W
Tenterden 29 51 4N 0 42 E
Tenterfield 139 29 0 S 152 0 E
Teófilo Otôni 171 17 50 S 41 30W
Tepa 120 6 57N 2 30W
Tepalcatepec, R. 164 18 35N 101 59W
Tepao 108 23 21N 106 33 E
Tepehuanes 164 25 21N 105 44W
Tepetongo 164 22 28N 103 9W
Tepic 164 21 30N 104 54W
Tepi'ng 107 37 28N 116 67 E
Teploklyuchenka 85 42 30N 78 30 E
Tepoca, C. 164 29 20N 112 25W
Tequila 164 20 54N 103 47W
Ter Apel 46 52 53N 7 5 E
Ter, R. 58 42 0N 2 30 E
Téra 121 14 0N 0 57 E
Tera, R. 56 41 54N 5 44W
Téramo 63 42 40N 13 40 E
Terang 140 38 15 S 142 55 E
Terawhiti, C. 142 41 16 S 174 38 E
Terborg 46 51 56N 6 22 E
Tercan 92 39 50N 40 30 E
Terceira 16 38 43N 27 13W
Tercero, R. 172 32 58 S 61 47W
Terdal 96 16 33N 75 9 E
Terebovlya 80 49 18N 25 44 E
Teregova 70 45 10N 22 16 E
Terek-Say 85 41 30N 71 11 E
Terembone Cr. 139 30 25 S 148 50 E
Terengganu □ 101 4 55N 103 0 E
Tereshka, R. 81 52 0N 46 36 E
Teresina 170 5 2 S 42 45W
Terewah L. 139 29 52 S 147 35 E
Terezinha 174 0 44N 69 27W
Terges, R. 57 37 49N 7 41W
Tergnier 43 49 40N 3 17 E
Terhazza 118 23 45N 4 59W
Terheijden 47 51 38N 4 45 E
Teriang 101 3 15N 102 26 E
Terkezi 117 18 27N 21 40 E
Terlizzi 65 41 8N 16 32 E
Termas de Chillan 172 36 50 S 71 31W
Terme 82 41 11N 37 0 E
Termez 85 37 0N 67 15 E
Términi Imerese 43 37 59N 13 51 E
Términos, Laguna de 165 18 35N 91 30W
Termoli 63 42 0N 15 0 E
Termon 38 55 3N 7 50W
Termonfeckin 38 53 47N 6 15W
Tern, oilfield 19 61 17N 0 55 E
Ternate 103 0 45N 127 25 E
Terneuzen 47 51 20N 3 50 E
Terney 77 45 3N 136 37 E
Terni 63 42 34N 12 38 E
Ternitz 52 47 43N 16 2 E
Ternopol 80 49 30N 25 40 E
Terowie, N.S.W., Austral. 139 32 27 S 147 52 E
Terowie, Vic., Austral. 140 33 10 S 138 50 E
Terra Bella 163 35 58N 119 3W
Terra Nova B. 13 74 50 S 164 40 E
Terrace 152 54 30N 128 35W
Terrace Bay 150 48 47N 87 10W
Terracina 64 41 17N 13 12 E
Terralba 64 39 42N 8 38 E
Terranuova 63 43 38N 11 35 E
Terrasini Favarotta 64 38 10N 13 4 E
Terrasson 44 45 7N 1 19 E
Terrebonne B. 159 29 15N 90 28W
Terrecht 118 20 10N 0 10W
Terrell 159 32 44N 96 19W
Terrenceville 151 47 40N 54 44W
Terrick Terrick 138 24 44 S 145 5 E
Terry 158 46 47N 105 20W
Terryglass 39 53 3N 8 14W
Terryville 162 41 41N 73 1W
Terschelling, I. 46 53 25N 5 20 E
Terskey Alatau, Khrebet 85 41 50N 77 0 E
Terter, R. 83 40 5N 46 15 E
Teruel 58 40 22N 1 8W
Teruel □ 58 40 48N 1 0W
Tervel 67 43 45N 27 28 E
Tervola 74 66 6N 24 49 E
Teryaweyna L. 140 32 18 S 143 22 E
Tešanj 66 44 38N 17 59 E
Teseney 123 15 5N 36 42 E
Tesha, R. 81 55 32N 43 0 E
Teshio 112 44 53N 141 44 E
Teshio-Gawa, R. 112 44 53N 141 45 E
Tešica 66 43 27N 21 45 E
Tesiyn Gol, R. 105 50 28N 93 4 E
Teslin 147 60 10N 132 43W
Teslin L. 152 60 15N 132 57W
Teslin, R. 152 61 34N 134 35W
Teslió 66 44 37N 17 54 E
Teso □ = Eastern □ 126 1 50N 33 45 E
Tessalit 121 20 12N 1 0 E
Tessaoua 121 13 47N 7 56 E
Tessenderlo 47 51 4N 5 5 E
Tessier 153 51 48N 107 26W
Tessin 48 54 2N 12 28 E
Tessit 121 15 13N 0 18 E
Test, R. 28 51 7N 1 30W
Testa del Gargano 65 41 50N 16 10 E
Teste, La 44 44 37N 1 8W
Tét 53 47 30N 17 33 E
Tetachuck L. 152 53 18N 125 55W
Tetas, Pta. 172 23 31 S 70 38W
Tetbury 28 51 37N 2 9W

Tete Tijibadok

Tete 127 16 13S 33 33E
Tete □ 127 15 15S 32 40E
Teterev, R. 80 50 30N 29 30E
Teteringen 47 51 37N 4 49E
Teterow 48 53 45N 12 34E
Teteven 67 42 58N 24 17E
Tethull, R. 152 60 35N 112 12W
Tetiyev 82 49 22N 29 38E
Tetlin 147 63 14N 142 50W
Tetlin Junction 147 63 29N 142 55W
Tetney 33 53 30N 0 1W
Teton, R. 160 47 58N 111 0W
Tétouan 118 35 35N 5 21W
Tetovo 66 42 1N 21 2E
Tettenhall 28 52 35N 2 7W
Tetuán = Tétouan 118 35 30N 5 25W
Tetyukhe 77 44 45N 135 40E
Teuco, R. 172 25 30S 60 25W
Teufen 51 47 24N 9 23E
Teulada 64 38 59N 8 47E
Teulon 153 50 23N 97 16W
Tevere, R. 63 42 30N 12 20E
Teviot, R. 35 55 21N 2 51W
Teviotdale 35 55 25N 2 50W
Teviothead 35 55 19N 2 55W
Tewantin 139 26 27S 153 3E
Tewkesbury 28 51 59N 2 8W
Texada I. 152 49 40N 124 25W
Texarkana, Ark., U.S.A. 159 33 25N 94 0W
Texarkana, Tex., U.S.A. 159 33 25N 94 3W
Texas 139 28 49S 151 15E
Texas □ 159 31 40N 98 30W
Texas City 159 27 20N 95 20W
Texel, I. 46 53 5N 4 50E
Texhoma 159 36 32N 101 47W
Texline 159 36 26N 103 0W
Texoma L. 159 34 0N 96 38W
Teyang 108 31 8N 104 24E
Teykovo 81 56 55N 40 30E
Teynham 29 51 19N 0 50E
Teyr Zebna 90 33 14N 35 23E
Teza, R. 81 56 41N 41 45E
Tezin 94 34 24N 69 30E
Teziutlán 165 19 50N 97 30W
Tezpur 98 26 40N 92 45E
Tezzeron L. 152 54 43N 124 30W
Tha-anne, R. 153 60 31N 94 37W
Tha Deua, Laos 100 17 57N 102 38E
Tha Deua, Laos 100 19 26N 101 50E
Tha Nun 101 8 12N 98 17E
Tha Pia 100 17 48N 100 32E
Tha Rua 100 14 34N 100 44E
Tha Sala 101 8 40N 99 56E
Tha Song Yang 101 17 34N 97 55E
Thaba Putsoa, mt. 129 29 45S 28 0E
Thabana Ntlenyana, Mt. 129 29 30S 29 9E
Thabazimbi 129 24 40S 26 4E
Thabeikkyin 98 22 53N 95 59E
Thai Binh 100 20 27N 106 20E
Thai Muang 101 8 24N 98 16E
Thai Nguyen 100 21 35N 105 46E
Thailand (Siam) ■ 100 16 0N 102 0E
Thakhek 100 17 25N 104 45E
Thakurgaon 98 26 2N 88 28E
Thal 94 33 28N 70 33E
Thal Desert 93 31 0N 71 30E
Thala 119 35 35N 8 40E
Thala La 99 28 25N 97 23E
Thalabarivat 100 13 33N 105 57E
Thalkirch 51 46 39N 9 17E
Thallon 139 28 30S 148 57E
Thalwil 51 47 17N 8 35E
Thame 29 51 44N 0 58W
Thame, R. 29 51 52N 0 47W
Thames 142 37 7S 175 34E
Thames, Firth of 142 37 0S 175 25E
Thames, R., Can. 150 42 20N 82 25W
Thames, R., N.Z. 142 37 32S 175 45E
Thames, R., U.K. 28 51 30N 0 35E
Thames, R., U.S.A. 162 41 18N 72 9W
Thāmit, W. 119 30 51N 16 14E
Than Uyen 100 22 0N 103 54E
Thana 96 19 12N 72 59E
Thanbyuzayat 98 15 58N 97 44E
Thanesar 94 30 1N 76 52E
Thanet, I. of 29 51 21N 1 20E
Thang Binh 101 15 50N 108 20E
Thangoo P.O. 136 18 10S 122 22E
Thangool 138 24 29S 150 35E
Thanh Hoa 100 19 48N 105 46E
Thanh Hung 101 9 55N 105 43E
Thanh Thuy 100 22 55N 104 51E
Thanjavur (Tanjore) 97 10 48N 79 12E
Thanlwin myit, R. 99 20 0N 98 0E
Thann 43 47 48N 7 5E
Thaon 43 48 15N 6 25E
Thap Sakae 101 11 30N 99 37E
Thap Than 100 15 27N 99 54E
Thar (Great Indian) Desert 94 28 25N 72 0E
Tharad 94 24 30N 71 30E
Thargomindah 139 27 58S 143 46E
Tharrawaddy 98 17 38N 95 48E
Tharrawaw 98 17 41N 95 28E
Tharthār, Bahr ath 92 34 0N 43 0E
Thasopoúla, I. 68 40 49N 24 45E
Thásos 68 40 50N 24 50E
Thásos, I. 68 40 40N 24 40E
That Khe 100 22 16N 106 28E
Thatcham 28 51 24N 1 17W
Thatcher, Ariz., U.S.A. 161 32 54N 109 46W
Thatcher, Colo., U.S.A. 161 37 38N 104 6W
Thaton 98 16 55N 97 22E
Thau, Étang de 44 43 23N 3 36E
Thaungdut 98 24 30N 94 40E
Thaxted 29 51 57N 0 20E
Thayer 159 36 34N 91 34W
Thayetmyo 98 19 20N 95 18E
Thayngen 51 47 49N 8 43E
Thazi 99 21 0N 96 5E
The Alberga, R. 139 27 6S 135 33E
The Bight 167 24 19N 75 24W
The Corrong 139 36 0S 139 30E
The Dalles 160 45 40N 121 11W
The Diamantina 139 26 45S 139 30E
The English Company's Is. 138 11 50S 136 32E
The Entrance 141 33 21S 151 30E
The Four Archers 138 15 31S 135 22E
The Frome, R. 139 29 8S 137 54E
The Granites 136 20 35S 130 21E
The Great Divide 141 35 0S 149 17E
The Grenadines, Is. 167 12 30N 61 30W
The Hague (s'Gravenhage) 47 52 7N 7 14E
The Hamilton, R. 139 26 40S 135 19E
The Johnston Lakes 137 32 25S 120 30E
The Lake 167 21 5N 73 34W
The Loup 38 54 42N 6 32W
The Macumba, R. 139 27 52S 137 12E
The Neales, R. 139 28 8S 136 47E
The Oaks 141 34 3S 150 34E
The Officer, R. 137 27 46S 129 46E
The Pas 153 53 45N 101 15W
The Range 127 19 2S 31 2E
The Rock 141 35 15S 147 2E
The Salt Lake 139 30 6S 142 8E
The Stevenson, R. 139 27 6S 135 33E
The Thumbs, Mts. 143 43 35S 170 40E
The Warburton, R. 139 28 4S 137 28E
Theale 28 51 26N 1 5W
Thebes 122 25 40N 32 35E
Thedford 158 41 59N 100 31W
Theebine 139 25 57S 152 34E
Thekulthili L. 153 61 3N 110 0W
Thelma, oilfield 19 58 25N 1 18E
Thelon, R. 153 62 35N 104 3W
Thénezay 42 46 44N 0 2W
Thenon 44 45 9N 1 4E
Theodore 138 24 55S 150 3E
Thepha 101 6 52N 100 58E
Thérain, R. 43 49 15N 2 27E
Thermaïkos Kólpos 68 40 15N 22 45E
Thermopílai P. 69 38 48N 22 45E
Thermopolis 160 43 14N 108 10W
Thesprotía □ 68 39 27N 20 22E
Thessalía □ 68 39 30N 22 0E
Thessalon 150 46 20N 83 30W
Thessaloníki 68 40 38N 23 0E
Thessaloníki □ 68 40 45N 23 0E
Thessaly = Thessalía 68 39 30N 22 0E
Thetford 29 52 25N 0 44E
Thetford Mines 151 46 8N 71 18W
Theun, R. 100 18 19N 104 0E
Theunissen 128 28 26S 26 43E
Theux 47 50 32N 5 49E
Thevenard 139 32 9S 133 38E
Thiámis, R. 68 39 34N 20 18E
Thiberville 42 49 8N 0 27E
Thicket Portage 153 55 19N 97 42W
Thief River Falls 159 48 15N 96 10W
Thiel 120 14 55N 15 5W
Thiene 63 45 42N 11 29E
Thierache 43 49 51N 3 45E
Thiers 44 45 52N 3 33E
Thies 120 14 50N 16 51W
Thiet 123 7 37N 28 49E
Thika 126 1 1S 37 5E
Thika □ 126 1 1S 37 5E
Thille-Boubacar 120 16 31N 15 5W
Thillot, Le 43 47 53N 6 46E
Thimphu (Tashi Chho Dzong) 98 27 31N 89 45E
þingvallavatn 74 64 11N 21 9W
Thionville 43 49 20N 6 10E
Thirá 69 36 23N 25 27E
Thirasiá, I. 69 36 26N 25 21E
Thirlmere, L. 32 54 32N 3 4W
Thirsk 33 54 15N 1 20W
Thisted 75 56 58N 8 40E
Thistle I. 140 35 0S 136 8E
Thistle, oilfield 19 61 20N 1 35E
Thitgy 98 18 15N 96 13E
Thitpokpin 98 19 24N 96 1E
Thiu Khao Phetchabun 101 16 20N 100 55E
Thívai 69 38 19N 23 19E
Thiviers 44 45 25N 0 54E
Thizy 45 46 2N 4 18E
þjorsa 74 63 47N 20 48W
Thlewiaza, R., Man., Can. 153 59 43N 100 5W
Thlewiaza, R., N.W.T., Can. 153 60 29N 94 40W
Thmar Puok 100 13 57N 103 4E
Tho Vinh 100 19 16N 105 42E
Thoa, R. 153 60 31N 109 47W
Thoen 100 17 36N 99 12E
Thoeng 100 19 41N 100 12E
Thoissey 45 46 12N 4 48E
Tholdi 95 35 5N 76 6E
Tholen 47 51 32N 4 13E
Thomas, Okla., U.S.A. 159 35 48N 98 48W
Thomas, W. Va., U.S.A. 156 39 10N 79 30W
Thomas, L. 139 26 4S 137 58E
Thomas Street 38 53 27N 8 15W
Thomastown 39 52 32N 7 10W
Thomasville, Ala., U.S.A. 157 31 55N 87 42W
Thomasville, Fla., U.S.A. 157 30 50N 84 0W
Thomasville, N.C., U.S.A. 157 35 5N 80 4W
Thommen 47 50 14N 6 5E
Thompson, Can. 153 55 45N 97 52W
Thompson, U.S.A. 162 41 52N 75 31W
Thompson Falls 160 47 37N 115 26W
Thompson Landing 153 62 56N 110 40W
Thompson, R., Can. 152 50 15N 121 24W
Thompson, R., U.S.A. 158 39 46N 93 37W
Thompsons 161 39 0N 109 50W
Thompsonville 162 42 0N 72 37W
Thomson, R. 138 25 11S 142 53E
Thomson's Falls = Nyahururu Falls 126 0 2N 36 27E
Thon Buri 100 13 43N 100 29E
Thonburi 101 13 50N 100 36E
Thônes 45 45 54N 6 18E
Thongwa 98 16 45N 96 33E
Thonon-les-Bains 45 46 22N 6 29E
Thonze 98 17 38N 95 47E
Thorez 83 48 4N 38 34E
þorlákshöfn 74 63 51N 21 22W
Thornaby on Tees 33 54 36N 1 19W
Thornborough 138 16 54S 145 2E
Thornbury, N.Z. 143 46 17S 168 9E
Thornbury, U.K. 28 51 36N 2 31W
Thorndon 29 52 16N 1 8E
Thorne, U.K. 33 53 36N 0 56W
Thorne, U.S.A. 163 38 36N 118 34W
Thorne Glacier 13 87 30N 150 0E
Thorney 29 52 37N 0 8W
Thornham 29 52 59N 0 35E
Thornhill 35 55 15N 3 46W
Thornthwaite 32 54 36N 3 13W
Thornton-Beresfield 141 32 50S 151 40E
Thornton Celveleys 32 53 52N 3 1W
Thornton Dale 33 54 14N 0 41W
Thorpe 29 52 38N 1 20E
Thorpe le Soken 29 51 50N 1 11E
Thouarcé 43 47 17N 0 30W
Thouin, C. 136 20 20S 118 10E
Thousand Oakes 163 34 10N 118 50W
Thrace = Thráki 68 41 10N 25 30E
Thráki 68 41 9N 25 30E
Thrakikón Pélagos 68 40 30N 25 0E
Thrapston 29 52 24N 0 32W
Three Bridges 29 51 7N 0 9W
Three Forks 160 45 5N 111 40W
Three Hills 152 51 43N 113 15W
Three Hummock I. 138 40 25S 144 55E
Three Kings Is. 142 34 10S 172 10E
Three Lakes 158 45 41N 89 10W
Three Pagodas P. 100 15 16N 98 23E
Three Points, C. 120 4 42N 2 6W
Three Rivers, Austral. 137 25 10S 119 5E
Three Rivers, Calif., U.S.A. 163 36 26N 118 54W
Three Rivers, Tex., U.S.A. 159 28 30N 98 10W
Three Sisters, Mt. 160 44 10N 121 52W
Threlkeld 32 54 37N 3 2W
Threshfield 32 54 5N 2 2W
þ ó risvatn 74 64 50N 19 26W
Throssell, L. 137 27 27S 124 16E
Throssell Ra. 136 17 24S 126 4E
þ ó rshöfn 74 66 12N 15 20W
Thrumster 37 58 24N 3 8W
Thuan Moa 101 8 58N 105 30E
Thubun Lakes 153 61 30N 112 0W
Thueyts 45 44 41N 4 9E
Thuillies 47 50 18N 4 20E
Thuin 47 50 20N 4 17E
Thuir 44 42 38N 2 45E
Thule 12 77 30N 69 0W
Thun 50 46 45N 7 38E
Thundelarra 137 28 53S 117 7E
Thunder B. 156 45 0N 83 20W
Thunder Bay 150 48 20N 89 0W
Thunder River 152 52 13N 119 20W
Thundulda 137 32 15S 126 3E
Thunersee 50 46 43N 7 39E
Thung Song 101 8 10N 99 40E
Thunkar 98 27 55N 91 0E
Thuong Tra 100 16 2N 107 42E
Thur, R. 51 47 32N 9 10E
Thurgau □ 51 47 34N 9 10E
Thüringer Wald 48 50 35N 11 0E
Thurlby 29 52 45N 0 21W
Thurles 39 52 40N 7 53W
Thurloo Downs 139 29 15S 143 30E
Thurmaston 28 52 40N 1 8W
Thurmont 162 39 37N 77 25W
Thurn P. 49 47 20N 12 15E
Thursby 32 54 40N 3 3W
Thursday I. 138 10 30S 142 3E
Thurso, Can. 150 45 36N 75 15W
Thurso, U.K. 37 58 34N 3 31W
Thurso, R. 37 58 36N 3 30W
Thurston I. 13 72 0S 100 0W
Thury-Harcourt 42 49 0N 0 30W
Thusis 51 46 42N 9 26E
Thutade L. 152 57 0N 126 55W
Thuy, Le 100 17 14N 106 49E
Thylungra 139 26 4S 143 28E
Thyolo 127 16 7S 35 5E
Thysville = Mbanza Ngungu 124 5 12S 14 53E
Ti-n-Amzi, O. 121 17 35N 4 20E
Ti-n-Barraouene, O. 121 18 40N 4 5E
Ti-n-Emensan 118 22 59N 4 45E
Ti-n-Geloulet 118 25 58N 4 2E
Ti-n-Medjerdam, O. 118 25 45N 1 30W
Ti-n-Tarabine, O. 119 21 37N 7 11E
Ti-n-Zaouaténe 118 48 55S 77 9W
Tia 141 31 10S 151 50E
Tiahualilo 164 26 20N 103 30W
Tianguá 170 3 44S 40 59W
Tiankoura 120 10 47N 3 17W
Tiaret (Tagdent) 118 35 28N 1 21E
Tiarra 141 32 46S 145 1E
Tiassalé 120 5 58N 4 57W
Tibagi 173 24 30S 50 24W
Tibagi, R. 173 22 47S 51 1W
Tibari 123 5 2N 31 48E
Tibati 121 6 22N 12 30E
Tiber = Tevere, R. 63 42 30N 12 20E
Tiber Res. 160 48 20N 111 15W
Tiberias 90 32 47N 35 32E
Tiberias, L. = Kinneret, Yam 90 32 49N 35 36E
Tibesti 119 21 0N 17 30E
Tibet 99 32 30N 86 0E
Tibet □ 105 32 30N 86 0E
Tibiri 121 13 34N 7 4E
Tibleş, mt. 70 47 32N 24 15E
Tibleş, Mţii 70 47 41N 24 6E
Tibnīn 90 33 12N 35 24E
Tibooburra 139 29 26S 142 1E
Tibro 73 58 28N 14 10E
Tibugá, Golfo de 174 5 45N 77 20W
Tiburón, I. 164 29 0N 112 30W
Ticehurst 29 51 2N 0 23E
Tichit 120 18 35N 9 20W
Ticino □ 51 46 20N 8 45E
Ticino, R. 62 45 23N 8 47E
Tickhill 33 53 25N 1 8W
Ticonderoga 162 43 50N 73 28W
Ticul 165 20 20N 89 50W
Tidaholm 73 58 12N 13 55E
Tiddim 98 23 20N 93 45E
Tideridjaouine, Adrar 118 23 0N 2 15E
Tideswell 33 53 17N 1 46W
Tidikelt 118 26 58N 1 30E
Tidjikdja 120 18 4N 11 35W
Tidore 103 0 40N 127 25E
Tidra, I. 120 19 45N 16 20W
Tiébélé 121 11 6N 0 59W
Tiébissou 120 7 9N 5 18W
Tiéboro 119 21 20N 17 7E
Tiefencastel 51 46 40N 9 33E
Tiego 120 12 6N 2 38E
T'iehling 107 42 17N 123 50E
Tiel 46 51 53N 5 26E
Tielt 47 51 0N 3 20E
Tien Shan 85 42 0N 80 0E
Tien Yen 100 21 20N 107 24E
T'iench'ang 107 32 41N 118 59E
T'ienchen 106 40 30N 114 6E
Tiench'eng 109 21 31N 111 18E
T'ienching 107 39 10N 117 15E
T'ienchu 108 26 55N 109 12E
T'iench'üan 108 30 4N 102 50E
T'ienchuangt'ai 107 40 49N 122 6E
Tienen 47 50 48N 4 57E
T'ienho 108 24 27N 108 42E
T'ienhsi 108 24 26N 106 5E
Tiénigbé 120 8 11N 5 43W
Tienkianghsien 69 30 25N 107 30E
T'ienlin 108 24 19N 106 15E
T'ienmen 109 30 37N 113 10E
T'ieno 108 25 9N 106 57E
Tienpai 109 21 30N 111 1E
T'ienshui 105 34 35N 105 15E
T'ient'ai 109 29 9N 121 2E
Tientsin = T'ienching 105 39 10N 117 15E
T'ientung 108 23 39N 107 8E
T'ienyang 108 23 43N 106 44E
Tierp 72 60 20N 17 30E
Tierra Alta 174 8 11N 76 4W
Tierra Amarilla 172 27 28S 70 18W
Tierra Colorada 165 17 10N 99 35W
Tierra de Barros 57 38 40N 6 30W
Tierra de Campos 56 42 10N 4 50W
Tierra del Fuego, I. Gr. de 176 54 0S 69 0W
Tiétar, R. 56 39 55N 5 50W
Tieté, R. 171 20 40S 51 35W
Tieyon 139 26 12S 133 52E
Tiffin 156 41 8N 83 10W
Tifi 123 6 12N 36 55E
Tiflèt 118 33 54N 6 20W
Tiflis = Tbilisi 83 41 50N 44 50E
Tifrah 90 31 19N 34 42E
Tifton 157 31 28N 83 32W
Tifu 103 3 39S 126 18E
Tigalda I. 147 54 9N 165 0W
Tighnabruaich 34 55 55N 5 13W
Tigil 77 58 0N 158 10E
Tignish 151 46 58N 64 2W
Tigre □ 123 13 35N 39 15E
Tigre, R. 174 3 30S 74 58W
Tigu 99 29 48N 91 38E
Tiguentourine 119 28 8N 8 58E
Tiguila 121 14 44N 1 50W
Tigveni 70 45 10N 24 31E
Tigyaing 98 23 45N 96 10E
Tih, Gebel el 122 29 32N 33 26E
Tihodaine, Dunes de 119 25 15N 7 15E
Tiji 119 32 0N 11 18E
Tijiamis 103 7 16S 108 29E
Tijibadok 103 6 53S 106 47E

Tijirit, O Tolox

Tijirit, O. 120 19 30N 6 15W
Tijuana 164 32 30N 117 3W
Tikal 166 17 2N 89 35W
Tikamgarh 95 24 44N 78 57E
Tikan 138 5 58S 149 2E
Tikhoretsk 83 45 56N 40 5E
Tikhvin 80 59 35N 33 30E
Tikkadouine, Adrar 118 24 28N 1 30E
Tiko 121 4 4N 9 20E
Tikrit 92 34 35N 43 37E
Tiksi 77 71 50N 129 0E
Tilamuta 103 0 40N 122 15E
Tilburg 47 51 31N 5 6E
Tilbury, Can. 150 42 17N 84 23W
Tilbury, U.K. 29 51 27N 0 24E
Tilcara 172 23 30S 65 23W
Tilden 158 42 3N 97 45W
Tilemsès 121 15 37N 4 44E
Tilemsi, Vallée du 121 17 42N 0 15E
Tilghman 162 38 42N 76 20W
Tilhar 95 28 0N 79 45E
Tilia, O. 118 27 32N 0 55E
Tilichiki 77 61 0N 166 5E
Tiligul, R. 82 47 35N 30 30E
Tililane 118 27 49N 0 6W
Tilin 98 21 41N 94 6E
Tilissos 69 38 15N 25 0E
Till, R. 35 55 35N 2 3W
Tillabéri 121 14 7N 1 28E
Tillamook 160 45 29N 123 55W
Tillberga 72 59 42N 16 39E
Tilley 152 50 28N 111 38W
Tillia 121 16 8N 4 47E
Tillicoultry 35 56 9N 3 44W
Tillsonburg 150 42 53N 80 44W
Tilmanstone 29 51 13N 1 18E
Tilos, I. 69 36 27N 27 27E
Tilpa 139 30 57S 144 24E
Tilrhemt 118 33 9N 3 22E
Tilsit = Sovetsk 80 55 6N 21 50E
Tilt, R. 37 56 50N 3 50W
Tilton 162 43 25N 71 36W
Timahoe 39 52 59N 7 12W
Timanskiy Kryazh 78 65 58N 50 5E
Timaru 143 44 23S 171 14E
Timashevo 84 53 22N 51 9E
Timashevsk 83 45 35N 39 0E
Timau 126 0 4N 37 15E
Timbákion 69 35 4N 24 45E
Timbaúba 170 7 31S 35 19W
Timbédra 120 16 17N 8 16W
Timber L. 158 45 29N 101 0W
Timber Mtn. 163 37 6N 116 28W
Timbío 174 2 20N 76 40W
Timbiqui 174 2 46N 77 42W
Timboon 140 38 30S 142 58E
Timbuktu = Tombouctou 120 16 50N 3 0W
Timdjaouine 118 21 47N 4 30E
Timétrine Montagnes 121 19 25N 1 0W
Timfi Óros 68 39 59N 20 45E
Timfristós, Óros 69 38 57N 21 50E
Timhadite 118 33 15N 5 4W
Timimoun 118 29 14N 0 16E
Timimoun, Sebkha de 118 28 50N 0 46E
Timiris, C. 120 19 15N 16 30W
Timiş □ 66 45 40N 21 30E
Timiş, R. 70 45 30N 21 0E
Timişoara 66 45 43N 21 15E
Timmins 150 48 28N 81 25W
Timmoudi 118 29 20N 1 8W
Timok, R. 66 44 10N 22 40E
Timoleague 39 51 40N 8 51W
Timolin 39 52 59N 6 49W
Timon 170 5 8S 42 52W
Timor □ 103 8 0S 126 30E
Timor, I. 103 9 0S 125 0E
Timor Sea 136 10 0S 127 0E
Timur □ 103 9 0S 125 0E
Tin Alkoum 119 24 30N 10 17E
Tin Gornai 121 16 38N 0 38W
Tin Mtn. 163 36 54N 117 28W
Tîna, Khalîg el 122 31 20N 32 42E
Tinaca Pt. 103 5 30N 125 25E
Tinaco 174 9 42N 68 26W
Tinafak, O. 119 27 10N 7 0W
Tinahely 39 52 48N 6 28W
Tinambacan 103 12 5N 124 32E
Tinapagee 139 29 25S 144 15E
Tinaquillo 174 9 55N 68 18W
Tinaroo Falls 138 17 5S 145 4E
Tinca 70 46 46N 21 58E
Tinchebray 42 48 47N 0 45W
Tindivanam 97 12 15N 79 35E
Tindouf 118 27 50N 8 4W
Tindzhe Dzong 95 28 20N 88 8E
Tineo 56 43 21N 6 27W
Tinerhir 118 31 29N 5 31W
Tinfouchi 118 28 58N 5 54W
T'ing Chiang, R. 109 24 24N 116 35E
Tingan 100 19 42N 110 18E
Tingch'u, R. 108 28 20N 99 12E
Tingewick 28 51 59N 1 4W
Tinggi, Pulau, Is. 101 2 18N 104 7E
Tinghai 109 30 0N 122 10E
Tinghsi 106 35 33N 104 32E
Tinghsiang 106 38 32N 112 59E
Tinghsien 106 38 30N 115 0E
Tingkawk Sakun 98 26 4N 96 44E
Tingk'ouchen 106 39 48N 106 36E
Tinglev 73 54 57N 9 13E
Tingnan 109 24 47N 115 2E
Tingo María 174 9 10S 76 0W
Tingpien 106 37 36N 107 38E
Tingshan 109 31 16N 119 51E
Tingsryd 73 56 31N 15 0E
Tingt'ao 106 35 4N 115 34E
Tingvalla 73 58 47N 12 2E
Tingyüan 109 32 32N 117 41E
Tinh Bien 101 10 36N 104 57E
Tinharé, I. de 171 13 30S 38 58W
Tinié 121 14 17N 1 30W
Tinioulig, Sebkra 118 22 30N 6 45W
Tinjoub 118 29 45N 5 40W
Tinkurrin 137 32 59S 117 46E
Tinnia 172 27 0S 62 45W
Tinnoset 71 59 45N 9 3E
Tinnsjø 71 59 55N 8 54E
Tinogasta 172 28 0S 67 40W
Tínos 69 37 33N 25 8E
Tiñoso, C. 59 37 32N 1 6W
Tinsukia 98 27 29N 95 26E
Tintagel 30 50 40N 4 45W
Tintagel Hd. 30 50 40N 4 46W
Tintern 31 51 42N 2 41W
Tintern Abbey 39 52 14N 6 50W
Tintigny 47 49 41N 5 31E
Tintina 172 27 2S 62 45W
Tintinara 140 35 48S 140 2E
Tinto, R. 57 37 30N 5 33W
Tinui 142 40 52S 176 5E
Tinwald 143 43 55S 171 43E
Tioga 162 41 54N 77 9W
Tioman, I. 101 2 50N 104 10E
Tioman, Pulau, Is. 101 2 50N 104 10E
Tionaga 150 48 0N 82 0W
Tione di Trento 62 46 3N 10 44E
Tior 123 6 26N 31 11E
Tioulilin 118 27 1N 0 2W
Tipongpani 99 27 20N 95 55E
Tipperary 39 52 28N 8 10W
Tipperary □ 39 52 37N 7 55W
Tipton, U.K. 28 52 32N 2 4W
Tipton, Calif., U.S.A. 163 36 3N 119 19W
Tipton, Ind., U.S.A. 156 40 17N 86 30W
Tipton, Iowa, U.S.A. 158 41 45N 91 12W
Tiptonville 159 36 22N 89 30W
Tiptree 29 51 48N 0 46E
Tiptur 97 13 15N 76 26E
Tira 90 32 14N 34 56E
Tiracambu, Serra do 170 3 15S 46 30W
Tirahart, O. 118 23 55N 2 0W
Tiran 93 32 45N 51 0E
Tirân 122 27 56N 34 35E
Tirana 68 41 18N 19 49E
Tirana-Durrësi □ 68 41 35N 20 0E
Tirano 62 46 13N 10 11E
Tirarer, Mont 121 19 35N 1 10W
Tiraspol 82 46 55N 29 35E
Tirat Carmel 90 32 46N 34 58E
Tirat Tsevi 90 32 26N 35 31E
Tirat Yehuda 90 32 1N 34 56E
Tiratimine 118 25 56N 3 37E
Tirdout 121 16 7N 1 5W
Tire 92 38 5N 27 50E
Tirebolu 92 40 58N 38 45E
Tiree, I. 34 56 31N 6 55W
Tiree, Passage of 34 56 30N 6 30W
Tirgoviste 70 44 55N 25 27E
Tîrgu Frumos 70 47 12N 27 2E
Tîrgu-Jiu 70 45 5N 23 19E
Tîrgu Mureş 70 46 31N 24 38E
Tîrgu Neamţ 70 47 12N 26 25E
Tîrgu Ocna 70 46 16N 26 39E
Tîrgu Secuiesc 70 46 0N 26 10E
Tirich Mir Mt. 93 36 15N 71 35E
Tiriola 65 38 57N 16 32E
Tiririca, Serra da 171 17 6S 47 6W
Tirlyanskiy 84 54 14N 58 35E
Tirna, R. 96 18 5N 76 30E
Tîrnava = Botoroaga 70 44 8N 25 32E
Tîrnava Mare, R. 70 46 15N 24 30E
Tîrnava Mica, R. 70 46 17N 24 30E
Tirnavos 68 39 45N 22 18E
Tîrnova 70 45 23N 22 1E
Tîrnăveni 70 46 19N 24 13E
Tirodi 96 21 35N 79 35E
Tirol □ 52 47 3N 10 43E
Tiros 171 19 0S 45 58W
Tirschenreuth 49 49 51N 12 20E
Tirso, L. 64 40 8N 8 56E
Tirso, R. 64 40 33N 9 12E
Tirstrup 73 56 18N 10 42E
Tirua 142 38 25S 174 40E
Tiruchchirappalli 97 10 45N 78 45E
Tiruchendur 97 8 30N 78 11E
Tiruchengodu 97 11 23N 77 56E
Tirumangalam 97 9 49N 77 58E
Tirunelveli (Tinnevelly) 97 8 45N 77 45E
Tirupati 97 13 45N 79 30E
Tiruppattur 97 12 30N 78 30E
Tiruppur 97 11 12N 77 22E
Tiruturaipundi 97 10 32N 79 41E
Tiruvadaimarudur 97 11 2N 79 27E
Tiruvallar 97 13 9N 79 57E
Tiruvannamalai 97 12 10N 79 12E
Tiruvarur (Negapatam) 97 10 46N 79 38E
Tiruvatipuram 97 12 39N 79 33E
Tiruvottiyur 97 13 10N 80 22E
Tisa, R. 66 45 30N 20 20E
Tisdale 153 52 50N 104 0W
Tiseirhatène, Mares de 118 22 51N 9 30W
Tishomingo 159 34 14N 96 38W
Tisjön 72 60 56N 13 0E
Tisnaren 72 58 58N 15 56E
Tisno 63 44 45N 15 41E
Tišnov 53 49 21N 16 25E
Tisovec 53 48 41N 19 56E
Tissemsilt 118 35 35N 1 50E
Tissit, O. 119 27 28N 9 58W
Tissø 73 55 35N 11 18E
Tista, R. 98 25 23N 89 43E
Tisted 73 56 58N 8 40E
Tisza, R. 53 47 38N 20 44E
Tiszaföldvár 53 47 0N 20 14E
Tiszafüred 53 47 38N 20 50E
Tiszalök 53 48 0N 21 10E
Tiszavasvári 53 47 58N 21 18E
Tit, Alg. 118 27 0N 1 37E
Tit, Alg. 119 23 0N 5 10E
Tit-Ary 77 71 50N 126 30E
Titaguas 58 39 53N 1 6W
Titahi Bay 142 41 6S 174 50E
Titai Damer 123 16 43N 37 25E
Titchfield 28 50 51N 1 13W
Titel 66 45 29N 20 18E
Tithwal 95 34 21N 73 50E
Titicaca, L. 174 15 30S 69 30W
Titilagarh 96 20 15N 83 5E
Tititira Head 98 43 38S 169 26E
Titiwa 121 12 14N 12 53E
Titlis 51 46 46N 8 27E
Titograd 66 42 30N 19 19E
Titov Veles 66 41 46N 21 47E
Titova Korenica 63 44 45N 15 41E
Titovo Uzice 66 43 55N 19 50E
Titule 126 3 15N 25 31E
Titumate 174 8 19N 77 5W
Titusville 156 41 35N 79 39W
Tiumpan Hd. 36 58 15N 6 10W
Tivaouane 120 14 56N 16 45W
Tivat 66 42 28N 18 43E
Tiveden 73 58 50N 14 30E
Tiverton 30 50 54N 3 30W
Tivoli 63 41 58N 12 45E
Tiwi 93 22 45N 59 12E
Tiyo 123 14 41N 40 57E
Tizga 118 32 1N 5 9W
Tizi n'Isly 118 32 28N 5 47W
Tizi Ouzou 119 36 42N 4 3E
Tizmín 165 21 0N 88 1W
Tiznados, R. 174 8 50N 67 50W
Tiznit 118 29 48N 9 45W
Tjalang 103 4 30N 95 43E
Tjangkuang, Tg. 102 7 0S 105 0E
Tjareme, G. 103 6 55S 108 27E
Tjeggelvas 74 66 37N 17 45E
Tjepu 103 7 12S 111 31E
Tjeukemeer 46 52 53N 5 48E
Tjiandjur 103 6 51S 107 7E
Tjibatu 103 7 8S 107 59E
Tjikadjang 103 7 25S 107 48E
Tjimahi 103 6 53S 107 33E
Tjirebon = Cirebon 103 6 45S 108 32E
Tjöllong 71 59 6N 10 3E
Tjöme 71 59 8N 10 26E
Tjonger Kanaal 46 52 52N 6 52E
Tjörn 73 58 0N 11 35E
Tjörnes 74 66 12N 17 9W
Tjuls 73 57 30N 18 15E
Tjurup 102 4 26S 102 13E
Tkibuli 83 42 26N 43 0E
Tkvarcheli 83 42 47N 41 52E
Tlacolula 165 16 57N 96 29W
Tlacotalpán 165 18 37N 95 40W
Tlaquepaque 164 20 39N 103 19W
Tlaxcala 165 19 20N 98 14W
Tlaxcala □ 165 19 30N 98 20W
Tlaxiaco 165 17 10N 97 40W
Tlell 152 53 34N 131 56W
Tlemcen 118 34 52N 1 15W
Tleta di Sidi Bouguedra 118 32 16N 8 58W
Tleta Sidi Bouguedra 118 32 16N 9 59W
Tlumach 80 48 46N 25 0E
Tłuszcz 54 52 25N 21 25E
Tlyarata 83 42 9N 46 26E
Tmassah 119 26 19N 15 51E
Tmisan 119 27 23N 13 30E
To Bong 100 12 45N 109 16E
T'o Chiang, R. 108 28 56N 105 33E
To-Shima 111 34 31N 139 17E
Toad, R. 152 59 25N 124 57W
Toay 172 36 50S 64 30W
Toba 111 34 30N 136 45E
Toba Kakar 94 31 30N 69 0E
Toba, L. 102 2 40N 98 50E
Toba Tek Singh 94 30 55N 72 25E
Tobago, I. 167 11 10N 60 30W
Tobarra 59 38 35N 1 41W
Tobelo 103 1 25N 127 56E
Tobercurry 38 54 3N 8 43W
Tobermore 38 54 49N 6 43W
Tobermorey 138 22 12S 138 0E
Tobermory, Can. 150 45 12N 81 40W
Tobermory, U.K. 34 56 37N 6 4W
Tobin, L. 136 21 45S 125 49E
Tobin L. 153 53 35N 103 30W
Toboali 102 3 0S 106 25E
Tobol 84 52 40N 62 39E
Tobol, R. 84 58 10N 68 12E
Toboli 103 0 38S 120 12E
Tobolsk 84 58 0N 68 10E
Tobruk = Tubruq 117 32 7N 23 55E
Tobyhanna 162 41 10N 75 15W
Tocantínia 170 9 33S 48 22W
Tocantinópolis 170 6 20S 47 25W
Tocantins, R. 170 14 30S 49 0W
Tocca 157 34 6N 83 17W
Toce, R. 62 46 5N 8 29E
Tochigi 111 36 25N 139 45E
Tochigi-ken □ 111 36 45N 139 45E
Tocina 57 37 37N 5 44W
Toconao 172 34 35N 83 19W
Toconhão, Serra do 171 14 30S 47 46W
Tocópero 174 11 30N 69 16W
Tocopilla 172 22 5S 70 10W
Tocumwal 141 35 45S 145 31E
Tocuyo, R. 174 10 50N 69 0W
Todd, R. 138 24 52S 135 48E
Toddington 29 51 57N 0 31W
Todeli 103 1 38S 124 34E
Todenyang 126 4 35N 35 56E
Todi 63 42 47N 12 24E
Tödi 51 46 48N 8 55E
Todjo 103 1 20S 121 15E
Todmorden 32 53 43N 2 7W
Todos os Santos, Baía de 171 12 48S 38 38W
Todos Santos 164 23 27N 110 13W
Todos Santos, Bahia de 164 31 48N 116 42W
Todtnau 49 47 50N 7 56E
Toe Hd., Ireland 39 51 29N 9 13W
Toe Hd., U.K. 36 57 50N 7 10W
Toecé 121 11 50N 1 16W
Toetoes B. 143 46 42S 168 41E
Tofield 152 53 25N 112 40W
Tofino 152 49 11N 125 55W
Töfsingdalems National Park 72 62 15N 12 44E
Tofta 73 57 11N 12 20E
Toftlund 73 55 11N 9 2E
Tōgane 111 35 33N 140 22E
Togba 120 17 26N 10 25W
Toggenburg 51 47 16N 9 9E
Togian, Kepulauan 103 0 20S 121 50E
Togliatti 81 53 37N 49 18E
Togo ■ 121 6 15N 1 35E
Toguzak, R. 84 54 3N 62 44E
Tōhoku □ 112 39 50N 141 45E
Toi 111 34 54N 134 47E
Toinya 123 6 17N 29 46E
Toiyabe Dome 163 38 51N 117 22W
Toiyabe, Ra. 163 39 10N 117 10W
Tōjō 110 34 53N 133 16E
Tok, R. 84 52 46N 52 22E
Tokaanu 142 38 58S 175 46E
Tokachi, R. 112 42 44N 143 42E
Tokaj 53 48 8N 21 27E
Tokala, G. 103 1 30S 121 40E
Tokanui 143 46 34S 168 56E
Tokarahi 143 44 56S 170 39E
Tokat 92 40 22N 36 35E
Tŏkchŏn 107 39 45N 126 18E
Tokelau Is. 130 9 0S 172 0W
Toki 111 35 18N 137 8E
Tokmak, Kirgizia, U.S.S.R. 84 42 55N 75 45E
Tokmak, Ukraine, U.S.S.R. 82 47 16N 35 42E
Toko Ra. 138 23 5S 138 20E
Tokomaru Bay 142 38 8S 178 22E
Tokombere 121 11 18N 3 30E
Tókomlós 53 46 24N 20 45E
Tokoname 111 34 53N 136 51E
Tokong 101 5 27N 100 23E
Tokoroa 142 38 20S 175 50E
Tokorozawa 111 35 47N 139 28E
T'ok'ot'o 106 40 15N 111 12E
Toktogul 85 41 50N 72 50E
Tokuii 110 34 11N 131 42E
Tokule 123 14 54N 38 26E
Tokunoshima 112 27 56N 128 55E
Tokushima 110 34 4N 134 34E
Tokushima-ken □ 110 35 50N 134 30E
Tokuyama 110 34 0N 131 50E
Tōkyō 111 35 45N 139 45E
Tōkyō-to □ 111 35 40N 139 30E
Tōkyō-Wan 111 35 25N 139 47E
Tolaerh 105 35 8N 81 33E
Tolaga Bay 142 38 21S 178 20E
Tolageak 147 70 2N 162 50W
Tolbukhin 67 43 37N 27 49E
Toledo, Spain 56 39 50N 4 2W
Toledo, Ohio, U.S.A. 156 41 37N 83 33W
Toledo, Oreg., U.S.A. 160 44 40N 123 59W
Toledo, Wash., U.S.A. 160 42 29N 122 58W
Toledo, Montes de 57 39 33N 4 20W
Tolentino 63 43 12N 13 17E
Tolfino 152 49 6N 125 54W
Tolga, Alg. 119 34 46N 5 22E
Tolga, Norway 71 62 26N 11 1E
Tolima □ 174 3 45N 75 15W
Tolima, Vol. 174 4 40N 75 19W
Tolitoli 103 1 5N 120 50E
Tolkamer 46 51 52N 6 6E
Tolkmicko 54 54 19N 19 31E
Tollarp 73 55 55N 13 58E
Tollesbury 29 51 46N 0 51E
Tolleson 161 33 29N 112 10W
Tollhouse 163 37 1N 119 24W
Tolmachevo 80 58 56N 29 57E
Tolmezzo 63 46 23N 13 0E
Tolmino 63 46 11N 13 45E
Tolna 53 46 25N 18 48E
Tolna □ 53 46 30N 18 30E
Tolne 73 57 28N 10 20E
Tolo 124 2 50S 18 40E
Tolo, Teluk 103 2 20S 122 10E
Tolokiwa I. 138 5 30S 147 30E
Tolon 121 9 26N 1 3W
Tolosa 58 43 8N 2 5W
Tolox 57 36 41N 4 54W

Tolsta Hd Tregnago

Tolsta Hd. 36 58 20N 6 10W
Toluca 165 19 20N 99 50W
Tolun 106 42 22N 116 30E
Tom Burke 129 23 5S 28 4E
Tomahawk 158 45 28N 89 40W
Tomakomai 112 42 38N 141 36E
Tomales 163 38 15N 122 53W
Tomales B. 163 38 15N 123 58W
Tomar 57 39 36N 8 25W
Tómaros Óros 68 39 29N 20 48E
Tomaszów Lubelski 54 50 29N 23 23E
Tomaszów Mazowiecki 54 51 30N 19 57E
Tomatin 37 57 20N 4 0W
Tomatlán 164 19 56N 105 15W
Tombé 123 5 53N 31 40E
Tombigbee, R. 157 32 0N 88 6W
Tombodor, Serra do 171 12 0S 41 30W
Tombouctou 120 16 50N 3 0W
Tombstone 161 31 40N 110 4W
Tomdoun 36 57 4N 5 2W
Tomé 172 36 36S 73 6W
Tomé-Açu 170 2 25S 48 9W
Tomelilla 73 55 33N 13 58E
Tomelloso 59 39 10N 3 2W
Tomingley 141 32 31S 148 16E
Tomini 103 0 30N 120 30E
Tomini, Teluk 103 0 10S 122 0E
Tominian 120 13 17N 4 35W
Tomiño 56 41 59N 8 46W
Tomintoul 37 57 15N 3 22W
Tomioka 111 36 15N 138 54E
Tomkinson Ranges 137 26 11S 129 5E
Tommot 77 58 50N 126 20E
Tomnavoulin 37 57 19N 3 18W
Tomnop Ta Suos 101 11 20N 104 15E
Tomo, Colomb. 174 2 38N 67 32W
Tomo, Japan 110 34 23N 133 23E
Tomobe 111 36 40N 140 41E
Toms Place 163 37 34N 118 41W
Toms River 162 39 59N 74 12W
Tomsk 76 56 30N 85 12E
Tomtabacken 73 57 30N 14 30E
Tonalá 165 16 8N 93 41W
Tonale, Passo del 62 46 15N 10 34E
Tonalea 161 36 17N 110 58W
Tonami 111 36 56N 136 58E
Tonantins 174 2 45S 67 45W
Tonasket 160 48 45N 119 30W
Tonawanda 156 43 0N 78 54W
Tonbridge 29 51 12N 0 18E
Tondano 103 1 35N 124 54E
Tondela 56 40 31N 8 5W
Tønder 73 54 58N 8 50E
Tondi 97 9 45N 79 4E
Tondi Kiwindi 121 14 28N 2 02E
Tondibi 121 16 39N 0 14W
Tone-Gawa, R. 111 35 44N 140 51E
Tone, R. 137 34 23S 116 25E
Tone R. 30 50 59N 3 15W
Tong 28 52 39N 2 18W
Tonga Is. ■ 130 20 0S 173 0W
Tonga Trench 143 18 0S 175 0W
Tongaat 129 29 33S 31 9E
Tongala 141 36 14S 144 56E
Tongaland 129 27 0S 32 0E
Tongareva I 143 9 0S 158 0W
Tongariro, mt. 142 39 7S 175 50E
Tongchŏnni 107 39 50N 127 25E
Tongeren 47 50 47N 5 28E
Tongio 141 37 14S 147 44E
Tongjosŏn Man 107 39 30N 128 0E
Tongking = Bac-Phan 101 21 30N 105 0E
Tongking, G. of 101 20 0N 108 0E
Tongnae 107 35 12N 129 5E
Tongobory 129 23 32S 44 20E
Tongoy 172 30 25S 71 40W
Tongres = Tongeren 47 50 47N 5 28E
Tongsa Dzong 98 27 31N 90 31E
Tongue 37 58 29N 4 25W
Tongue, Kyle of 37 58 30N 4 30W
Tongue, R. 160 48 30N 106 30W
Tongyang 107 39 9N 126 53E
Tonj 123 7 20N 28 44E
Tonk 94 26 6N 75 54E
Tonkawa 159 36 44N 67 22W
Tonkin = Bac-Phan 100 22 0N 105 0E
Tonkin, G. of 100 20 0N 108 0E
Tonlé Sap 100 13 0N 104 0E
Tonnay-Charente 44 45 56N 0 55W
Tonneins 44 44 24N 0 20E
Tonnerre 43 47 51N 3 59E
Tönning 48 54 18N 8 57E
Tonopah 163 38 4N 117 12W
Tonoshō 110 34 29N 134 11E
Tonosí 166 7 20N 80 20W
Tonsberg 71 59 19N 10 25E
Tonstad 71 58 40N 6 45E
Tonto Basin 61 33 58N 111 15W
Tonyrefail 31 51 35N 3 26W
Tonzang 98 23 36N 93 42E
Tonzi 98 24 39N 94 57E
Tooele 160 40 30N 112 20W
Toolonda 140 36 58S 141 5E
Toombeolo 38 53 26N 9 52W
Toomevara 39 52 50N 8 2W
Toompine 139 27 15S 144 19E
Toongi 141 32 28S 148 30E
Toonpan 138 19 28S 146 48E
Toora 141 38 39S 146 23E
Toora-Khem 77 52 28N 96 9E
Toormore 39 51 31N 9 41W
Toowoomba 139 27 32S 151 56E
Top 93 34 15N 68 35E
Top Ozero 78 65 35N 32 0E
Topalu 70 44 31N 28 3E
Topaz 163 38 41N 119 30W
Topeka 158 39 3N 95 40W
Topki 76 55 25N 85 20E
Topla, R. 53 49 0N 21 36E
Topley 152 54 32N 126 5W
Toplica, R. 66 43 15N 21 30E
Toplița 70 46 55N 25 27E
Topocalma, Pta. 172 34 10S 72 2W
Topock 161 34 46N 114 29W
Topola 66 44 17N 20 32E
Topoľčany 53 48 35N 18 12E
Topoli 83 47 59N 51 45E
Topolnitsa, R. 67 42 21N 24 0E
Topolobampo 164 25 40N 109 10W
Topolovgrad 67 42 5N 26 20E
TopolvǔT Mare 66 45 46N 21 41E
Toppenish 160 46 27N 120 16W
Topsham 30 50 40N 3 27W
Topusko 63 45 18N 15 59E
Toquima, Ra. 163 39 0N 117 0W
Tor Bay, Austral. 137 35 5S 117 50E
Tor Bay, U.K. 23 50 26N 3 31W
Tor Ness 37 58 47N 3 18W
Tor, oilfield 19 56 40N 3 35E
Torá 58 41 49N 1 25E
Tora Kit 123 11 2N 32 30E
Torata 174 17 3S 70 1W
Torbat-e Heydarīyeh 93 35 15N 59 12E
Torbat-e Jām 93 35 8N 60 35E
Torbay, Can. 151 47 40N 52 42W
Torbay, U.K. 30 50 26N 3 31W
Torchin 80 50 45N 25 0E
Tordal 71 59 10N 8 45E
Tordesillas 56 41 30N 5 0W
Tordoya 56 43 6N 8 36W
Töre 74 65 5S 22 40E
Töreboda 73 58 41N 14 7E
Torfajökull 74 63 54N 19 0W
Torgau 48 51 32N 13 0E
Torgelow 48 53 40N 13 59E
Torhout 47 51 5N 3 7E
Tori 123 7 53N 33 35E
Torigni-sur-Vire 42 49 3N 0 58W
Torija 58 40 44N 3 2W
Torin 164 27 33N 110 5W
Toriñana, C. 56 43 3N 9 17W
Torino 62 45 4N 7 40E
Torit 123 4 20N 32 55E
Torkovichi 80 58 51N 30 30E
Tormac 66 45 30N 21 30E
Tormentine 151 46 6N 63 46W
Tormes, R. 56 41 7N 6 0W
Tornado Mt. 152 49 55N 114 40W
Tornby 73 57 32N 9 56E
Torne älv 74 65 50N 24 12E
Torneå = Tornio 74 65 50N 24 12E
Torness 37 57 18N 4 22W
Torneträsk 74 68 24N 19 15E
Tornio 74 65 50N 24 12E
Tornionjoki 74 65 50N 24 12E
Tornquist 172 38 0S 62 15W
Toro 56 41 35N 5 24W
Torö 73 58 48N 17 50E
Toro, Cerro del 172 29 0S 69 50W
Toro Pk. 163 33 34N 116 24W
Törökszentmjklés 53 47 11N 20 27E
Toronátos Kólpos 68 40 5N 23 30E
Toronto, Austral. 141 33 0S 151 30E
Toronto, Can. 150 43 39N 79 20W
Toronto, U.S.A. 156 40 27N 80 36W
Toronto, L. 164 27 40N 105 30W
Toropets 80 56 30N 31 40E
Tororo 126 0 45N 34 12E
Toros Dağlari 92 37 0N 35 0E
Torphins 37 57 7N 2 37W
Torpoint 30 50 23N 4 12W
Torpshammar 72 62 29N 16 20E
Torquay, Austral. 140 38 20S 144 19E
Torquay, Can. 153 49 9N 103 30W
Torquay, U.K. 30 50 27N 3 31W
Torquemada 56 42 2N 4 19W
Torralba de Calatrava 57 39 1N 3 44W
Torran Rocks 34 56 14N 6 24W
Torrance 163 33 50N 118 19W
Torrão 57 38 16N 8 11W
Torre Annunziata 64 40 45N 14 26E
Tôrre de Moncorvo 56 41 12N 7 8W
Torre del Greco 65 40 47N 14 22E
Torre del Mar 57 36 44N 4 6W
Torre-Pacheco 29 37 44N 0 57W
Torre Pellice 62 44 49N 7 13E
Torreblanca 58 40 14N 0 12E
Torrecampo 57 38 29N 4 41W
Torrecilla en Cameros 58 42 15N 2 38W
Torredembarra 58 41 9N 1 24W
Torredonjimeno 57 37 46N 3 57W
Torrejoncillo 56 39 54N 6 28W
Torrelaguna 58 40 50N 3 38W
Torrelavega 56 43 20N 4 5W
Torremaggiore 65 41 42N 15 17E
Torremolinos 57 36 38N 4 30W
Torrens Cr. 138 22 23S 145 9E
Torrens Creek 138 20 48S 145 3E
Torrens, L. 140 31 0S 137 50E
Torrente 59 39 27N 0 28W
Torrenueva 59 38 38N 3 22W
Torreón 164 25 33N 103 25W
Torreperogil 59 38 2N 3 17W
Torres, Mexico 164 28 46N 110 47W
Torres, Spain 56 41 6N 5 0W
Tôrres Novas 57 39 27N 8 33W
Torres Strait 135 9 50S 142 20E
Torres Vedras 57 39 5N 9 15W
Torrevieja 59 37 59N 0 42W
Torrey 161 38 12N 111 30W
Torridge, R. 30 50 51N 4 10W
Torridon 36 57 33N 5 34W
Torridon, L. 36 57 35N 5 50W
Torrijos 56 39 59N 4 18W
Törring 73 55 52N 9 29E
Torrington, Conn., U.S.A. 162 41 50N 73 9W
Torrington, Wyo., U.S.A. 158 42 5N 104 8W
Torroboll 37 58 0N 4 23W
Torroella de Montgri 58 42 2N 3 8E
Torrox 57 36 46N 3 57W
Torsås 73 56 24N 16 0E
Torsby 72 60 7N 13 0E
Torsjok 72 57 5N 34 55E
Torsö 73 58 48N 13 45E
Torthorwald 35 55 7N 3 30W
Tortola, I. 147 18 19N 65 0W
Tórtoles de Esgueva 56 41 49N 4 2W
Tortona 62 44 53N 8 54E
Tortoreto 63 42 50N 13 55E
Tortorici 65 38 2N 14 48E
Tortosa 58 40 49N 0 31E
Tortosa C. 58 40 41N 0 52E
Tortosendo 56 40 15N 7 31W
Tortue, I. de la 167 20 5N 72 57W
Tortuga, Isla la 167 11 8N 67 2W
Torud 93 35 25N 55 5E
Torugart, Pereval 85 40 32N 75 24E
Torun 54 53 0N 18 39E
Torup 73 56 57N 13 5E
Torvastad 71 59 23N 5 15E
Torver 32 54 20N 3 7W
Tory I. 38 55 17N 8 12W
Torysa, R. 53 48 50N 21 15E
Torzhok 80 57 5N 34 55E
Tosa 110 33 24N 133 23E
Tosa-shimizu 110 32 52N 132 58E
Tosa-Wan 110 33 15N 133 30E
Tosa-yamada 110 33 36N 133 38E
Toscaig 36 57 23N 5 49W
Toscana 62 43 30N 11 5E
Tosno 80 59 30N 30 58E
Töss, R. 51 47 32N 8 39E
Tossa 58 41 43N 2 56E
Tostado 172 29 15S 61 50W
Tostedt 48 53 17N 9 42E
Tosu 110 33 22N 130 31E
Toszek 54 50 27N 18 32E
Totak 71 59 40N 7 45E
Totana 59 37 45N 1 30W
Toten 71 60 37N 10 53E
Toteng 128 20 22S 22 58E
Tôtes 42 49 41N 1 3E
Totland 28 50 41N 1 32W
Totley 33 53 18N 1 32W
Totma 81 60 0N 42 40E
Totnes 30 50 26N 3 41W
Totonicapán 166 14 50N 91 20W
Totskoye 84 52 32N 52 45E
Tottenham 141 32 14S 147 21E
Totton 28 50 55N 1 29W
Tottori 110 35 30N 134 15E
Tottori-ken □ 110 35 30N 134 12E
Touamotou, Archipel des 131 17 0S 144 0W
Touat 118 27 30N 0 30E
Touba 120 8 15N 7 40W
Toubkal, Djebel 118 31 0N 8 0W
Toubouai, Îles 131 25 0S 150 0W
Toucy 43 47 44N 3 15E
Tougan 120 13 11N 2 58W
Touggourt 119 33 10N 6 0E
Tougué 120 11 25N 11 50W
Toukmatine 119 24 49N 7 11E
Toul 43 48 40N 5 53E
Toulepleu 120 6 32N 8 24W
Toulon 45 43 10N 5 55E
Toulouse 44 43 37N 1 27E
Toummo 119 22 45N 14 8E
Toummo Dhoba 119 22 30N 14 31E
Toumodi 120 6 32N 5 4W
Tounan 109 23 41N 120 28E
Tounassine, Hamada 118 28 48N 5 0W
Toungoo 98 19 0N 96 30E
Touques, R. 42 49 22N 0 8E
Touquet, Le 42 50 30N 1 36E
Tour-du-Pin, La 45 45 33N 5 27E
Touraine 42 47 20N 0 30E
Tourane = Da Nang 100 16 4N 108 13E
Tourcoing 43 50 42N 3 10E
Tourcoingbam 121 13 23N 1 33W
Tournai 47 50 35N 3 25E
Tournan-en-Brie 43 48 44N 2 46E
Tournay 44 43 13N 0 13E
Tournon 45 45 4N 4 50E
Tournon-St.-Martin 42 46 45N 0 58E
Tournus 45 46 35N 4 54E
Touros 170 5 12S 35 28W
Tours 42 47 22N 0 40E
Touside, Pic 119 21 1N 16 18E
T'outaokou 107 42 44N 129 12E
Touwsrivier 128 33 20S 20 0E
Tovar 174 8 20N 71 46W
Tovarkovskiy 81 53 40N 38 5E
Tovdal 71 58 47N 8 10E
Tovdalselva 71 58 20N 8 16E
Towamba 141 37 6S 149 43E
Towanda 162 41 46N 76 30W
Towcester 29 52 7N 0 56W
Tower 158 47 49N 92 17W
Towerhill Cr. 138 22 28S 144 35E
Town Yetholm 35 55 33N 2 19W
Towner 158 48 25N 100 26W
Townsend 160 46 25N 111 32W
Townshend, C. 133 22 18S 150 30E
Townshend, I. 138 22 16S 150 31E
Townsville 138 19 15S 146 45E
Towson 162 39 26N 76 34W
Toyah 159 31 20N 103 48W
Toyahvale 159 30 58N 103 45W
Toyama 111 36 40N 137 15E
Toyama-ken □ 111 36 45N 137 30E
Tōyō 110 33 26N 134 16E
Toyohashi 111 34 45N 137 25E
Toyokawa 111 34 48N 137 27E
Toyonaka 111 34 50N 135 28E
Toyooka 110 35 35N 134 55E
Toyota 111 35 3N 137 7E
Toyoura 110 34 6N 130 57E
Toytepa 85 41 3N 69 20E
Tozeur 119 33 56N 8 8E
Tra On 101 9 58N 105 55E
Trabancos, R. 56 41 0N 5 3E
Trabzon 92 41 0N 39 45E
Tracadie 151 47 30N 64 55W
Tracy, Calif., U.S.A. 163 37 46N 121 27W
Tracy, Minn., U.S.A. 158 44 12N 95 3W
Tradate 62 45 43N 8 54E
Trafalgar 141 38 14S 146 12E
Trafalgar, C. 57 36 10N 6 2W
Traghan 119 26 0N 14 30E
Traian 70 45 2N 28 15E
Trail 152 49 5N 117 40W
Trainor L. 152 60 24N 120 17W
Traipu 171 9 58S 37 1W
Tralee 39 52 16N 9 42W
Tralee B. 39 52 17N 9 55W
Tramelan 50 47 13N 7 7E
Tramore 39 52 10N 7 10W
Tramore B. 39 52 9N 7 10W
Tran Ninh, Cao Nguyen 100 19 30N 103 10E
Tranas 73 58 3N 14 59E
Tranås 73 55 37N 13 59E
Trancas 172 26 20S 65 20W
Tranche-sur-Mer, La 42 46 20N 1 27W
Trancoso 56 40 49N 7 21W
Tranebjerg 73 55 51N 10 36E
Tranemo 73 57 30N 13 20E
Tranent 35 55 57N 2 58W
Trang 101 7 33N 99 38E
Trangahy 129 19 7S 44 43E
Trangan, I. 103 6 40S 134 20E
Trangie 141 32 4S 148 0E
Trångsviken 72 63 19N 14 0E
Trani 65 41 17N 16 24E
Tranoroa 129 24 42S 45 4E
Tranquebar 97 11 1N 79 54E
Tranqueras 173 31 8S 56 0W
Trans Nzoia □ 126 1 0N 35 0E
Transcona 153 49 50N 97 0W
Transilvania 70 46 19N 25 0E
Transkei □ 129 32 15S 28 15E
Transtrand 72 61 6N 13 20E
Transvaal □ 128 25 0S 29 0E
Transylvania = Transilvania 70 46 19N 25 0E
Transylvanian Alps 70 45 30N 25 0E
Trápani 64 38 1N 12 30E
Trappe Peak, Mt. 160 45 56N 114 29W
Traqowel 140 35 50S 144 0E
Traralgon 141 38 12S 146 34E
Traryd 73 56 35N 13 45E
Trarza □ 120 17 30N 15 0W
Tras os Montes e Alto-Douro □ 55 41 25N 7 20W
Trasacco 63 41 58N 13 30E
Trasimeno, L. 63 43 10N 12 5E
Träslöv 73 57 8N 12 21E
Trat 101 12 14N 102 33E
Traun 52 48 14N 14 15E
Traun-see 49 47 48N 13 45E
Traunstein 49 47 52N 12 40E
Tråvad 73 58 15N 13 5E
Traveller's L. 140 33 20S 142 0E
Travemünde 48 53 58N 10 52E
Travers, Mt. 143 42 1S 172 45E
Traverse City 156 44 45N 85 39W
Traverse I. 13 48 0S 28 0E
Travnik 66 44 17N 17 39E
Trawbreaga B. 38 55 20N 7 25W
Trawsfynydd 31 52 54N 3 55W
Trayning 137 31 7S 117 46E
Traynor 153 52 20N 108 32W
Trazo 56 43 0N 8 30W
Trbovlje 63 46 12N 15 5E
Trebbia, R. 62 44 52N 9 30E
Trebel, R. 48 54 0N 12 50E
Trebinje 66 42 44N 18 22E
Trebisacce 65 39 52N 16 32E
Trebišnica, R. 66 42 47N 18 8E
Trebišov 53 48 38N 21 41E
Trebizat 66 43 15N 17 30E
Třebon 52 48 59N 14 48E
Trebujena 57 36 52N 6 11W
Trecate 62 45 29N 8 42E
Tredegar 31 51 47N 3 16W
Trefeglwys 31 52 31N 3 31W
Trefriw 31 53 9N 3 50W
Tregaron 31 52 14N 3 56W
Trégastel-Plage 42 48 49N 3 31W
Tregnago 63 45 31N 11 10E

Tregrasse Is   Tullow

Tregrasse Is. 138 17 41 S 150 43 E
Trèguier 42 48 47 N 3 16 W
Trégunc 42 47 51 N 3 51 W
Tregynon 31 52 32 N 3 19 W
Treharris 31 51 40 N 3 17 W
Treherne 153 49 38 N 98 42 W
Trèia 63 43 30 N 13 20 E
Treig, L. 37 56 48 N 4 42 W
Treignac 44 45 32 N 1 48 E
Treinta y Tres 173 33 10 S 54 50 W
Treis 49 50 9 N 7 19 E
Trekveid 128 30 35 S 19 45 E
Trelde Næs 73 55 38 N 9 53 E
Trelech 31 51 56 N 4 28 W
Trelew 176 43 10 S 65 20 W
Trélissac 44 45 11 N 0 47 E
Trelleborg 73 55 20 N 13 10 E
Trélon 43 50 5 N 4 6 E
Tremadoc 31 52 57 N 4 9 W
Tremadoc, Bay 31 52 51 N 4 18 W
Tremblade, La 44 45 46 N 1 8 W
Tremelo 47 51 0 N 4 42 E
Trementina 159 35 27 N 105 30 W
Tremiti, I. 63 42 8 N 15 30 E
Tremonton 160 41 45 N 112 10 W
Tremp 58 42 10 N 0 52 E
Trenary 156 46 12 N 86 59 W
Trenčin 53 48 52 N 18 4 E
Trenche, R. 150 47 46 N 72 53 W
Trenggalek 103 8 5 S 111 44 E
Trenque Lauquen 172 36 0 S 62 45 W
Trent, R. 33 53 33 N 0 44 W
Trentham 32 52 59 N 2 12 W
Trentino-Alto Adige □ 62 46 5 N 11 0 E
Trento 62 46 5 N 11 8 E
Trenton, Can. 150 44 10 N 77 40 W
Trenton, Mo., U.S.A. 158 40 5 N 93 37 W
Trenton, Nebr., U.S.A. 158 40 14 N 101 4 W
Trenton, N.J., U.S.A. 162 40 15 N 74 41 W
Trenton, Tenn., U.S.A. 159 35 58 N 88 57 W
Trepassey 151 46 43 N 53 25 W
Tréport, Le 42 50 3 N 1 20 E
Treptow 48 53 42 N 13 15 E
Trepuzzi 65 40 26 N 18 4 E
Tres Arroyos 172 38 20 S 60 20 W
Três Corações 173 21 30 S 45 30 W
Três Lagoas 171 20 50 S 51 50 W
Tres Marías, Is. 164 21 25 N 106 28 W
Três Marias, Reprêsa 171 18 12 S 45 15 W
Tres Montes, C. 176 47 0 S 75 35 W
Tres Pinos 163 36 48 N 121 19 W
Três Pontas 173 21 23 S 45 29 W
Tres Puentes 172 27 50 S 70 15 W
Três Puntas, C. 176 47 0 S 66 0 W
Tres Rios 173 22 20 S 43 30 W
Tres Valles 165 18 15 N 96 8 W
Tresco I. 30 49 57 N 6 20 W
Treshnish Is. 34 56 30 N 6 25 W
Treska, R. 66 41 45 N 21 11 E
Treskavika Planina 66 43 40 N 18 20 E
Trespaderne 58 42 47 N 3 24 W
Tretower 31 51 53 N 3 11 W
Trets 45 43 27 N 5 41 E
Treuchtlingen 49 48 58 N 10 55 E
Treuddyn 31 53 7 N 3 8 W
Treuenbrietzen 48 52 6 N 12 51 E
Treungen 75 59 1 N 8 31 E
Treviglio 62 45 31 N 9 35 E
Trevinca, Peña 56 42 15 N 6 46 W
Treviso 63 45 40 N 12 15 E
Trevose Hd. 30 50 33 N 5 3 W
Trévoux 45 45 57 N 4 47 E
Trgovište 66 42 20 N 22 10 E
Triabunna 138 42 30 S 147 55 E
Triánda 69 36 25 N 28 10 E
Triang 101 3 13 N 102 27 E
Triangle 162 38 33 N 77 20 W
Triaucourt-en-Argonne 43 48 59 N 5 2 E
Tribsees 48 54 4 N 12 46 E
Tribulation, C. 138 16 5 S 145 29 E
Tribune 158 38 30 N 101 45 W
Tricárico 65 40 37 N 16 9 E
Tricase 65 39 56 N 18 20 E
Trichinopoly = Tiruchchirappalli 97 10 45 N 78 45 E
Trichur 97 10 30 N 76 18 E
Trida 141 33 1 S 145 1 E
Trier 49 49 45 N 6 37 E
Trieste 63 45 39 N 13 45 E
Trieste, G. di 63 45 37 N 13 40 E
Triggiano 65 41 4 N 16 58 E
Triglav 63 46 30 N 13 45 E
Trigno, R. 63 41 55 N 14 37 E
Trigueros 57 37 24 N 6 50 W
Trikeri 69 39 6 N 23 5 E
Trikhonis, Límni 69 38 34 N 21 30 E
Tríkkala 68 39 34 N 21 47 E
Tríkkala □ 68 39 41 N 21 30 E
Trikora, G. 103 4 11 S 138 0 E
Trilj 63 43 38 N 16 42 E
Trillick 38 54 27 N 7 30 W
Trillo 58 40 42 N 2 35 W
Trim 38 53 34 N 6 48 W
Trimdon 33 54 43 N 1 23 W
Trimley 29 51 59 N 1 19 E
Trincomalee 97 8 38 N 81 15 E
Trindade 171 16 40 S 49 30 W
Trindade, I. 15 20 20 S 29 50 W
Trinidad, Boliv. 174 14 54 S 64 50 W
Trinidad, Colomb. 174 5 25 N 71 40 W
Trinidad, Cuba 166 21 40 N 80 0 W
Trinidad, Uruguay 172 33 30 S 56 50 W
Trinidad, U.S.A. 159 37 15 N 104 30 W
Trinidad & Tobago ■ 167 10 30 N 61 20 W
Trinidad, I., Argent. 176 39 10 S 62 0 W
Trinidad, I., S. Amer. 167 10 30 N 61 15 W
Trinidad, R. 165 17 49 N 95 9 W
Trinitápoli 65 41 22 N 16 5 E
Trinity, Can. 151 48 22 N 53 29 W
Trinity, U.S.A. 159 30 50 N 95 20 W
Trinity B., Austral. 133 16 30 S 146 0 E
Trinity B., Can. 151 48 20 N 53 10 W
Trinity Mts. 159 40 20 N 118 50 W
Trinity R. 159 30 30 N 95 0 W
Trino 62 45 10 N 8 18 E
Trion 157 34 35 N 85 18 W
Trionto C. 65 34 38 N 16 47 E
Triora 62 44 0 N 7 46 E
Tripoli = Tarabulus 92 34 31 N 33 52 E
Tripoli = Tarābulus 119 32 49 N 13 7 E
Tripolis 69 37 31 N 22 25 E
Tripp 158 43 16 N 97 58 W
Tripura □ 98 24 0 N 92 0 E
Trischen, I. 48 54 3 N 8 32 E
Tristan da Cunha, I. 15 37 6 S 12 20 W
Trivandrum 97 8 31 N 77 0 E
Trivento 65 41 48 N 14 31 E
Trnava 53 48 23 N 17 35 E
Trobriand Is. 135 8 30 S 151 0 E
Trochu 152 51 50 N 113 13 W
Trodely I. 150 52 15 N 79 26 W
Trogir 63 43 32 N 16 15 E
Troglav, mt. 63 43 56 N 16 36 E
Trögstad 71 59 37 N 11 16 E
Tróia 65 41 22 N 15 19 E
Troilus, L. 150 50 50 N 74 35 W
Troina 65 37 47 N 14 34 E
Trois Fourches, Cap des 118 35 26 N 2 58 W
Trois Pistoles 151 48 5 N 69 10 W
Trois-Riviéres 150 46 25 N 72 40 W
Troisvierges 47 50 8 N 6 0 E
Troitsk 84 54 10 N 61 35 E
Troitskiy 84 55 29 N 37 18 E
Troitsko-Pechorsk 78 62 40 N 56 10 E
Trölladyngja 74 64 54 N 17 15 W
Trolladyngja 74 64 49 N 17 29 W
Trollhättan 73 58 17 N 12 20 E
Trollheimen 71 62 46 N 9 1 E
Tromöy 71 58 28 N 8 53 E
Troms fylke □ 74 68 56 N 19 0 E
Tromsø 74 69 40 N 18 56 E
Trona 163 35 46 N 117 23 W
Tronador, Mt. 176 41 53 S 71 0 W
Tröndelag, N. □ 74 65 0 N 12 0 E
Tröndelag, S. □ 71 62 0 N 10 0 E
Trondheim 71 63 25 N 10 25 E
Trondheimsfjorden 74 63 35 N 10 30 E
Trönninge 73 56 38 N 12 59 E
Trönö 72 61 22 N 16 54 E
Tronto, R. 63 42 50 N 13 46 E
Troodos, mt. 128 34 58 N 32 55 E
Troon 34 55 33 N 4 40 W
Tropea 65 38 40 N 15 53 E
Tropic 161 37 44 N 112 4 W
Tropoja 68 42 23 N 20 10 E
Trossachs, The 34 56 14 N 4 24 W
Trostan Mt. 38 55 4 N 6 10 W
Trostberg 49 48 2 N 12 33 E
Trotternish, dist. 36 57 32 N 6 15 W
Troup 159 32 10 N 95 3 W
Troup Hd. 37 57 41 N 2 18 W
Trout L., N.W. Terr., Can. 152 60 40 N 121 40 W
Trout L., Ont., Can. 153 51 20 N 93 15 W
Trout Lake 150 46 10 N 85 2 W
Trout, R. 152 61 19 N 119 51 W
Trout River 151 49 29 N 58 8 W
Trout Run 162 41 23 N 77 3 W
Trouville 42 49 21 N 0 5 E
Trowbridge 28 51 18 N 2 12 W
Troy, Turkey 92 39 55 N 26 20 E
Troy, Alabama, U.S.A. 157 31 50 N 85 58 W
Troy, Kans., U.S.A. 158 39 47 N 95 2 W
Troy, Mo., U.S.A. 158 38 56 N 90 59 W
Troy, Montana, U.S.A. 160 48 30 N 115 58 W
Troy, N.Y., U.S.A. 162 42 45 N 73 39 W
Troy, Ohio, U.S.A. 156 40 0 N 84 10 W
Troy, Pa., U.S.A. 162 41 47 N 76 47 W
Troyan 67 42 57 N 24 43 E
Troyes 43 48 19 N 4 3 E
Trpanj 66 43 1 N 17 15 E
Trstena 53 49 21 N 19 37 E
Trstenik 66 43 36 N 21 0 E
Trubchevsk 80 52 33 N 33 47 E
Truc Giang 101 10 14 N 106 22 E
Trucial States = Utd. Arab Emirates 93 24 0 N 54 30 E
Truckee 160 39 20 N 120 11 W
Trujillo, Colomb. 174 4 10 N 76 19 W
Trujillo, Hond. 166 16 0 N 86 0 W
Trujillo, Peru 174 8 0 S 79 0 W
Trujillo, Spain 57 39 28 N 5 55 W
Trujillo, U.S.A. 159 35 34 N 104 44 W
Trujillo, Venez. 174 9 22 N 70 26 W
Truk Is. 131 7 25 N 151 46 E
Trull 28 50 58 N 3 8 W
Trumann 159 35 42 N 90 32 W
Trumansburg 162 42 33 N 76 40 W
Trumbull, Mt. 161 36 25 N 113 32 W
Trumpington 29 52 11 N 0 6 E
Trún 66 42 51 N 22 38 E
Trun, France 42 48 50 N 0 2 E
Trun, Switz. 51 46 45 N 8 59 E
Trundle 141 32 53 S 147 42 E
Trung-Phan, reg. 100 16 0 N 108 0 E
Truro, Austral. 140 34 24 S 139 9 E
Truro, Can. 151 45 21 N 63 14 E
Truro, U.K. 30 50 17 N 5 2 W
Trûscǔu, Muntii 70 46 14 N 23 14 E
Truskmore, mt. 38 54 23 N 8 20 W
Truslove 137 33 20 S 121 45 E
Trustrup 73 56 20 N 10 46 E
Truth or Consequences 161 33 9 N 107 16 W
Trutnov 52 50 37 N 15 54 E
Truxton 162 42 45 N 76 2 W
Truyère, R. 44 44 38 N 2 34 E
Trwyn Cilan 31 52 47 N 4 31 W
Tryavna 67 42 54 N 25 25 E
Tryon 157 35 15 N 82 16 W
Trzciarka 54 53 3 N 16 25 E
Trzciel 54 52 23 N 15 50 E
Trzcinsko-Zdroj 54 52 58 N 14 35 E
Trzebiez 54 53 38 N 14 31 E
Trzebinia 54 50 11 N 19 30 E
Trzeblatów 54 54 3 N 15 18 E
Trzebnica 54 51 20 N 17 1 E
Trzemeszno 54 52 33 N 17 48 E
Tržič 63 46 22 N 14 18 E
Tsafriya 90 31 59 N 34 51 E
Tsaidam 105 37 0 N 95 0 E
Tsak'o 108 31 56 N 99 35 E
Tsamandás 68 39 46 N 20 21 E
Tsamkong = Chanchiang 109 21 15 N 110 20 E
Tsana Dzong 99 28 0 N 91 55 E
Tsanga 99 30 43 N 100 32 E
Ts'angchi 108 31 48 N 105 57 E
Ts'angchou 106 38 10 N 116 50 E
Tsangpo 99 29 40 N 89 0 E
Ts'angyüan 108 23 9 N 99 15 E
Ts'ao Ho, R. 107 40 32 N 124 11 E
Tsaochuang 107 34 30 N 117 49 E
Tsaochwang 174 35 11 N 115 28 E
Ts'aohsien 106 34 50 N 115 31 E
Tsaoyang 109 32 8 N 112 42 E
Tsaratanana 129 16 47 S 47 39 E
Tsaratanana, Mt. de 129 14 0 S 49 0 E
Tsarevo = Michurin 67 42 9 N 27 51 E
Tsaring Nor 99 34 40 N 97 20 E
Tsaritsáni 68 39 53 N 15 14 E
Tsau 128 20 8 S 22 29 E
Tsaukaib 128 26 37 S 15 39 E
Tsebrikovo 82 47 9 N 30 10 E
Ts'ehung 108 25 2 N 105 47 E
Tselinograd 76 51 10 N 71 30 E
Tsengch'eng 109 23 17 N 113 49 E
Ts'enkung 108 27 13 N 108 45 E
Tsetserleg 105 47 36 N 101 32 E
Tshabong 128 26 2 S 22 29 E
Tshane 125 24 5 S 21 54 E
Tshela 124 5 4 S 13 0 E
Tshesebe 129 20 43 S 27 32 E
Tshhinvali 83 42 14 N 44 1 E
Tshibeke 126 2 40 S 28 35 E
Tshibinda 126 2 23 S 28 30 E
Tshikapa 124 6 17 S 21 0 E
Tshilenge 126 6 12 S 23 40 E
Tshinsenda 127 12 15 N 28 0 E
Tshofa 124 5 8 S 25 8 E
Tshombe 129 25 18 S 45 29 E
Tshwane 128 22 24 S 22 1 E
Tsigara 128 20 22 S 25 54 E
Tsihombe 125 25 10 S 45 41 E
Tsilmamo 123 6 1 N 35 10 E
Tsimlyansk 83 47 45 N 42 0 E
Tsimlyanskoye Vdkhr. 83 48 0 N 43 0 E
Tsinan = Chinan 106 36 32 N 117 0 E
Tsineng 128 27 05 S 23 05 E
Tsinga, mt. 68 41 23 N 24 44 E
Tsinghai □ 105 36 0 N 96 0 E
Tsingtao = Ch'ingtao 107 36 5 N 120 25 E
Tsinjomitondraka 129 15 40 S 47 8 E
Tsiroanomandidy 129 18 46 S 46 2 E
Tsivilsk 81 55 50 N 47 25 E
Tsivory 129 24 4 S 46 5 E
Tskhinali 79 42 22 N 43 52 E
Tso Chiang, R. 108 22 52 N 108 5 E
Tso Morari, L. 95 32 50 N 78 20 E
Tsochou 108 22 36 N 107 36 E
Tsoch'üan 106 37 3 N 113 27 E
Tsodilo Hill 128 18 49 S 21 43 E
Tsogttsetsiy 106 43 43 N 105 35 E
Tsokung 108 29 55 N 97 44 E
Tsona Dzong 99 28 0 N 91 55 E
Tsoshui 106 33 40 N 109 9 E
Tsouhsien 106 35 24 N 116 58 E
Tsu 111 34 45 N 136 25 E
Tsu L. 152 60 40 N 111 52 W
Tsuchiura 111 36 12 N 140 15 E
Tsugaru-Kaikyō 112 41 35 N 141 0 E
Tsukumi 110 33 4 N 131 52 E
Tsukushi-Sanchi 110 33 25 N 130 30 E
Tsumeb 128 19 9 S 17 44 E
Tsumis 128 23 39 S 17 29 E
Tsuna 110 34 28 N 134 56 E
Ts'ungchiang 108 25 45 N 108 54 E
Tsunhua 107 40 12 N 117 56 E
Tsuni 108 27 43 N 106 52 E
Tsuno-Shima 110 34 21 N 130 52 E
Tsuru 111 35 31 N 138 57 E
Tsuruga 111 35 45 N 136 2 E
Tsuruga-Wan 111 35 50 N 136 3 E
Tsurugi 111 36 37 N 136 37 E
Tsurugi-San 110 33 51 N 134 6 E
Tsurumi-Saki 110 32 56 N 132 5 E
Tsuruoka 112 38 44 N 139 50 E
Tsurusaki 110 33 14 N 131 41 E
Tsushima 111 35 10 N 136 43 E
Tsushima, I. 110 34 20 N 129 20 E
Tsvetkovo 82 49 15 N 31 33 E
Tu, R. 98 22 50 N 97 15 E
Tua, R. 57 41 19 N 7 15 W
Tuai 143 38 47 S 177 15 E
Tuakau 142 37 16 S 174 59 E
Tual 103 5 30 S 132 50 E
Tuam 38 53 30 N 8 50 W
Tuamarina 143 41 25 S 173 59 E
Tuamgraney 39 52 54 N 8 32 W
Tuamotu Arch = Touamotou 131 17 0 S 144 0 W
Tuan 108 23 59 N 108 3 E
T'uanch'i 108 27 28 N 107 7 E
T'uanfeng 109 30 38 N 114 52 E
Tuao 103 17 47 S 121 30 E
Tuapse 83 44 5 N 39 10 E
Tuatapere 143 46 8 S 167 41 E
Tuath, Loch 34 56 30 N 6 15 W
Tuba City 161 36 8 N 111 12 W
Tubac 161 31 45 N 111 2 W
Tubai Is. = Toubouai, Îles 131 25 0 S 150 0 W
Tuban 102 6 57 S 112 4 E
Tubarão 173 28 30 S 49 0 W
Tubas 90 32 20 N 35 22 E
Tubau 102 3 10 N 113 40 E
Tubayq, Jabal at 122 29 30 N 27 30 E
Tubbergen 46 52 24 N 6 48 E
Tübingen 48 48 31 N 9 4 E
Tubize 47 50 42 N 4 13 E
Tubja, W. 122 25 27 N 38 55 E
Tubruq, (Tobruk) 117 32 7 N 23 55 E
Tubuai, Îles 131 25 0 S 150 0 W
Tuc Trung 101 11 1 N 107 12 E
Tucacas 174 10 48 N 68 19 W
Tucano 170 10 58 S 38 48 W
Tuch'ang 109 29 15 N 116 13 E
T'uch'ang 109 24 42 N 121 25 E
Tuchodi, R. 152 58 17 N 123 42 W
Tuchola 54 53 33 N 17 52 E
Tuchów 54 49 54 N 21 1 E
T'uch'üan 107 45 22 N 121 41 E
Tuckanarra 137 27 8 S 118 1 E
Tuckernuck I. 162 41 15 N 70 17 W
Tucson 161 32 14 N 110 59 W
Tucumán 172 26 50 S 65 20 W
Tucumán □ 172 26 48 S 66 2 W
Tucumcari 159 35 12 N 103 45 W
Tucupido 174 9 17 N 65 47 W
Tucupita 174 9 14 N 62 3 W
Tucuracas 174 11 45 N 72 22 W
Tucuruí 170 3 42 S 49 27 W
Tuczno 54 53 13 N 16 10 E
Tudela 58 42 4 N 1 39 W
Tudela de Duero 56 41 37 N 4 39 W
Tudor, Lac 151 55 50 N 65 25 W
Tudora 70 47 31 N 26 45 E
Tudweiliog 31 52 54 N 4 37 W
Tuella, R. 56 41 50 N 7 10 W
Tuen 139 28 33 S 145 37 E
Tueré, R. 170 2 48 S 50 59 W
Tufi 135 9 8 S 149 19 E
Tugidak I. 147 56 30 N 154 40 W
Tuguegarao 103 17 35 N 121 42 E
Tugur 77 53 50 N 136 45 E
Tugwa 128 17 27 S 18 33 E
Tukangbesi, Kepulauan 103 6 0 S 124 0 E
Tukarak I. 150 56 15 N 78 45 W
Tukobo 120 5 1 N 2 47 W
Tūkrah 119 32 30 N 20 37 E
Tuku, mt. 123 9 10 N 36 43 E
Tukums 80 57 2 N 23 3 E
Tukuyu 127 9 17 S 33 35 E
Tukzar 93 35 55 N 66 25 E
Tula, Hidalgo, Mexico 165 20 0 N 99 20 W
Tula, Tamaulipas, Mexico 165 23 0 N 99 40 W
Tula, Nigeria 121 9 51 N 11 27 E
Tula, U.S.S.R. 81 54 13 N 37 32 E
Tulak 93 33 55 N 63 40 E
Tulancingo 165 20 5 N 98 22 W
Tulanssu 105 36 52 N 98 24 E
Tulare 163 36 15 N 119 26 W
Tulare Basin 163 36 0 N 119 48 W
Tulare Lake 161 36 0 N 119 53 W
Tularosa 161 33 4 N 106 1 W
Tulbagh 128 33 16 S 19 6 E
Tulcán 174 0 48 N 77 43 W
Tulcea 70 45 13 N 28 46 E
Tulcea □ 70 45 0 N 29 0 E
Tulchin 82 48 41 N 28 55 E
Tuléar 129 23 21 S 43 40 E
Tuléar □ 129 21 0 S 45 0 E
Tulemalu L. 153 62 58 N 99 25 W
Tulgheş 70 4 58 N 25 45 E
Tuli, Indon. 103 1 24 S 122 26 E
Tuli, Rhod. 127 21 58 S 29 13 E
Tuliuchen 106 39 1 N 116 54 E
Tulkarm 90 32 19 N 35 10 E
Tulla, Ireland 39 52 53 N 8 45 W
Tulla, U.S.A. 159 34 35 N 101 44 W
Tulla, L. 34 56 33 N 4 47 W
Tullaghoge 38 54 36 N 6 43 W
Tullaghought 39 52 25 N 7 22 W
Tullahoma 157 35 23 N 86 12 W
Tullamore, Austral. 141 32 39 S 147 36 E
Tullamore, Ireland 39 53 17 N 7 30 W
Tullaroan 39 52 40 N 7 27 W
Tulle 44 45 16 N 0 47 E
Tullibigeal 141 33 25 S 146 44 E
Tullins 45 45 18 N 5 29 E
Tulln 52 48 20 N 16 4 E
Tullow 39 52 48 N 6 45 W

Tullus Uddingston

Tullus 123 11 7N 24 40E
Tully, Austral. 138 17 56S 145 55E
Tully, Ireland 38 53 44N 8 9W
Tully, U.S.A. 162 42 48N 76 7W
Tully Cross 38 53 35N 9 59W
Tŭlmaciu 70 45 38N 24 19E
Tulmaythah 117 32 40N 20 55E
Tulmur 138 22 40S 142 20E
Tulnici 70 45 51N 26 38E
Tulovo 67 42 33N 25 32E
Tulsa 159 36 10N 96 0W
Tulsequah 152 58 39N 133 35W
Tulsk 38 53 47N 8 15W
Tulu Milki 123 9 55N 38 14E
Tulu Welel, Mt. 123 8 56N 35 30E
Tulua 174 4 6N 76 11W
T'ulufan 105 42 56N 89 10E
Tulun 77 54 40N 100 10E
Tulungagung 103 8 5S 111 54E
Tum 103 3 28S 130 21E
Tuma 81 55 10N 40 30E
Tuma, R. 166 13 18N 84 50W
Tumaco 174 1 50N 78 45W
Tumatumari 174 5 20N 58 55W
Tumba 72 59 12N 17 48E
Tumba, L. 124 0 50S 18 0E
Tumbarumba 141 35 44S 148 0E
Tumbaya 172 23 50S 65 20W
Tumbes 174 3 30S 80 20W
Tumbwa 127 11 25S 27 15E
Tumby B. 140 34 21S 136 8E
T'umen 107 42 55N 129 50E
T'umen Kiang, R. 107 42 18N 130 41E
Tumeremo 174 7 18N 61 30W
Tumiritinga 171 18 58S 41 38W
Tumkur 97 13 18N 77 12E
Tumleberg 73 58 16N 12 52E
Tummel, L. 37 56 43N 3 55W
Tummel, R. 37 56 42N 4 5W
T'umot'eyuch'i 106 40 42N 111 8E
Tump 93 26 7N 62 16E
Tumpat 101 6 11N 102 10E
Tumsar 96 21 26N 79 45E
Tumu 120 10 56N 1 56W
Tumucumaque, Serra de 175 2 0N 55 0W
Tumut 141 35 16S 148 13E
Tumutuk 84 55 1N 53 19E
Tumwater 160 47 0N 122 58W
Tuna, Pta. 147 17 59N 65 53W
Tunas de Zaza 166 21 39N 79 34W
Tunbridge Wells 29 51 7N 0 16E
T'unch'i 105 29 50N 118 26E
Tuncurry 141 32 9S 152 29E
Tunduru 127 11 0S 37 25E
Tunduru □ 127 11 5S 37 22E
Tundzha, R. 67 42 0N 26 35E
Tune 71 59 16N 11 2E
Tung Chiang, R. 109 22 55N 113 35E
Tung-Pei 77 44 0N 126 0E
Tunga La 99 29 0N 94 14E
Tunga Pass 98 29 0N 94 14E
Tunga, R. 97 13 42N 75 20E
Tungabhadra Dam 97 15 21N 76 23E
Tungabhadra, R. 97 15 30N 77 0E
Tungachen 106 36 15N 165 12E
Tungan 109 26 24N 111 17E
T'ungan 109 24 44N 118 9E
T'ungcheng, Anhwei, China 109 31 3N 116 58E
T'ungcheng, Hupeh, China 109 29 15N 113 49E
Tungch'i 108 28 43N 106 42E
T'ungchiang, Heilungkiang, China 105 47 40N 132 30E
T'ungchiang, Szechwan, China 108 31 56N 107 15E
Tungchingch'eng 107 44 9N 129 7E
Tungchuan 105 35 4N 109 2E
T'ungch'uan 106 35 95N 109 5E
Tungch'uan 108 26 9N 103 7E
Tungfanghsien, (Paso) 100 18 50N 108 33E
Tungfeng 107 42 40N 125 34E
T'unghai 108 24 8N 102 43E
Tunghai Tao 109 21 2N 110 25E
Tunghsiang 109 28 14N 116 35E
T'unghsien 105 39 45N 116 43E
T'unghsin 106 37 9N 106 28E
T'unghua 107 41 45N 126 0E
Tungi 98 23 53N 90 24E
T'ungjen 105 27 43N 109 10E
Tungkan 108 23 22N 105 9E
Tungkou 107 39 52N 124 8E
Tungku 108 31 52N 100 14E
T'ungku 109 28 32N 114 23E
Tungkuan 109 23 0N 113 39E
T'ungkuan 105 34 37N 110 27E
Tungkuang 106 37 53N 116 32E
Tungla 166 13 24N 84 15W
Tunglan 108 24 30N 107 23E
T'ungliang 108 29 52N 106 2E
T'ungliao 107 43 37N 122 16E
Tungling 109 31 0N 117 54E
Tungliu 109 30 13N 116 55E
T'unglu 109 29 49N 119 40E
Tungnafellsjökull 74 64 45N 17 55W
T'ungnan 108 30 14N 105 48E
Tungning 107 44 3N 131 7E
T'ungpai 109 32 22N 113 24E
Tungp'ing 106 35 55N 116 18E
Tungpu 99 31 42N 98 19E
Tungshan 109 23 40N 117 31E
Tungshih 109 24 12N 120 43E
Tungsten, Can. 152 61 57N 128 16W
Tungsten, U.S.A. 160 40 50N 118 10W
Tungt'ai 109 32 50N 120 46E
T'ungtao 108 26 21N 109 36E
T'ungtien 108 26 40N 99 32E
Tungt'ing Hu 109 29 18N 112 45E
Tungtzu 108 28 8N 106 49E
Tunguchumuch'inch'i 106 45 33N 116 50E
Tunguska, Nizhmaya, R. 77 64 0N 95 0E
Tunguska, Podkammenaya, R. 77 61 0N 98 0E
T'ungwei 106 35 18N 105 10E
T'ungyü 107 44 48N 123 6E
Tunhua 107 43 20N 128 10E
Tunhuang 105 40 10N 94 50E
Tuni 96 17 22N 82 43E
Tunia 174 2 41N 76 31W
Tunica 159 34 43N 90 23W
Tunis 119 36 50N 10 11E
Tunis, Golfe de 119 37 0N 10 30E
Tunisia ■ 119 33 30N 9 10E
Tunja 174 5 40N 73 25W
Tunkhannock 162 41 32N 75 56W
T'unliu 106 36 19N 112 54E
Tunnsjøen 74 64 45N 13 25E
Tuno I. 73 55 58N 10 27E
T'unpuli Shan 105 35 0N 89 30E
Tunstall 29 52 7N 1 28E
Tuntatuliag 147 60 20N 162 45W
Tunungayualuk I. 151 56 0N 61 0W
Tunuyán 172 33 55S 69 0W
Tunuyán, R. 172 33 33S 67 30W
Tuolumne 163 37 59N 120 16W
Tuolumne, R. 163 37 36N 121 13W
Tuoy-Khaya 77 62 32N 111 18E
Tupã 173 21 57S 50 28W
Tupaciguara 171 18 35S 48 42W
Tuparro, R. 174 5 0N 68 40W
Tupelo 157 34 15N 88 42W
Tupik 77 54 26N 119 57E
Tupinambaranas, I. 174 3 0S 58 0W
Tupirama 170 8 58S 48 12W
Tupiratins 170 8 23S 48 8W
Tupiza 172 21 30S 65 40W
Tupman 163 35 18N 119 21W
Tupper 152 55 32N 120 1W
Tupper L. 156 44 18N 74 30W
Tupungato, Cerro 172 33 15S 69 50W
Tuque, La 150 47 30N 72 50W
Túquerres 174 1 5N 77 37W
Tur 90 31 47N 35 14E
Tura, India 98 25 30N 90 16E
Tura, U.S.S.R. 77 64 20N 99 30E
Tura, R. 84 57 12N 66 56E
Turaba, W. 122 21 15N 41 32E
Turagua, Serranía 174 7 20N 64 35W
Turaiyur 97 11 9N 78 38E
Turakina 142 40 3S 175 16E
Turakirae Hd. 142 41 26S 174 56E
Tūrān 93 35 45N 56 50E
Turan 77 51 38N 101 40E
Turbenthal 51 47 27N 8 51E
Tureburg 72 59 30N 17 58E
Turégano 56 41 9N 4 1W
Turek 54 52 3N 18 30E
Turen 174 9 17N 69 6W
Turfan Depression 105 42 45N 89 0E
Turgay 84 49 38N 63 30E
Turgay, R. 84 48 1N 62 45E
Tŭrgovishte 67 43 17N 26 38E
Turgutlu 92 38 30N 27 48E
Turhal 82 40 24N 36 19E
Turia, R. 58 39 43N 1 0W
TuriaçI 170 1 40S 45 28W
TuriaçI, R. 170 3 0S 46 0W
Turigshih 100 18 42N 109 27E
Turin = Torino 62 45 3N 7 40E
Turin Taber 152 49 47N 112 24W
Turinsk 84 58 3N 63 42E
Turkana □ 126 3 0N 35 30E
Turkana, L. 80 4 10N 32 10E
Turkestan 76 43 10N 68 10E
Turkestanskiy, Khrebet 85 39 35N 69 0E
Túrkeve 53 47 6N 20 44E
Turkey ■ 92 39 0N 36 0E
Turkey Creek P.O. 136 17 2S 128 12E
Turki 81 52 0N 43 15E
Turkmen S.S.R. □ 85 39 0N 59 0E
Turks Is. 167 21 20N 71 20W
Turks Island Passage 167 21 30N 71 20W
Turku (Åbo) 75 60 30N 22 19E
Turku-Pori □ 75 60 27N 22 15E
Turkwell, R. 126 2 30N 35 20E
Turlock 163 37 30N 120 55W
Turnagain, C. 142 40 28S 176 38E
Turnagain, R. 152 59 12N 127 35W
Turnberry, Can. 153 53 25N 101 45W
Turnberry, U.K. 34 55 19N 4 50W
Turneffe Is. 165 17 20N 87 50W
Turner 160 48 52N 108 25W
Turner Pt. 138 11 47S 133 32E
Turner River 136 17 52S 128 16E
Turner Valley 152 50 40N 114 17W
Turners Falls 162 42 36N 72 34W
Turnhout 47 51 19N 4 57E
Türnitz 52 47 55N 15 29E
Turnor L. 153 56 35N 108 35W
Turnov 52 50 34N 15 10E
Turnovo 67 43 5N 25 41E
Turnovo □ 67 43 4N 25 39E
Turnu Mŭgurele 70 43 46N 24 56E
Turnu Roşu Pasul 70 45 33N 24 17E
Turnu-Severin 70 44 39N 22 41E
Turö 73 55 2N 10 40E
Turon 159 37 48N 98 27W
Tuross Head 141 36 3S 150 8E
Turriff 37 57 32N 2 28W
Tursha 81 56 50N 47 45E
Tursi 65 40 15N 16 27E
Turtle Hd. I. 138 10 50S 142 37E
Turtle L., Can. 153 53 36N 108 38W
Turtle L., N.D., U.S.A. 158 47 30N 100 55W
Turtle L., Wis., U.S.A. 158 45 22N 92 10W
Turtleford 153 53 23N 108 57W
Turua 142 37 14S 175 35E
Turubah 92 28 20N 43 15E
Turukhansk 77 65 50N 87 50E
Turun ja Porin lääni □ 75 60 27N 22 15E
Turzovka 53 49 25N 18 41E
Tuscaloosa 157 33 13N 87 31W
Tuscánia 63 42 25N 11 53E
Tuscany = Toscana 62 43 28N 11 15E
Tuscola, Ill., U.S.A. 156 39 48N 88 15W
Tuscola, Tex., U.S.A. 159 32 15N 99 48W
Tuscumbia 157 34 42N 87 42W
Tushan 106 25 50N 107 33E
Tushino 81 55 44N 37 29E
Tuskar Rock 39 52 12N 6 10W
Tuskegee 157 32 24N 85 39W
Tŭšnad 70 47 30N 22 33E
Tustna 71 63 10N 8 5E
Tuszyn 54 51 36N 19 33E
Tutaryd 73 56 54N 13 59E
Tutbury 28 52 52N 1 41W
Tutikorin 97 8 50N 78 12E
Tutin 66 43 0N 20 20E
Tutóia 170 2 45S 42 20W
Tutoko Mt. 143 44 35S 168 1E
Tutong 102 4 47N 114 34E
Tutova, R. 70 46 20N 27 30E
Tutrakan 67 44 2N 26 40E
Tutshi L. 152 59 56N 134 30W
Tuttlingen 49 47 59N 8 50E
Tutuaia 103 8 25S 127 15E
Tutye 140 35 12S 141 29E
Tuva, A.S.S.R. □ 77 51 30N 95 0E
Tuxford 33 53 14N 0 52W
Tuxpan 165 20 50N 97 30W
Tuxtla Gutiérrez 165 16 50N 93 10W
Tuy 56 42 3N 8 39W
Tuy An 100 13 17N 109 16E
Tuy Doc 101 12 15N 107 27E
Tuy Hoa 100 13 5N 109 17E
Tuy Phong 101 11 14N 108 43E
Tuya L. 152 59 7N 130 35W
Tuyen Hoa 100 17 50N 106 10E
Tuyen Quang 100 21 50N 105 10E
Tuymazy 84 54 36N 53 42E
Tuyun 108 26 15N 107 32E
Tuz Gölü 92 38 45N 33 30E
Tuz Khurmatli 92 34 52N 44 41E
Tuz Khurmatu 92 34 50N 44 45E
Tuzkan, Ozero 85 40 35N 67 28E
Tuzla 66 44 34N 18 41E
Tuzlov, R. 83 47 28N 39 45E
Tvåaker 73 57 4N 12 25E
Tværsted 73 57 36N 10 12E
Tvarskog 73 56 34N 16 0E
Tved 73 56 12N 10 25E
Tvedestrand 71 58 38N 8 58E
Tveitsund 71 59 2N 8 31E
Tvelt 71 60 30N 7 11E
Tvyrditsa 67 42 42N 25 53E
Twain Harte 163 38 2N 120 14W
Twardogóra 54 51 23N 17 28E
Twatt 37 59 6N 3 15W
Tweed, R. 35 55 42N 2 10W
Tweede Exploërmond 46 52 55N 6 56E
Tweedmouth 35 55 46N 2 1W
Tweedshaws 35 55 26N 3 29W
Tweedsmuir Prov. Park 152 52 55N 126 20W
Twello 46 52 14N 6 6E
Twelve Pins 38 53 32N 9 50W
Twentynine Palms 163 34 10N 116 4W
Twillingate 151 49 42N 54 45W
Twin Bridges 160 45 33N 112 23W
Twin Falls 160 42 30N 114 30W
Twin Valley 158 47 18N 96 15W
Twinnge 98 21 58N 96 23E
Twisp 160 48 21N 120 5W
Twistringen 48 52 48N 8 38E
Two Harbors 158 47 1N 91 40W
Two Hills 152 53 43N 111 45W
Two Mile Borris 39 52 41N 7 43W
Two Rivers 156 44 10N 87 31W
Two Thumbs Ra. 143 43 45S 170 44E
Two Tree 138 18 25S 140 3E
Twofold B. 141 37 8S 149 59E
Twong 123 5 18N 28 29E
Twyford, Berks., U.K. 29 51 29N 0 51W
Twyford, Hants., U.K. 28 51 1N 1 19W
Ty 73 56 27N 8 32E
Tyborön 73 56 42N 8 12E
Tychy 54 50 9N 18 59E
Tyczyn 54 49 58N 22 2E
Tydd St. Mary 29 52 45N 0 9E
Tykocin 54 53 13N 22 46E
Tyldal 71 62 8N 10 48E
Tyldesley 32 53 31N 2 29W
Tyler, Minn., U.S.A. 158 44 18N 96 15W
Tyler, Tex., U.S.A. 159 44 18N 96 15W
Tylldal 71 62 7N 10 45E
Tylösand 73 56 33N 12 40E
Týn nad Vltavou 52 49 13N 14 26E
Tynagh 39 53 10N 8 22W
Tyndall, Mt. 143 43 15S 170 55E
Tyndinskiy 77 55 10N 124 43E
Tyndrum 34 56 26N 4 41W
Tyne & Wear □ 35 54 55N 1 35W
Tyne, R., Eng., U.K. 35 54 58N 1 28W
Tyne, R., Scot., U.K. 35 55 58N 2 45W
Tynemouth 35 55 1N 1 27W
Tynset 71 62 17N 10 47E
Tyre = Sūr 90 33 19N 35 16E
Tyrifjorden 71 60 2N 10 8E
Tyringe 73 56 9N 13 35E
Tyristrand 71 60 5N 10 5E
Tyrnyauz 83 43 21N 42 45E
Tyrol = Tirol 52 46 50N 11 20E
Tyrone □ 38 54 40N 7 15W
Tyrone, Co. 38 54 40N 7 15W
Tyrrell Arm 153 62 27N 97 30W
Tyrrell, L. 140 35 20S 142 50E
Tyrrell L. 153 63 7N 105 27W
Tyrrell, R. 140 35 26S 142 51E
Tyrrhenian Sea 60 40 0N 12 30E
Tysfjörden 74 68 10N 16 10E
Tysmenitsa 80 48 58N 24 50E
Tysnes 71 60 1N 5 30E
Tyssedal 71 60 7N 6 35E
Tystberga 73 58 51N 17 15E
Tyulgan 84 52 22N 56 12E
Tyumen 84 57 0N 65 18E
Tyumen-Aryk 85 44 2N 67 1E
Tyup 85 42 45N 78 20E
Tyvoll 71 62 43N 11 21E
Tywardreath 30 50 21N 4 40W
Tywi, R. 31 51 48N 4 20W
Tywyn 31 52 36N 4 5W
Tzaneen 129 23 47S 30 9E
Tzefa 90 31 7N 35 12E
Tzermíadhes Neapolis 69 35 11N 25 29E
Tzoumérka, Óros 68 39 30N 21 26E
Tzu Shui, R. 109 29 2N 112 55E
Tzuch'ang 106 37 12N 109 44E
Tzuch'eng 107 36 39N 117 56E
Tzuch'i 109 27 42N 116 58E
Tz'uch'i 109 29 59N 121 14E
Tzuchien 99 27 43N 98 34E
Tzuchin 109 23 38N 115 10E
Tzuchung 108 29 49N 104 55E
Tz'uhsien 106 36 22N 114 23E
Tzuhsing 109 25 58N 113 24E
Tzukuei 105 31 0N 110 38E
Tzukung 108 29 20N 104 50E
Tz'uli 109 29 25N 111 6E
Tzummarum 46 53 14N 5 32E
Tzupo 105 36 49N 118 5E
T'zuyang 108 32 31N 108 32E
Tzuyang 108 30 7N 104 39E
Tzuyün 108 25 45N 106 5E

U

U Taphao 100 12 35N 101 0E
Uad Erni, O. 118 26 30N 9 30W
Uainambi 174 1 43N 69 51W
Uanda 138 21 37S 144 55E
Uarsciek 91 2 28N 45 55E
Uasadi-jidi, Sierra 174 4 54N 65 18W
Uasin □ 126 0 30N 35 20E
Uassem 90 32 59N 36 2E
Uato-Udo 103 4 3S 126 6E
Uatumã, R. 174 1 30S 59 25W
Uauá 170 9 50S 39 28W
Uaupés 174 0 8S 67 5W
Uaxactún 166 17 25N 89 29W
Ub 66 44 28N 20 6E
Ubá 173 21 0S 43 0W
Ubaitaba 171 14 18S 39 20W
Ubangi, R. = Oubangi 124 1 0N 17 50E
Ubaté 174 5 19N 73 49W
Ubauro 94 28 15N 69 45E
Ube 110 33 56N 131 15E
Ubeda 59 38 3N 3 23W
Uberaba 171 19 50S 47 55W
Uberlândia 171 19 0S 48 20W
Ubiaja 121 6 41N 6 22E
Ubolratna Phong, L. 100 16 45N 102 30E
Ubombo 129 27 31S 32 4E
Ubon Ratchathani 100 15 15N 104 50E
Ubondo 126 0 55S 25 42E
Ubort, R. 80 51 45N 28 30E
Ubrique 57 36 41N 5 27W
Ubundi 126 0 22S 25 30E
Ucayali, R. 174 6 0S 75 0W
Uccle 47 50 48N 4 22E
Uchaly 84 54 19N 59 27E
Uchi Lake 153 51 10N 92 40W
Uchiko 110 33 33N 132 39E
Uchiura-Wan 112 42 25N 140 40E
Uchte 48 52 29N 8 52E
Uchterek 85 41 45N 73 12E
Uckerath 48 50 44N 7 22E
Uckfield 29 50 58N 0 6E
Ucluelet 152 48 57N 125 32W
Ucolta 107 32 56S 138 59E
Ucuriş 70 46 41N 21 58E
Uda, R. 77 54 42N 135 14E
Udaipur 94 24 36N 73 44E
Udaipur Garhi 95 27 0N 86 35E
Udamalpet 97 10 35N 77 15E
Udbina 63 44 31N 15 47E
Uddeholm 72 60 1N 13 38E
Uddel 46 52 15N 5 48E
Uddevalla 73 58 21N 11 55E
Uddingston 35 55 50N 4 3W

Uddjaur Ust Kuyga

Uddjaur	74	65 55N	17 50 E
Uden	47	51 40N	5 37 E
Udgir	96	18 25N	77 5 E
Udhampur	95	33 0N	75 5 E
Udi	121	6 23N	7 21 E
Udine	63	46 5N	13 10 E
Udine □	63	46 3N	13 13 E
Udipi	97	13 25N	74 42 E
Udmurt, A.S.S.R. □	84	57 30N	52 30 E
Udon Thani	100	17 29N	102 46 E
Udubo	121	11 52N	10 35 E
Udvoj Balken	67	42 50N	26 50 E
Udzungwa Range	127	11 15 S	35 10 E
Ueckermünde	48	53 45N	14 1 E
Ueda	111	36 24N	138 16 E
Uedineniya, Os.	12	78 0N	85 0 E
Uele, R.	124	3 50N	22 40 E
Uelen	77	66 10N	170 0W
Uelzen	48	53 0N	10 33 E
Ueno	111	34 53N	136 14 E
Uere, R.	124	3 45N	24 45 E
Uetendorf	50	46 47N	7 34 E
Ufa	84	54 45N	55 55 E
Ufa, R.	84	56 30N	58 10 E
Uffculme	30	50 45N	3 19W
Ufford	29	52 6N	1 22 E
Ugad R.	125	20 55 S	14 30 E
Ugalla, R.	126	6 0 S	32 0 E
Ugamas	128	28 0 S	19 41 E
Uganda ■	126	2 0N	32 0 E
Ugborough	30	50 22N	3 53W
Ugchelen	46	52 11N	5 56 E
Ugento	65	39 55N	18 10 E
Ugep	121	5 53N	8 2 E
Ugie	129	31 10 S	28 13 E
Ugijar	59	36 58N	3 7W
Ugine	45	45 45N	6 25 E
Ugla	122	25 40N	37 42 E
Uglich	81	57 33N	38 13 E
Ugljane	63	43 35N	16 46 E
Ugra, R.	80	54 45N	35 30 E
Ugurchin	67	43 6N	24 26 E
Uh, R.	53	48 40N	22 0 E
Uherske Hradiště	53	49 4N	17 30 E
Uhersky Brod	53	49 1N	17 40 E
Uhrichsville	156	40 23N	81 22W
Uig, Lewis, U.K.	36	58 13N	7 1W
Uig, Skye, U.K.	36	57 35N	6 20W
Uinta Mts.	160	40 45N	110 30W
Uitenhage	128	33 40 S	25 28 E
Uitgeest	46	52 32N	4 43 E
Uithoorn	46	52 14N	4 50 E
Uithuizen	46	53 24N	6 41 E
Uitkerke	47	51 18N	3 9 E
Ujda = Oujda	118	34 45N	2 0W
Ujfehértó	53	47 49N	21 41 E
Ujh, R.	95	32 40N	75 30 E
Ujhani	95	28 0N	79 6 E
Uji	111	34 53N	135 48 E
Ujjain	94	23 9N	75 43 E
Ujpest	53	47 22N	19 6 E
Ujszász	53	47 19N	20 7 E
Ujung Pandang	103	5 10 S	119 20 E
Uka	77	57 50N	162 0 E
Ukara I.	126	1 44 S	33 0 E
Ukehe	121	6 40N	7 24 E
Ukerewe □	126	2 0 S	32 30 E
Ukerewe Is.	126	2 0 S	33 0 E
Ukholovo	81	54 47N	40 30 E
Ukhrul	98	25 10N	94 25 E
Ukhta	78	63 55N	54 0 E
Ukiah	160	39 10N	123 9W
Ukki Fort	95	33 28N	76 54 E
Ukmerge	80	55 15N	24 45 E
Ukraine S.S.R. □	82	48 0N	35 0 E
Uksyanskoye	84	55 57N	63 1 E
Ukwi	128	23 29 S	20 30 E
Ulaanbaatar	105	47 55N	106 53 E
Ulaangom	105	49 58N	92 2 E
Ulak I.	147	51 24N	178 58W
Ulamambri	141	31 19 S	149 23 E
Ulamba	127	9 3 S	23 38 E
Ulan Bator = Ulaanbaatar	105	47 55N	106 53 E
Ulan Ude	77	52 0N	107 30 E
Ulanbel	85	44 50N	71 7 E
Ulanga □	127	8 40 S	36 50 E
Ulanów	54	50 30N	22 16 E
Ulaya, Morogoro, Tanz.	126	7 3 S	36 55 E
Ulaya, Shinyanga, Tanz.	126	4 25 S	33 30 E
Ulbster	37	58 21N	3 9W
Ulceby Cross	33	53 14N	0 6 E
Ulcinj	66	41 58N	19 10 E
Ulco	128	28 21 S	24 15 E
Ulefoss	71	59 17N	9 16 E
Ulëza	68	41 46N	19 57 E
Ulfborg	73	56 16N	8 20 E
Ulft	46	51 53N	6 23 E
Ulhasnagar	96	19 15N	73 10 E
Ulinda	141	31 35 S	149 30 E
Uljma	66	45 2N	21 10 E
Ulla, R.	56	42 45N	8 30W
Ulladulla	141	35 21 S	150 29 E
Ullånger	72	62 58N	18 16 E
Ullapool	36	57 54N	5 10W
Ullared	73	57 8N	12 42 E
Ulldecona	58	40 36N	0 20 E
Ullswater, L.	32	54 35N	2 52W
Ullvättern, L.	72	59 30N	14 21 E
Ulm	49	48 23N	10 0 E
Ulmarra	139	29 37 S	153 4 E
Ulmeni	70	45 4N	46 40 E
Ulricehamn	73	57 46N	13 26 E
Ulrum	46	53 22N	6 20 E
Ulsberg	71	62 45N	9 59 E
Ulsfeinvik	71	62 21N	5 53 E
Ulster □	38	54 45N	6 30W
Ulster Canal	38	54 15N	7 0W
Ulstrem	67	42 1N	26 27 E
Ultima	140	35 22 S	143 18 E
Ulubaria	95	22 31N	88 4 E
Ulugh Muztagh	99	36 40N	87 30 E
Uluguru Mts.	126	7 15 S	37 30 E
Ulva, I.	34	56 30N	6 12W
Ulvenhout	47	51 33N	4 48 E
Ulverston	32	54 13N	3 7W
Ulverstone	138	41 11 S	146 11 E
Ulvik	71	60 35N	6 54 E
Ulvo	73	56 40N	14 37 E
Ulya	77	59 10N	142 0 E
Ulyanovsk	81	54 25N	48 25 E
Ulyasutay	105	47 45N	96 49 E
Ulysses	159	37 39N	101 25W
Ulzio	62	45 2N	6 49 E
Um Qeis	90	32 40N	35 41 E
Umag	63	45 26N	13 31 E
Umala	174	17 25 S	68 5W
Uman	82	48 40N	30 12 E
Umánaé	12	70 40N	52 10W
Umánaé Fjord	10	70 40N	52 0W
Umaria	99	23 35N	80 50 E
Umarkhed	96	19 37N	77 38 E
Umarkot	93	25 15N	69 40 E
Umatilla	160	45 58N	119 17W
Umba	78	66 50N	34 20 E
Umbertide	63	43 18N	12 20 E
Umboi I.	135	5 40 S	148 0 E
Umbrella Mts.	143	45 35 S	169 5 E
Umbria □	63	42 53N	12 30 E
Ume, R.	74	64 45N	18 30 E
Umeå	74	63 45N	20 20 E
Umera	103	0 12 S	129 30 E
Umfuli, R.	127	17 50 S	29 40 E
Umgusa	127	19 29 S	27 52 E
Umi	110	33 34N	130 30 E
Umiat	147	69 25N	152 20W
Umka	66	44 40N	20 19 E
Umkomaas	129	30 13 S	30 48 E
Umm al Aranib	119	26 10N	14 54 E
Umm al Qaiwain	93	25 30N	55 35 E
Umm Arda	123	15 17N	32 31 E
Umm az Zamul	93	22 35N	55 18 E
Umm Bel	123	13 35N	28 0 E
Umm Digulgulaya	123	10 28N	24 58 E
Umm Dubban	123	15 23N	32 52 E
Umm el Fahm	90	32 31N	35 9 E
Umm Hagar	123	14 20N	36 41 E
Umm Koweika	123	13 10N	32 16 E
Umm Lajj	92	25 0N	37 23 E
Umm Merwa	122	18 4N	32 30 E
Umm Qurein	123	16 3N	28 49 E
Umm Rumah	122	25 50N	36 30 E
Umm Ruwaba	123	12 50N	31 10 E
Umm Said	93	25 0N	51 40 E
Umm Sidr	123	14 29N	25 10 E
Ummanz I.	48	54 29N	13 9 E
Umnak.	147	53 20N	168 20W
Umnak I.	147	53 0N	168 0W
Umniati, R.	127	18 0 S	29 0 E
Umpang	101	16 3N	98 54 E
Umpqua, R.	160	43 30N	123 30W
Umrer	96	20 51N	79 18 E
Umreth	94	22 41N	73 4 E
Umshandige Dam	127	20 10 S	30 40 E
Umtali	127	18 58 S	32 38 E
Umtata	129	31 36 S	28 49 E
Umuahia-Ibeku	121	5 33N	7 29 E
Umvukwe Ra..	127	16 45 S	30 45 E
Umvuma	127	19 16 S	30 30 E
Umzimvubu, R.	129	31 38 S	29 33 E
Umzingwane, R.	127	21 30 S	29 30 E
Umzinto	129	30 15 S	30 45 E
Una	94	20 46N	71 8 E
Una, Mt.	143	42 13 S	172 36 E
Una, R.	63	44 50N	16 15 E
Unac, R.	63	44 42N	16 15 E
Unadilla	162	42 20N	75 17W
Unalanaska I.	147	54 0N	164 30W
Uncastillo	58	42 21N	1 8W
Uncia	174	18 25 S	66 40W
Uncompahgce Pk., Mt.	161	38 5N	107 32W
Unden	73	58 45N	14 25 E
Underbool	140	35 10 S	141 51 E
Undersaker	72	63 19N	13 21 E
Undersvik	72	61 36N	16 20 E
Undredal	71	60 57N	7 6 E
Unecha	80	52 50N	32 37 E
Ungarie	141	33 38 S	146 56 E
Ungarra	140	34 12 S	136 2 E
Ungava B.	149	59 30N	67 30W
Ungava Pen.	50	60 0N	75 0W
Ungeny	82	47 11N	27 51 E
Unggi	105	42 16N	130 28 E
Ungwatiri	123	16 52N	36 10 E
Uni	84	56 44N	51 47 E
União	170	4 50 S	37 50W
União da Vitória	173	26 5 S	51 0W
União dos Palamares	170	9 10 S	36 2W
Uniejów	54	51 59N	18 46 E
Unije, I.	63	44 40N	14 15 E
Unimak I.	147	54 30N	164 30W
Unimak Pass.	148	53 30N	165 15W
Union, Mo., U.S.A.	158	38 25N	91 0W
Union, S.C., U.S.A.	157	34 49N	81 39W
Union City, N.J., U.S.A.	162	40 47N	74 5W
Union City, Ohio, U.S.A.	156	40 11N	84 49W
Union City, Pa., U.S.A.	156	41 53N	79 50W
Union Gap	157	46 38N	120 29W
Unión, La, Chile	176	40 10 S	73 0W
Unión, La, Colomb.	174	1 35N	77 5W
Unión, La, El Sal.	165	13 20N	87 50W
Union, La	164	17 58N	101 49W
Unión, La, Spain	59	37 38N	0 53W
Unión, La, Venez.	174	7 28N	67 53W
Union, Mt.	161	34 34N	112 21W
Union of Soviet Soc. Rep. ■	77	47 0N	100 0 E
Union Springs	157	32 9N	85 44W
Uniondale Road	128	33 39 S	23 7 E
Uniontown	156	39 54N	79 45W
Unirea	70	44 15N	27 35 E
United Arab Emirates ■	93	23 50N	54 0 E
United Arab Republic ■	113	27 5N	30 0 E
United Kingdom ■	27	55 0N	3 0W
United States of America ■	155	37 0N	96 0W
Unity	153	52 30N	109 5W
Unjha	94	23 46N	72 24 E
Unnao	95	26 35N	80 30 E
Uno, Ilha	120	11 15N	16 13W
Unshin, R.	38	54 8N	8 26W
Unst, I.	36	60 50N	0 55W
Unstrut, R.	48	51 16N	11 29 E
Unter-Engadin	51	46 48N	10 20 E
Unterägeri	51	47 8N	8 36 E
Unterkulm	50	47 18N	8 7 E
Unterseen	50	46 41N	7 50 E
Unterwalden nid dem Wald □	51	46 50N	8 25 E
Unterwalden ob dem Wald □	51	46 55N	8 15 E
Unterwaldner Alpen	51	46 55N	8 15 E
Unterwasser	51	46 32N	8 21 E
Unturán, Sierra de	174	1 35N	64 40W
Unuk, R.	152	56 5N	131 3W
Ünye	82	41 5N	37 15 E
Unzen-Dake	111	32 45N	130 17 E
Unzha	81	57 40N	44 8 E
Unzha, R.	81	58 0N	43 40 E
Uors	51	46 42N	9 12 E
Uozu	111	36 48N	137 24 E
Upa, R.	53	50 45N	16 15 E
Upal	123	6 56N	34 12 E
Upata	174	8 1N	62 24W
Upavon	28	51 17N	1 49W
Upemba, L.	127	8 30 S	26 20 E
Upernavik	12	72 49N	56 20W
Upington	128	28 25 S	21 15 E
Upleta	94	21 46N	70 16 E
Upolu Pt.	147	20 16N	155 52W
Upper Alkali Lake	160	41 47N	120 0W
Upper Arrow L.	152	50 30N	117 50W
Upper Austria = Oberösterreich	52	48 15N	14 10 E
Upper Chapel	31	52 3N	3 26W
Upper Foster L.	153	56 47N	105 20W
Upper Heyford	28	51 54N	1 16W
Upper Hutt	142	41 8 S	175 5 E
Upper Klamath L.	160	42 16N	121 55W
Upper L. Erne	38	54 14N	7 22W
Upper Lake	160	39 10N	122 55W
Upper Manilla	141	30 38 S	150 40 E
Upper Marlboro	162	38 49N	76 45W
Upper Musquodoboit	151	45 10N	62 58W
Upper Sandusky	156	40 50N	83 17W
Upper Volta ■	120	12 0N	0 30W
Upperchurch	39	52 43N	8 2W
Upphärad	73	58 9N	12 19 E
Uppingham	29	52 36N	0 43W
Uppsala	72	59 53N	17 38 E
Uppsala län □	72	60 0N	17 30 E
Upshi	95	33 48N	77 52 E
Upstart, C.	138	19 41 S	147 45 E
Upton, U.K.	32	53 14N	2 52W
Upton, U.S.A.	158	44 8N	104 35W
Upton-upon-Severn	28	52 4N	2 12W
Upwey	28	50 40N	2 29W
Ur	92	30 55N	46 25 E
Ura-Tyube	85	39 55N	69 1 E
Urabá, Golfo de	174	8 25N	76 53W
Uracará	174	2 20 S	57 50W
Urach	49	48 29N	9 25 E
Uraga-Suidō	111	35 13N	139 45 E
Urakawa	112	42 9N	142 47 E
Ural, Mt.	141	33 21 S	146 12 E
Ural Mts. = Uralskie Gory	78	60 0N	59 0 E
Ural, R.	84	49 0N	52 0W
Uralla	141	30 37 S	151 29 E
Uralsk	84	51 20N	51 20 E
Uralskie Gory	78	60 0N	59 0 E
Urambo	126	5 4 S	32 47 E
Urambo □	126	5 0 S	32 0 E
Urana	141	35 15 S	146 21 E
Urandangi	138	21 32 S	138 14 E
Uranium City	153	59 34N	108 37W
Uraricaá, R.	174	3 20N	61 56W
Uravakonda	97	14 57N	77 12 E
Urawa	111	35 50N	139 40 E
Uray	76	60 5N	65 15 E
Urbana, Ill., U.S.A.	156	40 7N	88 12W
Urbana, Ohio, U.S.A.	156	40 9N	83 44W
Urbana, La	174	7 8N	66 56W
Urbánia	63	43 40N	12 31 E
Urbano Santos	170	3 12 S	43 23W
Urbel, R.	58	42 30N	3 49W
Urbino	63	43 43N	12 38 E
Urbión, Picos de	58	42 1N	2 52W
Urcos	174	13 30 S	71 30W
Urda, Spain	57	39 25N	3 43W
Urda, U.S.S.R.	83	48 52N	47 23 E
Urdinarrain	172	32 37 S	58 52W
Urdos	44	42 51N	0 35W
Urdzhar	76	47 5N	81 38 E
Ure, R.	33	54 20N	1 25W
Uren	81	57 35N	45 55 E
Ures	164	29 30N	110 30W
Ureshino	110	33 6N	129 59 E
Urfa	92	37 12N	38 50 E
Urfahr	52	48 19N	14 17 E
Urgench	76	41 40N	60 30 E
Urgun	93	32 55N	69 12 E
Urgut	85	39 23N	67 15 E
Uri	95	34 8N	74 2 E
Uri □	51	46 43N	8 35 E
Uribante, R.	174	7 25N	71 50W
Uribe	174	3 13N	74 24W
Uribia	174	11 43N	72 16W
Urim	90	31 18N	34 32 E
Uriondo	172	21 41 S	64 41W
Urique	164	27 13N	107 55W
Urique, R.	164	26 29N	107 58W
Urirotstock	51	46 52N	8 32 E
Urk	46	52 39N	5 36 E
Urla	92	38 20N	26 55 E
Urlati	70	44 59N	26 15 E
Urlingford	39	52 43N	7 35W
Urmia, L.	92	37 30N	45 30 E
Urmia (Rezā'iyeh)	92	37 40N	45 0 E
Urmston	32	53 28N	2 22W
Urner Alpen	51	46 45N	8 45 E
Uroševac	66	42 23N	21 10 E
Urrao	174	6 20N	76 11W
Urshult	73	56 31N	14 50 E
Urso	123	9 35N	41 33 E
Ursus	54	52 21N	20 53 E
Uruaca	171	15 30 S	49 41W
Uruaçu	171	14 30 S	49 10W
Uruapán	164	19 30N	102 0W
Urubamba	174	13 5 S	72 10W
Urubamba, R.	174	11 0 S	73 0W
Uruçuca	171	14 35 S	39 16W
Uruçuí	170	7 20 S	44 28W
Uruçuí Prêto, R.	170	7 20 S	44 38W
Uruçuí, Serra do	170	9 0 S	44 45W
Urucuia, R.	171	16 8 S	45 5W
Uruguai, R.	173	24 0 S	53 30W
Uruguaiana	172	29 50 S	57 0W
Uruguay ■	172	32 30 S	55 30W
Uruguay, R.	172	28 0 S	56 0W
Urumchi = Wulumuchi	105	43 40N	87 50 E
Urup, I.	77	43 0N	151 0 E
Urup, R.	83	44 19N	41 30 E
Urutaí	171	17 28 S	48 12W
Uruyén	174	5 41N	62 25W
Uruzgan □	93	33 30N	66 0 E
Uryupinsk	81	50 45N	42 3 E
Urzhum	81	57 10N	49 56 E
Urziceni	70	44 46N	26 42 E
Usa	110	33 31N	131 21 E
Usa, R.	78	66 20N	56 0 E
Uşak	92	38 43N	29 28 E
Usakos	128	22 0 S	15 31 E
Usambara Mts.	126	4 50 S	38 20 E
Usedom	48	53 50N	13 55 E
Useko	124	5 8 S	32 24 E
Usfan	122	21 58N	39 27 E
Ush-Tobe	76	45 16N	78 0 E
Ushakova, O.	12	82 0N	80 0 E
Ushant = Ouessant, Île d'	42	48 25N	5 5W
Ushashi	126	1 59 S	33 57 E
Ushat	123	7 59N	29 28 E
Ushibuka	110	32 11N	130 1 E
Ushuaia	176	54 50 S	68 23W
Ushumun	77	52 47N	126 32 E
Usk	31	51 42N	2 53W
Usk, R.	31	51 37N	2 56W
Uskedal	71	59 56N	5 53 E
Üsküdar	92	41 0N	29 5 E
Uslar	48	51 39N	9 39 E
Usman	81	52 5N	39 48 E
Usoga □	126	0 5N	33 30 E
Usoke	126	5 7 S	32 19 E
Usolye Sibirskoye	77	52 40N	103 40 E
Usoro	121	5 33N	6 11 E
Uspallata, P. de	172	32 30 S	69 28W
Uspenskiy	76	48 50N	72 55 E
Usquert	46	53 24N	6 36 E
Ussel	44	45 32N	2 18 E
Ussuriysk	77	43 40N	131 50 E
Ust	52	50 41N	14 2 E
Ust Aldan = Batamay	77	63 30N	129 15 E
Ust Amginskoye = Khandyga	77	62 30N	134 50 E
Ust-Bolsheretsk	77	52 40N	156 30 E
Ust Buzulukskaya	81	50 8N	42 11 E
Ust Doneckij	83	47 35N	40 55 E
Ust Donetskiy	83	47 35N	40 55 E
Ust Ilga	77	55 5N	104 55 E
Ust Ilimpeya = Yukti	77	63 20N	105 0 E
Ust-Ilimsk	77	58 3N	102 39 E
Ust Ishim	76	57 45N	71 10 E
Ust Kamchatsk	77	56 10N	162 0 E
Ust Kamenogorsk	76	50 0N	82 20 E
Ust Karenga	77	54 40N	116 45 E
Ust Khayryuzova	77	57 15N	156 55 E
Ust Kut	77	56 50N	105 10 E
Ust Kuyga	77	70 1N	135 36 E

Ust Labinsk Vatoloha, Mt

Ust Labinsk 83 45 15N 39 50 E
Ust Luga 80 59 35N 28 26 E
Ust Maya 77 60 30N 134 20 E
Ust Mil 77 59 50N 133 0 E
Ust Nera 77 64 35N 143 15 E
Ust Olenek 77 73 0N 120 10 E
Ust-Omchug 77 61 9N 149 38 E
Ust Port 76 70 0N 84 10 E
Ust Tsilma 78 65 25N 52 0 E
Ust-Tungir 77 55 25N 120 15 E
Ust Urt = Ustyurt 76 44 0N 55 0 E
Ust Usa 78 66 0N 56 30 E
Ust-Uyskoye 84 54 16N 63 54 E
Ust Vorkuta 76 67 7N 63 35 E
Ustaoset 71 60 30N 8 2 E
Ustaritz 44 43 24N 1 27W
Uste 81 59 35N 39 40 E
Uster 51 47 22N 8 43 E
Ustí na Orlici 53 49 58N 16 38 E
Ustí nad Labem 52 50 41N 14 3 E
Ustica, I. 64 38 42N 13 10 E
Ustka 54 54 35N 16 55 E
Ustron 54 49 45N 18 48 E
Ustrzyki Dolne 54 49 27N 22 40 E
Ustye 77 55 30N 97 30 E
Ustyurt, Plato 76 44 0N 55 0 E
Ustyuzhna 81 58 50N 36 32 E
Ušće 66 43 43N 20 39 E
Usuki 110 33 8N 131 49 E
Usulután 166 13 25N 88 28W
Usumacinta, R. 165 17 0N 91 0W
Usva 84 58 41N 57 37 E
Uta 66 45 24N 21 13 E
Utah □ 160 39 30N 111 30W
Utah, L. 160 40 10N 111 58W
Ute Cr. 159 36 5N 103 45W
Utena 80 55 27N 25 40 E
Ütersen 48 53 40N 9 40 E
Utete 124 8 0S 38 45 E
Uthai Thani 100 15 22N 100 3 E
Uthal 94 25 44N 66 40 E
Uthmaniyah 92 25 5N 49 6 E
Utiariti 174 13 0S 58 10W
Utica 162 43 5N 75 18W
Utiel 58 39 37N 1 11W
Utik L. 153 55 15N 96 0W
Utikuma L. 152 55 50N 115 30W
Utinga 171 12 6S 41 5W
Uto 110 32 41N 130 40 E
Utrecht, Neth. 46 52 3N 5 8 E
Utrecht, S. Afr. 129 27 38S 30 20 E
Utrecht □ 46 52 6N 5 7 E
Utrera 57 37 12N 5 48W
Utsjoki 74 69 51N 26 59 E
Utsunomiya 111 36 30N 139 50 E
Uttar Pradesh □ 95 27 0N 80 0 E
Uttaradit 100 17 36N 100 5 E
Uttersberg 72 59 45N 15 39 E
Uttersley 73 54 56N 11 11 E
Uttoxeter 32 52 53N 1 50W
Utva, R. 84 51 28N 52 40 E
Ütze 48 52 28N 10 11 E
Uudenmaan lääni □ 75 60 25N 25 0 E
Uusikaarlepyy 74 63 32N 22 31 E
Uusikaupunki 75 60 47N 21 25 E
Uva 84 56 59N 52 13 E
Uvac, R. 66 43 35N 19 40 E
Uvalde 159 29 15N 99 48W
Uvarovo 81 51 59N 42 14 E
Uvat 76 59 5N 68 50 E
Uvelskiy 84 54 26N 61 22 E
Uvinza 126 5 5S 30 24 E
Uvira 126 3 22S 29 3 E
Uvlova, R. 52 49 34N 13 20 E
Uvs Nuur, L. 105 50 20N 92 45 E
Uwa 110 33 22N 132 31 E
Uwainhid 92 24 50N 46 0 E
Uwajima 110 33 10N 132 35 E
Uxmal 165 20 22N 89 46W
Uyeasound 36 60 42N 0 55W
Uyo 121 5 1N 7 53 E
Uyu, R. 98 24 51N 94 57 E
Uyuk 85 43 36N 71 16 E
Uyuni 172 20 35S 66 55W
Uyuni, Salar de 172 20 10S 68 0W
Uzbekistan S.S.R. □ 85 40 5N 65 0 E
Uzen, Bol. 81 50 0N 49 30 E
Uzen, Mal. 81 50 0N 48 30 E
Uzerche 44 45 25N 1 35 E
Uzès 45 44 1N 4 26 E
Uzgen 85 40 46N 73 18 E
Uzh, R. 80 51 15N 29 45 E
Uzhgorod 80 48 36N 22 18 E
Uzlovaya 81 54 0N 38 5 E
Uzun-Agach 85 43 35N 76 20 E
Uzunköprü 67 41 16N 26 43 E
Uzure 126 4 40S 34 22 E
Uzwil 51 47 26N 9 9 E

V

Vaal, R. 128 27 40S 25 30 E
Vaaldam 129 27 0S 28 14 E
Vaals 47 50 46N 6 1 E
Vaalwater 129 24 15S 28 8 E
Vaasa 74 63 16N 21 35 E
Vaasan lääni □ 74 63 2N 22 50 E
Vaassen 46 52 17N 5 58 E
Vabre 44 43 42N 2 24 E
Vác 53 47 49N 19 10 E
Vacaria 173 28 31S 50 52W
Vacaville 163 38 21N 122 0W
Vach, R. 76 60 56N 76 38 E
Vache, I.-à 167 18 2N 73 35W
Väddö 72 59 55N 18 50 E
Väderum 73 57 32N 16 11 E
Vadnagar 94 23 47N 72 40 E
Vado Ligure 62 44 16N 8 26 E
Vadodara 94 22 20N 73 10 E
Vadsø 74 70 3N 29 50 E
Vadstena 73 58 28N 14 54 E
Vaduz 51 47 8N 9 31 E
Vaerøy, Nordland Fylke, Norway 74 67 40N 12 40 E
Vaerøy, Sogn og Fjordane, Norway 71 61 17N 4 45 E
Vagney 43 48 1N 6 43 E
Vagnhärad 72 58 57N 17 33 E
Vagos 56 40 33N 8 42W
Vagsöy, I. 71 62 0N 5 0 E
Váh, R. 53 49 10N 18 20 E
Vaigach 76 70 10N 59 0 E
Vaigai, R. 97 9 47N 78 23 E
Vaiges 42 48 2N 0 30W
Vaihingen 49 48 44N 8 58 E
Vaihsel B. 13 75 0S 35 0W
Vaijapur 96 19 58N 74 45 E
Vaikam 97 9 45N 76 25 E
Vaila I. 36 60 12N 1 34W
Vailly Aisne 43 49 25N 3 30 E
Vaippar, R. 97 9 0N 78 25 E
Vaison 45 44 14N 5 4 E
Vajpur 96 21 24N 73 45 E
Vakarel 67 42 35N 23 40 E
Vakhsh, R. 85 37 6N 68 18 E
Vaksdal 71 60 29N 5 45 E
Vál 53 47 22N 18 40 E
Val d' Ajol, Le 43 47 55N 6 30 E
Val-de-Marne □ 43 48 45N 2 28 E
Val-d'Oise □ 43 49 5N 2 0 E
Val d'Or 150 48 7N 77 47W
Val Marie 153 49 15N 107 45W
Val-St.-Germain 47 48 34N 2 4 E
Valadares 56 41 5N 8 38W
Valahia 70 44 35N 25 0 E
Valais □ 50 46 12N 7 45 E
Valais, Alpes du 50 46 47N 7 30 E
Valandovo 66 41 19N 22 34 E
Valasské MeziříU5 53 49 29N 17 59 E
Valaxa, I. 69 38 50N 24 29 E
Valcheta 176 40 40S 66 20W
Valdagno 63 45 38N 11 18 E
Valdahon, Le 43 47 8N 6 20 E
Valday 80 57 58N 31 9 E
Valdayskaya Vozvyshennost 80 57 0N 33 40 E
Valdeazogues, R. 57 38 45N 4 55W
Valdemarsvik 73 58 14N 16 40 E
Valdepeñas, Ciudad Real, Spain 57 38 43N 3 25W
Valdepeñas, Jaén, Spain 57 37 33N 3 47W
Valderaduey, R. 56 42 30N 5 0W
Valderrobres 58 40 53N 0 9 E
Valdes Pen. 176 42 30S 63 45W
Valdez 147 61 14N 146 10W
Valdivia 176 39 50S 73 14W
Valdivia □ 176 40 0S 73 0W
Valdivia, La 172 34 43S 72 5W
Valdobbiádene 63 45 53N 12 0 E
Valdosta 157 30 50N 83 48W
Valdoviño 56 43 36N 8 8W
Valdres 71 60 55N 9 28 E
Vale, U.S.A. 160 44 0N 117 15W
Vale, U.S.S.R. 83 41 30N 42 58 E
Valea lui Mihai 70 47 32N 22 11 E
Valença, Brazil 171 13 20S 39 5W
Valença, Port. 56 42 1N 8 34W
Valença do Piauí 170 6 20S 41 45W
Valence 45 44 57N 4 54 E
Valence-d'Agen 44 44 8N 0 54 E
Valencia, Spain 59 39 27N 0 23W
Valencia, Venez. 174 10 11N 68 0W
Valencia □ 59 39 20N 0 40W
Valencia, Albufera de 59 39 20N 0 27W
Valencia de Alcántara 57 39 25N 7 14W
Valencia de Don Juan 56 42 17N 5 31W
Valencia des Ventoso 57 38 15N 6 29W
Valencia, G. de 59 39 30N 0 20 E
Valencia, L. de 167 10 13N 67 40W
Valenciennes 43 50 20N 3 34 E
Valensole 45 43 50N 5 59 E
Valentia Hr. 39 51 56N 10 17W
Valentia I. 39 51 54N 10 22W
Valentine, Nebr., U.S.A. 158 42 50N 100 35W
Valentine, Tex., U.S.A. 159 30 36N 104 28W
Valenton 160 48 45N 2 28 E
Valenza 62 45 2N 8 39 E
Våler 71 60 41N 11 50 E
Valera 174 9 19N 70 37W
Valguarnera Caropepe 65 37 30N 14 22 E
Valhall, oilfield 19 56 17N 3 25 E
Valier 160 48 15N 112 9W
Valinco, G. de 45 41 40N 8 52 E
Valjevo 66 44 18N 19 53 E
Valkeakoski 75 61 16N 24 2 E
Valkenburg 47 50 52N 5 50 E
Valkenswaard 47 51 21N 5 29 E
Vall de Uxó 58 40 49N 0 15W
Valla 72 59 2N 16 20 E
Valladolid, Mexico 165 20 30N 88 20W
Valladolid, Spain 56 41 38N 4 43W
Valladolid □ 56 41 38N 4 43W
Vallata 65 41 3N 15 16 E
Valldalssæter 71 59 56N 6 57 E
Valle 71 59 13N 7 33 E
Valle d'Aosta □ 62 45 45N 7 22 E
Valle de Arán 58 42 50N 0 55 E
Valle de Cabuérniga 56 43 14N 4 18W
Valle de la Pascua 174 9 13N 66 0W
Valle de Santiago 164 20 25N 101 15W
Valle de Zaragoza 164 27 28N 105 49W
Valle del Cauca □ 174 3 45N 76 30W
Valle Fértil, Sierra del 172 30 20S 68 0W
Valle Hermosa 165 25 35N 102 25 E
Valle Nacional 165 17 47N 96 19W
Vallecas 56 40 23N 3 41W
Valledupar 174 10 29N 73 15W
Vallejo 163 38 12N 122 15W
Vallenar 172 28 30S 70 50W
Valleraugue 44 44 6N 3 39 E
Vallet 42 47 10N 1 15W
Valletta 60 35 54N 14 30 E
Valley 31 53 17N 4 31W
Valley Center 163 33 13N 117 2W
Valley City 158 46 57N 98 0W
Valley Falls 160 42 33N 120 8W
Valley Okolona 159 34 0N 88 45W
Valley Springs 163 38 11N 120 50W
Valley View 162 40 39N 76 33W
Valleyfield 150 45 15N 74 8W
Valleyview 152 55 5N 117 17W
Valli di Comácchio 63 44 40N 12 15 E
Vallimanca, Arroyo 172 35 40S 59 10W
Vallo della Lucánia 65 40 14N 15 16 E
Vallon 45 44 25N 4 23 E
Vallorbe 50 46 42N 6 20 E
Valls 58 41 18N 1 15 E
Vallsta 72 61 31N 16 22 E
Valmaseda 58 43 11N 3 12W
Valmiera 80 57 37N 25 38 E
Valmont 42 49 45N 0 30 E
Valmontone 64 41 48N 12 55 E
Valmy 43 49 5N 4 45 E
Valnera, Mte. 58 43 9N 3 40W
Valognes 42 49 30N 1 28W
Valona (Vlora) 68 40 32N 19 28 E
Valongo 56 40 37N 8 27W
Valpaços 56 41 36N 7 17W
Valparaíso, Chile 172 33 2S 71 40W
Valparaíso, Mexico 164 22 50N 103 32W
Valparaiso 156 41 27N 87 2W
Valparaíso □ 172 33 2S 71 40W
Valpovo 66 45 39N 18 25 E
Valréas 45 44 24N 5 0 E
Vals 51 46 39N 10 11 E
Vals-les-Bains 45 44 42N 4 24 E
Vals, R. 128 27 28S 26 52 E
Vals, Tanjung 103 8 32S 137 32 E
Valsbaai 128 34 15S 18 40 E
Valskog 72 59 27N 15 57 E
Válta 68 40 3N 23 25 E
Valtellina 62 46 9N 10 2 E
Valverde del Camino 57 37 35N 6 47W
Valverde del Fresno 56 40 15N 6 51W
Valyiki 81 50 10N 38 5 E
Vama 70 47 34N 25 42 E
Vambarra Ra. 136 15 13S 130 24 E
Vamdrup 50 55 26N 9 10 E
Vammala 75 61 20N 22 55 E
Vámos 69 35 24N 24 13 E
Vamsadhara, R. 96 18 22N 84 15 E
Van 92 38 30N 43 20 E
Van Alstyne 159 33 25N 96 36W
Van Bruyssel 151 47 56N 72 9W
Van Buren, Can. 151 47 10N 67 55W
Van Buren, Ark., U.S.A. 159 35 28N 94 18W
Van Buren, Me., U.S.A. 157 47 10N 68 1W
Van Buren, Mo., U.S.A. 159 37 0N 91 0W
Van Canh 100 13 37N 109 0 E
Van der Kloof Dam 128 30 04S 24 40 E
Van Diemen, C., N.T., Austral. 136 11 9S 130 24 E
Van Diemen, C., Queens., Austral. 138 16 30S 139 46 E
Van Diemen G. 136 11 45S 131 50 E
Van Gölü 92 38 30N 43 0 E
Van Horn 161 31 3N 104 55W
Van Ninn 100 12 42N 109 14 E
Van Reenen P. 129 28 22S 29 27 E
Van Tassell 158 42 40N 104 3W
Van Tivu, I. 97 8 51N 78 15 E
Van Wert 156 40 52N 84 31W
Van Yen 100 21 4N 104 42 E
Vanavara 77 60 22N 102 16 E
Vancouver, Can. 152 49 20N 123 10W
Vancouver, U.S.A. 160 45 44N 122 41W
Vancouver, C. 137 35 2S 118 11 E
Vancouver I. 152 49 50N 126 0W
Vandalia, Ill., U.S.A. 158 38 57N 89 4W
Vandalia, Mo., U.S.A. 158 39 18N 91 30W
Vandeloos Bay 97 8 0N 81 45 E
Vandenburg 163 34 35N 120 44W
Vanderbijlpark 86 26 42S 27 54 E
Vanderhoof 152 54 0N 124 0W
Vanderlin I. 138 15 44S 137 2 E
Vandyke 138 24 10S 147 51 E
Vänern 73 58 47N 13 30 E
Vänersborg 73 58 26N 12 27 E
Vang Vieng 100 18 58N 102 32 E
Vanga 126 4 35S 39 12 E
Vangaindrano 129 23 21S 47 36 E
Vanguard 153 49 55N 107 20W
Vanier 150 45 27N 75 40W
Vanimo 135 2 42S 141 21 E
Vanivilasa Sagara 97 13 45N 76 30 E
Vaniyambadi 97 12 46N 78 44 E
Vankleek Hill 150 45 32N 75 40W
Vanna 74 70 6N 19 50 E
Vannas 74 63 58N 19 48 E
Vannes 42 47 40N 2 47W
Vanoise, Massif de la 45 45 25N 6 40 E
Vanrhynsdorp 128 31 36S 18 44 E
Vanrook 138 16 57S 141 57 E
Vans, Les 45 44 25N 4 7 E
Vansbro 72 60 32N 14 15 E
Vanse 71 58 6N 6 41 E
Vansittart B. 136 14 3S 126 17 E
Vanthli 94 21 28N 70 25 E
Vanua Levu, I. 130 16 33S 178 8 E
Vanwyksvlei 128 30 18S 21 49 E
Vanylven 71 62 5N 5 33 E
Vapnyarka 82 48 32N 28 45 E
Var □ 45 43 27N 6 18 E
Vara 73 58 16N 12 55 E
Varada, R. 97 14 46N 75 15 E
Varades 42 47 25N 1 1W
Varaita, R. 62 44 35N 7 15 E
Varaldsöy 71 60 6N 5 59 E
Varallo 62 45 50N 8 13 E
Varanasi (Benares) 95 25 22N 83 8 E
Varangerfjorden 74 70 3N 29 25 E
Varazdin 63 46 20N 16 20 E
Varazze 62 44 21N 8 36 E
Varberg 73 57 17N 12 20 E
Vardar, R. 66 41 25N 22 20 E
Varde 73 55 38N 8 29 E
Varde Å 73 55 35N 8 19 E
Vardø 74 70 23N 31 5 E
Varel 48 53 23N 8 9 E
Varella, Mui 100 12 54N 109 26 E
Varena 80 54 12N 24 30 E
Värendseke 73 57 4N 15 0 E
Varennes-sur-Allier 44 49 12N 5 0 E
Vareš 66 44 12N 18 23 E
Varese 62 45 49N 8 50 E
Varese Ligure 62 44 22N 9 33 E
Vårgårda 73 58 2N 12 49 E
Vargem Bonita 171 20 20S 46 22W
Vargem Grande 170 3 33S 43 56W
Varginha 173 21 33S 45 25W
Vargön 73 58 22N 12 20 E
Varhaug 71 58 37N 5 41 E
Varillas 172 24 0S 70 10W
Varing 73 58 30N 14 0 E
Värmdö, I. 72 59 18N 18 45 E
Värmeln 72 59 35N 13 0 E
Värmlands län □ 72 59 45N 13 20 E
Varmlandssaby 72 59 7N 14 15 E
Varna, Bulg. 67 43 13N 27 56 E
Varna, U.S.S.R. 84 53 24N 60 58 E
Varna, R. 96 17 13N 73 50 E
Varnamo 73 57 10N 14 3 E
Varnsdorf 52 49 56N 14 38 E
Värö 73 51 16N 12 15 E
Varpelev 73 55 22N 12 17 E
Värsjö 73 56 23N 13 27 E
Varsseveld 46 51 56N 6 29 E
Varteig 71 59 23N 11 12 E
Varto 92 39 10N 41 28 E
Vartofta 73 58 6N 13 40 E
Vartry Res. 39 53 3N 6 12W
Varvarin 66 43 43N 21 20 E
Varzaneh 93 32 25N 52 40 E
Várzea Alegre 170 6 47S 39 17W
Várzea da Palma 171 17 36S 44 44W
Varzi 62 44 50N 9 12 E
Varzo 62 46 12N 8 15 E
Varzy 43 47 22N 3 20 E
Vas □ 53 47 10N 16 55 E
Vasa 74 63 6N 21 38 E
Vasa Barris, R. 170 11 10S 37 10W
Vásárosnamény 53 48 9N 22 19 E
Väsby 73 56 13N 12 37 E
Vascâo, R. 57 37 44N 8 15W
Vascongadas 58 42 50N 2 45W
Vaşcŭu 70 46 28N 22 30 E
Väse 72 59 23N 13 52 E
Vasht = Khāsh 93 28 20N 61 6 E
Vasil Levski 67 43 23N 25 26 E
Vasilevichi 80 52 15N 29 50 E
Vasilikón 69 38 25N 23 40 E
Vasilkov 80 50 7N 30 28 E
Vaslui 70 46 38N 27 42 E
Vaslui □ 71 46 30N 27 30 E
Väsman 72 60 9N 15 5 E
Vassa 74 63 6N 21 38 E
Vassar, Can. 153 49 10N 95 55W
Vassar, U.S.A. 156 43 23N 83 33W
Vast Silen, L. 72 59 15N 12 15 E
Västerås 73 59 37N 16 38 E
Västerbottens län □ 74 64 58N 18 0 E
Västerdalälven 72 60 30N 13 25 E
Västernorrlands län □ 72 63 30N 17 40 E
Västervik 73 57 43N 16 43 E
Västmanland □ 72 59 55N 16 30 E
Vasto 63 42 8N 14 40 E
Vasvár 53 47 3N 16 47 E
Vatan 43 47 4N 1 50 E
Vaternish Pt. 36 57 36N 6 40W
Vatersay, I. 36 56 55N 7 32W
Vathí 69 37 46N 27 1 E
Váthia 69 36 29N 22 29 E
Vatican City ■ 63 41 54N 12 27 E
Vatin 66 45 12N 21 20 E
Vatnajökull 74 64 30N 16 48W
Vatnås 71 59 58N 9 37 E
Vatne 71 62 33N 6 38 E
Vatneyri 74 65 35N 24 0W
Vatoloha, Mt. 129 17 52S 47 48 E

Vatomandry **Vijayadurg**

Vatomandry	129	19 20 S	48 59 E
Vatra-Dornei	70	47 22 N	25 22 E
Vats	71	59 29 N	5 45 E
Vättern, L.	73	58 25 N	14 30 E
Vättis	51	46 55 N	9 27 E
Vaucluse □	45	44 3 N	5 10 E
Vaucouleurs	43	48 37 N	5 40 E
Vaud □	50	46 35 N	6 30 E
Vaughan	161	34 37 N	105 12 W
Vaughn	160	47 37 N	111 36 W
Vaulruz	50	46 38 N	7 0 E
Vaupés □	174	1 0 N	71 0 W
Vaupés, R.	174	1 0 N	71 0 W
Vauvert	45	43 42 N	4 17 E
Vauxhall	152	50 5 N	112 9 W
Vavincourt	43	48 49 N	5 12 E
Vavoua	120	7 23 N	6 29 W
Vaxholm	72	59 25 N	18 20 E
Växjö	73	56 52 N	14 50 E
Vaygach, Ostrov	76	70 0 N	60 0 E
Vaza Barris, R.	171	10 0 S	37 30 W
Veadeiros	171	14 7 S	47 31 W
Veagh L.	38	55 3 N	7 57 W
Vechta	48	52 47 N	8 18 E
Vechte, R.	46	52 34 N	6 6 E
Vecilla, La	56	42 51 N	5 27 W
Vecsés	53	47 26 N	19 19 E
Vedaraniam	97	10 25 N	79 50 E
Vedbæk	73	55 50 N	12 33 E
Veddige	73	57 17 N	12 20 E
Vedea, R.	70	44 0 N	25 20 E
Vedelgem	47	51 7 N	3 10 E
Vedia	172	34 30 S	61 31 W
Vedra, Isla del	59	38 52 N	1 12 E
Vedrin	47	50 30 N	4 52 E
Veendam	46	53 5 N	6 52 E
Veenendaal	46	52 2 N	5 34 E
Veenwouden	46	53 14 N	6 0 E
Veerle	47	51 4 N	4 59 E
Vefsna	74	65 48 N	13 10 E
Vega, Norway	74	65 40 N	11 55 E
Vega, U.S.A.	159	35 18 N	102 26 W
Vega Baja	147	18 27 N	66 23 W
Vega Fd.	74	65 37 N	12 0 E
Vega, I.	74	65 42 N	11 50 E
Vega, La	167	19 20 N	70 30 W
Vegadeo	56	43 27 N	7 4 W
Vegesack	48	53 10 N	8 38 E
Vegfjorden	74	65 37 N	12 0 E
Veggerby	73	56 54 N	9 39 E
Veggli	71	60 3 N	9 9 E
Veghel	47	51 37 N	5 32 E
Vegorritis, Limni	68	40 45 N	21 45 E
Vegreville	152	53 30 N	112 5 W
Vegusdal	71	58 32 N	8 10 E
Veii	63	42 0 N	12 24 E
Veinticino de Mayo	172	38 0 S	67 40 W
Veitch	140	34 39 S	140 31 E
Vejen	73	55 30 N	9 9 E
Vejer de la Frontera	57	36 15 N	5 59 W
Vejle	73	55 43 N	9 30 E
Vejle Amt □	73	55 2 N	11 22 E
Vejle Fjord	73	55 40 N	9 50 E
Vejlo	73	55 10 N	11 45 E
Vela Luka	63	42 59 N	16 44 E
Velanai I.	97	9 45 N	79 45 E
Velarde	161	36 11 N	106 1 W
Velas, C.	166	10 21 N	85 52 W
Velasco	159	29 0 N	95 20 W
Velasco, Sierra de.	172	29 20 S	67 10 W
Velay, Mts. du	44	45 0 N	3 40 E
Velb	46	52 0 N	5 59 E
Velddrif	128	32 42 S	18 11 E
Velden	47	51 25 N	6 10 E
Veldhoven	47	51 24 N	5 25 E
Veldwezelt	47	50 52 N	5 38 E
Velebit Planina	63	44 50 N	15 20 E
Velebitski Kanal	63	44 45 N	14 55 E
Veleka, R.	67	42 4 N	27 30 E
Velenje	63	46 23 N	15 8 E
Velestínon	68	39 23 N	22 43 E
Vélez	174	6 1 N	73 41 W
Velez	66	43 19 N	18 2 E
Vélez Blanco	57	37 41 N	2 5 W
Vélez Málaga	57	36 48 N	4 5 W
Vélez Rubio	59	37 41 N	2 5 W
Velhas, R.	171	17 13 S	44 49 W
Velika	66	45 27 N	17 40 E
Velika Goricá	63	45 44 N	16 5 E
Velika Kapela	63	45 10 N	15 5 E
Velika Kladuša	63	45 11 N	15 48 E
Velika Morava, R.	66	44 30 N	21 9 E
Velika Plana	66	44 20 N	21 1 E
Velikaya, R.	80	56 40 N	28 40 E
Veliké Kapušany	53	48 34 N	22 5 E
Velike Lašče	63	45 49 N	14 45 E
Veliki Backa Kanal	68	45 45 N	19 15 E
Veliki Jastrebac	66	43 25 N	21 30 E
Veliki Ustyug	78	60 47 N	46 20 E
Velikiye Luki	80	56 25 N	30 32 E
Veliko Turnovo	67	43 5 N	25 41 E
Velikonda Range	97	14 45 N	79 10 E
Velikoye, Oz.	81	55 15 N	40 0 E
Velingrad	67	42 4 N	23 58 E
Velino, Mt.	63	42 10 N	13 20 E
Velizh	80	55 30 N	31 11 E
Velké Karlovice	53	49 20 N	18 17 E
Velke Mezirici	52	49 21 N	16 1 E
Velký ostrov Zitný	53	48 5 N	17 20 E
Vellar, R.	97	11 30 N	79 36 E
Velletri	64	41 43 N	12 43 E
Velling	73	56 2 N	8 20 E
Vellinge	73	55 29 N	13 0 E
Vellir	74	65 55 N	18 28 W
Vellore	97	12 57 N	79 10 E
Velsen-Noord	46	52 27 N	4 40 E
Velsk	78	61 10 N	42 5 E
Velten	48	52 40 N	13 11 E
Veluwe Meer	46	52 24 N	5 44 E
Velva	158	48 6 N	100 56 W
Velvendós	68	40 15 N	22 6 E
Vem	73	56 21 N	8 21 E
Vembanad Lake	97	9 36 N	76 15 E
Veme	71	60 14 N	10 7 E
Ven	73	55 55 N	12 45 E
Vena	73	57 31 N	16 0 E
Venado	164	22 50 N	101 10 W
Venado Tuerto	172	33 50 S	62 0 W
Venafro	65	41 28 N	14 3 E
Venarey-les-Laumes	43	47 32 N	4 26 E
Venaria	62	45 12 N	7 39 E
Venčane	66	44 24 N	20 28 E
Vence	45	43 43 N	7 6 E
Vendas Novas	57	38 39 N	8 27 W
Vendée	42	46 50 N	1 35 W
Vendée □	44	46 40 N	1 20 W
Vendée, Collines de	42	46 35 N	0 45 W
Vendée, R.	42	46 30 N	0 45 W
Vendeuvre-sur-Barse	43	48 14 N	4 28 E
Vendôme	42	47 47 N	1 3 E
Vendrell	58	41 10 N	1 30 E
Vendsyssel	73	57 22 N	10 0 E
Veneta, Laguna	63	45 19 N	12 13 E
Venetie	147	67 0 N	146 30 W
Véneto □	63	45 30 N	12 0 E
Venev	81	54 22 N	38 17 E
Venézia	63	45 27 N	12 20 E
Venézia, Golfo di	63	45 20 N	13 0 E
Venezuela ■	174	8 0 N	65 0 W
Venezuela, Golfo de	174	11 30 N	71 0 W
Vengurla	97	15 53 N	73 45 E
Vengurla Rocks	97	15 50 N	73 22 E
Venice = Venézia	63	45 27 N	12 20 E
Vénissieux	45	45 43 N	4 53 E
Venjansjön	72	60 58 N	14 2 E
Venkatagiri	97	14 0 N	79 35 E
Venkatapuram	96	18 20 N	80 30 E
Venlo	47	51 22 N	6 11 E
Vennesla	71	58 15 N	8 0 E
Venø, Is.	73	56 33 N	8 38 E
Venraij	47	51 31 N	6 0 E
Venta de Cardeña	57	38 16 N	4 20 W
Venta de San Rafael	56	40 42 N	4 12 W
Venta, La	165	18 8 N	94 3 W
Ventana, Punta de la	164	24 4 N	109 48 W
Ventersburg	128	28 7 S	27 9 E
Ventimíglia	62	43 50 N	7 39 E
Ventnor	28	50 35 N	1 12 W
Ventotene, I.	64	40 48 N	13 25 E
Ventry	39	52 8 N	10 21 W
Ventspils	80	57 25 N	21 32 E
Ventuari, R.	174	5 20 N	66 0 W
Ventucopa	163	34 50 N	119 29 W
Ventura	163	34 16 N	119 18 W
Ventura, La	164	24 38 N	100 54 W
Venturosa, La	174	6 8 N	68 48 W
Venus B.	141	38 40 S	145 42 E
Veoy	71	62 45 N	7 30 E
Veoy Is.	71	62 45 N	7 30 E
Vera, Argent.	172	29 30 S	60 20 W
Vera, Spain	59	37 15 N	1 15 W
Veracruz	165	19 10 N	96 10 W
Veracruz □	165	19 0 N	96 15 W
Veraval	94	20 53 N	70 27 E
Verbánia	62	45 50 N	8 55 E
Verbicaro	65	39 46 N	15 54 E
Verbier	50	46 6 N	7 13 E
Vercelli	62	45 19 N	8 25 E
Verdalsøra	74	63 48 N	11 30 E
Verde Grande, R.	171	16 13 S	43 49 W
Verde Pequeno, R.	171	14 48 S	43 31 W
Verde, R., Argent.	176	41 55 S	66 0 W
Verde, R., Goiás, Brazil	171	18 1 S	50 14 W
Verde, R., Goiás, Brazil	171	19 11 S	50 44 W
Verde, R., Chihuahua, Mexico	164	26 59 N	107 58 W
Verde, R., Oaxaca, Mexico	164	15 59 N	97 50 W
Verde, R., Veracruz, Mexico	165	21 10 N	102 50 W
Verde, R., Parag.	172	23 9 S	57 37 W
Verden	48	52 58 N	9 18 E
Verdhikoúsa	68	39 47 N	21 59 E
Verdigre	158	42 38 N	98 0 W
Verdon-sur-Mer, Le	44	45 33 N	1 4 W
Verdun	43	49 12 N	5 24 E
Verdun-sur-le Doubs	43	46 54 N	5 0 E
Vereeniging	129	26 38 S	27 57 E
Vérendrye, Parc Prov. de	150	47 20 N	76 40 W
Vereshchagino	84	58 5 N	54 40 E
Verga, C.	120	10 30 N	14 10 W
Vergara	58	43 9 N	2 28 W
Vergato	62	44 18 N	11 8 E
Vergemont	138	23 33 S	143 1 E
Vergemont Cr.	138	24 16 S	143 16 E
[illegible]t	44	45 2 N	0 43 E
Veri[illegible]	56	41 57 N	7 27 W
Veri[illegible]a	56	43 32 N	5 43 W
Verkhnedvinsk	80	55 45 N	27 58 E
Verkhneuralsk	84	53 53 N	59 13 E
Verkhniy-Avzyan	84	53 32 N	57 33 E
Verkhniy Baskunchak	83	48 5 N	46 50 E
Verkhniy Tagil	84	57 22 N	59 56 E
Verkhniy Ufaley	84	56 4 N	60 14 E
Verkhniye Kigi	84	55 25 N	58 37 E
Verkhnyaya Salda	84	58 2 N	60 33 E
Verkhoturye	84	58 52 N	60 48 E
Verkhovye	81	52 55 N	37 15 E
Verkhoyansk	77	67 50 N	133 50 E
Verkhoyanskiy Khrebet	77	66 0 N	129 0 E
Verlo	153	50 19 N	108 35 W
Verma	71	62 21 N	8 3 E
Vermenton	43	47 40 N	3 42 E
Vermilion	153	53 20 N	110 50 W
Vermilion, B.	159	29 45 N	91 55 W
Vermilion Bay	153	49 50 N	93 20 W
Vermilion Chutes	152	58 22 N	114 51 W
Vermilion, R., Alta., Can.	153	53 22 N	110 51 W
Vermilion, R., Qué., Can.	150	47 38 N	72 56 W
Vermillion	158	42 50 N	96 56 W
Vermont □	156	43 40 N	72 50 W
Vern, oilfield	19	55 35 N	4 45 E
Vernal	160	40 28 N	109 35 W
Vernalis	163	37 36 N	121 17 W
Vernayez	50	46 8 N	7 3 E
Verner	150	46 25 N	80 8 W
Verneuil, Bois de	50	48 59 N	1 59 E
Verneuil-sur-Avre	42	48 45 N	0 55 E
Vernier	50	46 13 N	6 5 E
Vernon, Can.	152	50 20 N	119 15 W
Vernon, France	42	49 5 N	1 30 E
Vernon, U.S.A.	159	34 0 N	99 15 W
Vero Beach	157	27 39 N	80 23 W
Véroia	68	40 34 N	22 18 E
Verolanuova	62	45 20 N	10 5 E
Véroli	64	41 43 N	13 24 E
Verona	62	45 27 N	11 0 E
Veropol	77	66 0 N	168 0 E
Verrieres, Les	50	46 55 N	6 28 E
Versailles	43	48 48 N	2 8 E
Versoix	50	46 17 N	6 10 E
Vert, C.	120	14 45 N	17 30 W
Vertou	42	47 10 N	1 28 W
Vertus	43	48 54 N	4 0 E
Verulam	129	29 38 S	31 2 E
Verviers	47	50 37 N	5 52 E
Vervins	43	49 50 N	3 53 E
Verwood, Can.	153	49 30 N	105 40 W
Verwood, U.K.	28	50 53 N	1 53 W
Veryan	30	50 13 N	4 56 W
Veryan Bay	30	50 12 N	4 51 W
Verzej	63	46 34 N	16 13 E
Vesdre, R.	47	50 36 N	6 0 E
Veselí nad Luznicí	52	49 12 N	14 15 E
Veselie	67	42 18 N	27 38 E
Veselovskoye Vdkhr.	83	47 0 N	41 0 E
Veselyy Res.	83	47 0 N	41 0 E
Veshenskaya	83	49 35 N	41 44 E
Vesle, R.	43	49 17 N	3 50 E
Veslyana, R.	84	60 20 N	54 0 E
Vesoul	43	47 40 N	6 11 E
Vessigebro	73	56 58 N	12 40 E
Vest-Agder fylke □	71	58 30 N	7 15 E
Vest Fjorden	71	68 0 N	15 0 E
Vesta	166	9 43 N	83 3 W
Vestby	71	59 37 N	10 45 E
Vester Hassing	73	57 4 N	10 8 E
Vesterålen	74	68 45 N	14 30 E
Vestersche Veld	46	52 52 N	6 9 E
Vestfjorden	74	67 55 N	14 0 E
Vestfold fylke □	71	59 15 N	10 0 E
Vestmannaeyjar	74	63 27 N	20 15 W
Vestmarka	71	59 56 N	11 59 E
Vestnes	71	62 39 N	7 5 E
Vestone	62	45 43 N	10 25 E
Vestsjaellands Amt □	73	55 30 N	11 20 E
Vestspitsbergen	12	78 40 N	17 0 E
Vestvågøy	74	68 18 N	13 50 E
Vesuvio	65	40 50 N	14 22 E
Vesuvius, Mt. = Vesuvio	65	40 50 N	14 22 E
Veszprém	53	47 8 N	17 57 E
Veszprém □	53	47 5 N	17 55 E
Vésztö	53	46 55 N	21 16 E
Vetapalam	97	15 47 N	80 18 E
Vetlanda	73	57 24 N	15 3 E
Vetluga	81	57 53 N	45 45 E
Vetluzhskiy	81	57 17 N	45 12 E
Vetovo	67	43 42 N	26 16 E
Vetralla	63	42 20 N	12 2 E
Vetren	67	42 15 N	24 3 E
Vettore, Mte.	63	44 38 N	7 5 E
Veurne	47	51 5 N	2 40 E
Vevey	50	46 28 N	6 51 E
Vévi	68	40 47 N	21 38 E
Veys	92	31 30 N	49 0 E
Vézelise	43	48 30 N	6 5 E
Vezhen, mt.	67	42 50 N	24 20 E
Vi Thanh	101	9 42 N	105 26 E
Viacha	174	16 30 S	68 5 W
Viadana	62	44 55 N	10 30 E
Viana, Brazil	170	3 0 S	44 40 W
Viana, Port.	55	38 20 N	8 0 W
Viana, Spain	58	42 31 N	2 22 W
Viana do Castelo	56	41 42 N	8 50 W
Vianden	47	49 56 N	6 12 E
Vianen	46	51 59 N	5 5 E
Vianna do Castelo □	56	41 50 N	8 30 W
Vianópolis	171	16 40 S	48 35 W
Viar, R.	56	37 45 N	5 54 W
Viaréggio	62	43 52 N	10 13 E
Vibank	153	50 20 N	103 56 W
Vibey, R.	56	42 21 N	7 15 E
Vibo Valéntia	65	38 40 N	16 5 E
Viborg	73	56 27 N	9 23 E
Viborg Amt □	73	56 30 N	9 20 E
Vic-en-Bigorre	44	43 24 N	0 3 E
Vic-Fezensac	44	43 45 N	0 18 E
Vic Fézensac	44	43 47 N	0 19 E
Vic-sur-Cère	44	44 59 N	2 38 E
Vic-sur-Seille	43	48 45 N	6 33 E
Vicarstown	39	53 5 N	7 7 W
Vicenza	63	45 32 N	11 31 E
Vich	58	41 58 N	2 19 E
Vichada □	174	5 0 N	69 30 W
Vichuga	81	57 25 N	41 55 E
Vichy	44	46 9 N	3 26 E
Vickerstown	32	54 8 N	3 17 W
Vicksburg, Mich., U.S.A.	156	42 10 N	85 30 W
Vicksburg, Miss., U.S.A.	159	32 22 N	90 56 W
Vico, L. di	63	42 20 N	12 10 E
Viçosa, Min. Ger., Brazil	170	20 45 S	42 53 W
Viçosa, Pernambuco, Brazil	170	9 28 S	36 14 W
Viçosa do Ceará	170	3 34 S	41 5 W
Vicosoprano	51	46 22 N	9 38 E
Victor	158	38 43 N	105 7 W
Victor Emanuel Ra.	135	5 20 S	142 15 E
Victor Harbour	139	35 30 S	138 37 E
Victoria, Argent.	172	32 40 S	60 10 W
Victoria, Austral.	138	21 16 S	149 3 E
Victoria, Camer.	121	4 1 N	9 10 E
Victoria, Can.	152	48 30 N	123 25 W
Victoria, Chile	176	38 13 S	72 20 W
Victoria, Guin.	120	10 50 N	14 32 W
Victoria, H. K.	109	22 25 N	114 15 E
Victoria, Malay.	102	5 20 N	115 20 E
Victoria, Tex., U.S.A.	159	28 50 N	97 0 W
Victoria, Va., U.S.A.	158	38 52 N	99 8 W
Victoria □, Austral.	131	37 0 S	144 0 E
Victoria □, Rhod.	127	21 0 S	31 30 E
Victoria Beach	153	50 40 N	96 35 W
Victoria de las Tunas	166	20 58 N	76 59 W
Victoria Falls	127	17 58 S	25 45 E
Victoria, Grand L.	150	47 31 N	77 30 W
Victoria Harbour	150	44 45 N	79 45 W
Victoria I.	148	71 0 N	111 0 W
Victoria, L., N.S.W., Austral.	140	33 57 S	141 15 E
Victoria, L., Vic., Austral.	139	38 2 S	147 34 E
Victoria, L., E. Afr.	126	1 0 S	33 0 E
Victoria, La	174	10 14 N	67 20 W
Victoria Ld.	13	75 0 S	160 0 E
Victoria, Mt., Burma	98	21 15 N	93 55 E
Victoria, Mt., P.N.G.	135	8 55 S	147 32 E
Victoria Nile R.	126	2 25 N	31 50 E
Victoria, R.	136	15 10 S	129 40 E
Victoria R. Downs	136	16 25 S	131 0 E
Victoria Ra.	143	42 12 S	172 7 E
Victoria Res.	151	48 20 N	57 27 W
Victoria Taungdeik	99	21 15 N	93 55 E
Victoria West	128	31 25 S	23 4 E
Victoriaville	151	46 4 N	71 56 W
Victorica	172	36 20 S	65 30 W
Victorino	174	2 48 N	67 50 W
Victorville	163	34 32 N	117 18 W
Vicuña	172	30 0 S	70 50 W
Vicuña Mackenna	172	33 53 S	64 25 W
Vidalia	157	32 13 N	82 25 W
Vidauban	45	43 25 N	6 27 E
Videlv, R.	71	58 50 N	8 32 E
Vidigueira	57	38 12 N	7 48 W
Vidin	66	43 59 N	22 28 E
Vidio, Cabo	56	43 35 N	6 14 W
Vidisha (Bhilsa)	94	23 28 N	77 53 E
Vidöstern	73	57 5 N	14 0 E
Vidra	70	45 56 N	26 55 E
Viduša, mts.	66	42 55 N	18 21 E
Vidzy	80	54 40 N	26 37 E
Viedma	176	40 50 S	63 0 W
Viedma, L.	176	49 30 S	72 30 W
Vieira	56	41 38 N	8 8 W
Viejo Canal de Bahama	166	22 10 N	77 30 W
Viella	58	42 43 N	0 44 E
Vielsalm	47	50 17 N	5 54 E
Vien Pou Kha	101	20 45 N	101 5 E
Vienenburg	48	51 57 N	10 35 E
Vieng Pou Kha	100	20 41 N	101 4 E
Vienna, Illinois, U.S.A.	159	37 29 N	88 54 W
Vienna, Va., U.S.A.	162	38 54 N	77 16 W
Vienna = Wien	53	48 12 N	16 22 E
Vienne	45	45 31 N	4 53 E
Vienne □	44	45 53 N	0 42 E
Vienne, R.	42	47 5 N	0 30 E
Vientiane	100	17 58 N	102 36 E
Vieques, I.	147	18 8 N	65 25 W
Vierlingsbeek	47	51 36 N	6 1 E
Viersen	48	51 15 N	6 23 E
Vierwaldstättersee	51	47 0 N	8 30 E
Vierzon	43	47 13 N	2 5 E
Vieux-Boucau-les-Bains	44	43 48 N	1 23 W
Vif	45	45 5 N	5 41 E
Vigan	103	17 35 N	120 28 E
Vigan, Le	44	44 0 N	3 36 E
Vigevano	62	45 18 N	8 50 E
Vigia	170	0 50 S	48 5 W
Vigía Chico	165	19 46 N	87 35 W
Vignacourt	43	50 1 N	2 15 E
Vignemale, Pic du	44	42 47 N	0 10 W
Vigneulles	43	48 59 N	5 40 E
Vignola	62	44 29 N	11 0 E
Vigo	56	42 12 N	8 41 W
Vigo, Ría de	56	42 15 N	8 45 W
Vihiers	42	47 10 N	0 30 W
Vijayadurg	96	16 30 N	73 25 E

Vijayawada (Bezwada) Voitsberg

Vijayawada (Bezwada) 96 16 31N 80 39 E
Vijfhuizen 46 52 22N 4 41 E
Vikedal 71 59 30N 5 55 E
Viken, L. 73 58 40N 10 2 E
Vikersund 71 59 58N 10 2 E
Viking 152 53 7N 111 50W
Viking, gasfield 19 53 30N 2 20 E
Vikna 74 64 52N 10 57 E
Vikramasingapuram 97 8 40N 76 47 E
Viksjö 72 62 45N 17 26 E
Vikulovo 76 56 50N 70 40 E
Vila Alferes Chamusca 129 24 27 S 33 0 E
Vila Arriaga 125 14 35 S 13 30 E
Vila Bittencourt 174 1 20 S 69 20W
Vila Cabral = Lichinga 127 13 13 S 35 11 E
Vila Caldas Xavier 127 14 28 S 33 0 E
Vila Coutinho 127 14 37 S 34 19 E
Vila da Maganja 127 17 18 S 37 30 E
Vila da Ponte 125 14 35 S 16 40 E
Vila de Aljustrel 125 13 30 S 19 45 E
Vila de João Belo = Xai-Xai 129 25 6 S 33 31 E
Vila de Liquica 103 8 40 S 125 20 E
Vila de Manica 125 18 58 S 32 59 E
Vila de Rei 57 39 41N 8 9W
Vila de Sena = Sena 127 17 25 S 35 0 E
Vila do Bispo 57 37 5N 8 53W
Vila do Conde 56 41 21N 8 45W
Vila Fontes 125 17 51 S 35 24 E
Vila Fontes Velha 127 17 51 S 35 24 E
Vila Franca de Xira 57 38 57N 8 59W
Vila Gamito 127 14 12 S 33 0 E
Vila General Machado 125 11 58 S 17 22 E
Vila Gomes da Costa 129 24 20 S 33 37 E
Vila Henrique de Carvalho = Lunda 124 9 40 S 20 12 E
Vila Junqueiro 127 15 25 S 36 58 E
Vila Luiza 129 25 45 S 32 35 E
Vila Luso = Moxico 125 11 53 S 19 55 E
Vila Machado 127 19 15 S 34 14 E
Vila Marechal Carmona = Uige 124 7 30 S 14 40 E
Vila Mariano Machado 125 13 3 S 14 35 E
Vila Moatize 127 16 11 S 33 40 E
Vila Mouzinho 127 14 48 S 34 25 E
Vila Murtinho 174 10 20 S 65 20W
Vila Nova de Fozcôa 56 41 5N 7 9W
Vila Nova de Ourém 57 39 40N 8 35W
Vila Nova do Seles 125 11 35 S 14 22 E
Vila Novo de Gaia 56 41 4N 8 40W
Vila Paiva Couceiro 125 14 37 S 14 40 E
Vila Paiva de Andrada 127 18 37 S 34 2 E
Vila Pery = Chimoio 127 19 4 S 33 30 E
Vila Pouca de Aguiar 56 41 30N 7 38W
Vila Real 56 41 17N 7 48W
Vila Real de Santo Antonio 57 37 10N 7 28W
Vila Robert Williams 125 12 46 S 15 30 E
Vila Salazar, Angola 124 9 12 S 14 48 E
Vila Salazar, Indon. 103 5 25 S 123 50 E
Vila Teixeira da Silva 125 12 10 S 15 50 E
Vila Vasco da Gama 127 14 54 S 32 14 E
Vila Velha 173 20 20 S 40 17W
Vila Verissimo Sarmento 124 8 15 S 20 50 E
Vila Viçosa 57 38 45N 7 27W
Vilaboa 56 42 21N 8 39W
Vilaine, R. 42 47 35N 2 10W
Vilanculos 129 22 1 S 35 17 E
Vilar Formosa 56 40 38N 6 45W
Vilareal □ 56 41 36N 7 35W
Vileyka 80 54 30N 27 0 E
Vilhelmina 74 64 35N 16 39 E
Vilhena 174 12 30 S 60 0W
Viliga 77 60 2N 156 56 E
Viliya, R. 80 54 57N 24 35 E
Viljandi 80 58 28N 25 30 E
Villa Abecia 172 21 0 S 68 18W
Villa Ahumada 164 30 30N 106 40W
Villa Ana 172 28 28 S 59 40W
Villa Angela 172 27 34 S 60 45W
Villa Bella 174 10 25 S 65 30W
Villa Bens (Tarfaya) 116 27 55N 12 55W
Villa Cañas 172 34 0 S 61 35W
Villa Cisneros = Dakhla 116 23 50N 15 53W
Villa Colón 172 31 38 S 68 20W
Villa Constitución 172 33 15 S 60 20W
Villa de Cura 174 10 2N 67 29W
Villa de María 172 30 0 S 63 43W
Villa de Rosario 172 24 30 S 57 35W
Villa Dolores 172 31 58 S 65 15W
Villa Franca 172 26 14 S 58 20W
Villa Frontera 164 26 56N 101 27W
Villa Guillermina 172 28 15 S 59 29W
Villa Hayes 172 25 0 S 57 20W
Villa Iris 172 38 12 S 63 12W
Villa Julia Molina 167 19 5N 69 45W
Villa Madero 164 24 28N 104 10W
Villa María 172 32 20 S 63 10W
Villa Mazán 172 28 40 S 66 30W
Villa Mentes 172 21 10 S 63 30W
Villa Minozzo 62 44 21N 10 30 E
Villa Montes 172 21 10 S 63 30W
Villa Ocampo, Argent. 172 28 30 S 59 20W
Villa Ocampo, Mexico 164 26 29N 105 30W
Villa Ojo de Agua 172 29 30 S 63 44W
Villa San Agustín 172 30 35 S 67 30W
Villa San Giovanni 65 38 13N 15 38 E
Villa San José 172 32 12 S 58 15W
Villa San Martín 172 28 9 S 64 9W
Villa Santina 63 46 25N 12 55 E
Villa Unión 164 23 12N 106 14W
Villablino 56 42 57N 6 19W
Villabruzzi 91 3 3N 45 18 E
Villacampo, Pantano de 56 41 31N 6 0W
Villacañas 58 39 38N 3 20W
Villacarlos 58 39 53N 4 17 E
Villacarriedo 58 43 14N 3 48W
Villacarrillo 59 38 7N 3 3W
Villacastín 56 40 46N 4 25W
Villach 52 46 37N 13 51 E
Villaciaro 64 39 27N 8 45 E
Villada 56 42 15N 4 59W
Villadiego 56 42 31N 4 1W
Villadossóla 62 46 4N 8 16 E
Villafeliche 58 41 10N 1 30W
Villafranca 58 42 17N 1 46W
Villafranca de los Barros 57 38 35N 6 18W
Villafranca de los Caballeros 59 39 26N 3 21W
Villafranca del Bierzo 56 42 38N 6 50W
Villafranca del Cid 58 40 26N 0 16W
Villafranca del Panadés 58 41 21N 1 40 E
Villafranca di Verona 62 45 20N 10 51 E
Villagarcía de Arosa 56 42 34N 8 46W
Villagrán 165 24 29N 99 29W
Villaguay 172 32 0 S 58 45W
Villaharta 57 38 9N 4 54W
Villahermosa, Mexico 165 17 45N 92 50W
Villahermosa, Spain 59 38 46N 2 52W
Villaines-la-Juhel 42 48 21N 0 20W
Villajoyosa 59 38 30N 0 12W
Villalba 56 40 36N 3 59W
Villalba de Guardo 56 42 42N 4 49W
Villalón de Campos 56 42 5N 5 4W
Villalpando 56 41 51N 5 25W
Villaluenga 56 40 2N 3 54W
Villamañán 56 42 19N 5 35W
Villamartín 56 36 52N 5 38W
Villamayor 58 41 42N 0 43W
Villamblard 44 45 2N 0 32 E
Villanova Monteleone 64 40 30N 8 28 E
Villanueva, Colomb. 174 10 37N 72 59W
Villanueva, U.S.A. 161 35 16N 105 31W
Villanueva de Castellón 59 39 5N 0 31W
Villanueva de Córdoba 57 38 20N 4 38W
Villanueva de la Fuente 59 38 42N 2 42W
Villanueva de la Serena 57 38 59N 5 50W
Villanueva de la Sierra 56 40 12N 6 24W
Villanueva de los Castillejos 57 37 30N 7 15W
Villanueva del Arzobispo 59 38 10N 3 0W
Villanueva del Duque 57 38 20N 4 38W
Villanueva del Fresno 57 38 23N 7 10W
Villanueva y Geltrú 58 41 13N 1 40 E
Villaodrid 56 43 20N 7 11W
Villaputzu 64 39 28N 9 33 E
Villar del Arzobispo 58 39 44N 0 50W
Villar del Rey 57 39 7N 6 50W
Villarcayo 58 42 56N 3 34W
Villard 45 45 4N 5 33 E
Villard-Bonnot 45 45 14N 5 53 E
Villard-de-Lans 45 45 3N 5 33 E
Villarino de los Aires 56 41 18N 6 23W
Villarosa 65 37 36N 14 9 E
Villarramiel 56 42 2N 4 55W
Villarreal 58 39 55N 0 3W
Villarrica, Chile 176 39 15 S 72 30W
Villarrica, Parag. 172 25 40 S 56 30W
Villarrobledo 59 39 18N 2 36W
Villarroya de la Sierra 58 41 27N 1 46W
Villarrubia de los Ojos 59 39 14N 3 36W
Villars 45 46 0N 5 2 E
Villarta de San Juan 59 39 15N 3 25W
Villasayas 58 41 24N 2 39W
Villaseca de los Gamitos 56 41 2N 6 7W
Villastar 58 40 17N 1 9W
Villatobas 58 39 54N 3 20W
Villavicencio, Argent. 172 32 28 S 69 0W
Villavicencio, Colomb. 174 4 9N 73 37W
Villaviciosa 56 43 32N 5 27W
Villazón 172 22 0 S 65 35W
Ville de Paris □ 43 48 50N 2 20 E
Ville Marie 150 47 20N 79 30W
Ville Platte 159 30 45N 92 17W
Villedieu 42 48 50N 1 12W
Villefort 44 44 28N 3 56 E
Villefranche 43 47 19N 146 0 E
Villefranche-de-Lauragais 44 43 25N 1 44 E
Villefranche-de-Rouergue 44 44 21N 2 2 E
Villefranche-du-Périgord 44 44 38N 1 5 E
Villefranche-sur-Saône 45 45 59N 4 43 E
Villel 58 40 14N 1 12W
Villemaur 43 48 14N 3 40 E
Villemur-sur-Tarn 44 43 51N 1 31 E
Villena 59 38 39N 0 52W
Villenauxe 43 48 36N 3 30 E
Villenave 44 44 46N 0 33W
Villeneuve, France 43 48 42N 2 25 E
Villeneuve, Italy 62 45 40N 7 10 E
Villeneuve, Switz. 50 46 24N 6 56 E
Villeneuve-l'Archevèque 43 48 14N 3 32 E
Villeneuve-lès-Avignon 45 43 57N 4 49 E
Villeneuve-sur-Allier 44 46 40N 3 13 E
Villeneuve-sur-Lot 44 44 24N 0 42 E
Villeréal 44 44 38N 0 45 E
Villers Bocage 42 49 3N 0 40W
Villers Bretonneux 43 49 50N 2 30 E
Villers-Cotterets 43 49 15N 3 4 E
Villers-Farlay 47 47 0N 5 45 E
Villers-le-Bouillet 47 50 34N 5 15 E
Villers-le-Gambon 47 50 11N 4 37 E
Villers-sur-Mer 42 49 21N 0 2W
Villersexel 43 47 33N 6 26 E
Villerslev 73 56 49N 8 29 E
Villerupt 43 49 28N 5 55 E
Villerville 42 49 26N 0 5 E
Villiers 129 27 2 S 28 36 E
Villingen = Schwenningen 49 48 3N 8 29 E
Villisca 158 40 55N 94 59W
Villupuram 97 11 59N 79 31 E
Vilna 152 54 7N 111 55W
Vilnius 80 54 38N 25 25 E
Vils 52 47 33N 10 37 E
Vilsbiburg 49 48 27N 12 23 E
Vilslev 73 55 24N 8 42 E
Vilusi 66 42 44N 18 34 E
Vilvoorde 47 50 56N 4 26 E
Vilyuy, R. 77 63 58N 125 0 E
Vilyuysk 77 63 40N 121 20 E
Vimercate 62 45 38N 9 25 E
Vimiosa 56 41 35N 6 13W
Vimmerby 73 57 40N 15 55 E
Vimo 72 60 50N 14 20 E
Vimoutiers 42 48 57N 0 10 E
Vimperk 52 49 3N 13 46 E
Viña del Mar 172 33 0 S 71 30W
Vinaroz 58 40 30N 0 27 E
Vincennes 156 38 42N 87 29W
Vincent 163 34 33N 118 11W
Vinchina 172 28 45 S 68 15W
Vindel älv 74 64 20N 19 20 E
Vindeln 74 64 12N 19 43 E
Vinderup 73 56 29N 8 45 E
Vindhya Ra. 94 22 50N 77 0 E
Vinegar Hill 57 52 30N 6 28W
Vineland 162 39 30N 75 0W
Vinga 66 46 0N 21 14 E
Vingnes 71 61 7N 10 26 E
Vinh 100 18 45N 105 38 E
Vinh Linh 100 17 4N 107 2 E
Vinh Loi 101 9 20N 104 45 E
Vinh Long 101 10 16N 105 57 E
Vinh Yen 100 21 21N 105 35 E
Vinhais 56 41 50N 7 0W
Vinica 63 45 28N 15 16 E
Vinita 159 36 40N 95 12W
Vinkeveen 46 52 13N 4 56 E
Vinkovci 66 45 19N 18 48 E
Vinnitsa 82 49 15N 28 30 E
Vinstra 71 61 37N 9 44 E
Vinton, Iowa, U.S.A. 158 42 8N 92 1W
Vinton, La., U.S.A. 159 30 13N 93 35W
Vintu de Jos 70 46 0N 23 30 E
Viöl 48 54 32N 9 12 E
Violet Town 141 36 38 S 145 42 E
Vipava 63 45 51N 13 38 E
Vipiteno 63 46 55N 11 25 E
Viqueque 103 8 42 S 126 30 E
Vir 85 37 45N 72 5 E
Vir, I. 63 44 17N 15 3 E
Virac 103 13 30N 124 20 E
Virachei 100 13 59N 106 49 E
Virago Sd. 152 54 0N 132 42W
Virajpet 97 12 15N 75 50 E
Viramgam 94 23 5N 72 0 E
Virarajendrapet (Virajpet) 97 12 10N 75 50 E
Viravanallur 97 8 40N 79 30 E
Virden 153 49 50N 100 56W
Vire 42 48 50N 0 53W
Virgem da Lapa 171 16 49 S 42 21W
Virgenes, C. 176 52 19 S 68 21W
Virgin Gorda, I. 147 18 45N 64 26W
Virgin Is. 147 18 40N 64 30W
Virgin, R., Can. 153 57 2N 108 17W
Virgin, R., U.S.A. 161 36 50N 114 10W
Virginia, Ireland 38 53 50N 7 5W
Virginia, S. Afr. 128 28 8 S 26 55 E
Virginia, U.S.A. 158 47 30N 92 32W
Virginia □ 156 37 45N 78 0W
Virginia Beach 156 36 54N 75 58W
Virginia City, Mont., U.S.A. 160 45 25N 111 58W
Virginia City, Nev., U.S.A. 160 39 19N 119 39W
Virginia Falls 152 61 38N 125 42W
Virginiatown 150 48 9N 79 36W
Virgins, C. 176 52 10 S 68 30W
Virieu-le-Grand 45 45 51N 5 39 E
Virje 66 46 4N 16 59 E
Viroqua 158 43 33N 90 57W
Virovitica 66 45 51N 17 21 E
Virpaza, R. 66 42 14N 19 6 E
Virserum 73 57 20N 15 35 E
Virton 47 49 35N 5 32 E
Virtsu 80 58 32N 23 33 E
Virudhunagar 97 9 30N 78 0 E
Vis 63 43 0N 16 10 E
Vis, I. 63 43 0N 16 10 E
Vis Kanal 63 43 4N 16 5 E
Visalia 163 36 25N 119 18W
Visayan Sea 103 11 30N 123 30 E
Visby 73 57 37N 18 18 E
Viscount Melville Sd. 12 74 10N 108 0W
Visé 47 50 44N 5 41 E
Višegrad 66 43 47N 19 17 E
Viseu, Brazil 170 1 10 S 46 20W
Viseu, Port. 56 40 40N 7 55W
Vişeu 70 47 45N 24 25 E
Viseu □ 56 40 40N 7 55W
Vishakhapatnam 96 17 45N 83 20 E
Vishera, R. 84 59 55N 56 25 E
Vishnupur 95 23 8N 87 20 E
Visikoi I. 13 56 30 S 26 40 E
Visingsö 73 58 2N 14 20 E
Viskafors 73 57 37N 12 50 E
Vislanda 73 56 46N 14 30 E
Vislinskil Zaliv (Zalew Wislany) 54 54 20N 19 50 E
Visnagar 94 23 45N 72 32 E
Višnja Gora 63 45 58N 14 45 E
Viso del Marqués 59 38 32N 3 34W
Viso, Mte. 62 44 38N 7 5 E
Visoko 66 43 58N 18 10 E
Visp 50 46 17N 7 52 E
Vispa, R. 50 46 9N 7 48 E
Visselhovde 48 52 59N 9 36 E
Vissoie 50 46 13N 7 36 E
Vista 163 33 12N 117 14W
Vistonis, Limni 68 41 0N 25 7 E
Vistula, R. = Wisła, R. 54 53 38N 18 47 E
Vit, R. 67 43 30N 24 30 E
Vitanje 63 46 40N 15 18 E
Vitebsk 80 55 10N 30 15 E
Viterbo 63 42 25N 12 8 E
Viti Levu, I. 143 17 30 S 177 30 E
Vitiaz Str. 135 5 40 S 147 10 E
Vitigudino 56 41 1N 6 35W
Vitim 77 59 45N 112 25 E
Vitim, R. 77 58 40N 112 50 E
Vitina 69 37 40N 22 10 E
Vitina 66 43 17N 17 29 E
Vitória 171 20 20 S 40 22W
Vitoria 58 42 50N 2 41W
Vitória da Conquista 171 14 51 S 40 51W
Vitória de São Antão 170 8 10 S 37 20W
Vitorino Friere 170 4 4 S 45 10W
Vitré 42 48 8N 1 12W
Vitry-le-François 43 48 43N 4 33 E
Vitsi, Mt. 68 40 40N 21 25 E
Vittangi 74 67 41N 21 40 E
Vitteaux 43 47 24N 4 30 E
Vittel 43 48 12N 5 57 E
Vittória 65 36 58N 14 30 E
Vittório Véneto 63 45 59N 12 18 E
Vitu Is. 135 4 50 S 149 25 E
Vivegnis 47 50 42N 5 39 E
Viver 58 39 55N 0 36W
Vivero 56 43 39N 7 38W
Viviers 45 44 30N 4 40 E
Vivonne, Austral. 140 35 59 S 137 9 E
Vivonne, France 44 46 36N 0 15 E
Vivonne B. 140 35 59 S 137 9 E
Vizcaíno, Desierto de 164 27 40N 113 50W
Vizcaíno, Sierra 164 27 30N 114 0W
Vizcaya □ 58 43 15N 2 45W
Vizianagaram 96 18 6N 83 10 E
Vizille 45 45 5N 5 46 E
Vizinada 63 45 20N 13 46 E
Viziru 70 45 0N 27 43 E
Vizovice 53 49 12N 17 56 E
Vizzini 65 37 9N 14 43 E
Vlaardingen 46 51 55N 4 21 E
Vladicin Han 66 42 42N 22 1 E
Vladimir 81 56 0N 40 30 E
Vladimir Volynskiy 80 50 50N 24 18 E
Vladimirci 66 44 36N 19 45 E
Vladimirovac 66 45 1N 20 53 E
Vladimirovka, U.S.S.R. 83 44 37N 44 41 E
Vladimirovka, U.S.S.R. 83 48 27N 46 5 E
Vladimirovo 67 43 32N 23 22 E
Vladislavovka 82 45 15N 35 15 E
Vladivostok 82 43 10N 131 53 E
Vlamertinge 47 50 51N 2 49 E
Vlaming Head 137 21 48 S 114 5 E
Vlasenica 66 44 11N 18 59 E
Vlasim 52 49 40N 14 53 E
Vlasinsko Jezero 66 42 44N 22 37 E
Vlašić, mt. 66 44 19N 17 37 E
Vlasotinci 66 42 59N 22 7 E
Vleuten 46 52 6N 5 1 E
Vlieland, I. 46 53 30N 4 55 E
Vliestroom 46 53 19N 5 8 E
Vlijmen 47 51 42N 5 14 E
Vlissingen 47 51 26N 3 34 E
Vlora 68 40 32N 19 28 E
Vlora □ 68 40 12N 20 0 E
Vltava, R. 52 49 35N 14 10 E
Vlădeasa, mt. 70 46 47N 22 50 E
Vo Dat 101 11 9N 107 31 E
Vobarno 62 45 38N 10 30 E
Vočin 66 45 37N 17 33 E
Vodice 63 43 47N 15 47 E
Vodnany 52 49 9N 14 11 E
Vodnjan 63 44 59N 13 52 E
Voe 36 60 21N 1 15W
Voga 121 6 23N 1 30 E
Vogelkop = Doberai, Jazirah 103 1 25 S 133 0 E
Vogelsberg 48 50 37N 9 30 E
Voghera 62 44 59N 9 1 E
Vohémar 129 13 25 S 50 0 E
Vohipeno 129 22 22 S 47 51 E
Voi 126 3 25 S 38 32 E
Void 43 48 40N 5 36 E
Voil, L. 34 56 20N 4 25W
Voineşti, Iaşi, Rumania 70 47 5N 27 27 E
Voineşti, Ploeşti, Rumania 70 45 5N 25 14 E
Voiotia □ 69 38 20N 23 0 E
Voiron 45 45 22N 5 35 E
Voiseys B. 151 56 15N 61 50W
Voitsberg 52 47 3N 15 9 E

Voiviis Limni, L Walla Walla

Voiviis Limni, L. 68 39 30N 22 45 E
Vojens 73 55 16N 9 18 E
Vojmsjön 74 64 55N 16 40 E
Vojnió 63 45 19N 15 43 E
Vojvodina, Auton. Pokragina 66 45 20N 20 0 E
Vokhma 81 59 0N 46 45 E
Vokhma, R. 81 59 0N 46 44 E
Vokhtoga 81 58 46N 41 8 E
Volary 52 48 54N 13 52 E
Volborg 158 45 50N 105 44W
Volchansk 81 50 17N 36 58 E
Volchya, R. 82 48 0N 37 0 E
Volda 71 62 9N 6 5 E
Volendam 46 52 30N 5 4 E
Volga 81 57 58N 38 16 E
Volga Hts. = Privolzhskaya V.S. 79 51 0N 46 0 E
Volga, R. 83 52 20N 48 0 E
Volgodonsk 83 47 33N 42 5 E
Volgograd 83 48 40N 44 25 E
Volgogradskoye Vdkhr. 81 50 0N 45 20 E
Volgorechensk 81 57 28N 41 14 E
Volissós 69 38 29N 25 54 E
Volkerak 47 51 39N 4 18 E
Völkermarkt 52 46 39N 14 39 E
Volkhov 80 59 55N 32 15 E
Volkhov, R. 80 59 30N 32 0 E
Völklingen 49 49 15N 6 50 E
Volkovysk 80 53 9N 24 30 E
Volksrust 129 27 24S 29 53 E
Vollenhove 46 52 40N 5 58 E
Volnovakha 82 47 35N 37 30 E
Volo 140 31 37S 143 0 E
Volochayevka 77 48 40N 134 30 E
Volodary 81 56 12N 43 15 E
Vologda 81 59 25N 40 0 E
Volokolamsk 81 56 5N 36 0 E
Volokonovka 81 50 33N 37 58 E
Volontirovka 82 46 28N 29 28 E
Vólos 68 39 24N 22 59 E
Volosovo 80 59 27N 29 32 E
Volozhin 80 54 3N 26 30 E
Volsk 81 52 5N 47 28 E
Volstrup 73 57 19N 10 27 E
Volta, L. 121 7 30N 0 15 E
Volta, R. 121 8 0N 0 10W
Volta Redonda 173 22 31S 44 5W
Voltaire, C. 136 14 16S 125 35 E
Volterra 62 43 24N 10 50 E
Voltri 62 44 25N 8 43 E
Volturara Áppula 65 41 30N 15 2 E
Volturno, R. 65 41 18N 14 20 E
Volubilis 118 34 2N 5 33W
Vólvi, L. 68 40 40N 23 34 E
Volzhsk 81 55 57N 48 23 E
Volzhskiy 83 48 56N 44 46 E
Vondrozo 129 22 49S 47 20 E
Vónitsa 69 38 53N 20 58 E
Voorburg 46 52 5N 4 24 E
Voorne Putten 46 51 52N 4 10 E
Voorst 46 52 10N 6 8 E
Voorthuizen 46 52 11N 5 36 E
Vopnafjörður 74 65 45N 14 40W
Vorarlberg □ 52 47 20N 10 0 E
Vóras Óros 68 40 57N 21 45 E
Vorbasse 73 55 39N 9 6 E
Vorden 46 52 6N 6 19 E
Vorderrheim, R. 51 46 49N 9 25 E
Vordingborg 73 55 0N 11 54 E
Voreppe 45 45 18N 5 39 E
Voriai Sporádhes 69 39 15N 23 30 E
Vórios Evvoïkós Kólpos 69 38 45N 23 15 E
Vorkuta 78 67 48N 64 20 E
Vorma 71 60 9N 11 27 E
Vorona, R. 81 52 0N 42 20 E
Voronezh, R.S.S.R., U.S.S.R. 81 51 40N 39 10 E
Voronezh, Ukraine, U.S.S.R. 80 51 47N 33 28 E
Voronezh, R. 81 52 30N 39 30 E
Vorontsovo-Aleksandrovskoïe = Zelenokumsk. 83 44 30N 44 1 E
Voroshilovgrad 83 48 38N 39 15 E
Voroshilovsk = Kommunarsk 83 48 3N 38 40 E
Vorovskoye 77 54 30N 155 50 E
Vorselaar 47 51 12N 4 46 E
Vorskla, R. 82 49 30N 34 31 E
Vorukh 85 39 52N 70 35 E
Vorupør 73 56 58N 8 22 E
Vosges 43 48 20N 7 10 E
Vosges □ 43 48 12N 6 20 E
Voskopoja 68 40 40N 20 33 E
Voskresensk 81 55 27N 38 31 E
Voskresenskoye 81 56 51N 45 30 E
Voss 71 60 38N 6 26 E
Vosselaar 47 51 19N 4 52 E
Vostok I. 131 10 5S 152 23W
Vostotnyy Sayan 77 54 0N 96 0 E
Votice 52 49 38N 14 39 E
Votkinsk 84 57 0N 53 55 E
Votkinskoye Vdkhr. 78 57 30N 55 0 E
Vouga, R. 56 40 46N 8 10W
Voulte-sur-Rhône, La 45 44 48N 4 46 E
Vouvry 50 46 21N 6 21 E
Voúxa, Ákra 69 35 37N 20 32 E
Vouzela 56 40 43N 8 7W
Vouziers 43 49 22N 4 40 E
Voves 43 48 15N 1 38 E
Voxna 72 61 20N 15 30 E
Voy 37 59 1N 3 16W
Vozhe Oz. 78 60 45N 39 0 E
Vozhgaly 81 58 24N 50 1 E
Voznesensk 82 47 35N 31 15 E
Voznesenye 78 61 0N 35 45 E
Vráble 53 48 15N 18 16 E
Vrácevšnica 66 44 2N 20 34 E
Vrådal 71 59 20N 8 25 E
Vradiyevka 82 49 56N 30 38 E
Vraka 68 42 8N 19 28 E
Vrakhnéika 69 38 10N 21 40 E
Vrancea □ 70 45 50N 26 45 E
Vrancei, Munţi 70 46 0N 26 30 E
Vrangelja, Ostrov 77 71 0N 180 0 E
Vrangtjarn 72 62 14N 16 37 E
Vranica, mt. 66 43 59N 18 0 E
Vranje 66 42 34N 21 54 E
Vranjska Banja 66 42 34N 22 1 E
Vranov 53 48 53N 21 40 E
Vransko 63 46 17N 14 58 E
Vratsa 67 43 13N 23 30 E
Vratsa □ 67 43 30N 23 30 E
Vrbas 66 45 0N 17 27 E
Vrbas, R. 66 44 30N 17 10 E
Vrbnik 63 45 4N 14 32 E
Vrboviec 63 45 53N 16 28 E
Vrbovsko 63 45 24N 15 5 E
Vrchlabi 52 49 38N 15 37 E
Vrede 129 27 24S 29 6 E
Vredefort 128 27 0S 26 58 E
Vredenburg 128 32 51S 18 0 E
Vredendal 128 31 41S 18 35 E
Vreeswijk 46 52 1N 5 6 E
Vrena 73 58 54N 16 41 E
Vrgorac 66 43 12N 17 20 E
Vrhnika 63 45 58N 14 15 E
Vriddhachalam 97 11 30N 79 10 E
Vridi 120 5 15N 4 3W
Vridi Canal 120 5 15N 4 3W
Vries 46 53 5N 6 35 E
Vriezenveen 46 52 25N 6 38 E
Vrindaban 94 27 37N 77 40 E
Vrnograč 63 43 12N 17 20 E
Vrondádhes 69 38 25N 26 7 E
Vroomshoop 46 52 27N 6 34 E
Vrpolje 66 43 42N 16 1 E
Vršac 66 45 8N 21 18 E
Vršački Kanal 66 45 15N 21 0 E
Vrsheto 67 43 15N 23 23 E
Vryburg 128 26 55S 24 45 E
Vryheid 129 27 54S 30 47 E
Vsetin 53 49 20N 18 0 E
Vu Liet 100 18 43N 105 23 E
Vûcha, R. 67 41 53N 24 26 E
Vučitrn 66 42 49N 20 59 E
Vught 47 51 38N 5 20 E
Vuka, R. 66 45 28N 18 30 E
Vukovar 66 45 21N 18 59 E
Vulcan, Can. 152 50 25N 113 15W
Vulcan, Rumania 70 45 23N 23 17 E
Vulcan, U.S.A. 156 45 46N 87 51W
Vŭlcani 66 46 0N 20 26 E
Vulcano, I. 65 38 25N 14 58 E
Vulchedrŭma 67 43 42N 23 16 E
Vulci 63 42 23N 11 37 E
Vŭleni 70 44 15N 24 45 E
Vulkaneshty 82 45 35N 28 30 E
Vunduzi, R. 127 18 0S 33 45 E
Vung Tau 101 10 21N 107 4 E
Vûrbitsa 67 42 59N 26 40 E
Vutcani 70 46 26N 27 59 E
Vuyyuru 96 16 28N 80 50 E
Vvedenka 84 54 0N 63 53 E
Vyara 96 21 8N 73 28 E
Vyasniki 81 56 10N 42 10 E
Vyatka, R. 84 56 30N 51 0 E
Vyatskiye Polyany 84 56 5N 51 0 E
Vyazemskiy 77 47 32N 134 45 E
Vyazma 80 55 10N 34 15 E
Vyborg 78 60 43N 28 47 E
Vychegda R. 78 61 50N 52 30 E
Vychodné Beskydy 53 49 30N 22 0 E
Východočeský □ 52 50 20N 15 45 E
Východoslovenský □ 53 48 50N 21 0 E
Vyg-ozero 78 63 30N 34 0 E
Vyja, R. 81 41 53N 24 26 E
Vypin, I. 97 10 10N 76 15 E
Vyrnwy, L. 31 52 48N 3 30W
Vyrnwy, R. 31 52 43N 3 15W
Vyshniy Volochek 80 57 30N 34 30 E
Vyškov 53 49 17N 17 0 E
Vysoké Mýto 53 49 58N 16 23 E
Vysoké Tatry 53 49 30N 20 0 E
Vysokovsk 81 56 22N 36 30 E
Vysotsk 80 51 43N 36 32 E
Vyssi Brod 92 48 36N 14 20 E
Vytegra 52 61 15N 36 40 E

W

Wa 121 10 7N 2 25W
Waal, R. 46 51 59N 4 8 E
Waalwijk 47 51 42N 5 4 E
Waarschoot 47 51 10N 3 36 E
Waasmunster 47 51 6N 4 5 E
Wabag 135 5 32S 143 53 E
Wabakimi L. 150 50 38N 89 45W
Wabana 151 47 40N 53 0W
Wabasca 152 55 57N 113 45W
Wabash 156 40 48N 85 46W
Wabash, R. 156 39 10N 87 30W
Wabawng 98 25 18N 97 46 E
Wabeno 156 45 25N 88 40W
Wabi Gestro, R. 123 6 0N 41 35 E
Wabi, R. 123 7 35N 40 5 E
Wabi Shaballe, R. 123 8 0N 40 45 E
Wabigoon, L. 153 49 44N 92 34W
Wabowden 153 54 55N 98 38W
Wabrzezno 54 53 16N 18 57 E
Wabuk Pt. 150 55 20N 85 5W
Wabush City 151 52 55N 66 52W
Wabuska 160 39 16N 119 13W
W.A.C. Bennett Dam 152 56 2N 122 6W
Wachapreague 162 37 36N 75 41W
Wachtebeke 47 51 11N 3 52 E
Waco 159 31 33N 97 5W
Waconichi, L. 150 50 8N 74 0W
Wad ar Rimsa 92 26 5N 41 30 E
Wad Ban Naqa 123 16 32N 33 9 E
Wad Banda 123 13 10N 27 50 E
Wad el Haddad 123 13 50N 33 30 E
Wad en Nau 123 14 10N 33 34 E
Wad Hamid 123 16 20N 32 45 E
Wâd Medanî 123 14 28N 33 30 E
Wad Thana 94 27 22N 66 23 E
Wadayama 110 35 19N 134 52 E
Waddān 119 29 9N 16 45 E
Waddān, Jabal 119 29 0N 16 15 E
Waddeneilanden 46 53 25N 5 10 E
Waddenzee 46 53 6N 5 10 E
Wadderin Hill 137 32 0S 118 25 E
Waddesdon 29 51 50N 0 54W
Waddingham 33 53 28N 0 31W
Waddington 33 53 10N 0 31W
Waddington, Mt. 152 51 23N 125 15W
Waddinxveen 46 52 2N 4 40 E
Waddy Pt. 139 24 58S 153 21 E
Wadebridge 30 50 31N 4 51W
Wadena, Can. 153 51 57N 103 38W
Wadena, U.S.A. 158 46 25N 95 2W
Wädenswil 51 47 14N 8 30 E
Wadesboro 157 35 2N 80 2W
Wadhams 152 51 30N 127 30W
Wadhurst 29 51 3N 0 21 E
Wadi 121 13 5N 11 40 E
Wādī ash Shāfi' 119 27 30N 15 0 E
Wādī Banī Walīd 119 31 49N 14 0 E
Wadi Gemâl 122 24 35N 35 10 E
Wadi Halfa 122 21 53N 31 19 E
Wadi Masila 91 16 30N 49 0 E
Wadi Sabha 92 23 50N 48 30 E
Wadlew 54 51 31N 19 23 E
Wadowice 54 49 52N 19 30 E
Wadsworth 160 39 44N 119 22W
Waegwan 107 35 59N 128 23 E
Waenfawr 31 53 7N 4 10W
Wafou Hu 109 32 19N 116 56 E
Wafra 92 28 33N 48 3 E
Wagenberg 47 51 40N 4 46 E
Wageningen 46 51 58N 5 40 E
Wager B. 149 65 26N 88 40W
Wager Bay 149 65 56N 90 49W
Wagga Wagga 141 35 7S 147 24 E
Waghete 103 4 10S 135 50 E
Wagin, Austral. 137 33 17S 117 25 E
Wagin, Nigeria 137 12 42N 7 10 E
Wagon Mound 159 36 10N 105 0W
Wagoner 159 36 0N 95 20W
Wagrowiec 54 52 48N 17 19 E
Wah 94 33 45N 72 40 E
Wahai 103 2 48S 129 35 E
Wahiawa 147 21 30N 158 2W
Wahnai 94 32 40N 65 50 E
Wahoo 158 41 15N 96 35W
Wahpeton 158 46 20N 96 35W
Wahratta 140 31 58S 141 50 E
Wai 96 17 56N 73 57 E
Wai, Koh 101 9 55N 102 55 E
Waiai, R. 143 45 36S 167 45 E
Waianae 147 21 25N 158 8W
Waiau 143 42 39S 173 5 E
Waiau, R. 143 42 47S 173 22 E
Waiawe Ganga 97 6 15N 81 0 E
Waibeem 103 0 30S 132 50 E
Waiblingen 49 48 49N 9 20 E
Waidhofen, Niederösterreich, Austria 52 48 49N 15 17 E
Waidhofen, Niederösterreich, Austria 52 47 57N 14 46 E
Waigeo, I. 103 0 20S 130 40 E
Waihao Downs 143 44 48S 170 55 E
Waihao, R. 143 44 52S 171 11 E
Waiheke Islands 142 36 48S 175 6 E
Waihi 142 37 23S 175 52 E
Waihola 143 46 1S 170 8 E
Waihola L. 143 45 59S 170 8 E
Waihou, R. 143 37 15S 175 40 E
Waika 126 2 22S 25 42 E
Waikabubak 103 9 45S 119 25 E
Waikaka 143 45 55S 169 1 E
Waikaoti 131 45 36S 170 41 E
Waikare, L. 142 37 26S 175 13 E
Waikaremoana 142 38 42S 177 12 E
Waikaremoana L. 142 38 49S 177 9 E
Waikari 143 42 58S 172 41 E
Waikato, R. 142 37 23S 174 43 E
Waikawa Harbour 143 46 39S 169 9 E
Waikerie 140 34 9S 140 0 E
Waikiekie 142 35 57S 174 16 E
Waikokopu 142 39 3S 177 52 E
Waikokopu Harb. 142 39 4S 177 53 E
Waikouaiti 143 45 36S 170 41 E
Wailuku 147 20 53N 156 26W
Waimakariri, R. 143 42 23S 172 42 E
Waimangaroa 143 41 43S 171 46 E
Waimanola 147 21 19N 157 43W
Waimarie 143 41 35S 171 58 E
Waimarino 143 40 40S 175 20 E
Waimate 143 44 53S 171 3 E
Waimea 147 21 57N 159 39W
Waimea Plain 143 45 55S 168 35 E
Waimes 47 50 25N 6 7 E
Wainfleet All Saints 33 53 7N 0 16 E
Wainganga, R. 96 21 0N 79 45 E
Waingapu 103 9 35S 120 11 E
Waingmaw 98 25 21N 97 26 E
Wainiha 147 22 9N 159 34W
Wainuiomata 142 41 17S 174 56 E
Wainwright, Can. 153 52 50N 110 50W
Wainwright, U.S.A. 147 70 39N 160 10W
Waiotapu 142 38 21S 176 25 E
Waiouru 142 39 28S 175 41 E
Waipahi 143 46 6S 169 15 E
Waipahu 147 21 23N 158 1W
Waipapa Pt. 143 46 40S 168 51 E
Waipara 143 43 3S 172 46 E
Waipawa 142 39 56S 176 38 E
Waipiro 142 38 2S 176 22 E
Waipori 131 45 50S 169 52 E
Waipu 142 35 59S 174 29 E
Waipukurau 142 40 1S 176 33 E
Wairakei 142 38 37S 176 6 E
Wairarapa I. 142 41 14S 175 15 E
Wairau, R. 143 41 32S 174 7 E
Wairio 143 45 59S 168 3 E
Wairoa 142 39 3S 177 25 E
Wairoa, R. 142 36 5S 173 59 E
Waitaki Plains 143 44 22S 170 0 E
Waitaki, R. 143 44 23S 169 55 E
Waitara 142 38 59S 174 15 E
Waitchie 140 35 22S 143 8 E
Waitoa 142 37 37S 175 35 E
Waitotara 142 39 49S 174 44 E
Waitsburg 160 46 15N 118 10W
Waiuku 142 37 15S 174 45 E
Wajir 126 1 42N 40 20 E
Wajir □ 126 1 42N 40 20 E
Wakaia 143 45 44S 168 51 E
Wakasa 110 35 20N 134 24 E
Wakasa-Wan 111 34 45N 135 30 E
Wakatipu, L. 143 45 5S 168 33 E
Wakaw 153 52 39N 105 44W
Wakayama 111 34 15N 135 15 E
Wakayama-ken □ 111 33 50N 135 30 E
Wake 110 34 48N 134 8 E
Wake Forest 157 35 58N 78 30W
Wake I. 130 19 18N 166 36 E
Wakefield, N.Z. 143 41 24S 173 5 E
Wakefield, U.K. 33 53 41N 1 31W
Wakefield, Mass., U.S.A. 162 42 30N 71 3W
Wakefield, Mich., U.S.A. 158 46 28N 89 53W
Wakema 98 16 40N 95 18 E
Wakhan □ 93 37 0N 73 0 E
Wakkanai 112 45 28N 141 35 E
Wakkerstroom 129 27 24S 30 10 E
Wako 150 49 50N 91 22W
Wakool 140 35 28S 144 23 E
Wakool, R. 140 35 5S 143 33 E
Wakre 103 0 30S 131 5 E
Waku 135 6 5S 149 9 E
Wakuach L. 151 55 34N 67 32W
Walachia □ 70 44 40N 25 0 E
Walamba 127 13 30S 28 42 E
Walberswick 29 52 18N 1 39 E
Wałbrzych 54 50 45N 16 18 E
Walbury Hill 28 51 22N 1 28W
Walcha 141 30 55S 151 31 E
Walcha Road 141 30 55S 151 24 E
Walcheren, I. 46 51 30N 3 35 E
Walcott 160 41 50N 106 55W
Walcz 54 53 17N 16 27 E
Wald 51 47 17N 8 56 E
Waldbröl 48 50 52N 7 36 E
Waldeck 48 51 12N 9 4 E
Walden, Colo., U.S.A. 160 40 47N 106 20W
Walden, N.Y., U.S.A. 162 41 32N 74 13W
Waldenburg 50 47 23N 7 45 E
Waldorf 162 38 37N 76 54W
Waldport 160 44 30N 124 2W
Waldron, Can. 153 50 53N 102 35W
Waldron, U.K. 29 50 56N 0 13 E
Waldron, U.S.A. 159 34 52N 94 4W
Waldshut 49 47 37N 8 12 E
Waldya 123 11 50N 39 34 E
Walebing 137 30 40S 116 15 E
Walembele 120 10 30N 1 14W
Walensee 51 47 7N 9 13 E
Walenstadt 51 47 8N 9 19 E
Wales 147 65 38N 168 10W
Walewale 121 10 21N 0 50W
Walgett 133 30 0S 148 5 E
Walhalla, Austral. 141 37 56S 146 29 E
Walhalla, U.S.A. 153 48 55N 97 55W
Waliso 123 8 33N 38 1 E
Walkaway 137 28 59S 114 48 E
Walker 158 47 4N 94 35W
Walker L., Man., Can. 153 54 42N 96 57W
Walker L., Qué., Can. 151 50 20N 67 11W
Walker L., U.S.A. 163 38 56N 118 46W
Walkerston 138 21 11S 149 8 E
Wall 158 44 0N 102 14W
Walla Walla, Austral. 141 35 45S 146 54 E
Walla Walla, U.S.A. 160 46 3N 118 25W

Wallabadah Weaverham

Wallabadah 138 17 57S 142 15E
Wallace, Idaho, U.S.A. 160 47 30N 116 0W
Wallace, N.C., U.S.A. 157 34 50N 77 59W
Wallace, Nebr., U.S.A. 158 40 51N 101 12W
Wallaceburg 150 42 40N 82 23W
Wallacetown 143 46 21S 168 19E
Wallachia = Valahia 70 44 35N 25 0E
Wallal 139 26 32S 146 7E
Wallal Downs 136 19 47S 120 40E
Wallambin, L. 137 30 57S 117 35E
Wallaroo 140 33 56S 137 39E
Wallasey 32 53 26N 3 2W
Walldurn 49 49 34N 9 23E
Wallerawang 141 33 25S 150 4E
Wallhallow 138 17 50S 135 50E
Wallingford 162 43 27N 72 50W
Wallis Arch. 142 13 20S 176 20E
Wallisellen 51 47 25N 8 36E
Wallowa 160 45 40N 117 35W
Wallowa, Mts. 160 45 20N 117 30W
Walls 36 60 14N 1 32W
Wallsend, Austral. 141 32 55S 151 40E
Wallsend, U.K. 35 54 59N 1 30W
Wallula 160 46 3N 118 59W
Wallumbilla 139 26 33S 149 9E
Walmer, S. Afr. 128 33 57S 25 35E
Walmer, U.K. 29 51 12N 1 23E
Walmsley, L. 153 63 25N 108 36W
Walney, Isle of 32 54 5N 3 15W
Walnut Ridge 159 36 7N 90 58W
Walpeup 140 35 10S 142 2E
Walpole 29 52 44N 0 13E
Walsall 28 52 36N 1 59W
Walsenburg 159 37 42N 104 45W
Walsh, Austral. 138 16 40S 144 0E
Walsh, U.S.A. 159 37 28N 102 15W
Walsh, R. 138 16 31S 143 42E
Walshoutem 47 50 43N 5 4E
Walsoken 29 52 41N 0 12E
Walsrode 48 52 51N 9 37E
Waltair 96 17 44N 83 23E
Walterboro 157 32 53N 80 40W
Walters 159 34 25N 98 20W
Waltershausen 48 50 53N 10 33E
Waltham, Can. 150 45 57N 76 57W
Waltham, U.K. 29 53 32N 0 6W
Waltham, U.S.A. 34 42 22N 71 12W
Waltham Abbey 29 51 40N 0 1E
Waltham Forest 29 51 37N 0 2E
Waltham on the Wolds 29 52 49N 0 48W
Waltman 160 43 8N 107 15W
Walton 162 42 12N 75 9W
Walton-le-Dale 32 53 45N 2 41W
Walton-on-the-Naze 29 51 52N 1 17E
Walu 98 23 54N 96 57E
Walvis Ridge 15 30 0S 3 0E
Walvisbaai 128 23 0S 14 28E
Walwa 141 35 59S 147 44E
Wamaza 126 4 12S 27 2E
Wamba, Kenya 126 0 58N 37 19E
Wamba, Nigeria 126 8 58N 8 34E
Wamba, Zaïre 121 2 10N 27 57E
Wamego 158 39 14N 96 22W
Wamena 103 3 58S 138 50E
Wampo 99 31 30N 86 38E
Wamsasi 103 3 27S 126 7E
Wan Hat 98 20 14N 97 53E
Wan Kinghao 98 21 34N 98 17E
Wan Lai-Kam 98 21 21N 98 22E
Wan Tup 98 21 13N 98 42E
Wana 94 32 20N 69 32E
Wanaaring 139 29 38S 144 0E
Wanaka L. 143 44 33S 169 7E
Wanan 109 26 25N 114 50E
Wanapiri 103 4 30S 135 50E
Wanapitei 150 46 30N 80 45W
Wanapitei L. 150 46 45N 80 40W
Wanaque 162 41 3N 74 17W
Wanbi 140 34 46S 140 17E
Wanborough 28 51 33N 1 40W
Wanch'eng 108 22 51N 107 25E
Wanch'üan 106 35 26N 110 50E
Wanch'uan 106 40 50N 114 56E
Wandanian 141 35 6S 150 30E
Wanderer 127 19 36S 30 1E
Wandiwash 97 12 30N 79 30E
Wandoan 139 26 5S 149 55E
Wandre 47 50 40N 5 39E
Wandsworth 29 51 28N 0 15W
Wanfercée-Baulet 47 50 28N 4 35E
Wanfuchuang 107 40 10N 122 34E
Wang Kai (Ghâbat el Arab) 123 9 3N 29 23E
Wang Noi 100 14 13N 100 44E
Wang, R. 100 17 8N 99 2E
Wang Saphung 100 17 18N 101 46E
Wang Thong 100 16 50N 100 26E
Wanga 126 2 58N 29 12E
Wangal 103 6 8S 134 9E
Wanganella 141 35 6S 144 49E
Wanganui 142 39 35S 175 3E
Wanganui, R., N.I., N.Z. 142 39 25S 175 4E
Wanganui, R., S.I., N.Z. 143 43 3S 170 26E
Wangaratta 141 36 21S 146 19E
Wangchiang 109 30 7N 116 41E
Wangch'ing 107 43 14N 129 38E
Wangdu Phodrang 98 27 28N 89 54E
Wangerooge I. 48 53 47N 7 52E
Wangi 126 1 58S 40 58E
Wangiwangi, I. 103 5 22S 123 37E
Wangmo 108 25 14N 105 59E
Wangts'ang 108 32 12N 106 21E
Wangtu 106 38 42N 115 4E
Wanhsien, Hopeh, China 106 38 49N 115 7E
Wanhsien, Kansu, China 105 36 45N 107 24E
Wankaner 94 22 42N 71 0E
Wanki Nat. Park 128 19 0S 26 30E
Wankie 127 18 18S 26 30E
Wankie □ 127 18 18S 26 30E
Wanless 153 54 11N 101 21W
Wanna Lakes 137 28 30S 128 27E
Wannien 109 28 40N 116 55E
Wanon Niwar 100 17 38N 103 46E
Wanshengch'ang 108 28 58N 106 55E
Wanssum 47 51 32N 6 5E
Wanstead 143 40 8S 176 30E
Wantage 28 51 35N 1 25W
Wantsai 109 28 5N 114 22E
Wanyin 98 20 23N 97 15E
Wanyüan 108 32 4N 108 5E
Wanzarīk 119 27 3N 13 30E
Wanze 47 50 32N 5 13E
Wapakoneta 156 40 35N 84 10W
Wapato 160 46 30N 120 25W
Wapawekka L. 153 54 55N 104 40W
Wapikopa L. 150 42 50N 88 10W
Wapiti, R. 150 55 5N 118 18W
Wappingers Fs. 162 41 35N 73 56W
Wapsipinican, R. 158 41 44N 90 19W
Warabi 111 35 49N 139 41E
Warandab 91 7 20N 44 2E
Warangal 96 17 58N 79 45E
Waratah 138 41 30S 145 30E
Waratah B. 139 38 54S 146 5E
Warboys 29 52 25N 0 5W
Warburg 48 51 29N 9 10E
Warburton 141 37 47S 145 42E
Warburton, R. 143 27 30S 138 30E
Warburton Ra. 137 25 55S 126 28E
Ward, Ireland 38 53 25N 6 19W
Ward, N.Z. 143 41 49S 174 11E
Ward Cove 152 55 25N 132 10W
Ward Hunt, C. 135 8 2S 148 10E
Ward Hunt Str. 135 9 30S 150 0E
Ward Mtn. 163 37 12N 118 54W
Ward, R. 139 26 32S 146 6E
Warden 129 27 50S 29 0E
Wardha 96 20 45N 78 39E
Wardha, R. 93 19 57N 79 11E
Wardington 28 52 8N 1 17W
Wardle 32 53 7N 2 35W
Wardlow 152 50 56N 111 31W
Wardoan 133 25 59S 149 59E
Wards River 141 32 11S 151 56E
Ward's Stone, mt. 32 54 2N 2 39W
Ware, Can. 152 57 26N 125 41W
Ware, U.K. 29 51 48N 0 2W
Ware, U.S.A. 162 42 16N 72 15W
Waregem 47 50 53N 3 27E
Wareham, U.K. 28 50 41N 2 8W
Wareham, U.S.A. 162 41 45N 70 44W
Wareham, oilfield 19 50 40N 2 8W
Waremme 47 50 43N 5 15E
Waren 48 53 30N 12 41E
Warendorf 48 51 57N 8 0E
Warialda 139 29 29S 150 33E
Wariap 103 1 30S 134 5E
Warin Chamrap 100 15 12N 104 53E
Wark 35 55 5N 2 14W
Warkopi 103 1 12S 134 9E
Warkworth, N.Z. 142 36 24S 174 41E
Warkworth, U.K. 35 55 22N 1 38W
Warley 28 52 30N 2 0W
Warm Springs, Mont., U.S.A. 160 46 11N 112 56W
Warm Springs, Nev., U.S.A. 161 38 16N 116 32W
Warman 153 52 19N 106 30W
Warmbad, Namibia 128 19 14S 13 51E
Warmbad, Namibia 128 28 25S 18 42E
Warmbad, S. Afr. 129 24 51S 28 19E
Warmenhuizen 46 52 43N 4 44E
Warmeriville 43 49 20N 4 13E
Warminster 28 51 12N 2 11W
Warmond 46 52 12N 4 30E
Warnambool Downs 138 22 48S 142 52E
Warnemünde 48 54 9N 12 5E
Warner 152 49 17N 112 12W
Warner Range, Mts. 160 41 30S 120 20W
Warner Robins 157 32 41N 83 36W
Warneton 47 50 45N 2 57E
Warnow, R. 48 54 0N 12 9E
Warnsveld 46 52 8N 6 14E
Waroona 137 32 50S 115 58E
Warora 96 20 14N 79 1E
Warracknabeal 140 36 9S 142 26E
Warragul 141 38 10S 145 58E
Warrawaqine 136 20 51S 120 42E
Warrayelu 123 10 40N 39 28E
Warrego, R. 139 30 24S 145 21E
Warrego Ra. 138 25 15S 146 0E
Warren, Austral. 141 31 42S 147 51E
Warren, Ark., U.S.A. 159 33 35N 92 3W
Warren, Pa., U.S.A. 156 41 52N 79 10W
Warren, R.I., U.S.A. 156 41 43N 71 19W
Warrenpoint 38 54 7N 6 15W
Warrens Landing 153 53 40N 98 0W
Warrensburg 158 38 45N 93 45W
Warrenton, S. Afr. 128 28 9S 24 47E
Warrenton, U.S.A. 160 46 11N 123 59W
Warrenville 139 25 48S 147 22E
Warri 121 5 30N 5 41E
Warrie 136 22 12S 119 40E
Warrina 136 28 12S 135 50E
Warrington, N.Z. 143 45 43S 170 35E
Warrington, U.K. 32 53 25N 2 38W
Warrington, U.S.A. 157 30 22N 87 16W
Warrnambool 140 38 25S 142 30E
Warroad 158 49 0N 95 20W
Warsaw 156 41 14N 85 50W
Warsaw = Warszawa 54 52 13N 21 0E
Warsop 33 53 13N 1 9W
Warstein 48 51 26N 8 20E
Warszawa 54 52 13N 21 0E
Warszawa □ 54 52 30N 17 0E
Warta 54 51 43N 18 38E
Warta, R. 54 52 40N 16 10E
Waru 103 3 30S 130 36E
Warud 96 21 30N 78 16E
Warwick, Austral. 139 28 10S 152 1E
Warwick, U.K. 28 52 17N 1 36W
Warwick, N.Y., U.S.A. 162 41 16N 74 22W
Warwick, R.I., U.S.A. 162 41 43N 71 25W
Warwick □ 28 52 20N 1 30W
Wasa 152 49 45N 115 50W
Wasatch, Mt., Ra. 160 40 30N 111 15W
Wasbank 129 28 15S 30 9E
Wasbister 37 59 11N 3 2W
Wasco, Calif., U.S.A. 163 35 37N 119 16W
Wasco, Oreg., U.S.A. 160 45 45N 120 46W
Waseca 158 44 3N 93 31W
Wasekamio L. 153 56 45N 108 45W
Wash, The 33 52 58N 0 20W
Washburn, N.D., U.S.A. 158 47 23N 101 0W
Washburn, Wis., U.S.A. 158 46 38N 90 55W
Washford 28 51 9N 3 22W
Washington, U.K. 35 54 55N 1 30W
Washington, D.C., U.S.A. 162 38 52N 77 0W
Washington, Ga., U.S.A. 157 33 45N 82 45W
Washington, Ind., U.S.A. 156 38 40N 87 8W
Washington, Iowa, U.S.A. 158 41 20N 91 45W
Washington, Miss., U.S.A. 158 38 35N 91 20W
Washington, N.C., U.S.A. 157 35 35N 77 1W
Washington, N.J., U.S.A. 162 40 45N 74 59W
Washington, Ohio, U.S.A. 156 39 34N 83 26W
Washington, Pa., U.S.A. 156 40 10N 80 20W
Washington, Utah, U.S.A. 161 37 10N 113 30W
Washington □ 160 47 45N 120 30W
Washington Court House 156 39 34N 83 26W
Washington I., Pac. Oc. 131 4 43N 160 25W
Washington I., U.S.A. 156 45 24N 86 54W
Washington Mt. 156 44 15N 71 18W
Washir 93 32 15N 63 50E
Wasian 103 1 47S 133 19E
Wasilków 54 53 12N 23 13E
Wasior 103 2 43S 134 30E
Waskaiowaka, L. 153 56 33N 96 23W
Waskesiu Lake 153 53 55N 106 5W
Wasm 122 18 2N 41 32E
Waspik 47 51 41N 4 57E
Wassen 51 46 42N 8 36E
Wassenaar 46 52 8N 4 24E
Wasserburg 49 48 4N 12 15E
Wassy 43 48 30N 4 58E
Wast Water, L. 32 54 26N 3 18W
Waswanipi 150 49 40N 75 59W
Waswanipi, L. 150 49 35N 76 40W
Watangpone 103 4 29S 120 25E
Wataroa 143 43 18S 170 24E
Wataroa, R. 143 43 7S 170 16E
Watawaha, P. 103 6 30S 122 20E
Watchet 28 51 10N 3 20W
Water Park Pt. 138 22 56S 150 47E
Water Valley 159 34 9N 89 38W
Waterberg, Namibia 128 20 30S 17 18E
Waterberg, S. Afr. 129 24 14S 28 0E
Waterberg, mt. 128 20 26S 17 13E
Waterbury 162 41 32N 73 0W
Waterbury L. 153 58 10N 104 22W
Waterford, Ireland 39 52 16N 7 8W
Waterford, S. Afr. 128 33 6S 25 0E
Waterford, U.S.A. 163 37 38N 120 46W
Waterford □ 39 51 10N 7 40W
Waterford Harb. 39 52 10N 6 58W
Watergate Bay 30 50 26N 5 4W
Watergrasshill 39 52 1N 8 20W
Waterhen L., Man., Can. 153 52 10N 99 40W
Waterhen L., Sask., Can. 153 54 28N 108 25W
Wateringen 46 52 2N 4 16E
Waterloo, Belg. 47 50 43N 4 25E
Waterloo, Can. 150 43 30N 80 32W
Waterloo, S. Leone 120 8 26N 13 8W
Waterloo, U.K. 32 53 29N 3 2W
Waterloo, Ill., U.S.A. 158 38 22N 90 6W
Waterloo, Iowa, U.S.A. 158 42 27N 92 20W
Waterloo, N.Y., U.S.A. 162 42 54N 76 53W
Watermeal-Boitsford 47 50 48N 4 25E
Watermeet 158 46 15N 89 12W
Waternish 36 57 32N 6 35W
Waterton Lakes Nat. Park 152 49 5N 114 15W
Watertown, Conn., U.S.A. 162 41 36N 73 7W
Watertown, N.Y., U.S.A. 162 43 58N 75 57W
Watertown, S.D., U.S.A. 158 44 57N 97 5W
Watertown, Wis., U.S.A. 158 43 15N 88 45W
Waterval-Boven 129 25 40S 30 18E
Waterville, Ireland 39 51 49N 10 10W
Waterville, Me., U.S.A. 151 44 35N 69 40W
Waterville, N.Y., U.S.A. 162 42 56N 75 23W
Waterville, Wash., U.S.A. 160 47 45N 120 1W
Watervliet, Belg. 47 51 17N 3 38E
Watervliet, U.S.A. 162 42 46N 73 43W
Wates 103 7 53S 110 6E
Watford 29 51 38N 0 23W
Watford City 158 47 50N 103 23W
Wath 33 53 29N 1 20W
Wathaman, R. 153 57 16N 102 59W
Watheroo 137 30 15S 116 0W
Watien 109 32 45N 112 30E
Wat'ing 106 35 25N 106 46E
Watkins Glen 162 42 25N 76 55W
Watlings I. 167 24 0N 74 35W
Watlington, Norfolk, U.K. 29 52 40N 0 24E
Watlington, Oxford, U.K. 29 51 38N 1 0W
Watonga 159 35 51N 98 24W
Watou 47 50 51N 2 38E
Watraba 139 31 58S 133 13E
Watrous, Can. 153 51 40N 105 25W
Watrous, U.S.A. 159 35 50N 104 55W
Watsa 126 3 4N 29 30E
Watseka 156 40 45N 87 45W
Watson, Austral. 137 30 29S 131 31E
Watson, Can. 153 52 10N 104 30W
Watson Lake 147 60 6N 128 49W
Watsontown 162 41 5N 76 52W
Watsonville 163 36 55N 121 49W
Watten 37 21 1S 144 3E
Wattenwil 50 46 46N 7 30E
Wattiwarriganna Cr. 139 28 57S 136 10E
Watton 29 52 35N 0 50E
Wattwil 51 47 18N 9 6E
Watubela, Kepulauan 103 4 28S 131 54E
Wau 135 7 21S 146 47E
Waubach 47 50 55N 6 3E
Waubay 158 45 42N 97 17W
Waubra 140 37 21S 143 39E
Wauchope 141 31 28S 152 45E
Wauchula 157 27 35N 81 50W
Waugh 153 49 40N 95 20W
Waukegan 156 42 22N 87 54W
Waukesha 156 43 0N 88 15W
Waukon 158 43 14N 91 33W
Wauneta 158 40 27N 101 25W
Waupaca 158 44 22N 89 8W
Waupun 158 43 38N 88 44W
Waurika 159 34 12N 98 0W
Wausau 158 44 57N 89 40W
Wautoma 158 44 3N 89 20W
Wauwatosa 156 43 6N 87 59W
Wave Hill 136 17 32N 131 0E
Waveney, R. 29 52 24N 1 20E
Waver R. 32 54 50N 3 15W
Waverley 142 39 46S 174 37E
Waverly, Iowa, U.S.A. 158 42 40N 92 30W
Waverly, N.Y., U.S.A. 162 42 0N 76 33W
Wavre 47 50 43N 4 38E
Wavreille 47 50 7N 5 15E
Wâw 123 7 45N 28 1E
Waw an Namus 119 24 24N 18 11E
Wawa, Can. 150 47 59N 84 47W
Wawa, Nigeria 121 9 54N 4 27E
Wawa, Sudan 122 20 30N 30 22E
Wawanesa 153 49 36N 99 40W
Wawoi, R. 135 7 48S 143 16E
Wawona 163 37 32N 119 39W
Waxahachie 159 32 22N 96 53W
Waxweiler 49 50 6N 6 22E
Way, L. 137 26 45S 120 16E
Wayabula Rau 103 2 29N 128 17E
Wayatinah 138 42 19S 146 27E
Waycross 157 31 12N 82 25W
Wayi 123 5 8N 30 10E
Wayne, Nebr., U.S.A. 158 42 16N 97 0W
Wayne, W. Va., U.S.A. 156 38 15N 82 27W
Waynesboro, Miss., U.S.A. 157 31 40N 88 39W
Waynesboro, Pa., U.S.A. 156 39 46N 77 32W
Waynesboro, Va., U.S.A. 156 38 4N 78 57W
Waynesburg 156 39 54N 80 12W
Waynesville 157 35 31N 83 0W
Waynoka 159 36 38N 98 53W
Waza 94 33 22N 69 22E
Wāzin 119 31 58N 10 51E
Wazirabad, Afghan. 93 36 44N 66 47E
Wazirabad, Pak. 94 32 30N 74 8E
We 102 6 3N 95 56E
Weald, The 29 51 7N 0 9E
Wear, R. 35 54 55N 1 22W
Weardale 32 54 44N 2 5W
Wearhead 32 54 45N 2 14W
Weatherford, Okla., U.S.A. 159 35 30N 98 45W
Weatherford, Tex., U.S.A. 159 32 45N 97 48W
Weaver, R. 32 53 17N 2 35W
Weaverham 32 53 15N 2 30W

Webb City   Whitby

Webb City 159 37 9N 94 30W
Weber 142 40 24S 176 20E
Webera, Bale, Ethiopia 123 6 29N 40 33E
Webera, Shewa, Ethiopia 123 9 40N 39 0E
Webster, Mass., U.S.A. 162 42 4N 71 54W
Webster, S.D., U.S.A. 158 45 24N 97 33W
Webster, Wis., U.S.A. 158 45 53N 92 25W
Webster City 158 42 30N 93 50W
Webster Green 158 38 38N 90 20W
Webster Springs 156 38 30N 80 25W
Wecliniec 54 51 18N 15 10E
Weda 103 0 30N 127 50E
Weda, Teluk 103 0 30N 127 50E
Weddell I. 176 51 50S 61 0W
Weddell Sea 13 72 30S 40 0W
Wedderburn 140 36 20S 143 33E
Wedge I. 132 30 50S 115 11E
Wedgeport 151 43 44N 65 59W
Wedmore 28 51 14N 2 50W
Wednesbury 28 52 33N 2 1W
Wednesfield 28 52 36N 2 3W
Wedza 127 18 40S 31 33E
Wee Elwah 141 32 2S 145 14E
Wee Waa 139 30 11S 149 26E
Weed 160 41 29N 122 22W
Weedsport 162 43 3N 76 35W
Weemelah 139 29 2S 149 7E
Weenen 129 28 48S 30 7E
Weener 48 53 10N 7 23E
Weert 47 51 15N 5 43E
Weesen 51 47 7N 9 4E
Weesp 46 52 18N 5 2E
Weggis 51 47 2N 8 26E
Wegierska-Gorka 54 49 36N 19 7E
Wegorzewo 54 54 13N 21 43E
Wegrów 54 52 24N 22 0E
Wehl 46 51 58N 6 13E
Wei Ho, R., Honan, China 106 34 58N 113 32E
Wei Ho, R., Shensi, China 106 34 38N 110 20E
Wei-si 99 27 18N 99 18E
Weich'ang 107 41 56N 117 34E
Weichou Tao 108 21 3N 109 2E
Weich'uan 106 34 19N 114 0E
Weida 48 50 47N 12 3E
Weiden 49 49 40N 12 10E
Weifang 107 36 47N 119 10E
Weihai 107 37 30N 122 10E
Weihsi 108 27 18N 99 18E
Weihsin 108 27 48N 105 5E
Weilburg 48 50 28N 8 17E
Weilheim 49 47 50N 11 9E
Weimar 48 51 0N 11 20E
Weinan 106 34 30N 109 35E
Weinfelden 51 47 34N 9 6E
Weingarten 49 47 49N 9 39E
Weinheim 49 49 33N 8 40E
Weining 108 26 50N 104 19E
Weipa 138 12 24S 141 50E
Weir, R., Austral. 139 28 20S 149 50E
Weir, R., Can. 153 56 54N 93 21W
Weir River 153 56 49N 94 6W
Weisen 51 46 42N 9 43E
Weiser 160 44 10N 117 0W
Weishan, Shantung, China 107 34 49N 47 6E
Weishan, Yunnan, China 108 25 16N 100 21E
Weissenburg 49 49 2N 10 58E
Weissenfels 48 51 11N 11 58E
Weisshorn 50 46 7N 7 43E
Weissmies 50 46 8N 8 1E
Weisstannen 51 46 59N 9 22E
Weisswasser 48 51 30N 14 36E
Weiswampach 47 50 8N 6 5E
Wëitra 52 48 41N 14 54E
Weiyüan 106 35 6N 104 14E
Weiyuan 106 35 10N 104 20E
Weiz 52 47 13N 15 39E
Wejherowo 54 54 35N 18 12E
Wekusko 153 54 45N 99 45W
Wekusko L. 153 54 40N 99 50W
Welbourn Hill 139 27 21S 134 6E
Welby 153 50 33N 101 29W
Welch 156 37 29N 81 36W
Welcome 138 15 20S 144 40E
Weldon 35 55 16N 1 46W
Welega □ 123 9 25N 34 20E
Welford, Berks., U.K. 28 51 28N 1 24W
Welford, Northampton, U.K. 28 52 26N 1 5W
Welkenraedt 47 50 39N 5 58E
Welkite 123 8 15N 37 42E
Welkom 128 28 0S 26 50E
Welland 150 43 0N 79 10W
Welland, R. 29 52 43N 0 10W
Wellen 47 50 50N 5 21E
Wellesley Is. 138 17 20S 139 30E
Wellin 47 50 5N 5 6E
Wellingborough 29 52 18N 0 41W
Wellington, Austral. 141 32 35S 148 59E
Wellington, Can. 150 43 57N 77 20W
Wellington, N.Z. 142 41 19S 174 46E
Wellington, S. Afr. 128 33 38S 18 57E
Wellington, U.K. 28 50 58N 3 13W
Wellington, Col., U.S.A. 158 40 43N 105 0W
Wellington, Kans., U.S.A. 159 37 15N 97 25W
Wellington, Nev., U.S.A. 163 38 47N 119 28W
Wellington, Okla., U.S.A. 159 34 55N 100 13W
Wellington □ 143 40 8S 175 36E
Wellington Bridge 39 52 15N 6 45W
Wellington, I. 176 49 30S 75 0W
Wellington, L. 141 38 6S 147 20E
Wellington, Mt. 142 36 55S 174 52E
Wellington (Telford) 28 52 42N 2 31W
Wello, L. 137 26 43S 123 10E
Wellow 28 51 20N 2 22W
Wells, Norfolk, U.K. 29 52 57N 0 51E
Wells, Somerset, U.K. 28 51 12N 2 39W
Wells, Me., U.S.A. 162 43 18N 70 35W
Wells, Minn., U.S.A. 158 43 44N 93 45W
Wells, Nev., U.S.A. 160 41 8N 115 0W
Wells, N.Y., U.S.A. 162 43 24N 74 17W
Wells Gray Prov. Park 152 52 30N 120 15W
Wells L. 137 26 44S 123 15E
Wellsboro 156 41 46N 77 20W
Wellsford 142 36 16S 174 32E
Wellsville, Mo., U.S.A. 158 39 4N 91 30W
Wellsville, N.Y., U.S.A. 156 42 9N 77 53W
Wellsville, Ohio, U.S.A. 156 40 36N 80 40W
Wellsville, Utah, U.S.A. 160 41 35N 111 59W
Wellton 161 32 46N 114 6W
Welmel, W. 123 6 0N 40 20E
Welney 29 52 31N 0 15E
Welo □ 123 11 50N 39 48E
Wels 52 48 9N 14 1E
Welshpool 31 52 40N 3 9W
Welton 33 53 19N 0 29W
Welwel 91 7 5N 45 25E
Welwitschia 128 20 16S 14 59E
Welwyn 153 50 20N 101 30W
Welwyn Garden City 29 51 49N 0 11W
Wem 28 52 52N 2 45W
Wembere, R. 126 4 45S 34 0E
Wembury 30 50 19N 4 6W
Wemmel 47 50 55N 4 18E
Wemyss Bay 34 55 52N 4 54W
Wenatchee 160 47 30N 120 17W
Wench'ang 100 19 38N 110 42E
Wencheng 109 27 48N 120 5E
Wenchi 120 7 46N 2 8W
Wenchiang 108 30 43N 103 56E
Wenchou 109 28 1N 120 39E
Wench'uan 108 31 28N 103 35E
Wendell 160 42 50N 114 51W
Wendesi 103 2 30S 134 10E
Wendo 123 6 40N 38 27E
Wendover, U.K. 29 51 46N 0 45W
Wendover, U.S.A. 160 40 49N 114 1W
Wenduine 47 51 18N 3 5E
Wengan 108 27 0N 107 32E
Wengch'eng 109 24 22N 113 50E
Wenge 126 0 3N 24 0E
Wengen 50 46 37N 7 55E
Wengniut'ech'i 107 42 59N 118 48E
Wengpu 108 32 55N 98 30E
Wengyüan 109 24 21N 114 7E
Wenhsi 106 35 23N 111 8E
Wenhsiang 106 34 36N 110 34E
Wenhsien, Honan, China 106 34 56N 113 4E
Wenhsien, Kansu, China 106 58 0N 104 39E
Wenling 109 28 22N 121 18E
Wenlock 138 13 6S 142 58E
Wenlock Edge 23 52 30N 2 43W
Wenlock, R. 133 12 2S 141 55E
Wenshan 108 23 22N 104 13E
Wenshang 106 35 37N 116 33E
Wenshui, Kweichow, China 108 28 27N 106 31E
Wenshui, Shansi, China 106 37 25N 112 1E
Wensleydale 32 54 18N 2 0W
Wensu 105 41 15N 80 14E
Wenteng 107 37 10N 122 0E
Wentworth 140 34 2S 141 54E
Wentworth, Mt. 138 24 12S 147 1E
Wenut 103 3 11S 133 19E
Weobley 28 52 9N 2 52W
Weott 160 40 19N 123 56W
Wepener 128 29 42S 27 3E
Werbomont 47 50 23N 5 41E
Werda 128 25 24S 23 15E
Werdau 48 50 45N 12 20E
Werder, Ethiopia 91 6 58N 45 1E
Werder, Ger. 48 52 23N 12 56E
Werdohl 48 51 15N 7 47E
Weri 103 3 10S 132 30E
Werkendam 46 51 50N 4 53E
Werne 48 51 38N 7 38E
Wernigerode 48 51 49N 0 45E
Werribee 140 37 54S 144 40E
Werrimull 140 34 25S 141 38E
Werrington 30 50 31N 4 22W
Werris Creek 141 31 18S 150 38E
Wersar 103 1 30S 131 55E
Wertheim 49 49 44N 9 32E
Wervershoof 46 52 44N 5 10E
Wervik 47 50 47N 3 3E
Wesel 48 51 39N 6 34E
Weser, R. 48 53 33N 8 30E
Wesiri 103 7 30S 126 30E
Wesleyville 151 49 8N 53 36W
Wessel, C. 138 10 59S 136 46E
Wessel Is. 138 11 10S 136 45E
Wesselburen 48 54 11N 8 53E
Wessem 47 51 11N 5 49E
Wessington 158 44 30N 98 40W
Wessington Springs 158 44 10N 98 35W
West 159 31 50N 97 5W
West Auckland 33 54 38N 1 42W
West B. 151 45 53N 82 8W
West, B. 159 29 5N 89 27W
West Baines, R. 136 15 36S 129 58E
West Bend 156 43 25N 88 10W
West Bengal □ 95 25 0N 90 0E
West Branch 156 44 16N 84 13W
West Bridgford 33 52 56N 1 8W
West Bromwich 28 52 32N 2 1W
West Burra, I. 36 60 5N 1 21W
West Calder 35 55 51N 3 34W
West Canada Cr. 162 43 1N 74 58W
West Cape Howe 137 35 8S 117 36E
West Chester 162 39 58N 75 36W
West Coker 28 50 55N 2 40W
West Columbia 159 29 10N 95 38W
West Covina 163 34 4N 117 54W
West Derry 162 42 55N 71 19W
West Des Moines 158 41 30N 93 45W
West End 166 26 41N 78 58W
West Falkland Island 176 51 30S 60 0W
West Fen 33 53 5N 0 5W
West Frankfort 158 37 56N 89 0W
West Glamorgan □ 31 51 40N 3 55W
West Grinstead 29 50 58N 0 19W
West Haddon 28 52 21N 1 5W
West Harbour 131 45 51S 170 33E
West Hartford 162 41 45N 72 45W
West Haven 162 41 18N 72 57W
West Hazleton 162 40 58N 76 0W
West Helena 159 34 30N 90 40W
West Hurley 162 41 59N 74 7W
West Indies 158 15 0N 70 0W
West Kilbride 34 55 41N 4 50W
West Kirby 32 53 22N 3 11W
West Lavington 28 51 16N 1 59W
West Linton 35 55 45N 3 24W
West Looe 30 50 21N 4 29W
West Lulworth 28 50 37N 2 14W
West Lunga, R. 127 12 35S 24 45E
West Magpie R. 151 51 2N 64 42W
West Malling 29 51 16N 0 25E
West Memphis 159 35 5N 90 3W
West Meon 28 51 2N 1 3W
West Mersea 29 51 46N 0 55E
West Midlands □ 28 52 30N 1 55W
West Milton 162 41 1N 76 50W
West Monroe 159 32 32N 92 7W
West Nicholson 127 21 2S 29 20E
West Pakistan = Pakistan 93 27 0N 67 0W
West Palm Beach 157 26 44N 80 3W
West Paris 101 44 18N 70 30W
West Parley 28 50 46N 1 52W
West Plains 159 36 45N 91 50W
West Pt. 140 35 1S 135 56E
West Point, Can. 151 49 55N 64 30W
West Point, Jamaica 166 18 14N 78 30W
West Point, Ga., U.S.A. 157 32 54N 85 10W
West Point, Miss., U.S.A. 157 33 36N 88 38W
West Point, Nebr., U.S.A. 158 41 50N 96 43W
West Point, Va., U.S.A. 162 37 35N 76 47W
West Pokot □ 126 1 30N 35 40E
West, R. 162 42 52N 72 33W
West Rasen 33 53 23N 0 23W
West Reading 162 40 20N 75 57W
West Riding (□) 26 53 50N 1 30W
West Road R. 152 53 18N 122 53W
West Rutland 162 43 36N 73 3W
West Schelde = Westerschelde 47 51 23N 3 50E
West Sole, gasfield 19 53 40N 1 15E
West Spitsbergen 12 78 40N 17 0E
West Sussex □ 29 50 55N 0 30W
West-Terschelling 46 53 22N 5 13E
West Virginia □ 156 39 0N 18 0W
West-Vlaanderen □ 47 51 0N 3 0E
West Walker, R. 163 38 54N 119 9W
West Wittering 29 50 44N 0 53W
West Wyalong 141 33 56S 147 10E
West Yellowstone 160 44 47N 111 4W
West York 162 39 57N 76 46W
West Yorkshire □ 33 53 45N 1 40W
Westall 139 32 55S 134 4E
Westbank 152 49 50N 119 25W
Westbourne 29 50 53N 0 55W
Westbrook, Maine, U.S.A. 162 43 40N 70 22W
Westbrook, Tex., U.S.A. 159 32 25N 101 0W
Westbury, Austral. 138 41 30S 146 51E
Westbury, Salop, U.K. 28 52 40N 2 57W
Westbury, Wilts., U.K. 28 51 16N 2 11W
Westbury-on-Severn 28 51 49N 2 24W
Westby 158 48 52N 104 3W
Westend 163 35 42N 117 24W
Wester Ross, dist. 36 57 37N 5 0W
Westerbork 46 52 51N 6 37E
Westerham 29 51 16N 0 5E
Westerland 48 54 51N 8 20E
Western □, Kenya 126 0 30N 34 30E
Western □, Uganda 126 1 45N 31 30E
Western □, Zambia 127 13 15N 27 30E
Western Australia □ 137 25 0S 118 0E
Western Bay 151 46 50N 52 30W
Western Germany ■ 48 50 0N 8 0E
Western Ghats 97 15 30N 74 30E
Western Is. □ 36 57 40N 7 0W
Western River 140 35 42S 136 56E
Western Samoa ■ 130 14 0S 172 0W
Westernport 156 30 30N 79 5W
Westerschelde, R. 47 51 25N 4 0E
Westerstede 48 51 15N 7 55E
Westervoort 46 51 58N 5 59E
Westerwald, mts. 48 50 39N 8 0E
Westfield, U.K. 29 50 53N 0 30E
Westfield, U.S.A. 162 42 9N 72 49W
Westgat 47 51 39N 3 44E
Westhope 158 48 55N 101 0W
Westhoughton 32 53 34N 2 30W
Westkapelle, Belg. 47 51 19N 3 19E
Westkapelle, Neth. 47 51 31N 3 28E
Westland □ 143 43 33S 169 59E
Westland Bight 143 42 55S 170 5E
Westlock 152 54 9N 113 55W
Westmalle 47 51 18N 4 42E
Westmeath □ 38 53 30N 7 30W
Westmine 137 29 2S 116 8E
Westminster 162 39 34S 77 1W
Westmorland 161 33 2N 115 42W
Westmorland (□) 26 54 28N 2 40W
Weston, Malay. 102 5 10N 115 35E
Weston, U.K. 28 52 51N 2 2W
Weston, Oreg., U.S.A. 160 45 50N 118 30W
Weston, W. Va., U.S.A. 156 39 3N 80 29W
Weston I. 150 52 33N 79 36W
Weston-super-Mare 28 51 20N 2 59W
Westport, Ireland 38 53 44N 9 31W
Westport, N.Z. 143 41 46S 171 37E
Westport, U.S.A. 160 46 48N 124 4W
Westport B. 38 53 48N 9 38W
Westray 153 53 36N 101 24W
Westray Firth 37 59 15N 3 0W
Westray, I. 37 59 18N 3 0W
Westree 150 47 26N 81 34W
Westruther 35 55 45N 2 34W
Westview 152 49 50N 124 31W
Westville, Ill., U.S.A. 156 40 3N 87 36W
Westville, Okla., U.S.A. 159 36 0N 94 33W
Westward Ho 30 51 2N 4 16W
Westwood 160 40 26N 121 0W
Wetar, I. 103 7 30S 126 30E
Wetaskiwin 152 52 55N 113 24W
Wetherby 33 53 56N 1 23W
Wethersfield 162 41 43N 72 40W
Wetlet 98 21 13N 95 53E
Wettingen 51 47 28N 8 20E
Wetwang 33 54 2N 0 35W
Wetzikon 51 47 19N 8 48E
Wetzlar 48 50 33N 8 30E
Wevelgem 47 50 49N 3 12E
Wewak 135 3 38S 143 41E
Wewaka 159 35 10N 96 35W
Wexford 39 52 20N 6 28W
Wexford □ 39 52 20N 6 25W
Wexford Harb. 39 52 20N 6 25W
Wey, R. 29 51 19N 0 29W
Weybourne 29 52 57N 1 9E
Weybridge 29 51 22N 0 28W
Weyburn 153 49 40N 103 50W
Weyburn L. 152 63 0N 117 59W
Weyer 52 47 51N 14 40E
Weymouth, Can. 151 44 30N 66 1W
Weymouth, U.K. 28 50 36N 2 28W
Weymouth, U.S.A. 162 42 13N 70 53W
Weymouth, C. 133 12 37S 143 27E
Wezep 46 52 28N 6 0E
Whakamaru 142 38 23S 175 63E
Whakatane 142 37 57S 177 1E
Whale Cove 148 62 11N 92 36W
Whale Firth 36 60 40N 1 10W
Whale, R. 151 58 15N 67 40W
Whales 13 78 0S 165 0W
Whaley Bridge 32 53 20N 2 0W
Whalley 32 53 49N 2 25W
Whalsay, I. 36 60 22N 1 0W
Whalton 35 55 7N 1 46W
Whangamomona 142 39 8S 174 44E
Whangarei 142 35 43S 174 21E
Whangarei Harbour 142 35 45S 174 28E
Whangaroa 142 35 4S 173 46E
Whangumata 142 37 12S 175 53E
Whaplode 29 52 42N 0 3W
Wharanui 143 41 55S 174 6E
Wharfe, R. 33 53 55N 1 30W
Wharfedale 31 54 7N 2 4W
Wharton, N.J., U.S.A. 162 40 53N 74 36W
Wharton, Tex., U.S.A. 159 29 20N 96 6W
Whauphill 34 54 48N 4 31W
Whayjonta 139 29 40S 142 35E
Wheatland 158 42 4N 105 58W
Wheatley Hill 33 54 45N 1 23W
Wheaton, Md., U.S.A. 162 39 3N 77 3W
Wheaton, Minn., U.S.A. 158 45 50N 96 29W
Wheeler, Oreg., U.S.A. 160 45 45N 123 57W
Wheeler, Tex., U.S.A. 159 35 29N 100 15W
Wheeler Peak, Mt. 160 38 57N 114 15W
Wheeler, R. 153 57 34N 104 15W
Wheeler Ridge 163 35 0N 118 57W
Wheeling 156 40 2N 80 41W
Whichham 32 54 14N 3 22W
Whidbey I. 152 48 15N 122 40W
Whidbey Is. 136 34 30S 135 3E
Whiddy, I. 39 51 41N 9 30W
Whimple 30 50 46N 3 21W
Whipsnade 29 51 51N 0 32W
Whiskey Gap 152 49 0N 113 3W
Whiskey Jack L. 153 58 23N 101 55W
Whissendine 29 52 43N 0 46W
Whistleduck Cr. 138 20 15S 135 18E
Whistler 157 30 50N 88 10W
Whiston 32 53 25N 2 45W
Whitburn 35 55 52N 3 41W
Whitby 33 54 29N 0 37W

Whitchurch **Winterberg**

Whitchurch, U.K. **31** 51 32N 3 15W
Whitchurch, Devon, U.K. **30** 50 31N 4 7W
Whitchurch, Hants., U.K. **28** 51 14N 1 20W
Whitchurch, Here., U.K. **28** 51 51N 2 41W
Whitchurch, Salop, U.K. **32** 52 58N 2 42W
Whitcombe, Mt. **131** 43 12 S 171 0 E
Whitcombe, P. **131** 43 12 S 171 0 E
White B. **151** 50 0N 56 35W
White Bear Res. **151** 48 10N 57 05W
White Bird **160** 45 46N 116 21W
White Bridge **35** 57 11N 4 32W
White Butte **156** 46 23N 103 25W
White City **158** 38 50N 96 45W
White Cliffs, Austral. **140** 30 50 S 143 10 E
White Cliffs, N.Z. **143** 43 26 S 171 55 E
White Deer **159** 35 30N 101 8W
White Esk, R. **35** 55 14N 3 11W
White Hall **158** 39 25N 90 27W
White Haven **162** 41 3N 75 47W
White Horse Hill **28** 51 35N 1 35W
White I. **142** 37 30 S 177 13 E
White L., Austral. **136** 24 43 S 121 44 E
White L., U.S.A. **159** 29 45N 92 30W
White Mts. **163** 37 30N 118 15W
White Nile = Nîl el Abyad, Bahr **123** 9 30N 31 40 E
White Nile Dam **123** 15 24N 32 30 E
White Otter L. **150** 49 5N 91 55W
White Pass **147** 59 40N 135 3W
White Plains, Liberia **120** 6 28N 10 40W
White Plains, U.S.A. **162** 41 2N 73 44W
White, R., Ark., U.S.A. **159** 36 28N 93 55W
White, R., Colo., U.S.A. **160** 40 8N 108 52W
White, R., Ind., U.S.A. **156** 39 25N 86 30W
White, R., S.D., U.S.A. **158** 43 10N 102 52W
White River, Can. **150** 48 35N 85 20W
White River, S. Afr. **129** 25 20 S 31 00 E
White River, U.S.A. **158** 43 48N 100 5W
White River Junc. **162** 43 38N 72 20W
White Russia = Byelorussia, SSR **80** 53 30N 27 0 E
White Sea = Beloye More **78** 66 30N 38 0 E
White Sulphur Springs, Mont., U.S.A. **160** 46 35N 111 0W
White Sulphur Springs, W. Va., U.S.A. **160** 37 50N 80 16W
White Volta, R., (Volta Blanche) **121** 10 0N 1 0W
White Well **137** 31 25 S 131 3 E
Whiteadder Water, R. **35** 55 47N 2 20W
Whitecourt **152** 54 10N 115 45W
Whiteface **159** 33 35N 102 40W
Whitefish **160** 48 25N 114 22W
Whitefish L. **153** 62 41N 106 48W
Whitefish Pt. **156** 46 45N 85 0W
Whitegate, Clare, Ireland **39** 52 58N 8 24W
Whitegate, Cork, Ireland **39** 51 49N 8 15W
Whitegull, L. **151** 55 27N 64 17W
Whitehall, Ireland **39** 52 42N 7 2W
Whitehall, U.K. **37** 59 9N 2 36W
Whitehall, Mich., U.S.A. **156** 43 21N 86 20W
Whitehall, Mont., U.S.A. **160** 45 52N 112 4W
Whitehall, N.Y., U.S.A. **162** 43 32N 73 28W
Whitehall, Wis., U.S.A. **158** 44 20N 91 19W
Whitehaven **32** 54 33N 3 35W
Whitehead **38** 54 45N 5 42W
Whitehorse **147** 60 43N 135 3W
Whitehorse, Vale of **28** 51 37N 1 30W
Whitekirk **35** 56 2N 2 36W
Whiteman Ra. **135** 5 55 S 150 0 E
Whitemark **138** 40 7 S 148 3 E
Whitemouth **153** 49 57N 95 58W
Whiten Hd. **37** 58 34N 4 35W
Whitesail, L. **152** 53 35N 127 45W
Whitesand B. **30** 50 18N 4 20W
Whitesboro, N.Y., U.S.A. **162** 43 8N 75 20W
Whitesboro, Tex., U.S.A. **159** 33 40N 96 58W
Whiteshell Prov. Park **153** 50 0N 95 40W
Whitetail **158** 48 54N 105 15W
Whiteville **157** 34 20N 78 40W
Whitewater **156** 42 50N 88 45W
Whitewater Baldy, Mt. **161** 33 20N 108 44W
Whitewater L. **150** 50 50N 89 10W
Whitewood, Austral. **138** 21 28 S 143 30 E
Whitewood, Can. **153** 50 20N 102 20W
Whitfield **141** 36 42 S 146 24 E
Whithorn **162** 54 55N 4 25W
Whitianga **142** 36 47 S 175 41 E
Whitland **31** 51 49N 4 38W
Whitley Bay **35** 55 4N 1 28W
Whitman **162** 42 4N 70 55W
Whitmire **157** 34 33N 81 40W
Whitney **150** 45 31N 78 14W
Whitney, Mt. **163** 36 35N 118 14W
Whitney Pt. **162** 42 19N 75 59W
Whitstable **29** 51 21N 1 2 E
Whitsunday I. **138** 20 15 S 149 4 E
Whittier **147** 60 46N 148 48W
Whittington, Derby, U.K. **33** 53 17N 1 26W
Whittington, Salop, U.K. **28** 52 53N 3 0W
Whittle, C. **151** 50 11N 60 8W
Whittlesea **141** 37 27 S 145 9 E
Whittlesey **29** 52 34N 0 8W
Whittlesford **29** 52 6N 0 9 E
Whitton **33** 53 42N 0 39W
Whitwell, Derby, U.K. **33** 53 16N 1 11W
Whitwell, Isle of Wight, U.K. **28** 50 35N 1 19W
Whitwell, U.S.A. **157** 35 15N 85 30W
Whitwick **28** 52 45N 1 23W
Whitworth **32** 53 40N 2 11W
Whixley **33** 54 2N 1 19W
Wholdaia L. **153** 60 43N 104 20W
Whyalla **140** 33 2 S 137 30 E
Whyjonta **139** 29 41 S 142 28 E
Whyte Yarcowie **107** 33 13 S 138 54 E
Wiarton **150** 44 50N 81 10W
Wiawso **120** 6 10N 2 25W
Wiay I. **36** 57 24N 7 12W
Wiazow **54** 50 50N 17 10 E
Wibaux **158** 47 0N 104 13W
Wichian Buri **100** 15 39N 101 7 E
Wichita **159** 37 40N 97 29W
Wichita Falls **159** 33 57N 98 30W
Wick, Scot., U.K. **37** 58 26N 3 5W
Wick, Wales, U.K. **31** 51 24N 3 32W
Wick R. **37** 58 28N 3 14W
Wickenburg **161** 33 58N 112 45W
Wickepin **137** 32 50 S 117 30 E
Wickett **159** 31 37N 102 58W
Wickford **29** 51 37N 0 31 E
Wickham **28** 50 54N 1 11W
Wickham, C. **138** 39 35 S 143 57 E
Wickham Market **29** 52 9N 1 21 E
Wicklow **39** 53 0N 6 2W
Wicklow □ **39** 52 59N 6 25W
Wicklow Gap **39** 53 3N 6 23W
Wicklow Hd. **39** 52 59N 6 3W
Wicklow Mts. **39** 53 0N 6 30W
Wickwar **28** 51 35N 2 23W
Widawa **54** 51 27N 18 51 E
Widdrington **35** 55 15N 1 35W
Wide B. **138** 4 52 S 152 0 E
Wide Firth **37** 59 2N 3 0W
Widecombe **30** 50 34N 3 48W
Widemouth **30** 50 45N 4 34W
Widgiemooltha **137** 31 30 S 121 34 E
Widnes **32** 53 22N 2 44W
Wiek **48** 54 37N 13 17 E
Wielbark **54** 53 24N 20 55 E
Wielén **54** 52 53N 16 9 E
Wieliczka **54** 50 0N 20 5 E
Wielun **54** 51 15N 18 40 E
Wien **53** 48 12N 16 22 E
Wiener Neustadt **53** 47 49N 16 16 E
Wieprz, R., Koszalin, Poland **54** 54 26N 16 35 E
Wieprz, R., Lublin, Poland **54** 51 15N 22 50 E
Wierden **46** 52 22N 6 35 E
Wiers **47** 50 30N 3 32 E
Wieruszów **54** 51 19N 18 9 E
Wiesbaden **49** 50 7N 8 17 E
Wiesental **49** 49 15N 8 30 E
Wigan **32** 53 33N 2 38W
Wiggins, Colo., U.S.A. **158** 40 16N 104 3W
Wiggins, Miss., U.S.A. **159** 30 53N 89 9W
Wight, I. of **28** 50 40N 1 20W
Wigmore **28** 52 19N 2 51W
Wigston **28** 52 35N 1 6W
Wigton **32** 54 50N 3 9W
Wigtown **34** 54 52N 4 27W
Wigtown (□) **26** 54 53N 4 45W
Wigtown B. **34** 54 46N 4 15W
Wihéries **47** 50 23N 3 45 E
Wijangala **139** 33 57 S 148 59 E
Wijchen **46** 51 48N 5 44 E
Wijhe **46** 52 23N 6 8 E
Wijk bij Duurstede **46** 51 59N 5 21 E
Wil **51** 47 28N 9 3 E
Wilamowice **53** 49 55N 19 9 E
Wilangee **140** 31 28 S 141 20 E
Wilber **158** 40 34N 96 59W
Wilburton **159** 34 55N 95 15W
Wilcannia **140** 31 30 S 143 26 E
Wildbad **49** 48 44N 8 32 E
Wildervank **46** 53 5N 6 52 E
Wildeshausen **48** 52 54N 8 25 E
Wildhorn **50** 46 22N 7 21 E
Wildon **52** 46 52N 15 31 E
Wildrose, Calif., U.S.A. **163** 36 14N 117 11W
Wildrose, N. Dak., U.S.A. **158** 48 36N 103 17W
Wildspitze **52** 46 53N 10 53 E
Wildstrubel **50** 46 24N 7 32 E
Wildwood **162** 38 59N 74 46W
Wilgaroon **141** 30 52 S 145 42 E
Wilhelm II Coast **13** 67 0 S 90 0 E
Wilhelm Mt. **135** 5 50 S 145 1 E
Wilhelm-Pieck-Stadt Guben **48** 51 59N 14 48 E
Wilhelmina Kanaal **47** 51 36N 5 6 E
Wilhelmina, Mt. **175** 3 50N 56 30W
Wilhelmsburg, Austria **52** 48 6N 15 36 E
Wilhelmsburg, Ger. **48** 53 28N 10 1 E
Wilhelmshaven **48** 53 30N 8 9 E
Wilhelmstal **128** 21 58 S 16 21 E
Wilkes-Barre **162** 41 15N 75 52W
Wilkes Land **13** 69 0 S 120 0 E
Wilkesboro **157** 36 10N 81 9W
Wilkie **153** 52 27N 108 42W
Wilkinson Lakes **137** 29 40 S 132 39 E
Willamina **160** 45 9N 123 32W
Willamulka **140** 33 55 S 137 52 E
Willandra Billabong Creek **140** 33 22 S 145 52 E
Willapa, B. **160** 46 44N 124 0W
Willard, N. Mex., U.S.A. **161** 34 35N 106 1W
Willard, N.Y., U.S.A. **162** 42 40N 76 50W
Willard, Utah, U.S.A. **160** 41 28N 112 1W
Willaumez Pen. **138** 5 3 S 150 3 E
Willaura **140** 37 31 S 142 45 E
Willberforce, C. **138** 11 54 S 136 35 E
Willbriggie **141** 34 28 S 146 2 E
Willcox **161** 32 13N 109 53W
Willebroek **47** 51 4N 4 22 E
Willemstad **167** 12 5N 69 0W
Willenhall **28** 52 36N 2 3W
Willeroo **136** 15 14 S 131 37 E
Willesborough **29** 51 8N 0 55 E
Willet **162** 42 28N 75 55W
William Cr. **139** 28 58 S 136 22 E
William, Mt. **140** 37 17 S 142 35 E
William, R. **153** 59 8N 109 19W
Williambury **137** 23 45 S 115 12 E
Williams, Austral. **137** 33 2 S 116 52 E
Williams, U.S.A. **161** 35 16N 112 11W
Williams Lake **152** 52 2N 122 10W
Williamsburg, Ky., U.S.A. **157** 36 45N 84 10W
Williamsburg, Va., U.S.A. **162** 37 17N 76 44W
Williamsburg, Va., U.S.A. **162** 37 16N 79 43W
Williamson **156** 37 46N 82 17W
Williamsport **162** 41 18N 77 1W
Williamston **157** 35 50N 77 5W
Williamstown, Austral. **141** 37 51 S 144 52 E
Williamstown, Ireland **38** 53 41N 8 34W
Williamstown, Mass., U.S.A. **162** 42 43N 73 12W
Williamstown, N.Y., U.S.A. **162** 43 25N 75 53W
Williamstown, N.Y., U.S.A. **162** 43 25N 75 54W
Williamsville **159** 37 0N 90 33W
Willimantic **162** 41 45N 72 12W
Willingdon **29** 50 47N 0 17 E
Willis Group **138** 16 18 S 150 0 E
Willisau **50** 47 7N 8 0 E
Williston, S. Afr. **128** 31 20 S 20 53 E
Williston, Fla, U.S.A. **157** 29 25N 82 28W
Williston, N.D., U.S.A. **158** 48 10N 103 35W
Williston L. **152** 56 0N 124 0W
Williton **28** 51 9N 3 20W
Willits **160** 39 28N 123 17W
Willmar **158** 45 5N 95 0W
Willoughby **33** 53 14N 0 12 E
Willow Bunch **153** 49 20N 105 35W
Willow L. **152** 62 10N 119 8W
Willow Lake **158** 44 40N 97 40W
Willow River **152** 54 6N 122 28W
Willow Springs **159** 37 0N 92 0W
Willow Tree **141** 31 40 S 150 45 E
Willow Wall **107** 41 30N 120 40 E
Willowlake, R. **152** 62 42N 123 8W
Willowmore **128** 33 15 S 23 30 E
Willows, Austral. **138** 23 45 S 147 25 E
Willows, U.S.A. **160** 39 30N 122 10W
Wills Cr. **138** 22 43 S 140 2 E
Wills, L. **136** 21 25 S 128 51 E
Wills Pt. **159** 32 42N 95 57W
Willunga **140** 35 15 S 138 30 E
Wilmete **156** 42 6N 87 44W
Wilmington, Austral. **140** 32 39 S 138 7 E
Wilmington, U.K. **30** 50 46N 3 8W
Wilmington, Del., U.S.A. **162** 39 45N 75 32W
Wilmington, Ill., U.S.A. **156** 41 19N 88 10W
Wilmington, N.C., U.S.A. **157** 34 14N 77 54W
Wilmington, Ohio, U.S.A. **156** 39 29N 83 46W
Wilmington, Vt., U.S.A. **162** 42 52N 72 52W
Wilmslow **32** 53 19N 2 14W
Wilnecote **28** 52 36N 1 40W
Wilpena Cr. **140** 31 25 S 139 29 E
Wilrijk **47** 51 9N 4 22 E
Wilsall **160** 45 59N 110 4W
Wilson, U.S.A. **162** 40 41N 75 15W
Wilson, N.C., U.S.A. **157** 35 44N 77 54W
Wilson Bluff **137** 31 41 S 129 0 E
Wilson Inlet **137** 35 0 S 117 20 E
Wilson, Mt. **161** 37 55N 105 3W
Wilson, R., Queens., Austral. **139** 27 38 S 141 24 E
Wilson, R., W. Australia, Austral. **136** 16 48 S 128 16 E
Wilson's Promontory **141** 38 55 S 146 25 E
Wilster **48** 53 55N 9 23 E
Wilton, U.K. **28** 51 5N 1 52W
Wilton, U.S.A. **158** 47 12N 100 53W
Wilton, R. **138** 14 45 S 134 33 E
Wiltshire □ **28** 51 20N 2 0W
Wiltz **47** 49 57N 5 55 E
Wiluna **137** 26 36 S 120 14 E
Wimblington **29** 52 31N 0 5 E
Wimborne Minster **28** 50 48N 2 0W
Wimereux **43** 50 45N 1 37 E
Wimmera **133** 36 30 S 142 0 E
Wimmera, R. **140** 36 8 S 141 56 E
Winam G. **126** 0 20 S 34 15 E
Winburg **128** 28 30 S 27 2 E
Wincanton **28** 51 3N 2 24W
Winchelsea, Austral. **140** 38 10 S 144 1 E
Winchelsea, U.K. **29** 50 55N 0 43 E
Winchendon **162** 42 40N 72 3W
Winchester, N.Z. **143** 44 11 S 171 17 E
Winchester, U.K. **28** 51 4N 1 19W
Winchester, Conn., U.S.A. **162** 41 53N 73 9W
Winchester, Conn., U.S.A. **162** 41 55N 73 8W
Winchester, Idaho, U.S.A. **160** 46 11N 116 32W
Winchester, Ind., U.S.A. **156** 40 10N 84 56W
Winchester, Ky., U.S.A. **156** 38 0N 84 8W
Winchester, Mass., U.S.A. **162** 42 28N 71 10W
Winchester, N.H., U.S.A. **162** 42 47N 72 22W
Winchester, Tenn., U.S.A. **157** 35 11N 86 8W
Winchester, Va., U.S.A. **156** 39 14N 78 8W
Wind, R. **160** 43 30N 109 30W
Wind River Range, Mts. **160** 43 0N 109 30W
Windber **156** 40 14N 78 50W
Winder **157** 34 0N 83 40W
Windera **139** 26 17 S 151 51 E
Windermere **32** 54 24N 2 56W
Windermere, L. **32** 54 20N 2 57W
Windfall **152** 54 12N 116 13W
Windflower L. **152** 62 52N 118 30W
Windhoek **128** 22 35 S 17 4 E
Windischgarsten **52** 47 42N 14 21 E
Windmill Pt. **162** 37 35N 76 17W
Windom **158** 43 48N 95 3W
Windorah **138** 25 24 S 142 36 E
Window Rock **161** 35 47N 109 4W
Windrush, R. **28** 51 48N 1 35W
Windsor, Austral. **141** 33 37 S 150 50 E
Windsor, Newf., Can. **151** 48 57N 55 40W
Windsor, N.S., Can. **151** 44 59N 64 5W
Windsor, Ont., Can. **150** 42 18N 83 82W
Windsor, N.Z. **143** 44 59 S 170 49 E
Windsor, U.K. **29** 51 28N 0 36W
Windsor, Col., U.S.A. **158** 40 33N 104 55W
Windsor, Conn., U.S.A. **162** 41 50N 72 40W
Windsor, Miss., U.S.A. **158** 38 32N 93 31W
Windsor, N.Y., U.S.A. **162** 42 5N 75 37W
Windsor, Vt., U.S.A. **162** 43 30N 72 25W
Windsorton **128** 28 16 S 24 44 E
Windward Is. **167** 13 0N 63 0W
Windward Passage **167** 20 0N 74 0W
Windy L. **153** 60 20N 100 2W
Windygap **39** 52 28N 7 24W
Windygates **35** 56 12N 3 1W
Winefred L. **153** 55 30N 110 30W
Winejok **123** 9 1N 27 30 E
Winfield **159** 37 15N 97 0W
Wing **29** 51 54N 0 41W
Wingate Mts. **136** 14 25 S 130 40 E
Wingen **141** 31 54 S 150 54 E
Wingene **47** 51 3N 3 17 E
Wingham, Austral. **141** 31 48 S 152 22 E
Wingham, Can. **150** 43 55N 81 20W
Wingham, U.K. **29** 51 16N 1 12 E
Winifred **160** 47 30N 109 28W
Winisk **150** 55 20N 85 15W
Winisk L. **150** 52 55N 87 22W
Winisk, R. **150** 55 17N 85 5W
Wink **159** 31 49N 103 9W
Winkleigh **30** 50 49N 3 57W
Winkler **153** 49 15N 97 56W
Winklern **52** 46 52N 12 52 E
Winneba **121** 5 25N 0 36W
Winnebago **158** 43 43N 94 8W
Winnebago L. **156** 44 0N 88 20W
Winnecke Cr. **136** 18 35 S 131 34 E
Winnemucca **160** 41 0N 117 45W
Winnemucca, L. **160** 40 25N 19 21W
Winner **158** 43 23N 99 52W
Winnetka **156** 42 8N 87 46W
Winnett **160** 47 2N 108 28W
Winnfield **159** 31 57N 92 38W
Winnibigoshish L. **158** 47 25N 94 12W
Winning Pool **136** 23 9 S 114 30 E
Winnipeg **153** 49 50N 97 9W
Winnipeg Beach **153** 50 30N 96 58W
Winnipeg, L. **153** 52 0N 97 0W
Winnipeg, R. **153** 50 38N 96 19W
Winnipegosis **153** 51 39N 99 55W
Winnipegosis L. **153** 52 30N 100 0W
Winnipesaukee, L. **162** 43 38N 71 21W
Winnisquam L. **162** 43 33N 71 30W
Winnsboro, Lou, U.S.A. **159** 32 10N 91 41W
Winnsboro, S.C., U.S.A. **157** 34 23N 81 5W
Winnsboro, Tex., U.S.A. **158** 32 56N 95 15W
Winokapau, L. **151** 53 15N 62 50W
Winona, Miss., U.S.A. **159** 33 30N 89 42W
Winona, Wis., U.S.A. **158** 44 2N 91 45W
Winooski **156** 44 31N 73 11W
Winschoten **46** 53 9N 7 3 E
Winsen **48** 53 21N 10 11 E
Winsford **32** 53 12N 2 31W
Winslow, U.K. **29** 51 57N 0 52W
Winslow, U.S.A. **161** 35 2N 110 41W
Winstead **162** 41 55N 73 5W
Winster **33** 53 9N 1 42W
Winston-Salem **157** 36 7N 80 15W
Winsum **46** 53 20N 6 32 E
Winter Garden **157** 28 33N 81 35W
Winter Haven **157** 28 0N 81 42W
Winter Park **157** 28 34N 81 19W
Winterberg **48** 51 12N 8 30 E

Winterborne Abbas — Yaapeet

Winterborne Abbas 28 50 43N 2 30W
Winters 159 31 58N 99 58W
Winterset 158 41 18N 94 0W
Winterswijk 46 51 58N 6 43 E
Winterthur 51 47 30N 8 44 E
Winterton, Humberside, U.K. 33 53 39N 0 37W
Winterton, Norfolk, U.K. 29 52 43N 1 43 E
Winthrop, Minn., U.S.A. 158 44 31N 94 25W
Winthrop, Wash., U.S.A. 160 48 27N 120 6W
Winton, Austral. 138 22 24 S 143 3 E
Winton, N.Z. 143 46 8 S 168 20 E
Winton, U.S.A. 157 36 25N 76 58W
Wirksworth 33 53 5N 1 34W
Wirral 23 53 25N 3 0W
Wirraminna 140 31 12 S 136 13 E
Wirrulla 139 32 24 S 134 31 E
Wisbech 29 52 39N 0 10 E
Wisborough Green 29 51 2N 0 30W
Wisconsin □ 158 44 30N 90 0W
Wisconsin Dells 158 43 38N 89 45W
Wisconsin, R. 158 45 25N 89 45W
Wisconsin Rapids 158 44 25N 89 50W
Wisdom 147 45 36N 113 1W
Wiserman 147 67 25N 150 15W
Wishaw 35 55 46N 3 55W
Wishek 158 46 20N 99 35W
Wiske, R. 33 54 26N 1 27W
Wisła 53 49 38N 18 53 E
Wisła, R. 54 53 38N 18 47 E
Wisłok, R. 53 50 7N 22 25 E
Wisłoka, R. 53 49 50N 21 28 E
Wismar 48 53 53N 11 23 E
Wismar B. 48 54 0N 11 15 E
Wisner 158 42 0N 96 46W
Wissant 43 50 52N 1 40 E
Wissembourg 43 48 57N 7 57 E
Wissenkerke 47 51 35N 3 45 E
Wistoka, R. 54 49 50N 21 28 E
Witbank 129 25 51 S 29 14 E
Witchita 159 37 40N 97 22W
Witchyburn 37 57 37N 2 37W
Witdraai 128 26 58 S 20 48 E
Witham 29 51 48N 0 39 E
Witham, R. 33 53 3N 0 8W
Withern 33 53 19N 0 9 E
Withernsea 33 53 43N 0 2W
Witkowo 54 52 26N 17 45 E
Witley 29 51 9N 0 39W
Witmarsum 46 53 6N 5 28 E
Witney 28 51 47N 1 29W
Witnossob, R. 128 23 0 S 18 40 E
Wittdün 48 54 38N 8 23 E
Witten 48 51 26N 7 19 E
Wittenberg 48 51 51N 12 39 E
Wittenberge 48 53 0N 11 44 E
Wittenburg 48 53 30N 11 4 E
Wittenoom, W. Australia, Austral. 132 22 15 S 118 20 E
Wittenoom, W. Australia, Austral. 136 18 34 S 128 51 E
Wittersham 29 51 1N 0 42 E
Wittingen 48 52 43N 10 43 E
Wittlich 49 50 0N 6 54 E
Wittmund 48 53 39N 7 35 E
Wittow 48 54 37N 13 21 E
Wittstock 48 53 10N 12 30 E
Witzenhausen 48 51 20N 9 50 E
Wiveliscombe 28 51 2N 3 20W
Wivenhoe 29 51 51N 0 59 E
Wiyeb, W. 123 7 15N 40 15 E
Wladyslawowo 54 52 6N 18 28 E
Wlen 160 51 0N 15 39 E
Wlingi 103 8 5 S 112 25 E
Włocławek 54 52 40N 19 3 E
Włodawa 54 51 33N 23 31 E
Włoszczowa 54 50 50N 19 55 E
Woburn, U.K. 29 51 59N 0 37W
Woburn, U.S.A. 162 42 31N 71 7W
Woburn Sands 29 51 1N 0 38W
Wodonga 141 36 5 S 146 50 E
Wodzisław Sl. 54 50 1N 18 26 E
Woerden 46 52 5N 4 54 E
Woerht'ukou 106 42 35N 112 19 E
Woerth 43 48 57N 7 45 E
Woevre 43 49 15N 5 45 E
Wognum 46 52 40N 5 1 E
Wohlen 51 47 21N 8 17 E
Wokam, I. 103 5 45 S 134 28 E
Wokha 98 26 6N 94 16 E
Woking, Can. 152 55 35N 118 50W
Woking, U.K. 29 51 18N 0 33W
Wokingham 29 51 25N 0 50W
Wolbrom 54 50 24N 19 45 E
Woldegk 48 53 27N 13 35 E
Wolf Creek 160 47 1N 112 2W
Wolf L. 152 60 24N 133 42W
Wolf Point 158 48 6N 105 40W
Wolf, R. 152 60 17N 132 33W
Wolf Rock 30 49 56N 5 50W
Wolfe I. 150 44 7N 76 20W
Wolfeboro 162 43 35N 71 12W
Wolfenbüttel 48 52 10N 10 33 E
Wolfenden 152 52 0N 119 25W
Wolfheze 46 52 0N 5 48 E
Wolfram 138 17 6 S 145 0 E
Wolf's Castle 31 51 53N 4 57W
Wolfsberg 52 46 50N 14 52 E
Wolfsburg 48 52 27N 10 49 E
Wolgast 48 54 3N 13 46 E
Wolhusen 50 47 4N 8 4 E
Wolin 54 53 40N 14 37 E
Wollaston, Islas 176 55 40 S 67 30W
Wollaston L. 153 58 7N 103 10W
Wollaston Pen. 148 69 30N 115 0W
Wollogorang 138 17 13 S 137 57 E
Wollongong 141 34 25 S 150 54 E
Wolmaransstad 128 27 12 S 26 13 E
Wolmirstedt 48 52 15N 11 35 E
Wołomin 54 52 19N 21 15 E
Wołow 54 51 20N 16 38 E
Wolseley, Austral. 140 36 23 S 140 54 E
Wolseley, Can. 153 50 25N 103 15W
Wolseley, S. Afr. 128 33 26 S 19 7 E
Wolsingham 32 54 44N 1 52W
Wolstenholme Sound 12 74 30N 75 0W
Wolsztyn 54 52 8N 16 5 E
Wolvega 46 52 52N 6 0 E
Wolverhampton 28 52 35N 2 6W
Wolverton 29 52 3N 0 48W
Wolviston 33 54 39N 1 25W
Wombera 123 10 45N 35 49 E
Wombwell 33 53 31N 1 23W
Wommels 46 53 6N 5 36 E
Wonarah P.O. 138 19 55 S 136 20 E
Wonboyn 141 37 15 S 149 55 E
Wonck 47 50 46N 5 38 E
Wondai 139 26 20 S 151 49 E
Wondelgem 47 51 5N 3 44 E
Wonder Gorge 127 14 40 S 29 0 E
Wongalarroo L. 140 31 32 S 144 0 E
Wongan 137 30 51 S 116 37 E
Wongan Hills 137 30 53 S 116 42 E
Wongawal 137 25 5 S 121 55 E
Wonosari 103 7 38 S 110 36 E
Wŏnsan 107 39 11N 127 27 E
Wonston 28 51 9N 1 18W
Wonthaggi 141 38 37 S 145 37 E
Wonyulgunna Hill, Mt. 137 24 52 S 119 44 E
Woocalla 140 31 42 S 137 12 E
Wood Buffalo Nat. Park 152 56 28N 113 41W
Wood Green 138 22 26 S 134 12 E
Wood Is. 136 16 24 S 123 19 E
Wood L. 153 55 17N 103 17W
Wood Lake 158 42 38N 100 14W
Wood Mt. 153 49 14N 106 30W
Woodah I. 138 13 27 S 136 10 E
Woodanilling 137 33 31 S 117 24 E
Woodbine 162 39 14N 74 49W
Woodbourne 162 41 46N 74 35W
Woodbridge 29 52 6N 1 19 E
Woodburn 139 29 6 S 153 23 E
Woodbury, U.K. 30 50 40N 3 24W
Woodbury, U.S.A. 162 39 50N 75 9W
Woodchopper 147 65 25N 143 30W
Wooden Bridge 39 52 50N 6 13W
Woodend 140 37 20N 144 33 E
Woodford 39 53 3N 8 23W
Woodfords 163 38 47N 119 50W
Woodhall Spa. 33 53 10N 0 12W
Woodham Ferrers 29 51 40N 0 37 E
Woodlake 163 36 25N 119 6W
Woodland 160 38 40N 121 50W
Woodlands 137 24 46 S 118 8 E
Woodlark I. 135 9 10 S 152 50 E
Woodley 29 51 26N 0 54W
Woodpecker 152 53 30N 122 40W
Woodplumpton 32 53 47N 2 46W
Woodridge 153 49 20N 96 9W
Woodroffe, Mt. 137 26 20 S 131 45 E
Woodruff, Ariz., U.S.A. 161 34 51N 110 1W
Woodruff, Utah, U.S.A. 160 41 30N 111 4W
Woods, L., Austral. 138 17 50 S 133 30 E
Woods, L., Can. 151 54 30N 65 13W
Woods, Lake of the 153 49 30N 94 30W
Woodside, S. Australia, Austral. 140 34 58 S 138 52 E
Woodside, Victoria, Austral. 141 38 31 S 146 52 E
Woodstock, N.S.W., Austral. 141 33 45 S 148 53 E
Woodstock, Queens., Austral. 138 19 35 S 146 50 E
Woodstock, W.A., Austral. 136 21 41 S 118 57 E
Woodstock, N.B., Can. 151 46 11N 67 37W
Woodstock, Ont., Can. 150 43 10N 80 45W
Woodstock, U.K. 28 51 51N 1 20W
Woodstock, Ill., U.S.A. 158 42 17N 88 30W
Woodstock, Vt., U.S.A. 162 43 37N 72 31W
Woodstown 162 39 39N 75 20W
Woodville, N.Z. 142 40 20 S 175 53 E
Woodville, U.S.A. 159 30 45N 94 25W
Woodward 159 36 24N 99 28W
Woodward, Mt. 137 26 0 S 131 0 E
Woody 163 35 42N 118 50W
Wookey 28 51 13N 2 41W
Wookey Hole 28 51 13N 2 41W
Wool 28 50 41N 2 13W
Woolacombe 30 51 10N 4 12W
Woolamai, C. 141 38 30 S 145 23 E
Wooler 35 55 33N 2 0W
Woolgangie 137 31 12 S 120 35 E
Woolyeenyer, Mt. 137 32 16 S 121 47 E
Woombye 139 26 40 S 152 55 E
Woomera 140 31 11 S 136 47 E
Woonona 141 34 21 S 150 54 E
Woonsocket 162 42 0N 71 30W
Woonsockett 158 44 5N 98 15W
Wooramel 137 25 45 S 114 40 E
Wooramel, R. 137 25 30 S 114 30 E
Wooroloo 137 31 48 S 116 18 E
Wooroorooka 139 29 0 S 145 41 E
Wooster 156 40 38N 81 55W
Wootton Bassett 28 51 32N 1 55W
Wootton Wawen 28 52 16N 1 47W
Worb 50 46 56N 7 33 E
Worcester, S. Afr. 125 33 39 S 19 27 E
Worcester, U.K. 28 52 12N 2 12W
Worcester, Mass., U.S.A. 162 42 14N 71 49W
Worcester, N.Y., U.S.A. 162 42 35N 74 45W
Worcestershire (□) 26 52 13N 2 10W
Worfield 28 52 34N 2 22W
Wörgl 52 47 29N 12 3 E
Worikambo 121 10 43N 0 11W
Workington 32 54 39N 3 34W
Worksop 33 53 19N 1 9W
Workum 46 52 59N 5 26 E
Worland 160 44 0N 107 59W
Wormerveer 46 52 30N 4 46 E
Wormhoudt 43 50 52N 2 28 E
Wormit 35 56 26N 2 59W
Worms 49 49 37N 8 21 E
Worms Head 29 51 33N 4 19W
Worplesdon 29 51 16N 0 36W
Worsley 137 33 15 S 116 2 E
Wortham, U.K. 29 52 22N 1 3 E
Wortham, U.S.A. 159 31 48N 96 27W
Wörther See 52 46 37N 14 19 E
Worthing 29 50 49N 0 21W
Worthington 158 43 35N 95 30W
Wosi 103 0 15 S 128 0 E
Wota (Shoa Ghimirra) 123 7 4N 35 51 E
Wotton-under-Edge 28 51 37N 2 20W
Woubrugge 46 52 10N 4 39 E
Woudenberg 46 52 5N 5 25 E
Woudsend 46 52 56N 5 38 E
Wour 119 21 14N 16 0 E
Wouw 47 51 31N 4 23 E
Wowoni, I. 103 4 5 S 123 5 E
Woy Woy 141 33 30 S 151 19 E
Wragby 33 53 17N 0 18W
Wrangell 147 56 30N 132 25W
Wrangell, I. 152 56 20N 132 10W
Wrangell Mts. 147 61 40N 143 30W
Wrangle 33 53 3N 0 9 E
Wrath, C. 36 58 38N 5 0W
Wray 158 40 8N 102 18W
Wreck I. 162 37 12N 75 48W
Wrekin, The, Mt. 28 52 41N 2 35W
Wrens 157 33 13N 82 23W
Wrentham 29 52 24N 1 39 E
Wrexham 31 53 5N 3 0W
Wriezen 48 52 43N 14 9 E
Wright, Can. 152 51 52N 121 40W
Wright, Phil. 103 11 42N 125 2 E
Wright, Mt. 151 52 40N 67 25W
Wrightlington 28 51 18N 2 16W
Wrightson, Mt. 161 31 49N 110 56W
Wrightsville 162 40 2N 76 32W
Wrightwood 163 34 21N 117 38W
Wrigley 148 63 16N 123 27W
Writtle 29 51 44N 0 27 E
Wrocław 54 51 5N 17 5 E
Wrocław □ 54 51 0N 17 0 E
Wronki 54 52 41N 16 21 E
Wrotham 29 51 18N 0 20 E
Wroughton 28 51 31N 1 47W
Wroxham 29 52 42N 1 23 E
Września 54 52 21N 17 36 E
Wschowa 54 51 48N 16 20 E
Wu Chiang, R. 108 29 42N 107 20 E
Wu Shui, R. 109 27 7N 109 57 E
Wuan 106 36 45N 114 2 E
Wubin 137 30 6 S 116 37 E
Wuch'ang, Heilungkiang, China 107 44 55N 127 10 E
Wuch'ang, Hupeh, China 109 30 30N 114 15 E
Wuch'eng 108 30 48N 98 46 E
Wuch'i 108 31 28N 109 36 E
Wuchiang 109 31 10N 120 37 E
Wuchih Shan, mts. 100 18 45N 109 45 E
Wuch'ing 107 39 25N 117 7 E
Wuchou 105 23 33N 111 18 E
Wuch'uan, Inner Mong., China 106 41 8N 111 24 E
Wuch'uan, Kwangsi-Chuang, China 109 21 29N 110 49 E
Wuch'uan, Kweichow, China 108 28 30N 107 58 E
Wuchung 106 38 4N 106 12 E
Wufeng 109 30 12N 110 36 E
Wuhan 109 30 35N 114 15 E
Wuho 107 33 9N 117 53 E
Wuhsi 105 31 30N 120 20 E
Wuhsiang 106 36 50N 112 52 E
Wuhsing 109 30 49N 120 5 E
Wuhsüan 108 23 36N 109 39 E
Wuhu 105 31 18N 118 20 E
Wuhu (Wou-tou) 109 31 21N 118 30 E
Wui, Anhwei, China 109 28 53N 119 48 E
Wui, Hopeh, China 106 37 49N 115 54 E
Wui Shan, mts. 105 27 30N 117 30 E
Wukang 109 26 50N 110 15 E
Wukari 121 7 57N 9 42 E
Wulachieh 107 44 5N 126 27 E
Wulanhaot'e 105 46 5N 122 5 E
Wulanpulang 106 41 8N 110 56 E
Wulehe 121 3 42N 0 0 E
Wuliang Shan, mts. 108 24 0N 100 55 E
Wuliaru, I. 103 7 10 S 131 0 E
Wulien 107 35 45N 119 12 E
Wuluk'omushih Ling 105 36 25N 87 25 E
Wulumchi 105 43 40N 87 50 E
Wulunku Ho, R. 105 46 58N 87 28 E
Wum 121 6 40N 10 2 E
Wuming 108 23 11N 108 12 E
Wuneba 123 4 49N 30 22 E
Wuning 109 29 16N 115 0 E
Wunnummin L. 150 52 55N 89 10W
Wunsiedel 49 50 2N 12 0 E
Wunstorf 48 52 26N 9 29 E
Wuntho, Burma 98 21 44N 96 2 E
Wuntho, Burma 99 23 55N 95 45 E
Wupao 106 37 35N 110 45 E
Wup'ing 109 25 9N 116 5 E
Wuppertal, Ger. 48 51 15N 7 8 E
Wuppertal, S. Afr. 128 32 13 S 19 12 E
Wurarga 137 28 25 S 116 15 E
Würenlingen 51 47 32N 8 16 E
Wurung 138 19 13 S 140 38 E
Würzburg 49 49 46N 9 55 E
Wurzen 48 51 21N 12 45 E
Wushan, Kansu, China 106 34 42N 104 58 E
Wushan, Szechwan, China 108 31 3N 109 57 E
Wushench'i 106 38 57N 109 15 E
Wustrow . 48 54 4N 11 33 E
Wusu 105 44 27N 84 37 E
Wutai 106 38 44N 113 18 E
Wuti 107 37 46N 117 39 E
Wuting 108 25 33N 102 26 E
Wuting = Huimin 107 37 32N 117 33 E
Wuting Ho, R. 106 37 8N 110 25 E
Wut'ungch'iao 108 29 24N 104 0 E
Wutunghaolan 107 42 49N 120 11 E
Wuustwezel 47 51 23N 4 36 E
Wuwei, Anhwei, China 109 31 22N 117 55 E
Wuwei, Kansu, China 105 37 55N 102 48 E
Wuyang 106 33 25N 113 36 E
Wuyo 121 10 23N 11 50 E
Wuyüan, Inner Mong., China 106 41 6N 108 16 E
Wuyüan, Kiangsi, China 109 29 17N 117 54 E
Wuyün 105 49 17N 129 40 E
Wyaaba Cr. 138 16 27 S 141 35 E
Wyalkatchem 137 31 8 S 117 22 E
Wyalong 139 33 54 S 147 16 E
Wyalusing 162 41 40N 76 16W
Wyandotte 156 42 14N 83 13W
Wyandra 139 27 12 S 145 56 E
Wyangala Res. 141 33 54 S 149 0 E
Wyara, L. 139 28 42 S 144 14 E
Wych Farm, oilfield 19 50 38N 2 2W
Wycheproof 140 36 0N 143 17 E
Wye 29 51 11N 0 56 E
Wye, R. 28 52 0N 2 36W
Wyemandoo, Mt. 137 28 28 S 118 29 E
Wyk 48 54 41N 8 33 E
Wylfa Hd. 31 53 25N 4 28W
Wylye, R. 28 51 8N 1 53W
Wymondham, Leicester, U.K. 29 52 45N 0 42W
Wymondham, Norfolk, U.K. 29 52 34N 1 7 E
Wymore 158 40 10N 97 8W
Wynberg 128 34 2 S 18 28 E
Wynbring 139 30 33 S 133 32 E
Wyndham, Austral. 136 15 33 S 128 3 E
Wyndham, N.Z. 143 46 20 S 168 51 E
Wynne 159 35 15N 90 50W
Wynnstay 31 52 36N 3 33W
Wynnum 139 27 27 S 153 9 E
Wynyard 153 51 45N 104 10W
Wyola, L. 137 29 8 S 130 17 E
Wyoming □ 154 42 48N 109 0W
Wyong 141 33 14 S 151 24 E
Wyre Forest 28 52 24N 2 24W
Wyre, I. 37 59 7N 2 58W
Wyre, R. 37 53 52N 2 57W
Wyrzysk 54 53 10N 17 17 E
Wysoka 54 53 13N 17 2 E
Wyszków 54 52 36N 21 25 E
Wyszogród 54 52 23N 20 9 E
Wytheville 156 37 0N 81 3W

X

Xai-Xai 129 25 6 S 33 31 E
Xambioá 170 6 25 S 48 40W
Xanten 48 51 40N 6 27 E
Xanthí 68 41 10N 24 58 E
Xanthí □ 68 41 10N 24 58 E
Xapuri 174 10 35 S 68 35W
Xau 128 21 15 S 24 44 E
Xavantina 173 21 15 S 52 48W
Xenia 156 39 42N 83 57W
Xieng Khouang 100 19 17N 103 25 E
Xilókastron 69 38 4N 22 43 E
Xinavane 129 25 2 S 32 47 E
Xingu, R. 175 2 25 S 52 35W
Xiniás, L. 69 39 2N 22 12 E
Xique-Xique 170 10 50 S 42 40W
Xuan Loc 101 10 56N 107 14 E
Xuyen Moc 101 10 34N 107 25 E

Y

Ya 'Bud 90 32 27N 35 10 E
Yaamba 138 23 8 S 150 22 E
Yaan 108 30 0N 102 59 E
Yaapeet 140 35 45 S 142 3 E

Yabassi Yorktown

Yabassi	121	4 30N	9 57 E
Yabba North	141	36 13 S	145 42 E
Yabelo	123	4 57N	38 8 E
Yablanitsa	67	43 2N	24 5 E
Yablonovyy Khrebet	77	53 0N	114 0 E
Yabrīn	92	23 7N	48 52 E
Yach'i	108	27 35N	106 40 E
Yachiang	108	30 4N	101 7 E
Yacuiba	172	22 0 S	63 25W
Yadgir	96	16 45N	77 5 E
Yadkin, R.	157	36 15N	81 0W
Yadrin	81	55 57N	46 6 E
Yaeyama-Shotō	112	24 25N	124 0 E
Yagaba	121	10 14N	1 20W
Yagoua	124	10 20N	14 58 E
Yagur	90	32 45N	35 4 E
Yaha	101	6 29N	101 8 E
Yahk	152	49 6N	116 10W
Yahuma	124	1 0N	22 5 E
Yaihsien	100	18 14N	109 29 E
Yaizu	111	34 52N	138 20 E
Yajua	121	11 27N	12 49 E
Yakage	110	34 37N	133 35 E
Yakataga	147	60 5N	142 32W
Yakiang	99	30 4N	101 15 E
Yakima	160	46 42N	120 30W
Yakima, R.	160	47 0N	120 30W
Yako	120	12 59N	2 15W
Yakoruda	67	42 1N	23 29 E
Yakshur Bodya	84	57 11N	53 7 E
Yaku-Jima	112	30 20N	130 30 E
Yakut A.S.S.R. □	77	62 0N	130 0 E
Yakutat	147	59 50N	139 44W
Yakutsk	77	62 5N	129 40 E
Yala	101	6 33N	101 18 E
Yalabusha, R.	159	33 53N	89 50W
Yalbalgo	137	25 10 S	114 45 E
Yalboroo	138	20 50 S	148 40 E
Yalgoo	137	28 16 S	116 39 E
Yalikavak	69	37 6N	27 18 E
Yalinga	117	6 20N	23 10 E
Yalkubul, Punta	165	21 32N	88 37W
Y'allaq, G.	122	30 21N	33 31 E
Yalleroi	138	24 3 S	145 42 E
Yallourn	141	38 10 S	146 18 E
Yalpukh, Oz.	70	45 30N	28 41 E
Yalta	82	44 30N	34 10 E
Yalu Chiang, R.	107	39 45N	124 20 E
Yalung Chiang, R.	105	26 35N	101 45 E
Yalutorovsk	76	56 30N	65 40 E
Yam Kinneret	90	32 49N	35 36 E
Yamada	110	33 43N	130 49 E
Yamaga	110	33 1N	130 41 E
Yamagata	112	38 15N	140 15 E
Yamagata-ken □	112	38 30N	140 0 E
Yamagawa	110	31 12N	130 39 E
Yamaguchi	110	34 10N	131 32 E
Yamaguchi-ken □	110	34 20N	131 40 E
Yamal, Poluostrov	76	71 0N	70 0 E
Yamana	92	24 5N	47 30 E
Yamanaka	111	36 15N	136 22 E
Yamanashi-ken □	111	35 40N	138 40 E
Yamankhalinka	83	47 43N	49 21 E
Yamantau	78	54 20N	57 40 E
Yamantau, Gora	84	54 15N	58 6 E
Yamato	111	35 27N	139 25 E
Yamatotakada	111	34 31N	135 45 E
Yamazaki	110	35 0N	134 32 E
Yamba, N.S.W., Austral.	139	29 26 S	153 23 E
Yamba, S. Australia, Austral.	140	34 10 S	140 52 E
Yambah	138	23 10 S	133 50 E
Yâmbiô	123	4 35N	28 16 E
Yambol	67	42 30N	26 36 E
Yamdena	103	7 45 S	131 20 E
Yame	110	33 13N	130 35 E
Yamethin	98	20 29N	96 18 E
Yamil	121	12 53N	8 4 E
Yamma-Yamma L.	139	26 16 S	141 20 E
Yampa, R.	160	40 37N	108 0W
Yampi Sd.	136	16 8 S	123 38 E
Yampol	82	48 15N	28 15 E
Yamrat	121	10 11N	9 55 E
Yamrukohal, Mt.	67	42 44N	24 52 E
Yamun	90	32 29N	35 14 E
Yamuna (Jumna), R.	94	27 0N	78 30 E
Yan	121	10 5N	12 11 E
Yan Oya	97	9 0N	81 10 E
Yana, R.	77	69 0N	134 0 E
Yanac	140	36 8 S	141 25 E
Yanagawa	110	33 10N	130 24 E
Yanahara	110	34 58N	134 2 E
Yanam	96	16 47N	82 15 E
Yanaul	84	56 25N	55 0 E
Yanbu 'al Bahr	92	24 0N	38 5 E
Yancannia	139	30 12 S	142 35 E
Yanchep	137	31 30 S	115 45 E
Yanco	141	34 38 S	146 27 E
Yanco Cr.	141	35 14 S	145 35 E
Yandabome	138	7 1 S	145 46 E
Yandal	137	27 35 S	121 10 E
Yandanooka	137	29 18 S	115 29 E
Yandaran	138	24 43 S	152 6 E
Yandil	137	26 20 S	119 50 E
Yandoon	98	17 0N	95 40 E
Yanfolila	120	11 11N	8 9W
Yangambi	126	0 47N	24 20 E
Yangch'angtzukou	106	41 31N	109 1 E
Yangch'eng	106	35 32N	112 26 E
Yangchiang	109	21 55N	111 55 E
Yangchiaoch'iao	109	29 45N	112 45 E
Yangchiapa	106	42 6N	113 46 E
Yangchou	109	32 24N	119 26 E
Yangchoyung Hu	105	29 0N	90 40 E
Yangch'ü = T'aiyüan	106	37 55N	112 40 E
Yangch'üan	106	37 54N	113 36 E
Yangch'un	109	22 10N	111 47 E
Yanghsien	106	33 20N	107 30 E
Yanghsin	109	29 53N	115 10 E
Yangi-Yer	76	40 17N	68 48 E
Yangibazar	85	41 40N	70 53 E
Yangikishlak	85	40 25N	67 10 E
Yangiyul	85	41 0N	69 3 E
Yangku	106	36 8N	115 48 E
Yangliuch'ing	107	39 11N	117 9 E
Yangp'i	108	25 40N	100 0 E
Yangp'ing	109	31 13N	111 33 E
Yangp'ingkuan	106	33 2N	105 56 E
Yangshan	109	24 28N	112 38 E
Yangshuo	109	24 45N	110 24 E
Yangtze (Ch'ang Chiang)	109	1 48N	121 53 E
Yangyang	107	38 4N	128 38 E
Yangyüan	106	40 5N	114 12 E
Yanhee Res.	101	17 30N	98 45 E
Yanko Cr.	139	35 17 S	145 15 E
Yankton	158	42 55N	97 25W
Yanna	139	26 58 S	146 0 E
Yanonge	126	0 35N	24 38 E
Yantabulla	139	29 21 S	145 0 E
Yantra, R.	67	43 35N	25 37 E
Yany Kurgan	85	43 55N	67 15 E
Yao, Chad	117	12 56N	17 33 E
Yao, Japan	111	34 32N	135 36 E
Yao Yai, Ko	101	8 0N	98 35 E
Yaoan	108	25 32N	101 12 E
Yaoundé	121	3 50N	11 35 E
Yaowan	107	34 10N	118 3 E
Yap Is.	103	9 30N	138 10 E
Yapen	103	1 50 S	136 0 E
Yapen, Selat	103	1 20 S	136 10 E
Yapo, R.	174	0 30 S	77 0W
Yappar, R.	138	18 22 S	141 16 E
Yaqui, R.	164	28 28N	109 30W
Yar	84	58 14N	52 5 E
Yar-Sale	76	66 50N	70 50 E
Yaracuy □	174	10 20N	68 45W
Yaraka	138	24 53 S	144 3 E
Yaransk	81	57 13N	47 56 E
Yaratishky	80	54 3N	25 52 E
Yarcombe	30	50 51N	3 6W
Yarda	117	18 35N	19 0 E
Yardea P.O.	139	32 23 S	135 32 E
Yare, R.	29	52 36N	1 28 E
Yarensk	78	61 10N	49 8 E
Yarfa	122	24 40N	38 35 E
Yarí, R.	174	1 0N	73 40W
Yaringa North	137	25 53 S	114 30 E
Yaringa South	137	26 3 S	114 28 E
Yarkand = Soch'e	105	38 24N	77 20 E
Yarkhun, R.	95	36 30N	72 45 E
Yarm	33	54 31N	1 21W
Yarmouth, Can.	151	43 53N	65 45W
Yarmouth, U.K.	28	50 42N	1 29W
Yaroslavl	81	57 35N	39 55 E
Yarra Yarra Lakes	137	29 40 S	115 45 E
Yarraden	138	14 28 S	143 15 E
Yarraloola	136	21 33 S	115 52 E
Yarram	141	38 29 S	146 40 E
Yarraman	139	26 50 S	152 0 E
Yarraman Cr.	139	26 46 S	152 1 E
Yarranvale	139	26 50 S	145 20 E
Yarras	141	31 25 S	152 20 E
Yarrawonga	141	36 0 S	146 0 E
Yarrow	35	55 32N	3 0W
Yarrowee, R.	140	38 18 S	144 30 E
Yarto	140	35 28 S	142 16 E
Yartsevo	77	60 20N	90 0 E
Yarumal	174	6 58N	75 24W
Yaselda, R.	80	52 26N	25 30 E
Yashi	121	12 23N	7 54 E
Yashiro-Jima	110	33 55N	132 15 E
Yasin	95	36 24N	73 15 E
Yasinovataya	82	48 7N	37 57 E
Yasinski, L.	150	53 16N	77 35W
Yasnogorsk	81	54 32N	37 38 E
Yasothon	100	15 50N	104 10 E
Yass	141	34 49 S	148 54 E
Yasugi	110	35 26N	133 15 E
Yas'ur	90	32 54N	35 10 E
Yatagan	69	37 20N	28 10 E
Yate	28	51 32N	2 26W
Yates Center	159	37 53N	95 45W
Yates Pt.	143	44 29 S	167 49 E
Yathkyed L.	153	62 40N	98 0W
Yathong	141	32 37 S	145 33 E
Yatsuo	111	36 34N	137 8 E
Yatsushiro	110	32 30N	130 40 E
Yatsushiro-Kai	110	32 30N	130 25 E
Yatta	90	31 27N	35 6 E
Yatta Plat.	126	2 0 S	38 0 E
Yattah	90	31 27N	35 0 E
Yatton	28	51 23N	2 50W
Yauyos	174	12 10 S	75 50W
Yaval	96	21 10N	75 42 E
Yavan	85	38 19N	69 2 E
Yavari R.	174	4 50 S	72 0W
Yavorov	80	49 55N	23 20 E
Yawatahama	110	33 27N	132 24 E
Yawri B.	120	8 22N	13 0W
Yaxley	29	52 31N	0 14W
Yazagyo	98	23 30N	94 6 E
Yazd (Yezd)	93	31 55N	54 27 E
Yazdan	93	33 30N	60 50 E
Yazoo City	159	32 48N	90 28W
Yazoo, R.	159	32 35N	90 50W
Ybbs	52	48 12N	15 4 E
Yding Skovhøj	75	55 59N	9 46 E
Yea	141	37 14 S	145 26 E
Yealering	137	32 36 S	117 36 E
Yealmpton	30	50 21N	4 0W
Yearinan	141	31 10 S	149 11 E
Yebbi-Souma	119	21 7N	17 54 E
Yebbigué	119	22 30N	17 30 E
Yebel Jarris Tighzert, O.	118	28 10N	9 37W
Yebyu	99	14 15N	98 13 E
Yechŏn	107	36 39N	128 27 E
Yecla	59	38 35N	1 5W
Yécora	164	28 20N	108 58W
Yedashe	98	17 24N	95 50 E
Yeddou	118	28 5N	9 2W
Yeeda River	136	17 31 S	123 38 E
Yeelanna	139	34 9 S	135 45 E
Yefremov	81	53 15N	38 3 E
Yegorlyk, R.	83	46 15N	41 30 E
Yegorlykskaya	83	46 5N	40 35 E
Yegoryevsk	81	55 27N	38 55 E
Yegros	172	26 20 S	56 25W
Yehchih	108	27 39N	99 0 E
Yehsien	106	33 37N	113 20 E
Yehud	90	32 3N	34 53 E
Yehuda, Midbar	90	31 35N	34 57 E
Yei	123	4 3N	30 40 E
Yei, Nahr	123	5 50N	30 20 E
Yelan	81	50 55N	43 43 E
Yelan Kolenovski	81	51 16N	40 45 E
Yelandur	97	12 6N	77 0 E
Yelanskoye	77	61 25N	128 0 E
Yelarbon	139	28 33 S	150 49 E
Yelatma	81	55 0N	41 52 E
Yelets	81	52 40N	38 30 E
Yelimané	120	15 9N	22 49 E
Yell, I.	36	60 35N	1 5W
Yell Sd.	36	60 33N	1 15W
Yellamanchilli (Elamanchili)	96	17 26N	82 50 E
Yellow Sea	105	35 0N	123 0 E
Yellowdine	137	31 17 S	119 40 E
Yellowhead P.	152	52 53N	118 25W
Yellowknife	152	62 27N	114 21W
Yellowknife, R.	152	62 31N	114 19W
Yellowstone L.	160	44 30N	110 20W
Yellowstone National Park	160	44 35N	110 0W
Yellowstone, R.	158	46 35N	105 45W
Yelnya	80	54 35N	33 15 E
Yelsk	80	51 50N	29 3 E
Yelvertoft	138	20 13 S	138 53 E
Yelwa	122	10 49N	8 41 E
Yemanzhelinsk	84	54 58N	61 18 E
Yemen ■	91	15 0N	44 0 E
Yemen, South ■	74	15 0N	48 0 E
Yen Bai	100	21 42N	104 52 E
Yenakiyevo	82	48 15N	38 5 E
Yenan	106	36 42N	109 25 E
Yenangyaung	98	20 30N	95 0 E
Yenanma	98	19 46N	96 48 E
Yenchang	106	36 44N	110 2 E
Yench'eng, Honan, China	106	33 37N	114 0 E
Yench'eng, Kiangsu, China	107	33 24N	120 10 E
Yench'i	105	42 4N	86 34 E
Yenchi	107	42 53N	129 31 E
Yench'ih	106	37 47N	107 24 E
Yenchihsien	107	42 46N	129 24 E
Yenchin	108	28 4N	104 14 E
Yench'ing	106	40 28N	115 58 E
Yenching	108	29 7N	98 33 E
Yenchou	105	35 40N	116 50 E
Yench'uan	106	36 52N	110 11 E
Yenda	141	34 13 S	146 14 E
Yendéré	120	10 12N	4 59W
Yendi	121	9 29N	0 1W
Yenfeng	108	25 52N	101 5 E
Yenho	108	28 35N	108 28 E
Yenhsing	108	25 22N	101 44 E
Yenisaía	68	41 1N	24 57 E
Yenisey, R.	76	68 0N	86 30 E
Yeniseysk	77	58 39N	92 4 E
Yeniseyskiy Zaliv	76	72 20N	81 0 E
Yenne	45	45 43N	5 44 E
Yenotyevka	83	47 15N	47 0 E
Yenpien	108	26 54N	101 34 E
Yenshan, Hopeh, China	107	38 3N	117 12 E
Yenshan, Yunnan, China	108	23 40N	104 22 E
Yenshou	107	45 27N	128 19 E
Yent'ai	107	37 35N	121 25 E
Yent'ing	108	31 19N	105 20 E
Yenyüan	108	27 25N	101 33 E
Yenyuka	77	58 20N	121 30 E
Yeo, L.	137	28 0 S	124 30 E
Yeo, R.	28	51 1N	2 46W
Yeola	96	20 0N	74 30 E
Yeotmal	96	20 20N	78 15 E
Yeoval	141	32 41 S	148 39 E
Yeovil	28	50 57N	2 38W
Yepes	56	39 55N	3 39W
Yeppoon	138	23 5 S	150 47 E
Yeráki	69	37 0N	22 42 E
Yerbogachen	77	61 16N	108 0 E
Yerevan	83	40 10N	44 20 E
Yerilla	137	29 24 S	121 47 E
Yerington	163	38 59N	119 10W
Yerla, R.	96	17 35N	74 30 E
Yermakovo	77	52 35N	126 20 E
Yermo	163	34 58N	116 50W
Yermolayevo	78	52 58N	56 12 E
Yerofey Pavlovich	77	54 0N	122 0 E
Yerseke	47	51 29N	4 3 E
Yershov	81	51 15N	48 27 E
Yerūshalayim	90	31 47N	35 10 E
Yerville	42	49 40N	0 53 E
Yes Tor, Mt.	30	50 41N	3 59W
Yesagyo	98	21 38N	95 14 E
Yesan	107	36 41N	126 51 E
Yeşilirmak	82	41 0N	36 40 E
Yeso	159	34 29N	104 87W
Yessentuki	83	44 0N	42 45 E
Yeste	59	38 22N	2 19W
Yeu, I. d'	42	46 42N	2 20W
Yevlakh	83	40 39N	47 7 E
Yevpatoriya	82	45 15N	33 20 E
Yevstratovskiy	81	50 11N	39 2 E
Yeya, R.	83	46 40N	39 0 E
Yeysk Staro	82	46 40N	38 12 E
Yhati	172	25 45 S	56 35W
Yhú	173	25 0 S	56 0W
Yi, R.	172	33 7 S	57 8W
Yialí, I.	69	36 41N	27 11 E
Yiáltra	69	38 51N	22 59 E
Yianisádhes, I.	69	35 20N	26 10 E
Yiannitsa	68	40 46N	22 24 E
Yibal	91	22 10N	56 8 E
Yidhá	68	40 35N	22 53 E
Yinchiang	108	27 58N	108 20 E
Yinch'uan	105	38 30N	106 20 E
Yindarlgooda, L.	137	30 40 S	121 52 E
Ying Ho, R.	109	32 30N	116 32 E
Yingch'eng	109	30 55N	113 33 E
Yingchiang	108	24 48N	98 5 E
Yinghsien	106	39 36N	113 12 E
Yingk'ou	107	40 38N	122 30 E
Yingp'an, Chiang, G.	108	21 20N	109 30 E
Yingp'anshan	108	27 56N	105 34 E
Yingshan, Hupeh, China	109	31 37N	113 46 E
Yingshan, Hupeh, China	109	30 50N	115 45 E
Yingshan, Szechwan, China	108	31 6N	106 35 E
Yingshang	109	32 36N	116 16 E
Yingtan	105	28 12N	117 0 E
Yingte	109	24 10N	113 24 E
Yinkanie	140	34 22 S	140 17 E
Yinmabin	99	22 10N	94 55 E
Yinnietharra	137	24 39 S	116 12 E
Yioúra, I.	68	39 23N	24 10 E
Yipang	101	22 15N	101 26 E
Yirga Alem	124	6 34N	38 29 E
Yithion	69	36 46N	22 34 E
Yizre'el	90	32 34N	35 19 E
Ylitornio	74	66 19N	23 39 E
Ylivieska	74	64 4N	24 28 E
Yngaren	73	58 50N	16 35 E
Ynykchanskiy	77	60 15N	137 43 E
Yoakum	159	29 20N	97 10W
Yobuko	110	33 32N	129 54 E
Yog Pt.	103	13 55N	124 20 E
Yogyakarta	103	7 49 S	110 22 E
Yoho Nat. Park	152	51 25N	116 30W
Yojoa, L. de	166	14 53N	88 0W
Yŏju	107	37 20N	127 35 E
Yokadouma	124	3 35N	14 50 E
Yōkaichi	111	35 6N	136 12 E
Yōkaichiba	111	35 42N	140 33 E
Yokkaichi	111	35 0N	136 30 E
Yoko	121	5 50N	12 20 E
Yokohama	111	35 27N	139 39 E
Yokosuka	111	35 20N	139 40 E
Yokote	112	39 20N	140 30 E
Yola	121	9 10N	12 29 E
Yolaina, Cordillera de	166	11 30N	84 0W
Yom Mae Nam	101	15 15N	100 20 E
Yonago	110	35 25N	133 19 E
Yŏnan	107	37 55N	126 11 E
Yonezawa	112	37 57N	140 4 E
Yong Peng	101	2 0N	103 3 E
Yong Sata	101	7 8N	99 41 E
Yongampo	107	39 56N	124 23 E
Yŏngchon	107	35 58N	128 56 E
Yŏngdŏk	107	36 24N	129 22 E
Yŏngdŭngpo	107	37 31N	126 54 E
Yŏnghŭng	107	39 31N	127 18 E
Yŏngju	107	36 50N	128 40 E
Yŏngwŏl	107	37 11N	128 28 E
Yonibana	120	8 30N	12 19W
Yonker	153	52 40N	109 40W
Yonkers	162	40 57N	73 51W
Yonne □	43	47 50N	3 40 E
Yonne, R.	43	48 23N	2 58 E
Yonov	121	7 33N	8 42 E
Yoqueam	90	32 40N	35 6 E
York, Austral.	137	31 52 S	116 47 E
York, U.K.	33	53 58N	1 7W
York, Ala., U.S.A.	157	32 30N	88 18W
York, Nebr., U.S.A.	158	40 55N	97 35W
York, Pa., U.S.A.	162	39 57N	76 43W
York, C.	138	10 42 S	142 31 E
York Factory	153	57 0N	92 18W
York Haven	162	40 7N	76 46W
York, Kap	12	75 55N	66 25W
York, R.	162	37 15N	76 23W
York Sd.	136	14 50 S	125 5 E
York, Vale of	23	54 15N	1 25W
Yorke Pen.	140	34 50 S	137 40 E
Yorkshire Wolds	33	54 0N	0 30W
Yorkton	153	51 11N	102 28W
Yorktown, Tex., U.S.A.	159	29 0N	97 29W

Yorktown Zell

Yorktown, Va., U.S.A. **162** 37 14N 76 30W
Yornup **137** 34 2S 116 10E
Yoro **166** 15 9N 87 7W
Yosemite National Park **163** 38 0N 119 30W
Yosemite Village **163** 37 45N 119 35W
Yoshii **110** 33 16N 129 46E
Yoshimatsu **110** 32 0N 130 47E
Yoshkar Ola **81** 56 49N 47 10E
Yŏsu **107** 34 47N 127 45E
Youanmi **137** 28 37S 118 49E
Youbou **152** 48 53N 124 13W
Youghal **39** 51 58N 7 51W
Youghal B. **39** 51 55N 7 50W
Youkounkoun **120** 12 35N 13 11W
Young, Austral. **141** 34 19S 148 18E
Young, Can. **153** 51 47N 105 45W
Young, Uruguay **172** 32 44S 57 36W
Young, U.S.A. **161** 34 9N 110 56W
Young Ra. **143** 44 10S 169 30E
Younghusband, L. **140** 30 50S 136 5E
Younghusband Pen. **140** 36 0S 139 25E
Youngstown, Can. **153** 51 35N 111 10W
Youngstown, U.S.A. **156** 41 7N 80 41W
Youssoufia **118** 32 16N 8 31W
Yoweragabbie **137** 28 14S 117 39E
Yowrie **141** 36 17S 149 46E
Yoxall **28** 52 45N 1 49W
Yoxford **29** 52 16N 1 30E
Yozgat **92** 39 51N 34 47E
Ypané, R. **172** 23 29S 57 19W
Yport **42** 49 45N 0 15E
Ypres **47** 50 50N 2 52E
Ypsilanti **156** 42 18N 83 40W
Yreka **160** 41 44N 122 40W
Ysabel Chan. **135** 2 0S 150 0E
Ysbyty Ystwyth **31** 52 20N 3 50W
Ysleta **161** 31 45N 106 24W
Yssingeaux **45** 45 9N 4 8E
Ystad **73** 55 26N 13 50E
Ystalyfera **31** 51 46N 3 48W
Ystradgynlais **31** 51 47N 3 45W
Ystwyth, R. **31** 52 24N 4 2W
Ythan, R. **37** 57 26N 2 12W
Ytre Adal **71** 60 15N 10 14E
Ytterhogdal **72** 62 12N 14 56E
Ytyk-Kel **77** 62 20N 133 28E
Yü Chiang, R., China **105** 22 50N 108 6E
Yü Chiang, R., China **108** 22 50N 108 6E
Yu Shui, R. **108** 28 37N 110 23E
Yüan Chiang, R. **109** 29 0N 111 50E
Yüan Chiang, R (Hong.) **108** 29 12N 111 43E
Yüanan **109** 31 3N 111 34E
Yüanchiang, Hünan, China **109** 28 50N 112 23E
Yüanchiang, Yunnan, China **108** 23 40N 102 0E
Yüanch'ü **106** 35 18N 111 41E
Yüanli **109** 24 27N 120 39E
Yüanlin **109** 23 45N 120 30E
Yuanling **109** 28 30N 110 5E
Yüanmou **108** 25 42N 101 32E
Yuanyang **108** 23 10N 102 58E
Yüanyang **108** 35 3N 113 57E
Yuat, R. **135** 4 10S 143 52E
Yuba City **160** 39 12N 121 37W
Yūbari **112** 43 4N 141 59E
Yūbetsu **112** 43 13N 144 5E
Yucatán □ **165** 21 30N 86 30W
Yucatán Basin **14** 20 0N 84 0W
Yucatán Channel **166** 22 0N 86 30W
Yucca **161** 34 56N 114 6W
Yucca Valley **163** 34 8N 116 30W
Yücha **108** 26 55N 101 24E
Yucheng **106** 36 55N 116 40E
Yüch'i **108** 24 25N 102 35E
Yuch'i **109** 26 10N 118 11E
Yüchiang **109** 28 24N 116 53E
Yüch'ien **109** 30 12N 119 24E
Yüch'ing **108** 27 13N 107 54E
Yudino **76** 55 10N 67 55E
Yüehhsi, Anhwei, China **109** 30 54N 116 22E
Yüehhsi, Szechwan, China **108** 28 36N 102 35E
Yüehyang **109** 29 20N 113 7E
Yuendumu **136** 22 16S 131 49E
Yufu-Dake **110** 33 17N 131 33E
Yugoslavia ■ **66** 44 0N 20 0E
Yühsien **106** 34 10N 113 30E
Yuhsien, Hunan, China **109** 27 2N 113 20E
Yuhsien, Shansi, China **106** 38 5N 113 24E
Yühuan Tao, I. **109** 28 5N 121 15E
Yukan **109** 28 43N 116 35E
Yukhnov **80** 54 44N 35 15E
Yūki **111** 36 18N 139 53E
Yukon □ **147** 63 0N 135 0W
Yukon, R. **147** 65 30N 150 0W
Yukti **77** 63 20N 105 0E
Yukuhashi **110** 33 44N 130 59E
Yule, R. **136** 20 24S 118 12E
Yuli **122** 9 44N 10 12E
Yülin **100** 18 10N 109 31E
Yulin, Guangdong, China **109** 22 36N 110 7E
Yulin, Shensi, China **105** 38 15N 109 30E
Yuma, Ariz., U.S.A. **161** 32 45N 114 37W
Yuma, Colo., U.S.A. **158** 40 10N 102 43W
Yuma, B. de **167** 18 20N 68 35W
Yumali **140** 35 32S 139 45E
Yumbe **126** 3 28N 31 15E
Yumbi **126** 1 12S 26 15E
Yumbo **174** 3 35N 76 28W
Yümenhsien **105** 40 17N 97 12E
Yün Ho **107** 33 16N 118 45E
Yun Ho **109** 35 0N 117 0E
Yuna **137** 28 20S 115 0E
Yünan **109** 23 14N 111 31E
Yunaska I. **147** 52 40N 170 40W
Yünch'eng, Shansi, China **106** 35 1N 110 59E
Yünch'eng, Shantung, China **106** 35 35N 115 56E
Yunfou **109** 22 56N 112 2E
Yungan **109** 25 50N 117 25E
Yungas **174** 17 0S 66 0W
Yungay **172** 37 10S 72 5W
Yungch'eng **106** 33 56N 116 22E
Yungchi **106** 34 52N 110 26E
Yungch'ing **106** 39 19N 116 29E
Yungch'uan **108** 20 22N 105 52E
Yungch'un **109** 25 19N 118 17E
Yungfeng **109** 27 20N 115 27E
Yungfu **109** 24 59N 109 59E
Yungho **106** 36 44N 110 39E
Yunghsin **109** 16 55N 114 18E
Yunghsing **109** 26 8N 113 6E
Yunghsiu **109** 29 8N 115 42E
Yungjen **108** 26 4N 101 42E
Yungk'ang, Chekiang, China **109** 28 53N 120 2E
Yungk'ang, Kwangsi Chuang Aut. Region, China **108** 22 48N 107 51E
Yungnien **106** 36 49N 114 33E
Yungning, Kwangsi Chuang A. R., China **108** 22 45N 108 29E
Yungning, Ningsia Hui A. R., China **106** 38 18N 106 18E
Yungning, Yunnan, China **108** 27 50N 100 40E
Yungningchai **106** 36 35N 108 51E
Yungp'ing **108** 25 25N 99 36E
Yungshan **108** 28 11N 103 35E
Yungsheng **108** 26 42N 100 45E
Yungshun, Hunan, China **108** 29 3N 109 50E
Yungshun, Kwangsi Chuang, China **108** 22 48N 108 55E
Yungt'ai **109** 25 52N 118 55E
Yungteng **106** 36 44N 103 24E
Yungting **109** 24 49N 116 46E
Yunho = Lishui **109** 28 6N 119 34E
Yünhsi **109** 33 0N 110 22E
Yünhsiao **109** 24 1N 117 15E
Yünhsien, Hupeh, China **105** 32 50N 110 53E
Yünhsien, Yunnan, China **108** 24 25N 100 6E
Yünlin **109** 23 42N 120 31E
Yunling Shan, mts. **108** 28 30N 98 50E
Yunlung **99** 25 50N 99 25E
Yünmeng **109** 31 1N 113 39E
Yunnan □ **108** 25 0N 102 30E
Yunndaga **137** 29 45S 121 0E
Yunomae **110** 32 12N 130 59E
Yunotso **110** 35 5N 132 21E
Yunquera de Henares **58** 40 47N 3 11W
Yunta **140** 32 34S 139 36E
Yünyang **108** 30 55N 108 56E
Yüp'ing **108** 27 14N 108 54E
Yupyongdong **107** 41 49N 128 53E
Yur **77** 59 52N 137 49E
Yurga **76** 55 42N 84 51E
Yuria **84** 59 22N 54 10E
Yuribei **76** 71 20N 76 30E
Yurimaguas **174** 5 55S 76 0W
Yurya **81** 59 1N 49 13E
Yuryev Polskiy **81** 56 30N 59 47E
Yuryevets **81** 57 25N 43 2E
Yuryuzan **84** 54 27N 58 28E
Yuscarán **166** 13 58N 86 51W
Yusha, Jebel **90** 32 4N 35 41E
Yüshan **109** 28 40N 118 15E
Yüshanchen **108** 29 31N 108 25E
Yushe **106** 37 4N 112 58E
Yüshu **105** 33 1N 96 44E
Yushu **107** 44 46N 126 34E
Yüt'ai **106** 35 2N 116 40E
Yüt'ien **107** 39 53N 117 45E
Yütu **109** 26 0N 115 24E
Yütz'u **106** 37 42N 112 44E
Yüwang **106** 37 9N 106 28E
Yuyang **108** 28 44N 108 46E
Yüyang **109** 30 12N 119 56E
Yüyao **109** 30 3N 121 9E
Yuyao **109** 30 0N 121 20E
Yuyu **105** 40 20N 112 30E
Yuyü **106** 40 10N 112 25E
Yüyuan **109** 28 9N 121 11E
Yuzha **81** 56 40N 42 10E
Yuzhno-Sakhalinsk **77** 47 5N 142 5E
Yuzhno-Surkhanskoye Vodokhranilishehe **85** 37 53N 67 42E
Yuzhno-Uralsk **84** 54 26N 61 15E
Yuzhnyy Ural, mts. **84** 53 0N 58 0E
Yvelines □ **43** 48 40N 1 45E
Yverdon **50** 46 47N 6 39E
Yvetot **42** 49 37N 0 44E
Yvonand **50** 46 48N 6 44E

Z

Za, O. **118** 34 5N 2 30W
Zaalayskiy Khrebet **85** 39 20N 73 0E
Zaamslag **47** 51 19N 3 55E
Zaan, R. **46** 52 25N 4 52E
Zaandam **47** 52 26N 4 49E
Zab, Monts du **119** 34 55N 5 0E
Zabalj, Yugo. **66** 45 21N 20 5E
Zabalj, Yugo. **66** 45 23N 20 5E
Zabari **66** 44 22N 21 15E
Zabarjad **122** 23 40N 36 12E
Zabaykalskiy **77** 49 40N 117 10E
Zabkowice Slaskie **54** 50 22N 19 17E
Zabljak **66** 42 19N 19 10E
Zabludow **54** 53 0N 23 19E
Zabno **54** 50 9N 20 53E
Zābol **93** 31 0N 61 25E
Zābolī **93** 27 10N 61 35E
Zabré **121** 11 12N 0 36W
Zabrze **54** 50 24N 18 50E
Zacapa **166** 14 59N 89 31W
Zacapu **164** 19 50N 101 43W
Zacatecas **164** 22 49N 102 34W
Zacatecas □ **164** 23 30N 103 0W
Zacatecolua **166** 13 29N 88 51W
Zacaultipán **165** 20 39N 98 36W
Zacoalco **164** 20 10N 103 40W
Zadar **63** 44 8N 15 8E
Zadawa **121** 11 33N 10 19E
Zadetkyi Kyun **101** 10 0N 98 25E
Zadonsk **81** 52 25N 38 56E
Zafed **90** 32 58N 35 29E
Zafora, I. **69** 36 5N 26 24E
Zafra **57** 38 26N 6 30W
Zagan **54** 51 39N 15 22E
Zagazig **122** 30 40N 31 12E
Zaghouan **119** 36 23N 10 10E
Zaglivérion **68** 40 36N 23 15E
Zaglou **118** 27 17N 0 3W
Zagnanado **121** 7 18N 2 28E
Zagorá **68** 39 27N 23 6E
Zagora **118** 30 14N 5 51W
Zagórów **54** 52 10N 17 54E
Zagorsk **81** 56 20N 38 10E
Zagórz **54** 49 30N 22 14E
Zagreb **63** 45 50N 16 0E
Zāgros, Kudha-ye **93** 33 45N 47 0E
Zagubica **66** 44 15N 21 47E
Zaguinaso **120** 10 1N 6 14W
Zāhedān **93** 29 30N 60 50E
Zahirabad **96** 17 43N 77 37E
Zahlah **92** 33 52N 35 50E
Zahna **48** 51 54N 12 47E
Zahrez Chergui **118** 35 0N 3 30E
Zahrez Rharbi **118** 34 50N 2 55E
Zailiyskiy Alatau, Khrebet **85** 43 5N 77 0E
Zainsk **84** 55 18N 52 4E
Zaïr **118** 29 47N 5 51W
Zaïre, R. **124** 1 30N 28 0E
Zaïre, Rep. of ■ **124** 3 0S 23 0E
Zaječar **66** 43 53N 22 18E
Zakamensk **77** 50 23N 103 17E
Zakariya **90** 31 43N 34 57E
Zakataly **83** 41 38N 46 35E
Zakavkazye **83** 42 0N 44 0E
Zakhu **92** 37 10N 42 50E
Zákinthos **69** 37 47N 20 54E
Zåkinthos, I. **69** 37 45N 27 45E
Zakopane **54** 49 18N 19 57E
Zala □ **53** 46 42N 16 50E
Zala, R. **53** 46 53N 17 6E
Zalaegerszeg **53** 46 53N 16 47E
Zalakomár **53** 46 33N 17 10E
Zalalövö **53** 46 51N 16 35E
Zalamea de la Serena **57** 38 40N 5 38W
Zalamea la Real **57** 37 41N 6 38W
Zalau **121** 10 30N 8 58E
Zalazna **84** 58 39N 52 31E
Zalec **63** 46 16N 15 10E
Zaleshchiki **82** 48 45N 25 45E
Zalewo **54** 53 55N 19 41E
Zalingei **117** 13 5N 23 10E
Zalţan, Jabal **119** 28 46N 19 45E
Zaltbommel **46** 51 48N 5 15E
Zalŭ **121** 47 12N 23 5E
Zambeke **126** 2 8N 25 17E
Zambèze, R. **127** 18 46S 36 16E
Zambezi, R. **127** 18 46S 36 16E
Zambezia □ **127** 16 15S 37 30E
Zambia ■ **125** 15 0S 28 0E
Zamboanga **103** 6 59N 122 3E
Zambrano **174** 9 45N 74 49W
Zametchino **81** 53 30N 42 30E
Zamora, Mexico **164** 20 0N 102 21W
Zamora, Spain **56** 41 30N 5 45W
Zamora □ **56** 41 30N 5 46W
Zamosść **54** 50 50N 23 22E
Zamuro, Sierra del **174** 4 0N 62 30W
Zamzam, W. **119** 31 0N 14 30E
Zan **121** 9 26N 0 17W
Zanaga **124** 2 48S 13 48E
Záncara, R. **58** 39 20N 3 0W
Zandvoort **46** 52 22N 4 32E
Zanesville **156** 39 56N 82 2W
Zangue, R. **127** 18 5S 35 10E
Zanjan **92** 36 40N 48 35E
Zannone, I. **64** 40 38N 13 2E
Zante = Zákinthos **69** 37 47N 20 54E
Zanthus **137** 31 2S 123 34E
Zanzibar **126** 6 12S 39 12E
Zanzibar I. **126** 6 12S 39 12E
Zanzūr **119** 32 55N 13 1E
Zaouatalaz **119** 24 57N 8 16E
Zaouiet El Kahla **119** 27 10N 6 40E
Zaouiet Reggane **118** 26 32N 0 3E
Zapadna Morava, R. **66** 43 50N 20 15E
Zapadnaya Dvina **80** 56 15N 32 3E
Západné Beskydy **54** 49 30N 19 0E
Zapadočesky □ **52** 49 35N 13 0E
Západoslovenský □ **53** 48 30N 17 30E
Zapala **176** 39 0S 70 5W
Zapaleri, Cerro **172** 22 49S 67 11W
Zapata **159** 26 56N 92 17W
Zapatón, R. **57** 39 0N 6 49W
Zaporozhye **82** 47 50N 35 10E
Zapponeta **65** 41 27N 15 57E
Zara **92** 39 58N 37 43E
Zaragoza, Colomb. **174** 7 30N 74 52W
Zaragoza, Coahuila, Mexico **164** 28 30N 101 0W
Zaragoza, Nuevo León, Mexico **165** 24 0N 99 36W
Zaragoza, Spain **58** 41 39N 0 53W
Zaragoza □ **58** 41 35N 1 0W
Zarand **93** 30 46N 56 34E
Zarasai **80** 55 40N 26 12E
Zarate **172** 34 7S 59 0W
Zaraysk **81** 54 48N 38 53E
Zaraza **174** 9 21N 65 19W
Zarembo I. **152** 56 20N 132 50W
Zari **73** 13 8N 12 37E
Zaria **121** 11 0N 7 40E
Zarisberge **128** 24 30S 16 15E
Zarki **54** 50 38N 19 21E
Zarnów **54** 51 16N 20 9E
Zarnuqa **90** 31 53N 34 47E
Zarów **54** 50 56N 16 29E
Zarqa, R. **90** 32 10N 35 37E
Zaruma **174** 3 40S 79 30W
Zary **54** 51 37N 15 10E
Zarza de Alange **57** 38 49N 6 13W
Zarza de Granadilla **56** 40 14N 6 3W
Zarza, La **57** 37 42N 6 51W
Zarzaîtine **119** 28 32N 9 5E
Zarzal **174** 4 24N 76 4W
Zarzis **119** 33 31N 11 2E
Zas **56** 43 4N 8 53W
Zashiversk **77** 67 25N 142 40E
Zaskar Mountains **95** 33 15N 77 30E
Zaskar, R. **95** 33 55N 77 2E
Zastron **128** 30 18S 27 7E
Zatec **52** 50 20N 13 32E
Zator **54** 49 59N 19 28E
Zavala **66** 42 50N 17 59E
Zavareh **93** 33 35N 52 28E
Zaventem **47** 50 53N 4 28E
Zavetnoye **83** 47 13N 43 50E
Zavidovici **66** 44 27N 18 13E
Zavitinsk **77** 50 10N 129 20E
Zavodoski, I. **13** 56 0S 27 45W
Zavolzhye **81** 56 37N 43 18E
Zawadzkie **54** 50 37N 18 28E
Zawidów **54** 51 1N 15 1E
Zawiercie **54** 50 30N 19 13E
Zâwyet Shammâs **122** 31 30N 26 37E
Zâwyet Um el Rakham **122** 31 18N 27 1E
Zâwyet Ungeila **122** 31 23N 26 42E
Zayandeh, R. **93** 32 35N 32 0E
Zayarsk **77** 56 20N 102 55E
Zaysan **76** 47 28N 84 52E
Zaysan, Oz. **76** 48 0N 83 0E
Zāzamt, W. **119** 30 29N 14 30E
Zazir, O. **119** 22 0N 5 40E
Zázrivá **53** 49 16N 19 7E
Zbarazh **80** 49 43N 25 44E
Zbaszyn **54** 52 14N 15 56E
Zbaszynek **54** 52 16N 15 51E
Zblewo **54** 53 56N 18 19E
Zdandijk **46** 52 82N 4 49E
Zdolbunov **80** 50 30N 26 15E
Zdrelo **66** 44 16N 21 28E
Zdunska Wola **54** 51 37N 18 59E
Zduny **54** 51 39N 17 21E
Zeballos **152** 49 59N 126 50W
Zebediela **129** 24 20S 29 17E
Zedelgem **47** 51 8N 3 8E
Zeebrugge **47** 51 19N 3 12E
Zeehan **138** 41 52S 145 25E
Zeeland **47** 51 41N 5 40E
Zeeland □ **47** 51 30N 3 50E
Ze'elim **90** 31 13N 34 32E
Zeelst **47** 51 25N 5 25E
Zeerust **128** 25 31S 26 4E
Zefat **90** 32 58N 35 29E
Zegdou **118** 29 51N 4 53W
Zege **123** 11 43N 37 18E
Zegelsem **47** 50 49N 3 43E
Zegoua **120** 10 32N 5 35W
Zehdenick **48** 52 59N 13 20E
Zeil, Mt. **136** 23 24S 132 23E
Zeila **91** 11 15N 43 30E
Zeist **46** 52 5N 5 15E
Zeita **90** 32 23N 35 2E
Zeitz **48** 51 3N 12 9E
Zele **47** 51 4N 4 2E
Zelendolsk **81** 55 55N 48 30E
Zelengora, mts. **66** 43 22N 18 30E
Zelenika **66** 42 27N 18 37E
Zelenogradsk **80** 54 53N 20 29E
Zelenokumsk **83** 44 30N 44 1E
Zelenovski **83** 48 6N 50 45E
Zelhem **47** 52 0N 6 21E
Zell **49** 47 42N 7 50E

Place				
Zell am See	52	47 19N	12	47 E
Zella Mehlis	48	50 40N	10	41 E
Zelouane	86	35 1N	2	58W
Zelzate	47	51 13N	3	47 E
Zémio	126	5 2N	25	5 E
Zemmora	118	35 44N	0	51 E
Zemora, I.	119	37 5N	10	56 E
Zemoul, W.	118	29 15N	7	30W
Zemst	47	50 59N	4	28 E
Zemun	66	44 51N	20	25 E
Zenica	66	44 10N	17	57 E
Zenina	118	34 30N	2	37 E
Zentsūji	110	34 14N	133	47 E
Zepce	66	44 28N	18	2 E
Zeravshan	85	39 10N	68	39 E
Zeravshan, R.	85	39 32N	63	45 E
Zeravshanskiy, Khrebet	85	39 20N	69	0 E
Zerbst	48	51 59N	12	8 E
Zerhamra	118	29 58N	2	30W
Zerków	54	52 4N	17	32 E
Zermatt	50	46 2N	7	46 E
Zernez	51	46 42N	10	7 E
Zernograd	83	46 52N	40	11 E
Zeroud, O.	119	35 30N	9	30 E
Zerqani	68	41 30N	20	20 E
Zestafoni	83	42 6N	43	0 E
Zetel	48	53 33N	7	57 E
Zetland (□)	26	60 30N	0	15W
Zetten	46	51 56N	5	44 E
Zeulenroda	48	50 39N	12	0 E
Zeven	48	53 17N	9	19 E
Zevenaar	46	51 56N	6	5 E
Zevenbergen	47	51 38N	4	37 E
Zévio	62	45 23N	11	10 E
Zeya	77	54 2N	127	20 E
Zeya, R.	77	53 30N	127	0 E
Zeyse	123	5 44N	37	23W
Zeytin	92	37 53N	36	53 E
Zêzere, R.	56	40 0N	7	55W
Zgierz	54	51 45N	19	27 E
Zgorzelec	54	51 10N	15	0 E
Zhabinka	80	52 13N	24	2 E
Zhailma	84	51 30N	61	50 E
Zhalanash	85	43 3N	78	38 E
Zhamensk	80	54 37N	21	17 E
Zhanadarya	85	44 45N	64	40 E
Zhanatas	76	43 11N	81	18 E
Zharkol	84	49 57N	64	5 E
Zharkovskiy	80	55 56N	32	19 E
Zhashkov	82	49 15N	30	5 E
Zhdanov	82	47 5N	37	31 E
Zheleznogorsk-Ilimskiy	77	56 34N	104	8 E
Zherdevka	81	51 56N	41	21 E
Zhetykol, Ozero	84	51 2N	60	54 E
Zhigansk	77	66 35N	124	10 E
Zhigulevsk	81	53 28N	49	45 E
Zhirhovsk	81	50 57N	44	49 E
Zhitomir	80	50 20N	28	40 E
Zhizdra	80	53 45N	34	40 E
Zhlobin	80	52 55N	30	0 E
Zhmerinka	82	49 2N	28	10 E
Zhodino	80	54 5N	28	17 E
Zhovtnevoye	82	47 54N	32	2 E
Zhuantobe	85	43 43N	78	18 E
Zhukovka	80	53 35N	33	50 E
Zhupanovo	77	51 59N	15	9 E
Ziarat	94	30 25N	67	30 E
Zichem	47	51 2N	4	59 E
Ziebice	54	50 37N	17	2 E
Ziel, Mt.	136	23 20 S	132	30 E
Zielona Góra	54	51 57N	15	31 E
Zielona Góra □	54	51 57N	15	30 E
Zierikzee	47	51 40N	3	55 E
Ziesar	48	52 16N	12	19 E
Zifta	122	30 43N	31	14 E
Zigazinskiy	84	53 50N	57	20 E
Zigey	117	14 50N	15	50 E
Ziguinchor	120	12 25N	16	20W
Zihuatanejo	164	17 38N	101	33W
Zikhron Ya'Aqov	90	32 34N	34	56 E
Zile	92	40 15N	36	0 E
Zilfi	92	26 12N	44	52 E
Zilina	53	49 12N	18	42 E
Zillah	119	28 40N	17	41 E
Zillertaler Alpen	52	47 6N	11	45 E
Zima	77	54 0N	102	5 E
Zimane, Adrar in	118	22 10N	4	30 E
Zimapán	165	20 40N	99	20W
Zimba	127	17 20 S	26	25 E
Zimbabwe Rhodesia ■	127	20 16 S	31	0 E
Zimovniki	83	47 10N	42	25 E
Zinal	50	46 8N	7	38 E
Zinder	121	13 48N	9	0 E
Zinga	127	9 16 S	38	41 E
Zingem	47	50 54N	3	40 E
Zingst	48	54 24N	12	45 E
Zini, Yebel	118	28 0N	11	0W
Ziniaré	121	12 44N	1	10W
Zinjibar	91	13 5N	46	0 E
Zinkgruvan	73	58 50N	15	6 E
Zinnowitz	48	54 5N	13	54 E
Zion Nat. Park	161	37 25N	112	50W
Zipaquirá	174	5 0N	74	0W
Zippori	90	32 64N	35	16 E
Zirc	53	47 17N	17	42 E
Ziri	63	47 17N	11	14 E
Zirje, I.	63	43 39N	15	42 E
Zirl	52	47 17N	11	14 E
Zisterdorf	53	48 33N	16	45 E
Zitácuaro	164	19 20N	100	30W
Zitava, R.	53	48 14N	18	21 E
Zitiste	66	45 30N	2	32 E
Zitsa	68	39 47N	20	40 E
Zittau	48	50 54N	14	47 E
Zitundo	129	26 48 S	32	47 E
Zivinice	66	44 27N	18	36 E
Ziway, L.	123	8 0N	38	50 E
Ziz, Oued	118	31 40N	4	15W
Zizip	92	37 5N	37	50 E
Zlarin	63	43 42N	15	49 E
Zlatar	63	46 5N	16	3 E
Zlataritsa	67	43 2N	24	55 E
Zlatibor	66	43 45N	19	43 E
Zlatista	67	42 41N	24	7 E
Zlatna	70	46 8N	23	11 E
Zlatograd	67	41 22N	25	7 E
Zlatoust	78	55 10N	59	40 E
Zletovo	66	41 59N	22	17 E
Zlitan	119	32 25N	14	35 E
Złocieniec	54	53 30N	16	1 E
Złoczew	54	51 24N	18	35 E
Zlot	66	44 1N	22	0 E
Złotoryja	54	51 8N	15	55 E
Złotów	54	53 22N	17	2 E
Złoty Stok	54	50 27N	16	53 E
Zmeinogorsk	76	51 10N	82	13 E
Żmigród	54	51 28N	16	53 E
Zmiyev	82	49 45N	36	27 E
Znamenka	82	48 45N	32	30 E
Znin	54	52 51N	17	44 E
Znojmo	52	48 50N	16	2 E
Zoar	128	33 30 S	21	26 E
Zobia	126	3 0N	25	50 E
Zoetermeer	46	52 3N	4	30 E
Zofingen	50	47 17N	7	56 E
Zogno	62	45 49N	9	41 E
Zolder	47	51 1N	5	19 E
Zollikofen	50	47 0N	7	28 E
Zollikon	51	47 21N	8	34 E
Zolochev	80	49 45N	24	58 E
Zolotonosha	82	49 45N	32	5 E
Zomba	127	15 30 S	35	19 E
Zombi	126	3 35N	29	10 E
Zomergem	47	51 7N	3	33 E
Zongo	124	4 12N	18	0 E
Zonguldak	82	41 28N	31	50 E
Zonhoven	47	50 59N	5	23 E
Zorgo	121	12 22N	0	35W
Zorita	57	39 17N	5	39W
Zorleni	70	46 14N	27	44 E
Zornitsa	67	42 23N	26	58 E
Zorritos	174	3 50 S	80	40W
Zory	54	50 3N	18	44 E
Zorzor	120	7 46N	9	28W
Zossen	48	52 13N	13	28 E
Zottegam	47	50 52N	3	48 E
Zouar	119	20 30N	16	32 E
Zouérabe	116	22 35N	12	30W
Zousfana, O.	118	31 51N	1	30W
Zoutkamp	46	53 20N	6	18 E
Zqorzelec	54	51 9N	15	0 E
Zrenjanin	66	45 22N	20	23 E
Zuarungu	121	10 49N	0	52W
Zuba	121	9 11N	7	12 E
Zubair, Jazâir	123	15 0N	42	10 E
Zubia	57	37 8N	3	33W
Zubtsov	80	56 10N	34	34 E
Zueitina	119	30 58N	20	7 E
Zuénoula	120	7 34N	6	3W
Zuera	58	41 51N	0	49W
Zug	51	47 10N	8	31 E
Zug □	51	47 9N	8	35 E
Zugar	123	14 0N	42	40 E
Zugdidi	83	42 30N	41	48 E
Zugersee	51	47 7N	8	35 E
Zugspitze	49	47 25N	10	59 E
Zuid-Holland □	46	52 0N	4	35 E
Zuid-horn	46	53 15N	6	23 E
Zuidbeveland	47	51 30N	3	50 E
Zuidbroek	46	53 10N	6	52 E
Zuidelijk-Flevoland	46	52 22N	5	22 E
Zuidlaarder meer	46	53 8N	6	42 E
Zuidland	46	51 49N	4	15 E
Zuidlaren	46	53 6N	6	42 E
Zuidwolde	46	52 40N	6	26 E
Zújar	59	37 34N	2	50W
Zújar, Pantano del	57	38 55N	5	35W
Zújar, R.	59	38 30N	5	30 E
Zula	123	15 17N	39	40 E
Zulia □	174	10 0N	72	10W
Zülpich	48	50 41N	6	39 E
Zululand	129	43 19N	2	15W
Zumaya	58	43 19N	2	15W
Zumbo	127	15 35 S	30	26 E
Zummo	121	9 51N	12	59 E
Zumpango	165	19 48N	99	6W
Zundert	47	51 28N	4	39 E
Zungeru	121	9 48N	6	8 E
Zuni	161	35 7N	108	57W
Zupania	66	45 4N	18	43 E
Zur	66	42 13N	20	34 E
Zura	84	57 36N	53	24 E
Zŭrandului	70	46 14N	22	7 E
Zürich	51	47 22N	8	32 E
Zürich □	51	47 26N	8	40 E
Zürichsee	51	47 18N	8	40 E
Zuromin	54	53 4N	19	57 E
Zuru	121	11 27N	5	4 E
Zurzach	51	47 35N	8	18 E
Zut, I.	63	43 52N	15	17 E
Zutendaal	47	50 56N	5	35 E
Zutphen	46	52 9N	6	12 E
Zuwárrah	119	32 58N	12	1 E
Zuyevka	84	58 27N	51	10 E
Zuzemberk	63	45 52N	14	56 E
Zvenigorodka	82	49 4N	30	56 E
Zverinogolovskoye	84	55 0N	62	30 E
Zvezdets	67	42 6N	27	26 E
Zvolen	53	48 33N	19	10 E
Zvonce	66	42 57N	22	34 E
Zvornik	66	44 26N	19	7 E
Zwaag	46	52 40N	5	4 E
Zwanenburg	46	52 23N	4	45 E
Zwarte Meer	46	52 38N	5	57 E
Zwarte Waler	46	52 39N	6	1 E
Zwartemeer	46	52 43N	7	2 E
Zwartsluis	46	52 39N	6	4 E
Zwedru (Tchien)	120	5 59N	8	15W
Zweibrücken	49	49 15N	7	20 E
Zwenkau	48	51 13N	12	19 E
Zwetti	52	48 35N	15	9 E
Zwickau	48	50 43N	12	30 E
Zwijnaarde	47	51 0N	3	43 E
Zwijndrecht, Belg.	47	51 13N	4	20 E
Zwijndrecht, Neth.	46	51 50N	4	39 E
Zwolle	46	52 31N	6	6 E
Zymoelz, R.	152	54 33N	128	31W
Zyrardów	54	52 3N	20	35 E
Zywiec	54	44 42N	19	12 E

Alternative Spellings

NOTE: The following list gives the principal places where new names or spellings (given first) have been adopted. Earlier forms still in use are cross referenced to the new form. Place names of which the national spelling varies considerably from the English form, e.g. Livorno – Leghorn, are also included.

Aachen, Aix la Chapelle
Aalst: Alost
Abercorn, see Mbala
Abo, see Turku
Acre, see 'Akko
Adrianople, see Edirne
Affreville, see Khemis Miliana
Agram, see Zagreb
Agrigento: Girgenti
Ahvenanmaa: Åland Is.
Aix la Chapelle, see Aachen
Ain Mokra, see Berrahal
Ain Salah, see In Salah
Ain Touta: MacMahon
'Akko: Acre
Akmolinsk, see Tselinograd
Al Hoceima: Alhucemas, Villa Sanjurjo
Al Khalih: Hebron
Al Khums, see Homs
Al Lādhiqiyah: Latakia
Al Marj: Barce
Al Mawsil: Mosul
Al Mukha: Mocha
Al Qasabat: Cussabat
Al Quds: Jerusalem
Åland Is., see Ahvenanmaa
Alashantsoch'i: Payenhaot'e
Alba Iulia: Karlsburg
Albert, L., see Mobutu Sese Seko, L.
Albertville, see Kalemie
Alcazarquivir, see Ksar el Kebir
Aleppo, see Halab
Alexandretta, see İskenderun
Alexandria, see El Iskandarîya
Alhucemas, see Al Hoceima
Allenstein, see Olsztyn
Amraoti: Amravati
An Geata Mór: Binghamstown
An Nhon: Binh Dinh
An Uaimh: Navan
Andulo, see Macedo da Cavaleiros
Ankara: Angora
Annaba: Bône
Annobón, see Pagalu
Antakya: Antioch
Anvers: Antwerp, Antwerpen
Apollonia, see Marsa Susa
Ar Riyād: Riyadah
Arabian Gulf, see Persian G.
Arkhangelsk: Archangel
Arlon: Aarlen
Artemovsk: Bakhmut
Athínai: Athens
Augusto Cardosa: Metangula
Aumale, see Sour el Ghozlane
Auschwitz, see Oswiecim

Bac Lieu, see Vinh Loi
Bagenalstown, see Muine Bheag
Bahia, see Salvador
Baile Átha Cliath: Dublin
Baile Deasmhumhna: Ballydesmond
Bakhmut, see Artemovsk
Bakwanga, see Mbuji-Mayi
Ballydesmond, see Baile Deasmhumhna
Baltiysk: Pillau
Banaras, see Varanasi
Banda Aceh: Kutaradja
Bandar Maharani, see Muar
Bandar Penggarem, see Batu Pahat
Bandundu: Banningville
Banghāzī: Benghazi
Bangladesh: East Pakistan
Banjul: Bathurst
Barce, see Al Marj
Baroda, see Vadodara
Basel: Basle
Basutoland, see Lesotho
Batavia, see Jakarta
Batu Pahat: Bandar Penggarem
Bayan Tumen, see Choybalsan
Béchar: Colomb-Béchar
Bechuanaland Prot. see Botswana
Bedeau, see Ras el Ma
Bejaïa: Bougie
Belém: Pará
Belgard, see Białogard
Belize: British Honduras
Belogorsk: Kuibyshevka Vostochnaya
Benares, see Varanasi
Benghazi: Banghāzī
Benin: Dahomey
Beograd: Belgrade
Berdyansk: Osipenko
Bern: Berne
Berrahal: Ain Mokra
Bezwada, see Vijayawada
Bharat: India

Bharuch: Broach
Bhavnagar: Bhaunagar
Bhilsa, see Vidisha
Białogard: Belgrad
Binghamstown, see An Geata Mór
Binh Dinh, see An Nhon
Bir Mogrein: Fort Trinquet
Bitola: Monastir
Björneborg, see Pori
Bolzano: Bozen
Bône, see Annaba
Borgå, see Porvoo
Botswana: Bechuanaland Prot.
Bougie, see Bejaïa
Brahestad, see Raahe
Braniewo: Braunsberg
Bratislava: Pressburg
Braunsberg, see Braniewo
Breslau, see Wrocław
Bressanone: Brixen
Brest: Brest Litovsk
British Guiana, see Guyana
British Honduras, see Belize
Brixen, see Bressanone
Brno: Brünn
Broach, see Bharuch
Broken Hill, see Kabwe
Brugge: Bruges
Brunico: Bruneck
Brünn, see Brno
Brusa, see Bursa
Bruxelles: Brussel, Brussels
Bucureşti: Bucharest
Budweis, see České Budějovice
Bujumbura: Usumbura
Bukavu; Costermansville
Bunclody: Newtownbarry
Bursa: Brusa

Ca Mau, see Quang Long
Caesarea, see Qesari
Cairo, see El Qâhira
Calicut: Kozhikode
Cambridge: Galt
Candia, see Iráklion
Canton, see Kuangchou
Caporetto, see Kobarid
Caribrod, see Dimitrovgrad
Carlsbad, see Karlovy Vary
Carmona: Uige
Cattaro, see Kotor
Cawnpore, see Kanpur
Ceanannus Mór: Kells
Ceará, see Fortaleza
Celebes, see Sulawesi
Cerigo, see Kíthira
Cernauti, see Chernovtsy
České Budějovice: Budweis
Ceylon, see Sri Lanka
Chad: Tchad
Changan, see Hsian
Changchiak'ou: Kalgan
Charleville, see Rath Luirc
Chefoo, see Yent'ai
Chemnitz, see Karl Marx Stadt
Chemulpho, see Inch'ŏn
Cheribon, see Cirebon
Chernovtsy: Cernauti, Czernowitz
Chernyakhovsk: Insterberg
Ch'ich'ihaerh: Lungkiang
Chihli: Po Hai
Chilin: Yungki
Chilumba: Deep Bay
Chilung: Keelung
Chios, see Khíos
Chipata: Fort Jameson
Chisinau, see Kishinev
Chistyakovo, see Thorez
Chitipa: Fort Hill
Chkalov, see Orenburg
Choybalsan: Bayan Tumen
Chongjin: Seishin
Chtimba: Florence Bay
Churchill, R.: Hamilton R.
Cieszyn: Teschen
Cirebon: Cheribon
Cluj: Klausenburg
Coatzacoalcos: Pto. Mexico
Cocanada, see Kakinada
Colomb-Béchar, see Béchar
Cologne: Köln
Congo (Kinshasa), see Zaïre
Conjeeveram, see Kanchipuram
Constance, see Konstanz
Constanţa: Küstenje
Constantinople, see İstanbul
Copenhagen, see København
Coquilhatville, see Mbandaka
Corfu, see Kérkira
Corunna, see La Coruña
Costermansville, see Bukavu

Courtrai, see Kortrijk
Craigavon: Lurgan and Portadown
Crete, see Kríti
Cuamba, see Novo Freixo
Cussabat, see Al Qasabat
Cyclades, see Kikládhes
Cyrene, see Shahhat
Czernowitz, see Chernovtsy

Dahomey, see Benin
Dairen, see Lüta
Damascus, see Dimashq
Damietta, see Dumyât
Danzig, see Gdańsk
Daugavpils: Dvinsk
Deep Bay, see Chilumba
Deutsch Krone, see Wałcz
Dimashq: Damascus
Dimitrovgrad: Caribrod
Dimitrovo, see Pernik
Djerba: Houmt Souk
Djibouti: Fr. Terr. of the Afars & the Issas
Dnepropetrovsk: Yekaterinoslav
Dobrich, see Tolbukhin
Donetsk: Stalino
Dor: Tantura
Dorpat, see Tartu
Drissa, see Verchnedvinsk
Droichead Nua: Newbridge
Dublin, see Baile Átha Cliath
Dubrovnik: Ragusa
Dumyât: Damietta
Dunaújváros: Sztalinvaros
Dundo: Portugalia
Dunkerque: Dunquerque, Dunkirk
Durrësi: Durazzo
Dushanbe: Stalinbad
Dvinsk, see Daugavpils
Dzaudzhikau, see Ordzhonikidze

East Pakistan, see Bangladesh
Edirne: Adrianople
Edward, L., see Idi Amin Dada, L.
Eisenhüttenstadt: Stalinstadt, Furstenberg
El Asnam: Orléansville
El Bayadh: Géryville
El Eulma: St. Arnaud
El Harrach: Maison Carrée
El Iskandarîya: Alexandria
El Jadida: Mazagan
El Kala: La Calle
El Qâhira: Cairo
El Suweis: Suez
Elbiag: Elbing
Elizabethville, see Lubumbashi
Ellore: Eluru, Elluru
Escaut, see Schelde
Esfahân: Isfahan
Essaouira: Mogador
Evvoia: Euboea

Faizabad: Fyzabad
F'Dérik: Fort Gouraud
Fengtien, see Shenyang
Fernando Póo, see Macias Nguema Biyoga
Firenze: Florence
Fiume, see Rijeka
Flanders, see Vlaanderen
Florence Bay, see Chtimba
Florence, see Firenze
Flushing, see Vissingen
Formosa, see Taiwan
Fort de Polignac, see Illizi
Fort Flatters, see Zaouiet El-Kahla
Fort Gouraud, see F'Dérik
Fort Hall, see Muranga
Fort Jameson, see Chipata
Fort Lamy, see Ndjamena
Fort Rosebery, see Mansa
Fort Rousset, see Owando
Fort Rupert: Rupert House
Fort Hill, see Chitipa
Fort Manning, see Mchinji
Fort Trinquet, see Bir Mogrein
Fortaleza: Ceará
Fredrikshald, see Halden
French Terr. of the Afars & the Issas:, see Djibouti
Fribourg: Freiburg
Frunze: Pishpek
Fuchou: Minhow
Fünfkirchen, see Pécs
Fyzabad, see Faizabad

Gagarin: Gzhatsk
Gago Coutinho, see Lumbala
Gallipoli, see Gelibolu

Galt, see Cambridge
Gamlakarleby, see Kokkola
Gand, see Gent
Gävle: Gefle
Gdańsk: Danzig
Gelibolu: Gallipoli
Geneva (Lake), see Léman
Genève: Geneva (Town)
Genoa: Génova
Gent: Gand, Ghent
George River, see Port Nouveau-Québec
Géryville, see El Bayadh
Ghazaouet: Nemours
Ghent, see Gent
Girgenti, see Agrigento
Glatz, see Kłodzko
Gliwice: Gleiwitz
Glorenza: Glurns
Glubczyce: Leobschütz
Goleniów: Gollnow
Gorkiy: Nijni Novgorod
Gorodok, see Zakamensk
Göteborg: Gothenburg
Gottwaldov: Zlin
Great Whale River, see Poste de la Baleine
Grosswardein, see Oradea
Guardafui, C., see Ras Asir
Guinea-Bissau: Portuguese Guinea
Gunza: Porto Amboim
Guyana: British Guiana
Gzhatsk, see Gagarin

Haeju: Haiju
Haerhpin: Pinkiang
Hailaer; Hulun
Halab: Haleb, Aleppo
Halden: Fredrikshald
Haleb, see Halab
Halq el Qued: La Goulette
Hamadia: Victor Hugo
Hamilton R., see Churchill R.
Hämeenlinna: Tavastehus
Hannover: Hanover
Hebron, see Al Khalih
Heijo, see P'yöngyang
Helsinki: Helsingfors
Hermannstadt, see Sibiu
Hirschberg, see Jelenia Góra
Hollandia, see Jayapura
Homs: Al Khums, Leptis Magna
Hot Springs, see Truth or Consequences
Hot'ien: Khotan
Houmt Souk, see Djerba
Hovd: Jargalant, Kobdo
Hsian: Changan
Hulun, see Hailaer

Iaşi: Jassy
Ibiza: Iviza
Idi Amin Dada, L.: Edward, L.
Ieper: Ypres
Ighil Izane: Relizane
Ilebo: Port Francqui
Illizi: Fort de Polignac
In Salah: Ain Salah
Inch'ŏn: Chemulpho
India: Bharat
Inoucdjouac: Port Harrison
Insterberg, see Chernyakhovsk
Iráklion: Candia
Iran: Persia
Isfahan, see Esfahân
İskenderun: Alexandretta
Isiro: Paulis
İstanbul: Constantinople
Ivano-Frankovsk: Stanislav
Iviza, see Ibiza
Izmir: Smyrna

Jabalpur: Jubbulpore
Jadotville, see Likasi
Jaffa, see Tel Aviv-Yafo
Jakarta: Batavia
Jambi: Telanaipura
Jamnagar: Navanagar
Jargalant, see Hovd
Jassy, see Iaşi
Javhlant, see Ulyasutay
Jayapura: Sukarnapura, Hollandia
Jelenia Góra: Hirschberg
Jelgava: Mitau
Jerusalem: Al Quds
Jesselton, see Kota Kinabalu
João Pessoa: Paraiba
Jubbulpore, see Jabalpur

Kabwe: Broken Hill
Kakinada: Cocanada
Kalamata: Kalámai
Kalemie: Albertville

Kalgan, see Changchiak'ou
Kalinin: Tver
Kaliningrad: Königsberg
Kananga: Luluabourg
Kanchipuram: Conjeeveram
Kanchow: Kanhsien
Kanpur: Cawnpore
Kaolan, see Lanchou
Karl Marx Stadt: Chemnitz
Karlovac: Karlstadt
Karlsburg, see Alba Iulia
Karlstadt, see Karlovac
Karlovy Vary: Carlsbad
Kaschau, see Košice
Kaskinen, see Kaskö
Katowice: Stalinogrod
Kaunas: Kovno
Keelung, see Chilung
Keijo, see Sŏul
Kells, see Ceanannus Mór
Kendrapara: Kendlapara
Kenitra: Port Lyautey
Kérkira: Corfu
Khanh Hung: Soc Trang
Khemelnitski: Proskurov
Khemis Miliana, see Affreville
Khíos: Chios
Khodzhent, see Leninabad
Khotan, see Hot'ien
Kikládhes: Cyclades
Kinshasa: Leopoldville
Kirov: Viatka, Vyatka
Kirovgrad: Kirovo Yelisavetgrad, Zinovyevsk
Kisangani: Stanleyville
Kishinev: Chisinau
Kitakyūshū: Kokura, Moji, Tobata, Wakamatsu & Yawata
Kíthira: Cerigo
Klaipeda: Memel
Klausenburg, see Cluj
Kłodzko: Glatz
Kobarid: Caporetto
Kobdo, see Hovd
København: Copenhagen
Kokkola: Gamlakarleby
Kokura, see Kitakyūshū
Kolarovgrad, see Šumen
Kolchugino, see Leninsk Kuznetski
Köln, see Cologne
Kolobrzeg: Kolberg
Kommunarsk: Voroshilovsk, Stavropol
Königsberg, see Kaliningrad
Konstanz: Constance
Kortrijk: Courtrai
Košice: Kaschau
Koszalin: Köslin
Kota Kinabalu: Jesselton
Kotor: Cattaro
Kovna, see Kaunas
Kozhikode, see Calicut
Kraljevo: Rankovicevo
Krasnodar: Yekaterinodar
Kristiinankaupunki: Kristinestad
Kríti: Krete, Crete
Kropotkin: Romanovsk
Ksar Chellala: Reibell
Ksar el Kebir: Alcazarquivir
Kuangchou: Canton, Panyu
Kuçovè, see Qytet Stalin
Kuybyshev: Samara
Kuibyshevka Vostochnaya, see Belogorsk
K'unming: Yunnan
Küstenje, see Constanţa
Kutaraja, see Banda Aceh

La Calle, see El Kala
La Coruña: Corunna
La Goulette, see Halq el Qued
Laibach, see Ljubljana
Lanchou: Kaolan
Lappeenranta: Villmanstrand
Latakia, see Al Lādhiqiyah
Lauenburg, see Lebork
Lebork: Lauenburg
Leeu-Gamka: Fraserburg Road
Leghorn, see Livorno
Legnica: Liegnitz
Léman, Lake: Geneva, Lake
Lemberg, see Lvov
Leninabad: Khodzhent
Leninsk Kuznetski: Lenino, Kolchugino
Lensk: Mukhtuya
Leobschütz, see Glubczyce
Leopold II, L., see Mai-Ndombe, L.
Léopoldville, see Kinshasa
Leptis Magna, see Homs
Lesotho: Basutoland
Leuven: Louvain

Liberec: Reichenberg
Liegnitz, see Legnica
Liepaja: Libau
Likasi: Jadotville
Lisboa: Lisbon
Livorno: Leghorn
Llanelli: Llanelly
Ljubljana: Laibach
Lod: Lydda
Lourenço Marques, see Maputo
Louvain, see Leuven
Luau: Lunda
Lubumbashi: Elizabethville
Lucerne, see Luzern
Luena: Moxico
Lugansk, see Voroshilovgrad
Luluabourg, see Kananga
Lumbala: Gago Coutinho
Luofu: Lubero
Lurgan, see Craigavon
Lunda, see Luau
Lungkiang, see Ch'ich'ihaerh
Lüta: Port Arthur and Dairen
Luxembourg: Luxemburg
Luzern: Lucerne
Lvov: Lwow, Lemberg
Lydda, see Lod
Lyon: Lyons

Maas, see Meuse
Macedo da Cavaleira: Andulo
Machilipatnam: Masulipatnam
Macias Nguema Biyoga:
   Fernando Póo
MacMahon, see Ain Touta
Madura: Madurai
Magallanes, see Punta Arenas
Maghnia: Marnia
Mai-Ndombe, L.: Leopold II, L.
Maison Carrée, see El Harrach
Majorca, see Mallorca
Malawi: Nyasaland
Malawi, L.: L. Nyasa
Malbork: Marienburg
Malines, see Mechelen
Mallorca: Majorca
Mandsaur: Mandasor
Mansa: Fort Rosebery
Mantes-la-Jolie: Mantes
   Gassicourt
Mantova: Mantua
Maputo: Lourenço Marques
Maranhão, see São Luís
Marburg, see Maribor
Marchand, see Rommani
Marek, see Stanke Dimitrov
Maria Theresiopel, see Subotica
Mariánské Lázně: Marienbad
Maribor: Marburg
Maricourt: Wakeham Bay
Marienburg, see Malbork
Mariupol, see Zhdanov
Marnia, see Maghnia
Marsa Susa: Apollonia
Marseille: Marseilles
Masulipatnam, see Machilipatnam
Mathura: Muttra
Mayuram: Mayavaram
Mazagan, see El Jadida
Mbala: Abercorn
Mbandaka: Coquilhatville
Mbanza Congo: S. Salvador
   do Congo
Mbini, see Rio Muni
Mbuji-Mayi: Bakwanga
Mchinji: Fort Manning
Meathas Truim:
   Edgeworthstown
Mechelen: Malines
Memel, see Klaipeda
Menorca: Minorca
Menongue: Serpa Pinto
Me'ona: Tarshiha
Merano: Meran
Metangula, see
   Augusto Cardosa
Meuse: Maas
Mikkeli: Sankt Michel
Milano: Milan
Minhow, see Fuchou
Minorca, see Menorca
Misratah: Misurata
Mitau, see Jelgava
Mobutu Sese Seko, L.: Albert, L.
Mocha, see Al Mukha
Mogador, see Essaouira
Mohammedia: Perrégaux
Moji, see Kitakyūshū
Molotov, see Perm
Molotovsk, see Severodvinsk
Monastir, see Bitola
Montagnac, see Remchi
Montgomery, see Sahiwal
Moskva: Moscow
Mosul, see Al Mawsil
Moxico, see Luena
Muar: Bandar Maharani
Mukden, see Shenyang
Muine Bheag: Bagenalstown
Mukhtuya, see Lensk
München: Munich
Muranga: Fort Hall

Muscat & Oman, see Oman
Muttra, see Mathura

Najin: Rashin
Namibia: South West Africa
Namur: Namen
Nanning: Yungning
Nápoli: Naples
Navan, see An Uaimh
Navanagar, see Jamnagar
Ndalatando: Salazar
Ndjamena: Fort Lamy
Neemuch: Nimach
Neisse, see Nysa
Nemours, see Ghazaouet
Netherlands Guiana, see
   Surinam(e)
Neusatz, see Novi Sad
Neustettin, see Szczecinek
Newbridge (Ire.), see
   Droichead Nua
Newtonbarry, see Bunclody
Nictheroy, see Niteroi
Nieuwport: Nieuport
Nijni Novgorod, see Gorkiy
Nikolaistad, see Vaasa
Nimach, see Neemuch
Nisa, see Nysa
Niteroi: Nichteroy
Northern Rhodesia, see Zambia
Nouadhibou: Port Etienne
Nouveau Comptoir: Paint Hills
Nova Freixo: Cuamba
Novi Becej: Volosinovo
Novi Sad: Neusatz
Novokuznetsk: Stalinsk
Novomoskovsk: Stalinogorsk
Novosibirsk: Novo Nikolaevsk
Nsanje: Port Herald
Nürnberg: Nuremberg
Nyahururu: Thompson's Falls
Nyasa, L., see Malawi, L.
Nyasaland, see Malawi
Nykarleby, see Uusikaarlepyy
Nysa: Nisa, Neisse
Nyslott, see Savonlinna
Nystad, see Uusikaupunki

Odenburg, see Sopron
Olomouc: Olmutz
Olsztyn: Allenstein
Oman: Muscat & Oman
Ongiva: Va. Pereira d'Eça
Opole: Oppeln
Oporto, see Pôrto
Oradea: Grosswardein
Oran: Ouahran
Ordzhonikidze: Dzaudzihikau
Orléansville, see El Asnam
Orenburg: Chkalov
Osipenko, see Berdyansk
Ostende: Oostende, Ostend
Oswiecim: Auschwitz
Ouagadougou: Wagadugu
Ouargla: Wargla
Oulu: Uleåborg
Owando: Ft. Rousset

Pagalu: Annobón
Paint Hills, see
   Nouveau Comptoir
Pahangkaraya: Pahandut
Panyu, see Kuangchou
Paoshan: Yungchang
Paoting: Tsingyuan
Papua New Guinea: Papua, N. E.
   New Guinea
Pará, see Belém
Paraiba, see João Pessoa
Pátrai: Patras
Paulis, see Isiro
Payenhaot'e, see Alashantsoch'i
Pécs: Fünfkirchen
Peip'ing: Peking
Perm: Molotov
Pernambuco, see Recife
Pernik: Dimitrovo
Perrégaux, see Mohammedia
Persia, see Iran
Persian Gulf: Arabian G.
Phanh Bho Ho Chi Minh: Saigon
Philippeville, see Skikda
Philippopolis, see Plovdiv
Pillau, see Baltiysk
Pilsen, see Plzeň
Pinkiang, see Haerhpin
Piraevs: Piraeus, Peiraieus,
   Pireets
Pishpek, see Frunze
Plovdiv: Philippopolis
Plzeň, Pilsen
Podgorica, see Titograd
Po Hai, see Chihli
Pola, see Pula
Ponthierville, see Ubundı
Poona, see Pune
Pori: Björneborg
Port Arthur, see Lüta
Port Etienne, see Nouadhibou
Port Francqui, see Ilebo
Port Harrison, see Inoucdjouac
Port Herald, see Nsanje

Port Lyautey, see Kenitra
Port Nouveau-Québec:
   George River
Portadown, see Craigavon
Pôrto: Oporto
Porto Amboim, see Gunza
Portugalia, see Dundo
Portuguese Guinea, see Guinea-
   Bissau
Porvoo: Borgå
Poste de la Baleine:
   Great Whale River
Poznan: Posen
Praha: Prague
Pressburg, see Bratislava
Proskurov, see Khmelnitski
Puerto Mexico, see
   Coatzacoalcos
Pula: Pola
Pune: Poona
Punta Arenas: Magallanes
P'yŏngyang: Heijo

Qesari: Caesarea
Quang Long: Ca Mau
Quelpart, see Cheju-do
Qytet Stalin: Kuçovë

Raahe: Brahestad
Raciborz: Ratibor
Ragusa, see Dubrovnik
Rahaeng, see Tak
Rankovicevo, see Kraljevo
Ras Asir: Cape Guardafui
Ras el Ma: Bedeau
Rashïd: Rosetta
Rashin, see Najin
Rass el Oued: Tocqueville
Rath Luirc: Charleville
Ratibor, see Raciborz
Ratisbon, see Regensburg
Recife: Pernambuco
Regensburg: Ratisbon
Reibell, see Ksar Chellala
Reichenberg, see Liberec
Relizanne, see Ighil Izane
Remchi: Montagnac
Revel, see Tallinn
Rezā'iyeh, L.: Urmia, L.
Rhodes, see Rodhós
Rhodesia: Southern Rhodesia,
   Zimbabwe
Rijeka: Fiume
Rio Muni, see Mbini
Riyadah, see Ar Riyād
Rodhós: Rhodes
Roeselare: Roulers
Roma: Rome
Romanovsk, see Kropotkin
Rommani: Marchand
Roraima: Rio Branco
Rosetta: Rashid
Roulers, see Roeselare
Rovinj: Rovigno
Rudolf, L., see Turkana,L.
Rupert House, see Fort Rupert
Ruse: Ruschuk
Rybinsk: Shcherbakov

Saglouc: Sugluk
Sahiwal: Montgomery
Saïda: Sidon
Saigon, see Phanh Bho Ho Chi Minh
Saint Arnaud, see El Eulma
Saint Denis, see Sig
Saint Gall: Sankt Gallen
Saint Nicolas, see Sint Niklaas
Salazar, see Ndalatando
Salonika, see Thessaloníki
Salvador: Bahia
Samara, see Kuybyshev
Sambor: Sandan
Sankt Gallen, see Saint Gall
Sankt Michel: Mikkeli
Santo Domingo: Ciudad
   Trujillo
São Luís: Maranhão
S. Salvador do Congo, see
   Mbanza Congo
Saragossa, see Zaragoza
Savonlinna: Nyslott
Schässburg, see Sighişoara
Schelde: Escaut, Scheldt
Schweidnitz, see Świdnica
Scutari (Albania), see Shkodra
Scutari (Turkey), see Usküdar
Sedom: Sodom
Seishin, see Chongjin
Sept Iles: Seven Islands
Serpa Pinto, see Menongue
Severodvinsk: Molotovsk
Sevilla: Seville
's Gravenhage: The Hague
Shahhat: Cyrene
Shcherbakov, see Rybinsk
Sheki: Nukha
Shenyang: Mukden, Fengtien
Shetland: Zetland
Shkodra: Scutari
Siam, see Thailand
Sibiu: Hermannstadt
Sidon, see Saïda

Sig: St. Denis
Sighişoara: Schässburg
Simbirsk, see Ulyanovsk
Singora, see Songkhla
Sint Niklaas: Saint Nicolas
Siracusa: Syracuse
Skikda: Philippeville
Skopje: Skoptje, Usküb
Sliten, see Zlïtan
Smyrna, see Izmir
Soc Trang, see Khanh Hung
Soch'e: Yarkand
Sodom, see Sedom
Sofiya: Sofia
Sombor: Zombor
Songkhla: Singora
Sopron: Odenburg
Sŏul: Keijo
Sour el Ghozlane: Aumale
Sousse: Susa
South West Africa, see Namibia
Southern Rhodesia, see
   Rhodesia
Sovetsk: Tilsit
Split: Spalato
Sri Lanka: Ceylon
Stalin, see Varna
Stalinabad, see Dushanbe
Stalingrad, see Volgograd
Staliniri, see Tskhinvali
Stalino, see Donetsk
Stalinogorsk, see
   Novomoskovsk
Stalinogrod, see Katowice
Stalinsk, see Novokuznetsk
Stalinstad, see Eisenhüttenstadt
Stanislav, see Ivano-Frankovsk
Stanke Dimitrov: Marek
Stanleyville, see Kisangani
Stettin, see Szczecin
Sterzing: Vipiteno
Stolp, see Słupsk
Stolpmünde, see Ustka
Stuhlweissenburg, see
   Székesfehérvár
Subotica: Maria Theresiopel
Suchou: Wuhsien
Suez, see El Suweis
Sugluk, see Saglouc
Sukarnapura, see Jayapura
Sulawesi: Celebes
Šumen: Kolarovgrad
Sūr: Tyre
Surinam(e): Netherlands Guiana
Susa, see Sousse
Sverdlovsk: Yekaterinburg
Świdnica: Schweidnitz
Syracuse, see Siracusa
Szczecin: Stettin
Szczecinek: Neustettin
Székesfehérvár:
   Stuhlweissenburg
Sztalinvaros, see Dunaújváros

Tagdempt, see Tiaret
T'aipei: Taihoku
Taiwan: Formosa
T'aiyüan: Yangku
Tak: Rehaeng
Tallinn: Revel, Reval
Tampere: Tammefors
Tanganyika, see Tanzania
Tantura, see Dor
Tanzania: Tanganyika
   and Zanzibar
Tarābulus, see Tripoli
Tarshiha, see Me'ona
Tartu: Dorpat
Tavastehus, see Hämeenlinna
Tbilisi: Tiflis
Tchad, see Chad
Tel Aviv-Yafo: Jaffa, Tel Aviv
Telanaipura: Jambi
Tende: Tenda
Teschen, see Cieszyn
Thailand: Siam
Thebes, see Thívai
The Hague, see 's-Gravenhage
Thessaloníki: Salonika
Tiaret: Tagdempt
Thívai: Thebes
Thompson's Falls, see Nyahururu
Thorez: Christyakovo
Tiflis, see Tbilisi
Tihwa, see Wulumuchi
Tilsit, see Sovetsk
Timbuktu, see Tombouctou
Tiruchchirappalli: Trichinopoly
Tissemsilt: Vialar
Titograd: Podgorica
Tobata, see Kitakyūshū
Tocqueville, see Rass el Oued
Tolbukhin: Dobrich
Tombouctou: Timbuktu
Torino: Turin
Tornio: Tornea
Tournai: Doornik
Trèves: Trier
Trichinopoly, see
   Tiruchchirappalli
Tripoli: Tarābulus

Trucial States, see United Arab
   Emirates
Truth or Consequences:
   Hot Springs
Tselinograd: Akmolinsk
Tsingyuan, see Paoting
Tskhinvali: Staliniri
Turkana, L.: Rudolf, L.
Turku: Åbo
Turnovo: Veliko Tarnovo
Tver, see Kalinin
Tyre, see Sūr

Ubundi: Ponthierville
Uige, see Carmona
Ulan Ude: Verkhneudinsk
Uleåborg, see Oulu
Ulyanovsk: Simbitsk
Ulyasutay: Javhlant
United Arab Emirates: Trucial
   States
Urmia, L., see Rezā'iyeh, L.
Usküb, see Skopje
Usküdar: Scutari
Ussuryst: Voroshilov
Ustka: Stolpmünde
Usumbura, see Bujumbura
Uusikaarlepyy: Nykarleby
Uusikaupunki: Nystad

Vaasa: Nikolaistad
Vadodara: Baroda
Varanasi: Banaras, Benares
Varna: Stalin
Veliko Tarnovo, see Turnovo
Venézia: Venice
Ventspils: Windau, Vindava
Verchnedvinsk: Drissa
Verkhneudinsk, see Ulan Ude
Vialar, see Tissemsilt
Victor Hugo, see Hamadia
Viborg: Viipuri, Vyborg
Vidisha: Bhilsa
Vienna, see Wien
Vijayawada: Bezwada
Vila Pereira d'Eça, see Ongiva
Villa Sanjurjo, see Al Hoceima
Villmanstrand, see
   Lappeenranta
Vilnius: Vilna, Vilno
Vilnyus, Wilno
Vinh Loi: Bac Lieu
Vindava, see Ventspils
Vipiteno: Sterzing
Vishakhapatnam:
   Vizagapatnam,
   Visakhapatnam
Vlaanderen: Flanders
Vlissingen: Flushing
Volgograd: Stalingrad
Volosinovo, see Novi Becej
Voroshilov: Ussurysk
Voroshilovgrad: Lugansk
Voroshilovsk, see Kommunarsk
Vyatka, see Kirov

Wagadugu, see Oaugadougou
Wakamatsu, see Kitakyūshū
Wakeham Bay, see Maricourt
Walbrzych: Waldenburg
Walcz: Deutsch Krone
Wanchüan, see Kalgan
Warszawa: Warsaw
Wenchow: Yungkia
Wien: Vienna
Wilno, see Vilnius
Windau, see Ventspils
Wrocław: Breslau
Wuhsien, see Suchou
Wulumuchi: Tihwa

Yanam: Yonaon
Yangku, see T'aiyüan
Yarkand, see Soch'e
Yawata, see Kitakyūshū
Yekaterinburg, see Sverdlovsk
Yekaterinodar, see Krasnodar
Yekaterinoslav, see
   Dnepropetrovsk
Yelisavetgrad, see Kirovgrad
Yent'ai: Chéfoo
Ypres, see Ieper
Yungchang, see Paoshan
Yungki, see Chilin
Yunkia, see Wenchow
Yungning, see Nanning
Yunnan, see K'unming

Zadar: Zara
Zaïre: Congo (Kinshasa)
Zagreb: Agram
Zakamensk: Gorodok
Zambia: Northern Rhodesia
Zaouiet El-Kahla: Fort Flatters
Zaragoza: Saragossa
Zetland: Shetland
Zhdanov: Mariupol
Zimbabwe, see Rhodesia
Zinovievsk, see Kirovgrad
Zlin: Gottwaldov
Zlïtan: Sliten
Zombor, see Sombor

Geographical Terms

This is a list of some of the geographical words from foreign languages which are found in the place names on the maps and in the index. Each is followed by the language and the English meaning.

Afr. afrikaans
Alb. albanian
Amh. amharic
Ar. arabic
Ber. berber
Bulg. bulgarian
Bur. burmese

Chin. chinese
Cz. czechoslovakian
Dan. danish
Dut. dutch
Fin. finnish
Flem. flemish
Fr. french

Gae. gaelic
Ger. german
Gr. greek
Heb. hebrew
Hin. hindi
I.-C. indo-chinese
Ice. icelandic

It. italian
Jap. japanese
Kor. korean
Lapp. lappish
Lith. lithuanian
Mal. malay
Mong. mongolian

Nor. norwegian
Pash. pashto
Pers. persian
Pol. polish
Port. portuguese
Rum. rumanian
Russ. russian

Ser.-Cr. serbo-croat
Siam. siamese
Sin. sinhalese
Som. somali
Span. spanish
Swed. swedish
Tib. tibetan
Turk. turkish

A. (Ain) Ar. spring
–á Ice. river
a Dan., Nor., Swed. stream
–abad Pers., Russ. town
Abyad Ar. white
Ad. (Adrar) Ar., Ber. mountain
Ada, Adasi Tur. island
Addis Amh. new
Adrar Ar., Ber. mountain
Aïn Ar. spring
Ākra Gr. cape
Akrotíri Gr. cape
Alb Ger. mountains
Albufera Span. lagoon
–ålen Nor. islands
Alpen Ger. mountain pastures
Alpes Fr. mountains
Alpi It. mountains
Alto Port. high
–älv, –älven Swed. stream, river
Amt Dan. first-order administrative division
Appennino It. mountain range
Arch. (Archipiélago) Span. archipelago
Arcipélago It. archipelago
Arq. (Arquipélago) Port. archipelago
Arr. (Arroyo) Span. stream
–Ås, –åsen Nor., Swed. hill
Autonomna Oblast Ser.-Cr. autonomous region
Ayios Gr. island
Ayn Ar. well, waterhole

B(a). (Baía) Port. bay
B. (Baie) Fr. bay
B. (Bahía) Span. bay
B. (Ben) Gae. mountain
B. (Bir) Ar. well
B. (Bucht) Ger. bay
B. (Bugt.) Dan. bay
Baai, –baai Afr. bay
Bāb Ar. gate
Bäck, –bäcken Swed. stream
Back, backen, Swed. hill
Bad, –baden Ger. spa
Bādiya, -t Ar. desert
Baek Dan. stream
Baelt Dan. strait
Bahía Span. bay
Bahr Ar. sea, river
Bahra Ar. lake
Baía Port. bay
Baie Fr. bay
Bajo, –a, Span. lower
Bakke Nor. hill
Bala Pers. upper
Baltă Rum. marsh, lake
Banc Fr. bank
Bander Ar., Mal. port
Bandar Pers. bay
Banja Ser. Cr. spa, resort
Barat Mal. western
Barr. (Barrage) Fr. dam
Barracão Port. dam, waterfall
Bassin Fr. bay
Bayt Heb. house, village
Bazar Hin. market, bazaar
Be'er Heb. well
Beit Heb. village
Belo-, Belyy, Belaya,

Beloye, Russ. white
Ben Gae. mountain
Bender Somal. harbour
Berg,(e) –berg(e) Afr. mountain(s)
Berg, –berg Ger. mountain
–berg, –et Nor., Swed. hill, mountain, rock
Bet Heb. house, village
Bir, Bïr Ar. well
Birket Ar. lake, bay, marsh
Bj. (Bordj) Ar. port
–bjerg Dan. hill, point
Boca Span. river mouth
Bodden Ger. bay, inlet
Bogaz, Boğaz, –ı Tur. strait
Boka Ser.-Cr. gulf, inlet
Bol. (Bolshoi) Russ. great, large
Bordj Ar. fort
–borg Dan., Nor., Swed. castle, fort
–botn Nor. valley floor
bouche(s) Fr. mouth
Br. (Burnu) Tur. cape
Brațul Rum. distributary stream
–breen Nor. glacier
–bruck Ger. bridge
–brunn Swed. well, spring
Bucht Ger. bay
Bugt, –bugt Dan. bay
Buheirat Ar. lake
Bukit Mal. hill
Bukten Swed. bay
–bulag Mong. spring
Bûr Ar. port
Burg. Ar. fort
Burg, –burg Ger. castle
Burnu Tur. cape
Burun Tur. cape
Butt Gae. promontory
–by Dan., Nor., Swed. town
–byen Nor., Swed. town

C. (Cabo) Port., Span. headland, cape
C. (Cap) Fr. cape
C. (Capo) It. cape
Cabeza Span. peak, hill
Camp Port., Span. land, field
Campo Span. plain
Campos Span. upland
Can. (Canal) Fr., Span. canal
Canale It. canal
Canalul Ser.-Cr. canal
Cao Nguyên Thai. plateau, tableland
Cap Fr. cape
Capo It. cape
Cataracta Sp. cataract
Cauce Span. intermittent stream
Causse Fr. upland (limestone)
Cayi Tur. river
Cayo(s) Span. rock(s), islet(s)
Cerro Span. hill, peak
Ch. (Chaîne(s)) Fr. mountain range(s)
Ch. (Chott) Ar. salt lake
Chaco Span. jungle
Chaîne(s) Fr. mountain range(s)
Chap. (Chapada) Port. hills, upland

Chapa Span. hills, upland
Chapada Port. hills, upland
Chaung Bur. stream, river
Chen Chin. market town
Ch'eng Chin. town
Chiang Chin. river
Ch'ih Chin. pool
Ch'ŏn Kor. river
–chŏsuji Kor. reservoir
Chott Ar. salt lake, swamp
Chou Chin. district
Chu Tib. river
Chung Chin. middle
Chute Fr. waterfall
Co. (Cerro) Span. hill, peak
Coch. (Cochilla) Port. hills
Col Fr., It. Pass
Colline(s) Fr. hill(s)
Conca It. plain, basin
Cord. (Cordillera) Span. mountain chain
Costa It., Span. coast
Côte Fr. coast, slope, hill
Cuchillas Spain hills
Cu-Lao I.-C. island

D. (Dolok) Mal. mountain
Dágh Pers. mountain
Dağ(ı) Tur. mountain(s)
Dağları Tur. mountain range
Dake Jap. mountain
–dal Nor. valley
–dal, –e Dan., Nor. valley
–dal, –en Swed. valley, stream
Dalay Mong. sea, large lake
–dalir Ice. valley
–dalur Ice. valley
–damm, –en Swed. lake
Danau Mal. lake
Dao I.-O. island
Dar Ar. region
Darya Russ. river
Daryācheh Pers. marshy lake, lake
Dasht Pers. desert, steppe
Daung Bur. mountain, hill
Dayr Ar. depression, hill
Debre Amh. hill
Deli Ser.-Cr. mountain(s)
Denizi Tur. sea
Dépt. (Département) Fr. first-order administrative division
Desierto Span. desert
Dhar Ar. region, mountain chain
Dj. (Djebel) Ar. mountain
Dŏ Jap., Kor. island
Dong Kor. village, town
Dong Thai. jungle region
–dorf Ger. village
–dorp Afr. village
–drif Afr. ford
–dybet Dan. marine channel
Dzong Tib. town, settlement

Eil.-eiland(en) Afr., Dut. island(s)
–elv Nor. river
–'emeq Heb. plain, valley
'erg Ar. desert with dunes
Estrecho Span. strait
Estuario Span. estuary

Étang Fr. lagoon
–ey(jar) Ice. island(s)

F. (Fiume) It. river
F. Folyó Hung. river
Fd. (Fjord) Nor. Inlet of sea
–feld Ger. field
–fell Ice. mountain, hill
–feng Chin. mountain
Fiume It. river
Fj. (–fjell) Nor. mountain
–fjall Ice. mountain(s), hill(s)
–fjäll(et) Swed. hill(s), mountain(s), ridge
–fjällen Swed. mountains
–fjard(en) Swed. fjord, bay, lake
Fjeld Dan. mountain
–fjell Nor. mountain, rock
–fjord(en) Nor. inlet of sea
–fjorden Dan. bay, marine channel
–fjörður Ice. fjord
Fl. (Fleuve) Fr. river
Fl. (Fluss) Ger. river
–flói Ice. bay, marshy country
Fluss Ger. river
foce, –i It. mouth(s)
Folyó Hung. river
–fontein Afr. fountain, spring
–fors, –en, Swed. rapids, waterfall
Foss Ice., Nor. waterfall
–furt Ger. ford
Fylke Nor. first-order administrative division

G. (Gebel) Ar. mountain
G. (Gebirge) Ger. hills, mountains
G. (Golfe) Fr. gulf
G. (Golfo) It. gulf
G. (Gora) Bulg., Russ., Ser-Cr. mountain
G. (Gunong) Mal. mountain
–gang Kor. river
Ganga Hin., Sin. river
–gat Dan. sound
–gau Ger. district
Gave Fr. stream
–gawa Jap. river
Geb. (Gebirge) Ger. hills, mountains
Gebel Ar. mountain
Geziret Ar. island
Ghat Hin. range of hills
Ghiol Rum. lake
Ghubbat Ar. bay, inlet
Gji Alb. bay
Gjol Alb. lagoon, lake
Gl. (Glava) Ser.-Cr. mountain, peak
Glen. Gae. valley
Gletscher Ger. glacier
Gobi Mong. desert
Gol Mong. river
Golfe Fr. gulf
Golfo It., Span. gulf
Gomba Tib. settlement
Gora Bulg., Russ., Ser.-Cr. mountain
Góry Pol., Russ. mountain
Gölü Tur. lake
–gorod Russ. small town
Grad Bulg., Russ., Ser-Cr. town, city

Grada Russ. mountain range
Guba Russ. bay
–Guntō Jap. island group
Gunong Mal. mountain
Gurā Rum. passage

H. Hadabat Ar. plateau
–hafen Ger. harbour, port
Haff Ger. bay
Hai Chin. sea
Haihsia Chin. strait
–hale Dan. spit, peninsula
Hals Dan., Nor. peninsula, isthmus
Halvø Dan. peninsula
Halvøya Nor. peninsula
Hāmad, Hamada,
Hammādah Ar. stony desert, plain
–hamn Swed., Nor. harbour, anchorage
Hāmūn Ar. plain
Hāmūn Pers. low-lying marshy area
–Hantō Jap. peninsula
Harju Fin. hill
Hassi Ar. well
–haug Nor. hill
Hav Swed. gulf
Havet Nor. sea
–havn Dan., Nor. harbour
Hegyseg Hung. forest
Heide Ger. heath
Hi. (hassi) Ar. well
Ho Chin. river
–hø Nor. peak
Hochland Afr. highland
Hoek, –hoek Afr., Dut. cape
Höfn Ice. harbour, port
–hög, –en, –högar, –högarna Swed. hill(s), peak, mountain
Höhe Ger. hills
Holm Dan. island
–holm, –holme, –holzen, Swed. island
Hon I.-C. island
Hora Cz. mountain
–horn Nor. peak
Hory Cz. mountain range, forest
–hoved Dan. point, headland, peninsula
Hráun Ice. lava
–hsi Chin. mountain, stream
–hsiang Chin. village
–hsien Chin. district
Hu Chin. lake
Huk Dan., Ger. point
Huken Nor. head

I. (Île) Fr. island
I. (Ilha) Port. island
I. (Insel) Ger. island
I. (Isla) Span. island
I. (Isola) It. island
Idehan Ar., Ber. sandy plain
Île(s) Fr. island(s)
Ilha Port. island
Insel(n) Ger. island(s)
Irmak Tur. river
Is. (Inseln) Ger. islands
Is. (Islas) Span. islands
Is. (Isola) It. island
Isola, –e It. island(s)
Istmo Span. isthmus

J. (Jabal) Ar. mountain
J. (Jazira) Ar. island
J. (Jebel) Ar. mountain
J. (Jezioro) Pol. lake
Jabal Ar. mountain, range
–jaur Swed. lake
–järvi Fin. lake, bay, pond
Jasovir Bulg. reservoir
Jazâ'ir Ar. islands
Jazira Ar. island
Jazireh Pers. island
Jebel Ar. mountain
Jezero Ser.-Cr. lake
Jezioro Pol. lake
–Jima Jap. island
Jøkelen Nor. glacier
–joki Fin. stream
–jökull Ice. glacier
Jûras Licis Lat. bay, gulf

K. (Kap) Dan. cape
K (Khalig) Ar. gulf
K. (Kiang) Chin. river
K. (Kuala) Mal. confluence, estuary
Kaap Afr. cape
Kai Jap. sea
Kaikyō Jap. strait
Kamennyy Russ. stony
Kampong Mal. village
Kan. (Kanal) Ser.-Cr. channel, canal
Kanaal Dut., Flem. canal
Kanal Dan. channel, gulf
Kanal Ger., Swed. canal, stream
kanal Ser.-Cr. channel, canal
Kang Kor. river, bay
Kangri Tib. mountain glacier
Kap Dan., Ger. cape
Kapp Nor. cape
Kas I.-C. island
–kaupstaður Ice. market town
–kaupunki Fin. town
Kavir Pers. salt desert
Kébir Ar. great
Kéfar Heb. village, hamlet
–ken Jap. first-order administrative division
Kep Alb. cape
Kepulauan Mal. archipelago
Ketjil Mal. lesser, little
Khalig, Khalij Ar. gulf
khamba, –idg Tib. source, spring
Khawr Ar. wadi
Khirbat Ar. ruins
Kho Khot Thai. isthmus
Khôr Pers. creek, estuary
Khrebet Russ. mountain range
Kiang Chin. river
–klint Dan. cliff
–Klintar Swed. hills
Kloof Afr. gorge
Knude Dan. point
Ko Jap. lake
Ko Thai. island
Kohi Pash. mountains
Kol Russ. lake
Kolymskoye Russ. mountain range
Kólpos Gr., Tur. gulf, bay
Kompong Mal. landing place
–kop Afr. hill

-köping Swed. market town
Körfezi Tur. gulf
Kosa Russ. spit
-koski Fin. cataract, rapids
-kraal Afr. native village
Krasnyy Russ. red
Kryash Russ. ridge, hills
Kuala Mal. confluence, estuary
kuan Chin. pass
Kuh -hha Pers. mountains
Kul Russ. lake
Kulle Swed. hill, shoal
Kum Russ. sandy desert
Kumpu Fin. hill
Kurgan Russ. mound
Kwe Bur. bay, gulf
Kyst Dan. coast
Kyun, -zu, -umya Bur. island(s)

L. (Lac) Fr. lake
L. (Lacul) Rum. lake
L. (Lago) It., Span. lake, lagoon
L. (Lagoa) Port. lagoon
L. (Límni) Gr. lake
L. (Loch) Gae. (lake, inlet)
L. (Lough) Gae. (lake, inlet)
La Tib. pass
La (Lagoa) Port. lagoon
-laagte Afr. watercourse
Läani Fin. first-order administrative division
Län Swed. first-order administrative division
Lac Fr. lake
Lacul Rum. lake, lagoon
Lago It., Span. lake, lagoon
Lagoa Port. lagoon
Laguna It., Span. lagoon, intermittent lake
Lagune Fr. lake
Lahti Fin. bay, gulf, cove
Lakhti Russ. bay, gulf
Lampi Fin. lake
Land Ger. first-order administrative division
-land Dan. region
-land Afr., Nor. land, province
Lido It. beach, shore
Liehtao Chin. islands
Lilla Swed. small
Límni Gr. lake
Ling Chin. mountain range, ice
Linna Fin. historical fort
Llano Span. prairie, plain
Loch Gae. (lake)
Lough Gae. (lake)
Lum Alb. river
Lund Dan. forest
-lund, -en Swed. wood(s)

M. (Maj, Mai) Alb. mountain, peak
M. (Mont) Fr. mountain peak
M. (Mys) Russ. cape
Madîna(h) Ar. town, city
Madiq Ar. strait
Maj Alb. peak
Mäki Fin. hill, hillside
Mal Alb. mountain
Mal Russ. little, small
Mal/a, -i, -o Ser.-Cr. small, little
Man Kor. bay
Mar Span. lagoon, sea
Mare Rum. great
Marisma Span. marsh
-mark Dan., Nor. land
Marsâ Ar. anchorage, bay, inlet
Masabb Ar. river mouth
Massif Fr. upland, plateau
Mato Port. forest
Mazar Pers. shrine, tomb
Meer Afr., Dut., Ger. lake sea

Mi., Mti. (Monti) It. mountains
Miao Chin. temple, shrine
Midbar Heb. wilderness
Mif. (Massif) Fr. upland, plateau
Misaki Jap. cape, point
-mo Nor., Swed. heath, island
-mon Swed. heath
Mong Bur. town
Mont Fr. hill, mountain
Montagna It. mountain
Montagne Fr. hill, mountain
Montaña Span. mountain
Monte It., Port., Span. mountain
Monti It. mountains
More Russ. sea
Mörön Hung. river
Mt. (Mont) Fr. mountain
Mt. (Monti) It. mountain
Mt. (Montaña) Span. mountain range
Mte. (Monte) It., Port., Span. mountain
Mţi. (Munţi) Rum. mountain
Mts. (Monts) Fr. mountains
Muang Mal. town
Mui Ar., I.-C. cape
Mull Gae. (promontory)
Mund, -mund Afr. mouth
Munkhafed Ar. depression
Munte Rum. mount
Munţi(i) Rum. mountain(s)
Muong Mal. village
Myit Bur. river
Myitwanya Bur. mouths of river
-mýri Ice. bog
Mys Russ. cape

N. (Nahal) Heb. river
Naes Dan. point, cape
Nafûd Ar. sandy desert
Nahal Heb. river
Nahr Ar. river, stream
Najd Ar. plateau, pass
Nakhon Thai. town
Nam I.-C. river
-nam Kor. south
-näs Swed. cape
-nes Ice., Nor. cape
Ness, -ness Gae. promontory, cape
Nez Fr. cape
-niemi Fin. cape, point, peninsula, island
Nizhne, -iy Russ. lower
Nizmennost Russ. plain, lowland
Nísos, Nísoi Gr. island(s)
Nor Chin. lake
Nor Tib. peak
Nos Bulg., Russ. cape, point
Nudo Span. mountain
Nuruu Mong. mountain range
Nuur Mong. lake

O. (Ostrov) Russ. island
O (Ouâdî, Oued) Ar. wadi
-ö Swed. island, peninsula, point
-öar, (-na) Swed. islands
Oblast Russ. administrative division
Öbor Mong. inner
Occidental Fr., Span. western
Odde Dan., Nor. point, peninsula, cape
Oji Alb. bay
Ojo Span. spring
Oki Jap. bay
-ön Swed. island peninsula
Ondör Mong. high, tall

-ör Swed. island, peninsula, point
Orașul Rum. city
Ord Gae. point
Óri Gr. mountains
Oriental Span. eastern
Órmos Gr. bay
Óros Gr. mountain
Ort Ger. point, cape
Ostrov(a) Russ. island(s)
Otok(-i) Ser.-Cr. island(s)
Ouadi, -edi Ar. dry watercourse, wadi
Ouzan Pers. river
Ova (-si) Tur. plains, lowlands
-øy, (-a) Nor. island(s)
Oya Hin. point
Oya Sin. river
Oz. (Ozero, a) Russ. lake(s)

P. (Passo) It. pass
P. (Pasul) Rum. pass
P. (Pico) Span. peak
P. (Prokhod) Bulg. pass
-pää Fin. hill(s), mountain
Pahta Lapp. hill
Pampa, -s Span. plain(s) salt flat(s)
Pan. (Pantano) Span. Reservoir
Pantao Chin. peninsula
Parbat Urdu mountain
Pas Fr. gap
Paso Span. pass, marine channel
Pass Ger. pass
Passo It. pass
Pasul Rum. pass
Patam Hin. small village
Patna, -patnam Hin. small village
Pegunungan Mal. mountain, range
Pei, -pei Chin. north
Pélagos Gr. sea
Pen. (Península) Span. peninsula
Peña Span. rock, peak
Península Span. peninsula
Per. (Pereval) Russ. pass
Pertuis Fr. channel
Peski Russ. desert, sands
Phanom I.-C., Thai. mountain
Phnom I.-C. mountain
Phu I.-C. mountain
Pic Fr. peak
Pico(s) Span. peak(s)
Pik Russ. peak
Piz., pizzo It. peak
Pl. (Planina) Ser.-Cr. mountain, range
Plage Fr. beach
Plaine Fr. plain
Planalto Span. plateau
Planina Bulg., Ser.-Cr. mountain, range
Plat. (Plateau) Fr. level upland
Plato Russ. plateau
Playa Span. beach
P-ov. (Poluostrov) Russ. peninsula
Pointe Fr. point, cape
Pojezierze Pol. lakes plateau
Polder Dut. reclaimed farmland
-pólis Gr. city, town
Poluostrov Russ. peninsula
Połwysep Pol. peninsula
Pont Fr. bridge
Ponta Port. point, cape
Ponte It. bridge
Poort Afr. passage, gate
-poort Dut. port
Porta Port. pass
Porţil, -e Rum. gate
Portillo Span. pass
Porto It. port
Porto Port., Span. port

Pot. (Potámi, Potamós) Gr. river
Poulo I.-C. island
Pr. (Prŭsmyk) Cz. pass
Pradesh Hin. state
Presa Span. reservoir
Presqu'île Fr. peninsula
Prokhod Bulg. pass
Proliv Russ. strait
Prusmyk Cz. pass
Pso. (Passo) It. pass
Pta. (Ponta) Port. point, cape
Pta. (Punta) It., Span. point, cape, peak
Pte. (Pointe) Fr. point cape
Puerto Span. port, pass
Puig Cat. peak
Pulau Mal. island
Puna Span. desert plateau
Punta It., Span. point, peak
Puy Fr. hill

Qal'at Ar. fort
Qanal Ar. canal
Qasr Ar. fort
Qiryat Heb. town
Qolleh Pers. mountain

Ramla Ar. sand
Rann Hin. swampy region
Rao I.-C. river
Ras Amh. cape, headland
Rãs Ar. cape, headland
Recife(s) Port. reef(s)
Reka Bulg., Cz., Russ. river
Repede Rum. rapids
Represa Port. dam
Reshteh Pers. mountain range
-Rettõ Jap. group of islands
Ría Span. estuary, bay
Ribeirão Port. river
Rijeka Ser.-Cr. river
Rio Port. river
Río Span. river
Riv. (Riviera) It. coastal plain, coast, river
Riviera It. coast
Rivière Fr. river
Roche Fr. rock
Rog Russ. horn
-rück Ger. ridge
Rüd Pers. stream, river
Rudohorie Cz. ore mountains
Rzeka Pol. river

S. (Sungei) Mal. river
Sa. (Serra) It., Port. range of hills
Sa. (Sierra) Span. range of hills
-saari Fin. island
Sadd Ar. dam
Sagar, -ara Hin., Urdu lake
Saharã Ar. desert
Sahrâ Ar. desert
Sa'id Ar. highland
Sakar Fin. mountain
-Saki Jap. point
Sal. (Salar) Span. salt pan
Salina(s) Span. salt flat(s)
-salmi Fin. strait, sound, lake, channel
Saltsjöbad Swed. resort
Sammyaku Jap. mountain, range
Samut Thai. gulf
-San Jap. hill, mountain
Sap. (Sapadno) Russ. west
Sasso It. mountain
Se, Sé I.-C. river
Sebkha, -kra Ar. salt flats
See Ger. lake
-see Ger. sea
-şehir Turk. town
Selat Mal. strait
-selkä Fin. bay, lake, sound, ridge, hills

Selva Span. forest, wood
Seno Span. bay, sound
Serír Ar. desert of small stones
Serra It., Port. range of hills
Serranía Span. mountains
Sev. (Severo) Russ. north
-shahr Pers. city, town
Shan Chin. hills, mountains, pass
Shan-mo Chin. mountain range
Shatt Ar. river
-Shima Jap. island
Shimãli Ar. northern
-Shotõ Jap. group of islands
Shuik'u Chin. reservoir
Sierra Span. hill, range
Sjö, sjön Swed. lake, bay, sea
Sjøen Dan. sea
Skär Swed. island, rock, cape
Skog Nor. forest
-skog, -skogen Swed. wood(s)
-skov Dan. forest
Slieve Gae. range of hills
-sø Dan., Nor. lake
Sør Nor. south, southern
Solonchak Russ. salt lake, marsh
Souk Ar. market
Spitze Ger. peak, mountain
-spruit Afr. stream
-stad Afr., Nor., Swed. town
-stadt Ger. town
Staður Ice. town
Stausee Ger. reservoir
Stenón Gr. strait, pass
Step Russ. plain
Str. (Stretto) It. strait
-strand Dan., Nor. beach
-strede Nor. straits
Strelka Russ. spit
-strete Nor. straits
Stretto It. strait
Stroedet Dan. strait
-ström, -strömmen Swed. stream(s)
-stroom Afr. large river
Suidõ Jap. strait, channel
Sûn Bur. cape
Sund Dan. sound
-sund, -sundet Swed. sound, estuary, inlet
-sund(et) Nor. sound
Sungai, -ei Mal. river
Sungei Mal. river
Sur Span. south, southern
Sveti Bulg. pass
Syd Dan., Swed. south

Tai -tai Chin. tower
Tal Mong. plain, steppe
-tal Ger. valley
Tall Ar. hills, hummocks
Tandjung Mal. cape, headland
Tao Chin. island
Tassili Ar. rocky plateau
Tau Russ. mountain, range
Taung Bur. mountain, south
Taunggya Bur. pass
Têlok I.-C., Mal. bay bight
Teluk Mal. bay, gulf
Tg. (Tandjung) Mal. cape, headland
-thal Ger. valley
Thok Tib. town
Tierra Span. land, country
-tind Nor. peak
Tjärn, -en, -et Swed. lake
Tong Nor. village, town
Tong Bur., Thai. mountain range
Tonle I.-C. large river, lake
-träsk Swed. bog, swamp
Tsangpo Tib. large river
Tso Tib. lake

Tsu Jap. entrance, bay
Tulur Ar. hill
T'un Chin. village
Tung Chin. east
Tunnel Fr. tunnel
Tunturi Fin. hill(s), mountain(s), ridge

Uad Ar. dry watercourse, wadi
Udjung Mal. cape
Udd, udde, udden Swed. point, peninsula
Uebi Somal. river
Us Mong. water
Ust Russ. river mouth
Uul Mong., Russ. mountain, range

V. (Volcán) Span. volcano
-vaara Fin. hill, mountain, ridge, peak
-våg Nor. bay
Val Fr., It. valley
Valea Rum. valley
-vall, -vallen Swed. mountain
Valle Span. valley
Vallée Fr. valley
Valli It. lake, lagoon
Väst Swed. west
-vatn Ice., Nor. lake
Vatten Swed. lake
Vdkhr. (Vodokhranilishche) Russ. reservoir
-ved, -veden Swed. range, hills
Veld, -veld Afr. field
Velik/a, -e, -i, -o Ser.Cr. large
-vesi Fin. water, lake, bay sound, strait
Vest Dan., Nor. west
Vf. (vîrful) Rum. peak, mountain
-vidda Nor. plateau
Vig Dan. bay, inlet, cove, lagoon, lake, bight
-vik, -vika, -viken Nor., Swed. bay, cove, gulf, inlet, lake
Vila Port. small town
Villa Span. town
Ville Fr. town
Vinh I.-C. bay
Vîrful Rum. peak, mountain
-vlei Afr. pond, pool
Vodokhranilishche Russ. reservoir
Vol. (Volcán) Span. volcano, mountain
Vorota Russ. gate
Vostochnyy Russ. eastern
Vozyshennost Russ. heights, uplands
Vrata Bulg. gate, pass
Vrchovina Cz. mountainous country
Vrchy Cz. mountain range
Vung I.-C. gulf
-vuori Fin. mountain, hill

W. (Wâdi) Ar. dry watercourse
Wâhât Ar. oasis
Wald Ger. wood, forest
Wan Chin., Jap. bay
Webi Amh. river
Woestyn Afr. desert

Yam Heb. sea
Yang Chin. ocean
Yazovir Bulg. reservoir
Yoma Bur. mountain range
-yüan Chin. spring

-Zaki Jap. peninsula
Zalew Pol. lagoon, swamp
Zaliv Russ. bay
Zan Jap. mountain
Zatoka Pol. bay
Zee Dut. sea
Zemlya Russ. land, island(s)

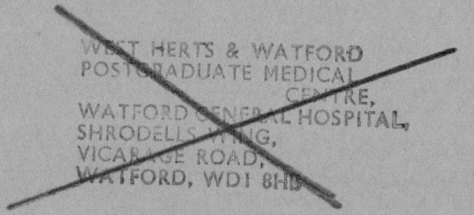